COMPACT SCHOOL & OFFICE EDITION

WEBSTER'S NEW WORLD DICTIONARY

David B. Guralnik, Editor in Chief

Webster's New World

Published by New World Dictionaries
A Division of Simon & Schuster, Inc.
Gulf + Western Building
One Gulf + Western Plaza
New York, New York 10023

Dictionary Editorial Offices:
New World Dictionaries
850 Euclid Avenue
Cleveland, Ohio 44114

PRENTICE HALL PRESS, TREE OF KNOWLEDGE, WEBSTER'S NEW WORLD
and colophons are trademarks of Simon & Schuster, Inc.

Manufactured in the United States of America

14   15   16   17

LIBRARY OF CONGRESS
CATALOG CARD NO.: 81-85762
Webster's New World Dictionary.

New York: Simon & Schuster
540 p. Compact School and Office ed.
8201   811119

ISBN: 0-671-41822-X hdbk.
ISBN: 0-671-44882-X pbk.

Previous editions of this book were published by
The World Publishing Company,
William Collins + World Publishing, Inc.
and William Collins Publishers, Inc.

WEBSTER'S NEW WORLD DICTIONARY, Compact School &
Office Edition is based on and includes material from WEBSTER'S
NEW WORLD DICTIONARY, Second College Edition, Copyright
© 1980 (newly revised), 1979, 1978, 1976, 1974, 1972 and 1970 by
Simon & Schuster, A Division of Gulf + Western Corporation

FOREWORD

This *Compact School and Office Edition* of WEBSTER'S NEW WORLD DICTIONARY has been prepared for those who need a simple, accurate, up-to-date dictionary as an aid to gaining a better working knowledge of the English language. It is an abridgment of the acclaimed *Second College Edition* of WEBSTER'S NEW WORLD DICTIONARY, and the entries have been carefully selected to include all the commonly used words that make up the basic vocabulary of English. In addition, a selection of the more frequently encountered specialized terms used in the sciences, the arts, business, and the professions are included, as well as the more common abbreviations and foreign words and phrases often found in English writings.

A special feature of this work not included in other dictionaries of its scope are the little word histories, or etymologies, that lend interest to the entries and often help put the current meanings of the words in sharper focus. Also included in this book are a number of useful reference supplements identified in the list of Contents below.

The type for this dictionary was created on the Fototronic CRT Typesetter, controlled by a Univac 1108 computer at Chi Corporation in Cleveland, Ohio. The typefaces used were 7 point Century Schoolbook and 8 point Helvetica Medium. The database for the dictionary was created and maintained by the publisher's staff in his own office using a video editing terminal connected via phone line to the Univac computer.

David B. Guralnik

CONTENTS

EDITORIAL STAFF

Editor in Chief	David B. Guralnik
Managing Editor	Thomas Layman
Editors	Clark C. Livensparger, Andrew N. Sparks, Christopher T. Hoolihan, Paul B. Murry, Ruth Kimball Kent, Jonathan L. Goldman, Roslyn Block
Assistants	Cynthia Sadonick, Angie West, Gertrude Tullar, Virginia C. Becker, Maureen Reister
Chief Proofreader	Shirley M. Miller

ABBREVIATIONS USED IN THIS DICTIONARY

abbrev. abbreviated; abbreviation
acc. accusative
adj. adjective
adv. adverb
Afr. African
Afrik. Afrikaans
alt. altered; alternative
Am, Am. American
Anat. Anatomy
Ar. Arabic
Aram. Aramaic
Archit. Architecture
Arith. Arithmetic
Assyr. Assyrian
Astron. Astronomy
Biol. Biology
Bot. Botany
Bret. Breton
Brit. British
Bulg. Bulgarian
C Celsius; Central
c. century; circa
Canad. Canadian
cap. capital
Celt. Celtic
cent. century; centuries
cf. compare
Ch. Church
Chem. Chemistry
Chin. Chinese
Colloq. colloquial
comp. compound; compounds
compar. comparative
conj. conjunction
contr. contracted; contraction
Dan. Danish
Dial., dial. dialectal
dim. diminutive
E eastern
E. East; English
Eccles. Ecclesiastical
Econ. Economics
Educ. Education
e.g. for example
Egypt. Egyptian
EInd. East Indian
Elec. Electricity
Eng. English
Esk. Eskimo
esp. especially
etym. etymology
Ex. example
F Fahrenheit
fem. feminine
ff. following
fig. figurative; figuratively
Finn. Finnish
Fl. Flemish
fl. flourished
Fr. French
Frank. Frankish
freq. frequentative; frequently
Fris. Frisian
fut. future
G. German
Gael. Gaelic
Gaul. Gaulish
gen. genitive
Geol. Geology
Geom. Geometry
Ger. German
Gmc. Germanic
Goth. Gothic

Gr. Greek
Gram. Grammar
Gym. Gymnastics
Haw. Hawaiian
Heb. Hebrew
Hung. Hungarian
hyp. hypothetical
Ice. Icelandic
i.e. that is
Ind. Indian
indic. indicative
inf. infinitive
infl. influenced
intens. intensive
interj. interjection
Ir, Ir. Irish
Iran. Iranian
It. Italian
Jav. Javanese
Jpn. Japanese
Kor. Korean
L Late
L. Latin
LGr. Late Greek
Linguis. Linguistics
lit. literally
Lith. Lithuanian
LL. Late Latin
LowG. Low German
M Medieval; Middle
masc. masculine
Math. Mathematics
MDu. Middle Dutch
ME. Middle English
Mech. Mechanics
Med. Medicine
Meteorol. Meteorology
Mex, Mex. Mexican
MFl. Middle Flemish
MFr. Middle French
MGr. Medieval Greek
MHG. Middle High German
mi. mile; miles
Mil. Military
ML. Medieval Latin
MLowG. Middle Low German
Mod, Mod. Modern
Mongol. Mongolic
Myth. Mythology
N northern
N. Norse; North
n. noun
Naut., naut. nautical
neut. neuter
nom. nominative
Norm, Norm. Norman
Norw. Norwegian
n.pl. noun plural
O Old
obj. objective
Obs., obs. obsolete
occas. occasionally
ODu. Old Dutch
OE. Old English
OFr. Old French
OHG. Old High German
ON. Old Norse
orig. origin; originally
OS. Old Saxon
p. page
pass. passive
Per. Persian
perf. perfect
pers. person
Peruv. Peruvian

Philos. Philosophy
Phoen. Phoenician
Phonet. Phonetics
Photog. Photography
phr. phrase
Physiol. Physiology
PidE. Pidgin English
pl. plural
Poet, Poetic
Pol. Polish
pop. population
Port. Portuguese
poss. possessive
pp. past participle
Pr. Provencal
prec. preceding
prep. preposition
pres. present
prob. probably
pron. pronoun
pronun. pronunciation
prp. present participle
Psychol. Psychology
pt. past tense
R.C.Ch. Roman Catholic Church
redupl. reduplication
refl. reflective
Rom. Roman
Russ. Russian
S southern
S. South
SAmInd. South American Indian
Sans. Sanskrit
Scand. Scandinavian
Scot, Scot. Scottish
Sem. Semitic
Serb. Serbian
sing. singular
Sinh. Sinhalese
Slav. Slavic
Sp. Spanish
sp. spelled; spelling
specif. specifically
sq. square
subj. subjunctive
superl. superlative
Sw. Swedish
Syr. Syrian
Tag. Tagalog
Tat. Tatar
Theol. Theology
Tibet. Tibetan
Turk. Turkish
ult. ultimately
unc. uncertain
v. verb
var. variant
v. aux. auxiliary verb
vi. intransitive verb
VL. Vulgar Latin
vt. transitive verb
W western
W. Welsh; West
WAfr. West African
WInd. West Indian
Yid. Yiddish
Zool. Zoology

‡ foreign word or phrase
+ plus
< derived from
? uncertain; possibly; perhaps
& and

A

A, a (ā) *n., pl.* **A's, a's** the first letter of the English alphabet
A (ā) *n.* **1.** a grade indicating excellence **2.** *Music* the sixth tone in the ascending scale of C major
a (ə; *stressed* ā) *adj.*, **indefinite article** [< *an*] **1.** one; one sort of **2.** each; any one **3.** per *[once a day]* A is used before words beginning with a consonant sound *[a child, a union, a history]*
a- *a prefix meaning:* **1.** [< OE.] *a)* in, into, on, at, to *[aboard] b)* the act or state of *[asleep] c)* up, out *[arise] d)* off, of *[akin]* **2.** [< Gr.] not *[agnostic]*
a. **1.** about **2.** acre(s) **3.** answer
aard·vark (ärd'värk') *n.* [< D. *aarde*, earth + *vark*, pig] an ant-eating African mammal
Aar·on (er'ən) *Bible* the older brother of Moses and first high priest of the Hebrews
ab- [L.] *a prefix meaning* away, from, off, down *[abdicate]*
a·back (ə bak') *adv.* [Archaic] backward — **taken aback** startled; surprised
ab·a·cus (ab'ə kəs) *n., pl.* **-cus·es, -cl'** (-sī') [< Gr. *abax*] a frame with sliding beads, for doing arithmetic
a·baft (ə baft') *adv.* [< OE. *on*, on + *be*, by + *æftan*, aft] aft —*prep. Naut.* behind
ab·a·lo·ne (ab'ə lō'nē) *n.* [AmSp.] a marine mollusk with a spiral shell
a·ban·don (ə ban'dən) *vt.* [< OFr. *mettre a bandon*, to put under (another's) ban] **1.** to give up completely **2.** to desert —*n.* unrestrained activity —**a·ban'don·ment** *n.*
a·ban'doned *adj.* **1.** forsaken; deserted **2.** wicked; immoral **3.** unrestrained
a·base (ə bās') *vt.* **a·based', a·bas'ing** [< ML. *abassare*, to lower] to humble or humiliate — **a·base'ment** *n.*
a·bash (ə bash') *vt.* [< L. *ex* + *bah* (interj.)] to make ashamed and ill-at-ease —**a·bash'ed·ly** (-id lē) *adv.* —**a·bash'ment** *n.*
a·bate (ə bāt') *vt.*, *vi.* **a·bat'ed, a·bat'ing** [< OFr. *abattre*, to beat down] **1.** to make or become less **2.** *Law* to end; terminate — **a·bate'ment** *n.*
ab·at·toir (ab'ə twär') *n.* [Fr.: see ABATE] a slaughterhouse
ab·ba·cy (ab'ə sē) *n., pl.* **-cles** an abbot's position, jurisdiction, or term of office
ab·bé (ä bā') *n.* [Fr.: see ABBOT] a French title of respect for a priest
ab·bess (ab'əs) *n.* [see ABBOT] a woman who is head of an abbey of nuns
ab·bey (ab'ē) *n.* **1.** a monastery or nunnery **2.** a church belonging to an abbey
ab·bot (ab'ət) *n.* [< Aram. *abbā*, father] a man who is head of an abbey of monks
abbrev. **1.** abbreviated **2.** abbreviation
ab·bre·vi·ate (ə brē'vē āt') *vt.* **-at'ed, -at'ing** [< L. *ad-*, to + *brevis*, short] to make shorter; esp., to shorten (a word) by leaving out letters —**ab·bre'vi·a'tor** *n.*
ab·bre·vi·a·tion (-ā'shən) *n.* **1.** a shortening **2.** a shortened form of a word or phrase, as *Mr.*

for *Mister*, *N.Y.* for *New York*
A B C (ā'bē'sē') *n., pl.* **A B C's 1.** [*usually pl.*] the alphabet **2.** the basic elements (of a subject)
ab·di·cate (ab'də kāt') *vt.*, *vi.* **-cat'ed, -cat'ing** [< L. *ab-*, off + *dicare*, to proclaim] to give up formally (a throne, etc.); surrender (a right) — **ab'di·ca'tion** *n.*
ab·do·men (ab'də mən, ab dō'-) *n.* [L.] the part of the body between the diaphragm and the pelvis, containing the intestines, etc.; belly —**ab·dom'i·nal** (-dä'mə n'l) *adj.*
ab·duct (ab dukt') *vt.* [< L. *ab-*, away + *ducere*, to lead] to kidnap —**ab·duc'tion** *n.* —**ab·duc'tor** *n.*
a·beam (ə bēm') *adv.*, *adj.* at right angles to a ship's length or keel
a·bed (ə bed') *adv.*, *adj.* in bed
A·bel (ā'b'l) *Bible* the second son of Adam and Eve, killed by his brother Cain
ab·er·ra·tion (ab'ər ā'shən) *n.* [< L. *ab-*, from + *errare*, to wander] **1.** a deviation from what is right, true, normal, etc. **2.** mental derangement —**ab·er·rant** (a ber'ənt) *adj.*
a·bet (ə bet') *vt.* **a·bet'ted, a·bet'ting** [< OFr. *a-*, to + *beter*, to bait] to incite or help, esp. in crime —**a·bet'ment** *n.* —**a·bet'tor, a·bet'ter** *n.*
a·bey·ance (ə bā'əns) *n.* [< OFr. *a-*, at + *bayer*, to gape] temporary suspension, as of an activity or ruling
ab·hor (ab hôr') *vt.* **-horred', -hor'ring** [< L. *ab-*, from + *horrere*, to shudder] to shrink from in disgust or hatred —**ab·hor'rence** *n.*
ab·hor'rent (-ənt) *adj.* causing disgust, hate, etc. —**ab·hor'rent·ly** *adv.*
a·bide (ə bīd') *vi.* **a·bode'** or **a·bid'ed, a·bid'ing** [OE. *abidan*] **1.** to remain **2.** [Archaic] to reside —*vt.* **1.** to await **2.** to endure —**abide by 1.** to live up to (a promise, etc.) **2.** to submit to and carry out
a·bid'ing *adj.* enduring; lasting
a·bil·i·ty (ə bil'ə tē) *n., pl.* **-tles 1.** a being able; power to do **2.** skill or talent
ab·ject (ab'jekt, ab jekt') *adj.* [< L. *ab-*, from + *jacere*, to throw] **1.** miserable; wretched **2.** degraded —**ab·jec'tion** *n.*
ab·jure (ab joor') *vt.* **-jured', -jur'ing** [< L. *ab-*, away + *jurare*, to swear] to give up (rights, allegiance, etc.) on oath; renounce —**ab·ju·ra·tion** (ab'joo rā'shən) *n.*
ab·la·tive (ab'lə tiv) *n.* [< L. *ablatus*, carried away] the case in Latin, etc. expressing removal, direction from, cause, etc.
a·blaze (ə blāz') *adj.* **1.** flaming **2.** very excited
a·ble (ā'b'l) *adj.* **a'bler, a'blest** [< L. *habere*, have] **1.** having enough power, skill, etc. (*to do* something) **2.** talented —**a'bly** *adv.*
-able [< L.] *a suffix meaning:* **1.** able to *[durable]* **2.** capable of being *[drinkable]* **3.** worthy of being *[lovable]* **4.** having qualities of *[comfortable]* **5.** tending to *[peaceable]*
a'ble-bod'ied *adj.* healthy and strong
ab·lu·tion (ab lōō'shən) *n.* [< L. *ab-*, off + *luere*, to wash] a washing of the body, esp. as

a religious ceremony —**ab·lu′tion·ar′y** *adj.*

-ably *an adv.-forming suffix corresponding to* **-ABLE**

ab·ne·gate (ab′nə gāt′) *vt.* **-gat′ed, -gat′ing** [< L. *ab-*, from + *negare*, deny] to deny and refuse; renounce —**ab′ne·ga′tion** *n.*

ab·nor·mal (ab nôr′m'l) *adj.* not normal, average, or typical —**ab·nor′mal·ly** *adv.*

ab·nor·mal·i·ty (ab′nôr mal′ə tē) *n.* **1.** an abnormal condition **2.** *pl.* **-ties** an abnormal thing

a·board (ə bôrd′) *adv., prep.* **1.** on or in (a ship, airplane, etc.) **2.** alongside

a·bode (ə bōd′) *pt. and pp. of* ABIDE —*n.* a home; residence

a·bol·ish (ə bäl′ish) *vt.* [< L. *abolere*, destroy] to do away with; put an end to

ab·o·li·tion (ab′ə lish′ən) *n.* **1.** an abolishing or being abolished **2.** [*occas.* A-] the abolishing of slavery in the U.S. —**ab′o·li′tion·ist** *n.*

A-bomb (ā′bäm) *n. same as* ATOMIC BOMB

a·bom·i·na·ble (ə bäm′ə nə b'l) *adj.* **1.** vile **2.** very bad —**a·bom′i·na·bly** *adv.*

a·bom·i·nate (ə bäm′ə nāt′) *vt.* **-nat′ed, -nat′-ing** [< L. *abominari*, regard as an ill omen] **1.** to hate; loathe **2.** to dislike greatly —**a·bom′i-na′tion** *n.*

ab·o·rig·i·nal (ab′ə rij′ə n'l) *adj.* **1.** existing (in a place) from the beginning; first **2.** of aborigines —*n.* an aborigine

ab′o·rig′i·ne′ (-ə nē′) *n., pl.* **-nes′** [L. < *ab-*, from + *origine*, the beginning] any of the first known inhabitants of a region

a·bort (ə bôrt′) *vi.* [< L. *aboriri*, miscarry] **1.** to have a miscarriage **2.** to fail to be completed —*vt.* **1.** to cause to have an abortion **2.** to cut short

a·bor·tion (ə bôr′shən) *n.* expulsion of a fetus from the womb before it is developed enough to survive —**a·bor′tion·ist** *n.*

a·bor′tive *adj.* **1.** unsuccessful; fruitless **2.** rudimentary **3.** causing abortion

a·bound (ə bound′) *vi.* [< L. *ab-*, away + *undare*, rise in waves] to be plentiful (often with *in* or *with*)

a·bout (ə bout′) *adv.* [< OE. *onbutan*, around] **1.** all around **2.** near **3.** in the opposite direction **4.** nearly [*about* ready] —*adj.* astir [he is up and *about*] —*prep.* **1.** on all sides of **2.** near to **3.** with **4.** intending; on the point of **5.** concerning

a·bout′-face′ (-fās′, -fās′) *n.* a reversal of position or opinion —*vi.* **-faced′, -fac′ing** to turn in the opposite direction

a·bove (ə buv′) *adv.* [OE. *abufan*] **1.** in a higher place; up **2.** earlier (in a piece of writing) **3.** higher in rank, etc. —*prep.* **1.** over; on top of **2.** better or more than [*above* average] —*adj.* mentioned earlier

a·bove′board′ *adv., adj.* without dishonesty

ab·ra·ca·dab·ra (ab′rə kə dab′rə) *n.* [LL.] **1.** a word supposed to have magic powers, used in incantations, etc. **2.** gibberish

ab·rade (ə brād′) *vt.* **-rad′ed, -rad′ing** [< L. *ab-*, away + *radere*, scrape] to rub off; wear away by scraping —**ab·rad′er** *n.*

A·bra·ham (ā′brə ham′) *Bible* the first patriarch of the Hebrews

ab·ra·sion (ə brā′zhən) *n.* **1.** an abrading **2.** an abraded spot

ab·ra′sive (-siv) *adj.* causing abrasion —*n.* a substance used for grinding, polishing, etc.

a·breast (ə brest′) *adv., adj.* **1.** side by side **2.** informed (*of*) or familiar (*with*)

a·bridge (ə brij′) *vt.* **a·bridged′, a·bridg′ing** [< L. *ad-*, to + *brevis*, short] **1.** to shorten, lessen, or curtail **2.** to shorten (a book, talk,

etc.) by using fewer words —**a·bridg′ment, a·bridge′ment** *n.*

a·broad (ə brôd′) *adv.* **1.** far and wide **2.** current [*rumors are abroad*] **3.** outdoors **4.** to or in foreign countries

ab·ro·gate (ab′rə gāt′) *vt.* **-gat′ed, -gat′ing** [< L. *ab-*, away + *rogare*, propose] to cancel or repeal; annul —**ab′ro·ga′tion** *n.*

a·brupt (ə brupt′) *adj.* [< L. *ab-*, off + *rumpere*, break] **1.** sudden; unexpected **2.** brusque **3.** very steep **4.** jerky and disconnected —**a·brupt′ly** *adv.*

Ab·sa·lom (ab′sə ləm) *Bible* David's favorite son, who rebelled against him

ab·scess (ab′ses) *n.* [< L. *ab(s)-*, from + *cedere*, go] an inflamed area in body tissues, containing pus —*vi.* to form an abscess

ab·scis·sa (ab sis′ə) *n., pl.* **-sas, -sae** (-ē) [< L. *ab-*, off + *scindere*, to cut] *Math.* the horizontal distance of a point from the vertical axis

ab·scond (ab skänd′) *vi.* [< L. *ab(s)-*, from + *condere*, to hide] to leave hastily and secretly to escape the law —**ab·scond′er** *n.*

ab·sence (ab′s'ns) *n.* **1.** a being absent **2.** the time of this **3.** a lack

ab·sent (ab′s'nt) *adj.* [< L. *ab-*, away + *esse*, to be] **1.** not present; away **2.** not existing; lacking **3.** not attentive —*vt.* (ab sent′) to keep (oneself) away

ab·sen·tee (ab′s'n tē′) *n.* one who is absent, as from work —*adj.* of, by, or from one who is absent —**ab′sen·tee′ism** *n.*

ab′sent-mind′ed *adj.* **1.** not attentive; preoccupied **2.** habitually forgetful

ab·sinthe, ab·sinth (ab′sinth) *n.* [Fr., ult. < OPer.] a green, bitter liqueur

ab·so·lute (ab′sə lōōt′) *adj.* [see ABSOLVE] **1.** perfect; complete **2.** not mixed; pure **3.** unrestricted [*absolute* rule] **4.** positive; definite **5.** actual; real [an *absolute* truth] **6.** not relative —*n.* something that is absolute —**the Absolute** *Philos.* that which is thought of as existing completely in and by itself —**ab′so·lute′ly** *adv.*

absolute zero the hypothetical point at which matter would have neither molecular motion nor heat: theoretically equal to −273.15°C or −459.67°F

ab·so·lu·tion (ab′sə lōō′shən) *n.* **1.** a formal freeing (*from* guilt); forgiveness **2.** remission (*of* sin or its penalty)

ab·so·lut·ism (ab′sə lōō′tiz'm) *n.* government in which the ruler has unlimited powers; despotism —**ab′so·lut′ist** *n., adj.*

ab·solve (əb zälv′, ab-; -sälv′) *vt.* **-solved′, -solv′ing** [< L. *ab-*, from + *solvere*, to loose] **1.** to free from guilt, a duty, etc. **2.** to give religious absolution to

ab·sorb (əb zôrb′, -sôrb′) *vt.* [< L. *ab-*, from + *sorbere*, drink in] **1.** to suck up; take in **2.** to interest greatly **3.** to pay for (costs, etc.) **4.** to take in and not reflect or recoil —**ab·sorb′ing** *adj.*

ab·sorb′ent *adj.* capable of absorbing moisture, etc. —*n.* a thing that absorbs —**ab·sorb′-en·cy** *n.*

ab·sorp·tion (əb zôrp′shən, -sôrp′-) *n.* **1.** an absorbing **2.** great interest —**ab·sorp′tive** *adj.*

ab·stain (əb stān′) *vi.* [< L. *ab(s)-*, from + *tenere*, hold] to do without voluntarily; refrain —**ab·sten′tion** (-sten′shən) *n.*

ab·ste·mi·ous (əb stē′mē əs) *adj.* [< L. *ab(s)-*, from + *temetum*, strong drink] eating and drinking sparingly

ab·sti·nence (ab′stə nəns) *n.* an abstaining from some or all food, liquor, etc. —**ab′sti·nent** *adj.*

ab·stract (ab strakt′, ab′strakt) *adj.* [< L.

ab(s)-, from + *trahere*, to draw] 1. thought of apart from material objects 2. expressing a quality so thought of 3. theoretical 4. *Art* not representing things realistically —*n.* (ab'strakt) a summary —*vt.* 1. (ab strakt') to take away 2. (ab'strakt) to summarize —**in the abstract** in theory as apart from practice —**ab·stract'ly** *adv.*

ab·stract'ed *adj.* absent-minded

ab·strac'tion *n.* 1. an abstracting 2. an abstract idea 3. mental withdrawal 4. an abstract painting, sculpture, etc.

ab·struse (ab strōōs') *adj.* [< L. *ab*(s)-, away + *trudere*, to thrust] hard to understand

ab·surd (əb surd') *adj.* [< Fr. < L. *absurdus*, not to be heard of] so unreasonable as to be ridiculous —**ab·surd'i·ty** *n., pl.* -ties —**ab·surd'ly** *adv.*

a·bun·dance (ə bun'dəns) *n.* [see ABOUND] a great supply; more than enough —**a·bun'dant** *adj.* —**a·bun'dant·ly** *adv.*

a·buse (ə byōōz') *vt.* **a·bused'**, **a·bus'ing** [< L. *ab-*, away + *uti*, to use] 1. to use wrongly 2. to mistreat 3. to insult; revile —*n.* (ə byōōs') 1. wrong use 2. mistreatment 3. a corrupt practice 4. insulting language —**a·bu'sive** (-byōōs'iv) *adj.* —**a·bu'sive·ly** *adv.*

a·but (ə but') *vi.* **a·but'ted**, **a·but'ting** [< OFr. *a-*, to + *bout*, end] to border (*on*) —*vt.* to border on

a·but'ment *n.* 1. an abutting 2. a part supporting an arch, bridge, etc.

a·bys·mal (ə biz'm'l) *adj.* 1. of or like an abyss 2. very bad —**a·bys'mal·ly** *adv.*

a·byss (ə bis') *n.* [< Gr. *a-*, without + *byssos*, bottom] 1. a bottomless gulf 2. anything too deep for measurement

-ac [< Fr. < Gr.] *a suffix meaning:* 1. relating to [*cardiac*] 2. affected by [*maniac*]

Ac *Chem.* actinium

AC, A.C., a.c. alternating current

a·ca·cia (ə kā'shə) *n.* [< Gr. *akakia*, thorny tree] 1. a tree or shrub with yellow or white flower clusters 2. the locust tree

ac·a·dem·ic (ak'ə dem'ik) *adj.* 1. of academies or colleges 2. having to do with liberal arts rather than technical education 3. formal 4. merely theoretical —**ac'a·dem'i·cal·ly** *adv.*

a·cad·e·mi·cian (ə kad'ə mish'ən, ak'ə də-) *n.* a member of an academy (sense 3)

a·cad·e·my (ə kad'ə mē) *n., pl.* -mies [< Gr. *akadēmeia*, place where Plato taught] 1. a private secondary school 2. a school offering training in a special field 3. an association of scholars, writers, etc. for advancing an art or science

a·can·thus (ə kan'thəs) *n., pl.* -thus·es, -thi (-thī) [< Gr. *akē*, a point] 1. a plant with lobed, often spiny leaves 2. *Archit.* a representation of these leaves

a cap·pel·la (ä' kə pel'ə) [It., in chapel style] unaccompanied: said of choral singing

ac·cede (ak sēd') *vi.* **-ced'ed**, **-ced'ing** [< L. *ad-*, to + *cedere*, to yield] 1. to enter upon the duties (of an office) 2. to assent; agree (*to*) —**ac·ced'ence** *n.*

ac·cel·er·an·do (ak sel'ə ran'dō, -rän'-) *adv., adj.* [It.] *Music* with gradually quickening tempo

ac·cel·er·ate (ək sel'ə rāt', ak-) *vt.* **-at'ed**, **-at'ing** [< L. *ad-*, to + *celerare*, hasten] 1. to increase the speed of 2. to cause to happen sooner —*vi.* to go faster —**ac·cel'er·a'tion** *n.* —**ac·cel'er·a'tor** *n.*

ac·cent (ak'sent) *n.* [Fr. < L. *ad-*, to + *canere*, sing] 1. the emphasis given a spoken syllable or word 2. a mark showing such emphasis or indicating pronunciation 3. a distinguishing manner of pronouncing [*an Irish accent*] 4. *Music & Verse* rhythmic stress —*vt.* (*also* ak sent') 1. to emphasize; stress 2. to mark with an accent

ac·cen·tu·ate (ak sen'chŏŏ wāt') *vt.* **-at'ed**, **-at'ing** to accent; esp., to emphasize —**ac·cen'·tu·a'tion** *n.*

ac·cept (ək sept') *vt.* [< L. *ad-*, to + *capere*, take] 1. to receive willingly 2. to approve 3. to agree to 4. to believe in 5. to say "yes" to 6. to agree to pay —**ac·cept'er** *n.*

ac·cept'a·ble *adj.* satisfactory —**ac·cept'a·bil'·i·ty** *n.* —**ac·cept'a·bly** *adv.*

ac·cept'ance *n.* 1. an accepting 2. approval 3. assent 4. a promise to pay

ac·cept·ed (ək sep'tid) *adj.* generally regarded as true, proper, etc.; conventional

ac·cess (ak'ses) *n.* [see ACCEDE] 1. approach or means of approach 2. the right to enter, use, etc. 3. an outburst

ac·ces'si·ble *adj.* 1. easy to approach or enter 2. obtainable 3. open to the influence of (with *to*) —**ac·ces'si·bil'i·ty** *n.*

ac·ces·sion (ak sesh'ən) *n.* 1. an attaining to a throne, power, etc.) 2. assent 3. *a*) increase by addition *b*) an item added

ac·ces·so·ry (ək ses'ər ē, ak-) *adj.* [see ACCEDE] 1. extra; additional 2. helping in an unlawful act —*n., pl.* -ries 1. something extra or complementary 2. one who, though absent, helps another to break the law

ac·ci·dent (ak'sə dənt) *n.* [< L. *ad-*, to + *cadere*, to fall] 1. an unintended happening 2. a mishap 3. chance

ac'ci·den'tal (-den't'l) *adj.* happening by chance —**ac'ci·den'tal·ly** *adv.*

ac·claim (ə klām') *vt.* [< L. *ad-*, to + *clamare*, to cry out] to greet or announce with loud approval; hail —*n.* loud approval

ac·cla·ma·tion (ak'lə mā'shən) *n.* 1. loud applause or strong approval 2. an approving vote by voice

ac·cli·mate (ak'lə māt', ə klī'mət) *vt., vi.* **-mat'ed**, **-mat'ing** [see AD- & CLIMATE] to accustom or become accustomed to a different climate or environment: also **ac·cli·ma·tize** (ə klī'mə tīz') **-tized'**, **-tiz'ing** —**ac'cli·ma'tion** *n.*

ac·cliv·i·ty (ə kliv'ə tē) *n., pl.* -ties [< L. *ad-*, up + *clivus*, hill] an upward slope

ac·co·lade (ak'ə lād') *n.* [Fr. < It. *accollare*, to embrace] an approving mention; award

ac·com·mo·date (ə käm'ə dāt') *vt.* **-dat'ed**, **-dat'ing** [< L. *ad-*, to + *com-*, with + *modus*, a measure] 1. to adjust; adapt 2. to supply (*with* something) 3. to do a favor for 4. to have room for

ac·com'mo·dat'ing *adj.* obliging

ac·com'mo·da'tion *n.* 1. adjustment 2. willingness to do favors 3. a help or convenience 4. [*pl.*] lodgings or space, as in a hotel, on a ship, etc.

ac·com·pa·ni·ment (ə kump'ni mənt) *n.* 1. anything that accompanies something else 2. an instrumental part supporting a solo voice, etc.

ac·com·pa·nist (ə kum'pə nist) *n.* one who plays an accompaniment

ac·com·pa·ny (ə kum'pə nē, ə kump'nē) *vt.* **-nied, -ny·ing** [see AD- & COMPANION] 1. to go with; attend 2. to add to; supplement 3. to play an accompaniment for or to

ac·com·plice (ə käm'plis) *n.* [< *a* (the article) + LL. *complex*, accomplice: see COMPLEX] one who knowingly helps another break a law

ac·com·plish (ə käm'plish) *vt.* [< L. *ad-*, intens. + *complere*, fill up] 2. an abstract idea

ac·com'plished *adj.* 1. done; completed 2. skilled; expert

ac·com'plish·ment *n.* 1. completion 2. work completed 3. a social art or skill

ac·cord (ə kôrd') *vt.* [< L. *ad-*, to + *cor*, heart] to grant —*vi.* to agree or harmonize (*with*) —*n.* mutual agreement; harmony —**of one's own accord** willingly

ac·cord'ance *n.* agreement; conformity —**ac·cord'ant** *adj.*

ac·cord'ing *adj.* in harmony —**according to** 1. in agreement with 2. as stated by

ac·cord'ing·ly *adv.* 1. in a way that is fitting and proper 2. therefore

ac·cor·di·on (ə kôr'dē ən) *n.* [< G., prob. < It. *accordare*, be in tune] a keyed musical instrument with a bellows which is pressed to force air through reeds —**ac·cor'di·on·ist** *n.*

ac·cost (ə kôst') *vt.* [< Fr. < L. *ad-*, to + *costa*, side] to approach and speak to, esp. boldly

ac·count (ə kount') *vt.* [< L. *computare*: see COMPUTE] to consider to be —*vi.* 1. to give a financial reckoning 2. to give reasons (*for*) —*n.* 1. a record of financial transactions 2. *same as:* *a*) BANK ACCOUNT *b*) CHARGE ACCOUNT 3. a credit customer 4. worth; importance 5. an explanation 6. a report —**on account** as partial payment —**on account of** because of —**on no account** under no circumstances —**take into account** to consider

ac·count'a·ble *adj.* 1. responsible; liable 2. explainable —**ac·count'a·bil'i·ty** *n.*

ac·count'ant (-'nt) *n.* one whose work is accounting —**ac·count'an·cy** *n.*

ac·count'ing *n.* the setting up and auditing of financial accounts

ac·cou·ter (ə kōōt'ər) *vt.* [Fr., prob. < L. *con-*, together + *suere*, sew] to equip or attire: also **ac·cou'tre -tred, -tring**

ac·cou'ter·ments (-mənts) *n.pl.* 1. clothes; dress 2. equipment; furnishings

ac·cred·it (ə kred'it) *vt.* [< Fr.: see CREDIT] 1. to authorize; certify 2. to believe in 3. to attribute

ac·cre·tion (ə krē'shən) *n.* [< L. *ad-*, to + *crescere*, to grow] 1. growth in size, esp. by addition 2. accumulated matter 3. a growing together of parts

ac·crue (ə krōō') *vi.* **-crued', -cru'ing** [see ACCRETION] to come as a natural growth or periodic increase, as interest on money

ac·cul·tu·ra·tion (ə kul'chə rā'shən) *n.* 1. adaptation to a new or different culture 2. mutual influence of different cultures

ac·cu·mu·late (ə kyōōm'yə lāt') *vt.*, *vi.* **-lat'ed, -lat'ing** [< L. *ad-*, to + *cumulare*, to heap] to pile up or collect —**ac·cu'mu·la'tion** *n.* —**ac·cu'mu·la'tive** *adj.*

ac·cu·ra·cy (ak'yər ə sē) *n.* the state of being accurate; precision

ac·cu·rate (ak'yər it) *adj.* [< L. *ad-*, to + *cura*, care] 1. careful and exact 2. free from errors —**ac'cu·rate·ly** *adv.*

ac·curs·ed (ə kur'sid, -kurst') *adj.* 1. under a curse 2. damnable Also **ac·curst'**

ac·cu·sa·tion (ak'yə zā'shən) *n.* 1. an accusing 2. what one is accused of

ac·cu·sa·tive (ə kyōō'zə tiv) *adj.* designating or in the case, as in Latin, of an object of a verb or preposition —*n.* 1. the accusative case 2. a word in this case

ac·cuse (ə kyōōz') *vt.* **-cused', -cus'ing** [< L. *ad-*, to + *causa*, a lawsuit] 1. to blame 2. to bring charges against (*of* breaking the law) —**the accused** *Law* the person charged with committing a crime —**ac·cus'er** *n.*

ac·cus·tom (ə kus'təm) *vt.* to make familiar by custom, habit, or use; habituate (*to*)

ac·cus'tomed *adj.* 1. customary; usual 2. used (*to*); in the habit of

ace (ās) *n.* [< L. *as*, unit] 1. a playing card, etc. with one spot 2. a point, as in tennis, won by a single stroke 3. an expert, esp. in combat flying —*adj.* [Colloq.] first-rate

ace in the hole [Slang] any advantage held in reserve

a·cerb (ə surb') *adj.* [< Fr. < L. *acerbus*, bitter] 1. sour in taste 2. sharp or bitter in temper, language, etc. —**a·cer·bi·ty** (ə sur'bə tē) *n.*

ac·e·tate (as'ə tāt') *n.* 1. a salt or ester of acetic acid 2. a fabric, etc. made of an acetate of cellulose

a·ce·tic (ə sēt'ik) *adj.* [< L. *acetum*, vinegar] of the sharp, sour liquid (**acetic acid**) found in vinegar

a·cet·i·fy (ə set'ə fī', -sēt'-) *vt.*, *vi.* **-fied', -fy'ing** to change into vinegar or acetic acid

ac·e·tone (as'ə tōn') *n.* [< ACETIC] a colorless liquid used as a solvent

a·cet·y·lene (ə set''l ēn') *n.* [< ACETIC + -YL + -ENE] a gas used for lighting and, with oxygen in a blowtorch, for welding, etc.

ac·e·tyl·sal·i·cyl·ic acid (ə set''l sal'ə sil'ik) aspirin

ache (āk) *vi.* **ached, ach'ing** [OE. *acan*] 1. to have or give dull, steady pain 2. [Colloq.] to yearn —*n.* a dull, continuous pain —**ach'y** *adj.* **-i·er, -i·est**

a·chene (ā kēn') *n.* [< Gr. *a-*, not + *chainein*, to gape] any small, dry, one-seeded fruit that ripens without bursting

a·chieve (ə chēv') *vt.* **a·chieved', a·chiev'ing** [< L. *ad-*, to + *caput*, head] 1. to do successfully 2. to get by effort —**a·chiev'a·ble** *adj.* —**a·chiev'er** *n.*

a·chieve'ment *n.* 1. an achieving 2. a thing achieved, esp. by skill, work, etc.; feat

A·chil·les (ə kil'ēz) *Gr. Myth.* Greek hero killed in the Trojan War

Achilles' heel (one's) vulnerable spot

ach·ro·mat·ic (ak'rə mat'ik) *adj.* [< Gr. *a-*, without + *chrōma*, color] refracting white light without breaking it up into its component colors

ac·id (as'id) *adj.* [< L. *acidus*, sour] 1. sour; sharp; tart 2. of an acid —*n.* 1. a sour substance 2. [Slang] *same as* LSD 3. *Chem.* any compound that reacts with a base to form a salt —**a·cid·i·ty** (ə sid'ə tē) *n.*, *pl.* **-ties** —**ac'id·ly** *adv.*

a·cid'i·fy' (-ə fī') *vt.*, *vi.* **-fied', -fy'ing** 1. to make or become sour or acid 2. to change into an acid —**a·cid'i·fi·ca'tion** *n.*

ac·i·do·sis (as'ə dō'sis) *n.* a condition in which the body's alkali reserve is below normal

acid test a crucial, final test

a·cid·u·late (ə sij'ōō lāt') *vt.* **-lat'ed, -lat'ing** to make somewhat acid or sour

a·cid'u·lous (-ləs) *adj.* 1. somewhat acid or sour 2. somewhat sarcastic

-acious [< L.] *a suffix meaning* inclined to, full of [*tenacious*]

-acity *a n.-forming suffix corresponding to* -ACIOUS [*tenacity*]

ac·knowl·edge (ək näl'ij) *vt.* **-edged, -edg·ing** [see KNOWLEDGE] 1. to admit as true 2. to recognize the authority or claims of 3. to respond to (a greeting, etc.) 4. to express thanks for 5. to state that one has received (a letter, etc.) —**ac·knowl'edg·ment, ac·knowl'edge·ment** *n.*

ac·me (ak′mē) *n.* [< Gr. *akmē,* a point, top] the highest point

ac·ne (ak′nē) *n.* [? < Gr.: see prec.] a skin disease causing pimples on the face, etc.

ac·o·lyte (ak′ə līt′) *n.* [< Gr. *akolouthos,* follower] **1.** an altar boy **2.** an attendant

ac·o·nite (ak′ə nīt′) *n.* [< Gr.] **1.** a poisonous plant with hoodlike flowers **2.** a drug made from its roots

a·corn (ā′kôrn′) *n.* [< OE. *æcern,* nut] the nut of the oak tree

acorn squash a kind of squash, acorn-shaped with a dark-green, ridged skin

a·cous·tic (ə kōōs′tik) *adj.* [< Fr. < Gr. *akouein,* to hear] **1.** having to do with hearing or acoustics **2.** designating a musical instrument whose tones are not electronically altered Also **a·cous′ti·cal** —**a·cous′ti·cal·ly** *adv.*

a·cous′tics (-tiks) *n.pl.* **1.** the qualities of a room, etc. that have to do with how clearly sounds can be heard in it **2.** [*with sing. v.*] the science dealing with sound

ac·quaint (ə kwānt′) *vt.* [< L. *ad,* to + *cognoscere,* know] **1.** to inform **2.** to make familiar (*with*)

ac·quaint′ance *n.* **1.** knowledge got from personal experience **2.** a person whom one knows slightly —**ac·quaint′ance·ship′** *n.*

ac·qui·esce (ak′wē es′) *vi.* -esced′, -esc′ing [< Fr. < L. *ad-,* to + *quiescere,* be at rest] to consent without protest —**ac′qui·es′cence** *n.* —**ac′qui·es′cent** *adj.*

ac·quire (ə kwīr′) *vt.* -quired′, -quir′ing [< L. *ad-,* to + *quaerere,* seek] **1.** to gain by one's own efforts **2.** to get as one's own —**ac·quire′ment** *n.*

ac·qui·si·tion (ak′wə zish′ən) *n.* **1.** an acquiring or being acquired **2.** something acquired

ac·quis·i·tive (ə kwiz′ə tiv) *adj.* eager to acquire money, etc.; grasping

ac·quit (ə kwit′) *vt.* -quit′ted, -quit′ting [< L. *ad,* to + *quietare,* to quiet] **1.** to release from a duty, etc. **2.** to declare not guilty of a charge **3.** to conduct (oneself); behave —**ac·quit′tal** *n.*

a·cre (ā′kər) *n.* [OE. *æcer,* field] **1.** a measure of land, 43,560 sq. ft. **2.** [*pl.*] lands

a·cre·age (ā′kər ij) *n.* acres collectively

ac·rid (ak′rid) *adj.* [< L. *acris,* sharp] **1.** sharp or bitter to the taste or smell **2.** sharp in speech, etc. —**ac′rid·ly** *adv.*

ac·ri·mo·ny (ak′rə mō′nē) *n., pl.* -nies [< L. *acer,* sharp] bitterness or harshness of manner or speech —**ac′ri·mo′ni·ous** *adj.*

ac·ro·bat (ak′rə bat′) *n.* [< Fr. < Gr. *akrobatos,* walking on tiptoe] a skilled gymnast, tumbler, etc. —**ac′ro·bat′ic** *adj.*

ac′ro·bat′ics (-iks) *n.pl.* [*also with sing. v.*] **1.** an acrobat's tricks **2.** any tricks requiring great skill

ac·ro·nym (ak′rə nim) *n.* [< Gr. *akros,* at the end + *onyma,* name] a word formed from the first (or first few) letters of several words, as *radar*

a·crop·o·lis (ə kräp′′l is) *n.* [< Gr. *akros,* at the top + *polis,* city] the fortified hill of an ancient Greek city, esp. [A-] that of Athens, on which the Parthenon was built

a·cross (ə krôs′) *adv.* **1.** crosswise **2.** from one side to the other —**prep. 1.** from one side to the other of **2.** on the other side of **3.** into contact with by chance

a·cros·tic (ə krôs′tik) *n.* [< Gr. *akros,* at the end + *stichos,* verse] a poem, etc. in which certain letters in each line, as the first or last, spell out a word, motto, etc.

a·cryl·ic fiber (ə kril′ik) [< ACR(ID) + -YL + -IC] any of a group of synthetic fibers made into fabrics

act (akt) *n.* [< Fr. < L. *agere,* to do] **1.** a thing done **2.** a doing **3.** a law **4.** a main division of a drama or opera **5.** a short performance on a variety program **6.** something done merely for show —*vt.* **1.** to play the part of **2.** to perform in (a play) —*vi.* **1.** to perform on the stage **2.** to behave **3.** to function **4.** to have an effect (*on*) **5.** to appear to be —**act up** [Colloq.] to misbehave

ACTH [*a*(*dreno*)*c*(*ortico*)*t*(*rophic*) *h*(*ormone*)] a pituitary hormone that stimulates the hormone production of the adrenal cortex

act·ing (ak′tiŋ) *adj.* **1.** functioning **2.** temporarily doing the duties of another —*n.* the art of an actor

ac·tin·ic (ak tin′ik) *adj.* [< Gr. *aktis,* ray] having to do with violet or ultraviolet rays that produce chemical changes

ac·tin·i·um (ak tin′ē əm) *n.* [< Gr. *aktis,* ray] a radioactive chemical element found in pitchblende: symbol, Ac

ac·tion (ak′shən) *n.* **1.** the doing of something **2.** a thing done **3.** [*pl.*] behavior **4.** an effect, as of a drug **5.** the way of working, as of a machine **6.** the moving parts, as of a gun **7.** the happenings, as in a story **8.** a lawsuit **9.** military combat **10.** [Slang] activity or excitement

ac·ti·vate (ak′tə vāt′) *vt.* -vat′ed, -vat′ing **1.** to make active **2.** to put (a military unit) on an active status **3.** to make radioactive **4.** to aerate (sewage) so as to purify it —**ac′ti·va′tion** *n.* —**ac′ti·va′tor** *n.*

activated carbon a highly porous carbon that can adsorb gases, vapors, and colloidal particles

ac·tive (ak′tiv) *adj.* **1.** acting, working, etc. **2.** causing motion or change **3.** lively **4.** requiring action [*active* sports] **5.** *Gram.* indicating the voice of a verb whose subject performs the action —*n. Gram.* the active voice —**ac′tive·ly** *adv.*

ac·tiv·ism (ak′tə viz′m) *n.* the policy of taking direct action, esp. for political or social ends —**ac′tiv·ist** *adj., n.*

ac·tiv·i·ty (ak tiv′ə tē) *n., pl.* -ties **1.** a being active **2.** liveliness **3.** a specific action [*outside activities*]

ac·tor (ak′tər) *n.* **1.** one who does something **2.** one who acts in plays, movies, etc. —**ac′tress** *n.fem.*

ac·tu·al (ak′chōō wal) *adj.* [< L. *agere,* to do] **1.** existing in reality **2.** existing at the time

ac′tu·al′i·ty (-wal′ə tē) *n.* **1.** reality **2.** *pl.* -ties an actual thing; fact

ac′tu·al·ize′ (-wə līz′) *vt.* -ized′, -iz′ing to make actual or real, or realistic

ac′tu·al·ly *adv.* really

ac·tu·ar·y (ak′chōō wer′ē) *n., pl.* -ies [< L. *actuarius,* a clerk] one who figures insurance risks, premiums, etc. —**ac′tu·ar′i·al** *adj.*

ac·tu·ate (ak′chōō wāt′) *vt.* -at′ed, -at′ing **1.** to put into action **2.** to cause to take action —**ac′tu·a′tion** *n.* —**ac′tu·a′tor** *n.*

a·cu·i·ty (ə kyōō′ə tē) *n.* [< Fr. < L. *acus,* a needle] keenness of thought or vision

a·cu·men (ə kyōō′mən) *n.* [< L. *acuere,* sharpen] keenness of mind; shrewdness

ac·u·punc·ture (ak′yoo puŋk′chər) *n.* [< L. *acus,* needle + PUNCTURE] the piercing of the body with needles to treat disease or relieve pain

a·cute (ə kyōōt′) *adj.* [< L. *acuere,* sharpen] **1.** sharp-pointed **2.** keen of mind; shrewd **3.** sensitive [*acute* hearing] **4.** severe or sharp, as pain **5.** severe but not chronic [an *acute* disease] **6.** very serious **7.** less than 90° [*acute* angles]—a·cute′ness *n.*

acute accent a mark (′) showing the quality of a vowel, stress, etc.

-acy [ult. < Gr.] *a suffix meaning* quality, condition, etc. [*celibacy*]

ad (ad) *n.* [Colloq.] an advertisement

ad- [L.] *a prefix meaning* motion toward, addition to, nearness to: also spelled **a-, ac-, af-, ag-, an-,** etc. before certain consonants

A.D. [L. *Anno Domini,* in the year of the Lord] of the Christian era: used with dates

ad·age (ad′ij) *n.* [Fr. < L. *ad-,* to + *aio,* I say] an old saying; proverb

a·da·gio (ə dä′jō, -zhō) *adv.* [It. *ad agio,* at ease] *Music* slowly —*adj.* slow —*n., pl.* **-gios 1.** a slow movement in music **2.** a slow ballet dance

Ad·am (ad′əm) [Heb. < *ādām,* human being] *Bible* the first man

ad·a·mant (ad′ə mənt, -mant′) *n.* [< Gr. *a-,* not + *daman,* subdue] a very hard substance —*adj.* **1.** too hard to be broken **2.** inflexible; unyielding

Adam's apple the projection of cartilage in the front of the throat, esp. of a man

a·dapt (ə dapt′) *vt.* [< Fr. < L. *ad-,* to + *aptare,* to fit] **1.** to make suitable by changing **2.** to adjust (oneself) to new circumstances —*vi.* to adjust oneself —a·dapt′a·bil′i·ty *n.* —a·dapt′a·ble *adj.* —a·dapt′er, a·dap′tor *n.*

ad·ap·ta·tion (ad′əp tā′shən) *n.* **1.** an adapting **2.** a thing or change resulting from adapting

a·dap·tive (ə dap′tiv) *adj.* **1.** showing adaptation **2.** able to adapt —a·dap′tive·ly *adv.*

add (ad) *vt.* [< L. *ad-,* to + *dare,* give] **1.** to join (*to*) so as to increase **2.** to state further **3.** to combine (numbers) into a sum —*vi.* **1.** to cause an increase (*to*) **2.** to find a sum —**add up to** to mean; signify

ad·dend (ad′end, ə dend′) *n.* [< ADDENDUM] a number or quantity to be added to another

ad·den·dum (ə den′dəm) *n., pl.* **-da** (-də) [L.] a thing added, as an appendix to a book

ad·der (ad′ər) *n.* [< OE. *nædre*] **1.** a small poisonous snake of Europe; common viper **2.** any of various other snakes

ad·dict (ə dikt′) *vt.* [< L. *addicere,* give assent] **1.** to give (oneself) up (*to* some strong habit): usually in the passive **2.** to make an addict of —*n.* (ad′ikt) one addicted —ad·dic′tion *n.*

ad·di·tion (ə dish′ən) *n.* **1.** an adding to get a sum **2.** a joining of one thing to another **3.** a part added —**in addition (to)** besides —ad·di′tion·al *adj.*

ad·di·tive (ad′ə tiv) *adj.* **1.** of addition **2.** to be added —*n.* something added

ad·dle (ad′'l) *vt., vi.* **-dled, -dling** [< OE. *adela,* dirt] **1.** to make or become rotten: said of an egg **2.** to make or become confused

ad·dress (ə dres′; *for n., esp.* 2 & 3, *also* ad′res) *vt.* [< L. *dirigere,* to direct] **1.** to direct (words *to*) **2.** to speak or write to **3.** to write the destination on (a letter, etc.) **4.** to apply or direct, as oneself —*n.* **1.** a speech **2.** the place where one lives or gets mail **3.** the destination indicated as on mail **4.** social skill and tact

ad·dress·ee (ad′res ē′) *n.* one to whom a letter, package, etc. is addressed

ad·duce (ə dōōs′, -dyōōs′) *vt.* **-duced′, -duc′ing** [< L. *adducere,* lead to] to give as a reason or proof; cite

-ade [ult. < L.] *a suffix meaning:* **1.** the act of [*blockade*] **2.** participant(s) [*brigade*] **3.** drink made from [*lemonade*]

ad·e·noids (ad′'n oidz′) *n.pl.* lymphoid growths, sometimes enlarged, in the throat behind the nose

ad·ept (ə dept′; *for n.* ad′ept) *adj.* [< L. *ad-,* to + *apisci,* attain] highly skilled; expert —*n.* an expert —ad·ept′ly *adv.*

ad·e·quate (ad′ə kwət) *adj.* [< L. *ad-,* to + *aequare,* make equal] meeting requirements; sufficient or suitable —ad′e·qua·cy, ad′e·quate·ness *n.* —ad′e·quate·ly *adv.*

ad·here (əd hir′, ad-) *vi.* **-hered′, -her′ing** [< L. *ad-,* to + *haerere,* to stick] **1.** to stick fast; stay attached **2.** to stay firm in supporting or approving —ad·her′ence *n.*

ad·her·ent *adj.* sticking fast; attached —*n.* a supporter or follower (*of* a cause, etc.)

ad·he·sion (-hē′zhən) *n.* **1.** a sticking or being stuck together **2.** devoted attachment **3.** *Physics* the force holding together the molecules of unlike substances in surface contact

ad·he·sive (-siv, -ziv) *adj.* **1.** sticking **2.** gummed; sticky —*n.* an adhesive substance, as glue —ad·he′sive·ness *n.*

adhesive tape tape sticky on one side, used in bandaging, etc.

ad hoc (ad′ häk′) [L., to this] for this case only

a·dieu (ə dyōō′, -dōō′; *Fr.* ä dyö′) *interj., n., pl.* **a·dieus′; Fr. a·dieux′** (-dyö′) [Fr.] goodbye

ad in·fi·ni·tum (ad in′fə nīt′əm) [L.] endlessly; forever; without limit

a·di·os (ä dyôs′) *interj.* [Sp.] goodbye

ad·i·pose (ad′ə pōs′) *adj.* [< L. *adeps,* fat] of or like animal fat; fatty —*n.* animal fat —ad′i·pos′i·ty (-päs′ə tē) *n.*

adj. 1. adjective **2.** adjutant

ad·ja·cent (ə jā′s'nt) *adj.* [< L. *ad-,* to + *jacere,* to lie] near or close (*to*); adjoining —ad·ja′cen·cy *n.* —ad·ja′cent·ly *adv.*

ad·jec·tive (aj′ik tiv) *n.* [< L. *adjicere,* add to] a word, as *big,* qualifying a noun or other substantive —*adj.* of or like an adjective —ad′jec·ti′val (-tī′v′l) *adj.*

ad·join (ə join′) *vt., vi.* [< L. *ad-,* to + *jungere,* join] to be next to (another) —ad·join′ing *adj.*

ad·journ (ə jurn′) *vt., vi.* [< L. *ad-,* to + *diurnus,* daily] to close (a meeting, session, etc.) for a time —ad·journ′ment *n.*

ad·judge (ə juj′) *vt.* **-judged′, -judg′ing** [< L. *ad-,* to + *judicare,* to judge] **1.** to decide by law **2.** to order or sentence by law

ad·ju·di·cate (ə jōō′də kāt′) *vt.* **-cat′ed, -cat′-ing** [see prec.] *Law* to hear and decide (a case) —*vi.* to act as a judge (*in* or *on*)

ad·junct (aj′uŋkt) *n.* [see ADJOIN] a secondary or nonessential addition

ad·jure (ə joor′) *vt.* **-jured′, -jur′ing** [< L. *ad-,* to + *jurare,* swear] **1.** to charge solemnly as under oath **2.** to beseech —ad′ju·ra′tion *n.*

ad·just (ə just′) *vt.* [< L. *ad,* to + *juxta,* near] **1.** to change so as to make fit, suitable, etc. **2.** to regulate, as a watch **3.** to settle rightly **4.** to decide the amount of, as an insurance claim —*vi.* to adapt oneself —ad·just′a·ble *adj.* —ad·just′ment *n.*

ad·ju·tant (aj′ə tənt) *n.* [< L. *adjuvare,* to help] **1.** an assistant **2.** *Mil.* a staff officer who assists the commanding officer **3.** a large stork of India and Africa

Adjutant General the U.S. Army general in charge of records, circulars, etc.

ad-lib (ad′lib′) *vt., vi.* **-libbed′, -lib′bing** [< L. *ad libitum,* at pleasure] [Colloq.] to improvise; extemporize

ad·man (ad′man′) *n., pl.* **-men′** a man whose work is advertising: also **ad man**

ad·min·is·ter (əd min′ə stər) *vt.* [< L. *ad-,* to + *ministrare,* serve] **1.** to manage; direct **2.** to give out, as punishment **3.** to apply, as medicine **4.** to tender, as an oath Also **ad·min′is-**

trate′ (-strāt′), **-trat′ed, -trat′ing** —*vi.* to furnish help (*to*)

ad·min′is·tra′tion (-strā′shən) *n.* **1.** management **2.** [*often* A-] the executive officials, as of a government, and their policies **3.** their term of office **4.** the administering (*of* punishment, medicine, etc.) —**ad·min′is·tra′tive** *adj.*

ad·min′is·tra′tor (-tər) *n.* **1.** one who administers **2.** *Law* one appointed to settle an estate

ad·mi·ra·ble (ad′mər ə b′l) *adj.* deserving admiration; excellent —**ad′mi·ra·bly** *adv.*

ad·mi·ral (ad′mər əl) *n.* [< Ar. *amir a′ ālî*, high leader] **1.** the commanding officer of a fleet **2.** a high-ranking naval officer

ad′mi·ral·ty (-tē) *n., pl.* **-ties** [*often* A-] a governmental department in charge of naval affairs, as in England

ad·mi·ra·tion (ad′mə rā′shən) *n.* **1.** an admiring **2.** pleased approval

ad·mire (əd mīr′) *vt.* **-mired′, -mir′ing** [< L. *ad-*, at + *mirari*, wonder] **1.** to regard with wonder and delight **2.** to have high regard for —**ad·mir′er** *n.*

ad·mis·si·ble (əd mis′ə b′l) *adj.* that can or should be admitted, as evidence

ad·mis′sion (-mish′ən) *n.* **1.** an admitting or being admitted **2.** an entrance fee **3.** a conceding, confessing, etc. **4.** a thing conceded, confessed, etc.

ad·mit (əd mit′) *vt.* **-mit′ted, -mit′ting** [< L. *ad-*, to + *mittere*, send] **1.** to permit or entitle to enter or use **2.** to allow; leave room for **3.** to have room for; hold **4.** to concede or confess — *vi.* to allow (with *of*) —**ad·mit′tance** *n.*

ad·mit′ted·ly *adv.* by admission or agreement

ad·mix·ture (ad miks′chər) *n.* [< L. *ad-*, to + *miscere*, mix] **1.** a mixture **2.** a thing or ingredient mixed in

ad·mon·ish (əd män′ish) *vt.* [< L. *ad-*, to + *monere*, warn] **1.** to warn; caution **2.** to reprove mildly **3.** to exhort —**ad·mo·ni·tion** (ad′mə nish′ən) *n.*

ad nau·se·am (ad′ nô′zē əm, -shē-, -sē-) [L.] to the point of disgust

a·do (ə dōō′) *n.* fuss; trouble

a·do·be (ə dō′bē) *n.* [Sp.] **1.** unburnt, sun-dried brick **2.** clay used for this **3.** a building of adobe

ad·o·les·cence (ad′′l es′′ns) *n.* the time of life between puberty and maturity; youth

ad′o·les′cent *adj.* [< L. *ad-*, to + *alescere*, grow up] of, typical of, or in adolescence —*n.* an adolescent person; teen-ager

A·don·is (ə dän′is, -dō′nis) *Gr. Myth.* a young man loved by Aphrodite —*n.* a very handsome young man

a·dopt (ə däpt′) *vt.* [< L. *ad-*, to + *optare*, choose] **1.** to take legally into one's own family and raise as one's own child **2.** to take as one's own **3.** to choose or accept —**a·dopt′a·ble** *adj.* —**a·dop′tion** *n.*

a·dop·tive (ə däp′tiv) *adj.* being such through adoption [*adoptive* parents]

a·dor·a·ble (ə dôr′ə b′l) *adj.* **1.** worthy of adoration **2.** [Colloq.] delightful

ad·o·ra·tion (ad′ə rā′shən) *n.* **1.** a worshiping **2.** great love or devotion

a·dore (ə dôr′) *vt.* **a·dored′, a·dor′ing** [< L. *ad-*, to + *orare*, speak] **1.** to worship as divine **2.** to love greatly **3.** [Colloq.] to like very much — **a·dor′ing·ly** *adv.*

a·dorn (ə dôrn′) *vt.* [< L. *ad-*, to + *ornare*, to ornament] **1.** to add beauty or distinction to **2.** to decorate —**a·dorn′ment** *n.*

ad·re·nal (ə drē′n′l) *adj.* [AD- + RENAL] **1.** near the kidneys **2.** of two endocrine glands

(**adrenal glands**) just above the kidneys —*n.* an adrenal gland

Ad·ren·al·in (ə dren′′l in) *a trademark for* EPINEPHRINE —*n.* [a-] epinephrine

a·drift (ə drift′) *adv., adj.* **1.** drifting **2.** devoid of aim or purpose

a·droit (ə droit′) *adj.* [Fr. *à*, to + *droit*, right] skillful and clever —**a·droit′ly** *adv.*

ad·sorb (ad sôrb′, -zôrb′) *vt.* [< L. *ad-*, to + *sorbere*, drink in] to collect, as a gas or liquid, in condensed form on a surface —**ad·sorp′tion** (-sôrp′shən, -zôrp′-) *n.*

ad·u·late (aj′ə lāt′) *vt.* **-lat′ed, -lat′ing** [< L. *adulari*, fawn upon] to flatter servilely —**ad′u·la′tion** *n.*

a·dult (ə dult′, ad′ult) *adj.* [see ADOLESCENT] grown-up; mature —*n.* a mature person, animal, or plant —**a·dult′hood** *n.*

a·dul·ter·ant (ə dul′tər ənt) *n.* an adulterating substance —*adj.* that adulterates

a·dul′ter·ate′ (-tə rāt′) *vt.* **-at′ed, -at′ing** [< L. *ad-*, to + *alter*, other] to make inferior, impure, etc. by adding a harmful or inferior substance —**a·dul′ter·a′tion** *n.*

a·dul·ter·y (ə dul′tər ē) *n., pl.* **-ies** [see ADULTERATE] sexual intercourse between a married person and another not the spouse — **a·dul′ter·er** *n.* —**a·dul′ter·ess** *n.fem.* —**a·dul′ter·ous** *adj.*

ad·um·brate (ad um′brāt, ad′əm brāt′) *vt.* **-brat·ed, -brat·ing** [< L. *ad-*, to + *umbra*, shade] **1.** to outline vaguely **2.** to overshadow —**ad′um·bra′tion** *n.*

adv. 1. adverb **2.** advertisement

ad·vance (əd vans′) *vt.* **-vanced′, -vanc′ing** [< L. *ab-*, from + *ante*, before] **1.** to bring forward **2.** to promote **3.** to propose **4.** to raise the rate of **5.** to lend —*vi.* **1.** to go forward **2.** to improve; progress **3.** to rise, as in rank —*n.* **1.** a moving forward **2.** an improvement **3.** a rise in value **4.** [*pl.*] approaches to get favor **5.** a payment before due —*adj.* **1.** in front [*advance* guard] **2.** beforehand —**in advance 1.** in front **2.** ahead of time —**ad·vance′ment** *n.*

ad·vanced′ *adj.* **1.** in front **2.** old **3.** ahead or higher in progress, price, etc.

ad·van·tage (əd van′tij) *n.* [< L. *ab ante*, from before] **1.** superiority **2.** a favorable circumstance, event, etc. **3.** gain; benefit —**take advantage of 1.** to use for one's own benefit **2.** to impose upon —**to advantage** to good effect —**ad·van·ta·geous** (ad′vən tā′jəs) *adj.*

Ad·vent (ad′vent) *n.* [< L. *ad-*, to + *venire*, come] **1.** the period including the four Sundays before Christmas **2.** [a-] a coming

ad·ven·ti·tious (ad′vən tish′əs) *adj.* [see ADVENT] not inherent; accidental

ad·ven·ture (əd ven′chər) *n.* [see ADVENT] **1.** an exciting or dangerous undertaking **2.** an unusual, stirring, often romantic experience —*vt., vi.* **-tured, -tur·ing** to risk; venture —**ad·ven′tur·ous, ad·ven′ture·some** *adj.* —**ad·ven′tur·ous·ly** *adv.*

ad·ven·tur·er *n.* **1.** one having or liking adventures **2.** *same as* SOLDIER OF FORTUNE **3.** one trying to get ahead by questionable schemes —**ad·ven′tur·ess** *n.fem.*

ad·verb (ad′vurb) *n.* [< L. *ad-*, to + *verbum*, word] a word used to modify a verb, adjective, or another adverb and expressing time, place, manner, degree, etc. —**ad·ver′bi·al** *adj., n.* —**ad·ver′bi·al·ly** *adv.*

ad·ver·sar·y (ad′vər ser′ē) *n., pl.* **-ies** [see ADVERT] an opponent; enemy

ad·verse (ad vurs′, ad′vurs) *adj.* [see ADVERT] **1.** opposed **2.** unfavorable **3.** opposite

ad·ver·si·ty (ad vur′sə tē) *n.* **1.** misfortune;

wretched or troubled state 2. *pl.* **-ties** a calamity; disaster

ad·vert (ad vurt′, əd-) *vi.* [< L. *ad-*, to + *vertere*, to turn] to call attention; refer (*to*)

ad·ver·tise (ad′vər tīz′) *vt.* **-tised′, -tis′ing** [see ADVERT] to describe or praise publicly, usually to promote for sale —*vi.* 1. to call public attention to things for sale 2. to ask (*for*) by public notice Also **advertize** —**ad′ver·tis′er** *n.*

ad·ver·tise·ment (ad′vər tīz′mənt, əd vur′tiz mənt) *n.* a public notice, usually paid for, as of things for sale: also **advertizement**

ad·vice (əd vīs′) *n.* [< L. *ad-*, to + *videre*, to look] 1. opinion given as to what to do; counsel 2. [*usually pl.*] information or report

ad·vis·a·ble (əd vīz′ə b'l) *adj.* to be advised; prudent —**ad·vis′a·bil′i·ty** *n.*

ad·vise (əd vīz′) *vt.* **-vised′, -vis′ing** 1. to give advice to; counsel 2. to offer as advice; recommend 3. to notify —*vi.* to consult (*with*) —**ad·vis′er, ad·vi′sor** *n.*

ad·vised′ *adj.* showing or resulting from thought or advice: now chiefly in *well-advised, ill-advised*

ad·vis·ed·ly (əd vīz′zid lē) *adv.* with due consideration; deliberately

ad·vise′ment (-vīz′mənt) *n.* careful consideration —**take under advisement** to consider carefully

ad·vi·so·ry (əd vī′zər ē) *adj.* 1. advising or empowered to advise 2. of advice —*n., pl.* **-ries** a warning about weather conditions

ad·vo·cate (ad′və kit, -kāt′) *n.* [< L. *ad-*, to + *vocare*, to call] one pleading for or supporting something —*vt.* (-kāt′) **-cat′ed, -cat′ing** to speak or write in support of —**ad′vo·ca·cy** (-kə sē) *n.*

advt. *pl.* **advts.** advertisement

adz, adze (adz) *n.* [OE. *adesa*] an axlike tool for trimming and smoothing wood

ae·gis (ē′jis) *n.* [< Gr. *aigis*, goatskin] 1. a protection 2. sponsorship; auspices

Ae·ne·as (i nē′əs) *Gr. & Rom. Myth.* a Trojan whose adventures are told in an epic poem (the **Aeneid**) by Virgil

ae·on (ē′ən, ē′än) *n. alt. sp. of* EON

aer·ate (er′āt′, ā′ər-) *vt.* **-at′ed, -at′ing** [AER(O)- + -ATE¹] 1. to expose to air 2. to charge (liquid) with gas, as in making soda water — **aer·a′tion** *n.*

aer·i·al (er′ē əl) *adj.* [< L. *aer*, air + -AL] 1. of or like air 2. unreal 3. of aircraft or flying —*n.* an antenna for radio or television

aer′i·al·ist (-ist) *n.* an acrobat who performs on a trapeze, tightrope, etc.

aer·ie (er′ē, ir′ē) *n.* [? < L. *ager*, field] the high nest of an eagle, etc.: also **aery**

aero- [< Gr. *aēr*, air] *a combining form meaning:* 1. air 2. aircraft or flying 3. gas

aer·o·bic (er ō′bik) *adj.* [< Gr. *aēr* + *bios*, life] able to live, grow, or take place only where free oxygen is present

aer·o·dy·nam·ics (er′ō dī nam′iks) *n.pl.* [*with sing. v.*] the branch of mechanics dealing with forces exerted by air or other gas in motion — **aer′o·dy·nam′ic** *adj.*

aer·o·nau·tics (er′ə nôt′iks) *n.pl.* [*with sing. v.*] [AERO- + Gr. *nautēs*, sailor + -ICS] the science of aircraft design or operation —**aer′o·nau′ti·cal** *adj.*

aer′o·plane′ (-plān′) *n. Brit. var. of* AIRPLANE

aer′o·sol′ (-sôl′, -säl′, -sōl′) *n.* [AERO- + SOL(UTION)] a suspension of colloidal particles in a gas —*adj.* of or from a container that aerates and ejects liquid as a spray or foam

aer·o·space (er′ō spās′) *n.* the earth's atmosphere and the space outside it

aes·thete (es′thēt′) *n.* [Gr. *aisthētēs*, one who perceives] a person who is or pretends to be highly sensitive to art and beauty

aes·thet·ic (-thet′ik) *adj.* 1. of aesthetics 2. of or sensitive to art and beauty —**aes·thet′i·cal·ly** *adv.*

aes·thet·ics (-iks) *n.pl.* [*with sing. v.*] the study or philosophy of art and beauty

a·far (ə fär′) *adv.* [Poet. or Archaic] at, to, or from a distance

af·fa·ble (af′ə b'l) *adj.* [< L. *ad-*, to + *fari*, speak] pleasant and friendly —**af′fa·bil′i·ty** *n.* —**af′fa·bly** *adv.*

af·fair (ə fer′) *n.* [< L. *ad-*, to + *facere*, do] 1. a thing to do 2. [*pl.*] matters of business 3. any matter, event, etc. 4. an amorous episode

af·fect (ə fekt′) *vt.* [< L. *ad-*, to + *facere*, do] 1. to have an effect on; influence 2. to move or stir the emotions of 3. to like to have, use, etc. 4. to make a pretense of feeling, liking, etc.

af·fec·ta·tion (af′ek tā′shən) *n.* 1. mere show or appearance; pretense 2. artificial behavior

af·fect′ed *adj.* 1. afflicted 2. influenced 3. emotionally moved 4. assumed for effect; artificial 5. behaving in an artificial way

af·fect′ing *adj.* emotionally moving

af·fec·tion (ə fek′shən) *n.* 1. fond or tender feeling 2. a disease

af·fec′tion·ate *adj.* tender and loving

af·fer·ent (af′ər ənt) *adj.* [< L. *ad-*, to + *ferre*, to bear] *Physiol.* bringing inward to a central part, as nerves: opposed to EFFERENT

af·fi·ance (ə fī′əns) *vt.* **-anced, -anc·ing** [< L. *ad-*, to + *fidere*, to trust] to betroth

af·fi·da·vit (af′ə dā′vit) *n.* [ML., he has made oath] a written statement made on oath, as before a notary public

af·fil·i·ate (ə fil′ē āt′) *vt.* **-at′ed, -at′ing** [< L. *ad-*, to + *filius*, son] 1. to take in as a member 2. to associate (oneself) —*vi.* to join —*n.* (-it) an affiliated person, club, etc.; member — **af·fil′i·a′tion** *n.*

af·fin·i·ty (ə fin′ə tē) *n., pl.* **-ties** [< L. *ad-*, to + *finis*, the end] 1. relationship by marriage 2. relationship; connection 3. a likeness implying common origin 4. a natural liking; also, mutual attraction 5. the attractive force between atoms

af·firm (ə furm′) *vt.* [< L. *ad-*, to + *firmare*, make firm] 1. to declare positively; assert 2. to confirm; ratify —*vi. Law* to declare solemnly but not under oath —**af·firm′a·ble** *adj.* —**af·fir·ma·tion** (af′ər mā′shən) *n.*

af·firm·a·tive (ə fur′mə tiv) *adj.* affirming; answering "yes" —*n.* 1. an expression of assent or agreement —the side upholding the proposition being debated

af·fix (ə fiks′) *vt.* [< L. *ad-*, to + *figere*, fasten] 1. to fasten; attach 2. to add at the end —*n.* (af′iks) 1. a thing affixed 2. a prefix or suffix

af·fla·tus (ə flāt′əs) *n.* [< L. *ad-*, to + *flare*, to blow] inspiration, as of an artist

af·flict (ə flikt′) *vt.* [< L. *ad-*, to + *fligere*, to strike] to cause pain or suffering to; distress greatly

af·flic·tion (ə flik′shən) *n.* 1. pain; suffering 2. any cause or source of this

af·flu·ence (af′lōo wəns) *n.* [< L. *ad-*, to + *fluere*, to flow] 1. abundance 2. wealth

af′flu·ent (-wənt) *adj.* 1. abundant 2. wealthy —*n.* a stream flowing into a river; tributary

af·ford (ə fôrd′) *vt.* [OE. *geforthian*, to advance] 1. to spare (money, time, etc.) without much inconvenience 2. to give; yield [*to afford pleasure*]

af·fray (ə frā′) *n.* [ME. *affrai* < OFr.] a noisy brawl; fray

af·front (ə frunt′) *vt.* [< L. *ad-*, to + *frons*, forehead] 1. to insult openly 2. to confront defiantly —*n.* an open insult

af·ghan (af′gan, -gən) *n.* [< *Afghanistan*] a crocheted or knitted blanket or shawl

a·fi·cio·na·do (ə fish′ə nä′dō) *n., pl.* -**dos** [Sp.] a devotee of some sport, etc.

a·field (ə fēld′) *adv.* 1. in, on, or to the field 2. away (from home); astray

a·fire (ə fīr′) *adv., adj.* on fire

a·flame (ə flām′) *adv., adj.* in flames

AFL-CIO American Federation of Labor and Congress of Industrial Organizations

a·float (ə flōt′) *adv.* 1. floating 2. at sea 3. flooded, as a ship's deck

a·flut·ter (ə flut′ər) *adv., adj.* in a flutter

a·foot (ə foot′) *adv.* 1. on foot 2. astir

a·fore (ə fôr′) *adv., prep., conj.* [Archaic or Dial. except in nautical use] before

a·fore′said′ (-sed′) *adj.* spoken of before

a·foul (ə foul′) *adv., adj.* in a collision or tangle —**run** (or **fall**) **afoul of** to get into trouble with

Afr. 1. Africa 2. African

a·fraid (ə frād′) *adj.* [ME. *affraied*] fearful; frightened: often merely indicating regret

a·fresh (ə fresh′) *adv.* again; anew

Af·ri·can (af′ri kən) *adj.* of Africa, its peoples, etc. —*n.* a native of Africa

Af·ri·kaans (af′ri känz′) *n.* [Afrik.] an official language of South Africa, developed from 17th-cent. Dutch

Af·ri·ka·ner (af′ri kän′ər) *n.* [Du.] a South African of European, esp. Dutch, ancestry

Af·ro (af′rō) *adj.* [< ff.] designating or of a bouffant hair style, as worn by some Negroes

Afro- *a combining form meaning* Africa(n)

Af·ro-A·mer·i·can (af′rō ə mer′ə kən) *adj.* of Negro Americans —*n.* a Negro American

aft (aft) *adv.* [< OE. *afta*, behind] at, near, or toward the stern of a ship or rear of an aircraft

af·ter (af′tər) *adv.* [OE. *æfter*] 1. behind 2. later —*prep.* 1. behind 2. later than 3. in search of 4. as a result of 5. in spite of 6. lower in rank or order than 7. in imitation of 8. for [named *after* Lincoln] 9. concerning —*conj.* following the time when —*adj.* 1. next; later 2. more aft

af′ter·birth′ *n.* the placenta and fetal membranes expelled after childbirth

af′ter·burn′er *n.* a device attached to some engines for burning or utilizing exhaust gases

af′ter·ef·fect′ *n.* a later or secondary effect

af′ter·glow′ *n.* a glow remaining, as after sunset

af′ter·math′ (-math′) *n.* [AFTER + OE. *mæth*, cutting of grass] a result or consequence, esp. an unpleasant one

af′ter·noon′ *n.* the time from noon to evening —*adj.* in the afternoon

af′ter·thought′ *n.* an added or later idea

af′ter·ward (-wərd) *adv.* later; subsequently: also **af′ter·wards**

Ag [L. *argentum*] *Chem.* silver

a·gain (ə gen′, -gān′) *adv.* [< OE. *on-*, up to + *gegn*, direct] 1. back into a former condition 2. once more 3. besides 4. on the other hand — **again and again** repeatedly

a·gainst (ə genst′) *prep.* [see prec.] 1. in opposition to 2. toward so as to strike 3. in contrast with 4. next to 5. in preparation for

Ag·a·mem·non (ag′ə mem′nän) *Gr. Myth.* commander in chief of the Greek army in the Trojan War

a·gape (ə gāp′) *adv., adj.* [A- + GAPE] 1. with the mouth wide open 2. wide open

ag·ate (ag′ət) *n.* [< Gr. *achatēs*] 1. a hard,

semiprecious stone with clouded coloring 2. a playing marble made of or like this

a·ga·ve (ə gä′vē) *n.* [< Gr. *agauos*, illustrious] a desert plant with tall flower stalks and thick, fleshy leaves

age (āj) *n.* [< L. *aetas*] 1. the length of time a person or thing has existed 2. a stage of life 3. old age 4. a historical or geological period 5. [*often pl.*] [Colloq.] a long time —*vi., vt.* **aged,** **ag′ing** or **age′ing** to grow or make old, or mature —**of age** of the age at which one has full legal rights

-age [< LL. *-aticum*] *a suffix meaning* act or state of, amount of, cost of, place of [usage, acreage, postage]

a·ged (ā′jid) *adj.* 1. old 2. (ājd) of the age of — **the aged** (ā′jid) old people

age·ism (āj′iz′m) *n.* [AGE + (RAC)ISM] discrimination against older people: also sp. **ag′-ism**

age′less *adj.* 1. not aging 2. eternal

a·gen·cy (ā′jən sē) *n., pl.* -**cies** [see AGENT] 1. action; power 2. means 3. a firm, etc. empowered to act for another 4. an administrative government division

a·gen·da (ə jen′də) *n., pl.* -**das** [< L. *agere*, do] a list of things to be dealt with, as at a meeting

a·gent (ā′jənt) *n.* [< L. *agere*, do] 1. an active force or substance producing an effect 2. a person, firm, etc. empowered to act for another 3. a representative of a government agency

age-old (āj′ōld′) *adj.* ages old; ancient

ag·er·a·tum (aj′ə rāt′əm) *n.* [< Gr. *a-*, not + *gēras*, old age] a plant with small, thick heads of usually bluish flowers

ag·glom·er·ate (ə gläm′ə rāt′) *vt., vi.* -**at′ed,** -**at′ing** [< L. *ad-*, to + *glomerare*, form into ball] to gather into a mass or ball —*adj.* (-ər it) gathered into a mass or ball —*n.* (-ər it) a jumbled heap, mass, etc.

ag·glu·ti·nate (ə gloot′'n it) *adj.* [< L. *ad-*, to + *gluten*, glue] stuck together —*vt., vi.* (-āt′) -**nat′ed,** -**nat′ing** to stick together —**ag·glu′ti·na′tion** *n.*

ag·gran·dize (ə gran′dīz′, ag′rən-) *vt.* -**dized′,** -**diz′ing** [< Fr. *a-*, to + *grandir*, to increase] 1. to make greater, richer, etc. 2. to make seem greater —**ag·gran′dize·ment** (-diz mənt) *n.*

ag·gra·vate (ag′rə vāt′) *vt.* -**vat′ed,** -**vat′ing** [< L. *ad-*, to + *gravis*, heavy] 1. to make worse 2. [Colloq.] to annoy —**ag′gra·va′tion** *n.*

ag·gre·gate (ag′rə gət) *adj.* [< L. *ad-*, to + *grex*, a herd] total —*n.* a mass of distinct things gathered together; total —*vt.* (-gāt′) -**gat′ed,** -**gat′ing** 1. to gather into a mass 2. to amount to; total —**ag′gre·ga′tion** *n.*

ag·gres·sion (ə gresh′ən) *n.* [Fr. < L. *aggredi*, to attack] 1. an unprovoked attack or warlike act 2. a being aggressive —**ag·gres′sor** *n.*

ag·gres·sive (ə gres′iv) *adj.* 1. boldly hostile; quarrelsome 2. bold and active; enterprising — **ag·gres′sive·ly** *adv.*

ag·grieve (ə grēv′) *vt.* -**grieved′,** -**griev′ing** [see AGGRAVATE] to cause grief or injury to; offend

a·ghast (ə gast′) *adj.* [< OE. *gast*, ghost] utterly horrified or dismayed

ag·ile (aj′'l) *adj.* [< L. *agere*, do] moving or thinking quickly and deftly; nimble —**ag′ile·ly** *adv.* —**a·gil·i·ty** (ə jil′ə tē) *n.*

ag·i·tate (aj′ə tāt′) *vt.* -**tat′ed,** -**tat′ing** [< L. *agere*, do] 1. to stir up; shake up 2. to excite; fluster —*vi.* to keep talking and writing so as to change things —**ag′i·ta′tion** *n.* —**ag′i·ta′tor** *n.*

a·glow (ə glō′) *adv., adj.* in a glow

ag·nos·tic (ag näs′tik) *n.* [< Gr. *a-*, not + base of *gignōskein*, know] one holding that it is impossible to know whether God exists — *adj.* of an agnostic —**ag·nos'ti·cal·ly** *adv.* —**ag·nos'ti·cism** (-tə siz'm) *n.*

a·go (ə gō') *adj.* [< OE. *agan,* pass away] gone by; past *[years ago]* —*adv.* in the past *[long ago]*

a·gog (ə gäg') *adv., adj.* [< OFr. *a- + gogue,* joke] with eagerness or excitement

ag·o·nize (ag'ə nīz') *vi.* -**nized', -niz'ing** 1. to struggle 2. to be in agony —*vt.* to torture —**ag'·o·niz'ing** *adj.*

ag·o·ny (ag'ə nē) *n., pl.* -**nies** [< Gr. *agōn,* a contest] 1. great mental or physical pain 2. death pangs

a·gou·ti, a·gou·ty (ə gōō'tē) *n., pl.* -**tis, -ties** [< SAmInd.] a rodent of tropical America, related to the guinea pig

a·grar·i·an (ə grer'ē ən) *adj.* [< L. *ager,* field] 1. of land or its ownership 2. of agriculture —*n.* one favoring equitable land division

a·gree (ə grē') *vi.* -**greed', -gree'ing** [< L. *ad-,* to + *gratus,* pleasing] 1. to consent (*to*) 2. to be in harmony 3. to be of the same opinion (*with*) 4. to arrive at an understanding (*about*) —*vt.* to grant

a·gree'a·ble *adj.* 1. pleasing 2. willing 3. conformable —**a·gree'a·bil'i·ty** *n.* —**a·gree'a·bly** *adv.*

a·gree'ment *n.* 1. an agreeing 2. a contract

ag·ri·busi·ness (ag'rə biz'nis) *n.* [AGRI(CULTURE) + BUSINESS] farming and the businesses and industries associated with farming

ag·ri·cul·ture (ag'ri kul'chər) *n.* [< L. *ager,* field + *cultura,* cultivation] the work of raising crops and livestock; farming —**ag'ri·cul'·tur·al** *adj.* —**ag'ri·cul'tur·ist, ag'ri·cul'tur·al·ist** *n.*

a·gron·o·my (ə grän'ə mē) *n.* [< Gr. *agros,* field + *nemein,* manage] the science and economics of raising crops —**a·gron'o·mist** *n.*

a·ground (ə ground') *adv., adj.* on or onto the shore, a reef, etc., as a ship

a·gue (ā'gyōō) *n.* [< ML. (*febris*) *acuta,* violent (fever)] 1. a fever, usually malarial, with regularly recurring chills 2. a fit of shivering

ah (ä) *interj.* an exclamation of pain, joy, etc.

a·ha (ä hä') *interj.* an exclamation as of triumph

a·head (ə hed') *adv., adj.* 1. in or to the front 2. onward 3. in advance 4. winning or profiting —**get ahead** to advance financially, etc. —**get ahead of** to outdo

a·hem (ə hem') *interj.* a coughlike sound made to get attention, fill a pause, etc.

a·hoy (ə hoi') *interj. Naut.* a call used in hailing

a·i (ä'ē) *n., pl.* **a'is** (-ēz) [< the animal's cry] a S. American sloth with three toes

aid (ād) *vt., vi.* [< L. *ad-,* to + *juvare,* to help] to help; assist —*n.* 1. help; assistance 2. a helper 3. an aide; aide-de-camp

aide (ād) *n.* [Fr.] 1. a helper 2. an aide-de-camp

aide-de-camp (ād'də kamp') *n., pl.* **aides'-de-camp'** [Fr., lit., camp assistant] a military officer serving as assistant to a superior

aid'man' *n., pl.* -**men'** an enlisted man in a medical corps attached to a combat unit

ai·grette, ai·gret (ā'gret, ā gret') *n.* an egret's plumes used, esp. formerly, as on a woman's hat

ail (āl) *vt.* [< OE. < *egle,* harmful] to pain, distress, or trouble —*vi.* to be ill

ai·le·ron (ā'lə rän') *n.* [Fr. < L. *ala,* wing] a hinged section of an airplane wing, for control

ail'ing *adj.* in poor health; sickly

ail'ment (-mənt) *n.* an illness, esp. a mild one

aim (ām) *vi., vt.* [< L. *ad-,* to + *aestimare,* to estimate] 1. to point (a weapon) or direct (a blow, remark, etc.) 2. to direct (one's efforts) 3. to intend —*n.* 1. an aiming 2. direction, as of a blow 3. intention —**take aim** to aim a weapon, etc.

aim'less *adj.* having no purpose

ain't (ānt) [< *amn't,* contr. of *am not*] [Colloq.] am not: also a dialectal or substandard contraction for *is not, are not, has not,* and *have not*

air (er) *n.* [< Gr. *aēr*] 1. the invisible mixture of gases surrounding the earth; atmosphere 2. a breeze; wind 3. an outward appearance *[an air of dignity]* 4. [*pl.*] affected, superior manners 5. public expression 6. transportation by aircraft 7. a tune —*adj.* of aviation —*vt.* 1. to let air into 2. to publicize —**in the air** 1. prevalent 2. not decided: also **up in the air** —**on** (or **off**) **the air** Radio & TV (not) broadcasting

air bag a bag of nylon, plastic, etc. that inflates automatically within an automobile at the impact of a collision, to protect riders

air base a base for military aircraft

air'borne' *adj.* 1. carried by air 2. aloft

air brake a brake operated by the action of compressed air on a piston

air conditioning regulation of air humidity and temperature in buildings, etc. —**air'-condi'tion** *vt.* —**air conditioner**

air'-cool' *vt.* to cool by passing air over, into, or through —**air'-cooled'** *adj.*

air'craft' *n., pl.* -**craft'** any machine for flying

aircraft carrier a warship with a large, flat deck for carrying aircraft

air·drome (er'drōm') *n.* [< AIR + Gr. *dromos,* course] the physical facilities of an air base

air'drop' *n.* the parachuting of supplies or troops from an aircraft —**air'drop'** *vt.*

Aire·dale (er'dāl') *n.* [< *Airedale,* valley in England] a large terrier with a wiry coat

air'field' *n.* a field where aircraft can take off and land

air·foil (er'foil') *n.* a wing, rudder, etc. of an aircraft

air force the aviation branch of a country's armed forces

air'lift' *n.* a system of transporting troops, supplies, etc. by aircraft

air'line' *n.* a system or company for moving passengers and freight by aircraft —*adj.* of, on, or by an airline

air'lin'er *n.* a large aircraft for passengers

air lock an airtight compartment, with adjustable air pressure, between places of unequal pressure

air'mail' *n.* mail transported by aircraft —*vt.* to send by airmail

air'man (-mən) *n., pl.* -**men** 1. an aviator 2. an enlisted person in the U.S. Air Force

air·plane (er'plān') *n.* a motor-driven or jet-propelled aircraft kept aloft by the forces of air upon its wings

air'port' *n.* a place where aircraft can take off and land, usually with facilities for repair, etc.

air rifle a compressed-air rifle shooting BB's, etc.

air'ship' *n.* a self-propelled aircraft that is lighter than air and can be steered

air'sick' *adj.* nauseated from traveling in an aircraft —**air'sick'ness** *n.*

air'strip' *n.* a temporary airplane runway

air'tight' *adj.* 1. too tight for air or gas to enter or escape 2. unassailable

air'waves' *n.pl.* the medium through which radio signals are transmitted

air'y *adj.* -**i·er, -i·est** 1. of air 2. open to the air;

breezy **3.** unsubstantial as air; visionary **4.** light as air; graceful **5.** lighthearted; gay **6.** flippant **7.** [Colloq.] putting on airs —**air′i·ly** *adv.* —**air′i·ness** *n.*

aisle (īl) *n.* [< L. *ala,* wing] a passageway, as between rows of seats —**aisled** (īld) *adj.*

a·jar (ə jär′) *adv., adj.* [< OE. *cier,* a turn] slightly open, as a door

a·kim·bo (ə kim′bō) *adv., adj.* [ON. < *keng,* bent + *bogi,* a bow] with hands on hips and elbows bent outward

a·kin (ə kin′) *adj.* **1.** of one kin; related **2.** having similar qualities

-al [L.] *a suffix meaning:* **1.** of, like, or suitable for *[comical]* **2.** the act or process of *[denial]*

Al *Chem.* aluminum

à la, a la (ä′lə) [Fr.] in the style of

al·a·bas·ter (al′ə bas′tər) *n.* [< Gr. *alabastros,* perfume vase] **1.** a translucent, whitish variety of gypsum **2.** a streaked or mottled variety of calcite

a la carte (ä′lə kärt′) [Fr.] with a separate price for each item on the menu

a·lack (ə lak′) *interj.* [A(H) + LACK] [Archaic] an exclamation of regret, surprise, etc.

a·lac·ri·ty (ə lak′rə tē) *n.* [< L. *alacer,* lively] eager willingness, with quick, lively action — **a·lac′ri·tous** *adj.*

A·lad·din (ə lad′′n) a boy in *The Arabian Nights* who found a magic lamp

à la king (ä′lə kiŋ′) served in a sauce containing mushrooms, pimentos, etc.

a la mode (al′ə mōd′, ä′lə) [Fr.] **1.** in fashion **2.** made or served in a certain style, as (pie) with ice cream Also **à la mode, alamode**

a·lar (ā′lər) *adj.* [< L. *ala,* a wing] **1.** of or like a wing **2.** having wings

a·larm (ə lärm′) *n.* [It. *all′arme,* to arms] **1.** [Archaic] a sudden call to arms **2.** a signal, sound, etc. to warn of danger **3.** a mechanism that warns of danger, arouses from sleep, etc. **4.** fear caused by danger —*vt.* **1.** to warn of danger **2.** to frighten

alarm clock a clock that sounds or flashes at a desired time, as to awaken a person

a·larm′ing *adj.* frightening

a·larm′ist *n.* **1.** one who habitually spreads alarming rumors **2.** one who anticipates the worst —*adj.* of or like an alarmist

a·las (ə las′) *interj.* an exclamation of sorrow, pity, regret, etc.

alb (alb) *n.* [< L. *albus,* white] a long, white linen robe worn by a priest at Mass

al·ba·core (al′bə kôr′) *n.* [< Ar. *al,* the + *bakūrah,* albacore] any of various related saltwater fishes, as the tuna or bonito

al·ba·tross (al′bə trôs′) *n.* [< Sp. < Ar. *al qādūs,* water container] any of several large, web-footed sea birds related to the petrel

al·be·it (ôl bē′it, al-) *conj.* [ME. *al be it,* al(though) it be] although; even though

al·bi·no (al bī′nō) *n., pl.* **-nos** [< L. *albus,* white] a person, animal, or plant lacking normal coloration: human albinos have white skin, whitish hair, and pink eyes —**al·bi·nism** (al′bə niz′m) *n.*

al·bum (al′bəm) *n.* [< L. *albus,* white] **1.** a book with blank pages for mounting pictures, stamps, etc. **2.** *a)* a booklike holder for phonograph records *b)* a single long-playing record or tape recording

al·bu·men (al byōō′mən) *n.* **1.** the white of an egg **2.** *same as* ALBUMIN

al·bu·min (al byōō′mən) *n.* [< L. *albus,* white] any of a class of water-soluble proteins found in milk, egg, muscle, blood, and in many plants —**al·bu·mi·nous** *adj.*

al·che·my (al′kə mē) *n.* [< Ar. < ? Gr. *cheein,* to pour] the chemistry of the Middle Ages, the chief aim of which was to change the baser metals into gold —**al·chem·ic** (al kem′ik) *adj.* —**al′che·mist** *n.*

al·co·hol (al′kə hôl′, -häl′) *n.* [< Ar. *al kuhl,* powder of antimony] **1.** a colorless, volatile, pungent liquid: it can be burned as fuel and is the intoxicating element in fermented liquors **2.** any such intoxicating liquor **3.** any of a series of similar organic compounds, as methyl (or wood) alcohol

al′co·hol′ic *adj.* **1.** of, containing, or caused by alcohol **2.** suffering from alcoholism —*n.* one who has chronic alcoholism

al′co·hol′ism *n.* a diseased condition caused by habitually drinking too much alcohol

al·cove (al′kōv) *n.* [< Ar. *al,* the + *qubba,* an arch] a recessed section of a room

al·de·hyde (al′də hīd′) *n.* [< AL(COHOL) + L. *de,* without + HYD(ROGEN)] a colorless fluid obtained from alcohol by oxidation

al·der (ôl′dər) *n.* [< OE. *alor*] a small tree or shrub of the birch family

al·der·man (ôl′dər mən) *n., pl.* **-men** [< OE. *eald,* old + *man*] in some cities, a municipal officer representing a certain district or ward —**al′der·man′ic** (-man′ik) *adj.*

Al·der·ney (ôl′dər nē) *n., pl.* **-neys** any of a breed of small dairy cattle

ale (āl) *n.* [< OE. *ealu*] a fermented drink made from malt and hops, similar to beer

a·lem·bic (ə lem′bik) *n.* [< Ar. *al,* the + *anbīq,* a still < Gr. *ambix,* a cup] **1.** an apparatus of glass or metal, formerly used for distilling **2.** anything that refines or purifies

a·lert (ə lurt′) *adj.* [< L. *erigere,* to ERECT] **1.** watchful; vigilantly ready **2.** active; nimble —*n.* an alarm; warning signal —*vt.* to warn, as to be ready —**on the alert** watchful; vigilant —**a·lert′ness** *n.*

al·ex·an·drine (al′ig zan′drin) *n.* [*occas.* A-] *Prosody* an iambic line having six feet

al·fal·fa (al fal′fə) *n.* [< Ar. *al-fasfaṣah,* the best fodder] a leguminous plant, used for fodder, pasture, and as a cover crop

al·gae (al′jē) *n.pl., sing.* **al′ga** (-gə) [L.] a group of plants, variously one-celled or colonial, containing chlorophyll and found in water or damp places

al·ge·bra (al′jə brə) *n.* [< Ar. *al,* the + *jabara,* to reunite] a mathematical system used to generalize certain arithmetical operations by use of letters or other symbols to stand for numbers —**al′ge·bra′ic** (-brā′ik) *adj.* —**al′ge·bra′i·cal·ly** *adv.*

-algia [< Gr. *algos,* pain] *a suffix meaning* pain

Al·gon·qui·an (al gän′kē ən, -kwē-) *adj.* designating or of a widespread family of N. American Indian languages —*n.* this family of languages

al·go·rithm (al′gər ith′m) *n.* [< *algorism,* Arabic system of numerals] *Math.* any special method of solving a certain kind of problem

a·li·as (ā′lē əs, āl′yəs) *n., pl.* **a′li·as·es** [< L., other] an assumed name —*adv.* otherwise named *[*Bell *alias* Jones*]*

A·li Ba·ba (ä′lē bä′bə, al′ē bab′ə) in *The Arabian Nights,* a poor woodcutter who finds the treasure of forty thieves in a cave

al·i·bi (al′ə bī′) *n., pl.* **-bis′** [L. < *alius ibi,* elsewhere] **1.** *Law* the plea that an accused person was elsewhere than at the scene of the crime **2.** [Colloq.] an excuse —*vi.* **-bied′, -bi′ing** [Colloq.] to offer an excuse

al·ien (āl′yən, -ē ən) *adj.* [< L. *alius,* other] **1.** foreign **2.** strange **3.** repugnant (*to*) **4.** of aliens

—n. 1. a foreigner **2.** a foreign-born resident who is not naturalized

al'ien·ate' (-āt') **vt. -at'ed, -at'ing 1.** to transfer the ownership of (property) to another **2.** to estrange **3.** to cause to transfer (affection) — **al'ien·a'tion** n.

al'ien·ist n. Law a psychiatrist

a·light' (ə līt') **vi. a·light'ed** or **a·lit', a·light'ing** [ME. alihtan] **1.** to get down or off **2.** to come down after flight

a·light² (ə līt') **adj.** lighted up; glowing

a·lign (ə līn') **vt.** [< Fr. < a, to + ligne, line] **1.** to bring into a straight line **2.** to bring (parts) into proper coordination **3.** to bring into agreement, etc. **—vi.** to line up Also sp. **aline** — **a·lign'ment** n.

a·like (ə līk') **adj.** [< OE. gelic] like one another; similar **—adv. 1.** similarly **2.** equally

al·i·ment (al'ə mənt) **n.** [< L. alere, to nourish] nourishment; food

al'i·men'ta·ry (-men'tər ē) **adj. 1.** of food or nutrition **2.** nourishing

alimentary canal (or **tract**) the passage in the body (from mouth to anus) that food goes through

al·i·mo·ny (al'ə mō'nē) **n.** [< L. alere, to nourish] an allowance paid, esp. to a woman, by the spouse or former spouse after a legal separation or divorce

a·lit (ə lit') **alt. pt. & pp. of** ALIGHT¹

a·live (ə līv') **adj.** [< OE. on, in + life, life] **1.** having life; living **2.** in existence, operation, etc. **3.** lively; alert **—alive to** fully aware of — **alive with** teeming with

al·ka·li (al'kə lī') **n., pl. -lies', -lis'** [< Ar. al, the + qili, ashes of a certain plant] **1.** any base, as soda, that is soluble in water and can neutralize acids **2.** any mineral salt that can neutralize acids

al'ka·line (-lin, -līn') **adj.** of, like, or containing an alkali **—al'ka·lin'i·ty** (-lin'ə tē) **n.**

al'ka·lize' (-līz') **vt. -lized', -liz'ing** to make alkaline **—al'ka·li·za'tion** n.

al'ka·loid' (-loid') **n.** any of a number of basic organic substances, as caffeine, quinine, etc., found in certain plants

all (ôl) **adj.** [OE. eall] **1.** the whole quantity or extent of **2.** every one of [all men] **3.** the greatest possible [in all sincerity] **4.** any [beyond all doubt] **5.** alone; only [all work and no play] **—pron. 1.** [with pl. v.] everyone [all are present] **2.** everything **3.** every part **—n. 1.** everything one has [give your all] **2.** a totality; whole **—adv. 1.** wholly; quite [all worn out] **2.** apiece [a score of two all] **—after all** nevertheless **—all but 1.** all except **2.** almost **—all in** [Colloq.] very tired **—all in all 1.** as a whole **2.** considering everything **—at all 1.** in the least **2.** in any way **3.** under any considerations **—for all** in spite of **—in all** altogether

all- a combining form meaning: **1.** wholly; entirely [all-absorbing] **2.** for every [all-purpose] **3.** of every part [all-inclusive]

Al·lah (al'ə, ä'lə) the Muslim name for GOD

all'-A·mer'i·can adj. chosen as the best in the U.S. **—n. 1.** a hypothetical football (or other) team of the best U.S. college players of the year **2.** a player on such a team

all'-a·round' adj. having many abilities, talents, or uses; versatile

al·lay (ə lā') **vt. -layed', -lay'ing** [< OE. a-, down + lecgan, to lay] **1.** to calm (fears, etc.) **2.** to lessen or relieve (pain, etc.)

all-clear (ôl'klir') **n.** a signal that an air raid is over

al·le·ga·tion (al'ə gā'shən) **n. 1.** an alleging **2.** an assertion, esp. one without proof

al·lege (ə lej') **vt. -leged', -leg'ing** [< L. ex-, out of + litigare, to dispute] **1.** to assert, esp. without proof **2.** to give as a plea

al·leg'ed·ly adv. according to allegation

al·le·giance (ə lē'jəns) **n.** [< OFr. liege, liege] **1.** the obligation of support and loyalty to one's ruler, country, etc. **2.** loyalty

al·le·go·ry (al'ə gôr'ē) **n., pl. -ries** [< Gr. < allos, other + agoreuein, to speak] a story in which people, things, and happenings have another meaning, often instructive, as in a fable **—al'le·gor'i·cal** adj.

al·le·gret·to (al'ə gret'ō) **adj., adv.** [It., dim. of ALLEGRO] Music moderately fast

al·le·gro (ə leg'rō, -lā'grō) **adj., adv.** [It.] Music fast

al·le·lu·ia (al'ə lōō'yə) **interj., n.** same as HALLELUJAH

al·ler·gen (al'ər jən) **n.** [G.] a substance inducing an allergic state or reaction **—al'ler·gen'ic** (-jen'ik) adj.

al·ler·gic (ə lur'jik) **adj.** of, caused by, or having an allergy

al·ler·gist (al'ər jist) **n.** a doctor who specializes in treating allergies

al·ler·gy (al'ər jē) **n., pl. -gies** [< Gr. allos, other + energēs, active] a hypersensitivity to a specific substance (as a food, pollen, etc.) or condition (as heat or cold)

al·le·vi·ate (ə lē'vē āt') **vt. -at'ed, -at'ing** [< L. ad-, to + levis, light] to lessen or relieve (pain, etc.) **—al·le'vi·a'tion** n.

al·ley (al'ē) **n., pl. -leys** [< OFr. aler, go] **1.** a narrow street **2.** a bowling lane

al'ley·way' n. an alley between buildings

al·li·ance (ə lī'əns) **n. 1.** an allying or close association, as of nations for a common objective or of families by marriage **2.** the countries, persons, etc. in such association

al·lied (ə līd', al'īd) **adj. 1.** united by kinship, treaty, etc. **2.** closely related

al·li·ga·tor (al'ə gāt'ər) **n.** [< Sp. < L. lacertus, lizard] a large crocodilelike lizard of the U.S., with a short, blunt snout

al·lit·er·ate (ə lit'ə rāt') **vi. -at'ed, -at'ing** to show or use alliteration

al·lit·er·a·tion (ə lit'ə rā'shən) **n.** [< L. ad-, to + littera, LETTER] repetition of an initial sound in two or more words of a phrase, etc.

al·lo·cate (al'ə kāt') **vt. -cat'ed, -cat'ing** [< L. ad-, to + locus, a place] **1.** to set apart for a specific purpose **2.** to distribute; allot **—al'lo·ca'tion** n.

al·lot (ə lät') **vt. -lot'ted, -lot'ting** [OFr. a-, to + lot, lot] **1.** to distribute in shares; apportion **2.** to assign (a share) **—al·lot'ment** n.

al·lot·ro·py (ə lät'rə pē) **n.** [< Gr. allos, other + tropos, manner] the property that certain chemical elements have of existing in two or more different forms, as carbon in charcoal, diamonds, etc.: also **al·lot'ro·pism**

all'-out' adj. complete or wholehearted

al·low (ə lou') **vt.** [< L. ad-, to + locus, a place] **1.** to permit; let [I'm not allowed to go] **2.** to let have [allowed no sweets] **3.** to acknowledge as valid **4.** to provide (an extra quantity) as for shrinkage, waste, etc. **—allow for** to keep in mind **—al·low'a·ble** adj.

al·low'ance (-əns) **n. 1.** an allowing **2.** something allowed **3.** an amount of money, food, etc. given regularly to a child, soldier, etc. **4.** a reduction in price, as for a trade-in **—make allowance(s) for** to excuse because of mitigating factors

al·loy (al'oi) **n.** [< L. ad-, to + ligare, bind] **1.** a metal that is a mixture of two or more metals **2.** a debasing addition —*vt.* (ə loi′) to make into an alloy

all right 1. satisfactory **2.** unhurt **3.** correct **4.** yes **5.** [Colloq.] certainly

all′-round′ *adj. same as* ALL-AROUND

all·spice (ôl′spīs′) *n.* a spice, combining the tastes of several spices, made from the berry of a West Indian tree

all′-star′ *adj.* made up entirely of outstanding or star performers

al·lude (ə lōōd′) *vi.* **-lud′ed, -lud′ing** [< L. *ad-*, to + *ludere*, to play] to refer indirectly (*to*)

al·lure (ə loor′) *vt., vi.* **-lured′, -lur′ing** [< OFr. *a-*, to + *lurer*, to LURE] to tempt with something desirable; attract —*n.* fascination; charm —**al·lure′ment** *n.*

al·lu·sion (ə lōō′zhən) *n.* **1.** an alluding **2.** an indirect or casual reference

al·lu·vi·um (ə lōō′vē əm) *n., pl.* **-vi·ums, -vi·a** (-vē ə) [< L. *ad-*, to + *luere*, wash] sand, clay, etc. deposited by flowing water —**al·lu′vi·al** *adj.*

al·ly (ə lī′) *vt.* **-lied′, -ly′ing** [< L. *ad-*, to + *ligare*, bind] **1.** to unite or join (*to* or *with*) for a specific purpose **2.** to relate by similarity of structure, etc. —*vi.* to become allied —*n.* (al′ī, ə lī′), *pl.* **-lies 1.** a country or person joined with another for a common purpose **2.** an associate

al·ma ma·ter (al′mə mät′ər, mät′ər) [L., fostering mother] **1.** the college or school that one attended **2.** its anthem

al·ma·nac (ôl′mə nak′) *n.* [< LGr. *almenichiaka*, calendar] **1.** a calendar with astronomical data, etc. **2.** a book published annually, with varied information

al·might·y (ôl mīt′ē) *adj.* all-powerful —**the Almighty** God —**al·might′i·ly** *adv.*

al·mond (ä′mənd, am′ənd) *n.* [< Gr. *amygdalē*] **1.** the edible, nutlike seed of a fruit like the peach **2.** the tree bearing this fruit —**al′mond·like′** *adj.*

al·most (ôl′mōst, ôl′mōst′) *adv.* very nearly

alms (ämz) *n., pl.* **alms** [< Gr. *eleos*, pity] money, food, etc. given to poor people

alms′house′ *n.* a poorhouse

al·oe (al′ō) *n., pl.* **-oes** [< Gr. *aloē*] **1.** a South African plant related to the lily **2.** [*pl., with sing. v.*] a laxative drug made from the juice of its fleshy leaves

a·loft (ə lôft′) *adv.* [< *a-*, on + *loft*] **1.** high up **2.** high above the deck of a ship

a·lo·ha (ə lō′ə, ä lō′hä) *n., interj.* [Haw., lit., love] a word used as a greeting or farewell

a·lone (ə lōn′) *adj., adv.* [< *all* + *one*] **1.** apart from anything or anyone else **2.** without any other person **3.** only —**let alone 1.** to refrain from bothering or interfering with **2.** not to speak of [we hadn't a dime, *let alone* a dollar]

a·long (ə lôŋ′) *prep.* [< OE. *and-*, over against + *-lang*, long] **1.** on or beside the length of **2.** in conformity with —*adv.* **1.** lengthwise **2.** progressively onward **3.** as a companion **4.** with one [take a book *along*] —**all along** from the beginning

a·long′side′ *adv.* at or by the side; side by side —*prep.* side by side with; beside

a·loof (ə lōōf′) *adv.* [< *a-*, on + Du. *loef*, to windward] at a distance but in view; apart —*adj.* cool and reserved —**a·loof′ness** *n.*

a·loud (ə loud′) *adv.* **1.** loudly **2.** in an audible voice [read the letter *aloud*]

alp (alp) *n.* [< Alps, mts. in SC Europe] a high mountain

al·pac·a (al pak′ə) *n.* [Sp. < SAmInd. *allpaca*] **1.** a S. American mammal related to the llama **2.** its long, fleecy wool **3.** a cloth woven from this wool

al·pha (al′fə) *n.* the first letter of the Greek alphabet (A, α)

al·pha·bet (al′fə bet′) *n.* [< Gr. *alpha* + *beta*] the letters used in writing a language, arranged in a traditional order —**al′pha·bet′i·cal** *adj.*

al·pha·bet·ize (al′fə bə tīz′) *vt.* **-ized′, -iz′ing** to arrange in alphabetical order

alpha particle a positively charged particle given off by certain radioactive substances

alpha ray a stream of alpha particles

al·pine (al′pīn, -pin) *adj.* of or like alps

al·read·y (ôl red′ē) *adv.* **1.** by or before the given or implied time **2.** even now or even then

al·right (ôl rīt′) *adv. var. of* ALL RIGHT: a disputed sp., but in common use

al·so (ôl′sō) *adv.* [< OE. *eal*, all + *swa*, so] in addition; too

al′so-ran′ (-ran′) *n.* [Colloq.] any loser in a race, competition, election, etc.

alt. 1. alternate **2.** altitude **3.** alto

al·tar (ôl′tər) *n.* [< L. *altus*, high] **1.** a platform where sacrifices are made to a god, etc. **2.** a table, stand, etc. used for sacred purposes —**lead to the altar** to marry

altar boy a boy or man who helps a priest, etc. at religious services, esp. at Mass

al·ter (ôl′tər) *vt., vi.* [< L. *alter*, other] to change; make or become different —**al′ter·a·ble** *adj.*

al′ter·a′tion *n.* **1.** an altering **2.** the result of this

al′ter·ca′tion *n.* [< L. *altercari*, to dispute] an angry argument; quarrel

al·ter e·go (ôl′tər ē′gō, eg′ō) [L., lit., other I] **1.** another aspect of oneself **2.** a very close friend

al·ter·nate (ôl′tər nit, al′-) *adj.* [< L. *alternus*, one after the other] **1.** succeeding each other **2.** every other —*n.* a substitute —*vt.* (-nāt′) **-nat′ed, -nat′ing** to do or use by turns —*vi.* **1.** to act, happen, etc. by turns **2.** to take turns regularly —**al′ter·nate·ly** *adv.* —**al′ter·na′tion** *n.*

alternating current an electric current that reverses its direction periodically

al·ter·na·tive (ôl tur′nə tiv, al-) *adj.* providing a choice between things —*n.* **1.** a choice between things **2.** any of the things to be chosen —**al·ter′na·tive·ly** *adv.*

al·ter·na·tor (ôl′tər nāt′ər) *n.* an electric generator or dynamo producing alternating current

al·though (ôl thō′) *conj.* in spite of the fact that; though: now sometimes sp. **altho**

al·tim·e·ter (al tim′ə tər, al′tə mēt′ər) *n.* an instrument for measuring altitude

al·ti·tude (al′tə tōōd′) *n.* [< L. *altus*, high] **1.** the height of a thing, esp. above sea level or the earth's surface **2.** a high place

al·to (al′tō) *n., pl.* **-tos** [It. < L. *altus*, high] **1.** the range of the lowest female voice **2.** a singer with this range —*adj.* of, in, for, or having this range

al·to·geth·er (ôl′tə geth′ər) *adv.* **1.** wholly; completely **2.** in all **3.** on the whole —**in the altogether** [Colloq.] nude

al·tru·ism (al′trōō iz′m) *n.* [< L. *alter*, other] unselfish concern for the welfare of others —**al′tru·ist** *n.* —**al′tru·is′tic** (-is′tik) *adj.* —**al′tru·is′ti·cal·ly** *adv.*

al·um (al′əm) *n.* [< L. *alumen*] a double sulfate, esp. of potassium and aluminum, used in medicine and in manufacturing

al·u·min·i·um (al′yōo min′yəm, -ē əm) *n. Brit. var. of* ALUMINUM

a·lu·mi·num (ə lōō′mə nəm) *n.* [< L. *alumen*,

alum] a silvery, lightweight metallic chemical element: symbol, Al

a·lum·nus (ə lum′nəs) *n., pl.* **-ni** (-nī) [L., foster son] a boy or man who has attended or is a graduate of a school, college, etc. **—a·lum′na** (-nə) *n.fem., pl.* **-nae** (-nē)

al·ways (ôl′wiz, -wāz) *adv.* [see ALL & WAY] 1. at all times 2. all the time; forever

a·lys·sum (ə lis′əm) *n.* [< Gr. *alyssos,* curing madness] 1. any of a number of garden plants, bearing white or yellow flowers 2. *same as* SWEET ALYSSUM

am (am, əm) [OE. *eom*] *1st pers. sing., pres. indic., of* BE

AM amplitude modulation

A.M., a.m., AM [L. *ante meridiem*] before noon: used to designate the time from midnight to noon

a·main (ə mān′) *adv.* [A-, on + MAIN] [Archaic] at or with great speed

a·mal·gam (ə mal′gəm) *n.* [< Gr. *malagma,* an emollient] 1. any alloy of mercury with another metal *[silver amalgam is used as a dental filling]* 2. any mixture or blend

a·mal′ga·mate′ (-gə māt′) *vt., vi.* **-mat′ed, -mat′ing** to unite; mix; combine **—a·mal′ga·ma′tion** *n.*

a·man·u·en·sis (ə man′yoo wen′sis) *n., pl.* **-ses** (-sēz) [L. < *a-,* from + *manus,* a hand + *-ensis,* relating to] a secretary

am·a·ranth (am′ə ranth′) *n.* [< Gr. *amarantos,* unfading] 1. any of a family of plants, usually with colorful leaves 2. [Poetic] an imaginary flower that never dies

am·a·ryl·lis (am′ə ril′əs) *n.* [< Gr. name for a shepherdess] a bulb plant with white to red lilylike flowers

a·mass (ə mas′) *vt.* [< Fr. < L. *a-,* to + *massare,* to pile up] to pile up; accumulate

am·a·teur (am′ə choor, -toor, -tyoor) *n.* [< Fr. < L. *amare,* to love] 1. one who does something for fun rather than for pay 2. one who does something unskillfully **—adj.** of or done by amateurs **—am′a·teur′ish** *adj.* **—am′a·teur·ism** *n.*

am·a·to·ry (am′ə tôr′ē) *adj.* [< L. *amare,* to love] of or showing sexual love

a·maze (ə māz′) *vt.* **a·mazed′, a·maz′ing** [see MAZE] to fill with great surprise or wonder; astonish **—a·maz′ing·ly** *adv.*

a·maze′ment *n.* great surprise or wonder

Am·a·zon (am′ə zän′) *n. Gr. Myth.* any of a race of female warriors

am·bas·sa·dor (am bas′ə dər) *n.* [< Pr. *ambaissador*] the highest-ranking diplomatic representative of one country to another **—am·bas′sa·do′ri·al** (-dôr′ē əl) *adj.* **—am·bas′sa·dor·ship′** *n.*

am·ber (am′bər) *n.* [< Ar. ′*anbar,* ambergris] 1. a brownish-yellow fossil resin used in jewelry, etc. 2. its color *adj.* amberlike or ambercolored

am′ber·gris′ (-grēs′, -gris′) *n.* [< Fr. *ambre gris,* gray amber] a waxy substance secreted by certain whales, used in making perfumes

am·bi- [< L. *ambo*] *a combining form meaning* both

am·bi·ance (am′bē əns) *n.* [Fr.: see AMBIENT] an environment or milieu: also **am′bi·ence**

am·bi·dex·trous (am′bə dek′strəs) *adj.* [see AMBI- & DEXTEROUS] able to use both hands with equal ease **—am′bi·dex·ter′i·ty** (-dek ster′ə tē) *n.*

am·bi·ent (am′bē ənt) *adj.* [< L. *ambire,* to go around] surrounding; on all sides

am·bi·gu·i·ty (am′bə gyōō′ə tē) *n.* 1. a being ambiguous 2. *pl.* **-ties** an ambiguous expression

am·big·u·ous (-yoo wəs) *adj.* [< L. *ambigere,* to wander around] 1. having two or more possible meanings 2. not clear; vague **—am·big′u·ous·ly** *adv.*

am·bi·tion (am bish′ən) *n.* [< L. *ambitio,* a going around (to solicit votes)] 1. a strong desire for fame, power, wealth, etc. 2. the thing so desired

am·bi′tious (-əs) *adj.* 1. full of or showing ambition 2. demanding great effort

am·biv·a·lence (am biv′ə ləns) *n.* [AMBI- + VALENCE] simultaneous conflicting feelings **—am·biv′a·lent** *adj.*

am·ble (am′b'l) *vi.* **-bled, -bling** [< L. *ambulare,* to walk] 1. to move at an easy gait: said of a horse, etc. 2. to walk in a leisurely manner **—n.** 1. a horse's ambling gait 2. a leisurely walking pace **—am′bler** *n.*

am·bro·sia (am brō′zhə) *n.* [< Gr. *a-,* not + *brotos,* mortal] 1. *Gr. & Rom. Myth.* the food of the gods 2. anything that tastes or smells delicious **—am·bro′sial** *adj.*

am·bu·lance (am′byə ləns) *n.* [< L. *ambulare,* to walk] a vehicle equipped for carrying the sick or wounded

am′bu·late′ (-lāt′) *vi.* **-lat′ed, -lat′ing** to move about; walk **—am′bu·lant** (-lənt) *adj.* **—am′bu·la′tion** *n.*

am′bu·la·to′ry (-lə tôr′ē) *adj.* 1. of or for walking 2. able to walk about

am·bus·cade (am′bəs kād′) *n., vt., vi.* **-cad′ed, -cad′ing** *same as* AMBUSH

am·bush (am′boosh) *n.* [< ML. *in-,* in + *boscus,* woods] 1. an arrangement of persons in hiding to make a surprise attack 2. their hiding place **—vt., vi.** to attack from hiding

a·me·ba (ə mē′bə) *n., pl.* **-bas, -bae** (-bē) *same as* AMOEBA **—a·me′bic** *adj.*

a·mel·io·rate (ə mēl′yə rāt′) *vt., vi.* **-rat′ed, -rat′ing** [< Fr. < L. *melior,* better] to make or become better; improve **—a·mel′io·ra′tion** *n.*

a·men (ā′men′, ä′-) *interj.* [< Heb. *āmēn,* truly] may it be so!: used after a prayer or to express approval

a·me·na·ble (ə mē′nə b'l, -men′ə-) *adj.* [< OFr. < L. *minare,* to drive (animals)] 1. responsible; answerable 2. responsive; submissive **—a·me′na·bil′i·ty** *n.*

a·mend (ə mend′) *vt.* [< L. *emendare*] 1. to correct; emend 2. to improve 3. to change or revise, as a law **—vi.** to improve one's conduct **—a·mend′a·ble** *adj.*

a·mend′ment *n.* 1. a correction of errors, faults, etc. 2. an improvement 3. a revision proposed or made in a bill, law, etc.

a·mends (ə mendz′) *n.pl.* [*sometimes with sing. v.*] something given or done to make up for injury, loss, etc.

a·men·i·ty (ə men′ə tē, -mē′nə-) *n., pl.* **-ties** [< L. *amoenus,* pleasant] 1. pleasantness 2. an attractive feature or convenience 3. [*pl.*] courteous acts

a·merce (ə murs′) *vt.* **a·merced′, a·merc′ing** [< OFr. *a merci,* at the mercy of] to punish, esp. by imposing a fine

A·mer·i·can (ə mer′ə kən) *adj.* 1. of or in America 2. of the U.S., its people, etc. **—n.** a native or inhabitant of America; specif., a citizen of the U.S.

A·mer′i·can·ism *n.* 1. a custom or belief originating in the U.S. 2. a word or idiom peculiar to American English 3. devotion or loyalty to the U.S., its customs, etc.

A·mer′i·can·ize′ (-īz′) *vt., vi.* **-ized′, -iz′ing** to make or become American in character, manners, etc. **—A·mer′i·can·i·za′tion** *n.*

am·e·thyst (am′ə thist) *n.* [< Gr. *amethystos,*

not drunken (from the notion that it prevented intoxication)] **1.** a purple variety of quartz or of corundum, used in jewelry **2.** purple or violet

a·mi·a·ble (ā′mē ə b'l) *adj.* [< L. *amicus*, friend] good-natured; friendly —**a′mi·a·bil′i·ty** *n.* —**a′mi·a·bly** *adv.*

am·i·ca·ble (am′i kə b'l) *adj.* [see AMIABLE] friendly in feeling; peaceable —**am′i·ca·bil′i·ty** *n.* —**am′i·ca·bly** *adv.*

a·mid (ə mid′) *prep.* among; in the middle of: also **a·midst** (ə midst′)

a·mid′ships′ *adv., adj.* in or toward the middle of a ship: also **a·mid′ship′**

a·mi·go (ə mē′gō) *n., pl.* -**gos** (-gōz) [Sp.] a friend

a·mi·no acids (ə mē′nō) [< AMMONIA] a group of nitrogenous organic compounds that are structural units of proteins

Am·ish (ä′mish, am′ish) *n.pl.* [< Jacob *Ammann* (or *Amen*), the founder] Mennonites of a sect founded in the 17th cent. —*adj.* of this sect

a·miss (ə mis′) *adv.* [see A- & MISS¹] **1.** astray **2.** wrongly —*adj.* wrong; improper

am·i·ty (am′ə tē) *n., pl.* -**ties** [< L. *amicus*, friend] friendly, peaceful relations

am·me·ter (am′mēt′ər) *n.* [AM(PERE) + -METER] an instrument for measuring an electric current in amperes

am·mo (am′ō) *n.* [Slang] ammunition

am·mo·nia (ə mōn′yə) *n.* [from a salt found near Libyan shrine of Jupiter *Ammon*] **1.** a colorless, pungent gas **2.** a water solution of this gas: also **ammonia water**

am·mu·ni·tion (am′yə nish′ən) *n.* [< L. *munire*, to fortify] **1.** bullets, shells, bombs, grenades, etc. **2.** any means of attack or defense

am·ne·sia (am nē′zhə, -zhē ə) *n.* [< Gr. *a-*, not + *mnasthai*, to remember] partial or total loss of memory

am·nes·ty (am′nəs tē) *n., pl.* -**ties** [< Gr. *amnēstia*, a forgetting] a general pardon, esp. for political offenses —*vt.* -**tied**, -**ty·ing** to grant amnesty to; pardon

a·moe·ba (ə mē′bə) *n., pl.* -**bas**, -**bae** (-bē) [< Gr. *ameibein*, to change] a microscopic, one-celled animal multiplying by fission —**a·moe′bic**, **a·moe′bold** *adj.*

a·mok (ə muk′) *adj., adv.* [Malay *amoq*] **1.** in a frenzy to kill **2.** in a violent rage

a·mong (ə muŋ′) *prep.* [< OE. *on*, in + *gemang*, a crowd] **1.** surrounded by [*among* friends] **2.** in the group of [best *among* books] **3.** with a share for each of [divided *among* us] **4.** by the joint action of

a·mongst (ə muŋst′) *prep. same as* AMONG

a·mor·al (ā môr′əl) *adj.* **1.** neither moral nor immoral **2.** without moral principles —**a·mor·al·i·ty** (ā′mə ral′ə tē) *n.*

am·o·rous (am′ər əs) *adj.* [< L. *amor*, love] **1.** fond of making love **2.** full of love **3.** of sexual love or lovemaking

a·mor·phous (ə môr′fəs) *adj.* [< Gr. *a-*, without + *morphē*, form] **1.** shapeless **2.** of no definite type **3.** *Chem.* not crystalline

am·or·tize (am′ər tīz′, ə môr′-) *vt.* -**tized**, -**tiz′ing** [< L. *ad*, to + *mors*, death] to put money aside at intervals for payment of (a debt, etc.) —**am′or·ti·za′tion** *n.*

a·mount (ə mount′) *vi.* [< L. *ad*, to + *mons*, mountain] **1.** to add up (*to* a sum) **2.** to be equal (*to*) in value, etc. —*n.* **1.** the sum of two or more quantities **2.** the whole value or effect **3.** a quantity

a·mour (ə moor′) *n.* [Fr. < L. *amor*, love] a love affair, esp. an illicit one

am·per·age (am′pər ij, am pir′-) *n.* the strength of an electric current in amperes

am·pere (am′pir) *n.* [after A. M. *Ampère* (1775–1836), Fr. physicist] the standard unit for measuring an electric current, equal to one coulomb per second

am·per·sand (am′pər sand′) *n.* [< *and per se and,* lit., (the sign) & by itself (is) *and*] a sign (&), meaning *and*

am·phet·a·mine (am fet′ə mēn′, -min) *n.* a drug used to overcome depression, fatigue, etc. and to lessen the appetite

am·phib·i·an (am fib′ē ən) *n.* [see ff.] **1.** any amphibious animal or plant **2.** an aircraft that can take off from or come down on either land or water **3.** a vehicle that can travel on either land or water —*adj. same as* AMPHIBIOUS

am·phib′i·ous (-əs) *adj.* [< Gr. *amphi-*, on both sides + *bios*, life] that can live or operate both on land and in water

am·phi·the·a·ter, **am·phi·the·a·tre** (am′fə thē′ə tər) *n.* [< Gr. *amphi-*, around + *theatron*, theater] a round or oval building with an open space (arena) surrounded by rising rows of seats

am·pho·ra (am′fər ə) *n., pl.* -**rae** (-ē), -**ras** [< Gr. *amphi-*, on both sides + *pherein*, to bear] a tall jar with a narrow neck and base and two handles, used by the ancient Greeks and Romans

am·ple (am′p'l) *adj.* -**pler**, -**plest** [< L. *amplus*] **1.** large in size, extent, etc. **2.** more than enough **3.** adequate —**am′ply** *adv.*

am·pli·fi·er (am′plə fī′ər) *n.* **1.** one that amplifies **2.** an electronic device used to increase electrical signal strength

am·pli·fy (am′plə fī′) *vt.* -**fied**, -**fy′ing** [< L. *amplus*, ample + *facere*, to make] **1.** to make stronger; esp., to strengthen (an electrical signal) **2.** to expand —*vi.* to expatiate —**am′pli·fi·ca′tion** *n.*

am·pli·tude (am′plə tōōd′) *n.* [see AMPLE] **1.** extent; largeness **2.** abundance **3.** scope or breadth **4.** the extreme range of a fluctuating quantity, from the average or mean to the extreme

amplitude modulation the changing of the amplitude of the transmitting radio wave in accordance with the signal being broadcast

am·pul (am′pool) *n.* [< Fr. < L. *ampulla*, bottle] a small glass container for one dose of a hypodermic medicine: also **am′pule** (-pyool), **am′poule** (-pool)

am·pu·tate (am′pyə tāt′) *vt.* -**tat′ed**, -**tat′ing** [< L. *am-*, for AMBI- + *putare*, to prune] to cut off (an arm, leg, etc.), esp. by surgery —**am′pu·ta′tion** *n.*

am·pu·tee (am′pyə tē′) *n.* a person who has had a limb or limbs amputated

amt. amount

Am·trak (am′trak′) *n.* [*Am(erican) tr(avel) (tr)a(c)k*] a nationwide system of passenger railroad service

a·muck (ə muk′) *adj., adv. same as* AMOK

am·u·let (am′yə lit) *n.* [< L.] something worn on the body as a charm against evil

a·muse (ə myōōz′) *vt.* **a·mused′**, **a·mus′ing** [< Fr. *à*, at + OFr. *muser*, to stare fixedly] **1.** to keep pleasantly occupied; entertain **2.** to make laugh, smile, etc.

a·muse′ment (-mənt) *n.* **1.** a being amused **2.** something that amuses

amusement park an outdoor place with devices for entertainment, as a merry-go-round, etc.

am·yl·ase (am′ə lās′) *n.* [< Gr. *amylon,* starch] an enzyme that helps change starch into sugar, found in saliva, etc.

an (ən; *stressed* an) *adj.,* **indefinite article** [< OE. *an,* one] **1.** one; one sort of **2.** each; any one **3.** per [two *an* hour] *An* is used before words beginning with a vowel sound [*an* eye, *an* honor, *an* ultimatum]

-an [< L. *-anus*] *a suffix meaning:* **1.** (one) belonging to [*diocesan*] **2.** (one) born in or living in [*American*] **3.** (one) believing in [*Mohammedan*]

a·nach·ro·nism (ə nak′rə niz′m) *n.* [< Gr. *ana-,* against + *chronos,* time] **1.** anything out of its proper time in history **2.** the representation of this —**a·nach′ro·nis′tic** *adj.* —**a·nach′ro·nis′ti·cal·ly** *adv.*

an·a·con·da (an′ə kän′də) *n.* [< ?] **1.** a large S. American snake of the boa family **2.** any similar snake that crushes its victim

a·nae·mi·a (ə nē′mē ə) *n. same as* ANEMIA

an·aer·o·bic (an′er ō′bik, -ə rō′-) *adj.* [< Gr. *an-,* without + *aero-,* AERO- + *bios,* life] that can live where there is no free oxygen

an·aes·the·sia (an′əs thē′zhə) *n. same as* ANESTHESIA —**an′aes·thet′ic** *adj., n.*

an·a·gram (an′ə gram′) *n.* [< Gr. *anagrammatizein,* transpose letters] **1.** a word or phrase made from another by rearranging its letters (Ex.: *now — won*) **2.** [*pl., with sing. v.*] a word game based on this

a·nal (ā′n′l) *adj.* of or near the anus

an·al·ge·si·a (an′′l jē′zē ə, -sē ə) *n.* [< Gr. *an-,* without + *algésia,* pain] a state of not feeling pain although fully conscious

an′al·ge′sic (-zik, -sik) *adj.* of or causing analgesia —*n.* a drug producing analgesia

analog computer an electronic computer that uses voltages to represent the numerical data of physical quantities

a·nal·o·gize (ə nal′ə jīz′) *vi., vt.* **-gized′, -giz′-ing** to use, or explain by, analogy

a·nal′o·gous (-gəs) *adj.* [see ANALOGY] similar or comparable in certain respects

an·a·logue, an·a·log (an′ə lôg′) *n.* a thing or part that is analogous —*adj.* of an analog computer: usually **analog**

a·nal·o·gy (ə nal′ə jē) *n., pl.* **-gies** [< Gr. *ana-,* according to + *logos,* ratio] **1.** similarity in some respects **2.** a comparing of something point by point with something similar

a·nal·y·sis (ə nal′ə sis) *n., pl.* **-ses′** (-sēz′) [Gr. < *ana-,* up + *lysis,* a loosing] **1.** a breaking up of a whole into its parts to find out their nature, etc. **2.** a statement of these findings **3.** *same as* PSYCHOANALYSIS **4.** *Chem.* the separation of compounds and mixtures into their constituents to determine their nature or proportion —**an·a·lyt·i·cal** (an′ə lit′i k′l) *adj.*

an·a·lyst (an′ə list) *n.* **1.** a person who analyzes **2.** *same as* PSYCHOANALYST

an′a·lyze′ (-līz′) *vt.* **-lyzed′, -lyz′ing 1.** to separate into parts so as to find out their nature, etc. **2.** to examine so as to determine the nature of **3.** to psychoanalyze —**an′a·lyz′a·ble** *adj.* —**an′a·lyz′er** *n.*

an·a·pest, an·a·paest (an′ə pest′) *n.* [< Gr. *ana-,* back + *paiein,* to strike] a metrical foot of three syllables, the first two unaccented and the third accented

an·ar·chism (an′ər kiz′m) *n.* **1.** the theory that all forms of government should be replaced by voluntary cooperation **2.** resistance, sometimes by terrorism, to government

an′ar·chist (-kist) *n.* **1.** a person who believes in anarchism **2.** a promoter of anarchy —**an′ar·chis′tic** *adj.*

an′ar·chy (-kē) *n.* [< Gr. *an-,* without + *archos,* leader] **1.** the complete absence of government **2.** political disorder and violence **3.** disorder; confusion —**an·ar′chic** (-är′kik), **an·ar′chi·cal** *adj.*

a·nath·e·ma (ə nath′ə mə) *n., pl.* **-mas** [< Gr., thing devoted to evil] **1.** a thing or person accursed **2.** anything greatly detested **3.** a formal curse, as in excommunicating a person **4.** any strong curse

a·nath′e·ma·tize′ (-tīz′) *vt., vi.* **-tized′, -tiz′ing** to utter an anathema (against)

a·nat·o·mize (ə nat′ə mīz′) *vt., vi.* **-mized′, -miz′ing 1.** to dissect (an animal or plant) in order to study the structure **2.** to analyze in detail —**a·nat′o·mist** *n.*

a·nat′o·my (-mē) *n., pl.* **-mies** [< Gr. *ana-,* up + *temnein,* to cut] **1.** the dissecting of an organism to study its structure **2.** the science of the structure of animals or plants **3.** the structure of an organism **4.** a detailed analysis —**an·a·tom·i·cal** (an′ə täm′i k′l), **an′a·tom′ic** *adj.*

-ance [< L.] *a suffix meaning:* **1.** the act of [*utterance*] **2.** a being [*vigilance*] **3.** a thing that [*conveyance*] **4.** a thing that is [*dissonance, inheritance*]

an·ces·tor (an′ses′tər) *n.* [< L. *ante-,* before + *cedere,* go] **1.** a person from whom one is descended; forebear **2.** an early type of animal from which later kinds have evolved **3.** a predecessor —**an′ces′tress** (-trəs) *n.fem.*

an·ces·tral (an ses′trəl) *adj.* of or inherited from ancestors —**an·ces′tral·ly** *adv.*

an·ces·try (an′ses′trē) *n., pl.* **-tries 1.** family lineage **2.** ancestors collectively

an·chor (aŋ′kər) *n.* [< Gr. *ankyra,* a hook] **1.** a heavy object, as an iron weight with flukes, lowered into the water by cable to keep a ship from drifting **2.** anything giving security or stability —*vt.* to hold secure as by an anchor —*vi.* **1.** to lower the anchor **2.** to become fixed —**at anchor** anchored

an′chor·age (-ij) *n.* **1.** an anchoring or being anchored **2.** a place to anchor

an·cho·rite (aŋ′kə rīt′) *n.* [< Gr. *ana-,* back + *chōrein,* retire] a religious recluse; hermit: also **an′cho·ret** (-rit)

anchor man *Radio & TV* a newscaster who coordinates various reports

an·cho·vy (an′chō′vē, -chə-; an′chō′vē) *n., pl.* **-vies, -vy** [< Port. *anchova*] a very small, herringlike fish

an·cient (ān′shənt) *adj.* [< L. *ante,* before] **1.** of times long past **2.** very old —*n.* an aged person —**the ancients** the people who lived in ancient times

an′cient·ly *adv.* in ancient times

an·cil·lar·y (an′sə ler′ē) *adj.* [< L. *ancilla,* maidservant] **1.** subordinate (*to*) **2.** auxiliary

and (ənd, ən, ′n; *stressed* and) *conj.* [OE.] **1.** also; in addition **2.** plus **3.** as a result **4.** [Colloq.] to [*try and* get it]

an·dan·te (än dän′tā, an dan′tē) *adj., adv.* [< It. *andare,* to walk] *Music* fairly slow

and·i·ron (and′ī′ərn) *n.* [< OFr. *andier*] either of a pair of metal supports for holding wood in a fireplace

and/or either *and* or *or,* according to what is meant [*personal and/or* real property]

an·dro·gen (an′drə jən) *n.* [< Gr. *andros,* man + -GEN] a male sex hormone that can give rise to masculine characteristics —**an′dro·gen′ic** (-jen′ik) *adj.*

an·ec·dote (an′ik dōt′) *n.* [< Gr. *anekdotos,* unpublished] a short, entertaining account of some event —**an′ec·dot′al** *adj.*

a·ne·mi·a (ə nē′mē ə) *n.* [< Gr. *a-,* without +

haima, blood] a condition in which the blood is low in red corpuscles or in hemoglobin, resulting in paleness, weakness, etc. **–a·ne′mic** (-mik) *adj.*

an·e·mom·e·ter (an′ə mäm′ə tər) *n.* [< Gr. *anemos*, the wind + -METER] a gauge for determining the force or speed of the wind

a·nem·o·ne (ə nem′ə nē′) *n.* [< Gr. *anemos*, the wind] **1.** a plant with white to red, cup-shaped flowers **2.** *same as* SEA ANEMONE

a·nent (ə nent′) *prep.* [< OE. *on efen*, lit., on even (with)] as regards; concerning

an·er·oid barometer (an′ər oid) [< Gr. *a-*, without + *nēros*, liquid + -OID] a barometer working by the bending of a metal plate, not by the rise or fall of mercury

an·es·the·sia (an′əs thē′zhə) *n.* [< Gr. *an-*, without + *aisthēsis*, feeling] a partial or total loss of the sense of pain, touch, etc.

an′es·thet′ic (-thet′ik) *adj.* **1.** of or with anesthesia **2.** producing anesthesia **–n.** a drug, gas, etc. used to produce anesthesia

an·es·the·tist (ə nes′thə tist) *n.* a person trained to administer anesthetics

an·es′the·tize′ (-tīz′) *vt.* **-tized′, -tiz′ing** to cause anesthesia in

an·eu·rysm, an·eu·rism (an′yər iz′m) *n.* [< Gr. *ana-*, up + *eurys*, broad] a sac formed by enlargement of an artery wall

a·new (ə nō͞o′) *adv.* again

an·gel (ān′j′l) *n.* [< Gr. *angelos*, messenger] **1.** *a*) a messenger of God *b*) a supernatural being **2.** an image of a human figure with wings and a halo **3.** a person regarded as beautiful, good, etc. **4.** [Colloq.] a financial backer, as for a play **–an·gel·ic** (an jel′ik) *adj.* **–an·gel′i·cal·ly** *adv.*

an·gel·fish (ān′j′l fish′) *n., pl.:* see FISH a bright-colored tropical fish with spiny fins

angel (food) cake a light, spongy, white cake made with egg whites

an·ger (aŋ′gər) *n.* [< ON. *angr*, distress] a feeling of displeasure and hostility resulting from injury, opposition, etc. **–vt.** to make angry **–vi.** to become angry

an·gi·na (pec·to·ris) (an jī′nə pek′tər is) [L., distress of the breast] a condition marked by pain in the chest, caused by a sudden decrease of blood to the heart

an·gle′ (aŋ′g′l) *n.* [< Gr. *ankylos*, bent] **1.** the shape or space formed by two straight lines or plane surfaces that meet **2.** the degrees of difference in direction between them **3.** a sharp corner **4.** a point of view **5.** [Colloq.] a tricky plan **–vt., vi. -gled, -gling 1.** to move or bend at an angle **2.** [Colloq.] to give a specific point of view to (a story, etc.)

an·gle² (aŋ′g′l) *vi.* **-gled, -gling** [OE. *angul*, fishhook] **1.** to fish with a hook and line **2.** to use tricks to get something [*angling* for attention] **–an′gler** *n.*

angle iron an angled piece of iron or steel used for joining or reinforcing two beams, etc.

An·gles (aŋ′g′lz) *n.pl.* a Germanic people that settled in E England in the 5th cent. A.D.

an′gle·worm′ *n.* an earthworm

An·gli·can (aŋ′gli kən) *adj.* [< ML. *Anglicus*, of the Angles] of the Church of England or any related church with the same faith and forms **–n.** a member of an Anglican church

An′gli·cize′ (-glə sīz′) *vt., vi.* **-cized′, -ciz′ing** to change to English pronunciation, customs, etc. **–An′gli·ci·za′tion** *n.*

Anglo- *a combining form meaning* English

An·glo-Sax·on (aŋ′glō sak′s′n) *n.* **1.** a member of the Germanic peoples living in England at the time of the Norman Conquest **2.** *same as*

OLD ENGLISH **3.** a person of English nationality or descent **–adj.** of the Anglo-Saxons or their language

An·go·ra (aŋ gôr′ə) *n.* [former name of *Ankara*, Turkey] **1.** a kind of cat with long, silky fur **2.** *a*) a kind of goat raised for its long, silky hair *b*) a cloth made from this

an·gry (aŋ′grē) *adj.* **-gri·er, -gri·est 1.** feeling or showing anger **2.** wild and stormy **–an′gri·ly** *adv.*

an·guish (aŋ′gwish) *n.* [< L. *angustus*, narrow] great mental or physical pain; agony **–vt., vi.** to feel or make feel anguish

an·gu·lar (aŋ′gyə lər) *adj.* **1.** having or forming an angle or angles; sharp-cornered **2.** lean; gaunt **3.** without ease or grace; stiff **–an′gu·lar′i·ty** (-ler′ə tē) *n., pl.* **-ties**

an·i·line (an′′l in, -ēn′) *n.* [< Ar. *al*, the + *nīl*, blue + -INE³] a colorless, oily liquid derivative of benzene, used in making dyes

an·i·mad·ver·sion (an′ə mad vur′zhən) *n.* a critical, esp. unfavorable, comment

an′i·mad·vert′ (-vurt′) *vi.* [< L. *animus*, mind + *ad-*, to + *vertere*, to turn] to comment adversely (*on* or *upon*)

an·i·mal (an′ə m′l) *n.* [< L. *anima*, breath, soul] **1.** any living organism except a plant or bacterium: most animals can move about **2.** any four-footed creature **3.** a brutish person **–adj. 1.** of or like an animal **2.** gross, bestial, etc. **–an′i·mal′i·ty** *n.*

an·i·mal·ism (an′ə m′l iz′m) *n.* the activity, appetites, nature, etc. of animals

an·i·mate (an′ə māt′) *vt.* **-mat′ed, -mat′ing** [see ANIMAL] **1.** to give life or motion to **2.** to make gay or spirited **3.** to inspire **–adj.** (-mit) **1.** living **2.** lively **–an′i·mat′ed** *adj.* **–an′i·ma′tor, an′i·mat′er** *n.*

animated cartoon a motion picture made by filming a series of drawings

an′i·ma′tion *n.* **1.** an animating or being animated **2.** life **3.** vivacity

an·i·mos·i·ty (an′ə mäs′ə tē) *n., pl.* **-ties** [see ANIMUS] a feeling of ill will; hostility

an·i·mus (an′ə məs) *n.* [L., passion] **1.** an animating force **2.** animosity; hostility

an·i·on (an′ī′ən) *n.* [< Gr. *ana-*, up + *ienai*, to go] a negatively charged ion

an·ise (an′is) *n.* [< Gr. *anēson*] **1.** a plant related to parsley **2.** its fragrant seed, used for flavoring: also **an·i·seed** (an′ə sēd′)

an·kle (aŋ′k′l) *n.* [OE. *ancleow*] **1.** the joint that connects the foot and the leg **2.** the part of the leg between the foot and calf

an′kle·bone′ *n.* the bone of the ankle

an·klet (aŋ′klit) *n.* **1.** an ornament, etc. worn around the ankle **2.** a short sock

an·nals (an′′lz) *n.pl.* [< L. *annus*, year] **1.** a written account of events year by year **2.** historical records; history **–an′nal·ist** *n.*

an·neal (ə nēl′) *vt.* [< OE. *an-*, on + *æl*, fire] to heat (glass, metals, etc.) and then cool slowly to prevent brittleness

an·nex (ə neks′) *vt.* [< L. *ad-*, to + *nectere*, to tie] **1.** to attach, esp. to something larger **2.** to incorporate into a state, etc. the territory of (another state, etc.) **–n.** (an′eks) something added on; esp., an addition to a building **–an′-nex·a′tion** *n.*

an·ni·hi·late (ə nī′ə lāt′) *vt.* **-lat′ed, -lat′ing** [< L. *ad-*, to + *nihil*, nothing] to destroy completely **–an·ni′hi·la′tion** *n.*

an·ni·ver·sa·ry (an′ə vur′sər ē) *n., pl.* **-ries** [< L. *annus*, year + *vertere*, to turn] **1.** the date on which some event occurred in an earlier year **2.** its celebration **–adj.** of or connected with an anniversary

an·no·tate (an'ə tāt') *vt., vi.* -tat'ed, -tat'ing [< L. *ad-*, to + *nota*, a sign] to provide explanatory notes for (a literary work, etc.) —**an'no·ta'tion** *n.* —**an'no·ta'tive** *adj.* —**an'no·ta'tor** *n.*

an·nounce (ə nouns') *vt.* -nounced', -nounc'ing [< L. *ad-*, to + *nuntiare*, to report] 1. to declare publicly; proclaim 2. to say 3. to make known the arrival, etc. of 4. to be an announcer for —*vi.* to act as an announcer —**announce'ment** *n.*

an·nounc'er *n.* 1. one who announces 2. one who introduces radio or television programs, identifies the station, etc.

an·noy (ə noi') *vt.* [< L. *in odio habere*, to have in hate] to irritate, bother, etc. —**an·noy'ance** *n.* —**an·noy'ing** *adj.*

an·nu·al (an'yoo wəl) *adj.* [< L. *annus*, year] 1. of or measured by a year 2. yearly 3. living only one year or season —*n.* 1. a yearly publication 2. a plant that lives only one year or season —**an'nu·al·ly** *adv.*

an·nu·i·ty (ə noo'ə tē) *n., pl.* -ties [see prec.] 1. a payment of a fixed sum of money at regular intervals, esp. yearly 2. an investment yielding such payments

an·nul (ə nul') *vt.* -nulled', -nul'ling [< LL. *annullare*, bring to nothing] to do away with; invalidate; cancel —**an·nul'ment** *n.*

an·nu·lar (an'yoo lər) *adj.* [< L. *anulus*, a ring] of, like, or forming a ring

an·nun·ci·a·tion (ə nun'sē ā'shən) *n.* 1. an announcing 2. [A-] *a*) the angel Gabriel's announcement to Mary that she was to give birth to Jesus *b*) the church festival (March 25) commemorating this

an·ode (an'ōd) *n.* [< Gr. *ana-*, up + *hodos*, way] 1. a positively charged electrode, as in an electrolytic cell, electron tube, etc. 2. the negative electrode in a battery supplying current

an·o·dyne (an'ə dīn') *adj.* [< Gr. *an-*, without + *odynē*, pain] relieving pain —*n.* anything that relieves pain or soothes

a·noint (ə noint') *vt.* [< L. *in-*, on + *ungere*, to smear] to put oil on, as in consecrating —**a·noint'ment** *n.*

a·nom·a·lous (ə näm'ə ləs) *adj.* [< Gr. *an-*, not + *homos*, the same] 1. deviating from the general rule; abnormal 2. inconsistent

a·nom'a·ly (-lē) *n., pl.* -lies 1. departure from the usual 2. anything anomalous

a·non (ə nän') *adv.* [OE. *on an*, in one] soon; shortly: now nearly archaic

anon. anonymous

a·non·y·mous (ə nän'ə məs) *adj.* [< Gr. *an-*, without + *onyma*, name] 1. with no name known 2. given, written, etc. by one whose name is withheld or unknown 3. lacking individuality —**an·o·nym·i·ty** (an'ə nim'ə tē) *n.* —**a·non'y·mous·ly** *adv.*

a·noph·e·les (ə näf'ə lēz') *n.* [< Gr. *anophelēs*, harmful] the mosquito that can transmit malaria

an·oth·er (ə nuth'ər) *adj.* 1. one more; an additional 2. a different —*pron.* 1. one additional 2. a different one 3. one of the same kind

ans. answer

an·swer (an'sər) *n.* [< OE. *and-*, against + *swerian*, swear] 1. a reply to a question, letter, etc. 2. any retaliation 3. a solution to a problem —*vi.* 1. to reply 2. to respond (*to*) [he *answers* to the name of Dick] 3. to be sufficient 4. to be responsible (*to* a person *for*) 5. to correspond (*to*) —*vt.* 1. to reply or respond to 2. to serve [to *answer* the purpose] 3. to refute (an accusation, etc.) 4. to suit [he *answers* the description] —**answer back** [Colloq.] to reply insolently —**an'swer·a·ble** *adj.*

ant (ant) *n.* [OE. *æmete*] any of a group of insects, generally wingless, that live in colonies with a complex division of labor

-ant [ult. < L.] *a suffix meaning:* 1. that has, shows, or does [*defiant*] 2. a person or thing that [*occupant*]

ant·ac·id (ant'as'id) *adj.* counteracting acidity —*n.* an antacid substance

an·tag·o·nism (an tag'ə niz'm) *n.* 1. a being opposed or hostile 2. an opposing force, principle, etc. —**an·tag'o·nis'tic** *adj.*

an·tag'o·nist *n.* an adversary; opponent

an·tag·o·nize (an tag'ə nīz') *vt.* -nized', -niz'-ing [< Gr. *anti-*, against + *agōn*, a contest] to incur the dislike of

ant·arc·tic (ant ärk'tik, -är'-) *adj.* [see ANTI- & ARCTIC] of or near the South Pole or the region around it

an·te (an'tē) *n.* [L., before] *Poker* the stake that each player must put into the pot before receiving cards —*vt., vi.* -ted or -teed, -te·ing *Poker* to put in (one's stake): also **ante up**

ante- [< L. *ante*, before] *a prefix meaning* before [*antecedent, anteroom*]

ant·eat·er (ant'ēt'ər) *n.* a mammal with a long snout, that feeds mainly on ants

an·te·bel·lum (an'ti bel'əm) *adj.* [L.] before the war; specif., before the American Civil War

an·te·ced·ent (an'tə sēd'nt) *adj.* [< L. *ante*, before + *cedere*, go] prior; previous —*n.* 1. any thing prior to another 2. [*pl.*] one's ancestry, past life, etc. 3. *Gram.* the word or phrase to which a pronoun refers

an·te·cham·ber (an'ti chām'bər) *n.* a smaller room leading into a larger room

an·te·date (an'ti dāt') *vt.* -dat'ed, -dat'ing 1. to put a date on that is earlier than the actual date 2. to come before

an·te·di·lu·vi·an (an'ti də loo'vē ən) *adj.* [< ANTE- + L. *diluvium*, a flood + -AN] 1. of the time before the Biblical Flood 2. very old or old-fashioned

an·te·lope (an'tə lōp') *n.* [< MGr. *antholops*, deer] a swift, cud-chewing, hollow-horned, deerlike animal related to oxen and goats

an·te me·ri·di·em (an'tē mə rid'ē əm) [L.] before noon: abbrev. **A.M., a.m., AM**

an·ten·na (an ten'ə) *n.* [< L. *antemna*, sail yard] 1. *pl.* -nae (-ē), -nas either of a pair of feelers on the head of an insect, crab, etc. 2. *pl.* -nas *Radio & TV* an arrangement of wires, rods, etc. used in sending and receiving electromagnetic waves

an·te·ri·or (an tir'ē ər) *adj.* [L., compar. of *ante*, before] 1. at or toward the front: opposed to POSTERIOR 2. previous; earlier

an·te·room (an'ti rōōm') *n.* a room leading to a larger one; waiting room

an·them (an'thəm) *n.* [< Gr. *anti-*, over against + *phōnē*, voice] 1. a religious choral song 2. a song of praise, as to a nation

an·ther (an'thər) *n.* [< Gr. *anthos*, a flower] the part of a stamen that contains the pollen

ant·hill (ant'hil') *n.* the soil heaped up by ants around their nest opening

an·thol·o·gy (an thäl'ə jē) *n., pl.* -gies [< Gr. *anthos*, flower + *legein*, to gather] a collection of poems, stories, etc. —**an·thol'o·gist** *n.*

an·thra·cite (an'thrə sīt') *n.* [< Gr. *anthrax*, coal] hard coal, which gives much heat but little flame and smoke

an·thrax (an'thraks) *n.* [< Gr., coal, carbuncle] an infectious disease of cattle, sheep, etc., which can be transmitted to man

anthropo- [< Gr. *anthrōpos*, man] *a combining form meaning* man, human

anthropoid   19   **antivivisectionist**

an·thro·poid (an′thrə poid′) *adj.* [ANTHROP(O)- + -OID] **1.** manlike; esp., designating or of any of the most highly developed apes, as the chimpanzee and gorilla **2.** apelike —*n.* any anthropoid ape —**an′thro·poi′dal** *adj.*

an·thro·pol·o·gy (an′thrə päl′ə jē) *n.* [ANTHROPO- + -LOGY] the study of the variety, distribution, characteristics, cultures, etc. of mankind —**an′thro·po·log′i·cal** (-pə läj′i k'l) *adj.* —**an′thro·pol′o·gist** *n.*

an′thro·po·mor′phism (-pə môr′fiz'm) *n.* [< ANTHROPO- + Gr. *morphē*, form + -ISM] the attributing of human shape to a god, object, etc. —**an′thro·po·mor′phic** *adj.*

an·ti (an′tī, -tē) *n., pl.* **-tis** [< ANTI-] [Colloq.] a person opposed to some policy, proposal, etc. —*prep.* [Colloq.] opposed to

anti- [< Gr. *anti*, against] *a prefix meaning:* **1.** against; hostile to **2.** that operates against **3.** that prevents, cures, or neutralizes **4.** opposite; reverse **5.** rivaling

an·ti·air·craft (an′tē er′kraft) *adj.* used for defense against hostile aircraft

an·ti·bac·te·ri·al (an′ti bak tir′ē əl) *adj.* that checks the growth or effect of bacteria

an′ti·bal·lis′tic missile (-bə lis′tik) a ballistic missile for intercepting an enemy ballistic missile

an′ti·bi·ot′ic (-bī ät′ik) *adj.* [< ANTI- + Gr. *biōsis*, way of life] destroying, or stopping the growth of, bacteria and other microorganisms —*n.* an antibiotic substance

an·ti·bod·y (an′ti bäd′ē) *n., pl.* **-ies** a protein produced in the body to neutralize an antigen

an·tic (an′tik) *adj.* [< L.: see ANTIQUE] odd and funny —*n.* a playful or silly act, etc.

An·ti·christ (an′ti krist′) *Bible* the great antagonist of Christ: I John 2:18

an·tic·i·pate (an tis′ə pāt′) *vt.* **-pat′ed, -pat′ing** [< L. *ante-*, before + *capere*, to take] **1.** to look forward to; expect **2.** to forestall **3.** to take care of, use, etc. in advance **4.** to be ahead of in doing something —**an·tic′i·pa′tion** *n.* —**an·tic′i·pa·to′ry** (-pə tôr′ē) *adj.*

an·ti·cler·i·cal (an′ti kler′ə k'l) *adj.* opposed to the influence of the clergy or church in public affairs

an′ti·cli′max (-klī′maks) *n.* **1.** a sudden drop from the important to the trivial **2.** a final event which is in disappointing contrast to those coming before —**an′ti·cli·mac′tic** (-mak′-tik) *adj.*

an′ti·co·ag′u·lant (-kō ag′yə lənt) *n.* a drug or substance that delays or prevents the clotting of blood

an′ti·de·pres′sant (-di pres′ənt) *adj.* lessening emotional depression —*n.* an antidepressant drug

an·ti·dote (an′tə dōt′) *n.* [< Gr. *anti-*, against + *dotos*, given] **1.** a remedy to counteract a poison **2.** anything that works against an evil —**an′ti·dot′al** *adj.*

an·ti·freeze (an′ti frēz′) *n.* a substance used, as in automobile radiators, to prevent freezing

an·ti·gen (an′tə jən) *n.* [ANTI- + -GEN] an enzyme, toxin, etc. to which the body reacts by producing antibodies

an·ti·he·ro (an′ti hir′ō) *n., pl.* **-roes** the protagonist of a novel, play, etc. who lacks the virtues of a traditional hero

an·ti·his·ta·mine (an′ti his′tə mēn′, -mən) *n.* any of several drugs used in treating allergic conditions, as hay fever and hives

an·ti·knock (an′ti näk′) *n.* a substance added to the fuel of internal-combustion engines to do away with noise caused by too rapid combustion

an·ti·ma·cas·sar (an′ti mə kas′ər) *n.* [ANTI- + *macassar* (*oil*), a former hair oil] a small cover to protect the back or arms of a chair, etc. from soiling

an·ti·mat·ter (an′ti mat′ər) *n.* a form of matter in which the electrical charge or other property of each constituent particle is the reverse of that in the usual matter of our universe

an′ti·mis′sile (-mis′'l) *adj.* designed as a defense against ballistic missiles

an·ti·mo·ny (an′tə mō′nē) *n.* [< ML.] a silvery-white metallic chemical element used to harden alloys, etc.: symbol, Sb

an·ti·pas·to (an′ti pas′tō, -päs′-) *n.* [It. < *anti-*, before + *pasto*, food] an appetizer of salted fish, meat, olives, etc.

an·tip·a·thy (an tip′ə thē) *n., pl.* **-thies** [< Gr. *anti-*, against + *pathein*, to feel] **1.** a strong dislike; aversion **2.** the object of this —**an·ti·pa·thet·ic** (an′ti pə thet′ik) *adj.* —**an′ti·pa·thet′i·cal·ly** *adv.*

an·ti·per·spir·ant (an′ti pur′spər ənt) *n.* a substance applied to the skin to reduce perspiration

an·ti·phon (an′tə fän′) *n.* [see ANTHEM] a hymn, etc. sung in responsive, alternating parts —**an·tiph′o·nal** (-tif′ə n'l) *adj.*

an·tip·o·des (an tip′ə dēz′) *n.pl.* [< Gr. *anti-*, opposite + *pous*, foot] two places directly opposite each other on the earth

an·ti·quar·i·an (an′tə kwer′ē ən) *adj.* **1.** of antiques or antiquities **2.** of antiquaries —*n.* an antiquary

an·ti·quar·y (an′tə kwer′ē) *n., pl.* **-ies** a collector or student of antiquities

an′ti·quate (-kwāt′) *vt.* **-quat′ed, -quat′ing** [see ANTIQUE] to make old or obsolete

an·tique (an tēk′) *adj.* [< L. *antiquus*, ancient] **1.** of ancient times **2.** out-of-date; old-fashioned **3.** of, or in the style of, a former period **4.** dealing in antiques —*n.* **1.** an ancient relic **2.** a piece of furniture, etc. of a former period —*vt.* **-tiqued′, -tiqu′ing** to make look antique

an·tiq·ui·ty (an tik′wə tē) *n., pl.* **-ties 1.** the early period of history, esp. before the Middle Ages **2.** great age **3.** [*pl.*] relics, monuments, etc. of the distant past

an·ti·Se·mit·ic (an′ti sə mit′ik) *adj.* **1.** having or showing prejudice against Jews **2.** discriminating against or persecuting Jews —**an′ti·Sem′ite** (-sem′īt) *n.* —**an′ti·Sem′i·tism** (-ə tiz′m) *n.*

an′ti·sep′tic (-sep′tik) *adj.* [ANTI- + SEPTIC] **1.** preventing infection, decay, etc.; effective against bacteria **2.** using antiseptics **3.** sterile —*n.* any antiseptic substance —**an′ti·sep′ti·cal·ly** *adv.*

an′ti·slav′er·y *adj.* against slavery

an′ti·so′cial (-sō′shəl) *adj.* **1.** not sociable **2.** harmful to the welfare of people

an·ti·tank (an′ti taŋk′) *adj.* for use against tanks in war

an·tith·e·sis (an tith′ə sis) *n., pl.* **-ses′** (-sēz′) [< Gr. *anti-*, against + *tithenai*, to place] **1.** a contrast or opposition, as of ideas **2.** the exact opposite —**an·ti·thet·i·cal** (an′tə thet′i k'l) *adj.*

an·ti·tox·in (an′ti täk′sin) *n.* **1.** an antibody formed by the body to act against a specific toxin **2.** a serum containing an antitoxin, injected into a person to prevent a disease —**an′-ti·tox′ic** *adj.*

an′ti·trust′ (-trust′) *adj.* opposed to or regulating trusts, or business monopolies

an′ti·viv′i·sec′tion·ist (-viv′ə sek′shən ist) *n.* one opposing vivisection

ant·ler (ant′lər) *n.* [< L. *ante-*, before + *ocularis*, of the eyes] the branched, deciduous horn of any animal of the deer family —**ant′-lered** *adj.*

an·to·nym (an′tə nim′) *n.* [< Gr. *anti-*, opposite + *onyma*, name] a word meaning the opposite of another word

an·trum (an′trəm) *n., pl.* **-tra** (-trə), **-trums** [< Gr. *antron*, cave] *Anat.* a cavity; esp., a sinus of the upper jaw

a·nus (ā′nəs) *n., pl.* **a′nus·es, a′ni** (-nī) [L.] the opening at the lower end of the alimentary canal

an·vil (an′vəl) *n.* [OE. *anfilt*] 1. an iron or steel block on which metal objects are hammered into shape 2. a bone in the ear

anx·i·e·ty (aŋ zī′ə tē) *n., pl.* **-ties** 1. worry or uneasiness about what may happen 2. an eager desire *[anxiety* to do well]

anx·ious (aŋk′shəs) *adj.* [< L. *angere*, choke] 1. uneasy in mind; worried 2. causing anxiety 3. eagerly wishing —**anx′ious·ly** *adv.* —**anx′-ious·ness** *n.*

an·y (en′ē) *adj.* [OE. *ænig*] 1. one, no matter which, of more than two *[any* pupil may answer] 2. some *[has he any* food?] 3. without limit *[any* number can play] 4. every *[any* child can do it] —*pron. sing. & pl.* any one or ones —*adv.* to any degree or extent

an′y·bod′y (-bud′ē, -bäd′ē) *pron.* 1. any person 2. an important person

an′y·how′ *adv. same as* ANYWAY

an′y·more′ *adv.* now; nowadays

an′y·one′ *pron.* any person; anybody

any one any single (person or thing)

an′y·place′ *adv. same as* ANYWHERE (sense 1)

an′y·thing *pron.* any object, event, fact, etc. — *n.* a thing, no matter of what kind —*adv.* in any way —**anything but** not at all

an′y·way′ *adv.* 1. in any manner 2. in any case 3. haphazardly; carelessly

an′y·where′ *adv.* 1. in, at, or to any place 2. [Colloq.] at all; to any extent —**get anywhere** [Colloq.] to have any success

A/O, a/o account of

A one (ā′ wun′) [Colloq.] first-class; first-rate; superior: also **A 1, A number 1**

a·or·ta (ā ôr′tə) *n., pl.* **-tas, -tae** (-tē) [< Gr. *aeirein*, to raise] the main artery of the body, carrying blood from the heart

a·pace (ə pās′) *adv.* at a fast pace; swiftly

A·pach·e (ə pach′ē) *n., pl.* **-es, -e** [prob. < Zuñi *ápachu*, enemy] a member of a tribe of SW U.S. Indians

a·part (ə pärt′) *adv.* [< L. *ad*, to + *pars*, part] 1. to one side; aside 2. away in place or time 3. separately in use, etc. *[viewed apart]* 4. in or to pieces —*adj.* separated —**apart from** other than; besides —**tell apart** to distinguish one from another

a·part·heid (ə pärt′hāt, -hīt) *n.* [Afrik., apartness] in South Africa, the policy of strict racial segregation

a·part·ment (ə pärt′mənt) *n.* [< Fr. < It. *parte*, part] a room or suite of rooms to live in —**apartment house** a building divided into apartments: also **apartment building**

ap·a·thy (ap′ə thē) *n., pl.* **-thies** [< Fr. < Gr. *a-*, without + *pathos*, emotion] 1. lack of emotion 2. indifference; lack of interest —**ap′a·thet′ic** (-thet′ik) —**ap′a·thet′i·cal·ly** *adv.*

ape (āp) *n.* [OE. *apa*] 1. a chimpanzee, gorilla, orangutan, or gibbon 2. any monkey 3. a coarse, uncouth person —*vt.* aped, ap′ing to imitate —**ape′like′** *adj.*

a·pe·ri·tif (ä′pā rə tēf′) *n.* [Fr.] an alcoholic drink taken before meals

ap·er·ture (ap′ər chər) *n.* [< L. *aperire*, to open] an opening; hole; gap

a·pex (ā′peks) *n., pl.* **-pex·es, ap·i·ces** (ap′ə sēz′, ā′pə-) [L.] 1. the highest point; peak 2. the pointed end; tip 3. a climax

a·pha·sia (ə fā′zhə) *n.* [Gr. < *a-*, not + *phanai*, speak] a total or partial loss of the power to use or understand words

a·phe·li·on (ə fē′lē ən) *n., pl.* **-li·ons, -li·a** (-ə) [< Gr. *apo*, from + *hēlios*, sun] the point farthest from the sun in the orbit of a planet, comet, or satellite

a·phid (ā′fid, af′id) *n.* [< Gr. *apheidēs*, lavish] a small insect that sucks the juice from plants

aph·o·rism (af′ə riz′m) *n.* [< Gr. *apo-*, from + *horizein*, to bound] 1. a concise statement of a principle 2. a maxim or adage —**aph′o·ris′tic** *adj.*

aph·ro·dis·i·ac (af′rə diz′ē ak′) *adj.* [< Gr. *Aphroditē*] arousing sexual desire —*n.* an aphrodisiac drug or other agent

Aph·ro·di·te (af′rə dīt′ē) the Greek goddess of love and beauty

a·pi·ar·y (ā′pē er′ē) *n., pl.* **-ies** [< L. *apis*, bee] a place where bees are kept

a·piece (ə pēs′) *adv.* [see A & PIECE] for each one

a·plen·ty (ə plen′tē) *adj., adv.* [Colloq.] in abundance

a·plomb (ə pläm′, -plum′) *n.* [< Fr.: see PLUMB] self-possession; poise

APO Army Post Office

a·poc·a·lypse (ə päk′ə lips′) *n.* [< Gr. *apokalyptein*, disclose] a religious writing depicting symbolically the end of evil; specif., [A-] *Bible* the book of REVELATION —**a·poc′a·lyp′tic** (-lip′tik) *adj.*

A·poc·ry·pha (ə päk′rə fə) [< Gr. *apo-*, away + *kryptein*, to hide] fourteen books of the Septuagint rejected in Protestantism and Judaism: eleven are accepted in the Roman Catholic Biblical canon

a·poc′ry·phal *adj.* 1. of doubtful authenticity 2. not genuine; false; counterfeit

ap·o·gee (ap′ə jē′) *n.* [< Gr. *apo-*, from + *gē*, earth] 1. the point farthest from a heavenly body, as the earth, in the orbit of a satellite around it 2. an apex

A·pol·lo (ə päl′ō) the Greek and Roman god of music, poetry, prophecy, and medicine —*n., pl.* **-los** a handsome young man

a·pol·o·get·ic (ə päl′ə jet′ik) *adj.* making apology; esp., expressing regret, as for a fault —**a·pol′o·get′i·cal·ly** *adv.*

a·pol·o·gist (ə päl′ə jist) *n.* one who defends or attempts to justify a doctrine, faith, action, etc.

a·pol′o·gize (-jīz′) *vi.* **-gized′, -giz′ing** to make an apology; esp., to express regret

a·pol·o·gy (ə päl′ə jē) *n., pl.* **-gies** [< Gr. *apo-*, from + *logos*, word] 1. a formal defense of some idea, doctrine, etc. 2. an expression of regret for a fault, wrong, etc. 3. an inferior substitute

ap·o·plec·tic (ap′ə plek′tik) *adj.* of, like, causing, or having apoplexy

ap·o·plex·y (ap′ə plek′sē) *n.* [< Gr. *apo-*, down + *plēssein*, to strike] sudden paralysis caused when a blood vessel in the brain breaks or becomes clogged; stroke

a·pos·ta·sy (ə päs′tə sē) *n., pl.* **-sies** [< Gr. *apo-*, away + *stasis*, standing] an abandoning of something that one once believed in, as a faith

a·pos′tate (-tāt′, -tit) *n.* a person guilty of apostasy; renegade —*adj.* guilty of apostasy

a pos·te·ri·o·ri (ā′ päs tir′ē ôr′ī, -ôr′ē) [ML.]

1. from effect to cause 2. based on observation or experience
A·pos·tle (ə päs''l) *n*. [< Gr. *apo-*, from + *stellein*, send] **1.** [*occas.* **a-**] any of the disciples of Jesus, esp. the original twelve **2.** [**a-**] the leader of a new reform movement
ap·os·tol·ic (ap'əs täl'ik) *adj*. **1.** of the Apostles, their teachings, work, etc. **2.** [*often* **A-**] of the Pope; papal
a·pos·tro·phe (ə päs'trə fē) *n*. [Fr. < Gr. *apo-*, from + *strephein*, to turn] the mark (') indicating: **1.** the omission of a letter or letters from a word (Ex.: *it's* for *it is*) **2.** the possessive case (Ex.: *Mary's* dress) **3.** certain plural forms (Ex.: *6's, t's*)
a·poth·e·car·y (ə päth'ə ker'ē) *n., pl.* **-ies** [< Gr. *apothēkē*, storehouse] a pharmacist
ap·o·thegm (ap'ə them') *n*. [< Gr. *apo-*, from + *phthengesthai*, to utter] a short, pithy saying
a·poth·e·o·sis (ə päth'ē ō'sis, ap'ə thē'ə-) *n., pl.* **-ses'** (-sēz') [< Gr. *apo-*, from + *theos*, god] **1.** the deifying of a person **2.** the glorification of a person or thing **3.** an ideal or exact type
ap·pall, ap·pal (ə pôl') *vt*. **-palled', -pal'ling** [< L. *pallidus*, pale] to fill with horror or dismay; shock **—ap·pal'ling** *adj*.
ap·pa·loo·sa (ap'ə loo'sə) *n*. [< *Palouse* Indians of NW U.S.] a breed of Western saddle horse with black or white spots on the rump and loins
ap·pa·ra·tus (ap'ə rat'əs, -rät'-) *n., pl.* **-tus, -tus·es** [< L. *ad-*, to + *parare*, prepare] **1.** the instruments, tools, etc. for a specific use **2.** any complex device, etc.
ap·par·el (ə per'əl) *n*. [< L. *apparare:* see prec.] clothing; attire **—vt.** **-eled** or **-elled, -el·ing** or **-el·ling** to clothe; dress
ap·par·ent (ə per'ənt, -par'-) *adj*. [see APPEAR] **1.** readily seen; visible **2.** evident; obvious **3.** appearing to be real or true; seeming **—ap·par'ent·ly** *adv*.
ap·pa·ri·tion (ap'ə rish'ən) *n*. [see APPEAR] **1.** anything that appears unexpectedly **2.** a ghost; phantom **3.** an appearing
ap·peal (ə pēl') *vt*. [< L. *ad-*, to + *pellere*, drive] to make an appeal of (a law case) **—vi.** **1.** to appeal a law case **2.** to make an urgent request (*to* a person *for* a decision, help, etc.) **3.** to be attractive or interesting **—n.** **1.** a request for help, etc. **2.** interest; attraction **3.** *Law* a request for the transference of a case to a higher court for rehearing **—ap·peal'ing** *adj*.
ap·pear (ə pir') *vi*. [< L. *ad-*, to + *parare*, come forth] **1.** to come into sight or being **2.** to become understood [*it appears* I lost] **3.** to seem; look **4.** to present oneself formally, as in court **5.** to come before the public [he will *appear* in Hamlet]
ap·pear'ance *n*. **1.** an appearing **2.** the outward aspect of anything **3.** an outward show; pretense **4.** [*pl.*] the way things seem to be **—put in an appearance** to be present for a short time, as at a party
ap·pease (ə pēz') *vt*. **-peased', -peas'ing** [< L. *pax*, peace] to make peaceful or quiet, esp. by giving in to the demands of **—ap·pease'ment** *n*.
ap·pel·lant (ə pel'ənt) *adj*. *Law* appealing **—n.** one who appeals, esp. to a higher court
ap·pel'late (-it) *adj*. *Law* relating to, or having jurisdiction to review, appeals
ap·pel·la·tion (ap'ə lā'shən) *n*. [see APPEAL] a name or title
ap·pend (ə pend') *vt*. [< L. *ad-*, to + *pendere*, suspend] to attach or affix; add

ap·pend'age *n*. **1.** anything appended; adjunct **2.** an external part, as a tail
ap·pen·dec·to·my (ap'ən dek'tə mē) *n., pl.* **-mies** [see -ECTOMY] the surgical removal of the appendix
ap·pen·di·ci·tis (ə pen'də sīt'əs) *n*. [see -ITIS] inflammation of the appendix
ap·pen·dix (ə pen'diks) *n., pl.* **-dix·es, -di·ces'** (-də sēz') [see APPEND] **1.** additional material at the end of a book **2.** a small sac (**vermiform appendix**) extending from the large intestine
ap·per·tain (ap'ər tān') *vi*. [< L. *ad-*, to + *pertinere*, to reach] to belong properly as a function, part, etc.; pertain
ap·pe·tite (ap'ə tīt') *n*. [< L. *ad-*, to + *petere*, seek] a desire, esp. for food
ap'pe·tiz'er (-tī'zər) *n*. a tasty food that stimulates the appetite
ap'pe·tiz'ing *adj*. stimulating the appetite; savory; tasty **—ap'pe·tiz'ing·ly** *adv*.
ap·plaud (ə plôd') *vt., vi*. [< L. *ad-*, to + *plaudere*, clap hands] **1.** to show approval (of) by clapping hands, etc. **2.** to praise
ap·plause (ə plôz') *n*. approval or praise, esp. as shown by clapping hands, etc.
ap·ple (ap'l) *n*. [OE. *æppel*] **1.** a round, firm, edible fruit **2.** the tree it grows on
apple butter jam made of stewed apples
ap'ple·jack' (-jak') *n*. brandy distilled from apple cider
ap'ple·sauce' (-sôs') *n*. apples cooked to a pulp in water and sweetened
ap·pli·ance (ə plī'əns) *n*. a device or machine, esp. one for household use
ap·pli·ca·ble (ap'li kə b'l) *adj*. that can be applied; appropriate **—ap'pli·ca·bly** *adv*.
ap·pli·cant (ap'li kənt) *n*. a person who applies, as for employment, help, etc.
ap·pli·ca·tion (ap'lə kā'shən) *n*. **1.** the act or a way of applying or being applied **2.** anything applied, as a remedy **3.** a request, or the form filled out in making a request **4.** continued effort **5.** relevance
ap'pli·ca'tor *n*. any device for applying medicine or paint, polish, etc.
ap·plied (ə plīd') *adj*. used in actual practice [*applied* science]
ap·pli·qué (ap'lə kā') *n*. [Fr. < L.: see APPLY] a decoration made of one material attached by sewing, etc. to another **—vt.** **-quéd', -qué'ing** to decorate with appliqué
ap·ply (ə plī') *vt*. **-plied', -ply'ing** [< L. *ad-*, to + *plicare*, to fold] **1.** to put on [*apply* glue] **2.** to use practically [*apply* your knowledge] **3.** to employ (oneself) diligently **—vi.** **1.** to make a formal request **2.** to be suitable or relevant **—ap·pli'er** *n*.
ap·point (ə point') *vt*. [< L. *ad-*, to + *punctum*, a point] **1.** to set (a date, place, etc.); decree **2.** to name for an office, etc. [*to appoint* a chairman] **3.** to furnish [well-*appointed*] **—ap·point'ee'** *n*.
ap·point'ive (-iv) *adj*. to which one is appointed, not elected [an *appointive* office]
ap·point'ment (-mənt) *n*. **1.** an appointing or being appointed **2.** a person appointed to an office, etc. **3.** an office held in this way **4.** an engagement to meet a person **5.** [*pl.*] furnishings
ap·por·tion (ə pôr'shən) *vt*. [see AD- & PORTION] to divide and distribute in shares **—ap·por'tion·ment** *n*.
ap·pose (ə pōz') *vt*. **-posed', -pos'ing** [< L. *ad-*, near + *ponere*, put] to put side by side or opposite **—ap·pos'a·ble** *adj*.
ap·po·site (ap'ə zit) *adj*. [see prec.] appropriate; apt **—ap'po·site·ly** *adv*.

ap·po·si·tion (ap'ə zish'ən) *n.* **1.** an apposing or the position resulting from this **2.** the placing of a word or expression beside another in explanation (Ex.: *Jim, my son,* is here) —**ap'·po·si'tion·al** *adj.*

ap·pos·i·tive (ə päz'ə tiv) *adj.* of or in apposition —*n.* a word, phrase, or clause in apposition

ap·prais·al (ə prā'z'l) *n.* **1.** an appraising **2.** an appraised value

ap·praise (ə prāz') *vt.* -praised', -prais'ing [< L. *ad,* to + *pretium,* price] **1.** to set a price for, esp. officially **2.** to estimate the quantity or quality of —**ap·prais'er** *n.*

ap·pre·ci·a·ble (ə prē'shə b'l, -shē ə-) *adj.* enough to be perceived; noticeable —**ap·pre'ci·a·bly** *adv.*

ap·pre·ci·ate (ə prē'shē āt') *vt.* -at'ed, -at'ing [see APPRAISE] **1.** to think well of; enjoy **2.** to be grateful for **3.** to estimate the quality or worth of **4.** to be fully or sensitively aware of **5.** to raise the price of —*vi.* to rise in value —**ap·pre'ci·a'tion** *n.* **1.** grateful recognition, as of a favor **2.** sensitive awareness, as of art **3.** a rise in value or price

ap·pre·ci·a·tive (ə prē'shə tiv, -shē ə-) *adj.* feeling or showing appreciation

ap·pre·hend (ap'rə hend') *vt.* [< L. *ad-,* to + *prehendere,* seize] **1.** to arrest (a suspect, etc.) **2.** to understand **3.** to fear; dread

ap'pre·hen'sion (-hen'shən) *n.* **1.** capture or arrest **2.** understanding **3.** anxiety or dread

ap'pre·hen'sive (-siv) *adj.* uneasy or fearful about the future —**ap'pre·hen'sive·ly** *adv.* —**ap'pre·hen'sive·ness** *n.*

ap·pren·tice (ə pren'tis) *n.* [see APPREHEND] **1.** a person working under a skilled craftsman to learn a trade **2.** any beginner —*vt.* -ticed, -tic·ing to place or accept as an apprentice —**ap·pren'tice·ship'** *n.*

ap·prise¹, ap·prize¹ (ə prīz') *vt.* -prised' or -prized', -pris'ing or -priz'ing [see APPREHEND] to inform or notify

ap·prize², ap·prise² (ə prīz') *vt.* -prized' or -prised', -priz'ing or -pris'ing *same as* APPRAISE

ap·proach (ə prōch') *vi.* [< L. *ad,* to + *prope,* near] to come closer —*vt.* **1.** to come nearer to **2.** to be similar to; approximate **3.** to make a proposal or request to **4.** to begin dealing with —*n.* **1.** a coming closer **2.** an approximation **3.** an advance or overture (*to* someone): *often used in pl.* **4.** a way of reaching; access **5.** *Golf* a shot from the fairway to the putting green —**ap·proach'a·bil'i·ty** *n.* —**ap·proach'a·ble** *adj.*

ap·pro·ba·tion (ap'rə bā'shən) *n.* [see APPROVE] official approval or permission

ap·pro·pri·ate (ə prō'prē āt') *vt.* -at'ed, -at'ing [< L. *ad-,* to + *proprius,* one's own] **1.** to take for one's own use, often improperly **2.** to set aside for a specific use [*to appropriate* funds for schools] —*adj.* (-it) suitable —**ap·pro'pri·ate·ly** (-it lē) *adv.*

ap·pro'pri·a'tion *n.* **1.** an appropriating **2.** money, etc. set aside for a specific use

ap·prov·al (ə prōō'v'l) *n.* **1.** an approving **2.** favorable opinion **3.** consent —**on approval** for the customer to examine and decide whether to buy or return

ap·prove (ə prōōv') *vt.* -proved', -prov'ing [< L. *ad-,* to + *probus,* good] **1.** to give one's consent to **2.** to judge to be good, satisfactory, etc. —*vi.* to have a favorable opinion (*of*) —**ap·prov'ing·ly** *adv.*

ap·prox·i·mate (ə präk'sə mit) *adj.* [< L. *ad-,* to + *prope,* near] **1.** near in position **2.** much like **3.** not exact, but almost so —*vt.* (-māt') -mat'ed, -mat'ing to come near to

ap·prox'i·ma'tion (-mā'shən) *n.* **1.** an approximating **2.** a fairly close estimate, etc.

ap·pur·te·nance (ə pur't'n əns) *n.* [see APPERTAIN] **1.** something added to a more important thing **2.** [*pl.*] accessories **3.** *Law* an additional, subordinate right or privilege —**ap·pur'te·nant** *adj., n.*

a·pri·cot (ap'rə kät', ā'prə-) *n.* [< L. *praecoquus,* early matured (fruit)] **1.** a small, yellowish-orange, peachlike fruit **2.** the tree it grows on

A·pril (ā'prəl) *n.* [< L.] the fourth month of the year, having 30 days: abbrev. **Apr.**

a pri·o·ri (ā'prē ôr'ē, ā'prī ôr'ī) [L.] **1.** from cause to effect **2.** based on theory instead of experience or experiment

a·pron (ā'prən) *n.* [< L. *mappa,* napkin] **1.** a garment worn over the front part of the body to protect one's clothes **2.** anything like this, as the part of a stage in front of the curtain —*vt.* to put an apron on

ap·ro·pos (ap'rə pō') *adv.* [Fr. *à propos,* to the purpose] at the right time; opportunely —*adj.* relevant —**apropos of** with regard to

apse (aps) *n.* [< Gr. *haptein,* fasten] a semicircular or polygonal projection of a church, with a domed or vaulted roof

apt (apt) *adj.* [< L. *apere,* fasten] **1.** appropriate; fitting **2.** tending or inclined **3.** quick to learn —**apt'ly** *adv.* —**apt'ness** *n.*

apt. *pl.* **apts.** apartment

ap·ti·tude (ap'tə tōōd') *n.* [see APT] **1.** suitability; fitness **2.** a natural tendency, ability, etc. **3.** quickness to learn

aq·ua (ak'wə, äk'-) *n., pl.* -uas, -uae (-wē) [L.] water —*adj.* [< AQUAMARINE] bluish-green

Aq·ua-lung (ak'wə luŋ', äk'-) [AQUA + LUNG] *a trademark for* a kind of self-contained underwater breathing apparatus —*n.* such an apparatus: usually **aq'ua·lung'**

aq·ua·ma·rine (ak'wə mə rēn', äk'-) *n.* [L. *aqua marina,* sea water] **1.** a transparent, pale bluish-green beryl **2.** its color —*adj.* bluish-green

aq·ua·naut (ak'wə nôt', äk'-) *n.* [AQUA + (ASTRO)NAUT] one trained to use a watertight underwater chamber as a base for undersea experiments

aq·ua·plane (ak'wə plān', äk'-) *n.* [AQUA + PLANE¹] a board on which one rides standing up as it is pulled by a motorboat

a·quar·ist (ə kwer'ist) *n.* the keeper of an aquarium

a·quar·i·um (ə kwer'ē əm) *n., pl.* -i·ums, -i·a (-ē ə) [< L. *aquarius,* of water] **1.** a tank, etc. for keeping live water animals and plants **2.** a place exhibiting these

A·quar·i·us (ə kwer'ē əs) [L., the water carrier] the eleventh sign of the zodiac

a·quat·ic (ə kwät'ik, -kwat'-) *adj.* **1.** growing or living in water **2.** done in or upon the water [*aquatic* sports]

aq·ue·duct (ak'wə dukt') *n.* [< L. *aqua,* water + *ducere,* to lead] **1.** a large pipe for bringing water from a distant source **2.** a bridgelike structure supporting this

a·que·ous (ā'kwē əs, ak'wē-) *adj.* of, like, or formed by water; watery

aq·ui·line (ak'wə līn', -lən) *adj.* [< L. *aquila,* eagle] **1.** of or like an eagle **2.** curved like an eagle's beak, as a nose

-ar [< L.] **1.** *a suffix meaning* of, relating to, like [*polar*] **2.** *a suffix denoting* agency [*vicar*]

Ar *Chem.* argon

Ar. **1.** Arabic **2.** Aramaic

Ar·ab (ar'əb) *n.* **1.** a native of Arabia **2.** any of a Semitic people originating in Arabia; commonly, a Bedouin —*adj.* of the Arabs —**A·ra·bi·an** (ə rā′bē ən) *adj., n.*

ar·a·besque (ar′ə besk′) *n.* [< Ar. *'arab*] an elaborate design of flowers, foliage, etc.

Arabian Nights, The a collection of ancient tales from Arabia, India, Persia, etc.

Ar·a·bic (ar′ə bik) *adj.* 1. of Arabia 2. of the Arabs —*n.* the Semitic language of the Arabs, spoken from Iraq to N Africa

Arabic numerals the figures 1, 2, 3, 4, 5, 6, 7, 8, 9, and the 0 (zero)

ar·a·ble (ar′ə b′l) *adj.* [Fr. < L. *arare*, to plow] suitable for plowing

a·rach·nid (ə rak′nid) *n.* [< Gr. *arachnē*, spider] any of a group of small animals, including spiders and scorpions, with eight legs

Ar·a·ma·ic (ar′ə mā′ik) *n.* a group of Semitic languages spoken in Biblical times

ar·bi·ter (är′bə tər) *n.* [L., a witness] arbitrator; judge; umpire

ar·bit·ra·ment (är bit′rə mənt) *n.* 1. arbitration 2. an arbitrator's verdict

ar·bi·trar·y (är′bə trer′ē) *adj.* [see ARBITER] 1. left to one's own choice 2. based on one's whim or notion 3. absolute; despotic —**ar′bi·trar′i·ly** *adv.* —**ar′bi·trar′i·ness** *n.*

ar·bi·trate (är′bə trāt′) *vt., vi.* -trat′ed, -trat′ing [see ARBITER] 1. to submit (a dispute) to arbitration 2. to decide (a dispute) as an arbitrator —**ar′bi·tra′tion** *n.* settlement of a dispute by an arbitrator

ar′bi·tra′tor *n.* one chosen to judge a dispute

ar·bor (är′bər) *n.* [< L. *herba*, herb] a place shaded by trees, shrubs, or vines

ar·bo·re·al (är bôr′ē əl) *adj.* [< L. *arbor*, tree] 1. of or like a tree 2. living in trees

ar·bo·re·tum (är′bə rēt′əm) *n., pl.* -tums, -ta (-ə) [L.] a place where many kinds of trees and shrubs are grown, as for study

ar·bor·vi·tae (är′bər vīt′ē) *n.* [L., tree of life] any of several evergreen trees, with flattened sprays of scalelike leaves

ar·bu·tus (är byōōt′əs) *n.* [L.] 1. a tree or shrub with dark-green leaves and berries like strawberries 2. a related trailing plant with clusters of white or pink flowers

arc (ärk) *n.* [< L. *arcus*, a bow, arch] 1. a bowlike curved line or object 2. the band of incandescent light formed when an electric discharge is conducted between two electrodes 3. a part of a curve, esp. of a circle —*vi.* arced or arcked, arc′ing or arck′ing 1. to move in a curved course 2. to form an arc

ar·cade (är kād′) *n.* [Fr. < L. *arcus*, arch] 1. a covered passageway, esp. one lined with shops 2. a line of arches and their supporting columns

ar·cane (är kān′) *adj.* [< L. *arcere*, shut up] 1. hidden or secret 2. esoteric

arch[1] (ärch) *n.* [< L. *arcus*, a bow, arch] 1. a curved structure used as a support over an open space, as in a doorway 2. the form of an arch 3. anything shaped like an arch —*vt., vi.* 1. to span with or as an arch 2. to form (into) an arch

arch[2] (ärch) *adj.* [< arch-] 1. main; chief 2. gaily mischievous; pert —**arch′ly** *adv.*

arch- [< Gr. *archos*, ruler] *a prefix meaning* main, chief [archbishop]

-arch [see ARCH] *a suffix meaning* ruler [matriarch]

arch. 1. archaic 2. architecture

ar·chae·ol·o·gy (är′kē äl′ə jē) *n.* [< Gr. *arche*, the beginning + -LOGY] the study of the life of ancient peoples, as by excavation of ancient cities: also sp. **archeology** —**ar′chae·o·log′i·cal** (-ə läj′i k′l) *adj.* —**ar′chae·ol′o·gist** *n.*

ar·cha·ic (är kā′ik) *adj.* [< Gr. *archaios*, ancient] 1. ancient 2. old-fashioned 3. seldom used except in poetry, the Bible, etc., as the word *thou* —**ar′cha·ism** *n.*

arch·an·gel (ärk′ān′j′l) *n.* a chief angel

arch·bish·op (ärch′bish′əp) *n.* a chief bishop

arch′dea′con (-dē′k′n) *n.* a church official ranking just below a bishop

arch′duke′ (-dōōk′) *n.* a chief duke

arch·en·e·my (ärch′en′ə mē) *n., pl.* -mies a chief enemy

arch·er (ärch′ər) *n.* [< L. *arcus*, a bow] one who shoots with bow and arrow

arch′er·y *n.* the practice, art, or sport of shooting with bow and arrow

ar·che·type (är′kə tīp′) *n.* [< Gr. *archos*, first + *typos*, a model] 1. an original pattern or model; prototype 2. a perfect example —**ar′che·typ′al** *adj.*

ar·chi·pel·a·go (är′kə pel′ə gō′) *n., pl.* -goes′, -gos′ [< Gr. *archi-*, chief + *pelagos*, sea] 1. a sea with many islands 2. such a group of islands

ar·chi·tect (är′kə tekt′) *n.* [< Gr. *archi-*, chief + *tektōn*, carpenter] 1. a person who designs buildings, etc. and administers their construction 2. any builder or creator

ar·chi·tec·ton·ics (är′kə tek tän′iks) *n.pl.* [*with sing. v.*] 1. the science of architecture 2. structural design, as of a symphony —**ar′chi·tec·ton′ic** *adj.*

ar·chi·tec·ture (är′kə tek′chər) *n.* 1. the science or profession of designing and constructing buildings, etc. 2. a style of construction 3. design and construction —**ar′chi·tec′·tur·al** *adj.* —**ar′chi·tec′tur·al·ly** *adv.*

ar·chives (är′kīvz) *n.pl.* [Fr. < Gr. *archē*, beginning] 1. a place where public records are kept 2. the records kept there

ar·chi·vist (är′kə vist, är′kī′vist) *n.* a person having charge of archives

arch·way (ärch′wā′) *n.* a passage under an arch

-archy [< Gr. *archein*, to rule] *a suffix meaning* a ruling [monarchy]

arc lamp a lamp in which the light is produced by an arc between electrodes: also **arc light**

arc·tic (ärk′tik, är′-) *adj.* [< Gr. *arktikos*, northern] 1. of or near the North Pole 2. very cold

arc′tics *n.pl.* [< ARCTIC] high, warm, waterproof overshoes, usually with buckles

-ard [< MHG. *hart*, bold] *a suffix meaning* one who carries an action to excess [sluggard]

ar·dent (är′d′nt) *adj.* [< L. *ardere*, burn] 1. passionate 2. zealous 3. glowing or burning —**ar′den·cy** (-d′n sē) *n.*

ar·dor (är′dər) *n.* [< L. *ardere*, burn] 1. emotional warmth; passion 2. zeal 3. intense heat Brit. sp. **ardour**

ar·du·ous (är′jōō wəs) *adj.* [L. *arduus*, steep] 1. difficult to do; laborious 2. using much energy; strenuous —**ar′du·ous·ly** *adv.*

are [OE. *aron*] *pl. & 2d pers. sing., pres. indic., of* BE

ar·e·a (er′ē ə) *n.* [L., vacant place] 1. a part of the earth's surface; region 2. the size of a surface, in square units 3. a particular part of a house, city, etc. 4. scope or extent —**ar′e·al** *adj.*

a·re·na (ə rē′nə) *n.* [L., sandy place] 1. the center of an ancient Roman amphitheater, for gladiatorial contests 2. any place like this 3. any sphere of struggle

arena theater a theater having a central stage surrounded by seats

aren't (ärnt) are not

Ar·es (er'ēz) *Gr. Myth.* the god of war

ar·gent (är'jənt) *adj.* [Fr. < L. *argentum,* silver] [Poet.] of silver

Ar·gen·tine (är'jən tēn', -tīn) *adj.* of Argentina, its people, etc. —*n.* a native or inhabitant of Argentina Also **Ar'gen·tin'e·an** (-tin'ē ən)

ar·gon (är'gän) *n.* [Gr., inert] a chemical element, a colorless, odorless gas found in the atmosphere: symbol, Ar

Ar·go·naut (är'gə nôt') *n.* [< Gr. *Argō,* Jason's ship + *nautēs,* sailor] *Gr. Myth.* any of the men who sailed with Jason to search for the Golden Fleece

ar·go·sy (är'gə sē) *n., pl.* **-sies** [< It. *Ragusea,* ship of Ragusa, ancient port] [Poet.] a large ship or a fleet of these

ar·got (är'gō, -gət) *n.* [Fr.] the specialized vocabulary of a particular group, as the secret jargon of criminals

ar·gue (är'gyōō) *vi.* **-gued, -gu·ing** [< L. *arguere,* prove] **1.** to give reasons (*for* or *against*) **2.** to dispute; quarrel —*vt.* **1.** to dispute about; debate **2.** to maintain; contend **3.** to persuade by giving reasons

ar'gu·ment (-gyə mənt) *n.* **1.** an arguing; debate **2.** a reason or reasons offered in arguing **3.** a dispute **4.** a summary

ar'gu·men·ta'tion (-men tā'shən) *n.* the process of arguing; debate

ar'gu·men'ta·tive (-tə tiv) *adj.* **1.** controversial **2.** apt to argue Also **ar'gu·men'tive**

ar·gyle (är'gīl) *adj.* [< *Argyll,* Scotland] knitted or woven in a diamond-shaped pattern, as socks

a·ri·a (är'ē ə, er'-) *n.* [It. < L. *aer,* air] a melody in an opera, etc., esp. for solo voice

-arian [< L.] *a suffix denoting* age, sect, social belief, occupation *[octogenarian]*

ar·id (ar'id, er'-) *adj.* [< L. *arere,* be dry] **1.** dry and barren **2.** not interesting; dull —**a·rid·i·ty** (ə rid'ə tē) *n.* —**ar'id·ly** *adv.*

Ar·i·es (er'ēz, ar'-; -i ēz') [L., the Ram] the first sign of the zodiac

a·right (ə rīt') *adv.* correctly

ar·il (ar'il) *n.* [< ML. *arillus,* dried grape] an additional covering on certain seeds after fertilization

a·rise (ə rīz') *vi.* **a·rose', a·ris'en** (-riz''n), **a·ris'ing** [OE. < *a-,* out + *risan,* to rise] **1.** to get up **2.** to rise; ascend **3.** to come into being **4.** to result (*from*)

ar·is·toc·ra·cy (ar'ə stäk'rə sē) *n., pl.* **-cies** [< Gr. *aristos,* best + *kratein,* to rule] **1.** government by a privileged minority, usually of inherited wealth **2.** a country with such government **3.** a privileged class; nobility

a·ris·to·crat (ə ris'tə krat', ar'is-) *n.* **1.** a member of the aristocracy **2.** one with the manners, beliefs, etc. of the upper class —**a·ris'to·crat'ic** *adj.*

a·rith·me·tic (ə rith'mə tik) *n.* [< Gr. *arithmos,* number] the science of computing by positive real numbers —*adj.* (ar'ith met'ik) of or using arithmetic: also **ar'ith·met'i·cal** —**a'rith·me·ti'cian** (-tish'ən) *n.*

ark (ärk) *n.* [< L. *arcere,* enclose] **1.** *Bible* the boat in which Noah, his family, and two of every kind of creature survived the Flood **2.** *same as* ARK OF THE COVENANT

ark of the covenant *Bible* the chest containing the stone tablets inscribed with the Ten Commandments

arm¹ (ärm) *n.* [OE. *earm*] **1.** *a)* an upper limb of the human body *b)* anything commonly in contact with this, as a sleeve, the support for the arm on a chair, etc. **2.** anything like an arm in structure, function, position, etc. —**at**

arm's length at a distance —**with open arms** cordially —**arm'less** *adj.*

arm² (ärm) *n.* [< L. *arma,* weapons] **1.** any weapon: *usually used in pl.* **2.** [*pl.*] warfare; fighting **3.** [*pl.*] heraldic insignia **4.** any branch of the military forces —*vt.* to provide with weapons, etc. —*vi.* to prepare for war —**up in arms 1.** prepared to fight **2.** indignant —**armed** *adj.*

ar·ma·da (är mä'də) *n.* [Sp. < L. *arma,* weapons] a fleet of warships or warplanes

ar·ma·dil·lo (är'mə dil'ō) *n., pl.* **-los** [Sp.: see prec.] a burrowing mammal of Texas and Central and South America, covered with bony plates

Ar·ma·ged·don (är'mə ged''n) *Bible* the place described as the scene of the last, deciding battle between good and evil

ar·ma·ment (är'mə mənt) *n.* **1.** [*often pl.*] all the military forces and equipment of a nation **2.** all the military equipment of a warship, fortification, etc. **3.** an arming or being armed for war

ar·ma·ture (är'mə chər) *n.* [see ARMADA] **1.** any protective covering **2.** the iron core wound with wire, usually a revolving part, in a generator or motor

arm'chair' *n.* a chair with supports at the sides for one's arms

armed forces all the military, naval, and air forces of a country

arm·ful (ärm'fool') *n., pl.* **-fuls** as much as the arms or one arm can hold

arm'hole' (-hōl') *n.* an opening for the arm in a garment

ar·mi·stice (är'mə stis) *n.* [Fr. < L. *arma,* arms + *sistere,* cause to stand] a temporary stopping of warfare by mutual agreement

Armistice Day *see* VETERANS DAY

arm·let (ärm'lit) *n.* an ornamental band worn around the upper arm

ar·mor (är'mər) *n.* [< L.: see ARMATURE] any defensive or protective covering —*vt., vi.* to put armor on Brit. sp. **armour**

ar·mor·er (är'mər ər) *n.* **1.** formerly, one who made or repaired armor **2.** a maker of firearms

ar·mo·ri·al (är môr'ē əl) *adj.* of coats of arms; heraldic

ar·mor·y (är'mər ē) *n., pl.* **-ies** [see ARM²] **1.** an arsenal **2.** a military drill hall **3.** an armaments factory

arm'pit' *n.* the hollow under the arm at the shoulder

ar·my (är'mē) *n., pl.* **-mies** [< L. *armata:* see ARMADA] **1.** a large, organized body of soldiers for waging war **2.** any large number of persons, animals, etc.

a·ro·ma (ə rō'mə) *n.* [< Gr. *arōma,* spice] a pleasant odor; fragrance

ar·o·mat·ic (ar'ə mat'ik) *adj.* of or having an aroma —*n.* an aromatic substance

a·rose (ə rōz') *pt. of* ARISE

a·round (ə round') *adv.* **1.** in a circle **2.** in every direction **3.** to the opposite direction, etc. **4.** [Colloq.] nearby [*stay around*] —*prep.* **1.** so as to encircle or envelop **2.** on the border of **3.** in various places in or on **4.** [Colloq.] about [*around 1890*]

a·rouse (ə rouz') *vt.* **a·roused', a·rous'ing 1.** to awaken **2.** to stir, as to action

ar·peg·gio (är pej'ō, -pej'ē ō) *n., pl.* **-gios** [< It. *arpa,* a harp] the playing of the notes of a chord in quick succession

ar·raign (ə rān') *vt.* [< L. *ad,* to + *ratio,* reason] **1.** to bring before a law court to answer charges **2.** to call to account; accuse —**ar·raign'ment** *n.*

ar·range (ə rānj′) *vt.* -ranged′, -rang′ing [< OFr. *a-*, to + *renc*, rank] 1. to put in the correct order 2. to classify 3. to prepare or plan 4. to settle or adjust (matters) 5. *Music* to adapt (a work) to particular instruments or voices — **ar·rang′er** *n.*

ar·range′ment *n.* 1. an arranging 2. a result or manner of arranging 3. [*usually pl.*] a plan 4. a settlement 5. *Music* an adaptation of a composition for particular instruments, voices, etc.

ar·rant (ar′ənt) *adj.* [var. of ERRANT] that is plainly such; out-and-out

ar·ras (ar′əs) *n.* [< *Arras*, Fr. city] 1. a kind of tapestry 2. a wall hanging of tapestry

ar·ray (ə rā′) *vt.* [ult. < L. *ad-*, to + Gmc. base *raid-*, order] 1. to put in order 2. to dress in finery —*n.* 1. an orderly grouping 2. an impressive display 3. fine clothes

ar·rears (ə rirz′) *n.pl.* [< L. *ad*, to + *retro*, behind] overdue debts —**in arrears** (or **arrear**) behind in paying a debt, etc.

ar·rest (ə rest′) *vt.* [< L. *ad-*, to + *restare*, to stop] 1. to stop or check 2. to seize by authority of the law 3. to catch and keep —*n.* an arresting or being arrested —**under arrest** in legal custody

ar·rest′ing *adj.* attracting attention

ar·riv·al (ə rī′v′l) *n.* 1. the act of arriving 2. a person or thing that arrives

ar·rive (ə rīv′) *vi.* -rived′, -riv′ing [< L. *ad*, to + *ripa*, shore] 1. to reach one's destination 2. to come 3. to attain fame, etc. —**arrive at** to reach by thinking, etc.

ar·ri·ve·der·ci (ä rē′ve der′chē) *interj.* [It.] until we meet again; goodbye

ar·ro·gance (ar′ə gəns) *n.* overbearing pride or self-importance

ar′ro·gant *adj.* [see ff.] full of or due to arrogance; haughty —**ar′ro·gant·ly** *adv.*

ar′ro·gate (-gāt′) *vt.* -gat′ed, -gat′ing [< L. *ad-*, for + *rogare*, ask] to claim or seize without right —**ar′ro·ga′tion** *n.*

ar·row (ar′ō) *n.* [OE. *arwe*] 1. a slender, usually pointed shaft, shot from a bow 2. a sign (←) used to indicate direction

ar′row·head′ (-hed′) *n.* 1. the pointed tip of an arrow 2. a plant with arrow-shaped leaves

ar′row·root′ *n.* [< use as antidote for poisoned arrows] 1. a tropical American plant with starchy roots 2. the edible starch made from its roots

ar·roy·o (ə roi′ō) *n., pl.* -os [Sp. < L. *arrugia*, mine pit] 1. a dry gully 2. a rivulet

ar·se·nal (är′s′n əl) *n.* [< Ar. *dār* (*eṣ*) *ṣinā′a*, workshop] a place for making and storing weapons and other munitions

ar·se·nic (är′s′n ik; *for adj.* är sen′ik) *n.* [ult. < Per. *zar*, gold] a silvery-white, brittle, very poisonous chemical element, compounds of which are used in insecticides, medicines, etc.: symbol, As —*adj.* of or containing arsenic

ar·son (är′s′n) *n.* [< L. *ardere*, to burn] the crime of purposely setting fire to a building — **ar′son·ist** *n.*

art¹ (ärt) *n.* [< L. *ars*] 1. creativity 2. skill 3. any specific skill or its application 4. any craft or its principles 5. a making of things that have form or beauty 6. any branch of this, as painting 7. paintings, statues, etc. 8. a branch of learning; specif., [*pl.*] same as LIBERAL ARTS 9. cunning 10. sly trick; wile: *usually used in pl.*

art² (ärt) *archaic 2d pers. sing., pres. indic.,* of BE: *used with* thou

art. 1. article 2. artificial

Ar·te·mis (är′tə mis) *Gr. Myth.* the goddess of the moon and hunting

ar·te·ri·o·scle·ro·sis (är tir′ē ō sklə rō′sis) *n.* [see ff. & SCLEROSIS] a hardening of the walls of the arteries, as in old age

ar·ter·y (är′tər ē) *n., pl.* -ies [prob. < Gr. *aeirein*, to raise] 1. any of the tubes carrying blood from the heart 2. a main road or channel —**ar·te′ri·al** (-tir′ē əl) *adj.*

ar·te·sian well (är tē′zhən) [< Fr. *Artois*, former Fr. province] a deep well in which water is forced up by underground pressure

art·ful (ärt′fəl) *adj.* 1. skillful or clever 2. cunning; crafty —**art′ful·ly** *adv.*

ar·thri·tis (är thrīt′is) *n.* [< Gr. *arthron*, a joint + -ITIS] inflammation of a joint or joints —**ar·thrit′ic** (-thrit′ik) *adj.*

ar·thro·pod (är′thrə päd′) *n.* [< Gr. *arthron*, a joint + -POD] an invertebrate animal with jointed legs and a segmented body

Ar·thur (är′thər) legendary 6th-cent. king of Britain —**Ar·thu′ri·an** (-thoor′ē ən) *adj.*

ar·ti·choke (är′tə chōk′) *n.* [ult. < Ar. *al-ḥaršūf*] 1. a thistlelike plant 2. its flower head, cooked as a vegetable

ar·ti·cle (är′ti k′l) *n.* [< L. *artus*, joint] 1. one of the sections of a document 2. a complete piece of writing, as in a newspaper, magazine, etc. 3. a separate item [an *article* of luggage] 4. a commodity 5. *Gram.* any one of the words *a*, *an*, or *the*, used as adjectives —*vt.* -cled, -cling to bind by the articles of an agreement

ar·tic·u·lar (är tik′yə lər) *adj.* [< L. *artus*, a joint] of the joints

ar·tic·u·late (är tik′yə lit) *adj.* [< L. *artus*, a joint] 1. jointed: usually **ar·tic′u·lat′ed** 2. spoken distinctly 3. able to speak 4. expressing oneself clearly —*vt.* (-lāt′) -lat′ed, -lat′ing 1. to put together by joints or in a connected way 2. to utter distinctly 3. to express clearly —*vi.* 1. to speak distinctly 2. to be jointed —**ar·tic′u·late·ly** *adv.* —**ar·tic′u·la′tion** *n.*

ar·ti·fact (är′tə fakt′) *n.* [see ff.] any object made by human work, as a primitive tool

ar·ti·fice (är′tə fis) *n.* [< L. *ars*, art + *facere*, make] 1. skill 2. trickery 3. a sly trick

ar·tif·i·cer (är tif′ə sər) *n.* 1. a skilled craftsman 2. an inventor

ar·ti·fi·cial (är′tə fish′əl) *adj.* [see ARTIFICE] made by human work or art; not natural 2. simulated [*artificial* teeth] 3. affected [an *artificial* smile] —**ar′ti·fi′ci·al′i·ty** (-fish′ē al′ə tē) *n., pl.* -ties

artificial respiration an artificial maintenance of breathing, as by forcing breath into the mouth

ar·til·ler·y (är til′ər ē) *n.* [< Pr. *artilla*, fortification] 1. mounted guns, as cannon 2. the science of guns; gunnery —**the artillery** the military branch using heavy mounted guns — **ar·til′ler·y·man** (-mən) *n., pl.* -men

ar·ti·san (är′tə z′n) *n.* [Fr. < It. < L. *ars*, art] a skilled workman; craftsman

art·ist (är′tist) *n.* 1. one who is skilled in any of the fine arts, esp. in painting, sculpture, etc. 2. one who does anything very well

ar·tis·tic (är tis′tik) *adj.* 1. of art or artists 2. done skillfully 3. sensitive to beauty —**ar·tis′ti·cal·ly** *adv.*

art·ist·ry (är′tis trē) *n.* artistic work or skill

art·less (ärt′lis) *adj.* 1. lacking skill or art 2. simple; natural 3. without guile or deceit; ingenuous —**art′less·ly** *adv.*

art·y (ärt′ē) *adj.* -i·er, -i·est [Colloq.] affectedly artistic —**art′i·ness** *n.*

ar·um (er′əm) *n.* [< Gr. *aron*] a plant bearing small flowers enclosed by a hoodlike leaf

-ary [< L.] *a suffix meaning:* 1. related to [*auxiliary*] 2. a place for [*granary*]

Ar·y·an (er'ē ən, ar'-) *n.* [< Sans. *ārya*, noble] 1. formerly, the hypothetical parent language of the Indo-European family 2. a person supposed to be a descendant of the prehistoric peoples who spoke this language *Aryan* has no validity as an ethnological term, as in Nazi use

as (az, əz) *adv.* [< ALSO] 1. to the same amount or degree; equally 2. for instance 3. when related in a specified way [this view *as* contrasted with that] —*conj.* 1. to the same amount or degree that 2. in the same manner that 3. while [pay *as* you go] 4. because 5. that the consequence is [so clear *as* to be obvious] 6. though [full *as* he was, he kept eating] —*pron.* 1. a fact that [he is tired, *as* you can see] 2. that (preceded by *such* or *the same*) [the same color *as* yours (is)] —*prep.* in the role or function of —**as for** (or **to**) concerning —**as if** (or **though**) as it (or one) would if —**as is** [Colloq.] just as it is —**as it were** as if it were so

As *Chem.* arsenic

as·a·fet·i·da, as·a·foet·i·da (as'ə fet'ə də) *n.* [< Per. *āzā*, gum + L. *f(o)etida*, fetid] a fetid resin formerly used in medicine

as·bes·tos, as·bes·tus (as bes'təs, az-) *n.* [< Gr. *a-*, not + *sbennynai*, to extinguish] a fire-resistant, fibrous mineral used in fireproofing, insulation, etc.

as·cend (ə send') *vi., vt.* [< L. *ad-*, to + *scandere*, to climb] 1. to go up; mount 2. to succeed to (a throne) —**as·cend'er** *n.*

as·cend'an·cy, as·cend'en·cy (-ən sē) *n.* a position of control or power; domination

as·cend'ant, as·cend'ent (-ənt) *adj.* 1. ascending 2. in control; dominant —*n.* ascendancy —**in the ascendant** at or nearing the height of power, fame, etc.

as·cen·sion (ə sen'shən) *n.* 1. an ascending 2. [A-] the fortieth day after Easter, celebrating the Ascension —**the Ascension** *Bible* the bodily ascent of Jesus into heaven

as·cent (ə sent') *n.* 1. an ascending or rising 2. an upward slope

as·cer·tain (as'ər tān') *vt.* [see AD- & CERTAIN] to find out with certainty

as·cet·ic (ə set'ik) *adj.* [< Gr. *askein*, to train the body] self-denying —*n.* one who leads a life of rigorous self-denial, esp. for religious purposes —**as·cet'i·cism** *n.*

a·scor·bic acid (ə skôr'bik) [A- (sense 2) + SCORB(UTIC) + -IC] a vitamin in citrus fruits, tomatoes, etc.; vitamin C: it prevents and cures scurvy

as·cot (as'kət) *n.* a necktie with very broad ends hanging from the knot

as·cribe (ə skrīb') *vt.* -**cribed', -crib'ing** [< L. *ad-*, to + *scribere*, to write] 1. to assign (*to* a supposed cause); attribute 2. to regard as belonging (*to*) or coming from someone —**as·crip·tion** (ə skrip'shən) *n.*

a·sep·tic (ā sep'tik, ə-) *adj.* not septic; free from disease-producing germs

a·sex·u·al (ā sek'shoo wəl) *adj.* 1. having no sex; sexless 2. of reproduction without the union of male and female germ cells —**a·sex'u·al·ly** *adv.*

ash[1] (ash) *n.* [OE. *æsce*] 1. the grayish powder left after something has burned 2. the gray color of wood ash 3. fine, volcanic lava See also ASHES

ash[2] (ash) *n.* [OE. *æsc*] 1. a shade tree of the olive family 2. its tough wood

a·shamed (ə shāmd') *adj.* 1. feeling shame 2. reluctant because fearing shame beforehand —**a·sham·ed·ly** (ə shā'mid lē) *adv.*

ash·en (ash'ən) *adj.* 1. of ashes 2. like ashes, esp. in color; pale; pallid

ash·es (ash'iz) *n.pl.* 1. the substance left after a thing has burned 2. human remains, esp. after cremation

a·shore (ə shôr') *adv., adj.* 1. to or on the shore 2. to or on land

Ash·to·reth (ash'tə reth') Astarte

ash'tray' *n.* a container for tobacco ashes

Ash Wednesday the first day of Lent: from the putting of ashes on the forehead in penitence

ash·y (ash'ē) *adj.* -**i·er, -i·est** 1. of, like, or covered with ashes 2. ashen; pale

A·sian (ā'zhən, -shən) *adj.* of Asia, its people, etc. —*n.* a native or inhabitant of Asia Also **A·si·at·ic** (ā'zhē at'ik)

a·side (ə sīd') *adv.* 1. on or to one side 2. away; in reserve [put this *aside* for me] 3. out of one's thoughts, etc. 4. apart; notwithstanding [joking *aside*] —*n.* words spoken by an actor and supposedly heard only by the audience —**aside from** 1. with the exception of 2. apart from

as·i·nine (as'ə nīn') *adj.* [< L. *asinus*, ass] like an ass; stupid, silly, etc. —**as'i·nine'ly** *adv.* —**as'i·nin'i·ty** (-nin'ə tē) *n., pl.* -**ties**

ask (ask) *vt.* [OE. *ascian*] 1. to use words in seeking the answer to (a question) 2. to put a question to (a person) 3. to request or demand 4. to invite —*vi.* 1. to make a request (*for*) 2. to inquire (*about*)

a·skance (ə skans') *adv.* [< ME. *a-*, on + *skwyn*, sidewise] 1. with a sidewise glance 2. with suspicion, disapproval, etc.

a·skew (ə skyōō') *adv.* to one side; awry —*adj.* on one side; awry

a·slant (ə slant') *adv.* on a slant —*prep.* on a slant across —*adj.* slanting

a·sleep (ə slēp') *adj.* 1. sleeping 2. inactive; dull 3. numb [my arm is *asleep*] 4. dead —*adv.* into a sleeping condition

a·so·cial (ā sō'shəl) *adj.* 1. not social; withdrawing from others 2. selfish

asp (asp) *n.* [< Gr. *aspis*] a small, poisonous snake of Africa and Europe

as·par·a·gus (ə spar'ə gəs) *n.* [< Gr. *asparagos*, a sprout] 1. a plant with small leaves and edible shoots 2. these shoots

as·pect (as'pekt) *n.* [< L. *ad-*, to + *specere*, to look] 1. the way one appears or looks 2. the appearance of a thing or idea from a specific viewpoint 3. a side facing in a given direction

as·pen (as'pən) *n.* [OE. *æspe*] a poplar tree whose leaves flutter in the least breeze

as·per·i·ty (as per'ə tē) *n., pl.* -**ties** [< L. *asper*, rough] 1. roughness or harshness 2. sharpness of temper

as·per·sion (ə spur'zhən) *n.* [< L. *ad-*, to + *spargere*, sprinkle] 1. a defaming 2. a damaging remark; slander

as·phalt (as'fôlt) *n.* [< Gr.] a brown or black tarlike substance mixed with sand or gravel, for paving, roofing, etc. —*vt.* to pave, roof, etc. with asphalt —**as·phal'tic** *adj.*

as·pho·del (as'fə del') *n.* [< Gr. *asphodelos*] a plant with white or yellow flowers

as·phyx·i·a (as fik'sē ə) *n.* [Gr. < *a-*, not + *sphyzein*, to throb] loss of consciousness from too little oxygen and too much carbon dioxide in the blood —**as·phyx'i·ant** *adj., n.*

as·phyx·i·ate (-āt') *vt.* **-at'ed, -at'ing** 1. to cause asphyxia in 2. to suffocate —**as·phyx'i·a'tion** *n.* —**as·phyx'i·a'tor** *n.*

as·pic (as'pik) *n.* [< OFr. *aspe*] a jelly of meat juice, tomato juice, etc. used as a relish, etc.

as·pir·ant (as′pər ənt, ə spīr′ənt) *adj.* aspiring —*n.* a person who aspires

as·pi·rate (as′pə rāt′; *for n. & adj.* -pər it) *vt.* -rat′ed, -rat′ing [< L.: see ASPIRE] **1.** to begin (a word or syllable) with the sound of English *h* **2.** to follow (a consonant) with an audible puff of breath —*n.* an aspirated sound —*adj.* aspirated

as′pi·ra′tion *n.* **1.** *a)* a strong desire or ambition *b)* the thing so desired **2.** an aspirating **3.** an aspirate

as′pi·ra′tor *n.* a suction apparatus for removing air, fluids, etc.

as·pire (ə spīr′) *vi.* -pired′, -pir′ing [< L. *ad*-, to + *spirare*, breathe] to be ambitious (*to* get or do something lofty); seek

as·pi·rin (as′pər in) *n.* [G.] a white powder used for reducing fever, relieving pain, etc.

ass (as) *n.* [< L. *asinus*] **1.** a horselike animal with long ears **2.** a silly person

as·sail (ə sāl′) *vt.* [< L. *ad*, to + *salire*, to leap] **1.** to attack physically and violently **2.** to attack with arguments, doubts, etc.

as·sail′ant (-ənt) *n.* an attacker

as·sas·sin (ə sas′'n) *n.* [Fr. < Ar. *ḥashshā-shin*, hashish users] a murderer who strikes suddenly; esp., the killer of a politically important person

as·sas′si·nate′ (-āt′) *vt.* -nat′ed, -nat′ing to murder (esp. a politically important person) — **as·sas′si·na′tion** *n.*

as·sault (ə sôlt′) *n.* [< L. *ad*, to + *saltare*, to leap] **1.** a violent attack; sometimes, specif., rape **2.** *Law* a threat or attempt to harm another physically —*vt., vi.* to make an assault (upon) —**as·sault′ive** *adj.*

assault and battery *Law* the carrying out of threatened physical harm

as·say (as′ā, a sā′) *n.* [< L. *ex*-, out + *agere*, to act] **1.** a testing **2.** the analysis of an ore, etc. to find out the nature and proportion of the ingredients **3.** a report of such analysis —*vt.* (a sā′, ə-) to make an assay of; test —**as·say′er** *n.*

as·sem·blage (ə sem′blij) *n.* **1.** an assembling or being assembled **2.** an assembly

as·sem·ble (ə sem′b'l) *vt., vi.* -bled, -bling [< L. *ad*-, to + *simul*, together] **1.** to gather into a group; collect **2.** to fit or put together the parts of

as·sem′bly (-blē) *n., pl.* -blies **1.** an assembling or being assembled **2.** a group of persons gathered together **3.** [A-] a legislative body **4.** a fitting together of parts to form a unit

assembly line an arrangement by which workers in succession perform single operations on the work as it moves along

as·sent (ə sent′) *vi.* [< L. *ad*-, to + *sentire*, to feel] to agree (*to*) —*n.* consent or agreement

as·sert (ə surt′) *vt.* [< L. *ad*-, to + *serere*, to join] **1.** to declare; affirm **2.** to maintain or defend (rights, etc.) —**assert oneself** to insist on one's rights, or on recognition

as·ser·tion (ə sur′shən) *n.* **1.** an asserting **2.** a positive statement; declaration

as·ser′tive (-tiv) *adj.* positive or confident in a persistent way

as·sess (ə ses′) *vt.* [< L. *ad*-, to + *sedere*, sit] **1.** to set an estimated value on (property, etc.) for taxation **2.** to set the amount of (a fine, etc.) **3.** to impose a fine, tax, etc. on —**as·sess′ment** *n.* —**as·ses′sor** *n.*

as·set (as′et) *n.* [< L. *ad*, to + *satis*, enough] **1.** anything owned that has value **2.** a desirable thing [charm is an *asset*] **3.** [*pl.*] all the property, accounts receivable, cash, etc. of a

person or business **4.** [*pl.*] *Law* property, as of a bankrupt

as·sid·u·ous (ə sij′oo wəs) *adj.* [< L. *ad*-, to + *sedere*, sit] diligent; persevering; careful —**as·si·du·i·ty** (as′ə dyoo̅′ə tē) *n., pl.* -ties

as·sign (ə sīn′) *vt.* [< L. *ad*-, to + *signare*, to sign] **1.** to set apart or mark for a specific purpose; designate **2.** to place at some task or duty **3.** to give out as a task; allot **4.** to ascribe (a motive, reason, etc.) **5.** *Law* to transfer (a claim, property, etc.)

as·sig·na·tion (as′ig nā′shən) *n.* **1.** an assignment **2.** an appointment to meet, esp. one made secretly by lovers

as·sign·ment (ə sīn′mənt) *n.* **1.** an assigning or being assigned **2.** anything assigned

as·sim·i·late (ə sim′ə lāt′) *vt.* -lat′ed, -lat′ing [< L. *ad*-, to + *similis*, like] **1.** to absorb (food) into the body **2.** to absorb and incorporate **3.** to make like or alike (with *to*) —*vi.* to become assimilated —**as·sim′i·la′tion** *n.*

as·sist (ə sist′) *vt., vi.* [< L. *ad*-, to + *stare*, to stand] to help; aid —*n.* an act or instance of helping —**assist at** to attend

as·sist′ance (-əns) *n.* help; aid

as·sist′ant (-ənt) *adj.* assisting —*n.* a helper

as·siz·es (ə sīz′iz) *n.pl.* [see ASSESS] **1.** court sessions held periodically in each county of England **2.** the time or place of these

as·so·ci·ate (ə sō′shē āt′, -sē-) *vt.* -at′ed, -at′-ing [< L. *ad*-, to + *socius*, companion] **1.** to connect; combine **2.** to bring into relationship as partner, etc. **3.** to connect in the mind —*vi.* to unite or join (*with*) as a partner, friend, etc. —*n.* (-it) **1.** a partner, colleague, friend, etc. **2.** anything joined with another **3.** a degree granted by a junior college at the end of a two-year course —*adj.* (-it) **1.** joined with others, as in some work **2.** of less than full status

as·so′ci·a′tion (-ā′shən) *n.* **1.** the act of associating **2.** fellowship; partnership **3.** an organization of persons having common purposes, etc.; society **4.** a connection between ideas, etc.

association football soccer

as·so·nance (as′ə nəns) *n.* [Fr. < L. *ad*-, to + *sonare*, to sound] likeness of sound without actual rhyme —**as′so·nant** *adj., n.*

as·sort (ə sôrt′) *vt.* [< L. *ad*-, to + *sors*, lot] to separate into classes according to kinds; classify —*vi.* to match (*with*)

as·sort′ed *adj.* **1.** various; miscellaneous **2.** classified **3.** matched

as·sort′ment *n.* **1.** an assorting or being assorted **2.** a miscellaneous group; variety

asst. assistant

as·suage (ə swāj′) *vt.* -suaged′, -suag′ing [< L. *ad*, to + *suavis*, sweet] **1.** to lessen (pain, etc.) **2.** to calm (anger, etc.) **3.** to satisfy or slake (thirst, etc.) —**as·suage′ment** *n.*

as·sume (ə soom′) *vt.* -sumed′, -sum′ing [< L. *ad*-, to + *sumere*, take] **1.** to take on (the appearance, role, etc. of) **2.** to seize; usurp **3.** to undertake **4.** to take for granted; suppose **5.** to feign

as·sum′ing *adj.* presumptuous

as·sump·tion (ə sump′shən) *n.* **1.** the act of assuming **2.** a supposition **3.** presumption **4.** [A-] *R.C.Ch. a)* the ascent of the Virgin Mary into heaven *b)* a festival on August 15 celebrating this

as·sur·ance (ə shoor′əns) *n.* **1.** the act of assuring **2.** a being assured; sureness; confidence **3.** a promise; guarantee **4.** self-confidence **5.** [Chiefly Brit.] insurance

as·sure (ə shoor′) *vt.* -sured′, -sur′ing [< L. *ad*,

to + *securus*, secure] **1.** to make (a person) sure of something; convince **2.** to give confidence to **3.** to promise confidently **4.** to guarantee **5.** [Brit.] to insure

as·sured′ *adj.* **1.** made sure; certain **2.** confident —**as·sur·ed·ly** (ə shoor′id lē) *adv.*

As·tar·te (as tär′tē) a Semitic goddess of fertility and sexual love

as·ter (as′tər) *n.* [< Gr. *astēr*, a star] any of a group of plants with variously colored daisylike flowers

as·ter·isk (as′tər isk) *n.* [< Gr. dim. of *astēr*, a star] a starlike sign (*) used in printing to indicate footnotes, omissions, etc.

a·stern (ə sturn′) *adv.* **1.** behind a ship **2.** at or toward the rear **3.** backward

as·ter·oid (as′tə roid′) *n.* [< Gr. *astēr*, star + -OID] **1.** any of the small planets between Mars and Jupiter **2.** a starfish

asth·ma (az′mə) *n.* [Gr.] a chronic disorder characterized by coughing, difficult breathing, etc. —**asth·mat′ic** (-mat′ik) *adj., n.*

a·stig·ma·tism (ə stig′mə tiz′m) *n.* [< Gr. *a-*, without + *stigma*, a mark + -ISM] an irregularity of a lens, esp. of the eye, so that rays do not meet in a single focal point —**as·tig·mat·ic** (as′tig mat′ik) *adj.*

a·stir (ə stur′) *adv., adj.* **1.** in motion **2.** out of bed

as·ton·ish (ə stän′ish) *vt.* [< L. *ex-*, out + *tonare*, to thunder] to fill with sudden surprise; amaze —**as·ton′ish·ing** *adj.* —**as·ton′ish·ing·ly** *adv.* —**as·ton′ish·ment** *n.*

as·tound (ə stound′) *vt.* [see prec.] to astonish greatly —**as·tound′ing** *adj.*

as·tra·khan (as′trə kən) *n.* [< *Astrakhan*, U.S.S.R. city] a loosely curled fur from the pelt of very young lambs

as·tral (as′trəl) *adj.* [< Gr. *astron*, star] of, from, or like the stars

a·stray (ə strā′) *adv.* off the right path or way

a·stride (ə strīd′) *adv.* with a leg on either side —*prep.* with a leg on either side of

as·trin·gent (ə strin′jənt) *adj.* [< L. *ad-*, to + *stringere*, to draw] **1.** that contracts body tissues and checks capillary bleeding, etc. **2.** harsh; severe —*n.* an astringent substance —**as·trin′gent·ly** *adv.*

as·trol·o·gy (ə sträl′ə jē) *n.* [< Gr. *astron*, star + -LOGY] a pseudoscience claiming to foretell the future by the supposed influence of the stars, planets, etc. on human affairs —**as·trol′o·ger** *n.* —**as·tro·log·i·cal** (as′trə läj′i k′l) *adj.*

as·tro·naut (as′trə nôt′) *n.* [< Fr.: see ff.] one trained to make flights in space

as·tro·nau·tics (as′trə nôt′iks) *n.pl.* [*with sing. v.*] [< Fr.: ult. < Gr. *astron*, star + *nautēs*, sailor] the science that deals with travel in outer space

as·tro·nom·i·cal (as′trə näm′i k′l) *adj.* **1.** of astronomy **2.** very large, as numbers

as·tron·o·my (ə strän′ə mē) *n.* [< Gr. *astron*, star + *nemein*, arrange] the science of the stars and other heavenly bodies, their motion, size, etc. —**as·tron′o·mer** *n.*

as·tro·phys·ics (as′trō fiz′iks) *n.pl.* [*with sing. v.*] the science of the physical properties and phenomena of the stars, etc. —**as·tro·phys′i·cist** (-ə sist) *n.*

as·tute (ə stōōt′) *adj.* [< L. *astus*, craft] shrewd; keen —**as·tute′ness** *n.*

a·sun·der (ə sun′dər) *adv.* [OE. *on sundran*] **1.** in or into pieces **2.** apart or separate

a·sy·lum (ə sī′ləm) *n.* [< Gr. *a-*, without + *sylē*, right of seizure] **1.** a place of safety; refuge **2.** *an old name for* a place for the care of the mentally ill, or of the aged, poor, etc.

a·sym·me·try (ā sim′ə trē) *n.* lack of symmetry —**a·sym·met·ri·cal** (ā′sə met′ri k′l), **a′sym·met′ric** *adj.*

at (at, ət) *prep.* [OE. *æt*] **1.** on; in; near; by *[at the office]* **2.** to or toward *[look at her]* **3.** attending *[at the party]* **4.** busy with *[at work]* **5.** in the state or manner of *[at war, at a trot]* **6.** because of *[sad at his death]* **7.** in the amount, etc. of **8.** on or near the age or time of *[at noon]*

At·a·brine (at′ə brin, -brēn′) [G. *atebrin*] a trademark for a synthetic drug used in treating malaria, etc. —*n.* [a-] this drug

at·a·vism (at′ə viz′m) *n.* [< Fr. < L. *atavus*, ancestor] reversion to remote ancestral characteristics —**at′a·vis′tic** *adj.*

a·tax·i·a (ə tak′sē ə) *n.* [< Gr. *a-*, not + *tassein*, arrange] inability to coordinate muscular movements —**a·tax′ic** *adj., n.*

ate (āt; *Brit., or U.S. dial.*, et) *pt. of* EAT

-ate¹ [< L. *-atus*, pp. ending] *a suffix meaning:* **1.** to become, cause to become, form, provide with *[maturate, vaccinate]* **2.** of or characteristic of, characterized by, having *[passionate]*

-ate² [< L. *-atus*, a noun ending] *a suffix denoting* a function, agent, or official *[potentate]*

at·el·ier (at′l yā′) *n.* [Fr.] a studio

a·the·ism (ā′thē iz′m) *n.* [< Gr. *a-*, without + *theos*, god] the belief that there is no God —**a′the·ist** *n.* —**a′the·is′tic** *adj.*

A·the·na (ə thē′nə) *Gr. Myth.* the goddess of wisdom, skills, and warfare

ath·e·nae·um, ath·e·ne·um (ath′ə nē′əm) **1.** a literary or scientific club **2.** a library; reading room

ath·er·o·scle·ro·sis (ath′ər ō sklə rō′sis) *n.* [< Gr. *athērōma*, grainy tumor + SCLEROSIS] formation of fatty nodules on hardening artery walls

a·thirst (ə thurst′) *adj.* **1.** [Archaic] thirsty **2.** eager; longing *[athirst for knowledge]*

ath·lete (ath′lēt′) *n.* [< Gr. *athlon*, a prize] a person trained in exercises or contests requiring physical strength, skill, speed, etc.

athlete's foot ringworm of the feet

ath·let·ic (ath let′ik) *adj.* **1.** of, like, or proper to athletes or athletics **2.** physically strong, skillful, etc. —**ath·let′i·cal·ly** *adv.*

ath·let·ics (-iks) *n.pl.* [*sometimes with sing. v.*] athletic sports, games, exercises, etc.

a·thwart (ə thwôrt′) *prep.* **1.** across **2.** against —*adv.* crosswise

-atic [Gr.] *a suffix meaning* of, of the kind of *[dramatic]*

a·tilt (ə tilt′) *adj., adv.* tilted

a·tin·gle (ə tin′g′l) *adj.* tingling; excited

-ation [< Fr. or L.] *a suffix meaning* act, condition, or result of *[compilation]*

-ative [< Fr. or L.] *a suffix meaning* of or relating to, serving to *[demonstrative]*

At·lan·tis (ət lan′tis) legendary sunken continent in the Atlantic

At·las (at′ləs) *Gr. Myth.* a Titan forced to hold the heavens on his shoulders —*n.* [a-] a book of maps

at·mos·phere (at′məs fir′) *n.* [< Gr. *atmos*, vapor + *sphaira*, sphere] **1.** all the air surrounding the earth **2.** the general mood or tone **3.** a unit of pressure equal to 14.69 lb. per sq. in. —**at′mos·pher′ic** (-fer′ik) *adj.* —**at′mos·pher′i·cal·ly** *adv.*

at·oll (a′tôl, ä′-) *n.* [< EInd. term] a coral island surrounding a lagoon

at·om (at′əm) *n.* [< Gr. *atomos*, uncut] **1.** a tiny particle; jot **2.** *Chem. & Physics* any of the smallest particles of an element that form

compounds with similar particles of other elements —**the atom** atomic energy
a·tom·ic (ə täm′ik) *adj.* 1. of an atom or atoms 2. of or using atomic energy 3. very small — **a·tom′i·cal·ly** *adv.*
atomic bomb, atom bomb a very destructive bomb, whose immense power derives from a chain reaction of nuclear fission
atomic energy the energy released from an atom in nuclear fission or fusion
at·om·ize (at′ə mīz′) *vt.* -ized′, -iz′ing 1. to separate into atoms 2. to reduce (a liquid) to a fine spray
at′om·iz′er (-mī′zər) *n.* a device used to shoot out a fine spray, as of medicine or perfume
a·to·nal·i·ty (ā′tō nal′ə tē) *n. Music* lack of tonality through intentional disregard of key — **a·ton·al** (ā tōn′'l) *adj.*
a·tone (ə tōn′) *vi.* **a·toned′, a·ton′ing** [< ME. *at one*, in accord] to make amends (for wrongdoing, etc.) —**a·ton′er** *n.*
a·tone′ment *n.* 1. an atoning 2. amends; expiation 3. [A-] *Theol.* the reconciliation of God with man through Jesus' death
a·top (ə täp′) *adv.* on or at the top —*prep.* on the top of
-atory [L.] *a suffix meaning* of, characterized by, or produced by [*exclamatory*]
a·tri·um (ā′trē əm) *n., pl.* **a′tri·a** (-ə), **a′tri·ums** [L.] 1. the main room of an ancient Roman house 2. an entrance hall 3. either of the upper chambers of the heart
a·tro·cious (ə trō′shəs) *adj.* [< L. *atrox*, fierce] 1. very cruel, evil, etc. 2. [Colloq.] offensive — **a·tro′cious·ly** *adv.*
a·troc·i·ty (ə träs′ə tē) *n., pl.* **-ties** 1. atrocious behavior 2. an atrocious act 3. [Colloq.] a very offensive thing
at·ro·phy (at′rə fē) *n.* [< Fr. < Gr. *a-*, not + *trephein*, nourish] a wasting away, or the failure to grow, of an organ, tissue, etc. —*vi.* **-phied, -phy·ing** to undergo atrophy
at·ro·pine (at′rə pēn′, -pin) *n.* [< Gr. *Atropos*, one of the Fates + -INE³] a poisonous alkaloid obtained from belladonna, used to relieve spasms
at·tach (ə tach′) *vt.* [< OFr. *estache*, a post] 1. to fasten by tying, etc. 2. to join (often used reflexively) 3. to connect by ties of affection 4. to affix (a signature, etc.) 5. to ascribe 6. *Law* to take (property, etc.) by writ —*vi.* to be joined; belong —**at·tach′a·ble** *adj.*
at·ta·ché (at′ə shā′; *chiefly Brit.* ə tash′ā) *n.* [Fr.: see prec.] a person with special duties on the staff of an ambassador, etc.
attaché case a flat, rectangular case for carrying documents, papers, etc.
at·tach′ment *n.* 1. the act of attaching something 2. anything that attaches; fastening 3. devotion 4. anything attached 5. an accessory for an electrical appliance, etc. 6. *Law* a taking of a person, property, etc. into custody
at·tack (ə tak′) *vt.* [< OFr.: see ATTACH] 1. to use force against in order to harm 2. to speak or write against 3. to undertake vigorously 4. to begin acting upon harmfully —*vi.* to make an assault —*n.* 1. an attacking 2. an onset of a disease —**at·tack′er** *n.*
at·tain (ə tān′) *vt.* [< L. *ad-*, to + *tangere*, to touch] 1. to gain; accomplish; achieve 2. to arrive at —**at·tain′a·bil′i·ty** *n.* —**at·tain′a·ble** *adj.* —**at·tain′ment** *n.*
at·tain·der (ə tān′dər) *n.* [OFr. *ataindre:* see prec.] loss of civil rights and property of one sentenced to death or outlawed
at·taint (ə tānt′) *vt.* to punish by attainder —*n.* an attainder

at·tar (at′ər) *n.* [< Ar. *'itr*, perfume] a perfume made from flower petals, esp. of roses
at·tempt (ə tempt′) *vt.* [< L. *ad-*, to + *temptare*, to try] to try to do, get, etc. —*n.* 1. a try 2. an attack, as on a person's life
at·tend (ə tend′) *vt.* [< L. *ad-*, to + *tendere*, to stretch] 1. to take care of 2. to go with 3. to accompany as a result 4. to be present at —*vi.* 1. to pay attention 2. to wait (*on* or *upon*) 3. to give care (*to*)
at·tend′ance *n.* 1. an attending 2. the number of persons attending
at·tend′ant *adj.* 1. attending or serving 2. being present 3. accompanying —*n.* one who attends or serves
at·ten·tion (ə ten′shən) *n.* 1. mental concentration or readiness for this 2. notice or observation 3. care or consideration 4. an act of courtesy: *usually used in pl.* 5. the erect posture of soldiers ready for a command
at·ten′tive (-tiv) *adj.* 1. paying attention 2. courteous, devoted, etc.
at·ten·u·ate (ə ten′yoo wāt′) *vt.* **-at′ed, -at′ing** [< L. *ad-*, to + *tenuis*, thin] 1. to make thin or slender 2. to dilute 3. to lessen or weaken —*vi.* to become thin, weak, etc. —**at·ten′u·a′tion** *n.*
at·test (ə test′) *vt.* [< L. *ad-*, to + *testari*, bear witness] 1. to declare to be true or genuine 2. to certify, as by oath 3. to serve as proof of —*vi.* to testify (*to*) —**at·tes·ta·tion** (at′es tā′shən) *n.*
at·tic (at′ik) *n.* [< Gr. *Attikos*, of Attica (ancient Gr. region): with reference to architectural style] the room or space just below the roof; garret
at·tire (ə tīr′) *vt.* **-tired′, -tir′ing** [< OFr. *a*, to + *tire*, order] to clothe; dress up —*n.* clothes; finery
at·ti·tude (at′ə tōōd′) *n.* [Fr. < It. < L. *aptus*, apt] 1. the posture of the body in connection with an action, mood, etc. 2. a way of acting, thinking, or feeling; one's disposition
at·tor·ney (ə tur′nē) *n., pl.* **-neys** [< OFr. *a-*, to + *torner*, to turn] any person having the legal power to act for another; esp., a lawyer: abbrev. **atty.**
attorney at law a lawyer
attorney general *pl.* **attorneys general, attorney generals** the chief law officer of a government
at·tract (ə trakt′) *vt.* [< L. *ad-*, to + *trahere*, to draw] 1. to draw to itself or oneself 2. to get the admiration, attention, etc. of; allure —*vi.* to be attractive
at·trac·tion (ə trak′shən) *n.* 1. an attracting or the power of attracting; esp., charm or fascination 2. anything that attracts 3. *Physics* the mutual action by which bodies, particles, etc. tend to cohere
at·trac·tive (-tiv) *adj.* that attracts; esp., charming, pretty, etc. —**at·trac′tive·ly** *adv.* —**at·trac′tive·ness** *n.*
at·trib·ute (ə trib′yoot) *vt.* **-ut·ed, -ut·ing** [< L. *ad-*, to + *tribuere*, assign] to think of as belonging to; assign or ascribe (*to*) —*n.* (a′trə byōōt′) a characteristic or quality of a person or thing —**at·trib′ut·a·ble** *adj.* —**at′tri·bu′tion** *n.*
at·trib·u·tive (-yoo tiv) *adj.* 1. attributing 2. preceding the noun it modifies: said of an adjective —*n.* an attributive adjective
at·tri·tion (ə trish′ən) *n.* [< L. *ad-*, to + *terere*, to rub] a wearing away by friction
at·tune (ə tōōn′) *vt.* **-tuned′, -tun′ing** 1. to tune 2. to bring into harmony
a·typ·i·cal (ā tip′i k'l) *adj.* not typical
Au [L. *aurum*] *Chem.* gold

au·burn (ô′bərn) *adj., n.* [< L. *albus*, white; infl. by ME *brun*, brown] reddish brown

auc·tion (ôk′shən) *n.* [< L. *augere*, to increase] a public sale where items are sold to the highest bidders —*vt.* to sell at auction

auc·tion·eer (ôk′shə nir′) *n.* one who sells things at auction —*vt.* to auction

au·da·cious (ô dā′shəs) *adj.* [< L. *audere*, to dare] **1.** bold or daring; fearless **2.** rudely bold; insolent —**au·da′cious·ly** *adv.*

au·dac·i·ty (ô das′ə tē) *n.* **1.** bold courage; daring **2.** brazen boldness; insolence **3.** *pl.* -**ties** an audacious act or remark

au·di·ble (ô′də b'l) *adj.* [< L. *audire*, hear] loud enough to be heard —**au′di·bil′i·ty** *n.* —**au′di·bly** *adv.*

au·di·ence (ô′dē əns) *n.* [< L. *audire*, hear] **1.** a group assembled to see and hear a play, concert, etc. **2.** all those reached by a radio or TV program, book, etc. **3.** the act of hearing **4.** a formal interview

au·di·o (ô′dē ō) *adj.* [< L. *audire*, hear] **1.** of frequencies corresponding to normally audible sound waves **2.** of the sound phase of television

au·di·ol·o·gy (ô′dē äl′ə jē) *n.* the science of aiding persons with hearing defects —**au′di·ol′o·gist** *n.*

au′di·o·vis′u·al (-vizh′ōō wəl) *adj.* involving both hearing and sight

au·dit (ô′dit) *n.* [< L. *audire*, to hear] an examination and adjustment of financial accounts —*vt., vi.* **1.** to check (accounts, etc.) **2.** to attend (a college course) as a listener receiving no credits

au·di·tion (ô dish′ən) *n.* **1.** the act or sense of hearing **2.** a hearing to try out an actor, singer, etc. —*vt., vi.* to try out in an audition

au·di·tor (ô′də tər) *n.* **1.** a hearer or listener **2.** one who audits accounts

au·di·to·ri·um (ô′də tôr′ē əm) *n.* **1.** a room where an audience sits **2.** a building or hall for concerts, speeches, etc.

au·di·to·ry (ô′də tôr′ē) *adj.* of hearing or the sense of hearing

‡**auf Wie·der·se·hen** (ouf vē′dər zā′ən) [G.] goodbye

au·ger (ô′gər) *n.* [< OE. *nafogar* < *nafu*, hub + *gar*, spear] a tool for boring holes

aught (ôt) *n.* [< OE. *a*, one + *wiht*, creature] **1.** anything whatever **2.** [< (N)AUGHT] a zero —*adv.* [Archaic] to any degree

aug·ment (ôg ment′) *vt., vi.* [< L. *augere*, to increase] to make or become greater —**aug′men·ta′tion** *n.*

au gra·tin (ō grät′'n) [Fr.] with a browned crust of bread crumbs and grated cheese

au·gur (ô′gər) *n.* [L.; prob. < *augere*, to increase] a fortuneteller; soothsayer —*vt., vi.* **1.** to foretell or prophesy **2.** to be an omen (of)

au·gu·ry (ô′gyər ē) *n., pl.* -**ries 1.** the practice of divination **2.** an omen; indication

Au·gust (ô′gəst) *n.* [L. < *Augustus*, Roman emperor] the eighth month of the year, having 31 days: abbrev. **Aug.**

au·gust (ô gust′) *adj.* [L. *augustus*] inspiring awe; imposing —**au·gust′ly** *adv.*

au jus (ō zhōō′, ō jōōs′) [Fr.] served in its natural juices: said of meat

auk (ôk) *n.* [< ON. *alka*] a diving bird of the northern seas, with webbed feet and short wings used as paddles

auld (ôld) *adj.* [Dial. & Scot.] old

auld lang syne (ôld′ laŋ′ zin′; sin′) [Scot., old long since] the good old days

aunt (ant) *n.* [< L. *amita*] **1.** a sister of one's

mother or father **2.** the wife of one's uncle Also **aunt′ie, aunt′y**

au·ra (ôr′ə) *n., pl.* -**ras, -rae** (-ē) [< Gr., akin to *aēr*, air] **1.** an invisible emanation **2.** a particular quality that seems to surround a person or thing

au·ral (ôr′əl) *adj.* [< L. *auris*, ear] of or received through the sense of hearing

au·re·ole (ôr′ē ōl′) *n.* [< L. *aurum*, gold] **1.** a halo **2.** the sun's corona

Au·re·o·my·cin (ôr′ē ō mīs′'n) [< L. *aureus*, golden + Gr. *mykēs*, fungus] *a trademark for* an antibiotic

au re·voir (ō′rə vwär′) [Fr.] goodbye

au·ri·cle (ôr′ə k'l) *n.* **1.** the external part of the ear **2.** loosely, an atrium of the heart **3.** an earlike part

au·ric·u·lar (ô rik′yōō lər) *adj.* **1.** of the ear or the sense of hearing **2.** said into the ear **3.** earshaped **4.** of an auricle

Au·ro·ra (ô rôr′ə) the Rom. goddess of dawn —*n.* [a-] **1.** *pl.* -**ras, -rae** (-ē) the dawn **2.** either of the luminous bands sometimes seen in the night sky: in the S Hemisphere, called the **aurora aus·tra·lis** (ô strā′lis), in the N Hemisphere, the **aurora bo·re·a·lis** (bôr′ē al′is)

aus·pice (ôs′pis) *n., pl.* -**pi·ces** (-pə sēz′) [< L. *auspicium*] **1.** an omen, esp. a favorable one **2.** [*pl.*] patronage

aus·pi·cious (ôs pish′əs) *adj.* **1.** favorable; propitious **2.** successful

aus·tere (ô stir′) *adj.* [< Gr. *austēros*, dry] **1.** stern; harsh **2.** showing strict self-discipline **3.** very plain —**aus·tere′ly** *adv.*

aus·ter·i·ty (ô ster′ə tē) *n., pl.* -**ties 1.** an austere quality, act, or practice **2.** tightened economy, as from shortages of goods

Aus·tral·ian (ô strāl′yən) *n.* a native or inhabitant of Australia

Aus·tri·an (ôs′trē ən) *n.* a native or inhabitant of Austria

au·tar·chy (ô′tär kē) *n., pl.* -**chies** [< Gr. *autos*, self + *archos*, ruler] **1.** absolute rule; autocracy **2.** a country under such rule —**au·tar′chic, au·tar′chi·cal** *adj.*

au·then·tic (ô then′tik) *adj.* [< Gr. *authentikos*, genuine] **1.** that can be believed; reliable **2.** genuine; real —**au·then′ti·cal·ly** *adv.* —**au·then·tic·i·ty** (ô′then tis′ə tē) *n.*

au·then′ti·cate′ (-tə kāt′) *vt.* -**cat′ed, -cat′ing** to establish as authentic, or true, valid, etc. —**au·then′ti·ca′tion** *n.*

au·thor (ô′thər) *n.* [< L. *augere*, to increase] **1.** one who makes or creates something **2.** the writer (*of* a book, etc.) —*vt.* to be the author of —**au′thor·ship′** *n.*

au·thor·i·tar·i·an (ə thôr′ə ter′ē ən) *adj.* believing in or characterized by absolute obedience to authority —*n.* an advocate or enforcer of such obedience —**au·thor′i·tar′i·an·ism** *n.*

au·thor′i·ta′tive (-tāt′iv) *adj.* **1.** having authority; official **2.** based on competent authority; reliable **3.** asserting authority; dictatorial —**au·thor′i·ta′tive·ly** *adv.*

au·thor·i·ty (ə thôr′ə tē) *n., pl.* -**ties** [see AUTHOR] **1.** the power or right to give commands, take action, etc.; jurisdiction **2.** [*pl.*] officials with this power **3.** influence resulting from knowledge, prestige, etc. **4.** a person, writing, etc. cited to support an opinion **5.** an expert

au·thor·ize (ô′thə rīz′) *vt.* -**ized′, -iz′ing 1.** to give official approval to **2.** to give power or authority to; empower **3.** to justify —**au′thor·i·za′tion** *n.* —**au′thor·iz′er** *n.*

Authorized Version the revised English translation of the Bible, published in 1611, authorized by King James

au·tism (ô′tiz'm) *n.* [AUT(O)- + -ISM] *Psychol.* a mental state marked by disregard of external reality —**au·tis′tic** *adj.*

au·to (ôt′ō) *n., pl.* **-tos** an automobile

auto- [Gr. *autos,* self] *a combining form meaning:* **1.** self **2.** by oneself or itself

au·to·bi·og·ra·phy (ôt′ə bī äg′rə fē) *n., pl.* **-phies** the story of one's own life written by oneself —**au′to·bi′o·graph′i·cal, au′to·bi′o·graph′ic** *adj.*

au·toc·ra·cy (ô täk′rə sē) *n., pl.* **-cies** [see AUTOCRAT] a government in which one person has supreme power; dictatorship

au·to·crat (ôt′ə krat′) *n.* [< Gr. *autos,* self + *kratos,* power] **1.** a ruler with absolute power; dictator **2.** any domineering person —**au′to·crat′ic** *adj.* —**au′to·crat′i·cal·ly** *adv.*

au·to·gi·ro, au·to·gy·ro (ôt′ə jī′rō) *n., pl.* **-ros** [orig. a trademark < AUTO- + Gr. *gyros,* a circle] an earlier kind of aircraft having both a propeller and a large horizontal rotor

au·to·graph (ôt′ə graf′) *n.* [< Gr. *autos,* self + *graphein,* write] a person's own signature or handwriting —*vt.* to write one's signature on or in

au·to·in·tox·i·ca·tion (ôt′ō in täk′sə kā′shən) *n.* poisoning by toxic substances (**autotoxins**) formed within the body

au·to·mat (ôt′ə mat′) *n.* [G.: see AUTOMATIC] a restaurant in which patrons get food from coin-operated compartments

au·to·mate (ôt′ə māt′) *vt.* **-mat′ed, -mat′ing** [< AUTOMATION] to convert to or use automation in

au′to·mat′ic (-mat′ik) *adj.* [Gr. *automatos,* self-moving] **1.** done without conscious thought or volition **2.** moving, operating, etc. by itself **3.** done with automatic equipment —*n.* an automatic rifle, pistol, etc. —**au′to·mat′i·cal·ly** *adv.*

au′to·ma′tion (-mā′shən) *n.* a manufacturing system in which many or all of the processes are automatically performed or controlled, as by electronic devices

au·tom·a·ton (ô täm′ə tän′) *n., pl.* **-tons′, -ta** (-tə) [see AUTOMATIC] **1.** an automatic device, esp. a robot **2.** a person acting in a mechanical way

au·to·mo·bile (ôt′ə mə bēl′, -mō′bēl) *n.* [see AUTO- & MOBILE] a passenger car propelled by an engine and used for traveling on streets or roads

au·to·mo·tive (ôt′ə mōt′iv) *adj.* [AUTO- + -MOTIVE] **1.** self-moving **2.** having to do with motor vehicles

au·ton·o·my (ô tän′ə mē) *n.* **1.** self-government **2.** *pl.* **-mies** any state that governs itself —**au·ton′o·mous** *adj.*

au·top·sy (ô′täp′sē) *n., pl.* **-sies** [< Gr. *autos,* self + *opsis,* a sight] an examination of a dead body to find the cause of death, etc.

au·tumn (ôt′əm) *n.* [< L. *autumnus*] the season between summer and winter; fall —**au·tum·nal** (ô tum′n'l) *adj.*

aux·il·ia·ry (ôg zil′yər ē) *adj.* [< L. *augere,* to increase] **1.** helping; assisting **2.** subsidiary **3.** supplementary —*n., pl.* **-ries** an auxiliary person, group, thing, etc.

auxiliary verb a verb that helps form tenses, moods, or voices of other verbs

a·vail (ə vāl′) *vi., vt.* [< L. *ad,* to + *valere,* be strong] to be of use, help, worth, or advantage (to) —*n.* effective use or help —**avail oneself of** to take advantage of

a·vail′a·ble *adj.* **1.** that can be used **2.** that

can be got or had; accessible —**a·vail′a·bil′i·ty** *n.* —**a·vail′a·bly** *adv.*

av·a·lanche (av′ə lanch′) *n.* [Fr. < L. *labi,* to slip] **1.** a large mass of loosened snow, earth, etc. sliding down a mountain **2.** an overwhelming amount

a·vant-garde (ä vänt′gärd′) *n.* [Fr.] the leaders in new movements, esp. in the arts; vanguard —*adj.* of such movements

av·a·rice (av′ər is) *n.* [< L. *avere,* to desire] greed; cupidity —**av·a·ri·cious** (av′ə rish′əs) *adj.* —**av′a·ri′cious·ness** *n.*

a·vast (ə vast′) *interj.* [< Du. *houd vast,* hold fast] *Naut.* stop! cease! halt!

av·a·tar (av′ə tär′) *n.* [Sans. *avatāra,* descent] **1.** *Hinduism* a god's coming in bodily form to earth **2.** any embodiment

a·vaunt (ə vônt′) *interj.* [< L. *ab,* from + *ante,* before] [Archaic] begone! go away!

A·ve Ma·ri·a (ä′vä mə rē′ə, -vē) [L.] *R.C.Ch.* **1.** "Hail, Mary," the first words of a prayer **2.** this prayer

a·venge (ə venj′) *vt., vi.* **a·venged′, a·veng′ing** [< L. *ad,* to + *vindicare,* to claim] **1.** to get revenge for (an injury, etc.) **2.** to take vengeance on behalf of, as for a wrong —**a·veng′er** *n.*

av·e·nue (av′ə nōō′) *n.* [< L. *ad-,* to + *venire,* come] **1.** a road, path, or drive **2.** a way of approach **3.** a street, esp. a wide, principal one: abbrev. **Ave., ave.**

a·ver (ə vur′) *vt.* **a·verred′, a·ver′ring** [< L. *ad,* to + *verus,* true] **1.** to declare to be true; affirm **2.** *Law* to state formally

av·er·age (av′rij, -ər ij) *n.* [< Fr. *avarie,* damage to ship: hence, idea of equal sharing of the loss] **1.** the result of dividing the sum of two or more quantities by the number of quantities **2.** the usual kind, amount, etc. —*adj.* **1.** being a numerical average **2.** usual; normal —*vi.* **-aged, -ag·ing** to be or amount to on the average —*vt.* **1.** to calculate the average of **2.** to do, take, etc. on the average **3.** to divide proportionately among more than two —**average out** to arrive at an average eventually —**on the (or an) average** as an average quantity, rate, etc.

a·verse (ə vurs′) *adj.* [see AVERT] unwilling

a·ver·sion (ə vur′zhən) *n.* **1.** a strong or definite dislike **2.** the object disliked

a·vert (ə vurt′) *vt.* [< L. *ab-,* from + *vertere,* to turn] **1.** to turn (the eyes, etc.) away **2.** to prevent —**a·vert′i·ble** *adj.*

a·vi·a·ry (ā′vē er′ē) *n., pl.* **-ies** [< L. *avis,* bird] a large cage for keeping many birds

a·vi·a·tion (ā′vē ā′shən) *n.* [see AVIARY] **1.** the science of flying airplanes **2.** the field of airplane design, construction, etc.

a′vi·a′tor *n.* an airplane pilot —**a′vi·a′trix** (-ā′triks) *n.fem.*

av·id (av′id) *adj.* [< L. *avere,* to desire] very eager or greedy —**a·vid·i·ty** (ə vid′ə tē) *n.*

av·o·ca·do (av′ə kä′dō) *n., pl.* **-dos** [< Mex.-Ind. *ahuacatl*] **1.** a thick-skinned, pear-shaped tropical fruit with yellow, buttery flesh **2.** the tree that it grows on

av·o·ca·tion (av′ə kā′shən) *n.* [< L. *ab-,* away + *vocare,* to call] something done in addition to regular work; hobby

a·void (ə void′) *vt.* [< ME. < OFr. *esvuidier,* to empty] to keep away from; shun —**a·void′a·ble** *adj.* —**a·void′ance** *n.*

av·oir·du·pois (av′ər də poiz′) *n.* [< OFr. *aveir de peis,* goods having weight] **1.** an English and American system of weights in which 16 oz. = 1 lb.: also **avoirdupois weight 2.** [Colloq.] weight, esp. of a person

a·vouch (ə vouch′) *vt.* [see ADVOCATE] **1.** to guarantee **2.** to declare the truth of; affirm **3.** to acknowledge openly

a·vow (ə vou′) *vt.* [see ADVOCATE] to declare openly; acknowledge —**a·vow′al** *n.* —**a·vowed′** *adj.*

aw (ô, ä) *interj.* an exclamation of protest, etc.

a·wait (ə wāt′) *vt.* [< Anglo-Fr. *a-*, to + *waitier*, wait] **1.** to wait for **2.** to be in store for — *vi.* to wait

a·wake (ə wāk′) *vt., vi.* **a·woke′** or **a·waked′**, **a·waked′**, **a·wak′ing** [< OE.] **1.** to rouse from sleep; wake **2.** to rouse from inactivity Also **a·wak′en** —*adj.* **1.** not asleep **2.** active or alert

a·wak′en·ing *n., adj.* **1.** (a) waking up **2.** (an) arousing, as of impulses, interest, etc.

a·ward (ə wôrd′) *vt.* [< ME. < ONormFr. *eswarder*] **1.** to give, as by legal decision **2.** to grant (a prize, etc.) —*n.* **1.** a decision, as by a judge **2.** a prize

a·ware (ə wer′) *adj.* [< OE. *wær*, cautious] knowing; conscious —**a·ware′ness** *n.*

a·wash (ə wôsh′) *adv., adj.* **1.** at a level where the water washes over the surface **2.** flooded **3.** afloat

a·way (ə wā′) *adv.* [< OE. *on*, on + *weg*, way] **1.** from any given place [run *away*] **2.** far [*away* behind] **3.** off; aside [turn *away*] **4.** from one's possession [give it *away*] **5.** at once [fire *away*] **6.** continuously [kept working *away*] —*adj.* **1.** absent; gone **2.** at a distance [a mile *away*] —*interj.* begone! —**away with** go, come, or take away —**do away with 1.** to get rid of **2.** to kill

awe (ô) *n.* [ON. *agi*] a mixed feeling of reverence, fear, and wonder —*vt.* **awed, aw′ing** to inspire awe in; fill with awe

a·weigh (ə wā′) *adj. Naut.* just clear of the bottom: said of an anchor being weighed

awe·some (ô′səm) *adj.* inspiring or showing awe —**awe′some·ly** *adv.* —**awe′some·ness** *n.*

awe-struck (ô′struk′) *adj.* filled with awe: also **awe′-strick′en** (-strik′ən)

aw·ful (ô′fəl) *adj.* [see AWE & -FUL] **1.** inspiring awe **2.** terrifying **3.** [Colloq.] very bad —*adv.* [Colloq.] very —**aw′ful·ness** *n.*

aw·ful·ly (ô′fə lē, -flē) *adv.* **1.** in a way to inspire awe **2.** [Colloq.] very

a·while (ə wīl′, -hwīl′) *adv.* for a short time

awk·ward (ôk′wərd) *adj.* [< ON. *ofugr*, turned backward + OE. *-weard*, -WARD] **1.** clumsy; bungling **2.** unwieldy **3.** uncomfortable [an *awkward* position] **4.** embarrassed or embarrassing [an *awkward* remark] —**awk′ward·ly** *adv.* —**awk′ward·ness** *n.*

awl (ôl) *n.* [< OE. *æl, awel*] a small, pointed tool for making holes in wood, leather, etc.

awn (ôn) *n.* [ON. *ǫgn*, chaff] the bristly fibers on a head of barley, oats, etc. —**awned** *adj.*

awn·ing (ô′niŋ) *n.* [< ? MFr. *auvent*, window shade] a structure, as of canvas, extended before a window, etc. as a protection from sun or rain

a·woke (ə wōk′) *pt. & occas. pp.* of AWAKE

A·WOL, a·wol (ā′wôl′) *adj.* absent without leave

a·wry (ə rī′) *adv., adj.* [see A- (sense 1) & WRY] **1.** with a twist to a side; askew **2.** wrong; amiss [our plans went *awry*]

ax, axe (aks) *n., pl.* **ax′es** [OE. *æx*] a tool with a long handle and a bladed head, for chopping wood, etc. —*vt.* **axed, ax′ing** to trim, split, etc. with an ax —**get the ax** [Colloq.] to be discharged from one's job —**have an ax to grind** [Colloq.] to have an object of one's own to gain or promote

ax·i·al (ak′sē əl) *adj.* **1.** of, like, or forming an axis **2.** around or along an axis

ax·i·om (ak′sē əm) *n.* [< Gr. *axios*, worthy] **1.** a statement universally accepted as true; maxim **2.** an established principle or law **3.** a self-evident truth —**ax′i·o·mat′ic** (-ə mat′ik) *adj.* —**ax′i·o·mat′i·cal·ly** *adv.*

ax·is (ak′sis) *n., pl.* **ax′es** (-sēz) [L.] **1.** a real or imaginary straight line on which an object rotates **2.** a central line around which the parts of a thing, system, etc. are evenly arranged

ax·le (ak′s'l) *n.* [< ON. *ǫxull*] **1.** a rod on or with which a wheel turns **2.** a bar connecting two opposite wheels, as of an automobile: also **ax′le·tree′**

Ax·min·ster (aks′min stər) *n.* [< *Axminster*, town in England] a varicolored, patterned carpet with a cut pile

aye¹ (ā) *adv.* [ON. *ei*] [Poet.] always; ever: also **ay**

aye² (ī) *adv.* [< ? prec.] yes; yea —*n.* an affirmative vote or voter Also **ay**

a·zal·ea (ə zāl′yə) *n.* [< Gr. *azaleos*, dry] **1.** a shrub related to the heath with flowers of various colors **2.** the flower of this plant

az·i·muth (az′ə məth) *n.* [< Ar. *al*, the + *samt*, way, path] *Astron.*, etc. distance in angular degrees in a clockwise direction from the north point or, in the Southern Hemisphere, south point

Az·tec (az′tek) *n.* **1.** *pl.* **-tecs, -tec** a member of a people who had an advanced civilization in Mexico before the Spanish conquest in 1519 **2.** their language —*adj.* of the Aztecs

az·ure (azh′ər) *adj.* [< Per. *lāzhuward*, lapis lazuli] sky-blue —*n.* **1.** sky blue **2.** [Poet.] the blue sky

B

B, b (bē) *n., pl.* **B's, b's** the second letter of the English alphabet

B (bē) *n.* **1.** a grade indicating above-average but not outstanding work **2.** *Chem.* boron **3.** *Music* the seventh tone in the scale of C major

B., b. 1. bachelor **2.** *Baseball a)* base *b)* baseman **3.** *Music* bass or basso **4.** bay **5.** book **6.** born **7.** brother

Ba *Chem.* barium

B.A. Bachelor of Arts

baa (bä) *n., vi.* [echoic] bleat

Ba·al (bā′əl, bāl) *n., pl.* **Ba′al·im** (-im), **Ba′als 1.** an ancient Semitic fertility god **2.** a false god; idol

bab·ble (bab′'l) *vi.* **-bled, -bling** [echoic] **1.** to make incoherent sounds **2.** to talk foolishly or too much **3.** to make a low, bubbling sound, as a brook —*vt.* to say incoherently or foolishly —*n.* **1.** confused, incoherent vocal sounds **2.** foolish talk **3.** a low, bubbling sound —**bab′bler** *n.*

babe (bāb) *n.* **1.** a baby **2.** a naive or helpless person: also **babe in the woods 3.** [Slang] a girl or young woman

Ba·bel (bā′b'l, bab′'l) *Bible* a city where people tried to build a tower to the sky and were caused suddenly to speak in different languages —*n.* [*also* **b-**] **1.** a confusion of voices, etc.; tumult **2.** a place of such confusion

ba·boon (ba bōōn′) *n.* [< OFr. *babuin*, ape, fool] a large and fierce, short-tailed monkey of Africa and Arabia, having a doglike snout

ba·bush·ka (bə bōōsh′kə) *n.* [Russ., grandmother] a woman's scarf worn on the head

ba·by (bā′bē) *n., pl.* **-bies** [ME. *babi*] **1.** a very young child; infant **2.** one who behaves like an infant **3.** a very young animal **4.** the youngest in a group **5.** [Slang] *a)* a girl or young woman *b)* any person or thing —*adj.* **1.** of or for an infant **2.** very young **3.** small of its kind **4.** childish —*vt.* **-bied, -by·ing 1.** to pamper **2.** [Colloq.] to handle with great care —**ba′by·hood′** *n.* —**ba′by·ish** *adj.* —**ba′by·like′** *adj.*

baby sitter a person hired to care for children, as when the parents are away —**ba′by-sit′** *vi., vt.* **-sat′, -sit′ting**

bac·ca·lau·re·ate (bak′ə lôr′ē it) *n.* [see BACHELOR] **1.** the degree of Bachelor of Arts (or Science, etc.) **2.** a speech at commencement

bac·cha·nal (bak′ə nəl, -nal′) *n.* **1.** a worshiper of Bacchus **2.** a drunken carouser **3.** a drunken orgy —**bac′cha·na′li·an** (-nā′lē ən) *adj., n.*

Bac·chus (bak′əs) an ancient Greek and Roman god of wine and revelry

bach·e·lor (bach′'l ər, bach′lər) *n.* [< ML. *baccalaris,* a squire] **1.** a man who has not married **2.** a person who is a BACHELOR OF ARTS (or SCIENCE, etc.) —**bach′e·lor·hood′** *n.*

Bachelor of Arts (or **Science,** etc.) **1.** a degree given by a college or university to one who has completed a four-year course in the humanities (or in science, etc.) **2.** one who has this degree

bachelor's button any of several plants having flowers shaped somewhat like buttons

ba·cil·lus (bə sil′əs) *n., pl.* **-cil′li** (-ī) [< L. *bacillum,* little stick] **1.** any of the rod-shaped bacteria **2.** [*usually pl.*] loosely, any bacterium

back (bak) *n.* [< OE. *bæk*] **1.** the rear part of the body from the nape of the neck to the end of the spine **2.** the backbone **3.** a part that supports or fits the back **4.** the rear part or reverse of anything **5.** *Sports* a player or position behind the front line —*adj.* **1.** at the rear **2.** distant **3.** of or for a time in the past *[back pay]* **4.** backward —*adv.* **1.** at, to, or toward the rear **2.** to or toward a former condition, time, etc. **3.** in reserve or concealment **4.** in return *[to pay one back]* —*vt.* **1.** to move backward **2.** to support **3.** to bet on **4.** to provide or be a back for —*vi.* to go backward —**back and forth** to and fro —**back down** to withdraw from a position, etc. —**back out (of) 1.** to withdraw from an enterprise **2.** to evade keeping a promise, etc. —**back up 1.** to support **2.** to move backward **3.** to accumulate because of restricted movement *[traffic backed up]* —**get** (or **put**) **one's back up** to make or be obstinate —**go back on** [Colloq.] **1.** to betray **2.** to fail to keep (a promise, etc.)

back′bite′ (-bīt′) *vt., vi.* **-bit′, -bit′ten** or **-bit′, -bit′ing** to slander (someone absent) —**back′-bit′er** *n.*

back′board′ *n. Basketball* a board or flat surface just behind the basket

back′bone′ *n.* **1.** the spine **2.** a main support **3.** willpower, courage, etc.

back′break′ing *adj.* very tiring

back′drop′ *n.* **1.** a curtain hung at the back of a stage **2.** background or setting

back′er *n.* **1.** a patron; supporter **2.** one who bets on a contestant

back′field′ *n. Football* the players behind the line; esp., the offensive unit

back′fire′ *n.* **1.** the burning out of a small area, as in a forest, to check the spread of a big fire **2.** a premature explosion in an internal-combustion engine **3.** reverse explosion in a gun —*vi.* **-fired′, -fir′ing 1.** to explode as a backfire **2.** to go wrong or boomerang, as a plan

back′gam′mon (-gam′ən) *n.* [BACK + ME. *gammen,* game] a game for two, with pieces moved according to the throw of dice

back′ground′ *n.* **1.** the part of a scene toward the back **2.** surroundings, sounds, data, etc. behind or subordinate to something **3.** one's training and experience **4.** events leading up to something

back′hand′ *n.* **1.** handwriting that slants up to the left **2.** a backhand catch, stroke, etc. —*adj.* **1.** done with the back of the hand turned inward, as for a baseball catch, or forward, as for a tennis stroke **2.** written in backhand —*adv.* in a backhand way

back′hand′ed *adj.* **1.** *same as* BACKHAND **2.** indirect or sarcastic; equivocal —*adv.* in a backhanded way

back′ing *n.* **1.** something forming a back for support **2.** support given to a person or cause **3.** supporters; backers

back′lash′ *n.* a sharp reaction; recoil

back′log′ (-lôg′) *n.* an accumulation or reserve —*vi., vt.* **-logged′, -log′ging** to accumulate as a backlog

back order an order not yet filled

back′pack′ *n.* a knapsack, often on a light frame, worn as by hikers —*vi.* to hike wearing a backpack —**back′pack′er** *n.*

back′ped′al *vi.* **-aled** or **-alled, -al·ing** or **-al·ling 1.** to pedal backward, as in braking a bicycle **2.** to move backward **3.** to retreat from an opinion

back′side′ *n.* **1.** the back part **2.** the rump

back′slide′ (-slīd′) *vi.* **-slid′, -slid′** or **-slid′den, -slid′ing** to slide backward in morals, religion, etc. —**back′slid′er** *n.*

back′stage′ *adv., adj.* behind and off the stage, as in the wings or dressing rooms

back′stretch′ *n.* the part of a race track farthest from the grandstand

back′stroke′ *n.* a stroke made by a swimmer lying face upward

back talk [Colloq.] insolent retorts

back′-to-back′ *adj.* [Colloq.] one right after another

back′track′ *vi.* **1.** to return by the same path **2.** to withdraw from a position, etc.

back′ward (-wərd) *adv.* **1.** toward the back **2.** with the back foremost **3.** in reverse order **4.** in a way contrary to normal **5.** into the past Also **back′wards** —*adj.* **1.** turned toward the rear or in the opposite way **2.** hesitant or shy **3.** slow or retarded —**back′ward·ly** *adv.* —**back′-ward·ness** *n.*

back′woods′ *n.pl.* [*occas. with sing. v.*] **1.** heavily wooded, remote areas **2.** any remote, thinly populated place

ba·con (bāk′n) *n.* [< OS. *baco,* side of bacon] salted and smoked meat from the back or sides of a hog

bac·te·ri·a (bak tir′ē ə) *n.pl., sing.* **-ri·um** (-əm) [< Gr. *baktron,* a staff] microorganisms which have no chlorophyll and multiply by simple division: some bacteria cause diseases, but others are necessary for fermentation, etc. —**bac·te′ri·al** *adj.*

bac·te'ri·cide' (-ə sīd') *n.* an agent that destroys bacteria —**bac·te'ri·ci'dal** *adj.*

bac·te'ri·ol'o·gy (-ē äl'ə jē) *n.* the science that deals with bacteria —**bac·te'ri·o·log'i·cal** (-ē ə läj'i k'l) *adj.* —**bac·te'ri·ol'o·gist** *n.*

bad' (bad) *adj.* **worse, worst** [ME.] **1.** not good; not as it should be **2.** inadequate or unfit **3.** unfavorable *[bad* news] **4.** rotten or spoiled **5.** incorrect or faulty **6.** *a)* wicked; immoral *b)* mischievous **7.** harmful **8.** severe *[a bad* storm] **9.** ill **10.** sorry; distressed *[he* feels *bad* about it] **11.** offensive **12.** [Slang] very good, etc. — *adv.* [Colloq.] badly —*n.* anything bad —**in bad** [Colloq.] in trouble or disfavor —**bad'ness** *n.*

bad² (bad) *archaic pt. of* BID

bade (bad; *occas.* bād) *pt. of* BID

badge (baj) *n.* [ME. *bage*] **1.** an emblem worn to show rank, membership, etc. **2.** any distinguishing sign, etc.

badg·er (baj'ər) *n.* [< ?] **1.** a burrowing animal with a broad back and thick, short legs **2.** its fur —*vt.* to nag at; torment

bad·i·nage (bad'ə näzh', bad'n ij) *n.* [Fr. < ML. *badare,* to gape] playful, teasing talk —*vt.* **-naged', -nag'ing** to tease

bad·lands (bad'landz') *n.pl.* an area of barren land with dry soil and soft rocks eroded into odd shapes

bad'ly *adv.* **1.** in a bad manner **2.** [Colloq.] very much; greatly

bad·min·ton (bad'min t'n) *n.* [< *Badminton,* Eng. estate] a game in which a shuttlecock is batted back and forth with rackets across a net

bad'-tem'pered *adj.* having a bad temper or cranky disposition; irritable

baf·fle (baf''l) *vt.* **-fled, -fling** [< ?] **1.** to confuse completely; confound **2.** to hinder; impede —*n.* a screen to deflect gases, sound waves, etc. — **baf'fle·ment** *n.* —**baf'fler** *n.* —**baf'fling** *adj.*

bag (bag) *n.* [ON. *baggi*] **1.** a nonrigid container of paper, plastic, etc., with a top opening that can be closed **2.** a satchel, suitcase, etc. **3.** a purse **4.** game taken in hunting **5.** a baglike shape or part **6.** [Slang] one's special interest **7.** [Slang] an unattractive woman **8.** *Baseball* a base —*vt.* **bagged, bag'ging 1.** to make bulge **2.** to capture **3.** to kill in hunting **4.** [Slang] to get —*vi.* **1.** to swell **2.** to hang loosely —**be left holding the bag** [Colloq.] to be left to suffer the bad consequences —**in the bag** [Slang] certain; assured

bag·a·telle (bag'ə tel') *n.* [Fr.] a trifle

ba·gel (bā'g'l) *n.* [Yid.] a hard, doughnut-shaped bread roll

bag·gage (bag'ij) *n.* [< ML. *baga,* chest, bag] **1.** the bags, etc. of a traveler; luggage **2.** the supplies and gear of an army

bag·gy (bag'ē) *adj.* **-gi·er, -gi·est 1.** puffed in a baglike way **2.** hanging loosely

bag'pipe' *n.* [*often pl.*] a shrill-toned musical instrument with reed pipes sounded by air forced from a leather bag: now chiefly Scottish —**bag'pip'er** *n.*

bah (bä) *interj.* an exclamation of contempt, scorn, or disgust

bail' (bāl) *n.* [< L. *bajulare,* bear a burden] **1.** money deposited with the court to get an arrested person temporarily released until his trial **2.** such a release **3.** the person giving bail —*vt.* **1.** to have (an arrested person) set free by giving bail **2.** to help out of financial or other difficulty Often with *out* —**bail'a·ble** *adj.*

bail² (bāl) *n.* [ME. *baille,* bucket] a bucket for dipping up water from a boat —*vi., vt.* to dip out (water) from (a boat) —**bail out** to parachute from an aircraft

bail³ (bāl) *n.* [< ON. *beygla*] a hoop-shaped handle for a bucket, etc.

bai·liff (bā'lif) *n.* [< L. *bajulus,* porter] **1.** a deputy sheriff **2.** a court officer who guards the jurors, keeps order in the court, etc. **3.** in England, *a)* a district administrative official *b)* a steward of an estate

bai·li·wick (bā'lə wik) *n.* [ME. < *bailif,* bailiff + *wik* < OE. *wic,* village] **1.** a bailiff's district **2.** one's particular area of activity, authority, etc.

bait (bāt) *vt.* [< ON. *beita,* make bite] **1.** to set dogs on for sport *[to bait* bears] **2.** to torment with unprovoked attacks **3.** to put food, etc. on (a hook or trap) as a lure for game **4.** to lure; entice —*n.* **1.** food, etc. put on a hook or trap as a lure **2.** any lure; enticement —**bait'er** *n.*

baize (bāz) *n.* [< L. *badius,* brown] a feltlike woolen cloth used on billiard tables

bake (bāk) *vt.* **baked, bak'ing** [OE. *bacan*] **1.** to cook (food) by dry heat, esp. in an oven **2.** to dry and harden (pottery) by heat; fire —*vi.* **1.** to bake bread, etc. **2.** to become baked —*n.* **1.** a baking **2.** a social affair at which a baked food is served

bak·er (bāk'ər) *n.* one whose work or business is baking bread, etc.

baker's dozen thirteen

bak'er·y *n.* **1.** *pl.* **-ies** a place where bread, pastries, etc. are baked or sold **2.** baked goods

baking powder a leavening agent containing baking soda and an acid substance

baking soda sodium bicarbonate, used as a leavening agent and as an antacid

bal·a·lai·ka (bal'ə lī'kə) *n.* [Russ.] a Russian stringed instrument somewhat like a guitar

bal·ance (bal'əns) *n.* [< LL. *bilanx,* having two scales] **1.** an instrument for weighing, esp. one with two matched hanging pans **2.** a state of equilibrium in weight, value, etc. **3.** bodily or mental stability **4.** harmonious proportion of elements in a design, etc. **5.** a weight, value, etc. that counteracts another **6.** equality of debits and credits, or the difference between them **7.** a remainder **8.** *same as* BALANCE WHEEL —*vt.* **-anced, -anc·ing 1.** to weigh in or as in a balance **2.** to compare as to relative value, etc. **3.** to counterpoise or counteract; offset **4.** to put or keep in a state of equilibrium; poise **5.** to make or be equal to in weight, value, etc. **6.** to find any difference between, or to equalize, the debits and credits of (an account) —*vi.* **1.** to be in equilibrium **2.** to be equal in weight, value, etc. **3.** to have the credits and debits equal —**in the balance** not yet settled

balance sheet a statement summarizing the financial status of a business

balance wheel a wheel to regulate the movement of a timepiece, etc.

bal·co·ny (bal'kə nē) *n., pl.* **-nies** [< It.] **1.** a platform projecting from a building and enclosed by a railing **2.** an upper floor of seats in a theater, etc. often jutting out over the main floor

bald (bôld) *adj.* [ME. *balled*] **1.** having white fur or feathers on the head, as some animals and birds **2.** lacking hair on the head **3.** not covered by natural growth **4.** plain or blunt — **bald'ness** *n.*

bald eagle a large eagle of N. America, with a white-feathered head

bal·der·dash (bôl'dər dash') *n.* [orig. a senseless mixture of liquids] nonsense

bald'-faced' (bôld'fāst') *adj.* brazen; shameless

bald'ing *adj.* becoming bald

bale[1] (bāl) *n.* [< OHG. *balla,* a ball] a large bundle, esp. a standardized quantity of goods, as cotton, compressed and bound —*vt.* **baled, bal′ing** to make into bales —**bal′er** *n.*

bale[2] (bāl) *n.* [OE. *bealu*] [Poetic] 1. evil; harm 2. sorrow; woe

bale·ful (bāl′fəl) *adj.* harmful or evil

balk (bôk) *n.* [OE. *balca,* a ridge] 1. a check, hindrance, etc. 2. *Baseball* an illegal motion by the pitcher entitling base runners to advance one base —*vt.* to obstruct or foil —*vi.* to stop and refuse to move or act —**balk′er** *n.*

Bal·kan (bôl′kən) *adj.* of the Balkans, their people, etc.

balk·y (bôk′ē) *adj.* **-i·er, -i·est** stubbornly resisting; balking —**balk′i·ness** *n.*

ball[1] (bôl) *n.* [ME. *bal*] 1. any round object; sphere; globe 2. *a)* a round or egg-shaped object used in various games *b)* any of several such games, esp. baseball 3. a throw or pitch of a ball *[a* fast *ball]* 4. a missile for a cannon, rifle, etc. 5. a rounded part of the body 6. *Baseball* a pitched ball that is not struck at and is not a strike —*vi., vt.* to form into a ball —**ball up** [Slang] to muddle or confuse —**be on the ball** [Slang] to be alert; be efficient

ball[2] (bôl) *n.* [< Fr. < Gr. *ballizein,* to dance] 1. a formal social dance 2. [Slang] a good time

bal·lad (bal′əd) *n.* [< OFr. *ballade,* dancing song] 1. a sentimental song with the same melody for each stanza 2. a narrative song or poem, usually anonymous, having short stanzas, simple words, and a refrain 3. a slow, sentimental popular song —**bal′lad·eer′** *n.* —**bal′-lad·ry** *n.*

bal·last (bal′əst) *n.* [< ODan. *bar,* bare + *last,* a load] 1. anything heavy carried in a ship, vehicle, etc. to give stability 2. crushed rock or gravel, used in railroad beds, etc. —*vt.* to furnish with ballast

ball bearing 1. a bearing in which the moving parts revolve on freely rolling metal balls 2. any of these balls

bal·le·ri·na (bal′ə rē′nə) *n.* [It. < L.: see BALL[2]] a woman ballet dancer

bal·let (bal′ā, ba lā′) *n.* [< Fr. < It. *ballo,* a dance] 1. an intricate group dance using pantomime and conventionalized movements to tell a story 2. ballet dancers

ballistic missile a long-range missile guided automatically in flight, but a free-falling projectile at its target

bal·lis·tics (bə lis′tiks) *n.pl.* [*with sing. v.*] 1. the science dealing with the motion and impact of projectiles 2. the study of the effects of firing on a firearm, bullet, etc. —**bal·lis′tic** *adj.*

bal·loon (bə lōōn′) *n.* [< Fr. < It. *palla,* a ball] 1. a large, airtight bag that rises when filled with a gas lighter than air 2. such a bag with a gondola for passengers or instruments 3. an inflatable rubber bag, used as a toy —*vi.* to swell; expand —*adj.* like a balloon —**bal·loon′ist** *n.*

bal·lot (bal′ət) *n.* [< It. *palla,* ball] 1. a ticket, paper, etc. by which a vote is registered 2. act, method, or right of voting, esp. by secret ballots 3. the total number of votes cast 4. a list of candidates for office —*vi.* to vote

ball′park′ *n.* a baseball stadium

ball′play′er *n.* a baseball player

ball point pen a fountain pen with a small ball bearing instead of a point

ball′room′ *n.* a large hall for dancing

bal·ly·hoo (bal′ē hōō′) *n.* [< ?] loud talk, sensational advertising, etc. —*vt., vi.* **-hooed′, -hoo′ing** [Colloq.] to promote with ballyhoo

balm (bäm) *n.* [< Gr. *balsamon*] 1. a fragrant healing ointment or oil 2. anything healing or soothing

balm′y *adj.* **-i·er, -i·est** 1. soothing, fragrant, etc. 2. [Slang] crazy

ba·lo·ney (bə lō′nē) *n.* [< ? *bologna*] 1. *same as* BOLOGNA 2. [Slang] nonsense

bal·sa (bôl′sə) *n.* [Sp.] 1. a tropical American tree having an extremely lightweight wood 2. the wood

bal·sam (bôl′səm) *n.* [see BALM] 1. an aromatic resin obtained from certain trees 2. an aromatic, resinous oil 3. balm 4. any of various trees yielding balsam

Bal·tic (bôl′tik) *adj.* of or near the Baltic Sea

bal·us·ter (bal′əs tər) *n.* [< Fr. < It. < Gr. *balaustion,* flower of the wild pomegranate: from the shape] any of the small posts of a railing, as on a staircase

bal·us·trade (bal′ə strād′) *n.* a railing held up by balusters

bam·boo (bam bōō′) *n.* [Malay *bambu*] a treelike tropical grass with jointed, often hollow stems used for furniture, canes, etc.

bam·boo·zle (bam bōō′z'l) *vt.* **-zled, -zling** [< ?] 1. to trick; cheat 2. to confuse

ban (ban) *vt.* **banned, ban′ning** [OE. *bannan,* summon] to prohibit or forbid, esp. officially —*n.* 1. a condemnation by church authorities 2. a curse 3. an official prohibition 4. strong public disapproval

ba·nal (bā′n'l; bə nal′) *adj.* [Fr.] trite; hackneyed —**ba·nal′i·ty** *n., pl.* **-ties** —**ba′nal·ly** *adv.*

ba·nan·a (bə nan′ə) *n.* [Sp. & Port.] 1. a treelike tropical plant with large clusters of edible fruit 2. the narrow, somewhat curved fruit, having a creamy flesh and a yellow or red skin

band[1] (band) *n.* [ON.] 1. something that binds, ties, or encircles, as a strip or ring of wood, rubber, metal, etc. 2. a stripe 3. a division on a long-playing phonograph record 4. a range of wavelengths or frequencies —*vt.* to put a band on or around

band[2] (band) *n.* [< Fr. < Goth. *bandwa,* a sign] 1. a group of people united for a common purpose 2. a group of musicians playing together, esp. upon wind and percussion instruments —*vi., vt.* to unite for a common purpose

band·age (ban′dij) *n.* [Fr. < *bande,* a strip] a strip of cloth or other dressing used to bind or cover an injury —*vt.* **-aged, -ag·ing** to put a bandage on

Band-Aid (band′dād′) [BAND(AGE) + AID] *a trademark for* a small prepared bandage of gauze and adhesive tape —*n.* [b- a-] a bandage of this type: also **band′aid′**

ban·dan·na, ban·dan·a (ban dan′ə) *n.* [Hindi *bāndhnū,* method of dyeing] a large, colored handkerchief, usually a print

band·box (band′bäks′) *n.* a light box, as of pasteboard, to hold hats, etc.

ban·deau (ban dō′) *n., pl.* **-deaux′** (-dōz′) [Fr.] 1. a narrow ribbon 2. a brassiere with little support

ban·dit (ban′dit) *n.* [It. *bandito*] a robber; highwayman —**ban′dit·ry** *n.*

band′mas′ter *n.* the leader of a musical band

ban·do·leer, ban·do·lier (ban′də lir′) *n.* [< Fr. < Sp. *banda,* scarf] a broad shoulder belt with pockets for carrying ammunition, etc.

band saw a power saw made as an endless, toothed steel belt running over pulleys

bands·man (bandz′mən) *n., pl.* **-men** a member of a band of musicians

band′stand′ *n.* a platform for a musical band, esp. one for outdoor concerts

band′wag′on *n.* a wagon for a band to ride in,

as in a parade —**on the bandwagon** [Colloq.] on the popular or winning side

ban·dy[1] (ban′dē) **vt. -died, -dy·ing** [Fr. *bander,* bandy at tennis] **1.** to toss or hit (a ball, etc.) back and forth **2.** to pass (gossip, etc.) about carelessly **3.** to exchange (words), as in arguing

ban·dy[2] (ban′dē) **adj.** [< Fr. *bander,* to bend] bent or curved outward

ban′dy-leg′ged (-leg′id, -legd′) **adj.** bowlegged

bane (bān) **n.** [OE. *bana,* slayer] **1.** the cause of harm, death, etc. **2.** deadly poison: obs. except in *ratsbane,* etc. —**bane′ful adj.**

bang[1] (baŋ) **vt.** [ON. *banga,* to pound] to hit, shut, etc. hard and noisily —**vi. 1.** to make a loud noise **2.** to strike sharply —**n. 1.** a hard, noisy blow **2.** a sudden, loud noise **3.** [Slang] a thrill —**adv. 1.** hard and noisily **2.** suddenly — **bang up** to damage

bang[2] (baŋ) **vt.** [< ?] to cut (hair) short and straight across —**n.** [usually pl.] banged hair worn across the forehead

ban·gle (baŋ′g'l) **n.** [Hindi *bangrī*] a decorative bracelet or anklet

bang-up (baŋ′up′) **adj.** [Colloq.] excellent

ban·ish (ban′ish) **vt.** [< OFr. *banir*] **1.** to exile **2.** to drive away; get rid of —**ban′ish·ment n.**

ban·is·ter (ban′əs tər) **n.** [< BALUSTER] [*often pl.*] a handrail, specif. one with balusters

ban·jo (ban′jō) **n., pl. -jos, -joes** [of Afr. origin] a musical instrument with a long neck, circular body, and strings that are plucked —**ban′-jo·ist n.**

bank[1] (baŋk) **n.** [< Fr. < It. < OHG. *bank,* a bench] **1.** an establishment for receiving or lending money **2.** a reserve supply —**vt., vi.** to put (money) into a bank —**bank on** [Colloq.] to rely on

bank[2] (baŋk) **n.** [< ON. *bakki*] **1.** a long mound or heap **2.** a steep slope **3.** a stretch of rising land at the edge of a stream, etc. **4.** a shallow place, as in a sea **5.** the lateral, slanting turn of an aircraft —**vt. 1.** to cover (a fire) with ashes and fuel so that it will burn longer **2.** to pile up so as to form a bank **3.** to slope (a curve in a road, etc.) **4.** to slope (an aircraft) laterally on a turn **5.** to strike (a billiard ball) so that it recoils from a cushion

bank[3] (baŋk) **n.** [< OHG. *bank,* bench] **1.** a row of oars **2.** a row or tier, as of keys in a keyboard —**vt.** to arrange in a bank

bank account money deposited in a bank and credited to the depositor

bank′book′ n. a book in which a bank depositor's account is recorded; passbook

bank′er n. one who owns or manages a bank

bank′ing n. the business of a bank

bank note a promissory note issued by a bank: it is a form of paper money

bank′roll′ n. a supply of money —**vt.** [Colloq.] to finance

bank·rupt (baŋk′rupt′) **n.** [< Fr. < It. *banca* + *rotta,* broken] a person legally declared unable to pay his debts —**adj. 1.** that is bankrupt; insolvent **2.** lacking in some quality —**vt.** to make bankrupt —**bank′rupt′cy n., pl. -cies**

ban·ner (ban′ər) **n.** [< OFr. *baniere*] **1.** a flag **2.** a headline extending across a newspaper page —**adj.** foremost

banns (banz) **n.pl.** [see BAN] the proclamation, generally made in church three times, of an intended marriage

ban·quet (baŋ′kwit) **n.** [Fr. < It. *banca,* table] **1.** a feast **2.** a formal dinner —**vt.** to honor with a banquet —**ban′quet·er n.**

ban·quette (baŋ ket′) **n.** [Fr. < Du. *bank,* bench] an upholstered bench along a wall

ban·shee, ban·shie (ban′shē) **n.** [< Ir. *bean,* woman + *sith,* fairy] *Ir. & Scot. Folklore* a female spirit whose wailing warns of impending death

ban·tam (ban′təm) **n.** [< *Bantam,* former province in Java] **1.** [*often* B-] any of several breeds of small domestic fowl **2.** a small, aggressive person

ban′tam-weight′ n. a boxer or wrestler weighing 113 to 118 lbs.

ban·ter (ban′tər) **vt.** [17th-c. slang] to tease playfully —**vi.** to exchange banter (*with* someone) —**n.** genial teasing —**ban′ter·er n.** — **ban′ter·ing·ly adv.**

Ban·tu (ban′tōo) **n.** [Bantu *ba-ntu,* mankind] **1. pl. -tus, -tu** any member of a group of African tribes **2.** any of their languages

ban·yan (ban′yən) **n.** [ult. < Sans.] an East Indian fig tree whose branches take root and become new trunks

bap·tism (bap′tiz'm) **n.** [< Gr. *baptizein,* to immerse] **1.** the rite of admitting a person into a Christian church by dipping him in water or sprinkling water on him **2.** an experience or trial that initiates, tests, etc. —**bap·tis′mal** (-tiz′m'l) **adj.**

Bap′tist (-tist) **n.** a member of a Protestant denomination practicing baptism by immersion

bap′tis·ter·y (-tis trē) **n., pl. -ies** a place, esp. in a church, for baptizing: also **bap′tis·try, pl. -tries**

bap·tize (bap′tīz, bap tīz′) **vt. -tized, -tiz·ing 1.** to administer baptism to **2.** to initiate **3.** to christen

bar (bär) **n.** [< ML. *barra,* barrier] **1.** any long, narrow piece of wood, metal, etc., often used as a barrier, lever, etc. **2.** an oblong piece [*bar* of soap*]* **3.** anything that obstructs or hinders **4.** a band, broad line, etc. **5.** a law court, esp. that part, enclosed by a railing, where the lawyers sit **6.** lawyers collectively **7.** the legal profession **8.** a counter at which alcoholic drinks are served **9.** a place with such a counter **10.** *Music a)* a vertical line dividing a staff into measures *b)* a measure —**vt. barred, bar′ring 1.** to fasten as with a bar **2.** to obstruct; close **3.** to oppose; prevent **4.** to exclude —**prep.** excluding —**cross the bar** to die

barb (bärb) **n.** [< L. *barba,* beard] **1.** a beard-like growth **2.** a sharp point projecting away from the main point of a fishhook, etc. **3.** a cutting remark —**vt.** to provide with a barb — **barbed adj.**

bar·bar·i·an (bär ber′ē ən) **n.** [see BARBAROUS] **1.** a member of a people considered primitive, savage, etc. **2.** a coarse or unmannerly person **3.** a cruel person —**adj.** uncivilized, cruel, etc. — **bar·bar′i·an·ism n.**

bar·bar·ic (-ik) **adj. 1.** uncivilized; primitive **2.** wild, crude, etc.

bar·bar·ism (bär′bər iz'm) **n. 1.** a word or expression not standard in a language **2.** the state of being primitive or uncivilized **3.** a barbarous act, custom, etc.

bar·bar·i·ty (bär ber′ə tē) **n., pl. -ties 1.** cruelty; brutality **2.** a cruel or brutal act **3.** a barbarous act, custom, etc.

bar′ba·rous (-bər əs) **adj.** [< Gr. *barbaros,* foreign] **1.** uncivilized **2.** crude, coarse, etc. **3.** cruel; brutal

bar·be·cue (bär′bə kyōo′) **n.** [Sp. *barbacoa*] **1.** *a)* a hog, steer, etc. roasted whole over an open fire *b)* any meat broiled over an open fire **2.** a party, picnic, or restaurant featuring this **3.** a portable outdoor grill —**vt. -cued′, -cu′ing** to roast or broil over an open fire, often with a highly seasoned sauce (**barbecue sauce**)

barbed wire twisted wire with barbs along it, used for barriers: also **barb′wire′** *n.*

bar·bel (bär′b′l) *n.* [see BARB] a threadlike growth from the lips or jaws of certain fishes

bar·bell (bär′bel′) *n.* [BAR¹ + (DUMB)BELL] a metal bar with varying weights attached at each end, used for weight-lifting exercises: also **bar bell**

bar·ber (bär′bər) *n.* [see BARB] a person whose work is cutting hair, shaving and trimming beards, etc. —*vt., vi.* to cut the hair (of), shave, etc.

bar·ber·ry (bär′ber′ē) *n., pl.* -**ries** [< Ar. *barbāris*] 1. a spiny shrub with sour, red berries 2. the berry

bar·bi·tu·rate (bär bich′ər it, bär′bə tyoor′it) *n.* [< G.] any salt or ester of a crystalline acid (**barbituric acid**), used as a sedative

bard (bärd) *n.* [Gael. & Ir.] a poet

bare (ber) *adj.* [OE. *bær*] 1. not covered or clothed; naked 2. without equipment or furnishings; empty 3. simple; plain 4. mere *[a bare wage]* —*vt.* bared, bar′ing to make bare; uncover —**lay bare** to uncover; expose —**bare′-ness** *n.*

bare′back′ *adv., adj.* on a horse with no saddle

bare′faced′ *adj.* 1. with the face uncovered 2. open; shameless

bare′foot′ *adj., adv.* without shoes and stockings —**bare′foot′ed** *adj.*

bare′hand′ed *adj., adv.* 1. with hands uncovered 2. without weapons or tools

bare′head′ed *adj., adv.* wearing no head covering

bare′leg′ged (-leg′id, -legd′) *adj., adv.* with the legs bare

bare′ly *adv.* 1. openly; plainly 2. only just; scarcely 3. scantily

bar·gain (bär′g′n) *n.* [< OFr. *bargaignier*, haggle] 1. a mutual agreement or contract 2. such an agreement in terms of its worth *[a bad bargain]* 3. something sold at a price favorable to the buyer —*vi.* 1. to haggle 2. to make a bargain —**bargain for** (or **on**) to expect; count on —**into the bargain** besides —**bar′-gain·er** *n.*

barge (bärj) *n.* [< ML. *barga*] 1. a large, flat-bottomed boat for carrying freight on rivers, etc. 2. a large pleasure boat —*vt.* **barged, barg′-ing** to carry by barge —*vi.* 1. to move slowly and clumsily 2. to come or go (*in* or *into*) in a rude, abrupt way

bar·i·tone (bar′ə tōn′) *n.* [< It. < Gr. *barys*, deep + *tonos*, tone] 1. the range of a male voice between bass and tenor 2. a singer or instrument with such a range 3. a part for a baritone

bar·i·um (ber′ē əm) *n.* [< Gr. *barys*, heavy] a silvery-white metallic chemical element: symbol, Ba

bark¹ (bärk) *n.* [ON. *bǫrkr*] the outside covering of trees and woody plants —*vt.* 1. to take the bark off (a tree) 2. [Colloq.] to scrape; skin *[to bark one's shins]*

bark² (bärk) *vi.* [OE. *beorcan*] 1. to make the sharp, abrupt cry of a dog or a similar sound 2. to speak sharply; snap —*n.* a sound made in barking

bar′keep′er *n.* 1. a bar owner 2. a bartender

bark·en·tine (bär′kən tēn′) *n.* [< Fr. *barque*, after BRIGANTINE] a sailing vessel with its foremast square-rigged and its other two masts rigged fore-and-aft

bark′er *n.* a person who attracts customers to a sideshow, etc. by loud talk

bar·ley (bär′lē) *n.* [< OE. *bere*] 1. a cereal grass 2. its grain

bar′maid′ *n.* a woman bartender

barn (bärn) *n.* [< OE. *bere*, barley + *ærn*, a building] a farm building for sheltering harvested crops, livestock, etc.

bar·na·cle (bär′nə k'l) *n.* [Fr. *bernicle*] a saltwater shellfish that attaches itself to ship bottoms, pilings, etc.

barn·storm (bärn′stôrm′) *vi., vt.* to tour small towns and rural areas, giving plays, speeches, etc.

barn′yard′ *n.* the yard near a barn —*adj.* of, like, or fit for a barnyard

ba·rom·e·ter (bə räm′ə tər) *n.* [< Gr. *baros*, weight + -METER] 1. an instrument for measuring atmospheric pressure, used in forecasting weather 2. anything that indicates change —**bar·o·met·ric** (bar′ə met′rik), **bar′o·met′ri·cal** *adj.*

bar·on (bar′ən) *n.* [OFr., man] 1. a member of the lowest rank of the British hereditary peerage 2. a magnate —**bar′on·age** *n.* —**bar′on·ess** *n.fem.* —**ba·ro·ni·al** (bə rō′nē əl) *adj.*

bar′on·et (-ə nit, -net′) *n.* a man holding the lowest hereditary British title, below a baron but above a knight —**bar′on·et·cy** (-sē) *n., pl.* -**cies**

ba·roque (bə rōk′) *adj.* [Fr. < Port. *barroco*, imperfect pearl] 1. *a)* very ornate and full of curved lines, as a style of architecture *b)* music having highly embellished melodies, fugues, etc. 2. overdecorated —*n.* baroque style, art, etc.

bar·racks (bar′iks) *n.pl.* [< Fr. < Sp. *barro*, clay] 1. a building or buildings for housing soldiers 2. any large, plain building

bar·ra·cu·da (bar′ə kōō′də) *n., pl.* -**da**, -**das** [Sp.] a fierce pikelike fish of tropical seas

bar·rage (bə räzh′) *n.* [Fr. < *barrer*, to stop] 1. a curtain of artillery fire 2. a prolonged attack —*vt., vi.* -**raged′**, -**rag′ing** to lay down a barrage (against)

barred (bärd) *adj.* 1. having bars or stripes 2. closed off with bars 3. forbidden or excluded

bar·rel (bar′əl) *n.* [< ML. *barillus*] 1. *a)* a large, wooden, cylindrical container with slightly bulging sides and flat ends *b)* its standard capacity (31 1/2 gal.) 2. any somewhat similar cylinder —*vt.* -**reled** or -**relled**, -**rel·ing** or -**rel·ling** to put in barrels —*vi.* [Slang] to go at a high speed

barrel organ a mechanical musical instrument played by turning a crank

bar·ren (bar′ən) *adj.* [< OFr. *baraigne*] 1. that cannot produce offspring; sterile 2. without vegetation; unfruitful 3. unproductive; unprofitable 4. boring; dull 5. devoid (*of*) —**bar′-ren·ness** *n.*

bar·rette (bə ret′) *n.* [Fr.] a bar or clasp for holding a girl's hair in place

bar·ri·cade (bar′ə kād′; *also, esp. for v.*, bar′ə kād′) *n.* [Fr. < It. *barricare*, to fortify] a barrier, esp. one put up hastily for defense —*vt.* -**cad′ed**, -**cad′ing** to block with a barricade

bar·ri·er (bar′ē ər) *n.* [< OFr. *barre*, BAR] 1. an obstruction, as a fence or wall 2. anything that holds apart *[racial barriers]*

bar·ring (bär′iŋ) *prep.* excepting

bar·ris·ter (bar′is tər) *n.* [< BAR (*n.* 5) + -*ister*, as in MINISTER] in England, a lawyer who pleads cases in court

bar′room′ *n.* a room with a bar at which alcoholic drinks are served

bar·row (bar′ō) *n.* [< OE. *beran*, BEAR¹] *same as:* 1. HANDBARROW 2. WHEELBARROW

bar·tend·er (bär′ten′dər) *n.* one who mixes and serves alcoholic drinks at a bar

bar·ter (bär′tər) *vi., vt.* [< ON. *baratta,* quarrel] to trade by exchanging (goods) without money —*n.* a bartering

bas·al (bā′s'l) *adj.* 1. of or at the base 2. basic; fundamental

basal metabolism the quantity of energy used by any organism at rest

ba·salt (bə sôlt′, bās′ôlt) *n.* [L. *basaltes,* dark marble] a dark, tough, heavy volcanic rock

base¹ (bās) *n.* [see BASIS] 1. the thing or part on which something rests 2. the principal element or essential ingredient 3. the part of a word to which affixes are attached 4. a basis 5. any of the four goals a baseball player must reach to score a run 6. a headquarters or source of supply 7. *Chem.* a substance that forms a salt when it reacts with an acid —*adj.* forming a base —*vt.* **based, bas′ing** 1. to make a base for 2. to establish

base² (bās) *adj.* [< VL. *bassus,* low] 1. ignoble; contemptible 2. menial; servile 3. inferior in quality 4. not precious [iron is a *base* metal] —**base′ness** *n.*

base′ball′ *n.* 1. a game played with a ball and bat by two opposing teams on a field with four bases forming a diamond 2. the ball used in this game

base′board′ *n.* a molding at the base of an interior wall

base hit *Baseball* a fair hit by which the batter gets safely on base

base′less *adj.* having no basis in fact

base line 1. *Baseball* the lane between any two consecutive bases 2. the back line at each end of a tennis court

base′ment (-mənt) *n.* the story of a building just below the main floor

bash (bash) *vt.* [echoic] [Colloq.] to hit hard —*n.* [Slang] a party

bash·ful (bash′fəl) *adj.* [(A)BASH + -FUL] timid; shy —**bash′ful·ness** *n.*

bas·ic (bā′sik) *adj.* 1. of or forming a base; fundamental 2. *Chem.* of or containing a base; alkaline —**bas′i·cal·ly** *adv.*

bas·il (baz′'l) *n.* [< Gr. *basilikon,* royal] a fragrant herb of the mint family

ba·sil·i·ca (bə sil′i kə) *n.* [< Gr. *basilikē* (*stoa*), royal (portico)] a church with a nave and side aisles

ba·sin (bās′'n) *n.* [< VL. *bacca,* water vessel] 1. a wide, shallow container for liquid 2. its contents or capacity 3. a sink 4. any large hollow, often with water in it 5. *same as* RIVER BASIN

ba·sis (bā′sis) *n., pl.* **-ses** (-sēz) [Gr., pedestal] 1. a base or foundation 2. a principal constituent 3. a basic principle

bask (bask) *vi.* [ME. *basken,* to wallow] to expose oneself pleasantly to warmth, another's favor, etc.

bas·ket (bas′kit) *n.* [ME.] 1. a container made of interwoven cane, strips of wood, etc. 2. its contents 3. *Basketball a)* the goal, a round, open net hanging from a ring *b)* a scoring toss of the ball through this

bas′ket·ball′ *n.* 1. a team game played on a floor with a raised basket on either end through which an inflated ball must be tossed 2. this ball

Basque (bask) *n.* 1. a member of a people living in the W Pyrenees 2. their language —*adj.* of the Basques or their language

bass¹ (bās) *n.* [< VL. *bassus,* low] 1. the range of the lowest male voice 2. a singer or instrument with this range; specif., *same as* DOUBLE BASS —*adj.* of, in, or for this range

bass² (bas) *n., pl.* **bass, bass′es** [OE. *bærs*] a spiny-finned food and game fish of fresh or salt water

bas·set (bas′it) *n.* [< OFr. *bas,* low] a hunting hound with a long body, short legs, and long ears

bas·si·net (bas′ə net′) *n.* [< Fr. *berceau,* a cradle] an infant's basketlike bed, often hooded and on wheels

bas·so (bas′ō) *n., pl.* **-sos** [It.] a bass voice or singer

bas·soon (bə sōōn′, ba-) *n.* [< Fr.] a double-reed bass woodwind musical instrument —**bas-soon′ist** *n.*

bass viol (bās) *same as* DOUBLE BASS

bast (bast) *n.* [OE. *bæst*] plant fiber used in ropes, mats, etc.

bas·tard (bas′tard) *n.* [< OFr.] an illegitimate child —*adj.* 1. of illegitimate birth 2. inferior, spurious, etc. —**bas′tard·ly** *adv.* —**bas′tard·y** *n.*

bas′tard·ize′ *vt.* **-ized′, -iz′ing** 1. to make, declare, or show to be a bastard 2. to make corrupt; debase —**bas′tard·i·za′tion** *n.*

baste¹ (bāst) *vt.* **bast′ed, bast′ing** [< OHG. *bastjan,* sew with bast] to sew temporarily with long, loose stitches —**bast′er** *n.*

baste² (bāst) *vt.* **bast′ed, bast′ing** [< OFr. *bassiner,* moisten] to moisten (roasting meat) with drippings, etc. —**bast′er** *n.*

baste³ (bāst) *vt.* **bast′ed, bast′ing** [ON. *beysta*] 1. to beat soundly 2. to attack with words

bas·tille, bas·tile (bas tēl′) *n.* [Fr.: see BASTION] a prison —**the Bastille** a prison in Paris destroyed July 14, 1789

bas·tion (bas′chən) *n.* [Fr. < It. < Gmc. *bastjan,* make with bast, build] 1. a projection from a fortification 2. any strong defense

bat¹ (bat) *n.* [OE. *batt*] 1. a stout club 2. a club used to strike the ball in baseball and cricket 3. [Colloq.] a blow or hit —*vt.* **bat′ted, bat′ting** to hit as with a bat —*vi.* to take a turn at batting —**go to bat for** [Colloq.] to defend

bat² (bat) *n.* [< Scand.] a nocturnal, mouselike, flying mammal with membranous wings —**blind as a bat** quite blind

bat³ (bat) *vt.* **bat′ted, bat′ting** [see BATTER¹] [Colloq.] to wink —**not bat an eye** [Colloq.] not show surprise

batch (bach) *n.* [OE. *bacan,* bake] 1. the amount (of bread, etc.) in one baking 2. a quantity or number made, etc. in one lot

bate (bāt) *vt., vi.* **bat′ed, bat′ing** [< ABATE] to lessen —**with bated breath** with the breath held in, as in fear

bath (bath) *n., pl.* **baths** (ba*th*z, baths) [OE. *bæth*] 1. a washing, esp. of the body, in water 2. water, etc. for bathing or for soaking something 3. a bathtub 4. a bathroom

bathe (bā*th*) *vt.* **bathed, bath′ing** [see prec.] 1. to put into a liquid; immerse 2. to give a bath to 3. to moisten 4. to cover as with a liquid [*bathed* in light] —*vi.* 1. to take a bath 2. to soak oneself in something —**bath′er** *n.*

bath′house′ *n.* 1. a public building for bathing 2. a building used by swimmers for changing clothes

Bath′i·nette′ (-ə net′) [after BASSINET] *a trademark for* a portable folding bathtub for babies

bathing suit a garment worn for swimming

ba·thos (bā′thäs) *n.* [Gr., depth] 1. an abrupt change from the lofty to the trivial; anticlimax 2. false pathos 3. triteness —**ba·thet·ic** (bə thet′ik) *adj.*

bath'robe' *n.* a long, loose coat for wear to and from the bath, in lounging, etc.

bath'room' *n.* a room with a bathtub, toilet, etc.

bath'tub' *n.* a tub to bathe in

bath·y·sphere (bath'ə sfir') *n.* [< Gr. *bathys*, deep + SPHERE] a round, watertight observation chamber lowered by cables into sea depths

ba·tik (bə tēk') *n.* [Malay] cloth with a design made by dyeing only the parts not covered with wax

ba·tiste (ba tēst', bə-) *n.* [Fr.: < supposed orig. maker, *Baptiste*] a fine cotton cloth

ba·ton (bə tän') *n.* [Fr.] 1. a staff serving as a symbol of office 2. a slender stick used in directing music 3. a metal rod twirled by a drum major or majorette

bat·tal·ion (bə tal'yən) *n.* [see BATTLE] a tactical military unit, part of a division

bat·ten[1] (bat'ʼn) *n.* [var. of BATON] 1. a sawed strip of wood 2. a strip of wood put over a seam between boards as a fastening or covering —*vt.* to fasten or supply with battens

bat·ten[2] (bat'ʼn) *vi.* [ON. *batna*, improve] to grow fat; thrive —*vt.* to fatten up

bat·ter[1] (bat'ər) *vt.* [< L. *battuere*, to beat] 1. to strike with blow after blow 2. to injure by hard wear —*vi.* to pound noisily

bat·ter[2] (bat'ər) *n.* the baseball or cricket player whose turn it is to bat: also, in cricket, **bats'man** (-mən), *pl.* **-men**

bat·ter[3] (bat'ər) *n.* [see BATTER[1]] a flowing mixture of flour, milk, etc. for making cakes, waffles, etc.

bat'ter·ing ram an ancient military machine having a heavy beam for battering down walls, etc.

bat·ter·y (bat'ər ē) *n., pl.* **-ies** [< Fr.: see BATTER[1]] 1. a battering or beating 2. a set of things used together 3. *Baseball* the pitcher and the catcher 4. *Elec.* a cell or group of cells storing an electrical charge and able to furnish a current 5. *Law* an illegal beating of another person 6. a set of heavy guns, rockets, etc.

bat·ting (bat'iŋ, -'n) *n.* [< BAT[1]] cotton, wool, etc. fibers wadded into sheets

bat·tle (bat'ʼl) *n.* [< L. *battuere*, to beat] 1. a large-scale fight between armed forces 2. armed fighting; combat 3. any fight or conflict —*vt., vi.* **-tled, -tling** to fight —*give* (or **do**) **battle** to fight —**bat'tler** *n.*

bat'tle-ax', bat'tle-axe' *n.* 1. a heavy ax formerly used as a weapon 2. [Slang] a harsh, domineering woman

bat·tle·dore (bat'ʼl dôr') *n.* [< ? Pr. *batedor*, beater] a racket used to hit a shuttlecock in a game like badminton

bat'tle·field' *n.* 1. the place where a battle is fought or was fought 2. any area of conflict Also **bat'tle·ground'**

bat'tle·ment (-mənt) *n.* [< OFr. *batailler*, fortify] a low wall, as on top of a tower, with open spaces for shooting

bat'tle·ship' *n.* any of a class of large warships with the biggest guns and very heavy armor

bat·ty (bat'ē) *adj.* **-ti·er, -ti·est** [< BAT[2] + -Y[2]] [Slang] 1. crazy 2. odd; eccentric

bau·ble (bô'b'l) *n.* [< L. *bellus*, pretty] a showy trifle; trinket

baux·ite (bôk'sīt) *n.* [Fr. < (*Les*) *Baux*, town in SE France] the claylike ore from which aluminum is obtained

bawd (bôd) *n.* [ME. *baude*] [Now Literary] a woman who keeps a brothel

bawd·y (bô'dē) *adj.* **-i·er, -i·est** indecent; obscene —**bawd'i·ness** *n.*

bawl (bôl) *vi., vt.* [< ML. *baulare*, to bark] 1. to shout or call out noisily; bellow 2. to weep loudly —*n.* 1. a bellow 2. a noisy weeping —**bawl out** [Slang] to scold angrily

bay[1] (bā) *n.* [< ML. *baia*] a wide inlet of a sea or lake, indenting the shoreline

bay[2] (bā) *n.* [< VL. *batare*, gape] 1. an alcove marked off by columns, etc. 2. a recess in a wall, as for a window 3. *same as* BAY WINDOW 4. a compartment for storage

bay[3] (bā) *vi.* [< VL. *batare*, gape] to bark in long, deep tones —*n.* 1. a baying 2. the situation of a hunted animal forced to turn and fight —**at bay** 1. with escape cut off 2. held off —**bring to bay** to force into a situation that makes escape impossible

bay[4] (bā) *n.* [< L. *baca*, berry] 1. the laurel tree 2. [*pl.*] honor; fame

bay[5] (bā) *adj.* [< L. *badius*] reddish-brown: said esp. of horses —*n.* 1. a horse, etc. of this color 2. reddish brown

bay·ber·ry (bā'ber'ē) *n., pl.* **-ries** 1. the wax myrtle 2. any of its wax-coated berries

bay leaf the aromatic leaf of the laurel tree, dried and used as a spice in cooking

bay·o·net (bā'ə nit, -net') *n.* [< Fr. < *Bayonne*, city in France] a detachable blade put on a rifle, for hand-to-hand fighting —*vt., vi.* **-net'ed** or **-net'ted, -net'ing** or **-net'ting** to stab with a bayonet

bay·ou (bī'ōō) *n.* [< AmInd.] in the southern U.S., a marshy inlet or outlet of a lake, river, etc.

bay window 1. a window or set of windows jutting out from a wall 2. [Slang] a large, protruding belly

ba·zaar (bə zär') *n.* [Per. *bāzār*] 1. in Oriental countries, a marketplace 2. a benefit sale for a club, church, etc.

ba·zoo·ka (bə zōōk'ə) *n.* [< name of a comic horn] a portable weapon of metal tubing, for launching armor-piercing rockets

bbl. *pl.* **bbls.** barrel

BB (shot) [designation of size] a size of shot (diameter, .18 in.) for an air rifle (**BB gun**) or shotgun

B.C. before Christ

be (bē, bi) *vi.* **was** or **were, been, be'ing** [OE. *beon*] 1. to exist; live 2. to happen; occur 3. to remain or continue *Note: be* is used to link its subject to a predicate complement [she *is* brave, let x *be* y] or as an auxiliary: (1) with a past participle: *a*) to form the passive voice [he will *be* paid] *b*) to form the perfect tense [Christ *is* risen] (2) with a present participle to express continuation [the motor *is* running] (3) with a present participle or infinitive to express futurity, possibility, obligation, intention, etc. [he *is* going next week, she *is* to walk the dog] *Be* is conjugated in the present indicative: (I) *am*, (he, she, it) *is*, (we, you, they) *are*; in the past indicative: (I, he, she, it) *was*, (we, you, they) *were*

be- [OE. < *be*, about] *a prefix meaning:* 1. around [*beset*] 2. completely [*bedeck*] 3. away [*betake*] 4. about [*bemoan*] 5. make [*besot*] 6. affect by [*becloud*]

Be *Chem.* beryllium

beach (bēch) *n.* [Eng. dial., pebbles] a sandy shore —*vt., vi.* to ground (a boat) on a beach

beach'comb'er (-kō'mər) *n.* one who loafs on beaches, living on what he can beg or find

beach'head' (-hed') *n.* a position established by invading troops on an enemy shore

bea·con (bēk'ʼn) *n.* [OE. *beacen*] 1. a light for

bead (bēd) *n.* [< OE. *biddan,* pray] **1.** a small ball of glass, etc., pierced for stringing **2.** [*pl.*] *a)* a string of beads *b)* a rosary **3.** any small, round object, as the front sight of a rifle **4.** a drop or bubble —*vt.* to decorate with beads — **say** (or **tell** or **count**) **one's beads** to say prayers with a rosary —**bead'ed** *adj.*

bea·dle (bē'd'l) *n.* [ME. *bidel*] formerly, a minor church officer who kept order

bead'y *adj.* **-i·er, -i·est** small, round, and glittering like a bead

bea·gle (bē'g'l) *n.* [< ? Fr. *bégueule,* wide-throat] a small hound with a smooth coat, short legs, and drooping ears

beak (bēk) *n.* [< L. *beccus*] **1.** a bird's bill **2.** the beaklike mouthpart of various insects, fishes, etc. —**beaked** (bēkt) *adj.*

beak·er (bē'kər) *n.* [< L. *bacar,* wine glass] **1.** a goblet **2.** a glass or metal container used by chemists, druggists, etc.

beam (bēm) *n.* [OE.] **1.** a long, thick piece of timber, metal, etc. **2.** the crossbar of a balance **3.** a ship's breadth at its widest point **4.** a slender shaft of light, etc. **5.** a radiant look, smile, etc. **6.** a steady radio or radar signal for guiding aircraft or ships —*vt.* **1.** to give out (shafts of light) **2.** to direct (a radio signal, etc.) —*vi.* **1.** to shine brightly **2.** to smile warmly

bean (bēn) *n.* [OE.] **1.** a plant with edible, kidney-shaped seeds **2.** any such seed **3.** a pod with such seeds **4.** [Slang] the head or brain — *vt.* [Slang] to hit on the head —**spill the beans** [Colloq.] to tell a secret

bear¹ (ber) *vt.* **bore, borne** or **born, bear'ing** [OE. *beran*] **1.** to carry **2.** to have or show **3.** to give birth to **4.** to produce or yield **5.** to support or sustain **6.** to withstand or endure **7.** to require *[this bears watching]* **8.** to carry or conduct (oneself) **9.** to give *[to bear witness]* — *vi.* **1.** to be productive **2.** to extend or move in a given direction **3.** to be relevant (with *on*) **4.** to put up patiently (with) —**bear down** (on) **1.** to exert pressure or effort (on) **2.** to approach —**bear out** to confirm —**bear up** to endure — **bear'er** *n.*

bear² (ber) *n.* [OE. *bera*] **1.** a large, heavy mammal with shaggy fur and a very short tail **2.** [B-] either of two N constellations (**Great Bear** and **Little Bear**) **3.** one who is clumsy, rude, etc. **4.** one who sells stocks, etc., hoping to buy them back later at a lower price —*adj.* falling in price *[a bear market]*

bear'a·ble *adj.* that can be endured

beard (bird) *n.* [OE.] **1.** the hair on the chin and cheeks of a man **2.** any beardlike part, as the awn of certain grains —*vt.* **1.** to oppose courageously **2.** to provide with a beard — **beard'ed** *adj.*

bear·ing (ber'iŋ) *n.* **1.** way of carrying and conducting oneself **2.** a supporting part **3.** a producing or the ability to produce **4.** endurance **5.** [*often pl.*] relative position or direction **6.** relation; relevance **7.** a part of a machine on which another part revolves, slides, etc.

bear'ish *adj.* **1.** like a bear; rude, surly, etc. **2.** directed toward or causing a lowering of prices in the stock exchange

beast (bēst) *n.* [< L. *bestia*] **1.** any large, four-footed animal **2.** a person who is brutal, gross, etc.

beast'ly *adj.* **-li·er, -li·est 1.** of or like a beast; brutal, etc. **2.** [Colloq.] disagreeable; unpleasant —**beast'li·ness** *n.*

beast of burden any animal used for carrying things

beat (bēt) *vt.* **beat, beat'en, beat'ing** [OE. *beatan*] **1.** to strike repeatedly **2.** to punish by so striking **3.** to dash repeatedly against **4.** to form (a path) by treading **5.** to mix by stirring **6.** to move (wings) up and down **7.** to outdo or defeat **8.** to mark (time) by tapping **9.** [Colloq.] *a)* to puzzle *b)* to cheat —*vi.* **1.** to strike repeatedly **2.** to throb —*n.* **1.** a beating, as of the heart **2.** any of a series of strokes **3.** a throb **4.** a habitual route **5.** the unit of musical rhythm —*adj.* **1.** [Slang] tired; exhausted **2.** of a group, esp. in the 1950's, who rejected social conventions —**beat down** to suppress —**beat it** [Slang] go away! —**beat off** to drive back — **beat up** (on) to give a beating to —**beat'er** *n.*

beat'en (-'n) *adj.* **1.** struck with repeated blows **2.** shaped by hammering **3.** flattened by treading **4.** defeated

be·a·tif·ic (bē'ə tif'ik) *adj.* **1.** making blissful or blessed **2.** full of bliss or joy

be·at·i·fy (bē at'ə fī') *vt.* **-fied', -fy'ing** [< Fr. < L. *beatus,* happy + *facere,* make] **1.** to make blissfully happy **2.** *R.C.Ch.* to declare one who has died to be among the blessed in heaven — **be·at'i·fi·ca'tion** *n.*

beat'ing *n.* **1.** the act of one that beats **2.** a whipping **3.** a throbbing **4.** a defeat

be·at·i·tude (bē at'ə tōōd') *n.* [< Fr. < L. *beatus,* happy] perfect blessedness or happiness —**the Beatitudes** the pronouncements in the Sermon on the Mount, which begin "Blessed are the poor in spirit"

beat·nik (bēt'nik) *n.* a member of the beat group

beau (bō) *n., pl.* **beaus, beaux** (bōz) [Fr. < L. *bellus,* pretty] a woman's sweetheart

beau·te·ous (byōōt'ē əs) *adj.* beautiful

beau·ti·cian (byōō tish'ən) *n.* one who works in a beauty shop

beau·ti·ful (byōōt'ə fəl) *adj.* having beauty

beau·ti·fy (-fī') *vt., vi.* **-fied', -fy'ing** to make or become beautiful —**beau'ti·fi·ca'tion** *n.* —**beau'-ti·fi'er** *n.*

beau·ty (byōōt'ē) *n., pl.* **-ties** [< L. *bellus,* pretty] **1.** the quality of being very pleasing, as in form, color, tone, behavior, etc. **2.** a thing having this quality **3.** good looks **4.** a very good-looking woman

beauty shop (or **salon** or **parlor**) a place where women go for hair styling, manicuring, etc.

bea·ver (bē'vər) *n.* [OE. *beofor*] **1.** an amphibious animal with webbed hind feet and a flat, broad tail **2.** its soft, brown fur **3.** a man's high silk hat

be·calm (bi käm') *vt.* **1.** to make calm **2.** to make (a ship) motionless from lack of wind

be·came (bi kām') *pt. of* BECOME

be·cause (bi kôz', -kuz') *conj.* [< ME. *bi,* by + CAUSE] for the reason or cause that; since — **because of** on account of

beck (bek) *n.* a beckoning gesture of the hand, head, etc. —**at the beck and call of** obedient to the wishes of

beck·on (bek''n) *vi., vt.* [< OE. *beacen,* a sign] to summon by a gesture, nod, etc.

be·cloud (bi kloud') *vt.* to cloud over

be·come (bi kum') *vi.* **-came', -come', -com'-ing** [OE. *becuman*] to come or grow to be —*vt.* to suit; be right for *[that hat becomes her]* — **become of** to happen to

be·com'ing *adj.* **1.** appropriate; seemly **2.** suitable to the wearer

bed (bed) *n.* [OE.] **1.** a piece of furniture for sleeping on **2.** a plot of soil where plants are raised **3.** the bottom of a river, lake, etc. **4.** any flat surface used as a foundation **5.** a geological layer —vt. **bed'ded, bed'ding 1.** to put to bed **2.** to embed **3.** to plant in a bed of earth **4.** to arrange in layers —vi. **1.** to go to bed; sleep **2.** to stratify

be·daz·zle (bi daz''l) vt. **-zled, -zling** to bewilder; confuse

bed'bug' n. a small, wingless, reddish-brown bloodsucking insect that infests beds, etc.

bed'cham'ber n. same as BEDROOM

bed'clothes' (-klōz', -klō*thz*') n.pl. sheets, blankets, etc. used on a bed

bed'ding (-iŋ) n. **1.** mattresses and bedclothes **2.** a bottom layer; base

be·deck (bi dek') vt. to adorn

be·dev·il (bi dev''l) vt. **-iled** or **-illed, -il·ing** or **-il·ling 1.** to plague; torment **2.** to confuse; bewilder —**be·dev'il·ment** n.

bed'fast' (-fast') adj. same as BEDRIDDEN

bed'fel'low (-fel'ō) n. **1.** a person who shares one's bed **2.** any associate

be·dim (bi dim') vt. **-dimmed', -dim'ming** to make dim; darken or obscure

bed·lam (bed'ləm) n. [< (the old London mental hospital of St. Mary of) *Bethlehem*] any noisy, confused place or condition

Bed·ou·in (bed'ōō win) n., pl. **-ins, -in** [< Fr. < Ar. *badāwīn*, desert dwellers] **1.** an Arab of the desert tribes of Arabia, Syria, or North Africa **2.** any wanderer

bed'pan' n. a shallow pan used as a toilet by one who is bedridden

be·drag·gle (bi drag''l) vt. **-gled, -gling** to make wet, limp, and dirty, as by dragging through mire —**be·drag'gled** adj.

bed'rid'den (-rid''n) adj. confined to bed, usually for a long time, by illness, infirmity, etc.

bed'rock' n. **1.** solid rock beneath the soil and superficial rock **2.** a secure foundation **3.** basic principles

bed'roll' n. a portable roll of bedding, generally for sleeping outdoors

bed'room' n. a room to sleep in

bed'side' n. the space beside a bed —adj. beside a bed

bed'sore' n. a body sore on a bedridden person, caused by chafing or pressure

bed'spread' n. an ornamental cover spread over the blanket on a bed

bed'spring' n. a framework of springs in a bed to support the mattress

bed'stead' (-sted') n. a framework for supporting the springs and mattress of a bed

bed'time' n. the time to go to bed

bee[1] (bē) n. [OE. *beo*] a four-winged, hairy insect that gathers pollen and nectar —**have a bee in one's bonnet** to be obsessed by an idea

bee[2] (bē) n. [< OE. *ben*, service] a meeting of people to work together or to compete

beech (bēch) n. [OE. *boece*] **1.** a tree with smooth, gray bark, hard wood, and edible nuts **2.** its wood —adj. of this tree

beech'nut' n. the small, three-cornered nut of the beech

beef (bēf) n., pl. **beeves;** also, and for 5 always, **beefs** [< L. *bos*, ox] **1.** a full-grown ox, cow, bull, or steer, esp. one bred for meat **2.** meat from such an animal **3.** [Colloq.] brawn **4.** [Slang] a complaint —vi. [Slang] to complain — **beef up** [Colloq.] to strengthen

beef'steak' (-stāk') n. a thick cut of beef for broiling or frying

beef'y adj. **-i·er, -i·est** fleshy and solid; brawny —**beef'i·ness** n.

bee·hive (bē'hīv') n. **1.** a hive of bees **2.** a place of great activity

bee'line' n. a straight, direct route

been (bin, ben, bēn) pp. of BE

beep (bēp) n. [echoic] the brief, high-pitched sound of a horn or electronic signal —vi., vt. to make or cause to make such a sound

beer (bir) n. [OE. *beor*] **1.** an alcoholic, fermented drink made from malt, hops, etc. **2.** a soft drink made from extracts of roots, etc.

bees'wax' n. wax secreted and used by bees to build their honeycombs

beet (bēt) n. [< L. *beta*] **1.** a plant with a thick, white or red root **2.** this root, used as a vegetable or as a source of sugar

bee·tle[1] (bēt''l) n. [< OE. *bitan*, to bite] an insect with hard front wings that cover the membranous hind wings when these are folded

bee·tle[2] (bēt''l) vi. **-tled, -tling** [prob. < BEETLE-BROWED] to project or jut; overhang —adj. jutting; overhanging: also **bee'tling**

bee-tle-browed (bēt''l broud') adj. [ME. < ? *bitel*, sharp + *brouwe*, brow] **1.** having bushy or overhanging eyebrows **2.** frowning; scowling

be·fall (bi fôl') vi., vt. **-fell', -fall'en, -fall'ing** [< OE. *be-* + *feallan*, fall] to happen or occur (to)

be·fit (bi fit') vt. **-fit'ted, -fit'ting** to be suitable or proper for —**be·fit'ting** adj.

be·fog (bi fôg', -fäg') vt. **-fogged', -fog'ging 1.** to envelop in fog **2.** to confuse

be·fore (bi fôr') adv. [< OE. *be-*, by + *foran*, before] **1.** ahead; in front **2.** in the past **3.** earlier; sooner —prep. **1.** ahead of in time, space, or order **2.** in front of **3.** to the sight, presence, or notice of [to stand *before* a judge, a bill *before* Congress] **3.** earlier than **4.** in preference to [death *before* dishonor] —conj. **1.** earlier than the time that [call *before* you go] **2.** rather than [I'd die *before* I'd tell]

be·fore'hand' (-hand') adv., adj. **1.** ahead of time **2.** in anticipation

be·foul (bi foul') vt. to dirty or sully

be·friend (bi frend') vt. to act as a friend to

be·fud·dle (bi fud''l) vt. **-dled, -dling** to confuse or stupefy —**be·fud'dle·ment** n.

beg (beg) vt., vi. **begged, beg'ging** [< MDu. *beggaert*, beggar] **1.** to ask for (alms) [he *begged* a dime] **2.** to ask earnestly; entreat — **beg off** to ask to be released from —**go begging** to be unwanted

be·gan (bi gan') pt. of BEGIN

be·get (bi get') vt. **-got'** or archaic **-gat'** (-gat'), **-got'ten** or **-got', -get'ting** [< OE. *begitan*, acquire] **1.** to become the father of **2.** to cause; produce —**be·get'ter** n.

beg·gar (beg'ər) n. **1.** a person who begs **2.** a very poor person —vt. **1.** to make poor; impoverish **2.** to make seem useless [beauty which *beggars* description]

beg'gar·ly adj. very poor, inadequate, etc.

be·gin (bi gin') vi. **-gan', -gun', -gin'ning** [OE. *beginnan*] **1.** to start **2.** to come into being —vt. **1.** to cause to start **2.** to originate

be·gin'ner n. one who is just beginning to do or learn something; novice

be·gin'ning n. **1.** a starting **2.** the time or place of starting; origin **3.** the first part **4.** [usually pl.] an early stage

be·gone (bi gôn', -gän') interj., vi. (to) be gone; go away; get out

be·gon·ia (bi gōn'yə) n. [< M. *Bégon* (1638-1710), Fr. patron of science] a plant with showy flowers and ornamental leaves

be·got (bi gät') pt. & alt. pp. of BEGET

be·got'ten (-'n) pp. of BEGET

be·grime (bi grīm') vt. **-grimed', -grim'ing** to cover with grime; soil

be·grudge (bi gruj′) *vt.* -grudged′, -grudg′ing 1. to resent another's possession of 2. to give with reluctance [he *begrudges* her every cent] —**be·grudg′ing·ly** *adv.*

be·guile (bi gīl′) *vt.* -guiled′, -guil′ing 1. to mislead or to deprive (of) by guile; deceive 2. to pass (time) pleasantly 3. to charm or delight — **be·guile′ment** *n.*

be·gun (bi gun′) *pp. of* BEGIN

be·half (bi haf′) *n.* [< OE. *be*, by + *healf*, side] support, side, interest, etc. —**in** (or **on**) **behalf of** in the interest of; for

be·have (bi hāv′) *vt., vi.* -haved′, -hav′ing [see BE- & HAVE] 1. to conduct (oneself) in a specified way 2. to conduct (oneself) properly

be·hav·ior (bi hāv′yər) *n.* way of behaving; conduct: Brit. sp. **behaviour** —**be·hav′ior·al** *adj.* —**be·hav′ior·al·ly** *adv.*

behavioral science any of the sciences, as sociology or psychology, that study human behavior

be·hav′ior·ism the doctrine that observed behavior provides the only valid data of psychology —**be·hav′ior·ist** *n., adj.*

be·head (bi hed′) *vt.* to cut off the head of

be·held (bi held′) *pt. & pp. of* BEHOLD

be·he·moth (bi hē′məth, bē′ə-) *n.* [< Heb.] 1. *Bible* a huge animal, assumed to be the hippopotamus 2. any huge animal or thing

be·hest (bi hest′) *n.* [OE. *behæs*, a vow] an order or earnest request

be·hind (bi hīnd′) *adv.* [OE. *behindan*] 1. in or to the rear 2. in a former time, place, etc. 3. into arrears 4. slow; late —*prep.* 1. in back of [sit *behind* me] 2. inferior to 3. later than [*behind* schedule] 4. beyond [*behind* the hill] 5. supporting [he is *behind* the plan] 6. hidden by [what's *behind* his smile?] —*adj.* that follows [the person *behind*] —*n.* [Colloq.] the buttocks

be·hind′hand (-hand′) *adv., adj.* late or slow in payment, time, or progress

be·hold (bi hōld′) *vt.* -held′, -held′ or archaic -hold′en, -hold′ing [OE. *bihealdan*, to hold] to look at; regard —*interj.* look! see! —**be·hold′er** *n.*

be·hold′en (-ən) *adj.* under obligation; indebted

be·hoof (bi hoof′) *n.* [OE. *behof*, profit] behalf, benefit, interest, sake, etc.

be·hoove (bi hoov′) *vt.* -hooved′, -hoov′ing [OE. *behofian*, to need] to be necessary for or incumbent upon [it *behooves* you to go]

beige (bāzh) *n.* [Fr.] grayish tan —*adj.* grayish-tan

be·ing (bē′iŋ) *n.* [see BE] 1. existence; life 2. essential nature 3. one that lives or exists [a human *being*] —**being as** (or **that**) [Dial. or Colloq.] since; because —**for the time being** for now

be·la·bor (bi lā′bər) *vt.* 1. to beat severely 2. to attack verbally 3. *same as* LABOR, *vt.*

be·lat·ed (bi lāt′id) *adj.* too late; tardy

be·lay (bi lā′) *vt., vi.* -layed′, -lay′ing [< OE. *belecgan*, make fast] 1. to make (a rope) secure by winding around a pin [belaying pin], cleat, etc. 2. [Naut. Colloq.] to hold; stop

belch (belch) *vi., vt.* [OE. *bealcian*] 1. to expel (gas) through the mouth from the stomach 2. to throw forth violently [the volcano *belched* flames] —*n.* a belching

bel·dam, bel·dame (bel′dəm) *n.* [see BELLE & DAME] an old woman, esp. a very ugly one; hag

be·lea·guer (bi lē′gər) *vt.* [< Du. *leger*, a camp] 1. to besiege by encircling 2. to beset; harass —**be·lea′guered** *adj.*

bel·fry (bel′frē) *n., pl.* -fries [ult. < OHG. *bergen*, protect + *frid*, peace] 1. a bell tower 2. the part of a tower that holds the bell(s)

Belg. 1. Belgian 2. Belgium

Bel·gian (bel′jən) *adj.* of Belgium, its people, etc. —*n.* a native of Belgium

be·lie (bi lī′) *vt.* -lied′, -ly′ing 1. to disguise or misrepresent 2. to leave unfulfilled 3. to show to be untrue

be·lief (bə lēf′) *n.* [OE. *geleafa*] 1. conviction that certain things are true 2. religious faith 3. trust or confidence 4. a creed, tenet, etc. 5. an opinion; expectation

be·lieve (bə lēv′) *vt.* -lieved′, -liev′ing [OE. *geliefan*] 1. to take as true, real, etc. 2. to have confidence in a statement or promise of 3. to suppose or think —*vi.* 1. to have confidence (*in*) 2. to have religious faith —**be·liev′a·ble** *adj.* —**be·liev′er** *n.*

be·lit·tle (bi lit′'l) *vt.* -tled, -tling to make seem little, less important, etc.

bell (bel) *n.* [OE. *belle*] 1. a hollow, cuplike object, as of metal, which rings when struck 2. the sound of a bell 3. anything shaped like a bell 4. *Naut.* a bell rung to mark the periods of the watch —*vt.* to attach a bell to —*vi.* to flare out like a bell

bel·la·don·na (bel′ə dän′ə) *n.* [< It., beautiful lady: from cosmetic use] 1. a poisonous plant of the nightshade family: source of atropine 2. atropine

bell′-bot′tom *adj.* designating trousers flaring at the ankles

bell buoy a buoy with a warning bell rung by the motion of the waves

belle (bel) *n.* [Fr., fem. of BEAU] a pretty woman or girl

belles-let·tres (bel let′rə) *n.pl.* [Fr.] nontechnical literature, as fiction, poetry, drama, etc. — **bel·let·rist** (bel let′rist) *n.*

bel·li·cose (bel′ə kōs′) *adj.* [< L. *bellicus*, of war] quarrelsome; warlike —**bel·li·cose′ly** *adv.* —**bel·li·cos′i·ty** (-käs′ə tē) *n.*

bel·lig·er·ent (bə lij′ər ənt) *adj.* [< L. *bellum*, war + *gerere*, carry on] 1. at war 2. of war 3. warlike 4. ready to fight or quarrel —*n.* a belligerent person or nation —**bel·lig′er·ence, bel·lig′er·en·cy** *n.*

bell·man (-mən) *n., pl.* -men a man or boy employed by a hotel, etc. to carry luggage and do errands: also **bellboy, bellhop**

bel·low (bel′ō) *vi.* [OE. *bylgan*] 1. to roar with a reverberating sound, as a bull 2. to cry out loudly, as in anger —*vt.* to utter loudly or powerfully —*n.* a bellowing sound

bel·lows (bel′ōz) *n. sing. & pl.* [see BELLY] 1. a device that produces a stream of air, used for blowing fires, in pipe organs, etc. 2. anything collapsible like a bellows

bell·weth·er (bel′weth′ər) *n.* a male sheep that leads the flock: it usually wears a bell

bel·ly (bel′ē) *n., pl.* -lies [OE. *belg*, leather bag] 1. the part of the body between the chest and thighs; abdomen 2. the underside of an animal's body 3. the stomach 4. the deep interior [the *belly* of a ship] —*vt., vi.* -lied, -ly·ing to swell out

bel′ly·ache′ (-āk′) *n.* pain in the abdomen —*vi.* -ached′, -ach′ing [Slang] to complain or grumble —**bel′ly·ach′er** *n.*

bel′ly·but′ton (-but′'n) *n.* [Colloq.] the navel

belly dance a dance characterized by a sinuous twisting of the abdomen and hips

be·long (bi lôŋ′) *vi.* [< ME.] 1. to have a proper place [it *belongs* here] 2. to be related (*to*) 3. to be a member (with *to*) 4. to be owned (with *to*)

be·long'ings *n.pl.* possessions

be·lov·ed (bi luv'id, -luvd') *adj.* dearly loved — *n.* a dearly loved person

be·low (bi lō') *adv., adj.* [see BE- & LOW¹] **1.** in or to a lower place; beneath **2.** at a later place (in a book, etc.) **3.** in hell **4.** on earth —*prep.* **1.** lower than, as in rank or worth **2.** unworthy of

belt (belt) *n.* [< L. *balteus,* a belt] **1.** a band of leather, etc. worn around the waist **2.** any encircling thing like this **3.** an endless band, as for transferring motion from one wheel to another **4.** a distinctive area *[the corn belt]* — *vt.* **1.** to encircle or fasten as with a belt **2.** [Slang] to hit hard **3.** [Colloq.] to sing *(out)* lustily —**below the belt** unfair(ly)

belt'way' *n.* an expressway passing around an urban area

be·moan (bi mōn') *vt., vi.* to lament

be·muse (bi myōoz') *vt.* **-mused', -mus'ing** [BE- + MUSE] to muddle; preoccupy

bench (bench) *n.* [OE. *benc*] **1.** a long, hard seat **2.** the place where judges sit in a court **3.** *[sometimes* B-*] a)* the status of a judge *b)* judges collectively *c)* a law court **4.** *same as* WORKBENCH —*vt.* *Sports* to take (a player) out of a game —**on the bench 1.** presiding in a law court **2.** *Sports* not taking part in the game

bend (bend) *vt.* **bent, bend'ing** [OE. *bendan,* bind] **1.** to make curved or crooked **2.** to turn from a straight line **3.** to make submit —*vi.* **1.** to turn from a straight line **2.** to yield by curving, as from pressure **3.** to curve the body; stoop *(over* or *down)* **4.** to give in; yield *[he bent* to her wishes] —*n.* **1.** a bending or being bent **2.** a curving part —**bend'a·ble** *adj.*

bend'er *n.* **1.** one that bends **2.** [Slang] a drinking bout; spree

be·neath (bi nēth') *adv., adj.* [< OE. *be-* + *neothan,* down] in a lower place; below; underneath —*prep.* **1.** lower than; below **2.** underneath **3.** unworthy of *[it is beneath* him to cheat]

ben·e·dict (ben'ə dikt') *n.* [< *Benedick,* in Shakespeare's *Much Ado About Nothing*] a newly married man, esp. one who seemed a confirmed bachelor

ben·e·dic·tion (ben'ə dik'shən) *n.* [< L. *bene,* well + *dicere,* speak] **1.** a blessing **2.** an invocation of divine blessing, esp. at the end of a church service —**ben'e·dic'to·ry** *adj.*

ben·e·fac·tion (ben'ə fak'shən) *n.* [< L. *bene,* well + *facere,* do] **1.** the act of helping those in need **2.** money or help given

ben·e·fac·tor (ben'ə fak'tər) *n.* one who has given financial or other help; patron —**ben'e·fac'tress** (-tris) *n.fem.*

ben·e·fice (ben'ə fis) *n.* [see BENEFACTION] an endowed church office providing a living for a vicar, rector, etc. —*vt.* **-ficed, -fic·ing** to provide with a benefice

be·nef·i·cence (bə nef'ə s'ns) *n.* [see BENEFACTION] **1.** a being kind or doing good **2.** a charitable act or generous gift

be·nef'i·cent (-s'nt) *adj.* showing beneficence; doing or resulting in good

ben·e·fi·cial (ben'ə fish'əl) *adj.* producing benefits; advantageous; favorable —**ben'e·fi'cial·ly** *adv.*

ben·e·fi·ci·ar·y (ben'ə fish'ē er'ē, -fish'ər ē) *n., pl.* **-ies** **1.** anyone receiving benefit **2.** a person named to receive an inheritance, income from an insurance policy, etc.

ben·e·fit (ben'ə fit) *n.* [see BENEFACTION] **1.** anything helping to improve conditions; advantage **2.** *[often pl.]* payments made by an insurance company, public agency, etc. as during sickness or retirement **3.** a public perform-

ance, dance, etc. whose proceeds go to help some person or cause —*vt.* **-fit·ed, -fit·ing** to help; aid —*vi.* to receive advantage; profit

be·nev·o·lence (bə nev'ə ləns) *n.* [< L. *bene,* well + *velle,* to wish] **1.** an inclination to do good; kindness **2.** a kindly, charitable act —**be·nev'o·lent** *adj.*

be·night·ed (bi nīt'id) *adj.* **1.** surrounded by darkness **2.** unenlightened; ignorant

be·nign (bi nīn') *adj.* [< *bene,* well + *genus,* birth] **1.** good-natured; kindly **2.** favorable; beneficial **3.** *Med.* not malignant —**be·nign'ly** *adv.*

be·nig·nant (bi nig'nənt) *adj.* [< prec.] **1.** kindly or gracious **2.** beneficial —**be·nig'nant·ly** *adv.*

be·nig·ni·ty (-nə tē) *n., pl.* **-ties** **1.** kindliness **2.** a kind act

ben·i·son (ben'ə z'n, -s'n) *n.* [< L.: see BENEDICTION] a blessing

ben·ny (ben'ē) *n., pl.* **-nies** [Slang] an amphetamine pill, esp. Benzedrine

bent¹ (bent) *pt. and pp. of* BEND —*adj.* **1.** curved or crooked **2.** strongly determined (with *on*) —*n.* **1.** a tendency **2.** a mental leaning; propensity *[a bent* for art]

bent² (bent) *n.* [OE. *beonot*] any of various low-growing grasses: also called **bent'grass**

be·numb (bi num') *vt.* **1.** to make numb **2.** to deaden the mind or feelings of

Ben·ze·drine (ben'zə drēn') *a trademark for* AMPHETAMINE —*n.* **[b-]** this drug

ben·zene (ben'zēn) *n.* [< BENZOIN] a flammable liquid obtained from coal tar and used as a solvent, in dyes, etc.

ben·zine (ben'zēn) *n.* [< BENZOIN] a flammable liquid obtained from petroleum and used as a motor fuel, in dry cleaning, etc.

ben·zo·ate (ben'zō āt') *n.* a salt or ester of benzoic acid

ben·zo·caine (ben'zə kān') *n.* [BENZO(IN) + (CO)CAINE] a white powder used in ointments as an anesthetic and to protect against sunburn

ben·zo·ic acid (ben zō'ik) [< BENZOIN] a white, crystalline acid used as an antiseptic, preservative, etc.

ben·zo·in (ben'zō in, -zoin) *n.* [< Fr. < It. < Ar. *lubān jāwi,* incense of Java] a resin from certain tropical Asiatic trees, used in medicine, perfumes, etc.

ben·zol (ben'zōl, -zôl) *n. same as* BENZENE

Be·o·wulf (bā'ə woolf') the hero of the Old English folk epic of that name (c.700 A.D.)

be·queath (bi kwēth', -kwēth') *vt.* [< OE. *be-* + *cwethan,* to say] **1.** to leave (property) to another by one's will **2.** to hand down; pass on —**be·queath'al** *n.*

be·quest (bi kwest') *n.* **1.** a bequeathing **2.** anything bequeathed

be·rate (bi rāt') *vt.* **-rat'ed, -rat'ing** [BE- + RATE²] to scold or rebuke severely

be·reave (bi rēv') *vt.* **-reaved'** or **-reft'** (-reft'), **-reav'ing** [< OE. *be-* + *reafian,* rob] **1.** to deprive: now usually in the pp. **(bereft)** *[bereft* of hope] **2.** to leave in a sad or lonely state, as by death —**be·reave'ment** *n.*

be·ret (bə rā') *n.* [< Fr. < L. *birrus,* a hood] a flat, round cap of felt, wool, etc.

ber·i·ber·i (ber'ē ber'ē) *n.* [Singh. *beri,* weakness] a disease caused by lack of thiamine (vitamin B₁) and characterized by nerve disorders, edema, etc.

berm, berme (bʉrm) *n.* [Fr. < MDu. *baerm*] a ledge or shoulder, as along the edge of a paved road

Ber·mu·da onion (bər myōō'də) a large onion

with a mild flavor, grown in Texas, California, etc.

Bermuda shorts knee-length trousers

ber·ry (ber'ē) *n., pl.* **-ries** [OE. *berie*] **1.** any small, fleshy fruit, as a raspberry **2.** the dry seed of various plants, as a coffee bean —*vi.* **-ried, -ry·ing 1.** to bear berries **2.** to pick berries

ber·serk (bər surk', -zurk') *adj., adv.* [ON. *berserkr,* warrior] in or into a violent rage or frenzy

berth (burth) *n.* [< base of BEAR¹] **1.** a place where a ship anchors **2.** a position, job, etc. **3.** a built-in bed on a ship, train, etc. —*vt.* to put into or furnish with a berth —*vi.* to occupy a berth —**give a wide berth to** to keep well clear of

ber·yl (ber'əl) *n.* [< Gr. *bēryllos*] a very hard mineral, as emerald and aquamarine

be·ryl·li·um (bə ril'ē əm) *n.* [< prec.] a hard, rare metallic chemical element: symbol, Be

be·seech (bi sēch') *vt.* **-sought'** or **-seeched', -seech'ing** [< OE. *be-,* + *secan,* seek] to ask (for) earnestly; entreat; beg

be·seem (bi sēm') *vi.* to be suitable (to)

be·set (bi set') *vt.* **-set', -set'ting** [< OE. *be-* + *settan,* to set] **1.** to set thickly with **2.** to harass **3.** to surround

be·set'ting *adj.* constantly harassing

be·side (bi sīd') *prep.* [OE. *bi sidan*] **1.** at the side of; near **2.** in comparison with *[beside his, her share seems tiny]* **3.** in addition to **4.** aside from —**beside oneself** wild or upset with fear, rage, etc.

be·sides (bi sīdz') *adv.* **1.** in addition **2.** except for that mentioned **3.** moreover —*prep.* **1.** in addition to **2.** other than; except

be·siege (bi sēj') *vt.* **-sieged', -sieg'ing 1.** to hem in with armed forces **2.** to close in on **3.** to overwhelm, as with requests

be·smear (bi smir') *vt.* to smear over; soil

be·smirch (bi smurch') *vt.* [BE- + SMIRCH] **1.** to soil **2.** to bring dishonor to; sully

be·sot (bi sät') *vt.* **-sot'ted, -sot'ting** to make a sot of; stupefy, as with liquor

be·sought (bi sôt') *pt. and pp. of* BESEECH

be·span·gle (bi span'g'l) *vt.* **-gled, -gling** to cover with or as with spangles

be·spat·ter (bi spat'ər) *vt.* to spatter, as with mud or slander

be·speak (bi spēk') *vt.* **-spoke', -spok'en** or **-spoke', -speak'ing 1.** to speak for in advance; reserve **2.** to be indicative of; show

Bes·se·mer process (bes'ə mər) [< H. *Bessemer,* 19th-c. Eng. inventor] a method of making steel by blasting air through molten iron in a large container

best (best) *adj. superl. of* GOOD [OE. *betst*] **1.** most excellent **2.** most suitable, desirable, etc. **3.** largest *[the best part of an hour]* —*adv. superl. of* WELL² **1.** in the most excellent manner **2.** in the highest degree —*n.* **1.** the most excellent person, thing, condition, etc. **2.** the utmost **3.** one's finest clothes —*vt.* to defeat or outdo —**all for the best** ultimately good —**at best** under the most favorable conditions —**get (or have) the best of 1.** to defeat **2.** to outwit —**had best** ought to —**make the best of** to do as well as one can with

bes·tial (bes'chəl, -tyəl) *adj.* [< L. *bestia,* beast] like a beast; savage, brutal, etc. —**bes'ti·al'i·ty** (-chē al'ə tē) *n., pl.* **-ties** —**bes'tial·ly** *adv.*

be·stir (bi stur') *vt.* **-stirred', -stir'ring** to stir to action; busy (oneself)

best man the principal attendant of the bridegroom at a wedding

be·stow (bi stō') *vt.* [see BE- & STOW] **1.** to present as a gift (often with *on* or *upon*) **2.** to apply; devote —**be·stow'al** *n.*

be·strew (bi strōō') *vt.* **-strewed', -strewed'** or **-strewn', -strew'ing 1.** to strew **2.** to scatter or lie scattered about

be·stride (bi strīd') *vt.* **-strode'** (-strōd'), **-strid'den** (-strid'n), **-strid'ing** to sit on, mount, or stand astride

best seller a book, phonograph record, etc. currently outselling most others

bet (bet) *n.* [prob. < ABET] **1.** an agreement that the person proved wrong will do or pay what is stipulated **2.** the thing or sum thus staked **3.** a person or thing likely to bring about a desired result —*vt., vi.* **bet** or **bet'ted, bet'ting 1.** to declare as in a bet **2.** to stake (money, etc.) in a bet

be·ta (bāt'ə) *n.* the second letter of the Greek alphabet (B, β)

be·take (bi tāk') *vt.* **-took', -tak'en, -tak'ing** to go (used reflexively)

beta particle an electron or positron ejected from the nucleus of an atom during radioactive disintegration

beta ray a stream of beta particles

be·tel (bēt'l) *n.* [Port. < Malay *vettilai*] a tropical Asian climbing plant: its leaf, along with lime and the fruit (**betel nut**) of a palm (**betel palm**), is chewed by some Asians

be·think (bi think') *vt.* **-thought', -think'ing** to remind (oneself)

be·tide (bi tīd') *vi., vt.* **-tid'ed, -tid'ing** [< BE- + OE. *tid,* time] to happen (to)

be·times (bi tīmz') *adv.* [ME. < *bi-,* by + TIME] **1.** early **2.** [Archaic] promptly

be·to·ken (bi tō'k'n) *vt.* **1.** to be a token or sign of **2.** to show beforehand

be·tray (bi trā') *vt.* [ult. < L. *tradere,* hand over] **1.** to help the enemy of (one's country, etc.) **2.** to fail to uphold *[to betray a trust]* **3.** to seduce and then desert **4.** to reveal unknowingly **5.** to reveal —**be·tray'al** *n.* —**be·tray'er** *n.*

be·troth (bi trōth', -trôth') *vt.* [< ME. < *be-* + OE. *treowth,* truth] to promise in marriage —**be·troth'al** *n.*

be·trothed' (-trōthd', -trôtht') *adj.* engaged to be married —*n.* the person to whom one is betrothed

bet·ter (bet'ər) *adj. compar. of* GOOD [< OE. *betera*] **1.** more excellent **2.** more suitable, desirable, etc. **3.** larger *[the better part of a day]* **4.** improved in health —*adv. compar. of* WELL² **1.** in a more excellent manner **2.** in a higher degree **3.** more —*n.* **1.** a person superior in position, etc. **2.** a more excellent thing, condition, etc. —*vt.* **1.** to outdo; surpass **2.** to improve —**better off** in a better condition —**get (or have) the better of 1.** to outdo **2.** to outwit

better half [Slang] one's wife or husband

bet·ter·ment (bet'ər mənt) *n.* a bettering; improvement

bet·tor, bet·ter (bet'ər) *n.* one who bets

be·tween (bi twēn') *prep.* [< OE. *be,* by + *tweon(um),* by twos] **1.** in the space, time, etc. separating (two things) **2.** that connects *[a bond between friends]* **3.** in the combined possession or action of **4.** from one or the other of *[choose between us]* —*adv.* in an intermediate space, time, etc.

be·twixt (bi twikst') *prep., adv.* [< OE. *betwix*] between: archaic except in **betwixt and between,** not altogether one nor altogether the other

bev·el (bev'l) *n.* [< ?] **1.** a tool for measuring or marking angles, etc. **2.** an angle other than a right angle **3.** a sloping edge between parallel surfaces —*adj.* sloped; beveled —*vt.* **-eled** or

-elled, -el·ing or -el·ling to cut to an angle other than a right angle —*vl.* to slope at an angle

bev·er·age (bev'rij, -ər ij) *n.* [< L. *bibere,* imbibe] any drink, esp. other than plain water

bev·y (bev'ē) *n., pl.* -ies [see BEVERAGE] 1. a group, esp. of girls or women 2. a flock: now chiefly of quail

be·wail (bi wāl') *vt.* to wail over or complain about; lament; mourn —**be·wail'er** *n.*

be·ware (bi wer') *vi., vt.* -wared', -war'ing [prob. < OE. < *be-* + *warian,* be wary] to be wary or careful (of)

be·wil·der (bi wil'dər) *vt.* [BE- + archaic *wilder,* to lose one's way] to confuse hopelessly; befuddle —**be·wil'der·ment** *n.*

be·witch (bi wich') *vt.* [< OE. *wicce,* witch] 1. to cast a spell over 2. to enchant; fascinate; charm —**be·witch'ing** *adj.*

be·yond (bi yänd') *prep.* [< OE. *be-* + *geond,* yonder] 1. farther on than 2. later than 3. outside the reach of [*beyond* help] 4. more or better than —*adv.* 1. farther away 2. in addition — **the (great) beyond** whatever follows death

bez·el (bez''l) *n.* [< OFr. *biais,* bias] 1. a sloping cutting edge, as of a chisel 2. the slanting face of a cut jewel 3. the groove and flange holding a gem or a watch crystal in place

bi- [L.] *a prefix meaning:* 1. having two 2. doubly 3. happening every two 4. happening twice during every 5. using two or both 6. joining or involving two

Bi *Chem.* bismuth

bi·an·nu·al (bī an'yoo wəl, -yool) *adj.* coming twice a year; semiannual

bi·as (bī'əs) *n., pl.* **bi'as·es** [Fr. *biais,* a slant] 1. a slanting or diagonal line, cut or sewn in cloth 2. partiality; prejudice —*adj.* slanting; diagonal —*adv.* diagonally —*vt.* -ased or -assed, -as·ing or -as·sing to prejudice —**on the bias** diagonally

bib (bib) *n.* [< L. *bibere,* to drink] 1. an apronlike cloth tied under a child's chin at meals 2. the upper part of an apron or overalls

Bib. 1. Bible 2. Biblical

Bi·ble (bī'b'l) *n.* [< Gr. *biblos,* papyrus] 1. the sacred book of Christianity; Old Testament and New Testament 2. the Holy Scriptures of Judaism; Old Testament 3. [**b-**] any book regarded as authoritative —**Bib·li·cal, bib·li·cal** (bib'li k'l) *adj.*

biblio- [< Gr. *biblion,* book] *a combining form meaning* book, of books

bib·li·og·ra·phy (bib'lē äg'rə fē) *n., pl.* -phies a list of writings on a given subject, by a given author, etc. —**bib'li·og'ra·pher** *n.* —**bib'li·o·graph'i·cal** (-ə graf'i k'l) *adj.*

bib·u·lous (bib'yoo ləs) *adj.* [< L. *bibere,* to drink] fond of alcoholic liquor

bi·cam·er·al (bī kam'ər əl) *adj.* [< BI- + L. *camera,* chamber] having two legislative chambers

bi·car·bon·ate (bī kär'bə nit, -nāt') *n.* an acid salt of carbonic acid

bicarbonate of soda *same as* SODIUM BICARBONATE

bi·cen·ten·ni·al (bī'sen ten'ē əl) *adj.* happening once every 200 years —*n.* a 200th anniversary or its celebration

bi·ceps (bī'seps) *n., pl.* -ceps or -ceps·es [L. < *bis,* two + *caput,* head] a muscle with two points of origin; esp., the large muscle in the front of the upper arm

bick·er (bik'ər) *vi., n.* [ME. *bikeren*] squabble; quarrel —**bick·er·er** *n.*

bi·cus·pid (bī kus'pid) *adj.* [< BI- + L. *cuspis,*

pointed end] having two points —*n.* any of eight adult teeth with two-pointed crowns

bi·cy·cle (bī'si k'l) *n.* [Fr.: see BI- & CYCLE] a vehicle consisting of a metal frame on two large wheels, one behind the other, and having handlebars and a saddlelike seat —*vi., vt.* -cled, -cling to ride on a bicycle —**bi'cy·clist, bi'cy·cler** *n.*

bid (bid) *vt.* **bade** (bad) or **bid, bid'den** or **bid, bid'ding** [< OE. *biddan,* to urge & *beodan,* to command] 1. to command or ask 2. *pt. & pp.* **bid** *a)* to offer (an amount) as the price for *b)* *Card Games* to state (a number of tricks) and declare (trump) 3. to express [to *bid* farewell] —*vi. pt. & pp.* **bid** to make a bid —*n.* 1. a bidding of an amount 2. the amount bid 3. a chance to bid 4. an attempt or try (*for*) 5. [Colloq.] an invitation —**bid fair** to seem likely —**bid'der** *n.*

bid'ding *n.* 1. a command or request 2. an invitation or summons

bid·dy (bid'ē) *n., pl.* -dies 1. a hen 2. [Slang] an elderly, gossipy woman

bide (bīd) *vi.* **bode** or **bid'ed, bid'ed, bid'ing** [OE. *bidan*] [Archaic or Dial.] 1. to stay; continue 2. to dwell 3. to wait —*vt.* [Archaic or Dial.] to endure —**bide one's time** *pt.* **bid'ed** to wait patiently for an opportunity

bi·det (bi dā') *n.* [Fr.] a low, bowl-shaped bathroom fixture for bathing the crotch

bi·en·ni·al (bī en'ē əl) *adj.* [< L. *bis,* twice + *annus,* year + -AL] 1. happening every two years 2. lasting for two years —*n.* 1. a biennial event 2. *Bot.* a plant that lasts two years —**bi·en'ni·al·ly** *adv.*

bier (bir) *n.* [OE. *bær,* a bed] a portable framework on which a coffin is placed

bi·fo·cal (bī fō'k'l, bī'fō'k'l) *adj.* adjusted to two different focal lengths —*n.* a lens with one part ground for close focus, and the rest ground for distant focus

bi'fo'cals *n.pl.* a pair of glasses with bifocal lenses

bi·fur·cate (bī'fər kāt') *vt., vi.* -cat'ed, -cat'ing [< L. *bi-* + *furca,* fork] to divide into two branches —*adj.* having two branches; forked — **bi'fur·ca'tion** *n.*

big (big) *adj.* **big'ger, big'gest** [akin to L. *bucca,* puffed cheek] 1. of great size, force, etc. 2. *a)* full-grown *b)* elder 3. loud 4. important 5. boastful; extravagant 6. noble [a *big* heart] — *adv.* [Colloq.] 1. boastfully [to talk *big*] 2. impressively —**big'ness** *n.*

big·a·my (big'ə mē) *n., pl.* -mies [< LL. *bis,* twice + Gr. *gamos,* marriage] the crime of marrying a second time while a previous marriage is still legally in effect —**big'a·mist** *n.* — **big'a·mous** *adj.*

big'heart'ed *adj.* generous or magnanimous

big'horn' *n.* an animal with large horns, esp. a large wild sheep of the Rocky Mountains

bight (bīt) *n.* [ME. *byht*] 1. a slack part in a rope 2. *a)* a curve in a coastline, etc. *b)* a bay formed by such a curve

big mouth [Slang] one who talks too much

big·ot (big'ət) *n.* [Fr. < OFr., a term of insult used of Normans] a narrow-minded person who is intolerant of other creeds, opinions, etc. —**big'ot·ry** (-ə trē) *n., pl.* -ries

big shot [Slang] an important, influential person: also **big noise, big wheel,** etc.

bike (bīk) *n., vt., vi.* **biked, bik'ing** [Colloq.] 1. bicycle 2. motorcycle

bi·ki·ni (bi kē'nē) *n.* [< *Bikini,* Pacific atoll] an extremely brief two-piece bathing suit for women

bi·lat·er·al (bī lat'ər əl) *adj.* 1. of, on, or having two sides, factions, etc. **2.** affecting both sides equally; reciprocal

bile (bīl) *n.* [Fr. < L. *bilis*] **1.** the bitter, greenish fluid secreted by the liver: it helps in digestion **2.** bitterness of spirit; anger

bilge (bilj) *n.* [var. of BULGE] **1.** the rounded, lower part of a ship's hold **2.** stagnant water that gathers there **3.** nonsense

bi·lin·gual (bī lin'gwəl) *adj.* [< L. *bis*, two + *lingua*, tongue] of, in, or speaking two languages —**bi·lin'gual·ly** *adv.*

bil·ious (bil'yəs) *adj.* **1.** of the bile **2.** having or resulting from some ailment of the liver **3.** bad-tempered; cross

bilk (bilk) *vt.* [? < BALK] to cheat or swindle; defraud —*n.* a bilking or being bilked

bill[1] (bil) *n.* [< ML. *bulla*, sealed document] **1.** a statement of charges for goods or services **2.** a list, as a menu or theater program **3.** a poster or handbill **4.** a draft of a proposed law **5.** a bill of exchange **6.** a piece of paper money **7.** *Law* a written declaration of charges and complaints filed —*vt.* **1.** to make out a bill of (items) **2.** to present a statement of charges to **3.** *a*) to advertise by bills *b*) to book (a performer) —**fill the bill** [Colloq.] to meet the requirements —**bill'a·ble** *adj.*

bill[2] (bil) *n.* [OE. *bile*] **1.** a bird's beak **2.** a beaklike mouthpart, as of a turtle —*vi.* to touch bills together —**bill and coo** to kiss, talk softly, etc. in a loving way

bill'board' *n.* a large signboard, usually outdoors, for advertising posters

bil·let (bil'it) *n.* [see BILL[1]] **1.** *a*) a written order to provide lodging for military personnel *b*) the lodging **2.** a position or job —*vt.* to assign to lodging by billet

bill·fold (bil'fōld') *n. same as* WALLET

bil·liards (bil'yərdz) *n.* [Fr. *billard*; orig., a cue] a game played with hard balls driven by a cue on an oblong table with raised, cushioned edges

bill·ing (bil'iŋ) *n.* the listing or order of listing of actors' names on a playbill, etc.

bil·lion (bil'yən) *n.* [Fr. < *bi-*, BI- + MILLION] **1.** a thousand millions **2.** formerly, in Great Britain, a million millions **3.** an indefinite but very large number —**bil'llonth** *adj., n.*

bill of exchange a written order to pay a certain sum of money to the person named

bill of fare a menu

bill of lading a receipt issued to a shipper by a carrier, listing the goods received for shipment

Bill of Rights the first ten amendments to the Constitution of the U.S., which guarantee civil liberties

bill of sale a written statement transferring ownership by sale

bil·low (bil'ō) *n.* [ON. *bylgja*] **1.** a large wave **2.** any large, swelling mass or surge, as of smoke —*vi., vt.* to surge or swell like a billow —**bil'low·y** *adj.*

bil·ly (bil'ē) *n., pl.* **-lies** [ult. < OFr. *bille*, tree trunk] a club, esp. one carried by a policeman

billy goat a male goat

bi·month·ly (bī munth'lē) *adj., adv.* **1.** once every two months **2.** loosely, twice a month —*n., pl.* **-lies** a publication appearing once every two months

bin (bin) *n.* [OE., manger] a box or enclosed space for storing foods, fuel, etc.

bi·na·ry (bī'nər ē) *adj.* [< L. *bis*, double] **1.** made up of two parts or things; twofold **2.** designating or of a number system that has 2 as its base —*n., pl.* **-ries** something made up of two parts or things

bin·au·ral (bī nôr'əl) *adj.* [see BI- & AURAL] **1.** involving the use of both ears **2.** of stereophonic sound recording

bind (bīnd) *vt.* **bound, bind'ing** [< OE. *bindan*] **1.** to tie together, as with rope **2.** to hold or restrain **3.** to encircle with a belt, etc. **4.** to bandage (often with *up*) **5.** to make stick together **6.** to constipate **7.** to reinforce with a band, as of tape **8.** to fasten together sheets of (a book) and enclose within a cover **9.** to obligate, as by duty **10.** to compel, as by legal restraint —*vi.* to be obligatory —*n.* [Colloq.] a difficult situation

bind'er *n.* **1.** one who binds **2.** a substance that binds, as tar **3.** a cover for holding sheets of paper together

bind·er·y (bīn'dər ē, -drē) *n., pl.* **-ies** a place where books are bound

bind'ing *n.* anything that binds, as *a*) a band, tape, etc. *b*) the covers and backing of a book —*adj.* that binds; esp., that holds one to an agreement, promise, etc.

binge (binj) *n.* [< ?] [Colloq.] a spree

bin·go (biŋ'gō) *n.* [< ?] a gambling game, like lotto, usually with many players

bin·oc·u·lar (bī näk'yə lər, bi-) *adj.* [< L. *bini*, double + *oculus*, an eye] using, or for, both eyes —*n.* [*usually pl.*] a binocular instrument, as field glasses

bi·no·mi·al (bī nō'mē əl) *n.* [< *bi-* + Gr. *nomos*, law] *Math.* an expression formed of two terms connected by a plus or minus sign

bio- [Gr. < *bios*, life] *a combining form meaning* life, of living things, biological [*biography*]

bi·o·chem·is·try (bī'ō kem'is trē) *n.* the branch of chemistry that deals with the life processes of plants and animals —**bi'o·chem'i·cal** *adj.* —**bi'o·chem'ist** *n.*

bi·o·de·grad·a·ble (-di grā'də b'l) *adj.* [BIO- + DEGRAD(E) + -ABLE] readily decomposed by bacterial action, as some detergents

bi·o·feed·back (-fēd'bak') *n.* a technique of seeking to control one's emotions by using electronic devices to train oneself to modify involuntary body functions, such as heartbeat

bi·og·ra·phy (bī äg'rə fē, bē-) *n., pl.* **-phies** [< Gr.: see BIO- & -GRAPHY] an account of a person's life written by another —**bi·og'ra·pher** *n.* —**bi·o·graph·i·cal** (bī'ə graf'i k'l), **bi'o·graph'ic** *adj.*

biol. **1.** biological **2.** biology

biological warfare the use of disease-spreading microorganisms, etc. in war

bi·ol·o·gy (bī äl'ə jē) *n.* [BIO- + -LOGY] the science dealing with the origin, history, life, structure, etc. of plants and animals —**bi·o·log·i·cal** (bī'ə läj'i k'l) *adj.* —**bi·ol'o·gist** *n.*

bi·on·ic (bī än'ik) *adj.* **1.** of bionics **2.** having artificial body parts, as in science fiction, so as to make a person very strong, skillful, etc. **3.** very strong, skillful, etc.

bi·on·ics (bī än'iks) *n.pl.* [*with sing. v.*] [< Gr. *bion*, living + -ICS] the science of designing instruments or systems modeled after living organisms

bi·o·phys·ics (bī'ō fiz'iks) *n.pl.* [*with sing. v.*] the study of biological phenomena in relation to physics —**bi'o·phys'i·cal** *adj.*

bi·op·sy (bī'äp'sē) *n., pl.* **-sies** [< BIO- + Gr. *opsis*, a sight] *Med.* the removal of living body tissue, etc. for diagnosis

bi·par·ti·san (bī pär'tə z'n) *adj.* of or representing two parties —**bi·par'ti·san·ship'** *n.*

bi·par·tite (bī pär'tīt) *adj.* [< L. *bi-*, two + *partire*, to divide] **1.** having two parts **2.** involving two

bi·ped (bī′ped) *n.* [< L. *bi-*, two + *pes*, foot] any two-footed animal

bi·plane (bī′plān′) *n.* an airplane with two sets of wings, one above the other

bi·ra·cial (bī rā′shəl) *adj.* consisting of or involving two races

birch (burch) *n.* [OE. *beorc*] 1. a tree having smooth bark in thin layers, and hard, close-grained wood 2. this wood 3. a bunch of birch twigs used for whipping —*vt.* to beat with a birch

bird (burd) *n.* [OE. *bridd*, young bird] 1. any of a group of warmblooded vertebrates with feathers and wings 2. [Slang] a person, esp. an eccentric one —**bird in the hand** something sure because already in one's possession —**birds of a feather** people with like characteristics or tastes —**for the birds** [Slang] ridiculous, etc.

bird·ie (bur′dē) *n. Golf* a score of one stroke under par for a hole

bird′lime′ (-līm′) *n.* a sticky substance spread on twigs to catch birds

bird's′-eye′ *adj.* 1. *a*) seen from above *b*) general 2. having markings like birds' eyes

birth (burth) *n.* [< OE. *beran*, to bear] 1. the act of bringing forth offspring 2. a being born 3. origin or descent 4. the beginning of anything 5. natural inclination [an actor by *birth*] —**give birth to** 1. to bring forth (offspring) 2. to originate

birth′day′ *n.* the anniversary of the day of a person's birth or a thing's beginning

birth′mark′ *n.* a skin blemish present at birth

birth′place′ *n.* the place of one's birth

birth′rate′ *n.* the number of births per year per 1000 of population in a given group

birth′right′ *n.* any rights that a person has by birth

bis·cuit (bis′kit) *n.*, *pl.* **-cuits, -cuit** [< L. *bis*, twice + *coquere*, to cook] 1. [Chiefly Brit.] a cracker or cookie 2. a quick bread baked in small pieces

bi·sect (bī′sekt) *vt.* [< BI- + L. *secare*, to cut] 1. to cut in two 2. *Geom.* to divide into two equal parts —*vi.* to divide; fork

bi·sex·ual (bī sek′shoo wəl) *adj.* of, or sexually attracted by, both sexes —*n.* one that is bisexual

bish·op (bish′əp) *n.* [< Gr. *epi-*, upon + *skopein*, to look] 1. a high-ranking clergyman, head of a diocese or church district 2. a chessman that can move only diagonally

bish·op·ric (bish′ə prik) *n.* the district, office, rank, etc. of a bishop

bis·muth (biz′məth) *n.* [< G.] a hard, brittle metallic chemical element used in low-melting alloys: symbol, Bi

bi·son (bīs′'n) *n.*, *pl.* **-sons** [Fr. < Gmc.] a four-legged bovine mammal with a shaggy mane and a humped back, as the American buffalo

bis·tro (bis′trō) *n.* [Fr.] a small café

bit¹ (bit) *n.* [< OE. *bite*, a bite] 1. the metal mouthpiece on a bridle, used for control 2. any curb or control 3. a drilling or boring tool for use in a brace, etc.

bit² (bit) *n.* [< OE. *bita*, a piece] 1. *a*) a small piece or quantity *b*) a limited degree [a *bit* of a bore] *c*) a short time 2. [Colloq.] 12 1/2 cents [two *bits*] —*adj.* very small [a *bit* role] —**bit by bit** gradually —**do one's bit** to do one's share

bitch (bich) *n.* [< OE. *bicce*] 1. the female of the dog, fox, etc. 2. a bad-tempered, malicious, etc. woman: a coarse term of contempt —*vi.* [Slang] to complain

bite (bīt) *vt.* **bit** (bit), **bit·ten** (bit′'n) or **bit, bit′·ing** [< OE. *bitan*] 1. to seize or cut with or as with the teeth 2. to cut into, as with a sharp weapon 3. to sting, as an insect 4. to hurt in a sharp, stinging way 5. to eat into; corrode —*vi.* 1. to press or snap the teeth (*into, at,* etc.) 2. to cause a biting sensation 3. to grip 4. to seize a bait 5. to be caught, as by a trick —*n.* 1. a biting 2. biting quality; sting 3. a wound or sting from biting 4. *a*) a mouthful *b*) a light meal 5. [Colloq.] an amount removed —**put the bite on** [Slang] to press for a loan, bribe, etc. —**bit′er** *n.*

bit·ing (bīt′iŋ) *adj.* 1. sharp 2. sarcastic

bit·ter (bit′ər) *adj.* [< OE. < base of *bitan*, to bite] 1. having a sharp, often unpleasant taste 2. causing or showing sorrow, pain, etc. 3. sharp; harsh 4. characterized by hatred, etc. —**bit′ter·ly** *adv.* —**bit′ter·ness** *n.*

bit·tern (bit′ərn) *n.* [prob. < L. *butio*] a wading bird of the heron family

bit′ters *n.pl.* a liquor containing bitter herbs, etc., used in some cocktails

bit′ter·sweet′ *n.* a N. American woody vine with orange fruits and red seeds —*adj.* 1. both bitter and sweet 2. pleasant and sad

bi·tu·men (bi too′mən) *n.* [L. < Celt.] any of several substances obtained as residue in the distillation of coal tar, petroleum, etc., or occurring as natural asphalt —**bi·tu′mi·nous** *adj.*

bituminous coal coal that yields pitch or tar when it burns; soft coal

bi·valve (bī′valv′) *n.* any mollusk having a shell of two parts, or valves, hinged together, as a clam —*adj.* having such a shell: also **bi′-valved′**

biv·ou·ac (biv′wak, -oo wak′) *n.* [Fr. < OHG. *bi-*, by + *wacht*, a guard] a temporary encampment (esp. of soldiers) in the open —*vi.* **-acked, -ack·ing** to encamp in the open

bi·week·ly (bī wēk′lē) *adj., adv.* 1. once every two weeks 2. semiweekly —*n.*, *pl.* **-lies** a biweekly publication

bi·zarre (bi zär′) *adj.* [Fr. < Basque *bizar*, beard] odd; grotesque; eccentric

bk. *pl.* **bks.** 1. bank 2. book

bl. 1. bale(s) 2. barrel(s)

B/L *pl.* **Bs/L** bill of lading

blab (blab) *vt., vi.* **blabbed, blab′bing** [echoic] 1. to give away (a secret) 2. to chatter —*n.* 1. gossip 2. one who blabs

black (blak) *adj.* [OE. *blæc*] 1. opposite to white; of the color of coal 2. having dark-colored skin and hair; esp., Negro 3. without light; dark 4. soiled; dirty 5. evil; wicked 6. sad; dismal 7. sullen —*n.* 1. black pigment, color, etc. 2. black clothes, esp. for mourning 3. [*also* B-] a Negro: *black* is now generally preferred —*vt., vi.* to blacken —**black out** to lose consciousness —**in the black** operating at a profit —**black′ness** *n.*

black′-and-blue′ *adj.* discolored, as by a bruise

black′ball′ *n.* a secret vote against —*vt.* 1. to vote against 2. to ostracize

black′ber′ry *n.*, *pl.* **-ries** 1. the dark, edible fruit of various brambles of the rose family 2. a bush or vine bearing this fruit

black′bird′ *n.* any of various birds the male of which is almost all black

black′board′ *n.* a smooth surface as of slate, on which to write with chalk

black′en ('n) *vi.* to become black or dark —*vt.* 1. to make black; darken 2. to slander

black eye a discoloration of the skin around an eye, caused by a blow

black′-eyed′ Su·san (-īd′ soo′z'n) a N. American wildflower with yellow rays about a dark center

black·guard (blag'ərd, -ärd) *n.* a scoundrel
black'head' *n.* a black-tipped plug of dried fatty matter in a skin pore
black'heart'ed *adj.* wicked; evil
black'ing *n.* a black polish, as for shoes
black'jack' (-jak') *n.* **1.** a small, leather-covered bludgeon with a flexible handle **2.** the card game TWENTY-ONE —*vt.* to hit with a blackjack
black'list' *n.* a list of censured persons being discriminated against —*vt.* to put on a blacklist
black lung (disease) a disease of the lungs caused by the continual inhalation of coal dust
black magic sorcery
black'mail' (-māl') *n.* [lit., black rent < ON. *mal*, discussion] payment extorted to prevent disclosure of information that could bring disgrace —*vt.* to get or try to get blackmail from —**black'mail'er** *n.*
black mark an unfavorable item in one's record
black market a system for selling goods illegally —**black'-mar'ket** *vt.*, *vi.* —**black mar·ket·eer** (mär'kə tir') (or **mar'ket·er)**
Black Muslim a member of a militant Islamic sect of American blacks
black'out' *n.* **1.** the extinguishing of all stage lights to end a scene **2.** a concealing of lights that might be visible to enemy aircraft **3.** temporary unconsciousness
black power political and economic power sought by black Americans in the struggle for civil rights
black sheep a person regarded as not so respectable by his family or group
black'smith' (-smith') *n.* one who works in iron, making and fitting horseshoes, etc.
black'thorn' *n.* a thorny shrub with blue-black, plumlike fruit; sloe
black'top' *n.* a bituminous mixture, usually asphalt, used as a surface for roads, etc.
black widow a black female spider with red underneath: it has a poisonous bite and eats its mate
blad·der (blad'ər) *n.* [OE. *blæddre*] **1.** a sac which holds urine flowing from the kidneys **2.** a bag, etc. resembling this
blade (blād) *n.* [OE. *blæd*] **1.** *a)* the leaf of a plant, esp. of grass *b)* the flat part of a leaf **2.** a broad, flat surface, as of an oar **3.** the cutting part of a knife, tool, etc. **4.** a sword **5.** a gay, dashing young man
blame (blām) *vt.* **blamed, blam'ing** [see BLASPHEME] **1.** to accuse of being at fault; condemn (*for*) **2.** to put the responsibility of (an error, etc. *on*) —*n.* **1.** a blaming **2.** responsibility for a fault —**be to blame** to deserve blame —**blame'less** *adj.*
blanch (blanch) *vt.* [see BLANK] **1.** to make white; bleach **2.** to make pale **3.** to scald (vegetables, etc.) —*vi.* to turn pale
bland (bland) *adj.* [< L. *blandus*, mild] **1.** agreeable **2.** mild **3.** insipid —**bland'ly** *adv.*
blan·dish (blan'dish) *vt.*, *vi.* [see BLAND] to flatter or coax —**blan'dish·ment** *n.*
blank (blaŋk) *adj.* [< Frank.] **1.** not written on (a *blank* paper) **2.** having an empty or vacant look **3.** empty of thought **4.** utter; complete (a *blank* denial) —*n.* **1.** an empty space, esp. one to be filled out in a printed form **2.** such a printed form **3.** an empty place or time **4.** a powder-filled cartridge without a bullet —*vt.* to hold (an opponent) scoreless —**draw a blank** [Colloq.] **1.** to be unsuccessful **2.** to be unable to remember something —**blank'ly** *adv.* —**blank'ness** *n.*
blan·ket (blaŋ'kit) *n.* [< OFr. dim. of *blanc*, white] **1.** a large, soft piece of cloth used for warmth, esp. as a bed cover **2.** anything like this (a *blanket* of snow) —*adj.* including many or all items (a *blanket* insurance policy) —*vt.* **1.** to cover, as with a blanket **2.** to suppress; obscure
blare (bler) *vt.*, *vi.* **blared, blar'ing** [ME. *bleren*, to bellow] to sound or exclaim loudly —*n.* a loud, brassy sound
blar·ney (blär'nē) *n.* [< *Blarney* stone in Ireland, traditionally kissed to gain skill in flattery] smooth talk used in flattery
bla·sé (blä zā') *adj.* [Fr.] satiated and bored
blas·pheme (blas fēm') *vt.* **-phemed', -phem'-ing** [< Gr. *blasphēmein*, speak evil of] **1.** to speak profanely of or to (God or sacred things) **2.** to curse —*vi.* to utter blasphemy —**blasphem'er** *n.*
blas'phe·my (-fə mē) *n.*, *pl.* **-mies 1.** profane abuse of God or sacred things **2.** anything irreverent —**blas'phe·mous** *adj.*
blast (blast) *n.* [< OE. *blæst*] **1.** a strong rush of air **2.** the sound of a sudden rush of air, as through a horn **3.** a blight **4.** an explosion, as of dynamite **5.** [Slang] a gay, hilarious time —*vi.* **1.** to make a loud, harsh sound **2.** to set off explosives, etc. —*vt.* **1.** to blight; wither **2.** to blow up; explode **3.** [Colloq.] to criticize sharply —**blast off** to take off: said of a rocket or missile —**(at) full blast** at full speed
blast furnace a smelting furnace in which a blast of air produces the intense heat
blast'off', blast'-off' *n.* the launching of a rocket, space vehicle, etc.
bla·tant (blāt'nt) *adj.* [prob. < L. *blaterare*, to babble] **1.** disagreeably loud; noisy **2.** very obtrusive —**bla'tan·cy** *n.*, *pl.* **-cies**
blath·er (blath'ər) *n.* [ON. *blathr*] foolish talk —*vi.*, *vt.* to chatter foolishly
blaze¹ (blāz) *n.* [< OE. *blæse*] **1.** a brilliant burst of flame; fire **2.** any very bright light **3.** a spectacular outburst **4.** a vivid display —*vi.* **blazed, blaz'ing 1.** to burn rapidly or shine brightly **2.** to be stirred, as with anger —**blaze away** to fire away rapidly
blaze² (blāz) *n.* [< ON. *blesi*] **1.** a white spot on an animal's face **2.** a mark made on a tree by cutting off a piece of bark —*vt.* **blazed, blaz'ing** to mark (a tree or trail) with blazes
blaz·er (blā'zər) *n.* a lightweight sports jacket, often brightly colored
bla·zon (blā'z'n) *n.* [OFr. *blason*, a shield] **1.** a coat of arms **2.** showy display —*vt.* **1.** to proclaim **2.** to adorn —**bla'zon·ry** *n.*
bldg. building
bleach (blēch) *vt.*, *vi.* [< OE. *blac*, pale] to make or become white or colorless —*n.* a substance for bleaching
bleach'ers *n.pl.* seats in tiers without a roof, for spectators at sporting events
bleak (blēk) *adj.* [< ON. *bleikr*, pale] **1.** exposed to wind and cold; bare **2.** cold; harsh **3.** cheerless; gloomy —**bleak'ly** *adv.*
blear (blir) *adj.* [< ME. *bleren*, to have watery eyes] **1.** made dim by tears, mucus, etc.: said of eyes **2.** blurred —*vt.* **1.** to dim with tears, mucus, etc. **2.** to blur —**blear'y** *adj.* **-i·er, -i·est**
bleat (blēt) *vi.* [< OE. *blætan*] to make the cry of a sheep, goat, or calf —*n.* a bleating
bleed (blēd) *vi.* **bled** (bled), **bleed'ing** [< OE. *blod*, blood] **1.** to emit or lose blood **2.** to feel pain, grief, or sympathy **3.** to ooze sap, juice, etc. —*vt.* **1.** to draw blood from **2.** to ooze (sap, juice, etc.) **3.** [Colloq.] to extort money from
bleep (blēp) *n.*, *vi.* [echoic] *same as* BEEP
blem·ish (blem'ish) *vt.* [< OFr. *blesmir*, injure] to mar —*n.* a flaw, defect, etc.

blench[1] (blench) *vt., vi. same as* BLANCH

blench[2] (blench) *vi.* [< OE. *blencan,* deceive] to shrink back, as in fear; flinch

blend (blend) *vt.* **blend′ed** or **blent, blend′ing** [< OE. *blendan*] 1. to mix or mingle (varieties of tea, tobacco, etc.) 2. to mix thoroughly —*vi.* 1. to mix or merge 2. to shade gradually into each other, as colors 3. to harmonize —*n.* 1. a blending 2. a mixture of varieties [a *blend* of coffee]

bless (bles) *vt.* **blessed** or **blest, bless′ing** [< OE. *bletsian,* consecrate with blood] 1. to make holy 2. to ask divine favor for 3. to endow (*with*) 4. to make happy 5. to praise 6. to protect from evil, harm, etc.

bless·ed (bles′id, blest) *adj.* 1. holy; sacred 2. blissful; fortunate 3. beatified 4. bringing joy —**bless′ed·ness** *n.*

bless′ing *n.* 1. an invocation or benediction 2. a grace said at meals 3. good wishes or approval 4. a special benefit

blew (bloo) *pt. of* BLOW[1] & BLOW[3]

blight (blīt) *n.* [? < ON. *blikja,* turn pale] 1. any insect, disease, etc. that destroys or stunts plants 2. anything that destroys, frustrates, etc. —*vt.* 1. to wither 2. to destroy

blimp (blimp) *n.* [echoic coinage] [Colloq.] a small, nonrigid or semirigid airship

blind (blīnd) *adj.* [OE.] 1. without the power of sight 2. of or for sightless persons 3. lacking insight 4. hard to see; hidden 5. closed at one end 6. not controlled by reason [*blind* fate] 7. *Aeron.* by the use of instruments only [*blind* flying] —*vt.* 1. to make sightless 2. to dazzle 3. to deprive of insight —*n.* 1. anything that obscures sight or keeps out light, as a window shade 2. a place of concealment 3. a decoy —**blind′ly** *adv.* —**blind′ness** *n.*

blind date [Colloq.] a date arranged for a man and a woman previously unacquainted

blind′er *n.* either of two flaps on a horse's bridle that shut out the side view

blind′fold′ (-fōld′) *vt.* [< ME. *blindfeld,* struck blind] to cover the eyes of, as with a cloth —*n.* something used to cover the eyes

blink (bliŋk) *vi.* [see BLENCH[2]] 1. to wink rapidly 2. to flash on and off; twinkle —*vt.* to cause (eyes, light, etc.) to wink or blink —*n.* 1. a blinking 2. a glimmer —**blink at** to ignore —**on the blink** [Slang] out of order

blink′er *n.* 1. a flashing warning light 2. *same as* BLINDER

blintz (blints) *n.* [< Yid. < Russ. *blin,* pancake] a thin pancake rolled with a filling of cottage cheese, etc.

bliss (blis) *n.* [OE. *bliths*] 1. great joy or happiness 2. spiritual joy —**bliss′ful** *adj.*

blis·ter (blis′tər) *n.* [< ON. *blastr*] 1. a raised patch of skin filled with watery matter and caused by burning or rubbing 2. anything like a blister —*vt.* 1. to raise blisters on 2. to lash with words —*vi.* to form blisters —**blis′ter·y** *adj.*

blithe (blīth) *adj.* [OE.] gay; carefree

blithe·some (blīth′səm) *adj.* blithe; gay

blitz (blits) *n.* [< ff.] a sudden, overwhelming attack —*vt.* to subject to a blitz

blitz′krieg′ (-krēg′) *n.* [G. < *blitz,* lightning + *krieg,* war] sudden, swift, large-scale offensive warfare

bliz·zard (bliz′ərd) *n.* [dial. *bliz,* violent blow + -ARD] a violent snowstorm with very cold winds

bloat (blōt) *vt., vi.* [< ON. *blautr,* soaked] 1. to swell, as with water or air 2. to puff up, as with pride

blob (bläb) *n.* [echoic] a small drop or mass

bloc (bläk) *n.* [Fr. < LowG. *block,* log] a bipar-

tisan group of legislators, or a group of nations, acting together in a common cause

block (bläk) *n.* [see BLOC] 1. a solid piece as of wood 2. a heavy stand on which chopping, etc. is done 3. an auctioneer's platform 4. an obstruction 5. a pulley in a frame 6. a city square 7. a group of buildings 8. a number of things regarded as a unit 9. *Printing* a piece of engraved wood, etc. with a design 10. *Sports* a legal thwarting of an opponent's play —*vt.* 1. to obstruct 2. to shape on a block 3. to support with blocks 4. to sketch roughly 5. *Sports* to hinder —**on the block** up for sale or auction —**block′age** *n.*

block·ade (blä käd′) *n.* [BLOCK + -ADE] 1. a shutting off of a place by troops or ships to prevent passage 2. any strategic barrier —*vt.* -ad′ed, -ad′ing to subject to a blockade

block and tackle pulley blocks and ropes, used for lifting large, heavy objects

block·bust·er (bläk′bus′tər) *n.* [Colloq.] a successful, heavily promoted movie, novel, etc.

block′bust′ing (-bus′tiŋ) *n.* the inducing of owners to sell their homes to escape a minority group

block′head′ (-hed′) *n.* a stupid person

block′house′ (-hous′) *n.* 1. formerly, a wooden fort 2. a reinforced structure for observers, as of missile launches

bloke (blōk) *n.* [< ?] [Chiefly Brit. Slang] a fellow

blond (bländ) *adj.* [Fr.] 1. having light-colored hair and skin 2. yellowish: said of hair 3. light-colored Also sp. **blonde** —*n.* a blond person —**blonde** *n.fem.*

blood (blud) *n.* [< OE. *blod*] 1. the red fluid circulating in the arteries and veins of vertebrates 2. bloodshed 3. the essence of life; life 4. the sap of a plant 5. passion, temperament, etc. 6. parental heritage; lineage 7. kinship 8. a dandy 9. people, esp. youthful people —**bad blood** hatred —**In cold blood** 1. with cruelty 2. deliberately

blood bank a supply of blood stored for future use in transfusion

blood count the number of red and white corpuscles in a given volume of blood

blood′cur′dling (-kurd′liŋ) *adj.* terrifying

blood′ed (-id) *adj.* of fine breed

blood′hound′ *n.* a large, keen-scented dog used in tracking fugitives, etc.

blood′less *adj.* 1. without bloodshed 2. anemic or pale —**blood′less·ly** *adv.*

blood′let′ting (-let′iŋ) *n.* the opening of a vein to remove blood

blood′mo·bile′ (-mō bēl′) *n.* a mobile unit collecting blood given for blood banks

blood money money paid for a murder

blood poisoning a diseased condition of the blood, due to certain microorganisms, etc.

blood pressure the pressure of the blood against the inner walls of the blood vessels

blood relation (or **relative**) a person related by birth

blood′shed′ *n.* killing; slaughter

blood′shot′ *adj.* red from swollen or broken small blood vessels: said of the eyes

blood′stream′ *n.* the circulating blood

blood′suck′er *n.* an animal that sucks blood, esp. a leech —**blood′suck′ing** *adj.*

blood′thirst′y *adj.* murderous; cruel

blood vessel an artery, vein, or capillary

blood′y *adj.* -i·er, -i·est 1. of or stained with blood 2. involving bloodshed 3. bloodthirsty 4. [Brit. Slang] cursed —*adv.* [Brit. Slang] very —*vt.* -led, -y·ing to stain with blood —**blood′i·ness** *n.*

bloom (bloom) *n.* [< ON. *blomi,* flowers] **1.** a flower; blossom **2.** a state or time of flowering **3.** a period of maximum health, vigor, etc. **4.** a healthy glow **5.** a powdery coating on some fruits or leaves —*vi.* 1. to blossom **2.** to be in one's prime **3.** to glow as with health

bloom·ers (bloo'mərz) *n.pl.* [< Amelia *Bloomer,* U.S. feminist] **1.** baggy trousers gathered at the knee, formerly worn by women for athletics **2.** a similar undergarment

bloom'ing *adj.* **1.** blossoming **2.** flourishing **3.** [Colloq.] complete

bloop·er (bloo'p'ər) *n.* [echoic] [Slang] **1.** a stupid mistake **2.** *Baseball* a fly that falls just beyond the infield for a hit

blos·som (bläs'əm) *n.* [< OE. *blostma*] **1.** a flower, esp. of a fruit-bearing plant **2.** a state or time of flowering —*vi.* **1.** to have or open into blossoms **2.** to begin to flourish; develop

blot (blät) *n.* [< ?] **1.** a spot or stain, esp. of ink **2.** anything that spoils or mars **3.** a moral stain —*vt.* **blot'ted, blot'ting** **1.** to spot; stain **2.** to disgrace **3.** to erase, obscure, or get rid of (with *out*) **4.** to dry, as with blotting paper — *vi.* **1.** to make blots **2.** to become blotted **3.** to be absorbent

blotch (bläch) *n.* [? < prec.] **1.** a skin discoloration **2.** any large blot or stain —*vt.* to mark with blotches —**blotch'y** *adj.* **-i·er, -i·est**

blot'ter *n.* **1.** a piece of blotting paper **2.** a book to record events

blotting paper a soft, absorbent paper used to dry a surface freshly written on in ink

blouse (blous, blouz) *n.* [Fr., workman's smock] **1.** a shirtlike garment worn by women and children **2.** a uniform coat worn by soldiers, etc. **3.** a sailor's jumper

blow¹ (blō) *vi.* **blew, blown, blow'ing** [< OE. *blawan*] **1.** to move with some force, as the wind **2.** to send forth air, as with the mouth **3.** to pant **4.** to sound by blowing **5.** to spout water and air, as whales do **6.** to be carried by the wind **7.** to storm **8.** to burst, as a tire, or melt, as a fuse **9.** [Colloq.] to brag **10.** [Slang] to go away —*vt.* **1.** to force air from, into, etc. **2.** to drive by blowing **3.** to sound by blowing **4.** to inflate **5.** to burst by an explosion **6.** to melt (a fuse, etc.) **7.** [Colloq.] to spend (money) freely **8.** [Slang] to bungle —*n.* **1.** a blowing **2.** a blast or gale —**blow over** to end, as trouble —**blow up 1.** to enlarge (a photograph) **2.** [Colloq.] to lose one's temper —**blow'er** *n.*

blow² (blō) *n.* [ME. *blowe*] **1.** a hard hit, as with the fist **2.** a sudden attack **3.** a sudden calamity; shock —**come to blows** to begin fighting

blow³ (blō) *vi.* **blew, blown, blow'ing** [OE. *blowan*] [Poet.] to bloom; blossom —*n.* a mass of blossoms

blow-by-blow (blō'bī'blō') *adj.* detailed

blow'-dry' *vt.* **-dried', -dry'ing** to dry (wet hair) with hot air blown from an electric device (**blow'-dry'er**)

blow'fly' *n., pl.* **-flies'** a fly that lays its eggs on meat, in wounds, etc.

blow'gun' *n.* a long, tubelike weapon through which darts or pellets are blown

blow'out' *n.* **1.** the bursting of a tire **2.** [Slang] a party, celebration, etc.

blow'pipe' *n.* a tube for forcing air into a flame to increase its heat

blow'torch' *n.* a small gasoline torch that shoots out a hot flame

blow'up' *n.* **1.** an explosion **2.** an enlarged photograph

blowz·y (blou'zē) *adj.* **-i·er, -i·est** [< obs.

blouze, wench] **1.** fat, ruddy, and coarse-looking **2.** slovenly; sloppy Also **blows'y**

blub·ber (blub'ər) *n.* [ME. *blober,* a bubble] fat as of the whale —*vi.* to weep loudly —*vt.* to say while blubbering —**blub'ber·er** *n.*

blu·cher (bloo'chər, -kər) *n.* [< von *Blücher* (1742–1819), Prussian field marshal] a kind of shoe with the vamp and tongue all one piece

bludg·eon (bluj'n) *n.* [? < MFr. *bouge,* a club] a short club with a thick or heavy end —*vt., vi.* **1.** to strike with a bludgeon **2.** to bully

blue (bloo) *adj.* [< Frank. *blao*] **1.** of the color of the clear sky **2.** livid: said of the skin **3.** gloomy **4.** puritanical **5.** [Colloq.] indecent —*n.* **1.** the color of the clear sky **2.** any blue pigment **3.** [*pl.*] [Colloq.] a depressed feeling (with *the*) **4.** [*pl., also with sing. v.*] Negro folk music with a slow tempo, melancholy words, etc. (often with *the*) —*vt.* **blued, blu'ing** or **blue'ing** **1.** to make blue **2.** to use bluing on or in —**out of the blue** unexpectedly —**the blue 1.** the sky **2.** the sea

Blue'beard' a legendary character who married and murdered one wife after another

blue'bell' *n.* any of various plants with blue, bell-shaped flowers

blue'ber'ry *n., pl.* **-ries** **1.** a small, edible, blue-black berry **2.** the shrub it grows on

blue'bird' *n.* a small N. American songbird, the male of which has a bluish back

blue blood **1.** descent from nobility **2.** an aristocrat: also **blue'blood'** *n.*

blue'bot'tle *n.* **1.** a plant with blue, bottle-shaped flowers **2.** a large blowfly with a steel-blue abdomen

blue cheese a cheese similar to Roquefort

blue'-col'lar *adj.* designating or of industrial workers

blue'fish' *n., pl.:* see FISH a bluish food fish of the Atlantic coast of N. America

blue'grass' *n.* **1.** a forage grass, as **Kentucky bluegrass 2.** [*often* B-] Southern folk music played on guitars, fiddles, banjos, etc.

blue'jack'et *n.* an enlisted man in the U.S. or British navy

blue jay a noisy American bird with a bluish upper part: also **blue'jay'** *n.*

blue'nose' *n.* [Colloq.] a puritanical person

blue'-pen'cil (-pen's'l) *vt.* **-ciled** or **-cilled, -cil·ing** or **-cil·ling** to edit, cut, or correct as with a blue pencil

blue'point' *n.* [< *Blue Point,* Long Island] a small oyster, usually eaten raw

blue'print' *n.* **1.** a photographic reproduction in white on a blue background, as of architectural plans **2.** any detailed plan or outline —*vt.* to make a blueprint of

blue'stock'ing *n.* a bookish woman

bluff¹ (bluf) *vt., vi.* [prob. < Du. *bluffen,* to baffle] to mislead or frighten by a false, bold front —*n.* **1.** a bluffing **2.** one who bluffs: also **bluff'er** *n.*

bluff² (bluf) *adj.* [< Du. *blaf,* flat] **1.** having a broad, flat front that slopes steeply **2.** having a rough, frank manner —*n.* a high, steep bank or cliff —**bluff'ly** *adv.*

blu·ing (bloo'iŋ) *n.* a blue rinse used on white fabrics to prevent yellowing: also sp. **blue'ing**

blu'ish (-ish) *adj.* somewhat blue

blun·der (blun'dər) *n.* [< ON. *blunda,* shut the eyes] **1.** to move clumsily **2.** to make a foolish mistake —*n.* a foolish mistake

blun'der·buss' (-bus') *n.* [Du. *donderbus,* thunder box] an obsolete short gun

blunt (blunt) *adj.* [< ?] **1.** slow to perceive; dull **2.** having a dull edge or point **3.** plain-spoken and abrupt —*vt., vi.* to make or become dull — **blunt'ly** *adv.*

blur (blur) *vt., vi.* **blurred, blur'ring** [? akin to BLEAR] **1.** to smear; blot **2.** to make or become indistinct in shape, etc. **3.** to dim —*n.* **1.** a being blurred **2.** an obscuring stain **3.** anything indistinct —**blur'ri·ness** *n.* —**blur'ry** *adj.*

blurb (blurb) *n.* [arbitrary coinage] [Colloq.] an exaggerated advertisement

blurt (blurt) *vt.* [prob. echoic] to say suddenly, without stopping to think (with *out*)

blush (blush) *vi.* [< OE. *blyscan,* to shine] **1.** to become red in the face, as from embarrassment **2.** to be ashamed (*at* or *for*) **3.** to become rosy —*n.* **1.** a reddening of the face, as from shame **2.** a rosy color —*adj.* rosy

blush'er *n.* **1.** one who blushes easily **2.** a facial cream, powder, etc. that gives color

blus·ter (blus'tər) *vi.* [< LowG. *blüstern*] **1.** to blow stormily: said of wind **2.** to speak in a noisy or swaggering way —*n.* **1.** noisy commotion **2.** noisy or swaggering talk —**blus'ter·y** *adj.*

blvd. boulevard

BO, B.O. body odor

bo·a (bō'ə) *n.* [L.] **1.** a tropical snake that crushes its prey **2.** a woman's long, fluffy scarf

boar (bôr) *n.* [OE. *bar*] **1.** an uncastrated male hog or pig **2.** a wild hog

board (bôrd) *n.* [< OE. *bord,* plank] **1.** a long, flat piece of sawed wood **2.** a flat piece of wood, etc. for some special use [a bulletin *board*] **3.** pasteboard **4.** *a)* a table for meals *b)* meals, esp. as provided regularly for pay **5.** a group of administrators; council **6.** the side of a ship —*vt.* **1.** to cover with boards **2.** to provide with meals, or room and meals, regularly for pay **3.** to come onto the deck of (a ship) **4.** to get on (an airplane, bus, etc.) —*vi.* to receive meals, or room and meals, regularly for pay — **go by the board** to be got rid of, lost, etc. —**on board** on a ship, aircraft, etc. —**the boards** the stage (of a theater) —**board'er** *n.*

board'ing·house' *n.* a house where meals, or room and meals, can be had for pay

board'walk' *n.* a walk made of thick boards

boast (bōst) *vi.* [< Anglo-Fr.] to talk, esp. about oneself, with too much pride; brag —*vt.* to brag about or glory in —*n.* **1.** a boasting **2.** anything boasted of —**boast'er** *n.* —**boast'ful** *adj.* —**boast'ful·ly** *adv.*

boat (bōt) *n.* [OE. *bat*] **1.** a small, open watercraft **2.** loosely, a ship **3.** a boat-shaped dish — *vi.* to go in a boat —**in the same boat** in the same unfavorable situation —**boat'man** (-mən) *n., pl.* -**men**

boat·er (bōt'ər) *n.* a stiff straw hat

boat'house' *n.* a building for storing boats

boat·swain (bō's'n) *n.* a ship's officer in charge of the deck crew, rigging, etc.

bob (bäb) *n.* [ME. *bobbe,* hanging cluster] **1.** any knoblike hanging weight **2.** a woman's or girl's short haircut **3.** a quick, jerky motion **4.** a float on a fishing line —*vt., vi.* **bobbed, bob'-bing** [ME. *bobben,* knock against] **1.** to move with jerky motions **2.** to cut (hair, etc.) short —**bob up** to appear suddenly

bob·bin (bäb'in) *n.* [Fr. *bobine*] a spool for thread, etc., used as in spinning

bob·by (bäb'ē) *n., pl.* -**bies** [after Sir Robert (*Bobby*) Peel (1788–1850)] [Brit. Colloq.] a policeman

bobby pin [< *bobbed* hair] a small metal hairpin with sides pressed close

bobby socks (or **sox**) [< BOB (*v.* 2)] [Colloq.] girls' ankle-length socks

bob'cat' *n.* a wildcat of the E U.S.

bob·o·link (bäb'ə liŋk') *n.* a migratory songbird of N. America

bob'sled' *n.* a long racing sled

bob·white (bäb'hwīt') *n.* [echoic] a small N. American quail

bock (beer) (bäk) [< *Einbeck,* German city where first brewed] a dark beer

bode' (bōd) *vt.* **bod'ed, bod'ing** [< OE. *boda,* messenger] to be an omen of —**bode ill** (or **well**) to be a bad (or good) omen

bode² (bōd) *pt. of* BIDE

bod·ice (bäd'is) *n.* [alt. < *bodies,* pl. of *body*] the upper part of a woman's dress

bod·i·ly (bäd''l ē) *adj.* **1.** physical **2.** of the body —*adv.* **1.** in person **2.** as a single body

bod·kin (bäd'k'n) *n.* [ME. *boidekyn* < ?] **1.** a pointed instrument for making holes in cloth **2.** a thick, blunt needle

bod·y (bäd'ē) *n., pl.* -**ies** [< OE. *bodig,* cask] **1.** the whole physical substance of a person, animal, or plant **2.** the trunk or torso **3.** a corpse **4.** [Colloq.] a person **5.** a group regarded as a unit **6.** the main part **7.** a mass of matter **8.** density or consistency, as of a liquid **9.** richness of tone or flavor

bod'y·guard' *n.* a person or persons assigned to guard someone

body politic the people who collectively constitute a political unit under a government

body stocking a tightfitting garment, usually of one piece, for the torso

Boer (bôr, boor) *n.* [Du. *boer,* peasant] a South African descended from Dutch colonists

bog (bäg, bôg) *n.* [< Gael. *bog,* soft] wet, spongy ground; small marsh —*vt., vi.* **bogged, bog'ging** to sink as in a bog —**bog'gy** *adj.*

bo·gey (bō'gē) *n., pl.* -**geys** **1.** *same as* BOGY **2.** [after an imaginary Colonel *Bogey*] *Golf* one stroke more than par on a hole: also sp. **bo'gie**

bog·gle (bäg''l) *vi.* -**gled, -gling** [< Scot. *bogle,* specter] to shy away, hesitate, or equivocate (*at*) —*vt.* to bungle —**a** boggling

bo·gus (bō'gəs) *adj.* [< ?] not genuine; fake

bo·gy (bō'gē, boog'ē) *n., pl.* -**gies** [see BOGGLE] an imaginary evil spirit; goblin: also sp. **bo'gie**

bo·gy·man, bo·gey·man (bō'gē man', boog'ē-) *n., pl.* -**men'** an imaginary frightful being

Bo·he·mi·an (bō hē'mē ən) *n.* **1.** a native of Bohemia **2.** *same as* CZECH (*n.* 2) **3.** [*often* b-] one living unconventionally —*adj.* **1.** of Bohemia, its people, etc. **2.** [*often* b-] like a Bohemian (*n.* 3)

boil' (boil) *vi.* [< L. *bulla,* a bubble] **1.** to bubble up and vaporize by being heated **2.** to seethe like boiling liquids **3.** to be agitated, as with rage **4.** to cook in boiling liquid —*vt.* **1.** to heat to the boiling point **2.** to cook in boiling liquid —*n.* the act or state of boiling —**boil down 1.** to lessen in quantity by boiling **2.** to condense

boil² (boil) *n.* [< OE. *byl*] an inflamed, painful, pus-filled swelling on the skin

boil'er *n.* **1.** a container to boil or heat things in **2.** a tank turning water to steam for heat or power **3.** a tank to heat and store water

boil'ing point the temperature at which a liquid boils: for water, 212°F (100°C)

bois·ter·ous (bois'tər əs) *adj.* [ME. *boistreous,* crude] **1.** turbulent **2.** *a)* noisy and unruly *b)* loud and exuberant

bold (bōld) *adj.* [< OE. *beald*] **1.** daring; fearless **2.** taking liberties; impudent **3.** prominent and clear —**bold'ly** *adv.*

bold'face' *n. Printing* type with heavy, dark lines

bole (bōl) *n.* [ON. *bolr*] a tree trunk

bo·le·ro (bə ler′ō) *n., pl.* **-ros** [Sp.] **1.** a Spanish dance in 3/4 time **2.** music for this **3.** a short, open vest

boll (bōl) *n.* [< OE. *bolla,* a bowl] the roundish pod of a plant, esp. of cotton or flax

boll weevil a small weevil whose larvae destroy cotton bolls

bo·lo·gna (bə lō′nē, -nyə) *n.* [< *Bologna,* It. city] a large, smoked sausage

Bol·she·vik (bōl′shə vik′, bäl′-) *n., pl.* **-viks′,** **-vi′ki** (-vē′kē) [Russ. < *bolshe,* the majority] [*also* **b-**] **1.** a member of a majority faction that came into power in Russia in 1917 **2.** a Communist, esp. of the Soviet Union —**Bol′-she·vism** *n.* —**Bol′she·vist** *n., adj.*

bol·ster (bōl′stər) *n.* [OE.] **1.** a long, narrow pillow **2.** any bolsterlike object or support —*vt.* to prop (*up*) as with a bolster

bolt¹ (bōlt) *n.* [OE.] **1.** a short, blunt arrow used with a crossbow **2.** a flash of lightning **3.** a sliding bar for locking a door, etc. **4.** a threaded metal rod used with a nut to hold parts together **5.** a roll (*of* cloth, paper, etc.) — *vt.* **1.** to say suddenly; blurt (*out*) **2.** to swallow (food) hurriedly **3.** to fasten as with a bolt **4.** to abandon (a party, group, etc.) —*vi.* **1.** to spring away suddenly; dart **2.** to withdraw support from one's party, etc. —*adv.* erectly [*to* sit *bolt* upright]

bolt² (bōlt) *vt.* [< OFr. *buleter*] to sift

bomb (bäm) *n.* [< Fr. < Gr. *bombos,* hollow sound] **1.** an explosive, incendiary, or chemical-filled container for dropping, hurling, etc. **2.** [Slang] a complete failure —*vt.* to attack or destroy with bombs —*vi.* [Slang] to fail utterly

bom·bard (bäm bärd′) *vt.* [< Fr. *bombarde,* mortar] to attack as with artillery or bombs — **bom·bard′ment** *n.*

bom·bar·dier (bäm′bə dir′) *n.* one who releases the bombs in a bomber

bom·bast (bäm′bast) *n.* [< Per. *pambak,* cotton] pompous talk or writing —**bom·bas′tic** *adj.* —**bom·bas′ti·cal·ly** *adv.*

bomb·er (bäm′ər) *n.* an airplane for dropping bombs

bomb′shell′ *n. same as* BOMB (*n.* 1) ˝

bo·na fi·de (bō′nə fīd′ *or* fī′dē) [L.] in good faith; without fraud

bo·nan·za (bə nan′zə) *n.* [Sp., prosperity] **1.** a rich vein of ore **2.** any source of wealth

bon·bon (bän′bän′) *n.* [Fr. *bon,* good] a small piece of usually creamy candy

bond (bänd) *n.* [ult. < Gothic *bindan,* bind] **1.** anything that binds, fastens, or unites **2.** [*pl.*] shackles **3.** a binding agreement **4.** the status of goods kept in a warehouse until taxes are paid **5.** an interest-bearing certificate issued by a government or business, redeemable on a specified date **6.** a written obligation to do or not do something **7.** an amount paid as surety or bail —*vt.* **1.** to fasten or unite **2.** to furnish a bond, or bail, for (someone) **3.** to place under bond **4.** to put under bonded debt

bond·age (bän′dij) *n.* [ult. < ON. *bua,* inhabit] serfdom; slavery

bond′man (-mən) *n., pl.* **-men** a serf; slave — **bond′wom′an** *n.fem., pl.* **-wom′en**

bonds·man (bändz′mən) *n., pl.* **-men 1.** *same as* BONDMAN **2.** one who furnishes bond, or surety

bone (bōn) *n.* [OE. *ban*] **1.** any of the pieces of hard tissue forming the skeleton of most vertebrates **2.** this hard tissue **3.** [*pl.*] the skeleton **4.** a bonelike substance or thing —*vt.* **boned, bon′ing** to remove the bones from —*vi.* [Slang] to study hard (usually with *up*) —**feel**

in one's bones to be certain without any real reason —**have a bone to pick** to have cause to quarrel —**make no bones about** [Colloq.] to admit freely —**bone′less** *adj.*

bone′-dry′ *adj.* very dry

bon·er (bōn′ər) *n.* [Slang] a blunder

bon·fire (bän′fīr′) *n.* [ME. *banefyre,* bone fire, pyre] an outdoor fire

bong (bôṇ, bäṇ) *n.* [echoic] a deep ringing sound —*vi.* to make this sound

bon·go (bäṇ′gō) *n., pl.* **-gos** [AmSp. < ?] either of a pair of small joined drums, of different pitch, struck with the fingers

bo·ni·to (bə nēt′ō) *n., pl.* **-tos, -toes, -to** [Sp.] any of several saltwater fishes related to the tuna

‡**bon·jour** (bôn zhōōr′) *interj.* [Fr.] good day; hello

bon·net (bän′it) *n.* [OFr. *bonet*] a woman's or child's hat with a chin ribbon

bon·ny, bon·nie (bän′ē) *adj.* **-ni·er, -ni·est** [< Fr. *bon,* good < L. *bonus*] [Chiefly Scot.] **1.** handsome **2.** fine; pleasant

bon·sai (bän sī′) *n., pl.* **-sai′** [Jpn.] a potted tree or shrub dwarfed by pruning, etc.

bo·nus (bō′nəs) *n., pl.* **-nus·es** [L., good] anything given as something extra

bon voy·age (bän′ voi äzh′) [Fr.] pleasant journey

bon·y (bō′nē) *adj.* **-i·er, -i·est 1.** of or like bones **2.** too thin —**bon′i·ness** *n.*

boo (bōō) *interj., n., pl.* **boos** a sound made to show, disapproval, to startle, etc. —*vi., vt.* **booed, boo′ing** to shout "boo" (at)

boo·by (bōō′bē) *n., pl.* **-bies** [prob. < Sp. *bobo*] a fool; nitwit: also [Slang] **boob** (bōōb)

book (book) *n.* [OE. *boc*] **1.** a printed work on sheets of paper bound together **2.** a main division of a literary work **3.** a record or account **4.** a libretto **5.** a booklike package, as of matches —*vt.* **1.** to record in a book; list **2.** to engage (rooms, etc.) ahead of time **3.** to record charges against on a police record —**by the book** according to the rules —**the (Good) Book** the Bible

book′bind′ing *n.* the art or work of binding books —**book′bind′er** *n.*

book′case′ *n.* a cabinet for books

book′end′ *n.* a support to keep books upright

book·ie (-ē) *n.* [Slang] *same as* BOOKMAKER

book′ish (-ish) *adj.* inclined to read and study

book′keep′ing *n.* the work of keeping a systematic record of business transactions — **book′keep′er** *n.*

book′let (-lit) *n.* a small book

book′mak′er *n.* a person in the business of taking bets, as on horse races

book′mark′ *n.* anything slipped between the pages of a book to mark a place

book′plate′ *n.* a label pasted in a book to name its owner

book′worm′ *n.* **1.** an insect larva that harms books by feeding on the binding, paste, etc. **2.** one who reads or studies much

boom¹ (bōōm) *vi., vt.* [echoic] to make, or say with, a deep hollow sound —*n.* this sound

boom² (bōōm) *n.* [Du., a beam] **1.** a spar extending from a mast to hold the bottom of a sail outstretched **2.** a long beam extending as from an upright to lift and guide something **3.** a barrier, as of logs, to prevent floating logs from dispersing —*vt.* to sail at top speed (usually with *along*)

boom³ (bōōm) *vi.* [< prec. *vi.*] to increase or grow rapidly —*vt.* to cause to flourish; promote —*n.* a prosperous period

boom·er·ang (bōōm′ə raṇ′) *n.* [< Australian

native name] **1.** a flat, curved stick that can be thrown so that it will return to the thrower **2.** a scheme, etc. that goes awry, to the disadvantage of the schemer —*vi.* to act as a boomerang

boon[1] (bōōn) *n.* [ON. *bon,* a petition] **1.** a welcome benefit **2.** [Archaic] a request

boon[2] (bōōn) *adj.* [< L. *bonus,* good] merry; convivial: now only in **boon companion**

boon·docks (bōōn'däks') *n.pl.* [< Tag. *bundok,* mountain] [Colloq.] **1.** a wilderness **2.** a rural region Used with *the*

boon·dog·gle (bōōn'dôg''l, -däg'-) *vi.* **-gled, -gling** [orig. dial., a strap] [Colloq.] to do trifling work —*n.* trifling work

boor (boor) *n.* [Du. *boer,* peasant] a rude, awkward, or ill-mannered person —**boor'ish** *adj.* —**boor'ish·ly** *adv.*

boost (bōōst) *vt.* [< ?] **1.** to raise as by a push from below **2.** to urge others to support —*n.* a boosting —**boost'er** *n.*

boot[1] (bōōt) *n.* [OFr. *bote*] **1.** a covering of leather, rubber, etc. for the foot and part or all of the leg **2.** a patch for the inside of a tire **3.** a kick **4.** [Slang] a navy or marine recruit — *vt.* **1.** to put boots on **2.** to kick

boot[2] (bōōt) *n., vt., vi.* [< OE. *bot,* advantage] [Archaic] profit —**to boot** besides

boot'black' *n.* one whose work is shining shoes and boots

boot·ee, boot·ie (bōōt'ē) *n.* a baby's soft, knitted or cloth shoe

booth (bōōth) *n., pl.* **booths** (bōō*th*z) [< ON. *bua,* dwell] a small structure or enclosure, as a stall for the sale of goods

boot'leg' *vt., vi.* **-legged', -leg'ging** [< hiding objects in a boot] to make or sell (esp. liquor) illegally —*adj.* bootlegged —*n.* something bootlegged —**boot'leg'ger** *n.*

boo·ty (bōōt'ē) *n.* [MLowG. *bute*] loot

booze (bōōz) *n.* [< MDu. *buse*] —*n.* [Colloq.] alcoholic liquor —**booz'y** *adj.* **-i·er, -i·est**

bop (bäp) *vt.* **bopped, bop'ping** [Slang] to hit; strike

bo·rate (bôr'āt) *n.* a salt or ester of boric acid —*vt.* **-rat·ed, -rat·ing** to treat with borax or boric acid —**bo'rat·ed** *adj.*

bo·rax (bôr'aks) *n.* [< Per. *būrah*] a white, crystalline salt used in glass, soaps, etc.

bor·der (bôr'dər) *n.* [< OHG. *bord,* margin] **1.** an edge or a part near an edge; margin **2.** a dividing line between countries, etc. **3.** a narrow strip along an edge —*vt.* **1.** to provide with a border **2.** to bound —*adj.* of or near a border — **border on** (or **upon**) to be next or close to

bor'der·land' *n.* **1.** land near a border **2.** a vague, uncertain condition

bor'der·line' *n.* a boundary —*adj.* on the boundary of what is acceptable, normal, etc.

bore[1] (bôr) *vt.* **bored, bor'ing** [< OE. *bor,* auger] **1.** to make a hole in with a drill, etc. **2.** to make (a hole, etc.) as by drilling **3.** to weary by being dull —*vi.* to bore a hole or passage — *n.* **1.** a hole made as by boring **2.** *a)* the hollow part of a tube, gun barrel, etc. *b)* its inside diameter **3.** a tiresome, dull person or thing — **bor'er** *n.*

bore[2] (bôr) *pt.* of BEAR[1]

bore·dom (bôr'dəm) *n.* the condition of being bored or uninterested

boric acid a white, crystalline, acid compound used as a mild antiseptic

born (bôrn) *alt. pp.* of BEAR[1] —*adj.* **1.** brought into being **2.** by birth or nature

born'-a·gain' *adj.* having a new or renewed faith or belief, as in evangelical Christianity

borne (bôrn) *pp.* of BEAR[1]

bo·ron (bôr'än) *n.* [< BORAX] a nonmetallic chemical element in borax, etc.: symbol, B

bor·ough (bur'ō) *n.* [< OE. *burg,* town] **1.** a self-governing, incorporated town **2.** any of the five administrative units of New York City

bor·row (bär'ō, bôr'ō) *vt., vi.* [OE. *borgian*] **1.** to take or receive (something), intending to return it **2.** to adopt (an idea, etc.) as one's own —**bor'row·er** *n.*

borsch (bôrsh) *n.* [Russ. *borshch*] beet soup: also **borsht** (bôrsht)

bosh (bäsh) *n., interj.* [Turk., empty] [Colloq.] nonsense

bos·om (booz'əm, bōō'zəm) *n.* [OE. *bosm*] **1.** the human breast **2.** the breast regarded as the source of feelings **3.** the interior; midst [in the *bosom* of one's family] **4.** the part of a garment that covers the breast —*adj.* close; intimate [a *bosom* companion]

boss[1] (bôs) *n.* [Du. *baas,* a master] **1.** an employer or supervisor **2.** one who controls a political organization —*vt.* **1.** to act as boss of **2.** [Colloq.] to order (a person) about —*adj.* **1.** [Colloq.] chief **2.** [Slang] excellent; fine

boss[2] (bôs) *n.* [< OFr. *boce,* a swelling] a protruding ornament, knob, or stud —*vt.* to stud

boss'y *adj.* **-i·er, -i·est** [Colloq.] domineering — **boss'i·ly** *adv.* —**boss'i·ness** *n.*

bo·sun (bōs''n) *n. same as* BOATSWAIN

bot·a·ny (bät''n ē) *n.* [< Gr. *botanē,* a plant] the science that deals with plants and plant life —**bot·an·i·cal** (bə tan'i k'l), **bo·tan'ic** *adj.* — **bot'a·nist** *n.*

botch (bäch) *vt.* [< ? Du. *botsen,* to patch] **1.** to patch clumsily **2.** to bungle —*n.* a bungled piece of work

both (bōth) *adj., pron.* [< OE. *ba tha,* both these] the two [both birds] —*conj.,* adv. equally (with *and*) [both tired and sick]

both·er (bä*th*'ər) *vt., vi.* [prob. < *pother*] **1.** to worry, annoy, etc. **2.** to trouble (oneself) —*n.* **1.** worry; trouble **2.** one who gives trouble — **both'er·some** (-səm) *adj.*

bot·tle (bät''l) *n.* [< LL. *buttis,* a cask] **1.** a narrow-necked container for liquids **2.** its contents —*vt.* **-tled, -tling** to put into a bottle — **bottle up 1.** to shut in **2.** to suppress (emotions) —**bot'tler** *n.*

bot'tle·neck' *n.* **1.** a narrow passage or road slowing traffic **2.** any hindrance

bot·tom (bät'əm) *n.* [< OE. *botm,* ground] **1.** the lowest part or place **2.** the part something rests on **3.** the side underneath **4.** a chair seat **5.** the ground beneath a body of water **6.** basis; cause; source **7.** [Colloq.] the buttocks — *adj.* lowest; last —**at bottom** fundamentally

bot·u·lism (bäch'ə liz'm) *n.* [< L. *botulus,* sausage] poisoning from the toxin of a bacillus in improperly preserved foods

bou·doir (bōōd'wär) *n.* [Fr., lit., pouting room] a woman's private room

bouf·fant (bōō fänt') *adj.* [< Fr. *bouffer,* puff out] puffed out; full, as some skirts

bough (bou) *n.* [OE. *bog,* shoulder] a branch of a tree, esp. a main branch

bought (bôt) *pt. & pp.* of BUY

bouil·lon (bool'yän, -yən) *n.* [Fr. < *bouillir,* to boil] a clear broth, esp. of beef

boul·der (bōl'dər) *n.* [ME. *bulder*] a large rock worn smooth by weather and water

boul·e·vard (bool'ə värd') *n.* [Fr. < MDu. *bolwerc,* bulwark] a broad street

bounce (bouns) *vi.* **bounced, bounc'ing** [ME. *bounsen,* to thump] **1.** to rebound **2.** to leap **3.** [Slang] to be returned: said of a worthless check —*vt.* **1.** to make bounce **2.** [Slang] to put (a person) out as by force —*n.* **1.** a bouncing **2.**

capacity for bouncing **3.** [Colloq.] energy; zest —**bounc'y** *adj.* **-i·er, -i·est**

bounc'er *n.* [Slang] one hired to remove disorderly people from a nightclub, etc.

bounc'ing *adj.* big, healthy, strong, etc.

bound¹ (bound) *vi.* [Fr. *bondir,* to leap] **1.** to move with a leap or leaps **2.** to bounce; rebound —*vt.* to cause to bound or bounce —*n.* **1.** a jump; leap **2.** a bounce; rebound

bound² (bound) *pt. & pp. of* BIND —*adj.* **1.** tied **2.** closely connected **3.** certain *[bound* to win*]* **4.** obliged *[legally bound* to pay*]* **5.** having a binding, as a book **6.** [Colloq.] determined; resolved

bound³ (bound) *adj.* [< ON. *bua,* prepare] going; headed *[bound* for home*]*

bound⁴ (bound) *n.* [< ML. *bodina*] **1.** a boundary **2.** *[pl.]* an area near a boundary —*vt.* to set a limit or boundary to —**out of bounds 1.** beyond the boundaries **2.** forbidden —**bound'·less** *adj.*

bound·a·ry (boun'drē, -dər ē) *n., pl.* **-ries** anything marking a limit or border

bound'en (-dən) *adj.* [old pp. of BIND] obligatory *[bounden* duty*]*

bound'er *n.* [< BOUND¹] [Chiefly Brit. Colloq.] an ill-mannered fellow; cad

boun·te·ous (boun'tē əs) *adj.* [see BOUNTY] **1.** generous **2.** abundant Also **boun'ti·ful** (-tə f'l)

boun'ty (-tē) *n., pl.* **-ties** [< L. *bonus,* good] **1.** generosity **2.** a generous gift **3.** a reward or premium

bou·quet (bō kā', boo-) *n.* [Fr.] **1.** a bunch of cut flowers **2.** aroma, as of wine

bour·bon (bur'bən, boor'-) *n.* [< *Bourbon* County, Ky.] *[sometimes* **B-**] a corn whiskey

bour·geois (boor zhwä') *n., pl.* **-geois'** [Fr. < LL. *burgus,* castle] a member of the bourgeoisie —*adj.* of the bourgeoisie; conventional, smug, etc.

bour·geoi·sie (boor'zhwä'zē') *n.* [*with sing. or pl. v.*] *same as* MIDDLE CLASS

bout (bout) *n.* [< OE. *bugan,* to bend] **1.** a contest or match **2.** a period; spell

bou·tique (boo tēk') *n.* [Fr. < Gr. *apothēkē,* storehouse] a small, elegant shop

bou·ton·niere, bou·ton·nière (boot''n ir', -yer') *n.* [Fr., buttonhole] a flower worn in a buttonhole

bo·vine (bō'vīn) *adj.* [< L. *bos,* ox] **1.** of or like an ox or cow **2.** slow, dull, etc. —*n.* an ox or related animal

bow¹ (bou) *vi.* [OE. *bugan,* to bend] **1.** to bend the head or body in respect, agreement, etc. **2.** to submit; yield —*vt.* **1.** to bend (the head), as in respect **2.** to weigh (*down*); overwhelm —*n.* a bending of the head or body, as in respect

bow² (bō) *n.* [see prec.] **1.** anything curved **2.** a flexible, curved strip, as of wood, with a taut cord connecting the ends, for shooting arrows **3.** a slender stick strung with horsehairs, for playing a violin, etc. **4.** *same as* BOWKNOT —*vt., vi.* **1.** to curve like a bow (sense 2) **2.** to play (a violin, etc.) with a bow

bow³ (bou) *n.* [< LowG. or Scand.] the front part of a ship or boat —*adj.* of or near the bow

bowd·ler·ize (boud'lə rīz') *vt.* **-ized', -iz'ing** [< Thomas *Bowdler,* who published an expurgated Shakespeare (1818)] to expurgate —**bowd'ler·ism** *n.*

bow·el (bou'əl) *n.* [< L. *botulus,* sausage] **1.** an intestine, esp. of a human being **2.** *[pl.]* the inside *[the bowels* of the earth*]* —**move one's bowels** to defecate

bow·er (bou'ər) *n.* [OE. *bur,* a dwelling] a place enclosed by boughs or vines; arbor

bow·ie knife (bōō'ē, bō'ē) *n.* [< Col. J. *Bowie*

(1799?-1836)] a long, single-edged knife of steel, orig. a weapon of frontiersmen

bow·knot (bō'nät') *n.* a decorative knot, usually with two loops and two ends

bowl¹ (bōl) *n.* [OE. *bolla*] **1.** a deep, rounded dish **2.** a large drinking cup **3.** a bowllike thing or part **4.** a stadium **5.** the contents of a bowl

bowl² (bōl) *n.* [< L. *bulla,* a bubble] **1.** a heavy ball used in the game of bowls **2.** a roll of the ball in bowling —*vt., vi.* **1.** to roll (a ball) or participate in bowling **2.** to move swiftly and smoothly —**bowl over 1.** to knock over **2.** [Colloq.] to astonish —**bowl'er** *n.*

bowl·der (bōl'dər) *n. alt. sp. of* BOULDER

bow·leg (bō'leg') *n.* a leg that has an outward curvature —**bow'leg'ged** (-leg'id, -legd') *adj.*

bowl'ing *n.* **1.** a game in which a heavy ball is bowled along a wooden lane (**bowling alley**) at large, wooden pins, now usually ten **2.** *same as* BOWLS

bowls (bōlz) *n.* a bowling game played on a smooth lawn (**bowling green**)

bow·man (bō'mən) *n., pl.* **-men** an archer

bow·sprit (bou'sprit, bō'-) *n.* [prob. < Du.] a tapered spar extending forward from the bow of a sailing ship

bow tie (bō) a necktie tied in a bowknot

box¹ (bäks) *n.* [< Gr. *pyxos,* boxwood] **1.** a container, usually rectangular and with a lid **2.** its contents **3.** a boxlike thing, as a booth or stall, or a small, enclosed section of seats as in a theater **4.** a reserved or special area, as for the batter or pitcher in baseball —*vt.* to put into a box —**box in** (or **up**) to shut in or confine —**box'like'** *adj.*

box² (bäks) *n.* [< ?] a blow struck with the hand, esp. on the ear —*vt., vi.* **1.** to strike with such a blow **2.** to fight in a boxing match

box³ (bäks) *n.* [< Gr. *pyxos*] an evergreen shrub with small leaves: also **box'wood'**

box'car *n.* an enclosed railroad freight car

box'er *n.* **1.** one that boxes; prizefighter **2.** a medium-sized dog with a smooth, brown coat

box'ing *n.* the skill or sport of fighting with the fists, esp. using padded leather mittens (**boxing gloves**)

box office 1. a place selling admission tickets, as in a theater **2.** [Colloq.] drawing power, in ticket sales, of a show or performer

boy (boi) *n.* [ME. *boie*] **1.** a male child **2.** any man: familiar term **3.** a male servant: patronizing term —*interj.* [Slang] an exclamation of pleasure, surprise, etc.: often **oh, boy!** —**boy'hood'** *n.* —**boy'ish** *adj.*

boy·cott (boi'kät) *vt.* [< a Capt. *Boycott* of Ireland, so treated in 1880] to join together in refusing to deal with, buy, etc. so as to coerce, etc. —*n.* a boycotting

boy scout a member of the **Boy Scouts,** a boys' club that stresses outdoor life

boy·sen·ber·ry (boi'z'n ber'ē) *n., pl.* **-ries** [< R. *Boysen,* U.S. horticulturist] a large, purple berry, developed by crossing the raspberry, loganberry, and blackberry

Br *Chem.* bromine

Br. 1. Britain **2.** British

br. 1. branch **2.** brother **3.** brown

bra (brä) *n.* [< BRASSIERE] an undergarment worn by women to support the breasts

brace (brās) *vt.* **braced, brac'ing** [< Gr. *brachīōn,* an arm] **1.** to tie or bind **2.** to strengthen as by supporting **3.** to equip with braces **4.** to make ready as for a shock **5.** to stimulate **6.** to get a firm hold with (the hands or feet) —*n.* **1.** a couple; pair **2.** a device that clasps or connects; fastener **3.** *[pl.]* [Brit.] suspenders **4.** a device to maintain tension **5.** either of the signs {} , used to connect words, lines, etc. **6.** *a)* a device that supports, props up, etc. *[a leg brace]* *b)* [*often pl.*] a device worn to correct faulty biting of the teeth **7.** a device for holding and rotating a drilling bit —**brace up** [Colloq.] to call forth one's courage, etc.

brace and bit a tool for boring, consisting of a removable drill (*bit*) in a rotating handle (*brace*)

brace·let (brās′lit) *n.* [see BRACE] **1.** an ornamental band or chain worn about the wrist or arm **2.** [Colloq.] a handcuff

brack·en (brak′'n) *n.* [< ON.] **1.** any large, coarse fern **2.** a growth of such ferns

brack·et (brak′it) *n.* [< Gaul. *braca*, pants] **1.** a support projecting from a wall **2.** any angle-shaped support **3.** either of the signs [ ], used to enclose words, figures, etc. **4.** a classification *[a $5 to $10 price bracket]* —*vt.* **1.** to support with brackets **2.** to enclose in brackets **3.** to classify together

brack·ish (brak′ish) *adj.* [< MDu. *brak*, salty] **1.** rather briny **2.** nauseating

bract (brakt) *n.* [L. *bractea*, thin metal plate] a usually small, scalelike leaf growing at the base of a flower

brad (brad) *n.* [ON. *broddr*, a spike] a thin wire nail

brae (brā) *n.* [ON. *bra*, eyelid, brow] [Scot.] a sloping bank; hillside

brag (brag) *vt., vi.* **bragged, brag′ging** [prob. < OFr. *braguer*] to boast —*n.* **1.** boastful talk **2.** [Colloq.] a boast —**brag′ger** *n.*

brag′gart (-ərt) *n.* an offensive boaster

Brah·ma (brä′mə) the chief member of the Hindu trinity (Brahma, Vishnu, and Siva) and creator of the universe

Brah·man (brä′mən) *n., pl.* **-mans** [Hindi < Sans., worship] **1.** *a)* a member of the priestly Hindu caste *b)* a cultured, upper-class person: also **Brahmin 2.** (brä′-) a breed of cattle related to the zebu

braid (brād) *vt.* [OE. *bregdan*, move quickly] **1.** to interweave three or more strands of (hair, straw, etc.) **2.** to make thus —*n.* **1.** a braided band or strip **2.** a woven band, as of ribbon, for binding or decorating

Braille (brāl) *n.* [< L. *Braille*, its 19th-c. Fr. inventor] [*also* **b-**] a system of printing for the blind, using raised dots for symbols

brain (brān) *n.* [OE. *brægen*] **1.** the mass of nerve tissue in the cranium **2.** [*often pl.*] intelligence **3.** [Colloq.] a very intelligent person — *vt.* to dash out the brains of

brain′child′ *n.* [Colloq.] an idea, plan, etc. produced by one's mental labor

brain′less *adj.* foolish or stupid

brain′storm′ *n.* [Colloq.] a sudden inspiration

brain′wash′ *vt.* [Colloq.] to indoctrinate so intensively as to make a radical change in beliefs, attitudes, etc.

brain′y *adj.* **-i·er, -i·est** [Colloq.] mentally bright; intelligent —**brain′i·ness** *n.*

braise (brāz) *vt.* **braised, brais′ing** [< Gmc. *brasa*, live coals] to brown (meat) in fat and then simmer in a covered pan

brake[1] (brāk) *n.* [< MLowG. or ODu.] a device used in a vehicle or machine to slow or stop movement —*vt., vi.* **braked, brak′ing** to slow down or stop as with a brake

brake[2] (brāk) *n.* [MLowG., stumps] a clump of brushwood, briers, etc.

brake′man (-mən) *n., pl.* **-men** formerly, a brake operator on a railroad train, now chiefly an assistant to the conductor

bram·ble (bram′b'l) *n.* [OE. *brom*, broom] a prickly shrub related to the rose, as the raspberry, blackberry, etc. —**bram′bly** *adj.*

bran (bran) *n.* [OFr. *bren*] the husks separated from grains of wheat, rye, oats, etc.

branch (branch) *n.* [< LL. *branca*, a paw] **1.** any woody extension from a tree or shrub; limb **2.** something branchlike; specif., *a)* a division or tributary of a river *b)* a subsidiary part or extension as of an organization, family, or field of study —*vi.* **1.** to put forth branches **2.** to come out (*from* the main part) as a branch —**branch off 1.** to separate into branches **2.** to diverge —**branch out** to extend one's interests, activities, etc. —**branch′like** *adj.*

brand (brand) *n.* [OE. < *biernan*, to burn] **1.** a burning or partially burned stick **2.** a mark burned on the skin with a hot iron, as on cattle to show ownership; also, the iron used **3.** a mark of disgrace; stigma **4.** *a)* an identifying mark or label; trademark *b)* the make of a commodity *[a brand of cigars] c)* a special kind —*vt.* **1.** to mark with a brand **2.** to put a stigma on

bran·dish (bran′dish) *vt.* [< Gmc. *brand*, sword] to wave or shake menacingly

brand name the name by which a brand or make of commodity is known —**brand′-name′** *adj.*

brand′-new′ *adj.* [orig., fresh from the fire] **1.** altogether new **2.** recently acquired

bran·dy (bran′dē) *n., pl.* **-dies** [< Du. *brandewijn*, distilled wine] an alcoholic liquor distilled from wine or from fermented fruit juice —*vt.* **-died, -dy·ing** to flavor with brandy

brant (brant) *n.* [< ?] a small, dark wild goose of Europe and N. America

brash (brash) *adj.* [< ?] **1.** reckless; rash **2.** bold; impudent —**brash′ness** *n.*

brass (bras) *n.* [OE. *bræs*] **1.** a yellowish metal, an alloy of copper and zinc **2.** [*often pl.*] brass-wind musical instruments **3.** [Colloq.] bold impudence **4.** [*often with pl. v.*] [Slang] high-ranking officers or officials —**brass′y** *adj.* **-i·er, -i·est**

bras·siere, bras·sière (brə zir′) *n.* [Fr. < *bras*, an arm] *same as* BRA

brass knuckles linked metal rings or a metal bar with finger holes, worn for rough fighting

brass tacks [Colloq.] basic facts

brass winds musical instruments made of coiled metal tubes and having a cup-shaped mouthpiece —**brass′-wind′** *adj.*

brat (brat) *n.* [< Gael. *bratt*, cloth] a child, esp. when impudent and unruly: scornful or playful term

brat·wurst (brat′wərst) *n.* [G. < OHG. < *brato*, lean meat + *wurst*, sausage] highly seasoned, fresh sausage of veal and pork

bra·va·do (brə vä′dō) *n.* [< Sp. < *bravo*, BRAVE] pretended courage or feigned confidence

brave (brāv) *adj.* **brav′er, brav′est** [Fr. < L. *barbarus*, barbarous] **1.** not afraid; courageous **2.** having a fine appearance —*n.* **1.** a brave man **2.** a N. American Indian warrior — *vt.* **braved, brav′ing 1.** to face with courage **2.** to defy; dare —**brave′ly** *adv.* —**brave′ness** *n.*

brav·er·y (brā′vər ē) *n.* braveness; courage

bra·vo (brä′vō) *interj.* [It.] well done! excellent! —*n., pl.* **-vos** a shout of "bravo!"

bra·vu·ra (brə vyoor′ə) *n.* [It. < *bravo*, brave] **1.** bold daring; dash **2.** a brilliant musical passage or technique

brawl (brôl) *vi.* [< ? Du. *brallen*, to boast] to quarrel or fight noisily —*n.* a noisy quarrel or fight —**brawl′er** *n.*

brawn (brôn) *n.* [< Frank. *brado*, meat] **1.** strong, well-developed muscles **2.** muscular strength —**brawn'y** *adj.* **-i·er, -i·est**

bray (brā) *vi.* [< VL. *bragire*, cry out] to make the loud, harsh cry of a donkey —*n.* such a cry

braze (brāz) *vt.* **brazed, braz'ing** [Fr. *braser*] to solder with a metal having a high melting point

bra·zen (brā'z'n) *adj.* [< OE. *bræs*, brass] **1.** of or like brass **2.** shameless **3.** harsh and piercing —**brazen it out** to act boldly as if not ashamed —**bra'zen·ly** *adv.* —**bra'zen·ness** *n.*

bra·zier[1] (brā'zhər) *n.* [see BRAISE] a metal container to hold live coals

bra·zier[2] (brā'zhər) *n.* a person who works in brass

Bra·zil·ian (brə zil'yən) *adj.* of Brazil, its people, etc. —*n.* a native of Brazil

Bra·zil nut (brə zil') the three-sided, oily, edible seed of a tall S. American tree

breach (brēch) *n.* [< OE. *brecan*, to break] **1.** a violation of a law, contract, rule of etiquette, etc. **2.** an opening broken through a wall, defense, etc. **3.** a break in friendly relations —*vt.* to make a breach in

breach of promise a breaking of a promise to marry

bread (bred) *n.* [OE., crumb] **1.** a food baked from dough made with flour or meal, water, yeast, etc. **2.** one's livelihood: also **bread and butter 3.** [Slang] money —*vt.* to cover with bread crumbs before cooking —**break bread** to eat

breadth (bredth) *n.* [< OE. *brad*, broad] **1.** width **2.** lack of narrowness; broadness

bread'win'ner *n.* one who supports dependents by his earnings

break (brāk) *vt.* **broke, bro'ken, break'ing** [OE. *brecan*] **1.** to split or crack into pieces by force; smash **2.** to cut open the surface of (soil, the skin, etc.) **3.** to make fail or end by force [to *break* a strike] **4.** to make useless as by cracking or shattering **5.** to tame as with force **6.** *a)* to cause to get rid (*of* a habit) *b)* to get rid of (a habit) **7.** to demote **8.** to make poor or bankrupt **9.** to surpass (a record) **10.** to violate, as a law **11.** to disrupt [to *break* ranks] **12.** to interrupt (a journey, electric circuit, etc.) **13.** to lessen the force of, as a fall, by interrupting **14.** to end suddenly, as a tie score **15.** to penetrate, as darkness **16.** to disclose **17.** to decipher or solve —*vi.* **1.** to split into pieces **2.** to force one's way (*through*) **3.** to stop associating (*with*) **4.** to become useless or ruined **5.** to change suddenly [his voice *broke*] **6.** to begin suddenly [*break* into song] **7.** to become disclosed **8.** to stop activity temporarily **9.** to fall apart or collapse —*n.* **1.** a breaking **2.** a broken place **3.** a beginning to appear [the *break* of day] **4.** an interruption of regularity **5.** an interval, gap, or rest **6.** a sudden change **7.** an escape **8.** [Slang] a piece of luck —**break down 1.** to go out of working order **2.** to collapse physically or emotionally **3.** to analyze —**break in 1.** to enter forcibly **2.** to interrupt **3.** to train (a beginner) **4.** to get the stiffness out of —**break off** to stop abruptly —**break out 1.** to escape **2.** to get pimples or a rash —**break up 1.** to separate; disperse **2.** to stop **3.** [Colloq.] to distress **4.** [Colloq.] to laugh or make laugh —**break'a·ble** *adj.*

break'age (-ij) *n.* **1.** a breaking **2.** things broken **3.** loss or damage due to breaking, or the sum allowed for this

break'down' *n.* **1.** a breaking down **2.** a failure of health **3.** an analysis

break'er *n.* **1.** one that breaks **2.** a wave breaking into foam

break·fast (brek'fəst) *n.* the first meal of the day —*vi.* to eat breakfast

break'neck' *adj.* dangerously fast

break'through' *n.* **1.** a breaking through against resistance **2.** a great discovery

break'up' *n.* **1.** dispersion **2.** disintegration **3.** collapse **4.** termination

break'wa'ter *n.* a barrier to break the impact of waves, as before a harbor

breast (brest) *n.* [OE. *breost*] **1.** either of two milk-secreting glands at the upper, front part of a woman's body **2.** the upper, front part of the body **3.** the part of a garment, etc. covering the breast **4.** the breast regarded as the center of emotions —*vt.* to face firmly; oppose —**make a clean breast of** to confess (crimes, faults, etc.) fully

breast'bone' *n. same as* STERNUM

breast'-feed' *vt.* **-fed', -feed'ing** to feed (a baby) milk from the breast; suckle

breast'plate' *n.* armor for the breast

breast stroke a swimming stroke with the arms brought out sideways from the chest

breast'work' *n.* a low wall put up quickly as a defense, esp. to protect gunners

breath (breth) *n.* [OE. *bræth*, odor] **1.** air taken into and let out of the lungs **2.** respiration **3.** power to breathe easily **4.** life; spirit **5.** a fragrant odor **6.** a slight breeze **7.** a whisper; murmur —**below** (or **under**) **one's breath** in a whisper —**catch one's breath 1.** to gasp **2.** to pause or rest —**out of breath** gasping, as from running

breathe (brēth) *vi., vt.* **breathed, breath'ing** [see prec.] **1.** to take (air) into the lungs and let out again; inhale and exhale **2.** to live **3.** to instill **4.** to speak or sing softly; whisper **5.** to rest

breath·er (brē'thər) *n.* **1.** one that breathes **2.** [Colloq.] a pause as for rest

breath·less (breth'lis) *adj.* **1.** lacking breath **2.** dead **3.** gasping **4.** unable to breathe easily because of emotion **5.** stifling —**breath'less·ly** *adv.*

breath'tak'ing *adj.* very exciting

bred (bred) *pt. & pp. of* BREED

breech (brēch) *n.* [OE. *brec*] **1.** the buttocks **2.** the part of a gun behind the barrel

breech'cloth' *n. same as* LOINCLOTH

breech·es (brich'iz) *n.pl.* **1.** trousers reaching to the knees **2.** [Colloq.] any trousers

breed (brēd) *vt.* **bred, breed'ing** [< OE. *brod*, fetus] **1.** to bring forth (offspring) **2.** to originate; produce **3.** to raise (animals) **4.** to rear; train —*vi.* **1.** to be produced **2.** to reproduce —*n.* **1.** a stock; strain **2.** a sort; type —**breed'er** *n.*

breed'ing *n.* **1.** the producing of young **2.** good upbringing **3.** the producing of plants and animals, esp. so as to improve the stock

breeze (brēz) *n.* [< Fr. *brise*] **1.** a gentle wind **2.** [Colloq.] an easy task —*vi.* **breezed, breez'ing** [Slang] to move or go briskly

breeze'way' *n.* a covered passageway, as between a home and a garage

breez·y (brēz'ē) *adj.* **-i·er, -i·est 1.** with breezes **2.** light and gay —**breez'i·ly** *adv.*

breth·ren (breth'rən) *n.pl.* brothers: now chiefly in religious use

breve (brev, brēv) *n.* [It. < L. *brevis*, brief] **1.** a mark (˘) put over a short vowel **2.** *Music* a note equal to two whole notes

bre·vet (brə vet') *n.* [< L. *brevis*, brief] *Mil.* a commission giving higher honorary rank without more pay —*vt.* **-vet'ted** or **-vet'ed, -vet'-ting** or **-vet'ing** to give a brevet to

bre·vi·ar·y (brē'vē er'ē, brĕv'yər ē) *n., pl.* **-ies** [< L. *brevis*, brief] *R.C.Ch.* a book of prayers, hymns, etc. to be said daily by priests and other clerics

brev·i·ty (brev'ə tē) *n.* [< L. *brevis*, brief] the quality of being brief or concise

brew (brōō) *vt.* [OE. *breowan*] **1.** to make (beer, ale, etc.) from malt and hops by boiling and fermenting **2.** to make (tea, coffee, etc.) by steeping or boiling **3.** to plot; scheme —*vi.* **1.** to brew beer, ale, etc. **2.** to begin to form: said of a storm, trouble, etc. —*n.* a brewed beverage — **brew'er** *n.*

brew'er·y (-ər ē) *n., pl.* **-ies** an establishment where beer, ale, etc. are brewed

bri·ar' (brī'ər) *n. same as* BRIER[1]

bri·ar' (brī'ər) *n.* **1.** *same as* BRIER[2] **2.** a tobacco pipe made of brierroot

bribe (brīb) *n.* [< OFr. *briber*, beg] anything given or promised as an inducement, esp. to do something illegal or wrong —*vt.* **bribed, brib'ing** to offer or give a bribe to —**brib'er** *n.* —**brib'er·y** *n.*

bric-a-brac (brik'ə brak') *n.* [< Fr. *à bric et à brac*, by hook or crook] small, ornamental objects used to decorate a room

brick (brik) *n.* [< MDu. *breken*] **1.** an oblong block of baked clay, used as in building; also, such blocks collectively **2.** anything bricklike in shape —*adj.* of or like brick —*vt.* to build or cover with brick

brick'bat' *n.* **1.** a piece of brick, esp. when used as a missile **2.** an unfavorable remark

brick'lay'ing *n.* the act or work of building or covering with bricks —**brick'lay'er** *n.*

brid·al (brīd''l) *adj.* [OE. *bryd ealo*, marriage feast] of a bride or wedding

bride (brīd) *n.* [OE. *bryd*] a woman just married or about to be married

bride'groom' *n.* [< OE. *bryd*, bride + *guma*, man] a man just married or about to be married

brides·maid (brīdz'mād') *n.* a young woman attending the bride at a wedding

bridge' (brij) *n.* [OE. *brycge*] **1.** a structure built over a river, etc. to provide a way across **2.** a thing providing connection, contact, etc. **3.** the bony part of the nose **4.** a raised platform on a ship **5.** a mounting for false teeth —*vt.* **bridged, bridg'ing** to build or be a bridge over

bridge' (brij) *n.* [< ? Russ.] a card game for two pairs of players in which they bid for the right to name the trump suit or declare no-trump

bridge'head' *n.* a fortified position established by an attacking force in enemy territory

bridge'work' *n.* a dental bridge or bridges

bri·dle (brīd''l) *n.* [< OE. *bregdan*, to pull] **1.** a head harness for guiding a horse **2.** anything that controls or restrains —*vt.* **-dled, -dling 1.** to put a bridle on **2.** to hold in check; restrain — *vi.* to draw one's head back as in anger

bridle path a path for horseback riding

brief (brēf) *adj.* [< L. *brevis*] **1.** short **2.** concise **3.** curt —*n.* **1.** a summary, specif. of the main points of a law case **2.** [*pl.*] legless underpants —*vt.* **1.** to summarize **2.** to give the pertinent facts to —**brief'ly** *adv.* —**brief'ness** *n.*

brief'case' *n.* a flat, flexible case for carrying papers, books, etc.

bri·er' (brī'ər) *n.* [OE. *brer*] a thorny bush, as a bramble —**bri'er·y** *adj.*

bri·er' (brī'ər) *n.* [Fr. *bruyère*] **1.** a heath of S Europe: its root (**brierroot**) is used for tobacco pipes **2.** *same as* BRIAR[2] (sense 2)

brig' (brig) *n.* [< It. *brigantino*, pirate ship] a two-masted ship with square sails

brig' (brig) *n.* [< ?] **1.** a prison on a U.S. warship **2.** [Mil. Slang] the guardhouse; jail

bri·gade (bri gād') *n.* [Fr. < It. *briga*, strife] **1.** a military unit composed of two or more battalions **2.** a group of people organized to do something [a fire *brigade*]

brig·a·dier (brig'ə dir') *n.* the commander of a brigade

brigadier general *U.S. Mil.* an officer ranking just above a colonel

brig·and (brig'ənd) *n.* [see BRIGADE] a bandit, esp. one of a roving band

bright (brīt) *adj.* [OE. *bryht*] **1.** full of light **2.** brilliant in color or sound **3.** lively; cheerful **4.** mentally quick; clever **5.** favorable **6.** illustrious —*adv.* in a bright way —**bright'ly** *adv.* — **bright'ness** *n.*

bright'en (-'n) *vt., vi.* to make or become bright or brighter

bril·liant (bril'yənt) *adj.* [Fr. < It. *brillare*, to sparkle] **1.** shining brightly **2.** vivid **3.** very splendid **4.** very intelligent, talented, etc. —*n.* a gem, esp. a diamond, cut with many facets to increase its sparkle —**bril'liance, bril'lian·cy** *n.* —**bril'liant·ly** *adv.*

brim (brim) *n.* [OE., sea] **1.** the topmost edge of a cup, glass, etc. **2.** a projecting rim, as of a hat —*vt., vi.* **brimmed, brim'ming** to fill or be full to the brim —**brim'less** *adj.*

brim'ful' *adj.* full to the brim

brim·stone (brim'stōn') *n.* [< OE. *biernan*, to burn + *stan*, a stone] *same as* SULFUR

brin·dle (brin'd'l) *adj. same as* BRINDLED —*n.* a brindled color

brin'dled (-d'ld) *adj.* [prob. < ME. *brennen*, to burn] gray or tawny, along with darker markings

brine (brīn) *n.* [OE.] **1.** water full of salt **2.** the sea or ocean —*vt.* **brined, brin'ing** to soak in or treat with brine —**brin'y** *adj.* **-i·er, -i·est**

bring (brin) *vt.* **brought, bring'ing** [OE. *bringan*] **1.** to carry or lead "here" or to where the speaker will be **2.** to make happen, be, etc. **3.** to lead to an action or belief **4.** to sell for [to *bring* a high price] —**bring about** to effect — **bring forth** to give birth to or produce —**bring off** to accomplish —**bring out 1.** to make clear; reveal **2.** to present publicly, as a new book or play —**bring to** to revive (one unconscious) — **bring up 1.** to rear (a child) **2.** to introduce, as into discussion **3.** to cough or vomit up

brink (brink) *n.* [MLowG. or Dan., shore] the edge, esp. at the top of a steep place; verge

bri·oche (brē ōsh', -ôsh') *n.* [Fr.] a light roll made with flour, butter, eggs, and yeast

bri·quette, bri·quet (bri ket') *n.* [Fr.] a brick as of pressed coal dust, for fuel

brisk (brisk) *adj.* [< ? Fr. *brusque*, brusque] **1.** quick in manner; energetic **2.** bracing, keen, sharp, etc. **3.** active; busy —**brisk'ly** *adv.* — **brisk'ness** *n.*

bris·ket (bris'kit) *n.* [ME. *brusket*] meat cut from the breast of an animal

bris·tle (bris''l) *n.* [OE. *byrst*] any short, stiff hair —*vi.* **-tled, -tling 1.** to stand up stiffly, like bristles **2.** to have the bristles stand up thus **3.** to stiffen as with fear or anger **4.** to be thickly covered (*with*) —**bris'tly** (-lē) *adj.* **-tli·er, -tli·est**

Brit. **1.** Britain **2.** British

britch·es (brich'iz) *n.pl.* [Colloq.] *same as* BREECHES (sense 2)

Brit·i·cism (brit'ə siz'm) *n.* a word or idiom characteristic of British English

Brit·ish (brit'ish) *adj.* **1.** of Great Britain or its people **2.** of the British Commonwealth —*n.* English as spoken and written in England — **the British** the people of Great Britain

British thermal unit a unit of heat equal to about 252 calories

Brit·on (brit′'n) *n.* **1.** a member of an early Celtic people of S Britain **2.** a native or inhabitant of Great Britain, esp. an Englishman

brit·tle (brit′'l) *adj.* [< OE. *breotan,* to break] easily broken or shattered —*n.* a brittle candy with nuts in it —**brit′tle·ness** *n.*

bro. *pl.* **bros.** brother

broach (brōch) *n.* [< ML. *brocca,* a spike] **1.** a tapered bit for enlarging holes **2.** same as BROOCH —*vt.* **1.** to make a hole in so as to let out liquid **2.** to start a discussion of

broad (brôd) *adj.* [OE. *brad*] **1.** of large extent from side to side; wide **2.** spacious [*broad* prairies] **3.** clear; open; full [*broad* daylight] **4.** obvious [a *broad* hint] **5.** ribald [a *broad* joke] **6.** tolerant; liberal **7.** wide in range **8.** main or general —*n.* the broad part of anything — **broad′ly** *adv.* —**broad′ness** *n.*

broad′cast′ (-kast′) *vt., vi.* -**cast′** or, in radio, occas. -**cast′ed, -cast′ing 1.** to scatter or spread widely **2.** to transmit by radio or TV —*adj.* **1.** widely scattered **2.** of, for, or by radio or TV broadcasting —*n.* **1.** a broadcasting **2.** a radio or TV program —*adv.* far and wide —**broad′-cast′er** *n.*

broad′cloth′ *n.* a fine, smooth cloth

broad′en (-'n) *vt., vi.* to widen; expand

broad jump *earlier term for* LONG JUMP

broad′loom′ *adj.* woven on a broad loom, as rugs

broad′-mind′ed *adj.* tolerant of unconventional ideas or behavior —**broad′-mind′ed·ly** *adv.* —**broad′-mind′ed·ness** *n.*

broad′side′ *n.* **1.** the side of a ship above the waterline **2.** the firing of all guns at once on one side of a ship **3.** a heavy critical attack **4.** a large printed sheet, as of advertising —*adv.* **1.** with the side facing **2.** indiscriminately

broad′sword′ *n.* a broad-bladed sword for slashing

bro·cade (brō kād′) *n.* [< Sp. < It. *broccare,* embroider] a rich cloth with a raised design woven into it —*vt.* -**cad′ed, -cad′ing** to weave such a design into

broc·co·li (bräk′ə lē) *n.* [It. < ML. *brocca,* a spike] a kind of cauliflower, with loose heads of tiny buds

bro·chette (brō shet′) *n.* [Fr.] a skewer for broiling chunks of meat

bro·chure (brō shoor′) *n.* [Fr. < *brocher,* to stitch] a pamphlet

brogue′ (brōg) *n.* [prob. < Ir. *barróg,* a hold] dialectal pronunciation, esp. that of English by the Irish

brogue² (brōg) *n.* [Ir. *brōg,* a shoe] a man's heavy oxford shoe

broil (broil) *vt., vi.* [< OFr. *bruillir*] to cook by exposing to direct heat —*n.* a broiling

broil′er *n.* **1.** a pan, stove part, etc. for broiling **2.** a chicken for broiling

broke (brōk) *pt. of* BREAK —*adj.* [Colloq.] **1.** having no money **2.** bankrupt

bro·ken (brō′k'n) *pp. of* BREAK —*adj.* **1.** splintered, fractured, etc. **2.** not in working order **3.** violated, as a promise **4.** disrupted as by divorce [a *broken* home] **5.** weakened or beaten **6.** interrupted **7.** imperfectly spoken [*broken* English] **8.** tamed —**bro′ken·ly** *adv.* —**bro′ken·ness** *n.*

bro′ken-down′ *adj.* **1.** sick or worn out, as by old age **2.** out of order; useless

bro′ken-heart′ed *adj.* crushed by sorrow, grief, etc.

bro·ker (brō′kər) *n.* [< OFr. *brochier,* to

broach] **1.** an agent for contracts or sales **2.** a stockbroker

bro′ker·age (-ij) *n.* **1.** a broker's business **2.** a broker's fee

bro·mide (brō′mīd) *n.* **1.** a compound of bromine with another element or a radical **2.** potassium bromide, used as a sedative **3.** a trite saying

bro·mine (brō′mēn) *n.* [< Gr. *brōmos,* stench] a chemical element, usually a reddish-brown, corrosive liquid: symbol, Br

bron·chi (brän′kī) *n. pl. of* BRONCHUS

bronchial tubes the bronchi and branching tubes

bron·chi′tis (-kīt′is) *n.* inflammation of the bronchial tubes

bron·chus (brän′kəs) *n., pl.* -**chi** (-kī) [< Gr. *bronchos,* windpipe] either of the two main branches of the trachea, or windpipe —**bron′-chi·al** (-kē əl) *adj.*

bron·co (brän′kō) *n., pl.* -**cos** [< Sp., rough] a wild or partially tamed horse or pony of the western U.S.: also sp. **bron′cho,** *pl.* -**chos**

bron′co·bust′er *n.* [Colloq.] a cowboy who tames broncos —**bron′co·bust′ing** *n.*

bron·to·sau·rus (brän′tə sôr′əs) *n., pl.* -**rus·es, -ri** (-ī) [< Gr. *brontē,* thunder + *sauros,* lizard] a huge American dinosaur

bronze (bränz) *n.* [Fr. < It. *bronzo*] **1.** an alloy of copper and tin **2.** a reddish-brown color — *adj.* of or like bronze —*vt.* **bronzed, bronz′ing** to color bronze

brooch (brōch, brōoch) *n.* [see BROACH] a large ornamental pin with a clasp

brood (brōod) *n.* [OE. *brod*] **1.** a group of birds hatched at one time **2.** the children in a family —*vt.* to sit on and hatch (eggs) —*vi.* **1.** to brood eggs **2.** to worry (often with *on, over,* or *about*)

brood′er *n.* **1.** one that broods **2.** a heated shelter for raising fowl

brook¹ (brook) *n.* [OE. *broc*] a small stream

brook² (brook) *vt.* [OE. *brucan,* to use] to put up with; endure

broom (brōom, broom) *n.* [OE. *brom,* brushwood] **1.** a shrub with yellow flowers **2.** a bundle of long, stiff fibers attached to a long handle (**broom′stick′**), used for sweeping

bros. brothers

broth (brôth) *n.* [OE.] a clear, thin soup made by boiling meat, etc. in water

broth·el (brôth′əl, bräth′-) *n.* [< OE. *broethan,* waste away] a house of prostitution

broth·er (bruth′ər) *n., pl.* -**ers;** chiefly religious, **breth′ren** [OE. *brothor*] **1.** a male as related to other children of his parents **2.** a brotherlike friend **3.** a male of the same race, creed, profession, etc. as one's own **4.** a lay member of a men's religious order

broth′er·hood′ *n.* **1.** the state of being a brother or brothers **2.** an association of men united in a common interest, work, etc.

broth′er-in-law′ *n., pl.* **broth′ers-in-law′ 1.** the brother of one's spouse **2.** the husband of one's sister **3.** the husband of the sister of one's spouse

broth′er·ly *adj.* **1.** of or like a brother **2.** friendly, kind, loyal, etc.

brougham (brōom, brōo′əm) *n.* [< Lord *Brougham,* 19th-c. Brit. statesman] **1.** a closed carriage with the driver's seat outside **2.** an early type of automobile

brought (brôt) *pt. & pp. of* BRING

brow (brou) *n.* [OE. *bru*] **1.** the eyebrow **2.** the forehead **3.** the edge of a cliff

brow′beat′ (-bēt′) *vt.* -**beat′, -beat′en, -beat′ing**

to intimidate with harsh, stern looks and talk —**brow'beat'er** *n.*

brown (broun) *adj.* [OE. *brun*] **1.** having the color of chocolate or coffee, a mixture of red, black, and yellow **2.** tanned or dark-skinned — *n.* brown color —*vt., vi.* to make or become brown —**brown'ish** *adj.*

brown·ie (broun'ē) *n.* **1.** a small, helpful elf **2.** [B-] a girl scout aged seven or eight **3.** a bar cut from a flat chocolate cake

brown'out' *n.* a dimming of lights in a city, as during an electric power shortage

brown'stone' *n.* a reddish-brown sandstone, used for building

brown study deep thought; reverie

brown sugar soft sugar with a brown coating

browse (brouz) *n.* [< OS. *brustian*, to sprout] leaves, shoots, etc. which animals feed on —*vt., vi.* browsed, brows'ing **1.** to nibble at (leaves, shoots, etc.) **2.** to examine (a book, articles for sale, etc.) casually

bruise (brōōz) *vt.* bruised, bruis'ing [< OE. *brysan*, crush] **1.** to injure and discolor (body tissue) without breaking the skin **2.** to injure the surface of (fruit, etc.) **3.** to hurt (the feelings, spirit, etc.) —*vi.* to be or become bruised —*n.* a bruised area, as of tissue

bruis'er *n.* a strong, pugnacious man

bruit (brōōt) *vt.* [< OFr. *bruire*, to rumble] to spread (*about*) a rumor of

brunch (brunch) *n.* [BR(EAKFAST) + (L)UNCH] [Colloq.] a combined breakfast and lunch

bru·net (brōō net') *adj.* [Fr. < OHG. *brun*, brown] **1.** having black or dark-brown hair, often with dark eyes and complexion **2.** having a dark color, as hair —*n.* a brunet person

bru·nette' (-net') *adj.* [Fr., fem. of prec.] same as BRUNET —*n.* a brunette woman or girl

brunt (brunt) *n.* [< ? ON. *bruni*, heat] **1.** the shock (of an attack) or the impact (of a blow) **2.** the heaviest or hardest part

brush' (brush) *n.* [< OFr. *broce*, bush] **1.** brushwood **2.** sparsely settled country **3.** a device for cleaning, painting, etc., having bristles, wires, etc. fastened into a back **4.** a brushing **5.** a light, grazing stroke **6.** a bushy tail, as of a fox —*vt.* **1.** to clean, paint, etc. with a brush **2.** to apply, remove, etc. as with a brush **3.** to graze in passing —*vi.* to graze past something —**brush off** [Slang] to dismiss — **brush up** to refresh one's memory

brush' (brush) *vi.* [ME. *bruschen*] to move with a rush; hurry —*n.* a short, quick fight

brush'off' *n.* [Slang] an abrupt dismissal: esp. in the phrase **give** (or **get**) **the brushoff**

brush'wood' *n.* **1.** chopped-off tree branches **2.** a thick growth as of shrubs

brusque (brusk) *adj.* [Fr. < ML. *bruscus*, brushwood] rough or abrupt in manner; curt: also **brusk** —**brusque'ly** *adv.* —**brusque'ness** *n.*

Brus·sels sprouts (brus''lz) **1.** a plant with small cabbagelike heads on an erect stem **2.** these edible heads

bru·tal (brōōt''l) *adj.* **1.** like a brute; savage, cruel, etc. **2.** very harsh —**bru'tal·ly** *adv.*

bru·tal·i·ty (brōō tal'ə tē) *n.* **1.** a being brutal **2.** *pl.* -**ties** a brutal act

bru'tal·ize' (-īz') *vt., vi.* -**ized', -iz'ing** to make or become brutal —**bru'tal·i·za'tion** *n.*

brute (brōōt) *adj.* [< L. *brutus*, irrational] **1.** not able to reason [a *brute* beast] **2.** of or like an animal; cruel, stupid, etc. —*n.* **1.** an animal **2.** a brutal person —**brut'ish** *adj.*

B.S., B.Sc. Bachelor of Science

b.s. 1. balance sheet **2.** bill of sale

B.t.u. British thermal unit(s): also **B.T.U.**

bu. 1. bureau **2.** bushel(s)

bub·ble (bub''l) *n.* [echoic] **1.** a film of liquid forming a ball around air or gas **2.** a tiny ball of air or gas in a liquid or solid **3.** a transparent dome **4.** a plausible scheme that proves worthless —*vi.* -**bled, -bling 1.** to make bubbles **2.** to make a gurgling sound —*vt.* to form bubbles in —**bub'bly** *adj.*

bubble gum a chewing gum used to blow bubbles

bu·bo (byōō'bō) *n., pl.* -**boes** [< Gr. *boubōn*, groin] an inflamed swelling of a lymph gland, esp. in the groin

bu·bon'ic plague (-bän'ik) a contagious disease marked by buboes, fever, and delirium

buc·ca·neer (buk'ə nir') *n.* [Fr. *boucanier*] a pirate, or sea robber

buck' (buk) *n.* [OE. *bucca*, male goat] **1.** a male deer, goat, etc. **2.** the act of bucking **3.** [Colloq.] a vigorous young man —*vi.* **1.** to rear upward quickly, as to throw off a rider: said of a horse **2.** [Colloq.] to resist something as if plunging against it —*vt.* **1.** to charge against, as in football **2.** to throw by bucking **3.** [Colloq.] to resist stubbornly —**buck for** [Slang] to work eagerly for (a promotion, etc.) —**buck up** [Colloq.] to cheer up

buck' (buk) *n.* [Du. *zaagbok*] **1.** a sawbuck; sawhorse **2.** a gymnastic apparatus for vaulting over

buck' (buk) *n.* [< ?] [Slang] a dollar —**pass the buck** [Colloq.] to shift the blame or responsibility to another

buck·a·roo (buk'ə rōō', buk'ə rōō') *n., pl.* -**roos'** [prob. < Gullah *buckra*, white man] a cowboy

buck'board' *n.* [< ?] an open carriage whose floorboards rest on the axles

buck·et (buk'it) *n.* [< OE. *buc*, pitcher] **1.** a round container with a curved handle, for carrying water, coal, etc. **2.** the amount held by a bucket: also **buck'et·ful'**, *pl.* -**fuls' 3.** a thing like a bucket, as the scoop on a steam shovel —**kick the bucket** [Slang] to die

bucket seat a single contoured seat with a movable back, as in sports cars

buck·eye (buk'ī') *n.* [BUCK¹ + EYE: from the appearance of the seed] **1.** a tree with large, spiny capsules enclosing shiny brown seeds **2.** the seed

buck·le' (buk''l) *n.* [< L. *buccula*, cheek strap of a helmet] **1.** a clasp for fastening a strap, belt, etc. **2.** a clasplike ornament —*vt., vi.* -**led, -ling** to fasten with a buckle —**buckle down** to apply oneself

buck·le' (buk''l) *vt., vi.* -**led, -ling** [prob. < Du. *bukken*, to bend] to bend or crumple —*n.* a bend, bulge, etc. —**buckle under** to yield

buck·ler (buk'lər) *n.* [OFr. *bocler*] a small, round shield worn on the arm

buck'-pass'er *n.* [Colloq.] one who regularly shifts blame or responsibility to someone else —**buck'-pass'ing** *n.*

buck·ram (buk'rəm) *n.* [prob. < *Bukhara*, city in Uzbek S.S.R.] a coarse, stiffened cloth used in bookbinding, etc.

buck·saw (buk'sô') *n.* [see BUCK²] a saw set in a frame and held with both hands in cutting wood

buck'shot' *n.* a large lead shot for shooting deer and other large game

buck'skin' *n.* **1.** a soft yellowish-gray leather made from the skins of deer or sheep **2.** [*pl.*] clothes made of buckskin

buck'tooth' *n., pl.* -**teeth'** a projecting front tooth —**buck'toothed'** *adj.*

buck'wheat' *n.* [< OE. *boc*, beech + WHEAT]

1. a plant with beechnut-shaped seeds **2.** a dark flour made from the seeds

bu·col·ic (byo͞o käl′ik) *adj.* [< Gr. *boukolos,* herdsman] **1.** of shepherds; pastoral **2.** of country life; rustic —*n.* a pastoral poem

bud (bud) *n.* [ME. *budde*] **1.** a small swelling on a plant, from which a shoot, leaf, or flower develops **2.** an early stage of development —*vi.* **bud′ded, bud′ding 1.** to put forth buds **2.** to begin to develop

Bud·dhism (boo͞od′iz'm, boo͞o′diz'm) *n.* [< *Buddha,* Indian founder in 6th c. B.C.] a religion of Asia teaching that by right living one achieves Nirvana —**Bud′dhist** *n., adj.*

bud·dy (bud′ē) *n., pl.* **-dies** [< ? Brit. dial.] [Colloq.] a comrade

budge (buj) *vt., vi.* **budged, budg′ing** [Fr. *bouger,* move] to move a little

budg·et (buj′it) *n.* [< L. *bulga,* a bag] **1.** a stock of items **2.** a plan adjusting expenses to income **3.** the estimated cost of living, operating, etc. —*vt.* **1.** to put on a budget **2.** to schedule *[budget* your time*]* —**budg′et·ar′y** *adj.* —**budg′et·er** *n.*

buff (buf) *n.* [< It. *bufalo,* BUFFALO] **1.** a heavy, soft, brownish-yellow leather **2.** a military coat made of this **3.** a dull brownish yellow **4.** [Colloq.] a devotee; fan —*adj.* **1.** made of buff **2.** of the color buff —*vt.* to clean or shine with leather or a leather-covered wheel —**in the buff** naked —**buff′er** *n.*

buf·fa·lo (buf′ə lō′) *n., pl.* **-loes′, -los′, -lo′** [< It. < Gr. *bous,* ox] **1.** any of various oxen, as the water buffalo of India **2.** popularly, the American bison —*vt.* **-loed′, -lo′ing** [Slang] to baffle, bluff, etc.

buff·er (buf′ər) *n.* [< OFr. *buffe,* a blow] anything that lessens shock, as of collision

buf·fet′ (buf′it) *n.* [OFr. < *buffe,* a blow] a blow or shock —*vt.* **1.** to punch or slap **2.** to thrust about —*vi.* to struggle

buf·fet² (bə fā′, boo-) *n.* [Fr.] **1.** a sideboard **2.** a sideboard or table at which guests serve themselves food **3.** a meal served thus

buf·foon (bə foon′) *n.* [< Fr. < It. *buffare,* to jest] a person who is always trying to be funny; clown —**buf·foon′er·y** *n.*

bug (bug) *n.* [prob. < W. *bwg,* hobgoblin] **1.** an insect with sucking mouthparts **2.** any insect **3.** [Colloq.] a germ or virus **4.** [Slang] a defect, as in a machine **5.** [Slang] a hidden microphone —*vt.* **bugged, bug′ging** [Slang] **1.** to hide a microphone in (a room, etc.) **2.** to annoy, anger, etc.

bug′a·boo (-ə boo͞o′) *n., pl.* **-boos′** a bugbear

bug′bear′ *n.* [BUG + BEAR²] **1.** an imaginary terror **2.** a cause of needless fear

bug·gy¹ (bug′ē) *n., pl.* **-gies** [< ?] **1.** a light, one-horse carriage with one seat **2.** a small carriage for a baby

bug·gy² (bug′ē) *adj.* **-gi·er, -gi·est 1.** infested with bugs **2.** [Slang] mentally ill

bu·gle (byo͞o′g'l) *n.* [< L. *buculus,* young ox] a brass-wind instrument like a small trumpet, usually without valves —*vi., vt.* **-gled, -gling** to signal by blowing a bugle

build (bild) *vt.* **built, build′ing** [< OE. *bold,* a house] **1.** to make by putting together material, parts, etc.; construct **2.** to establish; base *[build* a theory on facts*]* —*vi.* **1.** *a)* to put up buildings *b)* to have a house, etc. built **2.** to grow or intensify —*n.* form or figure *[*a stocky *build]* —**build′er** *n.*

build′ing *n.* **1.** anything that is built; structure **2.** the work or business of making houses, etc.

build′up′, build′-up′ *n.* [Colloq.] **1.** favorable publicity or praise **2.** growth or expansion

built′-in′ *adj.* **1.** made as part of a building **2.** inherent

bulb (bulb) *n.* [< Gr. *bolbos*] **1.** an underground bud with roots and a short, scaly stem, as in a lily or onion **2.** a corm, tuber, or tuberous root resembling a bulb, as in a crocus **3.** anything shaped like a bulb —**bul·bar** (bul′bər) *adj.* —**bul′bous** *adj.*

bulge (bulj) *n.* [< L. *bulga,* a bag] an outward swelling; protuberance —*vi., vt.* **bulged, bulg′ing** to swell out —**bulg′y** *adj.*

bulk (bulk) *n.* [ON. *bulki,* a heap] **1.** size, mass, or volume, esp. if great **2.** the main mass; largest part —*vi.* to have, or to increase in, size or importance —*adj.* **1.** aggregate **2.** not packaged —**bulk′y** *adj.* **-i·er, -i·est**

bulk·head (bulk′hed′) *n.* [< ON. *balkr,* partition + HEAD] **1.** an upright partition, as in a ship, for protection against fire or leakage **2.** a retaining wall

bull¹ (bool) *n.* [OE. *bula,* a steer] **1.** the adult male of any bovine animal, as the ox, or of certain other large animals, as the elephant, whale, etc. **2.** a person who buys stocks, etc. expecting, or seeking to bring about, a rise in their prices **3.** [Slang] insincere talk; nonsense —*adj.* **1.** male **2.** rising in price *[*a *bull* market*]* —**take the bull by the horns** to deal boldly with danger or difficulty —**bull′ish** *adj.*

bull² (bool) *n.* [< LL. *bulla,* a seal] an official document from the Pope

bull′dog′ *n.* a short-haired, square-jawed, heavily built dog noted for its stubborn grip —*adj.* like a bulldog; stubborn —*vt.* **-dogged′, -dog′ging** to throw (a steer) by seizing its horns and twisting its neck

bull′doze′ (-dōz′) *vt.* **-dozed′, -doz′ing** [< *bull,* a flogging + DOSE] **1.** [Colloq.] to force or frighten by threatening; intimidate **2.** to move, push, etc. with a bulldozer

bull′doz′er *n.* a tractor with a large, shovellike blade in front for pushing earth, etc.

bul·let (bool′it) *n.* [< L. *bulla,* a knob] a small, shaped piece of metal to be shot from a firearm

bul·le·tin (bool′ət 'n) *n.* [Fr. < It. < LL. *bulla,* a seal] **1.** a brief statement of late news **2.** a regular publication, as for members of a society

bul′let·proof′ *adj.* that bullets cannot pierce —*vt.* to make bulletproof

bull′fight′ (-fīt′) *n.* a public show in which a bull is provoked in various ways and then usually killed with a sword by a matador —**bull′-fight′er** *n.*

bull′finch′ *n.* a small European songbird

bull′frog′ *n.* a large N. American frog with a deep, loud croak

bull′head′ed (-hed′id) *adj.* blindly stubborn —**bull′head′ed·ness** *n.*

bull′horn′ *n.* a portable electronic voice amplifier

bul·lion (bool′yən) *n.* [< OFr. *billon,* small coin] ingots or bars of gold or silver

bull·ock (bool′ək) *n.* [< OE. dim. of *bula,* steer] a castrated bull; steer

bull′pen′ *n.* **1.** [Colloq.] a temporary detention room in a jail **2.** *Baseball* a practice area for relief pitchers

bull′s-eye (boolz′ī′) *n.* **1.** the central mark of a target **2.** a direct hit

bull terrier a strong, lean, white dog, a cross between the bulldog and the terrier

bul·ly¹ (bool′ē) *n., pl.* **-lies** [< MHG. *buole,* lover; later infl. by BULL¹] one who hurts or browbeats those who are weaker —*vt., vi.* **-lied,**

-ly·ing to act the bully (toward) —*adj., interj.*
[Colloq.] fine; very good
bul·ly² (bool'ē) *n.* [< Fr. *bouillir*, to boil]
canned or corned beef: also **bully beef**
bul·rush (bool'rush') *n.* [< OE. *bol*, tree trunk
+ *risc*, a rush] 1. a marsh plant of the sedge
family 2. *Bible* papyrus
bul·wark (bool'wərk) *n.* [MDu. *bolwerc*] 1. a
defensive wall; rampart 2. a defense or protection —*vt.* to be a bulwark for
bum (bum) *n.* [prob. < G. *bummeln*, go slowly]
[Colloq.] 1. a vagrant; beggar; loafer 2. a devotee, as of golf or tennis —*vi.* **bummed, bum'-
ming** [Colloq.] to live as a bum or by begging
—*vt.* [Slang] to get by sponging; cadge —*adj.*
bum'mer, bum'mest [Slang] 1. poor in quality
2. false 3. lame —**on the bum** [Colloq.] 1. living
as a vagrant 2. out of repair
bum·ble·bee (bum'b'l bē') *n.* [< ME.
bomblen, to buzz] a large, hairy, yellow-and-
black social bee
bum·bling (bum'bliŋ) *adj.* [< obs. *bumble*,
buzz] self-important in a blundering way
bum·mer (bum'ər) *n.* [Slang] an unpleasant
experience, esp. with drugs
bump (bump) *vt., vi.* [echoic] 1. to collide
(with); hit against 2. [Slang] to displace, as
from a job —*n.* 1. a light blow; jolt 2. a swelling, esp. one caused by a blow —**bump into**
[Colloq.] to meet unexpectedly —**bump off**
[Slang] to murder —**bump'y** *adj.* **-i·er, -i·est**
bump·er¹ (bum'pər) *n.* a device for absorbing
the shock of a collision, esp. a bar at the front
or back of an automobile
bump·er² (bum'pər) *n.* [prob. < obs. *bombard*,
liquor jug] a cup or glass filled to the brim —
adj. unusually abundant *[a bumper crop]*
bump·kin (bump'kən) *n.* [prob. < MDu. *bom-
mekijn*, small cask] an awkward or simple person from the country
bump'tious (-shəs) *adj.* [prob. < BUMP] disagreeably conceited or forward
bun (bun) *n.* [prob. < OFr. *buigne*, a swelling]
1. a small roll, often sweetened or spiced 2.
hair worn in a roll or knot
bunch (bunch) *n.* [< Fl. *boudje*, little bundle]
1. a cluster of similar things growing or
grouped together 2. [Colloq.] a group of people
—*vt., vi.* to collect in loose folds, wads, etc. —
bunch'y *adj.*
bun·combe (buŋ'kəm) *n.* [< *Buncombe*
County, N.C., loquaciously represented in 16th
Congress] [Colloq.] empty, insincere talk: also
bun'kum
bun·dle (bun'd'l) *n.* [prob. < MDu. *bondel*] 1.
a number of things bound together 2. a package 3. a bunch; collection —*vt.* **-dled, -dling** 1.
to make into a bundle 2. to send hastily
(*away, off, out,* or *into*) —**bundle up** to put on
plenty of warm clothing
bung (buŋ) *n.* [< MDu. *bonge*] a cork or other
stopper for the hole in a barrel, etc.
bun·ga·low (buŋ'gə lō') *n.* [< Hindi *bānglā*,
thatched house] a small, one-storied house
bun·gle (buŋ'g'l) *vt., vi.* **-gled, -gling** [< ?] to
spoil by clumsy work; botch —*n.* 1. a bungling
2. a clumsy piece of work
bun·ion (bun'yən) *n.* [prob. < OFr.: see BUN]
an inflammation and swelling at the base of
the big toe
bunk¹ (buŋk) *n.* [prob. < Scand. cognate of
BENCH] 1. a shelflike bed built against a wall,
as in a ship 2. [Colloq.] any sleeping place —*vi.*
to sleep in a bunk —*vt.* to provide a sleeping
place for
bunk² (buŋk) *n.* [Slang] *same as* BUNCOMBE
bunk'er *n.* [Scot. < ?] 1. a large bin, as for a

ship's fuel 2. an underground fortification 3. a
sand trap or mound of earth serving as an obstacle on a golf course
bunk'house' *n.* barracks for ranch hands, etc.
bun·ny (bun'ē) *n., pl.* **-nies** [dim. of dial. *bun*]
a rabbit: a child's term
Bun·sen burner (bun's'n) [< R. W. *Bunsen*,
19th-c. G. chemist] a small, tubular gas burner
that produces a hot, blue flame
bunt (bunt) *vt., vi.* [< ? Bret. *bounta*, to butt]
Baseball to bat (a pitched ball) lightly so that
it does not go beyond the infield —*n.* 1. the act
of bunting 2. a bunted ball
bunt·ing¹ (bun'tiŋ) *n.* [< ? ME. *bonting*, sifting (cloth)] 1. a thin cloth used in making
flags, etc. 2. decorative flags 3. a soft, warm,
baby's garment in the form of a hooded blanket
bunt·ing² (bun'tiŋ) *n.* [< ?] any of various
small, brightly colored birds having a stout
bill
buoy (boo'ē, boi) *n.* [< L. *boia*, fetter] 1. a
floating object anchored in water to warn of
rocks, etc. or to mark a channel 2. *short for*
LIFE BUOY —*vt.* 1. to mark with a buoy 2. to
keep afloat 3. to encourage
buoy·an·cy (boi'ən sē, boo'yən-) *n.* [< ? Sp.
boyar, to float] 1. the ability to float in liquid
or air 2. cheerfulness —**buoy'ant** *adj.*
bur (bur) *n.* [< Scand.] 1. a rough, prickly seed
capsule of certain plants 2. a plant with burs
3. *same as* BURR¹ & BURR²
bur·den¹ (burd''n) *n.* [< OE. *beran*, to bear] 1.
anything that is carried; load 2. a heavy load,
as of work, care, etc. 3. the carrying capacity
of a ship —*vt.* to put a burden on; oppress —
bur'den·some *adj.*
bur·den² (burd''n) *n.* [< OFr. *bourdon*, a
humming] 1. a chorus or refrain of a song 2. a
repeated, central idea; theme
bur·dock (bur'däk') *n.* [BUR + DOCK³] a plant
with purplish flower heads bearing prickles
bu·reau (byoor'ō) *n., pl.* **-reaus, -reaux** (-ōz)
[Fr., desk] 1. a chest of drawers for clothing,
etc. 2. an agency *[travel bureau]* 3. a government department
bu·reauc·ra·cy (byoo rä'krə sē) *n., pl.* **-cies** 1.
government by departmental officials follow-
ing an inflexible routine 2. the officials collectively 3. governmental officialism 4. the concentration of authority in administrative bu-
reaus —**bu·reau·crat** (byoor'ə krat') *n.* —**bu'-
reau·crat'ic** *adj.*
burg (burg) *n.* [var. of BOROUGH] [Colloq.] a
quiet or dull city or town
bur·geon (bur'jən) *vi.* [< OFr. *burjon*, a bud]
1. to put forth buds, etc. 2. to develop rapidly
-burger [< (HAM)BURGER] *a combining form
meaning:* 1. a sandwich of ground meat, fish,
etc. *[turkeyburger]* 2. hamburger and
[cheeseburger]
burgh (burg) *n.* [Scot. var. of BOROUGH] 1.
[Brit.] a borough 2. in Scotland, a chartered
town
burgh'er *n.* a citizen of a town
bur·glar (bur'glər) *n.* [< OFr. *burgeor*] one
who commits burglary
bur'glar·ize *vt.* **-ized', -iz'ing** [Colloq.] to commit burglary in
bur'gla·ry *n., pl.* **-ries** the act of breaking into
a dwelling at night to commit theft or other
felony
bur·go·mas·ter (bur'gə mas'tər) *n.* [< MDu.
burg, town + *meester*, master] the mayor of a
town in the Netherlands, Flanders, Austria, or
Germany
Bur·gun·dy (bur'gən dē) *n., pl.* **-dies** [*occas.* **b-**]

a red or white wine, orig. made in Burgundy, a region in SE France

bur·i·al (ber′ē əl) *n.* the burying of a dead body; interment

bur·lap (bur′lap) *n.* [< ? ME. *borel*] a coarse cloth made of jute or hemp

bur·lesque (bər lesk′) *n.* [Fr. < It. *burla,* a jest] **1.** any broadly comic or satirical imitation; parody **2.** a sort of vaudeville characterized by low comedy, striptease acts, etc. —*vt.,* *vi.* **-lesqued′, -lesqu′ing** to imitate comically

bur·ly (bur′lē) *adj.* **-li·er, -li·est** [ME. *borlich,* excellent] big and strong

burn (burn) *vt.* **burned** or **burnt, burn′ing** [OE. *biernan*] **1.** to set on fire **2.** to destroy by fire **3.** to injure by fire, friction, or acid **4.** to consume as a fuel **5.** to sunburn **6.** to cause by fire, heat, etc. **7.** to cause a sensation of heat in —*vi.* **1.** to be on fire; blaze **2.** to undergo combustion **3.** to give out light or heat; glow **4.** to be destroyed or injured by fire or heat **5.** to feel hot **6.** to be excited —*n.* **1.** an injury caused by fire, heat, etc. **2.** the process or result of burning —**burn down** to burn to the ground —**burn up** [Slang] to make or become angry —**burn′a·ble** *adj., n.*

burn′er *n.* the part of a stove, furnace, etc. from which the flame comes

burn′ing *adj.* **1.** that burns **2.** intense; critical *[a burning issue]*

bur·nish (bur′nish) *vt., vi.* [< OFr. *brun,* brown] to make or become shiny by rubbing —*n.* a gloss or polish —**bur′nish·er** *n.*

burnt (burnt) *alt. pt. and pp. of* BURN

burp (burp) *n., vi.* [echoic] [Colloq.] belch —*vt.* to cause (a baby) to belch

burr¹ (bur) *n.* [var. of BUR] **1.** a rough edge left on metal, etc. by drilling or cutting **2.** *same as* BUR

burr² (bur) *n.* [prob. echoic] **1.** the trilling of *r* as in Scottish speech **2.** a whirring sound

bur·ro (bur′ō) *n., pl.* **-ros** [Sp. < LL. *burricus,* small horse] a donkey

bur·row (bur′ō) *n.* [see BOROUGH] **1.** a hole dug in the ground by an animal **2.** any similar hole —*vi.* **1.** to make a burrow **2.** to live or hide in or as in a burrow

bur·sa (bur′sə) *n., pl.* **-sae** (-sē), **-sas** [< Gr. *byrsa,* a hide] *Anat.* a sac or cavity with a lubricating fluid, as between a tendon and bone

bur·sar (bur′sər) *n.* [< ML. *bursa,* a purse] a college treasurer

bur·si·tis (bər sīt′əs) *n.* [< BURSA + -ITIS] inflammation of a bursa

burst (burst) *vi.* **burst, burst′ing** [OE. *berstan*] **1.** to come apart suddenly and violently; explode **2.** to give sudden expression; break (*into* tears, laughter, etc.) **3.** to appear, start, etc. suddenly **4.** to be as full or crowded as possible —*vt.* to cause to burst —*n.* **1.** a bursting; explosion **2.** a break; rupture **3.** a sudden action; spurt **4.** a volley of shots

bur·y (ber′ē) *vt.* **-ied, -y·ing** [OE. *byrgan*] **1.** to put (a dead body) into the earth, a tomb, etc. **2.** to hide or cover **3.** to put away **4.** to immerse

bus (bus) *n., pl.* **bus′es, bus′ses** [< (OMNI)BUS] a large motor coach for many passengers, usually along a regular route —*vt.* **bused** or **bussed, bus′ing** or **bus′sing** to transport by bus —*vi.* **1.** to go by bus **2.** to do the work of a busboy

bus′boy′ *n.* a waiter's assistant who clears tables, brings water, etc.

bush (boosh) *n.* [ME.] **1.** a low woody plant with spreading branches; shrub **2.** anything like a bush **3.** uncleared land —*vi.* to grow

thickly —**beat around the bush** to talk around a subject without getting to the point —**bush′y** *adj.* **-i·er, -i·est**

bushed (boosht) *adj.* [Colloq.] tired; fatigued

bush·el (boosh′'l) *n.* [< OFr. *boisse,* grain measure] a unit of dry measure equal to 4 pecks or 32 quarts

bush·ing (boosh′iŋ) *n.* [< ML. *buxis,* a box] a removable metal sleeve for reducing friction on a bearing or other moving parts

bush league [Slang] *Baseball* a small or second-rate minor league —**bush′-league′** *adj.*

bush′man (-mən) *n., pl.* **-men** one who lives in the Australian bush

bush′mas′ter *n.* a large poisonous snake of Central and South America

bush′whack′er *n.* [prob. < BUSH + WHACK] a guerrilla fighter

bus·i·ly (biz′ə lē) *adv.* in a busy manner

busi·ness (biz′nis) *n.* [OE. *bisignes:* see BUSY] **1.** one's work; profession; occupation **2.** rightful concern **3.** a matter or affair **4.** commerce; trade **5.** a commercial or industrial establishment —*adj.* of or for business —**mean business** [Colloq.] to be in earnest

business college (or **school**) a school offering instruction in secretarial skills, etc.

busi′ness·like′ *adj.* efficient, methodical, etc.

busi′ness·man′ *n., pl.* **-men′** a man in business, esp. as an owner or executive —**busi′ness·wom′an** *n.fem., pl.* **-wom′en**

bus·ing, bus·sing (bus′iŋ) *n.* the act of transporting children by bus to a school outside of their neighborhood, esp. in order to desegregate the school

bus·kin (bus′kin) *n.* [< ? MDu. *brosekin,* small boot] **1.** a high, laced boot worn in ancient tragedy **2.** tragic drama

buss (bus) *n., vt., vi.* [< ?] [Archaic] kiss

bust¹ (bust) *n.* [< Fr. < It. *busto*] **1.** a sculpture of a person's head and shoulders **2.** a woman's bosom

bust² (bust) *vt., vi.* [< BURST] [Slang] **1.** to burst or break **2.** to make or become bankrupt or demoted **3.** to hit **4.** to arrest —*n.* [Slang] **1.** a failure **2.** a financial collapse **3.** a punch **4.** a spree **5.** an arrest —**bust′ed** *adj.*

bus·tle¹ (bus′'l) *vi., vt.* **-tled, -tling** [< ME. *busken,* prepare] to hurry busily —*n.* busy and noisy activity

bus·tle² (bus′'l) *n.* [< ? G. *buschel,* a pad] a framework or padding worn at the back by women to puff out the skirt

bus·y (biz′ē) *adj.* **-i·er, -i·est** [OE. *bisig*] **1.** active; at work **2.** full of activity **3.** in use, as a telephone **4.** too detailed —*vt.* **-ied, -y·ing** to make or keep busy

bus′y·bod′y (-bäd′ē) *n., pl.* **-ies** a meddler in the affairs of others

but (but) *prep.* [OE. *butan,* without] except; save *[nobody came but me]* —*conj.* **1.** yet; still *[it's good, but not great]* **2.** on the contrary *[I am old, but he is young]* **3.** unless *[it never rains but it pours]* **4.** that *[I don't doubt but you're right]* **5.** that...not *[I never gamble but I lose]* —*adv.* **1.** only *[if I had but known]* **2.** merely *[he is but a child]* **3.** just *[I heard it but now]* —*pron.* who...not; which...not *[not a man but felt it]* —**but for** if it were not for

bu·tane (byōō′tān) *n.* [< L. *butyrum,* butter] a hydrocarbon used as a fuel, etc.

butch·er (booch′ər) *n.* [< Frank. *bukk,* he-goat] **1.** one whose work is killing and dressing animals for meat **2.** one who cuts meat for sale **3.** a brutal killer —*vt.* **1.** to kill or dress (animals) for meat **2.** to kill brutally **3.** to botch —**butch′er·y** *n., pl.* **-ies**

but·ler (but′lər) *n.* [< OFr. *bouteille,* a bottle] a manservant, usually the head servant of a household

butt¹ (but) *n.* [< ?] **1.** the thick end of anything **2.** a stub or stump, as the unsmoked end of a cigar **3.** a target **4.** an object of ridicule or criticism **5.** [Slang] a cigarette —*vt., vi.* to join end to end

butt² (but) *vt., vi.* [< OFr. *buter,* to thrust against] **1.** to ram with the head **2.** to abut on —*n.* a butting —**butt in(to)** [Slang] to mix into (another's business, etc.)

butt³ (but) *n.* [< LL. *bottis,* cask] a large cask, as for wine or beer

butte (byo͞ot) *n.* [Fr., mound] a steep hill standing alone on a plain

but·ter (but′ər) *n.* [< L. *butyrum* < Gr. *bous,* cow + *tyros,* cheese] **1.** the solid, yellowish, edible fat obtained by churning cream **2.** any substance somewhat like butter —*vt.* **1.** to spread with butter **2.** [Colloq.] to flatter (often with *up*) —**but′ter·y** *adj.*

butter bean *same as* LIMA BEAN *or* WAX BEAN

but′ter·cup′ *n.* a plant with yellow, cup-shaped flowers

but′ter·fat′ *n.* the fatty part of milk, from which butter is made

but′ter·fin′gers *n.* one who often fumbles and drops things

but′ter·fly′ *n., pl.* -**flies′** [OE. *buttorfleoge*] an insect with a slender body and four broad, usually brightly colored wings

but′ter·milk′ *n.* the liquid left after churning butter from milk or cream

but′ter·nut′ *n.* **1.** a walnut tree of E N. America **2.** its edible, oily nut

but′ter·scotch′ (-skäch′) *n.* **1.** a hard, sticky candy made with brown sugar, butter, etc. **2.** a syrup with this flavor

but·tocks (but′əks) *n.pl.* [OE. *buttuc,* end] the fleshy, rounded parts of the hips; rump

but·ton (but′'n) *n.* [< OFr. *boton*] **1.** any small disk or knob used as a fastening, ornament, etc. on a garment **2.** anything small and shaped like a button —*vt., vi.* to fasten with buttons

but′ton·hole′ *n.* a slit or loop through which a button can be fastened —*vt.* -**holed′,** -**hol′ing 1.** to make buttonholes in **2.** to make (a person) listen to one

but·tress (but′ris) *n.* [< OFr. *buter:* see BUTT²] **1.** a structure built against a wall to support or reinforce it **2.** a support; prop —*vt.* **1.** to support with a buttress **2.** to bolster

bux·om (buk′səm) *adj.* [ME., humble] healthy, comely, plump, etc.: specif. said of a full-bosomed woman —**bux′om·ness** *n.*

buy (bī) *vt.* **bought, buy′ing** [< OE. *bycgan*] **1.** to get by paying money **2.** to get by an exchange **3.** to bribe **4.** [Slang] to accept as true [I can't *buy* his excuse] —*vi.* to be a buyer —*n.* **1.** a buying **2.** anything bought **3.** [Colloq.] a bargain —**buy off** to bribe —**buy out** to buy all the stock, rights, etc.

buy′er *n.* **1.** one who buys; consumer **2.** one whose work is to buy merchandise for a retail store

buzz (buz) *vi.* [echoic] **1.** to hum like a bee **2.** to gossip **3.** to be filled wih noisy activity or talk —*vt.* to fly an airplane low over —*n.* a sound like a bee's hum

buz·zard (buz′ərd) *n.* [< L. *buteo,* a kind of hawk] **1.** any of various hawks that are slow and heavy in flight **2.** *same as* TURKEY BUZZARD

buzz′er *n.* an electrical device that makes a buzzing sound as a signal

buzz saw a circular saw rotated by machinery

bx. box

by (bī) *prep.* [OE. *be, bi*] **1.** near; at [stand *by* the wall] **2.** *a)* in or during [to travel *by* night] *b)* for a fixed time [to work *by* the hour] *c)* not later than [back *by* noon] **3.** *a)* through; via [to Boston *by* Route 6] *b)* past; beyond [he walked right *by* me] **4.** in behalf of [he did well *by* me] **5.** through the agency of [gained *by* fraud] **6.** *a)* according to [*by* the book] *b)* in [to grow dark *by* degrees] *c)* following in series [march two *by* two] **7.** *a)* in or to the amount of [apples *by* the peck] *b)* and in another dimension [two *by* four] *c)* using (the given number) as multiplier or divisor —*adv.* **1.** close at hand [stand *by*] **2.** away; aside [put money *by*] **3.** past [he sped *by*] **4.** at someone's place [stop *by*] —**by and by** after a while —**by and large** considering everything —**by the by** incidentally

by- *a prefix meaning:* **1.** near **2.** secondary

bye (bī) *n.* [see BY] the advantage obtained by an unpaired contestant in a tournament, who advances to the next round without playing — *adj.* incidental —**by the bye** incidentally

bye′-bye′ *n., interj.* goodbye

by′-e·lec′tion *n.* [Chiefly Brit.] a special election between general elections

by·gone (bī′gôn′, -gän′) *adj.* past; former —*n.* anything gone or past

by·law (bī′lô′) *n.* [< ME. *bi,* town + *laue,* law] any of a set of rules adopted by an organization for governing its affairs

by′line′ *n.* a line above a newspaper article, etc. telling who wrote it

by′pass′ *n.* a way, pipe, channel, etc. between two points that avoids or is auxiliary to the main way —*vt.* **1.** to detour **2.** to furnish with a bypass **3.** to ignore

by′path′, by′-path′ *n.* a side path; byway

by′prod′uct, by′-prod′uct *n.* anything produced, as from residues, in the course of making another thing

by′stand′er *n.* a person who stands near but does not participate

by′way′ *n.* a side road or path

by′word′ *n.* **1.** a proverb **2.** a person or thing proverbial as being contemptible

C

C, c (sē) *n., pl.* **C's, c's** the third letter of the English alphabet

C (sē) *n.* **1.** a Roman numeral for 100 **2.** a grade indicating average work **3.** *Chem.* carbon **4.** *Music* the first tone in the scale of C major

C, C. 1. Celsius or centigrade **2.** Central

C. 1. Catholic **2.** Congress **3.** Corps

C., c. 1. carat **2.** catcher **3.** cent **4.** center **5.** centimeter **6.** century **7.** circa **8.** college **9.** copyright **10.** cubic **11.** cycle

Ca *Chem.* calcium

cab (kab) *n.* [< CABRIOLET] **1.** a carriage for public hire **2.** *short for* TAXICAB **3.** the place in a locomotive, truck, etc. where the operator sits

ca·bal (kə bal′) *n.* [Fr., intrigue] **1.** a small group joined in a secret intrigue **2.** such an intrigue

ca·ba·na (kə bän′ə, -ban′ə) *n.* [< Sp. < LL. *capanna*] **1.** a cabin or hut **2.** a small shelter for swimmers at a beach, pool, etc.

cab·a·ret (kab′ə rā′) *n.* [Fr.] a café with dancing, singing, etc. as entertainment

cab·bage (kab′ij) *n.* [? < L. *caput*, head] a vegetable with thick leaves formed into a round, compact head

cab·in (kab′n) *n.* [< LL. *capanna*, hut] **1.** a small, crudely or simply built house **2.** a room on a ship or boat **3.** the space for passengers in an aircraft

cab·i·net (kab′ə nit) *n.* [Fr. < ?] **1.** a case with drawers or shelves to hold or store things **2.** [*often* C-] a body of official advisers to a chief executive

cab′i·net·mak′er *n.* a workman who makes fine furniture —**cab′i·net·mak′ing** *n.*

cab′i·net·work′ *n.* articles made by a cabinetmaker: also **cab′i·net·ry** (-rē)

ca·ble (kā′b′l) *n.* [< L. *capere*, take hold] **1.** a thick, heavy rope, often of wire strands **2.** a bundle of insulated wires to carry an electric current **3.** a cablegram —*vt.* **-bled, -bling 1.** to fasten with a cable **2.** to transmit by undersea cable **3.** to send a cablegram to —*vi.* to send a cablegram

cable car a car drawn by a moving cable

ca′ble·gram′ (-gram′) *n.* a message sent by undersea cable

ca·boo·dle (kə boo͞′d′l) *n.* [< BOODLE] [Colloq.] lot; group [the whole *caboodle*]

ca·boose (kə boos′) *n.* [MDu. *kabuys*, cabin house] the trainmen's car at the rear of a freight train

cab·ri·o·let (kab′rē ə lā′) *n.* [< Fr. *cabriole*, a leap] a light, two-wheeled carriage drawn by one horse

ca·ca·o (kə kā′ō, -kä′ō) *n., pl.* **-os** [Sp. < Mex.-Ind. *cacauatl*] **1.** the seed of a tropical American tree, from which cocoa and chocolate are made: also **cacao bean 2.** this tree

cache (kash) *n.* [Fr. < L. *coactare*, constrain] **1.** a place in which stores of food, supplies, etc. are hidden **2.** anything so hidden —*vt.* **cached, cach′ing** to place in a cache

ca·chet (ka shā′) *n.* [Fr. < *cacher*, to hide] **1.** a seal on an official document **2.** a commemorative design, etc. stamped on mail

cack·le (kak′l) *vi.* **-led, -ling** [echoic] **1.** to make the shrill, broken sounds of a hen **2.** to laugh or chatter with similar sounds —*n.* a cackling

ca·coph·o·ny (kə käf′ə nē) *n., pl.* **-nies** [< Gr. *kakos*, bad + *phōnē*, voice] harsh, jarring sound; dissonance —**ca·coph′o·nous** *adj.*

cac·tus (kak′təs) *n., pl.* **-tus·es, -ti** (-tī) [< Gr. *kaktos*, kind of thistle] any of various desert plants with fleshy stems and spinelike leaves

cad (kad) *n.* [< CADET] a man whose behavior is not gentlemanly —**cad′dish** *adj.*

ca·dav·er (kə dav′ər) *n.* [L., prob. < *cadere*, to fall] a dead body; corpse, as for dissection

ca·dav′er·ous (-əs) *adj.* of or like a cadaver; pale, gaunt, haggard, etc.

cad·die, cad·dy[1] (kad′ē) *n.* [Scot. form of Fr. *cadet*: see CADET] **1.** one who attends a golfer, carrying his clubs, etc. **2.** a small, wheeled cart —*vi.* **-died, -dy·ing** to act as a caddie

cad·dy[2] (kad′ē) *n., pl.* **-dies** [< Malay *kati*, unit of weight] a small container for tea

-cade [< (CAVAL)CADE] *a suffix meaning* procession, parade [motorcade]

ca·dence (kād′ns) *n.* [< L. *cadere*, to fall] **1.** fall of the voice in speaking **2.** a rhythmic flow of sound **3.** measured movement, as in marching —**ca′denced** *adj.*

ca·den·za (kə den′zə) *n.* [It.: see prec.] an elaborate passage for the solo instrument in a concerto

ca·det (kə det′) *n.* [Fr. < L. dim. of *caput*, head] **1.** a student in training at an armed forces academy **2.** any trainee, as a practice teacher

cadge (kaj) *vt., vi.* **cadged, cadg′ing** [ME. *caggen*, to tie] to beg or get by begging —**cadg′er** *n.*

cad·mi·um (kad′mē əm) *n.* [< L. *cadmia*, zinc ore (in which it occurs)] a blue-white, metallic chemical element used in alloys, electroplating, etc.: symbol, Cd

ca·dre (kad′rē) *n.* [Fr. < L. *quadrum*, a square] a nucleus around which an expanded organization, as a military unit, can be built

ca·du·ce·us (kə doo͞′sē əs) *n., pl.* **-ce·i** (-sē ī′) [L.] the winged staff with two serpents twined about it, carried by Mercury: now a symbol of the medical profession

cae·cum (sē′kəm) *n. var. of* CECUM

Cae·sar (sē′zər) *n.* **1.** the title of the Roman emperors from Augustus to Hadrian **2.** any emperor or dictator

Cae·sar·e·an section (si zer′ē ən) [*also* c- s-] an operation for delivering a baby by cutting through the mother's abdominal and uterine walls: Julius Caesar was supposedly born this way

cae·su·ra (si zhoor′ə) *n., pl.* **-ras, -rae** (-ē) [L. < *caedere*, to cut] a break or pause in a line of verse, usually in the middle

ca·fé, ca·fe (ka fā′) *n.* [Fr. < It. *caffè*, coffee] a small restaurant or a barroom

caf·e·te·ri·a (kaf′ə tir′ē ə) *n.* [AmSp., coffee store] a restaurant in which food is displayed and patrons serve themselves

caf·feine, caf·fein (kaf′ēn, ka fēn′) *n.* [< G. < It. *caffè*, coffee + -*in*, -INE[3]] the alkaloid present in coffee, tea, etc.: it is a stimulant

cage (kāj) *n.* [< L. *cavus*, hollow] **1.** a structure of wires, bars, etc. for confining birds or animals **2.** any openwork structure —*vt.* **caged, cag′ing** to put in a cage

ca·gey, ca·gy (kā′jē) *adj.* **-gi·er, -gi·est** [< ?] [Colloq.] **1.** sly; tricky; cunning **2.** cautious —**ca′gi·ly** *adv.* —**ca′gi·ness** *n.*

ca·hoots (kə hoots′) *n.pl.* [< ?] [Slang] partnership; league: implying scheming in the phrase **in cahoots**

Cain (kān) *Bible* the oldest son of Adam and Eve: he killed his brother Abel —**raise Cain** [Slang] to cause a great commotion

cairn (kern) *n.* [Scot.] a conical heap of stones built as a monument or landmark

cais·son (kā′sän) *n.* [Fr. < It. < L. *capsa*, a box] **1.** a two-wheeled wagon with a chest for ammunition **2.** a watertight box for underwater construction work

cai·tiff (kāt′if) *n.* [< L. *captivus*, CAPTIVE] a mean, evil, or cowardly person —*adj.* mean, evil, or cowardly

ca·jole (kə jōl′) *vt., vi.* **-joled′, -jol′ing** [< Fr.] to coax with flattery and insincere talk —**ca·jol′er** *n.* —**ca·jol′er·y** *n.*

cake (kāk) *n.* [< ON.] **1.** a small, flat mass of baked or fried dough, batter, or hashed food **2.** a baked mixture of flour, eggs, sugar, etc., often covered with icing **3.** a shaped solid mass, as of soap **4.** a hard crust or deposit —*vt., vi.* **caked, cak′ing** to form into a hard mass or a crust —**take the cake** [Slang] to win the prize

cal·a·bash (kal′ə bash′) *n.* [< Fr. < Sp. *calabaza* < ?] 1. the gourdlike fruit of a tropical American tree 2. the bottle-shaped gourd of a tropical American vine, or a smoking pipe made from it

cal·a·boose (kal′ə bōōs′) *n.* [Sp. *calabozo*] [Slang] a jail

cal·a·mine (kal′ə mīn′) *n.* [Fr. < L. *cadmia*, zinc ore] a zinc-oxide powder used in skin lotions and ointments

ca·lam·i·ty (kə lam′ə tē) *n., pl.* **-ties** [< Fr. < L. *calamitas*] a great misfortune; disaster —**ca·lam′i·tous** *adj.* —**ca·lam′i·tous·ly** *adv.*

cal·car·e·ous (kal ker′ē əs) *adj.* [< L. *calx*, lime] of or like limestone, calcium, or lime

cal·cif·er·ous (kal sif′ər əs) *adj.* [< L. *calx*, lime + -FEROUS] containing calcite

cal·ci·fy (kal′sə fī′) *vt., vi.* **-fied′, -fy′ing** [< L. *calx*, lime + -FY] to change into a hard, stony substance by the deposit of lime or calcium salts —**cal′ci·fi·ca′tion** *n.*

cal′ci·mine′ (-mīn′) *n.* [< L. *calx*, lime] a white or colored liquid used as a wash for plastered walls —*vt.* **-mined′, -min′ing** to cover with calcimine

cal·cine (kal′sīn) *vt., vi.* **-cined, -cin·ing** [< ML. *calcinare*] to change to an ashy powder by heat —**cal′ci·na′tion** *n.*

cal·cite (kal′sīt) *n.* calcium carbonate, a mineral found as limestone, chalk, and marble

cal·ci·um (kal′sē əm) *n.* [< L. *calx*, lime] a soft, silver-white metallic chemical element found combined in limestone, chalk, etc.: symbol, Ca

calcium carbonate a white powder or crystalline compound found in limestone, chalk, marble, bones, shells, etc.

cal·cu·late (kal′kyə lāt′) *vt.* **-lat′ed, -lat′ing** [< L. *calculare*, reckon] 1. to determine by using mathematics; compute 2. to determine by reasoning; estimate 3. to plan; intend [words *calculated* to mislead us] —*vi.* 1. to make a computation 2. to rely (*on*) —**cal′cu·la·ble** (-lə b'l) *adj.*

cal′cu·lat′ed *adj.* deliberately planned or carefully considered

cal′cu·lat′ing *adj.* shrewd or scheming

cal′cu·la′tion *n.* 1. a calculating 2. something deduced by calculating 3. careful planning or forethought

cal′cu·la′tor *n.* 1. one who calculates 2. a machine for doing arithmetic rapidly

cal·cu·lus (kal′kyə ləs) *n., pl.* **-li′** (-lī′), **-lus·es** [L., pebble used in counting] 1. an abnormal stony mass in the body 2. a method of calculation or analysis in higher mathematics

cal·dron (kôl′drən) *n.* [< L. *calidus*, warm] a large kettle or boiler

cal·en·dar (kal′ən dər) *n.* [< L. *calendarium*, account book] 1. a system of determining the length and divisions of a year 2. a table that shows the days, weeks, and months of a given year 3. a schedule, as of pending court cases —*vt.* to enter in a calendar; schedule

cal·en·der (kal′ən dər) *n.* [< Fr. < Gr. *kylindein*, to roll] a machine with rollers for giving paper, cloth, etc. a smooth or glossy finish —*vt.* to process (paper, etc.) in a calender

cal·ends (kal′əndz) *n.pl.* [*often with sing. v.*] [< Gr. *kalein*, proclaim] the first day of each month in the ancient Roman calendar

calf[1] (kaf) *n., pl.* **calves**; *esp. for 3,* **calfs** [OE. *cealf*] 1. a young cow or bull 2. the young of some other large animals, as the elephant, seal, etc. 3. leather from a calf's hide —**kill the fatted calf** to make a feast of welcome

calf[2] (kaf) *n., pl.* **calves** [ON. *kalfi*] the fleshy back part of the leg below the knee

calf′skin′ *n.* 1. the skin of a calf 2. leather made from this

cal·i·ber, cal·i·bre (kal′ə bər) *n.* [< Fr. & Sp. < Ar. *qālib*, a mold] 1. the diameter of a cylindrical body, esp. of a bullet or shell 2. the diameter of the bore of a gun 3. quality or ability

cal·i·brate (kal′ə brāt′) *vt.* **-brat′ed, -brat′ing** 1. to determine the caliber of 2. to fix or correct the scale of (a measuring instrument) —**cal′i·bra′tion** *n.* —**cal′i·bra′tor** *n.*

cal·i·co (kal′ə kō′) *n., pl.* **-coes′, -cos′** [< *Calicut*, city in India] a kind of coarse, printed cotton cloth —*adj.* spotted like calico

cal·i·per (kal′ə pər) *n.* [var. of CALIBER] [*usually pl.*] an instrument consisting of a pair of hinged legs, for measuring thickness or diameter —*vt., vi.* to measure with calipers

ca·liph, ca·lif (kā′lif, kal′if) *n.* [< Ar. *khalifa*] supreme ruler: title taken by Mohammed's successors as heads of Islam

cal·is·then·ics (kal′əs then′iks) *n.pl.* [< Gr. *kallos*, beauty + *sthenos*, strength] athletic exercises —**cal′is·then′ic** *adj.*

calk[1] (kôk) *vt. same as* CAULK —**calk′er** *n.*

calk[2] (kôk) *n.* [< L. *calx*, a heel] a metal plate on the bottom of a shoe to prevent slipping

call (kôl) *vt.* [< ON. *kalla*] 1. to say in a loud tone; shout 2. to summon 3. to name; designate 4. to describe as specified 5. to awaken 6. to telephone 7. to give orders for 8. to stop (a game, etc.) 9. to demand payment of (a loan, etc.) 10. *Poker* to require (a player) to show his hand by equaling his bet —*vi.* 1. to shout 2. to visit for a short while 3. to telephone —*n.* 1. a calling 2. a loud utterance 3. the distinctive cry of an animal or bird 4. a summons to a meeting, etc. 5. an economic demand, as for a product 6. need [no *call* for tears] 7. a demand for payment 8. a brief visit 9. *Sports* an official's decision —**call down** [Colloq.] to scold —**call for** 1. to demand 2. to come and get —**call off** to cancel (a scheduled event) —**call on** to ask (a person) to speak —**call out** to shout —**call up** 1. to remember 2. to summon for duty 3. to telephone —**on call** available when summoned —**call′er** *n.*

cal·la (kal′ə) *n.* [< L., a kind of plant] a plant with a large, white leaf surrounding a yellow flower: also **calla lily**

call girl a prostitute who is called by telephone to make assignations

cal·lig·ra·phy (kə lig′rə fē) *n.* [< Gr. *kallos*, beauty + *graphein*, write] 1. beautiful handwriting 2. handwriting —**cal·lig′ra·pher** *n.* —**cal·li·graph·ic** (kal′ə graf′ik) *adj.*

call′ing *n.* 1. the act of one that calls 2. one's occupation, profession, or trade

cal·li·o·pe (kə lī′ə pē′, kal′ē ōp′) *n.* [< Gr. *kallos*, beauty + *ops*, voice] a musical instrument with a series of steam whistles, played like an organ

cal·los·i·ty (ka läs′ə tē, kə-) *n.* 1. a being callous or hardened 2. *pl.* **-ties** a callus on skin or bark

cal·lous (kal′əs) *adj.* [see CALLUS] 1. hardened 2. unfeeling; insensitive —**cal′lous·ly** *adv.* —**cal′lous·ness** *n.*

cal·low (kal′ō) *adj.* [OE. *calu*, bald] young and inexperienced —**cal′low·ness** *n.*

cal·lus (kal′əs) *n., pl.* **-lus·es** [L., hard skin] 1. a hardened, thickened place on the skin 2. tissue that develops over a wound on a plant —*vi.* to develop a callus

calm (käm) *n.* [< Gr. *kauma*, heat] stillness;

tranquillity —*adj.* still; not excited; tranquil —*vt., vi.* to make or become calm —**calm′ly** *adv.* —**calm′ness** *n.*

cal·o·mel (kal′ə mel′, -məl) *n.* [Fr. < Gr. *kalos*, beautiful + *melas*, black] a white powder, formerly used as a cathartic, etc.

ca·lor·ic (kə lôr′ik, -lär′-) *adj.* [see CALORIE] 1. of heat 2. of calories —**ca·lor′l·cal·ly** *adv.*

cal·o·rie (kal′ə rē) *n.* [Fr. < L. *calor*, heat] a unit for measuring heat, esp. for measuring energy produced by food when oxidized in the body: also sp. **cal′o·ry,** *pl.* **-ries**

cal·o·rif·ic (kal′ə rif′ik) *adj.* [< Fr. < L. *calor*, heat + *facere*, to make] producing heat

cal·o·rim·e·ter (kal′ə rim′ə tər) *n.* [< L. *calor*, heat + -METER] an apparatus for measuring heat

cal·u·met (kal′yə met′) *n.* [Fr. < L. *calamus*, a reed] a long-stemmed ceremonial tobacco pipe smoked by N. American Indians as a token of peace

ca·lum·ni·ate (kə lum′nē āt′) *vt., vi.* -at′ed, -at′ing [see CALUMNY] to slander —**ca·lum′nl·a′tlon** *n.* —**ca·lum′nl·a′tor** *n.*

cal·um·ny (kal′əm nē) *n., pl.* -nies [< Fr. < L. *calumnia*, slander] a false and malicious statement; slander

Cal·va·ry (kal′vər ē) *Bible* the place where Jesus was crucified

calve (kav) *vi., vt.* **calved, calv′ing** to give birth to (a calf)

calves (kavz) *n. pl. of* CALF

Cal·vin·ism (kal′vin iz′m) *n.* [< John *Calvin*, 16th-c. Fr. Protestant] the theological system of John Calvin and his followers: it emphasizes predestination —**Cal′vin·lst** *n., adj.* —**Cal′·vin·is′tlc** *adj.*

ca·lyp·so (kə lip′sō) *n.* [< ?] a highly syncopated, satirical ballad improvised and sung, originally, by natives of Trinidad

ca·lyx (kā′liks, kal′iks) *n., pl.* -lyx·es, -ly·ces′ (-lə sēz′) [L., pod] the outer whorl, or sepals, of a flower

cam (kam) *n.* [Du. *cam*, orig., a comb] a wheel, projection on a wheel, etc. which gives an irregular motion as to a wheel or shaft, or receives such motion from it

ca·ma·ra·de·rie (käm′ə räd′ər ē) *n.* [Fr.] loyalty and friendly feeling among comrades

cam·ber (kam′bər) *n.* [< L. *camur*, arched] a slight convex curve of a surface, as of a road —*vt., vi.* to arch slightly

cam·bi·um (kam′bē əm) *n.* [LL., change] a layer of formative cells between the wood and bark in woody plants, from which new wood and bark grow

cam·bric (kām′brik) *n.* [< *Cambrai*, Fr. city] a fine linen or cotton cloth

came (kām) *pt. of* COME

cam·el (kam′'l) *n.* [< Heb. *gāmāl*] a large, domesticated animal with a humped back and long neck: because it can store water in its body, it is used in Asian and African deserts

ca·mel·lia (kə mēl′yə) *n.* [It. < G. *Kamel* (d. 1706), missionary to the Far East] 1. an Asiatic evergreen tree or shrub with glossy, dark-green leaves and waxy, roselike flowers 2. the flower

ca·mel·o·pard (kə mel′ə pärd′) *n.* [< Gr. *kamelos*, camel + *pardalis*, leopard: from its neck and spots] *early name for* GIRAFFE

camel's hair 1. the hair of the camel 2. cloth made of this hair, sometimes mixed with wool, etc.

Cam·em·bert (cheese) (kam′əm ber′) [< *Camembert*, Fr. village] a soft, creamy, rich cheese

cam·e·o (kam′ē ō′) *n., pl.* -os′ [< It. < ML. *camaeus*] a gem carved with a figure raised in relief

cam·er·a (kam′ər ə) *n.* [L., a vault] 1. a device for taking photographs, a closed box containing a sensitized plate or film on which an image is formed when light enters through a lens 2. *TV* that part of the transmitter which receives the image and transforms it into electrical signals —**in camera** 1. in a judge's private office 2. in privacy or secrecy

cam·i·sole (kam′ə sōl′) *n.* [Fr. < Sp. < VL. *camisia*, shirt] 1. a woman's sleeveless underwaist 2. a woman's short negligee

cam·o·mile (kam′ə mīl′, -mēl′) *n. same as* CHAMOMILE

cam·ou·flage (kam′ə fläzh′, -fläj′) *n.* [Fr. < *camoufler*, to disguise] 1. the disguising of ships, guns, etc. to conceal them from the enemy 2. a disguise; deception —*vt., vi.* -flaged′, -flag′ing to disguise (a thing or person) in order to conceal

camp (kamp) *n.* [Fr. < It. < L. *campus*, field] 1. *a)* a place where temporary tents, huts, etc. are put up *b)* a group of such tents, etc. 2. the supporters of a particular cause 3. a recreational place in the country for vacationers, esp. children 4. the people living in a camp 5. [Slang] banality, artifice, etc. so extreme as to amuse or have a perversely sophisticated appeal —*adj.* [Slang] characterized by camp (*n.* 5) —*vi.* 1. to set up a camp 2. to live or stay in a camp (often with *out*) —**break camp** to pack up camping gear and depart

cam·paign (kam pān′) *n.* [< Fr. < L. *campus*, field] 1. a series of military operations with a particular objective 2. a series of planned actions, as for electing a candidate —*vi.* to participate in a campaign —**cam·paign′er** *n.*

cam·pa·ni·le (kam′pə nē′lē) *n., pl.* -les, -li (-lē) [It. < LL. *campana*, a bell] a bell tower

camp′er *n.* 1. one who vacations at a camp 2. a motor vehicle or trailer equipped for camping out

camp′fire′ *n.* 1. an outdoor fire at a camp 2. a social gathering around such a fire

cam·phor (kam′fər) *n.* [< Sans. *karpurah*, camphor tree] a crystalline substance with a strong odor, derived chiefly from an Oriental evergreen tree (camphor tree): used to repel moths, in medicine as a stimulant, etc. —**cam′phor·at′ed** *adj.*

camp meeting a religious gathering held outdoors or in a tent, etc.

cam·pus (kam′pəs) *n., pl.* -pus·es [L., field] the grounds, sometimes including the buildings, of a school or college —*adj.* of a school or college

camp′y *adj.* -i·er, -i·est [Slang] characterized by camp (*n.* 5)

can[1] (kan, kən) *vi. pt.* **could** [OE. *cunnan*, know] 1. to know how to 2. to be able to 3. to be likely to *[can* it be true?] 4. to have the right to 5. [Colloq.] to be permitted to; may —**can but** can only

can[2] (kan) *n.* [OE. *canne*, cup] 1. a container, usually metal, with a separate cover 2. a tinned metal container in which foods, etc. are sealed for preservation 3. the contents of a can 4. [Slang] *a)* a prison *b)* a toilet —*vt.* **canned, can′ning** 1. to put up in airtight cans or jars for preservation 2. [Slang] to dismiss

Ca·naan (kā′nən) *Bible* Promised Land of the Israelites

Ca·na·di·an (kə nā′dē ən) *adj.* of Canada, its people, etc. —*n.* a native of Canada

ca·naille (kə näl′) *n.* [Fr. < It. < L. *canis,* a dog] the mob; rabble

ca·nal (kə nal′) *n.* [< L. *canalis,* a channel] **1.** an artificial waterway for transportation or irrigation **2.** *Anat.* a tubular passage or duct — *vt.* **-nalled′** or **-naled′, -nal′ling** or **-nal′ing** to build a canal through

ca·na·pé (kan′ə pē, -pā′) *n.* [Fr.] a cracker, etc. spread with spiced meat, fish, cheese, etc., served as an appetizer

ca·nard (kə närd′) *n.* [Fr., a duck, hoax] a false, esp. malicious, report

ca·nar·y (kə ner′ē) *n., pl.* **-les** [< *Canary Islands*] **1.** a yellow songbird of the finch family **2.** a light yellow: also **canary yellow**

ca·nas·ta (kə nas′tə) *n.* [Sp., basket] a double-deck card game for two to six players

can·can (kan′kan′) *n.* [Fr.] a lively dance with much high kicking

can·cel (kan′s'l) *vt.* **-celed** or **-celled, -cel·ing** or **-cel·ling** [< L. *cancelli,* lattice] **1.** to cross out, as with lines **2.** to make invalid **3.** to do away with; abolish **4.** to neutralize or balance (often with *out*) —*n.* a canceling —**can′cel·la′-tion** *n.*

can·cer (kan′sər) *n.* [< L., a crab] [C-] the fourth sign of the zodiac —*n.* **1.** a malignant tumor: cancers tend to spread **2.** anything evil that spreads and destroys —**can′cer·ous** *adj.*

can·de·la·brum (kan′də lä′brəm, -lab′rəm) *n., pl.* **-bra** (-brə), **-brums** [< L. *candela,* candle] a large branched candlestick: also **can′de·la′bra** (-brə) *pl.* **-bras**

can·did (kan′did) *adj.* [< L. *candidus,* white, sincere] **1.** honest or frank **2.** unposed and informal [a candid photograph] —**can′did·ly** *adv.*

can·di·date (kan′də dāt′, -dit) *n.* [L. *candidatus,* white-robed, as Roman office seekers] one seeking, or proposed for, an office, award, etc. —**can′di·da·cy** *n., pl.* **-cies**

can·died (kan′dēd) *adj.* **1.** cooked in sugar **2.** sugary

can·dle (kan′d'l) *n.* [< L. *candela*] **1.** a cylinder of tallow or wax with a wick through it, which gives light when burned **2.** a unit of luminous intensity —*vt.* **-dled, -dling** to examine (eggs) for freshness, etc. by holding in front of a light —**burn the candle at both ends** to work or play so hard that one's energy is dissipated —**can′dler** *n.*

can′dle·pow′er *n.* the luminous intensity of a light source expressed in candles

can′dle·stick′ *n.* a cupped or spiked holder for a candle or candles

can·dor (kan′dər) *n.* [L., whiteness, openness] honesty or frankness in expressing oneself: Brit. sp. **can′dour**

can·dy (kan′dē) *n., pl.* **-dies** [< Per. *qand,* cane sugar] **1.** a sweet food, usually made of sugar or syrup, in small pieces, with flavoring, nuts, fruits, etc. **2.** a piece of this —*vt.* **-died, -dy·ing 1.** to cook in sugar or syrup, esp. to preserve or glaze **2.** to crystallize into sugar **3.** to sweeten; make pleasant

cane (kān) *n.* [< Gr. *kanna*] **1.** the slender, jointed stem of certain plants, as bamboo **2.** a plant with such a stem, as sugar cane **3.** the woody stem of a fruiting plant **4.** a stick used for flogging **5.** *same as* WALKING STICK **6.** split rattan —*vt.* **caned, can′ing 1.** to flog with a cane **2.** to make or furnish (chairs, etc.) with cane (*n.* 6)

cane·brake (kān′brāk′) *n.* [CANE + BRAKE²] a dense growth of cane plants

cane sugar sugar from sugar cane

ca·nine (kā′nīn) *adj.* [< L. *canis,* a dog] **1.** of or like a dog **2.** of the family of animals that includes dogs, wolves, and foxes —*n.* **1.** a dog or other canine animal **2.** any of the four sharp-pointed teeth next to the incisors: in full **canine tooth**

can·is·ter (kan′is tər) *n.* [< Gr. *kanistron,* wicker basket] a small box or can for coffee, tea, etc.

can·ker (kaŋ′kər) *n.* [< L.: see CANCER] an ulcerlike, spreading sore, esp. in the mouth — **can′ker·ous** *adj.*

can·na·bis (kan′ə bis) *n.* [L., hemp] **1.** hemp **2.** the female flowering tops of the hemp

canned (kand) *adj.* **1.** preserved in cans or jars **2.** [Slang] recorded, as music

can·nel (coal) (kan′'l) [< ? *candle coal*] a variety of bituminous coal that burns with a bright flame

can·ner·y (kan′ər ē) *n., pl.* **-les** a factory where foods are canned

can·ni·bal (kan′ə b'l) *n.* [Sp. *canibal*] **1.** a person who eats human flesh **2.** an animal that eats its own kind —*adj.* of or like cannibals — **can′ni·bal·ism** *n.* —**can′ni·bal·is′tic** *adj.*

can′ni·bal·ize′ (-īz′) *vt., vi.* **-ized′, -iz′ing** to strip parts from (old equipment) for use in other units —**can′ni·bal·i·za′tion** *n.*

can·ning (kan′iŋ) *n.* the process of preserving foods in cans or jars

can·non (kan′ən) *n., pl.* **-nons, -non** [< L. *canna,* cane] **1.** a large, mounted piece of artillery **2.** an automatic gun mounted on an aircraft

can′non·ade′ (-ād′) *n.* a continuous firing of artillery —*vt., vi.* **-ad′ed, -ad′ing** to fire artillery (at)

can′non·ball′ *n.* a heavy metal ball formerly used as a projectile in cannons: also **cannon ball**

can·not (kan′ät, kə nät′) can not —**cannot but** have no choice but to; must

can·ny (kan′ē) *adj.* **-ni·er, -ni·est** [< CAN¹] **1.** clever and cautious **2.** wise and well-informed —**can′ni·ly** *adv.*

ca·noe (kə nōō′) *n.* [< Sp. *canoa* < AmInd.] a narrow, light boat moved by paddles —*vi.* **-noed′, -noe′ing** to paddle, or go in, a canoe — **ca·noe′ist** *n.*

can·on (kan′ən) *n.* [< L., a rule] **1.** a law or body of laws of a church **2.** a basic rule, principle, or criterion **3.** an official list, as of books of the Bible **4.** a clergyman serving in a cathedral

ca·ñon (kan′yən) *n. same as* CANYON

ca·non·i·cal (kə nän′i k'l) *adj.* **1.** of or according to church law **2.** authoritative; accepted — **ca·non′i·cal·ly** *adv.*

ca·non′i·cals (-k'lz) *n.pl.* the prescribed clothes for a clergyman conducting services

can·on·ize (kan′ə nīz′) *vt.* **-ized′, -iz′ing 1.** to declare (a dead person) to be a saint **2.** to glorify **3.** to give church sanction to —**can′on·i·za′tion** *n.*

can·o·py (kan′ə pē) *n., pl.* **-pies** [< Gr. *kōnōpeion,* bed with mosquito nets] **1.** a covering of cloth, etc. fastened above a bed, throne, etc. or held over a person **2.** a rooflike projection —*vt.* **-pied, -py·ing** to place or form a canopy over

cant¹ (kant) *n.* [< L. *canere,* sing] **1.** the secret slang of beggars, thieves, etc.; argot **2.** the special vocabulary of those in a certain occupation; jargon **3.** insincere talk, esp. when pious or moral —*vi.* to use cant

cant² (kant) *n.* [< L. *cant(h)us,* tire of a wheel] **1.** an outside angle **2.** a beveled edge **3.** a tilt, slant, turn, etc. —*vt., vi.* to tilt; slant —*adj.* slanting

can't (kant) cannot

can·ta·bi·le (kän tä′bi lā′) *adj., adv.* [It. < L. *cantare*, sing] *Music* in a flowing manner; songlike —*n.* music in this style

can·ta·loupe, can·ta·loup (kan′tə lōp′) *n.* [< Fr. < It. *Cantalupo*, near Rome, where first grown in Europe] a muskmelon, esp. one with a hard, rough rind and juicy, orange flesh

can·tan·ker·ous (kan taŋ′kər əs) *adj.* [prob. < ME. *contakour*, troublemaker] bad-tempered; quarrelsome —**can·tan′ker·ous·ly** *adv.*

can·ta·ta (kən tät′ə) *n.* [It. < *cantare*, sing] a choral composition telling a story that is sung but not acted

can·teen (kan tēn′) *n.* [< Fr. < It. *cantina*, wine cellar] **1.** a recreation center for servicemen, teen-agers, etc. **2.** a small flask for carrying water

can·ter (kan′tər) *n.* [< *Canterbury gallop*, a riding pace] a moderate gallop —*vi., vt.* to ride at a canter

can·ti·cle (kan′ti k'l) *n.* [< L. *canere*, sing] **1.** a song or chant **2.** a liturgical hymn with words from the Bible

can·ti·le·ver (kan′t'l ē′vər, -ev′ər) *n.* [< ?] **1.** a bracket or block projecting as a support **2.** a projecting structure supported only at one end, which is anchored to a pier or wall —*vt.* to support by means of cantilevers

can·to (kan′tō) *n., pl.* **-tos** [It. < L. *canere*, sing] any of the main divisions of certain long poems

can·ton (kan′tən, kan tän′) *n.* [Fr. < It. < LL. *cantus*, corner] any of the states in the Swiss Republic —*vt.* **1.** to divide into cantons **2.** (kan tän′, -tōn′) to assign quarters to (troops, etc.)

Can·ton·ese (kan′tə nēz′) *adj.* of Canton, China, its people, or its language

can·ton·ment (kan tän′mənt, -tōn′-) *n.* [< Fr.: see CANTON] **1.** the assignment of troops to temporary quarters **2.** the quarters assigned

can·tor (kan′tər) *n.* [L., singer, poet] a singer of liturgical solos in a synagogue

can·vas (kan′vəs) *n.* [< L. *cannabis*, hemp] **1.** a coarse cloth of hemp, cotton, etc., used for tents, sails, etc. **2.** a sail, tent, etc. **3.** an oil painting on canvas —**under canvas 1.** in tents **2.** with sails unfurled

can·vas·back′ *n.* a N. American wild duck with a grayish back

can·vass (kan′vəs) *vt., vi.* [< *canvas:* ? because used for sifting] to go through (places) or among (people) asking for (votes, opinions, orders, etc.) —*n.* a canvassing or survey of votes, opinions, etc. —**can′vass·er** *n.*

can·yon (kan′yən) *n.* [Sp. *cañón,* tube < L. *canna,* reed] a long, narrow valley between high cliffs, often containing a stream

cap (kap) *n.* [< LL. *cappa,* cloak] **1.** any close-fitting head covering, brimless or visored **2.** a caplike thing; cover or top —*vt.* **capped, cap′-ping 1.** to put a cap on **2.** to cover the top or end of **3.** to match or surpass —**cap′per** *n.*

cap. 1. capacity **2.** *pl.* **caps.** capital

ca·pa·ble (kā′pə b'l) *adj.* [Fr. < L. *capere,* take] able; skilled; competent —**capable of 1.** admitting of **2.** having the qualities necessary for **3.** able to —**ca′pa·bil′i·ty** (-bil′ə tē) *n., pl.* **-ties** —**ca′pa·bly** *adv.*

ca·pa·cious (kə pā′shəs) *adj.* [< L. *capere,* take] roomy; spacious —**ca·pa′cious·ly** *adv.* —**ca·pa′cious·ness** *n.*

ca·pac·i·tor (kə pas′ə tər) *n.* a device for storing an electric charge; condenser

ca·pac′i·ty (-tē) *n., pl.* **-ties** [< L. *capere,* take] **1.** the ability to contain, absorb, or receive **2.** content or volume **3.** ability **4.** maximum output **5.** position; function

ca·par·i·son (kə par′ə s'n) *n.* [< Fr. < LL. *cappa,* cloak] an ornamental covering for a horse; trappings —*vt.* to adorn

cape¹ (kāp) *n.* [Fr. < LL. *cappa,* cloak] a sleeveless garment fastened at the neck and hanging over the back and shoulders

cape² (kāp) *n.* [< L. *caput,* head] a piece of land projecting into a body of water

ca·per¹ (kā′pər) *vi.* [prob. < Fr. *capriole,* a leap] to skip about in a playful manner —*n.* **1.** a gay, playful leap **2.** a prank **3.** [Slang] a robbery —**cut a caper** (or **capers**) **1.** to caper **2.** to play tricks

ca·per² (kā′pər) *n.* [< Gr. *kapparis*] the green flower bud of a Mediterranean bush, pickled and used as a seasoning

cap·il·lar·y (kap′ə ler′ē) *adj.* [< L. *capillus,* hair] very slender —*n., pl.* **-les 1.** a tube with a very small bore: also **capillary tube 2.** any of the tiny blood vessels connecting arteries with veins

capillary attraction (or **action**) the action by which liquids in contact with solids, as in a capillary tube, rise or fall: also **cap′il·lar′i·ty** (-ə tē) *n.*

cap·i·tal (kap′ə t'l) *adj.* [< L. *caput,* head] **1.** involving or punishable by death **2.** principal; chief **3.** being the seat of government **4.** of capital, or wealth **5.** excellent —*n.* **1.** *same as* CAPITAL LETTER **2.** a city that is the seat of government of a state, nation, etc. **3.** money or property owned or used in business **4.** an accumulation of such wealth **5.** [*often* C-] capitalists collectively **6.** the top part of a column —**make capital of** to make the most of; exploit

cap·i·tal·ism (-iz'm) *n.* **1.** the economic system in which the means of production and distribution are privately owned and operated for profit **2.** the principles, power, etc. of capitalists

cap·i·tal·ist *n.* **1.** an owner of wealth used in business **2.** an upholder of capitalism **3.** a wealthy person —**cap′i·tal·is′tic** *adj.* —**cap′i·tal·is′ti·cal·ly** *adv.*

cap·i·tal·ize (-īz′) *vt.* **-ized′, -iz′ing 1.** to use as or convert into capital **2.** to establish the capital stock of (a business) at a certain figure **3.** to supply capital to or for **4.** to begin (a word) with a capital letter —**capitalize on** to use to one's own advantage —**cap′i·tal·i·za′tion** *n.*

capital letter a large letter of a kind used to begin a sentence or proper name, as A, B, C, etc.

cap′i·tal·ly *adv.* in an excellent manner

capital punishment the death penalty

capital stock the capital of a corporation, divided into shares

cap·i·ta·tion (kap′ə tā′shən) *n.* [< L. *caput,* head] a tax or fee of so much per head

Cap·i·tol (kap′ə t'l) [< L. *Capitolium,* temple of Jupiter] the building in which the U.S. Congress meets, at Washington, D.C. —*n.* [*usually* c-] the building in which a State legislature meets

ca·pit·u·late (kə pich′ə lāt′) *vi.* **-lat′ed, -lat′ing** [< LL. *capitulare,* arrange conditions] to give up (*to* an enemy) on prearranged conditions —**ca·pit′u·la′tion** *n.*

ca·pon (kā′pän) *n.* [< L. *capo*] a castrated rooster fattened for eating

ca·price (kə prēs′) *n.* [Fr. < It.] **1.** a sudden, impulsive change in thought or action **2.** a capricious quality

ca·pri·cious (kə prish′əs) *adj.* subject to caprices; unpredictable —**ca·pri′cious·ly** *adv.* —**ca·pri′cious·ness** *n.*

Cap·ri·corn (kap'rə kôrn') [< L. *caper*, goat + *cornu*, horn] the tenth sign of the zodiac

cap·si·cum (kap'sə kəm) *n.* [< L. *capsa*, a box] **1.** any of various red peppers with pungent, fleshy pods **2.** these pods used as condiments or as a gastric stimulant

cap·size (kap'sīz) *vt., vi.* **-sized, -siz·ing** [< ?] to overturn or upset: said esp. of a boat

cap·stan (kap'stən) *n.* [< Fr. < L. *capere*, take] an upright drum, as on ships, around which cables are wound so as to haul them in

cap·stone (kap'stōn') *n.* the uppermost stone of a structure

cap·sule (kap's'l) *n.* [Fr. < L. *capsa*, chest] **1.** a small, soluble gelatin container for enclosing a dose of medicine **2.** a detachable compartment to hold men, instruments, etc. in a rocket **3.** *Bot.* a case, pod, or fruit containing seeds, spores, or carpels —*adj.* in a concise form —**cap'su·lar** *adj.*

cap·tain (kap'tən) *n.* [< L. *caput*, the head] **1.** a chief or leader **2.** the master of a ship **3.** the chief pilot of a commercial airplane **4.** the leader of a team, as in sports **5.** *U.S. Mil.* an officer ranking just above a first lieutenant **6.** *U.S. Navy* an officer ranking just above a commander Abbrev. **Capt.** —*vt.* to be captain of —**cap'tain·cy** (-sē), *pl.* **-cies, cap'tain·ship'** *n.*

cap·tion (kap'shən) *n.* [< L. *capere*, take] **1.** a heading, as of a newspaper article, or a legend, as under an illustration **2.** *same as* SUBTITLE (*n.* 2)

cap·tious (kap'shəs) *adj.* [see prec.] **1.** made for the sake of argument, as an objection **2.** quick to find fault —**cap'tious·ly** *adv.*

cap·ti·vate (kap'tə vāt') *vt.* **-vat'ed, -vat'ing** to capture the attention or affection of —**cap'ti·vat'ing·ly** *adv.* —**cap'ti·va'tion** *n.* —**cap'ti·va'tor** *n.*

cap·tive (kap'tiv) *n.* [< L. *capere*, take] a prisoner —*adj.* **1.** taken or held prisoner **2.** obliged to listen *[a captive audience]* —**cap·tiv'i·ty** *n., pl.* **-ties**

cap·tor (kap'tər) *n.* [L.] one who captures

cap·ture (kap'chər) *vt.* **-tured, -tur·ing** [< L. *capere*, take] **1.** to take or seize by force, surprise, etc. **2.** to represent in a more permanent form *[a picture capturing her charm]* —*n.* **1.** a capturing or being captured **2.** that which is captured

Cap·u·chin (kap'yŏŏ shin, -chin) *n.* [< Fr. *capuce*, cowl] **1.** a monk of a Franciscan order **2.** [c-] a new-world monkey with a hoodlike crown of hair

car (kär) *n.* [< L. *carrus*, chariot] **1.** any vehicle on wheels **2.** a vehicle that moves on rails **3.** an automobile **4.** *same as* ELEVATOR (*n.* 2)

ca·ra·bao (kär'ə bou') *n., pl.* **-baos', -bao'** [Sp. < Malay *karbau*] *same as* WATER BUFFALO

car·a·cul (kar'ə kəl) *n. same as* KARAKUL

ca·rafe (kə raf') *n.* [Fr.] a bottle of glass or metal for water, coffee, etc.

car·a·mel (kar'ə m'l, kär'm'l) *n.* [Fr.] **1.** burnt sugar used to color or flavor food **2.** chewy candy made from sugar, milk, etc.

car·a·pace (kar'ə pās') *n.* [Fr. < Sp.] an upper shell, as of the turtle

car·at (kar'ət) *n.* [Fr. < It. < Gr. *keration*] **1.** a unit of weight for precious stones, equal to 200 milligrams **2.** *same as* KARAT

car·a·van (kar'ə van') *n.* [< Fr. < Per. *kārwān*] **1.** a company of people traveling together for safety, as through a desert **2.** *same as* VAN²

car·a·van·sa·ry (kar'ə van'sə rē) *n., pl.* **-ries** [< Fr. < Per. *kārwān*, caravan + *sarāi*, palace] in the Orient, an inn for caravans

car·a·way (kar'ə wā') *n.* [< Ar. *karawiyā'*] the spicy seeds of an herb, used to flavor bread, cheese, etc.

car·bide (kär'bīd) *n.* a compound of an element, usually a metal, with carbon

car·bine (kär'bīn, -bēn) *n.* [< Fr. *scarabée*, beetle] **1.** a short-barreled rifle **2.** *U.S. Armed Forces* a semiautomatic or automatic .30-caliber rifle

carbo- *a combining form meaning* carbon: also **carb-**

car·bo·hy·drate (kär'bə hī'drāt) *n.* [CARBO- + HYDRATE] an organic compound, as a sugar or starch, composed of carbon, hydrogen, and oxygen

car·bol·ic acid (kär bäl'ik) *same as* PHENOL

car·bon (kär'bən) *n.* [< Fr. < L. *carbo*, coal] **1.** a nonmetallic chemical element found esp. in all organic compounds: diamond and graphite are pure carbon: symbol, C: a radioactive isotope (**carbon 14**) is used in dating fossils, etc. **2.** carbon paper **3.** a copy made with carbon paper: in full **carbon copy** —*adj.* of or like carbon

car·bo·na·ceous (kär'bə nā'shəs) *adj.* of, consisting of, or containing carbon

car·bon·ate (kär'bə nit) *n.* a salt or ester of carbonic acid —*vt.* (-nāt') **-at'ed, -at'ing** to charge with carbon dioxide —**car'bon·a'tion** *n.*

carbon black finely divided carbon produced by the incomplete burning of oil or gas

car'bon-date' (-dāt') *vt.* **-dat'ed, -dat'ing** to establish the approximate age of (fossils, etc.) by measuring the carbon 14 content

carbon dioxide a heavy, colorless, odorless gas: it passes out of the lungs in respiration

car·bon·ic acid (kär bän'ik) a weak, colorless acid formed by the solution of carbon dioxide in water

car·bon·if·er·ous (kär'bə nif'ər əs) *adj.* [< CARBON + -FEROUS] containing carbon or coal

car'bon·ize' (-nīz') *vt.* **-ized, -iz'ing 1.** to change into carbon, as by partial burning **2.** to treat or combine with carbon —**car'bon·i·za'tion** *n.*

carbon monoxide a colorless, odorless, highly poisonous gas

carbon paper thin paper coated on one side, as with a carbon preparation, used to make copies of letters, etc.

carbon tet·ra·chlo·ride (tet'rə klôr'īd) a nonflammable, colorless liquid used in fire extinguishers, cleaning mixtures, etc.

Car·bo·run·dum (kär'bə run'dəm) [CARB(ON) + (C)ORUNDUM] *a trademark for* a hard abrasive, esp. a carbide of silicon

car·boy (kär'boi) *n.* [< Per. *qarābah*] a large glass bottle to hold corrosive liquids, enclosed in a protective container

car·bun·cle (kär'buŋ k'l) *n.* [< L. dim. of *carbo*, coal] a painful, pus-bearing inflammation of tissue beneath the skin —**car·bun'cu·lar** (-kyŏŏ lər) *adj.*

car·bu·ret·or (kär'bə rāt'ər, -byŏŏ-) *n.* a device for mixing air with gasoline spray to make an explosive mixture in an internal-combustion engine

car·cass (kär'kəs) *n.* [< Fr. *carcasse*] **1.** the dead body of an animal **2.** a framework or shell Brit. var. **car'case** (-kəs)

car·cin·o·gen (kär sin'ə jən) *n.* [CARCINO(MA) + -GEN] any substance that produces cancer —**car'ci·no·gen'ic** *adj.*

car·ci·no·ma (kär'sə nō'mə) *n., pl.* **-mas, -ma·ta** (-mə tə) [L. < Gr. *karkinos*, a crab] a cancerous growth made up of epithelial cells

card¹ (kärd) *n.* [< Gr. *chartēs*, leaf of paper] **1.**

a flat, stiff piece of paper or pasteboard; specif., *a*) one of a pack of playing cards *b*) a card identifying a person, esp. as a member, agent, etc. *c*) a post card *d*) a card bearing a greeting *e*) any of a series of cards on which information is recorded **2.** an attraction *[a drawing card]* **3.** [Colloq.] a comical person — **put (or lay) one's cards on the table** to reveal something frankly

card² (kärd) *n.* [< L. *carere*, to card] a metal comb or a machine with wire teeth for combing fibers of wool, cotton, etc. —*vt.* to use a card on —**card'ing** *n., adj.*

card'board' *n.* stiff, thick paper, or pasteboard, used for cards, boxes, etc.

car·di·ac (kär'dē ak') *adj.* [< Fr. < Gr. *kardia*, heart] of or near the heart

car·di·gan (kär'də gən) *n.* [< 7th Earl of *Cardigan*] a sweater or jacket, usually knitted, that opens down the front

car·di·nal (kärd''n əl) *adj.* [< L. *cardo*, hinge] **1.** principal; chief **2.** bright-red —*n.* **1.** an official appointed by the Pope to his council **2.** bright red **3.** a bright-red American songbird: in full **cardinal bird 4.** *same as* CARDINAL NUMBER

cardinal number any number used in counting or showing how many (e.g., two, forty, 627, etc.): cf. ORDINAL

cardio- [< Gr. *kardia*, heart] *a combining form meaning* of the heart

car·di·o·gram (kär'dē ə gram') *n. same as* ELECTROCARDIOGRAM —**car'di·o·graph'** (-graf') *n.*

car'di·ol'o·gy (-äl'ə jē) *n.* the branch of medicine dealing with the heart —**car'di·ol'o·gist** *n.*

cards (kärdz) *n.pl.* **1.** any game played with a deck of cards, as poker **2.** card playing

card'sharp' *n.* [Colloq.] a professional cheater at cards: also **card shark, cardsharper**

care (ker) *n.* [< OE. *caru*, sorrow] **1.** *a*) worry or concern *b*) a cause of this **2.** close attention; heed **3.** a liking or regard (*for*) **4.** charge; protection **5.** something to watch over or attend to —*vi.* **cared, car'ing 1.** to feel concern **2.** to feel love or liking (*for*) **3.** to provide (*for*) **4.** to wish (*for*) —**(in) care of** at the address of —**take care of 1.** to be responsible for **2.** to provide for

ca·reen (kə rēn') *vi., vt.* [< Fr. < L. *carina*, keel] to lean or cause to lean sideways; tip; tilt; lurch —*n.* a careening

ca·reer (kə rir') *n.* [< Fr. < It. *carro*, car] **1.** a swift course **2.** one's progress through life **3.** a profession or occupation —*vi.* to rush wildly

ca·reer'ist *n.* a person excessively interested in his own professional ambitions

care'free' *adj.* without care or worry

care'ful *adj.* **1.** cautious; wary **2.** accurately or thoroughly done; painstaking —**care'ful·ly** *adv.* —**care'ful·ness** *n.*

care'less *adj.* **1.** carefree; untroubled **2.** not paying enough attention; inconsiderate **3.** done without enough attention, precision, etc. — **care'less·ly** *adv.* —**care'less·ness** *n.*

ca·ress (kə res') *vt.* [ult. < L. *carus*, dear] to touch lovingly or gently —*n.* an affectionate touch, kiss, etc. —**ca·ress'ing·ly** *adv.*

car·et (kar'it, ker'-) *n.* [L., there is lacking] a mark (Λ) used to show where something is to be added in a written or printed line

care'tak'er *n.* a person hired to take care of something, as a house, estate, etc.

care'worn' *adj.* showing the effects of troubles and worry; haggard

car·fare (kär'fer') *n.* the price of a ride on a streetcar, bus, etc.

car·go (kär'gō) *n., pl.* **-goes, -gos** [< Sp. *cargar*, to load] the load carried by a ship, truck, etc.

car'hop' *n.* [CAR + (BELL)HOP] one who serves customers in cars at a drive-in restaurant

car·i·bou (kar'ə bōō') *n.* [CanadFr.] a large, northern N. American deer

car·i·ca·ture (kar'ə kə chər) *n.* [Fr. < It. *caricare*, exaggerate] **1.** the exaggerated imitation of a person, literary style, etc. for satirical effect **2.** a picture, etc. in which this is done —*vt.* **-tured, -tur·ing** to depict as in a caricature — **car'i·ca·tur·ist** *n.*

car·ies (ker'ēz) *n.* [L., decay] decay of bones, or, esp., of teeth

car·il·lon (kar'ə län') *n.* [Fr., chime of four bells < L. *quattuor*, four] a set of bells tuned to the chromatic scale

car·i·ous (kar'ē əs) *adj.* having caries; decayed

car'load' *n.* a load that fills a car

car·min·a·tive (kär min'ə tiv) *adj.* [< L. *carminare*, cleanse] causing gas to be expelled from the stomach and intestines —*n.* a carminative medicine

car·mine (kär'min, -mīn) *n.* [< Ar. *qirmiz*, crimson] a red or purplish-red color —*adj.* red or purplish-red

car·nage (kär'nij) *n.* [Fr. < L. *caro*, flesh] bloody and extensive slaughter; massacre

car·nal (kär'n'l) *adj.* [< L. *caro*, flesh] **1.** of the flesh; material or worldly **2.** sensual; sexual — **car·nal'i·ty** (-nal'ə tē) *n.*

car·na·tion (kär nā'shən) *n.* [< L. *caro*, flesh] a plant related to the pink, with white, pink, or red flowers

car·nel·ian (kär nēl'yən) *n.* [< L. *carnis*, of flesh (color)] a red variety of chalcedony, used as a gem

car·ni·val (kär'nə vəl) *n.* [< Fr. or It.] **1.** the period of feasting and revelry just before Lent **2.** a reveling; festivity **3.** an entertainment with rides, games, etc.

car·ni·vore (kär'nə vôr') *n.* a carnivorous animal or plant

car·niv·o·rous (kär niv'ə rəs) *adj.* [< L. *caro*, flesh + *vorare*, eat] **1.** flesh-eating **2.** insect-eating, as certain plants **3.** of the carnivores — **car·niv'o·rous·ness** *n.*

car·ol (kar'əl) *n.* [< OFr. *carole*, kind of dance] a song of joy or praise; esp., a Christmas song —*vi., vt.* **-oled** or **-olled, -ol·ing** or **-ol·ling** to sing; warble —**car'ol·er, car'ol·ler** *n.*

car·om (kar'əm) *n.* [< Sp. *carambola*] **1.** Billiards a shot in which the cue ball successively hits the two object balls **2.** a hitting and rebounding —*vi.* **1.** to make a carom **2.** to hit and rebound

ca·rot·id (kə rät'id) *adj.* [Gr. *karōtis*] designating or of either of the two main arteries, one on each side of the neck, which convey blood to the head —*n.* a carotid artery

ca·rous·al (kə rou'zəl) *n. same as* CAROUSE

ca·rouse (kə rouz') *vi.* **-roused', -rous'ing** [< G. *gar aus(trinken)*, (to drink) up entirely] to engage in a noisy drinking party —*n.* a noisy drinking party —**ca·rous'er** *n.*

carp¹ (kärp) *n., pl.* **carp, carps** [< Gmc. *carpa*] an edible freshwater fish living in ponds

carp² (kärp) *vi.* [< ON. *karpa*, brag] to find fault pettily or unfairly —**carp'er** *n.*

car·pel (kär'pəl) *n.* [< Gr. *karpos*, fruit] a simple pistil, regarded as a modified leaf

car·pen·ter (kär'pən tər) *n.* [< L. *carpentum*, a cart] one who builds and repairs wooden articles, buildings, etc. —*vi.* to do a carpenter's work —**car'pen·try** (-trē) *n.*

car·pet (kär'pit) *n.* [< L. *carpere*, to card] **1.** a heavy fabric for covering a floor **2.** anything like a carpet **—vt.** to cover as with a carpet — **on the carpet** being reprimanded

car′pet·bag′ *n.* an old-fashioned traveling bag, made of carpeting

car′pet·bag′ger *n.* a Northerner who went South to profit from unsettled conditions after the Civil War

car′pet·ing *n.* carpets or carpet fabric

car pool an arrangement by a group to rotate the use of their cars

car′port′ (-pôrt′) *n.* an automobile shelter built as a roof at the side of a building

car·riage (kar′ij) *n.* [< L. *carrus,* wagon] **1.** a carrying; transportation **2.** manner of carrying oneself; bearing **3.** *a)* a four-wheeled, horse-drawn passenger vehicle *b)* *same as* BABY CARRIAGE **4.** a wheeled support **5.** a moving part (as on a typewriter) that supports and shifts something

car·ri·er (kar′ē ər) *n.* **1.** one that carries **2.** one in the transportation business **3.** one that transmits disease germs **4.** *same as* AIRCRAFT CARRIER

carrier pigeon *same as* HOMING PIGEON

car·ri·on (kar′ē ən) *n.* [< L. *caro,* flesh] decaying flesh of a dead body

car·rot (kar′ət) *n.* [< Gr. *karōton*] **1.** a plant with an edible, fleshy, orange-red root **2.** the root

car′rot·y *adj.* orange-red, as hair

car·rou·sel (kar′ə sel′, -zel′) *n.* [Fr.] *same as* MERRY-GO-ROUND

car·ry (kar′ē) *vt.* **-ried, -ry·ing** [< L. *carrus,* car] **1.** to hold or support **2.** to take from one place to another **3.** to lead or impel **4.** to transmit *[air carries* sounds*]* **5.** to transfer or extend **6.** to involve; imply **7.** to bear (oneself) in a specified way **8.** to win (an election, debate, etc.) **9.** *a)* to keep in stock *b)* to keep on one's account books, etc. **—vi. 1.** to act as a conductor, bearer, etc. **2.** to cover a range, as a voice **—n.,** *pl.* **-ries 1.** the distance covered by a gun, ball, etc. **2.** a portage **—be** (or **get**) **carried away** to become very emotional or enthusiastic — **carry on 1.** to engage in; conduct **2.** to continue **3.** [Colloq.] to behave wildly or childishly **—carry out** (or **through**) **1.** to put (plans, etc.) into practice **2.** to accomplish **—carry over** to postpone; continue

car′ry·all′ *n.* a large bag, basket, etc.

carrying charge interest paid on the balance owed in installment buying

car′ry·out′ *adj.* designating or of prepared food sold to be consumed elsewhere

car′ry-o′ver *n.* something carried over, as a remainder of crops or goods

car′sick′ *adj.* nauseated from riding in an automobile, bus, etc. **—car′sick′ness** *n.*

cart (kärt) *n.* [< ON. *kartr*] a small wagon **—vt., vi.** to carry in a cart, truck, etc.; transport — **cart′er** *n.*

cart·age (kär′tij) *n.* **1.** the work of carting **2.** the charge for this

carte blanche (kärt′ blänsh′) [Fr., blank card] full authority

car·tel (kär tel′) *n.* [G. *kartell* < Fr. *cartel:* see CARD[1]] an association of business firms establishing a national or international monopoly

car·ti·lage (kärt′'l ij) *n.* [< L. *cartilago*] a tough, elastic tissue forming part of the skeleton **—car′ti·lag′i·nous** (-aj′ə nəs) *adj.*

car·tog·ra·phy (kär täg′rə fē) *n.* [see CARD[1] & -GRAPHY] the art of making maps or charts — **car·tog′ra·pher** *n.*

car·ton (kärt′'n) *n.* [Fr. < It. *carta,* card] a cardboard box or container

car·toon (kär tōōn′) *n.* [< Fr.: see prec.] **1.** a drawing that caricatures some person or event **2.** *same as* COMIC STRIP **3.** *same as* ANIMATED CARTOON **—vi., vt.** to draw cartoons (of) **—cartoon′ist** *n.*

car·tridge (kär′trij) *n.* [< Fr. < It. *carta,* card] **1.** a cylindrical case of cardboard, metal, etc. containing the charge and primer, and usually the projectile, for a firearm **2.** a small container, as for camera film, a phonograph needle, etc.

cart·wheel (kärt′hwēl′, -wēl′) *n.* a kind of handspring performed sideways

carve (kärv) *vt.* **carved, carv′ing** [< OE. *ceorfan*] **1.** to make or shape by or as by cutting **2.** to decorate with cut designs **3.** to divide by cutting; slice **—vi. 1.** to carve statues or designs **2.** to carve meat **—carv′er** *n.* **—carv′ing** *n.*

carving knife a large knife for carving meat

car′wash′ *n.* a facility for washing and polishing automobiles

ca·sa·ba (kə sä′bə) *n.* [< *Kassaba,* town in Asia Minor] a cultivated melon with a hard, yellow rind

cas·cade (kas kād′) *n.* [Fr. < L. *cadere,* to fall] **1.** a small, steep waterfall **2.** a shower, as of sparks, etc. **—vi., vi. -cad′ed, -cad′ing** to fall or drop in a cascade

cas·car·a (kas ker′ə) *n.* [Sp., bark] **1.** a small buckthorn of the U.S. Pacific coast **2.** a laxative made from its bark

case[1] (kās) *n.* [< L. *casus,* accident < *cadere,* to fall] **1.** an example or instance *[case* of measles*]* **2.** a person being helped by a doctor, etc. **3.** any matter requiring study **4.** a statement of the facts, as in a law court **5.** convincing arguments *[he has no case]* **6.** a lawsuit **7.** a form taken by a noun, pronoun, or adjective to show its relation to neighboring words **—vt. cased, cas′ing** [Slang] to look over carefully — **in any case** anyhow **—in case** in the event that; if **—in case of** in the event of **—in no case** by no means; never

case[2] (kās) *n.* [< L. *capsa,* a box] **1.** a container, as a box **2.** a protective cover *[a watch case]* **3.** a frame, as for a window **—vt. cased, cas′ing 1.** to put in a container **2.** to cover or enclose

ca·sein (kā′sēn) *n.* [< L. *caseus,* cheese] a protein that is one of the chief constituents of milk and the basis of cheese

case·load (kās′lōd′) *n.* the number of cases being handled by a court, caseworker, etc.

case·ment (kās′mənt) *n.* [< OFr. *encassement,* a frame] a hinged window frame that opens outward

case′work′ *n.* social work in which guidance is given in cases of personal and family maladjustment **—case′work′er** *n.*

cash (kash) *n.* [< Fr. *caisse,* money box] **1.** money that one actually has; esp., ready money **2.** money, a check, etc. paid at the time of purchase **—vt.** to give or get cash for — *adj.* of or for cash **—cash in 1.** to turn into cash **2.** [Slang] to die

cash discount a discount allowed a purchaser paying within a specified period

cash·ew (kash′ōō, kə shōō′) *n.* [< Fr. < SAm-Ind. *acajú*] **1.** a tropical tree bearing edible, kidney-shaped nuts **2.** the nut

cash·ier[1] (ka shir′) *n.* [Fr. *caissier*] a person in charge of cash transactions for a bank, store, etc.

cash·ier[2] (ka shir′) *vt.* [< LL. *cassare,* destroy] to dismiss in dishonor

cash·mere (kazh′mir) *n.* [< *Kashmir,* region

in India] **1.** a fine carded wool from goats of N India and Tibet **2.** a soft, twilled cloth as of this wool

cash register a device, usually with a money drawer, that registers visibly the amount of a sale

cas·ing (kās′iŋ) *n.* **1.** a protective covering, as the skin of a sausage or the outer covering of a pneumatic tire **2.** a frame, as for a door or window

ca·si·no (kə sē′nō) *n., pl.* **-nos** [It. < L. *casa*, cottage] **1.** a room or building for dancing, gambling, etc. **2.** *same as* CASSINO

cask (kask) *n.* [< Sp. < L. *quassare*, shatter] **1.** a barrel of any size, esp. one for liquids **2.** the contents of a full cask

cas·ket (kas′kit) *n.* [prob. < OFr. *casse*, box] **1.** a small box or chest, as for valuables **2.** a coffin

Cas·san·dra (kə san′drə) *Gr. Myth.* a Trojan prophetess of doom whose prophecies were never believed

cas·sa·va (kə sä′və) *n.* [< Fr. < WInd. *casávi*] **1.** a tropical American plant with edible, starchy roots **2.** a starch made from the root, used in tapioca

cas·se·role (kas′ə rōl′) *n.* [Fr. < Gr. *kyathos*, a bowl] **1.** a covered baking dish in which food can be cooked and served **2.** food baked in such a dish

cas·sette (ka set′, kə-) *n.* [Fr. < L. *capsa*, a box] **1.** a case with roll film in it, for loading a camera quickly **2.** a similar case with magnetic tape, for use in a tape recorder

cas·sia (kash′ə) *n.* [ult. < Heb. *qeṣī′āh*] **1.** *a)* the bark of a tree of SE Asia: used as a source of cinnamon *b)* this tree **2.** any of various tropical plants whose leaves yield senna

cas·si·no (kə sē′nō) *n.* [see CASINO] a simple card game for two to four players

cas·sock (kas′ək) *n.* [< Fr. < Per. *kazh*, raw silk] a long, closefitting vestment, worn by clergymen

cast (kast) *vt.* **cast, cast′ing** [< ON. *kasta*] **1.** to throw with force; fling; hurl **2.** to deposit (a ballot or vote) **3.** to direct *[to cast* one's eyes*]* **4.** to project *[to cast* light*]* **5.** to throw off; shed (a skin, etc.) **6.** to form (molten metal, etc.) by pouring into a mold **7.** to select (an actor) for (a role or play) —*vi.* to throw; hurl — *n.* **1.** a casting; throw **2.** something formed in a mold, as a statue **3.** a plaster form for immobilizing a broken limb **4.** the set of actors in a play or movie **5.** an appearance, as of features **6.** kind; quality **7.** tinge; shade —**cast about** to search *(for)* —**cast aside** (or **away**) to discard — **cast off 1.** to discard **2.** to free a ship from a dock, etc.

cas·ta·nets (kas′tə nets′) *n.pl.* [< Sp. < L. *castanea*, chestnut: from the shape] a pair of small, hollow pieces of hard wood, ivory, etc., held in the hand and clicked in time to music

cast′a·way′ *n.* **1.** a person or thing cast off **2.** a shipwrecked person —*adj.* **1.** discarded **2.** shipwrecked

caste (kast) *n.* [Fr. < L. *castus*, pure] **1.** any of the hereditary Hindu social classes of a formerly segregated system of India **2.** any exclusive group **3.** class distinction based on birth, wealth, etc. —**lose caste** to lose social status

cast′er *n.* **1.** a container for serving vinegar, salt, etc. at the table **2.** a wheel, etc. set in a frame, for supporting and moving furniture Also **cas′tor**

cas·ti·gate (kas′tə gāt′) *vt.* **-gat′ed, -gat′ing** [< L. *castigare*] to rebuke severely, esp. by public

criticism —**cas′ti·ga′tion** *n.* —**cas′ti·ga′tor** *n.*

Cas·tile soap (kas tēl′) [< *Castile*, Spain, where first made] [*also* **c- s-**] a fine, mild, hard soap made from olive oil

cast′ing *n.* **1.** the action of one that casts **2.** anything, esp. of metal, cast in a mold

cast iron a hard, brittle alloy of iron made by casting —**cast′-i′ron** *adj.*

cas·tle (kas′'l) *n.* [< L. *castrum*, fort] **1.** a large building or group of buildings fortified as a stronghold **2.** any massive dwelling like this **3.** *Chess same as* ROOK² —*vt.* **-tled, -tling** *Chess* to move (a king) two squares and then set the castle in the square skipped by the king

cast′off′ *adj.* thrown away; discarded —*n.* a person or thing cast off

cas·tor-oil plant (kas′tər oil′) [< Gr. *kastōr*, beaver] a tropical plant with large, beanlike seeds which yield an oil (**castor oil**) used as a cathartic

cas·trate (kas′trāt) *vt.* **-trat·ed, -trat·ing** [< L. *castrare*] to remove the testicles of; emasculate —**cas·tra′tion** *n.*

cas·u·al (kazh′ōō wəl) *adj.* [< L. *casus*, chance] **1.** happening by chance; not planned **2.** occasional *[a casual* worker*]* **3.** careless or cursory **4.** nonchalant **5.** informal, or for informal use —**cas′u·al·ly** *adv.* —**cas′u·al·ness** *n.*

cas·u·al·ty (kazh′əl tē, -ōō wəl-) *n., pl.* **-ties 1.** an accident, esp. a fatal one **2.** a member of the armed forces killed, wounded, captured, etc. **3.** anyone hurt or killed in an accident

cas·u·ist·ry (kazh′ōō wis trē) *n., pl.* **-ries** [< Fr. < L. *casus*, CASE¹] subtle but false reasoning, esp. about moral issues; sophistry —**cas′u·ist** *n.*

cat (kat) *n.* [OE.] **1.** a small, soft-furred animal, often kept as a pet or for killing mice **2.** any flesh-eating mammal related to this, as the lion, tiger, leopard, etc. **3.** a spiteful woman **4.** [Slang] a man —**let the cat out of the bag** to let a secret be found out —**cat′like′** *adj.*

cat·a·clysm (kat′ə kliz′m) *n.* [< Gr. *kata-*, down + *klyzein*, to wash] **1.** a great flood **2.** any sudden, violent change, as in war —**cat′a·clys′mic** (-kliz′mik) *adj.*

cat·a·comb (kat′ə kōm′) *n.* [< ? L. *cata*, by + *tumba*, tomb] a gallery in an underground burial place: *usually used in pl.*

cat·a·falque (kat′ə falk′, -fôlk′) *n.* [Fr. < L. *cata-*, by + *fala*, scaffold] a wooden framework on which a body in a coffin lies in state

cat·a·lep·sy (kat′'l ep′sē) *n.* [< Gr. *katalēpsis*, a seizing] a condition of muscle rigidity and sudden, temporary loss of consciousness, as in epilepsy —**cat′a·lep′tic** *adj.*, *n.*

cat·a·log, cat·a·logue (kat′'l ôg′) *n.* [< Fr. < Gr. *kata-*, down + *legein*, to count] a complete list, as an alphabetical card file of the books in a library, a list of articles for sale, etc. —*vt., vi.* **-loged′** or **-logued′, -log′ing** or **-logu′ing** to arrange in a catalog —**cat′a·log′er** or **cat′a·logu′er** *n.*

ca·tal·pa (kə tal′pə) *n.* [< AmInd.] a tree with large, heart-shaped leaves and slender, beanlike pods

ca·tal·y·sis (kə tal′ə sis) *n., pl.* **-ses′** (-sēz′) [< Gr. *katalysis*, dissolution] the speeding up or, sometimes, slowing down of a chemical reaction by adding a substance which itself is not changed thereby —**cat·a·lyt·ic** (kat′'l it′ik) *adj.*, *n.*

cat·a·lyst (kat′'l ist) *n.* any substance serving as the agent in catalysis

cat·a·mount (kat′ə mount′) *n.* [< CAT + obs. *a*, of + MOUNT(AIN)] **1.** the puma **2.** the lynx

cat·a·pult (kat′ə pult′) *n.* [< Gr. *kata-*, down + *pallein*, hurl] 1. an ancient military device for throwing stones, etc. 2. a device for launching an airplane, rocket missile, etc. as from a deck or ramp —*vt.* to shoot as from a catapult —*vi.* to leap

cat·a·ract (kat′ə rakt′) *n.* [< Gr. *kata-*, down + *rhēgnynai*, to break] 1. a large waterfall 2. *a)* an eye disease in which the lens becomes opaque, causing partial or total blindness *b)* the opaque area

ca·tas·tro·phe (kə tas′trə fē) *n.* [< Gr. *kata-*, down + *strephein*, to turn] any sudden, great disaster —**cat·a·stroph·ic** (kat′ə sträf′ik) *adj.* — **cat′a·stroph′i·cal·ly** *adv.*

cat′bird′ *n.* a slate-gray N. American songbird that makes a mewing sound like a cat

cat′boat′ *n.* a sailboat with a single sail and mast set well forward

cat′call′ *n.* a shrill shout or whistle expressing derision, etc. —*vt., vi.* to make catcalls (at)

catch (kach) *vt.* **caught, catch′ing** [< L. *capere*, to take] 1. to seize and hold; capture 2. to take by a trap 3. to deceive 4. to surprise 5. to get to in time *[to catch a bus]* 6. to lay hold of; grab *[to catch a ball]* 7. to become infected with *[to catch a cold]* 8. to understand 9. to get entangled 10. [Colloq.] to see, hear, etc. — *vi.* 1. to become held, fastened, etc. 2. to burn 3. to keep hold, as a lock —*n.* 1. a catching 2. a thing that catches 3. something caught 4. one worth catching as a spouse 5. a break in the voice 6. [Colloq.] a tricky qualification —**catch at** to reach for eagerly —**catch on** 1. to understand 2. to become popular —**catch up** 1. to snatch 2. to overtake

catch′all′ (-ôl′) *n.* a place for holding all sorts of things

catch′er *n.* 1. one that catches 2. *Baseball* the player behind home plate, who catches pitched balls

catch′ing *adj.* 1. contagious 2. attractive

catch·up (kech′əp, kach′-) *n. same as* KETCHUP

catch′word′ *n.* 1. a word so placed as to catch attention, as either of the words at the top of this page 2. a word or phrase repeated so often that it becomes a slogan

catch′y *adj.* **-i·er, -i·est** 1. easily taken up and remembered *[a catchy tune]* 2. tricky

cat·e·chism (kat′ə kiz′m) *n.* [< Gr. *kata-*, thoroughly + *ēchein*, to sound] 1. a handbook of questions and answers for teaching the principles of a religion 2. a close questioning

cat′e·chize′ (-kīz′) *vt.* **-chized′, -chiz′ing** [see CATECHISM] to question searchingly: also **cat′-e·chise′** —**cat′e·chi·za′tion** *n.*

cat·e·gor·i·cal (kat′ə gôr′i k′l) *adj.* 1. unqualified; positive; explicit: said of a statement, etc. 2. of, as, or in a category —**cat′e·gor′i·cal·ly** *adv.*

cat·e·go·rize (kat′ə gə rīz′) *vt.* **-rized′, -riz′ing** to place in a category; classify

cat′e·go′ry (-gôr′ē) *n., pl.* **-ries** [< Gr. *katēgorein*, assert] a class or division in a scheme of classification

ca·ter (kā′tər) *vi.* [< L. *ad-*, to + *capere*, to take] 1. to provide food and service, as for parties 2. to seek to gratify another's desires (with *to*) —**ca′ter·er** *n.*

cat·er·cor·nered (kat′ē kôr′nərd) *adj.* [< OFr. *catre*, four + CORNERED] diagonal —*adv.* diagonally Also **cat′er·cor′ner**

cat·er·pil·lar (kat′ər pil′ər) *n.* [< L. *catta pilosus*, hairy cat] the wormlike larva of a butterfly, moth, etc. —[C-] *a trademark for* a tractor having an endless roller belt on each side, for moving over rough ground

cat·er·waul (kat′ər wôl′) *vi.* [prob. echoic] to make a shrill, howling sound like that of a cat; wail —*n.* such a sound

cat′fish′ *n., pl.*: see FISH a scaleless fish with long, whiskerlike barbels around the mouth

cat′gut′ *n.* a tough thread made from dried intestines, as of sheep, and used for surgical sutures, etc.

Cath. Catholic

ca·thar·sis (kə thär′sis) *n.* [< Gr. *katharos*, pure] 1. a purging, esp. of the bowels 2. a relieving of the emotions, esp. through the arts or psychotherapy

ca·thar′tic *adj.* purging —*n.* a medicine for purging the bowels; laxative

ca·the·dral (kə thē′drəl) *n.* [< Gr. *kata-*, down + *hedra*, a seat] 1. the main church of a bishop's see 2. any large church

cath·e·ter (kath′ə tər) *n.* [< Gr. *kata-*, down + *hienai*, send] a slender tube inserted into a body passage, etc., as for draining urine from the bladder —**cath′e·ter·ize′** (-īz′) *vt.* **-ized′, -iz′ing**

cath·ode (kath′ōd) *n.* [< Gr. *kata-*, down + *hodos*, way] 1. the negative electrode in an electrolytic cell, electron tube, etc. 2. the positive terminal in a battery

cathode rays streams of electrons projected from a cathode: they produce X-rays on striking solids

cath·o·lic (kath′ə lik, kath′lik) *adj.* [< Gr. *kata-*, completely + *holos*, whole] 1. all-inclusive; universal 2. broad in sympathies, tastes, etc.; liberal 3. [C-] of the Christian church headed by the Pope; Roman Catholic —*n.* [C-] *same as* ROMAN CATHOLIC —**Ca·thol·i·cism** (kə thäl′ə siz′m) *n.* —**cath·o·lic·i·ty** (kath′ə lis′ə tē) *n.*

cat·i·on (kat′ī′ən) *n.* [< Gr. *kata-*, down + *ienai*, to go] a positive ion: in electrolysis, cations move toward the cathode

cat·kin (kat′kin) *n.* [< Du. *katte*, cat] a drooping, scaly spike of flowers without petals, as on poplars or walnuts

cat·nap (kat′nap′) *n.* a short, light sleep —*vi.* **-napped′, -nap′ping** to take a catnap

cat′nip′ *n.* [CAT + nip (dial. for *catnip*) < L. *nepeta*] a plant of the mint family: cats like its odor

cat-o′-nine-tails (kat′ə nīn′tālz′) *n., pl.* **-tails′** a whip made of nine knotted cords attached to a handle

cat′s-paw′ (kats′pô′) *n.* a person used by another to do distasteful or unlawful work; dupe

cat·sup (kech′əp, kat′səp) *n. same as* KETCHUP

cat·tail (kat′tāl′) *n.* a tall marsh plant with long, brown, fuzzy spikes

cat·tle (kat′′l) *n.* [ult. < L. *caput*, the head] 1. [Archaic] farm animals 2. cows, bulls, steers, or oxen

cat·ty (kat′ē) *adj.* **-ti·er, -ti·est** 1. of or like a cat 2. spiteful, mean, malicious, etc. —**cat′ti·ly** *adv.* —**cat′ti·ness** *n.*

cat′ty-cor′nered *adj., adv. same as* CATER-CORNERED: also **cat′ty-cor′ner**

cat·walk (kat′wôk′) *n.* a high, narrow walk, as along a bridge or over an engine room

Cau·ca·sian (kô kā′zhən) *adj.* 1. of the Caucasus, its people, etc. 2. *same as* CAUCASOID —*n.* 1. a native of the Caucasus 2. *same as* CAUCASOID

Cau·ca·soid (kôk′ə soid′) *adj.* designating or of one of the major groups of mankind: loosely called the *white race* —*n.* a member of the Caucasoid group

cau·cus (kôk′əs) *n.* [< ?] a private meeting of

caudal

74

cell

a party to decide on policy, candidates, etc. —
vi. -cused or **-cussed, -cus·ing** or **-cus·sing** to
hold, or take part in, a caucus
cau·dal (kôd′'l) **adj.** [< L. *cauda,* tail] of, like,
at, or near the tail
caught (kôt) **pt. & pp.** of CATCH
caul (kôl) **n.** [OE. *cawl,* net] a membrane
sometimes enveloping the head of a child at
birth
caul·dron (kôl′drən) **n.** *same as* CALDRON
cau·li·flow·er (kôl′ə flou′ər, käl′-) **n.** [< It. <
L. *caulis,* cabbage] **1.** a variety of cabbage
with a compact white head of fleshy flower
stalks **2.** the head of this plant, eaten as a
vegetable
caulk (kôk) **vt.** [< L. *calx,* a heel] **1.** to make (a
boat, etc.) watertight by filling the seams with
oakum, tar, etc. **2.** to stop up (cracks) with a
filler **—caulk′er n.**
caus·al (kôz′'l) **adj. 1.** of, like, being, or expressing a cause **2.** relating to cause and effect
—cau·sal·i·ty (kô zal′ə tē) **n. —caus′al·ly adv.**
cau·sa·tion (kô zā′shən) **n. 1.** a causing **2.**
anything producing an effect; cause **—caus·a-
tive** (kôz′ə tiv) **adj.**
cause (kôz) **n.** [< L. *causa*] **1.** anything producing an effect or result **2.** a reason or motive
for some action, feeling, etc. **3.** any objective
or movement that people are interested in and
support **4.** a case to be resolved by a court **—vt.**
caused, caus′ing to be the cause of; bring
about **—cause′less adj.**
cause·way (kôz′wā′) **n.** [ult. < L. *calx,* limestone + WAY] **1.** a raised path or road, as
across a marsh **2.** a paved road; highway
caus·tic (kôs′tik) **adj.** [< Gr. *kaiein,* to burn]
1. that can burn or destroy tissue by chemical
action; corrosive **2.** cutting or sarcastic **—n.** a
caustic substance **—caus′ti·cal·ly adv.**
cau·ter·ize (kôt′ər iz′) **vt. -ized′, -iz′ing** [< Gr.
kautēr, branding iron] to burn with a hot iron
or needle, or with a caustic, so as to destroy
dead tissue, etc. **—cau′ter·i·za′tion n.**
cau′ter·y n., pl. -ies 1. an instrument or substance for cauterizing **2.** a cauterizing
cau·tion (kô′shən) **n.** [< L. *cautio*] **1.** a warning; admonition **2.** prudence; wariness **—vt.** to
warn; admonish
cau′tion·ar′y (-er′ē) **adj.** urging caution
cau·tious (kô′shəs) **adj.** full of caution; careful
to avoid danger; wary **—cau′tious·ly adv. —
cau′tious·ness n.**
cav·al·cade (kav′'l kād′) **n.** [Fr. < L. *caballus,*
horse] a procession, as of horsemen or car-
riages
cav·a·lier (kav′ə lir′) **n.** [Fr. < L. *caballus,*
horse] **1.** an armed horseman; knight **2.** a gallant gentleman, esp. a lady's escort **—adj. 1.**
free and easy **2.** casual **3.** arrogant **—cav′a-
lier′ly adv., adj.**
cav·al·ry (kav′'l rē) **n., pl. -ries** [< Fr.: see
CAVALIER] combat troops mounted originally
on horses but now often on motorized armored vehicles **—cav′al·ry·man** (-mən) **n., pl.
-men**
cave (kāv) **n.** [< L. *cavus,* hollow] a hollow
place inside the earth; cavern **—vt., vi. caved,
cav′ing** to collapse or make collapse (with *in*)
ca·ve·at emp·tor (kā′vē at′ emp′tôr) [L.] let
the buyer beware
cave-in′ n. 1. a caving in **2.** a place where the
ground, a mine, etc. has caved in
cave man a prehistoric human being of the
Stone Age who lived in caves
cav·ern (kav′ərn) **n.** [< L. *cavus,* hollow] a
cave, esp. a large cave

cav′ern·ous (-ər nəs) **adj. 1.** full of caverns **2.**
like a cavern
cav·i·ar, cav·i·are (kav′ē är′) **n.** [Fr. < Per.
khāviyār] the salted eggs of sturgeon, salmon,
etc. eaten as an appetizer
cav·il (kav′'l) **vi. -iled** or **-illed, -il·ing** or **-il·ling**
[< L. *cavilla,* a jest] to object unnecessarily;
carp **—n.** a trivial objection; quibble **—cav′il·er,
cav′il·ler n.**
cav·i·ty (kav′ə tē) **n., pl. -ties** [< L. *cavus,*
hollow] a hollow place, as in a tooth
ca·vort (kə vôrt′) **vi.** [< ?] **1.** to leap about;
prance **2.** to romp happily; frolic
caw (kô) **n.** [echoic] the harsh cry of a crow or
raven **—vi.** to make this sound
cay·enne (kī en′, kā-) **n.** [< SAmInd. *kynnha*]
a very hot red pepper made from the dried
fruit of a pepper plant: also **cayenne pepper**
cay·use (kī′ōōs, kī ōōs′) **n.** [< AmInd.] a small
Western horse used by cowboys
cc, c.c. cubic centimeter(s)
Cd *Chem.* cadmium
cease (sēs) **vt., vi. ceased, ceas′ing** [< L.
cedere, to yield] to end; stop; discontinue **—n.**
a ceasing
cease′-fire′ n. a temporary cessation of warfare; truce
cease′less (-lis) **adj.** unceasing; continual **—
cease′less·ly adv.**
ce·cum (sē′kəm) **n., pl. -ca** (-kə) [< L. *caecus,*
blind] the pouch at the beginning of the large
intestine
ce·dar (sē′dər) **n.** [< Gr. *kedros*] **1.** a pine tree
having durable, fragrant wood **2.** its wood
cede (sēd) **vt. ced′ed, ced′ing** [< L. *cedere,* to
yield] **1.** to give up one's rights in **2.** to transfer the ownership of
ce·dil·la (si dil′ə) **n.** [< Fr. < Sp. dim. of *zeda,*
the zeta] a mark put under *c* in some French
words (Ex.: *façade*) to show that it has an *s*
sound
ceil·ing (sēl′iŋ) **n.** [< L. *celare,* conceal] **1.** the
inside top part of a room, opposite the floor **2.**
an upper limit [a wage *ceiling*] **3.** *Aeron.* the
upper limit of visibility **—hit the ceiling** [Slang]
to become angry
cel·e·brate (sel′ə brāt′) **vt. -brat′ed, -brat′ing**
[< L. *celebrare,* to honor] **1.** to perform (a
ritual, etc.) **2.** to commemorate (an anniversary, etc.) with festivity **3.** to honor publicly **—
vi.** [Colloq.] to have a good time **—cel′e·brant**
(-brant) **n.**
cel·e·brat·ed (-id) **adj.** famous; renowned
cel·e·bra′tion n. 1. a celebrating **2.** that which
is done to celebrate
ce·leb·ri·ty (sə leb′rə tē) **n. 1.** fame **2.** *pl.* **-ties**
a famous person
ce·ler·i·ty (sə ler′ə tē) **n.** [< L. *celer,* swift]
swiftness in acting or moving; speed
cel·er·y (sel′ər ē) **n.** [< Fr. < Gr. *selinon,*
parsley] a plant with long, crisp leafstalks
eaten as a vegetable
ce·les·tial (sə les′chəl) **adj.** [< L. *caelum,*
heaven] **1.** of the heavens, or sky **2.** *a)* of
heaven; divine *b)* highest; perfect **—ce·les′-
tial·ly adv.**
cel·i·ba·cy (sel′ə bə sē) **n. 1.** the state of being
unmarried **2.** complete sexual abstinence
cel·i·bate (sel′ə bət) **adj.** [< L. *caelebs,*
unmarried] of or in a state of celibacy **—n.** a
celibate person
cell (sel) **n.** [< L. *cella*] **1.** a small room, as in a
convent or prison **2.** a small hollow, as in a
honeycomb **3.** a small unit of an organization
4. a small unit of protoplasm: all plants and
animals are made up of one or more cells **5.** a

receptacle for generating electricity by chemical reactions —**celled** (seld) *adj.*

cel·lar (sel′ər) *n.* [see prec.] a room or rooms below ground level and usually under a building

cel·lar·et (sel′ə ret′) *n.* [CELLAR + -ET] a cabinet for wine, liquor, glasses, etc.

cel·lo (chel′ō) *n., pl.* **-los, -li** (-ē) [< VIOLONCELLO] an instrument of the violin family, between the viola and double bass in size and pitch: also sp. **'cel'lo** —**cel′list** *n.*

cel·lo·phane (sel′ə fān′) *n.* [< CELLULOSE + Gr. *phainein,* appear] a thin, transparent material made from cellulose, used as a moistureproof wrapping

cel·lu·lar (sel′yoo lər) *adj.* of, like, or containing a cell or cells

Cel·lu·loid (sel′yoo loid′) [CELLUL(OSE) + -OID] *a trademark for* a flammable plastic substance made from nitrocellulose and camphor —*n.* [c-] this substance

cel·lu·lose (sel′yoo lōs′) *n.* [Fr. < L. *cella,* cell + -OSE¹] the chief substance in the cell walls of plants, used in making paper, textiles, etc.

cellulose acetate a cellulose resin used in making acetate fiber, plastics, etc.

Cel·si·us (sel′sē əs) *adj.* [< A. *Celsius* (1701–44), Swed. astronomer] designating or of a thermometer on which 0° is the freezing point and 100° is the boiling point of water; centigrade: abbrev. **C**

Celt (selt, kelt) *n.* [< L.] a person who speaks Celtic

Cel·tic (sel′tik, kel′-) *adj.* of the Celts, their languages, etc. —*n.* a group of languages including Gaelic and Welsh

ce·ment (si ment′) *n.* [< L. *caementum,* rough stone] **1.** a powdered substance of lime and clay, mixed with water, etc. to make mortar or concrete: it hardens upon drying **2.** any adhesive substance, as glue —*vt.* **1.** to join as with cement **2.** to cover with cement —*vi.* to be cemented —**ce·ment′er** *n.*

cem·e·ter·y (sem′ə ter′ē) *n., pl.* **-ies** [< Gr. *koiman,* put to sleep] a place for the burial of the dead; graveyard

cen·o·bite (sen′ə bīt′) *n.* [< Gr. *koinos,* common + *bios,* life] a member of a religious order in a monastery or convent

cen·o·taph (sen′ə taf′) *n.* [< Fr. < Gr. *kenos,* empty + *taphos,* tomb] a monument honoring a dead person whose body is somewhere else

cen·ser (sen′sər) *n.* [see INCENSE¹] a container in which incense is burned

cen·sor (sen′sər) *n.* [L. < *censere,* to value] an official with the power to examine literature, mail, etc. and remove or prohibit anything considered obscene, objectionable, etc. —*vt.* to act as a censor of (a book, writer, etc.) —**cen′sor·ship′** *n.*

cen·so·ri·ous (sen sôr′ē əs) *adj.* inclined to find fault; critical —**cen·so′ri·ous·ly** *adv.*

cen·sure (sen′shər) *n.* [see CENSOR] strong disapproval; condemnation —*vt.* **-sured, -sur·ing** to condemn as wrong —**cen′sur·a·ble** *adj.* —**cen′sur·er** *n.*

cen·sus (sen′səs) *n.* [L. < *censere,* enroll] an official count of population and recording of economic status, age, sex, etc.

cent (sent) *n.* [< L. *centum,* a hundred] a 100th part of a dollar, or a coin of this value; penny **cent. 1.** centigrade **2.** century

cen·taur (sen′tôr) *n.* [< Gr. *Kentauros*] *Gr. Myth.* a monster with a man's head, trunk, and arms, and a horse's body and legs

cen·ta·vo (sen tä′vō) *n., pl.* **-vos** [Sp.: see CENT] a small coin of the Philippines, Mexico,

and some S. American countries; one 100th of a peso

cen·te·nar·i·an (sen′tə ner′ē ən) *n.* a person at least 100 years old

cen·te·nar·y (sen ten′ər ē, sen′tə ner′ē) *adj.* [< L. *centum,* a hundred] **1.** of a century **2.** of a centennial —*n., pl.* **-ies 1.** a century **2.** *same as* CENTENNIAL

cen·ten·ni·al (sen ten′ē əl) *adj.* [< L. *centum,* a hundred + *annus,* year] **1.** of 100 years **2.** of a centennial —*n.* a 100th anniversary or its celebration —**cen·ten′ni·al·ly** *adv.*

cen·ter (sen′tər) *n.* [< Gr. *kentron,* a point] **1.** a point equally distant from all points on the circumference of a circle or surface of a sphere **2.** a pivot **3.** a focal point of activity **4.** the approximate middle point or part of anything **5.** *Sports* a player at the center of a line, floor, etc. **6.** [*often* C-] *Politics* a position between the left (liberals) and right (conservatives) —*vt.* **1.** to place in or near the center **2.** to gather to one place —*vi.* to be centered

center of gravity that point in a body around which its weight is evenly balanced

cen′ter·piece′ *n.* an ornament, bowl of flowers, etc. for the center of a table

centi- [L.] *a combining form meaning:* **1.** hundred **2.** a 100th part of

cen·ti·grade (sen′tə grād′) *adj.* [Fr. < L.: see CENTI- & GRADE] *same as* CELSIUS

cen′ti·gram′ (-gram′) *n.* [Fr.: see CENTI- & GRAM] a unit of weight, equal to 1/100 gram: chiefly Brit. sp. **cen′ti·gramme′**

cen·time (sän′tēm) *n.* [Fr.] the 100th part of a franc

cen·ti·me·ter (sen′tə mēt′ər) *n.* [< Fr.: see CENTI- & METER¹] a unit of measure, equal to 1/100 meter: chiefly Brit. sp. **cen′ti·me′tre**

cen·ti·pede (sen′tə pēd′) *n.* [Fr. < L. *centum,* a hundred + *pes,* foot] an arthropod with a pair of legs to each segment

cen·tral (sen′trəl) *adj.* **1.** in, near, or of the center **2.** equally accessible from various points **3.** main; basic **4.** of a controlling source in a system —**cen′tral·ly** *adv.*

cen′tral·ize′ (-trə līz′) *vt.* **-ized′,, -iz′ing 1.** to make central; bring to a center **2.** to organize under one control —*vi.* to become centralized —**cen′tral·i·za′tion** *n.*

cen·tre (sen′tər) *n., vt., vi.* **-tred, -tring** *chiefly Brit. sp. of* CENTER

centri- *same as* CENTRO-

cen·trif·u·gal (sen trif′yə gəl) *adj.* [< CENTRI- + L. *fugere,* flee] using or acted on by a force (**centrifugal force**) that tends to make rotating bodies move away from the center of rotation

cen·tri·fuge (sen′trə fyōōj′) *n.* a machine using centrifugal force to separate particles of varying density

cen·trip·e·tal (sen trip′ə t 'l) *adj.* [< CENTRI- + L. *petere,* seek] using or acted on by a force (**centripetal force**) that tends to make rotating bodies move toward the center of rotation

cen·trist (sen′trist) *n.* a member of a political party of the center

centro- [< L. *centrum,* CENTER] *a combining form meaning* center

cen·tu·ri·on (sen tyoor′ē ən) *n.* [see CENTURY] in ancient Rome, the commander of a military unit, originally of 100 men

cen·tu·ry (sen′chər ē) *n., pl.* **-ries** [< L. *centum,* a hundred] any period of 100 years, esp. as reckoned from 1 A.D.

ce·phal·ic (sə fal′ik) *adj.* [< Gr. *kephalē,* the head] **1.** of the head or skull **2.** in, on, or near the head

ce·ram·ic (sə ram′ik) *adj.* [< Gr. *keramos,*

clay] **1.** of pottery, tile, porcelain, etc. **2.** of ceramics —*n.* **1.** [*pl. with sing. v.*] the art or work of making objects of baked clay **2.** such an object —**ce·ram·ist** (sə ram'ist), **ce·ram'i·cist** (-ə sist) *n.*

ce·re·al (sir'ē əl) *adj.* [< L. *Cerealis*, of Ceres] of grain —*n.* **1.** any grain used for food, as wheat, oats, etc. **2.** any grass producing such grain **3.** food made from grain

cer·e·bel·lum (ser'ə bel'əm) *n., pl.* **-lums, -la** (-ə) [L., dim. of *cerebrum*, the brain] the section of the brain behind and below the cerebrum

cer·e·bral (ser'ə brəl, sə rē'-) *adj.* of the brain or the cerebrum

cerebral palsy spastic paralysis due to brain damage

cer·e·brate (ser'ə brāt') *vi.* **-brat'ed, -brat'ing** [see CEREBELLUM & -ATE¹] to use one's brain; think —**cer'e·bra'tion** *n.*

cer·e·brum (ser'ə brəm, sə rē'-) *n., pl.* **-brums, -bra** (-brə) [L.] the upper, main part of the brain

cer·e·ment (ser'ə mənt, sir'mənt) *n.* [< Gr. *kēros*, wax] **1.** a shroud **2.** [*usually pl.*] any burial clothes

cer·e·mo·ni·al (ser'ə mō'nē əl) *adj.* of, for, or consisting of ceremony; formal —*n.* **1.** a set system of forms or rites **2.** a rite

cer'e·mo'ni·ous (-nē əs) *adj.* **1.** full of ceremony **2.** very polite or formal

cer·e·mo·ny (ser'ə mō'nē) *n., pl.* **-nies** [L. *caerimonia*] **1.** a set of formal acts proper to a special occasion, as a religious rite **2.** behavior that follows rigid etiquette **3.** formality **4.** meaningless formality —**stand on ceremony** to insist on formality

Ce·res (sir'ēz) *Rom. Myth.* the goddess of agriculture

ce·rise (sə rēs', -rēz') *n., adj.* [Fr., a cherry] bright red; cherry red

cer·tain (surt'ʼn) *adj.* [< L. *cernere*, decide] **1.** fixed; settled **2.** inevitable **3.** reliable; dependable **4.** sure; positive **5.** not named, though definite [*a certain* person] **6.** some [*to a certain* extent] —**for certain** without doubt

cer'tain·ly *adv.* beyond a doubt; surely

cer'tain·ty (-tē) *n.* **1.** a being certain **2.** *pl.* **-ties** anything certain

cer·tif·i·cate (sur tif'ə kit) *n.* [see CERTIFY] a written statement testifying to a fact, qualification, etc. —*vt.* (-kāt') **-cat'ed, -cat'ing** to issue a certificate to or for

cer·ti·fied (sur'tə fīd') *adj.* **1.** guaranteed **2.** having, or attested to by, a certificate

cer·ti·fy (sur'tə fī') *vt.* **-fied', -fy'ing** [< L. *certus*, certain + *facere*, to make] **1.** to declare (a thing) true, accurate, etc. by formal statement **2.** to guarantee **3.** to issue a certificate to —**cer'ti·fi·ca'tion** *n.*

cer·ti·tude (sur'tə tōōd') *n.* **1.** a feeling absolutely sure **2.** inevitability

ce·ru·le·an (sə rōō'lē ən) *adj.* [< L., prob. < *caelum*, heaven] sky-blue; azure

cer·vix (sur'viks) *n., pl.* **-vi·ces'** (-və sēz'), **-vix·es** [L., the neck] a necklike part, esp. of the uterus —**cer'vi·cal** (-vi kəl) *adj.*

ce·si·um (sē'zē əm) *n.* [< L. *caesius*, bluish-gray] a soft, silver-white metallic chemical element: symbol, Cs

ces·sa·tion (se sā'shən) *n.* [< L. *cessare*, to cease] a ceasing; stop

ces·sion (sesh'ən) *n.* [< L. *cedere*, to yield] a ceding (of rights, etc.) to another

cess·pool (ses'pōōl') *n.* [< It. < L. *secessus*, place of retirement] a deep hole in the ground to receive drainage or sewage

ce·ta·cean (si tā'shən) *n.* [< Gr. *kētos*, whale] a water mammal as the whale and dolphin — *adj.* of the cetaceans

cf. [L. *confer*] compare

cg, cg., cgm, cgm. centigram(s)

Ch., ch. 1. chapter **2.** church

chafe (chāf) *vt.* **chafed, chaf'ing** [< L. *calere*, be warm + *facere*, to make] **1.** to rub so as to make warm **2.** to wear away or make sore by rubbing **3.** to annoy; irritate —*vi.* **1.** to rub (*on* or *against*) **2.** to be irritated —**chafe at the bit** to be impatient

chaff (chaf) *n.* [OE. *ceaf*] **1.** threshed or winnowed husks of grain **2.** anything worthless **3.** teasing —*vt., vi.* to tease

chaf·ing dish (chāf'iŋ) [see CHAFE] a pan with a heating apparatus beneath it, to cook food at the table or to keep food hot

cha·grin (shə grin') *n.* [Fr., grief] a feeling of embarrassment and distress caused by failure or disappointment —*vt.* **-grined', -grin'ing** to cause to feel chagrin

chain (chān) *n.* [< L. *catena*] **1.** a flexible series of joined links **2.** [*pl.*] *a*) bonds, shackles, etc. *b*) captivity **3.** a chainlike measuring instrument, as for surveying **4.** a connected series of things or events —*vt.* **1.** to fasten with chains **2.** to restrain

chain'-re·act' (-rē akt') *vi.* to be involved in or subjected to a chain reaction

chain reaction 1. a self-sustaining series of chemical or nuclear reactions in which reaction products keep the process going **2.** any sequence of events, each of which results in the following

chain saw a portable power saw with an endless chain carrying cutting teeth

chain store any of a chain of retail stores

chair (cher) *n.* [< L. *cathedra*: see CATHEDRAL] **1.** a piece of furniture with a back, for one person to sit on **2.** an important or official position **3.** a chairman —*vt.* **1.** to seat **2.** to preside over as chairman

chair'man (-mən) *n., pl.* **-men** a person who presides at a meeting or heads a committee, board, etc. —**chair'man·ship'** *n.* —**chair'wom'an** *n.fem., pl.* **-wom'en**

chaise (shāz) *n.* [Fr.] a lightweight carriage having two or four wheels

chaise longue (shāz' lôŋ', louŋj') *pl.* **chaise** (or **chaises**) **longues** (shāz' lôŋz', louŋ'jəz) [Fr., long chair] a couchlike chair with a long seat: also **chaise lounge**

chal·ced·o·ny (kal sed'ʼn ē, kal'sə dō'nē) *n., pl.* **-nies** [< Gr. *chalkēdōn*, a precious stone] a kind of colored quartz with the luster of wax

cha·let (sha lā', shal'ē) *n.* [Swiss-Fr.] a house with overhanging eaves

chal·ice (chal'is) *n.* [< L. *calix*, a cup] **1.** a cup; goblet **2.** the cup for the wine of Holy Communion **3.** a cup-shaped flower

chalk (chôk) *n.* [< L. *calx*, limestone] **1.** a soft, whitish limestone **2.** a piece of chalk or chalklike substance used for writing on a blackboard —*adj.* made with chalk —*vt.* to mark with chalk —**chalk up 1.** to score, get, or achieve **2.** to charge or credit —**chalk'y** *adj.* **-i·er, -i·est**

chal·lenge (chal'ənj) *n.* [< L. *calumnia*, CALUMNY] **1.** a demand for identification [*a* sentry gave the *challenge*] **2.** a calling into question [*a challenge* to an assertion] **3.** a call to a duel, contest, etc. **4.** anything that calls for special effort —*vt.* **-lenged, -leng·ing** to subject to a challenge —*vi.* to issue a challenge — **chal'lenge·a·ble** *adj.* —**chal'leng·er** *n.*

cham·ber (chām'bər) *n.* [< L. *camera*, a vault]

1. a room in a house, esp. a bedroom **2.** [pl.] a judge's office near the courtroom **3.** an assembly hall **4.** a legislative or judicial body **5.** a council [a chamber of commerce] **6.** an enclosed space in the body **7.** the part of a gun that holds the charge or cartridge

cham′ber·lain (-lin) n. [< OHG. chamarlinc] **1.** an officer in charge of the household of a ruler or lord **2.** a high official in certain royal courts **3.** [Brit.] a treasurer

cham′ber·maid′ n. a woman whose work is taking care of bedrooms, as in hotels

chamber music music for performance by a small group, as a string quartet

chamber of commerce an association established to further the business interests of its community

cham·bray (sham′brā) n. [< Cambrai, Fr. city] a cotton fabric made by weaving white threads across a colored warp

cha·me·leon (kə mēl′yən) n. [< Gr. chamai, on the ground + leōn, lion] a lizard that can change the color of its skin

cham·ois (sham′ē) n., pl. -ois [Fr.] **1.** a small, goatlike antelope of the mountains of Europe and the Caucasus **2.** a soft leather made from the skin of chamois, sheep, etc.: also sp. **cham′my,** pl. -mies

cham·o·mile (kam′ə mīl′, -mēl′) n. [< Gr. chamai, on the ground + mēlon, apple] a plant whose dried flowers have been used in a medicinal tea

champ¹ (champ) vt., vi. [prob. echoic] to chew hard and noisily; munch —**champ at the bit** to be restless

champ² (champ) n. [Slang] a champion

cham·pagne (sham pān′) n. **1.** an effervescent white wine, specif. one from Champagne, a region in NE France **2.** pale yellow

cham·pi·on (cham′pē ən) n. [< LL. campio, gladiator] **1.** one who fights for another or for a cause; defender **2.** a winner of first place in a competition —adj. excelling over all others — vt. to fight for; defend; support —**cham′pi·on·ship′** n.

chance (chans) n. [< L. cadere, to fall] **1.** the happening of events without apparent cause; luck **2.** an accidental happening **3.** a risk or gamble **4.** a ticket in a lottery **5.** an opportunity **6.** a possibility or probability —adj. accidental —vi. chanced, chanc′ing to have the fortune (to) —vt. to risk —**by chance** accidentally —**chance on** (or upon) to find by chance

chan·cel (chan′s'l) n. [< L. cancelli, lattices] that part of a church around the altar, reserved for clergy and the choir

chan·cel·ler·y (chan′sə lə rē) n., pl. -ies the position or office of a chancellor

chan′cel·lor (-lər) n. [< LL. cancellarius, secretary] **1.** the title of the president or a high officer in some universities **2.** the prime minister in certain countries **3.** a chief judge of a court of chancery or equity in some States **4.** a high church official —**chan′cel·lor·ship′** n.

chan·cer·y (chan′sər ē) n., pl. -ies [< ML. cancellaria] **1.** a court of equity **2.** a court of record

chan·cre (shaŋ′kər) n. [Fr.: see CANCER] a venereal sore or ulcer

chanc·y (chan′sē) adj. -i·er, -i·est risky

chan·de·lier (shan′də lir′) n. [Fr. < L. candela, candle] a lighting fixture hanging from a ceiling, with branches for candles, electric bulbs, etc.

chan·dler (chan′dlər) n. [< L. candela, candle] **1.** a maker of candles **2.** a retailer of supplies, equipment, etc. —**chan′dler·y** n., pl. -ies

change (chānj) vt. **changed, chang′ing** [< L. cambire, to barter < Celt.] **1.** to put or take (a thing) in place of something else; substitute [to change one's clothes] **2.** to exchange [let's change seats] **3.** to make different; alter —vi. **1.** to alter; vary [the scene changes] **2.** to leave one train, bus, etc. and board another **3.** to put on other clothes **4.** to make an exchange — n. **1.** a substitution, alteration, or variation **2.** variety **3.** another set of clothes **4.** a) money returned as the difference between the purchase price and the sum given in payment b) coins or bills that together equal the larger value of a single coin or bill c) small coins — **change′a·ble** adj. —**change′less** adj. —**chang′er** n.

change′ling (-liŋ) n. a child secretly exchanged for another, esp. in folk tales

change of life same as MENOPAUSE

change′o′ver n. a complete change, as in goods produced, equipment, etc.

chan·nel (chan′'l) n. [see CANAL] **1.** the bed or deeper part of a river, harbor, etc. **2.** a body of water joining two larger ones **3.** any means of passage or transmission **4.** [pl.] the official course of action [to request through channels] **5.** a long groove **6.** a frequency band assigned to a radio or television station —vt. **-neled** or **-nelled, -nel·ing** or **-nel·ling 1.** to make a channel in **2.** to send through a channel

chant (chant) n. [Fr. < L. canere, sing] **1.** a song, esp. one in which a number of words are sung to each tone **2.** a singsong way of speaking —vi., vt. to sing or say in a chant

chan·teuse (shan tooz′) n. [Fr.] a woman singer

chan·tey (shan′tē, chan′-) n., pl. -teys a song that sailors sing in rhythm with their motions at work: also **chan′ty,** pl. -ties

chan·ti·cleer (chan′tə klir′) n. [see CHANT & CLEAR] a rooster

cha·os (kā′äs) n. [< Gr. chaos, space] extreme confusion or disorder —**cha·ot′ic** (-ät′ik) adj.

chap¹ (chǎp, chap) n. [< ?] same as CHOP²

chap² (chap) n. [< Brit. chapman, peddler] [Colloq.] a man or boy; fellow

chap³ (chap) vt., vi. **chapped** or **chapt, chap′ping** [ME. chappen, to cut] to crack open or roughen, as skin —n. a chapped place in the skin

cha·peau (sha pō′) n., pl. -peaus′, -peaux′ (-pōz′) [Fr. < LL. cappa, hood] a hat

chap·el (chap′'l) n. [< LL. cappa, hood] **1.** a small church **2.** a small or private place of worship, as in a school

chap·er·on, chap·er·one (shap′ə rōn′) n. [Fr., hood] a person, esp. an older woman, who accompanies young unmarried people for propriety —vt., vi. **-oned′, -on′ing** to act as chaperon (to)

chap·lain (chap′lən) n. [see CHAPEL] a clergyman attached to a chapel **2.** a clergyman serving in a religious capacity with the armed forces —**chap′lain·ship′** n.

chap·let (chap′lit) n. [see CHAPEAU] **1.** a garland for the head **2.** a string of beads, esp. prayer beads

chaps (chaps, shaps) n.pl. [< MexSp. chaparejos] leather trousers worn over ordinary trousers by cowboys to protect their legs

chap·ter (chap′tər) n. [< L. caput, head] **1.** a main division, as of a book **2.** a local branch of an organization

char (chär) vt., vi. **charred, char′ring** [< CHARCOAL] to scorch

char·ac·ter (kar′ik tər) n. [< Gr. charattein, engrave] **1.** any figure, letter, or symbol used in writing and printing **2.** a distinctive trait **3.** kind or sort **4.** behavior typical of a person or group **5.** moral strength **6.** reputation **7.** status; position **8.** a person in a play, novel, etc. **9.** [Colloq.] an eccentric person —**in** (or **out of**) **character** consistent (or inconsistent)

char′ac·ter·is′tic (-tə ris′tik) *adj.* typical; distinctive —*n.* a distinguishing trait or quality — **char′ac·ter·is′ti·cal·ly** *adv.*

char′ac·ter·ize′ (-rīz′) *vt.* **-ized′, -iz′ing 1.** to describe the particular traits of **2.** to distinguish —**char′ac·ter·i·za′tion** *n.*

cha·rade (shə rād′) *n.* [Fr. < Pr. *charrar*, to gossip] [*often pl.*] a game in which words to be guessed are acted out in pantomime

char·coal (chär′kōl′) *n.* [prob. < ME. *charren*, to turn + *cole*, coal] **1.** a form of carbon made by partially burning wood, etc. in the absence of air **2.** a very dark gray

chard (chärd) *n.* [< Fr. < L. *carduus*, thistle] a beet with edible leaves and stalks

charge (chärj) *vt.* **charged, charg′ing** [< L. *carrus*, car] **1.** to load or fill (*with* something) **2.** to add an electrical charge to (a battery, etc.) **3.** to give as a duty, command, etc. to **4.** to accuse; censure **5.** to make liable for (an error, etc.) **6.** to ask as a price **7.** to record as a debt **8.** to attack vigorously —*vi.* **1.** to ask payment (*for*) [*to charge* for a service] **2.** to attack vigorously —*n.* **1.** the amount used to load something **2.** the amount of electrical energy stored in a battery, etc. **3.** responsibility or care (*of*) **4.** a person or thing entrusted to one's care **5.** instruction or command **6.** accusation; indictment **7.** cost **8.** a debt **9.** *same as* CHARGE ACCOUNT **10.** *a*) an attack, as by troops *b*) the signal for this —**in charge** having the responsibility or control —**charge′a·ble** *adj.*

charge account an arrangement by which a customer may pay for purchases within a specified future period

charg′er *n.* **1.** a person or thing that charges **2.** a horse ridden in battle

char·i·ot (char′ē ət) *n.* [see CHARGE] a horse-drawn, two-wheeled cart used in ancient times for war, racing, etc.

char′i·ot·eer′ (-ə tir′) *n.* a chariot driver

cha·ris·ma (kə riz′mə) *n., pl.* **-ma·ta** (-mə tə) [Gr.] **1.** a divinely inspired gift **2.** a special, inspiring quality of leadership —**char·is·mat·ic** (kar′iz mat′ik) *adj.*

char·i·ta·ble (char′i tə b'l) *adj.* **1.** generous to those in need **2.** of or for charity **3.** kind and forgiving

char′i·ty (-ə tē) *n., pl.* **-ties** [< L. *caritas*, affection] **1.** *Christian Theol.* love for one's fellow men **2.** kindness in judging others **3.** a giving of help to those in need **4.** a welfare institution, organization, etc.

char·la·tan (shär′lə t'n) *n.* [Fr. < It. < LL. *cerretanus*, seller of papal indulgences] a fake; impostor —**char′la·tan·ism, char′la·tan·ry** *n.*

char·ley horse (char′lē) [Colloq.] a cramp in the leg or arm muscles, caused by strain

charm (chärm) *n.* [< L. *carmen*] **1.** an object, action, or words assumed to have magic power **2.** a trinket on a bracelet, etc. **3.** a quality that attracts or delights —*vt., vi.* **1.** to act on as if by magic **2.** to fascinate; delight —**charm′er** *n.* —**charm′ing** *adj.*

char·nel (**house**) (chär′n'l) *n.* [< LL. *carnale*, graveyard] a building, etc. used for corpses and bones

Cha·ron (ker′ən) *Gr. Myth.* the boatman who ferried dead souls across the river Styx

chart (chärt) *n.* [< Gr. *chartēs*, leaf of paper] **1.** a map, esp. for use in navigation **2.** an information sheet with tables, graphs, etc. **3.** a table, graph, etc. —*vt.* **1.** to make a chart of **2.** to plan (a course of action)

char·ter (chär′tər) *n.* [see prec.] **1.** a franchise given by a government to a person, corporation, etc. **2.** a written statement of basic laws or principles; constitution **3.** written permission to form a local chapter of a society —*vt.* **1.** to grant a charter to **2.** to hire for exclusive use

charter member one of the founders or original members of an organization

char·treuse (shär trōoz′) *n.* [Fr.] pale, yellowish green

char′wom′an (chär′-) *n., pl.* **-wom′en** [see CHORE] a cleaning woman

char·y (cher′ē) *adj.* **-i·er, -i·est** [< OE. *cearu*, care] **1.** cautious **2.** sparing —**char′i·ly** *adv.* —**char′i·ness** *n.*

chase¹ (chās) *vt.* **chased, chas′ing** [ult. < L. *capere*, take] **1.** to follow so as to catch **2.** to run after; follow **3.** to drive away **4.** to hunt **5.** [Slang] to court; woo —*vi.* **1.** to go in pursuit **2.** [Colloq.] to rush —*n.* **1.** a chasing; pursuit **2.** the hunting of game for sport **3.** anything hunted; quarry —**give chase** to pursue

chase² (chās) *n.* [ult. < L. *capsa*, a box] **1.** a groove; furrow **2.** a rectangular metal frame in which pages or columns of type are locked —*vt.* **chased, chas′ing** to make a groove or furrow in

chase³ (chās) *vt.* **chased, chas′ing** [< Fr. *enchâsser*, enshrine] to ornament (metal) by engraving, etc.

chas′er *n.* [Colloq.] a mild drink, as water, taken after or with whiskey, rum, etc.

chasm (kaz′m) *n.* [< Gr. *chasma*] **1.** a deep crack in the earth's surface; abyss **2.** any break or gap **3.** a rift —**chas′mal** *adj.*

chas·sis (chas′ē, shas′ē) *n., pl.* **-sis** (-ēz) [Fr. < L. *capsa*, a box] **1.** the frame, wheels, etc. of a motor vehicle, but not the body and engine **2.** *Radio & TV a*) the framework to which the parts of a receiver, etc. are attached *b*) the assembled frame and parts

chaste (chāst) *adj.* [< L. *castus*, pure] **1.** not indulging in unlawful sexual activity **2.** celibate **3.** decent **4.** simple in style

chas·ten (chās′'n) *vt.* [< L. *castigare*, punish] **1.** to punish so as to correct; chastise **2.** to restrain from excess; subdue

chas·tise (chas tīz′) *vt.* **-tised′, -tis′ing** [see prec.] **1.** to punish, esp. by beating **2.** to scold sharply —**chas·tise′ment** *n.*

chas·ti·ty (chas′tə tē) *n.* **1.** virtuousness **2.** celibacy **3.** decency **4.** simplicity of style

chat (chat) *vi.* **chat′ted, chat′ting** [< CHATTER] to talk in a light, informal manner —*n.* a light, informal conversation

châ·teau (sha tō′) *n., pl.* **-teaux′** (-tōz′, -tō′), **-teaus′** [Fr. < L. *castellum*, castle] **1.** a French feudal castle **2.** a large country house, esp. in France Also **cha·teau′**

chat·e·laine (shat′'l ān′) *n.* [Fr., ult. < L. *castellum*, castle] **1.** the mistress of a large household **2.** an ornamental chain or clasp

chat·tel (chat′'l) *n.* [see CATTLE] a movable item of personal property

chat·ter (chat′ər) *vi.* [echoic] **1.** to make short, indistinct, rapid sounds, as birds, apes, etc. **2.** to talk much and foolishly **3.** to click together rapidly as teeth do from cold —*n.* **1.** a chattering **2.** foolish talk

chat′ter·box′ (-bäks′) *n.* an incessant talker

chat·ty (chat′ē) *adj.* **-ti·er, -ti·est** fond or full of chatting —**chat′ti·ly** *adv.*

chauf·feur (shō′fər, shō fur′) *n.* [Fr., lit.,

stoker] a person hired to drive a private automobile for someone else —*vt.* to act as a chauffeur to

chau·vin·ism (shō′və niz′m) *n.* [< N. *Chauvin,* fanatical Fr. patriot] 1. militant and fanatical patriotism 2. unreasoning devotion to one's race, sex, etc. —**chau′vin·ist** *n., adj.* —**chau′vin·is′tic** *adj.*

cheap (chēp) *adj.* [< OE. *ceap,* a bargain] 1. low in price 2. charging low prices 3. spending little 4. worth more than the price 5. easily got 6. of little value 7. contemptible 8. [Colloq.] stingy —*adv.* at a low cost —**cheap′ly** *adv.* —**cheap′ness** *n.*

cheap′en *vt., vi.* to make or become cheap or cheaper

cheap′skate′ *n.* [Slang] a stingy person

cheat (chēt) *n.* [< L. *ex-,* out + *cadere,* fall] 1. a fraud; swindle 2. a swindler —*vt.* 1. to defraud; swindle 2. to foil or elude [to *cheat* death] —*vi.* 1. to be dishonest or deceitful 2. [Slang] to be sexually unfaithful (often with *on*) —**cheat′er** *n.*

check (chek) *n.* [< OFr. *eschec,* a check at chess] 1. a sudden stop 2. any restraint of action 3. one that restrains 4. a supervision or test of accuracy, etc. 5. a mark (✓) to show verification of something 6. an identification ticket, token, etc. [a hat *check*] 7. one's bill, as at a restaurant 8. a written order to a bank to pay a sum of money 9. a pattern of squares, or one of the squares 10. *Chess* the state of a king that is in danger —*interj.* [Colloq.] agreed! right! —*vt.* 1. to stop suddenly 2. to hold back; restrain 3. to test, verify, etc. by investigation or comparison (often with *out*) 4. to mark with a check (often with *off*) 5. to mark with a pattern of squares 6. to deposit temporarily 7. to clear (esp. luggage) for shipment 8. *Chess* to place (an opponent's king) in check —*vi.* 1. to agree with one another, item for item (often with *out*) 2. to investigate or verify (often with *on, up on*) —**check in** to register at a hotel, etc. —**check out** 1. to pay and leave a hotel, etc. 2. to add up the prices of (items selected) for payment 3. to prove to be accurate, etc. —**in check** under control —**check′er** *n.*

check′book′ *n.* a book containing forms for writing checks on a bank

check′er·board′ *n.* a board with 64 squares of two alternating colors, used in checkers and chess

check′ered (-ərd) *adj.* 1. having a pattern of squares 2. varied

check′ers (-ərz) *n.pl.* 1. [*with sing. v.*] a game for two played with flat disks on a checkerboard 2. the disks

checking account a bank account against which the depositor can draw checks

check′list′ *n.* a list of things, names, etc. to be referred to: also **check list**

check′mate′ (-māt′) *n.* [ult. < Per. *shāh māt,* the king is dead] 1. *Chess a*) the winning move that puts the opponent's king in a position where it cannot be saved *b*) this position 2. total defeat, frustration, etc. —*vt.* **-mat′ed, -mat′ing** to subject to checkmate

check′out′ *n.* 1. the act or place of checking out purchases 2. the time by which one must check out of a hotel, etc.

check′point′ *n.* a place on a road, etc. where traffic is inspected

check′room′ *n.* a room in which to check (*vt.* 6) hats, coats, parcels, etc.

check′up′ *n.* a medical examination

Ched·dar (**cheese**) (ched′ər) [< *Cheddar,* England] [*often* c-] a hard, smooth cheese

cheek (chēk) *n.* [OE. *ceoke,* jaw] 1. either side of the face below the eye 2. [Colloq.] sauciness; impudence —(**with**) **tongue in cheek** in a humorous insincere way

cheek′bone′ *n.* the bone of the upper cheek, just below the eye

cheek′y *adj.* **-i·er, -i·est** [Colloq.] saucy; impudent —**cheek′i·ness** *n.*

cheep (chēp) *n.* [echoic] the short, shrill sound of a young bird —*vt., vi.* to chirp

cheer (chir) *n.* [< Gr. *kara,* the head] 1. a state of mind or feeling; spirit [be of good *cheer*] 2. gladness; joy 3. festive food or entertainment 4. encouragement 5. *a*) a glad, excited shout to urge on, greet, etc. *b*) a rallying cry —*vt.* 1. to comfort or gladden (often with *up*) 2. to urge on, greet, etc. with cheers —*vi.* 1. to become cheerful (usually with *up*) 2. to shout cheers

cheer′ful *adj.* 1. full of cheer; joyful 2. bright and attractive 3. willing [a *cheerful* helper] —**cheer′ful·ly** *adv.*

cheer′lead′er (-lē′dər) *n.* one who leads others in cheering for a football team, etc.

cheer′less *adj.* not cheerful; dismal —**cheer′less·ly** *adv.* —**cheer′less·ness** *n.*

cheer′y *adj.* **-i·er, -i·est** cheerful; lively

cheese (chēz) *n.* [ult. < L. *caseus*] a solid food made from milk curds

cheese′burg′er (-bur′gər) *n.* a hamburger topped with melted cheese

cheese′cake′ *n.* 1. a cake made with cottage cheese or cream cheese 2. [Slang] photographic display of the figure, esp. the legs, of a pretty girl

cheese′cloth′ *n.* [from its use as cheese wrapping] a thin cotton cloth with a loose weave

chees′y (-ē) *adj.* **-i·er, -i·est** 1. like cheese 2. [Slang] inferior; poor —**chees′i·ness** *n.*

chee·tah (chēt′ə) *n.* [< Hindi < Sans. *citra,* spotted] a swift, leopardlike animal of Africa and S Asia: it can be trained to hunt

chef (shef) *n.* [Fr. < *chef de cuisine,* head of the kitchen] 1. a head cook 2. any cook

‡chef-d'oeu·vre (she dë′vr′) *n., pl.* **chefs-d'oeu′vre** (she dë′vr′) [Fr., principal work] a masterpiece, as in art or literature

chem·i·cal (kem′i k'l) *adj.* 1. of, made by, or used in chemistry 2. made with or operated by chemicals —*n.* any substance used in or obtained by a chemical process —**chem′i·cal·ly** *adv.*

chemical engineering the science or profession of applying chemistry to industry

chemical warfare warfare using poisonous gases, etc.

che·mise (shə mēz′) *n.* [< VL. *camisia,* shirt] 1. a woman's undergarment somewhat like a loose, short slip 2. a straight, loose dress

chem·ist (kem′ist) *n.* [< (AL)CHEMIST] 1. a specialist in chemistry 2. [Brit.] a pharmacist, or druggist

chem·is·try (kem′is trē) *n.* [< CHEMIST] the science dealing with the composition and properties of substances, and with the reactions by which substances are produced from or converted into other substances

chem·ur·gy (kem′ər jē) *n.* [< CHEM(ISTRY) + -URGY] the branch of chemistry dealing with the industrial use of organic products, esp. from farms —**chem·ur′gic** (-ur′jik) *adj.*

che·nille (shi nēl′) *n.* [Fr., caterpillar] 1. a tufted, velvety yarn 2. a fabric filled or woven with this, as for rugs

cheque (chek) *n.* Brit. sp. of CHECK (*n.* 8)

cher·ish (cher′ish) *vt.* [< L. *carus,* dear] 1. to

hold dear 2. to protect; foster 3. to cling to the idea of

Cher·o·kee (cher′ə kē′) *n., pl.* **-kees′, -kee′** a member of an Indian tribe of the SW U.S.

che·root (shə rōōt′) *n.* [< Tamil *churuttu,* a roll] a cigar with both ends cut square

cher·ry (cher′ē) *n., pl.* **-ries** [< Gr. *kerasion*] 1. a small, fleshy fruit with a smooth, hard pit 2. the tree that it grows on 3. the wood of this tree 4. a bright red

cher·ub (cher′əb) *n., pl.* **-ubs;** for 1 usually **-u·bim** (-ə bim, -yoo bim) [< Heb. *kerūbh*] 1. any of an order of angels, often represented as a chubby, rosy-faced child with wings 2. an innocent or lovely child **—che·ru·bic** (chə rōō′bik) *adj.*

chess (ches) *n.* [< OFr. *eschec,* a check at chess] a game for two, each with 16 pieces (**chessmen**) moved variously on a checkerboard

chest (chest) *n.* [< Gr. *kistē,* a box] 1. a box with a lid 2. a cabinet with drawers; bureau 3. the part of the body enclosed by the ribs and breastbone

ches·ter·field (ches′tər fēld′) *n.* [< 19th-c. Earl of *Chesterfield*] a single-breasted topcoat, usually with a velvet collar

chest·nut (ches′nut′) *n.* [< Gr. *kastaneia*] 1. the edible nut of a tree of the beech family 2. this tree, or its wood 3. reddish brown 4. [Colloq.] a trite joke, etc.

chev·i·ot (shev′ē ət) *n.* [< *Cheviot* Hills, between England and Scotland] a rough, twilled wool fabric

chev·ron (shev′rən) *n.* [< OFr., rafter] a V-shaped bar on the sleeves of a uniform, showing rank

chew (chōō) *vt.* [< OE. *ceowan*] 1. to bite and crush with the teeth 2. [Slang] to rebuke severely (often with *out*) **—***vi.* to do chewing **—***n.* 1. a chewing 2. something chewed or for chewing **—chew′y** *adj.* **-i·er, -i·est**

chewing gum a sweet, flavored substance, as chicle, used for chewing

chg. *pl.* **chgs.** charge

chi (kī) *n.* the 22d letter of the Greek alphabet (Χ, χ)

Chi·an·ti (kē än′tē, -an′-) *n.* [It.] a dry, red wine

chi·a·ro·scu·ro (kē är′ə skyoor′ō) *n., pl.* **-ros** [It. < L. *clarus,* clear + *obscurus,* dark] 1. treatment of light and shade in a painting, drawing, etc. 2. a style or a painting, etc. emphasizing this

chic (shēk) *n.* [Fr. < MLowG. *schick,* skill] smart elegance **—***adj.* **chic·quer** (shēk′ər), **chic′-quest** (-ist) smartly stylish

chi·can·er·y (shi kān′ər ē) *n., pl.* **-ies** [< Fr.] 1. trickery 2. a trick

Chi·ca·no (chi kä′nō) *n., pl.* **-nos** [< AmSp.] [*also* c-] [Southwest] a U.S. citizen or inhabitant of Mexican descent

chi·chi, chi-chi (shē′shē, chē′chē) *adj.* [Fr.] extremely chic in an affected or showy way

chick (chik) *n.* [< CHICKEN] 1. a young chicken or bird 2. a child 3. [Slang] a young woman

chick·a·dee (chik′ə dē′) *n.* [echoic] a small bird related to the titmouse

chick·en (chik′ən) *n.* [< OE. *cycen,* lit., little cock] 1. a hen or rooster, esp. a young one 2. its edible flesh **—***adj.* 1. made of chicken 2. [Slang] timid or cowardly **—chicken out** [Slang] to quit from fear

chicken feed [Slang] a petty sum of money

chick′en-heart′ed *adj.* timid; cowardly

chicken pox an acute, contagious virus disease, esp. of children, with skin eruptions

chicken wire light, pliable wire fencing

chick′pea′ *n.* [< L. *cicer,* pea] 1. a bushy plant with hairy pods 2. the edible seeds

chick′weed′ *n.* a low-growing plant often found as a lawn weed

chic·le (chik′'l) *n.* [< MexInd.] a gumlike substance made from the sapodilla, used in chewing gum

chic·o·ry (chik′ə rē) *n., pl.* **-ries** [< Gr. *kichora*] 1. a weedy plant whose leaves are used for salad 2. its root, ground for mixing with coffee or as a coffee substitute

chide (chīd) *vt., vi.* **chid′ed** or **chid** (chid), **chid′ed** or **chid** or **chid·den** (chid′'n), **chid′ing** [OE. *cidan*] to scold; reprove mildly

chief (chēf) *n.* [< L. *caput,* the head] the head or leader of a group, organization, etc. **—***adj.* 1. highest in rank, office, etc. 2. main; principal **chief′ly** *adv.* 1. most of all 2. mainly **—***adj.* of or like a chief

chief′tain (-tən) *n.* [< L. *caput,* the head] a leader, esp. of a clan or tribe

chif·fon (shi fän′) *n.* [Fr. < *chiffe,* a rag] a sheer, silky cloth **—***adj.* 1. made of chiffon 2. made fluffy as with beaten egg whites

chif·fo·nier, chif·fon·nier (shif′ə nir′) *n.* [Fr. < prec.] a narrow, high chest of drawers, often with a mirror attached

chig·ger (chig′ər) *n.* [of Afr. origin] the tiny, red larva of certain mites, whose bite causes severe itching

chi·gnon (shēn′yän) *n.* [Fr. < L. *catena,* a chain] a coil of hair sometimes worn at the back of the neck by women

Chi·hua·hua (chi wä′wä) *n.* [< *Chihuahua,* a Mex. state] a breed of tiny dog with large, pointed ears, orig. from Mexico

chil·blain (chil′blān′) *n.* [CHIL(L) + *blain* < OE. *blegen,* a sore] a painful sore on the foot or hand, caused by exposure to cold

child (chīld) *n., pl.* **chil′dren** [< OE. *cild*] 1. an infant 2. a boy or girl before puberty 3. a son or daughter **—with child** pregnant **—child′less** *adj.*

child′birth′ *n.* the act of giving birth to a child

child′hood′ *n.* the state or time of being a child

child′ish *adj.* 1. of or like a child 2. immature; silly **—child′ish·ly** *adv.* **—child′ish·ness** *n.*

child′like′ *adj.* like a child, esp. in being innocent, trusting, etc.

chil·dren (chil′drən) *n. pl. of* CHILD

child's play anything simple to do

chil·i (chil′ē) *n., pl.* **-ies** [MexSp.] 1. the very hot dried pod of red pepper, often ground (**chili powder**) 2. a highly seasoned dish of beef, chilies or chili powder, beans, and often tomatoes: in full **chili con car·ne** (kən kär′nē) Also **chile**

chili sauce a spiced sauce of chopped tomatoes, sweet peppers, onions, etc.

chill (chil) *n.* [OE. *ciele*] 1. a feeling of coldness that makes one shiver 2. a moderate coldness 3. a discouraging influence 4. a sudden fear, etc. 5. unfriendliness **—***adj. same as* CHILLY **—***vi.* to become cool **—***vt.* 1. to make cold 2. to cause a chill in 3. to depress **—chill′ing·ly** *adv.*

chill factor the combined effect of wind and low temperature on loss of body heat

chill′y (-ē) *adj.* **-i·er, -i·est** 1. moderately cold 2. chilling 3. unfriendly 4. depressing **—chill′i·ness** *n.*

chime (chīm) *n.* [< L. *cymbalum,* cymbal] 1. [*usually pl.*] *a)* a set of tuned bells or metal tubes *b)* the musical sounds produced by these 2. a single bell in a clock, etc. **—***vi.* **chimed, chim′ing** 1. to sound as a chime 2. to agree **—**

vt. to indicate (time) by chiming —**chime in 1.** to join in **2.** to agree

Chi·me·ra (ki mir'ə, kī-) [< Gr. *chimaira*, she-goat] *Gr. Myth.* a fire-breathing monster with a lion's head, goat's body, and serpent's tail — *n.* [c-] an impossible fancy

chi·mer'i·cal (-mir'i k'l, -mer'-) *adj.* **1.** imaginary; unreal **2.** visionary

chim·ney (chim'nē) *n., pl.* **-neys** [ult. < Gr. *kaminos*, oven] **1.** the passage or structure through which smoke escapes from a fire, often extending above the roof **2.** a glass tube around the flame of a lamp

chim·pan·zee (chim'pan zē', chim pan'zē) *n.* [< Afr. native name] a medium-sized anthropoid ape of Africa, with large ears: also [Colloq.] **chimp** (chimp)

chin (chin) *n.* [OE. *cin*] the part of the face below the lower lip —*vt.* **chinned, chin'ning** to pull (oneself) up while hanging by the hands from a bar, until the chin is just above the bar

Chin. 1. China **2.** Chinese

chi·na (chī'nə) *n.* **1.** *a)* porcelain, orig. from China *b)* vitrified ceramic ware *c)* any earthenware **2.** dishes, etc. made of china Also **chi'na·ware'**

chinch (bug) (chinch) [< Sp. < L. *cimex*, bug] a small, white-winged, black bug that damages grain plants

chin·chil·la (chin chil'ə) *n.* [prob. dim. of Sp. *chinche*, chinch] **1.** *a)* a small rodent of the Andes *b)* its expensive, soft, pale-gray fur **2.** a heavy wool cloth used for making overcoats

Chi·nese (chī nēz', -nēs') *n.* **1.** *pl.* **-nese'** a native of China or one of Chinese descent **2.** the language of the Chinese —*adj.* of China, its people, etc.

chink[1] (chiŋk) *n.* [OE. *cine*] a crack; fissure

chink[2] (chiŋk) *n.* [echoic] a sharp, clinking sound —*vi., vt.* to make or cause to make this sound

chi·no (chē'nō, shē'-) *n.* [< ?] **1.** a strong, twilled cotton cloth **2.** [*pl.*] men's pants of chino

chintz (chints) *n.* [< Hindi *chhīnt*] a cotton cloth printed in colored designs and usually glazed

chintz'y *adj.* **-i·er, -i·est 1.** like chintz **2.** [Colloq.] cheap, stingy, etc.

chip (chip) *vt.* **chipped, chip'ping** [< OE.] to break or cut off small pieces from —*vi.* to break off in small pieces —*n.* **1.** a small piece of wood, etc. cut or broken off **2.** a place where a small piece has been chipped off **3.** a small disk used in poker, etc. as a counter **4.** a thin slice of food [a potato *chip*] —**chip in** [Colloq.] to contribute (money, etc.) —**chip on one's shoulder** [Colloq.] an inclination to fight —**in the chips** [Slang] wealthy

chip'munk (-muŋk') *n.* [< AmInd.] a small, striped N. American squirrel

chip'per *adj.* [< Brit. dial.] [Colloq.] in good spirits; lively

chiro- [< Gr. *cheir*, the hand] *a combining form meaning* hand

chi·rop·o·dy (kə räp'ə dē, kī-) *n.* [CHIRO- + -POD + -Y³] *same as* PODIATRY —**chi·rop'o·dist** *n.*

chi·ro·prac·tic (kī'rə prak'tik) *n.* [< CHIRO- + Gr. *praktikos*, practical] a method of treating disease by manipulation of the body joints, esp. of the spine —**chi'ro·prac'tor** *n.*

chirp (churp) *vi., vt.* [echoic] to make, or utter in, short, shrill tones, as some birds or insects do —*n.* a short, shrill sound

chir·rup (chur'əp, chir'-) *vi.* [< CHIRP] to chirp repeatedly —*n.* a chirruping sound

chis·el (chiz''l) *n.* [< L. *caedere*, to cut] a sharp-edged tool for cutting or shaping wood, stone, etc. —*vi., vt.* **-eled** or **-elled, -el·ing** or **-el·ling 1.** to cut or shape with a chisel **2.** [Colloq.] to take advantage of (someone) or get (something) as by cheating —**chis'el·er, chis'el·ler** *n.*

chit (chit) *n.* [< Hindi] a voucher of a small sum owed for food, drink, etc.

chit·chat (chit'chat') *n.* [< CHAT] **1.** light, informal talk **2.** gossip

chi·tin (kīt''n) *n.* [< Gr. *chitōn*, tunic] a tough, horny substance forming the outer covering of insects, crustaceans, etc.

chit·ter·lings, chit·lins, chit·lings (chit'lənz) *n.pl.* [< Gmc. base] the small intestines of pigs, used for food

chiv·al·rous (shiv''l rəs) *adj.* **1.** gallant, courteous, etc. like an ideal knight **2.** of chivalry Also **chiv·al·ric** (shi val'rik, shiv''l-) —**chiv'al·rous·ly** *adv.*

chiv·al·ry (shiv''l rē) *n.* [< OFr. *chevaler*, a knight] **1.** medieval knighthood **2.** the qualities of an ideal knight, as courage, honor, courtesy, etc.

chives (chīvz) *n.pl.* [< L. *cepa*, onion] a plant with small, hollow leaves having a mild onion odor, used for flavoring

chlo·ral (klôr'əl) *n.* **1.** a thin, oily, colorless, pungent liquid made from chlorine and alcohol **2.** *same as* CHLORAL HYDRATE

chloral hydrate a colorless, crystalline compound used as a sedative

chlor·dane (klôr'dān) *n.* a chlorinated, poisonous, volatile oil used as an insecticide: also **chlor'dan** (-dan)

chlo·ride (klôr'īd) *n.* a compound of chlorine and another element or radical

chlo·ri·nate (klôr'ə nāt') *vt.* **-nat'ed, -nat'ing** to treat (water or sewage) with chlorine for purification —**chlo'ri·na'tion** *n.*

chlo·rine (klôr'ēn, -in) *n.* [< Gr. *chlōros*, pale green] a greenish-yellow, poisonous gaseous chemical element with a disagreeable odor, used in bleaching, water purification, etc.: symbol, Cl

chlo·ro·form (klôr'ə fôrm') *n.* [< Fr.: see CHLORINE & FORMIC] a colorless, volatile liquid used as an anesthetic and solvent —*vt.* to anesthetize or kill with chloroform

chlo·ro·phyll, chlo·ro·phyl (klôr'ə fil') *n.* [< Gr. *chlōros*, green + *phyllon*, leaf] the green pigment of plants: it is involved in photosynthesis

chock (chäk) *n.* [ONormFr. *choque*, a block] a block or wedge placed under a wheel, etc. to prevent motion —*adv.* as close or tight as can be

chock'-full' *adj.* as full as possible

choc·o·late (chôk'lət, chäk'-; -ə lət) *n.* [< MexInd. *chocolatl*] **1.** a paste, powder, etc. made from roasted and ground cacao seeds **2.** a drink or candy made with chocolate **3.** reddish brown —*adj.* **1.** made of or flavored with chocolate **2.** reddish-brown

choice (chois) *n.* [< OFr. < Gothic *kausjan*, to taste] **1.** a choosing; selection **2.** the right or power to choose **3.** a person or thing chosen **4.** the best part **5.** a variety from which to choose **6.** an alternative —*adj.* **choic'er, choic'est 1.** of special excellence **2.** carefully chosen

choir (kwir) *n.* [< OFr. < L. *chorus*: see CHORUS] **1.** a group of singers, esp. in a church **2.** the part of a church they occupy

choke (chōk) *vt.* **choked, chok'ing** [< OE.

aceocian] **1.** to prevent from breathing by blocking the windpipe; strangle; suffocate **2.** to obstruct by clogging **3.** to hinder the growth or action of **4.** to fill up **5.** to cut off some air from the carburetor of (a gasoline engine) so as to make a richer gasoline mixture —*vi.* **1.** to be suffocated **2.** to be obstructed —*n.* **1.** the act or sound of choking **2.** the valve that chokes a carburetor —**choke back** to hold back (feelings, sobs, etc.) —**choke down** to swallow with difficulty —**choke up** [Colloq.] to be unable to speak, act efficiently, etc., as because of fear, tension, etc.

choke′cher′ry *n., pl.* **-ries 1.** a N. American wild cherry tree **2.** its astringent fruit

chok′er *n.* a closely fitting necklace

chol·er (käl′ər) *n.* [< Gr. *cholē*, bile] anger

chol·er·a (käl′ər ə) *n.* [see prec.] a severe, infectious disease characterized by profuse diarrhea, intestinal pain, etc.

chol′er·ic *adj.* [see CHOLER] easily angered

cho·les·ter·ol (kə les′tə rōl′, -rôl′) *n.* [< Gr. *cholē*, bile + *stereos*, solid] a crystalline alcohol found esp. in animal fats, blood, and bile

chomp (chämp) *vt., vi. same as* CHAMP[1]

choose (chōōz) *vt., vi.* **chose, cho′sen, choos′-ing** [OE. *ceosan*] **1.** to take as a choice; select **2.** to decide or prefer

choos′y, choos′ey *adj.* **-i·er, -i·est** [Colloq.] fussy in choosing

chop[1] (chäp) *vt.* **chopped, chop′ping** [ME. *choppen*] **1.** to cut by blows with a sharp tool **2.** to cut into small bits —*vi.* to make quick, cutting strokes —*n.* **1.** a short, sharp blow or stroke **2.** a slice of lamb, pork, etc. cut from the rib, loin, or shoulder **3.** a short, broken movement of waves

chop[2] (chäp) *n.* [var. of CHAP[1]] **1.** a jaw **2.** [*pl.*] the mouth and lower cheeks

chop·per (chäp′ər) *n.* **1.** one that chops **2.** [Colloq.] *a)* a helicopter *b)* a motorcycle

chop′py (-ē) *adj.* **-pi·er, -pi·est** [< CHOP[1]] **1.** rough with short, broken waves, as the sea **2.** making abrupt starts and stops; jerky —**chop′-pi·ness** *n.*

chop·sticks (chäp′stiks′) *n.pl.* [PidE.] two small sticks held together in one hand and used in some Asian countries to lift food to the mouth

chop su·ey (chäp′ sōō′ē) [< Chin. *tsa-sui*, lit., various pieces] a Chinese-American dish of meat, bean sprouts, celery, mushrooms, etc. in a sauce, served with rice

cho·ral (kôr′əl) *adj.* [Fr.] of, for, or sung by a choir or chorus —**cho′ral·ly** *adv.*

cho·rale, cho·ral (kə ral′, kô-) *n.* **1.** a hymn tune **2.** a choir

chord[1] (kôrd) *n.* [alt. (after L. *chorda*) < CORD] **1.** [Poet.] the string of a musical instrument **2.** a responsive feeling or emotion [to strike a sympathetic *chord*] **3.** *Geom.* a straight line joining any two points on an arc, curve, or circumference

chord[2] (kôrd) *n.* [< ACCORD] *Music* a combination of three or more tones sounded together in harmony

chore (chôr) *n.* [< OE. *cierr*, job] **1.** a routine task **2.** a hard or unpleasant task

cho·re·a (kô rē′ə) *n.* [< Gr. *choreia*, choral dance] a nervous disorder characterized by involuntary muscular contractions

chor·e·o·graph (kôr′ē ə graf′) *vt., vi.* [see ff.] to design or plan the movements of (a dance) —**chor′e·o·graph′ic** *adj.*

chor·e·og·ra·phy (kôr′ē äg′rə fē) *n.* [< Gr. *choreia*, dance + -GRAPHY] **1.** ballet dancing **2.**

the art of devising dances or ballets —**chor′e-og′ra·pher** *n.*

chor·is·ter (kôr′is tər) *n.* [see CHORUS] a member of a choir

chor·tle (chôr′t′l) *vi., vt.* **-tled, -tling** [coined by Lewis Carroll, prob. < CHUCKLE + SNORT] to make, or utter with, a gleeful chuckling or snorting sound —*n.* such a sound

cho·rus (kôr′əs) *n.* [< Gr. *choros*] **1.** a group of dancers and singers performing together **2.** the part of a drama, song, etc. performed by a chorus **3.** a group singing or speaking something together **4.** a simultaneous utterance by many **5.** music written for group singing **6.** the refrain of a song, following each verse —*vt., vi.* to sing, speak, or say in unison —**in chorus** in unison

chose (chōz) *pt. of* CHOOSE

cho·sen (chō′z′n) *pp. of* CHOOSE —*adj.* selected; choice

chow (chou) *n.* [< Chin.] **1.** any of a breed of medium-sized dog, originally from China **2.** [Slang] food

chow·der (chou′dər) *n.* [< Fr. *chaudière*, a pot] a thick soup of onions, potatoes, etc. and, often, clams and milk

chow mein (chou mān′) [Chin. *ch'ao*, to fry + *mien*, flour] a Chinese-American stew of meat, celery, bean sprouts, etc., served with fried noodles

Christ (krīst) [< Gr. *christos*, the anointed] Jesus of Nazareth, regarded by Christians as the prophesied Messiah

chris·ten (kris′'n) *vt.* [OE. *cristnian*] **1.** to take into a Christian church by baptism; baptize **2.** to give a name to, esp. at baptism —**chris′ten·ing** *n.*

Chris·ten·dom (kris′'n dəm) *n.* **1.** Christians collectively **2.** countries where most of the inhabitants profess Christianity

Chris·tian (kris′chən) *n.* a believer in Jesus as the Christ, or in the religion based on the teachings of Jesus —*adj.* **1.** of Jesus Christ **2.** of or professing the religion based on the teachings of Jesus **3.** having the qualities taught by Jesus, as love, kindness, etc. **4.** of Christians or Christianity

Chris·ti·an·i·ty (kris′chē an′ə tē) *n.* **1.** Christians collectively **2.** the Christian religion **3.** the state of being a Christian

Chris·tian·ize (kris′chə nīz′) *vt.* **-ized′, -iz′ing** to cause to be Christian

Christian name the baptismal name or given name, as distinct from the family name

Christian Science a religion and system of healing: official name, **Church of Christ, Scientist** —**Christian Scientist**

chris·tie, chris·ty (kris′tē) *n., pl.* **-ties** [< *Christiania*, former name of Oslo] a high-speed turn in skiing

Christ·mas (kris′məs) *n.* [see CHRIST & MASS] a holiday on Dec. 25 celebrating the birth of Jesus Christ

chro·mat·ic (krō mat′ik) *adj.* [< Gr. *chrōma*, color] **1.** of or having color or colors **2.** *Music* using or progressing by halftones —**chro·mat′i-cal·ly** *adv.*

chrome (krōm) *n.* [Fr. < Gr. *chrōma*, color] chromium or chromium alloy —*adj.* designating any of various pigments (**chrome red, chrome yellow**, etc.) made from chromium compounds

-chrome [< Gr. *chrōma*, color] a suffix meaning: **1.** color or coloring agent **2.** chromium

chro·mi·um (krō′mē əm) *n.* [see CHROME] a very hard metallic chemical element resistant to corrosion: symbol, Cr

chromo- [< Gr. *chrōma*, color] a combining

form meaning color or pigment *[chromosome]*
chro·mo·some (krō′mə sōm′) *n.* [CHROMO- +
-SOME²] any of the microscopic rod-shaped
bodies which carry the genes that convey
hereditary characteristics
chron·ic (krän′ik) *adj.* [< Fr. < Gr. *chronos*,
time] 1. lasting a long time or recurring: said
of a disease 2. having had an ailment or habit
for a long time —**chron′i·cal·ly** *adv.*
chron·i·cle (krän′i k'l) *n.* [< Gr. *chronika*,
annals] 1. a historical record of events in the
order of occurrence 2. a narrative; history —*vt.*
-cled, -cling to tell the history of —**chron′i·cler**
n.
chrono- [Gr. < *chronos*, time] *a combining
form meaning* time: also **chron-**
chron·o·log·i·cal (krän′ə läj′i k'l) *adj.* arranged in the order of occurrence —**chron′o·
log′i·cal·ly** *adv.*
chro·nol·o·gy (krə näl′ə jē) *n., pl.* -gies
[CHRONO- + -LOGY] 1. the science of measuring time and of dating events 2. an arrangement or list of events in the order of occurrence —**chro·nol′o·gist** *n.*
chro·nom·e·ter (krə näm′ə tər) *n.* [CHRONO-
+ -METER] a highly accurate kind of clock or
watch
chrys·a·lis (kris′'l əs) *n.* [< Gr. *chrysallis*] 1.
the pupa of a butterfly, encased in a cocoon 2.
the cocoon
chrys·an·the·mum (kri san′thə məm) *n.* [<
Gr. *chrysos*, gold + *anthemon*, a flower] 1. a
late-blooming plant of the composite family,
with showy flowers 2. the flower
chub (chub) *n.* [ME. *chubbe*] a small, freshwater fish related to the minnow and carp
chub′by *adj.* -bi·er, -bi·est [< prec.] round and
plump —**chub′bi·ness** *n.*
chuck¹ (chuk) *vt.* [< ? Fr. *choquer*, strike
against] 1. to tap playfully, esp. under the
chin 2. to toss 3. [Slang] to get rid of —*n.* 1. a
light tap under the chin 2. a toss
chuck² (chuk) *vt.* [? var. of CHOCK] 1. a cut of
beef from around the neck and shoulder blade
2. a clamplike holding device, as on a lathe
chuck′-full′ *adj. same as* CHOCK-FULL
chuck′hole′ *n.* [see CHOCK & HOLE] a rough
hole in a road
chuck·le (chuk′'l) *vi.* -led, -ling [prob. < *chuck*,
to cluck] to laugh softly in a low tone —*n.* a
soft, low-toned laugh
chuck wagon a wagon equipped as a kitchen
for feeding cowboys, etc.
chug (chug) *n.* [echoic] a puffing or explosive
sound, as of a steam locomotive —*vi.* chugged,
chug′ging to make, or move with, such sounds
chuk·ka (boot) (chuk′ə) [ult. < Sans. *cakra*,
wheel] a man's ankle-length, bootlike shoe
chum (chum) *n.* [prob. < *chamber (mate)*]
[Colloq.] a close friend —*vi.* chummed, chum′-
ming [Colloq.] to be close friends —chum′my
adj. -mi·er, -mi·est
chump (chump) *n.* [< ?] [Colloq.] a dupe; fool
chunk (chuŋk) *n.* [< ? CHUCK²] 1. a short, thick
piece 2. a fair portion
chunk′y *adj.* -i·er, -i·est 1. short and thick 2.
stocky —**chunk′i·ness** *n.*
church (chʉrch) *n.* [< Gr. *kyriakē (oikia)*,
Lord's (house)] 1. a building for public worship, esp. one for Christian worship 2. religious
service 3. [*usually* C-] *a)* all Christians *b)* a
particular Christian denomination 4. ecclesiastical, as opposed to secular, government
church′go′er *n.* a person who attends church,
esp. regularly
church′man (-mən) *n., pl.* -men 1. a clergyman
2. a member of a church

Church of England the episcopal church of
England: it is an established church with the
sovereign as its head
church′ward′en (-wôr′d'n) *n.* a lay officer who
attends to secular affairs of a church
church′yard′ *n.* the yard adjoining a church,
often used as a cemetery
churl (chʉrl) *n.* [OE. *ceorl*, freeman] 1. a peas-
ant 2. a surly, ill-bred, or miserly person —
churl′ish *adj.* —**churl′ish·ness** *n.*
churn (chʉrn) *n.* [OE. *cyrne*] a container in
which milk or cream is shaken to form butter
—*vt., vi.* 1. to stir and shake (milk or cream) in
a churn 2. to make (butter) thus 3. to stir up
or move vigorously
chute¹ (shoōt) *n.* [Fr., a fall] an inclined or vertical trough down which things may slide or
drop [a coal *chute*]
chute² (shoōt) *n.* [Colloq.] a parachute
chut·ney (chut′nē) *n., pl.* -neys [Hindi *chatnī*]
a relish of fruits, spices, and herbs
chutz·pah, chutz·pa (khoots′pə) *n.* [Heb. via
Yid.] [Colloq.] impudence; brass
CIA, C.I.A. Central Intelligence Agency
ci·ca·da (si kā′də) *n., pl.* -das, -dae (-dē) [L.] a
large flylike insect with transparent wings: the
male makes a shrill sound
cic·a·trix (sik′ə triks) *n., pl.* ci·cat·ri·ces (si
kat′rə sēz′) [L.] the contracted tissue at the
place where a wound heals
-cide [< L. *caedere*, to kill] *a suffix meaning:*
1. killer 2. killing
ci·der (sī′dər) *n.* [< Gr. *sikera*, intoxicant] the
juice pressed from apples, used as a beverage
or for making vinegar
ci·gar (si gär′) *n.* [< Sp. *cigarro*] a compact
roll of tobacco leaves for smoking
cig·a·rette (sig′ə ret′) *n.* [Fr., dim. of *cigare*,
cigar] a small roll of finely cut tobacco
wrapped in thin paper for smoking
cig′a·ril′lo (-ril′ō) *n., pl.* -los [Sp.] a small,
thin cigar
cil·i·a (sil′ē ə) *n.pl., sing.* -i·um (-əm) [L.] 1. the
eyelashes 2. *Biol.* small hairlike processes —
cil′i·ate (-it, -āt′) *adj.*
cil′i·ar′y (-er′ē) *adj.* of, like, or having cilia
cinch (sinch) *n.* [< Sp. < L. *cingulum*, a girdle]
1. a saddle or pack girth 2. [Slang] a thing
easy to do or sure to happen —*vt.* 1. to tighten
a girth on 2. [Slang] to make sure of
cin·cho·na (sin kō′nə) *n.* [< 17th-c. SAm.
Countess del *Chinchón*] 1. a tropical tree with
a bitter bark 2. the bark, from which quinine
is made
cinc·ture (siŋk′chər) *n.* [L. *cinctura*] a belt or
girdle —*vt.* -tured, -tur·ing to encircle with a
belt
cin·der (sin′dər) *n.* [OE. *sinder*] 1. a minute
piece of partly burned wood or coal 2. [*pl.*]
ashes from wood or coal
Cin·der·el·la (sin′də rel′ə) in a fairy tale, a
household drudge who eventually marries a
prince
cin·e·ma (sin′ə mə) *n.* [< Gr. *kinēma*, motion]
[Chiefly Brit.] a motion-picture theater —the
cinema motion pictures collectively —cin′e-
mat′ic *adj.*
cin·e·ma·tog·ra·phy (sin′ə mə täg′rə fē) *n.*
the art of photography in making motion pictures —**cin′e·ma·tog′ra·pher** *n.*
cin·na·bar (sin′ə bär′) *n.* [< Gr. *kinnabari*]
mercuric sulfide, a heavy, bright-red mineral,
the principal ore of mercury
cin·na·mon (sin′ə mən) *n.* [< Heb. *qinnāmōn*]
1. the light-brown spice made from the inner
bark of a laurel tree of the East Indies 2. this
bark

ci·pher (sī′fər) *n.* [< Ar. *ṣifr,* nothing] **1.** the symbol 0; naught; zero **2.** a nonentity **3.** *a)* secret writing based on a key *b)* the key to such a system

cir·ca (sur′kə) *prep.* [L.] about: used before an approximate date, figure, etc.

Cir·ce (sur′sē) in Homer's *Odyssey,* an enchantress who turned men into swine

cir·cle (sur′k'l) *n.* [< Gr. *kirkos*] **1.** a plane figure bounded by a single curved line every point of which is equally distant from the center **2.** this curved line **3.** anything like a circle, as a ring **4.** a complete or recurring series; cycle **5.** a group of people with common interests **6.** extent; scope, as of influence —*vt.* -cled, -cling **1.** to form a circle around **2.** to move around, as in a circle —*vi.* to go around in a circle

cir·clet (-klit) *n.* **1.** a small circle **2.** a circular band for the finger, head, etc.

cir·cuit (sur′kit) *n.* [< L. *circum-,* around + *ire,* to go] **1.** a boundary line or its length **2.** a going around something **3.** the regular journey of a person through a district in his work **4.** a chain or association, as of theaters or resorts **5.** a path over which electric current may flow —*vi.* to go in a circuit —*vt.* to make a circuit about

circuit breaker a device that automatically interrupts the flow of an electric current

cir·cu·i·tous (sər kyōō′ə təs) *adj.* roundabout; indirect —**cir·cu′i·tous·ly** *adv.*

cir·cuit·ry (sur′kə trē) *n.* the system or the components of an electric circuit

cir·cu·lar (sur′kyə lər) *adj.* **1.** in the shape of a circle; round **2.** moving in a circle **3.** roundabout; circuitous —*n.* a letter, advertisement, etc. for circulation among a number of people —**cir′cu·lar′i·ty** (-ler′ə tē) *n.* —**cir′cu·lar·ly** *adv.*

cir·cu·late (sur′kyə lāt′) *vt.* -lat′ed, -lat′ing [< L. *circulari,* form a circle] **1.** to move in a circle or circuit and return, as the blood **2.** to go from person to person or from place to place —*vt.* to make circulate —**cir′cu·la′tor** *n.* —**cir′cu·la·to′ry** (-lə tôr′ē) *adj.*

cir·cu·la′tion *n.* **1.** a circulating or moving around, as of the blood through the arteries and veins **2.** the distribution of newspapers, magazines, etc. among readers

circum- [< L. *circum*] *a prefix meaning* around, about, surrounding

cir·cum·cise (sur′kəm sīz′) *vt.* -cised′, -cis′ing [< L. *circum-,* around + *caedere,* to cut] to cut off all or part of the foreskin of —**cir′cum·ci′sion** (-sizh′ən) *n.*

cir·cum·fer·ence (sər kum′fər əns, -frəns) *n.* [< L. *circum-,* around + *ferre,* to carry] **1.** the line bounding a circle, ball, etc. **2.** the distance measured by this line

cir·cum·flex (sur′kəm fleks′) *n.* [< L. *circum-,* around + *flectere,* to bend] a mark (^, ˋ, ˜) used over certain vowels in some languages to indicate a specific sound

cir·cum·lo·cu′tion (-lō kyōō′shən) *n.* [< L.: see CIRCUM- & LOCUTION] a roundabout way of expressing something

cir·cum·nav′i·gate′ (-nav′ə gāt′) *vt.* -gat′ed, -gat′ing [< L.: see CIRCUM- & NAVIGATE] to sail or fly around (the earth, an island, etc.) —**cir′cum·nav′i·ga′tion** *n.*

cir′cum·scribe′ (-skrīb′) *vt.* -scribed′, -scrib′ing [< L.: see CIRCUM- & SCRIBE] **1.** to trace a line around; encircle **2.** to limit —**cir′cum·scrip′tion** (-skrip′shən) *n.*

cir′cum·spect′ (-spekt′) *adj.* [< L. *circum-,* around + *specere,* to look] cautious; discreet —**cir′cum·spec′tion** *n.*

cir′cum·stance′ (-stans′) *n.* [< L. *circum-,* around + *stare,* to stand] **1.** a fact or event accompanying another **2.** [*pl.*] conditions affecting a person, esp. financial conditions **3.** mere chance **4.** ceremony; show [pomp and *circumstance*] —**under no circumstances** never —**under the circumstances** conditions being what they are or were

cir′cum·stan′tial (-stan′shəl) *adj.* **1.** having to do with, or depending on, circumstances **2.** incidental **3.** detailed; complete

circumstantial evidence *Law* evidence offered to prove certain circumstances from which the fact at issue may be inferred

cir′cum·vent′ (-vent′) *vt.* [< L. *circum-,* around + *venire,* come] **1.** to go around **2.** to get the better of or prevent by craft or ingenuity —**cir′cum·ven′tion** *n.*

cir·cus (sur′kəs) *n.* [L., a circle] **1.** in ancient Rome, an amphitheater **2.** a traveling show of acrobats, trained animals, clowns, etc. **3.** [Colloq.] any riotously entertaining person, event, etc.

cir·rho·sis (sə rō′sis) *n.* [< Gr. *kirrhos,* tawny + -OSIS] a degenerative disease, esp. of the liver, marked by excess formation of connective tissue

cir·rus (sir′əs) *n., pl.* -rus [L., a curl] a formation of clouds in wispy filaments or feathery tufts

cis·tern (sis′tərn) *n.* [< L. *cista,* chest] a large tank for storing water, esp. rain water

cit·a·del (sit′ə d'l, -del′) *n.* [< L. *civitas,* city] **1.** a fortress **2.** a refuge

cite (sīt) *vt.* cit′ed, cit′ing [< L. *citare,* summon] **1.** to summon to appear before a court of law **2.** to quote **3.** to mention by way of example, proof, etc. **4.** to mention in an official report for meritorious service —**ci·ta′tion** *n.*

cit·i·fied (sit′i fīd′) *adj.* having the manners, dress, etc. attributed to city people

cit·i·zen (sit′ə zən) *n.* [< L. *civis,* citizen] a member of a state or nation who owes allegiance to it by birth or naturalization and is entitled to full civil rights —**cit′i·zen·ship′** *n.*

cit′i·zen·ry (-rē) *n.* all citizens as a group

cit·ric acid (si′trik) an acid obtained from citrus fruits

cit′ron (-trən) *n.* [Fr., lemon: see CITRUS] **1.** a yellow, thick-skinned fruit resembling a lemon **2.** its rind candied

cit·ron·el·la (si′trə nel′ə) *n.* [ModL.] a sharp-smelling oil used in perfume, insect repellents, etc.

cit·rus (si′trəs) *n.* [L.] **1.** any of the trees that bear oranges, lemons, limes, etc. **2.** any such fruit —*adj.* of these trees: also **cit′rous**

cit·y (sit′ē) *n., pl.* -ies [< L. *civis,* citizen] **1.** a large, important town **2.** in the U.S., an incorporated municipality with boundaries, powers, etc. defined by State charter **3.** the people of a city —*adj.* of a city

city hall a building housing a municipal government

civ·et (siv′it) *n.* [< Ar. *zabād*] **1.** the musky secretion of a catlike, flesh-eating mammal (**civet cat**) of Africa and S Asia: used in some perfumes **2.** the civet cat

civ·ic (siv′ik) *adj.* [< L. *civis,* citizen] of a city, citizens, or citizenship

civ·ics (-iks) *n.pl.* [*with sing. v.*] the study of civic affairs and the rights and duties of citizenship

civ·il (siv′'l) *adj.* [see CIVIC] **1.** of a citizen or citizens **2.** of a community of citizens **3.** civilized **4.** polite **5.** not military or religious —**civ′il·ly** *adv.*

civil disobedience nonviolent opposition to a law by refusing to comply with it, on the grounds of conscience

civil engineering engineering dealing with the construction of bridges, roads, etc. —**civil engineer**

ci·vil·ian (sə vil′yən) *n.* [see CIVIC] a person not in the armed forces —*adj.* of civilians

ci·vil′i·ty (-ə tē) *n., pl.* -**ties 1.** politeness **2.** a civil, or polite, act or utterance

civ·i·li·za·tion (siv′ə lə zā′shən) *n.* **1.** a civilizing or becoming civilized **2.** the total culture of a people, period, etc. **3.** the peoples considered to have reached a high social development

civ·i·lize (siv′ə līz′) *vt.* -**lized′**, -**liz′ing** [see CIVIC] **1.** to bring out of a primitive or savage condition to a higher level of civilization **2.** to improve in habits or manners; refine —**civ′i·lized′** *adj.*

civil law the body of law concerning private rights

civil liberties liberties guaranteed to the individual by law and custom; rights of thinking, speaking, and acting as one likes so long as one does not harm others

civil rights those rights guaranteed to the individual by the 13th, 14th, 15th, and 19th Amendments to the U.S. Constitution

civil service those employed in government service, esp. through public competitive examination —**civil servant**

civil war war between different factions of the same nation —**the Civil War** the war between the North and the South in the U.S. (1861–1865)

civ·vies, civ·ies (siv′ēz) *n.pl.* [Colloq.] civilian clothes

Cl *Chem.* chlorine

clack (klak) *vi., vt.* [prob. echoic < ON.] to make or cause to make a sudden, sharp sound —*n.* this sound —**clack′er** *n.*

clad (klad) *alt. pt. & pp. of* CLOTHE —*adj.* clothed; dressed

claim (klām) *vt.* [< L. *clamare*, cry out] **1.** to demand as rightfully belonging to one **2.** to require; deserve [to *claim* attention] **3.** to assert; maintain —*n.* **1.** a claiming **2.** a right to something **3.** something claimed, as land **4.** an assertion —**claim′a·ble** *adj.* —**claim′ant, claim′er** *n.*

clair·voy·ance (kler voi′əns) *n.* [Fr. < *clair,* clear + *voir,* see] the supposed ability to perceive things not in sight —**clair·voy′ant** *n., adj.*

clam (klam) *n.* [OE. *clamm,* fetter] a hard-shelled bivalve mollusk —*vi.* clammed, clam′ming to dig for clams —**clam up** [Colloq.] to refuse to talk

clam′bake′ *n.* **1.** a picnic at which steamed or baked clams, corn, and other foods are served **2.** [Colloq.] any large, noisy party

clam·ber (klam′bər) *vi.* [ME. *clambren*] to climb clumsily or with effort, using both hands and feet —*n.* a hard or clumsy climb

clam·my (klam′ē) *adj.* -**mi·er, -mi·est** [prob. < OE. *clay*] unpleasantly moist, cold, and sticky —**clam′mi·ness** *n.*

clam·or (klam′ər) *n.* [< L. *clamare,* cry out] **1.** a loud outcry; uproar **2.** a noisy demand or complaint **3.** a loud, sustained noise —*vi.* to make a clamor —**clam′or·ous** *adj.*

clamp (klamp) *n.* [< MDu. *klampe*] a device for clasping or fastening things together —*vt.* to fasten or brace with a clamp —**clamp down** (on) to become more strict (with)

clan (klan) *n.* [< Gael. < L. *planta,* offshoot] **1.** a group of families descended from a common ancestor **2.** a group of people with interests in common —**clans·man** (klanz′mən) *n., pl.* -**men**

clan·des·tine (klan des′t′n) *adj.* [< L. *clam,* secret] secret or hidden; furtive

clang (klaŋ) *vi., vt.* [echoic] to make or cause to make a loud, sharp, ringing sound, as by striking metal —*n.* this sound

clan·gor (klaŋ′ər) *n.* [L. < *clangere,* to clang] a continuous clanging sound —**clan′gor·ous** *adj.* —**clan′gor·ous·ly** *adv.*

clank (klaŋk) *n.* [echoic] a sharp metallic sound —*vi., vt.* to make or cause to make this sound

clan′nish *adj.* **1.** of a clan **2.** tending to associate closely with one's own group only —**clan′nish·ly** *adv.* —**clan′nish·ness** *n.*

clap (klap) *vi.* clapped, clap′ping [OE. *clæppan,* to beat] **1.** to make the explosive sound of two flat surfaces struck together **2.** to strike the hands together, as in applause —*vt.* **1.** to strike together briskly **2.** to strike with an open hand **3.** to put, move, etc. swiftly [clapped into jail] —*n.* **1.** the sound or act of clapping **2.** a slap

clap·board (klab′ərd, klap′bôrd′) *n.* [transl. of MDu. *klapholt* < *klappen,* to fit + *holt,* wood] a thin board with one thicker edge, used as siding —*vt.* to cover with clapboards

clap′per *n.* a thing that makes a clapping sound, as the tongue of a bell

clap′trap′ *n.* [CLAP + TRAP] insincere, empty talk intended to get applause

claque (klak) *n.* [Fr. < *claquer,* to clap] a group of people paid to applaud at a play, opera, etc.

clar·et (klar′it) *n.* [< L. *clarus,* clear] a dry red wine —*adj.* purplish-red

clar·i·fy (klar′ə fī′) *vt., vi.* -**fied′, -fy′ing** [< L. *clarus,* clear + *facere,* make] to make or become clear —**clar′i·fi·ca′tion** *n.*

clar·i·net (klar′ə net′) *n.* [< Fr.; ult. < L. *clarus,* clear] a single-reed woodwind instrument played by means of holes and keys —**clar′i·net′ist, clar′i·net′tist** *n.*

clar·i·on (klar′ē ən) *adj.* [< L. *clarus,* clear] clear, sharp, and ringing [a *clarion* call]

clar·i·ty (klar′ə tē) *n.* [< L. *clarus,* clear] clearness

clash (klash) *vi.* [echoic] **1.** to collide with a loud, harsh, metallic noise **2.** to conflict; disagree —*vt.* to strike with a clashing noise —*n.* **1.** the sound of clashing **2.** conflict

clasp (klasp) *n.* [ME. *claspe*] **1.** a fastening, as a hook, to hold things together **2.** a grasping; embrace **3.** a grip of the hand —*vt.* **1.** to fasten with a clasp **2.** to grasp firmly; embrace **3.** to grip with the hand

class (klas) *n.* [< L. *classis*] **1.** a number of people or things grouped together because of likenesses; kind; sort **2.** social or economic status [the middle *class*] **3.** *a)* a group of students taught together *b)* a meeting of such a group *c)* a group of students graduating together **4.** grade or quality **5.** [Slang] excellence —*vt.* to classify

clas·sic (klas′ik) *adj.* [< L. *classis,* class] **1.** being an excellent model of its kind **2.** of the art, literature, etc. of the ancient Greeks and Romans **3.** balanced, formal, restrained, etc. **4.** famous as traditional or typical —*n.* **1.** a writer, artist, etc. or a literary or artistic work recognized as excellent, authoritative, etc. **2.** a famous traditional event —**the classics** ancient Greek and Roman literature

clas′si·cal (-i k′l) *adj.* **1.** *same as* CLASSIC (senses 1, 2, 3) **2.** versed in Greek and Roman culture, literature, etc. **3.** designating or of music that conforms to certain standards of form, complexity, etc. **4.** standard and traditional *[classical* economics*]* —**clas′si·cal·ly** *adv.*

clas·si·cism (klas′ə siz′m) *n.* **1.** the aesthetic principles or qualities of ancient Greece and Rome **2.** adherence to these principles **3.** knowledge of classical art and literature — **clas′si·cist** *n.*

classified advertising advertising under such listings as *help wanted, lost and found,* etc. — **classified advertisement**

clas·si·fy (klas′ə fī′) *vt.* **-fied′, -fy′ing 1.** to arrange in classes according to a system **2.** to designate (government documents) as secret or restricted —**clas′si·fi·ca′tion** *n.*

class′mate′ *n.* a member of the same class at a school or college

clat·ter (klat′ər) *vi., vt.* [ME. *clateren*] to make or cause to make a clatter —*n.* **1.** a rapid succession of loud, sharp noises **2.** a tumult; hubbub

clause (klôz) *n.* [< L. *claudere,* to close] **1.** a group of words containing a subject and a verb: cf. MAIN CLAUSE, SUBORDINATE CLAUSE **2.** a particular article in a document

claus·tro·pho·bi·a (klôs′trə fō′bē ə) *n.* [< L. *claustrum,* enclosure + -PHOBIA] a fear of being in an enclosed place

clav·i·chord (klav′ə kôrd′) *n.* [< L. *clavis,* key + *chorda,* a string] a stringed musical instrument with a keyboard, predecessor of the piano

clav·i·cle (klav′ə k'l) *n.* [< Fr. < L. *clavis,* key] a bone connecting the sternum with the shoulder blade; collarbone

claw (klô) *n.* [OE. *clawu*] **1.** a sharp, hooked nail on a bird's or animal's foot **2.** the pincers of a crab, etc. —*vt., vi.* to scratch, clutch, etc. as with claws

clay (klā) *n.* [OE. *clæg*] **1.** a firm, plastic earth used in making pottery, etc. **2.** *a)* earth *b)* the human body —**clay′ey** *adj.* **clay′i·er, clay′i·est** —**clay′ish** *adj.*

clean (klēn) *adj.* [OE. *clæne*] **1.** free from dirt or impurities; unsoiled **2.** morally pure **3.** sportsmanlike **4.** neat and tidy **5.** free from flaws; clear **6.** thorough —*adv.* completely —*vt., vi.* to make or be made clean —**clean up 1.** to make clean or neat **2.** [Colloq.] to finish — **come clean** [Slang] to confess —**clean′ly** *adv.* — **clean′ness** *n.*

clean′-cut′ *adj.* **1.** clearly outlined **2.** well-formed **3.** trim, neat, etc.

clean′er *n.* a person or thing that cleans; esp., one who dry-cleans

clean·ly (klen′lē) *adj.* **-li·er, -li·est 1.** having clean habits **2.** always kept clean —**clean′li·ness** *n.*

cleanse (klenz) *vt.* **cleansed, cleans′ing** [OE. *clænsian*] to make clean, pure, etc. —**cleans′er** *n.*

clear (klir) *adj.* [< L. *clarus*] **1.** free from clouds; bright **2.** transparent **3.** easily seen or heard **4.** keen or logical *[a clear* mind*]* **5.** not obscure; obvious **6.** certain; positive **7.** free from guilt **8.** free from deductions; net **9.** free from debt **10.** free from obstruction; open — *adv.* in a clear manner —*vt.* **1.** to make clear **2.** to free from impurities, obstructions, etc. **3.** to make lucid **4.** to open *[clear* a path*]* **5.** to get rid of **6.** to prove the innocence of **7.** to pass or leap over, by, etc. **8.** to make as profit —*vi.* to become clear —**clear away** (or **off**) **1.** to remove so as to leave a cleared space **2.** to go away — **clear out** [Colloq.] to depart —**clear up** to make or become clear —**in the clear 1.** in the open **2.** [Colloq.] guiltless —**clear′ly** *adv.* —**clear′ness** *n.*

clear′ance (-əns) *n.* **1.** the clear space between

an object and that which it is passing **2.** *Banking* the adjustment of accounts in a clearinghouse

clear′-cut′ *adj.* **1.** clearly outlined **2.** distinct; plain

clear′ing *n.* an area of land cleared of trees

clear′ing·house′ *n.* an office maintained by several banks as a center for exchanging checks, balancing accounts, etc.

clear′sight′ed *adj.* **1.** seeing clearly **2.** understanding or thinking clearly

cleat (klēt) *n.* [ME.] a piece of wood or metal, often wedge-shaped, fastened to something to strengthen it or give secure footing

cleav·age (klē′vij) *n.* **1.** a cleaving; splitting; dividing **2.** a cleft; fissure

cleave¹ (klēv) *vt.* **cleaved** or **cleft** or **clove, cleaved** or **cleft** or **clo′ven, cleav′ing** [OE. *cleofan*] **1.** to divide by a blow; split **2.** to pierce

cleave² (klēv) *vi.* **cleaved, cleav′ing** [OE. *cleofian*] **1.** to adhere; cling (*to*) **2.** to be faithful (*to*)

cleav′er *n.* a heavy cleaving tool with a broad blade, used by butchers

clef (klef) *n.* [Fr. < L. *clavis,* a key] a symbol used in music to indicate the pitch of the notes on the staff

cleft (kleft) *alt. pt. & pp. of* CLEAVE¹ —*adj.* split; divided —*n.* **1.** an opening made by cleaving; crack; crevice **2.** a hollow between two parts

clem·a·tis (klem′ə tis) *n.* [< Gr. *klēma,* vine] a vine related to the buttercup, with bright-colored flowers

clem·en·cy (klem′ən sē) *n., pl.* **-cies** [see CLEMENT] **1.** leniency; mercy **2.** mildness, as of weather

clem·ent (klem′ənt) *adj.* [L. *clemens*] **1.** lenient; merciful **2.** mild, as weather

clench (klench) *vt.* [< OE. *(be)clencan,* make cling] **1.** to close (the teeth or fist) firmly **2.** to grip tightly —*n.* a firm grip

clere·sto·ry (klir′stôr′ē) *n., pl.* **-ries** [< ME. *cler,* CLEAR + *storie,* STORY²] the wall of a church rising above the roofs of the flanking aisles and containing windows

cler·gy (klur′jē) *n., pl.* **-gies** [see CLERK] ministers, priests, etc. collectively

cler′gy·man (-mən) *n., pl.* **-men** a member of the clergy; minister, priest, rabbi, etc.

cler·ic (kler′ik) *n.* [see CLERK] a clergyman — *adj.* of a clergyman or the clergy

cler′i·cal (-i k'l) *adj.* **1.** of a clergyman or the clergy **2.** of office clerks or their work —**cler′i·cal·ly** *adv.*

clerk (klurk) *n.* [< Gr. *klērikos,* priest] **1.** a layman with minor duties in a church **2.** an office worker who keeps records, types, files, etc. **3.** a public official who keeps the records of a court, town, etc. **4.** a salesclerk —*vi.* to work as a salesclerk

clev·er (klev′ər) *adj.* [? < Norw. *klöver*] **1.** skillful; adroit; dexterous **2.** intelligent; smart —**clev′er·ly** *adv.* —**clev′er·ness** *n.*

clew (kloō) *n.* [< OE. *cliwen*] **1.** a ball of thread or yarn **2.** *same as* CLUE **3.** a metal loop in the corner of a sail

cli·ché (klē shā′) *n.* [Fr. < *clicher,* to stereotype] a trite expression or idea

click (klik) *n.* [echoic] a slight, sharp sound like that of a door latch snapping into place — *vi., vt.* to make or cause to make a click

cli·ent (klī′ənt) *n.* [< L. *cliens,* follower] **1.** a person or company in whose behalf a lawyer, accountant, etc. works **2.** a customer

cli·en·tele (klī′ən tel′) *n.* [Fr. < L. *clientela*] all one's clients or customers, collectively

cliff (klif) *n.* [OE. *clif*] a high, steep face of rock, esp. on a coast; precipice

cli·mac·ter·ic (klī mak'tər ik) *n.* [< Gr. *klimax*, ladder] a crucial period in life, esp. the menopause —*adj.* crucial

cli·mate (klī'mət) *n.* [< Gr. *klima*, region] 1. the prevailing weather conditions of a place 2. a region with reference to its prevailing weather —**cli·mat'ic** (-mat'ik) *adj.*

cli·max (klī'maks) *n.* [< Gr. *klimax*, ladder] 1. the final, culminating element in a series; highest point of interest, excitement, etc. 2. the turning point of action in a drama, etc. — *vi., vt.* to reach, or bring to, a climax —**cli·mac'tic** (-mak'tik) *adj.*

climb (klīm) *vi., vt.* [OE. *climban*] 1. to go up by using the feet and often the hands 2. to ascend gradually 3. to move (*down, over, along,* etc.) using the hands and feet 4. to grow upward —*n.* 1. a climbing 2. a place to be climbed —**climb'er** *n.*

clime (klīm) *n.* [see CLIMATE] [Poet.] a region, esp. with reference to its climate

clinch (klinch) *vt.* [var. of CLENCH] 1. to fasten (a driven nail, etc.) by bending the projecting end 2. to settle (an argument, bargain, etc.) definitely —*vi.* 1. *Boxing* to grip the opponent's body with the arms 2. [Slang] to embrace —*n.* a clinching

clinch'er *n.* 1. one that clinches 2. a decisive point, argument, act, etc.

cling (kliŋ) *vi.* clung, cling'ing [OE. *clingan*] 1. to adhere; hold fast, as by embracing 2. to be or stay near 3. to be emotionally attached — **cling'er** *n.*

clin·ic (klin'ik) *n.* [< Gr. *klinē*, a bed] 1. the teaching of medicine by treating patients in the presence of students 2. a place where medical specialists practice as a group 3. an outpatient department, as of a hospital

clin'i·cal (-i k'l) *adj.* 1. of or connected with a clinic 2. having to do with the treatment and observation of patients, as distinguished from experimental study 3. scientifically impersonal —**clin'i·cal·ly** *adv.*

clink (kliŋk) *vi., vt.* [echoic] to make or cause to make a slight, sharp sound, as of glasses striking together —*n.* 1. such a sound 2. [Colloq.] a jail

clink'er *n.* [Du. *klinker*] a hard mass of fused matter, as from burned coal

clip¹ (klip) *vt.* clipped, clip'ping [< ON. *klippa*] 1. to cut as with shears 2. to cut short 3. to cut the hair of 4. [Colloq.] to hit sharply 5. [Slang] to cheat —*vi.* to move rapidly —*n.* 1. a clipping 2. a thing clipped 3. a rapid pace 4. [Colloq.] a quick, sharp blow

clip² (klip) *vi., vt.* clipped, clip'ping [OE. *clyppan,* to embrace] to grip tightly; fasten —*n.* anything that clips or fastens

clip·per (klip'ər) *n.* 1. [*usually pl.*] a tool for cutting or trimming 2. a sailing ship built for great speed

clip'ping *n.* a piece cut out or off, as an item clipped from a newspaper

clique (klēk, klik) *n.* [Fr. < *cliquer,* make a noise] a small, exclusive circle of people; coterie —**cliqu'ish** *adj.* —**cliqu'ish·ly** *adv.*

cli·to·ris (klit'ər əs) *n.* [< Gr. *kleitys,* hill] a small, erectile organ of the vulva

cloak (klōk) *n.* [< ML. *clocca,* a bell: from its shape] 1. a loose, usually sleeveless outer garment 2. something that covers or conceals —*vt.* 1. to cover as with a cloak 2. to hide; conceal

cloak'room' *n.* a room where hats, coats, umbrellas, etc. can be left temporarily

clob·ber (kläb'ər) *vt.* [< ?] [Slang] to beat or hit repeatedly; maul

cloche (klōsh) *n.* [Fr. < ML. *clocca,* bell] a closefitting, bell-shaped hat for women

clock¹ (kläk) *n.* [ME. *clokke,* orig., clock with bells < ML. *clocca,* bell] a device for measuring time, usually by means of pointers moving over a dial —*vt.* to record the time of (a race, etc.) with a stopwatch

clock² (kläk) *n.* [< ? prec., because orig. bell-shaped] a woven or embroidered ornament on the side of a stocking or sock

clock'wise' (-wīz') *adv., adj.* in the direction in which the hands of a clock rotate

clock'work' (-wurk') *n.* 1. the mechanism of a clock 2. any similar mechanism, with springs and gears —**like clockwork** regularly and precisely

clod (kläd) *n.* [OE.] 1. a lump, esp. of earth or clay 2. a dull, stupid fellow —**clod'dish** *adj.*

clod'hop'per *n.* [CLOD + HOPPER] 1. a plowman 2. a lout 3. a coarse, heavy shoe

clog (kläg) *n.* [ME. *clogge,* lump of wood] 1. anything that hinders or obstructs 2. a shoe with a thick, usually wooden sole —*vt.* **clogged, clog'ging** 1. to hinder 2. to obstruct (a passage); stop up —*vi.* to become stopped up

clois·ter (klois'tər) *n.* [< L. *claudere,* to close] 1. a place of religious seclusion; monastery or convent 2. a covered walk along an inside wall with a columned opening along one side —*vt.* to confine as in a cloister —**clois'tered** *adj.* — **clois'tral** *adj.*

clon·ing (klō'niŋ) *n.* [< Gr. *klōn,* a twig] the producing of an identical duplicate of an organism by replacing the nucleus of an unfertilized ovum with the nucleus of a body cell from the organism

close¹ (klōs) *adj.* clos'er, clos'est [see ff.] 1. confined or confining [*close* quarters] 2. hidden; secluded 3. secretive; reserved 4. miserly; stingy 5. oppressively warm and stuffy 6. with little space between; near together 7. compact; dense [a *close* weave] 8. near to the surface [a *close* shave] 9. intimate; familiar [a *close* friend] 10. strict; thorough; careful [*close* attention] 11. nearly equal or alike [*close* in age] —*adv.* in a close manner —**close'ly** *adv.* — **close'ness** *n.*

close² (klōz) *vt.* closed, clos'ing [< L. *claudere,* to close] 1. to shut 2. to block (an opening) 3. to finish; conclude —*vi.* 1. to become shut 2. to come to an end 3. to come close or together — *n.* an end; conclusion —**close down** (or **up**) to shut or stop entirely —**close in** to surround, cutting off escape

close call (klōs) [Colloq.] a narrow escape from danger: also **close shave**

close'-fist·ed (klōs'fis'tid) *adj.* stingy

close'fit'ting *adj.* fitting tightly

close'mouthed' (-mouthd', -moutht') *adj.* not talking much: also **close'lipped'**

clos·et (kläz'it) *n.* [< L. *claudere,* to close] a small room or cupboard for clothes, supplies, etc. —*vt.* to shut up in a private room for confidential talk

close-up (klōs'up') *n.* a photograph, TV shot, etc. taken at very close range

clo·sure (klō'zhər) *n.* [< L. *claudere,* to close] 1. a closing or being closed 2. a finish; end 3. anything that closes 4. *same as* CLOTURE

clot (klät) *n.* [OE. *clott*] a thickened mass or lump [a blood *clot*] —*vt., vi.* clot'ted, clot'ting to coagulate into a clot

cloth (klôth) *n., pl.* cloths (klôthz, klôths) [OE. *clath*] 1. a woven, knitted, or pressed fabric of fibrous material, as cotton, wool, silk, etc. 2. a tablecloth, washcloth, etc. —*adj.* made of cloth —**the cloth** the clergy

clothe (klō*th*) *vt.* **clothed** or **clad, cloth′ing** [see prec.] **1.** to provide with or dress in clothes **2.** to cover [*clothed* in glory]

clothes (klōz, klō*th*z) *n.pl.* [OE. *clathas*] **1.** clothing; wearing apparel **2.** bedclothes

clothes′pin′ *n.* a small clip, as of plastic or wood, for fastening clothes on a line

cloth·ier (klō*th*′yər) *n.* a dealer in clothes or cloth

cloth·ing (klō′*th*iŋ) *n.* **1.** clothes; wearing apparel **2.** a covering

clo·ture (klō′chər) *n.* [< Fr.: see CLOSURE] the ending of legislative debate by having the measure put to an immediate vote

cloud (kloud) *n.* [OE. *clud*, mass of rock] **1.** a visible mass of vapor in the sky **2.** a mass of smoke, dust, steam, etc. **3.** a great number of moving things [a *cloud* of bees] **4.** anything that darkens, obscures, etc. —*vt.* **1.** to darken or obscure as with clouds **2.** to make gloomy **3.** to sully —*vi.* to become cloudy, gloomy, etc. — **in the clouds 1.** impractical **2.** in a daydream — **under a cloud** under suspicion —**cloud′less** *adj.* —**cloud′y** *adj.* **-i·er, -i·est**

cloud′burst′ *n.* a sudden heavy rain

clout (klout) *n.* [OE. *clut,* a patch] [Colloq.] a blow, as with the hand —*vt.* [Colloq.] to strike, as with the hand; hit

clove[1] (klōv) *n.* [< L. *clavus,* nail: from its shape] **1.** the dried flower bud of a tropical evergreen tree, used as a pungent, fragrant spice **2.** the tree

clove[2] (klōv) *n.* [OE. *clufu*] a segment of a bulb, as of garlic

clove[3] (klōv) *alt. pt.* of CLEAVE[1]

clo·ven (klō′v'n) *alt. pp.* of CLEAVE[1] —*adj.* split

clo·ver (klō′vər) *n.* [OE. *clafre*] any of various herbs with leaves of three leaflets and small flowers in dense heads —**in clover** living in ease and luxury

clo′ver·leaf′ (-lēf′) *n., pl.* **-leafs′** a multiple highway interchange designed to let traffic flow freely in any of four directions through use of an overpass and curving ramps

clown (kloun) *n.* [< ? Fr. *colon,* farmer] **1.** a clumsy, boorish person **2.** a comedian who entertains with antics, tricks, etc., as in a circus —*vi.* to be, act like, or perform as a clown — **clown′ish** *adj.*

cloy (kloi) *vt., vi.* [< L. *clavus,* a nail] to surfeit by too much, esp. of anything too sweet, rich, etc. —**cloy′ing·ly** *adv.*

club (klub) *n.* [< ON. *klumba,* mass] **1.** a heavy stick used as a weapon **2.** any stick used in a game, as golf **3.** *a)* a group of people associated for a common purpose *b)* its meeting place **4.** *a)* [*pl.*] a suit of playing cards marked with a black trefoil (♣) *b)* a card of this suit —*vt.* **clubbed, club′bing** to strike as with a club —*vi.* to unite for a common purpose

club′foot′ *n., pl.* **-feet′** a congenitally misshapen, often clublike foot —**club′foot′ed** *adj.*

club′house′ *n.* **1.** a building used by a club **2.** a locker room used by an athletic team

club soda *same as* SODA WATER

cluck (kluk) *vi.* [echoic] to make low, sharp sounds, as of a hen calling her chicks —*n.* such a sound

clue (klōō) *n.* [see CLEW] a fact, object, etc. that helps solve a mystery or problem —*vt.* **clued, clu′ing** [Colloq.] to provide with information needed (often with *in*)

clump (klump) *n.* [< LowG. *klump*] **1.** a lump; mass **2.** a cluster, as of trees **3.** the sound of

heavy footsteps —*vi.* **1.** to walk heavily **2.** to form clumps

clum·sy (klum′zē) *adj.* **-si·er, -si·est** [ME. *clumsid,* numb] **1.** lacking grace or skill; awkward **2.** awkwardly shaped or made —**clum′si·ly** *adv.* —**clum′si·ness** *n.*

clung (kluŋ) *pt. & pp.* of CLING

clunk (kluŋk) *n.* a dull, metallic sound

clunk′er (-ər) *n.* [Slang] a battered old machine or automobile

clus·ter (klus′tər) *n.* [OE. *clyster*] a number of persons or things grouped together —*vi., vt.* to form or make into a cluster

clutch[1] (kluch) *vt.* [OE. *clyccan,* to clench] to grasp eagerly or tightly —*vi.* to snatch or seize (*at*) —*n.* **1.** [*usually pl.*] power; control **2.** a grasp; grip **3.** a device for engaging or disengaging a motor or engine

clutch[2] (kluch) *n.* [< ON. *klekja,* to hatch] **1.** a nest of eggs **2.** a brood of chicks

clut·ter (klut′ər) *n.* [< CLOT] a jumble; confusion —*vt.* to make untidy; litter (often with *up*)

Cm *Chem.* curium

cm, cm. centimeter(s)

co- *a prefix shortened from* COM-, *meaning:* **1.** together with [*cooperation*] **2.** joint [*coauthor*] **3.** equally [*coextensive*]

Co *Chem.* cobalt

Co., co. *pl.* **Cos., cos. 1.** company **2.** county

C/O, c.o. care of

C.O., CO Commanding Officer

coach (kōch) *n.* [< *Kócs,* village in Hungary] **1.** a large, covered, four-wheeled carriage **2.** a railroad passenger car **3.** the lowest-priced class of airline accommodations **4.** a bus **5.** an instructor or trainer as of athletes or actors — *vt., vi.* to instruct or train (someone)

coach′man (-mən) *n., pl.* **-men** the driver of a coach, or carriage

co·ag·u·late (kō ag′yōō lāt′) *vt.* **-lat′ed, -lat′ing** [< L. *co-,* together + *agere,* to drive] to cause (a liquid) to become semisolid; clot —*vi.* to become coagulated —**co·ag′u·lant** *n.* —**co·ag′u·la′tion** *n.*

coal (kōl) *n.* [OE. *col,* ember] **1.** a black, combustible mineral used as a fuel **2.** a piece of this **3.** an ember —*vt., vi.* to provide with or take in a supply of coal —**haul (rake,** etc.) **over the coals** to criticize sharply

co·a·lesce (kō′ə les′) *vi.* **-lesced′, -lesc′ing** [< L. *co-,* together + *alescere,* grow up] to unite into a single body or group —**co′a·les′cence** *n.* —**co′a·les′cent** *adj.*

co·a·li·tion (kō′ə lish′ən) *n.* [see prec.] a combination or union, esp. if temporary

coal oil kerosene

coal tar a black, thick liquid obtained by the distillation of coal, used as in dyes

coarse (kôrs) *adj.* **coars′er, coars′est** [< COURSE ("usual way")] **1.** of poor quality **2.** consisting of rather large particles **3.** rough; harsh **4.** unrefined; crude [a *coarse* joke] — **coarse′ly** *adv.* —**coarse′ness** *n.*

coars′en *vt., vi.* to make or become coarse

coast (kōst) *n.* [< L. *costa,* rib, side] **1.** land along the sea; seashore **2.** a slide down an incline, as on a sled —*vi.* **1.** to sail near or along a coast **2.** to slide down an incline, as on a sled **3.** to continue moving by momentum alone —**coast′al** *adj.*

coast′er *n.* **1.** one that coasts **2.** a small mat, disk, etc. put under a glass or bottle to protect the surface as of a table

coast guard a governmental force employed to defend a nation's coast, aid vessels in distress, etc.; specif., [**C- G-**] such a branch of the U.S. armed forces

coast'line' *n.* the outline of a coast

coat (kōt) *n.* [< ML. *cota,* tunic] **1.** a sleeved outer garment opening down the front **2.** the natural covering of an animal or plant **3.** a layer, as of paint, over a surface —*vt.* to cover with a coat

coat·ing (kōt'iŋ) *n. same as* COAT (sense 3)

coat of arms a design, as on a shield, used as the symbol of a family, etc.

coat'tail' (-tāl') *n.* either half of the divided lower back part of a coat

coax (kōks) *vt., vi.* [< obs. slang *cokes,* a fool] to urge or get with soft words, flattery, etc.

co·ax·i·al (kō ak'sē əl) *adj.* having a common axis: also **co·ax'al**

cob (käb) *n.* [prob. < LowG.] **1.** a corncob **2.** a male swan **3.** a short, thickset horse

co·balt (kō'bôlt) *n.* [< G. *kobold,* goblin] a hard, steel-gray metallic chemical element: symbol, Co

cobalt blue dark blue

cob·ble' (käb'l) *vt.* **-bled, -bling** [ME.] **1.** to mend or patch (shoes, etc.) **2.** to mend or put together clumsily or crudely

cob·ble² (käb'l) *n.* [< ?] a cobblestone —*vt.* **-bled, -bling** to pave with cobblestones

cob·bler (käb'lər) *n.* **1.** one who mends shoes **2.** a deep-dish fruit pie

cob'ble·stone' *n.* a rounded stone formerly used for paving streets

co·bra (kō'brə) *n.* [Port.] a very poisonous snake of Asia and Africa

cob·web (käb'web') *n.* [ME. *coppe,,* spider + WEB] **1.** a web spun by a spider **2.** anything flimsy, ensnaring, etc. like this

co·ca (kō'kə) *n.* [< SAmInd. name] a tropical S. American shrub whose dried leaves yield cocaine

co·caine, co·cain (kō kān') *n.* [< COCA] an alkaloid obtained from dried coca leaves: it is a narcotic and local anesthetic

coc·cus (käk'əs) *n., pl.* **coc·ci** (käk'sī) [< Gr. *kokkos,* berry] a spherical bacterium

coc·cyx (käk'siks) *n., pl.* **coc·cy'ges** (-sī'jēz) [< Gr. *kokkyx,* cuckoo: because shaped like its beak] a small, triangular bone at the end of the vertebral column

coch·i·neal (käch'ə nēl') *n.* [< L. *coccum,* a (red) berry] a red dye made from a dried Mexican insect

coch·le·a (käk'lē ə) *n., pl.* **-ae'** (-ē'), **-as** [< Gr. *kochlias,* snail] the spiral-shaped part of the inner ear —**coch'le·ar** *adj.*

cock' (käk) *n.* [OE. *coc*] **1.** a rooster or other male bird **2.** a faucet or valve **3.** a firearm hammer or its position for firing **4.** a jaunty tilt, as of a hat —*vt.* **1.** to tilt jauntily **2.** to raise or turn alertly **3.** to set the hammer of (a gun) in firing position

cock² (käk) *n.* [ME. *cokke*] a small, coneshaped pile, as of hay —*vt.* to pile in cocks

cock·ade (kä kād') *n.* [< Fr. < *coq,* a cock] a rosette or the like worn on the hat as a badge

cock·a·ma·mie (käk'ə mā'mē) *adj.* [< DECALCOMANIA] [Slang] of poor quality; inferior

cock-and-bull story (käk'n bool') an absurd tale

cock·a·too (käk'ə tōō') *n., pl.* **-toos'** [< Du. < Malay *kakatua*] a crested parrot of Australia and the East Indies

cocked hat a three-cornered hat

cock·er (spaniel) (käk'ər) [because a woodcock hunter] a small spaniel with silky hair and drooping ears

cock·eyed (käk'īd') *adj.* [< COCK¹ *v.* + EYE] **1.** cross-eyed **2.** [Slang] *a)* awry *b)* silly *c)* drunk

cock·fight (käk'fīt') *n.* a fight between gamecocks usually wearing metal spurs

cock·le' (käk'l) *n.* [< Gr. *konchē,* mussel] an edible shellfish with two heart-shaped shells — **cockles of one's heart** one's deepest emotions

cock·le² (käk'l) *n.* [OE. *coccel*] any of various weeds that grow in grainfields

cock'le·shell' *n.* the shell of a cockle

cock·ney (käk'nē) *n., pl.* **-neys** [ME. *cokenei,* spoiled child] [*often* C-] **1.** a native of the East End, London, speaking a characteristic dialect **2.** this dialect

cock·pit (käk'pit') *n.* **1.** a pit for cockfighting **2.** in a small airplane, the space for the pilot and, sometimes, passengers, or, in a large plane, for the pilot and crew

cock·roach (käk'rōch') *n.* [Sp. *cucaracha*] an insect with long feelers and a flat, soft body: a common household pest

cocks·comb (käks'kōm') *n.* **1.** the red, fleshy growth on the head of a rooster **2.** a plant related to the amaranth

cock·sure (käk'shoor') *adj.* [< COCK¹ + SURE] absolutely sure, esp. in an arrogant way

cock·tail (käk'tāl') *n.* [< ?] **1.** a mixed alcoholic drink, usually iced **2.** an appetizer, as fruit juice, diced fruits, or seafood

cock·y (käk'ē) *adj.* **-i·er, -i·est** [< COCK¹ + -Y²] [Colloq.] jauntily conceited

co·co (kō'kō) *n., pl.* **-cos** [Sp. < L. < Gr. *kokkos,* berry] **1.** *same as* COCONUT PALM **2.** *same as* COCONUT

co·coa (kō'kō) *n.* [see CACAO] **1.** powder made from roasted, ground cacao seeds **2.** a drink made by adding sugar and hot water or milk to this **3.** a reddish-yellow brown

cocoa butter a yellowish fat prepared from cacao seeds

co·co·nut, co·coa·nut (kō'kə nut') *n.* the fruit of a tropical tree (**coconut palm**), a thick, brown oval husk enclosing edible white meat and a sweet, milky fluid

co·coon (kə kōōn') *n.* [< Fr. < ML. *coco,* shell] the protective silky case that certain insect larvae spin about themselves before the pupa stage

cod (käd) *n., pl.* **cod, cods** a food fish of northern seas

C.O.D., c.o.d. collect on delivery

co·da (kō'də) *n.* [It. < L. *cauda,* a tail] *Music* a final passage

cod·dle (käd'l) *vt.* **-dled, -dling** [< ?] **1.** to cook (esp. eggs) gently in water not quite boiling **2.** to pamper

code (kōd) *n.* [< L. *codex,* wooden tablet] **1.** a body of laws arranged systematically **2.** any set of principles **3.** a set of signals for sending messages **4.** a system or set of symbols used as in secret writing —*vt.* **cod'ed, cod'ing** to put into a code

co·deine (kō'dēn) *n.* [< Gr. *kōdeia,* poppy head] an alkaloid derived from opium, used for pain relief and in cough medicines: also **co'dein**

co·dex (kō'deks) *n., pl.* **-di·ces** (-də sēz') [see CODE] an ancient manuscript

cod'fish' *n., pl.:* see FISH *same as* COD

codg·er (käj'ər) *n.* [< ?] [Colloq.] an eccentric, esp. elderly, fellow

cod·i·cil (käd'i s'l) *n.* [see CODE] an addition to a will

cod·i·fy (käd'ə fī', kō'də fī') *vt.* **-fied, -fy'ing** to arrange (laws, etc.) systematically —**cod'i·fi·ca'tion** *n.* —**cod'i·fi'er** *n.*

co·ed, co-ed (kō'ed') *n.* [Colloq.] a girl at-

tending a coeducational college —*adj.* [Colloq.]
1. coeducational **2.** of a coed

co·ed·u·ca·tion (kō'ej ə kā'shən) *n.* the educational system in which students of both sexes attend classes together —**co'ed·u·ca'-tion·al** *adj.*

co·ef·fi·cient (kō'ə fish'ənt) *n.* [CO- + EFFICIENT] **1.** a factor that contributes to produce a result or measures some physical property **2.** a multiplier of a variable or unknown quantity (as 6 in 6x)

co·e·qual (kō ē'kwəl) *adj., n.* equal

co·erce (kō urs') *vt.* -erced', -erc'ing [< L. *co-*, together + *arcere*, to confine] **1.** to restrain by force; curb **2.** to force; compel **3.** to enforce — **co·er'cion** (-ur'shən) *n.*

co·e·val (kō ē'v'l) *adj., n.* [< L. *co-*, together + *aevum*, an age] contemporary

co·ex·ist (kō'ig zist') *vi.* **1.** to exist together at the same time or in the same place **2.** to live together without conflict, despite differences — **co'ex·ist'ence** *n.* —**co'ex·ist'ent** *adj.*

cof·fee (kôf'ē) *n.* [< It. < Ar. *qahwa*] **1.** an aromatic drink made from the roasted and ground beanlike seeds of a tall tropical shrub related to the madder **2.** these seeds **3.** the shrub **4.** milky brown

coffee break a brief respite from work, when coffee, etc. is usually taken

cof'fee·cake' *n.* a kind of cake or roll for eating with coffee

coffee shop an informal restaurant where light refreshments or meals are served

coffee table a low table, typically in a living room, for serving refreshments

cof·fer (kôf'ər) *n.* [see COFFIN] **1.** a strongbox for money, jewelry, etc. **2.** [*pl.*] a treasury; funds —*vt.* to enclose in a coffer

cof·fin (kôf'in) *n.* [< Gr. *kophinos*, basket] the case in which a corpse is buried

cog (käg) *n.* [< Scand.] **1.** one of the teeth of a cogwheel **2.** a cogwheel

co·gent (kō'jənt) *adj.* [< L. *co-*, together + *agere*, to drive] forceful and to the point; compelling —**co'gen·cy** *n.*

cog·i·tate (käj'ə tāt') *vi., vt.* -tat'ed, -tat'ing [< L. *cogitari*, ponder] to think deeply (about); ponder —**cog'i·ta'tion** *n.*

co·gnac (kōn'yak) *n.* [Fr.] a brandy, specif. of Cognac, France

cog·nate (käg'nāt) *adj.* [< L. *co-*, together + (*g*)*nasci*, to be born] **1.** related by family **2.** derived from a common original form **3.** having the same nature —*n.* **1.** a person related to another **2.** a cognate word, language, or thing

cog·ni·tion (käg nish'ən) *n.* [< L. *co-*, together + (*g*)*noscere*, know] **1.** the process of knowing **2.** knowledge gained; perception —**cog'ni·tive** *adj.*

cog·ni·za·ble (käg'ni zə b'l) *adj.* **1.** that can be known or perceived **2.** *Law* within the jurisdiction of a court

cog·ni·zance (käg'nə zəns) *n.* perception; knowledge —**take cognizance of** to notice or recognize

cog'ni·zant (-zənt) *adj.* aware (*of*)

cog·no·men (käg nō'mən) *n.* [L. < *co-*, with + *nomen*, a name] **1.** a surname **2.** any name; esp., a nickname

cog'wheel' *n.* a wheel rimmed with teeth that mesh with those of another wheel, etc. to transmit or receive motion

co·hab·it (kō hab'it) *vi.* [< L. *co-*, together + *habitare*, dwell] to live together as husband and wife, esp. when not legally married —**co·hab'i·ta'tion** *n.*

co·heir (kō'er') *n.* a person who inherits jointly with another or others

co·here (kō hir') *vi.* -hered', -her'ing [< L. *co-*, together + *haerere*, to stick] **1.** to stick together **2.** to be connected logically

co·her'ent (-ənt) *adj.* **1.** sticking together **2.** logically consistent —**co·her'ence** *n.* —**co·her'ent·ly** *adv.*

co·he·sion (kō hē'zhən) *n.* a cohering; tendency to stick together —**co·he'sive** (-hēs'iv) *adj.* —**co·he'sive·ly** *adv.*

co·ho (kō'hō) *n., pl.* -ho, -hos [< ?] a small Pacific salmon, now also in N U.S. fresh waters

co·hort (kō'hôrt) *n.* [< L. *cohors*, enclosure] **1.** a band of soldiers **2.** any group or band **3.** an associate or supporter

coif (koif) *n.* [< LL. *cofea*, a cap] **1.** a cap that fits the head closely **2.** (*usually* kwäf) [< COIFFURE] a hair style

coif·fure (kwä fyoor') *n.* [Fr. < *coiffe*, COIF] **1.** a headdress **2.** a hair style

coil (koil) *vt., vi.* [< L. *com-*, together + *legere*, gather] to wind into a circular or spiral form — *n.* **1.** anything so wound **2.** the series of windings so formed, or one single turn **3.** *Elec.* a spiral of wire

coin (koin) *n.* [< L. *cuneus*, a wedge] **1.** a piece of stamped metal, issued by a government as money **2.** such pieces collectively —*vt.* **1.** to make (coins) by stamping (metal) **2.** to invent (a new word, phrase, etc.) —**coin'er** *n.*

coin'age (-ij) *n.* a coining or a thing coined

co·in·cide (kō'in sīd') *vi.* -cid'ed, -cid'ing [< Fr. < L. *co-*, together + *in-*, upon + *cadere*, to fall] **1.** to take up the same place in space **2.** to occur at the same time **3.** to correspond or agree exactly —**co·in'ci·dent** (-sə dənt) *adj.*

co·in·ci·dence (kō in'sə dəns) *n.* **1.** a coinciding **2.** a striking but merely accidental occurrence of events, ideas, etc. at the same time — **co·in'ci·den'tal** (-den't'l) *adj.* —**co·in'ci·den'tal·ly** *adv.*

co·i·tus (kō'it əs) *n.* [< L. *co-*, together + *ire*, to go] sexual intercourse: also **co·i·tion** (kō ish'ən) —**co'i·tal** *adj.*

coke (kōk) *n.* [ME. *colke*, a core] coal with most of its gases removed by heating: it burns with intense heat and little smoke

col- *same as* COM-: used before *l*

Col. Colonel

co·la¹ (kō'lə) *n.* [< WAfr. name] **1.** an African tree whose nuts yield an extract used in soft drinks and medicine **2.** a carbonated soft drink flavored with this extract

co·la² (kō'lə) *n. alt. pl. of* COLON²

col·an·der (kul'ən dər, käl'-) *n.* [prob. < L. *colum*, strainer] a perforated pan to drain off liquids

cold (kōld) *adj.* [OE. *cald*] **1.** of a low temperature **2.** chilled or chilling **3.** not cordial **4.** objective; detached [*cold* logic] **5.** faint or stale, as a scent in hunting **6.** [Colloq.] unprepared [to enter a game *cold*] **7.** [Slang] perfectly mastered, as a role **8.** [Slang] unconscious [knocked *cold*] —*adv.* altogether; completely [*cold* sober] —*n.* **1.** absence of heat or warmth, or the sensation produced **2.** a condition characterized by inflamed respiratory passages, a nasal discharge, etc. —**catch** (or **take**) **cold** to become ill with a cold —**have** (or **get**) **cold feet** [Colloq.] to be (or become) timid —**in the cold** neglected —**cold'ly** *adv.* —**cold'ness** *n.*

cold'blood'ed *adj.* **1.** having a body temperature that varies with the surrounding air, water, or land, as reptiles or fish **2.** pitiless; cruel

cold cream a creamy preparation for softening and cleansing the skin

cold front the forward edge of a cold air mass advancing into a warmer air mass

cold shoulder [Colloq.] a slight; snub; rebuff —**cold'-shoul'der** *vt.*

cold sore little blisters about the mouth during a cold or fever

cold turkey [Slang] **1.** abrupt and total withdrawal of drugs from an addict **2.** without preparation

cold war sustained hostility without actual warfare

cold wave an onset of colder weather

cole (kōl) *n.* [< L. *caulis*, cabbage] a plant of the mustard family; esp., rape

cole·slaw (kōl'slô') *n.* [< Du. *kool*, cabbage + *sla*, salad] a salad of shredded raw cabbage: also **cole slaw**

cole·wort (kōl'wurt') *n.* [COLE + WORT²] any cabbage with leaves not in a compact head

col·ic (käl'ik) *n.* [< Gr. *kōlon*, colon] acute abdominal pain —**col'ick·y** *adj.*

col·i·se·um (käl'ə sē'əm) *n.* [< L. *colosseum*] a large building or stadium

co·li·tis (kō līt'is) *n.* [< Gr. *kolon* + -ITIS] inflammation of the large intestine

col·lab·o·rate (kə lab'ə rāt') *vi.* -**rat'ed**, -**rat'ing** [< L. *com*-, with + *laborare*, to work] **1.** to work together, esp. in literary or scientific projects **2.** to cooperate with the enemy —**col·lab'o·ra'tion** *n.* —**col·lab'o·ra'tive** *adj.* —**col·lab'o·ra'tor** *n.*

col·lab'o·ra'tion·ist *n.* a person who cooperates with the enemy

col·lage (kə läzh') *n.* [Fr. < Gr. *kolla*, glue] an art form in which bits of objects are pasted on a surface

col·lapse (kə laps') *vi.* -**lapsed'**, -**laps'ing** [< L. *com*-, together + *labi*, to fall] **1.** to fall down or to pieces **2.** to break down suddenly **3.** to fold together compactly —*vt.* to make collapse —*n.* a collapsing —**col·laps'i·ble** *adj.*

col·lar (käl'ər) *n.* [< L. *collum*, neck] **1.** a garment part encircling the neck **2.** a band, as of leather, for an animal's neck **3.** anything like a collar —*vt.* **1.** to put a collar on **2.** to seize, as by the collar

col'lar·bone' *n.* the clavicle

col·lard (käl'ərd) *n.* [contr. < COLEWORT] a kind of kale, with coarse leaves

col·late (kä lāt') *vt.* -**lat'ed**, -**lat'ing** [< L. *com*-, together + *latus*, brought] to compare (texts) critically —**col·la'tor** *n.*

col·lat·er·al (kə lat'ər əl) *adj.* [< L. *com*-, together + *latus*, a side] **1.** parallel or corresponding **2.** accompanying or corroborating the main thing **3.** of the same ancestry but in a different line **4.** designating or of security given as a pledge for meeting an obligation — *n.* **1.** a collateral relative **2.** collateral security

col·la·tion (kə lā'shən) *n.* **1.** the act or result of collating **2.** a light meal

col·league (käl'ēg) *n.* [< Fr. < L. *com*-, together + *legare*, deputize] a fellow worker; associate

col·lect (kə lekt') *vt.* [< L. *com*-, together + *legere*, gather] **1.** to gather together **2.** to gather (stamps, etc.) as a hobby **3.** to call for and receive (money) for (bills, rent, etc.) **4.** to regain control of (oneself) —*vi.* to assemble or accumulate —*adj.*, *adv.* with payment to be made by the receiver [to telephone *collect*] —*n.* (käl'ekt) [*also* C-] a short prayer —**col·lec'tor** *n.*

col·lect'ed *adj.* **1.** gathered **2.** composed; calm

col·lect'i·ble, col·lect'a·ble *adj.* that can be or is collected —*n.* any of certain old things, not antiques, that people collect as a hobby

col·lec'tion *n.* **1.** a collecting **2.** things collected **3.** an accumulation **4.** a sum collected

col·lec'tive *adj.* **1.** formed by collecting **2.** of or as a group [*collective* effort] **3.** *Gram.* designating a noun, as *crowd*, singular in form but meaning a group —*n.* **1.** a collective enterprise or the people in it **2.** *Gram.* a collective noun —**col·lec'tive·ly** *adv.*

col·leen (käl'ēn, kə lēn') *n.* [< Ir. *caile*, girl] [Irish] a girl

col·lege (käl'ij) *n.* [see COLLEAGUE] **1.** an association of individuals with certain powers, duties, etc. [the electoral *college*] **2.** an institution of higher education granting degrees **3.** a school of a university **4.** a school for a specialized occupation [a secretarial *college*]

col·le·gian (kə lē'jən) *n.* a college student

col·le'giate (-jət) *adj.* of or like a college or collegians

col·lide (kə līd') *vi.* -**lid'ed**, -**lid'ing** [< L. *com*-, together + *laedere*, to strike] **1.** to strike violently together **2.** to clash

col·lie (käl'ē) *n.* [< ?] a large, long-haired Scottish sheep dog with a long, narrow head

col·lier (käl'yər) *n.* [see COAL & -IER] [Chiefly Brit.] **1.** a coal miner **2.** a ship for carrying coal

col'lier·y *n., pl.* -**ies** [Chiefly Brit.] a coal mine

col·li·sion (kə lizh'ən) *n.* a colliding

col·lo·cate (käl'ə kāt') *vt.* -**cat'ed**, -**cat'ing** [< L. *com*-, together + *locare*, to place] to place together, esp. side by side —**col'lo·ca'tion** *n.*

col·lo·di·on (kə lō'dē ən) *n.* [< Gr. *kolla*, glue + *eidos*, a form] a nitrocellulose solution that dries into a tough, elastic film

col·loid (käl'oid) *n.* [< Gr. *kolla*, glue + -OID] a substance made up of tiny, insoluble, nondiffusible particles that remain suspended in a medium of different matter —**col·loi'dal** *adj.*

colloq. **1.** colloquial(ly) **2.** colloquialism

col·lo·qui·al (kə lō'kwē əl) *adj.* [< L.: see COLLOQUY] **1.** of or like conversation **2.** designating or of the words, phrases, etc. characteristic of informal speech and writing —**col·lo'qui·al·ism** *n.* —**col·lo'qui·al·ly** *adv.*

col·lo·quy (käl'ə kwē) *n., pl.* -**quies** [< L. *com*-, together + *loqui*, speak] **1.** a conversation **2.** a conference

col·lu·sion (kə lōo'zhən) *n.* [< L. *com*-, with + *ludere*, to play] a secret agreement to do something illegal or fraudulent —**col·lu'sive** (-siv) *adj.*

co·logne (kə lōn') *n.* same as EAU DE COLOGNE

co·lon¹ (kō'lən) *n.* [< Gr. *kōlon*, limb] a mark of punctuation (:) used as before a long quotation or after the salutation of a formal letter

co·lon² (kō'lən) *n., pl.* -**lons**, -**la** (-lə) [< Gr. *kolon*] the part of the large intestine from the cecum to the rectum —**co·lon·ic** (kə län'ik) *adj.*

colo·nel (kur'n'l) *n.* [Fr. < It. < L. *columna*, column] a military officer ranking above a lieutenant colonel —**colo'nel·cy** (-sē) *n., pl.* -**cies**

co·lo·ni·al (kə lō'nē əl) *adj.* **1.** of or in a colony or colonies **2.** [often C-] of or in the thirteen British colonies that became the U.S. —*n.* an inhabitant of a colony —**co·lo'ni·al·ly** *adv.*

co·lo'ni·al·ism *n.* a system of having colonies, esp. for exploitation —**co·lo'ni·al·ist** *n., adj.*

col·o·nist (käl'ə nist) *n.* **1.** any of the original settlers of a colony **2.** a colonial

col'o·nize' (-nīz') *vt., vi.* -**nized'**, -**niz'ing** **1.** to found a colony (in) **2.** to settle in a colony — **col·o·ni·za'tion** *n.* —**col'o·niz'er** *n.*

col·on·nade (käl'ə näd') *n.* [Fr. < It. < L. *columna*, column] *Archit.* a series of regularly spaced columns

col·o·ny (käl'ə nē) *n., pl.* **-nies** [< L. *colere*, cultivate] **1.** a group of settlers in a distant land, under the jurisdiction of their native land **2.** the region settled **3.** any territory ruled by a distant state **4.** a community of the same nationality or pursuits, as within a city **5.** *Biol.* a group of similar animals or plants living or growing together

col·o·phon (käl'ə fän') *n.* [< Gr. *kolophōn*, top] a publisher's distinctive emblem

col·or (kul'ər) *n.* [L.] **1.** the property of reflecting light of a particular wavelength: the distinct colors of the spectrum are red, orange, yellow, green, blue, indigo, and violet **2.** any coloring matter; pigment; dye; paint **3.** facial color, esp. a healthy rosiness or a blush **4.** the color of the skin **5.** [*pl.*] an identifying colored badge, costume, etc. **6.** [*pl.*] a flag **7.** semblance; likeness **8.** vividness —*vt.* **1.** to give color to; paint, dye, etc. **2.** to change the color of **3.** to alter or influence, as by distorting [*prejudice colored* his views] —*vi.* **1.** to become colored **2.** to change color **3.** to flush or blush —**show one's colors** to reveal one's true self — **col'or·a'tion** *n.*

col·o·ra·tu·ra (kul'ər ə toor'ə) *n.* [It.] a soprano skilled at singing brilliant runs, trills, etc.: in full **coloratura soprano**

col'or·blind' *adj.* **1.** unable to perceive colors or to distinguish certain colors **2.** ignoring race —**col'or·blind'ness** *n.*

col'or·cast' *n.* a television broadcast in color —*vt., vi.* **-cast'** or **-cast'ed, -cast'ing** to televise in color

col'ored *adj.* **1.** having color **2.** non-Caucasoid; specif., Negro **3.** influenced

col'or·fast' (-fast') *adj.* that will keep its color without fading or running

col'or·ful *adj.* **1.** full of color **2.** varied, vivid, etc. —**col'or·ful·ly** *adv.*

col'or·ing *n.* **1.** something that imparts color **2.** the way a thing is colored **3.** false appearance

col'or·less *adj.* **1.** lacking color **2.** dull

color line a barrier of social, political, or economic restrictions imposed on Negroes or other nonwhites

co·los·sal (kə läs''l) *adj.* **1.** like a colossus in size; huge; gigantic **2.** [Colloq.] extraordinary —**co·los'sal·ly** *adv.*

co·los·sus (kə läs'əs) *n., pl.* **-los'si** (-ī), **-los'sus·es** [< Gr. *kolossos*] **1.** a huge statue **2.** any huge or important person or thing

col·our (kul'ər) *n., vt., vi.* Brit. sp. of COLOR

colt (kōlt) *n.* [OE.] a young male horse

col·ter (kōl'tər) *n.* [< L. *culter*, plowshare] a blade or disk on a plow, to cut soil vertically

col·um·bine (käl'əm bīn') *n.* [< L. *columba*, a dove] a plant related to the buttercup, with spurred flowers of various colors

col·umn (käl'əm) *n.* [< L. *columna*] **1.** a slender, upright structure, typically a supporting member in a building; pillar **2.** anything like a column [the spinal *column*] **3.** a formation in file, as of troops **4.** a vertical section of printed material on a page **5.** a regular feature article or department, as in a newspaper —**co·lum·nar** (kə lum'nər), **col'umned** (-əmd) *adj.*

col'um·nist (-əm nist, -ə mist) *n.* a person who writes or conducts a column, as in a newspaper

com- [L. < *cum*, with] *a prefix meaning* with,

together [*combine*] : also used as an intensive [*command*]

co·ma (kō'mə) *n.* [< Gr. *kōma*, deep sleep] a state of deep, prolonged unconsciousness, as from injury

co·make (kō'māk') *vt.* **-made', -mak'ing** same as COSIGN —**co'mak'er** *n.*

co·ma·tose (kō'mə tōs', käm'ə-) *adj.* **1.** of, like, or in a coma or stupor **2.** lethargic; torpid

comb (kōm) *n.* [OE. *camb*] **1.** a thin strip of plastic, metal, hard rubber, etc. with teeth, used as to arrange or clean the hair or to hold the hair in place **2.** anything used like or suggestive of a comb; specif., *a*) a tool for carding wool, cotton, etc. *b*) a red, fleshy outgrowth as on a rooster's head **3.** a honeycomb —*vt.* **1.** to arrange, straighten, clean, disentangle, etc. with or as if with a comb **2.** to search thoroughly

com·bat (kəm bat', käm'bat) *vi., vt.* **-bat'ed** or **-bat'ted, -bat'ing** or **-bat'ting** [< Fr. < L. *com-*, with + *battuere*, to beat, fight] to fight; struggle (against) —*n.* (käm'bat, kum'-) a battle; conflict —**com·bat·ant** (käm'bə tənt, kəm bat''nt) *adj., n.*

combat fatigue a neurotic condition characterized by anxiety, irritability, depression, etc., as after long combat in warfare

com·bat·ive (kəm bat'iv, käm'bə tiv) *adj.* disposed to fight; belligerent; pugnacious

comb·er (kō'mər) *n.* **1.** one that combs **2.** a large breaking wave

com·bi·na·tion (käm'bə nā'shən) *n.* **1.** a combining or being combined **2.** a thing formed by combining **3.** an association for a common purpose **4.** the series of numbers or letters to which the dial of a special lock (**combination lock**) is turned to open the lock

com·bine (kəm bīn') *vt., vi.* **-bined', -bin'ing** [< L. *com-*, together + *bini*, two by two] to bring or come into union; unite; join —*n.* (käm'bīn') **1.** a machine for harvesting and threshing grain **2.** an association, as of corporations, for purposes often unethical

comb·ings (kō'miŋz) *n.pl.* loose hair, wool, etc. removed in combing

combining form a word form occurring only in compounds or derivatives (Ex.: *cardio-* in *cardiograph*)

com·bo (käm'bō) *n., pl.* **-bos** [Colloq.] a combination; specif., a small jazz ensemble

com·bus·ti·ble (kəm bus'tə b'l) *adj.* easily igniting; flammable —*n.* a flammable substance

com·bus'tion (-chən) *n.* [< L. *com-*, intens. + *urere*, to burn] the act or process of burning

come (kum) *vi.* **came, come, com'ing** [OE. *cuman*] **1.** to move from "there" to "here" **2.** to arrive or appear **3.** to extend; reach **4.** to happen; occur [*success came* to her] **5.** to have a certain place or order [after 1 *comes 2*] **6.** to have a certain descent or origin **7.** to result **8.** to get to be [*it came* loose] **9.** to be available [*it comes* in two sizes] **10.** to amount —*interj.* now, now!: used as from impatience —**come about 1.** to occur **2.** to turn about —**come across 1.** to find by chance **2.** [Colloq.] to be effective, understood, etc. **3.** [Slang] to give or do what is wanted —**come around** (or **round**) **1.** to revive or recover **2.** to turn about **3.** to give in; yield —**come by 1.** to acquire **2.** to drop in for a visit —**come into 1.** to enter **2.** to inherit —**come off 1.** to get detached **2.** to occur — **come out 1.** to be disclosed **2.** to appear, be published, etc. **3.** to make a debut **4.** to end up —**come out for** to announce one's approval or endorsement of —**come through 1.** to complete or endure something successfully **2.** [Slang] to give or do what is wanted —**come to** to recover consciousness —**come up** to emerge for consideration, voting on, etc. —**come upon** to find or encounter by chance —**come up to** to meet (expectations, standards, etc.) —**come up with** to suggest, produce, find, etc. —**how come?** [Colloq.] why?

come′back′ *n.* [Colloq.] **1.** a return to a previous position of success, power, etc. **2.** a retort

co·me·di·an (kə mē′dē ən) *n.* an actor who plays comic parts —**co·me′di·enne′** (-en′) *n.fem.*

come′down′ *n.* a loss of status or position

com·e·dy (käm′ə dē) *n., pl.* **-dies** [< Gr. *kōmos,* festival + *aeidein,* sing] **1.** a drama or narrative with a happy ending or nontragic theme **2.** an amusing event

come·ly (kum′lē) *adj.* **-li·er, -li·est** [OE. *cymlic*] **1.** pleasant to look at; fair **2.** [Archaic] seemly; decorous; proper —**come′li·ness** *n.*

come′-on′ *n.* [Slang] an inducement

co·mes·ti·ble (kə mes′tə b'l) *n.* [Fr. < L. *com-,* intens. + *edere,* eat] [*usually pl.*] food

com·et (käm′ət) *n.* [< Gr. *komē,* hair] a heavenly body with a starlike nucleus and usually a long, luminous tail: comets orbit the sun

come·up·pance (kum′up′ns) *n.* [< COME + UP¹ + -ANCE] [Colloq.] deserved punishment; retribution

com·fit (kum′fit) *n.* [< L. *com-,* with + *facere,* to make] a candy; sweetmeat

com·fort (kum′fərt) *vt.* [< L. *com-,* intens. + *fortis,* strong] to soothe in distress or sorrow; console —*n.* **1.** relief from distress, grief, etc. **2.** one that comforts **3.** a state of ease and quiet enjoyment; also, something contributing to this —**com′fort·ing** *adj.* —**com′fort·less** *adj.*

com·fort·a·ble (kumf′tər b'l, kum′fər tə b'l) *adj.* **1.** providing comfort **2.** having comfort; at ease **3.** [Colloq.] sufficient to satisfy, as a salary; adequate —**com′fort·a·bly** *adv.*

com′fort·er *n.* **1.** one that comforts **2.** a quilted blanket

comfort station a public toilet; restroom

com·fy (kum′fē) *adj.* **-fi·er, -fi·est** [Colloq.] comfortable

com·ic (käm′ik) *adj.* **1.** of comedy **2.** amusing; funny —*n.* **1.** a comedian **2.** the humorous part of art or life **3.** *a*) *same as* COMIC STRIP or COMIC BOOK *b*) [*pl.*] a section of comic strips

com′i·cal *adj.* amusing; funny —**com′i·cal′i·ty** (-kal′ə tē) *n.* —**com′i·cal·ly** *adv.*

comic book a booklet of comic strips

comic strip a series of cartoons, as in a newspaper, telling a humorous or adventurous story

com′ing *adj.* **1.** approaching; next **2.** on the way to becoming successful, popular, important, etc. [it's the *coming* thing] —*n.* arrival; advent

com·i·ty (käm′ə tē) *n., pl.* **-ties** [< L. *comis,* polite] courteous behavior; politeness

comm. 1. commission **2.** committee

com·ma (käm′ə) *n.* [< Gr. *koptein,* cut off] a mark of punctuation (,) used to indicate a slight separation of sentence elements

com·mand (kə mand′) *vt.* [< L. *com-,* intens. + *mandare,* commit] **1.** to give an order to; direct **2.** to have authority over; control **3.** to have ready for use [to *command* a huge vocabulary] **4.** to deserve and get [to *command* respect] **5.** to control or look out over from a higher position —*vi.* to exercise authority —*n.* **1.** an order; direction **2.** authority to command **3.** power to control by position **4.** mastery **5.** a military or naval force, or district, under a specified authority

com·man·dant (käm′ən dant′, -dänt′) *n.* a commanding officer, as of a fort

com·man·deer (käm′ən dir′) *vt.* [< Fr. *commander,* to command] **1.** to seize (property) for military or governmental use **2.** [Colloq.] to take forcibly

com·mand′er *n.* **1.** one who commands **2.** *U.S. Navy* an officer ranking just above a lieutenant commander

commander in chief *pl.* **commanders in chief** the supreme commander of a nation's armed forces

commanding officer the officer in command of any of certain military units or installations

com·mand′ment *n.* a command or order; specif., any of the Ten Commandments

com·man·do (kə man′dō) *n., pl.* **-dos, -does** [Afrik. < Port.] a member of a small force trained to raid enemy territory

com·mem·o·rate (kə mem′ə rāt′) *vt.* **-rat′ed, -rat′ing** [< L. *com-,* intens. + *memorare,* remind] **1.** to honor the memory of, as by a ceremony **2.** to serve as a memorial to —**com·mem′o·ra′tion** *n.* —**com·mem′o·ra·tive** (-ər ə tiv, -ə rāt′iv) *adj.*

com·mence (kə mens′) *vi., vt.* **-menced′, -menc′ing** [< L. *com-,* together + *initiare,* begin] to begin; start —**com·menc′er** *n.*

com·mence′ment *n.* **1.** a beginning; start **2.** the ceremonies at which degrees or diplomas are conferred at a school

com·mend (kə mend′) *vt.* [see COMMAND] **1.** to put in the care of another; entrust **2.** to recommend **3.** to praise —**com·mend′a·ble** *adj.* —**com·mend′a·bly** *adv.* —**com·men·da·tion** (käm′ən dā′shən) *n.*

com·men·su·ra·ble (kə men′shər ə b'l, -sər-) *adj.* [see COMMENSURATE] measurable by the same standard or measure

com·men′su·rate (-shər it, -sər-) *adj.* [< L. *com-,* together + *mensura,* measurement] **1.** equal in measure or size **2.** proportionate **3.** *same as* COMMENSURABLE

com·ment (käm′ent) *n.* [< L. *com-,* intens. + *meminisse,* remember] **1.** an explanatory or critical note on something written or said **2.** a remark or observation **3.** talk; gossip —*vi.* to make comments (*on* or *upon*)

com·men·tar·y (käm′ən ter′ē) *n., pl.* **-ies** a series of remarks or explanatory notes

com′men·ta′tor (-tāt′ər) *n.* one who reports and analyzes news events, trends, etc., as on radio or TV

com·merce (käm′ərs) *n.* [Fr. < L. *com-,* together + *merx,* merchandise] trade on a large scale, as between countries

com·mer·cial (kə mur′shəl) *adj.* **1.** of commerce or business **2.** made or done for profit —*n. Radio & TV* a paid advertisement —**com·mer′cial·ly** *adv.*

com·mer′cial·ism *n.* the practices and spirit of commerce or business

com·mer′cial·ize′ (-īz′) *vt.* **-ized′, -iz′ing** to put on a business basis, esp. so as to make profit —**com·mer′cial·i·za′tion** *n.*

com·min·gle (kə miŋ′g'l) *vt., vi.* **-gled, -gling** to mingle together; blend

com·mis·er·ate (kə miz′ə rāt′) *vt.* **-at′ed, -at′ing** [< L. *com-,* intens. + *miserari,* to pity] to feel or show pity for —*vi.* to condole (*with*) —**com·mis·er·a′tion** *n.*

com·mis·sar (käm′ə sär′) *n.* [< Russ. < L. *committere,* commit] the head of a commissariat (sense 2): now called *minister*

com·mis·sar′i·at (-ser′ē ət) *n.* [Fr.] **1.** the branch of an army providing food and supplies

2. formerly, a government department in the U.S.S.R.: now called *ministry*

com·mis·sar·y (käm′ə ser′ē) *n., pl.* **-ies** [< L. *committere*, commit] a store, as in an army camp, where food and supplies are sold

com·mis·sion (kə mish′ən) *n.* [see COMMIT] **1.** a document authorizing certain duties or powers **2.** authority to act for another, or that which one is authorized to do **3.** a committing, as of a crime **4.** a group of people chosen to do something **5.** a government agency **6.** a percentage of money from sales, allotted to the agent **7.** *Mil.* an official certificate conferring rank as an officer —*vt.* **1.** to give a commission to **2.** to authorize **3.** *Naut.* to put (a vessel) into service —**in** (or **out of**) **commission** (not) in working order

com·mis′sion·er *n.* **1.** a member of a commission **2.** the top official of a government bureau, etc. **3.** one selected to regulate and control a professional sport

com·mit (kə mit′) *vt.* **-mit′ted, -mit′ting** [< L. *com-*, together + *mittere*, send] **1.** to give in charge; consign **2.** to put in custody or confinement [*committed* to prison] **3.** to do or perpetrate (an offense or crime) **4.** to pledge; bind —**com·mit′ment** *n.*

com·mit·tee (kə mit′ē) *n.* [see COMMIT] a group of people chosen to act upon a certain matter —**com·mit′tee·man** *n., pl.* **-men** —**com·mit′tee·wom′an** *n.fem., pl.* **-wom′en**

com·mode (kə mōd′) *n.* [Fr. < L.: see COM- & MODE] **1.** a chest of drawers **2.** a movable washstand **3.** a toilet

com·mo·di·ous (kə mō′dē əs) *adj.* [see prec.] spacious; roomy —**com·mo′di·ous·ly** *adv.*

com·mod·i·ty (kə mäd′ə tē) *n., pl.* **-ties** [see COMMODE] **1.** any useful thing **2.** anything bought and sold

com·mo·dore (käm′ə dôr′) *n.* [< Fr.: see COMMAND] *U.S. Navy* an officer ranking just above a captain

com·mon (käm′ən) *adj.* [< L. *communis*, shared by all or many] **1.** shared by all **2.** belonging to the community; public **3.** general; widespread **4.** familiar; usual **5.** not of the upper classes **6.** having no rank [a *common* soldier] **7.** vulgar; coarse **8.** designating a noun that refers to any of a group, as *book* —*n.* [*sometimes pl.*] land owned or used by all the inhabitants of a place —**in common** equally with all concerned —**com′mon·ly** *adv.* —**com′mon·ness** *n.*

com′mon·er *n.* one of the common people

common law law based on custom, usage, and judicial decisions

com′mon·place′ *n.* **1.** a trite remark; platitude **2.** anything common or ordinary —*adj.* obvious or ordinary

common pleas a State court having jurisdiction over civil and criminal trials

com·mons (käm′ənz) *n.pl.* **1.** the common people **2.** [*often with sing. v.*] [C-] *same as* HOUSE OF COMMONS **3.** [*often with sing. v.*] a dining room, as at a college

common sense sound practical judgment or good sense —**com′mon-sense′** *adj.*

com′mon·weal′ (-wēl′) *n.* the public good; the general welfare

com′mon·wealth′ (-welth′) *n.* **1.** the people of a nation or state **2.** a democracy or republic **3.** a federation of states

com·mo·tion (kə mō′shən) *n.* [< L. *com-*, together + *movere*, to move] **1.** violent motion; turbulence **2.** confusion; bustle

com·mu·nal (käm′yoon 'l, kə myoon′'l) *adj.* **1.** of a commune **2.** of or belonging to the community; public **3.** marked by common ownership of property —**com·mu′nal·ly** *adv.*

com·mune¹ (kə myoon′) *vi.* **-muned′, -mun′ing** [< OFr. *comuner*, to share] **1.** to converse intimately **2.** to be in close rapport

com·mune² (käm′yoon) *n.* [< L. *communis*, common] **1.** the smallest administrative district of local government in some European countries, as France **2.** a small group of people living communally

com·mu·ni·ca·ble (kə myoo′ni kə b'l) *adj.* that can be communicated, as an idea or a disease —**com·mu′ni·ca·bil′i·ty** *n.*

com·mu′ni·cant (-kənt) *n.* one who receives Holy Communion

com·mu·ni·cate (kə myoo′nə kāt′) *vt.* **-cat′ed, -cat′ing** [< L. *communicare*] **1.** to impart; transmit **2.** to give (information, etc.) —*vi.* **1.** to give or exchange information **2.** to be connected, as rooms

com·mu′ni·ca′tion *n.* **1.** a transmitting **2.** a giving or exchanging of information, etc. as by talk or writing **3.** a message, letter, etc. **4.** [*often pl.*] a means of communicating —**com·mu′ni·ca′tive** *adj.*

com·mun·ion (kə myoon′yən) *n.* [see COMMON] **1.** possession in common **2.** a communing **3.** a Christian denomination **4.** [C-] a celebrating of Holy Communion

com·mu·ni·qué (kə myoo′nə kā′) *n.* [Fr.] an official communication

com·mu·nism (käm′yə niz′m) *n.* [< Fr.: see COMMON] **1.** a theory or system of the ownership of all property by the community **2.** [*often* C-] *a)* socialism as formulated by Marx, Lenin, etc. *b)* any government or political movement supporting this

com′mu·nist (-nist) *n.* [< Fr.] **1.** an advocate or supporter of communism **2.** [C-] a member of a Communist party —*adj.* of or like communism —**com′mu·nis′tic** *adj.*

com·mu·ni·ty (kə myoo′nə tē) *n., pl.* **-ties** [see COMMON] **1.** *a)* any group living in the same area or having interests, work, etc. in common *b)* such an area **2.** society; the public **3.** a sharing or ownership in common

com·mute (kə myoot′) *vt.* **-mut′ed, -mut′ing** [< L. *com-*, intens. + *mutare*, to change] **1.** to exchange; substitute **2.** to change (an obligation, punishment, etc.) to one that is less severe —*vi.* **1.** to be a substitute **2.** to travel as a commuter —**com·mut′a·ble** *adj.* —**com′mu·ta′tion** *n.*

com·mut′er *n.* one who travels between two points regularly, esp. by train, bus, etc.

comp. **1.** comparative **2.** compound

com·pact (kəm pakt′; käm′pakt) *adj.* [< L. *com-*, together + *pangere*, fasten] **1.** closely and firmly packed; solid **2.** brief; terse **3.** designating or of a small, light model of automobile —*vt.* to pack firmly together —*n.* (käm′pakt) **1.** a small case containing face powder and a mirror **2.** a compact automobile **3.** an agreement; covenant —**com·pact′ly** *adv.* —**com·pact′ness** *n.*

com·pac′tor (-pak′tər) *n.* a device that compresses trash into small bundles

com·pan·ion (kəm pan′yən) *n.* [< L. *com-*, with + *panis*, bread] **1.** an associate; comrade **2.** a person paid to live or travel with another **3.** one of a pair or set —**com·pan′ion·a·ble** *adj.* —**com·pan′ion·ship′** *n.*

com·pan′ion·way′ *n.* a stairway from one deck of a ship to another

com·pa·ny (kum′pə nē) *n., pl.* **-nies** [see COMPANION] **1.** companionship; society **2.** a group of people gathered or associated for some purpose [a business *company*] **3.** a guest or guests **4.** a military unit composed of two or more platoons **5.** a ship's crew

com·pa·ra·ble (käm′pər ə b'l) *adj.* **1.** that can be compared **2.** worthy of comparison —**com′·pa·ra·bly** *adv.*

com·par·a·tive (kəm par′ə tiv) *adj.* **1.** involving comparison as a method *[comparative linguistics]* **2.** relative **3.** *Gram.* designating the second degree of comparison of adjectives and adverbs —*n. Gram.* the comparative degree *[finer* is the *comparative* of *fine]* —**com·par′a·tive·ly** *adv.*

com·pare (kəm per′) *vt.* -pared′, -par′ing [< L. *com*-, with + *par*, equal] **1.** to liken (*to*) **2.** to examine for similarities or differences **3.** *Gram.* to form the degrees of comparison of —*vi.* **1.** to be worth comparing (*with*) **2.** to make comparisons —**beyond** (or **without**) **compare** without equal

com·par·i·son (kəm par′ə s'n) *n.* **1.** a comparing or being compared **2.** likeness; similarity **3.** *Gram.* change in an adjective or adverb to show the positive, comparative, and superlative degrees —**In comparison with** compared with

com·part·ment (kəm pärt′mənt) *n.* [< Fr. < It. < L. *com*-, intens. + *partiri*, divide] any of the divisions into which a space is partitioned off —**com·part′men·tal·ize′** *vt.* -ized′, -iz′ing

com·pass (kum′pəs) *vt.* [< L. *com*-, together + *passus*, a step] **1.** to go around **2.** to surround **3.** to achieve or contrive —*n.* **1.** [*often pl.*] an instrument having two pivoted legs, for drawing circles, measuring, etc. **2.** a boundary **3.** an enclosed area **4.** range; scope **5.** an instrument for showing direction, esp. one with a swinging magnetic needle that points to the magnetic north

com·pas·sion (kəm pash′ən) *n.* [< L. *com*-, together + *pati*, suffer] deep sympathy; pity —**com·pas′sion·ate** (-it) *adj.*

com·pat·i·ble (kəm pat′ə b'l) *adj.* [see COMPASSION] getting along or going well together —**com·pat′i·bil′i·ty** *n.* —**com·pat′i·bly** *adv.*

com·pa·tri·ot (kəm pā′trē ət) *n.* [< Fr.: see COM- & PATRIOT] a fellow countryman

com·peer (käm′pir) *n.* [see COMPARE] **1.** an equal; peer **2.** a companion; comrade

com·pel (kəm pel′) *vt.* -pelled′, -pel′ling [< L. *com*-, together + *pellere*, to drive] to force or get by force —**com·pel′ling·ly** *adv.*

com·pen·di·ous (kəm pen′dē əs) *adj.* [see COMPENDIUM] containing all the essentials in brief form; concise —**com·pen′di·ous·ly** *adv.*

com·pen·di·um (kəm pen′dē əm) *n., pl.* -ums, -a (-ə) [< L. *com*-, together + *pendere*, weigh] a concise, comprehensive summary

com·pen·sate (käm′pən sāt′) *vt.* -sat′ed, -sat′ing [< L. *com*-, with + *pendere*, to weigh] **1.** to make up for; counterbalance **2.** to recompense; pay —*vi.* to make amends (*for*) —**com′·pen·sa′tion** *n.* —**com·pen·sa·to·ry** (kəm pen′sə tôr′ē) *adj.*

com·pete (kəm pēt′) *vi.* -pet′ed, -pet′ing [< L. *com*-, together + *petere*, seek] to be in rivalry; contend; vie (*in* a contest, etc.)

com·pe·tence (käm′pə təns) *n.* [Fr.: see prec.] **1.** sufficient means for one's needs **2.** ability; fitness Also **com′pe·ten·cy**

com·pe·tent (-tənt) *adj.* [see COMPETE] **1.** capable; fit **2.** sufficient; adequate —**com′pe·tent·ly** *adv.*

com·pe·ti·tion (käm′pə tish′ən) *n.* **1.** a competing; rivalry, esp. in business **2.** a contest or match **3.** those against whom one competes — **com·pet·i·tive** (kəm pet′ə tiv) *adj.*

com·pet·i·tor (kəm pet′ə tər) *n.* one who competes, as a business rival

com·pile (kəm pīl′) *vt.* -piled′, -pil′ing [< L. *com*-, together + *pilare*, to compress] **1.** to gather together (data, facts, etc.) in an orderly form **2.** to compose (a book, etc.) of materials from various sources —**com·pi·la·tion** (käm′pə lā′shən) *n.*

com·pla·cen·cy (kəm plās′'n sē) *n.* [< L. *com*-, intens. + *placere*, please] quiet satisfaction; often, specif., self-satisfaction or smugness: also **com·pla′cence** —**com·pla′cent** *adj.*

com·plain (kəm plān′) *vi.* [< L. *com*-, intens. + *plangere*, strike (the breast)] **1.** to express pain, displeasure, etc. **2.** to find fault **3.** to make an accusation or a formal charge —**com·plain′ant** *n.*

com·plaint′ (-plānt′) *n.* **1.** an utterance of pain, displeasure, etc. **2.** a cause for complaining **3.** an ailment **4.** *Law* a formal charge

com·plai·sant (kəm plā′z'nt, -s'nt) *adj.* [Fr.: see COMPLACENCY] willing to please; obliging — **com·plai′sance** *n.*

com·ple·ment (käm′plə mənt) *n.* [see COMPLETE] **1.** that which completes or perfects **2.** the amount needed to fill or complete **3.** a complete set —*vt.* (-ment′) to make complete — **com′ple·men′ta·ry** *adj.*

com·plete (kəm plēt′) *adj.* [< L. *com*-, intens. + *plere*, fill] **1.** lacking no parts **2.** finished **3.** thorough; absolute —*vt.* -plet′ed, -plet′ing **1.** to finish **2.** to make whole or perfect —**com·plete′ly** *adv.* —**com·plete′ness** *n.* —**com·ple′tion** (-plē′shən) *n.*

com·plex (kəm pleks′, käm′pleks) *adj.* [< L. *com*-, with + *plectere*, to weave] **1.** consisting of two or more related parts **2.** complicated — *n.* (käm′pleks) **1.** a complex whole **2.** a unified grouping, as of buildings **3.** *Psychoanalysis a)* a group of mostly unconscious attitudes toward something, strongly influencing behavior *b)* loosely, an obsession —**com·plex′i·ty** *n., pl.* -ties

com·plex·ion (kəm plek′shən) *n.* [see COMPLEX] **1.** the color, texture, etc. of the skin, esp. of the face **2.** nature; character; aspect

com·pli·ance (kəm plī′əns) *n.* **1.** a complying with a request, demand, etc. **2.** a tendency to give in to others —**In compliance with** complying with —**com·pli′ant** *adj.*

com·pli·cate (käm′plə kāt′) *vt., vi.* -cat′ed, -cat′ing [< L. *com*-, together + *plicare*, to fold] to make or become intricate, difficult, or involved —**com′pli·cat′ed** *adj.* —**com′pli·ca′tion** *n.*

com·plic·i·ty (kəm plis′ə tē) *n., pl.* -ties [Fr.: see COMPLEX] partnership in wrongdoing

com·pli·ment (käm′plə mənt) *n.* [Fr. < It. < Sp. < L.: see COMPLETE] **1.** a formal act of courtesy **2.** something said in praise **3.** [*pl.*] respects —*vt.* (-ment′) to pay a compliment to

com·pli·men·ta·ry (-men′tər ē) *adj.* **1.** paying or containing a compliment **2.** given free as a courtesy

com·ply (kəm plī′) *vi.* -plied′, -ply′ing [see COMPLETE] to act in accordance (*with* a request, order, etc.) —**com·pli′er** *n.*

com·po·nent (kəm pō′nənt) *adj.* [< L. *com*-, together + *ponere*, put] serving as one of the parts of a whole —*n.* a part, element, or ingredient

com·port (kəm pôrt′) *vt.* [< L. *com*-, together + *portare*, bring] to behave (oneself) in a specified manner —*vi.* to agree or accord (*with*) —**com·port′ment** *n.*

com·pose (kəm pōz′) *vt.* -posed′, -pos′ing [< OFr. *com*-, with + *poser*, to place] **1.** to make up; constitute **2.** to put in proper form **3.** to create (a musical or literary work) **4.** to adjust or settle **5.** to make calm **6.** to set (type) —*vi.* **1.** to create musical or literary works **2.** to set type

com·posed′ *adj.* calm; self-possessed

com·pos′er (-ər) *n.* a person who composes, esp. one who composes music

com·pos·ite (kəm päz′it) *adj.* [< L. *com-*, together + *ponere*, put] **1.** formed of distinct parts **2.** designating a family of plants, as the daisy, with flower heads composed of clusters of small flowers —*n.* a composite thing —**com·pos′ite·ly** *adv.*

com·po·si·tion (käm′pə zish′ən) *n.* **1.** a composing; specif., *a)* the art of writing *b)* the creation of musical works **2.** the makeup of a thing **3.** something composed **4.** the work of setting type

com·pos·i·tor (kəm päz′ə tər) *n.* a person who sets type; typesetter

com·post (käm′pōst) *n.* [see COMPOSITE] a mixture of decomposing vegetation, manure, etc. for fertilizing soil

com·po·sure (kəm pō′zhər) *n.* [see COMPOSE] calmness; self-possession

com·pote (käm′pōt) *n.* [Fr.: see COMPOSITE] **1.** a dish of stewed fruits **2.** a long-stemmed dish for candy, fruit, etc.

com·pound¹ (käm pound′, kəm-) *vt.* [see COMPOSITE] **1.** to mix or combine **2.** to make by combining parts —*adj.* (käm′pound, käm pound′) made up of two or more parts —*n.* (käm′pound) **1.** a thing formed by combining parts **2.** a substance containing two or more elements chemically combined in fixed proportions —**compound a felony** (or **crime**) to agree, for payment, not to prosecute a felony (or crime)

com·pound² (käm′pound) *n.* [< Malay *kampong*] in the Orient, an enclosed space with one or more buildings in it

compound fracture a fracture in which the broken bone pierces the skin

compound interest interest paid on both the principal and the accumulated interest

compound leaf a leaf divided into two or more leaflets with a common stalk

com·pre·hend (käm′prə hend′) *vt.* [< L. *com-*, with + *prehendere*, seize] **1.** to grasp mentally; understand **2.** to include; comprise — **com′pre·hen′si·ble** (-hen′sə b'l) *adj.* —**com′pre·hen′si·bly** *adv.*

com′pre·hen′sion (-hen′shən) *n.* **1.** an including or comprising **2.** the act of or capacity for understanding

com′pre·hen′sive *adj.* **1.** including much; inclusive **2.** able to understand —**com′pre·hen′-sive·ly** *adv.* —**com′pre·hen′sive·ness** *n.*

com·press (käm pres′) *vt.* [< L. *com-*, together + *premere*, to press] **1.** to press together and make more compact **2.** to put (air, etc.) under pressure —*n.* (käm′pres) a pad of folded cloth, often medicated or wet, applied to a part of the body —**com·pressed′** *adj.* —**com·pres′si·ble** *adj.* —**com·pres′sion** *n.*

com·pres′sor (-ər) *n.* a machine for compressing air, gas, etc.

com·prise (kəm prīz′) *vt.* **-prised′, -pris′ing** [see COMPREHEND] **1.** to include; contain **2.** to consist of **3.** to make up; form: a loose usage — **com·pris′al** *n.*

com·pro·mise (käm′prə mīz′) *n.* [< L. *com-*, together + *promittere*, to promise] **1.** a settlement in which each side makes concessions **2.** the result of such a settlement **3.** something midway —*vt., vi.* **-mised′, -mis′ing** **1.** to settle

by compromise **2.** to lay open to danger, suspicion, or disrepute

comp·trol·ler (kən trō′lər) *n.* [altered (after Fr. *compte*, an account) < CONTROLLER] same as CONTROLLER (sense 1) —**comp·trol′ler·ship′** *n.*

com·pul·sion (kəm pul′shən) *n.* a compelling or being compelled; force —**com·pul′sive** (-siv) *adj.* —**com·pul′sive·ly** *adv.*

com·pul·so·ry (-sər ē) *adj.* **1.** obligatory; required **2.** compelling

com·punc·tion (kəm puŋk′shən) *n.* [< L. *com-*, intens. + *pungere*, to prick] an uneasy feeling prompted by guilt —**com·punc′tious** *adj.*

com·pute (kəm pyŏot′) *vt., vi.* **-put′ed, -put′ing** [< L. *com-*, with + *putare*, reckon] to determine (an amount, number, etc.) by reckoning; calculate —**com·put′a·ble** *adj.* —**com·pu·ta·tion** (käm′pyŏo tā′shən) *n.*

com·put·er (kəm pyŏot′ər) *n.* a person or thing that computes; specif., an electronic machine that performs rapid, often complex calculations or compiles, correlates, and selects data

com·put′er·ize (-īz′) *vt.* **-ized′, -iz′ing** to equip with, or operate, produce, control, etc. by means of, an electronic computer —**com·put′er·i·za′tion** *n.*

com·rade (käm′rad) *n.* [< Fr. < Sp. *camarada*, chamber mate < L. *camera*, room] **1.** a friend; close companion **2.** an associate —**com′rade·ly** *adv.* —**com′rade·ship′** *n.*

com·sat (käm′sat) *n.* a communications satellite for relaying microwave transmissions, as of television

con¹ (kän) *adv.* [< L. *contra*] against [pro and *con*] —*n.* a reason, vote, etc. in opposition

con² (kän) *vt.* **conned, con′ning** [< OE. *cunnan*, know] to study carefully

con³ (kän) *adj.* [Slang] confidence [a con man] —*vt.* **conned, con′ning** [Slang] to swindle (a victim) by gaining his confidence

con⁴ (kän) *n.* [Slang] a convict

con- same as COM-: used before *c, d, f, g, j, n, q, s, t,* and *v*

con·cat·e·na·tion (kän kat′'n ā′shən) *n.* [< L. *com-*, together + *catena*, a chain] a connected series, as of events

con·cave (kän kāv′, kän′kāv) *adj.* [< L. *com-*, intens. + *cavus*, hollow] hollow and curved like the inside half of a hollow ball —**con·cav′-i·ty** (-kav′ə tē) *n., pl.* **-ties**

con·ceal (kən sēl′) *vt.* [< L. *com-*, together + *celare*, to hide] **1.** to hide **2.** to keep secret — **con·ceal′ment** *n.*

con·cede (kən sēd′) *vt.* **-ced′ed, -ced′ing** [< L. *com-*, with + *cedere*, cede] **1.** to admit as true or certain **2.** to grant as a right

con·ceit (kən sēt′) *n.* [see CONCEIVE] **1.** an exaggerated opinion of oneself, one's merits, etc.; vanity **2.** a fanciful or witty expression or notion

con·ceit′ed *adj.* vain

con·ceiv·a·ble (kən sē′və b'l) *adj.* that can be imagined —**con·ceiv′a·bil′i·ty** *n.*

con·ceive (kən sēv′) *vt.* **-ceived′, -ceiv′ing** [< L. *com-*, together + *capere*, take] **1.** to become pregnant with **2.** to form in the mind; imagine **3.** to understand —*vi.* **1.** to become pregnant **2.** to form an idea (*of*)

con·cen·trate (kän′sən trāt′) *vt.* **-trat′ed, -trat′-ing** [< L. *com-*, together + *centrum*, center + -ATE¹] **1.** to focus (one's thoughts, efforts, etc.) **2.** to increase the strength, density, etc. of —*vi.* to fix one's attention (*on* or *upon*) —*n.* a substance that has been concentrated —**con′cen·tra′tion** n.

concentration camp a place of confinement, as for political foes or minority groups

con·cen·tric (kən sen′trik) adj. [< L. com-, together + centrum, center] having a center in common, as circles —**con·cen′tri·cal·ly** adv.

con·cept (kän′sept) n. [see CONCEIVE] an idea; general notion

con·cep·tion (kən sep′shən) n. 1. a conceiving or being conceived in the womb 2. the beginning, as of a process 3. the formulation of ideas 4. a concept 5. an original idea or design —**con·cep′tive** adj.

con·cep′tu·al (-chōō wəl) adj. of conception or concepts —**con·cep′tu·al·ly** adv.

con·cern (kən surn′) vt. [< L. com-, with + cernere, sift] 1. to have a relation to 2. to engage or involve 3. to make uneasy —n. 1. a matter; affair 2. interest in or regard for a person or thing 3. relation; reference 4. worry; anxiety 5. a business firm —**as concerns** in regard to —**concern oneself** 1. to busy oneself 2. to be worried

con·cerned′ adj. 1. involved or interested (often with in) 2. uneasy or anxious

con·cern′ing prep. relating to; about

con·cert (kän′sərt) n. [Fr. < It. < L. com-, with + certare, strive] 1. mutual agreement; concord 2. a program of vocal or instrumental music —**In concert** in unison

con·cert·ed (kən sur′tid) adj. mutually arranged or agreed upon; combined

con·cer·ti·na (kän′sər tē′nə) n. [< CONCERT] a small accordion

con·cer·to (kən cher′tō) n., pl. **-tos, -tl** (-tē) [It.] a musical composition for one or more solo instruments and an orchestra

con·ces·sion (kən sesh′ən) n. 1. a conceding 2. a thing conceded; acknowledgment 3. a privilege granted by a government, company, etc., as the right to sell food at a park —**con·ces′sive** (-ses′iv) adj.

con·ces′sion·aire′ (-ə ner′) n. [< Fr.] the holder of a concession (sense 3)

conch (käŋk, känch) n., pl. **conchs** (käŋks), **conch′es** (kän′chəz) [< Gr. konchē] the spiral, one-piece shell of various sea mollusks

con·cil·i·ate (kən sil′ē āt′) vt. **-at′ed, -at′ing** [see COUNCIL] to win over; make friendly — **con·cil′i·a′tion** n. —**con·cil′i·a′tor** n. —**con·cil′i·a·to′ry** (-ə tôr′ē) adj.

con·cise (kən sīs′) adj. [< L. com-, intens. + caedere, to cut] brief and to the point; short and clear —**con·cise′ly** adv.

con·clave (kän′klāv, käŋ′-) n. [< L. com-, with + clavis, a key] a private meeting, specif. one held by the cardinals to elect a pope

con·clude (kən klōōd′) vt., vi. **-clud′ed, -clud′ing** [< L. com-, together + claudere, to shut] 1. to bring or come to an end; finish 2. to infer; deduce 3. to decide; determine 4. to arrange (a treaty, etc.)

con·clu·sion (kən klōō′zhən) n. 1. the end 2. a judgment or opinion formed after thought 3. an outcome 4. a concluding (of a treaty, etc.) —**In conclusion** lastly

con·clu′sive (-siv) adj. decisive; final —**con·clu′sive·ly** adv.

con·coct (kən käkt′, kän-) vt. [< L. com-, together + coquere, to cook] 1. to make by combining ingredients 2. to devise; plan —**con·coct′er** n. —**con·coc′tion** n.

con·com·i·tant (kən käm′ə tənt, kän-) adj. [< L. com-, together + comes, companion] accompanying; attendant —n. a concomitant condi-

tion, thing, etc. —**con·com′i·tance** (-təns) n. —**con·com′i·tant·ly** adv.

con·cord (kän′kôrd, käŋ′-) n. [< L. com-, together + cor, heart] 1. agreement; harmony 2. peaceful relations, as between nations 3. a treaty establishing this

con·cord·ance (kən kôr′d'ns, kän-) n. 1. agreement; harmony 2. an alphabetical list of the words in a book, with references to the passages where they occur

con·cord′ant adj. [Fr.] agreeing; harmonious

con·cor·dat (kən kôr′dat, kän-) n. [Fr.: see CONCORD] a compact; formal agreement

con·course (kän′kôrs, käŋ′-) n. [see CONCUR] 1. a crowd; throng 2. an open space where crowds gather, as in a park

con·crete (kän krēt′, kän′krēt) adj. [< L. com-, together + crescere, grow] 1. having a material existence; real; actual 2. specific, not general 3. made of concrete —n. (kän′krēt) 1. anything concrete 2. a hard building material made of sand, gravel, cement, and water —vt. **-cret′ed, -cret′ing** 1. to solidify 2. (kän′krēt) to cover with concrete —vi. to solidify —**con·crete′ly** adv.

con·cre′tion (-krē′shən) n. 1. a solidifying or being solidified 2. a solidified mass

con·cu·bine (käŋ′kyə bīn′, kän′-) n. [< L. com-, with + cubare, to lie down] in some societies, a secondary wife having inferior status

con·cu·pis·cence (kän kyōōp′ə s'ns) n. [< L. com-, intens. + cupere, to desire] strong sexual desire; lust —**con·cu′pis·cent** adj.

con·cur (kən kur′) vi. **-curred′, -cur′ring** [< L. com-, together + currere, to run] 1. to occur at the same time; coincide 2. to act together 3. to agree

con·cur′rence n. a concurring; esp., agreement; accord

con·cur′rent adj. 1. occurring at the same time 2. acting together; cooperating 3. Law having equal jurisdiction

con·cus·sion (kən kush′ən) n. [< L. com-, together + quatere, to shake] 1. a violent shaking; shock, as from impact 2. impaired functioning, esp. of the brain, caused by a violent blow or impact

con·demn (kən dem′) vt. [< L. com-, intens. + damnare, to harm] 1. to disapprove of strongly 2. to declare guilty 3. to inflict a penalty upon 4. to appropriate (property) for public use 5. to declare unfit for use —**con·dem·na·tion** (kän′dem nā′shən) n. —**con·demn′er** n.

con·dense (kən dens′) vt. **-densed′, -dens′ing** [< Fr. < L. com-, intens. + densus, dense] 1. to make more dense or compact 2. to express in fewer words 3. to change to a denser form, as from a gas to a liquid —vi. to become condensed —**con·den·sa·tion** (kän′dən sā′shən) n.

con·dens′er n. one that condenses; specif., a) an apparatus for liquefying gases or vapors b) a lens for concentrating light rays on an area c) Elec. same as CAPACITOR

con·de·scend (kän′də send′) vi. [< L. com-, together + descendere, descend] 1. to be gracious about doing a thing considered beneath one's dignity 2. to deal with others patronizingly —**con′de·scen′sion** n.

con·dign (kən dīn′) adj. [< L. com-, intens. + dignus, worthy] deserved; suitable: said esp. of punishment

con·di·ment (kän′də mənt) n. [< L. condire, to pickle] a seasoning or relish for food, as pepper, mustard, etc.

con·di·tion (kən dish′ən) n. [< L. com-, together + dicere, speak] 1. anything required for the performance, completion, or existence of something else; provision or prerequisite **2.** state of being **3.** *a*) [Colloq.] an illness *b*) a healthy state **4.** social position; rank —*vt.* **1.** to stipulate **2.** to impose a condition on **3.** to bring into fit condition **4.** to make accustomed (*to*) —**on condition that** provided that —**con·di'-tion·er** *n.*

con·di'tion·al *adj.* **1.** containing or dependent on a condition; qualified **2.** expressing a condition —**con·di'tion·al·ly** *adv.*

con·do (kän'dō) *n., pl.* **-dos, -does** *short for* CONDOMINIUM (sense 2)

con·dole (kən dōl') *vi.* **-doled', -dol'ing** [< L. *com-*, with + *dolere*, to grieve] to express sympathy; commiserate —**con·do'lence** (-dō'ləns), **con·dole'ment** *n.*

con·do·min·i·um (kän'də min'ē əm) *n.* [ModL. < L. *com-*, together + *dominium*, dominion] **1.** joint rule by two or more states **2.** *pl.* **-i·ums, -i·a** (-ə) an apartment building or multiple-dwelling-unit complex in which each tenant owns his own unit

con·done (kən dōn') *vt.* **-doned', -don'ing** [< L. *com-*, intens. + *donare*, give] to forgive or pardon (an offense) —**con·don'a·ble** *adj.*

con·dor (kän'dər) *n.* [Sp. < SAmInd. *cuntur*] **1.** a large vulture of the S. American Andes, with a bare head **2.** a similar vulture of California

con·duce (kən dōōs') *vi.* **-duced', -duc'ing** [< L. *com-*, together + *ducere*, to lead] to tend or lead (*to* an effect); contribute —**con·du'cive** *adj.*

con·duct (kän'dukt'; *for v.* kən dukt') *n.* [see prec.] **1.** management **2.** the way one acts; behavior —*vt.* **1.** to show the way to; lead **2.** to manage or control **3.** to direct (an orchestra, etc.) **4.** to behave (oneself) **5.** to be able to transmit [copper *conducts* electricity] —*vi.* **1.** to lead **2.** to act as a conductor —**con·duc'tion** *n.* —**con·duc'tive** *adj.*

con·duc·tiv·i·ty (kän'duk tiv'ə tē) *n.* the property of conducting heat, electricity, etc.

con·duc·tor (kən duk'tər) *n.* **1.** one who conducts; leader **2.** the director of an orchestra, etc. **3.** one in charge of passengers on a train, etc. **4.** a thing that conducts electricity, heat, etc.

con·duit (kän'dit, -dōō wit) *n.* [see CONDUCE] **1.** a pipe or channel for conveying fluids **2.** a tube for electric wires

cone (kōn) *n.* [< Gr. *kōnos*] **1.** a solid with a circle for its base and a curved surface tapering evenly to a point **2.** any cone-shaped object **3.** the woody, scaly fruit of evergreen trees

co·ney (kō'nē) *n., pl.* **-neys, -nies** [< L. *cuniculus*] **1.** a rabbit **2.** rabbit fur

con·fab (kän'fab') *n.* [ult. < L. *com-*, together + *fabulari*, to talk] [Colloq.] a chat

con·fec·tion (kən fek'shən) *n.* [< L. *com-*, with + *facere*, to make] any candy or other sweet preparation, as ice cream

con·fec'tion·er *n.* one who makes or sells candy and other confections

con·fec'tion·er'y (-er'ē) *n., pl.* **-ies** the shop or work of a confectioner

con·fed·er·a·cy (kən fed'ər ə sē) *n., pl.* **-cies** a league or alliance —**the Confederacy** the eleven Southern States that seceded from the U.S. in 1860 & 1861

con·fed·er·ate (kən fed'ər it) *adj.* [< L. *com-*, together + *foedus*, a league] **1.** united in an alliance **2.** [C-] of the Confederacy —*n.* **1.** an ally; associate **2.** an accomplice **3.** [C-] a Southern supporter of the Confederacy —*vt., vi.* (-ə rāt') **-at'ed, -at'ing** to unite in a confederacy; ally

con·fed'er·a'tion (-ə rā'shən) *n.* an alliance

con·fer (kən fur') *vt.* **-ferred', -fer'ring** [< L. *com-*, together + *ferre*, bring] to give; bestow —*vi.* to have a conference —**con·fer·ee** (kän'fə rē') *n.* —**con·fer'ment** *n.*

con·fer·ence (kän'fər əns, -frəns) *n.* [Fr.] **1.** a formal meeting for discussion **2.** an association, as of colleges, athletic teams, churches, etc.

con·fess (kən fes') *vt., vi.* [< L. *com-*, together + *fateri*, acknowledge] **1.** to admit or acknowledge (a fault, crime, belief, etc.) **2.** *a*) to tell (one's sins) to God *b*) to hear the confession of (a person): said of a priest

con·fes·sion (kən fesh'ən) *n.* **1.** a confessing **2.** something confessed **3.** a statement of religious beliefs **4.** a sect

con·fes'sion·al *n.* [Fr.] an enclosure in a church where a priest hears confessions

con·fes'sor *n.* **1.** one who confesses **2.** a priest authorized to hear confessions

con·fet·ti (kən fet'ē) *n.pl.* [*with sing. v.*] [It.] bits of colored paper scattered about at celebrations, etc.

con·fi·dant (kän'fə dant') *n.* [< Fr.] a close, trusted friend in whom one confides —**con'fi·dante'** *n.fem.*

con·fide (kən fīd') *vi.* **-fid'ed, -fid'ing** [< L. *com-*, intens. + *fidere*, to trust] to trust (*in* someone), esp. by sharing secrets —*vt.* **1.** to tell about as a secret **2.** to entrust (*to*)

con·fi·dence (kän'fə dəns) *n.* **1.** trust; reliance **2.** certainty; assurance **3.** belief in one's own abilities **4.** the belief that another will keep a secret **5.** a secret

confidence game a swindle effected by one (**confidence man**) who first gains the confidence of his victim

con'fi·dent (-dənt) *adj.* full of confidence; specif., *a*) assured; certain *b*) sure of oneself —**con'fi·dent·ly** *adv.*

con'fi·den'tial (-den'shəl) *adj.* **1.** secret **2.** of or showing confidence **3.** entrusted with private matters —**con'fi·den'ti·al'i·ty** *n.* —**con'fi·den'-tial·ly** *adv.*

con·fid·ing (kən fīd'iŋ) *adj.* trustful or inclined to trust —**con·fid'ing·ly** *adv.*

con·fig·u·ra·tion (kən fig'yə rā'shən) *n.* [< L. *com-*, together + *figurare*, to form] form, contour, or structure; outline

con·fine (kän/fīn') *n.* [< L. *com-*, with + *finis*, an end] [*usually pl.*] a boundary or bounded region —*vt.* (kən fīn') **-fined', -fin'ing** **1.** to keep within limits; restrict **2.** to keep shut up, as in prison, a sickbed, etc. —**con·fine'ment** *n.*

con·firm (kən furm') *vt.* [< L. *com-*, intens. + *firmus*, firm] **1.** to strengthen **2.** to give formal approval to **3.** to prove to be true **4.** to admit to full church membership

con·fir·ma·tion (kän'fər mā'shən) *n.* **1.** a confirming or being confirmed **2.** something that confirms **3.** a ceremony admitting a person to full church membership

con·firmed' *adj.* **1.** firmly established; habitual **2.** corroborated; proved

con·fis·cate (kän'fə skāt') *vt.* **-cat'ed, -cat'ing** [< L. *com-*, together + *fiscus*, treasury] **1.** to seize (private property) for the public treasury **2.** to seize as by authority; appropriate —**con'-fis·ca'tion** *n.*

con·fis·ca·to·ry (kən fis'kə tôr'ē) *adj.* **1.** of or effecting confiscation **2.** confiscating

con·fla·gra·tion (kän'flə grā'shən) *n.* [< L. *com-*, intens. + *flagrare*, burn] a big, destructive fire

con·flict (kən flikt'; *for n.,* kän'flikt) *vi.* [< L. *com-*, together + *fligere*, to strike] to be antagonistic, incompatible, etc. —*n.* **1.** a fight or war **2.** sharp disagreement, as of interests or ideas **3.** emotional disturbance

con·flu·ence (kän′flōō əns) *n.* [< L. *com*-, together + *fluere*, to flow] **1.** a flowing together, esp. of streams **2.** the place of this **3.** a coming together, as of people; crowd —**con′·flu·ent** *adj.*

con·form (kən fôrm′) *vt.* [see CON- & FORM] **1.** to make similar **2.** to bring into agreement; adapt —*vi.* **1.** to be or become similar **2.** to be in agreement **3.** to act in accordance with rules, customs, etc. —**con·form′ism** *n.* —**con·form′ist** *n.*

con·form′a·ble *adj.* **1.** that conforms; specif., *a)* similar *b)* in agreement *c)* adapted **2.** quick to conform; obedient

con·for·ma·tion (kän′fôr mā′shən) *n.* **1.** a symmetrical arrangement of the parts of a thing **2.** the structure or shape of a thing

con·form·i·ty (kən fôr′mə tē) *n., pl.* -**ties 1.** agreement; correspondence **2.** a conforming to rules, customs, etc. Also **con·form′ance**

con·found (kən found′, kän′-) *vt.* [< L. *com*-, together + *fundere*, pour] **1.** to confuse; bewilder **2.** to damn: a mild oath —**con·found′ed** *adj.*

con·frere (kän′frer, kōn′-) *n.* [OFr.] a colleague

con·front (kən frunt′) *vt.* [< Fr. < L. *com*-, together + *frons*, front] **1.** to face, esp. boldly or defiantly **2.** to bring face to face (*with*) — **con·fron·ta·tion** (kän′frən tā′shən) *n.*

con·fuse (kən fyōōz′) *vt.* -**fused′**, -**fus′ing** [see CONFOUND] **1.** to mix up; disorder **2.** to bewilder **3.** to embarrass **4.** to mistake the identity of —**con·fus′ed·ly** *adv.*

con·fu′sion (-fyōō′zhən) *n.* a confusing or being confused; disorder, bewilderment, etc.

con·fute (kən fyōōt′) *vt.* -**fut′ed**, -**fut′ing** [< L. *confutare*] to prove (a person, statement, etc.) to be in error or false —**con·fu·ta·tion** (kän′fyoo tā′shən) *n.*

con·geal (kən jēl′) *vt., vi.* [< L. *com*-, together + *gelare*, freeze] **1.** to freeze **2.** to thicken; coagulate —**con·geal′ment** *n.*

con·gen·ial (kən jēn′yəl) *adj.* [see CON- & GENIAL] **1.** kindred; compatible **2.** of the same temperament **3.** suited to one's needs —**con·ge′ni·al′i·ty** (-jēn′ē al′ə tē) *n.*

con·gen·i·tal (kən jen′ə t'l) *adj.* [< L.: see CON- & GENITAL] existing as such at birth — **con·gen′i·tal·ly** *adv.*

con·ger (eel) (käŋ′gər) [< Gr. *gongros*] a large, edible saltwater eel

con·gest (kən jest′) *vt.* [< L. *com*-, together + *gerere*, carry] **1.** to cause too much blood to accumulate in (a part of the body) **2.** to fill to excess; overcrowd —**con·ges′tion** *n.*

con·glom·er·ate (kən gläm′ə rāt′; *for adj. &* *n.* -ər it) *vt., vi.* -**at′ed**, -**at′ing** [< L. *com*-, together + *glomus*, ball] to form into a rounded mass —*adj.* **1.** formed into a rounded mass **2.** made up of substances collected into a single mass, esp. of rock fragments or pebbles cemented together by clay, silica, etc. —*n.* **1.** a conglomerate mass **2.** a large corporation formed by merging many diverse companies **3.** a conglomerate rock —**con·glom′er·a′tion** *n.*

con·grat·u·late (kən grach′ə lāt′) *vt.* -**lat′ed**, -**lat′ing** [< L. *com*-, together + *gratulari*, wish joy] to express to (a person) one's pleasure at his good fortune, success, etc. —**con·grat′u·la·to′ry** (-lə tôr′ē) *adj.*

con·grat·u·la′tion *n.* **1.** a congratulating **2.** [*pl.*] expressions of pleasure over another's good fortune or success

con·gre·gate (käŋ′grə gāt′) *vt., vi.* -**gat′ed**, -**gat′ing** [< L. *com*-, together + *grex*, a flock]

to gather into a mass or crowd; assemble — **con′gre·ga′tive** *adj.*

con′gre·ga′tion *n.* **1.** a gathering; assemblage **2.** an assembly of people for religious worship —**con′gre·gant** *n.*

con′gre·ga′tion·al *adj.* **1.** of or like a congregation **2.** [C-] of a Protestant denomination of self-governing churches

con·gress (käŋ′grəs) *n.* [< L. *com*-, together + *gradi*, to walk] **1.** an assembly or conference **2.** a legislature, esp. of a republic **3.** [C-] the U.S. legislature, consisting of the Senate and the House of Representatives —**con·gres·sion·al** (kən gresh′ən 'l) *adj.*

con′gress·man *n., pl.* -**men** [*often* C-] a member of Congress, esp. of the House of Representatives

con·gru·ent (käŋ′grōo wənt) *adj.* [< L. *congruere*, agree] corresponding; harmonious — **con′gru·ence, con′gru·en·cy** *n.*

con·gru·ous (käŋ′grōo wəs) *adj.* **1.** *same as* CONGRUENT **2.** fitting; suitable; appropriate — **con·gru·i·ty** (kən grōō′ə tē) *n., pl.* -**ties** —**con′·gru·ous·ly** *adv.*

con·i·cal (kän′i k'l) *adj.* of or like a cone: also **con′ic** —**con′i·cal·ly** *adv.*

co·ni·fer (kän′ə fər, kō′nə-) *n.* [< L. *conus*, cone + *ferre*, to bear] any of a group of cone-bearing trees and shrubs, mostly evergreens, as the pine, fir, etc. —**co·nif·er·ous** (kə nif′ər əs) *adj.*

conj. conjunction

con·jec·ture (kən jek′chər) *n.* [< L. *com*-, together + *jacere*, to throw] **1.** an inferring, theorizing, or predicting from incomplete evidence; guesswork **2.** a guess —*vt., vi.* -**tured**, -**tur·ing** to guess —**con·jec′tur·al** *adj.*

con·join (kən join′) *vt., vi.* [< L. *conjungere*] to join together; unite —**con·joint′** *adj.* —**con·joint′ly** *adv.*

con·ju·gal (kän′jə gəl) *adj.* [< L. *conjunx*, spouse] of marriage or the relation between husband and wife —**con′ju·gal·ly** *adv.*

con·ju·gate (kän′jə gət, -gāt′) *adj.* [< L. *com*-, together + *jugare*, join] joined together, esp. in a pair —*vt.* (-gāt′) -**gat′ed**, -**gat′ing** *Gram.* to give in order the inflectional forms of (a verb) —**con′ju·ga′tion** *n.* —**con′ju·ga′tive** *adj.*

con·junc·tion (kən juŋk′shən) *n.* [see CONJOIN] **1.** a joining together; union; combination **2.** coincidence **3.** a word used to connect words, phrases, or clauses (Ex.: *and, but, if,* etc.) — **con·junc′tive** *adj.*

con·junc·ti·vi·tis (kən juŋk′tə vīt′is) *n.* [see -ITIS] inflammation of the mucous membrane lining the eyelids

con·jure (kän′jər, kun′-; *for vt. 1* kən joor′) *vi.* -**jured**, -**jur·ing** [< L. *com*-, together + *jurare*, swear] **1.** to summon a demon, spirit, etc. by magic **2.** to practice magic —*vt.* **1.** to entreat solemnly **2.** to cause to appear, come (*up*), etc. as by magic —**con·ju·ra·tion** (kän′jə rā′shən) *n.* **con·jur·er, con·ju·ror** (kän′jər ər, kun′-) *n.* a magician; sorcerer

conk (käŋk) *n., vt.* [< CONCH] [Slang] hit on the head —**conk out** [Slang] **1.** to fail suddenly in operation **2.** to become tired

conn (kän) *vt.* **conned**, **con′ning** [see CONDUCE] *Naut.* to direct the course of (a vessel)

con·nect (kə nekt′) *vt.* [< L. *com*-, together + *nectere*, fasten] **1.** to join (two things together, or one thing *with* or *to* another); link; couple **2.** to show or think of as related; associate —*vi.* to be joined or related —**con·nec′tor, con·nect′er** *n.*

con·nec·tion (kə nek′shən) *n.* **1.** a joining or being joined **2.** a thing that joins **3.** a relation;

association 4. *a*) a relative, esp. by marriage *b*) an influential associate, etc.: *usually used in pl.* 5. [*usually pl.*] a transferring from one bus, airplane, etc. to another Brit. sp. con·nex′ion

con·nec′tive (-tiv) *adj.* connecting —*n.* that which connects, esp. a connecting word, as a conjunction

con·nip·tion (fit) (kə nip′shən) [pseudo-Latin] [Colloq.] a fit of anger, hysteria, etc.

con·nive (kə nīv′) *vi.* -nived′, -niv′ing [< L. *conivere*, to wink, connive] 1. to pretend not to look (*at* crime, etc.), thus giving tacit consent 2. to cooperate secretly (*with* someone), esp. in wrongdoing —con·niv′ance *n.* —con·niv′er *n.*

con·nois·seur (kän′ə sur′) *n.* [< L. ˊcognoscere*, know] one who has expert knowledge and keen discrimination in some field, esp. in the fine arts

con·note (kə nōt′) *vt.* -not′ed, -not′ing [< L. *com-*, together + *notare*, to mark] to suggest or convey (associations, overtones, etc.) in addition to the explicit, or denoted, meaning — con·no·ta·tion (kän′ə tā′shən) *n.* —con′no·ta′-tive *adj.*

con·nu·bi·al (kə nōō′bē əl) *adj.* [< L. *com-*, together + *nubere*, marry] of marriage

con·quer (käŋ′kər) *vt.* [< L. *com-*, intens. + *quaerere*, seek] 1. to get control of as by winning a war 2. to overcome; defeat —*vi.* to win; be victorious —con′quer·or *n.*

con·quest (kän′kwest, kän′-) *n.* 1. a conquering 2. something conquered 3. a winning of someone's love

con·quis·ta·dor (kän kwis′tə dôr′, -kēs′-) *n.*, *pl.* -dors′, -dores′ [Sp., conqueror] a 16th-c. Spanish conqueror of Mexico, Peru, etc.

con·san·guin·e·ous (kän′saŋ gwin′ē əs) *adj.* [see COM- & SANGUINE] closely related —con′-san·guin′i·ty *n.*

con·science (kän′shəns) *n.* [< L. *com-*, with + *scire*, know] an awareness of right and wrong, with a compulsion to do right

con·sci·en·tious (kän′shē en′shəs) *adj.* 1. governed by one's conscience; scrupulous 2. painstaking —con′sci·en′tious·ly *adv.*

conscientious objector one who from conscience refuses to take part in warfare

con·scious (kän′shəs) *adj.* [see CONSCIENCE] 1. having an awareness (*of* or *that*) 2. able to feel and think; awake 3. aware of oneself as a thinking being 4. intentional [*conscious* humor] 5. known to or felt by oneself —con′-scious·ly *adv.*

con′scious·ness *n.* 1. the state of being conscious; awareness 2. the totality of one's thoughts and feelings; mind

con·script (kən skript′; *for adj. & n.* kän′-skript) *vt.* [< L. *com-*, with + *scribere*, to write] to enroll for compulsory service in the armed forces; draft —*adj.* conscripted —*n.* a draftee —con·scrip′tion *n.*

con·se·crate (kän′sə krāt′) *vt.* -crat′ed, -crat′-ing [< L. *com-*, together + *sacer*, sacred] 1. to set apart as holy 2. to devote; dedicate —con′-se·cra′tion *n.*

con·sec·u·tive (kən sek′yə tiv) *adj.* [see CONSEQUENCE] following in uninterrupted order; successive —con·sec′u·tive·ly *adv.*

con·sen·sus (kən sen′səs) *n.* [see CONSENT] 1. general opinion 2. general agreement

con·sent (kən sent′) *vi.* [< L. *com-*, with + *sentire*, to feel] to agree, permit, or assent —*n.* 1. permission, approval, or assent 2. agreement [by common *consent*]

con·se·quence (kän′sə kwens′) *n.* [< L. *com-*, with + *sequi*, follow] 1. a result; effect 2. a

logical result or conclusion 3. importance — take the consequences to accept the results of one's actions

con′se·quent (-kwent′, -kwənt) *adj.* following as a result; resulting

con·se·quen·tial (kän′sə kwen′shəl) *adj.* 1. following as an effect 2. important

con′se·quent′ly *adv.* as a result; therefore

con·ser·va·tion (kän′sər vā′shən) *n.* 1. a conserving 2. the official care and protection of natural resources, as forests —con′ser·va′tion-ist *n.*

con·ser·va·tive (kən sur′və tiv) *adj.* 1. tending to conserve 2. tending to preserve established institutions, etc.; opposed to change 3. moderate; cautious —*n.* a conservative person —con-ser′va·tism *n.* —con·ser′va·tive·ly *adv.*

con·ser·va·to·ry (kən sur′və tôr′ē) *n.*, *pl.* -ries 1. a greenhouse 2. a school, as of music

con·serve (kən surv′) *vt.* -served′, -serv′ing [< L. *com-*, with + *servare*, to guard] 1. to keep from being damaged, lost, or wasted 2. to make (fruit) into preserves —*n.* (*usually* kän′-sərv) [*often pl.*] a preserve of two or more fruits

con·sid·er (kən sid′ər) *vt.* [< L. *com-*, with + *sidus*, a star] 1. to think about in order to understand or decide 2. to keep in mind 3. to be thoughtful of (others) 4. to regard as; think to be —*vi.* to think seriously

con·sid′er·a·ble *adj.* 1. worth considering; important 2. much or large —con·sid′er·a·bly *adv.*

con·sid′er·ate (-it) *adj.* having or showing regard for others and their feelings

con·sid·er·a′tion (-ə rā′shən) *n.* 1. the act of considering; deliberation 2. thoughtful regard for others 3. something considered in making a decision 4. a recompense; fee —take into consideration to keep in mind —under consideration being thought over

con·sid′ered (-ərd) *adj.* arrived at after careful thought

con·sid′er·ing *prep.* taking into account —*adv.* [Colloq.] all things considered

con·sign (kən sīn′) *vt.* [< L. *consignare*, to seal] 1. to hand over; deliver 2. to entrust 3. to assign; relegate 4. to send or deliver (goods) — con·sign′a·ble *adj.*

con·sign′ment (-mənt) *n.* 1. a consigning or being consigned 2. a shipment of goods sent to an agent for sale, etc. —on consignment with payment due after sale of the goods

con·sist (kən sist′) *vi.* [< L. *com-*, together + *sistere*, stand] 1. to be composed (*of*) 2. to be contained or inherent (*in*)

con·sis·ten·cy (-ən sē) *n.*, *pl.* -cies 1. *a*) firmness or thickness, as of a liquid *b*) degree of this 2. agreement; harmony 3. conformity with previous practice

con·sis′tent (-ənt) *adj.* 1. in harmony; compatible 2. holding to the same principles or practice —con·sis′tent·ly *adv.*

con·sis·to·ry (kən sis′tər ē) *n.*, *pl.* -ries [see CONSIST] 1. a church council, as the papal senate 2. a session of such a body

con·so·la·tion (kän′sə lā′shən) *n.* 1. comfort; solace 2. one that consoles

con·sole¹ (kən sōl′) *vt.* -soled′, -sol′ing [< Fr. < L. *com-*, with + *solari*, to solace] to make feel less sad; comfort

con·sole² (kän′sōl) *n.* [Fr.] 1. the desklike frame containing the keys, stops, etc. of an organ 2. a radio, television, or phonograph cabinet designed to stand on the floor 3. a control panel for operating aircraft, computers, electronic systems, etc.

con·sol·i·date (kən säl′ə dāt′) **vt., vi.** **-dat′ed, -dat′ing** [< L. *com-*, together + *solidus*, solid] **1.** to combine into one; unite **2.** to make or become strong, stable, etc. **—con·sol′i·da′tion** **n.**

con·som·mé (kän′sə mā′) **n.** [Fr.] a clear, strained meat soup

con·so·nance (kän′sə nəns) **n.** [< L. *com-*, with + *sonus*, sound] harmony, esp. of musical tones

con′so·nant (-nənt) **adj. 1.** in harmony or agreement **2.** harmonious in tone **—n.** a letter representing a speech sound made by obstructing the breath stream as *p, t, l, f,* etc. — **con·so·nan·tal** (kän′sə nant′'l) **adj.**

con·sort (kän′sôrt; *for v.* kən sôrt′) **n.** [< L. *com-*, with + *sors*, a share] a wife or husband, esp. of a reigning king or queen **—vt., vi.** to associate

con·sor·ti·um (kən sôr′shē əm) **n., pl.** **-ti·a** (-ə) [see prec.] an international alliance, as of business firms or banks

con·spic·u·ous (kən spik′yoo wəs) **adj.** [< L. *com-*, intens. + *specere*, to see] **1.** easy to see; obvious **2.** outstanding; striking **—con·spic′u·ous·ly adv.**

con·spir·a·cy (kən spir′ə sē) **n., pl.** **-cies 1.** a conspiring **2.** an unlawful plot **3.** the group taking part in such a plot

con·spire (kən spīr′) **vi.** **-spired′, -spir′ing** [< L. *com-*, together + *spirare*, to breathe] **1.** to plan together secretly, as to commit a crime **2.** to work together for any purpose or effect — **con·spir′a·tor** (-spir′ə tər) **n.**

con·sta·ble (kän′stə b'l, kun′-) **n.** [< LL. *comes stabuli,* lit., count of the stable] [Chiefly Brit.] a policeman

con·stab·u·lar·y (kən stab′yə ler′ē) **n., pl.** **-ies** constables, collectively

con·stant (kän′stənt) **adj.** [< L. *com-*, together + *stare*, stand] **1.** not changing; specif., *a)* resolute *b)* faithful *c)* regular; stable **2.** continual; persistent **—n.** anything that does not change or vary **—con′stan·cy n. —con′stant·ly adv.**

con·stel·la·tion (kän′stə lā′shən) **n.** [< L. *com-*, with + *stella*, star] **1.** a group of fixed stars **2.** any brilliant cluster

con·ster·na·tion (kän′stər nā′shən) **n.** [< L. *consternare*, terrify] great fear or shock

con·sti·pate (kän′stə pāt′) **vt.** **-pat′ed, -pat′ing** [< L. *com-*, together + *stipare*, cram] to cause constipation **—con′sti·pa′tion n.** infrequent and difficult movement of the bowels

con·stit·u·en·cy (kən stich′oo wən sē) **n., pl.** **-cies** the voters in a district

con·stit′u·ent (-wənt) **adj.** [see CONSTITUTE] **1.** necessary to the whole; component **2.** that can elect **3.** authorized to make or revise a constitution **—n. 1.** a voter in a district **2.** a component

con·sti·tute (kän′stə toot′) **vt.** **-tut′ed, -tut′ing** [< L. *com-*, together + *statuere*, to set] **1.** to establish (a law, government, etc.) **2.** to set up (an assembly, etc.) in a legal form **3.** to appoint **4.** to form

con′sti·tu′tion (-too′shən) **n. 1.** a constituting; establishment **2.** structure; organization **3.** *a)* the system of basic laws and principles of a government, society, etc. *b)* a document stating these; specif., **[C-]** the Constitution of the U.S.

con′sti·tu′tion·al adj. 1. of or in one's constitution; basic; essential **2.** of or in accordance with the constitution of a nation, society, etc. **—n.** a walk taken for one's health **—con′sti·tu′-**

tion·al′i·ty (-shə nal′ə tē) **n.** **—con′sti·tu′tion·al·ly adv.**

con·strain (kən strān′) **vt.** [< L. *com-*, together + *stringere*, draw tight] **1.** to confine **2.** to restrain **3.** to compel

con·straint′ n. 1. confinement or restriction **2.** compulsion or coercion **3.** forced, unnatural manner

con·strict (kən strikt′) **vt.** [see CONSTRAIN] **1.** to make smaller or narrower by squeezing, etc. **2.** to limit **—con·stric′tion n.**

con·struct (kən strukt′) **vt.** [< L. *com-*, together + *struere*, pile up] to build, form, or devise **—con·struc′tor n.**

con·struc·tion (kən struk′shən) **n. 1.** a constructing or manner of being constructed **2.** a structure **3.** an interpretation, as of a statement **4.** the arrangement of words in a sentence

con·struc′tive adj. helping to construct; leading to improvements *[constructive* criticism*]* — **con·struc′tive·ly adv.**

con·strue (kən stroo′) **vt., vi.** **-strued′, -stru′ing** [see CONSTRUCT] **1.** to analyze the grammatical construction of (a sentence, etc.) **2.** to translate **3.** to explain; interpret **—con·stru′a·ble adj.**

con·sul (kän′s'l) **n.** [< L. *consulere*, to deliberate] **1.** a chief magistrate of ancient Rome **2.** a government official appointed to live in a foreign city and serve his country's citizens and business interests there **—con′su·lar adj. —con′sul·ship′ n.**

con·su·late (-it) **n. 1.** the position, powers, etc. of a consul **2.** the office or residence of a consul

con·sult (kən sult′) **vi.** [< L. *consulere*, to deliberate] to talk things over; confer **—vt. 1.** to ask advice or information from **2.** to consider

con·sult′ant n. 1. a person who consults another **2.** one who gives professional or technical advice

con·sul·ta·tion (kän′s'l tā′shən) **n. 1.** a consulting **2.** a conference **—con·sul·ta·tive** (kən sul′tə tiv) **adj.**

con·sume (kən soom′) **vt.** **-sumed′, -sum′ing** [< L. *com-*, together + *sumere*, take] **1.** to destroy, as by fire **2.** to use up (time, money, etc.) **3.** to eat or drink up

con·sum′er n. one that consumes; specif., a person who buys goods or services for his own needs rather than to produce other goods

con·sum′er·ism (-iz′m) **n.** a movement for protecting the consumer against defective products, misleading business practices, etc.

con·sum·mate (kən sum′it) **adj.** [< L. *com-*, together + *summa*, a sum] **1.** complete or perfect **2.** highly expert **—vt.** (kän′sə māt′) **-mat′ed, -mat′ing 1.** to complete; finish **2.** to make (a marriage) actual by sexual intercourse **—con′sum·ma′tion n.**

con·sump·tion (kən sump′shən) **n. 1.** *a)* a consuming or being consumed; specif., the using up of goods or services *b)* the amount consumed **2.** a wasting disease; esp., tuberculosis of the lungs

con·sump′tive (-tiv) **adj. 1.** consuming or tending to consume **2.** of or having tuberculosis of the lungs **—n.** one who has tuberculosis of the lungs

cont., contd. continued

con·tact (kän′takt) **n.** [< L. *com-*, together + *tangere*, to touch] **1.** a touching or meeting **2.** the state of being in association (*with*) **3.** a connection **—vt. 1.** to place in contact **2.** to get in touch with **—vi.** to come into contact

contact lens a tiny, thin correctional lens placed in the fluid over the cornea

con·ta·gion (kən tā′jən) *n.* [see CONTACT] 1. the spreading of disease by contact 2. a contagious disease 3. the spreading of an emotion, idea, etc.

con·ta′gious (-jəs) *adj.* 1. spread by contact: said of diseases 2. carrying the causative agent of such a disease 3. spreading from person to person

con·tain (kən tān′) *vt.* [< L. *com-*, together + *tenere*, to hold] 1. to have in it; hold or include 2. to have the capacity for holding 3. to hold back or restrain within fixed limits —**con·tain′ment** *n.*

con·tain′er *n.* a thing for containing something; box, can, jar, etc.

con·tam·i·nate (kən tam′ə nāt′) *vt.* -nat′ed, -nat′ing [< L. *com-*, together + *tangere*, to touch] to make impure, corrupt, etc. by contact; pollute; taint —**con·tam′i·nant** *n.* —**con·tam′i·na′tion** *n.*

con·temn (kən tem′) *vt.* [< L. *com-*, intens. + *temnere*, to scorn] to despise; scorn

con·tem·plate (kän′təm plāt′) *vt.* -plat′ed, -plat′ing [< L. *contemplari*, observe] 1. to gaze at or think about intently 2. to expect or intend —*vi.* to muse —**con′tem·pla′tion** *n.* —**con·tem·pla·tive** (kən tem′plə tiv, kän′təm plāt′iv) *adj., n.*

con·tem·po·rar·y (kən tem′pə rer′ē) *adj.* [< L. *com-*, with + *tempus*, time] 1. living or happening in the same period 2. of about the same age 3. modern Also **con·tem′po·ra′ne·ous** (-rā′nē əs) —*n., pl.* -ies one of the same period as another or others

con·tempt (kən tempt′) *n.* [see CONTEMN] 1. the feeling of a person toward someone or something he considers low, worthless, etc. 2. the condition of being despised 3. *Law* a showing disrespect for the dignity of a court (or legislature)

con·tempt′i·ble *adj.* deserving contempt — **con·tempt′i·bly** *adv.*

con·temp·tu·ous (kən temp′choo wəs) *adj.* full of contempt; scornful

con·tend (kən tend′) *vi.* [< L. *com-*, together + *tendere*, stretch] 1. to fight 2. to argue 3. to compete; vie —*vt.* to assert —**con·tend′er** *n.*

con·tent¹ (kən tent′) *adj.* [see CONTAIN] 1. satisfied 2. assenting —*vt.* to satisfy —*n.* contentment

con·tent² (kän′tent) *n.* [see CONTAIN] 1. [*usually pl.*] *a)* all that is contained in something *b)* all that is dealt with in a writing or speech 2. meaning or substance 3. the amount contained

con·tent′ed *adj.* satisfied

con·ten·tion (kən ten′shən) *n.* [see CONTEND] 1. strife, dispute, etc. 2. a point argued for — **con·ten′tious** *adj.*

con·tent′ment *n.* a being contented

con·ter·mi·nous (kən tur′mə nəs) *adj.* [< L. *com-*, together + *terminus*, end] 1. having a common boundary 2. contained within the same boundaries or limits

con·test (kən test′) *vt.* [< L. *com-*, together + *testis*, witness] 1. to dispute 2. to fight for (a position, etc.) —*vi.* to struggle (*with* or *against*) —*n.* (kän′test) 1. a fight; struggle 2. a competitive race, game, etc.

con·test′ant *n.* [Fr.] 1. a competitor in a contest 2. one who contests a claim, etc.

con·text (kän′tekst) *n.* [< L. *com-*, together + *texere*, weave] the parts just before and after a word or passage, that determine its meaning —

con·tex·tu·al (kən teks′choo wəl) *adj.* —**con·tex′tu·al·ly** *adv.*

con·tig·u·ous (kən tig′yoo wəs) *adj.* [see CONTACT] 1. in contact; touching 2. near or adjacent —**con·ti·gu·i·ty** (kän′tə gyoo′ə tē) *n., pl.* -ties —**con·tig′u·ous·ly** *adv.*

con·ti·nence (känt′'n əns) *n.* [see CONTAIN] 1. self-restraint 2. self-restraint in sexual activity; esp., total abstinence —**con′ti·nent** *adj.*

con′ti·nent (-ənt) *n.* [see CONTAIN] any of the main large land areas of the earth —**the Continent** the mainland of Europe

con′ti·nen′tal (-en′t′l) *adj.* 1. of a continent 2. [*sometimes* C-] European 3. [C-] of the American colonies at the time of the American Revolution

con·tin·gen·cy (kən tin′jən sē) *n., pl.* -cies 1. dependence on chance 2. a possible or chance event

con·tin′gent *adj.* [see CONTACT] 1. possible 2. accidental 3. dependent (*on* or *upon* an uncertainty); conditional —*n.* 1. a chance happening 2. a share or quota, as of troops 3. a part of a large group

con·tin·u·al (kən tin′yoo wəl) *adj.* 1. repeated often 2. continuous —**con·tin′u·al·ly** *adv.*

con·tin′u·ance *n.* 1. a continuing 2. duration 3. an unbroken succession 4. *Law* postponement or adjournment

con·tin′u·a′tion (-wā′shən) *n.* 1. a continuing or being continued 2. a beginning again; resumption 3. a part added; sequel, etc.

con·tin·ue (kən tin′yoo) *vi.* -ued, -u·ing [< L. *continuare*, join] 1. to last; endure 2. to go on in a specified action or condition; persist 3. to extend 4. to stay 5. to resume after an interruption —*vt.* 1. to go on with 2. to extend 3. to resume 4. to cause to remain, as in office; retain 5. *Law* to postpone or adjourn to a later date

con·ti·nu·i·ty (kän′tə noo′ə tē) *n., pl.* -ties 1. a continuous state or quality 2. an unbroken, coherent whole 3. the script as for a motion picture

con·tin·u·ous (kən tin′yoo wəs) *adj.* going on uninterruptedly —**con·tin′u·ous·ly** *adv.*

con·tin′u·um (-yoo wəm) *n., pl.* -u·a (-wə), -u·ums [L.] a continuous whole, quantity, or series

con·tort (kən tôrt′) *vt., vi.* [< L. *com-*, together + *torquere*, to twist] to twist out of shape; distort —**con·tor′tion** *n.*

con·tor′tion·ist *n.* one who can twist his body into unnatural positions

con·tour (kän′toor) *n.* [Fr. < L. *com-*, intens. + *tornare*, to turn] the outline of a figure, land, etc. —*vt.* to shape to the contour of something

contra- [< L. *contra*] a prefix meaning against, opposite, opposed to

con·tra·band (kän′trə band′) *n.* [< Sp. < It.] smuggled goods —*adj.* illegal to import or export

con·tra·cep·tion (kän′trə sep′shən) *n.* [CONTRA- + (CON)CEPTION] prevention of the fertilization of the human ovum —**con′tra·cep′tive** *adj., n.*

con·tract (kän′trakt *for n. & usually for vt.* 1. *& vi.* 1; kən trakt′ *for v. generally*) *n.* [< L. *com-*, together + *trahere*, draw] an agreement, esp. a written one enforceable by law —*vt.* 1. to undertake by contract 2. to get or incur 3. to make smaller or shorter —*vi.* 1. to make a contract 2. to become smaller

con·trac·tile (kən trak′t′l) *adj.* having the power of contracting

con·trac′tion (-shən) *n.* 1. a contracting or

being contracted **2.** a shortened form (Ex.:
aren't for *are not*)
con·trac·tor (kän′trak tər, kən trak′-) *n.* one
who contracts to supply certain materials or
do certain work for a stipulated sum
con·trac·tu·al (kən trak′chōō wəl) *adj.* of or
constituting a contract
con·tra·dict (kän′trə dikt′) *vt.* [< L. *contra-*,
against + *dicere*, speak] **1.** to assert the opposite of **2.** to deny the statement of **3.** to be
contrary to —**con′tra·dic′tion** *n.* —**con′tra·dic′-
to·ry** *adj.*
con·tral·to (kən tral′tō) *n., pl.* **-tos, -ti** (-tē) [It.:
see CONTRA- & ALTO] **1.** the range of the lowest
female voice **2.** a singer with such a range —
adj. of or for a contralto
con·trap·tion (kən trap′shən) *n.* [< ?] [Colloq.]
a contrivance or gadget
con·tra·pun·tal (kän′trə pun′t'l) *adj.* [< It.
contrapunto, counterpoint] of or characterized
by counterpoint
con·trar·i·wise (kän′trer ē wīz′) *adv.* **1.** on the
contrary **2.** in the opposite way, etc.
con·trar·y (kän′trer ē; *for 4, often* kən trer′ē)
adj. [< L. *contra*, against] **1.** in opposition **2.**
opposite in nature, order, etc.; altogether different **3.** unfavorable **4.** always resisting; per-
verse —*n., pl.* **-ies** the opposite —**on the contrary**
as opposed to what has been said —**to the contrary** to the opposite effect —**con′trar·i·ly** *adv.* —
con′trar·i·ness *n.*
con·trast (kən trast′) *vt.* [< L. *contra*, against
+ *stare*, to stand] to compare so as to point
out the differences —*vi.* to show differences
when compared —*n.* (kän′trast) **1.** a contrasting or being contrasted **2.** a striking difference
between things being compared **3.** a person or
thing showing differences when compared with
another
con·tra·vene (kän′trə vēn′) *vt.* -**vened′**, -**ven′-
ing** [< L. *contra*, against + *venire*, come] **1.** to
go against; violate **2.** to contradict —**con′tra·
ven′tion** (-ven′shən) *n.*
con·trib·ute (kən trib′yōōt) *vt., vi.* -**ut·ed**, -**ut-
ing** [< L.: see CON- & TRIBUTE] **1.** to give
jointly with others to a common fund **2.** to
write (an article, poem, etc.) for a magazine,
newspaper, etc. **3.** to furnish (ideas, etc.) —
contribute to to have a share in bringing about
—**con·trib′u·tor** *n.* —**con·trib′u·to′ry** (-yōō tôr′ē)
adj.
con·tri·bu·tion (kän′trə byōō′shən) *n.* **1.** a
contributing **2.** something contributed
con·trite (kən trīt′) *adj.* [< L. *com-*, together
+ *terere*, to rub] feeling or showing remorse
or guilt —**con·tri′tion** (-trish′ən) *n.*
con·triv·ance (kən trī′vəns) *n.* **1.** a contriving
2. something contrived; device, etc.
con·trive (kən trīv′) *vt.* -**trived′**, -**triv′ing** [ult. <
VL. *contropare*, compare] **1.** to devise; plan **2.**
to invent or design **3.** to bring about; manage
—**con·triv′er** *n.*
con·trol (kən trōl′) *vt.* -**trolled′**, -**trol′ling** [<
ML. *contrarotulus*, a register] **1.** to regulate **2.**
to exercise authority over; direct **3.** to restrain
—*n.* **1.** power to direct or regulate **2.** a means
of controlling; check **3.** [*usually pl.*] an apparatus to regulate a mechanism —**con·trol′la-
ble** *adj.*
con·trol′ler *n.* **1.** one in charge of finances, as
in business, government (usually sp.
comptroller), etc. **2.** one controlling
con·tro·ver·sial (kän′trə vur′shəl) *adj.* of or
subject to controversy; debatable
con·tro·ver·sy (kän′trə vur′sē) *n., pl.* -**sies** [<
L. *contra*, against + *vertere*, to turn] **1.** a dis-

cussion in which opinions clash; debate **2.** a
quarrel
con′tro·vert′ (-vurt′) *vt.* **1.** to argue against;
deny **2.** to argue about; debate —**con′tro·vert′i-
ble** *adj.*
con·tu·ma·cy (kän′tōō mə sē) *n., pl.* -**cies** [<
L. *contumax*, stubborn] stubborn disobedience
—**con′tu·ma′cious** (-mā′shəs) *adj.*
con·tu·me·ly (kän′tōō mə lē) *n., pl.* -**lies** [< L.
contumelia, reproach] humiliating treatment
or scorn —**con′tu·me′li·ous** (-mē′lē əs) *adj.*
con·tu·sion (kən tōō′zhən) *n.* [< L. *com-*, intens. + *tundere*, to beat] a bruise
co·nun·drum (kə nun′drəm) *n.* [pseudo-L.] **1.**
a riddle whose answer is a pun **2.** any puzzling
problem
con·va·lesce (kän′və les′) *vi.* -**lesced′**, -**lesc′-
ing** [< L. *com-*, intens. + *valere*, be strong] to
regain strength and health —**con′va·les′cence**
n. —**con′va·les′cent** *adj., n.*
con·vec·tion (kən vek′shən) *n.* [< L. *com-*,
together + *vehere*, carry] **1.** a transmitting **2.**
a) movement of parts of a fluid within the
fluid because of differences in heat, etc. *b*)
heat transference by such movement
con·vene (kən vēn′) *vi., vt.* -**vened′**, -**ven′ing** [<
L. *com-*, together + *venire*, come] to assemble
for a meeting
con·ven·ience (kən vēn′yəns) *n.* [see
CONVENE] **1.** the quality of being convenient **2.**
comfort **3.** anything that adds to one's comfort
or saves work —**at one's convenience** at a time,
place, etc. that suits one
con·ven′ient (-yənt) *adj.* **1.** favorable to one's
comfort; easy to do, use, or get to; handy **2.**
[Colloq.] easily accessible (*to*); near (*to*) —**con-
ven′lent·ly** *adv.*
con·vent (kän′vənt, -vent) *n.* [see CONVENE] **1.**
a community of nuns or, sometimes, monks **2.**
the place where they live
con·ven·tion (kən ven′shən) *n.* **1.** an assembly
or the delegates **2.** an agreement as between
nations **3.** custom; usage
con·ven·tion·al *adj.* **1.** of a convention **2.** sanc-
tioned by or following custom or usage; cus-
tomary **3.** *a*) formal; not original, spontaneous,
etc. *b*) ordinary —**con·ven′tion·al′i·ty** (-shə
nal′ə tē) *n., pl.* -**ties** —**con·ven′tion·al·ly** *adv.*
con·verge (kən vurj′) *vi., vt.* -**verged′**, -**verg′ing**
[< L. *com-*, together + *vergere*, to turn] to
come or bring together at a point —**con·ver′-
gence** *n.* —**con·ver′gent** *adj.*
con·ver·sant (kən vur′s'nt, kän′vər-) *adj.* [see
CONVERSE[1]] familiar (*with*); versed (*in*)
con·ver·sa·tion (kän′vər sā′shən) *n.* a talking
together; conversing; specif., informal talk —
con′ver·sa′tion·al *adj.* —**con′ver·sa′tion·al·ist**
n.
conversation piece an unusual article of furniture, etc. that invites comment
con·verse[1] (kən vurs′) *vi.* -**versed′**, -**vers′ing** [<
L. *conversari*, to live with] to hold a conversation; talk —*n.* (kän′vərs) conversation
con·verse[2] (kän′vərs, kən vurs′) *adj.* [see
CONVERT] reversed in position, order, etc.; opposite —*n.* (kän′vərs) a converse thing; the opposite —**con·verse′ly** *adv.*
con·ver·sion (kən vur′zhən) *n.* a converting or
being converted
con·vert (kən vurt′) *vt.* [< L. *com-*, together +
vertere, to turn] **1.** to change; transform **2.** to
change from one belief, religion, etc. to
another **3.** to exchange for something equal in
value **4.** to misappropriate —*vi.* to be converted
—*n.* (kän′vərt) a person converted, as to a religion —**con·vert′er, con·ver′tor** *n.*
con·vert·i·ble (kən vurt′ə b'l) *adj.* that can be

converted —*n.* an automobile with a folding top —**con·vert'i·bil'i·ty** *n.*

con·vex (kän veks', kän'veks) *adj.* [< L. *com-,* together + *vehere,* bring] curving outward, like the surface of a sphere —**con·vex'i·ty** *n., pl.* **-ties**

con·vey (kən vā') *vt.* [< L. *com-,* together + *via,* way] **1.** to take from one place to another; carry **2.** to transmit —**con·vey'a·ble** *adj.* —**convey'or, con·vey'er** *n.*

con·vey'ance *n.* **1.** a conveying **2.** a means of conveying, esp. a vehicle

con·vict (kən vikt') *vt.* [see CONVINCE] to prove or find (a person) guilty —*n.* (kän'vikt) a convicted person serving a prison sentence

con·vic'tion (-vik'shən) *n.* **1.** a convicting or being convicted **2.** a being convinced **3.** a strong belief

con·vince (kən vins') *vt.* **-vinced', -vinc'ing** [< L. *com-,* intens. + *vincere,* conquer] to persuade by argument or evidence; make feel sure —**con·vinc'ing·ly** *adv.*

con·viv·i·al (kən viv'ē əl) *adj.* [< L. *com-,* together + *vivere,* to live] **1.** festive **2.** fond of eating, drinking, and good company; sociable —**con·viv'i·al'i·ty** *n.*

con·vo·ca·tion (kän'və kā'shən) *n.* **1.** a convoking **2.** an assembly

con·voke (kən vōk') *vt.* **-voked', -vok'ing** [< L. *com-,* together + *vocare,* to call] to call together; assemble —**con·vok'er** *n.*

con·vo·lut·ed (kän'və lōōt'id) *adj.* **1.** coiled **2.** involved; complicated

con·vo·lu'tion (-lōō'shən) *n.* [< L. *com-,* together + *volvere,* to roll] **1.** a twisting, coiling, or winding together **2.** a convoluted condition **3.** any of the irregular folds or ridges on the surface of the brain

con·voy (kän'voi, kən voi') *vt.* [see CONVEY] to escort in order to protect —*n.* (kän'voi) **1.** a convoying **2.** a protecting escort, as for ships **3.** ships, etc. being convoyed

con·vulse (kən vuls') *vt.* **-vulsed', -vuls'ing** [< L. *com-,* together + *vellere,* to pluck] **1.** to shake violently; agitate **2.** to cause to shake with laughter, rage, etc.

con·vul'sion (-vul'shən) *n.* **1.** a violent, involuntary contraction or spasm of the muscles: *often in pl.* **2.** a fit of laughter **3.** any violent disturbance —**con·vul'sive** *adj.*

co·ny (kō'nē) *n., pl.* **-nies** same as CONEY

coo (kōō) *vi.* [echoic] to make the soft, murmuring sound of pigeons —*n.* this sound

cook (kook) *n.* [< L. *coquere,* to cook] one who prepares food —*vt.* to prepare (food) by boiling, baking, frying, etc. —*vi.* **1.** to act as a cook **2.** to undergo cooking —**cook up** [Colloq.] to devise —**cook'er** *n.*

cook'book' *n.* a book with recipes and other information about preparing food

cook'er·y (-ər ē) *n.* [Chiefly Brit.] the art or practice of cooking

cook·ie, cook·y (kook'ē) *n., pl.* **-ies** [prob. < Du. *koek,* cake] a small, sweet, flat cake

cook'out' *n.* a meal cooked and eaten outdoors

cool (kōōl) *adj.* [OE. *col*] **1.** moderately cold **2.** tending to reduce the effects of heat [*cool clothes*] **3.** not excited; composed **4.** showing dislike or indifference **5.** calmly bold **6.** [Colloq.] without exaggeration [*a cool* $1,000] **7.** [Slang] pleasing —*n.* **1.** a cool time, place, etc. **2.** [Slang] dispassionate manner —*adv.* in a cool manner —*vt., vi.* to make or become cool —**cool'ly** *adv.* —**cool'ness** *n.*

cool'ant (-ənt) *n.* a fluid or other substance for cooling engines, etc.

cool'er *n.* **1.** a place for keeping things cool **2.** anything that cools **3.** [Slang] a jail

coo·lie (kōō'lē) *n.* [Hindi *qūlī,* servant] an unskilled native laborer, esp. formerly, in China, India, etc.

coon (kōōn) *n.* clipped form of RACCOON

coop (kōōp) *n.* [ult. < L. *cupa,* cask] **1.** a small cage or pen for poultry, etc. **2.** a place of confinement —*vt.* to confine as in a coop

co-op (kō'äp) *n.* [Colloq.] a cooperative

coop·er (kōōp'ər) *n.* [see COOP] one whose work is making or repairing barrels and casks

co·op·er·ate, co-op·er·ate (kō äp'ə rāt') *vi.* **-at'ed, -at'ing** [< L. *co-,* with + *opus,* work] to act or work with another or others for a common purpose: also **co·öp'er·ate' —co·op'er·a'-tion** *n.* —**co·op'er·a'tor** *n.*

co·op·er·a·tive, co-op·er·a·tive (kō äp'ər ə tiv, -ə rāt'iv) *adj.* **1.** cooperating or inclined to cooperate **2.** owned collectively by members who share in its benefits —*n.* a cooperative store, etc. Also **co·öp'er·a·tive**

co-opt (kō äpt') *vt.* [< L. *co-,* with + *optare,* choose] to elect or appoint as an associate

co·or·di·nate, co-or·di·nate (kō ôr'd'n it, -də nāt') *adj.* [< L. *co-,* with + *ordo,* order] **1.** of equal order or importance **2.** of coordination or coordinates —*n.* **1.** a coordinate person or thing **2.** any of a system of numbers used to define the position of a point, line, etc. —*vt.* (-də nāt') **-nat'ed, -nat'ing 1.** to make coordinate **2.** to bring into proper order or relation; adjust —*vi.* to become coordinate; function harmoniously Also **co·ör'di·nate —co·or'di·na'tor** *n.*

co·or'di·na'tion, co-or'di·na'tion *n.* **1.** a coordinating or being coordinated **2.** harmonious 'adjustment or action, as of muscles Also **co·ör'di·na'tion**

coot (kōōt) *n.* [< ? MDu. *koet*] **1.** a ducklike bird **2.** [Colloq.] a foolish person

coot·ie (kōōt'ē) *n.* [< Polynesian *kutu,* parasitic insect] [Slang] a louse

cop (käp) *vt.* **copped, cop'ping** [? ult. < L. *capere,* to take] [Slang] to seize, win, steal, etc. —*n.* [Slang] a policeman —**cop out** [Slang] **1.** to confess to the police **2.** *a)* to renege *b)* to quit

co·part·ner (kō pärt'nər) *n.* a partner, or associate —**co·part'ner·ship'** *n.*

cope[1] (kōp) *vi.* **coped, cop'ing** [< OFr. *coup,* a blow] to fight or contend (*with*) successfully

cope[2] (kōp) *n.* [< ML. *cappa*] a large, capelike vestment worn by priests

cop·i·er (käp'ē ər) *n.* **1.** one who copies **2.** a duplicating machine

co·pi·lot (kō'pī'lət) *n.* the assistant pilot of an aircraft

cop·ing (kō'piŋ) *n.* [< COPE[2]] the top layer of a masonry wall

co·pi·ous (kō'pē əs) *adj.* [< L. *copia,* abundance] plentiful; abundant —**co'pi·ous·ly** *adv.* —**co'pi·ous·ness** *n.*

cop-out (käp'out') *n.* [Slang] a copping out

cop·per (käp'ər) *n.* [< LL. *cuprum*] **1.** a reddish-brown, ductile metallic element: symbol, Cu **2.** [Chiefly Brit.] a penny **3.** a reddish brown —*adj.* **1.** of copper **2.** reddish-brown —**cop'per·y** *adj.*

cop'per·head' *n.* a poisonous N. American snake

co·pra (kō'prə, käp'rə) *n.* [Port. < Hindi *khoprā*] dried coconut meat

copse (käps) *n.* [< OFr. *couper,* to cut] a thicket of small trees: also **cop·pice** (käp'is)

cop·u·la (käp'yə lə) *n., pl.* **-las** [L. < *co-,* together + *apere,* to join] something that

links together; specif., *same as* LINKING VERB
—**cop′u·la′tive** (-lāt′iv, -lə tiv) *adj.*
cop′u·late′ (-lāt′) *vi.* **-lat′ed, -lat′ing** [see
COPULA] to have sexual intercourse —**cop′u·la′-
tion** *n.*
cop·y (käp′ē) *n., pl.* **-ies** [< L. *copia,* plenty] **1.**
a thing made just like another **2.** any of a
number of books, magazines, etc. having the
same contents **3.** matter to be set in type **4.**
the words of an advertisement —*vt., vi.* **-ied,
-y·ing 1.** to make a copy of **2.** to imitate —
cop′y·ist *n.*
cop′y·right′ *n.* the exclusive legal right to the
publication, sale, etc. of a literary or artistic
work —*vt.* to protect (a book, etc.) by copyright —*adj.* protected by copyright
cop′y·writ′er *n.* a writer of copy, esp. for advertisements
co·quet·ry (kōk′ə trē, kō ket′rē) *n., pl.* **-ries**
the behavior of a coquette
co·quette (kō ket′) *n.* [< Fr. *coq,* rooster] a girl
or woman flirt —**co·quet′tish** *adj.*
cor- *same as* COM-: used before *r*
cor·al (kôr′əl) *n.* [< Gr. *korallion*] **1.** the hard,
stony skeleton of some marine polyps, often in
masses forming reefs and atolls in tropical seas
2. any of such polyps **3.** a piece of coral **4.** yellowish red —*adj.* **1.** made of coral **2.** yellowish-
red
cor·bel (kôr′bəl) *n.* [< L. *corvus,* raven] a
bracket of stone, wood, etc. projecting from a
wall to support a cornice, etc.
cord (kôrd) *n.* [< Gr. *chordē*] **1.** thick string **2.**
a measure of wood cut for fuel (128 cu. ft.) **3.**
a) a rib on the surface of a fabric *b)* corduroy
4. *Anat.* any part like a cord **5.** *Elec.* a slender,
insulated cable with a plug —*vt.* **1.** to fasten
with a cord **2.** to stack (wood) in cords
cord′age (-ij) *n.* cords and ropes
cor·dial (kôr′jəl) *adj.* [< L. *cor,* heart] warm
and friendly; hearty —*n.* an aromatic, alcoholic
drink —**cor·di·al·i·ty** (kôr′jē al′ə tē, kôr jal′-)
n., pl. **-ties** —**cor′dial·ly** *adv.*
cord·ite (kôr′dīt) *n.* [< CORD: it is stringy] a
smokeless explosive made of nitroglycerin,
guncotton, etc.
cor·don (kôr′d′n) *n.* [see CORD] **1.** a line or circle of police, ships, etc. guarding an area **2.** a
cord, ribbon, or braid worn as a decoration
cor·do·van (kôr′də vən) *n.* [< *Córdoba,* Spain]
a soft, colored leather
cor·du·roy (kôr′də roi′) *n.* [prob. < CORD +
obs. *duroy,* coarse fabric] **1.** a heavy, ribbed
cotton fabric **2.** [*pl.*] trousers of this —*adj.* of,
or ribbed like, corduroy
core (kôr) *n.* [prob. < L. *cor,* heart] **1.** the central part of an apple, pear, etc. **2.** the central
part of anything **3.** the most important part —
vt. **cored, cor′ing** to remove the core of —**cor′er**
n.
co·re·spond·ent (kō′ri spän′dənt) *n.* [CO- +
RESPONDENT] *Law* a person charged with having committed adultery with the wife or husband from whom a divorce is sought
cork (kôrk) *n.* [< Sp. < L. *quercus,* oak] **1.** the
light, thick, elastic outer bark of an oak tree
(**cork oak**) **2.** a piece of cork; esp., a stopper
for a bottle, etc. **3.** any stopper —*vt.* to stop
with a cork
cork′screw′ *n.* a spiral-shaped device for pulling corks out of bottles
corm (kôrm) *n.* [< Gr. *kormos,* a log] the
fleshy, underground stem of certain plants, as
the gladiolus
cor·mo·rant (kôr′mə rənt) *n.* [< L. *corvus,*
raven + *marinus,* marine] a large, voracious,
diving bird with webbed toes

corn[1] (kôrn) *n.* [OE.] **1.** a small, hard seed, esp.
of a cereal grass; kernel **2.** a grain borne on
cobs enclosed in husks; maize **3.** [Brit.] grain
4. [Slang] ideas, humor, etc. considered old-
fashioned, trite, etc. —*vt.* to pickle (meat, etc.)
in brine
corn[2] (kôrn) *n.* [< L. *cornu,* a horn] a hard,
thick growth of skin, esp. on a toe
corn′cob′ (-käb′) *n.* **1.** the woody core of an
ear of corn **2.** a tobacco pipe (**corncob pipe**)
with a bowl made of such a core
cor·ne·a (kôr′nē ə) *n.* [< L. *cornu,* a horn] the
transparent outer coat of the eyeball —**cor′-
ne·al** *adj.*
cor·ner (kôr′nər) *n.* [< L. *cornu,* horn] **1.** the
point or place where lines or surfaces join and
form an angle **2.** the angle so formed **3.** the
angle at a street intersection **4.** a remote or secluded spot **5.** region; quarter **6.** an awkward
position hard to escape from **7.** a monopoly acquired on a stock or commodity to raise the
price —*vt.* **1.** to force into a corner (sense 6) **2.**
to get a monopoly on —*adj.* at, on, or for a corner —**cut corners** to cut down expenses, time,
etc.
cor′ner·stone′ (-stōn′) *n.* **1.** a stone laid in the
corner of a building, esp. at a ceremony for
beginning a building **2.** the basic part; foundation
cor·net (kôr net′) *n.* [< L. *cornu,* a horn] a
brass-wind musical instrument of the trumpet
class —**cor·net′ist, cor·net′tist** *n.*
corn′flow′er *n.* an annual plant of the composite family, with showy flowers
cor·nice (kôr′nis) *n.* [Fr. < Gr. *korōnis,*
wreath] a horizontal molding projecting along
the top of a wall, etc.
corn′meal′ *n.* meal made from maize
corn′starch′ (-stärch′) *n.* a starch made from
maize, used in cooking
cor·nu·co·pi·a (kôr′nə kō′pē ə, -nyōō-) *n.* [L.
cornu copiae, horn of plenty] **1.** a horn-shaped
container overflowing with fruits, flowers, and
grain **2.** an abundance
corn·y (kôr′nē) *adj.* **-i·er, -i·est** [Colloq.] unsophisticated, trite, etc. —**corn′i·ness** *n.*
co·rol·la (kə räl′ə, -rōl′-) *n.* [< L. *corona,*
crown] the petals of a flower
cor·ol·lar·y (kôr′ə ner′ē) *n., pl.* **-ies** [< L. *corol-
larium,* a gift] **1.** a proposition following from
one already proved **2.** an inference or deduction **3.** a normal result
co·ro·na (kə rō′nə) *n., pl.* **-nas, -nae** (-nē) [L.,
crown] **1.** a crown **2.** a ring of light around the
sun or moon; esp., the halo around the sun
during a total eclipse
cor·o·nar·y (kôr′ə ner′ē) *adj.* **1.** of or like a
crown **2.** of the arteries supplying blood to the
heart muscle —*n., pl.* **-ies** *same as* CORONARY
THROMBOSIS
coronary thrombosis the formation of an
obstructing clot in a coronary artery
cor·o·na·tion (kôr′ə nā′shən) *n.* the crowning
of a sovereign
cor·o·ner (kôr′ə nər) *n.* [ME., officer of the
crown] a public officer who must determine
the causes of any deaths not obviously due to
natural causes
cor·o·net (kôr′ə net′) *n.* [< OFr. *corone,*
crown] **1.** a small crown worn by nobility **2.** a
band of jewels, etc. for the head
corp., corpn. corporation
cor·po·ral[1] (kôr′pər əl) *n.* [< Fr. < It. < L.
caput, head] the lowest-ranking noncommissioned officer, just below a sergeant: abbrev.
Corp., Cpl

cor·po·ral[2] (kôr'pər əl) *adj.* [< L. *corpus*, body] of the body —**cor'po·ral·ly** *adv.*

cor·po·rate (kôr'pər it) *adj.* [< L. *corpus*, body] **1.** incorporated **2.** of a corporation **3.** shared; joint —**cor'po·rate·ly** *adv.*

cor·po·ra·tion (kôr'pə rā'shən) *n.* a group organized, as to operate a business, under a charter granting them as a body some of the legal rights, etc. of an individual

cor·po·re·al (kôr pôr'ē əl) *adj.* [< L. *corpus*, body] **1.** of the body **2.** material; physical — **cor·po're·al·ly** *adv.*

corps (kôr) *n., pl.* **corps** (kôrz) [< L. *corpus*, body] **1.** a body of people associated as in some work **2.** *Mil.* *a)* a specialized branch of the armed forces *b)* a tactical subdivision of an army

corpse (kôrps) *n.* [see CORPS] a dead body, esp. of a person

cor·pu·lence (kôr'pyoo ləns) *n.* [< L. *corpus*, body] fatness; obesity: also **cor'pu·len·cy** — **cor'pu·lent** *adj.*

cor·pus (kôr'pəs) *n., pl.* **-po·ra** (-pər ə) [L.] **1.** a body, esp. a dead one: used facetiously **2.** a collection, as of laws

cor·pus·cle (kôr'pəs 'l, -pus''l) *n.* [< L. *corpus*, body] any cell suspended in the blood, lymph, etc. of vertebrates

cor·ral (kə ral') *n.* [Sp. < L. *currere*, to run] an enclosure for horses, cattle, etc.; pen —*vt.* **-ralled', -ral'ling 1.** to drive into or confine in a corral **2.** to surround or capture

cor·rect (kə rekt') *vt.* [< L. *com-*, together + *regere*, lead straight] **1.** to make right **2.** to mark the errors of **3.** to scold or punish **4.** to cure or counteract (a defect) —*adj.* **1.** conforming to an established standard **2.** true; accurate; right —**cor·rec'tive** *adj., n.* —**cor·rect'ly** *adv.* —**cor·rect'ness** *n.* —**cor·rec'tor** *n.*

cor·rec·tion (kə rek'shən) *n.* **1.** a correcting or being corrected **2.** a change that corrects a mistake **3.** punishment to correct faults —**cor·rec'tion·al** *adj.*

cor·re·late (kôr'ə lāt') *vi., vt.* **-lat'ed, -lat'ing** [see COR- & RELATE] to be in or bring into mutual relation —**cor're·la'tion** *n.*

cor·rel·a·tive (kə rel'ə tiv) *adj.* **1.** having a mutual relationship **2.** *Gram.* expressing mutual relation and used in pairs, as *neither...nor* —*n.* a correlative word

cor·re·spond (kôr'ə spänd') *vi.* [< Fr. < L. *com-*, together + *respondere*, to answer] **1.** to be in agreement (*with* something); match **2.** to be similar or equal (*to*) **3.** to communicate by letters

cor're·spond'ence *n.* **1.** agreement; conformity **2.** similarity; analogy **3.** *a)* communication by exchange of letters *b)* the letters written or received

cor're·spond'ent *adj.* corresponding —*n.* **1.** a thing that corresponds **2.** one who exchanges letters with another **3.** one hired by a newspaper to send news regularly from a distant place

cor·ri·dor (kôr'ə dər, -dôr') *n.* [Fr. < L. *currere*, to run] a long passageway

cor·rob·o·rate (kə räb'ə rāt') *vt.* **-rat'ed, -rat'ing** [< L. *com-*, intens. + *robur*, strength] to confirm; support —**cor·rob'o·ra'tion** *n.* —**cor·rob'o·ra'tive** *adj.*

cor·rode (kə rōd') *vt., vi.* **-rod'ed, -rod'ing** [< L. *com-*, intens. + *rodere*, to gnaw] to eat into or wear away gradually, as by rusting

cor·ro·sion (-rō'zhən) *n.* a corroding or being corroded —**cor·ro'sive** (-siv) *adj., n.*

cor·ru·gate (kôr'ə gāt') *vt., vi.* **-gat'ed, -gat'ing** [< L. *com-*, intens. + *rugare*, to wrinkle] to

shape into parallel grooves and ridges; furrow —**cor'ru·ga'tion** *n.*

cor·rupt (kə rupt') *adj.* [< L. *com-*, together + *rumpere*, to break] **1.** evil; depraved **2.** taking bribes —*vt., vi.* to make or become corrupt — **cor·rupt'i·ble** *adj.*

cor·rup'tion *n.* **1.** a making, becoming, or being corrupt **2.** depravity **3.** bribery **4.** decay **5.** something corrupted

cor·sage (kôr säzh') *n.* [Fr.: see CORPS & -AGE] a small bouquet for a woman to wear, as at the waist or shoulder

cor·sair (kôr'ser) *n.* [< Fr. < L. *cursus*, COURSE] a pirate or pirate ship

cor·set (kôr'sit) *n.* [see CORPS] [*sometimes pl.*] a closefitting undergarment worn, chiefly by women, to give support to or shape the torso —*vt.* to dress in, or fit with, a corset

cor·tege, cor·tège (kôr tezh', -täzh') *n.* [Fr. < L. *cohors*] **1.** a group of attendants; retinue **2.** a ceremonial procession

cor·tex (kôr'teks) *n., pl.* **-ti·ces** (-tə sēz') [L., bark of a tree] **1.** the outer part of an internal organ; esp., the layer of gray matter over most of the brain **2.** the bark or rind of a plant — **cor'ti·cal** (-ti k'l) *adj.*

cor·ti·sone (kôrt'ə sōn', -zōn') *n.* [< CORTEX (of adrenals)] a hormone used in treating adrenal insufficiency, etc.

co·run·dum (kə run'dəm) *n.* [< Sans. *kuruvinda*, ruby] a hard mineral used for grinding and polishing

cor·us·cate (kôr'əs kāt') *vi.* **-cat'ed, -cat'ing** [< L. *coruscus*, vibrating] to glitter; sparkle — **cor'us·ca'tion** *n.*

cor·vette (kôr vet') *n.* [Fr.] a small, fast British warship for convoy duty

co·sign (kō'sīn') *vt., vi.* **1.** to sign (a promissory note) along with the maker, thus becoming responsible if the maker defaults **2.** to sign jointly —**co'sign'er** *n.*

cos·met·ic (käz met'ik) *adj.* [< Gr. *kosmos*, order] designed to beautify the complexion, hair, etc. —*n.* any cosmetic preparation

cos·mic (käz'mik) *adj.* [< Gr. *kosmos*, order] **1.** of the cosmos **2.** vast —**cos'mi·cal·ly** *adv.*

cosmic rays streams of highly penetrating charged particles that bombard the earth from outer space

cos·mog·o·ny (käz mäg'ə nē) *n.* [< Gr. *kosmos*, universe + *gignesthai*, produce] **1.** the origin of the universe **2.** *pl.* **-nies** a theory of this

cos·mol'o·gy (-mäl'ə jē) *n.* [< Gr. *kosmos*, universe + -LOGY] the study of the physical nature, form, etc. of the universe

cos·mo·naut (käz'mə nôt') *n.* [< Gr. *kosmos*, universe + *nautēs*, sailor] *same as* ASTRONAUT

cos·mo·pol·i·tan (käz'mə päl'ə t'n) *adj.* [< Gr. *kosmos*, world + *polis*, city] **1.** representative of all or many parts of the world **2.** at home in all countries or places —*n.* a cosmopolitan person

cos·mos (käz'məs, -mōs) *n.* [Gr. *kosmos*, universe] **1.** the universe considered as an orderly system **2.** any orderly system

Cos·sack (käs'ak, -ək) *n.* a member of a people of S Russia, famous as horsemen

cost (kôst) *vt.* **cost, cost'ing** [< L. *com-*, together + *stare*, to stand] **1.** to be obtained for (a certain price) **2.** to require the expenditure, loss, etc. of —*n.* **1.** the amount of money, labor, etc. required to get a thing; price **2.** loss; sacrifice —**at all costs** by any means required

cost·ly *adj.* **-li·er, -li·est 1.** costing much; dear **2.** magnificent; sumptuous —**cost'li·ness** *n.*

cos·tume (käs′tōōm) *n.* [Fr. < L. *consuetudo,* custom] **1.** *a)* style of dress as of a certain period *b)* a set of such clothes **2.** a set of outer clothes —*vt.* **-tumed, -tum·ing** to provide with a costume

co·sy (kō′zē) *adj.* **-si·er, -si·est** & *n., pl.* **-sies** *same as* COZY

cot[1] (kät) *n.* [< Hindi *khāt* < Sans.] a narrow bed, as of canvas on a folding frame

cot[2] (kät) *n.* [OE.] **1.** a small shelter **2.** a sheath, as for a hurt finger

cote (kōt) *n.* [see COT[2]] a small shelter for sheep, doves, etc.

co·te·rie (kōt′ər ē) *n.* [Fr. < OE. *cot,* hut] a group of friends with common interests

co·til·lion (kō til′yən, kə-) *n.* [< Fr.] **1.** a dance with intricate figures and changing of partners **2.** a formal ball

cot·tage (kät′ij) *n.* [< OFr. *cote* or ME. *cot,* hut] a small house, as a summer home

cottage cheese a soft, white cheese made from the curds of sour milk

cot·ter pin (kät′ər) a split pin fastened by spreading apart its ends after insertion

cot·ton (kät′'n) *n.* [< Ar. *quṭun*] **1.** the soft, white, fibrous substance around the seeds of certain mallow plants **2.** such a plant or plants **3.** thread or cloth of cotton —*adj.* of cotton — **cot′ton·y** *adj.*

cotton gin a machine for separating cotton fibers from the seeds

cot′ton·mouth′ *n. same as* WATER MOCCASIN

cot′ton·seed′ *n.* the seed of the cotton plant, yielding an edible oil

cot′ton·tail′ *n.* a common American rabbit with a short, fluffy tail

cot′ton·wood′ *n.* **1.** a poplar that has seeds covered with cottony hairs **2.** its wood

cot·y·le·don (kät′'l ēd′'n) *n.* [< Gr. *kotylē,* a cavity] a first leaf of the embryo of a flowering plant

couch (kouch) *n.* [< OFr. *couchier,* lie down] an article of furniture on which one may lie down; sofa —*vt.* **1.** to lay as on a couch **2.** to express in words —*vi.* to recline

cou·gar (kōō′gər) *n.* [< Fr. < SAmInd.] a large, tawny wildcat

cough (kôf) *vi.* [ME. *coughen*] to expel air suddenly and noisily from the lungs —*vt.* to expel by coughing —*n.* **1.** a coughing **2.** a condition of frequent coughing

could (kood) *v.* **1.** *pt. of* CAN[1] **2.** an auxiliary generally equivalent to *can,* expressing esp. a shade of doubt *[it could be so]*

could·n't (kood′'nt) could not

cou·lomb (kōō läm′) *n.* [< C. A. de *Coulomb* (1736–1806), Fr. physicist] the charge transported through a conductor by a current of one ampere flowing for one second

coun·cil (koun′s'l) *n.* [< L. *com-,* with + *calere,* to call] **1.** a group of people called together for consultation, advice, etc. **2.** an administrative or legislative body *[a city council]* —**coun′cil·man** (-mən) *n., pl.* **-men**

coun′ci·lor (-ər) *n.* a member of a council: also [Chiefly Brit.] **coun′cil·lor**

coun·sel (koun′s'l) *n.* [< L. *consilium*] **1.** a mutual exchange of ideas, etc.; discussion **2.** advice **3.** *a)* a lawyer or group of lawyers *b)* a consultant —*vt.* **-seled** or **-selled, -sel·ing** or **-sel·ling 1.** to give advice to **2.** to recommend (a plan, etc.) —*vi.* to give or take advice

coun′se·lor, coun′sel·lor (-ər) *n.* **1.** an adviser **2.** a lawyer

count[1] (kount) *vt.* [< L. *computare,* compute] **1.** to name or add up, unit by unit, so as to get a total **2.** to take account of; include **3.** to believe to be; consider —*vi.* **1.** to name numbers or add up items in order **2.** to be taken into account; have importance **3.** to have a specified value (often with *for*) **4.** to rely or depend (on or upon) —*n.* **1.** a counting, or adding up **2.** the total number **3.** a reckoning **4.** *Law* any of the charges in an indictment —**count out** to disregard; omit

count[2] (kount) *n.* [< L. *comes,* companion] a European nobleman equal in rank to an English earl

count′down′ *n.* **1.** the schedule of operations just before firing a rocket, etc. **2.** the counting off, in reverse order, of units of time in this schedule

coun·te·nance (koun′tə nəns) *n.* [< L. *continentia,* bearing] **1.** the facial expression **2.** the face; visage **3.** approval; support **4.** calm control —*vt.* **-nanced, -nanc·ing** to give support to; approve

count′er[1] *n.* **1.** a small piece of metal, wood, etc. for keeping score in some games **2.** an imitation coin **3.** a long table, board, etc. as in a store or kitchen, for displaying goods, serving, etc. **4.** one that counts

coun·ter[2] (koun′tər) *adv.* [< L. *contra,* against] in a contrary direction, manner, etc. —*adj.* opposed; contrary —*n.* **1.** the opposite **2.** a stiff leather piece around the heel of a shoe —*vt., vi.* **1.** to oppose (a person or thing) **2.** to say or do (something) in opposition

counter- [< L. *contra-,* against] *a combining form meaning:* **1.** opposite, contrary to *[counterclockwise]* **2.** in retaliation or return *[counterattack]* **3.** complementary, corresponding *[counterpart]*

coun′ter·act′ *vt.* to act against; neutralize the effect of —**coun′ter·ac′tion** *n.*

coun′ter·at·tack′ *n.* an attack made in opposition to another attack —*vt., vi.* to attack in opposition

coun′ter·bal′ance *n.* a weight, force, etc. that balances another —*vt.* **-anced, -anc·ing** to be a counterbalance to; offset

coun′ter·claim′ *n.* an opposing claim to offset another

coun′ter·clock′wise *adj., adv.* in a direction opposite to that in which the hands of a clock move

coun′ter·cul′ture *n.* the culture of those young people whose life style is opposed to the prevailing culture

coun′ter·es′pi·on·age′ *n.* actions to prevent or thwart enemy espionage

coun·ter·feit (koun′tər fit) *adj.* [< OFr. *contre-,* counter- + *faire,* to make] **1.** made in imitation of something genuine so as to defraud; forged *[counterfeit money]* **2.** pretended; sham —*n.* an imitation made to deceive —*vt., vi.* **1.** to make an imitation of (money, etc.) in order to defraud **2.** to pretend —**coun′ter·feit′er** *n.*

coun·ter·mand (koun′tər mand′) *vt.* [< L. *contra,* against + *mandare,* to command] **1.** to cancel (a command) **2.** to order back by a contrary order

coun′ter·pane′ (-pān′) *n.* [ult. < L. *culcita puncta,* embroidered quilt] a bedspread

coun′ter·part′ *n.* a person or thing that closely resembles another

coun′ter·point′ *n.* [< Fr. < It.: see COUNTER- & POINT, *n.*] the art of adding related but independent melodies to a basic melody, according to the rules of harmony

coun′ter·poise′ (-poiz′) *n.* [see COUNTER[2] & POISE] **1.** *same as* COUNTERBALANCE **2.** a state of balance —*vt.* **-poised'**, **-pois'ing** *same as* COUNTERBALANCE

coun·ter·rev'o·lu'tion *n.* **1.** a political movement to restore the system overthrown by a revolution **2.** a movement to combat revolutionary tendencies —**coun'ter·rev'o·lu'tion·ar'y** *adj., n.*

coun'ter·sign' *n.* **1.** a signature added to a previously signed document for confirmation **2.** a secret signal which must be given to a sentry in order to pass —*vt.* to confirm by signing —**coun'ter·sig'na·ture** *n.*

coun'ter·sink' *vt.* **-sunk'**, **-sink'ing 1.** to enlarge the top part of (a hole) to make the head of a bolt, screw, etc. fit into it **2.** to sink (a bolt, screw, etc.) into such a hole

coun'ter·ten'or *n.* **1.** the range of the highest male voice, above tenor **2.** a singer with this range

coun'ter·weigh' *vt. same as* COUNTERBALANCE —**coun'ter·weight'** *n.*

count·ess (koun'tis) *n.* the wife or widow of a count or earl

count'less (-lis) *adj.* too many to count

coun·tri·fied (kun'tri fīd') *adj.* **1.** rural; rustic **2.** having the appearance, etc. of country people Also sp. **coun'try·fied'**

coun·try (kun'trē) *n., pl.* **-tries** [< VL. *contrata*, that which is beyond] **1.** an area; region **2.** the whole territory or people of a nation **3.** the land of one's birth or citizenship **4.** land with farms and small towns; rural region —*adj.* rural; rustic

country club a club in the outskirts of a city, with a clubhouse, golf course, etc.

coun'try·man (-mən) *n., pl.* **-men 1.** a man who lives in the country **2.** a man of one's own country; compatriot

country music rural folk music, esp. of the Southern U.S.

coun'try·side' *n.* a rural region

coun·ty (koun'tē) *n., pl.* **-ties** [< L. *comitatus*, jurisdiction of a count] **1.** a small administrative district; esp., a subdivision of a State **2.** its people

coup (kōō) *n., pl.* **coups** (kōōz) [Fr. < L. *colaphus*, a blow] **1.** a sudden, successful move or action **2.** *same as* COUP D'ÉTAT

‡**coup de grâce** (kōō də gräs') [Fr., lit., stroke of mercy] the blow, shot, etc. that brings death to a sufferer

‡**coup d'é·tat** (dā tä') [Fr., lit., stroke of state] the sudden overthrow of a government

coupe (kōōp) *n.* [< Fr. *couper*, to cut] a closed, two-door automobile

cou·ple (kup''l) *n.* [< L. *copula*, a link] **1.** anything joining two things together; link **2.** two things or persons of the same sort; pair **3.** a man and woman who are engaged, married, etc. **4.** [Colloq.] a few —*vt.* **-pled**, **-pling** to link; connect —*vi.* **1.** to pair; unite **2.** to copulate

cou·plet (kup'lit) *n.* two successive, rhyming lines of poetry

cou'pling (-liŋ) *n.* **1.** a joining together **2.** a mechanical device for joining parts

cou·pon (kōō'pän, kyōō'-) *n.* [Fr. < *couper*, to cut] **1.** a detachable printed statement on a bond, specifying the interest due at a given time **2.** a certificate, ticket, etc. entitling one to cash, gifts, etc. or to be used in ordering goods or samples

cour·age (kur'ij) *n.* [< L. *cor*, heart] the quality of being brave; valor

cou·ra·geous (kə rā'jəs) *adj.* showing courage; brave —**cou·ra'geous·ly** *adv.*

cou·ri·er (koor'ē ər, kur'-) *n.* [< L. *currere*, to run] a messenger

course (kôrs) *n.* [< L. *currere*, to run] **1.** an onward movement; progress **2.** a way, path, or channel **3.** the direction taken **4.** a regular manner of procedure *[the law takes its course]* **5.** a series of like things in order **6.** a part of a meal served at one time **7.** *Educ. a)* a complete series of studies *b)* any of the studies — *vi.* **coursed**, **cours'ing** to run or race —**in due course** in the usual sequence (of events) —**in the course of** during —**of course 1.** naturally **2.** certainly

court (kôrt) *n.* [< L. *cohors*, enclosure] **1.** an uncovered space surrounded by buildings or walls **2.** a short street **3.** a playing area, as for tennis **4.** the palace, or the family and attendants, of a sovereign **5.** a sovereign and his councilors as a governing body **6.** any formal gathering held by a sovereign **7.** courtship **8.** *a)* a judge or judges *b)* a place where trials are held, investigations made, etc. *c)* a judicial assembly —*vt.* **1.** to pay attention to (a person) in order to get something **2.** to try to get the love of; woo **3.** to seek *[to court favor]* —*vi.* to woo —**pay court to** to court, as for favor or love

cour·te·ous (kur'tē əs) *adj.* [see COURT] polite and gracious —**cour'te·ous·ly** *adv.*

cour·te·san, cour·te·zan (kôr'tə zən, kur'-) *n.* [< Fr.] a prostitute

cour·te·sy (kur'tə sē) *n., pl.* **-sies 1.** courteous behavior **2.** a polite act or remark

court'house' *n.* **1.** a building in which law courts are held **2.** a building that houses the offices of a county government

cour·ti·er (kôr'tē ər, -tyər) *n.* an attendant at a royal court

court'ly *adj.* **-li·er**, **-li·est** suitable for a king's court; dignified; elegant —*adv.* in a courtly manner —**court'li·ness** *n.*

court'-mar'tial (-mär'shəl) *n., pl.* **courts'-mar'-tial 1.** a court of personnel in the armed forces to try offenses against military law **2.** a trial by a court-martial —*vt.* **-tialed** or **-tialled**, **-tial-ing** or **-tial·ling** to try by a court-martial

court'room' *n.* a room in which a law court is held

court'ship' *n.* the act, process, or period of courting, or wooing

court'yard' *n.* a space enclosed by walls, adjoining or in a large building

cous·in (kuz''n) *n.* [< L. *com-*, with + *soror*, sister] the son or daughter of one's uncle or aunt —**cous'in·ly** *adj., adv.*

cou·tu·rier (kōō toor'ē ā') *n.* [Fr.] a dress designer

cove (kōv) *n.* [< OE. *cofa*, cave, cell] **1.** a small bay or inlet **2.** a concave molding

cov·en (kuv'ən, kō'vən) *n.* [see CONVENE] a gathering or meeting, esp. of witches

cov·e·nant (kuv'ə nənt) *n.* [see CONVENE] **1.** a binding agreement made by two or more parties; compact **2.** a legal contract **3.** the promises made by God to man, as recorded in the Bible —*vt., vi.* to promise by or in a covenant

cov·er (kuv'ər) *vt.* [< L. *co-*, intens. + *operire*, to hide] **1.** to place something on or over **2.** to extend over **3.** to clothe **4.** to conceal; hide **5.** to protect as by shielding **6.** to protect financially *[to cover a loss]* **7.** to travel over **8.** to include or deal with **9.** to point a firearm at **10.** *Journalism* to get news, pictures, etc. of —*vi.* **1.** to spread over, as a liquid does **2.** to provide an excuse *(for)* —*n.* **1.** anything that covers, as a lid, top, etc. **2.** a shelter or a hiding place **3.** a tablecloth and a place setting **4.** *same as* COVER-UP —**take cover** to seek shelter —**under cover** in secrecy or concealment —**cov'er·er** *n.*

cov′er·age (-ij) *n.* the amount, extent, etc. covered by something

cov′er·all′ *n.* [*usually pl.*] a one-piece, outer garment, worn by mechanics, etc.

cover crop a crop, as clover, grown to keep soil fertile and uneroded

covered wagon a large wagon with an arched cover of canvas, used by pioneers

cov′er·ing *n.* anything that covers

cov·er·let (kuv′ər lit) *n.* [< OFr. *covrir,* COVER + *lit,* a bed] a bedspread

cov·ert (kuv′ərt) *adj.* [see COVER] concealed, hidden, or disguised —*n.* a shelter or hiding place, as for game —**cov′ert·ly** *adv.*

cov′er-up′ *n.* something used for hiding one's real activities, etc.

cov·et (kuv′it) *vt., vi.* [< L.: see CUPIDITY] to desire ardently (something that another has)

cov′et·ous (-əs) *adj.* greedy; avaricious —**cov′et·ous·ly** *adv.* —**cov′et·ous·ness** *n.*

cov·ey (kuv′ē) *n., pl.* **-eys** [< OFr. *cover,* to hatch] a small flock of birds, esp. partridges or quail

cow¹ (kou) *n.* [OE. *cu*] the mature female of domestic cattle, valued for its milk, or of certain other animals, as the buffalo or elephant

cow² (kou) *vt.* [< ON. *kūga,* to subdue] to make timid and submissive; overawe

cow·ard (kou′ərd) *n.* [ult. < L. *cauda,* tail] one who lacks courage or is shamefully afraid —*adj.* cowardly

cow′ard·ice (-is) *n.* lack of courage

cow′ard·ly *adj.* of or like a coward —*adv.* in the manner of a coward

cow′boy′ *n.* a ranch worker on horseback who herds cattle; also **cow′hand′**

cow·er (kou′ər) *vi.* [prob. < ON.] to crouch or huddle up, as from fear or cold; cringe

cow′hide′ *n.* 1. the hide of a cow 2. leather made from it 3. a leather whip

cowl (koul) *n.* [< L. *cucullus,* hood] 1. a monk's hood 2. a monk's cloak with a hood 3. the top front part of an automobile body, to which the windshield is attached —*vt.* to cover as with a cowl

cow′lick′ *n.* [< its looking as if licked by a cow] a tuft of hair that tends to stand up

cowl′ing *n.* [see COWL] a detachable metal covering as for an airplane engine

co′-work′er *n.* a fellow worker

cow-pox (kou′päks′) *n.* a disease of cows: its virus is used in vaccination against smallpox

cow·slip (kou′slip′) *n.* 1. a European primrose 2. same as MARSH MARIGOLD

cox (käks) *n., pl.* **cox′es** [Colloq.] a coxswain —*vt., vi.* to be coxswain for

cox·comb (käks′kōm′) *n.* [for *cock's comb*] a silly, vain, foppish fellow; dandy

cox·swain (käk′s'n, -swān′) *n.* [< *cock* (a small boat) + SWAIN] one who steers a boat or racing shell

coy (koi) *adj.* [< L. *quietus:* see QUIET] 1. bashful; shy 2. pretending to be innocent or shy —**coy′ly** *adv.* —**coy′ness** *n.*

coy·o·te (kī ōt′ē, kī′ōt) *n.* [< MexInd.] a small wolf of western N. American prairies

coz·en (kuz′'n) *vt., vi.* [< ME. *cosin,* fraud] to cheat, defraud, or deceive

co·zy (kō′zē) *adj.* **-zi·er, -zi·est** [< Scot. < ?] warm and comfortable; snug —*n., pl.* **-zies** a padded cover to keep a teapot hot —**co′zi·ly** *adv.* —**co′zi·ness** *n.*

CPA, C.P.A. Certified Public Accountant

Cpl, Cpl. Corporal

CPO, C.P.O. Chief Petty Officer

cps, c.p.s. cycles per second

Cr *Chem.* chromium

crab¹ (krab) *n.* [OE. *crabba*] a crustacean with four pairs of legs and a pair of pincers —*vi.* **crabbed, crab′bing** to catch crabs

crab² (krab) *n.* [akin ? to Scot. *scrabbe,* wild apple] 1. same as CRAB APPLE 2. a sour-tempered person —*vi.* **crabbed, crab′bing** [Colloq.] to complain —**crab′ber** *n.*

crab apple 1. a small, very sour apple 2. the tree it grows on: also **crab tree**

crab-bed (krab′id) *adj.* [< CRAB²] 1. peevish; cross 2. hard to read; illegible

crab′by *adj.* **-bi·er, -bi·est** [< CRAB²] peevish; cross —**crab′bi·ly** *adv.* —**crab′bi·ness** *n.*

crab grass a coarse, weedy grass

crack (krak) *vi.* [< OE. *cracian,* resound] 1. to make a sudden, sharp breaking noise 2. to break or split, usually without complete separation of parts 3. to rasp, as the voice 4. [Colloq.] to break down; collapse [to *crack* under the strain] —*vt.* 1. to cause to make a sharp, sudden noise 2. to cause to break or split 3. to break down (petroleum) by heat and pressure into gasoline, etc. 4. [Colloq.] to hit hard 5. to manage to solve 6. [Colloq.] to break open or into 7. [Slang] to make (a joke) —*n.* 1. a sudden, sharp noise 2. a break, usually partial 3. a chink; fissure 4. an erratic shift of vocal tone 5. [Colloq.] a sudden, sharp blow 6. [Colloq.] an attempt; try 7. [Slang] a joke —*adj.* [Colloq.] excelling; first-rate —**crack down (on)** to become strict (with) —**cracked up to be** [Colloq.] believed to be —**crack up 1.** to crash 2. [Colloq.] to break down physically or mentally

cracked (krakt) *adj.* 1. broken without complete separation into parts 2. harsh [a *cracked* voice] 3. [Colloq.] crazy

crack′er *n.* 1. one that cracks 2. a firecracker 3. a thin, crisp wafer

crack′er·jack′ *adj.* [Slang] excellent —*n.* [Slang] an excellent person or thing

crack·le (krak″l) *vi.* **-led, -ling** [< CRACK] to make slight, sharp, popping sounds —*vt.* to break with crackling sounds —*n.* crackling sounds

crack′pot′ *n.* [Colloq.] an eccentric person —*adj.* [Colloq.] eccentric

crack′up′ *n.* 1. a crash, esp. of an aircraft 2. [Colloq.] a mental or physical collapse

-cracy [< Gr. *kratos,* rule] *a combining form meaning* a (specified) type of government [autocracy]

cra·dle (krā′d'l) *n.* [OE. *cradol*] a baby's small bed, usually on rockers 2. infancy 3. the place of a thing's beginning 4. anything like a cradle —*vt.* **-dled, -dling** to place, rock, or hold in or as in a cradle

craft (kraft) *n.* [OE. *cræft,* power] 1. a special skill or art 2. a skilled trade, or its members 3. guile; slyness 4. *pl.* **craft** a boat, ship, or aircraft —*vt.* to make with skill

crafts·man (krafts′mən) *n., pl.* **-men** a skilled workman; artisan —**crafts′man·ship′** *n.*

craft′y *adj.* **-i·er, -i·est** sly; cunning —**craft′i·ly** *adv.* —**craft′i·ness** *n.*

crag (krag) *n.* [< Celt.] a steep rock projecting from a rock mass —**crag′gy** *adj.*

cram (kram) *vt.* **crammed, cram′ming** [OE. *crammian,* to stuff] 1. to pack full or too full 2. to stuff; force 3. to feed to excess —*vi.* 1. to eat too much or too quickly 2. to study a subject in a hurried, intensive way, for an examination —**cram′mer** *n.*

cramp¹ (kramp) *n.* [< OFr. *crampe,* bent] 1. a sudden, painful contraction of muscles, as from chill or strain 2. [*usually pl.*] abdominal spasms and pain —*vt.* to cause a cramp in

cramp² (kramp) *n.* [MDu. *krampe*, lit., bent in] anything that confines or hampers —*vt.* **1.** to confine or hamper **2.** to turn (the wheels as of a car) sharply

cran·ber·ry (kran′ber′ē, -bər ē) *n., pl.* **-ries** [< Du. *kranebere*] **1.** a firm, sour, edible, red berry of an evergreen shrub **2.** this shrub

crane (krān) *n.* [OE. *cran*] **1.** a large wading bird with very long legs and neck **2.** a machine for lifting and moving heavy weights, using a movable projecting arm or a horizontal traveling beam —*vt., vi.* **craned, cran′ing 1.** to raise or move as by a crane **2.** to stretch (the neck)

cra·ni·um (krā′nē əm) *n., pl.* **-ni·ums, -ni·a** (-ə) [< Gr. *kranion*] the skull, esp. the part containing the brain —**cra′ni·al** *adj.*

crank (kraŋk) *n.* [< OE. *cranc-*, as in *crancstæf*, yarn comb] **1.** a handle or arm at right angles to the shaft of a machine, to transmit motion **2.** [Colloq.] an eccentric or irritable person —*vt.* to start or operate by a crank —*vi.* to turn a crank

crank′case′ *n.* the metal casing of the crankshaft of an internal-combustion engine

crank′shaft′ *n.* a shaft having one or more cranks for transmitting or changing motion

crank′y *adj.* **-i·er, -i·est 1.** out of order **2.** irritable; cross **3.** eccentric

cran·ny (kran′ē) *n., pl.* **-nies** [< LL. *crena*, a notch] a crevice; crack

crap (krap) *n.* [< OFr., ordure] [Vulgar Slang] **1.** nonsense **2.** trash; junk —**crap′py** *adj.* **-pi·er, -pi·est**

crape (krāp) *n.* crepe; esp., black crepe as a sign of mourning

craps (kraps) *n.pl.* [*with sing. v.*] [Fr.] a gambling game played with two dice: also called **crap′shoot′ing** —**crap′shoot′er** *n.*

crash¹ (krash) *vi.* [prob. echoic] **1.** to fall, collide, or break with a loud, smashing noise **2.** to collapse; fail —*vt.* **1.** to cause to crash **2.** to force with a crashing noise (with *in, out,* etc.) **3.** [Colloq.] to get into (a party, etc.) without an invitation —*n.* **1.** a loud, smashing noise **2.** a crashing **3.** a sudden collapse —*adj.* [Colloq.] using all possible resources and effort

crash² (krash) *n.* [prob. < Russ. *krashenina,* linen] a coarse cloth of loose weave

crass (kras) *adj.* [L. *crassus,* gross] grossly stupid or dull —**crass′ly** *adv.*

-crat [< Gr. *kratos,* rule] *a combining form meaning* member or supporter of (a specified kind of) government or ruling body [*democrat, aristocrat*]

crate (krāt) *n.* [< L. *cratis,* wickerwork] a packing case made of slats of wood —*vt.* **crat′ed, crat′ing** to pack in a crate

cra·ter (krāt′ər) *n.* [< Gr. *kratēr,* bowl] **1.** a bowl-shaped cavity, as at the mouth of a volcano or on the moon **2.** a pit, as one made by an exploding bomb

cra·vat (krə vat′) *n.* [< Fr. *Cravate,* Croatian: from scarves worn by Croatian soldiers] **1.** a neckerchief **2.** a necktie

crave (krāv) *vt.* **craved, crav′ing** [OE. *crafian*] **1.** to ask for earnestly; beg **2.** to long for eagerly **3.** to need greatly —*vi.* to have an eager longing (*for*)

cra·ven (krā′vən) *adj.* [< L. *crepare,* to creak] very cowardly —*n.* a thorough coward

crav·ing (krā′viŋ) *n.* an intense desire or longing, as for affection or a food

craw (krô) *n.* [ME. *craue*] **1.** the crop of a bird **2.** the stomach of any animal

craw·fish (krô′fish′) *n., pl.:* see FISH *same as* CRAYFISH

crawl (krôl) *vi.* [< ON. *krafla*] **1.** to move slowly by drawing the body along the ground, like a worm **2.** to go on hands and knees **3.** to move slowly **4.** to swarm (*with* crawling things) **5.** to feel as if insects were crawling on one —*n.* **1.** slow movement **2.** an overarm swimming stroke

cray·fish (krā′fish′) *n., pl.:* see FISH [< OHG.] **1.** a freshwater crustacean somewhat like a little lobster **2.** *same as* SPINY LOBSTER

cray·on (krā′ən, -än′) *n.* [Fr. < *craie,* chalk] **1.** a small stick of chalk or colored wax, etc. used for drawing or writing **2.** a crayon drawing —*vt.* to draw with crayons

craze (krāz) *vt., vi.* **crazed, craz′ing** [ME. *crasen,* to crack < Scand.] to make or become insane —*n.* **1.** a mania **2.** a fad

cra·zy (krā′zē) *adj.* **-zi·er, -zi·est** [< CRAZE] **1.** mentally unbalanced **2.** [Colloq.] *a*) foolish or fantastic *b*) enthusiastic **3.** [Slang] fine; excellent —*n., pl.* **-zies** [Slang] a crazy person —**cra′zi·ly** *adv.* —**cra′zi·ness** *n.*

crazy bone *same as* FUNNY BONE

crazy quilt a patchwork quilt with no regular design

creak (krēk) *vi., vt.* [see CROAK] to make, or move with, a harsh, squeaking sound —*n.* such a sound —**creak′i·ly** *adv.* —**creak′i·ness** *n.* —**creak′y** *adj.* **-i·er, -i·est**

cream (krēm) *n.* [< Gr. *chrisma,* oil] **1.** the oily, yellowish part of milk **2.** a creamy cosmetic or emulsion **3.** the best part **4.** a yellowish white —*adj.* of, with, or like cream —*vt.* **1.** to add cream to **2.** to cook with cream **3.** to make creamy as by beating **4.** [Slang] to defeat soundly —**cream** of creamed purée of — **cream′i·ness** *n.* —**cream′y** *adj.* **-i·er, -i·est**

cream cheese a soft, white cheese made of cream or of milk enriched with cream

cream′er *n.* a small pitcher for cream

cream′er·y (-ər ē) *n., pl.* **-ies** a place where dairy products are processed or sold

crease (krēs) *n.* [see CREST] **1.** a line made by folding and pressing **2.** a fold; wrinkle —*vt.* **creased, creas′ing** to make a crease in —*vi.* to become creased

cre·ate (krē āt′) *vt.* **-at′ed, -at′ing** [< L. *creare*] **1.** to bring into being; originate, design, invent, etc. **2.** to bring about; cause

cre·a·tion (krē ā′shən) *n.* **1.** a creating or being created **2.** the universe **3.** anything created

cre·a·tive (-āt′iv) *adj.* **1.** creating or able to create **2.** inventive —**cre·a·tiv·i·ty** (krē′ā tiv′ə tē) *n.*

cre·a·tor (-āt′ər) *n.* **1.** one who creates **2.** [C-] God

crea·ture (krē′chər) *n.* [< L. *creatura*] **1.** a living being, animal or human **2.** one completely dominated by another

crèche (kresh, krāsh) *n.* [Fr.] **1.** a display representing the stable scene of Jesus' birth **2.** [Chiefly Brit.] a day nursery

cre·dence (krēd′ns) *n.* [< L. *credere,* believe] belief, esp. in another's testimony

cre·den·tial (kri den′shəl) *n.* [see prec.] [*usually pl.*] a paper showing one's right to a certain position or authority

cre·den·za (kri den′zə) *n.* [It.] a type of buffet, or sideboard

cred·i·ble (kred′ə b'l) *adj.* [< L. *credere,* believe] that can be believed; reliable —**cred′i·bil′i·ty** *n.* —**cred′i·bly** *adv.*

cred·it (kred′it) *n.* [< L. *credere,* believe] **1.** belief; confidence **2.** good reputation **3.** praise or approval **4.** a person or thing bringing approval **5.** acknowledgment of work done or help given **6.** the amount in a bank account **7.**

the entry in an account of payment on a debt **8.** *a)* trust in one's ability to meet payments *b)* the time allowed for payment **9.** *Éduc.* a completed unit of study —*vt.* **1.** to believe; trust **2.** to give credit to or praise for **3.** to give credit as in a bank account —**on credit** with the agreement to pay later

cred·it·a·ble *adj.* **1.** praiseworthy **2.** ascribable (*to*) —**cred′it·a·bly** *adv.*

credit card a card entitling one to charge bills at certain places

cred·i·tor (kred′it ər) *n.* a person who extends credit or to whom money is owed

credit union a cooperative association for pooling savings of members and making low-interest loans to them

cre·do (krē′dō, krā′dō) *n., pl.* **-dos** [L., I believe] *same as* CREED

cred·u·lous (krej′oo ləs) *adj.* [< L. *credere,* believe] tending to believe too readily —**cre·du·li·ty** (krə dōō′lə tē, -dyōō′-) *n.*

creed (krēd) *n.* [< L. *credo,* lit., I believe] **1.** a brief statement of religious belief, esp. one accepted by a church **2.** any statement of belief, principles, or the like

creek (krēk, krik) *n.* [< ON. *-kriki,* a winding] a small stream, somewhat larger than a brook

creel (krēl) *n.* [< OFr. *grail:* see GRIDDLE] a wicker basket for fishermen to carry fish in

creep (krēp) *vi.* **crept, creep′ing** [OE. *creopan*] **1.** to move with the body close to the ground, as on hands and knees **2.** to move slowly or stealthily **3.** to grow along the ground or a wall, as some plants —*n.* [Slang] an annoying person —**make one's flesh creep** to make one feel fear, disgust, etc. —**the creeps** [Colloq.] a feeling of fear, repugnance, etc. —**creep′er** *n.*

creep′y *adj.* **-i·er, -i·est** having or causing a feeling of fear or repugnance

cre·mate (krē′māt, kri māt′) *vt.* **-mat·ed, -mat·ing** [< L. *cremare,* to burn] to burn (a dead body) to ashes —**cre·ma′tion** *n.*

cre·ma·to·ry (krē′mə tôr′ē) *n., pl.* **-ries** a furnace for cremating: also **cre′ma·to′ri·um** (-ē əm), *pl.* **-ri·ums, -ri·a** (-ə) —*adj.* of or for cremation: also **cre′ma·to′ri·al**

crème de menthe (krem′də mänt′, menth′) [Fr.] a sweet, green, mint-flavored liqueur

Cre·ole, cre·ole (krē′ōl) *n.* [< Fr. < Sp. < L. *creare,* to create] **1.** a descendant of French settlers in Louisiana or of Spanish settlers in the Gulf States **2.** a person of mixed Creole and Negro descent —*adj.* **1.** of Creoles **2.** [*usually* c-] made with tomatoes, peppers, onions, etc.

cre·o·sote (krē′ə sōt′) *n.* [< Gr. *kreas,* flesh + *sōzein,* save] a pungent, oily liquid distilled from wood tar or coal tar: used as an antiseptic and a wood preservative

crepe, crêpe (krāp) *n.* [Fr. < L. *crispus,* curly] **1.** a thin, crinkled cloth, as of silk or wool **2.** *same as* CRAPE **3.** thin paper crinkled like crepe: also **crepe paper 4.** soft, wrinkled rubber: also **crepe rubber 5.** (*also* krep) a very thin pancake, rolled and filled

crept (krept) *pt. & pp. of* CREEP

cre·scen·do (krə shen′dō) *adj., adv.* [It. < L.: see CRESCENT] *Music* gradually getting louder —*n., pl.* **-dos** a gradual increase in loudness

cres·cent (kres′'nt) *n.* [< L. *crescere,* grow] **1.** the shape of the moon in its first or last quarter **2.** anything shaped like this —*adj.* shaped like a crescent

cress (kres) *n.* [OE. *cressa*] a plant, as watercress, with pungent leaves used in salads

crest (krest) *n.* [< L. *crista*] **1.** a comb, tuft, etc. on the head of some animals or birds **2.** a heraldic device, as on note paper, etc. **3.** the top; ridge **4.** the highest point or level —*vi.* to form or reach a crest —**crest′ed** *adj.*

crest·fall·en (krest′fôl′ən) *adj.* **1.** with bowed head **2.** dejected or humbled

cre·tin (krēt′'n) *n.* [< Fr. *chrétien,* Christian, hence human being] a person suffering from cretinism —**cre′tin·ous** *adj.*

cre′tin·ism *n.* a congenital thyroid deficiency with resulting deformity and idiocy

cre·tonne (krē′tän, kri tän′) *n.* [< Fr. < *Creton,* village in Normandy] a heavy, printed cotton or linen cloth, used as for curtains

cre·vasse (kri vas′) *n.* [Fr.: see CREVICE] a deep crack or fissure, esp. in a glacier

crev·ice (krev′is) *n.* [< OFr. < L. *crepare,* to creak] a narrow opening caused by a crack or split; fissure; cleft —**crev′iced** *adj.*

crew¹ (krōō) *n.* [< L. *crescere,* to grow] a group of people working together [*a ship's crew*]

crew² (krōō) *alt. pt. of* CROW² (sense 1)

crew·el (krōō′əl) *n.* [LME. *crule*] a fine worsted yarn used in embroidery (**crew′el·work′**)

crib (krib) *n.* [OE.] **1.** a rack or box for fodder; manger **2.** a small bed with high sides, for a baby **3.** an enclosure for storing grain **4.** a structure anchored under water, serving as a water intake, pier, etc. **5.** [Colloq.] a translation or other aid used, often dishonestly, in doing schoolwork —*vt.* **cribbed, crib′bing 1.** to confine **2.** to provide with a crib **3.** [Colloq.] to plagiarize —*vi.* [Colloq.] to use a crib for schoolwork —**crib′ber** *n.*

crib·bage (krib′ij) *n.* [< CRIB + -AGE] a card game in which the object is to form combinations that count for points

crick¹ (krik) *n.* [prob. ON.] a painful muscle cramp in the neck or back

crick² (krik) *n.* [Dial.] *same as* CREEK

crick·et¹ (krik′it) *n.* [< OFr. *criquer,* creak] a leaping insect related to the grasshoppers

crick·et² (krik′it) *n.* [prob. MDu. *cricke,* stick] **1.** an outdoor game played by two teams of eleven players, using a ball, bats, and wickets **2.** [Colloq.] fair play

cried (krīd) *pt. & pp. of* CRY

cri·er (krī′ər) *n.* **1.** one who cries **2.** a person who shouts out news, proclamations, etc.

crime (krīm) *n.* [< L. *crimen,* offense] **1.** an act committed or omitted in violation of a law **2.** a sin **3.** criminal acts, collectively

crim·i·nal (krim′ə n'l) *adj.* **1.** having the nature of crime **2.** relating to or guilty of crime —*n.* a person guilty of a crime —**crim′i·nal′i·ty** *n., pl.* **-ties** —**crim′i·nal·ly** *adv.*

crim·i·nol·o·gy (krim′ə näl′ə jē) *n.* the scientific study of crime and criminals —**crim′i·nol′o·gist** *n.*

crimp (krimp) *vt.* [< MDu. *crimpen,* to wrinkle] **1.** to press into narrow folds; pleat **2.** to curl (hair) **3.** to pinch together —*n.* **1.** a crimping **2.** anything crimped —**put a crimp in** [Colloq.] to hinder

crim·son (krim′z'n) *n.* [< Ar. *qirmiz*] deep red —*adj.* **1.** deep-red **2.** bloody —*vt., vi.* to make or become crimson

cringe (krinj) *vi.* **cringed, cring′ing** [< OE. *crin-gan,* to fall (in battle)] **1.** to draw back; crouch, as when afraid; cower **2.** to act servilely; fawn

crin·kle (kriŋ′k'l) *vi., vt.* **-kled, -kling** [see CRINGE] **1.** to wrinkle; ripple **2.** to rustle, as paper when crushed —*n.* a wrinkle —**crin′kly** *adj.* **-kli·er, -kli·est**

crin·o·line (krin′'l in) *n.* [Fr. < L. *crinis,* hair + *linum,* thread] **1.** a coarse, stiff cloth used as a lining in garments **2.** *same as* HOOP SKIRT

crip·ple (krip′'l) *n.* [< OE. *creopan*, to creep] one who is lame or otherwise disabled —*vt.* **-pled, -pling** to lame or disable —**crip′pler** *n.*

cri·sis (krī′sis) *n.*, *pl.* **-ses** (-sēz) [< Gr. *krinein*, to separate] **1.** the turning point in a disease, when it becomes clear whether the patient will recover or die **2.** any turning point **3.** a time of great trouble

crisp (krisp) *adj.* [< L. *crispus*, curly] **1.** brittle; easily crumbled **2.** fresh and firm **3.** fresh and tidy **4.** sharp and clear **5.** lively **6.** bracing *[crisp* air] **7.** curly and wiry Also **crisp′y** —*vt.*, *vi.* to make or become crisp —**crisp′ly** *adv.* —**crisp′ness** *n.*

criss·cross (kris′krôs′) *n.* [ME. *Christcros*, Christ's cross] a mark or pattern made of crossed lines —*adj.* marked by crossings —*vt.* to mark with crossing lines —*vi.* to move crosswise —*adv.* **1.** crosswise **2.** awry

cri·ter·i·on (krī tir′ē ən) *n.*, *pl.* **-i·a** (-ə), **-i·ons** [< Gr. *kritēs*, judge] a standard, rule, or test by which something can be judged

crit·ic (krit′ik) *n.* [< Gr. *krinein*, discern] **1.** one who writes judgments of books, plays, music, etc. professionally **2.** one who finds fault

crit′i·cal (-i k'l) *adj.* **1.** tending to find fault **2.** of critics or criticism **3.** of or forming a crisis; crucial —**crit′i·cal·ly** *adv.*

crit·i·cism (krit′ə siz′m) *n.* **1.** the act, art, or principles of criticizing, esp. literary or artistic work **2.** a review, article, etc. expressing this **3.** faultfinding

crit·i·cize (krit′ə sīz′) *vi.*, *vt.* **-cized′, -ciz′ing 1.** to analyze and judge as a critic **2.** to find fault (with)

cri·tique (kri tēk′) *n.* [Fr.] a critical analysis or evaluation as of a literary work

croak (krōk) *vi.* [echoic] **1.** to make a deep, hoarse sound *[frogs croak]* **2.** [Slang] to die —*vt.* to utter in deep, hoarse tones —*n.* a deep, hoarse sound

cro·chet (krō shā′) *n.* [Fr., small hook] needlework in which loops are made with a hooked needle —*vi.*, *vt.* **-cheted** (-shād′), **-chet′ing** to do, or make by, crochet

crock (kräk) *n.* [OE. *crocca*] an earthenware pot or jar

crock·er·y (kräk′ər ē) *n.* [< CROCK] earthenware pots, jars, dishes, etc.

croc·o·dile (kräk′ə dīl′) *n.* [< Gr. ? *krokē*, pebble + *drilos*, worm] a large, lizardlike reptile of tropical streams, having a long, narrow head with massive jaws

cro·cus (krō′kəs) *n.*, *pl.* **-cus·es, -ci** (-sī) [< Gr. *krokos*, saffron] a spring-blooming plant related to the iris, with a yellow, purple, or white flower

crois·sant (krə sänt′) *n.* [Fr., lit., CRESCENT] a roll in the shape of a crescent

Cro-Ma·gnon (krō mag′nən) *adj.* [< *Cro-Magnon* cave in France] of a prehistoric type of tall man on the European continent

crone (krōn) *n.* [prob. < MDu. *kronje*, old ewe] an ugly, withered old woman; hag

cro·ny (krō′nē) *n.*, *pl.* **-nies** [< ? Gr. *chronios*, long-continued] a close companion

crook (krook) *n.* [< ON. *krōkr*, hook] **1.** a hooked or curved staff, crosier, etc. **2.** a bend or curve **3.** [Colloq.] a swindler; thief —*vt.*, *vi.*

crooked (krookt), **crook′ing** to bend or curve

crook·ed (krookt; *for 2 & 3* krook′id) *adj.* **1.** having a crook or hook **2.** not straight; bent **3.** dishonest —**crook′ed·ly** *adv.* —**crook′ed·ness** *n.*

crook′neck′ *n.* a squash with a long, curved neck

croon (krōōn) *vi.*, *vt.* [< ME.] **1.** to sing in a low, gentle tone **2.** to sing (popular songs) in a sentimental manner —*n.* a low, gentle singing —**croon′er** *n.*

crop (kräp) *n.* [OE. *croppa*, cluster] **1.** a saclike part of a bird's gullet, in which food is stored before digestion **2.** any agricultural product, growing or harvested **3.** the yield of any product in one season or place **4.** a group **5.** the handle of a whip **6.** a short whip with a looped lash **7.** hair cut close to the head —*vt.* **cropped, crop′ping 1.** to cut or bite off the tops or ends of **2.** to reap **3.** to cut short —**crop out** (or **up**) to appear unexpectedly

crop′per *n.* **1.** one that crops **2.** a sharecropper —**come a cropper** [Colloq.] **1.** to fall heavily **2.** to fail

crop rotation a system of growing successive crops, as to prevent soil depletion

cro·quet (krō kā′) *n.* [Fr.: see CROTCHET] an outdoor game in which the players use mallets to drive a wooden ball through hoops in the ground

cro·quette (krō ket′) *n.* [Fr. < *croquer*, to crunch] a small mass of chopped meat, fish, etc., coated with crumbs and fried in deep fat

cro·sier (krō′zhər) *n.* [< OFr. *croce*] the staff of a bishop or abbot

cross (krôs) *n.* [< L. *crux*] **1.** an upright post with another across it, on which criminals were once executed **2.** [*often* C-] a representation of this, as a symbol of the crucifixion of Jesus, and hence of Christianity **3.** any trouble or affliction **4.** any mark made by intersecting lines **5.** a crossing of varieties or breeds —*vt.*, *vi.* **1.** to make the sign of the cross (upon) **2.** to place or lie across or crosswise **3.** to intersect **4.** to draw lines across (something) **5.** to go or extend across (something) **6.** to oppose **7.** to interbreed; hybridize **8.** to meet and pass (each other) —*adj.* **1.** lying or passing across **2.** contrary; opposed **3.** cranky; irritable **4.** of mixed variety or breed —**cross off** (or **out**) to cancel as by drawing lines across —**cross one's mind** to come to mind briefly

cross′bar′ *n.* a bar, line, or stripe placed crosswise

cross′beam′ *n.* a beam placed across another or from one wall to another

cross′bones′ *n.* a picture of two bones placed across each other: see SKULL AND CROSSBONES

cross′bow′ (-bō′) *n.* a medieval bow set transversely on a notched wooden stock

cross′breed′ *vt.*, *vi.* **-bred**, **-breed′ing** *same as* HYBRIDIZE —*n. same as* HYBRID

cross′-coun′try *adj.*, *adv.* across open country or fields, not by roads

cross′cut′ *adj.* **1.** used to cut across *[a crosscut* saw] **2.** cut across —*n.* a cut across —*vt.*, *vi.* **-cut′, -cut′ting** to cut across

cross′-ex·am′ine *vt.*, *vi.* **-ined, -in·ing 1.** to question closely **2.** *Law* to question (a witness already questioned by the opposing side) to determine the validity of his testimony —**cross′-ex·am′i·na′tion** *n.*

cross′-eye′ *n.* an abnormal condition in which the eyes are turned toward each other —**cross′-eyed′** *adj.*

cross′hatch′ *vt.*, *vi.* to shade with two sets of crossing parallel lines

cross′ing *n.* **1.** the act of passing across, thwarting, etc. **2.** an intersection, as of lines, streets, etc. **3.** a place where a street, river, etc. may be crossed

cross′piece′ *n.* a piece lying across another

cross′-pol′li·nate′ *vt.*, *vi.* **-nat′ed, -nat′ing** to transfer pollen from the anther of (one flower) to the stigma of (another)

cross′-pur′pose *n.* a contrary purpose —at **cross-purposes** having a misunderstanding as to each other's purposes

cross′-ref′er·ence *n.* a reference from one part of a book, index, etc. to another part

cross′road′ *n.* 1. a road that crosses another 2. [*usually pl.*] the place where roads intersect

cross section 1. *a*) a cutting through something *b*) a piece so cut off, or a representation of this 2. a representative part of a whole

cross′-stitch′ *n.* 1. a stitch made by crossing two stitches in the form of an X 2. needlework made with this stitch —*vt., vi.* to sew or embroider with this stitch

cross′-town′ *adj.* going across the main avenues of a city [a *cross-town* bus]

cross′walk′ *n.* a lane marked off for pedestrians to use in crossing a street

cross′wise′ (-wīz′) *adv.* so as to cross; across: also **cross′ways′** (-wāz′)

cross′word′ puzzle an arrangement of numbered squares to be filled in with words whose definitions are given as clues

crotch (kräch) *n.* [OE. *crycce,* a staff] 1. a pole forked on top 2. a place where two branches fork from a tree 3. the place where the legs fork from the human body

crotch·et (kräch′it) *n.* [< OFr. *croc,* a hook] a peculiar whim —**crotch′et·y** *adj.*

crouch (krouch) *vi.* [< OFr. *croc,* a hook] 1. to stoop low 2. to cringe —*n.* a crouching

croup (krōōp) *n.* [< obs. *croup,* speak hoarsely] an inflammation of the respiratory passages, with labored breathing and hoarse coughing — **croup′y** *adj.*

crou·pi·er (krōō′pē ā′, -ər) *n.* [Fr.] a person in charge of a gambling table

crou·ton (krōō′tän, krōō tän′) *n.* [< Fr.: see CRUST] any of the small pieces of toasted bread often served in soup, salads, etc.

crow′ (krō) *n.* [OE. *crawa*] a large, glossy-black bird with a harsh call —**as the crow flies** in a direct line —**eat crow** [Colloq.] to admit an error, recant, etc.

crow² (krō) *vi.* **crowed** or for 1 **crew** (krōō), **crowed, crow′ing** [OE. *crawan*] 1. to make the shrill cry of a rooster 2. to boast in triumph 3. to make a sound of pleasure —*n.* a crowing sound

crow·bar (krō′bär′) *n.* a long, metal bar used as a lever for prying, etc.

crowd (kroud) *vi.* [OE. *crudan*] 1. to push one's way (*into*) 2. to throng —*vt.* 1. to press or push 2. to fill too full; cram —*n.* 1. a large number of people or things grouped closely 2. [Colloq.] a set; clique

crow′foot′ *n., pl.* **-foots′** a plant related to the buttercup, with leaves resembling a crow's foot

crown (kroun) *n.* [< Gr. *korōnē,* wreath] 1. a wreath worn on the head in victory 2. a reward; honor 3. the head covering of a monarch 4. [*often* C-] *a*) the power of a monarch *b*) the monarch 5. the top part, as of the head, a hat, etc. 6. a British coin equal to five shillings 7. the highest quality, point, state, etc. of anything 8. *a*) the part of a tooth projecting beyond the gum line *b*) an artificial substitute for this —*vt.* 1. to put a crown on 2. to make (a person) a monarch 3. to honor or reward 4. to be at the top of 5. to be the highest part of 6. to put the finishing touch on

crown prince the male heir apparent to a throne

crow's-foot (krōz′foot′) *n., pl.* **-feet′** any of the wrinkles that often develop at the outer corners of the eyes: *usually used in pl.*

crow′s′-nest′ (-nest′) *n.* a lookout platform high on a ship's mast

cru·cial (krōō′shəl) *adj.* [Fr. < L. *crux,* a cross] 1. decisive; critical 2. very trying

cru·ci·ble (krōō′sə b'l) *n.* [< ML. *crucibulum,* lamp] 1. a heat-resistant container for melting ores, metals, etc. 2. a severe test

cru·ci·fix (krōō′sə fiks′) *n.* [< L. *crux,* a cross + *figere,* fasten] a representation of a cross with Jesus crucified on it

cru′ci·fix′ion (-fik′shən) *n.* 1. a crucifying 2. [C-] the crucifying of Jesus, or a representation of this

cru′ci·fy′ (-fī′) *vt.* **-fied′, -fy′ing** [see CRUCIFIX] 1. to execute by nailing or binding to a cross and leaving to die of exposure 2. to torment; torture

crude (krōōd) *adj.* [L. *crudus,* raw] 1. in a raw or natural state 2. lacking grace, taste, etc. 3. roughly made —**crude′ly** *adv.* —**cru·di·ty** (krōō′də tē), **crude′ness** *n.*

cru·el (krōō′əl) *adj.* [see prec.] 1. without mercy or pity 2. causing pain, distress, etc. — **cru′el·ly** *adv.* —**cru′el·ty** *n., pl.* **-ties**

cru·et (krōō′it) *n.* [< OFr. *crue,* earthen pot] a small glass bottle to hold vinegar, oil, etc. for the table

cruise (krōōz) *vi.* **cruised, cruis′ing** [< Du. *kruisen,* to cross] to sail or drive about from place to place, as for pleasure —*vt.* to sail or journey over or about —*n.* a cruising voyage

cruis′er *n.* 1. one that cruises, as a police car 2. a fast warship smaller than a battleship

crul·ler (krul′ər) *n.* [Du. < *krullen,* to curl] a kind of twisted doughnut

crumb (krum) *n.* [OE. *cruma*] 1. a small piece broken off, as of bread 2. any bit or scrap [*crumbs* of knowledge] 3. [Slang] a worthless person —*vt. Cooking* to cover with crumbs — **crumb′y** *adj.* **-i·er, -i·est**

crum·ble (krum′b'l) *vt.* **-bled, -bling** [< prec.] to break into crumbs or small pieces —*vi.* to fall to pieces; decay —**crum′bly** *adj.* **-bli·er, -bli·est**

crum·my (krum′ē) *adj.* **-mi·er, -mi·est** [Slang] cheap, shabby, inferior, etc.

crum·pet (krum′pit) *n.* [prob. < OE. *crompeht*] a batter cake baked on a griddle, usually toasted before serving

crum·ple (krum′p'l) *vt., vi.* **-pled, -pling** [< ME. *crimplen,* to wrinkle] to crush together into wrinkles

crunch (krunch) *vi., vt.* [echoic] to chew, press, grind, etc. with a noisy, crackling sound —*n.* 1. the act or sound of crunching 2. [Slang] *a*) a showdown *b*) a tight situation —**crunch′y** *adj.* **-i·er, -i·est**

crup·per (krup′ər, kroop′-) *n.* [< OFr. *crope,* rump] a leather strap attached to a harness and passed under a horse's tail

cru·sade (krōō sād′) *n.* [ult. < L. *crux,* a cross] 1. [*often* C-] any of the Christian military expeditions (11th–13th cent.) to recover the Holy Land from the Muslims 2. vigorous, concerted action for or against something —*vi.* **-sad′ed, -sad′ing** to engage in a crusade —**cru·sad′er** *n.*

crush (krush) *vt.* [< OFr. *croisir,* to break] 1. to press with force so as to break or put out of shape 2. to grind or pound into small bits 3. to subdue; overwhelm 4. to extract by squeezing —*vi.* to become crushed —*n.* 1. a crushing 2. a crowded mass of people 3. [Colloq.] an infatuation —**crush′er** *n.*

crust (krust) *n.* [< L. *crusta*] 1. the hard, outer part of bread 2. any dry, hard piece of bread 3. the pastry shell of a pie 4. any hard surface layer, as of snow **5.** [Slang] insolence —*vt., vi.* to cover or become covered with a crust

crus·ta·cean (krus tā'shən) *n.* [see prec.] any of a class of arthropods, as shrimps, crabs, lobsters, etc., with a hard outer shell

crust'y *adj.* -i·er, -i·est **1.** having a crust **2.** bad-tempered; surly

crutch (kruch) *n.* [OE. *crycce*, staff] **1.** a staff with a top crosspiece that fits under the armpit, used by the lame as an aid in walking **2.** any prop, support, etc. —*vt.* to prop up

crux (kruks) *n.* [L., a cross] **1.** a difficult problem **2.** the essential or deciding point

cry (krī) *vi.* **cried, cry'ing** [< L. *quiritare*, to wail] **1.** to make a loud sound, as for help **2.** to sob and shed tears; weep **3.** to plead (*for*), or show a great need (*for*) **4.** to utter its characteristic call: said of an animal —*vt.* **1.** to utter loudly; shout **2.** to call out (wares for sale, etc.) —*n., pl.* **cries 1.** a crying; call; shout **2.** an urgent appeal; plea **3.** a fit of weeping **4.** the characteristic call of an animal —**a far cry a** great distance or difference

cry'ba'by *n., pl.* **-bies** one who complains when he fails to win or get his own way

cry·o·gen·ics (krī'ə jen'iks) *n.pl.* [*with sing. v.*] [< Gr. *kryos*, cold + -GEN + -ICS] the science that deals with the effects of very low temperatures on matter

crypt (kript) *n.* [< Gr. *kryptein*] an underground vault, esp. one used for burial

cryp·tic (krip'tik) *adj.* **1.** hidden or mysterious **2.** obscure and curt

cryp·to·gram (krip'tə gram') *n.* [< Gr. *kryptos*, hidden + -GRAM] something written in code or cipher: also **cryp'to·graph'**

cryp·tog·ra·phy (krip täg'rə fē) *n.* [< Gr. *kryptos*, hidden + -GRAPHY] the art of writing or deciphering messages in code

crys·tal (kris't'l) *n.* [< Gr. *kryos*, frost] **1.** a clear, transparent quartz **2.** a very clear, brilliant glass **3.** articles of such glass, as goblets **4.** the covering over a watch face **5.** a solidified form of a substance having plane faces symmetrically arranged —*adj.* **1.** of crystal **2.** like crystal; clear

crys'tal·line (-tə lin) *adj.* **1.** made of crystal **2.** like crystal

crys'tal·lize (-līz') *vi., vt.* **-lized', -liz'ing 1.** to become or cause to become crystalline **2.** to take on or cause to take on a definite form — **crys'tal·li·za'tion** *n.*

Cs *Chem.* cesium

CST, C.S.T. Central Standard Time

ct. 1. *pl.* **cts.** cent **2.** court

Cu [L. *cuprum*] *Chem.* copper

cu. cubic

cub (kub) *n.* [< ? OIr. *cuib*, whelp] **1.** a young fox, bear, lion, etc. **2.** a novice

cub·by·hole (kub'ē hōl') *n.* [< Brit. dial. *cub*, little shed + HOLE] a small, enclosed space: also **cub'by**

cube (kyōōb) *n.* [< Gr. *kybos*] **1.** a solid with six equal, square sides **2.** the product obtained by multiplying a given number by its square [the *cube* of 3 is 27] —*vt.* **cubed, cub'ing 1.** to obtain the cube of (a number) **2.** to cut or shape into cubes

cube root the number of which a given number is the cube [the *cube root* of 8 is 2]

cu·bic (kyōō'bik) *adj.* **1.** having the shape of a cube: also **cu'bi·cal 2.** having three dimensions: a cubic foot is the volume of a cube one foot in length, width, and breadth

cu·bi·cle (kyōō'bi k'l) *n.* [< L. *cubare*, lie down] a small compartment

cub·ism (kyōō'biz'm) *n.* a school of modern

art characterized by the use of cubes and other geometric forms —**cub'ist** *n., adj.*

cu·bit (kyōō'bit) *n.* [< L. *cubitum*] an ancient measure of length, about 18–22 inches

cuck·old (kuk'·ld) *n.* [see CUCKOO] a man whose wife has committed adultery —*vt.* to make a cuckold of —**cuck'old·ry** (-rē) *n.*

cuck·oo (kōō'kōō', kook'ōō') *n.* [< OFr. *cucu*, echoic] **1.** a brown bird with a long, slender body: the European species lays its eggs in the nests of other birds **2.** its call —*adj.* [Slang] crazy; silly

cu·cum·ber (kyōō'kum bər) *n.* [< L. *cucumis*] a long fruit with green rind and firm white flesh, used in salads or pickled

cud (kud) *n.* [OE. *cudu*] a mouthful of swallowed food regurgitated from the first stomach of cattle and other ruminants and chewed a second time

cud·dle (kud''l) *vt.* **-dled, -dling** [< ?] to embrace and fondle —*vi.* to lie close and snug — **cud'dly** *adj.* **-dli·er, -dli·est**

cudg·el (kuj'əl) *n.* [OE. *cycgel*] a short, thick stick or club —*vt.* **-eled** or **-elled, -el·ing** or **-el·ling** to beat with a cudgel

cue[1] (kyōō) *n.* [< *q, Q* (? for L. *quando*, when), found in 16th-c. plays] **1.** a signal in dialogue, etc. for an actor's entrance or speech **2.** any signal to act **3.** a hint —*vt.* **cued, cu'ing** to **cue'ing** to give a cue to

cue[2] (kyōō) *n.* [< *queue*] **1.** same as QUEUE **2.** a long, tapering rod used in billiards, etc.

cuff (kuf) *n.* [< ME. *cuffe*, glove] **1.** a band at the wrist end of a sleeve **2.** a turned-up fold at the bottom of a trouser leg **3.** a handcuff **4.** a slap —*vt.* **1.** to put a cuff on **2.** to slap

cuff link a pair of linked buttons, etc. for keeping a shirt cuff closed

cui·sine (kwi zēn') *n.* [Fr. < L. *coquere*, to cook] **1.** a style of cooking or preparing food **2.** the food prepared

cul-de-sac (kul'də sak') *n., pl.* **-sacs'** [Fr., lit., bottom of a sack] a blind alley

-cule [< Fr. or L.] *a suffix meaning* small

cu·li·nar·y (kyōō'lə ner'ē, kul'ə-) *adj.* [< L. *culina*, kitchen] of cooking

cull (kul) *vt.* [< L. *colligere*, collect] to pick out; select and gather —*n.* something picked out for rejection as not up to standard

cul·mi·nate (kul'mə nāt') *vi.* **-nat'ed, -nat'ing** [< L. *culmen*, peak] to reach its highest point or climax —**cul'mi·na'tion** *n.*

cu·lotte (koo lät') *n.* [Fr.] [*often pl.*] women's trousers resembling a skirt

cul·pa·ble (kul'pə b'l) *adj.* [< L. *culpa*, fault] deserving blame —**cul'pa·bil'i·ty** *n.*

cul·prit (kul'prit) *n.* [< early law Fr. *culpable*, guilty + *prit*, ready (to prove)] a person accused, or found guilty, of a crime

cult (kult) *n.* [< L. *cultus*, care] **1.** a system of religious worship **2.** devoted attachment to a person, principle, etc. **3.** a sect

cul·ti·vate (kul'tə vāt') *vt.* **-vat'ed, -vat'ing** [see prec.] **1.** to prepare (land) for growing crops; till **2.** to grow (plants) **3.** to loosen the soil and kill weeds around (plants) **4.** to develop or improve [*cultivate* your mind] **5.** to seek to become familiar with —**cul'ti·va'tor** *n.*

cul'ti·va'tion *n.* **1.** the act of cultivating **2.** refinement, or culture

cul·ture (kul'chər) *n.* [see CULT] **1.** cultivation of the soil **2.** a growth of bacteria, etc. in a prepared substance **3.** improvement of the mind, manners, etc. **4.** development by special training or care **5.** the skills, arts, etc. of a given people in a given period; civilization —*vt.* **-tured, -tur·ing** to cultivate —**cul'tur·al** *adj.*

cul·vert (kul′vərt) *n.* [< ?] a drain or conduit under a road or embankment
cum·ber (kum′bər) *vt.* [< OFr. *combre*, obstruction] to hinder; hamper
cum′ber·some (-səm) *adj.* burdensome; unwieldy: also **cum′brous** (-brəs)
cum·in (kum′in) *n.* [< Gr. *kyminon*] 1. a plant related to the parsley 2. its aromatic fruits, used for flavoring
cu·mu·la·tive (kyōōm′yə lāt′iv, -lə tiv) *adj.* increasing in effect, size, etc. by successive additions —**cu′mu·la′tive·ly** *adv.*
cu·mu·lus (kyōōm′yə ləs) *n., pl.* -**li′** (-lī′) [L., a heap] a thick cloud type with a dark base and domelike upper parts
cu·ne·i·form (kyōō nē′ə fôrm′) *adj.* [< L. *cuneus*, a wedge + -FORM] wedge-shaped, as the characters used in ancient Assyrian inscriptions —*n.* cuneiform characters
cun·ning (kun′iŋ) *adj.* [< ME. *cunnen*, know] 1. sly; crafty 2. made with skill 3. pretty; cute —*n.* slyness; craftiness
cup (kup) *n.* [< L. *cupa*, tub] 1. a small, bowl-shaped container for beverages, often with a handle 2. a cup and its contents 3. a cupful 4. anything shaped like a cup —*vt.* **cupped, cup′ping** to shape like a cup
cup·board (kub′ərd) *n.* a closet or cabinet with shelves for dishes, food, etc.
cup′cake′ *n.* a small cake
cup′ful′ *n., pl.* -**fuls′** as much as a cup will hold; specif., eight ounces
Cu·pid (kyōō′pid) the Roman god of love —*n.* [c-] a representation of Cupid as a naked, winged cherub with bow and arrow
cu·pid·i·ty (kyōō pid′ə tē) *n.* [< L. *cupere*, to desire] strong desire for wealth; greed
cu·po·la (kyōō′pə lə) *n.* [It. < L. *cupa*, a tub] 1. a rounded roof or ceiling 2. a small dome or similar structure on a roof
cu·pro·nick·el (kyōō′prō nik′′l) *n.* [< L. *cuprum*, copper + NICKEL] an alloy of copper and nickel, used in some coins
cur (kur) *n.* [prob. < ON. *kurra*, to growl] 1. a mongrel dog 2. a contemptible person
cur·a·ble (kyoor′ə b′l) *adj.* that can be cured —**cur′a·bil′i·ty** *n.* —**cur′a·bly** *adv.*
cu·rate (kyoor′it) *n.* [< L. *cura*, care (of souls)] a clergyman who assists a vicar or rector —**cu′ra·cy** (-ə sē) *n., pl.* -**cies**
cur·a·tive (kyoor′ə tiv) *adj.* curing or having the power to cure —*n.* a remedy
cu·ra·tor (kyoo rāt′ər) *n.* [< L. *curare*, take care of] one in charge of a museum, etc.
curb (kurb) *n.* [< L. *curvus*, bent] 1. a chain or strap attached to a horse's bit, used to check the horse 2. anything that checks or restrains 3. a stone or concrete edging along a street 4. a market dealing in stocks and bonds not listed on the exchange —*vt.* to restrain; control
curb′ing *n.* 1. material for curbstones 2. a curb (sense 3)
curb′stone′ *n.* the stones making up a curb
curd (kurd) *n.* [< ME. *crud*, coagulated substance] [*often pl.*] the coagulated part of sour milk, from which cheese is made
cur·dle (kur′d′l) *vt., vi.* -**dled, -dling** to form into curd; coagulate —**curdle one's blood** to horrify or terrify one
cure (kyoor) *n.* [< L. *cura*, care] 1. a healing or being healed 2. a remedy 3. a method of medical treatment —*vt.* **cured, cur′ing** 1. to restore to health 2. to get rid of (an ailment, evil, etc.) 3. *a)* to preserve (meat), as by salting or smoking *b)* to process (tobacco, leather, etc.), as by drying

cure′-all′ *n.* something supposed to cure all ailments or evils
cur·few (kur′fyōō) *n.* [< OFr. *covrefeu*, lit., cover fire: orig. a nightly signal to cover fires and retire] a time in the evening beyond which children, etc. may not appear on the streets
cu·rie (kyoor′ē, kyoo rē′) *n.* [< Marie *Curie* (1867–1934), Pol. chemist in France] the unit used in measuring radioactivity
cu·ri·o (kyoor′ē ō′) *n., pl.* -**os′** [contr. of CURIOSITY] any unusual or rare article
cu·ri·os·i·ty (kyoor′ē äs′ə tē) *n., pl.* -**ties** 1. a desire to learn or know 2. anything curious or rare
cu·ri·ous (kyoor′ē əs) *adj.* [< L. *curiosus*, careful] 1. eager to learn or know; prying or inquisitive 2. unusual; strange
cu·ri·um (kyoor′ē əm) *n.* [see CURIE] a radioactive chemical element: symbol, Cm
curl (kurl) *vt.* [< ME. *crul*, curly] 1. to twist (hair, etc.) into ringlets 2. to bend around —*vi.* to become curled —*n.* 1. a ringlet of hair 2. anything with a curled shape —**curl up** 1. to gather into curls 2. to sit or lie with the legs drawn up —**curl′er** *n.* —**curl′y** *adj.* -**i·er, -i·est**
cur·lew (kur′lōō) *n.* [echoic] a large, brownish wading bird with long legs
curl·i·cue (kur′li kyōō′) *n.* [< CURLY + CUE²] a fancy curve, flourish, etc.
curl·ing (kur′liŋ) *n.* a game played on ice by sliding a heavy disk toward a target circle
cur·mudg·eon (kər muj′ən) *n.* [< ?] a surly, ill-mannered person
cur·rant (kur′ənt) *n.* [ult. < *Corinth*, ancient Gr. city] 1. a small, seedless raisin from the Mediterranean region 2. the sour berry of a large group of hardy shrubs
cur·ren·cy (kur′ən sē) *n., pl.* -**cies** [see CURRENT] 1. circulation 2. the money in circulation in any country 3. general use or acceptance
cur·rent (kur′ənt) *adj.* [< L. *currere*, to run] 1. of the present time 2. circulating 3. commonly accepted; in general use —*n.* 1. a flow of water or air in a definite direction 2. a general tendency or drift 3. the flow or rate of flow of electricity in a conductor —**cur′rent·ly** *adv.*
cur·ric·u·lum (kə rik′yə ləm) *n., pl.* -**la** (-lə), -**lums** [L., a course for racing] a series of required studies —**cur·ric′u·lar** *adj.*
cur·ry¹ (kur′ē) *vt.* -**ried, -ry·ing** [< OFr. *correier*, put in order] 1. to rub down and clean the coat of (a horse, etc.) with a comb or brush 2. to prepare (tanned leather) —**curry favor** to try to win favor by flattery, fawning, etc. —**cur′ri·er** *n.*
cur·ry² (kur′ē) *n., pl.* -**ries** [Tamil *kari*] 1. a powder prepared from various spices, or a sauce made with this 2. a stew made with curry —*vt.* -**ried, -ry·ing** to prepare with curry
curse (kurs) *n.* [OE. *curs*] 1. a calling on God or the gods to bring evil on some person or thing 2. a profane or obscene oath 3. evil that seems to come in answer to a curse —*vt.* **cursed** or **curst, curs′ing** 1. to call evil down on 2. to swear at 3. to afflict —*vi.* to swear; blaspheme
curs·ed (kur′sid, kurst) *adj.* 1. under a curse 2. deserving to be cursed; evil
cur·sive (kur′siv) *adj.* [ult. < L. *currere*, to run] designating or of writing in which the letters are joined
cur·so·ry (kur′sər ē) *adj.* [< L. *cursor*, runner] hastily, often superficially, done
curt (kurt) *adj.* [L. *curtus*, short] so brief as to be rude; brusque —**curt′ly** *adv.*

cur·tail (kər tāl′) *vt.* [< L. *curtus*, short] to cut short; reduce —**cur·tail′ment** *n.*

cur·tain (kur′t'n) *n.* [< L. *cors*, a court] a piece of cloth, etc. hung at a window, in front of a stage, etc. to decorate or conceal —*vt.* to provide as with a curtain

curt·sy (kurt′sē) *n., pl.* **-sies** [var. of COURTESY] a woman's bow of greeting, respect, etc. made by bending the knees and dipping the body slightly —*vi.* **-sied, -sy·ing** to make a curtsy Also sp. **curt′sey**

cur·va·ture (kur′və chər) *n.* 1. a curving or being curved 2. a curve or curved part

curve (kurv) *n.* [L. *curvus*, bent] 1. a line having no straight part; bend with no angles 2. something shaped like, or moving in, a curve —*vt., vi.* **curved, curv′ing** 1. to form a curve by bending 2. to move in a curve —**curv′y** *adj.* **-i·er, -i·est**

cur·vi·lin·e·ar (kur′və lin′ē ər) *adj.* consisting of or enclosed by curved lines

cush·ion (koosh′ən) *n.* [< ML. *coxinum*] 1. a pillow or pad 2. a thing like this in shape or use 3. something that absorbs shock —*vt.* to provide with a cushion

cusp (kusp) *n.* [L. *cuspis*, a point] a point, as on the chewing surface of a tooth

cus·pid (kus′pid) *n.* a canine tooth

cus·pi·dor (kus′pə dôr′) *n.* [< Port. *cuspir*, to spit] *same as* SPITTOON

cuss (kus) *n.* [Colloq.] 1. a curse 2. a person or animal regarded as queer or annoying —*vt., vi.* [Colloq.] to curse —**cuss′ed** *adj.*

cus·tard (kus′tərd) *n.* [< L. *crusta*, crust] 1. a mixture of eggs, milk, sugar, etc. boiled or baked 2. *same as* FROZEN CUSTARD

cus·to·di·an (kus tō′dē ən) *n.* 1. one who has the custody or care of something; keeper 2. a janitor —**cus·to′di·an·ship′** *n.*

cus·to·dy (kus′tə dē) *n., pl.* **-dies** [< L. *custos*, a guard] a guarding or keeping safe; care —**in custody** under arrest —**cus·to′di·al** (-tō′dē əl) *adj.*

cus·tom (kus′təm) *n.* [< L. *com-*, intens. + *suere*, be accustomed] 1. a usual practice; habit 2. social conventions carried on by tradition 3. [*pl.*] duties or taxes imposed on imported goods 4. the regular patronage of a business —*adj.* 1. made to order 2. making things to order

cus′tom·ar′y (-tə mer′ē) *adj.* in keeping with custom; usual —**cus′tom·ar′i·ly** *adv.*

cus′tom·er *n.* a person who buys, esp. one who buys regularly

cus′tom·house′ *n.* an office where customs or duties are paid: also **cus′toms·house′**

cus′tom·ize′ (-īz′) *vt., vi.* **-ized′, -iz′ing** to make according to individual specifications

cus′tom-made′ *adj.* made to order, according to the customer's specifications

cut (kut) *vt.* **cut, cut′ting** [ME. *cutten*] 1. to make an opening in with a sharp-edged instrument; gash 2. to pierce sharply so as to hurt 3. to have (a new tooth) grow through the gum 4. to divide into parts with a sharp-edged instrument 5. to hew 6. to reap 7. to pass across; intersect 8. to divide (a pack of cards) 9. to reduce; curtail 10. to trim; pare 11. to make or do as by cutting 12. [Colloq.] to pretend not to recognize (a person) 13. [Colloq.] to stay away from (a school class, etc.) 14. [Slang] to stop —*vi.* 1. to pierce, sever, gash, etc. 2. to take cutting [pine *cuts* easily] 3. to go (*across* or *through*) 4. to swing a bat, etc. (*at* a ball) 5. to change direction suddenly —*adj.* 1. that has been cut 2. made or formed by cutting —*n.* 1. a cutting or being cut 2. a stroke or opening

made by a sharp-edged instrument 3. a piece cut off, as of meat 4. a reduction 5. a passage or channel cut out 6. the style in which a thing is cut 7. an act, remark, etc. that hurts one's feelings 8. a block or plate engraved for printing, or the impression from this 9. [Colloq.] an unauthorized absence from school, etc. 10. [Slang] a share, as of profits —**cut and dried** 1. arranged beforehand 2. lifeless; dull —**cut down (on)** to reduce; lessen —**cut it out** [Colloq.] to stop what one is doing —**cut off** 1. to sever 2. to stop abruptly; shut off —**cut out for** suited for —**cut up** 1. to cut into pieces 2. [Slang] to clown, joke, etc.

cu·ta·ne·ous (kyōō tā′nē əs) *adj.* [< L. *cutis*, skin] of or on the skin

cut′a·way′ *n.* a man's formal coat cut so as to curve back to the tails

cut′back′ *n.* a reduction or stopping

cute (kyōōt) *adj.* **cut′er, cut′est** [< ACUTE] [Colloq.] 1. clever; shrewd 2. pretty or attractive, esp. in a dainty way

cu·ti·cle (kyōōt′i k'l) *n.* [L. *cuticula*, skin] 1. the outer layer of the skin 2. hardened skin, as at the base and sides of a fingernail

cut·lass, cut·las (kut′ləs) *n.* [< L. *culter*, knife] a short, thick, curved sword

cut·ler·y (kut′lər ē) *n.* [see prec.] 1. cutting implements, as knives 2. eating implements

cut·let (kut′lit) *n.* [< L. *costa*, a rib] 1. a small slice of meat from the ribs or leg, for frying or broiling 2. a small, flat croquette of chopped meat or fish

cut′off′ *n.* 1. the limit set for a process, etc. 2. a road that is a shortcut 3. any device for cutting off a flow or connection

cut′-rate′ *adj.* selling at a lower price

cut·ter (kut′ər) *n.* 1. a person or thing that cuts 2. a small, swift vessel

cut′throat′ *n.* a murderer —*adj.* ruthless

cut·ting (kut′iŋ) *n.* a shoot cut away from a plant for rooting or grafting —*adj.* 1. that cuts; sharp 2. chilling or piercing 3. sarcastic; harsh —**cut′ting·ly** *adv.*

cut′tle·fish′ (-fish′) *n., pl.*: see FISH [OE. *cudele*] a sea mollusk with ten sucker-bearing arms and a hard internal shell

cwt. hundredweight

-cy [< Gr. *-kia*] *a suffix meaning:* 1. quality, condition, or fact of being [*hesitancy*] 2. position, rank, or office of [*captaincy*]

cy·a·nide (sī′ə nīd′) *n.* a highly poisonous, white, crystalline compound

cy·ber·net·ics (sī′bər net′iks) *n.pl.* [*with sing. v.*] [< Gr. *kybernētēs*, helmsman] the comparative study of complex electronic computers and the human nervous system

cy·cla·mate (sī′klə māt′, sik′lə-) *n.* an organic compound with a sweet taste

cy·cla·men (sī′klə mən, sik′lə-) *n.* [< Gr. *kyklaminos*] a plant related to the primrose, with heart-shaped leaves

cy·cle (sī′k'l) *n.* [< Gr. *kyklos*, circle] 1. *a)* a period of time within which a round of regularly recurring events is completed *b)* a complete set of such events 2. a very long period of time 3. a series of poems or songs on the same theme 4. a bicycle, motorcycle, etc. —*vi.* **-cled, -cling** to ride a bicycle, etc. —**cy′clic** (-klik, sik′lik), **cy′cli·cal** *adj.*

cy·clist (sī′klist) *n.* one who rides a cycle

cyclo- [< Gr. *kyklos*, circle] *a combining form meaning of* a circle or wheel, circular

cy·clom·e·ter (sī kläm′ə tər) *n.* [CYCLO- + -METER] an instrument that records the revolutions of a wheel, for measuring distance traveled

cy·clone (sī′klōn) *n.* [< Gr. *kyklos,* circle] a storm with strong winds rotating about a moving center of low pressure
cy·clo·pe·di·a, cy·clo·pae·di·a (sī′klə pē′dē ə) *n. same as* ENCYCLOPEDIA
Cy·clops (sī′kläps) *n., pl.* **Cy·clo·pes** (sī klō′pēz) [< Gr. *kyklos,* circle + *ōps,* eye] *Gr. Myth.* any of a race of one-eyed giants
cy·clo·tron (sī′klə trän′) *n.* [CYCLO- + (ELEC)TRON] an apparatus for giving high energy to particles, as protons, etc.: used in atomic research
cyg·net (sig′nət) *n.* [< Gr. *kyknos,* swan] a young swan
cyl·in·der (sil′ən dər) *n.* [< Gr. *kylindein,* to roll] **1.** a solid figure described by the edge of a rectangle rotated around the parallel edge as axis **2.** anything with this shape; specif., *a)* the turning part of a revolver *b)* the piston chamber of an engine —**cy·lin·dri·cal** (sə lin′dri k'l) *adj.*
cym·bal (sim′b'l) *n.* [< Gr. *kymbē,* hollow of a vessel] *Music* a concave brass plate that makes a sharp, ringing sound when struck — **cym′bal·ist** *n.*
cyn·ic (sin′ik) *n.* [see CYNICAL] a cynical person —*adj. same as* CYNICAL
cyn′i·cal (-i k'l) *adj.* [< Gr. *kyōn,* dog] **1.** denying the sincerity of people or the value of life **2.** sarcastic, sneering, etc.
cyn′i·cism (-ə siz'm) *n.* **1.** the attitude or beliefs of a cynic **2.** a cynical remark, etc.
cy·no·sure (sī′nə shoor′, sin′ə-) *n.* [< Gr. *kynosoura,* dog's tail] a center of attention or interest
cy·press (sī′prəs) *n.* [< Gr. *kyparissos*] **1.** a dark-foliaged, cone-bearing evergreen **2.** its wood
cyst (sist) *n.* [< Gr. *kystis,* sac] any of certain saclike structures in plants or animals, esp. one filled with diseased matter
cy·tol·o·gy (sī täl′ə jē) *n.* [< Gr. *kytos,* a hollow + -LOGY] the branch of biology dealing with the study of cells
cy·to·plasm (sīt′ə plaz'm) *n.* [< Gr. *kytos,* a hollow + -PLASM] the protoplasm of a cell, exclusive of the nucleus: also **cy′to·plast′**
czar (zär) *n.* [< Russ. < L. *Caesar*] **1.** the title of any of the former emperors of Russia **2.** an autocrat —**cza·ri·na** (zä rē′nə) *n.fem.*
Czech (chek) *n.* **1.** a member of a Slavic people of central Europe **2.** the West Slavic language of the Czechs —*adj.* of Czechoslovakia, its people, or their language
Czech·o·slo·vak (chek′ə slō′väk) *adj.* of Czechoslovakia, its people, etc. —*n.* a Czech or Slovak living in Czechoslovakia Also **Czech′o·slo·vak′i·an** (-vä′kē ən)

D

D, d (dē) *n., pl.* **D's, d's** the fourth letter of the English alphabet
D (dē) *n.* **1.** a Roman numeral for 500 **2.** a grade for below-average work **3.** *Music* the second tone in the scale of C major
D. 1. December **2.** Democrat(ic) **3.** Dutch
d. 1. day(s) **2.** degree **3.** diameter **4.** died **5.** [L. *denarius,* pl. *denarii*] penny; pence
'd 1. *contracted form of* had *or* would *[I'd, they'd]* **2.** *contraction of* -ed *[foster'd]*
D.A. District Attorney
dab (dab) *vt., vi.* **dabbed, dab′bing** [ME. *dabben,* to strike] **1.** to touch lightly and quickly; pat **2.** to put on (paint, etc.) with light, quick strokes —*n.* **1.** a tap; pat **2.** a soft or moist bit of something
dab·ble (dab′'l) *vi.* **-bled, -bling** [< Du. *dabben,* to strike] **1.** to play in water, as with the hands **2.** to do something superficially (with *in* or *at*) —**dab′bler** *n.*
dace (dās) *n., pl.* **dace, dac′es** [< VL. *darsus*] a small freshwater fish of the carp family
dachs·hund (däks′hoond) *n.* [G. *dachs,* a badger + *hund,* a dog] a small dog with a long body and short legs
Da·cron (dā′krän, dak′rän) *a trademark for* a synthetic wrinkle-resistant fabric —*n.* [*also* d-] this fabric
dac·tyl (dak′t'l) *n.* [< Gr. *daktylos,* a finger] a metrical foot of three syllables, the first accented —**dac·tyl′ic** *adj.*
dad (dad) *n.* [< child's cry *dada*] [Colloq.] father: also **dad′dy** (dad′ē), *pl.* -**dies**
dad′dy-long′legs′ *n., pl.* -**long′legs′** a spiderlike animal with long legs
da·do (dā′dō) *n., pl.* -**does** [It. < L. *datum,* a die] **1.** the part of a pedestal between the cap and the base **2.** the lower part of a wall if decorated unlike the upper part
dae·mon (dē′mən) *n.* [< Gr. *daimōn*] **1.** *Gr.*
Myth. a secondary deity **2.** a guardian spirit **3.** *same as* DEMON
daf·fo·dil (daf′ə dil′) *n.* [< Gr. *asphodelos*] a narcissus with a yellow flower
daf·fy (daf′ē) *adj.* -**fi·er, -fi·est** [see DAFT] [Colloq.] crazy; silly —**daf′fi·ness** *n.*
daft (daft) *adj.* [< OE. *(ge)dæfte,* mild, gentle] **1.** silly; foolish **2.** insane; crazy
dag·ger (dag′ər) *n.* [< ML. *daggarius*] **1.** a weapon with a short, pointed blade, used for stabbing **2.** *Printing* a reference mark (†)
da·guerre·o·type (də ger′ə tīp′) *n.* [< C. L. J. M *Daguerre,* 19th-c. Fr. inventor] a photograph made by an early method on a chemically treated plate
dahl·ia (dal′yə, däl′-) *n.* [< A. *Dahl,* 18th-c. Swed. botanist] **1.** a perennial plant with large, showy flowers **2.** the flower
dai·ly (dā′lē) *adj.* done, happening, or published every (week)day —*n., pl.* -**lies** a daily newspaper —*adv.* every day; day after day
daily double a bet, the success of which depends on choosing both winners in two specified races on the same program
dain·ty (dān′tē) *n., pl.* -**ties** [< L. *dignitas,* worth] a delicacy —*adj.* -**ti·er, -ti·est 1.** delicious and choice **2.** delicately pretty **3.** *a)* of refined taste *b)* too fastidious; squeamish —**dain′ti·ness** *n.*
dair·y (der′ē) *n., pl.* -**ies** [< ME. *daie,* dairymaid] **1.** a place where milk and cream are made into butter, cheese, etc. **2.** a farm that produces, or a business that processes, milk **3.** a store that sells milk and milk products —**dair′y·maid′** *n.* —**dair′y·man** *n., pl.* -**men**
da·is (dā′is, dī′-) *n., pl.* **da′is·es** [< ML. *discus,* table] a raised platform
dai·sy (dā′zē) *n., pl.* -**sies** [< OE. *dæges eage,* lit., day's eye] a plant of the composite family,

bearing flowers with white rays around a yellow disk

dale (dāl) *n.* [OE. *dæl*] a valley

dal·ly (dal'ē) *vi.* **-lied, -ly·ing** [< OFr. *dalier*, to trifle] **1.** to play at love **2.** to deal lightly or carelessly (*with*) **3.** to waste time; loiter —**dal'·li·ance** (-ē əns) *n.*

Dal·ma·tian (dal mā'shən) *n.* a large, short-haired dog with dark spots on a white coat

dam[1] (dam) *n.* [ME.] a barrier built to hold back flowing water —*vt.* **dammed, dam'ming** **1.** to build a dam in **2.** to keep back or confine (usually with *up*)

dam[2] (dam) *n.* [see DAME] the female parent of any four-legged animal

dam·age (dam'ij) *n.* [< L. *damnum*] **1.** injury or harm resulting in a loss **2.** [*pl.*] *Law* money compensating for injury, loss, etc. —*vt.* **-aged, -ag·ing** to do damage to —**dam'age·a·ble** *adj.*

dam·ask (dam'əsk) *n.* [< It. < *Damascus*, Syria] **1.** a reversible fabric in figured weave, used for table linen, etc. **2.** steel decorated with wavy lines **3.** deep pink or rose —*adj.* **1.** made of or like damask **2.** deep-pink or rose

dame (dām) *n.* [< L. *domina*, lady] **1.** a lady **2.** [D-] in Great Britain, the title of a woman who has received an order of knighthood **3.** [Slang] a woman

damn (dam) *vt.* **damned, damn'ing** [< L. *damnare*, condemn] **1.** to condemn to hell **2.** to condemn as bad, inferior, etc. **3.** to swear at by saying "damn" —*n.* the saying of "damn" as a curse —*adj., adv.* [Colloq.] *short for* DAMNED —*interj.* an expression of anger, etc. — **not give** (or **care**) **a damn** [Colloq.] not care at all

dam·na·ble (dam'nə b'l) *adj.* **1.** deserving damnation **2.** deserving to be sworn at

dam·na'tion (-nā'shən) *n.* a damning or being damned —*interj.* an expression of anger, etc.

damned (damd) *adj.* **1.** condemned, as to hell **2.** [Colloq.] cursed; outrageous —*adv.* [Colloq.] very

Dam·o·cles (dam'ə klēz') *Gr. Legend* a man whose king seated him under a sword hanging by a hair to show him the perils of a ruler's life

Da·mon and Pyth·i·as (dā'mən ən pith'ē əs) *Classical Legend* two very devoted friends

damp (damp) *n.* [MDu., vapor] **1.** a slight wetness; moisture **2.** a harmful gas sometimes found in mines —*adj.* somewhat moist or wet —*vt.* **1.** to bank (a fire) **2.** to reduce or check (energy, action, etc.) —**damp'ness** *n.*

damp'-dry' *vt.* **-dried', -dry'ing** to dry (laundry) so that some moisture is retained —*adj.* designating laundry so treated

damp·en *vt.* **1.** to make damp; moisten **2.** to deaden, depress, or reduce —*vi.* to become damp —**damp'en·er** *n.*

damp·er *n.* **1.** anything that deadens or depresses **2.** a valve in a flue to control the draft **3.** a device to check vibration in the strings of a piano, etc.

dam·sel (dam'z'l) *n.* [see DAME] [Archaic] a girl; maiden

dam·son (dam'z'n) *n.* [< *Damascus*, Syria] a variety of small, purple plum

Dan. Danish

dance (dans) *vi.* **danced, danc'ing** [< OFr. *danser*] **1.** to move the body and feet in rhythm, ordinarily to music **2.** to move rapidly, lightly, gaily, etc. —*vt.* **1.** to perform (a dance) **2.** to cause to dance —*n.* **1.** rhythmic movement, ordinarily to music **2.** a particular kind of dance **3.** the art of dancing **4.** a party for dancing **5.** a piece of music for dancing **6.** rapid, lively movement —**danc'er** *n.*

dan·de·li·on (dan'də lī'ən) *n.* [< OFr. *dent*, tooth + *de*, of + *lion*, lion] a common weed with yellow flowers and jagged leaves

dan·der (dan'dər) *n.* [< ?] [Colloq.] anger or temper —**get one's dander up** [Colloq.] to become or make angry

dan·dle (dan'd'l) *vt.* **-dled, -dling** [< ?] to dance (a child) up and down on the knee or in the arms

dan·druff (dan'drəf) *n.* [< earlier *dandro* + dial. *hurf*, scab] little scales of dead skin on the scalp

dan·dy (dan'dē) *n., pl.* **-dies** [< ?] **1.** a man overly attentive to his clothes and appearance; fop **2.** [Colloq.] something very good —*adj.* **-di·er, -di·est** [Colloq.] very good

Dane (dān) *n.* a native of Denmark

dan·ger (dān'jər) *n.* [ult. < L. *dominus*, a master] **1.** liability to injury, damage, loss, or pain **2.** a thing that may cause injury, pain, etc.

dan'ger·ous *adj.* full of danger; unsafe

dan·gle (daŋ'g'l) *vi.* **-gled, -gling** [< Scand.] to hang swinging loosely —*vt.* to cause to dangle

Dan·iel (dan'yəl) *Bible* a Hebrew prophet whose faith saved him in the lion's den

Dan·ish (dā'nish) *adj.* of Denmark, the Danes, or their language —*n.* **1.** their language **2.** [*also* d-] fruit-filled pastry

dank (daŋk) *adj.* [ME.] disagreeably damp — **dank'ly** *adv.* —**dank'ness** *n.*

dap·per (dap'ər) *adj.* [< ? MDu.] **1.** small and active **2.** trim, neat, or smart

dap·ple (dap''l) *adj.* [< ON. *depill*, a spot] marked with spots; mottled: also **dap'pled** —*vt.* **-pled, -pling** to cover with spots

dare (der) *vt., vi.* **dared** or archaic **durst** (durst), **dared, dar'ing** [OE. *durran*] **1.** to have enough courage for (some act) **2.** to oppose and defy **3.** to challenge (someone) to do something —*n.* a challenge —**dare say** to think probable —**dar'er** *n.*

dare'dev'il (-dev''l) *adj.* bold and reckless —*n.* a bold, reckless person

dar'ing *adj.* fearless; bold —*n.* bold courage

dark (därk) *adj.* [< OE. *deorc*] **1.** entirely or partly without light **2.** almost black **3.** not light in color **4.** hidden **5.** gloomy **6.** evil; sinister **7.** ignorant —*n.* **1.** the state of being dark **2.** night —**in the dark** uninformed —**dark'ly** *adv.* — **dark'ness** *n.*

Dark Ages the Middle Ages, esp. the earlier part

dark'en *vi., vt.* to make or become dark

dark horse [Colloq.] an unexpected, almost unknown winner, nominee, etc.

dark'room' *n.* a darkened room for developing photographs

dar·ling (där'liŋ) *n.* [OE. *deorling*] a person much loved by another —*adj.* **1.** very dear; beloved **2.** [Colloq.] cute; attractive

darn[1] (därn) *vt., vi.* [< MFr. dial. *darner*] to mend (cloth, etc.) by sewing a network of stitches across the gap —*n.* a darned place in fabric —**darn'er** *n.*

darn[2] (därn) *vt., n., adj., adv., interj.* [Colloq.] a *euphemism for* DAMN (the curse)

dar·nel (där'n'l) *n.* [< Fr. dial. *darnelle*] a weedy rye grass which can become poisonous

dart (därt) *n.* [< OFr.] **1.** a small, pointed missile for throwing or shooting **2.** a sudden, quick movement **3.** a short, tapered seam —*vt., vi.* to send out or move suddenly and fast

Dar·win·i·an (där win'ē ən) *adj.* [< Charles *Darwin*, 19th-c. Eng. naturalist] of Charles

Darwin or his theory of evolution —*n.* a believer in this theory —**Dar'win·ism** *n.*

dash (dash) *vt.* [< Scand.] **1.** to smash; destroy **2.** to strike (something) violently against **3.** to throw or thrust (*away, down,* etc.) **4.** to splash —*vi.* **1.** to strike violently (*against* or *on*) **2.** to rush —*n.* **1.** a smash **2.** a splash **3.** a bit of something added **4.** a rush **5.** a short, fast race **6.** vigor; spirit **7.** the mark of punctuation (—) used to indicate a break, omission, etc. —**dash off 1.** to do, write, etc. hastily **2.** to rush away —**dash'er** *n.*

dash'board' *n.* a panel with instruments and gauges on it, as in an automobile

dash'ing *adj.* **1.** full of dash or spirit **2.** showy; stylish —**dash'ing·ly** *adv.*

das·tard (das'tərd) *n.* [ME.] a sneaky, cowardly evildoer

das'tard·ly *adj.* sneaky, cowardly, etc.

dat. dative

da·ta (dāt'ə, dat'ə) *n.pl.* [*often with sing. v.*] [see DATUM] facts or figures from which conclusions can be inferred

data base (or **bank**) a large collection of data in a computer, organized so that it can be expanded, updated, and retrieved rapidly: also **da'ta·base', da'ta·bank'** *n.*

data processing the handling of information by mechanical or electronic means

date' (dāt) *n.* [< L. *dare,* give] **1.** the time at which a thing happens **2.** the day or the month **3.** an appointment or social engagement —*vt.* **dat'ed, dat'ing 1.** to mark (a letter, etc.) with a date **2.** to find out or give the date of **3.** to make seem old-fashioned **4.** to have social engagements with —*vi.* **1.** to belong to a definite period in the past (usually with *from*) **2.** to date persons of the opposite sex —**out of date** old-fashioned —**up to date** modern

date² (dāt) *n.* [< Gr. *daktylos,* lit., a finger] the sweet, fleshy fruit of a palm (**date palm**)

date'line' *n.* the date and place of writing or issue, as given in a line in a newspaper, etc.

date line an imaginary line through the Pacific, largely along the 180th meridian: at this line, by international agreement, each calendar day begins at midnight, so that when it is Sunday just west of the line, it is Saturday just east of it

da·tive (dāt'iv) *adj.* [< L. *dare,* give] denoting that case which expresses the indirect object of a verb —*n.* **1.** the dative case **2.** a word or phrase in this case

da·tum (dāt'əm, dat'-) *n. sing. of* DATA

daub (dôb) *vt., vi.* [< L. *de-,* intens. + *albus,* white] **1.** to cover or smear with sticky, soft matter **2.** to paint badly —*n.* **1.** anything daubed on **2.** a daubing stroke **3.** a poorly painted picture

daugh·ter (dôt'ər) *n.* [OE. *dohtor*] **1.** a girl or woman as she is related to either or both parents **2.** a female descendant

daugh'ter-in-law' *n., pl.* **daugh'ters-in-law'** the wife of one's son

daunt (dônt, dänt) *vt.* [< L. *domare,* to tame] to frighten or discourage; dishearten

daunt'less *adj.* that cannot be daunted or intimidated; fearless —**daunt'less·ly** *adv.*

dau·phin (dô'fin) *n.* [Fr., dolphin] the eldest šon of the king of France: a title used from 1349 to 1830

dav·en·port (dav'ən pôrt') *n.* [< ?] a large couch or sofa

Da·vid (dā'vid) *Bible* the second king of Israel

dav·it (dav'it) *n.* [< OFr. dim. of *David*] either of a pair of uprights out over the side of a ship for suspending, lowering, or raising a boat

daw·dle (dôd''l) *vi., vt.* **-dled, -dling** [< ?] to waste (time) in trifling; loiter —**daw'dler** *n.*

dawn (dôn) *vi.* [< OE. *dæg,* day] **1.** to begin to be day; grow light **2.** to begin to appear, develop, etc. **3.** to begin to be understood or felt —*n.* **1.** daybreak **2.** the beginning (*of* something)

day (dā) *n.* [< OE. *dæg*] **1.** the period of light between sunrise and sunset **2.** the time (24 hours) that it takes the earth to revolve once on its axis **3.** [*also pl.*] a period; era **4.** a period of power, glory, etc. **5.** hours of work [an eight-hour *day*] —**call it a day** [Colloq.] to stop working for the day —**day after day** every day

day'break' *n.* the time in the morning when light first appears; dawn

day'dream' *n.* **1.** a pleasant, dreamlike thinking **2.** a pleasing but visionary notion —*vi.* to have daydreams —**day'dream'er** *n.*

day'light' *n.* **1.** the light of day **2.** dawn **3.** daytime **4.** understanding

day'light'-sav'ing time time that is one hour later than standard time

day nursery a nursery school for the daytime care of small children: also **day-care center**

day'time' *n.* the period of daylight

daze (dāz) *vt.* **dazed, daz'ing** [< ON. *dasi,* tired] **1.** to stun or bewilder **2.** to dazzle —*n.* a dazed condition —**daz'ed·ly** *adv.*

daz·zle (daz''l) *vt., vi.* **-zled, -zling** [< DAZE] **1.** to overpower or be overpowered by the glare of bright light **2.** to surprise or arouse admiration with brilliant qualities, display, etc. —*n.* a dazzling

DC, D.C., d.c. direct current

D.D. Doctor of Divinity

DDT a powerful insecticide

de- [< Fr. *de-* or L. *de*] *a prefix meaning:* **1.** away from, off [*derail*] **2.** down [*decline*] **3.** entirely [*defunct*] **4.** reverse the action of [*decode*]

dea·con (dēk''n) *n.* [< Gr. *diakonos,* servant] a church officer who helps the minister —**dea'con·ess** *n.fem.*

de·ac·ti·vate (dē ak'tə vāt') *vt.* **-vat'ed, -vat'ing 1.** to make (an explosive, chemical, etc.) inactive **2.** *Mil.* to disband (troops) —**de·ac'ti·va'tion** *n.*

dead (ded) *adj.* [OE.] **1.** no longer living **2.** without life **3.** deathlike **4.** lacking vitality, interest, warmth, etc. **5.** without feeling, motion, or power **6.** no longer used; obsolete **7.** unerring [a *dead* shot] **8.** complete [a *dead* stop] **9.** [Colloq.] very tired —*n.* the time of greatest darkness, most cold, etc. [the *dead* of night] —*adv.* **1.** completely **2.** directly —**the dead** those who have died —**dead'ness** *n.*

dead·beat (ded'bēt') *n.* [Slang] one who tries to evade paying his debts, etc.

dead·en (ded''n) *vt.* **1.** to lessen the vigor or intensity of; dull **2.** to make numb **3.** to make soundproof

dead end an end of a street, etc. that has no regular exit —**dead'-end'** *adj.*

dead heat a race in which two or more contestants finish even; tie

dead letter an unclaimed letter

dead'line' *n.* the latest time by which something must be done or completed

dead'lock' *n.* a standstill resulting from the action of equal and opposed forces —*vt., vi.* to bring or come to a deadlock

dead'ly *adj.* **-li·er, -li·est 1.** causing or likely to cause death **2.** to the death [*deadly* combat] **3.** as in death [*deadly* pale] **4.** extreme **5.** very boring —*adv.* **1.** as if dead **2.** extremely —**dead'li·ness** *n.*

dead′pan′ *n.* [Slang] an expressionless face
dead weight the weight of an inert person or thing
dead′wood′ (-wood′) *n.* 1. dead wood on trees 2. anything useless or burdensome
deaf (def) *adj.* [OE.] 1. unable to hear 2. unwilling to respond, as to a plea
deaf′en (-'n) *vt.* 1. to make deaf 2. to overwhelm with noise —**deaf′en·ing** *adj.*
deaf′-mute′ (-myōōt′) *n.* a person who is deaf and has not learned to speak
deal[1] (dēl) *vt.* dealt (delt), deal′ing [OE. *dælan*] 1. to portion out or distribute 2. to administer (a blow, etc.) —*vi.* 1. to have to do (*with*) [books *dealing* with fish] 2. to conduct oneself [*deal* fairly with others] 3. to attend to 4. to do business; trade (*with* or *in*) 5. to distribute playing cards to the players —*n.* 1. *a)* the distribution of playing cards *b)* a player's turn to deal 2. a business transaction 3. an agreement, esp. when underhanded 4. [Colloq.] conduct toward another —**deal′er** *n.*
deal[2] (dēl) *n.* [OE. *dæl*, a part] an indefinite or considerable amount —**a good** (or **great**) **deal** 1. a large amount 2. very much
deal′er·ship′ (-ship′) *n.* a franchise to market a product in an area
deal′ing *n.* 1. distribution 2. behavior 3. [*usually pl.*] transactions or relations
dean (dēn) *n.* [< LL. *decanus*, head of ten (monks, etc.)] 1. the presiding official of a cathedral 2. a college official in charge of the students or faculty 3. the senior member of a group —**dean′ship′** *n.*
dear (dir) *adj.* [OE. *deore*] 1. much loved 2. esteemed: a polite form of address [*Dear* Sir] 3. high-priced; costly 4. earnest [*our dearest* wish] —*n.* a loved person; darling —**interj.** an expression of distress, etc.
dearth (durth) *n.* [< ME. *dere*, dear] 1. famine 2. any scarcity or lack
death (deth) *n.* [OE.] 1. the act or fact of dying; ending of life 2. the state of being dead 3. any end resembling dying; total destruction 4. the cause of death —**put to death** to kill; execute —**death′like′** *adj.*
death′bed′ *n.* 1. the bed on which a person dies 2. one's last hours
death′blow′ *n.* 1. a blow that kills 2. a thing destructive or fatal (*to* something)
death′less *adj.* that cannot die; immortal —**death′less·ly** *adv.* —**death′less·ness** *n.*
death′ly *adj.* 1. causing death; deadly 2. like or characteristic of death —*adv.* 1. in a deathlike way 2. extremely [*deathly* ill]
death′trap′ *n.* an unsafe building, vehicle, etc.
death′watch′ *n.* a vigil beside a dead or dying person
de·ba·cle (di bäk′'l, -bak′-) *n.* [< Fr. *débâcler*, break up] 1. an overthrow; rout 2. a total, often ludicrous, failure
de·bar (dē bär′) *vt.* -barred′, -bar′ring [< Fr.: see DE- & BAR] 1. to exclude (*from* something); bar 2. to prevent or prohibit
de·bark (di bärk′) *vt., vi.* [< Fr. *dé*, from + *barque*, boat] to disembark —**de·bar·ka·tion** (dē′bär kā′shən) *n.*
de·base (di bās′) *vt.* -based′, -bas′ing [DE- + (A)BASE] to make lower in value, quality, dignity, etc. —**de·base′ment** *n.*
de·bate (di bāt′) *vi., vt.* -bat′ed, -bat′ing [< OFr.: see DE- & BATTER[1]] to engage in dispute (about); argue formally —*n.* 1. discussion of opposing reasons 2. a formal contest of skill in reasoned argument between opposing teams —**de·bat′a·ble** *adj.* —**de·bat′er** *n.*
de·bauch (di bôch′) *vt.* [Fr. *débaucher*, seduce]

to lead astray morally; corrupt —*vi.* to dissipate —*n.* an orgy —**de·bauch′er·y** *n., pl.* **-ies**
de·ben·ture (di ben′chər) *n.* [< L.: see DEBT] 1. a voucher acknowledging a debt 2. an interest-bearing bond
de·bil·i·tate (di bil′ə tāt′) *vt.* -tat′ed, -tat′ing [< L. *debilis*, weak] to make weak; enervate —**de·bil′i·ta′tion** *n.*
de·bil′i·ty (-tē) *n., pl.* **-ties** [< L. *debilis*, weak] bodily weakness; feebleness
deb·it (deb′it) *n.* [< L. *debere*, owe] 1. an entry in an account of money owed 2. the total of such entries —*vt.* to enter as a debit or debits
deb·o·nair, deb·o·naire (deb′ə ner′) *adj.* [< OFr. *de bon aire*, of good breed] 1. genial; affable 2. carefree; jaunty —**deb′o·nair′ly** *adv.*
de·bris, dé·bris (də brē′) *n.* [Fr. < OFr. *desbrisier*, break apart] 1. broken stone, wood, etc.; rubble 2. rubbish; litter
debt (det) *n.* [< L. *debere*, owe] 1. something owed to another 2. the condition of owing [to be in *debt*] 3. *Theol.* a sin
debt′or (-ər) *n.* one that owes a debt
de·bug (dē bug′) *vt.* -bugged′, -bug′ging [Slang] 1. to correct defects in 2. to find and remove hidden listening devices from
de·bunk (di buŋk′) *vt.* [DE- + BUNK[2]] [Colloq.] to expose the false or exaggerated claims, etc. of
de·but, dé·but (di byōō′, dā′byōō) *n.* [Fr. < *débuter*, lead off] 1. the first appearance before the public, as of an actor 2. the formal introduction of a girl into society
deb·u·tante (deb′yoo tänt′, deb′yoo tänt′) *n.* [< Fr.] a girl making a debut, esp. into society
deca- [< Gr. *deka*, ten] *a combining form meaning* ten: also **dec-**
dec·ade (dek′ād) *n.* [< Gr. *deka*, ten] 1. a group of ten 2. a period of ten years
dec·a·dence (dek′ə dəns, di kā′d'ns) *n.* [Fr. < L. *de-*, from + *cadere*, to fall] a process, condition, or period of decline, as in morals, art, etc.; deterioration —**dec′a·dent** *adj., n.*
dec·a·gon (dek′ə gän′) *n.* [see DECA- & -GON] a plane figure with ten sides and ten angles
dec·a·he·dron (dek′ə hē′drən) *n., pl.* **-drons, -dra** (-drə) [see DECA- & -HEDRON] a solid figure with ten plane surfaces
de·cal (di kal′) *n.* same as DECALCOMANIA
de·cal·co·ma·ni·a (di kal′kə mā′nē ə) *n.* [< Fr. < *décalquer*, to trace + *manie*, madness] a picture or design transferred from prepared paper onto glass, wood, etc.
Dec·a·logue, Dec·a·log (dek′ə lôg′) *n.* [< Gr.: see DECA- & -LOGUE] [*sometimes* d-] same as TEN COMMANDMENTS
de·camp (di kamp′) *vi.* [< Fr.: see DE- & CAMP] 1. to break camp 2. to go away suddenly and secretly
de·cant (di kant′) *vt.* [< Fr.: see DE- & CANT[2]] to pour off (a liquid) gently without stirring up the sediment
de·cant′er *n.* a decorative glass bottle, used for serving wine, etc.
de·cap·i·tate (di kap′ə tāt′) *vi.* -tat′ed, -tat′ing [Fr. < L. *de-*, off + *caput*, the head] to behead —**de·cap′i·ta′tion** *n.*
dec·a·pod (dek′ə päd′) *adj.* [see DECA- & -POD] ten-legged —*n.* any crustacean with ten legs
dec·a·syl·la·ble (dek′ə sil′ə b'l) *n.* a line of verse with ten syllables
de·cath·lon (di kath′län) *n.* [DEC(A)- + Gr. *athlon*, a contest] an athletic contest consisting of ten track and field events
de·cay (di kā′) *vi.* [see DECADENCE] 1. to lose strength, prosperity, etc. gradually; deteriorate 2. to rot 3. to undergo radioactive disintegra-

tion —*vt.* to cause to decay —*n.* **1.** deterioration **2.** a rotting **3.** radioactive disintegration

de·cease (di sēs') *n.* [< L. *de-*, from + *cedere*, go] death —*vi.* **-ceased'**, **-ceas'ing** to die

de·ceased' *adj.* dead —**the deceased** the dead person or persons

de·ceit (di sēt') *n.* **1.** a deceiving or lying **2.** a lie **3.** a deceitful quality

de·ceit'ful *adj.* **1.** apt to lie or cheat **2.** deceptive; false —**de·ceit'ful·ly** *adv.*

de·ceive (di sēv') *vt.* **-ceived'**, **-ceiv'ing** [< L. *decipere*] to make (a person) believe what is not true; mislead —*vi.* to use deceit

de·cel·er·ate (dē sel'ə rāt') *vt.*, *vi.* **-at'ed**, **-at'-ing** [DE- + (AC)CELERATE] to slow down

De·cem·ber (di sem'bər) *n.* [< L. *decem*, ten: tenth month in Rom. calendar] the twelfth and last month of the year, having 31 days: abbrev. **Dec.**

de·cen·cy (dē's'n sē) *n.*, *pl.* **-cies** a being decent; proper behavior, modesty, etc.

de·cen·ni·al (di sen'ē əl) *adj.* [< L. *decem*, ten + *annus*, year] **1.** of or lasting ten years **2.** occurring every ten years —*n.* a tenth anniversary

de·cent (dē's'nt) *adj.* [< L. *decere*, befit] **1.** proper and fitting **2.** not obscene **3.** respectable **4.** adequate *[decent* wages] **5.** fair and kind —**de'cent·ly** *adv.*

de·cen·tral·ize (dē sen'trə līz') *vt.* **-ized'**, **-iz'-ing** to break up (governmental authority, etc.) concentrated in a main center and distribute more widely —**de·cen'tral·i·za'tion** *n.*

de·cep·tion (di sep'shən) *n.* **1.** a deceiving or being deceived **2.** an illusion or fraud —**de·cep'tive** *adj.* —**de·cep'tive·ly** *adv.*

dec·i·bel (des'ə bel', -b'l) *n.* [< L. *decem*, ten + A. G. *Bell* (1847-1922)] a numerical expression of the relative loudness of a sound

de·cide (di sīd') *vt.* **-cid'ed**, **-cid'ing** [< L. *de-*, off + *caedere*, to cut] **1.** to end (a contest, dispute, etc.) by giving one side the victory **2.** to reach a decision about —*vi.* to arrive at a judgment or decision

de·cid'ed *adj.* **1.** definite; clear-cut **2.** unhesitating —**de·cid'ed·ly** *adv.*

de·cid·u·ous (di sij'oo wəs) *adj.* [< L. *de-*, + *cadere*, fall] **1.** falling off at a certain season, as some leaves or antlers **2.** shedding leaves annually

dec·i·mal (des'ə m'l) *adj.* [< L. *decem*, ten] of or based on the number 10 —*n.* a fraction with an unwritten denominator of 10 or some power of 10, shown by a point (**decimal point**) before the numerator (Ex.: .5 = 5/10)

dec·i·mate (des'ə māt') *vt.* **-mat'ed**, **-mat'ing** [< L. *decem*, ten] to destroy or kill a large part of —**dec'i·ma'tor** *n.*

de·ci·pher (di sī'fər) *vt.* [DE- + CIPHER] **1.** to translate from secret writing or code **2.** to make out the meaning of (a scrawl, etc.) —**de·ci'pher·a·ble** *adj.*

de·ci·sion (di sizh'ən) *n.* **1.** the act of deciding or settling a dispute or question **2.** the act of making up one's mind **3.** a judgment or conclusion **4.** determination

de·ci·sive (di sī'siv) *adj.* **1.** that settles a dispute, question, etc. **2.** showing decision

deck (dek) *n.* [MDu. *decken*, to cover] **1.** a floor of a ship **2.** a pack of playing cards —*vt.* to adorn; trim

deck'hand' *n.* a common sailor

deck·le edge (dek''l) [< G. *decke*, a cover] the rough, irregular edge on an untrimmed sheet of paper

de·claim (di klām') *vi.*, *vt.* [< L. *de-*, intens. + *clamare*, to shout] to recite or speak in a stud-

ied, dramatic, or impassioned way —**dec·la·ma·tion** (dek'lə mā'shən) *n.* —**de·clam·a·to·ry** (di klam'ə tôr'ē) *adj.*

dec·la·ra·tion (dek'lə rā'shən) *n.* **1.** a declaring; announcement **2.** a formal statement **3.** *Bridge* the winning bid

de·clar·a·tive (di klar'ə tiv) *adj.* making a statement or assertion

de·clare (di kler') *vt.* **-clared'**, **-clar'ing** [< L. *de-*, intens. + *clarus*, clear] **1.** to announce openly or formally **2.** to show or reveal **3.** to say emphatically **4.** *Card Games* to establish (trump or no-trump) by a successful bid —**declare oneself** to state strongly one's opinion —**de·clar'er** *n.*

de·clas·si·fy (dē klas'ə fī') *vt.* **-fied'**, **-fy'ing** to make (secret documents) available to the public

de·clen·sion (di klen'shən) *n.* [see DECLINE] **1.** a descent **2.** a decline **3.** *Gram.* the inflection of nouns, pronouns, or adjectives

de·cline (di klīn') *vi.* **-clined'**, **-clin'ing** [< L. *de-*, from + *clinare*, to bend] **1.** to bend or slope downward **2.** to deteriorate **3.** to refuse something —*vt.* **1.** to cause to bend or slope downward **2.** to refuse, esp. politely **3.** *Gram.* to give the inflected forms of (a noun, pronoun, or adjective) —*n.* **1.** a declining; deterioration; decay **2.** a period of decline **3.** a downward slope —**dec·li·na·tion** (dek'lə nā'shən) *n.*

de·cliv·i·ty (di kliv'ə tē) *n.*, *pl.* **-ties** [< L. *de-*, down + *clivus*, a slope] a downward slope

de·coct (di käkt') *vt.* [< L. *de-*, down + *coquere*, to cook] to extract the essence, flavor, etc. of by boiling —**de·coc'tion** *n.*

de·code (dē kōd') *vt.* **-cod'ed**, **-cod'ing** to translate (a coded message) into understandable language

dé·col·le·té (dā käl'ə tā') *adj.* [Fr. < L. *de*, from + *collum*, neck] cut low so as to bare the neck and shoulders

de·com·pose (dē'kəm pōz') *vt.*, *vi.* **-posed'**, **-pos'ing** [< Fr.] **1.** to break up into basic components or parts **2.** to rot —**de'com·po·si'tion** (-käm pə zish'ən) *n.*

de·con·gest·ant (dē'kən jes'tənt) *n.* a medication or treatment that relieves congestion, as in the nasal passages

de'con·tam'i·nate' (-tam'ə nāt') *vt.* **-nat'ed**, **-nat'ing** to rid of a harmful substance, as radioactive products

dé·cor, **de·cor** (dā kôr') *n.* [Fr.] a decorative scheme, as of a room

dec·o·rate (dek'ə rāt') *vt.* **-rat'ed**, **-rat'ing** [< L. *decus*, an ornament] **1.** to adorn; ornament **2.** to paint or wallpaper **3.** to give a medal or similar honor to —**dec'o·ra·tive** (-ər ə tiv, -ə rāt'iv) *adj.* —**dec'o·ra·tive·ly** *adv.* —**dec'o·ra'tor** *n.*

dec'o·ra'tion *n.* **1.** a decorating **2.** an ornament **3.** a medal or similar honor

Decoration Day *same as* MEMORIAL DAY

dec·o·rous (dek'ər əs, di kôr'əs) *adj.* having or showing decorum, good taste, etc.

de·co·rum (di kôr'əm) *n.* [< L. *decorus*, proper] **1.** whatever is suitable or proper **2.** propriety and good taste in behavior, speech, dress, etc.

de·cou·page, **dé·cou·page** (dā'kōō päzh') *n.* [Fr.] the art of cutting out designs from paper, foil, etc. and mounting them decoratively on a surface

de·coy (di koi'; *for n. also* dē'koi) *n.* [< Du. *de kooi*, the cage] **1.** an artificial or trained bird, etc. used to lure game into gun range **2.** a

thing or person used to lure into a trap —*vt.,
vi.* to lure or be lured into a trap

de·crease (di krēs′) *vi., vt.* -creased′, -creas′-
ing [< L. *de*-, from + *crescere*, grow] to
become or make gradually less, smaller, etc.;
diminish —*n.* (dē′krēs) 1. a decreasing 2.
amount of decreasing

de·cree (di krē′) *n.* [< L. *de*-, from + *cernere*,
see] an official order or decision —*vt.* -creed′,
-cree′ing to order by decree

de·crep·it (di krep′it) *adj.* [< L. *de*-, intens. +
crepare, creak] broken down or worn out by
old age or long use —**de·crep′i·tude′** (-ə tōōd′)
n.

de·cry (di krī′) *vt.* -cried′, -cry′ing [< Fr.: see
DE- & CRY] to denounce; censure

ded·i·cate (ded′ə kāt′) *vt.* -cat′ed, -cat′ing [<
L. *de*-, intens. + *dicare*, proclaim] 1. to set
aside for some purpose, esp. a religious one;
devote 2. to address (a book, etc.) to someone
as a sign of honor —**ded′i·ca′tion** *n.* —**ded′i·
ca′tor** *n.*

de·duce (di dōōs′) *vt.* -duced′, -duc′ing [< L.
de-, down + *ducere*, to lead] to infer by reasoning —**de·duc′i·ble** *adj.*

de·duct (di dukt′) *vt.* [see DEDUCE] to take
away or subtract (an amount or quantity) —
de·duct′i·ble *adj.*

de·duc′tion (-duk′shən) *n.* 1. a deducting or
being deducted 2. the amount deducted 3. reasoning from the general to the specific 4. a
conclusion —**de·duc′tive** *adj.*

deed (dēd) *n.* [OE. *dæd*] 1. a thing done; act 2.
a feat of courage, skill, etc. 3. a legal document
which transfers a property —*vt.* to transfer
(property) by such a document —**in deed** in
fact; really

deem (dēm) *vt., vi.* [OE. *deman*, to judge] to
think, believe, or judge

deep (dēp) *adj.* [OE. *deop*] 1. extending far
downward, inward, or backward 2. hard to understand; abstruse 3. serious 4. profound; wise
5. dark and rich [a *deep* red] 6. absorbed by
[*deep* in thought] 7. intense 8. of low pitch —*n.*
1. a deep place 2. the part that is darkest, etc.
[the *deep* of night] —*adv.* far down, far back,
etc. —**the deep** [Poet.] the ocean

deep′en (-′n) *vt., vi.* to make or become deep
or deeper

deep′-fry′ *vt.* -fried′, -fry′ing to fry in a deep
pan of boiling fat

deep′-root′ed *adj.* 1. having deep roots 2.
firmly fixed

deep′-seat′ed *adj.* 1. buried deep 2. firmly
fixed

deer (dir) *n., pl.* deer, occas. deers [OE. *deor*,
wild animal] a hoofed, cud-chewing animal,
the male of which bears antlers that are shed
annually

de·es·ca·late (dē es′kə lāt′) *vi., vt.* -lat′ed,
-lat′ing to reduce or lessen in scope, magnitude, etc. —**de·es·ca·la′tion** *n.*

de·face (di fās′) *vt.* -faced′, -fac′ing [see DE- &
FACE] to spoil the appearance of; mar —**de·
face′ment** *n.* —**de·fac′er** *n.*

de·fal·cate (di fal′kāt) *vi.* -cat·ed, -cat·ing [<
L. *defalcare*, to cut off] to embezzle —**de·fal·
ca·tion** (dē′fal kā′shən) *n.*

de·fame (di fām′) *vt.* -famed′, -fam′ing [< L.
dis-, from + *fama*, fame] to attack the reputation of; slander or libel —**def·a·ma·tion** (def′ə
mā′shən) *n.* —**de·fam·a·to·ry** (di fam′ə tôr′ē)
adj. —**de·fam′er** *n.*

de·fault (di fôlt′) *n.* [< L. *de*-, away + *fallere*,
fail] 1. failure to do or appear as required 2.
failure to pay money due —*vi., vt.* 1. to fail to

do, pay, etc. when required 2. to lose (a
contest) by default

de·feat (di fēt′) *vt.* [< L. *dis*-, from + *facere*,
do] 1. to win victory over 2. to bring to nothing; frustrate —*n.* a defeating or being defeated

de·feat′ist *n.* [< Fr.] one who too readily ac-
cepts defeat —**de·feat′ism** *n.*

def·e·cate (def′ə kāt′) *vi.* -cat·ed, -cat·ing [<
L. *de*-, from + *faex*, dregs] to excrete waste
matter from the bowels —**def′e·ca′tion** *n.*

de·fect (dē′fekt, di fekt′) *n.* [< L. *de*-, from +
facere, do] 1. lack of something necessary for
completeness 2. an imperfection; fault —*vi.* (di
fekt′) to forsake a party, cause, etc.; desert —
de·fec′tion *n.* —**de·fec′tor** *n.*

de·fec·tive (di fek′tiv) *adj.* having defects; imperfect; faulty —**de·fec′tive·ly** *adv.*

de·fend (di fend′) *vt.* [< L. *de*-, away + *fendere*, to strike] 1. to guard from attack;
protect 2. to support or justify 3. *Law* a) to
oppose (an action, etc.) b) to act as lawyer for
(an accused) —**de·fend′er** *n.*

de·fend·ant (di fen′dənt) *n. Law* the person
sued or accused

de·fense (di fens′) *n.* 1. a defending against
attack 2. something that defends 3. justification by speech or writing 4. *a)* the arguments
of a defendant *b)* the defendant and his counsel Brit. sp. **defence** —**de·fense′less** *adj.* —**de·
fen′si·ble** *adj.*

de·fen′sive *adj.* 1. defending 2. of or for defense —*n.* attitude or position of defense

de·fer′ (di fur′) *vt., vi.* -ferred′, -fer′ring [see
DIFFER] to postpone; delay —**de·fer′ment, de·
fer′ral** *n.*

de·fer² (di fur′) *vi.* -ferred′, -fer′ring [< L. *de*-,
down + *ferre*, to bear] to give in to the wish
or judgment of another

def·er·ence (def′ər əns) *n.* [< Fr.] 1. a yielding
in opinion, judgment, etc. 2. courteous respect

def·er·en·tial (-ə ren′shəl) *adj.* showing deference; very respectful

de·fi·ance (di fī′əns) *n.* a defying; open, bold
resistance to authority —**de·fi′ant** *adj.* —**de·fi′-
ant·ly** *adv.*

de·fi·cien·cy (di fish′ən sē) *n.* 1. a being deficient 2. *pl.* -cies a shortage

de·fi′cient (-ənt) *adj.* [see DEFECT] 1. lacking
in some essential; incomplete 2. inadequate in
amount, quality, etc.

def·i·cit (def′ə sit) *n.* [L. < *deficere*, to lack]
the amount by which a sum of money is less
than the required amount

de·file′ (di fīl′) *vt.* -filed′, -fil′ing [< OFr.
defouler, tread underfoot] 1. to make filthy 2.
to profane or sully —**de·file′ment** *n.*

de·file² (di fīl′, dē′fīl) *vi.* -filed′, -fil′ing [< Fr.
défiler, unravel] to march in single file —*n.* a
narrow passage, valley, etc.

de·fine (di fīn′) *vt.* -fined′, -fin′ing [< L. *de*-,
from + *finis*, boundary] 1. to determine the
limits or nature of; describe exactly 2. to state
the meaning of (a word, etc.) —**de·fin′a·ble** *adj.*

def·i·nite (def′ə nit) *adj.* [see prec.] 1. having
exact limits 2. precise in meaning; explicit 3.
certain; positive 4. *Gram.* limiting or specifying [''the'' is the *definite* article] —**def′i·nite·ly**
adv. —**def′i·nite·ness** *n.*

def·i·ni·tion (def′ə nish′ən) *n.* 1. a defining or
being defined 2. a statement of the meaning of
a word, etc.

de·fin·i·tive (di fin′ə tiv) *adj.* 1. conclusive 2.
most nearly complete and accurate 3. serving
to define —**de·fin′i·tive·ly** *adv.*

de·flate (di flāt′) *vt., vi.* -flat′ed, -flat′ing [DE-
+ (IN)FLATE] 1. to collapse by letting out air

or gas **2.** to lessen in amount, size, importance, etc.

de·fla'tion *n.* **1.** a deflating or being deflated **2.** a lessening of the amount of money in circulation, making it rise in value

de·flect (di flekt') *vt., vi.* [< L. *de-*, from + *flectere*, to bend] to turn or bend to one side — **de·flec'tion** *n.* —**de·flec'tive** *adj.*

de·flow·er (di flou'ər) *vt.* [see DE- & FLOWER] **1.** to make (a woman) no longer a virgin **2.** to ravage or spoil

de·fo·li·ant (dē fō'lē ənt) *n.* [< L. *de-*, from + *folium*, leaf] a chemical spray that strips growing plants of their leaves —**de·fo'li·ate'** (-āt') *vt.* -at'ed, -at'ing

de·for·est (dē fôr'ist, -fär'-) *vt.* to clear (land) of forests or trees

de·form (di fôrm') *vt.* [< L. *de-*, from + *forma*, form] **1.** to impair the form of **2.** to make ugly —**de·for·ma·tion** (dē'fôr mā'shən, def'ər-) *n.* — **de·form'er** *n.*

de·formed' *adj.* misshapen

de·form·i·ty (di fôr'mə tē) *n., pl.* -ties **1.** a deformed part, as of the body **2.** ugliness or depravity

de·fraud (di frôd') *vt.* to take property, rights, etc. from by fraud; cheat

de·fray (di frā') *vt.* [Fr. *défrayer*] to pay (the cost or expenses) —**de·fray'al** *n.*

de·frost (di frôst') *vt., vi.* to rid or become rid of frost or ice —**de·frost'er** *n.*

deft (deft) *adj.* [see DAFT] skillful in a quick, sure way —**deft'ly** *adv.*

de·funct (di funkt') *adj.* [< L. *defungi*, to finish] no longer existing; dead or extinct

de·fy (di fī') *vt.* -fied', -fy'ing [< L. *dis-*, from + *fidus*, faithful] **1.** to resist boldly or openly **2.** to dare (someone) to do or prove something

de·gen·er·ate (di jen'ər it) *adj.* [< L. *de-*, from + *genus*, race] having sunk below a former or normal condition, etc.; deteriorated —*n.* a degenerate person —*vi.* (-āt') -at'ed, -at'ing to lose former normal or higher qualities —**de·gen'er·a·cy** (-ə sē) *n.* —**de·gen'er·a'tion** *n.*

de·grade (di grād') *vt.* -grad'ed, -grad'ing [< L. *de-*, down + *gradus*, a step] **1.** to demote **2.** to lower in quality, moral character, etc. **3.** to dishonor; debase —**deg·ra·da·tion** (deg'rə dā'shən) *n.*

de·gree (di grē') *n.* [see prec.] **1.** any of the successive steps in a process **2.** social or official rank **3.** extent, amount, or intensity **4.** a rank given by a college or university to one who has completed a course of study, or to a distinguished person as an honor **5.** a grade of comparison of adjectives and adverbs [the superlative *degree*] **6.** *Law* the seriousness of a crime [murder in the first *degree*] **7.** a unit of measure for angles or arcs, 1/360 of the circumference of a circle **8.** a unit of measure for temperature —**by degrees** gradually —**to a degree** somewhat

de·hu·man·ize (dē hyōō'mə nīz') *vt.* -ized', -iz'ing to deprive of human qualities; make inhuman or machinelike

de·hu·mid·i·fy (dē'hyōō mid'ə fī') *vt.* -fied', -fy'ing to remove moisture from (the air, etc.) —**de'hu·mid'i·fi'er** *n.*

de·hy·drate (dē hī'drāt) *vt.* -drat·ed, -drat·ing to remove water from; dry —*vi.* to lose water — **de'hy·dra'tion** *n.*

de·i·fy (dē'ə fī') *vt.* -fied', -fy'ing [< L. *deus*, god + *facere*, to make] **1.** to make a god of **2.** to look upon as a god —**de'i·fi·ca'tion** (-fi kā'shən) *n.*

deign (dān) *vi.* [< L. *dignus*, worthy] to condescend (*to do* something)

de·ism (dē'iz'm) *n.* [< Fr. < L. *deus*, god] the belief that God exists and created the world but thereafter did not control it

de·i·ty (dē'ə tē) *n., pl.* -ties [< L. *deus*, god] **1.** the state of being a god **2.** a god or goddess — **the Deity** God

de·ject (di jekt') *vt.* [< L. *de-*, down + *jacere*, to throw] to dishearten; depress —**de·jec'tion** *n.*

de·ject'ed *adj.* in low spirits; depressed

de·lay (di lā') *vt.* [< OFr. *de-*, intens. + *laier*, to leave] **1.** to put off; postpone **2.** to make late; detain —*vi.* to stop for a while —*n.* a delaying or being delayed

de·lec·ta·ble (di lek'tə b'l) *adj.* [see DELIGHT] delightful or delicious

de·lec·ta·tion (dē'lek tā'shən) *n.* [see DELIGHT] delight; enjoyment

del·e·gate (del'ə gāt'; *also, for n.,* -git) *n.* [< L. *de-*, from + *legare*, send] a person authorized to act for others; representative —*vt.* -gat'ed, -gat'ing **1.** to appoint as a delegate **2.** to entrust (authority, etc.) to another

del'e·ga'tion *n.* **1.** a delegating or being delegated **2.** a group of delegates

de·lete (di lēt') *vt.* -let'ed, -let'ing [< L. *delere*, destroy] to take out (a word, etc.); cross out — **de·le'tion** *n.*

del·e·te·ri·ous (del'ə tir'ē əs) *adj.* [< Gr. *dēleisthai*, injure] harmful to health, well-being, etc.; injurious

delft·ware (delft'wer') *n.* [< *Delft*, city in the Netherlands] glazed earthenware, usually blue and white: also **delft, delf**

de·lib·er·ate (di lib'ər it) *adj.* [< L. *de-*, intens. + *librare*, weigh] **1.** carefully thought out, or done on purpose **2.** not rash or hasty **3.** unhurried —*vi., vt.* (-āt') -at'ed, -at'ing to consider carefully —**de·lib'er·ate·ly** *adv.* —**de·lib'er·a'tive** *adj.*

de·lib'er·a'tion *n.* **1.** a deliberating **2.** [*often pl.*] consideration and debate **3.** carefulness

del·i·ca·cy (del'i kə sē) *n., pl.* -cies **1.** the quality or state of being delicate; fineness, sensitivity, etc. **2.** a choice food

del·i·cate (del'i kit) *adj.* [< L. *delicatus*, delightful] **1.** pleasantly mild, light, etc. **2.** beautifully fine in texture, workmanship, etc. **3.** slight and subtle **4.** easily damaged, spoiled, etc. **5.** frail in health **6.** *a)* needing careful handling *b)* showing tact, consideration, etc. **7.** finely sensitive —**del'i·cate·ly** *adv.* —**del'i·cate·ness** *n.*

del·i·ca·tes·sen (del'i kə tes''n) *n.* [< G. pl. < Fr. *délicatesse*, delicacy] **1.** prepared cooked meats, fish, cheeses, salads, etc. **2.** a shop where such foods are sold

de·li·cious (di lish'əs) *adj.* [see DELIGHT] **1.** very enjoyable **2.** very pleasing to taste or smell —*n.* [**D-**] a sweet winter apple —**de·li'cious·ly** *adv.* —**de·li'cious·ness** *n.*

de·light (di līt') *vt.* [< L. *de-*, from + *lacere*, entice] to give great pleasure to —*vi.* **1.** to give great pleasure **2.** to be highly pleased —*n.* great pleasure, or a source of this —**de·light'ed** *adj.*

de·light'ful *adj.* giving delight; very pleasing — **de·light'ful·ly** *adv.*

De·li·lah (di lī'lə) *Bible* the mistress and betrayer of Samson

de·lim·it (di lim'it) *vt.* to set the limits or boundaries of —**de·lim'i·ta'tion** *n.*

de·lin·e·ate (di lin'ē āt') *vt.* -at'ed, -at'ing [< L. *de-*, from + *linea*, a line] **1.** to draw; sketch **2.** to depict in words; describe —**de·lin'e·a'tion** *n.* —**de·lin'e·a'tor** *n.*

de·lin·quent (di liŋ'kwənt) *adj.* [< L. *de-*, from

+ *linquere*, to leave] **1.** failing to do what duty or law requires **2.** overdue, as taxes —*n.* a delinquent person; esp., *same as* JUVENILE DELINQUENT —**de·lin′quen·cy** *n.*, *pl.* **-cies** —**delin′quent·ly** *adv.*

del·i·quesce (del′ə kwes′) *vi.* **-quesced′, -quesc′ing** [< L. *de-*, from + *liquere*, be liquid] **1.** to melt away **2.** to become liquid by absorbing moisture from the air —**del′i·ques′cence** *n.* —**del′i·ques′cent** *adj.*

de·lir·i·ous (di lir′ē əs) *adj.* **1.** in a state of delirium **2.** of or caused by delirium **3.** wildly excited —**de·lir′i·ous·ly** *adv.*

de·lir′i·um (-əm) *n.*, *pl.* **-ums, -a** (-ə) [< L. *de-*, from + *lira*, a line] **1.** a temporary mental disturbance, as during a fever, marked by confused speech and hallucinations **2.** uncontrollably wild excitement

de·liv·er (di liv′ər) *vt.* [< L. *de-*, from + *liberare*, to free] **1.** to set free or rescue **2.** to assist at the birth of **3.** to utter (a speech, etc.) **4.** to hand over **5.** to distribute (mail, etc.) **6.** to strike (a blow) **7.** to throw (a ball) —**de·liv′er·a·ble** *adj.*

de·liv′er·ance *n.* **1.** a freeing or being freed **2.** an opinion, etc. publicly expressed

de·liv′er·y *n.*, *pl.* **-ies 1.** a handing over **2.** a distributing, as of mail **3.** a giving birth; childbirth **4.** any giving forth **5.** the act or manner of giving a speech, throwing a ball, etc. **6.** something delivered

dell (del) *n.* [OE. *del*] a small, secluded valley or glen, usually a wooded one

del·phin·i·um (del fin′ē əm) *n.* [< Gr. *delphin*, dolphin] a tall plant bearing spikes of flowers, usually blue; larkspur

del·ta (del′tə) *n.* **1.** the fourth letter of the Greek alphabet (Δ, δ) **2.** a depósit of soil, usually triangular, formed at the mouth of some rivers

de·lude (di lōōd′) *vt.* **-lud′ed, -lud′ing** [< L. *de-*, from + *ludere*, to play] to mislead; deceive

del·uge (del′yōōj) *n.* [< L. *dis-*, off + *lavere*, to wash] **1.** a great flood **2.** a heavy rainfall — *vt.* **-uged, -ug·ing 1.** to flood **2.** to overwhelm

de·lu·sion (di lōō′zhən) *n.* **1.** a deluding or being deluded **2.** a false belief, specif. one not substantiated by objective evidence

de·luxe (di luks′, -lōōks′) *adj.* [Fr., lit., of luxury] of extra fine quality; elegant —*adv.* in a deluxe manner

delve (delv) *vi.* **delved, delv′ing** [OE. *delfan*] **1.** [Archaic] to dig **2.** to investigate; search (*into*) —**delv′er** *n.*

Dem. 1. Democrat **2.** Democratic

de·mag·net·ize (dē mag′nə tīz′) *vt.* **-ized′, -iz′-ing** to deprive of magnetic properties

dem·a·gogue, dem·a·gog (dem′ə gäg′) *n.* [< Gr. *dēmos*, the people + *agōgos*, leader] one who tries to stir up people's emotions so as to gain power —**dem′a·gog′y** (-gō′jē, -gäg′ē), **dem′a·gogu′er·y** (-gäg′ər ē) *n.*

de·mand (di mand′) *vt.* [< L. *de-*, from + *mandare*, entrust] **1.** to ask for boldly or urgently **2.** to ask for as a right **3.** to require; need —*vi.* to make a demand —*n.* **1.** a demanding **2.** a thing demanded **3.** a strong request **4.** an urgent requirement **5.** *Econ.* the desire for a commodity together with ability to pay for it; also, the amount people are ready to buy at a certain price —**in demand** asked for —**on demand** when presented for payment

de·mand′ing *adj.* making difficult demands on one's patience, energy, etc.

de·mar·ca·tion (dē′mär kā′shən) *n.* [< Sp. *de-*, from + *marcar*, to mark] **1.** the setting and marking of boundaries **2.** a boundary

de·mean′ (di mēn′) *vt.* [DE- + MEAN²] to degrade; lower

de·mean² (di mēn′) *vt.* [see DEMEANOR] to behave or conduct (oneself)

de·mean·or (di mēn′ər) *n.* [< OFr. *demener*, to lead] outward behavior; conduct

de·ment·ed (di ment′id) *adj.* [see DEMENTIA] mentally deranged; insane

de·men·tia (di men′shə) *n.* [< L. *de-*, out from + *mens*, the mind] loss or impairment of mental powers due to organic causes

de·mer·it (di mer′it) *n.* [< L. *de-*, intens. + *merere*, deserve, with *de-* taken as negative] **1.** a fault; defect **2.** a mark recorded against a student, etc. for poor conduct or work

de·mesne (di mān′, -mēn′) *n.* [see DOMAIN] a region or domain

De·me·ter (di mēt′ər) *Gr. Myth.* the goddess of agriculture

demi- [< L. *dimidius*, half] *a prefix meaning:* **1.** half **2.** less than usual in size, power, etc. *[demigod]*

dem·i·god (dem′ē gäd′) *n.* **1.** a minor deity **2.** a godlike person

dem′i·john′ (-jän′) *n.* [Fr. *dame-jeanne*] a large bottle of glass or earthenware in a wicker casing

de·mil·i·ta·rize (dē mil′ə tə rīz′) *vt.* **-rized′, -riz′ing** to free from military control or from militarism

dem·i·monde (dem′ē mänd′) *n.* [Fr. < *demi-*, DEMI- + *monde*, world] the class of women who have lost social standing because of sexual promiscuity

de·mise (di mīz′) *n.* [< Fr. < L. *de-*, down + *mittere*, send] **1.** *Law* a transfer of an estate by lease **2.** death —*vt.* **-mised′, -mis′ing** to transfer (an estate) by lease

dem·i·tasse (dem′ē tas′, -täs′) *n.* [Fr. < *demi-*, DEMI- + *tasse*, cup] a small cup of or for after-dinner black coffee

de·mo·bi·lize (dē mō′bə līz′) *vt.* **-lized′, -liz′ing** to disband (troops) —**de·mo′bi·li·za′tion** *n.*

de·moc·ra·cy (di mäk′rə sē) *n.*, *pl.* **-cies** [< Fr. < Gr. *dēmos*, the people + *kratein*, to rule] **1.** government by the people, directly or through representatives **2.** a country, etc. with such government **3.** equality of rights, opportunity, and treatment

dem·o·crat (dem′ə krat′) *n.* **1.** one who supports or practices democracy **2.** [D-] a member of the Democratic Party

dem′o·crat′ic *adj.* **1.** of or upholding (a) democracy **2.** of or for all or most people **3.** treating people of all classes in the same way **4.** [D-] of or belonging to the Democratic Party

Democratic Party one of the two major political parties in the U.S.

de·mod·u·la·tion (dē mäj′ōō lā′shən) *n.* *Radio* the recovery, at the receiver, of a signal modulated on a carrier wave

de·mog·ra·phy (di mäg′rə fē) *n.* [< Gr. *dēmos*, people + -GRAPHY] the statistical study of populations —**de·mog′ra·pher** *n.*

de·mol·ish (di mäl′ish) *vt.* [< Fr. < L. *de-*, down + *moliri*, build] to wreck —**dem·o·li·tion** (dem′ə lish′ən, dē′mə-) *n.*

de·mon (dē′mən) *n.* [< L. *daemon*] **1.** *same as* DAEMON **2.** a devil; evil spirit **3.** a person or thing regarded as evil, cruel, etc. —**de·mon·ic** (di män′ik) *adj.*

de·mon·e·tize (dē män′ə tīz′) *vt.* **-tized′, -tiz′-ing 1.** to deprive (currency) of its standard value **2.** to stop using as money

de·mo·ni·ac (di mō′nē ak′) *adj.* of or like a

demon; fiendish: also **de·mo·ni·a·cal** (dē'mə nī'ə k'l)

de·mon·stra·ble (di män'strə b'l) *adj.* that can be demonstrated, or proved —**de·mon'stra·bly** *adv.*

dem·on·strate (dem'ən strāt') *vt.* -**strat'ed**, -**strat'ing** [< L. *de-*, from + *monstrare*, to show] **1.** to show by reasoning; prove **2.** to explain by using examples, etc. **3.** to show the working of —*vi.* to show feelings or views publicly by taking part in meetings, parades, etc. —**dem'on·stra'tor** *n.*

dem'on·stra'tion *n.* **1.** a proving **2.** an explanation by example, etc. **3.** a showing of how something works **4.** a display, as of affection **5.** a public show of opinion, etc.

de·mon·stra·tive (di män'strə tiv) *adj.* **1.** showing clearly **2.** giving proof (*of*) **3.** showing feelings openly **4.** *Gram.* pointing out ["this" is a *demonstrative* pronoun]

de·mor·al·ize (di môr'ə līz') *vt.* -**ized'**, -**iz'ing 1.** to lower the morale of **2.** to throw into confusion

de·mote (di mōt') *vt.* -**mot'ed**, -**mot'ing** [DE- + (PRO)MOTE] to reduce to a lower grade; lower in rank —**de·mo'tion** *n.*

de·mul·cent (di mul's'nt) *adj.* [< L. *de-*, down + *mulcere*, to stroke] soothing —*n.* a soothing ointment

de·mur (di mur') *vi.* -**murred'**, -**mur'ring** [< L. *de-*, from + *mora*, a delay] to hesitate, as because of doubts; object —*n.* a demurring: also **de·mur'ral**

de·mure (di myoor') *adj.* [< *de-* (prob. intens.) + OFr. *mëur*, mature] **1.** modest; reserved **2.** affectedly modest; coy —**de·mure'ly** *adv.*

den (den) *n.* [OE. *denn*] **1.** the lair of a wild animal **2.** a haunt, as of thieves **3.** a small, cozy room where one can be alone to read, work, etc.

de·na·ture (dē nā'chər) *vt.* -**tured**, -**tur·ing 1.** to change the nature of **2.** to make (alcohol, etc.) unfit to drink

de·ni·al (di nī'əl) *n.* **1.** a denying; saying "no" (to a request, etc.) **2.** a contradiction **3.** a refusal to believe or accept (a doctrine, etc.) **4.** *same as* SELF-DENIAL

de·nier (den'yər) *n.* [< L. *deni*, by tens] a unit of weight for measuring the fineness of threads of silk, nylon, etc.

den·i·grate (den'ə grāt') *vt.* -**grat'ed**, -**grat'ing** [< L. *de-*, intens. + *nigrare*, blacken] to disparage the character of; defame —**den'i·gra'tion** *n.* —**den'i·gra'tor** *n.*

den·im (den'əm) *n.* [< Fr. (*serge*) *de Nîmes*, (serge) of Nîmes, Fr. town] a coarse, twilled cotton cloth

den·i·zen (den'i zən) *n.* [< L. *de intus*, from within] an inhabitant or frequenter of a particular place

de·nom·i·nate (di näm'ə nāt') *vt.* -**nat'ed**, -**nat'ing** [< L. *de-*, intens. + *nominare*, to name] to name; call

de·nom'i·na'tion (-nā'shən) *n.* **1.** the act of denominating **2.** a name **3.** a class or kind having a specific name or value [coins of different *denominations*] **4.** a religious sect

de·nom'i·na'tion·al *adj.* of, or under the control of, a religious sect

de·nom'i·na'tor (-nāt'ər) *n.* **1.** a shared characteristic **2.** *Math.* the term below the line in a fraction

de·note (di nōt') *vt.* -**not'ed**, -**not'ing** [< L. *de-*, down + *notare*, to mark] **1.** to indicate **2.** to signify explicitly; mean —**de·no·ta·tion** (dē'nō tā'shən) *n.*

de·noue·ment, dé·noue·ment (dā noo'män) *n.* [Fr.] the outcome or unraveling of a plot in a drama, story, etc.

de·nounce (di nouns') *vt.* -**nounced'**, -**nounc'-ing** [see DENUNCIATION] **1.** to accuse publicly; inform against **2.** to condemn strongly **3.** to give formal notice of the ending of (a treaty, etc.) —**de·nounce'ment** *n.* —**de·nounc'er** *n.*

dense (dens) *adj.* **dens'er, dens'est** [L. *densus*, compact] **1.** packed tightly together **2.** difficult to get through **3.** stupid —**dense'ly** *adv.* —**dense'ness** *n.*

den·si·ty (den'sə tē) *n.*, *pl.* -**ties 1.** the condition of being dense **2.** number per unit, as of area **3.** the ratio of the mass of an object to its volume

dent (dent) *n.* [ME., var. of DINT] **1.** a slight hollow made in a surface by a blow **2.** a slight impression —*vt.* to make a dent in —*vi.* to become dented

den·tal (den't'l) *adj.* [< L. *dens*, tooth] of or for the teeth or dentistry

den·tate (den'tāt) *adj.* [see DENTAL] having teeth or toothlike projections

den·ti·frice (den'tə fris) *n.* [< L. *dens*, tooth + *fricare*, to rub] any preparation for cleaning teeth

den·tin (den'tin) *n.* [see DENTAL] the hard, calcareous tissue under the enamel of a tooth: also **den'tine** (-tēn, -tin)

den·tist (den'tist) *n.* one whose profession is the care of teeth —**den'tist·ry** *n.*

den·ture (den'chər) *n.* [Fr. < L. *dens*, tooth] a set of artificial teeth

de·nude (di nōod') *vt.* -**nud'ed**, -**nud'ing** [< L. *de-*, off + *nudare*, to strip] to make bare or naked; strip

de·nun·ci·a·tion (di nun'sē ā'shən) *n.* [< L. *de-*, intens. + *nuntiare*, announce] the act of denouncing

de·ny (di nī') *vt.* -**nied**, -**ny'ing** [< L. *de-*, intens. + *negare*, deny] **1.** to declare (a statement) untrue **2.** to refuse to accept as true or right **3.** to refuse to acknowledge as one's own **4.** to refuse to give **5.** to refuse the request of —**deny oneself** to do without desired things

de·o·dor·ant (dē ō'dər ənt) *adj.* that can counteract undesired odors —*n.* any deodorant preparation

de·o'dor·ize' (-də rīz') *vt.* -**ized'**, -**iz'ing** to counteract the odor of or in

de·part (di pärt') *vi.* [< L. *dis-*, apart + *partire*, divide] **1.** to go away (*from*); leave **2.** to die **3.** to deviate (*from*)

de·part'ed *adj.* **1.** gone away **2.** dead —**the departed** the dead person or persons

de·part·ment (di pärt'mənt) *n.* **1.** a separate part or division, as of a government **2.** a field of knowledge or activity —**de·part'men'tal** (-men't'l) *adj.*

department store a retail store for the sale of various goods arranged in departments

de·par·ture (di pär'chər) *n.* **1.** a departing **2.** a starting out, as on a trip **3.** a deviation (*from* something)

de·pend (di pend') *vi.* [< L. *de-*, down + *pendere*, hang] **1.** to be determined by something else; be contingent (*on*) **2.** to rely (*on*) **3.** to rely (*on*) for support or aid

de·pend'a·ble *adj.* trustworthy; reliable —**de·pend'a·bil'i·ty** *n.*

de·pend'ence *n.* **1.** a being dependent **2.** reliance (*on*) for support or aid **3.** reliance

de·pend'en·cy *n.*, *pl.* -**cies 1.** *same as* DEPENDENCE **2.** something dependent **3.** a territory geographically distinct from the country governing it

de·pend'ent *adj.* **1.** hanging down **2.** influenced or determined by something else **3.** relying (*on*) for support, etc. **4.** subordinate — *n.* one relying on another for support, etc. Also sp., esp. for *n.*, **de·pend'ant**

de·pict (di pikt') *vt.* [< L. *de-*, intens. + *pingere*, to paint] **1.** to represent in a drawing, painting, etc. **2.** to picture in words; describe — **de·pic'tion** *n.*

de·pil·a·to·ry (di pil'ə tôr'ē) *adj.* [< L. *de-*, from + *pilus*, hair] serving to remove unwanted hair —*n., pl.* **-ries** a depilatory substance or device

de·plane (dē plān') *vi.* **-planed'**, **-plan'ing** to get out of an airplane after it lands

de·plete (di plēt') *vt.* **-plet'ed**, **-plet'ing** [< L. *de-*, from + *plere*, fill] **1.** to use up (resources, funds, etc.) **2.** to empty wholly or partly —**de·ple'tion** *n.*

de·plor·a·ble (di plôr'ə b'l) *adj.* regrettable or wretched —**de·plor'a·bly** *adv.*

de·plore (di plôr') *vt.* **-plored'**, **-plor'ing** [< Fr. < L. *de-*, intens. + *plorare*, weep] **1.** to regret deeply **2.** to regard as wretched

de·ploy (dē ploi') *vt., vi.* [< L. *dis-*, apart + *plicare*, to fold] *Mil.* to spread out so as to form a wider front —**de·ploy'ment** *n.*

de·pop·u·late (dē päp'yə lāt') *vt.* **-lat'ed**, **-lat'ing** to reduce the population of —**de·pop'u·la'tion** *n.*

de·port (di pôrt') *vt.* [< L. *de-*, from + *portare*, carry] **1.** to behave (oneself) in a specified way **2.** to expel (an alien) —**de·por·ta·tion** (dē'pôr tā'shən) *n.*

de·port'ment *n.* conduct; behavior

de·pose (di pōz') *vt.* **-posed'**, **-pos'ing** [< OFr. *de-*, from + *poser*, cease] **1.** to remove from office; oust **2.** *Law* to testify

de·pos·it (di päz'it) *vt.* [< L. *de-*, down + *ponere*, put] **1.** to place (money, etc.) for safekeeping, as in a bank **2.** to give as a pledge or partial payment **3.** to set down **4.** to leave (sediment, etc.) lying —*n.* **1.** something placed for safekeeping, as money in a bank **2.** a pledge or part payment **3.** something left lying —**de·pos'i·tor** *n.*

dep·o·si·tion (dep'ə zish'ən) *n.* **1.** a deposing or being deposed **2.** testimony **3.** something deposited

de·pos·i·to·ry (di päz'ə tôr'ē) *n., pl.* **-ries 1.** a place where things are put for safekeeping; storehouse **2.** a trustee

de·pot (dē'pō; *military & Brit.* dep'ō) *n.* [< Fr.: see DEPOSIT] **1.** a warehouse **2.** a railroad or bus station **3.** a storage place for military supplies

de·prave (di prāv') *vt.* **-praved'**, **-prav'ing** [< L. *de-*, intens. + *pravus*, crooked] to make morally bad; corrupt —**de·prav'i·ty** (-prav'ə tē) *n., pl.* **-ties**

dep·re·cate (dep'rə kāt') *vt.* **-cat'ed**, **-cat'ing** [< L. *de-*, off + *precari*, pray] **1.** to express disapproval of **2.** to belittle —**dep're·ca'tion** *n.* —**dep're·ca·to'ry** (-kə tôr'ē) *adj.*

de·pre·ci·ate (di prē'shē āt') *vt., vi.* **-at'ed**, **-at'ing** [< L. *de-*, from + *pretiare*, to value] **1.** to lessen in value **2.** to belittle —**de·pre'ci·a'tion** *n.*

dep·re·da·tion (dep'rə dā'shən) *n.* [< L. *de-*, intens. + *praedari*, to rob] a plundering

de·press (di pres') *vt.* [< L. *de-*, down + *premere*, to press] **1.** to press down **2.** to sadden **3.** to make less active **4.** to lower in value, price, etc. —**de·pres'sant** *n.*

de·pres·sion (di presh'ən) *n.* **1.** a depressing or being depressed **2.** a hollow or low place **3.** low spirits; dejection **4.** a decrease in force, activity, etc. **5.** a period of reduced business activity, much unemployment, etc. —**de·pres'sive** (-pres'iv) *adj.*

de·prive (di prīv') *vt.* **-prived'**, **-priv'ing** [< L. *de-*, intens. + *privare*, to separate] **1.** to take away from forcibly **2.** to keep from having, using, etc. —**dep·ri·va·tion** (dep'rə vā'shən) *n.*

dept. 1. department **2.** deputy

depth (depth) *n.* [< ME. *dep*, deep + -TH¹] **1.** the distance from the top downward, or from front to back **2.** deepness **3.** intensity **4.** profundity **5.** [*usually pl.*] the deepest part —**in depth** comprehensively

dep·u·ta·tion (dep'yoo tā'shən) *n.* **1.** a deputing or being deputed **2.** a delegation

de·pute (di pyoot') *vt.* **-put'ed**, **-put'ing** [< L. *de-*, from + *putare*, cleanse] **1.** to give (authority, etc.) to a deputy **2.** to appoint as one's substitute

dep·u·tize (dep'yə tīz') *vt.* **-tized'**, **-tiz'ing** to appoint as deputy

dep·u·ty (dep'yə tē) *n., pl.* **-ties** [see DEPUTE] a person appointed to substitute for or assist another

de·rail (di rāl') *vi., vt.* to run off the rails, as a train —**de·rail'ment** *n.*

de·range (di rānj') *vt.* **-ranged'**, **-rang'ing** [< Fr. < OFr. *des-*, apart + *rengier*, to range] **1.** to upset the order or working of **2.** to make insane —**de·range'ment** *n.*

Der·by (dur'bē; *Brit.* där'-) *n., pl.* **-bies 1.** any of certain famous horse races, as the one in England founded by an Earl of Derby **2.** [d-] a stiff felt hat with a round crown

der·e·lict (der'ə likt') *adj.* [< L. *de-*, intens. + *relinquere*: see RELINQUISH] **1.** deserted by the owner; abandoned **2.** negligent —*n.* **1.** a ship deserted at sea **2.** a destitute and rejected person

der·e·lic'tion (-lik'shən) *n.* **1.** an abandoning or being abandoned **2.** a neglect of, or failure in, duty

de·ride (di rīd') *vt.* **-rid'ed**, **-rid'ing** [< L. *de-*, down + *ridere*, to laugh] to laugh at in contempt or scorn; ridicule —**de·ri'sion** (-rizh'ən) *n.* —**de·ri'sive** (-rī'siv) *adj.*

der·i·va·tion (der'ə vā'shən) *n.* **1.** a deriving or being derived **2.** the source or origin of something **3.** the origin and development of a word

de·riv·a·tive (də riv'ə tiv) *adj.* **1.** derived **2.** not original —*n.* something derived

de·rive (di rīv') *vt.* **-rived'**, **-riv'ing** [< L. *de-*, from + *rivus*, a stream] **1.** to get or receive (*from* a source) **2.** to deduce or infer **3.** to trace from or to a source —*vi.* to come (*from* a source)

der·ma·ti·tis (dur'mə tīt'is) *n.* [< Gr. *derma*, the skin + -ITIS] inflammation of the skin

der·ma·tol'o·gy (-täl'ə jē) *n.* [< Gr. *derma*, the skin + -LOGY] the branch of medicine dealing with the skin and its diseases —**der'ma·tol'o·gist** *n.*

der·mis (dur'mis) *n.* [< LL. *epidermis*, EPIDERMIS] the layer of skin just below the epidermis

der·o·gate (der'ə gāt') *vi., vt.* **-gat'ed**, **-gat'ing** [< L. *de-*, from + *rogare*, ask] to detract or disparage —**der'o·ga'tion** *n.*

de·rog·a·to·ry (di räg'ə tôr'ē) *adj.* [see prec.] **1.** detracting **2.** disparaging; belittling Also **de·rog'a·tive**

der·rick (der'ik) *n.* [orig., a gallows, after T. *Derrick*, 17th-c. London hangman] **1.** a large apparatus for moving heavy objects **2.** a tall framework, as over an oil well, to support drilling machinery, etc.

der·ri·ère (der′ē er′) *n.* [Fr., back part < L. *de-*, from + *retro*, back] the buttocks

der·rin·ger (der′in jər) *n.* [< Henry *Deringer*, 19th-c. U.S. gunsmith] a short-barreled pistol of large caliber

der·vish (dur′vish) *n.* [< Per. *darvēsh*, beggar] a member of a Muslim ascetic order

de·sal·i·na·tion (dē sal′ə nā′shən) *n.* [DE- + SALIN(E) + -ATION] the removal of salt, esp. from sea water to make it drinkable: also **de·sal′i·ni·za′tion**

des·cant (des′kant, des kant′) *vi.* [< L. *dis-*, apart + *cantus*, song] 1. to discourse (*on* or *upon*) 2. to sing

de·scend (di send′) *vi.* [< L. *de-*, down + *scandere*, to climb] 1. to move down to a lower place 2. to pass from an earlier to a later time, from greater to less, etc. 3. to slope downward 4. to come down (*from* a source) 5. to stoop (*to* some act) 6. to make a sudden visit or attack (*on*) —*vt.* to move down, down along, or through

de·scend′ant *n.* an offspring of a certain ancestor, family, group, etc.

de·scent (di sent′) *n.* 1. a descending, or coming or going down 2. ancestry 3. a downward slope 4. a way down 5. a sudden attack 6. a decline

de·scribe (di skrīb′) *vt.* **-scribed′, -scrib′ing** [< L. *de-*, from + *scribere*, write] 1. to tell or write about 2. to trace the outline of —**de·scrib′er** *n.*

de·scrip·tion (di skrip′shən) *n.* 1. the act or technique of describing 2. a statement or passage that describes 3. sort or variety —**de·scrip′tive** (-tiv) *adj.*

de·scry (di skrī′) *vt.* **-scried′, -scry′ing** [< OFr. *descrier*, proclaim] 1. to catch sight of; discern 2. to detect

des·e·crate (des′ə krāt′) *vt.* **-crat′ed, -crat′ing** [DE- + (CON)SECRATE] to violate the sacredness of —**des′e·cra′tion** *n.*

de·seg·re·gate (dē seg′rə gāt′) *vt., vi.* **-gat′ed, -gat′ing** to abolish racial segregation in —**de·seg′re·ga′tion** *n.*

de·sen·si·tize (dē sen′sə tīz′) *vt.* **-tized′, -tiz′ing** to make less sensitive

de·sert[1] (di zurt′) *vt., vi.* [Fr. < L. *de-*, from + *serere*, join] 1. to abandon 2. to leave (one's military post, etc.) without permission and with no intent to return —**de·sert′er** *n.* —**de·ser′tion** (-zur′shən) *n.*

des·ert[2] (dez′ərt) *n.* [see prec.] 1. an uncultivated, uninhabited region; wilderness 2. a dry, barren, sandy region

de·sert[3] (di zurt′) *n.* [see DESERVE] [*often pl.*] deserved reward or punishment

de·serve (di zurv′) *vt., vi.* **-served′, -serv′ing** [< L. *de-*, intens. + *servire*, serve] to be worthy (of); merit —**de·serv′ed·ly** *adv.* —**de·serv′ing** *adj., n.*

des·ic·cate (des′i kāt′) *vt., vi.* **-cat′ed, -cat′ing** [< L. *de-*, intens. + *siccus*, dry] to dry up completely —**des′ic·ca′tion** *n.*

de·sid·er·a·tum (di sid′ə rät′əm, -zid′-) *n., pl.* **-ta** (-ə) [see DESIRE] something needed and wanted

de·sign (di zīn′) *vt.* [< L. *de-*, out + *signum*, a mark] 1. to sketch an outline for; plan 2. to contrive 3. to plan to do; intend —*vi.* to make original plans, etc. —*n.* 1. a plan; scheme 2. purpose; intention 3. a working plan; pattern 4. arrangement of form, parts, color, etc.; artistic invention —**by design** purposely —**de·sign′er** *n.*

des·ig·nate (dez′ig nāt′) *vt.* **-nat′ed, -nat′ing**

[see prec.] 1. to point out; specify 2. to name 3. to appoint —**des′ig·na′tion** *n.*

de·sign′ing *adj.* scheming; artful —*n.* the art of creating designs, patterns, etc.

de·sir·a·ble (di zir′ə b'l) *adj.* worth having; pleasing —**de·sir′a·bil′i·ty** *n.*

de·sire (di zīr′) *vt.* **-sired′, -sir′ing** [< L. *desiderare*] 1. to long for; crave 2. to ask for —*n.* 1. a wish or craving 2. sexual appetite 3. a request 4. a thing desired

de·sir′ous (-əs) *adj.* desiring; wanting

de·sist (di zist′) *vi.* [< L. *de-*, from + *stare*, to stand] to cease; stop

desk (desk) *n.* [< ML. *desca*, table] a table for writing, drawing, or reading

des·o·late (des′ə lit) *adj.* [< L. *de-*, intens. + *solus*, alone] 1. lonely; solitary 2. uninhabited 3. laid waste 4. forlorn —*vt.* (-lāt′) **-lat′ed, -lat′ing** 1. to rid of inhabitants 2. to lay waste 3. to make forlorn

des′o·la′tion (-lā′shən) *n.* 1. a making desolate 2. a desolate condition or place 3. misery 4. loneliness

de·spair (di sper′) *vi.* [< L. *de-*, without + *sperare*, to hope] to lose or give up hope —*n.* 1. loss of hope 2. a person or thing causing despair —**de·spair′ing** *adj.*

des·patch (di spach′) *vt., n.* *same as* DISPATCH

des·per·a·do (des′pə rä′dō, -rä′-) *n., pl.* **-does, -dos** [OSp. < L.: see DESPAIR] a dangerous criminal; bold outlaw

des·per·ate (des′pər it) *adj.* 1. rash or violent because of despair 2. having a very great need 3. very serious 4. drastic

des·per·a·tion (des′pə rā′shən) *n.* 1. a being desperate 2. recklessness resulting from despair

des·pi·ca·ble (des′pik ə b'l, di spik′-) *adj.* deserving to be despised; contemptible —**des′pi·ca·bly** *adv.*

de·spise (di spīz′) *vt.* **-spised′, -spis′ing** [< L. *de-*, down + *specere*, look at] to regard with scorn or great dislike

de·spite (di spīt′) *prep.* [see prec.] in spite of; notwithstanding

de·spoil (di spoil′) *vt.* [< L. *de-*, intens. + *spoliare*, to strip] to rob; plunder

de·spond·en·cy (di spän′dən sē) *n.* [< L. *de-*, from + *spondere*, to promise] loss of courage or hope; dejection: also **de·spond′ence** —**de·spond′ent** *adj.*

des·pot (des′pət) *n.* [< Gr. *despotēs*, a master] 1. an absolute ruler 2. a tyrant —**des·pot·ic** (de spät′ik) *adj.* —**des′pot·ism** *n.*

des·sert (di zurt′) *n.* [< OFr. *desservir*, to clear the table < L.] a final course of a meal, as of cake, fruit, etc.

des·ti·na·tion (des′tə nā′shən) *n.* 1. the end for which something or someone is destined 2. the place to which a person or thing is going

des·tine (des′tin) *vt.* **-tined, -tin·ing** [< L. *de-*, intens. + *stare*, to stand] 1. to predetermine, as by fate 2. to intend —**destined for** 1. bound for 2. intended for

des·tin·y (des′tə nē) *n., pl.* **-ies** [see prec.] 1. the seemingly inevitable succession of events 2. (one's) fate

des·ti·tute (des′tə tōōt′) *adj.* [< L. *de-*, down + *statuere*, to set] 1. lacking (*with of*) 2. living in complete poverty —**des′ti·tu′tion** *n.*

de·stroy (di stroi′) *vt.* [< L. *de-*, down + *struere*, build] 1. to tear down; demolish 2. to spoil completely; ruin 3. to kill

de·stroy′er *n.* 1. one that destroys 2. a small, fast warship

de·struct (di strukt′, dē′strukt′) *n.* a deliberate destruction, as of a launched, malfunctioning missile —*vt.*, *vi.* to destroy or be destroyed automatically

de·struct·i·ble (di struk′tə b'l) *adj.* that can be destroyed —**de·struct′i·bil′i·ty** *n.*

de·struc·tion (di struk′shən) *n.* 1. a destroying or being destroyed 2. a cause or means of destroying —**de·struc′tive** *adj.*

des·ue·tude (des′wi tōōd′) *n.* [< L. *de-*, from + *suescere*, be accustomed] disuse

des·ul·to·ry (des′'l tôr′ē) *adj.* [< L. *de-*, from + *salire*, to leap] 1. disconnected; aimless 2. random —**des′ul·to′ri·ly** *adv.*

de·tach (di tach′) *vt.* [< Fr.: see DE- & ATTACH] 1. to unfasten and remove; disconnect 2. to send (troops, etc.) on a special mission —**de·tach′a·ble** *adj.*

de·tached′ *adj.* 1. not connected; separate 2. aloof; disinterested; impartial

de·tach′ment *n.* 1. a detaching; separation 2. a unit of troops, etc. sent on special service 3. impartiality or aloofness

de·tail (di tāl′, dē′tāl) *n.* [< Fr. < *dé-*, from + *tailler*, to cut] 1. a dealing with things item by item 2. a minute account 3. a small part; item 4. *a*) one or more soldiers, etc. on special duty *b*) the duty —*vt.* 1. to tell, item by item 2. to assign to special duty —**de·tailed′** *adj.*

de·tain (di tān′) *vt.* [< L. *de-*, off + *tenere*, hold] 1. to keep in custody 2. to hold back — **de·tain′er** *n.* —**de·tain′ment** *n.*

de·tect (di tekt′) *vt.* [< L. *de-*, from + *tegere*, to cover] to discover (something hidden, not clear, etc.) —**de·tect′a·ble, de·tect′i·ble** *adj.* — **de·tec′tion** *n.* —**de·tec′tor** *n.*

de·tec′tive *n.* a person, usually on a police force, whose work is investigating crimes, getting needed evidence, etc.

dé·tente (dā tänt′) *n.* [Fr.] a lessening of tension, esp. between nations

de·ten·tion (di ten′shən) *n.* a detaining or being detained; forced delay

detention home a place where juvenile offenders are held in custody

de·ter (di tur′) *vt.* -terred′, -ter′ring [< L. *de-*, from + *terrere*, frighten] to keep or discourage (a person) from some action through fear, doubt, etc.

de·ter·gent (di tur′jənt) *adj.* [< L. *de-*, off + *tergere*, wipe] cleansing —*n.* a soaplike cleansing substance

de·te·ri·o·rate (di tir′ē ə rāt′) *vt.*, *vi.* -rat′ed, -rat′ing [< L. *deterior*, worse] to make or become worse —**de·te′ri·o·ra′tion** *n.*

de·ter·mi·nant (di tur′mi nənt) *n.* a thing or factor that determines

de·ter′mi·nate (-nit) *adj.* fixed; settled

de·ter·mi·na·tion (di tur′mə nā′shən) *n.* 1. a determining or being determined 2. a firm intention 3. firmness of purpose

de·ter·mine (di tur′mən) *vt.* -mined, -min·ing [< L. *de-*, from + *terminus*, a limit] 1. to set limits to; define 2. to settle conclusively 3. to decide or decide upon 4. to establish the nature, kind, or quality of 5. to find out exactly —*vi.* to decide

de·ter′mined *adj.* 1. having one's mind set; resolved 2. firm and unwavering

de·ter·rent (di tur′ənt) *adj.* deterring —*n.* a thing that deters —**de·ter′rence** *n.*

de·test (di test′) *vt.* [< Fr. < L. *detestari*, to curse by the gods] to dislike intensely; hate — **de·test′a·ble** *adj.* —**de·test′a·bly** *adv.*

de·tes·ta·tion (dē′tes tā′shən) *n.* 1. intense dislike; hatred 2. something detested

de·throne (dē thrōn′) *vt.* -throned′, -thron′ing to remove from a throne

det·o·nate (det′'n āt′) *vi.*, *vt.* -nat′ed, -nat′ing

[< L. *de-*, intens. + *tonare*, to thunder] to explode violently —**det′o·na′tion** *n.*

det′o·na′tor (-āt′ər) *n.* a fuse, percussion cap, etc. for setting off explosives

de·tour (dē′toor, di toor′) *n.* [< Fr.: see DE- & TURN] 1. a roundabout way 2. a route used when the regular route is closed —*vi.*, *vt.* to go or route on a detour

de·tract (di trakt′) *vt.* [< L. *de-*, from + *trahere*, to draw] to take away —*vi.* to take something desirable away (*from*) —**de·trac′tion** *n.* —**de·trac′tor** *n.*

det·ri·ment (det′rə mənt) *n.* [< L. *de-*, off + *terere*, to rub] 1. damage; injury 2. anything that causes this —**det′ri·men′tal** *adj.*

de·tri·tus (di trīt′əs) *n.* [L., a rubbing away: see prec.] rock fragments, etc. produced by disintegration or erosion

deuce (dōōs) *n.* [L. *duo*, two] 1. a playing card or side of a die with two spots 2. *Tennis* a tie score after which one side must score twice in a row to win 3. the devil: used in exclamations of annoyance, etc.

deu·ced (dōō′sid, dōōst) *adj.* devilish; extreme —*adv.* extremely: also **deu′ced·ly**

deu·te·ri·um (dōō tir′ē əm) *n.* [< Gr. *deuteros*, second] a heavy isotope of hydrogen, having an atomic weight of 2.0141: symbol, D

Deu·ter·on·o·my (dōōt′ər än′ə mē) [< Gr. *deuteros*, second + *nomos*, law] the fifth book of the Pentateuch in the Bible

de·val·ue (dē val′yōō) *vt.* -ued, -u·ing 1. to lessen the value of 2. to lower the exchange value of (a currency) Also **de·val′u·ate′** (-yoo wāt′) -at′ed, -at′ing —**de·val′u·a′tion** *n.*

dev·as·tate (dev′ə stāt′) *vt.* -tat′ed, -tat′ing [< L. *de-*, intens. + *vastare*, to make empty] 1. to lay waste; ravage; destroy 2. to overwhelm —**dev′as·ta′tion** *n.*

de·vel·op (di vel′əp) *vt.* [< Fr. < *dé-*, apart + OFr. *voloper*, to wrap] 1. to make fuller, better, stronger, etc. 2. to work out gradually; evolve 3. *Photog.* to put (a film, etc.) in chemical solutions so as to make the picture visible —*vi.* 1. to come into being or activity; occur 2. to become developed 3. to become known —**de·vel′op·er** *n.* —**de·vel′op·ment** *n.*

de·vi·ant (dē′vē ənt) *adj.* deviating from normal —*n.* one whose behavior is deviant

de·vi·ate (dē′vē āt′) *vi.*, *vt.* -at′ed, -at′ing [< L. *de-*, from + *via*, road] to turn aside (*from* a course, standard, etc.) —*adj.* (-it) *same as* DEVIANT —*n.* (-it) a deviant; esp., one whose sexual behavior is deviant —**de′vi·a′tion** *n.*

de·vice (di vīs′) *n.* [see DEVISE] 1. a plan, scheme, or trick 2. a mechanical contrivance 3. a design, as on a shield

dev·il (dev′'l) *n.* [ult. < Gr. *diabolos*, slanderer] 1. [*often* D-] *Theol. a*) the chief evil spirit; Satan (with *the*) *b*) any demon of hell 2. a very wicked person 3. a person who is mischievous, reckless, etc. 4. a wretched person —*vt.* -iled or -illed, -il·ing or -il·ling 1. to prepare (food) with hot seasoning 2. to annoy —**dev′il·ish** *adj.*

dev′il-may-care′ *adj.* reckless or carefree

dev′il·ment *n.* mischief

dev′il's-food′ cake reddish-brown chocolate cake

dev′il·try (-trē) *n.*, *pl.* -tries reckless mischief, fun, etc.: also **dev′il·ry**, *pl.* -ries

de·vi·ous (dē′vē əs) *adj.* [< L. *de-*, off + *via*, road] 1. roundabout 2. straying 3. not straightforward —**de′vi·ous·ly** *adv.*

de·vise (di vīz′) *vt.*, *vi.* -vised′, -vis′ing [< L. *dividere*, to divide] 1. to work out (something) by thinking; plan; invent 2. to bequeath (real property) by will —*n.* a bequest of real property

de·vi·tal·ize (dē vīt′'l īz′) *vt.* -**ized′**, -**iz′ing** to lower in vitality

de·void (di void′) *adj.* [see DE- & VOID] completely without; empty (*of*)

de·volve (di välv′) *vt., vi.* -**volved′**, -**volv′ing** [< L. *de-*, down + *volvere*, to roll] to pass (*on*) to another, as duties

de·vote (di vōt′) *vt.* -**vot′ed**, -**vot′ing** [< L. *de-*, from + *vovere*, to vow] to set apart; give; dedicate

de·vot′ed *adj.* very loving, loyal, or faithful — **de·vot′ed·ly** *adv.*

dev·o·tee (dev′ə tē′, -tā′) *n.* a person strongly devoted to something or someone

de·vo·tion (di vō′shən) *n.* **1.** a devoting or being devoted **2.** piety **3.** religious worship **4.** [*pl.*] prayers **5.** loyalty or deep affection —**de·vo′tion·al** *adj., n.*

de·vour (di vour′) *vt.* [< L. *de-*, intens. + *vorare*, swallow whole] **1.** to eat (up) hungrily **2.** to consume, engulf, or destroy **3.** to take in greedily, as with the eyes

de·vout (di vout′) *adj.* [see DEVOTE] **1.** very religious; pious **2.** earnest; sincere

dew (dōō) *n.* [OE. *deaw*] atmospheric moisture condensed in drops on cool surfaces at night — **dew′y** *adj.* -**i·er**, -**i·est**

dew′drop′ *n.* a drop of dew

dew′lap′ *n.* [OE. *deaw*, dew + *laeppa*, a fold] a loose fold of skin hanging from the throat of cattle, etc.

dex·ter·i·ty (dek ster′ə tē) *n.* [see ff.] skill in using one's hands, body, or mind

dex·ter·ous (dek′strəs, -stər əs) *adj.* [< L. *dexter*, right] skillful in using the hands, body, or mind: also **dex′trous**

dex·trose (dek′strōs) *n.* [see prec.] a glucose found in plants and animals

di-[1] [Gr. *di-* < *dis*, twice] *a prefix meaning* twice, double, twofold

di-[2] *same as* DIS-

di·a·be·tes (dī′ə bēt′is, -ēz) *n.* [< Gr. *dia-*, through + *bainein*, to go] a disease marked by excess sugar in the blood and urine, hunger, thirst, etc. —**di′a·bet′ic** (-bet′ik) *adj., n.*

di·a·bol·ic (dī′ə bäl′ik) *adj.* [see DEVIL] very wicked or cruel; fiendish; devilish: also **di′a·bol′i·cal** —**di′a·bol′i·cal·ly** *adv.*

di·ac·o·nate (dī ak′ə nit) *n.* the rank or office of a deacon

di·a·crit·ic (dī′ə krit′ik) *adj.* [< Gr. *dia-*, across + *krinein*, to separate] distinguishing: also **di′a·crit′i·cal** —*n.* a mark, as a macron or cedilla, added to a letter or symbol to show its pronunciation, etc.: in full **diacritical mark**

di·a·dem (dī′ə dem′) *n.* [< Gr. *dia-*, through + *dein*, to bind] **1.** a crown **2.** any ornamental band worn on the head

di·ag·nose (dī′əg nōs′, -nōz′) *vt., vi.* -**nosed′**, -**nos′ing** to make a diagnosis (of)

di·ag·no·sis (dī′əg nō′sis) *n., pl.* -**ses** (-sēz) [< Gr. *dia-*, through + *gignōskein*, know] **1.** the act or process of deciding the nature of a disease, problem, etc. by examination and analysis **2.** the resulting decision —**di′ag·nos′tic** (-näs′tik) *adj.* —**di′ag·nos·ti′cian** (-näs tish′ən) *n.*

di·ag·o·nal (dī ag′ə n'l) *adj.* [< Gr. *dia-*, through + *gōnia*, an angle] **1.** slanting as from one corner to the opposite one **2.** having slanting markings, lines, etc. —*n.* a diagonal line, plane, course, part, etc. —**di·ag′o·nal·ly** *adv.*

di·a·gram (dī′ə gram′) *n.* [< Gr. *dia-*, through + *graphein*, write] a sketch, plan, graph, etc. that explains a thing, as by outlining its parts —*vt.* -**gramed′** or -**grammed′**, -**gram′ing** or -**gram′ming** to make a diagram of —**di′a·gram·mat′ic** (-grə mat′ik) *adj.*

di·al (dī′əl, dīl) *n.* [< L. *dies*, day] **1.** the face of a clock, meter, etc. **2.** a graduated disk or strip, as on a radio, esp. for tuning in stations **3.** a rotating disk on a telephone, for making connections automatically —*vt., vi.* -**aled** or -**alled**, -**al·ing** or -**al·ling** to measure, select, tune in, telephone, etc. with a dial

dial. **1.** dialect(al) **2.** dialectic(al)

di·a·lect (dī′ə lekt′) *n.* [< Gr. *dia-*, between + *legein*, to talk] the form of a spoken language peculiar to a region, social group, etc. —**di′a·lec′tal** *adj.*

di′a·lec′tic (-lek′tik) *n.* **1.** [*often pl.*] a logical examination of ideas to determine their validity **2.** logical argumentation —**di′a·lec′ti·cal** *adj.*

di·a·logue, di·a·log (dī′ə lôg′) *n.* [see DIALECT] **1.** a conversation **2.** the passages of talk in a play, story, etc.

di·am·e·ter (dī am′ət ər) *n.* [< Gr. *dia-*, through + *metron*, a measure] **1.** a straight line through the center of a circle, etc. from one side to the other **2.** its length

di·a·met·ri·cal (dī′ə met′ri k'l) *adj.* **1.** of a diameter **2.** completely opposite Also **di′a·met′ric** —**di′a·met′ri·cal·ly** *adv.*

di·a·mond (dī′mənd, -ə mənd) *n.* [< Gr. *adamas*, adamant] **1.** a nearly pure, brilliant, crystalline carbon, the hardest mineral known **2.** a gem, etc. cut from this mineral **3.** *a*) the plane figure (◊) *b*) any of a suit of playing cards marked with this figure in red *c*) [*pl.*] this suit **4.** *Baseball* the infield or the whole field

Di·an·a (dī an′ə) *Rom. Myth.* the goddess of the moon and of hunting

di·a·pa·son (dī′ə pāz′'n) *n.* [< Gr. *dia-*, through + *pas*, all] an organ stop covering the instrument's complete range

di·a·per (dī′pər, dī′ə pər) *n.* [< ML. *diasprum*, flowered cloth] a soft, absorbent cloth folded around a baby's loins —*vt.* to put a diaper on (a baby)

di·aph·a·nous (dī af′ə nəs) *adj.* [< Gr. *dia-*, through + *phainein*, to show] gauzy or sheer

di·a·phragm (dī′ə fram′) *n.* [< Gr. *dia-*, through + *phragma*, a fence] **1.** the partition of muscles and tendons between the chest and the abdominal cavity **2.** a device to regulate light entering a camera lens **3.** a vibrating disk that makes or receives sound waves, as in a microphone **4.** a fitted, vaginal contraceptive device

di·ar·rhe·a, di·ar·rhoe·a (dī′ə rē′ə) *n.* [< Gr. *dia-*, through + *rhein*, to flow] too frequent and loose bowel movements

di·a·ry (dī′ə rē) *n., pl.* -**ries** [< L. *dies*, day] a daily written record of one's own experiences, thoughts, etc. —**di′a·rist** *n.*

di·as·to·le (dī as′tə lē′) *n.* [< Gr. *dia-*, apart + *stellein*, to put] rhythmic dilation of the heart —**di·a·stol·ic** (dī′ə stäl′ik) *adj.*

di·a·ther·my (dī′ə thur′mē) *n.* [< Gr. *dia-*, through + *thermē*, heat] medical treatment in which heat is produced in the tissues beneath the skin by a high-frequency electric current — **di′a·ther′mic** *adj.*

di·a·tom (dī′ə täm′, -ət əm) *n.* [< Gr. *diatomos*, cut in two] any of a number of related microscopic algae that are an important source of food for marine life

di·a·ton·ic (dī′ə tän′ik) *adj.* [< Gr. *dia-*, through + *teinein*, to stretch] *Music* designating or of any standard major or minor scale of eight tones

di·a·tribe (dī′ə trīb′) *n.* [< Gr. *dia-*, through + *tribein*, to rub] a bitter denunciation

dib·ble (dib′'l) *n.* [ME. *dibbel*] a pointed tool to make holes in the soil as for bulbs

dice (dīs) *n.pl., sing.* **die** or **dice** [see DIE²] small cubes marked on each side with from one to six dots and used in games of chance —*vi.* **diced, dic′ing** to play with dice —*vt.* to cut into small cubes

di·chot·o·my (dī kät′ə mē) *n., pl.* **-mies** [< Gr. *dicha*, in two + *temnein*, to cut] division into two usually opposed parts

dick·er (dik′ər) *vi.* [< earlier *dicker*, ten hides] to bargain or haggle

dick·ey (dik′ē) *n., pl.* **-eys** [< nickname *Dick*] **1.** a kind of bib or shirt front **2.** a small bird: in full **dickey bird** Also **dick′y,** *pl.* **-ies**

di·cot·y·le·don (dī′kät 'l ēd′'n) *n.* a flowering plant with two seed leaves (cotyledons) —**di′-cot·y·le′don·ous** *adj.*

Dic·ta·phone (dik′tə fōn′) [DICTA(TE) + -PHONE] *a trademark for* a machine that records and plays back speech for typed transcripts, etc. —*n.* this machine

dic·tate (dik′tāt, dik tāt′) *vt., vi.* **-tat·ed, -tat·ing** [< L. *dicere*, speak] **1.** to speak (something) aloud for someone else to write down **2.** to command expressly **3.** to give (orders) with authority —*n.* (dik′tāt) an authoritative command —**dic·ta′tion** *n.*

dic′ta·tor *n.* one who dictates; esp., an absolute ruler or tyrant —**dic′ta·to′ri·al** (-tə tôr′ē əl) *adj.* —**dic·ta′tor·ship′** *n.*

dic·tion (dik′shən) *n.* [< L. *dictio*, a speaking] **1.** manner of expression in words; choice of words **2.** enunciation

dic·tion·ar·y (dik′shə ner′ē) *n., pl.* **-ies** [see prec.] a book of alphabetically listed words with definitions, etc.

dic·tum (dik′təm) *n., pl.* **-tums, -ta** (-tə) [L. < *dicere*, speak] a formal statement of fact, opinion, principle, etc.; pronouncement

did (did) *pt. of* DO¹

di·dac·tic (dī dak′tik) *adj.* [< Gr. *didaskein*, teach] instructive: also **di·dac′ti·cal**

did·dle (did′'l) *vi., vt.* **-dled, -dling** [< ?] [Colloq.] **1.** to cheat or swindle **2.** to waste (time) in trifling —**did′dler** *n.*

did·n't (did′'nt) did not

di·do (dī′dō) *n., pl.* **-does, -dos** [< ?] [Colloq.] a mischievous trick; prank

die¹ (dī) *vi.* **died, dy′ing** [< ON. *deyja*] **1.** to stop living **2.** to stop functioning; end **3.** to lose force or activity **4.** to fade or wither away **5.** [Colloq.] to wish very much —**die away** (or **down**) to end gradually —**die off** to die one by one until all are gone —**die out** to stop existing

die² (dī) *n.* [< L. *dare*, give] **1.** *sing. of* DICE **2.** *pl.* **dies** (dīz) a tool for stamping, cutting, or shaping metal —*vt.* **died, die′ing** to stamp, cut, etc. with a die

die′-hard′, die′hard′ *n.* a person stubbornly resistant to new ideas or reform

di·e·lec·tric (dī′ə lek′trik) *n.* [< Gr. *dia-*, across + ELECTRIC] a substance that does not conduct electricity —*adj.* nonconducting

di·er·e·sis (dī er′ə sis) *n., pl.* **-ses′** (-sēz′) [< Gr. *dia-*, apart + *hairein*, to take] a mark (¨) placed over a vowel to show that it is pronounced separately

die·sel (dē′z'l, -s'l) *n.* [< R. *Diesel*, Ger. inventor] [*often* D-] an internal-combustion engine that burns oil ignited by heat from air compression

di·et¹ (dī′ət) *n.* [Gr. *diaita*, way of life] **1.** what

one usually eats or drinks **2.** a regimen of special or limited food and drink, as to lose weight —*vi.* to follow a diet —**di′e·tar′y** (-ə ter′ē) *adj.*

di·et² (dī′ət) *n.* [< ML. *dieta*] a formal assembly

di·e·tet·ic (dī′ə tet′ik) *adj.* of or for a particular diet of food and drink

di′e·tet′ics *n.pl.* [*with sing. v.*] the study of the foods needed for health

di·e·ti·tian, di·e·ti·cian (dī′ə tish′ən) *n.* a specialist in planning meals or diets

dif·fer (dif′ər) *vi.* [< L. *dis-*, apart + *ferre*, carry] **1.** to be different (*from*) **2.** to have opposite or unlike opinions; disagree

dif·fer·ence (dif′ər əns, dif′rəns) *n.* **1.** a being different or not alike **2.** the way in which people or things are different **3.** a differing in opinions; disagreement or quarrel **4.** the amount by which one quantity is greater or less than another

dif′fer·ent *adj.* **1.** not alike; dissimilar (with *from*, or, esp. colloquially, *than*, and, in Brit. usage, *to*) **2.** not the same; distinct **3.** various **4.** unusual —**dif′fer·ent·ly** *adv.*

dif·fer·en·tial (dif′ə ren′shəl) *adj.* of or constituting a difference —*n.* **1.** a differentiating amount, degree, etc. **2.** a gear arrangement connecting two axles in the same line to let the outside wheel turn faster around a curve than the inside wheel **3.** *Math.* an infinitesimal difference between values of a variable quantity

dif·fer·en′ti·ate′ (-ren′shē āt′) *vt.* **-at′ed, -at′ing 1.** to constitute a difference in or between **2.** to make unlike **3.** to distinguish the difference between —*vi.* **1.** to become different or differentiated **2.** to note a difference —**dif′fer·en′ti·a′tion** *n.*

dif·fi·cult (dif′i kəlt, -kult′) *adj.* **1.** hard to do, understand, etc. **2.** hard to satisfy, please, etc.

dif′fi·cul′ty *n., pl.* **-ties** [< L. *dis-*, not + *facilis*, easy] **1.** a being difficult **2.** something difficult; problem, obstacle, etc. **3.** trouble **4.** disagreement

dif·fi·dent (dif′ə dənt) *adj.* [< L. *dis-*, not + *fidere*, to trust] lacking confidence in oneself; timid; shy —**dif′fi·dence** *n.*

dif·frac·tion (di frak′shən) *n.* [< L. *dis-*, apart + *frangere*, to break] **1.** the breaking up of light into dark and light bands or into the colors of the spectrum **2.** a similar breaking up of other waves, as of sound

dif·fuse (di fyōos′) *adj.* [< L. *dis-*, apart + *fundere*, pour] **1.** spread out; not concentrated **2.** using more words than are needed —*vt., vi.* (-fyōoz′) **-fused′, -fus′ing** to pour or spread in every direction —**dif·fu′sion** *n.* —**dif·fu′sive** *adj.*

dig (dig) *vt.* **dug, dig′ging** [< Du. *dijk*, dike] **1.** to turn up or remove (ground, etc.) with a spade, the hands, etc. **2.** to make (a hole, etc.) by doing this **3.** to get out by digging **4.** to find out, as by careful study **5.** to jab **6.** [Slang] *a*) to understand *b*) to like —*vi.* **1.** to excavate **2.** [Colloq.] to work hard —*n.* **1.** an archaeological excavation **2.** [Colloq.] *a*) a jab *b*) a gibe —**dig′ger** *n.*

di·gest (dī′jest) *n.* [< L. *di-*, apart + *gerere*, to bear] a summary or synopsis —*vt.* (di jest′, dī-) **1.** to summarize **2.** to change (food), esp. in the stomach and intestines, into a form that can be absorbed by the body **3.** to absorb mentally —*vi.* to be digested —**di·gest′i·ble** *adj.*

di·ges·tion (di jes′chən, dī-) *n.* **1.** a digesting **2.** the ability to digest —**di·ges′tive** *adj.*

dig·it (dij′it) *n.* [L. *digitus*] **1.** a finger or toe **2.** any number from 0 to 9 —**dig′i·tal** *adj.*

digital computer a computer that uses numbers to perform calculations

dig·i·tal·is (dij'ə tal'is) *n.* [see DIGIT: from its flowers] 1. a plant with long spikes of thimble-like flowers; foxglove 2. a medicine made from the leaves of the purple foxglove, used as a heart stimulant

dig·ni·fied (dig'nə fīd') *adj.* having or showing dignity

dig·ni·fy (dig'nə fī') *vt.* -fied', -fy·ing [< L. *dignus*, worthy + *facere*, make] to give dignity to; honor, ennoble, etc.

dig·ni·tar·y (-ter'ē) *n., pl.* -ies a person holding a high, dignified position

dig·ni·ty (dig'nə tē) *n., pl.* -ties [< L. *dignus*, worthy] 1. worthiness 2. high repute; honor 3. a high position, rank, or title 4. stateliness 5. self-respect

di·graph (dī'graf) *n.* two letters that together represent one sound, as *ea* in *read*

di·gress (dī gres', di-) *vi.* [< L. *dis-*, apart + *gradi*, to go] to depart temporarily from the main subject in talking or writing —**di·gres'-sion** (-gresh'ən) *n.* —**di·gres'sive** *adj.*

dike (dīk) *n.* [OE. *dic*, ditch] an embankment or dam to prevent flooding by the sea or by a river

di·lap·i·dat·ed (di lap'ə dāt'id) *adj.* [< L. *dis-*, apart + *lapidare*, throw stones at] falling to pieces —**di·lap'i·da'tion** *n.*

di·late (dī lāt', di-) *vt., vi.* -lat'ed, -lat'ing [< L. *dis-*, apart + *latus*, wide] to make or become wider or larger; expand —**di·la'tion, dil·a·ta·tion** (dil'ə tā'shən) *n.* —**di·la'tor** *n.*

dil·a·to·ry (dil'ə tôr'ē) *adj.* [< L. *dilator*, one who delays] 1. causing delay 2. inclined to delay; slow; tardy

di·lem·ma (di lem'ə) *n.* [< Gr. *di-*, two + *lēmma*, proposition] a situation forcing a choice of unpleasant alternatives

dil·et·tante (dil'ə tänt', -tän'tē, -tan'tē) *n., pl.* -tantes', -tan'ti (-tē) [It. < L. *delectare*, to delight] one who dabbles in art, literature, etc.

dil·i·gent (dil'ə jənt) *adj.* [< L. *di-*, apart + *legere*, choose] 1. persevering and careful in work; industrious 2. done carefully —**dil'i-gence** *n.* —**dil'i·gent·ly** *adv.*

dill (dil) *n.* [OE. *dile*] an aromatic plant used to flavor pickles, etc.

dil·ly·dal·ly (dil'ē dal'ē) *vi.* -lied, -ly·ing [reduplicated form of DALLY] to dawdle

di·lute (di lōōt', dī-) *vt.* -lut'ed, -lut'ing [< L. *dis-*, off + *lavere*, to wash] to thin down or weaken as by mixing with water —*adj.* diluted —**di·lu'tion** *n.*

dim (dim) *adj.* **dim'mer, dim'mest** [OE.] 1. not bright; darkish or dull 2. not clear; vague, indistinct, etc. 3. not favorable *[dim* prospects*]* —*vt., vi.* **dimmed, dim'ming** to make or grow dim —**dim'ly** *adv.*

dim. 1. diminuendo 2. diminutive

dime (dīm) *n.* [< L. *decem*, ten] a coin of the U.S. and Canada equal to 10 cents

di·men·sion (də men'shən) *n.* [< L. *dis-*, off + *metiri*, to measure] 1. any measurable extent, as length 2. [*pl.*] measurements in length, width, and often depth 3. [*often pl.*] scope —**di·men'sion·al** *adj.*

dime store *same as* FIVE-AND-TEN-CENT STORE

di·min·ish (də min'ish) *vt., vi.* [< L. *de-*, from + *minuere*, lessen] to make or become smaller in size, degree, importance, etc. —**dim·i·nu·tion** (dim'ə nyōō'shən, -nōō'-) *n.*

di·min·u·en·do (də min'yōō wen'dō) *adj., adv.* [It.] *Music* with gradually diminishing volume

di·min·u·tive (də min'yōō tiv) *adj.* [see DIMINISH] very small; little —*n.* a word having

---

a suffix expressing smallness, endearment, etc., as *booklet* or *Jackie*

dim·i·ty (dim'ə tē) *n., pl.* -ties [< Gr. *dis-*, two + *mitos*, a thread] a thin, strong, corded cotton cloth

dim·ple (dim'p'l) *n.* [ME. *dimpel*] a small, natural hollow, as on the cheek —*vt., vi.* -pled, -pling to form dimples (in)

dim'wit' *n.* [Slang] a stupid person

din (din) *n.* [OE. *dyne*] a loud, continuous noise; confused clamor —*vt.* **dinned, din'ning** 1. to beset with a din 2. to repeat insistently or noisily —*vi.* to make a din

dine (dīn) *vi.* **dined, din'ing** [ult. < L. *dis-*, away + *jejunus*, fasting] to eat dinner —*vt.* to provide a dinner for

din·er (dī'nər) *n.* 1. a person eating dinner 2. a railroad car equipped to serve meals 3. a restaurant built to look like such a car

din·ette (dī net') *n.* an alcove or small room used as a dining room

ding (diŋ) *n.* [ME. *dingen*, to strike] the sound of a bell: also **ding'-dong'** (-dôŋ')

din·ghy (diŋ'gē) *n., pl.* -ghies [< Hindi] a small boat, as a ship's tender

din·gy (din'jē) *adj.* -gi·er, -gi·est [< ? DUNG] 1. not bright or clean 2. shabby

din·ky (diŋ'kē) *adj.* -ki·er, -ki·est [< Scot. *dink*, trim] [Colloq.] small

din·ner (din'ər) *n.* [see DINE] 1. the chief meal of the day 2. a banquet honoring a person or event

di·no·saur (dī'nə sôr') *n.* [< Gr. *deinos*, terrible + *sauros*, lizard] any of a group of extinct, often huge, four-limbed reptiles

dint (dint) *n.* [OE. *dynt*] 1. force; exertion: now chiefly in **by dint of** 2. a dent

di·o·cese (dī'ə sis, -sēs') *n.* [< Gr. *dioikein*, keep house] the district under a bishop's jurisdiction —**di·oc'e·san** (-äs'ə s'n) *adj.*

Di·o·ny·sus, Di·o·ny·sos (dī'ə nī'səs) *n.* the Greek god of wine and revelry

di·ox·ide (dī äk'sīd) *n.* an oxide with two atoms of oxygen per molecule

dip (dip) *vt.* **dipped, dip'ping** [OE. *dyppan*] 1. to put into liquid for a moment 2. to take out as by scooping up 3. to lower (a flag, etc.) and immediately raise again —*vi.* 1. to go down into a liquid and quickly come out 2. to sink suddenly 3. to slope down 4. to go (*into*) so as to dip something out *[to dip* into savings*]* 5. to look into or study something superficially (with *into*) —*n.* 1. a dipping or being dipped 2. a brief plunge 3. a liquid, sauce, etc. into which something is dipped 4. something dipped out 5. a downward slope

diph·the·ri·a (dif thir'ē ə, dip-) *n.* [< Gr. *diphthera*, leather] an acute infectious disease marked by high fever and formation of a membranelike obstruction to breathing

diph·thong (dif'thôŋ, dip'-) *n.* [< Gr. *di-*, two + *phthongos*, sound] a sound made by gliding from one vowel to another in one syllable, as (oi) in *boy*, formed by (ô) + (ē)

di·plo·ma (di plō'mə) *n.* [< Gr. *diplōma*, folded letter] a certificate issued by a school, college, etc. indicating graduation or conferring a degree

di·plo·ma·cy (di plō'mə sē) *n., pl.* -cies [< Fr.: see ff.] 1. the conducting of relations between nations 2. tact

dip·lo·mat (dip'lə mat') *n.* [< Fr. < L. *diploma*, DIPLOMA] 1. a representative of a government who conducts relations with another government 2. a tactful person

dip'lo·mat'ic *adj.* 1. of diplomacy 2. tactful —**dip'lo·mat'i·cal·ly** *adv.*

dip·per (dip′ər) *n.* **1.** a long-handled cup, etc. for dipping **2.** [**D-**] either of two groups of stars in the shape of a dipper (**Big Dipper** and **Little Dipper**)

dip·so·ma·ni·a (dip′sə mā′nē ə) *n.* [< Gr. *dipsa*, thirst + *mania*, madness] an abnormal and insatiable craving for alcoholic drink — **dip′so·ma′ni·ac′** (-ak′) *n.*

dire (dīr) *adj.* **dir′er, dir′est** [L. *dirus*] **1.** dreadful; terrible **2.** urgent [*dire* need]

di·rect (di rekt′, dī-) *adj.* [< L. *dirigere*, put straight] **1.** by the shortest way; straight **2.** straightforward; frank **3.** with nothing or no one between; immediate **4.** in unbroken line of descent; lineal **5.** exact; complete [the *direct* opposite] **6.** in the exact words [a *direct* quote] —*vt.* **1.** to manage; guide; conduct **2.** to order; command **3.** to turn or point; aim **4.** to tell (a person) the way to a place **5.** to address (words, etc.) to a specific person or group **6.** to supervise the action of (a play, etc.) **7.** to rehearse and conduct a (choir, orchestra, etc.) — *vi.* **1.** to give directions **2.** to be a director — *adv.* directly —**di·rect′ness** *n.*

direct current an electric current flowing in one direction

di·rec·tion (də rek′shən, dī-) *n.* **1.** a directing; management; supervision **2.** [*usually pl.*] instructions for doing, using, etc. **3.** an order or command **4.** the point faced or the line of movement or extension —**di·rec′tion·al** *adj.*

di·rec′tive (-tiv) *adj.* directing —*n.* a general order issued authoritatively

di·rect′ly *adv.* **1.** in a direct way or line; straight **2.** with nothing coming between **3.** exactly [*directly* opposite] **4.** right away

direct object the word or words denoting the receiver of the action of a verb (Ex.: *me* in *he hit me*)

di·rec′tor *n.* one who directs a school, corporation, etc. or a play, choir, etc.

di·rec′to·ry (-tə rē) *adj.* directing or advising — *n., pl.* **-ries** a book listing the names, addresses, etc. of a specific group of persons

dire·ful (dīr′fəl) *adj.* dreadful; terrible

dirge (durj) *n.* [< L. *dirige* (direct), first word of a funeral hymn] a song, poem, etc. expressing grief or mourning

dir·i·gi·ble (dir′i jə b′l, də rij′ə-) *adj.* [see DI-RECT & -IBLE] that can be steered —*n. same as* AIRSHIP

dirk (durk) *n.* [< ?] a short dagger

dirn·dl (durn′d′l) *n.* [< G. *dirne*, girl] a full skirt gathered at the waist

dirt (durt) *n.* [< ON. *dritr*, excrement] **1.** any unclean matter, as mud, trash, etc. **2.** earth; soil **3.** dirtiness, corruption, etc. **4.** obscenity **5.** malicious gossip

dirt′y *adj.* **-i·er, -i·est 1.** soiled; unclean **2.** obscene **3.** mean; nasty **4.** unfair; dishonest **5.** rough, as weather —*vt., vi.* **-ied, -y·ing** to make or become dirty; soil —**dirt′i·ly** *adv.* —**dirt′i·ness** *n.*

dis- [< L.] *a prefix denoting* separation, negation, or reversal [*dishonest, disown*]

dis·a·bil·i·ty (dis′ə bil′ə tē) *n., pl.* **-ties 1.** a disabled condition **2.** that which disables **3.** a legal disqualification

dis·a′ble (-ā′b′l) *vt.* **-bled, -bling 1.** to make unable, unfit, etc.; cripple **2.** to disqualify legally —**dis·a′ble·ment** *n.*

dis·a·buse (dis′ə byōōz′) *vt.* **-bused′, -bus′ing** to rid of false ideas; undeceive

dis·ad·van·tage (-əd van′tij) *n.* **1.** an unfavorable situation; drawback; handicap **2.** detriment —**dis·ad·van·ta′geous** (-ad′vən tā′jəs) *adj.*

dis·ad·van′taged *adj.* underprivileged

dis·af·fect (dis′ə fekt′) *vt.* to make unfriendly, discontented, or disloyal —**dis′af·fec′tion** *n.*

dis·a·gree′ (-ə grē′) *vi.* **-greed′, -gree′ing 1.** to be different **2.** to differ in opinion; specif., to quarrel or dispute **3.** to give distress [corn *disagrees* with me]

dis·a·gree′a·ble *adj.* **1.** unpleasant; offensive **2.** quarrelsome —**dis·a·gree′a·bly** *adv.*

dis·a·gree′ment *n.* **1.** refusal to agree **2.** difference; discrepancy **3.** difference of opinion **4.** a quarrel or dispute

dis·al·low′ (-ə lou′) *vt.* to refuse to allow; reject as invalid or illegal

dis·ap·pear′ (-ə pir′) *vi.* **1.** to cease to be seen; go out of sight **2.** to cease being —**dis·ap·pear′-ance** *n.*

dis·ap·point′ (-ə point′) *vt.* **1.** to fail to satisfy the expectations of **2.** to frustrate (hopes, etc.) —**dis·ap·point′ment** *n.*

dis·ap·pro·ba·tion (dis ap′rə bā′shən) *n.* disapproval

dis·ap·prove (dis′ə prōōv′) *vt., vi.* **-proved′, -prov′ing 1.** to have or express an unfavorable opinion (of) **2.** to refuse to approve —**dis′ap·prov′al** *n.*

dis·arm (dis ärm′) *vt.* **1.** to take away weapons from **2.** to make harmless **3.** to overcome the hostility of —*vi.* to reduce or do away with armed forces and armaments —**dis·ar′ma·ment** *n.*

dis·ar·range (dis′ə rānj′) *vt.* **-ranged′, -rang′ing** to make less neat; disorder —**dis′ar·range′-ment** *n.*

dis·ar·ray′ (-ə rā′) *vt.* to throw into disorder or confusion —*n.* disorder; confusion

dis·as·sem′ble (-ə sem′b′l) *vt.* **-bled, -bling** to take apart —**dis′as·sem′bly** *n.*

dis·as·so′ci·ate′ (-ə sō′shē āt′, -sē-) *vt.* **-at′ed, -at′ing** to sever association with; separate

dis·as·ter (di zas′tər) *n.* [< L. *dis-* + *astrum*, a star] any event causing great harm or damage; calamity —**dis·as′trous** *adj.*

dis·a·vow (dis′ə vou′) *vt.* to deny any knowledge of or responsibility for; disclaim — **dis′a·vow′al** *n.*

dis·band (dis band′) *vt., vi.* to break up as an organization —**dis·band′ment** *n.*

dis·bar′ (-bär′) *vt.* **-barred′, -bar′ring** to deprive (a lawyer) of the right to practice law —**dis·bar′ment** *n.*

dis·be·lieve′ *vt., vi.* **-lieved′, -liev′ing** to refuse to believe (*in*) —**dis′be·lief′** *n.*

dis·burse′ (-burs′) *vt.* **-bursed′, -burs′ing** [< OFr. *desbourser*] to pay out; expend —**dis·burse′ment** *n.*

disc (disk) *n.* **1.** *same as* DISK **2.** a phonograph record **3.** *Biol.* any disk-shaped part

dis·card (dis kärd′) *vt.* [< OFr.: see DIS- & CARD1] **1.** *Card Games* to throw away (undesired cards) **2.** to get rid of as no longer useful —*n.* (dis′kärd) **1.** a discarding or being discarded **2.** something discarded

dis·cern (di surn′, -zurn′) *vt., vi.* [< L. *dis-*, apart + *cernere*, to separate] to perceive or recognize clearly —**dis·cern′i·ble** *adj.* —**dis·cern′ment** *n.*

dis·cern′ing *adj.* having good judgment —**dis·cern′ing·ly** *adv.*

dis·charge (dis chärj′) *vt.* **-charged′, -charg′ing** [< L. *dis-*, from + *carrus*, wagon] **1.** to release or dismiss **2.** to unload (a cargo) **3.** to shoot (a gun or projectile) **4.** to emit **5.** to pay (a debt) or perform (a duty) **6.** *Elec.* to remove stored energy from (a battery, etc.) —*vi.* **1.** to get rid of a load, etc. **2.** to be released or thrown off **3.** to go off, as a gun —*n.* (*usually* dis′chärj) **1.** a discharging or being discharged 2. that which discharges or is discharged

dis·ci·ple (di sī'p'l) *n.* [< L. *dis-*, apart + *capere*, to hold] 1. a pupil or follower of any teacher or school 2. an early follower of Jesus, esp. one of the Apostles

dis·ci·pli·nar·i·an (dis'ə pli ner'ē ən) *n.* one who enforces strict discipline

dis·ci·pline (dis'ə plin) *n.* [see DISCIPLE] 1. training that develops self-control, efficiency, etc. 2. strict control to enforce obedience 3. orderly conduct 4. a system of rules 5. treatment that corrects or punishes —*vt.* **-plined, -plin·ing** 1. to train; control 2. to punish —**dis'ci·pli·nar'y** (-pli ner'ē) *adj.*

disc jockey one who plays recorded music on a radio program or at a disco

dis·claim (dis klām') *vt.* 1. to give up any claim to 2. to repudiate

dis·claim'er *n.* 1. a denial or renunciation, as of a claim or title 2. a disavowing

dis·close (-klōz') *vt.* **-closed', -clos'ing** 1. to bring into view; uncover 2. to reveal; make known —**dis·clo'sure** (-klō'zhər) *n.*

dis·co (dis'kō) *n., pl.* **-cos** [Fr. *discothèque*] a place for dancing to recorded music

dis·col'or *vt., vi.* to change in color by fading, streaking, or staining —**dis·col'or·a'tion** *n.*

dis·com·fit (dis kum'fit) *vt.* [< L. *dis-* + *conficere*, prepare] 1. to frustrate 2. to disconcert —**dis·com'fi·ture** (-fi chər) *n.*

dis·com'fort *n.* 1. lack of comfort; uneasiness 2. anything causing this —*vt.* to cause discomfort to

dis·com·mode (dis'kə mōd') *vt.* **-mod'ed, -mod'ing** [< DIS- + L. *commodare,* make suitable] to inconvenience

dis'com·pose' (-kəm pōz') *vt.* **-posed', -pos'ing** to disturb; fluster; disconcert —**dis'com·po'sure** (-pō'zhər) *n.*

dis'con·cert' (-kən surt') *vt.* 1. to upset (plans, etc.) 2. to upset the composure of

dis'con·nect' (-kə nekt') *vt.* to break the connection of —**dis'con·nec'tion** *n.*

dis'con·nect'ed *adj.* 1. separated 2. incoherent —**dis'con·nect'ed·ly** *adv.*

dis'con·so·late (dis kän'sə lit) *adj.* [see DIS- & CONSOLE¹] 1. inconsolable; dejected 2. cheerless

dis·con·tent (dis'kən tent') *adj. same as* DISCONTENTED —*n.* dissatisfaction: also **dis'con·tent'ment** —*vt.* to dissatisfy

dis'con·tent'ed *adj.* not contented; dissatisfied —**dis'con·tent'ed·ly** *adv.*

dis·con·tin·ue (dis'kən tin'yōō) *vt., vi.* **-ued, -u·ing** to stop; cease; give up —**dis'con·tin'u·ance, dis'con·tin'u·a'tion** *n.*

dis·cord (dis'kôrd) *n.* [< L. *dis-*, apart + *cor,* heart] 1. disagreement 2. a harsh or confused noise —**dis·cord'ant** *adj.*

dis·count (dis'kount) *n.* [see DIS- & COMPUTE] 1. a reduction as from a list price 2. the rate of interest charged on a discounted bill —*vt.* (*also* dis kount') 1. to pay or receive the value of (a promissory note, etc.) minus a deduction for interest 2. to deduct an amount from (a bill, price, etc.) 3. to sell at less than the regular price 4. *a)* to allow for exaggeration, bias, etc. in (a story, etc.) *b)* to disregard 5. to reckon with in advance

dis·coun·te·nance (dis koun'tə nəns) *vt.* **-nanced, -nanc·ing** 1. to discompose 2. to refuse approval or support to

dis·cour·age (dis kur'ij) *vt.* **-aged, -ag·ing** 1. to deprive of courage; dishearten 2. to persuade (a person) to refrain 3. to try to prevent by disapproving —**dis·cour'age·ment** *n.* —**dis·cour'ag·ing** *adj.*

dis·course (dis'kôrs) *n.* [< L. *dis-*, from + *currere,* to run] 1. talk; conversation 2. a formal treatment of a subject, spoken or written —*vi.* (dis kôrs') **-coursed', -cours'ing** to talk or write, esp. formally

dis·cour·te·ous (dis kur'tē əs) *adj.* impolite; ill-mannered —**dis·cour'te·ous·ly** *adv.*

dis·cour'te·sy (-tə sē) *n.* 1. impoliteness; rudeness 2. *pl.* **-sies** a rude or impolite act or remark

dis·cov·er (dis kuv'ər) *vt.* [see DIS- & COVER] 1. to be the first to find, see, or know about 2. to find out —**dis·cov'er·a·ble** *adj.* —**dis·cov'er·er** *n.*

dis·cov'er·y *n., pl.* **-ies** 1. a discovering 2. anything discovered

dis·cred·it (dis kred'it) *vt.* 1. to disbelieve 2. to cast doubt on 3. to disgrace —*n.* 1. loss of belief; doubt 2. disgrace

dis·creet (dis krēt') *adj.* [see DISCERN] careful about what one says or does; prudent

dis·crep·an·cy (dis krep'ən sē) *n., pl.* **-cies** [< L. *dis-*, from + *crepare,* to rattle] lack of agreement; inconsistency

dis·crete (dis krēt') *adj.* [see DISCERN] 1. separate and distinct 2. made up of distinct parts —**dis·crete'ly** *adv.*

dis·cre·tion (dis kresh'ən) *n.* 1. the freedom to make decisions 2. the quality of being discreet; prudence —**dis·cre'tion·ar'y** (-er'ē) *adj.*

dis·crim·i·nate (dis krim'ə nāt') *vi.* **-nat'ed, -nat'ing** [see DISCERN] 1. to distinguish 2. to show partiality or prejudice —**dis·crim'i·na'tion** *n.*

dis·crim'i·na·to'ry (-nə tôr'ē) *adj.* showing discrimination or bias

dis·cur·sive (dis kur'siv) *adj.* [see DISCOURSE] wandering from one topic to another; rambling —**dis·cur'sive·ness** *n.*

dis·cus (dis'kəs) *n.* [< Gr. *diskos*] a heavy disk, as of metal and wood, thrown in a contest of strength and skill

dis·cuss (dis kus') *vt.* [< L. *dis-*, apart + *quatere,* to shake] to talk or write about; consider the pros and cons of —**dis·cus'sion** (-kush'ən) *n.*

dis·dain (dis dān') *vt.* [< L. *dis-*, not + *dignari,* deign] to regard as beneath one's dignity; scorn —*n.* aloof contempt —**dis·dain'ful** *adj.*

dis·ease (di zēz') *n.* [see DIS- & EASE] 1. illness in general 2. a particular destructive process in an organism —**dis·eased'** *adj.*

dis·em·bark (dis'im bärk') *vt., vi.* to leave, or unload from, a ship, etc. —**dis'em·bar·ka'tion** *n.*

dis'em·bod'y (-im bäd'ē) *vt.* **-ied, -y·ing** to free from bodily existence

dis'em·bow'el (-im bou'əl) *vt.* **-eled** or **-elled, -el·ing** or **-el·ling** to take out the bowels of; eviscerate

dis'en·chant' (-in chant') *vt.* to free from an enchantment or illusion —**dis'en·chant'ment** *n.*

dis'en·cum'ber (-in kum'bər) *vt.* to free from a burden or hindrance

dis'en·gage' *vt., vi.* **-gaged', -gag'ing** to release or get loose from something that binds, holds, etc. —**dis'en·gage'ment** *n.*

dis'en·tan'gle (-in taŋ'g'l) *vt.* **-gled, -gling** to free from something that entangles, confuses, etc.; extricate —**dis'en·tan'gle·ment** *n.*

dis·fa·vor (dis fā'vər) *n.* 1. an unfavorable opinion; dislike; disapproval 2. the state of being disliked or disapproved of —*vt.* to regard or treat unfavorably

dis·fig·ure (-fig'yər) *vt.* **-ured, -ur·ing** to hurt the appearance of; deface

dis·fran·chise (-fran′chīz) *vt.* -chised, -chis·ing to deprive of a right, privilege, etc., esp. of the right to vote: also **dis′en·fran′chise**

dis·gorge′ (-gôrj′) *vt., vi.* -gorged′, -gorg′ing [< OFr.: see DIS- & GORGE] 1. to vomit 2. to pour forth (its contents)

dis·grace′ (-grās′) *n.* [< It. *dis-*, not + *grazia*, favor] 1. loss of favor or respect; dishonor; shame 2. a person or thing bringing shame — *vt.* -graced′, -grac′ing to bring shame upon

dis·grace′ful *adj.* causing or characterized by disgrace; shameful

dis·grun′tle (-grun′t'l) *vt.* -tled, -tling [ult. < DIS- & GRUNT] to make peevishly discontented

dis·guise′ (-gīz′) *vt.* -guised′, -guis′ing [< OFr.: see DIS- & GUISE] 1. to make appear, sound, etc. so different as to be unrecognizable 2. to hide the real nature of —*n.* 1. anything used for disguising 2. a disguising or being disguised

dis·gust′ (-gust′) *n.* [< DIS- + L. *gustus*, taste] a sickening dislike; deep aversion; repugnance —*vt.* to cause to feel disgust —**dis·gust′ed** *adj.* —**dis·gust′ing** *adj.*

dish (dish) *n.* [see DISCUS] 1. a shallow, concave container for holding food, as a plate, bowl, etc. 2. a particular kind of food 3. as much as a dish holds —*vt.* to serve in a dish (with *up* or *out*)

dis·ha·bille (dis′ə bēl′) *n.* [< Fr. < *dés-*, DIS- + *habiller*, to dress] the state of being dressed only partially or in night clothes

dis·har·mo·ny (dis här′mə nē) *n.* lack of harmony; discord

dis·heart·en (dis härt′n) *vt.* to discourage; depress —**dis·heart′en·ment** *n.*

di·shev·el (di shev′'l) *vt.* -eled or -elled, -el·ing or -el·ling [< OFr. *des-*, DIS- + *chevel*, hair] to cause (hair, clothes, etc.) to become disarranged; rumple

dis·hon′est *adj.* not honest; lying, cheating, etc. —**dis·hon′est·ly** *adv.*

dis·hon′es·ty *n.* 1. a being dishonest 2. *pl.* -ties a dishonest act

dis·hon′or *n.* 1. *a)* loss of honor, respect, etc. *b)* shame; disgrace 2. a cause of dishonor —*vt.* to insult or disgrace —**dis·hon′or·a·ble** *adj.* —**dis·hon′or·a·bly** *adv.*

dis·il·lu′sion *vt.* 1. to free from illusion 2. to take away the idealism of and make bitter, etc. —*n.* a disillusioning or being disillusioned: also **dis′il·lu′sion·ment**

dis·in·cline (dis′in klīn′) *vt.* -clined′, -clin′ing to make unwilling

dis′in·fect′ (-in fekt′) *vt.* to destroy the harmful bacteria, viruses, etc. in or on —**dis′in·fect′ant** *n.* —**dis′in·fec′tion** *n.*

dis·in·her′it (-in her′it) *vt.* to deprive of an inheritance —**dis′in·her′it·ance** *n.*

dis·in·te·grate (dis in′tə grāt′) *vt., vi.* -grat′ed, -grat′ing to separate into parts or fragments; break up —**dis·in′te·gra′tion** *n.* —**dis·in′te·gra′tor** *n.*

dis·in·ter (dis′in tur′) *vt.* -terred′, -ter′ring to dig up from a grave, etc.

dis·in·ter·est·ed (dis in′trist id, -tər ist-) *adj.* 1. impartial; unbiased 2. uninterested —**dis·in′ter·est·ed·ly** *adv.*

dis·joint′ *vt.* 1. to put out of joint; dislocate 2. to dismember 3. to destroy the unity, connections, etc. of —*vi.* to come apart at the joints —**dis·joint′ed** *adj.*

disk (disk) *n.* [see DISCUS] 1. a thin, flat, circular thing 2. *same as* DISC

disk jockey *same as* DISC JOCKEY

dis·like′ *vt.* -liked′, -lik′ing to have a feeling of not liking —*n.* a feeling of not liking; distaste

dis·lo·cate (dis′lō kāt′) *vt.* -cat′ed, -cat′ing 1. to displace (a bone) from its proper position at a joint 2. to disarrange —**dis′lo·ca′tion** *n.*

dis·lodge′ *vt., vi.* -lodged′, -lodg′ing to force from or leave a place where lodged, hiding, etc. —**dis·lodg′ment** *n.*

dis·loy′al *adj.* not loyal or faithful —**dis·loy′al·ty** *n., pl.* -ties

dis·mal (diz′m'l) *adj.* [< ML. *dies mali*, evil days] 1. causing gloom or misery 2. dark and gloomy; dreary —**dis′mal·ly** *adv.*

dis·man·tle (dis man′t'l) *vt.* -tled, -tling [see DIS- & MANTLE] 1. to strip of covering 2. to strip (a house, etc.) as of furniture 3. to take apart

dis·may′ (-mā′) *vt.* [< Anglo-Fr.] to make discouraged at the prospect of trouble; daunt —*n.* a loss of courage

dis·mem′ber (-mem′bər) *vt.* [see DIS- & MEMBER] 1. to cut or tear the limbs from 2. to cut or pull to pieces

dis·miss′ (-mis′) *vt.* [< L. *dis-*, from + *mittere*, to send] 1. to cause or allow to leave 2. to discharge from an office, employment, etc. 3. to put out of one's mind —**dis·miss′al** *n.*

dis·mount′ *vi.* to get off, as from a horse —*vt.* 1. to remove (a thing) from its mounting 2. to cause to get off 3. to take apart

dis·o·be·di·ence (dis′ə bē′dē əns) *n.* refusal to obey —**dis′o·be′di·ent** *adj.*

dis′o·bey′ *vt., vi.* to refuse or fail to obey

dis·or′der *n.* 1. a lack of order; confusion 2. a breach of public peace; riot 3. irregularity 4. an upset of normal function; ailment —*vt.* 1. to throw into disorder 2. to upset the normal functions of

dis·or′der·ly *adj.* 1. not orderly; untidy; unsystematic 2. unruly; riotous 3. violating public peace, safety, etc.

dis·or·gan·ize (dis ôr′gə nīz′) *vt.* -ized′, -iz′ing to break up the order or system of; disorder —**dis·or′gan·i·za′tion** *n.*

dis·o′ri·ent′ (-ôr′ē ent′) *vt.* 1. to cause to lose one's bearings 2. to confuse mentally

dis·own′ *vt.* to refuse to acknowledge as one's own; cast off

dis·par′age (-par′ij) *vt.* -aged, -ag·ing [< OFr. *des-* (see DIS-) + *parage*, rank] 1. to lower in esteem; discredit 2. to belittle —**dis·par′age·ment** *n.* —**dis·par′ag·ing** *adj.*

dis·pa·rate (dis′pər it) *adj.* [< L. *dis-*, not + *par*, equal] distinct or different in kind —**dis·par′i·ty** (-par′ə tē) *n., pl.* -ties

dis·pas′sion·ate *adj.* free from passion, emotion, or bias; calm; impartial —**dis·pas′sion·ate·ly** *adv.*

dis·patch′ (-pach′) *vt.* [< Sp. < L. *dis-*, not + LL. *impedicare*, to entangle] 1. to send promptly, as on an errand 2. to kill 3. to finish quickly —*n.* 1. a sending off 2. a killing 3. speed; promptness 4. a message 5. a news story sent to a newspaper, etc. —**dis·patch′er** *n.*

dis·pel′ (-pel′) *vt.* -pelled′, -pel′ling [< L. *dis-*, away + *pellere*, to drive] to scatter and drive away; disperse

dis·pen·sa·ble (-pen′sə b'l) *adj.* 1. that can be given out 2. that can be dispensed with

dis·pen′sa·ry (-sə rē) *n., pl.* -ries a room or place where medicines and first aid are available

dis·pen·sa′tion (-pən sā′shən) *n.* 1. a dispensing; distribution 2. anything distributed 3. an administrative system 4. a release from an obligation 5. *Theol. a)* the ordering of events under divine authority *b)* any religious system —**dis′pen·sa′tion·al** *adj.*

dis·pense' (-pens') *vt.* -pensed', -pens'ing [< L. *dis*-, out + *pendere*, weigh] 1. to give out; distribute 2. to prepare and give out (medicines, etc.) 3. to administer [to *dispense* the law] 4. to exempt; excuse —**dispense with** 1. to get rid of 2. to do without —**dis·pen'ser** *n.*

dis·perse' (-purs') *vt.* -persed', -pers'ing [< L. *dis*-, out + *spargere*, strew] 1. to break up and scatter 2. to dispel (mist, etc.) —*vi.* to scatter — **dis·per'sal** *n.* —**dis·pers'er** *n.* —**dis·per'sion** *n.*

dis·pir·it (di spir'it) *vt.* to depress; deject —**dis·pir'it·ed** *adj.*

dis·place' *vt.* -placed', -plac'ing 1. to move from its usual place 2. to discharge 3. to replace

displaced person one forced from his country, esp. in war, and left homeless

dis·place'ment *n.* 1. a displacing or being displaced 2. the weight or volume of air, water, etc. displaced by a floating object

dis·play' (-plā') *vt.* [< L. *dis*-, apart + *plicare*, to fold] 1. to unfold; spread out 2. to show off; exhibit 3. to disclose; reveal —*n.* 1. an exhibition 2. anything displayed 3. ostentation; show

dis·please' *vt., vi.* -pleased', -pleas'ing to fail to please; offend

dis·pleas'ure (-plezh'ər) *n.* a being displeased; dissatisfaction, annoyance, etc.

dis·port' (-pôrt') *vi.* [< OFr. *des-* (see DIS-) + *porter*, carry] to play; frolic —*vt.* to amuse (oneself)

dis·pose' (-pōz') *vt.* -posed', -pos'ing [see DIS- & POSITION] 1. to arrange 2. to settle (affairs) 3. to make willing —**dispose of** 1. to deal with; settle 2. to give away or sell 3. to get rid of — **dis·pos'a·ble** *adj.* —**dis·pos'al** *n.*

dis·pos'er *n.* a garbage-grinding device installed in a sink drain

dis·po·si·tion (dis'pə zish'ən) *n.* 1. arrangement 2. management of affairs 3. a selling or giving away 4. the power to dispose 5. a tendency 6. one's temperament

dis'pos·sess' *vt.* to deprive of the possession of land, a house, etc.; oust

dis'pro·por'tion *n.* lack of proportion —**dis'pro·por'tion·ate** *adj.*

dis·prove' *vt.* -proved', -prov'ing to prove to be false or in error —**dis·proof'** *n.*

dis·pu·ta·tion (dis'pyoo tā'shən) *n.* 1. a disputing; dispute 2. debate

dis'pu·ta'tious (-shəs) *adj.* inclined to dispute; fond of arguing

dis·pute (dis pyoot') *vi.* -put'ed, -put'ing [< L. *dis*-, apart + *putare*, think] 1. to argue; debate 2. to quarrel —*vt.* 1. to argue (a question) 2. to doubt 3. to oppose in any way —*n.* 1. a disputing; argument 2. a quarrel —**in dispute** not settled —**dis·pu'ta·ble** *adj.* —**dis·pu'tant** *adj., n.*

dis·qual'i·fy' *vt.* -fied', -fy'ing to make or declare unqualified, unfit, or ineligible —**dis·qual'i·fi·ca'tion** (-fi kā'shən) *n.*

dis·qui·et (-kwī'ət) *vt.* to make anxious or restless; disturb —*n.* restlessness; anxiety: also **dis·qui'e·tude'** (-ə tōōd')

dis·qui·si·tion (dis'kwə zish'ən) *n.* [< L. *dis*-, apart + *quaerere*, seek] a formal discourse; treatise

dis're·gard' *vt.* 1. to pay little or no attention to 2. to treat without due respect; slight —*n.* 1. lack of attention 2. lack of due regard or respect —**dis're·gard'ful** *adj.*

dis're·pair' *n.* the condition of needing repairs; state of neglect

dis·rep'u·ta·ble *adj.* 1. having or causing a bad reputation 2. not fit to be seen

dis're·pute' *n.* lack or loss of repute; bad reputation; disgrace

dis're·spect' *n.* lack of respect; discourtesy — **dis're·spect'ful** *adj.*

dis·robe (dis rōb') *vt., vi.* -robed', -rob'ing to undress —**dis·rob'er** *n.*

dis·rupt' (-rupt') *vt., vi.* [< L. *dis*-, apart + *rumpere*, to break] 1. to break apart 2. to disturb or interrupt —**dis·rup'tion** *n.* —**dis·rup'tive** *adj.*

dis·sat·is·fy' *vt.* -fied', -fy'ing to fail to satisfy —**dis·sat'is·fac'tion** *n.*

dis·sect (di sekt', dī-) *vt.* [< L. *dis*-, apart + *secare*, to cut] 1. to cut apart piece by piece, as a body for purposes of study 2. to analyze closely —**dis·sec'tion** *n.*

dis·sem·ble (di sem'b'l) *vt., vi.* -bled, -bling [< OFr. *dessembler*] 1. to conceal (the truth, one's feelings, etc.) under a false appearance 2. to feign —**dis·sem'blance** *n.*

dis·sem·i·nate (di sem'ə nāt') *vt.* -nat'ed, -nat'ing [< L. *dis*-, apart + *seminare*, to sow] to scatter about; spread widely —**dis·sem'i·na'tion** *n.* —**dis·sem'i·na'tor** *n.*

dis·sen·sion (di sen'shən) *n.* 1. a dissenting; disagreement 2. violent quarreling

dis·sent (di sent') *vi.* [< L. *dis*-, apart + *sentire*, feel] 1. to disagree 2. to reject the doctrines of an established church —*n.* a dissenting —**dis·sent'er** *n.*

dis·ser·ta·tion (dis'ər tā'shən) *n.* [< L. *dis*-, apart + *serere*, join] a formal discourse or treatise; thesis

dis·serv·ice (dis sur'vis) *n.* harm; injury

dis·sev·er (di sev'ər) *vt.* 1. to sever 2. to divide into parts —*vi.* to separate

dis·si·dence (dis'ə dəns) *n.* [< L. *dis*-, apart + *sidere*, sit] disagreement; dissent —**dis'si·dent** *adj., n.*

dis·sim·i·lar (di sim'ə lər) *adj.* not similar; different —**dis·sim'i·lar'i·ty** (-lar'ə tē) *n., pl.* -ties —**dis·sim'i·lar·ly** *adv.*

dis·si·mil·i·tude (dis'si mil'ə tōōd') *n.* dissimilarity; difference

dis·sim·u·late (di sim'yə lāt') *vt., vi.* -lat'ed, -lat'ing [see DIS- & SIMULATE] to dissemble — **dis·sim'u·la'tion** *n.*

dis·si·pate (dis'ə pāt') *vt.* -pat'ed, -pat'ing [< L. *dis*-, apart + *supare*, to throw] 1. to scatter 2. to make disappear 3. to waste or squander —*vi.* 1. to vanish 2. to indulge in pleasure to the point of harming oneself —**dis'si·pa'tion** *n.*

dis·so·ci·ate (di sō'shē āt', -sē-) *vt., vi.* -at'ed, -at'ing [< L. *dis*-, apart + *sociare*, join] to sever association (with); disunite —**dis·so'ci·a'tion** *n.*

dis·so·lute (dis'ə lōōt') *adj.* [see DISSOLVE] dissipated and immoral; debauched

dis·so·lu·tion (dis'ə lōō'shən) *n.* a dissolving or being dissolved; specif., *a*) a breaking up or into parts; disintegration *b*) a termination *c*) death

dis·solve (di zälv', -zôlv') *vt., vi.* -solved', -solv'ing [< L. *dis*-, apart + *solvere*, loosen] 1. to make or become liquid; melt 2. to pass or make pass into solution 3. to break up; decompose 4. to end as by breaking up; terminate 5. to disappear or make disappear —**dis·solv'a·ble** *adj.*

dis·so·nance (dis'ə nəns) *n.* [< L. *dis*-, apart + *sonus*, a sound] 1. an inharmonious combination of sounds 2. any lack of harmony or agreement —**dis'so·nant** *adj.*

dis·suade (di swād') *vt.* -suad'ed, -suad'ing [< L. *dis*-, away + *suadere*, persuade] to cause to turn aside (*from* a course, etc.) by persuasion or advice —**dis·sua'sion** *n.*

dis·taff (dis'taf) *n.* [< OE. *dis-*, flax + *stæf*, a staff] a staff on which flax, wool, etc. is wound for use in spinning —*adj.* female

dis·tance (dis'təns) *n.* [< L. *dis-*, apart + *stare*, to stand] 1. a being separated in space or time; remoteness 2. an interval between two points in space or time 3. a remoteness in behavior 4. a remote place —*vt.* -tanced, -tanc·ing to outdo

dis'tant (-tənt) *adj.* 1. far away in space or time 2. away [ten miles *distant*] 3. far apart in relationship [a *distant* cousin] 4. cool in manner; aloof 5. from or at a distance —**dis'tant·ly** *adv.*

dis·taste (dis tāst') *n.* dislike (*for*)

dis·tem·per (dis tem'pər) *n.* [< ML. *distemperare*, to disorder] an infectious virus disease of young dogs

dis·tend (dis tend') *vt., vi.* [< L. *dis-*, apart + *tendere*, to stretch] 1. to stretch out 2. to make or become swollen —**dis·ten'si·ble** *adj.* —**dis·ten'sion** *n.*

dis·till, dis·til (dis til') *vt., vi.* -tilled', -till'ing [< L. *de-*, down + *stillare*, to drip] 1. to fall or let fall in drops 2. to undergo, subject to, or produce by distillation —**dis·till'er** *n.*

dis·til·late (dis'tə lāt', -t'l it) *n.* a liquid obtained by distilling

dis·til·la·tion (dis'tə lā'shən) *n.* 1. the process of heating a mixture and condensing the resulting vapor to produce a more nearly pure substance 2. a distillate

dis·till'er·y *n., pl.* -ies a place where alcoholic liquors are distilled

dis·tinct (dis tiŋkt') *adj.* [see DISTINGUISH] 1. not alike; different 2. separate 3. clearly marked off; plain 4. unmistakable

dis·tinc'tion (-tiŋk'shən) *n.* 1. the act of making or keeping distinct 2. difference 3. a quality or feature that differentiates 4. fame 5. the quality that makes one seem superior 6. a mark of honor

dis·tinc'tive *adj.* making distinct; characteristic —**dis·tinc'tive·ness** *n.*

dis·tin·guish (dis tiŋ'gwish) *vt.* [< L. *dis-*, apart + *stinguere*, to prick] 1. to perceive or show the difference in 2. to characterize 3. to perceive clearly 4. to classify 5. to make famous —*vi.* to make a distinction (*between* or *among*) —**dis·tin'guish·a·ble** *adj.* —**dis·tin'guish·a·bly** *adv.*

dis·tin'guished *adj.* celebrated; famous

dis·tort (dis tôrt') *vt.* [< L. *dis-*, intens. + *torquere*, to twist] 1. to twist out of shape 2. to misrepresent —**dis·tor'tion** *n.*

dis·tract (dis trakt') *vt.* [< L. *dis-*, apart + *trahere*, to draw] 1. to draw (the mind, etc.) away in another direction; divert 2. to create conflict and confusion in

dis·trac'tion *n.* 1. a distracting or being distracted; confusion 2. anything that distracts confusingly or amusingly; diversion 3. great mental distress

dis·trait (dis trā') *adj.* [see DISTRACT] absentminded; inattentive

dis·traught' (-trôt') *adj.* [var. of prec.] 1. very troubled or confused 2. driven mad; crazed

dis·tress (dis tres') *vt.* [< L. *dis-*, apart + *stringere*, to stretch] to cause misery or suffering to —*n.* 1. pain, suffering, etc. 2. an affliction 3. a state of danger or trouble

dis·trib·ute (dis trib'yoot) *vt.* -ut·ed, -ut·ing [< L. *dis-*, apart + *tribuere*, allot] 1. to give out in shares 2. to spread out 3. to classify 4. to put (things) in various distinct places —**dis·tri·bu'tion** *n.*

dis·trib'u·tor *n.* one that distributes; specif., *a*)

a dealer that distributes goods to consumers *b*) a device for distributing electric current to spark plugs

dis·trict (dis'trikt) *n.* [Fr. < L. *dis-*, apart + *stringere*, to stretch] 1. a geographic or political division made for a specific purpose 2. any region

district attorney the prosecuting attorney for the State or Federal government in a specified district

dis·trust (dis trust') *n.* a lack of trust; doubt —*vt.* to have no trust in; doubt —**dis·trust'ful** *adj.*

dis·turb (dis turb') *vt.* [< L. *dis-*, intens. + *turbare*, to disorder] 1. to break up the quiet or settled order of 2. to make uneasy 3. to interrupt

dis·turb'ance *n.* 1. a disturbing or being disturbed 2. anything that disturbs 3. commotion; disorder

dis·u·nite (dis'yoo nīt') *vt.* -nit'ed, -nit'ing to destroy the unity of; separate —*vi.* to become separated —**dis·u'ni·ty** *n.*

dis·use (dis yoos') *n.* lack of use

ditch (dich) *n.* [OE. *dic*] a long, narrow channel dug into the earth, as for drainage —*vt.* 1. to make a ditch in 2. [Slang] to get rid of or away from

dith·er (dith'ər) *n.* [ME. *dideren*] an excited state

dit·to (dit'ō) *n., pl.* -tos [It. < L. *dicere*, speak] 1. the same (as above or before) 2. *same as* DITTO MARK —*adv.* as said before

ditto mark a mark (") used in lists or tables to show that the item above is to be repeated

dit·ty (dit'ē) *n., pl.* -ties [< L. *dicere*, speak] a short, simple song

di·u·ret·ic (dī'yoo ret'ik) *adj.* [< Gr. *dia-*, through + *ourein*, urinate] increasing the flow of urine —*n.* a diuretic substance

di·ur·nal (dī ur'n'l) *adj.* [< L. *dies*, day] 1. daily 2. of or in the daytime

div. 1. dividend 2. division 3. divorced

di·van (dī'van, di van') *n.* [< Per. *dīwān*] a large, low couch or sofa

dive (dīv) *vi.* dived or dove, dived, div'ing [OE. *dyfan*] 1. to plunge headfirst into water 2. to submerge 3. to plunge suddenly into something 4. to make a steep descent, as an airplane —*n.* 1. a plunge into water 2. any sudden plunge 3. a sharp descent, as of an airplane 4. [Colloq.] a cheap, disreputable bar, etc. —**div'er** *n.*

di·verge (də vurj', dī-) *vi.* -verged', -verg'ing [< L. *dis-*, apart + *vergere*, to turn] 1. to branch off or go in different directions 2. to differ, as in opinion —**di·ver'gence** *n.* —**di·ver'gent** *adj.*

di·vers (dī'vərz) *adj.* [OFr.: see DIVERSE] various

di·verse (dī vurs', də-) *adj.* [< L. *dis-*, apart + *vertere*, to turn] 1. different 2. varied —**di·verse'ly** *adv.*

di·vers·i·fy (də vur'sə fī') *vt.* -fied', -fy'ing to make diverse; vary —**di·ver'si·fi·ca'tion** *n.*

di·ver·sion (də vur'zhən, dī-) *n.* 1. a diverting, or turning aside 2. distraction of attention 3. a pastime

di·ver'sion·ar·y *adj.* serving to divert or distract [*diversionary* tactics]

di·ver·si·ty (də vur'sə tē, dī-) *n., pl.* -ties 1. difference 2. variety

di·vert' (-vurt') *vt.* [see DIVERSE] 1. to turn aside; deflect 2. to amuse

di·vest (də vest', dī-) *vt.* [< L. *dis-*, from + *vestire*, to dress] 1. to strip (*of* clothing, etc.) 2. to deprive (*of* rank, rights, etc.) 3. to rid (*of* something)

di·vide (də vīd') *vt.* -vid'ed, -vid'ing [< L.

dividere] **1.** to separate into parts; sever **2.** to classify **3.** to make or keep separate **4.** to apportion **5.** to cause to disagree **6.** *Math.* to separate into equal parts by a divisor —*vi.* **1.** to be or become separate **2.** to disagree **3.** to share **4.** *Math.* to do division —*n.* a ridge that divides two drainage areas —**di·vid'er** *n.*

div·i·dend (div'ə dend') *n.* **1.** the number or quantity to be divided **2.** *a)* a sum to be divided among stockholders, etc. *b)* a single share of this **3.** a bonus

div·i·na·tion (div'ə nā'shən) *n.* [see DIVINE] **1.** the practice of trying to foretell the future or the unknown **2.** a prophecy

di·vine (də vīn') *adj.* [< L. *divus*, a god] **1.** of, like, or from God or a god **2.** devoted to God; religious **3.** supremely great, good, etc. —*n.* a clergyman —*vt.* **-vined'**, **-vin'ing 1.** to prophesy **2.** to guess **3.** to find out by intuition —**di·vine'ly** *adv.*

divining rod a forked stick alleged to dip downward when held over underground water or minerals

di·vin·i·ty (də vin'ə tē) *n., pl.* **-ties 1.** a being divine **2.** a god **3.** theology

di·vis·i·ble (də viz'ə b'l) *adj.* that can be divided, esp. without leaving a remainder

di·vi·sion (də vizh'ən) *n.* **1.** a dividing or being divided **2.** a sharing **3.** a difference of opinion **4.** anything that divides; partition **5.** a segment, section, department, class, etc. **6.** the process of finding out how many times a number (the *divisor*) is contained in another (the *dividend*) **7.** a major military unit

di·vi·sor (də vī'zər) *n. Math.* the number by which the dividend is divided

di·vorce (də vôrs') *n.* [< L. *dis-*, apart + *vertere*, to turn] **1.** legal dissolution of a marriage **2.** complete separation —*vt.* **-vorced'**, **-vorc'ing 1.** to dissolve legally a marriage between **2.** to separate from (one's spouse) by divorce **3.** to separate

di·vor·cée, di·vor·cee (də vôr'sā', -sē') *n.* [Fr.] a divorced woman —**di·vor'cé'** *n.masc.*

div·ot (div'ət) *n.* [Scot.] a lump of turf dislodged by a golf club in making a stroke

di·vulge (də vulj') *vt.* **-vulged'**, **-vulg'ing** [< L. *dis-*, apart + *vulgare*, make public] to make known; reveal —**di·vul'gence** *n.*

div·vy (div'ē) *vt., vi.* **-vied**, **-vy·ing** [Slang] to share; divide (*up*)

Dix·ie (dik'sē) *n.* the Southern States of the U.S.

Dix'ie·land' *adj.* in, of, or like the style of jazz associated with New Orleans

diz·zy (diz'ē) *adj.* **-zi·er**, **-zi·est** [OE. *dysig*, foolish] **1.** feeling giddy or unsteady **2.** causing dizziness **3.** confused **4.** [Colloq.] silly —**diz'zi·ly** *adv.* —**diz'zi·ness** *n.*

D.J., DJ disc jockey

DNA [< *d(eoxyribo)n(ucleic) a(cid)*] an essential component of all living matter and the basic chromosomal material transmitting the hereditary pattern

do¹ (dōō) *vt.* **did**, **done**, **do'ing** [OE. *don*] **1.** to perform (an action, etc.) **2.** to finish; complete **3.** to cause [it *does* no harm] **4.** to exert [*do* your best] **5.** to deal with as required [*do* the ironing] **6.** to have as one's occupation; work at **7.** [Colloq.] to cheat **8.** [Colloq.] to serve (a jail term) —*vi.* **1.** to behave [he *does* well when praised] **2.** to be active [*do*, don't talk] **3.** to get along; fare [the patient is *doing* well] **4.** to be adequate [that necktie will *do*] **5.** to take place [anything *doing* tonight?] — Auxiliary uses of *do:* **1.** to give emphasis [please *do* stay] **2.** to ask a question [*did* you go?] **3.** to serve

as a substitute verb [love me as I *do* (love) you] —**do in** [Slang] to kill —**do over** [Colloq.] to redecorate —**do up** [Colloq.] to wrap up —**do with** to make use of —**do without** to get along without —**have to do with 1.** to be related to **2.** to deal with —**make do** to get along with what is available

do² (dō) *n.* [It.] *Music* the first or last tone of the diatonic scale

doc·ile (däs''l) *adj.* [Fr. < L. *docere*, teach] easy to discipline; tractable —**doc'ile·ly** *adv.* —**do·cil·i·ty** (dä sil'ə tē) *n.*

dock¹ (däk) *n.* [< It. *doccia*, canal] **1.** a large excavated basin for receiving ships between voyages **2.** a landing pier; wharf **3.** the water between two piers **4.** a platform for loading and unloading trucks, etc. —*vt.* to pilot (a ship) to a dock —*vi.* to come into a dock

dock² (däk) *n.* [< Fl. *dok*, cage] the place where the accused stands or sits in court

dock³ (däk) *n.* [OE. *docce*] a coarse weed related to buckwheat, with large leaves

dock⁴ (däk) *n.* [< ON. *dockr*] the solid part of an animal's tail —*vt.* **1.** to cut off the end of (a tail); bob **2.** to deduct from (wages, etc.)

dock·et (däk'it) *n.* [< *doggette*, a register] **1.** a list of cases to be tried by a law court **2.** an agenda —*vt.* to enter in a docket

dock'yard' *n.* a place with docks, machinery, etc. for repairing or building ships

doc·tor (däk'tər) *n.* [L., teacher] **1.** a person on whom a university has conferred a high degree, as a Ph.D. **2.** a physician or surgeon (M.D.) **3.** a person licensed to practice any of the healing arts —*vt.* [Colloq.] **1.** to try to heal **2.** to mend **3.** to tamper with —**doc'tor·al** *adj.*

doc'tor·ate (-it) *n.* the degree of doctor conferred by a university

doc·tri·naire (däk'trə ner') *adj.* [Fr.] adhering to a doctrine in a dogmatic way

doc·trine (däk'trən) *n.* [see DOCTOR] something taught as the principles of a religion, political party, etc.; tenet or tenets; dogma —**doc'tri·nal** *adj.*

doc·u·ment (däk'yə mənt) *n.* [< L. *documentum*, proof] anything written, printed, etc., relied upon to record or prove something —*vt.* (-ment') to provide with or support by documents —**doc'u·men·ta'tion** *n.*

doc'u·men'ta·ry (-men'tə rē) *adj.* **1.** of or supported by documents **2.** dramatically showing news events, social conditions, etc. in nonfictional form —*n., pl.* **-ries** a documentary film, TV show, etc.

dod·der (däd'ər) *vi.* [ME. *daderen*] **1.** to tremble, as from old age **2.** to totter

dodge (däj) *vi., vt.* **dodged**, **dodg'ing** [? akin to Scot. *dod*, to jog] **1.** to move quickly aside, or avoid by so moving **2.** to use tricks or evasions, or evade by so doing —*n.* **1.** a dodging **2.** a trick used in evading or cheating —**dodg'er** *n.*

do·do (dō'dō) *n., pl.* **-dos**, **-does** [Port. *doudo*, lit., stupid] a large flightless bird, now extinct

doe (dō) *n.* [OE. *da*] the female of the deer, antelope, rabbit, etc.

do·er (dōō'ər) *n.* **1.** one who does something **2.** one who gets things done

does (duz) *3d pers. sing., pres. indic.,* of DO¹

doe·skin (dō'skin') *n.* **1.** leather from the skin of a female deer **2.** a soft wool cloth

does·n't (duz'nt) does not

doff (däf, dôf) *vt.* [see DO¹ & OFF] **1.** to take off (one's hat, etc.) **2.** to discard

dog (dôg) *n.* [OE. *docga*] **1.** a domesticated animal related to the fox, wolf, and jackal **2.** a mean, contemptible fellow **3.** a mechanical de-

vice for holding or grappling **4.** [*pl.*] [Slang]
feet **5.** [Slang] anything unsatisfactory —*vt.*
dogged, dog′ging to follow or hunt like a dog
—*adv.* very [*dog*-tired] —**go to the dogs**
[Colloq.] to deteriorate
dog′-ear′ *n.* a turned-down corner of the leaf
of a book —**dog′-eared′** *adj.*
dog′fish′ *n., pl.:* see FISH any of various small
sharks
dog·ged (dôg′id) *adj.* persistent; stubborn
dog·ger·el (dôg′ər əl) *n.* [prob. < It. *doga,* barrel stave] trivial verse, poorly constructed and
usually comic
dog′gone′ *interj.* damn! darn! —*vt.* -**goned′,**
-**gon′ing** [Colloq.] to damn
dog′house′ *n.* a dog's shelter —**in the
doghouse** [Slang] in disfavor
do·gie, do·gy (dō′gē) *n., pl.* -**gies** [< ?] in the
western U.S., a stray calf
dog·ma (dôg′mə) *n., pl.* -**mas, -ma·ta** (-mə tə)
[< Gr. *dokein,* think] a doctrine; belief; esp., a
body of theological doctrines authoritatively
affirmed
dog·mat′ic (-mat′ik) *adj.* **1.** of or like dogma **2.**
asserted without proof **3.** stating opinion positively or arrogantly: also **dog·mat′i·cal** —**dog-
mat′i·cal·ly** *adv.*
dog′ma·tism (-tiz′m) *n.* dogmatic assertion of
opinion —**dog′ma·tist** *n.*
dog tag 1. a license tag for a dog **2.** [Slang] a
military identification tag
dog′tooth′ *n., pl.* -**teeth′** a canine tooth
dog′trot′ *n.* a slow, easy trot
dog′watch′ *n. Naut.* a duty period, either from
4 to 6 P.M. or from 6 to 8 P.M.
dog′wood′ *n.* a small tree bearing white or
pink flowers
doi·ly (doi′lē) *n., pl.* -**lies** [after a 17th-c. London draper] a small mat, as of lace or paper,
used to protect a surface
do·ings (dōō′inz) *n.pl.* actions
dol·drums (däl′drəmz, dōl′-) *n.pl.* [< ? DULL]
1. low spirits **2.** sluggishness **3.** equatorial
ocean regions noted for dead calms
dole (dōl) *n.* [OE. *dal*] **1.** money or food given
in charity **2.** anything given sparingly **3.**
money paid by a government to the unemployed —*vt.* **doled, dol′ing** to give sparingly or
as a dole
dole·ful (dōl′fəl) *adj.* [< L. *dolere,* suffer] sad;
mournful —**dole′ful·ly** *adv.*
doll (däl) *n.* [< nickname for *Dorothy*] **1.** a
child's toy made to resemble a human being **2.**
[Slang] any attractive or lovable person —*vt.,
vi.* [Colloq.] to dress stylishly or showily (with
up)
dol·lar (däl′ər) *n.* [< G. *thaler*] **1.** the monetary
unit of the U.S., equal to 100 cents **2.** the
monetary unit of various other countries, as
Canada **3.** a coin or paper bill of the value of a
dollar
dol·lop (däl′əp) *n.* [< ?] **1.** a soft mass **2.** a
quantity, often a small one
dol·ly (däl′ē) *n., pl.* -**lies 1.** a doll: child's word
2. a low, flat, wheeled frame for moving heavy
objects
do·lor·ous (dō′lər əs, däl′ər-) *adj.* [< L. *dolere,*
suffer] **1.** sorrowful; sad **2.** painful
dol·phin (däl′fən) *n.* [< Gr. *delphis*] a water-
dwelling mammal, often with a beaklike snout
dolt (dōlt) *n.* [< ? DULL] a stupid, slow-witted
person —**dolt′ish** *adj.*
-dom [OE. *dom,* state] *a suffix meaning:* **1.** the
rank, position, or dominion of [*kingdom*] **2.**
fact or state of being [*martyrdom*] **3.** a total of
all who are [*officialdom*]
do·main (dō mān′) *n.* [< L. *dominus,* master]

1. territory under one government or ruler **2.**
land belonging to one person; estate **3.** field of
activity or influence
dome (dōm) *n.* [< Gr. *dōma,* housetop] **1.** a
rounded roof or ceiling **2.** any dome-shaped
structure
do·mes·tic (də mes′tik) *adj.* [< L. *domus,*
house] **1.** of the home or family **2.** of or made
in one's country **3.** tame: said of animals **4.**
home-loving —*n.* a maid, cook, etc. —**do·mes′ti-
cal·ly** *adv.*
do·mes′ti·cate′ (-tə kāt′) *vt.* -**cat′ed, -cat′ing**
1. to accustom to home life **2.** to tame for
man's use —**do·mes′ti·ca′tion** *n.*
do·mes·tic·i·ty (dō′mes tis′ə tē) *n., pl.* -**ties**
home life, or devotion to it
dom·i·cile (däm′ə sīl′, -sil; dō′mə-) *n.* [< L.
domus, house] a home; residence
dom·i·nant (däm′ə nənt) *adj.* dominating —
dom′i·nance *n.* —**dom′i·nant·ly** *adv.*
dom′i·nate′ (-nāt′) *vt., vi.* -**nat′ed, -nat′ing** [<
L. *dominus,* master] **1.** to rule or control by
superior power **2.** to rise high above (the surroundings, etc.) —**dom′i·na′tion** *n.*
dom·i·neer (däm′ə nir′) *vi., vi.* [< Du. < L.:
see prec.] to rule (*over*) in a harsh or arrogant
way; tyrannize
dom′i·neer′ing *adj.* overbearing
do·min·ion (də min′yən) *n.* [see DOMAIN] **1.**
rule or power to rule **2.** a governed territory,
or, sometimes, a self-governing nation
dom·i·no (däm′ə nō′) *n., pl.* -**noes′, -nos′** [Fr.
& It.] **1.** a loose cloak with a hood and mask,
worn at masquerades **2.** a mask for the eyes **3.**
a small oblong tile marked with dots **4.** [*pl.,
with sing. v.*] a game played with such pieces
don¹ (dän) *n.* [Sp. < L. *dominus,* master] **1.**
[D-] Sir; Mr.: a Spanish title of respect **2.** a
Spanish gentleman **3.** [Colloq.] a tutor at a
British college
don² (dän) *vt.* **donned, don′ning** [contr. of *do
on*] to put on (a garment, etc.)
‡**do·ña** (dō′nyä) *n., pl.* -**ñas** (-nyäs) [Sp. < L.
domina, mistress] a lady: as a title [D-],
equivalent to *Lady, Madam*
do·nate (dō′nāt) *vt., vi.* -**nat·ed, -nat·ing** [prob.
< ff.] to give or contribute
do·na′tion *n.* [< L. *donum,* gift] **1.** the act of
donating **2.** a gift or contribution
done (dun) *pp.* of DO¹ —*adj.* **1.** completed **2.** sufficiently cooked **3.** acceptable
Don Ju·an (dän′ jōō′ən, dän′ wän′) **1.** *Sp.
Legend* a dissolute nobleman and seducer of
women **2.** any libertine
don·key (däŋ′kē, duŋ′-) *n., pl.* -**keys** [< ?] **1.**
the domesticated ass **2.** a stupid or stubborn
person **3.** a small steam engine
do·nor (dō′nər) *n.* one who donates
Don Qui·xo·te (dän′ kē hōt′ē, dän′ kwik′sət)
1. a satirical romance by Cervantes **2.** its chivalrous, unrealistic hero
don't (dōnt) do not
doo·dle (dōō′d'l) *vi.* -**dled, -dling** [G. *dudeln,* to
trifle] to scribble aimlessly —*n.* a mark made
in aimless scribbling
doom (dōōm) *n.* [OE. *dom*] **1.** a judgment; esp.,
a sentence of condemnation **2.** fate **3.** ruin or
death —*vt.* **1.** to condemn **2.** to destine to a
tragic fate
dooms·day (dōōmz′dā′) *n.* Judgment Day
door (dôr) *n.* [OE. *duru*] **1.** a movable structure
for opening or closing an entrance **2.** a doorway **3.** a means of access —**out of doors** outdoors
door′bell′ *n.* a bell rung by someone wishing
to enter a building or room
door′man′ (-man′, -mən) *n., pl.* -**men′** a man

whose work is opening the door of a building, hailing taxicabs, etc.

door'mat' *n.* a mat to wipe the shoes on before entering a house, etc.

door'nail' *n.* a large-headed nail used in studding some doors —**dead as a doornail** absolutely dead

door'step' *n.* a step leading from an outer door to a path, lawn, etc.

door'way' *n.* **1.** an opening in a wall that can be closed by a door **2.** any means of access

door'yard' *n.* a yard onto which a door of a house opens

dope (dōp) *n.* [Du. *doop,* sauce] **1.** any thick liquid or paste used as a lubricant, varnish, filler, etc. **2.** [Slang] *a)* any drug or narcotic *b)* a stupid person *c)* information —*vt.* **doped, dop'ing** to drug —**dope out** [Colloq.] to solve

dop·ey, dop·y (dō'pē) *adj.* **-i·er, -i·est** [Slang] **1.** under the influence of a narcotic **2.** lethargic or stupid —**dop'i·ness** *n.*

Dor·ic (dôr'ik) *adj.* designating or of a Greek style of architecture marked by fluted columns with simple capitals

dorm (dôrm) *n.* [Colloq.] a dormitory

dor·mant (dôr'mənt) *adj.* [< L. *dormire,* to sleep] **1.** sleeping **2.** inactive **3.** *Biol.* in a resting or torpid state —**dor'man·cy** *n.*

dor·mer (dôr'mər) *n.* [see prec.] a window set upright in a structure projecting from a sloping roof: also **dormer window**

dor·mi·to·ry (dôr'mə tôr'ē) *n., pl.* **-ries** [see DORMANT] **1.** a room with beds for a number of people **2.** a building, as at a college, with many rooms providing sleeping and living accommodations

dor·mouse (dôr'mous') *n., pl.* **-mice** (-mīs') [< ? OFr. *dormeuse,* sleepy] a small old-world rodent that resembles a squirrel

dor·sal (dôr's'l) *adj.* [< L. *dorsum,* the back] of, on, or near the back —**dor'sal·ly** *adv.*

do·ry (dôr'ē) *n., pl.* **-ries** [AmInd. (Central America) *dori,* a dugout] a small, flat-bottomed fishing boat with high sides

dose (dōs) *n.* [< Gr. *dosis,* a giving] an amount of medicine to be taken at one time —*vt.* **dosed, dos'ing** to give doses to —**dos'age** *n.*

dos·si·er (däs'ē ā', dôs'-) *n.* [Fr.] a collection of documents about some person or matter

dost (dust) *archaic 2d pers. sing., pres. indic., of* DO[1]: *used with* thou

dot (dät) *n.* [OE. *dott,* head of a boil] **1.** a tiny speck or mark **2.** a small, round spot —*vt.* **dot'ted, dot'ting** to mark as with a dot or dots —**on the dot** [Colloq.] at the exact time

dot·age (dōt'ij) *n.* < *doten,* to dote] **1.** feeble and childish state due to old age **2.** excessive affection

do·tard (dō'tərd) *n.* [see prec.] a foolish and doddering old person

dote (dōt) *vi.* **dot'ed, dot'ing** [ME. *doten*] **1.** to be weak-minded, esp. in old age **2.** to be excessively fond (with *on* or *upon*)

doth (duth) *archaic 3d pers. sing., pres. indic., of* DO[1]: chiefly in auxiliary uses

Dou·ay Bible (dōō ā') [< *Douai,* in France, where it was published in part (1609–10)] an English translation of the Bible from the Vulgate, for Roman Catholics

dou·ble (dub''l) *adj.* [< L. *duplus*] **1.** twofold **2.** having two layers **3.** having two of one kind **4.** being of two kinds [a *double* standard] **5.** having two meanings **6.** twice as much, as many, etc. —*adv.* **1.** twofold **2.** in a pair —*n.* **1.** anything twice as much, as many, etc. as normal **2.** a duplicate; counterpart **3.** a fold **4.** [*pl.*] a game of tennis, etc. with two players on each side **5.** *Baseball* a hit on which the batter reaches second base **6.** *Bridge* the doubling of an opponent's bid —*vt.* **-bled, -bling 1.** to make twice as much or many **2.** to fold **3.** to repeat or duplicate **4.** to be the double of **5.** *Bridge* to increase the point value or penalty of (an opponent's bid) —*vi.* **1.** to become double **2.** to turn sharply backward [to *double* on one's tracks] **3.** to serve as a double, serve two purposes, etc. —**double up 1.** to clench (one's fist) **2.** to bend over, as in pain **3.** to share a room, etc. with someone

double agent a spy who infiltrates an enemy espionage organization

dou'ble-bar'reled *adj.* **1.** having two barrels, as a kind of shotgun **2.** having a double purpose or meaning

double bass (bās) the largest and deepest-toned instrument of the violin family

double boiler a cooking utensil with an upper pan for food, fitting into a lower pan in which water is boiled

dou'ble-breast'ed *adj.* overlapping across the breast, as a coat

dou'ble-cross' *vt.* [Colloq.] to betray —**dou'-ble-cross'er** *n.*

double date [Colloq.] a social engagement shared by two couples —**dou'ble-date'** *vi., vt.* **-dat'ed, -dat'ing**

dou'ble-deal'ing *n.* duplicity

dou'ble-edged' *adj.* **1.** having two cutting edges **2.** applicable both ways, as an argument

dou·ble-en·ten·dre (dōō'blän tän'drə, dub''l än-) *n.* [Fr. (now obs.), double meaning] a word or phrase with two meanings, esp. when one of them is risqué

dou'ble-head'er *n.* two games played in succession on the same day

dou'ble-joint'ed *adj.* having joints that permit limbs, fingers, etc. to bend at other than the usual angles

dou'ble-knit' *adj.* knit with a double stitch that makes the fabric extra thick

dou'ble-park' *vt., vi.* to park (a vehicle) parallel to another parked alongside a curb

double play *Baseball* a play in which two players are put out

dou'ble-reed' *adj.* designating or of a woodwind instrument, as the oboe, having two reeds separated by a narrow opening —*n.* a double-reed instrument

double standard a system, code, etc. applied unequally; specif., a moral code stricter for women than for men

dou·blet (dub'lit) *n.* [< OFr. *double,* orig., something folded] **1.** a man's closefitting jacket of the 14th to 16th cent. **2.** either of a pair **3.** a pair

double take a delayed, startled reaction to some remark, situation, etc., following initial, unthinking acceptance

double talk 1. ambiguous and deceptive talk **2.** meaningless syllables like talk

double time a marching cadence of 180 three-foot steps a minute

dou·bloon (du blōōn') *n.* [< Fr. < Sp. < L. *duplus,* double] an obsolete Spanish coin

dou·bly (dub'lē) *adv.* **1.** twice **2.** two at a time

doubt (dout) *vi.* [< L. *dubitare*] to be uncertain or undecided —*vt.* **1.** to be uncertain about **2.** to tend to disbelieve —*n.* **1.** a lack of conviction or trust **2.** a condition of uncertainty **3.** an unsettled point or matter —**beyond doubt** certainly —**no doubt 1.** certainly **2.** probably

doubt'ful *adj.* **1.** uncertain **2.** giving rise to doubt **3.** feeling doubt; unsettled

doubt'less *adv.* **1.** certainly **2.** probably

douche (do͞osh) *n.* [Fr. < It. *doccia*] **1.** a jet of liquid applied externally or internally to some part of the body **2.** a device for douching —*vt.,* *vi.* **douched, douch'ing** to apply a douche (to)

dough (dō) *n.* [OE. *dag*] **1.** a mixture of flour, liquid, etc. worked into a soft, thick mass for baking **2.** [Slang] money

dough·boy (dō'boi') *n.* [Colloq.] a U.S. infantryman, esp. of World War I

dough'nut' *n.* a small, usually ring-shaped cake, fried in deep fat: also **do'nut'**

dough·ty (dout'ē) *adj.* **-ti·er, -ti·est** [< OE. *dugan,* to avail] valiant; brave: now humorous and somewhat archaic

dough·y (dō'ē) *adj.* **-i·er, -i·est** of or like dough; soft, pasty, etc. —**dough'i·ness** *n.*

dour (door, door, dour) *adj.* [< L. *durus,* hard] **1.** [Scot.] severe; stern **2.** sullen; gloomy — **dour'ly** *adv.* —**dour'ness** *n.*

douse (dous) *vt.* **doused, dous'ing** [?] **1.** to thrust suddenly into liquid **2.** to drench **3.** [Colloq.] to put out (a light or fire) quickly

dove¹ (duv) *n.* [< ? ON. *dūfa*] **1.** a bird of the pigeon family, with a cooing cry: a symbol of peace **2.** an advocate of peaceful international relationships

dove² (dōv) *alt. pt. of* DIVE

dove·cote (duv'kōt') *n.* a small box with compartments for nesting pigeons: also **dove'cot'** (-kät')

dove·tail (duv'tāl') *n.* a projecting part that fits into a corresponding indentation to form a joint —*vt., vi.* to join or fit together closely or by means of dovetails

dow·a·ger (dou'ə jər) *n.* [ult. < L. *dos,* dowry] **1.** a widow with a title or property derived from her dead husband **2.** an elderly woman of wealth and dignity

dow·dy (dou'dē) *adj.* **-di·er, -di·est** [< ME. *doude,* plain woman] not neat in dress; shabby —**dow'di·ness** *n.*

dow·el (dou'əl) *n.* [ME. *doule*] a peg of wood, etc., usually fitted into corresponding holes in two pieces to fasten them together

dow·er (dou'ər) *n.* [< L. *dos,* dowry] **1.** that part of a man's property which his widow inherits for life **2.** a dowry

down¹ (doun) *adv.* [OE. *adune,* from the hill] **1.** to, in, or on a lower place or level **2.** in or to a lower condition, amount, etc. **3.** from an earlier to a later period **4.** seriously *[get down to work]* **5.** in cash *[$5 down]* **6.** in writing *[take down notes]* —*adj.* **1.** descending **2.** in a lower place **3.** gone, brought, pulled, etc. down **4.** dejected **5.** ill **6.** in cash *[a down payment]* — *prep.* down toward, along, through, into, or upon —*vt.* to put or throw down —*n.* **1.** a misfortune *[ups and downs]* **2.** *Football* one of a series of plays in which a team tries to advance the ball —**down and out** penniless, ill, etc. —**down on** [Colloq.] angry with

down² (doun) *n.* [< ON. *dūnn*] **1.** soft, fine feathers **2.** soft, fine hair

down³ (doun) *n.* [OE. *dun,* hill] open, high, grassy land: *usually used in pl.*

down'cast' *adj.* **1.** directed downward **2.** sad; dejected

down'fall' *n.* **1.** *a)* a sudden fall, as from power *b)* the cause of this **2.** a sudden, heavy fall, as of snow

down'grade' *n.* a downward slope —*adj., adv.* downward —*vt.* **-grad'ed, -grad'ing** to demote — **on the downgrade** declining

down'heart'ed *adj.* discouraged

down'hill' *adv., adj.* **1.** toward the bottom of a hill **2.** to a poorer condition, status, etc.

down'pour' *n.* a heavy rain

down'right' *adv.* thoroughly; utterly —*adj.* **1.** absolute; utter **2.** plain; frank

Down's syndrome (dounz) [< J. *Down* (1828–96), Eng. physician] a congenital disease marked by mental deficiency, a broad face, slanting eyes, etc.

down'stage' *adj., adv.* of or toward the front of the stage

down'stairs' *adv.* **1.** down the stairs **2.** on or to a lower floor —*adj.* on a lower floor —*n.* a lower floor

down'stream' *adv., adj.* in the direction of the current of a stream

down'swing' *n.* **1.** a downward swing, as of a golf club **2.** a downward trend

down'town' *adj., adv.* in or toward the main business section of a city

down'trod'den *adj.* oppressed

down'ward (-wərd) *adv., adj.* toward a lower place, position, etc.: also **down'wards** *adv.*

down·y (doun'ē) *adj.* **-i·er, -i·est 1.** covered with soft, fine feathers or hair **2.** soft and fluffy, like down —**down'i·ness** *n.*

dow·ry (dou'rē) *n., pl.* **-ries** [see DOWER] **1.** the property that a woman brings to her husband at marriage **2.** a natural talent

dowse (douz) *vi.* **dowsed, dows'ing** [< ?] to search for water or minerals with a divining rod (**dowsing rod**) —**dows'er** *n.*

dox·ol·o·gy (däk säl'ə jē) *n., pl.* **-gies** [< Gr. *doxa,* praise + *legein,* speak] a hymn of praise to God

doze (dōz) *vi.* **dozed, doz'ing** [prob. < Scand.] to sleep fitfully; nap —*n.* a light sleep; nap

doz·en (duz'’n) *n., pl.* **-ens** or, esp. after a number, **-en** [< L. *duo,* two + *decem,* ten] a set of twelve: abbrev. **doz.**

DP, D.P. displaced person

Dr. Doctor

drab (drab) *n.* [< Fr. < VL. *drappus,* cloth] a dull yellowish brown —*adj.* **drab'ber, drab'best 1.** dull yellowish-brown **2.** dull

drach·ma (drak'mə) *n., pl.* **-mas, -mae** (-mē), **-mai** (-mī) [< Gr. *drachmē,* a handful] **1.** an ancient Greek silver coin **2.** the monetary unit of modern Greece

draft (draft) *n.* [< OE. *dragan,* to draw] **1.** a drawing, as of a vehicle or load **2.** *a)* a drawing in of a fish net *b)* the amount of fish caught in one draw **3.** *a)* a drinking or the amount taken at one drink *b)* [Colloq.] a portion of beer, etc. drawn from a cask **4.** an inhalation **5.** a rough sketch of a writing **6.** a plan or drawing of a work to be done **7.** a current of air **8.** a device for regulating the current of air in a heating system **9.** a written order for payment of money; check **10.** *a)* the taking of persons for compulsory military service *b)* those so taken **11.** the depth of water that a ship displaces —*vt.* **1.** to take, as for military service, by drawing from a group **2.** to make a sketch of or plans for —*adj.* **1.** used for pulling loads **2.** drawn from a cask *[draft beer]*

draft·ee (draf tē') *n.* a person drafted, esp. for service in the armed forces

drafts·man (drafts'mən) *n., pl.* **-men** one who draws plans of structures or machinery — **drafts'man·ship'** *n.*

draft'y *adj.* **-i·er, -i·est** letting in, having, or exposed to a draft or drafts of air —**draft'i·ly** *adv.* —**draft'i·ness** *n.*

drag (drag) *vt., vi.* **dragged, drag'ging** [OE. *dragan*] **1.** to pull or be pulled with effort, esp. along the ground **2.** to search the bottom of (a river, etc.), as with a net **3.** to draw (something) out over a period of time; move or pass too slowly —*n.* **1.** something dragged along the ground, as a harrow **2.** a grapnel, dragnet, etc. **3.** anything that hinders **4.** a dragging **5.** [Slang] influence **6.** [Slang] a puff of a cigarette, etc. **7.** [Slang] street *[the main drag]* **8.** [Slang] a dull person, situation, etc. — **drag on** (or **out**) to prolong or be prolonged tediously

drag·gle (drag′'l) *vt., vi.* **-gled, -gling** [< DRAG] to make or become wet or dirty by dragging in mud or water

drag′net′ *n.* **1.** a net dragged along a lake bottom, etc., as for catching fish **2.** an organized system or network for catching criminals

drag·o·man (drag′ə mən) *n., pl.* **-mans, -men** [< Ar. *targumān*] in the Near East, an interpreter

drag·on (drag′ən) *n.* [< Gr. *drakōn*] a mythical monster, typically a large, winged reptile breathing out fire and smoke

drag′on·fly′ *n., pl.* **-flies′** a large, long-bodied insect with narrow, transparent wings

dra·goon (drə gōōn′) *n.* [Fr.: see DRAGON] a heavily armed cavalryman —*vt.* to force (into) doing something; coerce

drag race [Slang] a race between hot-rod cars accelerating from a standstill on a short, straight course (**drag strip**)

drain (drān) *vt.* [< OE. *dryge*, dry] **1.** to draw off (liquid) gradually **2.** to draw liquid from gradually **3.** to exhaust (strength, resources, etc.) gradually —*vi.* **1.** to flow off; trickle **2.** to become dry by draining **3.** to discharge its waters —*n.* **1.** a channel, pipe, etc. for draining **2.** a draining —**drain′er** *n.*

drain′age (-ij) *n.* **1.** a draining **2.** a system of pipes, etc. for carrying off waste matter **3.** that which is drained off

drake (drāk) *n.* [ME.] a male duck

dram (dram) *n.* [< Gr. *drachma*, handful] **1.** *Apothecaries' Weight* a unit equal to 1/8 ounce **2.** *Avoirdupois Weight* a unit equal to 1/16 ounce **3.** *same as* FLUID DRAM

dra·ma (drä′mə, dram′ə) *n.* [< Gr.] **1.** a literary composition to be performed by actors; play **2.** the art of writing, acting, or producing plays **3.** a series of events as interesting, vivid, etc. as a play **4.** dramatic quality

dra·mat·ic (drə mat′ik) *adj.* **1.** of or connected with drama **2.** like a play **3.** vivid, exciting, etc. —**dra·mat′i·cal·ly** *adv.*

dra·mat·ics *n.pl.* [*usually with sing. v.*] the performing or producing of plays

dram·a·tis per·so·nae (dram′ə tis pər sō′nē) [ModL.] the characters in a play

dram·a·tist (dram′ə tist) *n.* a playwright

dram′a·tize′ (-tīz′) *vt.* **-tized′, -tiz′ing 1.** to make into a drama **2.** to regard or show dramatically —**dram′a·ti·za′tion** *n.*

drank (draŋk) *pt. & often colloq. pp.* of DRINK

drape (drāp) *vt.* **draped, drap′ing** [< VL. *drappus*, cloth] **1.** to cover or hang as with cloth in loose folds **2.** to arrange (a garment, cloth, etc.) in folds or hangings —*n.* cloth hanging in loose folds; esp., a drapery: *usually used in pl.*

drap·er (drā′pər) *n.* [Brit.] a dealer in cloth and dry goods

drap′er·y *n., pl.* **-ies 1.** hangings, etc. arranged in loose folds **2.** [*pl.*] curtains of heavy material

dras·tic (dras′tik) *adj.* [< Gr. *drastikos*, active] having a violent effect; severe; harsh —**dras′ti·cal·ly** *adv.*

draught (draft) *n., vt., adj. now chiefly Brit. sp.* of DRAFT

draughts (drafts) *n.pl.* [Brit.] the game of checkers

draw (drô) *vt.* **drew, drawn, draw′ing** [OE.

dragan] **1.** to make move toward one; pull **2.** to pull up, down, back, in, or out **3.** to need (a specified depth of water) to float in: said of a ship **4.** to attract **5.** to breathe in **6.** to elicit (a reply, etc.) **7.** to bring on; provoke **8.** to receive *[to draw* a salary*]* **9.** to withdraw (money) held in an account **10.** to write (a check or draft) **11.** to deduce **12.** to stretch **13.** to make (lines, pictures, etc.) as with a pencil —*vi.* **1.** to draw something (in various senses of the *vt.*) **2.** to be drawn **3.** to come; move *[to draw* near*]* **4.** to shrink **5.** to allow a draft, as of smoke, to move through —*n.* **1.** a drawing or being drawn **2.** the result of drawing **3.** a thing drawn **4.** a stalemate **5.** a ravine that water drains into —**draw out 1.** to extend **2.** to get (a person) to talk —**draw up 1.** to arrange in order **2.** to compose (a document) **3.** to stop

draw′back′ *n.* anything that lessens or prevents full satisfaction; shortcoming

draw′bridge′ *n.* a bridge that can be raised, lowered, or drawn aside

draw·er (drô′ər) *n.* **1.** one that draws **2.** (drôr) a sliding box in a table, chest, etc.

drawers (drôrz) *n.pl.* an undergarment for the lower part of the body

draw′ing *n.* **1.** the act of one that draws **2.** the art of making pictures, etc. as with a pencil **3.** a picture, design, etc. thus made **4.** a lottery

drawing card an entertainer, show, etc. that draws a large audience

drawing room [< *withdrawing room:* guests withdrew there after dinner] **1.** a room where guests are received or entertained **2.** a private compartment on a railroad sleeping car

drawl (drôl) *vt., vi.* [prob. < DRAW] to speak slowly, prolonging the vowels —*n.* a manner of speaking thus —**drawl′ing·ly** *adv.*

drawn (drôn) *pp.* of DRAW —*adj.* **1.** disemboweled **2.** tense; haggard

drawn butter melted butter

dray (drā) *n.* [< OE. *dragan*, to draw] a wagon for heavy loads —**dray′age** (-ij) *n.*

dread (dred) *vt.* [< OE. *ondrædan*] to anticipate with fear or distaste —*n.* **1.** intense fear **2.** fear mixed with awe —*adj.* **1.** dreaded or dreadful **2.** inspiring awe

dread′ful *adj.* **1.** inspiring dread; terrible **2.** [Colloq.] very bad, offensive, etc. —**dread′ful·ly** *adv.* —**dread′ful·ness** *n.*

dread′nought′, dread′naught′ (-nôt′) *n.* a large battleship with big guns

dream (drēm) *n.* [< OE., joy, music] **1.** a sequence of images, thoughts, etc. passing through a sleeping person's mind **2.** a daydream; reverie **3.** a fond hope **4.** anything like a dream —*vi., vt.* **dreamed** or **dreamt** (dremt), **dream′ing 1.** to have a dream or dreams (of) **2.** to have a remote idea (of) —**dream′er** *n.*

dream′y *adj.* **-i·er, -i·est 1.** filled with dreams **2.** visionary; impractical **3.** shadowy; vague **4.** soothing —**dream′i·ly** *adv.*

drear (drir) *adj.* [Poet.] dreary; melancholy

drear′y *adj.* **-i·er, -i·est** [< OE. *dreorig*, sad] gloomy; dismal —**drear′i·ness** *n.*

dredge[1] (drej) *n.* [prob. < MDu. *dregge*] an apparatus for scooping up mud, etc., as in deepening channels, harbors, etc. —*vt., vi.* **dredged, dredg′ing** to enlarge or clean out with a dredge

dredge[2] (drej) *vt.* **dredged, dredg′ing** [< ME. *dragge*, sweetmeat] to coat (food) with flour or the like

dregs (dregz) *n.pl.* [< ON. *dregg*] **1.** the particles that settle at the bottom of a liquid **2.** the most worthless part *[dregs* of society*]* — **dreg′gy** *adj.* **-gi·er, -gi·est**

drench (drench) *vt.* [< OE. *drincan,* to drink] to make wet all over; soak

dress (dres) *vt.* **dressed** or **drest, dress'ing** [< L. *dirigere,* lay straight] 1. to put clothes on; clothe 2. to trim; adorn 3. to arrange or do up (the hair) 4. to arrange (troops, etc.) in straight lines 5. to apply medicines and bandages to (a wound, etc.) 6. to prepare [to dress a fowl] 7. to smooth or finish (leather, stone, etc.) —*vi.* 1. to put on clothes 2. to wear formal clothes 3. to get into a straight line —*n.* 1. clothes 2. the common, one-piece, skirted garment of women —**dress up** to dress in formal or elegant clothes

dres·sage (drə säzh') *n.* [Fr., training] horsemanship in which slight movements are used to control the horse

dress'er *n.* 1. one who dresses (in various senses) 2. a chest of drawers for clothes

dress'ing *n.* 1. the act of one that dresses 2. bandages, etc. applied to a wound 3. a sauce for salads, etc. 4. a stuffing for roast fowl

dress'ing-down' *n.* a sound scolding

dressing gown a loose robe for wear when one is undressed or lounging

dress'mak'er *n.* one who makes women's dresses, suits, etc. to order —*adj.* not cut on severe, mannish lines —**dress'mak'ing** *n.*

dress rehearsal a final rehearsal, as of a play, performed exactly as it is to take place

dress'y *adj.* **-i·er, -i·est** 1. showy in dress or appearance 2. elegant; smart —**dress'i·ness** *n.*

drew (drōō) *pt.* of DRAW

drib·ble (drib''l) *vi., vt.* **-bled, -bling** [< DRIP] 1. to flow, or let flow, in drops 2. to drool 3. *Sports* to move (the ball or puck) along by repeated bouncing, kicking, etc. —*n.* 1. dribbling 2. a very small amount: also **drib'let** (-lit)

dried (drīd) *pt. & pp.* of DRY

dri·er (drī'ər) *n.* 1. a substance added to paint, etc. to make it dry fast 2. *same as* DRYER —*adj. compar.* of DRY

dri'est (-ist) *adj. superl.* of DRY

drift (drift) *n.* [< OE. *drifan,* to drive] 1. a being driven along, as by a current 2. the course on which something is driven 3. a tendency or trend 4. meaning; intent 5. a heap of snow, etc. piled up by the wind 6. rocks, gravel, etc. deposited by a glacier —*vi.* 1. to be carried along, as by a current 2. to go along aimlessly 3. to pile up in drifts —*vt.* to cause to drift —**drift'er** *n.*

drift'wood' *n.* wood drifting in the water, or that has been washed ashore

drill' (dril) *n.* [Du. *drillen,* to bore] 1. a tool for boring holes in wood, metal, etc. 2. systematic military or physical training 3. the method or practice of teaching by repeated exercises —*vt.* 1. to bore (a hole) with a drill 2. to train in, or teach by means of, drill 3. to instill (*into*) by repetition 4. [Colloq.] to cause to move swiftly and directly —*vi.* 1. to bore a hole 2. to undergo training or teaching by drill

drill² (dril) *n.* [< ?] a machine for making holes and dropping seeds into them

drill³ (dril) *n.* [< G. < L. *trilix,* three-threaded] a coarse, twilled linen or cotton cloth

dri·ly (drī'lē) *adv. same as* DRYLY

drink (driŋk) *vt.* **drank, drunk, drink'ing** [OE. *drincan*] 1. to swallow (liquid) 2. to absorb (liquid or moisture) 3. to swallow the contents of —*vi.* 1. to swallow liquid 2. to drink alcoholic liquor, esp. to excess —*n.* 1. any liquid for drinking 2. alcoholic liquor —**drink in** to take in eagerly with the senses or mind —**drink to** to drink a toast to —**drink'a·ble** *adj.* —**drink'er** *n.*

drip (drip) *vi., vt.* **dripped** or **dript, drip'ping** [OE. *dryppan*] to fall, or let fall, in drops —*n.* 1. a falling in drops 2. [Slang] a person regarded as dull, insipid, etc.

drip'-dry' *adj.* designating or of garments that dry quickly when hung wet and need little or no ironing —*vi.* **-dried', -dry'ing** to launder as a drip-dry garment does

drip'pings *n.* the juices that drip from roasting meat

drive (drīv) *vt.* **drove, driv'en, driv'ing** [OE. *drifan*] 1. to force to go; impel 2. to force into or from a state or act 3. to force to work, usually to excess 4. to hit (a ball) hard 5. to make penetrate 6. to control the movement of (a vehicle) 7. to transport in a vehicle 8. to push (a bargain, etc.) through —*vi.* 1. to advance violently 2. to try hard 3. to drive a blow, ball, etc. 4. to be driven: said of a motor vehicle 5. to operate a motor vehicle —*n.* 1. a driving 2. a trip in a vehicle 3. *a)* a road for automobiles, etc. *b)* a driveway 4. a rounding up of animals 5. a campaign to achieve some purpose 6. energy; push 7. a strong impulse or urge 8. the propelling mechanism of a machine, etc. —**drive at** to mean

drive'-in' *n.* a restaurant, movie theater, bank, etc. designed to serve people seated in their cars

driv·el (driv''l) *vi., vt.* **-eled** or **-elled, -el·ing** or **-el·ing** [< OE. *dreflian*] 1. to let (saliva) flow from the mouth; slobber 2. to speak or say in a silly, stupid way —*n.* silly, stupid talk

driv'er *n.* 1. one who drives an automobile, horse, etc. 2. a wooden-headed golf club used in hitting the ball from the tee

drive'way' *n.* a path for cars from a street to a garage, house, etc.

driz·zle (driz''l) *vi., vt.* **-zled, -zling** [prob. < ME.] to rain or let fall in fine, misty drops —*n.* a fine, misty rain —**driz'zly** *adj.*

drogue (drōg) *n.* [prob. < Scot. *drug,* drag] a funnel-shaped device towed behind an aircraft for drag effect

droll (drōl) *adj.* [< Fr. < MDu. *drol,* stout fellow] amusing in an odd or wry way —**droll'er·y** *n., pl.* **-ies** —**drol'ly** *adv.*

drom·e·dar·y (dräm'ə der'ē) *n., pl.* **-ies** [< Gr. *dramein,* to run] the one-humped or Arabian camel

drone¹ (drōn) *n.* [< OE. *dran*] 1. a male honeybee, which does no work 2. an idle parasite or loafer

drone² (drōn) *vi.* **droned, dron'ing** [< prec.] 1. to make a continuous humming sound 2. to talk in a monotonous way —*vt.* to utter in a monotonous tone —*n.* 1. a droning sound 2. a bagpipe

drool (drōōl) *vi.* [< DRIVEL] 1. to let saliva flow from one's mouth 2. to flow from the mouth, as saliva

droop (drōōp) *vi.* [< ON. *drūpa*] 1. to sink, hang, or bend down 2. to lose vitality 3. to become dejected —*vt.* to let sink or hang down —*n.* a drooping —**droop'y** *adj.*

drop (dräp) *n.* [OE. *dropa*] 1. a small quantity of liquid that is roundish, as when falling 2. a very small quantity of anything 3. anything like a drop in shape, size, etc. 4. a sudden fall, descent, slump, etc. 5. something that drops, as a curtain or trapdoor 6. the distance between a higher and lower level —*vi.* **dropped, drop'ping** 1. to fall in drops 2. *a)* to fall suddenly down *b)* to fall exhausted, wounded, or dead 3. to pass into a specified state [to drop off to sleep] 4. to come to an end [let the matter drop] —*vt.* 1. to let fall 2. to utter (a hint, etc.) casually 3. to send (a letter) 4. to stop, end, or dismiss **5.** to lower **6.** [Colloq.] to deposit at a specified place **—drop back** to be outdistanced: also **drop behind —drop in** to pay a casual visit **—drop out** to stop participating

drop curtain a theater curtain that is lowered and raised rather than drawn

drop kick *Football* a kick in which the ball is dropped to the ground and kicked just as it rebounds **—drop'-kick'** *vt., vi.*

drop'let (-lit) *n.* a very small drop

drop'out' (-out') *n.* a person who withdraws from school, esp. high school, before graduating

drop'per *n.* a small tube with a hollow rubber bulb at one end, used to release a liquid in drops

drop·sy (dräp'sē) *n.* [< Gr. *hydōr*, water] *an earlier term for* EDEMA

dross (drôs) *n.* [OE. *dros*, dregs] **1.** a scum formed on the surface of molten metal **2.** rubbish

drought (drout, drouth) *n.* [< OE. *drugian*, dry up] prolonged dry weather: also **drouth** (drouth, drout) **—drought'y** *adj.* **-i·er, -i·est**

drove[1] (drōv) *n.* [< OE. *drifan*, drive] **1.** a number of cattle, sheep, etc. driven or moving as a group; flock; herd **2.** a moving crowd of people

drove[2] (drōv) *pt. of* DRIVE

dro·ver (drō'vər) *n.* one who herds animals, esp. to market

drown (droun) *vi.* [< ON. *drukna*] to die by suffocation in water or other liquid **—vt. 1.** to kill by such suffocation **2.** to flood **3.** to be so loud as to overcome (another sound): usually with *out*

drowse (drouz) *vi.* **drowsed, drows'ing** [< OE. *drusian*, become sluggish] to sleep lightly; doze **—n.** a drowsing; doze

drow·sy (drou'zē) *adj.* **-si·er, -si·est** being or making sleepy or half asleep **—drow'si·ly** *adv.*

drub (drub) *vt.* **drubbed, drub'bing** [< Ar. *darb*, a beating] **1.** to beat as with a stick **2.** to defeat soundly **—drub'bing** *n.*

drudge (druj) *n.* [prob. < OE. *dreogan*, suffer] a person who does hard, menial, or tedious work **—vi.** **drudged, drudg'ing** to do such work **—drudg'er·y** *n., pl.* **-ies**

drug (drug) *n.* [< OFr. *drogue*] **1.** any substance used as or in a medicine **2.** a narcotic, hallucinogen, etc. **—vt. drugged, drug'ging 1.** to put a harmful drug in (a drink, etc.) **2.** to stupefy as with a drug **—drug on the market** a thing in much greater supply than demand

drug'gist (-ist) *n.* [Fr.] **1.** a dealer in drugs, medical equipment, etc. **2.** a pharmacist **3.** a drugstore owner or manager

drug'store' *n.* a store where drugs, medical supplies, and various items are sold and prescriptions are filled

dru·id (drōō'id) *n.* [Fr. < Celt.] [*often* D-] a member of a Celtic religious order in ancient Britain, Ireland, and France

drum (drum) *n.* [< Du. *trom*] **1.** a percussion instrument consisting of a hollow cylinder or hemisphere with a membrane stretched over the end or ends **2.** the sound produced by beating a drum **3.** any drumlike cylindrical object, as a metal container for oil, etc. **4.** the eardrum **—vi. drummed, drum'ming 1.** to beat a drum **2.** to tap continually, as with the fingers **—vt.** to instill (facts, etc. *into*) by repetition **— drum out** to expel from in disgrace

drum major a person who twirls a baton at the head of a marching band **—drum ma'jor·ette'** (-et') *fem.*

drum'mer *n.* **1.** a drum player **2.** [Colloq.] a traveling salesman

drum'stick' *n.* **1.** a stick for beating a drum **2.** the lower half of the leg of a cooked fowl

drunk (druŋk) *pp. of* DRINK **—adj.** overcome by alcoholic liquor; intoxicated **—n.** [Slang] **1.** a drunken person **2.** a drinking spree

drunk·ard (druŋ'kərd) *n.* a person who often gets drunk; inebriate

drunk'en *adj.* [*used before the noun*] **1.** intoxicated **2.** caused by or occurring during intoxication **—drunk'en·ness** *n.*

drupe (drōōp) *n.* [< Gr. *dryppa*, olive] any fruit with a soft, fleshy part around an inner stone that contains the seed, as a peach **—dru·pa·ceous** (drōō pā'shəs) *adj.*

dry (drī) *adj.* **dri'er, dri'est** [OE. *dryge*] **1.** not under water [*dry* land] **2.** not wet or damp **3.** lacking rain or water; arid **4.** thirsty **5.** not yielding milk **6.** solid; not liquid **7.** not sweet [*dry* wine] **8.** prohibiting or opposed to the sale of alcoholic liquors **9.** funny in a quiet but sharp way [*dry* wit] **10.** dull or boring **—n., pl. drys** [Colloq.] a prohibitionist **—vt., vi. dried, dry'ing** to make or become dry **—dry up 1.** to make or become thoroughly dry **2.** [Slang] to stop talking **—dry'ly** *adv.* **—dry'ness** *n.*

dry·ad (drī'əd) *n.* [< Gr. *drys*, tree] [*also* D-] *Classical Myth.* a tree nymph

dry battery 1. an electric battery made up of several connected dry cells **2.** a dry cell

dry cell a voltaic cell containing an absorbent so that its contents cannot spill

dry'-clean' *vt.* to clean (garments, etc.) with some solvent other than water, as naphtha or gasoline **—dry cleaner —dry cleaning**

dry dock a dock from which the water can be emptied, used for working on ships

dry'er *n.* an apparatus for drying (something) by heating or blowing air

dry goods cloth, cloth products, etc.

dry ice carbon dioxide solidified and compressed into snowlike cakes, used as a refrigerant

dry rot a fungous decay causing seasoned timber to crumble to powder

dry run [Slang] a practice exercise; rehearsal

dry wall a wall made of wallboard, etc. without using wet plaster **—dry'wall'** *adj.*

D.S.C., DSC Distinguished Service Cross

D.S.T., DST Daylight Saving Time

D.T.'s, d.t.'s (dē'tēz') [Slang] *same as* DELIRIUM TREMENS

du·al (dōō'əl) *adj.* [< L. *duo*, two] **1.** of two **2.** double; twofold **—du'al·ism** *n.* **—du·al'i·ty** (-al'ə tē) *n.* **—du'al·ly** *adv.*

dub[1] (dub) *vt.* **dubbed, dub'bing** [< OE. *dubbian*, to strike] **1.** to confer a title or name upon **2.** to make smooth, as by hammering, scraping, etc. **3.** [Slang] to bungle

dub[2] (dub) *vt.* **dubbed, dub'bing** [< DOUBLE] to insert (dialogue, music, etc.) in the sound track of a film (often with *in*)

du·bi·e·ty (dōō bī'ə tē) *n.* **1.** a being dubious; uncertainty **2.** *pl.* **-ties** a doubtful thing

du·bi·ous (dōō'bē əs) *adj.* [< L. *dubius*, uncertain] **1.** causing doubt **2.** feeling doubt; skeptical **3.** questionable **—du'bi·ous·ly** *adv.*

du·cal (dōō'k'l) *adj.* [< LL. *ducalis*, of a leader] of a duke or dukedom **—du'cal·ly** *adv.*

duc·at (duk'ət) *n.* [see DUCHY] **1.** any of several former European coins **2.** [Slang] a ticket

duch·ess (duch'is) *n.* **1.** the wife or widow of a duke **2.** a woman who, like a duke, rules a duchy

duch'y (-ē) *n., pl.* **-ies** [< L. *dux*, leader] the territory ruled by a duke or duchess

duck[1] (duk) *n.* [< OE. *duce,* lit., diver] **1.** a swimming bird with a flat bill, short neck, and webbed feet **2.** the flesh of a duck as food — **like water off a duck's back** with no effect or reaction

duck[2] (duk) *vt., vi.* [ME. *douken*] **1.** to plunge or dip under water for a moment **2.** to lower or move (the head, body, etc.) suddenly, as to avoid a blow **3.** [Colloq.] to avoid (a task, person, etc.) —*n.* a ducking

duck[3] (duk) *n.* [Du. *doek*] a cotton or linen cloth like canvas but finer and lighter

duck'bill' *n.* same as PLATYPUS

duck'ling *n.* a young duck

duck'pins' *n.pl.* **1.** [*with sing. v.*] a game like bowling, played with smaller pins and balls **2.** these pins

duck'weed' *n.* a minute flowering plant that floats on ponds and sluggish streams

duck'y *adj.* **-i·er, -i·est** [Slang] pleasing, delightful, etc.

duct (dukt) *n.* [< L. *ducere,* to lead] a tube, pipe, or channel, as for passage of a fluid — **duct'less** *adj.*

duc·tile (duk't'l) *adj.* [see prec.] **1.** that can be drawn and hammered thin without breaking: said of metals **2.** easily led; tractable —**duc·til'i·ty** (-til'ə tē) *n.*

ductless gland an endocrine gland

dud (dud) *n.* [prob. < Du. *dood,* dead] [Colloq.] **1.** a bomb or shell that fails to explode **2.** a failure

dude (dōōd) *n.* [< ?] **1.** a dandy; fop **2.** [Western Slang] a city fellow or tourist **3.** [Slang] any man

dudg·eon (duj'ən) *n.* [prob. < Anglo-Fr. *en digeon,* at the dagger hilt] anger or resentment: now chiefly in **in high dudgeon,** very angry or resentful

duds (dudz) *n.pl.* [prob. < ON. *dutha,* wrap up] [Colloq.] **1.** clothes **2.** belongings

due (dōō) *adj.* [< L. *debere,* owe] **1.** owed or owing as a debt; payable **2.** suitable; proper **3.** enough [*due care*] **4.** expected or scheduled to arrive —*adv.* exactly; directly [*due west*] —*n.* anything due; specif., [*pl.*] fees or other charges [membership *dues*] —**due to 1.** caused by **2.** [Colloq.] because of

du·el (dōō'əl) *n.* [< ML. *duellum,* war] **1.** a prearranged fight between two persons armed with deadly weapons **2.** any contest like this — *vi., vt.* **-eled** or **-elled, -el·ing** or **-el·ling** to fight a duel (with) —**du'el·ist** or **du'el·list, du'el·er** or **du'el·ler** *n.*

du·en·na (dōō en'ə) *n.* [< Sp. < L. *domina,* mistress] a chaperon or governess

due process (of law) the course of legal proceedings established to protect individual rights

du·et (dōō et') *n.* [< L. *duo,* two] *Music* **1.** a composition for two voices or instruments **2.** the two performers of such a composition

duf·fel (or **duf·fle**) **bag** (duf''l) [< *Duffel,* town in Belgium] a large cloth bag for carrying clothing and personal belongings

duf·fer (duf'ər) *n.* [< thieves' slang *duff,* to fake] [Slang] an incompetent person

dug[1] (dug) *pt. & pp.* of DIG

dug[2] (dug) *n.* [< Dan. *dægge,* suckle] a female animal's nipple or teat

dug'out' *n.* **1.** a boat hollowed out of a log **2.** a shelter, as in warfare, dug in the ground **3.** a covered shelter near a baseball diamond for the players to sit in

duke (dōōk) *n.* [< L. *ducere,* to lead] **1.** the ruler of an independent duchy **2.** a nobleman next in rank to a prince —**duke'dom** *n.*

dul·cet (dul'sit) *adj.* [< L. *dulcis,* sweet] soothing or pleasant to hear; melodious

dul·ci·mer (dul'sə mər) *n.* [< L. *dulce,* sweet + *melos,* a song] **1.** a musical instrument with metal strings, which are struck with two small hammers **2.** a violin-shaped stringed instrument plucked with a plectrum

dull (dul) *adj.* [< OE. *dol,* stupid] **1.** mentally slow; stupid **2.** physically slow; sluggish **3.** boring; tedious **4.** not sharp; blunt **5.** not feeling or felt keenly **6.** not vivid **7.** not glossy —*vt., vi.* to make or become dull —**dull'ness** *n.* —**dul'ly** *adv.*

dull'ard (-ərd) *n.* a stupid person

du·ly (dōō'lē) *adv.* in due manner; specif., *a*) rightfully *b*) when due *c*) as required

dumb (dum) *adj.* [OE.] **1.** lacking the power of speech; mute **2.** silent **3.** [G. *dumm*] [Colloq.] stupid —**dumb'ly** *adv.*

dumb·bell (dum'bel') *n.* **1.** a device used in pairs for muscular exercise: each one has round weights joined by a short bar **2.** [Slang] a stupid person

dumb·found, dum·found (dum'found') *vt.* [DUMB + (CON)FOUND] to make speechless by shocking; amaze

dumb show 1. formerly, a part of a play done in pantomime **2.** silent gestures

dumb'wait'er *n.* a small elevator for sending food, etc. from one floor to another

dum-dum (bullet) (dum'dum') [< *Dumdum,* arsenal near Calcutta, India] a soft-nosed bullet that expands when it hits

dum·my (dum'ē) *n., pl.* **-mies 1.** a figure made in human form, as for displaying clothing **2.** an imitation or sham **3.** [Slang] a stupid person **4.** *Bridge,* etc. the declarer's partner, whose hand is exposed on the board and played by the declarer —*adj.* sham

dump (dump) *vt.* [prob. < ON.] **1.** to unload in a heap or mass **2.** to throw away (rubbish, etc.) —*n.* **1.** a place for dumping rubbish **2.** *Mil.* a temporary storage center **3.** [Slang] a place that is unpleasant, ugly, etc. —**(down) in the dumps** in low spirits

dump'ling (-liŋ) *n.* [< ?] **1.** a small piece of dough, steamed or boiled and served with meat or soup **2.** a crust of baked dough filled with fruit

dump truck a truck that is unloaded by tilting the truck bed backward

dump·y (dum'pē) *adj.* **-i·er, -i·est 1.** short and thick; squat **2.** [Slang] ugly, run-down, etc. — **dump'i·ly** *adv.* —**dump'i·ness** *n.*

dun[1] (dun) *adj., n.* [OE.] dull grayish brown

dun[2] (dun) *vt., vi.* **dunned, dun'ning** [? dial. var. of DIN] to ask (a debtor) repeatedly for payment —*n.* an insistent demand for payment of a debt

dunce (duns) *n.* [< *Dunsman,* follower of *Duns Scotus,* 13th-c. Scot. scholar] a dull, ignorant person

dun·der·head (dun'dər hed') *n.* [< Du. *donder,* thunder] a stupid person; dunce

dune (dōōn) *n.* [Fr. < ODu. *duna*] a rounded hill or ridge of sand heaped by the wind

dune buggy [orig. used on sand dunes] a small automobile made from a standard, compact chassis and a prefabricated body

dung (duŋ) *n.* [OE.] animal excrement

dun·ga·ree (duŋ'gə rē') *n.* [Hindi *dungri*] **1.** a coarse cotton cloth **2.** [*pl.*] work trousers or overalls of this cloth

dun·geon (dun'jən) *n.* [< OFr. *donjon*] a dark, underground cell or prison

dung'hill' *n.* **1.** a heap of dung **2.** anything filthy

dunk (duŋk) *vt.* [G. *tunken*] **1.** to dip (bread, cake, etc.) into coffee, etc. before eating it **2.** to immerse briefly

du·o (dōō'ō) *n., pl.* **-os** [It.] **1.** *same as* DUET (esp. sense 2) **2.** a pair; couple

du·o·de·num (dōō'ə dē'nəm) *n., pl.* **-de'na** (-nə), **-de'nums** [< L. *duodeni,* twelve each: its length is about twelve fingers' breadth] the first section of the small intestine, below the stomach **—du'o·de'nal** *adj.*

dupe (dōōp) *n.* [Fr. < L. *upupa,* stupid bird] a person easily tricked or fooled **—vt. duped, dup'ing** to deceive or cheat

du·plex (dōō'pleks) *adj.* [L.] double **—n. 1.** an apartment with rooms on two floors **2.** a house of two separate family units

du·pli·cate (dōō'plə kit; *for v.* -kāt') *adj.* [< L. *duplicare,* to double] **1.** double **2.** corresponding exactly **—n.** an exact copy; facsimile **—vt. -cat'ed, -cat'ing 1.** to make an exact copy of **2.** to cause to happen again **—du'pli·ca'tion** *n.*

duplicating machine a machine for making copies of a letter, drawing, etc.: also **du'pli·ca'tor** *n.*

du·plic·i·ty (dōō plis'ə tē) *n., pl.* **-ties** [< LL. *duplicitas*] hypocritical cunning or deception; double-dealing

du·ra·ble (door'ə b'l) *adj.* [< L. *durare,* to last] **1.** lasting in spite of hard wear or frequent use **2.** stable **—du'ra·bil'i·ty** *n.*

du·ra·tion (doo rā'shən) *n.* [see DURABLE] the time that a thing continues or lasts

du·ress (doo res') *n.* [< L. *durus,* hard] **1.** imprisonment **2.** the use of force or threats

dur·ing (door'iŋ) *prep.* [see DURABLE] **1.** throughout the entire time of **2.** in the course of

durst (durst) *archaic pt. of* DARE

du·rum (wheat) (door'əm) [L. < *durus,* hard] a hard wheat that yields flour and semolina used in macaroni, spaghetti, etc.

dusk (dusk) *n.* [< OE. *dox,* dark-colored] **1.** the dim part of twilight **2.** gloom; dusky quality **— dusk'y** *adj.* **-i·er, -i·est**

dust (dust) *n.* [OE.] **1.** powdery earth or any finely powdered matter **2.** earth **3.** disintegrated mortal remains **4.** anything worthless **— vt. 1.** to sprinkle with dust, powder, etc. **2.** to rid of dust, as by wiping **—vi.** to remove dust, as from furniture **—bite the dust** to be killed, esp. in battle

dust bowl a region where eroded topsoil is blown away by winds during droughts

dust'er *n.* **1.** a person or thing that dusts **2.** a short, loose, lightweight housecoat

dust jacket a detachable paper cover for protecting the binding of a book

dust'pan' *n.* a shovellike receptacle into which dust or debris is swept from a floor

dust'y *adj.* **-i·er, -i·est 1.** covered with or full of dust **2.** like dust; powdery **3.** dust-colored **— dust'i·ly** *adv.* **—dust'i·ness** *n.*

Dutch (duch) *adj.* **1.** of the Netherlands, its people, language, etc. **2.** [Slang] German **—n.** the language of the Netherlands **—go Dutch** [Colloq.] to have each pay his own expenses **— in Dutch** [Colloq.] in trouble or disfavor **—the Dutch** the Dutch people

Dutch door a door with upper and lower halves that can be opened separately

Dutch oven a heavy metal pot with an arched lid, for cooking pot roasts, etc.

Dutch treat [Colloq.] any entertainment, etc. at which each pays his own expenses

Dutch uncle [Colloq.] one who bluntly and sternly lectures or scolds someone else

du·te·ous (dōōt'ē əs) *adj.* dutiful

du·ti·a·ble (dōōt'ē ə b'l) *adj.* necessitating payment of a duty or tax

du'ti·ful (-ə fəl) *adj.* **1.** showing, or resulting from, a sense of duty **2.** obedient

du·ty (dōōt'ē) *n., pl.* **-ties** [see DUE & -TY] **1.** obedience or respect to parents, elders, etc. **2.** conduct based on moral or legal obligation **3.** any action required by one's position **4.** a sense of obligation **5.** service, esp. military service **6.** a tax imposed on imports, etc. **—on** (or **off**) **duty** at (or having time off from) one's work or duty

dwarf (dwôrf) *n., pl.* **dwarfs, dwarves** (dwôrvz) [OE. *dweorg*] any abnormally small person, animal, or plant **—vt. 1.** to stunt the growth of **2.** to make seem small by comparison **—vi.** to become stunted or dwarfed **—adj.** undersized; stunted **—dwarf'ish** *adj.*

dwell (dwel) *vi.* **dwelt** or **dwelled, dwell'ing** [OE. *dwellan,* lead astray, hinder] to make one's home; reside **—dwell on** (or **upon**) to linger over in thought or speech **—dwell'er** *n.*

dwell'ing (place) a residence; abode

DWI, D.W.I. driving while intoxicated

dwin·dle (dwin'd'l) *vi., vt.* **-dled, -dling** [< OE. *dwinan,* wither] to become or make smaller or less; diminish; shrink

dyb·buk (dib'ək) *n.* [Heb. *dibbūq*] *Jewish Folklore* a spirit of one deceased that enters the body of a living person

dye (dī) *n.* [OE. *deag*] a substance or solution for coloring fabric, hair, etc.; also, the color produced **—vt., vi. dyed, dye'ing** to color as with dye **—dy'er** *n.*

dyed'-in-the-wool' *adj.* thoroughgoing; unchanging

dye'stuff' *n.* any substance constituting or yielding a dye

dy·ing (dī'iŋ) *prp. of* DIE[1] **—adj. 1.** about to die or end **2.** at death

dy·nam·ic (dī nam'ik) *adj.* [< Gr. *dynasthai,* be able] **1.** relating to energy or physical force in motion **2.** energetic; vigorous; forceful **—dy·nam'i·cal·ly** *adv.*

dy·nam'ics *n.pl.* [*with sing. v. for* 1] **1.** the branch of mechanics dealing with the motions of material bodies under the action of forces **2.** the various forces operating in any field

dy·na·mism (dī'nə miz'm) *n.* dynamic quality

dy·na·mite (dī'nə mīt') *n.* [see DYNAMIC] a powerful explosive made with nitroglycerin **— vt. -mit'ed, -mit'ing** to blow up with dynamite

dy·na·mo (dī'nə mō') *n., pl.* **-mos'** [see DYNAMIC] **1.** *earlier term for* GENERATOR **2.** a dynamic person

dy·nas·ty (dī'nəs tē) *n., pl.* **-ties** [< Gr. *dynasthai,* be strong] a succession of rulers, all of the same family **—dy·nas'tic** (-nas'tik) *adj.*

dys- [Gr.] *a prefix meaning* bad, ill, difficult, etc.

dys·en·ter·y (dis'n ter'ē) *n.* [< Gr. *dys-,* bad + *entera,* bowels] a painful intestinal inflammation characterized by diarrhea with bloody, mucous feces **—dys·en·ter'ic** *adj.*

dys·pep·si·a (dis pep'shə, -sē ə) *n.* [< Gr. *dys-,* bad + *peptein,* to digest] indigestion **—dys·pep'tic** *adj., n.*

dz. dozen; dozens

E

E, e (ē) *n., pl.* **E's, e's** the fifth letter of the English alphabet

E (ē) *n.* **1.** *Music* the third tone in the scale of C major **2.** *the symbol for* energy

e- *a prefix meaning* out, from, etc.: see EX-

E, E., e, e. 1. east **2.** eastern

each (ēch) *adj., pron.* [< OE. *ælc*] every one of two or more considered separately —*adv.* apiece [ten cents *each*] Abbrev. **ea.**

ea·ger (ē'gər) *adj.* [< L. *acer*, keen] keenly desiring; impatient or anxious —**ea'ger·ly** *adv.* —**ea'ger·ness** *n.*

ea·gle (ē'g'l) *n.* [< L. *aquila*] **1.** a large, strong bird of prey having sharp vision and powerful wings **2.** a representation of the eagle, esp. as the emblem of the U.S. **3.** a former U.S. $10 gold coin **4.** *Golf* a score of two below par on any hole

ea'gle-eyed' *adj.* having keen vision

ea·glet (ē'glit) *n.* a young eagle

ear¹ (ir) *n.* [OE. *eare*] **1.** the part of the body that perceives sound **2.** the external part of the ear **3.** one's sense of hearing or hearing ability **4.** anything like an ear —**be all ears** to listen attentively —**give** (or **lend**) **ear** to listen; heed —**play by ear** to play (music) without using notation —**play it by ear** [Colloq.] to improvise

ear² (ir) *n.* [< OE. *ær*] the grain-bearing spike of a cereal plant —*vi.* to sprout ears

ear'ache' *n.* an ache in an ear

ear'drum' *n. same as* TYMPANIC MEMBRANE

earl (url) *n.* [OE. *eorl*, warrior] a British nobleman ranking just above a viscount

ear·ly (ur'lē) *adv., adj.* **-li·er, -li·est** [< OE. *ær*, before + *-lice*, *-ly*] **1.** near the beginning **2.** before the expected or usual time **3.** in the distant past **4.** in the near future —**ear'li·ness** *n.*

ear'mark' *n.* **1.** a brand put on the ear of an animal **2.** an identifying mark or feature —*vt.* **1.** to set a distinctive mark upon **2.** to reserve for a special purpose

ear'muffs' (-mufs') *n.pl.* cloth or fur coverings for the ears in cold weather

earn (urn) *vt.* [OE. *earnian*] **1.** to receive (wages, etc.) for one's work **2.** to get as deserved **3.** to gain (interest, etc.) as profit

ear·nest¹ (ur'nist) *adj.* [OE. *eornoste*] **1.** serious and intense; not joking **2.** important —**in earnest 1.** serious **2.** with determination —**ear'nest·ly** *adv.* —**ear'nest·ness** *n.*

ear·nest² (ur'nist) *n.* [ult. < Heb. *'ērābōn*] money, etc. given as a pledge in binding a bargain

earn'ings *n.pl.* **1.** wages or other recompense **2.** profits, interest, dividends, etc.

ear'phone' *n.* a receiver for radio, etc. held to, or put into, the ear

ear'ring' *n.* a ring or other small ornament for the lobe of the ear

ear'shot' (-shät') *n.* the distance within which a sound can be heard

earth (urth) *n.* [OE. *eorthe*] **1.** [*occas.* E-] the planet we live on, the fifth largest of the solar system: see PLANET **2.** this world, as distinguished from heaven and hell **3.** land, as distinguished from sea or sky **4.** ground; soil —**down to earth** practical

earth'bound' (-bound') *adj.* confined to or by the earth or earthly things

earth'en *adj.* made of earth or clay

earth'en·ware' *n.* the coarser sort of containers, tableware, etc. made of baked clay

earth'ly *adj.* **1.** terrestrial **2.** worldly **3.** temporal **4.** conceivable —**earth'li·ness** *n.*

earth'nut' *n.* a root, tuber, or underground pod, as of the peanut

earth'quake' (-kwāk') *n.* a shaking of the crust of the earth, caused by underground shifting of rock

earth'ward (-wərd) *adv., adj.* toward the earth: also **earth'wards** *adv.*

earth'work' *n.* a defensive embankment made by piling up earth

earth'worm' *n.* a round, segmented worm that burrows in the soil

earth'y (ur'thē) *adj.* **-i·er, -i·est 1.** of or like earth or soil **2.** coarse; unrefined **3.** simple and natural —**earth'i·ness** *n.*

ease (ēz) *n.* [< L. *adjacens*, lying nearby] **1.** freedom from pain or trouble; comfort **2.** natural manner; poise **3.** freedom from difficulty; facility **4.** affluence —*vt.* **eased, eas'ing 1.** to free from pain or trouble; comfort **2.** to lessen (pain, anxiety, etc.) **3.** to facilitate **4.** to reduce the strain of **5.** to move by careful shifting, etc. —*vi.* to lessen in tension, pain, etc.

ea·sel (ē'z'l) *n.* [ult. < L. *asinus*, ass] an upright frame to hold an artist's canvas, etc.

ease·ment (ēz'mənt) *n.* **1.** an easing or being eased **2.** *Law* a right that one may have in another's land

eas·i·ly (ē'z'l ē) *adv.* **1.** in an easy manner **2.** without a doubt **3.** very likely

east (ēst) *n.* [OE. *east*] **1.** the direction in which sunrise occurs (90° on the compass, opposite west) **2.** a region in or toward this direction —*adj.* **1.** in, of, or toward the east **2.** from the east —*adv.* in or toward the east

East·er (ēs'tər) *n.* [< OE. *Eastre*, dawn goddess] an annual Christian festival in the spring celebrating the resurrection of Jesus

east'er·ly *adj., adv.* **1.** toward the east **2.** from the east

east'ern *adj.* **1.** in, of, or toward the east **2.** from the east **3.** [E-] of the East

east'ern·er *n.* a native or inhabitant of the east

east'ward (-wərd) *adv., adj.* toward the east: also **east'wards** *adv.*

eas·y (ē'zē) *adj.* **-i·er, -i·est** [see EASE] **1.** not difficult **2.** free from anxiety, pain, etc. **3.** comfortable; restful **4.** not stiff or awkward **5.** not strict; lenient **6.** compliant **7.** unhurried **8.** gradual —*adv.* [Colloq.] easily —**take it easy** [Colloq.] **1.** to refrain from anger, haste, etc. **2.** to relax; rest —**eas'i·ness** *n.*

easy chair a stuffed or padded armchair

eas'y·go'ing *adj.* dealing with things in a relaxed or lenient way

eat (ēt) *vt.* **ate, eat'en, eat'ing** [OE. *etan*] **1.** to chew and swallow (food) **2.** to consume or ravage (with *away* or *up*) **3.** to destroy, as acid does; corrode **4.** to make by eating [acid *eats* holes in cloth] **5.** [Slang] to bother —*vi.* to eat food

eat'a·ble *adj.* fit to be eaten —*n.* a thing fit to be eaten: *usually in pl.*

eat'er·y *n., pl.* **-ies** [Colloq.] a restaurant

eats (ēts) *n.pl.* [Colloq.] food; meals
eau de Co·logne (ō' də kə lōn') [Fr., lit., water of Cologne] a perfumed toilet water made of alcohol and aromatic oils
eaves (ēvz) *n.pl.* [< OE. *efes*] the projecting lower edge or edges of a roof
eaves'drop' (-dräp') *vi.* **-dropped', -drop'ping** [prob. < *eavesdropper*, one standing under eaves to overhear] to listen secretly to a conversation —**eaves'drop'per** *n.*
ebb (eb) *n.* [OE. *ebba*] **1.** the flow of the tide back toward the sea **2.** a lessening; decline —*vi.* **1.** to recede, as the tide **2.** to lessen; decline
eb·on·ite (eb'ən īt') *n.* same as VULCANITE
eb·on·y (eb'ən ē) *n., pl.* **-ies** [< Gr. *ebenos*] the hard, heavy, dark wood of certain tropical trees —*adj.* **1.** of ebony **2.** black
e·bul·lient (i bool'yənt) *adj.* [< L. *e-*, out + *bullire*, to boil] **1.** boiling; bubbling **2.** enthusiastic; exuberant —**e·bul'lience** *n.*
e·bul·li·tion (eb'ə lish'ən) *n.* **1.** a boiling or bubbling up **2.** a sudden outburst
ec·cen·tric (ik sen'trik) *adj.* [< Gr. *ek-*, out of + *kentron*, center] **1.** not having the same center, as two circles **2.** having its axis off center **3.** not exactly circular **4.** odd, as in conduct; unconventional —*n.* **1.** a disk set off center on a shaft, for converting circular motion into back-and-forth motion **2.** an eccentric person —**ec·cen'tri·cal·ly** *adv.* —**ec·cen·tric·i·ty** (ek'sen tris'ə tē, -sən-) *n., pl.* **-ties**
Ec·cle·si·as·tes (i klē'zē as'tēz) [< Gr. *ek-*, out + *kalein*, to call] a book of the Bible
ec·cle·si·as·tic (i klē'zē as'tik) *adj.* [see prec.] same as ECCLESIASTICAL —*n.* a clergyman
ec·cle'si·as'ti·cal *adj.* of the church or the clergy
ech·e·lon (esh'ə län') *n.* [< Fr. < L. *scala*, ladder] **1.** a steplike formation of ships, troops, aircraft, etc. **2.** a subdivision of a military force **3.** any of the levels of responsibility in an organization
ech·o (ek'ō) *n., pl.* **-oes** [< Gr. *ēchō*] **1.** the repetition of a sound by reflection of the sound waves from a surface **2.** a sound so produced —*vi.* **-oed, -o·ing 1.** to reverberate **2.** to make an echo —*vt.* to repeat (another's words, etc.)
e·cho·ic (e kō'ik) *adj.* imitative in sound, as the word *buzz* —**ech'o·ism** *n.*
é·clair (ā kler', ē-) *n.* [Fr., lit., lightning] a frosted pastry filled with custard, etc.
é·clat (ā klä') *n.* [Fr. < *éclater*, to burst (out)] **1.** brilliant success **2.** striking effect **3.** acclaim; fame
ec·lec·tic (i klek'tik, e-) *adj.* [< Gr. *ek-*, out + *legein*, to pick] selecting or selected from various sources —*n.* one who uses eclectic methods —**ec·lec'ti·cal·ly** *adv.*
e·clipse (i klips') *n.* [< Gr. *ek-*, out + *leipein*, to leave] **1.** the obscuring of the sun when the moon comes between it and the earth (**solar eclipse**), or of the moon when the earth's shadow is cast upon it (**lunar eclipse**) **2.** any obscuring of light, or of fame, glory, etc. —*vt.* **e·clipsed', e·clips'ing 1.** to cause an eclipse of **2.** to surpass
e·clip·tic (i klip'tik) *n.* the sun's apparent annual path, or orbit
ec·logue (ek'lôg) *n.* [see ECLECTIC] a short pastoral poem
e·co·cide (ē'kō sīd', ek'ō-) *n.* [< Gr. *oikos*, house + -CIDE] the destruction of the environment, as by defoliants, pollutants, etc.
e·col·o·gy (ē·käl'ə jē) *n.* [< Gr. *oikos*, house + *-logia*, -LOGY] the interrelationship of organisms and their environment, or the study of this —**e·col'o·gist** *n.*
econ. 1. economic(s) **2.** economy
e·co·nom·ic (ē'kə näm'ik, ek'ə-) *adj.* **1.** of the management of income, expenditures, etc. of a business, community, etc. **2.** of economics **3.** of the satisfaction of the material needs of people
e·co·nom'i·cal *adj.* **1.** not wasting money, time, etc.; thrifty **2.** of economics
e·co·nom'ics *n.pl.* [with sing. v.] **1.** the science that deals with the production, distribution, and consumption of wealth **2.** economic factors
e·con·o·mist (i kän'ə mist) *n.* a specialist in economics
e·con·o·mize' (-mīz') *vi.* **-mized', -miz'ing** to reduce waste or expenses —*vt.* to manage or use with thrift
e·con·o·my (-mē) *n., pl.* **-mies** [< Gr. *oikos*, house + *nomos*, managing] **1.** the management of the income, expenditures, etc. of a household, government, etc. **2.** careful management of wealth, etc.; thrift **3.** an instance of thrift **4.** an economic system of a specified kind, place, etc.
e·co·sys·tem (ē'kō sis'təm, ek'ō-) *n.* [< Gr. *oikos*, house + SYSTEM] a community of animals and plants and the environment with which it is interrelated
ec·ru (ek'rōō) *adj., n.* [< Fr. < L. *ex-*, intens. + *crudus*, raw] light tan; beige
ec·sta·sy (ek'stə sē) *n., pl.* **-sies** [< Gr. *ek-*, out + *histanai*, to place] overpowering joy; rapture —**ec·stat·ic** (ik stat'ik) *adj.*
-ectomy [< Gr. *ek-*, out + *temnein*, to cut] a combining form meaning a surgical excision of [appendectomy]
ec·u·men·i·cal (ek'yōō men'i k'l) *adj.* [< Gr. *oikoumenē* (gē), the inhabited (world)] **1.** general or universal; esp., of the Christian church as a whole **2.** furthering religious unity, esp. among Christian churches
ec'u·men·ism (-mə niz'm, e kyōō'-) *n.* the ecumenical movement, esp. among churches
ec·ze·ma (ek'sə mə, eg'zə-; ig zē'mə) *n.* [< Gr. *ek-*, out + *zein*, to boil] a skin disease characterized by inflammation, itching, and scaliness
-ed [OE.] a suffix used: **1.** to form the past tense and past participle of many verbs **2.** to form adjectives from nouns or verbs [cultured]
ed., *pl.* **eds. 1.** edition **2.** editor
ed·dy (ed'ē) *n., pl.* **-dies** [prob. < ON. *itha*] a little whirlpool or whirlwind —*vi.* **-died, -dy·ing** to move as in an eddy; whirl
e·del·weiss (ā'd'l vīs') *n.* [G. < *edel*, noble + *weiss*, white] a small, flowering plant, esp. of the Alps, with white, woolly leaves
e·de·ma (i dē'mə) *n.* [< Gr. *oidēma*, swelling] an abnormal accumulation of fluid in body tissues
E·den (ē'd'n) Bible the garden where Adam and Eve first lived; Paradise —*n.* any delightful place
edge (ej) *n.* [OE. *ecg*] **1.** the sharp, cutting part of a blade **2.** sharpness; keenness **3.** the brink or verge, as of a cliff **4.** a border; margin **5.** [Colloq.] advantage [you have the *edge* on me] —*vt., vi.* **edged, edg'ing 1.** to form an edge (on) **2.** to make (one's way) sideways **3.** to move gradually —**on edge** irritable or impatient —**take the edge off** to dull the force or pleasure of —**edg'er** *n.*
edge'ways' (-wāz') *adv.* with the edge foremost: also **edge'wise** (-wīz')
edg'ing *n.* trimming along an edge
edg·y (ej'ē) *adj.* **-i·er, -i·est** on edge; irritable —**edg'i·ness** *n.*

ed·i·ble (ed′ə b′l) *adj.* [< L. *edere,* eat] fit to be eaten —*n.* [*usually pl.*] food

e·dict (ē′dikt) *n.* [< L. *e-,* out + *dicere,* speak] a public order; decree

ed·i·fice (ed′ə fis) *n.* [see EDIFY] a building, esp. a large, imposing one

ed·i·fy (ed′ə fī′) *vt.* -fled′, -fy′ing [< L. *aedificare,* build] to instruct; esp., to instruct or improve morally —ed′i·fi·ca′tion *n.* —ed′i·fi′er *n.*

ed·it (ed′it) *vt.* [< EDITOR] 1. to prepare (a manuscript, etc.) for publication by arranging, revising, etc. 2. to control the policy and contents of (a newspaper, etc.) 3. to prepare (a film, tape, etc.) for presentation by cutting, dubbing, etc.

edit. 1. edited 2. edition 3. editor

e·di·tion (i dish′ən) *n.* [see EDITOR] 1. the size or form in which a book is published 2. the total number of copies of a book, etc. published at one time 3. one such copy

ed·i·tor (ed′i tər) *n.* [L. < *e-,* out + *dare,* give] 1. one who edits 2. the head of a department of a newspaper, etc.

ed·i·to·ri·al (ed′ə tôr′ē əl) *adj.* of or by an editor —*n.* a statement of opinion in a newspaper, etc. by an editor or publisher

ed′i·to′ri·al·ize′ (-īz′) *vi.* -ized′, -iz′ing to express editorial opinions

editor in chief *pl.* **editors in chief** the editor who heads the editorial staff of a publication

ed·u·cate (ej′ə kāt′) *vt.* -cat′ed, -cat′ing [< L. *e-,* out + *ducere,* to lead] 1. to train, teach, instruct, or develop, esp. by formal schooling 2. to pay for the schooling of —ed′u·ca′tor *n.*

ed′u·ca′tion *n.* 1. the process of educating; teaching 2. knowledge, etc. thus developed 3. formal schooling —ed′u·ca′tion·al *adj.*

e·duce (i do͞os′, ē-) *vt.* e·duced′, e·duc′ing [see EDUCATE] 1. to elicit 2. to deduce

-ee [< Anglo-Fr. pp. ending] *a suffix designating:* 1. the recipient of an action [*appointee*] 2. one in a specified condition [*absentee*]

eel (ēl) *n.* [OE. æl] a long, slippery, snakelike fish —eel′like′, eel′y *adj.*

e′er (er, ar) *adv.* [Poet.] ever

-eer [< L. *-arius*] *a suffix denoting* a person involved with or an action involving [*auctioneer, electioneer*]

ee·rie, ee·ry (ir′ē) *adj.* -ri·er, -ri·est [< OE. *earg,* timid] mysterious or weird

ef- *same as* EX-: used before *f* [*efferent*]

ef·face (i fās′, e-) *vt.* -faced′, -fac′ing [< L. *ex,* out + *facies,* face] 1. to blot out; erase 2. to make (oneself) inconspicuous

ef·fect (ə fekt′, i-) *n.* [< L. *ex-,* out + *facere,* do] 1. anything brought about by a cause; result 2. the power to cause results 3. influence 4. meaning [*he* spoke to this *effect*] 5. an impression made on the mind 6. a being operative or in force 7. [*pl.*] belongings; property —*vt.* to bring about; accomplish —in effect 1. actually 2. virtually 3. in operation —take effect to become operative

ef·fec′tive *adj.* 1. efficient 2. operative 3. impressive —ef·fec′tive·ly *adv.*

ef·fec·tu·al (ə fek′choo wəl, i-) *adj.* 1. producing, or able to produce, the desired effect 2. having legal force; valid

ef·fec′tu·ate′ (-wāt′) *vt.* -at′ed, -at′ing to bring about; effect

ef·fem·i·nate (i fem′ə nit) *adj.* [< L. *ex-,* out + *femina,* woman] showing qualities attributed to women, as weakness, delicacy, etc.; unmanly —ef·fem′i·na·cy (-nə sē) *n.*

ef·fer·ent (ef′ər ənt) *adj.* [< L. *ex-,* out +

ferre, to bear] designating nerves carrying impulses away from a nerve center

ef·fer·vesce (ef′ər ves′) *vi.* -vesced′, -vesc′ing [< L. *ex-,* out + *fervere,* to boil] 1. to give off gas bubbles, as soda water; bubble 2. to be lively —ef′fer·ves′cence *n.* —ef′fer·ves′cent *adj.*

ef·fete (e fēt′, i-) *adj.* [< L. *ex-,* out + *fetus,* productive] 1. no longer able to produce; sterile 2. decadent —ef·fete′ly *adv.*

ef·fi·ca·cious (ef′ə kā′shəs) *adj.* [see EFFECT & -OUS] that produces the desired effect —ef′fi·ca·cy (-kə sē) *n.*

ef·fi·cient (ə fish′ənt, i-) *adj.* [see EFFECT] producing the desired result with a minimum of effort, expense, or waste —ef·fi′cien·cy *n., pl.* -cies —ef·fi′cient·ly *adv.*

ef·fi·gy (ef′ə jē) *n., pl.* -gies [< L. *ex-,* out + *fingere,* to form] a statue or other image; esp., a crude representation (for hanging or burning) of one who is hated

ef·flu·ence (ef′loo wəns) *n.* [< L. *ex-,* out + *fluere,* to flow] 1. a flowing out 2. a thing that flows out —ef′flu·ent *adj., n.*

ef·flu·vi·um (e floo′vē əm, i-) *n., pl.* -vi·a (-ə), -vi·ums [see prec.] 1. an aura 2. a disagreeable or noxious vapor or odor

ef·fort (ef′ərt) *n.* [< L. *ex-,* intens. + *fortis,* strong] 1. the use of energy to do something 2. a try; attempt 3. a result of working or trying —ef′fort·less *adj.*

ef·fron·ter·y (e frun′tər ē, i-) *n., pl.* -ies [< L. *ex-,* from + *frons,* forehead] unashamed boldness; impudence; audacity

ef·ful·gence (e ful′jəns, i-) *n.* [< L. *ex-,* forth + *fulgere,* to shine] great brightness; radiance —ef·ful′gent *adj.*

ef·fuse (e fyo͞oz′, i-) *vt., vi.* -fused′, -fus′ing [< L. *ex-,* out + *fundere,* to pour] 1. to pour out or forth 2. to spread; diffuse

ef·fu′sion (-fyo͞o′zhən) *n.* 1. a pouring forth 2. unrestrained expression in speaking or writing —ef·fu′sive *adj.*

e.g. [L. *exempli gratia*] for example

e·gad (i gad′, ē-) *interj.* [prob. < *oh God*] a softened oath

e·gal·i·tar·i·an (i gal′ə ter′ē ən) *adj.* [< Fr. *égalité,* equality] advocating full political and social equality for all people

egg [1] (eg) *n.* [ON.] 1. the oval body laid by a female bird, fish, etc., containing the germ of a new individual 2. a female reproductive cell; ovum 3. a hen's egg, raw or cooked 4. something like an egg

egg [2] (eg) *vt.* [< ON. *eggja,* to give edge to] to urge or incite (with *on*)

egg′beat′er *n.* a kitchen utensil for beating eggs, cream, etc.

egg foo yong (or **young**) (eg′ fo͞o yuŋ′) a Chinese-American dish of eggs beaten and cooked with bean sprouts, onions, minced pork, etc.

egg′head′ *n.* [Slang] an intellectual

egg′nog′ (-näg′) *n.* [EGG[1] + *nog,* strong ale] a drink made of eggs, milk, sugar, and, often, whiskey

egg′plant′ *n.* a plant with a large, purple-skinned fruit, eaten as a vegetable

e·gis (ē′jis) *n. same as* AEGIS

eg·lan·tine (eg′lən tīn′, -tēn′) *n.* [< L. *aculeus,* a sting] a pink, European rose with sweet-scented leaves

e·go (ē′gō) *n., pl.* -gos [L., I] 1. the individual as aware of himself; the self 2. conceit 3. *Psychoanalysis* the part of the psyche which governs action rationally

e′go·cen′tric (-sen′trik) *adj.* viewing everything in relation to oneself —*n*. an egocentric person

e'go·ism *n*. **1.** selfishness; self-interest **2.** conceit —**e'go·ist** *n*. —**e'go·is'tic** *adj*.

e·go·tism (ē'gə tiz'm) *n*. **1.** excessive reference to oneself in speaking or writing **2.** conceit — **e'go·tist** *n*. —**e'go·tis'tic** *adj*.

ego trip an act, experience, etc. used for self-fulfillment or for increasing one's vanity

e·gre·gious (i grē'jəs) *adj*. [< L. *e-*, out + *grex*, a herd] remarkably bad; flagrant

e·gress (ē'gres) *n*. [< L. *e-*, out + *gradi*, go] a way out; exit

e·gret (ē'grit, eg'rit) *n*. [OFr. *aigrette*] **1.** a heronlike bird with long, white plumes **2.** such a plume

E·gyp·tian (i jip'shən, ē-) *adj*. of Egypt, its people, etc. —*n*. **1.** a native of Egypt **2.** the language of the ancient Egyptians

eh (ā, e) *interj*. a sound expressing: **1.** surprise **2.** doubt or inquiry

ei·der (ī'dər) *n*. [ult. < ON. *æthr*] **1.** a large sea duck of northern regions: often **eider duck 2.** *same as* EIDERDOWN

ei'der·down' *n*. the soft, fine down of the eider duck, used as a stuffing for quilts, pillows, etc.

eight (āt) *adj., n*. [OE. *eahta*] one more than seven; 8; VIII —**eighth** (ātth, āth) *adj., n*.

eight·een (ā'tēn') *adj., n*. eight more than ten; 18; XVIII —**eight'eenth'** *adj., n*.

eight·y (āt'ē) *adj., n., pl*. -**ies** eight times ten; 80; LXXX —**the eighties** the numbers or years, as of a century, from 80 through 89 —**eight'i·eth** (-ith) *adj., n*.

ei·ther (ē'thər, ī'-) *adj*. [OE. *æghwæther*] **1.** one or the other (of two) **2.** each (of two) —*pron*. one or the other —*conj*. a correlative used with *or* to denote a choice of alternatives [*either* go *or* stay] —*adv*. any more than the other; also [if you don't go, he won't *either*]

e·jac·u·late (i jak'yə lāt') *vt., vi*. -**lat'ed, -lat'-ing** [see EJECT] **1.** to eject (esp. semen) **2.** to utter suddenly; exclaim —**e·jac'u·la'tion** *n*.

e·ject (i jekt') *vt*. [< L. *e-*, out + *jacere*, to throw] to throw or drive out; expel; discharge —**e·jec'tion** *n*. —**e·jec'tor** *n*.

eke (ēk) *vt*. **eked, ek'ing** [OE. *eacan*, to increase] to make (a living) with difficulty (with *out*)

e·lab·o·rate (i lab'ər it) *adj*. [< L. *e-*, out + *labor*, work] developed in great detail; complicated —*vt*. (-ə rāt') -**rat'ed, -rat'ing** to work out in detail —*vi*. to add more details (usually with *on* or *upon*) —**e·lab'o·rate·ly** *adv*. —**e·lab'o·ra'tion** *n*.

é·lan (ā län') *n*. [Fr. < *élancer*, to dart] spirited self-assurance; dash

e·lapse (i laps') *vi*. **e·lapsed', e·laps'ing** [< L. *e-*, out + *labi*, to glide] to slip by; pass: said of time

e·las·tic (i las'tik) *adj*. [< Gr. *elaunein*, set in motion] **1.** able to return immediately to its original size, shape, etc. after being stretched, squeezed, etc.; flexible **2.** able to recover easily, as from dejection; buoyant **3.** adaptable —*n*. an elastic band or fabric —**e·las'tic'i·ty** (-tis'ə tē) *n*.

e·las'ti·cize' (-tə sīz') *vt*. -**cized', -ciz'ing** to make (fabric) elastic

e·late (i lāt', ē-) *vt*. -**lat'ed, -lat'ing** [< L. *ex-*, out + *ferre*, to bear] to raise the spirits of; make happy, etc. —**e·la'tion** *n*.

el·bow (el'bō) *n*. [see ELL² & BOW²] **1.** the joint between the upper and lower arm; esp., the outer angle made by a bent arm **2.** anything

bent like an elbow —*vt., vi*. to shove as with the elbows

elbow grease [Colloq.] hard work

el'bow·room' *n*. sufficient space or room

eld·er¹ (el'dər) *adj*. [< OE. *ald, old*] **1.** older **2.** of superior rank, position, etc. **3.** earlier; former —*n*. **1.** an older person **2.** an ancestor **3.** any of certain church officers

el·der² (el'dər) *n*. [OE. *ellern*] a shrub or tree with red or purple berries

el'der·ber'ry *n., pl*. -**ries 1.** *same as* ELDER² **2.** its berry, used for making wines

eld'er·ly *adj*. somewhat old

eld·est (el'dist) *adj*. oldest

El Do·ra·do, El·do·ra·do (el'də rä'dō) *pl*. -**dos** [Sp., the gilded] any place supposed to be rich in gold, opportunity, etc.

e·lect (i lekt') *adj*. [< L. *e-*, out + *legere*, choose] **1.** chosen **2.** elected but not yet installed in office [mayor-*elect*] **3.** *Theol*. chosen by God for salvation and eternal life —*vt., vi*. **1.** to select for an office by voting **2.** to choose

e·lec·tion (i lek'shən) *n*. **1.** a choosing or choice **2.** a choosing by vote

e·lec'tion·eer' (-shə nir') *vi*. to canvass votes, as for a candidate, in an election

e·lec'tive *adj*. **1.** filled by election [an *elective* office] **2.** chosen by election **3.** having the power to choose **4.** optional —*n*. an optional course in a school curriculum

e·lec'tor (-tər) *n*. **1.** one who elects; specif., a qualified voter **2.** a member of the electoral college —**e·lec'tor·al** *adj*.

electoral college an assembly elected by the voters to perform the formal duty of electing the president and vice president of the U.S.

e·lec'tor·ate (-it) *n*. all those qualified to vote in an election

E·lec·tra (i lek'trə) *Gr. Myth*. a daughter of Agamemnon: she incited her brother to kill their mother

e·lec·tric (i lek'trik) *adj*. [< Gr. *ēlektron*, amber: from the effect of friction on amber] **1.** of or charged with electricity **2.** producing, or produced by, electricity **3.** operated by electricity **4.** electrifying; exciting Also **e·lec'tri·cal** —**e·lec'tri·cal·ly** *adv*.

electric chair a chair used in electrocuting those sentenced to death

e·lec·tri·cian (i lek'trish'ən) *n*. a person whose work is the installation or repair of electric apparatus

e·lec'tric'i·ty (-tris'ə tē) *n*. **1.** a property of certain fundamental particles of all matter, as electrons (negative charges) and protons or positrons (positive charges): electric charge is generated by friction, induction, or chemical change **2.** an electric current **3.** electric current as a public utility for lighting, heating, etc.

e·lec·tri·fy (i lek'trə fī') *vt*. -**fied', -fy'ing 1.** to charge with electricity **2.** to excite; thrill; shock **3.** to equip for the use of electricity — **e·lec'tri·fi·ca'tion** *n*.

electro- *a combining form meaning* electric, electricity

e·lec·tro·car·di·o·gram (i lek'trō kär'dē ə gram') *n*. [ELECTRO- + CARDIO- + -GRAM] a tracing showing the changes in electric potential produced by heart contractions

e·lec'tro·car'di·o·graph' (-graf') *n*. an instrument for making electrocardiograms

e·lec'tro·cute' (i lek'trə kyōōt') *vt*. -**cut'ed, -cut'ing** [ELECTRO- + (EXE)CUTE] to kill or execute with electricity —**e·lec'tro·cu'tion** *n*.

e·lec·trode (i lek'trōd) *n*. [ELECTR(O)- + -ODE] any terminal that conducts electricity into or away from a battery, electron tube, etc.

e·lec·tro·dy·nam·ics (i lek'trō dī nam'iks) *n.pl.* [*with sing. v.*] the branch of physics dealing with the phenomena of electric currents and associated magnetic forces —**e·lec'tro·dy·nam'ic** *adj.*

e·lec'tro·en·ceph'a·lo·gram' (-en sef'ə lə gram') *n.* [< ELECTRO- + Gr. *enkephalos*, brain + -GRAM] a record of the changes in electric potential within the brain

e·lec'tro·en·ceph'a·lo·graph' (-graf') *n.* an instrument for making electroencephalograms

e·lec·trol·y·sis (i lek'träl'ə sis) *n.* [ELECTRO- + -LYSIS] 1. the decomposition of an electrolyte by an electric current passing through it 2. the removal of unwanted hair with an electrified needle

e·lec·tro·lyte (i lek'trə līt') *n.* [ELECTRO- + -LYTE] any substance which in solution can conduct an electric current by the movement of its dissociated ions —**e·lec'tro·lyt'ic** (-lit'ik) *adj.*

e·lec·tro·mag·net (i lek'trō mag'nit) *n.* a soft iron core that becomes a magnet when an electric current flows through a coil surrounding it

e·lec'tro·mag'net·ism (-nə tiz'm) *n.* 1. magnetism produced by an electric current 2. the branch of physics dealing with the relations between electricity and magnetism —**e·lec'tro·mag·net'ic** *adj.*

e·lec·tro·mo·tive (i lek'trə mōt'iv) *adj.* producing an electric current through differences in potential

e·lec·tron (i lek'trän) *n.* [see ELECTRIC] any of the negatively charged particles that form a part of all atoms

e·lec·tron·ic (i lek'trän'ik) *adj.* 1. of electrons 2. operating, produced, or done by the action of electrons —**e·lec'tron'i·cal·ly** *adv.*

e·lec'tron'ics *n.pl.* [*with sing. v.*] the science that deals with electronic action and the use of electron tubes, transistors, etc.

electron tube a sealed glass or metal tube with two or more electrodes and a gas or vacuum inside, through which electrons can flow

e·lec·tro·plate (i lek'trə plāt') *vt.* -plat'ed, -plat'ing to deposit a coating of metal on by electrolysis —*n.* anything so plated

e·lec'tro·type' (-tīp') *n. Printing* a facsimile plate made by electroplating a wax or plastic impression of the surface to be reproduced

el·ee·mos·y·nar·y (el i mäs'ə ner'ē, el'ē ə-) *adj.* [< Gr. *eleēmosynē*, pity] of, for, or supported by charity

el·e·gant (el'ə gənt) *adj.* [< Fr. < L. *e-*, out + *legere*, choose] 1. having dignified richness and grace, as of manner, design, dress, etc.; tastefully luxurious 2. [Colloq.] excellent —**el'e·gance** *n.* —**el'e·gant·ly** *adv.*

el·e·gi·ac (el'ə jī'ək, i lē'jē ak') *adj.* 1. of, like, or fit for an elegy 2. sad; mournful

el·e·gy (el'ə jē) *n., pl.* -gies [< Fr. < Gr. *elegos*, a lament] a mournful poem, esp. of lament and praise for the dead

el·e·ment (el'ə mənt) *n.* [< L. *elementum*] 1. the natural or suitable environment for a person or thing 2. a component part or quality, often one that is basic or essential 3. the wire coil, etc. that becomes glowing hot in an electric appliance 4. *Chem.* any substance that cannot be separated into different substances except by radioactive decay or by nuclear reactions: all matter is composed of such substances —**the elements** 1. the first principles; rudiments 2. wind, rain, etc.

el·e·men·tal (el'ə men't'l) *adj.* 1. of or like basic, natural forces; primal 2. *same as* ELEMENTARY (sense 2) 3. being an essential part or parts

el'e·men'ta·ry (-tər ē, -trē) *adj.* 1. *same as* ELEMENTAL 2. of first principles or fundamentals; basic; simple

elementary school a school of the first six (or eight) grades, where basic subjects are taught

el·e·phant (el'ə fənt) *n.* [< Gr. *elephas*] a huge, thick-skinned mammal with a long, flexible snout, or trunk, and, usually, two ivory tusks

el·e·phan·ti·a·sis (el'ə fən tī'ə sis) *n.* a chronic disease of the skin causing enlargement of certain bodily parts

el·e·phan·tine (el'ə fan'tēn, -tīn) *adj.* like an elephant; huge, slow, clumsy, etc.

el·e·vate (el'ə vāt') *vt.* -vat'ed, -vat'ing [< L. *e-*, out + *levare*, to lift] 1. to lift up; raise 2. to raise in rank 3. to raise to a higher moral level 4. to elate; exhilarate

el'e·va'tion *n.* 1. an elevating or being elevated 2. a high place or position 3. height above the surface of the earth or above sea level 4. a scale drawing of the front, rear, or side of a structure

el'e·va'tor *n.* 1. one that elevates, or lifts up 2. a suspended cage or enclosed boxlike structure for hoisting or lowering people or things 3. a warehouse for grain storage, etc. 4. a device like a horizontal rudder, for making an aircraft go up or down

e·lev·en (i lev'ən) *adj., n.* [OE. *endleofan*] one more than ten; 11; XI —**e·lev'enth** (-ənth) *adj., n.*

elf (elf) *n., pl.* **elves** (elvz) [OE. *ælf*] 1. *Folklore* a tiny, often mischievous fairy 2. a small, often mischievous child —**elf'in, elf'ish** *adj.*

e·lic·it (i lis'it) *vt.* [< L. *e-*, out + *lacere*, entice] to draw forth (a response, etc.)

e·lide (i līd') *vt.* **e·lid'ed, e·lid'ing** [< L. *e-*, out + *laedere*, to strike] to leave out; esp., to slur over (a letter, etc.) in pronunciation —**e·li·sion** (i lizh'ən) *n.*

el·i·gi·ble (el'i jə b'l) *adj.* [see ELECT] fit to be chosen; qualified; suitable —*n.* an eligible person —**el'i·gi·bil'i·ty** *n.*

e·lim·i·nate (i lim'ə nāt') *vt.* -nat'ed, -nat'ing [< L. *e-*, out + *limen*, threshold] 1. to get rid of; remove 2. to leave out of consideration; omit 3. to excrete —**e·lim'i·na'tion** *n.* —**e·lim'i·na'tor** *n.*

e·lite, é·lite (i lēt', ā-) *n.* [Fr. < L.: see ELECT] [*also used with pl. v.*] the group or part of a group regarded as the best, most powerful, etc.

e·lix·ir (i lik'sər) *n.* [Ar. *al-iksīr*] a hypothetical substance sought for by medieval alchemists to prolong life indefinitely: in full **elixir of life** 2. a panacea 3. a medicine made of drugs in alcoholic solution

E·liz·a·be·than (i liz'ə bē'thən, -beth'ən) *adj.* of or characteristic of the time of Elizabeth I (1533-1603) —*n.* an English person, esp. a writer, of that time

elk (elk) *n., pl.* **elk, elks** [OE. *eolh*] 1. a large, mooselike deer of N Europe and Asia, with broad antlers 2. *same as* WAPITI

ell' (el) *n.* something L-shaped; specif., an extension or wing at right angles to the main structure

ell² (el) *n.* [OE. *eln*, a forearm] a former English measure of length, equal to 45 in.

el·lipse (i lips') *n., pl.* -**lip'ses** (-lip'siz) [< Gr. *elleipein*, to fall short] a closed curve in the form of a symmetrical oval

el·lip·sis (i lip'sis) *n., pl.* -**ses** (-sēz) [see prec.] 1. the omission of a word or words understood in the context (Ex.: "if possible" for "if it is possible") **2.** a mark (...) indicating an omission of words or letters

el·lip·ti·cal (i lip′ti k′l) *adj.* **1.** having the form of an ellipse **2.** of or characterized by ellipsis Also **el·lip′tic** **—el·lip′ti·cal·ly** *adv.*

elm (elm) *n.* [OE.] **1.** a tall, hardy shade tree **2.** its hard, heavy wood

el·o·cu·tion (el′ə kyōō′shən) *n.* [see ELOQUENT] the art of public speaking **—el′o·cu′tion·ist** *n.*

e·lon·gate (i lôn′gāt) *vt., vi.* -gat·ed, -gat·ing [< L. *e-*, out + *longus*, long] to make or become longer; lengthen **—adj.** lengthened; stretched **— e·lon′ga′tion** *n.*

e·lope (i lōp′) *vi.* e·loped′, e·lop′ing [prob. < OE. *a-*, away + *hleapan*, to run] to run away secretly, esp. in order to get married **—e·lope′·ment** *n.* **—e·lop′er** *n.*

el·o·quent (el′ə kwənt) *adj.* [< L. *e-*, out + *loqui*, speak] **1.** vivid, forceful, fluent, etc. in speech or writing **2.** vividly expressive **—el′o·quence** *n.* **—el′o·quent·ly** *adv.*

else (els) *adj.* [OE. *elles*] **1.** different; other [somebody *else*] **2.** in addition [is there anything *else?*] **—adv.** **1.** differently; otherwise [where *else* can I go?] **2.** if not [study, (or) *else* you will fail]

else′where′ (-hwer′, -wer′) *adv.* in or to some other place; somewhere else

e·lu·ci·date (i lōō′sə dāt′) *vt., vi.* -dat·ed, -dat′·ing [< L. *e-*, out + *lucidus*, clear] to make clear; explain **—e·lu′ci·da′tion** *n.*

e·lude (i lōōd′) *vt.* e·lud·ed, e·lud′ing [< L. *e-*, out + *ludere*, to play] **1.** to avoid or escape from by quickness, cunning, etc.; evade **2.** to escape the mental grasp of **—e·lud′er** *n.* **—e·lu·sion** (i lōō′zhən) *n.*

e·lu·sive (i lōō′siv) *adj.* **1.** tending to elude **2.** hard to grasp mentally; baffling

elves (elvz) *n. pl. of* ELF

E·ly·si·um (i lizh′ē əm, -liz′-) *Gr. Myth.* the place where virtuous people dwell after death **—n.** any state of ideal bliss; paradise **—E·ly·sian** (i lizh′ən, -ē ən) *adj.*

em (em) *n.* **1.** the letter M, m **2.** *Printing* a unit of measure, as of column width

'em (əm, 'm) *pron.* [Colloq.] them

em- *same as* EN-: used before *p, b,* or *m*

e·ma·ci·ate (i mā′shē āt′, -sē-) *vt.* -at′ed, -at′·ing [< L. *e-*, out + *macies*, leanness] to cause to become abnormally lean; make lose much weight **—e·ma′ci·a′tion** *n.*

em·a·nate (em′ə nāt′) *vi.* -nat·ed, -nat′ing [< L. *e-*, out + *manare*, to flow] to come forth; issue **—em′a·na′tion** *n.*

e·man·ci·pate (i man′sə pāt′) *vt.* -pat′ed, -pat′ing [< L. *e-*, out + *manus*, the hand + *capere*, to take] **1.** to set free (a slave, etc.) **2.** to free from restraint **—e·man′ci·pa′tion** *n.* **— e·man′ci·pa′tor** *n.*

e·mas·cu·late (i mas′kyə lāt′) *vt.* -lat·ed, -lat′·ing [< L. *e-*, out + *masculus*, male] **1.** to castrate **2.** to weaken **—e·mas′cu·la′tion** *n.* **— e·mas′cu·la′tor** *n.*

em·balm (im bäm′) *vt.* [see EN- & BALM] to preserve (a dead body) with various chemicals **—em·balm′er** *n.*

em·bank (im baŋk′) *vt.* to protect, support, or enclose with a bank of earth, rubble, etc. **— em·bank′ment** *n.*

em·bar·go (im bär′gō) *n., pl.* -goes [Sp. < L. *in-*, in + ML. *barra*, a bar] **1.** a government order prohibiting the entry or departure of commercial ships at its ports **2.** any legal restriction of commerce **3.** any restriction or re-

straint **—vt.** -goed, -go·ing to put an embargo on

em·bark (im bärk′) *vt.* [Fr. < Sp. < L. *in-*, in + *barca*, small boat] to put or take aboard a ship, airplane, etc. **—vi.** **1.** to go aboard a ship, airplane, etc. **2.** to begin a journey **3.** to get started in an enterprise **—em·bar·ka·tion** (em′-bär kä′shən) *n.*

em·bar·rass (im ber′əs) *vt.* [Fr. < Sp. < It. *in-*, in + *barra*, a bar] **1.** to cause to feel self-conscious **2.** to hinder **3.** to cause to be in debt **—em·bar′rass·ment** *n.*

em·bas·sy (em′bə sē) *n., pl.* -sies [see AMBASSADOR] **1.** the official residence or offices of an ambassador **2.** an ambassador and his staff **3.** a person or group sent on an official mission

em·bat·tle[1] (im bat′'l) *vt.* -tled, -tling to provide with battlements

em·bat·tle[2] (im bat′'l) *vt.* -tled, -tling [< OFr.] [Rare, except in pp.] to prepare for battle

em·bed (im bed′) *vt.* -bed′ded, -bed′ding to set or fix firmly in a surrounding mass

em·bel·lish (im bel′ish) *vt.* [< OFr. *em-*, in + *bel*, beautiful] **1.** to decorate; adorn **2.** to improve (a story, etc.) by adding details, often fictitious **—em·bel′lish·ment** *n.*

em·ber (em′bər) *n.* [OE. *æmerge*] **1.** a glowing piece of coal, wood, etc. **2.** [pl.] the smoldering remains of a fire

em·bez·zle (im bez′'l) *vt.* -zled, -zling [< OFr. *en-*, in + *besillier*, destroy] to steal (money, etc. entrusted to one) **—em·bez′zle·ment** *n.* **— em·bez′zler** *n.*

em·bit·ter (im bit′ər) *vt.* to make bitter

em·bla·zon (im blā′z′n) *vt.* [see BLAZON] **1.** to decorate (*with* coats of arms, etc.) **2.** to display brilliantly **3.** to extol

em·blem (em′bləm) *n.* [< Gr. *en-*, in + *ballein*, to throw] a visible symbol of a thing, idea, etc.; sign; badge **—em′blem·at·ic** (-blə mat′ik) *adj.*

em·bod·y (im bäd′ē) *vt.* -ied, -y·ing **1.** to give bodily form to **2.** to give definite form to **3.** to form into, or make part of, an organized whole; incorporate **—em·bod′i·ment** *n.*

em·bold·en (im bōl′d′n) *vt.* to give courage to; cause to be bold or bolder

em·bo·lism (em′bə liz′m) *n.* [< Gr. *en-*, in + *ballein*, throw] the obstruction of a blood vessel by a blood clot or air bubble

em·bos·om (im booz′əm, -bōō′zəm) *vt.* **1.** to embrace; cherish **2.** to enclose; shelter

em·boss (im bôs′, -bäs′) *vt.* [see EN- & BOSS[2]] **1.** to decorate with raised designs, etc. **2.** to raise (a design, etc.) in relief

em·bou·chure (äm′bōō shoor′) *n.* [Fr. < L. *in*, in + *bucca*, cheek] the method of applying the lips to the mouthpiece of a wind instrument

em·bow·er (im bou′ər) *vt.* to enclose or shelter in or as in a bower

em·brace (im brās′) *vt.* -braced′, -brac′ing [< L. *im-*, in + *brachium*, an arm] **1.** to clasp in the arms lovingly; hug **2.** to accept readily **3.** to take up (a profession, etc.) **4.** to encircle **5.** to include **—vi.** to clasp each other in the arms **—n.** an embracing; hug **—em·brace′a·ble** *adj.*

em·bra·sure (im brā′zhər) *n.* [Fr. < *embraser*, widen an opening] **1.** an opening (for a door or window) wider on the inside than on the outside **2.** an opening in a wall for a gun, with the sides slanting outward

em·broi·der (im broi′dər) *vt., vi.* [< OFr. *en-*, on + *brosder*, embroider] **1.** to make (a design, etc.) on (fabric) with needlework **2.** to embellish (a story, etc.)

em·broi′der·y n., pl. -ies 1. the art of embroidering 2. embroidered work or fabric 3. embellishment, as of a story

em·broil (im broil′) vt. [see EN- & BROIL] 1. to confuse (affairs, etc.); muddle 2. to draw into a conflict or fight; involve in trouble —**em·broil′ment** n.

em·bry·o (em′brē ō′) n., pl. -os′ [< Gr. en-, in + bryein, to swell] 1. an animal in the earliest stages of its development in the uterus 2. the rudimentary plant contained in a seed 3. a) an early stage of something b) anything in such a stage —**em′bry·on′ic** (-än′ik) adj.

em′bry·ol′o·gy (-äl′ə jē) n. [EMBRYO + -LOGY] the branch of biology dealing with the formation and development of embryos —**em′bry·ol′o·gist** n.

em·cee (em′sē′) vt., vi. -ceed′, -cee′ing [< M.C.] [Colloq.] to act as master of ceremonies (for) —n. [Colloq.] a master of ceremonies

e·mend (i mend′) vt. [< L. emendare, to correct] to make scholarly corrections in (a text) —**e·men·da·tion** (ē′mən dā′shən) n.

em·er·ald (em′ər əld) n. [< Gr. smaragdos] 1. a bright-green, transparent precious stone 2. bright green —adj. bright-green

e·merge (i murj′) vi. e·merged′, e·merg′ing [< L. e-, out + mergere, to dip] 1. to rise as from a fluid 2. to become visible or apparent — **e·mer′gence** n.

e·mer·gen·cy (i mur′jən sē) n., pl. -cies [orig. sense, an emerging] a sudden, generally unexpected occurrence demanding immediate action

e·mer·i·tus (i mer′ə təs) adj. [L. < e-, out + mereri, to serve] retired from active service, usually for age, but retaining one's rank or title [professor emeritus]

em·er·y (em′ər ē) n. [< Gr. smyris] a dark, impure, coarse variety of corundum used for grinding, polishing, etc.

e·met·ic (i met′ik) adj. [< Gr. emein, to vomit] causing vomiting —n. an emetic medicine or other substance

-emia [< Gr. haima, blood] a suffix meaning a (specified) condition of the blood [leukemia]

em·i·grate (em′ə grāt′) vi. -grat′ed, -grat′ing [< L. e-, out + migrare, to move] to leave one country or region to settle in another —**em′i·grant** (-grənt) adj., n. —**em′i·gra′tion** n.

em·i·nence (em′ə nəns) n. [< L. eminere, stand out] 1. a high place, thing, etc. 2. superiority in rank, position, etc.; greatness 3. [E-] a title of honor of a cardinal

em′i·nent adj. [see prec.] 1. high; lofty 2. projecting; prominent 3. exalted; distinguished 4. outstanding

e·mir (i mir′) n. [< Ar. amara, to command] in certain Muslim countries, a ruler

em·is·sar·y (em′ə ser′ē) n., pl. -ies [see EMIT] a person, esp. a secret agent, sent on a specific mission

e·mis·sion (i mish′ən) n. 1. an emitting 2. something emitted; discharge

e·mit (i mit′) vt. e·mit′ted, e·mit′ting [< L. e-, out + mittere, send] 1. to send out; give forth 2. to utter (sounds, etc.)

e·mol·lient (i mäl′yənt) adj. [< L. e-, out + mollire, soften] softening; soothing —n. an emollient preparation, esp. for the surface tissues of the body

e·mol·u·ment (i mäl′yoo mənt) n. [< L. e-, out + molere, to grind] gain from employment; salary, fees, etc.

e·mote (i mōt′) vi. e·mot′ed, e·mot′ing [Colloq.] to display one's emotions dramatically

e·mo·tion (i mō′shən) n. [Fr. < L. e-, out + movere, to move] 1. strong feeling; excitement 2. any specific feeling, as love, hate, fear, anger, etc.

e·mo′tion·al adj. 1. of or showing emotion 2. easily aroused to emotion 3. appealing to the emotions

em·pa·thy (em′pə thē) n. [< Gr. en-, in + pathos, feeling] intellectual or emotional identification with another

em·per·or (em′pər ər) n. [< L. imperare, to command] the supreme ruler of an empire

em·pha·sis (em′fə sis) n., pl. -ses′ (-sēz′) [< Gr. en-, in + phainein, to show] 1. force of expression, action, etc. 2. special stress given to a syllable, word, etc. in speaking 3. importance; stress

em′pha·size′ (-sīz′) vt. -sized′, -siz′ing to give emphasis to; stress

em·phat·ic (im fat′ik) adj. 1. felt or done with emphasis 2. using emphasis in speaking, etc. 3. forcible —**em·phat′i·cal·ly** adv.

em·phy·se·ma (em′fə sē′mə) n. [< Gr. en-, in + physaein, to blow] a disease of the lungs in which the air sacs become distended and lose elasticity

em·pire (em′pīr) n. [see EMPEROR] 1. supreme rule 2. government by an emperor or empress 3. a group of states or territories under one sovereign power

em·pir·i·cal (em pir′i k'l) adj. [< Gr. en-, in + peira, trial] 1. relying or based on experiment and observation 2. relying on practical experience Also **em·pir′ic** —**em·pir′i·cism** (-ə siz′m) n.

em·place·ment (im plās′mənt) n. [Fr.] the prepared position from which a heavy gun or guns are fired

em·ploy (im ploi′) vt. [< L. in-, in + plicare, to fold] 1. to use 2. to keep busy or occupied 3. to engage the services of; hire —n. employment —**em·ploy′a·ble** adj.

em·ploy·ee, em·ploy·e (im ploi′ē, em′ploi ē′) n. a person employed by another for wages or salary

em·ploy′er n. one who employs others for wages or salary

em·ploy′ment n. 1. work; occupation; job 2. the number or percentage employed

em·po·ri·um (em pôr′ē əm) n., pl. -ri·ums, -ri·a (-ə) [< Gr. en-, in + poros, way] a store with a wide variety of merchandise

em·pow·er (im pou′ər) vt. 1. to give power to; authorize 2. to enable

em·press (em′pris) n. 1. an emperor's wife 2. a woman ruler of an empire

emp·ty (emp′tē) adj. -ti·er, -ti·est [< OE. æmettig, unoccupied] 1. having nothing or no one in it; unoccupied 2. worthless [empty pleasures] 3. insincere [empty promises] —vt. -tied, -ty·ing 1. to make empty 2. to remove (the contents) of something —vi. 1. to become empty 2. to pour out; discharge —n., pl. -ties an empty truck, bottle, etc. —**emp′ti·ness** n.

emp′ty-hand′ed adj. bringing or carrying away nothing

em·pyr·e·al (em pir′ē əl, em′pī rē′əl) adj. [< Gr. en-, in + pyr, a fire] of the empyrean

em·py·re·an (em′pī rē′ən, em pir′ē ən) n. [see prec.] 1. the highest heaven 2. the sky

e·mu (ē′myōō) n. [prob. < Port. ema, a crane] a large, nonflying Australian bird, similar to the ostrich but somewhat smaller

em·u·late (em′yə lāt′) vt. -lat′ed, -lat′ing [< L. aemulus, trying to equal] 1. to try to equal or surpass 2. to rival successfully —**em′u·la′tion** n. —**em′u·la′tor** n.

e·mul·si·fy (i mul′sə fī′) *vt., vi.* **-fied′, -fy′ing** to form into an emulsion —**e·mul′si·fi·ca′tion** *n.*
e·mul·sion (i mul′shən) *n.* [< L. *e-*, out + *mulgere*, to milk] a fluid formed by the suspension of one liquid in another; specif., *Pharmacy* a preparation of an oily substance suspended in a watery liquid
en (en) *n.* **1.** the letter N, n **2.** *Printing* a space half the width of an em
en- [< L. *in-*, in] *a prefix meaning:* **1.** to put or get into or on *[entrain]* **2.** to make *[enfeeble]* **3.** in or into *[enclose]*
-en [< OE.] *a suffix:* **1.** *meaning: a)* to become or cause to be *[weaken] b)* to cause to have *[strengthen] c)* made of *[woolen]* **2.** *used to form plurals [children]* **3.** *used to form diminutives [chicken]*
en·a·ble (in ā′b'l) *vt.* **-bled, -bling** to make able; provide with means, opportunity, power, etc. (*to* do something)
en·act (in akt′) *vt.* **1.** to make (a bill, etc.) into a law; pass (a law); decree **2.** to represent as in a play —**en·act′ment** *n.*
en·am·el (i nam′'l) *n.* [< OFr. *esmail*] **1.** a glassy, opaque substance fused to metal or the like as a protective coating **2.** the hard, white, glossy coating of teeth **3.** paint or varnish producing a hard, glossy surface —*vt.* **-eled** or **-elled, -el·ing** or **-el·ling** to coat with enamel
en·am′el·ware′ (-wer′) *n.* kitchen utensils, etc. made of enameled metal
en·am·or (in am′ər) *vt.* [ult. < L. *in-*, in + *amor*, love] to fill with love and desire; charm: mainly in the passive voice, with *of [enamored of her]*
en·camp (in kamp′) *vt., vi.* to set up, or put in, a camp —**en·camp′ment** *n.*
en·cap·su·late (in kap′sə lāt′, -syoo-) *vt.* **-lat′ed, -lat′ing** **1.** to enclose in a capsule **2.** to condense; abridge
en·case (in kās′) *vt.* **-cased′, -cas′ing** to enclose, as in a case
-ence [< L.] *a suffix meaning* act, quality, state, result, or degree *[conference]*
en·ceph·a·li·tis (en sef′ə līt′is, en′sef-) *n.* [< Gr. *enkephalos*, brain + -ITIS] inflammation of the brain
en·chant (in chant′) *vt.* [< L. *in-*, in + *cantare*, sing] **1.** to cast a spell over **2.** to charm greatly; delight —**en·chant′er** *n.* —**en·chant′ing** *adj.* —**en·chant′ment** *n.*
en·chi·la·da (en′chə lä′də) *n.* [AmSp.] a tortilla usually rolled with meat inside and served with a chili-flavored sauce
en·cir·cle (in sur′k'l) *vt.* **-cled, -cling** **1.** to surround **2.** to move in a circle around —**en·cir′cle·ment** *n.*
en·clave (en′klāv) *n.* [Fr. < L. *in*, in + *clavis*, a key] a territory surrounded by another country's territory
en·close (in klōz′) *vt.* **-closed′, -clos′ing** **1.** to shut in all around; fence in; surround **2.** to insert in an envelope, etc., often along with something else **3.** to contain
en·clo′sure (-klō′zhər) *n.* **1.** an enclosing or being enclosed **2.** something that encloses **3.** something enclosed, as in an envelope or by a wall
en·code (in kōd′) *vt.* **-cod′ed, -cod′ing** to put (information, etc.) into code
en·co·mi·um (en kō′mē əm) *n., pl.* **-mi·ums, -mi·a** (-ə) [< Gr. *en-*, in + *kōmos*, a revel] high praise; eulogy
en·com·pass (in kum′pəs) *vt.* **1.** to enclose; surround **2.** to contain; include
en·core (än′kôr) *interj.* [Fr.] again; once more —*n.* **1.** a demand by an audience, shown by ap-

plause, for further performance **2.** such further performance
en·coun·ter (in koun′tər) *vt.* [< L. *in*, in + *contra*, against] **1.** to meet unexpectedly **2.** to meet in conflict —*n.* **1.** a battle; fight **2.** an unexpected meeting —*adj.* designating or of a small group meeting to study personal relationships, with open exchange of feelings, etc.
en·cour·age (in kur′ij) *vt.* **-aged, -ag·ing** **1.** to give courage, hope, or confidence to **2.** to give support to; help —**en·cour′age·ment** *n.* —**en·cour′ag·ing** *adj.*
en·croach (in krōch′) *vi.* [< OFr. *en-*, in + *croc*, a hook] to trespass or intrude (*on* or *upon*) —**en·croach′ment** *n.*
en·crust (in krust′) *vt., vi.* same as INCRUST —**en′crus·ta′tion** *n.*
en·cum·ber (in kum′bər) *vt.* [see EN- & CUMBER] **1.** to hold back the motion or action of; hinder **2.** to load down; burden —**en·cum′brance** (-brəns) *n.*
-ency [L. *-entia*] *a suffix meaning* act, quality, state, result, or degree *[dependency]*
ency., encyc., encycl. encyclopedia
en·cyc·li·cal (in sik′li k'l, -sī′kli-) *n.* [< Gr. *en-*, in + *kyklos*, circle] a letter from the Pope to the bishops
en·cy·clo·pe·di·a, en·cy·clo·pae·di·a (in sī′klə pē′dē ə) *n.* [< Gr. *enkyklios*, general + *paideia*, education] a book or set of books with alphabetically arranged articles on all branches, or on one field, of knowledge —**en·cy′clo·pe′dic, en·cy′clo·pae′dic** *adj.*
en·cyst (en sist′) *vt., vi.* to enclose or become enclosed in a cyst, capsule, or sac
end (end) *n.* [OE. *ende*] **1.** a boundary; limit **2.** the last part of anything; finish; conclusion **3.** a ceasing to exist; death or destruction **4.** the part at or near an extremity; tip **5.** a purpose; intention **6.** an outcome; result **7.** a remnant **8.** *Football* a player at either end of the line —*vt., vi.* to bring or come to an end; finish; stop —*adj.* at the end; final —**make (both) ends meet** to keep one's expenses within one's income —**no end** [Colloq.] extremely —**put an end to 1.** to stop **2.** to do away with
en·dan·ger (in dān′jər) *vt.* to expose to danger, harm, or loss; imperil
en·dear (in dir′) *vt.* to make dear or beloved —**en·dear′ing** *adj.*
en·dear′ment *n.* **1.** affection **2.** an expression of affection
en·deav·or (in dev′ər) *vt.* [< EN- + OFr. *deveir*, duty] to try (*to* do something) —*n.* an earnest attempt or effort Brit. sp. **en·deav′our**
en·dem·ic (en dem′ik) *adj.* [< Fr. < Gr. *en-*, in + *dēmos*, people] **1.** native to a particular country, etc. **2.** restricted to and present in a particular country, etc.: said of a disease
end·ing (en′diŋ) *n.* **1.** the last part; finish **2.** death
en·dive (en′dīv, än′dēv) *n.* [< OFr. < Gr. *entybon*] a plant with curled, narrow leaves used in salads
end·less (end′lis) *adj.* **1.** having no end; eternal; infinite **2.** lasting too long *[an endless speech]* **3.** with the ends joined to form a closed unit *[an endless belt]* —**end′less·ly** *adv.*
end′most′ *adj.* at the end; farthest; last
endo- [< Gr. *endon*, within] *a combining form meaning* within, inner: also **end-**
en·do·crine (en′də krin, -krīn′) *adj.* [ENDO- + Gr. *krinein*, to separate] designating or of any gland producing an internal secretion carried by the blood to some body part whose functions it regulates
en·do·derm (en′də durm′) *n.* [< ENDO- + Gr.

derma, skin] the inner layer of cells of the embryo in its early stage

en·do·plasm (en′də plaz′m) *n.* the inner part of the cytoplasm of a cell

en·dorse (in dôrs′) *vt.* **-dorsed′, -dors′ing** [< L. *in,* on + *dorsum,* the back] **1.** to write on the back of (a document); specif., to sign (one's name) as payee on the back of (a check, etc.) **2.** to sanction —**en·dorse′ment** *n.* —**en·dors′er** *n.*

en·dow (in dou′) *vt.* [ult. < L. *in,* in + *dotare,* endow] **1.** to provide with some talent, quality, etc. *[endowed* with courage] **2.** to give money or property to (a college, etc.) —**en·dow′ment** *n.*

en·due (in dōō′) *vt.* **-dued′, -du′ing** [< L. *in-,* in + *ducere,* to lead] to provide (*with* qualities)

en·dur·ance (in door′əns) *n.* **1.** ability to last, continue, or remain **2.** ability to stand pain, fatigue, etc. **3.** duration

en·dure (in door′) *vt.* **-dured′, -dur′ing** [< L. *in-,* in + *durus,* hard] **1.** to stand (pain, fatigue, etc.) **2.** to tolerate —*vi.* **1.** to last; continue **2.** to bear pain, etc. without flinching —**en·dur′a·ble** *adj.*

en·dur·ing *adj.* lasting; permanent

end′ways′ (-wāz′) *adv.* **1.** on end; upright **2.** with the end foremost **3.** lengthwise **4.** end to end Also **end′wise′** (-wīz′)

-ene [after Gr. *-enos,* adj. suffix] a suffix used to form names for some hydrocarbons *[benzene]*

en·e·ma (en′ə mə) *n.* [< Gr. *en-,* in + *hienai,* send] the injection of a liquid, as a purgative, medicine, etc., into the rectum

en·e·my (en′ə mē) *n., pl.* **-mies** [< L. *in-,* not + *amicus,* friend] **1.** a person who hates another and wishes to injure him **2.** *a)* a nation hostile to another *b)* a soldier, citizen, etc. of a hostile nation **3.** one hostile to an idea, cause, etc. **4.** anything injurious —*adj.* of an enemy

en·er·get·ic (en′ər jet′ik) *adj.* having or showing energy; vigorous —**en′er·get′i·cal·ly** *adv.*

en·er·gize (en′ər jīz′) *vt.* **-gized′, -giz′ing** to give energy to; activate —**en′er·giz′er** *n.*

en·er·gy (en′ər jē) *n., pl.* **-gies** [< Gr. *en-,* in + *ergon,* work] **1.** force of expression **2.** *a)* inherent power; capacity for action *b)* [*often pl.*] such power, esp. in action **3.** effective power **4.** *Physics* the capacity for doing work and overcoming resistance

en·er·vate (en′ər vāt′) *vt.* **-vat′ed, -vat′ing** [< L. *e-,* out + *nervus,* a nerve] to deprive of strength, force, etc.; debilitate —**en′er·va′tion** *n.*

en·fee·ble (in fē′b'l) *vt.* **-bled, -bling** to make feeble —**en·fee′ble·ment** *n.*

en·fold (in fōld′) *vt.* **1.** to wrap in folds; envelop **2.** to embrace —**en·fold′er** *n.*

en·force (in fôrs′) *vt.* **-forced′, -forc′ing** **1.** to give force to **2.** to impose by force *[to enforce* one's will] **3.** to compel observance of (a law, etc.) —**en·force′a·ble** *adj.* —**en·force′ment** *n.* — **en·forc′er** *n.*

en·fran·chise (in fran′chīz) *vt.* **-chised, -chis·ing 1.** to free from slavery **2.** to admit to citizenship, esp. to the right to vote —**en·fran′·chise·ment** (-chiz mənt) *n.*

Eng. 1. England **2.** English

en·gage (in gāj′) *vt.* **-gaged′, -gag′ing** [see EN- & GAGE¹] **1.** to pledge (oneself); specif. (now only in the passive), to bind by a promise of marriage **2.** to hire **3.** to attract and hold (the attention, etc.) **4.** to enter into conflict with (the enemy) **5.** to mesh (gears, etc.) together —

vi. **1.** to pledge oneself **2.** to involve oneself **3.** to enter into conflict **4.** to mesh

en·gaged′ *adj.* **1.** pledged; esp., betrothed **2.** occupied; employed **3.** involved in combat, as troops **4.** meshed

en·gage′ment *n.* an engaging or being engaged; specif., *a)* a betrothal *b)* an appointment or commitment *c)* employment *d)* a conflict; battle *e)* state of being in gear

en·gag′ing *adj.* attractive; charming

en·gen·der (in jen′dər) *vt.* [< L. *in-,* in + *generare,* beget] to bring into being; cause; produce

en·gine (en′jən) *n.* [< L. *in-,* in + base of *gignere,* to produce] **1.** any machine that uses energy to develop·mechanical power **2.** a railroad locomotive **3.** any instrument or machine

en·gi·neer (en′jə nir′) *n.* **1.** one skilled in some branch of engineering **2.** one in charge of the operation of engines or technical equipment — *vt.* **1.** to plan, construct, etc. as an engineer **2.** to manage skillfully

en′gi·neer′ing *n.* the planning, designing, construction, etc. of machinery, roads, bridges, etc.

Eng·lish (iŋ′glish) *adj.* **1.** of England, its people, etc. **2.** of their language —*n.* **1.** the language of the people of England, the official language of the British Commonwealth, the U.S., etc. **2.** [*sometimes* e-] a spinning motion given to a ball —**the English** the people of England

English horn a double-reed instrument of the woodwind family

Eng′lish·man (-mən) *n., pl.* **-men** a native or inhabitant of England, esp. a man —**Eng′lish·wom′an** *n.fem., pl.* **-wom′en**

English sparrow the common sparrow, a small finch of European origin

en·gorge (in gôrj′) *vt.* **-gorged′, -gorg′ing 1.** to gorge **2.** *Med.* to congest (a blood vessel, tissue, etc.) with blood or other fluid —*vi.* to eat greedily

en·graft (in graft′) *vt.* to graft (a shoot, etc.) from one plant onto another

en·grave (in grāv′) *vt.* **-graved′, -grav′ing** [< Fr. *en-,* in + *graver,* to incise] **1.** to cut or etch (letters, designs, etc.) in or on (a metal plate, wooden block, etc.) **2.** to print from such a plate, etc. **3.** to impress deeply —**en·grav′er** *n.*

en·grav′ing *n.* **1.** the act or art of one who engraves **2.** an engraved plate, design, etc. **3.** a print made from an engraved surface

en·gross (in grōs′) *vt.* [< OFr. *engrossier,* become thick] to take the entire attention of; occupy wholly —**en·gross′ing** *adj.*

en·gulf (in gulf′) *vt.* [EN- + GULF] to swallow up; overwhelm

en·hance (in hans′) *vt.* **-hanced′, -hanc′ing** [ult. < L. *in,* in + *altus,* high] to make greater; heighten —**en·hance′ment** *n.* —**en·hanc′er** *n.*

e·nig·ma (ə nig′mə) *n., pl.* **-mas** [< Gr. *ainigma*] **1.** a riddle **2.** a perplexing or baffling matter, person, etc. —**e·nig·mat·ic** (en′ig mat′ik, ē′nig-), **e′nig·mat′i·cal** *adj.*

en·join (in join′) *vt.* [< L. *in-,* in + *jungere,* join] **1.** to command; order **2.** to prohibit, esp. by legal injunction

en·joy (in joi′) *vt.* [< OFr. *en-,* in + *joir,* rejoice] **1.** to get joy or pleasure from; relish **2.** to have the use or benefit of —**enjoy oneself** to have a good time —**en·joy′a·ble** *adj.* —**en·joy′·ment** *n.*

en·large (in lärj′) *vt.* **-larged′, -larg′ing 1.** to make larger; expand **2.** *Photog.* to reproduce on a larger scale —*vi.* **1.** to become. larger; increase **2.** to discuss at greater length (with *on* or *upon*) —**en·large′ment** *n.* —**en·larg′er** *n.*

en·light·en (in līt′'n) *vt.* **1.** to free from ignorance, prejudice, etc. **2.** to inform; instruct — **en·light′en·ment** *n.*

en·list (in list′) *vt., vi.* **1.** to enroll in some branch of the armed forces **2.** to engage in a cause or movement —**en·list′ee′** *n.* —**en·list′·ment** *n.*

en·liv·en (in lī′v'n) *vt.* to make active, vivacious, cheerful, etc. —**en·liv′en·ment** *n.*

en masse (en mas′) [Fr., lit., in mass] in a group; as a whole; all together

en·mesh (en mesh′) *vt.* to catch in or as in the meshes of a net; entangle

en·mi·ty (en′mə tē) *n., pl.* **-ties** [see ENEMY] the attitude or feelings of an enemy or enemies; hostility

en·no·ble (i nō′b'l) *vt.* **-bled, -bling** to give nobility to; dignify

en·nui (än′wē) *n.* [Fr.: see ANNOY] weariness and boredom

e·nor·mi·ty (i nôr′mə tē) *n., pl.* **-ties** [< Fr. < L. *e-*, out + *norma*, rule] **1.** great wickedness **2.** an outrageous act

e·nor·mous (i nôr′məs) *adj.* [see prec.] of great size, number, etc.; huge; vast

e·nough (i nuf′) *adj.* [OE. *genoh*] as much or as many as necessary; sufficient —*n.* the amount needed —*adv.* **1.** sufficiently **2.** fully; quite [oddly *enough*] **3.** tolerably

e·now (i nou′) *adj., n., adv.* [Archaic] enough

en·plane (en plān′) *vi.* **-planed′, -plan′ing** to board an airplane

en·quire (in kwīr′) *vt., vi.* **-quired′, -quir′ing** same as INQUIRE —**en·quir′y** *n., pl.* **-ies**

en·rage (in rāj′) *vt.* **-raged′, -rag′ing** to put into a rage; infuriate —**en·rage′ment** *n.*

en·rap·ture (in rap′chər) *vt.* **-tured, -tur·ing** to fill with delight

en·rich (in rich′) *vt.* to make rich or richer; give greater value, better quality, etc. to —**en·rich′ment** *n.*

en·roll, en·rol (in rōl′) *vt., vi.* **-rolled′, -roll′ing** **1.** to record or be recorded in a roll or list **2.** to enlist **3.** to make or become a member —**en·roll′ment, en·rol′ment** *n.*

en route (än rōōt′, en) [Fr.] on the way

en·sconce (in skäns′) *vt.* **-sconced′, -sconc′ing** [< Du. *schans*, small fort] to place or settle snugly or securely

en·sem·ble (än säm′b'l) *n.* [Fr. < L. *in-*, in + *simul*, at the same time] **1.** total effect **2.** a whole costume of matching parts **3.** *Music a)* a small group of musicians playing or singing together *b)* the performance of such a group, or of an orchestra, chorus, etc.

en·shrine (in shrīn′) *vt.* **-shrined′, -shrin′ing 1.** to enclose in a shrine **2.** to hold as sacred; cherish —**en·shrine′ment** *n.*

en·shroud (' -shroud′) *vt.* to cover as if with a shroud; hide; obscure

en·sign (en′sīn) *n.* [see INSIGNIA] **1.** a flag or banner **2.** (-s'n) *U.S. Navy* a commissioned officer of the lowest rank

en·si·lage (en′s'l ij) *n.* [Fr.] green fodder preserved in a silo

en·slave (in slāv′) *vt.* **-slaved′, -slav′ing 1.** to make a slave of **2.** to subjugate

en·snare ('-sner′) *vt.* **-snared′, -snar′ing** to catch as in a snare; trap

en·sue (in sōō′) *vi.* **-sued′, -su′ing** [< L. *in-*, in + *sequi*, follow] **1.** to follow immediately **2.** to result

en·sure (in shoor′) *vt.* **-sured′, -sur′ing 1.** to make sure **2.** to protect

-ent [< L. *-ens*, prp. ending] *a suffix meaning:* **1.** that has, shows, or does [insistent] **2.** a person or thing that [superintendent, solvent]

en·tail (in tāl′) *vt.* [< OFr. *taillier*, to cut] **1.** *Law* to limit the inheritance of (property) to a specific line of heirs **2.** to make necessary; require

en·tan·gle (in taŋ′g'l) *vt.* **-gled, -gling 1.** to involve in a tangle **2.** to involve in difficulty **3.** to confuse **4.** to complicate

en·tente (än tänt′) *n.* [Fr. < OFr. *entendre*, understand] **1.** an understanding or agreement, as between nations **2.** the parties to this

en·ter (en′tər) *vt.* [< L. *intra*, within] **1.** to come or go into **2.** to penetrate **3.** to insert **4.** to write down in a list, etc. **5.** to become a member of **6.** to get (someone) admitted **7.** to begin —*vi.* **1.** to come or go into some place **2.** to penetrate —**enter into 1.** to take part in **2.** to form a part of —**enter on** (or **upon**) to begin; start

en·ter·ic (en ter′ik) *adj.* [< Gr. *enteron*, intestine] intestinal

en·ter·prise (en′tər prīz′) *n.* [ult. < L. *inter*, in + *prehendere*, to take] **1.** an undertaking, esp. a bold, hard, or important one **2.** energy and initiative

en′ter·pris′ing *adj.* showing enterprise; full of energy and initiative; venturesome

en·ter·tain (en′tər tān′) *vt.* [ult. < L. *inter*, between + *tenere*, to hold] **1.** to amuse; divert **2.** to have as a guest **3.** to consider (an idea, etc.) —*vi.* to have guests

en′ter·tain′er *n.* one who entertains; esp., a popular singer, dancer, comedian, etc.

en′ter·tain′ing *adj.* interesting and pleasurable; amusing —**en′ter·tain′ing·ly** *adv.*

en′ter·tain′ment *n.* **1.** an entertaining or being entertained **2.** something that entertains; esp., a show or performance

en·thrall, en·thral (in thrôl′) *vt.* **-thralled′, -thrall′ing** [see EN- & THRALL] to fascinate; captivate; enchant

en·throne ('-thrōn′) *vt.* **-throned′, -thron′ing 1.** to place on a throne **2.** to revere; exalt —**en·throne′ment** *n.*

en·thuse ('-thōōz′) *vi.* **-thused′, -thus′ing** [Colloq.] to express enthusiasm —*vt.* [Colloq.] to make enthusiastic

en·thu·si·asm (in thōō′zē az′m) *n.* [< Gr. *en·thous*, inspired] intense or eager interest; zeal —**en·thu′si·ast′** (-ast′) *n.* —**en·thu′si·as′tic** *adj.*

en·tice (in tīs′) *vt.* **-ticed′, -tic′ing** [< L. *in*, in + *titio*, a firebrand] to attract by offering hope of reward or pleasure

en·tire (in tīr′) *adj.* [< L. *integer*, whole] not lacking any of the parts; whole; complete; intact —**en·tire′ly** *adv.*

en·tire·ty ('-tē) *n., pl.* **-ties 1.** the state or fact of being entire; wholeness **2.** an entire thing —**in its entirety** as a whole

en·ti·tle (in tīt′'l) *vt.* **-tled, -tling 1.** to give a title or name to **2.** to give a right or legal title to

en·ti·ty (en′tə tē) *n., pl.* **-ties** [ult. < L. *esse*, to be] **1.** existence **2.** a thing that has real, individual existence

en·tomb (in tōōm′) *vt.* to place in a tomb or grave; bury —**en·tomb′ment** *n.*

en·to·mol·o·gy (en′tə mäl′ə jē) *n.* [< Gr. *entomon*, insect + -LOGY] the branch of zoology that deals with insects —**en′to·mo·log′i·cal** (-mə läj′i k'l) *adj.* —**en′to·mol′o·gist** *n.*

en·tou·rage (än′tōō räzh′) *n.* [Fr. < *entourer*, to surround] a group of associates or attendants; retinue

en·trails (en′trālz, -trəlz) *n.pl.* [< L. *in-*

teraneus, internal] the inner organs of persons or animals; specif., the intestines; viscera

en·train (in trān') *vt., vi.* to put or go aboard a train —**en·train'ment** *n.*

en·trance[1] (en'trəns) *n.* **1.** the act of entering **2.** a place for entering; door, gate, etc. **3.** permission or right to enter; admission

en·trance[2] (in trans') *vt.* **-tranced', -tranc'ing 1.** to put into a trance **2.** to enchant; charm —**en·trance'ment** *n.*

en·trant (en'trənt) *n.* a person who enters

en·trap (in trap') *vt.* **-trapped', -trap'ping** to catch as in a trap

en·treat (in trēt') *vt., vi.* [< OFr. *en-,* in + *traiter:* see TREAT] to ask earnestly; beseech; implore —**en·treat'ing·ly** *adv.*

en·treat'y *n., pl.* **-ies** an earnest request

en·tree, en·trée (än'trā) *n.* [< Fr. < OFr. *entrer,* ENTER] **1.** the right to enter **2.** the main course of a meal

en·trench (in trench') *vt.* **1.** to surround with trenches **2.** to establish securely —**en·trench'-ment** *n.*

en·tre·pre·neur (än'trə prə nur') *n.* [Fr.: see ENTERPRISE] one who organizes a business undertaking, assuming the risk for the sake of profit

en·tro·py (en'trə pē) *n.* [< G. < Gr. *entropē,* a turning toward] **1.** a measure of the energy unavailable for useful work in a system **2.** the tendency of an energy system to run down

en·trust (in trust') *vt.* **1.** to charge with a trust or duty **2.** to assign the care of

en·try (en'trē) *n., pl.* **-tries** [< OFr.: see ENTER] **1.** an entering; entrance **2.** a way by which to enter **3.** an item or a note recorded in a list, journal, etc. **4.** one entered in a race, competition, etc.

en·twine (in twīn') *vt., vi.* **-twined', -twin'ing** to twine together or around

e·nu·mer·ate (i noo'mə rāt') *vt.* **-at'ed, -at'ing** [< L. *e-,* out + *numerare,* to count] **1.** to count **2.** to name one by one; specify, as in a list —**e·nu'mer·a'tion** *n.*

e·nun·ci·ate (i nun'sē āt', -shē-) *vt., vi.* **-at'ed, -at'ing** [< L. *e-,* out + *nuntiare,* announce] **1.** to state definitely **2.** to announce **3.** to pronounce (words) —**e·nun'ci·a'tion** *n.* —**e·nun'-ci·a'tor** *n.*

en·vel·op (in vel'əp) *vt.* [< OFr.: see EN- & DEVELOP] **1.** to cover completely **2.** to surround **3.** to conceal; hide —**en·vel'op·ment** *n.*

en·ve·lope (en'və lōp', än'-) *n.* **1.** a thing that envelops; covering **2.** a folded paper container for letters, etc., usually with a gummed flap

en·ven·om (in ven'əm) *vt.* **1.** to put venom or poison on or into **2.** to fill with hate

en·vi·a·ble (en'vē ə b'l) *adj.* worthy to be envied or desired —**en'vi·a·bly** *adv.*

en·vi·ous (en'vē əs) *adj.* feeling or showing envy —**en'vi·ous·ly** *adv.*

en·vi·ron·ment (in vī'rən mənt, -ərn mənt) *n.* [see ENVIRONS] **1.** surroundings **2.** all the conditions, etc. surrounding, and affecting the development of, an organism —**en·vi'ron·men'tal** (-men't'l) *adj.*

en·vi'ron·men'tal·ist *n.* a person working to solve environmental problems

en·vi·rons (in vī'rənz) *n.pl.* [< OFr. *en-,* in + *viron,* a circuit] **1.** the districts surrounding a city; suburbs **2.** vicinity

en·vis·age (en viz'ij) *vt.* **-aged, -ag·ing** [< Fr.: see EN- & VISAGE] to form an image of in the mind; visualize

en·vi·sion (en vizh'ən) *vt.* [EN- + VISION] to imagine (something not yet in existence)

en·voy (en'voi, än'-) *n.* [< Fr. < L. *in,* in +

via, way] **1.** a messenger; agent **2.** a diplomat ranking just below an ambassador

en·vy (en'vē) *n., pl.* **-vies** [< L. *invidia*] **1.** discontent and ill will over another's advantages, possessions, etc. **2.** desire for something that another has **3.** an object of such feeling —*vt.* **-vied, -vy·ing** to feel envy toward or because of

en·zyme (en'zīm) *n.* [< G. < Gr. *en-,* in + *zymē,* leaven] a proteinlike substance, formed in plant and animal cells, that acts as an organic catalyst in chemical reactions

e·on (ē'ən, ē'än) *n.* [< Gr. *aiōn,* an age] an extremely long, indefinite period of time

-eous [< L. *-eus*] *a suffix meaning* having the nature of, like *[beauteous]*

ep·au·let, ep·au·lette (ep'ə let') *n.* [< Fr.: see SPATULA] a shoulder ornament, as on military uniforms

e·pee, é·pée (e pā', ā-) *n.* [Fr. < Gr. *spathē,* blade] a sword, esp. a thin, pointed sword without a cutting edge, used in fencing

e·phed·rine (i fed'rin) *n.* [< Gr. *ephedra,* the plant horsetail] an alkaloid used to relieve nasal congestion and asthma

e·phem·er·al (i fem'ər əl) *adj.* [< Gr. *epi-,* upon + *hēmera,* a day] **1.** lasting only one day **2.** short-lived; transitory

e·phem'er·id (-id) *n.* [see prec.] *same as* MAYFLY

epi- [< Gr. *epi,* at, on] *a prefix meaning* on, upon, over, beside *[epiglottis, epidemic]*

ep·ic (ep'ik) *n.* [< Gr. *epos,* a word, song] a long narrative poem in a dignified style about the deeds of a hero or heroes —*adj.* of or like an epic; heroic; grand: also **ep'i·cal**

ep·i·cen·ter (ep'ə sen'tər) *n.* **1.** the area of the earth's surface directly above the place of origin of an earthquake **2.** a focal point

ep·i·cure (ep'i kyoor') *n.* [< *Epicurus,* ancient Gr. philosopher] one who has a discriminating taste for fine foods and drinks

ep·i·cu·re·an (ep'i kyoo rē'ən) *adj.* **1.** fond of sensuous pleasure **2.** having to do with an epicure —*n.* an epicure

ep·i·dem·ic (ep'ə dem'ik) *adj.* [< Fr. < Gr. *epi-,* among + *dēmos,* people] prevalent and spreading rapidly among many people in a community, as a contagious disease —*n.* **1.** an epidemic disease **2.** the spreading of such a disease —**ep'i·dem'i·cal·ly** *adv.*

ep·i·der·mis (ep'ə dur'mis) *n.* [< Gr. *epi-,* upon + *derma,* the skin] the outermost layer of the skin —**ep'i·der'mal** *adj.*

ep·i·glot·tis (ep'ə glät'is) *n.* [see EPI- & GLOTTIS] the thin lid of cartilage that covers the windpipe during swallowing

ep·i·gram (ep'ə gram') *n.* [< Gr. *epi-,* upon + *graphein,* write] a terse, witty, pointed statement —**ep·i·gram·mat·ic** (ep'i grə mat'ik) *adj.*

ep·i·lep·sy (ep'ə lep'sē) *n.* [< Gr. *epi-,* upon + *lambanein,* seize] a chronic nervous disease, characterized by convulsions, etc.

ep'i·lep'tic (-tik) *adj.* of or having epilepsy —*n.* a person who has epilepsy

ep·i·logue (ep'ə lôg') *n.* [< Gr. *epi-.* upon + *legein,* speak] **1.** a closing section of a novel, play, etc., providing further comment; specif., a speech to the audience by an actor **2.** the actor who speaks this

ep·i·neph·rine (ep'ə nef'rin) *n.* [< EPI- + Gr. *nephros,* kidney + -INE[3]] a hormone secreted by the adrenal gland, that stimulates the heart, etc.

E·piph·a·ny (i pif'ə nē) *n., pl.* **-nies** [< Gr. *epi-,* upon + *phainein,* to show] a Christian festival (Jan. 6) commemorating the revealing of Jesus as the Christ to the Gentiles

e·pis·co·pa·cy (i pis'kə pə sē) *n., pl.* **-cies** [< Gr. *epi-*, upon + *skopein*, to look] 1. church government by bishops 2. *same as* EPISCOPATE
e·pis'co·pal (-p'l) *adj.* 1. of or governed by bishops 2. [E-] designating or of any of various churches so governed
E·pis'co·pa'li·an (-pāl'yən, -pā'lē ən) *adj. same as* EPISCOPAL —*n.* a member of the Protestant Episcopal Church
e·pis'co·pate (-pit, -pāt') *n.* 1. the position, rank, or term of office of a bishop 2. a bishop's see 3. bishops collectively
ep·i·sode (ep'ə sōd') *n.* [< Gr. *epi-*, upon + *eisodos*, entrance] 1. any part of a novel, poem, etc. that is complete in itself; incident 2. any event or series of events complete in itself —**ep'i·sod'ic** (-säd'ik) *adj.*
e·pis·tle (i pis''l) *n.* [< Gr. *epi-*, to + *stellein*, send] 1. a letter 2. [E-] any of the letters of the Apostles in the New Testament
ep·i·taph (ep'ə taf') *n.* [< Gr. *epi-*, upon + *taphos*, tomb] an inscription, as on a tomb, in memory of a dead person
ep·i·the·li·um (ep'ə thē'lē əm) *n., pl.* **-li·ums**, **-li·a** (-ə) [< Gr. *epi-*, upon + *thēlē*, nipple] cellular tissue covering surfaces and lining most cavities of the body
ep·i·thet (ep'ə thet') *n.* [< Gr. *epi-*, on + *tithenai*, put] a word or phrase characterizing some person or thing
e·pit·o·me (i pit'ə mē) *n., pl.* **-mes** [< Gr. *epi-*, upon + *temnein*, to cut] 1. an abstract; summary 2. a person or thing that typifies a whole class
e·pit'o·mize' (-mīz') *vt.* **-mized'**, **-miz'ing** to make or be an epitome of
‡e plu·ri·bus u·num (ē' ploor'ə bəs yōō'nəm) [L.] out of many, one: a motto of the U.S.
ep·och (ep'ak) *n.* [< Gr. *epi-*, upon + *echein*, to hold] 1. the start of a new period of something 2. a period of time in terms of noteworthy events, persons, etc. —**ep'och·al** *adj.*
ep·ox·y (e päk'sē) *adj.* [EP(I)- + OXYGEN] designating a resin used in glues, etc. —*n., pl.* **-ies** an epoxy resin
ep·si·lon (ep'sə län') *n.* the fifth letter of the Greek alphabet (E, ε)
Ep·som salts (or **salt**) (ep'səm) [< *Epsom*, town in England] a white, crystalline salt, magnesium sulfate, used as a cathartic
eq·ua·ble (ek'wə b'l) *adj.* [see EQUAL] 1. steady; uniform 2. even; serene
e·qual (ē'kwəl) *adj.* [< L. *aequus*, even] 1. of the same quantity, size, value, etc. 2. having the same rights, ability, rank, etc. 3. evenly proportioned 4. having enough ability, strength, etc. (*to*) —*n.* any person or thing that is equal —*vt.* **e'qualed** or **e'qualled**, **e'qual·ing** or **e'qual·ling** 1. to be equal to 2. to do or make something equal to —**e·qual·i·ty** (i kwäl'ə tē, -kwôl'-) *n., pl.* **-ties** —**e'qual·ly** *adv.*
e·qual·ize (ē'kwə līz') *vt.* **-ized'**, **-iz'ing** to make equal or uniform —**e'qual·i·za'tion** *n.* —**e'qual·iz'er** *n.*
equal sign (or **mark**) the arithmetical sign (=), indicating equality (Ex.: 2 + 2 = 4)
e·qua·nim·i·ty (ek'wə nim'ə tē, ē'kwə-) *n.* [< L. *aequus*, even + *animus*, the mind] calmness of mind; composure
e·quate (i kwāt') *vt.* **e·quat'ed**, **e·quat'ing** 1. to make equal 2. to treat, regard, or express as equal
e·qua·tion (i kwā'zhən) *n.* 1. an equating or being equated 2. a statement of equality between two quantities, as shown by the equal sign (=)
e·qua·tor (i kwāt'ər) *n.* an imaginary circle

around the earth, equally distant from the North Pole and the South Pole —**e·qua·to·ri·al** (ē'kwə tôr'ē əl, ek'wə-) *adj.*
e·ques·tri·an (i kwes'trē ən) *adj.* [< L. *equus*, horse] 1. of horses or horsemanship 2. on horseback —*n.* a horseback rider, as in a circus
equi- *a combining form meaning* equal, equally [*equidistant*]
e·qui·an·gu·lar (ē'kwə aŋ'gyə lər) *adj.* having all angles equal
e'qui·dis'tant *adj.* equally distant
e'qui·lat'er·al (-lat'ər əl) *adj.* [< L. *aequus*, equal + *latus*, side] having all sides equal —*n.* a figure having equal sides
e·qui·lib·ri·um (ē'kwə lib'rē əm) *n., pl.* **-ri·ums**, **-ri·a** (-ə) [< L. *aequus*, equal + *libra*, a balance] a state of balance between opposing forces
e·quine (ē'kwīn, ek'wīn) *adj.* [< L. *equus*, horse] of or like a horse —*n.* a horse
e·qui·nox (ē'kwə näks') *n.* [< L. *aequus*, equal + *nox*, night] the time when the sun crosses the equator, making night and day of equal length in all parts of the earth
e·quip (i kwip') *vt.* **e·quipped'**, **e·quip'ping** [< OFr. *esquiper*, embark] to provide with what is needed
eq·ui·page (ek'wə pij) *n.* a carriage with horses and liveried servants
e·quip·ment (i kwip'mənt) *n.* 1. an equipping or being equipped 2. whatever one is equipped with; supplies, resources, etc.
eq·ui·poise (ek'wə poiz') *n.* [EQUI- + POISE] 1. state of equilibrium 2. counterbalance
eq·ui·ta·ble (ek'wit ə b'l) *adj.* fair; just
eq·ui·ty (ek'wət ē) *n., pl.* **-ties** [< L. *aequus*, equal] 1. fairness; justice 2. the value of property beyond the amount owed on it 3. *Law* a system of doctrines supplementing common and statute law
e·quiv·a·lent (i kwiv'ə lənt) *adj.* [< L. *aequus*, equal + *valere*, be strong] equal in quantity, value, force, meaning, etc. —*n.* an equivalent thing —**e·quiv'a·lence** *n.*
e·quiv·o·cal (i kwiv'ə k'l) *adj.* [< LL.: see EQUIVOCATE] 1. having two or more meanings; purposely ambiguous 2. uncertain; doubtful 3. suspicious; questionable
e·quiv'o·cate' (-kāt') *vi.* **-cat'ed**, **-cat'ing** [< L. *aequus*, equal + *vox*, voice] to use equivocal terms, as to deceive —**e·quiv'o·ca'tion** *n.* —**e·quiv'o·ca'tor** *n.*
-er [< OE.] 1. *a suffix meaning: a)* a person or thing having to do with [*hatter*] *b)* a person living in [*New Yorker*] *c)* a person or thing that [*sprayer*] *d)* repeatedly [*flicker*] 2. *a suffix forming the comparative degree* [*greater*]
e·ra (ir'ə, er'ə) *n.* [LL. *aera*] 1. a period of time measured from an important event 2. a period of time with some special characteristic
ERA 1. *Baseball* earned run average 2. Equal Rights Amendment
e·rad·i·cate (i rad'ə kāt') *vt.* **-cat'ed**, **-cat'ing** [< L. *e-*, out + *radix*, root] to uproot; wipe out; destroy —**e·rad'i·ca·ble** (-kə b'l) *adj.* —**e·rad'i·ca'tion** *n.* —**e·rad'i·ca'tor** *n.*
e·rase (i rās') *vt.* **e·rased'**, **e·ras'ing** [< L. *e-*, out + *radere*, to scrape] 1. to rub, scrape, or wipe out (writing, etc.) 2. to obliterate, as from the mind —**e·ras'a·ble** *adj.*
e·ras'er *n.* a thing that erases; specif., a rubber device for erasing ink or pencil marks, or a pad for removing chalk marks from a blackboard
e·ra·sure (i rā'shər) *n.* 1. an erasing 2. the place where a word, etc. has been erased
ere (er) *prep.* [< OE. *ær*] [Archaic or Poet.]

before (in time) —*conj.* [Archaic or Poet.] **1.** before **2.** rather than

e·rect (i rekt′) *adj.* [< L. *e-*, up + *regere*, make straight] upright —*vt.* **1.** to construct (a building, etc.) **2.** to set in an upright position **3.** to put together —**e·rec′tion** *n.* —**e·rect′ly** *adv.* — **e·rect′ness** *n.*

ere·long (er′lôṅ′) *adv.* [Archaic] before long

er·e·mite (er′ə mīt′) *n.* [see HERMIT] a religious recluse; hermit

erg (urg) *n.* [< Gr. *ergon*, work] *Physics* a unit of work or energy

ter·go (ur′gō) *conj., adv.* [L.] therefore

Er·in (er′in) [Poet.] Ireland

er·mine (ur′mən) *n.* [OFr.; prob. < OHG. *harmo*, weasel] **1.** a weasel whose fur is white in winter **2.** its white fur

e·rode (i rōd′) *vt.* **e·rod′ed, e·rod′ing** [< L. *e-*, out + *rodere*, gnaw] **1.** to wear away **2.** to form by wearing away gradually [the stream eroded a gully] —*vi.* to become eroded

E·ros (er′äs, ir′-) *Gr. Myth.* the god of love, son of Aphrodite

e·ro·sion (i rō′zhən) *n.* an eroding or being eroded —**e·ro′sive** *adj.*

e·rot·ic (i rät′ik) *adj.* [< Gr. *erōs*, love] of or arousing sexual feelings or desires; amatory — **e·rot′i·cal·ly** *adv.*

e·rot′i·cism (-ə siz′m) *n.* **1.** erotic quality **2.** sexual behavior **3.** preoccupation with sex

err (ur, er) *vi.* [< L. *errare*, wander] **1.** to be wrong or mistaken **2.** to deviate from the established moral code

er·rand (er′ənd) *n.* [OE. *ærende*] **1.** a short trip to do a thing, as for another **2.** the thing to be done

er·rant (er′ənt) *adj.* **1.** [< L. *iter*, a journey] roving or wandering in search of adventure **2.** [see ERR] erring; wrong —**er′rant·ly** *adv.* —**er′-rant·ry** *n.*

er·rat·ic (i rat′ik) *adj.* [< L. *errare*, wander] **1.** irregular; wandering **2.** eccentric; queer —*n.* an erratic person —**er·rat′i·cal·ly** *adv.*

er·ra·tum (e rät′əm, -rät′-) *n., pl.* **-ta** (-ə) [L. < *errare*, wander] an error in printing or writing

er·ro·ne·ous (ə rō′nē əs) *adj.* containing or based on error; wrong

er·ror (er′ər) *n.* [< L. *errare*, wander] **1.** the state of believing what is untrue **2.** a wrong belief **3.** something incorrect or wrong; mistake **4.** a transgression **5.** *Baseball* any misplay in fielding

er·satz (ur′zäts, er′-) *adj.* [G.] substitute or synthetic and inferior

erst (urst) *adv.* [< OE. *ær*, ere] [Archaic] formerly —*adj.* [Obs.] first

erst′while′ (-hwīl′) *adv.* [Archaic] formerly; some time ago —*adj.* former

e·ruct (i rukt′) *vt., vi.* [< L. *e-*, out + *ructare*, to belch] to belch

er·u·dite (er′yoo dīt′, -oo-) *adj.* [< L. *e-*, out + *rudis*, rude] learned; scholarly

er′u·di′tion (-dish′ən) *n.* learning acquired by reading and study; scholarship

e·rupt (i rupt′) *vi.* [< L. *e-*, out + *rumpere*, to break] **1.** to burst forth or out [the lava erupted] **2.** to throw forth lava, water, etc. **3.** to break out in a rash —*vt.* to cause to burst forth

e·rup·tion (i rup′shən) *n.* **1.** a bursting forth or out **2.** *a)* a breaking out in a rash *b)* a rash — **e·rup′tive** *adj.*

-ery [< LL. *-aria*] a suffix meaning: **1.** a place to [tannery] **2.** a place for [nunnery] **3.** the practice or act of [surgery] **4.** the product of [pottery] **5.** a collection of [crockery] **6.** the condition of [drudgery]

er·y·sip·e·las (er′ə sip″l əs, ir′-) *n.* [< Gr. *erythros*, red + *-pelas*, skin] an acute, infectious skin disease with local inflammation and fever

e·ryth·ro·cyte (i rith′rə sīt′) *n.* [< Gr. *erythros*, red + *kytos*, a hollow] a cell of human blood that carries oxygen

-es [< OE.] a suffix used: **1.** to form certain plurals [fishes] **2.** to form the third person singular, present indicative, of verbs [(he) kisses]

E·sau (ē′sô) *Bible* Isaac's son, who sold his birthright to his brother, Jacob

es·ca·late (es′kə lāt′) *vi.* **-lat′ed, -lat′ing 1.** to rise as on an escalator **2.** to expand, as from a limited conflict into a general war **3.** to increase rapidly, as prices

es′ca·la′tor (-ər) *n.* [< L. *scala*, ladder] a moving stairway on an endless belt

es·cal·lop, es·cal·op (e skäl′əp, -skal′-) *n., vt. same as* SCALLOP

es·ca·pade (es′kə pād′) *n.* [Fr.] a reckless adventure or prank

es·cape (ə skāp′, e-) *vi.* **-caped′, -cap′ing** [< L. *ex-*, out of + *cappa*, cloak] **1.** to get free **2.** to avoid harm, injury, etc. **3.** to leak away [gas is escaping] —*vt.* **1.** to get away from **2.** to avoid [to escape death] **3.** to come from involuntarily **4.** to slip away from [his name escapes me] —*n.* **1.** an escaping **2.** a means of escape **3.** a leakage **4.** a temporary mental release from reality —*adj.* providing an escape

es·cap·ee (ə skā′pē′, e-) *n.* a person who has escaped, esp. from confinement

es·cape′ment *n.* a notched wheel with a detaining catch to control the movement of a clock or watch

es·cap′ism (-iz′m) *n.* a tendency to escape from reality, responsibilities, etc. through the imagination —**es·cap′ist** *adj., n.*

es·ca·role (es′kə rōl′) *n.* [Fr. < L. *esca*, food] a kind of endive with wide leaves

es·carp·ment (e skärp′mənt) *n.* [< Fr.] a steep slope or cliff

-escence *a noun suffix corresponding to the adjective suffix* -ESCENT [obsolescence]

-escent [< L. *-escens*] *an adjective suffix meaning:* **1.** starting to be, being, or becoming [convalescent] **2.** giving off light or color [phosphorescent]

es·chew (es chōō′) *vt.* [< OHG. *sciuhan*, to fear] to keep away from; shun

es·cort (es′kôrt) *n.* [< L. *ex-*, out + *corrigere*, set right] **1.** one or more persons (or cars, ships, etc.) accompanying another to protect it or show honor **2.** a man accompanying a woman —*vt.* (i skôrt′) to go with as an escort

es·crow (es′krō) *n.* [OFr. *escroue*, scroll] *Law* the state of a bond, deed, etc. put in the care of a third party until certain conditions are fulfilled

es·cu·lent (es′kyoo lənt) *adj.* [< L. *esca*, food] edible —*n.* something fit for food

es·cutch·eon (i skuch′ən) *n.* [< L. *scutum*, shield] a shield on which a coat of arms is displayed

-ese [< L. *-ensis*] *a suffix meaning:* **1.** (a native or inhabitant) of [Portuguese] **2.** (in) the language of [Chinese]

Es·ki·mo (es′kə mō′) *n.* [< Fr. < Algonquian] **1.** *pl.* **-mos′, -mo′** a member of a native N. American people living in Greenland, N Canada, Alaska, etc. **2.** either of their two languages —*adj.* of the Eskimos, their language, etc. —**Es′ki·mo′an** *adj.*

Eskimo dog a strong breed of dog used by the Eskimos to pull sleds

e·soph·a·gus (i säf′ə gəs) *n., pl.* **-gi′** (-jī′) [< Gr. *oisein*, to be going to carry + *phagein*, eat] the passage for food from the pharynx to the stomach

es·o·ter·ic (es′ə ter′ik) *adj.* [< Gr. *esōteros*, inner] **1.** understood by only a chosen few **2.** confidential —**es′o·ter′i·cal·ly** *adv.*

ESP extrasensory perception

esp., espec. especially

es·pa·drille (es′pə dril′) *n.* [Fr. < Sp. *esparto*, coarse grass] a casual shoe with a canvas upper and a rope or rubber sole

es·pal·ier (es pal′yər) *n.* [Fr. < L. *spatula*, spatula] **1.** a lattice or trellis on which trees and shrubs are trained to grow flat **2.** a plant, tree, etc. so trained

es·pe·cial (ə spesh′əl) *adj.* special; particular; exceptional —**es·pe′cial·ly** *adv.*

Es·pe·ran·to (es′pə rän′tō, -ran′-) *n.* [after pseudonym of its inventor] an artificial language for international use

es·pi·o·nage (es′pē ə näzh′, -nij′) *n.* [< Fr. < It. *spia*, a spy] the act or practice of spying

es·pla·nade (es′plə nād′, -näd′) *n.* [Fr. < It. < L. *explanare*, to level] a level, open space of ground; esp., a public walk or roadway

es·pous·al (i spou′z'l) *n.* **1.** [*often pl.*] a wedding **2.** an espousing (of some cause, idea, etc.)

es·pouse (i spouz′) *vt.* **-poused′, -pous′ing** [see SPOUSE] **1.** to marry **2.** to support or advocate (some cause, idea, etc.)

es·pres·so (es pres′ō) *n., pl.* **-sos** [It.] coffee made by forcing steam through finely ground coffee beans

es·prit de corps (es prē′ də kôr′) [Fr.] group spirit; sense of pride, honor, etc. in shared activities

es·py (ə spī′, es pī′) *vt.* **-pied′, -py′ing** [see SPY] to catch sight of; spy

-esque [Fr.] *a suffix meaning:* **1.** in the manner or style of **2.** like [*picturesque*]

es·quire (es′kwīr, ə skwīr′) *n.* [< LL. *scutarius*, shield-bearer] **1.** formerly, an attendant for a knight **2.** in England, a member of the gentry ranking just below a knight **3.** [E-] a title of courtesy, usually abbrev. **Esq., Esqr.,** placed after a man's surname

-ess [< Gr.] *a suffix meaning* female [*lioness*]

es·say (e sā′) *vt.* [< L. *exagium*, a weighing] to try —*n.* **1.** (es′ā, e sā′) an attempt; trial **2.** (es′ā) a short, personal literary composition of an analytical or interpretive kind —**es′say·ist** *n.*

es·sence (es′'ns) *n.* [< L. *esse*, to be] **1.** the basic nature (of something) **2.** *a)* a concentrated substance that keeps the flavor, fragrance, etc. of the plant, drug, etc. from which it is extracted *b)* a perfume

es·sen·tial (ə sen′shəl) *adj.* **1.** of or constituting the essence of something; basic **2.** absolutely necessary; indispensable —*n.* something necessary or fundamental —**es·sen′tial·ly** *adv.*

-est [< OE.] a suffix forming the superlative degree [*greatest*]

EST, E.S.T. Eastern Standard Time

est. 1. established **2.** estimate(d)

es·tab·lish (ə stab′lish) *vt.* [< L. *stabilis*, stable] **1.** to enact (a law, statute, etc.) permanently **2.** to found (a nation, business, etc.) **3.** to bring about **4.** to set up in a business, etc. **5.** to cause to be accepted **6.** to prove; demonstrate

es·tab′lish·ment *n.* **1.** an establishing or being established **2.** a thing established, as a business, household, etc. —**the Establishment** an inner circle holding decisive power in a nation, institution, etc.

es·tate (ə stāt′) *n.* [< OFr. *estat*, state] **1.** a condition or stage of life **2.** property; posses-

sions **3.** an individually owned piece of land containing a residence

es·teem (ə stēm′) *vt.* [< L. *aestimare*, to value] **1.** to value highly; respect **2.** to consider —*n.* favorable opinion; high regard

es·ter (es′tər) *n.* [G. < *essig*, vinegar + *äther*, ether] an organic compound formed by the reaction of an acid and an alcohol

Es·ther (es′tər) *Bible* the Jewish wife of a Persian king: she saved her people from slaughter

es·thete (es′thēt′) *n. same as* AESTHETE —**es·thet′ic** (-thet′ik) *adj.*

es·thet′ics (-thet′iks) *n.pl. same as* AESTHETICS

es·ti·ma·ble (es′tə mə b'l) *adj.* worthy of esteem —**es′ti·ma·bly** *adv.*

es·ti·mate (es′tə māt′) *vt.* **-mat′ed, -mat′ing** [see ESTEEM] **1.** to form an opinion about **2.** to determine generally (size, cost, etc.) —*vi.* to make an estimate —*n.* (-mit) **1.** a general calculation; esp., an approximate computation of probable cost **2.** an opinion or judgment

es′ti·ma′tion *n.* **1.** an estimating **2.** an opinion or judgment **3.** esteem; regard

es·trange (ə strānj′) *vt.* **-tranged′, -trang′ing** [< L. *extraneus*, strange] to turn (a person) from an affectionate or friendly attitude to an indifferent or hostile one; alienate —**es·trange′ment** *n.*

es·tro·gen (es′trə jən) *n.* [< Gr. *oistros*, frenzy] any of several female sex hormones

es·tu·ar·y (es′chōō wer′ē) *n., pl.* **-ies** [< L. *aestus*, the tide] the wide mouth of a river, where the tide meets the current

-et [< OFr.] *a suffix meaning* little [*islet*]

e·ta (āt′ə, ēt′ə) *n.* the seventh letter of the Greek alphabet (H, η)

et al. [L. *et alii*] and others

et cet·er·a (et set′ər ə, set′rə) [L.] and others; and so forth: abbrev. **etc.**

etch (ech) *vt.* [< MHG. *ezzen*, to eat] to make (a drawing, design, etc.) on (metal plates, glass, etc.) by the action of an acid

etch′ing *n.* **1.** an etched plate, drawing, etc. **2.** a print made from an etched plate **3.** the art of making such drawings, etc.

e·ter·nal (i tur′n'l) *adj.* [< L. *aevum*, an age] **1.** without beginning or end **2.** forever the same **3.** seeming never to stop —**the Eternal** God — **e·ter′nal·ly** *adv.*

e·ter·ni·ty (i tur′nə tē) *n., pl.* **-ties 1.** the state or fact of being eternal **2.** infinite time **3.** a long period of time that seems endless **4.** the endless time after death

e·ther (ē′thər) *n.* [< Gr. *aithein*, to burn] **1.** the upper regions of space **2.** a volatile, colorless, highly flammable liquid, used as an anesthetic and a solvent **3.** an invisible substance once thought to pervade space

e·the·re·al (i thir′ē əl) *adj.* **1.** very light; airy; delicate **2.** not earthly; heavenly

eth·i·cal (eth′i k'l) *adj.* [< Gr. *ēthos*, character] **1.** having to do with ethics or morality; of or conforming to moral standards **2.** conforming to professional standards of conduct —**eth′i·cal·ly** *adv.*

eth·ics (eth′iks) *n.pl.* [see prec.] **1.** [*with sing. v.*] the study of standards of conduct and moral judgment **2.** the system of morals of a particular person, religion, group, etc.

E·thi·o·pi·an (ē′thē ō′pē ən) *adj.* of Ethiopia, its people, etc. —*n.* a native or inhabitant of Ethiopia

eth·nic (eth′nik) *adj.* [< Gr. *ethnos*, nation] of any of the basic divisions of mankind or of a heterogeneous population, as distinguished by customs, language, etc.: also **eth′ni·cal** —**eth′ni·cal·ly** *adv.*

eth·nol·o·gy (eth näl′ə jē) *n.* [< Gr. *ethnos*, nation + -LOGY] the branch of anthropology that deals with the distribution, characteristics, culture, etc. of various peoples —**eth′no·log′i·cal** (-nə läj′i k'l) *adj.* —**eth′no·log′i·cal·ly** *adv.* —**eth·nol′o·gist** *n.*

eth·yl (eth′'l) *n.* [< ETHER] the hydrocarbon radical which forms the base of common alcohol, ether, etc.

ethyl alcohol *same as* ALCOHOL (sense 1)

eth·yl·ene (eth′ə lēn′) *n.* [< ETHYL] a colorless, flammable, gaseous hydrocarbon, used as a fuel, an anesthetic, etc.

e·ti·ol·o·gy (ēt′ē äl′ə jē) *n., pl.* **-gies** [< Gr. *aitia*, cause + -LOGY] 1. the science of causes or origins 2. *Med.* the causes of a disease —**e′ti·o·log′ic** (-ə läj′ik) *adj.*

et·i·quette (et′i kət, -ket′) *n.* [Fr. *étiquette*, a ticket] the forms, manners, etc. conventionally acceptable or required in social relations

E·trus·can (i trus′kən) *adj.* of an ancient country (**Etruria**) in what is now WC Italy

et seq. [L. *et sequens*] and the following

-ette [Fr.] *a suffix meaning:* 1. little [*dinette*] 2. female [*majorette*]

é·tude (ā′tōōd) *n.* [Fr., STUDY] a musical composition for a solo instrument, designed to give practice in some special technique

ETV educational television

et·y·mol·o·gy (et′ə mäl′ə jē) *n., pl.* **-gies** [< Gr. *etymos*, true + -LOGY] 1. the origin and development of a word, phrase, etc. 2. the branch of linguistics dealing with this —Abbrev. etym. —**et′y·mo·log′i·cal** (-mə läj′ə k'l) *adj.* —**et′y·mol′o·gist** *n.*

eu- [Fr. < Gr.] *a prefix meaning* good, well [*eugenic*]

eu·ca·lyp·tus (yōō′kə lip′təs) *n., pl.* **-tus·es, -ti** (-tī) [< EU- + Gr. *kalyptos*, covered] an Australian evergreen related to the myrtle, valued for timber and oil

Eu·cha·rist (yōō′kə rist) *n.* [< Gr. *eucharistia*, gratitude] 1. *same as* HOLY COMMUNION 2. the consecrated bread and wine used in Holy Communion —**Eu′cha·ris′tic** *adj.*

eu·chre (yōō′kər) *n.* [< ?] a card game played with thirty-two cards

eu·gen·ics (yoo jen′iks) *n.pl.* [*with sing. v.*] [< Gr. *eu-*, good + *genesis*, birth] the movement to improve the human species by control of hereditary factors in mating —**eu·gen′ic** *adj.* —**eu·gen′i·cal·ly** *adv.*

eu·lo·gize (yōō′lə jīz′) *vt.* **-gized′, -giz′ing** to praise as in a eulogy —**eu′lo·gist** *n.*

eu′lo·gy (-jē) *n., pl.* **-gies** [< Gr. *eulegein*, speak well of] 1. speech or writing in praise; esp., a funeral oration 2. high praise —**eu′lo·gis′tic** (-jis′tik) *adj.* —**eu′lo·gis′ti·cal·ly** *adv.*

eu·nuch (yōō′nək) *n.* [< Gr. *eunē*, a bed + *echein*, keep] a castrated man

eu·phe·mism (yōō′fə miz′m) *n.* [< Gr. *eu-*, good + *phanai*, speak] 1. the use of a less direct word or phrase for one considered offensive 2. a word or phrase so substituted (Ex.: *remains* for *corpse*) —**eu′phe·mis′tic** *adj.* —**eu′phe·mis′ti·cal·ly** *adv.*

eu·pho·ni·ous (yoo fō′nē əs) *adj.* having a pleasant sound; harmonious

eu·pho·ny (yōō′fə nē) *n., pl.* **-nies** [< Gr. *eu-*, well + *phōnē*, voice] a pleasant combination of agreeable sounds, as in speech

eu·pho·ri·a (yoo fôr′ē ə) *n.* [< Gr. *eu-*, well + *pherein*, to bear] a feeling of well-being or high spirits —**eu·phor′ic** *adj.*

eu·phu·ism (yōō′fyoo wiz′m) *n.* [< *Euphues*, character in works by J. Lyly, 16th-c. Eng.

author] 1. a high-flown style of speaking or writing 2. an instance of this

Eur·a·sian (yoo rā′zhən) *adj.* of European and Asian descent —*n.* a Eurasian person

eu·re·ka (yoo rē′kə) *interj.* [< Gr.] I have found (it): an exclamation of triumphant achievement

Eu·ro·pe·an (yoor′ə pē′ən) *adj.* of Europe, its people, etc. —*n.* a native of Europe

eu·ryth·mics (yoo rith′miks) *n.pl.* [*with sing. v.*] [< Gr. *eu-*, well + *rhythmos*, rhythm] the art of performing bodily movements in rhythm

Eu·sta·chi·an tube (yoo stā′shən, -kē ən) [after B. *Eustachio*, 16th-c. It. anatomist] a slender tube between the middle ear and the pharynx

eu·tha·na·sia (yōō′thə nā′zhə) *n.* [< Gr. *eu-*, well + *thanatos*, death] act of causing death painlessly to end suffering

e·vac·u·ate (i vak′yoo wāt′) *vt.* **-at′ed, -at′ing** [< L. *e-*, out + *vacuus*, empty] 1. to make empty 2. to discharge (bodily waste) 3. to withdraw from; remove —*vi.* 1. to withdraw 2. to discharge bodily waste —**e·vac′u·a′tion** *n.* —**e·vac′u·ee′** (-wē′) *n.*

e·vade (i vād′) *vi., vt.* **e·vad′ed, e·vad′ing** [< Fr. < L. *e-*, out + *vadere*, go] 1. to avoid or escape (from) by deceit or cleverness 2. to avoid doing or answering directly

e·val·u·ate (i val′yoo wāt′) *vt.* **-at′ed, -at′ing** [< Fr. < L. *ex-*, out + *valere*, be worth] 1. to find the value or amount of 2. to appraise —**e·val′u·a′tion** *n.*

ev·a·nes·cent (ev′ə nes′'nt) *adj.* [< L. *e-*, out + *vanescere*, vanish] tending to fade away; vanishing; fleeting —**ev′a·nes′cence** *n.*

e·van·gel·i·cal (ē′van jel′i k'l, ev′ən-) *adj.* [< Gr. *eu-*, well + *angelos*, messenger] 1. of or according to the Gospels or the New Testament 2. of those Protestant churches that emphasize salvation by faith Also **e′van·gel·ic** —**e′van·gel′i·cal·ly** *adv.*

e·van′gel·ist *n.* 1. [E-] any of the four writers of the Gospels 2. anyone who evangelizes; esp., a traveling preacher; revivalist —**e·van′gel·ism** *n.*

e·van′gel·ize *vt.* **-ized′, -iz′ing** 1. to preach the gospel to 2. to convert to Christianity —*vi.* to preach the gospel

e·vap·o·rate (i vap′ə rāt′) *vt.* **-rat′ed, -rat′ing** [< L. *e-*, out + *vapor*, vapor] 1. to change (a liquid or solid) into vapor 2. to remove moisture from (milk, etc.), as by heating, so as to get a concentrated product —*vi.* 1. to become vapor 2. to give off vapor 3. to vanish —**e·vap′o·ra′tion** *n.* —**e·vap′o·ra′tor** *n.*

e·va·sion (i vā′zhən) *n.* 1. an evading; specif., an avoiding of a duty, question, etc. by deceit or cleverness 2. a way of doing this; subterfuge

e·va′sive (-siv) *adj.* 1. tending or seeking to evade; not straightforward; tricky 2. elusive —**e·va′sive·ness** *n.*

Eve (ēv) *Bible* Adam's wife, the first woman

eve (ēv) *n.* [< OE. *æfen*, evening] 1. [Poet.] evening 2. [*often* E-] the evening or day before a holiday 3. the period immediately before some event

e·ven′ (ē′vən, -v'n) *adj.* [OE. *efne, efen*] 1. flat; level; smooth 2. not varying; constant [an *even* tempo] 3. calm; tranquil [an *even* temper] 4. in the same plane or line [*even* with the rim] 5. equally balanced 6. owing and being owed nothing 7. revenged 8. just; fair [an *even* trade] 9. equal in number, quantity, etc. 10. exactly divisible by two 11. exact [an *even* mile] —*adv.* 1. however improbable; indeed **2.** exactly; just *[it happened even as I expected]* **3.** still; yet *[even worse]* —*vt., vi.* to make, become, or be even —**break even** [Colloq.] to finish as neither a winner nor a loser —**even if** though —**e'ven·ly** *adv.* —**e'ven·ness** *n.*

e·ven² (ē'vən) *n.* [Poet.] evening

e'ven·hand'ed (-han'did) *adj.* impartial

eve·ning (ēv'niŋ) *n.* [< OE. *æfen*] the last part of day and early part of night

e·vent (i vent') *n.* [< L. *e-,* out + *venire,* come] **1.** an occurrence, esp. when important **2.** a result **3.** a particular contest in a program of sports —**in any event** in any case —**in the event of** in case of

e·vent'ful *adj.* **1.** full of outstanding events **2.** having an important outcome

e·ven·tide (ē'vən tīd') *n.* [Archaic] evening

e·ven·tu·al (i ven'choo wəl) *adj.* happening in the end; final —**e·ven'tu·al·ly** *adv.*

e·ven'tu·al'i·ty (-wal'ə tē) *n., pl.* **-ties** a possible event, outcome, or condition

e·ven'tu·ate' (-wāt') *vi.* **-at'ed, -at'ing** to happen in the end; result

ev·er (ev'ər) *adv.* [< OE. *æfre*] **1.** always **2.** at any time *[do you ever see her?]* **3.** at all; by any chance *[how can I ever repay you?]* **4.** [Colloq.] truly *[was she ever tired!]* —**ever so** [Colloq.] very

ev'er·glade' (-glād') *n.* swampland

ev'er·green' *adj.* having green leaves all year —*n.* such a plant or tree

ev'er·last'ing *adj.* eternal —*n.* eternity

ev'er·more' *adv.* forever; constantly

e·vert (ē vurt') *vt.* [< L. *e-,* out + *vertere,* to turn] to turn outward or inside out

ev·er·y (ev'rē, -ər ē) *adj.* [< OE. *æfre ælc,* lit., ever each] **1.** each, individually and separately **2.** all possible *[he was given every chance]* **3.** each interval of *[a pill every three hours]* —**every now and then** from time to time: also [Colloq.] **every so often** —**every other** each alternate, as the first, third, fifth, etc. —**every which way** [Colloq.] in complete disorder

ev'er·y·bod'y (-bäd'ē, -bud'ē) *pron.* every person; everyone

ev'er·y·day' *adj.* **1.** daily **2.** suitable for ordinary days **3.** usual; common

ev'er·y·one (-wən, -wun') *pron.* everybody

every one every person or thing

ev'er·y·thing' *pron.* every thing; all

ev'er·y·where' *adv.* in or to every place

e·vict (i vikt') *vt.* [see EVINCE] to remove (a tenant) from leased premises by legal procedure —**e·vic'tion** *n.*

ev·i·dence (ev'ə dəns) *n.* **1.** the state of being evident **2.** something that makes another thing evident; sign **3.** *Law* a statement of a witness, an object, etc. bearing on or establishing the point in question —*vt.* **-denced, -denc·ing** to make evident

ev'i·dent (-dənt) *adj.* [< L. *e-,* from + *videre,* see] easy to see or perceive; clear

e·vil (ē'v'l) *adj.* [OE. *yfel*] **1.** morally bad or wrong; wicked **2.** harmful; injurious **3.** unlucky; disastrous —*n.* **1.** wickedness; sin **2.** anything causing harm, pain, etc.

e'vil·do'er (-dōō'ər) *n.* one who does evil

e·vince (i vins') *vt.* **e·vinced', e·vinc'ing** [< L. *e-,* intens. + *vincere,* conquer] to show plainly (a quality, feeling, etc.)

e·vis·cer·ate (i vis'ə rāt') *vt.* **-at'ed, -at'ing** [< L. *e-,* out + *viscera,* VISCERA] **1.** to remove the entrails from **2.** to deprive of an essential part —**e·vis'cer·a'tion** *n.*

e·voke (i vōk') *vt.* **e·voked', e·vok'ing** [< Fr. < L. *e-,* out + *vox,* the voice] to call forth; elicit

(a response, etc.) —**ev·o·ca·tion** (ev'ə kā'shən) *n.* —**e·voc·a·tive** (i väk'ə tiv) *adj.*

ev·o·lu·tion (ev'ə lōō'shən) *n.* [see EVOLVE] **1.** an unfolding; process of development **2.** a thing evolved **3.** a movement that is part of a series **4.** *Biol. a)* the development of a species, organism, etc. from its original to its present state *b)* a theory that all species developed from earlier forms —**ev'o·lu'tion·ar'y** *adj.* —**ev'·o·lu'tion·ist** *n., adj.*

e·volve (i välv') *vt., vi.* **e·volved', e·volv'ing** [< L. *e-,* out + *volvere,* to roll] **1.** to unfold; develop gradually **2.** to develop by evolution

ewe (yōō) *n.* [OE. *eowu*] a female sheep

ew·er (yōō'ər) *n.* [< L. *aqua,* water] a large, wide-mouthed water pitcher

ex- [< OFr. or L.] *a prefix meaning:* **1.** from, out *[expel]* **2.** beyond *[excess]* **3.** thoroughly *[exterminate]* **4.** upward *[exalt]* **5.** former *[ex-president]*

Ex. Exodus

ex. **1.** example **2.** except(ed)

ex·ac·er·bate (ig zas'ər bāt') *vt.* **-bat'ed, -bat'-ing** [< L. *ex-,* intens. + *acerbus,* harsh] **1.** to aggravate (disease, pain, etc.) **2.** to irritate —**ex·ac'er·ba'tion** *n.*

ex·act (ig zakt') *adj.* [< L. *ex-,* out + *agere,* to do] **1.** having or requiring accuracy **2.** without variation; precise —*vt.* **1.** to extort **2.** to demand and get —**ex·act'ly** *adv.* —**ex·act'ness** *n.*

ex·act'ing *adj.* **1.** making severe demands; strict **2.** demanding great care, effort, etc.; arduous —**ex·act'ing·ly** *adv.*

ex·ac'tion (-zak'shən) *n.* **1.** an exacting **2.** an extortion **3.** something exacted

ex·ac'ti·tude' (-tə tōōd') *n.* the quality of being exact; accuracy

ex·ag·ger·ate (ig zaj'ə rāt') *vt., vi.* **-at'ed, -at'-ing** [< L. *ex-,* out + *agger,* a heap] to think or tell of (something) as greater than it is; overstate —**ex·ag'ger·a'tion** *n.*

ex·alt (ig zôlt') *vt.* [< L. *ex-,* out + *altus,* high] **1.** to raise in status, dignity, etc. **2.** to praise; glorify **3.** to elate —**ex·al·ta·tion** (eg'zôl tā'shən) *n.*

ex·am·i·na·tion (ig zam'ə nā'shən) *n.* **1.** an examining or being examined **2.** a set of test questions: also [Colloq.] **ex·am'**

ex·am·ine (ig zam'ən) *vt.* **-ined, -in·ing** [< L. *examinare,* weigh] **1.** to look at critically or methodically; investigate; inspect **2.** to test by questioning —**ex·am'i·nee'** *n.* —**ex·am'in·er** *n.*

ex·am·ple (ig zam'p'l) *n.* [< L *eximere,* take out] **1.** something showing the character of the rest; sample **2.** a case that serves as a warning **3.** a model; pattern **4.** an instance illustrating a principle

ex·as·per·ate (ig zas'pə rāt') *vt.* **-at'ed, -at'ing** [< L. *ex-,* out + *asper,* rough] to annoy very much —**ex·as'per·a'tion** *n.*

ex·ca·vate (eks'kə vāt') *vt.* **-vat'ed, -vat'ing** [< L. *ex-,* out + *cavus,* hollow] **1.** to make a hole or cavity in **2.** to form (a tunnel, etc.) by hollowing out **3.** to unearth **4.** to dig out (earth, etc.) —**ex'ca·va'tion** *n.* —**ex'ca·va'tor** *n.*

ex·ceed (ik sēd') *vt.* [< L. *ex-,* out + *cedere,* go] **1.** to go or be beyond (a limit, etc.) **2.** to be more or greater than; surpass

ex·ceed'ing *adj.* surpassing; extraordinary; extreme —**ex·ceed'ing·ly** *adv.*

ex·cel (ik sel') *vt., vi.* **-celled', -cel'ling** [< L. *ex-,* out of + *-cellere,* to rise] to be better or greater than (another or others)

ex·cel·lence (ek's'l əns) *n.* **1.** an excelling; superiority **2.** a particular virtue **3.** [E-] *same as* EXCELLENCY

ex'cel·len·cy (-ən sē) *n., pl.* **-cies 1.** [E-] a title of honor for certain dignitaries, as an ambassador 2. *same as* EXCELLENCE

ex·cel·lent *adj.* [see EXCEL] outstandingly good of its kind; exceptional —**ex′cel·lent·ly** *adv.*

ex·cel·si·or (ek sel′sē ôr′) *interj.* [see EXCEL] onward and upward! —*n.* (ik sel′sē ər) long, thin wood shavings used for packing

ex·cept (ik sept′) *vt.* [< L. *ex-*, out + *capere*, take] to leave out or take out; exclude —*prep.* other than; but —*conj.* [Colloq.] were it not that; only —**except for** if it were not for **ex·cept′ing** *prep., conj. same as* EXCEPT

ex·cep′tion *n.* 1. an excepting 2. a person or thing different from others of the same class; case to which a rule does not apply 3. an objection

ex·cep′tion·a·ble *adj.* liable to exception

ex·cep′tion·al *adj.* 1. unusual; esp., unusually good 2. requiring special education, as because mentally handicapped —**ex·cep′tion·al·ly** *adv.*

ex·cerpt (ik surpt′) *vt.* [< L. *ex-*, out + *carpere*, to pick] to select or quote (passages from a book, etc.); extract —*n.* (ek′surpt′) a passage selected or quoted; extract

ex·cess (ik ses′, ek′ses′) *n.* [see EXCEED] 1. action that goes beyond a reasonable limit 2. an amount greater than is necessary 3. the amount by which one thing exceeds another; surplus —*adj.* (*usually* ek′ses′) extra or surplus —**in excess of** more than

ex·ces′sive *adj.* too much; immoderate

ex·change (iks chānj′) *vt., vi.* -**changed′**, -**chang′ing** [see EX- & CHANGE] 1. to give or receive (something) *for* another thing; trade; barter 2. to interchange (similar things) —*n.* 1. an exchanging; interchange, trade, etc. 2. a thing exchanged 3. a place for exchanging [a stock *exchange*] 4. a central office providing telephone service 5. the value of one currency in terms of another —**ex·change′a·ble** *adj.*

ex·cheq·uer (iks chek′ər, eks′chek-) *n.* [< ML. *scaccarium*, chessboard: accounts of revenue were kept on a squared board] 1. a national treasury 2. funds; finances

ex·cise[1] (ek′sīz) *n.* [ult. < L. *assidere*, assist (in office)] a tax on various commodities, as tobacco, within a country: also **excise tax**

ex·cise[2] (ik sīz′) *vt.* -**cised′**, -**cis·ing** [< L. *ex-*, out + *caedere*, to cut] to remove by cutting away —**ex·ci′sion** (-sizh′ən) *n.*

ex·cit·a·ble (ik sīt′ə b'l) *adj.* easily excited — **ex·cit′a·bil′i·ty** *n.* —**ex·cit′a·bly** *adv.*

ex·cite (ik sīt′) *vt.* -**cit′ed**, -**cit′ing** [< L. *ex-*, out + *ciere*, to call] 1. to make active; stimulate 2. to arouse; provoke 3. to arouse the feelings of —**ex·ci·ta·tion** (ek′sī tā′shən, -si-) —**ex·cit′ed** *adj.*

ex·cite′ment *n.* 1. an exciting or being excited 2. something that excites

ex·cit′ing *adj.* causing excitement; stirring, thrilling, etc. —**ex·cit′ing·ly** *adv.*

ex·claim (iks klām′) *vi., vt.* [< Fr. < L. *ex-*, out + *clamare*, to shout] to cry out; speak or say suddenly and excitedly

ex·cla·ma·tion (eks′klə mā′shən) *n.* 1. an exclaiming 2. something exclaimed —**ex·clam·a·to·ry** (iks klam′ə tôr′ē) *adj.*

exclamation mark (or **point**) a mark (!) used in punctuating to show surprise, strong feeling, etc.

ex·clude (iks klōōd′) *vt.* -**clud′ed**, -**clud′ing** [< L. *ex-*, out + *claudere*, to close] 1. to keep out; reject 2. to put out; force out; expel —**ex·clu′sion** (-klōō′zhən) *n.*

ex·clu·sive (-klōō′siv) *adj.* 1. excluding all others 2. not shared or divided; sole [an *exclusive* right] 3. excluding certain people, as for

social reasons —**exclusive of** not including —**ex·clu′sive·ly** *adv.*

ex·com·mu·ni·cate (eks′kə myōō′nə kāt′) *vt.* -**cat′ed**, -**cat′ing** to exclude from communion with a church —**ex′com·mu′ni·ca′tion** *n.*

ex·co·ri·ate (ik skôr′ē āt′) *vt.* -**at′ed**, -**at′ing** [< L. *ex-*, off + *corium*, the skin] to denounce harshly —**ex·co′ri·a′tion** *n.*

ex·cre·ment (eks′krə mənt) *n.* waste matter excreted from the bowels

ex·cres·cence (iks kres′'ns) *n.* [< L. *ex-*, out + *crescere*, grow] an abnormal outgrowth, as a bunion —**ex·cres′cent** *adj.*

ex·crete (iks krēt′) *vt., vi.* -**cret′ed**, -**cret′ing** [< L. *ex-*, out of + *cernere*, sift] to eliminate (body waste) —**ex·cre′tion** *n.* —**ex·cre·to·ry** (eks′krə tôr′ē) *adj.*

ex·cru·ci·at·ing (iks krōō′shē āt′iŋ) *adj.* [< L. *ex-*, intens. + *cruciare*, crucify] 1. intensely painful; agonizing 2. intense or extreme [*excruciating* care]

ex·cul·pate (eks′kəl pāt′) *vt.* -**pat′ed**, -**pat′ing** [< L. *ex-*, out + *culpa*, fault] to free from blame —**ex′cul·pa′tion** *n.*

ex·cur·sion (ik skur′zhən) *n.* [< L. *ex-*, out + *currere*, to run] 1. a short trip, as for pleasure 2. a round trip at reduced rates 3. a digression

ex·cuse (ik skyōōz′) *vt.* -**cused′**, -**cus′ing** [< L. *ex-*, from + *causa*, a charge] 1. to free of blame 2. to apologize or give reasons for 3. to overlook (an offense or fault) 4. to release from an obligation, etc. 5. to permit to leave 6. to justify —*n.* (-skyōōs′) 1. a defense of some action; apology 2. something that excuses 3. a pretext —**excuse oneself** 1. to apologize 2. to ask for permission to leave —**ex·cus′a·ble** *adj.*

ex·e·cra·ble (ek′si krə b'l) *adj.* [see EXECRATE] abominable —**ex′e·cra·bly** *adv.*

ex·e·crate (ek′si krāt′) *vt.* -**crat′ed**, -**crat′ing** [< L. *ex-*, out + *sacrare*, consecrate] 1. to denounce scathingly 2. to loathe; abhor —**ex′e·cra′tion** *n.*

ex·e·cute (ek′sə kyōōt′) *vt.* -**cut′ed**, -**cut′ing** [< L. *ex-*, intens. + *sequi*, follow] 1. to carry out; do 2. to administer (laws, etc.) 3. to put to death by legal sentence 4. to create in accordance with a plan, etc. 5. to make valid (a deed, will, etc.) —**ex′e·cu′tion** *n.*

ex′e·cu′tion·er *n.* one who carries out a court-imposed death penalty

ex·ec·u·tive (ig zek′yə tiv) *adj.* 1. of or capable of carrying out duties, managing affairs, etc. 2. empowered to administer (laws, government affairs, etc.) —*n.* 1. the branch of government administering the laws and affairs of a nation 2. one who administers or manages affairs

ex·ec·u·tor (ig zek′yə tər) *n.* a person appointed to carry out the provisions of another's will

ex·e·ge·sis (ek′sə jē′sis) *n., pl.* -**ses** (-sēz) [< Gr. *ex-*, out + *hēgeisthai*, to guide] analysis or interpretation of a word, passage, etc., as in the Bible

ex·em·plar (ig zem′plär, -plər) *n.* [< L. *exemplum*, EXAMPLE] 1. a model; pattern 2. a typical specimen

ex·em·pla·ry (-plə rē) *adj.* serving as a model or example [an *exemplary* life]

ex·em·pli·fy (ig zem′plə fī′) *vt.* -**fied′**, -**fy′ing** [< L. *exemplum*, example + *facere*, to make] to show by example —**ex·em′pli·fi·ca′tion** *n.*

ex·empt (ig zempt′) *vt.* [< L. *ex-*, out + *emere*, take] to free from a rule or obligation which applies to others —*adj.* freed from a usual rule, duty, etc. —**ex·emp′tion** *n.*

ex·er·cise (ek′sər sīz′) *n.* [< L. *exercere*, to

put to work] **1.** active use or operation **2.** performance (of duties, etc.) **3.** activity for developing the body or mind **4.** a task for developing a skill **5.** [*pl.*] a program of speeches, etc. —*vt.* -**cised′, -cis′ing 1.** to use; employ **2.** to use so as to develop or train **3.** to worry or perplex **4.** to exert (influence, etc.) — *vi.* to do exercises

ex·ert (ig zurt′) *vt.* [< L. *exserere*, stretch out] **1.** to put into action **2.** to apply (oneself) with great effort —**ex·er′tion** *n.*

ex·hale (eks hāl′) *vt., vi.* -**haled′, -hal′ing** [< Fr. < L. *ex-*, out + *halare*, breathe] **1.** to breathe forth (air) **2.** to give off (vapor, etc.) —**ex·ha·la·tion** (eks′hə lā′shən) *n.*

ex·haust (ig zôst′) *vt.* [< L. *ex-*, out + *haurire*, to draw] **1.** to draw off or let out (air, gas, etc.), as from a container **2.** to use up **3.** to empty completely; drain **4.** to tire out **5.** to deal with thoroughly —*n.* **1.** the discharge of used steam, gas, etc. from an engine **2.** the pipe through which such steam, etc. is released **3.** fumes, etc. given off —**ex·haust′i·ble** *adj.*

ex·haus·tion (ig zôs′chən) *n.* **1.** an exhausting **2.** great fatigue

ex·haus′tive *adj.* leaving nothing out

ex·hib·it (ig zib′it) *vt.* [< L. *ex-*, out + *habere*, to hold] **1.** to show; display **2.** to present to public view —*vi.* to put art objects, etc. on public display —*n.* **1.** a display **2.** a thing exhibited **3.** *Law* an object produced as evidence in court —**ex·hib′i·tor, ex·hib′it·er** *n.*

ex·hi·bi·tion (ek′sə bish′ən) *n.* **1.** an exhibiting **2.** that which is exhibited **3.** a public showing

ex′hi·bi′tion·ism *n.* **1.** a tendency to call attention to oneself or to show off **2.** *Psychol.* a tendency to expose bodily parts conventionally concealed —**ex′hi·bi′tion·ist** *n.*

ex·hil·a·rate (ig zil′ə rāt′) *vt.* -**rat′ed, -rat′ing** [< L. *ex-*, intens. + *hilaris*, glad] **1.** to make merry or lively **2.** to stimulate —**ex·hil′a·ra′tion** *n.*

ex·hort (ig zôrt′) *vt., vi.* [< L. *ex-*, out + *hortari*, to urge] to urge earnestly; entreat —**ex·hor·ta·tion** (eg′zôr tā′shən, ek′sər-) *n.*

ex·hume (ig zyōōm′) *vt.* -**humed′, -hum′ing** [< L. *ex-*, out + *humus*, the ground] to dig out of the earth; disinter —**ex·hu·ma·tion** (eks′hyōō mā′shən) *n.*

ex·i·gen·cy (ek′sə jən sē) *n., pl.* -**cies** [< L. *ex-*, out + *agere*, to do] **1.** urgency **2.** a situation calling for immediate attention **3.** [*pl.*] pressing needs —**ex′i·gent** *adj.*

ex·ile (eg′zīl, ek′sīl) *n.* [< L. *exul*, an exile] **1.** a prolonged living away from one's country, usually enforced; banishment **2.** a person in exile —*vt.* -**iled, -il·ing** to force into exile; banish

ex·ist (ig zist′) *vi.* [< Fr. < L. *ex-*, forth + *sistere*, to set, place] **1.** to have reality or being; be **2.** to occur or be present (*in*) **3.** to continue being; live —**ex·ist′ent** *adj.*

ex·ist′ence *n.* **1.** the state or fact of being **2.** life; living **3.** occurrence

ex·is·ten·tial (eg′zis ten′shəl) *adj.* **1.** of existence **2.** of existentialism

ex′is·ten′tial·ism *n.* a philosophical movement stressing individual existence and holding that man is totally free and responsible for his acts —**ex′is·ten′tial·ist** *adj., n.*

ex·it (eg′zit, ek′sit) *n.* [< L. *ex-*, out + *ire*, go] **1.** an actor's departure from the stage **2.** a going out; departure **3.** a way out —*vi.* to leave a place; depart

exo- [< Gr. *exō*] *a prefix meaning* outside, outer, outer part

ex·o·dus (ek′sə dəs) *n.* [< Gr. *ex-*, out +

hodos, way] a going out or forth —[E-] **1.** the departure of the Israelites from Egypt (with *the*) **2.** the second book of the Pentateuch, which describes this

ex of·fi·ci·o (eks′ ə fish′ē ō′) [L., lit., from office] by virtue of one's office, or position

ex·on·er·ate (ig zän′ə rāt′) *vt.* -**at′ed, -at′ing** [< L. *ex-*, out + *onerare*, to load] to declare or prove blameless —**ex·on′er·a′tion** *n.*

ex·or·bi·tant (ig zôr′bə tənt) *adj.* [< L. *ex-*, out + *orbita*, a track) going beyond what is reasonable, just, etc.; excessive —**ex·or′bi·tance** *n.* —**ex·or′bi·tant·ly** *adv.*

ex·or·cise, ex·or·cize (ek′sôr sīz′) *vt.* -**cised′** or -**cized′, -cis′ing** or -**ciz′ing** [< Gr. *ex-*, out + *horkos*, oath] **1.** to expel (an evil spirit) by ritual, incantation, etc. **2.** to free from such a spirit —**ex·or′cism** (-siz′m) *n.* —**ex·or′cist** *n.*

ex·ot·ic (ig zät′ik) *adj.* [< Gr. *exō*, outside] **1.** foreign **2.** strangely beautiful, enticing, etc. —**ex·ot′i·cal·ly** *adv.*

ex·pand (ik spand′) *vt., vi.* [< L. *ex-*, out + *pandere*, to spread] **1.** to spread out; unfold **2.** to increase in size, etc.; enlarge

ex·panse (ik spans′) *n.* a large, open area or unbroken surface; wide extent

ex·pan·sion *n.* **1.** an expanding or being expanded **2.** an expanded thing or part **3.** the extent or degree of expansion

ex·pan·sive *adj.* **1.** that can expand **2.** broad; extensive **3.** demonstrative; open and friendly —**ex·pan′sive·ly** *adv.*

ex·pa·ti·ate (ik spā′shē āt′) *vi.* -**at′ed, -at′ing** [< L. *ex(s)patiari*, wander] to speak or write at length —**ex·pa′ti·a′tion** *n.*

ex·pa·tri·ate (eks pā′trē āt′; *for n., usually* -it) *vt.* -**at′ed, -at′ing** [< L. *ex*, out of + *patria*, fatherland] to exile —*n.* an expatriated person —**ex·pa′tri·a′tion** *n.*

ex·pect (ik spekt′) *vt.* [< L. *ex-*, out + *spectare*, to look] **1.** to look for as likely to occur or appear **2.** to look for as proper or necessary **3.** [Colloq.] to suppose; guess —**be expecting** [Colloq.] to be pregnant

ex·pect′an·cy *n., pl.* -**cies 1.** expectation **2.** that which is expected, esp. statistically

ex·pect′ant *adj.* expecting

ex·pec·ta·tion (ek′spek tā′shən) *n.* **1.** an expecting **2.** a thing looked forward to **3.** [*also pl.*] a reason for expecting something

ex·pec·to·rant (ik spek′tər ənt) *n.* a medicine that helps to bring up phlegm

ex·pec·to·rate (ik spek′tə rāt′) *vt., vi.* -**rat′ed, -rat′ing** [< L. *ex-*, out + *pectus*, breast] **1.** to cough up and spit out (phlegm, etc.) **2.** to spit —**ex·pec′to·ra′tion** *n.*

ex·pe·di·en·cy (ik spē′dē ən sē) *n., pl.* -**cies 1.** a being expedient; suitability **2.** self-interest **3.** an expedient Also **ex·pe′di·ence**

ex·pe·di·ent (-ənt) *adj.* [see EXPEDITE] **1.** useful for effecting a desired result; convenient **2.** based on or guided by self-interest —*n.* an expedient thing; means to an end —**ex·pe′di·ent·ly** *adv.*

ex·pe·dite (ek′spə dīt′) *vt.* -**dit′ed, -dit′ing** [< L. *expedire*, lit., to free the feet] **1.** to speed up the progress of **2.** to do quickly —**ex′pe·dit′er** *n.*

ex·pe·di·tion (ek′spə dish′ən) *n.* [see EXPEDITE] **1.** a journey, voyage, etc., as for exploration **2.** those on such a journey **3.** efficient speed —**ex′pe·di′tion·ar′y** *adj.*

ex′pe·di′tious (-dish′əs) *adj.* efficient and speedy; prompt —**ex′pe·di′tious·ly** *adv.*

ex·pel (ik spel′) *vt.* -**pelled′, -pel′ling** [< L. *ex-*, out + *pellere*, to thrust] **1.** to drive out by force **2.** to dismiss by authority

ex·pend (ik spend′) *vt.* [< L. *ex-*, out + *pendere*, weigh] 1. to spend 2. to use up
ex·pend′a·ble *adj.* 1. for expending 2. *Mil.* designating equipment (or men) to be used up (or sacrificed) in service
ex·pend·i·ture (ik spen′də chər) *n.* 1. an expending of money, time, etc. 2. the amount expended
ex·pense (ik spens′) *n.* [see EXPEND] 1. financial cost 2. any cost or sacrifice 3. [*pl.*] charges met with as in one's work
ex·pen′sive *adj.* costly; high-priced
ex·pe·ri·ence (ik spir′ē əns) *n.* [< L. *experiri*, to try] 1. the act of living through an event 2. anything or everything observed or lived through 3. *a)* training and personal participation *b)* knowledge, skill, etc. resulting from this —*vt.* **-enced, -enc·ing** to have experience of; undergo
ex·pe′ri·enced *adj.* 1. having had much experience 2. having learned from experience
ex·per·i·ment (ik sper′ə mənt) *n.* [see EXPERIENCE] a practical test or trial —*vi.* (*also* -ment′) to make an experiment —**ex·per′i·men′tal** *adj.* —**ex·per′i·men·ta′tion** (-mən tā′shən) *n.*
ex·pert (ek′spərt, ik spurt′) *adj.* [see EXPERIENCE] 1. very skillful 2. of or from an expert —*n.* (ek′spərt) one who is very skillful or well-informed in some special field —**ex′pert·ly** *adv.* —**ex′pert·ness** *n.*
ex·pert·ise (ek′spər tēz′) *n.* [Fr.] the skill, knowledge, judgment, etc. of an expert
ex·pi·ate (ek′spē āt′) *vt.* **-at′ed, -at′ing** [< L. *ex-*, out + *piare*, appease] to make amends for (wrongdoing or guilt); atone for —**ex′pi·a′tion** *n.* —**ex′pi·a′tor** *n.*
ex·pire (ik spīr′) *vt.* **-pired′, -pir′ing** [< L. *ex-*, out + *spirare*, breathe] to exhale (air) —*vi.* 1. to exhale air 2. to die 3. to end —**ex·pi·ra·tion** (ek′spə rā′shən) *n.*
ex·plain (ik splān′) *vt.* [< L. *ex-*, out + *planus*, level] 1. to make plain or understandable 2. to give the meaning of; expound 3. to account for —*vi.* to give an explanation —**ex·plain′a·ble** *adj.*
ex·pla·na·tion (eks′plə nā′shən) *n.* 1. an explaining 2. something that explains; interpretation, meaning, etc.
ex·plan·a·to·ry (ik splan′ə tôr′ē) *adj.* explaining or intended to explain
ex·ple·tive (eks′plə tiv) *n.* [< L. *ex-*, out + *plere*, to fill] an oath or exclamation
ex·pli·ca·ble (eks′pli kə b'l, iks plik′ə-) *adj.* [see EXPLICATE] that can be explained
ex·pli·cate (eks′pli kāt′) *vt.* **-cat′ed, -cat′ing** [< L. *ex-*, out + *plicare*, to fold] to explain fully —**ex′pli·ca′tion** *n.*
ex·plic·it (ik splis′it) *adj.* [see prec.] 1. clearly stated; definite 2. outspoken 3. plain to see — **ex·plic′it·ly** *adv.*
ex·plode (ik splōd′) *vt.* **-plod′ed, -plod′ing** [orig., to drive off the stage < L. *ex-*, off + *plaudere*, applaud] 1. to expose as false 2. to make burst with a loud noise 3. to cause a rapid, violent change in, as by chemical reaction —*vi.* 1. to burst noisily 2. to break forth noisily [to *explode* with anger] 3. to increase very rapidly
ex·ploit (eks′ploit) *n.* [see EXPLICATE] a daring act; bold deed —*vt.* (*usually* ik sploit′) 1. to make use of; utilize 2. to make unethical use of for one's own profit —**ex′ploi·ta′tion** *n.*
ex·plore (ik splôr′) *vt., vi.* **-plored′, -plor′ing** [< L. *ex-*, out + *plorare*, to cry out] 1. to examine (something) carefully; investigate 2. to travel in (a little-known region) for discovery

—**ex·plo·ra·tion** (eks′plə rā′shən) *n.* —**ex·plor′a·to′ry** (-ə tôr′ē) *adj.* —**ex·plor′er** *n.*
ex·plo·sion (ik splō′zhən) *n.* 1. an exploding; esp., a blowing up 2. the noise made by exploding 3. a noisy outburst 4. a sudden, widespread increase
ex·plo′sive (-siv) *adj.* 1. of, causing, or like an explosion 2. tending to explode —*n.* a substance that can explode, as gunpowder
ex·po·nent (ik spō′nənt) *n.* [see EXPOUND] 1. one who expounds or promotes (principles, etc.) 2. an example or symbol (*of* something) 3. (*usually* ek′spō′nənt) *Algebra* a symbol placed at the upper right of another symbol to show how many times the latter is to be used as a factor (Ex.: b² = b x b) —**ex·po·nen·tial** (eks′pō nen′shəl) *adj.*
ex·port (ik spôrt′, eks′pôrt) *vt.* [< L. *ex-*, out + *portare*, carry] to send (goods, etc.) to another country, esp. for sale —*n.* (eks′pôrt) 1. something exported 2. an exporting Also **ex′·por·ta′tion** —**ex·port′er** *n.*
ex·pose (ik spōz′) *vt.* **-posed′, -pos′ing** [see EXPOUND] 1. to lay open (*to* danger, attack, etc.) 2. to reveal; exhibit; make known 3. *Photog.* to subject (a sensitized film or plate) to actinic rays
ex·po·sé (eks′pō zā′) *n.* [Fr.] a public disclosure of a scandal, crime, etc.
ex·po·si·tion (eks′pə zish′ən) *n.* [see EXPOUND] 1. a detailed explanation 2. writing or speaking that explains 3. a large public exhibition
ex·pos·i·tor (ik späz′ə tər) *n.* one who expounds or explains
ex·pos′i·to′ry (-tôr′ē) *adj.* of or containing exposition; explanatory
ex post fac·to (eks pōst fak′tō) [L., from (the thing) done afterward] done or made afterward, esp. if retroactive
ex·pos·tu·late (ik späs′chə lāt′) *vi.* **-lat′ed, -lat′ing** [< L. *ex-*, intens. + *postulare*, to demand] to reason with a person earnestly, opposing his actions or intentions —**ex·pos′tu·la′tion** *n.* —**ex·pos′tu·la′tor** *n.*
ex·po·sure (ik spō′zhər) *n.* 1. an exposing or being exposed 2. facing position of a house, etc. [an eastern *exposure*] 3. frequent appearance before the public 4. the time during which photographic film is exposed 5. a section of film for one picture
ex·pound (ik spound′) *vt.* [< L. *ex-*, out + *ponere*, put] 1. to set forth; state in detail 2. to explain
ex·press (ik spres′) *vt.* [< L. *ex-*, out + *premere*, to press] 1. to squeeze out (juice, etc.) 2. to put into words; state 3. to reveal; show 4. to signify or symbolize 5. to send by express —*adj.* 1. stated; explicit 2. specific 3. exact 4. fast and direct [an *express* bus, highway, etc.] 5. of express (*n.* 2) —*adv.* by express —*n.* 1. an express bus, etc. 2. a service to transport goods rapidly 3. things sent by express
ex·pres′sion (-spresh′ən) *n.* 1. a putting into words; stating 2. a manner of expressing, esp. with eloquence 3. a particular word or phrase 4. a showing of feeling, character, etc. 5. a look, intonation, etc. that conveys meaning 6. a mathematical symbol or set of symbols
ex·pres′sion·ism *n.* an early 20th-cent. movement in art, drama, etc., using symbols, stylization, etc. to express inner experience —**ex·pres′sion·ist** *adj., n.* —**ex·pres′sion·is′tic** *adj.*
ex·pres′sive *adj.* 1. that expresses; indicative (*of*) 2. full of meaning or feeling
ex·press′ly *adv.* 1. plainly; definitely 2. especially; particularly

ex·press′way *n.* a divided highway for high-speed, through traffic

ex·pro·pri·ate (eks prō′prē āt′) *vt.* -at′ed, -at′-ing [< L. *ex-*, out + *proprius*, one's own] to take (land, property, etc.) from its owner, esp. for public use —**ex·pro′pri·a′tion** *n.* —**ex·pro′pri·a′tor** *n.*

ex·pul·sion (ik spul′shən) *n.* an expelling or being expelled —**ex·pul′sive** (-siv) *adj.*

ex·punge (ik spunj′) *vt.* -punged′, -pung′ing [< L. *ex-*, out + *pungere*, to prick] to erase or remove completely; delete

ex·pur·gate (eks′pər gāt′) *vt.* -gat′ed, -gat′ing [< L. *ex-*, out + *purgare*, cleanse] to remove passages considered obscene, etc. from (a book, etc.) —**ex′pur·ga′tion** *n.*

ex·qui·site (eks′kwi zit, ik skwiz′it) *adj.* [< L. *ex-*, out + *quaerere*, ask] 1. carefully or elaborately done 2. very beautiful, esp. in a delicate way 3. of highest quality 4. very intense; keen —**ex′qui·site·ly** *adv.*

ex·tant (ek′stənt, ik stant′) *adj.* [< L. *ex-*, out + *stare*, to stand] still existing

ex·tem·po·ra·ne·ous (ik stem′pə rā′nē əs) *adj.* [see EXTEMPORE] done, spoken, or speaking without preparation —**ex·tem′po·ra′ne·ous·ly** *adv.*

ex·tem·po·re (ik stem′pə rē) *adv., adj.* [L. < *ex*, out of + *tempus*, time] with little preparation; offhand

ex·tem′po·rize (-rīz′) *vi., vt.* -rized′, -riz′ing to speak, perform, etc. extempore; improvise —**ex·tem′po·ri·za′tion** *n.*

ex·tend (ik stend′) *vt.* [< L. *ex-*, out + *tendere*, to stretch] 1. to make longer; prolong 2. to enlarge in area, scope, etc.; expand 3. to stretch forth 4. to offer; grant 5. to make (oneself) work or try hard —*vi.* 1. to be extended 2. to reach or stretch —**ex·tend′er** *n.* —**ex·ten′si·ble** (-sten′sə b'l), **ex·tend′i·ble** *adj.*

ex·ten′sion (-sten′shən) *n.* 1. an extending or being extended 2. range; extent 3. a part forming a continuation or addition

ex·ten′sive (-siv) *adj.* having great extent; vast; comprehensive —**ex·ten′sive·ly** *adv.*

ex·tent (ik stent′) *n.* 1. the space, amount, or degree to which a thing extends; size 2. scope; limits 3. an extended space

ex·ten·u·ate (ik sten′yoo wāt′) *vt.* -at′ed, -at′-ing [< L. *ex-*, out + *tenuis*, thin] to make (an offense, etc.) seem less serious

ex·te·ri·or (ik stir′ē ər) *adj.* [see EXTERNAL] 1. on the outside; outer 2. for use on the outside 3. coming from without —*n.* an outside or outside surface

ex·ter·mi·nate (ik stur′mə nāt′) *vt.* -nat′ed, -nat′ing [< L. *ex-*, out + *terminus*, boundary] to destroy entirely; wipe out —**ex·ter′mi·na′tion** *n.* —**ex·ter′mi·na′tor** *n.*

ex·ter·nal (ik stur′n'l) *adj.* [< L. *externus*] 1. on the outside; outer 2. existing apart from the mind; material 3. coming from without 4. superficial 5. foreign —*n.* an outside surface or part —**ex·ter′nal·ly** *adv.*

ex·tinct (ik stiŋkt′) *adj.* [see EXTINGUISH] 1. having died down or burned out 2. no longer in existence

ex·tinc′tion *n.* 1. an extinguishing 2. a destroying or being destroyed 3. a dying out, as of a species of animal

ex·tin·guish (ik stiŋ′gwish) *vt.* [< L. *ex-*, out + *stinguere*, to extinguish] 1. to put out (a fire, etc.) 2. to destroy —**ex·tin′guish·er** *n.* —**ex·tin′guish·ment** *n.*

ex·tir·pate (ek′stər pāt′) *vt.* -pat′ed, -pat′ing [< L. *ex-*, out + *stirps*, root] 1. to pull up by the

roots 2. to destroy completely —**ex′tir·pa′tion** *n.*

ex·tol, ex·toll (ik stōl′) *vt.* -tolled′, -tol′ling [< L. *ex-*, up + *tollere*, raise] to praise highly; laud

ex·tort (ik stôrt′) *vt.* [< L. *ex-*, out + *torquere*, to twist] to get (money, etc.) *from* someone by force or threats

ex·tor′tion (-stôr′shən) *n.* 1. an extorting 2. something extorted —**ex·tor′tion·ate** *adj.* —**ex·tor′tion·er, ex·tor′tion·ist** *n.*

ex·tra (eks′trə) *adj.* [< L. *extra*, more than] more or better than normal, expected, etc.; additional —*n.* an extra person or thing; specif., *a*) a special newspaper edition for important news *b*) an extra benefit *c*) an actor hired by the day for a minor part —*adv.* more than usually *[extra* hot*]*

extra- [see EXTERNAL] *a prefix meaning* outside, beyond, besides

ex·tract (ik strakt′) *vt.* [< L. *ex-*, out + *trahere*, draw] 1. to draw out by effort 2. to obtain by pressing, distilling, etc. 3. to deduce; derive 4. to copy out or quote (a passage, etc.) —*n.* (eks′trakt) something extracted; specif., *a*) a concentrate *[vanilla extract] b*) an excerpt —**ex·trac′tor** *n.*

ex·trac′tion *n.* 1. an extracting, specif. of a tooth 2. origin; descent

ex·tra·cur·ric·u·lar (eks′trə kə rik′yə lər) *adj.* not part of the required curriculum

ex·tra·dite (eks′trə dīt′) *vt.* -dit′ed, -dit′ing [< L. *ex*, out + *traditio*, a surrender] to turn over (an alleged criminal, etc.) to the jurisdiction of another country, State, etc. —**ex′tra·di′tion** (-dish′ən) *n.*

ex·tra·ne·ous (ik strā′nē əs) *adj.* [< L. *ex·traneus*, foreign] 1. coming from outside; foreign 2. not pertinent; irrelevant

ex·traor·di·nar·y (ik strôr′d'n er′ē) *adj.* [< L. *extra ordinem*, out of the usual order] 1. not usual or ordinary 2. very unusual; exceptional —**ex·traor′di·nar′i·ly** *adv.*

ex·trap·o·late (ik strap′ə lāt′) *vt., vi.* -lat′ed, -lat′ing [see EXTRA- & INTERPOLATE] to estimate (something unknown) on the basis of known facts —**ex·trap′o·la′tion** *n.*

ex·tra·sen·so·ry (eks′trə sen′sər ē) *adj.* apart from normal sense perception

ex·trav·a·gant (ik strav′ə gənt) *adj.* [< L. *extra*, beyond + *vagari*, wander] 1. going beyond reasonable limits; excessive 2. costing or spending too much; wasteful —**ex·trav′a·gance** *n.*

ex·trav·a·gan·za (ik strav′ə gan′zə) *n.* [< It. *estravaganza*, extravagance] a spectacular, elaborate theatrical production

ex·treme (ik strēm′) *adj.* [< L. *exterus*, outer] 1. farthest away; utmost 2. very great; excessive 3. unconventional or radical, as in politics 4. very severe; drastic —*n.* 1. either of two things that are as different or as far as possible from each other 2. an extreme act, degree, state, etc. —**go to extremes** to be immoderate in speech or action —**in the extreme** to the utmost degree —**ex·treme′ly** *adv.*

ex·trem′ism (-iz′m) *n.* a being extreme, esp. in politics —**ex·trem′ist** *n.*

ex·trem·i·ty (ik strem′ə tē) *n., pl.* -ties 1. the outermost part; end 2. the greatest degree 3. extreme need, danger, etc. 4. an extreme measure 5. *[pl.]* the hands and feet

ex·tri·cate (eks′trə kāt′) *vt.* -cat′ed, -cat′ing [< L. *ex-*, out + *tricae*, vexations] to set free (*from* a net, difficulty, etc.) —**ex′tri·ca·ble** *adj.* —**ex′tri·ca′tion** *n.*

ex·trin·sic (ek strin′sik) *adj.* [< L. *exter*,

ex·tro·vert (eks′trə vurt′) *n.* [< L. *extra-*, outside + *vertere*, to turn] one whose interest is more in his environment and in other people than in himself —**ex′tro·ver′sion** (-vur′zhən) *n.* —**ex′tro·vert′ed** *adj.*

ex·trude (ik strōōd′) *vt.* -**trud′ed**, -**trud′ing** [< L. *ex-*, out + *trudere*, to thrust] to push or force out, as through a small opening —*vi.* to be extruded; esp., to protrude —**ex·tru′sion** (-strōō′zhən) *n.*

ex·u·ber·ant (ig zōō′bər ənt, -zyōō′-) *adj.* [< Fr. < L. *ex-*, intens. + *uberare*, bear abundantly] 1. growing profusely; luxuriant 2. full of life, vitality, or high spirits —**ex·u′ber·ance** *n.* —**ex·u′ber·ant·ly** *adv.*

ex·ude (ig zōōd′, -zyōōd′) *vt., vi.* -**ud′ed**, -**ud′-ing** [< L. *ex-*, out + *sudare*, to sweat] 1. to pass out in drops, as through pores; ooze 2. to seem to radiate [to *exude* joy] —**ex·u·da·tion** (eks′yə dā′shən) *n.*

ex·ult (ig zult′) *vi.* [< Fr. < L. *ex-*, intens. + *saltare*, to leap] to rejoice greatly; be jubilant; glory —**ex·ult′ant** *adj.* —**ex·ul·ta·tion** (eg′zəl tā′shən, ek′səl-) *n.*

eye (ī) *n.* [OE. *eage*] 1. the organ of sight in man and animals 2. *a)* the eyeball *b)* the iris [blue *eyes*] 3. the area around the eye [a black *eye*] 4. [*often pl.*] sight; vision 5. a look; glance 6. attention; observation 7. the power of judging, etc. by eyesight [an *eye* for distances] 8. [*often pl.*] judgment; opinion [in the *eyes* of the law] 9. a thing like an eye in shape or function 10. [Slang] a detective: esp. in private eye —*vt.* eyed, eye′ing or ey′ing to look at; observe —**have an eye for** to have a keen appreciation of —**keep an eye on** to look after —**lay** (or **set** or **clap**) **eyes on** to see; look at —**make eyes at** to look at flirtatiously —**see eye to eye** to agree completely —**with an eye to** paying attention to; considering

eye′ball′ *n.* the ball-shaped part of the eye, enclosed by the socket and eyelids

eye′brow′ *n.* the bony arch over each eye, or the hair growing on this

eye′ful′ (-fōōl′) *n.* 1. a full look at something 2. [Slang] one that looks striking

eye′glass′ *n.* 1. a lens to help faulty vision 2. [*pl.*] a pair of such lenses in a frame

eye′lash′ *n.* any of the hairs on the edge of the eyelid

eye′let (-lit) *n.* 1. a small hole for receiving a cord, hook, etc. 2. a metal ring, etc. for lining such a hole 3. a small hole edged by stitching in embroidered work

eye′lid′ *n.* either of the two folds of flesh that cover and uncover the eyeball

eye liner a cosmetic applied in a thin line to the eyelid at the base of the eyelashes

eye′-o′pen·er (-ō′p'n ər) *n.* a surprising piece of news, sudden realization, etc.

eye′piece′ *n.* in a telescope, microscope, etc., the lens nearest the viewer's eye

eye shadow a cosmetic, usually green or blue, applied to the upper eyelids

eye′sight′ *n.* 1. the power of seeing; sight 2. the range of vision

eye′sore′ *n.* a thing unpleasant to look at

eye′strain′ *n.* a tired or strained condition of the eye muscles

eye′tooth′ *n., pl.* -**teeth′** a canine tooth of the upper jaw

eye′wit′ness *n.* one who has himself seen a specific thing happen

ey·rie, ey·ry (er′ē, ir′ē) *n., pl.* -**ries** same as AERIE

F

F, f (ef) *n., pl.* **F's, f's** the sixth letter of the English alphabet

F (ef) *n.* 1. a grade indicating failing work or, sometimes, fair or average work 2. *Chem.* fluorine 3. *Music* the fourth tone in the scale of C major

F, F. 1. Fahrenheit 2. Friday

F., f. 1. feminine 2. folio(s) 3. following 4. *Music* forte 5. franc(s)

fa (fä) *n.* [< ML.] *Music* the fourth tone of the diatonic scale

fa·ble (fā′b'l) *n.* [< L. *fabula*, a story] 1. a fictitious story, usually about animals, meant to teach a moral lesson 2. a myth or legend

fa′bled *adj.* 1. legendary 2. unreal

fab·ric (fab′rik) *n.* [< L. *fabrica*, workshop] 1. a framework or structure 2. a material made from fibers or threads by weaving, felting, etc.

fab·ri·cate (fab′rə kāt′) *vt.* -**cat′ed**, -**cat′ing** [see prec.] 1. to make, construct, etc.; manufacture 2. to make up (a story, reason, etc.); invent —**fab′ri·ca′tion** *n.*

fab·u·lous (fab′yoo ləs) *adj.* [see FABLE] 1. of or like a fable; fictitious 2. incredible 3. [Colloq.] wonderful —**fab′u·lous·ly** *adv.*

fa·çade, fa·cade (fə säd′) *n.* [Fr. < It.: see FACE] 1. the front of a building 2. an imposing appearance concealing something inferior

face (fās) *n.* [< L. *facies*] 1. the front of the head 2. the expression of the countenance 3. the main or front surface 4. the surface that is marked, as of a clock 5. appearance; outward aspect 6. dignity; self-respect: usually in lose (or save) face —*vt.* faced, fac′ing 1. to turn, or have the face turned, toward 2. to confront with courage, etc. 3. to cover with a new surface —*vi.* to turn, or have the face turned, in a specified direction —**face to face** 1. confronting each other 2. in the presence (with *with*) —**face up to** to confront with courage —**In the face of** 1. in the presence of 2. in spite of —**make a face** to grimace —**on the face of It** apparently

face′less (-lis) *adj.* 1. lacking a face 2. lacking a distinct character; anonymous

face lifting plastic surgery to remove wrinkles, etc. from the face: also **face lift**

fac·et (fas′it) *n.* [see FACE] 1. any of the polished plane surfaces of a cut gem 2. any of the sides or aspects, as of a personality —*vt.* -**et·ed** or -**et·ted**, -**et·ing** or -**et·ting** to cut or make facets on

fa·ce·tious (fə sē′shəs) *adj.* [< Fr. < L. *facetus*, witty] straining to be funny, esp. at the wrong time —**fa·ce′tious·ly** *adv.*

face value 1. the value shown as on a bill or bond 2. the seeming value

fa·cial (fā′shəl) *adj.* of or for the face —*n.* a cosmetic treatment for facial skin

facial tissue a sheet of soft tissue paper used as a handkerchief, etc.

fac·ile (fas′'l) *adj.* [Fr. < L. *facere*, do] 1. easily done, achieved, etc. **2.** effortless; quick [a *facile* wit] **3.** superficial

fa·cil·i·tate (fə sil'ə tāt') *vt.* **-tat'ed, -tat'ing** [see prec.] to make easy or easier

fa·cil'i·ty *n., pl.* **-ties 1.** absence of difficulty **2.** ready ability; skill **3.** [*usually pl.*] the means to do something **4.** a room, etc. for an activity

fac·ing (fās'iŋ) *n.* **1.** a lining along a garment edge **2.** exterior covering as on a wall surface

fac·sim·i·le (fak sim'ə lē) *n.* [< L. *facere*, make + *simile*, like] (an) exact reproduction or copy

fact (fakt) *n.* [< L. *facere*, do] **1.** a deed; act **2.** an actual or true thing **3.** reality; truth **4.** something stated as being true —**as a matter of fact** really: also **in fact**

fac·tion (fak'shən) *n.* [< L. *facere*, do] **1.** a group that is part of a larger group but that opposes the views of it or of other member groups **2.** dissension —**fac'tion·al** *adj.* —**fac'tion·al·ism** *n.*

fac'tious (-shəs) *adj.* of, characterized by, or producing faction

fac·ti·tious (fak tish'əs) *adj.* [< L. *facere*, do] forced or artificial

fac·tor (fak'tər) *n.* [< L. *facere*, do] **1.** one transacting business for another **2.** anything contributing to a result **3.** *Math.* any of the quantities forming a product when multiplied together —*vt. Math.* to resolve into factors

fac·to·ry (fak'tə rē) *n., pl.* **-ries** [< Fr.: see prec.] one or more buildings where manufacturing is done

fac·to·tum (fak tōt'əm) *n.* [< L. *facere*, do + *totum*, all] a handyman

fac·tu·al (fak'chōō wəl) *adj.* of or containing facts; real; actual —**fac'tu·al·ly** *adv.*

fac·ul·ty (fak''l tē) *n., pl.* **-ties** [< L. *facere*, do] **1.** any natural or specialized power of a living organism **2.** a special aptitude **3.** the teaching staff of a school or of one of its departments

fad (fad) *n.* [< Brit. dial.] an activity, fashion, etc. of widespread but brief popularity —**fad'dish** *adj.*

fade (fād) *vi.* **fad'ed, fad'ing** [< OFr. *fade*, pale] **1.** to lose color, intensity, power, etc. **2.** to wane, wither away, or die out —*vt.* to make fade —**fade in** (or **out**) *Motion Pictures, Radio & TV* to grow or make grow more (or less) distinct, as a scene

faer·ie, faer·y (fer'ē) *n.* [Archaic] **1.** fairyland **2.** *pl.* **-ies** a fairy

fag (fag) *vt., vi.* **fagged, fag'ging** [< ?] to make or become very tired by hard work —*n.* [Slang] a male homosexual: also **fag'got**

fag·ot, fag·got (fag'ət) *n.* [ult. < Gr. *phakelos*, a bundle] a bundle of sticks or twigs, esp. for use as fuel

Fahr·en·heit (fer'ən hīt', fär'-) *adj.* [< G. D. *Fahrenheit*, 18th-c. G. physicist] designating or of a thermometer on which 32° is the freezing point and 212° is the boiling point of water: abbrev. **F, Fah., Fahr.**

fail (fāl) *vi.* [< L. *fallere*, deceive] **1.** to be or become insufficient or lacking **2.** to weaken; die away **3.** to stop functioning **4.** to be deficient in meeting an obligation, expectation, etc. **5.** to be unsuccessful in gaining or achieving something **6.** to become bankrupt **7.** *Educ.* to get a grade of failure —*vt.* **1.** to be of no help to; disappoint **2.** to leave; abandon **3.** to neglect [he *failed* to go] **4.** *Educ. a)* to give a grade of failure to *b)* to get such a grade in —**without fail** for sure; positively

fail'ing *n.* **1.** a failure **2.** a weakness, defect, or fault —*prep.* without; lacking

faille (fīl, fāl) *n.* [Fr.] a ribbed, soft fabric of silk or rayon, for dresses, coats, etc.

fail'-safe' *adj.* designed to prevent unintended operation, as a nuclear device

fail·ure (fāl'yər) *n.* **1.** the act, state, or fact of failing **2.** a person or thing that fails **3.** *Educ.* a failing to pass, or a grade showing this

fain (fān) *adj., adv.* [OE. *fægen*, glad] [Archaic] glad(ly) or willing(ly)

faint (fānt) *adj.* [see FEIGN] **1.** weak; feeble **2.** timid **3.** feeling weak and dizzy **4.** dim; indistinct —*n.* a condition of brief unconsciousness —*vi.* to fall into a faint —**faint'ly** *adv.* —**faint'ness** *n.*

faint'heart'ed *adj.* cowardly; timid

fair¹ (fer) *adj.* [OE. *fæger*] **1.** attractive or beautiful **2.** unblemished [a *fair* name] **3.** light in color; blond **4.** clear and sunny **5.** easy to read [a *fair* hand] **6.** just and honest **7.** not violating the rules as of a game **8.** moderately large **9.** average [in *fair* condition] **10.** that may be hunted [*fair* game] **11.** *Baseball* that is not foul —*adv.* **1.** in a fair way [play *fair*] **2.** squarely —**fair and square** [Colloq.] with justice and honesty —**fair'ness** *n.*

fair² (fer) *n.* [< L. *feriae*, festivals] **1.** orig., a regular gathering for barter and sale of goods **2.** a festival featuring entertainment and things for sale **3.** an exhibition, as of farm products, manufactured goods, or international displays, usually also with various amusements

fair'-haired' *adj.* **1.** having blond hair **2.** [Colloq.] favorite

fair'ly *adv.* **1.** justly **2.** moderately **3.** completely or really [his voice *fairly* rang]

fair play observance of the rules, as in sports, or of honesty, etc., as in business

fair shake [Colloq.] fair, just, or equitable treatment

fair'-trade' *adj.* designating or of an agreement whereby the seller of a product charges no less than the minimum price set by the producer

fair'way' (-wā') *n.* on a golf course, the mowed part between a tee and a green

fair·y (fer'ē) *n., pl.* **-ies** [< OFr. *feie*] **1.** *Folklore* a tiny, graceful being in human form, with magic powers **2.** [Slang] a male homosexual —*adj.* **1.** of fairies **2.** fairylike

fair'y·land' *n.* **1.** the imaginary land where fairies live **2.** a lovely, enchanting place

fairy tale 1. a story about fairies, giants, etc. **2.** an untrue story

faith (fāth) *n.* [< L. *fidere*, to trust] **1.** unquestioning belief, esp. in God, religion, etc. **2.** a particular religion **3.** complete trust or reliance **4.** loyalty —**good** (or **bad**) **faith** (in)sincerity or (dis)honesty

faith'ful (-fəl) *adj.* **1.** loyal **2.** conscientious **3.** accurate; exact —**faith'ful·ly** *adv.* —**faith'ful·ness** *n.*

faith'less (-lis) *adj.* disloyal or dishonest —**faith'less·ly** *adv.* —**faith'less·ness** *n.*

fake (fāk) *vt., vi.* **faked, fak'ing** [< ? G. *fegen*, to clean] to practice deception by giving a false indication or appearance of (something); feign —*n.* a person or thing that is not genuine; fraud; sham; counterfeit —*adj.* not genuine; false; counterfeit —**fak'er** *n.*

fa·kir (fə kir') *n.* [Ar. *faqīr*, lit., poor] **1.** one of a Muslim holy sect of beggars **2.** a Hindu ascetic

fal·con (fal'kən, fôl'-, fô'-) *n.* [prob. < L. *falx*, sickle] a hawk trained to hunt small game —**fal'con·er** *n.* —**fal'con·ry** *n.*

fall (fôl) *vi.* **fell, fall'en, fall'ing** [OE. *feallan*] **1.** to come down by gravity, as when dropped **2.**

to come down suddenly from an upright position; tumble or collapse 3. to be wounded or killed in battle 4. to take a downward direction 5. to become lower, less, weaker, etc. 6. to lose power, status, etc. 7. to do wrong; sin 8. to be captured 9. to take on a sad look /his face *fell]* 10. to take place; occur 11. to come by inheritance, lot, etc. 12. to pass into a specified condition *[to fall ill]* 13. to be directed, esp. by chance 14. to be divided *(into)* 15. to hang down —*n.* 1. a dropping; descending 2. a coming down suddenly from an upright position 3. a downward direction or slope 4. a becoming lower or less 5. a capturing, overthrow, etc. 6. a loss of power, status, virtue, etc. 7. something fallen, as snow, or the amount of this 8. autumn 9. the distance something falls 10. [*pl., often with sing. v.*] water falling as over a cliff 11. a long tress of hair, added to a woman's hairdo —*adj.* of autumn —**fall back** to withdraw; retreat —**fall flat** to fail completely —**fall for** [Colloq.] 1. to fall in love with 2. to be tricked by —**fall in** 1. to agree 2. to line up in formation —**fall off** to become smaller, worse, etc. —**fall on** (or **upon**) to attack —**fall out** 1. to quarrel 2. to leave one's place in formation —**fall through** to fail —**fall to** to begin; esp., to begin eating

fal·la·cious (fə lā′shəs) *adj.* [see FALLACY] 1. erroneous 2. misleading or deceptive

fal·la·cy (fal′ə sē) *n., pl.* -**cies** [< L. *fallere*, deceive] 1. aptness to mislead 2. a mistaken idea; error 3. an error in reasoning

fall·en (fôl′ən) *adj.* that fell; dropped, prostrate, overthrown, ruined, etc.

fal·li·ble (fal′ə b'l) *adj.* [see FALLACY] capable of making mistakes or of being in error —**fal′li·bil′i·ty** *n.* —**fal′li·bly** *adv.*

fall′ing-out′ *n.* a quarrel

fall′off′ *n.* a decline

Fal·lo·pi·an tube (fə lō′pē ən) [< G. *Fallopius,* 16th-c. It. anatomist] either of two tubes that carry ova to the uterus

fall′out′ *n.* 1. the descent to earth of radioactive particles, as after a nuclear explosion 2. these particles

fal·low (fal′ō) *adj.* [OE. *fealh*] 1. left unplanted 2. inactive, as the mind

false (fôls) *adj.* **fals′er, fals′est** [< L. *fallere,* deceive] 1. not true or correct; wrong 2. untruthful; lying 3. disloyal 4. misleading 5. not real; artificial —*adv.* in a false way —**false′ly** *adv.* —**false′ness** *n.*

false′heart′ed *adj.* disloyal or deceitful

false′hood′ *n.* 1. falsity 2. a lie

fal·set·to (fôl set′ō) *n., pl.* -**tos** [It.: see FALSE] an artificially high vocal register —*adj., adv.* in this register

fal·si·fy (fôl′sə fī′) *vt.* -**fied′, -fy′ing** 1. to misrepresent 2. to alter (a record, etc.) fraudulently —**fal′si·fi·ca′tion** *n.*

fal·si·ty (fôl′sə tē) *n., pl.* -**ties** 1. the quality of being false 2. a lie

Fal·staff (fôl′staf) Sir **John** a character in some Shakespearean plays: he is a fat, jovial knight

fal·ter (fôl′tər) *vi.* [ME. *faltren*] 1. to move uncertainly or unsteadily 2. to stumble in speech 3. to act hesitantly; waver

fame (fām) *n.* [< L. *fama*] 1. reputation, esp. for good 2. the state of being well known —**famed** *adj.*

fa·mil·ial (fə mil′yəl) *adj.* of a family

fa·mil·iar (fə mil′yər) *adj.* [see FAMILY] 1. friendly; close; intimate 2. too friendly; unduly intimate 3. closely acquainted *(with)* 4.

common; ordinary —*n.* a close friend —**fa·mil′iar·ly** *adv.*

fa·mil′iar′i·ty (-yar′ə tē) *n., pl.* -**ties** 1. informality or intimacy, either acceptable or excessive, or an instance of this 2. close acquaintance *(with)*

fa·mil·iar·ize′ (-yə rīz′) *vt.* -**ized′, -iz′ing** 1. to make commonly known 2. to make fully acquainted —**fa·mil′iar·i·za′tion** *n.*

fam·i·ly (fam′ə lē) *n., pl.* -**lies** [< L. *famulus,* servant] 1. orig., all the people living in the same house 2. parents and their children 3. relatives 4. all those descended from a common ancestor; lineage 5. a group of related or similar things

family room a room in a home set apart for relaxation and recreation

fam·ine (fam′ən) *n.* [< L. *fames,* hunger] an acute and general shortage, specif. of food

fam·ish (fam′ish) *vt., vi.* [see prec.] to make or be very hungry

fa·mous (fā′məs) *adj.* 1. having fame; renowned 2. [Colloq.] very good or excellent —**fa′mous·ly** *adv.*

fan¹ (fan) *n.* [< L. *vannus,* basket to winnow grain] a device used to set up a current of air for ventilating or cooling —*vt., vi.* **fanned, fan′ning** 1. to move (air) as with a fan 2. to direct air (toward) as with a fan 3. to stir up; excite 4. *Baseball* to strike out —**fan out** to spread out

fan² (fan) *n.* [< FANATIC] [Colloq.] a person enthusiastic about a sport, performer, etc.

fa·nat·ic (fə nat′ik) *adj.* [< L. *fanum,* temple] unreasonably enthusiastic; overly zealous: also **fa·nat′i·cal** —*n.* a fanatic person —**fa·nat′i·cal·ly** *adv.* —**fa·nat′i·cism** *n.*

fan·ci·er (fan′sē ər) *n.* one especially interested in something *[a dog fancier]*

fan·ci·ful (fan′si fəl) *adj.* 1. full of fancy; imaginative 2. not real; imaginary

fan·cy (fan′sē) *n., pl.* -**cies** [< FANTASY] 1. imagination, esp. when light, playful, etc. 2. a mental image 3. a whim; caprice; notion 4. an inclination or fondness —*adj.* -**ci·er, -ci·est** 1. whimsical; capricious 2. extravagant *[a fancy price]* 3. highly decorated, elaborate, etc. 4. of superior skill or quality —*vt.* -**cied, -cy·ing** 1. to imagine 2. to like 3. to suppose —**fan′ci·ly** *adv.* —**fan′ci·ness** *n.*

fan′cy-free′ *adj.* 1. free to fall in love; unattached; uncommitted 2. carefree

fan′cy·work′ *n.* ornamental needlework

fan·dan·go (fan daŋ′gō) *n., pl.* -**gos** [Sp.] a lively Spanish dance

fan·fare (fan′fer′) *n.* [Fr.] 1. a loud blast of trumpets 2. noisy or showy display

fang (faŋ) *n.* [OE. < *fon,* seize] 1. one of the long, pointed teeth of meat-eating animals 2. one of the long, venom-injecting teeth of some snakes

fan·ta·size (fan′tə sīz′) *vt., vi.* -**sized′, -siz′ing** to evoke (mental images, illusions, etc.) in a fantasy, daydream, etc.

fan·tas·tic (fan tas′tik) *adj.* 1. existing in fantasy; imaginary; unreal 2. grotesque; odd 3. extravagant 4. seemingly impossible; incredible —**fan·tas′ti·cal·ly** *adv.*

fan·ta·sy (fan′tə sē) *n., pl.* -**sies** [< Gr. *phainein,* to show] 1. imagination or fancy 2. an odd or illusory mental image 3. a highly imaginative poem, play, etc.

FAO Food and Agriculture Organization (of the UN)

far (fär) *adj.* **far′ther, far′thest** [OE. *feorr*] 1. distant in space or time 2. more distant *[the far side]* —*adv.* 1. at or to a point distant in space or time 2. very much *[far* better*] —***as far as 1.** to the distance, extent, or degree that 2. [Colloq.] in regard to **—by far** very much: also **far and away —(in) so far as** to the extent that **—so far** up to this point

far·a·way′ *adj.* 1. distant in space or time 2. dreamy; abstracted

farce (färs) *n.* [Fr., stuffing < L. *farcire,* to stuff] 1. (an) exaggerated comedy based on highly unlikely situations 2. (an) absurd display, pretense, etc. **—far′ci·cal** *adj.*

fare (fer) *vi.* **fared, far′ing** [OE. *faran,* go] 1. [Poet.] to travel 2. to happen or result 3. to get along in a certain way *[to fare* worse*] —n.* 1. money paid for transportation 2. a passenger who pays a fare 3. food served, or consumed, esp. regularly

fare·well (fer′wel′; *for adj.* -wel′) *interj.* goodbye **—n. 1.** the expression of good wishes at parting 2. a departure **—adj.** parting; final *[a farewell* gesture*]*

far-fetched (fär′fecht′) *adj.* strained, as a comparison; forced; artificial

far′-flung′ *adj.* covering a wide area

fa·ri·na (fə rē′nə) *n.* [< L., meal] flour or meal made as from whole wheat or nuts and cooked to make a cereal or cereallike food

far·i·na·ceous (far′ə nā′shəs) *adj.* [see prec.] 1. of or made from flour or meal 2. mealy

farm (färm) *n.* [< ML. *firma,* fixed payment] a piece of land (with house, barns, etc.) on which crops or animals are raised; orig., such land let out to tenants **—vt. 1.** to cultivate (land) 2. to turn over to another for a fee **—vi.** to work on or operate a farm

farm′er *n.* one who operates or works on a farm

farm′hand′ *n.* a hired farm worker

farm′house′ *n.* a house on a farm

farm′ing *n.* the business of operating a farm; agriculture

farm′yard′ *n.* the yard surrounding or enclosed by the buildings on a farm

far·o (fer′ō) *n.* [Fr. *pharaon]* a gambling game played with cards

far-off (fär′ôf′) *adj.* distant; remote

far′-out′ *adj.* [Colloq.] nonconformist; esp., avant-garde

far·ra·go (fə rä′gō, -rä′-) *n., pl.* **-goes** [L., mixed fodder] a confused mixture; jumble

far′-reach′ing *adj.* having a wide range, extent, influence, or effect

far·ri·er (far′ē ər) *n.* [< L. *ferrum,* iron] [Brit.] a shoer of horses; blacksmith

far·row (far′ō) *n.* [OE. *fearh,* young pig] a litter of pigs **—vt., vi.** to give birth to (a litter of pigs)

far′sight′ed *adj.* 1. prudent and provident: also **far′see′ing.** 2. seeing distant objects better than near ones **—far′sight′ed·ness** *n.*

far·ther (fär′thər) *compar. of* FAR **—adj. 1.** more distant 2. additional; more **—adv. 1.** at or to a greater distance 2. to a greater degree 3. in addition Cf. FURTHER

far′ther·most′ *adj.* most distant; farthest

far·thest (fär′thist) *superl. of* FAR **—adj.** most distant **—adv. 1.** at or to the greatest distance 2. to the greatest degree

far·thing (fär′thiŋ) *n.* [OE. *feorthing]* a former British coin worth 1/4 penny

fas·ci·nate (fas′ə nāt′) *vt.* **-nat′ed, -nat′ing** [< L. *fascinum,* an enchanting] to hold spellbound; esp., to grip as by irresistible charm or interest **—fas′ci·na′tion** *n.*

fas·cism (fash′iz′m) *n.* [< It. < L. *fasces,* rods bound about an ax, ancient Roman symbol of authority] [*occas.* **F-**] a system of government

characterized by dictatorship, belligerent nationalism, militarism, etc.: first instituted in Italy (1922-43) **—fas′cist** *n., adj.*

fash·ion (fash′ən) *n.* [ult. < L. *facere,* make] 1. form or shape 2. way or manner 3. current style, as of dress **—vt. 1.** to make; form 2. to adapt *(to)* **—after** (or **in) a fashion** to some extent

fash′ion·a·ble *adj.* 1. in fashion; stylish 2. of stylish people **—fash′ion·a·bly** *adv.*

fast[1] (fast) *adj.* [OE. *fæst]* 1. firm; tightly fastened 2. loyal; devoted 3. unfading *[fast* colors*]* 4. speedy 5. ahead of time *[a fast* watch*]* 6. wild, dissolute, promiscuous, etc. 7. [Colloq.] glib **—adv. 1.** firmly; fixedly 2. sound *[fast* asleep*]* 3. speedily 4. ahead of time 5. wildly, dissolutely, etc.

fast[2] (fast) *vi.* [OE. *fæstan]* to abstain from all or certain foods **—n. 1.** a fasting 2. a time of fasting

fas·ten (fas′'n) *vt.* [see FAST[1]] 1. to attach; connect 2. to make secure, as by locking or buttoning 3. to fix (the attention, gaze, etc.) *on* a person or thing **—vi.** to become fastened **—fas′ten·er** *n.*

fas′ten·ing *n.* anything, as a clasp, used to fasten

fast′-food′ *adj.* designating a business offering food prepared and served quickly

fas·tid·i·ous (fas tid′ē əs) *adj.* [< L: *fastus,* disdain + *taedium:* see TEDIUM] 1. not easy to please 2. overly refined **—fas·tid′i·ous·ly** *adv.* **—fas·tid′i·ous·ness** *n.*

fast·ness (fast′nis) *n.* 1. the quality or condition of being fast 2. a stronghold

fat (fat) *adj.* **fat′ter, fat′test** [OE. *fætt]* 1. containing fat; oily; greasy 2. *a)* fleshy; plump *b)* obese 3. thick; broad 4. profitable *[a fat* job*]* 5. plentiful **—n. 1.** an oily material in animal tissue or plant seeds 2. the richest part of anything 3. anything superfluous **—chew the fat** [Slang] to chat

fa·tal (fāt′'l) *adj.* 1. fateful; decisive 2. bringing death 3. disastrous; ruinous **—fa′tal·ly** *adv.*

fa′tal·ism *n.* the belief that all events are determined by fate and hence inevitable **—fa′tal·ist** *n.* **—fa′tal·is′tic** *adj.*

fa·tal·i·ty (fə tal′ə tē, fā-) *n., pl.* **-ties 1.** subjection to fate 2. deadliness 3. a death caused as by an accident, fire, etc.

fat cat [Slang] a wealthy person

fate (fāt) *n.* [< L. *fatum,* oracle] 1. a supposed power making everything happen in a predetermined way; destiny 2. one's lot or destiny 3. final outcome 4. destruction or death **—the Fates** Gr. & Rom. Myth. three goddesses controlling human destiny

fat·ed (fāt′id) *adj.* 1. destined 2. doomed

fate′ful (-fəl) *adj.* 1. prophetic 2. full of consequences; crucial 3. controlled as if by fate 4. bringing death or destruction

fa·ther (fä′thər) *n.* [OE. *fæder]* 1. a male parent 2. [F-] God 3. an ancestor 4. a male originator, founder, or inventor 5. a Christian priest: used esp. as a title **—vt. 1.** to be the father of 2. to act as a father toward **—fa′ther·hood′** *n.* **—fa′ther·less** *adj.*

fa′ther-in-law′ *n., pl.* **fa′thers-in-law′** the father of one's wife or husband

fa′ther·land′ *n.* a person's native land

fa′ther·ly *adj.* of or like a father; kindly

fath·om (fath′əm) *n.* [OE. *fæthm,* the two arms outstretched] a nautical unit of depth or length, equal to 6 feet **—vt. 1.** to measure the depth of 2. to understand thoroughly **—fath′om·a·ble** *adj.* **—fath′om·less** *adj.*

fa·tigue (fə tēg′) *n.* [Fr. < L. *fatigare,* to

weary] **1.** exhaustion; weariness **2.** [*pl.*] soldiers' work clothing **3.** the tendency of a metal, etc. to break under stress —*vt., vl.*
-tigued', -tigu'ing to weary; tire
fat·ten (fat′'n) *n., vl.* to make or become fat
fat'ty *adj.* **-tl·er, -tl·est** of, like, or full of fat —**fat'tl·ness** *n.*
fat·u·ous (fach′ʊ wəs) *adj.* [L. *fatuus*] smugly stupid; asinine —**fat'u·ous·ly** *adv.*
fau·cet (fô′sit) *n.* [prob. < OFr. *faulser*, to breach] a device with a valve for regulating the flow of liquid as from a pipe; tap
fault (fôlt) *n.* [< L. *fallere*, deceive] **1.** something that mars; flaw; defect **2.** a misdeed or mistake **3.** responsibility for something wrong **4.** a fracture in rock strata —*vt.* to blame —**at fault** in the wrong —**find fault (with)** to criticize —**to a fault** excessively
fault'find'ing *n., adj.* criticizing
fault'less *adj.* perfect —**fault'less·ly** *adv.*
fault'y *adj.* **-l·er, -l·est** having a fault or faults; imperfect —**fault'l·ly** *adv.*
faun (fôn) *n.* [< L. *faunus*] any of a class of minor Roman deities, half man and half goat
fau·na (fô′nə) *n., pl.* **-nas, -nae** (-nē) [< LL. *Fauna*, Roman goddess] the animals of a specified region or time
Faust (foust) in legend and literature, a man who sold his soul to the devil for knowledge and power
faux pas (fō′ pä′) *pl.* **faux pas** (fō′ päz′) [Fr., lit., false step] a social blunder
fa·vor (fā′vər) *n.* [< L. *favere*, to favor] **1.** friendly regard; approval **2.** partiality **3.** a kind act **4.** a small gift or token —*vt.* **1.** to approve or like **2.** to be partial to **3.** to support; advocate **4.** to make easier; help **5.** to do a kindness for **6.** to look like; resemble [he *favors* his father] Brit. sp. **favour —in favor of 1.** approving **2.** to the advantage of
fa'vor·a·ble *adj.* **1.** approving **2.** helpful **3.** pleasing —**fa'vor·a·bly** *adv.*
fa·vor·ite (fā′vər it) *n.* **1.** a person or thing especially liked **2.** a contestant viewed as most likely to win —*adj.* highly regarded; preferred
fa'vor·it·ism *n.* partiality; bias
fawn[1] (fôn) *vl.* [< OE. *fægen*, glad] **1.** to show affection as by licking the hand: said of a dog **2.** to cringe and flatter
fawn[2] (fôn) *n.* [< L. *fetus*, FETUS] **1.** a deer less than a year old **2.** a pale, yellowish brown —*adj.* of this color
faze (fāz) *vt.* **fazed, faz'ing** [< OE. *fesan*, to drive] [Colloq.] to disturb; disconcert
FBI, F.B.I. Federal Bureau of Investigation
FCC, F.C.C. Federal Communications Commission
FDA, F.D.A. Food and Drug Administration
FDIC, F.D.I.C. Federal Deposit Insurance Corporation
Fe [L. *ferrum*] *Chem.* iron
fe·al·ty (fē′əl tē) *n., pl.* **-ties** [< L. *fidelitas*, fidelity] loyalty, esp. to a feudal lord
fear (fir) *n.* [OE. *fær*, danger] **1.** anxiety over real or possible danger, pain, etc.; fright **2.** awe; reverence **3.** apprehension; concern **4.** a cause for fear —*vt., vl.* **1.** to have fear (of) **2.** to be in awe (of) **3.** to expect with misgiving —**fear'less** *adj.* —**fear'less·ly** *adv.* —**fear'less·ness** *n.*
fear'ful *adj.* **1.** causing, feeling, or showing fear **2.** [Colloq.] very bad, great, etc.
fear'some *adj.* causing fear; frightful
fea·si·ble (fē′zə b'l) *adj.* [< L. *facere*, do] **1.** possible **2.** likely; probable **3.** suitable —**fea'si·bil'l·ty** *n.* —**fea'si·bly** *adv.*
feast (fēst) *n.* [< L. *festus*, festal] **1.** a festival

2. a rich, elaborate meal —*vl.* to dine richly —*vt.* **1.** to give a feast to **2.** to delight [to *feast* one's eyes on a sight]
feat (fēt) *n.* [< L. *factum*, a deed] a deed of unusual daring or skill
feath·er (feth′ər) *n.* [OE. *fether*] **1.** any of the soft, light outgrowths covering the body of a bird **2.** [*pl.*] *a)* plumage *b)* attire **3.** class; kind [birds of a *feather*] —*vt.* **1.** to provide or adorn as with feathers **2.** to turn (an oar or propeller blade) so that the edge is foremost —**feather in one's cap** a distinctive achievement —**feath'er·y** *adj.*
feath'er·bed'ding (-bed′iŋ) *n.* the practice of limiting work output or requiring extra workers so as to provide more jobs
feath'er·weight' *n.* **1.** a boxer weighing from 119 to 126 pounds **2.** a wrestler weighing from 124 to 134 pounds
fea·ture (fē′chər) *n.* [< L. *facere*, to make] **1.** *a)* [*pl.*] facial form or appearance *b)* any facial part **2.** a distinct or outstanding part or quality of something **3.** a special attraction, sale item, newspaper article, etc. **4.** a full-length motion picture —*vt.* **-tured, -tur·ing** to make a feature of
fe·brile (fē′brəl, -bril) *adj.* [< L. *febris*, fever] feverish
Feb·ru·ar·y (feb′rə wer′ē, feb′yoo wer′ē) *n.* [< L. *Februarius* (*mensis*), orig. month of expiation] the second month of the year, having 28 days (or 29 days in leap years): abbrev. **Feb., F.**
fe·ces (fē′sēz) *n.pl.* [< L. *faeces*, dregs] excrement —**fe'cal** (-kəl) *adj.*
feck·less (fek′lis) *adj.* [Scot. < *feck*, effect + -LESS] **1.** weak; ineffective **2.** careless
fe·cund (fē′kənd, fek′ənd) *adj.* [< L. *fecundus*] fertile; prolific —**fe·cun·di·ty** (fi kun′də tē) *n.*
fed (fed) *pt. & pp.* of FEED —**fed up** [Colloq.] having had enough to become disgusted, bored, etc.
Fed. 1. Federal **2.** Federation
fed·a·yeen (fed′ä yēn′) *n.pl.* [Ar., lit., self-sacrificers] Arab guerrillas
fed·er·al (fed′ər əl) *adj.* [< L. *foedus*, a league] **1.** designating or of a union of states, groups, etc. in which each member subordinates its power to a central authority **2.** designating or of such a central authority, specif. [*usually* F-] that of the U.S. government **3.** [F-] of a former U.S. political party (**Federalist Party**) which favored a strong centralized government **4.** [F-] of or for the U.S. government in the Civil War —*n.* [F-] **1.** a supporter of the U.S. government in the Civil War **2.** a Federal agent —**fed'er·al·ism** *n.* —**fed'er·al·ist** *adj., n.*
fed'er·al·ize' *vt.* **-ized', -iz'ing 1.** to unite in a federal union **2.** to put under the authority of a federal government —**fed'er·al·i·za'tion** *n.*
fed·er·ate (fed′ə rāt′) *vt., vl.* **-at'ed, -at'ing** to unite in a federal union —**fed'er·a'tion** *n.*
fe·do·ra (fə dôr′ə) *n.* [Fr.] a soft felt hat with the crown creased lengthwise
fee (fē) *n.* [< OFr. *feu*, fief & OE. *feoh*, cattle] **1.** a charge for professional services, licenses, tuition, etc. **2.** *Law* an inheritance in land
fee·ble (fē′b'l) *adj.* **-bler, -blest** [< L. *flere*, weep] lacking strength, force, vitality, effectiveness, etc.; weak —**fee'ble·ness** *n.* —**fee'bly** *adv.*
fee'ble·mind'ed *adj.* mentally subnormal
feed (fēd) *vt.* **fed, feed'ing** [OE. *fedan*] **1.** to give food to **2.** to supply with what maintains or furthers growth, development, operation, etc. **3.** to gratify —*vl.* **1.** to eat: said esp. of animals **2.** to flow steadily, as fuel into a machine

—*n.* 1. fodder 2. material supplied to a machine, or a machine part supplying it 3. [Colloq.] a meal —**feed on** (or **upon**) 1. to eat: said esp. of animals 2. to get satisfaction, support, etc. from —**feed'er** *n.*

feed'back' *n.* transfer of a part of the output back to the input, as of electricity or of information

feel (fēl) *vt.* **felt, feel'ing** [OE. *felan*] 1. to touch or handle and so examine 2. to sense physically, mentally, or emotionally 3. to experience or react strongly to (an emotion or condition) 4. to think or believe, often for unanalyzed reasons —*vi.* 1. to have physical sensation 2. to make a specified sensory impression [the rug *feels* soft] 3. to grope 4. to be aware of being [to *feel* happy] 5. to be moved to sympathy, pity, etc. (*for*) —*n.* 1. the act of feeling 2. the sense of touch 3. the sensory impression made or emotional response elicited by something —**feel like** [Colloq.] to have a desire for —**feel out** to try cautiously to find out the opinions of —**feel up to** [Colloq.] to feel capable of

feel'er *n.* 1. a specialized organ of touch, as the antenna of an insect 2. a remark, etc. made to find out another's attitude

feel'ing *n.* 1. the sense of touch 2. ability to experience physical sensation 3. awareness 4. emotion 5. [*pl.*] sensibilities 6. sympathy or pity 7. an opinion or sentiment

feet (fēt) *n. pl. of* FOOT

feign (fān) *vt., vi.* [< L. *fingere*, to shape] 1. to make up (a story, excuse, etc.) 2. to pretend

feint (fānt) *n.* [see prec.] 1. pretense 2. a misleading movement designed to confuse one's opponent —*vt., vi.* to make (a feint)

feist·y (fīst'ē) *adj.* **-i·er, -i·est** [ME. *fīst*, a breaking of wind] [Colloq.] 1. lively; energetic 2. pugnacious

feld·spar (feld'spär') *n.* [< G. *feld*, field + *spath*, spar] any of several crystalline and usually glassy minerals

fe·lic·i·tate (fə lis'ə tāt') *vt.* **-tat'ed, -tat'ing** [< L. *felix*, happy] to congratulate —**fe·lic'i·ta'tion** *n.*

fe·lic'i·tous (-təs) *adj.* [< FELICITY] appropriate; apt —**fe·lic'i·tous·ly** *adv.* —**fe·lic'i·tous·ness** *n.*

fe·lic'i·ty *n., pl.* **-ties** [< L. *felix*, happy] 1. happiness, or a cause of it 2. felicitousness

fe·line (fē'līn) *adj.* [< L. *felis*, cat] 1. of a cat or the cat family 2. catlike —*n.* any animal of the cat family

fell' (fel) *pt. of* FALL

fell² (fel) *vt.* [OE. *fellan*] 1. to knock down 2. to cut down (a tree)

fell³ (fel) *adj.* [< ML. *fello*] fierce; cruel

fell⁴ (fel) *n.* [OE. *fel*] an animal's hide or skin

fel·low (fel'ō, -ə) *n.* [OE. *feolaga*, partner] 1. an associate 2. one of the same rank; equal 3. either of a pair; mate 4. one holding a fellowship in a college, etc. 5. a member of a learned society 6. [Colloq.] a man or boy —*adj.* having the same position, work, etc. [*fellow* workers]

fel'low·ship' *n.* 1. companionship 2. mutual sharing 3. a group of people with the same interests 4. an endowment to support a person doing advanced study

fellow traveler a nonmember supporting the cause of a party

fel·on (fel'ən) *n.* [< ML. *felo*] one guilty of felony

fel'o·ny (-ə nē) *n., pl.* **-nies** [< ML. *felonia*, treason] a major crime, as murder, arson, etc. —**fe·lo·ni·ous** (fə lō'nē əs) *adj.*

felt' (felt) *n.* [OE.] a fabric of wool, often mixed as with fur or cotton, worked together as by

pressure and heat —*adj.* of felt —*vt.* to make into felt

felt² (felt) *pt. and pp. of* FEEL

fem. feminine

fe·male (fē'māl) *adj.* [< L. *femina*, woman] 1. designating or of the sex bearing offspring 2. of or suitable to this sex 3. having a hollow part for receiving an inserted part, as an electric socket —*n.* a female person, animal, or plant

fem·i·nine (fem'ə nin) *adj.* [see prec.] 1. of women or girls 2. having qualities viewed as typical of or suitable to women and girls 3. *Gram.* designating or of the gender of words referring to females or things orig. regarded as female —**fem'i·nin'i·ty** *n.*

fem'i·nism *n.* the movement to win political, economic, and social equality for women —**fem'i·nist** *n., adj.*

fe·mur (fē'mər) *n., pl.* **fe'murs, fem·o·ra** (fem'ər ə) [L., thigh] *same as* THIGHBONE —**fem'o·ral** *adj.*

fen (fen) *n.* [OE.] an area of low, flat, marshy land; swamp; bog

fence (fens) *n.* [< ME. *defens*, defense] 1. a protective or confining barrier as of posts, wire, etc. 2. one who deals in stolen goods —*vt.* **fenced, fenc'ing** 1. to enclose as with a fence (often with *in, off*, etc.) 2. to keep (*out*) as by a fence —*vi.* 1. to practice the art of fencing 2. to be evasive —**fenc'er** *n.*

fenc'ing *n.* 1. the art of fighting with a foil or other sword 2. material for making fences 3. a system of fences

fend (fend) *vi.* [< ME. *defenden*, defend] to resist; parry —**fend for oneself** to manage by oneself —**fend off** to ward off; parry

fend'er *n.* anything that fends off or protects something else, as any of the metal frames over the wheels of an automobile

fen·nel (fen'l) *n.* [< L. *fenum*, hay] an herb with aromatic seeds used in cooking, related to parsley

fe·ral (fir'əl) *adj.* [< L. *ferus*, fierce] 1. untamed; wild 2. savage; brutal

fer·ment (fur'ment) *n.* [< L. *fervere*, to boil] 1. something causing fermentation, as yeast 2. excitement; agitation —*vt.* (fər ment') 1. to cause fermentation in 2. to excite; agitate —*vi.* 1. to undergo fermentation 2. to be agitated

fer·men·ta·tion (fur'mən tā'shən, -men-) *n.* 1. the breakdown of complex molecules in organic compounds, caused by a ferment, as in the curdling of milk 2. agitation

fern (furn) *n.* [OE. *fearn*] any of a widespread class of nonflowering plants that have roots, stems, and fronds and that reproduce by spores

fe·ro·cious (fə rō'shəs) *adj.* [< L. *ferus*, wild] 1. violently cruel; fierce 2. [Colloq.] very great [a *ferocious* appetite] —**fe·ro'cious·ly** *adv.* —**fe·roc'i·ty** (-räs'ə tē) *n.*

-ferous [< L. *ferre*, to bear] *a suffix meaning* bearing, yielding [*coniferous*]

fer·ret (fer'it) *n.* [< L. *fur*, thief] a weasellike animal, tamed for hunting rabbits, rats, etc. —*vt.* 1. to force out of hiding with a ferret 2. to search (*out*)

Fer·ris wheel (fer'is) [< G. *Ferris* (1859-1896), U.S. engineer] a large, upright wheel revolving on a fixed axle, with suspended seats: used as an amusement ride

ferro- [< L. *ferrum*, iron] *a combining form meaning:* 1. iron 2. iron and

fer·rous (fer'əs) *adj.* [< L. *ferrum*, iron] of, containing, or derived from iron: also **fer'ric** (-ik)

fer·rule (fer′əl, -ool) *n.* [< L. *viriae*, bracelets] a metal ring or cap put around the end of a cane, tool, etc. to give added strength

fer·ry (fer′ē) *vt.*, *vi.* **-ried**, **-ry·ing** [OE. *ferian*, carry] 1. to take across or cross (a river, etc.) in a boat 2. to deliver (airplanes) by flying them 3. to transport by airplane —*n.*, *pl.* **-ries** 1. a system for carrying people, goods, etc. across a river, etc. 2. a boat (**ferryboat**) used for this —**fer′ry·man** (-mən) *n.*, *pl.* **-men**

fer·tile (fur′t'l) *adj.* [< L. *ferre*, to bear] 1. producing abundantly; fruitful 2. able to produce young, seeds, fruit, etc. 3. fertilized —**fer·til·i·ty** (fər til′ə tē) *n.*

fer·til·ize (-īz′) *vt.* **-ized′**, **-iz′ing** 1. to make fertile 2. to spread fertilizer on 3. to make (the female cell or female) fruitful by introducing the male germ cell; impregnate —**fer′til·i·za′-tion** *n.*

fer′til·iz′er *n.* manure, chemicals, etc. used to enrich the soil

fer·ule (fer′əl, -ool) *n.* [< L. *ferula*, a rod] a flat stick or ruler used for punishing children

fer·vent (fur′vənt) *adj.* [< L. *fervere*, to glow] showing great warmth of feeling; intensely earnest —**fer′vent·ly** *adv.*

fer·vid (fur′vəd) *adj.* [see prec.] impassioned; fervent —**fer′vid·ly** *adv.*

fer·vor (fur′vər) *n.* [see FERVENT] great warmth of emotion; ardor; zeal

-fest [< G. *fest*, a feast] *a combining form meaning* an occasion of much *[gabfest]*

fes·tal (fes′t'l) *adj.* [< L. *festum*, feast] of or like a joyous celebration; festive

fes·ter (fes′tər) *n.* [< L. *fistula*, ulcer] a small sore filled with pus —*vi.* 1. to form pus 2. to rankle

fes·ti·val (fes′tə v'l) *n.* [see FESTIVE] 1. a time or day of feasting or celebration 2. a celebration or series of performances 3. merrymaking

fes·tive (fes′tiv) *adj.* [< L. *festum*, feast] of or for a feast or festival; merry; joyous

fes·tiv·i·ty (fes tiv′ə tē) *n.*, *pl.* **-ties** 1. merrymaking; gaiety 2. a festival 3. [*pl.*] things done in celebration

fes·toon (fes toon′) *n.* [< It. *festa*, feast] a garland of flowers, etc. hanging in a curve —*vt.* to adorn with festoons

fe·tal (fēt′l) *adj.* of or like a fetus

fetch (fech) *vt.* [OE. *feccan*] 1. to go after and bring back; get 2. to cause to come 3. to sell for 4. [Colloq.] to deliver (a blow, etc.)

fetch′ing *adj.* attractive; charming

fete, fête (fāt) *n.* [Fr. *fête*: see FEAST] a festival; entertainment, esp. outdoors —*vt.* **fet′ed** or **fêt′ed**, **fet′ing** or **fêt′ing** to honor with a fete

fet·id (fet′id, fēt′-) *adj.* [< L. *f(o)etere*, to stink] having a bad smell; stinking

fet·ish (fet′ish, fēt′-) *n.* [< Port. *feitiço*] 1. any object believed to have magic power 2. anything to which one is irrationally devoted 3. any nonsexual object that abnormally excites erotic feelings Also **fet′ich** —**fet′ish·ism** *n.* —**fet′ish·ist** *n.*

fet·lock (fet′läk′) *n.* [< ME. *fet*, feet + *lok*, LOCK²] 1. a tuft of hair on the back of a horse's leg above the hoof 2. the joint bearing this tuft

fet·ter (fet′ər) *n.* [< OE. *fot*, foot] 1. a shackle or chain for the feet 2. any check or restraint —*vt.* 1. to bind with fetters 2. to restrain

fet·tle (fet′l) *n.* [ME. *fetlen*, make ready] condition; state *[he is in fine fettle]*

fe·tus (fēt′əs) *n.*, *pl.* **-tus·es** [L., a bringing forth] 1. the unborn young of an animal, esp. in its later stages 2. in man, the offspring from the womb from the fourth month until birth

feud (fyood) *n.* [< OFr.] a long-continued, deadly quarrel, esp. between clans or families —*vi.* to carry on a feud

feu·dal (fyood′'l) *adj.* [< OHG. *feho*, property] of or like feudalism

feu′dal·ism *n.* the social system in medieval Europe, in which land, worked by serfs, was held by vassals in exchange for military and other services to overlords

fe·ver (fē′vər) *n.* [< L. *febris*] 1. an abnormally increased body temperature 2. any disease marked by a high fever 3. a restless excitement —*vt.* to cause fever in —**fe′vered** *adj.* —**fe′ver·ish** *adj.*

fever blister (or **sore**) *same as* COLD SORE

few (fyoo) *adj.* [OE. *feawe*, pl.] not many — *pron.*, *n.* a small number —**quite a few** [Colloq.] a rather large number —**the few** the minority

fey (fā) *adj.* [OE. *fæge*] 1. [Archaic] fated 2. strange or unusual

fez (fez) *n.*, *pl.* **fez′zes** [< *Fez*, city in Morocco] a tapering felt hat worn, esp. formerly, by Turkish men

ff. 1. folios 2. following (pages, etc.)

FHA Federal Housing Administration

fi·an·cé (fē′än sā′) *n.* [Fr. < OFr. *fiance*, a promise] the man to whom a woman is engaged to be married

fi·an·cée (fē′än sā′) *n.* [Fr.: see prec.] the woman to whom a man is engaged to be married

fi·as·co (fē as′kō) *n.*, *pl.* **-coes**, **-cos** [Fr. < It. (*far*) *fiasco*, to fail] a complete, ridiculous failure

fi·at (fī′at, -ət) *n.* [L., let it be done] 1. a decree 2. a sanction

fib (fib) *n.* [? < *fable*] a lie about something unimportant —*vi.* **fibbed**, **fib′bing** to tell a fib — **fib′ber** *n.*

fi·ber, fi·bre (fī′bər) *n.* [< L. *fibra*] 1. a thread-like structure combining with others to form animal or vegetable tissue 2. any substance that can be separated into threadlike parts for weaving, etc. 3. texture 4. character; nature — **fi′brous** (-brəs) *adj.*

fi′ber·board′ *n.* a boardlike material made from pressed fibers of wood, etc.

Fi′ber·glas′ (-glas′) *a trademark for* finespun filaments of glass made into textiles or insulating material —*n.* [f-] this substance: usually **fiberglass**

fi·bril (fī′brəl) *n.* a small fiber

fi·bril·la·tion (fib′rə lā′shən) *n.* [< FIBRIL + -ATION] a rapid series of contractions of the heart, causing weak, irregular heartbeats

fi·broid (fī′broid) *adj.* like or composed of fibrous tissue, as a tumor

fi·bro·sis (fī brō′sis) *n.* an abnormal increase in the amount of fibrous connective tissue in an organ or tissue

fib·u·la (fib′yoo lə) *n.*, *pl.* **-lae** (-lē′), **-las** [L., a clasp] the long, thin outer bone of the lower leg

-fic [< L. *facere*, make] *a suffix meaning* making, creating *[terrific]*

-fication [see -FIC] *a suffix meaning* a making, creating *[glorification]*

fick·le (fik′'l) *adj.* [OE. *ficol*] changeable or unstable in affection, interest, etc.

fic·tion (fik′shən) *n.* [< L. *fingere*, to form] 1. an imaginary statement, story, etc. 2. any literary work with imaginary characters and events, as a novel, play, etc. 3. such works collectively —**fic′tion·al** *adj.*

fic·ti·tious (fik tish′əs) *adj.* 1. of or like fiction; imaginary 2. false 3. assumed for disguise *[a fictitious name]*

fid·dle (fid′'l) *n.* [OE. *fithele*] [Colloq.] a violin —*vi.* -dled, -dling 1. [Colloq.] to play on a violin 2. to tinker (*with*) nervously
fiddler crab a small, burrowing crab
fid′dle·sticks′ interj. nonsense!
fi·del·i·ty (fə del′ə tē, fī-) *n., pl.* -ties [< L. *fides*, faith] 1. faithful devotion to duty; loyalty 2. accuracy of reproduction
fidg·et (fij′it) *n.* [< ME. *fichen*] a restless or nervous state, esp. in the phrase **the fidgets** — *vi.* to make restless or nervous movements — **fidg′et·y adj.**
fi·du·ci·ar·y (fi dōō′shē er′ē) *adj.* [< L. *fiducia*, trust] holding or held in trust —*n., pl.* -ies a trustee
fie (fī) **interj.** for shame!
fief (fēf) *n.* [Fr.: see FEE] in feudalism, heritable land held by a vassal
field (fēld) *n.* [OE. *feld*] 1. a wide stretch of open land 2. a piece of cleared land for crops or pasture 3. a piece of land used for a particular purpose [a landing *field*] 4. any wide, unbroken expanse [a *field* of ice] 5. *a*) a battlefield *b*) a battle 6. a realm of knowledge or work 7. the background, as on a flag 8. all the entrants in a contest 9. *Physics* a space within which magnetic or electrical lines of force are active —*vt.* 1. to stop or catch and return (a baseball, etc.) 2. to put (a player) into active play —*vi.* to play a defensive position in baseball, etc. —**play the field** to expand one's activities to a broad area —**field′er n.**
field glass(es) a small, portable, binocular telescope
field goal *Football* a goal kicked from the field, scoring three points
field hand a hired farm laborer
field marshal in some armies, an officer of the highest rank
field′work′ *n.* the work of collecting scientific data in the field —**field′work′er n.**
fiend (fēnd) *n.* [OE. *feond*] 1. an evil spirit; devil 2. an inhumanly wicked person 3. [Colloq.] an addict [a dope *fiend*, fresh-air *fiend*] —**fiend′ish adj.**
fierce (firs) *adj.* **fierc′er, fierc′est** [< L. *ferus*, wild] 1. savage 2. violent 3. intensely eager 4. [Colloq.] very disagreeable —**fierce′ly adv.** — **fierce′ness n.**
fi·er·y (fī′ər ē) *adj.* **-i-er, -i-est** 1. like fire; glaring, hot, etc. 2. ardent 3. excitable —**fi′er·i·ness n.**
fi·es·ta (fi es′tə) *n.* [Sp. < L. *festus*, festal] 1. a religious festival 2. any gala celebration; holiday
fife (fīf) *n.* [G. *pfeife*] a small, shrill musical instrument like a flute
fif·teen (fif′tēn′) *adj., n.* [OE. *fiftene*] five more than ten; 15; XV —**fif′teenth′** (-tēnth′) *adj., n.*
fifth (fifth) *adj.* [< OE. *fif*, five] preceded by four others in a series; 5th —*n.* 1. the one following the fourth 2. any of the five equal parts of something; 1/5 3. a fifth of a gallon
Fifth Amendment the fifth amendment to the U.S. Constitution; specif., the clause protecting a person from being compelled to be a witness against himself
fif·ty (fif′tē) *adj., n., pl.* -ties [OE. *fiftig*] five times ten; 50; L —**the fifties** the numbers or years, as of a century, from 50 through 59 — **fif′ti·eth** (-ith) *adj., n.*
fif′ty-fif′ty adj. [Colloq.] even; equal —*adv.* [Colloq.] equally
fig (fig) *n.* [< L. *ficus*] 1. a small, sweet, pear-shaped fruit 2. the tree it grows on 3. a trifle [not worth a *fig*]
fig. 1. figurative(ly) 2. figure(s)

fight (fīt) *vi.* **fought, fight′ing** [OE. *feohtan*] to take part in a struggle, contest, etc., esp. against a foe or for a cause —*vt.* 1. to oppose physically or in battle 2. to struggle against 3. to engage in (a war, etc.) 4. to gain (one's way) by struggle —*n.* 1. any struggle, contest, or quarrel 2. power or readiness to fight
fight′er *n.* 1. one that fights; esp., a prizefighter 2. a fast, highly maneuverable combat airplane
fig·ment (fig′mənt) *n.* [< L. *fingere*, make] something imagined or made up in the mind
fig·u·ra·tion (fig′yə rā′shən) *n.* 1. a forming; shaping 2. form; appearance
fig·u·ra·tive (fig′yər ə tiv) *adj.* 1. representing by means of a figure or symbol 2. not in its usual or exact sense; metaphorical 3. using figures of speech
fig·ure (fig′yər) *n.* [< L. *fingere*, to form] 1. an outline or shape; form 2. the human form 3. a person thought of in a specified way [a historical *figure*] 4. a likeness of a person or thing 5. an illustration; diagram 6. a design 7. a pattern of musical notes 8. the symbol for a number [the *figure* 5] 9. [*pl.*] arithmetic 10. a sum of money 11. a surface or space bounded by lines or planes —*vt.* **-ured, -ur·ing** 1. to represent in definite form 2. to imagine 3. to ornament with a design 4. to compute with figures 5. [Colloq.] to believe; consider —*vi.* 1. to be conspicuous 2. to do arithmetic —**figure in** to include —**figure on** to rely on —**figure out** 1. to solve 2. to understand —**figure up** to total
fig′ure·head′ *n.* 1. a carved figure on the bow of a ship 2. one put in a position of leadership, but having no real power or authority
figure of speech an expression, as a metaphor or simile, using words in an unusual or non-literal sense
fig·u·rine (fig′yə rēn′) *n.* [Fr.] a small sculptured or molded figure; statuette
fil·a·ment (fil′ə mənt) *n.* [< L. *filum*, thread] a very slender thread or threadlike part; specif., the fine wire in a light bulb or electron tube
fil·bert (fil′bərt) *n.* [ME. *filberde*] the hazelnut or the tree it grows on
filch (filch) *vt.* [ME. *filchen*] to steal (usually something small or petty)
file¹ (fīl) *vt.* **filed, fil′ing** [< L. *filum*, thread] 1. to put (papers, etc.) in order for future reference 2. to dispatch (a news story) 3. to register (an application, etc.) 4. to put on public record —*vi.* 1. to move in a line 2. to register or apply (*for*) —*n.* 1. a folder, cabinet, etc. for keeping papers in order 2. an orderly arrangement of papers, etc. 3. a line of persons or things, one behind another
file² (fīl) *n.* [OE. *feol*] a steel tool with a rough, ridged surface for smoothing or grinding —*vt.* **filed, fil′ing** to smooth or grind, as with a file —**fil′er n.**
fi·let mi·gnon (fi lā′ min yōn′) [Fr., lit., tiny fillet] a thick, round cut of lean beef tenderloin broiled
fil·i·al (fil′ē əl, fil′yəl) *adj.* [< L. *filius*, son] of, suitable to, or due from a son or daughter
fil·i·bus·ter (fil′ə bus′tər) *n.* [< Sp. < MDu. *vrijbuiter*, freebooter] 1. a member of a legislature who obstructs a bill by making long speeches 2. such obstruction of a bill —*vt., vi.* to obstruct (a bill) by such methods —**fil′i·bus′ter·er n.**
fil·i·gree (fil′ə grē′) *n.* [< Fr. < It. < L. *filum*, thread + *granum*, grain] lacelike ornamental work of intertwined wire of gold, silver, etc. — *vt.* **-greed′, -gree′ing** to ornament with filigree

fil·ing (fīl′iŋ) *n.* a small piece scraped off with a file: *usually used in pl.*

Fil·i·pi·no (fil′ə pē′nō) *n., pl.* **-nos** [Sp.] a native of the Philippines —*adj.* Philippine

fill (fil) *vt.* [OE. *fyllan*] **1.** to put as much as possible into **2.** to occupy wholly *[the crowd filled the room]* **3.** to put a person into or to occupy (a position, etc.) **4.** to supply the things called for in (an order, etc.) **5.** to close or plug (holes, cracks, etc.) —*vi.* to become full —*n.* **1.** enough to make full or to satisfy **2.** anything that fills —**fill in 1.** to fill with some substance **2.** to complete by supplying something **3.** to be a substitute —**fill out 1.** to make or become larger, etc. **2.** to complete (a document, etc.) with data —**fill up** to make or become completely full —**fill′er** *n.*

fil·let (fil′it; *for n.* 2 & *v. usually* fil′ā, fi lā′) *n.* [< L. *filum*, thread] **1.** a thin strip or band **2.** a boneless, lean piece of meat or fish —*vt.* to bone and slice (meat or fish)

fill′-in′ *n.* **1.** one that fills a vacancy or gap **2.** [Colloq.] a brief summary of the pertinent facts

fill′ing *n.* a substance used to fill something, as gold in a tooth cavity

fil·lip (fil′əp) *n.* [< FLIP¹] **1.** a snap made by a finger held down by the thumb and then suddenly released **2.** something stimulating —*vt.* **1.** to strike or snap with a fillip **2.** to stimulate

fil·ly (fil′ē) *n., pl.* **-lies** [< ON. *fylja*] a young female horse

film (film) *n.* [OE. *filmen*] **1.** a fine, thin skin, coating, etc. **2.** a flexible cellulose material covered with a substance sensitive to light and used in photography **3.** a haze or blur **4.** a motion picture —*vt., vi.* **1.** to cover or be covered as with a film **2.** to make a motion picture (of) —**film′er** *n.*

film′strip′ *n.* a strip of film with stills of pictures, charts, etc., used in teaching, etc.

film′y *adj.* **-i·er, -i·est 1.** hazy, gauzy, etc. **2.** covered as with a film

fil·ter (fil′tər) *n.* [< ML. *filtrum*, FELT¹] **1.** a device or substance for straining out solid particles, impurities, etc. from a liquid or gas **2.** a device for absorbing certain light rays *[a lens filter]* —*vt., vi.* **1.** to pass through or as through a filter **2.** to remove with a filter —**fil′ter·a·ble, fil′tra·ble** (-trə b'l) *adj.*

filth (filth) *n.* [OE. *fylthe*] **1.** foul dirt **2.** obscenity —**filth′y** *adj.* **-i·er, -i·est**

fil·trate (fil′trāt) *vt.* **-trat·ed, -trat·ing** to filter — *n.* a filtered liquid —**fil·tra′tion** *n.*

fin (fin) *n.* [OE. *finn*] **1.** any of several winglike, membranous organs on the body of a fish, dolphin, etc. **2.** anything like this

fi·na·gle (fə nā′g'l) *vi., vt.* **-gled, -gling** [< ?] [Colloq.] to use, or get by, craftiness or trickery —**fi·na′gler** *n.*

fi·nal (fī′n'l) *adj.* [< L. *finis*, end] **1.** of or coming at the end; last **2.** deciding; conclusive —*n.* **1.** anything final **2.** [*pl.*] the last of a series of contests **3.** a final examination —**fi·nal′i·ty** (-nal′ə tē) *n., pl.* **-ties** —**fi′nal·ly** *adv.*

fi·na·le (fə nä′lē) *n.* [It.] the concluding part of a musical work, etc.

fi′nal·ist *n.* a contestant who competes in the finals

fi′nal·ize′ *vt.* **-ized′, -iz′ing** to make final; complete —**fi′nal·i·za′tion** *n.*

fi·nance (fə nans′, fī′nans) *n.* [< L. *finis*, end] **1.** [*pl.*] money resources, income, etc. **2.** the science of managing money matters —*vt.* **-nanced′, -nanc′ing** to supply or get money for —**fi·nan′cial** (-nan′shəl) *adj.*

fin·an·cier (fin′ən sir′, fī′nan-) *n.* [Fr.] one skilled in finance

finch (finch) *n.* [OE. *finc*] any of a group of small songbirds, including the canary, sparrow, etc.

find (fīnd) *vt.* **found, find′ing** [OE. *findan*] **1.** to discover by chance; come upon **2.** to get by searching **3.** to perceive; learn **4.** to recover (something lost) **5.** to consider; think **6.** to reach; attain **7.** to decide and declare to be — *vi.* to announce a decision *[the jury found for the accused]* —*n.* **1.** a finding **2.** something found —**find out** to discover; learn

find′er *n.* a camera device that shows what will appear in the photograph

find′ing *n.* **1.** discovery **2.** something found **3.** [*often pl.*] the verdict of a judge, scholar, etc.

fine (fīn) *adj.* **fin′er, fin′est** [< L. *finis*, end] **1.** very good; excellent **2.** with no impurities; refined **3.** clear and bright *[fine weather]* **4.** not heavy or coarse *[fine sand]* **5.** very thin or small *[fine print]* **6.** sharp *[a fine edge]* **7.** subtle; delicate *[a fine distinction]* **8.** too elegant —*adv.* **1.** in a fine manner **2.** [Colloq.] very well —*n.* a sum of money paid as a penalty —*vt.* **fined, fin′ing 1.** to make fine **2.** to order to pay a fine

fine arts any of certain art forms, esp. drawing, painting, sculpture, etc.

fin·er·y (fīn′ər ē) *n., pl.* **-ies** showy, elaborate clothes, jewelry, etc.

fi·nesse (fi nes′) *n.* [Fr.: see FINE] **1.** adroitness or skill **2.** the ability to handle delicate situations diplomatically **3.** cunning

fin·ger (fiŋ′gər) *n.* [OE.] **1.** any of the five jointed parts at the end of the hand, esp. one other than the thumb **2.** anything like a finger in shape or use —*vt.* **1.** to touch with the fingers; handle **2.** to play (an instrument) by using the fingers on strings, keys, etc. —**have (or keep) one's fingers crossed** to hope for something —**put one's finger on** to ascertain exactly

fin′ger·nail′ *n.* the horny substance on the upper part of the end joint of a finger

fin′ger·print′ *n.* an impression of the lines, etc. on a finger tip, used to identify a person —*vt.* to take the fingerprints of

finger tip the tip of a finger —**have at one's finger tips** to have available for instant use

fin·i·al (fin′ē əl) *n.* [ult. < L. *finis*, end] an ornament at the top of a spire, lamp, etc.

fin·ick·y (fin′i kē) *adj.* [< FINE] too particular; fussy: also **fin′i·cal** (-k'l), **fin′ick·ing**

fi·nis (fin′is, fī′nis) *n., pl.* **-nis·es** [L.] the end; finish

fin·ish (fin′ish) *vt.* [< L. *finis*, end] **1.** to bring to an end **2.** to come to the end of **3.** to use up **4.** to perfect **5.** to give a desired surface effect to —*vi.* to come to an end —*n.* **1.** the last part; end **2.** *a)* anything used to finish a surface, etc. *b)* the finished effect **3.** means or manner of completing or perfecting **4.** polish in manners, speech, etc. —**finish off 1.** to end **2.** to kill or ruin —**finish with** to bring to an end

fi·nite (fī′nīt) *adj.* [< L. *finis*, end] having definable limits; not infinite

Finn (fin) *n.* a native of Finland

fin·nan had·die (fin′ən had′ē) [prob. < *Findhorn* (Scotland) *haddock*] smoked haddock

Finn·ish (fin′ish) *adj.* of Finland, its people, their language, etc. —*n.* the language of the Finns

fiord (fyôrd) *n.* [Norw. < ON. *fjörthr*] a narrow inlet of the sea bordered by steep cliffs

fir (fur) *n.* [OE. *fyrh*] **1.** a cone-bearing evergreen tree related to the pine **2.** its wood

fire (fīr) *n.* [OE. *fyr*] **1.** the flame, heat, and light of combustion **2.** something burning, as fuel in a furnace **3.** a destructive burning *[a forest fire]* **4.** strong feeling; ardor **5.** a discharge of firearms —*vt., vi.* **fired, fir'ing 1.** to start burning **2.** to supply with fuel **3.** to bake (bricks, etc.) in a kiln **4.** to excite or become excited **5.** to shoot (a gun, bullet, etc.) **6.** to hurl or direct with force *[to fire questions]* **7.** to dismiss from a job; discharge —**catch (on) fire** to ignite —**on fire 1.** burning **2.** greatly excited —**under fire** under attack

fire'arm' *n.* any hand weapon from which a shot is fired by explosive force, as a rifle

fire'bomb' *n.* an incendiary bomb —*vt.* to attack or damage with a firebomb

fire'brand' *n.* **1.** a piece of burning wood **2.** one who stirs up strife or a revolt

fire'break' *n.* a strip of land cleared to stop the spread of fire, as in a forest

fire'bug' *n.* [Colloq.] one who deliberately sets fire to buildings, etc.; pyromaniac

fire'crack'er *n.* a roll of paper containing an explosive, set off at celebrations, etc.

fire'damp' *n.* a gas formed in coal mines, explosive when mixed with air

fire engine a motor truck with equipment for fighting fires

fire escape a ladder, outside stairway, etc. for escape from a burning building

fire'fly' *n., pl.* **-flies'** a winged beetle whose abdomen glows with a luminescent light

fire'man (-mən) *n., pl.* **-men 1.** a man whose work is fighting fires **2.** a man who tends a fire in a furnace, etc.

fire'place' *n.* a place for a fire, esp. an open place built in a wall

fire'plug' *n.* a street hydrant to which a hose can be attached for fighting fires

fire'proof' *adj.* not easily destroyed by fire —*vt.* to make fireproof

fire'side' *n.* **1.** the space around a fireplace **2.** home or home life

fire'storm' *n.* an intense fire over a wide area, as one caused by an atomic explosion

fire'trap' *n.* a building easily set afire or hard to escape from in case of fire

fire'wa'ter *n.* [Colloq.] alcoholic liquor

fire'wood' *n.* wood used as fuel

fire'works' *n.pl.* firecrackers, rockets, etc., used for noisy or brilliant displays: *sometimes used in sing.*

firing line 1. the line from which gunfire is directed at the enemy **2.** any vulnerable front position

firm[1] (furm) *adj.* [< L. *firmus*] **1.** solid; hard **2.** not moved easily; fixed **3.** not fluctuating; steady **4.** resolute; constant **5.** showing determination; strong **6.** definite *[a firm contract]* —*vt., vi.* to make or become firm —**firm'ly** *adv.* —**firm'ness** *n.*

firm[2] (furm) *n.* [< It. < L. *firmus*, firm] a business company

fir·ma·ment (fur'mə mənt) *n.* [< L. *firmus*, firm] the sky, viewed poetically as a solid arch or vault

first (furst) *adj.* [OE. *fyrst*] **1.** before any others; 1st **2.** earliest **3.** foremost in rank, importance, etc. —*adv.* **1.** before any other person or thing **2.** for the first time **3.** sooner; preferably —*n.* **1.** any person or thing that is first **2.** the beginning **3.** the winning place, as in a race **4.** low gear

first aid emergency treatment for injury, etc. before regular medical aid is available

first'born' *adj.* born first in a family; oldest —*n.* the firstborn child

first'-class' *adj.* **1.** of the highest class, quality, etc. **2.** designating or of the most expensive regular class of sealed mail —*adv.* **1.** with first-class accommodations **2.** by first-class mail

first'hand' *adj., adv.* from the original producer or source; direct

first lieutenant *U.S. Mil.* an officer ranking above a second lieutenant

first person that form of a pronoun or verb that refers to the speaker

first'-rate' *adj.* of the highest quality, class, etc. —*adv.* [Colloq.] very well

first'-string' *adj.* [Colloq.] *Sports* that is the first choice for regular play at the specified position

firth (furth) *n.* [< ON. *fjörthr*] a narrow inlet or arm of the sea

fis·cal (fis'kəl) *adj.* [< L. *fiscus*, public chest] **1.** relating to the public treasury or revenues **2.** financial —**fis'cal·ly** *adv.*

fish (fish) *n., pl.* **fish:** in referring to different species, **fish'es** [OE. *fisc*] **1.** any of a large group of coldblooded animals living in water and having backbones, gills for breathing, and fins **2.** the flesh of a fish used as food —*vi.* **1.** to catch or try to catch fish **2.** to try to get something indirectly (often with *for*) —*vt.* to grope for, find, and bring to view (often with *out*)

fish'er·man (-ər mən) *n., pl.* **-men** a person who fishes for sport or for a living

fish'er·y *n., pl.* **-ies 1.** the business of catching fish **2.** a place where fish are caught or bred

fish'hook' *n.* a hook, usually barbed, for catching fish

fish'ing *n.* the catching of fish for sport or for a living

fish'wife' *n., pl.* **-wives'** a coarse, scolding woman

fish'y *adj.* **-i·er, -i·est 1.** like a fish in odor, taste, etc. **2.** dull; without expression *[a fishy stare]* **3.** [Colloq.] questionable; odd

fis·sion (fish'ən) *n.* [< L. *findere*, to split] **1.** a splitting apart; cleavage **2.** *same as* NUCLEAR FISSION —**fis'sion·a·ble** *adj.*

fis·sure (fish'ər) *n.* [see prec.] a cleft or crack

fist (fist) *n.* [OE. *fyst*] a hand with the fingers closed tightly into the palm

fis·ti·cuffs (fis'ti kufs') *n.pl.* a fight, or the art of fighting, with the fists

fis·tu·la (fis'choo lə) *n., pl.* **-las, -lae'** (-lē') [L.] an abnormal hollow passage, as from an abscess, cavity, etc. to the skin

fit[1] (fit) *vt.* **fit'ted** or **fit, fit'ted, fit'ting** [ME. *fitten*] **1.** to be suitable to **2.** to be the proper size, shape, etc. for **3.** to adjust so as to fit **4.** to equip; outfit —*vi.* **1.** to be suitable or proper **2.** to have the proper size or shape —*adj.* **fit'ter, fit'test 1.** suited to some purpose, function, etc. **2.** proper; right **3.** healthy —*n.* the manner of fitting *[a tight fit]* —**fit'ly** *adv.* —**fit'ness** *n.* —**fit'ter** *n.*

fit[2] (fit) *n.* [OE. *fitt*, conflict] **1.** any sudden, uncontrollable attack *[a fit of coughing]* **2.** a temporary outburst, as of feeling **3.** a seizure involving convulsions or loss of consciousness —**by fits (and starts)** in an irregular way —**have (or throw) a fit** [Colloq.] to become very angry or upset

fit'ful (-fəl) *adj.* characterized by intermittent activity; spasmodic —**fit'ful·ly** *adv.*

fit'ting *adj.* suitable; proper —*n.* **1.** an adjustment or trying on of clothes, etc. for fit **2.** a part used to join or adapt other parts **3.** *[pl.]* fixtures —**fit'ting·ly** *adv.*

five (fīv) *adj., n.* [OE. *fif*] one more than four; 5; V

five′-and-ten′-cent′ store a store that sells a wide variety of inexpensive merchandise: also **five′-and-ten′** *n.*

fix (fiks) *vt.* [< L. *figere*, fasten] **1.** to fasten firmly **2.** to set firmly in the mind **3.** to direct (one's eyes) steadily **4.** to make rigid **5.** to make permanent **6.** to establish (a date, etc.) definitely **7.** to set in order **8.** to repair **9.** to prepare (food or meals) **10.** [Colloq.] to influence the result or action of (a race, jury, etc.) as by bribery **11.** [Colloq.] to punish —*vi.* **1.** to become fixed **2.** [Dial.] to prepare or intend —*n.* **1.** [Colloq.] a predicament **2.** [Slang] a situation that has been fixed (sense 10) **3.** [Slang] an injection of a narcotic by an addict —**fix up** [Colloq.] **1.** to repair **2.** to set in order; arrange

fix·a·tion (fik sā′shən) *n.* **1.** a fixing or being fixed **2.** an obsession

fix·a·tive (fik′sə tiv) *adj.* that is able or tends to make permanent, prevent fading, etc. —*n.* a fixative substance

fixed (fikst) *adj.* **1.** firmly in place **2.** clearly established **3.** resolute **4.** obsessive [a *fixed* idea] —**fix·ed·ly** (fik′sid lē) *adv.*

fix·ings (fik′siŋz) *n.pl.* [Colloq.] accessories or trimmings

fix·ture (fiks′chər) *n.* [see FIX] **1.** anything firmly in place **2.** any attached piece of equipment in a house, etc. **3.** a person long-established in a place or job

fizz (fiz) *n.* [echoic] **1.** a hissing, bubbling sound **2.** an effervescent drink —*vi.* **fizzed, fizz′ing 1.** to make a bubbling sound **2.** to effervesce

fiz·zle (fiz′'l) *vi.* **-zled, -zling** [< ME.] **1.** to make a hissing sound **2.** [Colloq.] to fail, esp. after a good start —*n.* **1.** a hissing sound **2.** [Colloq.] a failure

fjord (fyôrd) *n. same as* FIORD

fl. 1. [L. *floruit*] (he or she) flourished **2.** fluid

flab·ber·gast (flab′ər gast′) *vt.* [< ? FLABBY + AGHAST] [Colloq.] to amaze; dumbfound

flab·by (flab′ē) *adj.* **-bi·er, -bi·est** [< FLAP] **1.** limp and soft **2.** weak —**flab′bi·ness** *n.*

flac·cid (flak′sid, flas′id) *adj.* [< L. *flaccus*] flabby

‡**fla·con** (flä kōn′) *n.* [Fr.] a small flask with a stopper, for perfume, etc.

flag¹ (flag) *n.* [< ? FLAG⁴, to flutter] a cloth with colors, patterns, etc. used as a symbol of a nation, state, organization, etc., or as a signal —*vt.* **flagged, flag′ging** to signal as with a flag; esp., to signal to stop (often with *down*) —**flag′ger** *n.*

flag² (flag) *n.* [< ON. *flaga*, slab of stone] *same as* FLAGSTONE —*vt.* **flagged, flag′ging** to pave with flagstones

flag³ (flag) *n.* [ME. *flagge*] any of various irises with white, blue, or yellow flowers

flag⁴ (flag) *vi.* **flagged, flag′ging** [< ? ON. *flakka*, to flutter] **1.** to become limp **2.** to grow weak or tired

flag·el·late (flaj′ə lāt′) *vt.* **-lat′ed, -lat′ing** [< L. *flagellum*, a whip] to whip; flog —*adj.* having flagella or shaped like a flagellum —**flag′el·la′tion** *n.*

fla·gel·lum (flə jel′əm) *n., pl.* **-la** (-ə) **-lums** [L.: see prec.] *Biol.* a whiplike part serving as an organ of locomotion in certain cells, bacteria, etc.

flag·on (flag′ən) *n.* [< LL. *flasca*] a container for liquids, with handle, spout, and lid

flag′pole′ *n.* a pole on which a flag is raised and flown: also **flag′staff′**

fla·grant (flā′grənt) *adj.* [< L. *flagrare*, to blaze] glaringly bad; notorious; outrageous —**fla′gran·cy** (-grən sē), **fla′grance** *n.*

flag′ship′ *n.* the ship that carries the commander of a fleet or squadron

flag′stone′ *n.* a flat piece of paving stone

flail (flāl) *n.* [< L. *flagellum*, a whip] a farm tool for threshing grain by hand —*vt., vi.* **1.** to thresh with a flail **2.** to beat **3.** to move (one's arms) like flails

flair (fler) *n.* [< L. *fragrare*, to smell] **1.** a talent; knack **2.** [Colloq.] stylishness

flak (flak) *n.* [G. acronym] **1.** antiaircraft fire **2.** strong criticism: also **flack**

flake (flāk) *n.* [< Scand.] **1.** a small, thin mass **2.** a piece split off; chip —*vt., vi.* **flaked, flak′ing 1.** to form into flakes **2.** to chip off in flakes

flak·y *adj.* **-i·er, -i·est 1.** of flakes **2.** [Slang] very eccentric —**flak′i·ness** *n.*

flam·boy·ant (flam boi′ənt) *adj.* [Fr.: see FLAME] **1.** flamelike or brilliant **2.** too showy; ornate —**flam·boy′ance** *n.*

flame (flām) *n.* [< L. *flamma*] **1.** the burning gas of a fire, appearing as a tongue of light **2.** the state of burning with a blaze **3.** a thing like a flame **4.** an intense emotion **5.** a sweetheart: now humorous —*vi.* **flamed, flam′-ing 1.** to burst into flame **2.** to grow red or hot **3.** to become excited

flame′out′ *n.* a failure of combustion in a jet engine during flight

flame thrower [< G.] a military weapon that shoots flaming gasoline, oil, etc.

fla·min·go (flə miŋ′gō) *n., pl.* **-gos, -goes** [Port. < Sp. *flama*, flame] a tropical wading bird with long legs and pink or red feathers

flam·ma·ble (flam′ə b'l) *adj.* easily set on fire —**flam′ma·bil′i·ty** *n.*

flange (flanj) *n.* [< ? ME.] a projecting rim on a wheel, rail, etc., to hold it in place, give strength, etc. —*vt.* **flanged, flang′ing** to put a flange on

flank (flaŋk) *n.* [< OFr. *flanc*] **1.** the side of an animal between the ribs and the hip **2.** the side of anything **3.** the right or left side of a military force —*vt.* **1.** to be at the side of **2.** to attack, or pass around, the side of (enemy troops) —**flank′er** *n.*

flan·nel (flan′'l) *n.* [prob. < W. *gwlan*, wool] **1.** a soft, loosely woven cloth of wool or cotton **2.** [*pl.*] trousers, etc. made of this

flan·nel·ette, flan·nel·et (flan′ə let′) *n.* a soft, fleecy, cotton cloth

flap (flap) *n.* [ME. *flappe*] **1.** anything flat and broad hanging loose from one end **2.** the motion or sound of a swinging flap **3.** a slap **4.** [Slang] a commotion **5.** *Aeron.* a movable airfoil —*vt., vi.* **flapped, flap′ping 1.** to slap **2.** to move back and forth or up and down, as wings

flap′jack′ *n.* a pancake

flap·per (flap′ər) *n.* **1.** one that flaps **2.** [Colloq.] in the 1920's, a bold, unconventional young woman

flare (fler) *vi.* **flared, flar′ing** [ME. *fleare*] **1.** *a*) to blaze brightly *b*) to burn unsteadily **2.** to burst out suddenly, as in anger (with *up* or *out*) **3.** to curve outward, as a bell —*n.* **1.** a bright, unsteady blaze **2.** a brightly flaming signal light **3.** an outburst, as of emotion **4.** a curving outward, as of a skirt

flare′-up′ *n.* a sudden outburst of flame or of anger, trouble, etc.

flash (flash) *vi.* [ME. *flashen*, to splash] **1.** to send out a sudden, brief light **2.** to sparkle **3.** to come or pass suddenly —*vt.* **1.** to cause to flash **2.** to send (news, etc.) swiftly —*n.* **1.** a sudden, brief light **2.** a brief moment **3.** a sudden, brief display **4.** a brief news item sent by radio, etc. **5.** a gaudy display —**flash′er** *n.*

flash'back' *n.* an interruption in the continuity of a story, etc. by telling or showing an earlier episode

flash'bulb' *n.* an electric light bulb giving a brief, dazzling light, for taking photographs

flash'cube' *n.* a rotating cube containing a flashbulb in each of four sides

flash flood a sudden flood

flash'ing *n.* sheets of metal used to weatherproof joints, edges, etc., esp. of a roof

flash'light' *n.* a portable electric light, usually operated by batteries

flash'y *adj.* **-i·er, -i·est** 1. dazzling for a little while 2. gaudy; showy —**flash'i·ness** *n.*

flask (flask) *n.* [< LL. *flasca*, bottle] 1. any of various bottles used in laboratories, etc. 2. a small, flat pocket container for liquor, etc.

flat¹ (flat) *adj.* **flat'ter, flat'test** [< ON. *flatr*] 1. having a smooth, level surface 2. lying spread out 3. broad, even, and thin 4. absolute *[a flat* denial*]* 5. not fluctuating *[a flat* rate*]* 6. tasteless; insipid *[a flat* drink*]* 7. not interesting; dull 8. emptied of air *[a flat* tire*]* 9. without gloss *[flat* paint*]* 10. *Music* below the true pitch —*adv.* 1. in a flat manner or position 2. exactly 3. *Music* below the true pitch —*n.* 1. a flat surface or part 2. an expanse of level land 3. a deflated tire 4. *Music a)* a note one half step below another *b)* the symbol (♭) for such a note —*vt., vi.* **flat'ted, flat'ting** to make or become flat —**fall flat** to arouse no response

flat² (flat) *n.* [< Scot. dial. *flet*, a floor] an apartment or suite of rooms

flat'boat' *n.* a flat-bottomed boat, for carrying freight in shallow waters or on rivers

flat'fish' *n., pl.:* see FISH a flat-bodied fish with both eyes on the uppermost side, as the flounder

flat'foot' *n.* 1. a condition in which the instep arch is flattened 2. *pl.* **-foots'** [Slang] a policeman —**flat'-foot'ed** *adj.*

flat'i'ron *n. same as* IRON (sense 2)

flat'ten (-'n) *vt., vi.* to make or become flat or flatter

flat·ter (flat'ər) *vt.* [< Frank. *flat,* to smooth] 1. to praise insincerely 2. to try to please, as by praise 3. to make seem more attractive than is so 4. to gratify the vanity of —*vi.* to use flattery

flat'ter·y *n., pl.* **-ies** 1. a flattering 2. excessive or insincere praise

flat'top' *n.* [Slang] an aircraft carrier

flat·u·lent (flach'ə lənt, -yoo-) *adj.* [ult. < L. *flare,* to blow] 1. having or producing gas in the stomach or intestines 2. pompous —**flat'u·lence, flat'u·len·cy** *n.*

flaunt (flônt) *vi., vt.* [< ? dial. *flant,* to strut] to show off proudly or defiantly

fla·vor (flā'vər) *n.* [ult. < L. *flare,* to blow] 1. *a)* the combined taste and smell of something *b)* taste in general 2. *same as* FLAVORING 3. characteristic quality —*vt.* to give flavor to Brit. sp. **fla'vour**

fla'vor·ing *n.* an essence, extract, etc. that adds flavor to food or drink

flaw (flô) *n.* [prob. < Scand.] 1. a crack, as in a gem 2. a defect; fault —*vt., vi.* to make or become faulty

flax (flaks) *n.* [OE. *fleax*] 1. a slender, erect plant with delicate, blue flowers: the seed (**flax'seed'**) yields linseed oil 2. the fibers of this plant, spun into linen thread

flax'en (-'n) *adj.* 1. of or made of flax 2. paleyellow

flay (flā) *vt.* [OE. *flean*] 1. to strip off the skin of 2. to criticize harshly —**flay'er** *n.*

flea (flē) *n.* [OE. *fleah*] a small, wingless, jump-

ing insect that is a bloodsucking parasite as an adult

flea'-bit'ten *adj.* 1. bitten by or infested with fleas 2. wretched; shabby

fleck (flek) *n.* [ON. *flekkr*] a spot, speck, or flake —*vt.* to spot; speckle

fled (fled) *pt. & pp. of* FLEE

fledge (flej) *vi.* **fledged, fledg'ing** [< OE. *(un)flycge,* (un)fledged] to grow the feathers needed for flying —*vt.* to rear (a young bird) until it is able to fly

fledg·ling (flej'lin) *n.* 1. a young bird just fledged 2. a young, inexperienced person

flee (flē) *vi., vt.* **fled, flee'ing** [OE. *fleon*] to go swiftly or escape

fleece (flēs) *n.* [OE. *fleos*] the wool covering a sheep or similar animal —*vt.* **fleeced, fleec'ing** 1. to shear fleece from 2. to swindle —**fleec'er** *n.*

fleec'y *adj.* **-i·er, -i·est** of or like fleece; soft and light —**fleec'i·ness** *n.*

fleet¹ (flēt) *n.* [OE. *fleot*] 1. a number of warships under one command 2. any group of ships, trucks, airplanes, etc. under one control

fleet² (flēt) *adj.* [< OE. *fleotan,* to float] swift; rapid —**fleet'ness** *n.*

fleet'ing *adj.* passing swiftly

Flem·ish (flem'ish) *adj.* of Flanders, its people, or their language —*n.* the Low German language of Flanders

flesh (flesh) *n.* [OE. *flæsc*] 1. the soft substance of the body; esp., the muscular tissue 2. the pulpy part of fruits and vegetables 3. meat 4. the human body, as distinguished from the soul 5. all mankind 6. yellowish pink —**in the flesh** 1. alive 2. in person —**one's (own) flesh and blood** one's close relatives —**flesh'y** *adj.* **-i·er, -i·est**

flesh'pots' *n.pl.* places where luxuries and sensual pleasures are provided

fleur-de-lis (flur'də lē') *n., pl.* **fleurs-de-lis** (flur'də lēz') [< OFr., flower of the lily] a lily-like emblem, the coat of arms of the kings of France

flew (floo) *pt. of* FLY¹

flex (fleks) *vt., vi.* [< L. *flectere,* to bend] 1. to bend, as an arm 2. to contract, as a muscle

flex·i·ble (flek'sə b'l) *adj.* 1. able to bend without breaking; pliant 2. easily influenced 3. adjustable to change —**flex'i·bil'i·ty** *n.* —**flex'i·bly** *adv.*

flick¹ (flik) *n.* [echoic] a light, quick stroke —*vt.* to strike, remove, etc. with a light, quick stroke

flick² (flik) *n.* [< FLICKER¹] [Slang] a movie —**the flicks** a showing of a movie

flick·er (flik'ər) *vi.* [OE. *flicorian*] 1. to move with a quick, light, wavering motion 2. to burn or shine unsteadily —*n.* 1. a flickering 2. a dart of flame or light

fli·er (flī'ər) *n.* 1. a thing that flies 2. an aviator 3. a train, bus, etc. on a fast schedule 4. a handbill 5. [Colloq.] a gamble

flight¹ (flīt) *n.* [OE. *flyht*] 1. the act, manner, or power of flying 2. the distance flown 3. a group of things flying together 4. an airplane scheduled to fly a certain trip 5. a trip by airplane 6. a soaring above the ordinary *[a flight* of fancy*]* 7. a set of stairs, as between landings

flight² (flīt) *n.* [< OE. *fleon,* to flee] a fleeing, as from danger —**put to flight** to force to flee

flight'less *adj.* not able to fly

flight'y *adj.* **-i·er, -i·est** given to sudden whims; frivolous —**flight'i·ness** *n.*

flim·sy (flim'zē) *adj.* **-si·er, -si·est** [< ?] 1. easily broken or damaged; fragile 2. inadequate *[a flimsy excuse] —n.* a sheet of thin paper —**flim′si·ness** *n.*

flinch (flinch) *vi.* [< OFr. *flenchir*] to draw back from a blow or anything difficult or painful —*n.* a flinching

fling (fliŋ) *vt.* **flung, fling′ing** [< ON. *flengja,* to whip] **1.** to throw, esp. with force; hurl **2.** to put abruptly or violently **3.** to move (one's limbs, head, etc.) suddenly —*n.* **1.** a flinging **2.** a brief time of self-indulgence **3.** a spirited dance *[the Highland fling]* **4.** [Colloq.] a try

flint (flint) *n.* [OE.] a very hard, siliceous rock that makes sparks when struck with steel — **flint′y** *adj.* **-i·er, -i·est**

flip¹ (flip) *vt.* **flipped, flip′ping** [echoic] **1.** to toss with a quick jerk **2.** to snap (a coin) into the air with the thumb **3.** to turn or turn over —*vi.* **1.** to move jerkily **2.** [Slang] to lose self-control —*adj.* **flip′per, flip′pest** [Colloq.] flippant; saucy —*n.* a flipping

flip² (flip) *n.* [prob. < prec.] a sweetened, spiced drink of wine or liquor with egg

flip′-flop′ (-fläp′) *n.* **1.** an acrobatic spring backward from feet to hands to feet **2.** an abrupt reversal, as of opinion

flip′pant (-ənt) *adj.* [prob. < FLIP¹] frivolous and disrespectful; saucy —**flip′pan·cy** *n.*

flip·per (flip′ər) *n.* [< FLIP¹] **1.** a broad, flat limb, as of a seal, adapted for swimming **2.** a rubber paddle worn on each foot by swimmers

flirt (flurt) *vt.* [< ?] to move jerkily *[the bird flirted its tail]* —*vi.* **1.** to make love without serious intentions **2.** to toy, as with an idea — *n.* **1.** a quick, jerky movement **2.** one who plays at love

flir·ta·tion (flər tā′shən) *n.* a flirting, or playing at love —**flir·ta′tious** *adj.*

flit (flit) *vi.* **flit′ted, flit′ting** [< ON. *flytja*] to pass or fly lightly and rapidly

float (flōt) *n.* [< OE. *fleotan,* to float] **1.** anything that stays on the surface of a liquid, as a raft, a fishing-line cork, etc. **2.** a low, flat vehicle decorated for exhibit in a parade —*vi.* **1.** to stay on the surface of a liquid **2.** to drift gently on water, in air, etc. **3.** to move about aimlessly —*vt.* **1.** to cause to float **2.** to put into circulation *[to float a bond issue]* **3.** to arrange for (a loan) —**float′er** *n.*

flock (fläk) *n.* [OE. *flocc,* a troop] **1.** a group of certain animals, as sheep, birds, etc., living or feeding together **2.** any group, as of children — *vi.* to assemble or travel in a flock

flock·ing (fläk′iŋ) *n.* [< L. *floccus*] **1.** tiny fibers of wool, cotton, etc. applied to fabric, wallpaper, etc. as a velvetlike surface: also **flock 2.** such a fabric, etc.

floe (flō) *n.* [prob. < Norw. *flo,* layer] a piece of floating sea ice; ice floe

flog (fläg, flôg) *vt.* **flogged, flog′ging** [< ? L. *flagellare*] to beat with a stick, whip, etc. — **flog′ger** *n.*

flood (flud) *n.* [OE. *flod*] **1.** an overflowing of water on land normally dry; deluge **2.** the rising tide: also **flood tide 3.** a great outpouring, as of words —*vt.* to cover or fill, as with a flood —*vi.* to gush out in a flood —**the Flood** *Bible* the great flood in Noah's time

flood′light′ *n.* **1.** a lamp that casts a broad beam of bright light **2.** such a beam of light — *vt.* **-light′ed** or **-lit′, -light′ing** to illuminate by a floodlight

floor (flôr) *n.* [OE. *flor*] **1.** the inside bottom surface of a room **2.** any bottom surface *[the ocean floor]* **3.** a story in a building **4.** the right to speak in an assembly —*vt.* **1.** to furnish with a floor **2.** to knock down **3.** [Colloq.] to shock or confuse

floor′ing *n.* material for making a floor

floor show a show presenting singers, dancers, etc., as in a nightclub

floor′walk′er *n.* formerly, a department store employee supervising sales, etc.: now often **floor** (or **sales**) **manager**

flop (fläp) *vt.* **flopped, flop′ping** [var. of FLAP] to flap or throw noisily and clumsily —*vi.* **1.** to move, drop, or flap around loosely or clumsily **2.** [Colloq.] to fail —*n.* **1.** the act or sound of flopping **2.** [Colloq.] a failure —**flop′py** *adj.* **-pi·er, -pi·est**

flop′house′ *n.* [Colloq.] a cheap hotel

flo·ra (flôr′ə) *n.* [< L. *flos,* a flower] the plants of a specified region or time

flo′ral (-əl) *adj.* of, made of, or like flowers — **flo′ral·ly** *adv.*

flo·res·cence (flô res′'ns) *n.* [< L. *florere,* to bloom] a blooming or flowering —**flo·res′cent** *adj.*

flo·ret (flôr′it) *n.* [< L. *flos,* a flower] **1.** a small flower **2.** any of the small flowers making up the blossom of a composite plant

flor·id (flôr′id) *adj.* [< L. *flos,* a flower] **1.** ruddy: said of the complexion **2.** showy; ornate —**flor′id·ly** *adv.*

flor·in (flôr′in) *n.* [< L. *flos,* a flower] any of various European or S. African coins

flo·rist (flôr′ist) *n.* [< L. *flos,* a flower] one who cultivates or sells flowers

floss (flôs, fläs) *n.* [prob. < L. *floccus,* tuft of wool] **1.** the soft, downy waste fibers of silk **2.** a soft thread or yarn, as of silk, used. in embroidery **3.** a substance like this —**floss′y** *adj.* **-i·er, -i·est**

flo·ta·tion (flō tā′shən) *n.* **1.** a floating or launching **2.** the financing of a business, as by selling an entire issue of bonds

flo·til·la (flō til′ə) *n.* [Sp., dim. of *flota,* a fleet] **1.** a small fleet **2.** a fleet of boats or small ships

flot·sam (flät′səm) *n.* [< MDu. *vloten,* to float] the wreckage of a ship or its cargo found floating on the sea: chiefly in **flotsam and jetsam**

flounce¹ (flouns) *vi.* **flounced, flounc′ing** [prob. < Scand.] to move with quick, flinging motions of the body, as in anger —*n.* the act of flouncing

flounce² (flouns) *n.* [< OFr. *froncir,* to wrinkle] a wide ruffle, as on a skirt

floun·der¹ (floun′dər) *vi.* [? < FOUNDER] **1.** to struggle awkwardly, as in deep mud **2.** to speak or act in an awkward, confused way

floun·der² (floun′dər) *n.* [< Scand.] any of various flatfishes caught for food, as the halibut

flour (flour) *n.* [orig. flower (i.e., best) of meal] **1.** a fine, powdery substance produced by grinding and sifting grain, esp. wheat **2.** any finely powdered substance —*vt.* to put flour on or in —**flour′y** *adj.*

flour·ish (flur′ish) *vi.* [< L. *flos,* a flower] **1.** to grow vigorously; thrive **2.** to be at the peak of development, etc. —*vt.* to brandish (a sword, etc.) —*n.* **1.** anything done in a showy way **2.** a brandishing **3.** decorative lines in writing **4.** a musical fanfare

flout (flout) *vt., vi.* [prob. < ME. *flouten,* play the flute] to show scorn or contempt (for) —*n.* a flouting

flow (flō) *vi.* [OE. *flowan*] **1.** to move as a liquid does **2.** to move gently and smoothly **3.** to pour out **4.** to be derived; proceed **5.** to hang loose *[flowing hair]* **6.** to be plentiful —*n.* **1.** a flowing **2.** the rate of flow **3.** anything that flows

flow·er (flou′ər, flour) *n.* [< L. *flos]* **1.** the seed-

flowerpot 179 foam

producing structure of a flowering plant; blossom **2.** a plant cultivated for its blossoms **3.** the best or finest part —**vi. 1.** to produce blossoms **2.** to reach the best period —**in flower** flowering

flow′er·pot′ *n.* a container in which to grow plants

flow′er·y *adj.* **-i·er, -i·est 1.** covered or decorated with flowers **2.** full of ornate expressions and fine words

flown (flōn) *pp. of* FLY[1]

flu (flōō) *n.* **1.** *short for* INFLUENZA **2.** popularly, a respiratory or intestinal infection caused by a virus

fluc·tu·ate (fluk′chōō wāt′) *vi.* **-at′ed, -at′ing** [< L. *fluctus,* a wave] to be continually varying irregularly —**fluc′tu·a′tion** *n.*

flue (flōō) *n.* [< ? OFr. *fluie,* a flowing] a shaft for the passage of smoke, hot air, etc., as in a chimney

flu·ent (flōō′ənt) *adj.* [< L. *fluere,* to flow] **1.** flowing smoothly **2.** able to write or speak easily, expressively, etc.

fluff (fluf) *n.* [? blend of *flue,* soft mass + PUFF] **1.** soft, light down **2.** a loose, soft mass, as of dust —**vt. 1.** to shake or pat until loose and fluffy **2.** to bungle (one's lines), as in acting

fluff′y (-ē) *adj.* **-i·er, -i·est** like, or covered with, fluff; soft and feathery

flu·id (flōō′id) *adj.* [< L. *fluere,* to flow] **1.** that can flow; not solid **2.** not settled or fixed *[fluid plans]* **3.** available for investment or as cash — *n.* a liquid or gas —**flu·id′i·ty** *n.* —**flu′id·ly** *adv.*

fluid dram a liquid measure equal to 1/8 fluid ounce

fluke[1] (flōōk) *n.* [OE. *floc*] a flat, parasitic worm found as in sheep's livers

fluke[2] (flōōk) *n.* [prob. < prec.] **1.** either of the pointed blades on an anchor, which catch in the ground **2.** a barb of an arrow, harpoon, etc. **3.** either of the lobes of a whale's tail **4.** [Colloq.] a stroke of luck

flume (flōōm) *n.* [< L. *flumen,* river] an inclined chute for carrying water to transport logs, furnish power, etc.

flung (fluŋ) *pt. & pp. of* FLING

flunk (fluŋk) *vt., vi.* [< ?] [Colloq.] to fail, as in schoolwork

flun·ky (fluŋ′kē) *n., pl.* **-kies** [orig. Scot.] **1.** one who is servile to superiors **2.** one having menial tasks Also **flun′key,** *pl.* **-keys**

flu·o·res·cence (flōō′ə res′'ns) *n.* [ult. < L. *fluor,* flux] **1.** the property some substances have of producing light when acted upon by radiant energy **2.** light so produced —**flu′o·res′cent** *adj.*

fluorescent lamp (or **tube**) a glass tube coated on the inside with a fluorescent substance that gives off light (**fluorescent light**) when acted upon by a stream of electrons

fluor·i·date (flôr′ə dāt′, floor′-) *vt.* **-dat′ed, -dat′ing** to add fluorides to (a water supply) in order to reduce tooth decay —**fluor′i·da′tion** *n.*

flu·o·ride (floor′īd, flōō′ə rīd′) *n.* any of various compounds of fluorine

flu·o·rine (floor′ēn; flōō′ə rēn′, -rin) *n.* [< L. *fluor,* flux] a corrosive, greenish-yellow, gaseous chemical element: symbol, F

fluor·o·scope (floor′ə skōp′) *n.* a machine for examining internal structures by viewing the shadows cast on a fluorescent screen by objects through which X-rays are directed

flur·ry (flur′ē) *n., pl.* **-ries** [< ?] **1.** a sudden, brief rush of wind or fall of snow **2.** a sudden commotion —**vt. -ried, -ry·ing** to confuse; agitate

flush[1] (flush) *vi.* [blend of FLASH & ME. *flusshen,* fly up suddenly] **1.** to blush or glow **2.** to start up from cover: said of birds —**vt. 1.** to clean or empty with a sudden flow of water, etc. **2.** to make blush or glow **3.** to excite **4.** to drive (birds) from cover —**n. 1.** a rapid flow, as of water **2.** a sudden, vigorous growth **3.** sudden excitement **4.** a blush; glow **5.** a sudden feeling of heat, as in a fever —**adj. 1.** well supplied, esp. with money **2.** abundant **3.** level or even (*with*) **4.** direct; full

flush[2] (flush) *n.* [< L. *fluere,* to flow] a hand of cards all in the same suit

flus·ter (flus′tər) *vt., vi.* [prob. < Scand.] to make or be confused —*n.* a flustered state

flute (flōōt) *n.* [< Pr. *fläut*] **1.** a high-pitched wind instrument consisting of a long, slender tube with finger holes and keys **2.** a groove in the shaft of a column —**flut′ed** *adj.* —**flut′ing** *n.* —**flut′ist** *n.*

flut·ter (flut′ər) *vi.* [< OE. *fleotan,* to float] **1.** to flap the wings rapidly, without flying **2.** to wave, move, or beat rapidly and irregularly — *vt.* to cause to flutter —*n.* **1.** a fluttering movement **2.** an excited or confused state —**flut′ter·y** *adj.*

flu·vi·al (flōō′vē əl) *adj.* [< L. *fluere,* to flow] of, found in, or produced by a river

flux (fluks) *n.* [< L. *fluere,* to flow] **1.** a flowing **2.** a coming in of the tide **3.** a continual change **4.** any abnormal discharge from the body **5.** a substance used to help metals to fuse, as in soldering

fly[1] (flī) *vi.* **flew, flown, fly′ing** [OE. *fleogan*] **1.** to move through the air by using wings, as a bird, or in an aircraft **2.** to wave or float in the air **3.** to move swiftly **4.** to flee **5. flied, fly′ing** *Baseball* to hit a fly —**vt. 1.** to cause to float in air **2.** to operate (an aircraft) **3.** to flee from —*n., pl.* **flies 1.** a flap that conceals a zipper, buttons, etc. in a garment **2.** a flap serving as a tent door **3.** *Baseball* a ball batted high —**fly at** to attack as by springing forward —**let fly (at) 1.** to hurl (at) **2.** to unleash a verbal attack (at) —**on the fly** [Colloq.] while in a hurry

fly[2] (flī) *n., pl.* **flies** [OE. *fleoge*] **1.** any of a large group of insects with two transparent wings; esp., the housefly **2.** a fish lure made to resemble an insect

fly′-by-night′ *adj.* not trustworthy, esp. financially —*n.* an absconding debtor

fly′er *n. same as* FLIER

flying buttress a buttress connected with a wall by an arch, serving to resist outward pressure

flying fish a fish with winglike pectoral fins used in gliding through the air

fly′leaf′ *n., pl.* **-leaves** a blank leaf at the beginning or end of a book

fly′pa′per *n.* a sticky or poisonous paper set out to catch flies

fly′weight′ *n.* a boxer who weighs 112 pounds or less —*adj.* of flyweights

fly′wheel′ *n.* a heavy wheel on a machine, for regulating its speed

FM frequency modulation

foal (fōl) *n.* [OE. *fola*] a young horse, mule, etc.; colt or filly —*vt., vi.* to give birth to (a foal)

foam (fōm) *n.* [OE. *fam*] **1.** the whitish mass of bubbles formed on liquids by agitation, etc. **2.** something like foam, as frothy saliva **3.** a rigid or spongy cellular mass, made from liquid rubber, plastic, etc. —*vi.* to produce foam; froth —**foam at the mouth** to rage —**foam′y** *adj.* **-i·er, -i·est**

fob (fäb) *n.* [prob. < dial. G. *fuppe*, a pocket] **1.** a short ribbon or chain attached to a pocket watch **2.** any ornament worn on such a chain, etc.

F.O.B., f.o.b. free on board

fo·cal (fō′k'l) *adj.* of or at a focus

focal length the distance from the optical center of a lens to the point where the light rays converge

fo·cus (fō′kəs) *n., pl.* **-cus·es, -ci** (-sī) [L., hearth] **1.** the point where rays of light, heat, etc. come together; specif., the point where rays of reflected or refracted light meet **2.** *same as* FOCAL LENGTH **3.** an adjustment of this length to make a clear image **4.** any center of activity, attention, etc. —*vt.* **-cused** or **-cussed, -cus·ing** or **-cus·sing 1.** to bring into focus **2.** to adjust the focal length of (the eye, a lens, etc.) so as to make a clear image **3.** to concentrate —**in focus** clear; distinct —**out of focus** blurred

fod·der (fäd′ər) *n.* [< OE. *foda*, food] coarse food for cattle, horses, etc., as hay

foe (fō) *n.* [OE. *fah*, hostile] an enemy; opponent

foe·tus (fēt′əs) *n. same as* FETUS

fog (fôg, fäg) *n.* [prob. < Scand.] **1.** a large mass of water vapor condensed to fine particles, just above the earth's surface **2.** a state of mental confusion —*vt., vi.* **fogged, fog′ging** to make or become foggy, blurred, etc.

fog′gy *adj.* **-gi·er, -gi·est 1.** full of fog **2.** dim; blurred **3.** confused

fog′horn′ *n.* a horn blown to give warning to ships in a fog

fo·gy (fō′gē) *n., pl.* **-gies** [< ?] one who is old-fashioned or highly conservative: also **fo′gey,** *pl.* **-geys**

foi·ble (foi′b'l) *n.* [< Fr. *faible*, feeble] a small weakness in character; frailty

foil¹ (foil) *vt.* [< OFr. *fuler*, trample] to thwart; baffle

foil² (foil) *n.* [< L. *folium*, a leaf] **1.** a very thin sheet of metal [gold *foil*] **2.** one that sets off or enhances another by contrast **3.** [< ?] a long, thin, blunted fencing sword

foist (foist) *vt.* [prob. < dial. Du. *vuisten*, to hide in the hand] to put in slyly; palm off (*on* or *upon*)

fold¹ (fōld) *vt.* [OE. *faldan*] **1.** to double (material) upon itself **2.** to draw together and intertwine [*fold* your arms] **3.** to embrace **4.** to wrap up; envelop —*vi.* **1.** to be or become folded **2.** [Colloq.] to fail, as a play, business, etc. —*n.* a folded layer

fold² (fōld) *n.* [OE. *fald*] **1.** a pen for sheep **2.** a flock of sheep **3.** a group of people, esp. in a church

-fold [OE. *-feald*] *a suffix meaning:* **1.** having (a specified number of) parts **2.** (a specified number of) times as many or as much

fold′er *n.* **1.** a sheet of heavy paper folded as a holder for papers **2.** a booklet of folded, un-stitched sheets

fo·li·age (fō′lē ij) *n.* [< L. *folium*, a leaf] leaves, as of a plant or tree

fo·li·o (fō′lē ō′) *n., pl.* **-os′** [< L. *folium*, a leaf] **1.** a large sheet of paper folded once **2.** a book (the largest regular size) made of sheets so folded **3.** the number of a page in a book —*adj.* of folio size

folk (fōk) *n., pl.* **folk, folks** [OE. *folc*] **1.** *a)* a people; nation *b)* the common people **2.** [*pl.*] people; persons —*adj.* of the common people — (**one's**) **folks** [Colloq.] (one's) family

folk′lore′ *n.* the traditional beliefs, legends, etc. of a people

folk′sy (-sē) *adj.* **-si·er, -si·est** [Colloq.] friendly or sociable

fol·li·cle (fäl′i k'l) *n.* [< L. *follis*, bellows] any small sac, gland, etc. [a hair *follicle*]

fol·low (fäl′ō) *vt.* [< OE. *folgian*] **1.** to come or go after **2.** to chase **3.** to go along [*follow* the road] **4.** to take up (a trade, etc.) **5.** to result from **6.** to take as a model; imitate **7.** to obey **8.** to watch or listen to closely **9.** to understand —*vi.* **1.** to come or go after something else in place, time, etc. **2.** to result —**follow out** (or **up**) to carry out fully —**follow through** to continue and complete a stroke or action

fol′low·er *n.* **1.** one that follows another's teachings; disciple **2.** an attendant

fol′low·ing *adj.* that follows; next after —*n.* a group of followers —*prep.* after

fol′low-up′ *n.* a letter, visit, etc. that follows as a review or addition

fol·ly (fäl′ē) *n., pl.* **-lies** [see FOOL] **1.** a lack of sense; foolishness **2.** a foolish action or belief

fo·ment (fō ment′) *vt.* [< L. *fovere*, keep warm] to stir up; incite —**fo′men·ta′tion** *n.*

fond (fänd) *adj.* [< ME. *fonnen*, be foolish] **1.** foolishly tender; doting **2.** cherished [*fond* hopes] —**fond of** having a liking for —**fond′ly** *adv.* —**fond′ness** *n.*

fon·dant (fän′dənt) *n.* [Fr. < *fondre*, melt] a soft, creamy candy made of sugar

fon·dle (fän′d'l) *vt.* **-dled, -dling** [< obs. *fond, v.*] to stroke lovingly; caress

fon·due, fon·du (fän do̅o̅′) *n.* [Fr. < *fondre*, melt] melted cheese, etc., used for dipping cubes of bread

font¹ (fänt) *n.* [< L. *fons*, spring] **1.** a bowl to hold the water used in baptism **2.** a basin for holy water **3.** a source; origin

font² (fänt) *n.* [see FOUND³] *Printing* a complete assortment of type in one size and style

food (fo̅o̅d) *n.* [OE. *foda*] **1.** any substance, esp. a solid, taken in by a plant or animal to enable it to live and grow **2.** anything that nourishes [*food* for thought]

food stamp any of the Federal stamps sold below face value to low-income people for use in buying food

food′stuff′ *n.* any material made into or used as food

fool (fo̅o̅l) *n.* [< L. *follis*, windbag] **1.** a silly person; simpleton **2.** a jester **3.** a dupe —*vi.* **1.** to act like a fool **2.** to joke **3.** [Colloq.] to meddle (*with*) —*vt.* to trick; deceive —**fool around** [Colloq.] to trifle —**fool away** [Colloq.] to squander —**fool′er·y** *n.*

fool′har′dy *adj.* **-di·er, -di·est** foolishly daring; rash —**fool′har′di·ness** *n.*

fool′ish *adj.* silly; unwise; absurd

fool′proof′ *adj.* so harmless, simple, etc. as not to be mishandled, injured, etc. even by a fool

fools·cap (fo̅o̅lz′kap′) *n.* [< a watermark of a jester's cap] a size of writing paper, 13 by 16 in. in the U.S.

foot (foot) *n., pl.* **feet** [OE. *fot*] **1.** the end part of the leg, on which one stands **2.** the base or bottom [the *foot* of a page] **3.** a measure of length, equal to 12 inches: symbol ′ **4.** [Brit.] infantry **5.** a group of syllables serving as a unit of meter in verse —*vt.* **1.** to add (a column of figures) **2.** [Colloq.] to pay (costs, etc.) —**foot it** [Colloq.] to dance or walk —**on foot** walking —**put one's foot down** [Colloq.] to be firm — **under foot** in the way

foot′age (-ij) *n.* measurement in feet

foot′-and-mouth′ disease a contagious disease of cattle, deer, etc. characterized by blisters in the mouth and around the hoofs

foot′ball′ *n.* **1.** a field game played with an inflated leather ball by two teams **2.** the ball used

foot'-can'dle *n.* a unit of illumination, equal to the amount of direct light thrown by one candle (*n.* 2) on a square foot of surface one foot away

foot'fall' *n.* the sound of a footstep

foot'hill' *n.* a low hill at or near the foot of a mountain or mountain range

foot'hold' *n.* **1.** a place to put a foot down securely, as in climbing **2.** a secure position

foot'ing *n.* **1.** a secure placing of the feet **2.** *same as* FOOTHOLD **3.** a basis for relationship

foot'lights' *n.pl.* a row of lights along the front of a stage floor

foot'loose' *adj.* free to go wherever one likes or do as one likes

foot'man (-mən) *n., pl.* **-men** a male household servant who assists the butler

foot'note' *n.* a note of comment or reference at the bottom of a page

foot'path' *n.* a path for pedestrians

foot'-pound' *n.* a unit of energy, equal to the amount of energy needed to raise a one-pound weight a distance of one foot

foot'print' *n.* a mark left by a foot

foot'sore' *adj.* having sore or tender feet

foot'step' *n.* **1.** the distance covered in a step **2.** the sound of a step **3.** a footprint

foot'stool' *n.* a low stool for supporting the feet of a seated person

foot'work' *n.* the manner of using the feet, as in walking, boxing, dancing, etc.

fop (fäp) *n.* [ME. *foppe,* a fool] a silly, vain fellow; dandy —**fop'per·y** *n.*

for (fôr, fər) *prep.* [OE.] **1.** in place of [use a rope *for* a belt] **2.** in the interest of [acting *for* another] **3.** in favor of [vote *for* the levy] **4.** in honor of [a party *for* him] **5.** in order to have, get, keep, find, reach, etc. [walk *for* exercise, start *for* home] **6.** meant to be received by [flowers *for* a girl] **7.** suitable to [a room *for* sleeping] **8.** with regard to [so much *for* that] **9.** as being [know *for* a fact] **10.** considering the nature of [cool *for* July] **11.** because of [to cry *for* pain] **12.** in spite of [stupid *for* all her learning] **13.** to the length, amount, or duration of **14.** at the price of [two *for* a dollar] —*conj.* because

for- [OE.] *a prefix meaning* away, apart, off, etc. [forbid, forgo]

for·age (fôr'ij, fär'-) *n.* [< Frank. *fodr,* food] **1.** food for domestic animals **2.** a search for food —*vi.* **-aged, -ag·ing** to search for food —*vt.* to get or take food from; raid

fo·ra·men (fô rā'mən) *n., pl.* **-ram'i·na** (-ram'ə nə), **-ra'mens** [L., a hole] a small opening, as in a bone

for·ay (fôr'ā) *vt., vi.* [< OFr. *forrer,* to forage] to plunder —*n.* a raid, as for spoils

for·bear' (fôr ber') *vt.* **-bore', -borne', -bear'ing** [see FOR- & BEAR¹] to refrain from (doing, saying, etc.) —*vi.* **1.** to refrain or abstain **2.** to control oneself

for·bear² (fôr'ber') *n. same as* FOREBEAR

for·bear'ance (-əns) *n.* **1.** the act of forbearing **2.** self-control; patient restraint

for·bid (fər bid', fôr-) *vt.* **-bade'** (-bad') or **-bad', -bid'den, -bid'ding** [see FOR- & BID] to order not to do (something); prohibit

for·bid'ding *adj.* looking dangerous or disagreeable; repellent —**for·bid'ding·ly** *adv.*

force (fôrs) *n.* [< L. *fortis,* strong] **1.** strength; power **2.** physical coercion against a person or thing **3.** the power to control, persuade, etc.; effectiveness **4.** military power **5.** any group of people organized for some activity [a sales

force] **6.** energy that causes or alters motion — *vt.* **forced, forc'ing 1.** to make do something by force; compel **2.** to break open, into, or through by force **3.** to take by force; extort **4.** to drive as by force; impel **5.** to impose as by force (with *on* or *upon*) **6.** to produce as by force [to force a smile] **7.** to cause (plants, etc.) to develop faster by artificial means —**in force 1.** in full strength **2.** in effect; valid

forced (fôrst) *adj.* **1.** compulsory [forced labor] **2.** not natural; strained [a forced smile] **3.** due to need [a forced landing]

force'-feed' *vt.* **-fed', -feed'ing** to feed as by a tube through the throat

force'ful (-fəl) *adj.* full of force; powerful; vigorous; effective —**force'ful·ly** *adv.*

for·ceps (fôr'səps) *n., pl.* **for'ceps** [L. < *formus,* warm + *capere,* to take] tongs or pincers for grasping, pulling, etc.

for·ci·ble (fôr'sə b'l) *adj.* **1.** done by force **2.** having force —**for'ci·bly** *adv.*

ford (fôrd) *n.* [OE.] a shallow place in a stream, etc. that can be crossed by wading —*vt.* to cross at a ford —**ford'a·ble** *adj.*

fore (fôr) *adv., adj.* [OE.] at, in, or toward the front part, as of a ship —*n.* the front —*interj. Golf* a shout of warning that one is about to hit the ball

fore- [OE.] *a prefix meaning:* **1.** before in time, place, etc. [forenoon] **2.** the front part of [forearm]

fore'-and-aft' *adj. Naut.* from the bow to the stern; set lengthwise, as a rig

fore·arm¹ (fôr'ärm') *n.* the part of the arm between the elbow and the wrist

fore·arm² (fôr ärm') *vt.* to arm in advance

fore'bear' (-ber') *n.* [< FORE + BE + -ER] an ancestor

fore·bode (-bōd') *vt., vi.* **-bod'ed, -bod'ing** [see FORE- & BODE¹] **1.** to foretell; predict **2.** to have a presentiment of (something bad) —**fore·bod'ing** *n.*

fore'cast' *vt.* **-cast'** or **-cast'ed, -cast'ing 1.** to predict **2.** to serve as a prediction of —*n.* a prediction —**fore'cast'er** *n.*

fore·cas·tle (fōk's'l, fôr'kas·'l) *n.* [FORE- + CASTLE] **1.** the upper deck of a ship in front of the foremast **2.** the front part of a merchant ship, where the sailors' quarters are located

fore·close (fôr klōz') *vt.* **-closed', -clos'ing** [< OFr. *fors,* outside + *clore,* CLOSE²] to take away the right to redeem (a mortgage, etc.) — **fore·clo'sure** (-klō'zhər) *n.*

fore·doom' *vt.* to doom in advance

fore'fa'ther *n.* an ancestor

fore'fin'ger *n.* the finger nearest the thumb

fore'foot' *n., pl.* **-feet'** either of the front feet of an animal

fore'front' *n.* **1.** the extreme front **2.** the position of most activity, importance, etc.

fore·go¹ (fôr gō') *vt., vi.* **-went', -gone', -go'ing** to precede

fore·go² (fôr gō') *vt. same as* FORGO

fore·go'ing *adj.* previously said, written, etc.; preceding

fore·gone' *adj.* **1.** previous **2.** *a)* previously determined *b)* inevitable

fore'ground' *n.* the part of a scene, etc. nearest the viewer

fore'hand' *n.* a stroke, as in tennis, made with the palm of the hand turned forward —*adj.* done as with a forehand

fore·head (fôr'id, fär'-; fôr'hed') *n.* the part of the face between the eyebrows and the hairline

for·eign (fôr'in, fär'-) *adj.* [< L. *foras,* out-of-doors] **1.** situated outside one's own country, locality, etc. **2.** of, from, or characteristic of another country **3.** concerning the relations of one country to another *[foreign* affairs*]* **4.** not characteristic or belonging —**for'eign·ness** *n.*

for'eign-born' *adj.* born in another country

for'eign·er *n.* a person born in another country; alien

fore·know' *vt.* **-knew', -known', -know'ing** to know beforehand —**fore'knowl'edge** (-näl'ij) *n.*

fore'leg' *n.* either of the front legs of an animal

fore'lock' *n.* a lock of hair growing just above the forehead

fore'man (-mən) *n., pl.* **-men 1.** the chairman of a jury **2.** a man in charge of a group of workers, as in a factory

fore'mast' *n.* the mast nearest the bow of a ship

fore'most' *adj.* first in place, time, rank, etc. — *adv.* first

fore'named' *adj.* named before

fore'noon' *n.* the time from sunrise to noon

fo·ren·sic (fə ren'sik) *adj.* [< L. *forum,* marketplace] of or suitable for a law court or public debate —**fo·ren'si·cal·ly** *adv.*

fore'or·dain' *vt.* to ordain beforehand; predestine —**fore'or·di·na'tion** *n.*

fore'paw' *n.* a front paw

fore'quar'ter *n.* the front half of a side of beef, pork, etc.

fore'run'ner *n.* **1.** a herald **2.** a sign that tells or warns of something to follow **3.** *a)* a predecessor *b)* an ancestor

fore'sail' (-sāl', -s'l) *n.* the main sail on the foremast

fore·see' *vt.* **-saw', -seen', -see'ing** to see or know beforehand —**fore·see'a·ble** *adj.*

fore·shad'ow *vt.* to indicate or suggest beforehand; presage —**fore·shad'ow·er** *n.*

fore·short'en *vt. Drawing, Painting,* etc. to shorten some lines of (an object) to give the illusion of proper relative size

fore·show' *vt.* **-showed', -shown'** or **-showed', -show'ing** to indicate beforehand; foretell

fore'sight' *n.* **1.** *a)* a foreseeing *b)* the power to foresee **2.** prudent regard or provision for the future —**fore'sight'ed** *adj.*

fore'skin' *n.* the fold of skin that covers the end of the penis; prepuce

for·est (fôr'ist, fär'-) *n.* [< L. *foris,* out-of-doors] a thick growth of trees and underbrush covering a large tract of land —*adj.* of or in a forest —*vt.* to plant with trees

fore·stall (fôr stôl') *vt.* [< OE. *foresteall,* ambush] **1.** to prevent by doing something beforehand **2.** to act in advance of

for·est·a·tion (fôr'is tā'shən, fär'-) *n.* the planting or care of forests

for'est·er *n.* one trained in forestry

for'est·ry *n.* the science of planting and taking care of forests

fore'taste' *n.* a preliminary taste

fore·tell' *vt.* **-told', -tell'ing** to tell or indicate beforehand; prophesy; predict

fore'thought' *n.* **1.** a thinking or planning beforehand **2.** foresight; prudence

for·ev·er (fər ev'ər, fôr-) *adv.* **1.** for always; endlessly **2.** always; at all times Also **for·ev'-er·more'**

fore·warn' *vt.* to warn beforehand

fore'word' *n.* a brief or simple preface

for·feit (fôr'fit) *n.* [< OFr. *forfaire,* transgress] **1.** a fine or penalty for some crime, fault, or neglect **2.** the act of paying a forfeit —*adj.* lost or taken away as a forfeit —*vt.* to lose or be deprived of as a forfeit

for'fei·ture (-fə chər) *n.* **1.** a forfeiting **2.** anything forfeited; penalty or fine

for·gath·er (fôr gath'ər) *vi.* to come together; assemble: also **fore·gath'er**

for·gave (fər gāv', fôr-) *pt. of* FORGIVE

forge¹ (fôrj) *n.* [< L. *faber,* workman] **1.** a furnace for heating metal to be wrought **2.** a place where metal is heated and wrought; smithy —*vt., vi.* **forged, forg'ing 1.** to shape (metal) by heating and hammering **2.** to form; shape **3.** to imitate (a signature, etc.) fraudulently; counterfeit (a check, etc.) —**forg'er** *n.*

forge² (fôrj) *vt., vi.* **forged, forg'ing** [prob. altered < FORCE] to move forward steadily: often with *ahead*

for'ger·y *n., pl.* **-ies 1.** the act or legal offense of forging documents, signatures, etc. to deceive **2.** anything forged

for·get (fər get', fôr-) *vt., vi.* **-got', -got'ten** or **-got', -get'ting** [OE. *forgitan*] **1.** to be unable to remember **2.** to overlook or neglect —**forget oneself** to behave improperly —**for·get'ter** *n.*

for·get'ful *adj.* **1.** apt to forget **2.** negligent — **for·get'ful·ness** *n.*

for·get'-me-not' *n.* a plant with clusters of tiny blue, white, or pink flowers

for·give (fər giv', fôr-) *vt., vi.* **-gave', -giv'en, -giv'ing** [OE. *forgiefan*] to give up resentment against or the desire to punish; pardon (an offense or offender) —**for·giv'a·ble** *adj.* —**for·give'ness** *n.*

for·giv'ing *adj.* inclined to forgive

for·go (fôr gō') *vt.* **-went', -gone', -go'ing** [OE. *forgan*] to do without; abstain from

for·got (fər gät', fôr-) *pt. & alt. pp. of* FORGET

for·got'ten (-'n) *pp. of* FORGET

fork (fôrk) *n.* [< L. *furca*] **1.** an instrument with prongs at one end, for picking up or spearing **2.** something like a fork in shape **3.** the place where a road, etc. divides into branches **4.** any of these branches —*vi.* to divide into branches —*vt.* to use a fork on —**fork over** (or **out, up**) [Colloq.] to pay out; hand over —**forked** *adj.*

fork'lift' *n.* a device with projecting prongs, usually on a truck, for lifting heavy objects

for·lorn (fər lôrn', fôr-) *adj.* [< OE. *forleosan,* to lose utterly] **1.** abandoned; deserted **2.** wretched; miserable **3.** without hope

form (fôrm) *n.* [< L. *forma*] **1.** shape; general structure **2.** the figure of a person or animal **3.** a mold **4.** the combination of qualities making something what it is **5.** arrangement; style **6.** a way of doing something **7.** a customary way of behaving; ceremony **8.** a printed document with blanks to be filled in **9.** a particular kind or type **10.** condition of mind or body **11.** any of the changes in a word to show inflection, etc. **12.** type, etc. locked in a frame for printing —*vt.* **1.** to shape; fashion **2.** to train; instruct **3.** to develop (habits) **4.** to make up; create —*vi.* to be formed

-form [< L. *-formis*] *a suffix meaning* having the form of *[cuneiform]*

for·mal (fôr'məl) *adj.* [< L. *formalis*] **1.** according to fixed customs, rules, etc. **2.** stiff in manner **3.** *a)* designed for wear at ceremonies, etc. *b)* requiring clothes of this kind **4.** done or made in explicit, definite form *[a formal* contract*]* —*n.* **1.** a dance requiring formal clothes **2.** a woman's evening dress —**for'mal·ly** *adv.*

form·al·de·hyde (fôr mal'də hīd', fər-) *n.* [FORM(IC) + ALDEHYDE] a colorless, pungent gas, used in solution as a disinfectant and preservative

for′mal·ism *n.* strict attention to outward forms and customs —**for′mal·is′tic** *adj.*

for·mal·i·ty (fôr mal′ə tē) *n., pl.* **-ties 1.** *a)* an observing of customs, rules, etc.; propriety *b)* too careful attention to convention **2.** a formal act; ceremony

for·mal·ize (fôr′mə līz′) *vt.* **-ized′, -iz′ing 1.** to shape **2.** to make formal

for·mat (fôr′mat) *n.* [< L. *formatus,* formed] **1.** the size, shape, and arrangement of a book, etc. **2.** general plan, as of a TV program

for·ma·tion (fôr mā′shən) *n.* **1.** a forming or being formed **2.** a thing formed **3.** the way in which something is formed or arranged; structure **4.** an arrangement as of troops, ships, a football team, etc.

form·a·tive (fôr′mə tiv) *adj.* helping or involving formation or development

for·mer (fôr′mər) *adj.* [< OE. *formest,* foremost] **1.** previous; past **2.** first mentioned of two: used as a noun with *the*

for′mer·ly *adv.* in the past

for·mic (fôr′mik) *adj.* [< L. *formica,* an ant] designating a colorless acid, found in ants, etc.

for·mi·da·ble (fôr′mə də b'l) *adj.* [< L. *formidare,* to dread] **1.** causing fear, dread, or awe **2.** hard to handle or overcome

form′less *adj.* shapeless; amorphous

for·mu·la (fôr′myə lə) *n., pl.* **-las, -lae′** (-lē′) [L. < *forma,* form] **1.** a fixed form of words, esp. a conventional expression **2.** any conventional rule for doing something **3.** a prescription for a baby's food, a medicine, etc. **4.** a set of symbols expressing a mathematical rule **5.** *Chem.* an expression of the composition, as of a compound, using symbols and figures

for·mu·late (-lāt′) *vt.* **-lat′ed, -lat′ing 1.** to express in a formula **2.** to express in a definite way —**for′mu·la′tion** *n.*

for·ni·cate (fôr′nə kāt′) *vi.* **-cat′ed, -cat′ing** [< L. *fornix,* brothel] to commit fornication —**for′·ni·ca′tor** *n.*

for′ni·ca′tion *n.* voluntary sexual intercourse between unmarried persons

for·sake (fər sāk′, fôr-) *vt.* **-sook′** (-sook′), **-sak′en, -sak′ing** [< OE. *forsacan*] **1.** to give up (a habit, etc.) **2.** to abandon; desert

for·sooth (fər sooth′, fôr-) *adv.* [< OE. *for* + *soth,* truth] [Archaic] no doubt; indeed

for·swear (fôr swer′) *vt.* **-swore′, -sworn′, -swear′ing** to deny or renounce on oath —*vi.* to commit perjury

for·syth·i·a (fər sith′ē ə, fôr-) *n.* [< W. *Forsyth,* 18th-c. Eng. botanist] a shrub with yellow, bell-shaped flowers in early spring

fort (fôrt) *n.* [< L. *fortis,* strong] **1.** a fortified place for military defense **2.** a permanent army post

forte[1] (fôrt) *n.* [< Fr.: see FORT] that which one does particularly well

for·te[2] (fôr′tā, -tē) *adj., adv.* [It. < L. *fortis,* strong] *Music* loud

forth (fôrth) *adv.* [OE.] **1.** forward; onward **2.** out into view

forth′com′ing *adj.* **1.** about to appear; approaching **2.** ready when needed

forth′right′ *adj.* direct and frank —*adv.* straight forward; directly onward

forth′with′ *adv.* without delay

for·ti·fi·ca·tion (fôr′tə fi kā′shən) *n.* **1.** the act or science of fortifying **2.** a fort, defensive earthwork, etc. **3.** a fortified place

for·ti·fy (fôr′tə fī′) *vt.* **-fied′, -fy′ing** [< L. *fortis,* strong + *facere,* make] **1.** to strengthen physically, emotionally, etc. **2.** to strengthen against attack, as with forts **3.** to support; corroborate **4.** to strengthen (wine, etc.) by add-

ing alcohol **5.** to add vitamins, etc. to (milk, etc.)

for·tis·si·mo (fôr tis′ə mō′) *adj., adv.* [It. superl. of FORTE2] *Music* very loud

for·ti·tude (fôr′tə tood′, -tyood′) *n.* [< L. *fortis,* strong] firm courage; patient endurance of trouble, pain, etc.

fort·night (fôrt′nit′) *n.* [lit., fourteen nights] [Chiefly Brit.] two weeks

for·tress (fôr′trəs) *n.* [< L. *fortis,* strong] a fortified place; fort

for·tu·i·tous (fôr too′ə təs, -tyoo′-) *adj.* [< L. *fors,* luck] **1.** happening by chance; accidental **2.** lucky; fortunate —**for·tu′i·tous·ly** *adv.*

for·tu′i·ty *n., pl.* **-ties** chance; accident

for·tu·nate (fôr′chə nit) *adj.* **1.** having good luck **2.** coming by good luck —**for′tu·nate·ly** *adv.*

for·tune (fôr′chən) *n.* [< L. *fors,* luck] **1.** luck; chance; fate **2.** one's future lot, good or bad **3.** good luck; success **4.** wealth; riches

for′tune·tell′er *n.* one who professes to foretell events in other people's lives —**for′tune·tell′ing** *n., adj.*

for·ty (fôr′tē) *adj., n., pl.* **-ties** [OE. *feowertig*] four times ten; 40; XL —**the forties** the numbers or years, as of a century, from 40 through 49 —**for′ti·eth** (-ith) *adj., n.*

fo·rum (fôr′əm) *n.* [L.] **1.** the public square or marketplace of an ancient Roman city **2.** an assembly for the discussion of public matters

for·ward (fôr′wərd) *adj.* [OE. *foreweard*] **1.** at, toward, or of the front **2.** advanced **3.** onward **4.** prompt; ready **5.** bold; presumptuous **6.** of or for the future —*adv.* toward the front; ahead —*n. Basketball, Hockey,* etc. a player in a front position —*vt.* **1.** to promote **2.** to send on

for′wards *adv. same as* FORWARD

fos·sil (fäs′'l, fôs′-) *n.* [< L. *fossilis,* dug up] **1.** any hardened remains of a plant or animal of a previous geological period, preserved in the earth's crust **2.** a person who has outmoded, fixed ideas —*adj.* **1.** of or like a fossil **2.** obtained from the earth [coal is a *fossil* fuel] **3.** antiquated

fos′sil·ize (-īz′) *vt., vi.* **-ized′, -iz′ing 1.** to change into a fossil **2.** to make or become out of date, rigid, etc.

fos·ter (fôs′tər, fäs′-) *vt.* [OE. *fostrian,* nourish] **1.** to bring up; rear **2.** to help to develop; promote **3.** to cherish —*adj.* having a specified status in a family but not by birth [a *foster* brother]

fought (fôt) *pt. & pp. of* FIGHT

foul (foul) *adj.* [OE. *ful*] **1.** stinking; loathsome **2.** extremely dirty **3.** clogged with dirt, etc. **4.** indecent; profane **5.** wicked; abominable **6.** stormy [*foul* weather] **7.** tangled [a *foul* rope] **8.** not within the limits or rules set **9.** designating lines setting limits on the playing field **10.** dishonest **11.** [Colloq.] unpleasant, disagreeable, etc. —*adv.* in a foul way —*n. Sports* a hit, blow, move, etc. that is foul (*adj.* 8) —*vt.* **1.** to make filthy **2.** to dishonor **3.** to obstruct [grease *fouls* sink drains] **4.** to entangle (a rope, etc.) **5.** to make a foul against, as in a game **6.** *Baseball* to bat (the ball) foul —*vi.* to be or become fouled —**foul up** [Colloq.] to bungle —**foul′ly** *adv.* —**foul′ness** *n.*

fou·lard (foo lärd′) *n.* [Fr.] a lightweight fabric of silk, rayon, etc., usually figured

foul play 1. unfair play **2.** treacherous action or violence

foul′-up′ *n.* [Colloq.] a mix-up; mess

found[1] (found) *pt. & pp. of* FIND

found[2] (found) *vt.* [< L. *fundus,* bottom] **1.** to base [founded on fact] **2.** to begin to build or organize; establish —**found′er** n.

found³ (found) vt. [< L. fundere, pour] **1.** to melt and pour (metal) into a mold **2.** to make by pouring molten metal into a mold; cast

foun·da·tion (foun dā′shən) n. **1.** a founding or being founded; establishment **2.** an endowment to maintain an institution **3.** an institution so endowed **4.** basis **5.** the base of a wall, house, etc.

foun·der (foun′dər) vi. [< L. fundus, bottom] **1.** to stumble, fall, or go lame **2.** to fill with water and sink: said of a ship **3.** to break down

found·ling (found′liŋ) n. an infant of unknown parents, found abandoned

found·ry (foun′drē) n., pl. -ries a place where metal is cast

fount (fount) n. [< L. fons] **1.** [Poet.] a fountain or spring **2.** a source

foun·tain (foun′t'n) n. [< L. fons] **1.** a natural spring of water **2.** a source **3.** an artificial jet of water, or the device, basin, etc. where this flows **4.** a reservoir, as for ink

foun′tain·head′ n. the source, as of a stream

fountain pen a pen which is fed ink from its own reservoir or cartridge

four (fôr) adj., n. [OE. feower] one more than three; 4; IV

four′flush′er (-flush′ər) n. [< FLUSH²] [Colloq.] one who bluffs or tries to deceive

four′-in-hand′ n. a necktie tied in a slipknot with the ends left hanging

four′score′ adj., n. eighty

four′some (-səm) n. a group of four people

four′square′ adj. **1.** square **2.** unyielding; firm **3.** frank; forthright —adv. in a square form or manner

four′teen′ (-tēn′) adj., n. four more than ten; 14; XIV —**four′teenth′** adj., n.

fourth (fôrth) adj. [OE. feortha] preceded by three others in a series; 4th —n. **1.** the one following the third **2.** any of the four equal parts of something; 1/4

fourth′-class′ adj., adv. of or in a class of mail (parcel post) including parcels over 1 lb. in weight and books, films, etc.

fourth dimension a dimension in addition to those of length, width, and depth: in the theory of relativity, time is this dimension

Fourth of July see INDEPENDENCE DAY

fowl (foul) n. [OE. fugol] **1.** orig., any bird [fish or fowl] **2.** any of the domestic birds used as food, as the chicken, duck, etc. **3.** the flesh of these birds used for food

fox (fäks) n. [OE.] **1.** a small, wild mammal of the dog family, considered sly and crafty **2.** its fur **3.** a sly, crafty person —vt. to trick by craftiness

fox′glove′ n. same as DIGITALIS (sense 1)

fox′hole′ n. a hole dug in the ground as protection against enemy gunfire

fox terrier a small, active terrier, sometimes wire-haired, formerly trained to drive foxes out of hiding

fox trot a ballroom dance in 4/4 time, or music for it —**fox′-trot′** vi. -trot′ted, -trot′ting

fox·y (fäk′sē) adj. -i·er, -i·est **1.** foxlike; sly **2.** [Slang] attractive or sexy: said esp. of women

foy·er (foi′ər, foi yā′) n. [Fr. < L. focus, hearth] an entrance hall or lobby

Fr. 1. Father **2.** French **3.** Friday

fr. 1. fragment **2.** franc(s) **3.** from

fra·cas (frā′kəs) n. [Fr. < It. < fracassare, smash] a noisy dispute; brawl

frac·tion (frak′shən) n. [< L. frangere, to break] **1.** a small part, amount, etc.; fragment

2. Math. a quantity less than a whole, expressed as a decimal or with a numerator and denominator —**frac′tion·al** adj.

frac·tious (frak′shəs) adj. [< ?] **1.** unruly; rebellious **2.** irritable —**frac′tious·ly** adv.

frac·ture (frak′chər) n. [< L. frangere, to break] a breaking or break, esp. of a bone —vt., vi. -tured, -tur·ing to break; crack

frag·ile (fraj′'l) adj. [< L. frangere, to break] easily broken; frail; delicate

frag·ment (frag′mənt) n. [< L. frangere, to break] **1.** a part broken away **2.** an incomplete part, as of a novel —vt., vi. (also frag ment′) to break up —**frag′men·ta′tion** (-mən tā′shən) n.

frag′men·tar′y (-mən ter′ē) adj. made up of fragments; not complete

fra·grant (frā′grənt) adj. [< L. fragrare, emit a smell] having a pleasant odor —**fra′grance** n. — **fra′grant·ly** adv.

frail (frāl) adj. [see FRAGILE] **1.** easily broken; fragile **2.** slender and delicate **3.** easily tempted; morally weak

frail′ty (-tē) n. **1.** a being frail; esp., moral weakness **2.** pl. -ties a fault due to this

frame (frām) vt. framed, fram′ing [< OE. framian, be helpful] **1.** to form according to a pattern [to frame laws] **2.** to construct **3.** to put into words **4.** to enclose in a border, as a picture, etc. **5.** [Colloq.] to make appear guilty, as by falsifying evidence —n. **1.** a basic structure around which a thing is built; framework, as of a house **2.** body structure; build **3.** the structural case into which a window, door, etc. is set **4.** a border, as of a picture **5.** the way that anything is constructed; form **6.** mood; temper [a good frame of mind] **7.** one exposure in a filmstrip or movie film **8.** Bowling, etc. any of the divisions of a game —adj. having a wooden framework [a frame house]

frame′-up′ n. [Colloq.] **1.** a falsifying of evidence to make a person seem guilty **2.** a secret, deceitful scheme

frame′work′ n. **1.** a structure to hold together or to support something **2.** a basic structure or system

franc (fraŋk) n. [Fr. < L. Francorum rex, king of the French, formerly on the coin] the monetary unit of France, Belgium, Switzerland, Luxembourg, etc.

fran·chise (fran′chīz) n. [< OFr. franc, free] **1.** any special right or privilege granted by a government **2.** the right to vote; suffrage **3.** the right to sell a product or service —vt. -chised, -chis·ing to grant a franchise to

Franco- a combining form meaning: **1.** of France or the French **2.** France and

fran·gi·ble (fran′jə b'l) adj. [< L. frangere, to break] breakable —**fran′gi·bil′i·ty** n.

Frank (fraŋk) n. a member of the Germanic tribes whose 9th-c. empire extended over what is now France, Germany, and Italy

frank (fraŋk) adj. [< OFr. franc, free] free in expressing oneself; candid —vt. to send (mail) free of postage —n. **1.** the right to send mail free **2.** a mark indicating this right

Frank·en·stein (fraŋ′kən stīn′) the title character in a novel (1818), creator of a monster that destroys him —n. popularly, the monster

frank·furt·er (fraŋk′fər tər) n. [G. < Frankfurt, Germany] a smoked sausage of beef or beef and pork; wiener: also [Colloq.] frank

frank·in·cense (fraŋk′kən sens′) n. [see FRANK & INCENSE¹] a gum resin burned as incense

Frank·ish (fraŋ′kish) n. the West Germanic language of the Franks

fran·tic (fran′tik) adj. [< Gr. phrenitis,

madness] wild with anger, worry, etc. —**fran'ti·cal·ly** adv.

frap·pé (fra pā') n. [Fr. < frapper, to strike] **1.** a dessert of partly frozen fruit juices, etc. **2.** a beverage poured over shaved ice **3.** [Eastern] a milkshake Also **frappe** (frap)

fra·ter·nal (fra tur'n'l) adj. [< L. frater, brother] **1.** of brothers; brotherly **2.** designating or of a society based on fellowship

fra·ter·ni·ty (fra tur'na tē) n., pl. **-ties 1.** brotherliness **2.** a group of men joined together by common interests, for fellowship, etc., as in some colleges **3.** a group of people with the same beliefs, work, etc.

frat·er·nize (frat'ar nīz') vi. **-nized', -niz'ing** to associate in a brotherly way —**frat'er·ni·za'tion** n. —**frat'er·niz'er** n.

‡**Frau** (frou) n., pl. **Frau'en** (-ən) [G.] a married woman; lady: as a title, equivalent to Mrs. or Madam

fraud (frôd) n. [< L. fraus] **1.** deceit; trickery **2.** Law intentional deception **3.** a trick **4.** an impostor

fraud·u·lent (frô'ja lant) adj. **1.** based on or using fraud **2.** done or obtained by fraud —**fraud'u·lence** n.

fraught (frôt) adj. [< MDu. vracht, a load] filled (with) [a job fraught with danger]

‡**Fräu·lein** (froi'līn) n., pl. **-lein** [G.] an unmarried woman or girl; young lady: as a title, equivalent to Miss

fray¹ (frā) n. [< AFFRAY] a noisy fight

fray² (frā) vt., vi. [< L. fricare, to rub] to make or become worn or weak

fraz·zle (fraz''l) vt., vi. **-zled, -zling** [< dial. fazle] [Colloq.] **1.** to wear to tatters **2.** to tire —n. [Colloq.] a being frazzled

freak (frēk) n. [< ?] **1.** an odd notion; whim **2.** an unusual happening **3.** any abnormal animal, person, or plant **4.** [Slang] a) a drug user b) a devotee [a rock freak] —adj. queer; abnormal —**freak** (out) [Slang] **1.** to experience extreme reactions as from a psychedelic drug **2.** to become a hippie —**freak'ish** adj.

freak'out' n. [Slang] the act of freaking out

freck·le (frek''l) n. [< Scand.] a small, brownish spot on the skin —vt., vi. **-led, -ling** to make or become spotted with freckles —**freck'led, freck'ly** adj.

free (frē) adj. **fre'er, fre'est** [OE. freo] **1.** not under the control or power of another; having liberty; independent **2.** having civil liberties **3.** able to move in any direction; loose **4.** not burdened by obligations, discomforts, constraints, etc. **5.** not confined to the usual rules [free verse] **6.** not exact [a free translation] **7.** generous; profuse [free spending] **8.** with no charge or cost **9.** exempt from taxes, duties, etc. **10.** clear of obstructions [a free road] **11.** frank —adv. **1.** without cost **2.** in a free manner —vt. **freed, free'ing** to make free; specif., a) to release from bondage, arbitrary power, obligation, etc. b) to clear of obstruction, etc. —**free from** (or of) without —**make free with** to use freely —**free'ly** adv.

free·bie, free·by (frē'bē) n., pl. **-bies** [Slang] something given free of charge

free'boot'er (-bōōt'ar) n. [< Du. vrij, free + buit, plunder] a pirate; buccaneer

freed·man (frēd'mən) n., pl. **-men** a man legally freed from slavery or bondage

free·dom (frē'dəm) n. **1.** a being free **2.** a civil or political liberty [freedom of speech] **3.** exemption from a specified obligation, discomfort, etc. **4.** a being able to act, use, move, etc. without hindrance **5.** ease of movement; facility **6.** frankness

free'-for-all' n. a disorganized, general fight; brawl —adj. open to anyone

free'hand' adj. drawn by hand without the use of instruments, measurements, etc.

free'hold' n. **1.** an estate in land held for life or with the right to pass it on by inheritance **2.** such holding of land —**free'hold'er** n.

free lance a writer, artist, etc. who sells his services to individual buyers —**free'-lance'** adj., vi. **-lanced', -lanc'ing**

free'man (-mən) n., pl. **-men 1.** a person not in slavery or bondage **2.** a citizen

Free·ma·son (frē'mās''n) n. a member of a secret society based on brotherliness and mutual aid; Mason —**Free'ma'son·ry** n.

free on board delivered aboard the train, ship, etc. at the point of shipment, without extra charge

free'stone' n. a peach, etc. in which the pit does not cling to the pulp

free'think'er n. one who forms his opinions about religion independently

free trade trade conducted without quotas, protective tariffs, etc.

free'way' n. an expressway with interchanges for fully controlled access

free'will' adj. voluntary; spontaneous

freeze (frēz) vi. **froze, fro'zen, freez'ing** [OE. freosan] **1.** to be formed into, or become covered with, ice **2.** to become very cold **3.** to be damaged or killed by cold **4.** to become motionless **5.** to be made speechless by strong emotion **6.** to become formal or unfriendly —vt. **1.** to change into or cover with ice **2.** to make very cold **3.** to preserve (food) by rapid refrigeration **4.** to kill or damage by cold **5.** to make motionless **6.** to make formal or unfriendly **7.** to fix (prices, etc.) at a given level by authority —n. **1.** a freezing or being frozen **2.** a period of freezing weather

freeze'-dry' vt. **-dried', -dry'ing** to quick-freeze (food, vaccines, etc.) and then dry under high vacuum at low temperature

freez'er n. **1.** a machine for making ice cream **2.** a refrigerator, compartment, etc. for freezing and storing frozen foods

freezing point the temperature at which a liquid freezes: for water, it is 32°F or 0°C

freight (frāt) n. [< MDu. vracht, a load] **1.** the transportation of goods by water, land, or air **2.** the cost for such transportation **3.** the goods transported **4.** a railroad train for transporting goods: in full **freight train 5.** any load or burden —vt. **1.** to load with freight **2.** to load; burden **3.** to transport by freight

freight'er n. a ship for carrying freight

French (french) adj. of France, its people, etc. —n. the language of France —the French the people of France —**French'man** n., pl. **-men** — **French'wom'an** n.fem., pl. **-wom'en**

French cuff a shirt-sleeve cuff turned back on itself and fastened with a link

French dressing a salad dressing made of vinegar, oil, and various seasonings

French fry [often f- f-] to fry in very hot, deep fat until crisp: **French fried potatoes** (colloquially, **French fries**) are first cut into strips

French horn a brass-wind instrument with a coiled tube ending in a wide, flaring bell

French leave an unauthorized departure

French toast sliced bread dipped in a batter of egg and milk and fried

fre·net·ic (fra net'ik) adj. [< Gr. phrenētikos, mad] frantic; frenzied

fren·zy (fren'zē) n., pl. **-zies** [< Gr. phrenitis,

madness] wild excitement; brief delirium —
fren′zied *adj.* —**fren′zied·ly** *adv.*

fre·quen·cy (frē′kwən sē) *n., pl.* **-cies** 1. frequent occurrence 2. the number of times an event, value, etc. occurs in a given period or group 3. *Physics* the number of vibrations, waves, etc. in a unit of time

frequency modulation the changing of the frequency of the transmitting radio wave in accordance with the sound being broadcast

fre·quent (frē′kwənt) *adj.* [< L. *frequens,* crowded] 1. occurring often 2. constant; habitual —*vt.* (frē kwent′) to go to or be in habitually —**fre′quent·ly** *adv.*

fres·co (fres′kō) *n., pl.* **-coes, -cos** [It., fresh] 1. the art of painting with watercolors on wet plaster 2. a painting or design so made —*vt.* to paint in fresco

fresh[1] (fresh) *adj.* [OE. *fersc*] 1. recently made, grown, etc. *[fresh* coffee*]* 2. not spoiled 3. not tired; lively 4. not worn, soiled, etc. 5. new; recent 6. additional *[a fresh* start*]* 7. inexperienced 8. cool and refreshing *[a fresh* day*]* 9. brisk: said of wind 10. not salt: said of water —**fresh′ly** *adv.* —**fresh′ness** *n.*

fresh[2] (fresh) *adj.* [< G. *frech,* bold] [Slang] saucy; impudent

fresh′en (-ən) *vt., vi.* to make or become fresh —**fresh′en·er** *n.*

fresh′et (-it) *n.* a flooding of a stream because of melting snow or heavy rain

fresh′man (-mən) *n., pl.* **-men** 1. a beginner 2. a first-year student in a high school or college —*adj.* of or for freshmen

fresh′wa′ter *adj.* 1. of or living in water that is not salty 2. sailing only on inland waters 3. unskilled

fret[1] (fret) *vt., vi.* **fret′ted, fret′ting** [OE. *fretan,* eat up] 1. to gnaw, chafe, wear away, etc. 2. to make or become rough 3. to irritate or be irritated; worry —*n.* irritation; worry

fret[2] (fret) *n.* [< OFr. *frete* & OE. *frætwa*] an ornamental pattern of straight bars joining one another at right angles —*vt.* **fret′ted, fret′ting** to furnish with frets

fret[3] (fret) *n.* [OFr. *frette,* a band] any of the ridges across the fingerboard of a banjo, guitar, etc. to regulate the fingering

fret′ful *adj.* tending to fret; peevish

fret′work *n.* decorative openwork or carving

Freud·i·an (froi′dē ən) *adj.* of or according to Sigmund Freud, Austrian psychiatrist, or his theories —*n.* a follower of Freud

fri·a·ble (frī′ə b′l) *adj.* [< L. *friare,* to rub] easily crumbled —**fri′a·bil′i·ty** *n.*

fri·ar (frī′ər) *n.* [< L. *frater,* brother] *R.C.Ch.* a member of certain mendicant orders

fric·as·see (frik′ə sē′) *n.* [< Fr. *fricasser,* to cut up and fry] meat cut into pieces, stewed or fried, and served in its own gravy —*vt.* **-seed′, -see′ing** to prepare as a fricassee

fric·tion (frik′shən) *n.* [< L. *fricare,* to rub] 1. a rubbing of one object against another 2. conflict, as because of differing opinions 3. the resistance to motion of surfaces that touch — **fric′tion·al** *adj.*

Fri·day (frī′dē, -dā) *n.* [< *Frig,* Norse goddess] 1. the sixth day of the week: abbrev. **Fri., F.** 2. [< the devoted servant of ROBINSON CRUSOE] a faithful helper: usually **man** (or **girl**) **Friday**

fried (frīd) *pt. & pp.* of FRY[1]

fried·cake (frīd′kāk′) *n.* a small cake fried in deep fat; doughnut or cruller

friend (frend) *n.* [OE. *freond*] 1. a person whom one knows well and is fond of 2. an ally, supporter, or sympathizer 3. [F-] a member of a Christian sect, the Society of Friends; Quaker —**friend′less** *adj.*

friend′ly *adj.* **-li·er, -li·est** 1. of or like a friend; kindly 2. not hostile; amicable 3. supporting — **friend′li·ness** *n.*

friend′ship′ *n.* 1. the state of being friends 2. friendly feeling or attitude

frieze (frēz) *n.* [< ML. *frisium*] a horizontal band, usually with carved designs or sculpture, along a wall or around a room

frig·ate (frig′it) *n.* [< It. *fregata*] a fast, medium-sized sailing warship of the 18th & 19th cent.

fright (frīt) *n.* [OE. *fyrhto*] 1. sudden fear; alarm 2. an ugly or startling person or thing

fright′en *vt.* 1. to make suddenly afraid; scare 2. to drive (*away, off,* etc.) by frightening — **fright′ened** *adj.*

fright′ful *adj.* 1. causing fright; alarming 2. shocking 3. [Colloq.] *a*) unpleasant; annoying *b*) great *[a frightful* bore*]* —**fright′ful·ly** *adv.*

frig·id (frij′id) *adj.* [< L. *frigus,* coldness] 1. extremely cold 2. without warmth of feeling or manner 3. sexually unresponsive: said of a woman —**fri·gid′i·ty** *n.*

Frigid Zone either of two zones (**North** or **South Frigid Zone**) between the polar circles and the poles

frill (fril) *n.* [< ?] 1. an unnecessary ornament 2. a ruffle —**frill′y** *adj.* **-i·er, -i·est**

fringe (frinj) *n.* [< L. *fimbria*] 1. a border of cords or threads, loose or in bunches 2. an outer edge 3. a minor part —*vt.* **fringed, fring′ing** to be or make a fringe for —*adj.* 1. outer 2. additional 3. minor

frip·per·y (frip′ər ē) *n., pl.* **-ies** [< OFr. *frepe,* rag] 1. cheap, gaudy clothes 2. showy display in dress, manners, etc.

Fri·sian (frizh′ən) *n.* a West Germanic language spoken on islands (**Frisian Islands**) off N Netherlands, West Germany, & Denmark

frisk (frisk) *vi.* [< OHG. *frisc,* lively] to frolic — *vt.* [Slang] to search (a person) for weapons, etc. by passing the hands quickly over his clothing

frisk′y *adj.* **-i·er, -i·est** lively; frolicsome —**frisk′i·ly** *adv.* —**frisk′i·ness** *n.*

frit·ter[1] (frit′ər) *vt.* [< L. *frangere,* to break] to waste (money, time, etc.) bit by bit on petty things

frit·ter[2] (frit′ər) *n.* [< L. *frigere,* to fry] a small cake of fried batter

fri·vol·i·ty (fri väl′ə tē) *n.* 1. a frivolous quality 2. *pl.* **-ties** a frivolous act or thing

friv·o·lous (friv′ə ləs) *adj.* [L. *frivolus*] 1. trifling; trivial 2. silly and light-minded

frizz, friz (friz) *vt., vi.* **frizzed, friz′zing** [Fr. *friser*] to form into small, tight curls —*n.* something frizzed, as hair

friz·zle[1] (friz′'l) *vt., vi.* **-zled, -zling** [< FRY[1]] to fry, etc. with a sizzling sound

friz·zle[2] (friz′'l) *n., vt., vi.* **-zled, -zling** *same as* FRIZZ

friz′zly *adj.* **-zli·er, -zli·est** full of or covered with small, tight curls: also **friz′zy, -zi·er, -zi·est**

fro (frō) *adv.* [< ON. *frā*] backward: now only in *to and fro,* back and forth

frock (fräk) *n.* [OFr. *froc*] 1. a robe worn by friars, monks, etc. 2. a dress; gown —*vt.* to clothe in a frock

frog (frôg, fräg) *n.* [OE. *frogga*] 1. a tailless, leaping, four-legged amphibian with webbed feet 2. a braided loop used as a fastener on clothing 3. a device for keeping railroad cars on the proper rails at switches or intersections —**frog in the throat** hoarseness

frog'man' *n., pl.* **-men** a person trained and equipped for underwater work

frol·ic (fräl'ik) *n.* [< Du. < MDu. *vrō*, merry] **1.** a prank or trick **2.** a lively party or game **3.** merriment —*vi.* **-icked, -ick·ing 1.** to make merry; have fun **2.** to romp

frol'ic·some (-səm) *adj.* playful; merry

from (frum, främ) *prep.* [OE.] **1.** beginning at; starting with [he walked *from* the door] **2.** out of [*from* a closet] **3.** originating with [a letter *from* me] **4.** out of the possibility or use of [kept *from* going] **5.** at a place not near to [far *from* home] **6.** out of the whole of [take two *from* four] **7.** as not being like [to know good *from* evil] **8.** because of [to shake *from* fear]

frond (fränd) *n.* [L. *frons,* leafy branch] the leaf of a fern or palm

front (frunt) *n.* [< L. *frons,* forehead] **1.** *a)* outward behavior [a bold *front*] *b)* [Colloq.] an appearance of social standing, wealth, etc. **2.** the part facing forward **3.** the first part; beginning **4.** a forward or leading position **5.** the land bordering a lake, street, etc. **6.** the advanced battle area in warfare **7.** a broad coalition of parties, groups, etc. as for political purposes **8.** a person or group used to hide another's activity **9.** *Meteorol.* the boundary between two differing masses of air [a cold *front*] —*adj.* at, to, in, on, or of the front —*vt., vi.* **1.** to face **2.** to serve as a front (*for*) —**in front of** before —**fron'tal** *adj.*

front'age (-ij) *n.* **1.** the front part of a building **2.** the front boundary line of a lot **3.** land bordering a street, river, etc.

fron·tier (frun tir') *n.* [see FRONT] **1.** the border between two countries **2.** the part of a country which borders an unexplored region **3.** any new field of learning, etc. —*adj.* of or on the frontier —**fron·tiers'man** (-tirz'mən) *n., pl.* **-men**

fron·tis·piece (frun'tis pēs') *n.* [< L. *frons,* front + *specere,* to look] an illustration facing the first page or title page of a book

frost (frôst, fräst) *n.* [OE. < *freosan,* freeze] **1.** a temperature low enough to cause freezing **2.** frozen dew or vapor —*vt.* **1.** to cover with, or affect by, frost **2.** to cover with frosting **3.** to give a frostlike surface to (glass) —**frost'y** *adj.* **-i·er, -i·est**

frost'bite' *vt.* **-bit', -bit'ten, -bit'ing** to injure the tissues of (a body part) by exposure to intense cold —*n.* such injury

frost'ing *n.* **1.** a mixture of sugar, butter, eggs, etc. for covering a cake; icing **2.** a dull, frostlike finish on glass, metal, etc.

froth (frôth, fräth) *n.* [ON. *frotha*] **1.** foam **2.** foaming saliva **3.** light, trifling talk, ideas, etc. —*vi., vt.* to foam or cause to foam —**froth'y** *adj.* **-i·er, -i·est**

fro·ward (frō'ərd, -wərd) *adj.* [see FRO & -WARD] not easily controlled; willful

frown (froun) *vi.* [< OFr. *froigne,* sullen face] **1.** to contract the brows, as in displeasure or concentration **2.** to show disapproval (with *on* or *upon*) —*n.* a frowning

frow·zy (frou'zē) *adj.* **-zi·er, -zi·est** [< ?] dirty and untidy; slovenly: also sp. **frow'sy** —**frow'zi·ly** *adv.* —**frow'zi·ness** *n.*

froze (frōz) *pt.* of FREEZE

fro'zen (-'n) *pp.* of FREEZE —*adj.* **1.** turned into or covered with ice **2.** damaged or killed by freezing **3.** preserved by freezing, as food **4.** as if turned into ice **5.** kept at a fixed level **6.** not readily converted into cash

frozen custard a food like ice cream, but with less butterfat

fruc·ti·fy (fruk'tə fī') *vi., vt.* **-fied', -fy'ing** [< L. *fructificare*] to bear or cause to bear fruit

fru·gal (frōo'g'l) *adj.* [< L. *frugi,* fit for food] **1.** not wasteful; thrifty **2.** inexpensive or meager —**fru·gal'i·ty** (-gal'ə tē) *n., pl.* **-ties** —**fru'gal·ly** *adv.*

fruit (frōot) *n.* [< L. *fructus*] **1.** any plant product, as grain, vegetables, etc.: *usually used in pl.* **2.** a sweet and edible plant structure, consisting of a fruit (sense 4), usually eaten raw or as a dessert **3.** the result or product of any action [the *fruit* of labor] **4.** *Bot.* the mature ovary of a flowering plant, along with its contents, as the whole peach —*vi., vt.* to bear or cause to bear fruit

fruit'cake' *n.* a rich cake containing nuts, preserved fruit, citron, spices, etc.

fruit'ful *adj.* **1.** bearing much fruit **2.** productive **3.** profitable —**fruit'ful·ly** *adv.*

fru·i·tion (frōo ish'ən) *n.* **1.** the bearing of fruit **2.** a coming to fulfillment

fruit'less *adj.* **1.** without results; unsuccessful **2.** bearing no fruit; sterile

fruit'y *adj.* **-i·er, -i·est 1.** like fruit in taste or smell **2.** rich or mellow in tone

frump (frump) *n.* [< Du. *rompelen,* rumple] a dowdy woman —**frump'ish, frump'y** *adj.*

frus·trate (frus'trāt) *vt.* **-trat·ed, -trat·ing** [< L. *frustra,* in vain] **1.** to cause to have no effect; nullify **2.** to keep from an objective or from gratifying certain desires —**frus·tra'tion** *n.*

fry¹ (frī) *vt., vi.* **fried, fry'ing** [< L. *frigere*] to cook in fat or oil over direct heat —*n., pl.* **fries 1.** [*pl.*] fried potatoes **2.** a gathering where food is fried

fry² (frī) *n., pl.* **fry** [ME. *frie*] **1.** young fish **2.** offspring —**small fry** children

ft. fŏot; feet

fuch·sia (fyōo'shə) *n.* [< L. *Fuchs,* 16th-c. G. botanist] **1.** a shrubby plant with red or reddish flowers **2.** purplish red

fud·dle (fud''l) *vt.* **-dled, -dling** [< ?] to confuse or stupefy as with alcoholic liquor —*n.* a fuddled condition

fud·dy-dud·dy (fud'ē dud'ē) *n., pl.* **-dies** [Slang] a fussy or old-fashioned person

fudge (fuj) *n.* [? echoic] **1.** nonsense **2.** [< ?] a soft candy made of butter, milk, sugar, flavoring, etc. —*vi.* **fudged, fudg'ing 1.** to refuse to commit oneself **2.** to cheat

fu·el (fyōo'əl, fyōol) *n.* [ult. < L. *focus,* fireplace] **1.** coal, oil, gas, wood, etc. burned to supply heat or power **2.** material from which atomic energy can be obtained **3.** anything that intensifies strong feeling —*vt., vi.* **-eled or -elled, -el·ing or -el·ling** to supply with or get fuel

fuel cell a device converting chemical energy directly into electrical energy

fu·gi·tive (fyōo'jə tiv) *adj.* [< L. *fugere,* flee] **1.** fleeing as from danger, justice, etc. **2.** fleeting —*n.* one who flees as from justice

fugue (fyōog) *n.* [Fr. < L. *fugere,* flee] a musical composition in which a theme is developed contrapuntally —**fu'gal** *adj.*

-ful [< FULL¹] *a suffix meaning:* **1.** full of, having [joyful] **2.** having the qualities of or tendency to [helpful] **3.** *pl.* **-fuls** the quantity that fills [handful]

ful·crum (fool'krəm, ful'-) *n., pl.* **-crums, -cra** (-krə) [L., a support] the support on which a lever turns in raising something

ful·fill, ful·fil (fool fil') *vt.* **-filled', -fill'ing** [OE. *fullfyllan*] **1.** to carry out (something promised, etc.) **2.** to do (something required) **3.** to satisfy (a condition) **4.** to complete —**ful·fill'ment, ful·fil'ment** *n.*

full¹ (fool) *adj.* [OE.] **1.** having or occupying all there is space for **2.** having eaten all that one wants **3.** having a great deal (*of*) **4.** complete [*a full dozen*] **5.** having reached the greatest size, extent, etc. **6.** having clearness, volume, and depth [*a full tone*] **7.** plump; round **8.** with loose, wide folds; flowing [*a full skirt*] —*n.* the greatest amount, extent, etc. —*adv.* **1.** completely **2.** directly **3.** very [*full well*] —**in full 1.** to or for the full amount, etc. **2.** not abbreviated —**full′ness, ful′ness** *n.*

full² (fool) *vt., vi.* [< L. *fullo*, cloth fuller] to shrink and thicken (cloth) —**full′er** *n.*

full′back′ *n. Football* a member of the offensive backfield, behind the quarterback

full′-blood′ed *adj.* **1.** of unmixed breed or race; purebred: also **full′-blood′ 2.** vigorous

full′-blown′ *adj.* **1.** in full bloom; open **2.** fully developed; mature

full dress formal clothes

full′-fledged′ *adj.* completely developed or trained; of full rank or status

full moon the moon seen as a full disk

full′y *adv.* **1.** completely **2.** amply

ful·mi·nate (ful′mə nāt′) *vi., vt.* -nat′ed, -nat′ing [< L. *fulmen*, lightning] **1.** to explode **2.** to shout (denunciations, etc.) —**ful′mi·na′tion** *n.* —**ful′mi·na′tor** *n.*

ful·some (fool′səm, ful′-) *adj.* [see FULL¹ & -SOME¹, but infl. by ME. *ful*, foul] disgusting, esp. because excessive

fum·ble (fum′b'l) *vi., vt.* -bled, -bling [prob. < ON. *famla*, grope] **1.** to grope (*for*) or handle (a thing) clumsily **2.** to lose one's grasp on (a football, etc.) —*n.* a fumbling

fume (fyoom) *n.* [< L. *fumus*] [*often pl.*] a gas, smoke, or vapor, esp. if offensive —*vi.* fumed, fum′ing **1.** to give off fumes **2.** to show anger —*vt.* to expose to fumes

fu·mi·gate (fyoo′mə gāt′) *vt.* -gat′ed, -gat′ing [< L. *fumus*, smoke + *agere*, make] to expose to fumes, esp. to disinfect or kill the vermin in —**fu′mi·ga′tion** *n.* —**fu′mi·ga′tor** *n.*

fun (fun) *n.* [< ME. *fonne*, a fool] **1.** *a*) lively, gay play or playfulness *b*) pleasure **2.** a source of amusement —**like fun** [Slang] not at all —**make fun of** to ridicule

func·tion (funk′shən) *n.* [< L. *fungi*, perform] **1.** the normal or characteristic action of anything **2.** a special duty required in work **3.** a formal ceremony or social occasion **4.** a thing that depends on and varies with something else **5.** *Math.* a quantity whose value depends on that of another quantity or quantities —*vi.* **1.** to act in a required manner; work **2.** to be used (*as*)

func′tion·al *adj.* **1.** of a function **2.** performing a function **3.** *Med.* affecting a function of some organ without apparent organic changes —**func′tion·al·ly** *adv.*

func′tion·ar′y (-er′ē) *n., pl.* -ies an official performing some function

fund (fund) *n.* [L. *fundus*, bottom] **1.** a supply that can be drawn on; store **2.** *a*) a sum of money set aside for a purpose *b*) [*pl.*] ready money —*vt.* **1.** to put or convert into a long-term debt that bears interest **2.** to provide for with a fund

fun·da·men·tal (fun′də men′t'l) *adj.* [see FUND] of or forming a foundation or basis; basic —*n.* a principle, law, etc. serving as a basis —**fun′da·men′tal·ly** *adv.*

fun′da·men′tal·ism *n.* [*sometimes* F-] religious beliefs based on a literal interpretation of the Bible —**fun′da·men′tal·ist** *n., adj.*

fu·ner·al (fyoo′nər əl) *n.* [< L. *funus*] the rites connected with burial or cremation of the dead —*adj.* of or for a funeral

funeral director the manager of an estab-

lishment (**funeral home** or **parlor**) where funeral services can be held

fu·ne·re·al (fyoo nir′ē əl) *adj.* suitable for a funeral; sad and solemn; gloomy

fun·gi·cide (fun′jə sīd′) *n.* [< FUNGUS + -CIDE] any substance that kills fungi

fun·gus (fun′gəs) *n., pl.* **fun·gi** (fun′jī, fun′gī), **fun′gus·es** [L.] any of various plants, as molds, mildews, mushrooms, etc., that lack chlorophyll and leaves and reproduce by spores —**fun′gous** *adj.*

fu·nic·u·lar (fyoo nik′yoo lər) *n.* [< L. *funis*, a rope] a mountain railway on which cars are moved by cables

funk (funk) *n.* [< ? Fl. *fonck*, dismay] [Colloq.] **1.** a cowering through fear; panic **2.** a depressed mood

fun·nel (fun′'l) *n.* [ult. < L. *fundere*, to pour] **1.** a slender tube with a cone-shaped mouth, for pouring things into containers with small openings **2.** a cylindrical smokestack, as of a steamship —*vi., vt.* -neled or -nelled, -nel·ing or -nel·ling to move or pour as through a funnel

fun·ny (fun′ē) *adj.* -ni·er, -ni·est **1.** causing laughter **2.** [Colloq.] strange; queer —*n., pl.* -nies [Colloq.] *same as* COMIC STRIP: *usually in pl.* —**fun′ni·ness** *n.*

funny bone a place on the elbow where a sharp impact causes a tingling

fur (fur) *n.* [< OFr. *fuerre*, sheath] **1.** the soft, thick hair covering certain animals **2.** a processed skin bearing such hair

fur·be·low (fur′bə lō′) *n.* [var. of Fr. *falbala*] **1.** a flounce or ruffle **2.** [*usually pl.*] showy trimming

fur·bish (fur′bish) *vt.* [< OFr. *forbir*] **1.** to polish; burnish **2.** to renovate

Fu·ries (fyoor′ēz) *Gr. & Rom. Myth.* three female spirits who punished doers of unavenged crimes

fu·ri·ous (fyoor′ē əs) *adj.* [< L. *furiosus*] **1.** full of fury; violently angry **2.** violently overpowering **3.** very great; intense —**fu′ri·ous·ly** *adv.*

furl (furl) *vt.* [< L. *firmus*, FIRM¹ + *ligare*, to tie up] to roll up tightly and securely, as a flag —*n.* a roll of something furled

fur·long (fur′lôn) *n.* [< OE. *furh*, a furrow + *lang*, LONG¹] a measure of distance equal to 1/8 of a mile, or 220 yards

fur·lough (fur′lō) *n.* [< Du. *verlof*] a leave of absence, esp. for military enlisted personnel —*vt.* to grant a furlough to

fur·nace (fur′nəs) *n.* [< L. *fornus*, oven] an enclosed structure in which heat is produced as for heating a building

fur·nish (fur′nish) *vt.* [< OFr. *furnir*] to supply or provide, as with furniture

fur′nish·ings *n.pl.* **1.** furniture, as for a house **2.** things to wear

fur·ni·ture (fur′ni chər) *n.* [Fr. *fourniture*] **1.** movable things to equip a room, etc. for living, as chairs **2.** any equipment

fu·ror (fyoor′ôr) *n.* [< L. *furor*] **1.** fury; rage **2.** *a*) a widespread enthusiasm; craze *b*) a commotion or uproar

fur·ri·er (fur′ē ər) *n.* **1.** a dealer in furs **2.** one who processes furs

fur·ring (fur′in) *n.* thin strips of wood fixed on a wall, floor, etc. before adding boards or plaster

fur·row (fur′ō) *n.* [OE. *furh*] **1.** a narrow groove made in the ground by a plow **2.** anything like this, as a wrinkle —*vt.* to make furrows in —*vi.* to become wrinkled

fur·ry (fur′ē) *adj.* -ri·er, -ri·est **1.** of or like fur **2.** covered with fur —**fur′ri·ness** *n.*

fur·ther (fur′thər) *adj.* [OE. *furthra*] **1.** additional; more **2.** more distant; farther —*adv.* **1.** to a greater degree or extent **2.** in addition **3.** at or to a greater distance In sense 2 of the *adj.* and sense 3 of the *adv.*, FARTHER is more commonly used —*vt.* to give aid to; promote — **fur′ther·ance** *n.*

fur′ther·more′ *adv.* besides; moreover

fur·thest (fur′*th*ist) *adj.* most distant; farthest: also **fur′ther·most′** —*adv.* at or to the greatest distance or degree

fur·tive (fur′tiv) *adj.* [< Fr. < L. *fur*, thief] done or acting in a stealthy manner

fu·ry (fyoor′ē) *n., pl.* **-ries** [< L. *furere*, to rage] **1.** violent anger; wild rage **2.** violence; vehemence

furze (furz) *n.* [OE. *fyrs*] a prickly evergreen shrub of Europe, with yellow flowers

fuse[1] (fyōoz) *vt., vi.* **fused, fus′ing** [< L. *fundere*, to shed] **1.** to melt or to join by melting, as metals **2.** to unite or blend together —**fu′si·ble** *adj.*

fuse[2] (fyōoz) *n.* [< It. < L. *fusus*, hollow spindle] **1.** a tube or wick filled with combustible material for setting off an explosive charge **2.** *Elec.* a strip of easily melted metal placed in a circuit: it melts and breaks the circuit if the current becomes too strong

fu·se·lage (fyōo′sə läzh′) *n.* [Fr. < *fuselé,* tapering] the body of an airplane, exclusive of the wings, tail, and engines

fu·sil·lade (fyōo′sə lād′) *n.* [Fr. < *fusiller,* to shoot] a simultaneous discharge of many firearms

fu·sion (fyōo′zhən) *n.* **1.** a fusing **2.** *same as* NUCLEAR FUSION

fuss (fus) *n.* [prob. echoic] **1.** nervous activity or state **2.** [Colloq.] a quarrel **3.** [Colloq.] a showy display of approval, etc. —*vi.* **1.** to bustle about or worry over trifles **2.** to whine, as a baby

fuss′y *adj.* **-i·er, -i·est 1.** that fusses **2.** finicky —**fuss′i·ness** *n.*

fus·tian (fus′chən) *n.* [< L. *fustis*, wooden stick] pompous, pretentious talk or writing

fus·ty (fus′tē) *adj.* **-ti·er, -ti·est** [< OFr. *fust*, cask] **1.** musty **2.** old-fashioned

fu·tile (fyōot′'l) *adj.* [Fr. < L. *futilis*, that easily pours out] useless; vain —**fu′tile·ly** *adv.* —**fu·til·i·ty** (fyoo til′ə tē) *n., pl.* **-ties**

fu·ture (fyōo′chər) *adj.* [< L. *futurus*, about to be] **1.** that is to be or come **2.** *Gram.* indicating time to come —*n.* **1.** the time that is to come **2.** what is going to be **3.** prospective condition **4.** *Gram.* the future tense —**fu′tur·is′tic** *adj.*

fu·tu·ri·ty (fyoo toor′ə tē) *n., pl.* **-ties 1.** the future **2.** a future condition or event **3.** the quality of being future

fuze[1] (fyōoz) *vt., vi.* **fuzed, fuz′ing** *same as* FUSE[1]

fuze[2] (fyōoz) *n. same as* FUSE[2]

fuzz (fuz) *n.* [< ?] loose, light particles as of wool; fine hairs or fibers —**the fuzz** [Slang] a policeman or the police

fuzz′y *adj.* **-i·er, -i·est 1.** of, like, or covered with fuzz **2.** not clear or precise —**fuzz′i·ly** *adv.* —**fuzz′i·ness** *n.*

-fy [< L. *facere*, do] *a suffix meaning:* **1.** to make *[liquefy]* **2.** to cause to have *[glorify]* **3.** to become *[putrefy]*

G

G, g (jē) *n., pl.* **G's, g's 1.** the seventh letter of the English alphabet **2.** *Physics* gravity

G (jē) *n. Music* the fifth tone in the scale of C major

G., g. 1. gauge **2.** gram(s) **3.** gulf

gab (gab) *vi.* **gabbed, gab′bing** [< ON. *gabba,* to mock] [Colloq.] to talk much or idly; chatter —*n.* [Colloq.] chatter

gab·ar·dine (gab′ər dēn′) *n.* [< OFr. *gaverdine,* kind of cloak] a twilled cloth of wool, cotton, etc., with a fine, diagonal weave: also [Brit.] **gab′er·dine**

gab·ble (gab′'l) *vi., vt.* **-bled, -bling** [< GAB] to talk or utter rapidly and incoherently —*n.* rapid, incoherent talk

gab′by *adj.* **-bi·er, -bi·est** [Colloq.] talkative

gab′fest′ (-fest′) *n.* [Colloq.] an informal gathering to talk or gab

ga·ble (gā′b'l) *n.* [< Gmc.] the triangular wall enclosed by the sloping ends of a ridged roof — **ga′bled** *adj.*

Ga·bri·el (gā′brē əl) *Bible* an archangel, the herald of good news

Gad (gad) *interj.* [euphemism for GOD] [*also* g-] a mild oath

gad (gad) *vi.* **gad′ded, gad′ding** [? < OE. *gædeling,* companion] to wander about restlessly or idly

gad′a·bout′ *n.* [Colloq.] one who gads about, looking for fun, excitement, etc.

gad′fly′ *n., pl.* **-flies** [see GOAD & FLY[2]] **1.** a large fly that bites livestock **2.** one who annoys others

gadg·et (gaj′it) *n.* [< ?] any small mechanical device —**gadg′e·teer′** *n.* —**gadg′et·ry** *n.*

Gael (gāl) *n.* a Celt of Scotland, Ireland, or the Isle of Man

Gael′ic (-ik) *adj.* of the Gaels or any of their Celtic languages —*n.* any Celtic language spoken by the Gaels Abbrev. **Gael.**

gaff (gaf) *n.* [< Pr. *gaf* or Sp. *gafa*] **1.** a large hook on a pole for landing large fish **2.** a spar supporting a fore-and-aft sail —**stand the gaff** [Slang] to bear up well under difficulties, punishment, etc.

gaffe (gaf) *n.* [Fr.] a blunder

gag (gag) *vt.* **gagged, gag′ging** [echoic] **1.** to cause to retch **2.** to keep from speaking, as by stopping the mouth of —*vi.* to retch —*n.* **1.** something put into the mouth to prevent talking, etc. **2.** any restraint of free speech **3.** a joke

gage[1] (gāj) *n.* [< OFr., a pledge] **1.** something given as a pledge **2.** a glove, etc. thrown down as a challenge **3.** a challenge

gage[2] (gāj) *n., vt.* **gaged, gag′ing** *same as* GAUGE

gag·gle (gag′'l) *n.* [< ME. *gagelen,* to cackle] **1.** a flock of geese **2.** any group

gai·e·ty (gā′ə tē) *n., pl.* **-ties 1.** the quality of being gay; cheerfulness **2.** merrymaking **3.** showy brightness

gai·ly (gā′lē) *adv.* in a gay manner; specif., *a)* happily; merrily *b)* brightly

gain (gān) *n.* [< OFr. *gaaignier,* earn] **1.** an increase; specif., *a)* [*often pl.*] profit *b)* an increase in advantage **2.** acquisition —*vt.* **1.** to earn **2.** to win **3.** to get as an addition, profit, or advantage **4.** to make an increase in **5.** to get to; reach —*vi.* **1.** to make progress; improve, as in health **2.** to become heavier **—gain on** to draw nearer to (an opponent in a race, etc.)

gain·ful *adj.* producing gain; profitable

gain·say (gān'sā') *vt.* **-said'** (-sed', -sād'), **-say'ing** [< OE. *gegn,* against + *secgan,* to say] **1.** to deny **2.** to contradict **3.** to oppose — **gain'say'er** *n.*

gait (gāt) *n.* [< ON. *gata,* path] **1.** manner of walking or running **2.** any of various foot movements of a horse, as a trot, canter, etc. — **gait'ed** *adj.*

gai·ter (gāt'ər) *n.* [< Fr. *guêtre*] a cloth or leather covering for the instep, ankle, and lower leg

gal (gal) *n.* [Colloq.] a girl

gal. gallon; gallons

ga·la (gā'lə, gal'ə) *n.* [It. < OFr. *gale,* enjoyment] a festival **—adj.** festive

Gal·a·had (gal'ə had') in Arthurian legend, a knight successful in the quest for the Holy Grail because of his purity

gal·ax·y (gal'ək sē) [< Gr. *gala,* milk] [*often* G-] *same as* MILKY WAY **—n., pl. -ies 1.** any large group of stars **2.** a group of illustrious people **—ga·lac·tic** (gə lak'tik) *adj.*

gale (gāl) *n.* [< ?] **1.** a strong wind **2.** an outburst *[a gale* of laughter*]*

ga·le·na (gə lē'nə) *n.* [L., lead ore] native lead sulfide, a lead-gray mineral

gall¹ (gôl) *n.* [OE. *galla*] **1.** bile, the bitter liver secretion **2.** something distasteful **3.** bitter feeling **4.** [Colloq.] impudence

gall² (gôl) *n.* [see GALL³] a sore from chafing — *vt.* **1.** to make sore by rubbing **2.** to annoy

gall³ (gôl) *n.* [< L. *galla*] a plant tumor from fungi, insects, or bacteria

gal·lant (gal'ənt) *adj.* [< OFr.] **1.** stately; imposing **2.** brave and noble **3.** (gə lant', -länt') polite and attentive to women **—gal'lant·ry** *n., pl.* **-ries**

gall'blad'der *n.* a membranous sac attached to the liver: it stores gall, or bile

gal·le·on (gal'ē ən) *n.* [see GALLEY] a large Spanish ship of the 15th and 16th cent., with three or four decks at the stern

gal·ler·y (gal'ə rē) *n., pl.* **-ies** [< ML. *galeria*] **1.** a covered walk or porch open at one side **2.** a long, narrow, outside balcony **3.** *a)* a balcony as in a theater; esp., the highest balcony with the cheapest seats *b)* the people in these seats *c)* a group of spectators **4.** a long, narrow corridor or room **5.** an establishment for exhibiting art

gal·ley (gal'ē) *n., pl.* **-leys** [< MGr. *galaia*] **1.** a long, low ship of ancient times, using oars and sails **2.** a ship's kitchen **3.** *Printing a)* a shallow tray for holding composed type *b)* proof printed from such type: in full **galley proof**

Gal·lic (gal'ik) *adj.* **1.** of ancient Gaul or its people **2.** French

Gal·li·cism (gal'ə siz'm) *n.* [*also* g-] a French idiom, expression, etc.

Gal'li·cize' (-sīz') *vt., vi.* **-cized', -ciz'ing** [*also* g-] to make or become French or like the French in thought, language, etc.

gal·li·vant (gal'ə vant') *vi.* [< GALLANT] to go about in search of amusement

gal·lon (gal'ən) *n.* [< ML. *galo,* jug] a liquid measure, equal to 4 quarts

gal·lop (gal'əp) *vi., vt.* [< OFr. *galoper*] to go, or cause to go, at a gallop **—n.** the fastest gait of a horse, etc., consisting of a succession of leaping strides

gal·lows (gal'ōz) *n., pl.* **-lows·es, -lows** [OE. *galga*] an upright frame with a rope, for hanging condemned persons

gall'stone' *n.* a small, stony, abnormal mass in the gallbladder or bile duct

ga·lore (gə lôr') *adv.* [Ir. *go leór,* enough] in abundance; plentifully

ga·losh, ga·loshe (gə läsh') *n.* [< OFr. *galoche*] a high overshoe

gal·van·ic (gal van'ik) *adj.* **1.** of or producing an electric current **2.** startling

gal·va·nism (gal'və niz'm) *n.* [< Fr. < L. *Galvani,* 18th-c. It. physicist] electricity produced by chemical action

gal'va·nize' (-nīz') *vt.* **-nized', -niz'ing 1.** to apply an electric current to **2.** to startle; excite **3.** to plate (metal) with zinc

gal'va·nom'e·ter (-näm'ə tər) *n.* an instrument to measure a small electric current

gam·bit (gam'bit) *n.* [Fr. < Sp. *gambito,* a tripping] **1.** *Chess* an opening in which a pawn, etc. is sacrificed for an advantageous position **2.** any maneuver for advantage

gam·ble (gam'b'l) *vi.* **-bled, -bling** [OE. *gamenian,* to play] **1.** to play games of chance for money, etc. **2.** to take a risk for an advantage **—vt.** to bet; wager **—n.** a risky undertaking **—gam'bler** *n.*

gam·bol (gam'b'l) *n.* [< It. *gamba,* leg] a gamboling; frolic **—vi.** **-boled** or **-bolled, -bol·ing** or **-bol·ling** to jump and skip about in play; frolic

game¹ (gām) *n.* [OE. *gamen*] **1.** play; amusement **2.** *a)* a competitive amusement or sport *b)* a single contest **3.** the total points required for winning **4.** a project; scheme **5.** wild birds or animals hunted for sport or food **6.** [Colloq.] a business **—vi. gamed, gam'ing** to gamble **—adj. 1.** designating or of game (sense 5) **2.** *a)* plucky; courageous *b)* enthusiastic; ready (*for*) **—make game of** to make fun of **—the game is up** failure is certain **—game'ly** *adv.*

game² (gām) *adj.* [< ?] [Colloq.] lame

game'cock' *n.* a specially bred rooster trained for cockfights

games·man·ship (gāmz'mən ship') *n.* skill in using ploys to gain an advantage

game·ster (gām'stər) *n.* a gambler

gam·ete (gam'ēt, gə mēt') *n.* [< Gr. *gamos,* marriage] a reproductive cell that unites with another to form the cell that develops into a new individual

gam·in (gam'ən) *n.* [Fr.] **1.** a roaming, neglected child **2.** a girl with a roguish, saucy charm: also **ga·mine** (ga mēn')

gam·ma (gam'ə) *n.* the third letter of the Greek alphabet (Γ, γ)

gamma ray a strong electromagnetic radiation from a radioactive substance

gam·ut (gam'ət) *n.* [< Gr. letter *gamma,* for the lowest note of the medieval scale] **1.** any complete musical range **2.** the entire range or extent

gam·y (gā'mē) *adj.* **-i·er, -i·est 1.** having the strong flavor of cooked game **2.** slightly tainted **3.** plucky **4.** risqué

gan·der (gan'dər) *n.* [OE. *gan(d)ra*] **1.** a male goose **2.** [Slang] a look

gang (gaŋ) *n.* [< OE. *gang,* a going] a group — *vi.* to form a gang (with *up*) **—gang up on** [Colloq.] to attack as a group

gan·gling (gaŋ'gliŋ) *adj.* [< ?] tall, thin, and awkward; lanky: also **gan'gly**

gan·gli·on (gaŋ'glē ən) *n., pl.* **-gli·a** (-ə), **-gli·ons** [ult. < Gr., tumor] a mass of nerve cells from which nerve impulses are transmitted **—gan'gli·on'ic** (-än'ik) *adj.*

gang'plank' *n.* a narrow, movable platform by which to board or leave a ship

gan·grene (gaŋ'grēn, gaŋ grēn') *n.* [< Fr. <

Gr. *gran,* gnaw] decay of body tissue when the blood supply is obstructed as by injury, disease, etc. **—gan′gre·nous** (-grə nəs) *adj.*

gang·ster (gaŋ′stər) *n.* a member of a gang of criminals **—gang′ster·ism** *n.*

gang′way′ *n.* [OE. *gangweg*] a passageway; specif., *a*) an opening in a ship's side for freight or passengers *b*) a gangplank **—interj.** make room!

gan·net (gan′it) *n., pl.* **-nets, -net** [OE. *ganot*] a large, web-footed sea bird

gant·let (gônt′lit, gant′-) *n.* [< Sw. *gata,* lane + *lopp,* a run] **1.** a former punishment in which the offender ran between two rows of men who struck him **2.** a series of troubles

gan·try (gan′trē) *n., pl.* **-tries** [< L. *canterius,* beast of burden] **1.** a framework that spans a distance, as one on wheels that carries a traveling crane **2.** a wheeled framework with a crane, platforms, etc. for readying a rocket to be launched

gaol (jāl) *n. Brit. sp. of* JAIL

gap (gap) *n.* [< ON. *gapa,* to gape] **1.** a hole or opening made by breaking or parting **2.** a mountain pass or ravine **3.** a blank space **4.** a disparity; lag

gape (gāp) *vi.* **gaped, gap′ing** [< ON. *gapa*] **1.** to open the mouth wide, as in yawning **2.** to stare with the mouth open, as in wonder **3.** to open wide **—n. 1.** a gaping **2.** a wide opening

gar (gär) *n., pl.* **gar, gars** [< OE. *gar,* a spear] a long fish with a beaklike snout: also **gar′fish′**

ga·rage (gə räzh′, -räj′) *n.* [Fr. < *garer,* protect] **1.** a shelter for automobiles **2.** a business place where automobiles are repaired, stored, etc. **—vt.** **-raged′, -rag′ing** to put or keep in a garage

garb (gärb) *n.* [< It. *garbo,* elegance] **1.** clothing; style of dress **2.** external appearance **—vt.** to clothe

gar·bage (gär′bij) *n.* [ME., entrails of fowls] spoiled or waste food

gar·ban·zo (gär ban′zō) *n., pl.* **-zos** [Sp.] *same as* CHICKPEA

gar·ble (gär′b'l) *vt.* **-bled, -bling** [< It. < Ar. *ghirbāl,* a sieve] to distort or confuse (a story, etc.) so as to mislead

gar·den (gär′d'n) *n.* [< Frank.] **1.** a piece of ground for growing flowers, vegetables, etc. **2.** an area of fertile land **3.** [*often pl.*] a public parklike place, sometimes having displays of animals or plants **—vi.** to make, or work in, a garden **—gar′den·er** *n.*

gar·de·nia (gär dēn′yə) *n.* [< A. *Garden,* 18th-c. Am. botanist] a plant with glossy leaves and fragrant, waxy flowers

Gar·gan·tu·a (gär gan′choo wə) a giant king in a satire by Rabelais **—Gar·gan′tu·an, gar·gan′tu·an** *adj.*

gar·gle (gär′g'l) *vt., vi.* **-gled, -gling** [< Fr. < *gargouille,* throat] to rinse (the throat) with a liquid kept in motion by the slow expulsion of air from the lungs **—n.** a liquid for gargling

gar·goyle (gär′goil) *n.* [see prec.] a waterspout formed like a fantastic creature, projecting from the gutter of a building

gar·ish (ger′ish) *adj.* [prob. < ME. *gauren,* to stare] too bright or gaudy; showy

gar·land (gär′lənd) *n.* [< OFr. *garlande*] a wreath of flowers, leaves, etc. **—vt.** to decorate with garlands

gar·lic (gär′lik) *n.* [< OE. *gar,* a spear + *leac,* a leek] **1.** a plant of the lily family **2.** this strong-smelling bulb, used as seasoning **—gar′lick·y** *adj.*

gar·ment (gär′mənt) *n.* [see GARNISH] any article of clothing **—vt.** to clothe

gar·ner (gär′nər) *n.* [< L. *granum,* grain] a granary **—vt.** to gather up and store

gar·net (gär′nit) *n.* [< ML. *granatum*] **1.** any of a group of hard silicate minerals, chiefly crystalline: red varieties are used as gems **2.** a deep red

gar·nish (gär′nish) *vt.* [< OFr. *garnir,* furnish] **1.** to decorate; trim **2.** to decorate (food) to add color or flavor **3.** to garnishee **—n. 1.** a decoration **2.** something used to garnish food, as parsley

gar·nish·ee (gär′nə shē′) *vt.* **-eed′, -ee′ing** *Law* to attach (a debtor's property, wages, etc.) so as to pay the debt

gar·ret (gar′it) *n.* [< OFr. *garite,* watchtower] an attic

gar·ri·son (gar′ə s'n) *n.* [< OFr. *garir,* to watch] **1.** troops stationed in a fort **2.** a military post or station **—vt.** to station (troops) in (a fortified place) for its defense

gar·rote (gə rät′, -rōt′) *n.* [Sp.] **1.** a cord, thong, etc. used in strangling **2.** strangulation with a cord, thong, etc. **—vt.** **-rot′ed** or **-rot′ted, -rot′ing** or **-rot′ting** to execute or attack by such strangling Also sp. **ga·rotte′, gar·rotte′ —gar·rot′er** *n.*

gar·ru·lous (gar′ə ləs, -yoo-) *adj.* [< L. *garrire,* to chatter] talking too much **—gar·ru·li·ty** (gə rōō′lə tē) *n.*

gar·ter (gär′tər) *n.* [< OFr. *garet,* the back of the knee] an elastic band for holding a stocking in place **—vt.** to fasten with a garter

garter snake a small, harmless, striped snake common in N. America

gas (gas) *n.* [coined < Gr. *chaos,* chaos] **1.** the fluid form of a substance in which it can expand indefinitely; vapor **2.** any mixture of flammable gases used as for heating **3.** any gas used as an anesthetic **4.** any poisonous substance dispersed in the air, as in war **5.** [Colloq.] *a*) gasoline *b*) the accelerator in an automobile, etc. **—vt.** **gassed, gas′sing** to attack or kill by gas **—vi.** [Slang] to talk idly or boastfully **—gas′e·ous** (gas′ē əs, gash′əs) *adj.* **—gas′sy** *adj.* **-si·er, -si·est**

gash (gash) *vt.* [< OFr. *garser*] to make a long, deep cut in **—n.** a long, deep cut

gas·ket (gas′kit) *n.* [prob. < OFr. *garcette,* small cord] a piece or ring of rubber, metal, etc. placed around a piston or joint to make it leakproof

gas·o·hol (gas′ə hôl′) *n.* a mixture of gasoline and alcohol used as a motor fuel

gas·o·line (gas′ə lēn′, gas′ə lēn′) *n.* [< GAS + L. *oleum,* oil] a volatile, flammable liquid distilled from petroleum and used chiefly as a fuel in internal-combustion engines

gasp (gasp) *vi.* [< ON. *geispa,* to yawn] to inhale suddenly or breathe with effort **—vt.** to say with gasps **—n.** a gasping

gas station *same as* SERVICE STATION

gas·tric (gas′trik) *adj.* [GASTR(O)- + -IC] of, in, or near the stomach

gastric juice the acid digestive fluid produced by glands in the stomach lining

gas·tri·tis (gas trīt′is) *n.* [GASTR(O)- + -ITIS] inflammation of the stomach

gastro- [< Gr. *gastēr*] *a combining form meaning* the stomach (and)

gas·tron·o·my (gas trän′ə mē) *n.* [< Gr. *gastēr,* stomach + *nomos,* a rule] the art of good eating **—gas·tro·nom·ic** (-trə näm′ik), **gas′tro·nom′i·cal** *adj.*

gas·tro·pod (gas′trə päd′) *n.* [GASTRO- + -POD] any of a large group of mollusks having a single spiral shell, as snails, or no shell, as certain slugs: gastropods move by means of a broad, muscular, ventral foot

gate (gāt) *n.* [< OE. *geat*] **1.** a movable structure controlling passage through an opening in a fence or wall **2.** a gateway **3.** a structure controlling the flow of water, as in a canal **4.** the total paid admissions to a performance or exhibition —**to give (someone) the gate** [Slang] to get rid of

gate'way' *n.* **1.** an entrance in a wall, etc. fitted with a gate **2.** a means of access

gath·er (gath'ər) *vt.* [< OE. *gad(e)rian*] **1.** to bring together in one place or group **2.** to get gradually; accumulate **3.** to collect by picking; harvest **4.** to infer; conclude **5.** to draw into folds or pleats —*vi.* **1.** to assemble **2.** to increase —*n.* a pleat

gath'er·ing *n.* **1.** a meeting; crowd **2.** a series of folds in cloth

gauche (gōsh) *adj.* [Fr. < MFr. *gauchir*, become warped] awkward; tactless

gau·che·rie (gō'shə rē') *n.* gauche behavior or a gauche act

gaud (gôd) *n.* [ME. *gaude*, a trinket] a cheap, showy ornament

gaud'y *adj.* **-i·er, -i·est** bright and showy, but in bad taste —**gaud'i·ness** *n.*

gauge (gāj) *n.* [< ONormFr. *gaugier*, to gauge] **1.** a standard measure **2.** any device for measuring **3.** the distance between the rails of a railway **4.** the size of the bore of a shotgun —*vt.* **gauged, gaug'ing 1.** to measure the size, amount, etc. of **2.** to estimate; judge —**gaug'er** *n.*

Gaul (gôl) ancient division of the Roman Empire in W Europe —*n.* any of the people of Gaul

Gaul'ish *n.* the Celtic language spoken in ancient Gaul

gaunt (gônt) *adj.* [ME. *gawnte*] **1.** thin and bony; haggard, as from great hunger or age **2.** looking grim or forbidding —**gaunt'ly** *adv.* — **gaunt'ness** *n.*

gaunt·let' (gônt'lit, gänt'-) *n.* [< OFr. *gant*, glove] **1.** a medieval armored glove **2.** a long glove with a flaring cuff —**throw down the gauntlet** to challenge, as to combat

gaunt·let² (gônt'lit, gänt'-) *n.* same as GANT-LET

gauze (gôz) *n.* [Fr. *gaze*] any very thin, transparent, loosely woven material, as of cotton or silk —**gauz'y** *adj.* **-i·er, -i·est**

gave (gāv) *pt. of* GIVE

gav·el (gav'l) *n.* [< OE. *gafol*, a tool] a small mallet rapped on the table by a presiding officer in calling for attention

ga·votte (gə vät') *n.* [Fr.] a 17th-cent. dance like the minuet, but livelier

gawk (gôk) *vi.* [prob. < *gowk*, a simpleton] to stare stupidly

gawk'y *adj.* **-i·er, -i·est** clumsy; ungainly — **gawk'i·ly** *adv.* —**gawk'i·ness** *n.*

gay (gā) *adj.* [OFr. *gai*] **1.** joyous and lively; merry **2.** bright; brilliant [*gay* colors] **3.** [Slang] homosexual —**gay'ness** *n.*

gay·e·ty (gā'ə tē) *n. same as* GAIETY

gay·ly (gā'lē) *adv. same as* GAILY

gaze (gāz) *vi.* **gazed, gaz'ing** [< Scand.] to look steadily; stare —*n.* a steady look —**gaz'er** *n.*

ga·zelle (gə zel') *n.* [Fr. < Ar. *ghazāl*] a small, swift antelope of Africa and Asia, with horns and large, lustrous eyes

ga·zette (gə zet') *n.* [Fr. < It. dial. *gazeta*, a small coin, price of a newspaper] **1.** a newspaper **2.** in England, an official publication —*vt.* **-zet'ted, -zet'ting** [Chiefly Brit.] to announce or list in a gazette

gaz·et·teer (gaz'ə tir') *n.* a dictionary or index of geographical names

gear (gir) *n.* [prob. < ON. *gervi*, preparation] **1.** clothing; apparel **2.** equipment for some task, as a workman's tools, a harness, etc. **3.** *a)* [often *pl.*] a system of toothed wheels, disks, etc. meshed together to pass motion along *b)* a gearwheel *c)* a specific adjustment in motor-vehicle transmissions *d)* a part of a mechanism performing a specific function [the steering *gear*] —*vt.* **1.** to connect by or furnish with gears **2.** to adapt (one thing) to conform with another —**in** (or **out of**) **gear 1.** (not) connected to the motor **2.** (not) in proper working order

gear'shift' *n.* a device for connecting or disconnecting any of a number of sets of transmission gears to a motor, etc.

gear'wheel' *n.* a toothed wheel in a system of gears

gee' (jē) *interj., n.* a command to a horse, etc., meaning "turn right!" —*vt., vi.* **geed, gee'ing** to turn to the right

gee² (jē) *interj.* [< JE(SUS)] [Slang] an exclamation of surprise, wonder, etc.

geese (gēs) *n. pl. of* GOOSE

gee·zer (gē'zər) *n.* [< GUISE] [Slang] an eccentric old man

Gei·ger counter (gī'gər) [< H. *Geiger*, G. physicist] an instrument for detecting and counting ionizing particles, as from radioactive ores

gei·sha (gā'shə) *n., pl.* **-sha, -shas** [Jpn.] a Japanese girl trained as an entertainer to serve as a hired companion to men

gel (jel) *n.* [< GELATIN] a jellylike substance formed by a colloidal solution —*vi.* **gelled, gel'-ling** to form a gel

gel·a·tin, gel·a·tine (jel'ət 'n) *n.* [< L. *gelare*, freeze] a tasteless, odorless substance extracted by boiling bones, hoofs, etc., or a similar vegetable substance: dissolved and cooled, it forms a jellylike substance used in foods, photographic film, etc. —**ge·lat·i·nous** (jə lat'n əs) *adj.*

geld (geld) *vt.* **geld'ed** or **gelt, geld'ing** [< ON. *geldr*, barren] to castrate (esp. a horse)

geld'ing *n.* a gelded animal, esp. a horse

gel·id (jel'id) *adj.* [< L. *gelu*, frost] extremely cold; icy —**ge·lid·i·ty** (jə lid'ə tē) *n.*

gem (jem) *n.* [< L. *gemma*] **1.** a precious stone, cut for use as a jewel **2.** a highly valued person or thing —*vt.* **gemmed, gem'ming** to adorn with gems

Gem·i·ni (jem'ə nī', -nē') [L., twins] the third sign of the zodiac

-gen [< Gr. *gignesthai*, be born] a suffix meaning: **1.** something that produces [*oxygen*] **2.** something produced (in a specified way)

Gen. 1. General **2.** Genesis

gen·darme (zhän'därm) *n.* [Fr. < *gens d'armes*, men-at-arms] a policeman

gen·der (jen'dər) *n.* [< L. *genus*, origin] **1.** *Gram.* the classification by which words are grouped as masculine, feminine, or neuter **2.** [Colloq.] sex

gene (jēn) *n.* [see -GEN] any of the units in the chromosomes by which hereditary characters are transmitted

ge·ne·al·o·gy (jē'nē äl'ə jē, -al'-) *n., pl.* **-gies** [< Gr. *genea*, race + *-logia*, -LOGY] **1.** a recorded history of one's ancestry **2.** the study of family descent **3.** descent from an ancestor; lineage —**ge'ne·a·log'i·cal** (-ə läj'i k'l) *adj.* — **ge'ne·al'o·gist** *n.*

gen·er·a (jen'ər ə) *n. pl. of* GENUS

gen·er·al (jen'ər əl, jen'rəl) *adj.* [< L. *genus*,

class] **1.** of, for, or from all; not local or special **2.** of or for a whole genus, kind, etc. **3.** widespread *[general* unrest*]* **4.** most common; usual **5.** not precise; vague *[in* general terms*]* **6.** highest in rank *[an* attorney *general] —n.* **1.** a military officer ranking just above a lieutenant general: also **full general 2.** a military officer ranking above a colonel —**in general 1.** usually **2.** without specific details

General Assembly the legislative assembly of the United Nations

gen·er·al·is·si·mo (jen′ər ə lis′ə mō′) *n., pl.* -mos′ [It.] in some countries, the commander in chief of all the armed forces

gen·er·al·i·ty (jen′ə ral′ə tē) *n., pl.* -ties **1.** the quality of being general **2.** a nonspecific statement, idea, etc. **3.** the main body

gen′er·al·ize′ (-ə līz′) *vt.* -ized′, -iz′ing **1.** to state in terms of a general law **2.** to infer from (particular instances) **3.** to emphasize the general character of —*vi.* **1.** to formulate general principles **2.** to talk in generalities —**gen′er·al·i·za′tion** *n.*

gen′er·al·ly *adv.* **1.** widely; popularly **2.** usually **3.** not specifically

gen·er·ate (jen′ə rāt′) *vt.* -at′ed, -at′ing [< L. *genus,* race] **1.** to produce (offspring); beget **2.** to bring into being; produce —**gen′er·a·tive** (-ər ə tiv) *adj.*

gen′er·a′tion *n.* **1.** a generating; production **2.** a single stage in the succession of descent **3.** the average time (c. 30 years) between human generations **4.** all the people born about the same time

gen′er·a′tor *n.* a machine for changing mechanical energy into electrical energy; dynamo

ge·ner·ic (jə ner′ik) *adj.* [see GENUS & -IC] **1.** inclusive or general **2.** that is not a trademark **3.** of or characteristic of a genus —**ge·ner′i·cal·ly** *adv.*

gen·er·os·i·ty (jen′ə räs′ə tē) *n.* **1.** the quality of being generous **2.** *pl.* -ties a generous act

gen·er·ous (jen′ər əs) *adj.* [< L. *generosus,* noble] **1.** noble-minded; magnanimous **2.** willing to give or share; unselfish **3.** large; ample —**gen′er·ous·ly** *adv.*

gen·e·sis (jen′ə sis) *n., pl.* -ses′ (-sēz′) [< Gr.] a beginning; origin —[G-] the first book of the Bible

ge·net·ics (jə net′iks) *n.pl.* [*with sing. v.*] [< GENESIS] the branch of biology that deals with heredity and variation in animal and plant species —**ge·net′ic** *adj.* —**ge·net′i·cal·ly** *adv.* —**ge·net′i·cist** (-ə sist) *n.*

ge·nial (jēn′yəl) *adj.* [see GENIUS] **1.** promoting life and growth *[a* genial climate*]* **2.** cheerful and friendly; amiable —**ge·ni·al·i·ty** (jē′nē al′ə tē) *n.* —**ge′nial·ly** *adv.*

ge·nie (jē′nē) *n.* [Fr. *génie*] same as JINNI

gen·i·tal (jen′ə t'l) *adj.* [< L. *genere,* to beget] of reproduction or the sexual organs

gen′i·tals *n.pl.* the reproductive organs; esp., the external sex organs

gen·i·tive (jen′ə tiv) *adj.* [< Gr. *genos,* genus] designating or in the grammatical case expressing possession, source, etc. —*n.* the genitive case

ge·nius (jēn′yəs) *n.* [L., guardian spirit] **1.** particular spirit of a nation, place, age, etc. **2.** natural ability (*for*); strong inclination **3.** great mental capacity and inventive ability **4.** a person having this

gen·o·cide (jen′ə sīd′) *n.* [< Gr. *genos,* race + -CIDE] the systematic killing of a whole people or nation —**gen′o·ci′dal** *adj.*

gen·re (zhän′rə) *n.* [Fr. < L. *genus,* kind] **1.** a

kind or type **2.** painting in which subjects from everyday life are treated realistically

gent (jent) *n.* [Colloq.] a gentleman

gen·teel (jen tēl′) *adj.* [< Fr. *gentil*] **1.** formerly, well-bred or polite **2.** affectedly refined, polite, etc.

gen·tian (jen′shən) *n.* [< L. *gentiana*] a plant with blue, white, red, or yellow flowers

gen·tile (jen′tīl) *n.* [< L. *gentilis,* of the same clan] [*also* G-] any person not a Jew —*adj.* [*also* G-] not Jewish

gen·til·i·ty (jen til′ə tē) *n., pl.* -ties [see GENTLE] **1.** the condition of belonging by birth to the upper classes **2.** the quality of being genteel

gen·tle (jent′'l) *adj.* -tler, -tlest [< L. *gentilis,* of the same clan] **1.** of the upper classes **2.** refined; polite **3.** generous; kind **4.** tame *[a* gentle dog*]* **5.** kindly; patient **6.** not violent or harsh *[a* gentle tap*]* **7.** gradual *[a* gentle slope*]* —*vt.* -tled, -tling to tame or calm —**gen′tle·ness** *n.* —**gen′tly** *adv.*

gen′tle·folk′ *n.pl.* people of high social standing: also **gen′tle·folks′**

gen′tle·man (-mən) *n., pl.* -men **1.** a man of good family and social standing **2.** a well-bred, courteous man **3.** any man: polite term (chiefly in pl.) —**gen′tle·man·ly** *adj.* —**gen′tle·wom′an** *n.fem., pl.* -wom′en

gen·try (jen′trē) *n.* [see GENTLE] **1.** people of high social standing **2.** people of a particular class or group

gen·u·flect (jen′yə flekt′) *vi.* [< L. *genu,* knee + *flectere,* bend] to bend the knee, as in worship —**gen′u·flec′tion, gen′u·flex′ion** *n.*

gen·u·ine (jen′yoo wən) *adj.* [< L. *genuinus,* inborn] **1.** really being what it is said to be; true **2.** sincere —**gen′u·ine·ly** *adv.*

ge·nus (jē′nəs) *n., pl.* **gen·er·a** (jen′ər ə), **ge′nus·es** [L., race, kind] **1.** a class; kind; sort **2.** *Biol.* a classification of related plants or animals

geo- [< Gr. *gē*] *a combining form meaning* earth, of the earth *[geology]*

ge·o·des·ic (jē′ə des′ik) *adj.* **1.** same as GEODETIC (sense 1) **2.** designating the shortest line between two points on a curved surface **3.** having a surface formed of straight bars in a grid of polygons

ge′o·det′ic (-det′ik) *adj.* [< Gr. *gē,* earth + *daiein,* divide] **1.** of or concerned with the measurement of the earth and its surface **2.** same as GEODESIC (sense 2)

ge·og·ra·phy (jē äg′rə fē) *n., pl.* -phies [< Gr. *gē,* earth + *graphein,* to write] **1.** the science dealing with the earth's surface, continents, climates, plants, animals, resources, etc. **2.** the physical features of a region —**ge·og′ra·pher** *n.* —**ge′o·graph′i·cal** (-ə graf′i k'l), **ge′o·graph′ic** *adj.*

ge·ol·o·gy (jē äl′ə jē) *n., pl.* -gies [see GEO- & -LOGY] the science dealing with the development of the earth's crust, its rocks and fossils, etc. —**ge′o·log′ic** (-ə läj′ik), **ge′o·log′i·cal** *adj.* —**ge·ol′o·gist** *n.*

ge·om·e·try (jē äm′ə trē) *n., pl.* -tries [< Gr. *gē,* earth + *metrein,* measure] the branch of mathematics dealing with the properties, measurement, and relationships of points, lines, planes, and solids —**ge′o·met′ric** (-ə met′rik), **ge′o·met′ri·cal** *adj.*

ge·o·phys·ics (jē′ō fiz′iks) *n.pl.* [*with sing. v.*] the science dealing with the effects of weather, winds, tides, etc. on the earth —**ge′o·phys′i·cal** *adj.* —**ge′o·phys′i·cist** *n.*

ge·o·pol·i·tics (jē′ō päl′ə tiks) *n.pl.* [*with*

sing. v.] [< G. *geopolitik*] the interrelationship of politics and geography

ge·ra·ni·um (jə rā′nē əm) *n.* [< Gr. *geranion*, crane's-bill: its seed capsule is beaked] **1.** a plant with showy red, pink, or white flowers and many-lobed leaves **2.** a related wildflower

ger·bil (jur′b'l) *n.* [Fr. *gerbille*, ult. < Ar.] a small rodent with long hind legs

ger·i·at·rics (jer′ē at′riks) *n.pl.* [*with sing. v.*] [< Gr. *gēras*, old age + -IATRICS] the branch of medicine dealing with the diseases of old age

germ (jurm) *n.* [< L. *germen*, sprout] **1.** the rudimentary form from which a new organism is developed; seed, bud, etc. **2.** any microscopic disease-causing organism, esp. one of the bacteria **3.** an origin

Ger·man (jur′mən) *adj.* of Germany, its people, etc. —*n.* **1.** a native of Germany **2.** the language of the Germans

ger·mane (jər mān′) *adj.* [see GERM] truly relevant; pertinent

Ger·man·ic (jər man′ik) *adj.* **1.** German **2.** designating or of the original language of the German peoples or the languages descended from it —*n.* the Germanic branch of languages; Swedish, Dutch, English, etc.

ger·ma·ni·um (jər mā′nē əm) *n.* [< L. *Germania*, Germany] a rare, grayish-white, metallic chemical element: symbol, Ge

German measles *same as* RUBELLA

germ cell an egg or sperm cell

ger·mi·cide (jur′mə sīd′) *n.* [< GERM + -CIDE] anything used to destroy germs —**ger′mi·ci′dal** *adj.*

ger·mi·nal (jur′mə n'l) *adj.* **1.** of or like germs or germ cells **2.** in the first stage

ger′mi·nate′ (-nāt′) *vi., vt.* -nat′ed, -nat′ing [< L. *germen*, a sprout] to start developing; sprout, as from a seed —**ger′mi·na′tion** *n.*

ger·on·tol·o·gy (jer′ən täl′ə jē) *n.* [< Gr. *gerōn*, old man + -LOGY] the scientific study of aging and the problems of the aged

ger·ry·man·der (jer′i man′dər, ger′-) *vt., vi.* [< E. *Gerry*, governor of Mass. (1812) + SALAMANDER (the shape of the redistricted county)] to divide (a voting area) so as to give unfair advantage to one political party —*n.* redistricting of this kind

ger·und (jer′ənd) *n.* [< L. *gerere*, to do] *Gram.* a verbal noun ending in -*ing*

Ge·sta·po (gə stä′pō) *n.* [< G. *Ge(heime) Sta(ats)po(lizei)*, secret state police] the secret police of the German Nazi state

ges·tate (jes′tāt) *vt.* -tat·ed, -tat·ing [< L. *gerere*, to bear] to carry in the uterus during pregnancy —**ges·ta′tion** *n.*

ges·tic·u·late (jes tik′yə lāt′) *vi.* -lat′ed, -lat′ing [see GESTURE] to make or use gestures —**ges·tic′u·la′tion** *n.*

ges·ture (jes′chər) *n.* [< L. *gerere*, to bear] **1.** movement of part of the body to express or emphasize ideas, emotions, etc. **2.** any act or remark conveying a state of mind, intention, etc., often made merely for effect —*vi.* -tured, -tur·ing to make gestures

get (get) *vt.* **got, got** *or* **got′ten, get′ting** [< ON. *geta*] **1.** to come into the state of having; receive, obtain, etc. **2.** to arrive at [to *get* home early] **3.** to go and bring [*get* your books] **4.** to persuade [*get* him to go] **5.** to cause to be [he *got* his hands dirty] **6.** to prepare [to *get* lunch] **7.** [Colloq.] to be obliged to (with *have* or *has*) [he's *got* to pass] **8.** [Colloq.] to possess (with *have* or *has*) [he's *got* red hair] **9.** [Colloq.] to baffle or defeat **10.** [Colloq.] to understand **11.** [Slang] to cause an emotional re-

sponse in [her singing *gets* me] —*vi.* **1.** to come or arrive [to *get* to work on time] **2.** to be [I *got* into trouble] **3.** to contrive [to *get* to go] *Get* is used as an auxiliary for emphasis in passive constructions [we *got* beaten] —*n.* the young of an animal —**get around 1.** to move from place to place: also **get about 2.** to circumvent **3.** to influence as by flattery —**get away 1.** to go away **2.** to escape —**get away with** [Slang] to succeed in doing or taking without being discovered or punished —**get by** [Colloq.] to survive; manage —**get off 1.** to come off, down, or out of **2.** to leave **3.** to take off **4.** to escape or help to escape —**get on 1.** to go on or into **2.** to put on **3.** to proceed **4.** to grow older **5.** to succeed **6.** to agree —**get out 1.** to go out or away **2.** to take out **3.** to be disclosed **4.** to publish —**get over 1.** to recover from **2.** to forget —**get through 1.** to finish **2.** to manage to survive —**get together 1.** to assemble **2.** [Colloq.] to reach an agreement —**get up 1.** to rise (from sleep, etc.) **2.** to contrive; organize

get′a·way′ *n.* **1.** the act of starting, as in a race **2.** the act of escaping

Geth·sem·a·ne (geth sem′ə nē) *Bible* a garden outside Jerusalem, scene of the agony, betrayal, and arrest of Jesus

get′-up′ *n.* [Colloq.] costume; dress

gew·gaw (gyōō′gô) *n.* [< ME.] a trinket

gey·ser (gī′zər) *n.* [Ice. < ON. *gjosa*, to gush] a spring from which columns of boiling water and steam gush into the air at intervals

ghast·ly (gast′lē) *adj.* -li·er, -li·est [< OE. *gast*, ghost] **1.** horrible; frightful **2.** ghostlike; pale **3.** [Colloq.] very unpleasant —**ghast′li·ness** *n.*

gher·kin (gur′kin) *n.* [< Du. *gurken* < Pol. < Gr. < Per.] a small pickled cucumber

ghet·to (get′ō) *n., pl.* **-tos, -toes** [It.] **1.** a section of some European cities to which Jews were formerly restricted **2.** any section of a city in which many members of some minority group live

ghost (gōst) *n.* [OE. *gast*] **1.** the supposed disembodied spirit of a dead person, appearing as a pale, shadowy apparition **2.** a faint semblance [not a *ghost* of a chance] **3.** *Optics & TV* an unwanted secondary image —**give up the ghost** to die —**ghost′li·ness** *n.* —**ghost′ly** *adj.* -li·er, -li·est

ghost′writ′er (-rīt′ər) *n.* one who writes speeches, articles, etc. for another who professes to be the author —**ghost′write′** *vt., vi.*

ghoul (gōōl) *n.* [< Ar. *ghāla*, seize] **1.** *Oriental Folklore* an evil spirit that robs graves and feeds on the dead **2.** one who enjoys horrible things —**ghoul′ish** *adj.*

GHQ, G.H.Q. General Headquarters

GI (jē′ī′) *adj.* **1.** government issue: designating clothing, etc. issued to military personnel **2.** [Colloq.] of or characteristic of the U.S. armed forces —*n., pl.* **GI's, GIs** [Colloq.] a U.S. enlisted soldier

gi·ant (jī′ənt) *n.* [< Gr. *gigas*] **1.** an imaginary being of human form but of superhuman size **2.** a person or thing of great size, intellect, etc. —*adj.* of great size, strength, etc. —**gi′ant·ess** *n.fem.*

gib·ber (jib′ər, gib′-) *vi., vt.* [echoic] to speak or utter rapidly and incoherently

gib′ber·ish *n.* unintelligible chatter

gib·bet (jib′it) *n.* [< Frank. *gibb*, forked stick] **1.** a gallows **2.** a structure from which bodies of executed criminals were hung and exposed to public scorn

gib·bon (gib′ən) *n.* [Fr.] a small, slender, long-armed ape of India, S China, and the East Indies

gibe (jīb) *n., vi., vt.* **gibed, gib'ing** [< ? OFr. *giber*, handle roughly] jeer; taunt

gib·let (jib'lit) *n.* [< OFr. *gibelet*, stew made of game] any of the edible internal parts of a fowl, as the heart, gizzard, etc.

gid·dy (gid'ē) *adj.* **-di·er, -di·est** [OE. *gydig*, insane] **1.** having or causing a whirling, dazed sensation; dizzy **2.** frivolous

Gid·e·on (gid'ē ən) *Bible* a judge of Israel and victorious leader in battle

gift (gift) *n.* [< OE. *giefan*, to give] **1.** something given; present **2.** the act of giving **3.** a natural ability; talent

gift'ed *adj.* **1.** talented **2.** having superior intelligence —**gift'ed·ness** *n.*

gig¹ (gig) *n.* [prob. < Scand.] **1.** a light, two-wheeled, open carriage drawn by one horse **2.** a long, light ship's boat

gig² (gig) *n.* [< ?] [Slang] a job to play or sing jazz, rock, etc.

gi·gan·tic (jī gan'tik) *adj.* [see GIANT] huge; enormous; immense —**gi·gan'ti·cal·ly** *adv.*

gig·gle (gig''l) *vi.* **-gled, -gling** [prob. < Du. *giggelen*] to laugh with rapid, high-pitched sounds, suggestive of foolishness, etc. —*n.* such a laugh —**gig'gler** *n.* —**gig'gly** *adj.* **-gli·er, -gli·est**

gig·o·lo (jig'ə lō) *n., pl.* **-los** [Fr.] a man paid by a woman to be her escort

Gi·la monster (hē'lə) [< the *Gila* River, Ariz.] a stout, poisonous, black-and-orange lizard found in deserts of the SW U.S.

gild (gild) *vt.* **gild'ed** or **gilt, gild'ing** [OE. *gyldan*] **1.** to coat with gold leaf or a gold color **2.** to make (something) seem more attractive or valuable than it is

gill (gil) *n.* [prob. < Anglo-N.] the organ for breathing of most animals that live in water, as fish

gill² (jil) *n.* [< LL. *gillo*, cooling vessel] a liquid measure, equal to 1/4 pint

gilt (gilt) *alt. pt. & pp.* of GILD —*adj.* coated with gilt —*n.* gold leaf or a substance like gold, covering a surface

gilt'-edged *adj.* **1.** having gilded edges **2.** of the highest quality or value [*gilt-edged* securities] Also **gilt'-edge'**

gim·bals (gim'b'lz, jim'-) *n.pl.* [with *sing. v.*] [< L. *geminus*, twin] a pair of rings so pivoted that one swings freely within the other: used to keep a ship's compass level

gim·let (gim'lit) *n.* [< MDu. *wimpel*] a small boring tool with a spiral cutting edge

gim·mick (gim'ik) *n.* [< ?] [Slang] **1.** an attention-getting feature for promoting a product, etc. **2.** any clever gadget or ruse

gimp'y (gim'pē) *adj.* [< ?] [Colloq.] lame

gin¹ (jin) *n.* [< L. *juniperus*, juniper] a strong alcoholic liquor distilled from grain and usually flavored with juniper berries

gin² (jin) *n.* [< OFr. *engin*, ENGINE] **1.** a snare or trap, as for game **2.** a cotton gin —*vt.* **ginned, gin'ning 1.** to trap **2.** to remove seeds from (cotton) with a gin

gin·ger (jin'jər) *n.* [< L. *zingiber*] **1.** an Asiatic plant with rhizomes that are used as a spice and in medicine **2.** the spice made from the rhizome **3.** [Colloq.] vigor; spirit —**gin'ger·y** *adj.*

ginger ale a carbonated, sweet soft drink flavored with ginger

gin'ger·bread *n.* **1.** a cake flavored with ginger **2.** showy ornamentation

gin'ger·ly *adv.* carefully or cautiously —*adj.* careful; cautious —**gin'ger·li·ness** *n.*

ging·ham (giŋ'əm) *n.* [< Du. < Malay *ging-*

gang, striped] a cotton cloth, usually woven in stripes, checks, or plaids

gin·gi·vi·tis (jin'jə vīt'əs) *n.* [< L. *gingiva*, the gum + -ITIS] inflammation of the gums

gin rummy a variety of the card game rummy

gin·seng (jin'seŋ) *n.* [Chin. *jen shen*] a perennial plant with a thick, aromatic root, used medicinally

gip (jip) *n., vt., vi. same as* GYP

Gip·sy (jip'sē) *n. same as* GYPSY

gi·raffe (jə raf') *n.* [Fr. < It. < Ar. *zarāfa*] a large, cud-chewing animal of Africa, with a very long neck and legs

gird (gurd) *vt.* **gird'ed** or **girt, gird'ing** [OE. *gyrdan*] **1.** to encircle or fasten with a belt **2.** to encircle **3.** to prepare (oneself) for action

gird'er *n.* a large beam of timber or steel, for supporting the joists of a floor, a framework, etc.

gir·dle (gur'd'l) *n.* [OE. *gyrdel*] **1.** a belt for the waist **2.** anything that encircles **3.** an elasticized undergarment supporting waist and hips —*vt.* **-dled, -dling 1.** to bind, as with a girdle **2.** to encircle

girl (gurl) *n.* [ME. *girle*, youngster] **1.** a female child **2.** a young, unmarried woman **3.** a female servant **4.** [Colloq.] a sweetheart —**girl'-hood'** *n.* —**girl'ish** *adj.*

girl scout a member of the **Girl Scouts,** a girls' club stressing healthful activities

girt¹ (gurt) *alt. pt. & pp.* of GIRD

girt² (gurt) *vt.* **1.** to gird **2.** to fasten with a girth

girth (gurth) *n.* [< ON. *gjörth*] **1.** a band put around the belly of a horse, etc. to hold a saddle or pack **2.** the circumference, as of a tree trunk or person's waist —*vt.* to bind with a girth

gist ⟨jist⟩ *n.* [< OFr. *giste*, point at issue] the essence or main point, as of an article or argument

give (giv) *vt.* **gave, giv'en, giv'ing** [OE. *giefan*] **1.** to make a gift of **2.** to hand over [*he gave* the porter his bag] **3.** to sell (goods, etc.) or pay (a price) for goods, etc. **4.** to relay [*give* my regards] **5.** to cause to have **6.** to confer **7.** to act as host of (a party, etc.) **8.** to produce; supply [*cows give* milk] **9.** to sacrifice **10.** to concede; yield **11.** to offer **12.** to perform [to *give* a concert] **13.** to inflict (punishment, etc.) —*vi.* to bend, move, etc. from force or pressure —*n.* a bending, moving, etc. under pressure **2.** resiliency —**give away 1.** to make a gift of **2.** to give (the bride) ritually to the bridegroom **3.** [Colloq.] to reveal —**give forth** (or **off**) to emit —**give in** to yield —**give out 1.** to make public **2.** to distribute **3.** to become worn out, etc. —**give up 1.** to relinquish **2.** to stop **3.** to stop trying **4.** to lose hope for —**giv'er** *n.*

give'a·way *n.* [Colloq.] **1.** an unintentional revelation **2.** something given free or sold cheap

giv·en (giv'n) *pp.* of GIVE —*adj.* **1.** accustomed, as by habit **2.** stated **3.** assumed

given name a person's first name

giz·mo, gis·mo (giz'mō) *n., pl.* **-mos** [< ?] [Slang] **1.** any gadget or device **2.** a gimmick

giz·zard (giz'ərd) *n.* [< L. *gigeria*, cooked entrails of poultry] the muscular second stomach of a bird

gla·cé (gla sā') *adj.* [Fr.] **1.** having a smooth, glossy surface **2.** candied or glazed, as fruits — *vt.* **-céed, -cé'ing** to glaze (fruits)

gla·cial (glā'shəl) *adj.* **1.** of ice or glaciers **2.** of or produced by a glacial epoch

glacial epoch any period when much of the earth was covered with glaciers

gla·ci·ate (glā'shē āt') *vt.* **-at'ed, -at'ing 1.** to cover over with ice or a glacier **2.** to expose to or change by glacial action

gla·cier (glā'shər) *n.* [Fr. < L. *glacies,* ice] a large mass of ice and snow moving slowly down a mountain or valley

glad[1] (glad) *adj.* **glad'der, glad'dest** [OE. *glæd*] **1.** happy **2.** causing joy **3.** very willing **4.** bright or beautiful

glad[2] (glad) *n.* [Colloq.] a gladiolus

glad'den (-'n) *vt., vi.* to make or become glad

glade (glād) *n.* [ME.] **1.** an open space in a forest **2.** an everglade

glad·i·a·tor (glad'ē āt'ər) *n.* [L. < *gladius,* sword] in ancient Rome, a slave or paid performer who fought in an arena as a public show —**glad'i·a·to'ri·al** (-ə tôr'ē əl) *adj.*

glad·i·o·lus (glad'ē ō'ləs) *n., pl.* **-lus·es, -li** (-lī) [L., small sword] a plant with swordlike leaves and spikes of funnel-shaped flowers in various colors: also **glad'i·o'la**

glad'some (-səm) *adj.* joyful or cheerful

glair (gler) *n.* [< L. *clarus,* clear] raw white of egg, used in sizing —**glair'y** *adj.*

glam·our, glam·or (glam'ər) *n.* [Scot. var. of *grammar,* magic] seemingly mysterious allure; bewitching charm —**glam'or·ous, glam'our·ous** *adj.*

glance (glans) *vi.* **glanced, glanc'ing** [ME. *glansen*] **1.** to strike obliquely and go off at an angle **2.** to flash or gleam **3.** to take a quick look —*n.* **1.** a glancing off **2.** a flash or gleam **3.** a quick look

gland (gland) *n.* [Fr. < L. *glans,* acorn] any organ that separates certain elements from the blood and secretes them for the body to use or throw off —**glan·du·lar** (glan'jə lər) *adj.*

glare (gler) *vi.* **glared, glar'ing** [ME. *glaren*] **1.** to shine with a steady, dazzling light **2.** to stare fiercely —*vt.* to express with a glare —*n.* **1.** a steady, dazzling light **2.** a fierce or angry stare **3.** a smooth, bright, glassy surface, as of ice

glar'ing *adj.* **1.** dazzlingly bright **2.** too showy **3.** staring fiercely **4.** flagrant [a *glaring* mistake] Also **glar'y**

glass (glas) *n.* [OE. *glæs*] **1.** a hard, brittle substance, usually transparent, made by fusing silicates with soda, lime, etc. **2.** *same as* GLASSWARE **3.** *a*) an article made of glass, as a drinking container, mirror, etc. *b*) [*pl.*] eyeglasses or binoculars **4.** the quantity contained in a drinking glass —*vt.* to equip with glass —*adj.* of or made of glass —**glass'ful'** *n., pl.* **glass'fuls'**

glass'ware' *n.* articles made of glass

glass'y *adj.* **-i·er, -i·est 1.** like glass, as in smoothness **2.** expressionless or lifeless [a *glassy* stare] —**glass'i·ness** *n.*

glau·co·ma (glô kō'mə, glou-) *n.* [see GLAUCOUS] a disease of the eye marked by increased pressure in the eyeball

glau·cous (glô'kəs) *adj.* [< Gr. *glaukos,* gleaming] **1.** bluish-green or yellowish-green **2.** *Bot.* covered with a whitish bloom that can be rubbed off, as grapes, plums, etc.

glaze (glāz) *vt.* **glazed, glaz'ing** [< ME. *glas,* glass] **1.** to fit (windows, etc.) with glass **2.** to give a hard, glossy finish to (pottery, etc.) **3.** to cover (foods) with a coating of sugar syrup, etc. —*vi.* to become glassy or glossy —*n.* a glassy finish

gleam (glēm) *n.* [OE. *glæm*] **1.** a flash or beam of light **2.** a faint light **3.** a faint manifestation, as of hope, etc. —*vi.* **1.** to shine with a gleam **2.** to appear suddenly

glean (glēn) *vt., vi.* [< Celt.] **1.** to collect (grain

left by reapers) **2.** to collect (facts, etc.) gradually —**glean'er** *n.*

glee (glē) *n.* [OE. *gleo*] **1.** lively joy; merriment **2.** a part song for three or more voices —**glee'-ful** *adj.* —**glee'ful·ly** *adv.*

glee club a group singing part songs

glen (glen) *n.* [< ScotGael.] a narrow, secluded valley

glib (glib) *adj.* **glib'ber, glib'best** [< or akin to Du. *glibberig,* slippery] speaking or spoken smoothly and fluently, often too smoothly to be convincing —**glib'ly** *adv.*

glide (glīd) *vi.* **glid'ed, glid'ing** [OE. *glīdan*] **1.** to move smoothly and easily **2.** *Aeron. a*) to fly in a glider *b*) to descend at a normal angle with little or no engine power —*vt.* to cause to glide —*n.* **1.** the act of gliding **2.** a small disk or ball under furniture, etc. to allow easy sliding

glid'er *n.* **1.** one that glides **2.** an engineless aircraft carried along by air currents **3.** a porch swing suspended in a frame

glim·mer (glim'ər) *vi.* [< OE. *glæm,* gleam] **1.** to give a faint, flickering light **2.** to appear faintly —*n.* **1.** a faint, flickering light **2.** a faint manifestation

glimpse (glimps) *vt.* **glimpsed, glimps'ing** [see GLIMMER] to catch a quick view of —*vi.* to look quickly —*n.* **1.** a faint, fleeting appearance **2.** a quick view

glint (glint) *vi.* [prob. < Scand.] to gleam; flash —*n.* a gleam, flash, or glitter

glis·san·do (gli sän'dō) *n., pl.* **-di** (-dē), **-dos** [as if It. < Fr. *glisser,* to slide] *Music* a gliding effect

glis·ten (glis'n) *vi.* [OE. *glisnian*] to shine or sparkle with reflected light

glit·ter (glit'ər) *vi.* [prob. < ON. *glitra*] **1.** to shine; sparkle **2.** to be showy and bright —*n.* **1.** sparkling light **2.** showiness; brightness **3.** bits of glittering material

gloam·ing (glō'miŋ) *n.* [< OE. *glom*] evening dusk; twilight

gloat (glōt) *vi.* [prob. < ON. *glotta,* grin scornfully] to gaze or think with malicious pleasure

glob·al (glō'b'l) *adj.* worldwide

globe (glōb) *n.* [< L. *globus*] **1.** any ball-shaped thing; sphere **2.** the earth **3.** a spherical model of the earth **4.** anything shaped like a globe —**glo'bate** (-bāt) *adj.*

globe'-trot'ter *n.* one who travels widely about the world, esp. for pleasure

glob·u·lar (gläb'yə lər) *adj.* **1.** shaped like a globe **2.** made up of globules

glob'ule (-yool) *n.* [< L. *globus,* ball] a tiny ball; very small drop

glock·en·spiel (gläk'ən spēl') *n.* [G. < *glocke,* bell + *spiel,* play] a musical instrument with tuned metal bars in a frame, played with hammers

glom·er·ate (gläm'ər it) *adj.* [< L. *glomus,* ball] formed into a rounded mass

gloom (gloom) *n.* [prob. < Scand.] **1.** darkness; dimness **2.** sadness; dejection —**gloom'y** *adj.* **-i·er, -i·est**

glo·ri·fy (glôr'ə fī') *vt.* **-fied', -fy'ing** [< L. *gloria,* glory + *facere,* make] **1.** to give glory to **2.** to exalt as in worship **3.** to honor; extol **4.** to make seem better, greater, etc. than is so —**glo'ri·fi·ca'tion** *n.*

glo'ri·ous (-ē əs) *adj.* **1.** full of glory **2.** receiving or deserving glory **3.** splendid; magnificent —**glo'ri·ous·ly** *adv.*

glo·ry (glôr'ē) *n., pl.* **-ries** [< L. *gloria*] **1.** great honor or fame **2.** anything bringing this **3.** worship **4.** great splendor, success, etc. **5.** heavenly bliss **6.** *same as* HALO —*vi.* **-ried, -ry·ing** to exult (*in*)

gloss[1] (glôs) *n.* [< ? Scand.] **1.** the luster of a polished surface **2.** a deceptive outward appearance —*vt.* **1.** to give a shiny surface to **2.** to make (an error, etc.) seem right or trivial — **gloss'y** *adj.* **-i·er, -i·est**

gloss[2] (glôs) *n.* [< Gr. *glōssa,* tongue] a note of comment or explanation, as in a footnote —*vt.* to furnish (a text) with glosses

glos·sa·ry (gläs'ə rē, glôs'-) *n., pl.* **-ries** [see prec.] a list of difficult terms with explanations, as for a book, author, etc.

glos·so·la·li·a (gläs'ə lä'lē ə, glôs'-) *n.* [< Gr. *glōssa,* tongue + *lalein,* to speak] an uttering of unintelligible sounds, as in a religious ecstasy

glot·tal (glät'l) *adj.* of or produced in or at the glottis: also **glot'tic**

glot·tis (glät'is) *n.* [< Gr. *glōssa,* tongue] the opening between the vocal cords

glove (gluv) *n.* [OE. *glof*] **1.** a covering for the hand, with separate sheaths for the fingers and thumb **2.** a baseball player's mitt **3.** a boxing glove —*vt.* **gloved, glov'ing** to cover as with a glove

glow (glō) *vi.* [OE. *glowan*] **1.** to give off a bright light due to great heat **2.** to give out a steady light **3.** to be or feel hot **4.** to be enlivened by emotion **5.** to be bright with color —*n.* **1.** light given off, due to great heat **2.** steady, even light **3.** brightness, warmth, etc.

glow·er (glou'ər) *vi.* [prob. < ON.] to stare with sullen anger —*n.* a sullen, angry stare; scowl —**glow'er·ing·ly** *adv.*

glow'worm *n.* a wingless insect or insect larva that gives off a luminescent light

glu·cose (gl ō̄'kōs) *n.* [Fr. < Gr. *gleúkos,* sweetness] a crystalline sugar occurring naturally, as in fruits, or prepared commercially by the hydrolysis of starch

glue (glō̄) *n.* [< LL. *glus*] **1.** a sticky, viscous liquid made from animal gelatin, used as an adhesive **2.** any similar substance —*vt.* **glued, glu'ing** to make stick as with glue —**glue'y** *adj.*

glum (glum) *adj.* **glum'mer, glum'mest** [prob. < ME. *glomen,* look morose] gloomy; sullen — **glum'ly** *adv.*

glut (glut) *vt.* **glut'ted, glut'ting** [< L. *gluttire,* to swallow] to eat to excess —*vt.* **1.** to feed, fill, etc. to excess **2.** to supply (the market) beyond demand —*n.* **1.** a glutting or being glutted **2.** a supply that is greater than the demand

glu·ten (glōōt'n) *n.* [L., glue] a gray, sticky, nutritious protein substance found in wheat, etc. —**glu'ten·ous** *adj.*

glu·ti·nous (glōōt'n əs) *adj.* [< L. *gluten,* glue] gluey; sticky —**glu'ti·nous·ly** *adv.*

glut·ton (glut'n) *n.* [see GLUT] **1.** one who eats too much **2.** one who has a great capacity for something —**glut'ton·ous** *adj.* —**glut'ton·ous·ly** *adv.*

glut'ton·y *n., pl.* **-ies** the habit or act of eating too much

glyc·er·in, glyc·er·ine (glis'ər in) *n.* [< Fr. < Gr. *glykeros,* sweet] *popular and commercial name for* GLYCEROL

glyc·er·ol (glis'ər ōl', -ôl') *n.* [< prec.] a colorless, syrupy liquid made from fats and oils: used in skin lotions, in making explosives, etc.

gly·co·gen (glī'kə jən) *n.* [see GLYCERIN] a starchlike substance produced in animal tissues, that is changed into a simple sugar as needed by the body

gm. gram; grams

Gmc. Germanic

gnarl (närl) *n.* [< ME. *knorre*] a knot on a tree

trunk or branch —*vt.* to make knotted; twist — **gnarled, gnarl'y** *adj.*

gnash (nash) *vi., vt.* [prob. < ON.] to grind (the teeth) together, as in anger —*n.* a gnashing

gnat (nat) *n.* [OE. *gnæt*] any of various small, two-winged insects that bite or sting

gnaw (nô) *vt., vi.* [< OE. *gnagen*] **1.** to bite and wear away bit by bit; consume **2.** to torment, as by constant pain

gneiss (nīs) *n.* [< G. < OHG. *gneisto,* a spark] a granitelike rock formed of layers of feldspar, quartz, mica, etc.

gnome (nōm) *n.* [Fr. < Gr. *gnōmē,* thought] *Folklore* a dwarf who dwells in the earth and guards its treasures —**gnom'ish** *adj.*

gno·mon (nō'män) *n.* [< Gr. *gignōskein,* know] a column, pin on a sundial, etc. that casts a shadow indicating the time of day

GNP gross national product

gnu (nō̄) *n.* [< the native name] a large African antelope with an oxlike head and horns and a horselike mane and tail

go (gō) *vi.* **went, gone, go'ing** [OE. *gan*] **1.** to move along; travel; proceed **2.** to work properly; operate [the clock won't *go*] **3.** to act, sound, etc. as specified [the balloon *went* "pop"] **4.** to turn out; result [the game *went* badly] **5.** to pass: said of time **6.** to become [to *go* mad] **7.** to be expressed, sung, etc. [as the saying *goes*] **8.** to harmonize; agree [blue *goes* with gold] **9.** to be accepted, valid, etc. **10.** to leave; depart **11.** to fail [his hearing *went*] **12.** to be allotted or sold **13.** to reach, extend, etc. **14.** to attend [he *goes* to college] **15.** to be able to pass (*through*), fit (*into*), etc. **16.** to be capable of being divided (*into*) **17.** to belong [socks *go* in this drawer] —*vt.* **1.** to travel along [to *go* the wrong way] **2.** [Colloq.] *a*) to put up with *b*) to furnish (bail) for an arrested person —*n., pl.* **goes 1.** a success [make a *go* of marriage] **2.** [Colloq.] energy; animation **3.** [Colloq.] a try; attempt —**go along 1.** to continue **2.** to agree **3.** to accompany —**go back on** [Colloq.] **1.** to betray **2.** to break (a promise, etc.) —**go for 1.** to try to get **2.** [Colloq.] to be attracted by —**go in for** [Colloq.] to engage or indulge in —**go off 1.** to depart **2.** to explode — **go out 1.** to be extinguished, become outdated, etc. **2.** to attend social affairs, etc. —**go over 1.** to examine thoroughly **2.** to do again **3.** [Colloq.] to be successful —**go through 1.** to endure; experience **2.** to search —**go through with** to complete —**go together 1.** to harmonize **2.** [Colloq.] to be sweethearts —**go under** to fail, as in business —**let go 1.** to let escape **2.** to release one's hold —**let oneself go** to be unrestrained —**on the go** [Colloq.] in constant motion or action —**to go** [Colloq.] **1.** to be taken out: said of food in a restaurant **2.** still to be done, etc.

goad (gōd) *n.* [OE. *gad*] **1.** a sharp-pointed stick used in driving oxen **2.** any driving impulse; spur —*vt.* to drive as with a goad

go'-a·head' *n.* permission or a signal to proceed: usually with *the*

goal (gōl) *n.* [ME. *gol,* boundary] **1.** the place at which a race, trip, etc. ends **2.** an objective **3.** in some games, *a*) the line, net, etc. over or into which the ball or puck must go to score *b*) the score made

goal'keep'er *n.* in some games, a player stationed at a goal to block the ball or puck: also **goal'ie** (-ē), **goal'tend'er**

goat (gōt) *n.* [OE. *gat*] **1.** a cud-chewing mammal with hollow horns, related to the sheep **2.** a lecherous man **3.** [Colloq.] a scapegoat —**get one's goat** [Colloq.] to irritate one

goat·ee (gō tē′) *n.* a pointed beard
goat′herd′ *n.* one who herds goats
goat′skin′ *n.* the hide of a goat, or leather made from this
gob¹ (gäb) *n.* [< OFr. *gobe,* mouthful] 1. a soft lump or mass 2. [*pl.*] [Colloq.] a large quantity
gob² (gäb) *n.* [< ?] [Slang] a sailor in the U.S. Navy
gob·ble¹ (gäb′'l) *n.* [echoic] the throaty sound made by a male turkey —*vi.* -bled, -bling to make this sound —**gob′bler** *n.*
gob·ble² (gäb′'l) *vt., vi.* -bled, -bling [prob. < OFr. *gobe,* mouthful] 1. to eat quickly and greedily 2. to snatch (*up*)
gob′ble·dy·gook′ (-dē gook′) *n.* [? echoic] [Slang] pompous talk or writing
go′-be·tween′ *n.* one who makes arrangements between each of two sides; intermediary
gob·let (gäb′lit) *n.* [< OFr. *gobel*] a drinking glass with a base and stem
gob·lin (gäb′lin) *n.* [< ML. *gobelinus*] Folklore an evil or mischievous sprite
go-by (gō′bī′) *n.* [Colloq.] an intentional disregard or slight
god (gäd) *n.* [OE.] 1. any of various beings conceived of as supernatural, immortal, and having power over people or nature; deity, esp. a male one 2. an idol 3. a person or thing deified —[G-] in monotheistic religions, the creator and ruler of the universe; Supreme Being — **god′like′** *adj.*
god′child′ *n., pl.* -chil′dren the person for whom a godparent is sponsor
god′daugh′ter *n.* a female godchild
god′dess *n.* a female god
god′fa′ther *n.* a male godparent
god′head′ (-hed′) *n.* 1. *same as* GODHOOD 2. [G-] God (usually with *the*)
god′hood′ *n.* the state of being a god
god′less *adj.* 1. irreligious 2. wicked
god′ly *adj.* -li·er, -li·est devoted to God; devout —**god′li·ness** *n.*
god′moth′er *n.* a female godparent
god′par′ent *n.* sponsor of a child, accepting responsibility for its faith
god′send′ *n.* anything much wanted that comes unexpectedly, as if sent by God
god′son′ *n.* a male godchild
God′speed′ *n.* [contr. of *God speed you*] success; good luck: a wish made for travelers
go-get·ter (gō′get′ər) *n.* [Colloq.] an enterprising and aggressive person
gog·gle (gäg′'l) *vi.* -gled, -gling [ME. *gogelen*] to stare with bulging eyes —*n.* [*pl.*] large spectacles to protect the eyes as against wind — *adj.* bulging: said of the eyes
go-go (gō′gō′) *adj.* [< Fr. *à gogo,* in plenty] of rock-and-roll dancing performed in cafés, often in topless costumes
go·ing (gō′iŋ) *n.* 1. a departure 2. the condition of the ground or land as it affects traveling, walking, etc. —*adj.* 1. moving; working 2. commonly accepted —**be going to** will or shall
go′ing-o′ver *n.* [Colloq.] 1. a thorough inspection 2. a severe scolding or beating
go′ings-on′ *n.pl.* [Colloq.] actions or events, esp. when regarded with disapproval
goi·ter, goi·tre (goit′ər) *n.* [< L. *guttur,* throat] an enlargement of the thyroid gland, often seen as a swelling in the front of the neck
gold (gōld) *n.* [OE.] 1. a heavy, yellow metallic chemical element: it is a precious metal: symbol, Au 2. money; wealth 3. bright yellow — *adj.* 1. made of or like gold 2. bright-yellow
gold′brick′ *n.* [Mil. Slang] one who tries to

avoid work; shirker: also **gold′brick′er** —*vi.* [Mil. Slang] to avoid work
gold′en *adj.* 1. made of or containing gold 2. bright-yellow 3. very valuable; excellent 4. flourishing
golden ag·er (āj′ər) [Colloq.] [*also* G- A-] an elderly person, esp. one 65 or older and retired
Golden Fleece *Gr. Myth.* the fleece of gold captured by Jason
gold′en·rod′ *n.* a N. American plant with long, branching stalks bearing clusters of small, yellow flowers
golden rule the precept that one should act toward others as he would want them to act toward him
gold′-filled′ *adj.* made of a base metal overlaid with gold
gold′finch′ *n.* [OE. *goldfinc*] a small American finch, the male of which has a yellow body
gold′fish′ *n., pl.:* see FISH a small, golden-yellow or orange fish, often kept in aquariums
gold leaf gold beaten into very thin sheets, used for gilding —**gold′-leaf′** *adj.*
gold′smith′ *n.* a skilled worker who makes articles of gold
gold standard a monetary standard whose basic currency unit equals a specified quantity of gold
golf (gôlf, gälf) *n.* [< ? Scot. *gowf,* to strike] an outdoor game played on a tract of land (**golf course** or **golf links**) with a small, hard ball and long-handled clubs, the object being to hit the ball into each of 9 or 18 holes in the fewest possible strokes —*vi.* to play golf —**golf′er** *n.*
Go·li·ath (gə lī′əth) *Bible* the Philistine giant killed by David with a stone from a sling
gol·ly (gäl′ē) *interj.* an exclamation of surprise, etc.
-gon [< Gr. *gōnia,* an angle] *a combining form meaning* a figure having a (specified number of) angles
go·nad (gō′nad) *n.* [< Gr. *gonē,* seed] an animal organ that produces reproductive cells; ovary or testicle
gon·do·la (gän′də lə) *n.* [It.] 1. a long, narrow boat used on the canals of Venice 2. a railroad freight car with low sides and no top: also **gondola car** 3. a cabin suspended under a dirigible or balloon
gon′do·lier′ (-lir′) *n.* a man who rows or poles a gondola
gone (gôn, gän) *pp.* of GO —*adj.* 1. departed 2. ruined 3. lost 4. dead 5. consumed 6. ago; past —**far gone** deeply involved
gon′er *n.* [Colloq.] a person or thing certain to die, be ruined, etc.
gong (gôŋ, gäŋ) *n.* [< Malay; echoic] a slightly convex metallic disk that gives a loud, resonant tone when struck
gon·or·rhe·a, gon·or·rhoe·a (gän′ə rē′ə) *n.* [< Gr. *gonos,* semen + *rheein,* to flow] a venereal disease with inflammation of the genital organs
goo (gōō) *n.* [Slang] 1. anything sticky, or sticky and sweet 2. sentimentality —**goo′ey** *adj.* -i·er, -i·est
goo·ber (gōō′bər) *n.* [< Afr. *nguba*] [Chiefly South] a peanut
good (good) *adj.* bet′ter, best [OE. *god*] 1. suitable 2. beneficial 3. valid; real 4. healthy or sound 5. honorable [one's *good* name] 6. enjoyable, pleasant, etc. 7. thorough 8. virtuous, devout, kind, dutiful, etc. 9. skilled 10. considerable, etc. —*n.* something good; worth, virtue, benefit, etc. —*interj.* an exclamation as of satisfaction —*adv.* [Dial. or Colloq.] well; fully —**as good as** virtually; nearly —**for good (and all)**

permanently —**good and** [Colloq.] very or altogether —**good for 1.** able to endure or be used for (a period of time) **2.** worth **3.** able to pay or give —**make good 1.** to repay or replace **2.** to fulfill **3.** to succeed —**no good** useless; worthless —**to the good** as a profit or advantage

good′bye′, good′-bye′ (-bī′) *interj., n., pl.* **-byes′** [contr. of *God be with ye*] farewell: term used at parting: also **good′by′, good′-by′**

Good Friday the Friday before Easter, commemorating the crucifixion of Jesus

good′-heart′ed *adj.* kind; generous

good humor a cheerful, agreeable mood — **good′-hu′mored** *adj.*

good′-look′ing *adj.* handsome

good′ly *adj.* **-li·er, -li·est 1.** of good appearance or quality **2.** ample

good′-na′tured *adj.* pleasant; affable

good′ness *n.* the state or quality of being good; virtue, kindness, etc. —*interj.* an exclamation of surprise

goods (goodz) *n.pl.* **1.** movable personal property **2.** wares **3.** fabric; cloth —**get** (or **have**) **the goods on** [Slang] to discover (or know) something incriminating about

good Sa·mar·i·tan (sə mer′ə t'n) anyone who helps others unselfishly: Luke 10:30–37

good′-sized′ *adj.* fairly big; ample

good′-tem′pered *adj.* amiable

good turn a friendly, helpful act

good will 1. benevolence **2.** willingness **3.** the value of a business in patronage, reputation, etc. beyond its tangible assets Also **good′will′** *n.*

good′y *n., pl.* **-ies** [Colloq.] something good to eat, as a candy —*interj.* a child's exclamation of delight

goof (goof) *n.* [Slang] **1.** a stupid person **2.** a mistake; blunder —*vi.* [Slang] **1.** to err or blunder **2.** to waste time, shirk duties, etc. (with *off* or *around*) —**goof′y** *adj.* —**goof′i·ness** *n.*

goon (goon) *n.* [Slang] **1.** a ruffian or thug, esp. one hired as a strikebreaker **2.** a stupid person

goose (goos) *n., pl.* **geese** [OE. *gos*] **1.** a long-necked, web-footed bird like a duck but larger, esp. the female **2.** its flesh, used for food **3.** a silly person —**cook one's goose** [Colloq.] to spoil one's chances

goose′ber′ry *n., pl.* **-ries 1.** a small, round, sour berry used in preserves, pies, etc. **2.** the shrub it grows on

goose flesh (or **bumps** or **pimples**) a roughened condition of the skin, caused by cold, fear, etc.

goose′neck′ *n.* any of various mechanical devices shaped like a goose's neck, as a flexible support for a desk lamp

goose step a marching step in which the legs are raised high and kept unbent

GOP, G.O.P. Grand Old Party (Republican Party)

go·pher (gō′fər) *n.* [< ? Fr. *gaufre*, honeycomb: from its burrowing] **1.** a burrowing rodent with wide cheek pouches **2.** a striped ground squirrel of the prairies

gore¹ (gôr) *n.* [OE. *gor*, filth] blood from a wound; esp., clotted blood

gore² (gôr) *vt.* **gored, gor′ing** [OE. *gar*, a spear] **1.** to pierce as with a horn or tusk **2.** to insert a gore or gores in —*n.* a tapering piece of cloth inserted in a skirt, sail, etc. to give it fullness

gorge (gôrj) *n.* [< L. *gurges*, whirlpool] **1.** the gullet **2.** what has been swallowed **3.** a deep, narrow pass between steep heights —*vi., vt.* **gorged, gorg′ing** to stuff (oneself) with food; glut

gor·geous (gôr′jəs) *adj.* [< OFr. *gorgias*] **1.** brilliantly colored; magnificent **2.** [Slang] beautiful, delightful, etc.

go·ril·la (gə ril′ə) *n.* [< WAfr.] the largest and most powerful of the manlike apes, native to Africa

gor·mand·ize (gôr′mən dīz′) *vi., vt.* **-ized′, -iz′-ing** [< Fr. *gourmandise*, gluttony] to eat like a glutton —**gor′mand·iz′er** *n.*

gorse (gôrs) *n.* [OE. *gorst*] same as FURZE

gor·y (gôr′ē) *adj.* **-i·er, -i·est 1.** covered with gore; bloody **2.** with much bloodshed

gosh (gäsh) *interj.* an exclamation of surprise, wonder, etc.: a euphemism for *God*

gos·ling (gäz′liŋ) *n.* a young goose

gos·pel (gäs′p'l) *n.* [OE. *gōdspel*, good news] **1.** [*often* G-] the teachings of Jesus and the Apostles **2.** [G-] any of the first four books of the New Testament **3.** anything proclaimed or accepted as absolutely true: also **gospel truth**

gos·sa·mer (gäs′ə mər) *n.* [ME. *gosesomer*, lit., goose summer] **1.** a filmy cobweb **2.** a filmy cloth —*adj.* light and filmy

gos·sip (gäs′əp) *n.* [< OE. *godsibbe*, godparent] **1.** one who chatters idly about others **2.** such talk —*vi.* to indulge in gossip

got (gät) *pt. & alt. pp.* of GET

Goth (gäth) *n.* any member of a Germanic people that conquered most of the Roman Empire in the 3d, 4th, and 5th centuries A.D.

Goth′ic *adj.* **1.** of the Goths **2.** designating or of a style of architecture developed in W Europe between the 12th and 16th cent., with pointed arches, flying buttresses, etc. **3.** [*sometimes* g-] uncivilized —*n.* **1.** the East Germanic language of the Goths **2.** Gothic architecture

got·ten (gät′'n) *alt. pp.* of GET

gouge (gouj) *n.* [< LL. *gulbia*] **1.** a chisel for cutting grooves or holes in wood **2.** such a groove or hole —*vt.* **gouged, goug′ing 1.** to scoop out as with a gouge **2.** [Colloq.] to defraud or overcharge —**goug′er** *n.*

gou·lash (goo′läsh, -lash) *n.* [< Hung. *gulyás*] a beef or veal stew seasoned with paprika: also **Hungarian goulash**

gourd (gôrd, goord) *n.* [< L. *cucurbita*] **1.** any trailing or climbing plant of a family that includes the squash, melon, etc. **2.** the fruit of one species or its dried, hollowed-out shell, used as a cup, dipper, etc.

gour·mand (goor′mənd, goor mänd′) *n.* [OFr.] one who likes good food and drink, often to excess

gour·met (goor′mā) *n.* [Fr. < OFr., wine taster] one who likes and is an excellent judge of fine foods and drinks

gout (gout) *n.* [< L. *gutta*, a drop] a disease characterized by painful swelling of the joints, esp. in the big toe —**gout′y** *adj.*

gov., Gov. 1. government **2.** governor

gov·ern (guv′ərn) *vt., vi.* [< Gr. *kybernan*, to steer] **1.** to exercise authority over; rule, control, etc. **2.** to influence the action or conduct of; guide **3.** to determine

gov·ern·ess (-ər nəs) *n.* a woman employed in a private home to train and teach the children

gov·ern·ment (guv′ər mənt, -ərn mənt) *n.* **1.** the exercise of authority over a state, organization, etc.; control; rule **2.** a system of ruling, political administration, etc. **3.** those who direct the affairs of a state, etc.; administration —**gov′ern·men′tal** *adj.*

gov·er·nor (guv′ə nər, -ər nər) *n.* **1.** one who governs; esp., *a*) one appointed to govern a province, etc. *b*) the elected head of any State of the U.S. **2.** a mechanical device for automatically controlling the speed of an engine —**gov'er·nor·ship'** *n.*

govt., Govt. government

gown (goun) *n.* [< LL. *gunna*] **1.** a woman's formal dress **2.** a dressing gown **3.** a nightgown **4.** a long, flowing robe as of a judge —*vt.* to dress in a gown

Gr. Greek

gr. 1. grain(s) **2.** gram(s) **3.** gross

grab (grab) *vt.* **grabbed, grab'bing** [prob. < MDu. *grabben*] **1.** to snatch suddenly **2.** to get by unscrupulous methods **3.** [Slang] to affect; impress —*vi.* to grab or try to grab something —*n.* a grabbing

grab·by (grab'ē) *adj.* **-bi·er, -bi·est** grasping; avaricious

grace (grās) *n.* [< L. *gratus,* pleasing] **1.** beauty or charm as of form or manner **2.** good will; favor **3.** a delay granted to allow payment **4.** a short prayer of thanks for a meal **5.** [G-] a title, as of a duke **6.** the love and favor of God toward man —*vt.* **graced, grac'ing 1.** to decorate **2.** to dignify —**in the good (or bad) graces of** in favor (or disfavor) with —**grace'less** *adj.*

grace'ful *adj.* having beauty of form, movement, or expression —**grace'ful·ly** *adv.*

grace note an ornamental musical note

gra·cious (grā'shəs) *adj.* **1.** having or showing kindness, charm, courtesy, etc. **2.** compassionate **3.** polite to those held to be inferiors **4.** marked by luxury, ease, etc. *[gracious living]* —**gra'cious·ly** *adv.*

grack·le (grak''l) *n.* [< L. *graculus,* jackdaw] a blackbird somewhat smaller than a crow

gra·da·tion (grā dā'shən) *n.* **1.** an arranging in grades, or stages **2.** a gradual change by stages **3.** a step in a graded series

grade (grād) *n.* [Fr. < L. *gradus*] **1.** a stage or step in a progression **2.** *a)* a degree in a scale of quality, rank, etc. *b)* a group of people of the same rank, merit, etc. **3.** the degree of slope **4.** a sloping part **5.** any of the divisions in a school curriculum, by years **6.** a mark or rating as in a test —*vt.* **grad'ed, grad'ing 1.** to classify by grades of quality, etc.; sort **2.** to give a grade (sense 6) to **3.** to make (ground) level or evenly sloped, as for a road —*vi.* to change gradually —**make the grade** to succeed

grade crossing a place where a railroad intersects another railroad or a roadway on the same level

grade school *same as* ELEMENTARY SCHOOL

gra·di·ent (grā'dē ənt) *n.* [< L. *gradi,* to step] **1.** a slope, as of a road **2.** the degree of slope

grad·u·al (graj'oo wəl) *adj.* [< L. *gradus,* a step] taking place by degrees; developing little by little —**grad'u·al·ly** *adv.*

grad·u·ate (graj'oo wit; *for v.,* -wāt') *n.* [< L. *gradus,* a step] one who has completed a course of study at a school or college and received a degree or diploma —*vt.* **-at'ed, -at'ing 1.** to give a degree or diploma to upon completion of a course of study **2.** to mark with degrees for measuring **3.** to grade or sort as by size —*vi.* **1.** to become a graduate of a school, etc. **2.** to change by degrees —*adj.* **1.** graduated from a school, etc. **2.** of or for graduates

grad·u·a'tion *n.* **1.** a graduating from a school or college **2.** the ceremony connected with this

graf·fi·to (grə fēt'ō) *n., pl.* **-ti** (-ē) [It. < L. *graphium,* stylus] a crude inscription or drawing on a wall or other public surface

graft (graft) *n.* [< Gr. *grapheion,* stylus] **1.** *a)* a shoot or bud of one plant or tree inserted into another, where it grows permanently *b)* the inserting of such a shoot. **2.** *a)* a piece of skin, bone, etc. transplanted by surgery *b)* the transplanting **3.** *a)* dishonest use of one's position to gain money, etc. *b)* anything so gained —*vt., vi.* to insert (a graft)

gra·ham (grā'əm) *adj.* [< S. *Graham,* 19th-c. U.S. dietary reformer] designating or of finely ground whole-wheat flour

Grail (grāl) [< ML. *gradalis,* cup] *Medieval Legend* the cup used by Jesus at the Last Supper: also **Holy Grail**

grain (grān) *n.* [< L. *granum*] **1.** the small, hard seed of any cereal plant, as wheat, corn, etc. **2.** cereal plants **3.** a tiny, solid particle, as of salt or sand **4.** a tiny bit **5.** a unit of weight, equal to 0.0648 gram **6.** *a)* the arrangement of fibers, particles, etc. of wood, leather, etc. *b)* the markings or texture due to this **7.** disposition; nature —**against the** (or **one's**) **grain** contrary to one's feelings, nature, etc.

grain'field' *n.* a field of grain

grain'y *adj.* **-i·er, -i·est 1.** having a clearly defined grain, as wood **2.** coarsely textured; granular —**grain'i·ness** *n.*

gram (gram) *n.* [< Fr. < Gr. *gramma,* small weight] the basic unit of weight in the metric system, equal to about 1/28 of an ounce: chiefly Brit. sp. **gramme**

-gram [< Gr. *gramma,* writing] *a combining form meaning* something written *[telegram]*

gram·mar (gram'ər) *n.* [< Gr. *gramma,* writing] **1.** language study dealing with the forms of words and with their arrangement in sentences **2.** a system of rules for speaking or writing a given language **3.** a book of such rules **4.** one's manner of speaking or writing as judged by such rules —**gram·mar·i·an** (grə mer'ē ən) *n.* —**gram·mat·i·cal** (grə mat'i k'l) *adj.*

grammar school *earlier name for* ELEMENTARY SCHOOL

gran·a·ry (gran'ər ē, grā'nər ē) *n., pl.* **-ries** [< L. *granum,* grain] a building for storing grain

grand (grand) *adj.* [< L. *grandis,* large] **1.** higher in rank **2.** main *[the grand ballroom]* **3.** imposing in size, beauty, etc. **4.** illustrious **5.** inclusive *[the grand total]* **6.** [Colloq.] very good —*n.* [Slang] a thousand dollars —**grand'ly** *adv.*

grand- *a combining form meaning* of the generation older (or younger) than *[grandfather, grandson]*

grand'child' *n., pl.* **-chil'dren** a child of one's son or daughter

grand'daugh'ter *n.* a daughter of one's son or daughter

gran·dee (gran dē') *n.* [< Sp. & Port.: see GRAND] a man of high rank

gran·deur (gran'jər) *n.* [see GRAND] **1.** splendor; magnificence **2.** nobility; dignity

grand'fa'ther *n.* **1.** the father of one's father or mother **2.** a forefather

gran·dil·o·quent (gran dil'ə kwənt) *adj.* [< L. *grandis,* grand + *loqui,* speak] pompous; bombastic —**gran·dil'o·quence** *n.*

gran·di·ose (gran'dē ōs') *adj.* [Fr. < L. *grandis,* great] **1.** having grandeur; imposing **2.** pompous and showy

grand jury a jury that investigates accusations and indicts persons for trial if there is sufficient evidence

grand'ma (-mä) *n.* [Colloq.] grandmother

grand'moth'er *n.* **1.** the mother of one's father or mother **2.** a female ancestor

grand opera opera in which the whole text is set to music

grand'pa (-pä) *n.* [Colloq.] grandfather

grand′par′ent *n.* a grandfather or grand-mother

grand piano a large piano with strings set horizontally in a harp-shaped case

grand slam 1. *Baseball* a home run hit when there is a runner on each base **2.** *Bridge* the winning of all the tricks in a deal

grand′son′ *n.* a son of one's son or daughter

grand′stand′ *n.* the main seating structure for spectators at a sporting event, etc.

grange (grānj) *n.* [< L. *granum,* grain] **1.** a farm **2.** [G-] an association of farmers or a local lodge of this

gran·ite (gran′it) *n.* [< It. < L. *granum,* grain] a hard, crystalline rock consisting chiefly of feldspar and quartz

gran·ny, gran·nie (gran′ē) *n., pl.* -nies [Colloq.] **1.** a grandmother **2.** an old woman **3.** any fussy person

gran·o·la (grə nō′lə) *n.* [? < L. *granum,* grain] a breakfast cereal of rolled oats, wheat germ, sesame seeds, brown sugar or honey, nuts or dried fruit, etc.

grant (grant) *vt.* [< L. *credere,* believe] **1.** to give (what is requested, as permission) **2.** to give or transfer by legal procedure **3.** to admit as true —*n.* **1.** a granting **2.** something granted, as property —**take for granted** to accept as true, settled, etc.

gran·u·lar (gran′yə lər) *adj.* of, containing, or like grains or granules

gran′u·late′ (-lāt′) *vt., vi.* -lat′ed, -lat′ing to form into grains or granules

gran·ule (gran′yool) *n.* [< L. *granum,* grain] a small grain or particle

grape (grāp) *n.* [< OFr. *graper,* gather with a hook] **1.** a small, round, juicy berry, growing in clusters on a woody vine **2.** a grapevine **3.** a dark purplish red

grape′fruit′ *n.* a large, round, sour citrus fruit with a yellow rind

grape′vine′ *n.* **1.** a woody vine bearing grapes **2.** a secret means of information

graph (graf) *n.* [short for *graphic formula*] a diagram representing the successive changes in the value of a variable quantity or quantities —*vt.* to represent by a graph

-graph [< Gr. *graphein,* write] *a combining form meaning:* **1.** something that writes or records *[telegraph]* **2.** something written *[autograph]*

graph·ic (graf′ik) *adj.* [< Gr. *graphein,* write] **1.** realistic; vivid **2.** of arts (**graphic arts**) that include visual representation, esp. painting, drawing, etc. Also **graph′i·cal** —**graph′i·cal·ly** *adv.*

graph·ite (graf′īt) *n.* [< G. < Gr. *graphein,* write] a soft, black form of carbon used in pencils, lubricants, etc.

graph·ol·o·gy (gra fäl′ə jē) *n.* [< Fr.: see GRAPHIC & -LOGY] the study of handwriting, esp. as a clue to character, attitudes, etc. —**graph·ol′o·gist** *n.*

-graphy [< Gr. *graphein,* write] *a combining form meaning:* **1.** a process of writing or graphically representing *[lithography]* **2.** a descriptive science *[geography]*

grap·nel (grap′n'l) *n.* [< Pr. *grapa,* a hook] **1.** a small anchor with several flukes **2.** an iron bar with claws at one end for grasping things

grap·ple (grap′l) *n.* [OFr. *grapil*] **1.** *same as* GRAPNEL (sense 2) **2.** a hand-to-hand fight —*vt.* -pled, -pling to grip and hold —*vi.* **1.** to use a grapnel (sense 2) **2.** to wrestle **3.** to try to cope (*with*)

grappling iron (or **hook**) *same as* GRAPNEL (sense 2)

grasp (grasp) *vt.* [ME. *graspen*] **1.** to grip, as with the hand **2.** to take hold of eagerly; seize **3.** to comprehend —*vi.* to grab (with *at*) —*n.* **1.** a grasping; grip **2.** control; possession **3.** the power to hold or seize **4.** comprehension —**grasp′er** *n.*

grasp′ing *adj.* greedy; avaricious

grass (gras) *n.* [OE. *græs*] **1.** any of a family of plants with long, narrow leaves, jointed stems, and seedlike fruit, as wheat, rye, sugar cane, etc. **2.** any of various green plants with narrow leaves, growing densely in meadows, lawns, etc. **3.** pasture or lawn **4.** [Slang] marijuana —**grass′y** *adj.*

grass′hop′per *n.* any of a group of insects with two pairs of wings and powerful hind legs for jumping

grass roots [Colloq.] **1.** the common people **2.** a basic source or support

grass widow a woman divorced or separated from her husband —**grass widower**

grate¹ (grāt) *vt.* grat′ed, grat′ing [< OFr. *grater*] **1.** to grind into particles by scraping **2.** to rub against (an object) or grind (the teeth) together, with a harsh sound **3.** to irritate; annoy —*vi.* **1.** to rub with or make a rasping sound **2.** to be irritating —**grat′er** *n.*

grate² (grāt) *n.* [< L. *cratis,* a hurdle] **1.** *same as* GRATING **2.** a frame of metal bars to hold fuel in a fireplace **3.** a fireplace

grate·ful (grāt′fəl) *adj.* [obs. *grate* (< L. *gratus*), pleasing] **1.** thankful **2.** welcome —**grate′ful·ly** *adv.*

grat·i·fy (grat′ə fī′) *vt.* -fied′, -fy′ing [< Fr. < L. *gratus,* pleasing + *facere,* make] **1.** to please or satisfy **2.** to indulge; humor —**grat′i·fi·ca′-tion** *n.*

grat·ing (grāt′iŋ) *n.* a framework of bars set in a window, door, or other opening

gra·tis (grat′is, grāt′-) *adv., adj.* [L. < *gratia,* a favor] free of charge

grat·i·tude (grat′ə tōōd′) *n.* [< Fr. < L. *gratus,* thankful] a feeling of thankful appreciation for favors received

gra·tu·i·tous (grə tōō′ə təs) *adj.* [< L. *gratus,* pleasing] **1.** given free of charge **2.** uncalled-for —**gra·tu′i·tous·ly** *adv.*

gra·tu′i·ty (-tē) *n., pl.* -ties a gift of money, etc., esp. for a service; tip

grave¹ (grāv) *adj.* grav′er, grav′est [Fr. < L. *gravis,* heavy] **1.** important **2.** serious **3.** solemn —**grave′ly** *adv.*

grave² (grāv) *n.* [< OE. *grafan,* to dig] **1.** *a*) a place in the ground where a dead body is buried *b*) any burial place; tomb **2.** death —*vt.* graved, grav′en or graved, grav′ing **1.** to carve or sculpture **2.** to impress sharply —**grav′er** *n.*

grave accent a mark (`) showing the quality of a vowel, stress, etc.

grav·el (grav′l) *n.* [< OFr. *grave,* coarse sand] a loose mixture of pebbles and small rock fragments —*vt.* -eled or -elled, -el·ing or -el·ling to cover with gravel

grav′el·ly (-ē) *adj.* **1.** full of or like gravel **2.** harsh or rasping

grav·en (grāv′n) *alt. pp.* of GRAVE²

grave′stone′ *n.* a tombstone

grave′yard′ *n.* a cemetery

grav·i·tate (grav′ə tāt′) *vi.* -tat′ed, -tat′ing **1.** to move or tend to move in accordance with the force of gravity **2.** to be attracted (*toward*)

grav′i·ta′tion *n.* **1.** a gravitating **2.** *Physics* the force by which every mass attracts and is attracted by every other mass —**grav′i·ta′tion·al** *adj.*

grav·i·ty (grav′ə tē) *n., pl.* -ties [< L. *gravis,* heavy] **1.** the condition of being grave, or serious **2.** weight [specific *gravity*] **3.** gravitation; esp., the force that tends to draw all bodies in the earth's sphere toward the center of the earth

gra·vy (grā′vē) *n., pl.* **-vies** [ME. *grave*] **1.** the juice given off by meat in cooking **2.** a sauce made from this **3.** [Slang] money easily obtained

gray (grā) *n.* [< OE. *græg*] a color made by mixing black and white —*adj.* **1.** of the color gray **2.** having hair this color **3.** darkish or dreary **4.** vague —*vt., vi.* to make or become gray —**gray′ish** *adj.*

gray′ling (-liŋ) *n., pl.* **-ling, -lings** a freshwater game fish related to the salmon

gray matter 1. grayish nerve tissue of the brain and spinal cord **2.** [Colloq.] intelligence

graze¹ (grāz) *vt.* **grazed, graz′ing** [< OE. *græs,* grass] **1.** to feed on (growing grass, etc.) **2.** to put (livestock) out to graze —*vi.* to feed on growing grass, etc.

graze² (grāz) *vt., vi.* **grazed, graz′ing** [prob. < prec.] to scrape lightly in passing

Gr. Brit., Gr. Br. Great Britain

grease (grēs) *n.* [< L. *crassus,* fat] **1.** melted animal fat **2.** any thick, oily substance or lubricant —*vt.* (*also* grēz) **greased, greas′ing** to smear or lubricate with grease —**greas·y** (grē′sē, -zē) *adj.* **-i·er, -i·est**

grease′paint′ *n.* greasy coloring matter used by performers in making up for the stage

great (grāt) *adj.* [OE.] **1.** of much more than ordinary size, extent, etc. **2.** much above average; esp., *a)* intense *b)* eminent **3.** most important; main **4.** designating a relationship one generation removed [*great*-grandmother] **5.** [Colloq.] excellent —**great′ly** *adv.* —**great′ness** *n.*

Great Dane a large, powerful dog with short, smooth hair

great′-grand′child′ *n.* a child of any of one's grandchildren

great′-grand′par′ent *n.* a parent of any of one's grandparents

great′heart′ed *adj.* **1.** brave; fearless **2.** generous; unselfish

grebe (grēb) *n.* [Fr. *grèbe*] a diving and swimming bird related to the loons

Gre·cian (grē′shən) *adj., n.* Greek

Greco- *a combining form meaning:* **1.** Greek or Greeks **2.** Greek and or Greece and

greed (grēd) *n.* [< *greedy*] excessive desire, esp. for wealth; avarice

greed′y *adj.* **-i·er, -i·est** [OE. *grædig*] **1.** wanting or taking more than one needs or deserves; avaricious **2.** gluttonous; voracious —**greed′i·ly** *adv.* —**greed′i·ness** *n.*

Greek (grēk) *n.* **1.** a native or inhabitant of Greece **2.** the language of Greece —*adj.* of Greece, its people, language, or culture

green (grēn) *adj.* [OE. *grene*] **1.** of the color of growing grass **2.** sickly or bilious **3.** not ripe or mature **4.** inexperienced or naive **5.** not dried or seasoned **6.** [Colloq.] jealous —*n.* **1.** the color of growing grass **2.** [*pl.*] green leafy vegetables **3.** an area of smooth turf

green′back′ *n.* any piece of U.S. paper money printed in green on the back

green bean the edible, immature green pod of the kidney bean

green′er·y *n., pl.* **-ies** green vegetation

green′horn′ *n.* a beginner; novice

green′house′ *n.* a heated building, mainly of glass, for growing plants

green onion an immature onion with green leaves, eaten raw; scallion

green pepper the green, immature fruit of the sweet red pepper

green′sward′ (-swôrd′) *n.* green turf

green′wood′ *n.* a forest in leaf

greet (grēt) *vt.* [OE. *gretan*] **1.** to address with friendliness, etc. **2.** to meet or receive (a person, event, etc.) in a specified way **3.** to present itself to —**greet′er** *n.*

greet′ing *n.* **1.** the act or words of one who greets **2.** [*often pl.*] a message of regards

gre·gar·i·ous (grə ger′ē əs) *adj.* [< L. *grex,* herd] **1.** living in herds or flocks **2.** fond of the company of others; sociable

Gre·go·ri·an calendar (grə gôr′ē ən) the calendar now widely used, introduced by Pope Gregory XIII in 1582

grem·lin (grem′lən) *n.* [prob. < Dan. *græmling,* an imp] an imaginary small creature humorously blamed when things fail to work

gre·nade (grə nād′) *n.* [Fr. < L. *granum,* seed] a small bomb detonated by a fuse and usually thrown by hand

gren·a·dier (gren′ə dir′) *n.* [Fr. < *grenade*] **1.** orig., a soldier who threw grenades **2.** a member of a special regiment

gren·a·dine (gren′ə dēn′) *n.* [Fr.] a syrup made from pomegranate juice

grew (grōō) *pt. of* GROW

grey (grā) *n., adj., vt., vi.* Brit. *sp. of* GRAY

grey′hound′ *n.* a tall, slender, swift hound

grid (grid) *n.* [< GRIDIRON] **1.** a gridiron or grating **2.** a metallic plate in a storage battery **3.** an electrode, as of wire mesh, for controlling the flow of electrons in an electron tube

grid·dle (grid′'l) *n.* [< L. *craticula,* gridiron] a heavy, flat metal pan for cooking pancakes, etc.

grid′dle·cake′ *n.* a pancake

grid·i·ron (grid′ī′ərn) *n.* [see GRIDDLE] **1.** a framework of metal bars or wires for use in broiling **2.** anything resembling this, as a football field

grief (grēf) *n.* [see GRIEVE] **1.** intense emotional suffering caused by loss, disaster, etc.; deep sorrow **2.** a cause of such suffering —**come to grief** to fail or be ruined

griev·ance (grē′vəns) *n.* **1.** a circumstance thought to be unjust and ground for complaint **2.** complaint against a real or imagined wrong

grieve (grēv) *vi., vt.* **grieved, griev′ing** [< L. *gravis,* heavy] to feel or cause to feel grief

griev·ous (grē′vəs) *adj.* **1.** causing grief **2.** showing or full of grief **3.** severe **4.** deplorable; atrocious —**griev′ous·ly** *adv.*

grif·fin (grif′ən) *n.* [< Gr.] a mythical animal, part eagle and part lion

grill (gril) *n.* [see GRIDDLE] **1.** a gridiron **2.** grilled food **3.** a restaurant that specializes in grilled foods: also **grill′room′** —*vt.* **1.** to broil **2.** to question relentlessly

grille (gril) *n.* [see GRIDDLE] an open grating forming a screen to a door, window, etc.

grim (grim) *adj.* **grim′mer, grim′mest** [OE. *grimm*] **1.** fierce; cruel **2.** hard and unyielding; stern **3.** appearing forbidding, harsh, etc. **4.** frightful; ghastly

gri·mace (gri mās′) *n.* [Fr.] a wry or ugly expression of pain, disgust, etc. —*vi.* **-maced′, -mac′ing** to make grimaces

grime (grīm) *n.* [prob. < Fl. *grijm*] sooty dirt rubbed into a surface, as of the skin —*vt.* **grimed, grim′ing** to soil with grime —**grim′y** *adj.* **-i·er, -i·est**

grin (grin) *vi.* **grinned, grin′ning** [< OE.

grennian] to smile broadly, showing the teeth —*n.* such a smile

grind (grīnd) *vt.* **ground, grind'ing** [OE. *grindan*] **1.** to crush into fine particles; pulverize **2.** to oppress **3.** to sharpen or smooth by friction **4.** to rub together harshly or gratingly [to *grind* one's teeth] **5.** to operate by turning the crank of —*n.* **1.** a grinding **2.** the fineness of the particles ground **3.** long, difficult work or study —**grind'er** *n.*

grind'stone' *n.* a revolving stone disk for sharpening tools or polishing things —**keep one's nose to the grindstone** to work hard

grip (grip) *n.* [< OE. *gripan*, seize] **1.** a secure grasp; firm hold **2.** the way one holds a bat, golf club, etc. **3.** the power of grasping firmly **4.** mental grasp **5.** firm control; mastery **6.** a handle **7.** a small traveling bag —*vt.* **gripped** or **gript, grip'ping 1.** to take firmly and hold fast **2.** to get and hold the attention of —**come to grips** to struggle (*with*) —**grip'per** *n.*

gripe (grīp) *vt.* **griped, grip'ing** [OE. *gripan*, seize] **1.** formerly, to distress **2.** to cause sharp pain in the bowels of **3.** [Slang] to annoy —*vi.* [Slang] to complain —*n.* **1.** a pain in the bowels: *usually in pl.* **2.** [Slang] a complaint —**grip'er** *n.*

grippe (grip) *n.* [Fr., lit., a seizure] *earlier term for* INFLUENZA: also sp. **grip**

gris·ly (griz'lē) *adj.* **-li·er, -li·est** [OE. *grislic*] terrifying; ghastly

grist (grist) *n.* [OE.] grain that is to be or has been ground

gris·tle (gris''l) *n.* [OE.] cartilage, now esp. as found in meat —**gris'tly** *adj.*

grit (grit) *n.* [OE. *greot*] **1.** rough, hard particles of sand, etc. **2.** a coarse sandstone **3.** stubborn courage; pluck —*vt.* **grit'ted, grit'ting** to grind (the teeth) in anger or determination —**grit'ty** *adj.* **-ti·er, -ti·est** —**grit'ti·ness** *n.*

grits (grits) *n.pl.* [OE. *grytte*] coarsely ground grain, esp. corn

griz·zled (griz''ld) *adj.* [< OFr. *gris*, gray] **1.** gray or streaked with gray **2.** having gray hair

griz'zly (-lē) *adj.* **-zli·er, -zli·est** grayish; grizzled —*n., pl.* **-zlies** a grizzly bear

grizzly bear a large, ferocious, brown or grayish bear of W N. America

groan (grōn) *vi., vt.* [OE. *granian*] to utter (with) a deep sound expressing pain, distress, etc. —*n.* such a sound —**groan'er** *n.*

gro·cer (grō'sər) *n.* [< OFr. *grossier*] a dealer in food and household supplies

gro'cer·y *n., pl.* **-ies 1.** a grocer's store **2.** [*pl.*] the goods a grocer sells

grog (gräg) *n.* [< Old *Grog*, nickname of an 18th-c. Brit. admiral] **1.** rum mixed with water **2.** any alcoholic liquor

grog'gy *adj.* **-gi·er, -gi·est** [< prec.] **1.** orig., intoxicated **2.** shaky or dizzy

groin (groin) *n.* [< ? OE. *grynde*, abyss] **1.** the fold where the abdomen joins either thigh **2.** *Archit.* the sharp, curved edge where two ceiling vaults meet

groom (grōōm) *n.* [ME. *grom*, boy] **1.** one whose work is tending horses **2.** a bridegroom —*vt.* **1.** to clean and curry (a horse, dog, etc.) **2.** to make neat and trim **3.** to train (a person) for a particular purpose

groove (grōōv) *n.* [< ON. *grof*, a pit] **1.** a long, narrow furrow cut with a tool **2.** any channel or rut **3.** a settled routine —*vt.* **grooved, groov'ing** to make a groove in —*vi.* [Slang] to enjoy, appreciate, etc. in a relaxed way (usually with *on*)

groov'y *adj.* **-i·er, -i·est** [Slang] very pleasing

grope (grōp) *vi.* **groped, grop'ing** [< OE.

grapian, to touch] to feel or search about blindly or uncertainly —*vt.* to seek or find (one's way) by groping —**grop'er** *n.*

gros·beak (grōs'bēk') *n.* [< Fr.: see GROSS & BEAK] a finchlike bird with a thick, conical bill

gros·grain (grō'grān') *n.* [Fr., lit., coarse grain] a ribbed silk or rayon fabric

gross (grōs) *adj.* [< LL. *grossus,* thick] **1.** fat and coarse-looking **2.** flagrant; very bad **3.** dense; thick **4.** coarse; vulgar **5.** total; with no deductions —*n.* **1.** *pl.* **gross'es** overall total **2.** *pl.* **gross** twelve dozen —*vt., vi.* [Colloq.] to earn (a specified total amount) before expenses are deducted —**gross'ly** *adv.* —**gross'-ness** *n.*

gro·tesque (grō tesk') *adj.* [Fr. < It. *grotta,* grotto: from designs in Roman caves] **1.** distorted or fantastic in appearance, shape, etc. **2.** ridiculous; absurd

grot·to (grät'ō) *n., pl.* **-toes, -tos** [< It. < L. *crypta,* crypt] **1.** a cave **2.** a cavelike shrine, summerhouse, etc.

grouch (grouch) *vi.* [< OFr. *grouchier*] to grumble or complain sulkily —*n.* **1.** one who grouches continually **2.** a sulky mood **3.** a complaint —**grouch'y** *adj.* **-i·er, -i·est**

ground[1] (ground) *n.* [OE. *grund,* bottom] **1.** the solid surface of the earth **2.** soil; earth **3.** [*often pl.*] a tract of land [*grounds* of an estate] **4.** area, as of discussion **5.** [*often pl.*] *a*) basis; foundation *b*) valid reason or motive **6.** the background, as in a painting **7.** [*pl.*] dregs; sediment [coffee *grounds*] **8.** the connection of an electrical conductor with the ground —*adj.* of, on, or near the ground —*vt.* **1.** to set on the ground **2.** to cause to run aground **3.** to base; establish **4.** to instruct in the basic principles of **5.** to keep (an aircraft or pilot) from flying **6.** *Elec.* to connect (a conductor) with the ground —*vi.* **1.** to run ashore **2.** *Baseball* to be put out on a grounder (with *out*) —**gain** (or **lose**) **ground** to gain (or lose) in achievement, strength, etc. —**give ground** to retreat; yield —**hold** (or **stand**) **one's ground** to remain firm, not yielding —**run into the ground** [Colloq.] to overdo

ground[2] (ground) *pt. & pp. of* GRIND

ground'er *n.* *Baseball* a batted ball that travels along the ground: also **ground ball**

ground'hog' *n. same as* WOODCHUCK

ground'less *adj.* without reason or cause

ground squirrel any of various small, burrowing animals related to the tree squirrels and chipmunks

ground'swell' *n.* a wave of popular feeling

ground'work' *n.* foundation; basis

group (grōōp) *n.* [< It. *gruppo*] a number of persons or things gathered or classified together —*vt., vi.* to form into groups

group·er (grōōp'ər) *n.* [Port. *garoupa*] a large fish found in warm seas

group'ie (-ē) *n.* [Colloq.] a girl fan of rock groups, who follows them about

grouse[1] (grous) *n., pl.* **grouse** [< ?] a game bird with a round, plump body, feathered legs, and mottled feathers

grouse[2] (grous) *vi.* **groused, grous'ing** [< ?] [Colloq.] to complain —**grous'er** *n.*

grove (grōv) *n.* [OE. *graf*] a small wood or group of trees without undergrowth

grov·el (gruv''l, gräv''l) *vi.* **-eled** or **-elled, -el·ing** or **-el·ling** [ME. *grufelinge,* down on one's face] **1.** to lie or crawl in a prostrate position, esp. abjectly **2.** to behave humbly or abjectly

grow (grō) *vi.* **grew, grown, grow'ing** [OE. *growan*] **1.** to come into being; spring up **2.** to exist, develop, or thrive, as a living thing **3.** to

increase in size, quantity, etc. **4.** to become [to
grow weary] —*vt.* to cause to or let grow; raise;
cultivate —**grow up** to mature
growl (groul) *vi.* [< ? OFr. *grouler*] to make a
rumbling, menacing sound such as a dog
makes —*vt.* to utter in an angry or surly way
—*n.* the act or sound of growling
grown (grōn) *pp. of* GROW —*adj.* fully mature
grown-up (grōn'up'; *for n.* -up') *adj.* adult —*n.*
an adult: also **grown'up'**
growth (grōth) *n.* **1.** a growing or developing **2.**
degree or extent of increase in size, etc. **3.**
something that grows or has grown **4.** an abnormal mass of tissue, as a tumor
grub (grub) *vi.* **grubbed, grub'bing** [ME.
grubben] **1.** to dig in the ground **2.** to work
hard —*vt.* **1.** to clear (ground) of roots **2.** to uproot —*n.* **1.** a wormlike larva, esp. of a beetle **2.**
[Slang] food —**grub'ber** *n.*
grub'by *adj.* **-bi·er, -bi·est** dirty; messy
grub'stake' (-stāk') *n.* [GRUB, *n.* 2 + STAKE]
[Colloq.] money or supplies advanced as to a
prospector
grudge (gruj) *vt.* **grudged, grudg'ing** [< OFr.
grouchier] *same as* BEGRUDGE —*n.* resentment
or ill will over a grievance
gru·el (grōō'əl) *n.* [OFr., coarse meal] a thin
broth of meal cooked in water or milk
gru'el·ing, gru'el·ling *adj.* [prp. of obs. v.
gruel, punish] very trying; exhausting
grue·some (grōō'səm) *adj.* [< dial. *grue,* to
shudder + -SOME¹] causing horror or loathing;
grisly
gruff (gruf) *adj.* [Du. *grof*] **1.** rough or surly;
brusque **2.** harsh and throaty; hoarse
grum·ble (grum'b'l) *vi.* **-bled, -bling** [prob. <
Du. *grommelen*] **1.** to growl or rumble **2.** to
mutter or complain in a surly way —*vt.* to express by grumbling —*n.* a grumbling —**grum'-
bler** *n.*
grump·y (grum'pē) *adj.* **-i·er, -i·est** [prob.
echoic] grouchy; peevish —**grump'i·ness** *n.*
grunt (grunt) *vi., vt.* [< OE. *grunian*] to utter
(with) the deep sound of a hog
G-string (jē'strin') *n.* [< ?] **1.** a narrow loincloth **2.** a similar band worn by striptease
dancers
G-suit (jē'sōōt') *n.* [G for *gravity*] an
astronaut's or pilot's pressurized garment
gua·no (gwä'nō) *n., pl.* **-nos** [Sp. < SAmInd.]
manure of sea birds, used as fertilizer
guar·an·tee (gar'ən tē', gär'-) *n.* **1.** *same as*
GUARANTY (sense 1) **2.** *a)* a pledge to replace
something if it is not as represented *b)* assurance that something will be done as specified
3. a guarantor —*vt.* **-teed', -tee'ing 1.** to give a
guarantee for **2.** to promise: affirm
guar·an·tor (gar'ən tôr', -tər; gär'-) *n.* one
who gives a guaranty or guarantee
guar'an·ty (-tē) *n., pl.* **-ties** [< OFr. *garant,* a
warrant] **1.** a pledge or security for another's
debt or obligation **2.** an agreement that se-
cures the existence or maintenance of something
guard (gärd) *vt.* [< OFr. *garder*] **1.** to watch
over and protect; defend **2.** to keep from escape or trouble —*vi.* **1.** to keep watch (*against*)
2. to act as a guard —*n.* **1.** defense; protection
2. a posture of defense **3.** any device that
protects against injury or loss **4.** a person or
group that guards —**on** (one's) **guard** vigilant
guard'ed *adj.* **1.** watched over **2.** cautious; non-
committal —**guard'ed·ly** *adv.*
guard'house' *n. Mil.* **1.** a building used by a
guard when he is not walking a post **2.** a jail
for temporary confinement
guard'i·an (-ē ən) *n.* **1.** one who guards or

cares for another person, property, etc. **2.** a
person legally in charge of a minor or of someone incapable of managing his own affairs —
adj. protecting —**guard'i·an·ship'** *n.*
gua·va (gwä'və) *n.* [< SAmInd.] a yellow,
pear-shaped tropical fruit, used for jelly
gu·ber·na·to·ri·al (gōō'bər nə tôr'ē əl) *adj.* [L.
gubernator, governor] of a governor or his office
Guern·sey (gurn'zē) *n., pl.* **-seys** [< *Guernsey,*
one of the Channel Islands] any of a breed of
dairy cattle, usually fawn-colored with white
markings
guer·ril·la, gue·ril·la (gə ril'ə) *n.* [Sp., dim. of
guerra, war] a member of a small group of
fighters not part of the regular army, who
make surprise raids
guess (ges) *vt., vi.* [prob. < MDu. *gessen*] **1.** to
form a judgment or estimate of without actual
knowledge; surmise **2.** to judge correctly by
doing this **3.** to think or suppose —*n.* **1.** a
guessing **2.** something guessed
guess'work' *n.* **1.** a guessing **2.** a judgment,
result, etc. arrived at by guessing
guest (gest) *n.* [< ON. *gestr*] **1.** a person entertained at the home, club, etc. of another **2.**
any paying customer of a hotel, restaurant,
etc. —*adj.* **1.** for guests **2.** performing by invitation [a *guest* artist]
guff (guf) *n.* [echoic] [Slang] nonsensical, brash,
or insolent talk
guf·faw (gə fô') *n., vi.* [echoic] laugh in a loud,
coarse burst
guid·ance (gīd'ns) *n.* **1.** a guiding; direction;
leadership **2.** advice or counsel
guide (gīd) *vt.* **guid'ed, guid'ing** [< OFr. *guier*]
1. to point out the way for; lead **2.** to direct
the course of **3.** to manage; regulate —*n.* **1.** one
whose work is conducting tours, etc. **2.** a guiding or controlling device **3.** a book of basic information —**guid'a·ble** *adj.*
guide'book' *n.* a book containing directions
and information for tourists
guided missile a military missile whose
course is controlled by radar, etc.
guide'line' *n.* a principle by which to determine a course of action
guild (gild) *n.* [< OE. *gieldan,* to pay] any association for mutual aid and the promotion of
common interests
guil·der (gil'dər) *n.* [< MDu. *gulden,* golden]
monetary unit and coin of the Netherlands
guile (gīl) *n.* [OFr.] slyness and cunning; craftiness —**guile'less** *adj.*
guil·lo·tine (gil'ə tēn') *n.* [Fr. < J. *Guillotin,*
who advocated its use in the 18th c.] an instrument for beheading, having a heavy blade
dropped between two grooved uprights —*vt.*
(gil'ə tēn') **-tined', -tin'ing** to behead with a
guillotine
guilt (gilt) *n.* [OE. *gylt,* a sin] **1.** the fact of
having done a wrong or committed an offense
2. self-reproach from believing one has done a
wrong —**guilt'less** *adj.*
guilt'y *adj.* **-i·er, -i·est 1.** having guilt **2.** legally
judged an offender **3.** of, involving, or showing
guilt [a *guilty* look]
guin·ea (gin'ē) *n.* [< former Eng. gold coin,
orig. made of gold from *Guinea*] the sum of 21
English shillings
guinea fowl (or **hen**) [orig. from region of
Guinea] a domestic fowl with a rounded body
and speckled feathers
guinea pig [prob. orig. brought to England by
ships plying between England, *Guinea,* and S.
America] **1.** a small, fat rodent used in biologi-

cal experiments **2.** any subject used in an experiment

Guin·e·vere (gwin′ə vir′) *Legend* the wife of King Arthur and mistress of Lancelot

guise (gīz) *n.* [OFr. < OHG. *wisa,* manner] **1.** manner of dress; garb **2.** semblance **3.** a false appearance; pretense

gui·tar (gi tär′) *n.* [< Sp. < Gr. *kithara,* lyre] a musical instrument with strings, usually six, that are plucked with the fingers or a plectrum —**gui·tar′ist** *n.*

gulch (gulch) *n.* [prob. < dial. *gulch,* swallow greedily] a deep, narrow ravine

gulf (gulf) *n.* [ult. < Gr. *kolpos,* bosom] **1.** an area of ocean larger than a bay, indenting a coastline **2.** a wide, deep chasm **3.** a vast separation

gull[1] (gul) *n.* [< Celt.] a gray and white water bird with large wings and webbed feet

gull[2] (gul) *n.* [< ?] a person easily tricked; dupe —*vt.* to cheat; trick

Gul·lah (gul′ə) *n.* [< ? tribal names in W Africa] **1.** any of a group of Negroes living esp. on sea islands off S. Carolina and Georgia **2.** their English dialect

gul·let (gul′ət) *n.* [< L. *gula,* throat] **1.** the esophagus **2.** the throat

gul·li·ble (gul′ə b'l) *adj.* easily gulled or tricked; credulous —**gul′li·bil′i·ty** *n.*

gul·ly (gul′ē) *n., pl.* **-lies** [see GULLET] a channel or narrow ravine worn by water

gulp (gulp) *vt.* [prob. < Du. *gulpen*] **1.** to swallow hastily or greedily **2.** to choke back as if swallowing —*n.* **1.** a gulping **2.** the amount swallowed at one time

gum[1] (gum) *n.* [< L. *gumma*] **1.** a sticky substance found in certain trees and plants **2.** an adhesive **3.** *same as* CHEWING GUM —*vt.* **gummed, gum′ming** to coat or unite with gum —*vi.* to become sticky or clogged —**gum up** [Slang] to cause to go awry —**gum′my** *adj.* **-mi·er, -mi·est**

gum[2] (gum) *n.* [OE. *goma*] [*often pl.*] the firm flesh surrounding the base of the teeth —*vt.* **gummed, gum′ming** to chew with toothless gums

gum arabic a gum from certain acacia trees, used in medicine, candy, etc.

gum·bo (gum′bō) *n.* [< native African name for okra] a soup made thick with unripe okra pods

gum′drop′ *n.* a small, firm candy made of sweetened gum arabic or gelatin

gump·tion (gump′shən) *n.* [< Scot.] [Colloq.] courage and initiative; enterprise

gun (gun) *n.* [< ME. *gonnilde,* cannon < ON.] **1.** a weapon with a metal tube from which a projectile is discharged by the force of an explosive **2.** anything like this that shoots or squirts something —*vi.* **gunned, gun′ning** to shoot or hunt with a gun —*vt.* **1.** [Colloq.] to shoot (a person) **2.** [Slang] to advance the throttle of (an engine) —**jump the gun** [Slang] to begin before the proper time

gun′boat′ *n.* a small armed ship

gun′cot′ton *n.* nitrocellulose in a highly nitrated form, used as an explosive

gun′fire′ *n.* the firing of a gun or guns

gung-ho (guŋ′hō′) *adj.* [< Chin., lit., work together] enthusiastic

gun′man (-mən) *n., pl.* **-men** an armed gangster or hired killer

gun′ner *n.* **1.** a soldier, etc. who helps fire artillery **2.** a naval warrant officer in charge of a ship's guns

gun′ner·y *n.* the science of making or firing heavy guns and projectiles

gun·ny (gun′ē) *n.* [Hindi < Sans. *gōnī,* a sack] a coarse, heavy fabric of jute or hemp

gun′ny·sack′ *n.* a sack made of gunny

gun′play′ *n.* an exchange of gunshots, as between gunmen and police

gun′pow′der *n.* an explosive powder used in guns, for blasting, etc.

gun′run′ning *n.* the smuggling of guns and ammunition —**gun′run′ner** *n.*

gun′shot′ *n.* **1.** shot fired from a gun **2.** the range of fire

gun′smith′ *n.* one who makes or repairs small guns

gun·wale (gun′'l) *n.* [< supporting a ship's guns] the upper edge of the side of a ship or boat: also sp. **gunnel**

gup·py (gup′ē) *n., pl.* **-pies** [< R. *Guppy,* of Trinidad] a tiny, brightly colored tropical fish

gur·gle (gur′g'l) *vi.* **-gled, -gling** [prob. echoic] to make, or flow with, a bubbling sound —*n.* a gurgling sound

gu·ru (goor′oo, goo roo′) *n.* [Hindi < Sans. *guru-h,* venerable] in Hinduism, one's spiritual adviser or teacher

gush (gush) *vi.* [akin to ON. *gjosa*] **1.** to flow out plentifully **2.** to have a sudden flow **3.** to express with exaggerated feeling —*vt.* to cause to gush —*n.* a gushing

gush′er *n.* **1.** one who gushes **2.** an oil well from which oil spouts forth

gush′y *adj.* **-i·er, -i·est** given to or full of exaggerated feeling; effusive

gus·set (gus′it) *n.* [< OFr. *gousset*] a triangular or diamond-shaped piece inserted to make a garment stronger or roomier

gus·sie, gus·sy (gus′ē) *vt., vi.* **-sied, -sy·ing** [< *Gussie,* girl's nickname] [Slang] to dress (*up*) in a showy way

gust (gust) *n.* [< ON. *gustr*] **1.** a sudden, strong rush of wind, or of smoke, rain, etc. **2.** a sudden outburst of laughter, rage, etc. —**gust′y** *adj.* **-i·er, -i·est**

gus·ta·to·ry (gus′tə tôr′ē) *adj.* [< L. *gustus,* taste] of the sense of taste

gus·to (gus′tō) *n.* [It. & Sp. < L. *gustus,* taste] **1.** zest; relish **2.** great vigor

gut (gut) *n.* [< OE. *geotan,* pour] **1.** [*pl.*] the bowels or the stomach **2.** the intestine **3.** tough cord made of animal intestines **4.** [*pl.*] [Colloq.] the basic or inner parts **5.** [*pl.*] [Slang] daring; courage —*vt.* **gut′ted, gut′ting 1.** to remove the entrails from **2.** to destroy the interior of, as by fire —*adj.* [Slang] **1.** basic **2.** easy

gut′less *adj.* [Slang] lacking courage

guts·y (gut′sē) *adj.* **-i·er, -i·est** [Slang] courageous, forceful, etc.

gut·ta-per·cha (gut′ə pur′chə) *n.* [< Malay < *gētah,* gum + *pērchah,* the tree] a rubberlike gum from the latex of certain Asian trees

gut·ter (gut′ər) *n.* [< L. *gutta,* a drop] a trough or channel to carry off water, as along the eaves of a roof or the edge of a street —*vi.* to flow in a stream

gut·tur·al (gut′ər əl) *adj.* [< L. *guttur,* throat] **1.** of the throat **2.** produced in the throat; rasping —**gut′tur·al·ly** *adv.*

guy[1] (gī) *n.* [< OFr. *guier,* to guide] a wire, rope, etc. used to steady or guide something

guy[2] (gī) *n.* [< *Guy* Fawkes, Eng. conspirator] [Slang] a man or boy —*vt.* to tease

guz·zle (guz′'l) *vi., vt.* **-zled, -zling** [< ? OFr. *gosier,* throat] to drink greedily or immoderately —**guz′zler** *n.*

gym (jim) *n.* [Colloq.] *same as:* **1.** GYMNASIUM **2.** PHYSICAL EDUCATION

gym·na·si·um (jim nā′zē əm) *n., pl.* **-si·ums,**

-si·a (-ə) [< Gr. *gymnos*, naked] a room or building equipped for physical training and sports

gym·nas'tics *n.pl.* exercises to develop and train the muscles **—gym'nast** *n.*

gyn·e·col·o·gy (gī'nə käl'ə jē, jin'ə-, jī'nə-) *n.* [< Gr. *gynē*, woman + -LOGY] the branch of medicine dealing with the functions, diseases, etc. of women **—gyn'e·col'o·gist** *n.*

gyp (jip) *n.* [prob. < GYPSY] [Colloq.] **1.** a swindle **2.** a swindler: also **gyp'per** *—vt., vi.* **gypped, gyp'ping** [Colloq.] to swindle

gyp·sum (jip'səm) *n.* [< Gr. *gypsos*] a sulfate of calcium used to make plaster of Paris, to treat soil, etc.

Gyp·sy (jip'sē) *n., pl.* **-sies** [< earlier *Egipcien*,

Egyptian: orig. thought to be from Egypt] **1.** [*also* **g-**] a member of a wandering Caucasoid people, prob. orig. from India, with dark skin and black hair **2.** their language **3.** [g-] one who looks or lives like a Gypsy

gy·rate (jī'rāt) *vi.* **-rat·ed, -rat·ing** [< Gr. *gyros*, a circle] to move in a circular or spiral path; whirl **—gy·ra'tion** *n.*

gyro- [< Gr. *gyros*, a circle] *a combining form meaning:* **1.** gyrating [*gyroscope*] **2.** gyroscope

gy·ro·scope (jī'rə skōp') *n.* [GYRO- + -SCOPE] a wheel mounted in a ring so that its axis is free to turn in any direction: when the wheel is spun rapidly, it will keep its original plane of rotation

gyve (jīv) *n., vt.* **gyved, gyv'ing** [ME. *give*] [Archaic or Poet.] fetter; shackle

H

H, h (āch) *n., pl.* **H's, h's** the eighth letter of the English alphabet

H *Chem.* hydrogen

H., h. 1. height **2.** *Baseball* hits **3.** hour(s)

ha (hä) *interj.* an exclamation of wonder, surprise, anger, triumph, etc.

‡**ha·be·as cor·pus** (hā'bē əs kôr'pəs) [L., (that) you have the body] *Law* a writ requiring that a detained person be brought before a court to decide the legality of his detention or imprisonment

hab·er·dash·er (hab'ər dash'ər) *n.* [< ME.] a dealer in men's hats, shirts, gloves, etc. **—hab'er·dash'er·y** *n., pl.* **-ies**

ha·bil·i·ment (hə bil'ə mənt) *n.* [< MFr. *habiller*, clothe] **1.** [*usually pl.*] clothing; dress **2.** [*pl.*] furnishings or equipment; trappings

hab·it (hab'it) *n.* [< L. *habere*, have] **1.** a distinctive costume, as of a religious order **2.** disposition **3.** a thing done often and, hence, easily; custom **4.** a usual way of doing **5.** an addiction, esp. to narcotics

hab'it·a·ble *adj.* fit to be lived in

hab·i·tat (hab'ə tat') *n.* [L., it inhabits] **1.** native environment **2.** the place where a person or thing is ordinarily found

hab'i·ta'tion (-tā'shən) *n.* **1.** an inhabiting **2.** a dwelling; home

hab'it-form'ing *adj.* resulting in the formation of a habit or addiction

ha·bit·u·al (hə bich'ōō wəl) *adj.* **1.** done or acquired by habit **2.** steady; inveterate [*a habitual* smoker] **3.** much seen, done, or used; usual **—ha·bit'u·al·ly** *adv.*

ha·bit'u·ate' (-wāt') *vt.* **-at'ed, -at'ing** to accustom (*to*) **—ha·bit'u·a'tion** *n.*

hab·i·tude (hab'ə tōōd') *n.* **1.** habitual condition of mind or body; disposition **2.** custom

ha·bit·u·é (hə bich'ōō wā') *n.* [Fr.] a person who frequents a certain place

ha·ci·en·da (hä'sē en'də) *n.* [Sp. < L. *facere*, do] in Spanish America, a large estate, ranch, etc., or its main dwelling

hack' (hak) *vt.* [OE. *haccian*] to chop or cut roughly *—vi.* **1.** to make rough cuts **2.** to give harsh, dry coughs *—n.* **1.** a tool for hacking **2.** a gash or notch **3.** a harsh, dry cough **—hack'er** *n.*

hack² (hak) *n.* [< HACKNEY] **1.** a horse or a coach for hire **2.** an old, worn-out horse **3.** a literary drudge **4.** [Colloq.] a taxicab *—adj.* **1.** employed as a hack **2.** trite

hack·le (hak''l) *n.* [ME. *hechele*] **1.** all or any

of the neck feathers of a rooster, pigeon, etc. **2.** [*pl.*] the bristling hairs on a dog's neck and back

hack·ney (hak'nē) *n., pl.* **-neys** [< *Hackney*, England] **1.** a horse for ordinary driving or riding **2.** a carriage for hire

hack'neyed (-nēd') *adj.* made trite by overuse

hack·saw (hak'sô') *n.* a fine-toothed saw for cutting metal: also **hack saw**

had (had) *pt. & pp. of* HAVE

had·dock (had'ək) *n., pl.* **-dock, -docks** [ME. *hadok*] an Atlantic food fish, related to the cod

Ha·des (hā'dēz) *Gr. Myth.* the home of the dead *—n.* [*often* h-] [Colloq.] hell

had·n't (had''nt) had not

haft (haft) *n.* [OE. *hæft*] a handle or hilt of a knife, sword, ax, etc.

hag (hag) *n.* [< OE. *hægtes*] **1.** a witch **2.** an ugly, evil old woman **—hag'gish** *adj.*

hag·gard (hag'ərd) *adj.* [MFr. *hagard*, untamed] having a wild, wasted, worn look; gaunt **—hag'gard·ness** *n.*

hag·gle (hag''l) *vi.* **-gled, -gling** [< Scot. *hag*, to cut] to argue about terms, price, etc. *—n.* a haggling **—hag'gler** *n.*

hag'rid'den *adj.* harassed, as by fears

hah (hä) *interj. same as* HA

hail' (hāl) *vt.* [< ON. *heill*, whole, sound] **1.** to greet with cheers; acclaim **2.** to salute as **3.** to call out to *—n.* a greeting *—interj.* an exclamation of tribute, greeting, etc. **—hail from** to be from

hail² (hāl) *n.* [OE. *hægel*] **1.** frozen raindrops falling during thunderstorms **2.** a shower of or like hail *—vt., vi.* to pour down like hail

hail'stone' *n.* a pellet of hail

hail'storm' *n.* a storm with hail

hair (her) *n.* [OE. *hær*] **1.** any of the threadlike outgrowths from the skin **2.** a growth of these, as on the human head **3.** a very small space, degree, etc. **4.** a threadlike growth on a plant *—adj.* of or for hair **—get in one's hair** [Slang] to annoy one **—split hairs** to quibble **—hair'less** *adj.*

hair'breadth' (-bredth') *n.* a very small space or amount *—adj.* very narrow; close Also **hairs'breadth', hair's'-breadth'**

hair'cloth' *n.* cloth woven from horsehair, camel's hair, etc.: used esp. for upholstery

hair'cut' *n.* the act of, or a style of, cutting the hair

hair'do' *n., pl.* **-dos'** the style in which (a woman's) hair is arranged; coiffure
hair'dress'er *n.* a person whose work is dressing (women's) hair —**hair'dress'ing** *n., adj.*
hair'line' *n.* **1.** a very thin line **2.** the outline of the hair on the head
hair'pin' *n.* a small, usually U-shaped, piece of wire, etc. for keeping the hair in place —*adj.* U-shaped *[a hairpin turn]*
hair'-rais'ing *adj.* [Colloq.] shocking
hair'split'ting *adj., n.* making petty distinctions; quibbling —**hair'split'ter** *n.*
hair'spring' *n.* a slender, hairlike coil spring, as in a watch or clock
hair'y *adj.* **-i·er, -i·est 1.** of, like, or covered with hair **2.** [Slang] difficult —**hair'i·ness** *n.*
hake (hāk) *n., pl.* **hake, hakes** [prob. < ON.] a marine food fish related to the cod
hal·berd (hal'bərd) *n.* [< MHG. *helmbarte*] a combination spear and battle-ax of the 15th and 16th cent.: also **hal'bert** (-bərt)
hal·cy·on (hal'sē ən) *n.* [< Gr. *alkyōn*, kingfisher (fabled calmer of the sea)] tranquil, happy, idyllic, etc.: esp. in phrase **halcyon days**
hale[1] (hāl) *adj.* **hal'er, hal'est** [OE. *hal*] vigorous and healthy —**hale'ness** *n.*
hale[2] (hāl) *vt.* **haled, hal'ing** [< OFr. *haler*] to force (one) to go *[haled him into court]*
half (haf) *n., pl.* **halves** [OE. *healf*] **1.** either of the two equal parts of something **2.** either of the two equal periods of some games —*adj.* **1.** being a half **2.** incomplete; partial —*adv.* **1.** to the extent of a half **2.** [Colloq.] partly *[half convinced]* **3.** [Colloq.] at all: used with *not [not half bad]*
half'-and-half' *n.* something half one thing and half another, as a mixture of equal parts of milk and cream
half'-baked' *adj.* **1.** only partly baked **2.** not completely thought out
half brother a brother through one parent only
half'-cocked' *adj.* thoughtless or too hasty — **go off half-cocked** to speak or act thoughtlessly
half dollar a coin of the U.S. and Canada, worth 50 cents
half'heart'ed *adj.* with little enthusiasm, determination, interest, etc.
half'-life' *n.* the period required for the disintegration of half of the atoms in a radioactive substance: also **half life**
half'-mast' *n.* the position of a flag halfway down its staff, as in public mourning
half'-moon' *n.* **1.** the moon when only half its disk is clearly seen **2.** anything shaped like this
half note *Music* a note (♩) having one half the duration of a whole note
half·pen·ny (hā'pə nē, ·hāp'nē) *n., pl.* **-pence** (hā'pəns), **-pen·nies** a British coin equal to' half a penny
half sister a sister through one parent only
half sole a sole (of a shoe or boot) from the arch to the toe
half'track' *n.* an army truck, armored vehicle, etc. with a continuous tread instead of rear wheels
half'way' *adj.* **1.** midway between two points, etc. **2.** partial *[halfway measures]* —*adv.* **1.** to the midway point **2.** partially —**meet halfway** to be willing to compromise with
half'-wit' *n.* a stupid, silly, or imbecilic person —**half'-wit'ted** *adj.*
hal·i·but (hal'ə bət) *n., pl.* **-but, -buts** [ME. *hali*, holy + *butt*, a flounder: eaten on

holidays] a large, edible flatfish found in northern seas
hal·i·to·sis (hal'ə tō'sis) *n.* [< L. *halitus*, breath] bad-smelling breath
hall (hôl) *n.* [OE. *heall*] **1.** the main dwelling on an estate **2.** a public building with offices, etc. **3.** a large room for gatherings, exhibits, etc. **4.** a college or university building **5.** a vestibule at the entrance of a building **6.** a passageway
hal·le·lu·jah, hal·le·lu·iah (hal'ə lōō'yə) *interj.* [< Heb. *hallelū*, praise + *yāh*, Jehovah] praise (ye) the Lord! —*n.* a hymn of praise to God
hall·mark (hôl'märk') *n.* **1.** an official mark stamped on gold and silver articles orig. at Goldsmiths' Hall in London **2.** a mark or symbol of genuineness or high quality
hal·loo (hə lōō') *vi., vt.* **-looed', -loo'ing 1.** to call out in order to attract attention **2.** to shout —*interj., n.* a shout or call
hal·low (hal'ō) *vt.* [OE. *halgian*] to make or regard as holy
hal·lowed (hal'ōd; *in liturgy, often* hal'ə wid) *adj.* holy or sacred
Hal·low·een, Hal·low·e'en (hal'ə wēn', häl'-) *n.* [contr. < *all hallow even*] the evening of October 31, which is followed by All Saints' Day
hal·lu·ci·nate (hə lōō'sə nāt') *vi., vt.* **-nat'ed, -nat'ing** [< L. *hallucinari*, wander mentally] to have or cause to have hallucinations
hal·lu·ci·na·tion (hə lōō'sə nā'shən) *n.* the apparent perception of sights, sounds, etc. that are not actually present —**hal·lu'ci·na·to'ry** (-nə tôr'ē) *adj.*
hal·lu'ci·no·gen (-nə jen, hal'yoo sin'ə jen) *n.* a drug or other substance that produces hallucinations
hall·way (hôl'wā') *n.* a corridor
ha·lo (hā'lō) *n., pl.* **-los, -loes** [< Gr. *halōs*, circular threshing floor] **1.** a ring of light, as around the sun **2.** a symbolic ring of light around the head of a saint in pictures
hal·o·gen (hal'ə jən) *n.* [< Gr. *hals*, salt] any of the chemical elements, fluorine, chlorine, bromine, astatine, and iodine
halt[1] (hôlt) *n., vi., vt.* [< Fr. *faire halte* and G. *halt machen*] stop
halt[2] (hôlt) *vi.* [< OE. *healt*] **1.** [Archaic] to limp **2.** to hesitate —*adj.* lame —**the halt** those who are lame —**halt'ing·ly** *adv.*
hal·ter (hôl'tər) *n.* [OE. *hælftre*] **1.** a rope or strap for tying or leading an animal **2.** a hangman's noose **3.** a woman's upper garment, held up by a loop around the neck
halve (hav) *vt.* **halved, halv'ing 1.** to divide into two equal parts **2.** to reduce to half
halves (havz) *n. pl. of* HALF —**by halves 1.** halfway; imperfectly **2.** halfheartedly —**go halves** to share expenses equally
hal·yard (hal'yərd) *n.* [< ME. *halier* (see HALE[2])] a rope or tackle for raising or lowering a flag, sail, etc.: also sp. **halliard**
ham (ham) *n.* [OE. *hamm*] **1.** the back of the thigh **2.** the upper part of a hog's hind leg, salted, smoked, etc. **3.** [Colloq.] an amateur radio operator **4.** [Slang] an actor who overacts —**ham'my** *adj.* **-mi·er, -mi·est**
ham·burg·er (ham'bur'gər) *n.* [< *Hamburg*, Germany] **1.** ground beef **2.** a cooked patty of such meat, often eaten as a sandwich Also **ham'burg**
Ham·let (ham'lit) the title hero of a tragedy by Shakespeare
ham·let (ham'lit) *n.* [< LowG. *hamm*, enclosed area] a very small village
ham·mer (ham'ər) *n.* [OE. *hamor*] **1.** a tool for

pounding, having a metal head and a handle **2.** a thing like this in shape or use, as the part of a gun that strikes the firing pin **3.** a bone of the ear —*vt., vi.* **1.** to strike repeatedly as with a hammer **2.** to drive, force, or shape as with hammer blows —**hammer (away) at** to keep emphasizing

ham·mock (ham'ək) *n.* [Sp. *hamaca,* of WInd. orig.] a bed of canvas, etc. swung from ropes at both ends

ham·per¹ (ham'pər) *vt.* [ME. *hampren*] to hinder; impede; encumber

ham·per² (ham'pər) *n.* [< OFr. *hanap,* a cup] a large basket, usually with a cover

ham·ster (ham'stər) *n.* [G.] a ratlike animal, often used in scientific experiments

ham·string (ham'striŋ') *n.* a tendon at the back of the knee —*vt.* **-strung'**, **-string'ing** to disable, as by cutting a hamstring

hand (hand) *n.* [OE.] **1.** the part of the arm below the wrist, used for grasping **2.** a side or direction [at my right *hand*] **3.** possession or care [the land is in my *hands*] **4.** control [to strengthen one's *hand*] **5.** an active part [take a *hand* in the work] **6.** a promise to marry **7.** skill **8.** one having a special skill **9.** handwriting **10.** applause **11.** help [to lend a *hand*] **12.** a hired worker [a farm *hand*] **13.** a source [to get news at first *hand*] **14.** anything like a hand, as a pointer on a clock **15.** the breadth of a hand **16.** *Card Games a)* the cards held by a player at one time *b)* a round of play —*adj.* of, for, or controlled by the hand —*vt.* **1.** to give as with the hand **2.** to help or conduct with the hand —**at hand** near —**change hands** to pass to another's ownership —**from hand to mouth** with just enough for immediate needs —**hand in hand** together —**hand it to** [Slang] give deserved credit to —**hand over fist** [Colloq.] easily and in large amounts —**on hand 1.** near **2.** available **3.** present —**on the one** (or **other**) **hand** from one (or the opposed) point of view

hand'bag' *n.* **1.** a woman's purse **2.** a small suitcase

hand'ball' *n.* **1.** a game in which players bat a small ball against a wall or walls with the hand **2.** the small rubber ball

hand'bar'row *n.* a frame carried by two people, each holding a pair of handles at either end

hand'bill' *n.* a small printed notice, advertisement, etc. to be passed out by hand

hand'book' *n.* **1.** a compact reference book; manual **2.** a guidebook

hand'breadth' *n.* the breadth of the human palm, about four inches

hand'cart' *n.* a small cart, often with only two wheels, pulled or pushed by hand

hand'clasp' *n.* a clasping of each other's hand in greeting, farewell, etc.

hand'cuff' *n.* either of a pair of connected rings for shackling the wrists of a prisoner: *usually used in pl.* —*vt.* to put handcuffs on; manacle

hand'ed *adj.* having or involving (a specified kind or number of) hands [right-*handed,* two-*handed*]

hand'ful' *n., pl.* **-fuls'** **1.** as much or as many as the hand will hold **2.** a small number or amount **3.** [Colloq.] someone or something hard to manage

hand'gun' *n.* any firearm that is held and fired with one hand, as a pistol

hand·i·cap (han'dē kap') *n.* [< *hand in cap,* former kind of lottery] **1.** a competition in which difficulties are imposed on, or advantages given to, the various contestants to equalize their chances **2.** such a difficulty or advantage **3.** any hindrance —*vt.* **-capped'**, **-cap'ping 1.** to give a handicap to **2.** to hinder —**the handicapped** those who are physically disabled or mentally retarded —**hand'i·cap'per** *n.*

hand·i·craft (han'dē kraft') *n.* **1.** skill with the hands **2.** work calling for this, as weaving

hand'i·work' *n.* **1.** *same as* HANDWORK **2.** anything made or done by a particular person

hand·ker·chief (haŋ'kər chif) *n.* **1.** a small, square cloth for wiping the nose, face, etc. **2.** a kerchief

han·dle (han'd'l) *n.* [OE. < *hand*] **1.** that part of a tool, etc. by which it is held, turned, etc. **2.** a thing like a handle —*vt.* **-dled**, **-dling 1.** to touch, lift, operate, etc. with the hand **2.** to manage, control, etc. **3.** to deal with or treat **4.** to sell or deal in —*vi.* to respond to control [the car *handles* well]

han'dle·bar' *n.* [*often pl.*] a curved metal bar with handles on the ends, for steering a bicycle, etc.

hand'made' *adj.* made by hand, not by machine

hand'maid'en *n.* [Archaic] a woman or girl servant: also **hand'maid'**

hand'-me-down' *n.* [Colloq.] a used garment, etc. passed on to one

hand'out' *n.* **1.** a gift of food, clothing, etc., as to a beggar **2.** a leaflet handed out **3.** an official news release

hand'set' *n.* a telephone mouthpiece and receiver in a single unit, held in one hand

hand'shake' *n.* a gripping of each other's hand in greeting, agreement, etc.

hand·some (han'səm) *adj.* [orig., easily handled] **1.** considerable [a *handsome* sum] **2.** generous; gracious **3.** good-looking, esp. in a manly or dignified way

hand'spring' *n.* a spring in which one turns over in midair with one or both hands touching the ground

hand'-to-hand' *adj.* in close contact: said of fighting

hand'-to-mouth' *adj.* barely subsisting

hand'work' *n.* work done or made by hand, not by machine

hand'writ'ing *n.* **1.** writing done by hand, as with a pen **2.** a style of such writing

hand'y *adj.* **-i·er**, **-i·est 1.** close at hand; easily reached **2.** easily used; convenient **3.** clever with the hands —**hand'i·ly** *adv.*

han'dy·man' *n., pl.* **-men'** a man who does odd jobs

hang (haŋ) *vt.* **hung**, **hang'ing**; for *vt.* 3 & *vi.* 4 **hanged** is preferred *pt.* & *pp.* [OE. *hangian*] **1.** to attach from above with no support from below; suspend **2.** to attach (a door, etc.) so as to move freely **3.** to kill by suspending from a rope about the neck **4.** to paste (wallpaper) to walls **5.** to deadlock (a jury) —*vi.* **1.** to be suspended **2.** to hover in the air **3.** to swing freely **4.** to die by hanging **5.** to droop; bend —*n.* the way a thing hangs —**get** (or **have**) **the hang of 1.** to learn (or have) the knack of **2.** to understand the meaning of —**hang around** (or **about**) [Colloq.] to loiter around —**hang back** (or **off**) to be reluctant, as from shyness —**hang on 1.** to persevere **2.** to depend on **3.** to listen attentively to —**hang out** [Slang] to frequent —**hang up 1.** to put on a hanger, etc. **2.** to replace a telephone receiver

hang·ar (haŋ'ər) *n.* [Fr., a shed] a repair shed or shelter for aircraft

hang'dog' *adj.* sneaking or abject

hang′er *n.* **1.** one who hangs things **2.** a thing on which something is hung

hang gliding the sport of gliding through the air while hanging by a harness from a large type of kite (**hang glider**)

hang′ing *adj.* that hangs —*n.* **1.** a putting to death by hanging **2.** something hung, as a drapery

hang′man *n., pl.* **-men** one who hangs those condemned to die

hang′nail′ *n.* [< OE. *angnægl*, a corn] torn skin hanging next to a fingernail

hang′o′ver *n.* **1.** a survival **2.** sickness from drinking much alcoholic liquor

hang′-up′ *n.* [Slang] an emotional problem that cannot easily be resolved

hank (haŋk) *n.* [prob. < Scand.] a skein of yarn or thread

hank·er (haŋ′kər) *vi.* [prob. < Du. or LowG.] to crave or long (*for*) —**hank′er·ing** *n.*

han·ky-pan·ky (haŋ′kē paŋ′kē) *n.* [altered < HOCUS-POCUS] [Colloq.] trickery or deception

han·som (**cab**) (han′səm) [< J. A. *Hansom*, Eng. inventor] a two-wheeled covered carriage pulled by one horse

Ha·nu·ka (khä′nōō kä′, -kə; hä′-) *n.* [< Heb., dedication] a Jewish festival in early winter: also **Ha′nuk·kah′, Ha′nuk·ka′**

hap (hap) *n.* [< ON. *happ*] chance; luck

hap·haz·ard (hap′haz′ərd) *adj.* not planned; casual —*adv.* by chance —**hap′haz′ard·ly** *adv.*

hap·less (hap′lis) *adj.* unlucky

hap·pen (hap′n) *vi.* [ME. *happenen*] **1.** to take place; occur **2.** to be, occur, or come by chance **3.** to have the luck or occasion; chance [I happened to see it] —**happen on** (or **upon**) to meet or find by chance

hap′pen·ing *n.* an occurrence; event

hap·py (hap′ē) *adj.* **-pi·er, -pi·est** [< HAP] **1.** lucky; fortunate **2.** having, showing, or causing pleasure, joy, etc. **3.** suitable and clever [a *happy* idea] —**hap′pi·ly** *adv.* —**hap′pi·ness** *n.*

hap′py-go-luck′y *adj.* easygoing; trusting to luck —*adv.* haphazardly; by chance

ha·ra·ki·ri (hä′rə kir′ē) [Jpn. *hara*, belly + *kiri*, a cutting] ritual suicide by ripping out the bowels

ha·rangue (hə raŋ′) *n.* [< OIt. *aringo*, site for public assemblies] a long, blustering speech; tirade —*vt., vi.* **-rangued′, -rangu′ing** to speak or address in a harangue

har·ass (hə ras′, har′əs) *vt.* [< Fr. < OFr. *harer*, set a dog on] **1.** to worry or torment **2.** to trouble by repeated raids or attacks, etc. — **har·ass′er** *n.* —**har·ass′ment** *n.*

har·bin·ger (här′bin jər) *n.* [< OFr. *herberge*, a shelter] a forerunner; herald

har·bor (här′bər) *n.* [< OE. *here*, army + *beorg*, a shelter] **1.** a shelter **2.** a protected inlet for anchoring ships; port —*vt.* **1.** to shelter or house **2.** to hold in the mind [to *harbor* envy] —*vi.* to take shelter Brit. sp. **har′bour**

hard (härd) *adj.* [OE. *heard*] **1.** firm and unyielding to the touch; solid and compact **2.** powerful [a *hard* blow] **3.** difficult to do, understand, or deal with **4.** *a*) unfeeling [a *hard* heart] *b*) unfriendly [*hard* feelings] **5.** harsh; severe **6.** having mineral salts that interfere with lathering [*hard* water] **7.** energetic [a *hard* worker] **8.** strongly alcoholic [*hard* liquor] **9.** [Colloq.] addictive and harmful [*hard* drugs] —*adv.* **1.** energetically [work *hard*] **2.** with strength [hit *hard*] **3.** with difficulty [*hard*-earned] **4.** close; near [we live *hard* by] **5.** so as to be solid [frozen *hard*] **6.** sharply [turn *hard* right] —**hard and fast** invariable; strict —**hard of hearing** partially deaf —**hard up** [Colloq.] in

great need of money; very poor —**hard′ness** *n.*

hard′-bit′ten *adj.* tough; dogged

hard′-boiled′ *adj.* **1.** boiled until solid: said of an egg **2.** [Colloq.] unfeeling; callous

hard′-core′ *adj.* absolute; unqualified

hard·en (här′d'n) *vt., vi.* to make or become hard —**hard′en·er** *n.*

hard hat **1.** a protective helmet **2.** [Slang] a worker, as a miner, who wears such a hat

hard′head′ed *adj.* **1.** shrewd and unsentimental; practical **2.** stubborn

hard′heart′ed *adj.* unfeeling; pitiless

har·di·hood (här′dē hood′) *n.* boldness

hard′-line′ *adj.* aggressive; unyielding

hard′ly (härd′lē) *adv.* **1.** only just; scarcely **2.** probably not; not likely

hard sell high-pressure salesmanship

hard′ship′ *n.* **1.** hard circumstances of life **2.** a thing hard to bear, as poverty, pain, etc.

hard′tack′ (-tak′) *n.* unleavened bread made in very hard, large wafers

hard′ware′ (-wer′) *n.* **1.** articles made of metal, as tools, nails, fittings, etc. **2.** the mechanical, magnetic, and electronic devices of a computer

hard′wood′ *n.* any tough, heavy timber with a compact texture

har·dy (här′dē) *adj.* **-di·er, -di·est** [< OFr. *hardir*, make bold] **1.** bold and resolute **2.** too bold; rash **3.** robust; vigorous

hare (her) *n.* [OE. *hara*] a swift mammal related to the rabbit, with long ears, soft fur, etc.

hare′brained′ *adj.* giddy, rash, etc.

hare′lip′ *n.* a congenital deformity consisting of a cleft of the upper lip

ha·rem (her′əm) *n.* [Ar. *harīm*, prohibited (place)] **1.** that part of a Muslim's household in which the women live **2.** the women in a harem Also **ha·reem** (hä rēm′)

hark (härk) *vi.* [< ? OE. *heorcnian*, hearken] to listen carefully: usually in the imperative — **hark back** to go back; revert

hark·en (här′k'n) *vi.* same as HEARKEN

Har·le·quin (här′lə kwin, -kin) a traditional comic character in pantomime, who wears a mask and gay, spangled tights —*n.* [h-] a clown; buffoon

har·lot (här′lət) *n.* [OFr., rogue] a prostitute — **har′lot·ry** *n.*

harm (härm) *n.* [OE. *hearm*] **1.** hurt; injury **2.** moral wrong —*vt.* to do harm to; hurt

harm′ful *adj.* causing harm; hurtful

harm′less *adj.* causing no harm

har·mon·ic (här män′ik) *adj.* *Music* of or in harmony —*n.* same as OVERTONE

har·mon′i·ca (-i kə) *n.* a small wind instrument with a series of metal reeds that produce tones when air is blown or sucked across them

har·mo·ni·ous (här mō′nē əs) *adj.* **1.** having parts combined in an orderly or pleasing arrangement **2.** having similar ideas, interests, etc. **3.** having musical tones combined to give a pleasing effect

har·mo·nize (här′mə nīz′) *vi.* **-nized′, -niz′ing** to be or sing in harmony —*vt.* to make harmonious —**har′mo·niz′er** *n.*

har·mo·ny (här′mə nē) *n., pl.* **-nies** [< Gr. *harmos*, a fitting] **1.** pleasing agreement of parts in color, size, shape, etc. **2.** agreement in action, ideas, etc.; peaceable or friendly relations **3.** *Music* the pleasing combination of tones in a chord

har·ness (här′nis) *n.* [< OFr. *harneis*, armor] the leather straps and metal pieces by which a horse, mule, etc. is fastened to a vehicle, plow, etc. —*vt.* **1.** to put harness on **2.** to control so as to use the power of

harp (härp) *n.* [OE. *hearpe*] a musical instrument with strings stretched across a triangular frame, played by plucking —*vi.* **1.** to play a harp **2.** to persist in talking or writing tediously (*on* or *upon*) —**harp'ist** *n.*

har·poon (här pōōn') *n.* [< ON. *harpa*, to squeeze] a barbed spear with an attached line, used for spearing whales, etc. —*vt.* to strike or kill with a harpoon —**har·poon'er** *n.*

harp·si·chord (härp'si kôrd') *n.* [< It.: see HARP & CHORD] a stringed musical instrument with a keyboard like the piano

Har·py (här'pē) *n., pl.* **-pies** [< Gr. *harpazein*, seize] **1.** *Gr. Myth.* any of several hideous, winged monsters with the head and trunk of a woman and the tail and legs of a bird **2.** [h-] a greedy person

har·ri·dan (har'i d'n) *n.* [prob. < Fr. *haridelle*, worn-out horse] a disreputable, shrewish old woman

har·row (har'ō) *n.* [prob. < ON.] a heavy frame with spikes or disks, used for leveling and breaking up plowed ground, etc. —*vt.* **1.** to draw a harrow over (land) **2.** to cause mental distress to; vex —**har'row·ing** *adj.*

har·ry (har'ē) *vt.* **-ried, -ry·ing** [< OE. *here*, army] **1.** to raid and ravage or rob **2.** to torment; harass

harsh (härsh) *adj.* [ME. *harsk*] **1.** unpleasantly rough to the ear, eye, taste, or touch **2.** unpleasantly crude or abrupt **3.** severe; cruel —**harsh'ly** *adv.* —**harsh'ness** *n.*

hart (härt) *n.* [OE. *heorot*] a full-grown male European red deer; stag

har·um-scar·um (her'əm sker'əm) *adj.* [< ? HARE + SCARE + 'EM] reckless; rash

har·vest (här'vist) *n.* [OE. *hærfest*] **1.** the time of the year when grain, fruit, etc. are gathered in **2.** a season's crop **3.** the gathering in of a crop **4.** the outcome of any effort —*vt., vi.* to gather in (a crop, etc.) —**har'vest·a·ble** *adj.* —**har'vest·er** *n.*

has (haz) *3d pers. sing., pres. indic.,* of HAVE

has'-been' *n.* [Colloq.] a person or thing whose popularity is past

hash (hash) *vt.* [Fr. *hacher*, to chop] **1.** to chop (meat or vegetables) for cooking **2.** [Colloq.] to bungle —*n.* **1.** a chopped mixture of cooked meat and vegetables, usually baked **2.** a mixture **3.** a muddle

hash·ish (hash'ēsh, -ish) *n.* [Ar. *hashīsh*, dried hemp] a drug made from Indian hemp, chewed or smoked for its intoxicating or euphoric effects

has·n't (haz'nt) has not

hasp (hasp) *n.* [OE. *hæpse*] a hinged metal fastening for a door, window, etc.; esp., a metal piece fitted over a staple and fastened by a bolt or padlock

has·sle (has''l) *n.* [< ?] [Colloq.] **1.** a heated argument **2.** a troublesome situation —*vi.* **-sled, -sling** [Colloq.] to have a heated argument —*vt.* [Slang] to harass

has·sock (has'ək) *n.* [OE. *hassuc*, (clump of) coarse grass] a firmly stuffed cushion used as a footstool or seat

hast (hast) *archaic 2d pers. sing., pres. indic.,* of HAVE: *used with* thou

haste (hāst) *n.* [OFr.] quickness of motion; hurrying —**make haste** to hurry

has·ten (hās''n) *vt.* to make hurry; speed up —*vi.* to move swiftly; hurry

hast·y (hās'tē) *adj.* **-i·er, -i·est** **1.** done with haste; hurried **2.** done or made too quickly or rashly **3.** impetuous or impatient —**hast'i·ly** *adv.* —**hast'i·ness** *n.*

hat (hat) *n.* [OE. *hætt*] a head covering, usually with a brim and a crown —**pass the hat** to take up a collection —**talk through one's hat** [Colloq.] to talk nonsense

hatch[1] (hach) *vt.* [ME. *hacchen*] **1.** to bring forth (young) from (an egg or eggs) **2.** to contrive (a plan, plot, etc.) —*vi.* **1.** to bring forth young: said of eggs **2.** to emerge from the egg

hatch[2] (hach) *n.* [OE. *hæcc*, grating] **1.** *same as* HATCHWAY **2.** a lid for a hatchway

hatch[3] (hach) *vt.* [< OFr. *hache*, an ax] to mark or engrave with fine, crossed or parallel lines —**hatch'ing** *n.*

hatch'back' *n.* a car with a rear that swings up, giving entry to a storage area

hatch·er·y *n., pl.* **-ies** a place for hatching eggs, esp. those of fish or poultry

hatch·et (hach'it) *n.* [< OFr. *hache*, an ax] a small, short-handled ax —**bury the hatchet** to make peace

hatch'way' *n.* a covered opening in a ship's deck, or in a floor or roof

hate (hāt) *vt.* **hat'ed, hat'ing** [OE. *hatian*] **1.** to have strong dislike or ill will for **2.** to wish to avoid [to *hate* work] —*vi.* to feel hatred —*n.* **1.** a strong feeling of dislike or ill will **2.** a person or thing hated —**hat'er** *n.*

hate'ful *adj.* **1.** feeling or showing hate **2.** deserving hate —**hate'ful·ly** *adv.*

hath (hath) *archaic 3d pers. sing., pres. indic.,* of HAVE

ha·tred (hā'trid) *n.* strong dislike or ill will; hate

hat·ter (hat'ər) *n.* one who makes or sells hats

hau·berk (hô'bərk) *n.* [< Frank. *hals*, neck + *bergan*, protect] a medieval coat of armor

haugh·ty (hôt'ē) *adj.* **-ti·er, -ti·est** [< OFr. *haut*, high] having or showing great pride in oneself and contempt for others —**haugh'ti·ly** *adv.* —**haugh'ti·ness** *n.*

haul (hôl) *vt., vi.* [< ODu. *halen*, fetch] **1.** to move by pulling; drag **2.** to transport by wagon, truck, etc. —*n.* **1.** the act of hauling **2.** the amount gained, caught, etc. at one time **3.** the distance covered in transporting or traveling **4.** a load transported —**haul off** [Colloq.] to draw the arm back before hitting —**haul'er** *n.*

haunch (hônch, hänch) *n.* [< OFr. *hanche*] **1.** the hip, buttock, and upper thigh together **2.** an animal's loin and leg together

haunt (hônt, hänt) *vt.* [< OFr. *hanter*, to frequent] **1.** to visit (a place) often or continually **2.** to recur repeatedly to [memories *haunted* her] —*n.* a place often visited

haunt'ed *adj.* supposedly frequented by ghosts [a *haunted* house]

haunt'ing *adj.* recurring often to the mind

hau·teur (hō tur') *n.* [Fr. < *haut*, high] disdainful pride; haughtiness

have (hav) *vt.* **had, hav'ing** [OE. *habban*] **1.** to hold; own; possess [he *has* money] **2.** to possess as a part, etc. **3.** to experience [*have* a good time] **4.** to hold in mind [to *have* an idea] **5.** to get; take [*have* some tea] **6.** to beget (offspring) **7.** to engage in [to *have* a fight] **8.** to cause to; cause to be [*have* her leave] **9.** to permit; tolerate [I won't *have* this noise] **10.** [Colloq.] to hold at a disadvantage *Have* is used as an auxiliary to express completed action (Ex.: I *had* left), and with infinitives to express obligation or necessity (Ex.: we *have* to go) *Have got* often replaces *have*: see GET *Have* is conjugated in the present indicative: (I) *have*, (he, she, it) *has*, (we, you, they) *have* —*n.* a wealthy person or nation —**have it out** to settle a disagreement by fighting or discussion —**have on** to be wearing

ha·ven (hā′vən) *n.* [OE. *hæfen*] **1.** a port; harbor **2.** any sheltered place; refuge

have-not (hav′nät′) *n.* a person or nation with little wealth or resources

have·n't (hav′nt) have not

hav·er·sack (hav′ər sak′) *n.* [< Fr. < G. *habersack*, lit., sack of oats] a canvas bag for rations, worn over the shoulder, as by soldiers and hikers

hav·oc (hav′ək) *n.* [< OFr. *havot*, plunder] great destruction and devastation —**play havoc with** to devastate; ruin

haw[1] (hô) *n.* [OE. *haga*] **1.** the berry of the hawthorn **2.** same as HAWTHORN

haw[2] (hô) *interj., n.* a command to a horse, etc., meaning "turn left!" —*vt., vi.* to turn to the left

haw[3] (hô) *vi.* [echoic] to hesitate in speaking: in HEM AND HAW (see HEM[2])

hawk[1] (hôk) *n.* [OE. *hafoc*] **1.** a bird of prey with short, rounded wings, a long tail, and a hooked beak **2.** an advocate of war —*vi.* to hunt birds with the help of hawks

hawk[2] (hôk) *vt., vi.* [< HAWKER] to advertise or peddle (goods) in the street by shouting

hawk[3] (hôk) *vi., vt.* [echoic] to clear the throat (of) audibly

hawk′er *n.* [ult. < MLowG. *hoken*, peddle] one who hawks goods; huckster

hawk′-eyed′ *adj.* keen-sighted like a hawk

haw·ser (hô′zər) *n.* [ult. < L. *altus*, high] a rope or cable by which a ship is anchored, towed, etc.

haw·thorn (hô′thôrn′) *n.* [< OE. *haga*, hedge + *thorn*] a thorny shrub or small tree related to the rose, with red fruits (*haws*)

hay (hā) *n.* [OE. *hieg*] grass, clover, etc. cut and dried for fodder —*vi.* to mow and dry grass, etc. for hay

hay′cock′ (-käk′) *n.* a small, conical heap of hay drying in a field

hay fever an acute inflammation of the eyes and upper respiratory tract: an allergic reaction to some pollens

hay′loft′ *n.* a loft, or upper story, in a barn or stable, for storing hay

hay′mow′ (-mou′) *n.* same as HAYLOFT

hay′stack′ *n.* a large heap of hay piled up outdoors: also **hay′rick′** (-rik′)

hay′wire′ *adj.* [Slang] **1.** out of order; confused **2.** crazy: usually in **go haywire**

haz·ard (haz′ərd) *n.* [OFr. *hasard*, game of dice] **1.** chance **2.** risk; danger **3.** an obstacle on a golf course —*vt.* to risk

haz′ard·ous *adj.* risky; dangerous

haze[1] (hāz) *n.* [prob. < HAZY] **1.** a thin vapor of fog, smoke, dust, etc. in the air **2.** slight vagueness of mind —*vi., vt.* hazed, haz′ing to make or become hazy

haze[2] (hāz) *vt.* hazed, haz′ing [< ?] to force (fellow students) to do ridiculous or painful things, as in initiation

ha·zel (hā′z'l) *n.* [OE. *hæsel*] **1.** a tree or shrub related to the birch, bearing edible nuts **2.** a light brown —*adj.* light-brown

ha′zel·nut′ *n.* the small, edible, roundish nut of the hazel; filbert

ha·zy (hā′zē) *adj.* -zi·er, -zi·est [prob. < OE. *hasu*, dusky] **1.** somewhat foggy or smoky **2.** vague or obscure —**ha′zi·ness** *n.*

H-bomb (āch′bäm′) *n.* see HYDROGEN BOMB

he (hē) *pron. for pl.* see THEY [OE.] **1.** the man, boy, or male animal previously mentioned **2.** anyone [*he* who lags is left] —*n., pl.* **hes** a man, boy, or male animal

He *Chem.* helium

head (hed) *n.* [OE. *heafod*] **1.** the part of the body containing the brain, and the eyes, ears, nose, and mouth **2.** the mind; intelligence **3.** *pl.* **head** a unit of counting [ten *head* of cattle] **4.** [often *pl.*] the main side of a coin **5.** the uppermost part or thing; top **6.** the topic or title of a section, chapter, etc. **7.** the foremost or projecting part; front **8.** the part designed for holding, striking, etc. [the *head* of a nail] **9.** the recording or playing part of a tape recorder **10.** the membrane across the end of a drum **11.** the source of a river, etc. **12.** pressure [a *head* of steam] **13.** a position of leadership or honor **14.** a leader, ruler, etc. **15.** a large compact bud [a *head* of cabbage] **16.** [Slang] a habitual user of marijuana, LSD, etc. —*adj.* **1.** most important; principal **2.** at the top or front **3.** striking against the front [*head* winds] —*vt.* **1.** to be chief of or in charge of **2.** to lead; precede **3.** to cause to go in a specified direction —*vi.* to set out; travel [to *head* eastward] —**come to a head 1.** to be about to suppurate, as a boil **2.** to culminate — **go to one's head 1.** to confuse or intoxicate one **2.** to make one vain —**head off** to get ahead of and intercept —**head over heels** deeply; completely —**keep (or lose) one's head** to keep (or lose) one's poise, self-control, etc. — **make head or tail of** to understand —**over one's head** not understandable

head′ache′ (-āk′) *n.* **1.** a continuous pain in the head **2.** [Colloq.] a cause of worry, trouble, etc.

head′dress′ *n.* a covering or decoration for the head

-headed *a combining form meaning* having a head or heads [clearheaded, two-*headed*]

head′first′ *adv.* **1.** with the head in front; headlong **2.** recklessly; rashly

head′gear′ *n.* a hat, cap, bonnet, etc.

head′hunt′er *n.* a member of any of certain primitive tribes who remove and preserve the heads of slain enemies

head′ing *n.* **1.** something forming the head, top, or front **2.** the title, topic, etc., as of a chapter **3.** the direction in which a ship, plane, etc. is moving

head′land′ *n.* a point of land reaching out into the water; promontory

head′light′ *n.* a light with a reflector and lens, at the front of a vehicle: also **headlamp**

head′line′ *n.* printed lines at the top of a newspaper article, giving the topic —*vt.* **-lined′, -lin′ing 1.** to provide with a headline **2.** to give featured billing to

head′long′ (-lôŋ′) *adv., adj.* **1.** with the head first **2.** with uncontrolled speed and force **3.** reckless(ly); impetuous(ly)

head′mas′ter *n.* the principal of a private school —**head′mis′tress** *n.fem.*

head′-on′ *adj., adv.* with the head or front foremost [hit *head-on*]

head′phone′ *n.* a telephone or radio receiver held to the ear by a band over the head

head′pin′ *n.* the front pin of a triangle of bowling pins

head′quar′ters (-kwôr′tərz) *n.pl.* [often *with sing. v.*] **1.** the main office, or center of operations, of one in command, as in an army **2.** any main office

head′room′ *n.* space overhead

heads·man (hedz′mən) *n., pl.* **-men** one who executes by beheading

head′stone′ *n.* a stone marker placed at the head of a grave

head′strong′ *adj.* determined to do as one pleases

head'wa'ters *n.pl.* the small streams that are the sources of a river

head'way' *n.* **1.** forward motion **2.** progress in work, etc.

head·y (hed'ē) *adj.* **-i·er, -i·est 1.** impetuous; rash **2.** intoxicating —**head'i·ness** *n.*

heal (hēl) *vt., vi.* [OE. *hælan*] **1.** to make or become well or healthy again **2.** to cure (a disease) or mend, as a wound —**heal'er** *n.*

health (helth) *n.* [OE. *hælth*] **1.** physical and mental well-being; freedom from disease, etc. **2.** condition of body or mind [good *health*] **3.** a wish for a person's health and happiness, as in a toast

health food food thought to be very healthful, esp. organic food free of chemical additives

health'ful *adj.* helping to produce or maintain health —**health'ful·ly** *adv.*

health·y (hel'thē) *adj.* **-i·er, -i·est 1.** having good health **2.** showing or resulting from good health [a *healthy* appetite] **3.** healthful — **health'i·ness** *n.*

heap (hēp) *n.* [OE. *heap,* a troop] **1.** a pile or mass of things jumbled together **2.** [Colloq.] a large amount —*vt.* **1.** to make a heap of **2.** to give in large amounts **3.** to fill (a plate, etc.) full or to overflowing —*vi.* to rise in a heap

hear (hir) *vt.* **heard** (hurd), **hear'ing** [OE. *hieran*] **1.** to perceive or sense (sounds) by the ear **2.** to listen to **3.** to conduct a hearing of (a law case, etc.) **4.** to be informed of; learn —*vi.* to be able to hear sounds —**hear from** to get a letter, etc. from —**not hear of** not assent to

hear'ing *n.* **1.** the act or process of perceiving sounds **2.** the ability to hear **3.** opportunity to be heard **4.** an appearance before a judge, official board, etc. **5.** the distance sound will carry [within *hearing*]

heark·en (här'k'n) *vi.* [OE. *heorcnian*] to pay careful attention; listen carefully

hear·say (hir'sā') *n.* rumor; gossip

hearse (hurs) *n.* [< L. *hirpex,* a harrow] a funeral vehicle for carrying the corpse

heart (härt) *n.* [OE. *heorte*] **1.** the hollow, muscular organ that circulates the blood by alternate dilation and contraction **2.** the central, vital, or main part; core **3.** the human heart considered as the center of emotions, personality attributes, etc.; specif., *a)* inmost thought and feeling *b)* love, sympathy, etc. *c)* spirit or courage **4.** a conventionalized design of a heart (♥) **5.** *a)* any of a suit of playing cards marked with such symbols in red *b)* [*pl.*] this suit of cards —**after one's own heart** that pleases one perfectly —**at heart** in one's inmost nature —**by heart** by memorizing or from memory —**set one's heart on** to have a fixed desire for —**take heart** to cheer up

heart'ache' *n.* sorrow or grief

heart'break' *n.* overwhelming sorrow, grief, or disappointment —**heart'bro'ken** *adj.*

heart'burn' *n.* a burning, acid sensation beneath the breastbone, in the esophagus

heart'en (-'n) *vt.* to cheer up; encourage

heart'felt' *adj.* sincere; genuine

hearth (härth) *n.* [OE. *heorth*] **1.** the stone or brick floor of a fireplace **2.** *a)* the fireside *b)* the home

heart'less *adj.* unkind; unfeeling

heart'-rend'ing *adj.* causing much grief or mental anguish —**heart'-rend'ing·ly** *adv.*

heart'sick' *adj.* sick at heart; extremely unhappy or despondent: also **heart'sore'**

heart'strings' *n.pl.* deepest affections

heart'-to-heart' *adj.* intimate and candid

heart'y (-ē) *adj.* **-i·er, -i·est 1.** warm and friendly; cordial **2.** strongly felt or expressed [a *hearty* dislike] **3.** strong and healthy **4.** nourishing [a *hearty* meal] —*n., pl.* **-ies** [Archaic] a fellow sailor —**heart'i·ly** *adv.* —**heart'i·ness** *n.*

heat (hēt) *n.* [OE. *hætu*] **1.** the quality of being hot; hotness, or the perception of this **2.** much hotness **3.** hot weather or climate **4.** the warming of a house, etc. **5.** *a)* strong feeling; ardor, anger, etc. *b)* the period of this **6.** a single effort, bout, or trial **7.** the period of sexual excitement in animals, esp. females **8.** [Slang] coercion —*vt., vi.* **1.** to make or become warm **2.** to make or become excited

heat'ed *adj.* **1.** hot **2.** vehement or angry — **heat'ed·ly** *adv.*

heat'er *n.* a stove, furnace, radiator, etc. for heating a room, a car, water, etc.

heath (hēth) *n.* [OE. *hæth*] **1.** a tract of open wasteland, esp. in the British Isles **2.** any of various shrubs growing on heaths, as heather

hea·then (hē'than) *n., pl.* **-thens, -then** [OE. *hæthen*] **1.** anyone not a Jew, Christian, or Muslim **2.** a person regarded as uncivilized, irreligious, etc. —*adj.* **1.** pagan **2.** irreligious, etc. —**hea'then·ish** *adj.*

heath·er (heth'ər) *n.* [ME. *haddyr*] a low-growing shrub common in the British Isles, with small, purplish flowers

heat'stroke' *n.* a condition resulting from exposure to intense heat, characterized by high fever and collapse

heave (hēv) *vt.* **heaved** or (esp. *Naut.*) **hove, heav'ing** [< OE. *hebban*] **1.** to lift, esp. with effort **2.** to lift in this way and throw **3.** to utter (a sigh, etc.) with effort **4.** *Naut.* to raise, haul, etc. by pulling with a rope, etc. —*vi.* **1.** to swell up **2.** to rise and fall rhythmically **3.** *a)* to vomit *b)* to pant; gasp **4.** *Naut.* to haul (on or at a rope, etc.) —*n.* the act or effort of heaving —**heave to** *Naut.* to stop

heav·en (hev'n) *n.* [OE. *heofon*] **1.** [usually *pl.*] the visible sky; firmament **2.** *Theol.* [H-] *a)* the dwelling place of God and his angels, where the blessed go after death *b)* God **3.** any place or state of great happiness —**heav'en·ly** *adj.*

heav'en·ward *adv., adj.* toward heaven: also **heav'en·wards** *adv.*

heav·y (hev'ē) *adj.* **-i·er, -i·est** [OE. *hefig*] **1.** hard to lift because of its weight **2.** of more than the usual, expected, or defined weight **3.** larger, greater, or more intense than usual [a *heavy* blow, a *heavy* vote, *heavy* applause] **4.** to an unusual extent [a *heavy* drinker] **5.** hard to do [*heavy* work] **6.** sorrowful [a *heavy* heart] **7.** burdened with sleep, etc. [*heavy* eyelids] **8.** hard to digest [a *heavy* meal] **9.** cloudy; gloomy [a *heavy* sky] —*adv.* heavily —*n., pl.* **-ies** *Theater* a villain —**hang heavy** to pass tediously —**heav'i·ly** *adv.* —**heav'i·ness** *n.*

heav'y-du'ty *adj.* made to withstand great strain, bad weather, etc.

heav'y-hand'ed *adj.* **1.** clumsy; tactless **2.** cruel; tyrannical —**heav'y-hand'ed·ness** *n.*

heav'y-heart'ed *adj.* sad; depressed

heav'y·weight' *n.* a boxer or wrestler who weighs over 175 pounds

Heb. 1. Hebrew **2.** Hebrews

He·bra·ic (hi brā'ik) *adj.* of or characteristic of the Hebrews, their language, etc.; Hebrew

He·brew (hē'brōō) *n.* **1.** *a)* a member of an ancient Semitic people; Israelite *b)* a Jew **2.** *a)* the ancient Semitic language of the Israelites *b)* its modern form, the language of Israel — *adj.* of Hebrew or the Hebrews

heck (hek) *interj., n.* [Colloq.] *a* euphemism for HELL

heck·le (hek''l) *vt.* **-led, -ling** [< ME. *hechele*]

hectare 213 helpful

to harass (a speaker, etc.) with questions or taunts —**heck'ler** *n.*
hec·tare (hek'ter) *n.* [Fr.] metric measure of area, 10,000 square meters (2.471 acres)
hec·tic (hek'tik) *adj.* [< Gr. *hektikos,* habitual] 1. feverish; flushed 2. confused, rushed, etc. — **hec'ti·cal·ly** *adv.*
hec·to·graph (hek'tə graf') *n.* [< Gr. *hekaton,* hundred + -GRAPH] a duplicating device by which copies are taken from a sheet of gelatin
Hec·tor (hek'tər) *Gr. Myth.* a Trojan hero killed by Achilles: he was Priam's son —*vt., vi.* [h-] to browbeat; bully
he'd (hēd) 1. he had 2. he would
hedge (hej) *n.* [OE. *hecg*] 1. a dense row of shrubs, etc. forming a boundary 2. any fence or barrier 3. a hedging —*vt.* hedged, hedg'ing 1. to put a hedge around 2. to hinder or guard as with a barrier 3. to try to avoid loss in (a bet, etc.) as by making counterbalancing bets —*vi.* to refuse to commit oneself; avoid direct answers
hedge'hog' *n.* 1. a small insect-eating mammal of Europe, with sharp spines on the back 2. the American porcupine
hedge'hop' *vi.* -hopped', -hop'ping [Colloq.] to fly an airplane very close to the ground — **hedge'hop'per** *n.*
he·do·nism (hēd''n iz'm) *n.* [< Gr. *hēdonē,* pleasure] the doctrine that pleasure is the principal good —**he'do·nist** *n.*
-hedron [Gr.] *a combining form meaning* a figure or crystal with (a specified number of) surfaces
heed (hēd) *vt., vi.* [OE. *hedan*] to pay close attention (to) —*n.* close attention —**heed'ful** *adj.* —**heed'less** *adj.*
hee·haw (hē'hô') *vi., n.* [echoic] *same as* BRAY
heel¹ (hēl) *n.* [OE. *hela*] 1. the back part of the foot, under the ankle 2. that part of a stocking or shoe at the heel 3. anything like a heel in location, shape, etc. 4. [Colloq.] a despicable person —*vt.* 1. to furnish with a heel 2. to follow closely 3. [Colloq.] to provide with money —*vi.* to go along at the heels of someone — **down at the heel(s)** shabby; seedy
heel² (hēl) *vi.* [OE. *hieldan*] to lean to one side; list: said esp. of a ship —*vt.* to make (a ship) list
heft (heft) *n.* [< base of HEAVE] [Colloq.] 1. weight; heaviness 2. importance; influence —*vt.* [Colloq.] 1. to lift or heave 2. to estimate the weight of by lifting
heft·y (hef'tē) *adj.* -i·er, -i·est [Colloq.] 1. heavy 2. large and strong —**heft'i·ness** *n.*
he·gem·o·ny (hi jem'ə nē) *n., pl.* -nies [< Gr. *hēgemōn,* leader] leadership or dominance, esp. that of one nation over others
he·gi·ra (hi jī'rə) *n.* [< Ar. *hijrah,* flight] 1. [often H-] Mohammed's flight from Mecca in 622 A.D. 2. any journey as for escape
heif·er (hef'ər) *n.* [OE. *heahfore*] a young cow that has not borne a calf
height (hīt) *n.* [< OE. *heah,* high] 1. the topmost point 2. the highest limit; extreme 3. the distance from bottom to top 4. elevation above a given level; altitude 5. a relatively great distance above a given level 6. [often pl.] an eminence; hill
height'en (-'n) *vt., vi.* 1. to bring or come to a higher position 2. to make or become larger, greater, etc.
hei·nous (hā'nəs) *adj.* [< OFr. *haine,* hatred] outrageously evil —**hei'nous·ly** *adv.*
heir (er) *n.* [< L. *heres*] one who inherits or is entitled to inherit another's property, title, etc.

heir apparent the heir whose right to inherit cannot be denied if he outlives the ancestor
heir'ess (-is) *n.* a woman or girl who is an heir, esp. to great wealth
heir'loom' (-lōōm') *n.* [HEIR + LOOM¹] any possession handed down from generation to generation
heist (hīst) *n.* [< HOIST] [Slang] a robbery
held (held) *pt. & pp. of* HOLD¹
Helen of Troy *Gr. Legend* the beautiful wife of the king of Sparta: the Trojan War was started because Paris abducted her and took her to Troy
hel·i·cal (hel'i kəl) *adj.* of, or having the form of, a helix; spiral —**hel'i·cal·ly** *adv.*
hel·i·cop·ter (hel'ə käp'tər, hē'lə-) *n.* [< Gr. *helix,* a spiral + *pteron,* wing] a kind of aircraft lifted, moved, or kept hovering by revolving blades mounted horizontally
he·li·o·trope (hē'lē ə trōp') *n.* [< Gr. *hēlios,* the sun + *trepein,* to turn] 1. a plant with fragrant clusters of small, white or reddish-purple flowers 2. reddish purple
hel·i·port (hel'ə pôrt') *n.* a flat place where helicopters land and take off
he·li·um (hē'lē əm) *n.* [< Gr. *hēlios,* the sun] a chemical element, a very light, inert, colorless gas: it is used for inflating balloons, etc.: symbol, He
he·lix (hē'liks) *n., pl.* -lix·es, -li·ces' (hel'ə sēz') [Gr., a spiral] any spiral, as the thread of a screw, bolt, etc.
hell (hel) *n.* [< OE. *helan,* to hide] 1. [often H-] *Christianity* the place to which sinners and unbelievers go after death for punishment 2. any place or state of pain, cruelty, etc. —**catch (or get) hell** [Slang] to be severely scolded, punished, etc.
he'll (hēl) 1. he will 2. he shall
hell'bent' *adj.* [Slang] 1. recklessly determined 2. moving fast
hell'cat' *n.* an evil, spiteful woman
hel·le·bore (hel'ə bôr') *n.* [< Gr. *helleboros*] a plant related to the lily, whose rhizomes and roots were used in medicine
Hel·len·ic (hə len'ik) *adj.* 1. Greek 2. of the language, culture, etc. of the ancient Greeks — **Hel·len·ism** (hel'ən iz'm) *n.*
hel·lion (hel'yən) *n.* [Colloq.] a person fond of deviltry; troublemaker
hell'ish *adj.* 1. devilish; fiendish 2. [Colloq.] very unpleasant —**hell'ish·ly** *adv.*
hel·lo (he lō', hel'ō) *interj.* an exclamation of greeting
helm (helm) *n.* [OE. *helma*] 1. the wheel or tiller by which a ship is steered 2. control or leadership, as of an organization
hel·met (hel'mət) *n.* [< OFr. *helme*] a protective, rigid head covering for use in combat, certain sports, etc.
helms·man (helmz'mən) *n., pl.* -men one who steers a ship
hel·ot (hel'ət) *n.* [< Gr. *Heilotes,* serfs] a serf or slave
help (help) *vt.* [OE. *helpan*] 1. to make things easier or better for; aid; assist 2. to remedy [to *help* a cough] 3. *a)* to keep from; avoid [she can't *help* crying] *b)* to prevent [faults that can't be *helped*] 4. to serve or wait on (a customer, etc.) —*vi.* to give assistance; be useful — *n.* 1. a helping; aid; assistance 2. a remedy 3. one that helps; esp., a hired person or persons; servant(s), farmhand(s), etc. —**help oneself to** to take without asking —**help out** to help in getting or doing something —**help'er** *n.*
help'ful (-fəl) *adj.* giving help; useful —**help'ful·ly** *adv.* —**help'ful·ness** *n.*

help'ing (-iŋ) *n.* **1.** a giving of aid **2.** a portion of food served to one person

help'less *adj.* **1.** not able to help oneself; weak **2.** lacking help or protection —**help'less·ly** *adv.* —**help'less·ness** *n.*

help'mate' *n.* [< HELPMEET] a helpful companion; specif., a wife or husband

help'meet' *n.* [misreading of "an *help meet* for him" (Gen. 2:18)] *same as* HELPMATE

hel·ter-skel·ter (hel'tər skel'tər) *adv.* [arbitrary formation] in haste and confusion — *adj.* confused and disorderly

helve (helv) *n.* [OE. *helfe*] the handle of a tool, esp. of an ax or hatchet

hem¹ (hem) *n.* [OE.] the border on a garment, etc., made by folding and sewing down the edge —*vt.* **hemmed, hem'ming** to put a hem on —**hem in** (or **around** or **about**) to surround

hem² (hem) *interj., n.* the sound made in clearing the throat —*vi.* **hemmed, hem'ming 1.** to make this sound, as to get attention **2.** to grope about in speech for the right words: usually in **hem and haw**

he·ma·tol·o·gy (hē'mə täl'ə jē) *n.* [< Gr. *haima,* blood + -LOGY] the study of the blood and its diseases —**he'ma·tol'o·gist** *n.*

hemi- [Gr. *hēmi-*] *a prefix meaning* half [*hemisphere*]

hem·i·sphere (hem'ə sfir') *n.* **1.** half of a sphere or globe **2.** any of the halves (northern, southern, eastern, or western) of the earth — **hem'i·spher'i·cal** (-sfer'i kəl), **hem'i·spher'ic** *adj.*

hem·line (hem'līn') *n.* the bottom edge of a dress, coat, skirt, etc.

hem·lock (hem'läk) *n.* [OE. *hemlic*] **1.** a poisonous European plant, with small, white flowers: also **poison hemlock 2.** a poison made from this plant **3.** *a)* an evergreen tree related to the pine *b)* its wood

hemo- [< Gr. *haima*] *a combining form meaning* blood

he·mo·glo·bin (hē'mə glō'bin) *n.* [< prec. + GLOBULE] the red coloring matter of the red blood corpuscles

he·mo·phil·i·a (hē'mə fil'ē ə) *n.* [see HEMO- & -PHILE] a hereditary condition in which the blood fails to clot normally, causing prolonged bleeding from even minor injuries

hem·or·rhage (hem'ər ij, hem'rij) *n.* [< Gr. *haima,* blood + *rhēgnynai,* to break] the escape of blood from a blood vessel; heavy bleeding —*vi.* **-rhaged, -rhag·ing** to have a hemorrhage

hem·or·rhoid (hem'ə roid') *n.* [< Gr. *haima,* blood + *rhein,* to flow] a painful swelling of a vein in the region of the anus, often with bleeding: *usually used in pl.*

hemp (hemp) *n.* [OE. *hænep*] **1.** a tall Asiatic plant having tough fiber in its stem **2.** this fiber, used to make rope, sailcloth, etc. **3.** a substance, as marijuana, hashish, etc., made from its leaves and flowers

hem·stitch (hem'stich') *n.* an ornamental stitch, used esp. at a hem, made by pulling out several parallel threads and tying the cross threads into small bunches —*vt.* to put hemstitches on

hen (hen) *n.* [OE. *henn*] **1.** the female of the chicken (the domestic fowl) **2.** the female of various other birds

hence (hens) *adv.* [< OE. *heonan,* from here] **1.** from this place; away [go *hence*] **2.** from this time [a year *hence*] **3.** as a result; therefore **4.** [Archaic] from this source

hence'forth' *adv.* from this time on: also **hence'for'ward**

hench·man (hench'mən) *n., pl.* -men [OE. *hengest,* stallion + -*man*] a trusted follower

hen·na (hen'ə) *n.* [Ar. *hinnā'*] **1.** an old-world plant with white or red flowers **2.** a dye extracted from its leaves, used to tint the hair auburn **3.** reddish brown —*adj.* reddish-brown —*vt.* **-naed, -na·ing** to tint with henna

hen·peck (hen'pek') *vt.* to nag and domineer over (one's husband) —**hen'pecked'** *adj.*

he·pat·ic (hi pat'ik) *adj.* [< Gr. *hēpar,* liver] of, like, or affecting the liver

hep·a·ti·tis (hep'ə tīt'is) *n.* [< Gr. *hēpar,* liver + -ITIS] inflammation of the liver

her (hur) *pron.* [OE. *hire*] *objective case of* SHE —*poss. pronominal adj.* of, belonging to, or done by her

He·ra (hir'ə) *Gr. Myth.* the wife of Zeus and queen of the gods

her·ald (her'əld) *n.* [< OFr. *herault*] **1.** formerly, an official who made proclamations, carried state messages, etc. **2.** one who announces significant news **3.** a forerunner; harbinger —*vt.* to announce, foretell, etc.

he·ral·dic (hə ral'dik) *adj.* of heraldry or heralds

her'ald·ry *n., pl.* -ries **1.** the science dealing with coats of arms, genealogies, etc. **2.** ceremony or pomp

herb (urb, hurb) *n.* [< L. *herba*] **1.** any seed plant whose stem withers away annually **2.** any plant used as a medicine, seasoning, etc. —**her·ba·ceous** (hər bā'shəs, ər-) *adj.*

herb·age (ur'bij, hur'-) *n.* herbs collectively, esp. those used as pasturage; grass

her·bi·cide (hur'bə sīd', ur'-) *n.* any chemical substance used to destroy plants, esp. weeds — **her'bi·cid'dal** *adj.*

her'bi·vore' (-vôr') *n.* [Fr.] a herbivorous animal

her·biv·o·rous (hər biv'ər əs) *adj.* [< L. *herba,* herb + *vorare,* devour] feeding chiefly on plants

her·cu·le·an (hur'kyə lē'ən, hər kyōō'lē ən) *adj.* [*sometimes* H-] **1.** having the great size and strength of Hercules **2.** calling for great strength, size, or courage

Her·cu·les (hur'kyə lēz') *Gr. & Rom. Myth.* a hero famous for feats of strength —*n.* [h-] any very large, strong man

herd (hurd) *n.* [OE. *heord*] **1.** a number of cattle or other large animals feeding or living together **2.** a crowd **3.** the common people; masses: contemptuous term —*vt., vi.* to form into or move as a herd

herds·man (hurdz'mən) *n., pl.* -men one who keeps or tends a herd

here (hir) *adv.* [OE. *her*] **1.** at or in this place: often used as an intensive [John *here* is a good player] **2.** to or into this place [come *here*] **3.** at this point; now **4.** in earthly life — *n.* this place or point —**neither here nor there** irrelevant

here'a·bout' *adv.* in this general vicinity: also **here'a·bouts'**

here·af'ter *adv.* **1.** from now on; in the future **2.** following this —*n.* **1.** the future **2.** the state after death

here'by' *adv.* by this means

he·red·i·tar·y (hə red'ə ter'ē) *adj.* **1.** *a)* of, or passed down from, by inheritance from an ancestor *b)* having title, etc. by inheritance **2.** of or passed down by heredity

he·red·i·ty (hə red'ə tē) *n., pl.* -ties [< L. *heres,* heir] the transmission of characteristics from parents to offspring by means of genes

here·in (hir in') *adv.* **1.** in here **2.** in this writing **3.** in this matter, detail, etc.

here·of′ *adv.* of or concerning this

her·e·sy (her′ə sē) *n., pl.* **-sies** [< Gr. *hairesis,* selection, sect] **1.** a religious belief opposed to the orthodox doctrines of a church **2.** any opinion opposed to established views

her·e·tic (her′ə tik) *n.* one who professes a heresy; esp., a church member who holds beliefs opposed to church dogma —**he·ret·i·cal** (hə ret′i k'l) *adj.*

here′to·fore′ *adv.* up to now; before this

here′up·on′ *adv.* **1.** immediately following this **2.** concerning this

here·with′ *adv.* **1.** along with this **2.** by this method or means

her·it·a·ble (her′it ə b'l) *adj.* that can be inherited —**her′it·a·bil′i·ty** *n.*

her·it·age (her′ət ij) *n.* **1.** property that is or can be inherited **2.** a tradition, etc. derived from one's ancestors or the past

her·maph·ro·dite (hər maf′rə dīt′) *n.* [< *Hermaphroditos,* son of Hermes and Aphrodite, united in a single body with a nymph] a person, animal, or plant with the sexual organs of both the male and the female

Her·mes (hur′mēz) *Gr. Myth.* a god who served as messenger of the other gods

her·met·ic (hər met′ik) *adj.* [< prec. (reputed founder of alchemy)] airtight: also **her·met′i·cal** —**her·met′i·cal·ly** *adv.*

her·mit (hur′mit) *n.* [< Gr. *erēmos,* solitary] one who lives alone in seclusion; recluse

her′mit·age (-ij) *n.* a secluded retreat, as the place where a hermit lives

her·ni·a (hur′nē ə) *n., pl.* **-as, -ae′** (-ē′) [L.] the protrusion of an organ, esp. a part of the intestine, through a tear in the wall of the surrounding structure; rupture

her′ni·ate′ (-āt′) *vi.* **-at′ed, -at′ing** to protrude so as to form a hernia

he·ro (hir′ō, hē′rō) *n., pl.* **-roes** [< Gr. *hērōs*] **1.** a man of great courage, nobility, etc., or one admired for his exploits **2.** the central male character in a novel, play, etc.

he·ro·ic (hi rō′ik) *adj.* **1.** of or like a hero **2.** of or about heroes and their deeds **3.** daring and risky —*n.* [*pl.*] extravagant talk or action —**he·ro′i·cal·ly** *adv.*

her·o·in (her′ə win) *n.* [G., orig. a trademark] a habit-forming narcotic derived from morphine

her·o·ine (her′ə win) *n.* a girl or woman hero in life or literature

her′o·ism (-wiz′m) *n.* the qualities and actions of a hero or heroine; courage, etc.

her·on (her′ən) *n.* [< OFr. *hairon*] a wading bird with long legs, neck, and bill

her·pes (hur′pēz) *n.* [< Gr. *herpein,* to creep] a virus disease causing small blisters on the skin

her·pe·tol·o·gy (hur′pə täl′ə jē) *n.* [< Gr. *herpeton,* reptile + -LOGY] the branch of zoology dealing with reptiles

‡Herr (her) *n., pl.* **Herr′ren** (-ən) [G.] a man; gentleman: as a title, equivalent to *Mr.* or *Sir*

her·ring (her′iŋ) *n.* [OE. *hæring*] a small food fish of the N Atlantic

her′ring·bone′ *n.* anything having a pattern made up of rows of parallel, slanting lines resembling the ribs of a herring

hers (hurz) *pron.* that or those belonging to her [*hers* are better]

her·self (hər self′) *pron.* **1.** *the intensive form of* SHE [she went *herself*] **2.** *the reflexive form of* SHE [she hurt *herself*] **3.** her true self [she's not *herself* today]

hertz (hurts) *n., pl.* **hertz** [< H. R. *Hertz* (1857-94), G. physicist] the international unit of frequency, equal to one cycle per second

he's (hēz) **1.** he is **2.** he has

hes·i·tant (hez′ə tənt) *adj.* hesitating or undecided; doubtful —**hes′i·tan·cy,** *pl.* **-cies, hes′i·tance** *n.* —**hes′i·tant·ly** *adv.*

hes·i·tate (hez′ə tāt′) *vi.* **-tat′ed, -tat′ing** [< L. *haerere,* to stick] **1.** to stop in indecision; waver **2.** to pause **3.** to be reluctant [I *hesitate* to ask] **4.** to pause continually in speaking — **hes′i·ta′tion** *n.*

hetero- [Gr. < *heteros,* the other] *a combining form meaning* other, another, different

het·er·o·dox (het′ər ə däks′) *adj.* [< Gr. *hetero-,* other + *doxa,* opinion] opposed to the usual beliefs, esp. in religion; unorthodox — **het′er·o·dox′y** *n., pl.* **-ies**

het·er·o·ge·ne·ous (het′ər ə jē′nē əs) *adj.* [< Gr. *hetero-,* other + *genos,* a kind] **1.** differing in structure, quality, etc.; dissimilar **2.** composed of unlike parts

het·er·o·sex·u·al (het′ər ə sek′shoo wəl) *adj.* **1.** of or having sexual desire for those of the opposite sex **2.** *Biol.* of different sexes —*n.* a heterosexual individual

hew (hyoo) *vt.* **hewed** or **hewn, hew′ing** [OE. *heawan*] **1.** to chop or cut with an ax, knife, etc. **2.** to make or shape thus —*vi.* to conform (*to* a line, rule, etc.)

HEW (Department of) Health, Education, and Welfare

hex (heks) *n.* [< G. *hexe,* witch] something supposed to bring bad luck —*vt.* to cause to have bad luck

hexa- [< Gr. *hex,* six] *a combining form meaning* six

hex·a·gon (hek′sə gän′) *n.* [< Gr. *hex,* six + *gōnia,* an angle] a plane figure with six angles and six sides —**hex·ag′o·nal** (-sag′ə n'l) *adj.*

hex·am·e·ter (hek sam′ə tər) *n.* [see HEXA- & -METER1] **1.** a line of verse containing six metrical feet **2.** verse consisting of hexameters

hey (hā) *interj.* an exclamation used to attract attention, express surprise, etc.

hey·day (hā′dā′) *n.* [prob. < ME. *hey,* high + *dei,* day] the time of greatest vigor, success, etc.; prime

Hg [L. *hydrargyrum*] *Chem.* mercury

hi (hī) *interj.* an exclamation of greeting

hi·a·tus (hī ät′əs) *n., pl.* **-tus·es, -tus** [L. < *hiare,* to gape] a break or gap, as where a part is missing; lacuna

hi·ba·chi (hi bä′chē) *n., pl.* **-chis** [Jpn. < *hi,* fire + *bachi,* bowl] a charcoal-burning brazier and grill

hi·ber·nate (hī′bər nāt′) *vi.* **-nat′ed, -nat′ing** [< L. *hibernus,* wintry] to spend the winter in a dormant state —**hi′ber·na′tion** *n.*

hi·bis·cus (hī bis′kəs, hi-) *n.* [< L.] a plant, shrub, or small tree related to the mallow, with large, colorful flowers

hic·cup (hik′əp) *n.* [echoic] an involuntary contraction of the diaphragm that closes the glottis at the moment of breathing in so that a sharp sound is produced —*vi.* **-cuped** or **-cupped, -cup·ing** or **-cup·ping** to make a hiccup Also **hic·cough** (hik′əp)

hick (hik) *n.* [< *Richard*] [Colloq.] an awkward, unsophisticated person regarded as typical of rural areas; somewhat contemptuous term — *adj.* [Colloq.] of or like a hick

hick·o·ry (hik′ər ē) *n., pl.* **-ries** [< AmInd. *pawcohiccora*] **1.** N. American tree related to the walnut: its nut (**hickory nut**) is smooth-shelled and edible **2.** its hard wood

hide1 (hīd) *vt.* **hid** (hid), **hid·den** (hid′'n) or **hid, hid′ing** [OE. *hydan*] **1.** to put or keep out of sight; conceal **2.** to keep secret **3.** to keep from sight by obscuring, etc. —*vi.* to conceal oneself

hide² (hīd) *n.* [OE. *hid*] an animal skin or pelt, either raw or tanned

hide'a·way' (-ə wā') *n.* [Colloq.] a place where one can hide, be secluded, etc.

hide'bound' *adj.* obstinately conservative and narrow-minded

hid·e·ous (hid'ē əs) *adj.* [< OFr. *hide,* fright] horrible; very ugly or revolting

hide'-out' *n.* [Colloq.] a hiding place, as for gangsters

hie (hī) *vi., vt.* **hied, hie'ing** or **hy'ing** [OE. *higian*] to hurry or hasten

hi·er·ar·chy (hī'ə rär'kē) *n., pl.* **-chies** [< Gr. *hieros,* sacred + *archos,* ruler] **1.** church government by clergy in graded ranks **2.** the highest officials in such a system **3.** any group arranged in order of rank, grade, etc. —**hi'er·ar'chi·cal** *adj.*

hi·er·o·glyph·ic (hī'ər ə glif'ik, hī'rə-) *n.* [< Gr. *hieros,* sacred + *glyphein,* carve] **1.** a picture or symbol representing a word, sound, etc., in a system used by the ancient Egyptians and others **2.** a sign, symbol, etc. hard to understand —*adj.* of or like hieroglyphics

hi-fi (hī'fī') *n.* **1.** *same as* HIGH FIDELITY **2.** a radio, phonograph, etc. having high fidelity —*adj.* of or having high fidelity of sound reproduction

high (hī) *adj.* [OE. *heah*] **1.** lofty; tall **2.** extending upward a (specified) distance **3.** reaching to, situated at, or done from a height **4.** above others in rank, position, etc.; superior **5.** grave *[high* treason] **6.** greater in size, amount, cost, etc. than usual *[high* prices] **7.** luxurious *[high* living] **8.** raised or acute in pitch; shrill **9.** slightly tainted, as meat **10.** elated *[high* spirits] **11.** [Slang] *a)* drunk *b)* under the influence of a drug —*adv.* in or to a high level, degree, rank, etc. —*n.* **1.** a high level, place, etc. **2.** an area of high barometric pressure **3.** that gear of a motor vehicle, etc. producing the greatest speed **4.** [Slang] a euphoric state induced as by drugs —**high and low** everywhere —**on high** in heaven

high'ball' *n.* a drink of whiskey or brandy mixed with water, soda water, etc.

high'born' *adj.* of noble birth

high'boy' *n.* a high chest of drawers mounted on legs

high'brow' *n.* [Colloq.] one having or affecting highly cultivated tastes; intellectual —*adj.* [Colloq.] of or for highbrows

high'er-up' *n.* [Colloq.] a person of higher rank or position

high·fa·lu·tin(g) (hī'fə lŏot'n) *adj.* [Colloq.] pretentious or pompous

high fidelity in radio, sound recording, etc., nearly exact reproduction of a wide range of sound waves

high'-flown' (-flōn') *adj.* **1.** extravagantly ambitious **2.** bombastic

High German the West Germanic dialects spoken in C and S Germany

high'-grade' *adj.* of superior quality

high'hand'ed *adj.* overbearing —**high'hand'ed·ly** *adv.* —**high'hand'ed·ness** *n.*

high'-hat' *vt.* **-hat'ted, -hat'ting** [Slang] to snub

high'land (-lənd) *n.* a region containing many hills or mountains

high'light' *n.* **1.** a part on which light is brightest **2.** the most important or interesting part, scene, etc. —*vt.* **1.** to give highlights to **2.** to give prominence to

high'ly *adv.* **1.** very much **2.** favorably **3.** at a high level, wage, rank, etc.

high'-mind'ed *adj.* having high ideals, principles, etc.

high'ness *n.* **1.** height **2.** [H-] a title used in speaking to or of royalty

high'-pres'sure *adj.* **1.** having or withstanding high pressure **2.** using strongly persuasive methods —*vt.* **-sured, -sur·ing** [Colloq.] to urge with such methods

high'-rise' *n.* a tall apartment house, office building, etc. of many stories

high'road' *n.* **1.** [Chiefly Brit.] a main road; highway **2.** an easy or direct way

high school a secondary school that includes grades 10, 11, and 12, and sometimes 9

high seas open ocean waters outside the territorial limits of any nation

high'-spir'it·ed *adj.* **1.** courageous **2.** lively; spirited —**high'-spir'it·ed·ly** *adv.*

high'-strung' *adj.* nervous and tense; excitable

high'-ten'sion *adj.* having or carrying a high voltage

high tide 1. the highest level to which the tide rises **2.** any culminating point or time

high time none too soon

high'way' *n.* **1.** a public road **2.** a main road

high'way·man (-mən) *n., pl.* **-men** one who robs travelers on a highway

hi-jack (hī'jak') *vt.* [Colloq.] **1.** to steal (goods in transit, etc.) by force **2.** to force (an aircraft) to fly to a nonscheduled landing point —**hi'jack'er** *n.*

hike (hīk) *vi.* **hiked, hik'ing** [< dial. *heik*] to take a long, vigorous walk; tramp —*vt.* [Colloq.] **1.** to pull up; hoist **2.** to raise (prices, etc.) —*n.* **1.** a long walk **2.** [Colloq.] a rise —**hik'er** *n.*

hi·lar·i·ous (hi ler'ē əs, hī-) *adj.* [< Gr. *hilaros,* cheerful] **1.** noisily merry **2.** very funny —**hi·lar'i·ty** (-ə tē) *n.*

hill (hil) *n.* [OE. *hyll*] **1.** a natural raised part of the earth's surface, smaller than a mountain **2.** a small heap or mound *[an anthill]* **3.** a mound of soil heaped around plant roots *[a hill* of beans]

hill'bil'ly *n., pl.* **-lies** [< nickname *Billy*] [Colloq.] one who lives in or comes from the mountains or backwoods, esp. of the South: somewhat contemptuous term

hill'ock (-ək) *n.* a small hill; mound

hill'side' *n.* the side of a hill

hill'top' *n.* the top of a hill

hill'y *adj.* **-i·er, -i·est 1.** full of hills **2.** like a hill; steep —**hill'i·ness** *n.*

hilt (hilt) *n.* [OE.] the handle of a sword, tool, etc. —**(up) to the hilt** entirely

him (him) *pron.* [OE.] *objective case of* HE

him·self' *pron.* **1.** *the intensive form of* HE *[he went himself]* **2.** *the reflexive form of* HE *[he hurt himself]* **3.** his true self *[he is not himself today]*

hind¹ (hīnd) *adj.* **hind'er, hind'most'** or **hind'er·most'** [prob. < HINDER²] back; rear; posterior

hind² (hīnd) *n.* [OE.] the female red deer

hin·der¹ (hin'dər) *vt.* [OE. *hindrian*] **1.** to keep back; restrain; stop **2.** to thwart

hind'er² (hīn'dər) *adj.* [OE., behind] rear

Hin·di (hin'dē) *n.* the main (and official) language of India

hind'most' *adj.* farthest back; last

hind'quar'ter *n.* the hind half of a side of veal, beef, lamb, etc.

hin·drance (hin'drəns) *n.* **1.** a hindering **2.** a person or thing that hinders; obstacle

hind'sight' *n.* ability to see, after the event, what should have been done

Hin·du (hin'dōō) *n.* **1.** any of several peoples of India **2.** a follower of Hinduism —*adj.* **1.** of the Hindus, their language, etc. **2.** of Hinduism

Hin·du·ism *n.* the religion and social system of the Hindus

hinge (hinj) *n.* [< ME. *hengen,* hang] 1. a joint on which a door, lid, etc. swings 2. a natural joint, as of the shell of a clam —*vt.* **hinged, hing'ing** to attach by a hinge —*vi.* to depend (*on*)

hint (hint) *n.* [< OE. *hentan,* seize] a slight indication; indirect allusion —*vt., vi.* to give a hint (of)

hin·ter·land (hin'tər land') *n.* [G.] 1. the land behind that bordering a coast or river 2. a remote area

hip¹ (hip) *n.* [OE. *hype*] the part of the body around the joint formed by each thighbone and the pelvis

hip² (hip) *adj.* **hip'per, hip'pest** [< ?] [Slang] 1. sophisticated; knowing 2. fashionable 3. of hippies —**get** (or **be**) **hip to** [Slang] to become (or be) informed about

hip·pie (hip'ē) *n.* [< HIP² + -IE] [Slang] a young person who, in his alienation from conventional society, has turned to mysticism, psychedelic drugs, communal living, etc.: also **hip'py,** *pl.* **-pies**

hip·po (hip'ō) *n., pl.* **-pos** [Colloq.] *same as* HIPPOPOTAMUS

Hip·po·crat·ic oath (hip'ə krat'ik) the oath, attributed to Hippocrates, ancient Greek physician, generally taken by medical graduates: it sets forth their ethical code

hip·po·drome (hip'ə drōm') *n.* [< Fr. < Gr. *hippos,* horse + *dromos,* a course] an arena for a circus, games, etc.

hip·po·pot·a·mus (hip'ə pät'ə məs) *n., pl.* **-mus·es, -mi'** (-mī') [< Gr. *hippos,* horse + *potamos,* river] a large, plant-eating mammal with a heavy, thick-skinned body: it lives in or near rivers in Africa

hire (hīr) *n.* [OE. *hyr*] 1. the amount paid in hiring 2. a hiring —*vt.* **hired, hir'ing** to pay for the services of (a person) or the use of (a thing) —**hire out** to work for payment

hire'ling *n.* one who will follow anyone's orders for pay; mercenary

hir·sute (hur'sōōt, hir'-) *adj.* [L. *hirsutus*] hairy; shaggy

his (hiz) *pron.* [OE.] that or those belonging to him [*his* are better] —*poss. pronominal adj.* of, belonging to, or done by him

hiss (his) *vi.* [echoic] 1. to make a sound like that of a prolonged *s* 2. to show disapproval by hissing —*vt.* to say or indicate by hissing —*n.* the act or sound of hissing

hist (st, hist) *interj.* be quiet!

his·ta·mine (his'tə mēn') *n.* [< Gr. *histos,* tissue + AMMONIA] an ammonia derivative released by tissues in allergic reactions

his·tol·o·gy (his täl'ə jē) *n.* [< Gr. *histos,* tissue + -LOGY] the branch of biology concerned with the microscopic study of the structure of tissues

his·to·ri·an (his tôr'ē ən) *n.* a writer of, or authority on, history

his·tor·ic (his tôr'ik) *adj.* 1. *same as* HISTORICAL 2. famous in history

his·tor·i·cal (-i k'l) *adj.* 1. of or concerned with history 2. based on people or events of the past 3. established by history; factual

his·to·ry (his'tə rē) *n., pl.* **-ries** [< Gr. *histōr,* learned] 1. an account of what has happened, esp. in the life of a people, country, etc. 2. all recorded past events 3. the branch of knowledge that deals with the recording, analysis, etc. of past events 4. a known past [*this* coat has a *history*]

his·tri·on·ic (his'trē än'ik) *adj.* [< L. *histrio,* actor] 1. of acting or actors 2. overacted or overacting —**his'tri·on'i·cal·ly** *adv.*

his'tri·on'ics *n.pl.* [*sometimes with sing. v.*] 1. dramatics 2. an artificial or affected manner or outburst

hit (hit) *vt., vi.* **hit, hit'ting** [< ON. *hitta,* meet with] 1. to come against (something) with force; bump; knock 2. to give a blow (to); strike 3. to strike with a missile 4. to affect strongly [a town hard *hit* by floods] 5. to come (*on* or *upon*) by accident or after a search 6. to arrive at [stocks *hit* a new high] 7. *Baseball* to get (a base hit) —*n.* 1. a blow that strikes its mark 2. a collision 3. a successful and popular song, play, etc. 4. *Baseball same as* BASE HIT —**hit it off** to get along well together —**hit or miss** in a haphazard way —**hit'ter** *n.*

hit'-and-run' *adj.* hitting with a vehicle and then fleeing: also **hit'-skip'**

hitch (hich) *vi.* [ME. *hicchen*] 1. to move jerkily 2. to become fastened or caught 3. [Slang] to hitchhike —*vt.* 1. to move, pull, etc. with jerks 2. to fasten with a hook, knot, etc. 3. [Slang] to hitchhike —*n.* 1. a tug; jerk 2. a limp 3. a hindrance; obstacle 4. a catching or fastening 5. [Slang] a period of time served, as of military service 6. *Naut.* a kind of knot that can be easily undone

hitch'hike' (-hīk') *vi.* **-hiked', -hik'ing** to travel by asking for rides from motorists along the way —**hitch'hik'er** *n.*

hith·er (hith'ər) *adv.* [OE. *hider*] to this place; here —*adj.* nearer

hith'er·to' *adv.* until this time

hit man [Slang] a hired murderer

hive (hīv) *n.* [OE. *hyf*] 1. a shelter for a colony of domestic bees; beehive 2. the bees of a hive 3. a crowd of busy people 4. a place of great activity —*vt.* **hived, hiv'ing** to gather (bees) into a hive —*vi.* to enter a hive

hives (hīvz) *n.* [orig. Scot. dial.] an allergic skin condition characterized by itching and smooth, raised patches

H.M.S. 1. His (or Her) Majesty's Service 2. His (or Her) Majesty's Ship

hoard (hôrd) *n.* [OE. *hord*] a supply stored up and hidden —*vt., vi.* to accumulate and store away (money, goods, etc.)

hoar·frost (hôr'frôst') *n.* white, frozen dew on the ground, leaves, etc.; rime

hoarse (hôrs) *adj.* **hoars'er, hoars'est** [OE. *has*] 1. harsh and grating in sound 2. having a rough, husky voice —**hoarse'ness** *n.*

hoar·y (hôr'ē) *adj.* **-i·er, -i·est** 1. white or gray 2. having white or gray hair from old age 3. very old Also **hoar**

hoax (hōks) *n.* [< ? HOCUS-POCUS] a trick or fraud; esp., a practical joke —*vt.* to deceive with a hoax

hob (häb) *n.* [< *Robin* or *Robert*] [Eng. Dial.] an elf or goblin —**play** (or **raise**) **hob with** to make trouble for

hob·ble (häb''l) *vi.* **-bled, -bling** [ME. *hobelen*] to go haltingly; limp —*vt.* 1. to cause to limp 2. to hamper the movement of (a horse, etc.) by tying two legs together 3. to hinder —*n.* 1. a limp 2. a rope, strap, etc. used to hobble a horse

hob·by (häb'ē) *n., pl.* **-bies** [ME. *hoby*] 1. *same as* HOBBYHORSE 2. something that a person likes to do in his spare time —**hob'by·ist** *n.*

hob'by·horse' *n.* 1. a child's toy consisting of a stick with a horse's head 2. a rocking horse

hob·gob·lin (häb'gäb'lin) *n.* [HOB² + GOBLIN] 1. an elf or goblin 2. a bugbear

hob·nail' *n.* [*hob,* a peg + NAIL] a broadheaded nail put on the soles of heavy shoes to

prevent wear or slipping —*vt.* to put hobnails on —**hob'nailed'** *adj.*
hob'nob' (-näb') *vi.* -nobbed', -nob'bing [< ME. *habben*, have + *nabben*, not have] to be on close terms (*with*)
ho·bo (hō'bō) *n., pl.* -bos, -boes 1. a migratory worker 2. a vagrant; tramp
hock[1] (häk) *n.* [OE. *hoh*, the heel] the joint bending backward in the hind leg of a horse, ox, etc.
hock[2] (häk) *vt., n.* [< Du. *hok*, prison, debt] [Slang] *same as* PAWN[1]
hock·ey (häk'ē) *n.* [prob. < OFr. *hoquet*, bent stick] 1. a team game played on ice skates with curved sticks and a rubber disk (*puck*) 2. a similar game played on foot on a field with a small ball
hock'shop' *n.* [Slang] a pawnshop
ho·cus-po·cus (hō'kəs pō'kəs) *n.* [imitation L.] 1. meaningless words used as a formula by conjurers 2. *same as* SLEIGHT OF HAND 3. trickery
hod (häd) *n.* [prob. < MDu. *hodde*] 1. a long-handled wooden trough used for carrying bricks, mortar, etc. on the shoulder 2. a coal scuttle
hodge-podge (häj'päj') *n.* [< OFr. *hochepot*, a stew] a jumbled mixture; mess
hoe (hō) *n.* [< OHG. *houwan*, hew] a tool with a thin blade set across the end of a long handle, for weeding, loosening soil, etc. —*vt., vi.* **hoed, hoe'ing** to dig, cultivate, weed, etc. with a hoe
hoe'cake' (-kāk') *n.* a thin bread made of cornmeal
hog (hôg, häg) *n.* [OE. *hogg*] 1. a pig, esp. a full-grown pig raised for its meat 2. [Colloq.] a selfish, greedy, or filthy person —*vt.* hogged, **hog'ging** [Slang] to take all or an unfair share of —**go (the) whole hog** [Slang] to go all the way —**high on (or off) the hog** [Colloq.] in a luxurious or costly way —**hog'gish** *adj.* —**hog'gish·ly** *adv.*
ho·gan (hō'gôn, -gän) *n.* [< AmInd.] a Navaho Indian dwelling built of earth walls supported by timbers
hogs·head (hôgz'hed', hägz'-) *n.* 1. a large barrel or cask holding from 63 to 140 gallons 2. a liquid measure, esp. one equal to 63 gallons
hog'tie' *vt.* -tied', -ty'ing or -tie'ing 1. to tie the four feet or the hands and feet of 2. [Colloq.] to make incapable of effective action
hog'wash' *n.* 1. refuse fed to hogs; swill 2. insincere talk, writing, etc.
hoi pol·loi (hoi' pə loi') [Gr., the many] the common people; the masses
hoist (hoist) *vt.* [< Du. *hijschen*] to raise aloft; lift, esp. with a pulley, crane, etc. —*n.* 1. a hoisting 2. an apparatus for lifting; elevator or tackle
hoke (hōk) *vt.* hoked, hok'ing [< HOKUM] [Slang] to treat in a too sentimental or crudely comic way: usually with *up* —*n. same as* HOKUM —**hok'ey** *adj.*
ho·kum (hōk'əm) *n.* [< HOCUS-POCUS] [Slang] 1. crudely comic or mawkishly sentimental elements in a story, play, etc. 2. nonsense; humbug
hold[1] (hōld) *vt.* held, hold'ing [OE. *haldan*] 1. to keep in the hands, arms, etc.; grasp 2. to keep in a certain position or condition 3. to restrain or control; keep back 4. to possess; occupy [to *hold* an office] 5. to guard; defend [*hold* the fort] 6. to carry on (a meeting, etc.) 7. to contain [the jar *holds* a pint] 8. to regard; consider [I *hold* the story to be true] —

vi. 1. to go on being firm, loyal, etc. 2. to remain unbroken or unyielding [the rope *held*] 3. to be true or valid [a rule which still *holds*] 4. to continue [the wind *held* steady] —*n.* 1. a grasping or seizing; grip 2. a thing to hold on by 3. a controlling force [to have a *hold* over someone] —**get (catch, lay, or take) hold of** to take, seize, acquire, etc. —**hold forth** 1. to preach; lecture 2. to offer —**hold out** 1. to last; endure 2. to stand firm 3. to offer 4. [Colloq.] to refuse to give (what is to be given) —**hold over** 1. to postpone 2. to keep or stay for an additional period —**hold up** 1. to prop up 2. to show 3. to last; endure 4. to stop; delay 5. to stop forcibly and rob —**hold'er** *n.*
hold[2] (hōld) *n.* [< HOLE or MDu. *hol*] 1. the interior of a ship below decks, in which cargo is carried 2. the compartment for cargo in an aircraft
hold'ing *n.* 1. land, esp. a farm, rented from another 2. [*usually pl.*] property owned, esp. stocks and bonds
hold'o'ver *n.* [Colloq.] one staying on from a previous period
hold'up' *n.* 1. a delay 2. the act of stopping forcibly and robbing
hole (hōl) *n.* [OE. *hol*] 1. a hollow place; cavity 2. an animal's burrow 3. a small, dingy, squalid place 4. an opening in anything; gap; tear; rent 5. *Golf a*) a small cup in a green, into which the ball drops *b*) the tee, fairway, etc. leading to this —**hole up** [Colloq.] 1. to hibernate, as in a hole 2. to shut oneself in —**in the hole** [Colloq.] financially embarrassed or behind
hol·i·day (häl'ə dā') *n.* 1. a religious festival; holy day 2. a day of freedom from labor, often one set aside by law to celebrate some event 3. [*often pl.*] [Chiefly Brit.] a vacation —*adj.* of or suited to a holiday; joyous; gay
ho·li·ness (hō'lē nis) *n.* 1. a being holy 2. [H-] a title of the Pope (with *His* or *Your*)
hol·lan·daise sauce (häl'ən dāz') [Fr., of Holland] a creamy sauce, as for vegetables, made of butter, egg yolks, lemon juice, etc.
hol·ler (häl'ər) *vi., vt., n.* [Colloq.] yell
hol·low (häl'ō) *adj.* [OE. *holh*] 1. having a cavity inside; not solid 2. shaped like a bowl; concave 3. sunken [*hollow* cheeks] 4. empty or worthless 5. hungry 6. deep-toned and muffled —*adv.* in a hollow manner —*n.* 1. a hollow place; cavity 2. a valley —*vt., vi.* to make or become hollow
hol·ly (häl'ē) *n., pl.* -lies [OE. *holegn*] an evergreen shrub with glossy leaves and red berries
hol·ly·hock (häl'ē häk') *n.* [< OE. *halig*, holy + *hoc*, mallow] a tall plant related to the mallow, with large, showy flowers
hol·o·caust (häl'ə kôst', hō'lə-) *n.* [< Gr. *holos*, whole + *kaustos*, burnt] great destruction of life, esp. by fire
hol·o·graph (häl'ə graf') *adj.* [< Fr. < Gr. *holos*, whole + *graphein*, write] written in the handwriting of the person under whose name it appears —*n.* a holograph document
Hol·stein (hōl'stēn, -stīn) *n.* [< Schleswig-*Holstein*, Germany] any of a breed of large, black-and-white dairy cattle
hol·ster (hōl'stər) *n.* [Du.] a pistol case, usually of leather and attached to a belt
ho·ly (hō'lē) *adj.* -li·er, -li·est [< OE. *hal*, sound, whole] 1. dedicated to religious use; sacred 2. spiritually pure; sinless 3. deserving deep respect or reverence
Holy Communion a Christian rite in which bread and wine are partaken of as (symbols of) the body and blood of Jesus

Holy Spirit 1. the spirit of God **2.** the third person of the Trinity: also **Holy Ghost**

hom·age (häm′ij, äm′-) *n.* [< L. *homo,* a man] anything given or done to show reverence, honor, etc.

hom·burg (häm′bərg) *n.* [< *Homburg,* Prussia] a man's felt hat with the crown dented front to back and a stiff, upturned brim

home (hōm) *n.* [OE. *ham*] **1.** the place where one lives **2.** the city, state, etc. where one was born or reared **3.** a household and its affairs **4.** an institution for orphans, the aged, etc. **5.** the natural environment of an animal, plant, etc. **6.** in many games, the goal; esp., home plate — *adj.* **1.** of one's home or country; domestic **2.** central *[the home office] —adv.* **1.** at, to, or in the direction of home **2.** to the point aimed at *[to drive a nail home]* **3.** to the heart of the matter **—at home 1.** in one's home **2.** at ease — **bring (something) home to** to impress upon — **home (in) on** to be directed as by radar to (a destination) **—home′less** *adj.* **—home′like′** *adj.*

home economics the science and art of homemaking, including nutrition, etc.

home′land′ *n.* the country in which one was born or makes one's home

home′ly *adj.* **-li·er, -li·est 1.** suitable for home life; simple or plain **2.** crude **3.** unattractive — **home′li·ness** *n.*

home′made′ *adj.* made, or as if made, at home

home′mak′er *n.* a person who manages a home; esp., a housewife **—home′mak′ing** *n.*

home plate *Baseball* the slab the batter stands beside, the last base in a run

home run *Baseball* a safe hit that allows the batter to touch all the bases and score a run: also [Colloq.] **hom′er** *n.*

home′sick′ *adj.* longing for home **—home′sick′ness** *n.*

home′spun′ *n.* **1.** cloth made of yarn spun at home **2.** coarse cloth like this **—adj. 1.** spun at home **2.** made of homespun **3.** plain; homely

home′stead′ (-sted′) *n.* **1.** the place of a family's home, including the land and buildings **2.** a 160-acre tract of U.S. public land, granted as a farm **—home′stead′er** *n.*

home′stretch′ *n.* the part of a race track between the last turn and the finish line

home′ward (-wərd) *adv., adj.* toward home: also **home′wards** *adv.*

home′work′ *n.* **1.** work done at home **2.** schoolwork to be done outside class **3.** study or research to get ready for some project or activity: usually in **do one's homework**

home′y (-ē) *adj.* **hom′i·er, hom′i·est** comfortable, familiar, cozy, etc. **—home′y·ness** *n.*

hom·i·cide (häm′ə sīd′, hō′mə-) *n.* [< L. *homo,* man + *caedere,* to kill] **1.** the killing of one person by another **2.** a person who kills another **—hom′i·ci′dal** *adj.*

hom·i·let·ics (häm′ə let′iks) *n.pl.* [with sing. v.] [see HOMILY] the art of writing and preaching sermons **—hom′i·let′ic** *adj.*

hom·i·ly (häm′ə lē) *n., pl.* **-lies** [< Gr. *homilos,* assembly] **1.** a sermon **2.** a solemn, moralizing talk or writing

homing pigeon a pigeon trained to find its way home from distant places

hom·i·ny (häm′ə nē) *n.* [< AmInd.] dry corn hulled and coarsely ground: it is boiled for food

homo- [< Gr. *homos*] *a combining form meaning* same, equal, like

ho·mo·ge·ne·ous (hō′mə jē′nē əs, häm′ə-; -jēn′yəs) *adj.* [< Gr. *homos,* same + *genos,* kind] **1.** similar or identical in structure, quality, etc. **2.** composed of similar or identical parts **—ho′mo·ge·ne′i·ty** (-jə nē′ə tē) *n.*

ho·mog·e·nize (hə mäj′ə nīz′) *vt.* **-nized′, -niz′ing 1.** to make homogeneous **2.** to make more uniform throughout; specif., to process (milk) so that fat particles are so well emulsified that the cream does not separate **—ho·mog′e·ni·za′tion** *n.*

hom·o·graph (häm′ə graf′, hō′mə-) *n.* [HOMO- + -GRAPH] a word with the same spelling as another but with a different meaning and origin

ho·mol·o·gous (hō mäl′ə gəs) *adj.* [< Gr. *homos,* same + *legein,* to say] matching in structure, position, origin, etc.

hom·o·nym (häm′ə nim) *n.* [< Fr. < Gr. *homos,* same + *onyma,* a name] a word with the same pronunciation as another but with a different meaning, origin, and, usually, spelling (Ex.: *bore* and *boar*)

Ho·mo sa·pi·ens (hō′mō sā′pē enz′) [ModL. *homo,* man + *sapiens,* prp. of *sapere,* know] modern man; mankind; human being

ho·mo·sex·u·al (hō′mə sek′shoo wəl) *adj.* of or having sexual desire for those of one's own sex **—n.** a homosexual person **—ho′mo·sex′u·al′i·ty** *n.*

hom·y (hō′mē) *adj.* **-i·er, -i·est** *alt. sp. of* HOMEY **—hom′i·ness** *n.*

Hon., hon. 1. honorable **2.** honorary

hone (hōn) *n.* [< OE. *han,* a stone] a hard stone used to sharpen cutting tools **—vt.** **honed, hon′ing** to sharpen as with a hone

hon·est (än′əst) *adj.* [< L. *honor,* honor] **1.** trustworthy; truthful **2.** *a)* showing fairness and sincerity *b)* gained by fair methods **3.** genuine **4.** frank and open **—hon′est·ly** *adv.* — **hon′es·ty** *n.*

hon·ey (hun′ē) *n., pl.* **-eys** [OE. *hunig*] **1.** a sweet, syrupy substance that bees make as food from the nectar of flowers **2.** sweetness **3.** darling **4.** [Colloq.] something excellent

hon′ey·bee′ (-bē′) *n.* a bee that makes honey

hon′ey·comb′ (-kōm′) *n.* **1.** the structure of six-sided wax cells made by bees to hold their honey, eggs, etc. **2.** anything like this **—vt.** to fill with holes like a honeycomb

hon′ey·dew′ melon (-doo′) a melon with a smooth, whitish rind and sweet, green flesh

hon·eyed (hun′ēd) *adj.* **1.** sweetened with honey **2.** flattering *[honeyed words]*

hon′ey·moon′ *n.* the vacation spent together by a newly married couple **—vi.** to have or spend a honeymoon

hon′ey·suck′le (-suk′'l) *n.* any of a group of plants with small, fragrant flowers of red, yellow, or white

honk (hôŋk, häŋk) *n.* [echoic] **1.** the call of a wild goose **2.** a similar sound, as of an automobile horn **—vi., vt.** to make or cause to make such a sound

hon·ky-tonk (hôŋ′kē tôŋk′, häŋ′kē täŋk′) *n.* [< ?] [Slang] a cheap, noisy nightclub

hon·or (än′ər) *n.* [L.] **1.** high regard or respect; esp., *a)* glory; fame *b)* good reputation **2.** adherence to principles considered right; integrity **3.** chastity **4.** high rank; distinction **5.** [H-] a title of certain officials, as judges (with *His, Her,* or *Your*) **6.** something done or given as a token of respect **7.** a source of respect and fame **—vt. 1.** to respect greatly **2.** to show high regard for **3.** to do something in honor of **4.** to accept as good for payment, credit, etc. *[to honor credit cards]* **—do the honors** to act as host or hostess Brit. sp. **honour**

hon′or·a·ble *adj.* **1.** worthy of honor **2.** honest;

upright **3.** bringing honor *[honorable* mention*]* —**hon′or·a·bly** *adv.*

hon·o·ra·ri·um (än′ə rer′ē əm) *n., pl.* **-ri·ums,** **-ri·a** (-ə) [L.] a payment for professional services on which no fee is set

hon·or·ar·y (än′ə rer′ē) *adj.* **1.** given as an honor only *[an honorary degree]* **2.** designating or in an office held as an honor only, without service or pay

hon·or·if·ic (än′ə rif′ik) *adj.* [< L. *honor* + *facere,* to make] conferring honor; showing respect *[an honorific title]* —*n.* such a title, word, etc.

hood (hood) *n.* [OE. *hod*] **1.** a covering for the head and neck, often part of a cloak **2.** anything like a hood, as the metal cover over an automobile engine —*vt.* to cover as with a hood —**hood′ed** *adj.*

-hood [< OE. *had,* order, rank] *a suffix meaning:* **1.** state or quality *[childhood]* **2.** the whole group of *[priesthood]*

hood·lum (hood′ləm) *n.* [prob. < G. dial. *hudilump,* wretch] a wild, lawless person

hoo·doo (hoo′doo) *n., pl.* **-doos** [var. of VOODOO] **1.** *same as* VOODOO **2.** [Colloq.] bad luck or its cause

hood·wink (hood′wiŋk′) *vt.* [HOOD + WINK] **1.** orig., to blindfold **2.** to deceive; dupe

hoo·ey (hoo′ē) *Interj., n.* [echoic] [Slang] nonsense

hoof (hoof, hoof) *n., pl.* **hoofs, hooves** [OE. *hof*] the horny covering on the feet of cattle, horses, etc., or the entire foot —*vt., vi.* [Colloq.] to walk —**hoofed** *adj.*

hook (hook) *n.* [OE. *hoc*] **1.** a bent piece as of metal, used to catch, hold, or pull something **2.** something hooklike in shape **3.** the path of a hit ball that curves away to the left from a right-handed player or to the right from a left-handed player **4.** *Boxing* a short blow delivered with the arm bent —*vt.* **1.** to catch, fasten, strike, etc. with a hook **2.** to hit (a ball) in a hook —*vi.* **1.** to curve as a hook does **2.** to be fastened or caught by a hook —**by hook or by crook** by any means, honest or dishonest —**hook up** to connect, as a radio —**off the hook** [Colloq.] out of trouble —**on one's own hook** [Colloq.] by oneself; without help

hook·ah, hook·a (hook′ə) *n.* [Ar. *huqqah*] an Oriental tobacco pipe with a long tube by means of which the smoke is drawn through water so as to be cooled

hooked *adj.* **1.** like, having, or made by a hook **2.** [Slang] *a)* addicted (often with *on*) *b)* married

hook′er *n.* [Slang] a prostitute

hook′up′ *n.* **1.** the arrangement and connection of parts, circuits, etc., as in (a) radio **2.** [Colloq.] a connection or alliance

hook′worm′ *n.* a small, parasitic roundworm with hooks around the mouth, infesting the small intestine

hoo·li·gan (hoo′li gən) *n.* [< ? *Hooligan,* family name] [Slang] a hoodlum

hoop (hoop) *n.* [OE. *hop*] **1.** a circular band to hold barrel staves together **2.** anything similarly shaped, as a ring in a hoop skirt

hoop·la (hoop′lä) *n.* [< ?] [Colloq.] **1.** great excitement **2.** showy publicity

hoop skirt a skirt worn over a framework of hoops to make it spread out

hoo·ray (hoo rā′, hoo-) *Interj., n., vi.* hurrah

hoose·gow, hoos·gow (hoos′gou) *n.* [< Sp. *juzgado,* a court] [Slang] a jail

Hoo·sier (hoo′zhər) *n.* [Colloq.] a native or inhabitant of Indiana

hoot (hoot) *vi.* [echoic] **1.** to utter its characteristic hollow sound: said of an owl **2.** to make a sound like this **3.** to cry out, as in scorn —*vt.* to express (scorn) of (someone) by hooting —*n.* **1.** the cry of an owl **2.** any similar sound, as a shout of scorn

hop¹ (häp) *vi.* **hopped, hop′ping** [OE. *hoppian*] **1.** to make a short leap or leaps on one foot **2.** to leap on both or all feet, as a bird or frog does **3.** [Colloq.] to move quickly or in bounces —*vt.* **1.** to jump over **2.** to jump onto —*n.* **1.** a hopping **2.** [Colloq.] *a)* a dance *b)* a short flight in an airplane

hop² (häp) *n.* [< MDu. *hoppe*] **1.** a twining vine with cone-shaped flowers **2.** [*pl.*] the dried cones, used as for flavoring beer —**hop up** [Slang] **1.** to stimulate as with drugs **2.** to supercharge (an engine)

hope (hōp) *n.* [OE. *hopa*] **1.** a feeling that what is wanted will happen **2.** the object of this **3.** a reason for hope **4.** one on which hope may be based —*vt.* **hoped, hop′ing** to want and expect —*vi.* to have hope (*for*)

hope′ful *adj.* hoping or giving hope —*n.* one hoping or likely to succeed

hope′ful·ly *adv.* **1.** in a hopeful way **2.** it is to be hoped (that): regarded by some as a loose usage

hope′less *adj.* **1.** devoid of hope **2.** impossible to solve, deal with, etc.

hop·per (häp′ər) *n.* **1.** one that hops **2.** a box, tank, etc. allowing slow, even emptying

hop·sack·ing (häp′sak′iŋ) *n.* [lit., sacking for hops] **1.** a coarse material for bags **2.** a fabric somewhat like this, used as for suits Also **hop′sack′**

hop·scotch (häp′skäch′) *n.* [HOP¹ + *scotch,* line] a children's game, each player hopping to successive sections of a figure traced on the ground

horde (hôrd) *n.* [Fr., ult. < Tatar *urdu,* a camp] a large, swarming crowd; throng

hore·hound (hôr′hound′) *n.* [< OE. *har,* white + *hune,* horehound] **1.** a white-leaved, bitter plant related to the mint **2.** cough medicine or candy made from the juice of the leaves

ho·ri·zon (hə rī′z'n) *n.* [< Gr. *horos,* boundary] **1.** the line where the sky seems to meet the earth **2.** [*usually pl.*] one's limit as of experience

hor·i·zon·tal (hôr′ə zän′t'l) *adj.* **1.** parallel to the plane of the horizon **2.** flat and even; level —**hor′i·zon′tal·ly** *adv.*

hor·mone (hôr′mōn) *n.* [< Gr. *hormē,* impulse] a substance formed in a bodily organ and influencing another organ or tissue to which it is carried —**hor·mo′nal** *adj.*

horn (hôrn) *n.* [OE.] **1.** a hard, bony projection growing on the head of certain hoofed animals **2.** anything suggestive of this **3.** the substance horns are made of **4.** any brass-wind instrument or, *Jazz,* any wind instrument **5.** a signaling device with a sound like that of a horn —*adj.* made of horn —**horn in (on)** [Colloq.] to intrude or meddle (in) —**horned** *adj.* —**horn′less** *adj.*

hor·net (hôr′nit) *n.* [OE. *hyrnet*] any of several large, yellow-and-black wasps

horn of plenty *same as* CORNUCOPIA

horn′pipe′ *n.* **1.** a lively dance formerly popular with sailors **2.** music for this

horn′y *adj.* **-i·er, -i·est 1.** of or like horn **2.** having horns **3.** toughened and calloused **4.** [Slang] sexually aroused

ho·rol·o·gy (hô räl′ə jē) *n.* [< Gr. *hōra,* hour + -LOGY] the science or art of measuring time or making timepieces

hor·o·scope (hôr′ə skōp′, här′-) *n.* [Fr. < Gr.

hōra, hour + *skopein,* to view] a zodiacal chart by which astrologers profess to tell a person's future

hor·ren·dous (hô ren′dəs, hə-) *adj.* [see HORROR] horrible; frightful

hor·ri·ble (hôr′ə b'l, här′-) *adj.* [see HORROR] 1. causing horror; dreadful 2. [Colloq.] very bad —**hor′ri·bly** *adv.*

hor·rid (hôr′id, här′-) *adj.* 1. horrible; revolting 2. very bad —**hor′rid·ly** *adv.*

hor·ri·fy (hôr′ə fī′, här′-) *vt.* -**fied′,** -**fy′ing** 1. to cause to feel horror 2. [Colloq.] to shock greatly

hor·ror (hôr′ər, här′-) *n.* [< L. *horrere,* to bristle] 1. the strong feeling caused by something frightful or shocking 2. strong dislike 3. something causing horror

hors d'oeu·vre (ôr′ durv′, duv′), *pl.* **hors′ d'oeuvres′** (dŭrvz′, duvz′) [Fr., lit., outside of work] an appetizer, as a canapé, served before a meal

horse (hôrs) *n.* [OE. *hors*] 1. a large, four-legged, solid-hoofed animal with flowing mane and tail, domesticated for drawing loads, carrying riders, etc. 2. a supporting frame with legs —*vt.* **horsed, hors′ing** to supply with a horse or horses; put on horseback —**horse around** [Slang] to engage in horseplay —**on one's high horse** [Colloq.] arrogant

horse′back′ *n.* a horse's back —*adv.* on horseback

horse chestnut 1. a flowering tree with glossy brown seeds 2. one of the seeds

horse′fly′ *n., pl.* -**flies′** a large fly that sucks the blood of horses, cattle, etc.

horse′hair′ *n.* 1. hair, or a hair, from the mane or tail of a horse 2. a stiff fabric of such hair

horse′hide′ *n.* 1. the hide of a horse 2. leather made from this

horse′laugh′ *n.* a loud, coarse laugh

horse′man (-mən) *n., pl.* -**men** a man skilled in the riding or care of horses

horse′play′ *n.* rough, boisterous fun

horse′pow′er *n.* a unit for measuring the power of motors or engines, equal to 746 watts or to a rate of 33,000 foot-pounds per minute

horse′rad′ish *n.* 1. a plant of the mustard family, with a pungent, white root 2. a relish made by grating this root

horse sense [Colloq.] common sense

horse′shoe′ *n.* 1. a flat, U-shaped, protective metal plate nailed to a horse's hoof 2. anything shaped like this 3. [*pl.*] a game in which horseshoes are tossed at a stake

horse′whip′ *n.* a whip for driving horses —*vt.* -**whipped′,** -**whip′ping** to lash with a horsewhip

hors·y (hôr′sē) *adj.* -**i·er,** -**i·est** 1. of or like a horse 2. of or like people fond of horses, horse racing, etc. Also **hors′ey**

hor·ta·to·ry (hôr′tə tôr′ē) *adj.* [< L. *hortari,* incite] exhorting: also **hor′ta·tive**

hor·ti·cul·ture (hôr′tə kul′chər) *n.* [< L. *hortus,* a garden + *cultura,* culture] the art or science of growing flowers, fruits, etc. —**hor′ti·cul′tur·ist** *n.*

ho·san·na (hō zan′ə) *n., interj.* [< Heb. *hōshī′āh nnā,* save, we pray] an exclamation of praise to God

hose (hōz) *n., pl.* **hose;** for 2, usually **hos′es** [OE. *hosa*] 1. [*pl.*] stockings or socks 2. a flexible tube to convey fluid, esp. water from a hydrant —*vt.* **hosed, hos′ing** to water or drench with a hose

ho·sier·y (hō′zhər ē) *n.* stockings and socks

hos·pice (häs′pis) *n.* [Fr. < L. *hospes,* host, guest] a place of shelter for travelers

hos·pi·ta·ble (häs′pi tə b'l, häs pit′ə-) *adj.* [see prec.] friendly and solicitous toward guests —**hos′pi·ta·bly** *adv.*

hos·pi·tal (häs′pi t'l) *n.* [see HOSPICE] an institution for the treatment and care of the ill or injured

hos·pi·tal·i·ty (häs′pə tal′ə tē) *n., pl.* -**ties** the act, practice, or quality of being hospitable

hos·pi·tal·ize (häs′pi t'l īz′) *vt.* -**ized′,** -**iz′ing** to put in a hospital —**hos′pi·tal·i·za′tion** *n.*

host[1] (hōst) *n.* [< L. *hostia,* sacrifice] a wafer of the Eucharist; esp., [H-] a consecrated wafer

host[2] (hōst) *n.* [see HOSPICE] 1. *a*) a man entertaining guests in his own home or at his own expense *b*) *Radio & TV* the key personality conducting a show that typically features informal talk 2. a man who keeps an inn or hotel 3. any organism on or in which another (called a *parasite*) lives —*vi., vt.* to act as host (to)

host[3] (hōst) *n.* [< L. *hostis,* army] 1. an army 2. a multitude; great number

hos·tage (häs′tij) *n.* [< OFr.] a person kept or given as a pledge for the fulfillment of certain terms

hos·tel (häs′t'l) *n.* [see HOSPICE] a lodging place; inn: also **hos′tel·ry** (-rē), *pl.* -**ries**

host·ess (hōs′tis) *n.* 1. a woman entertaining guests in her own home or at her own expense; often, a host's wife 2. a stewardess, as on an airplane 3. a woman employed in a restaurant to supervise waitresses, seating, etc.

hos·tile (häs′t'l) *adj.* [< L. *hostis,* enemy] 1. of or characteristic of an enemy 2. unfriendly; antagonistic —**hos′tile·ly** *adv.*

hos·til·i·ty (häs til′ə tē) *n., pl.* -**ties** 1. a feeling of enmity, ill will, etc. 2. *a*) a hostile act *b*) [*pl.*] acts of war; warfare

hos·tler (häs′lər, äs′-) *n.* [contr. of *hosteler,* innkeeper] one who takes care of horses as at an inn

hot (hät) *adj.* **hot′ter, hot′test** [OE. *hat*] 1. of a high temperature 2. producing a burning sensation [*hot pepper*] 3. full of intense feeling or activity, as *a*) excitable [*a hot temper*] *b*) violent or angry [*a hot battle, hot words*] *c*) lustful *d*) controversial 4. following closely [*hot pursuit*] 5. *a*) electrically charged [*a hot wire*] *b*) highly radioactive 6. [Colloq.] *a*) recent; fresh [*hot news*] *b*) very popular [*a hot recording*] 7. [Slang] *a*) recently stolen or smuggled *b*) sought by the police 8. [Slang] good, funny, etc. —*adv.* in a hot manner —**make it hot for** [Colloq.] to make things uncomfortable for —**hot′ly** *adv.* —**hot′ness** *n.*

hot air [Slang] empty or pretentious talk

hot′bed′ *n.* 1. a bed of earth covered with glass and kept warm to make plants grow faster 2. any place that fosters rapid growth or much activity

hot′-blood′ed *adj.* fiery, reckless, etc.

hot cake a pancake —**sell like hot cakes** [Colloq.] to be sold rapidly

hot dog [Colloq.] a frankfurter or wiener, esp. one served in a soft roll

ho·tel (hō tel′) *n.* [< Fr.: see HOSPICE] an establishment providing lodging and often meals, as for travelers

hot′head′ed *adj.* 1. easily angered 2. impetuous —**hot′head′** *n.*

hot′house′ *n.* same as GREENHOUSE

hot line a telephone or telegraph line for immediate communication in a crisis

hot pepper any of various pungent peppers

hot plate a small gas or electric stove for cooking

hot rod [Slang] **1.** an old automobile with a supercharged engine **2.** its driver

hot'-tem'pered *adj.* easily angered

Hot·ten·tot (hät''n tät') *n.* **1.** a member of a nomadic people of SW Africa **2.** their language

hound (hound) *n.* [OE. *hund*] a dog; specif., any of several breeds of hunting dog —*vt.* **1.** to hunt or chase as with hounds **2.** to urge on

hour (our) *n.* [< Gr. *hōra*] **1.** one of the twenty-four equal parts of a day; sixty minutes **2.** the time, or one of the periods of time, during which something is done *[the dinner hour]* **3.** the time of day *[the hour is 2:30]* **4.** *Educ.* a credit, equal to each hour spent in class per week

hour'glass' *n.* an invertible device measuring time by the flow as of sand from an upper glass bulb to a lower bulb through a narrow interconnecting neck

hou·ri (hoor'ē, hou'rē) *n., pl.* -ris [< Ar.] a nymph of the Muslim paradise

hour·ly (our'lē) *adj., adv.* of, at, for, or throughout each hour or any hour

house (hous) *n., pl.* **hous·es** (hou'ziz) [OE. *hus*] **1.** a building to live in; specif., a building occupied by one family or person **2.** the people who live in a house; household **3.** a family, including kin, ancestors, and descendants **4.** a building or other shelter for storing things **5.** *a)* a theater *b)* the audience in it **6.** a business firm **7.** [*often* H-] a legislative assembly —*vt.* (houz) **housed, hous'ing 1.** to provide a house or lodging for **2.** to store, shelter, etc. —**keep house** to take care of the affairs of a home; run a house —**on the house** at the expense of the establishment

house'boat' *n.* a large, flat-bottomed boat used as a residence

house'break' *vt.* -broke', -bro'ken, -break'ing to train (a dog, cat, etc.) to void in the proper place —**house'bro'ken** *adj.*

house'break'ing *n.* a breaking into another's house as to commit theft

house'clean'ing *n.* a cleaning of the inside of a house —**house'clean'** *vi., vt.*

house'fly' *n., pl.* -flies' a two-winged fly found in and about houses

house'hold' *n.* **1.** all those living in one house **2.** the home and its affairs

house'hold·er *n.* **1.** one who owns or maintains a house **2.** the head of a household

house'keep·er *n.* one who manages a home, esp. a woman hired to do so —**house'keep'ing** *n.*

house'maid' *n.* a maid to do housework

house'moth'er *n.* a woman in charge of a sorority house, dormitory, etc., often as housekeeper

House of Commons the lower branch of the legislature of Great Britain or Canada

House of Lords the upper branch of the legislature of Great Britain

House of Representatives the lower branch of the U.S. legislature or of most States of the U.S.

house'top' *n.* the top of a house; roof

house'wares' *n.pl.* articles for household use, esp. in the kitchen

house'warm'ing *n.* a party given for or by someone moving into a new home

house'wife' *n., pl.* -wives' a married woman whose principal occupation is her household

house'work' *n.* the work involved in housekeeping, as cleaning or cooking

hous·ing (hou'ziŋ) *n.* **1.** the providing of shelter or lodging **2.** shelter or lodging **3.** houses collectively **4.** an enclosing frame, box, etc.

hove (hōv) *alt. pt. & pp. of* HEAVE

hov·el (huv''l, häv'-) *n.* [ME.] a small, miserable dwelling; hut

hov·er (huv'ər, häv'-) *vi.* [ME. *hoveren*] **1.** to stay suspended or flutter in the air near one place **2.** to linger close by **3.** to waver —*n.* a hovering

how (hou) *adv.* [OE. *hu*] **1.** in what manner or way **2.** in what state or condition **3.** for what reason **4.** to what effect **5.** to what extent, degree, etc. **6.** at what price **7.** [Colloq.] what? Also used as an intensive —*n.* the way of doing

how·be·it (hou bē'it) *adv.* [Archaic] however it may be; nevertheless

how·dah (hou'də) *n.* [< Hindi < Ar. *haudaj*] a canopied seat for riding on the back of an elephant or camel

how·ev·er (hou ev'ər) *adv.* **1.** in whatever way **2.** to whatever degree or extent **3.** nevertheless

how·itz·er (hou'it sər) *n.* [< Czech *haufnice*, a sling] a short cannon with a high trajectory

howl (houl) *vi.* [ME. *houlen*] **1.** to utter the long, wailing cry of wolves, dogs, etc. **2.** to utter a similar cry of pain, anger, grief, etc. **3.** to shout or laugh in scorn, mirth, etc. —*vt.* **1.** to utter with a howl **2.** to drive or effect by howling —*n.* **1.** a howling **2.** [Colloq.] something hilarious

howl'er *n.* **1.** one that howls **2.** [Colloq.] a ludicrous blunder

howl'ing *adj.* **1.** that howls **2.** [Slang] great *[a howling* success]

how·so·ev·er (hou'sō ev'ər) *adv.* **1.** to whatever degree or extent **2.** in whatever way

hoy·den (hoid''n) *n.* [< ?] a bold, boisterous girl

Hoyle (hoil) *n.* a book of rules for card games, orig. compiled by E. Hoyle (1672–1769) — **according to Hoyle** according to the rules and regulations

HP, H.P., hp, h.p. horsepower

HQ, H.Q., hq, h.q. headquarters

hr. *pl.* **hrs.** hour(s)

H.R. House of Representatives

H.R.H. His (or Her) Royal Highness

H.S., h.s. high school

ht. 1. heat **2.** *pl.* **hts.** height

hua·ra·ches (hə rä'chēz, wə rä'ches) *n.pl.* [MexSp.] flat sandals with straps or woven strips for uppers

hub (hub) *n.* [< ?] **1.** the wheel part attached to or turning on an axle **2.** a center, as of activity

hub·bub (hub'ub') *n.* [< ?] an uproar

hu·bris (hyoo'bris) *n.* [Gr. *hybris*] arrogance; insolence

huck·le·ber·ry (huk''l ber'ē) *n., pl.* -ries [< ?] **1.** a shrub of the heath family, with dark-blue berries **2.** this berry

huck·ster (huk'stər) *n.* [< MDu.] **1.** a peddler **2.** an aggressive merchant —*vt.* to peddle or sell

HUD (Department of) Housing and Urban Development

hud·dle (hud''l) *vi., vt.* -dled, -dling [< ?] **1.** to crowd close together **2.** to draw (oneself) up, as from cold **3.** [Slang] to confer privately **4.** *Football* to gather in a huddle —*n.* **1.** a confused crowd or heap **2.** [Slang] a private conference **3.** *Football* a grouping to get signals before a play

hue' (hyoo) *n.* [OE. *heow*] **1.** color **2.** a certain shade or tint of color

hue² (hyoo) *n.* [< OFr.] a shouting: now only in **hue and cry**, clamor

huff (huf) *vt.* [prob. echoic] to offend or anger —*vi.* to blow; puff —*n.* a condition of smoldering anger or resentment

huff′y *adj.* -**i**-**er**, -**i**-**est** **1.** easily offended; touchy **2.** piqued; ruffled

hug (hug) *vt.* **hugged**, **hug′ging** [prob. < ON. *hugga*, to comfort] **1.** to put the arms around and hold closely, esp. affectionately **2.** to cling to (a belief, opinion, etc.) **3.** to keep close to *[the bus hugged the curb]* —*vi.* to embrace —*n.* an embrace

huge (hyo͞oj, yo͞oj) *adj.* [OFr. *ahuge*] very large; immense —**huge′ly** *adv.* —**huge′ness** *n.*

Hu·gue·not (hyo͞o′gə nät′) *n.* a French Protestant of the 16th or 17th century

huh (hu, hun) *interj.* an exclamation used to express contempt, surprise, etc. or to ask a question

hu·la (ho͞o′lə) *n.* [Haw.] a native Hawaiian dance: also **hu′la-hu′la**

hulk (hulk) *n.* [OE. *hulc*] **1.** the body of a ship, esp. if dismantled **2.** a deserted wreck **3.** a big, clumsy person or thing

hulk′ing *adj.* big and heavy

hull (hul) *n.* [OE. *hulu*] **1.** *a)* an outer covering, specif. that of a seed or fruit, as a husk, pod, or nutshell *b)* the calyx as of a strawberry **2.** the frame or main body as of a ship —*vt.* to take the hulls off (nuts, etc.)

hul·la·ba·loo (hul′ə bə lo͞o′) *n.* [echoic] hubbub; uproar

hum (hum) *vi.* **hummed**, **hum′ming** [echoic] **1.** to make a low, continuous, murmuring sound **2.** to sing with closed lips **3.** [Colloq.] to be full of activity —*vt.* to sing (a tune) with closed lips —*n.* a continuous murmur

hu·man (hyo͞o′mən, yo͞o′) *adj.* [< L. *humanus*] of or characteristic of people or mankind —*n.* a person: also **human being**

hu·mane (hyo͞o mān′, yo͞o-) *adj.* [see prec.] **1.** kind, sympathetic, merciful, etc. **2.** civilizing; refining —**hu·mane′ly** *adv.*

hu·man·ism (hyo͞o′mə niz′m, yo͞o′-) *n.* **1.** any system of thought based on the interests and ideals of man **2.** [H-] the intellectual movement that stemmed from the study of Greek and Latin classics during the Middle Ages — **hu′man·ist** *n., adj.*

hu·man·i·tar·i·an (hyo͞o man′ə ter′ē ən, yo͞o-) *n.* one devoted to promoting human welfare; philanthropist —*adj.* philanthropic —**hu·man′i·tar′i·an·ism** *n.*

hu·man·i·ty (hyo͞o man′ə tē, yo͞o-) *n., pl.* -**ties** **1.** the fact or quality of being human or humane **2.** the human race —**the humanities** branches of learning other than the sciences, as literature, art, etc.

hu·man·ize (hyo͞o′mə nīz′, yo͞o′-) *vt., vi.* -**ized′**, -**iz′ing** to make or become human or humane —**hu′man·i·za′tion** *n.*

hu′man·kind′ *n.* the human race

hu′man·oid′ (-oid′) *adj.* nearly human —*n.* a nearly human creature

hum·ble (hum′b′l, um′-) *adj.* -**bler**, -**blest** [< L. *humilis*, low] **1.** having or showing awareness of one's defects; not proud; not self-assertive **2.** low in condition or rank; lowly —*vt.* -**bled**, -**bling** **1.** to lower in condition or rank **2.** to lessen or obliterate the pride of; make humble —**hum′bly** *adv.*

hum·bug (hum′bug′) *n.* [< ?] **1.** *a)* fraud; sham *b)* misleading or empty talk **2.** an impostor **3.** a spirit of trickery —*vt.* -**bugged′**, -**bug′-ging** to dupe; deceive —*interj.* nonsense!

hum·ding·er (hum′diŋ′ər) *n.* [Slang] a person or thing considered excellent

hum·drum (hum′drum′) *adj.* [echoic] monotonous; boring; dull

hu·mer·us (hyo͞o′mər əs) *n., pl.* -**mer·i′** (-ī′) [L.] the bone of the upper arm or forelimb, ex-tending from the shoulder to the elbow —**hu′-mer·al** *adj.*

hu·mid (hyo͞o′mid, yo͞o′-) *adj.* [< Fr. < L. *umere*, be moist] full of water vapor; damp

hu·mid′i·fy′ ‹(-ə fī′) *vt.* -**fied′**, -**fy′ing** to make humid —**hu·mid′i·fi′er** *n.*

hu·mid′i·ty (-tē) *n., pl.* -**ties** humid condition; specif., the amount of water vapor in the air

hu·mi·dor (hyo͞o′mə dôr′) *n.* a jar, case, etc., as for tobacco, designed to keep the contents moist

hu·mil·i·ate (hyo͞o mil′ē āt′) *vt.* -**at′ed**, -**at′ing** [< L. *humilis*, low] to hurt the pride or dignity of by making seem foolish or contemptible; mortify —**hu·mil′i·a′tion** *n.*

hu·mil′i·ty (-ə tē) *n.* the state or quality of being humble

hum·ming·bird (hum′iŋ burd′) *n.* a very small, brightly colored bird that feeds on nectar and has narrow wings that vibrate rapidly, often with a humming sound

hum·mock (hum′ək) *n.* [< ?] **1.** a low hill; knoll **2.** a ridge in a field of ice

hu·mor (hyo͞o′mər, yo͞o′-) *n.* [< L. *umor*, fluid, from former belief that four body fluids controlled one's disposition] **1.** mood; state of mind **2.** whim; caprice **3.** the quality of being funny **4.** *a)* ability to appreciate or express what is funny *b)* expression in speech or action of what is funny **5.** a bodily fluid, as lymph —*vt.* to comply with the mood or whim of Brit. sp. **humour** —**out of humor** not in a good mood

hu′mor·ist *n.* a person skilled in expressing what is funny

hu′mor·ous *adj.* amusing; funny

hump (hump) *n.* [prob. < LowG. *humpe*, thick piece] **1.** a rounded, protruding lump, as on a camel's back **2.** a hummock —*vt.* to hunch; arch

hump′back′ *n.* **1.** a humped, deformed back **2.** a person having a humped back

hu·mus (hyo͞o′məs) *n.* [L., earth] the brown or black organic part of the soil, resulting from the partial decay of plant and animal matter

Hun (hun) *n.* a member of a warlike Asiatic people who invaded Europe in the 4th and 5th centuries A.D.

hunch (hunch) *vt.* [< ?] to arch into a hump —*vi.* **1.** to move along jerkily **2.** to sit or stand with the back arched —*n.* **1.** a hump **2.** a chunk **3.** [Colloq.] a feeling that something is going to happen

hunch′back′ *n.* a humpback

hun·dred (hun′drid, -dərd) *adj., n.* [OE.] ten times ten; 100; C —**hun′dredth** (-dridth) *adj., n.*

hun′dred·fold′ *adj., adv., n.* a hundred times as much or as many

hun′dred·weight′ *n.* a unit of weight equal to 100 pounds in the U.S. and to 112 pounds in England

hung (huŋ) *pt. & pp.* of HANG —**hung over** [Slang] having an alcoholic hangover —**hung up (on)** [Slang] emotionally disturbed, frustrated, or obsessed (by)

Hung. 1. Hungarian **2.** Hungary

Hun·gar·i·an (huŋ ger′ē ən) *adj.* of Hungary, its people, etc. —*n.* **1.** a native of Hungary **2.** the language of the Hungarians

hun·ger (huŋ′gər) *n.* [OE. *hungor*] **1.** discomfort caused by a need for food **2.** starvation **3.** a need or appetite for food **4.** any strong desire —*vi.* **1.** to be hungry **2.** to crave —**hun′-gri·ly** *adv.* —**hun′gry** *adj.* -**gri·er**, -**gri·est**

hun·ker (huŋ′kər) *vi.* [prob. < ON. *hokra*, to creep] to settle down on one's haunches; squat

hunt (hunt) *vt., vi.* [OE. *huntian*] **1.** to kill or catch (game) for food or sport **2.** to search for; seek **3.** to pursue *—n.* **1.** a hunting **2.** a group of people who hunt together **3.** a search — **hunt′er, hunts′man** *n.*

hur·dle (hur′d'l) *n.* [OE. *hyrdel*] **1.** a framelike barrier for runners or horses to jump over in a race **2.** an obstacle *—vt.* **-dled, -dling 1.** to jump over **2.** to overcome (an obstacle) **—hur′dler** *n.*

hur·dy-gur·dy (hur′dē gur′dē) *n., pl.* **-gur′dies** [prob. echoic] *same as* BARREL ORGAN

hurl (hurl) *vt.* [prob. < ON.] **1.** to throw hard **2.** to cast down **3.** to utter vehemently *—vi.* [Colloq.] *Baseball* to pitch *—n.* a hard throw — **hurl′er** *n.*

hurl·y-burl·y (hur′lē bur′lē) *n., pl.* **-burl′ies** uproar; turmoil

hur·rah (hə rô′, -rä′) *interj., n.* [echoic] a shout of joy, approval, etc. *—vi.* to shout "hurrah" Also **hur·ray′** (-rā′)

hur·ri·cane (hur′ə kān′) *n.* [< WInd. *huracan*] a violent tropical cyclone

hur·ry (hur′ē) *vt.* **-ried, -ry·ing** [prob. akin to HURL] **1.** to move or send with haste **2.** to cause to occur or be done more rapidly or too rapidly **3.** to urge to act soon or too soon *—vi.* to move or act with haste *—n.* **1.** rush; haste **2.** eagerness to do, go, etc.

hurt (hurt) *vt.* **hurt, hurt′ing** [< OFr. *hurter*, to hit] **1.** to cause pain or injury to **2.** to harm **3.** to offend *—vi.* **1.** to cause pain, injury, etc. **2.** to have pain *—n.* **1.** a pain or injury **2.** harm or damage

hurt′ful *adj.* causing hurt; harmful

hur·tle (hur′t'l) *vi., vt.* **-tled, -tling** [ME. *hurtlen*] to move or throw with great speed or force

hus·band (huz′bənd) *n.* [< ON. *hūs*, house + *bondi*, freeholder] a married man *—vt.* to manage thriftily

hus′band·man (-mən) *n., pl.* **-men** [Archaic] a farmer

hus′band·ry *n.* **1.** thrifty care **2.** farming

hush (hush) *vt., vi.* [ME. *huscht*, quiet] **1.** to make or become quiet **2.** to calm *—n.* quiet; silence *—interj.* silence!

hush puppy [South] a cornmeal fritter

husk (husk) *n.* [prob. < MDu. *huus*, house] **1.** the dry outer covering of various fruits or seeds, as of corn **2.** any dry or useless covering *—vt.* to remove the husk from

hus·ky [1] (hus′kē) *n., pl.* **-kies** [< ? ESKIMO] [*sometimes* H-] a hardy dog used for pulling sleds in the Arctic

husk·y [2] (hus′kē) *adj.* **-i·er, -i·est 1.** dry in the throat; hoarse **2.** big and strong; robust — **husk′i·ly** *adv.***—husk′i·ness** *n.*

hus·sar (hŏŏ zär′) *n.* [< Serb. *husar*] a European light-armed cavalryman, brilliantly uniformed

hus·sy (huz′ē, hus′ē) *n., pl.* **-sies** [ME. *huswife*, housewife] **1.** a woman of low morals **2.** a bold, saucy girl

hus·tle (hus′'l) *vt.* **-tled, -tling** [< MDu. *hutsen*, to shake] **1.** to jostle **2.** to force in a rough, hurried manner *—vi.* **1.** to move hurriedly **2.** [Colloq.] to work energetically **3.** [Slang] to obtain money aggressively or immorally *—n.* **1.** a hustling **2.** [Colloq.] energetic action **—hus′-tler** *n.*

hut (hut) *n.* [< OHG. *hutta*] a crude little house or cabin

hutch (huch) *n.* [< ML. *hutica*, chest] **1.** a chest **2.** a china cabinet with open shelves on top **3.** a coop for small animals **4.** a hut

hy·a·cinth (hī′ə sinth′) *n.* [< Gr. *hyakinthos*] a plant related to the lily, with spikes of bell-shaped flowers

hy·brid (hī′brid) *n.* [L. *hybrida*] **1.** the offspring of two animals or plants of different species, varieties, etc. **2.** anything of mixed origin *—adj.* of or like a hybrid

hy′brid·ize′ (-brə dīz′) *vi., vt.* **-ized′, -iz′ing** to produce or cause to produce hybrids

hy·dran·ge·a (hī drān′jə, -dran′-; -jē ə) *n.* [< HYDRO- + Gr. *angeion*, vessel] a shrub with large, showy clusters of white, blue, or pink flowers

hy·drant (hī′drənt) *n.* [< Gr. *hydōr*, water] a large discharge pipe with a valve for drawing water from a water main; fireplug

hy·drate (hī′drāt) *n.* [HYDR(O)- + -ATE [1]] a chemical compound of water and another substance *—vt., vi.* **-drat·ed, -drat·ing** to combine with water

hy·drau·lic (hī drô′lik) *adj.* [< Gr. *hydōr*, water + *aulos*, tube] **1.** of hydraulics **2.** operated by the movement and force of liquid, as a brake **—hy·drau′li·cal·ly** *adv.*

hy·drau′lics *n.pl.* [*with sing. v.*] the science dealing with the mechanical properties of liquids, as water, and their application in engineering

hydro- [< Gr. *hydōr*, water] *a combining form meaning:* **1.** water [*hydrofoil*] **2.** hydrogen [*hydrocarbon*]

hy·dro·car·bon (hī′drə kär′bən) *n.* any compound containing only hydrogen and carbon

hy′dro·chlo′ric acid (-klôr′ik) a strong, highly corrosive acid that is a solution of the gas hydrogen chloride in water

hy′dro·e·lec′tric *adj.* producing, or relating to the production of, electricity by water power

hy·dro·foil (hī′drə foil′) *n.* [HYDRO- + (AIR)FOIL] **1.** a winglike structure that lifts and carries a watercraft just above the water at high speed **2.** such a watercraft

hy·dro·gen (hī′drə jən) *n.* [< Fr.: see HYDRO- & -GEN] a flammable, colorless, odorless gaseous chemical element, the lightest known substance; symbol, H

hy·dro·gen·ate (hī′drə jə nāt′, hī drāj′ə-) *vt.* **-at′ed, -at′ing** to combine or treat with hydrogen, as in producing a solid fat

hydrogen bomb an extremely destructive atom bomb in which atoms of hydrogen are fused by explosion of a nuclear-fission unit in the bomb

hydrogen peroxide an unstable liquid used as a bleach or disinfectant

hy·drol·y·sis (hī dräl′ə sis) *n., pl.* **-ses′** (-sēz′) [HYDRO- + -LYSIS] a chemical reaction in which a compound reacts with the ions of water to produce a weak acid, a weak base, or both

hy·drom·e·ter (hī dräm′ə tər) *n.* [HYDRO- + -METER] an instrument for determining the specific gravity of liquids

hy·dro·pho·bi·a (hī′drə fō′bē ə) *n.* [see HYDRO- & -PHOBIA] **1.** abnormal fear of water **2.** [from the symptomatic inability to swallow liquids] *same as* RABIES

hy·dro·plane (hī′drə plān′) *n.* [HYDRO- + PLANE [1]] **1.** a small, high-speed motorboat with hydrofoils or a flat bottom **2.** *same as* SEA-PLANE

hy·dro·pon·ics (hī′drə pän′iks) *n.pl.* [*with sing. v.*] [< HYDRO- + Gr. *ponos*, labor + -ICS] the science of growing plants in liquid mineral solutions

hy′dro·ther′a·py (-ther′ə pē) *n.* the treatment of disease, etc., esp. in physical therapy, by the use of water

hy·drous (hī′drəs) *adj.* [< HYDR(O)- + -OUS] containing water, as certain chemical compounds

hy·drox·ide (hī dräk′sīd) *n.* [< HYDR(O)- + OXIDE] a compound consisting of an element or radical combined with the radical OH

hy·e·na (hī ē′nə) *n.* [< Gr. *hys,* a hog] a wolflike, flesh-eating animal of Africa and Asia, with a shrill cry

hy·giene (hī′jēn) *n.* [< Fr. < Gr. *hygiēs,* healthy] **1.** a system of principles for preserving health **2.** sanitary practices; cleanliness —**hy·gi·en·ic** (hī′jē en′ik, -jē′nik, -jen′-) *adj.* —**hy′gi·en′i·cal·ly** *adv.*

hy·gi·en·ist (hī′jē ə nist, -jē nist; hī jē′nist) *n.* a specialist in hygiene

Hy·men (hī′mən) *Gr. Myth.* the god of marriage —*n.* [h-] [Poet.] **1.** marriage **2.** a wedding song

hy·men (hī′mən) *n.* [Gr. *hymēn,* membrane] the thin mucous membrane that usually closes part of the opening of the vagina in a virgin

hy·me·ne·al (hī′mə nē′əl) *adj.* [see HYMEN] of marriage —*n.* [Poet.] a wedding song

hymn (him) *n.* [< Gr. *hymnos*] a song of praise, esp. in honor of God —*vt.* to express or praise in a hymn

hym′nal (-nəl) *n.* a collection of religious hymns: also **hymn′book′** —*adj.* of hymns

hype (hīp) *n.* [Slang] **1.** a drug addict **2.** deception —*vt.* hyped, hyp′ing [Slang] **1.** to stimulate, as by drug injection: usually with *up* **2.** to promote in a sensational way

hyper- [Gr. *hyper,* over] *a prefix meaning* over, above, excessive *[hypercritical]*

hy·per·bo·la (hī pur′bə lə) *n., pl.* -las, -lae′ (-lē′) [< Gr. *hyper-,* over + *ballein,* to throw] a curve formed by the section of a cone cut by a plane more steeply inclined to the base than to the side of the cone

hy·per′bo·le (-bə lē) *n.* [L. < Gr.: see prec.] exaggeration for effect, not to be taken literally —**hy·per·bol·ic** (hī′pər bäl′ik) *adj.*

hy·per·crit·i·cal (hī′pər krit′i k'l) *adj.* too critical

hy·per·sen·si·tive (hī′pər sen′sə tiv) *adj.* excessively sensitive —**hy′per·sen′si·tiv′i·ty** *n.*

hy·per·ten·sion (hī′pər ten′shən) *n.* abnormally high blood pressure

hy·per·thy·roid·ism (hī′pər thī′roid iz′m) *n.* excessive activity of the thyroid gland, causing nervousness, rapid pulse, etc. —**hy′per·thy′roid** *adj., n.*

hy·per·tro·phy (hī pur′trə fē) *n.* [< HYPER- + Gr. *trophein,* nourish] an abnormal increase in the size of an organ or tissue —*vi., vt.* -phied, -phy·ing to undergo or cause to undergo hypertrophy

hy·phen (hī′f'n) *n.* [< Gr. *hypo-,* under + *hen,* one] a mark (-) used between the parts of a compound word or the syllables of a divided word, as at the end of a line —*vt. same as* HYPHENATE

hy′phen·ate′ (-āt′) *vt.* -at′ed, -at′ing to connect or write with a hyphen

hyp·no·sis (hip nō′sis) *n., pl.* -ses (-sēz) [< Gr. *hypnos,* sleep + -OSIS] a sleeplike condition artificially induced, in which the subject responds to the suggestions of the hypnotist

hyp·not·ic (hip nät′ik) *adj.* **1.** causing sleep; soporific **2.** of, like, or inducing hypnosis **3.** easily hypnotized —*n.* any agent causing sleep —**hyp·not′i·cal·ly** *adv.*

hyp·no·tism (hip′nə tiz′m) *n.* the act or practice of inducing hypnosis —**hyp′no·tist** *n.*

hyp′no·tize′ (-tīz′) *vt.* -tized′, -tiz′ing to induce hypnosis in

hypo- [Gr. *hypo,* under] *a prefix meaning:* **1.** under, beneath *[hypodermic]* **2.** less than, deficient in *[hypothyroid]*

hy·po·chon·dri·a (hī′pə kän′drē ə) *n.* [LL., pl., abdomen (supposed seat of this condition)] abnormal anxiety over one's health, often with imaginary illnesses

hy′po·chon′dri·ac′ (-ak′) *n.* [< Fr.] a person who has hypochondria

hy·poc·ri·sy (hi päk′rə sē) *n., pl.* -sies [< Gr. *hypokrisis,* acting a part] a pretending to be what one is not, or to feel what one does not; esp., a pretense of virtue, etc.

hyp·o·crite (hip′ə krit) *n.* [see prec.] one who pretends to be pious, virtuous, etc. without really being so —**hyp′o·crit′i·cal** *adj.* —**hyp′o·crit′i·cal·ly** *adv.*

hy·po·der·mic (hī′pə dur′mik) *adj.* [< HYPO- + Gr. *derma,* skin] injected under the skin —*n. same as:* **1.** HYPODERMIC INJECTION **2.** HYPODERMIC SYRINGE

hypodermic injection the injection of a medicine or drug under the skin

hypodermic syringe a syringe attached to a hollow needle (**hypodermic needle**), used for giving hypodermic injections

hy·pot·e·nuse (hī pät′'n ōōs′, -yōōs′) *n.* [< Gr. *hypo-,* under + *teinein,* stretch] the side of a right-angled triangle opposite the right angle: also **hy·poth′e·nuse′** (-päth′-)

hy·poth·e·sis (hī päth′ə sis, hi-) *n., pl.* -ses′ (-sēz′) [Gr. < *hypo-,* under + *tithenai,* to place] an unproved theory, etc. tentatively accepted to explain certain facts —**hy·poth′e·size′** (-sīz′) *vi., vt.* -sized′, -siz′ing

hy·po·thet·i·cal (hī′pə thet′i k'l) *adj.* based on a hypothesis; assumed; supposed: also **hy′po·thet′ic** —**hy′po·thet′i·cal·ly** *adv.*

hy·po·thy·roid·ism (hī′pō thī′roid iz′m) *n.* deficient activity of the thyroid gland, causing sluggishness, puffiness, etc. —**hy′po·thy′roid** *adj., n.*

hys·sop (his′əp) *n.* [< Heb. *ēzōbh*] a fragrant, blue-flowered plant related to the mint

hys·ter·ec·to·my (his′tə rek′tə mē) *n., pl.* -mies [< Gr. *hystera,* uterus + -ECTOMY] surgical removal of all or part of the uterus

hys·te·ri·a (his tir′ē ə, -ter′-) *n.* [< Gr. *hystera,* uterus: orig. attributed to disturbances of the uterus] **1.** a psychiatric condition characterized by excitability, anxiety, the simulation of organic disorders, etc. **2.** any outbreak of wild, uncontrolled behavior: also **hys·ter′ics** (-ter′iks) —**hys·ter′i·cal** (-ter′-), **hys·ter′ic** *adj.*

I

I, i (ī) *n., pl.* **I's, i's** the ninth letter of the English alphabet
I¹ (ī) *n.* **1.** a Roman numeral for 1 **2.** *Chem.* iodine
I² (ī) *pron., for pl. see* WE [OE. *ic*] the person speaking or writing
I., i. 1. island(s) **2.** isle(s)
-ial [L. *-ialis*] *same as* -AL
i·amb (ī'amb, -am) *n.* [< Fr. < Gr. *iambos*] a metrical foot of two syllables, the first unaccented and the other accented
i·am·bic (ī am'bik) *adj.* of or made up of iambs —*n.* **1.** an iamb **2.** an iambic verse
-iatrics [< Gr. *iatros*, physician] *a combining form meaning* treatment of disease [pediatrics]
-iatry [< Gr. *iatreia*, healing] *a combining form meaning* medical treatment [psychiatry]
i·bex (ī'beks) *n., pl.* **i'bex·es, i·bi·ces** (ib'ə sēz', ī'bə-) [L.] a wild goat of Europe, Asia, or Africa: the male has large, backward-curved horns
ibid. [L. *ibidem*] in the same place, i.e., the book, page, etc. just cited
i·bis (ī'bis) *n.* [< Egypt. *hīb*] a large wading bird related to the heron
-ible [L. *-ibilis*] *same as* -ABLE [legible]
-ic [< Gr. *-ikos*] *a suffix meaning:* **1.** *a)* of, having to do with [volcanic] *b)* like [angelic] *c)* produced by [photographic] *d)* consisting of [alcoholic] **2.** a person or thing *a)* having [paraplegic] *b)* supporting [Socratic] *c)* producing [hypnotic] Also **-ical**
ICBM intercontinental ballistic missile
ICC, I.C.C. Interstate Commerce Commission
ice (īs) *n.* [OE. *is*] **1.** water frozen solid by cold **2.** a frozen dessert of fruit juice, sugar, etc. **3.** [Slang] diamonds —*vt.* **iced, ic'ing 1.** to change into ice; freeze **2.** to cool with ice **3.** to cover with icing —*vi.* to freeze (often with *up* or *over*) —**break the ice** to make a start, as in getting acquainted —**cut no ice** [Colloq.] to have no effect
Ice. 1. Iceland **2.** Icelandic
ice age *same as* GLACIAL EPOCH
ice'berg' (-bʉrg') *n.* [prob. < Du. *ijsberg*, lit., ice mountain] a great mass of ice broken off from a glacier and floating in the sea
ice'boat' *n.* **1.** a light, often triangular frame, equipped with runners and driven over ice as by a sail **2.** an icebreaker
ice'bound' *adj.* **1.** held fast by ice, as a boat **2.** made inaccessible by ice, as a port
ice'box' *n.* a cabinet with ice in it for keeping foods, etc. cold; also, any refrigerator
ice'break'er *n.* a sturdy boat for breaking a channel through ice
ice'cap' *n.* a mass of glacial ice that spreads slowly out from a center
ice cream a sweet, frozen food made from flavored cream or milk —**ice'-cream'** *adj.*
ice floe a piece, large or small, of floating sea ice
Ice·lan·dic (īs lan'dik) *adj.* of Iceland, its people, etc. —*n.* the Germanic language of the Icelanders
ice·man (īs'man', -mən) *n., pl.* **-men'** a person who sells or delivers ice
ice skate *see* SKATE¹ (sense 1) —**ice'skate'** *vi.* **-skat'ed, -skat'ing**
ich·thy·ol·o·gy (ik'thē äl'ə jē) *n.* [< Gr.

ichthys, a fish + -LOGY] the branch of zoology dealing with fishes —**ich'thy·ol'o·gist** *n.*
i·ci·cle (ī'si k'l) *n.* [< OE. *is*, ice + *gicel*, piece of ice] a hanging piece of ice, formed by the freezing of dripping water
ic·ing (ī'siŋ) *n.* a mixture, as of sugar, butter, flavoring, etc., as for covering a cake; frosting
ick·y (ik'ē) *adj.* **-i·er, -i·est** [< STICKY] [Slang] **1.** too sticky or sweet **2.** distasteful
i·con (ī'kän) *n.* [< Gr. *eikōn*, image] **1.** an image; figure **2.** *Orthodox Eastern Ch.* a sacred image or picture of Jesus, Mary, etc.
i·con·o·clast (ī kän'ə klast') *n.* [< LGr. *eikōn*, image + *klaein*, to break] one who attacks venerated institutions or ideas —**i·con'o·clasm** *n.* —**i·con'o·clas'tic** *adj.*
-ics [see -IC] *a suffix meaning* art, science, study [physics, economics]
i·cy (ī'sē) *adj.* **i'ci·er, i'ci·est 1.** full of or covered with ice **2.** of ice **3.** like ice; slippery or very cold **4.** cold in manner; unfriendly —**i'ci·ly** *adv.* —**i'ci·ness** *n.*
id (id) *n.* [L., it] *Psychoanalysis* that part of the psyche which is the source of the instinctual drives
ID, I.D. identification
I'd (īd) **1.** I had **2.** I would **3.** I should
i·de·a (ī dē'ə) *n.* [< Gr. *idea*, appearance of a thing] **1.** a thought; mental conception or image **2.** an opinion or belief **3.** a plan or scheme **4.** a vague impression
i·de·al (ī dē'əl, ī dēl') *adj.* [see prec.] **1.** existing as an idea, model, etc. **2.** thought of as perfect **3.** existing only in the mind; imaginary **4.** of idealism —*n.* **1.** a conception of something in its most excellent form **2.** a perfect model **3.** a principle
i·de·al·ism *n.* **1.** behavior or thought based on a conception of things as one thinks they should be **2.** a striving to achieve one's ideals **3.** *Philos.* any theory which holds that the objects of perception are actually ideas of the perceiving mind —**i·de·al·ist** *n.* —**i·de·al·is'tic** *adj.* —**i·de·al·is'ti·cal·ly** *adv.*
i·de·al·ize (ī dē'ə līz') *vt.* **-ized', -iz'ing** to regard or show as perfect or more nearly perfect than is true —**i·de·al·i·za'tion** *n.*
i·de·al·ly *adv.* **1.** in an ideal manner; perfectly **2.** in theory
i·den·ti·cal (ī den'ti k'l) *adj.* [< L. *idem*, the same] **1.** the very same **2.** exactly alike —**i·den'ti·cal·ly** *adv.*
i·den·ti·fi·ca·tion (ī den'tə fi kā'shən) *n.* **1.** an identifying or being identified **2.** anything by which a person or thing can be identified
i·den·ti·fy (ī den'tə fī') *vt.* **-fied', -fy'ing 1.** to make identical; treat as the same **2.** to fix the identity of **3.** to associate closely —*vi.* to share another's feelings; sympathize (*with*) —**i·den'ti·fi'a·ble** *adj.*
i·den·ti·ty (-tē) *n., pl.* **-ties 1.** the state or fact of being the same **2.** *a)* the state or fact of being a specific person or thing; individuality *b)* the state of being as described
id·e·ol·o·gy (ī'dē äl'ə jē, id'ē-) *n., pl.* **-gies** [Fr. < Gr. *idea*, idea + *logos*, word] the doctrines, opinions, or way of thinking of an individual, class, etc. —**i'de·o·log'i·cal** (-ə läj'i k'l) *adj.*
ides (īdz) *n.pl.* [often with sing. v.] [Fr. < L.

idus] in the ancient Roman calendar, the 15th day of March, May, July, or October, or the 13th of the other months

id·i·o·cy (id′ē ə sē) *n.* 1. great foolishness or stupidity 2. *pl.* **-cies** an idiotic act or remark

id·i·om (id′ē əm) *n.* [< Fr. < Gr. *idios,* one's own] 1. the dialect of a people, region, etc. 2. the usual way in which words of a language are joined together to express thought 3. an accepted phrase or expression having a meaning different from the literal 4. a characteristic style

id·i·o·mat·ic (id′ē ə mat′ik) *adj.* 1. characteristic of a particular language 2. using idioms — **id′i·o·mat′i·cal·ly** *adv.*

id·i·o·syn·cra·sy (id′ē ə siŋ′krə sē) *n., pl.* **-sies** [< Gr. *idio-,* one's own + *synkrasis,* a mixture] any personal peculiarity, mannerism, etc. —**id′i·o·syn·crat′ic** (-sin krat′ik) *adj.*

id·i·ot (id′ē ət) *n.* [< Gr. *idiōtēs,* ignorant person] 1. a person having severe mental retardation: an obsolescent term 2. a very foolish or stupid person

id·i·ot·ic (id′ē ät′ik) *adj.* very foolish or stupid

i·dle (ī′d'l) *adj.* **i′dler, i′dlest** [OE. *idel,* empty] 1. worthless; futile 2. unfounded *[idle* rumors] 3. *a)* unemployed *b)* not in use 4. lazy —*vi.* **i′dled, i′dling** 1. to move slowly or aimlessly 2. to be unemployed or inactive 3. to operate without transmitting power, esp. with disengaged gears —*vt.* 1. to squander 2. to cause (a motor, etc.) to idle 3. to make inactive —**i′dle·ness** *n.* —**i′dler** *n.* —**i′dly** *adv.*

i·dol (ī′d'l) *n.* [< Gr. *eidōlon,* an image] 1. an image of a god, used as an object of worship 2. an object of excessive devotion or admiration

i·dol·a·try (ī däl′ə trē) *n., pl.* **-tries** 1. worship of idols 2. excessive devotion or reverence — **i·dol′a·ter** *n.* —**i·dol′a·trous** *adj.* —**i·dol′a·trous·ly** *adv.*

i·dol·ize (ī′d'l īz′) *vt.* **-ized′, -iz′ing** 1. to make an idol of 2. to love or admire excessively — **i′dol·i·za′tion** *n.*

i·dyll, i·dyl (ī′d'l) *n.* [< Gr. *eidos,* a form] 1. a short poem or prose work describing a simple, pleasant scene of rural or pastoral life 2. a scene or incident suitable for such a work — **i·dyl·lic** (ī dil′ik) *adj.*

-ie [earlier form of -Y¹] *a suffix meaning:* 1. small, little *[lassie]* 2. one that is as specified *[softie]*

i.e. [L. *id est]* that is (to say)

-ier [< L. *-arius] a suffix meaning* a person concerned with (a specified action or thing) *[bombardier]*

if (if) *conj.* [OE. *gif]* 1. on condition that; in case that *[if* I come, I'll see him] 2. granting that *[if* he was there, I didn't see him] 3. whether *[ask* him *if* he knows her] —**as if** as it would be if

if·fy (if′ē) *adj.* [Colloq.] doubtful

ig·loo (ig′lōo) *n., pl.* **-loos** [Esk. *igdlu]* an Eskimo house or hut, usually dome-shaped and built of blocks of packed snow

ig·ne·ous (ig′nē əs) *adj.* [< L. *ignis,* a fire] 1. of fire 2. produced by volcanic action or intense heat *[igneous* rock]

ig·nite (ig nīt′) *vt., vi.* **-nit′ed, -nit′ing** [< L. *ignis,* a fire] to start burning —**ig·nit′a·ble, ig·nit′i·ble** *adj.*

ig·ni·tion (ig nish′ən) *n.* 1. an igniting or means of igniting 2. the system for igniting the explosive mixture in the cylinder of an internal-combustion engine

ig·no·ble (ig nō′b'l) *adj.* [< L. *in-,* not + *(g)nobilis,* known] not noble; base; mean

ig·no·min·i·ous (ig′nə min′ē əs) *adj.* 1.

shameful; disgraceful 2. despicable 3. degrading —**ig′no·min′i·ous·ly** *adv.*

ig·no·min·y (ig′nə min′ē) *n., pl.* **-ies** [< Fr. < L. *in-,* without + *nomen,* name] loss of reputation; shame; disgrace

ig·no·ra·mus (ig′nə rā′məs, -ram′əs) *n., pl.* **-mus·es** an ignorant person

ig·no·rance (ig′nər əns) *n.* a being ignorant; lack of knowledge

ig′no·rant *adj.* [see IGNORE] 1. lacking knowledge or experience 2. caused by or showing lack of knowledge 3. unaware *(of)* —**ig′no·rant·ly** *adv.*

ig·nore (ig nôr′) *vt.* **-nored′, -nor′ing** [< Fr. < L. *in-,* not + *gnarus,* knowing] to disregard deliberately; pay no attention to

i·gua·na (i gwä′nə) *n.* [Sp. < SAmInd. *iuana]* a large, harmless, tropical American lizard

il- *same as:* 1. IN-¹ 2. IN-² Used before *l*

Il·i·ad (il′ē əd) [< Gr. *Ilios,* Troy] a long Greek epic poem, ascribed to Homer, about the final part of the Trojan War

-ility *pl.* **-ilities** *a suffix used in nouns formed from adjectives ending in* -ile, -il

ilk (ilk) *n.* [< OE. *ilca,* same] kind; sort; class: only in **of that** (or **his, her,** etc.) **ilk**

ill (il) *adj.* worse, worst [< ON. *illr]* 1. bad *[ill* repute, *ill* will, an *ill* omen] 2. not healthy; sick —*n.* anything causing harm, pain, etc.; evil —*adv.* worse, worst 1. badly 2. scarcely —**ill at ease** uneasy

I'll (īl) 1. I shall 2. I will

ill′-bred′ *adj.* badly brought up; rude

il·le·gal (i lē′gəl) *adj.* not lawful; against the law —**il·le·gal·i·ty** (il′ē gal′ə tē) *n., pl.* **-ties** —**il·le′gal·ly** *adv.*

il·leg·i·ble (i lej′ə b'l) *adj.* difficult or impossible to read because badly written or printed, faded, etc. —**il·leg′i·bil′i·ty** *n.* —**il·leg′i·bly** *adv.*

il·le·git·i·mate (il′ə jit′ə mit) *adj.* 1. born of parents not married to each other 2. not lawful 3. unsanctioned —**il′le·git′i·ma·cy** (-mə sē) *n.* —**il′le·git′i·mate·ly** *adv.*

ill′-fat′ed *adj.* 1. having or sure to have an evil fate or unlucky end 2. unlucky

ill′-fa′vored *adj.* ugly or unpleasant

ill′-got′ten *adj.* obtained by evil, unlawful, or dishonest means *[ill-gotten* gains]

ill humor a disagreeable, cross, or sullen mood —**ill′-hu′mored** *adj.*

il·lib·er·al (i lib′ər əl) *adj.* 1. narrow-minded 2. miserly

il·lic·it (i lis′it) *adj.* not allowed by law, custom, etc.; unlawful —**il·lic′it·ly** *adv.*

il·lim·it·a·ble (i lim′it ə b'l) *adj.* without limit or bounds —**il·lim′it·a·bly** *adv.*

il·lit·er·ate (i lit′ər it) *adj.* uneducated; esp., not knowing how to read or write —*n.* an illiterate person —**il·lit′er·a·cy** (-ə sē) *n.*

ill′-man′nered *adj.* rude; impolite

ill nature an unpleasant, disagreeable disposition —**ill′-na′tured** *adj.*

ill′ness *n.* the condition of being ill; sickness

il·log·i·cal (i läj′i k'l) *adj.* not logical or reasonable —**il·log′i·cal·ly** *adv.*

ill′-starred′ *adj.* unlucky; doomed

ill′-tem′pered *adj.* sullen; irritable

ill′-timed′ *adj.* inopportune

ill′-treat′ *vt.* to treat unkindly, cruelly, or unfairly; abuse —**ill′-treat′ment** *n.*

il·lu·mi·nate (i lōo′mə nāt′) *vt.* **-nat′ed, -nat′ing** [< L. *in-,* in + *luminare,* to light] 1. to give light to; light up 2. *a)* to make clear; explain *b)* to inform 3. to decorate with lights Also **il·lu′mine, -mined, -min·ing**

il·lu′mi·na′tion *n.* 1. an illuminating 2. the intensity of light per unit of area

illus., illust. illustration

ill·us·age (il′yoo̅′sij, -zij) *n.* unfair, unkind, or cruel treatment; abuse: also **ill usage**

ill′-use′ (-yoo̅z′) *vt.* -used′, -us′ing to subject to ill-usage —*n.* (-yoo̅s′) *same as* ILL-USAGE

il·lu·sion (i loo̅′zhən) *n.* [< L. *illudere*, to mock] 1. a false idea or conception 2. an unreal or misleading appearance or image —**il·lu′-so·ry** (-sər ē), **il·lu′sive** (-siv) *adj.*

il·lus·trate (il′ə strāt, i lus′trāt) *vt.* -trat′ed, -trat′ing [< L. *in-*, in + *lustrare*, illuminate] 1. to make clear or explain, as by examples or comparisons 2. to furnish (books, etc.) with explanatory or decorative pictures, etc. —**il′lus·tra′tor** *n.*

il′lus·tra′tion *n.* 1. an illustrating or being illustrated 2. an explanatory example, story, etc. 3. an explanatory or decorative picture, diagram, etc.

il·lus·tra·tive (i lus′trə tiv) *adj.* serving to illustrate —**il·lus′tra·tive·ly** *adv.*

il·lus·tri·ous (i lus′trē əs) *adj.* [< L. *illustris*, bright] very distinguished; famous

ill will hostility; hate; dislike

I′m (īm) I am

im- *same as:* 1. IN-¹ 2. IN-² Used before *b, m,* and *p*

im·age (im′ij) *n.* [< L. *imago*] 1. a representation of a person or thing; esp., a statue 2. the visual impression of something in a lens, mirror, etc. 3. a copy; likeness 4. a mental picture; idea 5. a figure of speech —*vt.* -aged, -ag·ing 1. to portray; delineate 2. to reflect 3. to imagine

im′age·ry (-rē) *n., pl.* -ries 1. mental images 2. descriptions and figures of speech

i·mag·i·na·ble (i maj′ə nə b′l) *adj.* that can be imagined —**i·mag′i·na·bly** *adv.*

i·mag′i·nar′y (-ner′ē) *adj.* existing only in the imagination; unreal

i·mag′i·na′tion (-nā′shən) *n.* 1. *a)* the act or power of forming mental images of what is not present *b)* the act or power of creating new ideas by combining previous experiences 2. responsiveness to the creations of others 3. resourcefulness

i·mag′i·na·tive (-nə tiv) *adj.* 1. having, using, or showing imagination 2. of or resulting from imagination

i·mag·ine (i maj′in) *vt., vi.* -ined, -in·ing [< L. *imago*, image] 1. to make a mental image (of); conceive in the mind 2. to suppose; think

im·be·cile (im′bə s′l) *n.* [< Fr. < L. *imbecilis*, feeble] 1. an adult mentally equal to a child between three and eight: an obsolescent term 2. a foolish or stupid person —*adj.* foolish or stupid: also **im′be·cil′ic** (-sil′ik) —**im′be·cil′i·ty** *n.*

im·bed (im bed′) *vt. same as* EMBED

im·bibe (im bīb′) *vt.* -bibed′, -bib′ing [< L. *in-*, in + *bibere*, drink] 1. to drink (esp. alcoholic liquor) 2. to drink in —*vi.* to drink —**im·bib′er** *n.*

im·bro·glio (im brōl′yō) *n., pl.* -glios [It. < *imbrogliare*, embroil] 1. an involved and confusing situation 2. a confused misunderstanding or disagreement

im·bue (im byoo̅′) *vt.* -bued′, -bu′ing [< L. *imbuere*, to wet] 1. to fill with color; dye 2. to permeate (*with* ideas, emotions, etc.)

im·i·tate (im′ə tāt′) *vt.* -tat′ed, -tat′ing [< L. *imitari*] 1. to follow the example of 2. to mimic 3. to copy the form, color, etc. of 4. to resemble —**im′i·ta′tor** *n.*

im′i·ta′tion *n.* 1. an imitating 2. the result of imitating; copy —*adj.* made to resemble something specified [*imitation* leather] —**im′i·ta′tive** *adj.*

im·mac·u·late (i mak′yə lit) *adj.* [< L. *in-*, not + *macula*, a spot] 1. perfectly clean 2. without flaw 3. pure; innocent; sinless —**im·mac′u·late·ly** *adv.*

im·ma·nent (im′ə nənt) *adj.* [< L. *in-*, in + *manere*, remain] 1. remaining within; inherent 2. present throughout the universe: said of God —**im′ma·nence** *n.*

im·ma·te·ri·al (im′ə tir′ē əl) *adj.* 1. spiritual 2. unimportant

im·ma·ture (im′ə toor′, -choor′, -tyoor′) *adj.* 1. not mature or ripe; not completely developed 2. not finished or perfected —**im′ma·tu′ri·ty** *n.*

im·meas·ur·a·ble (i mezh′ər ə b′l) *adj.* not measurable; boundless; vast —**im·meas′ur·a·bly** *adv.*

im·me·di·a·cy (i mē′dē ə sē) *n.* a being immediate; direct relevance to the present

im·me′di·ate (-it) *adj.* [see IN-² & MEDIATE] 1. not separated in space or time; closest 2. without delay; instant 3. next in order 4. directly or closely related —**im·me′di·ate·ly** *adv.*

im·me·mo·ri·al (im′ə môr′ē əl) *adj.* back beyond memory or record

im·mense (i mens′) *adj.* [Fr. < L. *in-*, not + *metiri*, to measure] very large; vast; huge

im·men′si·ty *n., pl.* -ties 1. great size or extent 2. infinite space or being

im·merse (i murs′) *vt.* -mersed′, -mers′ing [< L. *immergere*] 1. to plunge into or as if into a liquid 2. to baptize by dipping under water 3. to absorb deeply; engross [*immersed* in study] —**im·mer′sion** *n.*

im·mi·grant (im′ə grənt) *n.* one that immigrates —*adj.* immigrating

im′mi·grate′ (-grāt′) *vi.* -grat′ed, -grat′ing [see IN-¹ & MIGRATE] to come into a new country, etc. in order to settle there —**im′mi·gra′tion** *n.*

im·mi·nent (im′ə nənt) *adj.* [< L. *in-*, on + *minere*, to project] likely to happen soon: said of danger, evil, etc. —**im′mi·nence** *n.*

im·mis·ci·ble (i mis′ə b′l) *adj.* [< IN-² + MISCIBLE] that cannot be mixed, as oil and water

im·mo·bile (i mō′b′l) *adj.* 1. firmly placed; stable 2. motionless —**im′mo·bil′i·ty** *n.* —**im·mo′bi·lize′** *vt.* -lized′, -liz′ing

im·mod·er·ate (i mäd′ər it) *adj.* without restraint; excessive —**im·mod′er·ate·ly** *adv.*

im·mod·est (i mäd′ist) *adj.* 1. indecent; improper 2. bold; forward —**im·mod′est·ly** *adv.* —**im·mod′es·ty** *n.*

im·mo·late (im′ə lāt′) *vt.* -lat′ed, -lat′ing [< L. *immolare*, sprinkle with sacrificial meal] to kill as a sacrifice —**im′mo·la′tion** *n.*

im·mor·al (i môr′əl) *adj.* not moral; specif., unchaste; lewd —**im·mor′al·ly** *adv.*

im·mo·ral·i·ty (im′ə ral′ə tē) *n.* 1. a being immoral 2. *pl.* -ties an immoral act; vice

im·mor·tal (i môr′t′l) *adj.* 1. not mortal; living forever; enduring 2. having lasting fame —*n.* an immortal being —**im′mor·tal′i·ty** (-tal′ə tē) *n.* —**im·mor′tal·ly** *adv.*

im·mor′tal·ize′ (-tə līz′) *vt.* -ized′, -iz′ing to make immortal, as in fame

im·mov·a·ble (i moo̅′və b′l) *adj.* 1. firmly fixed 2. unyielding; steadfast

im·mune (i myoo̅n′) *adj.* [< L. *in-*, without + *munia*, duties] 1. exempt from or protected against something disagreeable or harmful 2. not susceptible to a specified disease —**im′mu·ni·za′tion** *n.* —**im′mu·nize′** *vt.* -nized′, -niz′ing

im·mu·ni·ty (i myoo̅n′ə tē) *n., pl.* -ties 1. exemption from something burdensome, as a legal obligation 2. resistance to a specified disease

im·mure (i myoor′) *vt.* -mured′, -mur′ing [< L. *im-*, in + *murus*, a wall] to shut up as within walls; confine

im·mu·ta·ble (i myoot′ə b'l) *adj.* unchangeable —**im·mu′ta·bly** *adv.*

imp (imp) *n.* [< Gr. *em-*, in + *phyton*, a plant] 1. a young demon 2. a mischievous child

im·pact (im pakt′) *vt.* [< L. *impingere*, press firmly together) to force tightly together —*n.* (im′pakt) 1. a striking together 2. the force of a collision; shock

im·pair (im per′) *vt.* [< L. *in-*, intens. + *pejor*, worse] to make worse, less, etc.; damage —**im·pair′ment** *n.*

im·pale (im pāl′) *vt.* -paled′, -pal′ing [< Fr. < L. *in-*, on + *palus*, pole] to pierce through with, or fix on, something pointed

im·pal·pa·ble (im pal′pə b'l) *adj.* 1. not perceptible to the touch 2. too subtle to be easily understood —**im·pal′pa·bly** *adv.*

im·pan·el (im pan′'l) *vt.* -eled or -elled, -el·ing or -el·ling 1. to enter the name or names of on a jury list 2. to choose (a jury) from such a list

im·part (im pärt′) *vt.* [see IN-¹ & PART] 1. to give a share of; give 2. to tell; reveal

im·par·tial (im pär′shəl) *adj.* without bias; fair —**im·par′ti·al′i·ty** (-shē al′ə tē) *n.*

im·pass·a·ble (im pas′ə b'l) *adj.* that cannot be passed, crossed, or traveled over

im·passe (im′pas, im pas′) *n.* [Fr.] a situation offering no escape; deadlock

im·pas·si·ble (im pas′ə b'l) *adj.* [< L. *im-*, not + *pati*, suffer] 1. that cannot feel pain 2. that cannot be moved emotionally

im·pas·sioned (im pash′ənd) *adj.* passionate; fiery; ardent —**im·pas′sioned·ly** *adv.*

im·pas·sive (im pas′iv) *adj.* 1. not feeling pain 2. not feeling or showing emotion; calm —**im·pas′sive·ly** *adv.*

im·pa·tience (im pā′shəns) *n.* 1. annoyance because of delay, opposition, etc. 2. restless eagerness to do something —**im·pa′tient** *adj.* —**im·pa′tient·ly** *adv.*

im·peach (im pēch′) *vt.* [< L. *in-*, in + *pedica*, a fetter] 1. to discredit (a person's honor, etc.) 2. to bring (a public official) before the proper tribunal on a charge of wrongdoing —**im·peach′ment** *n.*

im·pec·ca·ble (im pek′ə b'l) *adj.* [< L. *in-*, not + *peccare*, to sin] without defect or error; flawless —**im·pec′ca·bil′i·ty** *n.* —**im·pec′ca·bly** *adv.*

im·pe·cu·ni·ous (im′pi kyōō′nē əs) *adj.* [< L. *in-*, not + *pecunia*, money] having no money; poor

im·ped·ance (im pēd′'ns) *n.* [IMPED(E) + -ANCE] the total opposition in an electric circuit to the flow of an alternating current of a single frequency

im·pede (im pēd′) *vt.* -ped′ed, -ped′ing [< L. *in-*, in + *pes*, foot] to hinder

im·ped·i·ment (im ped′ə mənt) *n.* anything that impedes

im·pel (im pel′) *vt.* -pelled′, -pel′ling [< L. *in-*, on + *pellere*, to drive] 1. to drive or move forward 2. to force, compel, or urge

im·pend (im pend′) *vi.* [< L. *in-*, in + *pendere*, hang] to be about to happen

im·pen·e·tra·ble (im pen′i trə b'l) *adj.* 1. that cannot be penetrated 2. that cannot be solved or understood —**im·pen′e·tra·bil′i·ty** *n.* —**im·pen′e·tra·bly** *adv.*

im·pen·i·tent (im pen′ə tənt) *adj.* without regret or remorse —**im·pen′i·tence** *n.*

im·per·a·tive (im per′ə tiv) *adj.* [< L. *imperare*, to order] 1. indicating power or com-

mand 2. absolutely necessary; urgent 3. designating or of a verb mood expressing a command, etc. —*n.* a command

im·per·cep·ti·ble (im′pər sep′tə b'l) *adj.* not easily perceived; very slight, subtle, etc. —**im′per·cep′ti·bly** *adv.*

im·per′fect *adj.* 1. not complete 2. not perfect 3. designating a verb tense indicating incomplete or continuous past action

im·per·fec·tion (im′pər fek′shən) *n.* 1. a being imperfect 2. a shortcoming; defect

im·pe·ri·al (im pir′ē əl) *adj.* [< L. *imperium*, empire] 1. of an empire, emperor, or empress 2. having supreme authority 3. majestic; august 4. of great size or superior quality —*n.* a pointed beard

im·pe′ri·al·ism *n.* 1. imperial state, authority, or government 2. the policy of forming and maintaining an empire by conquest, domination, etc. —**im·pe′ri·al·ist** *n., adj.* —**im·pe′ri·al·is′tic** *adj.*

im·per·il (im per′əl) *vt.* -iled or -illed, -il·ing or -il·ling to put in peril

im·pe·ri·ous (im pir′ē əs) *adj.* [< L. *imperium*, empire] 1. arrogant; domineering 2. urgent —**im·pe′ri·ous·ly** *adv.*

im·per·ish·a·ble (im per′ish ə b'l) *adj.* that will not die or decay; indestructible

im·per·me·a·ble (im pur′mē ə b'l) *adj.* not permeable; not permitting passage, esp. of fluids —**im·per′me·a·bil′i·ty** *n.*

im·per·son·al (im pur′s'n əl) *adj.* 1. without reference to any particular person [an *impersonal* comment] 2. not existing as a person 3. designating a verb occurring only in the third person singular (Ex.: "it is snowing") —**im·per′son·al·ly** *adv.*

im·per·son·ate (im pur′sə nāt′) *vt.* -at′ed, -at′ing to assume the role of, theatrically or fraudulently; mimic —**im·per′son·a′tion** *n.* —**im·per′son·a′tor** *n.*

im·per′ti·nent *adj.* 1. not pertinent 2. insolent —**im·per′ti·nence** *n.*

im·per·turb·a·ble (im′pər tur′bə b'l) *adj.* that cannot be perturbed or excited

im·per·vi·ous (im pur′vē əs) *adj.* 1. impermeable 2. not affected by (with *to*)

im·pe·ti·go (im′pə ti′gō) *n.* [L.: see IMPETUS] a contagious skin disease with eruption of pustules

im·pet·u·ous (im pech′oo wəs) *adj.* [see IMPETUS] sudden and thoughtless; impulsive —**im·pet′u·os′i·ty** (-wäs′ə tē) *n.*

im·pe·tus (im′pə təs) *n., pl.* -tus·es [< L. *in-*, in + *petere*, rush at] 1. the force with which a body moves against resistance 2. a stimulus to action; incentive

im·pi·e·ty (im pi′ə tē) *n.* lack of piety, esp. toward God

im·pinge (im pinj′) *vi.* -pinged′, -ping′ing [< L. *in-*, in + *pangere*, to strike] 1. to strike or hit (*on, upon,* etc.) 2. to encroach (*on* or *upon*)

im·pi·ous (im′pē əs) *adj.* not pious; lacking reverence for God —**im′pi·ous·ly** *adv.*

imp·ish (im′pish) *adj.* of or like an imp; mischievous —**imp′ish·ly** *adv.*

im·plac·a·ble (im plak′ə b'l, -plā′kə-) *adj.* that cannot be appeased or pacified —**im·plac′a·bil′i·ty** *n.* —**im·plac′a·bly** *adv.*

im·plant (im plant′) *vt.* 1. to plant firmly 2. to fix firmly in the mind; instill

im·plau·si·ble (im plô′zə b'l) *adj.* not plausible —**im·plau′si·bly** *adv.*

im·ple·ment (im′plə mənt) *n.* [< L. *in-*, in + *plere*, fill] any tool, instrument, etc. used in a given activity —*vt.* (-ment′) 1. to fulfill; accomplish 2. to provide with implements —**Im′ple·men·ta′tion** n.

im·pli·cate (im′plə kāt′) vt. -cat′ed, -cat′ing [see IMPLY] 1. to involve in or associate with a crime, etc. 2. to imply

im′pli·ca′tion n. 1. an implicating or being implicated 2. something implied

im·plic·it (im plis′it) adj. [see IMPLY] 1. implied 2. without reservation; absolute

im·plore (im plôr′) vt. -plored′, -plor′ing [< L. in-, intens. + plorare, cry out] 1. to ask earnestly for 2. to beg (a person) to do something —**im·plor′ing·ly** adv.

im·ply (im plī′) vt. -plied′, -ply′ing [< L. in-, in + plicare, to fold] 1. to have as a necessary part, condition, or effect 2. to indicate indirectly; hint; suggest

im·po·lite (im′pə līt′) adj. not polite; discourteous; rude —**Im′po·lite′ly** adv.

im·pol·i·tic (im päl′ə tik) adj. not politic; unwise; injudicious —**Im·pol′I·tic·ly** adv.

im·pon·der·a·ble (im pän′dər ə b'l) adj. that cannot be weighed or measured —n. anything imponderable

im·port (im pôrt′, im′pôrt) vt. [< L. in-, in + portare, carry] 1. to bring (goods) from another country, esp. for selling 2. to mean; signify —vi. to be of importance; matter —n. (im′pôrt) 1. the importing of goods 2. something imported 3. meaning 4. importance —**Im′por·ta′tion** n. —**Im·port′er** n.

im·por·tant (im pôr′t'nt) adj. [see IMPORT] 1. of much meaning or consequence 2. having or seeming to have power, authority, etc. —**Im·por′tance** n. —**Im·por′tant·ly** adv.

im·por·tu·nate (im pôr′chə nit) adj. persistent in asking or demanding

im·por·tune (im′pôr tōōn′) vt., vi. -tuned′, -tun′ing [< Fr. < L. importunus, troublesome] to urge or entreat persistently and repeatedly —**Im′por·tu′nI·ty** n., pl. -tles

im·pose (im pōz′) vt. -posed′, -pos′ing [< Fr. < L. in-, on + ponere, to place] 1. to place (a burden, tax, etc. on or upon) 2. to force (oneself) on another —**Impose on** (or **upon**) 1. to bother unfairly for one's own benefit 2. to cheat —**Im′po·si′tion** n.

im·pos·ing adj. impressive because of great size, strength, dignity, etc.

im·pos·si·ble (im päs′ə b'l) adj. 1. not possible 2. intolerably disagreeable, unsuitable, etc. —**Im·pos′si·bll′I·ty** n., pl. -tles —**Im·pos′si·bly** adv.

im·post (im′pōst) n. [< L. in-, on + ponere, to place] a tax; esp., a duty on imports

im·pos·tor (im päs′tər) n. [see IMPOSE] one pretending to be what he is not; cheat

im·pos′ture (-chər) n. the act or practice of an impostor; fraud

im·po·tent (im′pə tənt) adj. 1. lacking physical strength 2. powerless 3. unable to engage in sexual intercourse: said of males —**Im′po·tence, Im′po·ten·cy** n.

im·pound (im pound′) vt. 1. to shut up (an animal) in a pound 2. to take into legal custody —**Im·pound′ment** n.

im·pov·er·ish (im päv′ər ish) vt. [< L. in-, in + pauper, poor] 1. to make poor 2. to deprive of strength, resources, etc. —**Im·pov′er·Ish·ment** n.

im·prac·ti·ca·ble (im prak′ti kə b'l) adj. 1. not capable of being carried out in practice 2. not capable of being used —**Im·prac′tI·ca·bly** adv.

im·prac·ti·cal (im prak′ti k'l) adj. not practical —**Im·prac′tI·cal′I·ty** n.

im·pre·ca·tion (im′prə kā′shən) n. [< L. in-, on + precari, pray] a curse

im·pre·cise (im′pri sīs′) adj. not precise —**Im′·pre·cI′sion** (-sizh′ən) n.

im·preg·na·ble (im preg′nə b'l) adj. [ult. < L. in-, not + prehendere, to take] 1. that cannot be captured or entered by force 2. unyielding —**Im·preg′na·bil′I·ty** n. —**Im·preg′na·bly** adv.

im·preg·nate (im preg′nāt) vt. -nat·ed, -nat·ing 1. to make pregnant; fertilize 2. to saturate 3. to imbue (with ideas, etc.) —**Im′preg·na′tion** n.

im·pre·sa·ri·o (im′prə sär′ē ō) n., pl. -os [It.] the manager of an opera

im·press[1] (im pres′) vt. [< IN-[1] + PRESS[2]] 1. to force into military service 2. to seize for public use —**Im·press′ment** n.

im·press[2] (im pres′) vt. [see IN-[1] & PRESS[1]] 1. to stamp; imprint 2. to affect strongly the mind or emotions of 3. to fix in the memory —n. (im′pres) 1. an impressing 2. an imprint

im·pres·sion (im presh′ən) n. 1. an impressing 2. a) an imprint b) a mental effect 3. a notion 4. an impersonation

im·pres′sion·a·ble adj. easily impressed or influenced; sensitive

im·pres′sion·ism n. a theory of art, music, etc. whose aim is to reproduce the immediate impression or mood —**Im·pres′sion·ist** n., adj. —**Im·pres′sion·Is′tic** adj.

im·pres·sive (im pres′iv) adj. tending to affect strongly the mind or emotions

im·pri·ma·tur (im′pri mät′ər, -mät′-) n. [ModL., let it be printed] license to publish or print a book, article, etc.

im·print (im print′) vt. [< L. in-, on + premere, to PRESS[1]] to mark or fix as by pressing or stamping; impress —n. (im′print) 1. a mark made by imprinting 2. a lasting effect 3. a note in a book giving facts of its publication

im·pris·on (im priz′'n) vt. to put in or as in prison —**Im·pris′on·ment** n.

im·prob·a·ble (im präb′ə b'l) adj. not probable; unlikely —**Im′prob·a·bll′I·ty** n., pl. -tles —**Im·prob′a·bly** adv.

im·promp·tu (im prämp′tōō) adj., adv. [Fr. < L. in promptu, in readiness] without preparation; offhand

im·prop·er (im präp′ər) adj. 1. not suitable; unfit 2. incorrect 3. not in good taste; indecent —**Im·prop′er·ly** adv.

im·pro·pri·e·ty (im′prə prī′ə tē) n., pl. -tles 1. a being improper 2. an improper action, usage, etc.

im·prove (im prōōv′) vt. -proved′, -prov′ing [< L. in-, in + prodesse, to profit] 1. to use (time, etc.) profitably 2. to make better 3. to add value to, as by cultivation —vi. to become better —**Improve on** (or **upon**) to do or make better than —**Im·prov′a·ble** adj.

im·prove′ment n. 1. an improving or being improved 2. a change that improves or adds value to something

im·prov·i·dent (im präv′ə dənt) adj. lacking foresight or thrift —**Im·prov′I·dence** n.

im·pro·vise (im′prə vīz′) vt., vi. -vised′, -vis′·ing [< Fr. < L. in-, not + providere, foresee] 1. to compose and perform without preparation 2. to make or do with whatever is at hand —**Im·prov·I·sa·tion** (im präv′ə zā′shən) n.

im·pru·dent (im prōōd′'nt) adj. not prudent; rash —**Im·pru′dence** n.

im·pu·dent (im′pyoo dənt) adj. [< L. in-, not + pudere, feel shame] shamelessly bold; insolent —**Im′pu·dence** n.

im·pugn (im pyōōn′) vt. [< L. in-, against + pugnare, to fight] to oppose as false

im·pulse (im′puls) n. [see IMPEL] 1. a) a driving forward *b*) an impelling force; impetus *c*) the motion or effect of such a force **2.** *a*) incitement to action by a stimulus *b*) a sudden inclination to act

im·pul·sive (im pul′siv) *adj.* **1.** driving forward **2.** of or from impulse

im·pu·ni·ty (im pyōō′nə tē) *n.* [< Fr. < L. *in-*, without + *poena*, punishment] exemption from punishment, penalty, or harm

im·pure (im pyoor′) *adj.* **1.** unclean; dirty **2.** immoral; obscene **3.** mixed with foreign matter; adulterated —**im·pure′ly** *adv.*

im·pu′ri·ty *n.* **1.** a being impure **2.** *pl.* **-ties** an impure thing or part

im·pute (im pyōōt′) *vt.* **-put′ed, -put′ing** [< L. *in-*, to + *putare*, to estimate] to attribute (esp. a fault or misconduct) to another; charge with —**im′pu·ta′tion** *n.*

in (in) *prep.* [OE.] **1.** contained by [in the room] **2.** wearing [in formal dress] **3.** during [done in a day] **4.** at the end of [due in an hour] **5.** perceptible to [in sight] **6.** amidst [in a storm] **7.** affected by [in trouble] **8.** employed at [in business] **9.** with regard to [in my opinion] **10.** using [speak in French] **11.** because of; for [to cry in pain] **12.** by way of [in recompense] **13.** into [come in the house] —*adv.* **1.** inside **2.** so as to be contained by a certain space, condition, etc. —*adj.* **1.** in power [the in group] **2.** inner; inside **3.** [Colloq.] currently smart [an in joke] —*n.* **1.** a person or group in power: *usually used in pl.* **2.** [Colloq.] special influence, power, etc. —**have it in for** [Colloq.] to hold a grudge against —**in for** certain to have [he's in for a shock] —**ins and outs** all the parts, details, and intricacies —**in that** because; since —**in with** associated with

in-¹ [< the prep. IN or L. *in*, in] *a prefix meaning* in, into, within, on, toward [infer, induct] : also used as an intensive [instigate, inflame]

in-² [< L. *in-*] *a prefix meaning* no, not, without, non- The following list includes some common compounds formed with *in-* that do not have special meanings; they will be understood if *not* or *lack of* is used with the meaning of the base word:

Inability	Indisputable
Inaccurate	Indistinct
Inactive	Indistinguishable
Inadequacy	Indivisible
Inadmissible	Inedible
Inadvisable	Ineffective
Inanimate	Ineffectual
Inapplicable	Inefficacious
Inappropriate	Inefficacy
Inaptitude	Ineligible
Inaudible	Inequality
Inauspicious	Inequity
Incapable	Inexcusable
Incivility	Inexpensive
Incommunicable	Inhospitable
Incomprehensible	Injudicious
Inconceivable	Inoperable
Inconclusive	Insensitive
Incontrovertible	Inseparable
Incorporeal	Insoluble
Incorrect	Insufficient
Incurable	Invariable

-in¹ [see -INE³] a suffix used in names of various compounds [albumin]

-in² a combining form used in terms formed by analogy with SIT-IN [teach-in]

in. inch; inches

in·ac·ces·si·ble (in′ək ses′ə b'l) *adj.* **1.** impossible to reach or enter **2.** that cannot be seen, talked to, etc. **3.** not obtainable

in·ac·ti·vate (in ak′tə vāt′) *vt.* **-vat′ed, -vat′ing** to make no longer active

in·ad·vert·ent (in′əd vur′tənt) *adj.* **1.** not attentive; negligent **2.** due to oversight —**in′ad·vert′ence** *n.* —**in′ad·vert′ent·ly** *adv.*

in·al·ien·a·ble (in āl′yən ə b'l) *adj.* [see ALIEN] that may not be taken away or transferred —**in·al′ien·a·bly** *adv.*

in·ane (in ān′) *adj.* [L. *inanis*] silly —**in·an′i·ty** (-an′ə tē) *n., pl.* **-ties**

in·ar·tic·u·late (in′är tik′yə lit) *adj.* **1.** without the articulation of normal speech [an *inarticulate* cry] **2.** unable to speak clearly or at all

in·as·much as (in′əz much′ əz) **1.** seeing that; since; because **2.** to the extent that

in·at·ten·tion (in′ə ten′shən) *n.* failure to pay attention —**in′at·ten′tive** *adj.*

in·au·gu·ral (in ô′gyə rəl) *adj.* [Fr.] of an inauguration —*n.* an inaugural ceremony or address

in·au′gu·rate′ (-rāt′) *vt.* **-rat′ed, -rat′ing** [< L. *inaugurare*, to practice augury] **1.** to induct into office formally **2.** to begin or dedicate formally —**in·au′gu·ra′tion** *n.*

in·board (in′bôrd′) *adv., adj.* **1.** inside the hull of a ship or boat **2.** close to the fuselage of an aircraft —*n.* a marine motor mounted inboard

in·born (in′bôrn′) *adj.* present in the organism at birth; innate; natural

in′bound′ *adj.* traveling or going inward

in·bred (in′bred′) *adj.* **1.** innate **2.** resulting from inbreeding

in·breed (in′brēd′) *vt., vi.* **-bred′, -breed′ing** to breed by continual mating with individuals of the same or closely related stocks

inc. **1.** inclosure **2.** including **3.** inclusive **4.** incorporated **5.** increase

In·ca (iŋ′kə) *n.* a member of the highly civilized Indian people that dominated Peru until the Spanish conquest —**In′can** *adj.*

in·cal·cu·la·ble (in kal′kyə lə b'l) *adj.* **1.** too great or too many to be calculated **2.** unpredictable —**in·cal′cu·la·bly** *adv.*

in·can·des·cent (in′kən des′'nt) *adj.* [< L. *in-*, in + *candere*, to shine] **1.** glowing with intense heat; red-hot or, esp., white-hot **2.** very bright —**in′can·des′cence** *n.*

incandescent lamp a lamp having a filament contained in a vacuum and heated to incandescence by an electric current

in·can·ta·tion (in′kan tā′shən) *n.* [< L. *in-*, in + *cantare*, to chant] **1.** words chanted in magic spells or rites **2.** this chanting

in·ca·pac·i·tate (in′kə pas′ə tāt′) *vt.* **-tat′ed, -tat′ing** **1.** to make unable or unfit; disable **2.** *Law* to disqualify

in′ca·pac′i·ty (-tē) *n., pl.* **-ties** **1.** lack of capacity, power, or fitness; disability **2.** legal ineligibility

in·car·cer·ate (in kär′sə rāt′) *vt.* **-at′ed, -at′ing** [< L. *in*, in + *carcer*, prison] to imprison —**in·car′cer·a′tion** *n.*

in·car·nate (in kär′nit) *adj.* [< L. *in-*, in + *caro*, flesh] endowed with a human body; personified —*vt.* (-nāt) **-nat′ed, -nat·ing** **1.** to embody or personify **2.** to make real —**in′car·na′tion** *n.*

in·cen·di·ar·y (in sen′dē er′ē) *adj.* [< L. *incendium*, a fire] **1.** having to do with willful destruction of property by fire **2.** designed to cause fires, as certain bombs **3.** willfully stirring up strife, riot, etc. —*n., pl.* **-ies** **1.** one who willfully stirs up strife, riot, etc. **2.** an incendiary bomb, etc.

in·cense¹ (in′sens) *n.* [see INCENSE²] **1.** any substance burned for its pleasant odor **2.** the fragrance from this **3.** any pleasant odor —*vt.*

-censed, -cens·ing to burn or offer incense to
in·cense[2] (in sens') *vt.* -censed', -cens'ing [<
L. *in-,* in + *candere,* to burn] to make very
angry; enrage —**in·cense'ment** *n.*
in·cen·tive (in sen'tiv) *adj.* [< L. *in-,* on +
canere, to sing] stimulating to action —*n.* a
stimulus; motive
in·cep·tion (in sep'shən) *n.* [see INCIPIENT] a
beginning; start; commencement
in·cer·ti·tude (in sur'tə tōōd') *n.* 1. doubt 2.
insecurity
in·ces·sant (in ses''nt) *adj.* [< L. *in-,* not +
cessare, cease] never ceasing; continuing or
repeated endlessly; constant
in·cest (in'sest) *n.* [< L. *in-,* not + *castus,*
chaste] sexual intercourse between persons too
closely related to marry legally —**in·ces·tu·ous**
(in ses'choo wəs) *adj.*
inch (inch) *n.* [< L. *uncia,* a twelfth] a measure
of length equal to 1/12 foot: symbol, " —*vt., vi.*
to move by degrees or very slowly —**every inch**
in all respects —**within an inch of** very close to
in·cho·ate (in kō'it) *adj.* [< L. *inchoare,* to
begin] just begun; rudimentary
in·ci·dence (in'si dəns) *n.* 1. a falling upon or
influencing 2. the degree or range of occurrence or effect
in'ci·dent (-dənt) *adj.* [< L. *in-,* on + *cadere,*
to fall] 1. likely to happen as a result 2. falling
upon or affecting —*n.* 1. an event, esp. a minor
one 2. a minor conflict
in'ci·den'tal (-den't'l) *adj.* 1. happening in
connection with a more important thing 2.
secondary or minor —*n.* 1. something incidental 2. [*pl.*] miscellaneous items
in'ci·den'tal·ly (-dent'lē, -den't'l ē) *adv.* 1. in
an incidental manner 2. as a new but related
point; by the way
in·cin·er·ate (in sin'ə rāt') *vt., vi.* -at'ed, -at'-
ing [< L. *in,* in + *cinis,* ashes] to burn to
ashes; burn up —**in·cin'er·a'tion** *n.*
in·cin'er·a'tor (-rāt'ər) *n.* a furnace for burning trash
in·cip·i·ent (in sip'ē ənt) *adj.* [< L. *in-,* on +
capere, to take] just beginning to exist or appear —**in·cip'i·ence** *n.*
in·cise (in sīz') *vt.* -cised', -cis'ing [< L. *in-,*
into + *caedere,* to cut] to cut into with a
sharp tool; engrave; carve
in·ci·sion (in sizh'ən) *n.* 1. an incising; cut 2.
incisive quality 3. *Surgery* a cut made into a
tissue or organ
in·ci·sive (in sī'siv) *adj.* 1. cutting into 2.
sharp; keen; acute —**in·ci'sive·ly** *adv.*
in·ci·sor (in sī'zər) *n.* any of the front cutting
teeth between the canines in either jaw
in·cite (in sīt') *vt.* -cit'ed, -cit'ing [< L. *in-,* on
+ *citare,* to urge] to urge to action; rouse —**incite'ment** *n.* —**in·cit'er** *n.*
incl. 1. inclosure 2. inclusive
in·clem·ent (in klem'ənt) *adj.* [< L. *in-,* not +
clemens, lenient] 1. rough; stormy 2. lacking
mercy; harsh —**in·clem'en·cy** *n.*
in·cli·na·tion (in'klə nā'shən) *n.* 1. an inclining 2. a slope; slant 3. *a)* a bias; tendency *b)* a
preference; liking
in·cline (in klīn') *vi.* -clined', -clin'ing [< L.
in-, on + *clinare,* to lean] 1. to lean; slope 2.
to bow the body or head 3. to have a tendency 4. to have a preference or liking —*vt.* 1. to
cause to lean, slope, etc. 2. to make willing; influence —*n.* (in'klīn, in klīn') a slope; grade
in·close (in klōz') *vt.* -closed', -clos'ing *same
as* ENCLOSE —**in·clo'sure** (-klō'zhər) *n.*
in·clude (in klōōd') *vt.* -clud'ed, -clud'ing [< L.
in-, in + *claudere,* to close] 1. to enclose 2. to
have as part of a whole; contain; comprise 3.

to put in a total, category, etc. —**in·clu'sion**
(-klōō'zhən) *n.*
in·clu'sive (-klōō'siv) *adj.* 1. taking everything
into account 2. including the terms or limits
mentioned —**in·clu'sive·ly** *adv.*
in·cog·ni·to (in'käg nēt'ō, in käg'ni tō') *adv.,
adj.* [It. < L. *in-,* not + *cognitus,* known] disguised under an assumed name, rank, etc. —*n.,
pl.* -tos 1. a person who is incognito 2. *a)* the
state of being incognito *b)* the disguise assumed
in·co·her·ent (in'kō hir'ənt) *adj.* 1. not logically connected; disjointed 2. characterized by
incoherent speech, thought, etc. —**in'co·her'-
ence** *n.* —**in'co·her'ent·ly** *adv.*
in·come (in'kum') *n.* the money or other gain
received for labor or services, or from
property, investments, etc.
in'com'ing *adj.* coming in or about to come in
in·com·mode (in'kə mōd') *vt.* -mod'ed, -mod'-
ing [< Fr. < L. *in-,* not + *commodus,*
convenient] to inconvenience; bother
in·com·mu·ni·ca·do (in'kə myōō'nə kä'dō)
adj. [Sp.] unable or not allowed to communicate with others
in·com·pa·ra·ble (in käm'pər ə b'l) *adj.* 1.
having no basis of comparison 2. beyond comparison; matchless
in·com·pat·i·ble (in'kəm pat'ə b'l) *adj.* not
getting along well together or not going well
together —**in'com·pat'i·bil'i·ty** *n.*
in·com·pe·tent (in käm'pə tənt) *adj.* without
adequate ability, knowledge, fitness, etc. —*n.*
an incompetent person —**in·com'pe·tence** *n.* —
in·com'pe·tent·ly *adv.*
in·com·plete (in'kəm plēt') *adj.* 1. lacking a
part or parts 2. unfinished; not concluded 3.
not perfect
in·con·gru·ous (in käŋ'groo wəs) *adj.* 1. lacking harmony or agreement of parts, etc. 2. unsuitable; inappropriate —**in·con·gru·i·ty** (in'kən
grōō'ə tē) *n., pl.* -ties
in·con·se·quen·tial (in kän'sə kwen'shəl) *adj.*
of no consequence; unimportant
in·con·sid·er·a·ble (in'kən sid'ər ə b'l) *adj.*
trivial; small
in·con·sid·er·ate (in'kən sid'ər it) *adj.*
without thought or consideration for others
in·con·sis·tent (in'kən sis'tənt) *adj.* 1. not in
accord 2. self-contradictory 3. changeable —**in'-
con·sis'ten·cy** *n., pl.* -cies
in·con·sol·a·ble (in'kən sōl'ə b'l) *adj.* that
cannot be consoled —**in'con·sol'a·bly** *adv.*
in·con·spic·u·ous (in'kən spik'yoo wəs) *adj.*
attracting little attention
in·con·stant (in kän'stənt) *adj.* not constant;
changeable, fickle, irregular, etc. —**in·con'-
stan·cy** *n.*
in·con·test·a·ble (in'kən tes'tə b'l) *adj.* un-
questionable; indisputable
in·con·ti·nent (in känt''n ənt) *adj.* 1. without
self-restraint, esp. in regard to sexual activity
2. unable to restrain a natural discharge, as of
urine —**in·con'ti·nence** *n.*
in·con·ven·ience (in'kən vēn'yəns) *n.* 1. lack
of comfort, ease, etc. 2. anything inconvenient
—*vt.* -ienced, -ienc·ing to trouble; bother
in'con·ven'ient (-yənt) *adj.* not favorable to
one's comfort; causing bother, etc.
in·cor·po·rate (in kôr'pə rāt') *vt.* -rat'ed, -rat'-
ing [see IN-[1] & CORPORATE] 1. to combine;
embody 2. to bring together into a single
whole; merge 3. to form into a corporation —
vi. 1. to unite into a single whole 2. to form a
corporation —**in·cor'po·ra'tion** *n.*
in·cor·ri·gi·ble (in kôr'i jə b'l) *adj.* [see IN-[2] &
CORRECT] that cannot be corrected or re-

formed, esp. because set in bad habits —**in-cor'ri-gi-bly** adv.

in·cor·rupt·i·ble (in′kə rup′tə b'l) adj. that cannot be corrupted, esp. morally

in·crease (in krēs′) vi., vt. -creased′, -creas′ing [< L. in-, in + crescere, grow] to become or make greater in size, etc. —n. (in′krēs) 1. an increasing 2. amount of increasing —on the in-crease increasing

in·creas'ing·ly adv. more and more

in·cred·i·ble (in kred′ə b'l) adj. not credible; seeming too unusual to be possible —**in·cred'i-bil'i·ty** n. —**in·cred'i·bly** adv.

in·cred·u·lous (in krej′oo ləs) adj. 1. unwilling to believe; doubting 2. showing doubt or disbe-lief —**in·cre·du·li·ty** (in′krə dōō′lə tē) n. —**in-cred'u·lous·ly** adv.

in·cre·ment (in′krə mənt, iŋ′-) n. an increase —**in'cre·men'tal** (-men′t'l) adj.

in·crim·i·nate (in krim′ə nāt′) vt. -nat'ed, -nat'ing [< L. in-, in + crimen, offense] 1. to accuse of a crime 2. to involve in, or make ap-pear guilty of, a crime or fault —**in·crim'i·na'-tion** n.

in·crust (in krust′) vt. 1. to cover as with a crust 2. to decorate, as with gems —vi. to form a crust —**in'crus·ta'tion** n.

in·cu·bate (iŋ′kyə bāt′) vt. -bat'ed, -bat'ing [< L. in-, on + cubare, to lie] 1. to sit on and hatch (eggs) 2. to keep (eggs, embryos, etc.) in a favorable environment for hatching or developing —vi. to undergo incubation —**in'cu-ba'tion** n.

in'cu·ba'tor n. 1. a heated container for hatch-ing eggs 2. a similar apparatus in which premature babies are kept for a period

in·cu·bus (iŋ′kyə bəs) n., pl. -bus·es, -bi′ (-bī′) [LL.] 1. a demon thought in medieval times to lie on sleeping women 2. a nightmare 3. an op-pressive burden

in·cul·cate (in kul′kāt, in′kul kāt′) vt. -cat·ed, -cat·ing [< L. in-, in + calcare, trample underfoot] to impress upon the mind by repe-tition or persistent urging —**in'cul·ca'tion** n.

in·cul·pate (in kul′pāt, in′kul pāt′) vt. -pat·ed, -pat·ing [< L. in-, on + culpa, blame] same as INCRIMINATE

in·cum·ben·cy (in kum′bən sē) n., pl. -cies 1. a duty or obligation 2. a term of office

in·cum'bent (-bənt) adj. [< L. in-, on + cubare, lie down] 1. resting (on or upon one) as a duty or obligation 2. currently in office —n. one who is currently in office

in·cum·ber (in kum′bər) vt. same as ENCUM-BER

in·cur (in kur′) vt. -curred′, -cur′ring [< L. in-, in + currere, to run] to bring upon oneself (something undesirable)

in·cur·sion (in kur′zhən) n. [see INCUR] an in-vasion or raid; inroad

Ind. 1. India 2. Indian 3. Indiana

ind. 1. independent 2. index

in·debt·ed (in det′id) adj. 1. in debt 2. obliged; owing gratitude

in·debt'ed·ness n. 1. a being indebted 2. the amount owed; all one's debts

in·de·cen·cy (in dē′s'n sē) n. 1. a being inde-cent 2. pl. -cies an indecent act or remark

in·de'cent (-s'nt) adj. not decent; specif., a) improper b) morally offensive —**in·de'cent·ly** adv.

in·de·ci·sion (in′di sizh′ən) n. inability to de-cide; vacillation

in'de·ci'sive (-sī′siv) adj. not decisive; vacillat-ing —**in'de·ci'sive·ly** adv.

in·deed (in dēd′) adv. certainly; truly —interj.

an exclamation of surprise, doubt, sarcasm, etc.

in·de·fat·i·ga·ble (in′di fat′i gə b'l) adj. [< L. in-, not + defatigare, tire out] not tiring

in·de·fen·si·ble (in′di fen′sə b'l) adj. 1. that cannot be defended 2. that cannot be justified

in·def·i·nite (in def′ə nit) adj. 1. having no exact limits 2. not precise in meaning; vague 3. not sure; uncertain 4. Gram. not limiting or specifying [a and an are indefinite articles]

in·del·i·ble (in del′ə b'l) adj. [< L. in-, not + delere, destroy] 1. that cannot be erased, washed out, etc. 2. leaving an indelible mark [indelible ink] —**in·del'i·bly** adv.

in·del·i·cate (in del′i kit) adj. lacking pro-priety or modesty; coarse —**in·del'i·ca·cy** n., pl. -cies —**in·del'i·cate·ly** adv.

in·dem·ni·fy (in dem′nə fī′) vt. -fied′, -fy′ing [< L. indemnis, unhurt + -FY] 1. to insure against loss, damage, etc. 2. to repay for (loss or damage) —**in·dem'ni·fi·ca'tion** n.

in·dem'ni·ty (-tē) n., pl. -ties 1. insurance against loss, damage, etc. 2. repayment for loss, damage, etc.

in·dent (in dent′) vt., vi. [< L. in, in + dens, tooth] 1. to notch 2. to make jagged in outline 3. to space (the beginning of a paragraph, etc.) in from the regular margin —**in'den·ta'tion** n.

in·den·ture (in den′chər) n. 1. a written con-tract 2. [often pl.] a contract binding one per-son to work for another —vt. -tured, -tur·ing to bind by indenture

in·de·pend·ence (in′di pen′dəns) n. a being independent; freedom from the control of another

Independence Day the Fourth of July, the anniversary of the American colonies' adop-tion of the Declaration of Independence on July 4, 1776

in'de·pend'ent (-dənt) adj. 1. free from the in-fluence or control of others; specif., a) self-governing b) self-confident; self-reliant c) not adhering to any political party d) not con-nected with others [an independent grocer] 2. not depending upon another for financial sup-port —n. one who is independent in thinking, action, etc.

in·de·scrib·a·ble (in′di skrī′bə b'l) adj. beyond the power of description

in·de·struct·i·ble (in′di struk′tə b'l) adj. that cannot be destroyed

in·de·ter·mi·na·ble (in′di tur′mi nə b'l) adj. that cannot be decided or ascertained

in'de·ter'mi·nate (-nit) adj. 1. indefinite; vague 2. unsettled; inconclusive

in·dex (in′deks) n., pl. -dex·es, -di·ces′ (-də sēz′) [L.: see INDICATE] 1. the forefinger: also **index finger** 2. a pointer, as the needle on a dial 3. an indication [an index of ability] 4. an alphabetical list of names, subjects, etc. indi-cating pages where found, as in a book 5. a figure showing ratio or relative change 6. [I-] R.C.Ch. formerly, a list of books forbidden to be read —vt. 1. to make an index of or for 2. to include in an index

India ink a black ink made of lampblack mixed with a gelatinous substance

In·di·an (in′dē ən) n. 1. a native of India or the East Indies 2. a member of any of the aboriginal peoples of N. America, S. America, or the West Indies: also **American Indian** —adj. 1. of India or the East Indies, their people, etc. 2. of the American Indians

Indian corn same as CORN¹ (sense 2)

Indian summer mild, warm, hazy weather fol-lowing the first frosts of late autumn

India paper a thin, strong, opaque printing paper, used as for some Bibles

in·dic. indicative

in·di·cate (in′də kāt′) *vt.* -cat′ed, -cat′ing [< L. *in-*, in + *dicare*, declare] 1. to direct attention to; point out 2. to be a sign of; signify 3. to show the need for 4. to state briefly —**in′di·ca′tion** *n.*

in·dic·a·tive (in dik′ə tiv) *adj.* 1. giving an indication 2. designating or of a verb mood used to express actuality or to ask a question

in·di·ca·tor (in′də kāt′ər) *n.* a person or thing that indicates; specif., a gauge, dial, etc. that measures something

in·dict (in dīt′) *vt.* [ult. < L. *in*, against + *dicere*, speak] to charge with a crime, esp. formally —**in·dict′ment** *n.*

in·dif′fer·ent *adj.* 1. having or showing no bias; neutral 2. unconcerned; apathetic 3. of no importance 4. fair; average —**in·dif′fer·ence** *n.*

in·dig·e·nous (in dij′ə nəs) *adj.* [< OL. *indu*, in + *gignere*, be born] born or growing naturally in a region or country; native

in·di·gent (in′di jənt) *adj.* [< OL. *indu*, in + *egere*, to need] poor; needy —**in′di·gence** *n.*

in·di·gest·i·ble (in′di jes′tə b′l) *adj.* not easily digested —**in′di·gest′i·bil′i·ty** *n.*

in·di·ges·tion (in′di jes′chən) *n.* difficulty in digesting food

in·dig·nant (in dig′nənt) *adj.* [< L. *in-*, not + *dignus*, worthy] feeling or expressing indignation —**in·dig′nant·ly** *adv.*

in·dig·na·tion (in′dig nā′shən) *n.* anger or scorn in reaction to injustice or meanness

in·dig·ni·ty (in dig′nə tē) *n., pl.* -ties an affront to one's dignity or self-respect

in·di·go (in′di gō′) *n., pl.* -gos′, -goes′ [Sp. < Gr. *Indikos*, Indian] 1. a blue dye obtained from certain plants or made synthetically 2. a deep violet blue —*adj.* of this color

in·di·rect (in′di rekt′) *adj.* 1. not straight 2. not straight to the point 3. devious 4. not immediate; secondary

in′di·rec′tion *n.* 1. roundabout act, procedure, or means 2. deceit; dishonesty

indirect object the word or words denoting the person or thing indirectly affected by the action of the verb (Ex.: *us* in *give us time*)

in·dis·creet (in′dis krēt′) *adj.* lacking prudence; unwise —**in′dis·creet′ly** *adv.*

in′dis·cre′tion (-kresh′ən) *n.* 1. lack of discretion 2. an indiscreet act or remark

in·dis·crim·i·nate (in′dis krim′ə nit) *adj.* 1. random 2. not making careful choices or distinctions

in·dis·pen·sa·ble (in′dis pen′sə b′l) *adj.* absolutely necessary

in·dis·posed (in′dis pōzd′) *adj.* 1. slightly ill 2. unwilling; disinclined —**in′dis·po·si′tion** (-pə zish′ən) *n.*

in·dis·sol·u·ble (in′di säl′yoo b′l) *adj.* that cannot be dissolved or destroyed; lasting

in·dite (in dīt′) *vt.* -dit′ed, -dit′ing [see INDICT] to compose and write

in·di·vid·u·al (in′di vij′oo wəl) *adj.* [< L. *individuus*, not divisible] 1. existing separately; single 2. of, for, by, or characteristic of a single person or thing —*n.* 1. a single thing or being 2. a person

in′di·vid′u·al·ism *n.* 1. the leading of one's life in one's own way 2. individuality 3. the doctrine that the state exists for the individual —**in′di·vid′u·al·ist** *n., adj.* —**in′di·vid′u·al·is′tic** *adj.*

in′di·vid′u·al′i·ty (-wal′ə tē) *n., pl.* -ties 1. the

sum of the characteristics that set one person or thing apart 2. separate existence

in′di·vid′u·al·ize′ (-vij′oo wə līz′) *vt.* -ized′, -iz′ing 1. to mark as different from others 2. to consider individually

in′di·vid′u·al·ly *adv.* 1. one at a time; separately 2. distinctively

in·doc·tri·nate (in däk′trə nāt′) *vt.* -nat′ed, -nat′ing to instruct in doctrines, theories, or beliefs —**in·doc′tri·na′tion** *n.*

In·do-Eu·ro·pe·an (in′dō yoor′ə pē′ən) *adj.* designating a family of languages including most of those of Europe and some of those of Asia —*n.* this family of languages

in·do·lent (in′də lənt) *adj.* [< L. *in-*, not + *dolere*, feel pain] idle; lazy —**in′do·lence** *n.*

in·dom·i·ta·ble (in däm′it ə b′l) *adj.* [< L. *in-*, not + *domare*, to tame] not easily discouraged or defeated —**in·dom′i·ta·bly** *adv.*

In·do·ne·sian (in′də nē′zhən) *adj.* 1. of Indonesia 2. designating or of the many related languages spoken in Indonesia, the Philippines, etc. —*n.* 1. a native of Indonesia, the Philippines, etc. 2. the Indonesian languages 3. the official Malay language of Indonesia

in·door (in′dôr′) *adj.* living, belonging, or carried on within a house or building

in·doors (in′dôrz′) *adv.* in or into a building

in·dorse (in dôrs′) *vt.* -dorsed′, -dors′ing *same as* ENDORSE

in·du·bi·ta·ble (in doo′bi tə b′l) *adj.* that cannot be doubted —**in·du′bi·ta·bly** *adv.*

in·duce (in doos′) *vt.* -duced′, -duc′ing [< L. *in-*, in + *ducere*, to lead] 1. to persuade 2. to bring on [to *induce* sleep with drugs] 3. to draw (a conclusion) from particular facts 4. to bring about (an electric or magnetic effect) in a body by placing it within a field of force

in·duce′ment *n.* 1. an inducing or being induced 2. a motive; incentive

in·duct (in dukt′) *vt.* [see INDUCE] 1. to place formally in an office, society, etc. 2. to enroll (esp. a draftee) in the armed forces

in·duct·ee (in duk′tē′) *n.* a person being inducted

in·duc·tion (in duk′shən) *n.* 1. an inducting or being inducted 2. reasoning from particular facts to a general conclusion 3. the inducing of an electric or magnetic effect by the influence of a field of force —**in·duc′tive** *adj.*

in·due (in doo′) *vt.* -dued′, -du′ing *same as* ENDUE

in·dulge (in dulj′) *vt.* -dulged′, -dulg′ing [L. *indulgere*, be kind to] 1. to satisfy (a desire) 2. to gratify the wishes of; humor —*vi.* to give way to one's desires

in·dul′gence (-dul′jəns) *n.* 1. an indulging or being indulgent 2. a thing indulged in 3. a favor or privilege 4. *R.C.Ch.* a remission of punishment still due for a sin after the guilt has been forgiven

in·dul′gent *adj.* indulging or inclined to indulge; kind or lenient, often to excess

in·dus·tri·al (in dus′trē əl) *adj.* 1. of, connected with, or resulting from industries 2. of or concerned with people working in industries —**in·dus′tri·al·ly** *adv.*

industrial arts the mechanical and technical skills used in industry

in·dus′tri·al·ism *n.* economic organization characterized by large industries, etc.

in·dus′tri·al·ist *n.* one who owns or manages an industrial enterprise

in·dus′tri·al·ize′ *vt.* -ized′, -iz′ing 1. to develop industrialism in 2. to organize as an industry

industrial park an area zoned for industrial

and business use, usually on the outskirts of a city

in·dus·tri·ous (in dus′trē əs) *adj.* hardworking; diligent —**In·dus′tri·ous·ly** *adv.*

in·dus·try (in′dəs trē) *n., pl.* **-tries** [< L. *industrius,* active] 1. earnest, steady effort 2. any branch of production, esp. manufacturing, or all of these collectively 3. the owners and managers of industry

-ine¹ [< L. *-inus*] *a suffix meaning* of, having the nature of, like [*divine, crystalline*]

-ine² [< L. *-ina*] *a suffix used to form certain abstract nouns [medicine, doctrine]*

-ine³ [< L. *-inus*] *a suffix used to form the chemical names of:* a) halogens [*iodine*] b) alkaloids or nitrogen bases [*morphine*] Often used to form commercial names [*Vaseline*]

in·e·bri·ate (in ē′brē āt′) *vt.* -at′ed, -at′ing [ult. < L. *in-,* intens. + *ebrius,* drunk] to make drunk; intoxicate —*n.* (-it) a drunkard —**In·e′·bri·a′tion** *n.*

in·ef·fa·ble (in ef′ə b'l) *adj.* [< L. *in-,* not + *effabilis,* utterable] 1. inexpressible 2. too sacred to be spoken —**In·ef′fa·bly** *adv.*

in·ef·fi·cient (in′ə fish′ənt) *adj.* 1. not producing the desired effect with a minimum of energy, time, etc. 2. incapable —**In′ef·fi′clen·cy** *n.*

in·e·luc·ta·ble (in′i luk′tə b'l) *adj.* [< L. *in-,* not + *eluctari,* to struggle] not to be avoided or escaped —**In′e·luc′ta·bly** *adv.*

in·ept (in ept′) *adj.* [< L. *in-,* not + *aptus,* fit] 1. unsuitable; unfit 2. absurd; foolish 3. clumsy; inefficient —**In·ept′I·tude′** (-ep′tə t̅o̅o̅d′), **in·ept′ness** *n.*

in·ert (in urt′) *adj.* [< L. *in-,* not + *ars,* skill] 1. without power to move or act 2. inactive; dull; slow 3. with few or no active properties —**In·ert′ly** *adv.*

in·er·tia (in ur′shə) *n.* [see INERT] 1. *Physics* the tendency of matter to remain at rest (or continue in a fixed direction) unless affected by an outside force 2. disinclination to move or act

in·es·cap·a·ble (in′ə skāp′ə b'l) *adj.* that cannot be escaped —**In′es·cap′a·bly** *adv.*

in·es·ti·ma·ble (in es′tə mə b'l) *adj.* too great to be properly estimated

in·ev·i·ta·ble (in ev′ə tə b'l) *adj.* [< L. *in-,* not + *evitabilis,* avoidable] that cannot be avoided; certain to happen —**In·ev′i·ta·bil′i·ty** *n.* —**In·ev′i·ta·bly** *adv.*

in·ex·haust·i·ble (in′ig zôs′tə b'l) *adj.* 1. that cannot be exhausted 2. tireless

in·ex·o·ra·ble (in ek′sər ə b'l) *adj.* [< L. *in-,* not + *exorare,* move by entreaty] 1. that cannot be influenced by persuasion or entreaty; unrelenting 2. that cannot be altered, checked, etc. —**In·ex′o·ra·bly** *adv.*

in·ex·pe·ri·ence (in′ik spir′ē əns) *n.* lack of experience or of the knowledge or skill resulting from experience —**In′ex·pe′ri·enced** *adj.*

in·ex·pert (in ek′spərt, in′ik spurt′) *adj.* not expert; unskillful —**In·ex′pert·ly** *adv.*

in·ex·pi·a·ble (in ek′spē ə b'l) *adj.* that cannot be expiated or atoned for

in·ex·pli·ca·ble (in eks′pli kə b'l) *adj.* that cannot be explained —**In·ex′pli·ca·bly** *adv.*

in·ex·press·i·ble (in′ik spres′ə b'l) *adj.* that cannot be expressed

in·ex·tin·guish·a·ble (in′ik stiŋ′gwish ə b'l) *adj.* that cannot be put out or stopped

‡**in ex·tre·mis** (in′ ik strē′mis) [L., in extremity] at the point of death

in·ex·tri·ca·ble (in eks′tri kə b'l) *adj.* 1. that one cannot extricate himself from 2. that cannot be disentangled or untied 3. insolvable — **In·ex′tri·ca·bly** *adv.*

inf. 1. infantry: also **Inf.** 2. infinitive

in·fal·li·ble (in fal′ə b'l) *adj.* [see IN-² & FALLIBLE] 1. incapable of error 2. dependable; reliable —**In·fal′II·bIl′I·ty** *n.*

in·fa·mous (in′fə məs) *adj.* 1. having a bad reputation; notorious 2. causing a bad reputation; scandalous

in·fa·my (in′fə mē) *n., pl.* **-mies** 1. very bad reputation; disgrace 2. great wickedness 3. an infamous act

in·fan·cy (in′fən sē) *n., pl.* **-cies** 1. the state or period of being an infant 2. the earliest stage of anything

in·fant (in′fənt) *n.* [< L. *in-,* not + *fari,* speak] a very young child; baby —*adj.* 1. of or for infants 2. in a very early stage

in·fan·tile (in′fən tīl′, -til) *adj.* 1. of infants 2. like an infant; babyish

infantile paralysis *same as* POLIOMYELITIS

in·fan·try (in′fən trē) *n., pl.* **-tries** [< It. *infante,* a youth] that branch of an army consisting of soldiers trained to fight on foot —**In′·fan·try·man** (-mən) *n., pl.* **-men**

in·fat·u·ate (in fach′o̅o̅ wāt′) *vt.* -at′ed, -at′ing [< L. *in-,* intens. + *fatuus,* foolish] to inspire with foolish love or affection —**In·fat′u·a′tion** *n.*

in·fect (in fekt′) *vt.* [< L. *inficere,* to stain] 1. to contaminate, or cause to become diseased, with a germ or virus 2. to imbue with one's feelings or beliefs, esp. so as to harm

in·fec·tion (in fek′shən) *n.* 1. an infecting or being infected 2. an infectious disease

in·fec′tious (-shəs) *adj.* 1. likely to cause infection 2. designating a disease caused by the presence in the body of certain microorganisms 3. tending to spread to others

in·fer (in fur′) *vt.* **-ferred′, -fer′ring** [< L. *in-,* in + *ferre,* bring] 1. to conclude by reasoning from something known or assumed 2. to imply: still sometimes regarded as a loose usage —**In′fer·ence** *n.*

in·fe·ri·or (in fir′ē ər) *adj.* [< L. *inferus,* low] 1. lower in space 2. lower in order, status, quality, etc. (with *to*) 3. poor in quality; below average —*n.* an inferior person or thing —**In·fe′ri·or′I·ty** (-ôr′ə tē) *n.*

in·fer·nal (in fur′n'l) *adj.* [< L. *inferus,* below] 1. of hell or Hades 2. hellish; fiendish

in·fer·no (in fur′nō) *n., pl.* **-nos** [It. < L.: see prec.] hell

in·fest (in fest′) *vt.* [< Fr. < L. *infestus,* hostile] 1. to overrun in large numbers, usually so as to be harmful 2. to be parasitic in or on —**In′fes·ta′tion** *n.*

in·fi·del (in′fə d'l) *n.* [< L. *in-,* not + *fidelis,* faithful] 1. one who does not believe in a particular, esp. the prevailing, religion 2. one who has no religion

in·fi·del·i·ty (in′fə del′ə tē) *n., pl.* **-ties** unfaithfulness, esp. in marriage

in·field (in′fēld′) *n.* 1. the area enclosed by the four base lines on a baseball field 2. the players (**Infielders**) whose field positions are there

in′fight′ing *n.* 1. fighting at close range 2. personal conflict within a group

in·fil·trate (in fil′trāt, in′fil trāt′) *vi., vt.* -trat·ed, -trat·ing 1. to filter or pass gradually through or into 2. to penetrate gradually, so as to seize control from within —**In′fII·tra′tion** *n.*

in·fi·nite (in′fə nit) *adj.* [see IN-² & FINITE] 1. lacking limits; endless 2. very great; vast —*n.* something infinite —**the Infinite (Being)** God

in·fin·i·tes·i·mal (in′fin ə tes′ə məl) *adj.* [< L. *infinitus,* infinite] too small to be measured; very minute

in·fin·i·tive (in fin′ə tiv) *n.* [see INFINITE] the form of a verb without reference to person,

number, or tense: usually following *to* (*to go*)
in·fin'i·tude' (-tōōd') *n.* **1.** a being infinite **2.**
an infinite quantity or extent
in·fin'i·ty (-tē) *n., pl.* **-ties** [< L. *infinitas*] **1.** a
being infinite **2.** unlimited space, time, etc. **3.**
an indefinitely large quantity
in·firm (in fưrm') *adj.* **1.** weak; feeble **2.** not
firm; unstable —**in·firm'ly** *adv.*
in·fir·ma·ry (in fưr'mə rē) *n., pl.* **-ries** a place
for the care of the sick, injured, etc.
in·fir'mi·ty (-mə tē) *n., pl.* **-ties 1.** physical
weakness or defect **2.** moral weakness
in·flame (in flām') *vt., vi.* **-flamed', -flam'ing**
[see IN-1 & FLAME] **1.** to arouse, excite, etc. or
become aroused, excited, etc. **2.** to undergo or
cause to undergo inflammation
in·flam·ma·ble (in flam'ə b'l) *adj.* **1.** *same as*
FLAMMABLE **2.** easily excited —*n.* anything
flammable —**in·flam'ma·bil'i·ty** *n.*
in·flam·ma·tion (in'flə mā'shən) *n.* **1.** an in-
flaming or being inflamed **2.** redness, pain,
heat, and swelling in some part of the body,
caused by injury or disease
in·flam·ma·to·ry (in flam'ə tôr'ē) *adj.* **1.** rousing or likely to rouse excitement, anger, etc. **2.**
of or caused by inflammation
in·flate (in flāt') *vt.* **-flat'ed, -flat'ing** [< L. *in-*,
in + *flare*, to blow] **1.** to blow full with air or
gas **2.** to puff up with pride **3.** to increase
beyond what is normal —*vi.* to become inflated
—**in·flat'a·ble** *adj.*
in·fla'tion *n.* **1.** an inflating or being inflated **2.**
an increase in the currency in circulation or a
marked expansion of credit, resulting in a fall
in currency value and a sharp rise in prices —
in·fla'tion·ar'y *adj.*
in·flect (in flekt') *vt.* [< L. *in-*, in + *flectere*, to
bend] **1.** to bend **2.** to vary the tone of (the
voice) **3.** to change the form of (a word) by inflection
in·flec·tion (in flek'shən) *n.* **1.** a bend **2.** a
change in the tone of the voice **3.** the change
in form of a word to indicate number, case,
gender, tense, etc. Brit. sp. **in·flex'ion** —**in·**
flec'tion·al *adj.*
in·flex·i·ble (in flek'sə b'l) *adj.* not flexible;
specif., *a*) rigid *b*) firm in mind; stubborn *c*)
unalterable —**in·flex'i·bil'i·ty** *n.*
in·flict (in flikt') *vt.* [< L. *in-*, on + *fligere*, to
strike] **1.** to cause (wounds, pain, etc.) as by
striking **2.** to impose (a punishment, etc. *on* or
upon) —**in·flic'tion** *n.*
in·flight (in'flīt') *adj.* done, shown, etc. while
an aircraft is in flight
in·flu·ence (in'floo wəns) *n.* [< L. *in-*, in +
fluere, to flow] **1.** the power to affect others **2.**
the ability to produce effects because of
wealth, high position, etc. **3.** one that has influence —*vt.* **-enced, -enc·ing** to have influence
or an effect on
in'flu·en'tial (-wen'shəl) *adj.* exerting influence, esp. great influence
in·flu·en·za (in'floo wen'zə) *n.* [It., an
influence] an acute, contagious virus infection,
characterized by inflammation of the respiratory tract, fever, muscular pain, etc.
in·flux (in'fluks') *n.* [Fr.: see INFLUENCE] a
flowing in or streaming in
in·fold (in fōld') *vt. same as* ENFOLD
in·form (in fôrm') *vt.* [see IN-1 & FORM] to give
knowledge of something to —*vi.* to give information, esp. in accusing another —**in·form'er** *n.*
in·for·mal (in fôr'məl) *adj.* not formal; specif.,
a) not according to fixed customs, rules, etc. *b*)
casual, relaxed, etc. *c*) not requiring formal
dress *d*) colloquial —**in'for·mal'i·ty** (-mal'ə tē)
n., pl. **-ties**

in·form·ant (in fôr'mənt) *n.* a person who
gives information
in·for·ma·tion (in'fər mā'shən) *n.* **1.** an in-
forming or being informed **2.** news or
knowledge **3.** data stored in or retrieved from
a computer —**in'for·ma'tion·al** *adj.*
in·form·a·tive (in fôr'mə tiv) *adj.* giving information; instructive
infra- [< L.] *a prefix meaning* below
in·frac·tion (in frak'shən) *n.* [see INFRINGE] a
violation of a law, pact, etc.
in·fra·red (in'frə red') *adj.* designating or of
those invisible rays just beyond the red of the
visible spectrum: they have a penetrating
heating effect
in'fra·struc'ture *n.* the basic facilities on
which a city, state, etc. depends, as roads or
schools
in·fre·quent (in frē'kwənt) *adj.* not frequent;
happening seldom; rare —**in·fre'quen·cy** *n.* —**in·**
fre'quent·ly *adv.*
in·fringe (in frinj') *vt.* **-fringed', -fring'ing** [< L.
in-, in + *frangere*, to break] to break or violate (a law or pact) —**infringe on** (or **upon**) to
encroach on (the rights, etc. of others) —**in·**
fringe'ment *n.*
in·fu·ri·ate (in fyoor'ē āt') *vt.* **-at'ed, -at'ing** [<
L. *in-*, in + *furia*, rage] to make very angry;
enrage —**in·fu'ri·a'tion** *n.*
in·fuse (in fyōōz') *vt.* **-fused', -fus'ing** [< L. *in-*,
in + *fundere*, pour] **1.** to instill or impart
(qualities, etc.) **2.** to fill; inspire **3.** to steep
(tea leaves, etc.) to extract the essence —**in·fu'-**
sion (-fyōō'zhən) *n.*
-ing [< OE.] *a suffix used to form the present
participle or verbal nouns [talking, painting]*
in·gen·ious (in jēn'yəs) *adj.* [< L. *in-*, in +
gignere, to produce] **1.** clever, resourceful, etc.
2. made or done cleverly or originally
in·gé·nue (an'zhə nōō', -jə-) *n.* [Fr.,
ingenuous] *Theater* the role of an inexperienced young woman, or an actress in this
role
in·ge·nu·i·ty (in'jə nōō'ə tē) *n.* ingenious quality; cleverness
in·gen·u·ous (in jen'yoo wəs) *adj.* [< L. *in-*, in
+ *gignere*, to produce] **1.** frank; open **2.** simple; naive —**in·gen'u·ous·ly** *adv.*
in·gest (in jest') *vt.* [< L. *in-*, into + *gerere*,
carry] to take (food, etc.) into the body, as by
swallowing —**in·ges'tion** *n.*
in·glo·ri·ous (in glôr'ē əs) *adj.* shameful; disgraceful —**in·glo'ri·ous·ly** *adv.*
in·got (iŋ'gət) *n.* [prob. < OPr. *lingo*, tongue] a
mass of metal cast into a bar or other convenient shape
in·grained (in grānd') *adj.* **1.** firmly established, as habits **2.** inveterate [*an ingrained
liar*]
in·grate (in'grāt) *n.* [< L. *in-*, not + *gratus*,
grateful] an ungrateful person
in·gra·ti·ate (in grā'shē āt') *vt.* **-at'ed, -at'ing**
[< L. *in-*, in + *gratia*, favor] to bring (oneself)
into another's favor —**in·gra'ti·at'ing·ly** *adv.* —
in·gra'ti·a'tion *n.*
in·grat·i·tude (in grat'ə tōōd') *n.* lack of gratitude; ungratefulness
in·gre·di·ent (in grē'dē ənt) *n.* [see INGRESS]
any of the things that make up a mixture;
component
in·gress (in'gres) *n.* [< L. *in-*, into + *gradi*,
go] **1.** the right to enter **2.** an entrance
in·grown (in'grōn') *adj.* grown inward, esp.
into the flesh, as a toenail
in·hab·it (in hab'it) *vt.* [< L. *in-*, in + *habi-*
tare, dwell] to live in

in·hab·it·ant (-i tənt) *n.* a person or animal that inhabits a specified place

in·hal·ant (in hāl′ənt) *adj.* used in inhalation —*n.* a medicine to be inhaled

in·hale (in hāl′) *vt., vi.* -haled′, -hal′ing [< L. *in-*, in + *halare*, breathe] to breathe in (air or smoke) —**in·ha·la·tion** (in′hə lā′shən) *n.*

in·here (in hir′) *vi.* -hered′, -her′ing [< L. *in-*, in + *haerere*, to stick] to be inherent

in·her·ent (in hir′ənt, -her′-) *adj.* [see prec.] existing in someone or something as a natural and inseparable quality, right, etc.

in·her·it (in her′it) *vt., vi.* [< L. *in*, in + *heres*, heir] 1. to receive (property, etc.) as an heir 2. to have (certain characteristics) by heredity —**in·her′i·tor** *n.*

in·her·it·ance *n.* 1. the action of inheriting 2. something inherited

in·hib·it (in hib′it) *vt.* [< L. *in-*, in + *habere*, to hold] to check or repress

in·hi·bi·tion (in′hi bish′ən, in′ə-) *n.* 1. an inhibiting or being inhibited 2. a mental process that restrains an action, emotion, or thought

in·hu·man (in hyōō′mən) *adj.* not having worthy human characteristics; cruel, brutal, etc. —**in′hu·man′i·ty** (-man′ə tē) *n.*

in·im·i·cal (in im′i k'l) *adj.* [< L. *in-*, not + *amicus*, friend] 1. hostile; unfriendly 2. in opposition; adverse

in·im·i·ta·ble (in im′ə tə b'l) *adj.* that cannot be imitated; matchless

in·iq·ui·ty (in ik′wə tē) *n.* [< L. *in-*, not + *aequus*, equal] 1. wickedness; sin 2. *pl.* -ties a wicked or unjust act —**in·iq′ui·tous** *adj.* —**in·iq′ui·tous·ly** *adv.*

in·i·tial (i nish′əl) *adj.* [< L. *in-*, in + *ire*, go] of or at the beginning; first —*n.* the first letter of a name —*vt.* -tialed or -tialled, -tial·ing or -tial·ling to mark with initials —**in·i′tial·ly** *adv.*

in·i·ti·ate (i nish′ē āt′) *vt.* -at′ed, -at′ing [see INITIAL] 1. to bring into practice or use 2. to teach the fundamentals of a subject to 3. to admit as a member into a fraternity, club, etc., esp. with a special or secret ceremony —**in·i′ti·a′tion** *n.*

in·i·ti·a·tive (i nish′ē ə tiv, -nish′ə-) *n.* 1. the action of taking the first step or move 2. ability in originating new ideas or methods 3. the introduction of proposed legislation, as to popular vote, by voters' petitions

in·ject (in jekt′) *vt.* [< L. *in-*, in + *jacere*, to throw] 1. to force (a fluid) into a vein, tissue, etc. by means of a syringe, etc. 2. to introduce (a remark, etc.) —**in·jec′tion** *n.*

in·junc·tion (in juŋk′shən) *n.* [< L. *in-*, in + *jungere*, join] 1. a command; order 2. a court order prohibiting or ordering a given action —**in·junc′tive** *adj.*

in·jure (in′jər) *vt.* -jured, -jur·ing [see INJURY] 1. to do harm or damage to; hurt 2. to wrong or offend

in·ju·ri·ous (in joor′ē əs) *adj.* injuring or likely to injure; harmful

in·ju·ry (in′jər ē) *n., pl.* -ries [< L. *in-*, not + *jus*, right] 1. physical harm to a person, etc. 2. an injurious act

in·jus·tice (in jus′tis) *n.* 1. a being unjust 2. an unjust act; wrong

ink (iŋk) *n.* [< Gr. *en-*, in + *kaiein*, to burn] a colored liquid used for writing, printing, etc. —*vt.* to cover, mark, or color with ink

ink·ling (iŋk′liŋ) *n.* [ME. *ingkiling*] 1. a hint; suggestion 2. a vague notion

ink′well′ *n.* a container for ink

ink′y *adj.* -i·er, -i·est 1. like very dark ink in color; black 2. covered with ink

in·laid (in′lād′, in lād′) *adj.* set into a surface or decorated, etc. by inlaying

in·land (in′lənd; *for n. & adv. usually* -land′) *adj.* of or in the interior of a country —*n.* inland areas —*adv.* into or toward the interior

in-law (in′lô′) *n.* [< (MOTHER)-IN-LAW, etc.] [Colloq.] a relative by marriage

in·lay (in′lā′; *for v., also in* lā′) *vt.* -laid′, -lay′-ing 1. to set (pieces of wood, metal, etc.) into a surface to make a design 2. to decorate thus —*n., pl.* -lays′ 1. inlaid decoration or material 2. a filling for a tooth made from a mold and cemented in

in·let (in′let) *n.* a narrow strip of water extending into a body of land

in·mate (in′māt′) *n.* a person confined with others in a prison, etc.

in me·mo·ri·am (in mə môr′ē əm) [L.] in memory (of)

in·most (in′mōst′) *adj.* 1. located farthest within 2. most intimate or secret

inn (in) *n.* [OE.] 1. a small hotel 2. a restaurant or tavern

in·nards (in′ərdz) *n.pl.* [< INWARDS] [Colloq.] inner organs or parts

in·nate (i nāt′, in′āt) *adj.* [< L. *in-*, in + *nasci*, be born] inborn; natural

in·ner (in′ər) *adj.* 1. located farther within; interior 2. intimate or secret

inner circle the small, exclusive, most influential part of a group

inner city the central sections of a large city, esp. when crowded or blighted

in′ner·most′ *adj. same as* INMOST

in′ner·sole′ *n. same as* INSOLE

in·ning (in′iŋ) *n.* [< OE. *innung*, getting in] *Baseball & (pl.) Cricket* 1. a team's turn at bat 2. a numbered round of play in which both teams have a turn at bat

inn′keep′er *n.* the owner of an inn

in·no·cent (in′ə sənt) *adj.* [< L. *in-*, not + *nocere*, to harm] 1. free from sin, evil, etc.; specif., not guilty of a specific crime 2. harmless 3. knowing no evil 4. without guile; artless 5. naive —*n.* an innocent person, as a child —**in′no·cence** *n.*

in·noc·u·ous (i näk′yoo wəs) *adj.* [see prec.] harmless —**in·noc′u·ous·ly** *adv.*

in·no·va·tion (in′ə vā′shən) *n.* [< L. *in-*, in + *novus*, new] 1. the process of making changes 2. a new method, custom, device, etc. —**in′no·vate′** *vi., vt.* -vat′ed, -vat′ing —**in′no·va′tor** *n.*

in·nu·en·do (in′yoo wen′dō) *n., pl.* -does, -dos [L. < in-, in + -nuere, to nod] a hint or sly remark, usually derogatory

in·nu·mer·a·ble (i nōō′mər ə b'l) *adj.* too numerous to be counted

in·oc·u·late (i näk′yoo lāt′) *vt.* -lat′ed, -lat′ing [< L. *inoculare*, to engraft a bud] to inject a serum or vaccine into, esp. in order to create immunity —**in·oc′u·la′tion** *n.* —**in·oc′u·la′tor** *n.*

in·of·fen·sive (in′ə fen′siv) *adj.* causing no harm or annoyance; unobjectionable

in·op·er·a·tive (in äp′ər ə tiv, -ə rāt′iv) *adj.* not working or functioning

in·or·di·nate (in ôr′d'n it) *adj.* [< L. *in-*, not + *ordo*, an order] excessive

in·or·gan·ic (in′ôr gan′ik) *adj.* not organic; specif. designating or of matter not animal or vegetable; not living

in·put (in′poot′) *n.* what is put in, as power into a machine, data into a computer, etc.

in·quest (in′kwest) *n.* [see INQUIRE] a judicial inquiry, esp. when held before a jury, as a coroner's investigation of a death

in·qui·e·tude (in kwī′ə tōōd′) *n.* restlessness; uneasiness

in·quire (in kwīr′) *vi.* -quired′, -quir′ing [< L. *in-*, into + *quaerere*, seek] **1.** to ask a question or questions **2.** to investigate (usually with *into*) —*vt.* to seek information about —**In·quir′er** *n.*

in·quir·y (in′kwə rē, in kwīr′ē) *n., pl.* -ies **1.** an inquiring; investigation **2.** a question

in·qui·si·tion (in′kwə zish′ən) *n.* **1.** an inquiry or investigation **2.** [I-] *R.C.Ch.* formerly, the tribunal for suppressing heresy and heretics **3.** any harsh suppression or relentless questioning

in·quis·i·tive (in kwiz′ə tiv) *adj.* **1.** inclined to ask many questions **2.** unnecessarily curious; prying —**in·quis′i·tive·ness** *n.*

in·quis′i·tor *n.* **1.** an investigator **2.** [I-] an official of the Inquisition —**in·quis′i·to′ri·al** (-tôr′ē əl) *adj.*

in re (in rē, rā) [L.] in the matter (of)

in·road (in′rōd′) *n.* **1.** a raid **2.** [*usually pl.*] any injurious encroachment

in·sane (in sān′) *adj.* **1.** mentally ill or deranged; mad **2.** of or for insane people **3.** very foolish; senseless —**in·sane′ly** *adv.* —**in·san′i·ty** (-san′ə tē) *n., pl.* -ties

in·sa·ti·a·ble (in sā′shə b′l, -shē ə-) *adj.* [see IN-[2] & SATIATE] that cannot be satisfied —**in·sa′ti·a·bly** *adv.*

in·scribe (in skrīb′) *vt.* -scribed′, -scrib′ing [< L. *in-*, in + *scribere*, write] **1.** to mark or engrave (words, symbols, etc.) on (a surface) **2.** to add (a person's name) to a list **3.** *a*) to dedicate (a book, etc.) *b*) to autograph **4.** to fix in the mind

in·scrip·tion (in skrip′shən) *n.* **1.** an inscribing **2.** something inscribed

in·scru·ta·ble (in skrōōt′ə b′l) *adj.* [< L. *in-*, not + *scrutari*, examine] not easily understood; enigmatic —**in·scru′ta·bil′i·ty** *n.*

in·sect (in′sekt) *n.* [< L. *insectum*, lit., notched] any of a large group of small, usually winged, invertebrates, as beetles, flies, etc., having three pairs of legs

in·sec·ti·cide (in sek′tə sīd′) *n.* any substance used to kill insects

in′sec·tiv′o·rous (-tiv′ər əs) *adj.* [< INSECT + L. *vorare*, devour] feeding chiefly on insects —**in·sec′ti·vore′** (-tə vôr′) *n.*

in·se·cure (in′si kyoor′) *adj.* **1.** not safe from danger **2.** feeling anxiety **3.** not firm or dependable —**in′se·cu′ri·ty** *n.*

in·sem·i·nate (in sem′ə nāt′) *vt.* -nat′ed, -nat′ing [< L. *in-*, in + *semen*, seed] **1.** to impregnate with semen **2.** to imbue (with ideas, etc.) —**in·sem′i·na′tion** *n.*

in·sen·sate (in sen′sāt, -sit) *adj.* **1.** not feeling sensation **2.** stupid **3.** without regard or feeling; cold —**in·sen′sate·ly** *adv.*

in·sen·si·ble (in sen′sə b′l) *adj.* **1.** unable to perceive with the senses **2.** unconscious **3.** unaware **4.** so slight as to be virtually imperceptible —**in·sen′si·bil′i·ty** *n.*

in·sert (in surt′) *vt.* [< L. *in-*, in + *serere*, join] to put or fit (something) into something else — *n.* (in′sərt) anything inserted or to be inserted —**in·ser′tion** *n.*

in·set (in set′) *vt.* -set′, -set′ting to set in; insert —*n.* (in′set) something inserted

in·side (in′sīd′, -sīd′; *for prep. & adv., usually* in′sīd′) *n.* **1.** the inner side, surface, or part **2.** [*pl.*] [Colloq.] the viscera —*adj.* **1.** internal **2.** secret —*adv.* **1.** on or in the inside; within **2.** indoors —*prep.* in or within —**inside of** within the space or time of —**inside out 1.** reversed **2.** [Colloq.] thoroughly

in·sid′er *n.* **1.** a person inside a given place or group **2.** one having secret or confidential information

in·sid·i·ous (in sid′ē əs) *adj.* [< L. *insidiae*, an ambush] **1.** characterized by treachery or slyness **2.** more dangerous than seems evident — **in·sid′i·ous·ly** *adv.*

in·sight (in′sīt′) *n.* **1.** the ability to see and understand clearly the inner nature of things **2.** an instance of such understanding

in·sig·ni·a (in sig′nē ə) *n.pl., sing.* -sig′ni·a, -sig′ne (-nē) [ult. < L. *in-*, in + *signum*, mark] distinguishing marks, as emblems of rank, membership, etc.

in·sig·nif·i·cant (in′sig nif′ə kənt) *adj.* **1.** meaningless **2.** unimportant; trivial **3.** small; unimposing —**in′sig·nif′i·cance** *n.*

in·sin·cere (in′sin sir′) *adj.* not sincere; deceptive or hypocritical —**in′sin·cere′ly** *adv.* —**in′sin·cer′i·ty** (-ser′ə tē) *n.*

in·sin·u·ate (in sin′yoo wāt′) *vt.* -at′ed, -at′ing [< L. *in-*, in + *sinus*, a curve] **1.** to introduce or work into gradually, indirectly, etc. **2.** to hint or suggest indirectly; imply —**in·sin′u·a′tion** *n.*

in·sip·id (in sip′id) *adj.* [< Fr. < L. *in-*, not + *sapidus*, savory] **1.** without flavor; tasteless **2.** not exciting; dull

in·sist (in sist′) *vi.* [< L. *in-*, on + *sistere*, to stand] to take and maintain a stand (often with *on* or *upon*) —*vt.* **1.** to demand strongly **2.** to declare firmly

in·sist′ent *adj.* **1.** insisting or demanding **2.** demanding attention —**in·sist′ence** *n.*

in·so·far (in′sə fär′) *adv.* to such a degree or extent (usually with *as*)

in·sole (in′sōl′) *n.* **1.** the inside sole of a shoe **2.** a removable sole put inside a shoe for comfort

in·so·lent (in′sə lənt) *adj.* [< L. *in-*, not + *solere*, be accustomed] boldly disrespectful; impudent —**in′so·lence** *n.*

in·sol·vent (in säl′vənt) *adj.* not solvent; unable to pay debts —**in·sol′ven·cy** *n.*

in·som·ni·a (in säm′nē ə) *n.* [< L. *in-*, without + *somnus*, sleep] abnormal inability to sleep —**in·som′ni·ac′** (-ak′) *n.*

in·so·much (in′sō much′) *adv.* **1.** to such an extent (*that*) **2.** inasmuch (*as*)

in·sou·ci·ant (in sōō′sē ənt) *adj.* [Fr. < *in-*, not + *soucier*, to care] calm and unbothered; carefree —**in·sou′ci·ance** *n.*

in·spect (in spekt′) *vt.* [< L. *in-*, at + *specere*, look at] **1.** to look at carefully **2.** to examine officially —**in·spec′tion** *n.*

in·spec′tor *n.* **1.** one who inspects; official examiner **2.** an officer on a police force, ranking next below a superintendent

in·spi·ra·tion (in′spə rā′shən) *n.* **1.** an inhaling **2.** an inspiring or being inspired mentally or emotionally **3.** *a*) any stimulus to creative thought or action *b*) an inspired idea, action, etc. —**in′spi·ra′tion·al** *adj.*

in·spire (in spīr′) *vt.* -spired′, -spir′ing [< L. *in-*, in + *spirare*, breathe] **1.** to inhale **2.** to stimulate, as to some creative effort **3.** to motivate by divine influence **4.** to arouse (a feeling) in (someone) **5.** to cause —*vi.* **1.** to inhale **2.** to give inspiration

Inst. **1.** Instant **2.** Institution

in·sta·bil·i·ty (in′stə bil′ə tē) *n.* lack of firmness, steadiness, determination, etc.

in·stall, in·stal (in stôl′) *vt.* -stalled′, -stall′ing [< ML. *in-*, in + *stallum*, a place] **1.** to place in an office, rank, etc. with formality **2.** to establish in a place **3.** to fix in position for use [*to install* new fixtures] —**in·stal·la·tion** (in′stə lā′shən) *n.*

in·stall′ment, in·stal′ment *n.* **1.** an installing or being installed **2.** any of the parts of a sum of money to be paid at regular specified times **3.** any of several parts, as of a magazine serial
installment plan a system by which purchases are paid for in installments
in·stance (in′stəns) *n.* [see INSTANT] **1.** an example; case **2.** a step in proceeding; occasion *[in the first instance] —vt.* **-stanced, -stanc·ing** to give as an example; cite *—for instance* as an example
in·stant (in′stənt) *adj.* [< L. *in-*, upon + *stare*, to stand] **1.** urgent; pressing **2.** of the current month: an old usage *[your letter of the 8th instant]* **3.** imminent **4.** immediate **5.** concentrated or precooked for quick preparation, as a food or beverage *—n.* **1.** a moment **2.** a particular moment *—the instant* as soon as
in·stan·ta·ne·ous (in′stən tā′nē əs) *adj.* done or happening in an instant; immediate
in′stant·ly *adv.* immediately
in·stead (in sted′) *adv.* [IN + STEAD] in place of the one mentioned *—instead of* in place of
in·step (in′step′) *n.* the upper surface of the arch of the foot, between the ankle and the toes
in·sti·gate (in′stə gāt′) *vt.* **-gat′ed, -gat′ing** [< L. *in-*, on + *stigare*, to prick] **1.** to urge on to an action **2.** to foment (rebellion) **—in′sti·ga′tion** *n.* **—in′sti·ga′tor** *n.*
in·still, in·stil (in stil′) *vt.* **-stilled′, -still′ing** [< L. *in-*, in + *stilla*, a drop] **1.** to put in drop by drop **2.** to put (an idea, feeling, etc.) *in* or *into* gradually
in·stinct (in′stiŋkt) *n.* [< L. *instinguere*, impel] **1.** (an) inborn tendency to behave in a way characteristic of a species **2.** a natural or acquired tendency; knack **—in·stinc′tive** *adj.* **—in·stinc′tive·ly** *adv.*
in·sti·tute (in′stə tōōt′) *vt.* **-tut′ed, -tut′ing** [< L. *in-*, in + *statuere*, set up] **1.** to set up; establish **2.** to start; initiate *—n.* something instituted; specif., *a)* an organization for the promotion of art, science, etc. *b)* a school or college specializing in some field
in′sti·tu′tion (-tōō′shən) *n.* **1.** an instituting or being instituted **2.** an established law, custom, etc. **3.** *a)* an organization having a social, educational, or religious purpose *b)* the building housing it **4.** [Colloq.] a well-established person or thing **—in′sti·tu′tion·al** *adj.*
in′sti·tu′tion·al·ize *vt.* **-ized′, -iz′ing 1.** to make into an institution **2.** to make institutional **3.** to place in an institution, as for treatment **—in′sti·tu′tion·al·i·za′tion** *n.*
in·struct (in strukt′) *vt.* [< L. *in-*, in + *struere*, pile up] **1.** to teach; educate **2.** to inform **3.** to order or direct
in·struc′tion (-struk′shən) *n.* **1.** an instructing; education **2.** something taught **3.** [*pl.*] orders or directions
in·struc′tive *adj.* giving knowledge
in·struc′tor *n.* **1.** a teacher **2.** a college teacher ranking below an assistant professor **—in·struc′tor·ship′** *n.*
in·stru·ment (in′strə mənt) *n.* [see INSTRUCT] **1.** a means of doing something **2.** a tool or implement **3.** a device for indicating, measuring, controlling, etc. **4.** any of various devices producing musical sound **5.** *Law* a formal document
in′stru·men′tal (-men′t'l) *adj.* **1.** serving as a means; helpful **2.** of, performed on, or written for a musical instrument
in′stru·men′tal·ist *n.* one who performs on a musical instrument

in′stru·men·tal′i·ty (-tal′ə tē) *n., pl.* **-ties** a means; agency
in′stru·men·ta′tion (-tā′shən) *n.* the writing or scoring of music for instruments
in·sub·or·di·nate (in′sə bôr′d'n it) *adj.* not submitting to authority; disobedient **—in′sub·or′di·na′tion** *n.*
in·sub·stan·tial (in′səb stan′shəl) *adj.* not substantial; specif., *a)* unreal *b)* flimsy
in·suf·fer·a·ble (in suf′ər ə b'l) *adj.* not sufferable; intolerable **—in·suf′fer·a·bly** *adv.*
in·su·lar (in′sə lər) *adj.* [< L. *insula*, island] **1.** of or like an island or islanders **2.** narrowminded; illiberal
in′su·late′ (-lāt′) *vt.* **-lat′ed, -lat′ing** [< L. *insula*, island] **1.** to set apart; isolate **2.** to cover with a nonconducting material in order to prevent the escape of electricity, heat, etc. **—in′su·la′tor** *n.*
in′su·la′tion *n.* **1.** an insulating or being insulated **2.** material used to insulate
in·su·lin (in′sə lin) *n.* [< L. *insula*, island: referring to islands of tissue in the pancreas] an extract from the pancreas of sheep, oxen, etc., used in treating diabetes
in·sult (in sult′) *vt.* [< L. *in-*, on + *salire*, to leap] to treat or speak to with scorn or disrespect *—n.* (in′sult) an insulting act, remark, etc. **—in·sult′ing** *adj.*
in·su·per·a·ble (in sōō′pər ə b'l) *adj.* [< L. *in-*, not + *superare*, overcome] that cannot be overcome **—in·su′per·a·bil′i·ty** *n.*
in·sup·port·a·ble (in′sə pôrt′ə b'l) *adj.* not supportable; unbearable
in·sur·ance (in shoor′əns) *n.* **1.** an insuring or being insured **2.** a contract (**insurance policy**) whereby compensation is guaranteed to the insured for a specified loss by fire, death, etc. **3.** the amount for which something is insured **4.** the business of insuring against loss
in·sure (in shoor′) *vt.* **-sured′, -sur′ing** [see IN-¹ & SURE] **1.** to take out or issue insurance on **2.** same as ENSURE **—in·sur′a·ble** *adj.*
in·sur·gent (in sur′jənt) *adj.* [< L. *in-*, upon + *surgere*, to rise] rising up against established authority *—n.* an insurgent person **—in·sur′gence** *n.*
in·sur·rec·tion (in′sə rek′shən) *n.* [see prec.] a rising up against established authority; revolt **—in′sur·rec′tion·ist** *n.*
int. 1. interest **2.** international
in·tact (in takt′) *adj.* [< L. *in-*, not + *tactus*, touched] unimpaired or uninjured; kept or left whole
in·tagl·io (in tal′yō) *n., pl.* **-los** [It. < *in-*, in + *tagliare*, to cut] a design carved or engraved below the surface
in·take (in′tāk′) *n.* **1.** a taking in **2.** amount taken in **3.** a place in a pipe, etc. where a fluid enters
in·tan·gi·ble (in tan′jə b'l) *adj.* **1.** that cannot be touched; incorporeal **2.** having value, but not material being or intrinsic value, as good will or stocks **3.** not easily defined; vague *—n.* something intangible **—in·tan′gi·bil′i·ty** *n.*
in·te·ger (in′tə jər) *n.* [L., whole] any whole number (as 5 or 10, or −5 or −10) or zero
in·te·gral (-grəl) *adj.* [see prec.] **1.** necessary for completeness; essential **2.** whole or complete **3.** forming a whole from parts
in·te·grate (-grāt′) *vt., vi.* **-grat′ed, -grat′ing** [< L. *integer*, whole] **1.** to make or become whole or complete **2.** to bring (parts) together into a whole **3.** *a)* to remove barriers imposing segregation upon (racial groups) *b)* to abolish segregation in **—in′te·gra′tion** *n.*
in·teg·ri·ty (in teg′rə tē) *n.* [see INTEGER] **1.**

completeness; wholeness **2.** unimpaired condition **3.** honesty, sincerity, etc.

in·teg·u·ment (in teg′yōo mənt) *n.* [< L. *in-*, upon + *tegere*, to cover] an outer covering; skin, shell, etc.

in·tel·lect (in′t'l ekt′) *n.* [< L. *inter-*, between + *legere*, choose] **1.** the ability to reason or understand **2.** high intelligence **3.** a very intelligent person

in·tel·lec·tu·al (in′t'l ek′chōō wəl) *adj.* **1.** of, involving, or appealing to the intellect **2.** requiring intelligence **3.** showing high intelligence —*n.* one who has intellectual interests — **in′tel·lec′tu·al·ly** *adv.*

in·tel·li·gence (in tel′ə jəns) *n.* [< L.: see INTELLECT] **1.** *a)* the ability to learn or understand *b)* the ability to cope with a new situation **2.** news or information **3.** those engaged in gathering secret information

in·tel′li·gent (-jənt) *adj.* having or showing intelligence; bright; clever

in·tel′li·gent′si·a (-jent′sē ə) *n.* [< Russ.] intellectuals collectively

in·tel·li·gi·ble (in tel′i jə b'l) *adj.* [< L.: see INTELLECT] that can be understood; clear; comprehensible —**in·tel′li·gi·bil′i·ty** *n.*

in·tem·per·ate (in tem′pər it) *adj.* **1.** not temperate or moderate; excessive **2.** drinking too much alcoholic liquor —**in·tem′per·ance** *n.* —**in·tem′per·ate·ly** *adv.*

in·tend (in tend′) *vt.* [< L. *in-*, at + *tendere*, to stretch] **1.** to plan; purpose **2.** to mean (something) to be or be used (*for*) **3.** to mean; signify —*vi.* to have a purpose

in·tend′ed *n.* [Colloq.] one's prospective wife or husband

in·tense (in tens′) *adj.* [see INTEND] **1.** very strong [an *intense* light] **2.** strained to the utmost; strenuous [*intense* thought] **3.** characterized by much action, emotion, etc. —**in·tense′ly** *adv.*

in·ten·si·fy (in tens′sə fī′) *vt., vi.* **-fied′, -fy′ing** to make or become more intense —**in·ten′si·fi·ca′tion** *n.* —**in·ten′si·fi′er** *n.*

in·ten′si·ty *n., pl.* **-ties 1.** a being intense **2.** great energy or vehemence, as of emotion **3.** the amount of force or energy of heat, light, sound, etc.

in·ten′sive *adj.* **1.** of or characterized by intensity; thorough **2.** designating very attentive hospital care given to patients, as after surgery **3.** *Gram.* giving force or emphasis (Ex.: "very" in "the very same man") —*n.* an intensive word, prefix, etc.

in·tent (in tent′) *adj.* [see INTEND] **1.** firmly directed; earnest **2.** having one's attention or purpose firmly fixed [*intent* on going] —*n.* **1.** an intending **2.** something intended; purpose —**to all intents and purposes** in almost every respect

in·ten·tion (in ten′shən) *n.* **1.** a determination to act in a specified way **2.** anything intended; purpose

in·ten′tion·al *adj.* done purposely

in·ter (in tur′) *vt.* **-terred′, -ter′ring** [< L. *in*, in + *terra*, earth] to put (a dead body) into a grave or tomb; bury

inter- [L.] *a combining form meaning:* **1.** between or among [*interstate*] **2.** with or on each other (or one another), mutual [*interact*]

in·ter·act (in′tər akt′) *vi.* to act on one another —**in′ter·ac′tion** *n.* —**in′ter·ac′tive** *adj.*

in′ter·breed′ *vt., vi.* **-bred′, -breed′ing** same as HYBRIDIZE

in′ter·cede′ (-sēd′) *vi.* **-ced′ed, -ced′ing** [< L. *inter-*, between + *cedere*, go] **1.** to plead in be-

half of another **2.** to intervene for the purpose of producing agreement; mediate

in·ter·cept (in′tər sept′) *vt.* [< L. *inter-*, between + *capere*, take] **1.** to seize, stop, or interrupt on the way [to *intercept* a message] **2.** *Math.* to mark off between two points, lines, or planes —**in′ter·cep′tion** *n.* —**in′ter·cep′tor,** **in′ter·cept′er** *n.*

in′ter·ces′sion (-sesh′ən) *n.* an interceding; mediation in behalf of another —**in′ter·ces′sor** (-ses′ər) *n.* —**in′ter·ces′so·ry** *adj.*

in′ter·change′ *vt.* **-changed′, -chang′ing 1.** to give and take mutually; exchange **2.** to put (each of two things) in the other's place **3.** to alternate —*vi.* to change places —*n.* (in′tər chānj′) **1.** an interchanging **2.** a place on a freeway where traffic can enter or depart —**in′ter·change′a·ble** *adj.*

in′ter·col·le′gi·ate *adj.* between or among colleges and universities

in·ter·com (in′tər käm′) *n.* a radio or telephone intercommunication system, as between rooms

in′ter·com·mu′ni·cate′ *vt., vi.* **-cat′ed, -cat′ing** to communicate with or to each other or one another

in′ter·con·nect′ *vt., vi.* to connect with one another

in·ter·course (in′tər kôrs′) *n.* [see INTER- & COURSE] **1.** communication or dealings between people, countries, etc. **2.** the sexual joining of two individuals; copulation: in full **sexual intercourse**

in′ter·de·pend′ence *n.* mutual dependence — **in′ter·de·pend′ent** *adj.*

in·ter·dict (in′tər dikt′) *vt.* [< L. *inter-*, between + *dicere*, say] **1.** to prohibit (an action) **2.** to restrain from doing or using something — *n.* (in′tər dikt′) an official prohibition or restraint —**in′ter·dic′tion** *n.*

in·ter·est (in′trist, in′tər ist) *n.* [< L. *inter-*, between + *esse*, be] **1.** a right to, or share in, something **2.** anything in which one has a share **3.** [often *pl.*] welfare; benefit **4.** [usually *pl.*] those having a common concern in some industry, cause, etc. [the steel *interests*] **5.** *a)* a feeling of concern, curiosity, etc. about something *b)* the power of causing this feeling *c)* something causing this feeling **6.** importance **7.** *a)* money paid for the use of money *b)* the rate of such payment —*vt.* **1.** to involve or excite the interest or attention of **2.** to cause to have an interest, or share, in —**in the interest(s) of** for the sake of

in′ter·est·ed *adj.* **1.** having an interest or share **2.** influenced by personal interest

in′ter·est·ing *adj.* exciting interest, curiosity, or attention —**in′ter·est·ing·ly** *adv.*

in′ter·face′ *n.* a surface that forms a boundary between two parts

in·ter·fere (in′tər fir′) *vi.* **-fered′, -fer′ing** [< L. *inter-*, between + *ferire*, to strike] **1.** to clash; collide **2.** *a)* to come between; intervene *b)* to meddle **3.** *Sports* to hinder an opposing player in any of various illegal ways —**interfere with** to hinder —**in′ter·fer′ence** *n.*

in·ter·im (in′tər im) *n.* [L. < *inter*, between] the period of time between; meantime —*adj.* temporary

in·te·ri·or (in tir′ē ər) *adj.* [< L. *inter*, between] **1.** situated within; inner **2.** inland **3.** private —*n.* **1.** the interior part, as of a room, country, etc. **2.** the domestic affairs of a country —**in·te′ri·or·ly** *adv.*

in·ter·ject (in′tər jekt′) *vt.* [< L. *inter-*, between + *jacere*, to throw] to throw in between; insert —**in′ter·jec′tor** *n.*

in·ter·jec′tion (-jek′shən) *n.* **1.** an interjecting **2.** something interjected **3.** *Gram.* an exclamation —Abbrev. **Interj.**

in′ter·lace′ *vt., vi.* **-laced′, -lac′ing 1.** to weave together **2.** to connect intricately

in′ter·lard′ *vt.* [see INTER- & LARD] to intersperse; diversify [to *interlard* a lecture with quotations]

in′ter·line′[1] *vt.* **-lined′, -lin′ing** to write or print (something) between the lines of (a text, etc.) —**in′ter·lin′e·ar** (-lin′ē ər) *adj.*

in′ter·line′[2] *vt.* **-lined′, -lin′ing** to put an inner lining under the ordinary lining of (a garment)

in′ter·lock′ *vt., vi.* to lock together; join with one another

in·ter·loc·u·tor (in′tər läk′yə tər) *n.* [< L. *inter*, between + *loqui*, to talk] **1.** a person taking part in a conversation **2.** the master of ceremonies in a minstrel show

in′ter·loc′u·to′ry (-tôr′ē) *adj.* **1.** conversational **2.** *Law* not final, as a decree

in·ter·lop·er (in′tər lō′pər) *n.* [prob. < INTER- + LOPE] one who meddles in others' affairs

in·ter·lude (in′tər lood′) *n.* [< L. *inter*, between + *ludus*, play] anything that fills time between two events, as music between acts of a play

in′ter·mar′ry *vi.* **-ried, -ry·ing** to become connected by marriage: said of persons of different races, religions, etc. —**in′ter·mar′riage** *n.*

in′ter·me′di·ar′y (-mē′dē er′ē) *adj.* **1.** acting as a mediator **2.** intermediate —*n., pl.* **-ies** a go-between; mediator

in′ter·me′di·ate (-mē′dē it) *adj.* [< L. *inter*-, between + *medius*, middle] being or happening between; in the middle —*n.* **1.** anything intermediate **2.** *same as* INTERMEDIARY

in·ter·ment (in tur′mənt) *n.* burial

in·ter·mez·zo (in′tər met′sō) *n., pl.* **-zos, -zi** (-sē, -zē) [It.] a short piece of music, as between parts of a composition

in·ter·mi·na·ble (in tur′mi nə b'l) *adj.* lasting, or seeming to last, forever; endless

in·ter·min·gle (in′tər miŋ′g'l) *vt., vi.* **-gled, -gling** to mix together; mingle

in′ter·mis′sion (-mish′ən) *n.* [< L. *inter*-, between + *mittere*, to send] an interval between periods of activity, as between acts of a play

in·ter·mit·tent (in′tər mit′'nt) *adj.* [see INTERMISSION] stopping and starting again at intervals; periodic —**in′ter·mit′tent·ly** *adv.*

in′ter·mix′ *vt., vi.* to mix together; blend

in·tern (in′tərn) *n.* [< L. *internus*, inward] **1.** a doctor serving as an assistant resident in a hospital, generally just after graduation from medical school **2.** an apprentice teacher, journalist, etc. Also *sp.* **Interne** —*vi.* to serve as an intern —*vt.* (in turn′) to detain and confine within an area [to *intern* aliens in time of war] —**in·tern′ment** *n.* —**in′tern·ship′** *n.*

in·ter·nal (in tur′n'l) *adj.* [< L. *internus*] **1.** of or on the inside; inner **2.** to be taken inside the body [*internal* remedies] **3.** intrinsic [*internal* evidence] **4.** domestic [*internal* revenue] —**in·ter′nal·ly** *adv.*

in·ter′nal-com·bus′tion engine an engine, as in an automobile, powered by the explosion of a fuel-and-air mixture within the cylinders

Internal revenue governmental income from taxes on income, profits, etc.

in·ter·na·tion·al (in′tər nash′ən 'l) *adj.* **1.** between or among nations **2.** concerned with the relations between nations **3.** for the use of all nations **4.** of or for people in various nations —**in′ter·na′tion·al·ize′** *vt.* **-ized′, -iz′ing**

in·ter·ne·cine (in′tər nē′sin, -sīn) *adj.* [< L.

inter-, between + *necare*, to kill] mutually destructive

in·ter·nist (in′tər nist, in tur′nist) *n.* a doctor who specializes in the nonsurgical treatment of diseases

in′ter·per′son·al *adj.* between persons

in′ter·plan′e·tar′y (-plan′ə ter′ē) *adj.* between planets

in′ter·play′ *n.* action or effect on each other

in·ter·po·late (in tur′pə lāt′) *vt.* **-lat′ed, -lat′ing** [< L. *inter*-, between + *polire*, to polish] **1.** to change (a text, etc.) by inserting new material **2.** to insert between or among others —**in·ter′po·la′tion** *n.*

in·ter·pose (in′tər pōz′) *vt., vi.* **-posed′, -pos′ing 1.** to place or come between **2.** to intervene (with) **3.** to interrupt (with)

in·ter·pret (in tur′prit) *vt.* [< L. *interpres*, negotiator] **1.** to explain or translate **2.** to construe **3.** to give one's own conception of, as a role in a play —*vi.* to translate —**in·ter′pre·ta′tion** *n.* —**in·ter′pret·er** *n.*

in·ter·ra·cial (in′tər rā′shəl) *adj.* between, among, or for persons of different races

in′ter·reg′num (-reg′nəm) *n., pl.* **-nums, -na** (-nə) [L. < *inter*-, between + *regnum*, a reign] **1.** an interval between two successive reigns, when the country has no sovereign **2.** any break in a series

in′ter·re·late′ *vt., vi.* **-lat′ed, -lat′ing** to make, be, or become mutually related —**in′ter·re·la′tion** *n.*

in·ter·ro·gate (in ter′ə gāt′) *vt., vi.* **-gat′ed, -gat′ing** [< L. *inter*-, between + *rogare*, ask] to question formally —**in·ter′ro·ga′tion** *n.* —**in·ter′ro·ga′tor** *n.*

in·ter·rog·a·tive (in′tə räg′ə tiv) *adj.* asking a question —*n.* an interrogative word, element, etc.

in·ter·rupt (in′tə rupt′) *vt.* [< L. *inter*-, between + *rumpere*, to break] **1.** to break into (a discussion, etc.) or break in upon (a speaker, worker, etc.) **2.** to make a break in the continuity of —*vi.* to interrupt an action, talk, etc. —**in′ter·rup′tion** *n.*

in′ter·scho·las′tic *adj.* between or among schools

in·ter·sect (in′tər sekt′) *vt.* [< L. *inter*-, between + *secare*, to cut] to divide into two parts by passing through or across —*vi.* to cross each other

in′ter·sec′tion *n.* **1.** an intersecting **2.** the point or line where two lines, surfaces, roads, etc. meet or cross

in·ter·sperse (in′tər spurs′) *vt.* **-spersed′, -spers′ing** [< L. *inter*-, among + *spargere*, scatter] **1.** to scatter among other things; put here and there **2.** to vary with things scattered here and there —**in′ter·sper′sion** *n.*

in′ter·state′ *adj.* between states of a federal government

in′ter·stel′lar *adj.* between or among the stars

in·ter·stice (in tur′stis) *n., pl.* **-stic·es** (-stis iz) [Fr. < L. *inter*-, between + *sistere*, to set] a crevice; crack —**in·ter·sti·tial** (in′tər stish′əl) *adj.*

in′ter·twine′ *vt., vi.* **-twined′, -twin′ing** to twine together

in′ter·ur′ban (-ur′bən) *adj.* between cities or towns —*n.* an interurban railway

in·ter·val (in′tər v'l) *n.* [< L. *inter*-, between + *vallum*, a wall] **1.** a space between things **2.** the time between events **3.** the difference in pitch between two tones —**at intervals 1.** now and then **2.** here and there

in·ter·vene (in′tər vēn′) *vi.* **-vened′, -ven′ing** [< L. *inter*-, between + *venire*, come] **1.** to come or be between **2.** to occur between two events, etc. **3.** to come in to modify, settle, or hinder some action, etc.

in·ter·ven·tion (-ven′shən) *n.* **1.** an intervening **2.** interference of one state in the affairs of another —**in′ter·ven′tion·ist** *n.*

in·ter·view (-vyōō′) *n.* **1.** a meeting of people face to face, as for evaluating a job applicant **2.** *a)* a meeting in which a person is asked about his views, etc., as by a reporter *b)* a published account of this —*vt.* to have an interview with —**in′ter·view′er** *n.*

in·ter·weave *vt., vi.* -wove′, -wo′ven, -weav′ing **1.** to weave together **2.** to connect closely

in·tes·tate (in tes′tāt, -tit) *adj.* [< L. *in-*, not + *testari*, make a will] having made no will — *n.* one who has died intestate

in·tes·tine (in tes′tin) *n.* [< L. *intus*, within] [*usually pl.*] the lower part of the alimentary canal, extending from the stomach to the anus and consisting of a convoluted upper part (**small intestine**) and a lower part of greater diameter (**large intestine**); bowel(s) —**in·tes′·tin·al** *adj.*

in·ti·mate (in′tə mit) *adj.* [< L. *intus*, within] **1.** most private or personal **2.** closely associated; very familiar **3.** fundamental —*n.* an intimate friend —*vt.* (-māt′) -mat′ed, -mat′ing to hint or imply —**in′ti·ma·cy** (-mə sē) *n., pl.* -cies —**in′ti·mate·ly** *adv.* —**in′ti·ma′tion** *n.*

in·tim·i·date (in tim′ə dāt′) *vt.* -dat′ed, -dat′-ing [< L. *in-*, in + *timidus*, afraid] to make afraid, as with threats —**in·tim′i·da′tion** *n.*

in·to (in′tōō, -too, -tə) *prep.* [OE.] **1.** toward and within [*into* a room] **2.** continuing to the midst of [to talk *into* the night] **3.** to the form, substance, or condition of [divided *into* parts] **4.** so as to strike [to run *into* a wall] **5.** [Colloq.] involved in [we are *into* jazz now]

in·tol·er·a·ble (in täl′ər ə b′l) *adj.* unbearable; too severe, painful, etc. to be endured

in·tol′er·ant (-ənt) *adj.* unwilling to tolerate others′ beliefs, etc. or persons of other races, etc. —**intolerant** of not able or willing to tolerate —**in·tol′er·ance** *n.*

in·to·na·tion (in′tə nā′shən) *n.* **1.** an intoning **2.** the manner of producing tones with regard to accurate pitch **3.** variations in pitch within an utterance

in·tone (in tōn′) *vt., vi.* -toned′, -ton′ing to speak or recite in a singing tone

in to·to (in tō′tō) [L.] as a whole

in·tox·i·cant (in täk′sə kənt) *n.* something that intoxicates; esp., alcoholic liquor

in·tox′i·cate (-kāt′) *vt.* -cat′ed, -cat′ing [< L. *in-*, in + *toxicum*, a poison] **1.** to make drunk **2.** to excite greatly —**in·tox′i·ca′tion** *n.*

intra- [L., within] *a combining form meaning* within, inside of

in·trac·ta·ble (in trak′tə b′l) *adj.* hard to manage; unruly or stubborn

in·tra·mu·ral (in′trə myoor′əl) *adj.* within the walls or limits of a city, college, etc.

in·tran·si·gent (in tran′sə jənt) *adj.* [ult. < L. *in-*, not + *transigere*, settle] refusing to compromise —*n.* one who is intransigent —**in·tran′·si·gence** *n.*

in·tran·si·tive (in tran′sə tiv) *adj.* not transitive; designating a verb that does not require a direct object to complete its meaning —**in·tran′si·tive·ly** *adv.*

in·tra·u·ter·ine (**contraceptive**) **device** (in′trə yōōt′ər in) *n.* a device, as a plastic loop, inserted in the uterus as a contraceptive

in′tra·ve′nous (-vē′nəs) *adj.* [INTRA- + VENOUS] in, or directly into, a vein

in·trep·id (in trep′id) *adj.* [< L. *in-*, not +

trepidus, alarmed] bold; fearless; brave —**In′·tre·pid′i·ty** *n.* —**in·trep′id·ly** *adv.*

in·tri·cate (in′tri kit) *adj.* [< L. *in-*, in + *tricae*, perplexities] **1.** hard to follow or understand because full of puzzling parts, details, etc. **2.** full of elaborate detail —**in′tri·ca·cy** (-kə sē) *n., pl.* -cies

in·trigue (in trēg′) *vi.* -trigued′, -trigu′ing [see INTRICATE] to plot secretly or underhandedly —*vt.* **1.** to get by secret plotting **2.** to excite the interest or curiosity of —*n.* **1.** secret or underhanded plotting **2.** a secret or underhanded plot or scheme **3.** a secret love affair —**in·trigu′er** *n.*

in·trin·sic (in trin′sik) *adj.* [< L. *intra-*, within + *secus*, close] belonging to the real nature of a thing; inherent —**in·trin′si·cal·ly** *adv.*

in·tro·duce (in′trə dōōs′, -dyōōs′) *vt.* -duced′, -duc′ing [< L. *intro-*, within + *ducere*, to lead] **1.** to put in; insert **2.** to add as a new feature **3.** to bring into use or fashion **4.** *a)* to make acquainted; present (*to*) [*introduce* me to her] *b)* to give experience of [they *introduced* him to music] **5.** to bring forward **6.** to begin [to *introduce* a talk with a joke]

in′tro·duc′tion (-duk′shən) *n.* **1.** an introducing or being introduced **2.** anything that introduces, as the preliminary section of a book or speech

in′tro·duc′to·ry (-tər ē) *adj.* serving to introduce; preliminary: also **in′tro·duc′tive**

in·tro·spec·tion (in′trə spek′shən) *n.* [< L. *intro-*, within + *specere*, to look] a looking into one′s own mind, feelings, etc. —**in′tro·spec′tive** *adj.*

in·tro·vert (in′trə vurt′) *n.* [< L. *intro*, within + *vertere*, to turn] one who is more interested in himself than in his environment or in other people —**in′tro·ver′sion** (-vur′zhən) *n.* —**in′tro·vert′ed** *adj.*

in·trude (in trōōd′) *vt., vi.* -trud′ed, -trud′ing [< L. *in-*, in + *trudere*, to thrust] to force (oneself) upon others without being asked or welcomed —**in·trud′er** *n.*

in·tru·sion (in trōō′zhən) *n.* an intruding —**in·tru′sive** (-siv) *adj.*

in·tu·i·tion (in′too wish′ən) *n.* [< L. *in-*, in + *tueri*, look at] the direct knowing or learning of something without conscious reasoning —**in·tu·i·tive** (in tōō′i tiv) *adj.*

in·un·date (in′ən dāt′) *vt.* -dat′ed, -dat′ing [< L. *in-*, in + *undare*, to flood] to cover as with a flood —**in′un·da′tion** *n.*

in·ure (in yoor′) *vt.* -ured′, -ur′ing [< ME. *in*, in + *ure*, work] to accustom to pain, trouble, etc. —*vi.* to take effect

in·vade (in vād′) *vt.* -vad′ed, -vad′ing [< L. *in-*, in + *vadere*, go] **1.** to enter forcibly, as to conquer **2.** to crowd into **3.** to intrude upon; violate —*vi.* to make an invasion —**in·vad′er** *n.*

in·va·lid[1] (in′və lid) *adj.* [< L. *in-*, not + *valere*, be strong] **1.** weak and sickly **2.** of or for invalids —*n.* one who is ill or disabled —*vt.* to disable or weaken —**in′va·lid·ism** *n.*

in·val·id[2] (in val′id) *adj.* not valid; having no force; null or void

in·val′i·date (-ə dāt′) *vt.* -dat′ed, -dat′ing to make invalid; deprive of legal force

in·val·u·a·ble (in val′yoo wə b′l) *adj.* too valuable to be measured; priceless

in·va·sion (in vā′zhən) *n.* an invading or being invaded, as by an army

in·vec·tive (in vek′tiv) *n.* [see INVEIGH] a violent verbal attack; insults, curses, etc.

in·veigh (in vā′) *vi.* [< L. *in-*, in + *vehere*, carry] to make a violent verbal attack; rail (*against*) —**in·veigh′er** *n.*

in·vei·gle (in vē′g'l, -vā′-) *vt.* -gled, -gling [< MFr. *aveugler,* to blind] to entice or trick into doing something

in·vent (in vent′) *vt.* [< L. *in-,* on + *venire,* come] 1. to think up [to *invent* excuses] 2. to think out or produce (a new device, etc.); originate —**in·ven′tor** *n.*

in·ven′tion (-ven′shən) *n.* 1. an inventing 2. the power of inventing; ingenuity 3. something invented

in·ven′tive (-tiv) *adj.* 1. of invention 2. skilled in inventing —**in·ven′tive·ly** *adv.*

in·ven·to·ry (in′vən tôr′ē) *n., pl.* -ries [see INVENT] 1. an itemized list of goods, property, etc., as of a business 2. the store of goods, etc. for such listing; stock —*vt.* -ried, -ry·ing to make an inventory of

in·verse (in vurs′, in′vurs′) *adj.* inverted; directly opposite —*n.* any inverse thing

in·ver·sion (in vur′zhən) *n.* 1. an inverting or being inverted 2. something inverted

in·vert (in vurt′) *vt.* [< L. *in-,* to + *vertere,* to turn] 1. to turn upside down 2. to reverse the order, position, direction, etc. of —**in·vert′i·ble** *adj.*

in·ver·te·brate (in vur′tə brit, -brāt′) *adj.* not vertebrate; having no backbone, or spinal column —*n.* any invertebrate animal

in·vest (in vest′) *vt.* [< L. *in-,* in + *vestis,* clothing] 1. to clothe 2. to install in office with ceremony 3. to furnish with power, authority, etc. 4. to put (money) into business, bonds, etc. in order to get a profit —*vi.* to invest money —**in·ves′tor** *n.*

in·ves·ti·gate (in ves′tə gāt′) *vt., vi.* -gat′ed, -gat′ing [< L. *in-,* in + *vestigare,* to track] to search (into); inquire —**in·ves′ti·ga′tive** *adj.* — **in·ves′ti·ga′tor** *n.*

in·ves′ti·ga′tion *n.* 1. an investigating 2. a careful inquiry

in·ves·ti·ture (in ves′tə chər) *n.* a formal investing with an office, power, etc.

in·vest·ment (in vest′mənt) *n.* 1. an investing or being invested 2. *a)* money invested *b)* anything in which money is or may be invested

in·vet·er·ate (in vet′ər it) *adj.* [< L. *in-,* in + *vetus,* old] firmly established; habitual —**in·vet′er·a·cy** *n.*

in·vid·i·ous (in vid′ē əs) *adj.* [< L. *invidia,* envy] such as to excite ill will; giving offense, as by discriminating unfairly

in·vig·or·ate (in vig′ə rāt′) *vt.* -at′ed, -at′ing to give vigor to; fill with energy

in·vin·ci·ble (in vin′sə b'l) *adj.* [< L. *in-,* not + *vincere,* overcome] that cannot be overcome; unconquerable —**in·vin′ci·bil′i·ty** (-bil′ə tē) *n.* —**in·vin′ci·bly** *adv.*

in·vi·o·la·ble (in vī′ə lə b'l) *adj.* 1. not to be violated; not to be profaned or injured; sacred 2. indestructible —**in·vi′o·la·bil′i·ty** *n.* —**in·vi′o·la·bly** *adv.*

in·vi′o·late (-lit, -lāt′) *adj.* not violated; kept sacred or unbroken

in·vis·i·ble (in viz′ə b'l) *adj.* 1. not visible; that cannot be seen 2. out of sight 3. imperceptible —**in·vis′i·bil′i·ty** *n.*

in·vi·ta·tion (in′və tā′shən) *n.* 1. an inviting 2. a message or note used in inviting

in′vi·ta′tion·al *adj.* participated in only by those invited, as an art show

in·vite (in vīt′) *vt.* -vit′ed, -vit′ing [< L. *invitare*] 1. to ask to come somewhere or do something 2. to make a request for 3. to give occasion for [action that *invites* scandal] 4. to tempt; entice —*n.* (in′vīt) [Colloq.] an invitation

in·vit′ing *adj.* tempting; enticing

in·vo·ca·tion (in′və kā′shən) *n.* an invoking of God, the Muses, etc.

in·voice (in′vois) *n.* [prob. < ME. *envoie,* message] an itemized list of goods shipped to a buyer, stating prices, etc. —*vt.* -voiced, -voic·ing to present an invoice for or to

in·voke (in vōk′) *vt.* -voked′, -vok′ing [< L. *in-,* on + *vocare,* to call] 1. to call on (God, the Muses, etc.) for blessing, help, etc. 2. to resort to (a law, penalty, etc.) as pertinent 3. to conjure 4. to beg for; implore

in·vol·un·tar·y (in väl′ən ter′ē) *adj.* 1. not done of one's own free will 2. unintentional 3. not consciously controlled [sneezing is *involuntary*] —**in·vol′un·tar′i·ly** *adv.*

in·vo·lute (in′və lōōt′) *adj.* [see INVOLVE] 1. intricate; involved 2. rolled up or curled in a spiral —**in′vo·lu′tion** *n.*

in·volve (in välv′) *vt.* -volved′, -volv′ing [< L. *in-,* in + *volvere,* to roll] 1. to make intricate or complicated 2. to entangle in difficulty, danger, etc.; implicate 3. to affect or include [a riot *involving* thousands] 4. to require [saving *involves* thrift] 5. to make busy; occupy [involved in research] —**in·volve′ment** *n.*

in·vul·ner·a·ble (in vul′nər ə b'l) *adj.* 1. that cannot be wounded or injured 2. proof against attack —**in·vul′ner·a·bly** *adv.*

in·ward (in′wərd) *adj.* 1. situated within; internal 2. mental or spiritual 3. directed toward the inside —*adv.* 1. toward the inside 2. into the mind or soul Also **in′wards** *adv.*

in′ward·ly *adv.* 1. in or on the inside 2. in the mind or spirit 3. toward the inside

i·o·dine (ī′ə dīn′, -din) *n.* [< Gr. *iōdēs,* violetlike] 1. a nonmetallic chemical element used in medicine: symbol, I 2. tincture of iodine, used as an antiseptic

i·o·dize (ī′ə dīz′) *vt.* -dized′, -diz′ing to treat with iodine

i·on (ī′ən, -än) *n.* [< Gr. *ienai,* go] an electrically charged atom or group of atoms

-ion [< L. *-io*] *a suffix meaning* the act, condition, or result of [translation, correction]

I·on·ic (ī än′ik) *adj.* designating or of a Greek style of architecture marked by ornamental scrolls on the capitals

i·on·ize (ī′ə nīz′) *vt., vi.* -ized′, -iz′ing to dissociate into ions, as a salt dissolved in water, or become electrically charged, as a gas under radiation —**i′on·i·za′tion** *n.*

i·on·o·sphere (ī än′ə sfir′) *n.* the outer layers of the earth's atmosphere, with appreciable electron and ion content

i·o·ta (ī ōt′ə) *n.* 1. the ninth letter of the Greek alphabet (I, ι) 2. a tiny quantity

IOU, I.O.U. (ī′ō′yōō′) 1. I owe you 2. a signed note bearing these letters, acknowledging a debt

-ious [see -OUS] *a suffix used to form adjectives meaning* having, characterized by [furious]

ip·e·cac (ip′ə kak′) *n.* [< SAmInd. name] a preparation made from the dried roots of a S. American plant, used to induce vomiting

ip·so fac·to (ip′sō fak′tō) [L.] by that very fact

IQ, I.Q. [intelligence quotient] a number that indicates a person's intelligence (mental age times 100 divided by chronological age)

ir- *same as:* 1. IN-¹ 2. IN-² Used before *r*

Ir. 1. Ireland 2. Irish

I·ra·ni·an (i rā′nē ən) *adj.* of Iran, its people, etc. —*n.* 1. a native of Iran 2. a group of languages, including Persian

I·ra·qi (i rä′kē, -rak′ē) *adj.* of Iraq, its people, etc. —*n.* 1. a native of Iraq 2. the Arabic dialect of the Iraqis

i·ras·ci·ble (i ras′ə b'l) *adj.* [see IRATE] easily angered; quick-tempered

i·rate (ī rāt′, ī′rāt) *adj.* [< L. *ira,* ire] angry; wrathful; incensed —**i·rate′ly** *adv.*

ire (īr) *n.* [< L. *ira*] anger; wrath

Ire. Ireland

ir·i·des·cent (ir′ə des′'nt) *adj.* [< Gr. *iris,* rainbow] having or showing an interplay of rainbowlike colors —**ir′i·des′cence** *n.*

i·ris (ī′ris) *n., pl.* **i′ris·es** [Gr., rainbow] **1.** the round, pigmented membrane surrounding the pupil of the eye **2.** a plant with sword-shaped leaves and showy flowers

I·rish (ī′rish) *adj.* of Ireland, its people, etc. —*n.* the English dialect of Ireland —**the Irish** the people of Ireland —**I′rish·man** *n., pl.* **-men** — **I′rish·wom′an** *n.fem., pl.* **-wom′en**

Irish Sea arm of the Atlantic between Ireland & Great Britain

irk (urk) *vt.* [ME. *irken,* be weary of] to annoy, disgust, tire out, etc.

irk′some (-səm) *adj.* tiresome or annoying

i·ron (ī′ərn) *n.* [OE. *iren*] **1.** a metallic chemical element, the most common of all the metals: symbol, Fe **2.** any device made of iron, as one with a flat undersurface, heated for pressing cloth **3.** [*pl.*] iron shackles **4.** firm strength; power **5.** a golf club with a metal head —*adj.* **1.** of iron **2.** like iron; strong **3.** cruel —*vt.,* *vi.* to press (clothes, etc.) with a hot iron —**iron out** to smooth out; eliminate

i′ron·clad′ *adj.* **1.** covered with iron **2.** difficult to change or break *[ironclad* rules*]*

iron curtain a barrier of secrecy'and censorship, esp. around the U.S.S.R.

i·ron·i·cal (ī rän′i k'l) *adj.* **1.** meaning the contrary of what is expressed **2.** using irony **3.** opposite to what might be expected Also **i·ron′ic** —**i·ron′i·cal·ly** *adv.*

iron lung a large metal respirator enclosing all of the body but the head

i′ron·stone′ *n.* a hard, white ceramic ware

i′ron·ware′ (-wer′) *n.* things made of iron

i·ro·ny (ī′rən ē, ī′ər nē) *n., pl.* **-nies** [< Gr. *eirōn,* dissembler in speech] **1.** expression in which the intended meaning of the words is the opposite of their usual sense **2.** an event or result that is the opposite of what is expected

Ir·o·quois (ir′ə kwoi′) *n., pl.* **-quois′** a member of a tribe of American Indians that lived in New York and Canada —*adj.* of the Iroquois — **Ir′o·quoi′an** *adj., n.*

ir·ra·di·ate (i rā′dē āt′) *vt.* **-at′ed, -at′ing 1.** to shine upon; light up **2.** to enlighten **3.** to radiate **4.** to expose to X-rays, ultraviolet rays, etc. —*vi.* to emit rays; shine —**ir·ra′di·a′tion** *n.*

ir·ra·tion·al (i rash′ən 'l) *adj.* **1.** lacking the power to reason **2.** senseless; unreasonable; absurd —**ir·ra′tion·al·ly** *adv.*

ir·re·claim·a·ble (ir′i klā′mə b'l) *adj.* that cannot be reclaimed

ir·rec·on·cil·a·ble (i rek′ən sīl′ə b'l) *adj.* that cannot be brought into agreement; incompatible —**ir·rec′on·cil′a·bly** *adv.*

ir·re·cov·er·a·ble (ir′i kuv′ər ə b'l) *adj.* that cannot be recovered, rectified, or remedied — **ir′re·cov′er·a·bly** *adv.*

ir·re·deem·a·ble (ir′i dēm′ə b'l) *adj.* **1.** that cannot be bought back **2.** that cannot be converted into coin, as certain paper money **3.** that cannot be changed or reformed —**ir′re·deem′a·bly** *adv.*

ir·ref·u·ta·ble (i ref′yoo tə b'l, ir′i fyoot′ə b'l) *adj.* indisputable

ir·re·gard·less (ir′i gärd′lis) *adj., adv. a substandard or humorous redundancy for* REGARD-LESS

ir·reg·u·lar (i reg′yə lər) *adj.* **1.** not conforming to established rule, standard, etc. **2.** not straight, even, or uniform **3.** *Gram.* not inflected in the usual way *[go* is an *irregular* verb*]* —**ir·reg′u·lar′i·ty** *n.*

ir·rel·e·vant (i rel′ə vənt) *adj.* not pertinent; not to the point —**ir·rel′e·vance, ir·rel′e·van·cy** *n.* —**ir·rel′e·vant·ly** *adv.*

ir·re·li·gious (ir′i lij′əs) *adj.* **1.** indifferent or hostile to religion **2.** profane; impious

ir·re·me·di·a·ble (ir′i mē′dē ə b'l) *adj.* that cannot be remedied; incurable

ir·rep·a·ra·ble (i rep′ər ə b'l) *adj.* that cannot be repaired, mended, remedied, etc.

ir·re·place·a·ble (ir′i plās′ə b'l) *adj.* not replaceable

ir′re·press′i·ble (-pres′ə b'l) *adj.* that cannot be repressed —**ir′re·press′i·bly** *adv.*

ir′re·proach′a·ble (-prō′chə b'l) *adj.* blameless; faultless —**ir′re·proach′a·bly** *adv.*

ir′re·sist′i·ble (-zis′tə b'l) *adj.* that cannot be resisted; too strong, fascinating, etc. to be withstood —**ir′re·sist′i·bly** *adv.*

ir·res·o·lute (i rez′ə loot′) *adj.* not resolute; wavering; indecisive —**ir·res′o·lu′tion** *n.*

ir·re·spec·tive (ir′i spek′tiv) *adj.* regardless (*of*) —**ir′re·spec′tive·ly** *adv.*

ir·re·spon·si·ble (ir′i spän′sə b'l) *adj.* **1.** not accountable for actions **2.** lacking a sense of responsibility —**ir′re·spon′si·bil′i·ty** *n.* —**ir′re·spon′si·bly** *adv.*

ir′re·triev′a·ble (-trēv′ə b'l) *adj.* that cannot be retrieved, recovered, restored, etc.

ir·rev·er·ence (i rev′ər əns) *n.* **1.** lack of reverence **2.** an act or statement showing this —**ir·rev′er·ent** *adj.* —**ir·rev′er·ent·ly** *adv.*

ir·re·vers·i·ble (ir′i vur′sə b'l) *adj.* not reversible; specif., that cannot be repealed or annulled —**ir′re·vers′i·bly** *adv.*

ir·rev·o·ca·ble (i rev′ə kə b'l) *adj.* that cannot be revoked or undone

ir·ri·ga·ble (ir′i gə b'l) *adj.* that can be irrigated

ir·ri·gate (ir′ə gāt′) *vt.* **-gat′ed, -gat′ing** [< L. *in-,* in + *rigare,* to water] **1.** to supply (land) with water by means of artificial ditches **2.** *Med.* to wash out (a cavity, wound, etc.) —**ir′ri·ga′tion** *n.*

ir·ri·ta·ble (ir′i tə b'l) *adj.* **1.** easily irritated or provoked **2.** *Med.* excessively sensitive to a stimulus —**ir′ri·ta·bil′i·ty** *n.* —**ir′ri·ta·bly** *adv.*

ir·ri·tant (-tənt) *adj.* causing irritation —*n.* something causing irritation

ir′ri·tate′ (-tāt′) *vt.* **-tat′ed, -tat′ing** [< L. *irritare,* excite] **1.** to provoke to anger; annoy **2.** to make (a part of the body) inflamed or sore —**ir′ri·ta′tion** *n.*

ir·rupt (i rupt′) *vi.* [< L. *in-,* in + *rumpere,* to break] **1.** to burst violently (*into*) **2.** *Ecol.* to increase abruptly in size of population —**ir·rup′tion** *n.*

is (iz) [OE.] *3d pers. sing., pres. indic.,* of BE

is. 1. island(s) **2.** isle(s)

I·saac (ī′zək) *Bible* one of the patriarchs, son of Abraham, and father of Jacob

I·sa·iah (ī zā′ə) *Bible* **1.** a Hebrew prophet of the 8th cent. B.C. **2.** the book containing his teachings: abbrev. **Isa.**

-ise *chiefly Brit. var. of* -IZE

-ish [OE. *-isc*] *a suffix meaning: a)* of (a specified people) *[Spanish] b)* like *[devilish] c)* somewhat *[tallish] d)* [Colloq.] approximately *[thirtyish]*

Ish·tar (ish′tär) the Babylonian and Assyrian goddess of love and fertility

i·sin·glass (ī′z'n glas′, -ziŋ-) *n.* [prob. < MDu. *huizen,* sturgeon + *blas,* bladder] **1.** a gelatin prepared from fish bladders **2.** mica, esp. in thin sheets

I·sis (ī'sis) the Egyptian goddess of fertility

Is·lam (is'läm, iz'-; is läm') *n.* [Ar. *islām*, lit., submission (to God's will)] **1.** the Muslim religion, a monotheistic religion founded by Mohammed **2.** Muslims collectively or the lands in which they predominate —**Is·lam'ic** (-lam'ik, -läm'-) *adj.*

is·land (ī'lənd) *n.* [< OE. *igland*, lit., island land: sp. after *isle*] **1.** a land mass not so large as a continent, surrounded by water **2.** anything like an island in position or isolation

is'land·er *n.* an inhabitant of an island

isle (īl) *n.* [< L. *insula*] a small island

is·let (ī'lit) *n.* a very small island

ism (iz'm) *n.* a doctrine, theory, system, etc., esp. one whose name ends in *-ism*

-ism [< Gr. *-ismos*] a suffix meaning: **1.** the act or result of *[terrorism]* **2.** the condition, conduct, or qualities of *[patriotism]* **3.** the theory of *[socialism]* **4.** devotion to *[nationalism]* **5.** an instance of *[witticism]* **6.** an abnormal condition caused by *[alcoholism]*

is·n't (iz''nt) is not

iso- [< Gr. *isos*, equal] a combining form meaning equal, similar, alike: also **is-**

i·so·bar (ī'sə bär') *n.* [< prec. + Gr. *baros*, weight] a line on a map connecting points of equal barometric pressure

i·so·late (ī'sə lāt') *vt.* **-lat'ed, -lat'ing** [< It. *isola* (< L. *insula*), island] to set apart from others; place alone —**i'so·la'tion** *n.*

i'so·la'tion·ist *n.* one who wants his country to avoid international alliances, etc. —*adj.* of isolationists —**i'so·la'tion·ism** *n.*

i·so·mer (ī'sə mər) *n.* [< Gr. *isos*, equal + *meros*, a part] any of two or more chemical compounds whose molecules contain the same atoms but in different arrangements

i·so·met·ric (ī'sə met'rik) *adj.* [< Gr. *isos*, equal + *metron*, a measure] **1.** of or having equality of measure: also **i'so·met'ri·cal 2.** of isometrics —*n.* [pl.] exercise in which muscles are briefly tensed in opposition to other muscles or to an immovable object

i·sos·ce·les (ī säs'ə lēz') *adj.* [< Gr. *isos*, equal + *skelos*, a leg] designating a triangle with two equal sides

i·so·tope (ī'sə tōp') *n.* [< ISO- + Gr. *topos*, place] any of two or more forms of an element having the same atomic number but different atomic weights

Is·ra·el (iz'rē əl) **1.** *Bible* Jacob **2.** the Jewish people

Is·rae·li (iz rā'lē) *adj.* of modern Israel or its people —*n., pl.* **-lis, -li** a native or inhabitant of modern Israel

Is·ra·el·ite (iz'rē ə līt') *n.* any of the people of ancient Israel

is·su·ance (ish'ōo wəns) *n.* an issuing; issue

is·sue (ish'ōo) *n.* [< L. *ex-*, out + *ire*, go] **1.** an outgoing; outflow **2.** an exit; outlet **3.** a result; consequence **4.** offspring **5.** a point under dispute **6.** a sending or giving out **7.** all that is put forth at one time **8.** *Med.* a discharge of blood, etc. —*vi.* **-sued, -su·ing 1.** to go or flow out; emerge **2.** to result (*from*) or end (*in*) **3.** to be published —*vt.* **1.** to let out; discharge **2.** to give or deal out (supplies, etc.) **3.** to publish — **at** (or **in**) **issue** in dispute —**take issue** to disagree —**is'su·er** *n.*

-ist [< Gr. *-istēs*] a suffix meaning: **1.** one who does or practices *[satirist]* **2.** one skilled in or occupied with *[druggist, violinist]* **3.** an adherent of *[anarchist]*

isth·mus (is'məs) *n., pl.* **-mus·es, -mi** (-mī) [<

Gr. *isthmos*, a neck] a narrow strip of land connecting two larger bodies of land

it (it) *pron. for pl. see* THEY [OE. *hit*] the animal or thing under discussion *It* is used as: *a*) the subject of an impersonal verb *[it is snowing]* *b*) a subject or object of indefinite sense in various idiomatic constructions *[it's all right, he lords it over us]* —*n.* the player, as in the game of tag, who must do some specific thing —**with it** [Slang] alert, informed, or hip

It., Ital. 1. Italian **2.** Italy

ital. italic (type)

I·tal·ian (i tal'yən) *adj.* of Italy, its people, etc. —*n.* **1.** a native of Italy **2.** the language of Italy

i·tal·ic (i tal'ik) *adj.* [< its early use in *Italy*] designating a type in which the letters slant upward to the right *[this is italic type]* —*n.* [usually *pl.*, sometimes with sing. *v.*] italic type

i·tal·i·cize (i tal'ə sīz') *vt.* **-cized', -ciz'ing** to print in italics

itch (ich) *vi.* [OE. *giccan*] **1.** to feel a tingling of the skin, with the desire to scratch **2.** to have a restless desire —*n.* **1.** an itching on the skin **2.** a restless desire —**the itch** an itching skin disorder —**itch'y** *adj.* **-i·er, -i·est**

-ite [< Gr. *-itēs*] a suffix meaning: **1.** an inhabitant of *[Akronite]* **2.** an adherent of *[laborite]* **3.** a manufactured product *[dynamite]*

i·tem (īt'əm) *n.* [< L. *ita*, so, thus] **1.** an article; unit; separate thing **2.** a bit of news or information

i'tem·ize (-īz') *vt.* **-ized, -iz'ing** to specify the items of; set down by items

it·er·ate (it'ə rāt') *vt.* **-at'ed, -at'ing** [< L. *iterum*, again] to utter or do again or repeatedly —**it'er·a'tion** *n.*

i·tin·er·ant (ī tin'ər ənt) *adj.* [< L. *iter*, a walk] traveling from place to place —*n.* a traveler

i·tin·er·ar·y (ī tin'ə rer'ē) *n., pl.* **-ies 1.** a route **2.** a record of a journey **3.** a detailed plan for a proposed journey

-itis [< Gr. *-itis*] a suffix meaning inflammation of (a specified part or organ) *[sinusitis]*

it'll (it''l) **1.** it will **2.** it shall

its (its) *pron.* that or those belonging to it — **possessive pronominal** *adj.* of, belonging to, or done by it

it's (its) **1.** it is **2.** it has

it·self (it self') *pron.* **1.** the intensive form of IT *[the work itself is easy]* **2.** the reflexive form of IT *[the dog bit itself]* **3.** its true self *[the cat is not itself today]*

it·ty-bit·ty (it'ē bit'ē) *adj.* [alteration < little bit] [Colloq.] very small; tiny: also **it·sy-bit·sy** (it'sē bit'sē)

-ity [< L. *-itas*] a suffix meaning state, condition *[chastity, possibility]*

IUD intrauterine device

I've (īv) I have

-ive [< Fr. *-if* < L. *-ivus*] a suffix meaning: **1.** of, related to, having the nature of *[substantive]* **2.** tending to *[creative]*

i·vo·ry (ī'vər ē, īv'rē) *n., pl.* **-ries** [ult. < Egypt. *ābu*, elephant] **1.** the hard, white substance forming the tusks of elephants, walruses, etc. **2.** a substance like ivory **3.** creamy white **4.** [pl.] [Slang] *a*) piano keys *b*) teeth *c*) dice — *adj.* **1.** of or like ivory **2.** creamy-white

ivory tower figuratively, a place of mental withdrawal from reality and action

i·vy (ī'vē) *n., pl.* **i'vies** [OE. *ifig*] **1.** a climbing vine with a woody stem and evergreen leaves **2.** any of various similar plants, as poison ivy

-ize [< Gr. *-izein*] a suffix meaning: **1.** to cause to be, make *[sterilize]* **2.** to become (like), change into *[crystallize]* **3.** to subject to, combine with *[oxidize]* **4.** to engage in *[theorize]*

J

J, j (jā) *n., pl.* **J's, j's** the tenth letter of the English alphabet

jab (jab) *vt., vi.* **jabbed, jab'bing** [< ME. *jobben,* to peck] **1.** to poke, as with a sharp instrument **2.** to punch with short, straight blows — *n.* a quick thrust or blow

jab·ber (jab'ər) *vi., vt.* [prob. echoic] to talk quickly, incoherently, or nonsensically — *n.* fast, incoherent, nonsensical talk

ja·bot (zha bō', ja-) *n.* [Fr., bird's crop] a trimming or frill, as of lace, attached to the neck or front of a blouse or shirt

jack (jak) *n.* [< the name *Jack*] **1.** [often **J-**] a man or boy **2.** any of various devices used to lift something heavy a short distance [an automobile *jack*] **3.** a plug-in receptacle used to make electric contact **4.** a playing card with a page boy's picture on it **5.** any of the small 6-pronged metal pieces tossed and picked up in the game of **jacks 6.** a small flag flown on the ship's bow as a signal or to show nationality **7.** [Old Slang] money — *vt.* to raise by means of a jack — **jack up** [Colloq.] to raise (prices, wages, etc.)

jack- [see prec.] *a combining form meaning:* **1.** male [*jackass*] **2.** large or strong [*jackknife*] **3.** boy, fellow [*jack-in-the-box*]

jack·al (jak'əl, -ôl) *n.* [< Sans.] a yellowish-gray wild dog of Asia and N Africa

jack·ass (jak'as') *n.* [JACK- + ASS] **1.** a male donkey **2.** a stupid or foolish person

jack·daw (jak'dô') *n.* [< *jack* + ME. *dawe,* jackdaw] a European black bird related to the crow, but smaller

jack·et (jak'it) *n.* [< Ar. *shakk*] **1.** a short coat **2.** an outer covering, as the removable paper cover on a book, the skin of a potato, etc. — *vt.* to put a jacket on

Jack Frost frost or cold weather personified

jack'-in-the-box' *n., pl.* **-box'es** a toy consisting of a box from which which a figure on a spring jumps up when the lid is lifted

jack'-in-the-pul'pit (-pool'pit) *n., pl.* **-pits** a plant with a flower spike partly arched over by a hoodlike covering

jack'knife' *n., pl.* **-knives' 1.** a large pocketknife **2.** a dive in which one keeps the knees unbent, touches the feet with the hands, and then straightens out — *vi.* **-knifed', -knif'ing** to bend at the middle as in a jackknife dive

jack'-of-all'-trades' *n., pl.* **jacks'-** [see JACK-] [often **J-**] one who can do many kinds of work acceptably

jack-o'-lan·tern (jak'ə lan'tərn) *n., pl.* **-terns** a hollow pumpkin cut to look like a face and used as a lantern

jack'pot' *n.* [JACK, *n.* 4 + POT] cumulative stakes, as in a poker game

jack rabbit a large hare of W N. America, with long ears and strong hind legs

Ja·cob (jā'kəb) *Bible* a son of Isaac

jade¹ (jād) *n.* [Fr. < Sp. *piedra de ijada,* stone of the side: supposed to cure pains in the side] **1.** a hard, ornamental stone, usually green **2.** a green color of medium hue

jade² (jād) *n.* [< ON. *jalda,* a mare] **1.** a worn-out, worthless horse **2.** a disreputable woman — *vt.* **jad'ed, jad'ing 1.** to tire **2.** to satiate

jag¹ (jag) *n.* [ME. *jagge*] a sharp, toothlike projection

jag² (jag) *n.* [< ?] [Slang] a drunken spree

jag·ged (jag'id) *adj.* having sharp projecting points or notches — **jag'ged·ly** *adv.*

jag·uar (jag'wär) *n.* [Port. < SAmInd.] a large, leopardlike cat, found from SW U.S. to Argentina

jai a·lai (hī'lī', hī'ə lī') [Sp. < Basque *jai,* celebration + *alai,* merry] a game like handball, played with a basketlike racket

jail (jāl) *n.* [ult. < L. *cavea,* a cage] a prison for those awaiting trial or convicted of minor offenses — *vt.* to put or keep in jail

jail'break' *n.* a breaking out of jail

jail'er, jail'or *n.* a person in charge of a jail or of prisoners

ja·lop·y (jə läp'ē) *n., pl.* **-ies** [< ?] [Slang] an old, ramshackle automobile

jal·ou·sie (jal'ə sē') *n.* [Fr.: see JEALOUS] a window, shade, or door of adjustable, horizontal slats of wood, metal, or glass

jam¹ (jam) *vt.* **jammed, jam'ming** [< ?] **1.** to squeeze into a confined space **2.** to crush **3.** to crowd **4.** to crowd into or block (a passageway, etc.) **5.** to wedge so that it cannot move **6.** to make (radio or radar signals) unintelligible, as by sending out others on the same wavelength — *vi.* **1.** to become wedged or stuck fast, esp. so as to become unworkable **2.** to push against one another in a confined space **3.** [Slang] *Jazz* to improvise — *n.* **1.** a jamming or being jammed [a traffic *jam*] **2.** [Colloq.] a difficult situation

jam² (jam) *n.* [< ? prec.] a food made by boiling fruit with sugar to a thick mixture

jamb (jam) *n.* [< LL. *gamba,* leg] a side post of an opening for a door, window, etc.

jam·bo·ree (jam'bə rē') *n.* [< ?] **1.** [Colloq.] a boisterous party or revel **2.** a large assembly of boy scouts

jam-packed (jam'pakt') *adj.* tightly packed; crammed

jan·gle (jaŋ'g'l) *vi.* **-gled, -gling** [< OFr. *jangler*] to make a harsh, inharmonious sound — *vt.* **1.** to cause to jangle **2.** to irritate [to *jangle* one's nerves] — *n.* a harsh sound — **jan'gler** *n.*

jan·i·tor (jan'i tər) *n.* [L., doorkeeper] the custodian of a building, who does routine maintenance — **jan'i·to'ri·al** (-ə tôr'ē əl) *adj.*

Jan·u·ar·y (jan'yoo wer'ē) *n., pl.* **-ies** [< L. < *Janus,* Roman god who was patron of beginnings and endings] the first month of the year, having 31 days: abbrev. **Jan., Ja.**

Jap. 1. Japan **2.** Japanese

ja·pan (jə pan') *n.* [orig. from Japan] a varnish giving a hard, glossy finish

Jap·a·nese (jap'ə nēz') *adj.* of Japan, its people, language, etc. — *n.* **1.** *pl.* **-nese'** a native of Japan **2.** the language of Japan

Japanese beetle a green-and-brown beetle, orig. from Japan, damaging to crops

jape (jāp) *n., vi.* **japed, jap'ing** [ME. *japen*] joke; trick

jar¹ (jär) *vi.* **jarred, jar'ring** [ult. echoic] **1.** to make a harsh sound; grate **2.** to have an irritating effect (*on* one) **3.** to vibrate from an impact **4.** to clash or quarrel — *vt.* to jolt or shock — *n.* **1.** a harsh, grating sound **2.** a vibration due to sudden impact **3.** a jolt or shock

jar² (jär) *n.* [< Fr. < Ar. *jarrah,* earthen

container] **1.** a container made of glass, earthenware, etc., with a large opening **2.** as much as a jar will hold: also **jar'ful'**

jar·di·niere (jär'd'n ir') *n.* [Fr. < *jardin,* a garden] an ornamental pot or stand for flowers or plants

jar·gon (jär'gən) *n.* [MFr., a chattering] **1.** unintelligible talk **2.** the specialized vocabulary and idioms of those in the same work, profession, etc.

jas·mine, jas·min (jaz'min; *chiefly Brit.* jas'-) *n.* [< Fr. < Per. *yāsamīn*] any of certain plants of warm regions, with fragrant flowers of yellow, red, or white

Ja·son (jās''n) *Gr. Myth.* a prince who led the Argonauts and got the Golden Fleece

jas·per (jas'pər) *n.* [< Gr. *iaspis*] an opaque variety of colored quartz

jaun·dice (jôn'dis) *n.* [ult. < L. *galbus,* yellow] a diseased condition in which the eyeballs, skin, and urine become abnormally yellow as a result of bile in the blood —*vt.* **-diced, -dic·ing 1.** to cause to have jaundice **2.** to make bitter or prejudiced through jealousy, envy, etc.

jaunt (jônt) *vi.* [< ?] to take a short trip for pleasure —*n.* such a trip; excursion

jaun·ty (jônt'ē) *adj.* **-ti·er, -ti·est** [< Fr. *gentil,* genteel] **1.** in fashion; chic **2.** gay and carefree; sprightly —**jaun'ti·ly** *adv.*

Ja·va (jä'və, jav'ə) *n.* [< *Java,* Indonesia] [*often* j-] [Slang] coffee

jav·e·lin (jav'lin, jav'ə lin) *n.* [< MFr. *javelot,* a spear] a light spear, esp. one thrown for distance in a contest

jaw (jô) *n.* [< ? OFr. *joue,* cheek] **1.** either of the two bony parts that hold the teeth and frame the mouth **2.** either of two movable parts that grasp or crush something, as in a vise —*vi.* [Slang] to talk

jaw'bone' *n.* a bone of a jaw, esp. of the lower jaw —*vt., vi.* **-boned', -bon'ing** to try to persuade by using the influence of one's high office

jaw'break'er *n.* **1.** a machine for crushing rocks, ore, etc. **2.** a hard, usually round candy **3.** [Slang] a word hard to pronounce

jay (jā) *n.* [< LL. *gaius,* a jay] **1.** any of several birds of the crow family **2.** *same as* BLUE JAY

jay·walk (jā'wôk') *vi.* to cross a street carelessly without obeying traffic rules

jazz (jaz) *n.* [< ?] **1.** a kind of music characterized by syncopation, melodic variations, etc. **2.** [Slang] remarks, acts, etc. regarded disparagingly —*adj.* of, in, or like jazz —*vt.* **1.** to play as jazz **2.** [Slang] to enliven or embellish (usually with *up*)

jazz'y *adj.* **-i·er, -i·est 1.** of or like jazz **2.** [Slang] lively, flashy, etc.

jeal·ous (jel'əs) *adj.* [see ZEAL] **1.** watchful in guarding [*jealous* of one's rights] **2.** *a)* resentfully suspicious [a *jealous* lover] *b)* resentfully envious *c)* resulting from such feelings [a *jealous* rage]

jeal'ous·y *n., pl.* **-ies** the quality, condition, or feeling of being jealous

jean (jēn) *n.* [< L. *Genua,* Genoa] **1.** a durable, twilled cotton cloth **2.** [*pl.*] trousers of this material or of denim

jeep (jēp) *n.* [< a creature in a comic strip by E. C. Segar] a small, rugged military automotive vehicle of World War II

jeer (jir) *vt., vi.* [< ? CHEER] to make fun of in a rude, sarcastic manner; scoff (at) —*n.* a jeering remark —**jeer'ing·ly** *adv.*

Je·ho·vah (ji hō'və) [< Heb. sacred name for God] God; (the) Lord

je·june (ji jōōn') *adj.* [L. *jejunus,* empty] **1.** not interesting **2.** not mature; childish

jell (jel) *vi., vt.* [< JELLY] **1.** to become, or make into, jelly **2.** [Colloq.] to crystallize [the plans didn't *jell*]

jel·ly (jel'ē) *n., pl.* **-lies** [< L. *gelare,* freeze] **1.** a soft, gelatinous food made from cooked fruit syrup or meat juice **2.** any substance like this —*vi., vt.* **-lied, -ly·ing** to jell (sense 1)

jel'ly·fish' *n., pl.:* see FISH **1.** a sea animal with an umbrella-shaped body of jellylike substance and long tentacles **2.** [Colloq.] a weak-willed person

jeop·ard·ize (jep'ər dīz') *vt.* **-ized', -iz'ing** to put in jeopardy; endanger

jeop·ard·y (jep'ər dē) *n., pl.* **-ies** [< OFr. *jeu parti,* lit., a game with even chances] great danger; peril

Jer·e·mi·ah (jer'ə mī'ə) *Bible* a Hebrew prophet

jerk (jurk) *n.* [< ?] **1.** a sharp, abrupt pull, twist, etc. **2.** a sudden muscular contraction **3.** [Slang] a person regarded as stupid, foolish, etc. —*vt., vi.* **1.** to move with a jerk; pull sharply **2.** to twitch

jerk'wa'ter *adj.* [Colloq.] small, unimportant, etc. [a *jerkwater* town]

jerk·y¹ (jurk'ē) *adj.* **-i·er, -i·est 1.** moving by jerks; spasmodic **2.** [Slang] stupid, foolish, etc. —**jerk'i·ly** *adv.* —**jerk'i·ness** *n.*

jer·ky² (jur'kē) *n.* [< Sp. *charqui*] meat, esp. beef, preserved by being sliced into strips and dried, as in the sun

jer·ry-built (jer'ē bilt') *adj.* built poorly, of cheap materials

Jer·sey (jur'zē) *n., pl.* **-seys** [< *Jersey,* one of the Channel Islands] **1.** any of a breed of reddish-brown dairy cattle **2.** [j-] *a)* a soft, elastic, knitted cloth *b)* any closefitting, knitted upper garment

jest (jest) *n.* [< L. *gerere,* perform] **1.** a mocking remark; taunt **2.** a joke **3.** fun; joking **4.** a thing to be laughed at —*vi.* **1.** to jeer; mock **2.** to joke

jest'er *n.* one who jests; esp., a man employed by a medieval ruler to amuse him

Jes·u·it (jezh'ŏo wit, jez'-) *n.* a member of the Society of Jesus, a R.C. religious order

Je·sus (jē'zəs) founder of the Christian religion: also called **Jesus Christ**

jet¹ (jet) *vt., vi.* **jet'ted, jet'ting** [< L. *jacere,* to throw] **1.** to gush out in a stream **2.** to travel or convey by a jet airplane —*n.* **1.** a stream of liquid or gas emitted, as from a spout **2.** a spout for emitting a jet **3.** a jet-propelled airplane: in full **jet (air)plane** —*adj.* jet-propelled

jet² (jet) *n.* [< Gr. *Gagas,* town in Asia Minor] **1.** a hard, black variety of lignite, used in jewelry **2.** a lustrous black —*adj.* **1.** made of jet **2.** black

jet'lin'er *n.* a commercial jet aircraft for carrying passengers

jet'port' *n.* an airport with long runways, for use by jet airplanes

jet propulsion a method of propelling airplanes, boats, etc. by the discharge of gases under pressure from a rear vent or vents —**jet'-pro·pelled'** (-prə peld') *adj.*

jet·sam (jet'səm) *n.* [var. of JETTISON] **1.** cargo thrown overboard to lighten a ship in danger **2.** such cargo washed ashore

jet set rich, fashionable people who travel widely for pleasure, esp. in jets

jet·ti·son (jet'ə s'n) *vt.* [< L. *jactare,* to throw] **1.** to throw (goods) overboard so as to lighten a ship in danger **2.** to discard

jet·ty (jet'ē) *n., pl.* **-ties** [see JET¹] **1.** a wall built out into the water to restrain currents, protect a harbor, etc. **2.** a landing pier

Jew (jōō) *n.* [< Heb. *yehūdī,* citizen of Judah] **1.** a person descended, or regarded as descended, from the ancient Hebrews **2.** a person whose religion is Judaism

jew·el (jōō′əl) *n.* [ult. < L. *jocus,* a joke] **1.** a precious stone; gem **2.** any person or thing very precious **3.** a small gem used as a bearing in a watch —*vt.* **-eled** or **-elled, -el·ing** or **-el·ling** to decorate or set with jewels

jew·el·er, jew·el·ler (-ər) *n.* one who makes or deals in jewelry, watches, etc.

jew′el·ry *n.* jewels collectively

Jew·ish (jōō′ish) *adj.* of or having to do with Jews or Judaism —*n.* [Colloq.] *same as* YIDDISH —**Jew′ish·ness** *n.*

Jew′ry (-rē) *n.* Jewish people collectively

Jez·e·bel (jez′ə bel′) *Bible* a wicked queen of Israel

jg, j.g. junior grade

jib (jib) *n.* [< Dan. *gibbe,* to jibe] a triangular sail projecting ahead of the foremast

jibe[1] (jīb) *vi.* **jibed, jib′ing** [< Du. *gijpen*] **1.** to shift from one side of a ship to the other, as a fore-and-aft sail **2.** to change the course of a ship so that the sails jibe **3.** [Colloq.] to be in agreement or accord

jibe[2] (jīb) *n., vi., vt. same as* GIBE

jif·fy (jif′ē) *n., pl.* **-fies** [< ?] [Colloq.] a very short time; instant: also **jiff**

jig (jig) *n.* [prob. < MFr. *gigue,* a fiddle] **1.** a fast, springy dance in triple time, or music for this **2.** a device used as a guide for a tool —*vi.,* *vt.* **jigged, jig′ging** to dance (a jig) —**in jig time** [Colloq.] very quickly —**the jig is up** [Slang] no chance is left

jig·ger (jig′ər) *n.* **1.** a small glass or cup, usually of 1 1/2 ounces, used to measure liquor **2.** the contents of a jigger

jig·gle (jig″l) *vt., vi.* **-gled, -gling** [< JIG] to move in quick, slight jerks —*n.* a jiggling

jig′saw′ *n.* a saw with a narrow blade set in a frame, used for cutting along curved or irregular lines: also **jig saw**

jigsaw puzzle a puzzle consisting of disarranged, irregularly cut pieces of a picture that are to be fitted together

jilt (jilt) *vt.* [< *Jill,* sweetheart] to reject or cast off (a previously accepted lover or sweetheart)

Jim Crow (jim′ krō′) [name of an early Negro minstrel song] [*also* **j- c-**] [Colloq.] the practice of discrimination against or segregation of blacks —**Jim′-Crow′** *vt., adj.*

jim·my (jim′ē) *n., pl.* **-mies** [< *James*] a short crowbar, used by burglars to pry open windows, etc. —*vt.* **-mied, -my·ing** to pry open with a jimmy, etc.

jin·gle (jiŋ′g'l) *vi.* **-gled, -gling** [echoic] to make light, ringing sounds, as small bells —*vt.* to cause to jingle —*n.* **1.** a jingling sound **2.** a catchy verse or song with easy rhythm, simple rhymes, etc.

jin·go·ism (jiŋ′gō iz'm) *n.* [< phr. *by jingo* in a patriotic Brit. song] chauvinistic advocacy of an aggressive, warlike foreign policy —**jin′go·ist** *n.*

jin·ni (ji nē′, jin′ē) *n., pl.* **jinn** [< Ar.] *Muslim Legend* a supernatural being that can influence human affairs

jin·rik·i·sha (jin rik′shô, -shä) *n.* [< Jpn. *jin,* a man + *riki,* power + *sha,* carriage] a small, two-wheeled carriage, pulled by one or two men: also sp. **jin·rick′sha**

jinx (jiŋks) *n.* [< Gr. *iynx,* the wryneck (bird used in black magic)] [Colloq.] a person or

thing supposed to bring bad luck —*vt.* [Colloq.] to bring bad luck to

jit·ney (jit′nē) *n., pl.* **-neys** [c.1903 < ? Fr. *jeton,* a token] a small bus or car that carries passengers for a low fare

jit·ter (jit′ər) *vi.* [? echoic] [Colloq.] to be nervous —**the jitters** [Colloq.] a very uneasy, nervous feeling —**jit′ter·y** *adj.*

jit′ter·bug′ *n.* [prec. + BUG] a fast, acrobatic dance for couples, esp. in the 1940's —*vi.* **-bugged′, -bug′ging** to dance the jitterbug

jive (jīv) *vt.* **jived, jiv′ing** [< JIBE[2]] [Slang] to speak to in a way that is exaggerated, insincere, etc., esp. so as to mislead —*n.* **1.** [Slang] talk used or like that used in jiving someone **2.** *former term* (c.1930–45) *for* JAZZ *or* SWING

Job (jōb) *Bible* a man who endured much suffering but did not lose his faith in God

job (jäb) *n.* [< ?] **1.** a piece of work done for pay **2.** a task; duty **3.** the thing or material being worked on **4.** employment; work —*adj.* hired or done by the job —*vt., vi.* **jobbed, job′bing 1.** to deal in (goods) as a jobber **2.** to sublet (work, etc.)

job·ber (jäb′ər) *n.* **1.** a wholesaler; middleman **2.** a person who does piecework

job lot an assortment of goods for sale as one quantity

jock·ey (jäk′ē) *n., pl.* **-eys** [< Scot. dim. of JACK] one whose job is riding horses in races —*vt., vi.* **-eyed, -ey·ing 1.** to cheat **2.** to maneuver for position or advantage

jock·strap (jäk′strap′) *n.* [*jock,* penis + STRAP] an elastic belt with a pouch to support the genitals, worn by men

jo·cose (jō kōs′) *adj.* [< L. *jocus,* a joke] joking or playful

joc·u·lar (jäk′yə lər) *adj.* [< L. *jocus,* a joke] joking; full of fun

joc·und (jäk′ənd, jō′kənd) *adj.* [< L. *jucundus,* pleasant] cheerful; genial; gay

jodh·purs (jäd′pərz) *n.pl.* [after *Jodhpur,* former state in India] riding breeches made loose and full above the knees and closefitting below

jog[1] (jäg) *vt.* **jogged, jog′ging** [ME. *joggen,* to spur] **1.** to give a little shake to **2.** to nudge **3.** to revive (a person's memory) —*vi.* to move along at a slow, steady, jolting pace —*n.* **1.** a little shake or nudge **2.** a slow, steady, jolting motion —**jog′ger** *n.*

jog[2] (jäg) *n.* [var. of JAG[1]] **1.** a projecting or notched part in a surface or line **2.** a sharp, brief change of direction

jog·gle (jäg″l) *vt., vi.* **-gled, -gling** [< JOG[1]] to shake or jolt slightly —*n.* a slight jolt

John (jän) *Bible* **1.** one of the twelve Apostles, reputed author of the fourth Gospel **2.** this book

john (jän) *n.* [Slang] a toilet

John Bull England, or an Englishman, personified

John Doe (dō) a fictitious name used in legal papers for an unknown person

John the Baptist *Bible* the forerunner and baptizer of Jesus

join (join) *vt., vi.* [< L. *jungere*] **1.** to bring or come together (with); connect; combine; unite **2.** to become a part or member of (a club, etc.) **3.** to participate (*in* a conversation, etc.)

join′er *n.* **1.** a carpenter who finishes interior woodwork **2.** [Colloq.] one who joins many organizations

joint (joint) *n.* [< L. *jungere,* join] **1.** a place where, or way in which, two things are joined **2.** a part of a jointed whole **3.** a large cut of meat with the bones still in it **4.** [Slang] *a)* a cheap bar, restaurant, etc. b) any building 5. [Slang] a marijuana cigarette —adj. 1. common to two or more [joint property] 2. sharing with another [a joint owner] —vt. 1. to fasten together by a joint or joints 2. to cut (meat) into joints —out of joint 1. dislocated 2. disordered

joint·ly adv. in common

joist (joist) n. [< OFr. giste, a bed] any of the parallel beams that hold up the planks of a floor or the laths of a ceiling

joke (jōk) n. [L. jocus] 1. anything said or done to arouse laughter; a funny anecdote 2. something done or said merely in fun 3. a person or thing to be laughed at —vi. joked, jok'ing to make jokes

jok'er n. 1. one who jokes 2. a hidden provision, as in a legal document, etc. to make it different from what it seems to be 3. an extra playing card used in some games

jol·li·ty (jäl'ə tē) n. a being jolly; gaiety

jol·ly (jäl'ē) adj. -li·er, -li·est [OFr. joli] 1. full of high spirits and good humor 2. [Colloq.] enjoyable —vt., vi. -lied, -ly·ing [Colloq.] 1. to try to make (a person) feel good, as by coaxing 2. to make fun of —jol'li·ly adv. —jol'li·ness n.

jolt (jōlt) vt. [< earlier jot] 1. to shake up or jar, as with a bumpy ride 2. to shock or surprise —vi. to move along in a bumpy manner —n. 1. a sudden jerk, bump, etc. 2. a shock or surprise

Jo·nah (jō'nə) Bible a Hebrew prophet: thrown overboard, he was swallowed by a big fish, but later cast up unharmed —n. one said to bring bad luck by his presence

jon·quil (jän'kwəl, jän'-) n. [< Fr. < L. juncus, a rush] a variety of narcissus having relatively small yellow flowers

Jo·seph (jō'zəf) Bible 1. Jacob's eleventh son, who became a high official in Egypt 2. the husband of Mary, mother of Jesus

josh (jäsh) vt., vi. [< ?] [Colloq.] to ridicule in a good-humored way; banter

Josh·u·a (jäsh'ōō wə) Bible Moses' successor, and leader of the Israelites into the Promised Land

jos·tle (jäs'l) vt., vi. -tled, -tling [see JOUST] to bump or push, as in a crowd —n. a jostling

jot (jät) n. [< Gr. iōta, the smallest letter] a very small amount —vt. jot'ted, jot'ting to make a brief note of (usually with down)

jounce (jouns) n., vt., vi. jounced, jounc'ing [< ?] jolt or bounce —jounc'y adj.

jour·nal (jur'n'l) n. [< L. diurnalis, daily] 1. a daily record of happenings, as a diary 2. a newspaper, magazine, or other periodical 3. Bookkeeping a book of original entry for recording transactions 4. Mech. the part of an axle or shaft that turns in a bearing

jour'nal·ism (-iz'm) n. the work of gathering, writing, and publishing or disseminating news, as through newspapers, etc. —jour'nal·ist n. —jour'nal·is'tic adj.

jour·ney (jur'nē) n., pl. -neys [< OFr. journee, ult. < L. dies, day] a traveling from one place to another; trip —vi. -neyed, -ney·ing to travel

jour'ney·man (-mən) n., pl. -men [ME. < journee, day's work + man] 1. a worker who has learned his trade 2. an experienced craftsman of only average ability

joust (joust, just) n. [< L. juxta, beside] a combat with lances between two knights on horseback —vi. to engage in a joust

jo·vi·al (jō'vē əl) adj. [Fr. < LL. Jovialis, of Jupiter: from astrological notion of planet's influence] full of hearty, playful good humor —jo'vi·al'i·ty (-al'ə tē) n.

jowl¹ (joul) n. [OE. ceafl, jaw] 1. the lower jaw 2. the cheek, esp. of a hog

jowl² (joul) n. [OE. ceole, throat] [often pl.] the fleshy, hanging part under the jaw

joy (joi) n. [< L. gaudium, joy] 1. a very glad feeling; happiness; delight 2. anything causing this —joy'less adj.

joy'ful adj. feeling, expressing, or causing joy; glad —joy'ful·ly adv.

joy'ous (-əs) adj. joyful; happy; gay

joy ride [Colloq.] an automobile ride merely for pleasure, often at reckless speeds

J.P. justice of the peace

Jpn. Japanese

Jr., jr. junior

ju·bi·lant (jōō'b'l ənt) adj. [< L. jubilum, wild shout] joyful and triumphant; elated

ju·bi·la·tion (jōō'bə lā'shən) n. 1. a rejoicing 2. a happy celebration

ju·bi·lee (jōō'bə lē') n. [< Heb. yōbēl, a ram's horn (trumpet)] 1. a 50th or 25th anniversary 2. a time or occasion of rejoicing 3. jubilation

Ju·dah (jōō'də) Bible one of Jacob's sons

Ju·da·ism (jōō'də iz'm) n. the Jewish religion —Ju·da'ic (-dā'ik) adj.

Ju·das (jōō'dəs) Bible the disciple who betrayed Jesus: in full Judas Is·car·i·ot (is ker'ē ət) —n. a traitor or betrayer

judge (juj) n. [< L. jus, law + dicere, say] 1. a public official with authority to hear and decide cases in a court of law 2. a person designated to determine the winner, settle a controversy, etc. 3. a person qualified to decide on the relative worth of anything —vt., vi. judged, judg'ing 1. to hear and pass judgment (on) in a court of law 2. to determine the winner of (a contest) or settle (a controversy) 3. to form an opinion about 4. to criticize or censure 5. to think; suppose —judge'ship' n.

judg·ment (juj'mənt) n. 1. a judging; deciding 2. a legal decision; order given by a judge, etc. 3. an opinion 4. the ability to come to an opinion 5. [J-] short for LAST JUDGMENT Also judge'ment —judg·men'tal (-men't'l) adj.

Judgment Day Theol. the time of God's final judgment of all people

ju·di·ca·to·ry (jōō'di kə tôr'ē) adj. [see JUDGE] having to do with administering justice —n., pl. -ries a law court, or law courts collectively

ju'di·ca·ture (-chər) n. 1. the administering of justice 2. jurisdiction of a judge or court 3. judges or courts collectively

ju·di·cial (jōō dish'əl) adj. 1. of judges, courts, or their functions 2. allowed, enforced, etc. by a court 3. befitting a judge 4. fair; unbiased —ju·di'cial·ly adv.

ju·di·ci·ar·y (jōō dish'ē er'ē, -dish'ər ē) adj. of judges or courts —n., pl. -ies 1. the part of government that administers justice 2. judges collectively

ju·di·cious (jōō dish'əs) adj. [see JUDGE] having or showing sound judgment

ju·do (jōō'dō) n. [Jpn. < jū, soft + dō, art] a form of jujitsu, esp. for self-defense

jug (jug) n. [a pet form of Judith or Joan] 1. a container for liquids, with a small opening and a handle 2. [Slang] a jail

jug·ger·naut (jug'ər nôt') n. [< Sans. Jagannātha, lord of the world] any terrible, irresistible force

jug·gle (jug''l) vt. -gled, -gling [< L. jocus, a joke] 1. to perform skillful tricks of sleight of hand with (balls, etc.) 2. to manipulate so as to cheat or deceive —vi. to toss up balls, etc. and keep them in the air —jug'gler n. —jug'gler·y n.

jug·u·lar (jug'yoo lər) adj. [< L. jugum, a

yoke] of the neck or throat —*n.* either of two large veins in the neck carrying blood from the head: in full **jugular vein**

juice (jōōs) *n.* [< L. *jus*, broth] **1.** the liquid part of a plant, fruit, etc. **2.** a liquid in or from animal tissue **3.** [Colloq.] energy; vitality **4.** [Slang] electricity —*vt.* **juiced, juic'ing** to extract juice from

juic·er (jōō'sər) *n.* a device for extracting juice from fruit

juic·y (jōō'sē) *adj.* **-i·er, -i·est 1.** full of juice **2.** [Colloq.] *a)* full of interest *b)* highly profitable —**juic'i·ness** *n.*

ju·jit·su (jōō jit'sōō) *n.* [< Jpn. < *jū*, soft + *jutsu*, art] a Japanese system of wrestling in which the strength and weight of an opponent are used against him: also sp. **ju·jut'su**

juke·box (jōōk'bäks') *n.* [< Am. Negro *juke*, wicked] a coin-operated electric phonograph

ju·lep (jōō'ləp) *n.* [< Per. *gul*, rose + *āb*, water] *same as* MINT JULEP

Jul·ian calendar (jōōl'yən) the calendar introduced by Julius Caesar in 46 B.C.: replaced by the Gregorian calendar

ju·li·enne (jōō'lē en') *adj.* [Fr.] *Cooking* cut into strips: said of vegetables

Ju·li·et (jōōl'yət, jōō'lē et') the heroine of Shakespeare's tragedy *Romeo and Juliet*

Ju·ly (joo lī', jōō-) *n., pl.* **-lies'** [< L. < *Julius* Caesar] the seventh month of the year, having 31 days: abbrev. **Jul.**

jum·ble (jum'b'l) *vt., vi.* **-bled, -bling** [? blend of JUMP + TUMBLE] to mix or be mixed in a confused heap —*n.* a confused mixture or heap

jum·bo (jum'bō) *n., pl.* **-bos** [< Am. Negro *jamba*, elephant] a very large person, animal, or thing —*adj.* very large

jump (jump) *vi.* [< ?] **1.** to spring or leap from the ground, a height, etc. **2.** to jerk; bob **3.** to move or act eagerly (often with *at*) **4.** to start in surprise **5.** to pass suddenly, as to a new topic **6.** to rise suddenly, as prices —*vt.* **1.** *a)* to leap over *b)* to pass over **2.** to cause to leap **3.** to leap upon **4.** to cause (prices, etc.) to rise **5.** [Colloq.] to attack suddenly **6.** to react to prematurely **7.** [Slang] to leave suddenly *[to jump town]* —*n.* **1.** a jumping **2.** a distance jumped **3.** a sudden transition **4.** a sudden rise, as in prices **5.** a sudden, nervous start or jerk —**get** (or **have**) **the jump on** [Slang] to get (or have) an advantage over —**jump ball** to forfeit bail by running away

jump·er (jum'pər) *n.* [< dial. *jump*, short coat] **1.** a loose jacket **2.** a sleeveless dress for wearing over a blouse, etc.

jump suit 1. a coverall worn as by paratroops **2.** any similar one-piece garment

jump'y *adj.* **-i·er, -i·est 1.** moving in jumps, etc. **2.** nervous; apprehensive

junc·tion (junk'shən) *n.* [< L. *jungere*, join] **1.** a joining or being joined **2.** a place of joining, as of highways

junc·ture (junk'chər) *n.* **1.** a joining or being joined **2.** a point of time

June (jōōn) *n.* [< L. *Junius*, of Juno] the sixth month of the year, having 30 days

jun·gle (jun'g'l) *n.* [< Hindi *jangal*, desert < Sans.] land densely covered with trees, vines, etc., as in the tropics

jun·ior (jōōn'yər) *adj.* [L. < *juvenis*, young] **1.** the younger: written *Jr.* after a son's name if it is the same as his father's **2.** of more recent position or lower rank *[a junior partner]* **3.** of juniors —*n.* **1.** one who is younger, of lower rank, etc. **2.** a student in the next-to-last year of a high school or college

junior college a school offering courses two years beyond the high school level

junior high school a school intermediate between elementary school and senior high school: it usually includes the 7th, 8th, and 9th grades

ju·ni·per (jōō'nə pər) *n.* [L. *juniperus*] a small evergreen shrub or tree with berrylike cones

junk¹ (junk) *n.* [< ?] **1.** old metal, paper, rags, etc. **2.** [Colloq.] useless stuff; trash **3.** [Slang] a narcotic drug; esp., heroin —*vt.* [Colloq.] to throw away or sell as junk; scrap —**junk'y** *adj.* **-i·er, -i·est**

junk² (junk) *n.* [< Indonesian *jon*] a Chinese flat-bottomed ship

Junk·er (yoon̄'kər) *n.* [G.] a Prussian of the militaristic landowning class

jun·ket (jun'kit) *n.* [ME. *joncate*, cream cheese] **1.** milk sweetened, flavored, and thickened into a curd **2.** a picnic **3.** an excursion, esp. one by an official at public expense —*vi.* to go on a junket —**junk'et·eer'** (-kə tir') *n.*

junk food snack food with chemical additives and little food value

junk·ie, junk·y (jun'kē) *n., pl.* **-ies** [Slang] a narcotics addict, esp. one addicted to heroin

Ju·no (jōō'nō) *Rom. Myth.* wife of Jupiter and queen of the gods

jun·ta (hoon'tə, jun'-) *n.* [Sp. < L. *jungere*, join] **1.** a Spanish or Latin-American legislative or administrative body **2.** a group of political intriguers, esp. military men in power after a coup d'état: also **jun·to** (jun'tō), *pl.* **-tos**

Ju·pi·ter (jōō'pə tər) *n.* **1.** the chief Roman god **2.** the largest planet of the solar system: see PLANET

ju·rid·i·cal (joo rid'i k'l) *adj.* [< L. *jus*, law + *dicere*, declare] of judicial proceedings or of law —**ju·rid'i·cal·ly** *adv.*

ju·ris·dic·tion (joor'is dik'shən) *n.* [see prec.] **1.** the administering of justice **2.** authority **3.** the range of authority —**ju'ris·dic'tion·al** *adj.*

ju·ris·pru·dence (joor'is prōō'd'ns) *n.* [< L. *jus*, law + *prudentia*, a foreseeing] **1.** the science or philosophy of law **2.** a division of law *[medical jurisprudence]*

ju·rist (joor'ist) *n.* [< L. *jus*, law] **1.** an expert in law or writer on law **2.** a judge

ju·ror (joor'ər) *n.* a member of a jury: also **ju'ry·man** (-mən), *pl.* **-men**

ju·ry (joor'ē) *n., pl.* **-ries** [< L. *jurare*, swear] **1.** a group sworn to hear evidence in a law case and to give a decision **2.** a committee that decides winners in a contest

just (just) *adj.* [< L. *jus*, law] **1.** right or fair *[a just decision]* **2.** righteous *[a just man]* **3.** deserved *[just praise]* **4.** lawful **5.** proper, fitting, etc. **6.** correct or true **7.** accurate; exact —*adv.* **1.** exactly *[just one o'clock]* **2.** almost at the point of *[just leaving]* **3.** only *[just a taste]* **4.** barely *[just missed him]* **5.** a very short time ago *[she just left]* **6.** immediately *[just to my right]* **7.** [Colloq.] quite; really *[feeling just fine]* —**just now** a moment ago —**just the same** [Colloq.] nevertheless —**just'ly** *adv.* —**just'ness** *n.*

jus·tice (jus'tis) *n.* **1.** a being righteous **2.** fairness **3.** rightfulness **4.** reward or penalty as deserved **5.** the use of authority to uphold what is just **6.** the administration of law **7.** *same as:* a) JUDGE (sense 1) b) JUSTICE OF THE PEACE —**do justice to** to treat fairly or with due appreciation

justice of the peace a local magistrate who decides minor cases, performs marriages, etc.

jus·ti·fy (jus'tə fī') *vt.* **-fied', -fy'ing** [< L. *justus*, just + *facere*, make] **1.** to show to be just, right, etc. **2.** *Theol.* to free from blame **3.** to supply good grounds for —**jus'ti·fi'a·ble** *adj.* —**jus'ti·fi'a·bly** *adv.* —**jus'ti·fi·ca'tion** (-fi kā'shən) *n.*

jut (jut) *vi., vt.* **jut'ted, jut'ting** [prob. var. of JET¹] to stick out; project —*n.* a part that juts

jute (jōot) *n.* [< Hindi < Sans. *jūṭa,* matted hair] **1.** a strong fiber used for making burlap, rope, etc. **2.** an East Indian plant yielding this fiber

ju·ven·ile (jōo'və n'l, -nīl') *adj.* [< L. *juvenis,* young] **1.** *a)* young *b)* immature; childish **2.** of or for young persons —*n.* **1.** a young person **2.** an actor who plays youthful roles **3.** a book for children

juvenile delinquency antisocial behavior by minors —**juvenile delinquent**

jux·ta·pose (juk'stə pōz') *vt.* **-posed', -pos'ing** [< Fr. < L. *juxta,* near + POSE] to put side by side or close together —**jux'ta·po·si'tion** *n.*

K

K, k (kā) *n., pl.* **K's, k's** the eleventh letter of the English alphabet

K [ModL. *kalium*] *Chem.* potassium

K., k. **1.** karat (carat) **2.** kilo **3.** king

kad·dish (käd'ish) *n.* [Aram. *qaddīsh,* holy] *Judaism* a hymn in praise of God, recited at the daily service or as a mourner's prayer

kaf·fee·klatsch (kä'fä kläch', kô'fē klach') *n.* [G. < *kaffee,* coffee + *klatsch,* gossip] [*also* K-] an informal gathering to drink coffee and chat

kai·ser (kī'zər) *n.* [< L. *Caesar*] emperor: the title [K-] of the former rulers of Austria and of Germany

kale (kāl) *n.* [Scot. var. of COLE] a hardy cabbage with loose, curled leaves

ka·lei·do·scope (kə lī'də skōp') *n.* [< Gr. *kalos,* beautiful + *eidos,* form + -SCOPE] **1.** a small tube containing bits of colored glass reflected by mirrors to form symmetrical patterns as the tube is rotated **2.** anything that changes constantly —**ka·lei'do·scop'ic** (-skäp'ik) *adj.*

kan·ga·roo (kaŋ'gə rōo') *n.* [< ?] a leaping, plant-eating mammal of Australia and nearby islands, with short forelegs and large, strong hind legs: the female has a pouch in which she carries her young

kangaroo court [Colloq.] an irregular or mock court illegally passing and executing judgment

ka·o·lin (kā'ə lin) *n.* [Fr. < Chin. name of hill where found] a white clay used in porcelain, etc.

ka·pok (kā'päk) *n.* [Malay *kapoq*] silky fibers from seeds of certain tropical trees: used for stuffing mattresses, etc.

kap·pa (kap'ə) *n.* the tenth letter of the Greek alphabet (K, κ)

ka·put (kä pōot') *adj.* [G. *kaputt*] [Slang] ruined, destroyed, etc.

kar·a·kul (kar'ə kəl) *n.* [< *Kara Kul,* lake in the U.S.S.R.] **1.** a sheep of C Asia **2.** the curly, black fur from the fleece of its newborn lambs

kar·at (kar'ət) *n.* [var. of CARAT] one 24th part (of pure gold)

ka·ra·te (kə rät'ē) *n.* [Jpn. < *kara,* empty + *te,* hand] a Japanese system of self-defense using blows struck by the side of the open hand and by the feet

kar·ma (kär'mə) *n.* [Sans., a deed] **1.** *Buddhism & Hinduism* a person's actions in one reincarnation thought of as determining his fate in the next **2.** loosely, fate

kart (kärt) *n.* [< CART] a small, flat, 4-wheeled, motorized vehicle for one person: used in special racing events

ka·ty·did (kāt'ē did') *n.* [echoic of its shrill sound] a large, green tree insect resembling the grasshopper

kay·ak (kī'ak) *n.* [Esk.] an Eskimo canoe made of skins covering a wooden frame

kay·o (kā'ō') *vt.* **-oed', -o'ing** [< KO] [Slang] *Boxing* to knock out —*n.* [Slang] *Boxing* a knockout

kc, kc. kilocycle; kilocycles

ke·bab (kə bäb') *n.* [Ar. *kabāb*] [*often pl.*] a dish consisting of small pieces of marinated meat broiled on a skewer, often with alternating pieces of onion, tomato, etc.

keel (kēl) *n.* [< ON.] the chief timber or steel piece extending along the length of the bottom of a ship or boat —**keel over** [Colloq.] **1.** to turn over; capsize **2.** to fall over suddenly, as in a faint —**on an even keel** upright and level, steady, stable, etc.

keen¹ (kēn) *adj.* [OE. *cene,* wise] **1.** having a sharp edge or point **2.** cutting; piercing [a *keen* wind] **3.** sharp and quick in seeing, hearing, etc.; acute **4.** sharp-witted; shrewd **5.** eager **6.** strong or intense [*keen* enjoyment] **7.** [Slang] good, excellent, etc.

keen² (kēn) *n.* [< Ir. *caoinim,* I wail] [Irish] a wailing for the dead —*vt., vi.* [Irish] to lament or wail for (the dead)

keep (kēp) *vt.* **kept, keep'ing** [OE. *cepan,* behold] **1.** to celebrate; observe [*keep* the Sabbath] **2.** to fulfill (a promise, etc.) **3.** to guard; tend **4.** to preserve; maintain **5.** to provide; support **6.** to make regular entries in [to *keep* a diary] **7.** to hold for future use or for a long time **8.** to have or hold and not let go; detain, restrain, etc. **9.** to stay in or at (a course, place, etc.) —*vi.* **1.** to stay in a specified state, position, etc. **2.** to continue; go on **3.** to refrain [to *keep* from laughing] **4.** to stay fresh; not spoil —*n.* **1.** care or custody **2.** the inner stronghold of a castle **3.** food and shelter; support —**for keeps** [Colloq.] **1.** with the winner keeping what he wins **2.** forever —**keep to oneself** **1.** to avoid others **2.** to refrain from telling —**keep up** **1.** to maintain in good condition **2.** to continue **3.** to maintain the pace **4.** to remain informed about (with *on* or *with*)

keep'er *n.* one that keeps; specif., *a)* a guard, as of prisoners *b)* a guardian *c)* a caretaker

keep'ing *n.* **1.** observance (of a rule, holiday, etc.) **2.** care; charge —**in keeping with** in conformity or accord with

keep'sake' *n.* something kept, or to be kept, in memory of the giver; memento

keg (keg) *n.* [< ON. *kaggi*] **1.** a small barrel **2.** a unit of weight for nails (100 lbs.)

kelp (kelp) *n.* [ME. *culp*] large, coarse, brown seaweed, rich in iodine

Kelt (kelt) *n. same as* CELT

ken (ken) *vt., vi.* **kenned, ken'ning** [OE. *cennan,* cause to know] [Scot.] to know (*of* or *about*) —*n.* range of knowledge

ken·nel (ken'l) *n.* [< L. *canis,* a dog] **1.** a

---

kept 252 **kiloliter**

doghouse 2. [often pl.] a place where dogs are bred or kept —vt. -neled or -nelled, -nel·ing or -nel·ling to keep in a kennel

kept (kept) pt. & pp. of KEEP —adj. maintained as a mistress [a kept woman]

ker·a·tin (ker'ət 'n) n. [< Gr. keras, horn + -IN¹] a tough, fibrous protein, the basic substance of hair, nails, horn, etc.

kerb (kurb) n. Brit. sp. of CURB (n. 3)

ker·chief (kur'chif) n. [< OFr. covrir, to cover + chef, the head] 1. a piece of cloth worn over the head or around the neck 2. a handkerchief

ker·nel (kur'n'l) n. [OE. cyrnel] 1. a grain or seed, as of corn 2. the inner, softer part of a nut, etc. 3. the central, most important part; essence

ker·o·sene (ker'ə sēn') n. [< Gr. kēros, wax] a thin oil distilled from petroleum, used as a fuel, solvent, etc.: also **kerosine**

kes·trel (kes'trəl) n. [echoic] a small European falcon that can hover in the air against the wind

ketch (kech) n. [ME. cache] a fore-and-aft rigged sailing vessel

ketch·up (kech'əp) n. [Malay kēchap, a fish sauce < Chin.] a sauce for meat, fish, etc.; esp., a thick sauce (**tomato ketchup**) of tomatoes, onions, spices, etc.

ket·tle (ket''l) n. [< L. catinus, a bowl] 1. a metal container for boiling or cooking things 2. a teakettle

ket·tle·drum' n. a hemispheric percussion instrument with a parchment top that can be tightened or loosened to change pitch

key¹ (kē) n., pl. **keys** [OE. cæge] 1. a device for moving the bolt of a lock and thus locking or unlocking something 2. any somewhat similar device, as a lever pressed down to operate a typewriter, piano, etc. 3. a thing that explains or solves 4. a controlling person or thing 5. style or mood of expression 6. Music a system of related tones based on a keynote and forming a given scale —adj. controlling; important —vt. keyed, key'ing 1. to furnish with a key 2. to regulate the tone or pitch of 3. to bring into harmony —key up to make tense or excited

key² (kē) n., pl. **keys** [Sp. cayo] a reef or low island

key'board' n. the row or rows of keys of a piano, typewriter, etc.

key'hole' n. an opening (in a lock) into which a key is inserted

key'note' n. 1. the lowest, basic note or tone of a musical scale 2. the basic idea or ruling principle, as of a speech, policy, etc. —vt. -not'ed, -not'ing 1. to give the keynote of 2. to give the keynote speech at (a convention, etc.)

key punch a machine with a keyboard for recording data by punching holes in cards for use in data processing

key'stone' n. 1. the central, topmost stone of an arch 2. the main part or principle

kg, kg. kilogram(s)

kha·ki (kak'ē, kä'kē) adj. [Hindi khākī, dusty] 1. dull yellowish-brown 2. made of khaki (cloth) —n., pl. -kis 1. a dull yellowish brown 2. strong twilled cloth of this color, used esp. for uniforms 3. [often pl.] a khaki uniform or trousers

khan (kän, kan) n. [< Turkic khān, lord] 1. a title of Tatar or Mongol rulers in the Middle Ages 2. a title of various dignitaries in Iran, Afghanistan, etc.

kHz kilohertz

kib·butz (ki boots', -boots') n., pl. **kib·but·zim** (kē'boo tsēm') [ModHeb.] an Israeli collective settlement, esp. a collective farm

kib·itz·er (kib'its ər) n. [Yid. < G. kiebitz] [Colloq.] an onlooker at a card game, etc., who volunteers advice —**kib'itz** vi.

ki·bosh (kī'bäsh) n. [< ?] [Slang] orig., nonsense: now usually in **put the kibosh on**, to put an end to; squelch, check, etc.

kick (kik) vi. [ME. kiken] 1. to strike out with the foot 2. to recoil, as a gun 3. [Colloq.] to complain 4. Football to kick the ball —vt. 1. to strike with the foot 2. to drive, force, etc. as by kicking 3. to score (a goal, etc.) by kicking 4. [Slang] to get rid of (a habit) —n. 1. a kicking 2. a sudden recoil 3. [Colloq.] a complaint 4. [Colloq.] a stimulating effect 5. [Colloq.] [often pl.] pleasure; thrill —kick in [Slang] to pay (one's share)

kick'back' n. [Slang] 1. a giving back of part of money received as payment 2. the money so returned

kick'off' n. Football a kick that puts the ball into play

kick'stand' n. a pivoted metal bar that can be kicked down to support a bicycle, motorcycle, etc. in an upright position

kid (kid) n. [ME. kide] 1. a young goat 2. leather from the skin of young goats: also **kid'skin'** 3. [Colloq.] a child or young person —adj. 1. made of kidskin 2. [Colloq.] younger [my kid sister] —vt., vi. **kid'ded, kid'ding** [Colloq.] to tease or fool playfully —**kid'der** n.

kid·dy, kid·die (kid'ē) n., pl. -dies [dim. of KID, n. 3] [Colloq.] a child

kid'nap' (-nap') vt. -napped' or -naped', -nap'ping or -nap'ing [KID, n. 3 + dial. nap, to snatch] 1. to steal (a child) 2. to seize and hold (a person) by force or fraud, often for ransom —**kid'nap'per, kid'nap'er** n.

kid·ney (kid'nē) n., pl. -neys [ME. kidenei] 1. either of a pair of glandular organs which separate waste products from the blood and excrete them as urine 2. an animal's kidney used as food 3. a) disposition b) kind; sort

kidney bean the kidney-shaped seed of the common garden bean

kidney stone a hard mineral deposit sometimes formed in the kidney

kiel·ba·sa (kēl bä'sə) n., pl. -si (-sē), -sas [Pol.] a smoked Polish sausage flavored with garlic

kil. kilometer(s)

kill (kil) vt. [ME. killen] 1. to cause the death of; slay 2. to destroy; put an end to 3. to defeat or veto (legislation) 4. to spend (time) on trivial matters —vi. to destroy life —n. 1. an act of killing 2. an animal or animals killed —**kill'er** n.

kill·deer (kil'dir') n. [echoic] a small N. American bird related to the plover

kill'ing adj. 1. causing death; deadly 2. exhausting; fatiguing —n. 1. slaughter; murder 2. [Colloq.] a sudden, great profit

kill'-joy' n. one who destroys or lessens other people's enjoyment: also **kill'joy'**

kiln (kil, kiln) n. [< L. culina, cooking stove] a furnace or oven for drying, burning, or baking bricks, pottery, grain, etc.

ki·lo (kē'lō, kil'ō) n., pl. -los [Fr.] short for: 1. KILOGRAM 2. KILOMETER

kilo- [Fr. < Gr. chilioi, thousand] a combining form meaning a thousand

kil·o·cy·cle (kil'ə sī'k'l) n. former name for KILOHERTZ

kil'o·gram' (-gram') n. a unit of weight and mass, equal to 1,000 grams (2.2046 lb.): chiefly Brit. sp. **kil'o·gramme'**

kil'o·hertz' (-hurts') n., pl. -hertz' one thousand hertz

kil'o·li·ter (-lēt'ər) n. a unit of capacity, equal

to 1,000 liters, or one cubic meter (264.18 gal.): chiefly Brit. sp. **kil′o·li′tre**

ki·lo·me·ter (ki läm′ə tər, kil′ə mēt′ər) *n.* a unit of length or distance, equal to 1,000 meters (3,280.8 ft.): chiefly Brit. sp. **ki·lo′me·tre** —**kil·o·met·ric** (kil′ə met′rik) *adj.*

kil·o·watt (kil′ə wät′) *n.* a unit of electrical power, equal to 1,000 watts

kilt (kilt) *n.* [prob. < Scand.] a knee-length, pleated tartan skirt worn sometimes by men of the Scottish Highlands

kil·ter (kil′tər) *n.* [< ?] [Colloq.] good condition; proper order: now chiefly in **out of kilter**

ki·mo·no (kə mō′nə) *n., pl.* -**nos** [Jpn.] 1. a loose outer garment with a sash, part of the traditional costume of Japanese men and women 2. a woman's dressing gown like this

kin (kin) *n.* [OE. *cynn*] relatives; family —*adj.* related, as by blood —(**near**) **of kin** (closely) related

-kin [< MDu. -*ken*] *a suffix meaning* little [*lambkin*]

kind (kīnd) *n.* [OE. *cynd*] 1. a natural group or division 2. essential character 3. sort; class —*adj.* 1. sympathetic, gentle, generous, etc. 2. cordial [*kind* regards] —**in kind** in the same way —**kind of** [Colloq.] somewhat; rather —**of a kind** alike

kin·der·gar·ten (kin′dər gär′t'n) *n.* [G. < *kinder,* children + *garten,* garden] a school or class for children, usually four to six years old, that develops basic skills and social behavior by games, handicraft, etc. —**kin′der·gart′ner, kin′der·gar′ten·er** *n.*

kind′heart′ed *adj.* sympathetic; kindly

kin′dle (kin′d'l) *vt.* -**dled,** -**dling** [< ON. *kynda*] 1. to set on fire; ignite 2. to excite (interest, feelings, etc.) —*vi.* 1. to catch fire 2. to become aroused or excited

kin·dling (kin′dliŋ) *n.* material, as bits of dry wood, for starting a fire

kind′ly *adj.* -**li·er,** -**li·est** 1. kind; gracious 2. agreeable; pleasant —*adv.* in a kind manner —**kind′li·ness** *n.*

kind′ness *n.* 1. the state, quality, or habit of being kind 2. a kind act

kin·dred (kin′drid) *n.* [< OE. *cynn,* kin + *ræden,* condition] *same as* KIN —*adj.* of like nature; similar [*kindred* spirits]

kine (kīn) *n.pl.* [< OE. *cy,* cows] [Archaic] cows; cattle

ki·net·ic (ki net′ik) *adj.* [< Gr. *kinein,* to move] of or resulting from motion

kin·folk (kin′fōk′) *n.pl.* relatives; kin: also **kin′-folks′**

king (kiŋ) *n.* [OE. *cyning*] 1. the male ruler of a state usually called a kingdom 2. a man who is supreme in some field 3. something supreme in its class 4. a playing card with a picture of a king on it 5. *Checkers* a piece that has moved the length of the board 6. *Chess* the chief piece —*adj.* chief (in size, importance, etc.): used often in combination —**king′ly** *adv.* —**king′ship′** *n.*

king′dom (-dəm) *n.* 1. a country headed by a king or queen; monarchy 2. a realm; sphere [the *kingdom* of poetry] 3. any of the three divisions into which all natural objects have been classified (the animal, vegetable, and mineral kingdoms)

king′fish′er *n.* a bright-colored bird with a large, crested head and a short tail

King James Version *same as* AUTHORIZED VERSION

King Lear (lir) the title character of a tragedy by Shakespeare

king′-size′ *adj.* [Colloq.] larger than the usual size: also **king′-sized′**

kink (kiŋk) *n.* [< Scand.] 1. a short twist or curl in a rope, hair, etc. 2. a painful cramp, as in the neck 3. a queer notion; eccentricity 4. a defect, as in a plan —*vi., vt.* to form or cause to form a kink or kinks —**kink′y** *adj.* -**i·er,** -**i·est**

kin·ship (kin′ship′) *n.* 1. family relationship 2. close connection

kins·man (kinz′mən) *n., pl.* -**men** a relative, esp. a male relative —**kins′wom′an** *n.fem., pl.* -**wom′en**

ki·osk (kē′äsk) *n.* [< Fr. < Per. *kūshk,* palace] a small, open structure used as a newsstand, etc.

kip·per (kip′ər) *vt.* [< ?] to cure (herring, salmon, etc.) by salting and then drying or smoking —*n.* a kippered herring, etc.

kirk (kurk; *Scot.* kirk) *n.* [Scot. & North Eng.] a church

kis·met (kiz′met) *n.* [< Turk. < Ar. *qasama,* to divide] fate; destiny

kiss (kis) *vt., vi.* [OE. *cyssan*] 1. to touch or caress with the lips as an act of affection, greeting, etc. 2. to touch lightly —*n.* 1. an act of kissing 2. a light, gentle touch 3. any of various candies

kiss′er *n.* 1. a person who kisses 2. [Slang] *a*) the mouth or lips *b*) the face

kit (kit) *n.* [ME. *kyt,* tub] 1. personal equipment 2. a set of tools, parts, etc. 3. a container for such equipment, tools, etc. —**the whole kit and caboodle** [Colloq.] everybody or everything

kitch·en (kich′ən) *n.* [< L. *coquere,* to cook] a room or place for the preparation and cooking of food

kitch′en·ette′ kitch′en·et′ (-et′) *n.* a small, compact kitchen

kitch′en·ware′ (-wer′) *n.* kitchen utensils

kite (kīt) *n.* [OE. *cyta*] 1. a bird related to the hawk, with long, pointed wings 2. a light, wooden frame covered with paper or cloth, to be flown in the wind at the end of a string —*vi.* **kit′ed, kit′ing** [Colloq.] to move lightly and rapidly

kith (kith) *n.* [OE. *cyth*] friends: now only in **kith and kin,** friends and relatives; also, often, relatives, or kin

kitsch (kich) *n.* [G., gaudy trash] pretentious but shallow art, writing, etc., designed for popular appeal —**kitsch′y** *adj.*

kit·ten (kit′'n) *n.* [< OFr. dim. of *chat,* cat] a young cat —**kit′ten·ish** *adj.*

kit·ty¹ (kit′ē) *n., pl.* -**ties** 1. a kitten 2. *a pet name for* a cat of any age

kit·ty² (kit′ē) *n., pl.* -**ties** [prob. < KIT] 1. in poker, etc., the stakes 2. money pooled

kit·ty-cor·nered (kit′ē kôr′nərd) *adj., adv. same as* CATER-CORNERED: also **kit′ty-cor′ner**

ki·wi (kē′wē) *n., pl.* -**wis** [Maori: echoic] a tailless New Zealand bird with undeveloped wings and hairlike feathers

K.K.K., KKK Ku Klux Klan

klep·to·ma·ni·a (klep′tə mā′nē ə) *n.* [< Gr. *kleptēs,* thief + -MANIA] an abnormal, persistent impulse to steal —**klep′to·ma′ni·ac′** (-ak′) *n.*

klieg light (klēg) [after A. & J. *Kliegl,* its inventors] a very bright arc light used to light motion-picture sets

km, km. kilometer(s)

knack (nak) *n.* [ME. *knak,* sharp blow] 1. a clever expedient 2. ability to do something easily

knack·wurst (näk′wurst′) *n.* [G.] a thick, highly seasoned sausage

knap·sack (nap′sak′) *n.* [< Du. *knappen,* eat + *zak,* a sack] a leather or canvas bag for carrying equipment, etc. on the back
knave (nāv) *n.* [OE. *cnafa,* boy] **1.** a tricky rascal; rogue **2.** a jack (the playing card) —**knav′ish** *adj.*
knead (nēd) *vt.* [OE. *cnedan*] **1.** to work (dough, clay, etc.) into a pliable mass by pressing and squeezing **2.** to massage
knee (nē) *n.* [OE. *cneow*] **1.** the joint between the thigh and the lower leg **2.** anything shaped like a bent knee —*vt.* **kneed, knee′ing** to hit or touch with the knee
knee′cap′ (-kap′) *n.* a movable bone at the front of the human knee
kneel (nēl) *vi.* **knelt** or **kneeled, kneel′ing** [< OE. *cneow*] to bend or rest on a knee or the knees —**kneel′er** *n.*
knell (nel) *vi.* [OE. *cnyllan*] **1.** to ring slowly; toll **2.** to sound ominously —*vt.* to call or announce as by a knell —*n.* **1.** the sound of a tolling bell **2.** an omen of death, failure, etc.
knelt (nelt) *alt. pt. and pp. of* KNEEL
knew (nōō) *pt. of* KNOW
knick·ers (nik′ərz) *n.pl.* [< D. *Knickerbocker,* fictitious Du. author of W. Irving's *History of New York*] short, loose trousers gathered just below the knees: also **knick′er·bock′ers** (-ər bäk′ərz)
knick·knack (nik′nak′) *n.* [< KNACK] a small ornamental article
knife (nīf) *n., pl.* **knives** (nīvz) [OE. *cnif*] **1.** a cutting instrument with a sharp-edged blade set in a handle **2.** a cutting blade, as in a machine —*vt.* **knifed, knif′ing** to cut or stab with a knife
knight (nīt) *n.* [OE. *cniht,* boy] **1.** in the Middle Ages, a man formally raised to honorable military rank and pledged to chivalrous conduct **2.** in Britain, a man who for some achievement is given honorary nonhereditary rank entitling him to use *Sir* before his given name **3.** a chessman shaped like a horse's head —*vt.* to make (a man) a knight
knight′-er′rant (-er′ənt) *n., pl.* **knights′-er′rant 1.** a medieval knight wandering in search of adventure **2.** a chivalrous or quixotic person —**knight′-er′rant·ry** (-rē) *n.*
knight′hood′ (-hood′) *n.* **1.** the rank or vocation of a knight **2.** knightly conduct **3.** knights collectively
knight′ly *adj.* **1.** of or like a knight; chivalrous, brave, etc. **2.** of knights
knit (nit) *vt., vi.* **knit′ted** or **knit, knit′ting** [< OE. *cnotta,* a knot] **1.** to make (a fabric or garment) by looping yarn or thread together with special needles **2.** to join closely and firmly **3.** to draw (the brows) together —*n.* fabric or a garment made by knitting —**knit′ter** *n.*
knit′ting *n.* knitted work
knob (näb) *n.* [ME. *knobbe*] **1.** a rounded lump or protuberance **2.** a handle, usually round, of a door, drawer, etc.
knob′by *adj.* **-bi·er, -bi·est 1.** covered with knobs **2.** like a knob
knock (näk) *vi.* [OE. *cnocian*] **1.** to strike a blow, as with the fist; rap, or to rap on a door **2.** to bump; collide **3.** to make a thumping noise, as an engine **4.** [Colloq.] to find fault —*vt.* **1.** to hit; strike **2.** to make by hitting [to *knock* a hole in the wall] **3.** [Colloq.] to find fault with —*n.* **1.** a knocking **2.** a hit; rap **3.** a thumping noise **4.** [Colloq.] an adverse criticism —**knock about** (or **around**) [Colloq.] to wander about —**knock down 1.** to strike down **2.** to take apart **3.** to indicate the sale of at an auction —**knock**

off 1. [Colloq.] to stop working **2.** [Colloq.] to deduct **3.** [Colloq.] to do **4.** [Slang] to kill, overcome, etc. —**knock out** to make unconscious or exhausted —**knock together** to make or compose hastily
knock′er *n.* one that knocks; specif., a hinged ring, etc. on a door, for knocking
knock′-kneed′ (-nēd′) *adj.* having legs which bend inward at the knee
knock′out′ *n.* **1.** a knocking out or being knocked out **2.** [Slang] a very attractive or striking person or thing **3.** *Boxing* a victory won when the opponent is knocked down and cannot rise before an official count of ten
knock·wurst (näk′wurst′) *n. alt. sp. of* KNACK-WURST
knoll (nōl) *n.* [OE. *cnoll*] a little rounded hill; mound
knot (nät) *n.* [OE. *cnotta*] **1.** a lump in a thread, etc. as formed by a tangle **2.** a fastening made by tying together pieces of string, rope, etc. **3.** an ornamental bow of ribbon, etc. **4.** a small group or cluster **5.** something that ties closely; esp., the bond of marriage **6.** a problem; difficulty **7.** a hard lump on a tree where a branch grows out, or a cross section of such a lump in a board **8.** *Naut.* a speed of one nautical mile an hour —*vt., vi.* **knot′ted, knot′ting 1.** to make or form a knot (in) **2.** to entangle or become entangled
knot′hole′ *n.* a hole in a board, etc. where a knot has fallen out
knot′ty *adj.* **-ti·er, -ti·est 1.** full of knots [a *knotty* board] **2.** hard to solve; puzzling [a *knotty* problem] —**knot′ti·ness** *n.*
know (nō) *vt.* **knew, known, know′ing** [OE. *cnawan*] **1.** to be well informed about **2.** to be aware of **3.** to have securely in the memory **4.** to be acquainted with **5.** to have understanding of or skill in **6.** to distinguish [to *know* right from wrong] —*vi.* **1.** to have knowledge **2.** to be sure or aware —**in the know** [Colloq.] having confidential information —**know′a·ble** *adj.*
know′-how′ (-hou′) *n.* [Colloq.] technical skill
know′ing *adj.* **1.** having knowledge **2.** shrewd; clever **3.** implying shrewd or secret understanding [a *knowing* look]
knowl·edge (näl′ij) *n.* **1.** the fact or state of knowing **2.** range of information or understanding **3.** what is known; learning —**to (the best of) one's knowledge** as far as one knows
knowl′edge·a·ble (-ə b'l) *adj.* having or showing knowledge or intelligence
known (nōn) *pp. of* KNOW
knuck·le (nuk′'l) *n.* [< ? MDu. or MLowG. *knokel,* little bone] **1.** a joint of the finger; esp., the joint connecting a finger to the rest of the hand **2.** the knee or hock joint of an animal, used as food —**knuckle down** to work hard —**knuckle under** to yield; give in
knuck′le·head′ (-hed′) *n.* [Colloq.] a stupid person
knurl (nurl) *n.* [prob. < ME. *knur,* a knot + GNARL] **1.** a knot, knob, etc. **2.** any of a series of small beads or ridges, as along the edge of a coin —*vt.* to make knurls on
KO (kā′ō′) *vt.* **KO'd, KO'ing** [Slang] *Boxing* to knock out —*n., pl.* **KO's** [Slang] *Boxing* a knockout Also **K.O., k.o.**
ko·a·la (kō ä′lə) *n.* [< the native name] an Australian tree-dwelling marsupial with thick, gray fur
kohl·ra·bi (kōl′rä′bē, kōl′rä′bē) *n., pl.* **-bies** [G. < It. *cavolo rapa*] a vegetable related to the cabbage, with an edible bulbous stem
ko·la (kō′lə) *n. same as* COLA¹ (sense 1)

kook (kōōk) *n.* [< ? *cuckoo*] [Slang] a person regarded as silly, eccentric, crazy, etc. **–kook′y, kook′le** *adj.*

ko·peck, ko·pek (kō′pek) *n.* [< Russ.] a monetary unit, and a coin, equal to 1/100 of a ruble

Ko·ran (kō ran′, kô rän′) *n.* [Ar. *qur'ān,* book] the sacred book of the Muslims

Ko·re·an (kô rē′ən) *adj.* of Korea, its people, their language, etc. **–n.** a native of Korea

ko·sher (kō′shər) *adj.* [Heb. *kāshēr,* proper] **1.** *Judaism* clean or fit to eat according to the dietary laws **2.** [Slang] right, proper, etc.

kow·tow (kou′tou′, kō′-) *vi.* [Chin. *k'o-t'ou,* lit., knock head] to show submissive respect (*to*)

KP, K.P. kitchen police, a detail to assist army cooks

Kr *Chem.* krypton

kraal (kräl) *n.* [Afrik.] **1.** a village of South African natives **2.** an enclosure for cattle or sheep in South Africa

Krem·lln (krem′lin) *n.* [Fr. < Russ. *kreml′*] **1.** the citadel of Moscow, formerly housing Soviet government offices **2.** the government of the Soviet Union

Krish·na (krish′nə) a Hindu god, an incarnation of Vishnu

kro·na (krō′nə) *n., pl.* **-nor** (-nôr) [Sw. < L. *corona,* crown] the monetary unit and a coin of Sweden

kro·ne (krō′nə) *n., pl.* **-ner** (-nər) [Dan. < L. *corona,* crown] the monetary unit and a coin of Denmark or Norway

kryp·ton (krip′tän) *n.* [< Gr. *kryptein,* to hide] a rare, inert gaseous chemical element: symbol, Kr

ku·chen (kōō′kən) *n.* [G., cake] a coffeecake made of yeast dough

ku·dos (kōō′däs, -dôs; kyōō′-) *n.* [Gr. *kydos*] [Colloq.] praise for achievement; glory; fame

Ku Klux Klan (kōō′ kluks′ klan′) [< Gr. *kyklos,* a circle] a U.S. secret terrorist society that is anti-Negro, anti-Semitic, anti-Catholic, etc.

küm·mel (kim′'l) *n.* [G., caraway] a liqueur flavored with caraway seeds, anise, etc.

kum·quat (kum′kwät) *n.* [< Chin. *chin-chü,* golden orange] **1.** a small, orange-colored, oval fruit with a sour pulp and a sweet rind **2.** the tree it grows on

kung fu (kooŋ′ fōō′, gōōŋ′) [< Chin.] a Chinese system of self-defense, like karate but with circular movements

kw. kilowatt(s)

L

L, l (el) *n., pl.* **L's, l's** the twelfth letter of the English alphabet

L (el) *n., pl.* **L's 1.** an object shaped like L **2.** a Roman numeral for 50

L. Latin

L., l. 1. lake **2.** latitude **3.** left **4.** length **5.** *pl.* **LL., ll.** line **6.** liter **7.** [L. *libra(e)*] pound(s)

la (lä) *n.* [< L.] *Music* the sixth tone of the diatonic scale

lab (lab) *n.* [Colloq.] a laboratory

la·bel (lā′b'l) *n.* [OFr., a rag] **1.** a card, paper, etc. marked and attached to an object to indicate its contents, destination, owner, producer, etc. **2.** a term of generalized classification **–vt.** **-beled** or **-belled, -bel·ing** or **-bel·ling 1.** to attach a label to **2.** to classify as; call

la·bl·al (lā′bē əl) *adj.* [see LABIUM] **1.** of the lips **2.** *Phonet.* formed mainly with the lips, as *b, m,* and *p*

la′bl·ate′ (-āt′, -it) *adj.* [see LABIUM] having, or formed like, a lip or lips

la·bl·um (lā′bē əm) *n., pl.* **-bl·a** (-ə) [L., a lip] *Anat., Bot.,* etc. a lip or liplike organ

la·bor (lā′bər) *n.* [L.] **1.** physical or mental exertion; work **2.** a specific task **3.** all wage-earning, esp. manual, workers **4.** labor unions collectively **5.** the process of childbirth **–vi. 1.** to work **2.** to work hard **3.** to move slowly and with difficulty **4.** to suffer (*under* a false idea, etc.) **5.** to be in childbirth **–vt.** to develop in too great detail

lab·o·ra·to·ry (lab′rə tôr′ē, -ər ə tôr′ē) *n., pl.* **-rles** [see LABOR] a room, building, etc. for scientific work or research

Labor Day the first Monday in September, a legal holiday honoring labor

la·bored (lā′bərd) *adj.* made or done with great effort; strained

la·bor·er (lā′bər ər) *n.* one who labors; esp., a wage-earning worker whose work is characterized by physical exertion

la·bo·rl·ous (lə bôr′ē əs) *adj.* **1.** involving hard work; difficult **2.** hard-working

labor union an association of workers to promote and protect the welfare, interests, and rights of its members

la·bour (lā′bər) *n., vi., vt. Brit. sp.* of LABOR

la·bur·num (lə bur′nəm) *n.* [L.] a small, poisonous tree or shrub of the legume family, with drooping yellow flowers

lab·y·rinth (lab′ə rinth′) *n.* [< Gr. *labyrinthos*] a structure containing winding passages hard to follow without losing one's way; maze **– lab′y·rln′thlne** (-rin′thin) *adj.*

lac (lak) *n.* [< Hindi < Sans. *lākṣā*] a resinous substance secreted on various trees in S Asia by a scale insect: the source of shellac

lace (lās) *n.* [< L. *laqueus,* noose] **1.** a string, etc. used to draw together and fasten the parts of a shoe, corset, etc. **2.** an openwork fabric of linen, etc., woven in ornamental designs **–vt. laced, lac′lng 1.** to fasten with a lace **2.** to weave together; intertwine **3.** to thrash; beat **–vi.** [Colloq.] to attack physically or verbally (with *into*)

lac·er·ate (las′ə rāt′) *vt.* **-at′ed, -at′lng** [< L. *lacer,* mangled] to tear jaggedly; mangle **– lac′er·a′tlon** *n.*

lace′work′ *n.* lace, or any openwork decoration like lace

lach·ry·mal (lak′rə məl) *adj.* [< L. *lacrima,* tear] **1.** of or producing tears **2.** *same as* LACRIMAL (sense 1)

lach′ry·mose′ (-mōs′) *adj.* **1.** inclined to shed tears; tearful **2.** causing tears; sad

lack (lak) *n.* [< or akin to MLowG. *lak*] **1.** the fact or state of not having enough or of not having any **2.** the thing that is lacking or needed **–vi., vt.** to be deficient in or entirely without

lack·a·dal·sl·cal (lak′ə dā′zi k'l) *adj.* [ult. < *alack the day*] showing lack of interest or spirit; listless

lack·ey (lak′ē) *n., pl.* **-eys** [< Sp. *lacayo*] **1.** a male servant of low rank **2.** a servile follower; toady

lack·lus·ter (lak′lus′tər) *adj.* lacking brightness; dull Also sp. **lack′lus′tre**

la·con·ic (lə kän′ik) *adj.* [< Gr. *Lakōn,* a Spartan] terse in expression; using few words —**la·con′i·cal·ly** *adv.*

lac·quer (lak′ər) *n.* [< Fr. < Port. *laca,* gum lac] 1. a coating substance made of shellac, gum resins, etc. dissolved in ethyl alcohol or other solvent that evaporates quickly 2. a resinous varnish obtained from certain Oriental trees 3. a wooden article coated with this —*vt.* to coat with lacquer

lac·ri·mal (lak′rə məl) *adj.* 1. of or near the glands that secrete tears 2. *same as* LACHRYMAL (sense 1)

la·crosse (lə krôs′) *n.* [CanadFr. < Fr. *la,* the + *crosse,* a crutch] a ball game played by two ten-member teams using long-handled, pouched rackets

lac·te·al (lak′tē əl) *adj.* [< L. *lac,* milk] of or like milk; milky

lac·tic (lak′tik) *adj.* [< L. *lac,* milk] of or obtained from milk

lactic acid a clear, syrupy acid formed when milk sours

lac·tose (lak′tōs) *n.* [< L. *lac,* milk] a white, crystalline sugar found in milk

la·cu·na (lə kyōō′nə) *n., pl.* **-nas, -nae** (-nē) [L., a ditch] a blank space; gap; hiatus

lac·y (lā′sē) *adj.* **-i·er, -i·est** of or like lace — **lac′i·ness** *n.*

lad (lad) *n.* [ME. *ladde*] a boy or youth

lad·der (lad′ər) *n.* [OE. *hlæder*] 1. a framework of two parallel sidepieces connected by rungs, for use in climbing up or down 2. any means of climbing

lad·die (lad′ē) *n.* [Chiefly Scot.] a lad

lade (lād) *vt., vi.* **lad′ed, lad′ed** or **lad′en, lad′ing** [OE. *hladan*] 1. to load 2. to bail; ladle

lad·en (lād′'n) *alt. pp.* of LADE —*adj.* 1. loaded 2. burdened; afflicted

la-di-da, la-de-da (lä′dē dä′) *adj.* [Colloq.] affectedly refined in speech, manners, etc.

lad·ing (lā′diŋ) *n.* a load; cargo; freight

la·dle (lā′d'l) *n.* [OE. *hlædel*] a long-handled, cuplike spoon for dipping —*vt.* **-dled, -dling** to dip out with, or carry in, a ladle

la·dy (lā′dē) *n., pl.* **-dies** [< OE. *hlaf,* loaf + base of *dæge,* kneader] 1. *a)* a woman of high social position *b)* a woman who is polite, refined, etc. 2. any woman 3. [L-] a British title given to women of certain ranks —*adj.* female [*a lady* barber]

la′dy·bug′ *n.* a small, roundish beetle with a spotted back: also **lady beetle**

la′dy·fin′ger *n.* a small spongecake shaped somewhat like a finger

la′dy-in-wait′ing *n., pl.* **la′dies-in-wait′ing** a woman attending, or waiting upon, a queen or princess

la′dy·like′ *adj.* like or suitable for a lady; refined; well-bred

la′dy·love′ *n.* a sweetheart

la′dy·ship′ *n.* 1. the rank or position of a lady 2. [*also* L-] a title used in speaking of or to a titled Lady: with *her* or *your*

lag (lag) *vi.* **lagged, lag′ging** [< ?] 1. to fall, move, or stay behind 2. to wane —*n.* 1. a falling behind or being retarded 2. the amount of this

la·ger (beer) (lä′gər) [G. *lagerbier,* lit., storehouse beer] a beer that is aged for several months after it has been brewed

lag·gard (lag′ərd) *n.* [< LAG + -ARD] a slow person, esp. one who falls behind —*adj.* slow or late in doing things

la·goon (lə gōōn′) *n.* [< Fr. & It. < L. *lacuna,* lake] 1. a shallow lake, esp. one connected with a larger body of water 2. the water enclosed by a circular coral reef 3. shallow salt water separated from the sea by dunes

la·ic (lā′ik) *adj.* [< Gr. *laos,* the people] secular; lay: also **la′i·cal** —*n.* a layman

laid (lād) *pt. & pp.* of LAY[1]

laid′-back′ *adj.* [Slang] relaxed, easygoing, etc.

lain (lān) *pp.* of LIE[1]

lair (ler) *n.* [OE. *leger*] the resting place of a wild animal; den

laird (lerd) *n.* [Scot. form of LORD] in Scotland, a landowner, esp. a wealthy one

lais·sez faire (les′ā fer′, lez′-) [Fr., let do] noninterference; specif., absence of governmental control over business

la·i·ty (lā′ət ē) *n., pl.* **-ties** [< LAY[3]] laymen collectively

lake (lāk) *n.* [< L. *lacus*] 1. a large, inland body of water 2. a pool of oil or other liquid

lam[1] (lam) *vt., vi.* **lammed, lam′ming** [< Scand.] [Slang] to beat; thrash

lam[2] (lam) *n.* [< ? prec.] [Slang] headlong flight —*vi.* **lammed, lam′ming** [Slang] to flee; escape —**on the lam** [Slang] in flight, as from the police

la·ma (lä′mə) *n.* [Tibetan *blama*] a priest or monk in Lamaism

La·ma·ism (lä′mə iz'm) *n.* a form of Buddhism practiced in Tibet and Mongolia

lamb (lam) *n.* [OE.] 1. a young sheep 2. its flesh used as food 3. lambskin 4. a gentle, innocent, or gullible person

lam·baste (lam bāst′, -bast′) *vt.* **-bast′ed, -bast′ing** [LAM[1] + BASTE[3]] [Colloq.] 1. to beat soundly 2. to scold severely

lamb·da (lam′də) *n.* the eleventh letter of the Greek alphabet (Λ, λ)

lam·bent (lam′bənt) *adj.* [< L. *lambere,* to lick] 1. playing lightly over a surface; flickering 2. softly glowing 3. light and graceful [*lambent* wit] —**lam′ben·cy** *n.*

lamb′kin *n.* a little lamb

lamb′skin′ *n.* the skin of a lamb, esp. with the fleece left on it

lame (lām) *adj.* [OE. *lama*] 1. crippled; esp., having an injured leg or foot that makes one limp 2. stiff and painful 3. poor, ineffectual, etc. [*a lame* excuse] —*vt.* **lamed, lam′ing** to make lame —**lame′ly** *adv.*

la·mé (la mā′) *n.* [< Fr. *lame,* metal plate] a cloth interwoven with metallic threads

lame duck an elected official whose term extends beyond the time of the election in which he was not reelected

la·ment (lə ment′) *vi., vt.* [< L. *lamentum,* a wailing] to feel or express deep sorrow (for); mourn —*n.* 1. a lamenting 2. an elegy, dirge, etc. mourning a loss, death, etc. —**lam·en·ta·ble** (lam′ən tə b'l, lə men′-) *adj.* —**lam′en·ta′tion** (-tā′shən) *n.*

lam·i·na (lam′ə nə) *n., pl.* **-nae** (-nē), **-nas** [L.] a thin flake, scale, or layer

lam·i·nate (lam′ə nāt′) *vt.* **-nat′ed, -nat′ing** 1. to cover with thin layers 2. to make by building up in layers —*adj.* (-nit) built in thin sheets or layers: also **lam′i·nat′ed** —**lam′i·na′tion** *n.*

lamp (lamp) *n.* [< Gr. *lampein,* to shine] 1. a container with a wick for burning oil, etc. to produce light or heat 2. any device for producing light or therapeutic rays 3. a holder or base for such a device

lamp′black′ *n.* fine soot used as a black pigment

lam·poon (lam pōōn′) *n.* [< Fr. *lampons,* let us drink (used as a refrain)] strongly satirical writing ridiculing someone —*vt.* to attack in a lampoon —**lam·poon′er** *n.*

lamp′post′ *n.* a post supporting a street lamp

lam·prey (lam′prē) *n., pl.* **-preys** [< ML. *lampreda*] an eellike parasitic fish with a funnel-shaped, sucking mouth

lance (lans) *n.* [< L. *lancea*] 1. a thrusting weapon consisting of a long wooden shaft with a sharp metal head 2. *same as: a)* LANCER *b)* LANCET 3. any instrument like a lance —*vt.* **lanced, lanc′ing** 1. to pierce with a lance 2. to cut open with a lancet

Lan·ce·lot (lan′sə lät′) the most celebrated of the Knights of the Round Table

lanc·er (lan′sər) *n.* a cavalry soldier armed with a lance

lan·cet (lan′sit) *n.* [< OFr. dim. of *lance,* LANCE] a small, pointed surgical knife, usually two-edged

land (land) *n.* [OE.] 1. the solid part of the earth's surface 2. a country or nation 3. ground or soil 4. real estate —*vt.* 1. to put on shore from a ship 2. to bring to a particular place [it *landed* him in jail] 3. to set (an aircraft) down on land or water 4. to catch 5. [Colloq.] to get or win 6. [Colloq.] to deliver (a blow) —*vi.* 1. to leave a ship and go on shore 2. to come to a port, etc.: said of a ship 3. to arrive at a specified place 4. to come to rest

land·ed (lan′did) *adj.* 1. owning land 2. consisting of land or real estate

land′fall′ *n.* 1. a sighting of land from a ship at sea 2. the land sighted

land′fill′ *n.* the disposal of garbage or rubbish by burying it in the ground

land grant a grant of public land by the government for a railroad, college, etc.

land′hold′er *n.* an owner or occupant of land —**land′hold′ing** *adj., n.*

land′ing *n.* 1. the act of coming to shore 2. the place where a ship is loaded or unloaded 3. a platform at the end of a flight of stairs 4. the act of alighting

landing gear the undercarriage of an aircraft, including wheels, etc.

land′la′dy *n., pl.* **-dies** a woman landlord

land′locked′ *adj.* 1. surrounded by land, as a bay 2. cut off from the sea and confined to fresh water [*landlocked* salmon]

land′lord′ *n.* 1. a person, esp. a man, who rents or leases land, houses, etc. to others 2. a man who keeps a rooming house, inn, etc.

land′lub′ber (-lub′ər) *n.* one who has had little experience at sea

land′mark′ *n.* 1. an object that marks the boundary of a piece of land 2. any prominent feature of the landscape, marking a locality 3. an important event in the development of something

land office a government office that handles the sales of public lands —**land′-of′fice busi·ness** [Colloq.] a booming business

land′scape′ (-skāp′) *n.* [< Du. *land,* land + *-schap,* -SHIP] 1. a picture representing natural, inland scenery 2. an expanse of natural scenery seen in one view —*vt.* **-scaped′, -scap′ing** to make (a plot of ground) more attractive, as by adding lawns, bushes, etc. —**land′scap′er** *n.*

land′slide′ *n.* 1. the sliding of a mass of rocks or earth down a slope 2. the mass sliding down 3. an overwhelming victory

land′ward (-wərd) *adv., adj.* toward the land: also **land′wards** *adv.*

lane (lān) *n.* [OE. *lanu*] 1. a narrow way, path, road, etc. 2. a path or strip designated, for reasons of safety, for ships, aircraft, automobiles, etc.

lan·guage (laŋ′gwij) *n.* [< L. *lingua,* tongue] 1. human speech or the written symbols for speech 2. *a)* any means of communicating *b)* a special set of symbols used in a computer 3. the speech of a particular nation, etc. [the French *language*] 4. the verbal expression characteristic of a particular group, writer, etc.

lan·guid (laŋ′gwid) *adj.* [< Fr. < L. *languere,* be faint] 1. without vigor or vitality; weak 2. listless; indifferent 3. sluggish; slow

lan′guish (-gwish) *vi.* [see LANGUID] 1. to become weak; droop 2. to long; pine 3. to put on a wistful air

lan·guor (laŋ′gər) *n.* [see LANGUID] 1. a lack of vigor or vitality; weakness 2. listlessness; sluggishness —**lan′guor·ous** *adj.*

lank (laŋk) *adj.* [OE. *hlanc*] 1. long and slender 2. straight and limp: said of hair

lank′y *adj.* **-i·er, -i·est** awkwardly tall and lean —**lank′i·ness** *n.*

lan·o·lin (lan′′l in) *n.* [< L. *lana,* wool + *oleum,* oil] a fatty substance obtained from wool and used in ointments, cosmetics, etc.

lan·tern (lan′tərn) *n.* [< Gr. *lampein,* to shine] a transparent case for holding and shielding a light

lan′tern-jawed′ *adj.* having long, thin jaws and sunken cheeks

lan·yard (lan′yərd) *n.* [< OFr. *lasne,* noose] a short rope used on board ship for holding or fastening something

lap¹ (lap) *n.* [OE. *læppa*] 1. *a)* the front part from the waist to the knees of a sitting person *b)* the part of the clothing covering this 2. that in which one is cared for, sheltered, etc. 3. *a)* an overlapping *b)* amount or place of this 4. one complete circuit around a race track — *vt.* **lapped, lap′ping** 1. to fold (*over* or *on*) 2. to wrap; enfold 3. to overlap 4. to get a lap ahead of (an opponent) in a race —*vi.* 1. to overlap 2. to extend beyond something in space or time (with *over*)

lap² (lap) *vi., vt.* **lapped, lap′ping** [OE. *lapian*] 1. to drink (a liquid) by dipping it up with the tongue as a dog does 2. to strike gently with a light splash, as waves —*n.* 1. a lapping 2. the sound of lapping —**lap up** [Colloq.] to take in eagerly

lap dog a pet dog small enough to hold in the lap

la·pel (lə pel′) *n.* [dim. of LAP¹] either of the front parts of a coat folded back and forming a continuation of the collar

lap·i·dar·y (lap′ə der′ē) *n., pl.* **-ies** [< L. *lapis,* a stone] a workman who cuts and polishes precious stones

lap·is laz·u·li (lap′is laz′yoo lī′) [< L. *lapis,* a stone + ML. *lazulus,* azure] an azure-blue, opaque, semiprecious stone

Lapp (lap) *n.* a member of a Mongoloid people living in Lapland: also **Lap′land·er**

lap·pet (lap′it) *n.* [dim. of LAP¹] a small fold or flap, as of a garment or of flesh

lapse (laps) *n.* [< L. *labi,* to slip] 1. a small error 2. *a)* a moral slip *b)* a falling into a lower condition 3. a passing, as of time 4. the termination as of a privilege through failure to meet requirements —*vi.* **lapsed, laps′ing** 1. to slip into a specified state [to *lapse* into a coma] 2. to backslide 3. to elapse 4. to become void because of failure to meet requirements

lar·board (lär′bərd) *n., adj.* [< OE. *hladan,* to lade + *bord,* side] port (left)

lar·ce·ny (lär′sə nē) *n., pl.* **-nies** [< L. *latro,* robber] the unlawful taking of another's property; theft —**lar′ce·nous** *adj.*

larch (lärch) *n.* [< L. *larix*] 1. a tree of the pine

family, that sheds its needles annually **2.** its tough wood

lard (lärd) *n.* [< L. *lardum*] the fat of hogs, melted and clarified —*vt.* **1.** to smear with lard, etc.; grease **2.** to put strips of fat pork, bacon, etc. on (meat, etc.) **3.** to embellish [a talk *larded* with jokes]

lard′er *n.* **1.** a place where food supplies are kept; pantry **2.** a supply of food

large (lärj) *adj.* **larg′er, larg′est** [< L. *largus*] **1.** big; great; bulky, spacious, of great extent or amount, etc. **2.** bigger than others of its kind **3.** operating on a big scale [a *large* producer] —*adv.* in a large way [write *large*] —**at large 1.** free; not confined **2.** fully; in detail **3.** representing no particular district [a congressman *at large*] —**large′ness** *n.* —**larg′ish** *adj.*

large′ly *adv.* **1.** much; in great amounts **2.** for the most part; mainly

large′-scale′ *adj.* **1.** drawn to a large scale **2.** of wide scope; extensive

lar·gess, lar·gesse (lär jes′, lär′jis) *n.* [see LARGE] **1.** generous giving **2.** a gift generously given

lar·go (lär′gō) *adj., adv.* [It., slow] *Music* slow and stately

lar·i·at (lar′ē it) *n.* [Sp. *la reata*, the rope] **1.** a rope for tethering grazing horses, etc. **2.** a lasso

lark[1] (lärk) *n.* [OE. *læwerce*] any of a large family of chiefly old-world songbirds; esp., the skylark

lark[2] (lärk) *vi.* [< ? ON. *leika*] to play or frolic —*n.* a frolic

lark·spur (lärk′spur′) *n.* *a common name for* DELPHINIUM

lar·va (lär′və) *n., pl.* **-vae** (-vē), **-vas** [L., ghost] the early form of any animal that changes structurally when it becomes an adult, as the tadpole —**lar′val** *adj.*

lar·yn·gi·tis (lar′ən jīt′əs) *n.* inflammation of the larynx, often with a temporary loss of voice

lar·ynx (lar′iŋks) *n., pl.* **lar′ynx·es, la·ryn·ges** (lə rin′jēz) [< Gr.] the structure at the upper end of the trachea, containing the vocal cords

la·sa·gna (lə zän′yə) *n.* [It., the noodle] a dish of wide noodles baked in layers with cheese, tomato sauce, and ground meat

las·civ·i·ous (lə siv′ē əs) *adj.* [< L. *lascivus*, wanton] **1.** characterized by or expressing lust **2.** tending to excite lust

la·ser (lā′zər) *n.* [l(ight) a(mplification by) s(timulated) e(mission of) r(adiation)] a device that amplifies focused light waves and concentrates them in a narrow, very intense beam

lash[1] (lash) *n.* [< ?] **1.** the flexible striking part of a whip **2.** a stroke as with a whip **3.** a sharp rebuke **4.** an eyelash —*vt.* **1.** to strike or drive as with a whip **2.** to switch energetically [the cat *lashed* its tail] **3.** to censure or rebuke —*vi.* to make strokes as with a whip —**lash out 1.** to strike out violently **2.** to speak angrily

lash[2] (lash) *vt.* [see LACE] to fasten or tie with a rope, etc.

lass (las) *n.* [prob. < ON. *lọskr*, weak] a young woman

las·sie (las′ē) *n.* [Scot.] a young girl

las·si·tude (las′ə tōōd′) *n.* [< L. *lassus*, faint] weariness; languor

las·so (las′ō, -ōō) *n., pl.* **-sos, -soes** [< Sp. < L. *laqueus*, noose] a long rope with a sliding noose at one end, used in catching cattle, etc. —*vt.* **-soed, -so·ing** to catch with a lasso —**las′-so·er** *n.*

last[1] (last) *alt. superl. of* LATE —*adj.* **1.** being or coming after all others in place or time; final

2. only remaining **3.** most recent [last month] **4.** least likely [the *last* person to suspect] **5.** conclusive [the *last* word] —*adv.* **1.** after all others **2.** most recently **3.** finally —*n.* the one coming last —**at (long) last** finally

last[2] (last) *vi.* [OE. *læstan*] to remain in existence or operation; endure —*vt.* **1.** to continue during **2.** to be enough for

last[3] (last) *n.* [< OE. *last*, footstep] a form shaped like a foot, used in making or repairing shoes —*vt.* to form on a last

last′ing *adj.* that lasts a long time; durable

Last Judgment *Theol.* the final judgment of mankind at the end of the world

last′ly *adv.* in conclusion; finally

last straw [< the last straw that broke the camel's back in the fable] a final annoyance or trouble that results in a defeat, loss of patience, etc.

Last Supper the last supper eaten by Jesus with his disciples before the Crucifixion

lat. latitude

latch (lach) *n.* [< OE. *læccan*] a fastening for a door, gate, or window; esp., a bar, etc. that fits into a notch —*vt., vi.* to fasten with a latch —**latch onto** [Colloq.] to get or obtain

late (lāt) *adj.* **lat′er** or **lat′ter, lat′est** or **last** [OE. *læt*] **1.** happening, coming, etc. after the usual or expected time, or at a time far advanced in a period [a *late* party, the *late* Middle Ages] **2.** *a*) recent *b*) having recently died —*adv.* **lat′er, lat′est** or **last 1.** after the expected time **2.** at or until an advanced time of the day, year, etc. **3.** toward the end of a period **4.** recently —**of late** recently —**late′ness** *n.*

late′ly *adv.* not long ago; recently

la·tent (lāt′nt) *adj.* [< L. *latere*, lurk] lying hidden and undeveloped in a person or thing —**la′ten·cy** *n.* —**la′tent·ly** *adv.*

lat·er·al (lat′ər əl) *adj.* [< L. *latus*, a side] of, at, from, or toward the side; sideways —**lat′er·al·ly** *adv.*

la·tex (lā′teks) *n.* [L., a fluid] a milky liquid in certain plants and trees: latex is the basis of rubber

lath (lath) *n., pl.* **laths** (lathz, laths) [< OE. *lætt*] **1.** any of the thin, narrow strips of wood used as a groundwork for plastering, etc. **2.** any framework for plaster

lathe (lāth) *n.* [prob. < MDu. *lade*] a machine for shaping wood, metal, etc. by holding and turning it rapidly against a cutting tool

lath·er (lath′ər) *n.* [OE. *leathor*, soap] **1.** the foam formed by soap and water **2.** foamy sweat **3.** [Slang] an excited state —*vt., vi.* to cover with or form lather —**lath′er·y** *adj.*

Lat·in (lat′n) *adj.* [< *Latium*, ancient country in C Italy] **1.** of ancient Rome, its people, their language, etc. **2.** designating or of the languages derived from Latin, the peoples who speak them, their countries, etc. —*n.* **1.** a native or inhabitant of ancient Rome **2.** the language of ancient Rome **3.** a person, as a Spaniard or Italian, whose language is derived from Latin

lat·i·tude (lat′ə tōōd′) *n.* [< L. *latus*, wide] **1.** extent; scope; range **2.** freedom from narrow restrictions **3.** *a*) distance north or south from the equator, measured in degrees *b*) a region with reference to this distance —**lat′i·tu′di·nal** *adj.*

la·trine (lə trēn′) *n.* [< L. *lavare*, to wash] a toilet for the use of many people, as in an army camp

lat·ter (lat′ər) *adj. alt. compar. of* LATE **1.** *a*) later; more recent *b*) nearer the end or close **2.** being the last mentioned of two

lat·ter·ly *adv.* lately; recently

lat·tice (lat′is) *n.* [< MHG. *latte,* lath] **1.** an openwork structure of crossed strips of wood, metal, etc. used as a screen, support, etc. **2.** a door, shutter, etc. formed of such a structure —*vt.* **-ticed, -tic·ing 1.** to arrange like a lattice **2.** to furnish with a lattice

lat′tice·work′ *n.* **1.** a lattice **2.** lattices collectively Also **lat′tic·ing**

laud (lôd) *n., vt.* [< L. *laus*] praise

laud′a·ble *adj.* praiseworthy

laud·a·num (lôd′'n əm) *n.* [< L. *ladanum,* a dark resin] **1.** formerly, any of various opium preparations **2.** a solution of opium in alcohol

laud·a·to·ry (lôd′ə tôr′ē) *adj.* expressing praise; commendatory

laugh (laf) *vi.* [< OE. *hleahhan*] to make the sounds and facial movements that express mirth, ridicule, etc. —*n.* **1.** the act or sound of laughing **2.** a cause of laughter —**laugh at 1.** to be amused by **2.** to make fun of —**laugh′er** *n.*

laugh′a·ble *adj.* amusing or ridiculous

laughing gas nitrous oxide used as an anesthetic: inhaling it may cause a reaction of laughter

laugh′ing·stock′ (-stäk′) *n.* an object of ridicule

laugh′ter (-tər) *n.* the action or sound of laughing

launch[1] (lônch) *vt.* [< L. *lancea,* lance] **1.** to hurl or send forth with some force [to *launch* a rocket] **2.** to slide (a vessel) into the water **3.** to set in operation or on some course [to *launch* an attack] —*vi.* **1.** *a)* to put to sea *b)* to begin something new With *out* or *forth* **2.** to plunge (*into*) —*n.* a launching —*adj.* designating or of facilities, sites, etc. used in launching spacecraft or missiles

launch[2] (lônch) *n.* [Sp. or Port. *lancha*] an open, or partly enclosed, motorboat

launch pad the platform from which a rocket, guided missile, etc. is launched: also **launching pad**

laun·der (lôn′dər) *vt., vi.* [< L. *lavare,* to wash] to wash, or wash and iron, (clothes, etc.) — **laun′der·er** *n.* —**laun′dress** (-dris) *n.fem.*

Laun·dro·mat (lôn′drə mat′) *a service mark for* a self-service laundry —*n.* [l-] such a laundry

laun·dry (lôn′drē) *n., pl.* **-dries 1.** a place for laundering **2.** clothes, etc. laundered or to be laundered

laun′dry·man (-mən) *n., pl.* **-men** a man who collects and delivers laundry

lau·re·ate (lôr′ē it) *adj.* [< L. *laurus,* laurel] honored, as with a crown of laurel —*n. same as* POET LAUREATE

lau·rel (lôr′əl) *n.* [< L. *laurus*] **1.** an evergreen tree or shrub of S Europe, with large, glossy leaves **2.** its foliage, esp. as woven into crowns **3.** [*pl.*] *a)* fame; honor *b)* victory **4.** a tree or shrub resembling the true laurel, as the mountain laurel

la·va (lä′və, lav′ə) *n.* [It. < L. *labi,* to slide] **1.** melted rock issuing from a volcano **2.** such rock when solidified by cooling

lav·a·liere, lav·a·lier (lav′ə lir′, lä′və-) *n.* [< Fr.] an ornament hanging from a chain, worn around the neck

lav·a·to·ry (lav′ə tôr′ē) *n., pl.* **-ries** [< L. *lavare,* to wash] **1.** a washbowl with faucets and drain **2.** a room with a washbowl and a toilet

lave (lāv) *vt., vi.* **laved, lav′ing** [< L. *lavare*] [Poet.] to wash; bathe

lav·en·der (lav′ən dər) *n.* [< ML. *lavandria*] **1.** a fragrant European mint with spikes of pale-

purplish flowers **2.** its dried flowers and leaves, used to perfume clothes, etc. **3.** a pale purple —*adj.* pale-purple

lav·ish (lav′ish) *adj.* [< OFr. *lavasse,* downpour] **1.** very generous; prodigal **2.** very abundant —*vt.* to give or spend liberally

law (lô) *n.* [OE. *lagu*] **1.** *a)* all the rules of conduct established by the authority or custom of a nation, etc. *b)* any one of such rules **2.** obedience to such rules **3.** the study of such rules; jurisprudence **4.** the seeking of justice in courts under such rules **5.** the profession of lawyers, judges, etc. **6.** *a)* a sequence of natural events occurring with unvarying uniformity under the same conditions *b)* the stating of such a sequence **7.** any rule expected to be observed —**the Law 1.** the Mosaic code, or the part of the Bible containing it **2.** [l-] [Colloq.] a policeman or the police

law′-a·bid′ing *adj.* obeying the law

law′break′er *n.* one who violates the law

law′ful *adj.* **1.** in conformity with the law **2.** recognized by law [*lawful* debts]

law′less *adj.* **1.** not regulated by the authority of law **2.** not in conformity with law; illegal **3.** not obeying the law; unruly

law′mak′er *n.* one who makes or helps to make laws; esp., a legislator

lawn[1] (lôn) *n.* [< OFr. *launde,* heath] land covered with grass kept closely mowed, esp. around a house

lawn[2] (lôn) *n.* [< *Laon,* city in France] a fine, sheer cloth of linen or cotton

lawn mower a hand-propelled or power-driven machine to cut lawn grass

law·ren·ci·um (lô ren′sē əm) *n.* [< E. O. *Lawrence* (1901–58), U.S. physicist] a radioactive chemical element produced by nuclear bombardment: symbol, Lr

law′suit′ (-soot′) *n.* a suit between private parties in a law court

law·yer (lô′yər) *n.* one whose profession is advising others in matters of law or representing them in lawsuits

lax (laks) *adj.* [< L. *laxus*] **1.** loose; slack; not tight **2.** not strict or exact

lax·a·tive (lak′sə tiv) *adj.* [see LAX] making the bowels loose and relieving constipation —*n.* any laxative medicine

lax′i·ty *n.* lax quality or condition

lay[1] (lā) *vt.* **laid, lay′ing** [< OE. *lecgan*] **1.** to cause to fall with force; knock down **2.** to place or put in a resting position (with *on* or *in*) **3.** to put down (bricks, carpeting, etc.) in the correct position or way **4.** to place; put; set [*lay* emphasis on accuracy] **5.** to produce (an egg) **6.** to allay, overcome, etc. **7.** to bet (a specified sum, etc.) **8.** to devise [to *lay* plans] **9.** to present or assert [to *lay* claim to property] —*n.* the way or position in which something is situated [the *lay* of the land] — **lay aside** to set aside for future use; save: also **lay away, lay by** —**lay in** to get and store away —**lay off 1.** to discharge (an employee), esp. temporarily **2.** [Slang] to cease —**lay open 1.** to cut open **2.** to expose —**lay out 1.** to spend **2.** to arrange according to a plan **3.** to spread out (clothes, etc.) ready for wear —**lay over** to stop a while in a place before going on —**lay up 1.** to store for future use **2.** to confine to a sickbed

lay[2] (lā) *pt. of* LIE[1]

lay[3] (lā) *adj.* [< Gr. *laos,* the people] **1.** of a layman **2.** not belonging to a given profession

lay[4] (lā) *n.* [ME. *lai*] **1.** a narrative poem for singing **2.** [Archaic] a song

lay′a·way′ plan a method of buying by making a deposit on something which is delivered only after full payment

lay·er *n.* **1.** a person or thing that lays **2.** a single thickness, coat, fold, etc.

lay·ette (lā et′) *n.* [< MDu. *lade*, chest] a complete outfit of clothes, bedding, etc. for a newborn baby

lay·man (lā′mən) *n., pl.* **-men** a person not of the clergy or of a given profession

lay·off (lā′ôf′) *n.* temporary unemployment, or the period of this

lay·out *n.* **1.** the manner in which anything is laid out; specif., the makeup of a newspaper, advertisement, etc. **2.** the thing laid out

lay·o·ver *n.* a stop during a journey

Laz·a·rus (laz′ə rəs) *Bible* a man raised from the dead by Jesus

laze (lāz) *vi., vt.* **lazed, laz′ing** to idle

la·zy (lā′zē) *adj.* **-zi·er, -zi·est** [prob. < MLowG. or MDu.] **1.** not eager or willing to work or exert oneself **2.** slow and heavy; sluggish —**la′zi·ly** *adv.* —**la′zi·ness** *n.*

la′zy·bones′ *n.* [Colloq.] a lazy person

Lazy Su·san (sōō′z′n) a revolving tray for food

lb. [L. *libra*, pl. *librae*] pound; pounds

lbs. pounds

l.c. 1. [L. *loco citato*] in the place cited **2.** *Printing* lower case

lea (lē) *n.* [OE. *leah*] [Chiefly Poet.] a meadow or grassy field

leach (lēch) *vt.* [prob. < OE. *leccan*, to water] **1.** to wash (wood ashes, etc.) with a filtering liquid **2.** to extract (a soluble substance) from some material —*vi.* to lose soluble matter through a filtering liquid

lead[1] (lēd) *vt.* **led, lead′ing** [OE. *lǣdan*] **1.** to direct, as by going before or along with, by physical contact, pulling a rope, etc.; guide **2.** to direct by influence **3.** to be the head of (an expedition, orchestra, etc.) **4.** to be at the head of [to *lead* one's class] **5.** to be ahead of in a contest **6.** to live; spend [to *lead* a full life] —*vi.* **1.** to show the way, as by going before **2.** to tend in a certain direction [with *to, from,* etc.] **3.** to bring as a result (with *to*) [hate *led* to war] **4.** to be or go first —*n.* **1.** the role or example of a leader **2.** first or front place **3.** the amount or distance ahead [to hold a safe *lead*] **4.** anything that leads, as a clue **5.** a principal role in a play, etc. **6.** the right of playing first in cards, or the card played —**lead off** to begin —**lead on** to lure —**lead up to** to prepare the way for

lead[2] (led) *n.* [OE.] **1.** a heavy, soft, bluish-gray metallic chemical element used for piping, etc.: symbol, Pb **2.** a weight for sounding depths at sea, etc. **3.** bullets **4.** a thin stick of graphite, used in pencils —*adj.* made of or containing lead —*vt.* to cover, line, or weight with lead

lead·en (led′′n) *adj.* **1.** made of lead **2.** heavy **3.** sluggish **4.** gloomy **5.** of a dull gray

lead·er (lē′dər) *n.* a person or thing that leads; guiding head —**lead′er·ship′** *n.*

lead·ing (lē′diŋ) *n.* direction; guidance —*adj.* **1.** that leads; guiding **2.** principal; chief

leading question a question put in such a way as to suggest the answer sought

lead time (lēd) the period of time needed from the decision to make a product to the start of production

leaf (lēf) *n., pl.* **leaves** (lēvz) [OE.] **1.** any of the flat, thin parts, usually green, growing from the stem of a plant **2.** a petal **3.** a sheet of paper **4.** a thin sheet of metal **5.** a hinged or removable section of a table top —*vi.* **1.** to bear

leaves **2.** to turn the pages of a book, etc. (with *through*)

leaf′let (-lit) *n.* **1.** a small or young leaf **2.** a separate sheet of printed matter, often folded

leaf′stalk′ (-stôk′) *n.* the part of a leaf that supports the blade and is attached to the stem

leaf′y *adj.* **-i·er, -i·est** having many or broad leaves —**leaf′i·ness** *n.*

league[1] (lēg) *n.* [< L. *ligare*, bind] **1.** an association of nations, groups, etc. for promoting common interests **2.** *Sports* a group of teams formed to play one another —*vt., vi.* **leagued, leagu′ing** to form into a league —**in league** allied —**leagu′er** *n.*

league[2] (lēg) *n.* [ult. < Celt.] a measure of distance, about 3 miles

League of Nations an association of nations (1920-46) succeeded by the UN

Le·ah (lē′ə) *Bible* the elder of the sisters who were wives of Jacob

leak (lēk) *vi.* [< ON. *leka*, to drip] **1.** to let a fluid out or in accidentally **2.** to enter or escape in this way, as a fluid **3.** to become known gradually, accidentally, etc. [the truth *leaked* out] —*vt.* to allow to leak —*n.* **1.** an accidental hole or crack that lets something out or in **2.** any accidental means of escape **3.** leakage —**leak′y** *adj.*

leak′age (-ij) *n.* **1.** a leaking; leak **2.** that which leaks or the amount that leaks

lean[1] (lēn) *vi.* **leaned** or **leant** (lent), **lean′ing** [OE. *hlinian*] **1.** to bend or slant from an upright position **2.** to bend the body and rest part of one's weight on something **3.** to rely (*on* or *upon*) **4.** to tend (*toward* or *to*) —*vt.* to cause to lean

lean[2] (lēn) *adj.* [OE. *hlǣne*] **1.** with little flesh or fat; thin; spare **2.** meager —*n.* meat containing little or no fat —**lean′ness** *n.*

lean′ing *n.* tendency; inclination

lean′-to′ *n., pl.* **-tos′** a structure whose sloping roof abuts a wall or building

leap (lēp) *vi.* **leaped** or **leapt** (lept, lēpt), **leap′ing** [OE. *hleapan*] **1.** to jump; spring; bound **2.** to accept eagerly something offered (with *at*) —*vt.* **1.** to pass over by a jump **2.** to cause to leap —*n.* **1.** a jump; spring **2.** the distance covered in a jump **3.** a sudden transition —**leap′er** *n.*

leap′frog′ *n.* a game in which each player in turn leaps over the bent backs of the others —*vt., vi.* **-frogged′, -frog′ging** to leap in or as in this way; skip (*over*)

leap year a year of 366 days, occurring every fourth year: the additional day is February 29

learn (lurn) *vt., vi.* **learned** (lurnd) or **learnt** (lurnt), **learn′ing** [OE. *leornian*] **1.** to get knowledge of or skill in (an art, trade, etc.) by study, experience, etc. **2.** to come to know; hear (*of* or *about*) **3.** to memorize —**learn′er** *n.*

learn·ed (lur′nid) *adj.* **1.** having or showing much learning **2.** (lurnd) acquired by study, experience, etc. [a *learned* response]

learn′ing *n.* **1.** the acquiring of knowledge or skill **2.** acquired knowledge or skill

lease (lēs) *n.* [< L. *laxus*, loose] a contract by which a landlord rents lands, buildings, etc. to a tenant for a specified time —*vt.* **leased, leas′ing** to give or get by a lease

leash (lēsh) *n.* [< L. *laxus*, loose] a cord, strap, etc. by which a dog, etc. is held in check —*vt.* to check or control as by a leash

least (lēst) *alt. superl.* of LITTLE —*adj.* [OE. *lǣst*] smallest in size, degree, etc. —*adv.* in the smallest degree —*n.* the smallest in amount, importance, etc. —**at (the) least 1.** with no less **2.** at any rate —**not in the least** not at all

least'wise' (-wīz') *adv.* [Colloq.] at least; anyway: also **least'ways'**
leath·er (leth'ər) *n.* [< OE. *lether-*] animal skin prepared for use by removing the hair and tanning —*adj.* of or made of leather
leath'er·neck' *n.* [< former leather-lined collar] [Slang] a U.S. Marine
leath'er·y *adj.* like leather; tough and flexible
leave¹ (lēv) *vt.* **left, leav'ing** [OE. *læfan,* let remain] **1.** to allow to remain [*leave* a sip for me, *leave* it open] **2.** to have remaining after one [he *leaves* a widow] **3.** to bequeath **4.** to go away from **5.** to abandon **6.** [Dial. or Slang] to let [*leave* us go] —*vi.* to go away or set out —**leave off** to stop —**leave out** to omit
leave² (lēv) *n.* [OE. *leaf*] **1.** permission **2.** *a)* permission to be absent from duty *b)* the period for which this is granted —**take leave of** to say goodbye to —**take one's leave** to depart
leave³ (lēv) *vi.* **leaved, leav'ing** to put forth, or bear, leaves; leaf
leav·en (lev''n) *n.* [< L. *levare,* raise] *same as* LEAVENING —*vt.* **1.** to make (dough) rise **2.** to spread through, causing a gradual change
leav'en·ing *n.* **1.** a substance, such as yeast, used to make dough rise **2.** any influence working to cause gradual change
leave of absence a leave from work or duty, esp. for a long time; also, the period of time
leaves (lēvz) *n. pl. of* LEAF
leave'-tak'ing *n.* a parting; farewell
leav·ings (lēv'iŋz) *n.pl.* things left over
lech·er (lech'ər) *n.* [OFr. *lechier,* live debauchedly] a lustful, grossly sensual man — **lech'er·ous** *adj.* —**lech'er·y** *n.*
lec·i·thin (les'ə thin) *n.* [< Gr. *lekithos,* egg yolk] a fatty compound found in nerve tissue, blood, egg yolk, etc. and plant cells
lec·tern (lek'tərn) *n.* [< L. *legere,* read] a reading stand
lec·ture (lek'chər) *n.* [< L. *legere,* read] **1.** an informative talk given before an audience, class, etc. **2.** a lengthy scolding —*vt., vi.* **-tured, -tur·ing 1.** to give a lecture (to) **2.** to scold — **lec'tur·er** *n.*
led (led) *pt. & pp. of* LEAD¹
ledge (lej) *n.* [ME. *legge*] **1.** a shelf **2.** a projecting ridge of rocks
ledg·er (lej'ər) *n.* [ME. *legger*] *Bookkeeping* a book of final entry, in which a record of debits, credits, etc. is kept
lee (lē) *n.* [OE. *hleo,* shelter] **1.** shelter **2.** *Naut.* the side or part away from the wind —*adj.* of or on the lee side
leech (lēch) *n.* [OE. *læce*] **1.** a bloodsucking worm living in water and used, esp. formerly, to bleed patients **2.** a person who is a parasite —*vi.* to act as a parasite
leek (lēk) *n.* [OE. *leac*] a vegetable that resembles a thick green onion
leer (lir) *n.* [OE. *hleor*] a sly, sidelong look showing lust, malicious triumph, etc. —*vi.* to look with a leer —**leer'ing·ly** *adv.*
leer·y (lir'ē) *adj.* **-i·er, -i·est** wary; suspicious
lees (lēz) *n.pl.* [< ML. *lia*] dregs or sediment, as of wine
lee·ward (lē'wərd; *naut.* lōō'ərd) *adj.* in the direction toward which the wind blows —*n.* the lee part or side —*adv.* toward the lee
lee·way (lē'wā') *n.* **1.** leeward drift of a ship or aircraft from its course **2.** [Colloq.] *a)* margin of time, money, etc. *b)* room for freedom of action
left¹ (left) *adj.* [< OE. *lyft,* weak] **1.** of that side toward the west when one faces north **2.** closer to the left side of one facing the thing mentioned —*n.* **1.** the left side **2.** [*often* L-] *Politics*

a radical or liberal position, party, etc. (often with *the*) —*adv.* on or toward the left hand or side
left² (left) *pt. & pp. of* LEAVE¹
left'-hand' *adj.* **1.** on or directed toward the left **2.** of, for, or with the left hand
left'-hand'ed *adj.* **1.** using the left hand more skillfully than the right **2.** done with or made for use with the left hand **3.** insincere or ambiguous [a *left-handed* compliment] —*adv.* with the left hand
left'ist *n., adj.* radical or liberal
left'o'ver *n.* something left over, as from a meal —*adj.* remaining unused, uneaten, etc.
left wing the more radical or liberal section of a political party, group, etc. —**left'-wing'** *adj.* — **left'-wing'er** *n.*
leg (leg) *n.* [ON. *leggr*] **1.** a body part by means of which men and animals stand and walk **2.** the part of a garment covering the leg **3.** anything like a leg in shape or use **4.** a stage of a journey —*vi.* **legged, leg'ging** [Colloq.] to walk or run: chiefly in the phrase **leg it** —**pull someone's leg** [Colloq.] to make fun of or fool one
leg·a·cy (leg'ə sē) *n., pl.* **-cies** [ult. < L. *lex, law*] **1.** money or property left to someone by a will **2.** anything handed down as from an ancestor
le·gal (lē'g'l) *adj.* [< L. *lex,* law] **1.** of or based on law **2.** permitted by law **3.** of or for lawyers —**le'gal·ly** *adv.*
legal holiday a holiday set by law
le'gal·ism *n.* strict or too strict adherence to the law —**le'gal·is'tic** *adj.*
le·gal·i·ty (li gal'ə tē) *n., pl.* **-ties** quality, condition, or instance of being legal or lawful
le·gal·ize (lē'gə līz') *vt.* **-ized', -iz'ing** to make legal or lawful —**le'gal·i·za'tion** *n.*
legal tender money acceptable by law in payment of an obligation
leg·ate (leg'it) *n.* [< L. *lex,* law] an envoy, esp. one officially representing the Pope
leg·a·tee (leg'ə tē') *n.* one to whom a legacy is bequeathed
le·ga·tion (li gā'shən) *n.* a diplomatic minister and his staff and headquarters
le·ga·to (li gät'ō) *adj., adv.* [< It. *legare,* to tie] *Music* in a smooth, even style, with no breaks between notes
leg·end (lej'ənd) *n.* [< L. *legere,* read] **1.** a story or body of stories handed down for generations and popularly believed to have a historical basis **2.** a notable person or the stories of his exploits **3.** an inscription on a coin, etc. **4.** a title, key, etc. accompanying an illustration or map
leg·end·ar·y (lej'ən der'ē) *adj.* of, based on, or presented in a legend or legends
leg·er·de·main (lej'ər di mān') *n.* [< MFr. *leger de main,* light of hand] **1.** sleight of hand; tricks of a stage magician **2.** trickery
leg·ged (leg'id, legd) *adj.* having (a specified number or kind of) legs [long-*legged*]
leg·ging (leg'iŋ) *n.* a covering for the leg: *usually used in pl.*
leg·horn (leg'hôrn, -ərn) *n.* [< *Leghorn,* It. seaport] [*often* L-] any of a breed of small chicken
leg·i·ble (lej'ə b'l) *adj.* [< L. *legere,* read] that can be read, esp. easily —**leg'i·bil'i·ty** *n.* —**leg'i·bly** *adv.*
le·gion (lē'jən) *n.* [< L. *legere,* to select] **1.** a large group of soldiers; army **2.** a large number; multitude —**le'gion·ar'y** *adj., n.* —**le'gion·naire'** (-jə ner') *n.*
leg·is·late (lej'is lāt') *vi.* **-lat'ed, -lat'ing** [see

LEGISLATION] to make or pass a law or laws — *vt.* to cause to be, go, etc. by making laws — **leg'is·la'tor** *n.*

leg·is·la'tion *n.* [< L. *lex*, law + *latio*, a bringing] 1. the making of laws 2. the law or laws made

leg·is·la'tive *adj.* 1. of legislation or a legislature 2. having the power to make laws

leg·is·la'ture (-chər) *n.* a body of persons given the power to make laws

le·git·i·mate (lə jit'ə mit) *adj.* [< L. *lex*, law] 1. born of parents married to each other 2. lawful 3. *a)* reasonable *b)* justifiable 4. conforming to accepted rules, standards, etc. 5. of stage plays, as distinguished from motion pictures, etc. —**le·git'i·ma·cy** (-mə sē) *n.*

le·git'i·mize (-mīz') *vt.* -**mized'**, -**miz'ing** to make or declare legitimate; legalize, authorize, justify, etc.: also **le·git'i·ma·tize'** (-mə tīz') -**tized'**, -**tiz'ing**

leg·man (leg'man') *n., pl.* -**men'** a reporter who turns in news from on the scene

leg'room' *n.* adequate space for the legs while seated, as in a car

leg·ume (leg'yoōm, li gyoōm') *n.* [< L. *legere*, gather] 1. any of a large family of plants having seeds growing in pods, including peas, beans, etc. 2. the pod or seed of such a plant —**le·gu·mi·nous** (li gyoō'min əs) *adj.*

leg'work' *n.* [Colloq.] necessary routine travel as part of a job

lei (lā, lā'ē) *n., pl.* **leis** [Haw.] in Hawaii, a wreath of flowers and leaves

lei·sure (lē'zhər, lezh'ər) *n.* [< L. *licere*, be permitted] free time during which one may indulge in rest, recreation, etc. —*adj.* free and unoccupied *[leisure* time]

lei'sure·ly *adj.* without haste; slow —*adv.* in an unhurried manner

lem·ming (lem'iŋ) *n.* [Dan. < ON. *læmingi*] a small arctic rodent with a short tail

lem·on (lem'ən) *n.* [< Per. *līmūn*] 1. a small, sour, pale-yellow citrus fruit 2. the spiny, semitropical tree that it grows on 3. [Slang] something that is defective —*adj.* 1. paleyellow 2. made with lemon

lem'on·ade' (-ə nād') *n.* a drink made of lemon juice, sugar, and water

le·mur (lē'mər) *n.* [< L. *lemures*, ghosts] a small primate related to the monkeys

lend (lend) *vt.* **lent**, **lend'ing** [< OE. *læn*, a loan] 1. to let another use or have (a thing) temporarily 2. to let out (money) at interest 3. to impart —*vi.* to make a loan —**lend itself** (or **oneself**) **to** to be useful for or open to —**lend'er** *n.*

length (leŋkth) *n.* [< OE. *lang*, long] 1. the distance from end to end of a thing 2. extent in space or time 3. a long stretch or extent 4. a piece of a certain length —**at length** 1. finally 2. in full

length'en *vt., vi.* to make or become longer

length'wise' (-wīz') *adv., adj.* in the direction of the length: also **length'ways'** (-wāz')

length'y *adj.* -**i·er**, -**i·est** long; esp., too long — **length'i·ly** *adv.*

le·ni·ent (lē'ni ənt, lēn'yənt) *adj.* [< L. *lenis*, soft] not harsh or severe; merciful —**le'ni·en·cy** *n.* —**le'ni·ent·ly** *adv.*

lens (lenz) *n.* [L., lentil: < its shape] 1. a curved piece of glass, plastic, etc. for bringing together or spreading rays of light passing through it: used in optical instruments to form an image 2. any device used to focus microwaves, sound waves, etc. 3. a transparent body of the eye: it focuses upon the retina light rays entering the pupil

Lent (lent) *n.* [OE. *lengten*, the spring] *Christianity* the forty weekdays of fasting and penitence, from Ash Wednesday to Easter — **Lent'en, lent'en** *adj.*

lent (lent) *pt. & pp. of* LEND

len·til (lent'l) *n.* [< L. *lens*] 1. a leguminous plant, with small, edible seeds 2. this seed

Le·o (lē'ō) [L., lion] the fifth sign of the zodiac

le·o·nine (lē'ə nīn') *adj.* [< L. *leo*, lion] of or like a lion

leop·ard (lep'ərd) *n.* [< Gr. *leōn*, lion + *pardos*, panther] 1. a large, wild animal of the cat family, with a black-spotted tawny coat, found in Africa and Asia 2. *same as* JAGUAR

le·o·tard (lē'ə tärd') *n.* [< J. *Léotard*, 19th-c. Fr. aerial performer] a tightfitting garment for acrobats, dancers, etc.

lep·er (lep'ər) *n.* [< Gr. *lepros*, scaly] a person having leprosy

lep·re·chaun (lep'rə kôn') *n.* [< OIr. *lu*, little + *corp*, body] *Ir. Folklore* a fairy who can reveal a buried crock of gold

lep·ro·sy (lep'rə sē) *n.* [see LEPER] a chronic infectious disease of the skin, flesh, nerves, etc., characterized by ulcers, white scaly scabs, deformities, etc. —**lep'rous** *adj.*

les·bi·an (lez'bē an) *n.* [< *Lesbos*, Gr. island home of the poetess Sappho] a homosexual woman —**les'bi·an·ism** *n.*

le·sion (lē'zhən) *n.* [< L. *laedere*, to harm] an injury of an organ or tissue resulting in impairment of function

less (les) *adj. alt. compar. of* LITTLE [OE. *læs(sa)*] not so much, so great, etc.; smaller; fewer —*adv. compar. of* LITTLE to a smaller extent —*n.* a smaller amount —*prep.* minus

-less [OE. *leas*, free] *a suffix meaning:* 1. without *[valueless]* 2. that does not *[tireless]* 3. that cannot be *[dauntless]*

les·see (les ē') *n.* [see LEASE] one to whom a lease is given; tenant

less·en (les''n) *vt., vi.* to make or become less; decrease, diminish, etc.

less·er (les'ər) *adj. alt. compar. of* LITTLE smaller, less, or less important

les·son (les''n) *n.* [< L. *legere*, to read] 1. an exercise for a student to learn 2. something learned for one's safety, etc. 3. [*pl.*] course of instruction 4. a selection read from the Bible 5. a rebuke; reproof

les·sor (les'ôr) *n.* [see LEASE] one who gives a lease; landlord

lest (lest) *conj.* [< OE. *thy læs the*, by the less that] for fear that

let¹ (let) *vt.* **let**, **let'ting** [OE. *lætan*, leave behind] 1. to leave: now only in **let alone** (or **let be**) 2. *a)* to rent *b)* to assign (a contract) 3. to cause to escape *[to let* blood] 4. to allow; permit Also used as an auxiliary in commands or suggestions *[let* us go] —*vi.* to be rented —**let down** 1. to lower 2. to slow up 3. to disappoint —**let off** 1. to give forth 2. to deal leniently with —**let on** [Colloq.] 1. to pretend 2. to indicate one's awareness —**let out** 1. to release 2. to rent out 3. to make a garment larger —**let up** 1. to relax 2. to cease

let² (let) *n.* [< OE. *lettan*, make late] an obstacle: used in **without let or hindrance**

-let [< MFr. *-el* + *-et*, dim. suffixes] *a suffix meaning* small *[ringlet]*

let'down' *n.* 1. a slowing up 2. the descent of an airplane about to land 3. a disappointment

le·thal (lē'thəl) *adj.* [< L. *letum*, death] causing death; fatal

leth·ar·gy (leth'ər jē) *n., pl.* -**gies** [< Gr. *lēthē*, oblivion + *argos*, idle] 1. an abnormal drowsi-

ness 2. sluggishness; apathy —**le·thar·gic** (li thär′jik) *adj.*
let's (lets) let us
let·ter (let′ər) *n.* [< L. *littera*] **1.** any character of the alphabet **2.** a written or printed message, usually sent by mail **3.** [*pl.*] *a*) literature *b*) learning; knowledge **4.** literal meaning —*vt.* to mark with letters
letter box *same as* MAILBOX
letter carrier *same as* MAIL CARRIER
let′tered *adj.* **1.** literate **2.** well-educated **3.** marked with letters
let′ter·head′ *n.* **1.** the name, address, etc. of a person or firm as a heading on stationery **2.** a sheet of such stationery
let′ter·ing *n.* **1.** the act of making letters or inscribing letters **2.** such letters
let′ter-per′fect *adj.* entirely correct
let·tuce (let′is) *n.* [< L. *lac*, milk] **1.** a plant with crisp, green leaves **2.** the leaves, much used for salads
let′up′ *n.* [Colloq.] **1.** a slackening **2.** a stop; pause
leu·ke·mi·a (loo kē′mē ə) *n.* [see LEUKOCYTE & -EMIA] a disease resulting in an abnormal increase in the production of leukocytes: also sp. **leu·kae′mi·a**
leu·ko·cyte (loo′kə sīt′) *n.* [< Gr. *leukos*, white + *kytos*, hollow] a white corpuscle in the blood: it destroys disease-causing organisms
lev·ee (lev′ē) *n.* [< Fr. < L. *levare*, to raise] an embankment to prevent a river from flooding bordering land
lev·el (lev′'l) *n.* [< L. *libra*, a balance] **1.** an instrument for determining the horizontal **2.** a horizontal plane or line [*sea level*] **3.** a horizontal area **4.** normal position with reference to height [*water seeks its level*] **5.** position in a scale of values [*income level*] —*adj.* **1.** perfectly flat and even **2.** not sloping **3.** even in height (*with*) **4.** not heaping [a *level* teaspoonful] **5.** equal in importance, advancement, quality, etc. **6.** calm or steady —*vt., vi.* **-eled** or **-elled, -el·ing** or **-el·ling 1.** to make or become level **2.** to demolish **3.** to raise and aim (a gun, etc.) — **level with** [Slang] to be honest with —**lev′el·er, lev′el·ler** *n.*
lev′el·head′ed *adj.* having an even temper and sound judgment —**lev′el·head′ed·ness** *n.*
lev·er (lev′ər, lē′vər) *n.* [< L. *levare*, raise] **1.** a bar used as a pry **2.** a means to an end **3.** *Mech.* a device consisting of a bar turning about a fixed point, using force at a second point to lift a weight at a third —*vt.* to lift with a lever —*vi.* to use a lever
lev′er·age (-ij) *n.* the action or mechanical power of a lever
le·vi·a·than (lə vī′ə thən) *n.* [< Heb. *liwyāthān*] **1.** *Bible* a sea monster **2.** any huge thing
Le·vi's (lē′vīz) [< *Levi* Strauss, the U.S. maker] *a trademark for* closefitting trousers of heavy denim
lev·i·ta·tion (lev′ə tā′shən) *n.* [< L. *levis*, LIGHT²] the illusion of raising a body in the air with no support
Le·vit·i·cus (lə vit′i kəs) the third book of the Bible
lev·i·ty (lev′ə tē) *n., pl.* **-ties** [< L. *levis*, LIGHT²] improper gaiety; frivolity
lev·y (lev′ē) *n., pl.* **-ies** [see LEVER] **1.** an imposing and collecting of a tax, fine, etc. **2.** the amount levied **3.** *a*) compulsory enlistment for military service *b*) a group so enlisted —*vt.* **-ied, -y·ing 1.** to impose (a tax, fine, etc.) **2.** to enlist (troops) **3.** to wage (war)
lewd (lood) *adj.* [OE. *lǣwede*, unlearned] show-

ing, or intended to excite, lust or sexual desire, esp. offensively —**lewd′ly** *adv.*
lex·i·cog·ra·phy (lek′sə käg′rə fē) *n.* [see LEXICON & -GRAPHY] the act, art, or work of writing or compiling a dictionary —**lex′i·cog′ra·pher** *n.*
lex·i·con (lek′si kən) *n.* [< Gr. *lexis*, a word] **1.** a dictionary **2.** a special vocabulary
Li *Chem.* lithium
li·a·bil·i·ty (lī′ə bil′ə tē) *n., pl.* **-ties 1.** the state of being liable **2.** anything for which a person is liable **3.** [*pl.*] *Accounting* the debts of a person or business **4.** something that works to one's disadvantage
li·a·ble (lī′ə b'l; *also, esp. for 3,* lī′b'l) *adj.* [< L. *ligare*, to bind] **1.** legally bound; responsible **2.** subject to [*liable* to heart attacks] **3.** likely (*to*) [*liable* to die]
li·ai·son (lē′ə zän′, -zōn′; lē ā′zän) *n.* [Fr. < L. *ligare*, bind] **1.** intercommunication, as between units of a military force **2.** an illicit love affair
li·ar (lī′ər) *n.* a person who tells lies
lib (lib) *n. clipped form of* LIBERATION
li·ba·tion (lī bā′shən) *n.* [< L. *libare*, pour out] **1.** the ritual of pouring out wine or oil in honor of a god **2.** the liquid poured out
li·bel (lī′b'l) *n.* [< L. *liber*, book] **1.** any written or printed matter tending to injure a person's reputation unjustly **2.** the act of publishing such a thing —*vt.* **-beled** or **-belled, -bel·ing** or **-bel·ling** to make a libel against —**li′bel·er, li′bel·ler** *n.* —**li′bel·ous, li′bel·lous** *adj.*
lib·er·al (lib′ər əl) *adj.* [< L. *liber*, free] **1.** generous **2.** ample; abundant **3.** not literal or strict **4.** tolerant; broad-minded **5.** favoring reform or progress —*n.* one who favors reform or progress —**lib′er·al·ism** *n.* —**lib′er·al·ly** *adv.* —**lib′er·al·ness** *n.*
liberal arts literature, philosophy, languages, history, etc. as courses of study
lib′er·al′i·ty (-ə ral′ə tē) *n., pl.* **-ties 1.** generosity **2.** tolerance; broad-mindedness
lib′er·al·ize′ (-ər ə līz′) *vt., vi.* **-ized′, -iz′ing** to make or become liberal —**lib′er·al·i·za′tion** *n.*
lib·er·ate (lib′ə rāt′) *vt.* **-at′ed, -at′ing** [< L. *liber*, free] **1.** to release from slavery, enemy occupation, etc. **2.** to secure equal rights for — **lib′er·a′tion** *n.* —**lib′er·a′tor** *n.*
lib·er·tar·i·an (lib′ər ter′ē ən) *n.* **1.** a believer in free will **2.** an advocate of full civil liberties
lib·er·tine (lib′ər tēn′) *n.* [< L. *liber*, free] a man who is sexually promiscuous —*adj.* licentious —**lib′er·tin·ism** *n.*
lib·er·ty (lib′ər tē) *n., pl.* **-ties** [< L. *liber*, free] **1.** freedom from slavery, captivity, etc. **2.** a particular right, freedom, etc. **3.** an impertinent attitude **4.** *U.S. Navy* permission for an enlisted person to be absent from duty for 72 hours or less —**at liberty 1.** not confined **2.** allowed (*to*) **3.** not busy or in use —**take liberties 1.** to be too familiar or impertinent **2.** to deal (*with* facts, etc.) in a distorting way
li·bid·i·nous (li bid′'n əs) *adj.* [see LIBIDO] lustful; lascivious —**li·bid′i·nous·ly** *adv.*
li·bi·do (li bē′dō, -bī′-) *n.* [L., desire] **1.** the sexual urge **2.** *Psychoanalysis* psychic energy generally; specif., that comprising the positive, loving instincts
Li·bra (lī′brə, lē′-) [L., a balance] the seventh sign of the zodiac
li·brar·i·an (lī brer′ē ən) *n.* a person in charge of a library or trained to work in a library
li·brar·y (lī′brer′ē) *n., pl.* **-ies** [< L. *liber*, book] **1.** a room or building where a collection of books, etc. is kept **2.** an institution in charge

of the care and circulation of such a collection **3.** a collection of books

li·bret·to (li bret′ō) *n., pl.* **-tos, -ti** (-ē) [It. < L. *liber,* book] the words, or text, of an opera, oratorio, etc. —**li·bret′tist** *n.*

lice (līs) *n. pl. of* LOUSE

li·cense (līs′'ns) *n.* [< L. *licere,* be permitted] **1.** formal or legal permission to do something specified **2.** a document indicating such permission **3.** freedom to deviate from rule, practice, etc. [poetic *license*] **4.** excessive freedom, constituting an abuse of liberty Brit. sp. **license** —*vt.* **-censed, -cens·ing** to permit formally

li′cen·see′ (-'n sē′) *n.* a person to whom a license is granted

li·cen·ti·ate (lī sen′shē it, -āt′) *n.* a person licensed to practice a specified profession

li·cen·tious (lī sen′shəs) *adj.* [see LICENSE] morally unrestrained; lascivious

li·chen (lī′kən) *n.* [< Gr. *leichein,* to lick] a mosslike plant growing in patches on rock, wood, soil, etc.

lick (lik) *vt.* [OE. *liccian*] **1.** to pass the tongue over **2.** to pass lightly over like a tongue **3.** [Colloq.] *a)* to whip *b)* to vanquish —*n.* **1.** a licking with the tongue **2.** a small quantity **3.** *short for* SALT LICK **4.** [Colloq.] *a)* a sharp blow *b)* a short, rapid burst of activity: also **lick and a promise 5.** [*often pl.*] [Slang] chance; turn —**lick up** to consume as by licking

lic·o·rice (lik′ər ish, -lik′rish) *n.* [< Gr. *glykys,* sweet + *rhiza,* root] **1.** the dried root or black flavoring extract of a European plant **2.** candy flavored with this extract

lid (lid) *n.* [OE. *hlid*] **1.** a movable cover, as for a box, etc. **2.** *short for* EYELID **3.** [Colloq.] a restraint —**lid′ded** *adj.*

lie[1] (lī) *vi.* **lay, lain, ly′ing** [OE. *licgan*] **1.** to be or put oneself in a horizontal or reclining position **2.** to rest on a support in a horizontal position **3.** to be in a specified condition **4.** to be situated [Canada *lies* to the north] **5.** to exist [love *lies* in her eyes] **6.** to be buried —*n.* the way in which something is situated; lay

lie[2] (lī) *vi.* **lied, ly′ing** [OE. *leogan*] to make a statement that one knows to be false —*vt.* to bring, put, accomplish, etc. by lying —*n.* a false statement made to deceive

lief (lēf) *adv.* [OE. *leof*] willingly; gladly: only in **would** (or **had**) **as lief,** etc.

liege (lēj) *adj.* [< OFr.] loyal; faithful —*n. Feudal Law* **1.** a lord or sovereign **2.** a subject or vassal

li·en (lēn, lē′ən) *n.* [Fr. < L. *ligare,* to bind] a legal claim on another's property as security for the payment of a debt

lieu (lōō) *n.* [< L. *locus,* place] place: now chiefly in **in lieu of,** instead of

lieu·ten·ant (lōō ten′ənt) *n.* [< MFr. *lieu,* place + *tenant,* holding] **1.** one who acts for a superior **2.** *U.S. Mil.* an officer ranking below a captain: see FIRST LIEUTENANT, SECOND LIEUTENANT **3.** *U.S. Navy* an officer ranking just above a lieutenant junior grade Abbrev. **Lieut., Lt.** —**lieu·ten′an·cy** (-ən sē) *n., pl.* **-cies**

lieutenant colonel *U.S. Mil.* an officer ranking above a major

lieutenant commander *U.S. Navy* an officer ranking above a lieutenant

lieutenant general *U.S. Mil.* an officer ranking above a major general

lieutenant governor an elected official of a State who ranks below and substitutes for the governor

lieutenant junior grade *U.S. Navy* an officer ranking above an ensign

life (līf) *n., pl.* **lives** [OE. *lif*] **1.** that property of plants and animals (ending at death) which makes it possible for them to take in food, get energy from it, grow, etc. **2.** the state of having this property **3.** a human being [100 *lives* were lost] **4.** living things collectively [plant *life*] **5.** the time a person or thing is alive or flourishing **6.** one's manner of living [a *life* of ease] **7.** the people and activities of a given time, place, etc. [military *life*] **8.** human existence [to learn from *life*] **9.** *a)* one's lifetime experiences *b)* a biography **10.** something essential to the continued existence of something else [freedom of speech is the *life* of democracy] **11.** the source of liveliness [the *life* of the party] **12.** vigor; liveliness

life belt a life preserver in the form of a belt

life′blood′ *n.* **1.** the blood necessary to life **2.** a vital element

life′boat′ *n.* any of the small rescue boats carried by a ship

life buoy *same as* LIFE PRESERVER

life′guard′ *n.* an expert swimmer employed at a beach, pool, etc. to prevent drownings

life insurance insurance in which a stipulated sum is paid at the death of the insured

life jacket (or **vest**) a life preserver in the form of a sleeveless jacket or vest

life′less *adj.* **1.** without life; specif., *a)* inanimate *b)* dead **2.** dull —**life′less·ly** *adv.*

life′like′ *adj.* resembling real life or a real person or thing

life′line′ *n.* **1.** the rope used to raise or lower a diver **2.** a commercial route, esp. maritime, of great importance

life′long′ *adj.* lasting or not changing during one's whole life

life net a strong net used by firemen, etc. as to catch people jumping from a burning building

life preserver a buoyant device for saving a person from drowning by keeping his body afloat

lif′er *n.* [Slang] a person sentenced to prison for the remainder of his life

life raft a small, inflatable raft or boat

life′sav′er *n.* **1.** a lifeguard **2.** [Colloq.] a help in time of need

life′-size′ *adj.* as big as the person or thing represented, as a statue, etc.: also **life′-sized′**

life style an individual's whole way of living

life′time′ *n.* the length of time that one lives, or that a thing lasts

life′work′ *n.* the work or task to which a person devotes his life

lift (lift) *vt.* [< ON. *lopt,* air] **1.** to bring up to a higher position; raise **2.** to raise in rank, condition, etc.; exalt **3.** to pay off (a mortgage, debt, etc.) **4.** to end (a blockade, etc.) **5.** [Slang] to steal —*vi.* **1.** to exert strength in raising something **2.** to rise; go up —*n.* **1.** a lifting or rising **2.** the amount lifted **3.** the distance something is lifted **4.** lifting force, influence, etc. **5.** elevation of mood, etc. **6.** elevated position or carriage **7.** a ride in the direction one is going **8.** help of any kind **9.** [Brit.] an elevator —**lift′er** *n.*

lift′off′ *n.* **1.** the vertical thrust of a spacecraft, missile, etc. at launching **2.** the time of this

lig·a·ment (lig′ə mənt) *n.* [< L. *ligare,* to bind] a band of tissue connecting bones or holding organs in place

lig·a·ture (lig′ə chər) *n.* [< L. *ligare,* bind] **1.** a tying or binding together **2.** a tie, bond, etc. **3.** two or more letters united, as æ, th **4.** *Surgery* a thread used to tie up an artery, etc.

light[1] (līt) *n.* [OE. *leoht*] **1.** *a)* the form of electromagnetic radiation acting on the retina of the eye to make sight possible *b)* ultraviolet or infrared radiation **2.** brightness; illumination **3.** a source of light, as the sun, a lamp, etc. **4.** daylight **5.** a thing used to ignite something **6.** a window or windowpane **7.** knowledge; enlightenment **8.** public view **9.** aspect *[presented in a favorable light]* **10.** an outstanding person —*adj.* **1.** having light; bright **2.** pale in color; fair —*adv.* palely *[a light blue color]* —*vt.* **light′ed** or **lit, light′ing 1.** to ignite *[to light a bonfire]* **2.** to cause to give off light **3.** to furnish with light **4.** to brighten; animate —*vi.* **1.** to catch fire **2.** to be lighted (usually with *up*) —**in the light of** considering

light² (līt) *adj.* [OE. *leoht*] **1.** having little weight; not heavy, esp. for its size **2.** less than the usual in weight, amount, force, etc. *[a light blow]* **3.** of little importance **4.** easy to bear *[a light tax]* **5.** easy to do *[light work]* **6.** gay; happy **7.** dizzy; giddy **8.** not serious *[light reading]* **9.** moderate *[a light meal]* **10.** moving with ease *[light on one's feet]* **11.** producing small products *[light industry]* —*adv.* lightly —*vi.* **light′ed** or **lit, light′ing 1.** to come to rest after traveling through the air **2.** to come or happen (*on* or *upon*) **3.** to strike suddenly, as a blow —**light out** [Colloq.] to depart suddenly —**make light of** to treat as unimportant

light′en¹ *vt., vi.* **1.** to make or become light or brighter **2.** to shine; flash

light′en² *vt., vi.* **1.** to make or become lighter in weight **2.** to make or become more cheerful

light′er¹ *n.* a person or thing that lights something or starts it burning

light′er² *n.* [< MDu. *licht*, LIGHT²] a large barge used in loading or unloading ships lying offshore

light′face′ *n. Printing* type with thin, light lines

light′-fin′gered *adj.* skillful at stealing, esp. by picking pockets

light′-foot′ed *adj.* stepping lightly and gracefully —**light′-foot′ed·ly** *adv.*

light′head′ed *adj.* **1.** giddy; dizzy **2.** flighty; frivolous —**light′head′ed·ness** *n.*

light′heart′ed *adj.* free from care; gay

light heavyweight a boxer or wrestler between a middleweight and heavyweight (in boxing, 161–175 lbs.)

light′house′ *n.* a tower with a bright light to guide ships at night

light′ing *n.* the act, manner, or art of giving light, or illuminating

light′ly *adv.* **1.** with little weight or pressure; gently **2.** to a small degree or amount **3.** nimbly; deftly **4.** cheerfully **5.** with indifference or neglect

light′-mind′ed *adj.* not serious; frivolous

light′ning (-niŋ) *n.* a flash of light in the sky caused by the discharge of atmospheric electricity

lightning bug (or **beetle**) *same as* FIREFLY

lightning rod a metal rod placed high on a building and grounded to divert lightning from the structure

light opera a short, amusing musical play

light′weight′ *n.* a boxer or wrestler between a featherweight and a welterweight (in boxing, 127–135 lbs.) —*adj.* light in weight

light′-year′ *n.* the distance that light travels in one year, c.6 trillion miles

lig·nite (lig′nīt) *n.* [Fr. < L. *lignum*, wood] a soft, brownish-black coal with the texture of the original wood

lik·a·ble (līk′ə b'l) *adj.* attractive, genial, etc.: also **likeable**

like¹ (līk) *adj.* [OE. *gelic*] having the same characteristics; similar; equal —*adv.* [Colloq.] likely *[like as not, he'll go]* —*prep.* **1.** similar to **2.** similarly to *[to sing like a bird]* **3.** characteristic of *[not like me to cry]* **4.** in the mood for *[to feel like sleeping]* **5.** indicative of *[it looks like rain]* **6.** as for example *[fruit, like pears and plums]* —*conj.* [Colloq.] **1.** as *[it's just like he said]* **2.** as if *[it looks like he's late]* —*n.* an equal or counterpart *[the like of it]* —**and the like** and others of the same kind —**like blazes** (or **crazy, the devil, mad,** etc.) [Colloq.] with furious energy, speed, etc. —**the like** (or **likes**) **of** [Colloq.] any person or thing like

like² (līk) *vt.* **liked, lik′ing** [OE. *lician*] to be so inclined *[do as you like]* —*vt.* **1.** to be pleased with; enjoy **2.** to wish *[I'd like to go]* —*n.* [*pl.*] preferences or tastes

-like a suffix meaning like, characteristic of *[doglike, homelike]*

like·li·hood (līk′lē hood′) *n.* (a) probability

like·ly (līk′lē) *adj.* **-li·er, -li·est** [OE. *geliclic*] **1.** credible *[a likely cause]* **2.** reasonably to be expected *[likely to rain]* **3.** suitable *[a likely man]* —*adv.* probably *[he will very likely go]*

like′-mind′ed *adj.* having the same ideas, tastes, etc. —**like′-mind′ed·ness** *n.*

lik·en (līk′'n) *vt.* to compare

like′ness *n.* **1.** a being like **2.** (the same) form or shape **3.** a copy, portrait, etc.

like′wise′ *adv.* [< *in like wise*] **1.** in the same manner **2.** also; too; moreover

lik′ing *n.* **1.** fondness; affection **2.** preference; taste; pleasure

li·lac (lī′lək, -läk) *n.* [Fr. < Per. *nīlak*, bluish] **1.** a shrub with large clusters of tiny, fragrant flowers **2.** a pale-purple color —*adj.* pale-purple

Lil·li·pu·tian (lil′ə pyōō′shən) *adj.* [< *Lilliput*, place in J. Swift's *Gulliver's Travels*] **1.** tiny **2.** petty

lilt (lilt) *vt., vi.* [ME. *lilten*] to sing, speak, or play with a light, graceful rhythm —*n.* a light, swingy rhythm or tune

lil·y (lil′ē) *n., pl.* **-ies** [< L. *lilium*] **1.** a plant grown from a bulb and having typically trumpet-shaped flowers **2.** its flower **3.** any similar plant, as the waterlily —*adj.* like a lily, as in whiteness, purity, etc.

lil′y-liv′ered (-liv′ərd) *adj.* cowardly

lily of the valley *pl.* **lilies of the valley** a low plant with a spike of fragrant, small, white, bell-shaped flowers

li·ma bean (lī′mə) [< *Lima*, capital of Peru] [*also* **L- b-**] **1.** a bean plant with broad pods **2.** its broad, flat, nutritious seed

limb (lim) *n.* [OE. *lim*] **1.** an arm, leg, or wing **2.** a large branch of a tree —**out on a limb** [Colloq.] in a precarious position

lim·ber (lim′bər) *adj.* [< ? LIMB] **1.** easily bent; flexible **2.** able to bend the body easily —*vt., vi.* to make or become limber

lim·bo (lim′bō) *n., pl.* **-bos** [< L. (in) *limbo*, (on) the border] **1.** [*often* **L-**] in some Christian theologies, a region bordering on hell, the abode after death of unbaptized children, etc. **2.** a place of oblivion or neglect **3.** an indeterminate state

Lim·bur·ger (**cheese**) (lim′bər gər) [< *Limburg*, Belgian province] a semisoft cheese with a strong odor

lime¹ (līm) *n.* [OE. *lim*] a white substance, calcium oxide, obtained by the action of heat on limestone and used in mortar and cement and to neutralize acid soil —*vt.* **limed, lim′ing** to treat with lime

lime² (līm) *n.* [Fr. < Ar. *līma*] a small, lemonshaped, greenish-yellow citrus fruit with a juicy, sour pulp

lime′ade′ (-ād′) *n.* a drink of lime juice and water, usually sweetened

lime′light′ *n.* **1.** a brilliant light created by the incandescence of lime, formerly used in theaters **2.** a prominent position before the public

lim·er·ick (lim′ər ik) *n.* [prob. < *Limerick*, Ir. county] a rhymed, nonsense poem of five lines

lime′stone′ *n.* rock consisting mainly of calcium carbonate

lim·it (lim′it) *n.* [< L. *limes*] **1.** the point, line, etc. where something ends or must end; boundary **2.** [*pl.*] bounds **3.** the greatest amount allowed —*vt.* to set a limit to; restrict —**lim′i·ta′tion** *n.* —**lim′it·less** *adj.*

lim·it·ed *adj.* **1.** confined within bounds; restricted **2.** making a restricted number of stops: said of a train, bus, etc.

limn (lim) *vt.* [< L. *illuminare*, make light] **1.** to paint or draw **2.** to describe

lim·ou·sine (lim′ə zēn′) *n.* [Fr., lit., a hood] a large, luxury automobile, esp. one driven by a chauffeur

limp (limp) *vi.* [< OE. *limpan*, befall] to walk with or as with a lame leg —*n.* a halt or lameness in walking —*adj.* lacking firmness; wilted, flexible, etc. —**limp′ly** *adv.* —**limp′ness** *n.*

limp·et (lim′pit) *n.* [< ML. *lempreda*] a mollusk which clings to rocks, timbers, etc.

lim·pid (lim′pid) *adj.* [< Fr. < L. *limpidus*] perfectly clear; transparent

lim·y (lī′mē) *adj.* **-i·er, -i·est** of, like, or containing lime —**lim′i·ness** *n.*

lin·age (lī′nij) *n.* the number of written or printed lines on a page

lin·den (lin′dən) *n.* [OE.] a tree with dense, heart-shaped leaves

line[1] (līn) *n.* [< L. *linea*, lit., linen thread] **1.** a cord, rope, wire, etc. **2.** any wire, pipe, etc., or system of these, conducting fluid, electricity, etc. **3.** a thin, threadlike mark **4.** a border or boundary **5.** a limit **6.** outline; contour **7.** a row of persons or things, as of printed characters across a page **8.** *same as* LINEAGE **9.** a succession of persons or things **10.** a transportation system of buses, ships, etc. **11.** the course a moving thing takes **12.** a course of conduct, action, explanation, etc. **13.** a person's trade or occupation **14.** a stock of goods **15.** a short letter, note, etc. **16.** a verse of poetry **17.** [*pl.*] all the speeches of one character in a play **18.** the forward combat position in warfare **19.** *Football* the players in the forward row **20.** *Math.* the path of a moving point —*vt.* **lined, lin′ing 1.** to mark with lines **2.** to bring into alignment (often with *up*) **3.** to form a line along —*vi.* to form a line (usually with *up*) — **bring** (or **come, get**) **into line** to bring (or come) into alignment —**down the line** completely; entirely —**draw the** (or **a**) **line** to set a limit —**hold the line** to stand firm

line[2] (līn) *vt.* **lined, lin′ing** [< L. *linum*, flax] to put, or be used as, a lining in

lin·e·age (lin′ē ij) *n.* [see LINE[1]] **1.** direct descent from an ancestor **2.** ancestry

lin·e·al (lin′ē əl) *adj.* **1.** in the direct line of descent from an ancestor **2.** hereditary **3.** linear —**lin′e·al·ly** *adv.*

lin·e·a·ment (lin′ē ə mənt) *n.* [< L. *linea*, LINE[1]] a distinctive feature, esp. of the face: *usually used in pl.*

lin·e·ar (lin′ē ər) *adj.* **1.** of, made of, or using a line or lines **2.** in a line

linear measure a system of measuring length in which 12 in. = 1 ft. or in which 100 cm. = 1 m.

line·back·er (līn′bak′ər) *n.* *Football* a defensive player directly behind the line

line drive a baseball hit in a straight line parallel to the ground

line′man (-mən) *n., pl.* **-men 1.** a person who sets up and repairs telephone or electric wires, etc. **2.** *Football* a player in the line Also **lines′man**

lin·en (lin′ən) *n.* [< OE. *lin*, flax: see LINE[2]] **1.** thread or cloth made of flax **2.** [*often pl.*] sheets, tablecloths, etc. of linen, or of cotton, etc.

lin·er (lī′nər) *n.* **1.** a steamship, airplane, etc. in regular service for a specific line **2.** *same as* LINE DRIVE **3.** a cosmetic applied in a fine line, as along the eyelid

line′up′ *n.* an arrangement of persons or things in or as in a line

-ling [OE.] *a suffix meaning:* **1.** small [*duckling*] **2.** contemptible [*hireling*]

lin·ger (liŋ′gər) *vi.* [< OE. *lengan*, to delay] **1.** to continue to stay, esp. through reluctance to leave **2.** to loiter

lin·ge·rie (län′zhə rā′, -rē′; -jə-) *n.* [Fr.] women's underwear

lin·go (liŋ′gō) *n., pl.* **-goes** [< L. *lingua*, tongue] language; esp., a dialect, jargon, etc. one is not familiar with

lin·gual (liŋ′gwəl) *adj.* [< L. *lingua*, the tongue] of, or pronounced with, the tongue

lin·guist (liŋ′gwist) *n.* [< L. *lingua*, the tongue] **1.** a specialist in linguistics **2.** *same as* POLYGLOT

lin·guis′tics *n.pl.* [*with sing. v.*] **1.** the science of language **2.** the study of a particular language —**lin·guis′tic** *adj.*

lin·i·ment (lin′ə mənt) *n.* [< L. *linere*, to smear] a medicated liquid to be rubbed on the skin for soothing sore or inflamed areas

lin·ing (lī′niŋ) *n.* [see LINE[2]] the material covering an inner surface

link (liŋk) *n.* [< Scand.] **1.** any of the series of loops forming a chain **2.** *a*) a section of something resembling a chain [a *link* of sausage] *b*) an element in a series [a weak *link* in the evidence] **3.** anything that connects [a *link* with the past] —*vt., vi.* to join; connect

link′age *n.* **1.** a linking or being linked **2.** a series or system of links

linking verb a verb that functions chiefly as a connection between a subject and a predicate complement (Ex.: *be, seem,* etc.)

links (liŋks) *n.pl.* [OE. *hlinc*, a slope] a golf course

link′up′ *n.* a linking together

lin·net (lin′it) *n.* [< L. *linum*, flax: it feeds on flaxseed] a small finch

li·no·le·um (li nō′lē əm) *n.* [< L. *linum*, flax + *oleum*, oil] a hard, washable floor covering made of a mixture of ground cork and linseed oil on a backing, as of canvas

lin·seed (lin′sēd′) *n.* [OE. *linsæd*] the seed of flax

linseed oil a yellowish oil extracted from flaxseed, used in oil paints, etc.

lint (lint) *n.* [prob. < *lin*, linen] **1.** scraped and softened linen **2.** bits of thread, fluff, etc. from cloth or yarn —**lint′y** *adj.*

lin·tel (lin′t'l) *n.* [ult. < L. *limen*, threshold] the horizontal crosspiece over a door, window, etc.

li·on (lī′ən) *n.* [< Gr. *leōn*] **1.** a large, powerful mammal of the cat family, found in Africa and SW Asia **2.** a person of great courage or strength **3.** a celebrity —**li′on·ess** *n.fem.*

li′on·heart′ed (-här′tid) *adj.* very brave

li·on·ize (lī′ə nīz′) *vt.* **-ized′, -iz′ing** to treat as a celebrity

lip (lip) *n.* [OE. *lippa*] **1.** either of the two fleshy folds forming the edges of the mouth **2.** anything like a lip, as the rim of a pitcher **3.** [Slang] insolent talk —*adj.* spoken, but insincere *[lip* service*]* —**keep a stiff upper lip** [Colloq.] to bear pain or distress bravely

lip′py *adj.* **-pi·er, -pi·est** [Slang] impudent or insolent —**lip′pi·ness** *n.*

lip reading recognition of a speaker's words, as by the deaf, by watching the movement of his lips —**lip′-read′** *vt., vi.*

lip′stick′ *n.* a small stick of cosmetic paste for coloring the lips

liq·ue·fy (lik′wə fī′) *vt., vi.* **-fied′, -fy′ing** [< Fr. < L. *liquere,* be liquid + *facere,* make] to change to a liquid —**liq′ue·fac′tion** (-fak′shən) *n.*

li·queur (li kur′) *n.* [Fr.] a sweet, syrupy, flavored alcoholic liquor

liq·uid (lik′wid) *adj.* [< L. *liquidus*] **1.** readily flowing; fluid **2.** clear; limpid **3.** flowing smoothly and gracefully, as verse **4.** readily convertible into cash —*n.* a substance that, unlike a solid, flows readily but, unlike a gas, does not expand indefinitely

liq·ui·date (lik′wə dāt′) *vt.* **-dat′ed, -dat′ing** [see LIQUID] **1.** to settle the accounts of (a business) by apportioning assets and debts **2.** to pay (a debt) **3.** to convert into cash **4.** to get rid of, as by killing —**liq′ui·da′tion** *n.* —**liq′ui·da′tor** *n.*

liq·uor (lik′ər) *n.* [L.] **1.** any liquid **2.** an alcoholic drink, esp. a distilled drink, as whiskey or rum

li·ra (lir′ə) *n., pl.* **-re** (-ā), *for 2* **-ras** [It. < L. *libra,* a balance] the monetary unit of **1.** Italy **2.** Turkey

lisle (līl) *n.* [< *Lisle* (now *Lille*), France] **1.** a fine, hard, extra-strong cotton thread **2.** a fabric, stockings, etc. woven of this

lisp (lisp) *vi.* [< OE. *wlisp,* a lisping] **1.** to substitute the sounds (th) and (*th*) for the sounds of *s* and *z* **2.** to speak imperfectly —*vt.* to utter with a lisp —*n.* the act or sound of lisping —**lisp′er** *n.*

lis·some, lis·som (lis′əm) *adj.* [< *lithesome*] lithe, limber, agile, etc.

list¹ (list) *n.* [< OE. *liste,* border] a series of names, words, etc. set forth in order —*vt.* to set forth or enter in a list, directory, etc.

list² (list) *vt., vi.* [< ?] to tilt to one side, as a ship —*n.* such a tilting

lis·ten (lis′n) *vi.* [OE. *hlysnan*] **1.** to make a conscious effort to hear **2.** to give heed; take advice —*n.* a listening —**lis′ten·er** *n.*

list·less (list′lis) *adj.* [LIST² + -LESS] indifferent because of illness, dejection, etc.; languid —**list′less·ly** *adv.*

list price retail price as given in a list

lists (lists) *n.pl.* [< ME. *liste,* border] a fenced area where knights jousted

lit (lit) *alt. pt. & pp. of* LIGHT

lit·a·ny (lit′'n ē) *n., pl.* **-nies** [< Gr. *litaneia*] prayer in which the congregation recites responses

li·tchi (lē′chē′) *n.* [Chin. *li-chih*] the raisinlike fruit of a Chinese evergreen tree, enclosed in a papery shell

li·ter (lēt′ər) *n.* [Fr. *litre* < Gr. *litra,* a pound] the basic unit of capacity in the metric system, equal to 1.0567 liquid quarts or .908 dry quart: Brit. sp. **li′tre**

lit·er·a·cy (lit′ər ə sē) *n.* the ability to read and write

lit·er·al (lit′ər əl) *adj.* [< L. *littera,* a letter] **1.** following the exact words of the original *[a literal* translation*]* **2.** in a basic or strict sense *[the literal* meaning*]* **3.** prosaic; matter-of-fact **4.** restricted to fact; real *[the literal* truth*]*

lit·er·ar·y (lit′ə rer′ē) *adj.* **1.** of or dealing with literature **2.** versed in literature

lit·er·ate (lit′ər it) *adj.* [< L. *littera,* a letter] **1.** able to read and write **2.** well-educated —*n.* a literate person

lit·e·ra·ti (lit′ə rät′ē, -rä′tī) *n.pl.* [It. < L.] scholarly or learned people

lit·er·a·ture (lit′ər ə chər) *n.* [< L. *littera,* a letter] **1.** *a)* all the writings of a particular time, country, etc., esp. those valued for excellence of form and expression *b)* all the writings on a particular subject **2.** [Colloq.] any printed matter

lithe (līth) *adj.* **lith′er, lith′est** [OE., soft] bending easily; supple; limber: also **lithe′some** (-səm) —**lithe′ness** *n.*

lith·i·um (lith′ē əm) *n.* [< Gr. *lithos,* stone] a soft, silver-white metallic chemical element, the lightest known metal: symbol, Li

lithium carbonate a white salt used in treating manic-depressive disorders

lith·o·graph (lith′ə graf′) *n.* a print made by lithography —*vt., vi.* to make (prints or copies) by lithography —**li·thog·ra·pher** (li thäg′rə fər) *n.*

li·thog·ra·phy (li thäg′rə fē) *n.* [< Gr. *lithos,* stone + -GRAPHY] printing from a flat stone or metal plate, parts of which have been treated to repel ink —**lith·o·graph·ic** (lith′ə graf′ik) *adj.*

lit·i·gant (lit′ə gənt) *n.* a party to a lawsuit

lit·i·gate (′ -gāt′) *vt., vi.* **-gat′ed, -gat′ing** [< L. *lis,* dispute + *agere,* do] to contest in a lawsuit —**lit′i·ga′tion** *n.*

lit·mus (lit′məs) *n.* [< ON. *litr,* color + *mosi,* moss] a purple coloring matter obtained from lichens: paper treated with it (**litmus paper**) turns blue in bases and red in acids

Litt.D. Doctor of Letters

lit·ter (lit′ər) *n.* [< L. *lectus,* a couch] **1.** a framework enclosing a couch on which a person can be carried **2.** a stretcher for carrying the sick or wounded **3.** straw, hay, etc. used as bedding for animals **4.** the young borne at one time by a dog, cat, etc. **5.** things lying about in disorder, esp. bits of rubbish —*vt.* **1.** to make untidy **2.** to scatter about carelessly

lit′ter·bug′ *n.* a person who litters a public place with trash, garbage, etc.

lit·tle (lit′'l) *adj.* **lit′tler** or **less** or **less′er, lit′tlest** or **least** [OE. *lytel*] **1.** small in size, amount, degree, etc. **2.** short in duration; brief **3.** small in importance or power *[the little* man*]* **4.** narrow-minded *[a little* mind*]* —*adv.* **less, least** **1.** slightly; not much **2.** not in the least —*n.* a small amount, degree, etc. —**little by little** gradually —**make** (or **think**) **little of** to treat as unimportant —**lit′tle·ness** *n.*

lit·to·ral (lit′ər əl) *adj.* [< L. *litus,* seashore] of, on, or along the shore —*n.* a shore zone

lit·ur·gy (lit′ər jē) *n., pl.* **-gies** [< Fr. < Gr. *leōs,* people + *ergon,* work] prescribed ritual for public worship —**li·tur·gi·cal** (li tur′jə k'l) *adj.*

liv·a·ble (liv′ə b'l) *adj.* **1.** fit or pleasant to live in, as a house **2.** endurable **3.** agreeable to live with Also sp. **liveable**

live¹ (liv) *vi.* **lived, liv′ing** [OE. *libban*] **1.** to have life **2.** *a)* to remain alive *b)* to endure **3.** to pass life in a specified manner **4.** to enjoy a full life **5.** to feed *[to live* on fruit*]* **6.** to reside —*vt.* **1.** to carry out in one's life *[to live* one's faith*]* **2.** to spend; pass *[to live* a useful life*]* —

live down to live so as to wipe out the shame of (a fault, etc.) —**live up to** to act in accordance with (ideals, promises, etc.)

live² (līv) *adj.* [< ALIVE] **1.** having life **2.** of the living state or living things **3.** of present interest [a *live* issue] **4.** still burning [a *live* spark] **5.** unexploded [a *live* shell] **6.** carrying electrical current [a *live* wire] **7.** *a)* transmitted during the actual performance *b)* recorded at a public performance *c)* in person **8.** *Sports* in play [a *live* ball]

-lived (līvd; *occas.* livd) *a combining form meaning* having (a specified kind of) life [short-*lived*]

live·li·hood (līv'lē hood') *n.* [< OE. *lif*, life + *-lad*, course] means of supporting life

live·long (liv'lôn') *adj.* [ME. *lefe longe*, lit., lief long: *lief* is merely intens.] long in passing; whole; entire [the *livelong* day]

live·ly (līv'lē) *adj.* **-li·er, -li·est** [OE. *liflic*] **1.** full of life; vigorous **2.** full of spirit; exciting **3.** gay; cheerful **4.** vivid; keen **5.** bounding back with great resilience [a *lively* ball] —**live'li·ness** *n.*

liv·en (līv'vən) *vt., vi.* to make or become lively or gay; cheer (*up*) —**liv'en·er** *n.*

liv·er (liv'ər) *n.* [OE. *lifer*] **1.** the largest glandular organ in vertebrate animals: it secretes bile and is important in metabolism **2.** this organ of an animal used as food

liv·er·ied (liv'ər ēd) *adj.* wearing a livery

liv·er·wurst (liv'ər wurst') *n.* [< G. *leber*, LIVER + *wurst*, sausage] a sausage containing ground liver

liv·er·y (liv'ər ē, liv'rē) *n., pl.* **-ies** [< OFr. *livree*, gift of clothes to a servant] **1.** an identifying uniform, as of a servant **2.** *a)* the care and feeding of horses for a fee *b)* the keeping of horses or vehicles for hire

lives (līvz) *n. pl. of* LIFE

live·stock (līv'stäk') *n.* domestic animals kept for use on a farm or raised for sale

liv·id (liv'id) *adj.* [L. *lividus*] **1.** discolored by a bruise; black-and-blue **2.** grayish-blue or pale [*livid* with rage]

liv·ing (liv'iŋ) *adj.* **1.** alive; having life **2.** in active operation or use [a *living* language] **3.** of persons alive [within *living* memory] **4.** true; lifelike **5.** of life [*living* conditions] —*n.* **1.** a being alive **2.** livelihood **3.** manner of existence —**the living** those that are still alive

living room a room in a home with sofas, chairs, etc., used for socializing, etc.

living wage a wage sufficient to maintain a reasonable level of comfort

liz·ard (liz'ərd) *n.* [< L. *lacerta*] any of a group of reptiles with a long, slender body and tail, a scaly skin, and four legs

LL., L.L. Late Latin

ll., ll lines

lla·ma (lä'mə) *n.* [Sp. < SAmInd. name] a S. American beast of burden related to the camel but smaller

lla·no (lä'nō) *n., pl.* **-nos** (-nōz) [Sp. < L. *planus*, plain] a grassy plain in the Southwest and in Spanish America

LL.B. Bachelor of Laws

LL.D. Doctor of Laws

lo (lō) *interj.* [OE. *la*] look! see!

load (lōd) *n.* [< OE. *lad*, a course] **1.** an amount carried at one time; burden **2.** something borne with difficulty **3.** [often *pl.*] [Colloq.] a great amount —*vt.* **1.** to put (something to be carried) into or upon (a carrier) **2.** to burden; oppress **3.** to supply in abundance **4.** to put ammunition into (a

firearm), film in (a camera), etc. —*vi.* to take on a load —**load'er** *n.*

load·stone (lōd'stōn') *n. var. sp. of* LODESTONE

loaf¹ (lōf) *n., pl.* **loaves** [OE. *hlaf*] **1.** a portion of bread baked in one piece **2.** any food baked in this shape

loaf² (lōf) *vi.* [prob. < LOAFER] to loiter or lounge about; idle, dawdle, etc.

loaf'er *n.* [prob. < G. *landläufer*, a vagabond] one who loafs; idler

loam (lōm) *n.* [OE. *lam*] a rich soil of clay, sand, and organic matter —**loam'y** *adj.*

loan (lōn) *n.* [< ON. *lān*] **1.** the act of lending **2.** something lent; esp., money lent at interest —*vt., vi.* to lend —**loan'er** *n.*

loan shark [Colloq.] a person who lends money at exorbitant rates of interest

loath (lōth) *adj.* [OE. *lath*, hostile] unwilling; reluctant [to be *loath* to depart]

loathe (lōth) *vt.* **loathed, loath'ing** [< OE. *lathian*, be hateful] to feel intense dislike or disgust for; abhor —**loath'er** *n.*

loath·ing (lōth'iŋ) *n.* intense dislike, disgust, or hatred; abhorrence

loath·some (lōth'səm) *adj.* causing loathing; disgusting —**loath'some·ness** *n.*

loaves (lōvz) *n. pl. of* LOAF¹

lob (läb) *vt., vi.* **lobbed, lob'bing** [ME. *lobbe-*, heavy] to toss or hit (a ball) in a high curve

lob·by (läb'ē) *n., pl.* **-bies** [LL. *lobia*: see LODGE] **1.** an entrance hall, as of a hotel, theater, etc. **2.** a group of lobbyists —*vi.* **-bied, -by·ing** to act as a lobbyist

lob'by·ist (-ist) *n.* one who tries to get legislators to support measures to benefit a special-interest group

lobe (lōb) *n.* [Gr. *lobos*] a rounded projection, as the lower end of the ear or any of the divisions of the brain, lung, or liver

lob·ster (läb'stər) *n.* [< OE. *loppe*, spider] an edible sea crustacean with four pairs of legs and a pair of large pincers

lo·cal (lō'k'l) *adj.* [< L. *locus*, a place] **1.** relating to place **2.** of, characteristic of, or confined to a particular place **3.** of or for a particular part of the body **4.** making all stops along its run [a *local* train] —*n.* **1.** a local train, bus, etc. **2.** a branch, as of a labor union —**lo'cal·ly** *adv.*

lo·cale (lō kal') *n.* [Fr. *local*] a locality, esp. with reference to associated events, etc.

lo·cal·i·ty (lō kal'ə tē) *n., pl.* **-ties** **1.** position with regard to surrounding objects, etc. **2.** a place

lo·cal·ize (lō'kə līz') *vt.* **-ized', -iz'ing** to limit, confine, or trace to a particular place or locality —**lo'cal·i·za'tion** *n.*

lo·cate (lō'kāt, lō kāt') *vt.* **-cat·ed, -cat·ing** [< L. *locus*, a place] **1.** to establish in a certain place [offices *located* downtown] **2.** to discover the position of **3.** to show the position of [to *locate* Guam on a map] —*vi.* [Colloq.] to settle

lo·ca'tion *n.* **1.** a locating or being located **2.** position; place —**on location** *Movies* away from the studio

loc. cit. [L. *loco citato*] in the place cited

loch (läk) *n.* [Gael. & OIr.] [Scot.] **1.** a lake **2.** an inlet of the sea

lock¹ (läk) *n.* [OE. *loc*, a bolt] **1.** a mechanical device for fastening a door, strongbox, etc. as with a key or combination **2.** an enclosed part of a canal, etc. equipped with gates so that the level of the water can be raised or lowered **3.** the mechanism of a firearm that explodes the charge —*vt.* **1.** to fasten with a lock **2.** to shut (*up, in,* or *out*); confine **3.** to fit; link [*lock* arms] **4.** to jam together so as to make immovable —*vi.* **1.** to become locked **2.** to interlock

lock² (läk) *n.* [OE. *loc*] **1.** a curl of hair **2.** a tuft of wool, etc.

lock'er *n.* **1.** a chest, closet, etc. that can be locked **2.** a large compartment for freezing and storing foods

locker room a room equipped with lockers

lock·et (läk'it) *n.* [< OFr. *loc*, a lock] a small, hinged case of gold, silver, etc., for holding a picture, lock of hair, etc.: it is usually worn on a necklace

lock'jaw' *n. same as* TETANUS

lock'smith' *n.* a person whose work is making or repairing locks and keys

lock·up (läk'up') *n.* a jail

lo·co (lō'kō) *adj.* [Sp., insane] [Slang] crazy; demented

lo·co·mo·tion (lō'kə mō'shən) *n.* [< L. *locus*, a place + MOTION] motion, or the power of moving, from one place to another

lo'co·mo'tive (-mōt'iv) *adj.* of locomotion —*n.* an electric, steam, or diesel engine on wheels, designed to push or pull a railroad train

lo·co·weed (lō'kō wēd') *n.* a plant of W N. America that causes a nervous disease in horses, cattle, etc.

lo·cust (lō'kəst) *n.* [< L. *locusta*] **1.** a large grasshopper often traveling in swarms and destroying crops **2.** *same as* SEVENTEEN-YEAR LOCUST **3.** a spiny tree of the E and C U.S., having clusters of fragrant white flowers

lo·cu·tion (lō kyōō'shən) *n.* [< L. *loqui*, speak] **1.** a word, phrase, or expression **2.** a particular style of speech

lode (lōd) *n.* [< OE. *lad*, a course] a vein, stratum, deposit, etc. of metallic ore

lode'star' *n.* a star by which one directs his course; esp., the North Star

lode'stone' *n.* a strongly magnetic variety of the mineral magnetite

lodge (läj) *n.* [< OFr. *loge*, arbor] **1.** a small house for special or seasonal use [a hunting *lodge*] **2.** a resort hotel or motel **3.** the local chapter or hall of a fraternal organization —*vt.* **lodged, lodg'ing 1.** to house, esp. temporarily **2.** to deposit; place **3.** to bring (a complaint) before legal authorities **4.** to confer (powers) upon (with *in*) —*vi.* **1.** to live in a place for a time **2.** to live (*with* or *in*) as a paying guest **3.** to come to rest (*in*) [a bone *lodged* in her throat]

lodg'er *n.* one who rents a room in another's home

lodg'ing *n.* **1.** a place to live in, esp. temporarily **2.** [*pl.*] a room or rooms rented in a private home

loft (lôft, läft) *n.* [< ON. *lopt*, upper room, air] **1.** the space just below the roof of a house, barn, etc. **2.** an upper story of a warehouse or factory **3.** a gallery [a choir *loft*] **4.** height given a ball hit or thrown —*vt., vi.* to give (a ball) loft

loft'y *adj.* **-i·er, -i·est 1.** very high **2.** elevated; noble **3.** haughty; arrogant

log¹ (lôg, läg) *n.* [ME. *logge*] **1.** a section of the trunk of a felled tree **2.** a device for measuring the speed of a ship **3.** a record of speed, progress, etc., specif. one kept on a ship's voyage or an aircraft's flight —*vt.* **logged, log'ging 1.** to saw (trees) into logs **2.** to enter in a ship's or an aircraft's log —*vi.* to cut down trees and remove the logs —**log'ger** *n.*

log² (lôg, läg) *n. short for* LOGARITHM

lo·gan·ber·ry (lō'gən ber'ē) *n., pl.* **-ries** [< J. H. *Logan* (1841–1928), U.S. horticulturist] **1.** a hybrid bramble developed from the blackberry

and the red raspberry **2.** its purplish-red fruit

log·a·rithm (lôg'ə rith'm, läg'-) *n.* [< Gr. *logos*, ratio + *arithmos*, number] the exponent indicating the power to which a fixed number must be raised to produce a given number — **log'a·rith'mic** *adj.*

loge (lōzh) *n.* [Fr.: see LODGE] a box or the forward section of a balcony in a theater, stadium, etc.

log'ging *n.* the work of felling trees, cutting them into logs, and transporting them to the sawmill

log·ic (läj'ik) *n.* [ult. < Gr. *logos*, word] **1.** the science of correct reasoning **2.** correct reasoning **3.** way of reasoning [poor *logic*] **4.** necessary connection or outcome, as of events

log'i·cal (-i k'l) *adj.* **1.** based on or using logic **2.** expected because of what has gone before — **log'i·cal·ly** *adv.*

lo·gi·cian (lō jish'ən) *n.* an expert in logic

lo·gis·tics (lō jis'tiks) *n.pl.* [with sing. *v.*] [< Fr. *loger*, to quarter] the military science of moving, supplying, and quartering troops

log'jam' *n.* an obstacle formed by an accumulation of many items to deal with

log'roll'ing *n.* **1.** mutual exchange of favors, esp. among legislators **2.** the sport of balancing oneself while revolving a floating log with one's feet

-logue [see LOGIC] *a combining form meaning* a (specified kind of) speaking or writing [monologue] : also **-log**

lo·gy (lō'gē) *adj.* **-gi·er, -gi·est** [< ? Du. *log*, dull] [Colloq.] dull or sluggish

-logy [see LOGIC] *a combining form meaning:* **1.** a (specified kind of) speaking [eulogy] **2.** science, doctrine, or theory of [biology, geology]

loin (loin) *n.* [< L. *lumbus*] **1.** [usually *pl.*] the lower part of the back between the hipbones and the ribs **2.** the front part of the hindquarters of beef, lamb, etc. **3.** [*pl.*] the hips and the lower abdomen regarded as the region of strength, etc.

loin'cloth' *n.* a cloth worn about the loins, as by some tribes in warm climates

loi·ter (loit'ər) *vi.* [< MDu. *loteren*] **1.** to spend time idly; linger **2.** to move slowly and indolently —*vt.* to spend (time) idly

loll (läl) *vi.* [< MDu. *lollen*] **1.** to lean or lounge about in a lazy manner **2.** to droop —*vt.* to let droop —**loll'er** *n.*

lol·li·pop, lol·ly·pop (läl'ē päp') *n.* [prob. < dial. *lolly*, the tongue + POP¹] a piece of hard candy on the end of a stick

lol·ly·gag (läl'ē gag') *vi.* **-gagged', -gag'ging** [< ?] [Colloq.] to waste time in trifling or aimless activity

lone (lōn) *adj.* [< ALONE] **1.** by oneself; solitary **2.** lonesome **3.** isolated

lone'ly *adj.* **-li·er, -li·est 1.** alone **2.** *a)* isolated *b)* unfrequented **3.** unhappy at being alone — **lone'li·ness** *n.*

lon·er (lō'nər) *n.* [Colloq.] one who avoids the company of others

lone'some *adj.* **1.** having or causing a lonely feeling **2.** unfrequented

long¹ (lôŋ) *adj.* [OE.] **1.** measuring much in space or time **2.** in length [six feet *long*] **3.** of greater than usual length, quantity, etc. [a *long* list] **4.** tedious; slow **5.** far-reaching [a *long* view of the matter] **6.** well supplied [*long* on excuses] —*adv.* **1.** for a long time **2.** for the duration of [all day *long*] **3.** at a remote time [*long* ago] —*n.* a long time —**as** (or **so**) **long as 1.** during the time that **2.** since **3.** provided that —**before long** soon

long² (lôŋ) *vi.* [OE. *langian*] to feel a strong yearning; wish earnestly

long. longitude

long distance a telephone service for calls to distant places —**long′-dis′tance** *adj., adv.*

lon·gev·i·ty (län jev′ə tē, lôn-) *n.* [< L. *longus*, long + *aevum*, age] long life

long′-faced′ *adj.* glum; disconsolate

long′hair′ *adj.* [Colloq.] of intellectuals or intellectual tastes

long′hand′ *n.* ordinary handwriting

long′horn′ *n.* any of a breed of long-horned cattle formerly raised in the Southwest

long′ing *n.* strong desire; yearning —*adj.* feeling or showing a yearning

lon·gi·tude (län′jə tōōd′) *n.* [< L. *longus*, long] angular distance, measured in degrees, east or west on the earth's surface from the prime meridian

lon′gi·tu′di·nal *adj.* 1. of or in length 2. running or placed lengthwise 3. of longitude

long jump an event in track and field that is a jump for distance rather than height

long-lived (lôŋ′līvd′, -livd′) *adj.* having or tending to have a long life span

long′-play′ing *adj.* designating a phonograph record that plays at 33 1/3 revolutions per minute

long′-range′ *adj.* taking the future into consideration

long′shore′man (-shôr′mən) *n., pl.* -men [< (a)*longshore* + MAN] a person whose work is loading and unloading ships

long shot [Colloq.] a betting choice that has little chance of winning and, hence, carries great odds

long′stand′ing *adj.* having continued for a long time

long′-suf′fer·ing *adj.* bearing trouble, etc. patiently for a long time

long′-term′ *adj.* for or extending over a long time

long ton 2,240 pounds: see TON

long′-wind′ed (-win′did) *adj.* 1. speaking or writing at great length 2. tiresomely long

look (look) *vi.* [OE. *locian*] 1. to direct one's eyes in order to see 2. to search 3. to appear; seem 4. to be facing in a specified direction — *vt.* 1. to direct one's eyes on 2. to have an appearance befitting [to *look* the part] —*n.* 1. the act of looking 2. outward aspect 3. [Colloq.] *a*) [*usually pl.*] appearance *b*) [*pl.*] personal appearance —*interj.* 1. see! 2. pay attention! — **look after** to take care of —**look down on** (or **upon**) to regard with contempt —**look for** to expect —**look forward to** to anticipate —**look in** (on) to pay a brief visit (to) —**look into** to investigate —**look out** to be careful —**look over** to examine —**look to** 1. to take care of 2. to rely upon —**look up** 1. to search for in a reference book 2. [Colloq.] to visit 3. [Colloq.] to improve —**look up to** to admire —**look′er** *n.*

look′er-on′ *n., pl.* **look′ers-on′** an observer or spectator; onlooker

looking glass a (glass) mirror

look′out′ *n.* 1. a careful watching 2. a place for keeping watch 3. a person detailed to watch

loom¹ (lōōm) *n.* [< OE. (ge)*loma*, tool] a machine for weaving thread or yarn into cloth

loom² (lōōm) *vi.* [< ?] to come into sight indistinctly, esp. in a large or threatening form

loon¹ (lōōn) *n.* [< ON. *lomr*] a fish-eating diving bird, noted for its weird cry

loon² (lōōn) *n.* [Scot. *loun*] a stupid or crazy person

loon·y (lōō′nē) *adj.* -i·er, -i·est [< LUNATIC] [Slang] crazy; demented

loop (lōōp) *n.* [ME. *loup*] 1. the figure of a line, thread, etc. that curves back to cross itself 2. anything forming this figure 3. an intrauterine contraceptive device —*vt.* 1. to make a loop of 2. to fasten with a loop —*vi.* to form a loop or loops

loop·hole (lōōp′hōl′) *n.* [prob. < MDu. *lupen*, to peer + HOLE] 1. a hole or slit in a wall 2. a means of evading an obligation, etc.

loose (lōōs) *adj.* [< ON.] 1. not confined or restrained; free 2. not firmly fastened 3. not tight or compact 4. not precise; inexact 5. sexually immoral —*adv.* loosely —*vt.* **loosed, loos′ing** 1. to set free; unbind 2. to make less tight, compact, etc. 3. to relax 4. to release [he *loosed* the arrow] —*vi.* to become loose — **loose′ly** *adv.*

loose′-leaf′ *adj.* having leaves or sheets that can easily be removed or inserted

loos·en (lōōs′'n) *vt., vi.* to make or become loose or looser —**loos′en·er** *n.*

loot (lōōt) *n.* [Hindi *lūt*] goods stolen or taken by force; plunder —*vt., vi.* to plunder —**loot′er** *n.*

lop¹ (läp) *vt.* **lopped, lop′ping** [OE. *loppian*] 1. to trim (a tree, etc.) by cutting off branches or twigs 2. to remove as by cutting off

lop² (läp) *vi.* **lopped, lop′ping** [prob. akin to LOB] to hang down loosely

lope (lōp) *vi.* **loped, lop′ing** [< ON. *hlaupa*, to leap] to move with a long, swinging stride or in an easy canter —*vt.* to cause to lope —*n.* a loping stride

lop′sid′ed (-sīd′id) *adj.* noticeably heavier, bigger, or lower on one side

lo·qua·cious (lō kwā′shəs) *adj.* [< L. *loqui*, to speak] very talkative —**lo·qua′cious·ly** *adv.* — **lo·quac′i·ty** (-kwas′ə tē) *n.*

lord (lôrd) *n.* [< OE. *hlaf*, loaf + *weard*, keeper] 1. a ruler; master 2. the head of a feudal estate 3. [L-] *a*) God *b*) Jesus Christ 4. in Great Britain, a titled nobleman —**lord it (over)** to domineer (over)

lord′ly *adj.* -li·er, -li·est 1. noble; grand 2. haughty —*adv.* in the manner of a lord

lord′ship′ *n.* 1. the rank or authority of a lord 2. rule; dominion 3. [*also* L-] a title used in speaking of or to a lord: with *his* or *your*

Lord's Prayer the prayer beginning *Our Father:* Matt. 6:9-13

lore (lôr) *n.* [OE. *lar*] knowledge or learning, esp. that of a traditional nature

lor·gnette (lôr nyet′) *n.* [Fr. < OFr. *lorgne*, squinting] a pair of eyeglasses, or an opera glass, attached to a handle

lorn (lôrn) *adj.* [ME. < *losen*, lose] [Archaic] forsaken, forlorn, bereft, or desolate

lor·ry (lôr′ē, lär′-) *n., pl.* -ries [< ?] [Brit.] a motor truck

lose (lōōz) *vt.* **lost, los′ing** [OE. *leosan*] 1. to become unable to find [I *lost* my key] 2. to have taken from one by accident, death, removal, etc. 3. to fail to keep [to *lose* one's temper] 4. to fail to see, hear, or understand 5. to fail to win 6. to fail to have, get, take, etc.; miss 7. to cause the loss of 8. to wander from (one's way, etc.) 9. to waste; squander —*vi.* to suffer (a) loss —**los′er** *n.*

loss (lôs) *n.* [< ? OE. *los*, ruin] 1. a losing or being lost 2. the damage, trouble, etc. caused by losing 3. that which is lost —**at a loss (to)** uncertain (how to)

lost (lôst, läst) *pt. & pp. of* LOSE —*adj.* 1. ruined; destroyed 2. not to be found; missing 3. no longer held, seen, heard, etc. 4. not gained or won 5. having wandered from the way 6. bewildered 7. wasted

lot (lät) *n.* [OE. *hlot*] **1.** the deciding of a matter by chance, as by drawing counters **2.** the decision thus arrived at **3.** one's share by lot **4.** fortune [his unhappy *lot*] **5.** a plot of ground **6.** a group of persons or things **7.** [*often pl.*] [Colloq.] a great amount **8.** [Colloq.] sort [he's a bad *lot*] —*adv.* very much: also **lots** —**draw** (or **cast**) **lots** to decide by lot
Lo·thar·i·o (lō ther′ē ō′) *n., pl.* **-i·os′** [< the rake in a play by N. Rowe (1674–1718)] [*often* l-] a lighthearted seducer of women
lo·tion (lō′shən) *n.* [< L. *lavare*, to wash] a liquid preparation used, as on the skin, for washing, soothing, healing, etc.
lot·ter·y (lät′ər ē) *n., pl.* **-ies** [see LOTTO] a game of chance in which people buy numbered chances on prizes, winners being chosen by lot
lot·to (lät′ō) *n.* [It. < Fr. < MDu. *lot*, lot] a game of chance played on cards with numbered squares: counters are placed on numbers chosen by lot
lo·tus, lo·tos (lōt′əs) *n.* [< Gr. *lōtos*] **1.** *Gr. Legend* a plant whose fruit induced forgetfulness **2.** any of several tropical waterlilies
loud (loud) *adj.* [OE. *hlud*] **1.** strongly audible: said of sound **2.** sounding with great intensity **3.** noisy **4.** emphatic [*loud* denials] **5.** [Colloq.] *a)* flashy *b)* vulgar —*adv.* in a loud manner —**loud′ness** *n.*
loud′speak′er *n.* a device for converting electrical energy to sound and amplifying it
lounge (lounj) *vi.* **lounged, loung′ing** [Scot. dial. < ? *lungis*, laggard] **1.** to stand, move, sit, etc. in a relaxed or lazy way **2.** to spend time in idleness —*n.* **1.** a room with comfortable furniture **2.** a couch
louse (lous) *n., pl.* **lice** [OE. *lus*] **1.** a small, wingless insect parasitic on man and other animals **2.** any similar insect parasitic on plants **3.** *pl.* **lous′es** [Slang] a mean, contemptible person —**louse up** [Slang] to botch; spoil; ruin
lous·y (lou′zē) *adj.* **-i·er, -i·est 1.** infested with lice **2.** [Slang] *a)* disgusting *b)* poor; inferior *c)* oversupplied (*with*)
lout (lout) *n.* [prob. < ME. *lutien*, to lurk] a clumsy, stupid fellow —**lout′ish** *adj.*
lou·ver (lōō′vər) *n.* [< MDu. *love*, theater gallery] **1.** an opening fitted with sloping slats (**louver boards**) so as to admit light and air but shed rain **2.** any of these slats **3.** any ventilating slit Also **lou′vre**
Lou·vre (lōō′vrə, lōōv) ancient royal palace in Paris, now an art museum
love (luv) *n.* [OE. *lufu*] **1.** a deep affection or liking for someone or something **2.** a passionate affection of one person for another **3.** the object of this; sweetheart **4.** *Tennis* a score of zero —*vt., vi.* **loved, lov′ing** to feel love (for) —**in love** feeling love —**make love 1.** to woo, embrace, etc. **2.** to have sexual intercourse —**lov′a·ble, love′a·ble** *adj.* —**love′less** *adj.*
love′lorn′ *adj.* pining from love
love′ly *adj.* **-li·er, -li·est 1.** very pleasing in looks or character; beautiful **2.** [Colloq.] highly enjoyable —**love′li·ness** *n.*
lov·er (luv′ər) *n.* **1.** a sweetheart **2.** [*pl.*] a couple in love with each other **3.** one who greatly enjoys some (specified) thing
love seat a small sofa for two
lov′ing *adj.* feeling or expressing love
loving cup a large drinking cup with two handles, often given as a trophy in sports
low (lō) *adj.* [< ON. *lagr*] **1.** not high or tall **2.** below the normal or usual surface or level [*low* ground] **3.** shallow **4.** less in amount, degree,

etc. than usual [*low* speed] **5.** deep in pitch **6.** depressed; melancholy **7.** not of high rank; humble **8.** vulgar; coarse **9.** poor; inferior **10.** not loud —*adv.* in or to a low level, degree, etc. —*n.* **1.** a low level, degree, etc. **2.** an arrangement of gears giving the lowest speed and greatest power **3.** *Meteorol.* an area of low pressure —**lay low** to overcome or kill —**lie low** to keep oneself hidden
low² (lō) *vi., n.* [OE. *hlowan*] same as MOO
low′born′ *adj.* of humble birth
low′boy′ *n.* a chest of drawers mounted on short legs
low′brow′ *n.* [Colloq.] one considered to lack intellectual tastes
low′down′ *n.* [Slang] the pertinent facts (with *the*) —*adj.* (lō′doun′) [Colloq.] mean; contemptible
low·er¹ (lō′ər) *adj. compar.* of LOW¹ below in place, rank, etc. —*vt.* **1.** to let or put down [to *lower* a window] **2.** to reduce in height, amount, etc. **3.** to weaken or lessen **4.** to demean —*vi.* to become lower
low·er² (lou′ər) *vi.* [ME. *louren*] **1.** to scowl or frown **2.** to appear dark and threatening —**low′er·ing** *adj.*
lower case small-letter type used in printing, as distinguished from capital letters (*upper case*) —**low′er-case′** *adj.*
Low German 1. the Germanic dialects of N Germany **2.** the branch of Germanic languages including English, Dutch, Flemish, etc.
low′-grade′ *adj.* of low quality or degree
low′-key′ *adj.* of low intensity, tone, etc.
low·land (lō′land, -land′) *n.* land below the level of the surrounding land
low′ly *adj.* **-li·er, -li·est 1.** of low position or rank **2.** humble; meek —*adv.* humbly
low′-mind′ed *adj.* having or showing a coarse, vulgar mind —**low′-mind′ed·ness** *n.*
low′-spir′it·ed *adj.* sad; melancholy
low tide the lowest level reached by the ebbing tide
lox (läks) *n.* [< Yid. < G. *lachs*, salmon] a variety of salty smoked salmon
loy·al (loi′əl) *adj.* [Fr.: see LEGAL] **1.** faithful to one's country, friends, ideals, etc. **2.** of or indicating loyalty —**loy′al·ly** *adv.* —**loy′al·ty** *n., pl.* **-ties**
loy′al·ist *n.* one who supports the government during a revolt —**loy′al·ism** *n.*
loz·enge (läz′′nj) *n.* [OFr. *losenge*] **1.** a diamond-shaped figure **2.** a cough drop, candy, etc., orig. in this shape
LP [*L(ong) P(laying)*] *a trademark for* a long-playing record —*n.* a long-playing record
Lr *Chem.* lawrencium
LSD [*l(y)s(ergic acid) d(iethylamide)*] a psychedelic drug that produces behavior and symptoms, as hallucinations, etc., like those of certain psychoses
Lt. Lieutenant
Ltd., ltd. limited
lu·au (lōō ou′, lōō′ou′) *n.* [Haw.] a Hawaiian feast, usually with entertainment
lub·ber (lub′ər) *n.* [< ME. *lobbe-*, heavy] **1.** a big, slow, clumsy person **2.** a landlubber
lube (lōōb) *n.* [Colloq.] a lubrication
lu·bri·cant (lōō′brə kənt) *adj.* reducing friction by providing a smooth surface film over parts that move against each other —*n.* a lubricant oil, grease, etc.
lu′bri·cate (-kāt′) *vt.* **-cat′ed, -cat′ing** [< L. *lubricus*, smooth] **1.** to make slippery or smooth **2.** to apply a lubricant to —**lu′bri·ca′tion** *n.* —**lu′bri·ca′tor** *n.*
lu·cid (lōō′sid) *adj.* [< L. *lucere*, to shine] **1.**

shining 2. transparent 3. sane 4. readily understood —**lu·cid′i·ty** *n.*

Lu·ci·fer (lo͞o′sə fər) [< L. *lux,* LIGHT[1] + *ferre,* to BEAR[1]] *Theol.* Satan

luck (luk) *n.* [prob. < MDu. *gelucke*] 1. the seemingly chance happening of events which affect one; fortune 2. good fortune —**luck out** [Colloq.] to be lucky —**luck′less** *adj.*

luck′y *adj.* -**i·er,** -**i·est** 1. having good luck 2. resulting fortunately 3. believed to bring good luck —**luck′i·ly** *adv.*

lu·cra·tive (lo͞o′krə tiv) *adj.* [< L. *lucrum,* riches] producing wealth or profit

lu·cre (lo͞o′kər) *n.* [< L. *lucrum,* riches] riches; money: chiefly derogatory

lu·cu·brate (lo͞o′kyo͞o brāt′) *vi.* -**brat′ed,** -**brat′-ing** [< L. *lucubrare,* to work by candlelight] to work or study laboriously, esp. late at night — **lu′cu·bra′tion** *n.*

lu·di·crous (lo͞o′di krəs) *adj.* [< L. *ludus,* a game] causing laughter because absurd or ridiculous —**lu′di·crous·ly** *adv.*

luff (luf) *vi.* [< ODu.] to turn the bow of a ship toward the wind

lug (lug) *vt.* **lugged, lug′ging** [prob. < Scand.] to carry or drag with effort —*n.* 1. an earlike projection by which a thing is held or supported 2. a heavy nut used with a bolt to secure a wheel to an axle

lug·gage (lug′ij) *n.* [< LUG + -AGE] suitcases, valises, trunks, etc.; baggage

lu·gu·bri·ous (lo͞o go͞o′brē əs) *adj.* [< L. *lugere,* mourn] mournful, esp. in a way that seems exaggerated or ridiculous

Luke (lo͞ok) *Bible* 1. a Christian disciple, reputed author of the third Gospel 2. this book

luke·warm (lo͞ok′wôrm′) *adj.* [ME. *luke,* tepid + *warm,* WARM] 1. barely or moderately warm 2. lacking enthusiasm

lull (lul) *vt.* [ME. *lullen*] 1. to calm by gentle sound or motion 2. to bring into a specified condition by soothing and reassuring 3. to allay —*vi.* to become calm —*n.* a short period of calm

lull·a·by (lul′ə bī′) *n., pl.* -**bies′** a song for lulling a baby to sleep

lum·ba·go (lum bā′gō) *n.* [< L. *lumbus,* loin] pain in the lower back

lum·bar (lum′bər, -bär) *adj.* [< L. *lumbus,* loin] of or near the loins

lum·ber[1] (lum′bər) *n.* [< ? pawnshop of *Lombardy,* in Italy] 1. discarded household articles, furniture, etc. 2. timber sawed into beams, boards, etc. —*vi.* to cut down timber and saw it into lumber

lum·ber[2] (lum′bər) *vi.* [< ? Scand.] to move heavily and noisily —**lum′ber·ing** *adj.*

lum·ber·jack (lum′bər jak′) *n.* a person whose work is cutting down timber and preparing it for the sawmill; logger

lum′ber·man (-mən) *n., pl.* -**men** 1. a logger; lumberjack 2. one who deals in lumber

lu·mi·nar·y (lo͞o′mə ner′ē) *n., pl.* -**ies** [< L. *lumen,* light] 1. a body that gives off light, such as the sun 2. a famous person

lu·mi·nous (lo͞o′mə nəs) *adj.* [< L. *lumen,* a light] 1. giving off light; bright 2. glowing in the dark 3. enlightening; clear —**lu′mi·nos′i·ty** (-näs′ə tē) *n., pl.* -**ties**

lum·mox (lum′əks) *n.* [< ?] [Colloq.] a clumsy, stupid person

lump[1] (lump) *n.* [ME. *lumpe*] 1. an indefinitely shaped mass of something 2. a swelling 3. [*pl.*] [Colloq.] hard blows, criticism, etc. —*adj.* in lumps —*vt.* 1. to put together in a lump or

lumps 2. to treat or deal with in a mass, or collectively —*vi.* to become lumpy

lump[2] (lump) *vt.* [Early ModE., to look sour] [Colloq.] to put up with (something disagreeable)

lump′y *adj.* -**i·er,** -**i·est** 1. full of lumps 2. covered with lumps —**lump′i·ness** *n.*

lu·na·cy (lo͞o′nə sē) *n., pl.* -**cies** [< LUNATIC] utter foolishness

lu·nar (lo͞o′nər)·*adj.* [< L. *luna,* the moon] of, on, or like the moon

lu·na·tic (lo͞o′nə tik) *adj.* [< L. *luna,* the moon] 1. of or for insane persons 2. utterly foolish —*n.* an insane person

lunch (lunch) *n.* [? < Sp. *lonja,* slice of ham] a light meal; esp., the midday meal between breakfast and dinner —*vi.* to eat lunch

lunch·eon (lun′chən) *n.* a lunch; esp., a formal lunch

lunch′eon·ette′ (-chə net′) *n.* a small restaurant where light lunches can be had

luncheon meat meat processed in loaves, sausages, etc. and ready to eat

lung (luŋ) *n.* [OE. *lungen*] either of the two spongelike breathing organs in the thorax of vertebrates

lunge (lunj) *n.* [< Fr. *allonger,* lengthen] 1. a sudden thrust, as with a sword 2. a sudden plunge forward —*vi., vt.* **lunged, lung′ing** to move, or cause to move, with a lunge —**lung′er** *n.*

lu·pine (lo͞o′pīn) *adj.* [< L. *lupus,* wolf] of or like a wolf —*n.* (-pin) a plant related to the pea, with long spikes of white, rose, or blue flowers

lurch[1] (lurch) *vi.* [< ?] 1. to pitch or sway suddenly to one side 2. to stagger —*n.* a lurching movement

lurch[2] (lurch) *n.* [prob. < OFr. *lourche,* duped] a difficult situation: only in **leave in the lurch**

lure (loor) *n.* [< OFr. *loirre*] 1. anything that tempts or entices 2. a bait used in fishing —*vt.* **lured, lur′ing** to attract; tempt; entice —**lur′er** *n.*

lu·rid (loor′id) *adj.* [L. *luridus,* ghastly] 1. glowing through a haze, as flames enveloped by smoke 2. shocking; sensational

lurk (lurk) *vi.* [ME. *lurken*] 1. to stay hidden, ready to attack, etc. 2. to be present as a latent threat 3. to move furtively

lus·cious (lush′əs) *adj.* [ME. *lucius*] 1. highly gratifying to taste or smell; delicious 2. delighting any of the senses

lush[1] (lush) *adj.* [< ? OFr. *lasche,* lax] 1. of or characterized by rich growth 2. rich, abundant, extravagant, etc. —**lush′ness** *n.*

lush[2] (lush) *n.* [Slang] an alcoholic

lust (lust) *n.* [OE., pleasure] 1. bodily appetite; esp., strong sexual desire 2. an intense desire [a *lust* for power] —*vi.* to feel an intense desire —**lust′ful** *adj.*

lus·ter (lus′tər) *n.* [< L. *lustrare,* illumine] 1. gloss; sheen 2. brightness; radiance 3. brilliant beauty or fame; glory Chiefly Brit. sp. **lustre**

lus′trous (-trəs) *adj.* having luster; shining —**lus′trous·ly** *adv.*

lust·y (lus′tē) *adj.* -**i·er,** -**i·est** full of vigor; strong; robust —**lust′i·ly** *adv.*

lute (lo͞ot) *n.* [ult. < Ar. *al′ūd,* the wood] an early stringed instrument with a rounded back and a long, fretted neck

Lu′ther·an *adj.* of the Protestant denomination founded by Martin Luther (1483-1546), leader of the German Reformation —*n.* a member of the Lutheran Church —**Lu′ther·an·ism** *n.*

lut·ist (lo͞ot′ist) *n.* a lute player: also **lu·ta·nist** (lo͞ot′'n ist)

lux·u·ri·ant (lug zhoor′ē ənt) *adj.* [see LUXURY]
1. growing with vigor and in abundance **2.**
richly varied, elaborate, etc. —**lux·u′ri·ance** *n.*
—**lux·u′ri·ant·ly** *adv.*
lux·u′ri·ate′ (-āt′) *vi.* -**at′ed, -at′ing 1.** to live in
great luxury **2.** to revel (*in*)
lux·u′ri·ous *adj.* **1.** fond of or indulging in luxury **2.** full of luxury; rich, comfortable, etc. —
lux·u′ri·ous·ly *adv.*
lux·u·ry (luk′shə rē, lug′zhə-) *n., pl.* -**ries** [< L.
luxus] **1.** the enjoyment of the best and most
costly things **2.** anything giving such enjoyment, usually something not a necessity
-**ly** [< OE. -*lic*] *a suffix meaning:* **1.** like or
characteristic of [*manly*] **2.** in a (specified)
manner, to a (specified) extent or direction, in
or at a (specified) time or place [*harshly, out-
wardly, hourly*] **3.** in sequence [*thirdly*] **4.** happening (once) every (specified) period)
[*monthly*]
ly·ce·um (lī sē′əm, lī′sē-) *n.* [< Gr. *Lykeion,*
grove at Athens where Aristotle taught] **1.** a
lecture hall **2.** an organization providing public
lectures, etc.
lye (lī) *n.* [OE. *leag*] any strongly alkaline substance, used in cleaning and in making soap
ly·ing[1] (lī′iŋ) *prp. of* LIE[1]
ly·ing[2] (lī′iŋ) *prp. of* LIE[2] —*adj.* false; not truthful —*n.* the telling of a lie
ly′ing-in′ *n.* confinement in childbirth —*adj.* of
or for childbirth
lymph (limf) *n.* [L. *lympha,* spring water] a
clear, yellowish fluid resembling blood plasma,
found in the lymphatic vessels
lym·phat·ic (lim fat′ik) *adj.* **1.** of, containing,
or conveying lymph **2.** sluggish

lymph node any of the compact structures
lying in groups along the course of the lymphatic vessels
lymph·oid (lim′foid) *adj.* of or like lymph or
the tissue of the lymph nodes
lynch (linch) *vt.* [< W. *Lynch,* vigilante in Virginia in 1780] to murder (an accused person)
by mob action, without lawful trial, as by
hanging —**lynch′ing** *n.*
lynx (liŋks) *n.* [< Gr. *lynx*] a wildcat found
throughout the N Hemisphere, having a short
tail and tufted ears
lynx′-eyed′ (-īd′) *adj.* very keen-sighted
ly·on·naise (lī′ə nāz′) *adj.* [Fr.] prepared with
sliced, fried onions
lyre (līr) *n.* [< Gr. *lyra*] a small stringed instrument resembling the harp, used by the an-
cient Greeks
lyr·ic (lir′ik) *adj.* [< Gr. *lyrikos*] **1.** suitable for
singing; specif., designating or of poetry expressing the poet's personal emotion **2.** of or
having a high voice with a light, flexible quality [*a lyric tenor*] —*n.* **1.** a lyric poem **2.**
[*usually pl.*] the words of a song
lyr′i·cal (-i k′l) *adj.* **1.** *same as* LYRIC **2.** expressing rapture or great enthusiasm
lyr′i·cist (-sist) *n.* a writer of lyrics, esp. for
popular songs
ly·ser·gic acid (lī sur′jik) [< Gr. *lysis,* a
loosening & ERGOT] *see* LSD
-**lysis** [< Gr. *lysis,* a loosening] *a combining
form meaning* a loosing, dissolution, dissolving,
destruction [*electrolysis, paralysis*]
-**lyte** [see -LYSIS] *a combining form meaning* a
substance undergoing a process of decomposition [*electrolyte*]

M

M, m (em) *n., pl.* **M's, m's** the thirteenth letter
of the English alphabet
M (em) *n.* a Roman numeral for 1,000
M. 1. Monday **2.** *pl.* **MM.** Monsieur
M., m. 1. male **2.** married **3.** masculine **4.**
mile(s) **5.** minute(s) **6.** month
m., m meter(s)
ma (mä) *n.* [Colloq.] mother
M.A. Master of Arts
ma'am (mam, mäm, məm) *n.* [Colloq.] madam:
used in direct address
ma·ca·bre (mə käb′rə, mə käb′) *adj.* [Fr. <
OFr. (*danse*) *Macabré,* (dance) of death]
gruesome; grim and horrible
mac·ad·am (mə kad′əm) *n.* [< J. L. *McAdam*
(1756-1836), Scot. engineer] small broken
stones, or a road made by rolling successive
layers of these, often with tar or asphalt —
mac·ad′am·ize′ *vt.* -**ized′, -iz′ing**
mac·a·ro·ni (mak′ə rō′nē) *n.* [It. *maccaroni,*
ult. < Gr. *makar,* blessed] pasta in the form of
tubes, etc.
mac·a·roon (mak′ə rōōn′) *n.* [see prec.] a
small cookie made of crushed almonds or coconut, and sugar
ma·caw (mə kô′) *n.* [< Port. < SAmInd. name]
a large, bright-colored, harsh-voiced parrot of
C. and S. America
Mac·beth (mək beth′) the title hero of a
tragedy by Shakespeare
Mace (mās) [< MACE[1]] *a trademark for* a combined tear gas and nerve gas
mace[1] (mās) *n.* [OFr. *masse*] **1.** a heavy, spiked
war club, used in the Middle Ages **2.** a staff

used as a symbol of authority by certain officials
mace[2] (mās) *n.* [< ML. *macis*] a spice made
from the dried husk of the nutmeg
mac·er·ate (mas′ə rāt′) *vt.* -**at′ed, -at′ing** [< L.
macerare, soften] **1.** to soften or separate the
parts of by soaking in liquid **2.** loosely, to tear,
chop, etc. into bits —**mac′er·a′tion** *n.*
mach. 1. machine **2.** machinery
ma·che·te (mə shet′ē, -chet′ē) *n.* [Sp. < L.
marcus, hammer] a large, heavy-bladed knife
used for cutting sugar cane, etc., esp. in C.
and S. America
Mach·i·a·vel·li·an (mak′ē ə vel′ē ən) *adj.* [<
N. *Machiavelli* (1469-1527), It. statesman]
crafty, deceitful, etc.
mach·i·na·tion (mak′ə nā′shən) *n.* [< L. *ma-
chinari,* to plot] a plot or scheme, esp. an evil
one: *usually used in pl.*
ma·chine (mə shēn′) *n.* [Fr. < Gr. *mēchos,*
contrivance] **1.** a vehicle, as an automobile: an
old-fashioned term **2.** a structure consisting of
a framework with various moving parts, for
doing some kind of work **3.** a person or organization functioning like a machine **4.** the controlling group in a political party **5.** a device,
as the lever or screw, that transmits, or
changes the application of, energy —*adj.* **1.** of
machines **2.** done by machinery —*vt.* -**chined′,
-chin′ing** to shape, etc. by machinery
machine gun an automatic gun, firing a rapid
stream of bullets
ma·chin·er·y (mə shēn′ər ē, -shēn′rē) *n., pl.*
-**ies 1.** machines collectively **2.** the working

parts of a machine **3.** any means by which something is kept in action [the *machinery* of government]

ma·chin'ist *n.* one who makes, repairs, or operates machinery

‡**ma·chis·mo** (mä chēz'mô) *n.* [Sp. < *macho,* masculine] assertive masculinity; virility

Mach (number) (mäk) [< E. *Mach* (1838–1916), Austrian physicist] [*also* **m-**] a number representing the ratio of the speed of an object to the speed of sound

mack·er·el (mak'ər əl) *n., pl.* **-el, -els** [< OFr. *makerel*] an edible fish of the North Atlantic

Mack·i·naw coat (mak'ə nô') [< *Mackinac* Is. in N Lake Huron] a short, heavy, double-breasted coat of wool, usually plaid: also **mackinaw** *n.*

mack·in·tosh (mak'in täsh') *n.* [< C. *Macintosh* (1766–1843), the Scot. inventor] a waterproof raincoat

mac·ra·mé (mak'rə mā') *n.* [Fr., ult. < Ar. *miqramah,* a veil] a coarse fringe or lace of thread or cord knotted in designs

macro- [< Gr. *makros,* long] a combining form meaning long, large

mac·ro·bi·ot·ics (mak'rō bī ät'iks) *n.pl.* [*with sing. v.*] [< prec. & Gr. *bios,* life] the art of prolonging life, as by a special diet —**mac'ro·bi·ot'ic** *adj.*

mac·ro·cosm (mak'rə käz'm) *n.* [see MACRO- & COSMOS] **1.** the universe **2.** any large, complex entity —**mac'ro·cos'mic** *adj.*

ma·cron (mā'krən, -krän) *n.* [< Gr. *makros,* long] a mark (¯) placed over a vowel to indicate its pronunciation

mad (mad) *adj.* **mad'der, mad'dest** [< OE. (*ge*)*mædan,* make mad] **1.** mentally ill; insane **2.** frantic [*mad* with fear] **3.** foolish and rash **4.** infatuated [she's *mad* about him] **5.** wildly amusing **6.** having rabies [a *mad* dog] **7.** angry —*n.* an angry mood —**mad'ly** *adv.* —**mad'ness** *n.*

mad·am (mad'əm) *n., pl.* **-ams**; for 1, usually **mes·dames** (mā däm') [< Fr., orig. *ma dame,* my lady] **1.** a woman; lady: a polite term of address **2.** a woman in charge of a brothel

mad·ame (mad'əm; *Fr.* mä däm') *n., pl.* **mes·dames** (mā däm') [Fr.] a married woman: title [**M-**] equivalent to *Mrs.*

mad·den (mad''n) *vt., vi.* to make or become mad; make or become insane, angry, or wildly excited —**mad'den·ing** *adj.*

mad·der (mad'ər) *n.* [OE. *mædere*] **1.** any of various plants; esp., a vine with yellow flowers and a red root **2.** a red dye made from the root

made (mād) *pt. & pp. of* MAKE —*adj.* **1.** constructed **2.** produced artificially **3.** sure of success

ma·de·moi·selle (mad'ə mə zel'; *Fr.* mäd mwä zel') *n., Fr. pl.* **mesde·moi·selles** (mäd mwä zel') [Fr. < *ma,* my + *demoiselle,* young lady] an unmarried woman or girl: title [**M-**] equivalent to *Miss*

made'-to-or'der *adj.* made to conform to the customer's specifications; custom-made

made'-up' *adj.* **1.** put together **2.** invented; false [a *made-up* story] **3.** with cosmetics applied

mad'house' *n.* **1.** [Archaic] a place of confinement for the mentally ill **2.** any place of turmoil, noise, etc.

mad'man' *n., pl.* **-men'** an insane person; lunatic —**mad'wom'an** *n.fem., pl.* **-wom'en**

Ma·don·na (mə dän'ə) [It. < *ma,* my + *donna,* lady] Mary, mother of Jesus —*n.* a picture or statue of Mary

ma·dras (mad'rəs, mə dras') *n.* [< *Madras,* India] a fine, firm cotton cloth, usually striped or plaid

mad·ri·gal (mad'ri gəl) *n.* [< It.] a part song, without accompaniment, popular in the 15th to 17th cent.

mael·strom (māl'strəm) *n.* [< Du. *malen,* grind + *stroom,* a stream] **1.** a large or violent whirlpool **2.** a violently agitated state of mind, affairs, etc.

ma·es·tro (mīs'trō, mä es'-) *n., pl.* **-tros, -tri** (-trē) [It. < L. *magister,* master] a master in any art; esp., a great composer, conductor, or teacher of music

Ma·fi·a, Maf·fi·a (mä'fē ə) *n.* [It. *maffia,* hostility to law] an alleged secret society of criminals

mag. 1. magazine **2.** magnetism

mag·a·zine (mag'ə zēn') *n.* [< Fr. < Ar. *makhzan,* granary] **1.** a warehouse or military supply depot **2.** a space in which explosives are stored, as in a fort **3.** a supply chamber, as in a rifle, camera, etc. **4.** a periodical publication containing stories, articles, etc.

ma·gen·ta (mə jen'tə) *n.* [< *Magenta,* town in Italy] **1.** a purplish-red dye **2.** purplish red —*adj.* purplish-red

mag·got (mag'ət) *n.* [ME. *magotte*] a wormlike larva, as of the housefly —**mag'got·y** *adj.*

Ma·gi (mā'jī) *n.pl., sing.* **-gus** (-gəs) [< OPer. *magus,* magician] *Douay Bible* the wise men who came bearing gifts to the infant Jesus

mag·ic (maj'ik) *n.* [< Gr. *magikos,* of the Magi] **1.** the use of charms, spells, etc. in seeking or pretending to control events **2.** any mysterious power [the *magic* of love] **3.** the art of producing illusions by sleight of hand, etc. —*adj.* **1.** of, produced by, or using magic **2.** producing extraordinary results, as by magic —**mag'i·cal** *adj.*

ma·gi·cian (mə jish'ən) *n.* [< OFr. *magicien*] an expert in magic

mag·is·te·ri·al (maj'is tir'ē əl) *adj.* **1.** of or for a magistrate **2.** authoritative

mag·is·trate (maj'is trāt') *n.* [< L. *magister,* master] **1.** a civil officer empowered to administer the law **2.** a minor official, as a justice of the peace

mag·ma (mag'mə) *n.* [L.] molten rock

Mag·na Char·ta (or **Car·ta**) (mag'nə kär'tə) [ML., great charter] the charter, granted in 1215, that guaranteed certain civil and political liberties to the English people

mag·nan·i·mous (mag nan'ə məs) *adj.* [< L. *magnus,* great + *animus,* soul] generous in overlooking injury or insult; rising above pettiness —**mag'na·nim'i·ty** (-nə nim'ə tē) *n.* —**mag·nan'i·mous·ly** *adv.*

mag·nate (mag'nāt) *n.* [< L. *magnus,* great] a very influential person

mag·ne·sia (mag nē'zhə, -shə) *n.* [< Gr. *Magnēsia,* district in ancient Greece] a white powder, magnesium oxide, used as a laxative and antacid

mag·ne'si·um (-zē əm, -zhē-) *n.* [< prec.] a light, silver-white metallic chemical element: symbol, Mg

mag·net (mag'nit) *n.* [see MAGNESIA] **1.** any piece of iron, steel, or lodestone that has the property of attracting iron or steel **2.** anything that attracts

mag·net·ic (mag net'ik) *adj.* **1.** having the properties of a magnet **2.** of, producing, or caused by magnetism **3.** of the earth's magnetism **4.** that can be magnetized **5.** powerfully attractive —**mag·net'i·cal·ly** *adv.*

magnetic field a region of space in which there is an appreciable magnetic force

magnetic tape a thin plastic ribbon with a magnetized coating for recording sound, digital computer data, etc.

mag·net·ism (mag′nə tiz′m) **n. 1.** the property or quality of being magnetic **2.** the force to which this is due **3.** personal charm

mag′net·ite′ (-tīt′) **n.** a black iron oxide, an important iron ore

mag′net·ize′ (-tīz′) **vt. -ized′, -iz′ing 1.** to give magnetic properties to (steel, iron, etc.) **2.** to charm (a person)

mag·ne·to (mag nēt′ō) **n., pl. -tos** a small generator in which permanent magnets produce the magnetic field

mag·nif·i·cent (mag nif′ə s'nt) **adj.** [< L. *magnus*, great + *facere*, do] **1.** beautiful and grand or stately; splendid, as in construction **2.** exalted: said of ideas, etc. **3.** [Colloq.] excellent — **mag·nif′i·cence n.** —**mag·nif′i·cent·ly adv.**

mag·ni·fy (mag′nə fī′) **vt., vi. -fied′, -fy′ing** [see MAGNIFICENT] **1.** to exaggerate **2.** to increase the apparent size of (an object), as (with) a lens —**mag′ni·fi·ca′tion** (-fi kā′shən) **n.** —**mag′ni·fi′er n.**

mag·ni·tude (mag′nə tōōd′) **n.** [< L. *magnus*, great] **1.** greatness of size, extent, or influence **2.** *a*) size *b*) importance **3.** the degree of brightness of a fixed star

mag·no·li·a (mag nō′lē ə, -nōl′yə) **n.** [< P. *Magnol* (1638–1715), Fr. botanist] **1.** a tree with large, fragrant flowers of white, pink, or purple **2.** the flower

mag·num (mag′nəm) **n.** [< L. *magnus*, great] a wine bottle holding about 2/5 of a gallon

‡**mag·num o·pus** (mag′nəm ō′pəs) [L.] **1.** a masterpiece **2.** a person's greatest work

mag·pie (mag′pī′) **n.** [< *Mag*, dim. of *Margaret* + *pie*, magpie] **1.** a noisy, black-and-white bird related to the crow **2.** one who chatters

Mag·yar (mag′yär) **n. 1.** a member of the main ethnic group in Hungary **2.** the Hungarian language

ma·ha·ra·jah, ma·ha·ra·ja (mä′hə rä′jə) **n.** [< Sans. *mahā*, great + *rājā*, king] formerly in India, a prince, specif. one who ruled any of the chief native states —**ma′ha·ra′ni, ma′ha·ra′nee** (-nē) **n.fem.**

ma·ha·ri·shi (mä′hä rish′ē) **n.** [< Hindi < *mahā*, great + *rshi*, sage] a Hindu teacher of mysticism and meditation

ma·hat·ma (mə hat′mə, -hät′-) **n.** [< Sans. *mahā*, great + *ātman*, soul] *Buddhism* any of a class of wise and holy persons held in special regard

mah-jongg, mah-jong (mä′jôŋ′) **n.** [< Chin. *ma-ch'iao*, sparrow (a figure on one of the tiles)] a game of Chinese origin, played with small tiles

ma·hog·a·ny (mə häg′ə nē, -hôg′-) **n., pl. -nies** [< ?] **1.** a tree of tropical America, with hard, reddish-brown wood **2.** the wood **3.** reddish brown —**adj.** reddish-brown

maid (mād) **n. 1.** *same as* MAIDEN **2.** a girl or woman servant

maid′en (-'n) **n.** [OE. *mægden*] **1.** a girl or young unmarried woman **2.** a virgin —**adj. 1.** of or suitable for a maiden **2.** unmarried or virgin **3.** untried; new **4.** first or earliest [a *maiden* voyage] —**maid′en·hood′ n.** —**maid′en·ly adj.**

maid′en·hair′ n. a fern with delicate fronds and slender stalks

maid′en·head′ (-hed′) **n.** the hymen

maiden name the surname that a woman had when not yet married

maid of honor an unmarried woman acting as chief attendant to a bride

maid′ser′vant n. a girl or woman servant

mail¹ (māl) **n.** [< OHG. *malaha*, wallet] **1.** letters, packages, etc. transported and delivered by the post office **2.** [*also pl.*] the postal system —**adj.** of mail —**vt.** to send by mail — **mail′er n.**

mail² (māl) **n.** [< L. *macula*, mesh of a net] a flexible body armor made of small metal rings, scales, etc. —**vt.** to cover as with mail

mail′box′ n. a box in which mail is put when delivered or a box into which mail is put for collection: also **mail box**

mail carrier one whose work is carrying and delivering mail; mailman; postman

mail′man′ n., pl. -men′ *same as* MAIL CARRIER

mail order an order for goods to be sent through the mail —**mail′-or′der adj.**

maim (mām) **vt.** [OFr. *mahaigner*] to cripple; mutilate; disable

main (mān) **n.** [OE. *mægen*, strength] **1.** a principal pipe in a distributing system for water, gas, etc. **2.** [Poet.] the ocean —**adj.** chief in size, importance, etc.; principal —**by main force** (or **strength**) by sheer force (or strength) —**in the main** mostly; chiefly —**with might and main** with all one's strength

main clause a clause that can function as a complete sentence by itself

main drag [Slang] the principal street of a city or town

main·land (mān′land′, -lənd) **n.** the principal land mass of a continent, as distinguished from nearby islands

main′line′ n. the principal road, course, etc. — **vt. -lined′, -lin′ing** [Slang] to inject (a narcotic drug) directly into a large vein

main′ly adv. chiefly; principally

main′mast (-məst, -mast′) **n.** the principal mast of a vessel

main′sail (-s'l, -sāl′) **n.** the principal sail of a vessel, set from the mainmast

main′spring′ n. 1. the principal spring in a clock, watch, etc. **2.** the chief motive, incentive, etc.

main′stay′ (-stā′) **n. 1.** the supporting line run forward from the mainmast **2.** a chief support

main′stream′ n. a major trend or line of thought, action, etc.

main·tain (mān tān′) **vt.** [< L. *manu tenere*, to hold in the hand] **1.** to keep or keep up; carry on **2.** to keep in continuance or in a certain state, as of repair **3.** to defend **4.** to affirm or assert **5.** to support by aid or influence **6.** to provide the means of existence for [to *maintain* a family]

main·te·nance (mān′t'n əns) **n. 1.** a maintaining or being maintained **2.** means of support

‡**maî·tre d'hô·tel** (me′tr′ dô tel′) [Fr., master of the house] **1.** a butler or steward **2.** a chief waiter

maize (māz) **n.** [< Sp. < WInd. *mahiz*] **1.** *same as* CORN¹ (sense 2) **2.** yellow

Maj. Major

ma·jes·tic (mə jes′tik) **adj.** grand; stately; dignified —**ma·jes′ti·cal·ly adv.**

maj·es·ty (maj′is tē) **n., pl. -ties** [< L. *magnus*, great] **1.** [**M-**] a title used in speaking to or of a sovereign, preceded by *His*, *Her*, or *Your* **2.** grandeur

ma·jol·i·ca (mə jäl′i kə) **n.** [< It.] a variety of Italian glazed pottery

ma·jor (mā′jər) **adj.** [L., compar. of *magnus*, great] **1.** greater in size, amount, importance, rank, etc. **2.** *Music a*) designating a scale with a half step between the 3d and 4th and between the 7th and 8th tones *b*) designating a regular interval on this scale —**vi.** *Educ.* to specialize (*in* a field of study) —*n.* **1.** *U.S. Mil.* an officer ranking just above a captain **2.** *Educ.* a principal field of study

ma′jor·do′mo (-dō′mō) *n., pl.* **-mos** [< Sp. or It. < L. *major*, greater + *domus*, house] a man in charge of a great household

major general *pl.* **major generals** *U.S. Mil.* an officer ranking just above a brigadier general

ma·jor·i·ty (mə jôr′ə tē, -jär′-) *n., pl.* **-ties** [< Fr. < L.: see MAJOR] **1.** the greater number; more than half of a total **2.** the excess of the larger number of votes cast for one candidate, bill, etc. over all the rest of the votes **3.** full legal age **4.** the military rank of a major

make (māk) *vt.* **made, mak′ing** [OE. *macian*] **1.** to bring into being; build, create, produce, etc. **2.** to cause to be or become [the news *made* her sad] **3.** to prepare for use [make the beds] **4.** to amount to [two pints *make* a quart] **5.** to have the qualities of [he *made* a good doctor] **6.** to acquire; earn **7.** to cause the success of [that venture *made* him] **8.** to understand [what do you *make* of that?] **9.** to execute, do, etc. [to *make* a speech] **10.** to cause or force [make him go] **11.** to arrive at; reach [the ship *made* port] **12.** [Colloq.] to get on or in [he *made* the team] —*vi.* **1.** to start (to do something) **2.** to behave as specified [to *make* merry] **3.** to cause something to be as specified [make ready] —*n.* **1.** the way in which something is made; style **2.** type; sort; brand —**make away with 1.** to steal **2.** to kill —**make believe** to pretend —**make for 1.** to go toward **2.** to attack **3.** to help effect —**make it** [Colloq.] to achieve a certain thing —**make off with** to steal —**make out 1.** to see with difficulty **2.** to understand **3.** to fill out (a blank form, etc.) **4.** to (try to) show or prove to be **5.** to succeed; get along —**make over 1.** to change; renovate **2.** to transfer the ownership of —**make up 1.** to put together **2.** to form; constitute **3.** to invent **4.** to provide (what is lacking) **5.** to compensate (*for*) **6.** to become friends again after a quarrel **7.** to put on cosmetics, etc. **8.** to decide (one's mind) —**mak′er** *n.*

make′-be·lieve′ *n.* **1.** pretense; feigning **2.** a pretender —*adj.* pretended; feigned

make′shift′ (-shift′) *n.* a temporary substitute or expedient —*adj.* that will do as a makeshift

make′up′, make′-up′ *n.* **1.** the way something is put together; composition **2.** nature; disposition **3.** the cosmetics, etc. used by an actor **4.** cosmetics generally

mal- [< L. *malus*, bad] a prefix meaning bad or badly, wrong, ill

mal·ad·just·ed (mal′ə jus′tid) *adj.* poorly adjusted, esp. to the environment —**mal′ad·just′ment** *n.*

mal·a·droit (mal′ə droit′) *adj.* [Fr.: see MAL- & ADROIT] awkward; clumsy; bungling

mal·a·dy (mal′ə dē) *n., pl.* **-dies** [< VL. *male habitus*, badly kept] a disease; illness; sickness

ma·laise (ma lāz′) *n.* [Fr. < *mal*, bad + *aise*, ease] a vague feeling of physical discomfort or uneasiness

mal·a·mute (mal′ə myōōt′) *n.* [< *Malemute*, an Eskimo tribe] a strong dog with a thick coat, developed as a sled dog by Eskimos

mal·a·prop·ism (mal′ə präp iz′m) *n.* [< Mrs. *Malaprop* in Sheridan's *The Rivals* (1775)] a ludicrous misuse of words that sound alike

ma·lar·i·a (mə ler′ē ə) *n.* [It. < *mala aria*, bad air] an infectious disease transmitted by the anopheles mosquito, characterized by intermittent chills and fever —**ma·lar′i·al, ma·lar′i·an, ma·lar′i·ous** *adj.*

ma·lar·key, ma·lar·ky (mə lär′kē) *n.* [< ?] [Slang] insincere talk; nonsense

mal·a·thi·on (mal′ə thī′än) *n.* [< chem. names] an organic insecticide

Ma·lay (mā′lā, mə lā′) *n.* **1.** a member of a large group of brown-skinned peoples living chiefly in the Malay Peninsula and the Malay Archipelago **2.** their language —*adj.* of the Malays, their language, etc. Also **Ma·lay′an**

mal·con·tent (mal′kən tent′) *adj.* [see MAL- & CONTENT[1]] dissatisfied or rebellious —*n.* a dissatisfied or rebellious person

male (māl) *adj.* [< L. *mas*, a male] **1.** designating or of the sex that fertilizes the ovum of the female **2.** of, like, or suitable for men or boys; masculine **3.** having a part shaped to fit into a corresponding hollow part —*n.* a male person, animal, or plant

mal·e·dic·tion (mal′ə dik′shən) *n.* [see MAL- & DICTION] a curse

mal·e·fac·tor (mal′ə fak′tər) *n.* [< L. *male*, evil + *facere*, do] an evildoer; criminal —**mal′e·fac′tion** *n.*

ma·lev·o·lent (mə lev′ə lənt) *adj.* [< L. *male*, evil + *velle*, to wish] wishing evil or harm to others —**ma·lev′o·lence** *n.*

mal·fea·sance (mal fē′z′ns) *n.* [< Fr. *mal*, evil + *faire*, do] wrongdoing, esp. by a public official —**mal·fea′sant** *adj.*

mal·for·ma·tion (mal′fôr mā′shən) *n.* faulty or abnormal formation of a body or part —**malformed′** *adj.*

mal·func·tion (mal fuŋk′shən) *vi.* to fail to function as it should —*n.* an instance of malfunctioning

mal·ice (mal′is) *n.* [< L. *malus*, bad] **1.** active ill will; desire to harm another **2.** *Law* evil intent

ma·li·cious (mə lish′əs) *adj.* having, showing, or caused by malice; spiteful

ma·lign (mə līn′) *vt.* [< L. *male*, ill + *genus*, born] to speak evil of; slander —*adj.* **1.** malicious **2.** evil; sinister **3.** very harmful

ma·lig′nant (-lig′nənt) *adj.* [see prec.] **1.** having an evil influence **2.** wishing evil **3.** very harmful **4.** causing or likely to cause death [a *malignant* growth] —**ma·lig′nan·cy, ma·lig′ni·ty** (-nə tē) *n.*

ma·lin·ger (mə liŋ′gər) *vi.* [< Fr. *malingre*, sickly] to pretend to be ill in order to escape duty or work —**ma·lin′ger·er** *n.*

mall (môl, mal) *n.* [< *maul*, mallet: from use in a game on outdoor lanes] **1.** a shaded walk or public promenade **2.** *a*) a shop-lined street for pedestrians only *b*) an enclosed shopping center

mal·lard (mal′ərd) *n.* [< OFr. *malart*] the common wild duck

mal·le·a·ble (mal′ē ə b'l) *adj.* [< L. *malleus*, hammer] **1.** that can be hammered, pounded, or pressed into various shapes without breaking **2.** adaptable —**mal′le·a·bil′i·ty** *n.*

mal·let (mal′it) *n.* [see prec.] **1.** a short-handled hammer with a wooden head, for driving a chisel, etc. **2.** a long-handled hammer, as for use in croquet or polo **3.** a small hammer for playing a xylophone, etc.

mal·low (mal′ō) *n.* [< L. *malva*] any of a family of plants, including the hollyhock, cotton, and okra, with large, showy flowers

mal·nour·ished (mal nur′isht) *adj.* improperly nourished

mal·nu·tri·tion (mal′nōō trish′ən) *n.* faulty or inadequate nutrition; poor nourishment

mal·oc·clu·sion (mal′ə klōō′zhən) *n.* a faulty position of the teeth so that they do not meet properly

mal·o·dor·ous (mal ō′dər əs) *adj.* having a bad odor; stinking

mal·prac·tice (mal prak′tis) *n.* professional misconduct or improper practice, esp. by a physician

malt (môlt) *n.* [OE. *mealt*] **1.** barley or other grain softened by soaking and then kiln-dried: used in brewing and distilling **2.** beer, ale, etc. —*adj.* made with malt —**malt′ed** *adj.* —**malt′y** *adj.* -**i·er**, -**i·est**

malted milk powdered malt and dried milk, used in a drink with milk, etc.

Mal·tese (môl tēz′) *adj.* of Malta, its inhabitants, etc. —*n.* **1.** *pl.* **-tese**′ a native of Malta **2.** the language spoken in Malta

mal·treat (mal trēt′) *vt.* [< Fr.: see MAL- & TREAT] to treat roughly or brutally —**mal·treat′ment** *n.*

mam·ma (mä′mə; *occas.* mə mä′) *n.* mother: a child's word: also **ma′ma**

mam·mal (mam′əl) *n.* [< L. *mamma*, breast] any of a group of vertebrates the females of which have milk-secreting glands for feeding their offspring —**mam·ma·li·an** (mə mā′lē ən) *adj., n.*

mam·ma·ry (mam′ər ē) *adj.* designating or of the milk-secreting glands

mam·mon (mam′ən) *n.* [< Aram. *māmōnā*, riches] [*often* M-] riches regarded as an object of worship and greedy pursuit —**mam′mon·ism** *n.*

mam·moth (mam′əth) *n.* [Russ. *mamont*] an extinct elephant with a hairy skin and long tusks —*adj.* very big; huge; enormous

man (man) *n., pl.* **men** (men) [OE. *mann*] **1.** a human being; person **2.** the human race; mankind **3.** an adult male person **4.** an adult male servant, employee, etc. **5.** a husband or lover **6.** a manly person **7.** any of the pieces used in chess, checkers, etc. —*vt.* **manned, man′ning 1.** to furnish with men for work, defense, etc. [to *man* a ship] **2.** to strengthen; brace —**as a** (or **one**) **man** in unison; unanimously —**to a man** with no exception

-man *a combining form meaning* man or person of a (specified) kind, in a (specified) activity, etc. [*Frenchman, sportsman*]

man·a·cle (man′ə k'l) *n.* [< L. *manus*, hand] **1.** a handcuff **2.** any restraint *Usually used in pl.* —*vt.* **-cled, -cling 1.** to put handcuffs on **2.** to restrain; hamper

man·age (man′ij) *vt.* **-aged, -ag·ing** [It. *maneggiare* < L. *manus*, hand] **1.** to control the movement or behavior of **2.** to have charge of; direct [to *manage* a household] **3.** to succeed in accomplishing —*vi.* **1.** to carry on business **2.** to contrive to get along —**man′age·a·ble** *adj.*

man′age·ment *n.* **1.** the act, art, or manner of managing, controlling, etc. **2.** the persons managing a business, institution, etc.

man′ag·er *n.* a person who manages the affairs of a business, institution, team, etc.

man·a·ge·ri·al (man′ə jir′ē əl) *adj.* of a manager or management

‡ma·ña·na (mä nyä′nä) *n., adv.* [Sp.] tomorrow or (at) some indefinite future time

man·a·tee (man′ə tē′) *n.* [< Sp. < native (Carib) name] a large, plant-eating aquatic mammal of tropical waters

Man·chu (man chōō′) *n.* **1.** *pl.* **-chus**′, **-chu**′ a member of a Mongolian people of Manchuria who ruled China from 1644 to 1912 **2.** their language —*adj.* of Manchuria, the Manchus, their language, etc.

man·da·rin (man′də rin) *n.* [< Port. < Sans. *mantra*, counsel] **1.** a high official of the former Chinese Empire **2.** a member of any

elite group **3.** [M-] the main dialect of Chinese **4.** a small orange with a loose rind

man·date (man′dāt) *n.* [< L. *mandare*, to command] **1.** an order or command **2.** *a*) formerly, a commission from the League of Nations to a country to administer some region, colony, etc. *b*) the area so administered **3.** the wishes of constituents expressed to a representative, etc.

man·da·to·ry (man′də tôr′ē) *adj.* **1.** of, like, or containing a mandate **2.** authoritatively commanded or required; obligatory

man·di·ble (man′də b'l) *n.* [< L. *mandere*, chew] the jaw; specif., *a*) the lower jaw of a vertebrate *b*) either jaw of a beaked animal

man·do·lin (man′d'l in′, man′də lin′) *n.* [< Fr. < LGr. *pandoura*, kind of lute] a musical instrument with four or five pairs of strings and a deep, rounded sound box

man·drake (man′drāk) *n.* [< L. < Gr. *mandragoras*] **1.** a poisonous plant of the nightshade family **2.** its thick root, formerly used in medicine as a narcotic

mane (mān) *n.* [OE. *manu*] the long hair growing from the top or sides of the neck of the horse, lion, etc. —**maned** *adj.*

man′-eat′er *n.* an animal that eats human flesh —**man′-eat′ing** *adj.*

ma·neu·ver (mə nōō′vər) *n.* [< Fr. < L. *manu operare*, to work by hand] **1.** a planned and controlled movement of troops, warships, etc. **2.** a stratagem; scheme —*vi., vt.* **1.** to perform or cause to perform maneuvers **2.** to manage or plan skillfully **3.** to move, get, make, etc. by some stratagem —**ma·neu′ver·a·ble** *adj.*

man·ful (man′fəl) *adj.* manly

man·ga·nese (maŋ′gə nēs′, -nēz′) *n.* [< Fr. < It. < ML. *magnesia*] a grayish-white metallic chemical element, used in various alloys: symbol, Mn

mange (mānj) *n.* [< OFr. *mangeue*, an itch] a skin disease of mammals, causing itching, hair loss, etc.

man·ger (mān′jər) *n.* [< L. *mandere*, to chew] a box or trough to hold hay, etc. for horses or cattle to eat

man·gle¹ (maŋ′g'l) *vt.* **-gled, -gling** [< OFr. *mehaigner*, maim] **1.** to mutilate by roughly cutting, hacking, etc. **2.** to spoil; botch; mar —**man′gler** *n.*

man·gle² (maŋ′g'l) *n.* [Du. *mangel* < Gr. *manganon*, war machine] a machine for pressing sheets, etc. between rollers —*vt.* **-gled, -gling** to press in a mangle —**man′gler** *n.*

man·go (maŋ′gō) *n., pl.* **-goes, -gos** [< Port. < Tamil *mān-kāy*] **1.** a yellow-red, somewhat acid tropical fruit **2.** the tree on which it grows

man·grove (maŋ′grōv) *n.* [< Port. < WInd. name] a tropical tree with branches that spread and send down roots, thus forming more trunks

man·gy (mān′jē) *adj.* **-gi·er, -gi·est 1.** having the mange **2.** shabby and filthy **3.** mean and low —**man′gi·ness** *n.*

man′han′dle *vt.* **-dled, -dling** to handle roughly

man′hole′ *n.* a hole through which one can enter a sewer, conduit, etc.

man′hood′ *n.* **1.** the state or time of being a man **2.** virility, courage, determination, etc. **3.** men collectively

man′-hour′ *n.* a time unit equal to one hour of work done by one person

man′hunt′ *n.* a hunt for a fugitive

ma·ni·a (mā′nē ə) *n.* [Gr.] **1.** wild or violent mental disorder **2.** an excessive enthusiasm; obsession

-mania [see prec.] *a combining form meaning* a

(specified) type of mental disorder [*kleptomania*]

ma·ni·ac (mā'nē ak') *adj.* wildly insane; raving —*n.* a violently insane person; lunatic — **ma·ni·a·cal** (mə nī'ə k'l) *adj.*

man·ic (man'ik) *adj.* having, characterized by, or like mania

man'ic-de·pres'sive *adj.* designating, of, or having a psychosis characterized by alternating periods of mania and mental depression — *n.* one who has this psychosis

man·i·cure (man'ə kyoor') *n.* [Fr. < L. *manus*, a hand + *cura*, care] a trimming, polishing, etc. of the fingernails —*vt.* -cured', -cur'ing to trim, polish, etc. (the fingernails) —**man'i·cur'-ist** *n.*

man·i·fest (man'ə fest') *adj.* [< L. *manifestus*, lit., struck by the hand] apparent to the senses or the mind; obvious —*vt.* to show plainly; reveal —*n.* an itemized list of a craft's cargo or passengers

man·i·fes·ta·tion (man'ə fes tā'shən) *n.* 1. a manifesting or being manifested 2. something that manifests

man·i·fes·to (man'ə fes'tō) *n., pl.* -toes [It. < L.: see MANIFEST] a public declaration of motives and intentions by a government or by an important person or group

man·i·fold (man'ə fōld') *adj.* [see MANY & -FOLD] 1. having many forms, parts, etc. 2. of many sorts 3. being such in many ways [a *manifold* villain] 4. operating several parts of one kind —*n.* a pipe with several outlets, as the cylinder exhaust system in an automobile —*vt.* to make a number of copies of, as with carbon paper

man·i·kin (man'ə k'n) *n.* [< Du. *manneken*] 1. a little man; dwarf 2. *same as* MANNEQUIN

Manila hemp [*often* m-] a strong fiber from the leafstalk of a Philippine plant, used for rope, etc.

Manila paper [*often* m-] strong, buff-colored paper, orig. made of Manila hemp

man in the street the average person

ma·nip·u·late (mə nip'yə lāt') *vt.* -lat'ed, -lat'-ing [ult. < Fr. < L. *manus*, a hand + *plere*, to fill] 1. to work or handle skillfully 2. to manage artfully or shrewdly, esp. in an unfair way 3. to alter (figures, accounts, etc.) for one's own purposes —**ma·nip'u·la'tion** *n.* —**ma·nip'u·la'tor** *n.*

man·kind *n.* 1. (man'kīnd') the human race 2. (-kīnd') all human males

man'ly *adj.* -li·er, -li·est having qualities regarded as befitting a man; strong, brave, etc. —*adv.* in a manly way

man'-made' *adj.* artificial; synthetic

man·na (man'ə) *n.* [< Heb. *mān*] 1. *Bible* food miraculously provided for the Israelites in the wilderness 2. any help that comes unexpectedly

man·ne·quin (man'ə kin) *n.* [Fr. < Du.: see MANIKIN] 1. a model of the human body, used by tailors, etc. 2. a woman who models clothes in stores, etc.

man·ner (man'ər) *n.* [< L. *manus*, a hand] 1. a way of doing something; mode of procedure 2. a way, esp. a usual way, of acting; habit 3. [*pl.*] *a)* ways of social behavior [good *manners*] *b)* polite ways of social behavior [to learn *manners*] 4. kind; sort

man'nered *adj.* 1. having manners of a specified sort [ill-*mannered*] 2. artificial or affected

man'ner·ism *n.* 1. excessive use of some distinctive manner in art, literature, etc. 2. a habitual peculiarity of manner in behavior, speech, etc.

man'ner·ly *adj.* polite —*adv.* politely

man·ni·kin (man'ə kin) *n. alt. sp. of* MANIKIN

man·nish (man'ish) *adj.* of, like, or fit for a man [she walks with a *mannish* stride]

ma·noeu·vre (mə nōō'vər) *n., vi., vt.* -vred, -vring *chiefly Brit. sp. of* MANEUVER

man of letters a writer, scholar, etc., esp. in the field of literature

man'-of-war' *n., pl.* men'-of-war' an armed naval vessel; warship

man·or (man'ər) *n.* [< L. *manere*, dwell] 1. in England, a landed estate 2. a mansion, as on an estate —**ma·no·ri·al** (mə nôr'ē əl) *adj.*

man'pow'er *n.* 1. power furnished by human strength 2. the collective strength or availability for work of the people in a given area, nation, etc. Also **man power**

man·sard (roof) (man'särd) [< F. *Mansard*, 17th-c. Fr. architect] a roof with two slopes on each of the four sides, the lower steeper than the upper

manse (mans) *n.* [< L. *manere*, dwell] a parsonage

man'ser'vant *n., pl.* men'ser'vants a male servant: also **man servant**

man·sion (man'shən) *n.* [< L. *manere*, dwell] a large, imposing house

man'-sized' *adj.* [Colloq.] of a size fit for a man; big: also **man'-size'**

man'slaugh'ter (-slôt'ər) *n.* the killing of a human being by another, esp. when unlawful but without malice

man·tel (man't'l) *n.* [see MANTLE] 1. the facing about a fireplace, including a shelf or slab above it 2. the shelf or slab: also called **man'-tel·piece'**

man·til·la (man til'ə) *n.* [Sp. < L. *mantellum*, a mantle] a woman's scarf worn over the hair and shoulders

man·tis (man'tis) *n., pl.* -tis·es, -tes (-tēz) [< Gr. *mantis*, prophet] an insect with forelegs held as if praying

man·tle (man't'l) *n.* [< L. *mantellum*] 1. a loose, sleeveless cloak 2. anything that envelops or conceals 3. a small, mesh hood which becomes white-hot over a flame and gives off light —*vt.* -tled, -tling to cover as with a mantle —*vi.* 1. to be or become covered 2. to blush or flush

man·tra (mun'trə, man'-) *n.* [Sans.] a chant of a Hindu hymn, text, etc.

man·u·al (man'yoo wəl) *adj.* [< L. *manus*, a hand] 1. of the hands 2. made, done, or worked by the hands 3. involving hard work with the hands —*n.* 1. a handy book of instructions, etc. for use as a guide 2. prescribed drill in the handling of a rifle

manual training training in practical arts and crafts, as metalworking, etc.

man·u·fac·ture (man'yə fak'chər) *n.* [Fr. < L. *manus*, a hand + *facere*, make] 1. the making of goods, esp. by machinery and on a large scale 2. anything so made 3. the making of something in a mechanical way —*vt.* -tured, -tur·ing 1. to make, esp. by machinery 2. to make up (excuses, etc.) —**man'u·fac'tur·er** *n.*

man·u·mit (man'yə mit') *vt.* -mit'ted, -mit'ting [< L. *manus*, a hand + *mittere*, send] to free from slavery —**man'u·mis'sion** (-mish'ən) *n.*

ma·nure (mə noor', -nyoor') *vt.* -nured', -nur'-ing [< OFr. *manouvrer*, to work with the hands] to put manure on or into —*n.* animal excrement, etc. used to fertilize soil

man·u·script (man'yə skript') *adj.* [< L. *manus*, hand + *scriptus*, written] 1. written by hand or typewritten 2. written with print-like letters —*n.* 1. a written or typewritten document, book, etc., as submitted to a publisher **2.** writing, not print

Manx (maŋks) *adj.* of the Isle of Man, its people, etc. —*n.* their language, now nearly extinct —**the Manx** the people of the Isle of Man

man·y (men′ē) *adj.* **more, most** [OE. *manig*] numerous —*n.* a large number (of persons or things) —*pron.* many persons or things

Ma·o·ri (mou′rē, mä′ō rē) *n.* **1.** *pl.* **-ris, -ri** any of the Polynesians native to New Zealand **2.** their language

map (map) *n.* [< L. *mappa*, napkin] **1.** a representation of all or part of the earth's surface, showing countries, bodies of water, etc. **2.** a representation of the sky, showing stars, etc. — *vt.* **mapped, map′ping 1.** to make a map of **2.** to plan

ma·ple (mā′p'l) *n.* [OE. *mapel(treo)*] **1.** any of a large group of trees grown for wood, sap, or shade **2.** its hard, light-colored wood **3.** the flavor of the syrup (**maple syrup**) or the sugar (**maple sugar**) made from its sap

mar (mär) *vt.* **marred, mar′ring** [OE. *mierran*, hinder] to hurt or spoil the looks, perfection, etc. of; impair; damage

Mar. March

mar·a·bou (mar′ə boo′) *n.* [Fr. < Ar. *murābit*, hermit] **1.** a large stork of Africa or India **2.** its plumes, used in millinery

ma·ra·ca (mə rä′kə) *n.* [< Port. < SAmInd. name] a percussion instrument made of a dried gourd or gourd-shaped rattle with loose pebbles in it

mar·a·schi·no (mar′ə skē′nō, -shē′-) *n.* [It. < *marasca*, cherry] a liqueur or cordial made from a kind of black wild cherry

maraschino cherries cherries in a syrup flavored with maraschino

mar·a·thon (mar′ə thän′) *n.* [< *Marathon*, in ancient Greece] **1.** a foot race of 26 miles, 385 yards **2.** any long-distance or endurance contest

ma·raud (mə rôd′) *vi., vt.* [< Fr. *maraud*, vagabond] to raid and plunder

mar·ble (mär′b'l) *n.* [< Gr. *marmaros*, white stone] **1.** a hard limestone, white or colored, which takes a high polish **2.** a piece of this stone, used in sculpture, etc. **3.** anything like marble in hardness, coldness, etc. **4.** *a*) a little ball of stone, glass, etc. *b*) [*pl., with sing. v.*] children's game played with such balls —*adj.* of or like marble —*vt.* **-bled, -bling 1.** to make (book edges) look mottled like marble **2.** to cause (meat) to be streaked with fat

mar′ble·ize′ *vt.* **-ized′, -iz′ing** to make look like marble

March (märch) *n.* [< L. *Mars*, Mars] the third month of the year, having 31 days

march[1] (märch) *vi.* [Fr. *marcher*] **1.** to walk with regular steps, as in military formation **2.** to advance steadily —*vt.* to make march or go —*n.* **1.** a marching **2.** a steady advance; progress **3.** a regular, steady step **4.** the distance covered in marching **5.** a piece of music for marching —**on the march** marching —**steal a march on** to get an advantage over secretly —**march′er** *n.*

march[2] (märch) *n.* [< OFr.] a boundary or frontier

March hare a hare in breeding time, proverbially an example of madness

marching orders orders to march, go, etc.

mar·chion·ess (mär′shə nis) *n.* **1.** the wife or widow of a marquess **2.** a lady of the rank of a marquess

Mar·di gras (mär′di grä′) [Fr., fat Tuesday]

the last day before Lent: a day of carnival, as in New Orleans

mare[1] (mer) *n.* [OE. *mere*] a fully mature female horse, mule, donkey, etc.

ma·re[2] (mer′ē) *n., pl.* **-ri·a** (-ē ə) [L., sea] a large, dark area on the moon or Mars

mare's-nest (merz′nest′) *n.* **1.** a hoax **2.** a mess

mar·ga·rine (mär′jə rin) *n.* [Fr.] a spread or cooking fat of vegetable oils processed to the consistency of butter, often churned with skim milk: also **mar′ga·rin**

mar·gin (mär′jən) *n.* [L. *margo*] **1.** a border or edge **2.** the blank border of a printed or written page **3.** *a*) an amount beyond what is needed *b*) provision for increase, advance, etc. **4.** the difference between the cost and selling price of goods —**mar′gin·al** *adj.*

ma·ri·a·chi (mär′ē ä′chē) *n., pl.* **-chis** [MexSp. < ?] **1.** one of a strolling band of musicians in Mexico **2.** such a band **3.** its music

mar·i·gold (mar′ə gōld′) *n.* [< Virgin *Mary* + *gold*] a plant of the composite family, with red, yellow, or orange flowers

ma·ri·jua·na, ma·ri·hua·na (mar′ə wä′nə) *n.* [AmSp.] **1.** *same as* HEMP (sense 1) **2.** its dried leaves and flowers, smoked for the psychological effects

ma·rim·ba (mə rim′bə) *n.* [< native Afr. name] a kind of xylophone with resonant tubes under the wooden bars

ma·ri·na (mə rē′nə) *n.* [It. & Sp., seacoast < L. *mare*, sea] a small harbor with docks, services, etc. for pleasure craft

mar·i·nade (mar′ə nād′) *n.* [Fr. < Sp. *marinar*, to pickle] **1.** a spiced pickling solution for steeping meat, fish, etc., often before cooking **2.** meat, etc. so steeped —*vt.* **-nad′ed, -nad′ing** *same as* MARINATE

mar·i·nate (mar′ə nāt′) *vt.* **-nat′ed, -nat′ing** [< It. *marinare*, to pickle] to steep (meat, etc.) in a marinade

ma·rine (mə rēn′) *adj.* [< L. *mare*, sea] **1.** of or found in the sea **2.** *a*) maritime; nautical *b*) naval —*n.* **1.** a member of a military force trained for service at sea **2.** [*often* M-] a member of the MARINE CORPS **3.** naval or merchant ships collectively

Marine Corps a branch of the U.S. armed forces trained for land, sea, and aerial combat

mar·i·ner (mar′ə nər) *n.* a sailor

mar·i·o·nette (mar′ē ə net′) *n.* [Fr. < *Marie*, Mary] a little jointed doll moved by strings or wires

mar·i·tal (mar′ə t'l) *adj.* [< L. *maritus*, a husband] of marriage —**mar′i·tal·ly** *adv.*

mar·i·time (mar′ə tīm′) *adj.* [< L. *mare*, sea] **1.** on, near, or living near the sea **2.** of navigation, shipping, etc. [*maritime law*]

mar·jo·ram (mär′jər əm) *n.* [? ult. < Gr. *amarakos*] a fragrant plant of the mint family, used in cooking

Mark (märk) *Bible* **1.** a Christian disciple, reputed author of the second Gospel **2.** this book

mark[1] (märk) *n.* [OE. *mearc*, boundary] **1.** a spot, scratch, etc. on a surface **2.** a printed or written symbol [*punctuation marks*] **3.** a brand or label on an article to show the maker, etc. **4.** an indication of some quality, character, etc. **5.** a grade [*a mark of B in Latin*] **6.** a standard of quality **7.** impression; influence **8.** an object of known position, serving as a guide **9.** a line, dot, etc. indicating position, as on a graduated scale **10.** a target or goal —*vt.* **1.** to put or make a mark or marks on **2.** to identify as by a mark **3.** to indicate by a mark **4.** to show plainly *[a smile marking joy]* **5.** to distinguish; characterize **6.** to take notice of; heed *[mark my words]* **7.** to grade; rate —**make one's mark** to achieve fame —**mark down** (or **up**) to mark for sale at a reduced (or an increased) price —**mark time 1.** to keep time while at a halt by lifting the feet as if marching **2.** to suspend progress for a time —**mark'er** *n.*

mark² (märk) *n.* [< ON. *mǫrk*, a half pound of silver] **1.** the monetary unit of East Germany **2.** the monetary unit of West Germany: in full **deut·sche mark** (doi′chə)

mark'down' *n.* **1.** a marking for sale at a reduced price **2.** the amount of reduction

marked (märkt) *adj.* **1.** having a mark or marks **2.** noticeable; distinct *[a marked change]* —**mark·ed·ly** (mär′kid lē) *adv.*

mar·ket (mär′kit) *n.* [ult. < L. *merx*, merchandise] **1.** a gathering of people for buying and selling things **2.** an open space or building with goods for sale from stalls, etc.: also **mar′ket·place′** **3.** a store selling provisions *[a meat market]* **4.** a region where goods can be bought and sold *[the European market]* **5.** buying and selling; trade **6.** demand (for goods, etc.) *[a good market for tea]* —*vt.* **1.** to offer for sale **2.** to sell —*vi.* to buy provisions — **mar′ket·a·bil′i·ty** *n.* —**mar′ket·a·ble** *adj.*

mark'ing *n.* **1.** a mark or marks **2.** the characteristic arrangement of marks, as on fur or feathers

marks·man (märks′mən) *n., pl.* **-men** a person who shoots, esp. with skill —**marks′man·ship′** *n.*

mark'up' *n.* **1.** a marking for sale at an increased price **2.** the amount of increase

mar·lin (mär′lin) *n., pl.* **-lin, -lins** [< MARLINESPIKE] a large, slender deep-sea fish

mar·line·spike, mar·lin·spike (mär′lin spīk′) *n.* [< Du. *marlijn*, small cord + SPIKE¹] a pointed iron instrument used in splicing rope

mar·ma·lade (mär′mə lād′) *n.* [ult. < Gr. *meli*, honey + *mēlon*, apple] a jamlike preserve of oranges or some other fruits and sugar

mar·mo·set (mär′mə zet′, -set′) *n.* [< OFr. *marmouset*, grotesque figure] a very small monkey of S. and C. America

mar·mot (mär′mət) *n.* [< Fr., prob. < L. *mus montanus*, mountain mouse] any of a group of thick-bodied rodents, as the woodchuck

ma·roon¹ (mə rōōn′) *n., adj.* [Fr. *marron*, chestnut] dark brownish red

ma·roon² (mə rōōn′) *vt.* [< Fr. < AmSp. *cimarrón*, wild] **1.** to put (a person) ashore in a desolate place and abandon him there **2.** to leave abandoned, helpless, etc.

mar·quee (mär kē′) *n.* [< Fr. *marquise*, orig. a canopy over an officer's tent] a rooflike projection or awning over an entrance, as to a theater

mar·quess (mär′kwis) *n.* [see MARQUIS] **1.** a British nobleman ranking above an earl **2.** *same as* MARQUIS

mar·que·try (mär′kə trē) *n.* [< Fr. *marque*, a mark] decorative inlaid work, as in furniture

mar·quis (mär′kwis; *Fr.* mär kē′) *n., pl.* **-quis·es;** *Fr.* **-quis′** (-kē′) [< ML. *marchisus*, a prefect] in some European countries, a nobleman ranking above an earl or count

mar·quise′ (-kēz′) *n.* **1.** the wife or widow of a marquis **2.** a lady of the rank of a marquis

mar·qui·sette (mär′ki zet′, -kwi-) *n.* [see MARQUEE] a thin, meshlike fabric used for curtains

mar·riage (mar′ij) *n.* **1.** the state of being married; wedlock **2.** a wedding **3.** any close union —**mar′riage·a·ble** *adj.*

mar′ried *adj.* **1.** being husband and wife **2.** having a husband or wife **3.** of marriage —*n.* a married person

mar·row (mar′ō) *n.* [OE. *mearg*] **1.** the soft, fatty tissue that fills the cavities of most bones **2.** the essential part

mar·ry (mar′ē) *vt.* **-ried, -ry·ing** [< L. *maritus*, a husband] **1.** to join as husband and wife **2.** to take as husband or wife **3.** to unite —*vi.* to get married —**marry off** to give in marriage

Mars (märz) **1.** *Rom. Myth.* the god of war **2.** a planet of the solar system: see PLANET

marsh (märsh) *n.* [OE. *merisc*] a tract of low, wet, soft land; swamp —**marsh′y** *adj.* **-i·er, -i·est** —**marsh′i·ness** *n.*

mar·shal (mär′shəl) *n.* [< OHG. *marah*, horse + *scalh*, servant] **1.** in various foreign armies, a general officer of the highest rank **2.** an official in charge of ceremonies, processions, etc. **3.** in the U.S., *a*) a Federal officer appointed to a judicial district with duties like those of a sheriff *b*) the head of some police or fire departments —*vt.* **-shaled** or **-shalled, -shal·ing** or **-shal·ling** **1.** to arrange (troops, ideas, etc.) in order **2.** *a*) to direct as a marshal *b*) to guide

marsh·mal·low (märsh′mel′ō, -mal′ō) *n.* [orig. made of the root of a mallow found in marshes] a soft, spongy confection of sugar, starch, gelatin, etc.

marsh marigold a marsh plant with bright-yellow flowers

mar·su·pi·al (mär sōō′pē əl) *adj.* [< Gr. *marsypos*, a pouch] of a group of mammals whose young are carried by the female for several months after birth in an external pouch of the abdomen —*n.* an animal of this kind, as a kangaroo, opossum, etc.

mart (märt) *n.* [MDu.] a market

mar·ten (mär′t′n) *n.* [< OFr. *martre*] **1.** a small mammal like a weasel but larger, with soft, thick fur **2.** the fur

mar·tial (mär′shəl) *adj.* [< L. *martialis*, of Mars] **1.** of or connected with war **2.** warlike; militaristic —**mar′tial·ly** *adv.*

martial law temporary rule by military authorities over civilians, as in time of war

Mar·tian (mär′shən) *adj.* of Mars —*n.* an imagined inhabitant of the planet Mars

mar·tin (mär′t′n) *n.* [Fr.] a bird of the swallow family

mar·ti·net (mär′t′n et′) *n.* [< *Martinet*, 17th-c. Fr. general] a very strict disciplinarian

mar·ti·ni (mär te′nē) *n., pl.* **-nis** [< ?] [*also* M-] a cocktail of gin (or vodka) and dry vermouth

mar·tyr (mär′tər) *n.* [< Gr. *martyr*, a witness] **1.** one tortured or killed because of his faith or beliefs **2.** one suffering great misery a long time —*vt.* to make a martyr of —**mar′tyr·dom** *n.*

mar·vel (mär′v'l) *n.* [< L. *mirari*, admire] a wonderful or astonishing thing —*vi.* **-veled** or **-velled, -vel·ing** or **-vel·ling** to be amazed; wonder —*vt.* to wonder at or about (followed by a clause)

mar·vel·ous (mär′v'l əs) *adj.* **1.** causing wonder; extraordinary, etc. **2.** [Colloq.] fine; splendid Also, chiefly Brit. sp., **mar′vel·lous** —**mar′vel·ous·ly** *adv.*

Marx·ism (märk′siz'm) *n.* the system of thought developed by Karl Marx, the founder of modern socialism, and Friedrich Engels — **Marx′ist, Marx′i·an** *adj., n.*

Mar·y (mer′ē) *Bible* mother of Jesus

Mary Mag·da·lene (mag′də lēn) *Bible* a woman out of whom Jesus cast devils

mar·zi·pan (mär'zi pan') *n.* [G. < It. *marzapane*] a pasty confection of ground almonds, sugar, and egg white

masc., mas. masculine

mas·ca·ra (mas kar'ə) *n.* [< Sp. < It. *maschera*] a cosmetic for coloring the eyelashes

mas·cot (mas'kät) *n.* [< Fr. < Pr. *masco*, sorcerer] any person, animal, or thing supposed to bring good luck by being present

mas·cu·line (mas'kyə lin) *adj.* [< L. *mas*, male] 1. male; of men or boys 2. suitable for or characteristic of men and boys; strong, vigorous, etc. 3. mannish: said of women 4. *Gram.* designating or of the gender of words referring to males or things orig. regarded as male —**mas'cu·lin'i·ty** *n.*

ma·ser (mā'zər) *n.* [m(icrowave) a(mplification by) s(timulated) e(mission of) r(adiation)] a device in which atoms, as in a gas, are raised to a higher energy level and emitted in a very narrow beam

mash (mash) *n.* [< OE. *mascwyrt*] 1. crushed malt or meal soaked in hot water for making wort 2. a mixture of bran, meal, etc. in warm water for feeding horses, etc. 3. any soft mass —*vt.* to change into a soft mass by beating, crushing, etc. —**mash'er** *n.*

mask (mask) *n.* [< Fr. < It. *maschera*] 1. a covering to conceal or protect the face 2. anything that conceals or disguises 3. a masque or masquerade 4. *a*) a molded likeness of the face *b*) a grotesque representation of a face, worn to amuse or frighten —*vt.* to conceal, cover, disguise, etc. as with a mask —**masked** *adj.* —**mask'er** *n.*

mas·och·ism (mas'ə kiz'm, maz'-) *n.* [< L. von Sacher-*Masoch*, 19th-c. Austrian writer] the getting of pleasure, specif. sexual pleasure, from being dominated or hurt —**mas'och·ist** *n.* —**mas'och·is'tic** *adj.*

ma·son (mā's'n) *n.* [< ML. *matio*] 1. one whose work is building with stone, brick, etc. 2. [M-] *same as* FREEMASON

Ma·son·ic (mə sän'ik) *adj.* [*also* m-] of Freemasons or Freemasonry

ma·son·ry (mā's'n rē) *n., pl.* **-ries** 1. the trade of a mason 2. something built by a mason; brickwork or stonework 3. [*usually* M-] *same as* FREEMASONRY

masque (mask) *n.* [see MASK] 1. *same as* MASQUERADE (sense 1) 2. a former kind of dramatic entertainment with a mythical or allegorical theme

mas·quer·ade (mas'kə rād') *n.* [see MASK] 1. a ball or party at which masks and fancy costumes are worn 2. *a*) a disguise *b*) an acting under false pretenses —*vi.* **-ad'ed, -ad'ing** 1. to take part in a masquerade 2. to act under false pretenses

Mass (mas) *n.* [< L. *missa* in *ite, missa est* (contio), go, (the meeting) is dismissed] [*also* m-] *R.C.Ch.* the service of the Eucharist

mass (mas) *n.* [< Gr. *maza*, barley cake] 1. a quantity of matter of indefinite shape and size; lump 2. a large quantity or number [*a mass* of bruises] 3. bulk; size 4. the main part 5. *Physics* the quantity of matter in a body as measured in its relation to inertia —*adj.* 1. of a large number 2. of or for the masses —*vt., vi.* to gather or form into a mass —**the masses** the great mass of common people

mas·sa·cre (mas'ə kər) *n.* [Fr. < OFr. *maçacre*, shambles] the indiscriminate, merciless killing of human beings or animals —*vt.* **-cred, -cr·ing** to kill in large numbers

mas·sage (mə säzh') *n.* [Fr. < Ar. *massa*, to touch] a rubbing, kneading, etc. of part of the body, as to stimulate circulation —*vt.* **-saged', -sag'ing** to give a massage to —**mas·sag'er** *n.*

mas·seur (ma sur') *n.* [Fr.] a man whose work is giving massages —**mas·seuse'** (-sooz', -sōōz') *n.fem.*

mas·sive (mas'iv) *adj.* [< Fr.] 1. forming or consisting of a large mass; big and solid 2. large and imposing 3. extensive

mass media those means of communication that reach and influence large numbers of people, esp. newspapers, television, etc.

mass production quantity production of goods, esp. by machinery and division of labor

mast (mast) *n.* [OE. *mæst*] 1. a tall vertical spar used to support the sails, yards, etc. on a ship 2. any vertical pole

mas·tec·to·my (mas tek'tə mē) *n., pl.* **-mies** surgical removal of a breast

mas·ter (mas'tər) *n.* [< L. *magister*] 1. a man who rules others or has control over something; specif., *a*) a man who is head of a household *b*) an employer *c*) an owner of an animal or slave *d*) the captain of a merchant ship *e*) [Chiefly Brit.] a male teacher 2. an expert; specif., *a*) a workman skilled in his trade *b*) an artist regarded as great 3. [M-] a title applied to: *a*) a boy too young to be addressed as *Mr.* *b*) one holding an advanced academic degree [*Master* of Arts] —*adj.* 1. being a master 2. of a master 3. chief; main; controlling —*vt.* 1. to become master of 2. to become an expert in (art, etc.)

mas'ter·ful *adj.* 1. acting the part of a master; imperious 2. expert; skillful

mas'ter·ly *adj.* expert; skillful —*adv.* in a masterly manner —**mas'ter·li·ness** *n.*

mas'ter·mind' *n.* a very intelligent person, esp. one with the ability to plan or direct a group project —*vt.* to be the mastermind of (a project)

master of ceremonies a person who presides over an entertainment

mas'ter·piece' *n.* 1. a thing made or done with masterly skill 2. the greatest work of a person or group Also **mas'ter·work'**

master sergeant *U.S. Mil.* a noncommissioned officer of high rank

mas'ter·y *n., pl.* **-ies** 1. control as by a master 2. ascendancy or victory 3. expert skill or knowledge

mast'head' *n.* 1. the top part of a ship's mast 2. that part of a newspaper or magazine stating its address, publishers, etc.

mas·ti·cate (mas'tə kāt') *vt.* **-cat'ed, -cat'ing** [ult. < *Gr. mastax*, mouth] to chew up (food, etc.) —**mas'ti·ca'tion** *n.*

mas·tiff (mas'tif) *n.* [ult. < L. *mansuetus*, tame] a large, powerful, smooth-coated dog with hanging lips and drooping ears

mas·to·don (mas'tə dän') *n.* [< Fr. < Gr. *mastos*, breast + *odous*, tooth: from the nipplelike processes on its molars] a large, extinct animal resembling the elephant but larger

mas·toid (mas'toid) *adj.* [< Gr. *mastos*, breast + *eidos*, form] designating, of, or near a projection of the temporal bone behind the ear —*n.* the mastoid projection

mas'toid·i'tis (-toi dīt'is) *n.* inflammation of the mastoid

mas·tur·bate (mas'tər bāt') *vi.* **-bat'ed, -bat'ing** [< L. *masturbari*] to manipulate the genitals for sexual gratification —**mas'tur·ba'tion** *n.* —**mas'tur·ba'tor** *n.*

mat[1] (mat) *n.* [< LL. *matta*] 1. a flat piece of cloth, woven straw, rubber, etc., variously used for protection, as under a vase, etc. or on the floor **2.** a thickly padded floor covering, as for wrestling, etc. **3.** anything growing or interwoven in a thick tangle —*vt., vi.* **mat′ted, mat′-ting** to interweave or tangle

mat² (mat) *adj.* [Fr. < OFr.] *same as* MATTE — *n.* **1.** *same as* MATTE **2.** a border, as of cardboard, put around a picture —*vt.* **mat′ted, mat′-ting 1.** to produce a dull finish on **2.** to frame (a picture) with a mat

mat·a·dor (mat′ə dôr′) *n.* [Sp. < *matar*, to kill] the bullfighter who kills the bull

match¹ (mach) *n.* [prob. < Gr. *myxa*, lamp wick] a slender piece of wood, cardboard, etc. tipped with a composition that catches fire by friction

match² (mach) *n.* [OE. (*ge*)*mæcca*, a mate] **1.** one that is equal or similar **2.** two that go well together **3.** a contest or game **4.** a marriage or mating —*vt.* **1.** to join in marriage; mate **2.** to put in opposition **3.** to be equal or similar to **4.** to make or get the counterpart or equivalent of **5.** to suit (one thing) to another —*vi.* to be equal, similar, etc.

match′book′ *n.* a folder of paper matches

match′less *adj.* having no equal; peerless

match′mak′ing *n.* the arranging of marriages for others —**match′mak′er** *n.*

mate¹ (māt) *n.* [MDu.] **1.** a companion or fellow worker **2.** one of a matched pair **3.** *a)* a husband or wife *b)* the male or female of paired animals **4.** an officer of a merchant ship, ranking below the captain —*vt., vi.* **mat′ed, mat′ing 1.** to pair **2.** to couple in marriage or sexually

mate² (māt) *n., interj., vt.* **mat′ed, mat′ing** *same as* CHECKMATE

ma·te·ri·al (mə tir′ē əl) *adj.* [< L. *materia*, matter] **1.** of matter; physical **2.** bodily; not spiritual **3.** important, essential, etc. —*n.* **1.** what a thing is made of; elements or parts **2.** fabric, as cloth **3.** [*pl.*] things used, as tools

ma·te′ri·al·ism (-iz′m) *n.* **1.** the doctrine that everything is explainable in terms of matter **2.** concern with material things rather than with spiritual values —**ma·te′ri·al·ist** *n., adj.* —**ma·te′ri·al·is′tic** *adj.*

ma·te′ri·al·ize′ (-ə līz′) *vt.* **-ized′, -iz′ing** to give material form to —*vi.* **1.** to become fact **2.** to take on bodily form —**ma·te′ri·al·i·za′tion** *n.*

ma·te′ri·al·ly *adv.* **1.** physically **2.** considerably

ma·te·ri·el, ma·té·ri·el (mə tir′ē el′) *n.* [Fr.: see MATERIAL] necessary materials and tools; specif., military weapons, equipment, supplies, etc.

ma·ter·nal (mə tur′n'l) *adj.* [< L. *mater*, mother] **1.** motherly **2.** of or from a mother **3.** on the mother's side of the family

ma·ter′ni·ty (-nə tē) *n.* the state of being a mother; motherhood —*adj.* for pregnant women

math (math) *n. short for* MATHEMATICS

math·e·mat·i·cal (math′ə mat′i k'l) *adj.* **1.** of or like mathematics **2.** rigorously exact; absolutely accurate

math′e·mat′ics (-iks) *n.pl.* [*with sing. v.*] [< Gr. *manthanein*, learn] sciences (arithmetic, geometry, etc.) dealing with quantities, forms, etc. by numbers and symbols —**math′e·ma·ti′-cian** (-mə tish′ən) *n.*

mat·in (mat′'n) *n.* [< L. *matutinus*, of the morning] **1.** [*pl.*] [*often* M-] a service of morning prayer **2.** [Poet.] a morning song

mat·i·nee, mat·i·née (mat′'n ā′) *n.* [see prec.] an afternoon performance, as of a play

ma·tri·arch (mā′trē ärk′) *n.* [< L. *mater*, a mother + -ARCH] a mother ruling her family

or tribe —**ma′tri·ar′chal** *adj.* —**ma′tri·ar′chy** *n., pl.* **-chies**

ma·tric·u·late (mə trik′yoo lāt′) *vt., vi.* **-lat′ed, -lat′ing** [see MATRIX] to enroll, esp. as a student in a college —**ma·tric′u·la′tion** *n.*

mat·ri·mo·ny (mat′rə mō′nē) *n., pl.* **-nies** [< L. *mater*, a mother] **1.** the ceremony or sacrament of marriage **2.** married state; wedlock —**mat′ri·mo′ni·al** *adj.*

ma·trix (mā′triks) *n., pl.* **-tri·ces′** (mā′trə sēz′, mat′rə-), **-trix·es** [ult. < L. *mater*, a mother] that within which something originates or takes form; specif., a die or mold for casting or shaping

ma·tron (mā′trən) *n.* [< L. *mater*, a mother] **1.** a wife or widow **2.** a woman superintendent of domestic arrangements in an institution **3.** a woman attendant or guard, as in a jail —**ma′-tron·ly** *adj.*

matte (mat) *n.* [var. of MAT²] a dull surface or finish —*adj.* not shiny; dull

mat·ted (mat′id) *adj.* closely tangled, as hair

mat·ter (mat′ər) *n.* [< L. *materia*] **1.** what a thing is made of; material **2.** whatever occupies space and is perceptible to the senses **3.** a specified substance [*coloring matter*] **4.** what is expressed or thought, apart from its style or form; content **5.** an amount or quantity **6.** *a)* a thing or affair *b)* a cause or occasion [*no laughing matter*] **7.** importance [*it's of no matter*] **8.** trouble [*what's the matter?*] **9.** pus —*vi.* to have importance —**as a matter of fact** in fact; really —**no matter 1.** it is not important **2.** regardless of

mat′ter-of-fact′ *adj.* sticking to facts; literal, practical, etc.

Mat·thew (math′yōō) *Bible* **1.** one of the twelve Apostles, reputed author of the first Gospel **2.** this book

mat·ting (mat′iŋ) *n.* **1.** a fabric, as of straw, for floor mats, padding, etc. **2.** mats collectively

mat·tock (mat′ək) *n.* [OE. *mattuc*] a tool like a pickax, used in loosening the soil, digging up roots, etc.

mat·tress (mat′ris) *n.* [< Ar. *matrah*, cushion] a casing of strong fabric filled with cotton, foam rubber, coiled springs, etc., used on a bed

ma·ture (mə toor′, -tyoor′) *adj.* [< L. *maturus*, ripe] **1.** fully grown, developed, ripened, etc. **2.** due, as a note or bond —*vt., vi.* **-tured′, -tur′ing** to make or become mature —**mat·u·ra·tion** (mach′oo rā′shən) *n.* —**ma·tu′ri·ty** *n.*

mat·zo (mät′sə, -sô) *n., pl.* **-zot, -zoth** (-sōt), **-zos** [Heb. *matstsāh*, unleavened] **1.** flat, thin, unleavened bread eaten by Jews during Passover **2.** a piece of this

maud·lin (môd′lin) *adj.* [< OFr. *Madeleine*, (Mary) Magdalene (often represented as weeping)] foolishly, often tearfully, sentimental

maul (môl) *n.* [< L. *malleus*, a hammer] a heavy hammer or mallet as for driving stakes —*vt.* **1.** to bruise or lacerate **2.** to handle roughly —**maul′er** *n.*

mau·so·le·um (mô′sə lē′əm, -zə-) *n., pl.* **-le′-ums, -le′a** (-lē′ə) [< the tomb of King *Mausolus*, in ancient Asia Minor] a large, imposing tomb

mauve (mōv, môv) *n.* [Fr., mallow < L. *malvea*] a delicate purple —*adj.* of such a color

mav·er·ick (mav′ər ik) *n.* [< S. *Maverick*, 19th-c. Texan whose cattle had no brand] **1.** an unbranded animal **2.** [Colloq.] an independent, as in politics

maw (mô) *n.* [OE. *maga*] **1.** orig., the stomach **2.** the oral cavity, jaws, or gullet, as of a beast

mawk·ish (mô′kish) *adj.* [< ON. *mathkr,* maggot] sickeningly sentimental
maxi- [< MAXIMUM] *a combining form meaning* maximum, very long, very large
max·il·la (mak sil′ə) *n., pl.* **-lae** (-ē) [L.] the upper jawbone
max·im (mak′sim) *n.* [< LL. *maxima* (*propositio*), the greatest (premise)] a concisely expressed principle or rule of conduct
max′i·mum (-məm) *n., pl.* **-mums, -ma** (-mə) [L., superl. of *magnus,* great] **1.** the greatest quantity, number, etc. possible **2.** the highest degree or point reached —*adj.* greatest possible, permissible, or reached
May (mā) *n.* [< L. *Maius*] the fifth month of the year, having 31 days
may (mā) *v.aux. pt.* **might** [OE. *mæg*] an auxiliary expressing: **1.** possibility [it *may* rain] **2.** permission [you *may* go] **3.** purpose, result, etc. [be quiet so that we *may* hear] **4.** wish or hope [*may* he win!]
Ma·ya (mä′yə) *n.* **1.** *pl.* **-yas, -ya** a member of a tribe of Indians of SE Mexico and Central America who had a highly developed civilization **2.** their language —*adj.* of the Mayas — **Ma′yan** *adj., n.*
may·be (mā′bē) *adv.* [ME. *it may be*] perhaps
May Day May 1: a traditional spring festival and, in many countries, a labor holiday
may·flow·er (mā′flou′ər) *n.* any of various plants flowering in May or early spring —[M-] the ship on which the Pilgrims came to America (1620)
may′fly′ *n., pl.* **-flies′** [see MAY & FLY²] a slender, short-lived insect with gauzy wings
may·hem (mā′hem, mā′əm) *n.* [see MAIM] **1.** *Law* the offense of maiming a person maliciously **2.** any deliberate destruction
may·o (mā′ō) *n.* [Colloq.] clip of MAYONNAISE
may·on·naise (mā′ə nāz′) *n.* [Fr., prob. < *Mahón,* port on a Sp. island] a creamy salad dressing made with egg yolks, oil, etc.
may·or (mā′ər, mer) *n.* [< L. *major,* greater] the chief administrative official of a municipality —**may′or·al** *adj.*
may′or·al·ty (-əl tē) *n., pl.* **-ties** the office or term of office of a mayor
maze (māz) *n.* [OE. *amasian,* amaze] **1.** a confusing, intricate network of pathways; labyrinth **2.** a state of confusion
‡maz·el tov (mä′z′l tôv′, tôf′) [Heb.] good luck: an expression of congratulation
ma·zur·ka (mə zur′kə) *n.* [Pol.] a lively Polish dance in 3/4 or 3/8 time
M.C. Master of Ceremonies
Mc·Coy (mə koi′), **the** (**real**) [< *Mackay,* Scottish clan name] [Slang] the real person or thing, not a substitute
M.D. [L. *Medicinae Doctor*] Doctor of Medicine
me (mē) *pron.* [OE.] *objective case of* I
ME. Middle English
mead¹ (mēd) *n.* [OE. *meodu*] an alcoholic drink made of fermented honey and water
mead² (mēd) *n.* [OE. *mæd*] [Poet.] a meadow
mead·ow (med′ō) *n.* [OE. *mæd*] **1.** a piece of land where grass is grown for hay **2.** low, level grassland near a stream, etc.
mea·ger (mē′gər) *adj.* [< L. *macer,* lean] **1.** thin; lean **2.** poor; not full or rich; inadequate —**mea′ger·ly** *adv.*
meal¹ (mēl) *n.* [OE. *mæl*] **1.** a time of eating; lunch, dinner, etc. **2.** the food then served
meal² (mēl) *n.* [OE. *melu*] **1.** any edible grain, coarsely ground **2.** anything ground or powdered —**meal′y** *adj.* **-i·er, -i·est**
meal′y-mouthed′ (-mouthd′, -moutht′) *adj.* not simple or direct in speech; euphemistic

mean¹ (mēn) *vt.* **meant** (ment), **mean′ing** [OE. *mænan*] **1.** to have in mind; intend **2.** to intend to express **3.** to denote; signify —*vi.* to have a (specified) degree of importance, effect, etc. —**mean well** to have good intentions
mean² (mēn) *adj.* [OE. (ge)*mæne*] **1.** low, as in quality; paltry; poor **2.** shabby in appearance **3.** ignoble; petty **4.** stingy **5.** bad-tempered, nasty, disagreeable, etc. **6.** [Slang] *a)* difficult *b)* expert —**mean′ly** *adv.* —**mean′ness** *n.*
mean³ (mēn) *adj.* [< L. *medius,* middle] **1.** halfway between extremes **2.** average —*n.* **1.** what is between extremes **2.** *Math.* an average or other intermediate quantity
me·an·der (mē an′dər) *vi.* [< Gr. *Maiandros,* a winding river of Asia Minor] to wander; ramble
mean′ing *n.* what is meant; significance; import —**mean′ing·ful** *adj.* —**mean′ing·less** *adj.*
means (mēnz) *n.pl.* [< MEAN³, *n.*] **1.** [*with sing. or pl. v.*] that by which something is done or obtained **2.** resources or wealth —**by all means 1.** without fail **2.** certainly —**by means of** by using —**by no means** certainly not
meant (ment) *pt. & pp. of* MEAN¹
mean′time′ *adv.* **1.** in or during the intervening time **2.** at the same time —*n.* the intervening time Also **mean′while′**
mea·sles (mē′z′lz) *n.pl.* [*with sing. v.*] [ME. *maseles*] **1.** an acute, infectious, communicable virus disease, usually of children, characterized by small red spots on the skin, high fever, etc. **2.** any of various similar but milder diseases; esp., rubella
mea·sly (mēz′lē) *adj.* **-sli·er, -sli·est 1.** infected with measles **2.** [Colloq.] contemptibly small, meager, or inferior
meas·ure (mezh′ər) *n.* [< L. *metiri,* to measure] **1.** the extent, dimensions, capacity, etc. of anything **2.** the determining of any of these; measurement **3.** *a)* a unit of measurement *b)* any standard of valuation **4.** a system of measurement **5.** an instrument used for measuring **6.** a definite quantity measured **7.** a course of action **8.** a statute; law **9.** a rhythmical pattern or unit; specif., the notes and rests between two bars on a staff of music —*vt.* **-ured, -ur·ing 1.** to determine the extent, dimensions, etc. of **2.** to mark off by measuring **3.** to be a measure of —*vi.* **1.** to determine extent, dimensions, etc. **2.** to be of specified extent, dimensions, etc. —**beyond** (or **above**) **measure** exceedingly —**in a measure** to some extent —**meas′ur·a·ble** *adj.* —**meas′ure·less** *adj.*
meas′ure·ment *n.* **1.** a measuring or being measured **2.** extent or quantity determined by measuring **3.** a system of measuring
meat (mēt) *n.* [OE. *mete*] **1.** food: archaic except in **meat and drink 2.** animal, esp. mammal, flesh used as food **3.** the edible part, as of a nut **4.** gist —**meat′y** *adj.* **-i·er, -i·est**
meat′ball′ *n.* a small ball of ground meat
meat′pack′ing *n.* the slaughtering of animals and the preparation of the meat for market
me·chan·ic (mə kan′ik) *n.* [< Gr. *mēchanē,* a machine] a worker skilled in using tools or repairing machines
me·chan′i·cal *adj.* **1.** involving machinery or tools **2.** produced or operated by machinery **3.** of the science of mechanics **4.** lacking spirit or expression; machinelike
me·chan′ics *n.pl.* [*with sing. v.*] **1.** the science of motion and the action of forces on bodies **2.** knowledge of machinery **3.** the technical aspect
mech·a·nism (mek′ə niz′m) *n.* [see MECHANIC] **1.** the working parts of a machine **2.** any sys-

tem of interrelated parts **3.** any physical or mental process by which a result is produced —**mech′a·nis′tic** *adj.*

mech′a·nize (-nīz′) *vt.* **-nized′, -niz′ing 1.** to make mechanical **2.** to equip (an industry) with machinery or (an army, etc.) with tanks, self-propelled guns, etc. —**mech′a·ni·za′tion** *n.*

med·al (med′'l) *n.* [< LL. *medialis,* medial] a small, flat piece of metal with a design or inscription on it, made in commemoration, given as an award, or used as a religious token

med′al·ist (-ist) *n.* one awarded a medal

me·dal·lion (mə dal′yən) *n.* [< Fr.: see MEDAL] **1.** a large medal **2.** a design, portrait, etc. shaped like a medal

med·dle (med′'l) *vi.* **-dled, -dling** [< L. *miscere,* to mix] to interfere in another's affairs —**med′-dler** *n.* —**med′dle·some** (-səm) *adj.*

me·di·a (mē′dē ə) *n. alt. pl.* of MEDIUM: see MEDIUM (*n.* 3)

me·di·al (mē′dē əl) *adj.* [< L. *medius,* middle] **1.** intermediate; middle **2.** average

me·di·an (mē′dē ən) *adj.* [see prec.] **1.** intermediate; middle **2.** designating the middle number in a series —*n.* a median number, point, line, etc.

me·di·ate (mē′dē āt′) *vi.* **-at′ed, -at′ing** [see MEDIAL] **1.** to be in an intermediate position **2.** to be an intermediary —*vt.* to settle (a dispute, etc.) by intervention —**me′di·a′tion** *n.* —**me′di·a′tor** *n.*

med·ic (med′ik) *n.* [L. *medicus*] [Colloq.] **1.** a physician or surgeon **2.** a member of a military medical corps

Med·i·caid (med′i kād′) *n.* [*also* m-] a State and Federal public health plan paying certain medical and hospital expenses of persons having a low income or no income

med·i·cal (med′i k'l) *adj.* of or involving the practice or study of medicine

Med·i·care (med′i ker′) *n.* [*also* m-] a Federal health program paying certain medical and hospital expenses esp. of the aged

med·i·cate (med′ə kāt′) *vt.* **-cat′ed, -cat′ing** [< L. *medicari,* heal] to treat with medicine — **med′i·ca′tion** *n.*

me·dic·i·nal (mə dis′'n 'l) *adj.* of, or having the properties, of medicine

med·i·cine (med′ə s'n) *n.* [< L. *medicus,* physician] **1.** the science and art of treating and preventing disease **2.** any substance, as a drug, used in treating disease, relieving pain, etc.

medicine man among N. American Indians, etc., a man supposed to have supernatural powers to cure disease and control spirits

med·i·co (med′i kō′) *n., pl.* **-cos′** [It.: see MEDICINE] [Colloq.] **1.** a doctor **2.** a medical student

me·di·e·val (mē′dē ē′v'l) *adj.* [< L. *medius,* middle + *aevum,* age] of, like, or typical of the Middle Ages —**me′di·e′val·ly** *adv.*

me·di·o·cre (mē′dē ō′kər) *adj.* [< Fr. < L. *medius,* middle + *ocris,* a peak] **1.** of middle quality; ordinary. **2.** not good enough; inferior —**me′di·oc′ri·ty** (-äk′rə tē) *n., pl.* **-ties**

med·i·tate (med′ə tāt′) *vt.* **-tat′ed, -tat′ing** [< L. *meditari*] to plan or intend —*vi.* to think deeply —**med′i·ta′tion** *n.* —**med′i·ta′tive** *adj.*

me·di·um (mē′dē əm) *n., pl.* **-di·ums:** also (except sense 5), and for sense 3 usually, **-di·a** (-ə) [L. < *medius,* middle] **1.** *a*) something intermediate *b*) a middle state or degree; mean **2.** an intervening thing through which a force acts **3.** any means, agency, etc.; specif., a means of communication, with advertising, directed toward the public: in this sense a sin-gular form **media** (*pl.* **medias**) is sometimes used **4.** a surrounding substance or environment **5.** one through whom communications are supposedly sent from the dead —*adj.* intermediate in quality, degree, amount, etc.

med·ley (med′lē) *n., pl.* **-leys** [see MEDDLE] **1.** a mixture of dissimilar things **2.** a musical piece made up of tunes or passages from various works

me·dul·la (mi dul′ə) *n., pl.* **-las, -lae** (-ē) [L., marrow] **1.** the medulla oblongata **2.** the inner substance of an organ

medulla ob·lon·ga·ta (äb′lôŋ gät′ə) the lowest part of the brain

meek (mēk) *adj.* [< ON. *miukr,* gentle] **1.** patient and mild **2.** too submissive

meer·schaum (mir′shəm, -shôm) *n.* [G. < *meer,* sea + *schaum,* foam] **1.** a white, claylike mineral used for tobacco pipes **2.** a pipe made of this

meet[1] (mēt) *vt.* **met, meet′ing** [OE. *metan*] **1.** to come upon; esp., to come face to face with **2.** to be present at the arrival of [*to meet a bus*] **3.** to come into contact with **4.** to be introduced to **5.** to contend with **6.** to be perceived by (the eye, ear, etc.) **7.** *a*) to satisfy (a demand, etc.) *b*) to pay (a bill, etc.) —*vi.* **1.** to come together, into contact, etc. **2.** to be introduced —*n.* a coming together as for a sports event —**meet (up) with 1.** to experience **2.** to receive

meet[2] (mēt) *adj.* [OE. (*ge*)*mæte*] [Now Rare] suitable; proper; fit

meet′ing *n.* **1.** a coming together **2.** a gathering; assembly **3.** a junction

mega- [Gr. < *megas,* great] *a combining form meaning:* **1.** large, powerful **2.** a million (of)

meg·a·hertz (meg′ə hurts′) *n., pl.* **-hertz′** [MEGA- + HERTZ] one million hertz: formerly **meg′a·cy′cle** (-sī′k'l)

meg·a·lo·ma·ni·a (meg′ə lō mā′nē ə) *n.* [< Gr. *megas,* large + -MANIA] a mental disorder characterized by delusions of grandeur, power, etc.

meg·a·lop·o·lis (meg′ə läp′ə ləs) *n.* [Gr., great city] a vast, populous, continuously urban area

meg·a·phone (meg′ə fōn′) *n.* [MEGA- + -PHONE] a funnel-shaped device to amplify and direct the voice

meg′a·ton′ (-tun′) *n.* [MEGA- + TON] the explosive force of a million tons of TNT

mel·a·mine (mel′ə mēn′) *n.* [G. *melamin*] a white crystalline compound used to make synthetic resins

mel·an·cho·li·a (mel′ən kō′lē ə) *n.* a mental disorder characterized by extreme depression, brooding, etc.

mel·an·chol·y (mel′ən käl′ē) *n.* [< Gr. *melas,* black + *cholē,* bile] sadness and depression of spirits —*adj.* **1.** sad and depressed **2.** causing sadness

Mel·a·ne·sian (mel′ə nē′zhən) *adj.* of Melanesia, its people, their language, etc.

mé·lange (mā länzh′, -länj′) *n.* [Fr. < *mêler,* to mix] a mixture or medley

mel·a·nin (mel′ə nin) *n.* [< Gr. *melas,* black] a brownish-black pigment found in skin, hair, etc.

Mel·ba toast (mel′bə) [< Nellie *Melba* (1861-1931), Australian soprano] [*also* m-] thin, dry toast

meld (meld) *vt., vi.* [G. *melden,* announce] *Card Games* to declare (a card combination), esp. by putting the cards face up on the table —*n.* **1.** a melding **2.** a card combination melded

me·lee, mê·lée (mā′lā, mā lā′) *n.* [Fr.] a confused hand-to-hand fight among a number of people

mel·io·rate (mēl′yə rāt′) *vt., vi.* -rat′ed, -rat′ing [< L. *melior*, better] to make or become better —mel′io·ra′tion *n.*

mel·lif·lu·ous (mə lif′loo wəs) *adj.* [< L. *mel*, honey + *fluere*, to flow] sounding sweet and smooth: also **mel·lif′lu·ent**

mel·low (mel′ō) *adj.* [prob. < OE. *melu*, MEAL²] 1. soft, sweet, etc. because ripe: said of fruit 2. full-flavored: said as of wine 3. rich, pure, etc.: said as of sound or light 4. grown gentle and understanding —*vt., vi.* to make or become mellow

me·lo′di·ous (-lō′dē əs) *adj.* 1. containing or producing melody 2. tuneful

mel·o·dra·ma (mel′ə drä′mə, -dram′ə) *n.* [< Fr. < Gr. *melos*, song + *drama*, drama] a shallow drama with stereotyped characters, exaggerated emotions, etc. —mel′o·dra·mat′ic (-drə mat′ik) *adj.*

mel·o·dy (mel′ə dē) *n., pl.* -dies [< Gr. *melos*, song + *aeidein*, sing] 1. a sequence of pleasing sounds 2. *a*) a tune, song, etc. *b*) the leading part in a harmonic composition —me·lod·ic (mə läd′ik) *adj.*

mel·on (mel′ən) *n.* [< Gr. *mēlon*, apple] the large, juicy, many-seeded fruit of certain trailing plants of the gourd family, as the cantaloupe

melt (melt) *vt., vi.* [OE. *m(i)eltan*] 1. to change from a solid to a liquid state, generally by heat 2. to dissolve 3. to disappear or make disappear gradually 4. to merge; blend 5. to soften

melting pot a place where immigrants of different nationalities and races are assimilated

mem·ber (mem′bər) *n.* [< L. *membrum*] 1. a limb or other part of a person, animal, or plant 2. a distinct part of a whole 3. one of the individuals belonging to a group

mem′ber·ship′ *n.* 1. the state of being a member 2. the members of a group 3. the total of these

mem·brane (mem′brān) *n.* [< L. *membrum*, member] a thin, soft layer of animal or plant tissue, covering or lining an organ or part — **mem′bra·nous** (-brə nəs) *adj.*

me·men·to (mə men′tō) *n., pl.* -tos, -toes [< L. *meminisse*, remember] a souvenir or other reminder

mem·o (mem′ō) *n., pl.* -os short for MEMORANDUM

mem·oirs (mem′wärz) *n.pl.* [< Fr. < L. *memoria*, memory] 1. an autobiography 2. a record of events that is based on the writer's personal knowledge

mem·o·ra·bil·i·a (mem′ər ə bil′ē ə) *n.pl.* [L.] noteworthy things remembered or collected

mem·o·ra·ble (mem′ər ə b′l) *adj.* worth remembering; notable —mem′o·ra·bly *adv.*

mem·o·ran·dum (mem′ə ran′dəm) *n., pl.* -dums, -da (-də) [L.] 1. a note written as a reminder 2. an informal written communication, as within an office

me·mo·ri·al (mə môr′ē əl) *adj.* [see MEMORY] serving as a remembrance —*n.* anything meant to help people remember a person, event, etc., as a monument —me·mo′ri·al·ize′ (-īz′) *vt.* —·ized′, -iz′ing

Memorial Day a legal holiday in the U.S. (the last Monday in May in most States) in memory of the dead servicemen of all wars

mem·o·rize (mem′ə rīz′) *vt.* -rized′, -riz′ing to commit to memory

mem·o·ry (mem′ər ē) *n., pl.* -ries [< L. *memor*, mindful] 1. the power or act of remembering

2. all that one remembers 3. something remembered 4. the period over which remembering extends 5. commemoration 6. reputation after death

men (men) *n. pl. of* MAN

men·ace (men′is) *n.* [< L. *minari*, threaten] a threat or danger —*vt., vi.* -aced, -ac·ing to threaten —men′ac·ing·ly *adv.*

mé·nage, me·nage (mā näzh′, mə-) *n.* [Fr. < L. *mansio*, a dwelling] a household

me·nag·er·ie (mə naj′ər ē) *n.* [< Fr.: see prec.] a collection of wild animals kept as in cages for exhibition

mend (mend) *vt.* [see AMEND] 1. to repair; fix 2. to reform —*vi.* 1. to improve, esp. in health 2. to heal, as a fracture —*n.* 1. a mending 2. a mended place —on the mend improving

men·da·cious (men dā′shəs) *adj.* [< L. *mendax*] untruthful —men·dac′i·ty (-das′ə tē) *n., pl.* -ties

men·di·cant (men′di kənt) *adj.* [< L. *mendicare*, beg] begging —*n.* 1. a beggar 2. a mendicant friar —men′di·can·cy *n.*

men′folk′, men′folks′ *n.pl.* [Dial. or Colloq.] men

me·ni·al (mē′nē əl) *adj.* [< L. *mansio*, a dwelling] 1. of or fit for servants 2. servile; low —*n.* 1. a domestic servant 2. a servile person — me′ni·al·ly *adv.*

me·nin·ges (mə nin′jēz) *n.pl.* [< Gr. *mēninx*, membrane] the three membranes enveloping the brain and the spinal cord

men·in·gi·tis (men′in jīt′is) *n.* inflammation of the meninges

Men·non·ite (men′ə nīt′) *n.* [< *Menno* Simons (1496?–1561?), a leader] a member of an evangelical Christian sect living and dressing plainly and rejecting military service, oath-taking, etc.

men·o·pause (men′ə pôz′) *n.* [< Gr. *mēn*, month + *pauein*, to end] the permanent cessation of menstruation

men·o·rah (mə nō′rə, -nôr′ə) *n.* [Heb., lamp stand] *Judaism* a candelabrum with seven (or nine) branches

men·ses (men′sēz) *n.pl.* [L., months] the periodic flow, usually monthly, of blood from the uterus

men·stru·ate (men′stroo wāt′, -strāt) *vi.* -at′ed, -at′ing [< L. *mensis*, month] to have a discharge of the menses —men′stru·al (-stroo wəl, -strəl) *adj.* —men′stru·a′tion *n.*

men·su·ra·tion (men′shə rā′shən, -sə-) *n.* [< L. *mensura*, a measure] a measuring —men′sur·a·ble *adj.*

-ment [< L. *-mentum*] a suffix meaning: 1. result [*improvement*] 2. means [*adornment*] 3. act, process [*movement*] 4. state of being [*disappointment*]

men·tal (men′t′l) *adj.* [< L. *mens*, the mind] 1. of, for, by, or in the mind 2. of or for the mentally ill —men′tal·ly *adv.*

men·tal·i·ty (men tal′ə tē) *n., pl.* -ties mental capacity, power, or activity

mental retardation congenitally low intelligence

men·thol (men′thôl, -thôl) *n.* [G. < L. *mentha*, MINT²] a white, waxy, pungent, crystalline alcohol from oil of peppermint, used as in medicine and cosmetics —men′tho·lat′ed (-thə lāt′id) *adj.*

men·tion (men′shən) *n.* [< L. *mens*, the mind] 1. a brief reference 2. a citing for honor —*vt.* to refer to briefly

men·tor (men′tər, -tôr) *n.* [< *Mentor*, friend of Odysseus] 1. a wise, loyal adviser 2. a teacher

men·u (men′yoo) *n., pl.* -us [Fr. < L. *minutus*,

small] a detailed list of the foods served at a meal

me·ow, me·ou (mē ou′) *n.* [echoic] the characteristic vocal sound of a cat —*vi.* to make this sound

mer·can·tile (mur′kən til, -tīl′) *adj.* [< Fr. < It. < L. *merx,* wares] of merchants or trade; commercial

mer·ce·nar·y (mur′sə ner′ē) *adj.* [< L. *merces,* wages] working or done only for payment —*n., pl.* **-ies** a soldier serving for pay in a foreign army

mer·cer (mur′sər) *n.* [< L. *merx,* wares] [Brit.] a dealer in textiles

mer·cer·ize (mur′sə rīz′) *vt.* **-ized′, -iz′ing** [< J. *Mercer,* 19th-c. Eng. calico dealer] to treat (cotton thread or fabric) with a solution of caustic soda to strengthen it, give it a silky luster, etc.

mer·chan·dise (mur′chən dīz′, -dīs′) *n.* [see MERCHANT] things bought and sold; goods; wares —*vt., vi.* (-dīz′) **-dised′, -dis′ing 1.** to buy and sell **2.** to promote the sale of (a product)

mer·chant (mur′chənt) *n.* [< L. *merx,* wares] **1.** one whose business is the buying and selling of goods **2.** a dealer at retail; storekeeper — *adj.* mercantile

mer′chant·man (-mən) *n., pl.* **-men** a merchant ship

merchant marine all the ships of a nation that are used in commerce

‡**mer·ci** (mer sē′) *interj.* [Fr.] thank you

mer·ci·ful (mur′si fəl) *adj.* having or showing mercy —**mer′ci·ful·ly** *adv.*

mer′ci·less *adj.* without mercy; pitiless

mer·cu·ri·al (mər kyoor′ē əl) *adj.* **1.** of mercury **2.** quick, changeable, fickle, etc.

Mer·cu·ro·chrome (mər kyoor′ə krōm′) [see MERCURY & -CHROME] *a trademark for* a red solution of a compound of mercury, used as an antiseptic

Mer·cu·ry (mur′kyoo rē) **1.** *Rom. Myth.* a god, the messenger of the other gods **2.** the smallest planet in the solar system: see PLANET —*n.* [m-] a heavy, silver-white metallic chemical element, liquid at ordinary temperatures, used in thermometers, dentistry, etc.: symbol, Hg

mer·cy (mur′sē) *n., pl.* **-cies** [< L. *merces,* payment] **1.** compassion or restraint with regard to the treatment of offenders, enemies, etc. **2.** a disposition to be kind or to forgive **3.** kind or compassionate treatment **4.** a thing to be grateful for —**at the mercy of** in the power of

mercy killing *same as* EUTHANASIA

mere (mir) *adj. superl.* **mer′est** [< L. *merus,* pure] being only or simply (what is specified)

mere′ly *adv.* only; simply; just

mer·e·tri·cious (mer′ə trish′əs) *adj.* [< L. *meretrix,* a prostitute] **1.** alluring but tawdry **2.** specious

mer·gan·ser (mər gan′sər) *n.* [< L. *mergus,* diver + *anser,* goose] a large, fish-eating, diving duck

merge (murj) *vi., vt.* **merged, merg′ing** [< L. *mergere,* to dip] **1.** to lose or make lose identity as by absorption **2.** to unite

merg′er *n.* a merging; specif., a combining of several companies into one

me·rid·i·an (mə rid′ē ən) *n.* [< L. *meridies,* noon] **1.** a zenith **2.** *a*) a great circle of the earth passing through the geographical poles and any given point on the earth's surface *b*) any of the lines of longitude

me·ringue (mə raŋ′) *n.* [Fr.] egg whites mixed

with sugar and beaten stiff, spread over a pie, etc.

me·ri·no (mə rē′nō) *n., pl.* **-nos** [Sp.] **1.** one of a breed of sheep with long, fine wool **2.** the wool **3.** a soft yarn or cloth of such wool

mer·it (mer′it) *n.* [< L. *mereri,* deserve] **1.** worth; value; excellence **2.** something deserving reward, praise, etc. **3.** [*pl.*] intrinsic rightness or wrongness —*vt.* to deserve

mer′i·to′ri·ous (-tôr′ē əs) *adj.* meriting reward, praise, etc.

Mer·lin (mur′lin) *Arthurian Legend* a magician and seer, helper of King Arthur

mer·maid (mur′mād′) *n.* [OE. *mere,* sea + MAID] an imaginary sea creature, half woman and half fish

mer·ry (mer′ē) *adj.* **-ri·er, -ri·est** [OE. *myrge*] full of fun and laughter —**make merry** to have fun —**mer′ri·ly** *adv.* —**mer′ri·ment** *n.*

mer′ry-go-round′ *n.* **1.** an amusement ride consisting of a revolving circular platform with artificial animals, usually moving up and down **2.** a whirl, as of work

mer′ry·mak′ing *n.* a making merry; joyous festivity —**mer′ry·mak′er** *n.*

me·sa (mā′sə) *n.* [Sp. < L. *mensa,* a table] a small, high plateau with steep sides

mes·cal (mes kal′) *n.* [Sp. *mezcal* < MexInd. *mexcalli*] a small cactus with buttonlike tops (**mescal buttons**) causing hallucinations when chewed

mes·ca·line (mes′kə lēn′, -lin) *n.* [< prec.] a psychedelic drug obtained from mescal buttons

mes·dames (mā däm′) *n. pl. of* MADAME, MADAM (sense 1), *or* MRS.

mesde·moi·selles (mād mwä zel′) *n. Fr. pl. of* MADEMOISELLE

mesh (mesh) *n.* [prob. < MDu. *maesche*] **1.** any of the open spaces of a net, screen, etc. **2.** a net or network **3.** a netlike material, as for stockings —*vt., vi.* **1.** to catch or be caught in or as in a net **2.** to fit together, as gears; interlock —**In mesh** with the gear teeth engaged

mes·mer·ize (mez′mər īz′, mes′-) *vt.* **-ized′, -iz′ing** [< Fr. < F. A. *Mesmer,* 18th-c. G. physician] to hypnotize or spellbind —**mes′-mer·ism** *n.* —**mes′mer·ist** *n.*

mes·quite, mes·quit (mes kēt′) *n.* [< MexInd. *mizquitl*] a thorny tree or shrub of the SW U.S. and Mexico

mess (mes) *n.* [< L. *missus,* course (at a meal)] **1.** a serving, as of porridge **2.** *a*) a group of people who regularly eat together, as in the army *b*) the meal they eat **3.** a jumble **4.** a state of trouble, confusion, untidiness, etc. —*vt.* to make dirty or untidy; also, to bungle; botch: often with *up* —*vi.* **1.** to eat as one of a mess **2.** to make a mess **3.** to putter or meddle (*in, with, around,* etc.) —**messy** *adj.* **-i·er, -i·est** —**mess′i·ness** *n.*

mes·sage (mes′ij) *n.* [< L. *mittere,* send] **1.** a communication sent between persons **2.** the chief idea that an artist, writer, etc. seeks to communicate in a work

mes·sen·ger (mes′′n jər) *n.* a person who carries messages or goes on errands

mess hall a room or building where soldiers, etc. regularly have meals

Mes·si·ah (mə sī′ə) [< Heb. *māshīah,* anointed] **1.** *Judaism* the expected deliverer of the Jews **2.** *Christianity* Jesus —**Mes·si·an·ic** (mes′ē an′ik) *adj.*

mes·sieurs (mes′ərz; Fr. mā syö′) *n. pl. of* MONSIEUR

mes·ti·zo (mes tē′zō) *n., pl.* **-zos, -zoes** [Sp. <

L. *miscere*, to mix] a person of mixed parentage, esp. Spanish and American Indian

met (met) *pt. & pp. of* MEET[1]

meta- [< Gr. *meta*, after] *a prefix meaning:* **1.** changed *[metamorphosis]* **2.** after, beyond, higher *[metaphysics]*

me·tab·o·lism (mə tab'ə liz'm) *n.* [< Gr. *meta*, beyond + *ballein*, to throw] the processes in organisms by which protoplasm is formed from food and broken down into waste matter, with the release of energy —**met·a·bol·ic** (met'ə bäl'ik) *adj.* —**me·tab'o·lize'** (-līz') *vt., vi.* **-lized', -liz'ing**

met·al (met''l) *n.* [< L. < Gr. *metallon*, metal, mine] **1.** *a)* any of a class of chemical elements, as iron, gold, copper, etc., that have luster, are malleable, can conduct heat and electricity, etc. *b)* an alloy of such elements, as brass, bronze, etc. **2.** anything consisting of metal **3.** material; stuff —**me·tal·lic** (mə tal'ik) *adj.*

met·al·lur·gy (met''l ur'jē) *n.* [< Gr. *metallon*, metal, mine + *ergon*, work] the science of separating metals from their ores and preparing them for use by smelting, refining, etc. —**met'al·lur'gi·cal, met'al·lur'gic** *adj.* —**met'al·lur'gist** *n.*

met·a·mor·phose (met'ə môr'fōz, -fōs) *vt., vi.* **-phosed, -phos·ing** to change in form or nature

met·a·mor·pho·sis (met'ə môr'fə sis, -môr fō'-) *n., pl.* **-ses'** (-sēz') [< Gr. *meta*, over + *morphē*, form] **1.** a change of form as, in myths, by magic **2.** the physical change undergone by some animals, as of tadpole to frog **3.** any marked change, as in character —**met'a·mor'phic** *adj.*

met·a·phor (met'ə fôr', -fər) *n.* [< Fr. < Gr. *meta*, over + *pherein*, to bear] a figure of speech in which one thing is spoken of as if it were another (Ex.: the curtain of night) —**met'a·phor'i·cal** *adj.*

met·a·phys·i·cal (met'ə fiz'i k'l) *adj.* **1.** of, or having the nature of, metaphysics **2.** very abstract or subtle **3.** supernatural

met'a·phys'ics (-iks) *n.pl.* [*with sing. v.*] [< Gr. *meta* (ta) *physika*, after (the) *Physics* (in Aristotle's work)] **1.** the branch of philosophy that seeks to explain the nature of being and reality **2.** speculative philosophy in general

me·tas·ta·sis (mə tas'tə sis) *n., pl.* **-ses'** (-sēz') [< Gr. *meta*, after + *histanai*, to place] the transfer, as of malignant cells, from one part of the body to another, as through the bloodstream —**me·tas'ta·size'** (-sīz') *vi.* **-sized', -siz'ing**

met·a·tar·sus (met'ə tär'səs) *n., pl.* **-si** (-sī) [< Gr. *meta*, over + *tarsos*, flat of the foot] the part of the foot between the ankle and the toes —**met'a·tar'sal** *adj., n.*

me·tath·e·sis (mə tath'ə sis) *n., pl.* **-ses'** (-sēz') [< Gr. *meta*, over + *tithenai*, to place] transposition, specif. of letters or sounds in a word

mete (mēt) *vt.* **met'ed, met'ing** [OE. *metan*] to allot; portion (*out*)

me·tem·psy·cho·sis (mi temp'si kō'sis, met'əm sī-) *n., pl.* **-ses** (-sēz) [< Gr. *meta*, over + *en*, in + *psychē*, soul] transmigration of souls

me·te·or (mēt'ē ər) *n.* [< Gr. *meta*, beyond + *eōra*, a hovering] **1.** the streak of light, etc. occurring when a meteoroid enters the earth's atmosphere **2.** loosely, a meteoroid or meteorite

me·te·or·ic (mēt'ē ôr'ik, -är'-) *adj.* **1.** of a meteor **2.** like a meteor in brilliance and swiftness

me·te·or·ite (mēt'ē ə rīt') *n.* a stone or metal mass remaining from a meteoroid fallen to earth

me'te·or·oid' (-roid') *n.* a small, solid body traveling through space, seen as a meteor when it enters the earth's atmosphere

me·te·or·ol·o·gy (mēt'ē ə räl'ə jē) *n.* [see METEOR & -LOGY] the science of the atmosphere and its phenomena; study of weather and climate —**me'te·or·o·log'i·cal** (-ər ə läj'i k'l) *adj.* —**me'te·or·ol'o·gist** *n.*

me·ter[1] (mēt'ər) *n.* [< Gr. *metron*, measure] **1.** rhythmic pattern in verse; measured arrangement of syllables according to stress **2.** rhythmic pattern in music **3.** [Fr.] the basic unit of length in the metric system, equal to 39.37 in.

me·ter[2] (mēt'ər) *n.* [< words ending in -METER] **1.** an apparatus for measuring and recording the quantity or rate of flow of gas, water, etc. passing through it **2.** *same as* PARKING METER

-meter [< Gr. *metron*, measure] *a suffix meaning:* **1.** a device for measuring (a specified thing) *[barometer]* **2.** having (a specified number of) metrical feet *[pentameter]*

meth·a·done (meth'ə dōn') *n.* [< its chemical name] a synthetic narcotic drug, less habit-forming than morphine, used in treating morphine addicts

meth·ane (meth'ān) *n.* [< METHYL] a colorless, odorless, flammable gas present in marsh gas, firedamp, and natural gas

me·thinks (mi thiŋks') *v.impersonal pt.* **me·thought'** [< OE. *me*, to me + *thyncth*, it seems] [Archaic] it seems to me

meth·od (meth'əd) *n.* [< Fr. < Gr. *meta*, after + *hodos*, a way] **1.** a way of doing anything, esp. an orderly way; process **2.** system in doing things or handling ideas

me·thod·i·cal (mə thäd'i k'l) *adj.* characterized by method; orderly; systematic: also **me·thod'ic** —**me·thod'i·cal·ly** *adv.*

Meth·od·ist (meth'ə dist) *n.* a member of a Protestant denomination developed from John Wesley's teachings —**Meth'od·ism** *n.*

meth·od·ol·o·gy (meth'ə däl'ə jē) *n., pl.* **-gies** a system of methods, as in a science

Me·thu·se·lah (mə thōō'zə lə) *Bible* a patriarch who lived 969 years

meth·yl (meth'əl) *n.* [< Fr. < Gr. *methy*, wine + *hylē*, wood] a hydrocarbon radical found in wood alcohol

me·tic·u·lous (mə tik'yoo ləs) *adj.* [< L. *metus*, fear] very careful or too careful about details; scrupulous or finicky

mé·tier (mā tyā') *n.* [Fr., a trade] work that one is particularly suited for

me·tre (mē'tər) *n. Brit. sp. of* METER[1]

met·ric (met'rik) *adj.* **1.** *same as* METRICAL **2.** of or in the metric system: see METRIC SYSTEM

met'ri·cal *adj.* **1.** of or composed in meter or verse **2.** of or used in measurement

met·ri·ca·tion (met'rə kā'shən) *n.* a changing over to the metric system

metric system a decimal system of weights and measures whose basic units are the gram, the meter, and the liter: see TABLES OF WEIGHTS AND MEASURES in Supplements

metric ton a measure of weight equal to 1,000 kilograms or 2,204.62 pounds

met·ro·nome (met'rə nōm') *n.* [< Gr. *metron*, measure + *nomos*, law] a device that can be set to beat time at different rates of speed, as for piano practice

me·trop·o·lis (mə träp''l is) *n., pl.* **-lis·es** [< Gr. *mētēr*, mother + *polis*, city] **1.** the main city, often the capital, of a country, state, etc.

2. any large or important city —**met·ro·pol·i·tan** (met′rə päl′ə t'n) *adj.*

met·tle (met′'l) *n.* [var.. of METAL] spirit or courage —**on one's mettle** prepared to do one's best

met′tle·some (-səm) *adj.* full of mettle; spirited, brave, etc.

mew¹ (myōō) *vt.* [< L. *mutare*, to change] to confine: see also MEWS

mew² (myōō) *n.* [echoic] the characteristic vocal sound made by a cat —*vi.* to make this sound

mewl (myōōl) *vi.* [< MEW²] to cry weakly, like a baby; whimper —**mewl′er** *n.*

mews (myōōz) *n.pl.* [*usually with sing. v.*] [< MEW¹] [Chiefly Brit.] stables or carriage houses, now often made into dwellings, in a court or alley

Mex. 1. Mexican 2. Mexico

Mex·i·can (mek′si kən) *adj.* of Mexico, its people, etc. —*n.* a native or inhabitant of Mexico

mez·za·nine (mez′ə nēn′) *n.* [Fr. < It. *mezzano*, middle] 1. a low-ceilinged story between two main stories, often a balcony jutting out over the main floor 2. the lowest balcony section of a theater

mez·zo-so·pra·no (met′sō sə pran′ō, mez′ō-) *n., pl.* **-nos, -ni** (-nē) [It. < *mezzo*, medium + SOPRANO] a voice or singer between soprano and contralto

mfg. manufacturing

mfr. *pl.* **mfrs.** manufacturer

Mg *Chem.* magnesium

mg, mg. milligram; milligrams

Mgr. Manager

MHz, Mhz megahertz

mi (mē) *n.* [< ML.] *Music* the third tone of the diatonic scale

mi. 1. mile(s) 2. mill(s)

mi·as·ma (mī az′mə, mē-) *n., pl.* **-mas, -ma·ta** (-mə tə) [Gr., pollution] a vapor as from marshes, formerly thought poisonous

mi·ca (mī′kə) *n.* [L., a crumb] a mineral that crystallizes in thin, flexible, easily separated layers resistant to heat

mice (mīs) *n. pl.* of MOUSE

micro- [< Gr. *mikros*, small] *a combining form meaning:* 1. very small [*microfilm*] 2. enlarging [*microscope*] 3. microscopic [*microchemistry*] 4. one millionth [*microgram*]

mi·crobe (mī′krōb) *n.* [Fr. < Gr. *mikros*, small + *bios*, life] a microorganism, esp. one causing disease

mi·cro·bi·ol·o·gy (mī′krō bī äl′ə jē) *n.* the branch of biology that deals with microorganisms

mi·cro·cosm (mī′krə käz′m) *n.* [see MICRO- & COSMOS] an organism or organization regarded as a world in miniature

mi′cro·fiche′ (-fēsh′) *n.* [Fr. < *micro-*, MICRO- + *fiche*, small card] a film card containing many pages of greatly reduced microfilm copy

mi′cro·film′ *n.* film on which documents, etc. are photographed in a reduced size for convenience —*vt., vi.* to photograph on microfilm

mi′cro·groove′ *n.* a very narrow needle groove, as for a long-playing phonograph record

mi·crom·e·ter (mī kräm′ə tər) *n.* [< Fr.: see MICRO- & -METER] an instrument for measuring very small distances, angles, etc.

mi·cron (mī′krän) *n.* [< Gr. *mikros*, small] one millionth of a meter

mi·cro·or·gan·ism (mī′krō ôr′gə niz'm) *n.* any microscopic animal or vegetable organism; esp., any of the bacteria, etc.

mi·cro·phone (mī′krə fōn′) *n.* [MICRO- +

-PHONE] an instrument that converts the mechanical energy of sound waves into an electric signal, as for radio

mi′cro·scope′ (-skōp′) *n.* [see MICRO- & -SCOPE] an instrument using a combination of lenses to make very small objects, as microorganisms, look larger

mi′cro·scop′ic (-skäp′ik) *adj.* 1. so small as to be invisible or obscure except through a microscope; minute 2. of, with, or like a microscope —**mi′cro·scop′i·cal·ly** *adv.*

mi′cro·wave′ *n.* an electromagnetic wave between 300,000 megahertz and 300 megahertz in frequency

mid¹ (mid) *adj.* [OE. *midd-*] middle

mid² (mid) *prep.* [Poet.] amid: also **'mid**

mid- *a combining form meaning* middle or middle part of [*midweek*]

mid′air′ *n.* any point not in contact with the ground or other surface

Mi·das (mī′dəs) *Gr. Myth.* a king with power to turn everything he touched into gold

mid′day′ *n., adj.* noon

mid·dle (mid′'l) *adj.* [OE. *middel*] 1. halfway between two given points, times, etc. 2. in between; intermediate 3. [M-] in a stage of language development intermediate between *Old* and *Modern* [*Middle* English] —*n.* 1. a point or part halfway between the ends; middle point, time, etc. 2. the middle part of the body; waist

middle age the time of life when one is neither young nor old —**mid′dle-aged′** *adj.*

Middle Ages the period of European history between ancient times and modern times, 476 A.D.–c.1450 A.D.

mid′dle·brow′ (-brou′) *n.* [Colloq.] one regarded as having conventional, middle-class tastes or opinions

middle class the social class between the aristocracy or very wealthy and the lower working class —**mid′dle-class′** *adj.*

middle ear the part of the ear including the eardrum and a cavity containing three small bones; tympanum

Middle English the English language between c.1100 and c.1500

mid′dle·man′ *n., pl.* **-men′** 1. a merchant who buys from a producer and sells at wholesale or retail 2. a go-between

mid′dle·most′ *adj. same as* MIDMOST

mid′dle-of-the-road′ *adj.* avoiding extremes, esp. of the political left or right

mid′dle·weight′ *n.* a boxer or wrestler between a welterweight and a light heavyweight (in boxing, 148–160 lbs.)

mid·dling (mid′liŋ) *adj.* of middle size, quality, state, etc.; medium —*adv.* [Colloq.] somewhat —**fair to middling** [Colloq.] moderately good or well

mid·dy (mid′ē) *n., pl.* **-dies** 1. [Colloq.] a midshipman 2. a girl's loose blouse with a sailor collar: in full **middy blouse**

midge (mij) *n.* [OE. *mycg*] a small, two-winged gnatlike insect

midg·et (mij′it) *n.* 1. a very small person 2. anything very small of its kind

mid·land (mid′lənd) *n.* the middle region of a country; interior —*adj.* in or of the midland; inland

mid′most′ *adj.* exactly in the middle, or nearest the middle

mid′night′ *n.* twelve o'clock at night —*adj.* of or at midnight

mid′point′ *n.* a point at or close to the middle or center

mid′riff (-rif) *n.* [< OE. *midd*, mid + *hrif*,

belly] **1.** *same as* DIAPHRAGM (sense 1) **2.** the middle part of the torso, between the abdomen and the chest

mid′ship′man (-ship′mən) *n., pl.* **-men** a student at the U.S. Naval Academy

midst[1] (midst) *n.* the middle; central part —**in our** (or **your, their) midst** among us (or you, them) —**in the midst of 1.** in the middle of **2.** during

midst[2] (midst) *prep.* [Poet.] in the middle of; amid

mid′stream′ *n.* the middle of a stream

mid′sum′mer *n.* **1.** the middle of summer **2.** the time of the summer solstice, about June 21 —*adj.* of, in, or like midsummer

mid′term′ *adj.* in the middle of the term —*n.* [Colloq.] a midterm examination

mid′way′ (-wā′) *n.* that part of a fair where sideshows, etc. are located —*adj., adv.* (also -wā′) in the middle

mid·wife (mid′wīf′) *n., pl.* **-wives′** [OE. *mid*, with + *wif*, wife] a woman who helps women in childbirth —**mid′wife′ry** (-wī′fə rē, -wīf′rē) *n.*

mid′win′ter *n.* **1.** the middle of winter **2.** the time of the winter solstice, about Dec. 22 —*adj.* of, in, or like midwinter

mid′year′ *adj.* in the middle of the year —*n.* [Colloq.] a midyear examination

mien (mēn) *n.* [< DEMEAN[2]] one's appearance, bearing, or manner

miff (mif) *vt.* [prob. echoic of cry of disgust] [Colloq.] to offend; displease

might[1] (mīt) *v.* [OE. *mihte*] **1.** *pt. of* MAY **2.** *an auxiliary generally equivalent to* MAY [it might rain]

might[2] (mīt) *n.* [OE. *miht*] great strength, force, or power

might′y *adj.* **-i-er, -i-est 1.** powerful; strong **2.** remarkably large, etc.; great —*adv.* [Colloq.] very —**might′i·ness** *n.*

mi·gnon·ette (min′yə net′) *n.* [< Fr. *mignon*, small] a plant with spikes of small, fragrant flowers

mi·graine (mī′grān) *n.* [Fr. < Gr. *hēmi-*, half + *kranion*, skull] an intense, periodic headache, usually limited to one side of the head

mi·grant (mī′grənt) *adj.* migrating —*n.* a person, bird, or animal that migrates

mi·grate (mī′grāt) *vi.* **-grat·ed, -grat·ing** [< L. *migrare*] **1.** to move from one country, etc. to another **2.** to move to another region with the change in seasons, as many birds **3.** to move from place to place to harvest seasonal crops —**mi·gra·to·ry** (mī′grə tôr′ē) *adj.*

mi·gra·tion (mī grā′shən) *n.* **1.** a migrating **2.** a group of people, birds, etc. migrating together

mi·ka·do (mi kä′dō) *n., pl.* **-dos** [Jpn. < *mi*, exalted + *kado*, gate] [*often* M-] the emperor of Japan: title no longer used

mike (mīk) *n.* [Colloq.] a microphone

mil (mil) *n.* [< L. *mille*, thousand] a unit of length, .001 inch

mil. 1. military **2.** militia

milch (milch) *adj.* [ME. *milche*] kept for milking [*milch* cows]

mild (mīld) *adj.* [OE. *milde*] **1.** gentle or moderate; not severe **2.** having a soft, pleasant flavor: said of tobacco, cheese, etc. —**mild′ly** *adv.* —**mild′ness** *n.*

mil·dew (mil′dōō′) *n.* [OE. *meledeaw*, lit., honeydew] a fungus that appears as a whitish, furry coating on plants or on damp cloth, paper, etc. —*vt., vi.* to affect or be affected with mildew

mile (mīl) *n.* [< L. *milia* (*passuum*), thousand (paces)] a unit of linear measure, equal to 5,280 ft.

mile·age (mīl′ij) *n.* **1.** an allowance per mile for traveling expenses **2.** total miles traveled **3.** rate per mile Also sp. **milage**

mile′post′ *n.* a signpost showing the distance in miles to or from a place

mil′er *n.* one who competes in mile races

mile′stone′ *n.* **1.** a stone set up as a milepost **2.** a significant event

mi·lieu (mēl yōō′) *n.* [Fr. < L. *medius*, middle + *locus*, a place] environment; esp., social setting

mil·i·tant (mil′i tənt) *adj.* [< L. *miles*, soldier] **1.** fighting **2.** ready to fight; aggressive in support of a cause —*n.* a militant person —**mil′i·tan·cy** *n.*

mil′i·ta·rism (-tər iz′m) *n.* **1.** military spirit **2.** a policy of aggressive military preparedness —**mil′i·ta·rist** *n.* —**mil′i·ta·ris′tic** *adj.*

mil′i·ta·rize (-tə rīz′) *vt.* **-rized′, -riz′ing** to equip and prepare for war

mil′i·tar·y (-ter′ē) *adj.* [< Fr. < L. *miles*, soldier] **1.** of, for, or by soldiers **2.** of, for, or fit for war **3.** of the army —**the military** armed forces

military police soldiers assigned to carry on police duties for the army

mil·i·tate (mil′ə tāt′) *vi.* **-tat·ed, -tat′ing** [< L. *militare*, be a soldier] to operate or work (*against*)

mi·li·tia (mə lish′ə) *n.* [< L. *miles*, soldier] an army composed of citizens called out in time of emergency —**mi·li′tia·man** (-mən) *n., pl.* **-men**

milk (milk) *n.* [OE. *meolc*] **1.** a white liquid secreted by the mammary glands of female mammals for suckling their young **2.** cow's milk **3.** any liquid like this [coconut *milk*] —*vt.* **1.** to squeeze milk from (a cow, goat, etc.) **2.** to extract (something), or extract something from, as if by milking [to *milk* a rich uncle for his money] —**milk′er** *n.*

milk′maid′ *n.* a girl or woman who milks cows or works in a dairy

milk′man′ *n., pl.* **-men′** a man who sells or delivers milk for a dairy

milk of magnesia a milky-white suspension of magnesium hydroxide in water, used as a laxative and antacid

milk′shake′ *n.* a drink of milk, flavoring, and ice cream, mixed until frothy

milk′sop′ (-säp′) *n.* a sissy

milk tooth any of the temporary, first teeth in a child or other young mammal

milk′weed′ *n.* a plant with a milky juice

milk′y *adj.* **-i-er, -i-est 1.** like milk; esp., white as milk **2.** of or containing milk

Milky Way a broad, faint band of light arching across the night sky, formed by billions of stars in our galaxy

mill[1] (mil) *n.* [< L. *mola*, millstone] **1.** a building with machinery for grinding grain into flour or meal **2.** any of various machines for grinding, crushing, cutting, etc. **3.** a factory [a steel *mill*] —*vt.* to grind, form, etc. by or in a mill —*vi.* to move (*around* or *about*) confusedly, as a crowd

mill[2] (mil) *n.* [< L. *millesimus*, thousandth] 1/10 of a cent: a money of account, used in taxation

mil·len·ni·um (mi len′ē əm) *n., pl.* **-ni·ums, -ni·a** (-ə) [< L. *mille*, thousand + *annus*, year] **1.** a period of 1,000 years **2.** *Theol.* the period of 1,000 years during which some believe Christ will reign on earth (with *the*): Rev. 20: 1–5 **3.** a period of great peace and happiness —**mil·len′ni·al** *adj.*

mil·ler (mil'ər) *n.* one who owns or operates a mill, esp. a flour mill

mil·let (mil'it) *n.* [< L. *milium*] **1.** a cereal grass whose grain is used for food in Europe and Asia **2.** any of several similar grasses used for forage

milli- [< L. *mille*, thousand] *a combining form meaning* one thousandth of (a specified unit)

mil·li·gram (mil'ə gram') *n.* [< Fr.] one thousandth of a gram: Brit. sp. **milligramme**

mil·li·me·ter (-mēt'ər) *n.* [< Fr.] one thousandth of a meter: Brit. sp. **millimetre**

mil·li·ner (mil'ə nər) *n.* [< *Milaner*, importer of dress wares from Milan] one who makes or sells women's hats

mil·li·ner·y (mil'ə ner'ē) *n.* **1.** women's hats **2.** the work of a milliner

mil·lion (mil'yən) *n., adj.* [< L. *mille*, thousand] a thousand thousands; 1,000,000 — **mil'lionth** *adj., n.*

mil'lion·aire' (-yə ner') *n.* [< Fr.] a person worth at least a million dollars, pounds, etc.

mill'stone' *n.* **1.** either of a pair of flat, round stones between which grain or the like is ground **2.** a heavy burden

milt (milt) *n.* [prob. < Scand.] the sex glands or sperm of male fishes

mime (mīm) *n.* [< Gr. *mimos*] **1.** the representation of an action, character, mood, etc. by gestures, not words **2.** a mimic or pantomimist —*vt.* **mimed, mim'ing** to mimic or pantomime

mim·e·o·graph (mim'ē ə graf') *n.* [< Gr. *mimeomai*, I imitate] a machine for making copies of written or typewritten matter by means of a stencil —*vt.* to make (such copies) of (specified matter)

mim·ic (mim'ik) *adj.* [< Gr. *mimos*, a mime] **1.** imitative **2.** make-believe —*n.* an imitator; esp., an actor skilled in mimicry —*vt.* **-icked, -ick·ing 1.** to imitate in speech or action, often so as to ridicule **2.** to copy or resemble closely

mim'ic·ry *n., pl.* **-ries** the practice, art, or way of mimicking

mi·mo·sa (mi mō'sə) *n.* [see MIME] a tree, shrub, or herb of warm regions, with spikes of small white or pink flowers

min. 1. minimum **2.** minute(s)

min·a·ret (min'ə ret') *n.* [Fr. < Ar. *manārah*, lighthouse] a high tower on a mosque

min·a·to·ry (min'ə tôr'ē) *adj.* [< L. *minari*, threaten] menacing; threatening

mince (mins) *vt.* **minced, minc'ing** [< L. *minutus*, small] **1.** to cut up into small bits; hash **2.** to express or do with affected daintiness **3.** to lessen the force of [to *mince* no words] —*vi.* to speak, act, or walk with affected daintiness

mince'meat' *n.* a mixture of chopped apples, raisins, suet, spices, etc., and sometimes meat, used as a filling for pie (**mince pie**)

mind (mīnd) *n.* [OE. (*ge*)*mynd*] **1.** memory [to bring to *mind*] **2.** opinion [to change one's *mind*] **3.** the seat of consciousness, where thinking, feeling, etc. take place **4.** intellect **5.** *same as* PSYCHE (*n.* 2) **6.** sanity —*vt.* **1.** to pay attention to; heed **2.** to obey **3.** to take care of [*mind* the baby] **4.** to be careful about [*mind* the stairs] **5.** to care about; object to [don't *mind* the noise] —*vi.* **1.** to pay attention **2.** to be obedient **3.** to be careful **4.** to care; object —**bear** (or **keep**) **in mind** to remember —**make up one's mind** to reach a decision —**out of one's mind 1.** insane **2.** frantic (*with* worry, grief, etc.)

mind'ed *adj.* **1.** having a (specified kind of) mind [high-*minded*] **2.** inclined [*minded* to go]

mind'ful *adj.* having in mind; aware or careful (*of*) —**mind'ful·ly** *adv.*

mind'less *adj.* **1.** without intelligence **2.** heedless (*of*) —**mind'less·ly** *adv.*

mind reader one who professes to be able to perceive another's thoughts

mind's eye the imagination

mine¹ (mīn) *pron.* [OE. *min*] that or those belonging to me [*mine* are better]

mine² (mīn) *n.* [< MFr. < ? Celt.] **1.** a large excavation made in the earth, from which to extract ores, coal, etc. **2.** a deposit of ore, coal, etc. **3.** any great source of supply **4.** *Mil. a)* a tunnel dug under an enemy's fort, etc., in which an explosive is placed *b)* an explosive hidden underground or in the sea, for destroying enemy troops, ships, etc. —*vt., vi.* **mined, min'ing 1.** to dig (ores, etc.) from (the earth) **2.** to dig or lay military mines in or under (a place) **3.** to undermine

min'er *n.* one whose work is digging coal, ore, etc. in a mine

min·er·al (min'ər əl) *n.* [< ML. *minera*, a mine] **1.** an inorganic substance found naturally in the earth, as ore, rock, etc. **2.** any substance neither vegetable nor animal —*adj.* of or containing minerals

min·er·al·o·gy (min'ə räl'ə jē, -ral'-) *n.* the scientific study of minerals —**min'er·al'o·gist** *n.*

mineral oil a colorless, tasteless oil derived from petroleum and used as a laxative

mineral water water containing mineral salts or gases

Mi·ner·va (mi nur'və) the Roman goddess of wisdom, etc.

mi·ne·stro·ne (min'ə strō'nē) *n.* [It.] a thick vegetable soup in a meat broth

min·gle (miŋ'g'l) *vt.* **-gled, -gling** [< OE. *mengan*, to mix] to mix together; blend —*vi.* **1.** to become mixed or blended **2.** to join or unite with others

mini- [< MINI(ATURE)] *a combining form meaning* miniature, very small, very short

min·i·a·ture (min'ē ə chər, min'i chər) *n.* [It. < L. *miniare*, paint red] **1.** a very small painting, esp. a portrait **2.** a copy or model on a very small scale —*adj.* very small —**in miniature** on a very small scale

min'i·a·tur·ize' (-īz') *vt.* **-ized', -iz'ing** to make in a small and compact form —**min'i·a·tur'i·za'tion** *n.*

min·i·bus (min'ē bus') *n.* a very small bus

min·im (min'im) *n.* [< L. *minimus*, least] **1.** the smallest liquid measure, about a drop **2.** [Brit.] *Music* a half note

min'i·mize' (-mīz') *vt.* **-mized', -miz'ing** to reduce to or estimate at the minimum

min'i·mum (-məm) *n., pl.* **-mums, -ma** (-mə) [L., least] **1.** the smallest quantity, number, etc. possible or permissible **2.** the lowest degree or point reached or recorded —*adj.* smallest possible, permissible, or reached: also **min'i·mal**

min·ing (mī'niŋ) *n.* the process or work of removing ores, coal, etc. from a mine

min·ion (min'yən) *n.* [Fr. *mignon*, darling] **1.** a favorite, esp. one who is a servile follower: term of contempt **2.** a subordinate official

min·is·cule (min'ə skyōōl') *adj. erroneous sp. of* MINUSCULE

min·i·skirt (min'ē skurt') *n.* a very short skirt ending well above the knee

min·is·ter (min'is tər) *n.* [L., a servant] **1.** a person appointed to head a department of government **2.** a diplomat representing his government in a foreign nation **3.** one authorized to conduct religious services in a church; pastor —*vi.* **1.** to serve as a minister in a church **2.** to give help *(to)* **—min′is·te′ri·al** (-tir′ē əl) *adj.* **—min′is·trant** (-trənt) *adj., n.*

min′is·tra′tion (-trā′shən) *n.* the giving of help or care

min′is·try (-trē) *n., pl.* **-tries 1.** the act of ministering, or serving **2.** *a)* the office or function of a clergyman *b)* the clergy **3.** *a)* the department under a minister of government *b)* his term of office *c)* the ministers of a government as a group

mink (miŋk) *n.* [< Scand.] **1.** a kind of weasel that lives in water part of the time **2.** its valuable fur, soft, thick, and white to brown in color

min·now (min′ō) *n.* [< OE. *myne*] any of a large number of usually small freshwater fishes, commonly used as bait

mi·nor (mī′nər) *adj.* [L.] **1.** lesser in size, amount, importance, rank, etc. **2.** under full legal age **3.** *Music* smaller than the corresponding major interval by a semitone **—***vi.* *Educ.* to have a secondary field of study *(in)* **—** *n.* **1.** a person under full legal age, not yet having all civil rights **2.** *Educ.* a minor field of study

mi·nor·i·ty (mə nôr′ə tē, mī-; -när′-) *n., pl.* **-ties 1.** the smaller number; less than half **2.** a racial, religious, ethnic, or political group that differs from the larger, controlling group **3.** the period or state of being under full legal age

Min·o·taur (min′ə tôr′) *Gr. Myth.* a monster, part man and part bull

min·strel (min′strəl) *n.* [see MINISTER] **1.** a traveling singer of the Middle Ages **2.** a member of a comic variety show (**minstrel show**) in which the performers blacken their faces **—min′strel·sy** (-sē) *n., pl.* **-sies**

mint[1] (mint) *n.* [< L. < Juno *Moneta*, whose temple was the mint] **1.** a place where money is coined by the government **2.** a large amount **—***adj.* new, as if freshly minted [in *mint* condition] **—***vt.* **1.** to coin (money) **2.** to invent or create **—mint′age** *n.*

mint[2] (mint) *n.* [< Gr. *mintha*] **1.** an aromatic plant whose leaves are used for flavoring **2.** a candy flavored with mint

mint julep an iced drink of whiskey or brandy, sugar, and mint leaves

min·u·end (min′yoo wend′) *n.* [< L. *minuere*, lessen] the number from which another is to be subtracted

min·u·et (min′yoo wet′) *n.* [< Fr. < *menu*, small: from the small steps taken] **1.** a slow, stately dance **2.** the music for this

mi·nus (mī′nəs) *prep.* [L. < *minor*, less] **1.** less [four *minus* two] **2.** [Colloq.] without [*minus* a toe] **—***adj.* **1.** involving subtraction [a *minus* sign] **2.** negative **3.** less than [a grade of A *minus*] **—***n.* a sign (–), indicating subtraction or negative quantity: in full **minus sign**

mi·nus·cule (mi nus′kyool, min′ə skyool′) *adj.* [Fr. < L. *minusculus*] very small

min·ute[1] (min′it) *n.* [< L. (*pars*) *minuta* (*prima*), (first) small (part)] **1.** the sixtieth part of an hour or of a degree or of an arc **2.** a moment **3.** a specific point in time **4.** [*pl.*] an official record of a meeting

mi·nute[2] (mī noot′) *adj.* [< L. *minutus*, small] **1.** very small **2.** of little importance **3.** of or attentive to tiny details; precise **—mi·nute′ly** *adv.*

min′ute·man′ *n., pl.* **-men′** a member of the American citizen army at the time of the Revolution

minute steak (min′it) a small, thin steak that can be cooked quickly

mi·nu·ti·ae (mi noo′shi ē′) *n.pl., sing.* **-ti·a**

(-shē ə, -shə) [see MINUTE[2]] small or unimportant details

minx (miŋks) *n.* [< ?] a pert, saucy young woman

mir·a·cle (mir′ə k'l) *n.* [< L. *mirus*, wonderful] **1.** an event or action that apparently contradicts known scientific laws **2.** a remarkable thing

mi·rac·u·lous (mi rak′yoo ləs) *adj.* **1.** having the nature of, or like, a miracle **2.** able to work miracles **—mi·rac′u·lous·ly** *adv.*

mi·rage (mi räzh′) *n.* [Fr. < VL. *mirare*, look at] an optical illusion, caused by the refraction of light, in which a distant object appears to be nearby

mire (mīr) *n.* [< ON. *myrr*] **1.** an area of wet, soggy ground **2.** deep mud or slush **—***vt.* **mired**, **mir′ing 1.** to cause to get stuck as in mire **2.** to soil with mud, etc. **—***vi.* to sink in mud

mir·ror (mir′ər) *n.* [< VL. *mirare*, look at] **1.** a smooth surface that reflects images; esp., a piece of glass coated on one side as with silver **2.** anything that truly pictures or describes **—***vt.* to reflect, as in a mirror

mirth (murth) *n.* [< OE. *myrig*, pleasant] joyfulness or gaiety, esp. when marked by laughter **—mirth′ful** *adj.* **—mirth′less** *adj.*

mis- [< OE. *mis-* or OFr. *mes-*] a prefix meaning: **1.** wrong(ly), bad(ly) **2.** no, not

mis·ad·ven·ture (mis′əd ven′chər) *n.* a mishap; bad luck

mis′al·li′ance *n.* an improper alliance; esp., an unsuitable marriage

mis·an·thrope (mis′ən thrōp′) *n.* [< Gr. *misein*, to hate + *anthrōpos*, a man] one who hates or mistrusts all people: also **mis·an′thro·pist** (-an′thrə pist) **—mis′an·throp′ic** (-thräp′ik) *adj.*

mis·an·thro·py (mis an′thrə pē) *n.* hatred or mistrust of all people

mis′ap·ply′ *vt.* **-plied′, -ply′ing** to apply or use badly or improperly

mis·ap·pre·hend (mis′ap rə hend′) *vt.* to misunderstand **—mis′ap·pre·hen′sion** (-hen′shən) *n.*

mis′ap·pro′pri·ate′ *vt.* **-at′ed, -at′ing** to appropriate to a wrong or dishonest use **—mis′ap·pro′pri·a′tion** *n.*

mis′be·got′ten *adj.* wrongly or unlawfully begotten; illegitimate

mis′be·have′ *vt., vi.* **-haved′, -hav′ing** to behave (oneself) wrongly **—mis′be·hav′ior** (-yər) *n.*

misc. miscellaneous

mis′cal′cu·late′ *vt., vi.* **-lat′ed, -lat′ing** to calculate incorrectly; miscount or misjudge **—mis′cal·cu·la′tion** *n.*

mis·call′ *vt.* to call by a wrong name

mis·car·riage (mis kar′ij) *n.* **1.** failure to carry out what was intended **2.** the expulsion of a fetus from the womb before it is developed enough to live

mis·car·ry (mis kar′ē) *vi.* **-ried, -ry·ing 1.** to go wrong; fail [the plan *miscarried*] **2.** to fail to arrive: said of mail, etc. **3.** to suffer a miscarriage of a fetus

mis·cast′ *vt.* **-cast′, -cast′ing** to cast (an actor or a play) unsuitably

mis·ce·ge·na·tion (mis′i jə nā′shən, mi sej′ə-) *n.* [coined c.1863 < L. *miscere*, to mix + *genus*, race] marriage or sexual relations between a man and woman of different races, esp. between a white and a black

mis·cel·la·ne·ous (mis′ə lā′nē əs) *adj.* [< L. *miscere*, to mix] consisting of various kinds or qualities

mis·cel·la·ny (mis′ə lā′nē) *n., pl.* **-nies** a miscellaneous collection, esp. of literary works

mis·chance' *n.* bad luck

mis·chief (mis'chif) *n.* [< OFr. *mes-*, mis- + *chief*, end] **1.** harm or damage, esp. that done by a person **2.** a cause of harm or annoyance **3.** *a)* a prank *b)* playful teasing

mis'chief-mak'er *n.* one who causes mischief, esp. by gossiping

mis·chie·vous (mis'chi vəs) *adj.* **1.** causing mischief; harmful **2.** prankish; teasing **3.** inclined to annoy with playful tricks

mis·ci·ble (mis'ə b'l) *adj.* [< L. *miscere*, to mix] that can be mixed —**mis'ci·bil'i·ty** *n.*

mis·con·ceive (mis'kən sēv') *vt., vi.* -**ceived'**, -**ceiv'ing** to misunderstand —**mis'con·cep'tion** (-sep'shən) *n.*

mis·con·duct (mis kän'dukt) *n.* **1.** bad or dishonest management **2.** improper behavior

mis·con·strue (mis'kən strōō') *vt.* -**strued'**, -**stru'ing** to misinterpret —**mis'con·struc'tion** *n.*

mis·count' *vt.* to count incorrectly —*n.* (*usually* mis'kount) an incorrect count

mis·cre·ant (mis'krē ənt) *adj.* [< OFr. *mes-*, mis- + *croire*, believe] villainous —*n.* a villain

mis·deal' *vt., vi.* -**dealt'**, -**deal'ing** to deal (playing cards) wrongly —*n.* (mis'dēl') a wrong deal

mis·deed (mis dēd') *n.* a wrong or wicked act; crime, sin, etc.

mis·de·mean·or (mis'di mēn'ər) *n.* [MIS- + DEMEANOR] *Law* any minor offense bringing a lesser punishment than a felony

mis'di·rect' *vt.* to direct wrongly or badly — **mis'di·rec'tion** *n.*

mis·do' *vt.* -**did'**, -**done'**, -**do'ing** to do wrongly

mi·ser (mī'zər) *n.* [L., wretched] a greedy, stingy person who hoards money, even at the expense of his own comfort —**mi'ser·li·ness** *n.* —**mi'ser·ly** *adv.*

mis·er·a·ble (miz'ər ə b'l) *adj.* **1.** in misery; wretched **2.** causing misery, discomfort, etc. **3.** bad; inadequate **4.** pitiable —**mis'er·a·bly** *adv.*

mis·er·y (miz'ər ē) *n., pl.* -**ies** [see MISER] **1.** a condition of great suffering; distress **2.** a cause of such suffering; pain, sorrow, poverty, etc.

mis·fea·sance (mis fē'z'ns) *n.* [< OFr. *mes-*, mis- + *faire*, do] *Law* wrongdoing; specif., the doing of a lawful act in an unlawful manner

mis·file' *vt.* -**filed'**, -**fil'ing** to file (papers, etc.) in the wrong place

mis·fire (mis fīr') *vi.* -**fired'**, -**fir'ing 1.** to fail to discharge or ignite properly **2.** to fail to have the desired effect —*n.* a misfiring

mis'fit' *n.* **1.** an improper fit **2.** a person not adjusted to his job, associates, etc.

mis·for'tune *n.* **1.** ill fortune; trouble **2.** an unlucky accident; mishap

mis·giv·ing (mis giv'iŋ) *n.* [*often pl.*] a disturbed feeling of fear, doubt, etc.

mis·gov'ern *vt.* to govern badly

mis·guide (mis gīd') *vt.* -**guid'ed**, -**guid'ing** to lead into error or misconduct; mislead

mis·han'dle *vt.* -**dled**, -**dling** to handle badly or roughly; abuse

mis·hap (mis'hap') *n.* an unlucky or unfortunate accident

mish·mash (mish'mash') *n.* a hodgepodge

mis'in·form' *vt.* to give false or misleading information to —**mis'in·for·ma'tion** *n.*

mis'in·ter'pret *vt.* to interpret wrongly; understand or explain incorrectly —**mis'in·ter'pre·ta'tion** *n.*

mis·judge' *vt., vi.* -**judged'**, -**judg'ing** to judge wrongly or unfairly

mis·la'bel *vt.* -**beled** or -**belled**, -**bel·ing** or -**bel·ling** to label incorrectly

mis·lay (mis lā') *vt.* -**laid'**, -**lay'ing 1.** to put in

a place afterward forgotten **2.** to put down or install improperly

mis·lead' *vt.* -**led'**, -**lead'ing 1.** to lead in a wrong direction **2.** to deceive or delude **3.** to lead into wrongdoing

mis·man'age *vt., vi.* -**aged**, -**ag·ing** to manage badly —**mis·man'age·ment** *n.*

mis·match' *vt.* to match badly or unsuitably — *n.* a bad or unsuitable match

mis·mate' *vt., vi.* -**mat'ed**, -**mat'ing** to mate badly or unsuitably

mis·name' *vt.* -**named'**, -**nam'ing** to give a wrong or inappropriate name to

mis·no·mer (mis nō'mər) *n.* [< OFr. *mes-*, mis- + *nommer*, to name] a name wrongly applied

mi·sog·y·ny (mi säj'ə nē) *n.* [< Gr. *misein*, to hate + *gynē*, woman] hatred of women —**mi·sog'y·nist** *n.* —**mi·sog'y·nous** *adj.*

mis·place' *vt.* -**placed'**, -**plac'ing 1.** to put in a wrong place **2.** to bestow (one's trust, etc.) unwisely **3.** *same as* MISLAY (sense 1) —**mis·place'ment** *n.*

mis·print' *vt.* to print incorrectly —*n.* (*usually* mis'print') an error in printing

mis'pro·nounce' *vt., vi.* -**nounced'**, -**nounc'ing** to pronounce differently from the accepted pronunciations

mis·quote' *vt., vi.* -**quot'ed**, -**quot'ing** to quote incorrectly —**mis'quo·ta'tion** *n.*

mis·read' (-rēd') *vt., vi.* -**read'** (-red'), -**read'ing** to read wrongly, esp. so as to misinterpret or misunderstand

mis'rep·re·sent' *vt.* to represent falsely; give an untrue idea of —**mis'rep·re·sen·ta'tion** *n.*

mis·rule' *vt.* -**ruled'**, -**rul'ing** to rule badly; misgovern —*n.* misgovernment

miss' (mis) *vt.* [OE. *missan*] **1.** to fail to hit, meet, catch, attend, do, see, hear, etc. **2.** to let (a chance, etc.) go by **3.** to avoid [he missed being hit] **4.** to notice, feel, or regret the absence or loss of —*vi.* **1.** to fail to hit **2.** to fail to be successful **3.** to misfire, as an engine —*n.* a failure to hit, obtain, etc.

miss' (mis) *n., pl.* **miss'es** [< MISTRESS] **1.** [M-] a title used before the name of an unmarried woman or girl **2.** a young, unmarried woman or girl **3.** [*pl.*] a series of sizes in clothing for women and girls of average proportions

mis·sal (mis''l) *n.* [< LL. *missa*, Mass] *R.C.Ch.* the official, liturgical book containing the prayers used in celebrating Mass throughout the year

mis·shape' *vt.* -**shaped'**, -**shap'ing** to shape badly; deform —**mis·shap'en** *adj.*

mis·sile (mis''l) *n.* [< L. *mittere*, send] an object, as a spear, bullet, rocket, etc., designed to be thrown or launched toward a target; often, specif., *same as* GUIDED MISSILE

mis'sile·ry, mis'sil·ry (-rē) *n.* **1.** the science of building and launching guided missiles **2.** guided missiles collectively

miss·ing (mis'iŋ) *adj.* absent; lost

mis·sion (mish'ən) *n.* [< L. *mittere*, send] **1.** a sending out or being sent out to perform a special duty **2.** *a)* a group of missionaries *b)* its headquarters **3.** a diplomatic delegation **4.** a group of technicians, specialists, etc. sent to a foreign country **5.** the special duty for which someone is sent **6.** the special task for which a person is apparently destined in life

mis'sion·ar'y (-er'ē) *adj.* of religious missions or missionaries —*n., pl.* -**ies** a person sent out by his church to preach and make converts in a foreign country

mis·sive (mis'iv) *n.* [Fr. < L. *mittere*, send] a letter or written message

mis·spell' *vt., vi.* **-spelled'** or **-spelt'**, **-spell'ing** to spell incorrectly
mis·spend' *vt.* **-spent'**, **-spend'ing** to spend improperly or wastefully
mis·state' *vt.* **-stat'ed**, **-stat'ing** to state incorrectly or falsely —**mis·state'ment** *n.*
mis·step' *n.* **1.** a wrong or awkward step **2.** a mistake in conduct
mist (mist) *n.* [OE.] **1.** a large mass of water vapor like a light fog **2.** a fine spray **3.** anything that dims or obscures —*vt., vi.* to make or become misty
mis·take (mi stāk') *vt.* **-took'**, **-tak'en**, **-tak'ing** [< ON. *mistaka,* take wrongly] to understand or perceive wrongly —*vi.* to make a mistake — *n.* a blunder; error —**mis·tak'a·ble** *adj.*
mis·tak'en *adj.* **1.** wrong; having an incorrect understanding **2.** incorrect: said of ideas, etc. — **mis·tak'en·ly** *adv.*
mis·ter (mis'tər) *n.* [< MASTER] **1.** [M-] a title used before the name of a man or his office and usually written *Mr.* **2.** [Colloq.] sir
mis·tle·toe (mis''l tō') *n.* [< OE. *mistel,* mistletoe + *tan,* a twig] a parasitic evergreen plant with yellowish flowers and white, poisonous berries
mis·took (mi stook') *pt. of* MISTAKE
mis·tral (mis'tral, mi sträl') *n.* [Fr. < Pr., master-wind] a cold, dry north wind that blows over the Mediterranean coast of France
mis·treat' *vt.* to treat wrongly or badly —**mis·treat'ment** *n.*
mis·tress (mis'tris) *n.* [< OFr. fem. of *maistre, master*] **1.** a woman who is head of a household or institution **2.** a woman, nation, etc. that has control or power **3.** a woman with whom a man is having a prolonged affair **4.** [M-] formerly, a title used before the name of a woman: now replaced by *Mrs.* or *Miss*
mis·tri·al (mis trī'əl) *n. Law* a trial made void as because of an error or because the jury cannot reach a verdict
mis·trust' *n.* lack of trust or confidence —*vt., vi.* to have no trust in; doubt —**mis·trust'ful** *adj.* —**mis·trust'ful·ly** *adv.*
mist·y (mis'tē) *adj.* **-i·er**, **-i·est** **1.** of, like, or covered with mist **2.** blurred, as by mist **3.** vague or obscure —**mist'i·ness** *n.*
mis'un·der·stand' *vt.* **-stood'**, **-stand'ing** to fail to understand correctly
mis'un·der·stand'ing *n.* **1.** a failure to understand; mistake of meaning or intention **2.** a quarrel; disagreement
mis·use (mis yōōz'; *for n.* -yōōs') *vt.* **-used'**, **-us'ing** **1.** to use improperly **2.** to treat badly or harshly; abuse —*n.* incorrect or improper use
mite (mīt) *n.* [OE.] **1.** a tiny arachnid, often parasitic upon animals or plants **2.** a very small sum of money **3.** a bit; a little **4.** a very small creature or object
mi·ter (mīt'ər) *n.* [< Gr. *mitra,* headband] **1.** a tall, ornamented cap worn by bishops and abbots **2.** *Carpentry* a joint formed by fitting together two pieces beveled so that they form a corner: also **miter joint**
mit·i·gate (mit'ə gāt') *vt., vi.* **-gat'ed**, **-gat'ing** [< L. *mitis,* mild + *agere,* to drive] to make or become less severe, less painful, etc. —**mit'i·ga'tion** *n.*
mitt (mit) *n.* [< MITTEN] **1.** a woman's glove covering part of the arm, the hand, and sometimes part of the fingers **2.** [Slang] a hand **3.** *a) Baseball* a padded glove, usually without separate and distinct sections for the four fingers *b)* a boxing glove

mit·ten (mit''n) *n.* [< OFr. *mitaine*] a glove with a single section for all four fingers
mix (miks) *vt.* **mixed** or **mixt**, **mix'ing** [prob. < Fr. < L. *miscere*] **1.** to blend together in a single mass **2.** to make by blending ingredients [to *mix* a cake] **3.** to combine [to *mix* work and play] —*vi.* **1.** to be mixed or blended **2.** to get along together —*n.* **1.** a mixture, as of ingredients for making something **2.** a beverage for mixing with alcoholic liquor —**mix up 1.** to mix thoroughly **2.** to confuse **3.** to involve (*in*) —**mix'er** *n.*
mixed (mikst) *adj.* **1.** blended **2.** made up of different parts, races, sexes, etc. **3.** confused
mix·ture (miks'chər) *n.* **1.** a mixing or being mixed **2.** something mixed
mix'-up' *n.* a confused condition; tangle
miz·zen·mast (miz''n məst, -mast') *n.* [< L. *medius,* middle] the mast nearest the stern in a ship with two or three masts
ML. Medieval (or Middle) Latin
Mlle. *pl.* **Mlles.** Mademoiselle
mm, mm. millimeter(s)
Mme. Madame
Mmes. Mesdames
Mn *Chem.* manganese
mne·mon·ic (nē män'ik) *adj.* [< Gr. *mnēmōn,* mindful] of or helping the memory
mne·mon·ics *n.pl.* [*with sing. v.*] a technique for improving memory
Mo *Chem.* molybdenum
mo. *pl.* **mos.** month
moan (mōn) *n.* [prob. < OE. *mænan,* complain] a low, mournful sound of sorrow or pain —*vt., vi.* **1.** to say with or utter a moan **2.** to complain or lament (about)
moat (mōt) *n.* [< OFr. *mote*] a deep, broad ditch, often filled with water, dug around a fortress or castle for protection
mob (mäb) *n.* [< L. *mobile* (*vulgus*), movable (crowd)] **1.** a disorderly, lawless crowd **2.** any crowd **3.** the masses: contemptuous term **4.** [Slang] a gang of criminals —*vt.* **mobbed**, **mob'bing 1.** to crowd around and attack, annoy, etc. **2.** to throng
mo·bile (mō'b'l, -bīl, -bēl) *adj.* [< L. *movere,* to move] **1.** moving or movable **2.** movable by means of a motor vehicle [a *mobile* X-ray unit] **3.** that can change rapidly or easily; adaptable —*n.* (*usually* -bēl) an abstract sculpture with parts that can move, as an arrangement of thin forms, rings, etc. suspended in midair —**mo·bil'i·ty** (-bil'ə tē) *n.*
mobile home a large trailer outfitted as a home
mo'bi·lize' (-bə līz') *vt., vi.* **-lized'**, **-liz'ing** to make or become organized and ready, as for war —**mo'bi·li·za'tion** *n.*
mob·ster (mäb'stər) *n.* [Slang] a gangster
moc·ca·sin (mäk'ə s'n) *n.* [< AmInd.] **1.** a heelless slipper of soft, flexible leather **2.** a similar slipper, but with a hard sole and heel **3.** *same as* WATER MOCCASIN
mo·cha (mō'kə) *n.* a choice grade of coffee grown orig. in Arabia —*adj.* flavored with coffee and, often, chocolate
mock (mäk) *vt.* [< OFr. *mocquer*] **1.** to ridicule **2.** to mimic, as in fun or derision **3.** to defy and make futile —*vi.* to express scorn, ridicule, etc. —*adj.* sham; imitation
mock'er·y *n., pl.* **-ies 1.** a mocking **2.** one receiving or deserving ridicule **3.** a false or derisive imitation **4.** futility
mock'ing·bird' *n.* an American bird that imitates the calls of other birds
mock-up (mäk'up') *n.* a scale model, usually a

full-sized replica, used for teaching, testing, etc.

mode (mōd) *n.* [< L. *modus*] **1.** a manner or way of acting, doing, or being **2.** customary usage or current fashion **3.** *Grammar same as* MOOD²

mod·el (mäd′'l) *n.* [< Fr. < L. *modus,* a measure] **1.** a small representation of a planned or existing object **2.** a person or thing regarded as a standard of excellence to be imitated **3.** a style or design **4.** *a)* one who poses for an artist or photographer *b)* one employed to display clothes by wearing them —*adj.* **1.** serving as a model **2.** representative of others of the same kind *[a model home]* —*vt.* **-eled** or **-elled, -el·ing** or **-el·ling 1.** *a)* to make a model of *b)* to plan or form after a model **2.** to display (clothes) by wearing —*vi.* to serve as a model (sense 4)

mod·er·ate (mäd′ər it) *adj.* [< L. *moderare,* restrain] **1.** within reasonable limits; avoiding extremes **2.** mild; calm **3.** of average or medium quality, range, etc. —*n.* one holding moderate opinions, as in politics —*vt., vi.* (-ə rāt′) **-at·ed, -at·ing 1.** to make or become moderate **2.** to preside over (a meeting, etc.) — **mod′er·ate·ly** *adv.*

mod·er·a′tion *n.* 1 a moderating **2.** avoidance of extremes **3.** calmness

mod·er·a·tor (mäd′ə rāt′ər) *n.* one who presides at a meeting, debate, etc.

mod·ern (mäd′ərn) *adj.* [< Fr. < L. *modo,* just now] **1.** of the present or recent times; specif., up-to-date **2.** [*often* **M-**] designating the most recent form of a language —*n.* a person living in modern times, having modern ideas, etc.

Modern English the English language since about the middle of the 15th century

mod′ern·ism *n.* modern ideas, practices, trends, etc. —**mod′ern·ist** *n., adj.* —**mod′ern·is′-tic** *adj.*

mo·der·ni·ty (mä dur′nə tē, mə-) *n.* a being modern

mod′ern·ize′ *vt., vi.* **-ized′, -iz′ing** to make or become modern —**mod′ern·i·za′tion** *n.*

mod·est (mäd′ist) *adj.* [< Fr. < L. *modus,* a measure] **1.** not vain or boastful; unassuming **2.** shy or reserved **3.** decorous or decent **4.** not extreme **5.** unpretentious —**mod′est·ly** *adv.* —**mod′es·ty** *n.*

mod·i·cum (mäd′i kəm) *n.* [L., moderate] a small amount; bit

mod·i·fy (mäd′ə fī′) *vt.* **-fied′, -fy′ing** [< L. *modificare,* to limit] **1.** to change slightly or partially in character, form, etc. **2.** to limit or lessen slightly **3.** *Gram.* to limit in meaning; qualify —**mod′i·fi·ca′tion** *n.* —**mod′i·fi′er** *n.*

mod·ish (mōd′ish) *adj.* stylish; fashionable

ModL. Modern Latin

mod·u·lar (mäj′ə lar) *adj.* of modules

mod·u·late (mäj′ə lāt′) *vt.* **-lat′ed, -lat′ing** [< L. *modus,* a measure] **1.** to regulate or adjust **2.** to vary the pitch, intensity, etc. of (the voice) **3.** to vary the amplitude, frequency, etc. of (a radio wave, etc.) —**mod′u·la′tion** *n.* —**mod′u·la′tor** *n.*

mod·ule (mäj′ōōl) *n.* [Fr. < L. *modus,* a measure] **1.** a standard or unit of measurement, as of building materials **2.** *a)* any of a set of units designed to be arranged in various ways *b)* a detachable unit with a specific function, as in a spacecraft

mo·gul (mō′gul, -g'l) *n.* [Per. *Mughul,* Mongol] a powerful or important person

mo·hair (mō′her) *n.* [< Ar. *mukhayyar*] **1.** the hair of the Angora goat **2.** yarn or a fabric made from this

Mo·ham·med·an (mō ham′i d'n) *adj.* of Mohammed or the Muslim religion —*n. same as* MUSLIM

Mo·ham′med·an·ism *n. same as* ISLAM

moi·e·ty (moi′ə tē) *n., pl.* **-ties** [< L. *medius,* middle] **1.** a half **2.** an indefinite part

moire (mwär, môr) *n.* [Fr.] a fabric, as silk, having a watered, or wavy, pattern: also **moi·ré** (mwä rā′, mô-)

moist (moist) *adj.* [< L. *mucus,* mucus] slightly wet; damp —**moist′ness** *n.*

mois·ten (mois′'n) *vt., vi.* to make or become moist

mois′ture (-chər) *n.* water or other liquid causing a slight wetness

mois′tur·ize′ (-iz′) *vt., vi.* **-ized′, -iz′ing** to add or restore moisture (to the skin, air, etc.) — **mois′tur·iz′er** *n.*

mo·lar (mō′lər) *adj.* [< L. *mola,* millstone] designating a tooth or teeth adapted for grinding —*n.* a molar tooth

mo·las·ses (mə las′iz) *n.* [< L. *mel,* honey] a thick, dark syrup produced from sugar

mold¹ (mōld) *n.* [< L. *modus,* a measure] **1.** a hollow form for shaping something plastic or molten **2.** a frame on which something is modeled **3.** a pattern; model **4.** something formed in or on a mold **5.** distinctive character —*vt.* to make or shape in or on, or as if in or on, a mold

mold² (mōld) *n.* [ME. *moul*] **1.** a fungus producing a furry growth on the surface of organic matter **2.** this growth —*vi.* to become moldy

mold³ (mōld) *n.* [OE. *molde,* earth] loose, soft soil rich with decayed organic matter

mold·er (mōl′dər) *vi.* [< OE. *molde,* dust] to crumble into dust; decay

mold·ing (mōl′diŋ) *n.* **1.** the act of one that molds **2.** something molded **3.** a shaped strip of wood, etc., as around the upper walls of a room

mold·y (mōl′dē) *adj.* **-i·er, -i·est 1.** covered with a growth of mold **2.** musty or stale

mole¹ (mōl) *n.* [OE. *mal*] a small, congenital spot on the human skin, usually dark-colored and raised

mole² (mōl) *n.* [ME. *molle*] a small, burrowing mammal with soft fur

mole³ (mōl) *n.* [< Fr. < L. *moles,* a dam] a breakwater

mol·e·cule (mäl′ə kyōōl′) *n.* [< Fr. < L. *moles,* a mass] **1.** the smallest particle of an element or compound that can exist in the free state and still retain the characteristics of the element or compound **2.** a small particle —**mo·lec·u·lar** (mə lek′yə lər) *adj.*

mole′hill′ *n.* a small ridge of earth formed by a burrowing mole

mole′skin′ *n.* **1.** the fur of the mole **2.** a strong cotton fabric with a soft nap

mo·lest (mə lest′, mō-) *vt.* [< L. *moles,* a burden] **1.** to annoy or to meddle with so as to trouble or harm **2.** to make improper sexual advances to —**mo·les·ta·tion** (mō′les tā′shən) *n.*

mol·li·fy (mäl′ə fī′) *vt.* **-fied′, -fy′ing** [< L. *mollis,* soft + *facere,* make] **1.** to soothe; appease **2.** to make less severe or violent

mol·lusk, mol·lusc (mäl′əsk) *n.* [< Fr. < L. *mollis,* soft] any of a group of invertebrates, as oysters, snails, etc., having a soft body often enclosed in a shell

mol·ly·cod·dle (mäl′ē käd′'l) *n.* [< the name *Molly* + CODDLE] a man or boy used to being coddled —*vt.* **-dled, -dling** to pamper

molt (mōlt) *vi.* [< L. *mutare,* to change] to shed

skin, feathers, horns, etc. prior to replacement by a new growth, as reptiles, birds, etc.

mol·ten (mōl't'n) *adj.* [archaic pp. of MELT] **1.** melted by heat **2.** made by being melted and cast in a mold

mo·lyb·de·num (mə lib'də nəm) *n.* [< Gr. *molybdos*, lead] a soft, silver-white metallic chemical element, used in alloys: symbol, Mo

mom (mäm) *n. colloq. var. of* MOTHER¹

mo·ment (mō'mənt) *n.* [< L. *momentum*, movement] **1.** an indefinitely brief period of time; instant **2.** a definite point in time **3.** a brief time of importance **4.** importance

mo·men·tar·i·ly (mō'mən ter'ə lē) *adv.* **1.** for a short time **2.** in an instant **3.** at any moment

mo·men·tar·y (mō'mən ter'ē) *adj.* lasting for only a moment; passing

mo·men·tous (mō men'təs) *adj.* of great moment; very important

mo·men·tum (mō men'təm) *n., pl.* -tums, -ta (-tə) [L.: see MOMENT] the impetus of a moving object, equal to the product of its mass and its velocity

mom·my (mäm'ē) *n., pl.* -mies *child's term for* MOTHER¹

Mon. 1. Monday **2.** Monsignor

mon·arch (män'ərk, -ärk) *n.* [< Gr. *monos*, alone + *archein*, to rule] a hereditary ruler; king, queen, etc. —**mo·nar·chi·cal** (mə när'ki k'l) *adj.*

mon'arch·ist (-ər kist) *n.* one who favors monarchy

mon·ar·chy (män'ər kē) *n., pl.* -chies a government or state headed by a monarch

mon·as·ter·y (män'ə ster'ē) *n., pl.* -ies [< Gr. *monos*, alone] the residence of a group of monks or nuns, esp. monks

mo·nas·tic (mə nas'tik) *adj.* of or characteristic of monks or nuns; ascetic: also **mo·nas'ti·cal** —*n.* a monk —**mo·nas'ti·cism** (-tə siz'm) *n.*

mon·au·ral (män ôr'l) *adj.* [MON(O)- + AURAL] designating or of sound reproduction using one channel to carry and reproduce sound

Mon·day (mun'dē, -dā) *n.* [OE. *monandæg*, moon's day] the second day of the week

mon·e·tar·y (män'ə ter'ē, mun'-) *adj.* [< L. *moneta*, a MINT¹] **1.** of the coinage or currency of a country **2.** of money

mon·ey (mun'ē) *n., pl.* -eys, -ies [< L. *moneta*, a MINT¹] **1.** stamped pieces of metal, or any paper notes, authorized by a government as a medium of exchange **2.** property; wealth —**in the money** [Slang] **1.** among the winners in a race, contest, etc. **2.** wealthy —**make money** to gain profits —**put money into** to invest money in

money belt a belt with a compartment to hold money

mon·eyed (mun'ēd) *adj.* wealthy; rich

mon'ey·mak'er *n.* **1.** one successful at acquiring money **2.** something financially profitable —**mon'ey·mak'ing** *adj., n.*

money order an order for the payment of a specified sum of money, as one issued at one post office or bank and payable at another

mon·ger (muŋ'gər, mäŋ'-) *n.* [< L. *mango*] [Chiefly Brit.] a dealer or trader

Mon·gol (mäŋ'gəl, -gōl) *adj., n. same as* MONGOLIAN

Mon·go'li·an *adj.* **1.** of Mongolia, its people, or their culture **2.** *same as: a)* MONGOLOID *b)* MONGOLIC —*n.* **1.** a native of Mongolia **2.** *same as: a)* MONGOLOID *b)* MONGOLIC

Mon·gol·ic (mäŋ gäl'ik) *adj.* designating or of a subfamily of languages spoken in Mongolia —*n.* any Mongolic language

Mon·gol·oid (mäŋ'gə loid') *adj.* **1.** of or characteristic of the natives of Mongolia **2.** designating or of one of the major groups of mankind, including most of the peoples of Asia —*n.* a member of the Mongoloid group

mon·goose (mäŋ'gōōs) *n., pl.* -goos·es [< native Indian name] a ferretlike, flesh-eating mammal that kills snakes, etc.

mon·grel (muŋ'grəl, mäŋ'-) *n.* [< OE. *mengan*, to mix] an animal or plant, esp. a dog, of mixed breed —*adj.* of mixed breed, race, character, etc.

mon·ied (mun'ēd) *adj. same as* MONEYED

mon·i·ker, mon·ick·er (män'i kər) *n.* [< ?] [Slang] a person's name

mo·ni·tion (mō nish'ən) *n.* [< L. *monere*, warn] admonition; warning

mon·i·tor (män'ə tər) *n.* [< L. *monere*, warn] **1.** in some schools, a student chosen to help keep order, record attendance, etc. **2.** a device for regulating the performance of a machine, aircraft, etc. **3.** *Radio & TV* a receiver for checking the quality of transmission —*vt., vi.* to watch or check on (a person or thing)

monk (muŋk) *n.* [< Gr. *monos*, alone] a man who joins a religious order living in retirement generally under vows of poverty, obedience, and chastity

mon·key (muŋ'kē) *n., pl.* -keys [prob. < Fr. or Sp. *mona*, ape + LowG. -*ke*, -KIN] any of the primates except man and the lemurs; specif., any of the smaller, long-tailed primates —*vi.* [Colloq.] to play or meddle

monkey business [Colloq.] foolish, mischievous, or deceitful tricks or behavior

mon'key·shines (-shīnz') *n.pl.* [Colloq.] mischievous tricks or pranks

monkey wrench a wrench with an adjustable jaw —**throw a monkey wrench into** [Colloq.] to disrupt the orderly functioning of

monks·hood (muŋks'hood') *n. same as* ACONITE (sense 1)

mon·o (män'ō) *adj. short for* MONOPHONIC —*n. short for* MONONUCLEOSIS

mono- [< Gr. *monos*, single] *a prefix meaning* one, alone, single

mon·o·cle (män'ə k'l) *n.* [Fr. < Gr. *monos*, single + L. *oculus*, eye] an eyeglass for one eye only

mon·o·cot·y·le·don (män'ə kät''l ē'd'n) *n.* a flowering plant with only one cotyledon — **mon'o·cot'y·le'don·ous** *adj.*

mo·nog·a·my (mə näg'ə mē) *n.* [< Fr. < Gr. *monos*, single + *gamos*, marriage] the practice or state of being married to only one person at a time —**mo·nog'a·mous** *adj.*

mon·o·gram (män'ə gram') *n.* [< Gr. *monos*, single + *gramma*, letter] the initials of a name combined in a single design

mon·o·graph (män'ə graf') *n.* [MONO- + -GRAPH] a book, article, etc., esp. a scholarly one, on a single subject

mon·o·lith (män'ə lith') *n.* [< Fr. < Gr. *monos*, single + *lithos*, stone] **1.** a single large block of stone, as one made into an obelisk, etc. **2.** something massive, unified, unyielding, etc. —**mon'o·lith'ic** *adj.*

mon·o·logue (män'ə lôg') *n.* [Fr. < Gr. *monos*, alone + *legein*, speak] **1.** a long speech **2.** a soliloquy **3.** a play, skit, etc. for one actor only

mon·o·ma·ni·a (män'ə mā'nē ə) *n.* an excessive interest in or enthusiasm for some one thing; craze

mon·o·nu·cle·o·sis (män'ə nōō'klē ō'sis) *n.*

[MONO- + NUCLE(US) + -OSIS] an acute disease, esp. of young people, with fever, swollen lymph nodes, sore throat, etc.

mon·o·phon·ic (män′ə fän′ik) *adj.* [< MONO- + Gr. *phōnē*, a sound] of sound reproduction using a single channel to carry and reproduce sounds

mo·nop·o·list (mə näp′ə list) *n.* one who has a monopoly or favors monopoly —**mo·nop′o·lis′tic** *adj.*

mo·nop′o·lize′ (-līz′) *vt.* **-lized′, -liz′ing 1.** to get, have, or exploit a monopoly of **2.** to get full control of

mo·nop′o·ly (-lē) *n., pl.* **-lies** [< Gr. *monos*, single + *pōlein*, sell] **1.** exclusive control of a commodity or service in a given market **2.** such control granted by a government **3.** something held as a monopoly **4.** a company that has a monopoly

mon·o·rail (män′ə rāl′) *n.* a railway with a single rail serving as a track for cars suspended from it or balanced on it

mon·o·syl·la·ble (män′ə sil′ə b'l) *n.* a word of one syllable —**mon′o·syl·lab′ic** (-si lab′ik) *adj.*

mon·o·the·ism (män′ə thē iz′m) *n.* [MONO- + THEISM] the doctrine or belief that there is only one God —**mon′o·the·ist** *n.* —**mon′o·the·is′tic** *adj.*

mon·o·tone (män′ə tōn′) *n.* [see MONO- & TONE] **1.** utterance of successive words without change of pitch or key **2.** tiresome sameness of style, color, etc. **3.** a single, unchanging musical tone

mo·not·o·nous (mə nät′'n əs) *adj.* **1.** going on in the same tone without variation **2.** having little or no variety **3.** tiresome because unvarying —**mo·not′o·ny** *n.*

mon·ox·ide (mə näk′sīd) *n.* an oxide with one atom of oxygen in each molecule

mon·sieur (mə syur′; *Fr.* mə syö′) *n., pl.* **mes·sieurs** (mes′ərz; *Fr.* mā syö′) [Fr., lit., my lord] a man; gentleman: as a title [**M-**], equivalent to *Mr.* or *Sir*

Mon·si·gnor (män sēn′yər) *n.* [It., lit., my lord] a title for certain Roman Catholic prelates

mon·soon (män sōōn′) *n.* [< Ar. *mausim*, a season] **1.** a seasonal wind of the Indian Ocean and S Asia **2.** the rainy season, when this wind blows from the southwest

mon·ster (män′stər) *n.* [< L. *monere*, warn] **1.** any greatly malformed plant or animal **2.** any grotesque imaginary creature **3.** a very wicked person **4.** any huge animal or thing

mon·strance (män′strəns) *n.* [< L. *monstrare*, to show] *R.C.Ch.* a receptacle in which the consecrated Host is exposed

mon·strous (män′strəs) *adj.* **1.** huge **2.** greatly malformed **3.** horrible; hideous **4.** hideously evil —**mon·stros·i·ty** (män sträs′ə tē) *n., pl.* **-ties**

mon·tage (män täzh′) *n.* [Fr. < *monter*, MOUNT²] **1.** a composite picture **2.** *Motion Pictures* a rapid sequence of photographic images, often superimposed

Mon·tes·so·ri method (or **system**) (män′tə sôr′ē) [< Maria *Montessori* (1870–1952), It. educator] a method of teaching young children, emphasizing training of the senses

month (munth) *n.* [OE. *monath*] **1.** any of the twelve divisions of the calendar year **2.** a period of four weeks or 30 days **3.** one twelfth of the solar year

month′ly *adj.* **1.** continuing for a month **2.** done, happening, payable, etc. every month —*n., pl.* **-lies** a periodical published once a month —*adv.* once a month; every month

mon·u·ment (män′yə mənt) *n.* [< L. *monere*, remind] **1.** something set up to keep alive the memory of a person or event, as a tablet, statue, etc. **2.** a work of enduring significance

mon′u·men′tal (-men′t'l) *adj.* **1.** of or serving as a monument **2.** like a monument; massive, enduring, etc. **3.** great; colossal

moo (mōō) *n., pl.* **moos** [echoic] the vocal sound made by a cow —*vi.* **mooed, moo′ing** to make this sound; low

mooch (mōōch) *vi., vt.* [ult. < OFr. *muchier*, to hide] [Slang] to get (food, money, etc.) by begging or sponging —**mooch′er** *n.*

mood¹ (mōōd) *n.* [OE. *mod*, mind] **1.** a particular state of mind or feeling **2.** a prevailing feeling or tone

mood² (mōōd) *n.* [< MODE] *Gram.* that aspect of verbs which indicates whether the action or state expressed is a fact, supposition, or command

mood′y *adj.* **-i·er, -i·est** subject to or characterized by gloomy or changing moods —**mood′i·ly** *adv.* —**mood′i·ness** *n.*

moon (mōōn) *n.* [OE. *mona*] **1.** the heavenly body that revolves around the earth once in 29 1/2 days and shines by reflected sunlight **2.** anything shaped like the moon (i.e., an orb or crescent) **3.** any satellite of a planet —*vi.* to behave in an idle or abstracted way

moon′beam′ *n.* a ray of moonlight

moon′light′ *n.* the light of the moon —*adj.* **1.** of moonlight **2.** lighted by the moon **3.** done or occurring by moonlight, or at night

moon′light′ing *n.* the practice of holding a second regular job, as at night, in addition to one's main job

moon′lit′ *adj.* lighted by the moon

moon′quake′ *n.* a trembling of the moon's surface, as because of internal rock shifting or meteorite impact

moon′shine′ *n.* **1.** moonlight **2.** nonsense **3.** [Colloq.] whiskey unlawfully made

moon′shot′ *n.* the launching of a rocket to the moon

moon′stone′ *n.* a translucent feldspar with a pearly luster, used as a gem

moon′struck′ *adj.* **1.** crazed; lunatic **2.** romantically dreamy **3.** dazed

Moor (moor) *n.* a member of a Muslim people of NW Africa —**Moor′ish** *adj.*

moor¹ (moor) *n.* [OE. *mor*] [Brit.] a tract of open wasteland, usually covered with heather and often marshy

moor² (moor) *vt.* [< ? MDu. *maren*, to tie] **1.** to hold (a ship, etc.) in place by cables or chains as to a pier or buoy **2.** to secure —*vi.* to moor a ship, etc.

moor′ing *n.* **1.** [*often pl.*] the lines, cables, etc. by which a ship is moored **2.** [*pl.*] a place where a ship is moored

moose (mōōs) *n., pl.* **moose** [< AmInd.] the largest animal of the deer family, native to the N U.S. and Canada

moot (mōōt) *adj.* [OE. (*ge*)*mot*, a meeting] **1.** debatable **2.** hypothetical —*vt.* to debate or discuss

mop (mäp) *n.* [< ? L. *mappa*, napkin] **1.** a bundle of rags, a sponge, etc. at the end of a stick, as for washing floors **2.** anything suggesting this, as a thick head of hair —*vt.* **mopped, mop′ping** to wash, wipe, or remove as with a mop —**mop up** [Colloq.] to finish

mope (mōp) *vi.* **moped, mop′ing** [akin to MDu. *mopen*] to be gloomy and apathetic —**mop′ey, mop′y, mop′ish** *adj.*

mop·pet (mäp′it) *n.* [< ?] [Colloq.] a little child: a term of affection

mo·raine (mə rān′) *n.* [Fr.] a mass of rocks, sand, etc. deposited by a glacier

mor·al (môr′əl, mär′-) *adj.* [< L. *mos*, pl. *mores*, morals] **1.** dealing with, or able to distinguish between, right and wrong conduct **2.** of, teaching, or in accordance with, the principles of right and wrong **3.** good in conduct or character; specif., sexually virtuous **4.** involving sympathy without action [moral support] **5.** virtually such because of its effects [a moral victory] **6.** based on strong probability [a moral certainty] —*n.* **1.** a moral lesson taught by a fable, event, etc. **2.** [pl.] principles or standards with respect to right and wrong in conduct; ethics —**mor′al·ly** *adv.*

mo·rale (mə ral′, mô-) *n.* [Fr.] moral or mental condition with respect to courage, discipline, confidence, etc.

mo·ral·i·ty (mə ral′ə tē, mô-) *n., pl.* **-ties** **1.** rightness or wrongness, as of an action **2.** right conduct **3.** ethics

mor·al·ize (môr′ə līz′, mär′-) *vi.* **-ized′, -iz′ing** [< Fr.] to consider or discuss moral matters, often self-righteously —**mor′al·iz′er, mor′al·ist** *n.* —**mor′al·is′tic** *adj.*

mo·rass (mə ras′, mô-) *n.* [< Du. < Frank. *marisk*] a bog; swamp

mor·a·to·ri·um (môr′ə tôr′ē əm) *n., pl.* **-ri·ums, -ri·a** (-ə) [< L. *mora*, a delay] **1.** a legal authorization to delay payment of money due **2.** any authorized delay

mo·ray (eel) (môr′ā) [< Port. < Gr. *myraina*] a voracious, brilliantly colored eel

mor·bid (môr′bid) *adj.* [< L. *morbus*, disease] **1.** of or caused by disease; diseased **2.** having or showing an interest in gruesome matters **3.** gruesome —**mor·bid′i·ty** *n.*

mor·dant (môr′d'nt) *adj.* [< L. *mordere*, to bite] caustic or sarcastic —*n.* a substance used in dyeing to fix the colors

more (môr) *adj. superl.* MOST [OE. *mara*] **1.** greater in amount or degree: compar. of MUCH **2.** greater in number: compar. of MANY **3.** additional [take more tea] —*n.* **1.** a greater amount or degree **2.** [with pl. v.] a greater number (of) **3.** something additional [more can be said] —*adv. superl.* MOST **1.** in or to a greater degree or extent **2.** in addition —**more or less 1.** somewhat **2.** approximately

more·o′ver (-ō′vər) *adv.* in addition to what has been said; besides

mo·res (môr′ēz, -āz) *n.pl.* [L., customs] behavior and customs that, through general observance, develop the force of law

morgue (môrg) *n.* [Fr.] **1.** a place where the bodies of unknown dead or those dead of unknown causes are temporarily kept **2.** a newspaper office's reference file

mor·i·bund (môr′ə bund′) *adj.* [< L. *mori*, die] **1.** dying **2.** coming to an end

Mor·mon (môr′mən) *n.* a member of the Church of Jesus Christ of Latter-day Saints, founded in 1830

morn (môrn) *n.* [OE. *morne*] [Poet.] morning

morn·ing (môr′niŋ) *n.* [OE. *morgen*] **1.** the first or early part of the day, from midnight, or esp. dawn, to noon **2.** dawn

morning glory a twining annual vine with trumpet-shaped flowers

mo·ron (môr′än) *n.* [coined (1910) < Gr. *mōros*, foolish] **1.** a person who is mentally retarded to a mild degree: an obsolescent term **2.** a very stupid person —**mo·ron′ic** *adj.*

mo·rose (mə rōs′) *adj.* [< L. *mos*, manner] gloomy, sullen, etc. —**mo·rose′ly** *adv.*

mor·pheme (môr′fēm) *n.* [< Fr. < Gr. *morphē*, form] the smallest meaningful language unit, as a base, affix, or inflectional ending

mor·phine (môr′fēn) *n.* [< G. or Fr. < *Morpheus*, Gr. god of dreams] an alkaloid derived from opium and used in medicine to relieve pain

mor·phol·o·gy (môr fäl′ə jē) *n.* [< G. < Gr. *morphē*, form + -LOGY] form and structure, as in biology or linguistics

mor·row (mär′ō, môr′ō) *n.* [< OE. *morgen*, morning] [Poet.] **1.** morning **2.** the next day

Morse (code) (môrs) [after S. F. B. *Morse*, its inventor] [often m-] a code, or alphabet, consisting of a system of dots and dashes, used in telegraphy, etc.

mor·sel (môr′s'l) *n.* [< L. *morsum*, a bite] **1.** a small portion of food **2.** a small piece

mor·tal (môr′t'l) *adj.* [< L. *mors*, death] **1.** that must eventually die **2.** of man as a being who must die **3.** of this world **4.** of death **5.** fatal **6.** very intense [mortal terror] —*n.* a human being —**mor′tal·ly** *adv.*

mor·tal·i·ty (môr tal′ə tē) *n.* **1.** the mortal nature of man **2.** death on a large scale, as from war **3.** the proportion of deaths to population; death rate

mor·tar (môr′tər) *n.* [< L. *mortarium*] **1.** a bowl in which substances are pulverized with a pestle **2.** [< Fr.] a short-barreled cannon which hurls shells in a high trajectory **3.** a mixture of cement or lime with sand and water, used between bricks or stones, or as plaster

mor·tar·board′ *n.* **1.** a square board with a handle beneath, for carrying mortar **2.** an academic cap with a square, flat top

mort·gage (môr′gij) *n.* [< OFr. *mort*, dead + *gage*, pledge] **1.** the pledging of property to a creditor as security for the payment of a debt **2.** the deed by which this is done —*vt.* **-gaged, -gag·ing 1.** to pledge (property) by a mortgage **2.** to put an advance claim on [he mortgaged his future] —**mort′ga·gor, mort′gag·er** *n.*

mort·ga·gee (môr′gə jē′) *n.* a person to whom property is mortgaged

mor·ti·cian (môr tish′ən) *n.* [< L. *mors*, death] *same as* FUNERAL DIRECTOR

mor·ti·fy (môr′tə fī′) *vt.* **-fied′, -fy′ing** [< L. *mors*, death + *facere*, to make] **1.** to control (physical desires) by self-denial, fasting, etc. **2.** to humiliate —**mor′ti·fi·ca′tion** (-fi kā′shən) *n.*

mor·tise (môr′tis) *n.* [< Ar. *murtazza*, joined] a notch or hole cut, as in a piece of wood, to receive a projecting part (tenon) shaped to fit

mor·tu·ar·y (môr′chōō wer′ē) *n., pl.* **-ies** [< L. *mortuus*, dead] a place where dead bodies are kept before burial or cremation

mos. months

Mo·sa·ic (mō zā′ik) *adj.* of Moses or the writings, laws, etc. attributed to him

mo·sa·ic (mō zā′ik) *n.* [< L. *musivus*, artistic < *musa*, MUSE] **1.** the making of pictures or designs by inlaying small bits of colored stone, glass, etc. in mortar **2.** a picture or design so made

Mo·ses (mō′ziz) *Bible* the leader who brought the Israelites out of slavery in Egypt

mo·sey (mō′zē) *vi.* [< var. of VAMOOSE] [Slang] **1.** to amble along **2.** to go away

Mos·lem (mäz′ləm, muz′-, mäs′-) *n., adj. var. of* MUSLIM

mosque (mäsk) *n.* [ult. < Ar. *sajada*, pray] a Muslim place of worship

mos·qui·to (mə skēt′ō) *n., pl.* **-toes, -tos** [Sp. & Port. < L. *musca*, a fly] a two-winged insect, the female of which bites animals and sucks their blood

moss (môs, mäs) *n.* [OE. *mos,* a swamp] a very small, green plant growing in velvety clusters on rocks, moist ground, etc. —**moss′y** *adj.*

most (mōst) *adj. compar.* MORE [OE. *mast*] **1.** greatest in amount or degree: superl. of MUCH **2.** greatest in number: superl. of MANY **3.** in the greatest number of instances —*n.* **1.** the greatest amount or degree **2.** [*with pl. v.*] the greatest number (*of*) —*adv. compar.* MORE in or to the greatest degree or extent

most′ly *adv.* **1.** for the most part; mainly **2.** chiefly; principally **3.** usually

mot (mō) *n.* [Fr., a word] a witty remark

mote (mōt) *n.* [OE. *mot*] a speck, as of dust

mo·tel (mō tel′) *n.* [MO(TORIST) + (HO)TEL] a hotel for those traveling by car

moth (môth) *n., pl.* **moths** (môthz, môths) [OE. *moththe*] a four-winged, chiefly night-flying insect related to the butterfly; specif., a moth **(clothes moth)** whose larvae eat holes in woolens, furs, etc.

moth′ball′ *n.* a small ball of naphthalene, the fumes of which repel clothes moths —**in mothballs** put into storage or reserve

moth·er (muth′ər) *n.* [OE. *modor*] **1.** a female parent **2.** an origin or source **3.** a woman who is the head **(mother superior)** of a religious establishment —*adj.* **1.** of or like a mother **2.** native [*mother* tongue] —*vt.* to be the mother of —**moth′er·hood′** *n.*

Mother Goose the imaginary creator of a collection of English nursery rhymes

moth′er-in-law′ (-ən lô′) *n., pl.* **moth′ers-in-law′** the mother of one's husband or wife

moth′er·land′ *n.* one's native land

moth′er·ly *adj.* of or like a mother; maternal —**moth′er·li·ness** *n.*

moth′er-of-pearl′ *n.* the hard, pearly internal layer of the shell of the pearl oyster, etc., used to make buttons, etc.

mo·tif (mō tēf′) *n.* [Fr.: see MOTIVE] **1.** a theme or subject that is repeated with various changes, as in a piece of music, a book, etc. **2.** a repeated figure in a design

mo·tile (mōt′'l) *adj.* [< L. *movere,* to move] *Biol.* capable of or exhibiting spontaneous motion

mo·tion (mō′shən) *n.* [< L. *movere,* to move] **1.** a moving from one place to another **2.** a moving of a part of the body; specif., a gesture **3.** a proposal formally made in an assembly —*vi.* to make a meaningful movement of the hand, etc. —*vt.* to direct by a meaningful gesture —**in motion** moving —**mo′tion·less** *adj.*

motion picture 1. a sequence of photographs or drawings projected on a screen in such rapid succession as to create the illusion of moving persons and objects **2.** a play, etc. in this form

mo·ti·vate (mōt′ə vāt′) *vt.* -**vat′ed,** -**vat′ing** to provide with, or affect as, a motive; incite —**mo′ti·va′tion** *n.*

mo·tive (mōt′iv) *n.* [< L. *movere,* to move] **1.** an inner drive, impulse, etc. that causes one to act; incentive **2.** *same as* MOTIF —*adj.* of or causing motion

-motive *a suffix meaning* moving, of motion [*locomotive*]

mot·ley (mät′lē) *adj.* [< ?] **1.** of many colors **2.** of many different elements [*a motley* group] **mo·tor** (mōt′ər) *n.* [L. < *movere,* to move] **1.** anything that produces motion **2.** an engine; esp., an internal-combustion engine **3.** a machine for converting electrical energy into mechanical energy —*adj.* **1.** producing motion **2.** of or powered by a motor **3.** of, by, or for motor vehicles **4.** for motorists **5.** of or involv-

ing muscular movements —*vi.* to travel by automobile

mo′tor·boat′ *n.* a boat propelled by a motor

mo·tor·cade (mōt′ər kād′) *n.* [MOTOR + (CAVAL)CADE] a procession of automobiles

mo′tor·car′ *n. same as* AUTOMOBILE

mo′tor·cy′cle (-sī′k'l) *n.* a two-wheeled vehicle propelled by an internal-combustion engine — **mo′tor·cy′clist** *n.*

motor hotel *same as* MOTEL: also **motor court, motor inn, motor lodge**

mo′tor·ist *n.* one who drives an automobile or travels by automobile

mo·tor·ize (mōt′ə rīz′) *vt.* -**ized′,** -**iz′ing** to equip with a motor or with motor-driven vehicles —**mo′tor·i·za′tion** *n.*

mo′tor·man (-mən) *n., pl.* -**men** one who drives an electric railway car

motor vehicle a vehicle on wheels having its own motor, as an automobile or bus

mot·tle (mät′'l) *vt.* -**tled,** -**tling** [< MOTLEY] to mark with blotches or streaks of different colors —**mot′tled** *adj.*

mot·to (mät′ō) *n., pl.* -**toes,** -**tos** [It., a word] a word or saying that expresses one's aims, ideals, or guiding rule

mould, mould′er, mould′ing, mould′y, moult (mōld, *etc.*) *chiefly Brit. sp. of* MOLD, MOLDER, MOLDING, MOLDY, MOLT

mound (mound) *n.* [< ? MDu. *mond,* protection] a heap or bank of earth, sand, etc. —*vt.* to heap up in a mound

mount¹ (mount) *n.* [< L. *mons*] a mountain

mount² (mount) *vi.* [< L. *mons,* mountain] **1.** to climb; ascend **2.** to climb up on something, as a horse **3.** to increase in amount —*vt.* **1.** to go up; ascend [*to mount* stairs] **2.** to get up on (a horse, platform, etc.) **3.** to set on or provide with a horse **4.** to fix (a jewel, picture, etc.) on or in the proper support, backing, setting, etc. **5.** to arrange (a dead animal, etc.) for exhibition **6.** to place (a gun) into position for use — *n.* **1.** the act of mounting **2.** a horse, etc. for riding **3.** the support, setting, etc. on or in which a thing is mounted

moun·tain (moun′t'n) *n.* [< L. *mons*] **1.** a natural raised part of the earth, larger than a hill **2.** a large pile, amount, etc. —*adj.* **1.** of or in mountains **2.** like a mountain

moun′tain·eer′ (-ir′) *n.* **1.** one who lives in a mountainous region **2.** a mountain climber —*vi.* to climb mountains

mountain goat *same as* ROCKY MOUNTAIN GOAT

mountain lion *same as* COUGAR

moun′tain·ous (-əs) *adj.* **1.** full of mountains **2.** like a mountain; esp., very large

moun·te·bank (moun′tə bank′) *n.* [< It. *montare,* to mount + *in,* on + *banco,* a bench] a charlatan, or quack

mount′ing *n.* something serving as a backing, support, setting, etc.

mourn (môrn) *vi., vt.* [OE. *murnan*] **1.** to feel or express sorrow for (something regrettable) **2.** to grieve for (someone dead)

mourn′ful *adj.* **1.** feeling or expressing grief or sorrow **2.** causing sorrow

mourn′ing *n.* **1.** a sorrowing; specif., the expression of grief at someone's death **2.** black clothes, etc., worn as a sign of grief

mouse (mous) *n., pl.* **mice** [OE. *mus*] **1.** any of numerous small rodents, esp. the **house mouse** which infests human dwellings **2.** a timid person **3.** [Slang] a dark, swollen bruise under the eye —*vi.* (mouz) moused, **mous′ing** to hunt for mice

mousse (moos) *n.* [Fr., foam] a light chilled

dessert made with egg white, whipped cream, etc., combined with fruit or flavoring
mous·tache (mə stash′, mus′tash) *n. var. of* MUSTACHE
mous·y, mous·ey (mou′sē, -zē) *adj.* -i·er, -i·est quiet, timid, drab, etc.
mouth (mouth) *n., pl.* **mouths** (mou*thz*) [OE. *muth*] **1.** the opening through which an animal takes in food and through which sounds are uttered **2.** any opening regarded as like the mouth *[the mouth of a river]* —*vt.* (mou*th*) **1.** to say, esp. in an insincere manner **2.** to form (a word) with the mouth soundlessly —**down in** (or **at**) **the mouth** [Colloq.] depressed; unhappy
mouth′ful′ *n., pl.* -**fuls′ 1.** as much as the mouth can hold **2.** the usual amount taken into the mouth **3.** a small amount **4.** [Slang] a pertinent remark: chiefly in **say a mouthful**
mouth organ *same as* HARMONICA
mouth′part′ *n.* a structure or organ around the mouth in arthropods, used for biting, grasping, etc.: *usually used in pl.*
mouth′piece′ *n.* **1.** a part, as of a musical instrument, held in or to the mouth **2.** a person, periodical, etc. used by others to express their views
mouth′wash′ *n.* a flavored liquid used for rinsing the mouth or gargling
mou·ton (mōō′tän) *n.* [Fr., sheep] lambskin, processed to resemble beaver, seal, etc.
mov·a·ble (mōō′və b'l) *adj.* that can be moved from one place to another —*n.* **1.** something movable **2.** *[usually pl.]* *Law* personal property, as furniture Also **move′a·ble**
move (mōōv) *vt.* **moved, mov′ing** [< L. *movere*] **1.** to change the place or position of **2.** to set or keep in motion **3.** to cause (*to act, do, say,* etc.) **4.** to arouse the emotions, etc. of **5.** to propose formally, as in a meeting —*vi.* **1.** to change place or position **2.** to change residence **3.** to be active **4.** to make progress **5.** to take action **6.** to be, or be set, in motion **7.** to make a formal application (*for*) **8.** to evacuate: said of the bowels **9.** to be sold: said of goods —*n.* **1.** the act of moving **2.** an action toward some goal **3.** *Chess, Checkers,* etc. the act of moving or one's turn to move —**on the move** [Colloq.] moving about
move′ment *n.* **1.** a moving or manner of moving **2.** an evacuation (of the bowels) **3.** a change in the location of troops, ships, etc. **4.** organized action by people working toward some goal **5.** the moving parts of a mechanism, as of a clock **6.** *Music a)* any of the principal divisions of an extended composition *b) same as* TEMPO *or* RHYTHM
mov′er *n.* one that moves; specif., one whose work is moving furniture, etc. for those changing residence
mov·ie (mōō′vē) *n.* [< MOVING PICTURE] a motion picture
mow[1] (mō) *vt., vi.* **mowed, mowed** or **mown, mow′ing** [OE. *mawan*] to cut down (grass, etc.) from (a lawn, etc.) as with a sickle or lawn mower —**mow down 1.** to cause to fall like cut grass **2.** to kill or destroy —**mow′er** *n.*
mow[2] (mou) *n.* [OE. *muga*] **1.** a heap of hay, grain, etc., esp. in a barn **2.** the part of a barn where hay or grain is stored
MP, M.P. Military Police
mpg, m.p.g. miles per gallon
mph, m.p.h. miles per hour
Mr. (mis′tər) *pl.* **Messrs.** (mes′ərz) mister: before a man's name or title
Mrs. (mis′iz) *pl.* **Mmes.** (mā däm′) mistress: before a married woman's name
MS., ms., ms *pl.* **MSS., mss., mss** manuscript

Ms. (miz, em′es′) a title, free of reference to marital status, used in place of either *Miss* or *Mrs.*
Msgr. Monsignor
MSgt, M/Sgt. Master Sergeant
MST, M.S.T. Mountain Standard Time
Mt., mt. *pl.* **mts. 1.** mount **2.** mountain
mu (myōō, mōō) *n.* the twelfth letter of the Greek alphabet (M, μ)
much (much) *adj.* **more, most** [OE. *mycel*] great in quantity, degree, etc. —*adv.* **1.** to a great degree or extent *[much* happier*]* **2.** nearly *[much* the same*]* —*n.* **1.** a great amount *[much* of it*]* **2.** something great, outstanding, etc. *[not much* to look at*]* —**make much of** to treat or consider as of great importance
mu·ci·lage (myōō′s'l ij) *n.* [< L. *mucere,* be moldy] **1.** a thick, sticky substance produced in certain plants **2.** any watery solution of gum, glue, etc. used as an adhesive —**mu′ci·lag′i·nous** (-sə laj′ə nəs) *adj.*
muck (muk) *n.* [< ON. *myki,* dung] **1.** moist manure **2.** black earth containing decaying matter, used as fertilizer **3.** dirt; filth —**muck′y** *adj.* -i·er, -i·est
muck′rake′ (-rāk′) *vi.* -**raked′**, -**rak′ing** [see MUCK & RAKE[1]] to search for and expose corruption in politics, business, etc. —**muck′rak′er** *n.*
mu·cous (myōō′kəs) *adj.* **1.** of, containing, or secreting mucus **2.** slimy
mucous membrane a mucus-secreting membrane lining body cavities
mu·cus (myōō′kəs) *n.* [L.] the slimy secretion that moistens and protects the mucous membranes
mud (mud) *n.* [prob. < a LowG. source] wet, soft, sticky earth
mud·dle (mud′'l) *vt.* -**dled, -dling** [< MUD] **1.** to mix up; bungle **2.** to confuse, as with liquor —*vi.* to act or think in a confused way —*n.* mess, confusion, etc.
mud′dy (-ē) *adj.* -**di·er, -di·est 1.** full of or spattered with mud **2.** cloudy *[muddy* coffee*]* **3.** confused, obscure, etc. —*vt., vi.* -**died, -dy·ing** to make or become muddy —**mud′di·ness** *n.*
mud′sling′ing *n.* unscrupulous attacks against an opponent, as in politics
mu·ez·zin (myōō ez′in) *n.* [< Ar. *adhana,* proclaim] a Muslim crier who calls the people to prayer at the proper hours
muff (muf) *n.* [Du. *mof* < Fr. *moufle,* mitten] **1.** a cylindrical covering of fur, etc. for keeping the hands warm **2.** *a) Baseball,* etc. a failure to hold the ball when catching it *b)* any bungling action —*vt., vi.* to do (something) badly or awkwardly
muf·fin (muf′'n) *n.* [< ?] a quick bread baked in a small, cup-shaped mold
muf·fle (muf′'l) *vt.* -**fled, -fling** [prob. < OFr. *moufle,* mitten] **1.** to wrap so as to hide, keep warm, etc. **2.** to cover so as to deaden sound **3.** to deaden (a sound)
muf′fler (-lər) *n.* **1.** a scarf worn around the throat, as for warmth **2.** a device for silencing noises
muf·ti (muf′tē) *n., pl.* -**tis** [Ar. < *āftā,* to judge] ordinary clothes, not a uniform
mug (mug) *n.* [prob. < Scand.] **1.** a cup of earthenware or metal, with a handle **2.** as much as a mug will hold **3.** [Slang] the face —*vt.* **mugged, mug′ging** to assault, usually with intent to rob —*vi.* [Slang] to grimace, esp. in overacting —**mug′ger** *n.*
mug·gy (mug′ē) *adj.* -**gi·er, -gi·est** [< ? ON. *mugga,* a drizzle] hot, damp, and close *[muggy* weather*]* —**mug′gi·ness** *n.*

mug·wump (mug′wump′) *n.* [< Algonquian *mugquomp*, chief] an independent, esp. in politics

mu·lat·to (mə lat′ō) *n., pl.* **-toes** [Sp. & Port. *mulato*, of mixed breed] a person who has one black parent and one white parent

mul·ber·ry (mul′ber′ē, -bər ē) *n., pl.* **-ries** [OE. *morberie*] **1.** a tree with edible, berrylike fruits **2.** this fruit **3.** purplish red

mulch (mulch) *n.* [ME. *molsh*, soft] leaves, peat, etc., spread around plants to prevent freezing of roots, etc. —*vt.* to apply mulch to

mulct (mulkt) *vt.* [< L. *multa*, a fine] **1.** to fine **2.** to extract (money) from (someone), as by fraud —*n.* a fine

mule¹ (myool) *n.* [< L. *mulus*] **1.** the (usually sterile) offspring of a male donkey and a female horse **2.** a machine that spins cotton fibers into yarn **3.** [Colloq.] a stubborn person

mule² (myool) *n.* [Fr. < L. *mulleus*, red shoe] a lounging slipper that bares the heel

mu·le·teer (myool′ə tir′) *n.* [< OFr.] a driver of mules

mul′ish *adj.* like a mule; stubborn

mull¹ (mul) *vt., vi.* [ME. *mullen*, to grind] [Colloq.] to ponder (*over*)

mull² (mul) *vt.* [< ?] to heat, sweeten, and flavor with spices (ale, cider, wine, etc.)

mul·lein (mul′in) *n.* [< L. *mollis*, soft] a tall plant with spikes of variously colored flowers

mul·let (mul′it) *n.* [< L. *mullus*] any of a group of edible, spiny-rayed fishes found in fresh and salt waters

mul·li·gan (stew) (mul′i g′n) [< ?] [Slang] a stew made of meat and vegetables

mul·li·ga·taw·ny (mul′i gə tô′nē) *n.* [Tamil *milagutannir*, pepper water] an East Indian soup of meat, etc., flavored with curry

mul·lion (mul′yən) *n.* [prob. < L. *medianus*, middle] a slender, vertical dividing bar between the lights of windows, panels, etc.

multi- [L. < *multus*, much, many] *a combining form meaning:* **1.** having many **2.** more than two **3.** many times more than

mul·ti·far·i·ous (mul′tə far′ē əs) *adj.* [< L.] having many kinds of parts or elements

mul′ti·mil′lion·aire′ *n.* a wealthy person worth many millions of dollars, francs, etc.

mul′ti·na′tion·al *adj.* **1.** of many nations **2.** designating or of a corporation with branches in many countries —*n.* a multinational corporation

mul·ti·ple (mul′tə p′l) *adj.* [Fr. < L. *multus*, many + *-plex*, -fold] having many parts, elements, etc. —*n.* a number that is a product of a specified number and another number

multiple sclerosis a disease of the central nervous system, with loss of coordination

mul′ti·plex′ (-pleks′) *adj.* [L.] designating a system for sending simultaneously two or more signals over a common circuit, etc.

mul·ti·pli·cand (mul′tə pli kand′) *n.* a number that is to be multiplied by another

mul′ti·pli·ca′tion (-pli kā′shən) *n.* a multiplying or being multiplied; specif., the process of finding the quantity obtained by repeating a specified quantity a specified number of times

mul′ti·plic′i·ty (-plis′ə tē) *n.* **1.** a being manifold or various **2.** a great number

mul′ti·pli′er (-plī′ər) *n.* **1.** one that multiplies **2.** the number by which another is to be multiplied

mul·ti·ply (mul′tə plī′) *vt., vi.* **-plied′, -ply′ing** [see MULTIPLE] **1.** to increase in number, degree, etc. **2.** to find the product (of) by multiplication

mul·ti·tude (mul′tə tood′) *n.* [< L. *multus*, many] a large number; host, myriad, etc.

mul′ti·tu′di·nous (-tood′′n əs) *adj.* many

mum¹ (mum) *n.* [Colloq.] a chrysanthemum

mum² (mum) *adj.* [ME. *momme*] silent

mum·ble (mum′b′l) *vt., vi.* **-bled, -bling** [ME. *momelen*] to speak or say indistinctly —*n.* a mumbled utterance —**mum′bler** *n.*

mum·bo jum·bo (mum′bō jum′bō) [of Afr. orig.] **1.** an idol or fetish **2.** meaningless ritual, etc.

mum·mer (mum′ər) *n.* [< OFr. *momo*, grimace] one who wears a mask or disguise, as for acting out pantomimes

mum′mer·y *n., pl.* **-ies 1.** performance by mummers **2.** a hypocritical show or ceremony

mum·mi·fy (mum′ə fī′) *vt., vi.* **-fied′, -fy′ing** to make or become a mummy

mum·my (mum′ē) *n., pl.* **-mies** [ult. < Per. *mum*, wax] a well-preserved dead body, esp. one preserved by embalming, as by the ancient Egyptians

mumps (mumps) *n.pl.* [*with sing. v.*] [pl. of obs. *mump*, a grimace] an acute communicable disease, caused by a virus and characterized by swelling of the salivary glands

munch (munch) *vt., vi.* [echoic] to chew steadily, often with a crunching sound

mun·dane (mun dān′, mun′dān) *adj.* [< L. *mundus*, world] **1.** of the world; worldly **2.** commonplace; everyday

mu·nic·i·pal (myoo nis′ə p′l) *adj.* [< L. *munia*, official duties + *capere*, to take] of or having to do with a city, town, etc. or its local government —**mu·nic′i·pal·ly** *adv.*

mu·nic′i·pal′i·ty (-pal′ə tē) *n., pl.* **-ties** a city, town, etc. having its own incorporated government

mu·nif·i·cent (myoo nif′ə s′nt) *adj.* [< L. *munus*, a gift + *facere*, to make] very generous in giving; lavish —**mu·nif′i·cence** *n.*

mu·ni·tions (myoo nish′ənz) *n.pl.* [< L. *munire*, fortify] war supplies; esp., weapons and ammunition

mu·ral (myoor′əl) *adj.* [Fr. < L. *murus*, a wall] of, on, or for a wall —*n.* a picture, esp. a large one, painted on a wall

mur·der (mur′dər) *n.* [OE. *morthor*] the unlawful and malicious or premeditated killing of a person —*vt.* **1.** to kill unlawfully and with malice **2.** to botch, as in performance [she *murdered* that song] —*vi.* to commit murder —**mur′der·er** *n.* —**mur′der·ess** *n.fem.*

mur·der·ous *adj.* **1.** of or characteristic of murder; brutal **2.** capable or guilty of, or intending, murder —**mur′der·ous·ly** *adv.*

murk (murk) *n.* [< ON. *myrkr*, dark] darkness; gloom

murk′y *adj.* **-i·er, -i·est** dark or gloomy

mur·mur (mur′mər) *n.* [< L.] **1.** a low, indistinct, continuous sound **2.** a mumbled complaint **3.** an abnormal sound in the body, esp. in the region of the heart —*vi.* to make a murmur —*vt.* to say in a murmur

mur·rain (mur′in) *n.* [< L. *mori*, to die] an infectious disease of cattle

mus·cat (mus′kət, -kat) *n.* [Fr. < LL. *muscus*, musk] a sweet European grape

mus·ca·tel (mus′kə tel′) *n.* a rich, sweet wine made from the muscat

mus·cle (mus′′l) *n.* [Fr. < L. *mus*, mouse] **1.** any body organ consisting of fibrous tissue that can be contracted and expanded to produce bodily movements **2.** this tissue **3.** muscular strength; brawn —*vi.* **-cled, -cling** [Colloq.] to force one's way (*in*)

mus′cle-bound′ *adj.* having some of the muscles enlarged and less elastic, as from too much exercise

mus·cu·lar (mus'kyə lər) *adj.* **1.** of or done by muscles **2.** having well-developed muscles — **mus'cu·lar'i·ty** (-lar'ə tē) *n.*

muscular dys·tro·phy (dis'trə fē) [< DYS- + Gr. *trephein*, nourish] a chronic disease characterized by a progressive wasting of the muscles

mus·cu·la·ture (mus'kyə lə chər) *n.* [Fr.] the arrangement of the muscles of a body, limb, etc.; muscular system

Muse (myōōz) *n.* [< Gr. *mousa*] **1.** *Gr. Myth.* any of the nine goddesses who presided over literature and the arts and sciences **2.** [m-] the spirit regarded as inspiring a poet or artist

muse (myōōz) *vi.* **mused, mus'ing** [< OFr. *muser*, to loiter] to think deeply; meditate —*vt.* to think or say meditatively

mu·se·um (myōō zē'əm) *n.* [ult. < Gr. *mousa,* Muse] a building, room, etc. for preserving and exhibiting artistic, historical, or scientific objects

mush¹ (mush) *n.* [prob. var. of MASH] **1.** a thick porridge of boiled cornmeal **2.** any thick, soft mass **3.** [Colloq.] maudlin sentimentality — **mush'y** *adj.* **-i·er, -i·est**

mush² (mush) *interj.* [? < Fr. *marcher,* go] a shout to urge on sled dogs —*vi.* to travel on foot over snow, usually with a dog sled

mush·room (mush'rōōm') *n.* [< LL. *mussirio*] any of various fleshy fungi, typically with a stalk capped by an umbrellalike top; esp., an edible variety —*adj.* of or like a mushroom —*vi.* to grow or spread rapidly

mu·sic (myōō'zik) *n.* [< Gr. *mousikē* (technē), (art) of the Muses] **1.** the art of combining tones to form expressive compositions **2.** such compositions **3.** any rhythmic sequence of pleasing sounds —**face the music** [Colloq.] to accept the consequences

mu'si·cal *adj.* **1.** of or for music **2.** melodious or harmonious **3.** fond of or skilled in music **4.** set to music —*n.* a light play or movie with dialogue, songs, and dances: often **musical comedy** —**mu'si·cal·ly** *adv.*

mu·si·cale (myōō'zə kal') *n.* [Fr.] a social affair featuring a musical program

mu·si·cian (myōō zish'ən) *n.* one skilled in music; esp., a professional performer

mu·si·col·o·gy (myōō'zi käl'ə jē) *n.* the study of the science, history, and methods of music —**mu'si·col'o·gist** *n.*

musk (musk) *n.* [< Sans. *mus,* mouse] an animal secretion having a strong odor: used in making perfumes —**musk'i·ness** *n.* —**musk'y** *adj.* **-i·er, -i·est**

mus·kel·lunge (mus'kə lunj') *n., pl.* **-lunge'** [< AmInd.] a large, edible pike of N. America: also called **mus'kie** (-kē)

mus·ket (mus'kit) *n.* [< L. *musca,* a fly] a former shoulder firearm, with a smooth bore

mus·ket·eer (mus'kə tir') *n.* a soldier armed with a musket

musk'mel'on *n.* any of various sweet, juicy melons, as the cantaloupe

musk·rat (musk'rat') *n.* **1.** a N. American water rodent with brown fur and a musky odor **2.** its fur

Mus·lim (muz'ləm, mooz'-, moos'-) *n.* [< Ar. < *aslama,* resign oneself (to God)] an adherent of Islam —*adj.* of Islam or the Muslims

mus·lin (muz'lin) *n.* [< Fr. < *Mosul,* city in Iraq] a strong cotton cloth; esp., a heavy kind used for sheets, etc.

muss (mus) *vt.* [prob. var. of MESS] to make

messy or disordered; disarrange —**muss'y** *adj.* **-i·er, -i·est**

mus·sel (mus''l) *n.* [ult. < L. *musculus*] any of various saltwater or freshwater bivalve mollusks

must (must) *v.aux. pt.* **must** [< OE. *moste*] an auxiliary expressing: **1.** necessity [I *must* go] **2.** probability [it *must* be Joe] **3.** certainty [all *must* die] —*n.* [Colloq.] something that must be done, had, etc.

mus·tache (mə stash', mus'tash) *n.* [< Fr. < Gr. *mastax,* mouth] the hair on the upper lip of men

mus·tang (mus'taŋ) *n.* [< Sp. *mesteño,* strayed] a small wild horse of the SW plains

mus·tard (mus'tərd) *n.* [< OFr.] **1.** a plant with yellow flowers and slender pods **2.** the yellow powder made from its ground seeds, often used in paste form as a condiment **3.** a dark yellow

mus·ter (mus'tər) *vt.* [< L. *monere,* to warn] **1.** to assemble (troops, etc.) **2.** to collect; summon [to *muster* up strength] —*vi.* to assemble, as troops —*n.* **1.** an assembling, as of troops for inspection **2.** the persons or things assembled —**muster in** (or **out**) to enlist in (or discharge from) military service —**pass muster** to measure up to the required standards

must·n't (mus''nt) must not

mus·ty (mus'tē) *adj.* **-ti·er, -ti·est** [< ? MOIST] **1.** having a stale, moldy smell or taste **2.** stale or trite; antiquated

mu·ta·ble (myōōt'ə b'l) *adj.* [< L. *mutare,* to change] **1.** that can be changed **2.** inconstant; fickle —**mu'ta·bil'i·ty** *n.*

mu·tant (myōōt''nt) *adj.* [see prec.] of mutation —*n.* an animal or plant with inheritable characteristics that differ from those of the parents

mu·tate (myōō'tāt) *vi., vt.* **-tat·ed, -tat·ing** [see MUTABLE] to change

mu·ta·tion (myōō tā'shən) *n.* **1.** a change, as in form, nature, etc. **2.** *a)* a sudden variation in some inheritable characteristic of an animal or plant *b)* a mutant

mute (myōōt) *adj.* [< L. *mutus*] **1.** not speaking; silent **2.** unable to speak —*n.* **1.** a deafmute **2.** *Music* a device that softens the tone of an instrument —*vt.* **mut'ed, mut'ing** to soften the sound of —**mute'ly** *adv.* —**mute'ness** *n.*

mu·ti·late (myōōt''l āt') *vt.* **-lat·ed, -lat·ing** [< L. *mutilus,* maimed] to cut off, damage, or spoil an important part of —**mu'ti·la'tion** *n.*

mu·ti·neer (myōōt''n ir') *n.* one guilty of mutiny

mu·ti·ny (myōōt''n ē) *n., pl.* **-nies** [ult. < L. *movere,* to move] revolt against constituted authority; esp., rebellion of soldiers or sailors against their officers —*vi.* **-nied, -ny·ing** to revolt —**mu'ti·nous** *adj.*

mutt (mut) *n.* [Slang] a mongrel dog

mut·ter (mut'ər) *vi., vt.* [ME. *moteren*] **1.** to speak or say in low, indistinct tones **2.** to grumble —*n.* **1.** a muttering **2.** something muttered

mut·ton (mut''n) *n.* [< ML. *multo,* sheep] the flesh of sheep, esp. a grown sheep, used as food

mu·tu·al (myōō'choo wəl) *adj.* [< L. *mutare,* to change] **1.** *a)* done, felt, etc. by each of two or more for or toward the other or others *b)* of each other **2.** shared in common [our *mutual* friend] —**mu'tu·al·ly** *adv.*

mutual fund a corporation that invests its shareholders' funds in diversified securities

muumuu 302 napalm

muu·muu (mōō′mōō) *n.* [Haw.] a long, loose dress of Hawaiian style
muz·zle (muz′'l) *n.* [< ML. *musum*] 1. the mouth, nose, and jaws of a dog, horse, etc. 2. a device put over the mouth of an animal to prevent its biting or eating 3. the front end of the barrel of a firearm —*vt.* -zled, -zling 1. to put a muzzle on (an animal) 2. to prevent from talking
my (mī) *possessive pronominal adj.* [OE. *min*] of, belonging to, or done by me
my·e·li·tis (mī′ə līt′is) *n.* [< Gr. *myelos*, marrow + -ITIS] inflammation of the spinal cord or the bone marrow
My·lar (mī′lär) *a trademark for* a polyester used for recording tapes, fabrics, etc. —*n.* [m-] this substance
my·na, my·nah (mī′nə) *n.* [Hindi *mainā*] a tropical bird of SE Asia related to the starling: some can mimic human speech
my·o·pi·a (mī ō′pē ə) *n.* [< Gr. *myein*, to close + *ōps*, eye] nearsightedness —**my·op′ic** (-äp′ik) *adj.*
myr·i·ad (mir′ē əd) *n.* [< Gr. *myrias*, ten thousand] a large number of persons or things —*adj.* very many
myr·mi·don (mur′mə dän′, -dən) *n.* [< name of a Greek tribe led by Achilles] an unquestioning follower
myrrh (mur) *n.* [ult. < Ar. *murr*] a fragrant gum resin from Arabia and E Africa, used in incense, perfume, etc.
myr·tle (mur′t'l) *n.* [< Gr. *myrtos*] 1. an evergreen shrub with white or pink, flowers and dark berries 2. any of various other plants, as the periwinkle

my·self (mī self′) *pron.* 1. *the intensive form of* I [I myself went] 2. *the reflexive form of* I [I hurt myself] 3. my true self [I am not myself today]
mys·te·ri·ous (mis tir′ē əs) *adj.* of, containing, or characterized by mystery
mys·ter·y (mis′tə rē) *n., pl.* -les [< Gr. *mystērion*, secret rite] 1. something unexplained, unknown, or kept secret 2. a novel or play about a secret crime, etc. [a murder mystery] 3. obscurity or secrecy
mys·tic (mis′tik) *adj.* [< Gr. *mystēs*, one initiated] 1. *same as* MYSTICAL 2. mysterious, secret, occult, etc. —*n.* one professing to undergo profound spiritual experiences
mys′ti·cal *adj.* 1. of mystics or mysticism 2. spiritually significant or symbolic 3. *same as* MYSTIC (sense 2)
mys·ti·cism (mis′tə siz'm) *n.* 1. the doctrine that knowledge of spiritual truths can be acquired by intuition and meditation 2. obscure thinking or belief
mys′ti·fy′ (-fī′) *vt.* -fied, -fy′ing 1. to puzzle or perplex 2. to involve in mystery
mys·tique (mis tēk′) *n.* [Fr., mystic] the quasi-mystical attitudes and feelings surrounding some person, institution, etc.
myth (mith) *n.* [< Gr. *mythos*] 1. a traditional story serving to explain some phenomenon, custom, etc. 2. mythology 3. any fictitious story 4. any imaginary person or thing —**myth′i·cal** *adj.*
my·thol·o·gy (mi thäl′ə jē) *n., pl.* -gies 1. the study of myths 2. myths collectively, esp. of a specific people —**myth·o·log·i·cal** (mith′ə läj′i k'l) *adj.* —**my·thol′o·gist** *n.*

N

N, n (en) *n., pl.* **N's, n's** the fourteenth letter of the English alphabet
N *Chem.* nitrogen
N, N., n, n. 1. north 2. northern
n. 1. net 2. neuter 3. noon 4. noun
Na [L. *natrium*] *Chem.* sodium
N.A. North America
nab (nab) *vt.* nabbed, nab′bing [prob. < dial. *nap*, to snatch] [Colloq.] 1. to seize suddenly; snatch 2. to arrest or catch (a felon or wrongdoer)
na·bob (nā′bäb) *n.* [< Ar. *nā'ib*, deputy] a very rich man
na·cre (nā′kər) *n.* [Fr. < Ar.] *same as* MOTHER-OF-PEARL —**na′cre·ous** (-krē əs) *adj.*
na·dir (nā′dər, -dir) *n.* [< Ar. *nazīr*, opposite] 1. the point opposite the zenith and directly below the observer 2. the lowest point
nae (nā) *adv.* [Scot.] no; not —*adj.* no
nag¹ (nag) *vt., vi.* nagged, nag′ging [< Scand.] 1. to annoy by continual scolding, faultfinding, etc. 2. to keep troubling —*n.* one who nags: also **nag′ger**
nag² (nag) *n.* [ME. *nagge*] an inferior horse, esp. an old one
nai·ad (nā′ad, nī′-) *n.* [< Gr. *naein*, to flow] [also N-] *Gr. & Rom. Myth.* any nymph living in springs, rivers, etc.
nail (nāl) *n.* [OE. *nægl*] 1. the thin, horny growth at the ends of fingers and toes 2. a slender, pointed piece of metal driven with a hammer to hold pieces of wood together —*vt.* 1. to attach, fasten, etc. with nails 2. [Colloq.] to catch or hit

na·ive, na·ïve (nä ēv′) *adj.* [Fr. < L. *nativus*, natural] unaffectedly simple; artless; unsophisticated —**na·ive′ly, na·ïve′ly** *adv.* —**na·ive·té′, na·ïve·té′** (-tā′) *n.*
na·ked (nā′kid) *adj.* [OE. *nacod*] 1. completely unclothed; nude 2. without covering [a naked sword] 3. without additions, disguises, etc.; plain [the naked truth]
nam·by-pam·by (nam′bē pam′bē) *adj.* [< nickname of *Ambrose Philips*, 18th-c. Eng. poet] weakly sentimental; insipid —*n., pl.* -bies a namby-pamby person
name (nām) *n.* [OE. *nama*] 1. a word or phrase by which a person, thing, or class is known; title 2. a word or phrase considered descriptive; epithet 3. a) reputation b) good reputation 4. appearance only, not reality [chief in name only] —*adj.* well-known —*vt.* named, nam′ing 1. to give a name to 2. to designate by name 3. to identify by the right name [name the oceans] 4. to appoint to an office, etc. 5. to specify (a day, price, etc.) —**in the name of** 1. in appeal to 2. by authority of
name′less *adj.* 1. not having a name 2. left unnamed 3. indescribable
name′ly *adv.* that is to say; to wit
name′sake′ *n.* a person with the same name as another, esp. if named after another
nap¹ (nap) *vi.* napped, nap′ping [OE. *hnappian*] to sleep lightly for a short time —*n.* a brief, light sleep
nap² (nap) *n.* [ME. *noppe*] the downy or hairy surface of cloth formed by short hairs or fibers
na·palm (nā′päm) *n.* [containing *na(phthene)*]

& *palm(itate)*] a jellylike substance with gasoline in it, used in fire bombs, etc.

nape (nāp) *n.* [ME.] the back of the neck

naph·tha (naf′thə, nap′-) *n.* [< Per. *neft,* pitch] a flammable liquid distilled from petroleum, coal tar, etc. and used as a fuel, solvent, etc.

naph′tha·lene′ (-lēn′) *n.* [< prec.] a white, crystalline hydrocarbon obtained from coal tar and used in moth repellents, dyes, etc.

nap·kin (nap′kin) *n.* [< L. *mappa,* cloth] **1.** a small cloth or piece of paper used while eating to protect the clothes or wipe the lips, etc. **2.** any small cloth, towel, etc.

narc, nark (närk) *n.* [Slang] a police agent who enforces narcotics laws

nar·cis·sism (när′sə siz′m) *n.* [see NARCISSUS] self-love —**nar′cis·sist** *n., adj.*

Nar·cis·sus (när sis′əs) *Gr. Myth.* a youth who fell in love with his own reflection in a pool and was changed into the narcissus —*n.* [n-] *pl.* **-cis′sus, -cis′sus·es, -cis′si** (-ī) a bulbous plant with white, yellow, or orange flowers

nar·co·sis (när kō′sis) *n.* unconsciousness caused by a narcotic

nar·cot·ic (när kät′ik) *n.* [< Gr. *narkē,* numbness] a drug, as opium, used to relieve pain and induce sleep —*adj.* **1.** of, like, or producing narcosis **2.** of, by, or for narcotic addicts

nar′co·tize′ (-tīz′) *vt.* **-tized′, -tiz′ing** to subject to a narcotic

nar·rate (nar′āt, na rāt′) *vt., vi.* **-rat·ed, -rat·ing** [< L. *narrare,* relate] to tell (a story), relate (events), etc. —**nar′ra·tor** *n.*

nar·ra·tion (na rā′shən) *n.* **1.** a narrating **2.** *same as* NARRATIVE

nar·ra·tive (nar′ə tiv) *adj.* in story form —*n.* **1.** a story; account **2.** the art or practice of narrating

nar·row (nar′ō) *adj.* [OE. *nearu*] **1.** small in width; not wide **2.** limited in meaning, size, amount, etc. [a *narrow* majority] **3.** limited in outlook; not liberal **4.** with barely enough space, time, etc. [a *narrow* escape] —*vi., vt.* to decrease or limit in width, extent, or scope —*n.* [*usually pl.*] a narrow passage; strait —**nar′row·ly** *adv.*

nar′row-mind′ed *adj.* limited in outlook; bigoted; prejudiced

nar·y (ner′ē) *adj.* [< *ne'er a,* never a] [Dial.] not any; no (with *a* or *an*) [*nary* a doubt]

NASA (nas′ə) National Aeronautics and Space Administration

na·sal (nā′z'l) *adj.* [< L. *nasus,* nose] **1.** of the nose **2.** produced by making breath go through the nose —**na′sal·ly** *adv.*

na′sal·ize′ *vt., vi.* **-ized′, -iz′ing** to pronounce or speak with a nasal sound

nas·cent (nas′'nt, nā′s'nt) *adj.* [< L. *nasci,* be born] **1.** coming into being **2.** beginning to form or develop —**nas′cen·cy** *n.*

na·stur·tium (nə stur′shəm) *n.* [< L. *nasus,* nose + *torquere,* to twist] **1.** a plant with red, yellow, or orange flowers and a pungent odor **2.** the flower

nas·ty (nas′tē) *adj.* **-ti·er, -ti·est** [< ?] **1.** very dirty; filthy **2.** morally offensive; obscene **3.** very unpleasant, mean, or harmful —**nas′ti·ly** *adv.* —**nas′ti·ness** *n.*

na·tal (nāt′'l) *adj.* [< L. *nasci,* be born] of or connected with one's birth

na·tes (nā′tēz) *n.pl.* [L.] the buttocks

na·tion (nā′shən) *n.* [< L. *nasci,* be born] **1.** a community of people with a territory, history, economic life, culture, and language in common **2.** people united under a single government; country

na·tion·al (nash′ə n'l) *adj.* of or affecting a nation as a whole —*n.* a citizen of a nation

National Guard in the U.S., the organized militia of individual States, part of the U.S. Army when called into active Federal service

na′tion·al·ism *n.* **1.** *a)* patriotism *b)* narrow, jingoist patriotism **2.** the advocacy of national independence —**na′tion·al·ist** *adj., n.* —**na′tion·al·is′tic** *adj.*

na·tion·al·i·ty (nash′ə nal′ə tē) *n., pl.* **-ties 1.** the status of belonging to a particular nation by birth or naturalization **2.** a national group

na·tion·al·ize (nash′ə nə līz′) *vt.* **-ized′, -iz′ing 1.** to make national **2.** to transfer ownership or control of (land, industries, etc.) to the nation —**na′tion·al·i·za′tion** *n.*

na′tion·wide′ *adj.* by or through the whole nation

na·tive (nāt′iv) *adj.* [< L. *nasci,* be born] **1.** inborn; innate **2.** belonging to a locality or country by birth, production, or growth **3.** being, or associated with, the place of one's birth [one's *native* land or language] **4.** found in nature; natural **5.** of or characteristic of the people born in a certain place —*n.* **1.** a person born in the region indicated **2.** an original inhabitant **3.** an indigenous plant or animal

na′tive-born′ *adj.* born in a specified place or country

na·tiv·i·ty (nə tiv′ə tē) *n., pl.* **-ties** [see NATIVE] birth —**the Nativity 1.** the birth of Jesus **2.** Christmas Day

natl. national

NATO (nā′tō) North Atlantic Treaty Organization

nat·ty (nat′ē) *adj.* **-ti·er, -ti·est** [< ? NEAT] trim and smart in appearance or dress

nat·u·ral (nach′ər əl) *adj.* [< L. *naturalis,* by birth] **1.** of or arising from nature **2.** produced or existing in nature; not artificial **3.** innate; not acquired **4.** true to nature; lifelike **5.** normal [a *natural* result] **6.** free from affectation **7.** *Music* neither sharped nor flatted —*n.* [Colloq.] a sure success —**nat′u·ral·ness** *n.*

natural gas a mixture of gaseous hydrocarbons, chiefly methane, used as fuel

nat′u·ral·ism *n.* **1.** action or thought based on natural desires **2.** *Literature, Art,* etc. faithful adherence to nature; realism

nat′u·ral·ist *n.* **1.** one who studies animals and plants **2.** an advocate of naturalism —**nat′u·ral·is′tic** *adj.*

nat′u·ral·ize′ (-ə līz′) *vt.* **-ized′, -iz′ing** to confer citizenship upon (an alien) —**nat′u·ral·i·za′tion** *n.*

nat′u·ral·ly *adv.* **1.** in a natural manner **2.** by nature; innately **3.** as one might expect; of course

natural resources the forms of wealth supplied by nature, as coal, oil, etc.

natural science the systematized knowledge of nature, including biology, chemistry, physics, etc.

na·ture (nā′chər) *n.* [< L. *nasci,* be born] **1.** the essential quality of a thing; essence **2.** inborn character **3.** kind; sort **4.** *a)* the entire physical universe *b)* [*sometimes* N-] the power, force, etc. that seems to regulate this **5.** the primitive state of man **6.** natural scenery —**by nature** inherently

naught (nôt) *n.* [< OE. *na wiht,* no person] **1.** nothing **2.** *Arith.* the figure zero (0)

naugh·ty (nôt′ē) *adj.* **-ti·er, -ti·est** [< obs. *naught,* wicked] **1.** not behaving properly; disobedient 2. indelicate —**naugh′ti·ly** *adv.* — **naugh′ti·ness** *n.*

nau·se·a (nô′shə, -sē ə) *n.* [< Gr. *nausia*, seasickness] 1. a feeling of sickness at the stomach, with an urge to vomit 2. disgust

nau·se·ate (nô′shē āt′, -sē-, -zē-) *vt., vi.* -**at′ed**, -**at′ing** to feel or cause to feel nausea

nau·seous (nô′shəs, -zē əs) *adj.* 1. causing nausea 2. [Colloq.] feeling nausea

nau·ti·cal (nôt′i k'l) *adj.* [< Fr. < Gr. *naus*, a ship] of sailors, ships, or navigation: abbrev. **naut.** —**nau′ti·cal·ly** *adv.*

nau·ti·lus (nôt′'l əs) *n., pl.* -**lus·es**, -**li′** (-ī′) [< Gr. *naus*, a ship] a tropical mollusk with a many-chambered, spiral shell

Nav·a·ho, Nav·a·jo (nav′ə hō′) *n., pl.* -**hos′**, -**ho′**, -**hoes′** a member of a tribe of SW U.S. Indians

na·val (nā′v'l) *adj.* [< L. *navis*, a ship] of, having, characteristic of, or for a navy, its ships, etc.

nave (nāv) *n.* [< L. *navis*, a ship] the main part of a church, from the chancel to the main entrance

na·vel (nā′v'l) *n.* [OE. *nafela*] the small depression in the abdomen, where the umbilical cord was attached to the fetus

navel orange a seedless orange having a navellike depression at its apex

nav·i·ga·ble (nav′i gə b'l) *adj.* 1. wide or deep enough to be traveled on by ships 2. that can be steered —**nav′i·ga·bil′i·ty** *n.*

nav·i·gate (nav′ə gāt′) *vt., vi.* -**gat′ed**, -**gat′ing** [< L. *navis*, a ship + *agere*, to lead] 1. to steer or direct (a ship or aircraft) 2. to travel through or over (water, air, etc.) in a ship or aircraft

nav′i·ga′tion (-gā′shən) *n.* a navigating; esp., the science of locating the position and plotting the course of ships and aircraft

nav′i·ga′tor *n.* one skilled in the navigation of a ship or aircraft

na·vy (nā′vē) *n., pl.* -**vies** [< L. *navis*, a ship] 1. all the warships of a nation 2. [*often* N-] the entire sea force of a nation, including its vessels, personnel, etc. 3. very dark blue: also **navy blue**

navy bean [from use in U.S. *Navy*] a small, white variety of kidney bean

nay (nā) *adv.* [< ON. *ne*, not + *ei*, ever] not only that, but beyond that [he is well-off, *nay* rich] —*n.* 1. a refusal or denial 2. a negative vote or voter

Na·zi (nät′sē) *adj.* [G., contr. of the party name] designating or of the German fascist political party that ruled Germany under Hitler (1933–45) —*n.* a party member

N.B., n.b. [L. *nota bene*] note well

NCO, N.C.O. noncommissioned officer

Ne *Chem.* neon

NE, N.E., n.e. 1. northeast 2. northeastern

Ne·an·der·thal (nē an′dər thôl′) *adj.* [< a G. valley] designating or of a form of primitive man of the early Stone Age

neap (nēp) *adj.* [OE. *nep*- in *nepflod*, neap tide] designating either of the two lowest monthly tides

Ne·a·pol·i·tan (nē′ə päl′ə t'n) *adj.* of Naples — *n.* a native or inhabitant of Naples

Neapolitan ice cream brick ice cream in layers of different colors and flavors

near (nir) *adv.* [OE. compar. of *neah*, nigh] 1. at a short distance in space or time 2. almost; nearly [near right] 3. closely; intimately —*adj.* 1. close in distance or time 2. close in relationship; akin 3. close in friendship; intimate 4. close in degree [a *near* escape] 5. short or di-

rect [the *near* way] —*prep.* close to —*vt., vi.* to draw near (to); approach —**near′ness** *n.*

near′by′ *adj., adv.* near; close at hand

near′ly *adv.* almost; not quite

near′sight′ed *adj.* seeing only near objects distinctly; myopic —**near′sight′ed·ness** *n.*

neat (nēt) *adj.* [< L. *nitere*, to shine] 1. clean and orderly 2. skillful and precise 3. unmixed 4. well-proportioned 5. cleverly phrased or done 6. [Slang] nice, pleasing, etc. —**neat′ly** *adv.* —**neat′ness** *n.*

′neath, neath (nēth) *prep.* [Poet.] beneath

neb·u·la (neb′yə lə) *n., pl.* -**lae′** (-lē′), -**las** [< L., fog] any of the cloudlike patches in the sky consisting of gaseous matter, far distant stars, or external galaxies —**neb′u·lar** *adj.*

neb′u·lous (-ləs) *adj.* unclear; vague; indefinite

nec·es·sar·i·ly (nes′ə ser′ə lē, nes′ə ser′-) *adv.* 1. because of necessity 2. as a necessary result

nec′es·sar′y (-ser′ē) *adj.* [< L. *ne-*, not + *cedere*, give way] 1. essential; indispensable 2. inevitable 3. required —*n., pl.* -**ies** a necessary thing

ne·ces·si·tate (nə ses′ə tāt′) *vt.* -**tat′ed**, -**tat′ing** 1. to make (something) necessary 2. to compel

ne·ces′si·ty (-tē) *n., pl.* -**ties** [see NECESSARY] 1. natural causation; fate 2. great need 3. something that cannot be done without 4. poverty —**of necessity** necessarily

neck (nek) *n.* [OE. *hnecca*] 1. that part of a man or animal joining the head to the body 2. that part of a garment nearest the neck 3. a necklike part; specif., *a*) a narrow strip of land *b*) the narrowest part of a bottle, vase, etc. *c*) a strait —*vt., vi.* [Slang] to kiss and caress in making love —**neck and neck** very close, as in a contest

neck·er·chief (nek′ər chif, -chēf′) *n.* a kerchief worn around the neck

neck′lace (-lis) *n.* [NECK + LACE, *n.* 1] an ornamental chain of gold, beads, etc. worn around the neck

neck′tie′ *n.* a decorative band for the neck, tied in front in a slipknot or bow

neck′wear′ *n.* articles worn about the neck, as neckties, scarfs, etc.

necro- [< Gr. *nekros*, dead body] *a combining form meaning* death, corpse

ne·crol·o·gy (ne kräl′ə jē) *n., pl.* -**gies** [see prec. & -LOGY] a list of people who have died

nec·ro·man·cy (nek′rə man′sē) *n.* [< Gr. *nekros*, corpse + *manteia*, divination] 1. divination by alleged communication with the dead 2. sorcery —**nec′ro·man′cer** *n.*

ne·cro·sis (ne krō′sis) *n., pl.* -**ses** (-sēz) [< Gr. *nekros*, dead body] the death or decay of tissue in a part of a body or plant

nec·tar (nek′tər) *n.* [< Gr. *nektar*, lit., that overcomes death] 1. *Gr. Myth.* the drink of the gods 2. any very delicious beverage 3. the sweetish liquid in many flowers, made into honey by bees

nec·tar·ine (nek′tə rēn′, nek′tə rēn′) *n.* [< prec.] a smooth-skinned variety of peach

nee, née (nā; *now often* nē) *adj.* [Fr.] born [Mrs. Helen Jones, *nee* Smith]

need (nēd) *n.* [OE. *nied*] 1. necessity 2. lack of something desired or required [the *need* of a rest] 3. something required or desired [one's daily *needs*] 4. *a*) a time or condition when help is required [a friend in *need*] *b*) poverty; want —*vt.* 1. to have need of; require 2. to be obliged [he *needs* to be careful] —*vi.* to be in need —**have need to** to be compelled to —**if need be** if it is required

need′ful *adj.* necessary; required

nee·dle (nēd''l) *n.* [OE. *nǣdl*] 1. a slender, sharp-pointed piece of steel with a hole for thread, used for sewing 2. a slender rod of steel, bone, etc. for crocheting or knitting 3. a short, pointed piece of metal, etc. that moves in phonograph-record grooves to transmit vibrations 4. the pointer of a compass, gauge, etc. 5. the thin, short leaf of the pine, spruce, etc. 6. the sharp, slender metal tube at the end of a hypodermic syringe —*vt.* -**dled, -dling** [Colloq.] 1. to goad; provoke 2. to tease
nee'dle·point' *n.* 1. lace made on a paper pattern with a needle 2. an embroidery of woolen threads on canvas, as in tapestry
need'less *adj.* not needed; unnecessary
nee'dle·work' *n.* work done with a needle; sewing or fancywork
need'n't (-'nt) need not
need·y (nēd'ē) *adj.* -**i·er, -i·est** in need; very poor; destitute —**need'i·ness** *n.*
ne'er (ner) *adv.* [Poet.] never
ne'er'-do-well' *n.* a shiftless, irresponsible person —*adj.* lazy, worthless, etc.
ne·far·i·ous (ni fer'ē əs) *adj.* [< L. *ne-,* not + *fas,* lawful] very wicked
ne·gate (ni gāt') *vt.* -**gat'ed, -gat'ing** [< L. *negare,* deny] 1. to deny the existence or truth of 2. to make ineffective
ne·ga·tion (ni gā'shən) *n.* 1. a denying; denial 2. the lack or opposite of something positive
neg·a·tive (neg'ə tiv) *adj.* [see NEGATE] 1. expressing denial or refusal; saying "no" 2. opposite to or lacking what is positive *[a negative personality]* 3. *Elec. a)* of electricity predominating in a body of resin that has been rubbed with wool *b)* charged with negative electricity *c)* having an excess of electrons 4. *Math.* designating a quantity less than zero, or one to be subtracted 5. *Photog.* reversing the light and shade of the original subject —*n.* 1. a negative word, phrase, etc. 2. the point of view opposing the affirmative 3. the plate in a voltaic battery where the lower potential is 4. *Photog.* an exposed and developed negative film from which positive prints are made —*vt.* -**tived, -tiv·ing** to refuse or deny —**in the negative** in refusal or denial of a plan, etc.
neg·lect (ni glekt') *vt.* [< L. *neg-,* not + *legere,* to gather] 1. to ignore or disregard 2. to fail to attend to properly 3. to leave undone — *n.* 1. a neglecting or being neglected 2. lack of proper care —**neg·lect'ful** *adj.*
neg·li·gee (neg'lə zhā') *n.* [< Fr. *négliger,* to neglect] 1. a woman's loosely fitting dressing gown 2. any informal attire
neg·li·gent (neg'li jənt) *adj.* 1. habitually failing to do the required thing 2. careless, inattentive, etc. —**neg'li·gence** *n.*
neg·li·gi·ble (-jə b'l) *adj.* that can be neglected or disregarded; trifling
ne·go·ti·ate (ni gō'shē āt') *vi.* -**at'ed, -at'ing** [< L. *negotium,* business] to discuss with a view to reaching agreement —*vt.* 1. to settle (a transaction, treaty, etc.) 2. to transfer or sell (checks, bonds, etc.) 3. to succeed in crossing, moving through, etc. —**ne·go'ti·a·ble** (-shē ə b'l, -shə b'l) *adj.* —**ne·go'ti·a'tion** *n.* —**ne·go'ti·a'tor** *n.*
Ne·gro (nē'grō) *n., pl.* -**groes** [< Sp. & Port. *negro,* black] 1. a member of the dominant group of mankind in Africa, characterized generally by a dark skin 2. a member of the Negroid group 3. any person with some Negro ancestors See BLACK (*n.* 3) —*adj.* of or for Negroes
Ne'groid (-groid) *adj.* designating or of one of the major groups of mankind, including most

of the peoples of Africa south of the Sahara
neigh (nā) *vi.* [OE. *hnǣgan*] to utter the characteristic cry of a horse —*n.* this cry
neigh·bor (nā'bər) *n.* [OE. *neah,* nigh + *gebur,* farmer] 1. one that lives or is situated near another 2. a fellow man —*adj.* nearby — *vt., vi.* to live or be situated near or nearby Brit. sp. **neigh'bour**
neigh'bor·hood' *n.* 1. a particular community, district, or area 2. the people living near one another —**in the neighborhood of** [Colloq.] 1. near (a place) 2. about; approximately
neigh'bor·ly *adj.* like or appropriate to neighbors; friendly —**neigh'bor·li·ness** *n.*
nei·ther (nē'thər, nī'-) *adj., pron.* [OE. *nahwæther,* lit., not whether] not either *[neither boy went; neither of them sings]* —*conj.* not either *[she could neither laugh nor cry]*
nem·e·sis (nem'ə sis) *n., pl.* -**ses'** (-sēz') [< Gr. *nemein,* deal out] 1. *a)* just punishment *b)* one who imposes it 2. anyone or anything that seems inevitably to defeat or frustrate one
neo- [< Gr. *neos*] *[often* N-] *a combining form meaning:* 1. new, recent 2. in a new or different way
ne·o·clas·sic (nē'ō klas'ik) *adj.* designating or of a revival of classic style in art, literature, etc.: also **ne'o·clas'si·cal**
ne·ol·o·gism (nē äl'ə jiz'm) *n.* [< Fr.: see NEO-, -LOGY, & -ISM] a new word or a new meaning for an established word
ne·on (nē'än) *n.* [< Gr. *neos,* new] a rare, inert gaseous chemical element: symbol, Ne
neon lamp a tube containing neon, which glows red when an electric current is sent through it
ne·o·phyte (nē'ə fīt') *n.* [< Gr. *neos,* new + *phyein,* to produce] 1. a new convert 2. a beginner; novice
ne'o·plasm (-plaz'm) *n.* [< NEO- + Gr. *plassein,* to form] an abnormal growth of tissue, as a tumor —**ne'o·plas'tic** *adj.*
ne'o·prene (-prēn') *n.* a synthetic rubber, highly resistant to oil, heat, light, etc.
ne·pen·the (ni pen'thē) *n.* [< Gr. *ne-,* not + *penthos,* sorrow] anything that causes forgetfulness of sorrow
neph·ew (nef'yōō) *n.* [< L. *nepos*] 1. the son of one's brother or sister 2. the son of one's brother-in-law or sister-in-law
ne·phri·tis (ne frīt'əs) *n.* [< Gr. *nephros,* kidney + -ITIS] disease of the kidneys, characterized by inflammation, etc.
ne plus ul·tra (nē plus ul'trə) [L., no more beyond] the highest point of perfection
nep·o·tism (nep'ə tiz'm) *n.* [< Fr. < L. *nepos,* nephew] favoritism shown to relatives, esp. in appointment to desirable positions
Nep·tune (nep'tōōn) 1. *Rom. Myth.* the god of the sea 2. the planet eighth in distance from the sun: see PLANET
nep·tu·ni·um (nep tōō'nē əm) *n.* a radioactive chemical element produced by irradiating uranium atoms: symbol, Np
nerd (nurd) *n.* [Slang] a person regarded as contemptibly dull, ineffective, etc.
nerve (nurv) *n.* [< L. *nervus*] 1. any of the cordlike fibers carrying impulses between body organs and the central nervous system 2. courage 3. strength; vigor 4. *[pl.]* nervousness 5. [Colloq.] impudent boldness —*vt.* **nerved, nerv'ing** to give strength or courage to —**get on one's nerves** [Colloq.] to make one irritable
nerve gas a poisonous gas causing paralysis
nerve'less *adj.* 1. without strength, courage, etc.; weak 2. not nervous; controlled
nerve'-rack'ing, nerve'-wrack'ing (-rak'iŋ)

adj. very trying to one's patience or equanimity

nerv·ous (nur'vəs) *adj.* **1.** vigorous in expression **2.** of or made up of nerves **3.** emotionally tense, restless, etc. **4.** fearful

nervous system all the nerve cells and nervous tissues in an organism, including, in the vertebrates, the brain, spinal cord, nerves, etc.

nerv'y *adj.* -**i**·er, -**i**·est **1.** full of courage; bold **2.** [Colloq.] brazen; impudent

-ness [OE. *-nes(s)*] *a suffix meaning* state, quality, or instance of being *[sadness]*

nest (nest) *n.* [OE.] **1.** the structure or place where a bird lays its eggs and shelters its young **2.** the place used by hornets, fish, etc. for spawning or breeding **3.** a cozy place; retreat **4.** a resort or its frequenters *[a nest of thieves]* **5.** a set of things, each fitting within the one next larger —*vi., vt.* to build or settle in (a nest)

nest egg money, etc. put aside as a reserve or to set up a fund

nes·tle (nes''l) *vi.* -**tled**, -**tling** [OE. *nestlian*] **1.** to settle down comfortably **2.** to press close for comfort or in affection **3.** to lie sheltered, as a house among trees —*vt.* to rest or press snugly

nest·ling (nest'liŋ, nes'-) *n.* a young bird not yet ready to leave the nest

net[1] (net) *n.* [OE. *nett*] **1.** an openwork fabric, as of string, used to snare birds, fish, etc. **2.** a trap; snare **3.** a meshed fabric, esp. one used to hold, protect, etc. *[a hairnet]* —*vt.* **net'ted**, **net'ting** to snare or enclose as with a net

net[2] (net) *adj.* [Fr., clear] remaining after deductions or allowances have been made —*n.* a net amount, profit, weight, etc. —*vt.* **net'ted**, **net'ting** to gain as profit, etc.

neth·er (neth'ər) *adj.* [OE. *neothera*] lower or under *[the nether world]*

neth·er·most (neth'ər mōst') *adj.* lowest

net'ting *n.* netted material

net·tle (net''l) *n.* [OE. *netele*] a weed with stinging hairs —*vt.* -**tled**, -**tling** to irritate; annoy; vex

net'work' *n.* **1.** an arrangement of parallel wires, etc. crossed at regular intervals by others so as to leave open spaces **2.** anything like this, as a system of interconnected roads, individuals, etc. **3.** *Radio & TV* a chain of transmitting stations

neu·ral (noor'əl, nyoor'-) *adj.* [NEUR(O)- + -AL] of a nerve, nerves, or the nervous system

neu·ral·gia (noo ral'jə, nyoo-) *n.* [see NEURO- & -ALGIA] severe pain along the course of a nerve —**neu·ral'gic** (-jik) *adj.*

neu·ras·the·ni·a (noor'əs thē'nē ə, nyoor'-) *n.* [< NEUR(O)- + Gr. *astheneia*, weakness] neurosis characterized by irritability, fatigue, anxiety, etc. —**neu'ras·then'ic** (-then'ik) *adj., n.*

neu·ri·tis (noo rīt'əs, nyoo-) *n.* [NEUR(O)- + -ITIS] inflammation of a nerve or nerves —**neu·rit'ic** (-rit'ik) *adj.*

neuro- [< Gr. *neuron*, nerve] *a combining form meaning* of a nerve or the nervous system: also **neur-**

neu·rol·o·gy (noo räl'ə jē, nyoo-) *n.* [prec. + -LOGY] the branch of medicine dealing with the nervous system and its diseases —**neu·ro·log·i·cal** (noor'ə läj'i k'l, nyoor'-) *adj.* —**neu·rol'o·gist** *n.*

neu·ron (noor'än, nyoor'-) *n.* the nerve cell body and all its processes

neu·ro·sis (noo rō'sis, nyoo-) *n., pl.* -**ses** (-sēz) [see NEURO- & -OSIS] a mental disorder characterized by anxiety, compulsions, obsessions, phobias, depression, etc.

neu·rot·ic (noo rät'ik, nyoo-) *adj.* of or having a neurosis —*n.* a neurotic person

neu·ter (noot'ər) *adj.* [< L. *ne-*, not + *uter*, either] **1.** *Biol. a*) having no sexual organs *b*) having undeveloped sexual organs in the adult **2.** *Gram.* designating or of the gender of words neither masculine nor feminine

neu·tral (noo'trəl) *adj.* [see prec.] **1.** supporting neither side in a quarrel or war **2.** of neither extreme in type, kind, etc.; indifferent **3.** having little or no decided color **4.** *Chem.* neither acid nor alkaline —*n.* **1.** a neutral person or nation **2.** a neutral color **3.** *Mech.* a disengaged position of gears

neu'tral·ism *n.* a policy of remaining neutral, esp. in a war —**neu'tral·ist** *adj., n.*

neu·tral'i·ty (-tral'ə tē) *n.* **1.** a being neutral **2.** the status or policy of a neutral nation

neu'tral·ize' (-trə līz') *vt.* -**ized'**, -**iz'ing** **1.** to declare (a nation, etc.) neutral in war **2.** to destroy or counteract the effectiveness, force, etc. of —**neu'tral·i·za'tion** *n.*

neu·tri·no (noo trē'nō) *n., pl.* -**nos** [It., little neutron] *Physics* an uncharged particle with almost no mass

neu·tron (noo'trän) *n.* [< NEUTRAL] an elementary, uncharged particle in an atomic nucleus

neutron bomb a thermonuclear bomb releasing radioactive neutrons that could kill people without destroying buildings, etc.

nev·er (nev'ər) *adv.* [< OE. *ne*, not + *æfre*, ever] **1.** not ever **2.** not at all

nev·er·more (nev'ər môr') *adv.* never again

never-never land an unreal or imaginary place or situation

nev·er·the·less (nev'ər thə les') *adv.* in spite of that; however

ne·vus (nē'vəs) *n., pl.* -**vi** (-vī) [< L. *naevus*] a birthmark or mole

new (noo) *adj.* [OE. *niwe*] **1.** appearing, thought of, discovered, made, etc. for the first time **2.** *a*) different *[a new hairdo] b*) strange; unfamiliar **3.** recently grown; fresh *[new potatoes]* **4.** unused **5.** modern; recent **6.** more; additional **7.** starting as a repetition of a cycle, series, etc. *[the new year]* **8.** having just reached a position, rank, place, etc. *[a new arrival]* —*adv.* **1.** again **2.** newly; recently —**new'ness** *n.*

new blood new people as a potential source of fresh ideas, renewed vigor, etc.

new'born' *adj.* **1.** recently born **2.** reborn

new'com'er *n.* a recent arrival

New Deal the principles and policies adopted by President F. D. Roosevelt to advance economic recovery and social welfare

new·el (noo'əl) *n.* [ult. < L. *nux*, nut] **1.** the upright pillar around which the steps of a winding staircase turn **2.** the post at the top or bottom of a flight of stairs, supporting the handrail: also **newel post**

new'fan'gled (-faŋ'g'ld) *adj.* [< ME. *newe*, new + *-fangel* < OE. *fon*, to take] new; novel: a humorously derogatory term

new'ly *adv.* **1.** recently; lately **2.** anew

new'ly·wed' *n.* a recently married person

new moon the moon when it is between the earth and the sun: it emerges as a crescent curving to the right

news (nooz) *n.pl.* [*with sing. v.*] **1.** new information **2.** reports of recent happenings

news'boy' *n.* a boy who sells or delivers newspapers

news'cast' *n.* a program of news broadcast over radio or TV —**news'cast'er** *n.*

news'deal'er *n.* a retailer of newspapers, magazines, etc.

news'let'ter *n.* a news bulletin issued regularly to a special group

news'man' (-man', -mən) *n., pl.* **-men'** (-men', -mən) **1.** *same as* NEWSDEALER **2.** one who gathers and reports news for a newspaper, TV station, etc.

news'pa'per *n.* a regular publication, usually daily or weekly, containing news, opinions, advertisements, etc.

news'print' *n.* a cheap paper used for newspapers, etc.

news'stand' *n.* a stand at which newspapers, magazines, etc. are sold

news'wor'thy (-wur'*th*ē) *adj.* timely and important or interesting

news'y *adj.* **-i·er, -i·est** [Colloq.] containing much news

newt (nōōt) *n.* [by merging of ME. *an eute* < OE. *efeta*, eft] any of various small amphibious salamanders

New Testament the part of the Bible containing the life and teachings of Jesus and his followers

new'-world' *adj.* of or from the Western Hemisphere

New Year's (Day) January 1

New Year's Eve the evening before New Year's Day

next (nekst) *adj.* [OE. *neahst*, superl. of *neah*, nigh] nearest; immediately preceding or following **—adv. 1.** in the nearest time, place, rank, etc. **2.** on the first subsequent occasion **—prep.** beside; nearest to

next-door (neks'dôr') *adj.* in or at the next house, building, etc.

nex·us (nek'səs) *n., pl.* **-us·es, nex'us** [L.] a connection or link

Ni *Chem.* nickel

ni·a·cin (nī'ə sin) *n.* [NI(COTINIC) AC(ID) + -IN¹] a member of the vitamin B complex

nib (nib) *n.* [< ME. *nebb*] **1.** a bird's beak **2.** a point, esp. a pen point

nib·ble (nib''l) *vt., vi.* **-bled, -bling** [LME. *nebyllen*] **1.** to eat (food) with quick, small bites **2.** to bite at with small, gentle bites **—n. 1.** a small bite or morsel **2.** a nibbling **—nib'-bler** *n.*

nice (nīs) *adj.* **nic'er, nic'est** [< L. *nescius*, ignorant] **1.** difficult to please; fastidious **2.** delicate; precise; subtle [a nice distinction] **3.** calling for care, tact, etc. **4.** *a)* finely discriminating *b)* minutely accurate **5.** *a)* pleasant *b)* attractive *c)* kind *d)* good **—nice'ly** *adv.*

ni·ce·ty (nī'sə tē) *n., pl.* **-ties 1.** precision; accuracy **2.** fastidiousness; refinement **3.** a subtle or minute detail, distinction, etc. **4.** something choice or dainty

niche (nich) *n.* [Fr., ult. < L. *nidus*, a nest] **1.** a recess in a wall for a statue, vase, etc. **2.** an especially suitable place or position

nick (nik) *n.* [prob. akin to *nocke*, notch] a small cut, chip, etc. made on a surface **—vt. 1.** to make a nick or nicks in **2.** to wound slightly **—in the nick of time** just before it is too late

nick·el (nik''l) *n.* [Sw. < G. *kupfernickel*, copper demon: the copperlike ore contains no copper] **1.** a hard, silver-white, metallic chemical element, used in alloys: symbol, Ni **2.** a U.S. or Canadian coin of nickel and copper, equal to five cents **—vt. -eled** or **-elled, -el·ing** or **-el·ling** to plate with nickel

nick·el·o·de·on (nik'ə lō'dē ən) *n.* [< NICKEL + Fr. *odéon*, concert hall] a coin-operated player piano or early jukebox

nick·er (nik'ər) *vi., n.* neigh; whinny

nick·name (nik'nām') *n.* [by merging of ME. *an ekename*, a surname] **1.** a substitute, often

descriptive name given in fun, etc., as "Shorty" **2.** a familiar form of a name, as "Dick" for "Richard" **—vt. -named', -nam'ing** to give a nickname to

nic·o·tine (nik'ə tēn', -tin) *n.* [Fr. < J. *Nicot*, 16th-c. Fr. diplomat who introduced tobacco into France] a poisonous alkaloid found in tobacco leaves

nic'o·tin'ic acid (-tin'ik, -tē'nik) *same as* NIACIN

niece (nēs) *n.* [< L. *neptis*] **1.** the daughter of one's brother or sister **2.** the daughter of one's brother-in-law or sister-in-law

nif·ty (nif'tē) *adj.* **-ti·er, -ti·est** [prob. < MAGNIFICENT] [Slang] attractive, smart, etc.

nig·gard (nig'ərd) *n.* [prob. < Scand.] a stingy person; miser **—adj.** stingy; miserly **—nig'-gard·ly** *adj., adv.*

nig·gle (nig''l) *vi.* **-gled, -gling** [prob. akin to Norw. dial. *nigla*] to work fussily; be finicky **—nig'gling** *adj., n.*

nigh (nī) *adj., adv., prep.* [OE. *neah*] [Chiefly Archaic or Dial.] near

night (nīt) *n.* [OE. *niht*] **1.** the period of darkness between sunset and sunrise **2.** any period or condition of darkness or gloom

night'cap' *n.* **1.** a cap worn in bed **2.** [Colloq.] an alcoholic drink taken at bedtime

night clothes clothes to be worn in bed, as pajamas

night'club' *n.* a place of entertainment open at night for drinking, dancing, etc.

night crawler any large earthworm that comes to the surface at night

night'fall' *n.* the close of day; dusk

night'gown' *n.* a loose gown worn in bed by women or girls

night'hawk' *n.* **1.** any of a group of night birds related to the whippoorwill **2.** *same as* NIGHT OWL

night'ie *n.* [Colloq.] a nightgown

night·in·gale (nīt''n gāl') *n.* [< OE. *niht*, night + *galan*, to sing] a small European thrush known for the melodious singing of the male, esp. at night

night'ly *adj.* **1.** of or like the night **2.** done or occurring every night **—adv. 1.** at night **2.** every night

night'mare' (-mer') *n.* [< ME. *niht*, night + *mare*, demon] **1.** a frightening dream **2.** any frightening experience **—night'mar'ish** *adj.*

night owl a person who works at night or otherwise stays up late

night'shade' (-shād') *n.* any of various flowering plants related to the potato and tomato; esp., a poisonous variety, as the belladonna

night'shirt' *n.* a long, loose, shirtlike garment, worn in bed, esp. formerly, by men or boys

night'spot' *n. colloq. var. of* NIGHTCLUB

night stick a heavy club carried by a policeman

night'time' *n.* the period of darkness from sunset to sunrise

night'wear' *n. same as* NIGHT CLOTHES

ni·hil·ism (nī'ə liz'm, nē'-, ni'hi-) *n.* [< L. *nihil*, nothing + -ISM] the general rejection of customary beliefs in morality, religion, etc. **—ni'hil·ist** *n.* **—ni'hil·is'tic** *adj.*

nil (nil) *n.* [L., contr. of *nihil*] nothing

nim·ble (nim'b'l) *adj.* **-bler, -blest** [< OE. *niman*, take] **1.** quick-witted; alert **2.** moving quickly and lightly **—nim'bly** *adv.*

nim·bus (nim'bəs) *n., pl.* **-bi** (-bī), **-bus·es** [L.] **1.** orig., any rain-producing cloud **2.** a halo surrounding the head of a saint, etc., as in a picture

nin·com·poop (nin'kəm po͞op', niŋ'-) *n.* [< ?] a stupid, silly person; fool

nine (nīn) *adj., n.* [OE. *nigon*] one more than eight; 9; IX —**ninth** (nīnth) *adj., n.*

nine'pins' *n.pl.* [*with sing. v.*] a British version of tenpins, using nine pins

nine'teen' (-tēn') *adj., n.* [OE. *nigontyne*] nine more than ten; 19; XIX —**nine'teenth'** (-tēnth') *adj., n.*

nine'ty (-tē) *adj., n., pl.* -**ties** nine times ten; 90; XC (or LXXXX) —**the nineties** the numbers or years, as of a century, from 90 through 99 —**nine'ti·eth** (-ith) *adj., n.*

nin·ny (nin'ē) *n., pl.* -**nies** [prob. by merging and contr. of *an innocent*] a fool; dolt

nip¹ (nip) *vt.* **nipped, nip'ping** [prob. < MLowG. *nippen*] **1.** to pinch or bite **2.** to sever (shoots, etc.) as by clipping **3.** to check the growth of **4.** to have a painful or injurious effect on because of cold —*n.* **1.** a nipping; pinch; bite **2.** a stinging quality, as in cold air **3.** stinging cold; frost —**nip and tuck** so close as to leave the outcome in doubt

nip² (nip) *n.* [prob. < Du. *nippen,* to sip] a small drink of liquor; sip —*vt., vi.* **nipped, nip'ping** to drink in nips

nip·per (nip'ər) *n.* **1.** anything that nips **2.** [*pl.*] pliers, pincers, etc. **3.** the claw of a crab or lobster

nip·ple (nip''l) *n.* [prob. < *neb* < OE. *nebb,* bird's beak] **1.** the small protuberance on a breast or udder, through which the milk passes; teat **2.** a teatlike part, as of rubber, for a baby's bottle

Nip·pon·ese (nip'ə nēz') *adj., n., pl.* -**ese'** [< Jpn. *Nippon,* Japan] Japanese

nip·py (nip'ē) *adj.* -**pi·er, -pi·est 1.** tending to nip **2.** cold in a stinging way

nir·va·na (nir vä'nə, nər-; -van'ə) *n.* [< Sans.] [*also* **N-**] **1.** *Buddhism* the state of perfect blessedness achieved by the absorption of the soul into the supreme spirit **2.** great peace or bliss

nit (nit) *n.* [OE. *hnitu*] **1.** the egg of a louse or similar insect **2.** a young louse, etc.

ni·ter (nīt'ər) *n.* [< Gr. *nitron*] *same as:* **1.** POTASSIUM NITRATE **2.** SODIUM NITRATE Also, chiefly Brit., **ni'tre**

nit-pick·ing (nit'pik'iŋ) *adj., n.* paying too much attention to petty details —**nit'-pick'er** *n.*

ni·trate (nī'trāt) *n.* a salt or ester of nitric acid —*vt.* -**trat·ed, -trat·ing** to treat or combine with nitric acid or a nitrate —**ni·tra'tion** *n.*

ni·tric acid (nī'trik) a colorless, corrosive acid containing nitrogen

ni·tro·cel·lu·lose (nī'trō sel'yoo lōs') *n.* a substance produced by treating wood, etc. with nitric acid: used for explosives, plastics, etc.

ni·tro·gen (nī'trə jən) *n.* [< Fr.: see NITER & -GEN] a colorless, tasteless, odorless gaseous chemical element forming nearly four fifths of the atmosphere: symbol, N —**ni·trog·e·nous** (nī träj'ə nəs) *adj.*

ni·tro·glyc·er·in, ni·tro·glyc·er·ine (nī'trə glis'ər in) *n.* a thick, explosive oil, prepared by treating glycerin with nitric and sulfuric acids: used in dynamite, etc.

ni·trous oxide (nī'trəs) a colorless, nonflammable gas containing nitrogen, used as an anesthetic and in aerosols

nit·ty-grit·ty (nit'ē grit'ē) *n.* [Slang] the actual, basic facts, issues, etc.

nit'wit' *n.* [? NIT + WIT¹] a stupid person

nix (niks) *adv.* [G. *nichts*] [Slang] **1.** no **2.** not at all —*interj.* [Slang] **1.** stop! **2.** I forbid, disagree, etc. —*vt.* [Slang] to disapprove of or stop

no (nō) *adv.* [< OE. *ne a,* not ever] **1.** not at all

[*no worse*] **2.** nay; not so: used to deny, refuse, or disagree —*adj.* not any [*no errors*] —*n., pl.* **noes, nos 1.** a refusal or denial **2.** a negative vote or voter

No., no. number

No·ah (nō'ə) *Bible* the patriarch commanded by God to build the ark: see ARK (sense 1)

No·bel prizes (nō bel') [< A. B. *Nobel,* 19th-c. Sw. inventor who established them] annual prizes given for distinction in physics, chemistry, medicine, and literature, and for the promotion of peace

no·bil·i·ty (nō bil'ə tē) *n., pl.* -**ties 1.** a being noble **2.** high rank in society **3.** the class of people of noble rank

no·ble (nō'b'l) *adj.* -**bler, -blest** [< L. *nobilis,* well-known] **1.** famous or renowned **2.** having high moral qualities **3.** excellent **4.** grand; stately [*a noble* view] **5.** of high rank or title —*n.* one having hereditary rank or title —**no'ble·ness** *n.* —**no'bly** *adv.*

no'ble·man (-mən) *n., pl.* -**men** a member of the nobility; peer —**no'ble·wom'an** *n.fem., pl.* -**wom'en**

no·blesse o·blige (nō bles' ō blēzh') [Fr., lit., nobility obliges] the obligation of people of high rank or social position to be kind and generous

no·bod·y (nō'bud'ē, -bäd'ē, -bəd ē) *pron.* not anybody; no one —*n., pl.* -**ies** a person of no importance

noc·tur·nal (näk tur'n'l) *adj.* [< L. *nox,* night] **1.** of, done, or happening in the night **2.** active during the night

noc·turne (näk'tərn) *n.* [Fr.] a romantic, dreamy musical composition, appropriate to night

nod (näd) *vi.* **nod'ded, nod'ding** [ME. *nodden*] **1.** to bend the head forward quickly, as in agreement, greeting, etc. **2.** to let the head fall forward because of drowsiness —*vt.* **1.** to bend (the head) forward quickly **2.** to signify (assent, etc.) by doing this —*n.* a nodding —**nod'der** *n.*

node (nōd) *n.* [L. *nodus,* knot] **1.** a knot; knob; swelling **2.** that part of a stem from which a leaf starts to grow —**nod'al** *adj.*

nod·ule (näj'o͞ol) *n.* [L. *nodulus*] a small knot or rounded lump

No·el, No·ël (nō el') *n.* [Fr. < L. *natalis,* natal] *same as* CHRISTMAS

no-fault (nō'fôlt') *adj.* of insurance in which the victim of an accident collects damages although blame for the accident is not established

nog·gin (näg'in) *n.* [prob. < *nog,* strong ale] **1.** a small cup or mug **2.** one fourth of a pint, as of liquor **3.** [Colloq.] the head

no'-good' *adj.* [Slang] contemptible

noise (noiz) *n.* [OFr.] **1.** *a*) loud shouting; clamor *b*) any loud, disagreeable sound **2.** sound —*vt.* **noised, nois'ing** to spread (a report, rumor, etc.)

noise'less *adj.* with little or no noise; silent —**noise'less·ly** *adv.*

noi·some (noi'səm) *adj.* [see ANNOY & -SOME] **1.** injurious to health **2.** foul-smelling; offensive —**noi'some·ly** *adv.*

nois'y *adj.* -**i·er, -i·est 1.** making noise **2.** full of noise —**nois'i·ly** *adv.*

no·mad (nō'mad) *n.* [< Gr. *nemein,* to pasture] **1.** any of a people having no permanent home, but moving about constantly, as in search of pasture **2.** a wanderer —*adj.* wandering: also **no·mad'ic**

no man's land the area on a battlefield separating the combatants

nom de plume (näm′ də plōōm′) *pl.* **noms′ de plume′** [Fr.] a pen name; pseudonym

no·men·cla·ture (nō′mən klā′chər) *n.* [< L. *nomen*, name + *calare*, to call] the system of names used in a branch of learning, or for the parts of a device

nom·i·nal (näm′i n′l) *adj.* [< L. *nomen*, a name] **1.** of or like a name **2.** in name only, not in fact [the *nominal* leader] **3.** relatively very small [a *nominal* fee]

nom·i·nate (näm′ə nāt′) *vt.* **-nat′ed, -nat′ing 1.** to appoint to an office or position **2.** to name as a candidate for election, an award, etc. — **nom′i·na′tion** *n.*

nom·i·na·tive (näm′ə nə tiv) *adj. Gram.* designating or of the case of the subject of a verb and the words that agree with it —*n.* **1.** this case **2.** a word in this case

nom·i·nee (näm′ə nē′) *n.* a person who is nominated

non- [< L. *non*] *a prefix meaning* not: less emphatic than *in-* and *un-*, which often give a word an opposite meaning The terms in the following list will be understood if *not* is used before the meaning of the base word

nonabrasive	non-English
nonabsorbent	nonessential
nonactive	nonexchangeable
nonaddictive	nonexclusive
nonadministrative	nonexempt
nonaggressive	nonexistence
nonalcoholic	nonexistent
nonallergenic	nonexplosive
nonassignable	nonfactual
nonattendance	nonfading
nonbasic	nonfat
nonbeliever	nonfatal
nonbelligerent	nonfiction
nonbreakable	nonfictional
nonburnable	nonflammable
non-Catholic	nonflowering
nonchargeable	nonfluctuating
nonclerical	nonflying
nonclinical	nonfunctional
noncollectable	nongovernmental
noncombustible	nongranular
noncommercial	nonhazardous
non-Communist	nonhereditary
noncompeting	nonhuman
noncompetitive	nonidentical
noncompliance	noninclusive
noncomplying	nonindependent
nonconducting	nonindustrial
nonconforming	noninfected
nonconsecutive	noninflammatory
nonconstructive	noninflationary
noncontagious	nonintellectual
noncontributory	noninterchangeable
noncontroversial	noninterference
nonconvertible	nonintoxicating
noncorroding	nonirritating
noncritical	nonjudicial
noncrystalline	nonlegal
noncumulative	nonliterary
nondelivery	nonmagnetic
nondepartmental	nonmalignant
nondepreciating	nonmember
nondestructive	nonmigratory
nondetachable	nonmilitant
nondisciplinary	nonmilitary
nondiscrimination	nonnarcotic
nondramatic	nonnegotiable
nondrinker	nonobjective
nondrying	nonobligatory
noneducational	nonobservance
noneffective	nonobservant
nonenforceable	nonoccupational

nonoccurrence	nonscoring
nonofficial	nonseasonal
nonoperational	nonsecular
nonoperative	nonsensitive
nonpaying	nonsmoker
nonpayment	nonsocial
nonperishable	nonspecializing
nonphysical	nonspiritual
nonpoisonous	nonstaining
nonpolitical	nonstandard
nonporous	nonstrategic
nonprejudicial	nonstriking
nonproductive	nonstructural
nonprofessional	nonsuccessive
nonprofitable	nonsupporting
nonpunishable	nonsustaining
nonracial	nonsympathizer
nonreciprocal	nontarnishable
nonreciprocating	nontaxable
nonrecoverable	nontechnical
nonrecurring	nonthinking
nonredeemable	nontoxic
nonrefillable	nontransferable
nonreligious	nontransparent
nonrenewable	nontropical
nonresidential	nonuser
nonresidual	nonvenomous
nonresistant	nonvirulent
nonreturnable	nonvocal
nonrhythmic	nonvocational
nonrigid	nonvoter
nonsalaried	nonvoting
nonscientific	nonyielding

non·age (nän′ij, nō′nij) *n.* [see NON- & AGE] the state of being under full legal age, usually twenty-one

non·a·ligned (nän′ə līnd′) *adj.* not aligned with either side in a conflict —**non′a·lign′ment** *n.*

nonce (näns) *n.* [by merging of ME. (*for then*) *ones*, lit., (for the) once] the present use, occasion, or time: chiefly in **for the nonce**

non·cha·lant (nän′shə länt′, nän′shə lənt) *adj.* [Fr., ult. < L. *non*, not + *calere*, be warm] **1.** without warmth or enthusiasm **2.** casually indifferent —**non′cha·lance′** *n.*

non·com (nän′käm′) *n.* [Colloq.] *short for* NONCOMMISSIONED OFFICER

non·com·bat·ant (nän käm′bə tənt, nän′kəm bat′ənt) *n.* **1.** a member of the armed forces not engaged in actual combat **2.** any civilian in wartime —*adj.* of noncombatants

non′com·mis′sioned officer (-kə mish′ənd) an enlisted person of any of various grades in the armed forces: in the U.S. Army, from corporal to sergeant major inclusive

non·com·mit·tal (nän′kə mit′′l) *adj.* not committing one to any point of view or course of action

non·con·duc·tor *n.* a substance that does not readily transmit electricity, sound, heat, etc.

non′con·form′ist *n.* one who does not conform to prevailing attitudes, behavior, etc.; esp., [N-] in England, a Protestant who is not an Anglican —**non′con·form′i·ty** *n.*

non·de·script (nän′di skript′) *adj.* [< L. *non*, not + *describere*, describe] belonging to no definite class or type; hard to classify or describe

none (nun) *pron.* [< OE. *ne*, not + *an*, one] **1.** no one; not anyone **2.** [*usually with pl. v.*] not any [*none* are his] —*n.* no part; nothing [I want *none* of it] —*adv.* not at all [*none* too soon]

non·en·ti·ty (nän en′tə tē) *n., pl.* **-ties** a person or thing of little or no importance.

none·such (nun'such') *n.* a person or thing unrivaled or unequaled; nonpareil

none·the·less (nun'thə les') *adv.* nevertheless: also **none the less**

non·in·ter·ven'tion *n.* the state or fact of not intervening; esp., a refraining by one nation from interference in the affairs of another

non·met'al *n.* an element lacking the characteristics of a metal, as oxygen, carbon, fluorine, etc. —**non'me·tal'lic** *adj.*

non·pa·reil (nän'pə rel') *adj.* [Fr. < *non,* not + *pareil,* equal] unequaled; peerless

non·par'ti·san *adj.* not partisan; esp., not connected with any single political party: also **non·par'ti·zan**

non·plus (nän plus', nän'plus') *vt.* **-plused'** or **-plussed'**, **-plus'ing** or **-plus'sing** [L. *non,* not + *plus,* more] to cause to be so perplexed that one cannot go, speak, or act further

non·prof'it *adj.* not intending or intended to earn a profit

non·res'i·dent *adj.* not residing in the locality where one works, attends school, etc. —*n.* a nonresident person

non're·stric'tive (-ri strik'tiv) *adj. Gram.* designating a clause, phrase, or word felt as not essential to the sense, usually set off by commas (Ex.: John, *who is six feet tall,* is younger than Bill)

non·sched'uled *adj.* licensed for commercial air flights as demand warrants rather than on a schedule

non'sec·tar'i·an (-sek ter'ē ən) *adj.* not confined to any specific religion

non·sense (nän'sens, -səns) *n.* words, actions, etc. that are absurd or meaningless —**non·sen'si·cal** *adj.*

non se·qui·tur (nän' sek'wi tər) [L., it does not follow] **1.** a conclusion that does not follow from the premises **2.** a remark not bearing on what has just been said

non'skid' *adj.* so constructed as to reduce skidding: said of a tire tread, etc.

non'stop' *adj., adv.* without a stop

non'sup·port' *n.* failure to provide for a legal dependent

non·un'ion *adj.* **1.** not belonging to a labor union **2.** not made or serviced under labor-union conditions **3.** refusing to recognize a labor union

non·vi'o·lence *n.* an abstaining from violence, as in opposing government policy —**non·vi'o·lent** *adj.*

noo·dle¹ (nōō'd'l) *n.* [< ?] [Slang] the head

noo·dle² (nōō'd'l) *n.* [G. *nudel*] a flat, narrow strip of dry dough, usually made with egg and served in soups, etc.

nook (nook) *n.* [ME. *nok*] **1.** a corner, esp. of a room **2.** a small secluded spot

noon (nōōn) *n.* [< L. *nona (hora),* ninth (hour) (orig. 3:00 P.M.)] twelve o'clock in the daytime; midday —*adj.* of or occurring at noon Also **noon'day'**, **noon'time'**

no one not anybody; nobody

noose (nōōs) *n.* [< L. *nodus,* a knot] a loop formed in a rope, etc. by means of a slipknot so that the loop tightens as the rope is pulled

nor (nôr) *conj.* [ME., contr. of *nother,* neither] and not; and not either [she neither hears *nor* sees]

Nor·dic (nôr'dik) *adj.* [OE. *north,* north] of a Caucasoid physical type exemplified by the tall, blond Scandinavians

norm (nôrm) *n.* [< L. *norma,* rule] a standard or model; esp., the standard of achievement of a large group

nor·mal (nôr'm'l) *adj.* **1.** conforming with an

acceptable standard or norm; natural; usual **2.** free from disease, disorder, etc.; sound in body or mind —*n.* **1.** anything normal **2.** the usual state, amount, etc. —**nor'mal·cy, nor·mal'i·ty** (-mal'ə tē) *n.* —**nor'mal·ize'** *vt., vi.* **-ized', -iz'-ing** —**nor'mal·i·za'tion** *n.*

nor'mal·ly *adv.* **1.** in a normal manner **2.** under normal circumstances; ordinarily

Nor·man (nôr'mən) *n.* [< OFr.] **1.** any of the people of Normandy who conquered England in 1066 **2.** a native of Normandy, France —*adj.* of Normandy, the Normans, their language, etc.

norm·a·tive (nôr'mə tiv) *adj.* of or establishing a norm, or standard

Norse (nôrs) *adj., n.* [prob. < Du. *noord,* north] Scandinavian, esp. (of) the Norwegian and Icelandic languages —**the Norse** the Scandinavians

Norse'man (-mən) *n., pl.* **-men** a member of the ancient Scandinavian people

north (nôrth) *n.* [OE.] **1.** the direction to the right of one facing the sunset (0° or 360° on the compass, opposite south) **2.** a region in or toward this direction **3.** [*often* N-] the northern part of the earth —*adj.* **1.** in, of, or toward the north **2.** from the north —*adv.* in or toward the north

north'east' *n.* **1.** the direction halfway between north and east **2.** a region in or toward this direction —*adj.* **1.** in, of, or toward the northeast **2.** from the northeast —*adv.* in, toward, or from the northeast —**north'east'er·ly** *adj., adv.* —**north'east'ern** *adj.* —**north'east'ward** (-wərd) *adv., adj.* —**north'east'wards** *adv.*

north·er·ly (nôr'thər lē) *adj., adv.* **1.** toward the north **2.** from the north

north·ern (nôr'thərn) *adj.* **1.** in, of, or toward the north **2.** from the north **3.** [N-] of the North —**north'ern·most'** *adj.*

north'ern·er *n.* a native or inhabitant of the north

northern lights *same as* AURORA BOREALIS

North Pole the northern end of the earth's axis

North Star Polaris, the bright star almost directly above the North Pole

north'ward (-wərd) *adv., adj.* toward the north: also **north'wards** *adv.*

north'west' *n.* **1.** the direction halfway between north and west **2.** a region in or toward this direction —*adj.* **1.** in, of, or toward the northwest **2.** from the northwest —*adv.* in, toward, or from the northwest —**north'west'-er·ly** *adj., adv.* —**north'west'ern** *adj.* —**north'-west'ward** (-wərd) *adv., adj.* —**north'west'wards** *adv.*

Norw. 1. Norway **2.** Norwegian

Nor·we·gian (nôr wē'jən) *adj.* of Norway, its people, language, etc. —*n.* **1.** a native or inhabitant of Norway **2.** the language of Norway

nose (nōz) *n.* [OE. *nosu*] **1.** the part of the face between the mouth and the eyes, having two openings for breathing and smelling: in animals, the snout, muzzle, etc. **2.** the sense of smell **3.** anything noselike in shape or position —*vt.* **nosed, nos'ing** **1.** to discover as by smell **2.** to rub with the nose **3.** to push (a way, etc.) with the front forward —*vi.* **1.** to pry inquisitively **2.** to move forward —**nose out** to defeat by a very small margin —**on the nose** [Slang] precisely; exactly —**turn up one's nose at** to sneer at; scorn —**under one's (very) nose** in plain view

nose'bleed' *n.* a bleeding from the nose

nose cone the cone-shaped foremost part of a rocket or missile

nose dive 1. a swift, downward plunge of an

airplane, nose first **2.** any sudden, sharp drop, as in prices **—nose′-dive′** *vi.* **-dived′, -div′ing**

nose drops medication administered through the nose with a dropper

nose′gay′ *n.* [NOSE + GAY (obs. "gay object")] a small bunch of flowers

nos·tal·gia (näs tal′jə) *n.* [< Gr. *nostos,* a return + -ALGIA] a longing for something far away or long ago **—nos·tal′gic** *adj.*

nos·tril (näs′trəl) *n.* [< OE. *nosu,* the nose + *thyrel,* hole] either of the openings into the nose

nos·trum (näs′trəm) *n.* [L., ours] **1.** a quack medicine **2.** a pet scheme for solving some problem

nos·y, nos·ey (nōz′ē) *adj.* **-i·er, -i·est** [Colloq.] prying; inquisitive

not (nät) *adv.* [< ME. *nought*] in no manner, degree, etc.: a word expressing negation or the idea of *no*

no·ta·ble (nōt′ə b'l) *adj.* [< L. *notare,* to note] worthy of notice; remarkable **—n.** a famous person **—no′ta·bly** *adv.*

no·ta·rize (nōt′ər īz′) *vt.* **-rized′, -riz′ing** to certify or attest (a document) as a notary

no·ta·ry (nōt′ər ē) *n., pl.* **-ries** [< L. *notare,* to note] an official authorized to certify or attest documents, take affidavits, etc.: in full **notary public**

no·ta·tion (nō tā′shən) *n.* [< L. *notare,* to note] **1.** the use of a system of signs or symbols for words, quantities, etc. **2.** any such system used in algebra, music, etc. **3.** a brief note **4.** a noting in writing

notch (näch) *n.* [by merging of ME. *an oche,* a notch] **1.** a V-shaped cut in an edge or surface **2.** a narrow, deep pass **3.** [Colloq.] a step; degree **—vt.** to cut notches in

note (nōt) *n.* [< L. *nota,* a mark] **1.** a distinguishing feature [a *note* of joy] **2.** importance or distinction [a person of *note*] **3.** a brief writing to aid the memory; memorandum **4.** a comment or explanation; annotation **5.** notice; heed [worthy of *note*] **6.** a short letter **7.** a written acknowledgment of a debt **8.** a cry or call, as of a bird **9.** *Music a*) a tone of definite pitch *b*) a symbol for a tone, indicating pitch and duration **—vt. not′ed, not′ing 1.** to heed; observe **2.** to set down in writing **3.** to mention specially **—compare notes** to exchange views

note′book′ *n.* a book in which notes, or memorandums, are kept

not·ed (nōt′id) *adj.* distinguished; eminent

note′wor′thy *adj.* worthy of note; outstanding; remarkable **—note′wor′thi·ness** *n.*

noth·ing (nuth′iŋ) *n.* [OE. *na thing*] **1.** no thing; not anything **2.** nothingness **3.** a thing that does not exist **4.** a person or thing considered of little or no importance **5.** a nought; zero **—adv.** not at all; in no way **—for nothing 1.** free; at no cost **2.** in vain **3.** without reason

noth′ing·ness *n.* **1.** nonexistence **2.** insignificance **3.** unconsciousness

no·tice (nōt′is) *n.* [see NOTE] **1.** an announcement or warning **2.** a short article about a book, play, etc. **3.** a written or printed sign giving some public information, warning, etc. **4.** attention; heed **5.** a formal warning of intention to end an agreement or contract at a certain time **—vt. -ticed, -tic·ing 1.** to refer to; mention **2.** to pay attention to; observe **—take notice** to observe

no′tice·a·ble *adj.* readily noticed; conspicuous **—no′tice·a·bly** *adv.*

no·ti·fy (nōt′ə fī′) *vt.* **-fied′, -fy′ing** [< L. *notus,* known + *facere,* to make] to give notice to;

inform; announce to **—no′ti·fi·ca′tion** (-fi kā′shən) *n.*

no·tion (nō′shən) *n.* [see NOTE] **1.** *a*) a mental image *b*) a vague thought **2.** a belief; opinion **3.** an inclination; whim **4.** an intention **5.** [*pl.*] small, useful articles, as needles, thread, etc., sold in a store

no·to·ri·e·ty (nōt′ə rī′ə tē) *n.* the quality or state of being notorious

no·to·ri·ous (nō tôr′ē əs) *adj.* [see NOTE] widely known, esp. unfavorably

no′-trump′ *adj. Bridge* with no suit being trumps **—n.** *Bridge* a no-trump bid or hand

not·with·stand·ing (nät′with stan′diŋ, -with-) *prep.* in spite of **—adv.** nevertheless **—conj.** although

nou·gat (nōō′gət) *n.* [Fr. < Pr. < L. *nux,* nut] a confection of sugar paste with nuts

nought (nôt) *n.* [< OE. *ne,* not + *awiht,* aught] **1.** nothing **2.** the figure zero (0)

noun (noun) *n.* [< L. *nomen,* a name] *Gram.* a word that names or denotes a person, thing, action, quality, etc.

nour·ish (nur′ish) *vt.* [< L. *nutrire*] **1.** to feed or sustain with substances necessary to life and growth **2.** to foster; promote **—nour′ish·ing** *adj.*

nour′ish·ment (-mənt) *n.* **1.** a nourishing or being nourished **2.** food

Nov. November

no·va (nō′və) *n., pl.* **-vae** (-vē), **-vas** [< L. *nova,* new] *Astron.* a star that brightens intensely and then gradually dims

nov·el (näv′'l) *adj.* [< L. dim. of *novus,* new] new and unusual **—n.** a relatively long fictional prose narrative

nov·el·ette (näv′ə let′) *n.* a short novel

nov′el·ist *n.* one who writes novels

nov′el·ty *n., pl.* **-ties 1.** the quality of being novel **2.** something new, fresh, or unusual **3.** a small, often cheap, cleverly made article: *usually used in pl.*

No·vem·ber (nō vem′bər) *n.* [< L. *novem,* nine: 9th month in Roman year] eleventh month of the year, having 30 days

no·ve·na (nō vē′nə) *n.* [< L. *novem,* nine] *R.C.Ch.* a nine-day period of devotions

nov·ice (näv′is) *n.* [< L. *novus,* new] **1.** a person on probation in a religious order before taking vows **2.** a person new to a particular activity, etc.; beginner

no·vi·ti·ate (nō vish′ē it) *n.* the period or state of being a novice

No·vo·cain (nō′və kān′) [L. *nov(us),* new + (c)OCAIN(E)] *a trademark for* an alkaloid compound used as a local anesthetic: also **Novocaine**

now (nou) *adv.* [OE. *nu*] **1.** *a*) at the present time *b*) at once **2.** at the time referred to; then; next **3.** very recently [he left just *now*] **4.** with things as they are [*now* I'll never know] **—conj.** since; seeing that **—n.** the present time [that's all for *now*] **—adj.** of the present time **—now and then** (or **again**) occasionally

now′a·days′ (-ə dāz′) *adv.* in these days; at the present time **—n.** the present time

no·way (nō′wā′) *adv.* by no means; not at all: now often **no′ way′,** used with the force of an interjection

no·where (nō′hwer′, -wer′) *adv.* not in, at, or to any place

no·wise (nō′wīz′) *adv.* in no manner; noway

nox·ious (näk′shəs) *adj.* [< L. *nocere,* to hurt] harmful to health or morals; injurious; unwholesome **—nox′ious·ly** *adv.*

noz·zle (näz′'l) *n.* [dim. of NOSE] the spout at the end of a hose, pipe, etc.

NT., NT, N.T. New Testament

nth (enth) *adj.* of the indefinitely large or small number represented by *n* —**to the nth degree** (or **power**) **1.** to an indefinite degree or power **2.** to an extreme

nt. wt. net weight

nu (nōō, nyōō) *n.* the thirteenth letter of the Greek alphabet (N, ν)

nu·ance (nōō'äns) *n.* [Fr. < *nuer*, to shade] a slight variation in tone, meaning, etc.

nub (nub) *n.* [var. of *knub*, knob] **1.** a lump or small piece **2.** [Colloq.] the gist

nub·bin (nub'in) *n.* [dim. of NUB] **1.** a small ear of Indian corn **2.** a small piece

nub·by (nub'ē) *adj.* -**bi·er**, -**bi·est** having a rough, knotted surface *[a nubby fabric]*

nu·bile (nōō'b'l, -bīl) *adj.* [Fr. < L. *nubere*, to marry] marriageable: said of a young woman who seems fully developed sexually

nu·cle·ar (nōō'klē ər) *adj.* **1.** of, like, or forming a nucleus **2.** of, involving, or using atomic nuclei or atomic energy, bombs, power, etc.

nuclear fission the splitting of the nuclei of atoms, with conversion of part of the mass into energy, as in the atomic bomb

nuclear fusion the fusion of atomic nuclei into a nucleus of heavier mass, with a resultant loss in the combined mass converted into energy, as in a hydrogen bomb

nuclear physics the branch of physics dealing with the structure of atomic nuclei, nuclear forces, etc.

nuclear reactor a device for creating a controlled nuclear chain reaction in a fissionable fuel, as to produce energy

nu·cle·us (nōō'klē əs) *n., pl.* -**cle·i'** (-ī'), -**cle·us·es** [L., a kernel] **1.** a central thing or part around which others are grouped **2.** any center of growth or development **3.** the central part of an atom **4.** the central mass of protoplasm in a cell

nude (nōōd) *adj.* [L. *nudus*] naked; bare —*n.* **1.** a nude human figure, esp. as in painting, sculpture, etc. **2.** the condition of being nude *[in the nude]* —**nu'di·ty** *n.*

nudge (nuj) *vt.* **nudged, nudg'ing** [< ?] to push gently, esp. with the elbow, in order to get attention, etc. —*n.* a gentle push

nud'ism *n.* the practice or cult of going nude —**nud'ist** *n., adj.*

nug·get (nug'it) *n.* [prob. < dial. *nug*, lump] a lump, esp. of native gold

nui·sance (nōō's'ns) *n.* [< L. *nocere*, annoy] an act, thing, person, etc. causing trouble, annoyance, or inconvenience

null (nul) *adj.* [< L. *nullus*, none] **1.** without legal force; invalid: usually in the phrase **null and void 2.** amounting to nought **3.** of no value, effect, etc.

nul·li·fy (nul'ə fī') *vt.* -**fied', -fy'ing** [< L. *nullus*, none + *facere*, make] **1.** to make legally null **2.** to cancel out —**nul'li·fi·ca'tion** *n.*

numb (num) *adj.* [< ME. *nimen*, take] deadened; insensible *[numb* with grief*]* —*vt.* to make numb —**numb'ly** *adv.*

num·ber (num'bər) *n.* [< L. *numerus*] **1.** a symbol or word showing how many or which one in a series (Ex.: 2, 27, four, sixth) **2.** *[pl.]* arithmetic **3.** the sum or total of persons or units **4.** *a)* *[often pl.]* many *b)* *[pl.]* numerical superiority **5.** quantity **6.** *a)* a single issue of a periodical *b)* a single song, dance, etc. in a program of entertainment **7.** [Colloq.] a person or thing singled out *[a smart *number]* **8.** *Gram.* the form of a word as indicating either singular or plural —*vt.* **1.** to count; enumerate **2.** to give a number to **3.** to include as one of a group **4.** to limit the number of **5.** to comprise; total —*vi.* to be numbered —**beyond** (or **without**) **number** too numerous to be counted —**the numbers** an illegal lottery based on certain numbers published in newspapers: also **numbers pool** (or **racket**)

num'ber·less *adj. same as* COUNTLESS

Num·bers (num'bərz) the 4th book of the Pentateuch in the Bible: abbrev. **Num.**

nu·mer·al (nōō'mər əl) *adj.* [< L. *numerus*, number] of or denoting a number or numbers —*n.* a figure, letter, or word expressing a number

nu·mer·a·tor (nōō'mə rāt'ər) *n. Math.* the term above the line in a fraction

nu·mer·i·cal (noo mer'i k'l) *adj.* **1.** of, or having the nature of, number **2.** in or by numbers **3.** expressed by numbers

nu·mer·ous (nōō'mər əs) *adj.* **1.** consisting of a great number **2.** very many

nu·mis·mat·ics (nōō'miz mat'iks, -mis-) *n.pl.* [*with sing. v.*] [< L. *numisma*, a coin] the study or collection of coins, medals, paper money, etc. —**nu·mis'ma·tist** (-mə tist) *n.*

num·skull, numb·skull (num'skul') *n.* [NUM(B) + SKULL] a stupid person; dunce

nun (nun) *n.* [< LL. *nonna*] a woman living in a convent under vows

nun·ci·o (nun'shē ō', -sē-) *n., pl.* -**os'** [< It. < L. *nuntius*, messenger] an ambassador of the Pope to a foreign government

nun·ner·y (nun'ər ē) *n., pl.* -**ies** *a former name for* CONVENT

nup·tial (nup'shəl, -chəl) *adj.* [< L. *nubere*, to marry] of marriage —*n.* [*pl.*] a wedding

nurse (nurs) *n.* [< L. *nutrire*, nourish] **1.** a woman hired to take care of another's children **2.** a person trained to take care of the sick, assist surgeons, etc. —*vt.* **nursed, nurs'ing 1.** to suckle (an infant) **2.** to take care of (a child, invalid, etc.) **3.** to nourish, foster, etc. **4.** to try to cure *[to *nurse* a cold]* **5.** to use or handle so as to protect or conserve —*vi.* **1.** to feed at the breast; suckle **2.** to serve as a nurse —**nurs'er** *n.*

nurse'maid' *n.* a woman hired to take care of a child or children

nurs·er·y (nur'sə rē) *n., pl.* -**ies 1.** a room in a home, set aside for the children **2.** *same as:* *a)* NURSERY SCHOOL *b)* DAY NURSERY **3.** a place where young trees or plants are raised for sale, etc.

nursery rhyme a poem for children

nursery school a prekindergarten school for young children aged usually 3 to 5

nursing home a residence providing care for the chronically ill, disabled, etc.

nur·ture (nur'chər) *n.* [< L. *nutrire*, nourish] **1.** food **2.** training; rearing —*vt.* -**tured, -tur·ing 1.** to feed or nourish **2.** to train, rear, foster, etc.

nut (nut) *n.* [OE. *hnutu*] **1.** a dry, one-seeded fruit, consisting of a kernel, often edible, in a woody shell, as the walnut **2.** the kernel itself **3.** loosely, any hard-shelled, relatively nonperishable fruit, as the peanut **4.** a small, usually metal block with a threaded hole, for screwing onto a bolt, etc. **5.** [Slang] *a)* a crazy or eccentric person *b)* a devotee; fan

nut'crack'er *n.* **1.** a device, usually hinged, for cracking nutshells **2.** a bird related to the crow, that feeds on nuts

nut'hatch' (-hach') *n.* a small, nut-eating bird with a sharp beak and short tail

nut'meat' *n.* the kernel of a nut

nut'meg' (-meg') *n.* [< L. *nux*, nut + LL. *muscus*, musk] the aromatic seed of an East Indian tree, used as a spice

nu·tri·a (nōō′trē ə) *n.* [Sp. < L. *lutra,* otter] 1. a S. American water rodent with webbed feet 2. its soft, brown fur

nu·tri·ent (nōō′trē ənt) *adj.* [< L. *nutrire,* nourish] nourishing; nutritious —*n.* anything nutritious

nu′tri·ment (-trə mənt) *n.* anything that nourishes; food

nu·tri·tion (nōō trish′ən) *n.* [see NUTRIENT] 1. the process by which an organism takes in and assimilates food 2. nourishment 3. the study of proper diet —**nu·tri′tion·al** *adj.* —**nu′-tri·tive** (-trə tiv) *adj.*

nu·tri′tious (-əs) *adj.* nourishing

nuts (nuts) *adj.* [Slang] crazy; foolish —*interj.* [Slang] an exclamation of disgust, scorn, etc.: often in the phrase **nuts to** (**someone** or **something**) —**be nuts about** [Slang] to be very enthusiastic about

nut′shell′ *n.* the shell enclosing the kernel of a nut —**in a nutshell** in concise form

nut′ty *adj.* **-ti·er, -ti·est** 1. containing or producing nuts 2. having a nutlike flavor 3. [Slang] *a*) very enthusiastic *b*) queer, crazy, etc. —**nut′-ti·ness** *n.*

nuz·zle (nuz′'l) *vt., vi.* **-zled, -zling** [< NOSE] 1. to push (against) or rub with the nose or snout 2. to nestle; snuggle

NW, N.W., n.w. 1. northwest 2. northwestern

ny·lon (nī′län) *n.* [arbitrary coinage] 1. an elastic, very strong synthetic material made into fiber, bristles, etc. 2. [*pl.*] stockings made of this

nymph (nimf) *n.* [< Gr. *nymphē*] 1. *Gr. & Rom. Myth.* any of a group of minor nature goddesses, living in rivers, trees, etc. 2. a lovely young woman 3. the young of an insect with incomplete metamorphosis

nym·pho·ma·ni·a (nim′fə mā′nē ə) *n.* abnormal and uncontrollable desire by a woman for sexual intercourse —**nym′pho·ma′ni·ac′** (-ak′) *n., adj.*

O

O, o (ō) *n., pl.* **O's, o's** 1. the fifteenth letter of the English alphabet 2. the numeral zero

O (ō) *interj.* 1. an exclamation in direct address *[O* Lord!*]* 2. oh

O 1. *Linguis.* Old *[OFr.]* 2. *Chem.* oxygen

O. 1. Ocean 2. October

oaf (ōf) *n.* [< ON. *alfr,* elf] a stupid, clumsy fellow; lout —**oaf′ish** *adj.*

oak (ōk) *n.* [OE. *ac*] 1. a large hardwood tree or bush bearing nuts called *acorns* 2. its wood —*adj.* of oak —**oak′en** *adj.*

oa·kum (ō′kəm) *n.* [< OE. *a-,* out + *camb,* a comb] stringy, hemp fiber got by taking apart old ropes: used in caulking

oar (ōr) *n.* [OE. *ar*] a long pole with a broad blade at one end, used in rowing —*vt., vi.* to row —**rest on one's oars** to stop to rest or relax —**oars·man** (ōrz′mən) *n., pl.* **-men**

oar′lock′ *n.* a device, often U-shaped, for holding an oar in place in rowing

OAS, O.A.S. Organization of American States

o·a·sis (ō ā′sis) *n., pl.* **-ses** (-sēz) [< Gr. *oasis*] a fertile place in a desert, due to the presence of water

oat (ōt) *n.* [OE. *ate*] [*usually pl.*] 1. a hardy cereal grass 2. its edible grain —**oat′en** *adj.*

oath (ōth) *n., pl.* **oaths** (ōthz, ōths) [OE. *ath*] 1. a declaration, as by appeal to God, that one will speak the truth, keep a promise, etc. 2. the profane use of God's name, as in anger 3. a swearword; curse

oat′meal′ *n.* 1. oats crushed into meal or flakes 2. a porridge made from this

ob- [< L. *ob*] *a prefix meaning:* 1. to, toward, before *[object]* 2. against *[obnoxious]* 3. upon, over *[obfuscate]* 4. completely *[obsolete]* In words of Latin origin, *ob-* assimilates to *o-* before *m, oc-* before *c, of-* before *f,* and *op-* before *p*

OB, O.B. 1. obstetrician 2. obstetrics

ob·bli·ga·to (äb′lə gät′ō) *n., pl.* **-tos, -ti** (-ē) [It., lit., obliged < L.] a musical accompaniment formerly required but now usually optional

ob·du·rate (äb′door ət, -dyoor-) *adj.* [< L. *ob-,* intens. + *durus,* hard] 1. hardhearted 2. stubborn; obstinate —**ob′du·ra·cy** *n.*

o·be·di·ent (ō bē′dē ənt) *adj.* obeying or willing to obey —**o·be′di·ence** *n.*

o·bei·sance (ō bā′s'ns, -bē′-) *n.* [< OFr. *obeir,* obey] 1. a gesture of respect, as a bow 2. homage; deference —**o·bei′sant** *adj.*

ob·e·lisk (äb′ə lisk, ō′bə-) *n.* [< Gr. *obelos,* needle] a tall, four-sided stone pillar tapering to its pyramidal top

o·bese (ō bēs′) *adj.* [< L. *ob-* (see OB-) + *edere,* eat] very fat; stout —**o·be′si·ty** (-ə tē) *n.*

o·bey (ō bā′) *vt.* [< L. *ob-* (see OB-) + *audire,* hear] 1. to carry out the orders of 2. to carry out (an order) 3. to be guided by *[to obey* one's conscience*]* —*vi.* to be obedient

ob·fus·cate (äb′fəs kāt′, äb fus′kāt) *vt.* **-cat′ed, -cat′ing** [< L. *ob-* (see OB-) + *fuscus,* dark] to obscure; confuse; bewilder —**ob′fus·ca′tion** *n.*

o·bit (ō′bit, äb′it) *n. same as* OBITUARY

o·bit·u·ar·y (ō bich′ōō wer′ē) *n., pl.* **-ies** [< L. *obire,* die] a notice of someone's death, usually with a brief biography

obj. 1. object 2. objective

ob·ject (äb′jikt) *n.* [< ML. *objectum,* thing thrown in the way < L. *ob-* (see OB-) + *jacere,* to throw] 1. a thing that can be seen or touched 2. a person or thing to which action, feeling, etc. is directed 3. purpose; goal 4. *Gram.* a noun or substantive that receives the action of a verb, or is governed by a preposition —*vt.* (əb jekt′, äb-) to state in opposition or disapproval —*vi.* to feel or express opposition or disapproval —**ob·jec′tor** *n.*

ob·jec·tion (əb jek′shən, äb-) *n.* 1. a feeling or expression of opposition or disapproval 2. a reason for objecting

ob·jec′tion·a·ble *adj.* 1. open to objection 2. disagreeable; offensive

ob·jec′tive *adj.* 1. existing as an object or fact, independent of the mind; real 2. concerned with the realities of the thing dealt with rather than the thoughts of the artist, writer, speaker, etc. 3. without bias or prejudice 4. *Gram.* designating or of the case of an object of a preposition or verb —*n.* something aimed at —**ob·jec′tive·ly** *adv.* —**ob·jec·tiv·i·ty** (äb′jek tiv′ə tē) *n.*

object lesson an actual demonstration or exemplification of some principle

ob·jet d'art (äb′zhä där′, ub′-) *pl.* **ob·jets d'art** (äb′zhä-, ub′-) [Fr.] a relatively small object of artistic value

ob·jur·gate (äb′jər gāt′) *vt.* **-gat′ed, -gat′ing** [< L. *ob-* (see OB-) + *jurgare*, chide] to upbraid sharply —**ob′jur·ga′tion** *n.*

ob·late (äb′lāt) *adj.* [< ModL. *oblatus*, thrust forward] flattened at the poles [an *oblate* spheroid]

ob·la·tion (ä blā′shən) *n.* [< L. *oblatus*, offered] an offering made to God or a god

ob·li·gate (äb′lə gāt′) *vt.* **-gat′ed, -gat′ing** [see OBLIGE] to bind by a contract, promise, sense of duty, etc.

ob′li·ga′tion *n.* **1.** an obligating or being obligated **2.** a legal or moral responsibility **3.** binding power of a contract, promise, etc. **4.** indebtedness for a favor, etc.

ob·lig·a·to·ry (ə blig′ə tôr′ē, äb′lig ə-) *adj.* legally or morally binding; required

o·blige (ə blīj′, ō-) *vt.* **o·bliged′, o·blig′ing** [< L. *ob-* (see OB-) + *ligare*, bind] **1.** to compel by moral, legal, or physical force **2.** to make indebted for a favor; do a favor for —*vi.* to do a favor

o·blig′ing *adj.* ready to do favors; helpful

ob·lique (ə blēk′, ō-; *also, esp. in mil. use,* -blīk′) *adj.* [< L. *ob-* (see OB-) + *liquis*, awry] **1.** slanting **2.** indirect or evasive —**ob·lique′ly** *adv.* —**ob·liq·ui·ty** (ə blik′wə tē), **ob·lique′ness** *n.*

ob·lit·er·ate (ə blit′ə rāt′) *vt.* **-at′ed, -at′ing** [< L. *ob-* (see OB-) + *litera*, a letter] **1.** to blot out; efface **2.** to destroy —**ob·lit′er·a′tion** *n.*

ob·liv·i·on (ə bliv′ē ən) *n.* [< L. *oblivisci*, forget] **1.** forgetfulness **2.** the state of being forgotten

ob·liv′i·ous *adj.* forgetful or unmindful (usually with *of* or *to*)

ob·long (äb′lôn) *adj.* [< L. *ob-* (see OB-) + *longus*, long] longer than broad; specif., rectangular and longer in one direction —*n.* an oblong figure

ob·lo·quy (äb′lə kwē) *n., pl.* **-quies** [< L. *ob-* (see OB-) + *loqui*, speak] **1.** verbal abuse; esp., widespread censure **2.** disgrace or infamy resulting from this

ob·nox·ious (əb näk′shəs, äb-) *adj.* [< L. *ob-* (see OB-) + *noxa*, harm] very unpleasant; offensive —**ob·nox′ious·ly** *adv.*

o·boe (ō′bō) *n.* [It. < Fr. *haut*, high (pitch) + *bois*, wood] a double-reed woodwind instrument having a high, penetrating tone —**o′bo·ist** *n.*

Obs., obs. obsolete

ob·scene (äb sēn′) *adj.* [< Fr. < L. *obscenus*, filthy] **1.** offensive to modesty or decency; lewd **2.** repulsive —**ob·scene′ly** *adv.* —**ob·scen′i·ty** (-sen′ə tē) *n., pl.* **-ties**

ob·scure (əb skyoor′, äb-) *adj.* [< L. *obscurus*, covered over] **1.** dim; dark; murky **2.** not easily seen; indistinct **3.** vague; ambiguous [an *obscure* answer] **4.** inconspicuous; hidden **5.** not well-known [an *obscure* actor] —*vt.* **-scured′, -scur′ing** to make obscure —**ob·scu′ri·ty** *n.*

ob·se·quies (äb′sə kwēz) *n.pl.* [< L. *obsequiae*, compliance, substituted for L. *exsequiae*, funeral] funeral rites

ob·se·qui·ous (əb sē′kwē əs, äb-) *adj.* [< L. *obsequi*, comply with] showing too great a willingness to serve or obey; fawning

ob·serv·ance (əb zur′vəns) *n.* **1.** the observing of a law, duty, custom, etc. **2.** a customary act, rite, etc.

ob·serv′ant *adj.* **1.** strict in observing a rule,

custom, etc. **2.** paying careful attention **3.** perceptive or alert

ob·ser·va·tion (äb′zər vā′shən) *n.* **1.** *a*) the act or power of observing *b*) something noticed **2.** a being seen or noticed **3.** a noting and recording of facts, as for research **4.** a comment; remark

ob·serv·a·to·ry (əb zur′və tôr′ē, äb-) *n., pl.* **-ries** a building equipped for scientific observation, esp. one with a large telescope for astronomical research

ob·serve (əb zurv′, äb-) *vt.* **-served′, -serv′ing** [< L. *ob-* (see OB-) + *servare*, keep] **1.** to adhere to (a law, custom, etc.) **2.** to celebrate (a holiday, etc.) **3.** *a*) to notice (something) *b*) to pay special attention to **4.** to arrive at as a conclusion **5.** to say casually; remark **6.** to examine scientifically —**ob·serv′er** *n.*

ob·sess (əb ses′, äb-) *vt.* [< L. *ob-* (see OB-) + *sedere*, sit] to haunt or trouble in mind; preoccupy —**ob·ses′sive** *adj.*

ob·ses′sion *n.* **1.** a being obsessed **2.** an idea, desire, etc. that obsesses one

ob·sid·i·an (əb sid′ē ən, äb-) *n.* [< one *Obsius*, its alleged discoverer] a hard, dark, volcanic glass

ob·so·les·cent (äb′sə les′'nt) *adj.* becoming obsolete —**ob′so·les′cence** *n.*

ob·so·lete (äb′sə lēt′) *adj.* [< L. *ob-* (see OB-) + *solere*, become accustomed] **1.** no longer in use; discarded **2.** out-of-date

ob·sta·cle (äb′sti k'l) *n.* [< L. *ob-* (see OB-) + *stare*, to stand] anything that stands in the way; obstruction

ob·stet·rics (əb stet′riks) *n.pl.* [*with sing. v.*] [< L. *obstetrix*, midwife] the branch of medicine concerned with the care and treatment of women during pregnancy and childbirth —**ob·stet′ric, ob·stet′ri·cal** *adj.* —**ob·ste·tri·cian** (äb′stə trish′ən) *n.*

ob·sti·nate (äb′stə nit) *adj.* [< L. *obstinare*, resolve on] **1.** determined to have one's own way; stubborn **2.** resisting treatment [an *obstinate* fever] —**ob′sti·na·cy** (-nə sē) *n.*

ob·strep·er·ous (əb strep′ər əs, äb-) *adj.* [< L. *ob-* (see OB-) + *strepere*, to roar] noisy or unruly, esp. in resisting

ob·struct (əb strukt′, äb-) *vt.* [< L. *ob-* (see OB-) + *struere*, pile up] **1.** to block (a passage) **2.** to hinder (progress, etc.) **3.** to block (the view) —**ob·struc′tive** *adj.*

ob·struc′tion (-struk′shən) *n.* **1.** an obstructing **2.** anything that obstructs; hindrance

ob·tain (əb tān′, äb-) *vt.* [< L. *ob-* (see OB-) + *tenere*, to hold] to get possession of by effort; procure —*vi.* to prevail [peace will *obtain*] —**ob·tain′a·ble** *adj.*

ob·trude (əb trood′, äb-) *vt.* **-trud′ed, -trud′ing** [< L. *ob-* (see OB-) + *trudere*, to thrust] **1.** to push out; eject **2.** to force (oneself, etc.) upon others unasked —*vi.* to obtrude oneself (*on* or *upon*) —**ob·tru′sion** (-trōō′zhən) *n.* —**ob·tru′sive** *adj.*

ob·tuse (äb tōōs′, əb-) *adj.* [< L. *ob-* (see OB-) + *tundere*, to strike] **1.** not sharp; blunt **2.** greater than 90 degrees and less than 180 degrees [an *obtuse* angle] **3.** slow to understand or perceive

ob·verse (äb vurs′, əb-; äb′vərs) *adj.* [< L. *ob-* (see OB-) + *vertere*, to turn] **1.** turned toward the observer **2.** forming a counterpart —*n.* (äb′vərs) **1.** the side, as of a coin or medal, bearing the main design **2.** a counterpart —**ob·verse′ly** *adv.*

ob·vi·ate (äb′vē āt′) *vt.* **-at′ed, -at′ing** [see OBVIOUS] to do away with or prevent by effective measures; make unnecessary —**ob'vi·a'tion** *n.*

ob·vi·ous (äb'vē əs) *adj.* [L. *obvius*, in the way] easy to see or understand; evident

oc- *see* OB-

oc·a·ri·na (äk'ə rē'nə) *n.* [It. < L. *auca*, a goose] a small, simple wind instrument with finger holes and a mouthpiece

occas. occasional(ly)

oc·ca·sion (ə kā'zhən) *n.* [< L. *ob-* (see OB-) + *cadere*, to fall] 1. a favorable time; opportunity 2. a fact or event that makes something else possible 3. *a)* a happening *b)* a particular time 4. a special time or event 5. need arising from circumstances —*vt.* to cause —**on occasion** sometimes

oc·ca'sion·al *adj.* 1. of or for special occasions 2. happening now and then; infrequent —**oc·ca'sion·al·ly** *adv.*

oc·ci·dent (äk'sə dənt) *n.* [< L. *occidere*, to fall: with reference to the setting sun] the west: now rare, except [O-] Europe and the Americas —**oc'ci·den'tal, Oc'ci·den'tal** *adj., n.*

oc·clude (ə klōōd') *vt.* **-clud'ed, -clud'ing** [< L. *ob-* (see OB-) + *claudere*, shut] 1. to close or block (a passage) 2. to shut in or out —*vi.* Dentistry to meet with the cusps fitting closely — **oc·clu·sion** (-klōō'zhən) *n.*

oc·cult (ə kult', ä'kult) *adj.* [< L. *occulere*, conceal] 1. hidden 2. secret 3. beyond human understanding 4. of such alleged mystic arts as astrology, etc. —**the occult** the occult arts —**oc·cult'ism** *n.*

oc·cu·pan·cy (äk'yə pən sē) *n., pl.* **-cies** an occupying; a taking or keeping in possession

oc'cu·pant *n.* one who occupies

oc·cu·pa·tion (äk'yə pā'shən) *n.* 1. an occupying or being occupied 2. (one's) trade, profession, or business —**oc'cu·pa'tion·al** *adj.*

oc·cu·py (äk'yə pī') *vt.* **-pied', -py'ing** [< L. *ob-* (see OB-) + *capere*, seize] 1. to take possession of by settlement or seizure 2. to hold possession of; specif., *a)* to dwell in *b)* to hold (a position or office) 3. to take up (space, time, etc.) 4. to busy (oneself, one's mind, etc.) — **oc'cu·pi'er** *n.*

oc·cur (ə kur') *vi.* **-curred', -cur'ring** [< L. *ob-* (see OB-) + *currere*, to run] 1. to exist 2. to come to mind 3. to happen

oc·cur'rence *n.* 1. the act or fact of occurring 2. an event; incident

o·cean (ō'shən) *n.* [< Gr. *Okeanos*] 1. the great body of salt water that covers about 71% of the earth's surface 2. any of its five principal divisions: the Atlantic, Pacific, Indian, Arctic, or Antarctic Ocean 3. a great quantity —**o·ce·an·ic** (ō'shē an'ik) *adj.*

o'cean·go'ing *adj.* of or for ocean travel

o·cean·ol·o·gy (ō'shə näl'ə jē) *n.* the study of the sea in all its aspects

o·cel·lus (ō sel'əs) *n., pl.* **-li** (-ī) [L. < *oculus*, an eye] the simple eye of certain invertebrates

o·ce·lot (äs'ə lät', ō'sə-) *n.* [Fr. < Mex. *ocelotl*, jaguar] a large, spotted cat of N. and S. America

o·cher, o·chre (ō'kər) *n.* [< Gr. *ōchros*, pale-yellow] 1. a yellow or reddish-brown clay containing iron, used as a pigment 2. the color of ocher; esp., dark yellow

-ock [OE. *-oc, -uc,* dim.] *a suffix used orig. to form the diminutive [hillock]*

o'clock (ə kläk', ō-) *adv.* of or according to the clock

Oct. October

octa- [< Gr. *oktō,* eight] *a combining form meaning eight:* also **oct-**

oc·ta·gon (äk'tə gän') *n.* [< Gr.: see OCTA- &

-GON] a plane figure with eight angles and eight sides —**oc·tag'o·nal** (-tag'ə n'l) *adj.*

oc·tane number (or **rating**) (äk'tān) a number representing the antiknock quality of a gasoline, etc.

oc·tave (äk'tiv, -tāv) *n.* [< L. *octavus,* eighth] *Music* 1. the eighth full tone above or below a given tone 2. the interval of eight degrees between a tone and either of its octaves 3. the series of tones within this interval, or the keys of an instrument producing such a series

oc·ta·vo (äk tā'vō, -tä'-) *n., pl.* **-vos** [< L. (in) *octavo,* (in) eight] 1. the page size (about 6 by 9 inches) of a book made up of printer's sheets folded into eight leaves 2. a book of such pages

oc·tet, oc·tette (äk tet') *n.* [< OCT(O)- + (DU)ET] *Music* 1. a composition for eight voices or eight instruments 2. the eight performers of this

Oc·to·ber (äk tō'bər) *n.* [< L. *octo,* eight: eighth month of the Roman year] the tenth month of the year, having 31 days

oc·to·ge·nar·i·an (äk'tə ji ner'ē ən) *adj.* [< L. *octoginta,* eighty] between the ages of eighty and ninety —*n.* a person of this age

oc·to·pus (äk'tə pəs) *n., pl.* **-pus·es, -pi'** (-pī') [< Gr. *oktō,* eight + *pous,* a foot] a mollusk with a soft body and eight arms covered with suckers

oc·u·lar (äk'yə lər) *adj.* [< L. *oculus,* the eye] 1. of, for, or like the eye 2. by eyesight

oc'u·list (-list) *n.* [< L. *oculus,* the eye] *earlier term for* OPHTHALMOLOGIST

OD, O.D. overdose

odd (äd) *adj.* [< ON. *oddi*] 1. remaining from a pair, set, etc. *[an odd glove]* 2. having a remainder of one when divided by two 3. left over after taking a round number 4. with a few more *[thirty odd years ago]* 5. occasional *[odd jobs]* 6. *a)* peculiar *b)* queer; eccentric — **odd'ly** *adv.*

odd'ball *n.* [Slang] an eccentric or nonconforming person —*adj.* [Slang] strange or unconventional

odd·i·ty (äd'ə tē) *n.* 1. peculiarity 2. *pl.* **-ties** an odd person or thing

odds (ädz) *n.pl.* 1. difference in favor of one side over the other; advantage 2. an equalizing advantage given by a bettor or competitor in proportion to the assumed chances in his favor —**at odds** quarreling —**by (all) odds** by far

odds and ends scraps; remnants

odds'-on' *adj.* having better than an even chance of winning *[an odds-on favorite]*

ode (ōd) *n.* [Fr. < Gr. *ōidē,* song] a lyric poem characterized by lofty feeling and dignified style

-ode [< Gr. *hodos*] *a suffix meaning* way, path

O·din (ō'din) *Norse Myth.* the chief god

o·di·ous (ō'dē əs) *adj.* [< L. *odium,* hatred] disgusting; offensive —**o'di·ous·ly** *adv.*

o'di·um (-əm) *n.* [L. < *odi,* I hate] 1. hatred 2. the disgrace brought on by hateful action

o·dom·e·ter (ō däm'ə tər) *n.* [< Fr. < Gr. *hodos,* way + *metron,* a measure] an instrument for measuring the distance traveled by a vehicle

o·dor (ō'dər) *n.* [L.] a smell; fragrance, stench, etc.: Brit. sp. **odour** —**be in bad** (or **ill**) **odor** to be in ill repute —**o'dor·less** *adj.* —**o'dor·ous** *adj.*

o·dor·if·er·ous (ō'dər if'ər əs) *adj.* giving off an odor, specif., a fragrant one

O·dys·se·us (ō dis'yōōs, -dis'ē əs) the hero of the *Odyssey,* one of the Greek leaders in the Trojan War

Od·ys·sey (äd′ə sē) an ancient Greek epic poem, ascribed to Homer, about the wanderings of Odysseus during the ten years after the fall of Troy —*n.* [*sometimes* o-] *pl.* -seys any extended wandering
OE., OE, O.E. Old English
Oed·i·pus (ed′ə pəs, ē′də-) *Gr. Myth.* a king who unwittingly killed his father and married his mother
o′er (ôr) *prep., adv.* [Poet.] over
of (uv, äv) *prep.* [OE.] 1. from; specif., *a*) coming from [men *of* Ohio] *b*) resulting from [to die *of* fever] *c*) at a distance from [east *of* the city] *d*) by [the poems *of* Poe] *e*) separated from [robbed *of* his money] *f*) from the whole constituting [part *of* the time] *g*) made from [a sheet *of* paper] 2. belonging to 3. *a*) possessing [a man *of* wealth] *b*) containing [a bag *of* nuts] 4. specified as [a height *of* six feet] 5. characterized by [a man *of* honor] 6. concerning; about 7. during [*of* late years]
of- *see* OB-
off (ôf) *adv.* [LME. variant of *of*, OF] 1. so as to be away or at a distance 2. so as to be no longer on, attached, etc. [take *off* your hat] 3. (a specified distance) away in space or time [20 yards *off*] 4. so as to be no longer in operation, etc. [turn the motor *off*] 5. so as to be less, etc. [5% *off* for cash] 6. away from one's work —*prep.* 1. no longer (or not) on, attached, etc. [*off* the road] 2. away from [to live *off* the campus] 3. from the substance of [to live *off* the land] 4. relieved from [*off* duty] 5. not up to the usual standard, etc. of [*off* one's game] —*adj.* 1. not on, attached, in operation, etc. 2. on the way [be *off* to bed] 3. away from work, etc. [we are *off* today] 4. not up to the usual standard, etc. 5. more remote [on the *off* chance] 6. in (specified) circumstances [to be well *off*] 7. not correct [his figures are *off*] —*interj.* go away! —**off and on** now and then
of·fal (ôf′l, äf′-) *n.* [ME. *ofall*, lit., off-fall] 1. [*with sing. or pl. v.*] the entrails, etc. of a butchered animal 2. refuse; garbage
off′beat′ *adj.* [< a rhythm in jazz music] [Colloq.] unconventional, unusual, etc.
off′-col′or *adj.* 1. varying from the standard color 2. not quite proper; risqué
of·fend (ə fend′) *vi.* [< L. *ob-* (see OB-) + *fendere*, to hit] 1. to commit a sin or crime 2. to create resentment, anger, etc. —*vt.* 1. to hurt the feelings of; make angry, etc. 2. to be displeasing to (the taste, sense, etc.) —**of·fend′er** *n.*
of·fense (ə fens′, ô′fens) *n.* 1. a sin or crime 2. a creating of resentment, anger, etc. 3. a feeling hurt, angry, etc. 4. something that causes anger, etc. 5. the act of attacking 6. the person, side, army, etc. that is attacking Brit. sp. **offence** —**take offense** to become offended; feel hurt, angry, etc.
of·fen′sive *adj.* 1. attacking or for attack 2. unpleasant; disgusting 3. causing resentment, anger, etc. —*n.* attitude or position of attack — **of·fen′sive·ly** *adv.*
of·fer (ôf′ər, äf′-) *vt.* [< L. *ob-* (see OB-) + *ferre*, bring] 1. to present in an act of worship [to *offer* prayers] 2. to present for acceptance 3. to show or give signs of [to *offer* resistance] 4. to bid (a price, etc.) —*vi.* to occur; present itself —*n.* the act of offering or thing offered
of′fer·ing *n.* 1. the act of making an offer 2. something offered; specif., *a*) a contribution *b*) a presentation made in worship
of′fer·to·ry (-tôr′ē) *n., pl.* -ries [*often* O-] 1. the offering of the Eucharistic bread and wine 2.

money collected at a church service, or a hymn sung during the collection
off′hand′ *adv.* without prior preparation —*adj.* 1. said or done offhand 2. casual, curt, etc. Also **off′hand′ed**
of·fice (ôf′is, äf′-) *n.* [< L. *officium*] 1. a service done for another 2. a duty, esp. as a part of one's work 3. a position of authority or trust, as in government 4. a place where work or business that is administrative, professional, etc. is carried on 5. a religious ceremony or rite
office boy a boy doing odd jobs in an office
of′fice·hold′er *n.* a government official
of·fi·cer (ôf′ə sər, äf′-) *n.* 1. anyone holding an office or position of authority in a government, business, club, etc. 2. a policeman 3. one holding a position of authority, esp. by commission, in the armed forces
of·fi·cial (ə fish′əl) *adj.* 1. of or holding an office, or position of authority 2. authorized or authoritative 3. formal —*n.* a person holding office —**of·fi′cial·dom** (-dəm) *n.*
of·fi·ci·ate (ə fish′ē āt′) *vi.* -at′ed, -at′ing 1. to perform official duties 2. to perform the functions of a priest, minister, etc.
of·fi·cious (ə fish′əs) *adj.* [see OFFICE] offering unwanted advice or services
off·ing (ôf′iŋ) *n.* [< OFF] the distant part of the sea visible from the shore —**in the offing 1.** far but in sight 2. at some indefinite future time
off′-key′ *adj.* 1. flat or sharp 2. not quite in accord with what is fitting, etc.
off′-lim′its *adj.* ruled a place not to be gone to by a specified group
off·set (ôf′set′) *n.* 1. anything that balances or compensates for something else 2. *same as* OFFSET PRINTING —*vt.* (ôf set′) -set′, -set′ting to balance, compensate for, etc.
offset printing a printing process in which the inked impression is first made on a rubber-covered roller, then transferred to paper
off′shoot′ *n.* 1. a shoot growing from the main stem of a plant 2. anything that branches off, or derives from, a main source
off′shore′ *adj.* 1. moving away from the shore 2. at some distance from shore —*adv.* away from the shore
off′side′ *adj. Sports* not in the proper position for play
off′spring′ *n., pl.* -spring′, -springs′ a child or children; progeny; young
off′-white′ *adj.* grayish-white or yellowish-white
oft (ôft) *adv.* [OE.] [Poet.] often
of·ten (ôf′n, ôf′t′n) *adv.* [ME. var. of prec.] many times; frequently: also **of′ten·times′**
o·gle (ō′g′l, ä′-) *vi., vt.* o′gled, o′gling [prob. < LowG. *oog*, the eye] to keep looking (at) boldly and with desire —*n.* an ogling look — **o′gler** *n.*
o·gre (ō′gər) *n.* [Fr.] 1. in fairy tales and folklore, a man-eating giant 2. a hideous or cruel man —**o′gre·ish, o′grish** *adj.*
oh (ō) *interj., n., pl.* oh's, ohs an exclamation of surprise, fear, wonder, pain, etc.
ohm (ōm) *n.* [< G. S. *Ohm* (1789–1854), G. physicist] the unit of electrical resistance
-oid [< Gr. *eidos*, a form] *a suffix meaning* like, resembling [*crystalloid*]
oil (oil) *n.* [< Gr. *elaion*, (olive) oil] 1. any of various greasy, combustible, normally liquid substances obtained from animal, vegetable, and mineral sources: oils are insoluble in water 2. *same as* PETROLEUM 3. *same as: a*) OIL COLOR *b*) OIL PAINTING —*vt.* to lubricate or

supply with oil —*adj.* of, from, or like oil —
oil′er *n.*
oil′cloth′ *n.* cloth made waterproof with oil or
with heavy coats of paint
oil color paint made by grinding a pigment in
oil
oil painting 1. a picture painted in oil colors **2.**
the art of painting in oil colors
oil′skin′ *n.* **1.** cloth made waterproof by treatment with oil **2.** [*often pl.*] a garment made of
this
oil well a well bored through layers of rock,
etc. to a supply of petroleum
oil′y *adj.* **-i-er, -i-est 1.** of, like, or containing oil
2. greasy **3.** too smooth; unctuous —**oil′i-ly** *adv.*
—**oil′i-ness** *n.*
oink (oiŋk) *n.* the grunt of a pig —*vi.* to make
this sound
oint-ment (oint′mənt) *n.* [< L. *unguentum:* see
UNGUENT] a fatty substance applied to the
skin as a salve or cosmetic
OK, O.K. (ō′kā′) *adj., adv., interj.* [abbrev. for
"oll korrect," jocular misspelling of *all correct*]
all right; correct —*n.* (ō′kā′) *pl.* **OK′s, O.K.′s**
approval —*vt.* (ō′kā′) **OK′d** or **O.K.′d, OK′ing** or
O.K.′ing to put an OK on; approve
o-kra (ō′krə) *n.* [< WAfr. name] **1.** a tall plant
with ribbed, sticky green pods **2.** the pods,
used as a vegetable
old (ōld) *adj.* **old′er** or **eld′er, old′est** or **eld′est**
[OE. *ald*] **1.** having lived or existed for a long
time **2.** of aged people **3.** of a certain age [ten
years *old*] **4.** not new **5.** worn out by age or
use **6.** former **7.** experienced [an *old* hand] **8.**
ancient **9.** of long standing **10.** designating the
earlier or earliest of two or more [the Old
World] —*n.* **1.** time long past [days of *old*] **2.**
something old (with *the*)
old country the country from which an immi-
grant came, esp. a country in Europe
old-en (ōl′d'n) *adj.* [Poet.] (of) old
Old English the Germanic language of the
Anglo-Saxons, spoken in England from c.400
to c.1100 A.D.
old′-fash′ioned *adj.* suited to or favoring the
styles, ideas, etc. of past times —*n.* [*also* O- F-]
a cocktail made with whiskey, soda water, bit-
ters, sugar, and fruit
Old French the French language as spoken
from the 9th to the 16th c.
Old Glory the flag of the U.S.
old hat [Slang] **1.** old-fashioned **2.** trite
Old High German the High German language
from the 8th to the 11th c.
old′ie, old′y *n., pl.* **old′ies** [Colloq.] an old
joke, song, movie, etc.
old lady [Slang] **1.** one's mother **2.** one's wife
Old Low German the Low German language
before the 12th c.
old maid 1. a woman, esp. an older woman,
who has never married **2.** a prim, prudish,
fussy person —**old′-maid′ish** *adj.*
old man [Slang] **1.** one's father **2.** one's husband **3.** [*usually* O- M-] a man in authority
Old Norse the Germanic language of the
Scandinavian peoples before the 14th c.
Old Saxon the Low German dialect of the
Saxons before the 10th c.
old′ster (-stər) *n.* [Colloq.] an old or elderly
person
Old Testament *Christian designation for* the
Holy Scriptures of Judaism, the first of the
two general divisions of the Christian Bible
old′-time′ *adj.* **1.** of or like past times **2.** of
long standing or experience
old′-tim′er *n.* [Colloq.] a longtime resident,
employee, etc.

old′-world′ *adj.* of the Eastern Hemisphere:
often with reference to European culture, customs, etc.
o-le-ag-i-nous (ō′lē aj′i nəs) *adj.* [< Fr. < L.
olea, olive tree] oily; unctuous
o-le-an-der (ō′lē an′dər, ō′lē an′dər) *n.* [ML.]
a poisonous evergreen shrub with fragrant
white, pink, or red flowers
o-le-o-mar-ga-rine (ō′lē ō mär′jə rin) *n.* [<
Fr. < L. *oleum,* an oil + MARGARINE] *full
name of* MARGARINE: also **o′le-o′**
ol-fac-to-ry (äl fak′tər ē, ōl-) *adj.* [< L. *olere,*
have a smell + *facere,* make] of the sense of
smell
ol-i-gar-chy (äl′ə gär′kē) *n., pl.* **-chies** [< Gr.
oligos, few + -ARCHY] **1.** (a) government with
the ruling power belonging to a few **2.** those
ruling —**ol′i-gar′chic, ol′i-gar′chi-cal** *adj.*
ol-ive (äl′iv) *n.* [< Gr. *elaia*] **1.** *a*) an evergreen
tree of S Europe and the Near East *b*) its
small, oval fruit, eaten green or ripe, or
pressed to extract its light-yellow oil (**olive oil**)
2. the yellowish-green color of the unripe fruit
olive branch the branch of the olive tree, a
symbol of peace
O-lym-pic games (ō lim′pik) [< *Olympia,*
plain in Greece, site of ancient games] an international athletic competition generally held
every four years: also **the O-lym′pics**
O-lym′pus (-pəs), **Mount** mountain in N
Greece: in Greek mythology, the home of the
gods —**O-lym′pi-an** (-pē ən) *n., adj.*
om-buds-man (äm′bədz mən) *n., pl.* **-men**
[Sw.] an appointed public official who investigates citizens' complaints against government
agencies
o-me-ga (ō mā′gə, -meg′ə, -mē′gə) *n.* the
twenty-fourth and final letter of the Greek alphabet (Ω, ω)
om-e-let, om-e-lette (äm′lit, äm′ə let) *n.* [<
Fr. < L. *lamella,* small plate] eggs beaten up,
often with milk or water, and cooked as a
pancake in a pan
o-men (ō′mən) *n.* [L.] a thing or happening
supposed to foretell a future event; augury
om-i-cron (äm′ə krän′, ō′mə-) *n.* the fifteenth
letter of the Greek alphabet (O, o)
om-i-nous (äm′ə nəs) *adj.* of or serving as an
evil omen; threatening
o-mis-sion (ō mish′ən) *n.* **1.** an omitting or
being omitted **2.** anything omitted
o-mit (ō mit′) *vt.* **o-mit′ted, o-mit′ting** [< L. *ob-*
(see OB-) + *mittere,* send] **1.** to fail to include;
leave out **2.** to fail to do; neglect
omni- [L. < *omnis,* all] *a combining form
meaning* all, everywhere
om-ni-bus (äm′nə bəs) *n., pl.* **-bus-es** [Fr. <
L., lit., for all] *same as* BUS —*adj.* providing for
many things at once
om-nip-o-tent (äm nip′ə tənt) *adj.* [< L.
omnis, all + *potens,* able] having unlimited
power or authority; all-powerful —**the Omnipo-
tent** God —**om-nip′o-tence** *n.*
om-ni-pres-ent (äm′ni prez′'nt) *adj.* present
in all places at the same time —**om′ni-pres′-
ence** *n.*
om-nis-cient (äm nish′ənt) *adj.* [< L. *omnis,*
all + *scire,* know] knowing all things —**om-
nis′cience** *n.*
om-niv-o-rous (äm niv′ər əs) *adj.* [< L. *omnis,*
all + *vorare,* devour] **1.** eating any sort of
food **2.** taking in everything indiscriminately
[an *omnivorous* reader]
on (än, ôn) *prep.* [OE.] **1.** in contact with, supported by, or covering **2.** in the surface of
[scars *on* it] **3.** near to [on my left] **4.** at the
time of [on Monday] **5.** connected with [on the

team/ **6.** engaged in /on a trip/ **7.** in a state of /on parole/ **8.** as a result of /a profit on the sale/ **9.** in the direction of /light shone on us/ **10.** through the use of /to live on bread/ **11.** concerning /an essay on war/ **12.** [Colloq.] chargeable to /a drink on the house/ **13.** [Slang] using; addicted to /on drugs/ —**adv. 1.** in a situation of contacting, being supported by, or covering **2.** in a direction toward /looked on/ **3.** forward /move on/ **4.** continuously /she sang on/ **5.** into operation or action /turn the light on/ —**adj.** in action or operation /the TV is on/ —**and so on** and more like the preceding —**on and off** intermittently

ON., ON, O.N. Old Norse

once (wuns) **adv.** [< OE. an, one] **1.** one time only **2.** at any time; ever **3.** formerly **4.** by one degree /a cousin once removed/ —**conj.** as soon as —**n.** one time /go this once/ —**at once 1.** immediately **2.** at the same time —**once (and) for all** finally —**once in a while** occasionally

once'-o'ver n. [Colloq.] **1.** a swiftly appraising glance **2.** a quick going-over

on·com·ing (än'kum'iŋ) **adj.** approaching

one (wun) **adj.** [OE. an] **1.** being a single thing **2.** united **3.** being uniquely such /the one solution/ **4.** the same **5.** a certain but unspecified /one day last week/ —**n. 1.** the first and lowest cardinal number; 1; I **2.** a single person or thing —**pron. 1.** a certain person or thing **2.** any person or thing —**at one** in accord

one'ness (-nis) n. **1.** singleness; unity **2.** unity of mind, feeling, etc. **3.** sameness

on·er·ous (än'ər əs, ō'nər-) **adj.** [< L. onus, a load] burdensome; oppressive

one·self (wun'self', wunz'-) **pron.** a person's own self: also **one's self** —**be oneself 1.** to function normally **2.** to be natural —**by oneself** alone; unaccompanied

one'-sid'ed (-sīd'id) **adj. 1.** on, having, or involving only one side **2.** unfair; favoring one side **3.** unequal /a one-sided race/

one'-time' adj. at a past time; former

one'-track' adj. [Colloq.] limited in scope /a one-track mind/

one'-way' adj. moving, or allowing movement, in one direction only

on'go'ing adj. going on; in process

on·ion (un'yən) n. [< L. unus, one] **1.** a plant of the lily family, with an edible bulb having a sharp smell and taste **2.** the bulb

on'ion·skin' n. a tough, thin, translucent paper

on'look'er n. a spectator

on·ly (ōn'lē) **adj.** [< OE. an, one + -lic, -LY] **1.** alone of its or their kind; sole **2.** alone in superiority; best —**adv. 1.** and no other; solely **2.** (but) in the end **3.** as recently as —**conj.** [Colloq.] except that; but —**if . . . only** I wish that —**only too** very

on·o·mat·o·poe·ia (än'ə mat'ə pē'ə) n. [< Gr. onoma, a name + poiein, make] formation of words by imitating sounds (Ex.: buzz) —**on'o·mat'o·poe'ic** adj.

on'rush' n. a headlong dash forward

on'set' n. **1.** an attack **2.** a beginning

on'slaught' (-slôt') n. [< Du. slagen, to strike] a violent, intense attack

on·to (än'tōō) **prep. 1.** to a position on **2.** [Slang] aware of Also **on to**

on·tog·e·ny (än täj'ə nē) n. [< Gr. einai, to be + -geneia, origin] the development of an individual organism

o·nus (ō'nəs) n. [L.] **1.** a burden, unpleasant duty, etc. **2.** blame

on·ward (än'wərd) **adv.** toward or at a position ahead: also **on'wards** —**adj.** advancing

on·yx (än'iks) n. [< Gr. onyx, fingernail] a type of agate with alternate colored layers

oo·dles (ōō'd'lz) **n.pl.** [< ?] [Colloq.] a great amount

ooze' (ōōz) n. [OE. wos, sap] an oozing or something that oozes —**vi. oozed, ooz'ing** to flow or leak out slowly —**vt.** to exude

ooze² (ōōz) n. [OE. wase] soft mud or slime, as at the bottom of a lake —**oo·zy** (ōō'zē) **adj.**

op- see OB-

o·pal (ō'p'l) n. [< Sans. upala, gem] a silica of various colors, typically iridescent: some varieties are semiprecious —**o·pal·es·cent** (ō'pə les''nt) **adj.**

o·paque (ō pāk') **adj.** [L. opacus, shady] **1.** not letting light through **2.** not reflecting light **3.** hard to understand **4.** slow in understanding — **o·paque'ly adv.**

op. cit. [L. opere citato] in the work cited

o·pen (ō'p'n) **adj.** [OE.] **1.** not closed, covered, clogged, or shut **2.** unenclosed **3.** spread out; unfolded **4.** having spaces, gaps, etc. **5.** free to be entered, used, etc. /an open meeting/ **6.** not decided /an open question/ **7.** not prejudiced or narrow-minded **8.** generous **9.** free from legal or discriminatory restrictions /open season, open housing/ **10.** not conventional or customary /open marriage/ **11.** not yet taken /the job is open/ **12.** not secret; public **13.** frank; candid —**vt., vi. 1.** to cause to be, or to become, open **2.** to spread out; expand; unfold **3.** to make or become available for use, etc. without restriction **4.** to begin; start **5.** to start operating — **open to 1.** willing to receive, discuss, etc. **2.** available to —**the open 1.** the outdoors **2.** public knowledge —**o'pen·er** n. —**o'pen·ly adv.** —**o'pen·ness** n.

open air the outdoors —**o'pen-air'** adj.

o'pen-and-shut' adj. easily decided

o'pen-end'ed adj. unrestricted

o'pen-hand'ed adj. generous

o'pen-heart'ed adj. **1.** not reserved; frank **2.** kindly; generous

o'pen-hearth' adj. designating or using a furnace with a wide hearth and low roof, for making steel

open house informal reception of visitors freely coming and going, at one's home, a school, etc.

o'pen·ing n. **1.** a becoming or making open **2.** an open place; hole; gap **3.** a clearing **4.** a) a beginning b) a first performance **5.** an opportunity **6.** a job available

o'pen-mind'ed adj. open to new ideas; not biased —**o'pen-mind'ed·ness** n.

o'pen·work' n. ornamental work, as in cloth, with openings in the material

op·er·a' (äp'ər ə) n. [It. < L., a work] a play with the text sung to orchestral accompaniment —**op'er·at'ic** (-ə rat'ik) **adj.**

o·pe·ra² (ō'pə rə, äp'ər ə) n. pl. of OPUS

op·er·a·ble (äp'ər ə b'l) **adj.** [see OPERATE] **1.** practicable **2.** treatable surgically

opera glasses a small binocular telescope used at the opera, in theaters, etc.

op·er·ate (äp'ə rāt') **vi. -at'ed, -at'ing** [< L. operari, to work] **1.** to be in action; work **2.** to produce a certain effect **3.** to perform a surgical operation —**vt. 1.** to put or keep in action **2.** to manage **3.** [Colloq.] to perform surgery on

op·er·a·tion (äp'ə rā'shən) n. **1.** the act or method of operating **2.** a being in action or at work **3.** any of a series of procedures in some work **4.** any specific plan, project, etc. **5.** any surgical procedure to remedy a physical ailment —**op'er·a'tion·al adj.**

op·er·a·tive (äp'ə rā'tiv, äp'ər ə-) **adj. 1.** capable of or in operation **2.** effective **3.** connected with physical work or mechanical action

op′er·a′tor (-tər) *n.* **1.** one who operates a machine **2.** a person engaged in commercial or industrial operations

op·er·et·ta (äp′ə ret′ə) *n.* [It. < OPERA[1]] a light, amusing opera with spoken dialogue

oph·thal·mic (äf thal′mik) *adj.* [< Gr. *ophthalmos,* the eye] of the eye; ocular

oph·thal·mol·o·gy (äf′thal mäl′ə jē; äp′-; -thə-) *n.* the branch of medicine dealing with the structure, functions, and diseases of the eye —**oph′thal·mol′o·gist** *n.*

o·pi·ate (ō′pē it, -āt′) *n.* **1.** any medicine containing opium or any of its derivatives **2.** anything quieting

o·pine (ō pīn′) *vt., vi.* **o·pined′, o·pin′ing** [< L. *opinari,* think] to think; suppose: now usually humorous

o·pin·ion (ə pin′yən) *n.* [< L. *opinari,* think] **1.** a belief not based on certainty but on what seems true or probable **2.** an evaluation, estimation, etc. **3.** an expert's formal judgment **4.** a judge's formal statement of the law bearing on a case

o·pin′ion·at′ed (-āt′id) *adj.* holding obstinately to one's opinions

o·pi·um (ō′pē əm) *n.* [L. < Gr. *opos,* vegetable juice] a narcotic drug made from the seed of a certain poppy

o·pos·sum (ə päs′əm) *n.* [< AmInd.] a small, tree-dwelling American marsupial

op·po·nent (ə pō′nənt) *n.* [< L. *ob-* (see OB-) + *ponere,* to set] one who opposes, as in a fight, game, etc.; adversary

op·por·tune (äp′ər tōōn′) *adj.* [< L. *opportunus,* lit., before the port] **1.** suitable: said of time **2.** timely

op′por·tun′ism *n.* the adapting of one's actions, judgments, etc. to circumstances, as in politics, without regard for principles —**op′por·tun′ist** *n.*

op·por·tu·ni·ty (äp′ər tōō′nə tē) *n., pl.* **-ties 1.** a combination of circumstances favorable for the purpose **2.** a good chance

op·pose (ə pōz′) *vt.* **-posed′, -pos′ing** [see OB- & POSITION] **1.** to place opposite, in balance or contrast **2.** to contend with

op·po·site (äp′ə zit) *adj.* [see OB- & POSITION] **1.** set against, facing, or back to back **2.** entirely different; exactly contrary —*n.* anything opposed or opposite —*prep.* across from —**op′po·site·ly** *adv.*

op′po·si′tion (-zish′ən) *n.* **1.** an opposing **2.** resistance, contrast, etc. **3.** anything that opposes **4.** [*often* O-] a political party opposing the party in power

op·press (ə pres′) *vt.* [< L. *ob-* (see OB-) + *premere,* to press] **1.** to weigh heavily on the mind, spirits, or senses of **2.** to keep down by the cruel or unjust use of authority —**op·pres′sor** *n.*

op·pres·sion (ə presh′ən) *n.* **1.** an oppressing or being oppressed **2.** a thing that oppresses **3.** physical or mental distress

op·pres·sive (ə pres′iv) *adj.* **1.** hard to put up with **2.** tyrannical **3.** distressing —**op·pres′sive·ly** *adv.*

op·pro·bri·ous (ə prō′brē əs) *adj.* expressing opprobrium; abusive

op·pro′bri·um (-əm) *n.* [< L. *opprobrare,* to reproach] **1.** disgrace; scorn **2.** anything bringing shame

opt (äpt) *vi.* [< Fr. < L. *optare*] to make a choice

op·tic (äp′tik) *adj.* [< Fr. < Gr. *optikos*] of the eye or sense of sight

op′ti·cal (-′l) *adj.* **1.** of the sense of sight; visual **2.** of optics **3.** made to give help in seeing —**op′ti·cal·ly** *adv.*

op·ti·cian (äp tish′ən) *n.* one who makes or sells eyeglasses, etc.

op·tics (äp′tiks) *n.pl.* [*with sing. v.*] the branch of physics dealing with light and vision

op·ti·mism (äp′tə miz′m) *n.* [< Fr. < L. *optimus,* best] **1.** the belief that good ultimately prevails over evil **2.** the tendency to take the most hopeful or cheerful view of matters —**op′ti·mist** *n.* —**op′ti·mis′tic** *adj.*

op′ti·mum (-məm) *n.* [see prec.] the best or most favorable degree, condition, etc. —*adj.* best; most favorable

op·tion (äp′shən) *n.* [Fr. < L. *optare,* to wish] **1.** a choosing **2.** the right of choosing **3.** something that is or can be chosen **4.** the right to buy or sell something at a set price within a set time —**op′tion·al** *adj.*

op·tom·e·try (äp täm′ə trē) *n.* [< Gr. *optikos,* optic + *metron,* measure] the science or profession of testing the vision and fitting glasses to correct eye defects —**op·tom′e·trist** *n.*

op·u·lent (äp′yə lənt) *adj.* [< L. *ops,* wealth] **1.** wealthy; rich **2.** abundant —**op′u·lence** *n.* —**op′u·lent·ly** *adv.*

o·pus (ō′pəs) *n., pl.* **o·pe·ra** (ō′pə rə, äp′ər ə), **o′pus·es** [L., a work] a work; composition; esp., any of the numbered musical works of a composer

or (ôr, ər) *conj.* [< OE. *oththe*] a coordinating conjunction introducing: *a)* an alternative [red or blue] *b)* a synonymous term [ill, or sick]

-or [< L. *-or*] *a suffix meaning:* **1.** a person or thing that [inventor] **2.** quality or condition [error]

or·a·cle (ôr′ə k'l, är′-) *n.* [< L. *orare,* to pray] **1.** in ancient Greece and Rome, the place where, or medium by which, deities were consulted **2.** the revelation of a medium or priest **3.** *a)* any person of great wisdom *b)* statements of such a person —**o·rac·u·lar** (ô rak′yoo lər) *adj.*

o·ral (ôr′əl) *adj.* [< L. *os,* mouth] **1.** uttered; spoken **2.** of or near the mouth

or·ange (ôr′inj, är′-) *n.* [ult. < Sans. *naranga*] **1.** a reddish-yellow, round citrus fruit with a sweet, juicy pulp **2.** the evergreen tree it grows on **3.** reddish yellow —*adj.* **1.** reddish-yellow **2.** of oranges

or′ange·ade′ (-ād′) *n.* a drink made of orange juice and water, usually sweetened

o·rang·u·tan (ô rang′oo tan′, ə-; -taŋ′) *n.* [< Malay *oran,* man + *utan,* forest] a large ape of Borneo and Sumatra, with shaggy, reddish-brown hair and a hairless face

o·rate (ô rāt′, ôr′āt) *vi.* **o·rat′ed, o·rat′ing** to make an oration; speak pompously: a humorously derogatory term

o·ra·tion (ô rā′shən) *n.* [< L. *orare,* speak] a formal speech, as at a ceremony

or·a·tor (ôr′ət ər, är′-) *n.* an eloquent public speaker

or·a·to·ri·o (ôr′ə tôr′ē ō′, är′-) *n., pl.* **-os′** [It., small chapel] a long, dramatic musical work, usually on a religious theme, presented without stage action

or·a·to·ry (ôr′ə tôr′ē, är′-) *n., pl.* **-ries** [< L. *oratoria*] skill in public speaking —**or′a·tor′i·cal** *adj.*

orb (ôrb) *n.* [L. *orbis,* a circle] **1.** a globe; sphere **2.** any heavenly sphere, as the sun

or·bit (ôr′bit) *n.* [< L. *orbis,* a circle] the path of a heavenly body, artificial satellite, or spacecraft in its revolution around another body —*vi.*, *vt.* to go or put into an orbit in space —**or'bit·al** *adj.*

or·chard (ôr'chərd) *n.* [< L. *hortus*, a garden + OE. *geard*, enclosure] 1. an area where fruit trees are grown 2. such trees

or·ches·tra (ôr'kis trə, -kes'-) *n.* [< Gr. *orchēstra*, space for the chorus] 1. the space in front of the stage, where the musicians sit: in full **orchestra pit** 2. the main floor of a theater 3. *a)* a group of musicians playing together *b)* their instruments —**or·ches'tral** (-kes'trəl) *adj.*

or·ches·trate' (-trāt') *vt.*, *vi.* **-trat'ed, -trat'ing** to compose or arrange (music) for an orchestra —**or'ches·tra'tion** *n.*

or·chid (ôr'kid) *n.* [< Gr. *orchis*, testicle: from the shape of its roots] 1. a plant having flowers with three petals, one lip-shaped 2. the flower 3. a light bluish red —*adj.* of this color

or·dain (ôr dān') *vt.* [< L. *ordo*, an order] 1. to decree; establish; enact 2. to invest with the office of a minister, priest, or rabbi —*vi.* to command

or·deal (ôr dēl') *n.* [OE. *ordal*] a painful or severe experience

or·der (ôr'dər) *n.* [< L. *ordo*, straight row] 1. social position 2. a state of peace; orderly conduct 3. arrangement of things or events; series 4. a definite plan; system 5. a military, monastic, or fraternal brotherhood 6. a condition in which everything is in its place and functioning properly 7. condition in general [in working *order*] 8. an authoritative command, instruction, etc. 9. a class; kind 10. an established method, as of conduct in meetings, etc. 11. *a)* a request to supply something *b)* the thing supplied 12. written instructions to pay money or surrender property 13. [*pl.*] the position of ordained minister —*vt.*, *vi.* 1. to put or keep (things) in order; arrange 2. to command 3. to request (something to be supplied) —**in** (or **out of**) **order** 1. in (or out of) proper position 2. in (or not in) working condition —**in order that** so that —**in order to** as a means to —**in short order** without delay —**on the order of** similar to

or'der·ly *adj.* 1. neat or tidy 2. well-behaved; law-abiding —*adv.* in proper order —*n.*, *pl.* **-lies** 1. an enlisted man assigned as a personal attendant 2. a male hospital attendant —**or'der·li·ness** *n.*

or·di·nal (ôr'd'n əl) *adj.* [< L. *ordo*, an order] expressing order in a series —*n.* any number showing order in a series (e.g., ninth, 25th, etc.): in full **ordinal number**

or·di·nance (ôr'd'n əns) *n.* [< L. *ordo*, an order] a statute, esp. a municipal one

or·di·nar·i·ly (ôr'd'n er'ə lē) *adv.* 1. usually; as a rule 2. in an ordinary way

or·di·nar·y (ôr'd'n er'ē) *adj.* [< L. *ordo*, an order] 1. customary; usual 2. *a)* unexceptional; common *b)* relatively inferior —**out of the ordinary** unusual

or·di·nate (ôr'd'n it, -āt') *n.* [< L. *ordo*, an order] *Math.* the vertical distance of a point from the horizontal axis

or·di·na·tion (ôr'd'n ā'shən) *n.* an ordaining or being ordained

ord·nance (ôrd'nəns) *n.* [< ORDINANCE] 1. artillery 2. all weapons and ammunition used in warfare

or·dure (ôr'jər, -dyoor) *n.* [< OFr. *ord*, filthy] dung; excrement

ore (ôr) *n.* [OE. *ar*, brass] any natural combination of minerals, esp. one from which a metal or metals can be profitably extracted

o·reg·a·no (ô reg'ə nō, ə-) *n.* [< Sp., ult. < Gr.

origanon] a plant with fragrant leaves used for seasoning

or·gan (ôr'gən) *n.* [< Gr. *organon*, an instrument] 1. a keyboard musical instrument with sets of graduated pipes through which compressed air is passed, causing sound by vibration 2. in animals and plants, a part adapted to perform a specific function 3. a means for performing some action 4. a means of communicating ideas, as a periodical

or·gan·dy, or·gan·die (ôr'gən dē) *n.*, *pl.* **-dies** [Fr. *organdi*] a very sheer, crisp cotton fabric

or·gan·ic (ôr gan'ik) *adj.* 1. of or having to do with an organ 2. inherent; inborn 3. systematically arranged 4. designating or of any chemical compound containing carbon 5. of, like, or derived from living organisms 6. grown with only animal or vegetable fertilizers —**or·gan'i·cal·ly** *adv.*

or·gan·ism (ôr'gə niz'm) *n.* any living thing

or'gan·ist *n.* one who plays the organ

or·gan·i·za·tion (ôr'gə ni zā'shən) *n.* 1. an organizing or being organized 2. an organized group, as a club, union, etc. —**or'gan·i·za'tion·al** *adj.*

or·gan·ize (ôr'gə nīz') *vt.* **-ized, -iz'ing** 1. to provide with an organic structure; systematize 2. to arrange 3. to establish —*vi.* to become organized —**or'gan·iz'er** *n.*

or·gan·za (ôr gan'zə) *n.* [< ?] a stiff, sheer fabric

or·gasm (ôr'gaz'm) *n.* [< Fr. < Gr. *organ*, to swell] the climax of a sexual act

or·gy (ôr'jē) *n.*, *pl.* **-gies** [< Fr. < Gr. *orgia*, secret rites] 1. any wild merrymaking 2. overindulgence in any activity —**or'gi·as'tic** (-as'tik) *adj.*

o·ri·ent (ôr'ē ənt; *also*, *esp. for v.* -ent') *n.* [< L. *oriri*, arise: used of the rising sun] [O-] the East, or Asia; esp., the Far East —*vt.* to adjust (oneself) to a particular situation —**o'ri·en·ta'tion** *n.*

O'ri·en'tal (-en't'l) *adj.* of the Orient, its people, etc. —*n.* a member of a people native to the Orient

or·i·fice (ôr'ə fis, är'-) *n.* [Fr. < L. *os*, mouth + *facere*, make] an opening; mouth or outlet

orig. 1. origin 2. original 3. originally

or·i·gin (ôr'ə jin, är'-) *n.* [< L. *oriri*, to rise] 1. a coming into existence or use; beginning 2. parentage; birth 3. source; root

o·rig·i·nal (ə rij'ə n'l) *adj.* 1. first; earliest 2. never having been before; new; novel 3. capable of creating something new; inventive 4. being that from which copies are made —*n.* 1. a primary type that has given rise to varieties 2. an original work, as of art or literature —**o·rig'i·nal'i·ty** (-nal'ə tē) *n.*

o·rig·i·nate (ə rij'ə nāt') *vt.* **-nat'ed, -nat'ing** to bring into being; esp., to invent —*vi.* to come into being; begin; start —**o·rig'i·na'tion** *n.* —**o·rig'i·na'tor** *n.*

o·ri·ole (ôr'ē ōl') *n.* [ult. < L. *aurum*, gold] any of a group of American birds, with orange and black plumage, that build hanging nests

O·ri·on (ō rī'ən, ô-) a very bright equatorial constellation

Or·lon (ôr'län) *a trademark for* a synthetic fiber somewhat similar to nylon

or·na·ment (ôr'nə mənt) *n.* [< L. *ornare*, adorn] 1. anything that adorns; decoration 2. one whose character or talent adds luster to his society, etc. —*vt.* (-ment') to decorate —**or'na·men'tal** *adj.* —**or'na·men·ta'tion** *n.*

or·nate (ôr nāt') *adj.* [< L. *ornare*, adorn] 1. heavily ornamented 2. flowery

or·ner·y (ôr'nər ē) *adj.* [< ORDINARY] [Chiefly

Dial.] **1.** having an ugly disposition **2.** obstinate —**or′ner·i·ness** *n.*

or·ni·thol·o·gy (ôr′nə thäl′ə jē) *n.* [< Gr. *ornis,* bird + -LOGY] the branch of zoology dealing with birds —**or′ni·thol′o·gist** *n.*

o·ro·tund (ôr′ə tund′) *adj.* [< L. *os,* mouth + *rotundo,* round] **1.** clear, strong, and deep: said of the voice **2.** bombastic

or·phan (ôr′fən) *n.* [< Gr. *orphanos*] a child whose parents are dead —*adj.* **1.** being an orphan **2.** of or for orphans —*vt.* to cause to become an orphan

or′phan·age (-ij) *n.* an institution for orphans

or·ris (ôr′is, är′-) *n.* [prob. < L. *iris,* iris] a European iris having a fragrant rootstock (**or′-ris·root′**), used in perfumery, etc.

ortho- [< Gr. *orthos,* straight] *a combining form meaning:* **1.** straight *[orthodontics]* **2.** correct *[orthography]* Also **orth-**

or·tho·don·tics (ôr′thə dän′tiks) *n.pl.* [*with sing. v.*] [< ORTH(O)- + Gr. *odōn,* tooth + -ICS] the branch of dentistry concerned with correcting tooth irregularities: also **or′tho·don′-ti·a** —**or′tho·don′tist** *n.*

or·tho·dox (ôr′thə däks′) *adj.* [< Fr. < Gr. *orthos,* correct + *doxa,* opinion] conforming to the usual beliefs or established doctrines, esp. in religion; conventional —**or′tho·dox′y** *n., pl.* -**ies**

Orthodox Eastern Church the Christian church dominant in E Europe, W Asia, and N Africa

or·thog·ra·phy (ôr thäg′rə fē) *n., pl.* -**phies** [see ORTHO- & -GRAPHY] **1.** correct spelling **2.** spelling as a subject of study —**or·tho·graph·ic** (ôr′thə graf′ik) *adj.*

or·tho·pe·dics (ôr′thə pē′diks) *n.pl.* [*with sing. v.*] [< Fr. < ORTHO- + Gr. *pais,* child] the branch of surgery concerned with deformities, diseases, and injuries of the bones, joints, etc. —**or′tho·pe′dic** *adj.* —**or′tho·pe′dist** *n.*

-ory [< L. *-orius*] *a suffix meaning:* **1.** of, having the nature of *[contradictory]* **2.** a place or thing for *[directory]*

Os *Chem.* osmium

OS., OS, O.S. Old Saxon

os·cil·late (äs′ə lāt′) *vi.* -**lat′ed,** -**lat′ing** [< L. *oscillare,* to swing] **1.** to swing to and fro **2.** to vacillate **3.** *Physics* to vary between maximum and minimum values, as electric current —**os′-cil·la′tion** *n.* —**os′cil·la′tor** *n.*

os·cil·lo·scope (ä sil′ə skōp′, ə-) *n.* [< L. *oscillare,* to swing + -SCOPE] an instrument that visually records an electrical wave on a fluorescent screen

os·cu·late (äs′kyə lāt′) *vt., vi.* -**lat′ed,** -**lat′ing** [< L. *osculum,* a kiss] to kiss

-ose[1] [Fr. < (*gluc*)*ose*] *a suffix designating:* **1.** a carbohydrate *[cellulose]* **2.** the product of a protein hydrolysis

-ose[2] [L. *-osus*] *a suffix meaning* full of, like *[bellicose, morose]*

o·sier (ō′zhər) *n.* [< ML. *ausaria,* bed of willows] a willow whose wood is used for baskets and furniture

-osis [< Gr. *-ōsis*] *a suffix meaning:* **1.** state, condition, action *[osmosis]* **2.** an abnormal or diseased condition *[neurosis]*

os·mi·um (äz′mē əm) *n.* [< Gr. *osmē,* odor] a bluish metallic chemical element, occurring as an alloy with platinum: symbol, Os

os·mo·sis (äs mō′sis, äz-) *n.* [< Gr. *ōsmos,* impulse] the tendency of fluids to pass through a somewhat porous membrane so as to equalize concentrations on both sides

os·prey (äs′prē) *n., pl.* -**preys** [< L. *os,* a bone

+ *frangere,* to break] a large hawk that feeds solely on fish

os·si·fy (äs′ə fī′) *vt., vi.* -**fied′,** -**fy′ing** [< L. *os,* a bone + -FY] **1.** to change or develop into bone **2.** to fix rigidly in a custom, etc. —**os′si-fi·ca′tion** *n.*

os·ten·si·ble (äs ten′sə b'l, əs-) *adj.* [Fr. < L. *ostendere,* to show] apparent; seeming —**os-ten′si·bly** *adv.*

os·ten·ta·tion (äs′tən tā′shən) *n.* [see prec.] showy display —**os′ten·ta′tious** *adj.*

osteo- [< Gr. *osteon*] *a combining form meaning* a bone or bones *[osteopath]*

os·te·op·a·thy (äs′tē äp′ə thē) *n.* [see OSTEO- & -PATHY] a school of medicine and surgery that emphasizes the relationship of the muscles and bones to all other body systems —**os′-te·o·path′** (-path′) *n.*

os·tra·cize (äs′trə sīz′) *vt.* -**cized′,** -**ciz′ing** [< Gr. *ostrakon,* a shell (cast as a ballot)] to banish from society, etc. —**os′tra·cism** *n.*

os·trich (ôs′trich, äs′-) *n.* [< L. *avis,* bird + *struthio,* ostrich] a large, swift-running, nonflying bird of Africa and the Near East

OT., OT, O.T. Old Testament

O·thel·lo (ə thel′ō, ō-) a tragedy by Shakespeare in which the title character kills his wife because he wrongly believes her unfaithful

oth·er (u*th*′ər) *adj.* [OE.] **1.** being the remaining one or ones *[Bill and the other boy(s)]* **2.** different or distinct from that or those implied *[some other girl]* **3.** additional *[he has no other coat]* —*pron.* **1.** the other one **2.** some other one *[do as others do]* —*adv.* otherwise *[I can't do other than go]*

oth·er·wise′ *adv.* **1.** in another manner; differently *[to believe otherwise]* **2.** in all other respects *[an otherwise intelligent man]* **3.** in other circumstances —*adj.* different

oth′er·world′ly (-wurld′lē) *adj.* being apart from earthly interests

o·ti·ose (ō′shē ōs′) *adj.* [< L. *otium,* leisure] **1.** idle **2.** futile **3.** useless

ot·ter (ät′ər) *n.* [OE. *oter*] **1.** a furry, swimming mammal related to the weasel **2.** its fur

ot·to·man (ät′ə mən) *n.* [< Fr.] a low, cushioned seat or footstool

ouch (ouch) *interj.* an exclamation of pain

ought (ôt) *v.aux.* [< OE. *agan,* owe] an auxiliary used to express obligation or duty *[he ought to pay rent]* or desirability *[you ought to rest]* or probability *[he ought to be here soon]*

‡oui (wē) *adv.* [Fr.] yes

ounce (ouns) *n.* [< L. *uncia,* a twelfth] **1.** a unit of weight equal to 1/16 pound avoirdupois, or 1/12 pound troy **2.** a fluid ounce, 1/16 pint **3.** any small amount

our (our, är) *possessive pronominal adj.* [OE. *ure*] of, belonging to, made, or done by us

ours (ourz, ärz) *pron.* that or those belonging to us *[a friend of ours]*

our·selves (our selvz′) *pron.* **1.** the intensive form of WE *[we went ourselves]* **2.** the reflexive form of WE *[we hurt ourselves]* **3.** our true selves *[we are not ourselves today]*

-ous [< L. *-osus*] *a suffix meaning* having, full of, characterized by *[outrageous]*

oust (oust) *vt.* [< OFr. *ouster*] to force out; expel, dispossess, etc.

oust′er *n.* an ousting or being ousted

out (out) *adv.* [OE. *ut*] **1.** away or forth from a place, position, etc. **2.** into the open air **3.** into existence or activity *[disease broke out]* **4.** *a)* to a conclusion *[argue it out]* *b)* completely *[tired out]* **5.** into sight or notice *[the moon came *out]* **6.** from existence or activity *[fade out]* **7.** aloud *[sing out]* **8.** beyond a regular surface, condition, etc. *[stand out]* **9.** into disuse *[long skirts went out]* **10.** from a number or stock *[pick out]* **11.** [Slang] into unconsciousness **12.** *Baseball,* etc. in a manner producing an out *[to fly out]* —*adj.* **1.** external: usually in combination *[outpost]* **2.** beyond regular limits **3.** away from work, etc. **4.** in error **5.** not in operation, use, etc. **6.** [Colloq.] having suffered a loss *[out five dollars]* **7.** *Baseball* having failed to get on base —*prep.* out of —*n.* **1.** something that is out **2.** [Slang] a way out; excuse **3.** *Baseball* the failure of a player to reach base safely —*vi.* to come out — **on the outs** [Colloq.] on unfriendly terms —**out for** trying to get or do —**out of 1.** from inside of **2.** from the number of **3.** beyond **4.** from (material, etc.) **5.** because of *[out of* spite*]* **6.** having no *[out of* gas*]* **7.** so as to deprive *[cheat out of* money*]* —**out to** trying to

out- *a combining form meaning:* **1.** at or from a point away, outside *[outbuilding]* **2.** going away or forth, outward *[outbound]* **3.** better or more than *[outdo]*

out·age (out′ij) *n.* an accidental suspension of operation, as of electric power

out′-and-out′ *adj.* complete; thorough

out′back′ *n.* any remote, sparsely settled region viewed as uncivilized

out·bid′ *vt.* **-bid′, -bid′ding** to bid or offer more than (another)

out′board′ (-bôrd′) *adj.* outside the hull of a watercraft *[an outboard motor]*

out′bound′ *adj.* outward bound

out′break′ *n.* a breaking out; sudden occurrence, as of disease, war, rioting, etc.

out′build′ing *n.* a structure, as a garage, separate from the main building

out′burst′ *n.* a sudden release, as of emotion or energy

out′cast′ *adj.* driven out; rejected —*n.* a person or thing cast out or rejected

out·class′ *vt.* to surpass; excel

out′come′ *n.* result; consequence

out′crop′ *n.* the emergence of a mineral at the earth's surface

out′cry′ *n., pl.* **-cries′ 1.** a crying out **2.** a strong protest or objection

out′dat′ed *adj.* no longer popular

out·dis′tance *vt.* **-tanced, -tanc·ing** to leave behind, as in a race

out·do′ *vt.* **-did′, -done′, -do′ing** to exceed; surpass —**outdo oneself** to do better than expected

out′door′ (-dôr′) *adj.* **1.** being or occurring outdoors **2.** of, or fond of, the outdoors

out′doors′ (-dôrz′) *adv.* in or into the open; outside —*n.* the outdoor world

out′er *adj.* farther out; exterior

outer space space beyond the earth's atmosphere or beyond the solar system

out′field′ *n. Baseball* **1.** the playing area beyond the infield **2.** the players (**outfielders**) positioned there

out′fit′ *n.* **1.** the equipment used in any craft or activity **2.** clothing worn together **3.** a group of people associated in some activity —*vt.* **-fit′-ted, -fit′ting** to equip —**out′fit′ter** *n.*

out′flank′ *vt.* **1.** to go around and beyond the flank of (enemy troops) **2.** to thwart

out′fox′ (-fäks′) *vt.* to outwit; outsmart

out′go′ *n., pl.* **-goes′** that which is paid out; expenditure

out′go′ing *adj.* **1.** going out; leaving **2.** sociable, friendly, etc.

out′grow′ *vt.* **-grew′, -grown′, -grow′ing 1.** to grow faster or larger than **2.** to lose or get rid

of by becoming mature **3.** to grow too large for

out′growth′ *n.* **1.** a growing out **2.** a result; consequence **3.** an offshoot

out′guess′ (-ges′) *vt.* to outwit

out′house′ *n.* a small outbuilding with a toilet over a pit; privy

out′ing *n.* **1.** a pleasure trip **2.** an outdoor walk, ride, etc.

out·land·ish (out lan′dish) *adj.* **1.** very odd; fantastic **2.** remote; secluded

out·last′ *vt.* to endure longer than

out·law (out′lô′) *n.* **1.** orig., a person deprived of legal rights and protection **2.** a notorious criminal —*vt.* **1.** orig., to declare to be an outlaw **2.** to declare illegal

out′lay′ (-lā′) *n.* **1.** a spending (of money, energy, etc.) **2.** money, etc. spent

out′let′ *n.* **1.** a passage for letting something out **2.** a means of expression *[an outlet for rage]* **3.** a market for goods

out′line′ *n.* **1.** a line bounding the limits of an object **2.** a sketch showing only contours **3.** a general plan **4.** a systematic summary —*vt.* **-lined′, -lin′ing 1.** to draw in outline **2.** to make an outline of

out·live′ *vt.* **-lived′, -liv′ing 1.** to live longer than; survive **2.** to outlast

out′look′ *n.* **1.** the view from a place **2.** viewpoint **3.** prospect; probable result

out′ly·ing (-lī′iŋ) *adj.* relatively far out from a certain point; remote

out′ma·neu′ver, out′ma·noeu′vre *vt.* **-vered** or **-vred, -ver·ing** or **-vring** to maneuver with better effect than; outwit

out·match′ (-mach′) *vt.* to surpass; outdo

out′mod′ed (-mōd′id) *adj.* no longer in fashion or accepted; obsolete

out′num′ber *vt.* to exceed in number

out′-of-date′ *adj.* not current; old-fashioned

out′-of-doors′ *adv., n. same as* OUTDOORS

out′-of-the-way′ *adj.* **1.** secluded **2.** unusual **3.** not conventional

out′pa′tient *n.* a patient, not an inmate, receiving treatment at a hospital

out′play′ *vt.* to play better than

out′post′ *n.* **1.** *Mil. a)* a small group stationed at a distance beyond the main force *b)* the station so occupied **2.** a frontier settlement

out′put′ *n.* **1.** the work done or amount produced, esp. over a given period **2.** information delivered by a computer **3.** *Elec.* the useful current delivered

out·rage (out′rāj′) *n.* [ult. < L. *ultra,* beyond] **1.** an extremely vicious or violent act **2.** a deep insult or offense **3.** great anger, etc. aroused by this —*vt.* -raged′, -rag′ing **1.** to commit an outrage upon **2.** to cause outrage in

out·ra′geous (-rā′jəs) *adj.* **1.** involving or doing great injury or wrong **2.** very offensive or shocking —**out·ra′geous·ly** *adv.*

out′rank′ *vt.* to exceed in rank

out·reach′ (out′rēch′) *vt., vi.* **1.** to surpass **2.** to reach out —*n.* (out′rēch′) a reaching out —*adj.* designating or of a branch away from the main office of a social agency, etc.

out′rid′er *n.* **1.** an attendant on horseback who accompanies a stagecoach, etc. **2.** a cowboy who rides over a range to prevent cattle from straying

out′rig′ger *n.* **1.** a timber rigged out from the side of a canoe to prevent tipping **2.** a canoe of this type

out·right (out′rīt′) *adj.* **1.** utter; downright **2.** complete; whole —*adv.* (out′rīt′) **1.** entirely **2.** openly **3.** at once

out′run′ *vt.* **-ran′, -run′, -run′ning 1.** to run faster or farther than **2.** to exceed

out·sell' *vt.* **-sold'**, **-sell'ing** to sell in greater amounts than

out·set' *n.* a setting out; beginning

out·shine' *vt.* **-shone'** or **-shined'**, **-shin'ing** 1. to shine brighter or longer than 2. to surpass; excel —*vi.* to shine forth

out·side' *n.* 1. the outer side; exterior 2. outward aspect 3. any area not inside —*adj.* 1. outer 2. coming from or situated beyond given limits [*outside* help] 3. extreme 4. slight; mere [an *outside* chance] —*adv.* 1. on or to the outside 2. outdoors —*prep.* 1. on or to the outer side of 2. beyond the limits of —**outside of** 1. outside 2. [Colloq.] other than

out·sid'er *n.* one not a member of a given group

out·size' *n.* an odd or very large size

out·skirts' (-skurts') *n.pl.* the outer areas, as of a city

out·smart' *vt.* [Colloq.] to overcome by cunning or cleverness; outwit

out·spo'ken *adj.* 1. unrestrained in speech; frank 2. spoken boldly or candidly

out·spread' *adj.* spread out; extended

out·stand'ing *adj.* 1. projecting 2. distinguished 3. unpaid 4. issued and sold

out·stretch' *vt.* 1. to extend 2. to stretch beyond

out·strip' *vt.* **-stripped'**, **-strip'ping** 1. to go at a faster pace than 2. to excel

out·vote' *vt.* **-vot'ed**, **-vot'ing** to defeat or surpass in voting

out·ward (out'wərd) *adj.* 1. having to do with the outside; outer 2. visible 3. to or toward the outside —*adv.* toward the outside: also **out'-wards** —**out'ward·ly** *adv.*

out·wear' *vt.* **-wore'**, **-worn'**, **-wear'ing** 1. to wear out 2. to be more lasting than

out·weigh' *vt.* 1. to weigh more than 2. to be more important than

out·wit' *vt.* **-wit'ted**, **-wit'ting** to get the better of by cunning or cleverness

o·va (ō'və) *n. pl. of* OVUM

o·val (ō'v'l) *adj.* [< Fr. < L. *ovum*, an egg] 1. elliptical 2. having the form of an egg —*n.* anything oval

o·va·ry (ō'vər ē) *n., pl.* **-ries** [< L. *ovum*, an egg] 1. either of two female reproductive glands producing eggs 2. *Bot.* the enlarged hollow part of the pistil, containing ovules — **o·var·i·an** (ō ver'ē ən) *adj.*

o·va·tion (ō vā'shən) *n.* [< L. *ovare*, celebrate a triumph] an enthusiastic public welcome, burst of applause, etc.

ov·en (uv'ən) *n.* [OE.] a compartment or receptacle for baking, drying, etc. by means of heat

o·ver (ō'vər) *prep.* [OE. *ofer*] 1. in, at, or to a position above 2. across and down from 3. so as to cover 4. upon, as an effect 5. above in authority, power, etc. 6. on or to the other side of 7. through all or many parts of 8. during [over the year] 9. more than 10. in preference to 11. concerning —*adv.* 1. a) above or across b) across the brim 2. more; beyond 3. from start to finish [read it *over*] 4. a) from an upright position b) upside down [turn the cup *over*] 5. again 6. at or on the other side 7. from one side, etc. to another [win him *over*] —*adj.* 1. upper, outer, superior, excessive, or extra 2. finished; past 3. having reached the other side 4. [Colloq.] as a surplus

over- *a combining form meaning:* 1. above in position, rank, etc. [*overlord*] 2. passing across or beyond [*overrun*] 3. excessive, too much [*overload*] : the list below includes some common compounds formed with *over-* that can

be understood if *too* or *too much* is added to the meaning of the base word

overabundance	overexpose
overactive	overheat
overambitious	overindulgence
overanxious	overload
overburden	overpay
overcautious	overpopulate
overconfident	overproduce
overcook	overproduction
overcritical	overrefined
overcrowd	overripe
overdevelop	oversell
overeager	oversensitive
overeat	overspecialize
overemphasize	overstimulate
overenthusiastic	overstock
overexercise	overstrict
overexert	overtire

o'ver·act' *vt., vi.* to act with exaggeration

o·ver·age' (ō'vər āj') *adj.* over the age fixed as a standard

o·ver·age² (ō'vər ij) *n.* a surplus, as of goods

o'ver·all' *adj.* 1. from end to end 2. total —*adv.* (ō'vər ôl') 1. from end to end 2. in general

o'ver·alls' *n.pl.* loose trousers, often with an attached bib, worn over other clothing to protect against dirt and wear

o'ver·awe' *vt.* **-awed'**, **-aw'ing** to overcome or subdue by inspiring awe

o'ver·bal'ance *vt.* **-anced**, **-anc·ing** 1. to outweigh 2. to throw off balance

o'ver·bear'ing (-ber'iŋ) *adj.* arrogant or domineering

o·ver·blown (ō'vər blōn') *adj.* 1. overdone; excessive 2. pompous; bombastic

o'ver·board' *adv.* 1. over a ship's side 2. from a ship into the water —**go overboard** [Colloq.] to go to extremes

o'ver·cast' (-kast') *n.* a covering, esp. of clouds —*adj.* cloudy: said of the sky

o'ver·charge' *vt., vi.* **-charged'**, **-charg'ing** 1. to charge too high a price 2. to overload —*n.* (ō'vər chärj') 1. an excessive charge 2. too full a load

o'ver·cloud' *vt., vi.* to make or become cloudy, gloomy, etc.

o'ver·coat' *n.* a coat, esp. a heavy coat, worn over the usual clothing for warmth

o'ver·come' *vt.* **-came'**, **-come'**, **-com'ing** 1. to get the better of in competition, etc. 2. to suppress, prevail over, overwhelm, etc. —*vi.* to win

o'ver·do' *vt.* **-did'**, **-done'**, **-do'ing** 1. to do too much 2. to spoil by exaggerating 3. to cook too long —*vi.* to do too much

o'ver·dose' *n.* too large a dose

o'ver·draw' *vt.* **-drew'**, **-drawn'**, **-draw'ing** to draw on in excess of the amount credited to the drawer —**o'ver·draft'** *n.*

o'ver·dress' *vt., vi.* to dress too warmly, too showily, or too formally

o'ver·due' *adj.* past or delayed beyond the time set for payment, arrival, etc.

o'ver·es'ti·mate' (-es'tə māt') *vt.* **-mat'ed**, **-mat'ing** to set too high an estimate on or for —*n.* (-mit) an estimate that is too high —**o'ver·es'ti·ma'tion** *n.*

o'ver·flow' *vt.* 1. to flow across; flood 2. to flow over the brim of 3. to fill beyond capacity —*vi.* 1. to run over 2. to be superabundant —*n.* (ō'vər flō') 1. an overflowing 2. the amount that overflows 3. a vent for overflowing liquids

o'ver·grow' *vt.* **-grew'**, **-grown'**, **-grow'ing** to overspread so as to cover, as with foliage —*vi.* to grow too fast or beyond normal size —**o'ver·grown'** *adj.* —**o'ver·growth'** *n.*

o′ver·hand′ *adj., adv.* with the hand raised above the elbow

o′ver·hang′ *vt., vi.* -hung′, -hang′ing 1. to hang or project over or beyond (something) —*n.* (ō′vər haŋ′) the projection of one thing over another

o′ver·haul′ (-hôl′) *vt.* 1. *a*) to check thoroughly for needed repairs, adjustments, etc. *b*) to make such repairs, etc., as on a motor 2. to catch up with —*n.* (ō′vər hôl′) an overhauling

o′ver·head′ *adj.* 1. above the head 2. in the sky 3. on a higher level, with reference to related objects —*n.* the general, continuing costs of a business, as of rent, etc. —*adv.* (ō′vər hed′) above the head; aloft

o′ver·hear′ *vt.* -heard′, -hear′ing to hear (something spoken or a speaker) without the speaker's knowledge or intention

o′ver·joy′ *vt.* to give great joy to; delight

o′ver·kill′ *n.* the capacity of a nation's nuclear weapon stockpile to kill many times the total population of any given nation

o′ver·land′ *adv., adj.* by, on, or across land

o′ver·lap′ *vt., vi.* -lapped′, -lap′ping to lap over; extend over (something or each other) so as to coincide in part

o′ver·lay′ *vt.* -laid′, -lay′ing 1. to lay or spread over 2. to cover, as with a decorative layer

o′ver·look′ *vt.* 1. to look at from above 2. to give a view of from above 3. to rise above 4. *a*) to look beyond and not see *b*) to ignore; neglect 5. to excuse in an indulgent way 6. to supervise

o′ver·lord′ *n.* a lord ranking above other lords

o′ver·ly (-lē) *adv.* too much; excessively

o′ver·night′ *adv.* 1. during the night 2. very suddenly —*adj.* (ō′vər nīt′) 1. done or going on during the night 2. for one night [an *overnight* guest] 3. of or for a brief trip [an *overnight* bag]

o′ver·pass′ *n.* a bridge or other passageway over a road, railway, etc.

o′ver·pow′er *vt.* to subdue; overwhelm

o′ver·rate′ *vt.* -rat′ed, -rat′ing to rate or estimate too highly

o′ver·reach′ *vt.* 1. to reach beyond or above 2. to reach too far for and miss —**overreach oneself** to fail because of trying more than one can do

o′ver·re·act′ *vi.* to react in an extreme, highly emotional way

o′ver·ride′ *vt.* -rode′, -rid′den, -rid′ing 1. to ride over 2. to prevail over 3. to disregard or nullify

o′ver·rule′ *vt.* -ruled′, -rul′ing 1. to rule out or set aside, as by higher authority 2. to prevail over —**o′ver·rul′ing** *adj.*

o′ver·run′ *vt.* -ran′, -run′, -run′ning 1. to spread out over so as to cover 2. to swarm over, as vermin 3. to run beyond (certain limits) —*vi.* to overflow

o′ver·seas′ *adv.* over or beyond the sea —*adj.* 1. foreign 2. over or across the sea Chiefly Brit., **o′ver·sea′**

o′ver·see′ *vt.* -saw′, -seen′, -see′ing to supervise; superintend —**o′ver·se′er** *n.*

o′ver·shad′ow *vt.* 1. to cast a shadow over 2. to darken 3. to be more important than

o′ver·shoe′ *n.* a boot of rubber or fabric, worn over the regular shoe to protect from cold or dampness

o′ver·shoot′ *vt.* -shot′, -shoot′ing 1. to shoot or pass over or beyond 2. to exceed —*vi.* to shoot or go too far

o′ver·sight′ (-sīt′) *n.* a careless mistake or omission

o′ver·sim′pli·fy′ *vt., vi.* -fied′, -fy′ing to simplify so much as to distort —**o′ver·sim′pli·fi·ca′tion** *n.*

o′ver·size′ *adj.* 1. too large 2. larger than the normal or usual

o′ver·sleep′ *vi.* -slept′, -sleep′ing to sleep past the intended time for getting up

o′ver·spread′ *vt., vi.* -spread′, -spread′ing to spread or cover over

o′ver·state′ (-stāt′) *vt.* -stat′ed, -stat′ing to exaggerate —**o′ver·state′ment** *n.*

o′ver·step′ (-step′) *vt.* -stepped′, -step′ping to go beyond the limits of; exceed

o′ver·strung′ *adj.* too highly strung; tense

o′ver·stuff′ *vt.* 1. to stuff with too much of something 2. to upholster (furniture) with deep stuffing

o·vert (ō vurt′, ō′vurt) *adj.* [< L. *aperire*, to open] 1. not hidden; open 2. *Law* done publicly, without attempt at concealment — **o·vert′ly** *adv.*

o′ver·take′ *vt.* -took′, -tak′en, -tak′ing 1. to catch up with 2. to come upon suddenly

o′ver·tax′ *vt.* 1. to tax too heavily 2. to make excessive demands on

o′ver·throw′ *vt.* -threw′, -thrown′, -throw′ing 1. to throw or turn over 2. to conquer; bring to an end —*n.* (ō′vər thrō′) 1. an overthrowing or being overthrown 2. destruction; end

o′ver·time′ *n.* 1. time beyond the established limit, as of working hours 2. pay for work done in such time —*adj., adv.* of, for, or during (an) overtime

o′ver·tone′ *n.* 1. any of the attendant higher tones heard with a fundamental musical tone 2. an implication: *usually used in pl.*

o·ver·ture (ō′vər chər) *n.* [< L. *apertura*, APERTURE] 1. an introductory offer or proposal 2. a musical introduction to an opera, etc.

o′ver·turn′ *vt.* 1. to turn over 2. to conquer — *vi.* to tip over; capsize

o′ver·ween′ing (-wē′niŋ) *adj.* [< OE. *oferwenan:* see OVER- & WEEN] 1. arrogant 2. excessive

o′ver·weight′ *adj.* above the normal or allowed weight

o′ver·whelm′ (-hwelm′) *vt.* [see OVER- & WHELM] 1. to pour down on and bury beneath 2. to crush; overpower —**o′ver·whelm′ing** *adj.*

o′ver·work′ *vt.* to work or use to excess —*vi.* to work too hard or too long —*n.* (ō′vər wurk′) severe or burdensome work

o′ver·wrought′ (-rôt′) *adj.* 1. very nervous or excited 2. too elaborate; ornate

ovi- [< L. *ovum*, an egg] *a combining form* meaning egg or ovum

o·vi·duct (ō′vi dukt′) *n.* [see OVI- & DUCT] a duct or tube through which the ovum passes from an ovary to the uterus or to the outside

o·vip·a·rous (ō vip′ər əs) *adj.* [< L. *ovum*, egg + *parere*, produce] producing eggs which hatch after leaving the body

o·void (ō′void) *adj.* [OV(I)- + -OID] egg-shaped —*n.* anything of ovoid form

o·vu·late (ō′vyə lāt′) *vi.* -lat′ed, -lat′ing [< L. *ovum*, egg] to produce and discharge ova from the ovary —**o′vu·la′tion** *n.*

o·vule (ō′vyōōl) *n.* [Fr. < L. *ovum*, egg] 1. *Bot.* the part of a plant which develops into a seed 2. *Zool.* the immature ovum —**o′vu·lar** *adj.*

o·vum (ō′vəm) *n., pl.* **o·va** (ō′və) [L., an egg] *Biol.* a mature female germ cell

owe (ō) *vt.* **owed, ow′ing** [< OE. *agan*, to own] 1. to be indebted to (someone) for (a specified amount or thing) 2. to feel the need to do, give, etc. —*vi.* to be in debt

ow·ing (ō′iŋ) *adj.* 1. that owes 2. due; unpaid —**owing to** because of; as a result of

owl (oul) *n.* [OE. *ule*] **1.** a night bird of prey, having a large head, large eyes, and a short, hooked beak **2.** a person of nocturnal habits, solemn appearance, etc.

owl'et (-it) *n.* a young or small owl

own (ōn) *adj.* [< OE. *agan,* to possess] belonging or relating to oneself or itself [his *own* book] —*n.* that which belongs to oneself [the car is her *own*] —*vt.* **1.** to possess; have **2.** to admit; acknowledge —*vi.* to confess (*to*) —**on one's own** [Colloq.] by one's own efforts —**own'er** *n.* —**own'er·ship'** *n.*

ox (äks) *n., pl.* **ox'en** [OE. *oxa*] **1.** any of several bovine mammals, as the buffalo, yak, etc. **2.** a castrated bull

ox·blood (äks'blud') *n.* a deep-red color

ox'bow' (-bō') *n.* the U-shaped part of an ox yoke which passes under and around the animal's neck

ox·ford (äks'fərd) *n.* [< *Oxford,* England] [*sometimes* O-] a low shoe laced over the instep: also **oxford shoe**

ox·i·da·tion (äk'sə dā'shən) *n.* an oxidizing or being oxidized —**ox'i·dant** (-dənt) *n.*

ox·ide (äk'sīd) *n.* [< Gr. *oxys,* sour + Fr. (*ac*)*ide,* acid] a compound of oxygen with another element or a radical

ox·i·dize (äk'sə dīz') *vt.* **-dized', -diz'ing** to unite with oxygen, as in burning or rusting — *vi.* to become oxidized —**ox'i·diz'er** *n.*

oxy- [< Gr. *oxys,* sharp] *a combining form meaning:* **1.** sharp, acid **2.** oxygen

ox·y·a·cet·y·lene (äk'sē ə set''l ēn') *adj.* of or using a mixture of oxygen and acetylene, as for producing a hot flame used in welding

ox·y·gen (äk'si jən) *n.* [< Fr.: see OXY- & -GEN] a colorless, odorless gaseous chemical element, the most abundant of all elements: it is essential to life processes and to combustion: symbol, O

ox'y·gen·ate' (-jə nāt') *vt.* **-at'ed, -at'ing** to mix or combine with oxygen —**ox'y·gen·a'tion** *n.*

oxygen tent a transparent enclosure supplied with oxygen, fitted around a bed patient to help him breathe

oys·ter (oi'stər) *n.* [< Gr. *ostreon*] an edible marine mollusk with an irregular, bivalve shell

oz. *pl.* **oz., ozs.** ounce

o·zone (ō'zōn) *n.* [Fr. < Gr. *ozein,* to smell] **1.** a form of oxygen with a strong odor, formed by an electrical discharge in air and used as a bleaching agent, water purifier, etc. **2.** [Slang] pure, fresh air

P

P, p (pē) *n., pl.* **P's, p's** the sixteenth letter of the English alphabet —**mind one's p's and q's** to be careful what one does

P *Chem.* phosphorus

p. 1. *pl.* **pp.** page **2.** participle **3.** past **4.** per **5.** pint

pa (pä; *dial. often* pô) *n.* [Colloq.] father

P.A. public address (system)

pace (pās) *n.* [< L. *passus,* a step] **1.** a step in walking, running, etc. **2.** the length of a step or stride **3.** the rate of speed in walking, etc. **4.** rate of progress, etc. **5.** a gait **6.** the gait of a horse in which both legs on the same side are raised together —*vt.* **paced, pac'ing 1.** to walk back and forth across **2.** to measure by paces **3.** to set the pace for (a runner, etc.) —*vi.* **1.** to walk with regular steps **2.** to move at a pace: said of a horse —**put through one's paces** to test one's abilities, etc. —**pac'er** *n.*

pace'mak'er *n.* **1.** a runner, horse, etc. that sets the pace, as in a race: also **pace'set'ter 2.** an electronic device implanted in the body to regulate the heartbeat

pach·y·derm (pak'ə durm') *n.* [< Gr. *pachys,* thick + *derma,* skin] a large, thick-skinned, hoofed animal, as the elephant, rhinoceros, etc.

pach·y·san·dra (pak'ə san'drə) *n.* [< ModL. name of genus] a low, hardy evergreen plant often grown as a ground cover

pa·cif·ic (pə sif'ik) *adj.* [see PACIFY] **1.** making or tending to make peace **2.** peaceful; calm; tranquil —**pa·cif'i·cal·ly** *adv.*

pac·i·fi·er (pas'ə fi'ər) *n.* **1.** a person or thing that pacifies **2.** a nipple or teething ring for babies

pac'i·fism (-fiz'm) *n.* opposition to the use of force under any circumstances; specif., refusal to participate in war —**pac'i·fist** *n., adj.*

pac·i·fy (pas'ə fi') *vt.* **-fied', -fy'ing** [Fr. < L. *pax,* peace + *facere,* make] **1.** to make peaceful or calm; appease **2.** to secure peace in (a nation, etc.)

pack' (pak) *n.* [ult. < MFl. *pac*] **1.** a bundle of things tied up for carrying **2.** a package of a standard number, as cigarettes, playing cards, etc. **3.** a group of wild animals living together —*vt.* **1.** to make a pack of **2.** *a)* to put together in a box, trunk, etc. *b)* to fill (a box, etc.) **3.** to crowd; cram [to *pack* the hall] **4.** to fill in tightly, as for prevention of leaks **5.** to carry in a pack **6.** to send (*off*) **7.** [Slang] *a)* to carry (a gun, etc.) *b)* to deliver (a blow) with force — *vi.* **1.** to make up packs **2.** to put one's clothes, etc. into luggage for a trip **3.** to crowd together **4.** to settle into a compact mass —*adj.* used for carrying packs, etc. [a *pack* animal] —**send packing** to dismiss (a person) abruptly

pack² (pak) *vt.* to choose (a jury, etc.) dishonestly so as to get desired results

pack·age (pak'ij) *n.* **1.** a wrapped or boxed thing; parcel **2.** a number of items, plans, etc. offered as a unit —*vt.* **-aged, -ag·ing** to put into a package

package store a store where alcoholic liquor is sold by the bottle to be drunk elsewhere

pack'er *n.* one who packs, as in a packing house

pack'et (-it) *n.* **1.** a small package **2.** a boat that travels a regular route carrying passengers, freight, and mail

pack'ing *n.* **1.** the act or process of a person or thing that packs **2.** any material used to pack

packing house a plant where meats, etc. are processed and packed for future sale

pack rat a North American rat that often hides small articles in its nest

pack'sad'dle *n.* a saddle with fastenings to secure and balance the load carried by a pack animal

pact (pakt) *n.* [< L. *pax,* peace] an agreement

pad' (pad) *n.* [echoic] the dull thud of a footstep —*vi.* **pad'ded, pad'ding** to walk, esp. with a soft step

pad² (pad) *n.* [prob. var. of POD] **1.** anything soft used to protect from friction, blows, etc.;

cushion **2.** the cushionlike sole of an animal's paw **3.** the floating leaf of a waterlily **4.** a tablet of paper for writing on **5.** [Slang] the place where one lives —*vt.* **pad'ded, pad'ding 1.** to stuff or cover with soft material **2.** to lengthen (a speech, etc.) with unnecessary material **3.** to fill (an expense account, etc.) with fraudulent entries

pad'ding *n.* any material used to pad

pad·dle' (pad''l) *n.* [< ?] **1.** a short oar with a wide blade, used without an oarlock **2.** any similar implement used in flogging, etc. —*vt., vi.* **-dled, -dling 1.** to propel (a canoe, etc.) with a paddle **2.** to beat with a paddle; spank — **pad'dler** *n.*

pad·dle² (pad''l) *vi.* **-dled, -dling** [prob. < PAD¹] to move hands or feet in shallow water; dabble

paddle wheel a wheel with paddles around it for propelling a steamboat

pad·dock (pad'ak) *n.* [< OE. *pearruc*, enclosure] **1.** a small enclosure near a stable, where horses are exercised **2.** an enclosure near a race track, where horses are assembled before a race

pad·dy (pad'ē) *n., pl.* **-dies** [Malay *padi*] a rice field: often **rice paddy**

pad·lock (pad'läk') *n.* [< ME.] a removable lock with a hinged link to be passed through a staple, chain, or eye —*vt.* to fasten as with a padlock

pa·dre (pä'drā) *n.* [Sp., It., Port. < L. *pater*, father] **1.** father: the title of a priest in Italy, Spain, etc. **2.** [Slang] a chaplain

pae·an (pē'ən) *n.* [< Gr. *Paian*, epithet of Apollo] a song of joy, triumph, etc.

pa·gan (pā'gən) *n.* [< L. *paganus*, a peasant] **1.** anyone not a Christian, Muslim, or Jew; heathen **2.** one who has no religion —*adj.* **1.** of pagans **2.** not religious —**pa'gan·ism** *n.*

page' (pāj) *n.* [Fr. < L. *pangere*, to fasten] **1.** *a)* one side of a leaf of a book, newspaper, etc. *b)* the entire leaf **2.** [*often pl.*] a record of events —*vt.* **paged, pag'ing** to number the pages of

page² (pāj) *n.* [< It. *paggio*] a young attendant who runs errands, carries messages, etc., as in a hotel, legislature, etc. —*vt.* **paged, pag'ing** to try to find (a person) by calling his name, as a hotel page does

pag·eant (paj'ənt) *n.* [< ME. *pagent*, stage scene] **1.** a spectacular exhibition, parade, etc. **2.** an outdoor drama celebrating historical events

pag'eant·ry *n., pl.* **-ries 1.** grand spectacle, gorgeous display **2.** empty display

pa·go·da (pə gō'də) *n.* [< Port., prob. < Per. *but*, idol + *kadah*, house] in the Orient, a several-storied temple in the form of a pyramidal tower

paid (pād) *pt. & pp. of* PAY

pail (pāl) *n.* [< OE. *pægel*, wine vessel] **1.** a cylindrical container, usually with a handle, for holding liquids, etc.; bucket **2.** the amount held by a pail: also **pail'ful'** *pl.* **-fuls'**

pain (pān) *n.* [< Gr. *poinē*, penalty] **1.** physical or mental suffering caused by injury, disease, tribulation, etc. **2.** [*pl.*] great care [take *pains* with the work] **3.** [Slang] an annoyance —*vt.* to cause pain to —**on** [upon *or* under] **pain of** with the threat of (penalty) —**pain'less** *adj.* — **pain'less·ly** *adv.*

pain'ful *adj.* **1.** causing or having pain; hurting **2.** irksome —**pain'ful·ly** *adv.*

pains·tak·ing (pānz'tā'kiŋ) *adj.* requiring or showing great care or diligence

paint (pānt) *vt.* [< L. *pingere*] **1.** *a)* to make (a picture) in colors applied to a surface *b)* to depict with paints **2.** to describe vividly **3.** to cover or decorate with paint —*vi.* to paint pictures —*n.* a mixture of pigment with oil, water, etc. used as a covering or coloring

paint'er *n.* **1.** an artist who paints pictures **2.** one whose work is covering surfaces, as walls, with paint

paint'ing *n.* a picture made with paints

pair (per) *n., pl.* **pairs**; sometimes, after a number, **pair** [< L. *par*, equal] **1.** two corresponding things associated or used together [a *pair* of shoes] **2.** a single thing with two corresponding parts [a *pair* of pants] **3.** any two persons or animals regarded as a unit —*vt., vi.* **1.** to form a pair or pairs (of); match **2.** to mate

pais·ley (pāz'lē) *adj.* [< *Paisley*, Scotland] [*also* P-] designating an elaborate, colorful pattern of intricate, curved figures

pa·ja·mas (pə jam'əz, -jä'məz) *n.pl.* [< Per. *pāi*, leg + *jāma*, garment] a loosely fitting sleeping or lounging suit consisting of jacket and trousers

Pa·ki·stan·i (pä'ki stä'nē) *adj.* of Pakistan or its people —*n.* a native of Pakistan

pal (pal) *n.* [Eng. Romany < Sans. *bhrātr*, brother] [Colloq.] a close friend

pal·ace (pal'is) *n.* [< L. *Palatium*, one of the seven hills in Rome] **1.** the official residence of a king, etc. **2.** any large, magnificent building

pal·at·a·ble (pal'it ə b'l) *adj.* **1.** pleasant to the taste **2.** acceptable to the mind

pal·ate (pal'it) *n.* [L. *palatum*] **1.** the roof of the mouth **2.** taste —**pal'a·tal** (-'l) *adj.*

pa·la·tial (pə lā'shəl) *adj.* [see PALACE] **1.** of, suitable for, or like a palace **2.** large and ornate; magnificent —**pa·la'tial·ly** *adv.*

pal·a·tine (pal'ə tīn', -tin) *adj.* [see PALACE] having royal privileges —*n.* a nobleman having royal privileges in his own territory

pa·lav·er (pə lav'ər) *n.* [Port. *palavra*, a speech] talk; esp., idle talk —*vi.* to talk glibly

pale' (pāl) *adj.* [< L. *pallere*, to be pale] **1.** of a whitish or colorless complexion **2.** lacking intensity, as color, light, etc. **3.** feeble —*vi., vt.* **paled, pal'ing** to become or make pale —**pale'ly** *adv.* —**pale'ness** *n.*

pale² (pāl) *n.* [< L. *palus*, a stake] **1.** a pointed stake used in fences; picket **2.** a boundary; enclosure: now chiefly figurative

pale'face' *n.* a white person: a term allegedly first used by N. American Indians

pa·le·on·tol·o·gy (pā'lē än täl'ə jē) *n.* [< Gr. *palaios*, ancient + *ōn*, a being + -LOGY] the branch of geology that deals with prehistoric life through the study of fossils —**pa'le·on·tol'o·gist** *n.*

pal·ette (pal'it) *n.* [Fr. < L. *pala*, a shovel] a thin board on which an artist mixes paints

pal·ing (pāl'iŋ) *n.* **1.** a fence made of pales **2.** a pale, or pales collectively

pal·i·sade (pal'ə sād') *n.* [< Fr. < L. *palus*, a stake] **1.** any of a row of large pointed stakes set in the ground to form a fence as for fortification **2.** such a fence **3.** [*pl.*] a line of steep cliffs

pall' (pôl) *vi.* **palled, pall'ing** [ME. *pallen*] **1.** to become cloying, insipid, etc. **2.** to become satiated or bored

pall² (pôl) *n.* [< L. *pallium*, a cover] **1.** a piece of velvet, etc. used to cover a coffin, hearse, etc. **2.** a dark or gloomy covering

pall·bear·er (pôl'ber'ər) *n.* [PALL² + BEARER] one of the persons who bear the coffin at a funeral

pal·let' (pal'it) *n.* [see PALETTE] a low, portable platform for storing goods in warehouses, etc.

pal·let² (pal'it) *n.* [< L. *palea*, chaff] a small, inferior bed or a mattress filled as with straw and used on the floor

pal·li·ate (pal'ē āt') *vt.* -at'ed, -at'ing [< L. *pallium*, a cloak] 1. to lessen the severity of without curing; alleviate 2. to make appear less serious or offensive; excuse —**pal'li·a'tive** *adj., n.*

pal·lid (pal'id) *adj.* [< L. *pallidus*, PALE¹] faint in color; pale —**pal'lid·ly** *adv.*

pal·lor (pal'ər) *n.* [L. < *pallere*, be pale] unnatural paleness, as of the face

palm¹ (päm; *occas.* pälm) *n.* [< L. *palma*: from its handlike fronds] 1. any of several tropical or subtropical trees with a tall, branchless trunk and a bunch of large leaves at the top 2. a leaf of this tree carried as a symbol of victory 3. victory —**palm'y** *adj.*

palm² (päm; *occas.* pälm) *n.* [< L. *palma*] the inner surface of the hand between the fingers and wrist —*vt.* to hide (something) in the palm, as in a sleight-of-hand trick —**palm off** to pass off by fraud or deceit

pal·met·to (pal met'ō) *n., pl.* -tos, -toes a small palm tree with fan-shaped leaves

palm·is·try (päm'is trē, päl'mis-) *n.* [< ME., prob. < *paume*, PALM² + *maistrie*, mastery] fortunetelling by means of the lines, etc. on the palm of a person's hand —**palm'ist** *n.*

Palm Sunday the Sunday before Easter, commemorating Jesus' triumphal entry into Jerusalem

pal·o·mi·no (pal'ə mē'nō) *n., pl.* -nos [AmSp. < Sp., dove-colored, ult. < L. *palumbes*, pigeon] a pale-yellow horse with white mane and tail

pal·pa·ble (pal'pə b'l) *adj.* [< L. *palpare*, to touch] 1. that can be touched; felt, etc. 2. easily perceived by the senses; perceptible 3. obvious; plain —**pal'pa·bly** *adv.*

pal·pi·tate (pal'pə tāt') *vi.* -tat'ed, -tat'ing [< L. *palpare*, to feel] 1. to beat rapidly or flutter, as the heart 2. to throb; quiver —**pal'pi·ta'tion** *n.*

pal·sy (pôl'zē) *n., pl.* -sies [see PARALYSIS] paralysis of any voluntary muscle, sometimes accompanied by uncontrollable tremors —*vt.* -sied, -sy·ing to paralyze

pal·try (pôl'trē) *adj.* -tri·er, -tri·est [prob. < LowG. *palte*, rag] trifling; petty

pam·pas (pam'pəz) *n.pl.* [AmSp. < SAmInd. *pampa*, plain] the extensive treeless plains of Argentina

pam·per (pam'pər) *vt.* [< LowG.] to be overindulgent with; coddle —**pam'per·er** *n.*

pam·phlet (pam'flit) *n.* [< OFr. *Pamphilet*, popular name of a ML. poem] a small, unbound booklet, often on some topic of current interest —**pam'phlet·eer'** (-flə tir') *n.*

Pan (pan) *Gr. Myth.* a god of fields, forests, flocks, and shepherds, represented with the legs of a goat

pan¹ (pan) *n.* [OE. *panne*] 1. any broad, shallow container used in cooking, etc. 2. a pan-shaped part or object 3. [Slang] a face —*vt., vi.* **panned, pan'ning** 1. [Colloq.] to criticize unfavorably 2. *Mining* to wash (gravel) in a pan in order to separate (gold, etc.) —**pan out** [Colloq.] to turn out; esp., to turn out well

pan² (pan) *vt., vi.* **panned, pan'ning** [< PAN(ORAMA)] to move (a motion-picture or television camera) so as to get a panoramic effect —*n.* the act of panning

pan- [< Gr. *pan*, all] *a combining form meaning:* 1. all [*pantheism*] 2. [P-] of, comprising, or uniting every [*Pan-American*]

pan·a·ce·a (pan'ə sē'ə) *n.* [< Gr. *pan*, all + *akeisthai*, to cure] a supposed remedy or cure for all ills

pa·nache (pə nash') *n.* [Fr., ult. < LL. *pinnaculum*, plume] carefree self-confidence or style

Pan'-A·mer'i·can *adj.* of North, Central, and South America, collectively

pan·cake (pan'kāk') *n.* a thin, flat cake of batter fried on a griddle or in a pan

pan·chro·mat·ic (pan'krō mat'ik) *adj.* sensitive to light of all colors [*panchromatic film*]

pan·cre·as (pan'krē əs, pan'-) *n.* [< Gr. *pan*, all + *kreas*, flesh] a large gland that secretes a digestive juice into the small intestine —**pan'cre·at'ic** (-at'ik) *adj.*

pan·da (pan'də) *n.* [Fr. < native name] 1. a reddish, raccoonlike mammal of the Himalayas 2. a black-and-white, bearlike mammal of China and Tibet: also **giant panda**

pan·dem·ic (pan dem'ik) *adj.* [< Gr. *pan*, all + *dēmos*, people] epidemic over a large region

pan·de·mo·ni·um (pan'də mō'nē əm) *n.* [< name of demon's abode in Milton's *Paradise Lost* < Gr. *pan-* + *daimōn*, demon] wild disorder or noise

pan·der (pan'dər) *n.* [< L. *Pandarus*, lovers' go-between in a medieval story] 1. a procurer; pimp 2. one who helps others to satisfy their vices, etc. Also **pan'der·er** —*vi.* to act as pander (*to*)

Pan·do·ra (pan dôr'ə) [< Gr. *pan*, all + *dōron*, a gift] *Gr. Myth.* the first mortal woman: she opened a box letting all human ills into the world

pane (pān) *n.* [< L. *pannus*, piece of cloth] a sheet of glass in a window, door, frame, etc.

pan·e·gyr·ic (pan'ə jir'ik) *n.* [< Gr. *panēgyris*, public meeting] 1. a formal speech or writing praising a person or event 2. high praise —**pan'e·gyr'i·cal** *adj.*

pan·el (pan''l) *n.* [see PANE] 1. *a*) a section or division, usually rectangular, set off on a wall, door, etc. *b*) a board for instruments or controls 2. a strip inserted in a skirt, etc. 3. a list of persons summoned for jury duty 4. a group of persons selected for judging, discussing, etc. —*vt.* -eled or -elled, -el·ing or -el·ling to provide with panels

pan'el·ing, pan'el·ling *n.* panels collectively

pan'el·ist *n.* a member of a panel (*n.* 4)

pang (pan) *n.* [< ?] a sudden, sharp, brief pain, physical or emotional

pan'han'dle¹ *n.* [*often* P-] a strip of land like the handle of a pan

pan'han'dle² *vt., vi.* -dled, -dling [Colloq.] to beg (from), esp. on the streets —**pan'han'dler** *n.*

pan·ic (pan'ik) *n.* [< Fr. < Gr. *panikos*, of Pan, as inspirer of sudden fear] a sudden, unreasoning fear, often spreading quickly —*vi.* -icked, -ick·ing 1. to affect with panic 2. [Slang] to delight as with comedy —*vi.* to give way to panic —**pan'ick·y** *adj.*

pan'ic-strick'en *adj.* stricken with panic; badly frightened: also **panic-struck**

pan·nier, pan·ier (pan'yər, -ē ər) *n.* [< L. *panis*, bread] a large basket for carrying loads on the back

pan·o·ply (pan'ə plē) *n., pl.* -plies [< Gr. *pan*, all + *hopla*, arms] 1. a complete suit of armor 2. any magnificent array

pan·o·ra·ma (pan'ə ram'ə) *n.* [< PAN- + Gr. *horama*, a view] 1. an open view in all directions 2. a constantly changing scene —**pan'o·ram'ic** *adj.*

pan·sy (pan'zē) *n., pl.* -sies [Fr. *pensée*, a

thought] a small, flowering plant with flat, broad, velvety petals in many colors

pant (pant) *vi.* [ult. < L. *phantasia*, nightmare] 1. to breathe rapidly and heavily, as from running fast 2. to yearn eagerly (with *for* or *after*) —*vt.* to gasp out —*n.* any of a series of rapid, heavy breaths; gasp

pan·ta·loons (pan't'l ōōnz') *n.pl.* [It., ult. after St. *Pantalone*] trousers

pan·the·ism (pan'thē iz'm) *n.* the belief that God is the sum of all beings, forces, etc. in the universe —**pan'the·ist** *n.* —**pan'the·is'tic** *adj.*

pan·the·on (pan'thē än') *n.* [< Gr. *pan*, all + *theos*, a god] 1. a temple for all the gods 2. [often P-] a building in which the famous dead of a nation are entombed

pan·ther (pan'thər) *n.* [< Gr. *panthēr*] 1. a leopard 2. a cougar 3. a jaguar

pant·ies (pan'tēz) *n.pl.* women's or children's short underpants: also **pant'ie, pant'y**

pan·to·mime (pan'tə mīm') *n.* [< Gr.: see PAN- & MIME] 1. a drama without words, using actions and gestures only 2. actions and gestures without words —*vt., vi.* -**mimed**', -**mim'ing** to express or act in pantomime —**pan'to·mim'ic** (-mim'ik) *adj.*

pan·try (pan'trē) *n., pl.* -**tries** [< L. *panis*, bread] a small room off the kitchen, where cooking ingredients, china, etc. are kept

pants (pants) *n.pl.* [< PANTALOONS] 1. trousers 2. drawers or panties —An adjective or in compounds, usually **pant** [*pant* legs]

pant·suit (pant'sōōt') *n.* a woman's outfit of a matched jacket and pants: also **pants suit**

panty hose a woman's undergarment combining panties with hose

pant'y·waist' (-wāst') *n.* [Slang] a sissy

pan·zer (pan'zər; G. pän'tsər) *adj.* [G., armor] armored [a *panzer* division]

pap (pap) *n.* [orig. < baby talk] 1. any soft food for babies or invalids 2. any oversimplified writing, etc.

pa·pa (pä'pə; *now less freq.* pə pä') *n.* father: a child's word

pa·pa·cy (pä'pə sē) *n., pl.* -**cies** [< ML. *papa*, pope] 1. the position or authority of the Pope 2. the period during which a pope rules 3. [P-] the government of the Roman Catholic Church, headed by the Pope

pa·pal (pä'pəl) *adj.* 1. of the Pope or the papacy 2. of the Roman Catholic Church

pa·paw (pô'pô) *n.* [prob. < PAPAYA] 1. a tree of central and southern U.S. bearing a yellowish, edible fruit 2. its fruit

pa·pa·ya (pə pä'yə) *n.* [Sp. < SAmInd.] 1. a tropical American tree bearing a large, yellowish-orange fruit 2. its fruit

pa·per (pā'pər) *n.* [see PAPYRUS] 1. a thin, flexible material in sheets, made from rags, wood pulp, etc. and used to write or print on, wrap, etc. 2. a single sheet of this 3. an official document 4. an essay, dissertation, etc. 5. a newspaper 6. wallpaper 7. [*pl.*] credentials —*adj.* 1. of, or made of, paper 2. like paper; thin —*vt.* to cover with wallpaper —**pa'per·y** *adj.*

pa'per·back' *n.* a book bound in paper

pa'per·boy' *n.* a boy who sells or delivers newspapers

pa'per·hang'er *n.* one whose work is covering walls with wallpaper

pa'per·weight' *n.* any small, heavy object set on papers to keep them from being scattered

paper work the keeping of records, filing of reports, etc. incidental to some task

pa·pier-mâ·ché (pā'pər mə shā') *n.* [Fr. < *papier*, paper + *mâcher*, to chew] a material made of paper pulp mixed with size, glue, etc.

and molded into various objects when moist

pa·pil·la (pə pil'ə) *n., pl.* -**lae** (-ē) [L. < *papula*, pimple] a small bulge of flesh, as on the tongue —**pap·il·lar·y** (pap'ə ler'ē) *adj.*

pa·poose (pa pōōs') *n.* [< AmInd.] a North American Indian baby

pa·pri·ka (pa prē'kə, pap'ri-) *n.* [Hung. < Gr. *peperi*, pepper] a red condiment ground from the fruit of certain peppers

Pap test (pap) [< G. *Papanicolaou*, 20th-c. U.S. anatomist] a test for uterine cancer

pa·py·rus (pə pī'rəs) *n., pl.* -**ri** (-rī), -**rus·es** [< Gr. *papyros*] 1. a tall water plant of Egypt 2. a writing material made from the pith of this plant by the ancients

par (pär) *n.* [L., an equal] 1. the established value of a currency in foreign-exchange rates 2. an equal status, level, etc.: usually in **on a par (with)** 3. the average state, condition, etc. [work that is above *par*] 4. the face value of stocks, bonds, etc. 5. *Golf* the number of strokes established as a skillful score for a hole or course —*adj.* 1. of or at par 2. average

par·a·ble (par'ə b'l) *n.* [< Gr. *para-*, beside + *ballein*, to throw] a short, simple story teaching a moral or religious lesson

pa·rab·o·la (pə rab'ə lə) *n.* [see prec.] *Math.* a plane curve formed by the intersection of a cone with a plane parallel to its side —**par·a·bol·ic** (par'ə bäl'ik) *adj.*

par·a·chute (par'ə shōōt') *n.* [Fr. < *para-*, protecting + *chute*, a fall] a large cloth contrivance, umbrella-shaped when unfolded, used to retard the speed of one dropping from an airplane, etc. —*vt., vi.* -**chut'ed**, -**chut'ing** to drop by parachute —**par'a·chut'ist** *n.*

pa·rade (pə rād') *n.* [Fr. < Sp. < L. *parare*, to prepare] 1. ostentatious display 2. a review of troops 3. any organized procession or march, as for display 4. a public walk or promenade —*vt.* -**rad'ed**, -**rad'ing** 1. to march or walk through (the streets, etc.), as for display 2. to show off [he *parades* his knowledge] —*vi.* 1. to march in a parade 2. to show off

par·a·digm (par'ə dim, -dīm') *n.* [< Fr. < Gr. *para*, beside + *deigma*, example] 1. a pattern, example, or model 2. *Gram.* an example of a declension or conjugation, giving all the inflectional forms of a word

par·a·dise (par'ə dīs') *n.* [< Gr. *paradeisos*, a garden] 1. [P-] the garden of Eden 2. *same as* HEAVEN (sense 2 *a*) 3. any place or state of perfection, happiness, etc.

par·a·dox (par'ə däks') *n.* [< Gr. *para-*, beyond + *doxa*, opinion] 1. a statement that seems contradictory, absurd, etc. but may be true in fact 2. a statement that contradicts itself and is false —**par'a·dox'i·cal** *adj.* —**par'a·dox'i·cal·ly** *adv.*

par·af·fin (par'ə fin) *n.* [G. < L. *parum*, too little + *affinis*, akin: from its inertness] a white, waxy substance distilled from petroleum and used for making candles, sealing jars, etc.

par·a·gon (par'ə gän', -gən) *n.* [< It. *paragone*, touchstone] a model of perfection or excellence

par·a·graph (par'ə graf') *n.* [< Gr. *para-*, beside + *graphein*, write] 1. a distinct section of a writing, begun on a new line and often indented 2. a mark (¶) used to indicate a new paragraph 3. a brief item in a newspaper or magazine —*vt.* to arrange in paragraphs

par·a·keet (par'ə kēt') *n.* [see PARROT] a small, slender parrot with a long tail

par·a·le·gal (par'ə lē'gəl) *adj.* designating or of persons trained to aid lawyers but not licensed to practice law —*n.* such a person

par·al·lax (par′ə laks′) *n.* [< Fr. < Gr. *para-*, beyond + *allassein*, to change] the apparent change in the position of an object resulting from a change in the viewer's position

par·al·lel (par′ə lel′) *adj.* [< Fr. < Gr. *para-*, side by side + *allēlos*, one another] 1. extending in the same direction and at a constant distance apart, so as never to meet 2. similar or corresponding —*n.* 1. a parallel line, surface, etc. 2. any person or thing similar to another; counterpart 3. any comparison showing likeness 4. any of the imaginary lines parallel to the equator and representing degrees of latitude (**parallel of latitude**) —*vt.* **-leled′** or **-lelled′**, **-lel′ing** or **-lel′ling** 1. to be parallel with /the road *parallels* the river/ 2. to compare 3. to match; equal —**par′al·lel′ism** (-iz′m) *n.*

par·al·lel′o·gram′ (-ə gram′) *n.* a four-sided plane figure having the opposite sides parallel and equal

pa·ral·y·sis (pə ral′ə sis) *n., pl.* **-ses′** (-sēz′) [< Gr. *para-*, beside + *lyein*, to loose] 1. partial or complete loss of the power of motion or sensation in some or all of the body 2. a condition of helpless inactivity —**par·a·lyt·ic** (par′ə lit′ik) *adj., n.*

par·a·lyze (par′ə līz′) *vt.* **-lyzed′**, **-lyz′ing** 1. to cause paralysis in 2. to make ineffective or powerless

par·a·me·ci·um (par′ə mē′shē əm, -sē əm) *n., pl.* **-ci·a** (-ə) [< Gr. *paramēkēs*, oval] a one-celled, elongated protozoan that moves by means of cilia

par·a·med·i·cal (par′ə med′i k′l) *adj.* [< Gr. *para-*, beside + MEDICAL] of auxiliary medical personnel, as midwives, nurses' aides, etc.

par·a·mount (par′ə mount′) *adj.* [< OFr. *par*, by + *amont*, uphill] chief; supreme

par·a·mour (par′ə moor′) *n.* [< OFr. *par amour*, with love] a lover; esp., the illicit sexual partner of a married person

par·a·noi·a (par′ə noi′ə) *n.* [< Gr. *para-*, beside + *nous*, the mind] a mental disorder characterized by delusions, as of grandeur or, esp., persecution —**par′a·noid′** *adj., n.*

par·a·pet (par′ə pit, -pet′) *n.* [Fr. < It. *parare*, to guard + *petto*, breast] 1. a wall or bank for screening troops from enemy fire 2. a low wall or railing, as on a balcony

par·a·pher·na·li·a (par′ə fər nāl′yə, -fə nā′lē ə) *n.pl.* [*often with sing. v.*] [< Gr. *para-*, beyond + *phernē*, a dowry] 1. personal belongings 2. equipment

par·a·phrase (par′ə frāz′) *n.* [Fr. < Gr. *para-*, beyond + *phrazein*, tell] a rewording of the meaning of something spoken or written —*vt., vi.* **-phrased′**, **-phras′ing** to reword

par·a·ple·gi·a (par′ə plē′jē ə, -jə) *n.* [< Gr. *para-*, beside + *plēgē*, a stroke] paralysis of the entire lower half of the body —**par′a·ple′gic** (-plē′jik, -plej′ik) *adj., n.*

par′a·psy·chol′o·gy (-sī käl′ə jē) *n.* [PARA- + PSYCHOLOGY] the study of psychic phenomena such as telepathy

par·a·site (par′ə sīt′) *n.* [< Gr. *para-*, beside + *sitos*, food] 1. one who lives at others' expense without making any useful return 2. a plant or animal that lives on or within another —**par′a·sit′ic** (-sit′ik) *adj.*

par·a·sol (par′ə sôl′) *n.* [Fr. < It. *parare*, ward off + *sole*, the sun] a light umbrella used as a sunshade

par·a·troops (par′ə trōōps′) *n.pl.* [< PARA(CHUTE) + TROOP] troops trained and equipped to parachute into a combat area —**par′a·troop′er** *n.*

par·boil (pär′boil′) *vt.* [< L. *per*, through + *bullire*, to boil: infl. by *part*] to boil until partly cooked

par·cel (pär′s′l) *n.* [see PARTICLE] 1. a small, wrapped bundle; package 2. a piece, as of land —*vt.* **-celed** or **-celled**, **-cel·ing** or **-cel·ling** to separate into parts and distribute (with *out*)

parcel post a postal service for carrying and delivering parcels (fourth-class mail)

parch (pärch) *vt.* [< ?] 1. to expose (corn, etc.) to great heat, so as to dry or roast 2. to make hot and dry 3. to make very thirsty —*vi.* to become very hot, dry, etc.

parch·ment (pärch′mənt) *n.* [ult. < L. (*charta*) *Pergamena*, (paper) of *Pergamum*, city in Asia Minor] 1. the skin of a sheep, goat, etc. prepared as a surface for writing 2. paper treated to resemble this 3. a manuscript on parchment

par·don (pär′d′n) *vt.* [< L. *per-*, through + *donare*, give] 1. to release from punishment 2. to forgive (an offense) 3. to excuse (a person) for a minor fault, etc. —*n.* 1. forgiveness 2. an official document granting a pardon —**par′don·a·ble** *adj.*

pare (per) *vt.* **pared, par′ing** [< L. *parare*, prepare] 1. to cut or trim away (the rind, skin, etc.) of; peel 2. to reduce gradually

par·e·gor·ic (par′ə gôr′ik) *n.* [< Gr. *parēgoros*, consoling] a camphorated tincture of opium, used to relieve diarrhea

par·ent (per′ənt) *n.* [< L. *parere*, beget] 1. a father or mother 2. any organism in relation to its offspring 3. a source; origin —**pa·ren·tal** (pə ren′t′l) *adj.* —**pa·ren′tal·ly** *adv.* —**par′ent·hood′** *n.*

par′ent·age (-ij) *n.* descent; lineage; origin

pa·ren·the·sis (pə ren′thə sis) *n., pl.* **-ses′** (-sēz′) [< Gr. *para-*, beside + *entithenai*, insert] 1. a word, clause, etc. added as an explanation or comment within a sentence 2. either or both of the curved lines ( ) used to set this off —**par·en·thet·i·cal** (par′ən thet′i k′l), **par′en·thet′ic** *adj.*

par′ent·ing (-iŋ) *n.* the work of a parent in raising a child or children

pa·re·sis (pə rē′sis) *n.* [Gr. < *parienai*, relax] 1. partial paralysis 2. a syphilitic brain disease marked by paralytic attacks

par·fait (pär fā′) *n.* [Fr., perfect] a frozen dessert of cream and eggs, or ice cream, fruit, etc. in a tall, slender glass

pa·ri·ah (pə rī′ə) *n.* [< Tamil *paraiyan*] 1. a member of one of the lowest social castes in India 2. any outcast

par·i·mu·tu·el (par′ə myōō′chōō wəl) *n.* [Fr., lit., a mutual bet] a system of betting on races in which the winning bettors share the net of each pool in proportion to their wagers

par·ing (per′iŋ) *n.* a thin piece pared off

Par·is (par′is) *Gr. Legend* a prince of Troy: see HELEN OF TROY

par·ish (par′ish) *n.* [< LGr. *paroikia*, diocese] 1. a part of a diocese under the charge of a priest or minister 2. the congregation of a church 3. a civil division in Louisiana, corresponding to a county

pa·rish·ion·er (pə rish′ə nər) *n.* a member of a parish

par·i·ty (par′ə tē) *n.* [< Fr. < L. *par*, equal] 1. equality in power, value, etc. 2. equality of value at a given ratio between different kinds of money, etc.

park (pärk) *n.* [< ML. *parricus*] 1. wooded land held as part of a private estate or as a hunting preserve 2. an area of public land, with playgrounds, etc., for recreation —*vt., vi.* 1. to leave (a vehicle) in a certain place temporarily 2. to maneuver (a vehicle) into a space for parking

par·ka (pär′kə) *n.* [Aleutian < Russ., fur coat] a hip-length hooded jacket

parking meter a coin-operated device for showing the length of time a parking space may be occupied

park′way′ *n.* a broad roadway edged or divided with plantings of trees, bushes, etc.

parl·ance (pär′ləns) *n.* [< OFr. *parler*, speak] a style of speaking or writing; idiom /military *parlance]*

par·lay (pär′lā, -lē; *for v., also* pär lā′) *vt., vi.* [< Fr. < It. *paro*, a pair] to bet (an original wager plus its winnings) on another race, etc. —*n.* a parlayed bet

par·ley (pär′lē) *vi.* [< Fr. *parler*, speak] to confer, esp. with an enemy —*n., pl.* **-leys** a conference, as to settle a dispute

par·lia·ment (pär′lə mənt) *n.* [< OFr. *parler*, speak] **1.** an official government council **2.** [P-] the national legislative body of certain countries, esp. Great Britain

par′lia·men·tar′i·an (-men ter′ē ən) *n.* one skilled in parliamentary rules or debate

par′lia·men′ta·ry (-men′tər ē) *adj.* **1.** of or by a parliament **2.** conforming to the rules of a parliament

par·lor (pär′lər) *n.* [< OFr. *parler*, speak] **1.** a living room **2.** a business establishment, esp. one with specialized services /a beauty *parlor]* Brit. sp. **parlour**

Par·me·san (cheese) (pär′mə zän′) [Fr. < It. < *Parma*, city in Italy] a hard, dry Italian cheese, usually grated

pa·ro·chi·al (pə rō′kē əl) *adj.* [see PARISH] **1.** of or in a parish **2.** narrow; provincial —**pa·ro′chi·al·ism** *n.*

parochial school a school supported and controlled by a church

par·o·dy (par′ə dē) *n., pl.* **-dies** [< Fr. < Gr. *para-*, beside + *ōidē*, song] a nonsensical imitation of a literary or musical work or style — *vt.* **-died, -dy·ing** to make a parody of —**par′o·dist** *n.*

pa·role (pə rōl′) *n.* [Fr. < LL. *parabola*, a speech] the release of a prisoner before his sentence has expired, on condition of future good behavior —*vt.* **-roled′, -rol′ing** to release on parole —**on parole** at liberty under conditions of parole

par·ox·ysm (par′ək siz′m) *n.* [< Fr. < Gr. *para-*, beyond + *oxynein*, sharpen] **1.** a sudden attack of a disease **2.** a sudden outburst, as of laughter

par·quet (pär kā′) *n.* [Fr. < MFr. *parc*, a park] **1.** the main floor of a theater: usually called *orchestra* **2.** a flooring of parquetry —*vt.* **-queted′** (-kād′), **-quet′ing** (-kā′iŋ) to make (a floor) of parquetry

par·quet·ry (pär′kə trē) *n.* [< Fr.] inlaid flooring in geometric forms

par·ri·cide (par′ə sīd′) *n.* [Fr. < L. *paricida*, kin + *caedere*, kill] **1.** one who murders his parent or another near relative **2.** the act of a parricide

par·rot (par′ət) *n.* [Fr. dial. *perrot]* **1.** a bird with a hooked bill and brightly colored feathers: some parrots can learn to imitate human speech **2.** a person who mechanically repeats the words of others —*vt.* to repeat or imitate without understanding

par·ry (par′ē) *vt.* **-ried, -ry·ing** [< L. *parare*, prepare] **1.** to ward off (a blow, etc.) **2.** to evade (a question, etc.) —*vi.* to make a parry — *n., pl.* **-ries** a warding off or evasion

parse (pärs) *vt., vi.* parsed, pars′ing [< L. *pars* (*orationis*), part (of speech)] to break (a

sentence) down, giving the grammatical form and function of each part

par·si·mo·ny (pär′sə mō′nē) *n.* [< L. *parcere*, to spare] stinginess; extreme frugality —**par′si·mo′ni·ous** *adj.*

pars·ley (pärs′lē) *n.* [< Gr. *petros*, a rock + *selinon*, celery] a plant with aromatic leaves used to flavor or garnish some foods

pars·nip (pär′snip) *n.* [< L. *pastinare*, dig up] **1.** a plant with a long, thick, sweet, white root used as a vegetable **2.** its root

par·son (pär′s'n) *n.* [see PERSON] **1.** a clergyman in charge of a parish **2.** any clergyman

par′son·age (-ij) *n.* the dwelling provided by a church for the use of its parson

part (pärt) *n.* [< L. *pars*] **1.** a portion, segment, etc. of a whole /part of a book] **2.** an essential, separable element /an automobile part] **3.** a share assigned or given; specif., *a*) duty /to do one's part] *b*) [*usually pl.*] talent; ability /a man of *parts] c*) a role in a play *d*) any voice or instrument in a musical ensemble, or the score for it **4.** a region; esp., [*usually pl.*] a district **5.** one of the sides in a conflict, etc. **6.** a dividing line formed in combing the hair —*vt.* **1.** to break or divide into parts **2.** to comb (the hair) so as to leave a part **3.** to break or hold apart —*vi.* **1.** to break or divide into parts **2.** to separate and go different ways **3.** to cease associating **4.** to go away (*from*) —*adj.* partial —**for one's part** so far as one is concerned —**for the most part** mostly —**in part** partly —**part with** to relinquish —**take part** to participate

par·take (pär tāk′) *vi.* **-took′, -tak′en, -tak′ing** [< *part taker*] **1.** to participate (*in* an activity) **2.** to eat or drink, esp. with others (usually with *of*)

par·the·no·gen·e·sis (pär′thə nō jen′ə sis) *n.* [< Gr. *parthenos*, virgin + *genesis*, origin] reproduction by the development of an unfertilized ovum, seed, or spore, as in certain insects, algae, etc.

Par·the·non (pär′thə nän′) [< Gr. *parthenos*, virgin (i.e., Athena)] the Doric temple of Athena on the Acropolis

par·tial (pär′shəl) *adj.* [< L. *pars*, a part] **1.** favoring one person, faction, etc. more than another; biased **2.** not complete —**partial to** fond of —**par′ti·al′i·ty** (-shē al′ə tē) *n.* —**par′tial·ly** *adv.*

par·tic·i·pant (pär tis′ə pənt) *adj.* participating —*n.* a person who participates

par·tic′i·pate′ (-pāt′) *vi.* **-pat′ed, -pat′ing** [< L. *pars*, a part + *capere*, to take] to have or take a share with others (*in* an activity, etc.) —**par·tic′i·pa′tion** *n.* —**par·tic′i·pa′tor** *n.*

par·ti·ci·ple (pär′tə sip′'l) *n.* [see prec.] a verbal form having the qualities of both verb and adjective —**par′ti·cip′i·al** (-sip′ē əl) *adj.*

par·ti·cle (pär′ti k'l) *n.* [< L. *pars*, part] **1.** a tiny fragment or trace **2.** a short, uninflected part of speech, as an article, preposition, etc.

par·ti·col·ored (pär′tē kul′ərd) *adj.* [< Fr. *parti*, divided + COLORED] **1.** having different colors in different parts **2.** diversified

par·tic·u·lar (pər tik′yə lər) *adj.* [see PARTICLE] **1.** of or belonging to a single group, person, or thing **2.** regarded separately; specific **3.** unusual **4.** hard to please; exacting —*n.* a distinct fact, item, detail, etc. —**in particular** especially —**par·tic′u·lar′i·ty** (-lar′ə tē) *n., pl.* **-ties**

par·tic′u·lar·ize′ (-lə rīz′) *vt., vi.* **-ized, -iz′ing** to give particulars or details (of)

par·tic′u·lar·ly *adv.* **1.** in detail **2.** especially **3.** specifically

part′ing *adj.* **1.** dividing; separating **2.** departing **3.** given, spoken, etc. at parting —*n.* **1.** a breaking or separating **2.** a leave-taking or departure

par·ti·san (pärt′ə z'n) *n.* [< L. *pars,* part] **1.** a strong supporter of a side, party, etc. **2.** a guerrilla fighter —*adj.* of or like a partisan Also sp. **par′ti·zan —par′ti·san·ship′** *n.*

par·ti·tion (pär tish′ən) *n.* [< L. *partitio*] **1.** division into parts **2.** something that divides, as a wall separating rooms —*vt.* **1.** to divide into parts **2.** to divide by a partition

part′ly *adv.* in part; not fully

part·ner (pärt′nər) *n.* [< ME.] one who takes part in an activity with another or others; specif., *a)* one of two or more persons heading the same business *b)* a spouse *c)* either of two persons dancing together *d)* a player on the same side or team

part′ner·ship′ *n.* **1.** the state of being a partner **2.** the relationship of partners; joint interest

part of speech any of the classes to which words can be assigned by form, function, etc., as noun, verb, etc.

par·took (pär took′) *pt. of* PARTAKE

par·tridge (pär′trij) *n.* [< Gr. *perdix*] any of several game birds, as the grouse, pheasant, etc.

part′-time′ *adj.* of or engaged in work, study, etc. for periods of less time than in a full schedule

par·tu·ri·tion (pär′choo rish′ən) *n.* [< L. *parere,* to produce] childbirth

part′way′ *adv.* to a degree but not fully

par·ty (pär′tē) *n., pl.* **-ties** [< L. *pars,* part] **1.** a group working to promote a political platform or slate, a cause, etc. **2.** a group acting together to accomplish something *[a surveying party]* **3.** a gathering for social entertainment **4.** one concerned in an action, plan, lawsuit, etc. *[a party* to the action*]* **5.** [Colloq.] a person —*vi.* **-tied, -ty·ing** to attend social parties — *vt.* to give a party for

party line 1. a single circuit connecting two or more telephone users with the exchange **2.** the policies of a political party

par·ve·nu (pär′və noo′, -nyoo′) *n.* [Fr. < L. *parvenire,* arrive] a newly rich person who is considered an upstart

pas·chal (pas′k'l) *adj.* [< Heb. *pesah,* Passover] **1.** of Passover **2.** of Easter

pa·sha (pə shä′, pä′shə, pash′ə) *n.* [Turk. *pasha*] formerly, in Turkey, a title of honor placed after the name

pass (pas) *vi.* [< L. *passus,* a step] **1.** to go or move forward, through, etc. **2.** to go or be conveyed from one place, condition, etc. to another **3.** *a)* to cease *b)* to depart **4.** to die (usually with *away, on,* or *out*) **5.** to go by **6.** to elapse *[an hour passed]* **7.** to make a way (*through* or *by*) **8.** to be accepted without question **9.** to be approved, as by a legislative body **10.** to go through a test, course, etc. successfully **11.** to give a sentence, judgment, etc. **12.** *Card Games* to decline a chance to bid —*vt.* **1.** to go by, beyond, over, or through; specif., *a)* to leave behind *b)* to go through (a test, course, etc.) successfully **2.** to cause or allow to go, move, proceed, etc.; specif., *a)* to ratify; enact *b)* to spend (time) *c)* to excrete **3.** to make move from place to place; circulate **4.** to give (an opinion or judgment) —*n.* **1.** an act of passing; passage **2.** a condition or situation *[a strange pass]* **3.** *a)* a ticket, etc. giving one free entry or exit *b)* Mil. a brief leave of absence **4.** a motion of the hands **5.** a tentative attempt **6.** a narrow passage, etc., esp. between moun-

tains **7.** [Slang] an overfamiliar attempt to embrace or kiss **8.** *Sports* a transfer of a ball, etc. to another player during play —**come** (or **bring) to pass** to (cause to) happen —**pass for** to be accepted as —**pass off** to cause to be accepted through deceit —**pass out 1.** to distribute **2.** to faint —**pass over** to disregard; ignore —**pass up** [Colloq.] to refuse or let go by — **pass′er** *n.*

pass′a·ble *adj.* **1.** that can be passed, traveled over, etc. **2.** adequate; fair

pas·sage (pas′ij) *n.* **1.** a passing; specif., *a)* migration *b)* transition *c)* the enactment of a law **2.** permission or right to pass **3.** a voyage **4.** a way or means of passing; road, passageway, etc. **5.** an interchange, as of blows **6.** a portion of a book, composition, etc.

pas′sage·way′ *n.* a narrow way for passage, as a hall, corridor, or alley

pass′book′ *n. same as* BANKBOOK

pas·sé (pa sä′) *adj.* [Fr., past] **1.** out-of-date; old-fashioned **2.** rather old

pas·sel (pas′'l) *n.* [< PARCEL] [Colloq.] a group, esp. a fairly large one

pas·sen·ger (pas′'n jər) *n.* [< OFr. *passage,* passage] a person traveling in a vehicle

pass′er-by′ *n., pl.* **pass′ers-by′** one who passes by

pass′ing *adj.* **1.** going by, beyond, etc. **2.** fleeting **3.** casual *[a passing* remark*]* **4.** satisfying requirements *[a passing* grade*]* —*n.* the act of one that passes; specif., death —**in passing** incidentally

pas·sion (pash′ən) *n.* [< L. *pati,* suffer] **1.** [P-] the suffering of Jesus during the Crucifixion or after the Last Supper **2.** any emotion, as hate, love, etc. **3.** extreme emotion, as rage, enthusiasm, lust, etc. **4.** the object of strong desire

pas′sion·ate (-it) *adj.* **1.** having or showing strong emotions **2.** hot-tempered **3.** intense; ardent **4.** sensual —**pas′sion·ate·ly** *adv.*

pas·sive (pas′iv) *adj.* [see PASSION] **1.** not active, but acted upon **2.** not resisting; submissive **3.** inactive **4.** *Gram.* denoting the voice of a verb whose subject receives the action —*n.* the passive voice —**pas′sive·ly** *adv.* —**pas′sive-ness, pas·siv′i·ty** *n.*

passive resistance opposition to a government, by refusal to comply or by nonviolent acts, as fasting

Pass·o·ver (pas′ō′vər) *n.* a Jewish holiday commemorating the ancient Hebrews' deliverance from slavery in Egypt

pass′port′ *n.* a government document issued to a citizen traveling abroad, certifying identity and citizenship

pass′word′ *n.* a secret word or phrase used for identification, as in passing a guard

past (past) *rare pp. of* PASS —*adj.* **1.** gone by; ended **2.** of a former time **3.** just gone by *[the past* week*]* **4.** *Gram.* indicating a time gone by *[the past* tense*]* —*n.* **1.** time gone by **2.** the history of a person, group, etc. **3.** a hidden or questionable personal background —*prep.* beyond in time, space, amount, etc. —*adv.* to and beyond

pas·ta (päs′tə) *n.* [It.] **1.** the flour paste of which spaghetti, etc. is made **2.** spaghetti, macaroni, etc. cooked in some way

paste (pāst) *n.* [< Gr. *pastē,* porridge] **1.** dough for making rich pastry **2.** any soft, moist, smooth preparation *[toothpaste,* almond *paste]* **3.** a mixture of flour or starch, water, etc. used as an adhesive **4.** a hard, brilliant glass used for artificial gems —*vt.* **past′ed, past′ing 1.** to make adhere, as with paste **2.** [Slang] to hit

paste'board' *n.* a stiff material made of layers of paper pasted together

pas·tel (pas tel') *n.* [Fr. < LL. *pasta*, paste] **1.** a crayon of ground coloring matter **2.** a picture drawn with such crayons **3.** a soft, pale shade of color

pas·tern (pas'tərn) *n.* [< OFr. < *pasture*, a tether] the part of a horse's foot between the fetlock and the hoof

pas·teur·ize (pas'chə rīz', -tə-) *vt.* **-ized', -iz'-ing** [< L. *Pasteur*, 19th-c. Fr. bacteriologist] to destroy bacteria in (milk, etc.) by heating to a prescribed temperature for a specified time — **pas'teur·i·za'tion** *n.*

pas·tiche (pas tēsh') *n.* [Fr.] **1.** an artistic composition drawn from various sources **2.** a hodgepodge

pas·time (pas'tīm') *n.* a way of spending spare time pleasantly

pas·tor (pas'tər) *n.* [L., a shepherd] a clergyman in charge of a congregation

pas'to·ral *adj.* **1.** of shepherds or their work, etc. **2.** of rural life idealized as peaceful, simple, etc. **3.** of a pastor or his duties

pas'tor·ate (-it) *n.* the position, rank, or term of office of a pastor

past participle a participle used: *a*) to indicate a past time or state (as *gone* in "he has gone") *b*) as an adjective (as *grown* in "a grown man")

pas·tra·mi (pə strä'mē) *n.* [Yid. < Romanian] highly spiced, smoked beef

pas·try (pās'trē) *n., pl.* **-tries** [see PASTE] **1.** pies, tarts, etc. with crusts baked from flour dough made with shortening **2.** all fancy baked goods

pas·tur·age (pas'chər ij) *n. same as* PASTURE

pas·ture (pas'chər) *n.* [< L. *pascere*, to feed] **1.** grass, etc. used as food by grazing animals **2.** ground suitable for grazing —*vt.* **-tured, -tur·ing** to put (cattle, etc.) out to graze in a pasture — *vi.* to graze

past·y (pās'tē) *adj.* **-i·er, -i·est** of or like paste in color or texture —**past'i·ness** *n.*

pat (pat) *n.* [prob. echoic] **1.** a gentle tap or stroke with a flat surface **2.** the sound made by this **3.** a small lump, as of butter —*vt.* **pat'ted, pat'ting 1.** to tap or stroke gently with the hand or a flat surface **2.** to shape, apply, etc. by patting —*adj.* **1.** exactly suitable *[a pat hand in poker]* **2.** so glib as to seem contrived —**have (down) pat** [Colloq.] to know thoroughly —**stand pat** to stick to an opinion, etc.

pat. 1. patent **2.** patented

patch (pach) *n.* [ME. *pacche*] **1.** a piece of material to cover or mend a hole or tear or to strengthen a weak spot **2.** a dressing for a wound **3.** an area; spot *[patches of blue sky]* **4.** a small plot of ground **5.** a scrap; bit —*vt.* **1.** to put a patch on **2.** to produce crudely or hurriedly (often with *up* or *together*) —**patch up** to settle (a quarrel, etc.) —**patch'y** *adj.* **-i·er, -i·est**

patch'work' *n.* needlework, as a quilt, made of odd patches of cloth

pate (pāt) *n.* [< ?] the top of the head: a humorous term

pâ·té (pä tā') *n.* [Fr.] a meat paste

pa·tel·la (pə tel'ə) *n., pl.* **-las, -lae** (-ē) [L., a pan] *same as* KNEECAP

pat·ent (pat''nt; *also, for adj. 1 & 2,* pāt'-) *adj.* [< L. *patere*, be open] **1.** open, accessible, etc. **2.** obvious; plain **3.** protected by a patent —*n.* **1.** a document granting the exclusive right to produce or sell an invention, etc. for a certain time **2.** *a*) the right so granted *b*) the thing so protected —*vt.* to get a patent for

patent leather leather with a hard, glossy finish: formerly patented

patent medicine a trademarked medical preparation obtainable without a prescription

pa·ter·nal (pə tur'n'l) *adj.* [< L. *pater*, father] **1.** fatherly **2.** inherited from a father **3.** on the father's side of the family

pa·ter'nal·ism *n.* the system of controlling a country, employees, etc. as a father might his children —**pa·ter'nal·is'tic** *adj.*

pa·ter'ni·ty (-nə tē) *n.* **1.** the state of being a father **2.** male parentage

pa·ter·nos·ter (pät'ər nôs'tər, pät'-) *n.* [L., our father] the Lord's Prayer, esp. in Latin: often **Pater Noster**

path (path) *n.* [OE. *pæth*] **1.** a way worn by footsteps **2.** a walk for use by people on foot **3.** a line of movement **4.** a course of conduct —**path'less** *adj.*

pa·thet·ic (pə thet'ik) *adj.* [< Gr. *pathos*, suffering] **1.** arousing pity, sympathy, etc.; pitiful **2.** pitifully unsuccessful, etc. —**pa·thet'i·cal·ly** *adv.*

path·o·gen·ic (path'ə jen'ik) *adj.* causing disease

pa·thol·o·gy (pə thäl'ə jē) *n.* [< Fr. < Gr. *pathos*, suffering + -LOGY] **1.** the branch of medicine that deals with the nature of disease, esp. with structural and functional effects **2.** any abnormal variation from a sound condition —**path·o·log·i·cal** (path'ə läj'i k'l) *adj.* —**pa·thol'o·gist** *n.*

pa·thos (pā'thäs, -thôs) *n.* [Gr., suffering] the quality in something which arouses pity, sorrow, sympathy, etc.

path'way' *n. same as* PATH

-pathy [< Gr. *pathos*, suffering] *a combining form meaning:* **1.** feeling *[antipathy]* **2.** disease *[osteopathy]*

pa·tience (pā'shəns) *n.* the state, quality, or fact of being patient

pa'tient (-shənt) *adj.* [< L. *pati*, suffer] **1.** enduring pain, trouble, etc. without complaint **2.** calmly tolerating insult, delay, etc. **3.** diligent; persevering —*n.* one receiving medical care —**pa'tient·ly** *adv.*

pat·i·na (pat''n ə, pə tē'nə) *n.* [Fr. < It.] a fine greenish crust formed by oxidation on bronze or copper

pa·ti·o (pat'ē ō') *n., pl.* **-os'** [Sp.] **1.** a courtyard open to the sky **2.** a paved area, as one next to a house, for outdoor lounging, dining, etc.

pat·ois (pat'wä) *n., pl.* **-ois** (-wäz) [Fr.] a nonstandard form of a language, as a provincial dialect

pat. pend. patent pending

pa·tri·arch (pā'trē ärk') *n.* [< Gr. *patēr*, father + *archein*, to rule] **1.** the father and ruler of a family or tribe, as Abraham, Isaac, or Jacob in the Bible **2.** a man of great age and dignity **3.** a high-ranking bishop, as in the Orthodox Eastern Church —**pa'tri·ar'chal** *adj.*

pa'tri·ar'chy (-kē) *n., pl.* **-chies** a social organization in which the father is head of the family, descent being traced through the male line

pa·tri·cian (pə trish'ən) *n.* [< L. *pater*, father] an aristocrat

pat·ri·mo·ny (pat'rə mō'nē) *n., pl.* **-nies** [< L. *pater*, father] property inherited from one's father or ancestors —**pat'ri·mo'ni·al** *adj.*

pa·tri·ot (pā'trē ət) *n.* [< Fr. < Gr. *patris*, fatherland] one who loves and zealously supports his country —**pa'tri·ot'ic** (-ät'ik) *adj.* —**pa'tri·ot'i·cal·ly** *adv.* —**pa'tri·ot·ism** *n.*

pa·trol (pə trōl') *vt., vi.* **-trolled', -trol'ling** [<

Fr. < OFr. *patouiller*, to paddle] to make a regular, repeated circuit of in guarding —*n.* **1.** a patrolling **2.** a person or group patrolling

pa·trol'man (-mən) *n., pl.* **-men** a policeman assigned to patrol a specific area

pa·tron (pā'trən) *n.* [< L. *pater*, father] **1.** a protector; benefactor **2.** one who sponsors and supports some person, activity, etc. **3.** a regular customer —**pa'tron·ess** *n.fem.*

pa·tron·age (pā'trən ij, pat'rən-) *n.* **1.** support, encouragement, etc. given by a patron **2.** condescension **3.** *a)* customers *b)* business; trade **4.** *a)* the power to grant political favors *b)* such favors

pa·tron·ize (pā'trə nīz', pat'rə-) *vt.* **-ized', -iz'- ing 1.** to sponsor; support **2.** to treat kindly but as an inferior **3.** to be a regular customer of (a store, etc.)

patron saint a saint looked upon as a special guardian

pat·ro·nym·ic (pat'rə nim'ik) *n.* [< Gr. *patēr*, father + *onyma*, a name] a name showing descent from a given person (e.g., *Stevenson*, son of Steven)

pat·sy (pat'sē) *n., pl.* **-sies** [< ?] [Slang] a person easily imposed upon

pat·ter' (pat'ər) *vi.* [< PAT] to make, or move so as to make, a patter —*n.* a series of quick, light taps

pat·ter² (pat'ər) *vt., vi.* [< PATERNOSTER] to speak rapidly or glibly —*n.* glib, rapid speech, as of salesmen

pat·tern (pat'ərn) *n.* [< OFr. *patron*] **1.** a person or thing worthy of imitation **2.** a model, plan, etc. used in making things **3.** a design **4.** a regular way of acting or doing —*vt.* to make or do in imitation of a model or pattern (with *on, upon,* or *after*)

pat·ty (pat'ē) *n., pl.* **-ties** [Fr. *pâté*, a pie] a small, flat cake of ground meat, fish, etc., usually fried

pau·ci·ty (pô'sə tē) *n.* [< L. *paucus*, few] **1.** fewness; small number **2.** scarcity

Paul (pôl) *Bible* the Apostle of Christianity to the Gentiles, author of many Epistles

Paul Bun·yan (bun'yən) *American Folklore* a giant lumberjack who performed superhuman feats

paunch (pônch) *n.* [< L. *pantex*, belly] the abdomen, or belly; esp., a potbelly —**paunch'y** *adj.*

pau·per (pô'pər) *n.* [L.] an extremely poor person, esp. one who lives on charity —**pau'per·ism** *n.*

pause (pôz) *n.* [< Gr. *pauein*, to stop] a temporary stop or rest —*vi.* **paused, paus'ing** to make a pause; stop

pave (pāv) *vt.* **paved, pav'ing** [< L. *pavire*, beat] to cover the surface of (a road, etc.), as with concrete or asphalt —**pave the way (for)** to prepare the way (for)

pave'ment *n.* a paved surface, as of concrete; specif., a paved street or road

pa·vil·ion (pə vil'yən) *n.* [< L. *papilio*, tent] **1.** a large tent **2.** a building, often partly open, for exhibits, etc., as at a fair or park **3.** any of a group of related buildings

paw (pô) *n.* [< OFr. *poue*] **1.** the foot of a four-footed animal having claws **2.** [Colloq.] a hand —*vt., vi.* **1.** to touch, dig, strike, etc. with the paws or feet **2.** to handle clumsily, roughly, or overintimately

pawl (pôl) *n.* [akin ? to Du. *pal*, pole] a device, as a hinged tongue which engages cogs in a wheel, allowing motion in only one direction

pawn' (pôn) *n.* [< MFr. *pan*] **1.** anything given as security, as for a debt; pledge **2.** the state

of being pledged —*vt.* to give as security — **pawn'er, paw'nor** *n.*

pawn² (pôn) *n.* [< ML. *pedo*, foot soldier] **1.** a chessman of the lowest value **2.** a person used to advance another's purposes

pawn'bro'ker *n.* a person licensed to lend money at interest on personal belongings left with him as security —**pawn'bro'king** *n.*

pawn'shop' *n.* a pawnbroker's shop

paw·paw (pô'pô') *n.* same as PAPAW

pay (pā) *vt.* **paid, pay'ing** [< L. *pacare*, pacify] **1.** to give (a person) what is due, as for goods or services **2.** to give (what is due) in return, as for goods or services **3.** to settle (a debt, etc.) **4.** *a)* to give (a compliment, etc.) *b)* to make (a visit, etc.) **5.** to be profitable to —*vi.* **1.** to give due compensation **2.** to be profitable — *n.* **1.** a paying or being paid **2.** money paid; esp., wages or salary —*adj.* **1.** operated by depositing a coin [a *pay* telephone] **2.** designating a service, etc. paid for by fees [*pay* TV] — **in the pay of** employed and paid by —**pay back 1.** to repay **2.** to retaliate upon —**pay off** to pay all that is owed —**pay out** (*pt.* **payed out**) to let out (a rope, cable, etc.) —**pay up** to pay in full or on time —**pay'er** *n.*

pay'a·ble *adj.* **1.** that can be paid **2.** that is to be paid (on a specified date); due

pay'check' *n.* a check in payment of wages, etc.

pay'day' *n.* the day on which wages, etc. are paid

pay dirt soil, ore, etc. rich enough in minerals to make mining profitable

pay·ee (pā ē') *n.* one to whom a check, note, money, etc. is payable

pay'load' *n.* **1.** a cargo **2.** the warhead of a ballistic missile, the spacecraft launched by a rocket, etc.

pay'mas'ter *n.* the official in charge of paying employees —**pay'mis'tress** *n.fem.*

pay'ment *n.* **1.** a paying or being paid **2.** something paid **3.** penalty or reward

pay'off' *n.* **1.** settlement, reckoning, or payment **2.** [Colloq.] a bribe **3.** [Colloq.] an unexpected climax

pay·o·la (pā ō'lə) *n.* [Slang] a bribe, as to a disc jockey for promoting a song unfairly

pay phone (or **station**) a public telephone, usually coin-operated

pay'roll' *n.* **1.** a list of employees to be paid, with the amount due each **2.** the total amount needed for this

Pb [L. *plumbum*] *Chem.* lead

PBX, P.B.X. [< *p*(*rivate*) *b*(*ranch*) *ex*(*change*)] a telephone system within an organization, having outside lines

p.c. percent: also **pct.**

pd. paid

pea (pē) *n., pl.* **peas**, archaic **pease** [< ME. *pese*, a pea, mistaken as *pl.*; ult. < Gr. *pison*] **1.** a climbing plant with green seed pods **2.** its small, round seed, eaten as a vegetable

peace (pēs) *n.* [< L. *pax*] **1.** freedom from war **2.** an agreement to end war **3.** law and order **4.** harmony; concord **5.** serenity, calm, or quiet —**hold (or keep) one's peace** to be silent — **peace'a·ble** *adj.*

peace'ful *adj.* **1.** not quarrelsome **2.** free from disturbance; calm —**peace'ful·ly** *adv.*

peace'mak'er *n.* one who makes peace, as by settling the quarrels of others

peace'time' *n.* a time of peace —*adj.* of or characteristic of such a time

peach (pēch) *n.* [< L. *Persicum* (*malum*), Persian (apple)] **1.** a tree with round, juicy, orange-yellow fruit having a fuzzy skin and a rough pit **2.** its fruit **3.** the color of this fruit **4.** [Slang] any person or thing well liked

pea·cock (pē'käk') *n.* [< L. *pavo*, peacock] the male of a pheasantlike bird (**pea'fowl'**), with a long, showy tail which can be spread out like a fan —**pea'hen'** *n.fem.*

pea jacket [< Du. *pijjekker*] a short, heavy woolen coat, worn by seamen: also **pea'coat'**

peak (pēk) *n.* [var. of *pike* (summit)] **1.** a pointed end or top, as of a cap, roof, etc. **2.** *a*) the summit of a mountain ending in a point *b*) a mountain with such a summit **3.** the highest point of anything —*vt., vi.* to come or bring to a peak

peak·ed (pē'kid) *adj.* [< ?] thin and drawn, as from illness

peal (pēl) *n.* [< ME. *apele*, appeal] **1.** the loud ringing of a bell or bells **2.** a set of bells **3.** a loud, prolonged sound, as of gunfire, laughter, etc. —*vt., vi.* to ring or resound

pea·nut *n.* **1.** a vine of the legume family, with underground pods containing edible seeds **2.** the pod or its seed

peanut butter a paste or spread made by grinding roasted peanuts

pear (per) *n.* [< L. *pirum*] **1.** a tree with soft, juicy fruit, round at the base and narrowing toward the stem **2.** this fruit

pearl (purl) *n.* [ult. < L. *perna*, a sea mussel] **1.** a smooth, hard, usually white or bluish-gray, roundish growth formed within the shell of some oysters and other mollusks: it is used as a gem **2.** *same as* MOTHER-OF-PEARL **3.** anything pearllike in shape, beauty, value, etc. **4.** bluish gray —**pearl'y** *adj.* **-i·er, -i·est**

peas·ant (pez''nt) *n.* [< LL. *pagus*, district] a small farmer or farm laborer, as in Europe or Asia —**peas'ant·ry** *n.*

peat (pēt) *n.* [< ML. *peta*, piece of turf] partly decayed plant matter found in ancient swamps, dried and used for fuel

peat moss peat composed of residues of mosses, used as a mulch

peb·ble (peb''l) *n.* [< OE. *papol(stan)*, pebble (stone)] a small stone worn smooth and round, as by running water —**peb'bly** *adj.*

pe·can (pi kan', -kän') *n.* [< AmInd.] **1.** an olive-shaped, edible nut with a thin shell **2.** the N. American tree on which it grows

pec·ca·dil·lo (pek'ə dil'ō) *n., pl.* **-loes, -los** [Sp. < L. *peccare*, to sin] a small fault or offense

pec·ca·ry (pek'ər ē) *n., pl.* **-ries** [< SAmInd. name] a piglike animal of N. and S. America, with sharp tusks

peck¹ (pek) *vt.* [< ME. *picken*, to pick] **1.** to strike, as with a beak **2.** to make by doing this *[to peck a hole]* **3.** to pick up or get by pecking —*vi.* to make strokes as with a beak —*n.* **1.** a stroke made as with a beak **2.** [Colloq.] a quick, casual kiss —**peck at** [Colloq.] to eat very little of

peck² (pek) *n.* [< OFr. *pek*] **1.** a unit of dry measure equal to 1/4 bushel, or 8 quarts **2.** [Colloq.] a large amount, as of trouble

pec·tin (pek'tin) *n.* [< Gr. *pēktos*, congealed] a carbohydrate obtained from certain fruits, which yields a gel that is the basis of jellies and jams

pec·to·ral (pek'tər əl) *adj.* [< L. *pectus*, breast] of or located in or on the chest or breast —*n.* a pectoral muscle

pec·u·late (pek'yə lāt') *vt., vi.* **-lat'ed, -lat'ing** [< L. *peculari*] to embezzle

pe·cu·liar (pi kyōōl'yər) *adj.* [< L. *peculium*, private property] **1.** of only one person, thing,

etc.; exclusive **2.** particular; special **3.** odd; strange —**pe·cul'iar·ly** *adv.*

pe·cu·li·ar·i·ty (pi kyōō'lē ar'ə tē) *n.* **1.** a being peculiar **2.** *pl.* **-ties** something that is peculiar, as a trait

pe·cu·ni·ar·y (pi kyōō'nē er'ē) *adj.* [< L. *pecunia*, money] of or involving money

ped·a·gogue, ped·a·gog (ped'ə gäg', -gôg') *n.* [< Gr. *pais*, child + *agein*, to lead] a teacher; often specif., a pedantic teacher

ped'a·go'gy (-gō'jē, -gäj'ē) *n.* the art or science of teaching —**ped'a·gog'ic** (-gäj'ik), **ped'a·gog'i·cal** *adj.* —**ped'a·gog'i·cal·ly** *adv.*

ped·al (ped''l) *adj.* [< L. *pes*, foot] of the foot or feet —*n.* a lever operated by the foot, as on a bicycle, organ, etc. —*vt., vi.* **-aled** or **-alled, -al·ing** or **-al·ling** to operate by pedals; use the pedals (of)

ped·ant (ped''nt) *n.* [< Fr. < It., ult. < Gr. *paidagōgos*, teacher] **1.** one who emphasizes trivial points of learning **2.** a narrow-minded teacher who insists on exact adherence to rules —**pe·dan·tic** (pi dan'tik) *adj.* —**pe·dan'ti·cal·ly** *adv.* —**ped'ant·ry** *n.*

ped·dle (ped''l) *vi., vt.* **-dled, -dling** [< ? ME. *ped*, basket] to go from place to place selling (small articles) —**ped'dler, ped'lar** *n.*

-pede [< L. *pes*, foot] *a combining form meaning* foot or feet *[centipede]*

ped·es·tal (ped'is t'l) *n.* [< Fr. < It. *piè*, foot + *di*, of + *stal*, a rest] the bottom support of a column, statue, etc.

pe·des·tri·an (pə des'trē ən) *adj.* [< L. *pes*, foot] **1.** going or done on foot **2.** for pedestrians **3.** ordinary and dull; prosaic —*n.* a walker —**pe·des'tri·an·ism** *n.*

pe·di·at·rics (pē'dē at'riks) *n.pl. [with sing. v.]* [< Gr. *pais*, child + -IATRICS] the branch of medicine dealing with the care of infants and children —**ped'di·at'ric** *adj.* —**pe'di·a·tri'cian** (-ə trish'ən) *n.*

ped·i·cab (ped'i kab') *n.* [< L. *pes*, foot + CAB] a three-wheeled carriage, esp. in SE Asia, pedaled by the driver

ped·i·cure (ped'i kyoor') *n.* [< Fr. < L. *pes*, foot + *cura*, care] a trimming, cleaning, etc. of the toenails

ped·i·gree (ped'ə grē') *n.* [< MFr. *pie de grue*, crane's foot: from lines in genealogical tree] **1.** a list of ancestors **2.** descent; lineage **3.** a recorded line of descent, esp. of a purebred animal —**ped'i·greed'** *adj.*

ped·i·ment (ped'ə mənt) *n.* [< earlier *periment*, prob. < PYRAMID] an ornamental gable or triangular piece on the front of a building, over a doorway, etc.

pe·dom·e·ter (pi däm'ə tər) *n.* [< L. *pes*, foot + Gr. *metron*, a measure] an instrument carried to measure the distance walked

peek (pēk) *vi.* [< ?] to glance or look quickly and furtively, as through an opening —*n.* such a glance

peel (pēl) *vt.* [< L. *pilare*, make bald] to cut away (the skin, rind, etc.) of —*vi.* **1.** to shed skin, etc. **2.** to come off, as old paint —*n.* the rind or skin of fruit —**peel off** *Aeron.* to veer away from a flight formation abruptly —**peel'er** *n.*

peel·ing *n.* a rind, etc. peeled off

peep¹ (pēp) *vi.* [echoic] to make the short, high-pitched cry of a young bird —*n.* a peeping sound —**peep'er** *n.*

peep² (pēp) *vi.* [ME. *pepen*] **1.** to look through a small opening or from a place of hiding **2.** to show gradually or partially —*n.* a brief look; furtive glimpse —**peep'er** *n.*

peep'hole' *n.* a hole to peep through

peeping Tom [< the legendary English tailor who peeped at Lady Godiva] one who gets sexual pleasure from furtively watching others

peer¹ (pir) *n.* [< L. *par*, equal] 1. one that has the same rank, value, etc.; specif., an equal before the law 2. a British noble —**peer′age** (-ij) *n.* —**peer′ess** *n.fem.*

peer² (pir) *vi.* [< ? APPEAR] 1. to look closely, as in trying to see more clearly 2. to show slightly

peer′less *adj.* without equal

peeve (pēv) *vt.* **peeved, peev′ing** [< ff.] [Colloq.] to make peevish —*n.* [Colloq.] an annoyance

pee′vish *adj.* [< ?] irritable; fretful; cross

pee-wee (pē′wē′) *n.* [prob. < WEE] [Colloq.] an unusually small person or thing

peg (peg) *n.* [ME. *pegge*] 1. a short pin or bolt used to hold parts together, hang things on, mark the score of a game, etc. 2. a step or degree —*vt.* **pegged, peg′ging** 1. to fasten, secure, mark, etc. as with pegs 2. to maintain (prices, etc.) at a fixed level 3. [Colloq.] to throw (a ball) —**peg away (at)** to work steadily (at)

Peg·a·sus (peg′ə səs) 1. *Gr. Myth.* a winged horse 2. a northern constellation

peign·oir (pān wär′, pān′wär; pen-) *n.* [Fr. < L. *pecten*, a comb] a short negligee

pe·jo·ra·tion (pē′jə rā′shən, pej′ə-) *n.* [< L. *pejor*, worse] a worsening —**pe·jo·ra·tive** (pi jôr′ə tiv) *adj., n.*

Pe·king·ese (pē′kə nēz′) *n., pl.* -**ese′** a small dog with long, silky hair, short legs, and a pug nose: also **Pe′kin·ese′**

pe·koe (pē′kō) *n.* [< Chin. *pek-ho*, white down (on the young leaves used)] a black, small-leaved tea of Sri Lanka and India

pe·lag·ic (pi laj′ik) *adj.* [< Gr. *pelagos*, sea] of the open sea or ocean

pelf (pelf) *n.* [akin to MFr. *pelfre*, booty] 1. orig., booty 2. wealth regarded with contempt

pel·i·can (pel′i kən) *n.* [< Gr. *pelekan*] a large water bird with webbed feet and an expandable pouch in the lower bill for scooping up fish

pel·la·gra (pə lag′rə, -lā′grə) *n.* [It. < *pelle*, skin + *-agra* < Gr. *agra*, seizure] a chronic disease caused by a deficiency of niacin in the diet and characterized by skin eruptions and mental disorders

pel·let (pel′ət) *n.* [< L. *pila*, a ball] 1. a little ball, as of clay or medicine 2. a bullet, small lead shot, etc.

pell-mell, pell·mell (pel′mel′) *adv., adj.* [< Fr. < OFr. *mesler*, to mix] 1. in a confused mass or manner 2. in reckless haste

pel·lu·cid (pə lōō′sid) *adj.* [< L. *per*, through + *lucere*, to shine] 1. transparent; clear 2. clear and simple in style

pelt¹ (pelt) *vt.* [? ult. < L. *pillare*, to drive] 1. to throw things at 2. to beat repeatedly 3. to throw (missiles) —*vi.* to strike heavily or steadily, as hard rain

pelt² (pelt) *n.* [prob. < OFr. *pel*, a skin] the skin of a fur-bearing animal, esp. when stripped from the carcass

pel·vis (pel′vis) *n., pl.* -**vis·es, -ves** (-vēz) [L., a basin] 1. the basinlike cavity in the posterior part of the trunk in man and many other vertebrates 2. the bones forming this cavity — **pel′vic** *adj.*

pem·mi·can (pem′i kən) *n.* [< AmInd.] a concentrated food of dried beef, suet, raisins, etc.

pen¹ (pen) *n.* [OE.] a small enclosure, as for domestic animals —*vt.* **penned** or **pent, pen′ning** to enclose as in a pen

pen² (pen) *n.* [< L. *penna*, feather] 1. a device used in writing or drawing with ink, often

with a metal point split into two nibs 2. the metal point —*vt.* **penned, pen′ning** to write as with a pen

pen³ (pen) *n.* [Slang] a penitentiary

pe·nal (pē′n′l) *adj.* [< L. *poena*, punishment] of, for, constituting, or deserving punishment —**pe′nal·ly** *adv.*

pe·nal·ize (pē′n′l īz′, pen′′l-) *vt.* -**ized′, -iz′ing** to impose a penalty on; punish

pen·al·ty (pen′′l tē) *n., pl.* -**ties** 1. punishment 2. the handicap, fine, etc. imposed on an offender 3. *Sports* a loss of yardage, etc. imposed for breaking a rule

pen·ance (pen′əns) *n.* [see PENITENT] voluntary self-punishment, reparation, etc. to show repentance for wrongdoing

pence (pens) *n.* [Brit.] *pl. of* PENNY

pen·chant (pen′chənt) *n.* [Fr. < L. *pendere*, hang] a strong liking; inclination

pen·cil (pen′s′l) *n.* [< L. *penis*, tail] a pointed, rod-shaped instrument with a core of graphite or crayon, used for writing, drawing, etc. —*vt.* -**ciled** or -**cilled, -cil·ing** or -**cil·ling** to write, draw, etc. as with a pencil

pend (pend) *vi.* [< L. *pendere*, hang] to await judgment or decision

pend·ant (pen′dənt) *n.* [see prec.] 1. an ornamental hanging object, as an earring 2. a decorative piece suspended from a ceiling or a roof —*adj. same as* PENDENT

pend·ent (pen′dənt) *adj.* [see PEND] 1. suspended 2. overhanging 3. undecided; pending —*n. same as* PENDANT

pend′ing *adj.* 1. not decided 2. impending —*prep.* 1. during 2. while awaiting; until

pen·du·lous (pen′joo ləs) *adj.* [see PEND] 1. hanging freely 2. drooping

pen′du·lum (-ləm) *n.* [see PEND] a body hung from a fixed point so that it can swing freely to and fro: often used to regulate clock movements

Pe·nel·o·pe (pə nel′ə pē) Odysseus's wife, who waited faithfully for his return

pen·e·trate (pen′ə trāt′) *vt., vi.* -**trat′ed, -trat′ing** [< L. *penitus*, inward] 1. to enter by piercing 2. to have an effect throughout 3. to affect deeply 4. to understand —**pen′e·tra′tion** *n.*

pen′e·trat′ing *adj.* 1. sharp; piercing 2. acute; discerning Also **pen′e·tra′tive**

pen·guin (peŋ′gwin) *n.* [prob. < W.] a flightless bird of the S Hemisphere with webbed feet and paddlelike flippers for swimming

pen·i·cil·lin (pen′ə sil′in) *n.* [< L. *penicillus*, brush] an antibiotic obtained from certain molds or produced synthetically

pen·in·su·la (pə nin′sə lə, -syoo-) *n.* [< L. *paene*, almost + *insula*, isle] a land area almost entirely surrounded by water —**pen·in′su·lar** *adj.*

pe·nis (pē′nis) *n., pl.* -**nis·es, -nes** (-nēz) [L., a tail] the male organ of sexual intercourse

pen·i·tent (pen′ə tənt) *adj.* [< L. *paenitere*, repent] sorry for having done wrong and willing to atone —*n.* a penitent person —**pen′i·tence** *n.* —**pen′i·ten′tial** (-ten′shəl) *adj.* —**pen′i·tent·ly** *adv.*

pen·i·ten·tia·ry (pen′ə ten′shə rē) *adj.* making one liable to imprisonment in a penitentiary — *n., pl.* -**ries** a State or Federal prison for persons convicted of serious crimes

pen′knife′ (-nīf′) *n., pl.* -**knives′** (-nīvz′) a small pocketknife

pen′man (-mən) *n., pl.* -**men** 1. one skilled in penmanship 2. an author

pen′man·ship′ (-ship) *n.* 1. handwriting as an art or skill 2. a style of handwriting

pen name a pseudonym

pen·nant (pen′ənt) *n.* [< PENNON] **1.** any long, narrow flag **2.** such a flag symbolizing a championship, as in baseball

pen·ni·less (pen′i lis) *adj.* without even a penny; extremely poor

pen·non (pen′ən) *n.* [< L. *penna*, feather] **1.** a flag or pennant **2.** a pinion; wing

pen·ny (pen′ē) *n., pl.* **-nies;** for 1 (esp. collectively) **pence** [< OE. *pening*] **1.** in the United Kingdom, *a)* formerly, 1/12 shilling *b)* a 1/100 part of a pound: in full **new penny 2.** a U.S. or Canadian cent —**a pretty penny** [Colloq.] a large sum of money

pen′ny·weight′ *n.* a unit of weight equal to 1/20 ounce troy weight

pe·nol·o·gy (pē näl′ə jē) *n.* [< Gr. *poinē*, penalty + -LOGY] the study of prison management and reform —**pe·nol′o·gist** *n.*

pen·sion (pen′shən) *n.* [< L. *pensio*, a paying] a regular payment, not wages, to one who is retired or disabled —*vt.* to grant a pension to — **pen′sion·er** *n.*

pen·sive (pen′siv) *adj.* [< L. *pensare*, consider] thinking deeply, often of sad or melancholy things —**pen′sive·ly** *adv.*

pent (pent) *alt. pt. & pp. of* PEN[1] —*adj.* held or kept in; penned (often with *up*)

penta- [< Gr. *pente*, five] *a combining form meaning* five: also **pent-**

pen·ta·cle (pen′tə k'l) *n.* [< prec.] a five-pointed star formerly used as a symbol in magic: also **pen′ta·gram′** (-gram′)

pen·ta·gon (pen′tə gän′) *n.* [< Gr.: see PENTA- & -GON] a plane figure with five angles and five sides —**the Pentagon** the pentagonal office building of the Defense Department, near Washington, D.C. —**pen·tag′o·nal** (-tag′ə n'l) *adj.*

pen·tam·e·ter (pen tam′ə tər) *n.* [see PENTA- & -METER] a line of verse containing five metrical feet

Pen·ta·teuch (pen′tə tōōk′) *n.* [< Gr. *pente*, five + *teuchos*, book] the first five books of the Bible

Pen·te·cost (pen′tə kôst′, -käst′) *n.* [< Gr. *pentēkostē* (*hēmera*), the fiftieth (day)] a Christian festival on the seventh Sunday after Easter —**Pen′te·cos′tal** *adj.*

pent·house (pent′hous′) *n.* [< L. *appendere*, append] a house or apartment on the roof of a building

pe·nu·che, pe·nu·chi (pə nōō′chē) *n.* [< AmSp. *panocha*, ult. < L. *panis*, bread] a fudgelike candy made of brown sugar, etc.

pe·nu·ri·ous (pə nyoor′ē əs, -noor′-) *adj.* **1.** miserly; stingy **2.** destitute

pen·u·ry (pen′yə rē) *n.* [< L. *penuria*, want] destitution; extreme poverty

pe·on (pē′än, -ən) *n.* [< Sp. < ML. *pedo*, foot soldier] **1.** in Latin America, a person of the laboring class **2.** an exploited laborer —**pe′on·age** (-ə nij) *n.*

pe·o·ny (pē′ə nē) *n., pl.* **-nies** [< Gr. *Paiōn*, Apollo as god of medicine: from its former medicinal use] **1.** a plant with large pink, white, red, or yellow, showy flowers **2.** the flower

peo·ple (pē′p'l) *n., pl.* **-ple;** for 1 **-ples** [< L. *populus*, nation] **1.** all the persons of a racial or ethnic group; nation, race, etc. **2.** the persons of a certain place, group, or class **3.** the persons under the leadership or control of a particular person or body **4.** one's relatives; family **5.** the populace **6.** persons considered indefinitely [what will *people* say?] —*vt.* **-pled, -pling** to populate

pep (pep) *n.* [< PEPPER] [Colloq.] energy; vigor

—*vt.* **pepped, pep′ping** [Colloq.] to fill with pep; invigorate (with *up*) —**pep′py** *adj.* **-pi·er, -pi·est** —**pep′pi·ness** *n.*

pep·per (pep′ər) *n.* [< Gr. *peperi*] **1.** *a)* a pungent condiment ground from the dried fruits of an East Indian plant *b)* this plant **2.** the fruit of the red pepper plant, red, yellow, or green, sweet or hot —*vt.* **1.** to season with ground pepper **2.** to pelt with small objects

pep′per·corn′ *n.* the dried berry of the black pepper

pep′per·mint′ *n.* **1.** a plant related to the mint that yields a pungent oil used in flavoring **2.** the oil **3.** a candy flavored with this oil

pep·per·o·ni (pep′ə rō′nē) *n., pl.* **-nis, -ni** [< It. *peperoni*] a highly spiced Italian sausage

pep′per·y *adj.* **-i·er, -i·est 1.** of, like, or highly seasoned with pepper **2.** sharp or fiery, as words **3.** hot-tempered

pep·sin (pep′s'n) *n.* [G. < Gr. *peptein*, to digest] a stomach enzyme, aiding in the digestion of proteins

pep·tic (-tik) *adj.* **1.** of or aiding digestion **2.** caused by digestive secretions [a *peptic* ulcer]

per (pur, pər) *prep.* [L.] **1.** through; by; by means of **2.** for each [fifty cents *per* yard]

per- [< L. *per*, through] *a prefix meaning:* **1.** through, throughout **2.** thoroughly, very

Per. 1. Persia **2.** Persian

per·ad·ven·ture (pur′əd ven′chər) *adv.* [< OFr. *par*, by + *aventure*, chance] [Archaic] **1.** possibly **2.** by chance —*n.* [Archaic] chance

per·am·bu·late (pər am′byoo lāt′) *vt., vi.* **-lat′ed, -lat′ing** [< L. *per*, through + *ambulare*, to walk] to walk (through, over, etc.) — **per·am′bu·la′tion** *n.*

per·am′bu·la′tor (-lāt′ər) *n.* [Chiefly Brit.] a baby carriage

per an·num (pər an′əm) [L.] by the year; yearly

per·cale (pər kāl′) *n.* [Fr. < Per.] closely woven cotton cloth, used for sheets, etc.

per cap·i·ta (pər kap′ə tə) [ML., lit., by heads] for each person

per·ceive (pər sēv′) *vt., vi.* **-ceived′, -ceiv′ing** [< L. *per*, through + *capere*, take] **1.** to grasp mentally **2.** to become aware (of) through the senses —**per·ceiv′a·ble** *adj.*

per·cent (pər sent′) *adv., adj.* [< It. < L. *per centum*] in, to, or for every hundred: symbol, %: also **per cent** —*n.* [Colloq.] percentage

per·cent·age (-ij) *n.* **1.** a given part in every hundred **2.** part; portion

per·cen·tile (pər sen′til, -sent′'l) *n.* Statistics any of 100 divisions of a series, each of equal frequency

per·cep·ti·ble (pər sep′tə b'l) *adj.* that can be perceived —**per·cep′ti·bly** *adv.*

per·cep·tion (-shən) *n.* **1.** the mental grasp of objects, etc. through the senses **2.** insight **3.** knowledge, etc. gained by perceiving

per·cep′tive *adj.* **1.** of or capable of perception **2.** able to perceive quickly

perch[1] (purch) *n., pl.* **perch, perch′es** [< Gr. *perkē*] **1.** a small, spiny-finned, freshwater food fish **2.** a similar marine fish

perch[2] (purch) *n.* [< L. *pertica*, pole] **1.** a horizontal pole, branch, etc. serving as a roost for birds **2.** any high resting place **3.** a measure of length, equal to 5 1/2 yards —*vt., vi.* to rest or place on or as on a perch

per·chance (pər chans′) *adv.* [< OFr. *par*, by + *chance*, chance] [Archaic] **1.** by chance **2.** perhaps

per·cip·i·ent (pər sip′ē ənt) *adj.* perceiving, esp. keenly —*n.* one who perceives

per·co·late (pur′kə lāt′) *vt.* **-lat′ed, -lat′ing** [<

L. *per*, through + *colare*, to strain] **1.** to pass (a liquid) through a porous substance; filter **2.** to brew (coffee) in a percolator —*vi.* to ooze through a porous substance —**per'co·la'tion** *n.*

per·co·la·tor *n.* a coffeepot in which boiling water bubbles up through a tube and filters back down through ground coffee

per·cus·sion (pər kush'ən) *n.* [< L. *percutere*, to strike] the hitting of one body against another, as the hammer of a firearm against a powder cap (**percussion cap**)

percussion instrument a musical instrument producing a tone when struck, as a drum, cymbal, etc.

per di·em (pər dē'əm, dī'-) [L.] daily

per·di·tion (pər dish'ən) *n.* [< L. *perdere*, lose] *Theol.* **1.** the loss of the soul **2.** *same as* HELL

per·e·gri·nate (per'ə gri nāt') *vt.*, *vi.* -**nat'ed**, -**nat'ing** [see PILGRIM] to travel, esp. walk (through) —**per'e·gri·na'tion** *n.*

per·e·grine (**falcon**) (per'ə grin, -grēn') [see prec.] a very swift European falcon

per·emp·to·ry (pə remp'tər ē) *adj.* [< L. *perimere*, destroy] **1.** *Law* barring further action; final **2.** that cannot be denied, delayed, etc., as a command **3.** imperious; dogmatic —**per·emp'·to·ri·ness** *n.*

per·en·ni·al (pə ren'ē əl) *adj.* [< L. *per*, through + *annus*, year] **1.** lasting throughout the whole year **2.** continuing for a long time **3.** living more than two years: said of plants —*n.* a perennial plant

per·fect (pur'fikt; *for v. usually* pər fekt') *adj.* [< L. *per*, through + *facere*, to do] **1.** complete in all respects; flawless **2.** excellent, as in skill or quality **3.** completely accurate; exact **4.** utter; absolute *[a perfect fool]* **5.** *Gram.* expressing a state or action completed at the time of speaking —*vt.* **1.** to complete **2.** to make perfect or nearly perfect —*n.* **1.** the perfect tense **2.** a verb form in this tense —**per'·fect·ly** *adv.*

per·fec·tion (pər fek'shən) *n.* **1.** the act of perfecting **2.** a being perfect **3.** a person or thing that is the perfect embodiment of some quality —**to perfection** perfectly

per·fec'tion·ist *n.* one who strives for perfection

per·fi·dy (pur'fə dē) *n.*, *pl.* -**dies** [< Fr. < L. *per*, through + *fides*, faith] betrayal of trust; treachery —**per·fid·i·ous** (pər fid'ē əs) *adj.*

per·fo·rate (pur'fə rāt') *vt.*, *vi.* -**rat'ed**, -**rat'ing** [< L. *per*, through + *forare*, bore] **1.** to make a hole or holes through **2.** to pierce with holes in a row, as a pattern, computer tape, sheet of postage stamps, etc. —**per'fo·ra'tion** *n.*

per·force (pər fôrs') *adv.* [< OFr.: see PER & FORCE] of necessity; necessarily

per·form (pər fôrm') *vt.* [< OFr.] **1.** to do (a task, etc.) **2.** to fulfill (a promise, etc.) **3.** to render or enact (a piece of music, dramatic role, etc.) —*vi.* to execute an action or process; esp., to dance, act in a play, etc. —**per·form'er** *n.*

per·form'ance *n.* **1.** the act of performing **2.** functional effectiveness **3.** a deed or feat **4.** *a)* a formal exhibition or presentation, as a play *b)* one's part in this

per·fume (pər fyōōm') *vt.* -**fumed'**, -**fum'ing** [< L. *per*-, intens. + *fumare*, to smoke] to scent with perfume —*n.* (*usually* pur'fyōōm) **1.** a sweet scent; fragrance **2.** a substance producing a pleasing odor; esp., a volatile oil extracted from flowers

per·fum'er·y (-ər ē) *n.*, *pl.* -**ies** **1.** perfumes collectively **2.** a place where perfume is made or sold

per·func·to·ry (pər fuŋk'tər ē) *adj.* [< L. *per*-, intens. + *fungi*, to perform] **1.** done merely as a routine; superficial **2.** without concern; indifferent —**per·func'to·ri·ly** *adv.*

per·go·la (pur'gə lə) *n.* [It. < L. *pergula*] an arbor with a latticework roof

per·haps (pər haps') *adv.* [PER- + pl. of *hap*, chance] possibly; maybe

peri- [< Gr. *peri*] *a prefix meaning:* **1.** around; about *[periscope]* **2.** near *[perigee]*

per·i·gee (per'ə jē') *n.* [< Fr. < Gr. *peri*-, near + *gē*, earth] the point nearest the moon, the earth, or another planet, in the orbit of a satellite or spacecraft around it

per·i·he·li·on (per'ə hē'lē ən) *n.*, *pl.* -**li·ons**, -**li·a** (-ə) [< Gr. *peri*-, around + *hēlios*, the sun] the point nearest the sun in the orbit around it of a planet, comet, or man-made satellite

per·il (per'əl) *n.* [< L. *periculum*, danger] **1.** exposure to harm or injury **2.** something that may cause harm —*vt.* -**iled** or -**illed**, -**il·ing** or -**il·ling** to expose to danger

per'il·ous *adj.* involving peril or risk; dangerous —**per'il·ous·ly** *adv.*

pe·rim·e·ter (pə rim'ə tər) *n.* [< Gr. *peri*-, around + *metron*, a measure] **1.** the outer boundary of a figure or area **2.** the total length of this

pe·ri·od (pir'ē əd) *n.* [< Gr. *periodos*, cycle] **1.** the interval between successive occurrences of an event **2.** a portion of time characterized by certain processes, etc. *[a period of change]* **3.** any of the portions of time into which a game, school day, etc. is divided **4.** the menses **5.** an end or conclusion **6.** *a)* the pause in speaking or a mark of punctuation (.) used at the end of a sentence *b)* the dot (.) following many abbreviations

pe·ri·od·ic (pir'ē äd'ik) *adj.* **1.** appearing or recurring at regular intervals **2.** intermittent

pe'ri·od'i·cal *adj.* **1.** periodic **2.** published at regular intervals, as monthly, etc. —*n.* a periodical publication

per·i·o·don·tal (per'ē ə dän't'l) *adj.* [< PERI- + Gr. *odōn*, tooth] occurring around a tooth or affecting the gums

per·i·pa·tet·ic (per'i pə tet'ik) *adj.* [< Fr. < Gr. *peri*-, around + *patein*, to walk] **1.** [P-] of the philosophy or followers of Aristotle **2.** walking or moving about; itinerant

pe·riph·er·y (pə rif'ər ē) *n.*, *pl.* -**ies** [< Gr. *peri*-, around + *pherein*, to bear] **1.** an outer boundary, esp. of a rounded figure **2.** surrounding space —**pe·riph'er·al** *adj.*

pe·riph·ra·sis (pə rif'rə sis) *n.*, *pl.* -**ses'** (-sēz') [< Gr. *peri*-, around + *phrazein*, speak] the use of many words where a few would do

per·i·scope (per'ə skōp') *n.* [PERI- + -SCOPE] an optical instrument that allows one to see around or over an obstacle: used on submarines, etc.

per·ish (per'ish) *vi.* [< L. *per*-, intens. + *ire*, go] **1.** to be destroyed or ruined **2.** to die, esp. violently

per'ish·a·ble *adj.* that may perish; esp., liable to spoil, as some foods

per·i·to·ne·um (per'it 'n ē'əm) *n.*, *pl.* -**ne'a** (-ə), -**ne'ums** [< Gr. *peri*-, around + *teinein*, to stretch] the serous membrane lining the abdominal cavity

per·i·to·ni·tis (per'it 'n īt'əs) *n.* inflammation of the peritoneum

per·i·wig (per'ə wig') *n.* [< Fr. *perruque*] a wig worn by men in the 17th & 18th cent.

per·i·win·kle (per'ə wiŋ'k'l) *n.* [< L.

pervinca] a creeping plant with blue, white, or pink flowers

per·i·win·kle² (per'ə wiŋ'k'l) *n.* [OE. *pinewincle*] a small saltwater snail with a thick, cone-shaped shell

per·jure (pur'jər) *vt.* **-jured, -jur·ing** [< L. *per,* through + *jurare,* swear] to make (oneself) guilty of perjury —**per'jur·er** *n.*

per'ju·ry (-jər ē) *n., pl.* **-ries** [< L. *perjurus,* false] the willful telling of a lie while under oath

perk (purk) *vt.* [ME. *perken*] **1.** to raise (the head, ears, etc.) briskly **2.** to make smart in appearance (often with *up*) —*vi.* to become lively (with *up*) —**perk'y** *adj.* **-i·er, -i·est** — **perk'i·ness** *n.*

per·ma·frost (pur'mə frôst', -fräst') *n.* [PERMA(NENT) + FROST] permanently frozen subsoil

per·ma·nent (pur'mə nənt) *adj.* [< L. *per,* through + *manere,* remain] lasting or intended to last indefinitely or for a long time — *n.* a permanent wave —**per'ma·nence** *n.* —**per'ma·nent·ly** *adv.*

permanent wave a long-lasting hair wave produced by use of chemicals or heat

per·me·a·ble (pur'mē ə b'l) *adj.* that can be permeated, as by fluids —**per'me·a·bil'i·ty** *n.*

per·me·ate (pur'mē āt') *vt., vi.* **-at'ed, -at'ing** [< L. *per,* through + *meare,* to glide] to spread or diffuse; penetrate (*through* or *among*) —**per'me·a'tion** *n.*

per·mis·si·ble (pər mis'ə b'l) *adj.* that can be permitted —**per·mis'si·bly** *adv.*

per·mis·sion (pər mish'ən) *n.* the act of permitting; esp., formal consent

per·mis·sive (pər mis'iv) *adj.* allowing freedom; lenient —**per·mis'sive·ness** *n.*

per·mit (pər mit') *vt.* **-mit'ted, -mit'ting** [< L. *per,* through + *mittere,* send] **1.** to allow to be done; consent to **2.** to allow [*permit* me to go] —*vi.* to give opportunity [if time *permits*] —*n.* (usually pur'mit) a document granting permission; license

per·mu·ta·tion (pur'myoo tā'shən) *n.* **1.** any radical alteration **2.** *Math.* any of the total number of groupings into which a group of elements can be arranged

per·ni·cious (pər nish'əs) *adj.* [< Fr. < L. *per,* thoroughly + *necare,* kill] causing great injury, destruction, etc.; deadly

per·o·ra·tion (per'ə rā'shən) *n.* [< L. *per,* through + *orare,* speak] the concluding part of a speech, including a summing up

per·ox·ide (pə räk'sid) *n.* [PER- + OXIDE] any oxide containing the oxygen (O_2) group linked by a single bond; specif., hydrogen peroxide — *vt.* **-id·ed, -id·ing** to bleach with hydrogen peroxide

per·pen·dic·u·lar (pur'pən dik'yə lər) *adj.* [< L. *perpendiculum,* plumb line] **1.** at right angles to a given line or plane **2.** exactly upright; vertical —*n.* a line at right angles to another line or plane

per·pe·trate (pur'pə trāt') *vt.* **-trat'ed, -trat'ing** [< L. *per,* thoroughly + *patrare,* to effect] **1.** to do (something evil, criminal, etc.) **2.** to commit (a blunder), impose (a hoax), etc. —**per'pe·tra'tion** *n.* —**per'pe·tra'tor** *n.*

per·pet·u·al (pər pech'oo wəl) *adj.* [< L. *perpetuus,* constant] **1.** lasting forever or for a very long time **2.** continuing without interruption; constant —**per·pet'u·al·ly** *adv.*

per·pet'u·ate (-wāt') *vt.* **-at'ed, -at'ing** to make perpetual; cause to continue or be remembered —**per·pet'u·a'tion** *n.*

per·pe·tu·i·ty (pur'pə tōō'ə tē, -tyōō'-) *n.* un-

limited time; eternity —**in perpetuity** forever

per·plex (pər pleks') *vt.* [< L. *per,* through + *plectere,* to twist] to make (a person) uncertain, hesitant, etc.; confuse —**per·plex'ing** *adj.* —**per·plex'i·ty** *n.*

per·qui·site (pur'kwə zit) *n.* [< L. *per-,* intens. + *quaerere,* seek] **1.** something in addition to one's regular pay for one's work, as a tip **2.** a privilege or benefit

per se (pur' sē', sā') [L.] by (or in) itself; intrinsically

per·se·cute (pur'sə kyōot') *vt.* **-cut'ed, -cut'ing** [< L. *per,* through + *sequi,* follow] to afflict constantly so as to injure or distress, esp. for reasons of religion, race, etc. —**per'se·cu'tion** *n.* —**per'se·cu'tor** *n.*

Per·seph·o·ne (pər sef'ə nē) *Gr. Myth.* the daughter of Demeter, abducted by Pluto to be his wife

Per·seus (pur'syōos, -sē əs) *Gr. Myth.* a son of Zeus and the slayer of Medusa

per·se·vere (pur'sə vir') *vi.* **-vered', -ver'ing** [< L. *per-,* intens. + *severus,* severe] to continue doing something in spite of difficulty, opposition, etc.; persist —**per'se·ver'ance** *n.*

Per·sian (pur'zhən) *adj.* of Persia, its people, language, etc.; Iranian —*n.* the Iranian language of the Persians

Persian lamb the pelt of karakul lambs

per·si·flage (pur'sə fläzh') *n.* [Fr. < L. *per,* through + *sifilare,* to whistle] light, frivolous talk or writing; banter

per·sim·mon (pər sim'ən) *n.* [< AmInd.] **1.** a hardwood tree with plumlike fruit **2.** the fruit, sour when green, but sweet when ripe

per·sist (pər sist', -zist') *vi.* [< L. *per,* through + *sistere,* cause to stand] **1.** to refuse to give up, esp. when faced with opposition **2.** to continue insistently **3.** to endure; remain; last

per·sist'ent *adj.* **1.** continuing, esp. in the face of opposition, etc. **2.** continuing to exist or endure **3.** constantly repeated —**per·sist'ence, per·sist'en·cy** *n.*

per·snick·e·ty (pər snik'ə tē) *adj.* [< Scot. dial.] [Colloq.] too particular; fussy

per·son (pur's'n) *n.* [< L. *persona*] **1.** a human being **2.** the human body **3.** personality; self **4.** *Gram.* division into three sets of pronouns, and, usually, corresponding verb forms, to identify the subject: see FIRST PERSON, SECOND PERSON, THIRD PERSON —**in person** actually present

-person *a combining form meaning* person in a specified activity: used to avoid the masculine implications of *-man* [*chairperson*]

per'son·a·ble (-ə b'l) *adj.* having a pleasing appearance and personality

per'son·age (-ij) *n.* **1.** an important person; notable **2.** any person

per'son·al (-əl) *adj.* **1.** private; individual **2.** done in person **3.** involving human beings **4.** of the body or physical appearance **5.** *a)* concerning the character, conduct, etc. of a person [a *personal* remark] *b)* tending to make personal remarks **6.** *Gram.* indicating person **7.** *Law* of property (**personal property**) that is movable

per·son·al·i·ty (pur'sə nal'ə tē) *n., pl.* **-ties 1.** the quality or fact of being a particular person **2.** distinctive individual qualities of a person, collectively **3.** a notable person **4.** [*pl.*] offensive remarks aimed at a person

per·son·al·ize (pur's'n ə līz') *vt.* **-ized', -iz'ing** to make personal

per'son·al·ly *adv.* **1.** in person **2.** as a person [I dislike him *personally*] **3.** in one's own opinion **4.** as though directed at oneself [to take a remark *personally*]

per·son·i·fy (pər sän′ə fī′) *vt.* **-fied′, -fy′ing** [< Fr.] **1.** to think of or represent (a thing) as a person **2.** to be a perfect example of; typify — **per·son′i·fi·ca′tion** *n.*

per·son·nel (pur′sə nel′) *n.* [Fr.] persons employed in any work, enterprise, service, etc. — *adj.* of or in charge of personnel

per·spec·tive (pər spek′tiv) *n.* [< L. *per*, through + *specere*, to look] **1.** the art of picturing objects so as to show relative distance or depth **2.** the appearance of objects as determined by their relative distance and positions **3.** a sense of proportion

per·spi·ca·cious (pur′spə kā′shəs) *adj.* [see PERSPECTIVE] having keen judgment; discerning —**per′spi·cac′i·ty** (-kas′ə tē) *n.*

per·spic·u·ous (pər spik′yoo wəs) *adj.* [see PERSPECTIVE] easily understood; lucid —**per·spi·cu·i·ty** (pur′spə kyoo′ə tē) *n.*

per·spi·ra·tion (pur′spə rā′shən) *n.* **1.** the act of perspiring **2.** sweat

per·spire (pər spīr′) *vt., vi.* **-spired′, -spir′ing** [< Fr. < L. *per*, through + *spirare*, breathe] to sweat

per·suade (pər swād′) *vt.* **-suad′ed, -suad′ing** [< L. *per-*, intens. + *suadere*, to urge] to cause to do or believe something, esp. by reasoning, urging, etc.; convince

per·sua·sion (pər swā′zhən) *n.* **1.** a persuading or being persuaded **2.** power of persuading **3.** a strong belief **4.** a particular religious belief

per·sua·sive *adj.* having the power, or tending, to persuade —**per·sua′sive·ly** *adv.*

pert (purt) *adj.* [< L. *apertus*, open] bold; impudent; saucy —**pert′ly** *adv.*

per·tain (pər tān′) *vi.* [< L. *per-*, intens. + *tenere*, to hold] **1.** to belong; be associated **2.** to have reference

per·ti·na·cious (pur′tə nā′shəs) *adj.* [< L. *per-*, intens. + *tenax*, holding fast] **1.** holding firmly to some purpose, belief, etc. **2.** hard to get rid of —**per′ti·na′cious·ly** *adv.* —**per′ti·nac′i·ty** (-nas′ə tē) *n.*

per·ti·nent (pur′t′n ənt) *adj.* [see PERTAIN] of or connected with the matter at hand —**per′ti·nence** *n.* —**per′ti·nent·ly** *adv.*

per·turb (pər turb′) *vt.* [< L. *per-*, intens. + *turbare*, disturb] to cause to be alarmed, agitated, or upset —**per·tur·ba·tion** (pur′tər bā′shən) *n.*

pe·rus·al (pə roo′z′l) *n.* a perusing

pe·ruse (pə rooz′) *vt.* **-rused′, -rus′ing** [prob. < L. *per-*, intens. + ME. *usen*, to use] **1.** to read carefully; study **2.** to read

per·vade (pər vād′) *vt.* **-vad′ed, -vad′ing** [< L. *per*, through + *vadere*, go] to spread or be prevalent throughout —**per·va′sion** (-vā′zhən) *n.* —**per·va′sive** *adj.*

per·verse (pər vurs′) *adj.* [see PERVERT] **1.** deviating from what is considered right or good **2.** stubbornly contrary **3.** obstinately disobedient —**per·ver′si·ty** *n., pl.* **-ties**

per·ver·sion (-vur′zhən) *n.* **1.** a perverting or being perverted **2.** something perverted **3.** any sexual act or practice considered abnormal

per·vert (pər vurt′) *vt.* [< L. *per-*, intens. + *vertere*, to turn] **1.** to lead astray; corrupt **2.** to misuse **3.** to distort **4.** to debase —*n.* (pur′vərt) a perverted person; esp., one who practices sexual perversions

pes·ky (pes′kē) *adj.* **-ki·er, -ki·est** [prob. < PEST + -Y²] [Colloq.] annoying; troublesome —**pes′ki·ness** *n.*

pe·so (pā′sō) *n., pl.* **-sos** [Sp. < L. *pendere*, weigh] the monetary unit and a coin of various Spanish-speaking countries

pes·si·mism (pes′ə miz′m) *n.* [< Fr. < L.

pejor, worse] **1.** the belief that the evil in life outweighs the good **2.** the tendency to expect the worst outcome —**pes′si·mist** *n.* —**pes′si·mis′tic** *adj.*

pest (pest) *n.* [< Fr. < L. *pestis*, plague] a person or thing that causes trouble, annoyance, etc.; specif., an insect, weed, rat, etc.

pes·ter (pes′tər) *vt.* [< OFr. *empestrer*, entangle] to annoy with petty irritations

pes·ti·cide (pes′tə sīd′) *n.* any chemical used for killing insects, weeds, etc.

pes·tif·er·ous (pes tif′ər əs) *adj.* [< L. *pestis*, plague + *ferre*, to bear] **1.** orig., carrying disease **2.** [Colloq.] annoying

pes·ti·lence (pes′t′l əns) *n.* **1.** any virulent, contagious or infectious disease, esp. one that is epidemic **2.** anything harmful —**pes′ti·len′tial** (-tə len′shəl) *adj.*

pes′ti·lent *adj.* [see PEST] **1.** deadly **2.** dangerous to society **3.** annoying

pes·tle (pes′′l) *n.* [< L. *pinsere*, to pound] a tool used to pound or grind substances, esp. in a mortar

pet¹ (pet) *n.* [orig. Scot. dial.] **1.** an animal that is domesticated and kept as a companion or treated with fondness **2.** a person treated with particular indulgence —*adj.* **1.** kept or treated as a pet **2.** especially liked; favorite **3.** particular *[a pet peeve]* —*vt.* **pet′ted, pet′ting** to stroke or pat gently; caress —*vi.* [Colloq.] to kiss, embrace, etc. amorously

pet² (pet) *n.* [< ?] a sulky mood

pet·al (pet′′l) *n.* [< Gr. *petalos*, outspread] any of the leaflike parts of a blossom

pet·cock (pet′käk′) *n.* [< L. *pedere*, break wind + COCK¹] a small valve for draining pipes, boilers, etc.

Pe·ter (pēt′ər) *Bible* **1.** one of the twelve Apostles; reputed author of two Epistles **2.** either of these books

pe·ter (pēt′ər) *vi.* [< ?] [Colloq.] to become gradually smaller, weaker, etc. and then cease (with *out*)

pe·tite (pə tēt′) *adj.* [Fr.] small and trim in figure: said of a woman

pe·ti·tion (pə tish′ən) *n.* [< L. *petere*, ask] **1.** a solemn, earnest request; entreaty **2.** a formal document embodying such a request —*vt.* **1.** to address a petition to **2.** to ask for —*vi.* to make a petition

pet·rel (pet′rəl) *n.* [< ? Saint *Peter*: see Matt. 14:29] a small, dark sea bird with long wings

pet·ri·fy (pet′rə fī′) *vt.* **-fied′, -fy′ing** [< Fr. < L. *petra*, a rock + *facere*, make] **1.** to turn into stone **2.** to harden or deaden **3.** to paralyze, as with fear —**pet′ri·fac′tion** (-fak′shən) *n.*

pet·ro·chem·i·cal (pet′rō kem′i k′l) *n.* a chemical derived ultimately from petroleum

pet·rol (pet′rəl) *n.* [< Fr.: see PETROLEUM] *Brit. term for* GASOLINE

pet·ro·la·tum (pet′rə lāt′əm) *n.* [< PETROLEUM] a greasy, jellylike substance derived from petroleum and used for ointments, etc.: also **petroleum jelly**

pe·tro·le·um (pə trō′lē əm) *n.* [< L. *petra*, a rock + *oleum*, oil] an oily, liquid solution of hydrocarbons occurring naturally in certain rock strata: it yields kerosene, gasoline, etc.

pet·ti·coat (pet′i kōt′) *n.* [< PETTY + COAT] a woman's underskirt —*adj.* of or by women

pet·tish (pet′ish) *adj.* [< PET²] peevish; petulant —**pet′tish·ly** *adv.*

pet·ty (pet′ē) *adj.* **-ti·er, -ti·est** [OFr. *petit*] **1.** relatively unimportant **2.** narrow-minded, mean, etc. **3.** relatively low in rank —**pet′ti·ness** *n.*

petty cash a cash fund for incidentals

petty officer a naval enlisted man whose grade corresponds to that of a noncommissioned army officer

pet·u·lant (pech′oo lənt) ***adj.*** [< L. *petere,* to attack] impatient or irritable, esp. over a petty annoyance —**pet′u·lance** ***n.***

pe·tu·ni·a (pə tōōn′yə, -ē ə) ***n.*** [< SAmInd. *petun,* tobacco] a plant with variously colored, funnel-shaped flowers

pew (pyōō) ***n.*** [< Gr. *pous,* foot] any of the benches with a back that are fixed in rows in a church

pew·ter (pyōōt′ər) ***n.*** [OFr. *peautre*] **1.** a dull, silvery-gray alloy of tin with lead, etc. **2.** articles made of pewter

pe·yo·te (pā ōt′ē) ***n.*** [AmSp. < AmInd. *peyotl,* caterpillar] *same as* MESCAL

Pfc, Pfc., PFC Private First Class

pg. page

pha·lanx (fā′laŋks) ***n.,*** *pl.* **-lanx·es, pha·lan·ges** (fə lan′jēz) [Gr., line of battle] **1.** an ancient military formation of infantry in close ranks with shields together **2.** any massed group **3.** *pl.* **-lan′ges** any of the bones of the fingers or toes

phal·lus (fal′əs) ***n.,*** *pl.* **-li** (-ī), **-lus·es** [< Gr. *phallos*] an image of the penis as the reproductive organ —**phal′lic** ***adj.***

phan·tasm (fan′taz′m) ***n.*** [< Gr. *phantazein,* to show] **1.** a figment of the mind; esp., a specter, or ghost **2.** a deceptive likeness

phan·tas·ma·go·ri·a (fan taz′mə gôr′ē ə) ***n.*** [< Fr. < Gr. *phantasma,* phantasm + *ageirein,* assemble] a rapidly changing series of things seen or imagined, as in a dream

phan·ta·sy (fan′tə sē) ***n.,*** *pl.* **-sies** *same as* FANTASY

phan·tom (fan′təm) ***n.*** [see FANTASY] **1.** an apparition; specter **2.** an illusion —***adj.*** of or like a phantom; illusory

Phar·aoh (fer′ō) ***n.*** the title of the rulers of ancient Egypt

Phar·i·see (far′ə sē′) ***n.*** **1.** a member of an ancient Jewish sect that rigidly observed both the written and the oral law **2.** [**p-**] a self-righteous, hypocritical person

phar·ma·ceu·ti·cal (fär′mə sōōt′i k′l) ***adj.*** [< Gr. *pharmakon,* a medicine] of pharmacy or drugs: also **phar′ma·ceu′tic** —***n.*** a drug or medicine

phar′ma·ceu′tics (-iks) ***n.pl.*** [*with sing. v.*] *same as* PHARMACY (sense 1)

phar·ma·cist (fär′mə sist) ***n.*** one licensed to practice pharmacy

phar′ma·col′o·gy (-käl′ə jē) ***n.*** [< Gr. *pharmakon,* a drug] the science dealing with the effect of drugs on living organisms —**phar′ma·col′o·gist** ***n.***

phar′ma·co·pe′ia, phar′ma·co·poe′ia (-kə pē′ə) ***n.*** [< Gr. *pharmakon,* a drug + *poiein,* to make] an official book listing drugs and medicines

phar·ma·cy (fär′mə sē) ***n.,*** *pl.* **-cies** [< Gr. *pharmakon,* a drug] **1.** the art or profession of preparing and dispensing drugs and medicines **2.** a drugstore

phar·yn·gi·tis (far′in jīt′əs) ***n.*** inflammation of the pharynx; sore throat

phar·ynx (far′iŋks) ***n.,*** *pl.* **phar′ynx·es, pha·ryn·ges** (fə rin′jēz) [Gr.] the cavity leading from the mouth and nasal passages to the larynx and esophagus —**pha·ryn·ge·al** (fə rin′jē əl) ***adj.***

phase (fāz) ***n.*** [< Gr. *phasis*] **1.** any stage in the illumination or appearance of the moon or a planet **2.** any stage in a series of changes, as in development **3.** an aspect or side, as of a problem —***vt.*** **phased, phas′ing** to introduce, carry out, etc. in stages (often with *in, into,* etc.) —**in** (or **out of**) **phase** in (or not in) synchronization —**phase out** to bring to an end by stages

Ph.D. Doctor of Philosophy

pheas·ant (fez′nt) ***n.*** [< Gr. *phasianos,* (bird) of *Phasis,* river in Asia] a chickenlike game bird with a long tail and brightly colored feathers

phe·no·bar·bi·tal (fē′nə bär′bə tôl′) ***n.*** a white crystalline powder used as a sedative

phe·nol (fē′nōl, -nôl) ***n.*** a white crystalline compound, corrosive and poisonous, used to make explosives, synthetic resins, etc. and, in dilute solution (*carbolic acid*), as an antiseptic

phe·nom·e·non (fi näm′ə nän′) ***n.,*** *pl.* **-na** (-nə); also, esp. for 2 & usually for 3, **-nons′** [< Gr. *phainesthai,* appear] **1.** any observable fact or event that can be scientifically described **2.** anything extremely unusual **3.** [Colloq.] an extraordinary person; prodigy —**phe·nom′e·nal** ***adj.***

phi (fī, fē) ***n.*** the 21st letter of the Greek alphabet (Φ, φ)

phi·al (fī′əl) ***n.*** [< Gr. *phialē,* shallow bowl] a small glass bottle; vial

phi·lan·der (fi lan′dər) ***vi.*** [< Gr. *philos,* loving + *anēr,* a man] to engage lightly in love affairs: said of a man —**phi·lan′der·er** ***n.***

phi·lan·thro·py (fi lan′thrə pē) ***n.*** [< Gr. *philein,* to love + *anthrōpos,* man] **1.** a desire to help mankind, esp. as shown by gifts to charitable institutions **2.** *pl.* **-pies** a philanthropic act, gift, etc. —**phil·an·throp·ic** (fil′ən thräp′ik) ***adj.*** —**phi·lan′thro·pist** ***n.***

phi·lat·e·ly (fi lat′'l ē) ***n.*** [< Fr. < Gr. *philos,* loving + *ateleia,* exemption from (further) tax (i.e., postage prepaid)] the collection and study of postage stamps, postmarks, etc. —**phi·lat′e·list** ***n.***

-phile [< Gr. *philos,* loving] *a combining form meaning* loving, liking

phil·har·mon·ic (fil′här män′ik) ***adj.*** [< Fr. < It. < Gr. *philos,* loving + *harmonia,* harmony] loving or devoted to music —***n.*** a society sponsoring a symphony orchestra

Phil·ip·pine (fil′ə pēn′) ***adj.*** of the Philippine Islands or their people

phil·is·tine (fil′is tēn′, fi lis′tin) ***n.*** [after an ancient people of SW Palestine] a person who is smugly conventional, lacking in culture, etc.

phil·o·den·dron (fil′ə den′drən) ***n.*** [< Gr. *philos,* loving + *dendron,* tree] a tropical American vine

phi·los·o·pher (fi läs′ə fər) ***n.*** [< Gr. *philos,* loving + *sophos,* wise] **1.** one who is learned in philosophy **2.** one who lives by or expounds a system of philosophy **3.** one who meets difficulties with calm composure

phil·o·soph·ic (fil′ə säf′ik) ***adj.*** **1.** of a philosophy or a philosopher **2.** devoted to or learned in philosophy **3.** calm; rational Also **phil′o·soph′i·cal**

phi·los·o·phize (fi läs′ə fīz′) ***vi.*** **-phized′, -phiz′ing** **1.** to think or reason like a philosopher **2.** to moralize, express truisms, etc.

phi·los′o·phy (-fē) ***n.,*** *pl.* **-phies** [see PHILOSOPHER] **1.** theory or analysis of the principles underlying conduct, thought, knowledge, and the nature of the universe **2.** the general principles of a field of knowledge **3.** a particular system of ethics

phil·ter (fil′tər) ***n.*** [< Gr. *philein,* to love] a potion or charm thought to arouse sexual love

phle·bi·tis (fli bīt′is) ***n.*** [< Gr. *phleps,* vein + -ITIS] inflammation of a vein

phlegm (flem) ***n.*** [< LL. < Gr. *phlegma,*

inflammation] thick mucus discharged from the throat, as during a cold

phleg·mat·ic (fleg mat'ik) *adj.* [see prec.] sluggish or unexcited

phlo·em (flō'em) *n.* [G. < Gr. *phloos*, bark] the cell tissue through which food is distributed in a plant

phlox (fläks) *n.* [Gr., a flame] a N. American plant with clusters of white, red, or bluish flowers

-phobe [Fr. < Gr. *phobos*, a fear] *a suffix meaning* one who fears or hates

pho·bi·a (fō'bē ə) *n.* [< Gr. *phobos*, a fear] an irrational, excessive, and persistent fear of some thing or situation —**pho'bic** *adj.*

-phobia [see prec.] *a combining form meaning* fear, dread, hatred *[claustrophobia]*

phoe·be (fē'bē) *n.* [echoic, with sp. after *Phoebe*, Gr. goddess of the moon] a small, crested American bird that catches insects in flight

phoe·nix (fē'niks) *n.* [< Gr. *phoinix*] *Egyptian Myth.* a bird which lived for 500 years and then consumed itself in fire, rising renewed from the ashes

phone (fōn) *n.*, *vt.*, *vi.* **phoned, phon'ing** *colloq.* short for TELEPHONE

-phone [< Gr. *phōnē*, a sound] *a combining form meaning:* **1.** a device producing or transmitting sound **2.** a telephone

pho·net·ics (fə net'iks) *n.pl.* [*with sing. v.*] [< Gr. *phōnē*, a sound] the study of the production and written representation of speech sounds —**pho·net'ic** *adj.* —**pho·ne·ti·cian** (fō'nə tish'ən) *n.*

pho·no·graph (fō'nə graf') *n.* [< Gr. *phōnē*, a sound + -GRAPH] an instrument for reproducing sound recorded in a spiral groove on a disk —**pho'no·graph'ic** *adj.*

pho·ny (fō'nē) *adj.* **-ni·er, -ni·est** [< Brit. thieves' argot *fawney*, gilt ring] [Colloq.] not genuine; false —*n., pl.* **-nies** something or someone not genuine; fake; fraud Also sp. **phoney** —**pho'ni·ness** *n.*

phos·phate (fäs'fāt) *n.* [Fr.] **1.** a salt or ester of phosphoric acid **2.** a fertilizer containing phosphates **3.** a flavored carbonated beverage

phos·pho·res·cence (fäs'fə res''ns) *n.* **1.** the property of giving off light without noticeable heat, as phosphorus does **2.** such light —**phos'·pho·res'cent** *adj.*

phos·phor·ic acid (fäs fôr'ik) any of several oxygen acids of phosphorus

phos·pho·rus (fäs'fər əs) *n.* [< Gr. *phōs*, a light + *pherein*, to bear] a nonmetallic chemical element, a phosphorescent, waxy solid that ignites spontaneously at room temperature: symbol, P

pho·to (fōt'ō) *n., pl.* **-tos** short for PHOTOGRAPH

photo- *a combining form meaning:* **1.** [< Gr. *phōs*, a light] of or produced by light **2.** [< PHOTOGRAPH] of photography

pho·to·cop·y (fōt'ə käp'ē) *n., pl.* **-ies** a photographic reproduction, as of a book page, made by a special device (**pho'to·cop'i·er**)

pho·to·e·lec·tric cell (fōt'ō i lek'trik) any device in which light controls an electric circuit which operates a mechanical device, as for opening doors

pho·to·en·grav·ing (fōt'ō in grā'viŋ) *n.* **1.** a process by which photographs are reproduced in relief on printing plates **2.** such a plate **3.** a print made from such a plate —**pho'to·en·grave'** *vt.* **-graved', -grav'ing** —**pho'to·en·grav'er** *n.*

photo finish a race finish so close that the

winner can be determined only from a photograph of the finish

pho·to·flash (fōt'ə flash') *adj.* designating a flashbulb, etc. electrically synchronized with the camera shutter

pho·to·gen·ic (fōt'ə jen'ik) *adj.* [PHOTO- + -GEN + -IC] that looks or is likely to look attractive in photographs

pho·to·graph (fōt'ə graf') *n.* a picture made by photography —*vt.* to take a photograph of —*vi.* to appear (as specified) in photographs — **pho·tog·ra·pher** (fə täg'rə fər) *n.*

pho·tog·ra·phy (fə täg'rə fē) *n.* [PHOTO- + -GRAPHY] the art or process of producing pictorial images on a surface (as film in a camera) sensitive to light or other radiant energy —**pho·to·graph·ic** (fōt'ə graf'ik) *adj.* — **pho'to·graph'i·cal·ly** *adv.*

pho·ton (fō'tän) *n.* [PHOT(O)- + (ELECTR)ON] a quantum of electromagnetic energy

pho·to·off·set (fōt'ō ôf'set') *n.* a method of offset printing in which the text or pictures are photographically transferred to a metal plate from which inked impressions are made on the roller

Pho·to·stat (fōt'ə stat') [PHOTO- + -STAT] *a trademark for* a device for making copies of printed matter, drawings, etc. directly as positives on special paper —*n.* [p-] a copy so made —*vt.* [p-] **-stat'ed** or **-stat'ted, -stat'ing** or **-stat'-ting** to make a photostat of —**pho'to·stat'ic** *adj.*

pho·to·syn·the·sis (fōt'ə sin'thə sis) *n.* the formation in green plants of organic substances, chiefly sugars, from carbon dioxide and water by the action of light on the chlorophyll

pho'to·syn'the·size' (-sīz') *vt., vi.* **-sized', -siz'ing** to carry on, or produce by, photosynthesis

phrase (frāz) *n.* [< Gr. *phrazein*, speak] **1.** a short, colorful expression **2.** a group of words, not a full sentence or clause, conveying a single thought **3.** a short, distinct musical passage —*vt.* **phrased, phras'ing** to express in words or in a phrase —**phras·al** (frā'z'l) *adj.*

phra·se·ol·o·gy (frā'zē äl'ə jē) *n., pl.* **-gies** choice and pattern of words

phre·nol·o·gy (fri näl'ə jē) *n.* [< Gr. *phrēn*, mind + -LOGY] a system, now rejected, of analyzing character and mental faculties by studying the shape of the head

phy·log·e·ny (fī läj'ə nē) *n., pl.* **-nies** [< Gr. *phylon*, tribe + -geneia, origin] the origin and evolution of a group or race of animals or plants

phy·lum (fī'ləm) *n., pl.* **-la** (-lə) [< Gr. *phylon*, tribe] a main division of the animal kingdom or, loosely, of the plant kingdom

phys·ic (fiz'ik) *n.* [< Gr. *physis*, nature] a medicine, esp. a cathartic —*vt.* **-icked, -ick·ing** to dose with this

phys·i·cal (fiz'i k'l) *adj.* [see prec.] **1.** of nature and all matter; material **2.** of or according to the laws of nature **3.** of, or produced by the forces of, physics **4.** of the body —*n.* a general medical examination

physical education instruction in the exercise and care of the body; esp., a course in gymnastics, etc.

physical therapy the treatment of disease, injury, etc. by physical means, as exercise, massage, etc.

phy·si·cian (fə zish'ən) *n.* [see PHYSIC] a doctor of medicine

phys·ics (fiz'iks) *n.pl.* [see PHYSIC] [*with sing. v.*] the science dealing with the properties, changes, interactions, etc. of matter and energy —**phys'i·cist** (-ə sist) *n.*

phys·i·og·no·my (fiz'ē äg'nə mē) *n., pl.* **-mies** [< Gr. *physis*, nature + *gnōmōn*, one who knows] facial features and expression

phys·i·ol·o·gy (fiz'ē äl'ə jē) *n.* [< Fr. < Gr. *physis*, nature + -LOGY] the science dealing with the functions and vital processes of living organisms —**phys'i·o·log'i·cal** (-ə läj'i k'l) *adj.* —**phys'i·ol'o·gist** *n.*

phys·i·o·ther·a·py (fiz'ē ō ther'ə pē) *n.* *same as* PHYSICAL THERAPY

phy·sique (fi zēk') *n.* [Fr.] the structure, strength, or appearance of the body

pi¹ (pī) *n., pl.* **pies** [see PIE] **1.** jumbled printing type **2.** any jumble —*vt.* **pied, pie'ing** or **pi'ing** to jumble

pi² (pī) *n.* **1.** the sixteenth letter of the Greek alphabet (II, π) **2.** the symbol (π) designating the ratio of the circumference of a circle to its diameter, about 3.1416

pi·a·nis·si·mo (pē'ə nis'ə mō') *adj., adv.* [It.] *Music* very soft

pi·an·ist (pē an'ist, pyan'-, pē'ən-) *n.* [< Fr.] one who plays the piano

pi·an·o¹ (pē an'ō, pyan'ō) *n., pl.* **-os** [It. < PIANOFORTE] a large, stringed keyboard instrument: each key operates a felt-covered hammer that strikes a corresponding steel wire or set of wires

pi·an·o² (pē ä'nō, pyä'-) *adj., adv.* [It.] *Music* soft

pi·an·o·for·te (pē an'ə fôrt', pē an'ə fôr'tē) *n.* [It. < *piano*, soft + *forte*, loud] *same as* PIANO¹

pi·as·ter (pē as'tər) *n.* [< Fr. < It., ult. < L. *emplastrum*, plaster] a unit of currency in Egypt, Lebanon, Syria, Turkey, etc.

pi·az·za (pē at'sə, pyät'-) *n.* [It.] **1.** in Italy, a public square **2.** (pē az'ə) a large, covered porch

pi·ca (pī'kə) *n.* [< ? ML., directory] a size of type, 12 point

pic·a·yune (pik'ē ōōn') *adj.* [< Fr. *picaillon*, small coin] trivial; petty

pic·co·lo (pik'ə lō') *n., pl.* **-los'** [It., small] a small flute, pitched an octave above the ordinary nary flute

pick¹ (pik) *n.* [OE. *pic*, PIKE²] **1.** any of several pointed tools for picking, esp. a heavy one used in breaking up soil, rock, etc. **2.** *same as* PLECTRUM

pick² (pik) *vt.* [ME. *picken*] **1.** to pierce, dig up, etc. with something pointed **2.** to probe, scratch at, etc. in trying to remove, or to clear something from **3.** to gather (flowers, berries, etc.) **4.** to prepare (a fowl) by removing the feathers **5.** to pull (fibers, rags, etc.) apart **6.** to choose; select **7.** to provoke *[to pick a fight]* **8.** to pluck (the strings) of (a guitar, etc.) **9.** to open (a lock) with a wire, etc. instead of a key **10.** to steal from (another's pocket, etc.) —*vi.* **1.** to use a pick **2.** to select, esp. in a fussy way —*n.* **1.** the act of choosing or the choice made **2.** the best —**pick at** to eat sparingly of —**pick off 1.** to remove by picking **2.** to hit with a carefully aimed shot —**pick on** [Colloq.] to single out for criticism, abuse, etc. —**pick out** to choose —**pick up 1.** to grasp and lift **2.** to get or learn, esp. by chance **3.** to stop for and take along **4.** to gain (speed) **5.** to improve

pick·a·back (pik'ə bak') *adv., adj.* [ult. < PACK¹] *same as* PIGGYBACK

pick·ax, pick·axe (pik'aks') *n.* [< OFr. *picquois*] a pick with a point at one end of the head and a chisellike edge at the other

pick·er·el (pik'ər əl) *n., pl.* **-el, -els** [ME. *pik,*

PIKE³ + dim. *-rel*] any of various small N. American freshwater fishes

pick·et (pik'it) *n.* [Fr. *piquet*] **1.** a pointed stake used as in a fence **2.** a soldier or soldiers stationed to guard against a surprise attack **3.** a person, as a member of a striking labor union, stationed outside a factory, etc. to demonstrate protest —*vt.* **1.** to enclose with a picket fence **2.** to hitch (an animal) to an upright stake **3.** to post as a military picket **4.** to station a picket or serve as a picket at (a factory, etc.)

pick'ings *n.pl.* **1.** something picked **2.** leftovers; scraps **3.** profit; returns **4.** spoils

pick·le (pik''l) *n.* [< MDu. *pekel*] **1.** a brine, vinegar, etc. used to preserve or marinate food **2.** a vegetable, specif. a cucumber, so preserved **3.** [Colloq.] an awkward situation —*vt.* **-led, -ling** to put in a pickle solution

pick'pock'et *n.* one who steals from pockets

pick'up' *n.* **1.** a picking up **2.** the process or power of increasing in speed **3.** a small delivery truck **4.** a device for producing electric currents from the vibrations of a phonograph needle **5.** [Colloq.] a casual acquaintance **6.** [Colloq.] improvement

pick'y *adj.* **-i·er, -i·est** [Colloq.] fussy

pic·nic (pik'nik) *n.* [Fr. *pique-nique*] a pleasure outing, with an outdoor meal —*vi.* **-nicked, -nick·ing** to have a picnic —**pic'nick·er** *n.*

pi·cot (pē'kō) *n., pl.* **-cots** (-kōz) [Fr. < *pic,* a point] any of the small loops forming an ornamental edging on lace, ribbon, etc.

pic·to·ri·al (pik tôr'ē əl) *adj.* of, in, with, or like a picture or pictures —*n.* a periodical with many pictures

pic·ture (pik'chər) *n.* [< L. *pictus,* painted] **1.** a likeness made by drawing, photographing, etc. **2.** a perfect likeness or image *[the picture of health]* **3.** anything suggestive of a beautiful painting, drawing, etc. **4.** a vivid description **5.** *same as* MOTION PICTURE **6.** the image on a television screen —*vt.* **-tured, -tur·ing 1.** to make a picture of **2.** to show visibly **3.** to describe **4.** to imagine

pic'tur·esque' (-chə resk') *adj.* like a picture; scenic, quaint, vivid, etc.

picture window a large window that seems to frame the outside view

pid·dle (pid''l) *vi., vt.* **-dled, -dling** [< ?] to dawdle or trifle

pidg·in (pij'in) *n.* [supposed Chin. pronun. of BUSINESS] a jargon for trade purposes, using words and grammar from different languages: **pidgin English** uses English words and Chinese or Melanesian syntax

pie (pī) *n.* [ME.] a baked dish, as of fruit, with an under or upper crust or both —(**as**) **easy as pie** [Colloq.] very easy

pie·bald (pī'bôld') *adj.* [*pie*, magpie + BALD] covered with patches of two colors —*n.* a piebald horse, etc.

piece (pēs) *n.* [OFr. *pece*] **1.** a part broken or separated from the whole **2.** a part of a whole, regarded as complete in itself **3.** a single thing, as an artistic work, a firearm, a coin, one of a set, etc. —*vt.* **pieced, piec'ing 1.** to add pieces to, as in repairing **2.** to join the pieces of, as in mending —**go to pieces 1.** to fall apart **2.** to lose self-control

piece'meal' (-mēl') *adv.* [< ME. *pece,* a piece + *-mele,* a measure] piece by piece —*adj.* made or done piecemeal

piece'work' *n.* work paid for at a fixed rate (**piece rate**) per piece of work done

pied (pīd) *adj.* [< *pie*, magpie] covered with patches of two or more colors

pier   343   pin

pier (pir) *n.* [< ML. *pera*] **1.** a structure supporting the spans of a bridge **2.** a structure built out over water and supported by pillars: used as a landing place, pavilion, etc. **3.** *Archit.* a heavy supporting column

pierce (pirs) *vt.* **pierced, pierc'ing** [< L. *per*, through + *tundere*, to strike] **1.** to pass into or through as a pointed instrument does; stab **2.** to make a hole in **3.** to break into or through **4.** to penetrate with the sight or mind —*vi.* to penetrate

pi·e·tism (pī'ə tiz'm) *n.* religious piety, esp. if exaggerated —**pi'e·tis'tic** *adj.*

pi·e·ty (pī'ə tē) *n., pl.* **-ties** [< L. *pius*, pious] **1.** devotion to religious duties and practices **2.** devotion to parents, family, etc. **3.** a pious act

pif·fle (pif''l) *n.* [Colloq.] anything considered trivial or nonsensical

pig (pig) *n.* [ME. *pigge*] **1.** a domesticated animal with a broad snout and a fat body; swine; hog **2.** a young hog **3.** a gluttonous or filthy person **4.** an oblong casting of metal poured from the smelting furnace

pi·geon (pij'ən) *n.* [< L. *pipire*, to peep] any of various related birds with a small head, plump body, and short legs

pi'geon·hole' *n.* a small, open compartment, as in a desk, for filing papers —*vt.* **-holed', -hol'ing 1.** to put in a pigeonhole **2.** to put aside indefinitely **3.** to categorize; classify

pi'geon-toed' (-tōd') *adj.* having the toes or feet turned in

pig·gish (pig'ish) *adj.* like a pig; gluttonous or filthy —**pig'gish·ly** *adv.*

pig'gy (-ē) *n., pl.* **-gies** a little pig —*adj.* **-gi·er, -gi·est** same as PIGGISH

pig'gy·back' (-bak') *adv., adj.* [alt. of PICKABACK] **1.** (carried or carrying) on the shoulders or back **2.** of or by the carrying of truck trailers on flatcars

pig'head'ed *adj.* stubborn; obstinate

pig iron [see PIG, sense 4] crude iron, smelted for casting in molds

pig·ment (pig'mənt) *n.* [L. *pigmentum*] **1.** coloring matter used to make paints **2.** coloring matter in the cells and tissues of animals or plants

pig'men·ta'tion (-mən tā'shən) *n.* coloration in animals or plants due to their natural pigment

Pig·my (pig'mē) *adj., n., pl.* **-mies** alt. sp. of PYGMY

pig'pen' *n.* a pen where pigs are confined: also **pig'sty'** (-stī') *pl.* **-sties'**

pig'skin' *n.* **1.** leather made from the skin of a pig **2.** [Colloq.] a football

pig'tail' (-tāl') *n.* a long braid of hair hanging at the back of the head

pike¹ *n.* short for TURNPIKE

pike² (pīk) *n.* [Fr. *pique*] a former weapon consisting of a metal spearhead on a long wooden shaft

pike³ (pīk) *n., pl.* **pike, pikes** [ME. *pik*] a freshwater game fish with a narrow, pointed head and a slender body

pik·er (pī'kər) *n.* [< ? *Pike* County, Mo.] [Slang] a person who is petty, stingy, etc.

pi·laf, pi·laff (pi läf', pē'läf) *n.* [Per. & Turk. *pilāw*] rice boiled in a seasoned liquid: also **pi·lau'** (-lô')

pi·las·ter (pi las'tər) *n.* [< Fr. < It. < L. *pila*, a pile] a columnlike rectangular support projecting partially from a wall

pile¹ (pīl) *n.* [< L. *pila*, pillar] **1.** a mass of things heaped together **2.** a heap, as of wood, on which a corpse or sacrifice is burned **3.** a large building **4.** [Colloq.] a large amount —*vt.*

piled, pil'ing 1. to heap up **2.** to load —*vi.* **1.** to form a pile **2.** to move confusedly in a mass (with *in, out,* etc.)

pile² (pīl) *n.* [< L. *pilus*, a hair] a soft, velvety, raised surface of yarn loops, as on a rug —**piled** *adj.*

pile³ (pīl) *n.* [OE. *pil*] a long, heavy beam driven into the earth to support a structure

pile driver (or **engine**) a machine for driving piles by raising and dropping a heavy weight on them

piles (pīlz) *n.pl.* [< L. *pila*, a ball] hemorrhoids

pile'up' *n.* **1.** a piling up **2.** [Colloq.] a collision involving several vehicles

pil·fer (pil'fər) *vt., vi.* [< MFr. *pelfre*, booty] to steal (esp. small sums or petty objects)

pil·grim (pil'grəm) *n.* [< L. *peregrinus*, foreigner] **1.** a wanderer **2.** a traveler to a holy place **3.** [P-] one of the English Puritan founders of Plymouth Colony in 1620

pil'grim·age (-ij) *n.* **1.** a pilgrim's journey to a holy place **2.** any long journey

pill (pil) *n.* [< L. *pila*, a ball] a small ball, tablet, etc. of medicine to be swallowed whole — **the pill** (or **Pill**) [Colloq.] a contraceptive drug taken as a pill by women

pil·lage (pil'ij) *n.* [< MFr. *piller*, rob] **1.** a plundering **2.** loot —*vt., vi.* **-laged, -lag·ing** to plunder

pil·lar (pil'ər) *n.* [< L. *pila*, column] **1.** a slender, vertical structure used as a support; column **2.** a main support of something

pill'box' *n.* **1.** a small box for pills **2.** an enclosed gun emplacement of concrete

pil·lion (pil'yən) *n.* [< L. *pellis*, a skin] an extra seat behind the saddle on a horse or motorcycle

pil·lo·ry (pil'ər ē) *n., pl.* **-ries** [< OFr. *pilori*] a wooden board with holes for the head and hands, in which petty offenders were formerly locked and exposed to public scorn —*vt.* **-ried, -ry·ing 1.** to put in a pillory **2.** to expose to public scorn

pil·low (pil'ō) *n.* [OE. *pyle*] a cloth case filled with feathers and used as a support, as for the head during sleep —*vt.* to rest as on a pillow —**pil'low·y** *adj.*

pil'low·case' *n.* a removable cloth case to cover a pillow: also **pil'low·slip'**

pi·lot (pī'lət) *n.* [< Gr. *pēdon*, oar blade] **1.** a steersman; specif., one licensed to steer ships as into or out of a harbor **2.** an aircraft operator **3.** a guide; leader —*vt.* **1.** to act as a pilot of **2.** to guide; lead —*adj.* serving as a test unit

pilot film (or **tape**) a film (or videotape) of a single segment of a projected television series

pi'lot·house' *n.* an enclosed place on the upper deck of a ship, for the helmsman

pilot light a small gas burner kept lighted to rekindle a principal burner when needed

pi·men·to (pi men'tō) *n., pl.* **-tos** [< Sp. < L. *pigmentum*, pigment] a variety of sweet red pepper: also **pi·mien'to** (-myen'-, -men'-)

pimp (pimp) *n.* [< ?] a prostitute's agent —*vi.* to act as a pimp

pim·ple (pim'p'l) *n.* [< ?] a small, often inflamed swelling of the skin —**pim'ply** *adj.*

pin (pin) *n.* [OE. *pinn*] **1.** a peg, as of wood or metal, used as a fastening, support, etc. **2.** a pointed piece of stiff wire, used for fastening **3.** anything pinlike **4.** an ornament or badge with a pin or clasp for fastening to clothes **5.** *Bowling* any of the clubs at which the ball is rolled —*vt.* **pinned, pin'ning 1.** to fasten as with a pin **2.** to hold firmly in one position —**pin down 1.** to get (someone) to be definite or specific **2.** to establish (a fact, details, etc.) —

pin (something) on someone [Colloq.] to lay the blame for (something) on someone

pin·a·fore (pin′ə fôr′) *n.* [PIN + AFORE] a sleeveless garment worn over a dress

pince-nez (pans′nā′, pins′-) *n., pl.* **pince′-nez′** (-nāz′) [Fr., nose-pincher] eyeglasses without sidepieces, kept in place by a spring gripping the bridge of the nose

pin·cers (pin′sərz) *n.pl.* [*occas. with sing. v.*] [< OFr. *pincier,* to pinch] **1.** a tool with two pivoted parts, for gripping things **2.** a grasping claw, as of a lobster

pinch (pinch) *vt.* [see prec.] **1.** to squeeze as between finger and thumb **2.** to nip off the end of (a plant shoot) **3.** to press painfully upon (a bodily part) **4.** to make thin, cramped, etc., as by hunger or cold **5.** [Slang] *a)* to steal *b)* to arrest —*vi.* **1.** to squeeze painfully **2.** to be stingy —*n.* **1.** a pinching or being pinched **2.** an amount grasped between finger and thumb **3.** an emergency

pinch′ers *n.pl. same as* PINCERS

pinch′-hit′ *vi.* **-hit′, -hit′ting 1.** *Baseball* to bat in place of the batter whose turn it is **2.** to substitute in an emergency (*for*) —**pinch hitter**

pin′cush′ion *n.* a small cushion to stick pins in to keep them handy

pine[1] (pīn) *n.* [< L. *pinus*] **1.** an evergreen tree with needlelike leaves and woody cones **2.** the wood

pine[2] (pīn) *vi.* **pined, pin′ing** [< L. *poena,* a pain] **1.** to waste (*away*) from grief, longing, etc. **2.** to yearn

pine·ap·ple (pīn′ap′'l) *n.* [ME. *pinappel,* pine cone] **1.** a juicy, edible tropical fruit shaped somewhat like a pine cone **2.** the plant it grows on

pin′feath′er *n.* an undeveloped, emerging feather

ping (piŋ) *n.* [echoic] a sharp sound as of a bullet striking metal —*vi., vt.* to make or cause to make this sound

Ping-Pong (piŋ′pôŋ′, piŋ′päŋ′) [echoic] *a trademark for* table tennis equipment —*n.* [p-p-] table tennis

pin·ion (pin′yən) *n.* [< Fr. < L. *pinna,* a feather] **1.** a cogwheel engaging with a larger one **2.** the end joint of a bird's wing **3.** a wing **4.** a wing feather —*vt.* to bind the wings or arms of

pink[1] (piŋk) *n.* [< ?] **1.** any of certain plants with pink, red, or white flowers **2.** the flower **3.** pale red **4.** the finest example, condition, etc. —*adj.* pale-red —**in the pink** [Colloq.] healthy; fit

pink[2] (piŋk) *vt.* [ME. *pynken*] **1.** to cut a sawtoothed edge on (cloth, etc.) **2.** to prick or stab

pink′eye′ *n.* a contagious eye infection in which the eyeball and the lining of the eyelid are red and inflamed

pink·ie, pink·y (piŋ′kē) *n., pl.* **-ies** [prob. < Du. *pinkje*] the smallest finger

pink′ing shears shears with notched blades, for making edges of cloth

pin money money for miscellaneous small expenses

pin·na·cle (pin′ə k'l) *n.* [< L. *pinna,* a wing] **1.** a small turret or spire **2.** a slender, pointed formation, as a mountain peak **3.** the highest point

pin·nate (pin′āt, -it) *adj.* [< L. *pinna,* a feather] *Bot.* with leaflets on each side of a common stem

pi·noch·le, pi·noc·le (pē′nuk′'l) *n.* [< G. < Fr. *binocle,* pince-nez] a card game using a double deck of all cards above the eight

pin′point′ *vt.* to locate precisely

pint (pīnt) *n.* [ME. *pynte*] a measure of capacity (liquid or dry) equal to 1/2 quart

pin·to (pin′tō) *n., pl.* **-tos** [AmSp., spotted] a horse with patches of white and another color

pinto (bean) a mottled kidney bean of the SW U.S.

pin′up′ *adj.* **1.** designed or suitable for pinning up on a wall **2.** [Colloq.] designating an attractive girl whose picture is often pinned up on walls

pin′wheel′ *n.* **1.** a small wheel with vanes of paper, etc., pinned to a stick so as to revolve in the wind **2.** a whirling firework

pi·o·neer (pī′ə nir′) *n.* [Fr. *pionnier,* ult. < L. *pes,* foot] one who goes before, preparing the way for others, as an early settler —*vi.* to be a pioneer —*vt.* to be a pioneer in or of

pi·ous (pī′əs) *adj.* [L. *pius*] **1.** of, showing, or prompted by real or feigned religious devotion **2.** sacred —**pi′ous·ly** *adv.*

pip[1] (pip) *n.* [< PIPPIN] a small seed, as of an apple

pip[2] (pip) *n.* [< ?] any of the figures or dots used as on playing cards or dominoes

pip[3] (pip) *n.* [< L. *pituita,* phlegm] a contagious disease of fowl

pipe (pīp) *n.* [< L. *pipare,* to chirp] **1.** a tube into which air is blown to make musical sounds; specif., [*pl.*] *same as* BAGPIPE **2.** a long tube for conveying water, oil, etc. **3.** a tubular part, organ, etc. **4.** a tube with a small bowl at one end, for smoking tobacco, etc. —*vi.* **piped, pip′ing 1.** to play a pipe **2.** to make shrill sounds —*vt.* **1.** to play (a tune) on a pipe **2.** to utter shrilly **3.** to bring, call, etc. by playing pipes **4.** to convey (water, oil, etc.) by pipes **5.** to trim (a dress, coat, etc.) with piping —**pipe down** [Slang] to shout or talk less —**pip′er** *n.*

pipe dream [Colloq.] a wild idea, vain hope, etc.

pipe′line′ *n.* **1.** a line of pipes for conveying water **2.** any channel of conveyance

pipe organ *same as* ORGAN (sense 1)

pip·ing (pīp′iŋ) *n.* **1.** music made by pipes **2.** a shrill sound **3.** a system of pipes **4.** a narrow, rounded trimming on seams or edges —**piping hot** so hot as to sizzle

pip·pin (pip′in) *n.* [< OFr. *pepin,* a seed] any of a number of varieties of apple

pip·squeak (pip′skwēk′) *n.* [Colloq.] one contemptibly insignificant

pi·quant (pē′kənt) *adj.* [Fr. < *piquer,* to prick] **1.** agreeably pungent to the taste **2.** exciting interest; stimulating —**pi′quan·cy** *n.*

pique (pēk) *n.* [see prec.] resentment; ruffled pride —*vt.* **piqued, piqu′ing 1.** to make resentful **2.** to excite; arouse

pi·qué (pē kā′) *n.* [see PIQUANT] a firmly woven cotton fabric with wales: also **pi·que′**

pi·ra·cy (pī′rə sē) *n., pl.* **-cies 1.** robbery of ships on the high seas **2.** unauthorized use of copyrighted or patented work

pi·ra·nha (pi rän′yə, -ran′-) *n.* [< SAmInd. *piro,* a fish + *sainha,* tooth] a small, fierce, voracious freshwater fish of S. America

pi·rate (pī′rət) *n.* [< Gr. *peirān,* to attack] one that practices piracy —*vt., vi.* **-rat·ed, -rat·ing 1.** to take (something) by piracy **2.** to publish or reproduce (a book, recording, etc.) in violation of a copyright

pi·ro·gi (pi rō′gē) *n.pl.* [Russ., pies] small pastry turnovers filled with meat, cheese, etc.: also **pi·rosh′ki** (-räsh′kē), **pi·ro′gen** (-rō′gən)

pir·ou·ette (pir′oo wet′) *n.* [Fr., spinning top] a whirling on one foot or on the point of the toe —*vi.* **-et′ted, -et′ting** to do a pirouette

pis·ca·to·ri·al (pis'kə tôr'ē əl) *adj.* [< L. *pis-cis,* a fish] of fishermen or fishing
Pis·ces (pī'sēz, pis'ēz) [L., pl. of *piscis,* a fish] the twelfth sign of the zodiac
pis·mire (pis'mīr', piz'-) *n.* [ME. *pisse,* urine + *mire,* ant] an ant
pis·ta·chi·o (pi stä'shē ō', -stash'ē-) *n., pl.* **-os'** [< It. < OPer. *pistah*] **1.** a small tree related to the cashew **2.** its edible greenish seed (**pistachio nut**)
pis·til (pis't'l) *n.* [Fr. < L. *pistillum,* pestle] the seed-bearing organ of a flower
pis·tol (pis't'l) *n.* [< Fr. < G. < Czech *pišt'al*] a small firearm held and fired with one hand
pis·ton (pis't'n) *n.* [Fr. < L. *pinsere,* to beat] a disk or short cylinder fitted into a hollow cylinder and moved back and forth by the pressure of a fluid to transmit motion to a rod (**piston rod**) or moved by the rod to exert pressure on the fluid
piston ring a split ring placed around a piston to make it fit the cylinder closely
pit¹ (pit) *n.* [Du. < MDu. *pitte*] the hard stone, as of a peach, containing the seed —*vt.* **pit'ted, pit'ting** to remove the pit from
pit² (pit) *n.* [< L. *puteus,* a well] **1.** a hole in the ground **2.** an abyss **3.** a pitfall **4.** an enclosed area in which animals are kept or made to fight **5.** a small hollow in a surface **6.** the section for the orchestra, in front of the stage — *vt.* **pit'ted, pit'ting** **1.** to put in a pit **2.** to make pits in **3.** to set in competition (*against*) —*vi.* to become marked with pits —**the pits** [Slang] the worst possible thing, place, etc.
pi·ta (**bread**) (pē'tä) [< ?] a round, flat bread of the Middle East, with a pocket for a filling
pit·a·pat (pit'ə pat') *adv.* with rapid beating — *n.* a rapid succession of beats
pitch¹ (pich) *n.* [< L. *pix*] **1.** a black, sticky substance formed from coal tar, petroleum, etc. and used for waterproofing, etc. **2.** any of certain bitumens, as asphalt
pitch² (pich) *vt.* [ME. *picchen*] **1.** to set up [to *pitch* a tent] **2.** to throw; toss **3.** to fix at a certain point, level, degree, etc. **4.** *Baseball a)* to throw (the ball) to the batter *b)* to serve as pitcher for (a game) —*vi.* **1.** to pitch something, as a ball **2.** to plunge forward or dip downward **3.** to rise and fall, as a ship in rough water —*n.* **1.** act or manner of pitching **2.** a throw; toss **3.** anything pitched **4.** a point or degree [feelings were at a high *pitch*] **5.** the degree of slope **6.** [Slang] a line of talk for persuading **7.** *Music,* etc. the highness or lowness of sound determined by frequency vibrations —**pitch in** [Colloq.] to begin working hard —**pitch into** [Colloq.] to attack
pitch'-black' *adj.* very black
pitch'blende' (-blend') *n.* [< G. *pech,* PITCH¹ + *blenden,* deceive] a brown to black lustrous mineral, the chief ore of uranium
pitch'-dark' *adj.* very dark
pitched battle (picht) **1.** a battle in which positions are previously fixed **2.** a fierce combat
pitch·er¹ (pich'ər) *n.* [< L. *bacar,* wineglass] a container, usually with handle and lip, for holding and pouring liquids
pitch·er² (pich'ər) *n.* one that pitches; esp., *Baseball* the player pitching to the batters
pitch'fork' *n.* a large, long-handled fork for lifting and tossing hay, straw, etc.
pitch'man (-mən) *n., pl.* **-men** **1.** a hawker of goods **2.** [Slang] any high-pressure salesman
pitch pipe a small pipe producing a fixed tone used as a standard of pitch, esp. for singers
pit·e·ous (pit'ē əs) *adj.* arousing or deserving pity —**pit'e·ous·ly** *adv.*

pit'fall' *n.* [ME. *pit,* PIT² + *falle,* a trap] **1.** a covered pit to trap animals **2.** a hidden danger
pith (pith) *n.* [OE. *pitha*] **1.** the soft, spongy tissue in the center of certain plant stems **2.** gist
pith'y (-ē) *adj.* **-i·er, -i·est** **1.** of, like, or full of pith **2.** terse and full of meaning
pit·i·ful (pit'i fəl) *adj.* **1.** arousing or deserving pity **2.** contemptible Also **pit'i·a·ble** (-ē ə b'l) —**pit'i·ful·ly** *adv.*
pit'i·less (-lis) *adj.* without pity; merciless
pi·ton (pē'tän) *n.* [Fr. < MFr., a spike] a spike with an eye for a rope, driven into rock or ice to support a mountain climber
pit·tance (pit''ns) *n.* [ult. < L. *pius,* pious] a small amount, share, or allotment
pit·ter-pat·ter (pit'ər pat'ər) *n.* [echoic] a rapid succession of light tapping sounds
pi·tu·i·tar·y (pi tōō'ə ter'ē) *adj.* [< L. *pituita,* phlegm] of a small, oval endocrine gland (**pituitary gland**) attached to the brain: it secretes hormones affecting growth, etc.
pit·y (pit'ē) *n., pl.* **-ies** [ult. < L. *pius,* pious] **1.** sorrow for another's suffering or misfortune **2.** a cause for sorrow —*vt., vi.* **-ied, -y·ing** to feel pity (for)
piv·ot (piv'ət) *n.* [Fr.] **1.** a point, shaft, etc. on which something turns **2.** that on which something depends **3.** a pivoting movement —*vt.* to provide with a pivot —*vi.* to turn as on a pivot —**piv'ot·al** *adj.*
pix·ie, pix·y (pik'sē) *n., pl.* **-ies** [< Brit. dial.] a fairy or sprite
pi·zazz, piz·zazz (pə zaz') *n.* [< ?] [Slang] **1.** vigor **2.** flair, style, etc.
piz·za (pēt'sə) *n.* [It.] an Italian dish made of a thin layer of dough covered with tomatoes, cheese, etc. and baked
piz·zi·ca·to (pit'sə kät'ō) *adj.* [It.] *Music* plucked: a direction to pluck the strings as of a violin
pk. *pl.* **pks.** **1.** pack **2.** park **3.** peck
pkg. package; packages
pl. **1.** place **2.** plural
plac·ard (plak'ärd, -ərd) *n.* [< MDu. *placke,* a piece] a notice for display; poster —*vt.* to put placards on or in
pla·cate (plā'kāt, plak'āt) *vt.* **-cat·ed, -cat·ing** [< L. *placare*] to appease; pacify
place (plās) *n.* [< Gr. *plateia,* street] **1.** a city square or court **2.** a short street **3.** space; room **4.** region **5.** *a)* an occupied part of space *b)* situation **6.** a city, town, etc. **7.** a residence **8.** a building or space devoted to a special purpose **9.** a particular spot, part, position, etc. **10.** a step or point in a sequence **11.** the customary or proper position, time, etc. **12.** a seat, location, etc. reserved or occupied by someone **13.** an office; employment **14.** the duties of any position **15.** *Racing* the second position at the finish —*vt.* **placed, plac'ing** **1.** *a)* to put in a particular place, condition, relation, etc. *b)* to identify **2.** to find employment for **3.** to repose (trust) *in* **4.** to finish in (a specified position) in a race —*vi.* to finish second or among the first three in a race —**take place** to occur
pla·ce·bo (plə sē'bō) *n., pl.* **-bos, -boes** [L., I shall please] *Med.* a neutral preparation given as to humor a patient
place mat a small mat serving as an individual table cover for a person at a meal
place'ment *n.* **1.** a placing or being placed **2.** location or arrangement
pla·cen·ta (plə sen'tə) *n., pl.* **-tas, -tae** (-tē) [< Gr. *plax,* flat object] an organ developed

within the uterus and nourishing a fetus through the umbilical cord

plac·er (plas′ər) *n.* [AmSp., ult. < Gr. *plateia*, street] a deposit of gravel or sand with particles of gold, platinum, etc. in it that can be washed out

place setting the china, silverware, etc. for setting one place at a table for a meal

plac·id (plas′id) *adj.* [L. *placidus*] calm; quiet —**pla·cid·i·ty** (plə sid′ə tē) *n.*

plack·et (plak′it) *n.* [< ?] a slit at the waist as of a skirt to make a garment easy to put on and take off

pla·gia·rize (plā′jə rīz′) *vt., vi.* -**rized**′, -**riz**′**ing** [< L. *plagiarius*, kidnapper] to take (ideas, writings, etc.) from (another) and pass them off as one's own —**pla′gia·rism** *n.* —**pla′gia·rist**, **pla′gia·riz′er** *n.*

plague (plāg) *n.* [< Gr. *plēgē*, misfortune] 1. any affliction or calamity 2. any deadly epidemic disease —*vt.* **plagued, plagu′ing** to afflict, vex, etc.

plaid (plad) *n.* [Gael. *plaide*, a blanket] 1. cloth with a crossbar pattern 2. such a pattern

plain (plān) *adj.* [< L. *planus*, flat] 1. open; clear [in *plain* view] 2. evident 3. direct; frank 4. not fancy 5. simple 6. homely 7. pure; unmixed 8. common; ordinary —*n.* an extent of level country —*adv.* clearly —**plain′ly** *adv.* —**plain′ness** *n.*

plain′clothes′ man a detective or policeman who wears civilian clothes while on duty: also **plain′clothes′man** (-mən) *n., pl.* -**men**

plaint (plānt) *n.* [< L. *plangere*, to lament] 1. [Poet.] lamentation 2. a complaint

plain·tiff (plān′tif) *n.* [see prec.] one who brings a suit into a court of law

plain·tive (plān′tiv) *adj.* [see PLAINT] mournful; sad —**plain′tive·ly** *adv.*

plait (plāt) *n.* [< L. *plicare*, to fold] 1. *same as* PLEAT 2. a braid of hair, etc. —*vt.* 1. *same as* PLEAT 2. to braid

plan (plan) *n.* [Fr.] 1. a diagram showing the arrangement as of a structure 2. a scheme for making, doing, or arranging something 3. any outline or sketch —*vt., vi.* **planned, plan′ning** to make or have in mind a plan of or for (something) —**plan′ner** *n.*

plane[1] (plān) *adj.* [L. *planus*, flat] flat; level —*n.* 1. a surface wholly containing every straight line joining any two points in it 2. a flat or level surface 3. a level of existence, development, etc. 4. an airplane 5. an airfoil

plane[2] (plān) *n.* [< L. *planus*, level] a carpenter's tool for smoothing or leveling wood —*vt.* **planed, plan′ing** to smooth or level as with a plane —**plan′er** *n.*

plan·et (plan′it) *n.* [< Gr. *planan*, wander] any heavenly body revolving about the sun: the major planets, in their order from the sun, are Mercury, Venus, Earth, Mars, Jupiter, Saturn, Uranus, Neptune, and Pluto —**plan′e·tar′y** (-ə ter′ē) *adj.*

plan·e·tar·i·um (plan′ə ter′ē əm) *n., pl.* -**i·ums**, -**i·a** (-ə) a room or building with a large dome on the inner side of which the images of the sun, moon, planets, and stars are optically projected by an instrument that revolves to show celestial motions

plank (plaŋk) *n.* [< LL. *planca*] 1. a long, broad, thick board 2. any of the principles in a platform as of a political party —*vt.* 1. to cover, lay, etc. with planks 2. to broil and serve on a board 3. [Colloq.] to set (*down*) with force

plank·ton (plaŋk′tən) *n.* [G. < Gr. *planktos*, wandering] floating microscopic animal and plant life used as food by fish

plant (plant) *n.* [< L. *planta*, a sprout] 1. a living organism that has no sense organs, cannot move voluntarily, and synthesizes food from carbon dioxide 2. a soft-stemmed organism of this kind, as distinguished from a tree or shrub 3. the machinery, buildings, etc. of a factory, etc. —*vt.* 1. to put into the ground to grow 2. to set firmly in position 3. to settle 4. [Slang] to place (a person or thing) so as to trick or trap

plan·tain[1] (plan′tin) *n.* [< L. *plantago*] a plant with leaves at the base of the stem and spikes of tiny, greenish flowers

plan·tain[2] (plan′tin) *n.* [< Sp. < L. *platanus* < Gr. *platys*, broad] 1. a tropical banana plant with a coarse fruit 2. the fruit

plan·ta·tion (plan tā′shən) *n.* [< L. *plantare*, to plant] 1. an estate in a warm climate, cultivated by workers living on it 2. a large, cultivated planting of trees

plant′er *n.* 1. a plantation owner 2. a person or machine that plants 3. a container for house plants

plaque (plak) *n.* [Fr. < MDu. *placke*, disk] 1. a thin, flat, decorated or lettered piece as of metal, placed as on a wall 2. a bacterial film on teeth

plash (plash) *vt., vi., n.* [echoic] splash

plas·ma (plaz′mə) *n.* [G. < Gr. *plassein*, to form] 1. the fluid part of blood, lymph, etc. 2. protoplasm 3. a high-temperature, ionized, electrically neutral gas

plas·ter (plas′tər) *n.* [< Gr. *emplassein*, to daub] 1. a pasty mixture of lime, sand, and water, hard when dry, for coating walls, ceilings, etc. 2. a medicinal preparation spread as on cloth for application —*vt.* 1. to cover as with plaster 2. to apply like a plaster 3. to make lie smooth and flat

plas′ter·board′ *n.* a thin board formed of layers of plaster of Paris and paper

plaster of Paris calcined gypsum which, combined with water, forms a thick, pasty, quick-setting mixture used as in making casts and statuary

plas·tic (plas′tik) *adj.* [< Gr. *plassein*, to form] 1. that molds or shapes matter; formative 2. that can be molded or shaped 3. made of a plastic —*n.* any of various nonmetallic, synthetic compounds that can be molded and hardened —**plas·tic′i·ty** (-tis′ə tē) *n.*

plastic surgery surgery to repair deformed bodily parts as by skin transfer

plat (plat) *n.* [var. of PLOT] 1. a small piece of ground 2. a map or plan as of subdivided land —*vt.* **plat′ted, plat′ting** to make a map or plan of

plate (plāt) *n.* [< Gr. *platys*, flat] 1. a smooth, flat, thin piece as of metal 2. an impression taken from engraved metal 3. dishes, utensils, etc. of, or plated with, gold or silver 4. a shallow dish 5. the food in a dish; course 6. *Baseball short for* HOME PLATE 7. *Dentistry* a denture, specif. the part fitted to the gums 8. *Photog.* a sheet as of glass, with a light-sensitive coating 9. *Printing* a cast made as from a mold of set type —*vt.* **plat′ed, plat′ing** 1. to coat with metal 2. to cover with metal plates

pla·teau (pla tō′) *n., pl.* -**teaus**′, -**teaux**′ (-tōz′) [Fr. < Gr. *platys*, flat] 1. an elevated tract of level land 2. a period of stability or little progress

plate glass polished, clear glass in thick sheets, for shop windows, mirrors, etc.

plat·en (plat′'n) *n.* [see PLATE] 1. in a printing press, a flat metal plate which presses the

paper against the inked type 2. in a type-writer, the roller against which the keys strike
plat·form (plat'fôrm') *n.* [Fr. *plate-forme*, lit., flat form] 1. a raised horizontal surface, as a stage for speakers, etc. 2. a statement of policy, as of a political party
plat·i·num (plat''n əm) *n.* [< Sp. *plata*, silver] a steel-gray metallic chemical element, resistant to corrosion: used for jewelry, etc.: symbol, Pt
plat·i·tude (plat'ə tōōd') *n.* [Fr. < *plat*, flat, after *latitude*, etc.] a trite remark
Pla·ton·ic (plə tän'ik) *adj.* 1. of Plato, an ancient Gr. philosopher, or his philosophy 2. [*usually* p-] not sexual, but purely spiritual or intellectual [*platonic* love]
pla·toon (plə tōōn') *n.* [Fr. *peloton*, a ball, group] 1. a military unit composed of two or more squads 2. a group like this
plat·ter (plat'ər) *n.* [< OFr. *plat:* see PLATE] a large, shallow dish, usually oval, for serving food
plat·y·pus (plat'ə pəs) *n., pl.* **-pus·es, -pi'** (-pī') [< Gr. *platys,* flat + *pous,* a foot] a small, aquatic, egg-laying mammal of Australia, with webbed feet and a bill like a duck's: in full **duckbill platypus**
plau·dit (plô'dit) *n.* [< L. *plaudere,* applaud] [*usually pl.*] 1. applause 2. any expression of approval
plau·si·ble (plô'zə b'l) *adj.* [< L. *plaudere,* applaud] seemingly true, trustworthy, etc. – **plau'si·bil'i·ty** *n.* –**plau'si·bly** *adv.*
play (plā) *vi.* [OE. *plegan*] 1. to move lightly, rapidly, etc. [sunlight *playing* on the water] 2. to have fun 3. to take part in a game or sport 4. to gamble 5. to trifle (*with*) 6. to perform on a musical instrument 7. to give out sounds 8. to act in a specified way [to *play* fair] 9. to perform on the stage, etc. 10. to impose (*on* another's feelings, etc.) –*vt.* 1. to take part in (a game or sport) 2. to oppose (a person, etc.) in a game 3. to do, as in fun [to *play* tricks] 4. to bet (on) 5. to cause to move, etc.; wield 6. to cause [to *play* havoc] 7. to perform (music, a drama, etc.) 8. to perform on (an instrument) 9. to act the part of [to *play* Iago] –*n.* 1. motion or activity, esp. when free and rapid 2. freedom for motion or action 3. sport, games, etc. 4. fun; joking 5. the playing of a game 6. a move or act in a game 7. a dramatic composition or performance; drama –**play down** to minimize –**played out** exhausted –**play up** to give prominence to –**play up to** [Colloq.] to try to please by flattery
play'back' *n.* the playing of a phonograph record or tape
play'bill' *n.* a program of a play
play'boy' *n.* a pleasure-seeking man of means
play'er *n.* 1. one who plays a game, instrument, etc. 2. an actor
play'ful *adj.* 1. fond of play or fun; frisky 2. jocular –**play'ful·ly** *adv.*
play'go'er *n.* one who attends plays regularly
play'ground' *n.* a place, often part of a schoolyard, for outdoor games and play
play'house' *n.* 1. a theater 2. a small house for children to play in 3. a doll house
playing cards cards used in playing various games, arranged in decks of four suits
play'mate' *n.* a companion in games and recreation: also **play'fel'low**
play'-off' *n.* a contest to break a tie or decide a championship
play on words a pun or punning
play'thing' *n.* a toy
play'wright' (-rīt') *n.* a writer of plays

pla·za (plä'zə, plaz'ə) *n.* [Sp. < L.: see PLACE] 1. a public square in a city or town 2. *same as* SHOPPING CENTER 3. a service area along a superhighway
plea (plē) *n.* [< L. *placere,* please] 1. a statement in defense; excuse 2. an appeal; entreaty 3. *Law* a defendant's statement, answering the charges against him
plea bargaining pretrial bargaining in which a defendant agrees to plead guilty to lesser charges if more serious charges are dropped
plead (plēd) *vi.* **plead'ed** or **pled** or **plead** (pled), **plead'ing** 1. to present a plea in a law court 2. to make an appeal; beg –*vt.* 1. to argue (a law case) 2. to answer (guilty or not guilty) to a charge 3. to offer as an excuse –**plead'er** *n.*
pleas·ant (plez''nt) *adj.* [< MFr. *plaisir,* please] 1. agreeable to the mind or senses; pleasing 2. having an agreeable manner, appearance, etc. –**pleas'ant·ly** *adv.*
pleas'ant·ry (-'n trē) *n., pl.* **-ries** 1. a humorous remark 2. a polite social remark
please (plēz) *vt.* **pleased, pleas'ing** [< L. *placere*] 1. to be agreeable to; satisfy 2. to be the wish of [it *pleased* him to go] –*vi.* 1. to be agreeable; satisfy 2. to have the wish; like [to do as one *pleases*] *Please* is also used in polite requests [*please* sit]
pleas'ing *adj.* giving pleasure; agreeable
pleas·ur·a·ble (plezh'ər ə b'l) *adj.* pleasant; enjoyable –**pleas'ur·a·bly** *adv.*
pleas·ure (plezh'ər) *n.* 1. a pleased feeling; delight 2. one's wish, will, or choice 3. a thing that gives delight or satisfaction
pleat (plēt) *n.* [see PLAIT] a flat double fold in cloth, etc., pressed or stitched in place –*vt.* to lay and press (cloth, etc.) in a pleat or pleats
ple·be·ian (pli bē'ən) *n.* [< L. *plebs,* common people] 1. one of the common people 2. a vulgar, coarse person –*adj.* vulgar, coarse, or common
pleb·i·scite (pleb'ə sīt') *n.* [< Fr. < L. *plebs,* common people + *scitum,* decree] a direct vote of the people on a political issue
plec·trum (plek'trəm) *n., pl.* **-trums, -tra** (-trə) [< Gr. *plēssein,* to strike] a thin piece of metal, bone, etc. for plucking the strings of a guitar, mandolin, etc.
pled (pled) *alt. pt. & pp. of* PLEAD
pledge (plej) *n.* [prob. < OS. *plegan,* to guarantee] 1. the condition of being given or held as security for a contract, payment, etc. 2. a person or thing given or held as such security 3. a promise or agreement 4. something promised, esp. money –*vt.* **pledged, pledg'ing** 1. to give as security 2. to bind by a promise 3. to promise to give
ple·na·ry (plē'nə rē, plen'ə-) *adj.* [< L. *plenus,* full] 1. full; complete 2. for attendance by all members
plen·i·po·ten·ti·ar·y (plen'i pə ten'shē er'ē, -shə rē) *adj.* [< L. *plenus,* full + *potens,* powerful] having or giving full authority –*n., pl.* **-ies** a diplomat given full authority
plen·i·tude (plen'ə tōōd') *n.* [< L. *plenus,* full] 1. fullness; completeness 2. abundance; plenty
plen·te·ous (plen'tē əs) *adj.* plentiful
plen·ti·ful (plen'ti fəl) *adj.* 1. having or yielding plenty 2. abundant
plen·ty (plen'tē) *n.* [< L. *plenus,* full] 1. prosperity; opulence 2. an ample supply 3. a large number –*adv.* [Colloq.] quite
pleth·o·ra (pleth'ə rə) *n.* [< Gr. *plēthos,* fullness] an overabundance
pleu·ri·sy (ploor'ə sē) *n.* [< Gr. *pleura,* a rib] inflammation of the thin membrane which

lines the chest and covers the lungs, characterized by painful breathing

Plex·i·glas (plek′sə glas′) [< L. *plexus*, a twining + GLASS] *a trademark for* a lightweight, transparent thermoplastic substance —*n.* this material: also **plex′i·glass**

plex·us (plek′səs) *n., pl.* **-us·es, -us** [< L. *plectere*, to twine] a network, as of blood vessels or nerves

pli·a·ble (plī′ə b'l) *adj.* [< L. *plicare*, to fold] 1. easily bent; flexible 2. easily influenced or persuaded 3. adaptable —**pli′a·bil′i·ty, pli′a·ble·ness** *n.*

pli·ant (plī′ənt) *adj.* 1. easily bent; pliable 2. compliant —**pli′an·cy** *n.*

pli·ers (plī′ərz) *n.pl.* [< PLY¹] small pincers for gripping small objects, bending wire, etc.

plight¹ (plīt) *n.* [< OFr. *pleit*, a fold] a distressing situation

plight² (plīt) *vt.* [< OE. *pliht*, danger] to pledge, or bind by a pledge

plinth (plinth) *n.* [< Gr. *plinthos*, a brick] the square block at the base of a column, pedestal, etc.

plod (pläd) *vi.* **plod′ded, plod′ding** [prob. echoic] 1. to move heavily and laboriously 2. to work steadily —**plod′der** *n.*

plop (pläp) *vt., vi.* **plopped, plop′ping** [echoic] to drop with a sound like that of something flat falling into water —*n.* the sound of plopping —*adv.* with a plop

plot (plät) *n.* [OE.] 1. a small area of ground 2. a secret, usually evil, scheme 3. the plan of action of a play, novel, etc. —*vt.* **plot′ted, plot′ting** 1. to draw a map, plan, etc. of 2. to make secret plans for —*vi.* to scheme —**plot′ter** *n.*

plough (plou) *n., vt., vi. chiefly Brit.* sp. of PLOW

plov·er (pluv′ər, plō′vər) *n.* [< L. *pluvia*, rain] a shore bird with a short tail and long, pointed wings

plow (plou) *n.* [OE. *ploh*] 1. a farm implement used to cut and turn up the soil 2. anything like this, as a snowplow —*vt.* 1. to cut and turn up (soil) with a plow 2. to make as if by plowing [he *plowed* his way in] —*vi.* 1. to use a plow 2. to move (*through, into*, etc.) with force 3. to plod 4. to begin work vigorously (with *into*) —**plow′man** (-mən) *n., pl.* **-men**

plow′share′ (-sher′) *n.* the cutting blade of a plow

ploy (ploi) *n.* [? < (EM)PLOY] an action intended to outwit another person

pluck (pluk) *vt.* [OE. *pluccian*] 1. to pull off or out; pick 2. to pull feathers or hair from 3. to pull at (a taut string, etc.) and release quickly —*vi.* to pull (*at*) —*n.* 1. a pulling 2. courage

pluck′y *adj.* **-i·er, -i·est** brave; spirited; resolute —**pluck′i·ness** *n.*

plug (plug) *n.* [MDu. *plugge*] 1. an object used to stop up a hole, etc. 2. a cake of tobacco 3. an electrical device, as with prongs, for making contact or closing a circuit 4. *same as: a)* SPARK PLUG *b)* FIREPLUG 5. [Colloq.] a free boost, advertisement, etc. —*vt.* **plugged, plug′ging** 1. to stop up (a hole, etc.) with a plug 2. to insert a plug of 3. [Colloq.] to advertise with a plug 4. [Slang] to shoot a bullet into — *vi.* [Colloq.] to work doggedly

plum (plum) *n.* [OE. *plume*] 1. *a)* a tree bearing a smooth-skinned, edible fruit with a flattened stone *b)* the fruit 2. a raisin 3. the dark bluish-red color of some plums 4. something choice or desirable

plum·age (plo͞o′mij) *n.* [< L. *plumbe*, a feather] a bird's feathers

plumb (plum) *n.* [< L. *plumbum*, LEAD²] a lead

weight (**plumb bob**) hung at the end of a line (**plumb line**), used to determine how deep water is or whether a wall, etc. is vertical — *adj.* perfectly vertical —*adv.* 1. straight down 2. [Colloq.] entirely [*plumb* crazy] —*vt.* 1. to test or sound with a plumb 2. to discover the facts of —**out of** (or **off**) **plumb** not vertical

plumb·er (plum′ər) *n.* [< L. *plumbum*, LEAD²] a worker who installs and repairs pipes, fixtures, etc., as of water or gas systems

plumb·ing (plum′iŋ) *n.* 1. the work of a plumber 2. the pipes and fixtures with which a plumber works

plume (plo͞om) *n.* [< L. *pluma*] 1. a feather, esp. a large, showy one 2. a cluster of these — *vt.* **plumed, plum′ing** 1. to adorn with plumes 2. to preen

plum·met (plum′it) *n.* [see PLUMB] 1. a plumb 2. a thing that weighs heavily —*vi.* to fall or drop straight downward

plump¹ (plump) *adj.* [< MDu. *plomp*, bulky] full and rounded in form; chubby —*vt., vi.* to fill out (sometimes with *up* or *out*)

plump² (plump) *vi.* [echoic] 1. to fall or bump (*against*) 2. to offer strong support (*for*) —*vt.* to drop or put down heavily or suddenly —*n.* a fall or the sound of this —*adv.* 1. suddenly or heavily 2. straight down —*adj.* blunt; direct

plun·der (plun′dər) *vt., vi.* [< G. *plunder*, baggage] 1. to rob by force, esp. in warfare 2. to take (property) by force or fraud —*n.* 1. the act of plundering 2. goods taken by force or fraud —**plun′der·er** *n.*

plunge (plunj) *vt.* **plunged, plung′ing** [< L. *plumbum*, LEAD²] to thrust or throw suddenly (*into*) —*vi.* 1. to dive or rush into 2. to move violently and rapidly downward or forward 3. [Colloq.] to gamble heavily —*n.* 1. a dive or fall 2. a swim —**take the plunge** to start on some uncertain enterprise

plung′er *n.* 1. one who plunges 2. a large, rubber suction cup used to free clogged drains 3. any cylindrical device that operates with a plunging motion, as a piston

plunk (pluŋk) *vt.* [echoic] 1. to strum (a banjo, guitar, etc.) 2. to throw or put down heavily; plump —*vi.* 1. to give out a twanging sound 2. to fall heavily —*n.* the act or sound of plunking

plu·ral (ploor′əl) *adj.* [< L. *plus*, more] more than one —*n. Gram.* the form of a word designating more than one (Ex.: *hands, men*)

plu·ral·i·ty (ploo ral′ə tē) *n., pl.* **-ties** 1. a being plural or numerous 2. a majority 3. the excess of votes in an election that the leading candidate has over his nearest rival

plu·ral·ize (ploor′ə līz′) *vt., vi.* **-ized′, -iz′ing** to make or become plural

plus (plus) *prep.* [L., more] 1. added to [2 *plus* 2] 2. in addition to —*adj.* 1. designating a sign (**plus sign, +**) indicating addition 2. positive [a *plus* quantity] 3. higher than [a grade of B *plus*] 4. [Colloq.] and more [personality *plus*] —*n., pl.* **plus′es, plus′ses** 1. a plus sign 2. something added or favorable

plush (plush) *n.* [< L. *pilus*, hair] a fabric with a soft, thick pile —*adj.* [Slang] luxurious — **plush′y** *adj.* **-i·er, -i·est**

Plu·to (plo͞ot′ō) 1. *Gr. & Rom. Myth.* the god ruling the lower world 2. the outermost planet of the solar system: see PLANET

plu·toc·ra·cy (plo͞o täk′rə sē) *n., pl.* **-cies** [< Gr. *ploutos*, wealth + *kratein*, to rule] 1. government by the wealthy 2. a group of wealthy people who control a government

plu·to·crat (plo͞ot′ə krat′) *n.* 1. a member of a

wealthy ruling class **2.** one whose wealth gives him control or influence

plu·to·ni·um (ploo tō′nē əm) *n.* [< *Pluto* (planet)] a radioactive metallic chemical element: symbol, Pu

plu·vi·al (ploo′vē əl) *adj.* [< L. *pluvia,* rain] of, or having much, rain

ply[1] (plī) *n., pl.* **plies** [< L. *plicare,* to fold] **1.** a thickness or layer, as of plywood, cloth, etc. **2.** a twisted strand in rope, etc.

ply[2] (plī) *vt.* **plied, ply′ing** [contr. < APPLY] **1.** to work with (a tool, faculty, etc.) **2.** to work at (a trade) **3.** to keep supplying, assailing, etc. (*with*) **4.** to sail back and forth across —*vi.* **1.** to keep busy or work **2.** to travel regularly (*between* places): said of ships, buses, etc.

ply′wood[′] *n.* [PLY[1] + WOOD] a material made of thin layers of wood glued and pressed together

P.M., p.m., PM [L. *post meridiem*] after noon: used to designate time from noon to midnight

pneu·mat·ic (noo mat′ik) *adj.* [< Gr. *pneuma,* breath] **1.** of or containing wind, air, or gases **2.** worked by or filled with compressed air — **pneu·mat′i·cal·ly** *adv.*

pneu·mo·nia (noo mōn′yə, nyoo-) *n.* [< Gr. *pnein,* to breathe] inflammation or infection of the lungs, caused by bacteria, viruses, etc.

P.O., p.o. post office

poach[1] (pōch) *vt.* [< MFr. *poche,* a pocket: the yolk is "pocketed" in the white] to cook (fish, an egg without its shell, etc.),in or over water near the boiling point

poach[2] (pōch) *vt., vi.* [< Fr. < MHG. *puchen,* to plunder] **1.** to trespass on (private property), esp. for hunting or fishing **2.** to hunt or catch (game or fish) illegally

pock (päk) *n.* [OE. *pocc*] **1.** a pustule caused by smallpox, etc. **2.** *same as* POCKMARK

pock·et (päk′it) *n.* [< OFr. *poque,* a bag] **1.** a little bag or pouch, esp. when sewn into or on clothing, for carrying small articles **2.** a pouchlike cavity or hollow **3.** a small area or group [a *pocket* of poverty] **4.** *Geol.* a cavity filled with ore, oil, etc. —*adj.* **1.** that can be carried in a pocket **2.** small —*vt.* **1.** to put into a pocket **2.** to envelop; enclose **3.** to take dishonestly, as money **4.** to suppress [*pocket* one's pride] —**pock′et·ful**[′] *n., pl.* **-fuls**[′]

pock′et·book[′] *n.* **1.** a woman's purse **2.** monetary resources

pock′et·knife[′] *n., pl.* **-knives**[′] a knife with blades that fold into the handle

pock·mark (päk′märk′) *n.* a scar or pit left by a pustule, as of smallpox

pod (päd) *n.* [< ?] a dry fruit or seed vessel, as a legume

-pod [< Gr. *pous,* a foot] *a combining form meaning:* **1.** foot **2.** (one) having (a specified number or kind of) feet Also **-pode**

po·di·a·try (pō dī′ə trē, pə-) *n.* [< Gr. *pous,* foot + -IATRY] the profession dealing with the treatment of foot disorders —**po·di′a·trist** *n.*

po·di·um (pō′dē əm) *n., pl.* **-di·ums, -di·a** (-ə) [< Gr. *pous,* foot] a low platform, esp. for the conductor of an orchestra

po·em (pō′əm) *n.* [< Gr. *poiein,* to make] an arrangement of words, esp. a rhythmical composition, sometimes rhymed, in a style more imaginative than ordinary speech

po·e·sy (pō′ə sē′, -zē′) *n.* old-fashioned var. of POETRY

po·et (pō′ət) *n.* **1.** one who writes poems **2.** one who expresses himself with beauty of thought and language —**po′et·ess** [Now Rare] *n.fem.*

poet. **1.** poetic **2.** poetry

po·et·as·ter (pō′ə tas′tər) *n.* [< POET + L.

-*aster,* dim. suffix] a writer of mediocre verse

po·et·ic (pō et′ik) *adj.* **1.** of, like, or for poets or poetry **2.** having the beauty, imagination, etc. of poetry Also **po·et′i·cal**

poetic license disregard of strict fact or of rigid form, for artistic effect

poet laureate the official poet of a nation, appointed to write poems celebrating national events, etc.

po·et·ry (pō′ə trē) *n.* **1.** the art or structure of poems **2.** poems **3.** poetic qualities

po·grom (pō gräm′) *n.* [Russ., devastation] an organized massacre of a minority group, esp. of Jews (as in Czarist Russia)

poi (poi, pō′ē) *n.* [Haw.] a Hawaiian food made of mashed, fermented taro root

poign·ant (poin′yənt) *adj.* [< L. *pungere,* to prick] **1.** sharp to the smell **2.** sharply painful to the feelings **3.** biting [*poignant* wit] — **poign′an·cy** *n.*

poin·ci·a·na (poin′sē an′ə, -ā′nə) *n.* [< M. de *Poinci,* a governor of the Fr. West Indies] a small tropical tree with showy red, orange, or yellow flowers

poin·set·ti·a (poin set′ē ə, -set′ə) *n.* [< J. R. *Poinsett,* 19th-c. U.S. ambassador to Mexico] a tropical plant with yellow flowers and petal-like red leaves

point (point) *n.* [< L. *pungere,* to prick] **1.** a dot in writing, etc., as a decimal point **2.** position, location, etc. [all *points* south] **3.** the exact moment **4.** a condition reached [a boiling *point*] **5.** an item [*point* by *point*] **6.** a distinguishing characteristic **7.** a unit, as of value, game scores, etc. **8.** a sharp end **9.** a projecting piece of land; cape **10.** the essential fact or idea **11.** aim; purpose **12.** an impressive argument or fact **13.** a helpful hint **14.** a mark showing direction on a compass **15.** a measuring unit for printing type, about 1/72 of an inch —*vt.* **1.** to sharpen to a point **2.** to give (a story, etc.) emphasis (usually with *up*) **3.** to show (usually with *out*) [*point* the way] **4.** to aim —*vi.* **1.** to direct one's finger or the like (*at* or *to*) **2.** to call attention (*to*) **3.** to be directed (*to* or *toward*) —**at the point of** very close to — **beside the point** irrelevant —**to the point** pertinent; apt: also **in point**

point′-blank′ *adj., adv.* [POINT + *blank,* white center of a target] **1.** (aimed) straight at a mark **2.** direct(ly); blunt(ly)

point′ed *adj.* **1.** having a sharp end **2.** sharp; incisive **3.** aimed at someone, as a remark **4.** very evident

point′er *n.* **1.** a long, tapered rod for pointing to things **2.** an indicator on a meter, etc. **3.** a large, lean hunting dog with a smooth coat **4.** [Colloq.] a helpful hint

point′less *adj.* **1.** without a point **2.** without meaning or force; senseless

point of view 1. the way in which something is viewed **2.** a mental attitude

point′y *adj.* **-i·er, -i·est 1.** that comes to a sharp point **2.** having many points

poise (poiz) *n.* [< L. *pendere,* weigh] **1.** balance; stability **2.** ease and dignity of manner **3.** carriage, as of the body —*vt., vi.* **poised, pois′ing 1.** to balance or be balanced **2.** to suspend or be suspended

poi·son (poi′z'n) *n.* [< L. *potio,* potion] a substance which in small quantities can cause illness or death —*vt.* **1.** to harm or destroy with poison **2.** to put poison on or into **3.** to influence wrongly —*adj.* poisonous

poison ivy a plant with leaves of three leaflets and ivory-colored berries: it can cause a severe rash on contact

poi'son·ous *adj.* that can injure or kill by or as by poison —**pol'son·ous·ly** *adv.*

poke[1] (pōk) *vt.* **poked, pok'ing** [MDu. or LowG. *poken*] **1.** *a)* to jab with a stick, etc. *b)* [Slang] to hit **2.** to make (a hole, etc.) by poking —*vi.* **1.** to jab (*at*) **2.** to search (*about* or *around*) **3.** to move slowly (*along*) —*n.* **1.** a jab; thrust **2.** [Slang] a blow with the fist —**poke fun (at)** to ridicule

poke[2] (pōk) *n.* [< Frank.] [Dial.] a sack

pok·er[1] (pō'kər) *n.* [< ?] a card game in which the players bet on the value of their hands, forming a pool to be taken by the winner

pok·er[2] (pō'kər) *n.* a bar, as of iron, for stirring a fire

poker face [Colloq.] an expressionless face, as of a poker player hiding the nature of his hand

pok·y (pō'kē) *adj.* **-i·er, -i·est** [see POKE[1]] **1.** slow; dull **2.** small and uncomfortable [a *poky* room] Also **pok'ey**

Pol. 1. Poland **2.** Polish

po·lar (pō'lər) *adj.* **1.** of or near the North or South Pole **2.** of a pole or poles **3.** opposite in character, direction, etc.

polar bear a large, white bear of the arctic regions

Po·lar·is (pō lar'is) *same as* NORTH STAR

po·lar·i·ty (pō lar'ə tē) *n., pl.* **-ties 1.** the property of having opposite magnetic poles **2.** any tendency to turn, feel, etc. in a certain way, as if magnetized

po·lar·i·za·tion (pō'lər i zā'shən) *n.* **1.** the producing or acquiring of polarity **2.** *Optics* a condition, or the production of a condition, of light in which the vibrations of the waves are confined to one plane or one direction

po·lar·ize (pō'lə rīz') *vt.* **-ized', -iz'ing** to give polarity to —*vi.* to acquire polarity; specif., to separate into opposed groups, viewpoints, etc.

Po·lar·oid (pō'lə roid') *a trademark for:* **1.** a transparent material capable of polarizing light **2.** a camera that develops and prints snapshots: in full **Polaroid (Land) camera**

Pole (pōl) *n.* a native of Poland

pole[1] (pōl) *n.* [< L. *palus*, a stake] a long, slender piece of wood, metal, etc. —*vt., vi.* **poled, pol'ing** to propel (a boat or raft) with a pole

pole[2] (pōl) *n.* [< Gr. *polos*] **1.** either end of any axis, as of the earth **2.** either of two opposed forces, parts, etc., as the ends of a magnet, terminals of a battery, etc.

pole·cat (pōl'kat') *n.* [prob. < OFr.: see PULLET & CAT] **1.** a small, weasellike carnivore of Europe **2.** *same as* SKUNK

po·lem·ic (pə lem'ik, pō-) *adj.* [< Fr. < Gr. *polemos*, a war] of or involving dispute: also **po·lem'i·cal** —*n.* (a) controversy

po·lem'ics *n.pl.* [*with sing. v.*] the art or practice of disputation —**po·lem'i·cist** (-ə sist) *n.*

pole'star' *n.* **1.** the North Star **2.** a guiding principle

pole vault a leap for height by vaulting over a bar with the aid of a long pole —**pole'-vault'** *vi.*

po·lice (pə lēs') *n.* [Fr. < Gr. *polis*, city] **1.** the governmental department (of a city, state, etc.) for keeping order and investigating crime **2.** [*with pl. v.*] the members of such a department —*vt.* **-liced', -lic'ing 1.** to control, protect, etc. with police or the like **2.** to keep (a military camp, etc.) clean and orderly

po·lice'man (-mən) *n., pl.* **-men** a member of a police force —**po·lice'wom'an** *n.fem., pl.* **-wom'en**

police state a government that uses police to suppress political opposition

pol·i·cy[1] (päl'ə sē) *n., pl.* **-cies** [see POLICE] **1.**

wise or prudent management **2.** any governing principle, plan, etc.

pol·i·cy[2] (päl'ə sē) *n., pl.* **-cies** [< Gr. *apodeixis*, proof] a written insurance contract

po·li·o·my·e·li·tis (pō'lē ō mī'ə līt'əs) *n.* [< Gr. *polios*, gray + *myelos*, marrow] an acute infectious disease caused by a virus inflammation of the gray matter of the spinal cord, often resulting in muscular paralysis: also **po'li·o'**

Po·lish (pō'lish) *adj.* of Poland, its people, their language, etc. —*n.* the Slavic language of the Poles

pol·ish (päl'ish) *vt.* [< L. *polire*] **1.** to smooth and brighten, as by rubbing **2.** to refine (manners, style, etc.) —*vi.* to take a polish —*n.* **1.** a surface gloss **2.** elegance; refinement **3.** a substance used for polishing —**polish off** [Colloq.] to finish or get rid of —**pol'ished** *adj.*

po·lite (pə lit') *adj.* [< L. *polire*, to polish] **1.** cultured; refined **2.** having good manners —**po·lite'ly** *adv.* —**po·lite'ness** *n.*

pol·i·tic (päl'ə tik) *adj.* [see POLICE] **1.** having practical wisdom; prudent **2.** expedient [a *politic* plan] —*vi.* **-ticked, -tick·ing** to campaign in politics

po·lit·i·cal (pə lit'i k'l) *adj.* **1.** of, concerned with, or engaged in government, politics, etc. **2.** of or characteristic of political parties or politicians

political science the science of the principles, organization, and methods of government

pol·i·ti·cian (päl'ə tish'ən) *n.* one actively engaged in politics: often used with implications of seeking personal or partisan gain, scheming, etc.

po·lit·i·co (pə lit'i kō') *n., pl.* **-cos'** [Sp. or It.] *same as* POLITICIAN

pol·i·tics (päl'ə tiks) *n.pl.* [*with sing. or pl. v.*] **1.** the science of government **2.** political affairs **3.** political methods, tactics, etc. **4.** political opinions, principles, etc. **5.** factional scheming for power

pol'i·ty *n., pl.* **-ties** [see POLICE] **1.** the governmental organization of a state, church, etc. **2.** a society with a government; state

pol·ka (pōl'kə) *n.* [Czech < Pol. *Polak*, a Pole] **1.** a fast dance for couples **2.** music for this dance —*vi.* to dance the polka

pol·ka dot (pō'kə) any of a pattern of small round dots on cloth

poll (pōl) *n.* [ME. *pol*] **1.** the head **2.** a counting, listing, etc. of persons, esp. of voters **3.** the number of votes recorded **4.** [*pl.*] a place where votes are cast **5.** a canvassing of people's opinions on some question —*vt.* **1.** to cut off or cut short **2.** to register the votes of **3.** to receive (a certain number of votes) **4.** to cast (a vote) **5.** to canvass in a poll (sense 5)

pol·len (päl'ən) *n.* [L., dust] the yellow, powderlike male sex cells on the stamens of a flower

pollen count the number of grains of pollen, esp. of ragweed, in a given volume of air at a specified time and place

pol·li·nate (päl'ə nāt') *vt.* **-nat'ed, -nat'ing** to transfer pollen from a stamen to a pistil of (a flower) —**pol'li·na'tion** *n.*

pol·li·wog (päl'ē wäg') *n.* [< ME.: see POLL & WIGGLE] a tadpole: also sp. **pol'ly·wog'**

poll·ster (pōl'stər) *n.* a person whose work is taking public opinion polls

pol·lute (pə lōōt') *vt.* **-lut'ed, -lut'ing** [< L. *polluere*] to make unclean, impure, or corrupt; defile —**pol·lu'tant** *n.* —**pol·lut'er** *n.* —**pol·lu'tion** *n.*

po·lo (pō'lō) *n.* [prob. < Tibet. *pulu*, the ball] a

game played on horseback by two teams using a wooden ball and long-handled mallets
po·lo·naise (päl'ə nāz') *n.* [Fr. < fem. of *polonais,* Polish] a stately Polish dance
pol·troon (päl trōōn') *n.* [< Fr. < It. *poltrone*] a thorough coward
poly- [< Gr. *polys*] *a combining form meaning* much, many
pol·y·clin·ic (päl'ē klin'ik) *n.* [POLY- + CLINIC] a clinic or hospital treating various kinds of disease
pol·y·es·ter (päl'ē es'tər) *n.* [POLY(MER) + ESTER] a polymeric synthetic resin used in making plastics, fibers, etc.
pol·y·eth·yl·ene (päl'ē eth'ə lēn') *n.* [POLY(MER) + ETHYLENE] a thermoplastic resin used in making plastics, etc.
po·lyg·a·my (pə lig'ə mē) *n.* [< Fr. < Gr. *poly-,* many + *gamos,* marriage] the practice of having two or more wives or husbands at the same time —**po·lyg'a·mist** *n.*
pol·y·glot (päl'i glät') *adj.* [< Gr. *poly-,* many + *glōtta,* tongue] 1. speaking or writing several languages 2. written in several languages —*n.* a polyglot person
pol·y·gon (päl'i gän') *n.* [< Gr.: see POLY- & -GON] a closed plane figure with several angles and sides, usually more than four —**po·lyg·o·nal** (pə lig'ə n'l) *adj.*
pol'y·graph' (-graf') *n.* an instrument for recording changes in blood pressure, pulse rate, etc., used on persons suspected of lying
pol·y·mer (päl'i mər) *n.* [G. < Gr. *poly-,* many + *meros,* a part] a substance consisting of giant molecules formed from smaller molecules of the same substance —**pol'y·mer'ic** (-mer'ik) *adj.*
Pol·y·ne·sian (päl'ə nē'zhən) *adj.* of Polynesia, a group of Pacific islands, its people, languages, etc. —*n.* 1. a native of Polynesia 2. the group of languages of Polynesia
pol·yp (päl'ip) *n.* [< Fr. < Gr. *poly-,* many + *pous,* a foot] 1. a small water animal with tentacles at the top of a tubelike body 2. a projecting growth of mucous membrane inside the nose, bladder, etc.
po·lyph·o·ny (pə lif'ə nē) *n.* [< Gr. *poly-,* many + *phōnē,* a sound] *Music* a combining of a number of harmonious melodies; counterpoint —**pol·y·phon·ic** (päl'i fän'ik) *adj.*
pol·y·syl·lab·ic (päl'i si lab'ik) *adj.* 1. having four or more syllables 2. characterized by polysyllabic words —**pol'y·syl'la·ble** (-sil'ə b'l) *n.*
pol·y·tech·nic (päl'i tek'nik) *adj.* [< Fr. < Gr. *poly-,* many + *technē,* an art] of or providing instruction in many scientific and technical subjects
pol·y·the·ism (päl'i thē iz'm) *n.* [< Fr. < Gr. *poly-,* many + *theos,* god] belief in more than one god —**pol'y·the·is'tic** *adj.*
pol·y·un·sat·u·rat·ed (päl'i un sach'ə rāt'id) *adj.* designating any of certain vegetable and animal fats and oils with a low cholesterol content
po·made (pä mād', -mäd') *n.* [< Fr. < It. *pomo,* apple (orig. an ingredient)] a perfumed preparation, as for the hair
pome·gran·ate (päm'gran'it, päm'ə-; pum'-) *n.* [ult. < L. *pomum,* fruit + *granum,* seed] 1. a round, red, pulpy fruit with a thick rind and many seeds 2. the bush or tree that bears it
pom·mel (pum''l, päm'-) *n.* [< L. *pomum,* fruit] the rounded, upward-projecting front part of a saddle —*vt.* -meled *or* -melled, -mel·ing *or* -mel·ling *same as* PUMMEL
pomp (pämp) *n.* [< Gr. *pompē,* solemn

procession] 1. stately display 2. ostentatious show or display
pom·pa·dour (päm'pə dôr') *n.* [< Mme. *Pompadour,* mistress of Louis XV] a hairdo in which the hair is brushed up high from the forehead
pom·pa·no (päm'pə nō') *n., pl.* -no', -nos' [< Sp.] a spiny-finned, saltwater food fish of N. America and the West Indies
pom·pon (päm'pän', -päm') *n.* [Fr.] 1. an ornamental tuft, as of silk or wool, worn as on hats or waved by cheerleaders: also **pom-pom** (päm'päm') 2. a chrysanthemum, dahlia, etc. with small, round flowers
pom·pous (päm'pəs) *adj.* 1. full of pomp 2. pretentious; self-important —**pom·pos'i·ty** (-päs'ə tē) *n., pl.* -ties
pon·cho (pän'chō) *n., pl.* -chos [< SAmInd.] 1. a cloak like a blanket with a hole for the head 2. a raincoat like this
pond (pänd) *n.* [< ME. var. of POUND³] a body of standing water smaller than a lake
pon·der (pän'dər) *vt., vi.* [< L. *ponderare,* weigh] to think deeply (about); deliberate
pon'der·ous *adj.* 1. very heavy; unwieldy 2. labored; dull, as in style
pone (pōn) *n.* [< AmInd.] [Chiefly Southern] corn bread in small, oval loaves
pon·gee (pän jē') *n.* [< Chin. dial. *pen-chi,* domestic loom] a soft, thin silk cloth, usually in natural tan
pon·iard (pän'yərd) *n.* [< Fr., ult. < L. *pugnus,* fist] a dagger
pon·tiff (pän'tif) *n.* [< L. *pontifex,* high priest] 1. a bishop 2. [P-] the Pope
pon·tif·i·cal (pän tif'i k'l) *adj.* 1. of a pontiff 2. papal 3. pompous or dogmatic
pon·tif'i·cate (-i kit) *n.* the office or term of a pontiff —*vi.* (-i kāt') -cat'ed, -cat'ing 1. to officiate as a pontiff 2. to be pompous or dogmatic
pon·toon (pän tōōn') *n.* [< Fr. < L. *pons,* a bridge] 1. a flat-bottomed boat 2. any of a row of boats, floating cylinders, etc., used to support a temporary bridge 3. a boatlike float on an aircraft's landing gear
po·ny (pō'nē) *n., pl.* -nies [< Scot., prob. < L. *pullus,* foal] 1. a horse of any small breed 2. a small liqueur glass 3. a literal translation of a foreign work, used in doing schoolwork
pooch (pōōch) *n.* [< ?] [Slang] a dog
poo·dle (pōō'd'l) *n.* [G. *pudel*] a dog with a solid-colored, curly coat
pooh (pōō) *interj.* an exclamation of disdain, disbelief, or impatience
pooh-pooh (pōō'pōō') *vt.* to make light of; belittle
pool¹ (pōōl) *n.* [OE. *pol*] 1. a small pond 2. a puddle 3. a tank for swimming 4. a deep, still spot in a river
pool² (pōōl) *n.* [< Fr. < LL. *pulla,* hen] 1. a game of billiards played on a table with six pockets 2. *a)* a combination of resources, funds, supplies, etc. for some common purpose *b)* the parties forming such a combination —*vt., vi.* to contribute to a common fund
poop¹ (pōōp) *n.* [< L. *puppis,* stern of a ship] a raised deck at the stern of a sailing ship: also **poop deck**
poop² (pōōp) *vt.* [Slang] to exhaust; tire
poor (poor) *adj.* [< L. *pauper,* poor] 1. having little or no means to support oneself; needy 2. lacking in some quality; specif., *a)* inadequate *b)* inferior *c)* contemptible 3. worthy of pity; unfortunate —**the poor** poor, or needy, people —**poor'ly** *adv.*

poor'house' *n.* formerly, an institution for paupers, supported from public funds

poor'-mouth' *vi.* [Colloq.] to complain about one's lack of money

pop[1] (päp) *n.* [echoic] **1.** a sudden, light, explosive sound **2.** any carbonated, nonalcoholic beverage —*vi.* **popped, pop'ping 1.** to make, or burst with, a pop **2.** to move, go, etc. suddenly **3.** to bulge: said of the eyes **4.** *Baseball* to hit the ball high into the infield —*vt.* **1.** to cause (corn) to pop, as by roasting **2.** to put suddenly [he popped his head in]

pop[2] (päp) *n.* [< PAPA] [Slang] father

pop[3] (päp) *adj.* short for POPULAR

pop. 1. popular **2.** population

pop (art) a realistic art style using techniques and subjects from commercial art, comic strips, posters, etc.

pop'corn' *n.* **1.** a variety of corn with hard grains which pop open into a white, puffy mass when heated **2.** the popped grains

pope (pōp) *n.* [< Gr. *pappas,* father] [usually **P-**] *R.C.Ch.* the bishop of Rome and head of the Church

pop'gun' *n.* a toy gun that shoots pellets by air compression, with a pop

pop·in·jay (päp'in jā') *n.* [< Ar. *babaghā,* parrot] a talkative, conceited person

pop·lar (päp'lər) *n.* [< L. *populus*] **1.** a tall tree related to the willow, having soft, fibrous wood **2.** its wood

pop·lin (päp'lən) *n.* [< Fr., prob. < *Poperinge,* city in Flanders] a sturdy ribbed fabric of cotton, silk, etc.

pop·o·ver (päp'ō'vər) *n.* a puffy, hollow muffin

pop·py (päp'ē) *n., pl.* **-ples** [< L. *papaver*] a plant with a milky juice and showy, variously colored flowers

pop'py·cock' (-käk') *n.* [Du. *pappekak,* dung] [Colloq.] foolish talk; nonsense

poppy seed the small, dark seed of the poppy, used in baking, etc.

pop·u·lace (päp'yə lis) *n.* [Fr. < It. < L. *populus,* people] **1.** the common people; the masses **2.** *same as* POPULATION (sense 1 *a*)

pop·u·lar (päp'yə lər) *adj.* [< L. *populus,* the people] **1.** of, carried on by, or intended for people generally **2.** not expensive [popular prices] **3.** prevalent **4.** liked by many people — **pop'u·lar'i·ty** (-lar'ə tē) *n.* —**pop'u·lar·ly** *adv.*

pop·u·lar·ize (päp'yə lə rīz') *vt.* **-ized', -iz'ing** to make popular

pop·u·late (päp'yə lāt') *vt.* **-lat'ed, -lat'ing** [< L. *populus,* the people] **1.** to inhabit **2.** to supply with inhabitants

pop'u·la'tion *n.* **1.** *a*) all the people in a country, region, etc. *b*) the number of these **2.** a populating or being populated

pop·u·lous (päp'yə ləs) *adj.* full of people; thickly populated —**pop'u·lous·ness** *n.*

por·ce·lain (pôr's'l in) *n.* [< Fr. < It. *porcellana*] a hard, white, translucent variety of ceramic ware

porch (pôrch) *n.* [< L. *porta,* gate] **1.** a covered entrance to a building **2.** an open or enclosed gallery or room on the outside of a building

por·cine (pôr'sin, -sin) *adj.* [< Fr. < L. *porcus,* a hog] of or like pigs or hogs

por·cu·pine (pôr'kyə pīn') *n.* [< L. *porcus,* pig + *spina,* spine] a rodent having coarse hair mixed with long, stiff, sharp spines

pore[1] (pôr) *vi.* **pored, por'ing** [< ?] **1.** to study carefully (with *over*) **2.** to ponder (with *over*)

pore[2] (pôr) *n.* [< Gr. *poros,* passage] a tiny opening, as in plant leaves, skin, etc., for absorbing or discharging fluids

pork (pôrk) *n.* [< L. *porcus,* pig] the flesh of a pig or hog used as food

pork barrel [Colloq.] government money spent for political patronage

pork'y *adj.* **-i·er, -i·est 1.** of or like pork **2.** [Slang] saucy, cocky, etc.

por·no (pôr'nō) *n., adj.* [Slang] *short for* PORNOGRAPHY, PORNOGRAPHIC: also **porn** (pôrn)

por·nog·ra·phy (pôr nägʹrə fē) *n.* [< Gr. *pornē,* a prostitute + *graphein,* to write] writings, pictures, etc. intended primarily to arouse sexual desire —**por'no·graph'ic** (-nə graf'ik) *adj.*

po·rous (pôr'əs) *adj.* full of pores, through which fluids, air, or light may pass —**po·ros·i·ty** (pô räs'ə tē) *n.*

por·phy·ry (pôr'fər ē) *n., pl.* **-ries** [< Gr. *porphyros,* purple] any igneous rock with large, distinct crystals

por·poise (pôr'pəs) *n.* [< L. *porcus,* pig + *piscis,* a fish] **1.** a small whale with a blunt snout **2.** a dolphin

por·ridge (pôr'ij) *n.* [< POTTAGE by confusion with VL. *porrata,* leek broth] [Chiefly Brit.] a soft food made of cereal or meal boiled in water or milk

por·rin·ger (pôr'in jər) *n.* [< Fr. *potager,* soup dish: infl. by prec.] a bowl for porridge, cereal, etc.

port[1] (pôrt) *n.* [< L. *portus,* haven] **1.** a harbor **2.** a city with a harbor where ships load or unload cargo

port[2] (pôrt) *n.* [< *Oporto,* city in Portugal] a sweet, dark-red wine

port[3] (pôrt) *vt.* [< L. *portare,* carry] to hold (a rifle, etc.) diagonally in front of one, as for inspection

port[4] (pôrt) *n.* [prob. < PORT[1]] the left side of a ship, etc. as one faces the bow —*adj.* of or on the port —*vt., vi.* to turn (the helm) to the port side

port[5] (pôrt) *n.* [< L. *porta,* door] **1.** a porthole **2.** an opening, as in a valve face, for the passage of steam, gas, etc.

Port. 1. Portugal **2.** Portuguese

port·a·ble (pôr'tə b'l) *adj.* [< L. *portare,* carry] **1.** that can be carried **2.** easily carried —*n.* something portable —**port'a·bil'i·ty** *n.*

por·tage (pôr'tij) *n.* [< L. *portare,* carry] **1.** a carrying of boats and supplies overland between navigable rivers, lakes, etc. **2.** any route over which this is done

por·tal (pôr't'l) *n.* [< L. *porta,* door] a doorway, gate, or entrance

port·cul·lis (pôrt kul'is) *n.* [< MFr. *porte,* a gate + *coleïce,* sliding] a large iron grating lowered to bar the gateway of a castle or fortified town

por·tend (pôr tend') *vt.* [< L. *por-,* through + *tendere,* to stretch] **1.** to be an omen of; presage **2.** to signify

por·tent (pôr'tent) *n.* **1.** something that portends an event; omen **2.** significance

por·ten·tous (pôr ten'təs) *adj.* **1.** being a portent; ominous **2.** amazing **3.** pompous

por·ter[1] (pôr'tər) *n.* [< L. *porta,* gate] a doorman or gatekeeper

por·ter[2] (pôr'tər) *n.* [< L. *portare,* carry] **1.** a man who carries luggage, etc. for hire **2.** a man who sweeps, cleans, etc. in a bank, store, etc. **3.** a railroad attendant for passengers in a sleeper **4.** a dark-brown beer

por'ter·house' (-hous') *n.* [orig., a tavern: see PORTER[2], sense 4] a choice cut of beef from the loin just before the sirloin: in full **porterhouse steak**

port·fo·li·o (pôrt fō'lē ō') *n., pl.* **-os'** [< L. *por-*

tare, carry + *folium*, leaf] **1.** a flat, portable case for loose papers, etc.; briefcase **2.** the office of a minister of state **3.** a list of an investor's securities

port·hole (pôrt'hōl') *n.* an opening in a ship's side to admit light and air

por·ti·co (pôr'tə kō') *n., pl.* **-coes', -cos'** [It. < L. *porticus*] a porch or covered walk, consisting of a roof supported by columns

por·tiere, por·tière (pôr tyer') *n.* [Fr. < *porte*, door] a curtain hung in a doorway

por·tion (pôr'shən) *n.* [< L. *portio*] **1.** a part, esp. that allotted to a person; share **2.** a dowry **3.** destiny —*vt.* **1.** to divide into portions **2.** to give as a portion to

port·ly (pôrt'lē) *adj.* **-li·er, -li·est 1.** massive and stately **2.** stout; corpulent

port·man·teau (pôrt man'tō) *n., pl.* **-teaus, -teaux** (-tōz) [< Fr. *porter*, carry + *manteau*, cloak] a stiff suitcase that opens like a book into two compartments

por·trait (pôr'trit, -trāt) *n.* [see PORTRAY] **1.** a painting, photograph, etc. of a person, esp. of his face **2.** a description

por·trai·ture (pôr'tri chər) *n.* **1.** the practice or art of portraying **2.** a portrait

por·tray (pôr trā') *vt.* [< L. *pro-*, forth + *trahere*, draw] **1.** to make a portrait of **2.** to describe graphically **3.** to play the part of in a play, movie, etc. —**por·tray'al** *n.*

Por·tu·guese (pôr'chə gēz') *adj.* of Portugal, its people, language, etc. —*n.* **1.** *pl.* **-guese'** a native of Portugal **2.** the Romance language of Portugal and Brazil

pose (pōz) *vt.* **posed, pos'ing** [< LL. *pausare*, to rest] **1.** to propose (a question, etc.) **2.** to put (an artist's model, etc.) in a certain attitude —*vi.* **1.** to assume a certain attitude, as in modeling for an artist **2.** to strike attitudes for effect **3.** to set oneself up (*as*) —*n.* **1.** a bodily attitude, esp. one held for an artist, etc. **2.** behavior assumed for effect; pretense

Po·sei·don (pō sī'd'n) *Gr. Myth.* god of the sea

pos·er (pō'zər) *n.* **1.** one who poses; affected person: also **po·seur** (pō zur') **2.** a baffling question

posh (päsh) *adj.* [< ?] [Colloq.] luxurious and fashionable —**posh'ness** *n.*

po·si·tion (pə zish'ən) *n.* [< L. *ponere*, to place] **1.** the way in which a person or thing is placed or arranged **2.** one's attitude or opinion **3.** the place where one is; location **4.** the usual or proper place **5.** rank, esp. high rank **6.** a job; office —*vt.* to put in a certain position

pos·i·tive (päz'ə tiv) *adj.* [see prec.] **1.** definitely set; explicit [*positive* instructions] **2.** *a)* having the mind set; confident *b)* overconfident or dogmatic **3.** showing agreement; affirmative **4.** constructive [*positive* criticism] **5.** regarded as having real existence [a *positive* good] **6.** based on facts [*positive* proof] **7.** *Elec. a)* of electricity predominating in a glass body after it has been rubbed with silk *b)* charged with positive electricity *c)* having a deficiency of electrons **8.** *Gram.* of an adjective or adverb in its uncompared degree **9.** *Math.* greater than zero **10.** *Photog.* with the relation of light and shade the same as in the thing photographed —*n.* something positive, as a degree, quality, quantity, photographic print, etc. —**pos'i·tive·ly** *adv.*

pos·i·tron (päz'ə trän') *n.* [POSI(TIVE) + (ELEC)TRON] a particle opposite in charge to an electron, having about the same mass and magnitude of charge

poss. possessive

pos·se (päs'ē) *n.* [L., be able] a body of men summoned by a sheriff to assist him in keeping the peace

pos·sess (pə zes') *vt.* [< L. *possidere*] **1.** to have as something that belongs to one; own **2.** to have as an attribute, quality, etc. **3.** to gain control over [*possessed* by an idea] —**pos·ses'sor** *n.*

pos·sessed' *adj.* **1.** owned **2.** controlled as if by a demon; crazed

pos·ses·sion (pə zesh'ən) *n.* **1.** a possessing or being possessed; ownership **2.** anything possessed **3.** [*pl.*] property; wealth **4.** territory ruled by an outside country

pos·ses'sive (-zes'iv) *adj.* **1.** of possession **2.** showing or desiring possession **3.** *Gram.* designating or of a case, form, or construction indicating possession (Ex.: *my, Bill's*) —*n. Gram.* the possessive case or form —**pos·ses'sive·ly** *adv.*

pos·si·ble (päs'ə b'l) *adj.* [< L. *posse*, be able] **1.** that can be or exist **2.** that may or may not happen **3.** that can be done, chosen, etc. **4.** permissible —**pos'si·bil'i·ty** (-bil'ə tē) *n., pl.* **-ties**

pos'si·bly (-blē) *adv.* **1.** by any possible means **2.** perhaps; maybe

pos·sum (päs'əm) *n.* [Colloq.] *same as* OPOSSUM —**play possum** to pretend to be asleep, dead, ill, etc.

post' (pōst) *n.* [< L. *postis*] **1.** a piece of wood, metal, etc. set upright to support a sign, fence, etc. **2.** the starting point of a horse race —*vt.* **1.** to put up (a notice, etc.) on (a wall, etc.) **2.** to announce by posting notices **3.** to warn against trespassing on (grounds, etc.) by posted notices **4.** to put (a name) on a posted or published list

post² (pōst) *n.* [< Fr. < It. *posto*] **1.** the place where a soldier, guard, etc. is stationed **2.** *a)* a place where troops are stationed *b)* the troops there **3.** the place assigned to one **4.** a position, job, or duty —*vt.* **1.** to assign to a post **2.** to put up (a bond, etc.)

post³ (pōst) *n.* [< Fr. < It. *posta*] [Chiefly Brit.] (the) mail —*vi.* to travel fast; hasten —*vt.* **1.** [Chiefly Brit.] to mail **2.** to inform [keep me *posted*]

post- [L. < *post*, after] *a prefix meaning:* **1.** after in time, following [*postgraduate*] **2.** after in space, behind [*postnasal*]

post·age (pōs'tij) *n.* the amount charged for mailing a letter, etc., esp. as represented by stamps

post·al (pōs't'l) *adj.* [Fr.] of mail or post offices —*n.* [Colloq.] a postal card

postal card a card with a printed postage stamp, for use in the mails

post card a card, often a picture card, that can be sent through the mail when a postage stamp is affixed

post'date' *vt.* **-dat'ed, -dat'ing 1.** to assign a later date to than the actual date **2.** to be subsequent to

post·er (pōs'tər) *n.* a large advertisement or notice posted publicly

pos·te·ri·or (päs tir'ē ər, pōs-) *adj.* [L. < *post*, after] **1.** later; following **2.** at or toward the rear —*n.* the buttocks

pos·ter·i·ty (päs ter'ə tē) *n.* [see prec.] **1.** all of a person's descendants **2.** all future generations

post'grad'u·ate *adj.* of or taking a course of study after graduation —*n.* a student taking such courses

post'haste' *adv.* with great haste

post·hu·mous (päs'choo məs) *adj.* [< L. *post-*

umus, last] **1.** born after the father's death **2.** published after the author's death **3.** arising or continuing after one's death —**post'hu·mous·ly** *adv.*

pos·til·ion, pos·til·lion (pōs til'yən, päs-) *n.* [Fr. < It. *posta*, POST³] one who rides the leading left-hand horse of a team drawing a carriage

post·lude (pōst'lōōd') *n.* [POST- + (PRE)LUDE] a concluding musical section

post'man (-mən) *n., pl.* -**men** a mailman

post'mark' *n.* a post-office mark stamped on mail, canceling the postage stamp and recording the date and place —*vt.* to stamp with a postmark

post'mas'ter *n.* a person in charge of a post office —**post'mis'tress** *n.fem.*

postmaster general *pl.* **postmasters general, postmaster generals** the head of a government's postal system

post me·ri·di·em (mə rid'ē əm) [L.] after noon: abbrev. **P.M., p.m., PM**

post-mor·tem (pōst'môr'təm) *adj.* [L.] **1.** after death **2.** of a post-mortem —*n.* an examination of a body after death

post·na·sal drip (pōst'nā'z'l) a discharge of mucus from behind the nose onto the pharynx, due to a cold, etc.

post'na'tal (-nāt''l) *adj.* after birth

post office 1. the governmental department in charge of the mails **2.** a place where mail is sorted, postage stamps are sold, etc.

post'op'er·a·tive (-äp'ər ə tiv) *adj.* of or occurring after a surgical operation

post'paid' *adj.* with the postage prepaid

post·pone (pōst pōn') *vt.* -**poned'**, -**pon'ing** [< L. *post-*, after + *ponere*, put] to put off until later —**post·pone'ment** *n.*

post·script (pōst'skript') *n.* [< L. *post-*, after + *scribere*, write] a note added below the signature of a letter

pos·tu·late (päs'chə lāt') *vt.* -**lat'ed**, -**lat'ing** [< L. *postulare*, to demand] **1.** to assume to be true, real, etc., esp. as a basis for argument **2.** to take for granted —*n.* (-lit) **1.** something postulated **2.** a prerequisite **3.** a basic principle

pos·ture (päs'chər) *n.* [< L. *ponere*, to place] **1.** the position or carriage of the body **2.** a position assumed as in posing **3.** an official stand or position —*vi.* -**tured**, -**tur·ing** to pose or assume an attitude: also **pos'tur·ize'** -**ized'**, -**iz'·ing**

post'war' *adj.* after the (or a) war

po·sy (pō'zē) *n., pl.* -**sies** [< POESY] a flower or bouquet: old-fashioned usage

pot (pät) *n.* [OE. *pott*] **1.** a round vessel for holding liquids, cooking, etc. **2.** a pot with its contents **3.** [Colloq.] all the money bet at a single time **4.** [Slang] marijuana —*vt.* **pot'ted, pot'ting 1.** to put into a pot **2.** to cook or preserve in a pot —**go to pot** to go to ruin — **pot'ful'** *n.*

po·ta·ble (pōt'ə b'l) *adj.* [Fr. < L. *potare*, to drink] drinkable —*n.* something drinkable — **po'ta·bil'i·ty** *n.*

pot·ash (pät'ash') *n.* [< Du. *pot*, pot + *asch*, ASH¹] any potassium compound used in fertilizers, soaps, etc.

po·tas·si·um (pə tas'ē əm) *n.* [see prec.] a soft, silver-white metallic chemical element: its salts are used in fertilizers, glass, etc.: symbol, K —**po·tas'sic** *adj.*

potassium nitrate a crystalline compound, used in fertilizers, gunpowder, etc.

po·ta·to (pə tāt'ō) *n., pl.* -**toes** [Sp. *patata* < WInd.] **1.** the starchy tuber of a widely cultivated plant, cooked as a vegetable **2.** this plant

potato chip a very thin slice of potato fried crisp and then salted

pot'bel'ly *n., pl.* -**lies** a protruding belly —**pot'bel'lied** *adj.*

pot'boil'er *n.* a piece of writing, etc., often inferior, done quickly for money

po·tent (pōt''nt) *adj.* [< L. *posse*, be able] **1.** having authority or power **2.** convincing; cogent **3.** effective, as a drug **4.** able to engage in sexual intercourse: said of a male —**po'ten·cy** *n., pl.* -**cies**

po·ten·tate (pōt''n tāt') *n.* a ruler; monarch

po·ten·tial (pə ten'shəl) *adj.* [see POTENT] that can come into being; possible; latent —*n.* **1.** something potential **2.** the relative voltage at a point in an electric circuit with respect to some reference point in the same circuit —**po·ten'ti·al'i·ty** (-shē al'ə tē) *n., pl.* -**ties**

poth·er (päth'ər) *n.* [< ?] a fuss; commotion —*vt., vi.* to fuss or bother

pot'hold'er *n.* a small pad or piece of cloth for handling hot pots, etc.

pot'hook' *n.* **1.** an S-shaped hook for hanging a pot over a fire **2.** a curved mark in writing

po·tion (pō'shən) *n.* [< L. *potare*, to drink] a drink, as of medicine, poison, or a supposedly magic substance

pot'luck' *n.* whatever the family meal happens to be [invited in to take *potluck*]

pot'pie' *n.* **1.** a meat pie made in a pot or deep dish **2.** a stew with dumplings

pot·pour·ri (pō'poo rē', pät poor'ē) *n.* [Fr. < *pot*, a pot + *pourrir*, to rot] a medley or miscellany; mixture

pot·sherd (pät'shurd') *n.* [see POT & SHARD] a piece of broken pottery

pot'shot' *n.* **1.** an easy shot **2.** a random shot **3.** a haphazard try

pot·tage (pät'ij) *n.* [< Du. *pot*, a pot] a kind of thick soup or stew

pot·ter (pät'ər) *n.* a maker of earthenware pots, dishes, etc.

potter's field [cf. Matt. 27:7] a burial ground for paupers or unknown persons

potter's wheel a rotating, horizontal disk upon which clay is molded into bowls, etc.

pot'ter·y *n., pl.* -**ies 1.** a potter's workshop **2.** the art of a potter **3.** pots, bowls, etc. made of clay hardened by heat

pouch (pouch) *n.* [< MFr. *poche*] **1.** a small bag or sack, as for pipe tobacco **2.** a mailbag **3.** a saclike structure, as that on the abdomen of the kangaroo, etc. for offspring

poul·tice (pōl'tis) *n.* [< ML. *pultes*, pap] a hot, soft, moist mass applied to a sore part of the body —*vt.* -**ticed**, -**tic·ing** to apply a poultice to

poul·try (pōl'trē) *n.* [< L. *pullus*, chicken] domestic fowls, as chickens

pounce (pouns) *n.* [ME. *pownce*, talon] a pouncing —*vi.* **pounced, pounc'ing** to swoop down or leap (*on*, *upon*, or *at*) as if to seize

pound¹ (pound) *n., pl.* **pounds**, collectively **pound** [< L. *pondus*, a weight] **1.** a unit of weight, equal to 16 oz. avoirdupois or 12 oz. troy: abbrev. **lb. 2.** the monetary unit of the United Kingdom and of various other countries: symbol £

pound² (pound) *vt.* [OE. *punian*] **1.** to beat to a pulp, powder, etc.; pulverize **2.** to hit hard — *vi.* **1.** to deliver repeated, heavy blows (*at* or *on*) **2.** to move with heavy steps **3.** to throb

pound³ (pound) *n.* [< OE. *pund-*] a municipal enclosure for stray animals

pound'cake' *n.* a rich cake made (orig. with a pound each) of flour, butter, sugar, etc.

pour (pôr) *vt.* [ME. *pouren*] **1.** to cause to flow in a continuous stream **2.** to emit, utter, etc. profusely or steadily —*vi.* **1.** to flow freely, etc. **2.** to rain heavily

pout (pout) *vi.* [ME. *pouten*] **1.** to thrust out the lips, as in sullenness **2.** to sulk —*n.* a pouting

pov·er·ty (päv′ər tē) *n.* [< L. *pauper*, poor] **1.** the condition or quality of being poor; need **2.** inferiority; inadequacy **3.** scarcity

pov′er·ty-strick′en *adj.* very poor

POW, P.O.W. prisoner of war

pow·der (pou′dər) *n.* [< L. *pulvis*] **1.** any dry substance in the form of fine, dustlike particles, produced by crushing, grinding, etc. **2.** a specific kind of powder [bath *powder*] —*vt.* **1.** to put powder on **2.** to make into powder — **pow′der·y** *adj.*

powder room a lavatory for women

pow·er (pou′ər) *n.* [ult. < L. *posse*, be able] **1.** ability to do or act **2.** vigor; force; strength **3.** *a)* authority; influence *b)* legal authority **4.** physical force or energy [electric *power*] **5.** a person or thing having great influence, force, or authority **6.** a nation, esp. one dominating others **7.** the result of multiplying a quantity by itself **8.** the degree of magnification of a lens —*vt.* to supply with power —*adj.* **1.** operated by electricity, a fuel engine, etc. [*power* tools] **2.** served by an auxiliary system that reduces effort [*power* steering] **3.** carrying electricity

pow′er·ful *adj.* strong; mighty; influential

pow′er·house′ *n.* **1.** a building where electric power is generated **2.** [Colloq.] a strong or energetic person, team, etc.

pow′er·less *adj.* without power; weak; unable

power of attorney a written statement legally authorizing a person to act for one

pow-wow (pou′wou′) *n.* [< AmInd.] **1.** a conference of or with N. American Indians **2.** [Colloq.] any conference

pox (päks) *n.* [for *pocks*: see POCK] **1.** a disease characterized by skin eruptions, as smallpox **2.** syphilis

pp. 1. pages **2.** past participle

ppd. 1. postpaid **2.** prepaid

ppr., p.pr. present participle

P.P.S., p.p.s. [L. *post postscriptum*] an additional postscript

Pr. Provençal

pr. 1. pair(s) **2.** present **3.** price

P.R., PR public relations

prac·ti·ca·ble (prak′ti kə b'l) *adj.* **1.** that can be put into practice; feasible **2.** that can be used —**prac′ti·ca·bil′i·ty** *n.*

prac·ti·cal (prak′ti k'l) *adj.* **1.** of or obtained through practice or action **2.** useful **3.** concerned with application to useful ends, rather than theory [*practical* science] **4.** given to actual practice [a *practical* farmer] **5.** that is so in practice; virtual **6.** matter-of-fact —**prac′ti·cal′i·ty** (-kal′ə tē) *n., pl.* -ties

practical joke a trick played in fun

prac′ti·cal·ly *adv.* **1.** in a practical manner **2.** from a practical viewpoint **3.** in effect; virtually **4.** [Colloq.] almost; nearly

prac·tice (prak′tis) *vt.* -ticed, -tic·ing [< Gr. *prassein*, do] **1.** to do or engage in regularly; make a habit of **2.** to do repeatedly so as to gain skill **3.** to work at, esp. as a profession — *vi.* **1.** to do something repeatedly so as to gain skill **2.** to work at a profession —*n.* **1.** a practicing; habit, custom, etc. **2.** *a)* repeated action for gaining skill *b)* the skill so acquired **3.** the actual doing of something **4.** *a)* the exercise of

a profession *b)* a business based on this — **prac′tic·er** *n.*

prac′ticed *adj.* skilled; expert

prac·ti·tion·er (prak tish′ən ər) *n.* one who practices a profession, art, etc.

prag·mat·ic (prag mat′ik) *adj.* [< Gr. *pragma*, thing done] **1.** practical **2.** testing the validity of all concepts by their practical results Also **prag·mat′i·cal** —**prag·mat′i·cal·ly** *adv.* —**prag′ma·tism** (-mə tiz′m) *n.* —**prag′ma·tist** *n.*

prai·rie (prer′ē) *n.* [Fr., meadowland] a large area of level or rolling grassy land

prairie dog a small, squirrellike, burrowing rodent of N. America, with a barking cry

prairie schooner a covered wagon

praise (prāz) *vt.* **praised, prais′ing** [< L. *pretium*, worth] **1.** to commend the worth of **2.** to glorify (God, etc.), as in song —*n.* a praising or being praised; acclaim

praise′wor′thy *adj.* worthy of praise

pra·line (prā′lēn, prä′-) *n.* [Fr.] a crisp or soft candy made with nuts

pram (pram) *n.* [Brit. Colloq.] a perambulator

prance (prans) *vi.* **pranced, pranc′ing** [< ?] **1.** to rise up, or move along, on the hind legs: said of a horse **2.** to caper or strut —*n.* a prancing —**pranc′er** *n.*

prank (praŋk) *n.* [< ?] a playful or mischievous trick —**prank′ster** *n.*

prate (prāt) *vi., vt.* **prat′ed, prat′ing** [< MDu. *praten*] to talk much and foolishly; chatter

prat·tle (prat′'l) *vi., vt.* **-tled, -tling** [MLowG. *pratelen*] to prate or babble —*n.* chatter or babble —**prat′tler** *n.*

prawn (prôn) *n.* [< ?] an edible, shrimplike crustacean

pray (prā) *vt.* [< L. *prex*, prayer] **1.** to implore [(I) *pray* (you) tell me] **2.** to ask for by prayer —*vi.* to say prayers, as to God

prayer (prer) *n.* **1.** the act of praying **2.** an entreaty; supplication **3.** *a)* a humble request, as to God *b)* a set of words used in praying **4.** [often *pl.*] a religious prayer service **5.** something prayed for —**prayer′ful** *adj.* —**prayer′ful·ly** *adv.*

pre- [< L. *prae*, before] *a prefix meaning* before in time, place, or rank [*prewar*]

preach (prēch) *vi.* [< L. *prae-*, before + *dicare*, to proclaim] **1.** to give a sermon **2.** to give moral advice, esp. in a tiresome way —*vt.* **1.** to advocate or urge as by preaching **2.** to deliver (a sermon) —**preach′ment** *n.*

preach′er *n.* one who preaches; esp., a clergyman

pre·am·ble (prē′am′b'l) *n.* [< L. *prae-*, before + *ambulare*, go] an introduction, esp. one to a constitution, statute, etc., stating its purpose

pre·ar·range (prē′ə rānj′) *vt.* **-ranged′, -rang′ing** to arrange beforehand

prec. preceding

pre·car·i·ous (pri ker′ē əs) *adj.* [see PRAY] dependent upon circumstances or chance; uncertain; risky —**pre·car′i·ous·ly** *adv.*

pre·cau·tion (pri kô′shən) *n.* [< Fr. < L. *prae-*, before + *cavere*, take care] care taken beforehand, as against danger, failure, etc. —**pre·cau′tion·ar′y** *adj.*

pre·cede (pri sēd′) *vt., vi.* **-ced′ed, -ced′ing** [see PRE- & CEDE] to be, come, or go before in time, place, order, rank, etc.

prec·e·dence (pres′ə dəns, pri sēd′'ns) *n.* the act, right, or fact of preceding in time, place, order, rank, etc.: also **prec′e·den·cy**

prec·e·dent (pres′ə dənt) *adj.* preceding —*n.* (pres′ə dənt) an act, statement, etc. that may serve as an example or justification for a later one

pre·ced'ing *adj.* that precedes

pre·cept (prē'sept) *n.* [< L. *prae-*, before + *capere*, take] a rule of moral conduct

pre·cep·tor (pri sep'tər) *n.* a teacher

pre·cinct (prē'siŋkt) *n.* [< L. *praecingere*, encompass] **1.** [*usually pl.*] an enclosure between buildings, walls, etc. **2.** [*pl.*] environs **3.** *a)* a police district *b)* a subdivision of a voting ward **4.** a limited area

pre·ci·os·i·ty (presh'ē äs'ə tē) *n., pl.* **-ties** [see PRECIOUS] affectation in language

pre·cious (presh'əs) *adj.* [< L. *pretium*, a price] **1.** of great price or value; costly **2.** beloved; dear **3.** very fastidious, affected, etc. —**pre'cious·ly** *adv.* —**pre'cious·ness** *n.*

prec·i·pice (pres'ə pis) *n.* [< Fr. < L. *prae-*, before + *caput*, a head] a vertical or overhanging rock face

pre·cip·i·tant (pri sip'ə tənt) *adj.* [see prec.] *same as* PRECIPITATE

pre·cip'i·tate' (-tāt'; *also, for adj. & n.,* -tit) *vt.* **-tat'ed, -tat'ing** [see PRECIPICE] **1.** to hurl downward **2.** to cause to happen before expected, needed, etc. **3.** *Chem.* to separate (a dissolved substance) out from a solution —*vi.* **1.** *Chem.* to be precipitated **2.** to condense and fall as rain, snow, etc. —*adj.* **1.** falling steeply **2.** acting hastily or rashly **3.** very sudden or abrupt —*n.* a substance precipitated out from a solution —**pre·cip'i·tate·ly** *adv.*

pre·cip'i·ta'tion *n.* **1.** a precipitating or being precipitated **2.** sudden or rash haste **3.** *a)* rain, snow, etc. *b)* the amount of this **4.** *Chem.* a precipitating or a precipitate

pre·cip'i·tous (-ə təs) *adj.* **1.** steep like a precipice **2.** rash —**pre·cip'i·tous·ly** *adv.*

pré·cis (prā sē', prā'sē) *n., pl.* **-cis'** (-sēz', -sēz) [Fr.: see PRECISE] a concise abridgment; summary

pre·cise (pri sīs') *adj.* [< L. *prae-*, before + *caedere*, to cut] **1.** accurately stated; definite **2.** minutely exact **3.** scrupulous; fastidious **4.** finicky —**pre·cise'ly** *adv.*

pre·ci·sion (pri sizh'ən) *n.* the quality of being precise; exactness —**pre·ci'sion·ist** *n.*

pre·clude (pri klōōd') *vt.* **-clud'ed, -clud'ing** [< L. *prae-*, before + *claudere*, to close] to make impossible, esp. in advance; prevent —**pre·clu'sion** *n.* —**pre·clu'sive** *adj.*

pre·co·cious (pri kō'shəs) *adj.* [< L. *prae-*, before + *coquere*, to cook] matured earlier than usual, as a child —**pre·co'cious·ness, pre·coc'i·ty** (-käs'ə tē) *n.*

pre·cog·ni·tion (prē'käg nish'ən) *n.* [see PRE- & COGNITION] the supposed extrasensory perception of a future event —**pre·cog'ni·tive** *adj.*

pre-Co·lum·bi·an (prē'kə lum'bē ən) *adj.* of any period in the Americas before Columbus's voyages

pre·con·ceive (prē'kən sēv') *vt.* **-ceived', -ceiv'ing** to form an idea or opinion of beforehand —**pre'con·cep'tion** (-sep'shən) *n.*

pre·cur·sor (pri kur'sər) *n.* [< L. *praecurrere*, run ahead] **1.** a forerunner **2.** a predecessor —**pre·cur'so·ry** *adj.*

pred·a·to·ry (pred'ə tôr'ē) *adj.* [< L. *praeda*, a prey] **1.** of or living by plundering **2.** preying on other animals —**pred'a·tor** (-tər) *n.*

pred·e·ces·sor (pred'ə ses'ər, pred'ə ses'ər) *n.* [< L. *prae-*, before + *decedere*, go away] a person preceding another, as in office

pre·des·ti·na·tion *n.* **1.** *Theol.* the doctrine that *a)* God foreordained everything that would happen *b)* God predestines souls to salvation or to damnation **2.** destiny

pre·des·tine (prē des'tin) *vt.* **-tined, -tin·ing** to destine or decree beforehand

pre·de·ter·mine (prē'di tur'mən) *vt.* **-mined, -min·ing** to determine or decide beforehand —**pre'de·ter'mi·na'tion** *n.*

pre·dic·a·ment (pri dik'ə mənt) *n.* [see PREACH] a difficult or embarrassing situation

pred·i·cate (pred'i kāt') *vt.* **-cat'ed, -cat'ing** [see PREACH] **1.** to affirm as a quality or attribute **2.** to base (something) *on* or *upon* facts, conditions, etc. —*n.* (-kit) *Gram.* the word or words that make a statement about the subject —*adj.* (-kit) *Gram.* of or involved in a predicate

pre·dict (pri dikt') *vt., vi.* [< L. *prae-*, before + *dicere*, tell] to state (what one believes will happen); foretell —**pre·dict'a·ble** *adj.* —**pre·dic'tion** *n.*

pre·di·gest (prē'di jest', -dī-) *vt.* to treat (food) as with enzymes for easier digestion when eaten —**pre'di·ges'tion** *n.*

pre·di·lec·tion (pred''l ek'shən) *n.* [< Fr. < L. *prae-*, before + *diligere*, prefer] a preconceived liking; partiality (*for*)

pre·dis·pose (prē'dis pōz') *vt.* **-posed', -pos'ing** to make susceptible (*to*); incline —**pre'dis·po·si'tion** *n.*

pre·dom·i·nant (pri däm'ə nənt) *adj.* **1.** having authority or influence over others; superior **2.** most frequent; prevailing —**pre·dom'i·nance** *n.*

pre·dom'i·nate' (-nāt') *vi.* **-nat'ed, -nat'ing 1.** to have influence or authority (*over* others) **2.** to prevail; preponderate —**pre·dom'i·na'tion** *n.*

pre·em·i·nent, pre-em·i·nent (prē em'ə nənt) *adj.* eminent above all others; surpassing: also **pre·ĕm'i·nent** —**pre·em'i·nence** *n.*

pre·empt', pre-empt' (-empt') *vt.* [< L. *prae-*, before + *emere*, buy] **1.** to gain the right to buy (public land) by settling on it **2.** to seize before anyone else can **3.** *Radio & TV* to replace (a scheduled program) Also **pre·ĕmpt'** —**pre·emp'tion** *n.*

preen (prēn) *vt.* [< ME. *proinen*, PRUNE[2]] **1.** to clean and trim (the feathers) with the beak: said of birds **2.** to dress up or adorn (oneself) **3.** to pride (oneself) —*vi.* to primp

pre·ex·ist, pre-ex·ist (prē'ig zist') *vt., vi.* to exist previously or before (another person or thing): also **pre'ĕx·ist'** —**pre'ex·ist'ence** *n.*

pre·fab·ri·cate (prē fab'rə kāt') *vt.* **-cat'ed, -cat'ing** to make (houses, etc.) in standardized sections for shipment and quick assembly —**pre'fab·ri·ca'tion** *n.*

pref·ace (pref'is) *n.* [< L. *prae-*, before + *fari*, speak] an introduction to a book, speech, etc. —*vt.* **-aced, -ac·ing 1.** to furnish with a preface **2.** to be a preface to —**pref'a·to'ry** (-ə tôr'ē) *adj.*

pre·fect (prē'fekt) *n.* [< L. *praeficere*, to set over] any of various administrators —**pre'fec·ture** (-fek chər) *n.*

pre·fer (pri fur') *vt.* **-ferred', -fer'ring** [< L. *prae-*, before + *ferre*, BEAR[1]] **1.** to promote; advance **2.** to put before a court, etc. for consideration **3.** to like better

pref·er·a·ble (pref'ər ə b'l) *adj.* more desirable —**pref'er·a·bly** *adv.*

pref·er·ence (pref'ər əns) *n.* **1.** a preferring or being preferred **2.** something preferred **3.** advantage given to one person, country, etc. over others —**pref'er·en'tial** (-ə ren'shəl) *adj.* —**pref'er·en'tial·ly** *adv.*

pre·fer·ment (pri fur'mənt) *n.* an advancement in rank, etc.; promotion

pre·fix (prē'fiks) *n.* [< L. *prae-*, before + *figere*, to fix] a syllable or syllables fixed at the beginning of a word to alter its meaning, etc. —*vt.* (*also* prē fiks') to add as a prefix

preg·nant (preg′nənt) *adj.* [< L. *pregnans*] **1.** having (an) offspring developing in the uterus; with young **2.** mentally fertile; inventive **3.** full of meaning, etc. **4.** filled (*with*) —**preg′-nan·cy** *n., pl.* -**cies**

pre·hen·sile (pri hen′s'l) *adj.* [< Fr. < L. *prehendere*, take] adapted for seizing or grasping, esp. by wrapping around something, as a monkey's tail

pre·his·tor·ic (prē′his tôr′ik) *adj.* of the period before recorded history: also **pre′his·tor′i·cal** — **pre′his·tor′i·cal·ly** *adv.*

pre·judge (prē juj′) *vt.* -**judged′**, -**judg′ing** to judge beforehand, or without all the evidence —**pre·judg′ment, pre·judge′ment** *n.*

prej·u·dice (prej′ə dis) *n.* [< L. *prae-*, before + *judicium*, judgment] **1.** a preconceived, usually unfavorable, idea **2.** an opinion held in disregard of facts that contradict it; bias **3.** intolerance or hatred of other races, etc. **4.** injury or harm —*vt.* -**diced, -dic·ing 1.** to harm or damage **2.** to cause to have prejudice; bias — **prej′u·di′cial** (-dish′əl) *adj.*

prel′ate (-it) *n.* [< L. *praeferre*, place before] a high-ranking ecclesiastic, as a bishop —**prel′-a·cy** (-ə sē) *n.*

pre·lim·i·nar·y (pri lim′ə ner′ē) *adj.* [< Fr. < L. *prae-*, before + *limen*, threshold] leading up to the main action, etc.; preparatory —*n., pl.* -**ies** [*often pl.*] a preliminary step, procedure, test, etc.

prel·ude (prel′yo͞od, prā′lo͞od) *n.* [< Fr. < L. *prae-*, before + *ludere*, to play] **1.** a preliminary part; preface **2.** *Music* an introductory section of a suite, fugue, etc. —*vt., vi.* -**ud·ed, -ud·ing** to serve as or be a prelude (to)

pre·mar·i·tal (prē mar′ə t'l) *adj.* before marriage

pre·ma·ture (prē′mə to͞or′, -choor′) *adj.* [< L.: see PRE- & MATURE] happening, done, arriving, etc. before the proper or usual time; too early —**pre′ma·ture′ly** *adv.*

pre·med·i·tate (pri med′ə tāt′) *vt., vi.* -**tat′ed, -tat′ing** to think out or plan beforehand —**pre-med′i·ta′tion** *n.*

pre·mier (pri mir′, -myir′) *adj.* [< L. *primus*, first] **1.** first in importance; chief **2.** first in time —*n.* a chief official; specif., *a*) a prime minister *b*) the governor of a Canadian province —**pre·mier′ship** *n.*

pre·mière, pre·miere (pri myer′, -mir′) *n.* [Fr., fem. of *premier*] a first performance of a play, etc.

prem·ise (prem′is) *n.* [< L. *prae-*, before + *mittere*, send] **1.** a previous statement serving as a basis for an argument **2.** [*pl.*] a piece of real estate —*vt.* (*also* pri mīz′) -**ised, -is·ing 1.** to state as a premise **2.** to preface (a discourse, etc.)

pre·mi·um (prē′mē əm) *n., pl.* -**ums** [< L. *prae-*, before + *emere*, take] **1.** a reward or prize, esp. as an inducement to buy **2.** an amount paid in addition to the regular charge, etc. **3.** a payment, as for an insurance policy **4.** very high value [to put a *premium* on honesty] —**at a premium** very valuable, as because of scarcity

pre·mo·ni·tion (prē′mə nish′ən, prem′ə-) *n.* [< L. *prae-*, before + *monere*, warn] **1.** a forewarning **2.** a foreboding —**pre·mon·i·to·ry** (pri män′ə tôr′ē) *adj.*

pre·na·tal (prē nāt′'l) *adj.* [PRE- + NATAL] before birth —**pre·na′tal·ly** *adv.*

pre·oc·cu·py (prē äk′yə pī′) *vt.* -**pied′, -py′ing** [< L.: see PRE- & OCCUPY] **1.** to occupy the thoughts of; engross **2.** to take possession of

before someone else or beforehand —**pre·oc′cu-pa′tion** (-pā′shən) *n.*

pre·or·dain (prē′ôr dān′) *vt.* to ordain or decree beforehand —**pre′or·di·na′tion** *n.*

prep. 1. preparatory **2.** preposition

pre·paid (prē pād′) *pt. & pp. of* PREPAY

prep·a·ra·tion (prep′ə rā′shən) *n.* **1.** a preparing or being prepared **2.** a preparatory measure **3.** something prepared, as a medicine, cosmetic, etc.

pre·par·a·to·ry (pri par′ə tôr′ē) *adj.* **1.** introductory **2.** designating a school that prepares students for college entrance

pre·pare (pri par′) *vt.* -**pared′, -par′ing** [< L. *prae-*, before + *parare*, get ready] **1.** to make ready **2.** to equip or furnish **3.** to put together; construct [to *prepare* a dinner] —*vi.* **1.** to make things ready **2.** to make oneself ready

pre·par′ed·ness *n.* the state of being prepared, esp. for waging war

pre·pay (prē pā′) *vt.* -**paid′, -pay′ing** to pay or pay for in advance —**pre·pay′ment** *n.*

pre·pon·der·ate (pri pän′də rāt′) *vi.* -**at′ed, -at′ing** [< L. *prae-*, before + *ponderare*, weigh] to be greater in amount, power, influence, etc.; predominate —**pre·pon′der·ance** *n.* —**pre·pon′-der·ant** *adj.*

prep·o·si·tion (prep′ə zish′ən) *n.* [< L. *prae-*, before + *ponere*, to place] a relation word, as *in, by, to*, etc., that connects a noun or pronoun to another word —**prep′o·si′tion·al** *adj.*

pre·pos·sess (prē′pə zes′) *vt.* **1.** to prejudice **2.** to impress favorably at once

pre′pos·sess′ing *adj.* that impresses favorably; pleasing —**pre′pos·sess′ing·ly** *adv.*

pre·pos·ter·ous (pri päs′tər əs) *adj.* [< L. *prae-*, before + *posterus*, coming after] contrary to nature, reason, etc.; absurd

pre·req·ui·site (pri rek′wə zit) *adj.* required beforehand as a necessary condition —*n.* something prerequisite

pre·rog·a·tive (pri räg′ə tiv) *n.* [< L. *praerogare*, ask before] an exclusive privilege, esp. one peculiar to a rank, class, etc.

Pres. President

pres. present

pres·age (pres′ij; *for v.* pri sāj′) *n.* [< L. *prae-*, before + *sagire*, perceive] **1.** a warning or portent **2.** a foreboding —*vt.* -**aged′, -ag′ing 1.** to give warning of **2.** to predict

pres·by·ter (prez′bi tər) *n.* [see PRIEST] **1.** in the Presbyterian Church, an elder **2.** in the Episcopal Church, a priest or minister

Pres·by·te·ri·an (prez′bə tir′ē ən) *adj.* designating or of a church of a Protestant denomination governed by presbyters —*n.* a member of a Presbyterian church

pre·sci·ence (prē′shē əns, presh′əns) *n.* [< L. *praescire*, know beforehand] apparent knowledge of things before they happen

pre·scribe (pri skrīb′) *vt.* -**scribed′, -scrib′ing** [< L. *prae-*, before + *scribere*, write] **1.** to order; direct **2.** to order or advise as a medicine or treatment: said of physicians

pre·scrip·tion (pri skrip′shən) *n.* **1.** something prescribed; order **2.** a doctor's written direction for the preparation and use of a medicine **3.** a medicine so prescribed

pres·ence (prez′ns) *n.* **1.** the fact or condition of being present **2.** immediate surroundings [in his *presence*] **3.** one's bearing or appearance **4.** a spirit felt to be present

presence of mind ability to think and act quickly in an emergency

pres·ent (prez′nt) *adj.* [< L. *prae-*, before + *esse*, be] **1.** being at the specified place **2.** existing or happening now **3.** *Gram.* indicating action or state now or action that is always true (Ex.: man *is* mortal) —*n.* **1.** the present time or occasion **2.** the present tense or a verb in it **3.** a gift —*vt.* (pri zent') **1.** to introduce (a person) **2.** to exhibit; show **3.** to offer for consideration **4.** to give (a gift, etc.) to (a person, etc.) —**present arms** *Mil.* to hold a rifle vertically in front of the body

pre·sent·a·ble (pri zen'tə b'l) *adj.* **1.** suitable for presentation **2.** properly dressed for meeting people

pre·sen·ta·tion (prē'zen tā'shən, prez''n-) *n.* **1.** a presenting or being presented **2.** something presented

pre·sen·ti·ment (pri zen'tə mənt) *n.* [see PRE- & SENTIMENT] a feeling that something, esp. of an unfortunate nature, is about to take place

pres'ent·ly *adv.* **1.** soon **2.** now

pre·sent·ment (pri zent'mənt) *n.* same as PRESENTATION

present participle a participle used: *a)* to express a present action or state (as "he is *growing*") *b)* as an adjective (as "a *growing* boy")

pre·serv·a·tive (pri zur'və tiv) *adj.* preserving —*n.* anything that preserves *[a preservative added to foods]*

pre·serve (pri zurv') *vt.* **-served'**, **-serv'ing** [< L. *prae-*, before + *servare*, keep] **1.** to protect from harm, danger, etc. **2.** to keep from spoiling **3.** to prepare (food), as by canning, for future use **4.** to keep up; maintain —*n.* **1.** [*usually pl.*] fruit preserved by cooking with sugar **2.** a place where game, fish, etc. are maintained —**pres·er·va·tion** (prez'ər vā'shən) *n.*

pre·side (pri zīd') *vi.* **-sid'ed**, **-sid'ing** [< Fr. < L. *prae-*, PRE- + *sedere*, sit] **1.** to be chairman **2.** to have control or authority

pres·i·dent (prez'i dənt) *n.* [see PRESIDE] **1.** the highest officer of a company, club, etc. **2.** [*often* P-] the chief executive, or formal head, of a republic —**pres'i·den·cy** *n.* —**pres'i·den'tial** (-den'shəl) *adj.*

press[1] (pres) *vt.* [< L. *premere*]. **1.** to act on with steady force or weight; push against; squeeze **2.** to squeeze (juice, etc.) from **3.** *a)* to compress *b)* to iron (clothes, etc.) **4.** to embrace closely **5.** to force; compel **6.** to entreat persistently **7.** to try to impose **8.** to emphasize **9.** to distress *[pressed for time]* **10.** to urge on —*vi.* **1.** to weigh down **2.** to go forward with determination **3.** to crowd —*n.* **1.** pressure, urgency, etc. **2.** a crowd **3.** any machine for crushing, stamping, smoothing, etc. **4.** *a) short for* PRINTING PRESS *b)* the art or business of printing *c)* newspapers, magazines, etc., or the persons who write for them *d)* publicity, etc., as in newspapers **5.** an upright closet for clothes, etc.

press[2] (pres) *vt.* [< L. *praes,* surety + *stare,* to stand] to force into service, esp. military or naval service

press agent one whose work is to get publicity for an individual, organization, etc.

press'ing *adj.* calling for immediate attention

press'man (-mən) *n., pl.* **-men** an operator of a printing press

pres·sure (presh'ər) *n.* **1.** a pressing or being pressed **2.** a state of distress **3.** a compelling influence *[social pressure]* **4.** urgency **5.** *Physics* force per unit of area exerted upon a surface, etc. —*vt.* **-sured**, **-sur·ing** to exert pressure on

pres'sur·ize' (-īz') *vt.* **-ized'**, **-iz'ing** to keep

nearly normal air pressure inside of (an airplane, etc.), as at high altitudes

pres·ti·dig·i·ta·tion (pres'tə dij'i tā'shən) *n.* [Fr. < It. *presto,* quick + L. *digitus,* a finger] sleight of hand —**pres'ti·dig'i·ta'tor** *n.*

pres·tige (pres tēzh', -tēj') *n.* [Fr. < L. *praestigium,* illusion] **1.** the power to impress or influence **2.** reputation based on high achievement, character, etc. —**pres·ti'gious** (-tij'əs, -tē'jəs) *adj.*

pres·to (pres'tō) *adv., adj.* [It., quick] fast

pre·sume (pri zōōm', -zyōōm') *vt.* **-sumed'**, **-sum'ing** [< L. *prae-,* before + *sumere,* take] **1.** to dare (to say or do something) **2.** to take for granted; suppose —*vi.* to act presumptuously; take liberties —**pre·sum'a·ble** *adj.* —**pre·sum'a·bly** *adv.*

pre·sump·tion (pri zump'shən) *n.* **1.** a presuming; specif., *a)* forwardness; effrontery *b)* a taking of something for granted **2.** the thing presumed **3.** a reason for presuming —**pre·sump'tive** *adj.*

pre·sump·tu·ous (-chōō wəs) *adj.* too bold or forward; taking too much for granted

pre·sup·pose (prē'sə pōz') *vt.* **-posed'**, **-pos'ing 1.** to suppose or assume beforehand **2.** to require or imply as a preceding condition —**pre'sup·po·si'tion** *n.*

pre·teen (prē'tēn') *n.* a child nearly a teenager

pre·tend (pri tend') *vt.* [< L. *prae-,* before + *tendere,* to stretch] **1.** to feign; simulate *[to pretend illness]* **2.** to make believe *[pretend I'm you]* —*vi.* **1.** to lay claim (*to*) **2.** to make believe

pre·tense (pri tens', prē'tens) *n.* **1.** a claim; pretension **2.** a false claim **3.** a false show of something **4.** a pretending, as at play **5.** a pretext **6.** pretentiousness Brit. sp. **pretence**

pre·ten·sion (pri ten'shən) *n.* **1.** a pretext **2.** a claim **3.** assertion of a claim **4.** pretentiousness

pret·er·it, pret·er·ite (pret'ər it) *adj.* [< L. *praeter-,* beyond + *ire,* go] *Gram.* expressing past action or state —*n.* **1.** the past tense **2.** a verb in it

pre·ter·nat·u·ral (prēt'ər nach'ər əl) *adj.* [< L. *praeter-,* beyond + *naturalis,* natural] **1.** not ordinary; abnormal **2.** supernatural

pre·text (prē'tekst) *n.* [< L. *prae-,* before + *texere,* weave] a false reason put forth to hide the real one; excuse

pret·ty (prit'ē, pur'tē) *adj.* **-ti·er, -ti·est** [< OE. *prættig,* crafty] pleasing; attractive in a dainty or graceful way —*adv.* fairly; somewhat —*vt.* **-tied, -ty·ing** to make pretty (usually with *up*) —**pret'ti·ly** *adv.*

pret·zel (pret's'l) *n.* [G. *brezel*] a hard, brittle biscuit usually in the form of a loose knot or stick, sprinkled with salt

pre·vail (pri vāl') *vi.* [< L. *prae-,* before + *valere,* be strong] **1.** to be victorious (*over* or *against*) **2.** to succeed **3.** to be or become stronger or more widespread; predominate **4.** to be prevalent —**prevail on** (or **upon, with**) to persuade

pre·vail'ing *adj.* **1.** superior in strength, influence, etc. **2.** predominant **3.** prevalent

prev·a·lent (prev'ə lənt) *adj.* [see PREVAIL] widely existing, practiced, or accepted; common —**prev'a·lence** *n.*

pre·var·i·cate (pri var'ə kāt') *vi.* **-cat'ed, -cat'ing** [< L. *prae-,* before + *varicare,* straddle] **1.** to evade the truth **2.** to lie —**pre·var'i·ca'tion** *n.* —**pre·var'i·ca'tor** *n.*

pre·vent (pri vent') *vt.* [< L. *prae-,* before + *venire,* come] to stop or keep from doing or happening; hinder —**pre·vent′a·ble, pre·vent′i·ble** *adj.* —**pre·ven′tion** *n.*

pre·ven′tive *adj.* preventing or serving to prevent; esp., preventing disease —*n.* anything that prevents Also **pre·vent′a·tive**

pre·view (prē′vyoo) *n.* **1.** an advance, restricted showing, as of a movie **2.** a showing of scenes from a movie, etc. to advertise it Also **pre′vue** (-vyoo)

pre·vi·ous (prē′vē əs) *adj.* [< L. *prae-*, before + *via*, a way] occurring or going before — **previous to** before

pre·war (prē′wôr′) *adj.* before the war

prey (prā) *n.* [< L. *praeda*, plunder] **1.** an animal hunted for food by another animal **2.** a victim **3.** the act of preying on other animals [a bird of *prey*] —*vi.* **1.** to plunder **2.** to hunt other animals for food **3.** to weigh as an obsession Generally used with *on* or *upon*

price (prīs) *n.* [< L. *pretium*] **1.** the amount of money, etc. asked or paid for something; cost **2.** value or worth **3.** the cost, as in life, labor, etc., of obtaining some benefit —*vt.* **priced, pric′ing 1.** to fix the price of **2.** [Colloq.] to find out the price of —**at any price** no matter what the cost

price′less *adj.* **1.** too valuable to be measured by price **2.** [Colloq.] very amusing or absurd

prick (prik) *n.* [OE. *prica*, a dot] **1.** a tiny puncture made by a sharp point **2.** [Archaic] a pointed object **3.** a sharp pain caused as by being pricked —*vt.* **1.** to make (a hole) in (something) with a sharp point **2.** to pain sharply —**prick up one's (or its) ears 1.** to raise the ears erect **2.** to listen closely

prick·le (prik′'l) *n.* [< OE. *prica*, prick] **1.** any sharp point, as a thornlike growth on a plant **2.** a tingling sensation —*vt., vi.* **-led, -ling** to tingle —**prick′ly** *adj.*

prickly heat an itching skin eruption caused by inflammation of the sweat glands

pride (prīd) *n.* [< OE. *prut*, proud] **1.** *a)* an overhigh opinion of oneself *b)* haughtiness; arrogance **2.** dignity and self-respect **3.** satisfaction in one's achievements, etc. **4.** a person or thing that one is proud of —**pride oneself on** to be proud of

priest (prēst) *n.* [< Gr. *presbys*, old] **1.** one whose function is to perform religious rites **2.** in some Christian churches, a clergyman authorized to administer the sacraments **3.** any clergyman —**priest′ess** *n.fem.* —**priest′hood′** *n.* —**priest′ly** *adj.*

prig (prig) *n.* [< 16th-c. slang] one who smugly affects great propriety or morality —**prig′gish** *adj.* —**prig′gish·ly** *adv.*

prim (prim) *adj.* **prim′mer, prim′mest** [< ?] stiffly formal, precise, moral, etc.; proper — **prim′ly** *adv.*

pri·ma·cy (prī′mə sē) *n., pl.* **-cies** [see PRIMATE] **1.** a being first in time, order, rank, etc. **2.** the rank of a primate

pri·ma don·na (prē′mə dän′ə) *pl.* **pri′ma don′nas** [It., first lady] the principal woman singer, as in an opera

pri·ma fa·ci·e (prī′mə fā′shi ē′, fā′shē) [L., at first view] adequate to establish a fact unless refuted: said of evidence

pri·mal (prī′m'l) *adj.* [< L. *primus*, first] **1.** first in time; original **2.** first in importance; chief — **pri′mal·ly** *adv.*

pri·ma·ri·ly (prī mer′ə lē, prī′mer′-) *adv.* **1.** at first; originally **2.** principally

pri·ma·ry (prī′mer′ē, -mər ē) *adj.* [< L. *primus*, first] **1.** first in time or order; original **2.** from which others are derived; fundamental **3.** first in importance; chief **4.** designating the basic

colors, as red, green, and blue in color photography, or red, yellow, and blue in painting — *n., pl.* **-ries 1.** something first in order, quality, etc. **2.** a preliminary election at which candidates are chosen for the final election

pri·mate (prī′māt; *also, for 1*, -mit) *n.* [< L. *primus*, first] **1.** an archbishop, or the highest-ranking bishop in a province, etc. **2.** any of a group of mammals, including man, the apes, etc. —**pri′mate·ship′** *n.*

prime (prīm) *adj.* [< L. *primus*, first] **1.** first in time; original **2.** first in rank or importance; chief; principal **3.** first in quality **4.** fundamental **5.** *Math.* that can be evenly divided by no other whole number than itself or 1 —*n.* **1.** the first or earliest part **2.** the best or most vigorous period **3.** the best part —*vt.* **primed, prim′ing 1.** to make ready; prepare **2.** to get (a pump) into operation by pouring water into it **3.** to undercoat (a surface)

prime meridian the meridian from which longitude is measured east and west; 0°

prime minister in parliamentary governments, the chief executive

prim·er¹ (prim′ər) *n.* [< L. *primus*, first] **1.** a simple book for teaching reading to children **2.** any elementary textbook

prim·er² (prī′mər) *n.* **1.** a thing that primes **2.** an explosive cap, etc. used to fire the main charge **3.** a first coat of paint, etc.

prime time *Radio & TV* the hours when the largest audience is available

pri·me·val (prī mē′v'l) *adj.* [< L. *primus*, first + *aevum*, age] of the earliest times or ages; primordial —**pri·me′val·ly** *adv.*

prim·ing (prī′miŋ) *n.* the explosive used to set off the charge in a gun, etc.

prim·i·tive (prim′ə tiv) *adj.* [< L. *primus*, first] **1.** of the earliest time; original **2.** crude; simple **3.** primary; basic —*n.* a primitive person or thing

pri·mo·gen·i·ture (prī′mə jen′i chər) *n.* [< L. *primus*, first + *genitura*, a begetting] **1.** the condition of being the firstborn of the same parents **2.** the right of inheritance of the eldest son

pri·mor·di·al (prī môr′dē əl) *adj.* [< L. *primus*, first + *ordiri*, begin] **1.** primitive **2.** fundamental; original

primp (primp) *vt., vi.* [prob. < PRIM] to groom or dress up in a fussy way

prim·rose (prim′rōz′) *n.* [alt. (after *rose*) < ML. *primula*] a small plant with tubelike, often yellow flowers

prince (prins) *n.* [< L. *princeps*, chief] **1.** a ruler ranking below a king: head of a principality **2.** a son of a sovereign **3.** a preeminent person in a group

prince′ly *adj.* **-li·er, -li·est 1.** of a prince **2.** magnificent; generous

prin·cess (prin′sis, -ses) *n.* **1.** orig., any female monarch **2.** a daughter of a sovereign **3.** the wife of a prince

prin·ci·pal (prin′sə pəl) *adj.* [see PRINCE] first in rank, importance, etc. —*n.* **1.** a principal person or thing **2.** a governing officer, as of a school **3.** the amount of a debt, etc. minus the interest —**prin′ci·pal·ly** *adv.*

prin·ci·pal·i·ty (prin′sə pal′ə tē) *n., pl.* **-ties** the territory ruled by a prince

principal parts the principal inflected forms of a verb: in English, the present infinitive, the past tense, and past participle (*drink, drank, drunk*)

prin·ci·ple (prin′sə pəl) *n.* [see PRINCE] **1.** a fundamental truth, law, etc., upon which others are based **2.** *a)* a rule of conduct *b)* ad-

herence to such rules; integrity **3.** the scientific law that explains a natural action **4.** the method of a thing's operation
print (print) *n.* [< L. *premere*, to press] **1.** a mark made on a surface by pressing or stamping **2.** cloth printed with a design **3.** the impression of letters, designs, etc. made by inked type or from a plate, block, etc. **4.** a photograph made by passing light through a negative onto sensitized paper —*vt., vi.* **1.** to stamp (a mark, letter, etc.) on a surface **2.** to produce on (paper, etc.) the impression of inked type, plates, etc. **3.** to produce (a book, etc.) **4.** to write in letters resembling printed ones **5.** to make (a photographic print) **6.** in computers, to deliver (information) by means of a printing device: often with *out* —**in** (or **out of**) **print** still (or no longer) for sale by the publisher: said of books, etc. —**print′er** *n.* —**print′ing** *n.*
printing press a machine for printing from inked type, plates, or rolls
print′out′ *n.* the printed output of a computer
pri·or (prī′ər) *adj.* [L.] **1.** preceding in time; earlier **2.** preceding in order or importance —*n.* the head of a priory —**pri′or·ess** *n.fem.*
pri·or·i·tize (prī ôr′ə tīz′) *vt.* -**tized′**, -**tiz′ing** to arrange in order of importance
pri·or·i·ty (prī ôr′ə tē, -är′-) *n., pl.* -**ties 1.** a being prior; precedence **2.** a prior right **3.** something given prior attention
pri′o·ry *n., pl.* -**ries** a monastery governed by a prior, or a convent governed by a prioress
prism (priz′′m) *n.* [< Gr. *prizein*, to saw] **1.** a solid figure whose ends are equal and parallel polygons and whose sides are parallelograms **2.** a transparent prism whose ends are triangles: used to disperse light into the spectrum —**pris·mat·ic** (priz mat′ik) *adj.* —**pris·mat′i·cal·ly** *adv.*
pris·on (priz′′n) *n.* [< L. *prehendere*, take] a place of confinement, esp. for those convicted by or awaiting trial
pris′on·er *n.* one held captive or confined, esp. in prison
pris·sy (pris′ē) *adj.* -**si·er, -si·est** [prob. < PR(IM) + (S)ISSY] [Colloq.] very prim; fussy
pris·tine (pris′tēn, -tin) *adj.* [< L. *pristinus*, former] **1.** characteristic of the earliest period; original **2.** uncorrupted; unspoiled
prith·ee (prith′ē) *interj.* [< *pray thee*] [Archaic] I pray thee; please
pri·va·cy (prī′və sē) *n.* **1.** a being private; seclusion **2.** secrecy **3.** one's private life
pri·vate (prī′vit) *adj.* [< L. *privus*, separate] **1.** of or concerning a particular person or group **2.** not open to, intended for, or controlled by the public *[a private school]* **3.** for an individual person *[a private room]* **4.** not holding public office *[a private citizen]* **5.** secret *[a private matter]* —*n.* an enlisted man of the lowest rank in the U.S. Army or Marine Corps —**in private** not publicly —**pri′vate·ly** *adv.*
pri·va·teer (prī′və tir′) *n.* **1.** a privately owned ship commissioned in war to capture enemy ships, esp. merchant ships **2.** a commander or crew member of a privateer
pri·va·tion (prī vā′shən) *n.* lack of the ordinary necessities or comforts
priv·et (priv′it) *n.* [< ?] an evergreen shrub used for hedges
priv·i·lege (priv′′l ij) *n.* [< L. *privus*, separate + *lex*, a law] a special right, favor, etc. granted to some person or group —*vt.* -**leged, -leg·ing** to grant a privilege to
priv·y (priv′ē) *adj.* private: now only in such phrases as **privy council**, a body of confidential advisers named by a ruler —*n., pl.* -**ies** an outhouse —**privy to** privately informed about

prize[1] (prīz) *vt.* **prized, priz′ing** [see PRICE] to value highly; esteem —*n.* **1.** something offered or given to the winner of a contest, etc. **2.** anything worth striving for —*adj.* **1.** that has received a prize **2.** worthy of a prize **3.** given as a prize
prize[2] (prīz) *n.* [< L. *prehendere*, to take] something, esp. a warship, captured in war —*vt.* **prized, priz′ing** to pry, as with a lever
prize′fight′ *n.* a professional boxing match
pro[1] (prō) *adv.* [L., for] on the affirmative side —*adj.* favorable —*n., pl.* **pros** a vote, position, etc. in favor of something
pro[2] (prō) *adj., n., pl.* **pros** *short form of* PROFESSIONAL
pro-[1] [Gr. < *pro*, before] *a prefix meaning* before in place or time
pro-[2] [L. < *pro*, forward] *a prefix meaning:* **1.** forward or ahead *[progress]* **2.** forth *[produce]* **3.** substituting for *[pronoun]* **4.** supporting, favoring *[prolabor]*
prob. 1. probably **2.** problem
prob·a·bil·i·ty (präb′ə bil′ə tē) *n., pl.* -**ties 1.** a being probable; likelihood **2.** something probable
prob·a·ble (präb′ə b′l) *adj.* [< L. *probare*, prove] **1.** likely to occur or be **2.** reasonably so, but not proved —**prob′a·bly** *adv.*
pro·bate (prō′bāt) *n.* [see PROBE] the act or process of probating —*adj.* having to do with probating —*vt.* -**bat·ed, -bat·ing** to establish officially the validity of (a will)
pro·ba·tion (prō bā′shən) *n.* [see PROBE] **1.** a testing or trial, as of character, ability, etc. **2.** the conditional suspension of a convicted person's sentence —**pro·ba′tion·ar′y, pro·ba′tion·al** *adj.*
pro·ba′tion·er *n.* a person on probation
probe (prōb) *n.* [< L. *probare*, to test] **1.** a surgical instrument for exploring a wound, etc. **2.** a searching investigation **3.** an instrumented spacecraft for exploring outer space, etc. —*vt.* **probed, prob′ing 1.** to explore (a wound, etc.) with a probe **2.** to investigate thoroughly —*vi.* to search
prob·i·ty (prō′bə tē, präb′ə-) *n.* [< L. *probus*, good] honesty; integrity
prob·lem (präb′ləm) *n.* [< Gr. *problēma*] **1.** a question to be worked out **2.** a perplexing or difficult matter, person, etc.
prob·lem·at·ic (präb′lə mat′ik) *adj.* **1.** of the nature of a problem **2.** uncertain Also **prob′lem·at′i·cal** —**prob′lem·at′i·cal·ly** *adv.*
pro·bos·cis (prō bäs′is) *n., pl.* -**cis·es** [< Gr. *pro-*, before + *boskein*, to feed] an elephant's trunk, or a long, flexible snout
pro·ce·dure (prə sē′jər) *n.* the act or method of proceeding in some action —**pro·ce′dur·al** *adj.*
pro·ceed (prə sēd′) *vi.* [< L. *pro-*, forward + *cedere*, go] **1.** to go on, esp. after stopping **2.** to carry on some action **3.** to take legal action (*against*) **4.** to come forth or issue (*from*)
pro·ceed′ing *n.* **1.** a going on with what one has been doing **2.** a course of action **3.** [*pl.*] a record of transactions **4.** [*pl.*] legal action
pro·ceeds (prō′sēdz) *n.pl.* the sum or profit derived from a sale, venture, etc.
proc·ess (präs′es) *n.* [see PROCEED] **1.** a series of changes by which something develops *[the process of growth]* **2.** a method of doing something with all the steps involved **3.** *Biol.* a projecting part **4.** *Law* a written order, as a court summons —*vt.* to prepare by or subject to a special process —**in process** in the course of being done —**in (the) process of** in or during the course of —**proc′es·sor, proc′ess·er** *n.*

procession   361   progression

pro·ces·sion (prə sesh′ən) n. [see PROCEED] a number of persons or things moving forward, as in a parade

pro·ces′sion·al n. a hymn sung at the beginning of a church service during the entrance of the clergy

pro·claim (prō klām′) vt. [< L. pro-, before + clamare, cry out] to announce officially; announce to be

proc·la·ma·tion (präk′lə mā′shən) n. 1. a proclaiming 2. something that is proclaimed

pro·cliv·i·ty (prō kliv′ə tē) n., pl. -ties [< L. pro-, before + clivus, a slope] a natural tendency or inclination

pro·cras·ti·nate (prō kras′tə nāt′) vi., vt. -nat′ed, -nat′ing [< L. pro-, forward + cras, tomorrow] to put off doing (something) until later; delay —pro·cras′ti·na′tion n. —pro·cras′ti·na′tor n.

pro·cre·ate (prō′krē āt′) vt., vi. -at′ed, -at′ing [< L. pro-, before + creare, create] to produce (young); beget —pro′cre·a′tion n. —pro′cre·a′tive adj. —pro′cre·a′tor n.

proc·tor (präk′tər) n. [see PROCURE] a college official who maintains order, supervises examinations, etc. —vt. to supervise (an examination)

pro·cure (prō kyoor′) vt. -cured′, -cur′ing [< L. pro-, for + curare, attend to] to get; obtain — pro·cur′a·ble adj. —pro·cure′ment n.

pro·cur′er n. same as PIMP

prod (präd) vt. prod′ded, prod′ding [< ?] 1. to jab or poke as with a pointed stick 2. to urge or stir into action —n. 1. a prodding 2. something that prods —prod′der n.

prod·i·gal (präd′i gəl) adj. [< L. pro-, forth + agere, to drive] 1. wasteful in a reckless way 2. extremely abundant —n. a spendthrift —prod′i·gal′i·ty (-gal′ə tē) n., pl. -ties

pro·di·gious (prə dij′əs) adj. [see PRODIGY] 1. wonderful; amazing 2. enormous; huge —pro·di′gious·ly adv.

prod·i·gy (präd′ə jē) n., pl. -gies [< L. prodigium, omen] an extraordinary person or thing; specif., a child of genius

pro·duce (prə dōōs′) vt. -duced′, -duc′ing [< L. pro-, forward + ducere, to lead] 1. to bring to view; show [to produce identification] 2. to bring forth; bear 3. to make or manufacture 4. to cause 5. to get ready and present (a play, etc.) —vi. to yield something —n. (präd′ōōs, prō′dōōs) something produced; esp., fresh fruits and vegetables —pro·duc′er n.

prod·uct (präd′əkt) n. 1. something produced by nature or by man 2. result; outgrowth 3. Math. the quantity obtained by multiplying two or more quantities together

pro·duc·tion (prə duk′shən) n. a producing or something produced

pro·duc′tive adj. 1. fertile 2. marked by abundant production 3. bringing as a result (with of) [war is productive of misery] —pro·duc′tive·ly adv. —pro·duc·tiv·i·ty (prō′dək tiv′ə tē), pro·duc′tive·ness n.

Prof. Professor

pro·fane (prə fān′) adj. [< L. pro-, before + fanum, temple] 1. not connected with religion; secular 2. showing disrespect or contempt for sacred things —vt. -faned′, -fan′ing 1. to treat (sacred things) with disrespect or contempt 2. to debase; defile —prof·a·na·tion (präf′ə nā′shən) n. —pro·fane′ly adv. —pro·fane′ness n.

pro·fan·i·ty (-fan′ə tē) n. 1. a being profane 2. pl. -ties profane language; swearing

pro·fess (prə fes′) vt. [< L. pro-, before + fateri, avow] 1. to declare openly; affirm 2. to claim to have (some feeling, knowledge, etc.) 3. to declare one's belief in

pro·fes·sion (prə fesh′ən) n. 1. a professing or declaring; avowal 2. a) an occupation requiring advanced education and training, as medicine, law, etc. b) all the people in such an occupation

pro·fes′sion·al adj. 1. of, engaged in, or worthy of the standards of, a profession 2. engaging in some sport or in a specified occupation for pay —n. one who is professional —pro·fes′sion·al·ly adv.

pro·fes·sor (prə fes′ər) n. a teacher; specif., a college teacher of the highest rank —pro·fes·so·ri·al (prō′fə sôr′ē əl) adj. —pro′fes·so′ri·al·ly adv. —pro·fes′sor·ship′ n.

prof·fer (präf′ər) vt. [< OFr.: see PRO-² & OFFER] to offer (usually something intangible) [to proffer friendship] —n. an offer

pro·fi·cient (prə fish′ənt) adj. [< L. pro-, forward + facere, make] highly competent; skilled —pro·fi′cien·cy (-ən sē) n., pl. -cies

pro·file (prō′fīl) n. [< It. < L. pro-, before + filum, a thread] 1. a) a side view of the face b) a drawing of this 2. an outline 3. a short, vivid biography

prof·it (präf′it) n. [see PROFICIENT] 1. advantage; gain 2. [often pl.] financial gain; esp., the sum remaining after deducting costs —vt., vi. to be of advantage (to); benefit —prof′it·a·ble adj. —prof′it·a·bly adv.

prof·i·teer (präf′ə tir′) n. one who makes an unfair profit by charging exorbitant prices when there is a short supply —vi. to be a profiteer

prof·li·gate (präf′lə git) adj. [< L. pro-, forward + fligere, to drive] 1. dissolute 2. recklessly wasteful —n. a profligate person —prof′li·ga·cy (-gə sē) n.

pro·found (prə found′) adj. [< L. pro-, forward + fundus, bottom] 1. very deep [profound sleep, grief, etc.] 2. having intellectual depth 3. complete; thorough —pro·found′ly adv. —pro·fun′di·ty (-fun′də tē) n., pl. -ties

pro·fuse (prə fyōōs′) adj. [< L. pro-, forth + fundere, pour] giving or given freely and abundantly —pro·fu′sion (-fyōō′zhən) n.

pro·gen·i·tor (prō jen′ə tər) n. [< L. pro-, forth + gignere, beget] 1. an ancestor in direct line 2. a precursor

prog·e·ny (präj′ə nē) n., pl. -nies [see prec.] children, descendants, or offspring

prog·no·sis (präg nō′sis) n., pl. -no′ses (-sēz) [< Gr. pro-, before + gignōskein, know] a prediction, esp. of the probable course of a disease —prog·nos′tic (-näs′tik) n., adj.

prog·nos′ti·cate′ (-näs′tə kāt′) vt. -cat′ed, -cat′ing [see prec.] to foretell, predict, or foreshadow —prog·nos′ti·ca′tion n.

pro·gram (prō′gram, -grəm) n. [< Fr. < Gr. pro-, before + graphein, write] 1. a list of the acts, speeches, musical pieces, etc. that make up an entertainment 2. a scheduled broadcast on radio or television 3. a plan or procedure 4. a) a logical sequence of operations to be performed by an electronic computer b) the coded instructions and data for this —vt. -grammed or -gramed, -gram·ming or -gram·ing 1. to schedule in a program 2. to plan a computer program for 3. to furnish (a computer) with a program Brit. sp. pro′gramme

prog·ress (präg′res) n. [< L. pro-, before + gradi, to step] 1. a moving forward 2. development 3. improvement —vi. (prə gres′) 1. to move forward 2. to advance toward a goal; develop or improve

pro·gres·sion (prə gresh′ən) n. 1. a moving forward 2. a succession, as of events 3. Math. a

series of numbers increasing or decreasing by a constant difference between terms
pro·gres'sive (-gres'iv) *adj.* **1.** moving forward **2.** continuing by successive steps **3.** of or favoring progress, reform, etc. —*n.* a person who is progressive
pro·hib·it (prō hib'it) *vt.* [< L. *pro-*, before + *habere*, have] **1.** to forbid by law or by an order **2.** to prevent; hinder —**pro·hib'i·tive, pro·hib'i·to'ry** *adj.*
pro·hi·bi·tion (prō'ə bish'ən) *n.* **1.** a prohibiting **2.** the forbidding by law of the manufacture or sale of alcoholic liquors —**pro'hi·bi'tion·ist** *n.*
proj·ect (präj'ekt) *n.* [< L. *pro-*, before + *jacere*, to throw] **1.** a proposal or plan **2.** an organized undertaking **3.** a complex of apartments or houses, usually publicly owned or financed —*vt.* (prə jekt') **1.** to propose (a plan) **2.** to throw forward **3.** to cause to jut out **4.** to cause (a shadow, image, etc.) to fall upon a surface —*vi.* to jut out —**pro·jec'tion** *n.*
pro·jec·tile (prə jek't'l, -tīl) *n.* **1.** an object designed to be shot forward, as a bullet **2.** anything thrown or hurled forward
pro·jec'tion·ist *n.* the operator of a slide or movie projector
pro·jec'tor *n.* a machine for projecting pictures or movies on a screen
pro·le·tar·i·at (prō'lə ter'ē ət) *n.* [< Fr. < L. *proletarius*, a citizen of the lowest class] the working class; esp., the industrial working class —**pro'le·tar'i·an** *adj., n.*
pro·lif·er·ate (prō lif'ə rāt') *vi., vt.* -at'ed, -at'ing [< Fr. < L. *proles*, offspring + *ferre*, to bear] to increase rapidly —**pro·lif'er·a'tion** *n.*
pro·lif·ic (prə lif'ik) *adj.* [< Fr. < L. *proles*, offspring + *facere*, make] **1.** producing many young or much fruit **2.** creating many products of the mind
pro·lix (prō liks', prō'liks) *adj.* [< L. *prolixus*, extended] wordy or long-winded —**pro·lix'i·ty** *n.*
pro·logue (prō'lôg) *n.* [< Gr. *pro-*, before + *logos*, a discourse] **1.** an introduction to a poem, play, etc. **2.** any preliminary act, event, etc.
pro·long (prə lôn') *vt.* [< L. *pro-*, forth + *longus*, long] to lengthen in time or space: also **pro·lon'gate** (-gāt) -gat·ed, -gat·ing —**pro'lon·ga'tion** *n.*
prom (präm) *n.* [< PROMENADE] [Colloq.] a dance, as of the senior class at a school or college
prom·e·nade (präm'ə nād', -näd') *n.* [Fr. < L. *pro-*, forth + *minare*, to herd] **1.** a leisurely walk taken for pleasure, display, etc. **2.** a public place for walking **3.** a ball, or dance —*vi., vt.* -nad'ed, -nad'ing to take a promenade (along or through)
Pro·me·the·us (prə mē'thē əs, -thyōōs) *Gr. Myth.* a Titan who stole fire from heaven to benefit mankind
prom·i·nent (präm'ə nənt) *adj.* [< L. *prominere*, to project] **1.** sticking out; projecting **2.** noticeable at once; conspicuous **3.** widely and favorably known —**prom'i·nence** *n.* —**prom'i·nent·ly** *adv.*
pro·mis·cu·ous (prə mis'kyōō wəs) *adj.* [< L. *pro-*, forth + *miscere*, to mix] **1.** consisting of different elements indiscriminately mixed **2.** showing a lack of discrimination, esp. in sexual liaisons —**pro·mis·cu·i·ty** (präm'is kyōō'ə tē), *n., pl.* -ties
prom·ise (präm'is) *n.* [< L. *pro-*, forth + *mittere*, send] **1.** an agreement to do or not to do something **2.** indication, as of a successful fu-

ture **3.** something promised —*vi., vt.* -ised, -is·ing **1.** to make a promise of (something) **2.** to give a basis for expecting (something) —**prom'is·ing** *adj.*
Promised Land *Bible* Canaan, promised by God to Abraham and his descendants: Gen. 17:8
prom·is·so·ry (präm'i sôr'ē) *adj.* containing a promise
prom·on·to·ry (präm'ən tôr'ē) *n., pl.* -ries [prob. < L. *prominere*, to project] a peak of high land that juts out into a body of water; headland
pro·mote (prə mōt') *vt.* -mot'ed, -mot'ing [< L. *pro-*, forward + *movere*, to move] **1.** to raise to a higher rank, position, or grade **2.** to further the establishment, growth, sales, etc. of —**pro·mo'tion** *n.*
pro·mot'er *n.* one who organizes and furthers a new enterprise
prompt (prämpt) *adj.* [< L. *pro-*, forth + *emere*, take] **1.** ready, punctual, etc. **2.** done, spoken, etc. without delay —*vt.* **1.** to urge into action **2.** to remind of something that has been forgotten; specif., to help (an actor, etc.) with a cue **3.** to inspire —**prompt'er** *n.* —**prompt'ly** *adv.* —**prompt'ness, promp·ti·tude** (prämp'tə tōōd') *n.*
prom·ul·gate (präm'əl gāt', prō mul'gāt) *vt.* -gat'ed, -gat'ing [< L., ? ult. < *pro-*, before + *vulgus*, the people] **1.** to make known officially **2.** to make widespread —**prom'ul·ga'tion** *n.*
pron. **1.** pronoun **2.** pronunciation
prone (prōn) *adj.* [< L. *pronus*] **1.** lying face downward or prostrate **2.** disposed or inclined (*to*) [*prone* to err]
prong (prôn) *n.* [akin to MLowG. *prangen*, to press] **1.** any of the pointed ends of a fork **2.** any pointed projecting part, as on an antler —**pronged** *adj.*
pro·noun (prō'noun) *n.* [< L. *pro*, for + *nomen*, noun] a word used in place of a noun (Ex.: *I, he, ours*, etc.) —**pro·nom'i·nal** (-näm'i n'l) *adj.*
pro·nounce (prə nouns') *vt.* -nounced', -nounc'ing [< L. *pro-*, before + *nuntiare*, announce] **1.** to declare officially, solemnly, etc. [*pronounced* man and wife] **2.** to utter or articulate (a sound or word) —**pro·nounce'a·ble** *adj.*
pro·nounced' *adj.* clearly marked; definite [a *pronounced* change]
pro·nounce'ment *n.* a formal statement, as of an opinion or judgment
pron·to (prän'tō) *adv.* [Sp.: see PROMPT] [Slang] at once; quickly
pro·nun·ci·a·tion (prə nun'sē ā'shən) *n.* **1.** the act or way of pronouncing words **2.** *a)* any of the accepted or standard pronunciations of a word *b)* the representation in phonetic symbols of such a pronunciation
proof (prōōf) *n.* [< L. *probare*, to test] **1.** a proving or testing of something **2.** evidence that establishes the truth of something **3.** the relative strength of alcohol **4.** *Photog.* a trial print of a negative **5.** *Printing* a trial impression taken for checking errors, etc. —*adj.* of tested strength in resisting (with *against*)
-proof *a combining form meaning:* **1.** impervious to [*waterproof*] **2.** protected from [*foolproof*]
proof'read' (-rēd') *vt., vi.* -read' (-red'), -read'ing to read and mark corrections on (printers' proofs, etc.) —**proof'read'er** *n.*
prop[1] (präp) *n.* [MDu. *proppe*] a support, as a pole, placed under or against something: often used figuratively —*vt.* **propped, prop'ping 1.** to

support, as with a prop (often with *up*) **2.** to lean (something) *against* a support

prop² (präp) *n. same as* PROPERTY (sense 4)

prop³ (präp) *n. same as* PROPELLER

prop. **1.** proposition **2.** proprietor

prop·a·gan·da (präp′ə gan′də) *n.* [see PROPAGATE] **1.** any widespread promotion of particular ideas, doctrines, etc. **2.** ideas, etc. so spread —**prop′a·gan′dist** *n., adj.* —**prop′a·gan′-dize** *vt., vi.* -**dized,** -**diz·ing**

prop·a·gate (präp′ə gāt′) *vt.* -**gat′ed,** -**gat′ing** [< L. *propago,* slip (of a plant)] **1.** to cause (a plant or animal) to reproduce itself **2.** to reproduce (itself): said of a plant or animal **3.** to spread (ideas, customs, etc.) —*vi.* to reproduce, as plants or animals —**prop′a·ga′tion** *n.*

pro·pane (prō′pān) *n.* a gaseous hydrocarbon, used as a fuel

pro·pel (prə pel′) *vt.* -**pelled′,** -**pel′ling** [< L. *pro-,* forward + *pellere,* drive] to drive forward —**pro·pel′lant** *n.*

pro·pel′ler *n.* a device consisting of blades in a rotating hub for propelling a ship or aircraft

pro·pen·si·ty (prə pen′sə tē) *n., pl.* -**ties** [< L. *pro-,* before + *pendere,* hang] a natural inclination or tendency; bent

prop·er (präp′ər) *adj.* [< L. *proprius,* one's own] **1.** specially suitable; appropriate; fitting **2.** naturally belonging (*to*) **3.** conforming to a standard; correct **4.** decent; decorous **5.** in the most restricted sense [Boston *proper* (i.e., apart from its suburbs)] **6.** Gram. naming a specific individual, place, etc. [*Jane, Asia,* and *Paris* are *proper* nouns] —**prop′er·ly** *adv.*

prop·er·ty (präp′ər tē) *n., pl.* -**ties** [< L. *proprius,* one's own] **1.** ownership **2.** something owned, esp. real estate **3.** a characteristic or attribute **4.** any of the movable articles used in a stage setting

proph·e·cy (präf′ə sē) *n., pl.* -**cies** **1.** prediction of the future **2.** something predicted

proph′e·sy′ (-sī′) *vt., vi.* -**sied′,** -**sy′ing** **1.** to predict as by divine guidance **2.** to predict in any way —**proph′e·si′er** *n.*

proph·et (präf′it) *n.* [< Gr. *pro-,* before + *phanai,* speak] **1.** a religious leader regarded as, or claiming to be, divinely inspired **2.** one who predicts the future —**proph′et·ess** *n.fem.*

pro·phet·ic (prə fet′ik) *adj.* **1.** of or like a prophet **2.** of, like, or containing a prophecy —**pro·phet′i·cal·ly** *adv.*

pro·phy·lac·tic (prō′fə lak′tik) *adj.* [< Gr. *pro-,* before + *phylassein,* to guard] preventive or protective; esp., preventing disease —*n.* a prophylactic medicine, device, etc.

pro′phy·lax′is (-sis) *n., pl.* -**lax′es** (-sēz) *Dentistry* a cleaning of the teeth to remove plaque and tartar

pro·pin·qui·ty (prō piŋ′kwə tē) *n.* [< L. *propinquus,* near] nearness

pro·pi·ti·ate (prə pish′ē āt′) *vt.* -**at′ed,** -**at′ing** [see PROPITIOUS] to win or regain the good will of; appease —**pro·pi′ti·a′tion** *n.* —**pro·pi′ti·a·to′ry** (-ə tôr′ē) *adj.*

pro·pi·tious (prə pish′əs) *adj.* [< L. *pro-,* before + *petere,* seek] **1.** favorably inclined **2.** favorable [a *propitious* omen]

pro·po·nent (prə pō′nənt) *n.* [< L. *pro-,* forth + *ponere,* to place] one who espouses or supports a cause, etc.

pro·por·tion (prə pôr′shən) *n.* [< L. *pro-,* for + *portio,* a part] **1.** the comparative relation in size, amount, etc. between things; ratio **2.** a part, share, etc., esp. in its relation to the whole **3.** symmetry or balance **4.** [*pl.*] dimensions —*vt.* **1.** to put in proper relation or balance **2.** to arrange the parts of in a har-

monious way —**pro·por′tion·al, pro·por′tion·ate** (-shə nit) *adj.*

pro·pos·al (prə pō′z'l) *n.* **1.** a proposing **2.** a proposed plan **3.** an offer of marriage

pro·pose (prə pōz′) *vt.* -**posed′,** -**pos′ing** [< L. *pro-,* forth + *ponere,* to place] **1.** to put forth for consideration or acceptance **2.** to plan or intend **3.** to present as a toast in drinking —*vi.* to offer marriage

prop·o·si·tion (präp′ə zish′ən) *n.* **1.** something proposed; plan **2.** [Colloq.] a proposed deal, as in business **3.** a subject to be debated **4.** *Math.* a problem to be solved

pro·pound (prə pound′) *vt.* [see PROPOSE] to set forth for consideration

pro·pri·e·tar·y (prə prī′ə ter′ē) *adj.* [see PROPERTY] belonging to a proprietor, as under a patent, trademark, or copyright

pro·pri·e·tor (prə prī′ə tər) *n.* an owner —**pro·pri′e·tor·ship′** *n.* —**pro·pri′e·tress** *n.fem.*

pro·pri·e·ty (prə prī′ə tē) *n., pl.* -**ties** [see PROPER] **1.** the quality of being proper, fitting, etc. **2.** conformity with accepted standards of behavior

pro·pul·sion (prə pul′shən) *n.* [see PROPEL] **1.** a propelling or being propelled **2.** propelling force —**pro·pul′sive** *adj.*

pro·rate (prō rāt′, prō′rāt′) *vt., vi.* -**rat′ed,** -**rat′-ing** [< *pro rata*] to divide or assess proportionately

pro·sa·ic (prō zā′ik) *adj.* [< L. *prosa,* PROSE] commonplace; dull

pro·sce·ni·um (prō sē′nē əm) *n., pl.* -**ni·ums,** -**ni·a** (-ə) [< Gr. *pro-,* before + *skēnē,* a tent] the arch framing a conventional stage

pro·scribe (prō skrīb′) *vt.* -**scribed′,** -**scrib′ing** [< L. *pro-,* before + *scribere,* write] **1.** to outlaw **2.** to banish; exile **3.** to denounce or forbid the use, etc. of —**pro·scrip′tion** (-skrip′shən) *n.* —**pro·scrip′tive** *adj.*

prose (prōz) *n.* [< L. *prosa,* direct] ordinary language, not poetry

pros·e·cute (präs′ə kyōot′) *vt.* -**cut′ed,** -**cut′ing** [< L. *pro-,* before + *sequi,* follow] **1.** to carry on; engage in **2.** to conduct legal proceedings against —**pros′e·cu′tion** *n.* —**pros′e·cu′tor** *n.*

pros·e·lyte (präs′ə līt′) *n.* [< Gr. *prosēlytos*] one who has been converted from one religion, belief, etc. to another —*vt., vi.* -**lyt′ed,** -**lyt′ing** to try to make a convert (of): also **pros′e·lyt·ize′** (-li tīz′) -**ized′,** -**iz′ing** —**pros′e·lyt·ism** (-li tiz′m) *n.*

pros·o·dy (präs′ə dē) *n., pl.* -**dies** [< Gr. *prosōidia,* accent] versification; study of meter, rhyme, etc.

pros·pect (präs′pekt) *n.* [< L. *pro-,* forward + *specere,* to look] **1.** a broad view; scene **2.** viewpoint; outlook **3.** anticipation **4.** *a)* something expected *b)* [*usually pl.*] apparent chance for success **5.** a likely customer, candidate, etc. —*vt., vi.* to explore or search (*for* gold, oil, etc.) —**pros′pec·tor** *n.*

pro·spec·tive (prə spek′tiv) *adj.* expected; likely

pro·spec·tus (prə spek′təs) *n.* [L.: see PROSPECT] a statement of the features of a new work, enterprise, etc.

pros·per (präs′pər) *vi.* [< L. *prosperus,* favorable] to succeed, thrive, grow, etc.

pros·per·i·ty (prä sper′ə tē) *n.* prosperous condition; wealth, success, etc.

pros·per·ous (präs′pər əs) *adj.* **1.** prospering; flourishing **2.** well-to-do; well-off **3.** conducive to success —**pros′per·ous·ly** *adv.*

pros·tate (präs′tāt) *adj.* [< Gr. *prostatēs,* one standing before] designating or of a gland surrounding the male urethra at the base of the bladder —*n.* the prostate gland

pros·ti·tute (präs′tə tōōt′) *n.* [< L. *pro-*, before + *statuere*, cause to stand] a woman who engages in promiscuous sexual intercourse for pay —*vt.* -tut′ed, -tut′ing 1. to offer (oneself or another) as a prostitute 2. to sell (oneself, one's talents, etc.) for base purposes —**pros′ti·tu′tion** *n.*

pros·trate (präs′trāt) *adj.* [< L. *pro-*, before + *sternere*, stretch out] 1. lying face downward 2. lying prone or supine 3. overcome; laid low —*vt.* -trat·ed, -trat·ing 1. to lay in a prostrate position 2. to lay low; subjugate —**pros·tra′tion** *n.*

pros·y (prō′zē) *adj.* -i·er, -i·est 1. like prose 2. prosaic; dull

pro·tag·o·nist (prō tag′ə nist) *n.* [< Gr. *prōtos*, first + *agōnistēs*, actor] the main character in a drama, novel, etc.

pro·tect (prə tekt′) *vt.* [< L. *pro-*, before + *tegere*, to cover] to shield from injury, danger, or loss; defend —**pro·tec′tor** *n.*

pro·tec′tion *n.* 1. a protecting or being protected 2. a person or thing that protects

pro·tec′tive *adj.* 1. protecting 2. intended to protect domestic industry from foreign competition [*protective* tariffs]

pro·tec′tor·ate (-tər it) *n.* a weak state under the control and protection of a stronger state

pro·té·gé (prōt′ə zhā′) *n.* [Fr. < L.: see PROTECT] a person guided and helped in his career by another

pro·tein (prō′tēn, prōt′ē in) *n.* [G., ult. < Gr. *prōtos*, first] any of a class of complex nitrogenous substances occurring in all living matter and essential to the diet

pro tem·po·re (prō tem′pə rē′) [L.] for the time being; temporarily: shortened to **pro tem**

pro·test (prə test′) *vt.* [< L. *pro-*, forth + *testari*, affirm] 1. to state positively 2. to speak strongly against —*vi.* to express disapproval; object —*n.* (prō′test) 1. an objection 2. a formal statement of objection —**prot·es·ta·tion** (prät′is tā′shən) *n.*

Prot·es·tant (prät′is tənt) *n.* [see prec.] a member of any of the Christian churches resulting or derived from the Reformation —**Prot′es·tant·ism** *n.*

proto- [< Gr. *prōtos*, first] *a combining form meaning:* 1. first in time, original 2. first in importance

pro·to·col (prōt′ə kôl′, -käl′) *n.* [< LGr. *prōtokollon*, contents page] 1. an original draft or record of a document, negotiation, etc. 2. the code of ceremonial forms in official dealings, as between heads of state or diplomats

pro·ton (prō′tän) *n.* [< Gr. *prōtos*, first] an elementary particle in the nucleus of all atoms, carrying a unit positive charge of electricity

pro·to·plasm (prōt′ə plaz′m) *n.* [see PROTO- & PLASMA] a semifluid, viscous colloid, the essential living matter of all animal and plant cells —**pro′to·plas′mic** *adj.*

pro·to·type (prōt′ə tīp′) *n.* the first thing or being of its kind; original

pro·to·zo·an (prōt′ə zō′ən) *n.* [< Gr. *prōtos*, first + *zōion*, animal] any of a large group of mostly microscopic, one-celled animals: also **pro′to·zo′on** (-än), *pl.* -**zo′a** (-ə)

pro·tract (prō trakt′) *vt.* [< L. *pro-*, forward + *trahere*, to draw] to draw out; prolong —**pro·trac′tion** *n.*

pro·trac′tor *n.* a graduated, semicircular instrument for plotting and measuring angles

pro·trude (prō trōōd′) *vt., vi.* -trud′ed, -trud′ing [< L. *pro-*, forth + *trudere*, to thrust] to

thrust or jut out; project —**pro·tru′sion** (-trōō′zhən) *n.*

pro·tu·ber·ance (prō tōō′bər əns) *n.* [< L. *pro-*, forth + *tuber*, a bump] a part or thing that sticks out; bulge —**pro·tu′ber·ant** *adj.*

proud (proud) *adj.* [< LL. *prode*, beneficial] 1. having or showing a proper pride in oneself 2. haughty; arrogant 3. feeling or causing great pride or joy 4. caused by pride 5. stately; splendid —**proud of** highly pleased with —**proud′ly** *adv.*

prove (prōōv) *vt.* proved, proved or prov′en, prov′ing [< L. *probare*, to test] 1. to test by experiment, a standard, etc. 2. to establish as true —*vi.* to be shown to be [her guess *proved* right] —**prov′a·ble** *adj.*

Pro·ven·çal (prō′vən säl′, präv′ən-) *n.* the vernacular of S France, a Romance language of literary importance in its medieval form

prov·en·der (präv′ən dər) *n.* [< L. *prae-*, before + *habere*, have] 1. dry food for livestock 2. [Colloq.] food; provisions

prov·erb (präv′ərb) *n.* [< L. *pro-*, before + *verbum*, a word] a short, popular saying that expresses an obvious truth —**pro·ver·bi·al** (prə vur′bē əl) *adj.* **pro·ver′bi·al·ly** *adv.*

pro·vide (prə vīd′) *vt.* -vid′ed, -vid′ing [< L. *pro-*, before + *videre*, see] 1. to make available; supply 2. to supply with 3. to stipulate —*vi.* 1. to prepare (*for* or *against* a possible situation or event) 2. to furnish support (*for*) —**pro·vid′er** *n.*

pro·vid′ed *conj.* on the condition or understanding (often with *that*)

prov·i·dence (präv′ə dəns) *n.* 1. provident management 2. the benevolent guidance of God or nature 3. [P-] God

prov′i·dent *adj.* [see PROVIDE] 1. providing for the future 2. prudent or economical

prov′i·den′tial (-den′shəl) *adj.* of, by, or as if decreed by divine providence —**prov′i·den′tial·ly** *adv.*

pro·vid·ing (prə vīd′iŋ) *conj. same as* PROVIDED

prov·ince (präv′ins) *n.* [< L. *provincia*] 1. an administrative division of a country, specif. of Canada 2. *a)* a district; territory *b)* [*pl.*] the parts of a country removed from the major cities 3. range of duties or functions 4. a field of knowledge

pro·vin·cial (prə vin′shəl) *adj.* 1. of a province 2. having the ways, speech, etc. of a certain province 3. countrified 4. narrow; limited —**pro·vin′cial·ism** *n.*

pro·vi·sion (prə vizh′ən) *n.* 1. a providing or supplying 2. something provided for the future; specif., [*pl.*] a stock of food 3. a stipulation; proviso —*vt.* to supply with provisions

pro·vi′sion·al *adj.* conditional or temporary —**pro·vi′sion·al·ly** *adv.*

pro·vi·so (prə vī′zō) *n., pl.* -sos, -soes [ML. *proviso* (*quod*), provided (that)] a clause, as in a document, making some condition; stipulation

prov·o·ca·tion (präv′ə kā′shən) *n.* 1. a provoking 2. something that provokes, or angers, incites, etc.

pro·voc·a·tive (prə väk′ə tiv) *adj.* provoking or tending to provoke to action, thought, anger, etc. —**pro·voc′a·tive·ly** *adv.*

pro·voke (prə vōk′) *vt.* -voked′, -vok′ing [< L. *pro-*, forth + *vocare*, to call] 1. to excite to some action or feeling 2. to anger or irritate 3. to stir up (action or feeling) 4. to evoke —**pro·vok′ing** *adj.*

pro·vost (prō′vōst) *n.* [< L. *praepositus*, chief]

any of various officials, as in some churches or colleges

pro·vost guard (prō′vō) a detail of military police under the command of an officer (**provost marshal**)

prow (prou) *n.* [< Fr., ult. < Gr. *prōira*] the forward part of a ship or boat

prow·ess (prou′is) *n.* [< OFr. *prouesse*] 1. bravery; valor 2. superior ability, skill, etc.

prowl (proul) *vi., vt.* [< ?] to roam about furtively, as in search of prey or loot —*n.* a prowling —**prowl′er** *n.*

prox·im·i·ty (präk sim′ə tē) *n.* [< L. *prope*, near] nearness in space, time, etc.

prox·y (präk′sē) *n., pl.* **-ies** [< ME. *procuracie*, office of a procurator] 1. the authority to act for another 2. a person so authorized

prude (prōōd) *n.* [Fr. < *prudefemme*, excellent woman] one who is overly modest or proper in behavior, dress, speech, etc. —**prud′er·y** *n.* —**prud′ish** *adj.*

pru·dence (prōōd′ns) *n.* 1. a being prudent 2. careful management —**pru·den·tial** (prōō den′shəl) *adj.*

pru·dent (prōōd′nt) *adj.* [< L. *providens*, provident] 1. exercising sound judgment in practical matters 2. cautious in conduct; not rash 3. managing carefully —**pru′dent·ly** *adv.*

prune[1] (prōōn) *n.* [< Gr. *proumnon*, plum] a dried plum

prune[2] (prōōn) *vt., vi.* pruned, prun′ing [< MFr., prob. ult. < L. *propago*, a plant slip] 1. to trim dead or living parts from (a plant) 2. to remove (unnecessary parts) from (something) —**prun′er** *n.*

pru·ri·ent (proor′ē ənt) *adj.* [< L. *prurire*, to itch] tending to excite lust; lewd —**pru′ri·ence** *n.* —**pru′ri·ent·ly** *adv.*

pry[1] (prī) *n., pl.* **pries** [< PRIZE[2]] a lever or crowbar —*vt.* pried, pry′ing 1. to raise or move with a pry 2. to draw forth with difficulty

pry[2] (prī) *vi.* pried, pry′ing [< ?] to look closely or inquisitively; snoop

P.S., PS 1. postscript: also **p.s.** 2. Public School

psalm (säm) *n.* [< Gr. *psallein*, to pluck (a harp)] 1. a sacred song or poem 2. [*usually* P-] any of the sacred songs that make up the Book of Psalms in the Bible

Psalms (sämz) a book of the Bible, consisting of 150 psalms: also **Book of Psalms**,

pseu·do (sōō′dō) *adj.* [see PSEUDO-] sham; false; spurious

pseudo- [< Gr. *pseudēs*, false] *a prefix meaning* sham, counterfeit

pseu·do·nym (sōō′də nim′) *n.* [< Fr. < Gr. *pseudēs*, false + *onyma*, a name] a fictitious name, as assumed by an author; pen name

pshaw (shô) *interj., n.* an exclamation of impatience, disgust, contempt, etc.

psi (sī, psē) *n.* the twenty-third letter of the Greek alphabet (Ψ, ψ)

pso·ri·a·sis (sə rī′ə sis) *n.* [< Gr. *psōra*, an itch] a chronic skin disease characterized by scaly patches

psst (pst) *interj.* a sound made to get someone's attention quietly

psych (sīk) *vt.* psyched, psych′ing [< PSYCHOANALYZE] [Slang] to figure out the motives of, esp. so as to outwit or control (often with *out*)

psych. psychology

Psy·che (sī′kē) [< Gr. *psychē*, soul] *Rom. Myth.* the wife of Cupid —*n.* [p-] 1. the soul 2. the mind, esp. as a functional entity governing the total organism and its interactions with the environment

psy·che·del·ic (sī′kə del′ik) *adj.* [< prec. +

Gr. *delein*, make manifest] 1. of or causing extreme changes in the conscious mind 2. of or like the auditory or visual effects experienced with psychedelic drugs

psy·chi·a·try (sə kī′ə trē, sī-) *n.* [see PSYCHO- & -IATRY] the branch of medicine dealing with disorders of the mind, including psychoses, neuroses, etc. —**psy·chi·at·ric** (sī′kē at′rik) *adj.* —**psy·chi′a·trist** *n.*

psy·chic (sī′kik) *adj.* [< Gr. *psychē*, soul] 1. of the psyche, or mind 2. beyond known physical processes 3. apparently sensitive to forces beyond the physical world Also **psy′chi·cal** —*n.* one who is supposedly psychic (sense 3) — **psy′chi·cal·ly** *adv.*

psy·cho (sī′kō) *adj., n. colloq.* shortened form of PSYCHOTIC, PSYCHOPATH, PSYCHOPATHIC

psycho- [< Gr. *psychē*, soul] *a combining form meaning* the mind or mental processes [*psychology*] : also **psych-**

psy·cho·a·nal·y·sis (sī′kō ə nal′ə sis) *n.* a method of treating neuroses and some other mental disorders through analysis of emotional conflicts, repressions, etc. by getting the patient to talk freely, analyzing his dreams, etc. —**psy′cho·an′a·lyst** (-an′əl ist) *n.* —**psy′cho·an′a·lyze** (-īz′) *vt.* -lyzed′, -lyz′ing

psy·chol·o·gy (sī käl′ə jē) *n., pl.* -gies [see PSYCHO- & -LOGY] 1. the science dealing with the mind and with mental and emotional processes 2. the science of human and animal behavior —**psy′cho·log′i·cal** (-kə läj′i k'l) *adj.* —**psy·chol′o·gist** *n.*

psy·cho·path (sī′kə path′) *n.* [see PSYCHO- & -PATHY] a person with serious personality defects, whose behavior, often criminal, is largely amoral, irresponsible, and impulsive —**psy′cho·path′ic** *adj.*

psy·cho·sis (sī kō′sis) *n., pl.* -ses (-sēz) [see PSYCHO- & -OSIS] any major mental disorder in which the personality is very seriously disorganized —**psy·chot′ic** (-kät′ik) *adj., n.*

psy·cho·so·mat·ic (sī′kō sō mat′ik) *adj.* [PSYCHO- + SOMATIC] designating or of a physical disorder originating in or aggravated by emotional processes

psy·cho·ther·a·py (-ther′ə pē) *n.* [PSYCHO- + THERAPY] treatment of mental disorders by counseling, psychoanalysis, etc. —**psy′cho·ther′a·pist** *n.*

Pt *Chem.* platinum

pt. *pl.* **pts.** 1. part 2. pint 3. point

pt., p.t. past tense

P.T.A. Parent-Teacher Association

ptar·mi·gan (tär′mə gən) *n.* [< Scot. *tarmachan*] a northern grouse

pto·maine (tō′mān) *n.* [< It. < Gr. *ptōma*, corpse] an alkaloid substance, often poisonous, formed in decaying matter

Pu *Chem.* plutonium

pub (pub) *n.* [< *pub(lic house)*] [Chiefly Brit. Colloq.] a bar or tavern

pu·ber·ty (pyōō′bər tē) *n.* [< L. *puber*, adult] the physical stage at which sexual reproduction first becomes possible

pu·bes·cent (pyōō bes′nt) *adj.* [see prec.] reaching or having reached puberty

pu·bic (pyōō′bik) *adj.* [see PUBERTY] of or in the region of the genitals

pub·lic (pub′lik) *adj.* [ult. < L. *populus*, the people] 1. of the people as a whole 2. for the use or benefit of all [a *public* park] 3. acting officially for the people [a *public* prosecutor] 4. known by most people —*n.* 1. the people as a whole 2. a specific part of the people [the reading *public*] —**in public** openly —**pub′lic·ly** *adv.*

pub·li·can (pub′li kən) *n.* **1.** in ancient Rome, a tax collector **2.** [Brit.] a person who manages a bar or tavern

pub·li·ca·tion (pub′lə kā′shən) *n.* [see PUBLISH] **1.** public notification **2.** the printing and distributing for sale of books, magazines, etc. **3.** something published, as a book or periodical

public domain the condition of being free from copyright or patent

pub·li·cist (pub′lə sist) *n.* one whose business is publicity; press agent

pub·lic·i·ty (pə blis′ə tē) *n.* **1.** *a)* any information or action that brings a person, place, or thing to the attention of the public *b)* the work of getting such attention **2.** notice by the public

pub·li·cize (pub′lə sīz′) *vt.* **-cized′, -ciz′ing** to give publicity to

public relations relations of an organization with the public through publicity

public school 1. in the U.S., an elementary or secondary school maintained by public taxes and supervised by local authorities **2.** in England, a private boarding school for boys

public servant a government official or a civil-service employee

pub′lic-spir′it·ed *adj.* having or showing zeal for the public welfare

public utility an organization that supplies water, electricity, transportation, etc. to the public

pub·lish (pub′lish) *vt.* [< L. *publicare*] **1.** to make publicly known; announce **2.** to issue (a printed work) for sale —*vi.* to write books, etc. that are published —**pub′lish·a·ble** *adj.* —**pub′·lish·er** *n.*

puck¹ (puk) *n.* [akin to POKE¹] the hard rubber disk used in ice hockey

puck² (puk) *n.* [OE. *puca*] a mischievous sprite or elf —**puck′ish** *adj.*

puck·er (puk′ər) *vt., vi.* [< POKE²] to draw up into wrinkles or small folds —*n.* such a wrinkle or fold

pud·ding (pood′iŋ) *n.* [akin ? to OE. *puduc,* a swelling] a soft, sweet food variously made with flour, eggs, milk, fruit, etc.

pud·dle (pud′'l) *n.* [< OE. *pudd,* ditch] a small pool of water, esp. stagnant or muddy water —*vt.* **-dled, -dling** to treat (iron) by puddling —**pud′dler** *n.*

pud′dling (-liŋ) *n.* the making of wrought iron from pig iron by heating and stirring it along with oxidizing agents

pudg·y (puj′ē) *adj.* **-i·er, -i·est** [? < Scot. *pud,* belly] short and fat —**pudg′i·ness** *n.*

pueb·lo (pweb′lō) *n., pl.* **-los** [Sp. < L. *populus,* people] an Indian village of the SW U.S. in which the Indians live communally in terraced structures of stone or adobe

pu·er·ile (pyōō′ər əl) *adj.* [< Fr. < L. *puer,* boy] childish; silly —**pu′er·il′i·ty** *n.*

puff (puf) *n.* [OE. *pyff*] **1.** a short, sudden gust or expulsion of wind, breath, smoke, etc. **2.** a draw at a cigarette, etc. **3.** a light pastry filled with whipped cream, etc. **4.** a soft pad [a powder *puff]* **5.** exaggerated praise, as of a book —*vi.* **1.** to blow in puffs **2.** to breathe rapidly **3.** to swell (*out* or *up*) **4.** to take puffs on a cigarette, etc. —*vt.* **1.** to blow, smoke, etc. in or with puffs **2.** to inflate; swell **3.** to praise unduly —**puff′i·ness** *n.* —**puff′y** *adj.* **-i·er, -i·est**

puff′ball′ *n.* a round, white-fleshed fungus that bursts at the touch when mature

puf·fin (puf′in) *n.* [ME. *poffin*] a northern sea bird with a triangular beak

pug (pug) *n.* [< ? PUCK²] a small, short-haired dog with a snub nose

pu·gil·ism (pyōō′jə liz'm) *n.* [< L. *pugil,* boxer] same as BOXING —**pu′gil·ist** *n.* —**pu′gil·is′tic** *adj.*

pug·na·cious (pug nā′shəs) *adj.* [< L. *pugnare,* to fight] eager and ready to fight; quarrelsome —**pug·nac′i·ty** (-nas′ə tē) *n.*

pug nose a short, thick, turned-up nose

puke (pyōōk) *n., vi., vt.* **puked, puk′ing** [< ?] same as VOMIT: avoided by some as vulgar

pul·chri·tude (pul′krə tōōd′) *n.* [< L. *pulcher,* beautiful] physical beauty

pule (pyōōl) *vi.* **puled, pul′ing** [echoic] to whine or whimper, as a fretful child

pull (pool) *vt.* [OE. *pullian,* to pluck] **1.** to exert force on so as to move toward the source of the force **2.** to pluck out (a tooth, etc.) **3.** to rip; tear **4.** to strain (a muscle) **5.** [Colloq.] to carry out; perform [to *pull* a raid] **6.** [Colloq.] to restrain [to *pull·* a punch] **7.** [Colloq.] to draw (a gun, etc.) —*vi.* **1.** to exert force in dragging, tugging, etc. **2.** to be capable of being pulled **3.** to move (*away, ahead,* etc.) —*n.* **1.** the act or force of pulling **2.** a hard, steady effort **3.** something to be pulled, as a handle **4.** [Colloq.] *a)* influence *b)* drawing power —**pull for** [Colloq.] to cheer on —**pull off** [Colloq.] to accomplish —**pull through** [Colloq.] to get over (an illness, difficulty, etc.) —**pull up** to stop —**pull′er** *n.*

pul·let (pool′it) *n.* [< L. *pullus,* chicken] a young hen, usually not more than a year old

pul·ley (pool′ē) *n., pl.* **-leys** [< Gr. *polos,* axis] a small wheel with a grooved rim in which a rope, belt, etc. runs, as to raise weights or transmit power

Pull·man (car) (pool′mən) [< G. M. *Pullman* (1831-97), U.S. inventor] a railroad car with private compartments or berths for sleeping

pull′o′ver *adj.* that is pulled on over the head —*n.* a pullover sweater, shirt, etc.

pull′up′ *n.* the act of chinning oneself

pul·mo·nar·y (pul′mə ner′ē) *adj.* [< L. *pulmo,* a lung] of or affecting the lungs

Pul·mo·tor (pool′mōt′ər, pul′-) [< L. *pulmo,* a lung + MOTOR] *a trademark for* an apparatus for applying artificial respiration —*n.* [**p-**] such an apparatus

pulp (pulp) *n.* [< Fr. < L. *pulpa,* flesh] **1.** a soft, moist, formless mass **2.** the soft, juicy part of a fruit **3.** the soft pith of a plant stem **4.** the sensitive substance under the dentine of a tooth **5.** ground-up, moistened fibers of wood, rags, etc., used to make paper —**pulp′i·ness** *n.* —**pulp′y** *adj.*

pul·pit (pool′pit) *n.* [< L. *pulpitum,* a stage] **1.** a raised platform from which a clergyman preaches in a church **2.** preachers as a group

pul·sar (pul′sär) *n.* [PULS(E) + -AR] any of several small heavenly objects in the Milky Way that emit radio pulses regularly

pul·sate (pul′sāt) *vi.* **-sat·ed, -sat·ing** [< L. *pulsare,* to beat] **1.** to beat or throb rhythmically, as the heart **2.** to vibrate; quiver —**pul·sa′tion** *n.* —**pul′sa′tor** *n.*

pulse (puls) *n.* [< L. *pulsus,* a beating] **1.** the regular beating in the arteries, caused by the heart pulsating **2.** any regular beat —*vi.* **pulsed, puls′ing** to pulsate; throb

pul·ver·ize (pul′və rīz′) *vt., vi.* **-ized′, -iz′ing** [< L. *pulvis,* dust] to grind or be ground into a powder —**pul′ver·i·za′tion** *n.*

pu·ma (pyōō′mə) *n.* [AmSp.] same as COUGAR

pum·ice (pum′is) *n.* [< L. *pumex*] a light, porous, volcanic rock used in solid or powdered form to scour, smooth, and polish

pum·mel (pum′'l) *vt.* -meled or -melled, -mel·ing or -mel·ling [< POMMEL] to hit with repeated blows

pump[1] (pump) *n.* [< Sp. *bomba*] a machine that forces a liquid or gas into, or draws it out of, something —*vt.* 1. to move (fluids) with a pump 2. to remove water, etc. from 3. to drive air into, as with a pump 4. to force in, draw out, move up and down, etc. like a pump 5. [Colloq.] *a)* to question persistently *b)* to get (information) thus —**pump′er** *n.*

pump[2] (pump) *n.* [< ? Fr. *pompe,* an ornament] a low-cut shoe without straps or ties

pump·er·nick·el (pum′pər nik′'l) *n.* [G.] a coarse, dark, sour rye bread

pump·kin (pum′kin, pump′-, puŋ′-) *n.* [< Gr. *pepōn,* ripe] 1. a large, round, orange-yellow, gourdlike fruit 2. the vine it grows on

pun (pun) *n.* [< ? It. *puntiglio,* fine point] the humorous use of words that have the same sound or spelling, but have different meanings —*vi.* **punned, pun′ning** to make a pun or puns —**pun′ner** *n.*

punch[1] (punch) *n.* [see PUNCHEON[1]] a tool driven against a surface that is to be pierced, shaped, or stamped —*vt.* to pierce, stamp, etc. or make (a hole, etc.) with a punch

punch[2] (punch) *vt.* [ME. *punchen*] 1. to prod with a stick 2. to herd (cattle) as by prodding 3. to hit with the fist —*n.* 1. a blow with the fist 2. [Colloq.] force; vigor

punch[3] (punch) *n.* [< a Hindi word for "five": it orig. had five ingredients] a sweet drink of fruit juices, sherbet, etc., often mixed with wine or liquor

punch′-drunk′ *adj.* dazed, confused, unsteady, etc., as from many blows to the head in boxing

pun·cheon[1] (pun′chən) *n.* [< L. *pungere,* to prick] 1. a short, upright wooden post 2. a heavy piece of timber roughly dressed

pun·cheon[2] (pun′chən) *n.* [OFr. *poinçon*] a large cask (72–120 gal.), for beer, wine, etc.

punc·til·i·ous (puŋk til′ē əs) *adj.* [< Fr. < It. < L. *punctum,* a point] 1. very careful about every detail of behavior 2. very exact; scrupulous

punc·tu·al (puŋk′choo wəl) *adj.* [< L. *punctus,* a point] on time; prompt —**punc′tu·al′i·ty** (-wal′ə tē) *n.* —**punc′tu·al·ly** *adv.*

punc·tu·ate (puŋk′choo wāt′) *vt.* -at′ed, -at′ing [< L. *punctus,* a point] 1. to use certain standardized marks (**punctuation marks**) as the period, comma, etc. in (written or printed matter) 2. to interrupt 3. to emphasize — **punc′tu·a′tion** *n.*

punc·ture (puŋk′chər) *n.* [< L. *pungere,* pierce] 1. a piercing 2. a hole made by a sharp point —*vt., vi.* -tured, -tur·ing to pierce or be pierced as with a sharp point

pun·dit (pun′dit) *n.* [< Sans. *paṇḍita*] a person who has great learning

pun·gent (pun′jənt) *adj.* [< L. *pungere,* to prick] 1. producing a sharp sensation of taste or smell 2. sharp, biting, or stimulating —**pun′gen·cy** *n.* —**pun′gent·ly** *adv.*

pun·ish (pun′ish) *vt.* [< L. *punire*] 1. to cause to undergo pain, loss, etc., as for a crime 2. to impose a penalty for (an offense) —**pun′ish·a·ble** *adj.*

pun′ish·ment *n.* 1. a punishing or being punished 2. the penalty imposed

pu·ni·tive (pyoo′nə tiv) *adj.* inflicting, or concerned with, punishment

punk[1] (puŋk) *n.* [var. of SPUNK] any substance, as decayed wood, that smolders when ignited, used as tinder, or to light fireworks, etc.

punk[2] (puŋk) *n.* [< ?] [Slang] 1. a young hoodlum 2. a youngster regarded as inexperienced, insignificant, etc. —*adj.* [Slang] poor or bad in quality

pun·ster (pun′stər) *n.* one fond of making puns

punt[1] (punt) *n.* [< ? *bunt,* kick] *Football* a kick in which the ball is dropped from the hands and kicked before it strikes the ground —*vt., vi.* to kick (a football) in a punt

punt[2] (punt) *n.* [< L. *pons,* a bridge] a flat-bottomed boat with square ends —*vt., vi.* to propel (a boat) with a long pole

pu·ny (pyoo′nē) *adj.* -ni·er, -ni·est [< Fr. < OFr. *puis,* after + *né,* born] of inferior size, strength, or importance; weak

pup (pup) *n.* 1. a young dog; puppy 2. a young fox, seal, etc.

pu·pa (pyoo′pə) *n., pl.* -pae (-pē), -pas [< L., a doll] an insect in the stage between the larval and adult forms —**pu′pal** *adj.*

pu·pil[1] (pyoo′p'l) *n.* [< L. *pupillus,* ward] a person taught by a teacher or tutor, as in school

pu·pil[2] (pyoo′p'l) *n.* [< Fr. < L. *pupilla,* figure reflected in the eye] the contractile circular opening in the center of the iris of the eye

pup·pet (pup′it) *n.* [< L. *pupa,* doll] 1. a small, humanlike figure, moved with the hands or by strings in a performance (**puppet show**) 2. one whose actions, ideas, etc. are controlled by another —**pup′pet·eer′** *n.* —**pup′pet·ry** *n.*

pup·py (pup′ē) *n., pl.* -ples [< MFr. *popee,* doll] a young dog —**pup′py·ish** *adj.*

pup tent a small, portable tent

pur·blind (pur′blīnd′) *adj.* [ME. *pur blind,* quite blind] 1. partly blind 2. slow in understanding

pur·chase (pur′chəs) *vt.* -chased, -chas·ing [< OFr. *pour,* for + *chacier,* to chase] to buy —*n.* 1. anything bought 2. a buying 3. a fast hold applied to move something heavy or to keep from slipping —**pur′chas·a·ble** *adj.* —**pur′chas·er** *n.*

pure (pyoor) *adj.* [< L. *purus*] 1. free from any adulterant or anything harmful 2. simple; mere 3. utter; absolute 4. faultless 5. blameless 6. virgin or chaste 7. abstract or theoretical [*pure* physics] —**pure′ly** *adv.*

pu·rée (pyoo rā′, pyoor′ā) *n.* [Fr. < L. *purus,* pure] 1. cooked food put through a sieve or blender to make it soft and smooth 2. a thick soup of this —*vt.* -reed′, -rée′ing to make a purée of Also sp. **puree**

pur·ga·tive (pur′gə tiv) *adj.* purging —*n.* a substance that purges; specif., a cathartic

pur·ga·to·ry (pur′gə tôr′ē) *n., pl.* -ries [see PURGE] [often P-] *Christian Theol.* a state or place after death for expiating sins by suffering —**pur′ga·to′ri·al** *adj.*

purge (purj) *vt.* purged, purg′ing [< L. *purus,* clean + *agere,* to do] 1. to cleanse of impurities, etc. 2. to cleanse of sin 3. to rid (a nation, party, etc.) of (individuals held to be disloyal) 4. to empty (the bowels) —*n.* 1. a purging 2. that which purges; esp., a cathartic —**purg′er** *n.*

pu·ri·fy (pyoor′ə fī′) *vt.* -fied′, -fy′ing [< L. *purus,* pure + *facere,* make] 1. to rid of impurities, etc. 2. to free from guilt, sin, etc. —*vi.* to be purified —**pu′ri·fi·ca′tion** *n.*

pur·ism (pyoor′iz'm) *n.* strict observance of precise usage or style, as in language —**pur′ist** *n.*

Pu·ri·tan (pyoor′ə t'n) *n.* [< PURITY] 1. a member of an English Protestant group who, in the 16th and 17th centuries, wanted to simplify the Church of England worship service **2.** [**p-**] a person regarded as very strict in morals and religion —**pu'ri·tan'i·cal** (-tan'i k'l) *adj.*

pu·ri·ty (pyoor'ə tē) *n.* [< LL. *puritas*] a being pure; specif., *a*) freedom from ·adulterants *b*) cleanness *c*) innocence or chastity

purl' (purl) *vi.* [< ? Scand.] to move in ripples or with a murmuring sound —*n.* the murmuring sound of purling water

purl² (purl) *vt., vi.* [< ?] to invert (stitches) in knitting —*n.* an inversion of knitting stitches

pur·lieu (pur'lōō) *n.* [< OFr. pur-, through + *aler,* to go] **1.** an outlying part **2.** [*pl.*] environs

pur·loin (pər loin') *vt., vi.* [< OFr. pur-, for + *loin,* far] to steal —**pur·loin'er** *n.*

pur·ple (pur'p'l) *n.* [< Gr. *porphyra,* fish yielding purple dye] **1.** a dark bluish red **2.** crimson cloth or clothing: a former emblem of royalty —*adj.* **1.** bluish-red **2.** imperial **3.** ornate *[purple prose]* **4.** vigorous; strong *[purple language]* — **pur'plish** *adj.*

pur·port (pər pôrt'; *for n.* pur'pôrt) *vt.* [< OFr. *por-,* forth + *porter,* to bear] **1.** to profess as its meaning **2.** to give the appearance, often falsely, of being, intending, etc. —*n.* **1.** meaning; sense **2.** intention

pur·pose (pur'pəs) *vt., vi.* -posed, -pos·ing [< OFr. *porposer:* see PROPOSE] to plan or intend —*n.* **1.** what one plans to get or do; aim **2.** determination **3.** the reason or use for something —**on purpose** intentionally —**pur'pose·ful** *adj.* —**pur'pose·less** *adj.*

pur'pose·ly *adv.* with a definite purpose; intentionally; deliberately

purr (pur) *n.* [echoic] a low, vibratory sound made by a cat when it seems to be pleased — *vi., vt.* to make, or express by, such a sound

purse (purs) *n.* [< Gr. *byrsa,* a hide] **1.** a small bag for carrying money **2.** finances; money **3.** a sum of money given as a present **4.** a woman's handbag —*vt.* pursed, purs'ing to pucker (one's lips, etc.)

purs·er (pur'sər) *n.* [ME., purse bearer] a ship's officer in charge of accounts, tickets, etc., esp. on a passenger vessel

pur·su·ance (pər sōō'əns) *n.* a pursuing, or carrying out, as of a project, plan, etc.

pur·su'ant *adj.* [Now Rare] pursuing — **pursuant to** in accordance with

pur·sue (pər sōō') *vt.* -sued', -su'ing [< L. *pro-,* forth + *sequi,* follow] **1.** to follow in order to overtake or capture; chase **2.** to follow (a specified course, action, etc.) **3.** to strive for **4.** to keep on harassing —**pur·su'er** *n.*

pur·suit (-sōōt') *n.* **1.** a pursuing **2.** one's career, interest, etc.

pu·ru·lent (pyoor'ə lənt, -yoo lənt) *adj.* [Fr. < L. *pus, pus*] of, like, containing, or discharging pus —**pu'ru·lence** *n.*

pur·vey (pər vā') *vt.* [see PROVIDE] to supply (esp. food) —**pur·vey'or** *n.*

pur·view (pur'vyōō) *n.* [< Anglo-Fr. *purveu (est),* (it is) provided] scope or extent, as of control, activity, etc.

pus (pus) *n.* [L.] the yellowish-white matter produced by an infection —**pus'sy** *adj.*

push (poosh) *vt., vi.* [< L. *pulsare,* to beat] **1.** to press against so as to move **2.** to urge on; impel **3.** to promote the use, sale, etc. of —*n.* **1.** a pushing **2.** a vigorous effort **3.** an advance against opposition **4.** [Colloq.] enterprise; drive —**push'er** *n.*

push'o'ver *n.* [Slang] **1.** anything easy to do **2.** a person, group, etc. easily persuaded, defeated, etc.

push'y *adj.* **-i·er, -i·est** [Colloq.] annoyingly aggressive and persistent —**push'i·ness** *n.*

pu·sil·lan·i·mous (pyōō's'l an'ə məs) *adj.* [< L. *pusillus,* tiny + *animus,* the mind] timid or cowardly —**pu'sil·la·nim'i·ty** (-ə nim'ə tē) *n.*

puss (poos) *n.* [< ?] a cat: pet name: also **puss'y,** *pl.* **-ies, puss'y·cat'**

puss'y·foot' *vi.* [Colloq.] **1.** to move with stealth or caution, like a cat **2.** to avoid committing oneself

pussy willow a willow bearing silvery, velvetlike catkins before the leaves appear

pus·tule (pus'chōōl) *n.* [L. *pustula*] a small swelling in the skin, containing pus —**pus'tu·lar** *adj.*

put (poot) *vt.* put, put'ting [< OE. *potian,* to push] **1.** to drive; thrust **2.** to throw with an overhand thrust *[put the shot]* **3.** to make be in a specified place, condition, relation, etc.; place; set **4.** to·impose (a tax, etc.) **5.** to attribute; ascribe **6.** to express·*[put* it plainly] **7.** to present for decision *[put* the question] **8.** to bet (money) *on* —*vi.* to go (*in, out,* etc.) —*adj.* [Colloq.] fixed *[stay put]* —**put across** [Colloq.] to make understood, accepted, successful, etc. —**put aside** (or **by**) to keep for later use —**put down 1.** to crush; repress **2.** to write down **3.** [Slang] to belittle or humiliate —**put in for** to apply for —**put it** (or **something**) **over** on [Colloq.] to deceive; trick —**put off 1.** to postpone **2.** to evade; divert —**put on 1.** to clothe oneself with **2.** to pretend **3.** to stage (a play) **4.** [Slang] to hoax —**put out 1.** to expel; dismiss **2.** to extinguish (a fire or light) **3.** to inconvenience **4.** *Baseball* to retire (a batter or runner) —**put through 1.** to carry out **2.** to cause to do or undergo —**put up 1.** to offer **2.** to preserve (fruits, etc.) **3.** to provide lodgings for **4.** to provide (money) **5.** to arrange (the hair) with rollers, etc. **6.** [Colloq.] to incite (a person) *to* some action —**put upon** to impose on —**put up with** to tolerate

put'·down' *n.* [Slang] a belittling remark or crushing retort

pu·tre·fy (pyōō'trə fī') *vt., vi.* -fied', -fy'ing [< L. *putris,* putrid + *facere,* make] to make or become putrid; rot —**pu'tre·fac'tion** (-fak'shən) *n.*

pu·tres·cent (pyōō tres'nt) *adj.* putrefying; rotting —**pu·tres'cence** *n.*

pu·trid (pyōō'trid) *adj.* [< Fr. < L. *putrere,* be rotten] rotten and foul-smelling

putt (put) *n.* [< PUT, *v.*] *Golf* a light stroke made on the putting green to put the ball into the hole —*vt., vi.* to hit (the ball) with a putt

putt·er' (put'ər) *n. Golf* a short, straight-faced club used in putting

put·ter² (put'ər) *vi.* [< OE. *potian,* to push] to busy oneself in an ineffective way (often with *around,* etc.) —*vt.* to fritter (*away*)

putt·ing green (put'iŋ) *Golf* the area of smooth turf in which the hole is sunk

put·ty (put'ē) *n.* [< Fr. *potée,* lit., potful] **1.** a soft, plastic mixture of powdered chalk and linseed oil, used to fill small cracks, etc. **2.** any similar substance —*vt.* -tied, -ty·ing to cement, fill, etc. with putty

puz·zle (puz'l) *vt.* -zled, -zling [< ?] to perplex; bewilder —*vi.* **1.** to be perplexed, etc. **2.** to exercise one's mind, as on a problem —*n.* **1.** a puzzling problem, etc. **2.** a toy or problem to test skill or ingenuity —**puzzle out** to solve by deep thought —**puz'zle·ment** *n.*

Pvt. *Mil.* Private

PX post exchange

Pyg·my (pig'mē) *n., pl.* **-mies** [< Gr. *pygmaios,* of the length of the forearm] **1.** a member of any of several African and Asian peoples of small stature 2. [p-] any very small person or thing —*adj.* 1. of Pygmies 2. [p-] very small

py·ja·mas (pə jam′əz, -jä′məz) *n.pl. Brit. sp. of* PAJAMAS

py·lon (pī′län) *n.* [Gr. *pylōn*, gateway] 1. a gateway, as of an Egyptian temple 2. a tower-like structure, as for supporting electric lines

py·lo·rus (pī lôr′əs) *n., pl.* **-ri** (-ī) [< Gr. *pylōros*, gatekeeper] the opening from the stomach into the duodenum —**py·lor′ic** *adj.*

py·or·rhe·a, py·or·rhoe·a (pī′ə rē′ə) *n.* [< Gr. *pyon*, pus + *rhein*, to flow] an infection of the gums and tooth sockets, with formation of pus and loosening of the teeth

pyr·a·mid (pir′ə mid) *n.* [< Gr. *pyramis*] 1. a huge structure with a square base and four triangular sides meeting at the top, as a royal tomb of ancient Egypt 2. *Geom.* a solid figure with a polygonal base, whose sides are the bases of triangular surfaces meeting at a common vertex —*vi., vt.* to build up as in a pyramid —**py·ram·i·dal** (pi ram′ə d'l) *adj.*

pyre (pīr) *n.* [< Gr. *pyr*, a fire] a pile of wood, for burning a corpse in a funeral rite

Py·rex (pī′reks) [coined < PIE] *a trademark for* a heat-resistant glassware for cooking, etc.

py·rite (pī′rīt) *n., pl.* **py·ri·tes** (pə rit′ēz, pī′rīts) [< Gr. *pyritēs*, flint] iron sulfide, a lustrous, yellow mineral

pyro- [< Gr. *pyr*, a fire] *a combining form meaning* fire, heat: also **pyr-**

py·ro·ma·ni·a (pī′rə mā′nē ə) *n.* [PYRO- + -MANIA] a compulsion to start destructive fires —**py′ro·ma′ni·ac′** (-nē ak′) *n., adj.*

py·ro·tech·nics (pī′rə tek′niks) *n.pl.* [< Fr. < Gr. *pyr*, fire + *technē*, art] 1. a display of fire-works 2. a dazzling display, as of wit —**py′ro·tech′nic** *adj.*

Pyr·rhic victory (pir′ik) [< *Pyrrhus*, Gr. king who defeated the Romans after heavy losses] a victory that is too costly

py·thon (pī′thän, -thən) *n.* [< Gr. *Pythōn*, a serpent slain by Apollo] a large, nonpoisonous snake of Asia and Africa that crushes its prey to death

pyx (piks) *n.* [< Gr. *pyxis*, a box] a container for Eucharistic wafers

Q

Q, q (kyoō) *n., pl.* **Q's, q's** the seventeenth letter of the English alphabet

q. 1. quart 2. queen 3. question

Q.E.D. [L. *quod erat demonstrandum*] which was to be proved

QM, Q.M. Quartermaster

qt. 1. quantity 2. quart(s)

Q.T., q.t. [Slang] quiet: usually in **on the Q.T.** (or **q.t.**), in secret

quack[1] (kwak) *vi.* [echoic] to utter the sound or cry of a duck —*n.* this sound

quack[2] (kwak) *n.* [< earlier *quacksalver* (< MDu. *quacken*, to brag + *zalf*, salve)] 1. an untrained person who practices medicine fraudulently 2. any person who pretends to have knowledge or skill he does not have —*adj.* fraudulent —**quack′er·y** *n.*

quad (kwäd) *n. same as:* 1. QUADRANGLE (of a college) 2. QUADRAPHONIC 3. QUADRUPLET

quad·ran·gle (kwäd′raŋ′g'l) *n.* [see QUADRI- & ANGLE[1]] 1. a plane figure with four angles and four sides 2. an area surrounded on its four sides by buildings —**quad·ran′gu·lar** (-gyə lər) *adj.*

quad·rant (kwäd′rənt) *n.* [< L. *quadrans*, fourth part] 1. an arc of 90° 2. a quarter section of a circle 3. an instrument for measuring altitudes in astronomy and navigation

quad·ra·phon·ic (kwäd′rə fän′ik) *adj.* [< L. *quadra*, a square + Gr. *phōnē*, a sound] using four channels to record and reproduce sound

quad·rat·ic (kwäd rat′ik) *adj. Algebra* involving a quantity or quantities that are squared but none that are raised to a higher power

quad·ren·ni·al (kwäd ren′ē əl) *adj.* [< L. *quadri-* (see QUADRI-) + *annus*, a year] lasting four years

quadri- [L. < *quattuor*, four] *a combining form meaning* four times: also **quadr-**

quad·ri·lat·er·al (kwäd′rə lat′ər əl) *adj.* [see QUADRI- & LATERAL] four-sided —*n.* a plane figure having four sides and four angles

qua·drille (kwə dril′, kwä-) *n.* [Fr.; ult. < L. *quadra*, a square] 1. a square dance performed by four couples 2. music for this

quad·ru·ped (kwäd′roo ped′) *n.* [< L. *quadru-*, four + *pes*, a foot] an animal, esp. a mammal, with four feet

quad·ru·ple (kwä drōō′p'l, kwäd′roo-) *adj.* [< L. *quadru-*, four + *-plus*, -fold] 1. consisting of four 2. four times as much or as many —*n.* an amount four times as much or as many —*vt., vi.* **-pled, -pling** to make or become four times as much or as many

quad·ru·plet (kwä drup′lit, -drōō′plit; kwäd′roo plit) *n.* 1. any of four offspring born at a single birth 2. a group of four, usually of one kind

quad·ru·pli·cate (kwä drōō′plə kāt′; *for adj. & n., usually* -kit) —*vt.* **-cat′ed, -cat′ing** [< L. *quadru-*, four + *plicare*, to fold] to make four identical copies of —*adj.* 1. fourfold 2. being the fourth of identical copies —*n.* any of four identical copies

quaff (kwäf, kwaf) *vt., vi.* [prob. < LowG. *quassen*, overindulge] to drink deeply and heartily —*n.* a quaffing

quag·mire (kwag′mīr′) *n.* [< *quag*, bog + MIRE] wet, boggy ground

qua·hog, qua·haug (kwô′hôg, kō′-) *n.* [< AmInd.] a hard-shelled clam

quail[1] (kwāl) *vi.* [prob. < L. *coagulare*, coagulate] to draw back in fear; cower

quail[2] (kwāl) *n.* [< OFr.] a small game bird that resembles the partridge

quaint (kwānt) *adj.* [< OFr. < L. *cognitus*, known] 1. pleasingly odd or old-fashioned 2. unusual; curious 3. fanciful; whimsical —**quaint′ly** *adv.* —**quaint′ness** *n.*

quake (kwāk) *vi.* **quaked, quak′ing** [OE. *cwacian*] 1. to tremble or shake 2. to shiver, as from fear or cold —*n.* 1. a quaking 2. an earthquake —**quak′y** *adj.*

Quak·er (kwāk′ər) *n.* [< founder's admonition to "quake" at the word of the Lord] a member of the SOCIETY OF FRIENDS

qual·i·fi·ca·tion (kwäl′ə fi kā′shən) *n.* 1. a qualifying or being qualified 2. a modification or restriction 3. any skill, etc. that fits one for a job, office, etc.

qual·i·fied (kwäl′ə fĭd′) *adj.* 1. fit; competent 2. limited; modified

qual′i·fy′ (-fī′) *vt.* -fied′, -fy′ing [< Fr. < L. *qualis,* of what kind + *facere,* make] 1. to make fit for a job, etc. 2. to make legally capable 3. to modify; restrict 4. to moderate; soften 5. *Gram.* to modify the meaning of (a word) —*vi.* to be or become qualified —**qual′i·fi′er** *n.*

qual′i·ta·tive (-tāt′iv) *adj.* having to do with quality —**qual′i·ta′tive·ly** *adv.*

qual·i·ty (kwäl′ə tē) *n., pl.* -ties [< L. *qualis,* of what kind] 1. that which makes something what it is; characteristic 2. basic nature; kind 3. the degree of excellence of a thing 4. superiority

qualm (kwäm) *n.* [OE. *cwealm,* disaster] 1. a sudden feeling of sickness, faintness, etc. 2. a doubt; misgiving 3. a twinge of conscience; scruple —**qualm′ish** *adj.*

quan·da·ry (kwän′drē, -dər ē) *n., pl.* -ries [< ? L. *quande,* how much] a state of perplexity; dilemma

quan·ti·ta·tive (kwän′tə tāt′iv) *adj.* having to do with quantity

quan·ti·ty (kwän′tə tē) *n., pl.* -ties [< L. *quantus,* how much] 1. an amount; portion 2. any indeterminate bulk or number 3. [*also pl.*] a great amount 4. that property of a thing which can be measured 5. a number or symbol expressing this property

quan·tum (kwän′təm) *n., pl.* -ta (-tə) [L., how much] *Physics* an elemental unit, as of energy: the **quantum theory** states that energy is absorbed or radiated discontinuously in quanta

quar·an·tine (kwôr′ən tēn′, kwär′-) *n.* [< It. < L. *quadraginta,* forty] 1. the period, orig. 40 days, during which a vessel suspected of carrying contagious disease is detained in port 2. any isolation imposed to keep contagious diseases, etc. from spreading 3. a place for such isolation —*vt.* -tined′, -tin′ing to place under quarantine

quark (kwôrk) *n.* [arbitrary coinage] any of three hypothetical particles assumed as the basic units of matter

quar·rel (kwôr′əl, kwär′-) *n.* [< L. *queri,* complain] 1. a cause for dispute 2. a dispute, esp. an angry one —*vi.* -reled or -relled, -rel·ing or -rel·ling 1, to complain 2. to dispute heatedly 3. to have a breach in friendship — **quar′rel·er** *n.*

quar′rel·some (-səm) *adj.* inclined to quarrel —**quar′rel·some·ness** *n.*

quar·ry[1] (kwôr′ē, kwär′ē) *n., pl.* -ries [< OFr. *curer,* eviscerate] an animal, etc. being hunted down

quar·ry[2] (kwôr′ē, kwär′ē) *n., pl.* -ries [< L. *quadrare,* to square] a place where stone or slate is excavated —*vt.* -ried, -ry·ing to excavate from a quarry

quart (kwôrt) *n.* [< L. *quartus,* fourth] 1. a liquid measure, equal to 1/4 gallon 2. a dry measure, equal to 1/8 peck

quar·ter (kwôr′tər) *n.* [< L. *quartus,* fourth] 1. any of the four equal parts of something; fourth 2. one fourth of a year 3. one fourth of an hour 4. one fourth of a dollar; 25 cents, or a coin of this value 5. any leg of a four-legged animal, with the adjoining parts 6. a particular district or section 7. [*pl.*] lodgings 8. a particular source [*news from high quarters*] —*vt.* 1. to divide into four equal parts 2. to provide lodgings for —*adj.* constituting a quarter —**at close quarters** at close range

quar′ter·back′ *n. Football* the back who calls the signals and directs the plays

quar′ter-deck′, quar′ter·deck′ *n.* the after part of the upper deck of a ship, usually for officers

quar′ter·ly *adv.* occurring regularly four times a year —*adj.* once every quarter of the year — *n., pl.* -lies a publication issued every three months

quar′ter·mas′ter *n.* 1. *Mil.* an officer who provides troops with quarters, clothing, equipment, etc. 2. *Naut.* a petty officer or mate who attends to navigation, signals, etc.

quarter note *Music* a note (♩) having one fourth the duration of a whole note

quar·tet, quar·tette (kwôr tet′) *n.* [< Fr. < L. *quartus,* a fourth] 1. a group of four 2. *Music a)* a composition for four voices or instruments *b)* the four performers of this

quar·to (kwôr′tō) *n., pl.* -tos [< L. (*in*) *quarto,* (in) a fourth] 1. the page size (about 9 by 12 in.) of a book made up of sheets folded into four leaves 2. such a book

quartz (kwôrts) *n.* [G. *quarz*] a crystalline mineral, usually colorless and transparent

qua·sar (kwā′sär, -sər) *n.* [< *quas*(*i-stell*)*ar* (*radio source*)] a distant, starlike, celestial object that emits much light or powerful radio waves

quash[1] (kwäsh) *vt.* [< L. *cassus,* empty] *Law* to annul or set aside (an indictment)

quash[2] (kwäsh) *vt.* [< L. *quatere,* to break] to put down; suppress [*to quash an uprising*]

qua·si (kwā′sī, -zī; kwä′sē, -zē) *adv.* [L. < *quam,* as + *si,* if] as if; seemingly —*adj.* seeming Often hyphenated as a prefix

quat·rain (kwä′trān) *n.* [Fr. < L. *quattuor,* four] a stanza or poem of four lines

qua·ver (kwā′vər) *vi.* [ME. *cwafien*] 1. to shake or tremble 2. to be tremulous: said of the voice —*vt.* to utter in a tremulous voice —*n.* a tremulous quality in a voice, etc.

quay (kē) *n.* [MFr. *cai* < Celt.] a wharf, usually of stone or concrete

quea·sy (kwē′zē) *adj.* -si·er, -si·est [< Scand.] 1. causing or feeling nausea 2. squeamish; easily nauseated 3. uneasy —**quea′si·ly** *adv.* — **quea′si·ness** *n.*

queen (kwēn) *n.* [OE. *cwen*] 1. the wife of a king 2. a woman monarch in her own right 3. a woman noted for her beauty or accomplishments 4. the fully developed, reproductive female in a colony of bees, ants, etc. 5. a playing card with a picture of a queen on it 6. [Slang] a male homosexual 7. *Chess* the most powerful piece —**queen′ly** *adj.*

queer (kwir) *adj.* [< ? G. *quer,* crosswise] 1. differing from what is usual; odd; strange 2. slightly ill 3. [Colloq.] eccentric —*vt.* [Slang] to spoil the success of —*n.* [Slang] a homosexual —**queer′ly** *adv.*

quell (kwel) *vt.* [OE. *cwellan,* kill] 1. to crush; subdue 2. to quiet; allay

quench (kwench) *vt.* [OE. *cwencan*] 1. to extinguish [*water quenched the fire*] 2. to satisfy [*he quenched his thirst*] 3. to cool (hot steel, etc.) suddenly by plunging into water, etc. — **quench′less** *adj.*

quer·u·lous (kwer′ə ləs, -yə-) *adj.* [< L. *queri,* complain] 1. inclined to find fault 2. full of complaint; peevish

que·ry (kwir′ē) *n., pl.* -ries [< L. *quaerere,* ask] 1. a question; inquiry 2. a question mark —*vt., vi.* -ried, -ry·ing to question

quest (kwest) *n.* [< L. *quaerere,* seek] 1. a seeking; hunt 2. a journey for adventure

ques·tion (kwes′chən) *n.* [< L. *quaerere,* ask] 1. an asking; inquiry 2. something asked 3. doubt; uncertainty 4. a matter open to discussion **5.** a matter of difficulty [not a *question* of money] **6.** a point being debated, as before an assembly —*vt.* **1.** to ask questions of **2.** to express uncertainty about; doubt **3.** to dispute; challenge —*vi.* to ask questions —**out of the question** impossible —**ques'tion·er** *n.*

ques'tion·a·ble *adj.* **1.** that can be questioned **2.** suspected of being immoral, dishonest, etc. —**ques'tion·a·bly** *adv.*

question mark a mark of punctuation (?) put after a sentence or word to indicate a direct question, or to express doubt, uncertainty, etc.

ques'tion·naire' (-chə ner') *n.* [Fr.] a written or printed list of questions used in gathering information from persons

queue (kyoo) *n.* [Fr. < L. *cauda*, tail] **1.** a pigtail **2.** [Chiefly Brit.] a line, as of persons waiting to be served —*vi.* **queued, queu'ing** [Chiefly Brit.] to form in a queue, or line (often with *up*)

quib·ble (kwib''l) *n.* [< L. *qui*, who] **1.** a petty evasion; cavil **2.** a petty objection or criticism —*vi.* -**bled, -bling** to resort to a quibble —**quib'-bler** *n.*

quick (kwik) *adj.* [OE. *cwicu*, living] **1.** *a)* rapid; swift [a *quick* walk] *b)* prompt [a *quick* reply] **2.** prompt to understand or learn **3.** easily stirred [a *quick* temper] —*adv.* quickly; rapidly —*n.* **1.** the living [the *quick* and the dead] **2.** the sensitive flesh under the nails **3.** the deepest feelings [cut to the *quick*] — **quick'ly** *adv.* —**quick'ness** *n.*

quick bread any bread leavened with baking powder, soda, etc. and baked as soon as the batter or dough is mixed

quick'en *vt., vi.* **1.** to animate; revive **2.** to move more rapidly; hasten **3.** to show signs of life, as a fetus

quick'-freeze' *vt.* -**froze', -fro'zen, -freez'ing** to subject (food) to sudden freezing for long storage at low temperatures

quick'ie (-ē) *n.* [Slang] anything done or made quickly and, often, cheaply

quick'lime' (-līm') *n.* unslaked lime

quick'sand' *n.* [< ME.: see QUICK & SAND] a deep deposit of loose, wet sand, easily engulfing heavy objects

quick'sil'ver *n.* the metal mercury

quick'-wit'ted *adj.* nimble of mind

quid (kwid) *n.* [var. of *cud*] a piece, as of tobacco, to be chewed

quid pro quo (kwid' prō kwō') [L.] **1.** one thing in return for another **2.** a substitute

qui·es·cent (kwī es''nt) *adj.* [< L. *quiescere*, become quiet] quiet; still; inactive —**qui·es'-cence** *n.* —**qui·es'cent·ly** *adv.*

qui·et (kwī'ət) *adj.* [L. *quies*, rest] **1.** still; calm; motionless **2.** *a)* not noisy; hushed *b)* not speaking; silent **3.** gentle **4.** not easily excited **5.** not bright or showy **6.** unobtrusive —*n.* **1.** a quiet state; calmness, stillness, etc. **2.** a quiet or peaceful quality —*vt., vi.* to make or become quiet —**qui'et·ly** *adv.*

qui·e·tude (kwī'ə tōōd', -tyōōd') *n.* a state of being quiet; rest; calmness

qui·e·tus (kwī ēt'əs) *n.* [< ML. *quietus* (*est*), (he is) quit] **1.** discharge from debt, etc. **2.** release from life; death

quill (kwil) *n.* [prob. < MLowG. or MDu.] **1.** a large, stiff feather **2.** *a)* the hollow stem of a feather *b)* anything made from this, as a pen **3.** a spine of a porcupine or hedgehog

quilt (kwilt) *n.* [< L. *culcita*, a bed] a cover for a bed, filled with down, wool, etc. and stitched together in lines or patterns —*vt.* to stitch as or like a quilt —*vi.* to make a quilt —**quilt'er** *n.*

quince (kwins) *n.* [< Gr. *kydōnion*] **1.** a yellow-

---

ish, hard, apple-shaped fruit used in preserves **2.** the tree it grows on

qui·nine (kwī'nīn) *n.* [< *quina*, cinchona bark] a bitter, crystalline substance extracted from cinchona bark, used esp. for treating malaria

quinine water *same as* TONIC (*n.* 2)

quin·sy (kwin'zē) *n.* [< Gr. *kyōn*, dog + *anchein*, to choke] *an earlier term for* TONSILLITIS

quint (kwint) *n. short for* QUINTUPLET

quin·tes·sence (kwin tes''ns) *n.* [< ML. *quinta essentia*, fifth essence] **1.** the pure essence of something **2.** a perfect example — **quin'tes·sen'tial** (-tə sen'shəl) *adj.*

quin·tet, quin·tette (kwin tet') *n.* [< L. *quintus*, a fifth] **1.** a group of five **2.** *Music a)* a composition for five voices or five instruments *b)* the five performers of this

quin·tu·ple (kwin tōō'p'l, -tyōō'-) *adj.* [< L. *quintus*, a fifth + *-plex*, -fold] **1.** consisting of five **2.** five times as much or as many —*vt., vi.* -**pled, -pling** to make or become five times as much or as many

quin·tu·plet (kwin tup'lit, -tōō'plit) *n.* [dim. of prec.] **1.** any of five offspring born at a single birth **2.** a group of five

quip (kwip) *n.* [< L. *quippe*, indeed] a witty or sarcastic remark; jest —*vi.* **quipped, quip'ping** to utter quips —**quip'ster** *n.*

quire (kwīr) *n.* [< L. *quaterni*, four each] a set of 24 or 25 sheets of the same paper

quirk (kwurk) *n.* [< ?] **1.** a sudden twist, etc. **2.** a peculiar mannerism

quirt (kwurt) *n.* [AmSp. *cuarta*] a riding whip with a braided leather lash and a short handle

quis·ling (kwiz'liŋ) *n.* [< V. *Quisling*, Norw. collaborationist with the Nazis] a traitor

quit (kwit) *vt.* **quit** or **quit'ted, quit'ting** [< ML. *quietus*, free] **1.** to free (oneself) *of* **2.** to give up **3.** to leave; depart from **4.** to stop; resign from —*vi.* **1.** to stop doing something **2.** to give up one's job; resign —*adj.* clear, free, or rid

quit'claim' (kwit'klām') *n.* a deed relinquishing a claim to property or some right

quite (kwīt) *adv.* [< QUIT, *adj.*] **1.** completely; entirely **2.** really; truly **3.** to a considerable degree —**quite a few** (or **bit,** etc.) [Colloq.] more than a few (or bit, etc.)

quits (kwits) *adj.* [see QUIETUS] on even terms, as by paying a debt, retaliating, etc. —**call it quits** [Colloq.] to stop working, being friendly, etc.

quit·tance (kwit''ns) *n.* [see QUIT] **1.** *a)* payment of a debt, etc. *b)* a document certifying this **2.** recompense; repayment

quit'ter *n.* [Colloq.] one who quits or gives up easily, without trying hard

quiv·er (kwiv'ər) *vi.* [see QUICK] to shake; tremble —*n.* a quivering; tremor

quiv·er (kwiv'ər) *n.* [OFr. *coivre*] **1.** a case for holding arrows **2.** its contents

quix·ot·ic (kwik sät'ik) *adj.* [< DON QUIXOTE] extravagantly chivalrous or romantically idealistic; impractical

quiz (kwiz) *n., pl.* **quiz'zes** [prob. < L. *quis*, what?] a questioning; esp., a short examination to test one's knowledge —*vt.* **quizzed, quiz'zing** to ask questions of, as in interrogating

quiz·zi·cal (kwiz'i k'l) *adj.* **1.** odd; comical **2.** perplexed —**quiz'zi·cal·ly** *adv.*

quoin (koin, kwoin) *n.* [var. of COIN] **1.** the external corner of a building; esp., any of the stones forming the corner **2.** a wedge-shaped block

quoit (kwoit, koit) *n.* [prob. < OFr. *coite*, a cushion] **1.** a ring thrown, in a game, to encircle an upright peg **2.** [*pl.*, *with sing. v.*] this game

quon·dam (kwän′dəm) *adj.* [L.] former [*a quondam* pacifist]

Quon·set hut (kwän′sit) [< *Quonset* Point, R.I., where first made] a *trademark for* a prefabricated, metal shelter like a half cylinder on its flat side

quo·rum (kwôr′əm) *n.* [< L. *qui*, who] the minimum number of members who must be present at an assembly before it can validly transact business

quo·ta (kwōt′ə) *n.* [< L. *quota pars*, how large a part] a share or proportion assigned to each of a number

quo·ta·tion (kwō tā′shən) *n.* **1.** a quoting **2.** the words or passage quoted **3.** the current quoted price of a stock, bond, etc.

quotation mark either of a pair of punctuation marks ("...") used to enclose a direct quotation

quote (kwōt) *vt.* **quot′ed, quot′ing** [< ML. *quotare*, to number (chapters)] **1.** to repeat a passage from or statement of **2.** to repeat (a passage, statement, etc.) **3.** to state (the price of something) —*n.* [Colloq.] *same as:* **1.** QUOTATION **2.** QUOTATION MARK —*quot′a·ble adj.*

quoth (kwōth) *vt.* [< OE. *cwethan*, speak] [Archaic] said

quo·tid·i·an (kwō tid′ē ən) *adj.* [< L. *quotidie*] **1.** daily **2.** ordinary —*n.* anything, esp. a fever, that recurs daily

quo·tient (kwō′shənt) *n.* [< L. *quot*, how many] the number obtained when one number is divided by another

q.v. [L. *quod vide*] which see

R

R, r (är) *n., pl.* **R's, r's** the eighteenth letter of the English alphabet

R *Elec.* resistance —**the three R's** reading, writing, and arithmetic, regarded as the basic studies

r *Math.* radius

R., r. **1.** radius **2.** railroad **3.** right **4.** river **5.** road **6.** *Baseball* runs

Ra *Chem.* radium

rab·bi (rab′ī) *n., pl.* **-bis, -bies** [< Heb. *rabbī*, my master] a teacher of the Jewish law, now usually the ordained leader of a synagogue — **rab.bin·i·cal** (rə bin′i k′l) *adj.*

rab·bit (rab′it) *n.* [ME. *rabette*] **1.** a burrowing mammal that is usually smaller than the hare, having soft fur and long ears **2.** its fur

rabbit ears [Colloq.] an indoor TV antenna with two rods that form a V shape

rabbit punch *Boxing* a sharp blow to the back of the neck

rab·ble (rab′′l) *n.* [< ME. < ?] a crowd; mob

rab′ble-rous′er (-rouz′ər) *n.* one who tries to arouse people to violent action by appeals to emotions, prejudices, etc.

rab·id (rab′id) *adj.* [< L. *rabere*, to rage] **1.** violent; raging **2.** fanatical **3.** of or having rabies —**rab′id·ly** *adv.*

ra·bies (rā′bēz) *n.* [L., madness] an infectious virus disease of mammals, passed on to man by the bite of an infected animal: it causes choking, convulsions, etc.

rac·coon (ra kōōn′) *n.* [< AmInd. *ärakun*, lit., scratcher] **1.** a small, tree-climbing mammal of N. America, having yellowish-gray fur and a black-ringed tail **2.** its fur

race¹ (rās) *n.* [< ON. *rās*, a running] **1.** a competition of speed, as in running **2.** any contest like a race [the *race* for mayor] **3.** a swift current of water, or its channel —*vi.* **raced, rac′ing 1.** to take part in a race **2.** to go or move swiftly —*vt.* **1.** to compete with in a race **2.** to enter (a horse, etc.) in a race **3.** to make go fast —**rac′er** *n.*

race² (rās) *n.* [Fr. < It. *razza*] **1.** any of the different varieties of mankind, mainly the Caucasoid, Mongoloid, and Negroid groups **2.** any geographical, national, or tribal ethnic grouping **3.** any distinct group of people

race′horse′ *n.* a horse bred and trained for racing

ra·ceme (rā sēm′, rə-) *n.* [L. *racemus*, cluster of grapes] a flower cluster with individual flowers growing on small stems at intervals along one central stem

race track a course prepared for racing

race′way′ *n.* **1.** a narrow channel **2.** a race track, as for harness races or for drag races

Ra·chel (rā′chəl) *Bible* the younger of the two wives of Jacob

ra·chi·tis (rə kīt′əs) *n.* [< Gr. *rhachis*, spine] *same as* RICKETS

ra·cial (rā′shəl) *adj.* **1.** of a race, or ethnic group **2.** of or between races

rac·ism (rā′siz'm) *n.* the practice of racial discrimination, segregation, etc. —**rac′ist** *n., adj.*

rack¹ (rak) *n.* [prob. < MDu. *recken*, to stretch] **1.** a framework, stand, etc. for holding things [clothes *rack*] **2.** a toothed bar that meshes with a cogwheel, etc. **3.** an instrument of torture which stretches the victim's limbs **4.** any great torment —*vt.* **1.** to torture on a rack **2.** to torment —**on the rack** in a painful situation — **rack one's brains** to try hard to think of something —**rack up** [Slang] to score or achieve

rack² (rak) *n.* [var. of WRACK] destruction: now only in **go to rack and ruin,** to become ruined

rack·et¹ (rak′it) *n.* [prob. echoic] **1.** a noisy confusion **2.** *a*) an obtaining of money illegally *b*) [Colloq.] any dishonest scheme

rack·et² (rak′it) *n.* [< MFr. < Ar. *rāhah*, palm of the hand] a light bat for tennis, etc., with a network of catgut, nylon, etc. in a frame attached to a handle: also **rac′quet**

rack·et·eer (rak′ə tir′) *n.* one who gets money illegally, as by fraud or extortion —**rack′et·eer′ing** *n.*

rac·on·teur (rak′än tur′) *n.* [Fr. < *raconter*, to recount] a person skilled at telling stories or anecdotes

rac′quet·ball′ *n.* a game played like handball, but with a racket

rac·y (rā′sē) *adj.* **-i·er, -i·est** [< RACE²] **1.** lively; spirited **2.** pungent **3.** risqué

ra·dar (rā′där) *n.* [*ra(dio) d(etecting) a(nd) r(anging)*] a system or device that transmits radio waves to a reflecting object, as an aircraft, to determine its location, speed, etc. by the reflected waves

ra′dar·scope′ (-skōp′) *n.* an instrument that displays on a screen the reflected radio waves picked up by radar

ra·di·al (rā′dē əl) *adj.* [see RADIUS] **1.** of or like a ray or rays; branching out from a center **2.** of a radius

radial (ply) tire an automobile tire with ply cords nearly at right angles to the center line of the tread

ra·di·ant (rā′dē ənt) *adj.* [see RADIUS] **1.** shining brightly **2.** showing joy, love, etc. **3.** issuing (from a source) in or as in rays —**ra′di·ance** *n.* —**ra′di·ant·ly** *adv.*

ra·di·ate (rā′dē āt′) *vi.* -**at′ed,** -**at′ing** [see RADIUS] **1.** to send out rays of heat, light, etc. **2.** to branch out in lines from a center —*vt.* **1.** to send out (heat, light, etc.) in rays **2.** to give forth (happiness, love, etc.)

ra′di·a′tion *n.* **1.** a radiating **2.** the rays sent out **3.** nuclear particles

ra′di·a′tor *n.* an apparatus for radiating heat, as into a room or from an automobile engine

rad·i·cal (rad′i k′l) *adj.* [< L. *radix,* a root] **1.** of or from the root; fundamental **2.** favoring basic change, as in the social structure —*n.* **1.** a person having radical views **2.** *Chem.* a group of two or more atoms acting as a single atom **3.** *Math.* the sign (√) used with a quantity to show that its root is to be extracted —**rad′i·cal·ism** *n.* —**rad′i·cal·ly** *adv.*

ra·di·i (rā′dē ī′) *n. pl. of* RADIUS

ra·di·o (rā′dē ō′) *n., pl.* -**os′** [ult. < L. *radius:* see RADIUS] **1.** the transmission of sounds or signals by electromagnetic waves through space, without wires, to a receiving set **2.** such a set **3.** broadcasting by radio as an industry, entertainment, etc. —*adj.* of, using, used in, or sent by radio —*vt., vi.* -**oed′,** -**o′ing** to transmit, or communicate with, by radio

radio- [Fr. < L.: see RADIUS] *a combining form meaning:* **1.** ray, raylike **2.** by radio **3.** by means of radiant energy [*radiotherapy*]

ra′di·o·ac′tive *adj.* giving off radiant energy in particles or rays by the disintegration of atomic nuclei —**ra′di·o·ac′tive·ly** *adv.* —**ra′di·o·ac·tiv′i·ty** *n.*

ra′di·o·gram′ (-gram′) *n.* a message sent by radio: also **ra′di·o·tel′e·gram′**

ra′di·o·i′so·tope′ *n.* a radioactive isotope of a chemical element

ra′di·ol′o·gy (-äl′ə jē) *n.* the science dealing with X-rays and other radiant energy, esp. as used in medicine and radiotherapy —**ra′di·ol′o·gist** *n.*

ra′di·o·ther′a·py *n.* the treatment of disease by X-rays or by rays from a radioactive substance

rad·ish (rad′ish) *n.* [< L. *radix,* a root] **1.** a plant of the mustard family, with an edible root **2.** the pungent root, eaten raw

ra·di·um (rā′dē əm) *n.* [< L. *radius,* a ray] a radioactive metallic chemical element, found in uranium minerals, which undergoes spontaneous atomic disintegration: symbol, Ra

ra·di·us (rā′dē əs) *n., pl.* -**di·i′** (-ī′), -**us·es** [L., spoke (of a wheel), hence ray] **1.** a straight line from the center to the periphery of a circle or sphere **2.** the circular area within the sweep of such a line [*within a radius of five miles*]

RAF, R.A.F. Royal Air Force

raf·fi·a (raf′ē ə) *n.* [< native name] **1.** a palm tree of Madagascar, with large leaves **2.** fiber from its leaves, used for weaving

raff·ish (raf′ish) *adj.* [(RIFF)RAFF + -ISH] **1.** disreputable, rakish, etc. **2.** tawdry; vulgar

raf·fle (raf′'l) *n.* [MFr. *rafle,* dice game] a lottery in which a chance or chances to win a prize are bought —*vt.* -**fled,** -**fling** to offer as a prize in a raffle (often with *off*)

raft[1] (raft) *n.* [< ON. *raptr,* a log] **1.** a floating structure of logs, boards, etc. fastened together **2.** an inflatable boat

raft[2] (raft) *n.* [< Brit. dial. *raff,* rubbish] [Colloq.] a large number or quantity

raft·er (raf′tər) *n.* [OE. *ræfter*] any of the beams that slope from the ridge of a roof to the eaves and support the roof

rag[1] (rag) *n.* [ult. < ON. *rögg,* tuft of hair] **1.** a waste piece of cloth, esp. an old or torn one **2.** a small cloth for dusting, etc. **3.** [*pl.*] old, worn clothes —*adj.* made of rags —**chew the rag** [Slang] to chat

rag[2] (rag) *vt.* **ragged, rag′ging** [< ?] [Slang] **1.** to tease **2.** to scold

rag[3] (rag) *n.* **1.** *short for* RAGTIME **2.** a composition in ragtime

rag·a·muf·fin (rag′ə muf′in) *n.* [ME. *Ragamoffyn,* name of a demon] a dirty, ragged person; esp., a poor, ragged child

rage (rāj) *n.* [< L. *rabies,* madness] **1.** furious, uncontrolled anger **2.** violence or intensity —*vi.* **raged, rag′ing** **1.** to show violent anger, as in speech **2.** to be violent, uncontrolled, etc. **3.** to spread unchecked, as a disease —(**all**) **the rage** a fad or craze

rag·ged (rag′id) *adj.* **1.** shabby or torn from wear **2.** wearing shabby or torn clothes **3.** uneven; rough **4.** shaggy [*ragged* hair]

rag′ged·y (-ē) *adj.* somewhat ragged

rag·lan (rag′lən) *n.* [< Lord *Raglan,* 19th-c. Brit. general] a loose coat with each sleeve (**raglan sleeve**) continuing in one piece to the collar

ra·gout (ra gōō′) *n.* [< Fr. *ragoûter,* revive the appetite of] a highly seasoned stew of meat and vegetables

rag·time (rag′tīm′) *n.* [prob. < *ragged time*] **1.** a type of strongly syncopated American music in fast, even time, popular 1890–1915 **2.** its rhythm

rag′weed′ *n.* [< the tattered appearance of the leaves] a weed whose pollen is a major cause of hay fever

rah (rä) *interj.* hurrah: used as a cheer

raid (rād) *n.* [< ROAD, in obs. sense "a riding"] **1.** a sudden, hostile attack, as by troops, bandits, etc. **2.** a sudden invasion of a place by police, to discover violations of the law —*vt., vi.* to make a raid (on) —**raid′er** *n.*

rail[1] (rāl) *n.* [< L. *regula,* a rule] **1.** a bar of wood, metal, etc. placed between posts as a barrier or support **2.** any of the parallel metal bars forming a track, as for railroad cars **3.** a railroad —*vt.* to supply with rails

rail[2] (rāl) *vi.* [ult. < LL. *ragere,* to bellow] to complain violently; inveigh

rail[3] (rāl) *n.* [< MFr. *raaler,* to screech] a small wading bird living in marshes

rail′ing *n.* **1.** material for rails **2.** rails collectively **3.** a fence or balustrade

rail·ler·y (rāl′ər ē) *n., pl.* -**ies** [see RAIL[2]] **1.** light ridicule; banter **2.** a teasing remark

rail′road′ *n.* **1.** a road laid with parallel steel rails along which locomotives draw cars **2.** a complete system of such roads —*vt.* **1.** to transport by railroad **2.** [Colloq.] to rush through (a bill) or convict (a person) hastily, without careful consideration —*vi.* to work on a railroad —**rail′road′er** *n.*

rail′way′ *n.* **1.** [Brit.] a railroad **2.** any track with rails for guiding wheels

rai·ment (rā′mənt) *n.* [see ARRAY & -MENT] [Archaic] clothing

rain (rān) *n.* [OE. *regn*] **1.** water falling in drops condensed from the atmosphere **2.** the falling of such drops **3.** a rapid falling of many small objects —*vi.* **1.** to fall: said of rain [it is *raining]* **2.** to fall like rain —*vt.* **1.** to pour down (rain, etc.) **2.** to give in large quantities —**rain out** to cause (an event) to be canceled because of rain —**rain'y** *adj.* **-i-er, -i-est**

rain'bow' (-bō') *n.* an arc containing the colors of the spectrum in bands, formed in the sky by the refraction of the sun's rays in falling rain or mist —*adj.* of many colors

rain check the stub of a ticket to a ball game, etc., entitling the holder to future admission if the original event is rained out

rain'coat' *n.* a waterproof or water-repellent coat

rain'drop' *n.* a single drop of rain

rain'fall' *n.* **1.** a falling of rain **2.** the amount of water falling as rain, snow, etc. over a given area during a given time

rain'storm' *n.* a storm with a heavy rain

rain'wa'ter *n.* water that is falling or has fallen as rain

raise (rāz) *vt.* **raised, rais'ing** [< ON. *reisa*] **1.** to make rise; lift **2.** to construct; build **3.** to increase in amount, degree, intensity, etc. *[raise prices, raise* one's voice*]* **4.** to produce; provoke **5.** to present for consideration *[to raise* a question*]* **6.** to collect (an army, money, etc.) **7.** to end (a siege) **8.** *a)* to cause to grow *b)* to rear (children) —*n.* **1.** a raising **2.** an increase in amount, as in salary or wages

rai·sin (rā'z'n) *n.* [< L. *racemus,* cluster of grapes] a sweet, dried grape

ra·jah, ra·ja (rä'jə) *n.* [< Hindi < Sans. *rāj,* to rule] a prince in India, etc.

rake¹ (rāk) *n.* [OE. *raca*] a long-handled tool with teeth at one end, for gathering loose grass, leaves, etc. —*vt.* **raked, rak'ing 1.** to gather or smooth with a rake **2.** to search through carefully **3.** to direct gunfire along (a line of troops, etc.)

rake² (rāk) *n.* [contr. of *rakehell]* a dissolute man; debauchee

rake³ (rāk) *vi., vt.* **raked, rak'ing** [? akin to Sw. *raka,* to project] to be or put at a slant —*n.* a slanting or inclining

rake'-off' *n.* [Slang] a commission or rebate, esp. one gained in a shady deal

rak·ish (rā'kish) *adj.* [< RAKE³ + -ISH] **1.** having a trim appearance suggesting speed: said of a ship **2.** dashing; jaunty —**rak'ish·ly** *adv.* — **rak'ish·ness** *n.*

ral·ly¹ (ral'ē) *vt., vi.* **-lied, -ly·ing** [< OFr. *re-,* again + *alier,* join] **1.** to gather together (retreating troops) and restore to a state of order **2.** to bring or come together for a common purpose **3.** to revive; recover —*n., pl.* **-lies** a rallying or being rallied; specif., a mass meeting

ral·ly² (ral'ē) *vt., vi.* **-lied, -ly·ing** [Fr. *rallier,* to RAIL²] to tease playfully

ram (ram) *n.* [OE. *ramm]* **1.** a male sheep **2.** *same as* BATTERING RAM —*vt.* **rammed, ram'ming 1.** to strike against with great force **2.** to force into place

ram·ble (ram'b'l) *vi.* **-bled, -bling** [< ME. *romen,* to roam] **1.** to roam about; esp., to stroll about idly **2.** to talk or write aimlessly **3.** to spread in all directions, as a vine —*n.* a rambling, esp. a stroll

ram'bler *n.* **1.** a person or thing that rambles **2.** any of certain climbing roses

ram·bunc·tious (ram buŋk'shəs) *adj.* [< *robustious]* wild, boisterous, unruly, etc. —**rambunc'tious·ly** *adv.*

ram·e·kin, ram·e·quin (ram'ə kin) *n.* [< Fr. < MDu. *rammeken,* cheese dish] a small, individual baking dish

ram·i·fy (ram'ə fī') *vt., vi.* **-fied', -fy'ing** [< Fr.

< L. *ramus,* a branch + *facere,* make] to divide or spread out into branches or branchlike divisions —**ram'i·fi·ca'tion** *n.*

ramp (ramp) *n.* [< OFr. *ramper,* to climb] **1.** a sloping walk, plank, etc. joining different levels **2.** a wheeled staircase for boarding an airplane

ram·page (ram pāj') *vi.* **-paged', -pag'ing** [prob. akin to prec.] to rush violently about; rage —*n.* (ram'pāj) a rampaging: chiefly in **on the** (or **a**) **rampage**

ramp·ant (ram'pənt) *adj.* [see RAMP] **1.** growing unchecked; rife **2.** violent and uncontrollable

ram·part (ram'pärt, -pərt) *n.* [< Fr. *re-,* again + *emparer,* fortify] **1.** a defensive embankment around a castle, fort, etc., with a parapet at the top **2.** any defense

ram'rod' *n.* a rod for ramming down the charge in a muzzle-loading gun

ram·shack·le (ram'shak'l) *adj.* [< RANSACK] loose and rickety; likely to fall apart

ran (ran) *pt. of* RUN

ranch (ranch) *n.* [< AmSp. *rancho]* **1.** a large farm, esp. in western States, for raising cattle, horses, or sheep **2.** a house with all the rooms on one floor: in full **ranch house** —*vi.* to work on or manage a ranch —**ranch'er, ranch'man** (-mən) *n., pl.* **-men**

ran·cid (ran'sid) *adj.* [< L. *rancere,* to be rank] having the bad smell or taste of spoiled fats or oils

ran·cor (raŋ'kər) *n.* [< L. *rancere,* to be rank] a continuing and bitter hate or ill will: Brit. sp. **ran'cour** —**ran'cor·ous** *adj.*

R & D, R and D research and development

ran·dom (ran'dəm) *adj.* [< OFr. *randir,* run violently] made, done, etc. in a haphazard way —**at random** haphazardly

rang (raŋ) *pt. of* RING¹

range (rānj) *vt.* **ranged, rang'ing** [< OFr. *renc,* a row] **1.** to put in order, esp. in a row or rows **2.** to place with others in a cause, etc. **3.** to roam about —*vi.* **1.** to extend in a given direction **2.** to roam **3.** to vary between stated limits —*n.* **1.** a row, line, or series **2.** a series of connected mountains **3.** the firing distance of a weapon **4.** *a)* a place for shooting practice *b)* a place for testing rockets in flight **5.** extent; scope **6.** a large open area for grazing livestock **7.** the limits within which there are differences in amount, degree, etc. *[a wide range* in price*]* **8.** a cooking stove

rang'er *n.* **1.** a member of a special military or police force that patrols a region **2.** a warden who patrols forests

rang·y (rān'jē) *adj.* **-i·er, -i·est** long-limbed and slender —**rang'i·ness** *n.*

rank¹ (raŋk) *n.* [< OFr. *renc]* **1.** a row, line, or series **2.** a social class **3.** a high position in society **4.** an official grade *[the rank* of major*]* **5.** a relative position as measured by quality, etc. *[a poet of the first rank]* **6.** a row of soldiers, etc., side by side **7.** *[pl.]* all those in an organization, as the army, who are not officers or leaders: also **rank and file** —*vt.* **1.** to place in a rank **2.** to assign a position to **3.** to outrank — *vi.* to hold a certain position

rank² (raŋk) *adj.* [OE. *ranc,* strong] **1.** growing vigorously and coarsely *[rank* grass*]* **2.** very bad in smell or taste **3.** coarse; indecent **4.** utter; extreme *[rank* injustice*]* —**rank'ness** *n.*

rank'ing *adj.* **1.** of the highest rank **2.** prominent or outstanding

ran·kle (raŋ'k'l) *vi., vt.* **-kled, -kling** [< ML. *dracunculus,* a fester] **1.** orig., to fester **2.** to fill with or cause long-lasting rancor, anger, etc.

ran·sack (ran′sak) *vt.* [< ON. *rann*, a house + *sækja*, to search] **1.** to search thoroughly **2.** to plunder; pillage

ran·som (ran′səm) *n.* [see REDEEM] **1.** the redeeming of a captive by paying money or meeting other demands **2.** the price so paid or demanded —*vt.* to get (a captive) released by paying the demanded price —**ran′som·er** *n.*

rant (rant) *vi., vt.* [< obs. Du. *ranten*] to talk in a loud, wild way; rave —*n.* ranting talk

rap (rap) *vt.* **rapped, rap′ping** [prob. echoic] **1.** to strike quickly and sharply; tap **2.** [Slang] to criticize sharply —*vi.* **1.** to knock sharply **2.** [Slang] to talk —*n.* **1.** a quick, sharp knock **2.** [Slang] blame or punishment

ra·pa·cious (rə pā′shəs) *adj.* [< L. *rapere*, to seize] **1.** greedy; voracious **2.** predatory —**ra·pac·i·ty** (rə pas′ə tē) *n.*

rape[1] (rāp) *n.* [< L. *rapere*, to seize] **1.** *a)* the crime of having sexual intercourse with a woman forcibly and without her consent, or (**statutory rape**) with a girl below the age of consent *b)* any sexual assault **2.** any violent or outrageous assault —*vt., vi.* **raped, rap′ing** to commit rape (on) —**rap′ist** *n.*

rape[2] (rāp) *n.* [L. *rapa*, turnip] a plant of the mustard family, with leaves used for fodder

rap·id (rap′id) *adj.* [< L. *rapere*, to rush] moving or done with speed; swift —*n.* [*usually pl.*] a part of a river where the current is swift —**ra·pid·i·ty** (rə pid′ə tē), **rap′id·ness** *n.* —**rap′id·ly** *adv.*

rapid transit a system of rapid public transportation in an urban area, using electric trains on an unimpeded right of way

ra·pi·er (rā′pē ər) *n.* [Fr. *rapière*] a light, sharp-pointed sword used for thrusting

rap·ine (rap′in) *n.* [< L. *rapere*, to seize] plunder; pillage

rap·port (ra pôr′, -pôrt′) *n.* [Fr. < L. *ad-*, to + *portare*, to carry] sympathetic relationship; agreement; harmony

rapt (rapt) *adj.* [< L. *rapere*, to seize] **1.** carried away with joy, love, etc.; full of rapture **2.** absorbed (*in*)

rap·ture (rap′chər) *n.* **1.** the state of being carried away with joy, love, etc. **2.** an expression of this —**rap′tur·ous** *adj.*

rare[1] (rer) *adj.* **rar′er, rar′est** [< L. *rarus*] **1.** not often seen, done, found, etc.; uncommon **2.** unusually good; excellent **3.** not dense [*rare atmosphere*] —**rare′ness** *n.*

rare[2] (rer) *adj.* **rar′er, rar′est** [OE. *hrere*] not fully cooked; partly raw

rare·bit (rer′bit) *n.* same as WELSH RABBIT

rar·e·fy (rer′ə fī′) *vt., vi.* **-fied′, -fy′ing** [< L. *rarus*, rare + *facere*, make] to make or become less dense —**rar′e·fac′tion** (-fak′shən) *n.*

rare·ly (rer′lē) *adv.* **1.** not often; seldom **2.** uncommonly

rar·i·ty (rer′ə tē) *n.* **1.** a being rare; specif., *a)* scarcity *b)* lack of density **2.** *pl.* **-ties** a rare or uncommon thing

ras·cal (ras′k'l) *n.* [OFr. *rascaille*, scrapings] **1.** a rogue **2.** a mischievous child —**ras·cal′i·ty** (-kal′ə tē) *n.* —**ras′cal·ly** *adj., adv.*

rash[1] (rash) *adj.* [ME. *rasch*] too hasty and careless; reckless —**rash′ly** *adv.*

rash[2] (rash) *n.* [MFr. *rasche*] **1.** a breaking out of red spots on the skin **2.** a sudden appearance of a large number

rash·er (rash′ər) *n.* [< ? obs. *rash*, to cut] a thin slice of bacon, etc., or a serving of several such slices

rasp (rasp) *vt.* [< OHG. *raspon*, scrape together] **1.** to scrape as with a file **2.** to grate upon; irritate —*vi.* **1.** to grate **2.** to make a rough, grating sound —*n.* **1.** a type of rough file **2.** a rough, grating sound —**rasp′y** *adj.* -i-er, -i-est

rasp·ber·ry (raz′ber′ē, -bər ē) *n., pl.* **-ries** [< earlier *raspis*] **1.** a small, red or purple, juicy fruit of various brambles **2.** the bramble bearing this **3.** [Slang] a sound of derision

rat (rat) *n.* [OE. *ræt*] **1.** a long-tailed rodent resembling, but larger than, the mouse **2.** [Slang] a sneaky, contemptible person; informer, etc. —*vi.* **rat′ted, rat′ting** [Slang] to inform (*on*)

ratch·et (rach′it) *n.* [< Fr. < It. *rocca*, distaff] **1.** a toothed wheel or bar, that catches and holds a pawl, preventing backward movement **2.** such a pawl

rate[1] (rāt) *n.* [< L. *reri*, reckon] **1.** the amount, degree, etc. of anything in relation to units of something else [*the rate of pay*] **2.** price, esp. per unit of some commodity, service, etc. **3.** a class or rank [*of the first rate*] —*vt.* **rat′ed, rat′ing 1.** to appraise **2.** to consider; esteem **3.** [Colloq.] to deserve —*vi.* to have value, status, etc. —**at any rate 1.** in any event **2.** anyway

rate[2] (rāt) *vt., vi.* **rat′ed, rat′ing** [ME. *raten*] to scold severely; chide

rath·er (rath′ər) *adv.* [< OE. *hrathe*, quickly] **1.** more willingly; preferably **2.** with more justice, reason, etc. [*I, rather than you, should pay*] **3.** more accurately [*my son, or rather, stepson*] **4.** on the contrary [*somewhat* —**rather than** instead of

rat·i·fy (rat′ə fī′) *vt.* **-fied′, -fy′ing** [< L. *ratus* (see RATE[1]) + *facere*, make] to approve; esp., to give official sanction to —**rat′i·fi·ca′tion** *n.* —**rat′i·fi′er** *n.*

rat·ing (rāt′iŋ) *n.* **1.** a rank or grade, as of military or naval personnel **2.** a placement in a certain rank or class **3.** an evaluation

ra·tio (rā′shō, -shē ō′) *n., pl.* **-tios** [L.: see REASON] **1.** a fixed relation in degree, number, etc. between two similar things; proportion **2.** *Math.* a fraction

ra·ti·o·ci·nate (rash′ē ō′sə nāt′, -ās′ə-) *vi.* **-nat′ed, -nat′ing** [see RATIO] to reason, esp. using formal logic —**ra′ti·o′ci·na′tion** *n.*

ra·tion (rash′ən, rā′shən) *n.* [see RATIO] **1.** a fixed portion; share **2.** a fixed allowance of food, as a daily allowance for one soldier —*vt.* **1.** to give rations to **2.** to distribute (food, clothing, etc.) in rations, as in a time of scarcity —**ra′tion·ing** *n.*

ra·tion·al (rash′ən 'l) *adj.* [see RATIO] **1.** of or based on reasoning **2.** able to reason **3.** sensible or sane —**ra′tion·al′i·ty** (-ə nal′ə tē) *n.* —**ra′tion·al·ly** *adv.*

ra·tion·ale (rash′ə nal′) *n.* [L., rational] **1.** the rational basis for something **2.** an explanation of reasons or principles

ra·tion·al·ize (rash′ən ə līz′) *vt.* **-ized′, -iz′ing 1.** to make rational or reasonable **2.** to devise explanations for (one's acts, beliefs, etc.), usually in self-deception —*vi.* to rationalize one's acts, beliefs, etc. —**ra′tion·al·i·za′tion** *n.*

rat·line (rat′lin) *n.* [< ?] any of the small ropes which join the shrouds of a ship and serve as a ladder: also sp. **rat′lin**

rat·tan (ra tan′) *n.* [< Malay *raut*, to strip] **1.** a climbing palm with long, slender, tough stems **2.** these stems, used in wickerwork, canes, etc.

rat·tle (rat′'l) *vi.* **-tled, -tling** [prob. echoic] **1.** to make a series of sharp, short sounds **2.** to chatter (often with *on*) —*vt.* **1.** to cause to rattle **2.** to confuse or upset —*n.* **1.** a series of sharp, short sounds **2.** the series of horny rings at the end of a rattlesnake's tail **3.** a baby's toy, etc. that rattles when shaken —**rat′tly** (-lē, -′l ē) *adj.*

rat′tle·brain′ *n.* a silly, talkative person

rat′tler *n.* a rattlesnake

rat′tle·snake′ *n.* a poisonous American snake with horny rings at the end of the tail that rattle when shaken

rat′tle·trap′ *n.* a rickety, old car

rat·ty (rat′ē) *adj.* **-ti·er, -ti·est** [Slang] shabby or run-down

rau·cous (rô′kəs) *adj.* [L. *raucus*] **1.** hoarse **2.** loud and rowdy —**rau′cous·ness** *n.*

raun·chy (rôn′chē) *adj.* **-chi·er, -chi·est** [< ?] [Slang] **1.** dirty, sloppy, etc. **2.** risqué, lustful, etc. —**raun′chi·ness** *n.*

rav·age (rav′ij) *n.* [Fr.: see RAVISH] destruction; ruin —*vt.* **-aged, -ag·ing** to destroy violently; ruin —*vi.* to commit ravages

rave (rāv) *vi.* **raved, rav′ing** [prob. < OFr. *raver*] **1.** to talk incoherently or wildly **2.** to talk with great enthusiasm (*about*) —*n.* [Colloq.] a very enthusiastic commendation

rav·el (rav′'l) *vt., vi.* **-eled or -elled, -el·ing or -el·ling** [MDu. *ravelen*] to separate into its parts, esp. threads; untwist; fray —*n.* a raveled part or thread

ra·ven (rā′vən) *n.* [OE. *hræfn*] a large, black bird related to the crow —*adj.* black and lustrous

rav·e·nous (rav′ə nəs) *adj.* [see RAVISH] **1.** greedily hungry **2.** rapacious

ra·vine (rə vēn′) *n.* [Fr., flood: ult. < L.] a long, deep hollow in the earth, esp. one worn by a stream; gorge

rav·ing (rā′viŋ) *adj.* **1.** that raves; delirious **2.** [Colloq.] exciting enthusiastic admiration [a *raving* beauty] —*adv.* in a raving way

ra·vi·o·li (rav′ē ō′lē) *n.pl.* [*with sing. v.*] [It.] small casings of dough containing ground meat, cheese, etc., usually served in a tomato sauce

rav·ish (rav′ish) *vt.* [< L. *rapere*, seize] **1.** to seize and carry away forcibly **2.** to rape **3.** to fill with great joy or delight —**rav′ish·er** *n.* —**rav′ish·ment** *n.*

rav·ish·ing *adj.* giving much delight

raw (rô) *adj.* [OE. *hreaw*] **1.** not cooked **2.** in its natural condition; not processed [*raw* silk] **3.** inexperienced [a *raw* recruit] **4.** with the skin rubbed off; sore and inflamed **5.** uncomfortably cold and damp [a *raw* wind] **6.** indecent, bawdy, etc. **7.** [Colloq.] harsh or unfair [a *raw* deal] —**raw′ly** *adv.* —**raw′ness** *n.*

raw′boned′ (-bōnd′) *adj.* lean; gaunt

raw′hide′ *n.* **1.** an untanned or partially tanned cattle hide **2.** a whip made of this

ray[1] (rā) *n.* [see RADIUS] **1.** any of the thin lines, or beams, of light that appear to come from a bright source **2.** any of several lines radiating from a center **3.** a beam of radiant energy, radioactive particles, etc. **4.** a tiny amount

ray[2] (rā) *n.* [< L. *raia*] a fish with a broad, flat body, widely expanded fins at each side, and a whiplike tail

ray·on (rā′än) *n.* [coined < RAY[1]] **1.** a textile fiber made from a cellulose solution **2.** a fabric of such fibers

raze (rāz) *vt.* **razed, raz′ing** [< L. *radere*, to scrape] to tear down completely; demolish

ra·zor (rā′zər) *n.* [see RAZE] a sharp-edged instrument for shaving **2.** *same as* SHAVER (sense 2)

razz (raz) *vt., vi.* [< RASPBERRY] [Slang] to tease, ridicule, heckle, etc.

raz·zle-daz·zle (raz′'l daz′'l) *n.* [Slang] a flashy, deceptive display

rbi, RBI, r.b.i. *Baseball* run(s) batted in

R.C. 1. Red Cross **2.** Roman Catholic

Rd., rd. 1. road **2.** rod

R.D. Rural Delivery

re[1] (rā) *n.* [It.] *Music* the second tone of the diatonic scale

re[2] (rē, rā) *prep.* [L. < *res*, thing] in the case or matter of; as regards

re- [< Fr. or L.] *a prefix meaning:* **1.** back [*repay*] **2.** again, anew [*reappear*] It is used with a hyphen: 1) to distinguish between a word in which the prefix means simply *again* or *anew* and a word having a special meaning (Ex.: *re-cover, recover*) 2) esp. formerly, before a word beginning with an *e* The following list contains some of the common words in which *re-* means *again* or *anew*

reaccustom	reeducate	reopen
reacquaint	reelect	reorder
reacquire	reemerge	repack
readdress	reemphasize	repaint
readjust	reenact	repave
readmit	reenlist	rephrase
reaffirm	reenter	replant
reappear	reestablish	replaster
reapply	reevaluate	replay
reappoint	reexamine	republish
rearm	refashion	reread
reassemble	refasten	reschedule
reassert	refinance	reseal
reassess	reformulate	resell
reassign	refuel	reshuffle
reawaken	refurnish	restate
rebroadcast	reheat	restring
rebuild	rehire	restudy
recharge	reinfect	restyle
recheck	reinsert	resubscribe
reclassify	reinspect	resupply
recommence	reinstall	retell
reconvene	reinvest	retest
recook	reinvestigate	rethink
recopy	reissue	retrain
re-cover	rekindle	retype
redecorate	relearn	reunite
rededicate	reload	reupholster
redesign	remarry	reuse
redirect	rename	revisit
rediscover	renominate	rewash
redistribution	renumber	reweigh
redraw	reoccupy	rework
reedit	reoccur	rezone

reach (rēch) *vt.* [OE. *ræcan*] **1.** to thrust out or extend (the hand, etc.) **2.** to extend to, or touch, by thrusting out, etc. **3.** to obtain and hand over [*reach* me the salt] **4.** to go as far as; attain **5.** to influence; affect **6.** to get in touch with, as by telephone —*vi.* **1.** to thrust out the hand, etc. **2.** to extend in influence, space, time, etc. **3.** to carry, as sight, sound, etc. **4.** to try to get something —*n.* **1.** a stretching or thrusting out **2.** the power of, or the extent covered in, stretching, obtaining, etc. **3.** a continuous extent, esp. of water

re·act (rē akt′) *vi.* **1.** to act in return or reciprocally **2.** to go back to a former condition, stage, etc. **3.** to respond to a stimulus **4.** *Chem.* to act with another substance in producing a chemical change

re·act·ant (rē ak′tənt) *n.* any substance involved in a chemical reaction

re·ac·tion (rē ak′shən) *n.* **1.** a return or opposing action, etc. **2.** a response, as to a stimulus **3.** a movement back to a former or less advanced condition **4.** a chemical change

re·ac′tion·ar′y (-shə ner′ē) *adj.* of, showing, or

favoring reaction, esp. in politics —*n., pl.* **-ies** a reactionary person
re·ac·ti·vate (rē ak'tə vāt') *vt.* **-vat'ed, -vat'ing** to make active again; specif., to restore to active military status —**re·ac'ti·va'tion** *n.*
re·ac'tive (-tiv) *adj.* **1.** tending to react **2.** of, from, or showing reaction
re·ac·tor (rē ak'tər) *n. same as* NUCLEAR REACTOR
read[1] (rēd) *vt.* **read** (red), **read'ing** (rēd'iŋ) [OE. *rædan,* to counsel] **1.** to get the meaning of (writing) by interpreting the characters **2.** to utter aloud (something written) **3.** to understand or interpret **4.** to foretell (the future) **5.** to study *[to read* law*]* **6.** to register, as a gauge —*vi.* **1.** to read something written **2.** to learn by reading (with *about* or *of*) **3.** to be phrased in certain words —**read into** (or **in**) to attribute (a particular meaning) to —**read out of** to expel from (an organization)
read[2] (red) *pt. & pp. of* READ[1] —*adj.* informed by reading *[well-read]*
read'er *n.* **1.** one who reads **2.** *a)* a book for teaching how to read *b)* an anthology
read'ing *n.* **1.** the act of one who reads **2.** any material to be read **3.** the amount measured by a barometer, etc. **4.** a particular interpretation or performance
read·out (rēd'out') *n.* **1.** the retrieving of information from a computer **2.** the information retrieved
read·y (red'ē) *adj.* **-i·er, -i·est** [OE. *ræde*] **1.** prepared to act or be used immediately **2.** willing **3.** likely or liable immediately *[ready* to cry*]* **4.** skillful; dexterous **5.** prompt *[a ready* reply*]* **6.** available immediately *[ready* cash*]* —*vt.* **-ied, -y·ing** to make ready; prepare —**make ready** to prepare —**read'i·ly** *adv.* —**read'i·ness** *n.*
read'y-made' *adj.* made so as to be ready for immediate use or sale
re·a·gent (rē ā'jənt) *n. Chem.* a substance used to detect, measure, or react with another substance
re·al (rē'əl, rēl) *adj.* [< L. *res,* thing] **1.** existing as or in fact; actual **2.** genuine **3.** *Law* of or relating to immovable things *[real* property*]* —*adv.* [Colloq.] very —**for real** [Slang] real or really
real estate land, including the buildings or improvements on it and its natural assets
re·al·ism (rē'ə liz'm) *n.* **1.** a tendency to face facts and be practical **2.** portrayal of people and things as they really are —**re'al·ist** *n.* —**re'al·is'tic** *adj.* —**re'al·is'ti·cal·ly** *adv.*
re·al·i·ty (rē al'ə tē) *n., pl.* **-ties 1.** the quality or fact of being real **2.** a person or thing that is real; fact —**in reality** in fact; actually
re·al·ize (rē'ə līz') *vt.* **-ized', -iz'ing** [< Fr.] **1.** to make real; bring into being **2.** to understand fully **3.** to convert (assets, rights, etc.) into money **4.** to gain; obtain *[to realize* a profit*]* **5.** to be sold for (a specified sum) —**re'al·i·za'tion** *n.*
re'al·ly *adv.* **1.** in reality; actually **2.** truly *[really* hot*]* —*interj.* indeed
realm (relm) *n.* [see REGAL] **1.** a kingdom **2.** a region; sphere
Re·al·tor (rē'əl tər) *n.* a real estate broker who is a member of the National Association of Real Estate Boards
re·al·ty (rē'əl tē) *n. same as* REAL ESTATE
ream[1] (rēm) *n.* [< Ar. *rizma,* a bale] **1.** a quantity of paper varying from 480 to 516 sheets **2.** *[pl.]* [Colloq.] a great amount
ream[2] (rēm) *vt.* [< OE. *reman,* widen] to enlarge or taper (a hole) as with a reamer

ream'er *n.* **1.** a sharp-edged tool for enlarging or tapering holes **2.** a device with a ridged cone-shaped part on which oranges, etc. are squeezed for juice
reap (rēp) *vt., vi.* [OE. *ripan*] **1.** to cut (grain) with a scythe, reaper, etc. **2.** to gather (a harvest) **3.** to get (something) as a result of action, work, etc.
reap'er *n.* **1.** one who reaps **2.** a machine for reaping grain
re·ap·por·tion (rē'ə pôr'shən) *vt.* to apportion again; specif., to adjust the representation pattern of (a legislature) —**re'ap·por'tion·ment** *n.*
rear[1] (rir) *n.* [see ARREAR(S)] **1.** the back part **2.** the position behind or at the back **3.** the part of an army, etc. farthest from the battle front —*adj.* of, at, or in the rear —**bring up the rear** to come at the end
rear[2] (rir) *vt.* [OE. *ræran*] **1.** to put upright; elevate **2.** to build; erect **3.** to grow or breed **4.** to bring to maturity by educating, nourishing, etc. *[to rear* a child*]* —*vi.* **1.** to rise on the hind legs, as a horse **2.** to rise (*up*) in anger, etc.
rear admiral *U.S. Navy* an officer ranking just above a captain
rear guard a military detachment to protect the rear of a main force
rear'most' (-mōst') *adj.* farthest in the rear
re'ar·range' *vt.* **-ranged', -rang'ing** to arrange again or in a different manner —**re'ar·range'ment** *n.*
rear'ward (-wərd) *adj.* at, in, or toward the rear —*adv.* toward the rear: also **rear'wards**
rea·son (rē'z'n) *n.* [< L. *reri,* think] **1.** an explanation of an act, idea, etc. **2.** a cause or motive **3.** the ability to think, draw conclusions, etc. **4.** good sense **5.** sanity —*vt., vi.* **1.** to think logically (about); analyze **2.** to argue or infer —**stand to reason** to be logical —**rea'son·ing** *n.*
rea'son·a·ble *adj.* **1.** able to reason **2.** just; fair **3.** sensible; wise **4.** not excessive —**rea'son·a·bly** *adv.*
re'as·sure' *vt.* **-sured', -sur'ing 1.** to assure again **2.** to restore to confidence —**re'as·sur'ance** *n.* —**re'as·sur'ing·ly** *adv.*
re·bate (rē'bāt) *vt.* **-bat·ed, -bat·ing** [< OFr.: see RE- & ABATE] to give back (part of a payment) —*n.* a return of part of a payment
Re·bec·ca, Re·bek·ah (ri bek'ə) *Bible* the wife of Isaac
reb·el (reb''l) *n.* [< L. *re-,* again + *bellare,* wage war] one in rebellion —*adj.* rebellious —*vi.* (ri bel') **-elled', -el'ling 1.** to be a rebel **2.** to feel or show strong aversion
re·bel·lion (ri bel'yən) *n.* **1.** armed resistance to one's government **2.** defiance of any authority
re·bel·lious (-yəs) *adj.* **1.** in rebellion **2.** of or like rebels or rebellion; defiant
re·birth (ri burth', rē'burth') *n.* **1.** a new or second birth **2.** a reawakening; revival
re·bound (ri bound') *vi.* to spring back, as upon impact —*n.* (rē'bound') a rebounding
re·buff (ri buf') *n.* [< It. *rabbuffo*] **1.** an abrupt refusal of offered advice, help, etc. **2.** any repulse —*vt.* **1.** to refuse bluntly **2.** to repulse
re·buke (ri byōōk') *vt.* **-buked', -buk'ing** [< OFr. *re-,* back + *buchier,* to beat] to blame or scold in a sharp way; reprimand —*n.* a sharp reprimand
re·bus (rē'bəs) *n.* [L., lit., by things] a kind of puzzle consisting of pictures, etc. combined to suggest words or phrases
re·but (ri but') *vt.* **-but'ted, -but'ting** [< OFr. *re-,* back + *buter,* to push] to contradict or oppose, esp. in a formal manner by argument, proof, etc. —**re·but'tal** *n.*

re·cal·ci·trant (ri kal'si trənt) *adj.* [< L. *re-*, back + *calcitrare*, to kick] refusing to obey — **re·cal'ci·trance** *n.*

re·call (ri kôl') *vt.* **1.** to call back **2.** to remember **3.** to take back; revoke **4.** to cause to be aware, alert, etc. again —*n.* (*also* rē'kôl') **1.** a recalling **2.** memory **3.** the removal of, or right to remove, an official from office by popular vote

re·cant (ri kant') *vt., vi.* [< L. *re-*, back + *canere*, sing] to renounce formally (one's former beliefs, statements, etc.) —**re·can·ta·tion** (rē'kan tā'shən) *n.*

re·cap[1] (rē kap', rē'kap') *vt.* **-capped', -cap'ping** to cement and vulcanize a strip of rubber on the outer surface of (a worn tire) —*n.* (rē'kap') a recapped tire

re·cap[2] (rē'kap') *n.* a recapitulation, or summary —*vt., vi.* **-capped', -cap'ping** to recapitulate

re·ca·pit·u·late (rē'kə pich'ə lāt') *vi., vt.* **-lat'ed, -lat'ing** [see RE- & CAPITULATE] to repeat briefly; summarize —**re'ca·pit'u·la'tion** *n.*

re·cap'ture *vt.* **-tured, -tur·ing 1.** to capture again; retake **2.** to remember —*n.* a recapturing or being recaptured

recd., rec'd. received

re·cede (ri sēd') *vi.* **-ced'ed, -ced'ing** [see RE- & CEDE] **1.** to go or move back [the flood *receded*] **2.** to slope backward **3.** to lessen, dim, etc.

re·ceipt (ri sēt') *n.* [see RECEIVE] **1.** *old term for* RECIPE **2.** a receiving or being received **3.** a written acknowledgment that something has been received **4.** [*pl.*] the amount received —*vt.* **1.** to mark (a bill) paid **2.** to write a receipt for

re·ceiv·a·ble (ri sē'və b'l) *adj.* **1.** that can be received **2.** due from customers

re·ceive (ri sēv') *vt.* **-ceived', -ceiv'ing** [< L. *re-*, back + *capere*, take] **1.** to take or get (something given, sent, thrown, etc.) **2.** to react to as specified **3.** to learn [to *receive* news] **4.** to let in or greet (visitors, etc.) —*vi.* **1.** to be a recipient **2.** to greet visitors, etc.

re·ceiv'er *n.* **1.** one who receives **2.** in radio, TV, telephony, etc., a device converting electrical impulses to sounds or images **3.** *Law* one appointed to administer or hold in trust property in bankruptcy or in a lawsuit

re·cent (rē's'nt) *adj.* [< L. *recens*] **1.** done, made, etc. just before the present; new **2.** of a time just before the present —**re'cent·ly** *adv.*

re·cep·ta·cle (ri sep'tə k'l) *n.* [see RECEIVE] a container

re·cep·tion (ri sep'shən) *n.* **1.** *a)* a receiving or being received *b)* the manner of this **2.** a social function for the receiving of guests **3.** *Radio & TV* the receiving of signals, with reference to the quality of reproduction

re·cep'tion·ist *n.* an office employee who receives callers, gives information, etc.

re·cep'tive *adj.* able or ready to receive requests, suggestions, new ideas, etc.

re·cess (rē'ses; *also, and for v. usually,* ri ses') *n.* [< L. *recedere*, recede] **1.** a hollow place, as in a wall **2.** a secluded or inner place **3.** a temporary halting of work, a session, etc. —*vt.* **1.** to place in a recess **2.** to form a recess in —*vi.* to take a recess

re·ces·sion (ri sesh'ən) *n.* **1.** a going back or receding; withdrawal **2.** a temporary falling off of business activity

re·ces'sion·al (-'l) *n.* a hymn sung at the end of a church service as the clergy and choir march out

re·ces'sive *adj.* receding

rec·i·pe (res'ə pē) *n.* [L. < *recipere*, receive] **1.** a list of ingredients and directions for preparing a dish or drink **2.** any procedure for bringing about a desired result

re·cip·i·ent (ri sip'ē ənt) *n.* [see RECEIVE] one that receives —*adj.* able to receive

re·cip·ro·cal (ri sip'rə k'l) *adj.* [< L. *reciprocus*, returning] **1.** done, felt, given, etc. in return **2.** mutual **3.** corresponding but reversed **4.** corresponding or complementary —*n.* **1.** a complement, counterpart, etc. **2.** *Math.* the quantity resulting from the division of 1 by the given quantity [the *reciprocal* of 7 is 1/7]

re·cip'ro·cate' (-kāt') *vt., vi.* **-cat'ed, -cat'ing 1.** to give and get reciprocally **2.** to give, do, feel, etc. in return **3.** to move alternately back and forth —**re·cip'ro·ca'tion** *n.*

rec·i·proc·i·ty (res'ə präs'ə tē) *n., pl.* **-ties** [< Fr.] **1.** reciprocal state or relationship **2.** mutual exchange; esp., exchange of special privileges between two countries

re·cit·al (ri sīt''l) *n.* **1.** a reciting **2.** the story, etc. told **3.** a musical or dance program, as by a soloist —**re·cit'al·ist** *n.*

rec·i·ta·tion (res'ə tā'shən) *n.* **1.** *same as* RECITAL (senses 1 & 2) **2.** *a)* the speaking aloud in public of something memorized *b)* a piece so presented **3.** a reciting by pupils of answers to questions on a prepared lesson

rec·i·ta·tive (res'ə tə tēv') *n.* [< It.: see RECITE] a type of declamatory singing, as in the dialogue of operas

re·cite (ri sīt') *vt., vi.* **-cit'ed, -cit'ing** [see RE- & CITE] **1.** to speak aloud (something memorized) **2.** to tell in detail

reck'less *adj.* [OE. *reccan*] heedless; rash

reck·on (rek'ən) *vt.* [OE. *-recenian*] **1.** to count; compute **2.** to regard as being **3.** to estimate **4.** [Colloq. or Dial.] to suppose —*vi.* **1.** to count up **2.** to rely (*on*) —**reckon with** to take into consideration

reck'on·ing *n.* **1.** count or computation **2.** the settlement of an account

re·claim (ri klām') *vt.* [see RE- & CLAIM] **1.** to bring back from error, vice, etc. **2.** to make (wasteland, etc.) usable **3.** to recover (useful materials) from waste products —**rec·la·ma·tion** (rek'lə mā'shən) *n.*

re·cline (ri klīn') *vt., vi.* **-clined', -clin'ing** [< L. *re-*, back + *clinare*, to lean] to lie or cause to lie back or down; lean back

rec·luse (rek'lōōs, ri klōōs') *n.* [< L. *re-*, back + *claudere*, shut] one who lives a secluded, solitary life —**re·clu·sive** (ri klōō'siv) *adj.*

rec·og·ni·tion (rek'əg nish'ən) *n.* **1.** a recognizing or being recognized **2.** identification of a person or thing as being known

re·cog·ni·zance (ri käg'ni zəns, -kän'i-) *n.* [< L. *re-*, again + *cognoscere*, know] *Law* a bond binding one to some act

rec·og·nize (rek'əg nīz') *vt.* **-nized', -niz'ing** [< prec.] **1.** to identify as known **2.** to know by some detail, as of appearance **3.** to perceive **4.** to accept as a fact; admit **5.** to acknowledge as commendable **6.** to acknowledge the legal standing of (a government or state) **7.** to grant the right to speak, as at a meeting —**rec'og·niz'a·ble** *adj.*

re·coil (ri koil') *vi.* [< L. *re-*, back + *culus*, buttocks] **1.** to draw back, as in fear **2.** to spring or kick back, as a gun when fired —*n.* (*also* rē'koil') a recoiling

rec·ol·lect (rek'ə lekt') *vt., vi.* [see RE- & COLLECT] to remember, esp. with some effort —**rec'ol·lec'tion** *n.*

rec·om·mend (rek'ə mend') *vt.* [see RE- & COMMEND] **1.** to entrust to **2.** to suggest favorably as suited to some position, etc. **3.** to make acceptable **4.** to advise; counsel —**rec'om·men·da'tion** *n.*

rec·om·pense (rek'əm pens') *vt.* **-pensed'**, **-pens'ing** [see RE- & COMPENSATE] **1.** to repay or reward **2.** to compensate (a loss, etc.) —*n.* **1.** requital, reward, etc. **2.** compensation, as for a loss

rec·on·cile (rek'ən sīl') *vt.* **-ciled'**, **-cil'ing** [see RE- & CONCILIATE] **1.** to make friendly again **2.** to settle (a quarrel, etc.) **3.** to make (facts, ideas, etc.) consistent **4.** to make acquiescent (*to*) —**rec'on·cil'a·ble** *adj.* —**rec'on·cil'i·a'tion** (-sil'ē ā'shən) *n.*

rec·on·dite (rek'ən dīt') *adj.* [< L. *re-*, back + *condere*, to hide] beyond ordinary understanding; abstruse

re·con·di·tion (rē'kən dish'ən) *vt.* to put back in good condition by cleaning, repairing, etc.

re·con·nais·sance (ri kän'ə səns, -zəns) *n.* [Fr.: see RECOGNIZANCE] an exploratory survey, as in seeking out information about enemy positions

rec·on·noi·ter (rē'kə noit'ər, rek'ə-) *vi., vt.* to make a reconnaisance (of): Brit. sp., **rec'on·noi'tre, -tred, -tring**

re·con·sid·er (rē'kən sid'ər) *vt., vi.* to consider again; think (a matter) over, as with a view to changing a decision

re·con'sti·tute' *vt.* **-tut'ed, -tut'ing** to constitute again; specif., to restore (a dried or condensed substance) to its original form by adding water

re'con·struct' *vt.* **1.** to construct again; remake **2.** to build up again in its original form, as from remaining parts

re'con·struc'tion *n.* **1.** a reconstructing **2.** [R-] the period or process, after the Civil War, of reestablishing the Southern States in the Union

re·cord (ri kôrd'; *for n. & adj.* rek'ərd) *vt.* [< L. *recordari*, remember] **1.** to write down for future use **2.** to register, as on a graph **3.** to register (sound or visual images) on a disc, tape, etc. for later reproduction —*n.* **1.** a being recorded **2.** anything serving as evidence of an event, etc. **3.** the known facts about anyone or anything **4.** a grooved disc for playing on a phonograph **5.** the best performance, etc. achieved —*adj.* being the best, largest, etc. —**off the record** confidential(ly) —**on (the) record** recorded

re·cord'er *n.* **1.** an official who keeps records **2.** a machine or device that records; esp., *same as* TAPE RECORDER **3.** an early form of flute

re·cord'ing *n.* **1.** what is recorded, as on a disc or tape **2.** the disc, tape, etc.

re·count (ri kount') *vt.* [see RE- & COUNT¹] to tell in detail; narrate

re·count (rē'kount') *vt.* to count again —*n.* (rē'kount') a second count, as of votes: also written **recount**

re·coup (ri kōōp') *vt.* [< Fr. *re-*, again + *couper*, to cut] **1.** to make up for [to recoup a loss] **2.** to regain —*n.* a recouping

re·course (rē'kôrs, ri kôrs') *n.* [see RE- & COURSE] **1.** a turning for aid, safety, etc. **2.** that to which one turns seeking aid, safety, etc.

re·cov·er (ri kuv'ər) *vt.* [< L. *recuperare*] **1.** to get back (something lost, etc.) **2.** to regain (health, etc.) **3.** to make up for [to recover losses] **4.** to save (oneself) from a fall, etc. **5.** to reclaim (land from the sea, etc.) **6.** *Sports* to regain control of (a fumbled or wild ball, etc.) —*vi.* **1.** to regain health, balance, control, etc. **2.** *Sports* to recover a ball, etc.

re·cov·er·y *n., pl.* **-ies** a recovering; specif., *a*) a return to health *b*) a regaining of something lost, balance, etc. *c*) a retrieval of a capsule, nose cone, etc. after a spaceflight

rec·re·ant (rek'rē ənt) *adj.* [< OFr. *recreire*, surrender allegiance] **1.** cowardly **2.** disloyal — *n.* **1.** a coward **2.** a traitor

rec·re·a·tion (rek'rē ā'shən) *n.* [< L. *recreare*, refresh] any form of play, amusement, etc. used for refreshment of body or mind —**rec're·a'tion·al** *adj.*

re·crim·i·nate (ri krim'ə nāt') *vi.* **-nat'ed, -nat'ing** [< L. *re-*, back + *crimen*, offense] to answer an accuser by accusing him in return —**re·crim'i·na'tion** *n.*

re·cruit (ri krōōt') *vt., vi.* [< Fr. < L. *re-*, again + *crescere*, grow] **1.** to enlist (personnel) into an army or navy **2.** to enlist (new members) for an organization —*n.* **1.** a recently enlisted or drafted soldier, sailor, etc. **2.** a new member of any group —**re·cruit'er** *n.* —**re·cruit'ment** *n.*

rec·tal (rek't'l) *adj.* of, for, or near the rectum —**rec'tal·ly** *adv.*

rec·tan·gle (rek'taŋ'g'l) *n.* [Fr. < L. *rectus*, straight + *angulus*, a corner] any four-sided plane figure with four right angles —**rec·tan'gu·lar** (-gyə lər) *adj.*

rec·ti·fy (rek'tə fī') *vt.* **-fied', -fy'ing** [< L. *rectus*, straight + *facere*, make] **1.** to put right; correct **2.** *Elec.* to convert (alternating current) to direct current —**rec'ti·fi·ca'tion** *n.*

rec·tor (rek'tər) *n.* [< L. *regere*, to rule] **1.** in some churches, a clergyman in charge of a parish **2.** the head of certain schools, colleges, etc.

rec·to·ry (rek'tər ē) *n., pl.* **-ries** the residence of a clergyman who is a rector

rec·tum (rek'təm) *n., pl.* **-tums, -ta** (-tə) [< L. *rectum (intestinum)*, straight (intestine)] the lowest segment of the large intestine

re·cum·bent (ri kum'bənt) *adj.* [< L. *re-*, back + *cumbere*, to bend] lying down

re·cu·per·ate (ri kōō'pə rāt') *vt., vi.* **-at'ed, -at'ing** [< L. *recuperare*, recover] **1.** to recover (losses, health, etc.) **2.** to get well again —**re·cu'per·a'tion** *n.* —**re·cu'per·a'tive** *adj.*

re·cur (ri kur') *vi.* **-curred', -cur'ring** [< L. *re-*, back + *currere*, run] **1.** to return in thought, talk, etc. [to recur to a topic] **2.** to occur again or at intervals —**re·cur'rence** *n.* —**re·cur'rent** *adj.*

re·cy·cle (rē sī'k'l) *vt.* **-cled, -cling 1.** to pass through a cycle again **2.** to use again and again

red (red) *n.* [OE. *read*] **1.** the color of blood **2.** any red pigment **3.** [*often* R-] a political radical; esp., a communist —*adj.* **red'der, red'dest 1.** of the color red **2.** [*often* R-] politically radical; esp., communist —**in the red** losing money —**see red** [Colloq.] to become angry —**red'dish** *adj.*

red'-blood'ed *adj.* vigorous, lusty, etc.

red'cap' *n.* a porter in a railroad station, air terminal, etc.

red carpet a very grand welcome and entertainment (with *the*) —**red'-car'pet** *adj.*

red'coat' *n.* a British soldier in a uniform with a red coat

Red Cross an international society for the relief of suffering in time of war or disaster

red deer a deer native to Europe and Asia

red·den (red'ʼn) *vt.* to make red —*vi.* to become red; esp., to blush or flush

re·deem (ri dēm') *vt.* [< L. *re(d)-*, back + *emere*, get] **1.** to get or buy back; recover **2.** to pay off (a mortgage, etc.) **3.** to turn in (trading stamps or coupons) for premiums **4.** to ransom

5. to deliver from sin **6.** to fulfill (a promise) **7.** *a*) to make amends or atone for *b*) to restore (oneself) to favor —**re·deem′a·ble** *adj.* —**re-deem′er** *n.* —**re·demp·tion** (ri demp′shən) *n.*

re·de·ploy (rē′di ploi′) *vt., vi.* to move (troops, etc.) from one area to another —**re′de·ploy′-ment** *n.*

re′de·vel′op *vt.* **1.** to develop again **2.** to re-build or restore (a run-down area)

red′-hand′ed *adv., adj.* in the very commission of crime or wrongdoing

red·head (red′hed′) *n.* a person with red hair —**red′head′ed** *adj.*

red herring [< herring drawn across the trace in hunting to distract the hounds] something used to divert attention from the basic issue

red′-hot′ *adj.* **1.** hot enough to glow **2.** very ex-cited, angry, etc. **3.** very new

re·dis′trict *vt.* to divide anew into districts

red′-let′ter *adj.* designating a memorable or joyous day or event

red′lin′ing (-lī′nin) *n.* [from outlining of such areas in red on a map] the refusal by some banks and companies to issue loans or insur-ance on property in certain neighborhoods

re·do′ *vt.* **-did′, -done′, -do′ing 1.** to do again **2.** to redecorate (a room, etc.)

red·o·lent (red′'l ənt) *adj.* [< L. *re*(*d*)-, intens. + *olere,* to smell] **1.** sweet-smelling **2.** smelling (*of*) **3.** suggestive (*of*) —**red′o·lence** *n.*

re·dou·ble (rē dub′'l) *vt., vi.* **-bled, -bling 1.** to double again **2.** to make or become twice as much or twice as great

re·doubt (ri dout′) *n.* [< Fr. < It.: see REDUCE] **1.** a breastwork **2.** any stronghold

re·doubt·a·ble (ri dout′ə b'l) *adj.* [< L. *re*-, in-tens. + *dubitare,* to doubt] **1.** formidable **2.** commanding respect —**re·doubt′a·bly** *adv.*

re·dound (ri dound′) *vi.* [< L. *re*(*d*)-, intens. + *undare,* to surge] **1.** to have a result (*to* the credit or discredit of) **2.** to come back; react (*upon*)

red pepper 1. a plant with a red, many-seeded fruit **2.** the fruit **3.** the ground fruit or seeds, used for seasoning

re·dress (ri dres′) *vt.* [see RE- & DRESS] to rec-tify, as by making compensation for (a wrong, etc.) —*n.* (*usually* rē′dres) **1.** compensation **2.** a redressing

red snapper a reddish, deep-water food fish

red tape [< tape used for tying official papers] rigid adherence to routine and regulations, causing delay

re·duce (ri dōōs′) *vt.* **-duced′, -duc′ing** [< L. *re*-, back + *ducere,* to lead] **1.** to lessen, as in size, price, etc. **2.** to change to a different form **3.** to lower, as in rank or condition **4.** to sub-due or conquer **5.** to compel by need [*reduced* to stealing] —*vi.* to lose weight, as by dieting

re·duc·tion (ri duk′shən) *n.* **1.** a reducing or being reduced **2.** anything made by reducing **3.** the amount by which something is reduced

re·dun·dant (ri dun′dənt) *adj.* [see REDOUND] **1.** excess; superfluous **2.** wordy **3.** unnecessary to the meaning: said of words —**re·dun′dan·cy** *n.* —**re·dun′dant·ly** *adv.*

red′wood′ *n.* **1.** a giant evergreen of the Pacific coast **2.** its reddish wood

re·ech·o, re-ech·o (rē ek′ō) *vt., vi.* **-oed, -o·ing** to echo back or again —*n., pl.* **-oes** the echo of an echo

reed (rēd) *n.* [OE. *hreod*] **1.** a tall, slender grass **2.** a musical pipe made from a hollow stem **3.** a thin strip of wood, etc. placed against the mouthpiece, as of a clarinet, and vibrated by the breath to produce a tone —**reed′y** *adj.* **-i·er, -i·est**

reef[1] (rēf) *n.* [prob. < ON. *rif,* a rib] a ridge of rock, coral, or sand at or near the surface of the water

reef[2] (rēf) *n.* [ME. *riff*] a part of a sail which can be folded and tied down to reduce the area exposed to the wind —*vt., vi.* to reduce (a sail) by taking in part of it

reek (rēk) *n.* [OE. *rec*] a strong, unpleasant smell —*vi.* to have a strong, offensive smell

reel[1] (rēl) *n.* [OE. *hreol*] **1.** a spool on which wire, film, fishing line, etc. is wound **2.** the quantity of wire, film, etc. usually wound on one reel —*vt.* to wind on a reel —*vi.* **1.** to sway or stagger, as from drunkenness or dizziness **2.** to spin; whirl —**reel in 1.** to wind on a reel **2.** to pull in (a fish) by winding a line on a reel —**reel off** to tell, write, etc. fluently —**reel out** to unwind from a reel

reel[2] (rēl) *n.* [prob. < prec.] a lively dance

re·en·try, re-en·try (rē en′trē) *n., pl.* **-tries** a coming back, as of a space vehicle, into the earth's atmosphere

ref (ref) *n., vt., vi. same as* REFEREE

re·fec·tion (ri fek′shən) *n.* [< L. *re-,* again + *facere,* make] a light meal

re·fec′to·ry (-tər ē) *n., pl.* **-ries** a dining hall, as in a monastery

re·fer (ri fur′) *vt.* **-ferred′, -fer′ring** [< L. *re-,* back + *ferre,* to bear] **1.** to submit (a quarrel, etc.) for settlement **2.** to direct (*to* someone or something) for aid, information, etc. —*vi.* **1.** to relate or apply (*to*) **2.** to direct attention (*to*) **3.** to turn (*to*) for information, aid, etc.

ref·er·ee (ref′ə rē′) *n.* **1.** a person to whom something is referred for decision **2.** an official who enforces the rules in certain sports con-tests —*vt., vi.* **-eed′, -ee′ing** to act as referee (in)

ref·er·ence (ref′ər əns) *n.* **1.** a referring or being referred **2.** relation [*in reference* to his letter] **3.** *a*) the directing of attention to a per-son or thing *b*) a mention **4.** *a*) an indication, as in a book, of some other work to be con-sulted *b*) any such work **5.** *a*) one who can offer information or recommendation *b*) a statement giving the qualifications, abilities, etc. of someone seeking a position **6.** a book, etc. referred to for information —**make refer-ence to** to refer to; mention

ref·er·en·dum (ref′ə ren′dəm) *n., pl.* **-dums, -da** (-də) [L.: see REFER] **1.** the submission of a law to a direct vote of the people **2.** the right of the people to vote on such laws

re·fer′ral (ri fur′əl) *n.* **1.** a referring or being re-ferred **2.** a person who is referred to another person

re·fill (rē fil′) *vt., vi.* to fill again —*n.* (rē′fil) **1.** a unit to refill a special container **2.** a refilling of a medical prescription —**re·fill′a·ble** *adj.*

re·fine (ri fīn′) *vt., vi.* **-fined′, -fin′ing** [RE- + *fine,* make fine] **1.** to free or become free from impurities, etc. **2.** to make or become more polished or elegant

re·fined′ *adj.* **1.** purified **2.** cultivated; elegant **3.** subtle, precise, etc.

re·fine′ment *n.* **1.** a refining or being refined *b*) the result of this **2.** delicacy or elegance of manners, speech, etc. **3.** an improvement **4.** a subtlety

re·fin′er·y *n., pl.* **-ies** a plant for purifying raw materials as oil, sugar, etc.

re·fin·ish (rē fin′ish) *vt.* to put a new surface on (wood, metal, etc.)

re·fit (rē fit′) *vt., vi.* **-fit′ted, -fit′ting** to make or be made fit for use again by repairing, reequipping, etc.

re·flect (ri flekt′) *vt.* [< L. *re-,* back + *flectere,* to bend] **1.** to throw back (light, heat, or sound) **2.** to give back an image of; mirror **3.** to bring as a result *[to reflect* honor*]* —*vi.* **1.** to throw back light, heat, etc. **2.** to give back an image **3.** to think seriously (*on* or *upon*) **4.** to cast discredit (*on* or *upon*) —**re·flec'tive** *adj.*

re·flec'tion *n.* **1.** a reflecting or being reflected **2.** anything reflected **3.** contemplation **4.** an idea or remark **5.** discredit

re·flec'tor *n.* a surface, object, or device that reflects light, sound, heat, etc.

re·flex (rē'fleks) *adj.* [see REFLECT] designating or of an involuntary action, as a sneeze, due to the direct transmission of a stimulus to a muscle or gland —*n.* a reflex action

re·flex·ive (ri flek'siv) *adj.* **1.** designating a verb whose subject and object are identical (Ex.: he *hurt* himself) **2.** designating a pronoun used as the object of such a verb

re·for·est (rē fôr'ist, -fär'-) *vt., vi.* to plant new trees on (land once forested) —**re'for·est·a'tion** *n.*

re·form (ri fôrm') *vt.* [see RE- & FORM] **1.** to make better as by stopping abuses; improve **2.** to cause (a person) to behave better —*vi.* to become better in behavior —*n.* an improvement; correction of faults

re-form (rē'fôrm') *vt., vi.* to form again

ref·or·ma·tion (ref'ər mā'shən) *n.* **1.** a reforming or being reformed **2.** [R-] the 16th-cent. religious movement that resulted in establishing the Protestant churches

re·form·a·to·ry (ri fôr'mə tôr'ē) *n., pl.* -ries **1.** a prison to which young law offenders are sent to be reformed: also **reform school 2.** a penitentiary for women

re·form·er (ri fôr'mər) *n.* one who seeks to bring about political or social reform

re·fract (ri frakt') *vt.* [< L. *re-*, back + *frangere*, to break] to cause (a ray of light, heat, etc.) to undergo refraction

re·frac'tion *n.* the bending of a ray or wave of light, heat, or sound as it passes from one medium into another

re·frac·to·ry (ri frak'tər ē) *adj.* [see REFRACT] hard to manage; obstinate

re·frain' (ri frān') *vi.* [< L. *re-*, back + *frenare*, to curb] to hold back; keep oneself (*from* doing something)

re·frain² (ri frān') *n.* [see REFRACT] **1.** a phrase or verse repeated at intervals in a song or poem **2.** music for this

re·fresh (ri fresh') *vt.* **1.** to make fresh by cooling, wetting, etc. **2.** to make (a person) feel cooler, stronger, etc., as by food, sleep, etc. **3.** to replenish; renew **4.** to stimulate —*vi.* to revive

re·fresh'ment *n.* **1.** a refreshing or being refreshed **2.** that which refreshes **3.** [*pl.*] food or drink or both

re·frig·er·ate (ri frij'ə rāt') *vt.* -at'ed, -at'ing [< L. *re-*, intens. + *frigus*, cold] to make or keep cool or cold, as for preserving —**re·frig'er·ant** *adj., n.* —**re·frig'er·a'tion** *n.*

re·frig'er·a'tor *n.* a box, cabinet, or room in which food, drink, etc. are kept cool

ref·uge (ref'yōōj) *n.* [< L. *re-*, back + *fugere*, flee] (a) shelter or protection from danger, difficulty, etc.

ref·u·gee (ref'yoo jē', ref'yoo jē') *n.* one who flees from his home or country to seek refuge elsewhere

re·ful·gent (ri ful'jənt) *adj.* [< L. *re-*, back + *fulgere*, shine] shining; radiant —**re·ful'gence** *n.*

re·fund (ri fund') *vt., vi.* [< L. *re-*, back + *fundere*, pour] to give back (money, etc.); repay —

n. (rē'fund') a refunding or the amount refunded

re·fur·bish (ri fur'bish) *vt.* [RE- + FURBISH] to freshen or polish up again; renovate

re·fuse' (ri fyōoz') *vt., vi.* -fused', -fus'ing [< L. *re-*, back + *fundere*, pour] **1.** to decline to accept; reject **2.** to decline (*to* do, grant, etc.) — **re·fus'al** *n.*

ref·use² (ref'yōōs, -yōoz) *n.* [see prec.] waste; rubbish

re·fute (ri fyōot') *vt.* -fut'ed, -fut'ing [< L. *refutare*, repel] to prove to be false or wrong —**ref·u·ta·tion** (ref'yə tā'shən) *n.*

re·gain (ri gān') *vt.* **1.** to get back again; recover **2.** to get back to

re·gal (rē'gəl) *adj.* [< L. *rex*, king] of, like, or fit for a king; royal —**re'gal·ly** *adv.*

re·gale (ri gāl') *vt., vi.* -galed', -gal'ing [< Fr. *ré-* (see RE-) + OFr. *gale*, joy] to entertain as with a feast —**re·gale'ment** *n.*

re·ga·li·a (ri gāl'yə, -gā'lē ə) *n.pl.* [see REGAL] **1.** royal insignia **2.** the insignia of a society, etc. **3.** finery

re·gard (ri gärd') *n.* [see RE- & GUARD] **1.** a steady look; gaze **2.** consideration; concern **3.** respect and affection **4.** reference; relation *[in regard* to this matter*]* **5.** [*pl.*] good wishes *[he sends his *regards]* —*vt.* **1.** to look at attentively **2.** to hold in affection and respect **3.** to consider **4.** to concern or involve —**as regards** concerning

re·gard'ing *prep.* concerning; about

re·gard'less *adj.* without regard; careless — *adv.* [Colloq.] without regard for objections, etc. —**regardless of** in spite of

re·gat·ta (ri gät'ə, -gat'-) *n.* [It.] **1.** a boat race **2.** a series of boat races

re·gen·er·ate (ri jen'ər it) *adj.* [< L.: see RE- & GENERATE] renewed or restored —*vt.* (-ə rāt') -at'ed, -at'ing **1.** to cause to be spiritually reborn **2.** to cause to be completely reformed **3.** to bring into existence again; reestablish —**re·gen'er·a'tion** *n.* —**re·gen'er·a'tive** *adj.*

re·gent (rē'jənt) *n.* [< L. *regere*, to rule] **1.** a person appointed to rule when a monarch is absent, too young, etc. **2.** a member of a governing board, as of a university —**re'gen·cy** *n.* —**re'gent·ship'** *n.*

reg·gae (reg'ā) *n.* [< ?] a form of popular Jamaican music influenced by rock-and-roll and calypso

re·gime, ré·gime (ri zhēm', rā-) *n.* [see REGIMEN] **1.** a political or ruling system **2.** a social system **3.** *same as* REGIMEN

reg·i·men (rej'ə mən) *n.* [< L. *regere*, to rule] a system of diet, exercise, rest, etc. for improving the health

reg·i·ment (rej'ə mənt) *n.* [< L. *regere*, to rule] a military unit consisting of two or more battalions —*vt.* (-ment') **1.** to organize systematically **2.** to subject to strict discipline and control —**reg'i·men'tal** *adj.* —**reg'i·men·ta'tion** *n.*

re·gion (rē'jən) *n.* [see REGAL] **1.** a large, indefinite part of the earth's surface **2.** any division or part, as of an organism *[the abdominal *region]* —**re'gion·al** *adj.* —**re'gion·al·ly** *adv.*

reg·is·ter (rej'is tər) *n.* [< L. *regerere*, to record] **1.** *a)* a list of names, items, etc. *b)* a book in which this is kept **2.** a device for recording *[a cash *register]* **3.** an opening into a room by which the amount of air passing through can be controlled **4.** *Music* a part of the range of a voice or instrument —*vt.* **1.** to enter in a list **2.** to indicate as on a scale **3.** to show, as by facial expression *[to register* joy*]*

4. to safeguard (mail) by having its committal to the postal system recorded, for a fee —*vi.* 1. to enter one's name in a list, as of voters 2. to make an impression —reg′is·trant *n.*

registered nurse a trained nurse who has passed a State examination

reg·is·trar (rej′i strär′) *n.* an official who keeps records, as in a college

reg·is·tra·tion (rej′i strā′shən) *n.* 1. a registering or being registered 2. an entry in a register 3. the number of persons registered

reg′is·try (-is trē) *n., pl.* -tries 1. *same as* REGISTRATION 2. an office where registers are kept 3. *same as* REGISTER (*n.* 1)

re·gress (ri gres′) *vi.* [< L. *re-*, back + *gradi*, go] to go back —re·gres′sion *n.* —re·gres′sive *adj.*

re·gret (ri gret′) *vt.* -gret′ted, -gret′ting [< OFr. *regreter*, mourn] to feel sorrow or remorse over (an occurrence, one's acts, etc.) —*n.* sorrow, esp. over one's acts or omissions —(one's) regrets a polite expression of regret, as at declining an invitation —re·gret′ful *adj.* —re·gret′table *adj.*

reg·u·lar (reg′yə lər) *adj.* [< L. *regula*, a rule] 1. conforming to a rule, type, etc.; orderly; symmetrical 2. conforming to a fixed principle or procedure 3. customary or established 4. consistent *[a regular* customer*]* 5. functioning in a normal way *[a regular* pulse*]* 6. properly qualified *[a regular* doctor*]* 7. designating one of the standing army of a country 8. [Colloq.] *a)* thorough; complete *[a regular* nuisance*]* *b)* pleasant, friendly, etc. —*n.* a regular soldier or player —reg′u·lar′i·ty (-lar′ə tē) *n.* —reg′u·lar·ize′ *vt.* -ized′, -iz′ing —reg′u·lar·ly *adv.*

reg·u·late (reg′yə lāt′) *vt.* -lat′ed, -lat′ing [see prec.] 1. to control or direct according to a rule, principle, etc. 2. to adjust to a standard, rate, etc. 3. to adjust (a clock, etc.) so as to make work accurately —reg′u·la′tive *adj.* —reg′u·la′tor *n.*

reg·u·la·tion *n.* 1. a regulating or being regulated 2. a rule or law by which conduct, etc. is regulated —*adj.* usual; normal

re·gur·gi·tate (ri gur′jə tāt′) *vi., vt.* -tat′ed, -tat′ing [< ML. *re-*, back + LL. *gurgitare*, to surge] to bring (partly digested food) from the stomach back to the mouth —re·gur′gi·ta′tion *n.*

re·ha·bil·i·tate (rē′hə bil′ə tāt′) *vt.* -tat′ed, -tat′ing [< ML. *rehabilitare*, to restore] 1. to restore to rank, reputation, etc. which one has lost 2. to put back·in good condition 3. to bring or restore to a state of health or constructive activity —re′ha·bil′i·ta′tion *n.* —re′ha·bil′i·ta′tive *adj.*

re·hash (rē hash′) *vt.* [RE- + HASH] to work up again or go over again —*n.* (rē′hash) the act or result of rehashing

re·hearse (ri hurs′) *vt., vi.* -hearsed′, -hears′ing [< OFr. *re-*, again + *hercer*, to harrow] 1. to recite, esp. in detail 2. to practice (a play, etc.) for public performance —re·hears′al *n.*

reign (rān) *n.* [< L. *regere*, to rule] 1. royal power 2. dominance or sway 3. the period of rule, dominance, etc. —*vi.* 1. to rule as a sovereign 2. to prevail *[peace reigns]*

re·im·burse (rē′im burs′) *vt.* -bursed′, -burs′ing [RE- + archaic *imburse*, to pay] to pay back —re′im·burse′ment *n.*

rein (rān) *n.* [see RETAIN] 1. [*usually pl.*] a narrow strap of leather attached in pairs to a horse's bit and manipulated to control the animal 2. [*pl.*] a means of controlling —*vt.* to guide or control as with reins —give (free) rein to to free from restraint

re·in·car·na·tion (rē′in kär nā′shən) *n.* [see RE- & INCARNATE] rebirth of the soul in another body —re′in·car′nate *vt.* -nat·ed, -nat·ing

rein·deer (rān′dir′) *n., pl.* -deer′, occas. -deers′ [< ON. *hreinn*, reindeer + *dȳr*, deer] a large deer with branching antlers, found in northern regions and domesticated there as a beast of burden

re·in·force (rē′in fôrs′) *vt.* -forced′, -forc′ing [RE- + var. of ENFORCE] 1. to strengthen (a military or naval force) with more troops, ships, etc. 2. to strengthen, as by propping, adding new material, etc. —re·in·force′ment *n.*

re·in·state (rē′in stāt′) *vt.* -stat′ed, -stat′ing to restore to a former state, position, etc. —re′in·state′ment *n.*

re·it·er·ate (rē it′ə rāt′) *vt.* -at′ed, -at′ing [see RE- & ITERATE] to say or do again or repeatedly —re·it′er·a′tion *n.* —re·it′er·a′tive *adj.*

re·ject (ri jekt′) *vt.* [< L. *re-*, back + *jacere*, to throw] 1. to refuse to take, agree to, use, believe, etc. 2. to discard —*n.* (rē′jekt) a rejected person or thing —re·jec′tion *n.*

re·joice (ri jois′) *vi., vt.* -joiced′, -joic′ing [< OFr. *rejoir*] to be or make glad or happy —re·joic′ing *n.*

re·join (rē join′) *vt., vi.* 1. to join again; reunite 2. to answer

re·join·der (ri join′dər) *n.* [see RE- & JOIN] 1. an answer to a reply 2. any answer

re·ju·ve·nate (ri jōō′və nāt′) *vt.* -nat′ed, -nat′-ing [< RE- + L. *juvenis*, young] to make feel or seem young again —re·ju′ve·na′tion *n.*

re·lapse (ri laps′) *vi.* -lapsed′, -laps′ing [see RE- & LAPSE] to slip back into a former state, esp. into illness after apparent recovery —*n.* (*also* rē′laps) a relapsing

re·late (ri lāt′) *vt.* -lat′ed, -lat′ing [< L. *relatus*, brought back] 1. to tell the story of; narrate 2. to connect, as in thought or meaning —*vi.* to have reference or some relation (*to*) —re·lat′er, re·la′tor *n.*

re·lat′ed *adj.* connected or associated, as by origin, kinship, marriage, etc.

re·la′tion *n.* 1. a narrating 2. what is narrated; recital 3. connection, as in thought, meaning, etc. 4. connection by origin or marriage; kinship 5. a relative 6. [*pl.*] the connections between or among persons, nations, etc. —in (or with) relation to concerning —re·la′tion·ship′ *n.*

rel·a·tive (rel′ə tiv) *adj.* 1. related each to the other 2. having to do with; relevant 3. comparative *[relative* comfort*]* 4. meaningful only in relationship *["cold" is a relative* term*]* 5. Gram. that refers to an antecedent *[a relative* pronoun*]* —*n.* a person related to others by kinship

rel·a·tiv·i·ty (rel′ə tiv′ə tē) *n.* 1. a being relative 2. *Physics* the theory of the relative, rather than absolute, character of motion, velocity, mass, etc., and the interdependence of matter, time, and space

re·lax (ri laks′) *vt., vi.* [< L. *re-*, back + *laxare*, loosen] 1. to make or become less firm, tense, etc. 2. to rest, as from work

re·lax′ant *adj.* causing relaxation, esp. of muscular tension —*n.* a relaxant drug

re·lax·a·tion (rē′lak sā′shən) *n.* 1. a relaxing or being relaxed 2. a lessening of or rest from work, worry, etc. 3. recreation

re·lay (rē′lā) *n.* [< MFr. *re-*, back + *laier*, to leave] 1. a fresh supply of horses, etc., as for a stage of a journey 2. a relief crew of workers; shift 3. a race (in full **relay race**) between teams, each member of which goes a part of the distance —*vt.* (*also* ri lā′) -**layed**, -**lay·ing** to convey as by relays [to *relay* news]

re·lease (ri lēs′) *vt.* -**leased**′, -**leas′ing** [see RELAX] **1.** to set free, as from confinement, work, pain, etc. **2.** to let (a missile, etc.) go **3.** to permit to be issued, published, etc. —*n.* **1.** a releasing, as from prison, work, pain, etc. **2.** a device for releasing a catch, etc., as on a machine **3.** a book, news item, etc. released to the public **4.** *Law* a written surrender of a claim, etc.

rel·e·gate (rel′ə gāt′) *vt.* -**gat′ed**, -**gat′ing** [< L. *re-*, away + *legare*, send] **1.** to exile or banish (*to*) **2.** to consign or assign, esp. to an inferior position **3.** to refer or hand over for decision — **rel′e·ga′tion** *n.*

re·lent (ri lent′) *vi.* [< L. *re-*, again + *lentus*, pliant] to become less severe, stern, or stubborn; soften —**re·lent′less** *adj.* —**re·lent′less·ly** *adv.*

rel·e·vant (rel′ə vənt) *adj.* [see RELIEVE] relating to the matter under consideration; pertinent —**rel′e·vance, rel′e·van·cy** *n.*

re·li·a·ble (ri lī′ə b′l) *adj.* that can be relied on; dependable —**re·li′a·bil′i·ty** *n.* —**re·li′a·bly** *adv.*

re·li·ance (ri lī′əns) *n.* **1.** trust, dependence, or confidence **2.** a thing relied on —**re·li′ant** *adj.*

rel·ic (rel′ik) *n.* [< OFr.: see RELINQUISH] **1.** an object, custom, etc. surviving from the past **2.** a souvenir **3.** [*pl.*] ruins **4.** the venerated remains, etc. of a saint, martyr, etc.

re·lief (ri lēf′) *n.* **1.** a relieving, as of pain, anxiety, a burden, etc. **2.** anything that eases tension, or offers a pleasing change **3.** aid, esp. by a public agency to the needy **4.** *a*) release from work or duty *b*) those bringing such release **5.** the projection of sculptured forms from a flat surface **6.** the differences in height, collectively, of land forms, shown as by lines on a map (**relief map**) —**in relief** carved or molded so as to project from a surface

re·lieve (ri lēv′) *vt.* -**lieved**′, -**liev′ing** [< L. *re-*, again + *levare*, to raise] **1.** to ease or reduce (pain, anxiety, etc.) **2.** to free from pain, distress, a burden, etc. **3.** to give or bring aid to **4.** to set free from duty or work by replacing **5.** to make less tedious, etc. by providing a pleasing change

re·li·gion (ri lij′ən) *n.* [< L. *religio*] **1.** belief in God or gods to be worshiped, usually expressed in conduct and ritual **2.** any specific system of belief, worship, etc.

re·li·gious (-əs) *adj.* **1.** devout; pious **2.** of or concerned with religion **3.** conscientiously exact; scrupulous

re·lin·quish (ri liŋ′kwish) *vt.* [< L. *re-*, from + *linquere*, to leave] **1.** to give up (a plan, etc.) **2.** to surrender (property, a right, etc.) **3.** to let go (a grasp, etc.) —**re·lin′quish·ment** *n.*

rel·ish (rel′ish) *n.* [< OFr. *relais*, something remaining] **1.** an appetizing flavor **2.** enjoyment; zest [to listen with *relish*] **3.** pickles, olives, etc. served with a meal or as an appetizer —*vt.* to enjoy; like

re·live (rē liv′) *vt.* -**lived**′, -**liv′ing** to experience again (a past event) as in the imagination

re·lo·cate (rē lō′kāt) *vt., vi.* -**cat·ed**, -**cat·ing** to move to a new location

re·luc′tant (-tənt) *adj.* [< L. *re-*, against + *luctari*, to struggle] **1.** unwilling; disinclined **2.** marked by unwillingness [a *reluctant* answer] —**re·luc′tance** *n.*

re·ly (ri lī′) *vi.* -**lied**′, -**ly′ing** [< L. *re-*, back + *ligare*, bind] to trust; depend (with *on* or *upon*)

re·main (ri mān′) *vi.* [< L. *re-*, back +

manere, to stay] **1.** to be left over when the rest has been taken away, etc. **2.** to stay **3.** to continue [he *remained* a cynic] **4.** to be left to be dealt with, done, etc.

re·main′der *n.* **1.** those remaining **2.** what is left when a part is taken away **3.** what is left when a smaller number is subtracted from a larger

re·mains′ *n.pl.* **1.** what is left after use, destruction, etc. **2.** a dead body

re·mand (ri mand′) *vt.* [< L. *re-*, back + *mandare*, to order] to send back, as a prisoner into custody

re·mark (ri märk′) *vt., vi.* [< Fr. < *re-*, again + *marquer*, to mark] to notice, observe, or comment; make (as) an observation —*n.* a brief comment

re·mark′a·ble *adj.* worthy of notice; extraordinary —**re·mark′a·bly** *adv.*

re·me·di·al (ri mē′dē əl) *adj.* **1.** providing a remedy **2.** intended to correct deficiencies, as certain study courses

rem·e·dy (rem′ə dē) *n., pl.* -**dies** [< L. *re-*, again + *mederi*, heal] **1.** any medicine or treatment for a disease **2.** something to correct a wrong or evil —*vt.* -**died**, -**dy·ing** to cure, correct, etc.

re·mem·ber (ri mem′bər) *vt.* [< L. *re-*, again + *memorare*, bring to mind] **1.** to think of again **2.** to bring back to mind by an effort; recall **3.** to be careful not to forget **4.** to mention (a person) to another as sending regards —*vi.* to bear in mind or call back to mind

re·mem′brance (-brəns) *n.* **1.** a remembering or being remembered **2.** the power to remember **3.** a souvenir or keepsake

re·mind (ri mīnd′) *vt., vi.* to put (a person) in mind (of something); cause to remember —**re·mind′er** *n.* —**re·mind′ful** *adj.*

rem·i·nisce (rem′ə nis′) *vi.* -**nisced**′, -**nisc′ing** [< REMINISCENCE] to think, talk, or write about past events

rem′i·nis′cence (-nis′′ns) *n.* [Fr. < L. *re-*, again + *memini*, remember] **1.** a remembering **2.** memory **3.** [*pl.*] an account of remembered experiences —**rem′i·nis′cent** *adj.* —**rem′i·nis′cent·ly** *adv.*

re·miss (ri mis′) *adj.* [see REMIT] careless; negligent —**re·miss′ness** *n.*

re·mis·sion (ri mish′ən) *n.* [see REMIT] **1.** forgiveness or pardon, as of sins **2.** release from a debt, tax, etc. **3.** a lessening or disappearance of pain or symptoms, etc.

re·mit (ri mit′) *vt.* -**mit′ted**, -**mit′ting** [< L. *re-*, back + *mittere*, send] **1.** to forgive or pardon **2.** to free someone from (a debt, tax, penalty, etc.) **3.** to slacken; lessen **4.** to send (money) in payment —*vi.* **1.** to slacken **2.** to send money in payment —**re·mit′tance** *n.* —**re·mit′tent** *adj.*

rem·nant (rem′nənt) *n.* [see REMAIN] what is left over, as a piece of cloth at the end of a bolt

re·mod·el (rē mäd′′l) *vt.* -**eled** or -**elled**, -**el·ing** or -**el·ling** **1.** to model again **2.** to make over; rebuild

re·mon·strate (ri män′strāt) *vt.* -**strat·ed**, -**strat·ing** [< L. *re-*, again + *monstrare*, to show] to say in protest, objection, etc. —*vi.* to protest; object —**re·mon′strance** (-strəns) *n.* —**re·mon′strant** *adj., n.*

re·morse (ri môrs′) *n.* [< L. *re-*, again + *mordere*, to bite] a torturing sense of guilt for one's actions —**re·morse′ful** *adj.* —**re·morse′less** *adj.*

re·mote (ri mōt′) *adj.* -**mot′er**, -**mot′est** [< L. *remotus*, removed] **1.** distant in space or time **2.** distant in relation, connection, etc. **3.** distantly related *[a remote cousin]* **4.** slight *[a remote chance]* —**re·mote′ly** *adv.* —**re·mote′ness** *n.*

re·move (ri mōōv′) *vt.* -**moved′, -mov′ing** [see RE- & MOVE] **1.** to move (something) from where it is; take away or off **2.** to dismiss, as from office **3.** to get rid of **4.** to kill —*vi.* to move away, as to another residence —*n.* a step or degree away *[only one remove from war]* — **re·mov′a·ble** *adj.* —**re·mov′al** *n.*

re·mu·ner·ate (ri myōō′nə rāt′) *vt.* -**at′ed, -at′-ing** [< L. *re-*, again + *munus*, gift] to pay (a person) for (a service, loss, etc.) —**re·mu′ner·a·ble** *adj.* —**re·mu′ner·a′tion** *n.* —**re·mu′ner·a′tive** *adj.*

ren·ais·sance (ren′ə säns′, -zäns′) *n.* [Fr. < *re-*, again + *naître*, be born] **1.** a rebirth; revival **2.** [R-] the great revival of art and learning in Europe in the 14th, 15th, and 16th centuries

re·nal (rē′n′l) *adj.* [< Fr. < L. *renes*, kidneys] of or near the kidneys

re·nas·cence (ri nas′′ns, -nās′-) *n.* [*also* R-] a rebirth; revival —**re·nas′cent** *adj.*

rend (rend) *vt., vi.* **rent, rend′ing** [OE. *rendan*] to tear or split apart with violence

ren·der (ren′dər) *vt.* [ult. < L. *re(d)-*, back + *dare*, give] **1.** to submit, as for approval, payment, etc. **2.** to give in return or pay as due *[render* thanks] **3.** to cause to be **4.** to give (aid) or do (a service) **5.** to depict, as by drawing **6.** to play (music), act (a role), etc. **7.** to translate **8.** to melt down (fat)

ren·dez·vous (rän′dā vōō′) *n., pl.* -**vous′** (-vōōz′) [< Fr. *rendez-vous*, betake yourself] **1.** a meeting place **2.** an agreement to meet **3.** such a meeting —*vi., vt.* -**voused′** (-vōōd′), -**vous′ing** (-vōō′iŋ) to bring or come together at a rendezvous

ren·di·tion (ren dish′ən) *n.* a rendering; performance, translation, etc.

ren·e·gade (ren′ə gād′) *n.* [< Sp. < L. *re-*, again + *negare*, deny] one who abandons a party, movement, etc. to join the other side; turncoat

re·nege (ri nig′) *vi.* -**neged′, -neg′ing** [see prec.] **1.** to go back on a promise **2.** to play a card not of the suit called for —**re·neg′er** *n.*

re·new (ri nōō′) *vt.* **1.** to make new or fresh again **2.** to reestablish **3.** to resume **4.** to put in a fresh supply of **5.** to give or get an extension of *[renew* a lease] —**re·new′a·ble** *adj.* —**re·new′al** *n.*

ren·net (ren′it) *n.* [ME. *rennen*, coagulate] an extract from the stomach of calves, etc., used to curdle milk

re·nounce (ri nouns′) *vt.* -**nounced′, -nounc′ing** [< L. *re-*, back + *nuntiare*, tell] **1.** to give up formally (a claim, etc.) **2.** to give up (a habit, etc.) **3.** to disown —**re·nounce′ment** *n.*

ren·o·vate (ren′ə vāt′) *vt.* -**vat′ed, -vat′ing** [< L. *re-*, again + *novus*, new] to make as good as new; repair, rebuild, etc. —**ren′o·va′tion** *n.* — **ren′o·va′tive** *adj.* —**ren′o·va′tor** *n.*

re·nown (ri noun′) *n.* [< OFr. *re-*, again + *nom(m)er*, to name] great fame or reputation —**re·nowned′** *adj.*

rent¹ (rent) *n.* [< L. *reddita*, paid] a stated payment at fixed intervals for the use of a house, land, etc. —*vt.* to get or give use of in return for rent —*vi.* to be let for rent

rent² (rent) *pt. & pp. of* REND —*n.* a hole or gap made by tearing

rent·al (ren′t′l) *n.* **1.** an amount paid or received as rent **2.** a house, car, etc. for rent **3.** a renting —*adj.* of, in, or for rent

re·nun·ci·a·tion (ri nun′sē ā′shən) *n.* a renouncing, as of a right

re·or·gan·ize (rē ôr′gə nīz′) *vt., vi.* -**ized′, -iz′-ing** to organize anew —**re·or′gan·i·za′tion** *n.* — **re·or′gan·iz′er** *n.*

rep (rep) *n.* [Fr. *reps* < Eng. *ribs*] a ribbed fabric of silk, wool, cotton, etc.

Rep. 1. Representative **2.** Republican

re·paid (ri pād′) *pt. & pp. of* REPAY

re·pair¹ (ri per′) *vt.* [< L. *re-*, again + *parare*, prepare] **1.** to put back in good condition; fix; renew **2.** to make amends for (a wrong, etc.) — *n.* **1.** a repairing **2.** [*usually pl.*] work done in repairing **3.** the state of being repaired *[kept in repair]* —**re·pair′a·ble** *adj.*

re·pair² (ri per′) *vi.* [< L. *re-*, back + *patria*, native land] to go (*to* a place)

rep·a·ra·tion (rep′ə rā′shən) *n.* [see REPAIR¹] **1.** a making of amends **2.** [*usually pl.*] compensation, as for war damage

rep·ar·tee (rep′ər tē′, -tā′) *n.* [< Fr. *re-*, back + *partir*, to part] **1.** a quick, witty reply **2.** quick, witty conversation

re·past (ri past′) *n.* [< OFr. *re-*, RE- + *past*, food] food and drink; a meal

re·pa·tri·ate (rē pā′trē āt′) *vt., vi.* -**at′ed, -at′-ing** [see REPAIR²] to send back or return to the country of birth, citizenship, etc. —**re·pa′tri·a′-tion** *n.*

re·pay (ri pā′) *vt.* -**paid′, -pay′ing 1.** to pay back **2.** to make return to for (a favor, etc.) — **re·pay′a·ble** *adj.* —**re·pay′ment** *n.*

re·peal (ri pēl′) *vt.* [see RE- & APPEAL] to revoke; cancel; annul, as a law —*n.* revocation, abrogation, etc. —**re·peal′a·ble** *adj.*

re·peat (ri pēt′) *vt.* [< L. *re-*, again + *petere*, seek] **1.** to say again **2.** to say from memory **3.** to say (something) as said by someone else **4.** to tell to someone else *[repeat* a secret] **5.** to do or make again (*vi.* to say or do again —*n.* **1.** a repeating **2.** anything said or done again **3.** *Music a)* a passage repeated in playing *b)* a symbol for this —**re·peat′er** *n.*

re·peat′ed *adj.* said, made, or done again or often —**re·peat′ed·ly** *adv.*

re·pel (ri pel′) *vt.* -**pelled′, -pel′ling** [< L. *re-*, back + *pellere*, to drive] **1.** to drive or force back **2.** to refuse or reject **3.** to cause dislike in; disgust **4.** to be resistant to (water, etc.) — *vi.* to cause dislike, etc. —**re·pel′lent** *adj., n.* — **re·pel′ler** *n.*

re·pent (ri pent′) *vi., vt.* [< L. *re-*, again + *paenitere*, repent] **1.** to feel sorry for (an error, sin, etc.) **2.** to feel such regret over (an action, intention, etc.) as to change one's mind —**re·pent′ance** *n.* —**re·pent′ant** *adj.*

re·per·cus·sion (rē′pər kush′ən) *n.* [see RE- & PERCUSSION] **1.** reflection, as of sound **2.** a reaction to some event or action: *usually used in pl.* —**re′per·cus′sive** *adj.*

rep·er·toire (rep′ər twär′) *n.* [< Fr. < L. *reperire*, discover] the stock of plays, songs, etc. that a company, singer, etc. is prepared to perform

rep′er·to′ry (-tôr′ē) *n., pl.* -**ries 1.** *same as* REPERTOIRE **2.** the system of alternating several plays throughout a season with a permanent acting group

rep·e·ti·tion (rep′ə tish′ən) *n.* [< L. *repetitio*] **1.** a repeating **2.** something repeated —**rep′e·ti′tious** *adj.* —**re·pet·i·tive** (ri pet′ə tiv) *adj.*

re·pine (ri pīn′) *vi.* -**pined′, -pin′ing** [RE- + PINE²] to feel or express discontent

re·place (ri plās′) *vt.* -**placed′, -plac′ing 1.** to put back in a former or the proper place **2.** to take the place of **3.** to provide an equivalent for —**re·place′ment** *n.*

re·plen·ish (ri plen'ish) *vt.* [< L. *re-*, again + *plenus*, full] **1.** to make full or complete again **2.** to supply again —**re·plen'ish·ment** *n.*

re·plete (ri plēt') *adj.* [< L. *re-*, again + *plere*, to fill] **1.** filled; plentifully supplied **2.** stuffed, as with food —**re·ple'tion** *n.*

rep·li·ca (rep'li kə) *n.* [< It.: see REPLY] a copy of a work of art, etc.

re·ply (ri plī') *vi.* -**plied'**, -**ply'ing** [< L. *re-*, back + *plicare*, to fold] to answer or respond —*n.*, *pl.* -**plies'** an answer

re·port (ri pôrt') *vt.* [< L. *re-*, back + *portare*, carry] **1.** to give an account of **2.** to carry and repeat (a message, etc.) **3.** to announce formally **4.** to make a charge about (something) or against (someone) to one in authority —*vi.* **1.** to make a report **2.** to present oneself, as for work —*n.* **1.** rumor **2.** a statement or account **3.** a formal presentation of facts **4.** the noise of an explosion —**re·port'ed·ly** *adv.*

re·port'er *n.* one who reports; specif., one who gathers information and writes reports as for a newspaper

re·pose[1] (ri pōz') *vt.* -**posed'**, -**pos'ing** [< L. *re-*, again + LL. *pausare*, to rest] to lay to rest —*vi.* **1.** to lie at rest **2.** to rest —*n.* **1.** *a*) rest *b*) sleep **2.** composure **3.** calm

re·pose[2] (ri pōz') *vt.* -**posed'**, -**pos'ing** [see REPOSITORY] **1.** to place (trust, etc.) *in* someone **2.** to place (power, etc.) *in* the control of some person or group

re·pos·i·to·ry (ri päz'ə tôr'ē) *n., pl.* -**ries** [< L. *re-*, back + *ponere*, to place] a box, room, etc. in which things may be put for safekeeping

re·pos·sess (rē'pə zes') *vt.* to get possession of again —**re'pos·ses'sion** *n.*

rep·re·hend (rep'ri hend') *vt.* [< L. *re-*, back + *prehendere*, take] **1.** to reprimand; rebuke **2.** to blame; censure

rep're·hen'si·ble (-hen'sə b'l) *adj.* deserving to be reprehended

rep·re·sent (rep'ri zent') *vt.* [see RE- & PRESENT, v.] **1.** to present to the mind **2.** to present a likeness of **3.** to describe **4.** to be a symbol for **5.** to be the equivalent of **6.** to act (a role) **7.** to act in place of, esp. by conferred authority **8.** to serve as a specimen, example, etc. of

rep're·sen·ta'tion *n.* **1.** a representing or being represented **2.** legislative representatives, collectively **3.** a likeness, image, picture, etc. **4.** [*often pl.*] a statement of claims, protest, etc. —**rep're·sen·ta'tion·al** *adj.*

rep're·sent'a·tive *adj.* **1.** representing **2.** of or based on representation of the people by elected delegates **3.** typical —*n.* **1.** an example; type **2.** one authorized to act for others **3.** [R-] a member of the lower house of Congress or of a State legislature

re·press (ri pres') *vt.* [see RE- & PRESS[1]] **1.** to hold back; restrain **2.** to put down; subdue **3.** *Psychiatry* to force (painful ideas, etc.) into the unconscious —**re·pres'sion** *n.* —**re·pres'sive** *adj.*

re·prieve (ri prēv') *vt.* -**prieved'**, -**priev'ing** [< Fr. *reprendre*, take back] **1.** to postpone the execution of (a condemned person) **2.** to give temporary relief to —*n.* a reprieving or being reprieved

rep·ri·mand (rep'rə mand') *n.* [< L. *reprimere*, repress] a severe or formal rebuke —*vt.* to rebuke severely or formally

re·pris·al (ri prī'z'l) *n.* [see REPREHEND] injury done for injury received; retaliation, esp. in war

re·proach (ri prōch') *vt.* [< L. *re-*, back + *prope*, near] to accuse of a fault; rebuke —*n.* **1.**

shame, disgrace, etc., or a cause of this **2.** censure; rebuke

rep·ro·bate (rep'rə bāt') *adj.* [< LL. *reprobare*, reprove] depraved; corrupt —*n.* a depraved person —**rep'ro·ba'tion** *n.*

re·pro·duce (rē'prə dōōs') *vt.* -**duced'**, -**duc'ing** to produce again; specif., *a*) to bring forth others of (its kind) *b*) to make a copy of —*vi.* to produce offspring

re'pro·duc'tion (-duk'shən) *n.* **1.** a copy, imitation, etc. **2.** the process by which animals and plants produce new individuals —**re'pro·duc'tive** *adj.*

re·proof (ri prōōf') *n.* a reproving; rebuke

re·prove (ri prōōv') *vt.* -**proved'**, -**prov'ing** [see RE- & PROVE] to rebuke or censure —**re·prov'ing·ly** *adv.*

rep·tile (rep't'l, -tīl) *n.* [< L. *repere*, to creep] a coldblooded, creeping or crawling vertebrate, as a snake, lizard, turtle, etc. —**rep·til·i·an** (rep til'ē ən) *adj., n.*

re·pub·lic (ri pub'lik) *n.* [< L. *res publica*, public thing] a state or government in which the power is exercised by representatives elected by citizens entitled to vote

re·pub'li·can (-li kən) *adj.* **1.** of or like a republic **2.** [R-] of or belonging to the Republican Party —*n.* **1.** one who favors a republic **2.** [R-] a member of the Republican Party —**re·pub'li·can·ism** *n.*

Republican Party one of the two major political parties in the U.S.

re·pu·di·ate (ri pyōō'dē āt') *vt.* -**at'ed**, -**at'ing** [< L. *repudium*, separation] **1.** to disown **2.** to refuse to acknowledge; deny —**re·pu'di·a'tion** *n.* —**re·pu'di·a'tor** *n.*

re·pug·nant (ri pug'nənt) *adj.* [< L. *re-*, back + *pugnare*, to fight] **1.** contradictory or opposed **2.** distasteful; offensive —**re·pug'nance** *n.* —**re·pug'nant·ly** *adv.*

re·pulse (ri puls') *vt.* -**pulsed'**, -**puls'ing** [see REPEL] **1.** to drive back (an attack, etc.) **2.** to refuse or reject with discourtesy, etc.; rebuff —*n.* **1.** a repelling or being repelled **2.** a refusal or rebuff

re·pul'sion *n.* **1.** a repelling or being repelled **2.** strong dislike, distaste, etc.

re·pul'sive *adj.* causing strong dislike or aversion; disgusting —**re·pul'sive·ness** *n.*

rep·u·ta·ble (rep'yoo tə b'l) *adj.* having a good reputation; respectable —**rep'u·ta·bil'i·ty** *n.* —**rep'u·ta·bly** *adv.*

rep·u·ta·tion (rep'yoo tā'shən) *n.* [see REPUTE] **1.** estimation in which a person or thing is commonly held **2.** favorable estimation **3.** fame

re·pute (ri pyōōt') *vt.* -**put'ed**, -**put'ing** [< L. *re-*, again + *putare*, think] to consider to be as specified [he is *reputed* to be rich] —*n.* same *as* REPUTATION

re·quest (ri kwest') *n.* [see REQUIRE] **1.** an asking for something **2.** something asked for **3.** state of being asked for; demand —*vt.* **1.** to ask for **2.** to ask (a person) to do something

Re·qui·em (rek'wē əm, rāk'-) *n.* [L., rest] [*also* r-] *R.C.Ch.* **1.** a Mass for the repose of the dead **2.** its musical setting

re·quire (ri kwīr') *vt.* -**quired'**, -**quir'ing** [< L. *re-*, again + *quaerere*, ask] **1.** to insist upon; demand; order **2.** to need —**re·quire'ment** *n.*

req·ui·site (rek'wə zit) *adj.* [see REQUIRE] required; necessary; indispensable —*n.* something requisite

req·ui·si·tion (rek'wə zish'ən) *n.* **1.** a requiring, as by authority **2.** a formal written request, as for equipment —*vt.* to demand or take, as by authority

re·quite (ri kwīt') *vt.* -**quit'ed**, -**quit'ing** [RE- +

quite, obs. var. of QUIT] to repay for (a benefit, service, etc., or an injury, wrong, etc.) —**re·quit′al** *n.* —**re·quit′er** *n.*

re·run (rē′run′) *n.* a repeat showing of a motion picture, television show, etc.

re·sale (rē′sāl′) *n.* a selling again, specif. to a third party

re·scind (ri sind′) *vt.* [< L. *re-*, back + *scindere*, to cut] to revoke or cancel, as a law

res·cue (res′kyōō) *vt.* **-cued, -cu·ing** [ult. < L. *re-*, again + *ex-*, off + *quatere*, to shake] to free or save from danger, evil, etc. —*n.* a rescuing —**res′cu·er** *n.*

re·search (ri surch′, rē′surch) *n.* [see RE- & SEARCH] [*sometimes pl.*] systematic investigation in a field of knowledge, to establish facts or principles —*vi., vt.* to do research (on or in) —**re·search′er** *n.*

re·sec·tion (ri sek′shən) *n.* [< L. *re-*, back + *secare*, to cut] the surgical removal of part of an organ, bone, etc.

re·sem·blance (ri zem′bləns) *n.* similarity of appearance, character, etc.; likeness

re·sem·ble (ri zem′b'l) *vt.* **-bled, -bling** [ult. < L. *re-*, again + *simulare*, to feign] to be like or similar to

re·sent (ri zent′) *vt.* [< L. *re-*, again + *sentire*, feel] to feel or show a bitter hurt or indignation at (a person, act, etc.) —**re·sent′ful** *adj.* —**re·sent′ment** *n.*

res·er·va·tion (rez′ər vā′shən) *n.* **1.** a reserving **2.** something reserved or withheld **3.** a limiting condition **4.** public land set aside for some special use, as for Indians **5.** a reserving, as of a hotel room, theater ticket, etc. until called for

re·serve (ri zurv′) *vt.* **-served′, -serv′ing** [< L. *re-*, back + *servare*, to hold] **1.** to keep back; set apart for later or special use **2.** to retain for oneself —*n.* **1.** something reserved **2.** a limitation [*without reserve*] **3.** the practice of keeping one's thoughts, feelings, etc. to oneself **4.** reticence; silence **5.** [*pl.*] troops not on active duty but subject to call —**in reserve** reserved for later use

re·served′ *adj.* **1.** set apart for some person, purpose, etc. **2.** aloof or reticent

res·er·voir (rez′ər vwär′) *n.* [Fr.: see RESERVE] **1.** a place where water is collected and stored for use **2.** a reserve supply

re·side (ri zīd′) *vi.* **-sid′ed, -sid′ing** [< L. *re-*, back + *sedere*, to sit] **1.** to dwell for some time; live (*in* or *at*) **2.** to be present or inherent (*in*): said of qualities, etc.

res·i·dence (rez′i dəns) *n.* **1.** a residing **2.** the place where one resides; home —**res′i·den′tial** (-den′shəl) *adj.*

res′i·den·cy (-dən sē) *n., pl.* **-cies** a period of advanced training for a doctor at a hospital

res′i·dent (-dənt) *adj.* residing; esp., living in a place while working, etc. there —*n.* **1.** one who lives in a place, not a visitor **2.** a doctor who is serving a residency

re·sid·u·al (ri zij′oo wəl) *adj.* of or like a residue; remaining —*n.* **1.** something remaining **2.** [*pl.*] fees paid for reruns, as on TV

res·i·due (rez′ə dōō′) *n.* [< L. *residuus*, remaining] what is left after part is removed; remainder

re·sign (ri zīn′) *vt., vi.* [< L. *re-*, back + *signare*, to sign] to give up (a claim, office, position, etc.) —**resign oneself (to)** to submit (to) —**res·ig·na·tion** (rez′ig nā′shən) *n.* **1.** a resigning **2.** formal notice of this **3.** patient submission

re·signed (ri zīnd′) *adj.* feeling or showing resignation —**re·sign′ed·ly** (-zīn′id lē) *adv.*

re·sil·ient (ri zil′yənt, -ē ənt) *adj.* [< L. *re-*,

back + *salire*, to jump] **1.** springing back into shape or position; elastic **2.** recovering strength, spirits, etc. quickly —**re·sil′ience, re·sil′ien·cy** *n.*

res·in (rez′'n) *n.* [L. *resina*] **1.** a substance exuded from various plants and trees and used in medicines, varnish, etc. **2.** same as ROSIN —**res′in·ous** *adj.*

re·sist (ri zist′) *vt.* [< L. *re-*, back + *sistere*, to set] **1.** to withstand; fend off **2.** to oppose actively; fight against —*vi.* to oppose or withstand something —**re·sist′er** *n.* —**re·sist′i·ble** *adj.*

re·sist′ance *n.* **1.** a resisting **2.** power to resist; specif., the ability of an organism to ward off disease **3.** opposition of some force, thing, etc. to another, as to the flow of an electric current —**re·sist′ant** *adj., n.*

re·sis′tor *n.* a device used in an electric circuit to produce resistance

res·o·lute (rez′ə lōōt′) *adj.* [see RE- & SOLVE] having or showing a fixed, firm purpose; determined —**res′o·lute′ly** *adv.*

res′o·lu′tion *n.* **1.** the act or result of resolving something **2.** the thing determined upon; decision as to future action **3.** a resolute quality of mind **4.** a formal statement of opinion or determination by an assembly **5.** a solving or answering

re·solve (ri zälv′) *vt.* **-solved′, -solv′ing** [see RE- & SOLVE] **1.** to break up into separate parts; analyze **2.** to reach as a decision; determine **3.** to solve (a problem) **4.** to decide by vote —*vi.* **1.** to be resolved, as by analysis **2.** to come to a decision —*n.* **1.** a fixed purpose **2.** a formal resolution —**re·solv′a·ble** *adj.*

re·solved′ *adj.* firm and fixed in purpose

res·o·nant (rez′ə nənt) *adj.* [< L. *resonare*, to resound] **1.** resounding **2.** producing resonance [*resonant* walls] **3.** vibrant; sonorous [a *resonant* voice] —**res′o·nance** *n.* —**res′o·nate′** (-nāt′) *vi., vt.* **-nat′ed, -nat′ing**

re·sort (ri zôrt′) *vi.* [< OFr. *re-*, again + *sortir*, go out] to have recourse; turn (*to*) for help, support, etc. —*n.* **1.** a place to which people go often, as on vacation **2.** a source of help, support, etc.; recourse

re·sound (ri zound′) *vi.* [< L. *re-*, again + *sonare*, to sound] to make a loud, echoing sound; reverberate —**re·sound′ing** *adj.*

re·source (rē′sôrs, ri sôrs′) *n.* [< Fr. < OFr. *re-*, again + *sourdre*, spring up] **1.** something ready for use or available as needed **2.** [*pl.*] wealth; assets **3.** resourcefulness

re·source′ful *adj.* able to deal effectively with problems, etc. —**re·source′ful·ness** *n.*

re·spect (ri spekt′) *vt.* [< L. *re-*, back + *specere*, look at] **1.** to feel or show honor or esteem for **2.** to show consideration for —*n.* **1.** high regard; esteem **2.** courteous consideration **3.** [*pl.*] expressions of regard **4.** a particular detail **5.** reference; relation [with *respect* to him] —**re·spect′ful** *adj.* —**re·spect′ful·ly** *adv.*

re·spect′a·ble *adj.* **1.** worthy of respect or esteem **2.** correct; proper **3.** of moderate quality or size **4.** presentable —**re·spect′a·bil′i·ty** *n.* —**re·spect′a·bly** *adv.*

re·spect′ing *prep.* concerning; about

re·spec′tive *adj.* as relates individually to each of two or more —**re·spec′tive·ly** *adv.*

res·pi·ra·tion (res′pə rā′shən) *n.* act or process of breathing —**res·pi·ra·to·ry** (res′pər ə tôr′ē) *adj.*

res′pi·ra′tor *n.* **1.** a mask, as of gauze, worn to prevent the inhaling of harmful substances **2.** an apparatus for giving artificial respiration

re·spire (ri spīr′) *vi., vt.* **-spired′, -spir′ing** [< L. *re-*, back + *spirare*, breathe] to breathe
res·pite (res′pit) *n.* [see RESPECT] **1.** a delay or postponement **2.** temporary relief, as from pain, work, etc.; rest
re·splend·ent (ri splen′dənt) *adj.* [< L. *re-*, again + *splendere*, to shine] shining brightly; dazzling —**re·splend′ence** *n.*
re·spond (ri spänd′) *vi.* [< L. *re-*, back + *spondere*, to pledge] **1.** to answer; reply **2.** to react **3.** to react favorably —*vt.* to say in answer
re·spond′ent *adj.* responding —*n.* **1.** one who responds **2.** *Law* a defendant
re·sponse (ri späns′) *n.* **1.** something said or done in responding; reply **2.** words said or sung by the congregation or choir in answer to the clergyman **3.** any reaction to a stimulus
re·spon·si·bil·i·ty (ri spän′sə bil′ə tē) *n., pl.* **-ties 1.** a being responsible **2.** a thing or person that one is responsible for
re·spon′si·ble (-sə b'l) *adj.* **1.** obliged to account (*for*); answerable (*to*) **2.** involving obligation or duties **3.** accountable for one's behavior or for an act **4.** trustworthy; dependable —**re·spon′si·bly** *adv.*
re·spon′sive (-siv) *adj.* reacting readily, as to appeal —**re·spon′sive·ly** *adv.*
rest[1] (rest) *n.* [OE.] **1.** sleep or repose **2.** ease or inactivity after exertion **3.** relief from anything distressing, tiring, etc. **4.** absence of motion **5.** a resting place **6.** a thing that supports **7.** *Music* an interval of silence between tones, or a symbol for this —*vi.* **1.** to get refreshed by sleeping, ceasing work, etc. **2.** to be at ease **3.** to be quiet or still **4.** to lie, sit, or lean **5.** to be or lie (where specified) *[the fault rests with him]* **6.** to rely; depend —*vt.* **1.** to refresh by rest **2.** to put for ease, etc. *[rest your head here]*
rest[2] (rest) *n.* [< L. *restare*, remain] **1.** what is left; remainder **2.** *[with pl. v.]* the others —*vi.* to go on being *[rest assured]*
res·tau·rant (res′tə rənt, -ränt′) *n.* [Fr.: see RESTORE] a place where meals can be bought and eaten
res·tau·ra·teur (res′tər ə tur′) *n.* [Fr.] a person who owns or operates a restaurant
rest·ful (rest′fəl) *adj.* **1.** full of or giving rest **2.** quiet; tranquil —**rest′ful·ly** *adv.*
res·ti·tu·tion (res′tə tōō′shən) *n.* [L. *re-*, again + *statuere*, to set up] **1.** restoration to the rightful owner of something lost or taken away **2.** a making good for loss or damage; reimbursement
res·tive (res′tiv) *adj.* [< OFr. < L.: see REST[2]] **1.** hard to control; balky, etc. **2.** nervous under restraint; restless
rest′less *adj.* **1.** unable to relax **2.** giving no rest; disturbed *[restless sleep]* **3.** rarely still; active **4.** seeking change
res·to·ra·tion (res′tə rā′shən) *n.* **1.** a restoring or being restored **2.** something restored, as by rebuilding
re·stor·a·tive (ri stôr′ə tiv) *adj.* restoring health, consciousness, etc. —*n.* something that restores
re·store (ri stôr′) *vt.* **-stored′, -stor′ing** [< L. *re-*, again + *-staurare*, to place] **1.** to give back (something taken, lost, etc.) **2.** to bring back to a former or normal state, or to a position, rank, use, etc. **3.** to bring back to health, strength, etc.
re·strain (ri strān′) *vt.* [< L. *re-*, back + *stringere*, draw tight] to check; curb
re·straint (ri strānt′) *n.* **1.** a restraining or

being restrained **2.** a means of restraining **3.** confinement **4.** control of emotions, etc.
re·strict (ri strikt′) *vt.* [see RESTRAIN] to confine; limit —**re·stric′tion** *n.*
re·stric′tive *adj.* **1.** restricting **2.** *Gram.* designating a clause, phrase, or word felt as limiting what it modifies and so not set off by commas (Ex.: *the woman who spoke to us* is a scientist)
rest′room′ *n.* a room in a public building, with toilets, washbowls, etc.: also **rest room**
re·sult (ri zult′) *vi.* [< L. *resultare*, to rebound] **1.** to happen as an effect of some cause **2.** to end as a consequence (*in* something) —*n.* **1.** anything that issues as an effect **2.** the number, etc. obtained by mathematical calculation —**re·sult′ant** *adj.*
re·sume (ri zōōm′) *vt.* **-sumed′, -sum′ing** [< L. *re-*, again + *sumere*, take] **1.** to take or occupy again **2.** to continue after interruption —*vi.* to begin again or go on again —**re·sump·tion** (ri zump′shən) *n.*
ré·su·mé (rez′oo mā′, rā′zoo-) *n.* [Fr.: see RESUME] a summary, esp. of employment experience: also written **resume, resumé**
re·sur·face (rē sur′fis) *vt.* **-faced, -fac·ing** to put a new surface on —*vi.* to come to the surface again
re·sur·gent (ri sur′jənt) *adj.* rising or tending to rise again —**re·sur′gence** *n.*
res′ur·rec′tion *n.* [< L. *resurgere*, rise again] **1.** *Theol.* a rising from the dead; specif., [the R-] the rising of Jesus from the dead **2.** a coming back into use, etc.; revival —**res′ur·rect′** *vt.*
re·sus·ci·tate (ri sus′ə tāt′) *vt., vi.* **-tat′ed, -tat′ing** [< L. *re-*, again + *suscitare*, revive] to revive when unconscious, apparently dead, etc. —**re·sus′ci·ta′tion** *n.*
re·tail (rē′tāl) *n.* [< OFr. *re-*, again + *tailler*, to cut] the sale of goods in small quantities directly to the consumer —*adj.* of or engaged in such sale —*adv.* in small amounts or at a retail price —*vt., vi.* to sell or be sold at retail —**re′tail·er** *n.*
re·tain (ri tān′) *vt.* [< L. *re-*, back + *tenere*, to hold] **1.** to keep in possession, use, etc. **2.** to keep in mind **3.** to engage (a lawyer, etc.) by an advance fee
re·tain′er *n.* **1.** a person or thing that retains **2.** a person serving someone of rank or wealth **3.** a fee paid to engage a lawyer's services
retaining wall a wall built to keep back earth or water
re·take (rē tāk′) *vt.* **-took′, -tak′en, -tak′ing 1.** to take again; recapture **2.** to photograph again —*n.* (rē′tāk′) a scene, etc. photographed again
re·tal·i·ate (ri tal′ē āt′) *vi.* **-at′ed, -at′ing** [< L. *re-*, back + *talio*, punishment in kind] to return like for like, esp. injury for injury —**re·tal′i·a′tion** *n.* —**re·tal′i·a·to′ry** *adj.*
re·tard (ri tärd′) *vt.* [< L. *re-*, back + *tardare*, hinder] to hinder, delay, or slow the progress of —**re·tar·da·tion** (rē′tär dā′shən) *n.*
re·tard′ant *n.* a substance that delays a chemical reaction —*adj.* that retards
retch (rech) *vi.* [< OE. *hræcan*, to spit] to make a straining effort to vomit, esp. without bringing anything up
re·ten·tion (ri ten′shən) *n.* **1.** a retaining or being retained **2.** capacity for retaining **3.** memory —**re·ten′tive** *adj.*
ret·i·cent (ret′ə s'nt) *adj.* [< L. *re-*, again + *tacere*, be silent] disinclined to speak; reserved —**ret′i·cence** *n.*
ret·i·na (ret′'n ə) *n., pl.* **-nas, -nae** (-ē′) [prob. < L. *rete*, net] the innermost coat of the back

part of the eyeball, on which the image is formed —**ret′i·nal** *adj.*

ret·i·nue (ret′'n ōō′) *n.* [see RETAIN] a group of persons attending a person of rank

re·tire (ri tīr′) *vi.* **-tired′, -tir′ing** [< Fr. *re-,* back + *tirer,* draw] 1. to withdraw to a secluded place 2. to go to bed 3. to retreat, as in battle 4. to give up one's work, career, etc., esp. because of advanced age —*vt.* 1. to withdraw (troops) 2. to pay off (bonds, etc.) 3. to cause to retire from a job, etc. 4. *Baseball,* etc. to end the batting turn of (a batter, side, etc.) — **re·tir′ee′** *n.* —**re·tire′ment** *n.*

re·tir′ing *adj.* reserved; modest; shy

re·tool (rē tōōl′) *vt., vi.* to adapt the machinery of (a factory) for making a different product

re·tort¹ (ri tôrt′) *vt., vi.* [< L. *re-,* back + *torquere,* to twist] 1. to return in kind (an insult, etc. received) 2. to answer back, esp. in a sharp, quick, or clever way —*n.* a retorting or the response so made

re·tort² (ri tôrt′) *n.* [< ML. *retorta:* see prec.] a container for distilling, usually of glass and with a long tube

re·touch (rē tuch′) *vt.* to touch up details in (a painting, photograph, etc.)

re·trace (ri trās′) *vt.* **-traced′, -trac′ing** [see RE- & TRACE¹] to go back over again [to *retrace* one's steps]

re·tract (ri trakt′) *vt., vi.* [< L. *re-,* back + *trahere,* draw] 1. to draw back or in 2. to withdraw (a statement, charge, etc.); recant —**re·tract′a·ble, re·trac′tile** (-t'l) *adj.* —**re·trac′tion** *n.*

re·tread (rē tred′; *for n.* rē′tred′) *vt., n. same as* RECAP¹

re·treat (ri trēt′) *n.* [< L. *re-,* back + *trahere,* to draw] 1. a withdrawal, as from danger 2. a safe, quiet place 3. a period of seclusion, esp. for contemplation 4. *a)* the forced withdrawal of troops under attack *b)* a signal for this *c)* a signal by drum or bugle at sunset for lowering the national flag —*vi.* to withdraw; go back

re·trench (ri trench′) *vt., vi.* [see RE- & TRENCH] to cut down or reduce (esp. expenses); curtail; economize —**re·trench′ment** *n.*

ret·ri·bu·tion (ret′rə byōō′shən) *n.* [< L. *re-,* back + *tribuere,* to pay] deserved reward or, esp., punishment —**re·trib·u·tive** (ri trib′yōō tiv), **re·trib′u·to′ry** (-tôr′ē) *adj.*

re·trieve (ri trēv′) *vt.* **-trieved′, -triev′ing** [< OFr. *re-,* again + *trouver,* to find] 1. to get back; recover 2. to restore 3. to set right (a loss, error, etc.) 4. to recover (information) from data stored in a computer 5. to find and bring back (killed or wounded game): said of dogs —*vi.* to retrieve game —**re·triev′al** *n.*

re·triev′er *n.* 1. one who retrieves 2. a dog trained to retrieve game

retro- [< L.] *a combining form meaning* backward, back, behind

ret·ro·ac·tive (ret′rō ak′tiv) *adj.* applying to, or going into effect as of, the preceding period —**ret′ro·ac′tive·ly** *adv.*

ret·ro·grade (ret′rə grād′) *adj.* [see RETRO- & GRADE] 1. moving backward 2. going back to a worse condition —*vi.* **-grad′ed, -grad′ing** 1. to go backward 2. to worsen

ret·ro·gress (ret′rə gres′) *vi.* [< L.: see RETROGRADE] to move backward, esp. into a worse condition —**ret′ro·gres′sion** *n.*

ret·ro·rock·et, ret·ro·rock·et (ret′rō räk′it) *n.* a small rocket, as on a spacecraft, used to produce thrust against flight direction so as to reduce speed

ret·ro·spect (ret′rə spekt′) *n.* [< L. *retro-,* back + *specere,* to look] contemplation of the

past —**ret′ro·spec′tion** *n.* —**ret′ro·spec′tive** *adj.* —**ret′ro·spec′tive·ly** *adv.*

re·turn (ri turn′) *vi.* [see RE- & TURN] 1. to go or come back 2. to reply —*vt.* 1. to bring, send, or put back 2. to do in reciprocation [to *return* a visit] 3. to yield, as a profit 4. to report officially 5. to elect or reelect —*n.* 1. a coming or going back 2. a bringing, sending, or putting back 3. something returned 4. repayment; requital 5. [*often pl.*] yield or profit, as from investments 6. a reply 7. an official report [election *returns*] 8. a form for reporting income tax due —*adj.* 1. of or for returning 2. given, sent, done, etc. in return —**in return** as a return

re·un·ion (rē yōōn′yən) *n.* a coming together again after separation

rev (rev) *vt., vi.* **revved, rev′ving** [< *revolution* of an engine] [Colloq.] to speed up (an engine, motor, etc.)

Rev. *pl.* **Revs.** Reverend

re·vamp (rē vamp′) *vt.* 1. to put a new vamp on 2. to make over; revise

re·veal (ri vēl′) *vt.* [< L. *re-,* back + *velum,* veil] 1. to make known (something hidden or secret) 2. to expose to view

re·veil·le (rev′ə lē) *n.* [< Fr. < L. *re-,* again + *vigilare,* to watch] a signal on a bugle, drum, etc. in the morning to waken soldiers or sailors

rev·el (rev′'l) *vi.* **-eled** *or* **-elled, -el·ing** *or* **-el·ling** [see REBEL] 1. to be noisily festive 2. to take much pleasure (*in*) —*n.* merrymaking —**rev′el·ry** *n., pl.* **-ries**

rev·e·la·tion (rev′ə lā′shən) *n.* 1. a revealing 2. something disclosed, esp. a striking disclosure 3. *Theol.* God's revealing of himself to man — [R-] the last book of the New Testament: also **Revelations**

re·venge (ri venj′) *vt.* **-venged′, -veng′ing** [< OFr. *re-,* again + *vengier,* take vengeance] to inflict harm in return for (an injury, etc.) —*n.* 1. a revenging 2. what is done in revenging 3. desire to take vengeance —**re·venge′ful** *adj.*

rev·e·nue (rev′ə nōō′) *n.* [< OFr. *re-,* back + *venir,* come] income of a government from taxes, licenses, etc.

re·ver·ber·ate (ri vur′bə rāt′) *vt., vi.* **-at′ed, -at′ing** [< L. *re-,* again + *verberare,* to beat] to throw back (sound); reecho —**re·ver′ber·a′tion** *n.*

re·vere (ri vir′) *vt.* **-vered′, -ver′ing** [< Fr. < L. *re-,* again + *vereri,* to fear] to regard with deep respect, love, and awe

rev·er·ence (rev′ər əns) *n.* a feeling of deep respect, love, and awe —*vt.* **-enced, -enc·ing** to treat with reverence —**rev′er·ent, rev′er·en′tial** (-ə ren′shəl) *adj.*

rev′er·end (-ər ənd, -rənd) *adj.* worthy of reverence: used [*usually* the R-] as a title of respect for a clergyman

rev·er·ie, rev·er·y (rev′ər ē) *n., pl.* **-ies** [< Fr. *rever,* to wander] 1. daydreaming 2. a fanciful notion

re·vers (ri vir′, -ver′) *n., pl.* **-vers′** (-virz′, -verz′) [Fr.: see REVERSE] a part (of a garment) turned back to show the reverse side, as a lapel: also **re·vere′** (-vir′)

re·verse (ri vurs′) *adj.* [see REVERT] 1. turned backward; opposite or contrary 2. causing movement in the opposite direction —*n.* 1. the opposite or contrary 2. the back of a coin, medal, etc. 3. a change from good fortune to bad 4. a mechanism for reversing, as a gear on a machine —*vt.* **-versed′, -vers′ing** 1. to turn about, upside down, or inside out 2. to change to the opposite 3. *Law* to revoke or annul (a decision, etc.) —*vi.* to go or turn in the opposite direction —**re·ver'sal** (-vur's'l) *n.* —**re·vers'-i·ble** *adj.*

re·vert (ri vurt') *vi.* [< L. *re-*, back + *vertere*, to turn] **1.** to go back, as to a former practice, subject, etc. **2.** *Biol.* to return to an earlier type **3.** *Law* to go back to a former owner or his heirs —**re·ver'sion** (-vur'zhən) *n.* —**re·vert'-i·ble** *adj.*

re·view (ri vyōō') *n.* [< L. *re-*, again + *videre*, see] **1.** a looking at or looking over again **2.** a general survey or report **3.** a looking back, as on past events **4.** reexamination, as of the decision of a lower court **5.** a critical report of a book, play, etc. **6.** a formal inspection, as of troops on parade —*vt.* **1.** to look back on **2.** to survey **3.** to inspect (troops, etc.) formally **4.** to give or write a critical report of (a book, play, etc.) —**re·view'er** *n.*

re·vile (ri vīl') *vt., vi.* -**viled'**, -**vil'ing** [see RE- & VILE] to use abusive language (to or about) — **re·vile'ment** *n.*

re·vise (ri vīz') *vt.* -**vised'**, -**vis'ing** [< Fr. < L. *re-*, back + *visere*, to survey] **1.** to read over (a manuscript, etc.) to correct and improve **2.** to change or amend —**re·vi'sion** (-vizh'ən) *n.*

Revised Standard Version a mid-20th-cent. revision of the Bible

re·viv·al (ri vī'v'l) *n.* **1.** a reviving or being revived **2.** a bringing or coming back into use, being, etc. **3.** a new presentation of an earlier play, etc. **4.** restoration to vigor and activity **5.** a meeting led by an evangelist to stir up religious feeling —**re·viv'al·ist** *n.*

re·vive (ri vīv') *vi., vt.* -**vived'**, -**viv'ing** [< L. *re-*, again + *vivere*, to live] **1.** to return to life or consciousness **2.** to return to health and vigor **3.** to come or bring back into use, attention, exhibition, etc.

re·viv·i·fy (ri viv'ə fī') *vt., vi.* -**fied'**, -**fy'ing** to give or get new life or vigor —**re·viv'i·fi·ca'tion** *n.*

re·voke (ri vōk') *vt.* -**voked'**, -**vok'ing** [< L. *re-*, back + *vocare*, to call] to withdraw, repeal, or cancel (a law, etc.) —**rev·o·ca·ble** (rev'ə kə b'l), **re·vok·a·ble** (ri vō'kə b'l) *adj.* —**rev·o·ca·tion** (rev'ə kā'shən) *n.*

re·volt (ri vōlt') *n.* [< Fr.: see REVOLVE] a rebellion against the government or any authority —*vi.* **1.** to rebel against authority **2.** to be disgusted (with *at* or *against*) —*vt.* to disgust — **re·volt'ing** *adj.*

rev·o·lu·tion (rev'ə lōō'shən) *n.* [see REVOLVE] **1.** movement of a body in an orbit **2.** a turning around a center or axis; rotation **3.** a complete cycle **4.** a complete change **5.** complete overthrow of a government or social system — **rev'o·lu'tion·ar'y** (-er'ē) *adj., n., pl.* -**ies** —**rev'o·lu'tion·ist** *n.*

rev·o·lu·tion·ize (-īz') *vt.* -**ized'**, -**iz'ing** to make a complete and basic change in

re·volve (ri välv') *vt.* -**volved'**, -**volv'ing** [< L. *re-*, back + *volvere*, to roll] **1.** to turn over in the mind **2.** to cause to travel in a circle or orbit **3.** to cause to rotate —*vi.* **1.** to move in a circle or orbit **2.** to rotate **3.** to recur at intervals

re·volv'er *n.* a handgun with a revolving cylinder holding several bullets

re·vue (ri vyōō') *n.* [Fr.: see REVIEW] a musical show with skits, songs, and dances, often parodying recent events, etc.

re·vul·sion (ri vul'shən) *n.* [< L. *re-*, back + *vellere*, to pull] an abrupt, strong reaction; esp., disgust

re·ward (ri wôrd') *n.* [< OFr. *regarde*] **1.** something given in return for something done **2.** money offered, as for capturing a criminal —*vt.*

to give a reward to (someone) for (service, etc.)

re·wind (rē wīnd') *vt.* -**wound'**, -**wind'ing** to wind (film, tape, etc.) back on the reel

re·word' *vt.* to change the wording of

re·write (rē rīt') *vt., vi.* -**wrote'**, -**writ'ten**, -**writ'ing** **1.** to write again **2.** to revise **3.** to write (news turned in) in a form suitable for publication

RFD, R.F.D. Rural Free Delivery

rhap·so·dize (rap'sə dīz') *vi., vt.* -**dized'**, -**diz'-ing** to speak, write, etc. in a rhapsodic manner —**rhap'so·dist** *n.*

rhap'so·dy (-dē) *n., pl.* -**dies** [< Gr. *rhaptein*, to stitch together + *ōidē*, song] **1.** any ecstatic or enthusiastic speech or writing **2.** an instrumental composition of free, irregular form, suggesting improvisation —**rhap·sod'ic** (-säd'ik), **rhap·sod'i·cal** *adj.*

rhe·a (rē'ə) *n.* [< Gr.] a large S. American non-flying bird

rhe·o·stat (rē'ə stat') *n.* [< Gr. *rheos*, current + -STAT] a device for varying the resistance of an electric circuit, used as to dim or brighten electric lights

rhe·sus (monkey) (rē'səs) [< Gr. proper name] a small, brownish monkey of India, used in medical research and kept in zoos

rhet·o·ric (ret'ər ik) *n.* [< Gr. *rhētōr*, orator] **1.** the art of using words effectively; esp., the art of prose composition **2.** artificial eloquence — **rhe·tor·i·cal** (ri tôr'i k'l) *adj.* —**rhet'o·ri'cian** (-ə rish'ən) *n.*

rhetorical question a question asked only to produce an effect, no answer being expected

rheum (rōōm) *n.* [< Gr. *rheuma*, a flow] watery discharge from the eyes, nose, etc., as in a cold —**rheum'y** *adj.*

rheumatic fever a disease, usually of children, with fever, painful joints, and inflammation of the heart

rheu·ma·tism (rōō'mə tiz'm) *n.* [see RHEUM] *a popular term for* a painful condition of the joints and muscles —**rheu·mat'ic** (-mat'ik) *adj., n.* —**rheu'ma·toid'** (-mə toid') *adj.*

rheumatoid arthritis a chronic disease with painful swelling of joints

Rh factor (är'āch') [first discovered in *rh*esus monkeys] a group of antigens, usually present in human blood: people who have this factor are **Rh positive**; those who do not are **Rh negative**

rhine·stone (rīn'stōn') *n.* an artificial gem of colorless, bright glass, often cut to look like a diamond

rhi·ni·tis (rī nīt'əs) *n.* [< Gr. *rhis*, nose + -ITIS] inflammation of the mucous membrane of the nose

rhi·no (rī'nō) *n., pl.* -**nos**, -**no** *short for* RHINOCEROS

rhi·noc·er·os (rī näs'ər əs) *n.* [< Gr. *rhis*, nose + *keras*, horn] a large, thick-skinned, plant-eating mammal of Africa and Asia, with one or two upright horns on the snout

rhi·zome (rī'zōm) *n.* [< Gr. *rhiza*, a root] a horizontal, rootlike stem, which usually sends out roots below and leafy shoots above the ground

rho (rō) *n.* the seventeenth letter of the Greek alphabet (P, ρ)

rho·do·den·dron (rō'də den'drən) *n.* [< Gr. *rhodon*, a rose + *dendron*, a tree] a tree or shrub, usually evergreen, with showy pink, white, or purple flowers

rhom·boid (räm'boid) *n.* [see RHOMBUS & -OID] a parallelogram with oblique angles and only the opposite sides equal

rhom·bus (räm'bəs) *n., pl.* -**bus·es**, -**bi** (-bī) [<

Gr. *rhombos,* turnable object] an equilateral parallelogram, esp. one with oblique angles: also **rhomb**

rhu·barb (roo'bärb) *n.* [< Gr. *rhëon,* rhubarb + *barbaron,* foreign] **1.** a plant whose thick, sour stalks are cooked into a sauce, etc. **2.** [Slang] a heated argument

rhyme (rïm) *n.* [prob. < L. *rhythmus,* rhythm] **1.** likeness of sounds at the ends of words or lines of verse **2.** a word that has the same end sound as another **3.** poetry or (a) verse employing this —*vi.* rhymed, rhym'ing **1.** to make rhyming verse **2.** to form a rhyme *["more" rhymes* with "door"] —*vt.* **1.** to put into rhyme **2.** to use as a rhyme

rhythm (rith'm, -əm) *n.* [< Fr. < Gr. *rhythmos,* measure] **1.** movement characterized by a regular recurrence, as of a beat, accent, etc. **2.** the pattern of this in music, verse, etc. — **rhyth'mic, rhyth'mi·cal** *adj.*

rib (rib) *n.* [OE.] **1.** any of the curved bones attached to the spine and enclosing the chest cavity **2.** anything like a rib in appearance or function —*vt.* ribbed, rib'bing **1.** to form with ribs **2.** [Slang] to tease —**ribbed** *adj.* —**rib'less** *adj.*

rib·ald (rib'əld) *adj.* [< OFr. *ribaud,* debauchee] coarsely joking; esp., joking about sex in an earthy way —**rib'ald·ry** *n.*

rib·bon (rib'ən) *n.* [MFr. *riban*] **1.** a narrow strip as of silk or rayon, used for decorating, etc. **2.** [*pl.*] torn shreds **3.** a strip of cloth inked for use in a typewriter, etc.

ri·bo·fla·vin (rï'bə flā'vin) *n.* [< *ribose,* á sugar + L. *flavus,* yellow] a factor of the vitamin B complex found in milk, eggs, liver, fruits, leafy vegetables, etc.

rice (rïs) *n.* [ult. < Gr. *oryza*] **1.** a cereal grass of warm climates, planted in ground under water **2.** its starchy seeds or grain, used as food —*vt.* riced, ric'ing to form (cooked potatoes, etc.) into ricelike granules

rich (rich) *adj.* [OE. *rice,* noble] **1.** having much money or property; wealthy **2.** well supplied (*with*); abounding (*in*) **3.** valuable or costly **4.** full of choice ingredients, as butter, sugar, etc. **5.** *a*) full and mellow: said of sound *b*) deep; vivid: said of colors *c*) very fragrant **6.** abundant **7.** yielding in abundance, as soil, etc. **8.** [Colloq.] very amusing —**the rich** wealthy people collectively —**rich'ness** *n.*

rich·es (rich'iz) *n.pl.* [< OFr. *richesse*] much money, property, etc.; wealth

rick (rik) *n.* [OE. *hreac*] a stack of hay, straw, etc. —*vt.* to pile into ricks

rick·ets (rik'its) *n.* [? < Gr. *rhachis,* spine] a disease, chiefly of children, characterized by a softening and, often, bending of the bones: it is caused by lack of vitamin D

rick·et·y (rik'it ē) *adj.* **1.** having rickets **2.** feeble; weak; shaky —**rick'et·i·ness** *n.*

rick·shaw, rick·sha (rik'shô) *n. same as* JINRIKISHA

ric·o·chet (rik'ə shā') *n.* [Fr.] the rebound or skipping of an object after striking a surface at an angle —*vi.* -cheted' (-shād'), -chet'ing (-shā'iŋ) to make a ricochet

rid (rid) *vt.* rid or rid'ded, rid'ding [< ON. *rythja,* to clear (land)] to free or relieve, as of something undesirable —**get rid of** to dispose of

rid·dance (rid'ns) *n.* a ridding or being rid; clearance or removal

rid·den (rid'n) *pp. of* RIDE

rid·dle¹ (rid''l) *n.* [< OE. *rædan,* to guess] **1.** a puzzling question, etc. requiring some ingenuity to answer **2.** any puzzling person or thing

rid·dle² (rid''l) *vt.* -dled, -dling [OE. *hriddel*] **1.** to make many holes in **2.** to affect every part of *[riddled* with errors]

ride (rïd) *vi.* rode, rid'den, rid'ing [OE. *ridan*] **1.** to be carried along (by a horse, *in* a vehicle, etc.) **2.** to be supported in motion (*on* or *upon*) *[tanks ride* on treads] **3.** to admit of being ridden *[the car rides* smoothly] **4.** to move or float on the water **5.** [Colloq.] to continue undisturbed *[let the matter ride]* —*vt.* **1.** to sit on or in so as to move along **2.** to move over, along, or through (a road, area, etc.) by horse, car, etc. **3.** to control, dominate, etc. *[ridden* by fear] **4.** [Colloq.] to torment, as with ridicule —*n.* **1.** a riding **2.** a thing to ride at an amusement park

rid'er *n.* **1.** one who rides **2.** an addition or amendment to a document

ridge (rij) *n.* [OE. *hrycg*] **1.** the long, narrow crest of something, as of a wave **2.** a long, narrow elevation of land **3.** any narrow, raised strip, as on a fabric **4.** the horizontal line formed by the meeting of two sloping surfaces —*vt., vi.* ridged, ridg'ing to form into or mark with a ridge or ridges

rid·i·cule (rid'ə kyool') *n.* [Fr. < L. *ridere,* to laugh] **1.** the act of making one the object of scornful laughter **2.** words or actions used in doing this —*vt.* -culed', -cul'ing to make fun of; deride

ri·dic·u·lous (ri dik'yə ləs) *adj.* deserving ridicule —**ri·dic'u·lous·ly** *adv.*

rife (rïf) *adj.* [OE. *ryfe*] **1.** frequently occurring; widespread **2.** abounding *[rife* with error]

riff (rif) *n.* [prob. < REFRAIN²] *Jazz* a constantly repeated musical phrase —*vi.* to perform a riff

rif·fle (rif''l) *n.* [< ?] **1.** a ripple in a stream, produced by a reef, etc. **2.** a certain way of shuffling cards

riff·raff (rif'raf') *n.* [< OFr.: see RIFLE² & RAFFLE] those people regarded as worthless or disreputable

ri·fle¹ (rï'f'l) *vt.* -fled, -fling [< Fr. *rifler,* to scrape] to cut spiral grooves within (a gun barrel, etc.) —*n.* a shoulder gun with a rifled barrel: see RIFLING

ri·fle² (rï'f'l) *vt.* -fled, -fling [< OFr. *rifler,* to plunder] **1.** to ransack in order to rob **2.** to take as plunder; steal

ri'fle·man (-mən) *n., pl.* -men a soldier armed with a rifle

ri·fling (rï'fliŋ) *n.* **1.** the cutting of spiral grooves within a gun barrel to make the bullet spin **2.** a system of such grooves

rift (rift) *n.* [< Dan. *rive,* to tear] an opening caused by splitting; cleft —*vt., vi.* to split

rig (rig) *vt.* rigged, rig'ging [< Scand.] **1.** to fit (a ship, mast, etc.) with (sails, shrouds, etc.) **2.** to equip **3.** to arrange dishonestly **4.** [Colloq.] to dress (with *out*) —*n.* **1.** the arrangement of sails, etc. on a vessel **2.** equipment **3.** a tractor-trailer

rig·a·ma·role (rig'ə mə rōl') *n. var. of* RIGMAROLE

rig'ging *n.* the chains, ropes, etc. that support and work masts, sails, etc.

right (rït) *adj.* [< OE. *riht,* straight] **1.** with a straight or perpendicular line **2.** upright; virtuous **3.** correct **4.** fitting; suitable **5.** designating the side meant to be seen **6.** mentally or physically sound **7.** *a*) designating or of that side toward the east when one faces north *b*) closer to the right side of one facing the thing mentioned —*n.* **1.** what is right, just, etc. **2.** a power, privilege, etc. belonging to one by law, nature, etc. **3.** the right side **4.** [*often* R-] *Politics* a conservative or reactionary position, party, etc. (often with *the*) —*adv.* **1.** in a straight line; directly *[go right home]* **2.** in a way that is correct, proper, just, etc. **3.** completely **4.** exactly *[right here]* **5.** on or toward the right hand **6.** very: in certain titles *[the right reverend]* —*vt.* **1.** to put upright **2.** to correct **3.** to put in order —**right away** (or **off**) at once —**right on!** [Slang] precisely! exactly! —**right'ly** *adv.*

right'a·bout'-face' *n. same as* ABOUT-FACE

right angle an angle of 90 degrees

right·eous (rī'chəs) *adj.* **1.** acting justly; upright; virtuous **2.** morally right or justifiable **3.** [Slang] good, satisfying, etc.

right'ful *adj.* **1.** fair and just; right **2.** having a lawful claim —**right'ful·ly** *adv.*

right'-hand' *adj.* **1.** on or directed toward the right **2.** of, for, or with the right hand **3.** most helpful or reliable *[my right-hand man]*

right'-hand'ed *adj.* **1.** using the right hand more skillfully than the left **2.** done with or made for use with the right hand —*adv.* with the right hand

right'ist *n., adj.* conservative or reactionary

right'-mind'ed *adj.* having correct views or sound principles —**right'-mind'ed·ness** *n.*

right of way 1. the right to move first at intersections **2.** land over which a road, power line, etc. passes Also **right'-of-way'**

right wing the more conservative or reactionary section of a political party, group, etc. —**right'-wing'** *adj.*

rig·id (rij'id) *adj.* [< L. *rigere*, be stiff] **1.** not bending or flexible; stiff **2.** not moving; set **3.** severe or strict **4.** allowing no change: said of a dirigible —**ri·gid·i·ty** (ri jid'ə tē) *n.* —**rig'id·ly** *adv.*

rig·ma·role (rig'mə rōl') *n.* [< ME. *rageman rolle*, a document] **1.** rambling talk; nonsense **2.** a fussy or time-wasting procedure

rig·or (rig'ər) *n.* [see RIGID] severity; strictness; hardship: Brit. sp. **rig'our** —**rig'or·ous** *adj.* —**rig'or·ous·ly** *adv.*

rig·or mor·tis (rig'ər môr'tis, rī'gôr) [ModL., stiffness of death] the stiffening of the muscles after death

rile (rīl) *vt.* **riled, ril'ing** [var. of ROIL] [Colloq. or Dial.] to anger; irritate

rill (ril) *n.* [< Du. *ril*] a little brook

rim (rim) *n.* [OE. *rima*, an edge] **1.** an edge, border, or margin, esp. of something circular **2.** the outer part of a wheel —*vt.* **rimmed, rim'ming** to put a rim on

rime¹ (rīm) *n., vt., vi.* **rimed, rim'ing** *same as* RHYME —**rim'er** *n.*

rime² (rīm) *n.* [OE. *hrim*] hoarfrost

rind (rīnd) *n.* [OE.] a hard outer layer or coating, as on fruit, cheese, bacon, etc.

ring¹ (riŋ) *vi.* **rang** or chiefly dial. **rung, rung, ring'ing** [OE. *hringan*] **1.** to give forth the resonant sound of a bell **2.** to seem *[to ring true]* **3.** to sound a bell, esp. as a summons **4.** to resound *[to ring with laughter]* **5.** to have a ringing sensation, as the ears —*vt.* **1.** to cause (a bell, etc.) to ring **2.** to signal, announce, etc. as by ringing **3.** to call by telephone —*n.* **1.** the sound of a bell **2.** a characteristic quality *[the ring of truth]* **3.** the act of ringing a bell **4.** a telephone call

ring² (riŋ) *n.* [OE. *hring*] **1.** an ornamental circular band worn on a finger **2.** any similar band *[a key ring]* **3.** a circular line, mark, or figure **4.** a group of people or things in a circle **5.** a group working to advance its own interests, esp. dishonestly **6.** an enclosed area for contests, exhibitions, etc. *[a circus ring]* **7.** prizefighting (with *the*) —*vt.* **ringed, ring'ing 1.**

to encircle **2.** to form into, or furnish with, a ring or rings —**run rings around** [Colloq.] **1.** to outrun easily **2.** to excel greatly

ring'er¹ *n.* a horseshoe, etc. thrown so that it encircles the peg

ring'er² *n.* **1.** one that rings a bell, etc. **2.** [Slang] *a)* a person or thing closely resembling another *b)* a fraudulent substitute in a competition

ring'lead'er *n.* one who leads others, esp. in unlawful acts, etc.

ring'let (-lit) *n.* **1.** a little ring **2.** a curl of hair, esp. a long one

ring'mas'ter *n.* a man who directs the performances in a circus ring

ring'side' *n.* the place just outside the ring, as at a boxing match

ring'worm' *n.* a contagious skin disease caused by a fungus

rink (riŋk) *n.* [< OFr. *renc*, a rank] **1.** a smooth expanse of ice for skating **2.** a smooth floor for roller-skating

rinse (rins) *vt.* **rinsed, rins'ing** [ult. < L. *recens*, fresh] **1.** to wash or flush lightly **2.** to remove soap, etc. from with clean water —*n.* **1.** a rinsing or the liquid used **2.** a solution for coloring hair

ri·ot (rī'ət) *n.* [< OFr. *rihoter*, to make a disturbance] **1.** wild or violent disorder, confusion, etc.; esp., a violent disturbance of the peace **2.** a bright display *[a riot of color]* **3.** [Colloq.] something very amusing —*vi.* to take part in a public disturbance —**ri'ot·er** *n.* —**ri'ot·ous** *adj.* —**ri'ot·ous·ly** *adv.*

rip (rip) *vt.* **ripped, rip'ping** [LME. *rippen*] **1.** *a)* to cut or tear apart roughly *b)* to remove in this way (with *off, out,* etc.) *c)* to sever (stitches) so as to open (a seam, etc.) **2.** to saw (wood) along the grain —*vi.* **1.** to become torn **2.** [Colloq.] to rush; speed —*n.* a torn place or burst seam —**rip off** [Slang] **1.** to steal or rob **2.** to cheat, exploit, etc. —**rip'per** *n.*

rip cord a cord, etc. pulled to open a parachute during descent

ripe (rīp) *adj.* [OE.] **1.** ready to be harvested, as grain or fruit **2.** of sufficient age, etc. to be used *[ripe cheese]* **3.** highly developed; mature **4.** fully prepared *[ripe for marriage]* —**ripe'ly** *adv.* —**ripe'ness** *n.*

rip·en (rī'pən) *vi., vt.* to become or make ripe; mature; age, cure, etc.

rip'-off' *n.* [Slang] a stealing, robbing, cheating, exploiting, etc.

ri·poste, ri·post (ri pōst') *n.* [< Fr. < L. *respondere,* to answer] a sharp, swift retort

rip·ple (rip''l) *vi., vt.* **-pled, -pling** [prob. < RIP] to form or have little waves on the surface (of) —*n.* a small wave, or a movement, appearance, etc. like this —**rip'ply** (-lē) *adj.* **-pli·er, -pli·est**

rip'-roar'ing (-rôr'iŋ) *adj.* [Slang] boisterous; uproarious

rip'saw' *n.* a saw with coarse teeth, for cutting wood along the grain

rise (rīz) *vi.* **rose, ris·en** (riz'n), **ris'ing** [OE. *risan*] **1.** to stand or sit up after sitting, lying, etc. **2.** to rebel; revolt **3.** to go up; ascend **4.** to appear above the horizon *[the moon rose]* **5.** to attain a higher level, status, rank, etc. **6.** to extend, slant, or move upward **7.** to increase in amount, degree, etc. **8.** to expand and swell, as dough with yeast **9.** to originate; begin —*vt.* to cause to rise —*n.* **1.** upward motion; ascent **2.** an advance in status, rank, etc. **3.** a slope upward **4.** an increase in degree, amount, etc. **5.** a beginning, origin, etc. —**give rise to** to bring about

ris'er *n.* **1.** a person or thing that rises **2.** a vertical piece between the steps in a stairway

ris·i·ble (riz′ə b′l) *adj.* [Fr. < L. *ridere,* to laugh] causing laughter; funny —**ris′i·bil′i·ty** *n., pl.* **-ties**

risk (risk) *n.* [< Fr. < It. *risco*] the chance of injury, damage, or loss; hazard —*vt.* **1.** to expose to risk /to *risk* one's life/ **2.** to take the chance of /to *risk* a fight/ —**risk′y** *adj.* **-i·er, -i·est**

ris·qué (ris kā′) *adj.* [Fr. < *risquer,* to risk] very close to being improper or indecent; suggestive

rite (rīt) *n.* [L. *ritus*] a solemn or ceremonial act, as in religious use

rit·u·al (rich′oo wəl) *adj.* of, like, or done as a rite —*n.* a system or form of rites, religious or otherwise —**rit′u·al·ly** *adv.*

ri·val (rī′v'l) *n.* [Fr. < L. *rivalis*] **1.** one who tries to get the same thing as another, or to equal or surpass another; competitor **2.** an equal or a satisfactory substitute —*adj.* being a rival; competing —*vt.* **-valed** or **-valled, -val·ing** or **-val·ling 1.** to try to equal or surpass **2.** to equal —**ri′val·ry** *n., pl.* **-ries**

rive (rīv) *vt., vi.* **rived, riv·en** (riv′'n) or **rived, riv′ing** [ON. *rifa*] **1.** to rend **2.** to split; cleave

riv·er (riv′ər) *n.* [< L. *ripa,* a bank] a natural stream of water larger than a creek, emptying into an ocean, lake, etc.

river basin the area drained by a river and its tributaries

riv′er·side′ *n.* the bank of a river

riv·et (riv′it) *n.* [< MFr. *river,* to clinch] a metal bolt with a head and a plain end that is flattened after the bolt is passed through parts to be held together —*vt.* to fasten firmly, as with rivets —**riv′et·er** *n.*

riv·u·let (riv′yoo lit) *n.* [< It. < L. *rivus,* a brook] a little stream

rm. *pl.* **rms. 1.** ream **2.** room

R.N., RN Registered Nurse

RNA [< *r(ibo)n(ucleic) a(cid)*] an essential component of all living matter: one form carries genetic information

roach¹ (rōch) *n. same as* COCKROACH

roach² (rōch) *n., pl.* **roach, roach′es** [< OFr. < *roche*] a freshwater fish related to the carp

road (rōd) *n.* [OE. *rad,* a ride] **1.** a way made for traveling; highway **2.** a way; course /the *road* to fortune/ **3.** [*often pl.*] a place near shore where ships can ride at anchor

road′bed′ *n.* the foundation laid for railroad tracks or for a highway, etc.

road′block′ *n.* a blockade set up in a road to prevent movement of vehicles

road runner a long-tailed, crested desert bird of the SW U.S. and N Mexico, that can run swiftly

road′show′ *n.* **1.** a touring theatrical show **2.** a reserved-seat film showing

road′side′ *n.* the side of a road —*adj.* on or at the side of a road

road′way′ *n.* **1.** a road **2.** the part of a road along which cars, trucks, etc. move

roam (rōm) *vt., vi.* [ME. *romen*] to wander aimlessly (over or through) —**roam′er** *n.*

roan (rōn) *adj.* [< OSp. *roano*] bay, black, etc., with a thick sprinkling of white hairs —*n.* a roan horse

roar (rôr) *vi.* [OE. *rarian*] **1.** to make a loud, deep, rumbling sound **2.** to laugh boisterously —*vt.* to utter with a roar —*n.* a loud, deep, rumbling sound —**roar′er** *n.*

roast (rōst) *vt.* [< OFr. *rostir*] **1.** to cook (meat, etc.) with little or no moisture, as in an oven **2.** to process (coffee, etc.) by exposure to heat **3.** to expose to great heat **4.** [Colloq.] to criticize severely —*vi.* **1.** to undergo roasting **2.** to be or become very hot —*n.* **1.** roasted meat **2.** a cut of meat for roasting **3.** a picnic at which food is roasted —*adj.* roasted

rob (räb) *vt.* **robbed, rob′bing** [< OFr. *rober*] **1.** to take property from unlawfully by force **2.** to deprive of something unjustly or injuriously —*vi.* to commit robbery —**rob′ber** *n.* —**rob′ber·y** *n., pl.* **-ies**

robe (rōb) *n.* [< OFr.] **1.** a long, loose outer garment; specif., *a*) such a garment worn to show rank or office, as by a judge *b*) a bathrobe or dressing gown **2.** a covering or wrap /a lap *robe*/ —*vt., vi.* **robed, rob′ing** to dress in or cover with a robe

rob·in (räb′in) *n.* [< OFr. dim. of *Robert*] a large N. American thrush with a dull-red breast: also **robin redbreast**

Robin Hood *Eng. Legend* the leader of a band of outlaws that robbed the rich to help the poor

Rob·in·son Cru·soe (räb′in s'n kroo′sō) the title hero of Defoe's novel (1719) about a shipwrecked sailor

ro·bot (rō′bət, -bät) *n.* [< Czech < OBulg. *rabu,* servant] **1.** a mechanical device operating in a seemingly human way **2.** a person acting or working mechanically

ro·bust (rō bust′, rō′bust) *adj.* [< L. *robur,* a hard oak] strong and healthy; hardy

rock¹ (räk) *n.* [< OFr. *roche*] **1.** a large mass of stone **2.** broken pieces of stone **3.** mineral matter formed in masses in the earth's crust **4.** anything like a rock; esp., a firm support, etc. **5.** [Colloq.] a stone —**on the rocks** [Colloq.] **1.** ruined **2.** bankrupt **3.** served over ice cubes: said of liquor, etc.

rock² (räk) *vt., vi.* [OE. *roccian*] **1.** to move back and forth or from side to side **2.** to sway strongly; shake —*n.* **1.** a rocking motion **2.** *a*) *same as* ROCK-AND-ROLL *b*) popular music evolved from rock-and-roll, folk music, country music, etc.

rock-and-roll (räk′'n rōl′) *n.* a form of popular music with a strong, regular beat, which evolved from jazz and the blues

rock bottom the lowest level

rock′-bound′ *adj.* surrounded or covered by rocks

rock′er *n.* **1.** either of the curved pieces on which a cradle, etc. rocks **2.** a chair mounted on such pieces: also **rocking chair**

rock·et (räk′it) *n.* [It. *rocchetta,* a spool] any device driven forward by gases escaping through a rear vent, as a firework, projectile, or the propulsion mechanism of a spacecraft —*vi.* to soar

rock′et·ry (-ə trē) *n.* the science of designing, building, and launching rockets

rocking horse a child's toy horse mounted on rockers or springs

rock′-ribbed′ *adj.* **1.** having rocky ridges **2.** firm; unyielding

rock salt common salt in solid masses

rock wool a fibrous material made from molten rock, used for insulation

rock·y¹ (räk′ē) *adj.* **-i·er, -i·est 1.** full of rocks **2.** consisting of rocks **3.** like a rock; firm, hard, etc. —**rock′i·ness** *n.*

rock·y² (räk′ē) *adj.* **-i·er, -i·est** inclined to rock; unsteady —**rock′i·ness** *n.*

Rocky Mountain goat a white, goatlike antelope of the mountains of northwest N. America

ro·co·co (rə kō′kō) *n.* [Fr. < *rocaille,* shell work] an elaborate style of architecture and

decoration, imitating foliage, scrolls, etc. —*adj.*
1. of or in rococo **2.** too elaborate
rod (räd) *n.* [OE. *rodd*] **1.** a straight stick, bar,
etc. **2.** a stick for beating as punishment **3.** a
scepter carried as a symbol of office **4.** a measure of length equal to 5 1/2 yards **5.** a pole for
fishing
rode (rōd) *pt. of* RIDE
ro·dent (rōd′nt) *n.* [< L. *rodere*, gnaw] any of
various gnawing mammals, including rats,
mice, beavers, etc. —*adj.* gnawing
ro·de·o (rō′dē ō′, rō dā′ō) *n., pl.* -**os**′ [Sp. < L.
rotare, to turn] a public exhibition of the skills
of cowboys, as broncobusting, lassoing, etc.
roe¹ (rō) *n.* [ME. *rowe*] fish eggs
roe² (rō) *n., pl.* **roe, roes** [< OE. *ra*] a small,
agile European and Asian deer
roe·buck (rō′buk′) *n.* the male roe deer
roent·gen (rent′gən) *n.* [< W. K. *Roentgen*
(1845–1923), Ger. physicist] the unit for
measuring the radiation of X-rays (**Roentgen
rays**) or gamma rays
Rog·er (räj′ər) *interj.* [< name of signal flag for
R] [*also* r-] **1.** received: used to indicate reception of a radio message **2.** [Colloq.] right! OK!
rogue (rōg) *n.* [< ?] **1.** a scoundrel **2.** a fun-
loving, mischievous person —**ro·guer·y** (rō′gər
ē) *n.* —**ro·guish** (rō′gish) *adj.*
roil (roil) *vt.* [< Fr. < L. *robigo*, rust] **1.** to
make (a liquid) cloudy, muddy, etc. by stirring
up the sediment **2.** to make angry
roist·er (rois′tər) *vi.* [see RUSTIC] **1.** to swagger
2. to be lively and noisy
role, rôle (rōl) *n.* [Fr. *rôle*, a roll: from roll containing actor's part] **1.** a part, or character,
that an actor plays **2.** a function assumed by
someone [an advisory *role*]
roll (rōl) *vi.* [< L. *rota*, wheel] **1.** to move by
turning over and over **2.** to move on wheels **3.**
to pass [the years *rolled* by] **4.** to extend in
gentle swells **5.** to make a loud, rising and falling sound [thunder *rolls*] **6.** to move or rock
from side to side —*vt.* **1.** to move by turning
over and over **2.** to move on wheels or rollers
3. to utter with a full, flowing sound **4.** to say
with a trill [to *roll* one's r's] **5.** to give a swaying motion to **6.** to move around or from side
to side [to *roll* one's eyes] **7.** to wind into a
ball or cylinder [to *roll* a cigarette] **8.** to flat-
ten or spread —*n.* **1.** a rolling **2.** a scroll **3.** a
list of names **4.** something rolled into a cylinder **5.** a small, shaped piece of bread **6.** a
swaying motion **7.** a loud, reverberating sound,
as of thunder **8.** a slight swell on a surface
roll call the reading aloud of a roll to find out
who is absent
roll′er *n.* **1.** one that rolls **2.** a cylinder on
which something is rolled, or a heavy one used
to crush, smooth, or spread something **3.** a
long, heavy wave
roller coaster an amusement ride in which
small cars move on tracks that dip and curve
sharply
roller skate a skate with wheels: see SKATE¹
(sense 2) —**roll′er-skate**′ *vi.* -**skat′ed**, -**skat′ing**
rol·lick (räl′ik) *vi.* [< ? FROLIC] to play or
behave in a gay, carefree way —**rol′lick·ing** *adj.*
rolling pin a heavy, smooth cylinder of wood,
glass, etc., used to roll out dough
rolling stock all the vehicles of a railroad or a
trucking company
ro·ly-po·ly (rō′lē pō′lē) *adj.* [< ROLL] short and
plump; pudgy
Rom. Roman
ro·maine (rō mān′) *n.* [Fr., Roman] a kind of
lettuce with long leaves forming a long, slender head

Ro·man (rō′mən) *adj.* **1.** of or characteristic of
ancient or modern Rome, its people, etc. **2.** of
the Roman Catholic Church **3.** [*usually* r-]
designating or of the usual upright style of
printing types —*n.* **1.** a native or inhabitant of
ancient or modern Rome **2.** [*usually* r-] roman
type or characters
Roman candle a firework consisting of a long
tube that sends out balls of fire, etc.
Roman Catholic 1. of the Christian church
(**Roman Catholic Church**) headed by the Pope
2. a member of this church
ro·mance (rō mans′; *also, for n.*, rō′mans) *adj.*
[ult. < L. *Romanicus*, Roman] designating or
of any of the languages derived from Vulgar
Latin, as Italian, Spanish, French, etc. —*n.* **1.** a
long poem or tale, orig. written in a Romance
language, about knights, adventure, and love
2. a novel of love, adventure, etc. **3.** excitement, love, etc. of the kind found in such
literature **4.** a love affair —*vt., vi.* -**manced**′,
-**manc′ing** [Colloq.] ·to woo; court —**ro·manc′er**
n.
Roman Empire empire of the ancient Romans
(27 B.C.–395 A.D.)
Roman numerals Roman letters used as numerals: I = 1, V = 5, X = 10, L = 50, C =
100, D = 500, and M = 1,000
ro·man·tic (rō man′tik) *adj.* **1.** of, like, or
characterized by romance **2.** fanciful or ·ficti-
tious **3.** not practical; visionary **4.** full of
thoughts, feelings, etc. of romance **5.** suited for
romance **6.** [*often* R-] of a 19th-cent. cultural
movement characterized by freedom of form
and spirit, emphasis on feeling and originality,
etc. —*n.* a romantic person —**ro·man′ti·cal·ly**
adv. —**ro·man′ti·cism** (-tə siz′m) *n.*
Rom·a·ny (räm′ə nē, rō′mə-) *n.* [< Gypsy *rom*,
a man] the language of the Gypsies
Ro·me·o (rō′mē ō′) the young lover in
Shakespeare's tragedy *Romeo and Juliet*
romp (rämp) *n.* [prob. < OFr. *ramper*, climb]
boisterous, lively play —*vi.* to play in a boisterous, lively way
romp′er *n.* **1.** one who romps **2.** [*pl.*] a loose,
one-piece outer garment with bloomerlike
pants, for a small child
Rom·u·lus (räm′yoo ləs) *Rom. Myth.* founder
and first king of Rome: he and his twin
brother Remus were suckled by a she-wolf
rood (rōōd) *n.* [OE. *rod*] **1.** a crucifix **2.** a measure of area usually equal to 1/4 acre
roof (rōōf, roof) *n., pl.* **roofs** [OE. *hrof*] **1.** the
outside top covering of a building **2.** anything
like this [the *roof* of the mouth] —*vt.* to cover
as with a roof
roof′er *n.* a builder or repairer of roofs
roof′ing *n.* material for roofs
rook¹ (rook) *n.* [OE. *hroc*] a crowlike European
bird —*vt., vi.* to swindle; cheat
rook² (rook) *n.* [< Per. *rukh*] *Chess* a piece
moving only horizontally or vertically
rook·er·y (rook′ər ē) *n., pl.* -**ies** a breeding
place or colony of rooks
rook·ie (rook′ē) *n.* [< ?] [Slang] **1.** an inexperienced army recruit **2.** any novice
room (rōōm, room) *n.* [OE. *rum*] **1.** space to
contain something **2.** opportunity [*room* for
doubt] **3.** an interior space enclosed or set
apart by walls **4.** [*pl.*] living quarters **5.** the
people in a room —*vi., vt.* to have, or provide
with, lodgings —**room′ful**′ *n.* —**room′y** *adj.* -**i·er**,
-**i·est**
room and board lodging and meals
room′er *n.* one who rents lodgings; lodger
room·ette (rōō met′) *n.* a small compartment
in a railroad sleeping car

rooming house a house with furnished rooms for rent

room'mate' *n.* a person with whom one shares a room or rooms

roost (rōōst) *n.* [OE. *hrost*] 1. a perch on which birds, esp. domestic fowls, can rest or sleep 2. a place with perches for birds 3. a place for resting, sleeping, etc. —*vi.* 1. to sit, sleep, etc. on a perch 2. to settle down, as for the night

roost·er (rōōs'tər) *n.* the male of the chicken

root' (rōōt, root) *n.* [< ON. *rot*] 1. the part of a plant, usually underground, that anchors the plant, draws water and food from the soil, etc. 2. the embedded part of a tooth, hair, etc. 3. a source or cause 4. a supporting or essential part 5. a quantity that, multiplied by itself a specified number of times, produces a given quantity 6. *same as* BASE (*n.* 3) —*vi.* to take root —*vt.* 1. to fix the roots of in the ground 2. to establish; settle —**take root** 1. to begin growing by putting out roots 2. to become settled

root² (rōōt, root) *vt.* [< OE. *wrot*, snout] to dig (*up* or *out*) as with the snout —*vi.* 1. to search about; rummage 2. [Colloq.] to encourage a team, etc.: usually with *for*

root beer a carbonated drink made of extracts from the roots of certain plants, etc.

root'let (-lit) *n.* a little root

rope (rōp) *n.* [OE. *rap*] 1. a thick, strong cord made of intertwisted strands of fiber, etc. 2. a ropelike string of things —*vt.* **roped, rop'ing** 1. to fasten or tie with a rope 2. to mark off or enclose with a rope 3. to catch with a lasso — **know the ropes** [Colloq.] to know the procedures —**rope in** [Slang] to trick into doing something

Roque·fort (cheese) (rōk'fərt) [< *Roquefort*, France, where orig. made] a strong cheese with a bluish mold

Ror·schach test (rôr'shäk)' [< H. *Rorschach* (1884-1922), Swiss psychiatrist] *Psychol.* a personality test in which responses to various inkblot designs are interpreted

ro·sa·ry (rō'zər ē) *n., pl.* **-ries** [ML. *rosarium*] *R.C.Ch.* a string of beads used to keep count in saying prayers

rose¹ (rōz) *n.* [< L. *rosa*] 1. a shrub with prickly stems and flowers of red, pink, white, yellow, etc. 2. its flower 3. pinkish red or purplish red —*adj.* rose-colored

rose² (rōz) *pt. of* RISE

ro·sé (rō zā') *n.* [Fr.] a light, pink wine

ro·se·ate (rō'zē it, -āt') *adj.* rose-colored

rose'bud' *n.* the bud of a rose

rose'bush' *n.* a shrub that bears roses

rose·mar·y (rōz'mer'ē) *n.* [ult. < L. *ros marinus*, dew of the sea] an evergreen shrub of the mint family, with fragrant leaves used in cooking, etc.

ro·sette (rō zet') *n.* [Fr.] an ornament, arrangement, etc. suggesting a rose

rose water a preparation consisting of water and attar of roses, used as a perfume

rose'wood' *n.* [< its odor] 1. a hard, reddish wood, used in furniture, etc. 2. a tropical tree yielding such wood

Rosh Ha·sha·na (rōsh' hə shô'nə, -shä'-) the Jewish New Year: also **Rosh Hashona**

ros·in (räz'n) *n.* [see RESIN] the hard, brittle resin left after the distillation of crude turpentine: it is rubbed on violin bows, used in making varnish, etc.

ros·ter (räs'tər) *n.* [< Du. *rooster*] a list or roll, as of military personnel

ros·trum (räs'trəm) *n., pl.* **-trums, -tra** (-trə) [L., (ship's) beak] a platform for public speaking — **ros'tral** *adj.*

ros·y (rō'zē) *adj.* **-i·er, -i·est** 1. rose-red or pink [*rosy cheeks*] 2. bright, promising, etc. [*a rosy future*] —**ros'i·ness** *n.*

rot (rät) *vi., vt.* **rot'ted, rot'ting** [OE. *rotian*] to decompose; decay —*n.* 1. a rotting 2. something rotten 3. a plant or animal disease causing decay 4. [Slang] nonsense

ro·ta·ry (rōt'ər ē) *adj.* [< L. *rota*, wheel] 1. turning around a central point or axis, as a wheel 2. having rotating parts [*a rotary press*]

ro·tate (rō'tāt) *vi., vt.* **-tat·ed, -tat·ing** [< L. *rota*, wheel] 1. to turn around an axis 2. to change in regular succession —**ro·ta'tion** *n.* — **ro'ta·to'ry** (-tə tôr'ē) *adj.*

ROTC, R.O.T.C. Reserve Officers' Training Corps

rote (rōt) *n.* [< ?] a fixed, mechanical way of doing something —**by rote** by memory alone, without thought

ro·tis·ser·ie (rō tis'ər ē) *n.* [Fr. < MFr. *rostir*, to roast] a grill with an electrically turned spit

ro·to·gra·vure (rōt'ə grə vyoor') *n.* [< L. *rota*, wheel + Fr. *gravure*, engraving] 1. a process of printing pictures, etc. on a rotary press using cylinders etched from photographic plates 2. a newspaper pictorial section printed by this process

ro·tor (rōt'ər) *n.* [< ROTATE] 1. the rotating part of a motor, dynamo, etc. 2. a system of rotating airfoils, as on a helicopter

rot·ten (rät''n) *adj.* [ON. *rotinn*] 1. decayed; spoiled 2. smelling of decay 3. morally corrupt 4. unsound, as if decayed within 5. [Slang] very bad, disagreeable, etc.

ro·tund (rō tund') *adj.* [L. *rotundus*] round or rounded out; plump —**ro·tun'di·ty** *n.*

ro·tun·da (rō tun'də) *n.* [< It. < L. *rotundus*, rotund] a round building, hall, or room, esp. one with a dome

rou·é (rōō ā') *n.* [Fr. < *rouer*, to break on the wheel] a dissipated man; rake

rouge (rōōzh) *n.* [Fr., red] 1. a reddish cosmetic powder, paste, etc. for coloring the cheeks and lips 2. a reddish powder for polishing jewelry, etc. —*vi., vt.* **rouged, roug'ing** to use cosmetic rouge (on)

rough (ruf) *adj.* [OE. *ruh*] 1. not smooth or level; uneven 2. shaggy [*a rough coat*] 3. *a*) stormy [*rough weather*] *b*) disorderly [*rough play*] 4. harsh or coarse 5. lacking comforts and conveniences 6. not polished or finished; crude 7. approximate [*a rough guess*] 8. [Colloq.] difficult [*a rough time*] —*n.* 1. rough ground, material, condition, etc. 2. *Golf* any part of the course where grass, etc. grows uncut —*adv.* in a rough manner —*vt.* 1. to make rough 2. to treat roughly (often with *up*) 3. to make or shape roughly (usually with *in* or *out*) —*vi.* to behave roughly —**rough it** to live without comforts —**rough'ly** *adv.* —**rough'ness** *n.*

rough'age (-ij) *n.* rough or coarse food or fodder, as bran, straw, etc.

rough'en *vt., vi.* to make or become rough

rough'-hew' *vt.* **-hewed', -hewed'** or **-hewn', -hew'ing** 1. to hew (timber, stone, etc.) roughly, or without smoothing 2. to form roughly Also **roughhew**

rough'house' (-hous') *n.* [Slang] rough or boisterous play, fighting, etc. —*vt., vi.* **-housed', -hous'ing** [Slang] to treat or act roughly

rough'neck' *n.* [Slang] a rowdy

rough'shod' *adj.* shod with horseshoes having metal points to prevent slipping —**ride roughshod over** to treat harshly

rou·lette (rōō let') *n.* [Fr. < L. *rota*, wheel] a gambling game played by rolling a small ball around a shallow bowl with a revolving inner disk (**roulette wheel**) with red and black numbered compartments

round (round) *adj.* [< L. *rotundus*, rotund] **1.** shaped like a ball, circle, or cylinder **2.** plump **3.** full; complete [a *round* dozen] **4.** expressed by a whole number, or in tens, hundreds, etc. **5.** large; considerable [a *round* sum] **6.** brisk; vigorous [a *round* pace] —*n.* **1.** something round **2.** the part of a beef animal between the rump and the leg **3.** movement in a circular course **4.** a series or succession [a *round* of parties] **5.** [*often pl.*] a regular, customary circuit, as by a watchman **6.** *a*) a single shot from a rifle, etc. or from a number of rifles fired together *b*) ammunition for such a shot **7.** a single outburst, as of applause **8.** a single period of action in certain games **9.** a short song which one group begins singing when another has reached the second phrase, etc. —*vt.* **1.** to make round **2.** to make plump **3.** to express as a round number (usually with *off*) **4.** to complete; finish **5.** to go or pass around —*vi.* **1.** to make a circuit **2.** to turn; reverse direction **3.** to become plump —*adv.* **1.** in a circle **2.** through a recurring period of time [to work the year *round*] **3.** from one to another [the peddler came *round*] **4.** in circumference [ten feet *round*] **5.** on all sides **6.** about; near **7.** in a roundabout way **8.** here and there **9.** with a rotating movement **10.** in the opposite direction —*prep.* **1.** so as to encircle **2.** on all sides of **3.** in the vicinity of **4.** in a circuit; through In the U.S., *round* (*adv. & prep.*) is generally superseded by *around* —**in the round 1.** in an arena theater **2.** in full, rounded form: said of sculpture **3.** in full detail —**round about** in or to the opposite direction —**round up** to collect in a herd, group, etc. —**round'ness** *n.*

round'a·bout' *adj.* **1.** indirect; circuitous **2.** encircling; enclosing

roun·de·lay (roun'də lā') *n.* [< OFr. *rondel*, a short lyrical poem] a simple song in which some phrase, line, etc. is continually repeated

round'house' *n.* a circular building with a turntable, for storing and repairing locomotives

round'ly *adv.* **1.** in a round form **2.** vigorously **3.** fully; completely

round'-shoul'dered *adj.* stooped because the shoulders are bent forward

Round Table 1. the table around which King Arthur and his knights sat **2.** [r- t-] an informal discussion group

round'-the-clock' *adj., adv.* continuous(ly)

round trip a trip to a place and back again —**round'-trip'** *adj.*

round'up' *n.* **1.** a driving together of cattle, etc. on the range, as for branding **2.** any similar collecting **3.** a summary

round'worm' *n.* a hookworm or similar round, unsegmented worm

rouse (rouz) *vt., vi.* **roused, rous'ing** [LME. *rowsen*] **1.** to stir up; excite or become excited **2.** to wake

roust·a·bout (roust'ə bout') *n.* [< ROUSE + ABOUT] an unskilled or transient laborer, as in circuses

rout[1] (rout) *n.* [< L. *rupta*, broken] **1.** a rabble **2.** a disorderly flight **3.** an overwhelming defeat —*vt.* **1.** to put to flight **2.** to defeat overwhelmingly

rout[2] (rout) *vt.* [< ROOT[2]] to force out —**rout out 1.** to scoop, gouge, or hollow out **2.** to make (a person) get out

route (root, rout) *n.* [< L. *rupta* (*via*), broken (path)] **1.** a road, etc. for traveling; esp., a

highway **2.** a regular course, as in delivering mail, etc. —*vt.* **rout'ed, rout'ing 1.** to send by a specified route **2.** to fix the order of procedure of

rou·tine (roo tēn') *n.* [see prec.] a regular procedure, customary or prescribed —*adj.* like or using routine —**rou·tine'ly** *adv.*

rove (rōv) *vt., vi.* **roved, rov'ing** [< ?] to wander about; roam —**rov'er** *n.*

row[1] (rō) *n.* [OE. *ræw*] **1.** a number of people or things in a line **2.** any of the lines of seats in a theater, etc.

row[2] (rō) *vt., vi.* [OE. *rowan*] **1.** to propel (a boat) with oars **2.** to carry in a rowboat —*n.* a trip by rowboat —**row'er** *n.*

row[3] (rou) *n., vi.* [< ? ROUSE] quarrel, squabble, or brawl

row'boat' *n.* a boat made to be rowed

row·dy (rou'dē) *n., pl.* **-dies** [< ? ROW[3]] a rough, quarrelsome, and disorderly person; hoodlum —*adj.* **-di·er, -di·est** rough, quarrelsome, etc. —**row'di·ness** *n.*

row·el (rou'əl) *n.* [ult. < L. *rota*, wheel] a small wheel with sharp points, forming the end of a spur

roy·al (roi'əl) *adj.* [< L. *regalis*] **1.** of a king or queen **2.** of a kingdom **3.** suitable for a king or queen; magnificent, stately, etc. —**roy'al·ly** *adv.*

roy'al·ist *n.* one who supports a monarch or monarchy, esp. in times of revolution

roy·al·ty *n., pl.* **-ties 1.** the rank or power of a king or queen **2.** a royal person or persons **3.** royal quality **4.** a share of the proceeds from a patent, book, etc. paid to the owner, author, etc.

rpm, r.p.m. revolutions per minute

R.R., RR railroad

R.S.V.P., r.s.v.p. [Fr. *répondez s'il vous plaît*] please reply

rub (rub) *vt.* **rubbed, rub'bing** [ME. *rubben*] **1.** to move (one's hand, a cloth, etc.) back and forth over (something) firmly **2.** to spread (polish, salve, etc.) on a surface **3.** to move (things) over each other with pressure and friction **4.** to make sore by rubbing **5.** to remove by rubbing (*out, off*, etc.) —*vi.* **1.** to move with pressure and friction (*on, against*, etc.) **2.** to rub something —*n.* **1.** a rubbing **2.** an obstacle, difficulty, or source of irritation —**rub down 1.** to massage **2.** to smooth, polish, etc. by rubbing —**rub the wrong way** to annoy or irritate

rub·ber[1] (rub'ər) *n.* **1.** one that rubs **2.** [from use as an eraser] an elastic substance made from the milky sap of various tropical plants, or synthetically **3.** something made of this substance; specif., a low-cut overshoe —*adj.* made of rubber —**rub'ber·y** *adj.*

rub·ber[2] (rub'ər) *n.* [< ?] the deciding game in a series: usually **rubber game**

rubber band a narrow, continuous band of rubber as for holding objects together

rubber cement an adhesive of unvulcanized rubber in a solvent that quickly evaporates when exposed to air

rub'ber·ize' (-īz') *vt.* **-ized', -iz'ing** to coat or impregnate with rubber

rubber plant 1. any plant yielding latex **2.** a house plant with large, glossy, leathery leaves

rubber stamp 1. a stamp of rubber, inked for printing signatures, dates, etc. **2.** [Colloq.] *a*) a person, bureau, etc. that approves something in a routine way *b*) any routine approval —**rub'ber-stamp'** *vt., adj.*

rub·bish (rub'ish) *n.* [ult. < base of RUB] **1.** any material thrown away as worthless; trash **2.** nonsense

rub·ble (rub′'l) *n.* [akin to RUBBISH] rough, broken pieces of stone, brick, etc.

rub′down′ *n.* a massage

rube (rōōb) *n.* [< name *Reuben*] a country person regarded as simple, unsophisticated, etc.

ru·bel·la (rōō bel′ə) *n.* [< L. *ruber*, red] a contagious virus disease, characterized by small red spots on the skin

ru·bi·cund (rōō′bi kund′) *adj.* [< L. *ruber*, red] reddish; ruddy

ru·ble (rōō′b'l) *n.* [Russ. *rubl′*] the monetary unit of the U.S.S.R.

ru·bric (rōō′brik) *n.* [< L. *ruber*, red] **1.** a section heading, direction, etc. often in red (as in a prayerbook) **2.** any rule, explanatory comment, etc.

ru·by (rōō′bē) *n., pl.* **-bies** [< L. *rubeus*, reddish] **1.** a clear, deep-red variety of corundum, valued as a precious stone **2.** deep red — *adj.* deep-red

ruck·sack (ruk′sak) *n.* [G. < *rücken*, the back + *sack*, a sack] a kind of knapsack

ruck·us (ruk′əs) *n.* [prob. a merging of earlier *ruction*, uproar & RUMPUS] [Colloq.] noisy confusion; disturbance; row

rud·der (rud′ər) *n.* [OE. *rother*, steering oar] a broad, flat, movable piece hinged to the rear of a ship or aircraft, used for steering

rud·dy (rud′ē) *adj.* **-di·er, -di·est** [OE. *rudig*] **1.** having a healthy red color **2.** red or reddish — **rud′di·ness** *n.*

rude (rōōd) *adj.* **rud′er, rud′est** [< L. *rudis*] **1.** crude; rough **2.** barbarous **3.** unrefined; uncouth **4.** discourteous **5.** primitive —**rude′ly** *adv.* —**rude′ness** *n.*

ru·di·ment (rōō′də mənt) *n.* [< L. *rudis*, rude] **1.** a first principle or element, as of a subject to be learned **2.** a first slight beginning of something —**ru′di·men′ta·ry** (-men′tər ē) *adj.*

rue¹ (rōō) *vt., vi.* rued, ru′ing [OE. *hreowan*] to feel sorrow or remorse (for); regret; repent —*n.* [Archaic] sorrow —**rue′ful** *adj.* —**rue′ful·ly** *adv.*

rue² (rōō) *n.* [< Gr. *rhytē*] a strong-scented herb with bitter leaves

ruff (ruf) *n.* [< RUFFLE] **1.** a high, frilled, stiff collar of the 16th-17th cent. **2.** a ring of feathers or fur standing out about the neck of an animal

ruf·fi·an (ruf′ē ən, ruf′yən) *n.* [< It. *ruffiano*, a pander] a brutal, lawless person

ruf·fle (ruf′'l) *vt.* **-fled, -fling** [< ON. or MLowG.] **1.** to disturb the smoothness of **2.** to gather into ruffles **3.** to make (feathers, etc.) stand up **4.** to disturb or annoy —*vi.* **1.** to become uneven **2.** to become disturbed, annoyed, etc. —*n.* **1.** a pleated strip of cloth, lace, etc. for trimming **2.** a disturbance **3.** a ripple

rug (rug) *n.* [< Scand.] **1.** a piece of thick fabric used as a floor covering **2.** [Chiefly Brit.] a lap robe

rug·ged (rug′id) *adj.* [ME., prob. < Scand.] **1.** uneven; rough **2.** stormy **3.** harsh; severe; hard **4.** not polished or refined **5.** strong; robust — **rug′ged·ly** *adv.*

ru·in (rōō′in) *n.* [< L. *ruere*, to fall] **1.** [*pl.*] the remains of something destroyed, decayed, etc. **2.** anything destroyed, etc. **3.** downfall, destruction, etc. **4.** anything causing this —*vt., vi.* to bring or come to ruin —**ru′in·a′tion** *n.* —**ru′in·ous** *adj.*

rule (rōōl) *n.* [< L. *regere*, lead straight] **1.** an established regulation or guide for conduct, procedure, usage, etc. **2.** custom **3.** the customary course **4.** government; reign **5.** a ruler (sense 2) —*vt., vi.* **ruled, rul′ing 1.** to have an influence over; guide **2.** to govern **3.** to settle by decree **4.** to mark lines (on) as with a ruler —**as a rule** usually —**rule out** to exclude

rule of thumb a practical, though crude and unscientific, method

rul′er *n.* **1.** one who governs **2.** a thin strip of metal, wood, etc. with a straight edge, used in drawing lines, measuring, etc.

rum (rum) *n.* [< ?] an alcoholic liquor made from fermented sugar cane, molasses, etc.

rum·ba (rum′bə) *n.* [AmSp.] **1.** a dance of Cuban Negro origin **2.** music for this dance

rum·ble (rum′b'l) *vi., vt.* **-bled, -bling** [prob. < MDu. *rommelen*] **1.** to make or cause to make a deep, continuous, rolling sound **2.** to move with such a sound —*n.* **1.** a rumbling sound **2.** [Slang] a gang fight

ru·mi·nant (rōō′mə nənt) *adj.* [see RUMINATE] **1.** chewing the cud **2.** meditative —*n.* any of a group of four-footed, cud-chewing mammals, as the cattle, sheep, deer, etc.

ru′mi·nate′ (-nāt′) *vt., vi.* **-nat′ed, -nat′ing** [< L. *ruminare*] **1.** to chew (the cud) **2.** to meditate (on); muse —**ru′mi·na′tion** *n.* —**ru′mi·na′tive** *adj.*

rum·mage (rum′ij) *n.* [< MFr. *run*, ship's hold] **1.** odds and ends **2.** a rummaging —*vt., vi.* **-maged, -mag·ing** to search through (a place) thoroughly

rummage sale a sale of contributed miscellaneous articles, as for charity

rum·my (rum′ē) *n.* [< ?] any of certain card games whose object is to match sets and sequences

ru·mor (rōō′mər) *n.* [L., noise] **1.** general talk not based on definite knowledge **2.** an unconfirmed report, story, etc. in general circulation —*vt.* to tell or spread by rumor Brit. sp. **ru′·mour**

rump (rump) *n.* [< ON. *rumpr*] **1.** the hind part of an animal where the legs and back join **2.** the buttocks **3.** the remnant

rum·ple (rum′p'l) *n.* [< MDu. *rompe*] an uneven crease; wrinkle —*vt., vi.* **-pled, -pling** to wrinkle; muss —**rum′ply** *adj.*

rum·pus (rum′pəs) *n.* [< ?] [Colloq.] noisy disturbance; uproar

run (run) *vi.* **ran, run, run′ning** [< ON. & OE.] **1.** to go by moving the legs faster than in walking **2.** to move swiftly **3.** to go, move, etc. easily and freely **4.** to make a quick trip (*up to, down to,* etc.) **5.** to flee **6.** to compete in a race, election, etc. **7.** to go, as on a schedule **8.** to climb or creep, as a vine **9.** to ravel, as a stocking **10.** to operate, as a machine **11.** to flow **12.** to spread over cloth, etc. when moistened, as colors **13.** to discharge pus, etc. **14.** to continue **15.** to pass into a specified condition [to *run* into trouble] **16.** to be written, etc. in a specified way **17.** to be at a specified size, price, etc. [meat *runs* high] —*vt.* **1.** to follow (a specified course) **2.** to travel over **3.** to perform as by running [to *run* a race] **4.** to incur (a risk) **5.** to get past [to *run* a blockade] **6.** to make run, move, compete, etc. **7.** to force into a specified condition **8.** to drive (an object) into, against, etc. (something) **9.** to make flow in a specified way, place, etc. **10.** to manage [to *run* a household] **11.** to trace **12.** to undergo (a fever, etc.) **13.** to publish (a story, etc.) as in a newspaper —*n.* **1.** an act or period of running **2.** the distance covered in running **3.** a trip; journey **4.** a continuous course or period **5.** a continuous course of performances, etc., as of a play **6.** a continued series of demands, as for specified goods **7.** a flow or rush of water **8.** a small, swift stream **9.** the output during a period of operation **10.** a kind or class; esp., the average kind **11.** an enclosed area for domestic animals **12.** freedom to move about at will [the *run* of the house] **13.** a large number of fish migrating together **14.** a ravel, as in a stocking **15.** *Baseball* a scoring point, made by a successful circuit of the bases —**in the long run** ultimately —**on the run** running or running away —**run across** to encounter by chance: also **run into** —**run down 1.** to stop operating **2.** to run against so as to knock down **3.** to pursue and capture or kill **4.** to speak of disparagingly —**run out** to come to an end; expire —**run out of** to use up —**run over 1.** to ride over **2.** to overflow to ride over **2.** to overflow **3.** to examine, rehearse, etc. rapidly —**run through 1.** to use up quickly or recklessly **2.** to pierce —**run up** to raise, rise, or accumulate rapidly

run′a·round′ *n.* [Colloq.] a series of evasive excuses, delays, etc.

run′a·way′ *n.* **1.** a fugitive **2.** a horse, etc. that runs away —*adj.* **1.** running away or having run away **2.** easily won, as a race **3.** rising rapidly, as prices

run′down′ *n.* a concise summary

run′-down′ *adj.* **1.** not wound and therefore not running, as a clock **2.** in poor physical condition, as from overwork **3.** fallen into disrepair

rune (rōōn) *n.* [OE. *run*] **1.** any of the characters of an ancient Germanic alphabet **2.** any poem, song, etc. that is mystical or obscure —**ru′nic** *adj.*

rung′ (ruŋ) *n.* [OE. *hrung*, a staff] a rod forming a step of a ladder, a crosspiece on a chair, etc.

rung² (ruŋ) *pp. of* RING¹

run′-in′ *n.* **1.** *Printing* matter added without a break or new paragraph **2.** [Colloq.] a quarrel, fight, etc.

run′ner *n.* **1.** one that runs, as a racer, messenger, etc. **2.** a long, narrow cloth or rug **3.** a ravel, as in hose **4.** a long, trailing stem, as of a strawberry plant **5.** either of the long, narrow pieces on which a sled, etc. slides

run′ner-up′ *n., pl.* **-ners-up′** a person or team that finishes second in a contest

run′ning *n.* the act of one that runs; racing, managing, etc. —*adj.* **1.** that runs (in various senses) **2.** measured in a straight line [a *running* foot] **3.** continuous; unbroken [a *running* commentary] —*adv.* in succession [for five days *running*]

running mate a candidate for a lesser office in his or her relationship to the candidate for the greater office

run′ny *adj.* **-ni·er, -ni·est 1.** flowing, esp. too freely **2.** discharging mucus [a *runny* nose]

run′-off′ *n.* a deciding, final contest

run′-of-the-mill′ *adj.* ordinary

runt (runt) *n.* [< ?] a stunted animal, plant, or (in a contemptuous sense) person —**runt′y** *adj.* **-i·er, -i·est**

run′-through′ *n.* a complete rehearsal, from beginning to end

run′way′ *n.* a channel, track, etc. in, on, or along which something moves; esp., a strip of leveled ground used by airplanes in taking off and landing

ru·pee (rōō pē′) *n.* [< Hindi < Sans. *rūpya*, wrought silver] the monetary unit of India, Pakistan, etc.

rup·ture (rup′chər) *n.* [< L. *rumpere*, to break] **1.** a breaking apart or being broken apart;

breach **2.** a hernia —*vt., vi.* **-tured, -tur·ing** to cause or suffer a rupture

ru·ral (roor′əl) *adj.* [< L. *rus*, the country] of, like, or living in the country; rustic

ruse (rōōz) *n.* [Fr. < OFr. *reuser*, deceive] a stratagem or trick

rush′ (rush) *vt., vi.* [< OFr. *reuser*, deceive, repel] **1.** to move, dash, etc. impetuously **2.** to make a sudden attack (on) **3.** to pass, come, go, etc. swiftly or suddenly **4.** *Football* to advance (the ball) by a running play —*n.* **1.** a rushing **2.** an eager movement of many people to get to a place **3.** intense activity; haste **4.** a sudden attack **5.** a press, as of business, requiring unusual haste

rush² (rush) *n.* [OE. *risc*] a grasslike marsh plant with round stems used in making mats

rush hour a time of day when business, traffic, etc. are heavy

rusk (rusk) *n.* [< Sp. *rosca*, twisted bread roll] **1.** a sweet, raised bread or cake toasted until brown and crisp **2.** a piece of this

Russ. 1. Russia **2.** Russian

rus·set (rus′it) *n.* [< L. *russus*, reddish] **1.** yellowish (or reddish) brown **2.** a winter apple with a mottled skin

Rus·sian (rush′ən) *adj.* of Russia, its people, language, etc. —*n.* **1.** a native of Russia **2.** the Slavic language of the Russians

rust (rust) *n.* [OE.] **1.** the reddish-brown coating formed on iron and steel exposed to air and moisture **2.** any stain resembling this **3.** reddish brown **4.** a plant disease caused by parasitic fungi, spotting stems and leaves —*vi., vt.* **1.** to form rust (on) **2.** to deteriorate, as through disuse

rus·tic (rus′tik) *adj.* [< L. *rus*, the country] **1.** of the country; rural **2.** unsophisticated or uncouth —*n.* a country person —**rus′ti·cal·ly** *adv.* —**rus·tic′i·ty** (-tis′ə tē) *n.*

rus·ti·cate (rus′ti kāt′) *vi., vt.* **-cat′ed, -cat′ing 1.** to go or send to live in the country **2.** to become or make rustic

rus·tle′ (rus′'l) *vi., vt.* **-tled, -tling** [ult. echoic] to make or cause to make soft sounds, as of leaves moved by a breeze —*n.* a series of such sounds

rus·tle² (rus′'l) *vi., vt.* **-tled, -tling** [< ?] [Colloq.] to steal (cattle, etc.) —**rustle up** [Colloq.] to collect or get together —**rus′tler** *n.*

rust′proof′ *adj.* resistant to rust

rust·y (rus′tē) *adj.* **-i·er, -i·est 1.** coated with rust, as a metal **2.** *a)* impaired by disuse, neglect, etc. *b)* having lost skill through lack of practice **3.** rust-colored

rut′ (rut) *n.* [< ? MFr. *route*, route] **1.** a groove, track, etc. as made by wheels **2.** a fixed, routine procedure, way of acting, etc. —*vt.* **rut′ted, rut′ting** to make ruts in

rut² (rut) *n.* [< L. *rugire*, to roar] the periodic sexual excitement of some male mammals —*vi.* **rut′ted, rut′ting** to be in rut

ru·ta·ba·ga (rōōt′ə bā′gə) *n.* [Sw. dial. *rotabagge*] a turnip with a large, yellow root

Ruth (rōōth) *Bible* a widow deeply devoted to her mother-in-law, Naomi

ruth·less (rōōth′lis) *adj.* [< OE. *hreowan*, to rue] without pity or compassion

Rwy., Ry. Railway

ry·a rug (rē′ə) [< Sw.] a decorative, hand-woven, thick rug of Scandinavian origin

rye (rī) *n.* [OE. *ryge*] **1.** a hardy cereal grass **2.** its grain or seeds, used for making flour, etc. **3.** whiskey distilled from this grain

S

S, s (es) *n., pl.* **S's, s's** the nineteenth letter of the English alphabet

S *Chem.* sulfur —*adj.* (es) shaped like S

-s [alt. of -ES] **1.** the plural ending of most nouns [*lips*] **2.** the ending of the third person singular, present indicative, of verbs

-'s¹ [OE. *-es*] the ending of the possessive singular of nouns (and some pronouns) and of the possessive plural of nouns not ending in *s* [*boy's, one's, men's*]

-'s² *the assimilated form of:* **1.** is [*he's here*] **2.** has [*she's gone*] **3.** does [*what's it matter?*] **4.** us [*let's go*]

S, S., s, s. **1.** south **2.** southern

S., s. 1. *pl.* **SS., ss.** saint **2.** school

s. 1. second(s) **2.** shilling(s)

S.A. South America

Sab·bath (sab'əth) *n.* [< Heb. *shābath*, to rest] **1.** the seventh day of the week (Saturday), observed as a day of rest and worship by Jews **2.** Sunday as the usual Christian day of rest and worship

Sab·bat·i·cal (sə bat'i k'l) *adj.* **1.** of the Sabbath **2.** [s-] bringing a period of rest [*a sabbatical leave*] —*n.* [s-] a sabbatical year or leave

sabbatical year a period of absence with pay, for study, travel, etc., given as to teachers, orig. every seven years

sa·ber, sa·bre (sā'bər) *n.* [< Fr. < MHG. *sabel*] a heavy cavalry sword with a slightly curved blade

Sa·bin vaccine (sā'bin) [< Dr. A. B. *Sabin* (1906–), its U.S. developer] a polio vaccine taken orally

sa·ble (sā'b'l) *n.* [< Russ. *sobol*] **1.** same as MARTEN **2.** its costly fur

sa·bot (sab'ō, sa bō') *n.* [Fr., ult. < Ar. *sabbât*, sandal] a shoe shaped from a single piece of wood

sab·o·tage (sab'ə täzh') *n.* [Fr. < *sabot:* from damage done to machinery by wooden shoes] intentional destruction of machines, etc. by employees in labor disputes or of railroads, bridges, etc. by enemy agents or an underground resistance —*vt., vi.* **-taged', -tag'ing** to commit sabotage (on) —**sab'o·teur'** (-tur') *n.*

sac (sak) *n.* [see SACK¹] a pouchlike part in a plant or animal

SAC, S.A.C. Strategic Air Command

sac·cha·rin (sak'ə rin) *n.* [< Gr. *sakcharon*] a white, crystalline coal-tar compound used as a sugar substitute

sac'cha·rine (-rin) *adj.* **1.** of or like sugar **2.** too sweet [*a saccharine voice*]

sac·er·do·tal (sas'ər dōt'l) *adj.* [< L. *sacerdos,* priest] of priests or the office of priest

sa·chem (sā'chəm) *n.* [AmInd.] among some N. American Indian tribes, the chief

sa·chet (sa shā') *n.* [Fr.] a small bag, pad, etc. filled with perfumed powder (**sachet powder**) and placed with stored clothes

sack¹ (sak) *n.* [ult. < Heb. *śaq*] **1.** a bag, esp. a large one of coarse cloth **2.** [Slang] dismissal from a job (with *the*) **3.** [Slang] a bed —*vt.* **1.** to put into sacks **2.** [Slang] to dismiss from a job

sack² (sak) *n.* [see prec.] the plundering of a captured city, etc. —*vt.* to plunder or loot (a city, etc.)

sack³ (sak) *n.* [< Fr. (*vin*) *sec,* dry (wine)] a dry, white Spanish wine

sack'cloth' *n.* **1.** a coarse cloth used for sacks: also **sack'ing 2.** coarse cloth worn as a symbol of mourning or penitence

sac·ra·ment (sak'rə mənt) *n.* [< L. *sacer,* sacred] **1.** any of certain Christian rites, as baptism, Holy Communion, etc. **2.** something regarded as sacred —**sac'ra·men'tal** *adj.*

sa·cred (sā'krid) *adj.* [< L. *sacer,* holy] **1.** consecrated to a god or God; holy **2.** having to do with religion **3.** hallowed; venerated **4.** inviolate —**sa'cred·ly** *adv.*

sac·ri·fice (sak'rə fīs') *n.* [< L. *sacer,* holy + *facere,* to make] **1.** an offering, as of a life or object, to a deity **2.** a giving up of one thing for the sake of another **3.** a loss incurred in selling —*vt., vi.* **-ficed', -fic'ing 1.** to offer as a sacrifice to a deity **2.** to give up (one thing) for the sake of another **3.** to sell at less than value —**sac'ri·fi'cial** (-fish'əl) *adj.*

sac·ri·lege (sak'rə lij) *n.* [< L. *sacer,* sacred + *legere,* take away] a desecrating of anything held sacred —**sac'ri·le'gious** (-lij'əs, -lē'jəs) *adj.* —**sac'ri·le'gious·ly** *adv.*

sac·ro·sanct (sak'rō saŋkt') *adj.* [< L. *sacer,* sacred + *sanctus,* holy] very sacred, holy, or inviolable

sad (sad) *adj.* **sad'der, sad'dest** [OE. *sæd,* sated] **1.** having or expressing low spirits; unhappy; sorrowful **2.** causing dejection, sorrow, etc. —**sad'ly** *adv.* —**sad'ness** *n.*

sad'den *vt., vi.* to make or become sad

sad·dle (sad'l) *n.* [OE. *sadol*] **1.** a seat for a rider on a horse, bicycle, etc., usually padded and of leather **2.** a cut of lamb, etc. including part of the backbone —*vt.* **-dled, -dling 1.** to put a saddle on **2.** to encumber; burden —**in the saddle** in control

sad'dle·bag' *n.* **1.** a large bag, usually one of a pair, hung behind the saddle on a horse, etc. **2.** a similar bag on a bicycle, etc.

saddle horse a horse trained for riding

saddle shoes white oxford shoes with a contrasting band across the instep

Sad·du·cee (saj'oo sē') *n.* a member of an ancient Jewish party that accepted only the written law

sad·ism (sad'iz'm, sā'diz'm) *n.* [< marquis de *Sade,* 18th-c. Fr. writer] the getting of pleasure from mistreating others —**sad'ist** *n.* —**sa·dis'tic** *adj.* —**sa·dis'ti·cal·ly** *adv.*

sa·fa·ri (sə fär'ē) *n., pl.* **-ris** [< Ar. *safara,* to travel] a journey or hunting expedition, esp. in Africa

safe (sāf) *adj.* **saf'er, saf'est** [< L. *salvus*] **1.** free from danger, damage, etc. **2.** having escaped injury; unharmed **3.** giving protection **4.** trustworthy **5.** prudent; cautious —*n.* a locking metal container for valuables —**safe'ly** *adv.* — **safe'ness** *n.*

safe'-con'duct *n.* permission, usually written, to travel safely through enemy regions

safe'-de·pos'it *adj.* designating or of a box or vault, esp. in a bank, for storing valuables

safe'guard' *n.* a protection; precaution —*vt.* to protect or guard

safe'keep'ing *n.* a keeping or being kept in safety; protection or custody

safe·ty (sāf'tē) *n., pl.* **-ties 1.** a being safe;

security **2.** a device to prevent accident **3.** *Football a)* the grounding of the ball by the offense behind its own goal line *b)* a defensive back farthest from the line of scrimmage —*adj.* giving safety

safety glass shatterproof glass

safety match a match that strikes only on a prepared surface

safety pin a pin bent back on itself and having the point held in a guard

safety razor a razor with guards for the blade to protect the skin from cuts

safety valve an automatic valve for a boiler, etc. that releases steam if the pressure is too great

saf·flow·er (saf′lou′ər) *n.* [ult. < Ar.] a flowering thistlelike plant whose seeds yield an edible oil

saf·fron (saf′rən) *n.* [< Du. < It. < Ar. *za'farān*] **1.** a plant having orange stigmas **2.** the dried stigmas, used as a dye and flavoring **3.** orange yellow

S. Afr. 1. South Africa **2.** South African

sag (sag) *vi.* **sagged, sag′ging** [prob. < Scand.] **1.** to sink, esp. in the middle, from weight or pressure **2.** to hang down unevenly **3.** to lose firmness, strength, etc.; weaken —*n.* **1.** a sagging **2.** a sagging place

sa·ga (sä′gə) *n.* [ON., a tale] **1.** a medieval Scandinavian story telling of battles, legends, etc. **2.** any long story of heroic deeds

sa·ga·cious (sə gä′shəs) *adj.* [< L. *sagax,* wise] keenly perceptive; shrewd —**sa·ga′-cious·ly** *adv.* —**sa·gac′i·ty** (-gas′ə tē) *n.*

sage[1] (sāj) *adj.* **sag′er, sag′est** [ult. < L. *sapere,* know] having or showing wisdom or good judgment —*n.* a very wise man

sage[2] (sāj) *n.* [< L. *salvus,* safe: it reputedly had healing powers] **1.** a plant related to the mint with leaves used in flavoring meat, etc. **2.** *same as* SAGEBRUSH

sage′brush′ *n.* a plant with aromatic leaves, common in dry areas of the W U.S.

sag′gy *adj.* **-gi·er, -gi·est** tending to sag —**sag′gi·ness** *n.*

Sag·it·ta·ri·us (saj′i ter′ē əs) [L., archer] the ninth sign of the zodiac

sa·gua·ro (sə gwä′rō) *n., pl.* **-ros** [MexSp. < native name] a giant cactus of the SW U.S. and N Mexico

sa·hib (sä′ib) *n.* [Hindi < Ar.] sir; master: title formerly used in India when speaking to or of a European

said (sed) *pt. & pp. of* SAY —*adj.* aforesaid

sail (sāl) *n.* [OE. *segl*] **1.** a sheet, as of canvas, spread to catch the wind so as to drive a vessel forward **2.** sails collectively **3.** a trip in a ship or boat **4.** anything like a sail —*vi.* **1.** to be moved forward by means of sails **2.** to travel on water **3.** to begin a trip by water **4.** to manage a sailboat **5.** to glide or move smoothly, like a ship in full sail —*vt.* **1.** to move upon (a body of water) in a vessel **2.** to manage (a vessel) —**sail into** [Colloq.] to attack vigorously —**set sail** to begin a trip by water — **under sail** sailing

sail′boat′ *n.* a boat propelled by a sail or sails

sail′cloth′ *n.* canvas or similar cloth used in making sails, tents, etc.

sail′fish′ *n., pl.:* see FISH a large, tropical marine fish with a large, saillike dorsal fin

sail′or *n.* **1.** one who makes his living by sailing **2.** an enlisted man in the navy **3.** a hat with a low, flat crown and flat brim

saint (sānt) *n.* [< L. *sanctus,* holy] **1.** a holy person **2.** a person who is unusually charitable, patient, etc. **3.** in certain Christian churches, a person officially recognized and venerated for having attained heaven after a very holy life —**saint′li·ness** *n.* —**saint′ly** *adj.* **-li·er, -li·est**

Saint Ber·nard (bər närd′) a large dog of a breed once used in the Swiss Alps to rescue lost travelers

Saint Pat′rick's Day March 17, observed by the Irish in honor of their patron saint

Saint Valentine's Day February 14, observed in honor of a martyr of the 3d cent. and as a day for sending valentines to sweethearts, etc.

saith (seth) *archaic 3d pers. sing., pres. indic., of* SAY

sake[1] (sāk) *n.* [OE. *sacu,* suit at law] **1.** reason; motive *[for the sake of money]* **2.** behalf *[for my sake]*

sa·ke[2] (sä′kē) *n.* [Jpn.] a Japanese alcoholic beverage made from rice: also sp. **saki**

sa·laam (sə läm′) *n.* [Ar. *salām,* peace] an Oriental greeting made by bowing low while placing the right hand on the forehead —*vt., vi.* to greet with, or make, a salaam

sal·a·ble (sāl′ə b'l) *adj.* that can be sold; marketable: also **sale′a·ble**

sa·la·cious (sə lā′shəs) *adj.* [< L. *salire,* to leap] **1.** lecherous; lustful **2.** obscene

sal·ad (sal′əd) *n.* [< L. *salata,* salted] a dish, usually cold, of vegetables, usually raw, or fruits, served with a dressing, or molded in gelatin

salad dressing a preparation of oil, vinegar, spices, etc. put on a salad

sal·a·man·der (sal′ə man′dər) *n.* [< Gr. *salamandra*] **1.** a mythological reptile said to live in fire **2.** a scaleless, tailed amphibian with a soft, moist skin

sa·la·mi (sə lä′mē) *n.* [It. < L. *sal,* salt] a spiced, salted sausage

sal·a·ry (sal′ə rē) *n., pl.* **-ries** [< L. *salarium,* orig. part of a Roman soldier's pay for buying salt < *sal,* salt] a fixed payment at regular intervals for work or services —**sal′a·ried** (-rēd) *adj.*

sale (sāl) *n.* [< ON. *sala*] **1.** a selling **2.** opportunity to sell; market **3.** an auction **4.** a selling at prices lower than usual —**for** (or **on**) **sale** to be sold

sales·clerk (sālz′klurk′) *n.* a person employed to sell goods in a store

sales′man (-mən) *n., pl.* **-men** a man employed to sell goods —**sales′man·ship′** *n.*

sales′per·son *n.* a person employed to sell goods; esp., a salesclerk

sales talk 1. talk aimed at selling something **2.** any talk to persuade

sales tax a tax on sales

sales′wom′an *n., pl.* **-wom′en** a woman salesclerk: also **sales′la′dy,** *pl.* **-dies, sales′girl′**

sal·i·cyl·ic acid (sal′ə sil′ik) [< *salicin* (substance from certain willows) < Fr.] a white, crystalline compound, used in aspirin

sa·lient (sāl′yənt, sā′lē ənt) *adj.* [< L. *salire,* to leap] **1.** pointing outward; projecting **2.** noticeable; prominent —*n.* a salient angle, part, etc. —**sa′lience** *n.* —**sa′lient·ly** *adv.*

sa·line (sā′līn, -lēn) *adj.* [< L. *sal,* salt] of, like, or containing salt; salty

sa·li·va (sə lī′və) *n.* [L.] a thin, watery fluid secreted by glands in the mouth: it aids in digestion —**sal·i·var·y** (sal′ə ver′ē) *adj.*

sal·i·vate (sal′ə vāt′) *vi.* **-vat′ed, -vat′ing** [< L. *salivare*] to secrete saliva

sal·low (sal′ō) *adj.* [OE. *salu*] of a sickly, pale-yellowish complexion

sal·ly (sal′ē) *n., pl.* **-lies** [< L. *salire,* to leap] **1.** a sudden rushing forth, as to attack **2.** any sudden start into activity **3.** a quick witticism;

quip **4.** an excursion; jaunt —*vi.* **-lled, -ly·ing** to rush or set (*forth* or *out*) on a sally

salm·on (sam'ən) *n., pl.* **-on, -ons** [< L. *salmo*] **1.** a game and food fish whose flesh is pink when cooked: salmon spawn in fresh water but usually live in salt water **2.** yellowish pink: also **salmon pink**

sal·mo·nel·la (sal'mə nel'ə) *n., pl.* **-lae** (-ē), **-la, -las** [< D. *Salmon* (d. 1914), U.S. veterinarian] any of certain bacilli that cause typhoid fever, food poisoning, etc.

sa·lon (sə län', sal'än) *n.* [Fr.: see SALOON] **1.** a large reception hall or drawing room **2.** a regular gathering of distinguished guests **3.** a parlor or shop [a beauty *salon*]

sa·loon (sə loon') *n.* [< Fr. < It. *sala,* hall] **1.** any large room or hall for receptions, exhibitions, etc. **2.** a place where alcoholic drinks are sold; bar

salt (sôlt, sält) *n.* [OE. *sealt*] **1.** sodium chloride, a white crystalline substance found in natural beds, in sea water, etc., and used for seasoning food, etc. **2.** a chemical compound derived from an acid by replacing hydrogen with a metal **3.** piquancy; esp., pungent wit **4.** [*pl.*] mineral salts used as a cathartic, restorative, etc. **5.** [Colloq.] a sailor —*adj.* containing, preserved with, or tasting of salt —*vt.* to sprinkle, season, or preserve with salt —**salt away** [Colloq.] to store or save (money, etc.) —**with a grain of salt** with allowance or reserve —**salt'i·ness** *n.* —**salt'y** *adj.* **-i·er, -i·est**

salt'cel'lar (-sel'ər) *n.* [< *salt* + MFr. *salière,* saltcellar] a small dish or shaker for salt

salt·ine (sôl tēn') *n.* [SALT + -INE³] a flat, crisp cracker sprinkled with salt

salt lick a natural deposit or a block of rock salt which animals come to lick

salt'pe'ter (-pēt'ər) *n.* [< L. *sal,* salt + *petra,* a rock] *same as* POTASSIUM NITRATE

salt pork pork cured in salt

salt'shak'er *n.* a container for salt, with a perforated top

salt'wa'ter *adj.* of, having to do with, or living in salt water or the sea

sa·lu·bri·ous (sə loo'brē əs) *adj.* [< L. *salus,* health] healthful, wholesome, etc.

sal·u·tar·y (sal'yoo ter'ē) *adj.* [< L. *salus,* health] **1.** healthful **2.** beneficial

sal·u·ta·tion (sal'yoo tā'shən) *n.* [see SALUTE] **1.** the act of greeting or addressing **2.** a form of greeting, as "Dear Sir" in a letter

sa·lute (sə loot') *vt., vi.* **-lut'ed, -lut'ing** [< L. *salus,* health] **1.** to greet in a friendly way, as by bowing **2.** to honor ceremonially and officially by firing cannon, raising the hand to the head, etc. —*n.* an act, remark, or gesture made in saluting

sal·vage (sal'vij) *n.* [see SAVE¹] **1.** *a)* the rescue of a ship and cargo from shipwreck, etc. *b)* compensation paid for such rescue **2.** *a)* the rescue of any property from destruction or waste *b)* the property saved —*vt.* **-vaged, -vag·ing** to save or rescue from shipwreck, fire, etc.

sal·va·tion (sal vā'shən) *n.* [< L. *salvare,* to save] **1.** a saving or being saved **2.** a person or thing that saves or rescues **3.** *Theol.* spiritual rescue from sin and death

Salvation Army a Christian organization for helping the very poor

salve (sav) *n.* [OE. *sealf*] **1.** any soothing or healing ointment for wounds, burns, etc. **2.** anything that soothes or heals —*vt.* **salved, salv'ing** to soothe

sal·ver (sal'vər) *n.* [< Fr. < Sp. < L. *salvare,* to save] a tray

sal·vo (sal'vō) *n., pl.* **-vos, -voes** [< L. *salve,*

hail!] a discharge of a number of guns, either in salute or at a target

sam·ba (sam'bə) *n.* [Port.] a Brazilian dance of African origin, or music for it —*vi.* to dance the samba

same (sām) *adj.* [ON. *samr*] **1.** being the very one; identical **2.** alike in kind, quality, amount, etc. **3.** unchanged [to keep the *same* look] **4.** before-mentioned —*pron.* the same person or thing —*adv.* in the same way —**same'·ness** *n.*

sam·o·var (sam'ə vär') *n.* [Russ.] a Russian metal urn with an internal tube for heating water for tea

sam·pan (sam'pan) *n.* [Chin. *san-pan*] a small boat used in China and Japan, rowed with a scull from the stern

sam·ple (sam'p'l) *n.* [see EXAMPLE] a part that shows what the whole thing or group is like; specimen or example —*vt.* **-pled, -pling** to take or test a sample of

sam'pler *n.* **1.** one who samples **2.** a cloth embroidered with designs, mottoes, etc. in different stitches

Sam·son (sam's'n) *Bible* an Israelite with great strength: Judges 13-16

Sam·u·el (sam'yoo wəl, -yool) *Bible* a Hebrew judge and prophet

sam·u·rai (sam'ə rī') *n., pl.* **-rai'** [Jpn.] a member of a military caste in feudal Japan

san·a·to·ri·um (san'ə tôr'ē əm) *n., pl.* **-ri·ums, -ri·a** (-ə) [< L. *sanare,* heal] *chiefly Brit. var. of* SANITARIUM

sanc·ti·fy (saŋk'tə fī') *vt.* **-fied', -fy'ing** [< L. *sanctus,* holy + *facere,* make] **1.** to set apart as holy; consecrate **2.** to make free from sin —**sanc'ti·fi·ca'tion** *n.*

sanc·ti·mo·ni·ous (saŋk'tə mō'nē əs) *adj.* pretending to be very pious

sanc'ti·mo'ny *n.* [< L. *sanctus,* holy] affected piety or righteousness

sanc·tion (saŋk'shən) *n.* [< L. *sanctus,* holy] **1.** authorization **2.** support; approval **3.** [*usually pl.*] a boycott or other coercive measure, as against a nation defying international law —*vt.* **1.** to ratify or confirm **2.** to authorize or permit

sanc·ti·ty (saŋk'tə tē) *n., pl.* **-ties** [< L. *sanctus,* holy] **1.** saintliness **2.** sacredness

sanc·tu·ar·y (saŋk'choo wer'ē) *n., pl.* **-ies** [< L. *sanctus,* sacred] **1.** a holy place; specif., a church, temple, etc. **2.** a place of refuge or protection **3.** refuge; protection

sanc·tum (saŋk'təm) *n., pl.* **-tums, -ta** (-tə) [L.] **1.** a sacred place **2.** a private room where one is not to be disturbed

sand (sand) *n.* [OE.] **1.** loose, gritty grains of disintegrated rock, as on beaches, in deserts, etc. **2.** [*usually pl.*] an area of sand —*vt.* **1.** to sprinkle or fill with sand **2.** to smooth or polish, as with sandpaper

san·dal (san'd'l) *n.* [< Gr. *sandalon*] **1.** a shoe made of a sole fastened to the foot by straps **2.** any of various low slippers

san'dal·wood' *n.* [ult. < Sans. *candana*] **1.** the hard, sweet-smelling heartwood of an Asiatic tree **2.** this tree

sand'bag' *n.* a bag filled with sand and used for ballast, in fortifications, etc. —*vt.* **-bagged', -bag'ging** to place sandbags in or around

sand bar a ridge of sand formed in a river or along a shore

sand'blast' *n.* a current of air or steam carrying sand at a high velocity, used in cleaning metal, stone, etc. —*vt.* to clean with a sandblast —**sand'blast'er** *n.*

sand'box' *n.* a box containing sand for children to play in

sand'hog' *n.* a laborer in underground or underwater construction projects

sand'lot' *adj.* having to do with games, esp. baseball, played by amateurs, orig. on a sandy lot —**sand'lot'ter** *n.*

sand'man' *n.* a mythical person supposed to make children sleepy by dusting sand in their eyes

sand'pa'per *n.* paper coated on one side with sand, used for smoothing and polishing —*vt.* to smooth or polish with sandpaper

sand'pip'er (-pī'pər) *n.* a small shore bird with a long, soft-tipped bill

sand'stone' *n.* a sedimentary rock consisting largely of sand grains cemented together by silica, etc.

sand'storm' *n.* a windstorm in which large quantities of sand are blown about

sand trap a hollow filled with sand, serving as a hazard on a golf course

sand·wich (sand'wich, san'-) *n.* [< 4th Earl of *Sandwich* (1718–92)] slices of bread with meat, cheese, etc. between them —*vt.* to place between other persons, things, etc.

sand·y (san'dē) *adj.* -**i·er**, -**i·est** 1. of or like sand 2. pale reddish-yellow

sane (sān) *adj.* **san'er**, **san'est** [L. *sanus*, healthy] 1. mentally healthy; rational 2. showing good sense; sensible *[a sane policy]* —**sane'ly** *adv.*

San·for·ize (san'fə rīz') *vt.* -**ized'**, -**iz'ing** [< *Sanford* L. Cluett (1874–1968), the inventor] to preshrink (cloth) permanently by a patented process before making garments

sang (saŋ) *pt. of* SING

san·gui·nar·y (saŋ'gwi ner'ē) *adj.* [see SANGUINE] 1. with much bloodshed or killing 2. bloodthirsty

san·guine (saŋ'gwin) *adj.* [< L. *sanguis*, blood] 1. of the color of blood; ruddy 2. cheerful; confident —**san'guine·ly** *adv.*

san·i·tar·i·um (san'ə ter'ē əm) *n., pl.* -**i·ums**, -**i·a** (-ə) [< L. *sanitas*, health] a nursing home, hospital, etc. for the care of invalids or convalescents

san·i·tar·y (san'ə ter'ē) *adj.* [< L. *sanitas*, health] 1. of health or the rules and conditions of health; esp., of absence of dirt and agents of disease 2. clean; hygienic

sanitary napkin an absorbent pad worn by women during menstruation

san·i·ta·tion (san'ə tā'shən) *n.* 1. the science and work of producing hygienic conditions 2. drainage and disposal of sewage

san·i·tize (san'ə tīz') *vt.* -**tized'**, -**tiz'ing** to make sanitary, as by sterilizing

san·i·ty (san'ə tē) *n.* 1. the state of being sane 2. soundness of judgment

sank (saŋk) *pt. of* SINK

sans (sanz; *Fr.* sän) *prep.* [Fr. < L. *sine*] without; lacking

San·skrit, San·scrit (san'skrit) *n.* the classical literary language of ancient India

San·ta Claus, San·ta Klaus (san'tə klôz') [< Du. *Sant Nikolaas*, St. Nicholas] *Folklore* a fat, white-bearded, jolly old man in a red suit, who distributes gifts at Christmas

sap¹ (sap) *n.* [OE. *sæp*] 1. the juice that circulates through a plant, bearing water, food, etc. 2. vigor; energy 3. [Slang] a stupid person

sap² (sap) *vt.* **sapped**, **sap'ping** [< MFr. < It. *zappe*, a hoe] 1. to undermine by digging away foundations 2. to weaken; exhaust

sa·pi·ent (sā'pē ənt) *adj.* [< L. *sapere*, to taste,

know] full of knowledge; wise —**sa'pi·ence** *n.* —**sa'pi·ent·ly** *adv.*

sap·ling (sap'liŋ) *n.* a young tree

sap·o·dil·la (sap'ə dil'ə) *n.* [< Sp. < Central AmInd. *tzapotl*] a tropical American evergreen tree yielding chicle

sap·phire (saf'īr) *n.* [< Gr. *sappheiros*] 1. a hard precious stone of a clear, deep-blue corundum 2. its color —*adj.* deep-blue

sap·py (sap'ē) *adj.* -**pi·er**, -**pi·est** 1. full of sap; juicy 2. [Slang] foolish; silly —**sap'pi·ness** *n.*

sap'suck'er *n.* a small American woodpecker that often drills holes in maples, apple trees, etc. and drinks the sap

Sar·a·cen (sar'ə s'n) *n.* any Arab or any Muslim, esp. during the Crusades

Sar·ah (ser'ə, sar'ə) *Bible* the wife of Abraham and mother of Isaac

sa·ran (sə ran') *n.* [a coinage] a thermoplastic substance used in making various fabrics, a transparent wrapping material, etc.

sar·casm (sär'kaz'm) *n.* [< Gr. *sarkazein*, to tear flesh] 1. a taunting or sneering remark, generally ironical 2. the making of such remarks 3. sarcastic quality

sar·cas·tic (sär kas'tik) *adj.* 1. of, like, or full of sarcasm; sneering 2. using sarcasm —**sar·cas'ti·cal·ly** *adv.*

sar·co·ma (sär kō'mə) *n., pl.* -**mas**, -**ma·ta** (-mə tə) [< Gr. *sarx*, flesh] a malignant tumor that begins in connective tissue

sar·coph·a·gus (sär käf'ə gəs) *n., pl.* -**gi'** (-jī'), -**gus·es** [< Gr. *sarx*, flesh + *phagein*, to eat: limestone coffins hastened disintegration] a stone coffin, esp. one on display, as in a monumental tomb

sar·dine (sär dēn') *n.* [< L. *sarda*, a fish] any of various small ocean fishes preserved in tightly packed cans for eating

sar·don·ic (sär dän'ik) *adj.* [< Gr. *sardanios*, bitter] disdainfully or bitterly sarcastic *[a sardonic smile]* —**sar·don'i·cal·ly** *adv.*

sa·ri (sä'rē) *n.* [< Sans.] an outer garment of Hindu women, a long cloth wrapped around the body with one end over the shoulder

sa·rong (sə rôŋ') *n.* [Malay *särung*] a garment of men and women in the East Indies, etc., a long cloth worn like a skirt

sar·sa·pa·ril·la (sas'pə ril'ə, särs'-, sär'sə-) *n.* [< Sp. *zarza*, bramble + *parra*, vine] 1. a tropical American plant with fragrant roots 2. a carbonated drink flavored with an extract from the dried roots

sar·to·ri·al (sär tôr'ē əl) *adj.* [< LL. *sartor*, a tailor] 1. of tailors or their work 2. of men's dress —**sar·to'ri·al·ly** *adv.*

sash¹ (sash) *n.* [Ar. *shāsh*, muslin] an ornamental ribbon or scarf worn over the shoulder or around the waist

sash² (sash) *n.* [< Fr. *châssis*, a frame] a frame for holding the glass pane of a window or door, esp. a sliding frame

sa·shay (sa shā') *vi.* [< Fr. *chassé*, a dance] [Colloq.] to walk or go, esp. casually

sass (sas) *n.* [var. of SAUCE] [Colloq.] impudent talk —*vt.* [Colloq.] to talk impudently to

sas·sa·fras (sas'ə fras') *n.* [Sp. *sasafras*] 1. a small N. American tree bearing small, bluish fruits 2. the dried root bark of this tree, used as a flavoring

sass·y (sas'ē) *adj.* -**i·er**, -**i·est** [dial. var. of SAUCY] [Colloq.] impudent; saucy

sat (sat) *pt. & pp. of* SIT

Sat. 1. Saturday 2. Saturn

Sa·tan (sāt''n) [< Heb. *sāṭan*, to plot against] the Devil

sa·tan·ic (sā tan′ik, sə-) *adj.* like Satan; devilish; wicked —**sa·tan′i·cal·ly** *adv.*

satch·el (sach′əl) *n.* [< L. *saccus*, a sack] a small bag for carrying clothes, books, etc.

sate (sāt) *vt.* **sat′ed, sat′ing** [prob. < L. *satiare*, to fill full] **1.** to satisfy (an appetite, desire, etc.) to the full **2.** to satiate

sa·teen (sa tēn′) *n.* [< SATIN] a smooth, glossy cotton cloth, made to imitate satin

sat·el·lite (sat′'l īt′) *n.* [Fr. < L. *satelles*, an attendant] **1.** an attendant of some important person **2.** *a)* a small heavenly body revolving around a larger one *b)* a man-made object put into orbit around the earth, the moon, etc. **3.** a small state economically dependent on a larger state

sa·tia·ble (sā′shə b'l, -shē ə-) *adj.* that can be sated or satiated —**sa′tia·bil′i·ty** *n.*

sa·ti·ate (sā′shē āt′) *vt.* **-at′ed, -at′ing** [< L. *satis*, enough] to provide with more than enough, so as to weary or disgust; glut

sa·ti·e·ty (sə tī′ə tē) *n.* the state of being satiated

sat·in (sat′'n) *n.* [< Ar. *zaitūnī*, of *Zaitūn*, former name of a Chinese seaport] a fabric of silk, nylon, etc. with a smooth, glossy finish on one side —**sat′in·y** *adj.*

sat′in·wood′ *n.* **1.** a smooth wood used in fine furniture **2.** a tree yielding such wood

sat·ire (sa′tīr) *n.* [Fr. < L. *satira*] **1.** a literary work in which vices, follies, etc. are held up to ridicule and contempt **2.** the use of ridicule, sarcasm, etc. to attack vices, follies, etc. —**sa·tir·i·cal** (sə tir′i k'l), **sa·tir′ic** *adj.* —**sat·i·rist** (sat′ə rist) *n.*

sat·i·rize (sat′ə rīz′) *vt.* **-rized′, -riz′ing** to attack with satire —**sat′i·riz′er** *n.*

sat·is·fac·tion (sat′is fak′shən) *n.* **1.** a satisfying or being satisfied **2.** something that satisfies; specif., *a)* anything that brings pleasure or contentment *b)* settlement of debt

sat′is·fac′to·ry (-tə rē, -trē) *adj.* satisfying; fulfilling a need, wish, etc. —**sat′is·fac′to·ri·ly** *adv.* —**sat′is·fac′to·ri·ness** *n.*

sat·is·fy (sat′is fī′) *vt.* **-fied′, -fy′ing** [< L. *satis*, enough + *facere*, to make] **1.** to fulfill the needs or desires of; gratify **2.** to fulfill the requirements of **3.** to free from doubt; convince **4.** *a)* to give what is due to *b)* to discharge (a debt, etc.) —*vi.* to be adequate, sufficient, etc.

sa·trap (sā′trap, sat′rap) *n.* [< OPer.] a petty tyrant

sat·u·rate (sach′ə rāt′) *vt.* **-rat′ed, -rat′ing** [< L. *satur*, full] **1.** to cause to be thoroughly soaked **2.** to cause to be so completely filled or supplied that no more can be taken up —**sat′u·ra′tion** *n.*

Sat·ur·day (sat′ər dē, -dā′) *n.* [OE. *Sæterdæg*, Saturn's day] the seventh and last day of the week

Sat·urn (sat′ərn) **1.** *Rom. Myth.* the god of agriculture **2.** a planet in the solar system: see PLANET

sat·ur·nine (sat′ər nīn′) *adj.* [< supposed influence of planet Saturn] sluggish, grave, taciturn, etc. —**sat′ur·nine′ly** *adv.*

sat·yr (sāt′ər, sat′-) *n.* [< Gr. *satyros*] **1.** *Gr. Myth.* a lecherous woodland deity, represented as a man with a goat's ears, horns, and legs **2.** a lecherous man

sauce (sôs) *n.* [< L. *sal*, salt] **1.** *a)* a liquid or soft dressing served with food as a seasoning *b)* a flavored syrup put on ice cream **2.** stewed or preserved fruit **3.** [Colloq.] impudence —*vt.* **sauced, sauc′ing 1.** to flavor with a sauce **2.** [Colloq.] to be saucy to

sauce′pan′ *n.* a small pot with a projecting handle, used for cooking

sau·cer (sô′sər) *n.* [see SAUCE] a shallow dish, esp. one designed to hold a cup

sau·cy (sô′sē) *adj.* **-ci·er, -ci·est** [SAUC(E) + -Y²] **1.** rude; impudent **2.** pert; sprightly —**sau′ci·ly** *adv.* —**sau′ci·ness** *n.*

sauer·kraut (sour′krout′) *n.* [G. *sauer*, sour + *kraut*, cabbage] chopped cabbage fermented in brine

Saul (sôl) *Bible* the first king of Israel

sau·na (sou′nə, sô′-) *n.* [Finn.] **1.** a Finnish bath with exposure to hot, dry air **2.** the enclosure for such a bath

saun·ter (sôn′tər) *vi.* [< ?] to walk about idly; stroll —*n.* a leisurely walk

sau·ri·an (sôr′ē ən) *adj.* [< Gr. *sauros*, a lizard] of or like lizards

sau·sage (sô′sij) *n.* [see SAUCE] pork or other meat, chopped fine, seasoned, and often stuffed into a casing

sau·té (sō tā′, sô-) *adj.* [Fr. < *sauter*, to leap] fried quickly in a little fat —*vt.* **-téed′, -té′ing** to fry quickly in a little fat

sau·terne (sō turn′, sô-) *n.* [< *Sauternes*, town in France] a white table wine

sav·age (sav′ij) *adj.* [< L. *silva*, a wood] **1.** wild; uncultivated [a *savage* jungle] **2.** fierce; untamed [a *savage* tiger] **3.** primitive; barbarous [a *savage* tribe] **4.** cruel; pitiless —*n.* **1.** a member of a primitive or uncivilized society **2.** a brutal person —**sav′age·ly** *adv.* —**sav′age·ry** *n.*

sa·vant (sə vänt′, sav′ənt) *n.* [Fr. < L. *sapere*, to know] a learned person

save¹ (sāv) *vt.* **saved, sav′ing** [< L. *salvus*, safe] **1.** to rescue or preserve from harm or danger **2.** to preserve for future use **3.** to prevent loss or waste of [to *save* time] **4.** to avoid or lessen [to *save* wear] **5.** *Theol.* to deliver from sin —*vi.* **1.** to avoid expense, waste, etc. **2.** to hoard money or goods —**sav′a·ble, save′a·ble** *adj.* —**sav′er** *n.*

save² (sāv) *prep., conj.* [< OFr. *sauf*, lit., SAFE] except; but: also **sav′ing**

sav·ing (sā′viŋ) *adj.* that saves; specif., *a)* economical *b)* redeeming —*n.* **1.** the act of one that saves **2.** [*often pl. with sing. v.*] any reduction in time, expense, etc. **3.** [*pl.*] sums of money saved

sav·ior, sav·iour (sāv′yər) *n.* [< LL. *salvare*, to save] one who saves —**the Saviour** (or **Savior**) Jesus Christ

sa·voir-faire (sav′wär fer′) *n.* [Fr., to know (how) to do] ready knowledge of what to do or say

sa·vor (sā′vər) *n.* [< L. *sapor*] **1.** the taste or smell of something **2.** characteristic quality —*vi.* to have the particular taste, smell, or quality (*of*) —*vt.* to taste with delight Brit. sp. **savour**

sa′vor·y *adj.* **-i·er, -i·est 1.** pleasing to the taste or smell **2.** pleasant, agreeable, etc. Brit. sp. **savoury** —**sa′vor·i·ness** *n.*

sav·vy (sav′ē) *vi.* **-vied, -vy·ing** [< Sp. *sabe* (*usted*), do (you) know] [Slang] to understand —*n.* [Slang] shrewd understanding

saw¹ (sô) *n.* [OE. *sagu*] a cutting tool having a thin, metal blade or disk with sharp teeth —*vt.* **sawed, sawed** or **sawn, saw′ing** to cut or shape with a saw —*vi.* **1.** to cut with or as a saw **2.** to be cut with a saw

saw² (sô) *n.* [OE. *sagu*] an old saying; maxim

saw³ (sô) *pt.* of SEE¹

saw·buck (sô′buk′) *n.* [Du. *zaagbok*] **1.** a sawhorse **2.** [Slang] a ten-dollar bill

saw′dust′ (-dust′) *n.* tiny bits of wood formed in sawing

saw′horse′ (-hôrs′) *n.* a rack on which wood is placed while being sawed

saw′mill′ (-mil′) *n.* a place where logs are sawed into boards

saw′-toothed′ (-tootht′) *adj.* having notches like the teeth of a saw; serrate: also **saw′-tooth′**

saw·yer (sô′yər) *n.* one whose work is sawing wood, as into planks and boards

sax (saks) *n.* [Colloq.] a saxophone

Sax·on (sak′s'n) *n.* 1. a member of an ancient Germanic people of N Germany, some of whom settled in England 2. *same as* ANGLO-SAXON (*n.* 1 & 3) 3. any dialect of the Saxons —*adj.* of the Saxons, their language, etc.

sax·o·phone (sak′sə fōn′) *n.* [Fr., after A. J. *Sax*, 19th-c. Belgian inventor + -PHONE] a single-reed, keyed, metal wind instrument — **sax′o·phon′ist** *n.*

say (sā) *vt.* **said, say′ing** [OE. *secgan*] 1. to utter; speak 2. to express in words; state 3. to state positively or as an opinion [I cannot *say* who won] 4. to recite [*say* your prayers] 5. to estimate [he is, I'd *say*, forty] —*n.* 1. a chance to speak [to have one's *say*] 2. authority, as to make a final decision: often with *the* —**that is to say** in other words

say′ing *n.* something said; esp., an adage, proverb, or maxim

say-so (sā′sō′) *n.* [Colloq.] 1. (one's) word, assurance, etc. 2. right of decision

Sb [L. *stibium*] *Chem.* antimony

scab (skab) *n.* [ON. *skabb*] 1. a crust forming over a sore during healing 2. a worker who refuses to join a union, or who replaces a striking worker —*vi.* **scabbed, scab′bing** 1. to become covered with a scab 2. to act as a scab —**scab′by** *adj.* -**bi·er,** -**bi·est**

scab·bard (skab′ərd) *n.* [? < OHG. *scar*, sword + *bergan*, to hide] a sheath for the blade of a sword, dagger, etc. —*vt.* to sheath

sca·bies (skā′bēz, -bē ēz) *n.* [< L. *scabere*, to scratch] a contagious skin disease caused by mites, characterized by intense itching

scab·rous (skab′rəs, skā′brəs) *adj.* [< L. *scabere*, to scratch] 1. scaly or scabby 2. indecent, scandalous, etc.

scad (skad) *n.* [< ?] [*usually pl.*] [Colloq.] a very large amount [*scads* of money]

scaf·fold (skaf′'ld, -ōld) *n.* [OFr. *escafalt*] 1. a temporary framework for supporting people working on a building, etc. 2. a raised platform on which criminals are executed 3. any raised framework

scaf′fold·ing *n.* 1. the materials that form a scaffold 2. a scaffold or scaffolds

scal·a·wag (skal′ə wag′) *n.* [< ?] a rascal

scald (skôld) *vt.* [< L. *ex-*, intens. + *calidus*, hot] 1. to burn with hot liquid or steam 2. to heat almost to the boiling point 3. to use boiling liquid on, as in sterilizing —*n.* a burn caused by scalding

scale¹ (skāl) *n.* [< L. *scala*, a ladder] 1. *a*) a series of marks along a line used in measuring [the *scale* of a thermometer] *b*) any instrument so marked 2. the proportion that a map, etc. bears to the thing it represents [a *scale* of one inch to a mile] 3. *a*) a series of degrees classified by size, amount, etc. [a wage *scale*] *b*) any degree in such a series 4. *Music* a sequence of tones, rising or falling in pitch, according to a system of intervals —*vt.* **scaled, scal′ing** 1. to climb up or over 2. to make according to a scale —**scale down** (or **up**) to reduce (or increase) according to a ratio

scale² (skāl) *n.* [< OFr. *escale*, husk] 1. any of the thin, flat, horny plates covering many fishes and reptiles 2. any thin, platelike layer or piece —*vt.* **scaled, scal′ing** to scrape scales from —*vi.* to flake or peel off in scales —**scal′y** *adj.* -**i·er,** -**i·est**

scale³ (skāl) *n.* [ON. *skāl*, bowl] 1. either pan of a balance 2. [*often pl.*] a balance or other weighing device —*vt.* **scaled, scal′ing** to weigh

scale insect any of various small insects destructive to plants: the females secrete a wax scale

sca·lene (skā lēn′, skā′lēn) *adj.* [< Gr. *skalēnos*, uneven] having unequal sides and angles: said of a triangle

scal·lion (skal′yən) *n.* [< L. (*caepa*) *Ascalonia*, (onion of) Ascalon (Philistine city)] any of various onions, as the leek or a green onion with an almost bulbless root

scal·lop (skäl′əp, skal′-) *n.* [OFr. *escalope*] 1. a kind of edible mollusk with two curved, hinged shells 2. one of the shells 3. any of a series of curves, etc. forming an ornamental edge —*vt.* 1. to cut the edge of in scallops 2. to bake with a milk sauce and bread crumbs

scalp (skalp) *n.* [< Scand.] the skin on the top and back of the head, usually covered with hair —*vt.* 1. to cut or tear the scalp from 2. [Colloq.] to buy (theater tickets, etc.) and resell them at higher prices —**scalp′er** *n.*

scal·pel (skal′pəl) *n.* [< L. *scalpere*, to cut] a small, sharp, straight knife used in surgery and anatomical dissections

scamp (skamp) *n.* [< MFr. *escamper*, to flee] a mischievous fellow; rascal —**scamp′ish** *adj.*

scam·per (skam′pər) *vi.* [see SCAMP] to run or go quickly —*n.* a scampering

scam·pi (skam′pē) *n., pl.* -**pi,** -**pies** [It.] a large prawn, valued as food

scan (skan) *vt.* **scanned, scan′ning** [< L. *scandere*, to climb] 1. to analyze (verse) by marking off the metrical feet 2. to look at closely 3. to glance at quickly 4. *TV* to traverse (a surface) rapidly with a beam of light or electrons as in reproducing an image —*vi.* to be in a certain poetic meter —*n.* a scanning

Scan., Scand. Scandinavian

scan·dal (skan′d'l) *n.* [< Fr. < Gr. *skandalon*, a snare] 1. anything that offends morals and leads to disgrace 2. shame, outrage, etc. caused by this 3. disgrace 4. wicked gossip

scan′dal·ize′ *vt.* -**ized′,** -**iz′ing** to outrage the moral feelings of by improper conduct

scan′dal·mon′ger (-muŋ′gər, -mäŋ′-) *n.* one who gossips maliciously

scan′dal·ous *adj.* 1. causing scandal; shameful 2. spreading slander; libelous

Scan·di·na·vi·an (skan′də nā′vē ən) *adj.* of Scandinavia, its people, languages, etc. —*n.* 1. any of the people of Scandinavia 2. the sub-branch of Germanic languages spoken by them

scant (skant) *adj.* [< ON. *skammr*, short] 1. inadequate; meager 2. not quite up to full measure —*vt.* to stint —**scant′ness** *n.*

scant′y *adj.* -**i·er,** -**i·est** 1. barely sufficient; meager 2. insufficient; not enough —**scant′i·ly** *adv.* —**scant′i·ness** *n.*

scape·goat (skāp′gōt′) *n.* [(E)SCAPE + GOAT: see Lev. 16:7–26] one who bears the blame for the mistakes or crimes of others

scape′grace′ *n.* [(E)SCAPE + GRACE] a graceless, unprincipled fellow; scamp; rogue

scap·u·la (skap′yoo lə) *n., pl.* -**lae′** (-lē′), -**las** [L.] the shoulder blade

scar (skär) *n.* [< Gr. *eschara*, fireplace] a mark left after a wound, burn, etc. has healed —*vt.,*

vi. scarred, scar′ring to mark with or form a scar
scar·ab (skar′əb) *n.* [< Fr. < L. *scarabaeus*] **1.** a beetle **2.** a carved image of a beetle
scarce (skers) *adj.* [ult. < L. *excerpere,* to select] **1.** not common; rarely seen **2.** not plentiful; hard to get —*adv. literary var. of* SCARCELY —**scarce′ness** *n.*
scarce′ly *adv.* **1.** hardly; not quite **2.** probably not or certainly not
scar·ci·ty (sker′sə tē) *n., pl.* **-ties 1.** a being scarce; inadequate supply **2.** rarity; uncommonness
scare (sker) *vt.* **scared, scar′ing** [< ON. *skjarr,* timid] to fill with sudden fear —*vi.* to become frightened —*n.* a sudden fear —**scare up** [Colloq.] to produce or gather quickly
scare′crow′ *n.* a human figure made with sticks, old clothes, etc., put in a field to scare birds from crops
scarf (skärf) *n., pl.* **scarfs, scarves** (skärvz) [< ONormFr. *escarpe,* purse hung from the neck] **1.** a long or broad piece of cloth worn about the neck, head, etc. **2.** a long, narrow covering for a table, etc.
scar·let (skär′lit) *n.* [< ML. *scarlatum,* scarlet cloth] very bright red —*adj.* **1.** of this color **2.** sinful
scarlet fever an acute contagious disease characterized by sore throat, fever, and a scarlet rash
scar·y (sker′ē) *adj.* **-i·er, -i·est** [Colloq.] **1.** causing fear **2.** easily frightened —**scar′i·ness** *n.*
scat¹ (skat) *vi.* **scat′ted, scat′ting** [? a hiss + CAT] [Colloq.] to go away: usually in the imperative
scat² (skat) *adj.* [< ?] Jazz using improvised, meaningless syllables in singing —*n.* such singing —*vi.* **scat′ted, scat′ting** to sing scat
scath·ing (skā′thiŋ) *adj.* [< ON. *skathi,* harm] searing; harsh or caustic [*scathing* remarks] —**scath′ing·ly** *adv.*
scat·ter (skat′ər) *vt.* [ME. *skateren*] **1.** to throw here and there; sprinkle **2.** to separate and drive in many directions; disperse —*vi.* to move apart in several directions —*n.* a scattering
scat′ter·brain′ *n.* one who is not able to think in a serious way
scatter rug a small rug for covering only a limited area
scav·eng·er (skav′in jər) *n.* [< ONormFr. *escauwer,* inspect] **1.** one who gathers things discarded by others **2.** any animal that eats refuse and decaying matter —**scav′enge** (-inj) *vt., vi.* **-enged, -eng·ing**
sce·nar·i·o (si ner′ē ō′) *n., pl.* **-os′** [It. < L. *scaena,* SCENE] **1.** the working script of a motion picture **2.** an outline of a proposed series of events —**sce·nar′ist** *n.*
scene (sēn) *n.* [< Gr. *skēnē,* stage] **1.** the place where an event occurs **2.** the setting of a play, story, etc. **3.** a division of a play, usually part of an act **4.** a particular incident, as of a story **5.** *same as* SCENERY (sense 1) **6.** a view of people or places **7.** a display of strong feeling [to make a *scene*] **8.** [Colloq.] the locale for a specified activity
sce·ner·y (sē′nər ē) *n., pl.* **-ies 1.** painted screens, backdrops, etc., used on the stage to represent places **2.** the general appearance of a place; features of a landscape
sce·nic (sē′nik) *adj.* **1.** of the stage and its scenery, lighting, etc. **2.** of natural scenery; having beautiful scenery —**sce′ni·cal·ly** *adv.*
scent (sent) *vt.* [< L. *sentire,* to feel] **1.** to smell **2.** to suspect **3.** to fill with an odor; perfume —

n. **1.** a smell; odor **2.** the sense of smell **3.** a perfume **4.** an odor left by an animal, by which it is tracked
scep·ter (sep′tər) *n.* [< Gr. *skēptron,* staff] a staff held by a ruler as a symbol of sovereignty: Brit. sp. **scep′tre**
scep·tic (skep′tik) *n., adj. chiefly Brit. sp. of* SKEPTIC —**scep′ti·cal** *adj.* —**scep′ti·cism** *n.*
sched·ule (skej′ool, -əl) *n.* [< L. *scheda,* a leaf of paper] **1.** a list of details **2.** a list of times of recurring events; timetable **3.** a timed plan for a project —*vt.* **-uled, -ul·ing 1.** to place in a schedule **2.** to plan for a certain time
sche·mat·ic (skē mat′ik) *adj.* of or like a scheme, outline, diagram, etc.
scheme (skēm) *n.* [< Gr. *schēma,* a form] **1.** a systematic program for attaining some object **2.** an orderly combination of things on a definite plan **3.** a diagram **4.** a plot; intrigue —*vt., vi.* schemed, schem′ing to devise; plot; contrive —**schem′er** *n.*
scher·zo (sker′tsō) *n., pl.* **-zos, -zi** (-tsē) [It., a jest] a lively movement as of a sonata, in 3/4 time
schism (siz′m; *now occas.* skiz′m) *n.* [< Gr. *schizein,* to cleave] a split, esp. in a church, because of a difference of opinion, doctrine, etc. —**schis·mat′ic** (-mat′ik) *adj., n.*
schist (shist) *n.* [< Fr. < Gr. *schizein,* cleave] a crystalline rock easily split into layers
schiz·o·phre·ni·a (skit′sə frē′nē ə, skiz′ə-) *n.* [< Gr. *schizein,* cleave + *phrēn,* the mind] a mental disorder characterized by separation between thought and emotion, delusions, etc. —**schiz′oid** (-soid), **schiz′o·phren′ic** (-fren′ik) *adj., n.*
schmaltz (shmälts) *n.* [< G. *schmalz,* melted fat] anything very sentimental —**schmaltz′y** *adj.*
schnapps (shnäps) *n.* [G., a dram] any strong alcoholic liquor: also sp. **schnaps**
schnau·zer (shnou′zər) *n.* [G. < *schnauzen,* to snarl] a small active dog with a wiry coat
schol·ar (skäl′ər) *n.* [< L. *schola,* SCHOOL¹] **1.** a learned person **2.** a student or pupil —**schol′ar·ly** *adj., adv.*
schol′ar·ship′ *n.* **1.** the systematized knowledge of a scholar **2.** a gift of money, etc. to help a student
scho·las·tic (skə las′tik) *adj.* of schools, colleges, students, teachers, etc.; academic —**scho·las′ti·cal·ly** *adv.*
school¹ (skool) *n.* [< Gr. *scholē*] **1.** a place or institution, with its buildings, etc., for teaching and learning **2.** all of its students and teachers **3.** a regular session of teaching **4.** the process of being educated [he likes *school*] **5.** any situation through which one gains knowledge [the *school* of hard knocks] **6.** a particular division of a university **7.** a group following the same beliefs, methods, etc. —*vt.* **1.** to teach; instruct **2.** to discipline; control —*adj.* of a school or schools
school² (skool) *n.* [Du., a crowd] a group of fish, etc. swimming together
school board a group of people in charge of local public schools
school′book′ *n.* a textbook
school′boy′ *n.* a boy attending school —**school′girl′** *n.fem.*
school′house′ *n.* a building used as a school
school′ing *n.* training or education; esp., formal instruction at school
school′marm′ (-märm′, -mäm′) *n.* [Colloq.] **1.** a woman schoolteacher **2.** any person who tends to be old-fashioned and prudish

school'mas'ter *n.* a man who teaches in, or is head of, a school —**school'mis'tress** *n.fem.*

school'mate' *n.* a person going to the same school at the same time as another

school'room' *n.* a classroom in a school

school'teach'er *n.* one who teaches in a school

school year the part of a year when school is in session

schoon·er (skōō'nər) *n.* [< ?] 1. a ship with two or more masts, rigged fore and aft 2. a large beer glass

schuss (shoos) *n.* [G., shot, rush] a straight run down a hill in skiing —*vi.* to make such a run

schwa (shwä) *n.* [G. < Heb. *sh'wā*] 1. the neutral vowel sound of most unstressed syllables in English, as of *a* in *ago* 2. the symbol (ə) for this

sci·at·i·ca (sī at'i kə) *n.* [< Gr. *ischion*, hip] any painful condition in the hip or thigh; esp., neuritis of the long nerve (**sciatic nerve**) down the back of the thigh

sci·ence (sī'əns) *n.* [< L. *scire*, know] 1. systematized knowledge derived from observation, study, etc. 2. a branch of knowledge, esp. one that systematizes facts, principles, and methods 3. skill or technique

science fiction highly imaginative fiction typically involving real or imagined scientific phenomena

sci·en·tif·ic (sī'ən tif'ik) *adj.* 1. of or dealing with science 2. based on, or using, the principles and methods of science; systematic and exact —**sci'en·tif'i·cal·ly** *adv.*

sci'en·tist *n.* a specialist in science, as in biology, chemistry, etc.

scim·i·tar, scim·i·ter (sim'ə tər) *n.* [It. *scimitarra*] a short, curved sword used by Turks, Arabs, etc.

scin·til·la (sin til'ə) *n.* [L.] 1. a spark 2. a trace

scin·til·late (sin't'l āt') *vi.* -lat'ed, -lat'ing [< L. *scintilla*, a spark] 1. to sparkle or twinkle 2. to be brilliant and witty —**scin'til·la'tion** *n.*

sci·on (sī'ən) *n.* [OFr. *cion*] 1. a shoot or bud of a plant, used for grafting 2. a descendant

scis·sors (siz'ərz) *n.pl.* [< LL. *cisorium*, cutting tool] a cutting instrument with two opposing blades pivoted together so that they work against each other: also **pair of scissors**

scle·ro·sis (skli rō'sis) *n., pl.* -ses (-sēz) [< Gr. *sklēros*, hard] an abnormal hardening of body tissues —**scle·rot'ic** (-rät'ik) *adj.*

scoff (skôf, skäf) *n.* [prob. < Scand.] an expression of scorn or derision; jeer —*vt., vi.* to mock or jeer (*at*) —**scoff'er** *n.*

scold (skōld) *n.* [< ON. *skald*, poet (prob. because of satirical verses)] a woman who habitually uses abusive language —*vt.* to find fault with angrily; rebuke —*vi.* 1. to find fault angrily 2. to use abusive language —**scold'er** *n.* —**scold'ing** *adj., n.*

scol·lop (skäl'əp) *n., vt. var. of* SCALLOP

sconce (skäns) *n.* [ult. < L. *abscondere*, to hide] a wall bracket as for holding a candle

scone (skōn) *n.* [Scot. < ? MDu. *schoonbrot*, fine bread] a tea cake resembling a baking powder biscuit

scoop (skōōp) *n.* [< MDu. *schope*, bucket & *schoppe*, a shovel] 1. any of various small, shovellike utensils used for taking up flour, ice cream, etc. 2. the deep shovel of a dredge or steam shovel 3. a scooping, or the amount scooped up at one time 4. a motion as of scooping 5. [Colloq.] a publishing of news before a rival newspaper —*vt.* 1. to take up or out as with a scoop 2. to hollow (*out*) 3. [Colloq.] to publish news before (a rival) —**scoop'ful'** *n., pl.* -fuls'

scoot (skōōt) *vi., vt.* [prob. < ON. *skjōta*, to shoot] [Colloq.] to go quickly; scurry off

scoot'er *n.* 1. a child's two-wheeled vehicle moved by pushing one foot against the ground 2. a similar vehicle propelled by a motor: in full **motor scooter**

scope (skōp) *n.* [< It. < Gr. *skopos*, watcher] 1. the extent of the mind's grasp 2. range or extent of action, observation, inclusion, etc. 3. room for action or thought

-scope [< Gr. *skopein*, to see] *a combining form meaning* an instrument, etc. for seeing or observing

scor·bu·tic (skôr byōōt'ik) *adj.* [< ML. *scorbutus*, scurvy] of, like, or having scurvy

scorch (skôrch) *vt.* [< ? Scand.] 1. to burn slightly or on the surface 2. to parch or shrivel by heat —*vi.* to become scorched —*n.* a superficial burn

score (skôr) *n.* [< ON. *skor*] 1. a scratch, mark, notch, incision, etc. 2. a debt or account 3. a grudge 4. a reason or ground 5. the number of points made, as in a game 6. a grade, as on a test 7. twenty people or objects 8. [*pl.*] very many 9. a copy of a musical composition, showing all parts for the instruments or voices 10. [Colloq.] the actual facts [to know the *score*] —*vt.* **scored, scor'ing** 1. to mark or mark out with notches, lines, etc. 2. *a)* to make (runs, points, etc.) in a game *b)* to record the score of 3. to achieve, as a success 4. to grade, as in testing 5. to arrange a musical score 6. to upbraid —*vi.* 1. to make points, as in a game 2. to keep score in a game 3. to succeed in getting what one wants —**scor'er** *n.*

score'board' *n.* a large board for posting scores, etc., as in a stadium

scorn (skôrn) *n.* [< OFr. *escharnir*, to scorn] great contempt, often with anger —*vt.* 1. to regard with scorn 2. to refuse or reject with scorn —**scorn'ful** *adj.* —**scorn'ful·ly** *adv.*

Scor·pi·o (skôr'pē ō') [L., scorpion] the eighth sign of the zodiac

scor'pi·on (-ən) *n.* [< Gr. *skorpios*] an arachnid found in warm regions, with a long tail ending in a poisonous sting

scot (skät) *n.* a native of Scotland

Scot. 1. Scotch 2. Scotland 3. Scottish

Scotch (skäch) *adj.* of Scotland: cf. SCOTTISH — *n. same as:* 1. SCOTTISH 2. SCOTCH WHISKY

scotch (skäch) *vt.* [prob. < OFr. *coche*, a notch] 1. to cut or maim 2. to put an end to; stifle [to *scotch* a rumor]

Scotch'man *n., pl.* -men *var. of* SCOTSMAN

Scotch tape [< *Scotch*, a trademark] a thin, transparent, cellulose adhesive tape

Scotch whisky whiskey distilled in Scotland from malted barley

scot-free (skät'frē') *adj.* [orig., free from payment of *scot* (early term for tax)] unharmed or unpunished; free from penalty

Scotland Yard the London police headquarters, esp. its detective bureau

Scots (skäts) *adj., n. same as* SCOTTISH

Scots'man (-mən) *n., pl.* -men a native of Scotland: *Scotsman* or *Scot* is preferred to *Scotchman* in Scotland

Scot·tish (skät'ish) *adj.* of Scotland, its people, their English dialect, etc. *Scottish* is formal usage, but with some words, *Scotch* is used (e.g., tweed, whisky), with others, *Scots* (e.g., law) —*n.* the English spoken in Scotland —**the Scottish** the Scottish people

scoun·drel (skoun'drəl) *n.* [prob. ult. < L. *ab-*

scondere, ABSCOND] a mean, immoral, or wicked person

scour[1] (skour) *vt., vi.* [< L. *ex-,* intens. + *curare,* take care of] **1.** to clean by vigorous rubbing, as with abrasives **2.** to remove dirt and grease from (wool, etc.)

scour[2] (skour) *vt.* [prob. < L. *ex-,* out + *currere,* to run] to pass over quickly, or range over, as in search [to scour a library for a book]

scourge (skurj) *n.* [< L. *ex,* off + *corrigia,* a whip] **1.** a whip **2.** any cause of great suffering [the *scourge* of war] —*vt.* scourged, scourg'ing **1.** to whip; flog **2.** to punish or afflict severely

scout (skout) *n.* [< L. *auscultare,* listen] **1.** a soldier, plane, etc. sent to spy out the enemy's strength, movements, etc. **2.** a person sent out to search for new talent, etc. **3.** a Boy Scout or Girl Scout —*vt., vi.* **1.** to reconnoiter **2.** to go in search of (something)

scout'mas'ter *n.* the adult leader of a troop of Boy Scouts

scow (skou) *n.* [Du. *schouw*] a large, flat-bottomed boat with square ends, used for carrying freight, often towed by a tug

scowl (skoul) *vi.* [prob. < Scand.] to look angry, sullen, etc. as by contracting the eyebrows —*n.* a scowling; angry frown

scrab·ble (skrab'l) *vi.* -bled, -bling [< Du. *schrabben,* to scrape] **1.** to scratch, scrape, etc. as though looking for something **2.** to struggle

scrag·gly (skrag'lē) *adj.* -gli·er, -gli·est [prob. < ON.] sparse, scrubby, ragged, etc.

scram (skram) *vi.* scrammed, scram'ming [< SCRAMBLE] [Slang] to get out

scram·ble (skram'b'l) *vi.* -bled, -bling [< ?] **1.** to climb, crawl, or clamber hurriedly **2.** to scuffle or struggle for something —*vt.* **1.** to mix haphazardly **2.** to make (transmitted signals) unintelligible in transit **3.** to stir and cook (slightly beaten eggs) —*n.* **1.** a hard climb or advance **2.** a disorderly struggle, as for something prized

scrap[1] (skrap) *n.* [< ON. *skrap*] **1.** a small piece; fragment **2.** discarded material **3.** [pl.] bits of food —*adj.* **1.** in the form of pieces, leftovers, etc. **2.** used and discarded —*vt.* scrapped, scrap'ping **1.** to make into scrap **2.** to discard; junk

scrap[2] (skrap) *n., vi.* scrapped, scrap'ping [prob. < SCRAPE] [Colloq.] fight or quarrel —**scrap'per** *n.* —**scrap'pi·ness** *n.* —**scrap'py** *adj.* -pi·er, -pi·est

scrap'book' *n.* a book of blank pages for mounting clippings, pictures, etc.

scrape (skrāp) *vt.* scraped, scrap'ing [< ON. *skrapa*] **1.** to make smooth or clean by rubbing with a tool or abrasive **2.** to remove in this way (with *off, out,* etc.) **3.** to scratch, abrade, etc. **4.** to gather slowly and with difficulty [to scrape up some money] —*vi.* **1.** to rub against something harshly; grate **2.** to manage to get by (with *along, by,* etc.) —*n.* **1.** a scraping **2.** a scraped place **3.** a harsh, grating sound **4.** a predicament —**scrap'er** *n.*

scratch (skrach) *vt.* [prob. a fusion of ME. *scratten* & *cracchen*] **1.** to scrape or cut the surface of slightly **2.** to tear or dig with the nails or claws **3.** to scrape lightly to relieve itching **4.** to scrape with a grating noise **5.** to write or draw hurriedly or carelessly **6.** to strike out (writing, etc.) **7.** *Sports* to withdraw a contestant —*vi.* **1.** to use nails or claws in digging or wounding **2.** to scrape —*n.* **1.** the act of scratching **2.** a mark, tear, etc. made by scratching **3.** a grating or scraping sound —*adj.* used for hasty notes, figuring, etc. [scratch

paper] —from scratch from nothing; without advantage —up to scratch [Colloq.] up to a standard —**scratch'y** *adj.* -i·er, -i·est

scrawl (skrôl) *vt., vi.* [< ?] to write or draw hastily, carelessly, etc. —*n.* a sprawling handwriting, often illegible —**scrawl'y** *adj.* -i·er, -i·est

scraw·ny (skrô'nē) *adj.* -ni·er, -ni·est [prob. < Scand.] very thin

scream (skrēm) *vi.* [ME. *screamen*] **1.** to utter a shrill, piercing cry as in pain or fright **2.** to shout, laugh, etc. wildly —*vt.* to utter as with a scream —*n.* **1.** a sharp, piercing cry or sound **2.** [Colloq.] a hilariously funny person or thing

screech (skrēch) *vi.* [ON. *skraekja*] to utter (with) a shrill, high-pitched cry —*n.* such a cry —**screech'y** *adj.* -i·er, -i·est

screen (skrēn) *n.* [< OFr. *escren*] **1.** a curtain or partition used to separate, conceal, protect, etc. **2.** anything that shields, conceals, etc. [a smoke *screen*] **3.** a coarse mesh of wire, etc. used as a sieve **4.** a frame covered with a mesh, used, as on a window, to keep insects out **5.** a surface upon which movies, slides, etc. are projected **6.** the movie industry —*vt.* **1.** to separate, conceal, etc., as with a screen **2.** to sift through a screen **3.** to interview or test in order to separate according to skills, etc. **4.** to project (movies, etc.) upon a screen

screen'play' *n.* a story written in a form suitable for production as a movie

screw (skrōō) *n.* [< OFr. *escroue,* hole in which a screw turns] **1.** a naillike metal piece grooved in an advancing spiral, for fastening things by being turned **2.** any spiral thing like this **3.** any of various devices operating or threaded like a screw —*vt.* **1.** to twist; turn **2.** to fasten, tighten, etc. as with a screw **3.** to contort **4.** [Slang] to cheat; swindle —*vi.* **1.** to go together or come apart by being turned like a screw [a lid screws on] **2.** to be fitted for screws —**put the screws on** (or **to**) to subject to force or pressure

screw'ball' *n.* [Slang] an erratic, irrational, or unconventional person

screw'driv'er *n.* a tool used for turning screws

screw'y *adj.* -i·er, -i·est [Slang] irrational, peculiar, absurd, etc.

scrib·ble (skrib'l) *vt., vi.* -bled, -bling [< L. *scribere,* write] **1.** to write carelessly, hastily, etc. **2.** to make meaningless or illegible marks (on) —*n.* scribbled writing

scribe (skrīb) *n.* [< L. *scribere,* write] **1.** one who copied manuscripts before the invention of printing **2.** a writer; author

scrim·mage (skrim'ij) *n.* [< SKIRMISH] **1.** a confused struggle **2.** *Football* a) the play that follows the pass from center b) a practice game —*vi.* -maged, -mag·ing to take part in a scrimmage

scrimp (skrimp) *vt.* [prob. < Scand.] **1.** to make too small, short, etc. **2.** to treat stingily —*vi.* to be sparing and frugal

scrip (skrip) *n.* [< SCRIPT] a certificate of a right to receive something, as stocks, money, etc.

script (skript) *n.* [< L. *scribere,* write] **1.** handwriting **2.** a copy of the text of a play, movie, TV show, etc.

scrip·ture (skrip'chər) *n.* [see SCRIPT] **1.** [S-] [often pl.] a) the sacred writings of the Jews, identical with the Old Testament of the Christians b) the Christian Bible **2.** any sacred writing —**scrip'tur·al** *adj.*

scrod (skräd) *n.* [prob. < MDu. *schrode,* strip] a young codfish, split and prepared for cooking

scrof·u·la (skräf′yə lə) *n.* [< L. *scrofa,* a sow] tuberculosis of the lymphatic glands, esp. of the neck —**scrof′u·lous** *adj.*

scroll (skrōl) *n.* [< ME. *scrowe*] 1. a roll of parchment or paper, usually with writing on it 2. an ornamental design in coiled or spiral form

scro·tum (skrōt′əm) *n., pl.* **-ta** (-ə), **-tums** [L.] in most male mammals, the pouch of skin containing the testicles

scrounge (skrounj) *vt.* **scrounged, scroung′ing** [< ?] [Colloq.] 1. to get by begging or sponging 2. to pilfer —*vi.* [Colloq.] to search (*around*) for something

scrub[1] (skrub) *n.* [dial. var. of SHRUB] 1. a thick growth of stunted trees or bushes 2. any person or thing smaller than the usual, or inferior 3. *Sports* a substitute player —*adj.* 1. poor; inferior 2. undersized —**scrub′by** *adj.* **-bi·er, -bi·est**

scrub[2] (skrub) *vt., vi.* **scrubbed, scrub′bing** [prob. < Scand.] 1. to clean or wash by rubbing hard 2. to rub hard —*n.* a scrubbing —**scrub′ber** *n.*

scruff (skruf) *n.* [< ON. *skrufr*] the nape of the neck

scruff·y (skruf′ē) *adj.* **-i·er, -i·est** [< dial. *scruff,* var. of SCURF] shabby; unkempt

scrump·tious (skrump′shəs) *adj.* [altered < SUMPTUOUS] [Colloq.] very pleasing

scru·ple (skrōō′p′l) *n.* [< L. *scrupulus,* small stone] 1. a very small quantity 2. a doubt arising from difficulty in deciding what is right, proper, etc. —*vt., vi.* **-pled, -pling** to hesitate (at) from doubt

scru·pu·lous (skrōō′pyə ləs) *adj.* 1. having or showing scruples; conscientiously honest 2. careful of details; precise

scru·ti·nize (skrōōt′'n īz′) *vt.* **-nized′, -niz′ing** to look at carefully; examine closely

scru·ti·ny (-′n ē) *n., pl.* **-nies** [< L. *scrutari,* examine] a close examination

scu·ba (skōō′bə) *n.* [*s*(*elf*-)*c*(*ontained*) *u*(*nderwater*) *b*(*reathing*) *a*(*pparatus*)] a diver's apparatus with compressed-air tanks for breathing under water

scud (skud) *vi.* **scud′ded, scud′ding** [prob. < ON.] 1. to move swiftly 2. to be driven before the wind —*n.* 1. a scudding 2. spray, clouds, etc. driven by the wind

scuff (skuf) *vt.* [prob. < ON. *skufa,* to shove] 1. to scrape (the ground, etc.) with the feet 2. to wear a rough place on the surface of —*vi.* 1. to walk without lifting the feet; shuffle —*n.* 1. a scuffing 2. a worn or rough spot 3. a loose-fitting house slipper

scuf·fle (skuf′'l) *vi.* **-fled, -fling** [< SCUFF] 1. to struggle or fight in rough confusion 2. to drag one's feet —*n.* 1. a rough, confused fight 2. a shuffling of feet

scull (skul) *n.* [prob. < Scand.] 1. an oar worked from side to side over the stern of a boat to propel it 2. a light rowboat for racing —*vt., vi.* to propel with a scull —**scull′er** *n.*

scul·ler·y (skul′ər ē) *n., pl.* **-ies** [< L. *scutella,* tray] a room where kitchen utensils are cleaned

scul·lion (skul′yən) *n.* [ult. < L. *scopa,* broom] [Archaic] a servant who does rough kitchen work

sculpt (skulpt) *vt., vi. same as* SCULPTURE

sculp·tor (skulp′tər) *n.* an artist who creates works of sculpture —**sculp′tress** *n.fem.*

sculp′ture (-chər) *n.* [< L. *sculpere,* carve] 1. the art of forming stone, clay, wood, etc. into statues, figures, or the like 2. a work or works of sculpture —*vt., vi.* **-tured, -tur·ing** 1. to carve,

chisel, etc. (statues, figures, etc.) 2. to make or form like sculpture —**sculp′tu·ral** *adj.*

scum (skum) *n.* [< MDu. *schum*] 1. a thin layer of impurities on the top of a liquid 2. refuse 3. low, despicable people —**scum′my** *adj.* **-mi·er, -mi·est**

scup·per (skup′ər) *n.* [< ?] an opening in a ship's side to let water run off the deck

scurf (skurf) *n.* [< ON.] 1. little, dry scales shed by the skin, as dandruff 2. any scaly coating —**scurf′y** *adj.* **-i·er, -i·est**

scur·ril·ous (skur′ə ləs) *adj.* [< L. *scurra,* buffoon] coarse; vulgar; abusive —**scur·ril·i·ty** (skə ril′ə tē) *n., pl.* **-ties**

scur·ry (skur′ē) *vi.* **-ried, -ry·ing** [< ?] to run hastily —*n.* a scurrying

scur·vy (skur′vē) *adj.* **-vi·er, -vi·est** [< SCURF] low; mean —*n.* a disease resulting from a vitamin C deficiency, causing weakness, anemia, spongy gums, etc. —**scur′vi·ly** *adv.*

scutch·eon (skuch′ən) *n. same as* ESCUTCHEON

scut·tle[1] (skut′'l) *n.* [< L. *scutella,* a dish] a bucket for carrying coal

scut·tle[2] (skut′'l) *vi.* **-tled, -tling** [prob. < SCUD] to scurry —*n.* a scurry

scut·tle[3] (skut′'l) *n.* [< Sp. *escotilla*] a small, covered opening in the hull or deck of a ship —*vt.* **-tled, -tling** to cut holes through the lower hull of (a ship) to sink it

scut′tle·butt′ (-but′) *n.* [< *scuttled butt,* lidded cask] 1. *Naut.* a drinking fountain on shipboard 2. [Colloq.] rumor or gossip

scuz·zy (skuz′ē) *adj.* **-zi·er, -zi·est** [Slang] dirty, shabby, etc.

scythe (sīth) *n.* [OE. *sithe*] a tool with a long, single-edged blade on a bent wooden shaft, for cutting grass, grain, etc. by hand

Se *Chem.* selenium

SE, S.E., s.e. 1. southeast 2. southeastern

sea (sē) *n.* [OE. *sæ*] 1. the ocean 2. a large body of salt water [the Red *Sea*] 3. a large body of fresh water [the *Sea* of Galilee] 4. the condition of the ocean's surface [a calm *sea*] 5. a heavy wave 6. a very great amount —**at sea** 1. on the open sea 2. uncertain; bewildered

sea anemone a sea polyp having a firm, gelatinous body and petallike tentacles

sea′board′ *n.* land bordering on the sea —*adj.* bordering on the sea

sea′coast′ *n.* land bordering on the sea

sea′far′er *n.* a traveler by sea —**sea′far′ing** *adj.*

sea′food′ *n.* food prepared from or consisting of saltwater fish or shellfish

sea′go′ing *adj.* 1. made for use on the open sea 2. *same as* SEAFARING

sea gull *same as* GULL[1]

sea horse a small, semitropical fish with a slender tail, plated body, and a head somewhat like that of a horse

seal[1] (sēl) *n.* [< L. *sigillum*] 1. *a*) a design or initial impressed, often over wax, on a letter or document as a mark of authenticity *b*) a stamp or ring for making such an impression 2. a piece of paper, etc. bearing an impressed design recognized as official 3. something that seals or closes tightly 4. something that guarantees; pledge 5. an ornamental paper stamp [Christmas *seals*] —*vt.* 1. to mark with a seal, as to authenticate or certify 2. to close or shut tight as with a seal [an envelope *sealed* with glue, a *sealed* door] 3. to confirm the truth of (a promise, etc.) 4. to settle finally

seal[2] (sēl) *n.* [OE. *seolh*] 1. a sea mammal with a sleek coat and four flippers: it lives in cold water and eats fish 2. the fur of a fur seal 3. leather made from sealskin —*vi.* to hunt seals —**seal′er** *n.*

seal·ant (sēl′ənt) *n.* a substance, as a wax, plastic, etc., used for sealing

sea legs the ability to walk without loss of balance on board ship, esp. in a rough sea

sea level the mean level of the sea between high and low tide

sea lion a large seal of the N Pacific

seal′skin′ *n.* **1.** the pelt of the fur seal **2.** a garment made of this

seam (sēm) *n.* [OE.] **1.** a line formed by sewing together two pieces of material **2.** any line marking joining edges **3.** a mark like this, as a scar, wrinkle, etc. **4.** a stratum of ore, coal, etc. —*vt.* **1.** to join together so as to form a seam **2.** to mark with a seamlike line, etc. —**seam′less** *adj.*

sea·man (sē′mən) *n., pl.* **-men 1.** a sailor **2.** an enlisted man ranking below a petty officer in the navy —**sea′man·ship′** *n.*

seam·stress (sēm′stris) *n.* a woman who makes her living by sewing

seam′y *adj.* **-i·er, -i·est** unpleasant, squalid, or sordid —**seam′i·ness** *n.*

sé·ance (sā′äns) *n.* [Fr. < OFr. < L. *sedere,* to sit] a meeting at which spiritualists seek to communicate with the dead

sea′plane′ *n.* any airplane designed to land on and take off from water

sea′port′ *n.* **1.** a port or harbor used by ocean ships **2.** a city having such a port

sear (sir) *vt.* [OE.] **1.** to wither **2.** to burn the surface of **3.** to make callous

search (surch) *vt.* [< LL. *circare,* go about] **1.** to go over and look through in order to find something **2.** to examine (a person) for something concealed **3.** to examine carefully; probe —*vi.* to make a search —*n.* a searching —**in search of** trying to find by searching

search′ing *adj.* **1.** examining thoroughly **2.** keen; piercing —**search′ing·ly** *adv.*

search′light′ *n.* **1.** an apparatus on a swivel, that projects a strong beam of light **2.** such a beam

search warrant a legal document authorizing a police search, as for stolen articles

sea′scape′ *n.* [SEA + (LAND)SCAPE] **1.** a view of the sea **2.** a picture of this

sea′shell′ *n.* a saltwater mollusk shell

sea′shore′ *n.* land along the sea; seacoast

sea′sick′ness *n.* nausea, dizziness, etc. caused by the rolling of a ship at sea —**sea′sick′** *adj.*

sea′side′ *n.* seashore

sea·son (sē′z'n) *n.* [< VL. *satio,* sowing time] **1.** any of the four divisions of the year; spring, summer, fall, or winter **2.** the time when something takes place, is popular, permitted, etc. **3.** the fitting time —*vt.* **1.** to make (food) more tasty by adding salt, spices, etc. **2.** to add zest to **3.** to make more fit for use, as by aging **4.** to accustom —*vi.* to become seasoned

sea′son·a·ble *adj.* **1.** suitable to the season **2.** timely; opportune

sea′son·al *adj.* of or depending on the season —**sea′son·al·ly** *adv.*

sea′son·ing *n.* any flavoring added to food

seat (sēt) *n.* [ON. *sæti*] **1.** a place to sit **2.** a thing to sit on; chair, etc. **3.** the buttocks **4.** the part of a chair, garment, etc. that one sits on **5.** the right to sit as a member **6.** the chief location, or center —*vt.* **1.** to set in or on a seat **2.** to have seats for [the car *seats* six]

seat belt anchored straps buckled across the hips, to protect a seated passenger

sea′ward (sē′wərd) *adv., adj.* toward the sea

sea′way′ *n.* an inland waterway to the sea for ocean ships

sea′weed′ *n.* a sea plant, esp. any alga

sea′wor′thy (-wur′thē) *adj.* fit for travel on the open sea: said of a ship

se·ba·ceous (si bā′shəs) *adj.* [< L. *sebum,* tallow] of, like, or secreting fat, etc.

SEC, S.E.C. Securities and Exchange Commission

sec. 1. second(s) **2.** secretary

se·cede (si sēd′) *vi.* **-ced′ed, -ced′ing** [< L. *se-,* apart + *cedere,* to go] to withdraw formally from a larger group

se·ces·sion (si sesh′ən) *n.* **1.** a seceding **2.** [*often* S-] the withdrawal of the Southern States from the Federal Union (1860–61) —**se·ces′sion·ist** *n.*

se·clude (si klood′) *vt.* **-clud′ed, -clud′ing** [< L. *se-,* apart + *claudere,* shut] to shut off from others; isolate

se·clu·sion (si kloo′zhən) *n.* retirement; isolation; privacy —**se·clu′sive** *adj.*

sec·ond[1] (sek′ənd) *adj.* [< L. *sequi,* follow] **1.** coming next after the first; 2d or 2nd **2.** another of the same kind; other [a *second* chance] **3.** next below the first in rank, value, etc. —*n.* **1.** one that is second **2.** an article or merchandise not of first quality **3.** an aid or assistant, as to a boxer **4.** the second forward gear —*vt.* **1.** to assist **2.** to indicate formal support of (a motion, etc.) so that it can be discussed or voted on —*adv.* in the second place, group, etc.

sec·ond[2] (sek′ənd) *n.* [< ML. *minuta secunda,* lit., second minute] **1.** 1/60 of a minute of time or of angular measurement **2.** a very short time; instant

sec·ond·ar·y (sek′ən der′ē) *adj.* **1.** second in order, rank, importance, etc. **2.** subordinate; minor **3.** not primary; derivative

secondary school a school, as a high school, coming after elementary school

sec′ond-class′ *adj.* **1.** of the class, rank, etc. next below the highest **2.** of a class of mail consisting of newspapers, magazines, etc. **3.** inferior —*adv.* by second-class mail or travel arrangements

sec′ond-guess′ *vt., vi.* [Colloq.] to use hindsight in criticizing (someone), remaking (a decision), etc.

sec′ond-hand′ *adj.* **1.** not direct from the original source **2.** used before; not new **3.** of or dealing in used merchandise

second lieutenant a commissioned officer of the lowest rank

sec′ond·ly *adv.* in the second place; second

second nature acquired habits, etc. deeply fixed in a person's nature

second person that form of a pronoun (as *you*) or verb (as *are*) which refers to the person(s) spoken to

sec′ond-rate′ *adj.* **1.** second in quality, etc. **2.** inferior —**sec′ond-rat′er** *n.*

second wind **1.** the return of normal breathing following severe exertion **2.** the recovered capacity for continuing any effort

se·cre·cy (sē′krə sē) *n., pl.* **-cies 1.** a being secret **2.** the practice or habit of being secretive

se·cret (sē′krit) *adj.* [< L. *se-,* apart + *cernere,* sift] **1.** kept from or acting without the knowledge of others **2.** beyond general understanding; mysterious **3.** concealed from sight; hidden —*n.* a secret cause, fact, process, etc. —**se′cret·ly** *adv.*

sec·re·tar·i·at (sek′rə ter′ē ət) *n.* the office, position, or quarters of a secretary of high position in a government, etc.

sec·re·tar·y (sek′rə ter′ē) *n., pl.* **-ies** [< ML. *secretarius,* one entrusted with secrets] **1.** one who keeps records, handles correspondence, etc. for an organization or person **2.** the head of a government department **3.** a writing desk —**sec′re·tar′i·al** *adj.*

se·crete (si krēt′) *vt.* -**cret′ed**, -**cret′ing** [see SECRET] **1.** to hide; conceal **2.** to form and release (a specified secretion) as a gland, etc. does

se·cre·tion (si krē′shən) *n.* **1.** a hiding or concealing **2.** a substance secreted by an animal or plant

se·cre·tive (sē′krə tiv) *adj.* reticent; not frank or open —**se′cre·tive·ly** *adv.*

Secret Service a U.S. government service for uncovering counterfeiters, guarding the President, etc.

sect (sekt) *n.* [< L. *sequi*, follow] **1.** a religious denomination **2.** a group of people having a common leadership, philosophy, etc.

sec·tar·i·an (sek ter′ē ən) *adj.* **1.** of or devoted to some sect **2.** narrow-minded

sec·tion (sek′shən) *n.* [< L. *secare*, to cut] **1.** a cutting **2.** a part cut off; slice; division **3.** any distinct or separate part **4.** a drawing, etc. of a thing as it would appear if cut straight through —*vt.* to divide into sections

sec′tion·al *adj.* **1.** of or devoted to a given section or district **2.** made up of sections —**sec′·tion·al·ism** *n.*

sec·tor (sek′tər) *n.* [< L. *secare*, to cut] **1.** part of a circle bounded by any two radii and the included arc **2.** any of the districts into which an area is divided for military operations **3.** a section; segment

sec·u·lar (sek′yə lər) *adj.* [< L. *saeculum*, age] **1.** not religious; not connected with a church **2.** not bound by a monastic vow *[secular clergy]* —**sec′u·lar·ism** *n.*

sec′u·lar·ize′ (-lə rīz′) *vt.* -**ized′**, -**iz′ing** to change from religious to civil ownership or use —**sec′u·lar·i·za′tion** *n.*

se·cure (si kyoor′) *adj.* [< L. *se-*, free from + *cura*, care] **1.** free from fear, care, etc. **2.** free from danger; safe **3.** firm; stable *[make the knot secure]* **4.** reliable —*vt.* -**cured′**, -**cur′ing** **1.** to make safe; protect **2.** to make certain; guarantee, as with a pledge *[to secure a loan]* **3.** to make firm, fast, etc. **4.** to obtain

se·cu·ri·ty (si kyoor′ə tē) *n., pl.* -**ties** **1.** a feeling of being free from fear, doubt, etc. **2.** protection or defense, as against attack **3.** something given as a pledge of repayment, etc. **4.** a stock certificate or bond: *usually used in pl.*

secy., sec′y. secretary

se·dan (si dan′) *n.* [< ?] a closed car with two or four doors and front and rear seats

se·date¹ (si dāt′) *adj.* [< L. *sedare*, to settle] **1.** calm; composed **2.** serious; dignified —**se·date′ly** *adv.*

se·date² (si dāt′) *vt.* -**dat′ed**, -**dat′ing** to dose with a sedative —**se·da′tion** *n.*

sed·a·tive (sed′ə tiv) *adj.* [see SEDATE¹] tending to soothe or quiet; lessening excitement, irritation, etc. —*n.* a sedative medicine

sed·en·tar·y (sed′′n ter′ē) *adj.* [< Fr. < L. *sedere*, sit] involving much sitting

Se·der (sā′dər) *n.* [Heb. *sēdher*, service] *Judaism* the feast of Passover

sedge (sej) *n.* [OE. *secg*] a grasslike plant often found on wet ground or in water

sed·i·ment (sed′ə mənt) *n.* [< Fr. < L. *sedere*, sit] **1.** matter settled to the bottom of a liquid **2.** *Geol.* matter deposited by water or wind —**sed′i·men′ta·ry** (-men′tər ē), **sed′i·men′tal** *adj.*

sed′i·men·ta′tion (-men tā′shən, -mən-) *n.* the depositing of sediment

se·di·tion (si dish′ən) *n.* [< L. *sed-*, apart + *itio*, a going] a stirring up of rebellion against

the government —**se·di′tion·ist** *n.* —**se·di′tious** *adj.*

se·duce (si doos′) *vt.* -**duced′**, -**duc′ing** [< L. *se-*, apart + *ducere*, to lead] **1.** to tempt to wrongdoing **2.** to induce to engage in unlawful sexual intercourse **3.** to entice —**se·duc′er** *n.* —**se·duc′tion** *n.* —**se·duc′tive** *adj.*

sed·u·lous (sej′oo ləs) *adj.* [< *sedulus*] working hard and steadily; diligent

see¹ (sē) *vt.* **saw, seen, see′ing** [OE. *seon*] **1.** to get knowledge of through the eyes; look at **2.** to understand **3.** to find out; learn **4.** to experience **5.** to make sure *[see that he goes]* **6.** to escort *[I'll see you home]* **7.** to encounter **8.** to visit or consult **9.** to receive *[too busy to see anyone]* —*vi.* **1.** to have the power of sight **2.** to understand **3.** to think *[let's see, where is it?]* —**see after** to take care of —**see through 1.** to perceive the true nature of **2.** to finish **3.** to help through difficulty —**see to** (or **about**) to attend to

see² (sē) *n.* [< L. *sedes*, a seat] the official seat, or center of authority, of a bishop

seed (sēd) *n., pl.* **seeds, seed** [OE. *sæd*] **1.** the plant part containing the embryo of a new plant **2.** seeds collectively **3.** an origin; source **4.** ancestry or posterity **5.** sperm or semen —*vt.* **1.** to plant as with seed **2.** to remove seeds from **3.** to distribute (tournament contestants) so as to avoid matching the best too early —*vi.* to produce seed —**go to seed** (or **run**) **to seed 1.** to shed seed **2.** to deteriorate

seed′ling (-liŋ) *n.* **1.** a plant grown from a seed **2.** a young tree

seed money money to begin a long-term project or get more funds for it

seed′y *adj.* -**i·er**, -**i·est 1.** full of seed **2.** gone to seed **3.** shabby, run-down, etc. —**seed′i·ness** *n.*

seek (sēk) *vt.* **sought, seek′ing** [OE. *secan*] **1.** to try to find; look for **2.** to try for; aim at **3.** to attempt *[to seek to please]* —**seek′er** *n.*

seem (sēm) *vi.* [prob. < ON. *sæma*, conform to] **1.** to appear to be *[to seem glad]* **2.** to appear *[he seems to know]* **3.** to have the impression *[I seem to have lost it]*

seem′ing *adj.* that seems real, true, etc.; apparent

seem′ly *adj.* -**li·er**, -**li·est** proper, fitting, etc. —**seem′li·ness** *n.*

seen (sēn) *pp.* of SEE¹

seep (sēp) *vi.* [OE. *sipian*, to soak] to leak; ooze —*n.* a seeping —**seep′age** (-ij) *n.*

seer (sir) *n.* one supposedly able to foretell the future

seer·suck·er (sir′suk′ər) *n.* [< Hindi < Per. *shir u shakar*, lit., milk and sugar] a crinkled fabric of linen, cotton, etc.

see·saw (sē′sô′) *n.* [redupl. of SAW¹] **1.** a plank balanced at the middle and ridden by children for fun, one plank end going up when the other goes down **2.** any up-and-down or back-and-forth movement —*vt., vi.* to ride or move as on a seesaw

seethe (sēth) *vi.* **seethed, seeth′ing** [OE. *sēothan*] **1.** to boil **2.** to surge, be agitated, etc. as if boiling

seg·ment (seg′mənt) *n.* [< L. *secare*, to cut] any of the parts into which something is separated; section —*vt., vi.* (-ment) to divide into segments —**seg′men·ta′tion** *n.*

seg·re·gate (seg′rə gāt′) *vt.* -**gat′ed**, -**gat′ing** [< L. *se-*, apart + *grex*, a flock] to set apart from others; specif., to impose segregation on (racial groups, social facilities, etc.) —**seg′re·ga′tion** *n.*

se·gue (seg′wā, sā′gwā) *vi.* -**gued**, -**gue·ing** [It. < L. *sequi*, follow] to continue without break *(to or into)* what follows, as in music —*n.* a segueing

seine (sān) *n.* [< Gr. *sagēnē*] a large fishing net with weights along the bottom —*vt., vi.* **seined, sein'ing** to fish with a seine

seis·mic (sīz'mik) *adj.* [< Gr. *seiein,* to shake] of, like, or from an earthquake

seis'mo·graph' (-graf') *n.* an instrument that records the intensity and duration of earthquakes —**seis'mo·graph'ic** *adj.*

seize (sēz) *vt.* **seized, seiz'ing** [< ML. *sacire*] **1.** *a)* to take forcible legal possession of *b)* to capture and put into custody; apprehend **2.** to take hold of forcibly, suddenly, or quickly **3.** to attack or afflict suddenly *[he was seized with pain]* —**sei·zure** (sē'zhər) *n.*

sel·dom (sel'dəm) *adv.* [OE. *seldan,* rare] not often

se·lect (sə lekt') *adj.* [< L. *se-,* apart + *legere,* choose] **1.** chosen in preference to others **2.** choice; excellent **3.** careful in choosing **4.** exclusive —*vt., vi.* to choose

se·lec·tion (sə lek'shən) *n.* **1.** a selecting or being selected **2.** that or those selected —**se·lec'tive** *adj.* —**se·lec'tiv'i·ty** *n.*

selective service compulsory military service according to age, physical fitness, etc.

se·lect'man (-mən) *n., pl.* **-men** one of a board of governing officers in most New England towns

se·le·ni·um (sə lē'nē əm) *n.* [< Gr. *selēnē,* the moon] a gray nonmetallic chemical element: used as in photoelectric devices: symbol, Se

self (self) *n., pl.* **selves** [OE.] **1.** the identity, character, etc. of a person or thing **2.** one's own person as distinct from all others **3.** one's own welfare or advantage —*pron.* [Colloq.] myself, himself, etc.

self- *a prefix meaning* of, by, in, to, with, or for oneself or itself The following list includes some common compounds formed with *self-* that do not have special meanings:

self-abasement	self-improvement
self-abnegation	self-incrimination
self-advancement	self-indulgence
self-appointed	self-inflicted
self-assertion	self-justification
self-deception	self-knowledge
self-defeating	self-love
self-delusion	self-moving
self-destruction	self-perpetuating
self-discipline	self-pity
self-effacement	self-preservation
self-employed	self-protection
self-examination	self-questioning
self-help	self-regulating
self-imposed	self-reproach

self'-ad·dressed' *adj.* addressed to oneself

self'-as·sur'ance *n.* confidence in oneself; self-confidence —**self'-as·sured'** *adj.*

self'-cen'tered *adj.* occupied or concerned only with one's own affairs; selfish

self'-con·ceit' *n.* too high an opinion of oneself; vanity —**self'-con·ceit'ed** *adj.*

self'-con'fi·dence *n.* confidence in one's own ability, etc. —**self'-con'fi·dent** *adj.*

self'-con'scious *adj.* unduly conscious of oneself as an object of notice; ill at ease

self'-con·tained' *adj.* **1.** keeping one's affairs to oneself **2.** showing self-control **3.** complete within oneself or itself

self'-con'tra·dic'tion *n.* **1.** contradiction of oneself or itself **2.** a statement or idea with contradictory elements —**self'-con'tra·dic'to·ry** *adj.*

self'-con·trol' *n.* control of one's own emotions, desires, actions, etc. —**self'-con·trolled'** *adj.*

self'-de·fense' *n.* defense of oneself or of one's rights, beliefs, etc.

self'-de·ni'al *n.* denial or sacrifice of one's own desires or pleasures

self'-de·struct' *vt., vi. same as* DESTRUCT

self'-de·ter'mi·na'tion *n.* **1.** determination according to one's own mind; free will **2.** the right of a people to choose its own form of government

self'-ed'u·cat'ed *adj.* educated by oneself, with little or no formal schooling

self'-es·teem' *n.* **1.** belief in oneself; self-respect **2.** undue pride in oneself; conceit

self'-ev'i·dent *adj.* evident without need of proof or explanation

self'-ex·plan'a·to'ry *adj.* explaining itself; obvious without explanation

self'-ex·pres'sion *n.* expression of one's own personality, as in art

self'-ful·fill'ing *adj.* **1.** bringing about fulfillment of one's aspirations **2.** fulfilled chiefly as an effect of having been expected or predicted

self'-gov'ern·ment *n.* government of a group by its own members —**self'-gov'ern·ing** *adj.*

self'-im'age *n.* one's concept of oneself and one's identity, abilities, worth, etc.

self'-im·por'tant *adj.* having an exaggerated opinion of one's own importance; pompous or officious —**self'-im·por'tance** *n.*

self'-in'ter·est *n.* **1.** one's own interest or advantage **2.** exaggerated regard for this

self'ish *adj.* overly concerned with one's own interests, etc. and having little concern for others —**self'ish·ly** *adv.*

self'less *adj.* devoted to others' welfare; unselfish —**self'less·ness** *n.*

self'-made' *adj.* **1.** made by oneself or itself **2.** successful, rich, etc. through one's own efforts

self'-pos·ses'sion *n.* full control of one's feelings, actions, etc.; composure —**self'-possessed'** *adj.*

self'-re·li'ance *n.* reliance on one's own abilities, judgment, etc. —**self'-re·li'ant** *adj.*

self'-re·spect' *n.* proper respect for oneself —**self'-re·spect'ing** *adj.*

self'-re·straint' *n.* restraint imposed on oneself by oneself —**self'-re·strained'** *adj.*

self'-right'eous *adj.* filled with or showing smug conviction of one's own righteousness

self'-sac'ri·fice' *n.* sacrifice of oneself or of one's own interests for the benefit of others —**self'-sac'ri·fic'ing** *adj.*

self'same' *adj.* (the) very same; identical

self'-sat'is·fied' *adj.* filled with or showing satisfaction with oneself —**self'-sat'is·fac'tion** *n.*

self'-seek'er *n.* a person seeking only or mainly to further his own interests —**self'-seek'ing** *n., adj.*

self'-serv'ice *n.* the practice of serving oneself and then paying a cashier

self'-serv'ing *adj.* serving one's own interests

self'-start'er *n.* a device for automatically starting an internal-combustion engine

self'-styled' *adj.* so named by oneself

self'-suf·fi'cient *adj.* getting along without help; independent —**self'-suf·fi'cien·cy** *n.*

self'-taught' *adj.* **1.** having taught oneself **2.** learned by teaching oneself

self'-willed' *adj.* stubborn; willful

self'-wind'ing *adj.* winding itself automatically

sell (sel) *vt.* **sold, sell'ing** [OE. *sellan,* give] **1.** to exchange (goods or services) for money, etc. **2.** to offer for sale **3.** to promote the sale of — *vi.* **1.** to engage in selling **2.** to be sold *(for or* *at*) —**sell out 1.** to dispose of completely by selling **2.** [Colloq.] to betray —**sell'er** *n.*

Selt·zer (water) (selt'sər) [< *Niederselters,* Germany] **1.** an effervescent natural mineral water **2.** [*often* **s-**] carbonated water

sel·vage, sel·vedge (sel'vij) *n.* [< SELF + EDGE] an edge woven to keep cloth from raveling

selves (selvz) *n. pl. of* SELF

se·man·tics (sə man'tiks) *n.pl.* [*with sing. v.*] [< Fr. < Gr. *sēma,* a sign] the study of the development and changes of the meanings of words —**se·man'tic** *adj.*

sem·a·phore (sem'ə fôr') *n.* [< Fr. < Gr. *sēma,* a sign + *pherein,* to bear] any apparatus or system for signaling, as by lights or flags

sem·blance (sem'bləns) *n.* [< L. *similis,* like] **1.** outward appearance **2.** resemblance **3.** a copy, representation, etc.

se·men (sē'mən) *n.* [L., a seed] the fluid secreted by the male reproductive organs

se·mes·ter (sə mes'tər) *n.* [G. < L. *sex,* six + *mensis,* month] either of the two terms in a school year

sem·i (sem'ī) *n., pl.* **-is** *short for* SEMITRAILER (sense 2)

semi- [L.] *a prefix meaning:* **1.** half **2.** partly **3.** twice in a (specified period)

sem·i·an·nu·al (sem'ē an'yoo wəl) *adj.* **1.** happening, done, etc. every half year **2.** lasting half a year —**sem'i·an'nu·al·ly** *adv.*

sem·i·cir·cle (sem'i sur'k'l) *n.* a half circle — **sem'i·cir'cu·lar** (-kyə lər) *adj.*

sem·i·co·lon (sem'i kō'lən) *n.* a mark of punctuation (;) to show separation ·greater than that marked by the comma

sem·i·con·duc'tor *n.* a substance with a poor conductivity that can be improved by adding certain substances or by applying heat, light, or voltage

sem·i·con'scious *adj.* not fully conscious

sem·i·fi'nal *adj.* coming just before the final match, as of a tournament —*n.* a semifinal match, etc.

sem·i·month'ly *adj.* appearing, done, etc. twice a month —*adv.* twice monthly

sem·i·nal (sem'ə n'l) *adj.* [see SEMEN] **1.** of seed or semen **2.** being a source

sem·i·nar (sem'ə när') *n.* [see ff.] **1.** a group of supervised students doing advanced study **2.** the study itself

sem·i·nar·y (sem'ə ner'ē) *n., pl.* **-ies** [< L. *seminarium,* seed plot] **1.** a school, esp. a private school for young women: an old-fashioned term **2.** a school for training priests, ministers, or rabbis

sem·i·pre·cious (sem'i presh'əs) *adj.* designating gems, as garnets or opals, of lower value than those classified as precious

sem·i·pro·fes'sion·al *adj.* engaging in a sport, etc. for pay but not as a regular occupation —*n.* a semiprofessional player, etc. Also [Colloq.] **sem'i·pro'**

Sem·ite (sem'īt) *n.* [prob. < Fr. *Sémite:* see SEMITIC] a member of any people speaking a Semitic language, as a Hebrew or Arab

Se·mit·ic (sə mit'ik) *adj.* [< G. *semitisch* < Heb.] **1.** of or like the Semites **2.** designating or of a group of related languages of SW Asia and N Africa that includes Hebrew and Arabic

sem·i·tone (sem'i tōn') *n. Music* the difference in pitch between any two immediately adjacent keys on the piano

sem'i·trail'er *n.* **1.** a trailer partly supported by the rear of a tractor (sense 2), being at-

tached to the tractor by a coupling **2.** a truck made up of such a trailer and tractor; semi

sem'i·trop'i·cal *adj.* partly tropical

sem'i·week'ly *adj.* appearing, done, etc. twice a week —*adv.* twice weekly

Sen., sen. 1. senate **2.** senator **3.** senior

sen·ate (sen'it) *n.* [< L. *senex,* old] **1.** a lawmaking assembly **2.** [**S-**] the upper branch of the U.S. legislature or of most U.S. State legislatures

sen·a·tor (sen'ə tər) *n.* a member of a senate —**sen'a·to'ri·al** (-tôr'ē əl) *adj.*

send (send) *vt.* **sent, send'ing** [OE. *sendan*] **1.** to cause to go or be carried; dispatch **2.** to impel; drive **3.** to make happen, come, etc. **4.** [Slang] to excite; thrill —*vi.* to send a message, messenger, etc. —**send for 1.** to summon **2.** to place an order for —**send'er** *n.*

send'-off' *n.* [Colloq.] **1.** a display of friendship or affection for someone starting out as on a trip **2.** the act of getting someone or something started

se·nile (sē'nīl) *adj.* [< L. *senex,* old] **1.** of old age **2.** showing signs of old age, such as an impaired memory —**se·nil·i·ty** (si nil'ə tē) *n.*

sen·ior (sēn'yər) *adj.* [L. < *senex,* old] **1.** older: written *Sr.* after a father's name if his son's name is the same **2.** of higher rank or longer service **3.** of or for seniors —*n.* **1.** one who is older, of higher rank, etc. **2.** a student in the last year of a high school or college

senior high school high school (usually grades 10, 11, & 12)

sen·ior·i·ty (sēn yôr'ə tē) *n., pl.* **-ties 1.** a being senior **2.** status, priority, etc. achieved by length of service in a given job

sen·na (sen'ə) *n.* [< Ar. *sanā*] **1.** any of certain cassias **2.** their dried leaves, used as a laxative

‡**se·ñor** (se nyôr') *n., pl.* **-ño'res** (-nyô'res) [Sp.] a man; gentleman: as a title [**S-**], equivalent to *Mr.* or *Sir*

‡**se·ño·ra** (se nyô'rä) *n., pl.* **-ras** (-räs) [Sp.] a married woman; lady: as a title [**S-**], equivalent to *Mrs.* or *Madam*

‡**se·ño·ri·ta** (se'nyô rē'tä) *n.* [Sp.] an unmarried woman or girl; young lady: as a title [**S-**], equivalent to *Miss*

sen·sa·tion (sen sā'shən) *n.* [< L. *sensus,* sense] **1.** the receiving of sense impressions through hearing, seeing, etc. **2.** a conscious sense impression **3.** a generalized feeling, as of joy **4.** *a*) a reaction of general excitement *b*) the cause of this

sen·sa'tion·al *adj.* **1.** intensely interesting **2.** intended to excite, startle, etc. **3.** [Colloq.] exceptionally fine, good, etc. —**sen·sa'tion·al·ism** *n.*

sense (sens) *n.* [< Fr. < L. *sentire,* to feel] **1.** any faculty of receiving impressions through body organs; specif., sight, hearing, taste, smell, or touch **2.** *a*) perception through such faculties *b*) a generalized feeling or reaction **3.** an ability to understand some quality [*a sense* of humor] **4.** normal intelligence and judgment **5.** meaning, as of a word —*vt.* **sensed, sens'ing** **1.** to perceive **2.** to detect, as by sensors —**in a sense** to some extent —**make sense** to be intelligible or logical

sense'less *adj.* **1.** unconscious **2.** stupid; foolish **3.** meaningless

sen·si·bil·i·ty (sen'sə bil'ə tē) *n., pl.* **-ties 1.** the capacity for physical sensation **2.** [*often pl.*] the capacity for being affected emotionally, intellectually, or aesthetically

sen·si·ble (sen'sə b'l) *adj.* [see SENSE] **1.** that can cause physical sensation **2.** easily perceived **3.** having or showing good sense; wise — **sen′si·bly** *adv.*

sen·si·tive (sen′sə tiv) *adj.* **1.** sensory **2.** keenly susceptible to stimuli **3.** easily hurt; tender **4.** highly responsive intellectually, emotionally, etc. **5.** easily offended, shocked, etc. —**sen′si·tiv′i·ty** *n.*

sen′si·tize′ (-tīz′) *vt.* **-tized′, -tiz′ing** to make sensitive, as to light

sen·sor (sen′sər, -sôr) *n.* a device designed to detect, measure, or record physical phenomena and to respond in various ways

sen·so·ry (sen′sər ē) *adj.* of the senses or sensation: also **sen·so′ri·al** (-sôr′ē əl)

sen·su·al (sen′shoo wəl) *adj.* [see SENSE] **1.** of the body and the senses as distinguished from the intellect **2.** connected or preoccupied with sexual pleasures —**sen′su·al′i·ty** (-wal′ə tē) *n.* —**sen′su·al·ly** *adv.*

sen·su·ous (sen′shoo wəs) *adj.* **1.** of, from, or appealing to the senses **2.** enjoying sense impressions —**sen′su·ous·ly** *adv.*

sent (sent) *pt. & pp. of* SEND

sen·tence (sen′t′ns) *n.* [< L. *sententia,* opinion] **1.** *a)* a decision, as of a court; esp., the determination by a court of a punishment *b)* the punishment **2.** *Gram.* a group of words expressing a statement, question, etc. and usually containing a subject and predicate —*vt.* **-tenced, -tenc·ing** to pronounce punishment upon

sen·ten·tious (sen ten′shəs) *adj.* [see prec.] full of, or fond of using, maxims, proverbs, etc.; often, pompously trite

sen·tient (sen′shənt) *adj.* [see SENSE] of or having feeling; conscious

sen·ti·ment (sen′tə mənt) *n.* [see SENSE] **1.** a complex combination of feelings and opinions **2.** an opinion, attitude, etc.: *often used in pl.* **3.** susceptibility to emotional appeal **4.** appeal to the emotions **5.** maudlin emotion; sentimentality

sen′ti·men′tal (-men′t′l) *adj.* **1.** full of tender, gentle, often mawkish feeling **2.** emotional rather than rational —**sen′ti·men′tal·ism** *n.* —**sen′ti·men′tal·ist** *n.* —**sen′ti·men·tal′i·ty** (-tal′ə tē) *n.*

sen′ti·men′tal·ize′ *vi., vt.* **-ized′, -iz′ing** to be or make sentimental

sen·ti·nel (sen′ti n′l) *n.* [< Fr. < L. *sentire,* to sense] one set to guard a group and warn of danger

sen·try (sen′trē) *n., pl.* **-tries** [< ?] a sentinel; esp., a soldier acting as a sentinel

se·pal (sē′p′l) *n.* [< Fr. < Gr. *skepē,* a covering + L. *petalum,* petal] a leaflike part of a calyx

sep·a·ra·ble (sep′ər ə b′l) *adj.* that can be separated —**sep′a·ra·bly** *adv.*

sep·a·rate (sep′ə rāt′) *vt.* **-rat′ed, -rat′ing** [< L. *se-,* apart + *parare,* arrange] **1.** to set apart into sections, groups, etc.; divide **2.** to set apart or keep apart —*vi.* **1.** to withdraw **2.** to part, become disconnected, etc. —*adj.* (-ər it) **1.** set apart from the other or others **2.** distinct; individual —**sep′a·rate·ly** *adv.* —**sep′a·ra′tor** *n.*

sep′a·ra′tion (-ə rā′shən) *n.* **1.** a separating or being separated **2.** the place where this occurs; break; division **3.** an arrangement by which a man and wife live apart by agreement or court decree

sep′a·ra·tism (-ər ə tiz′m) *n.* the advocacy of political, religious, or racial separation —**sep′a·ra·tist** *n.*

se·pi·a (sē′pē ə) *n., adj.* [< Gr., cuttlefish] (of) dark reddish brown

sep·sis (sep′sis) *n.* [< Gr. *sēpein,* make putrid]

poisoning caused by absorption of certain microorganisms into the blood

Sep·tem·ber (sep tem′bər) *n.* [< L. *septem,* seven: seventh month in ancient Rom. calendar] the ninth month of the year, having 30 days: abbrev. **Sept.**

sep·tic (sep′tik) *adj.* [see SEPSIS] causing, or resulting from, sepsis or putrefaction

septic tank an underground tank in which waste matter is decomposed by bacteria

Sep·tu·a·gint (sep′too wə jint) *n.* [< L. *septuaginta,* seventy: in tradition, done by 70 or 72 translators] a Greek translation of the Hebrew Scriptures

sep·ul·cher (sep′′l kər) *n.* [< L. *sepelire,* bury] a vault for burial; grave; tomb

se·pul·chral (sə pul′krəl) *adj.* **1.** of sepulchers, burial, etc. **2.** suggestive of the grave or burial; dismal; gloomy **3.** deep and melancholy: said of sound —**se·pul′chral·ly** *adv.*

seq. [L. *sequentes* or *sequentia*] the following

se·quel (sē′kwəl) *n.* [< L. *sequi,* follow] **1.** something that follows; continuation **2.** a result or consequence **3.** a literary work continuing an earlier work but complete in itself

se·quence (sē′kwəns) *n.* [see prec.] **1.** *a)* the coming of one thing after another; succession *b)* the order of this **2.** a series **3.** a result or consequence **4.** *Motion Pictures* a succession of shots forming one uninterrupted episode

se·ques·ter (si kwes′tər) *vt.* [< LL. *sequestrare,* to remove] **1.** to set apart; separate **2.** to confiscate **3.** to seclude —**se·ques·tra·tion** (sē′kwes trā′shən) *n.*

se·quin (sē′kwin) *n.* [Fr. < It. < Ar. *sikkah,* a stamp] a small, shiny spangle, as a metal disk, esp. one of many sewn on fabric for decoration

se·quoi·a (si kwoi′ə) *n.* [< *Sequoya,* AmInd. inventor of Cherokee writing] a giant evergreen tree of the W U.S.

se·rag·lio (si ral′yō, -räl′-) *n., pl.* **-lios** [< It. < L. *sera,* a lock] *same as* HAREM (sense 1)

se·ra·pe (sə rä′pē) *n.* [MexSp.] a woolen blanket worn as an outer garment by men in Spanish-American countries

ser·aph (ser′əf) *n., pl.* **-aphs, -a·phim** (-ə fim′) [< Heb.] *Theol.* a heavenly being or one of the highest orders of angels —**se·raph·ic** (sə raf′ik) *adj.*

Serb (surb) *n.* **1.** a native or inhabitant of Serbia **2.** *same as* SERBIAN (*n.* 1) —*adj. same as* SERBIAN

Ser·bi·an (sur′bē ən) *adj.* of Serbia, the Serbs, or their language —*n.* **1.** Serbo-Croatian as spoken in Serbia **2.** *same as* SERB (*n.* 1)

Ser·bo-Cro·a·tian (sur′bō krō ā′shən) *n.* the major Slavic language of Yugoslavia

sere (sir) *adj.* [var. of SEAR] [Poet.] withered

ser·e·nade (ser′ə nād′) *n.* [< Fr. < It. < L. *serenus,* serene] music played or sung at night, esp. by a lover under his sweetheart's window —*vt., vi.* **-nad′ed, -nad′ing** to play or sing a serenade (to)

ser·en·dip·i·ty (ser′ən dip′ə tē) *n.* [< a Per. tale, *The Three Princes of Serendip*] a seeming gift for finding good things accidentally —**ser′en·dip′i·tous** *adj.*

se·rene (sə rēn′) *adj.* [L. *serenus*] **1.** clear; unclouded **2.** undisturbed; calm —**se·rene′ly** *adv.* —**se·ren′i·ty** (-ren′ə tē) *n.*

serf (surf) *n.* [< L. *servus,* a slave] a person in feudal servitude, bound to his master's land and transferred with it to a new owner —**serf′dom** *n.*

serge (surj) *n.* [< L. *sericus,* silken] a strong twilled fabric

ser·geant (sär′jənt) *n.* [< L. *servire,* to serve]

1. a noncommissioned officer ranking just above a corporal 2. a police officer ranking next below a captain or lieutenant
ser′geant-at-arms′ *n., pl.* **ser′geants-at-arms′** an officer appointed to keep order as in a court
sergeant major *pl.* **sergeants major** *U.S. Army & Marine Corps* the highest ranking noncommissioned officer
se·ri·al (sir′ē əl) *adj.* [< L. *series,* series] of or in a series —*n.* a story, movie, etc. issued in successive parts
se′ri·al·ize *vt.* **-ized′, -iz′ing** to arrange or issue in successive parts —**se′ri·al·i·za′tion** *n.*
serial number one of a series of numbers assigned for identification
se·ries (sir′ēz) *n., pl.* **-ries** [< L. *serere,* join] a number of similar things or individuals in a row, sequence, or related group
ser·if (ser′if) *n.* [Du. *schreef,* a line] *Printing* a fine line projecting from a main stroke of a letter
se·ri·ous (sir′ē əs) *adj.* [< L. *serius*] 1. earnest, grave, etc. 2. not joking; sincere 3. requiring careful consideration; important 4. dangerous *[a serious wound]*
ser·mon (sur′mən) *n.* [< L. *sermo*] 1. a speech on religion or morals, esp. by a clergyman 2. any serious talk on behavior, duty, etc., esp. a tedious one —**ser′mon·ize′** *vi.* **-ized′, -iz′ing**
Sermon on the Mount the sermon given by Jesus to his disciples
se·rous (sir′əs) *adj.* 1. of or containing serum 2. like serum; thin and watery
ser·pent (sur′pənt) *n.* [< L. *serpere,* to creep] a snake
ser′pen·tine′ (-pən tēn′, -tīn′) *adj.* of or like a serpent; esp., *a*) cunning; treacherous *b*) turning often; winding
ser·rate (ser′āt, -it) *adj.* [< L. *serra,* a saw] notched like a saw: also **ser·rat′ed**
ser·ried (ser′ēd) *adj.* [< L. *sera,* a lock] placed close together
se·rum (sir′əm) *n., pl.* **-rums, -ra** (-ə) [L., whey] 1. any watery animal fluid; esp., the yellowish fluid (**blood serum**) separating from clotted blood 2. blood serum from an immunized animal, used as an antitoxin
serv·ant (sur′vənt) *n.* [< L. *servus*] 1. a person hired to work in another's home as a maid, cook, etc. 2. a person devoted to another or to a cause, creed, etc.
serve (surv) *vt.* **served, serv′ing** [< L. *servire*] 1. to work for as a servant 2. to do services for; aid; help 3. to do military or naval service for 4. to spend (a term of imprisonment, etc.) 5. to provide (customers) with (goods or services) 6. to set (food or drink) before (someone) 7. to meet the needs of 8. to function for *[if memory serves me well]* 9. to treat *[you've been ill served]* 10. to deliver (a summons, etc.) to 11. to hit (a tennis ball, etc.) so as to start play —*vi.* 1. to work as a servant 2. to do service *[he served* in the navy] 3. to carry out the duties of an office 4. to be of service 5. to meet needs 6. to wait on table 7. to hit a tennis ball, etc. so as to start play —*n.* the act of serving a tennis ball, handball, etc.; also, one's turn for this —**serve (someone) right** to be what (someone) deserves —**serv′er** *n.*
serv·ice (sur′vis) *n.* [< L. *servus,* a slave] 1. the occupation of a servant 2. *a*) public employment *b*) a branch of this; specif., the armed forces 3. work done for others 4. a religious ceremony *a*) helpful or useful action *b*) benefit; advantage *c*) [*pl.*] friendly help; also, professional aid 6. *a*) the serving of food

or drink *b*) the articles used 7. a system or method of providing people with some utility, as water or gas 8. the serve, as in tennis —*vt.* **-iced, -ic·ing** 1. to furnish with a service; supply 2. to make fit for service, as by repairing —**in** (or **out of**) **service** in (or not in) use or usable condition —**of service** helpful; useful
serv′ice·a·ble *adj.* 1. that is or can be of service; useful 2. wearing well; durable
serv′ice·man′ *n., pl.* **-men′** 1. a member of the armed forces 2. a person whose work is repairing something: also **service man**
service mark a symbol, word, etc. used by a supplier of services to distinguish the services from those of competitors: usually registered and protected by law
service station a place providing gasoline, maintenance, etc. for motor vehicles
ser·vile (sur′v'l, -vīl) *adj.* [< L. *servus,* a slave] 1. of a slave 2. like that of a slave 3. humbly submissive —**ser′vile·ly** *adv.* —**ser·vil·i·ty** (sər vil′ə tē) *n.*
ser·vi·tor (sur′və tər) *n.* a servant
ser·vi·tude (sur′və tōōd′) *n.* [see SERVILE] 1. slavery 2. work imposed as punishment for crime
ser·vo (sur′vō) *n., pl.* **-vos** short for: 1. SERVOMECHANISM 2. SERVOMOTOR
ser′vo·mech′a·nism *n.* an automatic control system regularly checking output against input so as to achieve the desired control
ser′vo·mo′tor *n.* a device controlled by an amplified signal from a low-power actuator
ses·a·me (ses′ə mē) *n.* [< Gr.] 1. an East Indian or African plant with flat seeds that yield an edible oil 2. the seeds
ses·qui·cen·ten·ni·al (ses′kwi sen ten′ē əl) *adj.* [L. *sesqui-,* more by a half + CENTENNIAL] of a period of 150 years —*n.* a 150th anniversary
ses·sion (sesh′ən) *n.* [< L. *sedere,* sit] 1. a meeting or series of meetings, as of a legislature or court 2. a period of study, classes, etc. 3. a period of any activity —**in session** meeting
set (set) *vt.* **set, set′ting** [OE. *settan*] 1. to cause to sit; seat 2. to put in a specified place, condition, etc. 3. to put in order, as *a*) to put (a trap) into position *b*) to adjust (a clock, dial, etc.) *c*) to arrange (a table) for a meal *d*) to put (a fractured bone) into position for healing *e*) to arrange (hair) in a desired style 4. to make firm, fixed, settled, etc. *[pectin sets jelly]* 5. to direct 6. to appoint, establish, etc. *[to set limits]* 7. to estimate or value *[to set* all at naught*]* 8. to fit (words *to* music or music *to* words) 9. to arrange (type) for printing —*vi.* 1. to sit on eggs: said of a fowl 2. to become firm, fixed, etc. *[the concrete has set]* 3. to start moving (with *out, off,* etc.) 4. to have a certain direction; tend 5. to seem to descend *[the setting* sun] —*adj.* 1. fixed, established, etc. *[a set time]* 2. deliberately thought out 3. immovable; inflexible; rigid 4. ready *[get set]* —*n.* 1. a setting or being set 2. the way a thing is set *[the set* of his jaw] 3. direction or tendency 4. something set, as stage scenery 5. the act or a style of arranging hair 6. a number of persons or things grouped or classed together 7. assembled equipment for radio or television reception 8. *Tennis* a group of six or more games won by a margin of at least two —**set about** (or **in, to**) to start doing; begin —**set down** to put in writing —**set forth** to present or state —**set off** 1. to make prominent by contrast 2. to make explode —**set on** (or **upon**) to attack —**set up** 1. to erect 2. to establish; found

set'back' *n.* a reversal in progress

set·tee (se tē') *n.* **1.** a seat or bench with a back **2.** a small sofa

set'ter *n.* **1.** one that sets **2.** a long-haired hunting dog trained to find game

set'ting *n.* **1.** the act of one that sets **2.** the position of a dial, etc. that has been set **3.** a mounting, as of a gem **4.** the time, place, etc. of a play or novel **5.** actual physical surroundings

set·tle (set''l) *vt.* **-tled, -tling** [OE. *setlan*] **1.** to put in order; arrange, as one's affairs **2.** to set in place firmly or comfortably **3.** to colonize **4.** to cause to sink and become more compact **5.** to free (the nerves, etc.) from disturbance **6.** to decide (a dispute, etc.) **7.** to pay (a debt, etc.) —*vi.* **1.** to stop moving and stay in one place **2.** to descend and spread *[fog settled over the city]* **3.** to become localized, as pain **4.** to take up permanent residence **5.** to sink *[the building is settling]* **6.** to become denser by sinking, as sediment **7.** to become more stable **8.** to reach an agreement or decision *(with* or *on)* — **set'tler** *n.*

set'tle·ment *n.* **1.** a settling or being settled **2.** a new colony **3.** a village **4.** an agreement **5.** payment **6.** a community center for the underprivileged

set'up' *n.* **1.** the way something is set up; specif., the makeup or arrangement as of an organization **2.** [Colloq.] a contest, etc. arranged to make winning easy

sev·en (sev''n) *adj., n.* [OE. *seofon*] one more than six; 7; VII —**sev'enth** *adj., n.*

seven seas all the oceans of the world

sev'en·teen' (-tēn') *adj., n.* seven more than ten; 17; XVII —**sev'en·teenth'** (-tēnth') *adj., n.*

sev'en·teen'-year' locust a cicada which lives underground for 13-17 years before emerging as an adult

seventh heaven a state of perfect happiness

sev·en·ty (sev''n tē) *adj., n., pl.* **-ties** seven times ten; 70; LXX —**the seventies** the numbers or years, as of a century, from 70 through 79 —**sev'en·ti·eth** (-ith) *adj., n.*

sev·er (sev'ər) *vt., vi.* [< L. *separare*] to separate, divide, or break off —**sev'er·ance** *n.*

sev·er·al (sev'ər əl) *adj.* [< L. *separ*] **1.** separate; distinct **2.** different; respective **3.** more than two but not many; few —*n. [with pl. v.]* a small number *(of)* —*pron. [with pl. v.]* a few —**sev'er·al·ly** *adv.*

se·vere (sə vir') *adj.* **-ver'er, -ver'est** [< L. *severus*] **1.** harsh or strict, as in treatment; stern **2.** serious; grave, as in expression **3.** rigidly accurate or demanding **4.** extremely plain *[a severe style]* **5.** keen; intense *[severe pain]* **6.** difficult; rigorous *[a severe test]* —**se·vere'ly** *adv.* —**se·vere'ness, se·ver'i·ty** (-ver'ə tē) *n.*

sew (sō) *vt., vi.* **sewed, sewn** (sōn) or **sewed, sew'ing** [OE. *siwian*] **1.** to join or fasten with stitches made with needle and thread **2.** to make, mend, etc. by sewing —**sew up** [Colloq.] **1.** to get full control of **2.** to make sure of success in —**sew'er** *n.*

sew·age (sōō'ij) *n.* the waste matter carried off by sewers or drains

sew·er (sōō'ər) *n.* [ult. < L. *ex*, out + *aqua*, water] a pipe or drain, usually underground, for carrying off water and waste matter

sew'er·age (-ij) *n.* **1.** a system of sewers **2.** same as SEWAGE

sew·ing (sō'iŋ) *n.* **1.** the act of one who sews **2.** material for sewing

sewing machine a machine with a mechanically driven needle for sewing

sex (seks) *n.* [< L. *sexus*] **1.** either of the two divisions, male or female, of persons, animals, or plants **2.** the character of being male or female **3.** the attraction of one sex for another **4.** sexual intercourse

sex- [< L. *sex*, six] *a combining form meaning* six

sex appeal the physical charm that attracts members of the opposite sex

sex·ism (sek'siz'm) *n.* exploitation and domination of one sex by the other, specif. of women by men —**sex'ist** *adj., n.*

sex·tant (seks'tənt) *n.* [< L. *sextans*, a sixth part (of a circle)] an instrument for measuring the angular distance of the sun, a star, etc. from the horizon, as to determine position at sea

sex·tet, sex·tette (seks tet') *n.* [< L. *sex*, six] **1.** a group of six **2.** *Music a)* a composition for six voices or instruments *b)* the six performers of this

sex·ton (seks'tən) *n.* [ult. < L. *sacer*, sacred] a church official in charge of the maintenance of church property

sex·u·al (sek'shōō wəl) *adj.* of or involving sex, the sexes, the sex organs, etc. —**sex'u·al'i·ty** (-wal'ə tē) *n.* —**sex'u·al·ly** *adv.*

sex'y *adj.* **-i·er, -i·est** [Colloq.] exciting or intended to excite sexual desire

Sgt., Sgt. Sergeant

sh (sh) *interj.* hush! be quiet!

shab·by (shab'ē) *adj.* **-bi·er, -bi·est** [< OE. *sceabb*, a scab] **1.** run-down; dilapidated **2.** *a)* ragged; worn *b)* wearing worn clothing **3.** mean; shameful *[shabby treatment]*

shack (shak) *n.* [< ?] a small, crudely built cabin; shanty

shack·le (shak''l) *n.* [OE. *sceacel*] **1.** a metal fastening, usually in pairs, for the wrist or ankle of a prisoner; fetter **2.** *[usually pl.]* anything that restrains freedom, as of expression **3.** a device for fastening or coupling —*vt.* **-led, -ling** to bind, fasten, or hinder with or as with shackles

shad (shad) *n., pl.* **shad, shads** [OE. *sceadd*] a herringlike saltwater fish that spawns in rivers

shade (shād) *n.* [OE. *sceadu*] **1.** slight darkness caused by cutting off rays of light **2.** an area less brightly lighted than its surroundings **3.** degree of darkness of a color **4.** *a)* a small difference *[shades* of opinion*] b)* a slight amount or degree **5.** a device used to screen from light *[a* window *shade*, lamp *shade]* **6.** *[pl.]* [Slang] sunglasses —*vt.* **shad'ed, shad'ing 1.** to screen from light **2.** to darken; dim **3.** to represent shade in (a painting, etc.) —*vi.* to change slightly or by degrees

shad'ing (-iŋ) *n.* **1.** a shielding against light **2.** the representation of light or shade in a picture **3.** any small variation

shad·ow (shad'ō) *n.* [< OE. *sceadu*, shade] **1.** the darkness or the dark shape cast by something cutting off light **2.** gloom or that which causes gloom **3.** a shaded area in a picture **4.** a ghost **5.** a remnant or trace —*vt.* **1.** to throw a shadow upon **2.** to follow closely, esp. in secret —**shad'ow·y** *adj.*

shad·y (shād'ē) *adj.* **-i·er, -i·est 1.** giving shade **2.** shaded, as from the sun; full of shade **3.** [Colloq.] of questionable character —**on the shady side of** beyond (a given age) —**shad'i·ness** *n.*

shaft (shaft) *n.* [OE. *sceaft*] **1.** an arrow or spear, or its stem **2.** anything hurled like a missile *[shafts* of wit*]* **3.** a long, slender part or object, as a pillar, either of the two poles between which an animal is harnessed to a vehicle, a bar transmitting motion to a mechanical part, etc. **4.** a long, narrow opening sunk into the earth **5.** a vertical opening passing through a building, as for an elevator —**vt.** [Slang] to cheat, trick, exploit, etc.

shag¹ (shag) **n.** [OE. *sceacga*] **1.** a long, heavy coarse nap, as on some rugs **2.** fabric with such a nap

shag² (shag) **vt. shagged, shag′ging** [< ?] to chase after and retrieve (baseballs hit in batting practice)

shag′gy adj. -gi·er, -gi·est 1. covered with long, coarse hair **2.** carelessly groomed; unkempt **3.** having a rough nap or surface

shah (shä) **n.** [Per. *shāh*] a title of the ruler of Iran

shake (shāk) **vt., vi. shook, shak′en, shak′ing** [OE. *sceacan*] **1.** to move quickly up and down, back and forth, etc. **2.** to bring, force, mix, etc. by brisk movement **3.** to tremble or cause to tremble **4.** *a)* to become or cause to become unsteady *b)* to unnerve or become unnerved **5.** to clasp (another's hand), as in greeting —**n. 1.** an act of shaking **2.** *short for* MILKSHAKE **3.** [*pl.*] [Colloq.] a convulsive trembling (usually with *the*) **4.** [Colloq.] deal [*a fair shake*] —**no great shakes** [Colloq.] not unusual —**shake down 1.** to cause to fall by shaking **2.** [Slang] to extort money from —**shake off** to get rid of —**shak′y adj. -i·er, -i·est**

shake′down′ n. [Colloq.] **1.** an extortion of money, as by blackmail **2.** a thorough search —**adj.** for testing new equipment, etc. [*a shakedown cruise*]

shak′er n. 1. a person or thing that shakes **2.** a device used in shaking

shake′-up′ n. a shaking up; specif., an extensive reorganization

shale (shāl) **n.** [OE. *scealu*, a shell] a rock formed of hardened clay, that splits into thin layers

shall (shal) **v., pt. should** [OE. *sceal*] an auxiliary sometimes used to express futurity in the first person and determination, obligation, etc. in the second and third persons *Shall* and *will* are used interchangeably in prevailing usage

shal·lot (shə lät′) **n.** [< OFr. *eschaloigne*, scallion] **1.** a small onion whose bulbs are used for flavoring **2.** *same as* GREEN ONION

shal·low (shal′ō) **adj.** [ME. *shalow*] **1.** not deep **2.** lacking depth of character —**n.** [*usually pl.*] a shoal —**shal′low·ness n.**

shalt (shalt) *archaic 2d pers. sing., pres. indic., of* SHALL: *used with* thou

sham (sham) **n.** [< ? SHAME] something false or fake; one that is a fraud —**adj.** false or fake —**vt., vi. shammed, sham′ming** to fake

sham·ble (sham′b'l) **vi. -bled, -bling** [< obs. use in "*shamble* legs," bench legs] to walk clumsily; shuffle —**n.** a shambling walk

sham′bles (-b'lz) **n.pl.** [*with sing. v.*] [ult. < L. *scamnum*, a bench] **1.** a slaughterhouse **2.** a scene of great slaughter, destruction, or disorder

shame (shām) **n.** [OE. *scamu*] **1.** a painful feeling of having lost the respect of others because of improper behavior, etc. **2.** dishonor or disgrace **3.** something unfortunate or outrageous —**vt. shamed, sham′ing 1.** to cause to feel shame **2.** to dishonor or disgrace **3.** to force by a sense of shame —**put to shame 1.** to cause to feel shame **2.** to surpass —**shame′ful adj.**

shame′faced′ adj. 1. shy or bashful **2.** showing a feeling of shame; ashamed

shame′less adj. having or showing no shame, modesty, or decency; brazen

sham·poo (sham pōō′) **vt. -pooed′, -poo′ing** [< Hindi *chāmpnā*, to press] **1.** to wash (the hair)

2. to wash the hair of **3.** to wash (a rug, etc.) —**n. 1.** a shampooing **2.** a liquid soap, etc. used for this —**sham·poo′er n.**

sham·rock (sham′räk′) **n.** [< Ir. *seamar*, clover] a cloverlike plant with leaflets in groups of three: the emblem of Ireland

shang·hai (shaŋ′hī′) **vt. -haied′, -hai′ing** [< such kidnapping for crews on the China run] to kidnap, usually by drugging, for service aboard ship

shank (shaŋk) **n.** [OE. *scanca*] **1.** the part of a leg between the knee and the ankle in man, or a corresponding part in animals **2.** the whole leg **3.** the part of a tool between the handle and the working part —**shank of the evening** early evening

shan't (shant) shall not

shan·tung (shan′tuŋ′) **n.** [< *Shantung*, province of China] a fabric of silk, rayon, etc. with an uneven surface

shan·ty (shan′tē) **n.,** *pl.* **-ties** [< CanadFr. *chantier*, workshop] a small, shabby dwelling; hut

shape (shāp) **n.** [< OE. (*ge*)*sceap*, form] **1.** the way a thing looks because of its outline; outer form **2.** the contour of the body **3.** definite or regular form [*to begin to take shape*] **4.** [Colloq.] physical condition —**vt. shaped, shap′ing 1.** to give definite shape to **2.** to arrange, express, etc. in definite form **3.** to adapt [*shaped* to our needs] —**shape up** [Colloq.] to develop to a definite or satisfactory form, etc. —**take shape** to begin to have definite form —**shape′less adj.**

shape′ly adj. -li·er, -li·est having a pleasing shape; well-proportioned

shard (shärd) **n.** [OE. *sceard*] a fragment or broken piece, esp. of pottery; potsherd

share¹ (sher) **n.** [OE. *scearu*] **1.** a portion that belongs to an individual **2.** any of the equal parts of the capital stock of a corporation —**vt. shared, shar′ing 1.** to distribute in shares **2.** to have or use in common with others —**vi.** to have a share (*in*)

share² (sher) **n.** [OE. *scear*] a plowshare

share′crop′ vi., vt. -cropped′, -crop′ping to work (land) for a share of the crop —**share′-crop′per n.**

share′hold′er n. one who owns shares of stock

shark¹ (shärk) **n.** [prob. < G. *schurke*, scoundrel] **1.** a swindler **2.** [Slang] an expert

shark² (shärk) **n.** [< ?] a large, predatory sea fish with a tough, slate-gray skin

shark′skin′ n. a cloth of cotton, wool, rayon, etc. with a smooth, silky surface

sharp (shärp) **adj.** [OE. *scearp*] **1.** having a fine edge or point for cutting or piercing **2.** having a point or edge; not rounded **3.** not gradual; abrupt **4.** clearly defined; distinct [*a sharp contrast*] **5.** quick in perception; clever **6.** attentive; vigilant **7.** crafty; underhanded **8.** harsh or severe [*sharp criticism*] **9.** violent [*a sharp attack*] **10.** brisk; active **11.** intense [*a sharp pain*] **12.** pungent **13.** cold [*a sharp wind*] **14.** [Slang] attractively dressed or groomed **15.** *Music* above true pitch —**n. 1.** [Colloq.] an expert **2.** *Music a)* a tone one half step above another *b)* the symbol (♯) indicating this —**vt., vi.** *Music* to make or become sharp —**adv. 1.** in a sharp manner; specif., *a)* abruptly or briskly *b)* attentively or alertly *c) Music* above true pitch **2.** precisely [*one o'clock sharp*] —**sharp′ly adv.**

sharp′en vt., vi. to make or become sharp or sharper —**sharp′en·er n.**

sharp′er n. a swindler or cheat

sharp'-eyed' *adj.* having keen sight or perception: also **sharp'-sight'ed**
sharp'ie (-ē) *n.* [Colloq.] a shrewd, cunning person
sharp'shoot'er *n.* a good marksman
sharp'-tongued' (-tuŋd') *adj.* using sharp or harshly critical language
sharp'-wit'ted (-wit'id) *adj.* having or showing keen intelligence —**sharp'-wit'ted·ness** *n.*
shat·ter (shat'ər) *vt., vi.* [ME. *schateren*, to scatter] 1. to break or burst into pieces 2. to damage or be damaged severely
shave (shāv) *vt.* **shaved, shaved** or **shav'en, shav'ing** [OE. *sceafan*] 1. to cut away thin slices or sections from 2. *a*) to cut off (hair) at the surface of the skin *b*) to cut the hair to the surface of (the face, etc.) *c*) to cut the beard of (a person) 3. to barely touch in passing; graze —*vi.* to cut off hair with a razor, etc. —*n.* the act or result of shaving
shav'er *n.* 1. one who shaves 2. an instrument used in shaving, esp. one with electrically operated cutters 3. [Colloq.] a boy; lad
shav'ing *n.* 1. the act of one who shaves 2. a thin piece of wood, etc. shaved off
shawl (shôl) *n.* [< Per. *shāl*] an oblong or square cloth worn, esp. by women, as a covering for the head or shoulders
she (shē) *pron., for pl. see* THEY [< OE. *seo*] the woman, girl, or female animal previously mentioned —*n., pl.* **shes** a woman, girl, or female animal
sheaf (shēf) *n., pl.* **sheaves** [OE. *sceaf*] 1. a bundle of cut stalks of grain, etc. 2. a collection, as of papers, bound in a bundle
shear (shir) *vt.* **sheared, sheared** or **shorn, shear'ing** [OE. *scieran*] 1. to cut as with shears 2. to clip (hair) from (the head), (wool) from (sheep), etc. 3. to strip (*of* a power, right, etc.) —*n.* 1. a machine used in cutting metal 2. a shearing
shears *n.pl.* [*also with sing. v.*] 1. large scissors 2. a large tool or machine with two opposed blades, used to cut metal, etc.
sheath (shēth) *n., pl.* **sheaths** (shēthz, shēths) [OE. *sceath*] 1. a case for the blade of a knife, sword, etc. 2. a covering or receptacle resembling this
sheathe (shēth) *vt.* **sheathed, sheath'ing** 1. to put into a sheath 2. to enclose in a case or covering
sheath·ing (shē'thiŋ) *n.* something that sheathes, as boards, etc. forming the base for roofing or siding
sheaves (shēvz) *n. pl. of* SHEAF
she-bang (shə baŋ') *n.* [Colloq.] an affair, business, contrivance, etc.: chiefly in **the whole shebang**
shed¹ (shed) *n.* [OE. *scead*] a small structure for shelter or storage
shed² (shed) *vt.* **shed, shed'ding** [OE. *sceadan*, to separate] 1. to pour out 2. to cause to flow [to *shed* tears] 3. to radiate [to *shed* confidence] 4. to repel [oilskin *sheds* water] 5. to cast off (a natural growth, as hair, etc.) —*vi.* to shed hair, etc. —**shed blood** to kill violently
she'd (shēd) 1. she had 2. she would
sheen (shēn) *n.* [< OE. *sciene*, beautiful] brightness
sheep (shēp) *n., pl.* **sheep** [OE. *sceap*] 1. a cud-chewing mammal related to the goats, with heavy wool and edible flesh 2. one who is meek, stupid, timid, etc.
sheep dog any dog trained to herd sheep
sheep'ish *adj.* 1. embarrassed or chagrined 2. shy or bashful —**sheep'ish·ly** *adv.*
sheep'skin' *n.* 1. the skin of a sheep 2. parch-

ment or leather made from the skin of a sheep 3. [Colloq.] *same as* DIPLOMA
sheer¹ (shir) *vi., vt.* [var. of SHEAR] to change or cause to change course suddenly
sheer² (shir) *adj.* [< ON. *skærr*, bright] 1. very thin; transparent: said of textiles 2. absolute; downright [*sheer* persistence] 3. extremely steep —*adv.* 1. completely; utterly 2. very steeply
sheet¹ (shēt) *n.* [OE. *sceat*] 1. a large piece of cotton, linen, etc., used on a bed 2. *a*) a single piece of paper *b*) [Colloq.] a newspaper 3. a broad, continuous surface, as of flame, water, etc. 4. a broad, thin piece of any material, as glass, metal, etc.
sheet² (shēt) *n.* [OE. *sceatline*] a rope for controlling the set of a sail
sheet·ing (shēt'iŋ) *n.* 1. material of cotton, linen, etc. used for making sheets 2. material used in covering or lining a surface [copper *sheeting*]
sheet metal metal rolled thin in sheet form
sheet music music printed on unbound sheets of paper
sheik, sheikh (shēk) *n.* [Ar. *shaikh*, lit., old man] the chief of an Arab family, tribe, or village
shek·el (shek''l) *n.* [< Heb. *shāqal*, weigh] 1. a gold or silver coin of the ancient Hebrews 2. [*pl.*] [Slang] money
shelf (shelf) *n., pl.* **shelves** [prob. < MLowG. *schelf*] 1. a thin, flat board fixed horizontally to a wall, etc., used for holding things 2. something like a shelf; specif., *a*) a ledge *b*) a sand bar or reef —**on the shelf** out of use, circulation, etc.
shell (shel) *n.* [OE. *sciel*] 1. a hard outer covering, as of a turtle, egg, nut, etc. 2. something like a shell in being hollow, empty, a covering, etc. 3. a woman's pullover, sleeveless knit blouse 4. a light, narrow racing boat rowed by a team 5. an explosive artillery projectile 6. a small-arms cartridge —*vt.* 1. to remove the shell or covering from [to *shell* peas] 2. to bombard —**shell out** [Colloq.] to pay out (money)
she'll (shēl) 1. she shall 2. she will
shel·lac, shel·lack (shə lak') *n.* [SHEL(L) + LAC] 1. a resin usually produced in thin, flaky layers 2. a thin varnish containing this resin and alcohol —*vt.* **-lacked', -lack'ing** 1. to apply shellac to 2. [Slang] *a*) to beat *b*) to defeat decisively
-shelled *a combining form meaning* having a (specified kind of) shell
shell'fish' *n., pl.*: see FISH any aquatic animal with a shell, as the clam or lobster
shel·ter (shel'tər) *n.* [< ? OE. *scield*, shield + *truma*, a troop] 1. something that protects, as from the elements, danger, etc. 2. a being covered, protected, etc. —*vt.* to provide shelter for; protect —*vi.* to find shelter
shelve (shelv) *vt.* **shelved, shelv'ing** 1. to furnish with shelves 2. to put on a shelf or shelves 3. to lay aside [to *shelve* a discussion]
shelves (shelvz) *n. pl. of* SHELF
shelv'ing *n.* 1. material for shelves 2. shelves collectively
she·nan·i·gan (shi nan'i g'n) *n.* [< ?] [*usually pl.*] [Colloq.] trickery; mischief
shep·herd (shep'ərd) *n.* [see SHEEP & HERD²] 1. a person who herds sheep 2. a clergyman —*vt.* to herd, guard, lead, etc. as a shepherd —**shep'herd·ess** *n.fem.*
sher·bet (shur'bət) *n.* [< Ar. *sharbah*, a drink] a frozen dessert like an ice, but with gelatin and, often, milk added

sher·iff (sher'if) *n.* [< OE. *scir,* shire + *gerafa,* a chief officer] the chief law-enforcement officer of a county

sher·ry (sher'ē) *n., pl.* **-ries** [< *Jerez,* Spain] 1. a strong, yellow or brown ·Spanish wine 2. any similar wine made elsewhere

she's (shēz) 1. she is 2. she has

shew (shō) *n., vt., vi.* **shewed, shewn** or **shewed, shew'ing** *archaic sp. of* SHOW

shib·bo·leth (shib'ə ləth) *n.* [< Heb. *shibbōleth,* a stream] 1. *Bible* the test word used to distinguish the enemy: Judg. 12:4–6 2. any password 3. any phrase, custom, etc. peculiar to a certain class, faction, etc.

shied (shīd) *pt. & pp. of* SHY

shield (shēld) *n.* [OE. *scield*] 1. a piece of armor worn on the forearm to ward off blows, etc. 2. one that guards, protects, etc. 3. anything shaped like a shield 4. an escutcheon — *vt., vi.* to defend; protect

shift (shift) *vt.* [OE. *sciftan,* divide] 1. to move from one person, place, etc. to another 2. to replace by another or others 3. to change the arrangement of (gears) —*vi.* 1. to change position, direction, etc. 2. to get along *[to shift* for oneself*]* —*n.* 1. a shifting; change 2. a plan of conduct, esp. for an emergency 3. an evasion; trick 4. *short for* GEARSHIFT 5. *a)* a group of people working in relay with other groups *b)* the work period involved —**make shift** to do the best one can (*with* the means at hand)

shift'less *adj.* lazy or careless

shift'y *adj.* **-i·er, -i·est** of a tricky nature; evasive —**shift'i·ness** *n.*

shill (shil) *n.* [< ?] [Slang] the confederate of a gambler, auctioneer, etc. who pretends to buy, bet, etc. so as to lure others

shil·le·lagh, shil·la·lah (shi lā'lē, -lə) *n.* [< *Shillelagh,* Ir. village] a cudgel

shil·ling (shil'iŋ) *n.* [OE. *scylling*] a British money of account and coin: coinage discontinued in 1971

shil·ly-shal·ly (shil'ē shal'ē) *vi.* **-lied, -ly·ing** [< *shall I?*] to be irresolute; vacillate, esp. over trifles

shim (shim) *n.* [< ?] a thin piece of wood, etc. used for filling space, leveling, etc.

shim·mer (shim'ər) *vi.* [OE. *scymrian*] to shine with an unsteady light —*n.* a shimmering light —**shim'mer·y** *adj.*

shim·my (shim'ē) *n.* [< a jazz dance < CHEMISE] a shaking or wobbling, as in a car's wheels —*vi.* **-mied, -my·ing** to shake or wobble

shin (shin) *n.* [OE. *scinu*] the front part of the leg between the knee and the ankle —*vt., vi.* **shinned, shin'ning** to climb (a rope, etc.) gripping with hands and legs

shin'bone' *n. same as* TIBIA

shin·dig (shin'dig') *n.* [< colloq. *shindy,* commotion] [Colloq.] a dance, party, or other social affair

shine (shīn) *vi.* **shone** or, esp. for vt. 2, **shined, shin'ing** [OE. *scinan*] 1. to emit or reflect light 2. to excel; be eminent 3. to show itself clearly *[love shone* from her face*]* —*vt.* 1. to direct the light of 2. to make shiny by polishing —*n.* 1. brightness; radiance 2. luster; polish 3. splendor —**take a shine to** [Slang] to take a liking to

shin'er (-ər) *n.* 1. a silvery minnow 2. [Slang] a black eye, as from a blow

shin·gle[1] (shiŋ'g'l) *n.* [prob. < Scand.] [Chiefly Brit.] 1. coarse gravel worn smooth by water, as on a beach 2. an area covered with this

shin·gle[2] (shiŋ'g'l) *n.* [< OE. *scindel*] 1. a thin, flat tile of asphalt, asbestos, etc. laid with others in a series of overlapping rows as a covering for roofs, etc. 2. [Colloq.] a small sign-

board, as that of a doctor —*vt.* **-gled, -gling** to cover (a roof, etc.) with shingles

shin·gles (shiŋ'g'lz) *n.* [< L. *cingere,* to gird] an acute virus disease with eruption of blisters on the skin along a nerve

shin'guard' *n.* a padded guard worn to protect the shin in some sports

shin·ny (shin'ē) *vi.* **-nied, -ny·ing** *same as* SHIN

Shin·to (shin'tō) *n.* [Jpn. < Chin. *shin,* god + *tao,* way] a religion of Japan, emphasizing ancestor worship —**Shin'to·ism** *n.*

shin·y (shīn'ē) *adj.* **-i·er, -i·est** 1. bright; shining 2. highly polished; glossy

ship (ship) *n.* [OE. *scip*] 1. any large vessel navigating deep water 2. a ship's officers and crew 3. an aircraft —*vt.* **shipped, ship'ping** 1. to put or take on board a ship 2. to send or transport by any carrier *[to ship* coal by rail*]* 3. to take in (water) over the side, as in a heavy sea 4. to put in place on a vessel *[ship* the oars*]* 5. to hire for work on a ship —*vi.* 1. to go aboard ship; embark 2. to be hired to serve on a ship —**ship'per** *n.*

-ship [OE. *-scipe*] *a suffix meaning:* 1. the quality or state of *[friendship]* 2. *a)* the rank or office of *[governorship]* *b)* one having the rank of *[lordship]* 3. skill as *[leadership]* 4. all persons (of a specified group)· collectively *[readership]*

ship'board' *n.* a ship: chiefly in **on shipboard,** aboard a ship

ship'build'er *n.* one whose business is building ships —**ship'build'ing** *n.*

ship'mate' *n.* a fellow sailor

ship'ment *n.* 1. the shipping or transporting of goods 2. goods shipped

ship'ping *n.* 1. the act or business of transporting goods 2. ships collectively, as of a nation or port, esp. with reference to tonnage

ship'shape' *adj.* having everything neatly in place; trim —*adv.* in a shipshape manner

ship'wreck' *n.* 1. the remains of a wrecked ship 2. the loss of a ship through storm, etc. 3. any ruin or destruction —*vt.* to cause to undergo shipwreck

ship'yard' *n.* a place where ships are built and repaired

shire (shīr) *n.* [OE. *scir,* office] in Great Britain, a county

shirk (shurk) *vt., vi.* [< ?] to neglect or evade (a duty, etc.) —**shirk'er** *n.*

shirr (shur) *n.* [< ?] *same as* SHIRRING —*vt.* 1. to make shirring in (cloth) 2. to bake (eggs) with crumbs in small buttered dishes

shirr'ing *n.* a gathering made in cloth by drawing the material up on parallel rows of short stitches

shirt (shurt) *n.* [OE. *scyrte*] 1. a garment worn by men on the upper part of the body 2. an undershirt —**keep one's shirt on** [Slang] to be patient or calm

shirt'tail' (-tāl') *n.* the part of a shirt extending below the waist

shirt'waist' (-wāst') *n.* a woman's blouse tailored like a shirt

shish ke·bab (shish' kə bäb') [< Arm. < Ar. *shīsh,* skewer + *kebāb,* kebab] a dish of kebabs, esp. of lamb

shiv·er[1] (shiv'ər) *n.* [ME. *schivere*] a fragment or splinter —*vt., vi.* to break into fragments or splinters

shiv·er[2] (shiv'ər) *vi.* [< ? OE. *ceafl,* a jaw] to shake, tremble, etc., as from fear or cold —*n.* a shaking, trembling, etc. —**shiv'er·y** *adj.*

shoal[1] (shōl) *n.* [OE. *scolu*] 1. a large group; crowd 2. a large school of fish

shoal[2] (shōl) *n.* [OE. *sceald,* shallow] 1. a shallow place in a river, sea, etc. **2.** a sand bar forming a shallow place

shock[1] (shäk) *n.* [< Fr. < MDu. *schokken,* collide] **1.** a sudden, powerful blow, shake, etc. **2.** *a)* a sudden emotional disturbance *b)* the cause of this **3.** the violent effect on the body of an electric current passing through it **4.** a disorder caused by severe injury, loss of blood, etc., and marked by a sharp drop in blood pressure, etc. —*vt.* **1.** to disturb emotionally **2.** to produce electric shock in —*vi.* to be shocked

shock[2] (shäk) *n.* [ME. *schokke*] bundles of grain stacked together to cure and dry

shock[3] (shäk) *n.* [< ? prec.] a thick, bushy or tangled mass, as of hair

shock absorber a device, as on the springs of a car, that lessens or absorbs the force of shocks

shock'ing *adj.* causing great surprise, horror, disgust, etc. —**shock'ing·ly** *adv.*

shock'proof' *adj.* able to absorb shock without being damaged

shock troops troops especially chosen, trained, and equipped to lead an attack

shod (shäd) *alt. pt. & pp. of* SHOE

shod·dy (shäd'ē) *n., pl.* **-dies** [< ?] **1.** an inferior woolen cloth made from used fabrics **2.** anything worth less than it seems to be —*adj.* **-di·er, -di·est 1.** made of inferior material **2.** poorly made **3.** sham

shoe (shōō) *n.* [OE. *sceoh*] **1.** an outer covering for the foot **2.** a horseshoe **3.** the part of a brake that presses against a wheel **4.** the casing of a pneumatic tire —*vt.* **shod** or **shoed, shoe'ing** to furnish with shoes —**fill one's shoes** to take one's place

shoe'horn' *n.* an implement inserted at the back of a shoe to help slip the heel in

shoe'lace' *n.* a length of cord, leather, etc. used for lacing and fastening a shoe

shoe'mak'er *n.* one whose business is making and repairing shoes —**shoe'mak'ing** *n.*

shoe'shine' *n.* the polishing of shoes

shoe'string' *n.* **1.** a shoelace **2.** a small amount of capital

shoe tree a form put into a shoe to stretch it or preserve its shape

shone (shōn) *pt. & pp. of* SHINE

shoo (shōō) *interj.* away! get out! —*vt.* **shooed, shoo'ing** to drive away, as by crying "shoo"

shoo'-in' *n.* [Colloq.] one expected to win easily in an election, race, etc.

shook (shook) *pt. of* SHAKE —**shook up** [Slang] upset; disturbed

shoot (shōōt) *vt.* **shot, shoot'ing** [OE. *sceotan*] **1.** to move swiftly over, by, etc. [*to shoot* the rapids] **2.** to variegate (*with* another color) **3.** to thrust or put forth (a branch, etc.) **4.** to discharge or fire (a bullet, gun, arrow, etc.) **5.** to send forth swiftly or with force **6.** to hit, wound, etc. with a bullet, arrow, etc. **7.** to photograph or film **8.** [Slang] to inject (a narcotic drug) **9.** *Sports a)* to throw or drive (a ball, etc.) toward the objective *b)* to score (a goal, points, etc.) —*vi.* **1.** to move swiftly **2.** to be felt suddenly, as pain **3.** to grow rapidly **4.** to jut out **5.** to fire a missile, gun, etc. **6.** to use guns, etc., as in hunting **7.** [Slang] to inject a narcotic drug —*n.* **1.** a shooting trip, contest, etc. **2.** a new growth; sprout —**shoot at** (or **for**) [Colloq.] to strive for —**shoot'er** *n.*

shooting star *same as* METEOR

shop (shäp) *n.* [OE. *sceoppa,* booth] **1.** a place where things are offered for sale; esp., a small store **2.** a place where a particular kind of work is done —*vi.* **shopped, shop'ping** to visit

shops to examine or buy goods —**talk shop** to discuss one's work

shop'keep'er *n.* one who operates a shop, or store

shop'lift'er *n.* one who steals articles during shopping hours —**shop'lift'** *vt., vi.*

shop'per *n.* **1.** one who shops **2.** one hired by a store to shop for others **3.** one hired by a store to compare competitors' prices, etc.

shopping center a complex of stores, restaurants, etc. with a common parking area

shop'talk' *n.* **1.** the specialized vocabulary of a particular occupation, etc. **2.** conversation about one's work, esp. after hours

shop'worn' *adj.* **1.** soiled, faded, etc. from having been displayed in a shop **2.** trite

shore[1] (shôr) *n.* [ME. *schore*] land at the edge of a body of water

shore[2] (shôr) *n.* [ME. *schore*] a beam, etc. used as a prop —*vt.* **shored, shor'ing** to support as with shores (usually *with up*)

shore patrol a detail of the U.S. Navy, Coast Guard, or Marine Corps acting as military police on shore

shorn (shôrn) *alt. pp. of* SHEAR

short (shôrt) *adj.* [OE. *scort*] **1.** not extending far from end to end **2.** not great in range or scope **3.** not tall **4.** brief; concise **5.** not retentive [a *short* memory] **6.** curt; brusque **7.** less than a sufficient or correct amount **8.** tending to crumble, as pastry **9.** designating a sale of securities, etc. which the seller expects to buy later at a lower price —*n.* **1.** something short **2.** [*pl.*] *a)* short trousers *b)* a man's undergarment like these **3.** *same as* SHORT CIRCUIT —*adv.* **1.** abruptly; suddenly **2.** briefly; concisely **3.** so as to be short —*vt., vi.* **1.** to give less than what is needed, usual, etc. **2.** *same as:* *a)* SHORTCHANGE *b)* SHORT-CIRCUIT —*fall* (or **come**) **short** to fail to reach, suffice, etc. —**in short** briefly —**run short** to have less than enough —**short of** less than or lacking —**short'ness** *n.*

short'age (-ij) *n.* a deficiency in the amount needed or expected; deficit

short'bread' *n.* a rich, crumbly cake or cookie made with much shortening

short'cake' *n.* a light biscuit or a sweet cake served with fruit, etc. as a dessert

short'change' *vt., vi.* **-changed', -chang'ing** [Colloq.] **1.** to give less money than is due in change **2.** to cheat

short circuit 1. a low-resistance connection between two points in an electric circuit, that deflects the current or causes excessive current flow **2.** popularly, a disrupted electric circuit resulting from this —**short'-cir'cuit** *vt., vi.*

short'com'ing *n.* a deficiency or defect

short cut 1. a shorter route **2.** a way of saving time, effort, etc.

short'en *vt., vi.* to make or become short or shorter

short'en·ing *n.* fat used to make pastry, etc. crisp or flaky

short'hand' *n.* any system of speed writing using symbols for sounds, words, etc. —*adj.* written in or using shorthand

short'-hand'ed *adj.* short of workers

short'horn' *n.* any of a breed of cattle with short, curved horns

short'-lived' (-līvd', -livd') *adj.* having a short life span or existence

short'ly *adv.* **1.** briefly **2.** soon **3.** abruptly

short order any food that can be cooked quickly when ordered, as at a lunch counter —**short'-or'der** *adj.*

short'-range' *adj.* reaching over a short distance or period of time

short ribs rib ends of beef from the forequarter

short shrift very little care or attention —**make short shrift of** to make short work of

short'sight'ed *adj.* 1. *same as* NEARSIGHTED 2. lacking in foresight

short'stop' *n. Baseball* the infielder between second and third base

short'-tem'pered *adj.* easily angered

short'wave' *n.* a radio wave 60 meters or less in length

short'-wind'ed (-win'did) *adj.* easily put out of breath by exertion

shot[1] (shät) *n.* [OE. *sceot*] 1. the act of shooting 2. range; scope 3. an attempt; try 4. a pointed, critical remark 5. the path of an object thrown, etc. 6. *a*) a projectile for a gun *b*) projectiles collectively 7. small pellets of lead for a shotgun 8. the heavy metal ball used in the shot put 9. a marksman 10. a photograph or continuous film sequence 11. a hypodermic injection, as of vaccine 12. a drink of liquor —**call the shots** to direct or control what happens

shot[2] (shät) *pt. & pp. of* SHOOT —*adj.* 1. variegated, streaked, etc. with another color or substance 2. [Colloq.] ruined or worn out

shot'gun' *n.* a gun for firing small shot at close range

shot put a contest in which a heavy metal ball is propelled with an overhand thrust from the shoulder —**shot'-put'ter** *n.*

should (shood) *v.* [OE. *sceolde*] 1. *pt. of.* SHALL 2. an auxiliary used to express: *a*) obligation, duty, etc. /he *should* help/ *b*) expectation or probability /he *should* be here soon/ *c*) a future condition /if I *should* die/

shoul·der (shōl'dər) *n.* [OE. *sculdor*] 1. *a*) the joint connecting the arm or forelimb with the body *b*) the part of the body including this joint 2. [*pl.*] the two shoulders and the part of the back between them 3. a shoulderlike projection 4. the land along the edge of a road —*vt.* 1. to push through, as with the shoulder 2. to carry upon the shoulder 3. to assume the burden of —**straight from the shoulder** without reserve; frankly —**turn (or give) a cold shoulder to** to snub or shun

shoulder blade either of the two flat bones in the upper back

shoulder harness an anchored strap passing across the upper body, used with a seat belt, as in a car

should·n't (shood''nt) should not

shout (shout) *n.* [ME. *schoute*] a loud, sudden cry, call, etc. —*vt., vi.* to utter in a shout or cry out loudly —**shout'er** *n.*

shove (shuv) *vt., vi.* **shoved, shov'ing** [OE. *scufan*] 1. to push, as along a surface 2. to push roughly —*n.* a push —**shove off** 1. to push (a boat) away from shore 2. [Colloq.] to leave

shov·el (shuv''l) *n.* [OE. *scofl*] a tool with a broad scoop and a long handle: used in lifting and moving loose material —*vt.* **-eled** or **-elled, -el·ing** or **-el·ling** 1. to lift and move with a shovel 2. to dig out with a shovel —**shov'el·ful'** *n., pl.* **-fuls'**

show (shō) *vt.* **showed, shown** or **showed, show'ing** [OE. *sceawian*, to look] 1. to bring or put in sight 2. to guide; conduct 3. to point out 4. to reveal /to *show* anger/ 5. to prove; demonstrate 6. to grant (favor, mercy, etc.) —*vi.* 1. to be or become seen; appear 2. to be noticeable 3. to finish third in a horse race —*n.* 1. a showing or demonstration 2. a public display or exhibition 3. a pompous display 4. a pretense /her sorrow was a mere *show*/ 5. a presentation of entertainment —**show off** to make a display of, esp. a vain display —**show up** 1. to expose 2. to arrive 3. [Colloq.] to surpass

show'boat' *n.* a boat with a theater and actors aboard who play river towns

show'case' *n.* a glass-enclosed case for displaying things, as in a store

show'down' *n.* [Colloq.] an action that brings matters to a climax

show·er (shou'ər) *n.* [OE. *scur*] 1. a brief fall of rain, sleet, etc. 2. a sudden, abundant fall, as of sparks 3. a party at which gifts are presented to the guest of honor 4. a bath in which the body is sprayed with fine streams of water —*vt.* 1. to spray with water, etc. 2. to pour forth as in a shower —*vi.* 1. to fall or come as a shower 2. to take a shower (sense 4) —**show'er·y** *adj.*

show'ing *n.* 1. an exhibition 2. a performance

show·man (shō'mən) *n., pl.* **-men** 1. one whose business is producing shows 2. a person skilled at presenting anything in a striking manner —**show'man·ship'** *n.*

shown (shōn) *alt. pp. of* SHOW

show'off' *n.* one who shows off

show'place' *n.* 1. a place that is exhibited to the public for its beauty, etc. 2. any beautiful place

show'room' *n.* a room where merchandise is displayed, as for advertising or sale

show'y *adj.* **-i·er, -i·est** 1. of striking appearance 2. attracting attention in a gaudy way —**show'i·ly** *adv.* —**show'i·ness** *n.*

shrank (shraŋk) *alt. pt. of* SHRINK

shrap·nel (shrap'n'l) *n.* [< Gen. *Shrapnel* (1761-1842), its Brit. inventor] 1. an artillery shell filled with an explosive charge and small metal balls 2. these balls or the shell fragments scattered on explosion

shred (shred) *n.* [OE. *screade*] 1. a long, narrow strip cut or torn off 2. a fragment /not a *shred* of truth/ —*vt.* **shred'ded** or **shred, shred'ding** to cut or tear into shreds —**shred'der** *n.*

shrew (shrōō) *n.* [OE. *screawa*] 1. a small, mouselike mammal with a long snout 2. a nagging, bad-tempered woman —**shrew'ish** *adj.* —**shrew'ish·ness** *n.*

shrewd (shrōōd) *adj.* [ME. *schrewe*, shrew] clever or sharp in practical affairs; astute

shriek (shrēk) *vi., vt.* [prob. < ON.] to make or utter with a loud, piercing cry; screech —*n.* such a cry

shrift (shrift) *n.* [< OE. *scrifan*, to shrive] [Archaic] confession to and absolution by a priest

shrike (shrīk) *n.* [OE. *scric*] a shrill-voiced bird of prey with a hooked bill

shrill (shril) *adj.* [echoic] producing a high, thin, piercing sound —*vt., vi.* to utter (with) a shrill sound —**shrill'ness** *n.* —**shril'ly** *adv.*

shrimp (shrimp) *n.* [< OE. *scrimman*, to shrink] 1. a small, long-tailed crustacean, valued as food 2. [Colloq.] a small, slight person

shrine (shrīn) *n.* [< L. *scrinium*, box] 1. a container holding sacred relics 2. a saint's tomb 3. any hallowed place

shrink (shriŋk) *vi.* **shrank** or **shrunk, shrunk** or **shrunk'en, shrink'ing** [OE. *scrincan*] 1. to contract, as from heat, cold, wetness, etc. 2. to lessen, as in amount 3. to draw back —*vt.* to cause to shrink

shrink'age *n.* 1. a shrinking 2. the amount of shrinking, decrease, etc.

shrinking violet a very shy person

shrive (shrīv) *vt., vi.* **shrived** or **shrove** (shrōv), **shriv'en** (shriv''n) or **shrived, shriv'ing** [< L. *scribere,* write] [Archaic] to hear the confession of and give absolution

shriv·el (shriv''l) *vt., vi.* **-eled** or **-elled, -el·ing** or **-el·ling** [prob. < Scand.] to shrink and wrinkle or wither

shroud (shroud) *n.* [OE. *scrud*] **1.** a cloth used to wrap a corpse for burial **2.** something that covers, protects, etc. **3.** any of the ropes stretched from a ship's side to a masthead —*vt.* to hide; cover

Shrove·tide (shrōv'tīd') *n.* the three days before Ash Wednesday (**Shrove Sunday, Monday,** and **Tuesday**)

shrub (shrub) *n.* [OE. *scrybb,* brushwood] a low, woody plant with several stems; bush — **shrub'by** *adj.*

shrub'ber·y *n., pl.* **-ies** shrubs collectively

shrug (shrug) *vt., vi.* **shrugged, shrug'ging** [ME. *shruggen*] to draw up (the shoulders), as in doubt, indifference, etc. —*n.* the gesture so made

shrunk (shruŋk) *alt. pt. & pp. of* SHRINK

shrunk'en *alt. pp. of* SHRINK —*adj.* contracted in size

shtick (shtik) *n.* [Yid.] [Slang] a comic bit or special talent

shuck (shuk) *n.* [< ?] a shell, pod, or husk —*vt.* **1.** to remove shucks from **2.** to remove like a shuck *[to shuck* one's clothes*]*

shucks (shuks) *interj.* [prob. < prec.] an exclamation of disappointment, embarrassment, etc.

shud·der (shud'ər) *vi.* [ME. *schoderen*] to shake or tremble violently, as in horror —*n.* a shuddering —**shud'der·ing·ly** *adv.*

shuf·fle (shuf''l) *vt., vi.* **-fled, -fling** [prob. < LowG. *schuffeln*] **1.** to move (the feet) with a dragging gait **2.** to mix (playing cards) **3.** to mix together in a jumbled mass —*n.* a shuffling —**shuf'fler** *n.*

shuf'fle·board' *n.* [< *shovel board*] a game in which disks are pushed with a cue toward numbered squares

shun (shun) *vt.* **shunned, shun'ning** [OE. *scunian*] to keep away from; avoid strictly

shunt (shunt) *vt., vi.* [< ? prec.] **1.** to move or turn to one side **2.** to switch, as a train, from one track to another —*n.* **1.** a shunting **2.** a railroad switch

shush (shush) *interj.* [echoic] hush! be quiet! —*vt.* to say "shush" to ·

shut (shut) *vt.* **shut, shut'ting** [OE. *scyttan*] **1.** to move (a door, lid, etc.) so as to close (an opening, container, etc.) **2.** to prevent entrance to or exit from **3.** to fold up the parts of (an umbrella, book, etc.) —*vi.* to be or become shut —*adj.* closed, fastened, etc. —**shut down** to cease or cause to cease operating —**shut in** to surround or enclose —**shut off** to prevent passage of or through —**shut out 1.** to exclude (a sound, view, etc.) **2.** to prevent from scoring —**shut up 1.** to enclose or confine **2.** [Colloq.] to stop or make stop talking

shut'down' *n.* a stoppage of work or activity, as in a factory

shut'eye' *n.* [Slang] sleep

shut'-in' *n.* a person who is too ill, weak, etc. to go out —*adj.* not able to go out

shut'out' *n.* a preventing of the opposing side or team from scoring

shut'ter *n.* **1.** a person or thing that shuts **2.** a movable cover for a window **3.** a device for opening and closing the aperture of a camera lens —*vt.* to close with shutters

shut·tle (shut''l) *n.* [OE. *scytel*] **1.** a device that carries thread back and forth, as in weaving **2.** a bus, etc. that makes frequent trips back and forth over a short route —*vt., vi.* **-tled, -tling** to move by or as if by a shuttle

shut'tle·cock' *n.* a rounded piece of cork having a flat end stuck with feathers: used in badminton

shy' (shī) *adj.* **shy'er** or **shi'er, shy'est** or **shi'est** [OE. *sceoh*] **1.** easily frightened; timid **2.** not at ease with others; bashful **3.** distrustful; wary **4.** [Slang] lacking —*vi.* **shied, shy'ing 1.** to move suddenly when startled **2.** to be or become cautious —**shy'ly** *adv.* —**shy'ness** *n.*

shy² (shī) *vt., vi.* **shied, shy'ing** [< ?] to fling, esp. sideways with a jerk

shy·ster (shī'stər) *n.* [< ? G. *scheisser,* defecator] [Slang] an unethical lawyer

Si *Chem.* silicon

Si·a·mese (sī'ə mēz') *adj., n., pl.* **-mese'** *same as* THAI

Siamese twins [after such a pair born in Siam (now Thailand)] any pair of twins born joined to each other

sib·i·lant (sib''l ənt) *adj.* [< L. *sibilare,* to hiss] having or making a hissing sound —*n.* a sibilant consonant, as (s) or (z)

sib·ling (sib'liŋ) *n.* [< OE. *sibling,* a relative] a brother or sister

sib·yl (sib''l) *n.* [< Gr. *sibylla*] a prophetess of ancient Greece or Rome

‡**sic'** (sik) *adv.* [L.] thus; so: used within brackets, [*sic*], to show that a quoted passage, esp. one containing some error, is exactly reproduced

sic² (sik) *vt.* **sicked, sick'ing** [< SEEK] to incite (a dog) to attack

Si·cil·i·an (si sil'yən, -ē ən) *adj.* of Sicily, its people, etc. —*n.* a native of Sicily

sick' (sik) *adj.* [OE. *seoc*] **1.** suffering from disease; ill **2.** having nausea **3.** of or for sick people *[sick* leave*]* **4.** deeply disturbed, as by grief **5.** disgusted by an excess *[sick* of excuses*]* **6.** [Colloq.] morbid *[a sick* joke*]* —**the sick** sick people

sick² (sik) *vt. same as* SIC²

sick'bed' *n.* the bed of a sick person

sick'en *vt., vi.* to make or become sick, disgusted, etc. —**sick'en·ing** *adj.*

sick·le (sik''l) *n.* [ult. < L. *secare,* to cut] a tool having a crescent-shaped blade with a short handle, for cutting tall grass, etc.

sick·ly (sik'lē) *adj.* **-li·er, -li·est 1.** in poor health **2.** of or produced by sickness *[a sickly* pallor*]* **3.** faint; feeble *[a sickly* light*]* **4.** weak; insipid

sick'ness *n.* **1.** a being sick or diseased **2.** a particular disease **3.** nausea

sick'room' *n.* the room of a sick person

side (sīd) *n.* [OE.] **1.** the right or left half, as of a body **2.** a position beside one **3.** *a)* any of the lines or surfaces that bound something *b)* either of the two bounding surfaces of an object that are not the front, back, top, or bottom **4.** either of the two surfaces of paper, cloth, etc. **5.** an aspect *[his cruel side]* **6.** any location with reference to a central point **7.** the ideas, position, etc. of one person or faction opposing another **8.** one of the parties in a contest, conflict, etc. **9.** a line of descent — *adj.* **1.** of, at, or on a side **2.** of or from one side *[a side* glance*]* **3.** secondary *[a side* issue*]* —*vt.* **sid'ed, sid'ing** to furnish with sides or siding —**side by side** beside each other —**side with** to support (a faction, etc.) —**take sides** to support a faction, etc.

arms weapons worn at the side or waist, a sword, pistol, etc.

ide'board' *n.* a piece of furniture for holding able linen, silverware, etc.

de·burns (sīd'bʉrnz') *n.pl.* [reversed < *burn-sides,* side whiskers worn by A. E. *Burnside,* Civil War general] the hair growing on a man's face, just in front of the ears

side dish any food served along with the main course, as in a separate dish

side'kick' *n.* [Slang] 1. a close friend 2. a partner

ide'light' *n.* incidental information

side'line' *n.* 1. either of two lines marking the side limits of a playing area, as in football 2. a secondary line of merchandise, work, etc.

ide'long' *adv.* toward the side —*adj.* directed to the side, as a glance

side'piece' *n.* a piece forming, or attached to, the side of something

si·de·re·al (sī dir'ē əl) *adj.* [< L. *sidus,* a star] of, or expressed in reference to, the stars

side'show' *n.* a small show apart from the main show

side'slip' *vi., vt.* **-slipped', -slip'ping** to slip or cause to slip sideways —*n.* a slip or skid to the side

side'split'ting *adj.* 1. very hearty: said of laughter 2. causing hearty laughter

side'step' *vt., vi.* **-stepped', -step'ping** to dodge as by stepping aside

side'swipe' (-swīp') *vt., vi.* **-swiped', -swip'ing** to hit along the side in passing —*n.* such a blow

side'track' *vt., vi.* 1. to switch (a train) to a siding 2. to turn away from the main issue

side'walk' *n.* a path for pedestrians, usually paved, along the side of a street

side'ways' (-wāz') *adj., adv.* 1. from the side 2. with one side forward Also **side'wise'** (-wīz')

sid·ing (sīd'iŋ) *n.* 1. boards, etc. for covering the outside of a frame building 2. a short railroad track, for unloading, etc., connected with a main track by a switch

si·dle (sī'd'l) *vi.* **-dled, -dling** [< *sideling,* sideways] to move sideways, esp. shyly or stealthily

siege (sēj) *n.* [< L. *sedere,* sit] 1. the encirclement of a fortified place by an enemy intending to take it 2. a persistent effort to win something 3. a long, distressing period [a siege of illness] —**lay siege to** to subject to a siege

si·en·na (sē en'ə) *n.* [It. *terra di Siena,* earth of Siena, city in Italy] 1. a yellowish-brown earth pigment 2. a reddish-brown pigment made by burning this

si·er·ra (sē er'ə) *n.* [Sp. < L. *serra,* a saw] a range of mountains with a saw-toothed appearance

si·es·ta (sē es'tə) *n.* [Sp. < L. *sexta (hora),* sixth (hour), noon] a nap or rest after the noon meal

sieve (siv) *n.* [OE. *sife*] a utensil with many small openings for straining, sifting, etc.

sift (sift) *vt.* [OE. *siftan*] 1. to pass through a sieve so as to separate the coarse from the fine particles 2. to examine with care; weigh (evidence, etc.) 3. to separate [to sift fact from fable] —*vi.* to pass through or as through a sieve

sigh (sī) *vi.* [< OE. *sican*] 1. to take in and let out a long, deep, sounded breath, as in sorrow, relief, etc. 2. to long or lament (for) —*n.* the act or sound of sighing

sight (sīt) *n.* [< OE. *seon,* to see] 1. something seen or worth seeing 2. the act of seeing 3. a device to aid the eye in aiming a gun, etc. 4.

aim or observation taken, as with a gun, sextant, etc. 5. the ability to see; eyesight 6. range of vision 7. [Colloq.] anything that looks unpleasant, odd, etc. —*vt.* 1. to observe 2. to glimpse 3. to adjust the sights of 4. to aim (a gun, etc.) at —*vi.* to look carefully [sight along the line] —**a sight for sore eyes** [Colloq.] a welcome sight —*at* (or *on*) **sight** as soon as seen —**by sight** by appearance —**not by a long sight** 1. not nearly 2. not at all

sight'less *adj.* blind

sight'ly *adj.* **-li·er, -li·est** pleasant to the sight —**sight'li·ness** *n.*

sight'see'ing *n.* a visiting of places of interest —**sight'se'er** *n.*

sig·ma (sig'mə) *n.* the eighteenth letter of the Greek alphabet (Σ, σ, ς)

sign (sīn) *n.* [< L. *signum*] 1. something that indicates a fact, quality, etc. [black is a sign of mourning] 2. a gesture that tells something specified 3. a mark or symbol having a specific meaning [the sign ¢ for cent(s)] 4. a publicly displayed board, etc. bearing information, advertising, etc. 5. any visible trace or indication [the signs of spring] —*vt.* 1. to write (one's name) on (a letter, check, contract, etc.) 2. to hire by written contract —*vi.* to write one's signature —**sign off** to stop broadcasting —**sign'er** *n.*

sig·nal (sig'n'l) *n.* [< L. *signum,* a sign] 1. any sign, event, etc. that initiates action 2. a gesture, device, etc. that conveys command, warning, etc. 3. *Radio, TV,* etc. the electrical impulses, etc. transmitted or received —*adj.* 1. not ordinary; notable 2. used as a signal —*vt., vi.* **-naled** or **-nalled, -nal·ing** or **-nal·ling** 1. to make a signal or signals (to) 2. to communicate by signals

sig'nal·ize' (-īz') *vt.* **-ized', -iz'ing** 1. to make notable 2. to draw attention to

sig·na·to·ry (sig'nə tôr'ē) *adj.* having joined in the signing of something —*n., pl.* **-ries** a signatory person, nation, etc.

sig·na·ture (sig'nə chər) *n.* [< L. *signare,* to sign] 1. a person's name written by himself 2. *Music* signs placed at the beginning of a staff to show key or time

sign·board (sīn'bôrd') *n.* a board bearing a sign, esp. one advertising something

sig·net (sig'nit) *n.* [< OFr. *signe,* a sign] a small seal used in marking documents as official, etc.

sig·nif·i·cance (sig nif'ə kəns) *n.* 1. that which is signified; meaning 2. the quality of being significant; expressiveness 3. importance; consequence

sig·nif'i·cant (-kənt) *adj.* [< L. *significare,* signify] 1. having or expressing a meaning 2. full of meaning 3. important; momentous

sig·ni·fy (sig'nə fī') *vt.* **-fied', -fy'ing** [< L. *signum,* a sign + *facere,* make] 1. to be an indication of 2. to make known by a sign, words, etc. —**sig'ni·fi·ca'tion** *n.*

‡**si·gnor** (sē nyôr') *n., pl.* **-gno'ri** (-nyô'rē) [It.] a man; gentleman: as a title [**S-**], equivalent to *Mr.* or *Sir*

‡**si·gno·ra** (sē nyô'rä) *n., pl.* **-re** (-re) [It.] a married woman; lady: as a title [**S-**], equivalent to *Mrs.* or *Madam*

‡**si·gno·ri·na** (sē'nyô rē'nä) *n., pl.* **-ne** (-ne) [It.] an unmarried woman or girl: as a title [**S-**], equivalent to *Miss*

sign'post' *n.* 1. a post bearing a sign 2. an obvious clue, symptom, etc.

si·lage (sī'lij) *n.* green fodder stored in a silo

si·lence (sī'ləns) *n.* 1. a keeping silent 2. absence of sound 3. omission of mention —*vt.*

-lenced, -lenc·ing 1. to make silent **2.** to put down; repress —*interj.* be silent!

si'lenc·er *n.* **1.** one that silences **2.** a device for muffling the report of a firearm

si·lent (sī'lənt) *adj.* [< L. *silere*, be silent] **1.** making no vocal sound; mute **2.** not talkative **3.** quiet; still **4.** not spoken, expressed, etc. **5.** not active [factories now *silent*] —**si'lent·ly** *adv.*

sil·hou·ette (sil'ōo wet') *n.* [< E. de *Silhouette*, 18th-c. Fr. minister of finance] **1.** a solid, usually black, outline drawing, esp. a profile **2.** any dark shape seen against a light background —*vt.* **-et'ted, -et'ting** to show or project in silhouette

sil·i·ca (sil'i kə) *n.* [< L. *silex*, flint] a hard, glassy mineral found in various forms, as in quartz, sand, etc.

sil·i·cate (sil'i kit, -kāt') *n.* a salt or ester derived from silica

sil·i·con (sil'i kən, -kän) *n.* [< L. *silex*, flint] a nonmetallic chemical element found always in combination: symbol, Si

sil'i·cone' (-kŏn') *n.* an organic silicon compound highly resistant to heat, water, etc. and used in resins, lubricants, etc.

sil'i·co'sis (-ə kō'sis) *n.* [< SILICON + -OSIS] a chronic lung disease caused by inhaling silica dust over a period of time

silk (silk) *n.* [OE. *seoluc*] **1.** the fine, soft fiber produced by silkworms **2.** thread or fabric made from this **3.** any silklike substance —*adj.* of or like silk: also **silk'en** —**silk'y** *adj.* **-i·er, -i·est**

silk'worm' (-wurm') *n.* any of certain moth caterpillars that produce cocoons of silk fiber

sill (sil) *n.* [OE. *syll*] a horizontal piece supporting a house wall, etc. or forming the bottom member of an upright frame for a door or window opening

sil·ly (sil'ē) *adj.* **-li·er, -li·est** [< OE. *sælig*, happy] having or showing little sense or judgment; foolish, absurd, etc. —**sil'li·ly** *adv.* —**sil'li·ness** *n.*

si·lo (sī'lō) *n., pl.* **-los** [Fr. < Sp. < Gr. *siros*] an airtight pit or tower in which green fodder is stored

silt (silt) *n.* [prob. < Scand.] a fine-grained, earthy sediment made up of particles carried or laid down by water —*vt., vi.* to fill or choke up with silt —**silt'y** *adj.* **-i·er, -i·est**

sil·ver (sil'vər) *n.* [< OE. *seolfor*] **1.** a white, precious metallic chemical element that is very ductile and malleable: symbol, Ag **2.** silver coin **3.** silverware **4.** a lustrous, grayish white —*adj.* **1.** of or containing silver **2.** silvery —*vt.* to cover with or as with silver

sil'ver·fish' *n.* a wingless insect with silvery scales, found in damp, dark places

silver lining anything seen as hopeful or comforting in the midst of despair

silver nitrate a colorless crystalline salt used in photography, as an antiseptic, etc.

sil'ver·smith' *n.* a skilled worker who makes articles of silver

sil'ver·ware' *n.* **1.** articles, esp. tableware, made of or plated with silver **2.** any metal tableware

sil'ver·y *adj.* **1.** of, like, or containing silver **2.** soft and clear in tone

sim·i·an (sim'ē ən) *adj.* [< L. *simia*, an ape] of or like an ape or monkey —*n.* an ape or monkey

sim·i·lar (sim'ə lər) *adj.* [< L. *similis*] nearly but not exactly the same or alike —**sim'i·lar'·i·ty** (-lar'ə tē) *n., pl.* **-ties**

sim·i·le (sim'ə lē) *n.* [L., a likeness] a figure of

speech likening one thing to another by using *like, as,* etc. (Ex.: a voice like thunder)

si·mil·i·tude (sə mil'ə tōōd') *n.* [< L. *similitudo*] likeness; resemblance

sim·mer (sim'ər) *vi.* [echoic] **1.** to remain at or just below the boiling point **2.** to be about to break out, as in anger —*vt.* to keep at or just below the boiling point —*n.* a simmering

si·mon-pure (sī'mən pyoor') *adj.* [< *Simon Pure,* a character in an 18th-c. play] genuine; authentic

si·mo·ny (sī'mə nē, sim'ə-) *n.* [< *Simon Magus,* a magician in the Bible: Acts 8:9–24] the buying or selling of sacred things, as church offices

sim·pa·ti·co (sim pät'i kō) *adj.* [< It. or Sp.] compatible or congenial

sim·per (sim'pər) *vi.* [Early ModE.] to smile in a silly or affected way —*n.* such a smile

sim·ple (sim'p'l) *adj.* **-pler, -plest** [< L. *simplex*] **1.** having only one or a few parts, features, etc.; uncomplicated **2.** easy to do or understand, as a task **3.** without additions [the *simple* facts] **4.** not ornate or luxurious; plain **5.** without guile or deceit **6.** not showy; natural **7.** of low rank or position; ordinary **8.** stupid; foolish

simple interest interest computed on principal alone, not on principal plus interest

sim'ple-mind'ed *adj.* **1.** foolish **2.** feebleminded

sim·ple·ton (sim'p'l tən) *n.* a fool

sim·plic·i·ty (sim plis'ə tē) *n., pl.* **-ties 1.** a simple state or quality; freedom from complexity, etc. **2.** absence of elegance, luxury, etc. **3.** artlessness **4.** foolishness

sim·pli·fy (sim'plə fī') *vt.* **-fied', -fy'ing** to make simpler or less complex —**sim'pli·fi·ca'tion** *n.*

sim·plis·tic (sim plis'tik) *adj.* making complex problems unrealistically simple

sim·ply (sim'plē) *adv.* **1.** in a simple way **2.** merely [*simply* trying to help] **3.** completely [*simply* overwhelmed]

sim·u·late (sim'yoo lāt') *vt.* **-lat'ed, -lat'ing** [< L. *simulare*] **1.** to give a false appearance of; feign **2.** to look or act like —**sim'u·la'tion** *n.*

si·mul·ta·ne·ous (sī'm'l tā'nē əs) *adj.* [< L. *simul,* at the same time] occurring, done, etc. at the same time

sin (sin) *n.* [OE. *synne*] **1.** the willful breaking of religious or moral law **2.** any offense or fault —*vi.* **sinned, sin'ning** to commit a sin —**sin'ful** *adj.* —**sin'ner** *n.*

Si·nai (sī'nī), **Mount** *Bible* the mountain where Moses received the Law from God

since (sins) *adv.* [ult. < OE. *sith,* after + *thæt,* that] **1.** from then until now [he came Monday and has been here ever *since*] **2.** at some time between then and now [he was ill last week but has *since* recovered] **3.** before now; ago [gone long *since*] —*prep.* **1.** continuously from (then) until now [out walking *since* noon] **2.** during the period following [he's written twice *since* May] —*conj.* **1.** after the time that [two years *since* they met] **2.** continuously from the time when [lonely ever *since* he left] **3.** because [*since* you're tired, let's go]

sin·cere (sin sir') *adj.* **-cer'er, -cer'est** [< L. *sincerus,* pure] **1.** without deceit or pretense **2.** genuine [*sincere* affection] —**sin·cere'ly** *adv.* —**sin·cer'i·ty** (-ser'ə tē) *n.*

si·ne·cure (sī'nə kyoor', sin'ə-) *n.* [< L. *sine,* without + *cura,* care] any position that brings profit while requiring little or no work

si·ne di·e (sī'nē dī'ē) [LL., without a day] for an indefinite period

si·ne qua non (sī'nē kwä nän') [L., without which not] something essential or indispensable

sin·ew (sin'yōō) *n.* [< OE. *seonu*] **1.** a tendon **2.** muscular power; strength —**sin'ew·y** (-yōō wē) *adj.*

sing (siŋ) *vi.* **sang** or now rarely **sung, sung, sing'ing** [OE. *singan*] **1.** to produce musical sounds with the voice **2.** to use song in praise [of thee I *sing*] **3.** to produce musical sounds, as a songbird **4.** to hum, buzz, etc., as a bee **5.** [Slang] to confess to a crime, esp. implicating others —*vt.* **1.** to render (a song, etc.) by singing **2.** to extol, etc. in song **3.** to bring or put by singing [to *sing* to sleep] —*n.* [Colloq.] a singing by a group —**sing'a·ble** *adj.* —**sing·er** (siŋ'ər) *n.*

sing. singular

singe (sinj) *vt.* **singed, singe'ing** [OE. *sengan*] **1.** to burn superficially or slightly **2.** to expose (a carcass) to flame in removing feathers, etc. —*n.* **1.** a singeing **2.** a slight burn —**sing·er** (sin'jər) *n.*

sin·gle (siŋ'g'l) *adj.* [< L. *singulus*] **1.** *a*) one only *b*) separate and distinct [every *single* time] **2.** alone **3.** of or for one person or family **4.** between two persons only [*single* combat] **5.** unmarried **6.** having only one part; not multiple **7.** unbroken —*vt.* **-gled, -gling** to select from others (usually with *out*) —*vi.* Baseball to hit a single —*n.* **1.** a single person or thing **2.** Baseball a hit by which the batter reaches first base **3.** [*pl.*] Tennis, etc. a match with only one player on each side

sin'gle-breast'ed *adj.* overlapping over the breast just enough to be fastened, as a coat

single file a single column of persons or things, one behind another

sin'gle-hand'ed *adj., adv.* **1.** using only one hand **2.** done or working alone

sin'gle-mind'ed *adj.* **1.** honest; sincere **2.** with only one aim or purpose

sin'gle·ton (-tən) *n.* **1.** a playing card that is the only one of a suit held by a player **2.** a single thing

sin·gle·tree (siŋ'g'l trē') *n.* [< ME. *swingle*, a rod + *tre*, a tree] a crossbar at the front of a wagon, etc. to which the traces of a horse's harness are hooked

sin·gly (siŋ'glē) *adv.* **1.** alone **2.** one by one **3.** unaided

sing'song' *n.* **1.** an unvarying rise and fall of tone **2.** speech, etc. marked by this

sin·gu·lar (siŋ'gyə lər) *adj.* [< L. *singulus*, single] **1.** unique **2.** extraordinary; remarkable **3.** strange; odd **4.** Gram. designating only one —*n.* Gram. the singular number or form of a word —**sin'gu·lar'i·ty** (-lar'ə tē) *n.* —**sin'gu·lar·ly** *adv.*

Sin·ha·lese (sin'hə lēz', -lēs') *adj.* of Sri Lanka, its principal people, their language, etc. —*n.* **1.** *pl.* **-lese'** any of the Sinhalese people **2.** their language

sin·is·ter (sin'is tər) *adj.* [< L. *sinister*, left-hand] **1.** orig., on or to the left-hand side **2.** threatening harm, etc. **3.** evil

sink (siŋk) *vi.* **sank** or **sunk, sunk, sink'ing** [OE. *sincan*] **1.** to go beneath the surface of water, etc. **2.** to go down slowly **3.** to appear to descend, as the sun **4.** to become lower, as in level, degree, value, etc. **5.** to become hollow, as the cheeks **6.** to pass gradually (*into* sleep, etc.) **7.** to approach death —*vt.* **1.** to make sink **2.** to make (a well, design, etc.) by digging, cutting, etc. **3.** to invest **4.** to defeat; undo —*n.* **1.** a cesspool or sewer **2.** a basin, as in a kitchen, with a drainpipe **3.** an area of sunken land

sink'er *n.* **1.** one that sinks **2.** a lead weight for fishing

Sino- [Fr. < Gr. *Sinai*] a combining form meaning Chinese and

sin·u·ous (sin'yōō wəs) *adj.* [< L. *sinus*, a bend] **1.** bending or winding in and out **2.** not straightforward; devious

si·nus (sī'nəs) *n.* [L., a bent surface] a cavity, hollow, etc.; specif., any of the air cavities in the skull opening into a nasal cavity

si·nus·i·tis (sī'nə sīt'əs) *n.* inflammation of a sinus, esp. of the skull

-sion [< L. *-sio*] a suffix meaning act, state, or result of [*discussion, confusion*]

Sioux (sōō) *n., pl.* **Sioux** (sōō, sōōz) a member of a group of Indian tribes of the N U.S. and S America —*adj.* of these tribes: also **Siou·an** (sōō'ən)

sip (sip) *vt., vi.* **sipped, sip'ping** [akin to LowG. *sippen*] to drink a little at a time —*n.* **1.** a sipping **2.** a small quantity sipped —**sip'per** *n.*

si·phon (sī'fən) *n.* [Fr. < Gr. *siphōn*, a tube] **1.** a bent tube for carrying liquid out over the edge of a container to a lower level, through the force of air pressure on the liquid **2.** a sealed bottle from which carbonated water may be released —*vt., vi.* to draw off, or pass, through a siphon

sir (sur) *n.* [see SIRE] **1.** [sometimes S-] a respectful term of address used to a man: not followed by the name **2.** [S-] a title used before the name of a knight or baronet

sire (sīr) *n.* [< L. *senior*, comp. of *senex*, old] **1.** a title of respect used in addressing a king **2.** [Poet.] a father or forefather **3.** the male parent of an animal —*vt.* **sired, sir'ing** to beget: said esp. of animals

si·ren (sī'rən) *n.* [< Gr. *Seirēn*] **1.** Gr. & Rom. Myth. any of several sea nymphs whose singing lured sailors to their death on rocky coasts **2.** a seductive woman **3.** a warning device, etc. producing a wailing sound

sir·loin (sur'loin) *n.* [< OFr. *sur*, over + *loigne*, loin] a choice cut of beef from the loin end just in front of the rump

si·roc·co (sə räk'ō) *n., pl.* **-cos** [It. < Ar. *sharq*, the east] a hot, oppressive wind blowing from the Libyan deserts into S Europe

sir·ree, sir·ee (sə rē') *interj.* [< SIR] an interjection used for emphasis after *yes* or *no*

sir·up (sir'əp, sur'-) *n. same as* SYRUP

sis (sis) *n. colloq.* form of SISTER

si·sal (sī's'l) *n.* [< *Sisal*, in SE Mexico] **1.** a strong fiber obtained from the leaves of an agave **2.** this agave

sis·sy (sis'ē) *n., pl.* **-sies** [dim. of SIS] [Colloq.] **1.** an effeminate man or boy **2.** a coward —**sis'si·fied'** *adj.*

sis·ter (sis'tər) *n.* [ON. *systir*] **1.** a female as related to other children of her parents **2.** a friend who is like a sister **3.** a female of the same race, creed, profession, etc. as one's own **4.** a nun **5.** one of the same kind, model, etc. —**sis'ter·ly** *adj.*

sis'ter·hood' *n.* —**sis'ter·ly** *adj.*

sis'ter-in-law' *n., pl.* **sis'ters-in-law'** **1.** the sister of one's spouse **2.** the wife of one's brother **3.** the wife of the brother of one's spouse

sit (sit) *vi.* **sat, sit'ting** [OE. *sittan*] **1.** to rest the body on the buttocks, as on a chair **2.** to rest on the haunches with the forelegs braced, as a dog **3.** to perch, as a bird **4.** to cover eggs for hatching, as a hen **5.** *a*) to occupy a seat as a judge, legislator, etc. *b*) to be in session, as a court **6.** to pose, as for a portrait **7.** to be located **8.** to rest or lie [cares *sit* lightly on him] **9.** *same as* BABY-SIT —*vt.* **1.** to cause to sit **2.** to stay seated on (a horse, etc.) —**sit down** to take a seat —**sit in (on)** to attend —**sit up 1.** to sit erect **2.** to put off going to bed **3.** [Colloq.] to become suddenly alert —**sit'ter** *n.*

si·tar (si tär′) *n.* [Hindi *sitār*] a lutelike instrument of India with a long, fretted neck

sit'-down' *n.* a strike in which strikers stay inside a factory, etc. refusing to work

site (sīt) *n.* [< L. *situs*, position] the location or scene of anything

sit'-in' *n.* a demonstration, as for civil rights, in which a group sits down inside a public place and refuses to leave

sit'ting *n.* **1.** the act or position of one that sits **2.** a session, as of a court **3.** a period of being seated

sit·u·ate (sich′oo wāt′) *vt.* -at'ed, -at'ing [see SITE] to put in a certain place; locate

sit'u·a'tion *n.* **1.** location; position; place **2.** condition with regard to circumstances **3.** a state of affairs **4.** a job; position

situation comedy a comic TV series with episodes involving stock characters

sit'-up', sit'up' *n.* an exercise of sitting up from a lying position

Si·va (sē′və) Hindu god of destruction and reproduction: see BRAHMA

six (siks) *adj., n.* [OE. *sex*] one more than five; 6; VI —**sixth** (siksth) *adj., n.*

six'teen' (-tēn′) *adj., n.* [OE. *syxtene*] six more than ten; 16; XVI —**six'teenth'** (-tēnth′) *adj., n.*

sixth sense intuitive power

six·ty (siks′tē) *adj., n., pl.* **-ties** [OE. *sixtig*] six times ten; 60; LX —**the sixties** the numbers or years, as of a century, from 60 through 69 —**six'ti·eth** (-ith) *adj., n.*

siz·a·ble (sī′zə b'l) *adj.* quite large or bulky: also **size'a·ble**

size¹ (sīz) *n.* [ult. < L. *sedere*, sit] **1.** that quality of a thing which determines how much space it occupies; dimensions **2.** any of a series of graded classifications of goods [size ten shoes] **3.** extent, amount, etc. —*vt.* **sized, siz'ing** to make or arrange according to size —**size up** [Colloq.] **1.** to estimate; judge **2.** to meet requirements

size² (sīz) *n.* [ME. *syse*] a thin, pasty substance used as a glaze or filler on paper, cloth, etc. —*vt.* **sized, siz'ing** to stiffen or glaze with size

-sized *a combining form meaning* of (a specified) size [small-*sized*]: also **-size**

siz·ing (sī′zin) *n.* **1.** *same as* SIZE² **2.** the act or process of applying size

siz·zle (siz′'l) *vi.* **-zled, -zling** [echoic] **1.** to make a hissing sound when in contact with heat **2.** to be extremely hot —*n.* a sizzling sound

skate¹ (skāt) *n.* [< OFr. *eschace*, stilt] **1.** *a)* a bladelike metal runner in a frame, fastened to a shoe for gliding on ice *b)* a shoe with such a runner attached Also **ice skate 2.** a frame or shoe with two pairs of small wheels, for gliding on a floor, sidewalk, etc.: also **roller skate** —*vi.* **skat'ed, skat'ing** to move along on skates —**skat'er** *n.*

skate² (skāt) *n.* [< ON. *skata*] a fish of the ray family with a broad, flat body

skate'board' *n.* a short, oblong board with two wheels at each end, ridden as down an incline —*vi.* to ride on a skateboard

skeet (skēt) *n.* [< ON. *skeyti*, projectile] trapshooting in which the shooter fires from different angles

skein (skān) *n.* [< MFr. *escaigne*] a quantity of thread or yarn in a coil

skel·e·ton (skel′ə t'n) *n.* [< Gr. *skeletos*, dried up] **1.** the hard framework of bones of an animal body **2.** a supporting framework **3.** an outline, as of a book —**skel'e·tal** *adj.*

skeleton key a key with a slender bit that can open many simple locks

skep·tic (skep′tik) *adj.* [< Gr. *skeptikos*, inquiring] *var. of* SKEPTICAL —*n.* **1.** an adherent of skepticism **2.** one who habitually questions matters generally accepted **3.** one who doubts religious doctrines

skep'ti·cal (-ti k'l) *adj.* doubting; questioning —**skep'ti·cal·ly** *adv.*

skep'ti·cism (-siz'm) *n.* **1.** the doctrine that the truth of all knowledge must always be in question **2.** skeptical attitude **3.** doubt about religious doctrines

sketch (skech) *n.* [< Du. < Gr. *schedios*, extempore] **1.** a rough drawing or design, done rapidly **2.** a brief outline **3.** a short, light story, play, etc. —*vi., vt.* to make a sketch (of) —**sketch'y** *adj.* **-i·er, -i·est**

skew (skyoo) *vi., vt.* [see ESCHEW] to slant or set at a slant —*adj.* slanting —*n.* a slant or twist

skew·er (skyoo′ər) *n.* [< ON. *skifa*, a slice] a long pin used to hold meat together while cooking —*vt.* to fasten as with skewers

ski (skē) *n., pl.* **skis, ski** [Norw. < ON. *skith*, snowshoe] either of a pair of long runners of wood, etc. fastened to the shoes for gliding over snow —*vi.* **skied, ski'ing** to glide on skis —**ski'er** *n.*

skid (skid) *n.* [< ON. *skith*, snowshoe] **1.** a plank, log, etc. used as a track upon which to slide a heavy object **2.** a low, movable platform for holding loads **3.** a runner on an aircraft landing gear **4.** a sliding wedge used to brake a wheel **5.** the act of skidding —*vt., vi.* **skid'ded, skid'ding 1.** to slide or slip, as a vehicle on ice **2.** to decline sharply —**be on** (or **hit**) **the skids** [Slang] to be on the downgrade

skid row [< *skid road*, trail to skid logs along] a city area where vagrants gather

skiff (skif) *n.* [< It. *schifo*] **1.** a light rowboat **2.** a long rowboat, esp. one with a small sail

ski lift an endless cable, typically with seats, for carrying skiers up a slope

skill (skil) *n.* [ON. *skil*, distinction] **1.** great ability or proficiency **2.** an art, craft, etc., esp. one involving the use of the hands or body **3.** ability in such an art, etc. —**skilled** *adj.* —**skill'ful, skil'ful** *adj.*

skil·let (skil′it) *n.* [< ? L. *scutra*, a dish] a shallow pan with a handle, for frying food

skim (skim) *vt., vi.* **skimmed, skim'ming** [ME. *skimen*] **1.** to remove (floating matter) from (a liquid) **2.** to look through (a book, etc.) hastily **3.** to glide lightly (over)

skim milk milk with the cream removed

skimp (skimp) *vi., vt.* [Colloq.] *same as* SCRIMP

skimp'y *adj.* **-i·er, -i·est** [Colloq.] barely enough; scanty —**skimp'i·ness** *n.*

skin (skin) *n.* [ON. *skinn*] **1.** the outer covering of the animal body **2.** a pelt **3.** something like skin, as fruit rind, etc. —*vt.* **skinned, skin'ning 1.** to remove the skin of **2.** to injure by scraping (one's knee, etc.) **3.** [Colloq.] to swindle —**get under one's skin** [Colloq.] to irritate one —**skin'less** *adj.*

skin diving underwater swimming with air supplied by snorkel or scuba gear —**skin'-dive'** *vi.* **-dived', -div'ing** —**skin diver**

skin'flick' (-flik′) *n.* [Slang] a pornographic motion picture

skin'flint' *n.* [lit., one who would skin a flint for economy] a miser

skinned (skind) *adj.* having skin (of a specified kind) *[dark-skinned]*

skin·ny (skin′ē) *adj.* **-ni·er, -ni·est** emaciated; thin **—skin′ni·ness** *n.*

skin′ny-dip′ (-dip′) *vi.* **-dipped′, -dip′ping** [Colloq.] to swim in the nude

skin′tight′ *adj.* tightfitting *[skintight jeans]*

skip (skip) *vi., vt.* **skipped, skip′ping** [ME. *skippen*] **1.** to leap lightly (over) **2.** to ricochet or bounce **3.** to pass to another point, omitting or ignoring (something) **4.** [Colloq.] to leave (a place) hurriedly **—n. 1.** a skipping **2.** a gait alternating light hops on each foot

skip·per (skip′ər) *n.* [< MDu. *schip*, a ship] the captain of a ship

skir·mish (skur′mish) *n.* [< It. *schermire*, to fight < Gmc.] **1.** a brief fight between small groups, as in a battle **2.** any slight conflict **—vi.** to take part in a skirmish

skirt (skurt) *n.* [< ON. *skyrt*, shirt] **1.** that part of a dress, coat, etc. that hangs below the waist **2.** a woman's garment that hangs down from the waist **3.** something like a skirt **—vi., vt.** to be on, or move along, the edge (of)

ski run a slope or course used for skiing

skit (skit) *n.* [prob. < ON. *skjota*, to shoot] a short, humorous sketch, as in the theater

ski tow an endless cable for towing skiers up a slope on their skis

skit·tish (skit′ish) *adj.* [see SKIT & -ISH] **1.** lively; playful **2.** easily frightened; jumpy **3.** fickle **—skit′tish·ly** *adv.*

skiv·vy (skiv′ē) *n., pl.* **-vies** [< ?] [Slang] **1.** a man's, esp. a sailor's, short-sleeved undershirt: usually **skivvy shirt 2.** [*pl.*] men's underwear

skoal (skōl) *interj.* [< Dan. & Norw. < ON. *skāl*, a bowl] to your health: a toast

skul·dug·ger·y, skull·dug·ger·y (skul dug′ər ē) *n.* [< ?] [Colloq.] sneaky, dishonest behavior

skulk (skulk) *vi.* [ME. *sculken*] to move about in a stealthy manner; slink **—skulk′er** *n.*

skull (skul) *n.* [< Scand.] **1.** the bony framework of the head, enclosing the brain **2.** the head or mind

skull and crossbones a representation of two bones under a human skull, used to label poisons, etc.

skull′cap′ *n.* a light, closefitting, brimless cap, usually worn indoors

skunk (skuŋk) *n.* [< AmInd. *segonku*] **1.** a small, bushy-tailed mammal having black fur with white stripes down the back: it ejects a foul-smelling liquid when molested **2.** its fur **3.** [Colloq.] a despicable person

sky (skī) *n., pl.* **skies** [< ON., a cloud] **1.** [*often pl.*] the upper atmosphere *[blue skies]* **2.** the firmament **3.** heaven

sky′cap′ *n.* a porter at an air terminal

sky′-high′ *adj., adv.* very high

sky′jack′ (-jak′) *vt.* [Colloq.] to hijack (an aircraft) **—sky′jack′er** *n.*

sky′lark′ *n.* a lark of Europe and Asia, famous for the song it utters as it soars

sky′light′ *n.* a window in a roof or ceiling

sky′line′ *n.* **1.** the visible horizon **2.** the outline of a city, etc. seen against the sky

sky′rock′et *n.* a firework rocket that explodes in midair **—vi., vt.** to rise or cause to rise rapidly

sky′scrap′er *n.* a very tall building

sky′ward (-wərd) *adv., adj.* toward the sky: also **sky′wards** *adv.*

sky′ways′ *n.pl.* routes of air travel

sky′writ′ing *n.* the tracing of words in the sky by trailing smoke from an airplane

slab (slab) *n.* [ME. *sclabbe*] a flat, broad, fairly thick piece

slack¹ (slak) *adj.* [OE. *slæc*] **1.** slow; sluggish **2.** not busy; dull *[a slack period]* **3.** loose; not tight **4.** careless *[a slack workman]* **—vt., vi.** *same as* SLACKEN **—n. 1.** a part that hangs loose **2.** a lack of tension **3.** a dull period; lull **—slack off** to slacken **—slack up** to go more slowly

slack² (slak) *n.* [ME. *sleck*] a mixture of small pieces of coal, coal dust, and dirt left from the screening of coal

slack·en (slak′'n) *vt., vi.* **1.** to make or become less active, brisk, etc. **2.** to loosen or relax, as rope

slack′er *n.* one who shirks his work or duty

slacks (slaks) *n.pl.* trousers for men or women

slag (slag) *n.* [< MLowG. *slagge*] the fused refuse separated from a metal in smelting

slain (slān) *pp. of* SLAY

slake (slāk) *vt.* **slaked′, slak′ing** [< OE. *slæc*, slack] **1.** to make (thirst, etc.) less intense by satisfying **2.** to produce a chemical change in (lime) by combination with water

sla·lom (slä′ləm) *n.* [Norw., sloping trail] a downhill skiing race over a zigzag course

slam¹ (slam) *vt., vi.* **slammed, slam′ming** [prob. < Scand.] **1.** to shut, hit, throw, put, etc. with force and noise **2.** [Colloq.] to criticize severely **—n. 1.** the act or sound of slamming **2.** [Colloq.] a severe criticism

slam² (slam) *n.* [< ?] *Bridge* shortened form of GRAND SLAM *or* LITTLE SLAM

slam·mer (slam′ər) *n.* [Slang] a prison or jail

slan·der (slan′dər) *n.* [see SCANDAL] **1.** the utterance of a falsehood damaging to another's reputation **2.** such a spoken falsehood **—vt.** to utter such a falsehood about **—slan′der·er** *n.* **—slan′der·ous** *adj.* **—slan′der·ous·ly** *adv.*

slang (slaŋ) *n.* [< ?] highly informal language, usually short-lived, that is outside of standard usage **—slang′y** *adj.* **-i·er, -i·est**

slant (slant) *vt., vi.* [< Scand.] **1.** to incline; slope **2.** to write or tell so as to express a particular bias **—n. 1.** an oblique surface, line, etc.; slope **2.** a point of view or attitude **—adj.** sloping

slap (slap) *n.* [echoic] **1.** a blow with something flat, as the palm of the hand **2.** an insult; rebuff **—vt. slapped, slap′ping 1.** to strike with something flat **2.** to put, hit, etc. with force **—vi.** to make a dull, sharp noise, as upon impact **—adv.** [Colloq.] directly

slap′dash′ (-dash′) *adv.* in a hasty, careless manner **—adj.** hasty, careless, etc.

slap′-hap′py *adj.* [Slang] **1.** dazed, as by blows to the head **2.** silly or giddy

slap′stick′ *n.* crude comedy full of horseplay **—adj.** of or like such comedy

slash (slash) *vt.* [< ? OFr. *esclachier*, to break] **1.** to cut with sweeping strokes, as of a knife **2.** to cut slits in **3.** to reduce drastically, as prices **—vi.** to make a sweeping stroke as with a knife **—n. 1.** a slashing **2.** a cut made by slashing

slat (slat) *n.* [< OFr. *esclat*, a fragment] a thin, narrow strip of wood, etc. **—vt. slat′ted, slat′ting** to provide with slats

slate (slāt) *n.* [see SLAT] **1.** a hard rock that cleaves into thin, smooth layers **2.** its bluish-gray color **3.** a roofing tile, etc. made of slate **4.** a list of proposed candidates **—vt. slat′ed, slat′ing 1.** to cover with slate **2.** to designate, as for candidacy **—a clean slate** a record showing no faults, mistakes, etc.

slat·tern (slat′ərn) *n.* [< dial. *slatter*, to slop] a slovenly or sluttish woman **—slat′tern·ly** *adj.*

slaugh·ter (slôt′ər) *n.* [< ON. *slātr*, lit., slain

flesh] 1. the killing of animals for food 2. the brutal killing of a person 3. the killing of people in large numbers —vt. 1. to kill (animals) for food 2. to kill (people) brutally or in large numbers

slaugh'ter·house' n. a place where animals are butchered for food

Slav (släv, slav) n. a member of a group of peoples of E and SE Europe, including the Russians, Serbs, Czechs, Poles, Slovaks, etc. —adj. same as SLAVIC

Slav. Slavic

slave (släv) n. [< LGr. Sklabos: first applied to captive Slavs] 1. a human being who is owned by another 2. one who is dominated by some influence, habit, etc. 3. one who slaves; drudge —vi. **slaved, slav'ing** to work like a slave; drudge

slave driver 1. one who oversees the work of slaves 2. any merciless taskmaster

slav·er (slav'ər) vi. [< Scand.] to drool —n. saliva drooling from the mouth

slav·er·y (slä'və rē, släv'rē) n. 1. the owning of slaves as a practice 2. the condition of a slave; bondage 3. drudgery

Slav·ic (släv'ik, slav'-) adj. of the Slavs, their languages, etc. —n. a family of languages, including Russian, Bulgarian, Polish, Czech, etc.

slav·ish (slä'vish) adj. 1. of or like slaves; servile 2. blindly dependent or imitative

slaw (slô) n. short for COLESLAW

slay (slā) vt. **slew, slain, slay'ing** [OE. slean] to kill in a violent way

slea·zy (slē'zē) adj. **-zi·er, -zi·est** [< Slesia, var. of Silesia, region in E Europe] 1. flimsy in texture [a sleazy fabric] 2. shoddy, cheap, etc. — **slea'zi·ness** n.

sled (sled) n. [ME. sledde] a vehicle on runners for moving over snow, ice, etc. —vt., vi. **sled'ded, sled'ding** to carry or ride on a sled — **sled'der** n.

sledge¹ (slej) n. [OE. slecge] same as SLEDGEHAMMER

sledge² (slej) n. [MDu. sleedse] a large, heavy sled for carrying loads

sledge'ham'mer n. [see SLEDGE¹] a long, heavy hammer, usually held with both hands

sleek (slēk) adj. [< SLICK] 1. smooth and shiny; glossy 2. of well-fed or well-groomed appearance 3. suave —vt. to make sleek —**sleek'ly** adv. —**sleek'ness** n.

sleep (slēp) n. [OE. slæp] 1. a natural, regularly recurring state of rest for the body and mind, during which there is little or no conscious thought 2. any state like sleep —vi. **slept, sleep'ing** to be in the state of, or a state like, sleep —vt. to provide sleeping accommodations for —**sleep off** to rid oneself of by sleeping —**sleep'less** adj.

sleep'er n. 1. one who sleeps 2. a railroad car with berths for passengers to sleep in: also **sleeping car** 3. something that achieves an unexpected success

sleeping bag a warmly lined, zippered bag for sleeping in, esp. outdoors

sleeping sickness an infectious, usually fatal disease, esp. in Africa, characterized by lethargy, prolonged coma, etc.

sleep'walk'ing n. the act or practice of walking while asleep —**sleep'walk'er** n.

sleep'wear' n. same as NIGHT CLOTHES

sleep'y adj. **-i·er, -i·est** 1. ready or likely to fall asleep; drowsy 2. dull; quiet [a sleepy town] — **sleep'i·ness** n.

sleet (slēt) n. [ME. slete] 1. partly frozen rain 2. a mixture of rain with snow —vi. to shower in the form of sleet —**sleet'y** adj.

sleeve (slēv) n. [OE. sliefe] 1. that part of a garment that covers the arm 2. a tubelike part fitting around another part —**up one's sleeve** hidden but ready to be used —**sleeve'less** adj.

sleigh (slā) n. [Du. slee] a light vehicle on runners, for travel over snow and ice

sleight of hand (slīt) [< ON. slœgr, crafty] 1. skill with the hands, esp. in deceiving onlookers by magic tricks 2. such tricks

slen·der (slen'dər) adj. [< ?] 1. long and thin 2. having a slim figure 3. small in amount, size, etc. —**slen'der·ness** n.

slen'der·ize' vt., vi. **-ized', -iz'ing** to make or become slender

slept (slept) pt. & pp. of SLEEP

sleuth (slōōth) n. [< ON. sloth, a track] [Colloq.] a detective

slew¹ (slōō) n. [Ir. sluagh, a host] [Colloq.] a large number or amount

slew² (slōō) pt. of SLAY

slice (slīs) n. [< Frank. slizzan] 1. a thin, broad piece cut from something 2. a part or share 3. a hit ball, or its path, curving away to the right from a right-handed player or to the left from a left-handed player —vt. **sliced, slic'ing** 1. to cut into slices 2. to cut off as in a slice (with off, from, away, etc.) 3. to hit (a ball) in a slice —vi. to cut (through) like a knife —**slic'er** n.

slick (slik) vt. [OE. slician] 1. to make smooth 2. [Colloq.] to make smart, neat, etc. (with up) —adj. 1. sleek; smooth 2. slippery 3. [Colloq.] smooth but superficial, tricky, etc. —n. a smooth area on the water, as from a film of oil

slick'er n. a loose, waterproof coat

slide (slīd) vi. **slid** (slid), **slid'ing** [OE. slidan] 1. to move along in constant contact with a smooth surface, as on ice 2. to glide 3. to slip [it slid from his grasp] —vt. 1. to cause to slide 2. to place quietly or deftly (with in or into) — n. 1. a sliding 2. a smooth, often inclined surface for sliding 3. something that works by sliding 4. a photographic transparency for use with a projector or viewer 5. a small glass plate on which objects are mounted for microscopic study 6. the fall of a mass of rock, snow, etc. down a slope —**let slide** to neglect

slide fastener a zipper or zipperlike device with two grooved plastic edges joined or separated by a slide

slide rule an instrument for rapid calculations, consisting of a ruler with a central sliding piece, both marked with logarithmic scales

slight (slīt) adj. [OE. sliht] 1. a) light in build; slender b) frail; fragile 2. lacking strength, importance, etc. 3. small in amount or extent — vt. 1. to neglect 2. to treat with disrespect 3. to treat as unimportant —n. a slighting or being slighted —**slight'ly** adv.

slim (slim) adj. **slim'mer, slim'mest** [< Du., bad] 1. small in girth; slender 2. small in amount, degree, etc.; slight —vt., vi. **slimmed, slim'ming** to make or become slim —**slim'ly** adv. —**slim'ness** n.

slime (slīm) n. [OE. slim] any soft, moist, slippery, often sticky matter —**slim'y** adj.

sling (slin) n. [< ON. slyngva, to throw] 1. a primitive instrument whirled by hand for throwing stones 2. a cast; throw; fling 3. a supporting band, strap, etc. as for raising a heavy object 4. a cloth looped from the neck under an injured arm for support —vt. **slung, sling'ing** 1. to throw, cast, etc. 2. to hang in a sling; suspend

sling'shot' n. a Y-shaped piece of wood,

metal, etc. with an elastic band attached to the upper tips for shooting stones, etc.

slink (sliŋk) *vi.* **slunk, slink'ing** [OE. *slincan*, to creep] to move in a furtive or sneaky way, or as if ashamed

slink'y *adj.* **-i·er, -i·est 1.** sneaky; furtive **2.** [Slang] sinuous in movement, line, etc.

slip¹ (slip) *vi.* **slipped, slip'ping** [MLowG. *slippen*] **1.** to go quietly or secretly [to *slip* out of a room] **2.** to pass smoothly or easily **3.** to escape from one's memory, etc. **4.** to slide accidentally, lose footing, etc. **5.** to make a mistake; err **6.** to become worse —*vt.* **1.** to put or move quickly or easily **2.** to escape (one's mind) **3.** to get loose from —*n.* **1.** a space between piers, where ships can dock **2.** a woman's undergarment, about the length of a dress **3.** a pillowcase **4.** a slipping or falling down **5.** an error or mistake —**let slip** to say without intending to —**slip up** to make a mistake

slip² (slip) *n.* [< MDu. *slippen*, to cut] **1.** a stem, root, etc. of a plant, used for planting or grafting **2.** a young, slim person **3.** a small piece of paper

slip'cov·er *n.* a removable, fitted cloth cover for a sofa, armchair, etc.

slip'knot' *n.* a knot made so that it will slip along the rope around which it is tied

slipped disk a ruptured cartilaginous disk between vertebrae, esp. in the lumbar region

slip·per (slip'ər) *n.* a light, low shoe easily slipped onto the foot, esp. for indoor wear

slip·per·y (slip'ə rē) *adj.* **-i·er, -i·est 1.** liable to cause slipping, as a wet surface **2.** tending to slip away, as from a grasp **3.** unreliable; tricky —**slip'per·i·ness** *n.*

slip·shod (slip'shäd') *adj.* [after obs. *slip-shoe*, a slipper] careless or slovenly

slip'-up' *n.* [Colloq.] an error; oversight

slit (slit) *vt.* **slit, slit'ting** [ME. *slitten*] **1.** to cut or split open, esp. by a lengthwise incision **2.** to cut into strips —*n.* a straight, narrow cut, opening, etc.

slith·er (slith'ər) *vi.* [< OE. *slidan*, to slide] to slip, slide, or glide along —*n.* a slithering

sliv·er (sliv'ər) *n.* [OE. *slifan*, to cut] a thin, sharp piece cut or split off; splinter —*vt., vi.* to cut or split into slivers

slob (släb) *n.* [< Ir. *slab*, mud < Scand.] [Colloq.] a sloppy or coarse person

slob·ber (släb'ər) *vi.* [prob. < LowG. *slubberen*, to swig] **1.** to drool **2.** to speak in a maudlin way —*n.* slaver

sloe (slō) *n.* [OE. *sla*] **1.** the blackthorn **2.** its small, plumlike fruit

sloe'-eyed' *adj.* **1.** having large, dark eyes **2.** having almond-shaped eyes

slog (släg) *vt., vi.* **slogged, slog'ging** [ME. *sluggen*, go slowly] **1.** to make (one's way) with great effort; plod **2.** to work hard (*at*)

slo·gan (slō'gən) *n.* [< Gael. *sluagh*, a host + *gairm*, a call: orig., a battle cry] **1.** a catchword or motto associated with a political party, etc. **2.** a catch phrase used to advertise a product

sloop (slōōp) *n.* [< Du. < LowG. *slupen*, to glide] a small sailing vessel with a single mast and a jib

slop (släp) *n.* [OE. *sloppe*] **1.** watery snow or mud **2.** a puddle of spilled liquid **3.** unappetizing liquid or semiliquid food **4.** [*often pl.*] liquid waste of any kind —*vt., vi.* **slopped, slop'ping** to spill or splash

slope (slōp) *n.* [< OE. *slupan*, to glide] **1.** rising or falling ground **2.** any inclined line, surface, etc.; slant **3.** the amount or degree of this —*vi.*

sloped, slop'ing to have an upward or downward inclination; incline; slant —*vt.* to cause to slope

slop·py (släp'ē) *adj.* **-pi·er, -pi·est 1.** splashy; slushy **2.** *a)* slovenly *b)* slipshod **3.** [Colloq.] gushingly sentimental

slosh (släsh) *vi.* [var. of SLUSH] **1.** to splash through water, mud, etc. **2.** to splash about: said of a liquid

slot (slät) *n.* [< OFr. *esclot*, hollow between the breasts] **1.** a narrow opening, as to receive a coin **2.** [Colloq.] a position in a group —*vt.* **slot'ted, slot'ting** to make a slot in

sloth (slôth, slōth, släth) *n.* [< OE. *slaw*, slow] **1.** disinclination to work or exert oneself; laziness **2.** a slow-moving, tree-dwelling S. American mammal —**sloth'ful** *adj.*

slouch (slouch) *n.* [< ON. *slōka*, to droop] **1.** a lazy or incompetent person **2.** a drooping posture —*vi.* to stand, walk, etc. in a slouch

slough¹ (sluf) *n.* [ME. *slouh*] a castoff layer or covering, as the skin of a snake —*vi.* to be shed; come off (often with *off*) —*vt.* to shed; get rid of (often with *off*)

slough² (slou) *n.* [OE. *sloh*] **1.** a place full of soft, deep mud **2.** deep discouragement

Slo·vak (slō'väk, -vak) *n.* **1.** any of a Slavic people living chiefly in E Czechoslovakia **2.** their language —*adj.* of the Slovaks, their language, etc.

slov·en (sluv'ən) *n.* [prob. < MDu. *slof*, lax] a dirty or untidy person —**slov'en·ly** *adj.*

Slo·ve'ni·an *n.* **1.** any of a Slavic people living chiefly in NW Yugoslavia **2.** their language —*adj.* of Slovenians or their language Also **Slo·vene** (slō'vēn)

slow (slō) *adj.* [OE. *slaw*] **1.** not quick in understanding **2.** taking a longer time than is usual **3.** marked by low speed, etc.; not fast **4.** behind the correct time, as a clock **5.** passing tediously; dull —*vt., vi.* to make or become slow or slower (often with *up* or *down*) —*adv.* in a slow manner —**slow'ly** *adv.* —**slow'ness** *n.*

slow'-mo'tion *adj.* **1.** moving slowly **2.** designating a filmed or taped sequence with the original action slowed down

slow'-wit'ted *adj.* mentally slow; dull

sludge (sluj) *n.* [var. of *slutch*, mud] **1.** mud, mire, or ooze **2.** any heavy, slimy deposit, sediment, etc.

slue (slōō) *vt., vi.* **slued, slu'ing** [< ?] to turn or swing around a fixed point

slug¹ (slug) *n.* [ME. *slugge*, clumsy one] a small mollusk like a snail without a shell

slug² (slug) *n.* [prob. < prec.] **1.** a small piece of metal; specif., a bullet **2.** a piece of metal used illegally in place of a coin in automatic coin machines

slug³ (slug) *n.* [prob. < Dan. *sluge*, to gulp] [Slang] a single drink, esp. of alcoholic liquor

slug⁴ (slug) *vt.* **slugged, slug'ging** [ON. *slag*] [Colloq.] to hit hard, esp. with the fist or a bat —*n.* [Colloq.] a hard blow or hit —**slug'ger** *n.*

slug·gard (slug'ərd) *n.* [< ME. *sluggen*, be lazy] a lazy person —*adj.* lazy: also **slug'gard·ly**

slug·gish (slug'ish) *adj.* [< SLUG¹] **1.** lacking energy; lazy **2.** slow or slow-moving **3.** lacking normal vigor —**slug'gish·ly** *adv.* —**slug'gish·ness** *n.*

sluice (slōōs) *n.* [< L. *excludere*, to shut out] **1.** an artificial channel for water, with a gate to regulate the flow **2.** such a gate: also **sluice gate 3.** any channel for excess water **4.** a sloping trough with water, as for washing gold ore

—*vt.* **sluiced, sluic′ing 1.** to draw off through a sluice **2.** to wash with water from a sluice

slum (slum) *n.* [< ?] a populous area characterized by poverty, poor housing, etc. —*vi.* **slummed, slum′ming** to visit slums

slum·ber (slum′bər) *vi.* [< OE. *sluma,* slumber] **1.** to sleep **2.** to be inactive —*n.* **1.** sleep **2.** an inactive state —**slum′ber·ous** *adj.*

slump (slump) *vi.* [prob. < MLowG. *slumpen,* occur by accident] **1.** to fall or sink suddenly **2.** to have a drooping posture —*n.* **1.** a sudden decline **2.** a drooping posture **3.** a period of performing below normal

slung (slun) *pt. & pp.* of SLING

slunk (slunk) *pt. & pp.* of SLINK

slur (slur) *vt.* **slurred, slur′ring** [prob. < MDu. *sleuren,* to drag] **1.** to pronounce indistinctly **2.** to disparage **3.** *Music* to produce (successive notes) by gliding without a break —*n.* **1.** a slurring **2.** a slurred pronunciation **3.** a disparaging remark **4.** *Music* a symbol (⌢) or (⌣) connecting notes to be slurred —**slur over** to pass over quickly and carelessly

slush (slush) *n.* [prob. < Scand.] **1.** partly melted snow **2.** soft mud **3.** sentimentality —**slush′y** *adj.* **-i·er, -i·est**

slut (slut) *n.* [ME. *slutte*] **1.** a dirty, slovenly woman **2.** a sexually immoral woman

sly (slī) *adj.* **sly′er** or **sli′er, sli′est** or **sly′est** [< ON. *slœgr*] **1.** tricky; crafty **2.** cunningly underhanded **3.** playfully mischievous —**on the sly** secretly —**sly′ly** *adv.* —**sly′ness** *n.*

smack¹ (smak) *n.* [OE. *smæc*] **1.** a slight taste or flavor **2.** a trace; bit —*vi.* to have a smack (*of*)

smack² (smak) *n.* [< ?] **1.** a sharp noise made by parting the lips suddenly **2.** a loud kiss **3.** a slapping blow —*vt.* **1.** to part (the lips) so as to make a smack **2.** to kiss or slap loudly —*adv.* **1.** with a smack **2.** directly; squarely

smack³ (smak) *n.* [prob. < Du. *smak*] a fishing vessel fitted with a well for keeping fish alive

small (smôl) *adj.* [OE. *smæl*] **1.** comparatively little in size; not large **2.** little in quantity, extent, duration, etc. **3.** of little importance; trivial **4.** young [*small* children] **5.** mean; petty —*n.* the small part [the *small* of the back] —**feel small** to feel shame —**small′ness** *n.*

small′-mind′ed (-mīn′did) *adj.* selfish, petty, prejudiced, etc. —**small′-mind′ed·ness** *n.*

small′pox′ (-päks′) *n.* an acute, contagious virus disease characterized by fever and pustular eruptions that often leave scars

small talk light conversation; chitchat

smart (smärt) *vi.* [OE. *smeortan*] **1.** *a*) to cause sharp, stinging pain, as a slap *b*) to feel such pain **2.** to feel mental distress —*n.* a smarting sensation —*adj.* **1.** causing sharp pain [a *smart* blow] **2.** sharp, as pain **3.** brisk; lively [a *smart* pace] **4.** intelligent, clever, etc. **5.** neat; trim **6.** stylish **7.** [Colloq.] impertinent or saucy —**smart′ly** *adv.* —**smart′ness** *n.*

smart′en (-′n) *vt., vi.* to make or become smart or smarter: usually with *up*

smash (smash) *vt., vi.* [prob. < MASH] **1.** to break into pieces with noise or violence **2.** to hit, move, or collide with force **3.** to destroy or be destroyed —*n.* **1.** a hard, heavy blow **2.** a violent, noisy breaking **3.** a violent collision **4.** total failure, esp. in business **5.** a great popular success

smash′up′ *n.* **1.** a violent wreck or collision **2.** total failure; ruin

smat·ter·ing (smat′ər in) *n.* [ME. *smateren,* to chatter] **1.** superficial knowledge **2.** a small number

smear (smir) *vt.* [OE. *smerian,* anoint] **1.** to

cover or soil with something greasy, sticky, etc. **2.** to apply (something greasy, etc.) **3.** to slander —*vi.* to be or become smeared —*n.* **1.** a mark made by smearing **2.** slander —**smear′y** *adj.* **-i·er, -i·est**

smell (smel) *vt.* **smelled** or **smelt, smell′ing** [ME. *smellen*] **1.** to be aware of through the nose; detect the odor of **2.** to sense the presence of [to *smell* trouble] —*vi.* **1.** to use the sense of smell; sniff **2.** to have an odor [to *smell* fresh] **3.** to have an unpleasant odor —*n.* **1.** the sense by which odors are perceived **2.** odor; scent **3.** an act of smelling

smell′y *adj.* **-i·er, -i·est** having an unpleasant odor

smelt¹ (smelt) *n.* [OE.] a small, silvery food fish found in northern seas

smelt² (smelt) *vt.* [< MDu. *smelten*] **1.** to melt or fuse (ore, etc.) so as to separate impurities from pure metal **2.** to refine (metal) in this way

smelt′er *n.* **1.** one whose work is smelting **2.** a place where smelting is done

smile (smīl) *vi.* **smiled, smil′ing** [ME. *smilen*] **1.** to show pleasure, amusement, affection, etc. by an upward curving of the mouth **2.** to regard with favor (with *on* or *upon*) —*vt.* to express with a smile —*n.* the act or expression of smiling

smirch (smurch) *vt.* [prob. < OFr. *esmorcher,* to hurt] **1.** to soil or smear **2.** to dishonor —*n.* **1.** a smudge; smear **2.** a stain on a reputation

smirk (smurk) *vi.* [OE. *smearcian,* to smile] to smile in a conceited or complacent way —*n.* such a smile

smite (smīt) *vt.* **smote, smit·ten** (smit′'n) or **smote, smit′ing** [OE. *smitan*] **1.** [Now Rare] to strike hard **2.** to attack with disastrous effect **3.** to affect strongly or favorably

smith (smith) *n.* [OE.] **1.** one who makes or repairs metal objects **2.** a blacksmith

smith·er·eens (smith′ə rēnz′) *n.pl.* [Ir. *smidirín*] [Colloq.] small fragments; bits

smith·y (smith′ē) *n., pl.* **-ies** the workshop of a smith, esp. a blacksmith

smock (smäk) *n.* [OE. *smoc* or ON. *smokkr*] a loose, shirtlike outer garment worn to protect the clothes

smock′ing *n.* decorative stitching used to gather cloth and make it hang in folds

smog (smôg, smäg) *n.* [SM(OKE) + (F)OG] a mixture of fog and smoke —**smog′gy** *adj.* **-gi·er, -gi·est**

smoke (smōk) *n.* [OE. *smoca*] **1.** the vaporous matter arising from something burning **2.** any vapor, etc. like this **3.** an act of smoking tobacco, etc. **4.** a cigarette, cigar, etc. —*vi.* **smoked, smok′ing 1.** to give off smoke **2.** to draw in and exhale the smoke of tobacco; use cigarettes, etc. —*vt.* **1.** to cure (meat, etc.) with smoke **2.** to use (tobacco, a pipe, etc.) in smoking —**smoke out** to force out of hiding, secrecy, etc. —**smoke′less** *adj.* —**smok′er** *n.*

smoke′house′ *n.* a building where meats, fish, etc. are cured with smoke

smoke screen a cloud of smoke spread to screen the movements of troops, ships, etc.

smoke′stack′ (-stak′) *n.* a pipe for discharging smoke from a factory, etc.

smok·y (smō′kē) *adj.* **-i·er, -i·est 1.** giving off smoke **2.** of, like, or of the color of, smoke **3.** filled with smoke

smol·der (smōl′dər) *vi.* [ME. *smoldren*] **1.** to burn and smoke without flame **2.** to exist in a suppressed state

smooch (smōōch) *n., vt., vi.* [Slang] kiss

smooth (smōōth) *adj.* [OE. *smoth*] **1.** having an

even surface, with no roughness **2.** without lumps **3.** even or gentle in movement *[a smooth voyage]* **4.** free from interruptions, difficulties, etc. **5.** calm; serene **6.** pleasing to the taste; bland **7.** polished or ingratiating, esp. in an insincere way —*vt.* **1.** to make level or even **2.** to remove lumps or wrinkles from **3.** to free from difficulties, etc. **4.** to make calm; soothe **5.** to polish or refine —*adv.* in a smooth manner —**smooth over** to make light of —**smooth′ly** *adv.* —**smooth′ness** *n.*

smor·gas·bord, smör·gås·bord (smôr′gəs bôrd′, smur′-) *n.* [Sw.] **1.** a wide variety of appetizers, cheeses, meats, etc. served buffet style **2.** a restaurant serving these

smote (smōt) *pt. & alt. pp. of* SMITE

smoth·er (smu*th*′ər) *vt.* [< ME. *smorther*, dense smoke] **1.** to keep from getting air; suffocate **2.** to cover (a fire), to put it out **3.** to cover over thickly **4.** to stifle, as a yawn —*vi.* to be suffocated

smudge (smuj) *vt., vi.* smudged, smudg′ing [ME. *smogen*] to make or become dirty; smear —*n.* **1.** a dirty spot **2.** a fire made to produce dense smoke **3.** such smoke, used to protect plants from frost, etc.

smug (smug) *adj.* **smug′ger, smug′gest** [prob. < LowG. *smuk*, neat] annoyingly self-satisfied —**smug′ly** *adv.* —**smug′ness** *n.*

smug·gle (smug′'l) *vt., vi.* **-gled, -gling** [< LowG. *smuggeln*] **1.** to bring into or take out of a country secretly or illegally **2.** to bring, take, etc. secretly —**smug′gler** *n.*

smut (smut) *n.* [< LowG. *smutt*] **1.** sooty matter **2.** a soiled spot **3.** indecent talk or writing **4.** a fungous disease of plants —**smut′ti·ness** *n.* —**smut′ty** *adj.* **-ti·er, -ti·est**

Sn [L. *stannum*] *Chem.* tin

snack (snak) *n.* [< ME. *snaken*, to bite] a light meal between regular meals

snaf·fle (snaf′'l) *n.* [prob. < ODu. *snabbe*, bill of a bird] a bit, usually jointed, attached to a bridle and having no curb

snag (snag) *n.* [< Scand.] **1.** a sharp point or projection **2.** an underwater tree stump or branch **3.** a tear, as in fabric, made by a snag **4.** an unexpected or hidden difficulty —*vt.* snagged, snag′ging **1.** to damage on a snag **2.** to hinder; impede

snail (snāl) *n.* [OE. *snægl*] a slow-moving mollusk with a wormlike body and a spiral protective shell

snake (snāk) *n.* [OE. *snaca*] **1.** a long, scaly, limbless reptile with a tapering tail **2.** a treacherous or deceitful person —*vi.* **snaked, snak′ing** to move, twist, etc. like a snake

snak·y (snā′kē) *adj.* **-i·er, -i·est 1.** of or like a snake or snakes **2.** winding; twisting **3.** cunningly treacherous

snap (snap) *vi., vt.* **snapped, snap′ping** [< MDu. *snappen*] **1.** to bite or grasp suddenly (often with *at*) **2.** to speak or say sharply (often with *at*) **3.** to break suddenly **4.** to make or cause to make a sudden, cracking sound **5.** to close, fasten, etc. with this sound **6.** to move or cause to move suddenly and smartly *[to snap to attention]* **7.** to take a snapshot (of) —*n.* **1.** a sudden bite, grasp, etc. **2.** a sharp, cracking sound **3.** a short, angry utterance **4.** a brief period of cold weather **5.** a fastening that closes with a click **6.** [Colloq.] alertness or vigor **7.** [Slang] an easy job, problem, etc. —*adj.* **1.** made or done quickly *[a snap decision]* **2.** that fastens with a snap **3.** [Slang] easy —**snap out of it** to improve or recover quickly —**snap′per** *n.* —**snap′pish** *adj.*

snap bean a green bean or wax bean

snap′drag′on *n.* [SNAP + DRAGON: from the mouth-shaped flowers] a plant with spikes of saclike two-lipped flowers

snap′py *adj.* **-pi·er, -pi·est 1.** irritable; cross **2.** that snaps **3.** [Colloq.] *a)* brisk or lively *b)* sharply chilly **4.** [Colloq.] stylish; smart

snap′shot′ *n.* a photograph taken with brief exposure, using a hand camera

snare (sner) *n.* [< ON. *snara*] **1.** a trap for small animals **2.** anything dangerous, etc. that tempts or attracts **3.** a length of spiraled wire or of gut across the bottom of a drum —*vt.* **snared, snar′ing** to catch as in a snare; trap

snarl¹ (snärl) *vi.* [< earlier *snar*, to growl] **1.** to growl fiercely, baring the teeth, as a dog **2.** to speak sharply, as in anger —*vt.* to utter with a snarl —*n.* **1.** a fierce growl **2.** a harsh utterance

snarl² (snärl) *vt., vi., n.* [ME. *snarlen*] tangle

snatch (snach) *vt.* [ME. *snacchen*] to take suddenly, without right, etc.; grab —*vi.* to try to seize a thing suddenly; grasp (*at* something) —*n.* **1.** a snatching **2.** a short time **3.** a fragment; bit

sneak (snēk) *vi., vt.* **sneaked** or colloq. **snuck, sneak′ing** [OE. *snican*] to move, act, give, put, take, etc. secretly or stealthily —*n.* **1.** one who sneaks **2.** an act of sneaking —*adj.* without warning —**sneak′y** *adj.* **-i·er, -i·est**

sneak′er *n.* a cloth shoe with a heelless, soft rubber sole

sneer (snir) *vi.* [ME. *sneren*] **1.** to look scornful **2.** to express derision, etc. in speech or writing —*n.* **1.** an act of sneering **2.** a sneering look, etc.

sneeze (snēz) *vi.* **sneezed, sneez′ing** [< OE. *fneosan*] to exhale breath from the nose and mouth in a sudden, uncontrolled way —*n.* an act of sneezing

snick·er (snik′ər) *vi.* [echoic] to laugh in a sly or partly stifled manner —*n.* a snickering laugh

snide (snīd) *adj.* [prob. < Du. dial.] slyly malicious or derisive —**snide′ly** *adv.*

sniff (snif) *vi., vt.* [echoic] **1.** to draw in (air) forcibly through the nose **2.** to express (disdain, etc.) by sniffing **3.** to smell by sniffing —*n.* **1.** an act or sound of sniffing **2.** something sniffed

snif·fle (snif′'l) *vi.* **-fled, -fling** to sniff repeatedly, as in checking mucus running from the nose —*n.* an act or sound of sniffling —**the sniffles** [Colloq.] a head cold

snig·ger (snig′ər) *vi., n.* [echoic] snicker

snip (snip) *vt., vi.* **snipped, snip′ping** [Du. *snippen*] to cut or cut off in a short, quick stroke —*n.* **1.** a small piece cut off **2.** [Colloq.] a young or impudent person

snipe (snīp) *n.* [ON. *snipa*] a long-billed wading bird —*vi.* **sniped, snip′ing 1.** to hunt snipe **2.** to shoot at individuals from a hidden position **3.** to direct a sly attack (*at* someone)

snip·pet (snip′it) *n.* [dim. of SNIP] a small scrap, specif. of information

snip·py (snip′ē) *adj.* **-pi·er, -pi·est** [Colloq.] insolently curt, sharp, etc.

snitch (snich) *vt.* [Slang] to steal —*vi.* [Slang] to tattle (*on*) —*n.* an informer

sniv·el (sniv′'l) *vi.* **-eled** or **-elled, -el·ing** or **-el·ling** [ME. *snivelen*] **1.** to cry and sniffle **2.** to complain **3.** to make a tearful, often false display of grief

snob (snäb) *n.* [< ?] one who attaches great importance to wealth, social position, etc., having contempt for those he considers inferior —**snob′ber·y, snob′bish·ness** *n.* —**snob′bish** *adj.*

snood (snood) *n.* [OE. *snod*] a baglike net

worn at the back of a woman's head to hold the hair

snoop (sno͞op) *vi.* [Du. *snoepen*, to eat snacks on the sly] [Colloq.] to pry about in a sneaking way —*n.* [Colloq.] one who snoops — **snoop'y** *adj.* -i·er, -i·est

snoot (sno͞ot) *n.* [see SNOUT] [Colloq.] 1. the nose 2. a face

snoot'y *adj.* -i·er, -i·est [Colloq.] haughty; snobbish —**snoot'i·ness** *n.*

snooze (sno͞oz) *n.* [< ? LowG. *snusen*, to snore] [Colloq.] a brief sleep; nap —*vi.* **snoozed, snooz'ing** [Colloq.] to nap; doze

snore (snôr) *vi.* **snored, snor'ing** [echoic] to breathe, while asleep, with harsh sounds —*n.* a snoring —**snor'er** *n.*

snor·kel (snôr'k'l) *n.* [G. *schnörkel*, spiral] a breathing tube extending above the surface of the water, used in swimming just below the surface

snort (snôrt) *vi.* [akin to SNORE] 1. to force breath from the nose noisily 2. to express scorn, etc. by a snort —*n.* 1. the act of snorting 2. [Slang] a drink of straight liquor, taken in one gulp

snot (snät) *n.* [OE. (*ge*)*snot*, mucus)] 1. nasal mucus: a vulgar term 2. [Slang] a young person who is insolent —**snot'ty** *adj.* -ti·er, -ti·est

snout (snout) *n.* [prob. < MDu. *snute*] the projecting nose and jaws of an animal

snow (snō) *n.* [OE. *snaw*] 1. frozen particles of water vapor that fall to earth as white, crystalline flakes 2. a falling of snow 3. a mass of fallen snow —*vi.* to fall as or like snow —*vt.* 1. to cover or obstruct with snow (with *in, under*) 2. [Slang] to deceive or mislead —**snow under** 1. to overwhelm with work, etc. 2. to defeat decisively —**snow'y** *adj.* -i·er, -i·est

snow'ball' *n.* a mass of snow packed together into a ball —*vi.* to increase rapidly like a rolling ball of snow

snow'bank' *n.* a large mound of snow

snow'bound' *adj.* blocked off by snow

snow'drift' *n.* a smooth heap of snow blown together by the wind

snow'drop' *n.* a low-growing, bulbous plant with small, bell-shaped white flowers

snow'fall' *n.* 1. a fall of snow 2. the amount of snow falling in a given area or time

snow'flake' *n.* a single crystal of snow

snow'man' *n., pl.* -**men'** a crude human figure made of snow packed together

snow'mo·bile' (-mō bēl') *n.* a motor vehicle for traveling over snow, with steerable runners in front and tractor treads at the rear

snow'plow' *n.* a plowlike machine used to clear snow off a road, etc.

snow'shoe' *n.* a racket-shaped wooden frame crisscrossed with leather, etc., worn on the feet to prevent sinking in deep snow

snow'storm' *n.* a storm with heavy snow

snow tire a tire with a deep tread for added traction on snow or ice

snub (snub) *vt.* **snubbed, snub'bing** [ON. *snubba*, chide] 1. to treat with scorn, disregard, etc. 2. to check suddenly the movement of —*n.* scornful treatment —*adj.* short and turned up: said of the nose

snub'-nosed' *adj.* having a snub nose

snuff[1] (snuf) *vt.* [< ?] 1. to trim off the charred end of (a wick) 2. to put out (a candle) —**snuff out** 1. to extinguish 2. to destroy —**snuff'er** *n.*

snuff[2] (snuf) *vt., vi.* [MDu. *snuffen*] to sniff or smell —*n.* 1. a sniff 2. powdered tobacco taken up into the nose or applied to the gums —**up to snuff** [Colloq.] up to the usual standard

snuf·fle (snuf''l) *n., vi.* **-fled, -fling** [< SNUFF[2]] sniffle

snug (snug) *adj.* **snug'ger, snug'gest** [prob. < Scand.] 1. warm and cozy 2. neat; trim [a *snug* cabin] 3. tight in fit [a *snug* coat] 4. hidden [to lie *snug*] —**snug'ly** *adv.* —**snug'ness** *n.*

snug'gle (-'l) *vi.* **-gled, -gling** [< SNUG] to cuddle; nestle

so (sō) *adv.* [OE. *swa*] 1. as shown or described [hold the bat *so*] 2. *a*) to such an extent [why are you *so* late?] *b*) very [they are *so* happy] *c*) [Colloq.] very much 3. therefore [they were tired, and *so* left] 4. more or less [fifty dollars or *so*] 5. also; likewise [I'm going and so are you] 6. then [and *so* to bed] —*conj.* 1. in order (*that*) 2. [Colloq.] with the result that —*pron.* that which has been specified or named —*interj.* an exclamation of surprise, triumph, etc. —*adj.* true [that's *so*] —**and so on** (or **forth**) and the rest; et cetera —**so as** with the purpose or result —**so what?** [Colloq.] even if so, what then?

soak (sōk) *vt.* [OE. *socian*] 1. to make thoroughly wet 2. to take in; absorb (with *up*) 3. [Colloq.] to overcharge —*vi.* 1. to stay immersed in liquid for wetting, etc. 2. to penetrate —*n.* 1. a soaking or being soaked 2. [Slang] a drunkard

so-and-so (sō'ən sō') *n., pl.* **so'-and-sos'** [Colloq.] some person or thing not specified: often euphemistic

soap (sōp) *n.* [OE. *sape*] 1. a substance used with water to produce suds for washing: made by the action of an alkali, as potash, on fats 2. [Slang] *same as* SOAP OPERA: also **soap'er** —*vt.* to scrub with soap —**no soap** [Slang] (it is) not acceptable —**soap'i·ness** *n.* —**soap'y** *adj.* -i·er, -i·est

soap'box' *n.* any improvised platform used in speaking to a street audience

soap opera [Colloq.] a daytime radio or TV serial drama of a melodramatic, sentimental nature

soap'stone' *n.* a soft, impure talc in rock form, used as an abrasive, etc.

soap'suds' *n.pl.* foamy, soapy water

soar (sôr) *vi.* [ult. < L. *ex-*, out + *aura*, air] 1. to rise or fly high into the air 2. to glide along high in the air 3. to rise above the ordinary level

sob (säb) *vi.* **sobbed, sob'bing** [ME. *sobben*] to weep aloud with short, gasping breaths —*vt.* to utter with sobs —*n.* the act or sound of sobbing —**sob'bing·ly** *adv.*

so·ber (sō'bər) *adj.* [< L. *sobrius*] 1. temperate, esp. in the use of liquor 2. not drunk 3. serious, solemn, sedate, etc. 4. quiet; plain, as color, clothes, etc. —*vt., vi.* to make or become sober (often with *up* or *down*) —**so'ber·ly** *adv.* —**so'ber·ness** *n.*

so·bri·e·ty (sə brī'ə tē, sō-) *n.* a being sober; specif., *a*) temperance, esp. in the use of liquor *b*) seriousness; sedateness

so·bri·quet (sō'brə kā') *n.* [Fr.] 1. a nickname 2. an assumed name

Soc., soc. 1. socialist 2. society

so'-called' *adj.* 1. known by this term 2. inaccurately regarded as such

soc·cer (säk'ər) *n.* [< (AS)SOC(IATION FOOTBALL)] a kind of football played by kicking a round ball

so·cia·ble (sō'shə b'l) *adj.* [Fr.: see SOCIAL] 1. friendly; affable 2. characterized by informal conversation and companionship —*n.* a social — **so'cia·bil'i·ty** *n.*

so·cial (sō'shəl) *adj.* [< L. *socius*, companion] 1. of or having to do with human beings in their living together **2.** living in this way [man as a *social* being] **3.** of or having to do with society, esp. fashionable society **4.** sociable **5.** of or for companionship **6.** of or engaged in welfare work *—n.* an informal gathering; party **—so′cial·ly** *adv.*

so′cial·ism (-iz′m) *n.* **1.** a theory of the ownership and operation of the means of production and distribution by society, with all members sharing in the work and the products **2.** [*often* **S-**] a political movement for establishing such a system **—so′cial·ist** *n., adj.* **—so′cial·is′tic** *adj.*

so·cial·ite (sō′shə līt′) *n.* a person who is prominent in fashionable society

so′cial·ize′ (-līz′) *vt.* **-ized′, -iz′ing 1.** to make social **2.** to put under government ownership *—vi.* to take part in social activity **—so′cial·i·za′-tion** *n.*

social science sociology, history, or any study of social structure

social security a Federal system of old-age, unemployment, or disability insurance

social work the promotion of the welfare of the community and the individual, as through counseling agencies, recreation centers, etc. **— social worker**

so·ci·e·ty (sə sī′ə tē) *n., pl.* **-ties** [< L. *socius*, companion] **1.** a group of persons forming a single community **2.** a particular system of group living **3.** all people, collectively **4.** companionship **5.** an organized group with some interest in common **6.** the wealthy, dominant class **—so·ci′e·tal** *adj.*

Society of Friends a Christian religious sect which has no formal creed and rejects violence in human relations

so·ci·ol·o·gy (sō′sē äl′ə jē, -shē-) *n.* [see -LOGY] the science of social relations, organization, and change **—so′ci·o·log′i·cal** (-ə läj′i k'l) *adj.* **—so·ci·ol′o·gist** *n.*

sock[1] (säk) *n., pl.* **socks, sox** [< L. *soccus*, light shoe] a short stocking

sock[2] (säk) *vt.* [Slang] to hit with force *—n.* [Slang] a blow *—adv.* [Slang] directly

sock·et (säk′it) *n.* [< OFr. *soc*, plowshare] a hollow part into which something fits

sock·eye (säk′ī′) *n.* [< AmInd.] a salmon of the N Pacific, with red flesh

sod (säd) *n.* [prob. < MDu. *sode*] **1.** a surface layer of earth containing grass; turf **2.** a piece of this layer *—vt.* **sod′ded, sod′ding** to cover with sod

so·da (sō′də) *n.* [ult. < Ar. *suwwād*, a plant burned to produce soda] **1.** *same as: a)* SODIUM BICARBONATE *b)* SODIUM CARBONATE *c)* SODIUM HYDROXIDE **2.** *a) same as* SODA WATER *b)* a confection of soda water, syrup, and ice cream

soda cracker a light, crisp cracker, usually salted, made orig. with baking soda

soda fountain a counter for making and serving soft drinks, sodas, sundaes, etc.

soda pop a flavored, carbonated soft drink

soda water water charged under pressure with carbon dioxide gas

sod·den (säd′'n) *adj.* [obs. pp. of SEETHE] **1.** soaked through **2.** soggy from improper cooking **3.** dull or stupefied, as from liquor

so·di·um (sō′dē əm) *n.* [< SODA] an alkaline metallic chemical element: symbol, Na

sodium bicarbonate a crystalline compound used in baking powder, as an antacid, etc.

sodium carbonate a hydrated carbonate of sodium, used in washing

sodium chloride common salt

sodium hydroxide a white, strongly caustic substance

sodium nitrate a clear, crystalline salt, used in explosives, fertilizers, etc.

Sod·om and Go·mor·rah (säd′əm and gə môr′ə) *Bible* two sinful cities destroyed by fire

sod′om·y (-ē) *n.* [< SODOM] any sexual intercourse held to be abnormal, as between two persons of the same sex

so·fa (sō′fə) *n.* [Fr. < Ar. *ṣuffah*] an upholstered couch with fixed back and arms

soft (sôft) *adj.* [OE. *softe*] **1.** giving way easily under pressure **2.** easily cut, worked, etc. [a *soft* metal] **3.** not as hard as is normal, desirable, etc. [*soft* butter] **4.** smooth to the touch **5.** easy to digest: said of a diet **6.** nonalcoholic: said of drinks **7.** having few of the mineral salts that keep soap from lathering: said of water **8.** mild, as a breeze **9.** weak; not vigorous **10.** easy [a *soft* job] **11.** kind; lenient **12.** not bright: said of color or light **13.** gentle; low: said of sound *—adv.* gently; quietly **— soft′ly** *adv.*

soft′ball′ *n.* **1.** a game like baseball played with a larger and softer ball **2.** the ball used

soft′-boiled′ *adj.* boiled only a short time so that the yolk is soft: said of an egg

sof·ten (sôf′'n) *vt., vi.* to make or become soft or softer **—sof′ten·er** *n.*

soft′heart′ed *adj.* **1.** full of compassion **2.** not strict or severe, as in discipline

soft palate the soft, fleshy part at the rear of the roof of the mouth; velum

soft′-ped′al *vt.* **-aled** or **-alled, -al·ing** or **-al·ling** [from pedal action in piano, etc.] [Colloq.] to make less emphatic

soft sell selling that relies on subtle suggestion **—soft′-sell′** *adj.*

soft soap [Colloq.] flattery or smooth talk **— soft′-soap′** *vt.*

soft′ware′ (-wer′) *n.* the programs, data, etc. for a computer

soft′y *n., pl.* **-ies** [Colloq.] one who is overly sentimental or trusting

sog·gy (säg′ē, sôg′ē) *adj.* **-gi·er, -gi·est** [prob. < ON. *sog*, a sucking] **1.** soaked **2.** sodden **—sog′-gi·ness** *n.*

soil[1] (soil) *n.* [< L. *solum*] **1.** the surface layer of earth, supporting plant life **2.** country [foreign soil] **3.** ground or earth

soil[2] (soil) *vt.* [ult. < L. *sus*, pig] **1.** to make dirty; stain **2.** to disgrace *—vi.* to become soiled *—n.* **1.** a soiled spot **2.** excrement

soi·ree, soi·rée (swä rā′) *n.* [< Fr. *soir*, evening] an evening party or gathering

so·journ (sō′jurn; *also, for v.,* sō jurn′) *vi.* [< L. *sub-*, under + *diurnus*, of a day] to live somewhere temporarily *—n.* a brief stay

sol (sōl) *n.* [< ML.] *Music* the fifth tone of the diatonic scale

sol·ace (säl′is) *n.* [< L. *solari*, to comfort] **1.** an easing of grief, loneliness, etc. **2.** something that relieves; comfort *—vt.* **-aced, -ac·ing** to comfort; console

so·lar (sō′lər) *adj.* [< L. *sol*, the sun] **1.** of or having to do with the sun **2.** produced by or coming from the sun

so·lar·i·um (sō ler′ē əm, sə-) *n., pl.* **-i·a** (-ə) [L. < *sol*, the sun] a glassed-in porch, room, etc. where people sun themselves

solar plexus a network of nerves in the abdominal cavity behind the stomach

solar system the sun and all the heavenly bodies that revolve around it

sold (sōld) *pt. & pp. of* SELL

sol·der (säd′ər) *n.* [< L. *solidare*, make firm] a metal alloy used when melted to join or patch metal parts, etc. *—vt., vi.* to join (things) with solder **—sol′der·er** *n.*

sol·dier (sōl′jər) *n.* [< LL. *solidus*, a coin] **1.** a member of an army **2.** an enlisted man, as distinguished from an officer **3.** one who works for a specified cause —*vi.* **1.** to serve as a soldier **2.** to shirk one's duty, as by feigning illness —**sol′dier·ly** *adj.*

soldier of fortune a mercenary soldier, esp. one seeking adventure or excitement

sole¹ (sōl) *n.* [ult. < L. *solum*, a base] **1.** the bottom surface of the foot **2.** the part of a shoe, sock, etc. corresponding to this —*vt.* **soled, sol′ing** to furnish (a shoe, etc.) with a sole

sole² (sōl) *adj.* [< L. *solus*] without another; single; one and only

sole³ (sōl) *n.* [< L. *solea*, SOLE¹: from its shape] a sea flatfish valued as food

sol·e·cism (säl′ə siz′m) *n.* [< Gr. *soloikos*, speaking incorrectly] a violation of the conventional usage, grammar, etc. of a language — **sol′e·cis′tic** *adj.*

sole·ly (sōl′lē) *adv.* **1.** alone **2.** only, exclusively, merely, or altogether

sol·emn (säl′əm) *adj.* [< L. *sollus*, all + *annus*, year] **1.** sacred **2.** formal **3.** serious; deeply earnest **4.** awe-inspiring

so·lem·ni·ty (sə lem′nə tē) *n., pl.* -ties **1.** solemn ritual **2.** seriousness; gravity

sol·em·nize (säl′əm nīz′) *vt.* -nized′, -niz′ing **1.** to celebrate formally or according to ritual **2.** to perform (a ceremony)

so·le·noid (sō′lə noid′) *n.* [< Fr. < Gr. *sōlēn*, a channel + *eidos*, a form] a coil of wire carrying an electric current and acting like a magnet

so·lic·it (sə lis′it) *vt., vi.* [see SOLICITOUS] **1.** to appeal to (persons) for (aid, donations, etc.) **2.** to entice or lure —**so·lic′i·ta′tion** *n.*

so·lic′i·tor (-ər) *n.* **1.** one who solicits trade, contributions, etc. **2.** in England, a lawyer other than a barrister **3.** the official law officer for a city, department, etc.

so·lic·i·tous (sə lis′ə təs) *adj.* [< L. *sollus*, whole + *ciere*, set in motion] **1.** showing care or concern [*solicitous* for her welfare] **2.** eager —**so·lic′i·tous·ly** *adv.*

so·lic′i·tude′ (-tōōd′) *n.* a being solicitous; care, concern, etc.

sol·id (säl′id) *adj.* [< L. *solidus*] **1.** relatively firm or compact; neither liquid nor gaseous **2.** not hollow **3.** having three dimensions **4.** firm and strong **5.** having no breaks or divisions **6.** of one color, material, etc. throughout **7.** showing unity; unanimous **8.** firm or dependable — *n.* **1.** a solid substance, not a liquid or gas **2.** an object having length, breadth, and thickness

sol·i·dar·i·ty (säl′ə dar′ə tē) *n., pl.* -ties complete unity, as of purpose, feeling, etc.

so·lid·i·fy (sə lid′ə fī′) *vt., vi.* -fied′, -fy′ing **1.** to make or become solid, firm, etc. **2.** to crystallize —**so·lid′i·fi·ca′tion** *n.*

so·lid′i·ty (-tē) *n.* a being solid

sol′id-state′ *adj.* designating electronic devices that can control current without heated filaments, moving parts, etc.

so·lil·o·quy (sə lil′ə kwē) *n., pl.* -quies [< L. *solus*, alone + *loqui*, speak] **1.** a talking to oneself **2.** lines in a drama spoken by a character as if to himself —**so·lil′o·quize′** (-kwīz′) *vi., vt.* -quized′, -quiz′ing

sol·i·taire (säl′ə ter′) *n.* [Fr.: see SOLITARY] **1.** a single gem, esp. a diamond, set by itself **2.** a card game for one person

sol′i·tar′y (-ter′ē) *adj.* [< L. *solus*, alone] **1.** living or being alone **2.** single; only [a *solitary*

example] **3.** lonely; remote **4.** done in solitude —**sol′i·tar′i·ness** *n.*

sol′i·tude′ (-tōōd′) *n.* [see prec.] **1.** a being solitary, or alone **2.** a secluded place

so·lo (sō′lō) *n., pl.* -los [It. < L. *solus*, alone] **1.** a musical piece or passage to be performed by one person **2.** any performance by one person alone —*adj.* for or by a single performer —*adv.* alone —*vi.* to perform a solo —**so′lo·ist** *n.*

Sol·o·mon (säl′ə mən) *Bible* king of Israel; son of David: noted for his wisdom

so long *colloq. term for* GOODBYE

sol·stice (säl′stis, sōl′-) *n.* [< L. *sol*, the sun + *sistere*, to halt] the time of the year when the sun reaches the point farthest north (June 21 or 22) or farthest south (Dec. 21 or 22) of the equator: in the Northern Hemisphere, the **summer solstice** and **winter solstice**, respectively

sol·u·ble (säl′yōō b'l) *adj.* [see SOLVE] **1.** that can be dissolved **2.** that can be solved —**sol′u·bil′i·ty** *n.* —**sol′u·bly** *adv.*

so·lu·tion (sə lōō′shən) *n.* [see SOLVE] **1.** *a)* the solving of a problem *b)* an answer, explanation, etc. **2.** *a)* the dispersion of one or more substances in another, usually a liquid, so as to form a homogeneous mixture *b)* the mixture so produced

solve (sälv) *vt.* **solved, solv′ing** [< L. *se-*, apart + *luere*, let go] to find an answer for (a problem, etc.); explain —**solv′a·ble** *adj.*

sol·vent (säl′vənt) *adj.* [see SOLVE] **1.** able to pay all one's debts **2.** that can dissolve another substance —*n.* a substance that can dissolve another one —**sol′ven·cy** *n.*

so·mat·ic (sō mat′ik) *adj.* [< Gr. *sōma*, the body] of the body; physical

som·ber (säm′bər) *adj.* [< Fr. < L. *sub*, under + *umbra*, shade] **1.** dark and gloomy or dull **2.** melancholy **3.** solemn —**som′ber·ly** *adv.*

som·bre·ro (säm brer′ō) *n., pl.* -ros [Sp. < *sombra*, shade: see SOMBER] a broad-brimmed hat worn in Mexico, the Southwest, etc.

some (sum) *adj.* [OE. *sum*] **1.** certain but not specified or known [*some* people smoke] **2.** of a certain unspecified quantity, degree, etc. [have *some* butter] **3.** about [*some* ten of us] **4.** [Colloq.] remarkable, striking, etc. [it was *some* fight] —*pron.* a certain unspecified number, quantity, etc. [take *some*] —*adv.* **1.** about [*some* ten men] **2.** [Colloq.] to some extent [slept *some*] **3.** [Colloq.] to a great extent [must run *some* to catch up] —**and then some** [Colloq.] and more than that

-some¹ [OE. *-sum*] *a suffix meaning* like, tending to (be) [*tiresome, lonesome*]

-some² [< Gr. *sōma*, body] *a combining form meaning* body [*chromosome*]

some·bod·y (sum′bud′ē, -bäd′ē) *pron.* a person unknown or not named; some person —*n., pl.* -ies a person of importance

some′day′ (-dā′) *adv.* at some future time

some′how′ (-hou′) *adv.* in a way not known, stated, or understood

some′one′ *pron. same as* SOMEBODY

som·er·sault (sum′ər sôlt′) *n.* [< L. *supra*, over + *saltus*, a leap] an acrobatic stunt done by turning the body one revolution, heels over head —*vi.* to do a somersault

some·thing (sum′thiŋ) *n.* **1.** a thing not definitely known, understood, etc. [*something* went wrong] **2.** a definite but unspecified thing [have *something* to eat] **3.** a bit; a little **4.** [Colloq.] a remarkable person or thing —*adv.* **1.** somewhat **2.** [Colloq.] really [sounds *something* awful] —**make something of 1.** to find a use for **2.** to treat as very important **3.**

[Colloq.] to treat as a point of dispute — **something else** [Slang] one that is quite remarkable
some'time' *adv.* at some unspecified or future time —*adj.* **1.** former **2.** occasional
some'times' *adv.* at times; occasionally
some'way' *adv.* in some way or manner: also **some'ways'**
some'what' *n.* some degree, amount, part, etc. —*adv.* to some extent, degree, etc.
some'where' *adv.* **1.** in, to, or at some place not known or specified **2.** at some time, degree, age, figure, etc. (with *about, around, in,* etc.)
som·nam·bu·lism (säm nam'byoo liz'm) *n.* [< L. *somnus,* sleep + *ambulare,* walk] sleepwalking —**som·nam'bu·list** *n.*
som·no·lent (säm'nə lənt) *adj.* [< L. *somnus,* sleep] **1.** sleepy **2.** causing drowsiness —**som'no·lence** *n.*
son (sun) *n.* [OE. *sunu*] **1.** a boy or man as he is related to either or both parents **2.** a male descendant
so·nar (sō'när) *n.* [*so*(und) *n*(*avigation*) *a*(*nd*) *r*(*anging*)] an apparatus for transmitting sound waves through water: used to locate submarines, find depths, etc.
so·na·ta (sə nät'ə) *n.* [It. < L. *sonare,* to SOUND¹] a musical composition for one or two instruments, usually in three or four movements in different tempos, etc.
song (sôŋ) *n.* [OE. *sang*] **1.** the act or art of singing **2.** a piece of music for singing **3.** *a*) poetry *b*) a ballad or lyric set to music **4.** a singing sound —**for a song** cheaply
song'bird' *n.* a bird that makes vocal sounds that are like music
song'fest' (-fest') *n.* [SONG + -FEST] an informal gathering of people for singing songs, esp. folk songs
song'ster (-stər) *n.* [OE. *sangestre*] a singer — **song'stress** *n.fem.*
son·ic (sän'ik) *adj.* [< L. *sonus,* SOUND¹] of sound or the speed of sound
son'-in-law' *n., pl.* **sons'-in-law'** the husband of one's daughter
son·net (sän'it) *n.* [Fr. < It. < L. *sonus,* SOUND¹] a poem normally of fourteen lines in any of several rhyme schemes
so·no·rous (sə nôr'əs, sän'ər əs) *adj.* [< L. *sonor,* a sound] **1.** producing sound; resonant **2.** full, deep, or rich in sound —**so·nor·i·ty** (sə nôr'ə tē, sō-) *n.*
soon (sōōn) *adv.* [OE. *sona,* at once] **1.** in a short time [we will *soon* be there] **2.** promptly; quickly [as *soon* as possible] **3.** ahead of time; early [he left too *soon*] **4.** readily; willingly [I'd as *soon* go as stay] —**sooner or later** eventually
soot (soot, sōōt) *n.* [OE. *sot*] a black substance, chiefly carbon particles, formed by the incomplete combustion of burning matter —**soot'y** *adj.* -i·er, -i·est
sooth (sōōth) *adj.* [OE. *soth*] [Archaic] truth
soothe (sōōth) *vt.* **soothed, sooth'ing** [< OE. *soth,* truth] **1.** to make calm or composed, as by gentleness, flattery, etc. **2.** to relieve (pain, etc.) —**sooth'er** *n.*
sooth·say·er (sōōth'sā'ər) *n.* one who claims to foretell the future —**sooth'say'ing** *n.*
sop (säp) *n.* [OE. *sopp*] **1.** a piece of food, as bread, soaked in milk, etc. **2.** something given to appease; bribe —*vt., vi.* **sopped, sop'ping 1.** to soak, steep, etc. **2.** to take (*up*), as water, by absorption
soph·ism (säf'iz'm) *n.* [< Gr. *sophos,* clever] clever and plausible argument that is faulty or misleading

soph'ist (-ist) *n.* one who uses clever, specious reasoning
so·phis·ti·cate (sə fis'tə kāt') *vt.* -cat'ed, -cat'ing [see SOPHISM] to change from being natural, naive, etc. to being artificial, worldly-wise, etc. —*n.* (*usually* -kit) a sophisticated person
so·phis'ti·cat'ed *adj.* **1.** not naive **2.** for sophisticates **3.** highly complex, refined, etc. — **so·phis'ti·ca'tion** *n.*
soph·is·try (säf'is trē) *n., pl.* -tries unsound or misleading but subtle reasoning
soph·o·more (säf'ə môr') *n.* [< obs. *sophumer,* sophist] a student in the second year of college or tenth grade at high school
soph'o·mor'ic *adj.* of or like sophomores; opinionated, etc. though immature
-sophy [< Gr. *sophia,* skill, wisdom] *a combining form meaning* knowledge [*philosophy*]
sop·o·rif·ic (säp'ə rif'ik, sō'pə-) *adj.* [< L. *sopor,* sleep + -FIC] **1.** causing sleep **2.** sleepy —*n.* a drug, etc. that causes sleep
sop'py *adj.* -pi·er, -pi·est **1.** very wet: also **sop'ping 2.** [Colloq.] sentimental
so·pra·no (sə pran'ō, -prä'nō) *n., pl.* -nos, -ni (-prä'nē) [It. < *sopra,* above] **1.** the highest singing voice of women and children **2.** a singer or instrument with such a range **3.** a part for a soprano —*adj.* of, for, or having the range of, a soprano
sor·cer·y (sôr'sər ē) *n., pl.* -ies [< L. *sors,* fate] the supposed use of evil magic power; witchcraft —**sor'cer·er** *n.* —**sor'cer·ess** *n.fem.*
sor·did (sôr'did) *adj.* [< L. *sordes,* filth] **1.** dirty; filthy **2.** squalid; wretched **3.** base; ignoble —**sor'did·ly** *adv.* —**sor'did·ness** *n.*
sore (sôr) *adj.* **sor'er, sor'est** [OE. *sar*] **1.** giving or feeling pain; painful **2.** *a*) filled with grief *b*) causing sadness, grief, etc. [*sore* hardships] **3.** provoking irritation [a *sore* point] **4.** [Colloq.] angry; offended —*n.* a sore, usually infected spot on the body —*adv.* [Archaic] sorely —**sore'ness** *n.*
sore'head' *n.* [Colloq.] one who is angry, resentful, etc., or one easily made so
sore'ly *adv.* **1.** grievously; painfully [*sorely* vexed] **2.** urgently [*sorely* needed]
sor·ghum (sôr'gəm) *n.* [< It. *sorgo*] **1.** a cereal grass grown for grain, syrup, fodder, etc. **2.** a syrup made from its juices
so·ror·i·ty (sə rôr'ə tē) *n., pl.* -ties [< L. *soror,* sister] a group of women or girls joined together for social or professional reasons, as in some colleges
sor·rel¹ (sôr'əl, sär'-) *n.* [< Frank. *sur,* sour] a plant with sour leaves
sor·rel² (sôr'əl, sär'-) *n.* [< ML. *saurus,* light brown] **1.** light reddish brown **2.** a horse, etc. of this color —*adj.* light reddish-brown
sor·row (sär'ō) *n.* [OE. *sorg*] **1.** mental suffering caused by loss, disappointment, etc. **2.** that which produces grief —*vi.* to grieve —**sor'row·ful** *adj.*
sor·ry (sär'ē) *adj.* -ri·er, -ri·est [< OE. *sar,* sore] **1.** full of sorrow, pity, or regret **2.** *a*) inferior; poor *b*) wretched
sort (sôrt) *n.* [< L. *sors,* a lot] **1.** any group of related things; kind; class **2.** quality or type — *vt.* to arrange according to class or kind —**of sorts** of an inferior kind: also **of a sort** —**out of sorts** [Colloq.] cross or ill —**sort of** [Colloq.] somewhat
sor·tie (sôr'tē) *n.* [Fr. < *sortir,* to issue] **1.** a sudden attack by troops from a besieged place **2.** one mission by a single military plane
SOS (es'ō'es') signal of distress (. . . . .) used in wireless telegraphy

so-so (sō'sō') *adv.* just passably —*adj.* just fair; neither good nor bad Also **so so**

sot (sät) *n.* [< VL. *sottus,* a fool] a drunkard

sot·to vo·ce (sät'ō vō'chē) [It., under the voice] in an undertone, so as not to be overheard

souf·flé (soo flā', soo'flā) *adj.* [Fr. < *souffler,* to blow] made light and puffy in cooking: also **souf·fléed'** (-flād') —*n.* a baked food made light and puffy by adding beaten egg whites before baking

sought (sôt) *pt. & pp. of* SEEK

soul (sōl) *n.* [OE. *sawol*] **1.** the part of one's being that is thought of as the center of feeling, thinking, will, etc. apart from the body **2.** the moral or emotional nature of man **3.** spiritual or emotional warmth, force, etc. **4.** vital or essential part, quality, etc. **5.** a person [a town of 1,000 *souls*] **6.** [Colloq.] among U.S. blacks, a sense of racial pride and social and cultural solidarity

soul food [Colloq.] items of food popular among U.S. blacks, as chitterlings, ham hocks, turnip greens, etc.

soul'ful *adj.* full of or showing deep feeling

sound[1] (sound) *n.* [< L. *sonus*] **1.** that which is heard, resulting from stimulation of auditory nerves by vibrations in the air **2.** the distance within which a sound may be heard **3.** the impression made by something said, etc. —*vi.* **1.** to make a sound **2.** to seem through sound [to *sound* sad] —*vt.* **1.** *a*) to cause to sound *b*) to utter distinctly [to *sound* one's *r's*] **2.** to express, signal, etc. —**sound'less** *adj.*

sound[2] (sound) *adj.* [OE. (*ge*)*sund*] **1.** free from defect, damage, or decay **2.** healthy [a *sound* body] **3.** firm and safe [a *sound* bank] **4.** based on valid reasoning; sensible **5.** thorough, complete, etc. **6.** deep and undisturbed: said of sleep **7.** honest, loyal, etc. —*adv.* deeply [*sound* asleep]

sound[3] (sound) *n.* [< OE. & ON. *sund*] **1.** a wide channel linking two bodies of water or separating an island from the mainland **2.** a long arm of the sea

sound[4] (sound) *vt., vi.* [< L. *sub,* under + *unda,* a wave] **1.** *a*) to measure the depth of (water), esp. with a weighted line *b*) to probe (the air or space) for data **2.** to try to find out the opinions of (a person): often with *out* — **sound'ing** *n.*

sounding board 1. a board, etc. used to reflect sound **2.** a person on whom one tests one's ideas, opinions, etc.

sound'proof' *adj.* able to keep sound from coming through —*vt.* to make soundproof

sound track the sound record along one side of a motion-picture film

soup (soop) *n.* [< OFr. *soupe*] a liquid food made by cooking meat, vegetables, etc. in water, milk, etc. —**soup up** [Slang] to increase the power, capacity for speed, etc. of (an engine, etc.) —**soup'y** *adj.* **-i·er, -i·est**

soup·çon (soop sôn', soop'sôn') *n.* [Fr.] **1.** a slight trace, as of a flavor **2.** a bit

sour (sour) *adj.* [OE. *sur*] **1.** having a sharp, acid taste, as vinegar **2.** spoiled by fermentation **3.** cross, bitter, etc. **4.** distasteful or unpleasant —*vt., vi.* to make or become sour — **sour'ly** *adv.* —**sour'ness** *n.*

source (sôrs) *n.* [< L. *surgere,* to rise] **1.** a spring, etc. from which a stream arises **2.** a place of origin **3.** a person, book, etc. that provides information

sour'dough' *n.* **1.** [Dial.] fermented dough kept for use as leaven **2.** a prospector in the western U.S. or Canada

sour grapes a scorning of something only because it cannot be had

souse (sous) *n.* [< OHG. *sulza,* brine] **1.** a pickled food, as pig's feet **2.** liquid for pickling; brine **3.** a plunging into a liquid **4.** [Slang] a drunkard —*vt., vi.* **soused, sous'ing 1.** to pickle **2.** to plunge in a liquid **3.** to make or become soaking wet

south (south) *n.* [OE. *suth*] **1.** the direction to the left of one facing the sunset (180° on the compass, opposite north) **2.** [*often* S-] a region in or toward this direction —*adj.* **1.** in, of, or toward the south **2.** from the south —*adv.* in or toward the south

south'east' *n.* **1.** the direction halfway between south and east **2.** a region in or toward this direction —*adj.* **1.** in, of, or toward the southeast **2.** from the southeast —*adv.* in, toward, or from the southeast —**south'east'-er·ly** *adj., adv.* —**south'east'ern** *adj.* —**south'-east'ward** (-wərd) *adv., adj.* —**south'east'wards** *adv.*

south·er·ly (su*th*'ər lē) *adj., adv.* **1.** toward the south **2.** from the south

south·ern (su*th*'ərn) *adj.* **1.** in, of, or toward the south **2.** from the south **3.** [S-] of the South —**south'ern·most** *adj.*

south·ern·er (su*th*'ər nər, -ə nər) *n.* a native or inhabitant of the south

south·paw (south'pô') *n.* [Slang] a person who is left-handed; esp., a left-handed baseball pitcher

South Pole the southern end of the earth's axis

south'ward (-wərd) *adv., adj.* toward the south: also **south'wards** *adv.*

south'west' *n.* **1.** the direction halfway between south and west **2.** a region in or toward this direction —*adj.* **1.** in, of, or toward the southwest **2.** from the southwest —*adv.* in, toward, or from the southwest —**south'west'-er·ly** *adj., adv.* —**south'west'ern** *adj.* —**south'-west'ward** (-wərd) *adv., adj.* —**south'west'wards** *adv.*

sou·ve·nir (soo'və nir') *n.* [Fr. < L. *subvenire,* come to mind] something kept as a reminder; keepsake; memento

sov·er·eign (säv'rən, -ər in) *adj.* [< L. *super,* above] **1.** above all others; greatest **2.** supreme in power, rank, etc. **3.** independent of all others [a *sovereign* state] —*n.* **1.** a monarch or ruler **2.** esp. formerly, a British gold coin worth one pound

sov'er·eign·ty (-tē) *n., pl.* **-ties 1.** the status, rule, etc. of a sovereign **2.** supreme and independent political authority

so·vi·et (sō'vē it, -et') *n.* [Russ., lit., council] in the Soviet Union, any of various elected governing councils, ranging from village and town soviets to the Supreme Soviet —*adj.* [S-] of or connected with the Soviet Union

sow[1] (sou) *n.* [OE. *sugu*] an adult female pig or hog

sow[2] (sō) *vt.* **sowed, sown** (sōn) or **sowed, sow'ing** [OE. *sawan*] **1.** to scatter or plant (seed) for growing **2.** to plant (a field, etc.) with seed **3.** to spread —*vi.* to sow seed

soy (soi) *n.* [Jpn. < Chin. *chiang,* salted bean + *yu,* oil] a dark, salty sauce made from fermented soybeans: also **soy sauce**

soy'bean' *n.* **1.** a plant widely grown for its seeds, rich in protein and oil **2.** its seed

Sp. 1. Spain **2.** Spaniard **3.** Spanish

spa (spä) *n.* [< *Spa,* resort in Belgium] **1.** a mineral spring **2.** a resort having a mineral spring

space (spās) *n.* [< L. *spatium*] **1.** the boundless

expanse within which all things exist 2. *same as* OUTER SPACE 3. distance, area, etc. between or within things 4. room for something *[parking space]* 5. an interval of time —*vt.* **spaced, spac'ing** to arrange with spaces between —**spac'er** *n.*

space'craft' *n., pl.* **-craft'** a spaceship or satellite for use in outer space

space'flight' *n.* a flight through outer space

space'man' *n., pl.* **-men'** an astronaut

space'ship' *n.* a rocket-propelled vehicle for travel in outer space

spa·cious (spā'shəs) *adj.* 1. having more than enough space; vast 2. large

spade[1] (spād) *n.* [OE. *spadu*] a long-handled digging tool with a flat blade that is pressed with the foot —*vt., vi.* **spad'ed, spad'ing** to dig with a spade

spade[2] (spād) *n.* [Sp. *espada*, sword < L. *spatha*, SPATULA] 1. the black figure (♠) marking one of the four suits of playing cards 2. a card of this suit

spade'work' *n.* any tiresome work necessary to make a beginning

spa·ghet·ti (spə get'ē) *n.* [It. < *spago*, small cord] long, thin strings of pasta, boiled or steamed and served with a sauce

spake (spāk) *archaic pt. of* SPEAK

span (span) *n.* [OE. *sponn*] 1. the distance (about 9 in.) between the tips of the thumb and little finger when extended 2. the full extent between any two limits 3. a part between two supports 4. the full duration, as of attention 5. [< Du.] a team of two animals used together —*vt.* **spanned, span'ning** 1. to measure, esp. by the span of the hand 2. to extend, reach, or pass over or across

span·gle (spaŋ'g'l) *n.* [< OE. *spang*, a clasp] a small piece of bright metal sewn on fabric for decoration —*vt.* **-gled, -gling** to cover with spangles

Span·iard (span'yərd) *n.* a native of Spain

span·iel (span'yəl) *n.* [< MFr. *espagnol*, Spanish] any of several breeds of dog with a silky coat, drooping ears, and short legs

Span·ish (span'ish) *adj.* of Spain, its people, their language, etc. —*n.* the Romance language of Spain and of Spanish America —**the Spanish** the people of Spain

spank (spaŋk) *vt.* [echoic] to strike with something flat, as the open hand, esp. on the buttocks, as in punishment —*n.* a smack given in spanking

spank'ing *adj.* 1. rapid 2. brisk: said of a breeze —*adv.* [Colloq.] altogether *[spanking new]* —*n.* a series of spanks

spar[1] (spär) *n.* [< ON. *sparri*] any pole, as a mast or yard, supporting the sails on a ship

spar[2] (spär) *vi.* **sparred, spar'ring** [< It. *parare*, to parry] 1. to box with caution, landing few heavy blows 2. to dispute; argue

spare (sper) *vt.* **spared, spar'ing** [OE. *sparian*] 1. to refrain from killing, hurting, etc. 2. to save or free (a person) from (something) 3. to avoid using or use frugally 4. to do without; give up, as time or money —*adj.* 1. not in regular use; extra 2. free: said of time 3. meager; scanty 4. lean; thin —*n.* 1. an extra part, thing, etc. 2. *Bowling* a knocking down of all the pins in two rolls of the ball —**spare'ness** *n.*

spare'ribs' *n.pl.* a cut of pork, consisting of the thin end of the ribs

spar'ing *adj.* 1. frugal 2. scanty; meager

spark (spärk) *n.* [OE. *spearca*] 1. a glowing bit of matter, esp. one thrown off by a fire 2. any flash or sparkle 3. a particle or trace 4. the brief flash of light accompanying an electric

discharge —*vi.* to make sparks —*vt.* to stir into action

spar·kle (spär'k'l) *vi.* **-kled, -kling** 1. to throw off sparks 2. to glitter 3. to effervesce —*n.* 1. a spark 2. a glittering 3. brilliance —**spar'kler** (-klər)

spark plug a piece fitted into a cylinder of an internal-combustion engine to make sparks that ignite the fuel mixture within

spar·row (spar'ō) *n.* [OE. *spearwa*] a common N. American bird with a striped breast

sparse (spärs) *adj.* [< L. *spargere*, scatter] thinly spread; not dense —**sparse'ly** *adv.* —**sparse'ness, spar·si·ty** (spär'sə tē) *n.*

Spar·tan (spär'tən) *adj.* 1. of ancient Sparta, its people, culture, etc. 2. like the Spartans; brave, disciplined, strict, etc. —*n.* a Spartan person —**Spar'tan·ism** *n.*

spasm (spaz'm) *n.* [< Gr. *span*, to pull] 1. a sudden, involuntary muscular contraction 2. any short, sudden burst of activity, feeling, etc.

spas·mod·ic (spaz mäd'ik) *adj.* [see prec. & -OID] of or like spasms; fitful

spas·tic (spas'tik) *adj.* of or characterized by muscular spasms —*n.* one having a spastic condition

spat[1] (spat) *n.* [prob. echoic] [Colloq.] a brief, petty quarrel —*vi.* **spat'ted, spat'ting** [Colloq.] to have a spat

spat[2] (spat) *n.* [< *spatterdash*, a legging] a short gaiter for the instep and ankle

spat[3] (spat) *alt. pt. & pp. of* SPIT[2]

spat[4] (spat) *n.* [< ?] the spawn of the oyster or other bivalve shellfish

spate (spāt) *n.* [ME. < ?] a large outpour, as of words

spa·tial (spā'shəl) *adj.* [< L. *spatium*, space] of, or existing in, space

spat·ter (spat'ər) *vt., vi.* [< ?] 1. to scatter or spurt in drops 2. to splash —*n.* 1. a spattering 2. a mark made by spattering

spat·u·la (spach'ə lə) *n.* [L. < *spatha*, flat blade] an implement with a broad, flexible blade for spreading or blending foods, paints, etc.

spav·in (spav'in) *n.* [MFr. *esparvain*] a disease of horses affecting the hock joint and causing lameness —**spav'ined** *adj.*

spawn (spôn) *vt., vi.* [< L. *ex-*, out + *pandere*, spread] 1. to produce or deposit (eggs, sperm, or young) 2. to produce prolifically —*n.* 1. the mass of eggs produced by fishes, mollusks, etc. 2. something produced, esp. in great quantity, as offspring

spay (spā) *vt.* [< Gr. *spathē*, flat blade] to sterilize (a female animal) by removing the ovaries

speak (spēk) *vi.* **spoke** or archaic **spake, spo'ken, speak'ing** [OE. *sp(r)ecan*] 1. to utter words; talk 2. to communicate as by talking 3. to make a request *(for)* 4. to make a speech —*vt.* 1. to make known as by speaking 2. to use (a given language) in speaking 3. to utter (words) orally —**so to speak** that is to say —**speak out** (or **up**) to speak clearly or freely

speak·eas·y (spēk'ē'zē) *n., pl.* **-ies** [Slang] a place where alcoholic drinks are sold illegally

speak'er *n.* 1. one who speaks or makes speeches 2. the presiding officer of a lawmaking body, specif. [S-] of the U.S. House of Representatives 3. a loudspeaker

spear (spir) *n.* [OE. *spere*] 1. a weapon with a long shaft and sharp head, for thrusting 2. [var. of SPIRE] a long blade or shoot, as of grass —*vt.* to pierce or stab as with a spear

spear'head' *n.* 1. the point of a spear 2. the

leading person or group, as in an attack —*vt.* to lead (an attack, etc.)

spear'mint' *n.* [< its flower spikes] a fragrant plant of the mint family, used for flavoring

spe·cial (spesh'əl) *adj.* [< L. *species*, kind] 1. distinctive or unique 2. exceptional; extraordinary 3. highly regarded 4. of or for a particular purpose 5. not general; specific —*n.* a special person or thing

special delivery delivery of mail by special postal messenger, for an extra fee

spe'cial·ist *n.* one who specializes in a particular study, work, etc.

spe'cial·ize' *vi.* -ized', -iz'ing to concentrate on a special study or special branch of a profession —**spe'cial·i·za'tion** *n.*

spe'cial·ty *n., pl.* -ties 1. a special quality, feature, etc. 2. a special study, branch of a profession, etc. 3. an article or product with special features, etc.

spe·cie (spē'shē, -sē) *n.* [< L. *species*, kind] coin, as distinguished from paper money

spe'cies (-shēz, -sēz) *n., pl.* -cies [L., appearance] 1. a distinct kind; sort 2. a single, distinct kind of plant or animal, having certain distinguishing characteristics

specif. specifically

spe·cif·ic (spi sif'ik) *adj.* [see SPECIFY] 1. definite; explicit 2. peculiar to or characteristic of something 3. of a particular sort 4. specially indicated as a cure for some disease —*n.* 1. a specific cure 2. a particular —**spe·cif'i·cal·ly** *adv.*

spec·i·fi·ca·tion (spes'ə fi kā'shən) *n.* 1. a specifying 2. [*usually pl.*] an enumeration of particulars, as to size, materials, etc. 3. something specified

specific gravity the ratio of the weight of a given volume of a substance to that of an equal volume of another substance (as water) used as a standard

spec·i·fy (spes'ə fī') *vt.* -fied', -fy'ing [< L. *species*, kind + *facere*, to make] to mention or describe in detail; state explicitly

spec·i·men (spes'ə mən) *n.* [L. < *specere*, see] a part or individual used as a sample of a whole or group

spe·cious (spē'shəs) *adj.* [< L. *species*, appearance] seeming good, sound, etc. but not really so —**spe'cious·ly** *adv.*

speck (spek) *n.* [OE. *specca*] 1. a small spot 2. a tiny bit —*vt.* to mark with specks

speck·le (spek''l) *n.* a small speck —*vt.* -led, -ling to mark with speckles

specs (speks) *n.pl.* [Colloq.] 1. eyeglasses 2. specifications: see SPECIFICATION (sense 2)

spec·ta·cle (spek'tə k'l) *n.* [< L. *specere*, see] 1. something remarkable to look at 2. a grand public show 3. [*pl.*] eyeglasses: an old-fashioned term

spec·tac·u·lar (spek tak'yə lər) *adj.* of or like a spectacle; strikingly grand or unusual

spec·ta·tor (spek'tāt ər) *n.* [L. < *spectare*, behold] one who watches without taking an active part

spec·ter (spek'tər) *n.* [< L. *spectare*, behold] a ghost; apparition: Brit. sp. **spectre** —**spec'tral** *adj.* —**spec'tral·ly** *adv.*

spec·tro·scope (spek'trə skōp') *n.* an optical instrument for breaking up light into a spectrum so it can be studied —**spec'tro·scop'ic** (-skäp'ik) *adj.*

spec·trum (spek'trəm) *n., pl.* -tra (-trə), -trums [< L., appearance] 1. the series of colored bands diffracted and arranged in order of their respective wavelengths by the passage of

white light through a prism, etc. 2. a continuous range or entire extent

spec·u·late (spek'yə lāt') *vi.* -lat'ed, -lat'ing [< L. *specere*, see] 1. to think reflectively; ponder; esp., to conjecture 2. to engage in a risky business venture on the chance of making huge profits —**spec'u·la'tion** *n.* —**spec'u·la'tive** (-lāt'iv, -lə tiv) *adj.* —**spec'u·la'tor** *n.*

speech (spēch) *n.* [< OE. *sp(r)ecan*, speak] 1. the act or manner of speaking 2. the power to speak 3. what is spoken; utterance, talk, etc. 4. a talk given to an audience 5. the language of a certain people

speech'less *adj.* 1. incapable of speech 2. silent, as from shock —**speech'less·ly** *adv.*

speed (spēd) *n.* [OE. *spæd*, success] 1. rapid motion; swiftness 2. rate of movement; velocity 3. [Slang] any of various amphetamine compounds —*vi.* **sped** (sped) or **speed'ed, speed'ing** to go fast, esp. faster than the legal limit —*vt.* 1. to help succeed; aid 2. to cause to go, move, etc. swiftly —**speed up** to increase in speed —**speed'er** *n.*

speed'boat' *n.* a motorboat built for speed

speed·om·e·ter (spi däm'ə tər) *n.* a device attached to a motor vehicle, etc. to indicate speed

speed'way' *n.* 1. a track for racing cars or motorcycles 2. a road for high-speed traffic

speed'y *adj.* -i·er, -i·est 1. rapid; swift 2. without delay; prompt [a *speedy* reply] —**speed'i·ly** *adv.*

spell¹ (spel) *n.* [OE., a saying] 1. a word or formula supposed to have some magic power 2. irresistible influence; magical charm; fascination

spell² (spel) *vt.* **spelled** or **spelt, spell'ing** [< OFr. *espeller*, explain] 1. to name, write, etc., esp. correctly, the letters of (a word, etc.) 2. to make up (a word): said of specified letters 3. to mean [red *spells* danger] —*vi.* to spell words —**spell out** to explain in detail

spell³ (spel) *vt.* **spelled, spell'ing** [OE. *spelian*] [Colloq.] to work in place of (another) while he rests; relieve —*n.* 1. a period of work, duty, etc. 2. a period of anything [a *spell* of crying] 3. [Colloq.] a fit of illness

spell'bind' *vt.* -bound', -bind'ing to hold or affect as by a spell; fascinate; enchant

spell'down' *n.* a contest in spelling: also **spelling bee**

spell'er *n.* 1. one who spells words 2. a textbook used to teach spelling

spell'ing *n.* 1. the act of one who spells words 2. the way a word is spelled

spe·lunk·er (spi luŋ'kər) *n.* [< obs. *spelunk*, cave, ult. < Gr. *spēlynx*] one who explores caves as a hobby

spend (spend) *vt.* **spent, spend'ing** [< L. *expendere*, EXPEND] 1. to use up, exhaust, etc. [his fury was *spent*] 2. to pay out (money) 3. to devote (time, effort, etc.) to something 4. to pass (time) 5. to waste; squander —*vi.* to pay out or use up money, etc. —**spend'er** *n.*

spend'thrift' *n.* one who spends money carelessly; squanderer —*adj.* wasteful

spent (spent) *pt. & pp.* of SPEND —*adj.* 1. tired out; physically exhausted 2. used up; worn out

sperm (spurm) *n.* [< Gr. *sperma*, seed] 1. the fluid from the male reproductive organs; semen 2. *same as* SPERMATOZOON

sper·mat·o·zo·on (spər mat'ə zō'än) *n., pl.* -zo'a (-ə) [< Gr. *sperma*, seed + *zōion*, animal] the male germ cell, found in semen: it penetrates and fertilizes the egg of the female

spew (spyo͞o) *vt., vi.* [OE. *spiwan*] 1. to throw

up from or as from the stomach; vomit **2.** to gush forth

sphere (sfir) *n.* [< Gr. *sphaira*] **1.** any round body with a surface equally distant from the center at all points; globe; ball **2.** place or range of action, knowledge, etc. —**spher·i·cal** (sfer'i k'l, sfir'-) *adj.*

sphe·roid (sfir'oid) *n.* a body that is almost but not quite a sphere —*adj.* of this shape: also **sphe·roi'dal**

sphinc·ter (sfiŋk'tər) *n.* [< Gr. *sphingein*, to draw close] a ring-shaped muscle at a body orifice

sphinx (sfiŋks) *n.* [< Gr. *sphinx*, strangler] **1.** [S-] a statue with a lion's body and man's head, near Cairo, Egypt **2.** [S-] *Gr. Myth.* a winged monster with a lion's body and a woman's head: it strangled passers-by unable to answer its riddle **3.** one who is hard to know or understand

spice (spīs) *n.* [< L. *species*, sort] **1.** an aromatic vegetable substance, as clove, pepper, etc., used to season food **2.** that which gives zest or piquancy —*vt.* **spiced, spic'ing 1.** to season with spice **2.** to add zest to —**spic'y** *adj.* **-i·er, -i·est**

spick-and-span (spik'n span') *adj.* [< SPIKE[1] + ON. *spānn*, a chip] **1.** new or fresh **2.** neat and clean

spi·der (spī'dər) *n.* [< OE. *spinnan*, spin] **1.** any of various small arachnids that have eight legs and spin webs **2.** a frying pan

spiel (spēl) *n.* [G., play] [Slang] a talk or harangue, as by a salesman —**spiel'er** *n.*

spig·ot (spig'ət, spik'-) *n.* [ME. *spigote*] **1.** a plug to stop the vent in a cask, etc. **2.** a faucet

spike[1] (spīk) *n.* [prob. < ON. *spīkr*] **1.** a long, heavy nail **2.** a sharp-pointed projection, as on the sole of a shoe to prevent slipping —*vt.* **spiked, spik'ing 1.** to fasten or fit as with spikes **2.** to pierce with, or impale on, a spike **3.** to thwart (a scheme, etc.) **4.** [Slang] to add alcoholic liquor to (a drink) —**spik'y** *adj.*

spike[2] (spīk) *n.* [L. *spica*] **1.** an ear of grain **2.** a long flower cluster

spill (spil) *vt.* **spilled** or **spilt, spill'ing** [< OE. *spillan*, destroy] **1.** to allow (a fluid), esp. unintentionally, to run, scatter, or flow over from a container **2.** to shed (blood) **3.** [Colloq.] to make (a rider, etc.) fall off —*vi.* to be spilled — *n.* **1.** a spilling **2.** [Colloq.] a fall

spill'way' *n.* a channel to carry off excess water

spin (spin) *vt.* **spun, spin'ning** [OE. *spinnan*] **1.** to draw out and twist fibers of (wool, cotton, etc.) into thread **2.** to make (thread, etc.) thus **3.** to make (a web, cocoon, etc.): said of spiders, etc. **4.** to draw *out* (a story) at great length **5.** to rotate swiftly —*vi.* **1.** to spin thread, etc. **2.** to whirl **3.** to seem to be spinning from dizziness **4.** to move along swiftly and smoothly —*n.* **1.** a whirling or rotating movement **2.** a ride in a motor vehicle **3.** a descent of an airplane, nose first along a spiral path —**spin'ner** *n.*

spin·ach (spin'ich, -ij) *n.* [< OSp. < Ar. < Per. *aspanākh*] a plant with dark-green, juicy, edible leaves

spi·nal (spī'n'l) *adj.* of the spine or spinal cord —**spi'nal·ly** *adv.*

spinal column the series of joined vertebrae forming the axial support for the skeleton; spine

spinal cord the thick cord of nerve tissue in the spinal column

spin·dle (spin'd'l) *n.* [< OE. *spinnan*, spin] **1.** a slender rod or pin for twisting, winding, or holding the thread in spinning **2.** something shaped like a spindle **3.** any rod, pin, or shaft that revolves or serves as an axis for a revolving part

spin·dly (spin'dlē) *adj.* **-dli·er, -dli·est** long or tall and very thin or slender: also **spin'dling** (-dliŋ)

spine (spīn) *n.* [< L. *spina*, thorn] **1.** a sharp, stiff projection, as a thorn of the cactus or a porcupine's quill **2.** anything like this **3.** the spinal column **4.** anything like this, as the back of a book —**spin'y** *adj.* **-i·er, -i·est**

spine'less *adj.* **1.** having no spine or spines **2.** lacking courage, willpower, etc.

spin·et (spin'it) *n.* [It., prob. < *spina*, thorn] a small upright piano

spinning wheel a simple spinning machine with one spindle driven by a large wheel

spin-off (spin'ôf') *n.* a secondary product, benefit, development, program, etc.

spin·ster (spin'stər) *n.* [ME. < *spinnen*, to spin] an unmarried woman, esp. an older one; old maid —**spin'ster·hood'** *n.*

spiny lobster a sea crustacean like the common lobster, but lacking large pincers and having a spiny shell

spi·ral (spī'rəl) *adj.* [< Gr. *speira*] circling around a point in constantly increasing (or decreasing) curves, or in constantly changing planes —*n.* a spiral curve or coil —*vi.*, *vt.* **-raled** or **-ralled, -ral·ing** or **-ral·ling** to move or form (into) a spiral —**spi'ral·ly** *adv.*

spire (spīr) *n.* [OE. *spir*] **1.** a sprout, spike, or stalk of a plant **2.** the top part of a pointed, tapering object **3.** anything that tapers to a point, as a steeple

spi·re·a (spī rē'ə) *n.* [< Gr. *speira*, a coil] a shrub of the rose family, with clusters of small pink or white flowers: also sp. **spi·rae'a**

spir·it (spir'it) *n.* [< L. *spirare*, breathe] **1.** the soul **2.** [*also* S-] life, will, thought, etc., regarded as separate from matter **3.** a supernatural being, as a ghost, angel, etc. **4.** an individual [a brave *spirit*] **5.** [*often pl.*] disposition; mood [high *spirits*] **6.** vivacity, courage, etc. **7.** enthusiastic loyalty [school *spirit*] **8.** true intention [the *spirit* of the law] **9.** an essential quality or prevailing tendency [the *spirit* of the times] **10.** [*usually pl.*] distilled alcoholic liquor —*vt.* to carry (away or off) secretly and swiftly —**spir'it·less** *adj.*

spir'it·ed *adj.* lively; vigorous

spir·it·u·al (spir'i choo wəl) *adj.* **1.** of the spirit or soul **2.** of or consisting of spirit; not corporeal **3.** religious; sacred —*n.* a religious folk song of U.S. Negro origin —**spir'it·u·al'i·ty** (-wal'ə tē) *n., pl.* **-ties** —**spir'it·u·al·ly** *adv.*

spir·it·u·al·ism *n.* the belief that the dead survive as spirits which can communicate with the living —**spir'it·u·al·ist** *n.*

spi·ro·chete (spī'rə kēt') *n.* [< Gr. *speira*, a spiral + *chaitē*, hair] any of various spiral-shaped bacteria

spit[1] (spit) *n.* [OE. *spitu*] **1.** a thin, pointed rod on which meat is roasted over a fire **2.** a narrow point of land extending into a body of water —*vt.* **spit'ted, spit'ting** to impale as on a spit

spit[2] (spit) *vt.* **spit** or **spat, spit'ting** [OE. *spittan*] **1.** to eject from the mouth **2.** to eject explosively —*vi.* to eject saliva from the mouth —*n.* **1.** a spitting **2.** saliva —**spit and image** [Colloq.] perfect likeness

spite (spīt) *n.* [< DESPITE] ill will; malice; grudge —*vt.* **spit'ed, spit'ing** to show one's spite for by hurting, frustrating, etc. —**in spite of** regardless of —**spite'ful** *adj.*

spit·tle (spit′'l) *n.* spit; saliva

spit·toon (spi tōōn′) *n.* a container to spit into

splash (splash) *vt.* [< PLASH] **1.** to cause (a liquid) to scatter **2.** to dash a liquid, mud, etc. on, so as to wet or soil —*vi.* to move, strike, etc. with a splash —*n.* **1.** the act or sound of splashing **2.** a spot made as by splashing — **make a splash** [Colloq.] to attract great attention —**splash′y** *adj.* -i·er, -i·est

splash·down (splash′doun′) *n.* the landing of a spacecraft on water

splat·ter (splat′ər) *n., vt., vi.* spatter; splash

splay (splā) *adj.* [< ME. *displaien,* to DISPLAY] spreading out —*vt., vi.* to spread out

splay′foot *n., pl.* -feet a foot that is flat and turned outward

spleen (splēn) *n.* [Gr. *splēn*] **1.** a large, vascular organ in the upper left part of the abdomen: it modifies the blood structure **2.** malice; spite —**spleen′ful** *adj.*

splen·did (splen′did) *adj.* [< L. *splendere,* to shine] **1.** shining; brilliant **2.** magnificent; gorgeous **3.** grand; glorious **4.** [Colloq.] very good; fine —**splen′did·ly** *adv.*

splen·dor (splen′dər) *n.* [< L. *splendere,* to shine] **1.** great luster; brilliance **2.** magnificent richness or glory Brit. sp. **splen′dour** —**splen′-dor·ous, splen′drous** *adj.*

sple·net·ic (spli net′ik) *adj.* **1.** of the spleen **2.** irritable; peevish

splice (splīs) *vt.* **spliced, splic′ing** [MDu. *splissen*] **1.** to join (ropes) by weaving together the end strands **2.** to join (pieces of wood) by overlapping the ends **3.** to fasten the ends of (wire, magnetic tape, etc.) together, as by soldering, cementing, etc. —*n.* a joint made by splicing —**splic′er** *n.*

splint (splint) *n.* [MDu. or MLowG. *splinte*] **1.** a thin strip of wood or cane woven with others to make baskets, chair seats, etc. **2.** a strip of wood, etc. used to hold a broken bone in place

splin·ter (splin′tər) *vt., vi.* [see SPLINT] to break or split into thin, sharp pieces —*n.* a thin, sharp piece of wood, bone, etc., made by splitting —**splin′ter·y** *adj.*

split (split) *vt., vi.* **split, split′ting** [MDu. *splitten*] **1.** to separate lengthwise into two or more parts **2.** to break or tear apart **3.** to divide into shares **4.** to disunite **5.** *a*) to break into atoms: said of a molecule *b*) to produce nuclear fission in or undergo nuclear fission: said of an atom —*n.* **1.** a splitting **2.** a break; crack **3.** a division in a group, etc. —*adj.* separated

split′-lev′el *adj.* designating a type of house in which each floor level is about a half story above or below the adjacent one

split′ting *adj.* **1.** that splits **2.** severe or sharp, as a headache

splotch (spläch) *n.* [prob. < SPOT & BLOTCH] an irregular spot, splash, or stain —*vt.* to mark with splotches —**splotch′y** *adj.*

splurge (splurj) *n.* [echoic] [Colloq.] **1.** any showy display or effort **2.** a spending spree — *vi.* **splurged, splurg′ing** [Colloq.] **1.** to show off **2.** to spend money freely

splut·ter (splut′ər) *vi.* [var. of SPUTTER] **1.** to make hissing or spitting sounds **2.** to speak hurriedly and confusedly —*n.* a spluttering

spoil (spoil) *vt.* **spoiled** or **spoilt, spoil′ing** [< L. *spolium,* plunder] **1.** to damage so as to make useless, etc. **2.** to impair the enjoyment, etc. of **3.** to cause to expect too much by overindulgence —*vi.* to become spoiled; decay, etc., as food —*n.* [*usually pl.*] plunder; booty —**spoil′-age** *n.*

spoil′sport′ *n.* one whose actions spoil the pleasure of others

spoils system the treating of public offices as the booty of the successful political party

spoke[1] (spōk) *n.* [OE. *spaca*] **1.** any of the braces extending from the hub to the rim of a wheel **2.** a ladder rung

spoke[2] (spōk) *pt. of* SPEAK

spo·ken (spō′k'n) *pp. of* SPEAK —*adj.* **1.** uttered; oral **2.** having a (specified kind of) voice [*soft-spoken*]

spokes·man (spōks′mən) *n., pl.* -men one who speaks for another or others

spo·li·a·tion (spō′lē ā′shən) *n.* [< L. *spoliatio*] robbery; plundering

sponge (spunj) *n.* [< Gr. *spongia*] **1.** a plant-like sea animal with a porous structure **2.** the highly absorbent skeleton of such animals, used for washing surfaces, etc. **3.** a piece of spongy plastic, etc. —*vt.* **sponged, spong′ing 1.** to wipe, dampen, absorb, etc. as with a sponge **2.** [Colloq.] to get as by begging, imposition, etc. —*vi.* [Colloq.] to be a parasite —**spong′er** *n.* —**spon′gy** *adj.* -gi·er, -gi·est

sponge bath a bath taken by using a wet sponge or cloth without getting into water

sponge′cake′ *n.* a light cake of porous texture: also **sponge cake**

spon·sor (spän′sər) *n.* [L. < *spondere,* promise solemnly] **1.** one who assumes responsibility as surety for, or endorser of, some person or thing **2.** a godparent **3.** a business firm, etc. that pays for a radio or TV program advertising its product —*vt.* to act as sponsor for — **spon′sor·ship′** *n.*

spon·ta·ne·i·ty (spän′tə nē′ə tē, -nā′-) *n.* **1.** a being spontaneous **2.** *pl.* -ties a spontaneous movement, action, etc.

spon·ta·ne·ous (spän tā′nē əs) *adj.* [< L. *sponte,* of free will] **1.** moved by a natural feeling or impulse, without constraint, effort, etc. **2.** acting by internal energy, force, etc. —**spon-ta′ne·ous·ly** *adv.*

spontaneous combustion the process of catching fire as a result of heat generated by internal chemical action

spoof (spōōf) *n.* [Slang] **1.** a hoax or joke **2.** a light satire —*vt., vi.* [Slang] **1.** to fool; deceive **2.** to satirize playfully

spook (spōōk) *n.* [Du.] [Colloq.] a ghost —*vt., vi.* [Colloq.] to startle or be startled, frightened, etc. —**spook′y** *adj.*

spool (spōōl) *n.* [< MDu. *spoele*] a cylinder upon which thread, wire, etc. is wound

spoon (spōōn) *n.* [OE. *spon,* a chip] **1.** a utensil consisting of a small, shallow bowl with a handle, used for eating or stirring **2.** something shaped like a spoon, as a fishing lure —*vt.* to take up with a spoon

spoon·er·ism (spōōn′ər iz'm) *n.* [< Rev. W. A. *Spooner* of Oxford] an unintentional interchange of sounds in words (Ex.: It is kistomary to cuss the bride)

spoon′-feed′ *vt.* -fed′, -feed′ing **1.** to feed with a spoon **2.** to pamper; coddle

spoor (spoor, spôr) *n.* [Afrik. < MDu.] the track or trail of a wild animal

spo·rad·ic (spô rad′ik, spə-) *adj.* [< Gr. *sporas,* scattered] **1.** happening at intervals **2.** appearing singly or in isolated instances —**spo·rad′i-cal·ly** *adv.*

spore (spôr) *n.* [< Gr. *spora,* a seed] a small reproductive body produced by bacteria, mosses, ferns, etc. and capable of giving rise to a new individual —*vi.* **spored, spor′ing** to develop spores

sport (spôrt) *n.* [< DISPORT] **1.** any recreational

activity; specif., a game, competition, etc. requiring bodily exertion **2.** fun; play **3.** a thing joked about **4.** [Colloq.] a sportsmanlike person **5.** [Colloq.] a pleasure-loving, flashy person **6.** *Biol.* a plant or animal markedly different from the normal type —*vt.* [Colloq.] to display [to *sport* a loud tie] —*vi.* **1.** to play **2.** to joke —*adj.* **1.** of or for sports **2.** suitable for casual wear: also **sports** [a *sport*(s) coat] —**in** (or **for**) **sport** in jest —**make sport of** to ridicule

sport'ing *adj.* **1.** of or interested in sports **2.** sportsmanlike; fair **3.** of games, etc. involving gambling

spor·tive (spôr'tiv) *adj.* **1.** full of sport or fun **2.** done in fun —**spor'tive·ly** *adv.*

sports (or **sport**) **car** a low, small automobile with a high-compression engine

sports'cast' *n.* a radio or TV broadcast of sports news —**sports'cast'er** *n.*

sports'man *n., pl.* -**men 1.** a man who takes part in sports, esp. hunting, fishing, etc. **2.** one who plays fair and can lose without complaint or win without gloating —**sports'man·like'** *adj.* —**sports'man·ship'** *n.*

sport'y *adj.* -**i·er, -i·est** [Colloq.] **1.** sporting or sportsmanlike **2.** flashy or showy

spot (spät) *n.* [< MDu. *spotte*] **1.** a small area differing from the surrounding area, as in color **2.** a stain, speck, etc. **3.** a flaw, as in character **4.** a locality; place —*vt.* **spot'ted, spot'ting 1.** to mark with spots **2.** to stain; blemish **3.** to place; locate **4.** to see; recognize **5.** [Colloq.] to allow as a handicap —*vi.* **1.** to become marked with spots **2.** to make a stain, as ink —*adj.* **1.** ready [*spot* cash] **2.** made at random [a *spot* survey] —**hit the spot** [Colloq.] to satisfy a craving —**in a (bad) spot** [Slang] in trouble —**on the spot** [Slang] in trouble or in a demanding situation —**spot'less** *adj.* —**spot'ted** *adj.*

spot'-check' *vt.* to check or examine at random —*n.* such a checking

spot'light' *n.* **1.** a strong beam of light focused on a particular person, thing, etc. **2.** a lamp used to project such a light

spot'ty *adj.* -**ti·er, -ti·est 1.** having, occurring in, or marked with spots **2.** not uniform or consistent —**spot'ti·ness** *n.*

spouse (spous) *n.* [< L. *sponsus*, betrothed] (one's) husband or wife

spout (spout) *n.* [< ME. *spouten*, to spout] **1.** a projecting tube by which a liquid is poured **2.** a stream, etc. as of liquid from a spout —*vt., vi.* **1.** to shoot out (liquid, etc.) as from a spout **2.** to speak or utter in a loud, pompous, or hasty manner

sprain (sprān) *vt.* [< ? L. *ex-*, out + *premere*, to press] to wrench a ligament or muscle of (a joint) without dislocating the bones —*n.* an injury resulting from this

sprang (spraŋ) *alt. pt. of* SPRING

sprat (sprat) *n.* [OE. *sprott*] a small European fish of the herring family

sprawl (sprôl) *vi.* [OE. *spreawlian*] **1.** to sit or lie with the limbs in a relaxed or awkward position **2.** to spread out awkwardly, as handwriting, etc. —*vt.* to cause to sprawl —*n.* a sprawling movement or position

spray[1] (sprā) *n.* [< MDu. *spraeien*, to spray] **1.** a mist of fine liquid particles **2.** *a)* a jet of such particles, as from a spray gun *b)* a device for spraying **3.** something likened to a spray — *vt., vi.* **1.** to direct a spray (upon) **2.** to shoot out in a spray —**spray'er** *n.*

spray[2] (sprā) *n.* [ME.] a small branch of a tree, etc., with leaves, flowers, etc.

spray gun a gunlike device that shoots out a spray of liquid, as paint or insecticide

spread (spred) *vt., vi.* **spread, spread'ing** [OE. *sprædan*] **1.** to open or stretch out; unfold **2.** to move apart (the fingers, wings, etc.) **3.** to distribute or be distributed over an area **4.** to extend in time **5.** to make or be made widely known, felt, etc. **6.** to cover or be covered (*with* something), as in a thin layer **7.** to set (a table) for a meal **8.** to push or be pushed apart —*n.* **1.** the act or extent of spreading **2.** an expanse **3.** a cloth cover for a table, bed, etc. **4.** jam, butter, etc. used on bread **5.** [Colloq.] a meal with a wide variety of food

spree (sprē) *n.* [< earlier *spray*] **1.** a noisy frolic **2.** a drinking bout **3.** a period of unrestrained activity [a shopping *spree*]

sprig (sprig) *n.* [ME. *sprigge*] a little twig or spray

spright·ly (sprīt'lē) *adj.* -**li·er, -li·est** [see SPRITE] gay, lively, brisk, etc. —*adv.* in a sprightly manner —**spright'li·ness** *n.*

spring (spriŋ) *vi.* **sprang** or **sprung, sprung, spring'ing** [OE. *springan*] **1.** to leap; bound **2.** to come, appear, etc. suddenly **3.** to bounce **4.** to arise from some source; grow or develop **5.** to become warped, split, etc. **6.** to rise up above surrounding objects Often followed by *up* —*vt.* **1.** to cause to leap forth suddenly **2.** to cause (a trap, etc.) to snap shut **3.** to cause to warp, split, etc. **4.** to make known suddenly **5.** [Slang] to get (someone) released from jail —*n.* **1.** a leap, or the distance so covered **2.** a sudden flying back **3.** elasticity; resilience **4.** a device, as a coil of wire, that returns to its original form after being forced out of shape **5.** a flow of water from the ground **6.** a source or origin **7.** that season of the year following winter, in which plants begin to grow again **8.** any period of beginning —*adj.* **1.** of, for, appearing in, or planted in the spring **2.** having, or supported on, springs **3.** coming from a spring [*spring* water] —**spring a leak** to begin to leak suddenly

spring'board' *n.* a flexible, springy board used as a takeoff in leaping or diving

spring fever the listlessness that many people feel in early days of spring

spring'time' *n.* the season of spring

spring'y *adj.* -**i·er, -i·est** elastic

sprin·kle (spriŋ'k'l) *vt., vi.* -**kled, -kling** [ME. *sprinklen*] **1.** to scatter in drops or particles **2.** to scatter drops or particles (upon) **3.** to rain lightly —*n.* **1.** a sprinkling **2.** a light rain — **sprin'kler** *n.*

sprin'kling *n.* a small number or amount, esp. when thinly distributed

sprint (sprint) *vi., n.* [< Scand.] run or race at full speed for a short distance —**sprint'er** *n.*

sprite (sprīt) *n.* [< L. *spiritus*, spirit] an elf, pixie, fairy, or goblin

sprock·et (spräk'it) *n.* [< ?] **1.** any of the teeth, as on a wheel rim, arranged to fit the links of a chain **2.** such a wheel: in full **sprocket wheel**

sprout (sprout) *vi.* [OE. *sprutan*] to begin to grow; give off shoots or buds —*vt.* to cause to sprout —*n.* **1.** a young growth on a plant; shoot **2.** a new growth from a bud, etc.

spruce[1] (sproos) *n.* [ME. *Spruce*, Prussia] **1.** an evergreen tree having slender needles **2.** its wood

spruce[2] (sproos) *adj.* **spruc'er, spruc'est** [< *Spruce* leather (see prec.)] neat and trim; smart —*vt., vi.* **spruced, spruc'ing** to make or become spruce

sprung (spruŋ) *pp. & alt. pt. of* SPRING

spry (sprī) *adj.* **spri'er** or **spry'er, spri'est** or **spry'est** [< Scand.] full of life; active and agile —**spry'ly** *adv.*
spud (spud) *n.* [Colloq.] a potato
spume (spyo͞om) *n.* [< L. *spuma*] foam, froth, or scum —*vt., vi.* **spumed, spum'ing** to foam or froth
spu·mo·ni (spə mō'nē) *n.* [It.] an Italian ice cream in variously flavored layers
spun (spun) *pt. & pp. of* SPIN —*adj.* formed by or as if by spinning
spunk (spuŋk) *n.* [IrGael. *sponc,* tinder] [Colloq.] courage; spirit —**spunk'y** *adj.* -i·er, -i·est —**spunk'i·ness** *n.*
spur (spur) *n.* [OE. *spura*] **1.** a pointed device worn on the heel by horsemen, used to urge the horse forward **2.** a stimulus **3.** any spurlike projection **4.** a short railroad track connected with the main track —*vt.* **spurred, spur'ring 1.** to prick with spurs **2.** to urge or incite —*vi.* to hurry; hasten —**on the spur of the moment** abruptly and impulsively
spu·ri·ous (spyoor'ē əs) *adj.* [L. *spurius*] not true or genuine; false
spurn (spurn) *vt.* [OE. *spurnan*] to reject scornfully
spurt (spurt) *vt., vi.* [OE. *sprutan,* to sprout] **1.** to gush forth in a stream or jet **2.** to show a sudden, brief burst of energy —*n.* **1.** a sudden shooting forth; jet **2.** a sudden, brief burst of energy, activity, etc.
sput·nik (spoot'nik, sput'-) *n.* [Russ., lit., co-traveler] an artificial satellite of the earth, esp. any of the U.S.S.R.
sput·ter (sput'ər) *vi., vt.* [Du. *sputteren*] **1.** to spit or throw out (bits or drops) in an explosive manner **2.** to speak or say in a confused, explosive manner **3.** to make sharp, sizzling sounds, as frying fat —*n.* a sputtering
spu·tum (spyo͞ot'əm) *n., pl.* **-ta** (-ə) [< L. *spuere,* to spit] saliva, usually mixed with mucus, spit out
spy (spī) *vt.* **spied, spy'ing** [< OHG. *spehōn,* examine] to catch sight of; see —*vi.* to watch closely and secretly; act as a spy —*n., pl.* **spies 1.** one who keeps close and secret watch on others **2.** a person employed by a government to get secret information on the military affairs, etc. of another government —**spy out** to discover or seek to discover by looking carefully
spy'glass' *n.* a small telescope
sq. square
squab (skwäb) *n.* [prob. < Scand.] a very young pigeon
squab·ble (skwäb'l) *vi.* **-bled, -bling** [< Scand.] to quarrel noisily over a small matter; wrangle —*n.* a noisy, petty quarrel
squad (skwäd) *n.* [< Fr. < It. or Sp.: see SQUARE] **1.** a small group of soldiers, often a subdivision of a platoon **2.** any small group of people working together
squad car a police patrol car
squad'ron (-rən) *n.* [< It. *squadra,* a square] a unit of warships, cavalry, military aircraft, etc.
squal·id (skwäl'id) *adj.* [< L. *squalere,* be foul] **1.** foul; filthy **2.** wretched
squall[1] (skwôl) *n.* [< Scand.] a brief, violent windstorm, usually with rain or snow —*vi.* to storm briefly —**squall'y** *adj.*
squall[2] (skwôl) *vi., vt.* [ON. *skvala,* cry out] to cry and scream loudly or harshly —*n.* a harsh, shrill cry or loud scream
squal·or (skwäl'ər) *n.* [L., foulness] a being squalid; filth and wretchedness
squan·der (skwän'dər) *vt., vi.* [prob. < dial. *squander,* scatter] to spend or use wastefully

square (skwer) *n.* [< L. *ex-,* out + *quadrare,* to square] **1.** a plane figure having four equal sides and four right angles **2.** anything shaped like or nearly like this **3.** an area bounded by streets on four sides **4.** any side of such an area **5.** an open area bounded by several streets, used as a park, etc. **6.** an instrument used for drawing or testing right angles **7.** the product of a number multiplied by itself **8.** [Slang] a person who is square (*adj.* 10) —*vt.* **squared, squar'ing 1.** to make into a square **2.** to make straight, even, right-angled, etc. **3.** to settle; adjust [to *square* accounts] **4.** to bring into agreement [to *square* a statement with the facts] **5.** to multiply (a quantity) by itself —*vi.* to fit; agree; accord (*with*) —*adj.* **1.** having four equal sides and four right angles **2.** forming a right angle **3.** straight, level, even, etc. **4.** leaving no balance; balanced **5.** just; fair **6.** direct; straightforward **7.** designating or of a unit of surface measure in the form of a square with sides of a specified length **8.** solid; thickset [a *square* build] **9.** [Colloq.] satisfying; substantial [a *square* meal] **10.** [Slang] old-fashioned or unsophisticated —*adv.* in a square manner —**square off** (or **away**) to get in position for attacking or defending
square dance a lively dance with various steps, the couples forming squares, etc.
square'-rigged' *adj.* having square sails as principal sails —**square'-rig'ger** *n.*
square root the number that when squared will produce a given number [3 is the *square root* of 9]
squash[1] (skwäsh) *vt.* [< L. *ex-,* intens. + *quatere,* to shake] **1.** to crush into a soft or flat mass; press **2.** to suppress; quash —*vi.* **1.** to be squashed **2.** to make a sound of squashing —*n.* **1.** something squashed **2.** the act or sound of squashing **3.** a game played in a four-walled court with rackets and a rubber ball
squash[2] (skwäsh) *n.* [< Algonquian] the fleshy fruit of various plants of the gourd family, cooked as a vegetable
squash'y (-ē) *adj.* -i·er, -i·est **1.** soft and wet; mushy **2.** easily squashed
squat (skwät) *vi.* **squat'ted, squat'ting** [< L. *ex-,* intens. + *cogere,* to force] **1.** to crouch, with the knees bent and the weight on the balls of the feet **2.** to crouch close to the ground **3.** to settle on land without any right or title to it **4.** to settle on public land so as to get title to it —*adj.* short and thick: also **squat'ty** —*n.* the position of squatting —**squat'ter** *n.*
squaw (skwô) *n.* [< Algonquian] a N. American Indian woman, esp. a wife
squawk (skwôk) *vi.* [echoic] **1.** to utter a loud, harsh cry **2.** [Colloq.] to complain or protest —*n.* **1.** a squawking cry **2.** [Colloq.] a complaint —**squawk'er** *n.*
squeak (skwēk) *vi.* [ME. *squeken*] to make or utter a sharp, high-pitched sound or cry —*vt.* to say in a squeak —*n.* a short, shrill sound or cry —**narrow** (or **close**) **squeak** [Colloq.] a narrow escape —**squeak through** (or **by,** etc.) [Colloq.] to barely manage to succeed, survive, etc. —**squeak'y** *adj.* -i·er, -i·est
squeal (skwēl) *vi.* [ME. *squelen*] **1.** to make or utter a long, shrill sound or cry **2.** [Slang] to inform against someone —*vt.* to utter with a squeal —*n.* a long, shrill sound or cry —**squeal'er** *n.*
squeam·ish (skwēm'ish) *adj.* [ME. *squaimous*] **1.** easily nauseated **2.** easily shocked or offended; prudish **3.** too fastidious
squee·gee (skwē'jē) *n.* [prob. < SQUEEZE] a

T-shaped tool with a blade of rubber, etc. for wiping liquid off a surface

squeeze (skwēz) *vt.* **squeezed, squeez'ing** [OE. *cwysan*] **1.** to press hard, esp. from two or more sides **2.** to extract (juice, etc.) from (fruit, etc.) **3.** to force (*into, out,* etc.) by pressing **4.** to embrace closely; hug —*vi.* **1.** to yield to pressure **2.** to exert pressure **3.** to force one's way by pushing —*n.* **1.** a squeezing or being squeezed **2.** a close embrace; hug **3.** the state of being closely pressed or packed; crush **4.** a period of scarcity, hardship, etc.

squelch (skwelch) *n.* [< ?] [Colloq.] a crushing retort, rebuke, etc. —*vt.* [Colloq.] to suppress or silence completely

squib (skwib) *n.* [prob. echoic] **1.** a firecracker that hisses before exploding **2.** a short, witty writing that criticizes, etc.

squid (skwid) *n.* [prob. akin to SQUIRT] a long, slender sea mollusk with ten arms, two longer than the others

squig·gle (skwig''l) *n.* [SQU(IRM) + (W)IGGLE] a short, wavy line or illegible scrawl —*vt., vi.* **-gled, -gling** to write as, or make, squiggles

squint (skwint) *vi.* [akin to Du. *schuin,* sideways] **1.** to peer with the eyes partly closed **2.** to look sideways or askance **3.** to be cross-eyed —*n.* **1.** a squinting **2.** a being cross-eyed **3.** [Colloq.] a glance, often sidelong

squire (skwīr) *n.* [< ESQUIRE] **1.** a young man of high birth who attended a knight **2.** in England, the owner of a large rural estate **3.** a title of respect for a justice of the peace, etc. **4.** an attendant; esp., a man escorting a woman —*vt., vi.* **squired, squir'ing** to act as a squire (to)

squirm (skwurm) *vi.* [prob. echoic] **1.** to twist and turn the body; wriggle **2.** to show or feel distress —*n.* a squirming —**squirm'y** *adj.* **-i·er, -i·est**

squir·rel (skwur'əl) *n.* [< Gr. *skia,* a shadow + *oura,* tail] **1.** a small, tree-dwelling rodent with heavy fur and a long, bushy tail **2.** its fur

squirt (skwurt) *vt., vi.* [prob. < LowG. *swirtjen*] **1.** to shoot out (a liquid) in a jet; spurt **2.** to wet with liquid so shot out —*n.* **1.** a jet of liquid **2.** [Colloq.] a small, esp. impudent, person

Sr *Chem.* strontium

Sr. Senior

S.R.O. standing room only

S.S., SS, S/S steamship

SST supersonic transport

St. 1. Saint **2.** Strait **3.** Street

stab (stab) *n.* [prob. < ME. *stubbe,* stub] **1.** a wound made by stabbing **2.** a thrust, as with a knife **3.** a sharp pain —*vt., vi.* **stabbed, stab'-bing 1.** to pierce or wound as with a knife **2.** to thrust (a knife, etc.) into something **3.** to pain sharply —**make** (or **take**) **a stab at** to make an attempt at

sta·bil·i·ty (stə bil'ə tē) *n., pl.* **-ties 1.** a being stable; steadiness **2.** firmness of purpose, etc. **3.** permanence

sta·bi·lize (stā'bə līz') *vt.* **-lized', -liz'ing 1.** to make stable, or firm **2.** to keep from changing, as in price **3.** to give stability to (a plane, ship, etc.) —**sta'bi·li·za'tion** *n.*

sta·ble[1] (stā'b'l) *adj.* **-bler, -blest** [< L. *stare,* to stand] **1.** *a)* firm *b)* not likely to break down, fall apart, etc. **2.** firm in character, purpose, etc. **3.** enduring

sta·ble[2] (stā'b'l) *n.* [< L. *stare,* to stand] **1.** a building in which horses or cattle are sheltered and fed **2.** all the racehorses of one owner —*vt., vi.* **-bled, -bling** to keep or be kept in a stable

stac·ca·to (stə kät'ō) *adj.* [It., detached]

Music with distinct breaks between successive tones

stack (stak) *n.* [ON. *stakkr*] **1.** a large, neatly arranged pile of straw, hay, etc. **2.** any orderly pile **3.** a smokestack **4.** [*pl.*] the main area for shelving books in a library —*vt.* **1.** to pile in a stack **2.** to arrange underhandedly for a desired result

stack'up' *n.* an arrangement of circling aircraft at various altitudes awaiting their turn to land

sta·di·um (stā'dē əm) *n.* [< Gr. *stadion,* unit of length, c.607 ft.] a large structure for football, baseball, etc. with tiers of seats for spectators

staff (staf) *n., pl.* **staffs;** also, for senses 1 & 4, **staves** [OE. *stæf*] **1.** a stick or rod used for support, a weapon, a symbol of authority, etc. **2.** a group of people assisting a leader **3.** a specific group of workers *[a teaching staff]* **4.** *Music* the five horizontal lines and four intermediate spaces on which music is written —*vt.* to provide with a staff, as of workers

staff'er *n.* a member of a staff

stag (stag) *n.* [OE. *stagga*] a full-grown male deer —*adj.* for men only *[a stag party]*

stage (stāj) *n.* [< L. *stare,* to stand] **1.** a platform **2.** *a)* an area or platform upon which plays, etc. are presented *b)* the theater, or acting as a profession (with *the*) **3.** the scene of an event **4.** a stopping place, or the distance between stops, on a journey **5.** short for STAGECOACH **6.** a period or degree in a process of development, etc. *[the larval stage]* **7.** any of the propulsion units used in sequence in spacecraft, etc. —*vt.* **staged, stag'ing 1.** to present as on a stage **2.** to plan and carry out *[stage* an attack*]*

stage'coach' *n.* formerly, a horse-drawn public coach that traveled a regular route

stage'hand' *n.* one who sets up scenery, operates the curtain, etc. on a stage

stage'-struck' *adj.* having an intense desire to act in the theater

stag·ger (stag'ər) *vi.* [ON. *stakra,* to totter] to totter or reel, as from a blow, fatigue, etc. —*vt.* **1.** to make stagger **2.** to affect strongly, as with astonishment **3.** to make zigzag or alternating **4.** to arrange (duties, vacation, etc.) so as to avoid crowding —*n.* [*pl., with sing. v.*] a disease of horses, causing staggering, etc.

stag·nant (stag'nant) *adj.* [< L. *stagnare,* to stagnate] **1.** not flowing or moving **2.** foul from lack of movement; said of water, etc. **3.** lacking activity, etc.; sluggish

stag'nate (-nāt) *vi., vt.* **-nat·ed, -nat·ing** to become or make stagnant —**stag·na'tion** *n.*

staid (stād) *archaic pt. & pp.* of STAY[3] —*adj.* sober; sedate —**staid'ly** *adv.*

stain (stān) *vt.* [< L. *dis-,* from + *tingere,* to color] **1.** to spoil by discoloring or spotting **2.** to disgrace or dishonor **3.** to color (wood, etc.) with a dye —*n.* **1.** a discoloration, spot, etc. resulting from staining **2.** a moral blemish **3.** a dye for staining wood, etc. —**stain'less** *adj.*

stainless steel steel alloyed with chromium, etc., virtually immune to rust and corrosion

stair (ster) *n.* [OE. *stæger*] **1.** [*usually pl.*] a staircase **2.** one of a series of steps leading from one level to another

stair'case' *n.* a flight of stairs with a handrail: also **stair'way'**

stair'well' *n.* a vertical shaft (in a building) containing a staircase

stake (stāk) *n.* [OE. *staca*] **1.** a length of wood or metal, pointed for driving into the ground **2.** the post to which a person was tied for execution by burning **3.** [*often pl.*] money, etc. risked as in a wager **4.** [*often pl.*] the winner's prize in a race, etc. —*vt.* **staked, stak′ing 1.** to mark the boundaries of [*to stake* out a claim] **2.** to fasten to a stake **3.** to risk; gamble **4.** [Colloq.] to furnish with money, etc. —**at stake** being risked —**pull up stakes** [Colloq.] to change one's residence, etc. —**stake out** to put under police surveillance

sta·lac·tite (stə lak′tīt) *n.* [< Gr. *stalaktos*, dripping] an icicle-shaped lime deposit hanging from the roof of a cave

sta·lag·mite (stə lag′mīt) *n.* [< Gr. *stalagmos*, a dropping] a cone-shaped deposit on the floor of a cave, often beneath a stalactite

stale (stāl) *adj.* **stal′er, stal′est** [prob. < LowG.] **1.** having lost freshness; flat, dry, stagnant, etc. **2.** trite, as a joke **3.** out of condition, bored, etc. —*vt., vi.* **staled, stal′ing** to make or become stale

stale·mate (stāl′māt′) *n.* [< OFr. *estal, a* fixed location + MATE²] **1.** *Chess* a situation in which a player cannot move, resulting in a draw **2.** a deadlock —*vt.* **-mat′ed, -mat′ing** to bring into a stalemate

stalk¹ (stôk) *vi., vt.* [< OE. *stealc,* steep] **1.** to walk (through) in a stiff, haughty manner **2.** to advance grimly **3.** to pursue (game, etc.) stealthily —*n.* **1.** a stiff, haughty stride **2.** a stalking of game, etc.

stalk² (stôk) *n.* [OE. *stela*] **1.** the stem of a plant **2.** any part like this

stall¹ (stôl) *n.* [OE. *steall*] **1.** a compartment for one animal in a stable **2.** *a)* a booth, etc. as at a market *b)* a pew in a church **3.** a stop or standstill, esp. when due to a malfunction —*vt., vi.* **1.** to keep or be kept in a stall **2.** to bring or come to a standstill, esp. unintentionally

stall² (stôl) *vi., vt.* [< obs. *stale,* a decoy] to act evasively or hesitantly so as to deceive or delay —*n.* [Colloq.] any trick used in stalling

stal·lion (stal′yən) *n.* [< Gmc. *stal,* a stall] an uncastrated male horse

stal·wart (stôl′wərt) *adj.* [< OE. *stathol,* foundation + *wyrthe,* worth] **1.** sturdy; robust **2.** valiant **3.** resolute; firm —*n.* a stalwart person —**stal′wart·ly** *adv.*

sta·men (stā′mən) *n.* [< L., a thread] a pollen-bearing organ in a flower

stam·i·na (stam′ə nə) *n.* [L., pl. of *stamen*] resistance to fatigue, illness, hardship, etc.

stam·mer (stam′ər) *vt., vi.* [OE. *stamerian*] to speak or say with involuntary pauses and rapid repetitions —*n.* a stammering —**stam′-mer·er** *n.*

stamp (stamp) *vt.* [ME. *stampen*] **1.** to bring (the foot) down forcibly **2.** to crush or pound with the foot **3.** to imprint or cut out (a design, etc.) **4.** to cut (*out*) by pressing with a die **5.** to put a stamp on **6.** to characterize —*vi.* **1.** to bring the foot down forcibly **2.** to walk with loud, heavy steps —*n.* **1.** a stamping **2.** a machine, tool, or die for stamping **3.** a mark or form made by stamping **4.** any of various seals, gummed pieces of paper, etc. used to show that a fee, as for postage, has been paid **5.** any similar seal [a trading *stamp*] **6.** kind; class —**stamp out 1.** to crush by treading on forcibly **2.** to suppress

stam·pede (stam pēd′) *n.* [< AmSp. < Sp. *estampar,* to stamp] a sudden, headlong rush or flight, as of a herd of cattle —*vi.* **-ped′ed, -ped′ing** to move in a stampede —*vt.* to cause to stampede

stance (stans) *n.* [< L. *stare,* to stand] **1.** the way one stands, esp. the placement of the feet **2.** the attitude taken in a situation

stanch (stônch, stanch) *vt., vi., adj. see* STAUNCH

stan·chion (stan′chən) *n.* [see STANCE] **1.** an upright post or support **2.** a device to confine a cow

stand (stand) *vi.* **stood, stand′ing** [OE. *standan*] **1.** to be in, or assume, an upright position, as on the feet **2.** to be supported on a base, pedestal, etc. **3.** to take or be in a (specified) position, attitude, etc. **4.** to have a (specified) height when standing **5.** to be placed or situated **6.** to gather and remain, as water **7.** to remain unchanged **8.** to make resistance **9.** *a)* to halt *b)* to be stationary —*vt.* **1.** to place upright **2.** to endure **3.** to withstand **4.** to undergo [to *stand* trial] —*n.* **1.** a standing; esp., a halt or stop **2.** a position; station **3.** a view, opinion, etc. **4.** a structure to stand or sit on **5.** a place of business **6.** a rack, small table, etc. for holding things **7.** a growth of trees, etc. —**stand by 1.** to be near and ready if needed **2.** to aid —**stand for 1.** to represent **2.** [Colloq.] to tolerate —**stand off** to keep at a distance —**stand on 1.** to be founded on **2.** to insist upon —**stand out 1.** to project **2.** to be distinct, prominent, etc. —**stand up 1.** to rise to a standing position **2.** to prove valid, durable, etc. **3.** [Slang] to fail to keep a date with

stand·ard (stan′dərd) *n.* [< OFr. *estendard*] **1.** a flag, banner, etc. as an emblem of a military unit, etc. **2.** something established as a rule or basis of comparison in measuring quantity, quality, value, etc. **3.** an upright support —*adj.* **1.** used as or conforming to an established rule, model, etc. **2.** generally accepted as reliable or authoritative **3.** ordinary; typical

stand′ard-bear′er *n.* **1.** one carrying the flag **2.** a leader of a political party, etc.

stand′ard·ize′ *vt.* **-ized′, -iz′ing** to make standard or uniform —**stand′ard·i·za′tion** *n.*

standard time the time in any of the 24 time zones, each an hour apart, into which the earth is divided: in North America there are eight zones

stand′by′ *n., pl.* **-bys′** a person or thing that is dependable, a possible substitute, etc.

stand·ee (stan dē′) *n.* [Colloq.] one who stands, usually because no seats are vacant

stand′ing *n.* **1.** status or reputation [in good *standing*] **2.** duration [of long *standing*] —*adj.* **1.** that stands; upright **2.** in or from a standing position [a *standing* jump] **3.** stagnant, as water **4.** permanent [a *standing* order] **5.** not in use

stand′off′ *n.* a tie in a contest

stand′off′ish *adj.* reserved and cool; aloof

stand′point′ *n.* point of view

stand′still′ *n.* a stop or halt

stank (staŋk) *alt. pt. of* STINK

stan·za (stan′zə) *n.* [It.: ult. < L. *stare,* to stand] a group of lines of verse forming a division of a poem or song

staph·y·lo·coc·cus (staf′ə lō käk′əs) *n., pl.* **-coc′ci** (-käk′sī) [< Gr. *staphylē,* bunch of grapes + *kokkos,* a grain] any of certain spherical bacteria in clusters or chains that cause pus to form in abscesses

sta·ple¹ (stā′p'l) *n.* [< MDu. *stapel,* mart] **1.** a chief commodity made, grown, etc. in a particular place **2.** raw material **3.** a regularly stocked item of trade, as salt **4.** the fiber of cotton, wool, etc. —*adj.* **1.** regularly stocked, produced, or used **2.** chief; main

sta·ple² (stā′p'l) *n.* [OE. *stapol,* a post] a U-shaped piece of metal with sharp ends, driven into wood, etc., as to hold a hook, wire, etc., or through papers as a binding —*vt.* **-pled, -pling** to fasten with a staple —**sta′pler** *n.*

star (stär) *n.* [OE. *steorra*] **1.** any heavenly body seen as a small fixed point of light, esp. a distant sun **2.** a flat figure with usually five or six points **3.** anything like such a figure **4.** an asterisk **5.** a planet, etc. regarded as influencing human fate **6.** one who excels, esp. in a sport **7.** a leading actor or actress —*vt.* **starred, star′ring 1.** to mark with stars as a decoration, etc. **2.** to present (a performer) in a leading role —*vi.* **1.** to excel, esp. in a sport **2.** to have a leading role —*adj.* **1.** excelling [a star athlete] **2.** of a star or stars

star·board (stär′bərd, -bôrd′) *n.* [< OE. *steoran*, to steer (with a large oar on the ship's right side) + *bord*, board] the right side of a ship, etc. as one faces forward —*adj.* of or on the starboard

starch (stärch) *n.* [< OE. *stearc*, stiff] **1.** a white, tasteless, odorless food substance found in potatoes, grain, etc. **2.** a powdered form of this, used in laundering to stiffen cloth, etc. —*vt.* to stiffen as with starch —**starch′y** *adj.* **-i·er, -i·est**

star′dom (-dəm) *n.* the status of a star of stage, screen, etc.

stare (ster) *vi.* **stared, star′ing** [OE. *starian*] to gaze steadily and intently —*vt.* to look fixedly at —*n.* a staring look

star′fish′ *n., pl.*: see FISH a small, star-shaped sea animal

star′gaze′ *vi.* **-gazed′, -gaz′ing 1.** to gaze at the stars **2.** to daydream —**star′gaz′er** *n.*

stark (stärk) *adj.* [OE. *stearc*] **1.** rigid, as a corpse **2.** sharply outlined **3.** bleak; desolate **4.** sheer; utter —*adv.* utterly

stark′-nak′ed *adj.* entirely naked

star′let (-lit) *n.* a young actress being promoted as a possible future star

star′light′ *n.* light from the stars —**star′lit′** *adj.*

star·ling (stär′liŋ) *n.* [OE. *stær*] any of a family of old-world birds, esp. the **common starling**, with iridescent plumage, introduced into the U.S.

star′ry *adj.* **-ri·er, -ri·est 1.** shining; bright **2.** lighted by or full of stars

Stars and Stripes the U.S. flag

star′-span′gled *adj.* studded or spangled with stars

Star-Spangled Banner 1. the U.S. flag **2.** the U.S. national anthem

start (stärt) *vi.* [OE. *styrtan*] **1.** to make a sudden or involuntary movement **2.** to go into action or motion; begin; commence **3.** to spring into being, activity, etc. —*vt.* **1.** to flush (game) **2.** to displace, loosen, etc. **3.** to set into motion, action, etc. **4.** to begin doing, etc. **5.** to cause to be an entrant in a race, etc. —*n.* **1.** a sudden, brief shock or startled movement **2.** a starting or beginning **3.** *a)* a place or time of beginning *b)* a lead or other advantage **4.** an opportunity to begin a career, etc. —**start out** (or **off**) to start a journey, project, etc. — **start′er** *n.*

star·tle (stärt′'l) *vt.* **-tled, -tling** [< ME. *sterten*, to start] to surprise, frighten, or alarm suddenly; esp., to cause to start —*vi.* to be startled

starve (stärv) *vi.* **starved, starv′ing** [< OE. *steorfan*, to die] **1.** to die from lack of food **2.** to suffer from hunger **3.** [Colloq.] to suffer great need (with *for*) —*vt.* **1.** to cause to starve **2.** to force by starving —**star·va·tion** (stär vā′shən) *n.*

stash (stash) *vt.* [prob. a blend of STORE & CACHE] [Colloq.] to hide in a secret or safe

place —*n.* [Slang] **1.** a place for hiding things **2.** something hidden away

-stat [< Gr. *-statēs*] *a combining form meaning* stationary [*thermostat*]

state (stāt) *n.* [< L. *stare*, to stand] **1.** a set of circumstances, etc. characterizing a person or thing; condition **2.** condition as regards structure, form, etc. **3.** rich display; pomp **4.** [*sometimes* S-] a body of people politically organized under one government; nation **5.** [*usually* S-] any of the political units that together form a federal government, as in the U.S. **6.** civil government [church and *state*] — *adj.* **1.** formal; ceremonial **2.** [*sometimes* S-] of the government or a state —*vt.* **stat′ed, stat′ing 1.** to establish by specifying **2.** *a)* to set forth in words *b)* to express —**in a state** [Colloq.] in an agitated emotional condition —**lie in state** to be displayed formally before burial —**the States** the United States —**state′hood′** *adj.*

state′ly *adj.* **-li·er, -li·est** dignified, imposing, grand, etc. —**state′li·ness** *n.*

state′ment *n.* **1.** *a)* the act of stating *b)* the thing stated **2.** a summary of a financial account

state′room′ *n.* **1.** a private cabin on a ship **2.** a private room in a railroad car

state′side′ *adj.* [Colloq.] of or in the U.S. (as viewed from abroad) —*adv.* [Colloq.] in, to, or toward the U.S.

states′man *n., pl.* **-men** one who is wise or experienced in the business of government — **states′man·ship′** *n.*

stat·ic (stat′ik) *adj.* [< Gr. *statikos*, causing to stand] **1.** of masses, forces, etc. at rest or in equilibrium **2.** at rest; inactive **3.** designating, of, or producing stationary electrical charges, as from friction **4.** of or having to do with static —*n.* **1.** atmospheric electrical charges causing noise on radio or TV **2.** such noise **3.** [Slang] adverse criticism

sta·tion (stā′shən) *n.* [< L. *stare*, to stand] **1.** the place or building where one stands or is located; esp., an assigned post **2.** a regular stopping place, as on a bus line or railroad **3.** social standing **4.** a place equipped for radio and TV transmission, or its frequency —*vt.* to assign to a station

sta·tion·ar·y (stā′shə ner′ē) *adj.* [see STATION] **1.** not moving; fixed **2.** unchanging

station break a pause in radio or TV programs for station identification

sta·tion·er (stā′shə nər) *n.* [< ML. *stationarius*, shopkeeper] a dealer in office supplies, etc.

sta·tion·er·y (-ner′ē) *n.* writing materials; specif., paper and envelopes

station wagon an automobile with folding or removable rear seats and a tailgate that can be opened

sta·tis·tics (stə tis′tiks) *n.pl.* [< L. *status*, standing] **1.** numerical facts assembled and classified so as to present significant information **2.** [*with sing. v.*] the science of compiling such facts —**sta·tis′ti·cal** *adj.* —**stat·is·ti·cian** (stat′is tish′ən) *n.*

stat·u·ar·y (stach′ oo wer′ē) *n., pl.* **-ies** statues collectively

stat·ue (stach′oo) *n.* [< L. *statuere*, to place] the form of a person or animal carved in stone, etc., modeled in clay, etc., or cast in metal, etc.

stat·u·esque (stach′oo wesk′) *adj.* of or like a statue; tall and well-proportioned

stat′u·ette (-wet′) *n.* a small statue

stat·ure (stach′ər) *n.* [< L. *statura*] **1.** the

standing height of the body **2.** growth or level of attainment *[moral stature]*

sta·tus (stāt′əs, stat′-) *n., pl.* **-tus·es** [L., standing] **1.** legal condition *[the status of a minor]* **2.** position; rank **3.** high position; prestige **4.** state, as of affairs

status quo (kwō′) [L., the state in which] the existing state of affairs

status symbol a possession regarded as a sign of (high) social status

stat·ute (stach′ōōt) *n.* [see STATUE] **1.** an established rule **2.** a law passed by a legislative body

stat·u·to·ry (stach′oo tôr′ē) *adj.* **1.** fixed or authorized by statute **2.** punishable by statute, as an offense

staunch (stônch, stänch) *vt.* [< L. *stare*, to stand] to check the flow of (blood, etc.) from (a wound, etc.) —*vi.* to stop flowing —*adj.* **1.** seaworthy **2.** steadfast; loyal **3.** strong; solid — **staunch′ly** *adv.*

stave (stāv) *n.* [< *staves*, pl. of STAFF] **1.** one of the shaped strips of wood that form the wall of a barrel, bucket, etc. **2.** a stick or staff **3.** a stanza —*vt.* **staved** or **stove, stav′ing** to puncture, as by breaking in staves —**stave off** to ward off or hold off

staves (stāvz) *n.* **1.** *alt. pl.* of STAFF **2.** *pl.* of STAVE

stay¹ (stā) *n.* [OE. *stæg*] a heavy rope or cable used as a brace, as for a mast of a ship

stay² (stā) *n.* [MFr. *estaie*] **1.** a support; prop **2.** a strip of stiffening material used in a corset, shirt collar, etc. —*vt.* to support, or prop up

stay³ (stā) *vi.* [< L. *stare*, to stand] **1.** to continue in the place or condition specified; remain **2.** to live; dwell **3.** to stop; halt **4.** to pause; delay **5.** [Colloq.] to endure; last —*vt.* **1.** to stop or check **2.** to hinder or detain **3.** to postpone (legal action) **4.** to satisfy (thirst, etc.) for a time **5.** to remain to the end of —*n.* **1.** *a)* a stopping or being stopped *b)* a halt or pause **2.** a postponement in legal action **3.** the action of remaining, or the time spent, in a place —**stay put** [Colloq.] to remain in place or unchanged

Ste. [Fr. *Sainte*] Saint (female)

stead (sted) *n.* [OE. *stede*] the place or position of a person or thing as filled by a substitute — **stand (one) in good stead** to give (one) good service

stead·fast (sted′fast′) *adj.* [OE. *stedefæste*] **1.** firm; fixed **2.** constant

stead·y (sted′ē) *adj.* **-i·er, -i·est** [see STEAD & -Y²] **1.** not shaky; firm; stable **2.** constant, regular, or uniform **3.** constant in behavior, loyalty, etc. **4.** calm and controlled *[steady nerves]* **5.** sober; reliable —*vt., vi.* **-ied, -y·ing** to make or become steady —*n.* [Colloq.] one's sweetheart —*adv.* in a steady manner —**go steady** [Colloq.] to be sweethearts —**stead′i·ly** *adv.*

steak (stāk) *n.* [< ON. *steikja*, to roast on a spit] a thick slice of meat, esp. beef, or fish, for broiling or frying

steal (stēl) *vt.* **stole, stol′en, steal′ing** [OE. *stælan*] **1.** to take (another's property, etc.) dishonestly, esp. in a secret manner **2.** to take (a look, etc.) slyly **3.** to gain slyly or artfully *[he stole her heart]* **4.** to move, put, etc. stealthily *(in, from,* etc.) **5.** *Baseball* to gain (a base) safely without the help of a hit, walk, or error —*vi.* **1.** to be a thief **2.** to move stealthily —*n.* [Colloq.] **1.** a stealing **2.** an extraordinary bargain

stealth (stelth) *n.* [< ME. *stelen*, to steal] secret or furtive action —**stealth′i·ly** *adv.* — **stealth′y** *adj.* **-i·er, -i·est**

steam (stēm) *n.* [OE.] **1.** water as converted into a vapor by being heated to the boiling point **2.** the power of steam under pressure **3.** condensed water vapor **4.** [Colloq.] driving force; energy —*adj.* **1.** using or operated by steam **2.** containing or conducting steam —*vi.* **1.** to give off steam **2.** to become covered with condensed steam **3.** to move by steam power — *vt.* to expose to steam, as in cooking —**steam′y** *adj.*

steam′boat′ *n.* a small steamship

steam engine an engine using steam under pressure to supply mechanical energy

steam′er *n.* **1.** something operated by steam, as a steamship **2.** a container for cooking, cleaning, etc. with steam

steam fitter a mechanic whose work (**steam fitting**) is installing boilers, pipes, etc. in steam-pressure systems

steam′roll′er *n.* a heavy, steam-driven roller used in road building, etc. —*vt., vi.* to move, crush, override, etc. as (with) a steamroller

steam′ship′ *n.* a ship driven by steam

steam shovel a large, mechanically operated digger, powered by steam

steed (stēd) *n.* [OE. *steda*] a horse

steel (stēl) *n.* [OE. *stiele*] **1.** a hard, tough alloy of iron with carbon, etc. **2.** a thing of steel **3.** great strength or hardness —*adj.* of or like steel —*vt.* to make hard, tough, etc. —**steel′y** *adj.* **-i·er, -i·est**

steel wool long, thin shavings of steel in a pad, used for scouring, etc.

steel′yard′ (-yärd′, -yərd) *n.* [STEEL + obs. *yard*, rod] a balance scale consisting of a metal arm suspended from above

steep¹ (stēp) *adj.* [OE. *steap*, lofty] **1.** having a sharp rise or slope; precipitous **2.** [Colloq.] excessive; extreme —**steep′ly** *adv.*

steep² (stēp) *vt., vi.* [akin to ON. *steypa*] to soak, saturate, imbue, etc.

stee·ple (stē′p'l) *n.* [OE. *stepel*] **1.** a tower rising above the main structure, as of a church **2.** *same as* SPIRE

stee′ple·chase′ *n.* a horse race over a course obstructed with ditches, hedges, etc.

stee′ple·jack′ *n.* one who builds, paints, or repairs steeples, smokestacks, etc.

steer¹ (stir) *vt., vi.* [OE. *stieran*] **1.** to guide (a ship, etc.) with a rudder **2.** to direct the course of (an automobile, etc.) **3.** to follow (a course)

steer² (stir) *n.* [OE. *steor*] **1.** a castrated male of the cattle family **2.** loosely, any male of beef cattle

steer′age (-ij) *n.* **1.** a steering **2.** formerly, a section in a ship occupied by passengers paying the lowest fare

steers·man (stirz′mən) *n., pl.* **-men** one who steers a ship or boat; helmsman

stein (stīn) *n.* [G.] a beer mug

stel·lar (stel′ər) *adj.* [< L. *stella*, star] **1.** of a star **2.** excellent **3.** leading; chief

stem¹ (stem) *n.* [OE. *stemn*] **1.** the main stalk of a plant **2.** any stalk supporting leaves, flowers, or fruit **3.** a stemlike part, as of a pipe, goblet, etc. **4.** the prow of a ship; bow **5.** the part of a word to which inflectional endings are added —*vt.* **stemmed, stem′ming** to make headway against *[to stem the tide]* —*vi.* to originate or derive

stem² (stem) *vt.* **stemmed, stem′ming** [< ON. *stemma*] to stop or check by or as if by damming up

stench (stench) *n.* [OE. *stenc*] an offensive smell; stink

sten·cil (sten's'l) *vt.* -**ciled** or -**cilled**, -**cil·ing** or -**cil·ling** [ult. < L. *scintilla*, a spark] to make or mark with a stencil —*n.* 1. a thin sheet, as of paper, cut through so that when ink, etc. is applied, designs, letters, etc. form on the surface beneath 2. a design, etc. so made

ste·nog·ra·phy (stə näg′rə fē) *n.* [< Gr. *stenos*, narrow + -GRAPHY] shorthand writing for later transcription in typewriting —**ste·nog′ra·pher** *n.* —**sten·o·graph·ic** (sten′ə graf′ik) *adj.*

sten·to·ri·an (sten tôr′ē ən) *adj.* [< *Stentor*, a Greek herald in the *Iliad*] very loud

step (step) *n.* [OE. *stepe*] 1. a single movement of the foot, as in walking 2. the distance covered by such a movement 3. a short distance 4. a manner of stepping 5. the sound of stepping 6. a rest for the foot in climbing, as a stair 7. a degree; level; stage 8. any of a series of acts, processes, etc. —*vi.* **stepped, step′ping** 1. to move by executing a step 2. to walk a short distance 3. to move briskly (*along*) 4. to enter (*into* a situation, etc.) 5. to press the foot down (*on*) —*vt.* to measure by taking steps (with *off*) —**in** (or **out of**) **step** (not) conforming to a marching rhythm, a regular procedure, etc. —**step up** 1. to advance 2. to increase, as in rate

step·broth·er (step′bruth′ər) *n.* one's stepparent's son by a former marriage

step′child′ *n., pl.* -**chil′dren** [OE. *steop*-, orphaned] a child (**stepdaughter** or **stepson**) by a former marriage of one's spouse

step′lad′der *n.* a four-legged ladder having broad, flat steps

step′par′ent *n.* the person (**stepfather** or **stepmother**) who has married one's parent after the death or divorce of the other parent

steppe (step) *n.* [< Russ. *step*′] any of the great plains of SE Europe and Asia, having few trees

step′ping·stone′ *n.* 1. a stone used to step on, as in crossing a stream, etc. 2. a means of bettering oneself Also **stepping stone**

step·sis·ter (step′sis′tər) *n.* one's stepparent's daughter by a former marriage

step′-up′ *n.* an increase, as in amount

-**ster** [OE. *-estre*] *a suffix meaning* one who is, does, creates, or is associated with (something specified) [*trickster, gangster*]

ster·e·o (ster′ē ō′, stir′-) *n., pl.* -**os′** 1. a stereophonic record player, radio, system, etc. 2. a stereoscope —*adj. short for* STEREOPHONIC

stereo- [< Gr. *stereos*, hard] *a combining form meaning* solid, firm, three-dimensional [*stereoscope*]

ster·e·o·phon·ic (ster′ē ə fän′ik, stir′-) *adj.* [< prec. + Gr. *phōnē*, a sound] designating sound reproduction using two or more channels to carry and reproduce through separate speakers a blend of sounds from separate sources

ster′e·o·scope′ (-skōp′) *n.* [STEREO- + -SCOPE] an instrument with two eyepieces that gives a three-dimensional effect to photographs viewed through it

ster′e·o·type′ (-tīp′) *n.* [< Fr.: see STEREO- & -TYPE] 1. a printing plate cast from a mold, as of a page of set type 2. a fixed idea or popular conception —*vt.* -**typed′**, -**typ′ing** to make a stereotype of

ster·ile (ster′'l) *adj.* [L. *sterilis*] 1. incapable of producing offspring, fruit, etc.; barren 2. free from living microorganisms —**ste·ril·i·ty** (stə ril′ə tē) *n.*

ster′i·lize′ (-ə līz′) *vt.* -**lized′**, -**liz′ing** to make sterile; specif., *a*) to make incapable of reproduction *b*) to free from living microorganisms —**ster′i·li·za′tion** *n.*

ster·ling (stur′liŋ) *n.* [ME. *sterlinge*, Norman coin] 1. sterling silver 2. British money —*adj.* 1. designating silver that is at least 92.5 percent pure 2. of British money 3. made of sterling silver 4. excellent [*sterling* principles]

stern[1] (sturn) *adj.* [OE. *styrne*] 1. severe; strict [*stern* measures] 2. grim [a *stern* face] 3. relentless; firm —**stern′ly** *adv.*

stern[2] (sturn) *n.* [< ON. *styra*, to steer] the rear end of a ship, boat, etc.

ster·num (stur′nəm) *n., pl.* -**nums**, -**na** (-nə) [< Gr. *sternon*] a flat, bony structure to which most of the ribs are attached in the front of the chest; breastbone

stet (stet) [L.] let it stand: a printer's term used to indicate that matter previously struck out is to remain —*vt.* **stet′ted, stet′ting** to mark with "stet"

steth·o·scope (steth′ə skōp′) *n.* [< Fr. < Gr. *stēthos*, the chest + -SCOPE] *Med.* an instrument placed against the body for examining the heart, lungs, etc. by listening to the sounds they make

ste·ve·dore (stē′və dôr′) *n.* [< Sp. < L. *stipare*, to cram] a person employed at loading or unloading ships

stew (stōō) *vt., vi.* [ult. < L. *ex*-, out + Gr. *typhos*, steam] 1. to cook by simmering or boiling slowly 2. to worry —*n.* 1. a dish, esp. of meat and vegetables, cooked by stewing 2. a state of worry

stew·ard (stōō′ərd) *n.* [< OE. *stig*, hall + *weard*, keeper] 1. a person put in charge of a large estate 2. an administrator, as of finances and property 3. one responsible for the food and drink, etc. in a club, restaurant, etc. 4. an attendant on a ship, airplane, etc. —**stew′ard·ship′** *n.*

stew·ard·ess (-ər dis) *n.* a woman steward, esp. on an airplane

stick (stik) *n.* [OE. *sticca*] 1. a twig or branch broken or cut off 2. a long, slender piece of wood, as a club, cane, etc. 3. any sticklike piece [a *stick* of gum] —*vt.* **stuck, stick′ing** 1. to pierce, as with a pointed instrument 2. to pierce with (a knife, pin, etc.) 3. to thrust (*in, into, out,* etc.) 4. to attach by gluing, pinning, etc. 5. to obstruct, detain, etc. [the wheels were *stuck*] 6. [Colloq.] to put, set, etc. 7. [Colloq.] to puzzle; baffle 8. [Slang] *a*) to impose a burden, etc. upon *b*) to defraud —*vi.* 1. to be fixed by a pointed end, as a nail 2. to adhere; remain 3. to persevere [to *stick* at a job] 4. to remain firm and resolute [he *stuck* with us] 5. to become embedded, jammed, etc. 6. to be puzzled 7. to hesitate; scruple [he'll *stick* at nothing] 8. to protrude or project (*out, up,* etc.) —**stick by** to remain loyal to —**stick up for** [Colloq.] to uphold; defend —**the sticks** [Colloq.] the rural districts

stick′er *n.* a person or thing that sticks; specif., a gummed label

stick′-in-the-mud′ *n.* [Colloq.] a person who resists change or progress

stick·ler (stik′lər) *n.* [< OE. *stihtan*, arrange] 1. one who insists on a certain way of doing things [a *stickler* for discipline] 2. [Colloq.] something difficult to solve

stick′pin′ *n.* an ornamental pin worn in a cravat or necktie

stick shift a gearshift, as on a car, operated manually by a lever

stick′up′ *n. slang term for* HOLDUP (sense 2)

stick′y *adj.* -**i·er, -i·est** 1. that sticks; adhesive 2. [Colloq.] hot and humid 3. [Colloq.] troublesome 4. [Colloq.] maudlin

stiff (stif) *adj.* [OE. *stif*] 1. hard to bend or

move; rigid; firm **2.** sore or limited in movement: said of joints or muscles **3.** not fluid; thick **4.** strong; powerful *[a stiff breeze]* **5.** harsh *[a stiff punishment]* **6.** difficult *[a stiff climb]* **7.** constrained or awkward **8.** [Colloq.] high *[a stiff price]* —**stiff'ly** *adv.*

stiff'en *vt., vi.* to make or become stiff or stiffer —**stiff'en·er** *n.*

stiff'-necked' (-nekt') *adj.* stubborn

sti·fle (stī'f'l) *vt.* **-fled, -fling** [< MFr. *estouffer,* smother] **1.** to suffocate; smother **2.** to suppress or check; stop *[to stifle a sob]* —*vi.* to die or suffer from lack of air

stig·ma (stig'mə) *n., pl.* **-mas, stig·ma'ta** (-mät'ə) [L. < Gr., a mark] **1.** a mark of disgrace or reproach **2.** a spot on the skin, esp. one that bleeds in certain nervous tensions **3.** the upper tip of the pistil of a flower, receiving the pollen —**stig·mat'ic** (-mat'ik) *adj.*

stig'ma·tize' *vt.* **-tized', -tiz'ing 1.** to brand with a stigma **2.** to mark as disgraceful —**stig'-ma·ti·za'tion** *n.*

stile (stīl) *n.* [< OE. *stigan,* to climb] **1.** a step or set of steps used in climbing over a fence or wall **2.** *short for* TURNSTILE

sti·let·to (sti let'ō) *n., pl.* **-tos, -toes** [It. < L. *stilus,* pointed tool] a small dagger with a slender, tapering blade

still[1] (stil) *adj.* [OE. *stille*] **1.** without sound; silent **2.** not moving; motionless **3.** calm; tranquil **4.** designating or of a single photograph taken from a motion-picture film —*n.* **1.** silence; quiet **2.** a still photograph —*adv.* **1.** at or up to the time indicated **2.** even; yet *[still colder]* **3.** nevertheless; yet *[rich but still unhappy]* —*conj.* nevertheless; yet —*vt., vi.* to make or become still —**still'ness** *n.*

still[2] (stil) *n.* [< obs. *still,* to distill] an apparatus used for distilling liquids, esp. alcoholic liquors

still'born' *adj.* dead when born

still life a picture of inanimate objects, as fruit, flowers, etc.

stilt (stilt) *n.* [ME. *stilte*] **1.** either of a pair of poles, each with a footrest somewhere along its length, used for walking, as in play **2.** a long post used to hold a building, etc. above the ground or out of the water

stilt·ed (stil'tid) *adj.* artificially formal or dignified; pompous —**stilt'ed·ness** *n.*

stim·u·lant (stim'yə lənt) *adj.* stimulating —*n.* anything, as a drug, that stimulates

stim'u·late' (-lāt') *vt.* **-lat'ed, -lat'ing** [< L. *stimulus,* a goad] **1.** to stir up or spur on; excite **2.** to invigorate —**stim'u·la'tion** *n.*

stim'u·lus (-ləs) *n., pl.* **-li'** (-lī') [L., a goad] **1.** an incentive **2.** any action or agent that causes an activity in an organism, organ, etc.

sting (stiŋ) *vt.* **stung, sting'ing** [OE. *stingan*] **1.** to prick or wound with a sting **2.** to cause sudden, smarting pain to **3.** to cause to suffer mentally **4.** to stimulate suddenly and sharply **5.** [Slang] to cheat —*vi.* to cause or feel sharp, smarting pain —*n.* **1.** a stinging **2.** a pain or wound resulting from stinging **3.** a sharp-pointed organ, as in insects and plants, that pricks, wounds, etc. —**sting'er** *n.*

stin·gy (stin'jē) *adj.* **-gi·er, -gi·est** [akin to STING] **1.** giving or spending grudgingly; miserly **2.** less than needed; scanty —**stin'gi·ly** *adv.* —**stin'gi·ness** *n.*

stink (stiŋk) *vi.* **stank** or **stunk, stunk, stink'ing** [OE. *stincan*] to give off a strong, unpleasant smell —*n.* a strong, unpleasant smell; stench —**stink'er** *n.*

stint (stint) *vt.* [< OE. *styntan,* to blunt] to restrict to a certain quantity, often small —*vi.* to

be sparing in giving or using —*n.* **1.** restriction; limit **2.** an assigned task

sti·pend (stī'pend) *n.* [< L. *stips,* small coin + *pendere,* to pay] a regular or fixed payment, as a salary or an allowance

stip·ple (stip''l) *vt.* **-pled, -pling** [< Du. *stippel,* a speckle] to paint, draw, or engrave in small dots —**stip'pling** *n.*

stip·u·late (stip'yə lāt') *vt.* **-lat'ed, -lat'ing** [< L. *stipulari,* to bargain] **1.** to arrange definitely, as in a contract **2.** to specify as an essential condition of an agreement —**stip'u·la'-tion** *n.*

stir (stur) *vt., vi.* **stirred, stir'ring** [OE. *styrian*] **1.** to move, esp. slightly **2.** to rouse from sleep, lethargy, etc. **3.** to make active or be active **4.** to mix (a liquid, etc.) by moving a spoon, etc. around **5.** to excite the feeling (of) **6.** to incite (often with *up*) —*n.* **1.** a stirring **2.** movement; activity **3.** commotion —**stir'rer** *n.*

stir'-fry' *vt.* **-fried', -fry'ing** to fry (diced or sliced vegetables, meat, etc.) quickly in a wok, with a little oil, stirring constantly

stir'ring *adj.* **1.** active; busy **2.** rousing; exciting *[stirring music]*

stir·rup (stur'əp, stir'-) *n.* [OE. *stigrap*] **1.** a flat-bottomed ring hung from a saddle and used as a footrest **2.** a stirrup-shaped bone in the middle ear

stitch (stich) *n.* [OE. *stice,* a puncture] **1.** a single complete in-and-out movement of a needle in sewing, knitting, etc. **2.** a loop, etc. made by stitching **3.** a particular kind of stitch or stitching **4.** a sudden, sharp pain **5.** a bit or piece —*vi., vt.* to make stitches (in); sew —**stitch'er** *n.*

stoat (stōt) *n.* [ME. *stote*] a large European weasel, esp. in its brown summer coat

stock (stäk) *n.* [OE. *stocc*] **1.** the trunk of a tree **2.** *a)* descent; ancestry *b)* a strain, race, etc. of animals or plants **3.** a supporting or main part of an implement, etc., as the part of a rifle holding the barrel **4.** [*pl.*] a wooden frame with holes for confining the ankles or wrists, formerly used for punishment **5.** raw material **6.** water in which meat, fish, etc. has been boiled, used in soups **7.** livestock **8.** a supply of goods on hand in a store, etc. **9.** shares of corporate capital, or the certificates showing such ownership **10.** *same as* STOCK COMPANY (sense 2) —*vt.* **1.** to furnish (a farm, shop, etc.) with stock **2.** to keep a supply of, as for sale or for future use —*vi.* to put in a stock, or supply (with *up*) —*adj.* **1.** kept in stock *[stock sizes]* **2.** common or trite *[a stock joke]* **3.** that deals with stock **4.** relating to a stock company —**in** (or **out of**) **stock** (not) available for sale or use —**take stock 1.** to inventory the stock on hand **2.** to make an appraisal, as of probabilities —**take** (or **put**) **stock in** [Colloq.] to have faith in

stock·ade (stä kād') *n.* [< Fr. < Pr. *estaca,* a stake] **1.** a defensive barrier of stakes driven into the ground side by side **2.** an enclosure, as a fort, made with such stakes

stock'bro'ker *n.* a broker who buys and sells stocks and bonds

stock car a standard automobile, modified in various ways for use in racing

stock company 1. a company whose capital is divided into shares **2.** a theatrical company that presents a repertoire of plays

stock exchange 1. a place where stocks and bonds are bought and sold **2.** an association of stockbrokers

stock'hold'er (-hōl'dər) *n.* one owning stock or shares in a given company

stock·ing (stäk'iŋ) *n.* [< obs. sense of STOCK] a closefitting covering, usually knitted, for the foot and leg

stock market *same as* STOCK EXCHANGE

stock'pile' (-pīl') *n.* a reserve supply of goods, raw material, etc. —*vt., vi.* -**piled'**, -**pil'ing** to accumulate a stockpile (of)

stock'-still' *adj.* perfectly motionless

stock'y *adj.* -**i·er**, -**i·est** heavily built; short and thickset —**stock'i·ness** *n.*

stock'yard' *n.* an enclosure for keeping cattle, hogs, etc. to be slaughtered

stodg·y (stäj'ē) *adj.* -**i·er**, -**i·est** [< dial. *stodge*, heavy food] dull; uninteresting

Sto·ic (stō'ik) *n.* [< Gr. *stoa*, colonnade: the Stoics met in a colonnade] 1. a member of an ancient Greek school of philosophy 2. [s-] a stoical person —*adj.* [s-] *same as* STOICAL — **Sto'i·cism, sto'i·cism** *n.*

sto·i·cal (stō'i k'l) *adj.* showing indifference to joy, grief, pain, etc.; impassive

stoke (stōk) *vt., vi.* **stoked, stok'ing** [< Du. *stoken*, to poke] 1. to stir up and feed fuel to (a fire) 2. to tend (a furnace, etc.)

stole' (stōl) *n.* [< Gr. *stolē*, garment] 1. a long strip of cloth worn like a scarf by some clergymen 2. a woman's long scarf of cloth or fur worn around the shoulders

stole² (stōl) *pt. of* STEAL

stol·en (stō'lən) *pp. of* STEAL

stol·id (stäl'id) *adj.* [L. *stolidus*, slow] having or showing little or no emotion; unexcitable — **sto·lid·i·ty** (stə lid'ə tē) *n.*

stom·ach (stum'ək) *n.* [ult. < Gr. *stoma*, mouth] 1. the saclike, digestive organ into which food passes from the esophagus 2. the abdomen; belly 3. appetite for food 4. desire or inclination —*vt.* 1. to be able to eat or digest 2. to tolerate; bear

stom'ach·ache' *n.* pain in the stomach or abdomen

stomp (stämp) *vt., vi. var. of* STAMP

stone (stōn) *n.* [OE. *stan*] 1. the hard, solid, nonmetallic mineral matter of rock 2. a piece of rock 3. the seed of certain fruits 4. a precious gem 5. *pl.* **stone** in Great Britain, 14 pounds avoirdupois 6. an abnormal stony mass formed in the kidney, gall bladder, etc. —*vt.* **stoned, ston'ing** 1. to throw stones at 2. to remove the stone from (a peach, etc.) —*adj.* of stone

stone- [< prec.] *a combining form meaning completely* [*stone*-blind]

Stone Age the early period in human culture when stone implements were used

stoned (stōnd) *adj.* [Slang] 1. drunk; intoxicated 2. under the influence of a drug

stone's throw a relatively short distance

stone'wall' *vi.* [Colloq.] to obstruct a debate, investigation, etc.

ston·y (stō'nē) *adj.* -**i·er**, -**i·est** 1. full of stones 2. of or like stone; specif., unfeeling; pitiless — **ston'i·ly** *adv.* —**ston'i·ness** *n.*

stood (stood) *pt. & pp. of* STAND

stooge (stōōj) *n.* [< ?] [Colloq.] 1. an actor who aids a comedian by being the victim of his jokes, pranks, etc. 2. anyone who acts as a foil, underling, etc.

stool (stōōl) *n.* [OE. *stol*] 1. a single seat having no back or arms 2. feces

stool pigeon [Colloq.] a spy or informer, esp. for the police

stoop' (stōōp) *vi.* [OE. *stupian*] 1. to bend the body forward 2. to carry the head and shoulders habitually bent forward 3. to demean oneself —*n.* the position of stooping

stoop² (stōōp) *n.* [Du. *stoep*] a small porch or platform at the door of a house

stoop labor work done by stooping, as in picking crops from low-growing plants

stop (stäp) *vt.* **stopped, stop'ping** [< L. *stuppa*, stop up] 1. to close by filling, shutting off, etc. 2. to cause to cease motion, activity, etc. 3. to block; intercept; prevent 4. to desist from; cease [*stop* talking] —*vi.* 1. to cease moving, etc.; halt 2. to leave off doing something 3. to cease operating 4. to become clogged 5. to tarry or stay —*n.* 1. a stopping or being stopped 2. a finish; end 3. a stay or sojourn 4. a place stopped at, as on a bus route 5. an obstruction, plug, etc. 6. a finger hole in a wind instrument, closed to produce a desired tone 7. a pull, lever, etc. for controlling a set of organ pipes —**stop off** to stop for a while en route to a place

stop'cock' *n.* a cock or valve to stop or regulate the flow of a liquid

stop'gap' *n.* a person or thing serving as a temporary substitute

stop'o'ver *n.* a brief stop or stay at a place in the course of a journey

stop'page (-ij) *n.* 1. a stopping or being stopped 2. an obstructed condition; block

stop'per *n.* something inserted to close an opening; plug —*vt.* to close with a stopper

stop'watch' *n.* a watch with a hand that can be started and stopped instantly, for timing races, etc.

stor·age (stôr'ij) *n.* 1. a storing or being stored 2. a place or space for storing goods 3. the cost of storing goods

storage battery a battery of cells for generating electric current: the cells can be recharged

store (stôr) *vt.* **stored, stor'ing** [< L. *instaurare*, restore] 1. to put aside for use when needed 2. to furnish with a supply 3. to put in a warehouse, etc. for safekeeping —*n.* 1. a supply (*of* something) for use when needed; reserve 2. [*pl.*] supplies, esp. of food, clothing, etc. 3. a retail establishment where goods are offered for sale 4. a storehouse —**in store** set aside for the future; in reserve —**set** (or **put** or **lay**) **store by** to value

store'front' *n.* a front room on the ground floor of a building, designed for use as a retail store

store'house' *n.* a place where things are stored; esp., a warehouse

store'keep'er *n.* 1. a person in charge of stores, or supplies 2. a retail merchant

store'room' *n.* a room where things are stored

stork (stôrk) *n.* [OE. *storc*] a large, long-legged wading bird, having a long neck and bill

storm (stôrm) *n.* [OE.] 1. a strong wind, with rain, snow, thunder, etc. 2. any heavy fall of rain, snow, etc. 3. a strong emotional outburst 4. any strong disturbance 5. a sudden, strong attack on a fortified place —*vi.* 1. to blow violently; rain, snow, etc. 2. to rage 3. to rush violently [to *storm* into a room] —*vt.* to attack vigorously

storm door (or **window**) a door (or window) placed outside the regular one as added protection

storm'y *adj.* -**i·er**, -**i·est** 1. of or characterized by storms 2. violent, raging, etc.

sto·ry' (stôr'ē) *n., pl.* -**ries** [< Gr. *historia*, narrative] 1. the telling of an event or series of events; account; narration 2. a joke 3. a fictitious narrative shorter than a novel 4. the plot of a novel, play, etc. 5. [Colloq.] a falsehood 6. *Journalism* a news report

sto·ry² (stôr'ē) *n., pl.* -**ries** [< prec.] a horizontal division of a building, from a floor to the ceiling above it

sto′ry·book′ *n.* a book of stories, esp. one for children

sto′ry·tell′er *n.* one who narrates stories —**sto′ry·tell′ing** *n.*

stoup (stoōp) *n.* [ON. *staup*, cup] a basin for holy water in a church

stout (stout) *adj.* [< OFr. *estout*, bold] 1. courageous; brave 2. strong; sturdy; firm 3. powerful; forceful 4. fat; thickset —*n.* heavy, dark-brown beer —**stout′ly** *adv.*

stout′heart′ed *adj.* courageous; brave

stove[1] (stōv) *n.* [MDu., heated room] an apparatus for heating, cooking, etc.

stove[2] (stōv) *alt. pt. & pp. of* STAVE

stow (stō) *vt.* [OE. *stow*, a place] to pack in an orderly way —**stow away** 1. to put or hide away 2. to be a stowaway

stow′a·way′ *n.* one who hides aboard a ship, airplane, etc. to get free passage, etc.

strad·dle (strad′'l) *vt., vi.* -**dled, -dling** [< STRIDE] 1. to sit or stand astride of, or stand with the legs wide apart 2. to appear to take both sides of (an issue) —*n.* a straddling —**strad′dler** *n.*

strafe (sträf) *vt.* **strafed, straf′ing** [< G. *Gott strafe England* (God punish England)] to attack with machine-gun fire from low-flying aircraft

strag·gle (strag′'l) *vi.* -**gled, -gling** [prob. < ME. *straken*, to roam] 1. to wander from the main group 2. to be scattered over a wide area 3. to hang in an unkempt way, as hair —**strag′gler** *n.* —**strag′gly** *adj.*

straight (strāt) *adj.* [< ME. *strecchen*, to stretch] 1. having the same direction throughout its length; not crooked, bent, etc. 2. direct; undeviating 3. in order; properly arranged, etc. 4. honest; sincere 5. unmixed; undiluted [*straight* whiskey] 6. [Slang] normal or conventional —*adv.* 1. in a straight line 2. upright; erectly 3. without detour, delay, etc. —*n. Poker* a hand of five cards in sequence —**straight away** (or **off**) without delay

straight′en *vt., vi.* to make or become straight —**straighten out** 1. to make or become less confused, easier to deal with, etc. 2. to reform —**straight′en·er** *n.*

straight face a facial expression showing no amusement or other emotion —**straight′-faced′** *adj.*

straight′for′ward *adj.* 1. moving or leading straight ahead; direct 2. honest; frank —*adv.* in a straightforward manner

straight′way′ *adv.* at once

strain[1] (strān) *vt.* [< L. *stringere*] 1. to draw or stretch tight 2. to exert, use, etc. to the utmost 3. to injure by overexertion [to *strain* a muscle] 4. to stretch beyond the normal limits 5. to pass through a screen, sieve, etc.; filter —*vi.* 1. to strive hard 2. to filter, ooze, etc. —*n.* 1. a straining or being strained 2. great effort, exertion, etc. 3. a bodily injury from overexertion 4. stress or force 5. a great demand on one's resources, etc.

strain[2] (strān) *n.* [< OE. *strynan*, to produce] 1. ancestry; lineage 2. race; stock; line 3. a group of individuals different from others in its species 4. an inherited tendency 5. a trace; streak 6. [*often pl.*] a musical tune

strain′er *n.* a device for straining, sifting, or filtering; sieve, filter, etc.

strait (strāt) *adj.* [< L. *stringere*, draw tight] [Archaic] narrow or strict —*n.* [*often pl.*] 1. a narrow waterway connecting two large bodies of water 2. difficulty

strait′en *vt.* 1. esp. formerly, to make strait or narrow 2. to bring into difficulties: esp. in **in straitened circumstances,** lacking sufficient money

strait′jack′et *n.* a coatlike device used to restrain a person

strait′-laced′ (-lāst′) *adj.* narrowly strict in behavior or moral views

strand[1] (strand) *n.* [OE.] shore, esp. ocean shore —*vt., vi.* 1. to run or drive aground, as a ship 2. to put or be put into a helpless position [*stranded* in a desert]

strand[2] (strand) *n.* [< ?] 1. any of the threads, fibers, wires, etc. that are twisted together to form a string, rope, or cable 2. a ropelike length of anything [a *strand* of pearls]

strange (strānj) *adj.* **strang′er, strang′est** [< L. *extraneus*, foreign] 1. not previously known, seen, etc.; unfamiliar 2. unusual; extraordinary 3. peculiar; odd 4. reserved; distant 5. unaccustomed (*to*)

stran·ger (strān′jər) *n.* 1. a newcomer 2. a person not known to one

stran·gle (straŋ′g'l) *vt., vi.* -**gled, -gling** [< Gr. *strangos*, twisted] 1. to choke to death 2. to suppress; stifle

stran′gle·hold′ *n.* 1. an illegal wrestling hold choking an opponent 2. any force that restricts or suppresses freedom

stran·gu·late (straŋ′gyə lāt′) *vt.* -**lat′ed, -lat′ing** *Med.* to block (a tube) by constricting —**stran′gu·la′tion** *n.*

strap (strap) *n.* [dial. form of STROP] a narrow strip of leather, etc. for tying or holding things —*vt.* **strapped, strap′ping** to fasten with a strap —**strap′less** *adj.*

strapped (strapt) *adj.* [Colloq.] without money

strap·ping (strap′iŋ) *adj.* [Colloq.] tall and sturdy

stra·ta (strāt′ə, strat′ə) *n. alt. pl. of* STRATUM

strat·a·gem (strat′ə jəm) *n.* [< Gr. *stratos*, army + *agein*, to lead] 1. a trick, plan, etc. for deceiving an enemy in war 2. any tricky ruse

stra·te·gic (strə tē′jik) *adj.* 1. of strategy 2. sound in strategy 3. essential to effective military strategy Also **stra·te′gi·cal** —**stra·te′gi·cal·ly** *adv.*

strat·e·gy (strat′ə jē) *n., pl.* -**gies** 1. the science of planning and directing military operations 2. a plan or action based on this 3. skill in managing or planning, esp. by using stratagems —**strat′e·gist** *n.*

strat·i·fy (strat′ə fī′) *vt., vi.* -**fied′, -fy′ing** to form or arrange in layers or strata —**strat′i·fi·ca′tion** *n.*

strat·o·sphere (strat′ə sfir′) *n.* [< Fr. < ModL. *stratum*, layer + Fr. *sphère*, sphere] the atmospheric zone lying between c.6 and c.30 miles above the earth's surface

stra·tum (strāt′əm, strat′-) *n., pl.* -**ta** (-ə), -**tums** [< L. *stratus*, a spreading] 1. a horizontal layer of material; specif., *Geol.* a single layer of sedimentary rock 2. a level of society

stra′tus (-əs) *n., pl.* -**ti** (-ī) [see prec.] a long, low, gray cloud layer

straw (strô) *n.* [OE. *streaw*] 1. hollow stalks of grain after threshing 2. a single one of these 3. a tube used for sucking beverages 4. a trifle —*adj.* 1. straw-colored; yellowish 2. made of straw 3. worthless

straw′ber′ry (-ber′ē, -bər ē) *n., pl.* -**ries** [prob. from the strawlike particles on the fruit] 1. the small, red, fleshy fruit of a vinelike plant related to the rose 2. this plant

straw boss [Colloq.] an overseer of work with little or no authority

straw vote an unofficial vote for sampling popular opinion on an issue, etc.

stray (strā) *vi.* [prob. < L. *extra vagari,* wander outside] **1.** to wander from a given place, course, etc. **2.** to deviate (*from* what is right) — *n.* one that strays; esp., a lost domestic animal —*adj.* **1.** having strayed; lost **2.** isolated [a few *stray* words]

streak (strēk) *n.* [OE. *strica*] **1.** a long, thin mark; stripe **2.** a thin layer, as of fat in meat or ore in rock **3.** a tendency in one's nature [a jealous *streak*] **4.** a period, as of luck —*vt.* to mark with streaks —*vi.* **1.** to become streaked **2.** to move swiftly —**streak′y** *adj.*

stream (strēm) *n.* [OE.] **1.** a current of water; specif., a small river **2.** a steady flow, as of air, light, etc. **3.** a continuous series [a *stream* of cars] —*vi.* **1.** to flow as in a stream **2.** to flow (*with*) [eyes *streaming* with tears] **3.** to move swiftly

stream′er *n.* **1.** a long, narrow flag **2.** any long, narrow flowing strip

stream′line *vt.* -**lined′,** -**lin′ing** to make streamlined —*adj.* same as STREAMLINED

stream′lined *adj.* **1.** having a contour designed to offer the least resistance in moving through air, water, etc. **2.** efficient, simplified, trim, etc.

street (strēt) *n.* [< L. *strata* (*via*), paved (road)] **1.** a public road in a city or town, esp. a paved one **2.** such a road apart from its sidewalks **3.** the people living, working, etc. along a given street

street′car′ *n.* a car on rails that provides public transportation on city streets

street′walk′er *n.* a prostitute

strength (strenkth) *n.* [OE. *strengthu*] **1.** the state or quality of being strong; force **2.** toughness; durability **3.** the power to resist attack **4.** potency, as of drugs **5.** intensity, as of sound **6.** force of an army, etc. as measured in numbers —**on the strength of** based or relying on

strength′en *vt., vi.* to make or become stronger —**strength′en·er** *n.*

stren·u·ous (stren′yoo wəs) *adj.* [L. *strenuus*] requiring or characterized by great effort or energy —**stren′u·ous·ly** *adv.*

strep (strep) *n.* short for STREPTOCOCCUS

strep·to·coc·cus (strep′tə käk′əs) *n., pl.* -**coc′ci** (-käk′sī) [< Gr. *streptos,* twisted + *kokkos,* kernel] any of a group of spherical bacteria that occur generally in chains: some cause serious diseases

strep′to·my′cin *n.* [< Gr. *streptos,* twisted + *mykēs,* fungus] an antibiotic drug obtained from molds: used in treating various bacterial diseases

stress (stres) *n.* [< L. *strictus,* strict] **1.** strain; specif., force that strains or deforms **2.** emphasis; importance **3.** *a*) mental or physical tension *b*) urgency, pressure, etc. causing this **4.** the relative force of utterance given a syllable or word; accent —*vt.* **1.** to put stress or pressure on **2.** to accent **3.** to emphasize

stretch (strech) *vt.* [OE. *streccan*] **1.** to reach out; extend **2.** to pull or spread out to full extent or to a greater size **3.** to cause to extend too far; strain **4.** to strain in interpretation, scope, etc. —*vi.* **1.** *a*) to spread out to full extent or beyond normal limits *b*) to extend over a given distance or time **2.** *a*) to extend the body or limbs to full length *b*) to lie down (usually with *out*) **3.** to become stretched —*n.* **1.** a stretching or being stretched **2.** an unbroken period [a ten-year *stretch*] **3.** an unbroken length, tract, etc. [a *stretch* of beach] **4.** short

for HOMESTRETCH —*adj.* made of elasticized fabric —**stretch′a·ble** *adj.*

stretch′er *n.* **1.** one that stretches **2.** a light frame covered with canvas, etc. for carrying the sick or injured

strew (strōō) *vt.* **strewed, strewed** or **strewn, strew′ing** [OE. *streawian*] **1.** to scatter; spread here and there **2.** to cover as by scattering

stri′at·ed *adj.* [< L. *striare,* to groove] marked with thin, parallel lines

strick·en (strik′'n) *alt. pp. of* STRIKE —*adj.* **1.** struck or wounded **2.** suffering, as from pain, etc.

strict (strikt) *adj.* [< L. *stringere,* draw tight] **1.** exact; precise **2.** perfect; absolute **3.** *a*) enforcing rules carefully *b*) closely enforced —**strict′ly** *adv.* —**strict′ness** *n.*

stric·ture (strik′chər) *n.* [see prec.] **1.** strong criticism; censure **2.** an abnormal narrowing of a duct or passage in the body

stride (strīd) *vi., vt.* **strode, strid·den** (strid′'n), **strid′ing** [OE. *stridan*] **1.** to walk with long steps **2.** to cross with a single, long step **3.** to straddle —*n.* **1.** a long step **2.** the distance covered by a stride **3.** [usually *pl.*] progress; advancement

stri·dent (strīd′'nt) *adj.* [< L. *stridere,* to rasp] harsh-sounding; shrill; grating

strife (strīf) *n.* [< OFr. *estrif*] **1.** contention **2.** a fight or quarrel; struggle

strike (strīk) *vt.* **struck, struck** or **strick′en, strik′ing** [OE. *strican,* to go] **1.** to give (a blow, etc.) to **2.** to make by stamping, etc. [to *strike* coins] **3.** to announce (time), as with a bell: said of clocks, etc. **4.** to ignite (a match) or produce (a light, etc.) by friction **5.** to crash into [the stone *struck* his arm] **6.** to attack **7.** to come upon; find, notice, etc. **8.** to afflict, as with disease, pain, etc. **9.** to affect as if by a blow, etc.; specif., to occur to [*struck* by an idea] **10.** to remove (*from* a list, record, etc.) **11.** to make (a bargain, truce, etc.) **12.** to lower (a sail, flag, etc.) **13.** to assume (a pose, etc.) — *vi.* **1.** to hit (*at*) **2.** to attack **3.** to make sounds as by being struck: said of a bell, clock, etc. **4.** to collide; hit (*against, on,* or *upon*) **5.** to seize a bait: said of a fish **6.** to come suddenly (*on* or *upon*) **7.** to refuse to continue to work until demands are met **8.** to proceed in a new direction —*n.* **1.** a striking; blow **2.** a refusal by employees to go on working, in an attempt to gain better working conditions **3.** a finding of a rich deposit of oil, coal, etc. **4.** *Baseball* a pitched ball which is struck at but missed, delivered through the strike zone but not struck at, etc. **5.** *Bowling* a knocking down of all the pins on the first bowl —**strike out 1.** to erase **2.** to start out **3.** *Baseball* to put out, or be put out, on three strikes —**strike up** to begin —**strik′er** *n.*

strik′ing *adj.* impressive, outstanding, etc.

string (strin) *n.* [OE. *streng*] **1.** a thin line of fiber, wire, etc. used for tying, pulling, etc. **2.** a length of things on a string [a *string* of pearls] **3.** a line, row, or series of things [a *string* of houses] **4.** *a*) a slender cord stretched on a violin, guitar, etc. and bowed, plucked, or struck to make a musical sound *b*) [*pl.*] all the stringed instruments of an orchestra **5.** a fiber of a plant **6.** [Colloq.] a condition attached to a plan, offer, etc.: *usually used in pl.* —*vt.* **strung, string′ing 1.** to provide with strings **2.** to thread on a string **3.** to tie, hang, etc. with a string **4.** to remove the strings from (beans, etc.) **5.** to arrange in a row **6.** to extend [*string* a cable] —**pull strings** to use influence, often secretly, to gain advantage —**string′y** *adj.* **-i·er, -i·est**

string bean *same as* SNAP BEAN

stringed (strind) *adj.* having strings

strin·gent (strin′jənt) *adj.* [see STRICT] strict; severe —**strin′gen·cy** *n.*

strip¹ (strip) *vt.* **stripped, strip′ping** [< OE. *strypan*] **1.** to remove (the clothing, etc.) from (a person) **2.** to dispossess of (honors, titles, etc.) **3.** to plunder; rob **4.** to take off (a covering) from (something) **5.** to make bare by taking away removable parts **6.** to break the thread of (a bolt, etc.) or the teeth of (a gear) —*vi.* to take off all clothing —**strip′per** *n.*

strip² (strip) *n.* [< STRIPE] **1.** a long, narrow piece, as of land **2.** a runway for airplanes

stripe (strip) *n.* [< MDu.] **1.** a long, narrow band or mark differing as in color from the area around it **2.** a strip of cloth on a uniform to show rank, years served, etc. **3.** kind; sort —*vt.* **striped, strip′ing** to mark with stripes

strip·ling (strip′lin) *n.* a youth

strip·tease (strip′tēz′) *n.* an act in which a woman takes off her clothes slowly, usually to music —**strip′teas′er** *n.*

strive (strīv) *vi.* **strove, striv·en** (striv′'n) or **strived, striv′ing** [< OFr. *estrif*, effort] **1.** to make great efforts; try very hard **2.** to struggle [to *strive* against tyranny]

strobe (light) (strōb) [< Gr. *strobos*, a twisting around] an electronic tube emitting rapid, brief, and brilliant flashes of light: used in photography, the theater, etc.

strode (strōd) *pt. of* STRIDE

stroke (strōk) *n.* [ME.] **1.** the act of striking; blow of an ax, whip, etc. **2.** a sudden action resulting as if from a blow [a *stroke* of luck] **3.** a sudden attack, esp. of apoplexy **4.** a single, strong effort **5.** the sound of striking, as of a clock **6.** *a)* a single movement, as with some tool, pen, etc. *b)* any of a series of motions made against water, air, etc. **7.** a mark made by a pen, etc. —*vt.* **stroked, strok′ing** to draw one's hand, etc. gently over the surface of

stroll (strōl) *vi.* [prob. < G. dial. *strolen*] **1.** to walk in an idle, leisurely manner; saunter **2.** to wander —*vt.* to stroll along or through —*n.* a leisurely walk

stroll′er *n.* **1.** one who strolls **2.** a light, chair-like baby carriage

strong (strôn) *adj.* [OE. *strang*] **1.** *a)* physically powerful *b)* healthy; sound **2.** morally or intellectually powerful [a *strong* will] **3.** firm; durable **4.** powerful in wealth, numbers, etc. **5.** of a specified number [a force 6,000 *strong*] **6.** having a powerful effect **7.** intense in degree or quality [*strong* coffee, *strong* light, etc.] **8.** forceful, vigorous, etc.

strong′-arm′ *adj.* [Colloq.] using physical force —*vt.* [Colloq.] to use force upon

strong′box′ *n.* a heavily made box or safe for storing valuables

strong′hold′ *n.* a place having strong defenses

strong′-mind′ed *adj.* determined; unyielding: also **strong′-willed′**

stron·ti·um (strän′shē əm, -tē-) *n.* [< *Strontian*, Scotland, where first found] a pale-yellow metallic chemical element resembling calcium in properties: symbol, Sr

strop (sträp) *n.* [OE.] a thick leather strap for sharpening razors —*vt.* **stropped, strop′ping** to sharpen on a strop

strove (strōv) *alt. pt. of* STRIVE

struck (struk) *pt. & pp. of* STRIKE —*adj.* closed or affected by a labor strike

struc·ture (struk′chər) *n.* [< L. *struere*, arrange] **1.** something built or constructed, as

a building **2.** the arrangement of all the parts of a whole **3.** something composed of parts —*vt.* **-tured, -tur·ing** to put together systematically —**struc′tur·al** *adj.*

stru·del (strōō′d'l) *n.* [G.] a pastry made of a thin sheet of dough filled with apples, etc. and rolled

strug·gle (strug′'l) *vi.* **-gled, -gling** [ME. *strogelen*] **1.** to fight violently with an opponent **2.** to make great efforts; strive —*n.* **1.** a great effort **2.** conflict

strum (strum) *vt., vi.* **strummed, strum′ming** [echoic] to play (a guitar, etc.) unskillfully or idly —*n.* a strumming

strum·pet (strum′pit) *n.* [ME.] a prostitute

strung (strun) *pt. & alt. pp. of* STRING —**strung out** [Slang] suffering from the effects of narcotics addiction

strut (strut) *vi.* **strut′ted, strut′ting** [< OE. *strutian*, stand rigid] to walk swaggeringly —*n.* **1.** a strutting walk **2.** a brace fitted into a framework to resist pressure

strych·nine (strik′nin, -nīn, -nēn) *n.* [Fr. < Gr. *strychnos*, nightshade] a highly poisonous crystalline alkaloid: used in small doses as a stimulant

stub (stub) *n.* [OE. *stybb*] **1.** a tree stump **2.** a short piece left over **3.** any short projection **4.** a short piece of a ticket, bank check, etc. kept as a record —*vt.* **stubbed, stub′bing** to strike (one's toe, etc.) against something

stub·ble (stub′'l) *n.* [< L. *stipula*, a stalk] **1.** short stumps of grain left standing after harvesting **2.** any growth like this

stub·born (stub′ərn) *adj.* [? < OE. *stybb*, a stub] **1.** refusing to yield or comply; obstinate **2.** done in an obstinate or persistent way **3.** hard to handle, etc.

stub·by (stub′ē) *adj.* **-bi·er, -bi·est 1.** covered with stubs or stubble **2.** short and dense **3.** short and thickset —**stub′bi·ness** *n.*

stuc·co (stuk′ō) *n., pl.* **-coes, -cos** [It.] plaster or cement for surfacing walls, etc. —*vt.* **-coed, -co·ing** to cover with stucco

stuck (stuk) *pt. & pp. of* STICK

stuck′-up′ *adj.* [Colloq.] snobbish

stud¹ (stud) *n.* [OE. *studu*, a post] **1.** any of a series of small knobs used to ornament a surface **2.** a small buttonlike device for fastening shirt collars, etc. **3.** an upright piece in a building frame to which laths, etc. are nailed —*vt.* **stud′ded, stud′ding 1.** to set or decorate with studs, etc. **2.** to set thickly on [rocks *stud* the hillside]

stud² (stud) *n.* [OE. *stod*] **1.** *same as* STUD-HORSE **2.** any male animal used for breeding

stu·dent (stōōd′'nt) *n.* [< L. *studere*, to study] **1.** one who studies something **2.** one who is enrolled for study in a school, etc.

stud′horse′ *n.* a stallion kept for breeding

stud·ied (stud′ēd) *adj.* **1.** prepared by careful study **2.** deliberate

stu·di·o (stōō′dē ō′) *n., pl.* **-os′** [It., a study] **1.** a place where an artist, etc. works or where dancing lessons, etc. are given **2.** a place where movies, radio or TV programs, etc. are produced

studio couch a couch that can be opened into a full-sized bed

stu·di·ous (stōō′dē əs) *adj.* **1.** fond of study **2.** attentive; zealous

stud·y (stud′ē) *n., pl.* **-ies** [< L. *studere*, to study] **1.** the seeking of knowledge, as by reading, etc. **2.** careful examination of a subject, event, etc. **3.** a branch of learning **4.** [*pl.*] education; schooling **5.** earnest effort or deep thought **6.** a room for study, etc. —*vt.* **-ied,**

-y·ing 1. to try to learn by reading, etc. **2.** to investigate carefully **3.** to read (a book, etc.) intently **—vi. 1.** to study something **2.** to be a student **3.** to meditate

stuff (stuf) **n.** [< OFr. *estoffe*] **1.** the material out of which anything is made **2.** essence; character **3.** matter in general **4.** cloth, esp. woolen cloth **5.** objects; things **6.** worthless objects; junk **7.** [Colloq.] superior ability, skill, etc. **—vt. 1.** to fill or pack; specif., *a)* to fill the skin of (a dead animal) in taxidermy *b)* to fill (a fowl, etc.) with seasoning, bread crumbs, etc. before roasting **2.** to fill too full **3.** to plug; block **—vi.** to eat too much

stuffed shirt [Slang] a pompous, pretentious person

stuff′ing n. something used to stuff, as padding in upholstery, a seasoned mixture for stuffing fowl, etc.

stuff′y adj. -i·er, -i·est 1. poorly ventilated; close **2.** having the nasal passages stopped up, as from a cold **3.** dull; stodgy **4.** pompous **— stuff′i·ness n.**

stul·ti·fy (stul′tə fī′) **vt. -fied′, -fy′ing** [< L. *stultus,* foolish + *facere,* make] **1.** to cause to appear foolish, stupid, etc. **2.** to make worthless, etc. **—stul′ti·fi·ca′tion n.**

stum·ble (stum′b′l) **vi. -bled, -bling** [< Scand.] **1.** to trip in walking, running, etc. **2.** to walk unsteadily **3.** to do in a blundering way **4.** to do wrong **5.** to come by chance **—n.** a stumbling

stumbling block a difficulty

stump (stump) **n.** [prob. < MLowG. *stump*] **1.** the lower end of a tree or plant left in the ground after removal of the upper part **2.** the part of a leg, tooth, etc. left after the rest has been removed **3.** the place where a political speech is made **—vt. 1.** to travel over (a district) making political speeches **2.** [Colloq.] to puzzle; baffle **—vi. 1.** to walk heavily **2.** to travel about making political speeches

stun (stun) **vt. stunned, stun′ning** [< L. *ex-,* intens. + *tonare,* to crash] **1.** to make unconscious, as by a blow **2.** to shock

stung (stuŋ) *pt. & pp. of* STING

stunk (stuŋk) *pp. & alt. pt. of* STINK

stun·ning (stun′iŋ) **adj.** [Colloq.] remarkably attractive, excellent, etc.

stunt¹ (stunt) **vt.** [OE., stupid] **1.** to check the growth or development of **2.** to hinder (growth, etc.)

stunt² (stunt) **n.** [< ?] something done to show one's skill or daring, attract attention, etc. **—vi.** to perform a stunt

stu·pe·fy (stoo′pə fī′) **vt. -fied′, -fy′ing** [< L. *stupere,* be stunned + *facere,* to make] **1.** to make lethargic; stun **2.** to amaze; bewilder **— stu′pe·fac′tion n.**

stu·pen·dous (stoo pen′dəs) **adj.** [< L. *stupere,* be stunned] astonishingly great

stu·pid (stoo′pid) **adj.** [see prec.] **1.** lacking normal intelligence **2.** foolish; silly **3.** dull; tiresome **—stu·pid′i·ty,** *pl.* **-ties, stu′pid·ness n. — stu′pid·ly adv.**

stu·por (stoo′pər) **n.** [L.] a state in which the mind and senses are dulled

stur·dy (stur′dē) **adj. -di·er, -di·est** [< OFr. *estourdi,* stunned] **1.** firm; resolute **2.** strong; hardy **—stur′di·ness n.**

stur·geon (stur′jən) **n.** [< OFr. *esturjon*] a large food fish: a source of caviar

stut·ter (stut′ər) **n., vt., vi.** [< ME. *stutten*] *same as* STAMMER **—stut′ter·er n.**

sty¹ (stī) **n.,** *pl.* **sties** [< OE. *sti,* hall] **1.** a pen for pigs **2.** any foul place

sty², **stye** (stī) **n.,** *pl.* **sties** [ult. < OE. *stigan,* to rise] a small, inflamed swelling on the rim of the eyelid

style (stīl) **n.** [< L. *stilus,* pointed writing tool] **1.** a stylus **2.** *a)* manner of expression in language *b)* characteristic manner of expression, design, etc. in any art, period, etc. **3.** excellence of expression **4.** *a)* fashion *b)* something stylish **—vt. styled, styl′ing 1.** to name; call **2.** to design the style of

styl′ish adj. conforming to current style in dress, decoration, etc.; fashionable

styl′ist n. a writer, etc. whose work has style and distinction **—sty·lis′tic adj.**

styl′ize (-īz) **vt. -ized, -iz·ing** to make conform to a given style; make conventional **—styl′i·za′tion n.**

sty·lus (stī′ləs) **n.,** *pl.* **-lus·es, -li** (-lī) [< L. *stilus,* pointed tool] **1.** a sharp, pointed marking device **2.** *a)* a pointed device for cutting the grooves of a phonograph record *b)* a phonograph needle

sty·mie (stī′mē) **n.** [prob. < Scot., person partially blind] *Golf* a situation in which a ball to be putted is blocked by another ball **—vt. -mied, -mie·ing** to block; impede Also **sty′my -mied, -my·ing**

styp·tic (stip′tik) **adj.** [< Gr. *styphein,* to contract] that halts bleeding; astringent

Sty·ro·foam (stī′rə fōm′) *a trademark for* a rigid, foamy-looking, lightweight plastic

Styx (stiks) *Gr. Myth.* the river crossed by dead souls entering Hades

suave (swäv) **adj.** [< L. *suavis,* sweet] smoothly gracious or polite; polished **—suave′ly adv. —suav′i·ty, suave′ness n.**

sub (sub) **n.** *short for:* **1.** SUBMARINE **2.** SUBSTITUTE **—vi. subbed, sub′bing** [Colloq.] to be a substitute (*for* someone)

sub- [< L. *sub,* under] *a prefix meaning:* **1.** beneath [*subsoil*] **2.** lower than [*subaltern*] **3.** to a lesser degree than [*subtropical*]

sub. 1. substitute(s) **2.** suburb(an)

sub·al·tern (sab ôl′tərn) **n.** [< L. *sub-,* under + *alternus,* alternate] a subordinate

sub′branch′ n. a branch division

sub′com′pact n. a model of automobile smaller than a compact

sub·con′scious adj. occurring with little or no conscious perception on the part of the individual: said of mental processes **—the subconscious** subconscious mental activity

sub·con′ti·nent n. a large land mass smaller than a continent

sub·con′tract n. a secondary contract undertaking some or all obligations of another contract **—vt., vi.** to make a subcontract (for) **— sub·con′trac·tor n.**

sub′cul′ture n. 1. a distinctive social group within a larger group **2.** its distinct cultural patterns

sub·cu·ta·ne·ous (sub′kyoo tā′nē əs) **adj.** beneath the skin

sub·dea′con n. a cleric ranking just below a deacon

sub′di·vide′ vt., vi. -vid′ed, -vid′ing 1. to divide further **2.** to divide (land) into small parcels **— sub′di·vi′sion n.**

sub·due (sab doo′) **vt. -dued′, -du′ing** [< L. *subducere,* to remove] **1.** to conquer **2.** to overcome; control **3.** to make less intense; diminish; soften

subj. 1. subject **2.** subjunctive

sub·ject (sub′jikt) **adj.** [< L. *sub-,* under + *jacere,* to throw] **1.** under the authority or control of another **2.** having a tendency [*subject* to anger] **3.** exposed [*subject* to censure] **4.** contingent upon [*subject* to approval**7** —*n.* **1.** a person under the authority or control of another **2.** one undergoing a treatment, experiment, etc. **3.** something dealt with in discussion, study, etc.; theme **4.** *Gram.* the word or words in a sentence about which something is said —*vt.* (səb jekt′) **1.** to bring under the authority or control of **2.** to cause to undergo something —**sub·jec′tion** *n.*

sub·jec·tive (səb jek′tiv) *adj.* of or resulting from the feelings of the person thinking; not objective; personal —**sub·jec·tiv·i·ty** (sub′jek tiv′ə tē) *n.*

sub·join (səb join′) *vt.* [see SUB- & JOIN] to add (something) at the end; append

sub·ju·gate (sub′jə gāt′) *vt.* -gat′ed, -gat′ing [< L. *sub-*, under + *jugum,* a yoke] to conquer or make subservient —**sub′ju·ga′tion** *n.* —**sub′-ju·ga′tor** *n.*

sub·junc·tive (səb juŋk′tiv) *adj.* [< L. *subjungere,* subjoin] designating or of that mood of a verb used to express supposition, desire, possibility, etc., rather than to state a fact

sub·lease (sub′lēs′) *n.* a lease granted by a lessee —*vt.* (sub lēs′) -leased′, -leas′ing to grant or hold a sublease of

sub·let (sub let′, sub′let′) *vt.* -let′, -let′ting **1.** to let to another (property which one is renting) **2.** to let out (work) to a subcontractor

sub·li·mate (sub′lə māt′) *vt., vi.* -mat′ed, -mat′ing **1.** to sublime (a substance) **2.** to express (unacceptable impulses) in ways that are acceptable —**sub′li·ma′tion** *n.*

sub·lime (sə blīm′) *adj.* [< L. *sub-*, up to + *limen,* lintel] **1.** noble; exalted **2.** inspiring awe or admiration —*vt.* -limed′, -lim′ing to purify (a solid) by heating to a gaseous state and condensing the vapor back into solid form —**the sublime** something sublime —**sub·lim′i·ty** (-blim′ə tē) *n.*

sub·lim·i·nal (sub lim′ə n′l) *adj.* [see prec.] below the threshold of consciousness

sub·ma·chine gun (sub′mə shēn′) a portable, automatic firearm

sub·mar·gi·nal (sub mär′ji n′l) *adj.* below minimum standards

sub·ma·rine (sub′mə rēn′) *adj.* being, living, etc. underwater —*n.* (sub′mə rēn′) a warship that can operate under water

sub·merge (səb murj′) *vt., vi.* -merged′, -merg′ing [< L. *sub-*, under + *mergere,* to plunge] to place or sink beneath the surface, as of water —**sub·mer′gence** *n.*

sub·merse′ (-murs′) *vt.* -mersed′, -mers′ing *same as* SUBMERGE —**sub·mer′sion** *n.*

sub·mis·sion (səb mish′ən) *n.* **1.** a submitting or surrendering **2.** resignation; obedience — **sub·mis′sive** *adj.*

sub·mit′ (-mit′) *vt.* -mit′ted, -mit′ting [< L. *sub-*, under + *mittere,* to send] **1.** to present to others for consideration, etc. **2.** to yield to the control of another **3.** to offer as an opinion —*vi.* to yield

sub·nor·mal (sub nôr′m′l) *adj.* below the normal, esp. in intelligence

sub·or·di·nate (sə bôr′də nit) *adj.* [< L. *sub-*, under + *ordinare,* to order] **1.** below another in rank, importance, etc. **2.** under the authority of another **3.** *Gram.* functioning as a noun, adjective, or adverb within a sentence —*n.* a subordinate person or thing —*vt.* (-nāt′) -nat′ed, -nat′ing to place in a subordinate position —**sub·or′di·na′tion** *n.*

subordinate clause a clause that cannot function syntactically as a complete sentence by itself

sub·orn (sə bôrn′) *vt.* [< L. *sub-*, under + *or-*

nare, furnish] to induce (another) to commit perjury

sub·poe·na (sə pē′nə) *n.* [< L. *sub poena,* under penalty] a written legal order directing a person to appear in court to testify, etc. —*vt.* -naed, -na·ing to summon with such an order Also sp. **sub·pe′na**

sub ro·sa (sub rō′zə) [L., under the rose] secretly

sub·scribe (səb skrīb′) *vt., vi.* -scribed′, -scrib′-ing [< L. *sub-*, under + *scribere,* write] **1.** to sign (one's name) on a document, etc. **2.** to give support or consent (*to*) **3.** to promise to contribute (money) **4.** to agree to receive and pay for a periodical, etc. (with *to*) —**sub·scrib′er** *n.*

sub·scrip·tion (səb skrip′shən) *n.* **1.** a subscribing **2.** money subscribed **3.** a formal agreement to receive and pay for a periodical, theater tickets, etc.

sub·se·quent (sub′si kwənt, -kwent′) *adj.* [< L. *sub-*, after + *sequi,* follow] coming after; following —**subsequent to** after

sub·ser·vi·ent (səb sur′vē ənt) *adj.* **1.** that is of service, esp. in a subordinate capacity **2.** submissive; servile —**sub·ser′vi·ence** *n.*

sub·side (səb sīd′) *vi.* -sid′ed, -sid′ing [< L. *sub-*, under + *sidere,* settle] **1.** to sink to a lower level or to the bottom **2.** to become less active, intense, etc.

sub·sid·i·ar·y (səb sid′ē er′ē) *adj.* [see SUBSIDY] **1.** giving aid, service, etc. **2.** being in a subordinate relationship —*n., pl.* -ies one that is subsidiary; specif., a company controlled by another company

sub·si·dize (sub′sə dīz′) *vt.* -dized′, -diz′ing to support with a subsidy —**sub′si·di·za′tion** *n.* — **sub′si·diz′er** *n.*

sub·si·dy (sub′sə dē) *n., pl.* -dies [< L. *subsidium,* auxiliary forces] a grant of money, as from a government to a private enterprise

sub·sist (səb sist′) *vi.* [< L. *sub-*, under + *sistere,* to stand] **1.** to continue to be; exist **2.** to continue to live (*on* or *by*)

sub·sist′ence *n.* **1.** a subsisting **2.** the act of providing sustenance **3.** means of support or livelihood, esp. the barest means

sub·soil (sub′soil′) *n.* the layer of soil beneath the surface soil

sub·son·ic (sub sän′ik) *adj.* designating or of speeds less than that of sound

sub·stance (sub′stəns) *n.* [< L. *substare,* exist] **1.** the real or essential part of anything **2.** the physical matter of which a thing consists **3.** *a)* a solid quality *b)* consistency **4.** the real meaning **5.** wealth

sub·stand′ard *adj.* below standard

sub·stan·tial (səb stan′shəl) *adj.* **1.** of or having substance **2.** real; true **3.** strong; solid **4.** ample; large **5.** important **6.** wealthy **7.** with regard to essential elements

sub·stan·ti·ate (səb stan′shē āt′) *vt.* -at′ed, -at′ing [see SUBSTANCE] to show to be true or real by giving evidence —**sub·stan′ti·a′tion** *n.*

sub·stan·tive (sub′stən tiv) *adj.* [see SUBSTANCE] essential —*n.* a noun or any word or group of words functioning as a noun

sub·sti·tute (sub′stə tōōt′) *n.* [ult. < L. *sub-*, under + *statuere,* to put] a person or thing acting or used in place of another —*vt., vi.* -tut′ed, -tut′ing to put, use, or serve in place of another —*adj.* being a substitute —**sub′sti·tu′-tion** *n.*

sub·stra·tum (sub′strāt′əm) *n., pl.* -ta (-ə) -tums [see SUB- & STRATUM] a part, substance, etc. that lies beneath and supports another

sub·struc·ture (-struk′chər) *n.* a structure acting as a support, base, or foundation

sub·sume (səb so͞om′) *vt.* **-sumed′, -sum′ing** [< L. *sub-*, under + *sumere*, take] to include within a larger class, group, etc.

sub·teen′ *n.* a child nearly a teen-ager

sub·ter·fuge (sub′tər fyo͞oj′) *n.* [< L. *subter-*, below + *fugere*, flee] any plan, action, etc. used to hide one's objective, etc.

sub·ter·ra·ne·an (sub′tə rā′nē ən) *adj.* [< L. *sub-*, under + *terra*, earth] **1.** underground **2.** secret

sub·ti′tle *n.* **1.** a secondary title of a book, play, etc. **2.** a line or lines of dialogue shown on a movie or TV screen —*vt.* **-tl′tled, -tl′tling** to add a subtitle or subtitles to

sub·tle (sut′'l) *adj.* **-tler, -tlest** [< L. *subtilis*, fine, thin] **1.** thin; not dense **2.** mentally keen **3.** delicately skillful **4.** crafty; sly **5.** not obvious —**sub′tle·ty** *n., pl.* **-ties** —**sub′tly** *adv.*

sub·tract (səb trakt′) *vt., vi.* [< L. *sub-*, under + *trahere*, to draw] to take away or deduct (a part from a whole) or (one quantity from another) —**sub·trac′tion** *n.*

sub·tra·hend (sub′trə hend′) *n.* a quantity to be subtracted from another

sub·trop′i·cal *adj.* of, or characteristic of, or bordering on the tropics

sub·urb (sub′ərb) *n.* [< L. *sub-*, under + *urbs*, town] a district on the outskirts of a city — **sub·ur·ban** (sə bur′bən) *adj.*

sub·ur′ban·ite′ (-īt′) *n.* a person living in a suburb

sub·ur·bi·a (sə bur′bē ə) *n.* the suburbs or suburbanites collectively

sub·ven·tion (səb ven′shən) *n.* [< L. *sub-*, under + *venire*, come] a subsidy

sub·ver·sive (səb vur′siv) *adj.* tending to subvert —*n.* a subversive person

sub·vert (səb vurt′) *vt.* [< L. *sub-*, under + *vertere*, to turn] **1.** to overthrow or destroy (something established) **2.** to corrupt, as in morals —**sub·ver′sion** *n.*

sub·way (sub′wā′) *n.* an underground, metropolitan electric railway

suc- *same as* SUB-: used before *c*

suc·ceed (sək sēd′) *vi.* [< L. *sub-*, under + *cedere*, to go] **1.** to follow, as in office **2.** to be successful —*vt.* **1.** to follow into office, etc. **2.** to come after

suc·cess (sək ses′) *n.* **1.** a favorable outcome **2.** the gaining of fame, wealth, etc. **3.** a successful person or thing

suc·cess′ful *adj.* **1.** turning out as was hoped for **2.** having gained wealth, fame, etc.

suc·ces·sion (sək sesh′ən) *n.* **1.** a succeeding or coming after another **2.** the right to succeed to an office, etc. **3.** a number of persons or things coming one after another

suc·ces·sive (-ses′iv) *adj.* coming one after another —**suc·ces′sive·ly** *adv.*

suc·ces′sor *n.* one who follows or succeeds another, as to an office

suc·cinct (sək siŋkt′) *adj.* [< L. *sub-*, under + *cingere*, to gird] clearly and briefly stated; terse —**suc·cinct′ly** *adv.*

suc·cor (suk′ər) *vt.* [< L. *sub-*, under + *currere*, to run] to help in time of need or distress —*n.* aid; relief

suc·co·tash (suk′ə tash′) *n.* [< AmInd.] a dish of lima beans and corn kernels cooked together

suc·cu·lent (suk′yoo lənt) *adj.* [< L. *sucus*, juice] **1.** juicy **2.** interesting —**suc′cu·lence, suc′cu·len·cy** *n.* —**suc′cu·lent·ly** *adv.*

suc·cumb (sə kum′) *vi.* [< L. *sub-*, under +

cumbere, to lie] **1.** to give way (*to*); yield **2.** to die

such (such) *adj.* [OE. *swilc*] **1.** of the kind mentioned or implied **2.** of the same or a similar kind **3.** whatever **4.** so extreme, so much, etc. *[such fun!]* —*adv.* to so great a degree — *pron.* such a one or ones —**as such 1.** as being what is indicated **2.** in itself —**such as** for example

such′like′ *adj.* of such a kind —*pron.* persons or things of such a kind

suck (suk) *vt.* [OE. *sucan*] **1.** to draw (liquid) into the mouth **2.** to take in as if by sucking **3.** to suck liquid from (fruit, etc.) **4.** to hold in the mouth so that it dissolves **5.** to hold in the mouth and draw on —*vi.* to suck something — *n.* the act of sucking

suck′er *n.* **1.** one that sucks **2.** a carplike freshwater fish **3.** a part used, as by the leech, for sucking or holding fast to something **4.** a shoot from the roots or stem of a plant **5.** a lollipop **6.** [Slang] one easily fooled or cheated

suck·le (suk′'l) *vt., vi.* **-led, -ling 1.** to feed at the breast or udder **2.** to nourish

suck′ling *n.* an unweaned child or young animal

su·crose (so͞o′krōs) *n.* [< Fr. *sucre*, sugar + (GLUC)OSE] a sugar found in sugar cane, sugar beets, etc.

suc·tion (suk′shən) *n.* [< L. *sugere*, to suck] **1.** a sucking **2.** production of a partial vacuum so that surrounding fluid, etc. is sucked in —*adj.* operating by suction

sud·den (sud′'n) *adj.* [ult. < L. *sub-*, under + *ire*, go] **1.** happening or coming unexpectedly **2.** abrupt **3.** done quickly —**all of a sudden** without warning; quickly

suds (sudz) *n.pl.* [prob. < MDu. *sudse*, marsh water] **1.** soapy water **2.** foam, froth, or lather —**suds′y** *adj.* **-i·er, -i·est**

sue (so͞o) *vt., vi.* **sued, su′ing** [< L. *sequi*, follow] **1.** to appeal (to); petition **2.** to prosecute in a court in seeking redress of wrongs, etc. —**su′er** *n.*

′suede, suède (swād) *n.* [< Fr. *gants de Suède*, Swedish gloves] **1.** tanned leather with the flesh side buffed into a nap **2.** a cloth like this

su·et (so͞o′it) *n.* [< L. *sebum*, fat] the hard fat of cattle and sheep: used in cooking and to make tallow —**su′et·y** *adj.*

suf- *same as* SUB-: used before *f*

suf·fer (suf′ər) *vt., vi.* [< L. *sub-*, under + *ferre*, to bear] **1.** to undergo or endure (pain, injury, loss, etc.) **2.** to undergo (any process) **3.** to allow; tolerate —**suf′fer·er** *n.* —**suf′fer·ing** *n.*

suf′fer·ance *n.* **1.** capacity to endure pain, etc. **2.** consent, sanction, etc. implied by failure to prohibit

suf·fice (sə fīs′) *vi.* **-ficed′, -fic′ing** [< L. *sub-*, under + *facere*, make] to be enough

suf·fi·cient (sə fish′'nt) *adj.* as much as is needed; enough —**suf·fi′cien·cy** *n.*

suf·fix (suf′iks) *n.* [< L. *sub-*, under + *figere*, fix] a syllable or syllables added at the end of a word to alter its meaning. (Ex.: *-ish* in *smallish*)

suf·fo·cate (suf′ə kāt′) *vt.* **-cat′ed, -cat′ing** [< L. *sub-*, under + *fauces*, throat] **1.** to kill by cutting off the supply of air for breathing **2.** to smother, suppress, etc. —*vi.* **1.** to die by being suffocated **2.** to choke, stifle, etc. —**suf′fo·ca′tion** *n.*

suf·frage (suf′rij) *n.* [< L. *suffragium*] **1.** a vote or voting **2.** the right to vote

suf·fra·gette (suf′rə jet′) *n.* a woman advocate of female suffrage

suf·fuse (sə fyo͞oz′) *vt.* **-fused′, -fus′ing** [< L.

sub-, under + *fundere*, pour] to overspread, as with light —**suf·fu'sion** *n.*

sug·ar (shoog'ər) *n.* [< Sans. *sárkarâ*] any of a class of sweet, soluble carbohydrates, as sucrose, glucose, etc.; specif., sucrose from sugar cane and sugar beets —*vt.* **1.** to put sugar in or on **2.** to make seem less unpleasant —*vi.* to form sugar —**sug'ar·less** *adj.* —**sug'ar·y** *adj.*

sugar beet a beet having a white root, used as a source of common sugar

sugar cane a very tall tropical grass, cultivated as the main source of sugar

sug'ar·coat' *vt.* **1.** to coat with sugar **2.** to make seem less unpleasant

sug'ar·plum' (-plum') *n.* a round piece of sugary candy

sug·gest (səg jest') *vt.* [< L. *sub-*, under + *gerere*, carry] **1.** to bring (a thought, etc.) to the mind for consideration **2.** to call to mind by association of ideas **3.** to propose as a possibility **4.** to imply; intimate

sug·gest'i·ble (-jes'tə b'l) *adj.* easily influenced by suggestion —**sug·gest'i·bil'i·ty** *n.*

sug·ges'tion (-jes'chən) *n.* **1.** a suggesting or being suggested **2.** something suggested **3.** a faint hint; trace

sug·ges'tive *adj.* **1.** that tends to suggest ideas **2.** tending to suggest something considered improper or indecent

su·i·cide (sōō'ə sid') *n.* [L. *sui*, of oneself + -CIDE] **1.** the intentional killing of oneself **2.** one who commits suicide —**su'i·ci'dal** *adj.*

suit (sōōt) *n.* [< L. *sequi*, follow] **1.** a set of clothes; esp., a coat and trousers (or skirt) **2.** any of the four sets of playing cards **3.** action to secure justice in a court of law **4.** an act of suing, pleading, etc. —*vt.* **1.** to meet the needs of **2.** to make fit; adapt **3.** to please; satisfy — **follow suit** to follow the example set —**suit oneself** to do as one pleases

suit'a·ble *adj.* right for a given purpose —**suit'a·bil'i·ty** *n.* —**suit'a·bly** *adv.*

suit'case' *n.* a flat, rectangular travel case with two compartments

suite (swēt) *n.* [Fr.: see SUIT] **1.** a group of attendants; retinue **2.** a unit of connected rooms **3.** (*occas.* sōōt) a set of matched furniture for a room

suit'ing *n.* cloth for making suits

suit·or (sōōt'ər) *n.* a man courting a woman

su·ki·ya·ki (sōō'kē yä'kē) *n.* [Jpn.] a Japanese dish of thinly sliced meat and vegetables, cooked quickly

Suk·kot, Suk·koth (soo kōt', sook'ōs) *n.* [Heb., lit., tabernacles] a Jewish fall festival commemorating the wandering of the Hebrews after the Exodus

sul·fa (sul'fə) *adj.* designating or of a family of drugs, used against some bacterial infections

sul·fate (sul'fāt) *n.* a salt or ester of sulfuric acid

sul·fide (sul'fīd) *n.* a compound of sulfur with another element or a radical

sul·fur (sul'fər) *n.* [L. *sulphur*] a pale-yellow nonmetallic chemical element: it burns with a blue flame and a stifling odor: symbol, S

sul·fu·ric (sul fyoor'ik) *adj.* of or containing sulfur

sulfuric acid an oily, colorless, corrosive liquid used in explosives, fertilizers, etc.

sul·fu·rous (sul'fər əs) *adj.* **1.** (*usually* sul fyoor'əs) of or containing sulfur **2.** like burning sulfur in odor, color, etc.

sulk (sulk) *vi.* [< SULKY] to be sulky —*n.* a sulky mood, state, or person

sulk·y (sul'kē) *adj.* -i·er, -i·est [prob. < OE.

solcen, idle] sullen; peevish —*n.*, *pl.* -ies a light, two-wheeled carriage for one person —**sulk'i·ly** *adv.* —**sulk'i·ness** *n.*

sul·len (sul'ən) *adj.* [< L. *solus*, alone] **1.** silent and keeping to oneself because one feels angry, bitter, hurt, etc. **2.** gloomy; dismal — **sul'len·ly** *adv.*

sul·ly (sul'ē) *vt.* -lied, -ly·ing [prob. < OFr. *souiller*] to soil, stain, etc., now esp. by disgracing

sul·phur (sul'fər) *n.* *var. of* SULFUR

sul·tan (sul't'n) *n.* [Fr. < Ar. *sulṭān*] a Muslim ruler

sul·tan·a (sul tan'ə) *n.* a sultan's wife, mother, sister, or daughter

sul·tan·ate (sul't'n it, -āt') *n.* the authority, office, or dominion of a sultan

sul·try (sul'trē) *adj.* -tri·er, -tri·est [< SWELTER] **1.** oppressively hot and moist **2.** inflamed, as with passion

sum (sum) *n.* [< L. *summus*, highest] **1.** an amount of money **2.** the whole amount **3.** gist; summary **4.** the result gotten by adding numbers or quantities **5.** a problem in arithmetic — *vt.* summed, sum'ming **1.** to add up **2.** to summarize Usually with *up*

su·mac, su·mach (shōō'mak, sōō'-) *n.* [Ar. *summāq*] any of various plants with compound leaves and cone-shaped clusters of hairy, red fruit

sum·ma·rize (sum'ə riz') *vt.* -rized', -riz'ing to make or be a summary of

sum·ma·ry (sum'ə rē) *adj.* [< L. *summa*, a sum] **1.** concise; condensed **2.** prompt and informal **3.** hasty and arbitrary —*n.*, *pl.* -ries a brief account covering the main points; digest —**sum·mar·i·ly** (sə mer'ə lē) *adv.*

sum·ma·tion (sə mā'shən) *n.* a final summing up of arguments, as in a court trial

sum·mer (sum'ər) *n.* [OE. *sumor*] the warmest season of the year, following spring —*adj.* of or for summer —*vi.* to pass the summer —**sum'mer·y** *adj.*

sum'mer·house' *n.* an open structure in a garden, park, etc. providing a shady rest

sum'mer·time' *n.* the season of summer

sum·mit (sum'it) *n.* [< L. *summus*, highest] **1.** the highest point; top **2.** the highest degree or state; acme

sum·mon (sum'ən) *vt.* [< L. *sub-*, secretly + *monere*, warn] **1.** to call together; order to convene **2.** to call or send for with authority **3.** to call forth; rouse [*summon* (up) strength] — **sum'mon·er** *n.*

sum'mons (-ənz) *n.*, *pl.* -mons·es [see SUMMON] **1.** an order to come or do something **2.** *Law* an official order to appear in court

sump·tu·ous (sump'choo wəs) *adj.* [< L. *sumptus*, expense] **1.** costly; lavish **2.** magnificent, as in furnishings

sun (sun) *n.* [OE. *sunne*] **1.** the self-luminous, gaseous sphere about which the earth and other planets revolve **2.** the heat or light of the sun **3.** any star that is the center of a planetary system —*vt.*, *vi.* sunned, sun'ning to warm, dry, tan, bleach, etc. in the sunlight — **sun'less** *adj.*

Sun. Sunday

sun bath exposure of the body to sunlight

sun'bathe' (-bāth') *vi.* -bathed', -bath'ing to take a sun bath —**sun'bath'er** *n.*

sun'beam' *n.* a ray or beam of sunlight

Sun'belt' *n.* those States of the South and Southwest with a sunny climate and expanding economy: also **Sun Belt**

sun'bon'net *n.* a bonnet for shading the face and neck from the sun

sun'burn' (-burn') *n.* inflammation of the skin from prolonged exposure to the sun or a sunlamp —*vi., vt.* -burned' or -burnt', -burn'ing to give or get a sunburn

sun'burst' (-burst') *n.* a decoration, as a brooch, suggesting the sun and its rays

sun·dae (sun'dē, -dā) *n.* [prob. < SUNDAY] a serving of ice cream covered with syrup, fruit, nuts, etc.

Sun·day (sun'dē, -dā) *n.* [< OE. *sunnandæg*, day of the sun] the first day of the week, observed by most Christians as a day of worship or rest

sun·der (sun'dər) *vt., vi.* [< OE. *sundor*, asunder] to break apart; separate

sun·di·al (sun'dī'əl, -dīl') *n.* an instrument that shows time by the shadow of a pointer cast by the sun on a dial marked in hours

sun'down' *n.* same as SUNSET

sun·dries (sun'drēz) *n.pl.* sundry items

sun'dry (-drē) *adj.* [< OE. *sundor*, apart] various; miscellaneous

sun'fish' *n., pl.:* see FISH 1. any of several freshwater fishes 2. a large, sluggish, ocean fish with a thick body

sun'flow'er *n.* a tall plant having yellow, daisylike flowers containing edible seeds

sung (suŋ) *pp. & rare pt. of* SING

sun'glass'es *n.pl.* eyeglasses with tinted lenses to shade the eyes from glare

sunk (suŋk) *pp. & alt. pt. of* SINK

sunk·en (suŋk'ən) *adj.* 1. submerged 2. below the general level *[a sunken patio]* 3. hollow *[sunken cheeks]* 4. dejected

sun'lamp' *n.* an electric lamp that radiates ultraviolet rays like those of sunlight

sun'light' *n.* the light of the sun

sun'lit' *adj.* lighted by the sun

sun'ny (-ē) *adj.* -ni·er, -ni·est 1. full of sunshine 2. bright and cheerful 3. of or like the sun — **sun'ni·ness** *n.*

sun'rise' (-rīz') *n.* 1. the daily appearance of the sun above the eastern horizon 2. the time of this

sun'set' (-set') *n.* 1. the daily disappearance of the sun below the western horizon 2. the time of this

sun'shine' *n.* 1. the shining of the sun, or its light and heat 2. cheerfulness, joy, etc., or a source of this —**sun'shin'y** *adj.*

sun'spot' *n.* any temporarily cooler region appearing from time to time as a dark spot on the sun

sun'stroke' *n.* heatstroke caused by excessive exposure to the sun —**sun'struck'** *adj.*

sun'tan' *n.* a darkened skin caused by exposure to the sun or a sunlamp

sun'up' *n.* same as SUNRISE

sup (sup) *vi.* supped, sup'ping [< OFr. *soupe*, soup] to have supper

su·per (sōo'pər) *n.* [< SUPER-] short for: 1. SUPERNUMERARY 2. SUPERINTENDENT —*adj.* 1. outstanding; fine 2. extreme

super- [L. < *super*, above] *a prefix meaning:* 1. over, above *[superstructure]* 2. superior to *[supervisor]* 3. surpassing *[superabundant]* 4. greater than others of its kind *[supermarket]* 5. extra *[supertax]*

su·per·a·bun·dant (sōo'pər ə bun'dənt) *adj.* overly abundant —**su'per·a·bun'dance** *n.* —**su'per·a·bun'dant·ly** *adv.*

su'per·an'nu·at'ed (-an'yoo wāt'id) *adj.* [< L. *super*, beyond + *annus*, year] 1. too old for further work 2. retired because of old age or infirmity 3. obsolete

su·perb (soo purb', sōo-) *adj.* [< L. *super*,

above] 1. noble; majestic 2. rich; splendid 3. excellent —**su·perb'ly** *adv.*

su·per·car·go (sōo'pər kär'gō) *n., pl.* -goes, -gos [< Sp.] an officer on a merchant ship who has charge of the cargo

su·per·charge (sōo'pər chärj') *vt.* -charged', -charg'ing to increase the power of (an engine) as with a device (**supercharger**) that forces air into the cylinders

su·per·cil·i·ous (sōo'pər sil'ē əs) *adj.* [< L. *super-*, above + *cilium*, eyelid (with reference to raised brows)] showing pride or contempt; haughty

su·per·e·go (sōo'pər ē'gō) *n., pl.* -gos *Psychoanalysis* that part of the psyche which enforces moral standards

su'per·er'o·ga'tion (-er'ə gā'shən) *n.* [< LL. *super*, above + *erogare*, pay out] a doing more than is needed —**su'per·e·rog'a·to'ry** (-i räg'ə tôr'ē) *adj.*

su'per·fi'cial (-fish'əl) *adj.* [< L. *super-*, above + *facies*, face] 1. of or being on the surface 2. concerned with and understanding only the obvious; shallow 3. quick and cursory 4. merely apparent —**su'per·fi'ci·al'i·ty** (-ē al'ə tē) *n., pl.* -ties —**su'per·fi'cial·ly** *adv.*

su·per·flu·ous (soo pur'floo wəs) *adj.* [< L. *super-*, above + *fluere*, to flow] unnecessary or excessive —**su·per·flu·i·ty** (sōo'pər floo'ə tē) *n., pl.* -ties

su'per·high'way' *n.* same as EXPRESSWAY

su'per·hu'man *adj.* 1. having a nature above that of man; divine 2. greater than normal for a human being

su'per·im·pose' *vt.* -posed', -pos'ing 1. to put on top of something else 2. to add as a dominant feature

su'per·in·tend' *vt.* to act as superintendent of; supervise

su'per·in·tend'ent *n.* [see SUPER- & INTEND] 1. a person in charge of a department, institution, etc. 2. the custodian of a building, etc.

su·pe·ri·or (sə pir'ē ər, soo-) *adj.* [< L. *superus*, that is above] 1. higher in space 2. higher in order, status, quality, etc. (with *to*) 3. above average; excellent 4. haughty —*n.* 1. a superior person or thing 2. the head of a religious community —**su·pe'ri·or'i·ty** (-ôr'ə tē) *n.*

superl. superlative

su·per·la·tive (sə pur'lə tiv, soo-) *adj.* [< L. *super-*, above + *latus*, pp. of *ferre*, carry] 1. excelling all others; supreme 2. *Gram.* designating the extreme degree of comparison of adjectives and adverbs —*n.* 1. the highest degree; acme 2. *Gram.* the superlative degree

su·per·man (sōo'pər man') *n., pl.* -men' an apparently superhuman man

su'per·mar'ket *n.* a large, self-service, retail food store, often one of a chain

su·per·nal (soo pur'n'l) *adj.* [< L. *supernus*, upper] celestial, heavenly, or divine

su·per·nat·u·ral (sōo'pər nach'ər əl) *adj.* existing outside the known laws of nature; specif., of or involving God or ghosts, etc.

su'per·nu'mer·ar'y (-nōo'mə rer'ē) *adj.* [< L. *super-*, above + *numerus*, number] extra —*n., pl.* -ies 1. an extra person or thing 2. an actor with a small, nonspeaking part, as in a mob scene

su'per·pose' (-pōz') *vt.* -posed', -pos'ing [see SUPER- & POSE] to lay or place on, over, or something else

su·per·sat·u·rate (sōo'pər sach'ə rāt') *vt.* -rat'ed, -rat'ing to saturate beyond the normal point for the given temperature

su'per·scribe' (-skrīb') *vt.* -scribed, -scrib'ing [< L. *super-*, above + *scribere*, write] to write

(something) on the top or outer surface of — **su′per·scrip′tion** *n.*
su·per·script (sōō′pər skript′) *n.* a figure, letter, or symbol written above and to the side of another (Ex.: 2 in x²)
su·per·sede (sōō′pər sēd′) *vt.* **-sed′ed, -sed′ing** [< L. *super-*, above + *sedere*, sit] **1.** to set aside as inferior or obsolete; displace **2.** to replace, succeed, or supplant
su′per·son′ic (-sän′ik) *adj.* [< SUPER + L. *sonus*, sound] **1.** of or moving at a speed greater than sound **2.** ultrasonic
su′per·star′ *n.* a prominent performer considered to have exceptional skill and talent
su·per·sti·tion (sōō′pər stish′ən) *n.* [< L. *super-*, over + *stare*, to stand] **1.** any belief that is not in accord with known facts or rational thought, esp. such a belief in charms, omens, the supernatural, etc. **2.** any action or practice based on such a belief —**su′per·sti′tious** *adj.*
su′per·struc′ture *n.* **1.** a structure built on top of another, as above the main deck of a ship **2.** that part of a building above the foundation
su·per·vene (sōō′pər vēn′) *vi.* **-vened′, -ven′ing** [< L. *super-*, over + *venire*, come] to come or happen as something added or unexpected — **su′per·ven′tion** (-ven′shən) *n.*
su·per·vise (sōō′pər vīz′) *vt., vi.* **-vised′, -vis′ing** [< L. *super-*, over + *videre*, see] to oversee or direct (work, workers, a project, etc.); superintend —**su′per·vi′sion** (-vizh′ən) *n.* —**su′per·vi′sor** *n.* —**su′per·vi′so·ry** *adj.*
su·pine (soo pīn′) *adj.* [L. *supinus*] **1.** lying on the back, face upward **2.** showing no concern or doing nothing about matters
supp., suppl. supplement
sup·per (sup′ər) *n.* [OFr. *souper*] an evening meal, or a late, light meal
sup·plant (sə plant′) *vt.* [< L. *sub-*, under + *planta*, sole of the foot] **1.** to take the place of, esp. by force or plotting **2.** to remove and replace with something else
sup·ple (sup′'l) *adj.* [< L. *supplex*, humble] **1.** bending easily; flexible **2.** lithe; limber **3.** easily influenced; adaptable
sup·ple·ment (sup′lə mənt) *n.* [see SUPPLY¹] **1.** something added, esp. to make up for a lack **2.** a section of additional material in a book, newspaper, etc. —*vt.* (-ment′) to provide a supplement to —**sup′ple·men′ta·ry** (-men′tər ē), **sup′ple·men′tal** *adj.*
sup·pli·ant (sup′lē ənt) *n.* one who supplicates —*adj.* supplicating Also **sup′pli·cant** (-lə kənt)
sup·pli·cate (sup′lə kāt′) *vt., vi.* **-cat′ed, -cat′ing** [< L. *sub-*, under + *plicare*, to fold] **1.** to ask for (something) humbly **2.** to make a humble request (of) —**sup′pli·ca′tion** *n.* —**sup′pli·ca′tor** *n.*
sup·ply (sə plī′) *vt.* **-plied′, -ply′ing** [< L. *sub-*, under + *plere*, fill] **1.** to furnish; provide **2.** to meet the needs of **3.** to make up for (a deficiency, etc.) —*n., pl.* **-plies 1.** a supplying **2.** an amount available for use or sale; stock **3.** [*pl.*] needed materials, etc. —**sup·pli′er** *n.*
sup·port (sə pôrt′) *vt.* [< L. *sub-*, under + *portare*, carry] **1.** to carry the weight of; hold up **2.** to encourage; help **3.** to advocate; uphold **4.** to maintain (a person, institution, etc.) **5.** to help prove or vindicate **6.** to endure **7.** to keep up; maintain **8.** to act a subordinate role with (a star) in a play —*n.* **1.** a supporting or being supported **2.** a person or thing that supports **3.** a means of support —**sup·port′er** *n.*
sup·pose (sə pōz′) *vt.* **-posed′, -pos′ing** [< L. *sub-*, under + *ponare*, put] **1.** to assume to be true, as for the sake of argument **2.** to believe,

think, etc. **3.** to consider as a possibility **4.** to expect [she's *supposed* to telephone] —*vi.* to conjecture —**sup·posed′** *adj.* —**sup·pos′ed·ly** *adv.*
sup·po·si·tion (sup′ə zish′ən) *n.* **1.** a supposing **2.** something supposed
sup·pos·i·to·ry (sə päz′ə tôr′ē) *n., pl.* **-ries** [see SUPPOSE] a small piece of medicated substance inserted into the rectum, vagina, etc., where it melts
sup·press (sə pres′) *vt.* [< L. *sub-*, under + *premere*, to press] **1.** to put down by force; quell **2.** to keep from being known, published, etc. **3.** to keep back; restrain **4.** *Psychiatry* to consciously dismiss from the mind —**sup·pres′sion** (-presh′ən) *n.*
sup·pu·rate (sup′yoo rāt′) *vi.* **-rat′ed, -rat′ing** [< L. *sub-*, under + *pus*, pus] to form or discharge pus —**sup′pu·ra′tion** *n.*
su·prem·a·cist (sə prem′ə sist, soo-) *n.* one who believes in the supremacy of a particular group
su·prem·a·cy (sə prem′ə sē, soo-) *n., pl.* **-cies** supreme power or authority
su·preme (sə prēm′, soo-) *adj.* [< L. *superus*, that is above] **1.** highest in rank, power, etc. **2.** highest in quality, achievement, etc. **3.** highest in degree **4.** final
Supreme Being God
Supreme Court 1. the highest Federal court **2.** the highest court in most States
Supt., supt. Superintendent
sur-¹ [< L. *super*, over] *a prefix meaning* over, upon, above, beyond
sur-² *same as* SUB-: used before *r*
sur·cease (sur′sēs) *n.* [< L. *supersedere*, refrain from] end; cessation
sur·charge (sur chärj′) *vt.* **-charged′, -charg′ing 1.** to overcharge **2.** to overload **3.** to mark (a postage stamp) with a surcharge —*n.* (sur′chärj) **1.** an additional charge **2.** a new face value printed over the old on a postage stamp
sur·cin·gle (sur′siŋ′g'l) *n.* [< MFr. *sur-*, over + L. *cingulum*, a belt] a strap passed around a horse's body and over a saddle, pack, etc.
sure (shoor) *adj.* **sur′er, sur′est** [< L. *securus*] **1.** that will not fail; reliable [a *sure* method] **2.** that cannot be doubted, questioned, etc. **3.** having no doubt; confident [*sure* of one's facts] **4.** bound to be or happen [a *sure* defeat] **5.** bound to do, etc. [*sure* to lose] —*adv.* [Colloq.] surely —**for sure** certain(ly) —**sure enough** [Colloq.] without doubt —**sure′ness** *n.*
sure′-foot′ed *adj.* not likely to stumble, fall, or err —**sure′-foot′ed·ly** *adv.*
sure·ly *adv.* **1.** with confidence **2.** certainly
sure·ty (shoor′ə tē, shoor′tē) *n., pl.* **-ties 1.** a being sure **2.** something that makes sure, protects, etc. **3.** one who makes himself responsible for another
surf (surf) *n.* [prob. < *sough*, rustle] the waves of the sea breaking, as on the shore —*vi.* to engage in surfing —**surf′er** *n.*
sur·face (sur′fis) *n.* [< Fr. *sur-*, over + *face*, a face] **1.** *a)* the exterior of an object *b)* any of the faces of a solid **2.** superficial features —*adj.* **1.** of, on, or at the surface **2.** superficial —*vt.* **-faced, -fac·ing** **1.** to give a surface to, as in paving —*vi.* to rise to the surface of the water
surf′board′ *n.* a long, narrow board used in the sport of surfing
sur·feit (sur′fit) *n.* [< OFr. < *sur-*, over + *faire*, make] **1.** too great an amount or supply **2.** overindulgence, esp. in food or drink **3.** disgust, nausea, etc. resulting from this —*vt.* to supply to excess
surf·ing (sur′fiŋ) *n.* the sport of riding in

toward shore on the crest of a wave, esp. on a surfboard

surge (surj) *n.* [prob. < L. *surgere,* to rise] **1.** a large wave of water, or its motion **2.** any sudden strong rush, as of energy, electric power, etc. —*vi.* **surged, surg'ing** to move in a surge

sur·geon (sur'jən) *n.* a doctor who specializes in surgery

sur·ger·y (sur'jər ē) *n., pl.* **-ies** [ult. < Gr. *cheir,* the hand + *ergein,* to work] **1.** the treatment of disease, injury, etc. by manual or instrumental operations **2.** the operating room of a surgeon or hospital

sur'gi·cal (-ji k'l) *of* surgeons or surgery

sur·ly (sur'lē) *adj.* **-li·er, -li·est** [earlier *sirly,* imperious < SIR] bad-tempered; sullenly rude; uncivil —**sur'li·ness** *n.*

sur·mise (sər mīz') *n.* [< OFr. *sur-,* upon + *metre,* put] a conjecture; guess —*vt., vi.* **-mised', -mis'ing** to guess

sur·mount (sər mount') *vt.* [see SUR-¹ & MOUNT²] **1.** to overcome (a difficulty) **2.** to be or rise above **3.** to climb up and across (a height, etc.)

sur·name (sur'nām') *n.* [< OFr. *sur-,* over + *nom,* name] the family name; last name

sur·pass (sər pas') *vt.* [< OFr. *sur-,* over + *passer,* to PASS] **1.** to be better than; excel **2.** to go beyond the limit, capacity, etc. of —**sur·pass'ing** *adj.*

sur·plice (sur'plis) *n.* [ult. < L. *super-,* above + *pelliceum,* fur robe] a loose, white, wide-sleeved outer vestment worn by the clergy and choir in some churches

sur·plus (sur'plus) *n.* [OFr. < *sur-,* above + L. *plus,* more] a quantity over what is needed or used —*adj.* forming a surplus

sur·prise (sər prīz') *vt.* **-prised', -pris'ing** [< OFr. *sur-,* above + *prendre,* take] **1.** to come upon suddenly or unexpectedly; take unawares **2.** to attack without warning **3.** to amaze; astonish —*n.* **1.** a being surprised **2.** something that surprises

sur·re·al·ism (sə rē'ə liz'm) *n.* [< Fr. *sur-,* above + *réalisme,* REALISM] a modern movement in the arts, trying to portray the workings of the subconscious mind —**sur·re'al·ist** *adj., n.* —**sur·re'al·is'tic** *adj.*

sur·ren·der (sə ren'dər) *vt.* [< MFr. *sur-,* up + *rendre,* RENDER] **1.** to give up possession of; yield to another on compulsion **2.** to give up or abandon —*vi.* to give oneself up, esp. as a prisoner —*n.* the act of surrendering

sur·rep·ti·tious (sur'əp tish'əs) *adj.* [< L. *sub-,* under + *rapere,* to seize] done, got, made, acting, etc. in a secret, stealthy way

sur·rey (sur'ē) *n., pl.* **-reys** [< *Surrey,* county in England] a light, four-wheeled carriage with two seats

sur·ro·gate (sur'ə gāt) *n.* [< L. *sub-,* in place of + *rogare,* to elect] **1.** a deputy or substitute for another person **2.** in some States, a probate court judge

sur·round (sə round') *vt.* [< L. *super-,* over + *undare,* to rise] to encircle on all or nearly all sides

sur·round'ings *n.pl.* the things, conditions, etc. that surround one; environment

sur·tax (sur'taks) *n.* an extra tax on something already taxed

sur·veil·lance (sər vā'ləns) *n.* [Fr. < *sur-,* over + *veiller,* to watch] **1.** watch kept over a person, esp. a suspect **2.** supervision

sur·vey (sər vā'; *for n.* sur'vā) *vt.* [< OFr. *sur-,* over + *veoir,* see] **1.** to examine or consider in detail or comprehensively **2.** to determine the location, form, or boundaries of (a tract of

land) —*n., pl.* **-veys 1.** a detailed study made by gathering and analyzing information **2.** a comprehensive study **3.** the process of surveying an area **4.** a written description of the area surveyed —**sur·vey'or** *n.*

sur·vive (sər vīv') *vt.* **-vived', -viv'ing** [< L. *super-,* above + *vivere,* to live] to remain alive or in existence after —*vi.* to continue living —**sur·viv'al** *n.* —**sur·vi'vor** *n.*

sus·cep·ti·ble (sə sep'tə b'l) *adj.* [< L. *sub-,* under + *capere,* take] easily affected emotionally —**susceptible of** admitting; allowing —**susceptible to** easily influenced or affected by —**sus·cep'ti·bil'i·ty** *n.*

sus·pect (sə spekt') *vt.* [< L. *sub-,* under + *spicere,* to look] **1.** to believe to be guilty on little or no evidence **2.** to believe to be bad, wrong, etc.; distrust **3.** to suppose —*adj.* (*usually* sus'pekt) suspected —*n.* (sus'pekt) one suspected, esp. of a crime

sus·pend (sə spend') *vt.* [< L. *sub-,* under + *pendere,* hang] **1.** to exclude for a time from a position, school, team, etc. as a punishment **2.** to make inoperative for a time **3.** to hold back (judgment, a sentence, etc.) **4.** to hang by a support from above **5.** to hold (dust in the air, etc.) in suspension —*vi.* to stop temporarily

sus·pend·ers (sə spen'dərz) *n.pl.* **1.** a pair of straps passed over the shoulders to support the trousers **2.** [Brit.] garters

sus·pense (sə spens') *n.* [< L. *suspendere,* SUSPEND] **1.** the state of being uncertain **2.** excitement that builds as a climax nears, as in a story, play, etc.

sus·pen·sion (sə spen'shən) *n.* **1.** a suspending or being suspended **2.** a supporting device upon or from which something is suspended

suspension bridge a bridge suspended from cables anchored at either end and supported by towers at intervals

sus·pi·cion (sə spish'ən) *n.* [< L. *suspicere,* to SUSPECT] **1.** a suspecting or being suspected **2.** the feeling or state of mind of one who suspects **3.** a very small amount; trace —*vt.* [Dial.] to suspect

sus·pi'cious *adj.* **1.** arousing suspicion **2.** showing or feeling suspicion

sus·tain (sə stān') *vt.* [< L. *sub-,* under + *tenere,* hold] **1.** to keep in existence; maintain or prolong **2.** to provide nourishment for **3.** to support; carry the weight of **4.** to endure; withstand **5.** to suffer (an injury, loss, etc.) **6.** to uphold the validity of **7.** to confirm; corroborate

sus·te·nance (sus'ti nəns) *n.* **1.** a sustaining or being sustained **2.** means of livelihood **3.** that which sustains life; food

su·ture (sōō'chər) *n.* [< L. *suere,* sew] **1.** the line of junction of two bones, esp. of the skull **2.** *a*) the stitching together of the two edges of a wound or incision *b*) any of the stitches of gut, etc. so made

svelte (svelt, sfelt) *adj.* [Fr.] **1.** slender and graceful **2.** suave, polished, etc.

SW, S.W., s.w. southwest(ern)

Sw. 1. Sweden **2.** Swedish

swab (swäb) *n.* [< ModDu. *zwabben,* do dirty work] **1.** a mop for scrubbing **2.** a small piece of cotton, etc. used to medicate or clean the throat, mouth, etc. —*vt.* **swabbed, swab'bing** to use a swab on

swad·dle (swäd''l) *vt.* **-dled, -dling** [OE. *swethel*] to wrap (a newborn baby) in long, narrow bands of cloth

swag (swag) *n.* [prob. < Norw.] [Slang] loot

swag·ger (swag'ər) *vi.* [prob. < Norw. *svagga,* to sway] **1.** to walk with a bold, arrogant stride; strut **2.** to boast or brag loudly —*n.* a swaggering walk or manner

swain (swān) *n.* [ON. *sveinn,* boy.] [Archaic] a young man who is courting or wooing; suitor

swal·low[1] (swäl'ō) *n.* [OE. *swealwe*] any of a group of small, swift-flying birds with long, pointed wings and a forked tail

swal·low[2] (swäl'ō) *vt.* [OE. *swelgan*] **1.** to pass (food, etc.) from the mouth into the stomach **2.** to absorb (often with *up*) **3.** to retract (words said) **4.** to put up with [to *swallow* insults] **5.** to suppress [to *swallow* one's pride] **6.** [Colloq.] to accept as true without question —*vi.* to move the throat muscles as in swallowing something —*n.* **1.** a swallowing **2.** the amount swallowed at one time

swam (swam) *pt. of* SWIM

swamp (swämp, swômp) *n.* [prob. < LowG.] a piece of wet, spongy land; bog —*vt.* **1.** to plunge in a swamp, water, etc. **2.** to flood as with water **3.** to overwhelm [*swamped* by debts] **4.** to sink (a boat) by filling with water —**swamp'y** *adj.* **-i·er, -i·est**

swamp buggy a vehicle for traveling over swampy land, often amphibious

swan (swän, swôn) *n.* [OE.] a large, web-footed water bird, usually white, with a long, graceful neck

swank (swaŋk) *n.* [akin to OE. *swancor,* supple] [Colloq.] ostentatious display —*adj.* [Colloq.] ostentatiously stylish: also **swank'y, -i·er, -i·est**

swan's'-down' *n.* **1.** the soft down of the swan, used for trimming clothes, etc. **2.** a soft, thick flannel

swan song [after the song supposedly sung by a dying swan] the last act or final work of a person

swap (swäp, swôp) *n., vt., vi.* **swapped, swap'ping** [ME. *swappen,* to strike] [Colloq.] exchange, trade, or barter

sward (swôrd) *n.* [< OE. *sweard,* skin] turf

swarm (swôrm) *n.* [OE. *swearm*] **1.** a large number of bees, with a queen, leaving a hive to start a new colony **2.** a colony of bees in a hive **3.** a moving mass or crowd —*vi.* **1.** to fly off in a swarm, as bees do **2.** to move, be present, etc. in large numbers **3.** to be filled or crowded

swarth·y (swôr'*th*ē, -thē) *adj.* **-i·er, -i·est** [< OE. *sweart*] having a dark skin

swash (swäsh, swôsh) *vi.* [echoic] to dash, strike, etc. with a splash

swash'buck'ler (-buk'lər) *n.* [prec. + BUCKLER] a blustering, swaggering fighting man —**swash'buck'ling** *n., adj.*

swas·ti·ka (swäs'ti kə) *n.* [< Sans. < *svasti,* well-being] **1.** an ancient design of a cross with four equal arms, each bent in a right angle **2.** this design with the arms bent clockwise, used as the Nazi emblem

swat (swät) *vt.* **swat'ted, swat'ting** [echoic] [Colloq.] to hit with a quick, sharp blow —*n.* [Colloq.] a quick, sharp blow —**swat'ter** *n.*

swatch (swäch) *n.* [orig., a cloth tally < ?] a sample piece of cloth, etc.

swath (swäth, swôth) *n.* [OE. *swathu,* a track] **1.** the width covered by one cut of a scythe or other mowing device **2.** a strip, row, etc. mowed

swathe (swā*th*) *vt.* **swathed, swath'ing** [OE. *swathian*] **1.** to wrap up in a bandage **2.** to envelop —*n.* a bandage or wrapping

sway (swā) *vi.* [ON. *sveigja*] **1.** *a)* to swing or move from side to side or to and fro *b)* to vacillate in position, opinion, etc. **2.** to lean to one side; veer —*vt.* **1.** to cause to sway **2.** to in-

fluence or divert [his threats *swayed* us] —*n.* **1.** a swaying or being swayed **2.** influence or control [under the *sway* of greed]

sway'backed' (-bakt') *adj.* having an abnormal sagging of the spine, as some horses

swear (swer) *vi.* **swore, sworn, swear'ing** [OE. *swerian*] **1.** to make a solemn declaration, supporting it with an appeal to God **2.** to make a solemn promise; vow **3.** to use profane language; curse —*vt.* **1.** to declare, pledge, or vow on oath **2.** to administer a legal oath to —**swear off** to renounce —**swear out** to obtain (a warrant for someone's arrest) by making a charge under oath

swear'word' *n.* a profane word or phrase

sweat (swet) *vt., vi.* **sweat** or **sweat'ed, sweat'ing** [OE. *swat*] **1.** to give forth or cause to give forth a salty moisture through the pores of the skin; perspire **2.** to give forth or condense (moisture) on its surface **3.** to work so hard as to cause sweating —*n.* **1.** the salty liquid given forth in perspiration **2.** moisture that collects in droplets on a surface **3.** a condition of eagerness, anxiety, etc. —**sweat out** [Slang] **1.** to suffer through (something) **2.** to wait anxiously for —**sweat'y** *adj.*

sweat'er *n.* a knitted or crocheted outer garment for the upper part of the body

sweat shirt a heavy cotton jersey, worn to absorb sweat during or after exercise

sweat'shop' *n.* a shop or factory where employees work long hours at low wages under poor working conditions

Swed. 1. Sweden **2.** Swedish

Swede (swēd) *n.* a native of Sweden

Swed·ish (swē'dish) *adj.* of Sweden, its people, their language, etc. —*n.* the Germanic language of the Swedes

sweep (swēp) *vt.* **swept, sweep'ing** [OE. *swapan*] **1.** to clean (a floor, etc.) as by brushing with a broom **2.** to remove (dirt, etc.) as with a broom **3.** to strip, carry away, or destroy with forceful movement **4.** to touch in moving across [hands *sweeping* the keyboard] **5.** to pass swiftly over or across **6.** to win overwhelmingly —*vi.* **1.** to clean a floor, etc. as with a broom **2.** to move steadily with speed, force, or gracefulness **3.** to extend in a long curve or line [a road *sweeping* up a hill] —*n.* **1.** the act of sweeping, as with a broom **2.** a sweeping movement **3.** range or scope **4.** an extent or stretch, as of land **5.** a sweeping line, curve, or contour **6.** one whose work is sweeping **7.** a complete victory

sweep'ings *n.pl.* things swept up, as dirt from the floor

sweep'stakes' *n., pl.* **-stakes'** a lottery in which the winner or winners of the common fund of stakes are determined by a horse race or other contest

sweet (swēt) *adj.* [OE. *swete*] **1.** having a taste of, or like that of, sugar **2.** *a)* pleasant in taste, smell, sound, etc. *b)* gratifying *c)* friendly, kindly, etc. **3.** *a)* not rancid or sour *b)* not salty or salted —*n.* a sweet food —**sweet'ish** *adj.* —**sweet'ness** *n.*

sweet alyssum a short garden plant with small spikes of tiny flowers

sweet'bread' (-bred') *n.* the thymus or pancreas of a calf, etc., when used as food

sweet'bri'er, sweet'bri'ar (-brī'ər) *n. same as* EGLANTINE

sweet corn any of various strains of corn eaten unripe as a table vegetable

sweet·en (swēt''n) *vt.* **1.** to make sweet **2.** to make pleasant or agreeable

sweet′en·er *n.* a sweetening agent, esp. a synthetic one, as saccharin
sweet′heart′ *n.* a loved one; lover
sweet′meat′ (-mēt′) *n.* a candy
sweet pea a climbing plant with fragrant, butterfly-shaped flowers
sweet pepper 1. a red pepper producing a large, mild fruit **2.** the fruit
sweet potato 1. a tropical trailing plant with a fleshy, orange or yellow, tuberlike root used as a vegetable **2.** its root
sweet′-talk′ *vt., vi.* [Colloq.] to flatter
sweet tooth [Colloq.] a craving for sweets
swell (swel) *vi., vt.* **swelled, swelled** or **swol′len, swell′ing** [OE. *swellen*] **1.** to expand as a result of pressure from within **2.** to curve out; bulge **3.** to fill (*with* pride, etc.) **4.** to increase in size, force, intensity, etc. *—n.* **1.** a part that swells; specif., a large, rolling wave **2.** an increase in size, amount, degree, etc. **3.** a crescendo *—adj.* [Slang] fine, excellent, grand, elegant, etc.
swelled head [Colloq.] an exaggerated opinion of oneself *—swell′head′ed adj.*
swell′ing *n.* **1.** an increase in size, force, etc. **2.** a swollen part, as on the body
swel·ter (swel′tər) *vi.* [OE. *sweltan*, to die] to sweat and wilt from great heat
swel′ter·ing *adj.* very hot, sweaty, etc.
swept (swept) *pt. & pp. of* SWEEP
swept′back′ *adj.* having a backward slant, as the wings of some aircraft
swerve (swurv) *vt., vi.* **swerved, swerv′ing** [OE. *sweorfan*, to scour] to turn aside suddenly from a straight line, course, etc. *—n.* a swerving motion
swift (swift) *adj.* [OE.] **1.** moving with great speed; fast **2.** coming, acting, etc. quickly *—n.* a swift-flying bird resembling the swallow *—* **swift′ly** *adv.* **—swift′ness** *n.*
swig (swig) *vt., vi.* **swigged, swig′ging** [< ?] [Colloq.] to drink in big gulps *—n.* [Colloq.] a big gulp, esp. of liquor
swill (swil) *vt., vi.* [OE. *swilian*] to drink greedily or in large quantities *—n.* liquid garbage used for feeding pigs, etc.
swim¹ (swim) *vi.* **swam, swum, swim′ming** [OE. *swimman*] **1.** to move through water by moving the arms, legs, fins, etc. **2.** to move along smoothly **3.** to float on or in a liquid **4.** to overflow [eyes *swimming* with tears] *—vt.* to swim in or across *—n.* an act of swimming **—in the swim** active in what is popular at the moment *—swim′mer n.*
swim² (swim) *n.* [OE. *swima*] a dizzy spell *—vi.* **swam, swum, swim′ming** to be dizzy
swin·dle (swin′d′l) *vt.* **-dled, -dling** [< G. *schwindeln*, to cheat] to cheat or trick out of money or property; defraud *—n.* an act of swindling; fraud *—swin′dler n.*
swine (swin) *n., pl.* **swine** [OE. *swin*] **1.** a pig, hog, or boar: usually used collectively **2.** a vicious, contemptible person *—swin′ish adj. —swin′ish·ly adv.*
swing (swiŋ) *vt., vi.* **swung, swing′ing** [OE. *swingan*] **1.** to sway or move back and forth **2.** to strike (*at*) **3.** to walk, trot, etc. with relaxed movements **4.** to turn, as on a hinge **5.** to hang **6.** to move in a curve [*swing* the car around] **7.** [Colloq.] to cause to come about successfully [to *swing* an election] **8.** [Slang] to be sophisticated, active, etc., esp. in the pursuit of pleasure *—n.* **1.** a swinging **2.** the arc through which something swings **3.** the manner of swinging a golf club, etc. **4.** a relaxed motion, as in walking **5.** a sweeping blow or stroke **6.** the course of some activity **7.** rhythm, as of music **8.** a seat hanging from

ropes or chains, on which one can swing **9.** a trip or tour **10.** jazz music c.1935-45, using large bands, strong rhythms, etc.
swing′er *n.* [Slang] one who swings (*v.* 8)
swing shift [Colloq.] a work shift from about midafternoon to about midnight
swipe (swip) *n.* [prob. var. of SWEEP] [Colloq.] a hard, sweeping blow *—vt.* **swiped, swip′ing 1.** [Colloq.] to hit with a swipe **2.** [Slang] to steal
swirl (swurl) *vi., vt.* [prob. < Norw. *svirla*, to whirl] to move or cause to move with a whirling motion *—n.* **1.** a whirl; eddy **2.** a twist; curl *—swirl′y adj.*
swish (swish) *vi., vt.* [echoic] **1.** to move with a sharp, hissing sound, as a cane swung through the air **2.** to rustle, as skirts *—n.* a swishing sound or movement
Swiss (swis) *adj.* of Switzerland, its people, etc. *—n., pl.* **Swiss** a native of Switzerland
Swiss (cheese) a pale-yellow, hard cheese with many large holes
Swiss steak a thick cut of round steak pounded with flour and braised
switch (swich) *n.* [prob. < LowG.] **1.** a thin, flexible stick used for whipping **2.** a tress of detached hair used as part of a coiffure **3.** a sharp lash, as with a whip **4.** a device used to open, close, or divert an electric circuit **5.** a device used in transferring a train from one track to another **6.** a shift; change *—vt.* **1.** to whip, as with a switch **2.** to swing sharply **3.** to shift; change **4.** to turn (an electric light, etc.) *on* or *off* **5.** to transfer (a train, etc.) to another track **6.** [Colloq.] to exchange [to *switch* places] *—vi.* to shift
switch′board′ (-bôrd′) *n.* a panel for controlling a system of electric circuits, as in a telephone exchange
switch′-hit′ter *n.* a baseball player who bats right-handed or left-handed
swiv·el (swiv′′l) *n.* [< OE. *swifan*, to revolve] a coupling device that allows free turning of the parts attached to it *—vi., vt.* **-eled or -elled, -eling** or **-el·ling** to turn or cause to turn as on a swivel or pivot
swiz·zle stick (swiz′′l) [< ?] a small rod for stirring mixed drinks
swol·len (swō′lən) *alt. pp. of* SWELL *—adj.* blown up; distended; bulging
swoon (swoon) *vi., n.* [OE. *geswogen*, unconscious] *same as* FAINT
swoop (swoop) *vi.* [OE. *swapan*, sweep along] to pounce or sweep (*down, upon*, etc.), as a bird in hunting *—n.* a swooping
sword (sôrd) *n.* [OE. *sweord*] a hand weapon having a long, sharp-pointed blade set in a hilt **—at swords′ points** ready to quarrel or fight
sword′fish′ *n., pl.*: see FISH a large marine food and game fish with the upper jawbone extending in a long, swordlike point
sword′play′ (-plā′) *n.* the act or skill of using a sword, as in fencing
swords·man (sôrdz′mən) *n., pl.* **-men 1.** one who uses a sword in fencing or fighting **2.** one skilled in using a sword
swore (swôr) *pt. of* SWEAR
sworn (swôrn) *pp. of* SWEAR *—adj.* bound or pledged as by an oath [*sworn* friends]
swum (swum) *pp. of* SWIM
swung (swuŋ) *pt. & pp. of* SWING
syb·a·rite (sib′ə rit′) *n.* [< *Sybaris*, ancient Gr. city in S Italy] anyone very fond of luxury and pleasure *—syb′a·rit′ic* (-rit′ik) *adj.*
syc·a·more (sik′ə môr′) *n.* [< Gr. *sykomoros*] **1.** a shade tree of Egypt and Asia Minor, with

figlike fruit **2.** a maple tree of Europe and Asia

syc·o·phant (sik'ə fənt) *n.* [< Gr. *sykophantēs*, informer] one who seeks favor by flattering people of wealth or influence

syl·lab·i·fy (si lab'ə fī') *vt.* -**fled'**, -**fy'ing** to divide into syllables —**syl·lab'i·fi·ca'tion** *n.*

syl·la·ble (sil'ə b'l) *n.* [< Gr. *syn-*, together + *lambanein*, to hold] **1.** a word or part of a word pronounced with a single, uninterrupted sounding of the voice **2.** any of the parts into which a written word is divided, more or less like its spoken syllables —**syl·lab·ic** (si lab'ik) *adj.*

syl·la·bus (sil'ə bəs) *n., pl.* -**bus·es**, -**bi** (-bī') [< Gr. *sillybos*, parchment label] a summary, esp. of a course of study

syl·lo·gism (sil'ə jiz'm) *n.* [< Gr. *syn-*, together + *logizesthai*, to reason] a form of reasoning in which two premises are made and a logical conclusion drawn from them

sylph (silf) *n.* [ModL. *sylphus*, a spirit < ?] a slender, graceful woman or girl

syl·van (sil'vən) *adj.* [< L. *silva*, a woods] **1.** of or in the woods or forests **2.** wooded

sym·bol (sim'b'l) *n.* [< Gr. *syn-*, together + *ballein*, to throw] **1.** a thing that represents another [the dove is a *symbol* of peace] **2.** a written or printed mark, letter, etc. standing for a quality, process, etc., as in music or chemistry —**sym·bol·ic** (-bäl'ik), **sym·bol'i·cal** *adj.*

sym·bol·ism (sim'b'l iz'm) *n.* **1.** representation by symbols **2.** a system of symbols **3.** symbolic meaning —**sym'bol·ist** *n.*

sym·bol·ize' *vt.* -**ized'**, -**iz'ing 1.** to be a symbol of; stand for **2.** to represent by a symbol or symbols —**sym'bol·i·za'tion** *n.*

sym·me·try (sim'ə trē) *n., pl.* -**tries** [< Gr. *syn-*, together + *metron*, a measure] **1.** correspondence of opposite parts in size, shape, and position **2.** balance or beauty of form resulting from this —**sym·met·ri·cal** (si met'ri k'l) *adj.*

sym·pa·thet·ic (sim'pə thet'ik) *adj.* **1.** of, feeling, or showing sympathy **2.** in agreement with one's tastes, mood, etc. —**sym'pa·thet'i·cal·ly** *adv.*

sym'pa·thize' (-thīz') *vi.* -**thized'**, -**thiz'ing 1.** to share the feelings or ideas of another **2.** to feel or express sympathy

sym·pa·thy (sim'pə thē) *n., pl.* -**thies** [< Gr. *syn-*, together + *pathos*, feeling] **1.** sameness of feeling **2.** agreement in qualities; accord **3.** a mutual liking or understanding **4.** ability to share another's ideas, feelings, etc.; esp., [*often pl.*] pity or compassion

sym·pho·ny (sim'fə nē) *n., pl.* -**nies** [< Gr. *syn-*, together + *phōnē*, a sound] **1.** harmony, as of sounds, color, etc. **2.** a long musical composition in several movements, for full orchestra **3.** a large orchestra for playing such works: in full **symphony orchestra 4.** [Colloq.] a symphony concert —**sym·phon'ic** (-fän'ik) *adj.*

sym·po·si·um (sim pō'zē əm) *n., pl.* -**si·ums**, -**si·a** (-ə) [< Gr. *syn-*, together + *posis*, a drinking] **1.** a conference for discussing some subject **2.** a collection of opinions or essays on some subject

symp·tom (simp'təm) *n.* [< Gr. *syn-*, together + *piptein*, to fall] any circumstance or condition that indicates the existence of something, esp. of a particular disease; sign —**symp'to·mat'ic** (-tə mat'ik) *adj.*

syn- [Gr.] *a prefix meaning* with, together, at the same time

syn·a·gogue (sin'ə gäg', -gôg') *n.* [< Gr. *syn-*, together + *agein*, to bring] **1.** an assembly of Jews for worship and religious study **2.** a building or place for such an assembly

syn·apse (si naps') *n.* [< Gr. *syn-*, together + *apsis*, a joining] the point of contact where nerve impulses are transmitted from one neuron to another

syn·chro·nize (siŋ'krə nīz') *vt.* -**nized'**, -**niz'ing** [< Gr. *syn-*, together + *chronos*, time] to move or occur at the same time or rate —*vt.* to cause to agree in time or rate of speed —**syn'·chro·ni·za'tion** *n.*

syn'chro·nous (-nəs) *adj.* happening at the same time or at the same rate

syn·co·pate (siŋ'kə pāt') *vt.* -**pat'ed**, -**pat'ing** [< Gr. *syn-*, together + *koptein*, to cut] to shift (the regular accent) as by beginning a tone on an unaccented beat and continuing it through the next accented beat —**syn'co·pa'·tion** *n.*

syn·di·cate (sin'də kit) *n.* [< Gr. *syn-*, together + *dikē*, justice] **1.** an association of individuals or corporations formed for a project requiring much capital **2.** any group, as of criminals, organized for some undertaking **3.** an organization that sells articles or features to a number of newspapers —*vt.* (-kāt') -**cat'ed**, -**cat'ing 1.** to manage as or form into a syndicate **2.** to publish (articles, etc.) through a syndicate — **syn'di·ca'tion** *n.*

syn·drome (sin'drōm) *n.* [< Gr. *syn-*, with + *dramein*, to run] a set of symptoms characterizing a disease or condition

syn·od (sin'əd) *n.* [< Gr. *syn-*, together + *hodos*, way] a council of churches or church officials

syn·o·nym (sin'ə nim) *n.* [< Gr. *syn-*, together + *onyma*, name] a word having the same or nearly the same meaning as another in the same language —**syn·on·y·mous** (si nän'ə məs) *adj.*

syn·op·sis (si näp'sis) *n., pl.* -**ses** (-sēz) [< Gr. *syn-*, together + *opsis*, a seeing] a short outline or review of the main points, as of a story; summary

syn·tax (sin'taks) *n.* [< Fr. < Gr. *syn-*, together + *tassein*, arrange] the way words are put together and related to one another in sentences —**syn·tac'ti·cal** *adj.*

syn·the·sis (sin'thə sis) *n., pl.* -**ses'** (-sēz') [< Gr. *syn-*, together + *tithenai*, to place] the combining of parts or elements so as to form a whole, a compound, etc. —**syn'the·size'** (-sīz') *vt.* -**sized'**, -**siz'ing**

syn·thet'ic (-thet'ik) *adj.* **1.** of or involving synthesis **2.** produced by chemical synthesis, rather than of natural origin **3.** not real; artificial —*n.* a synthetic substance —**syn·thet'i·cal·ly** *adv.*

syph·i·lis (sif'ə lis) *n.* [< *Syphilus*, hero of a L. poem (1530)] an infectious venereal disease — **syph'i·lit'ic** (-lit'ik) *adj., n.*

Syr·i·an (sir'ē ən) *adj.* of Syria, its people, language, etc. —*n.* **1.** a member of the Semitic people of Syria **2.** their Arabic dialect

syr·inge (sə rinj', sir'inj) *n.* [< Gr. *syrinx*, a pipe] a device consisting of a tube with a rubber bulb or piston at one end, for drawing in a liquid and then ejecting it in a stream: used to inject fluids into or cleanse body cavities, etc.

syr·up (sir'əp, sur'-) *n.* [< Ar. *sharāb*, a drink] a sweet, thick liquid made by boiling sugar with water, often flavored or, in pharmacy, medicated —**syr'up·y** *adj.*

sys·tem (sis'təm) *n.* [< Gr. *syn-*, together + *histanai*, to set] **1.** a group of things or parts connected in some way so as to form a whole *[the solar system, school system]* **2.** a set of facts, rules, etc. that make up an orderly plan **3.** orderly procedure; method **4.** the body, or a number of bodily organs, functioning as a unit **sys'tem·at'ic** (-tə mat'ik) *adj.* **1.** constituting or based on a system **2.** according to a system; orderly —**sys'tem·at'i·cal·ly** *adv.*

sys'tem·a·tize' (-təm ə tīz') *vt.* **-tized', -tiz'ing** to form into a system; arrange in a systematic way
sys·tem·ic (sis tem'ik) *adj.* of or affecting the body as a whole —**sys·tem'i·cal·ly** *adv.*
sys·to·le (sis'tə lē') *n.* [< Gr. *syn-*, together + *stellein*, send] the usual rhythmic contraction of the heart —**sys·tol'ic** (-täl'ik) *adj.*

T

T, t (tē) *n., pl.* **T's, t's** the twentieth letter of the English alphabet —**to a T** to perfection; exactly **T.** tablespoon(s)
t. **1.** teaspoon(s) **2.** temperature **3.** ton(s)
tab[1] (tab) *n.* [< ?] **1.** a small, flat loop or strip on something for opening it, hanging it up, etc. **2.** a projecting piece on a card, useful in filing
tab[2] (tab) *n.* [prob. < TABULATION] [Colloq.] **1.** a bill, as at a restaurant **2.** total cost —**keep tabs** (or **a tab**) **on** to check on
tab·by (tab'ē) *n., pl.* **-bies** [< Fr., ult. < Ar.] any pet cat, esp. a female
tab·er·na·cle (tab'ər nak''l) *n.* [< L. *tabernaculum*, a tent] **1.** the portable sanctuary carried by the Jews in their wanderings from Egypt **2.** a large place of worship
ta·ble (tā'b'l) *n.* [< L. *tabula*, board] **1.** a thin slab of metal, stone, etc. **2.** *a)* a piece of furniture having a flat top set on legs *b)* such a table set with food *c)* food served *d)* the people seated at a table **3.** *a)* a systematic list of details, contents, etc. *b)* an orderly arrangement of facts, figures, etc. **4.** any flat, horizontal surface, piece, etc. —*vt.* **-bled, -bling 1.** to put on a table **2.** to postpone consideration of (a motion, bill, etc.) —**at table** at a meal —**turn the tables** to reverse a situation
tab·leau (tab'lō) *n., pl.* **-leaux** (-lōz), **-leaus** [Fr. < OFr. dim. of *table*, TABLE] a representation of a scene by persons depicted in costume
ta'ble·cloth' *n.* a cloth for covering a table
ta·ble d'hôte (tä'b'l dōt') [Fr., table of the host] a complete meal with courses as specified, served at a restaurant for a set price
ta'ble·land' *n.* a high, broad, flat region
ta'ble·spoon' *n.* a large spoon for serving, measuring, etc., holding 1/2 fluid ounce —**ta'-ble·spoon'ful** *n., pl.* **-fuls**
tab·let (tab'lit) *n.* [see TABLE] **1.** a flat, thin piece of metal, stone, etc. with an inscription **2.** a writing pad of paper sheets glued together at one edge **3.** a small, flat, hard mass, as of medicine
table tennis a game somewhat like tennis, played on a table with a small plastic ball
ta'ble·ware' (-wer') *n.* dishes, glassware, silverware, etc. for use at meals
tab·loid (tab'loid) *n.* [TABL(ET) + -OID] a newspaper, usually half size, with many pictures and short news stories
ta·boo (ta boo', tə-) *n.* [S Pacific native term *tabu*] **1.** among some Polynesian peoples, etc., a sacred prohibition making certain people or things untouchable, etc. **2.** any conventional social restriction —*adj.* prohibited by taboo —*vt.* **1.** to put under taboo **2.** to prohibit or forbid Also **tabu**
tab·u·lar (tab'yə lər) *adj.* [see TABLE] **1.** flat **2.** *a)* of or arranged in columns in a table *b)* calculated by using tables

tab'u·late' (-lāt') *vt.* **-lat'ed, -lat'ing** to put (facts, statistics, etc.) in a table —**tab'u·la'tion** *n.* —**tab'u·la'tor** *n.*
ta·chom·e·ter (ta käm'ə tər, tə-) *n.* [< Gr. *tachos*, speed + -METER] a device that indicates or measures the revolutions per minute of a revolving shaft
tac·it (tas'it) *adj.* [Fr. *tacite* < L. *tacere*, to be silent] **1.** unspoken; silent **2.** not openly expressed, but implied or understood —**tac'it·ly** *adv.*
tac·i·turn (tas'ə turn') *adj.* [see prec.] usually silent; not liking to talk
tack (tak) *n.* [< MDu. *tacke*, twig] **1.** a short nail with a sharp point and a large, flat head **2.** a temporary stitch **3.** a change of direction made by a sailboat in sailing a course against the wind **4.** a zigzag course **5.** a course of action —*vt.* **1.** to fasten with tacks **2.** to attach or add **3.** to maneuver (a boat) by a tack —*vi.* to change course suddenly
tack·le (tak''l) *n.* [< MDu. *takel*] **1.** equipment; gear **2.** a system of ropes and pulleys for moving weights **3.** a tackling, as in football **4.** *Football* the player next to either end on the line —*vt.* **-led, -ling 1.** to take hold of; seize **2.** to try to do; undertake **3.** *Football* to bring down (the ball carrier) —**tack'ler** *n.*
tack·y (tak'ē) *adj.* **-i·er, -i·est 1.** sticky, as glue **2.** [Colloq.] shabby
ta·co (tä'kō) *n., pl.* **-cos** [AmSp. < Sp., a plug, wad] a fried, folded tortilla filled with chopped meat, shredded lettuce, etc.
tact (takt) *n.* [< L. *tangere*, to touch] a sense of the right thing to say or do without offending —**tact'ful** *adj.* —**tact'ful·ly** *adv.* —**tact'less** *adj.* —**tact'less·ly** *adv.*
tac·tics (tak'tiks) *n.pl.* [< Gr. *tassein*, arrange] **1.** [*with sing. v.*] the science of maneuvering military and naval forces **2.** any methods used to gain an end —**tac'ti·cal** *adj.* —**tac·ti'cian** (-tish'ən) *n.*
tac·tile (tak't'l) *adj.* [Fr. < L. *tangere*, to touch] of or perceived by the sense of touch
tad·pole (tad'pōl') *n.* [ME. *tadde*, toad + *poll*, head] the larva of a frog or toad, having gills and a tail and living in water
taf·fe·ta (taf'i tə) *n.* [< Per. *tāftan*, to weave] a fine, stiff fabric of silk, nylon, etc., with a sheen
taf·fy (taf'ē) *n.* [< ?] a chewy candy made of sugar or molasses boiled down and pulled
tag (tag) *n.* [prob. < Scand.] **1.** a hanging end or part **2.** a hard-tipped end on a cord or lace **3.** a card, etc. attached as a label **4.** an epithet **5.** the last line or lines of a speech, story, etc. **6.** a children's game in which one player chases the others until he touches one —*vt.* **tagged, tag'ging 1.** to provide with a tag **2.** to choose; select **3.** to touch in playing tag **4.** [Colloq.] to follow close behind —*vi.* [Colloq.] to follow closely (with *along, after*, etc.)

Ta·ga·log (tä gä′läg, -lôg) *n.* **1.** *pl.* **-logs, -log** a member of a Malayan people of the Philippine Islands **2.** their Indonesian language

Ta·hi·tian (tə hēsh′ən) *adj.* of Tahiti, its people, language, etc. *—n.* **1.** a native of Tahiti **2.** the Tahitian language

tail (tāl) *n.* [OE. *tægel*] **1.** the rear end of an animal's body, esp. when a distinct appendage **2.** anything like an animal's tail in form or position **3.** the hind, bottom, last, or inferior part of anything **4.** [*often pl.*] the reverse side of a coin **5.** [*pl.*] [Colloq.] full-dress attire for men **6.** [Colloq.] a person that follows another, esp. in surveillance *—adj.* **1.** at the rear **2.** from the rear [a *tail* wind] *—vt., vi.* [Colloq.] to follow close behind

tail′gate′ *n.* the hinged or removable gate at the back of a wagon, truck, etc. *—vi., vt.* **-gat′ed, -gat′ing** to drive too closely behind (another vehicle) *—tail′gat′er n.*

tail′light′ *n.* a light, usually red, at the rear of a vehicle to warn vehicles coming from behind

tai·lor (tā′lər) *n.* [< LL. *taliare*, to cut] one who makes, repairs, and alters clothes *—vi.* to work as a tailor *—vt.* **1.** to make by tailor's work **2.** to form, alter, etc. for a certain purpose [a novel *tailored* for TV]

tail′pipe′ *n.* an exhaust pipe at the rear of an automotive vehicle

tail′spin′ *n. same as* SPIN (*n.* 3)

taint (tānt) *vt.* [ult. < L. *tingere*, to wet] **1.** to affect with something injurious, unpleasant, etc.; infect **2.** to make morally corrupt *—vi.* to become tainted *—n.* a trace of corruption, disgrace, etc.

take (tāk) *vt.* **took, tak′en, tak′ing** [< ON. *taka*] **1.** to get possession of; capture, seize, etc. **2.** to get hold of **3.** to capture the fancy of **4.** to obtain, acquire, assume, etc. **5.** to use, consume, etc. **6.** to buy, rent, subscribe to, etc. **7.** to join or support (one side in a disagreement, etc.) **8.** to choose; select **9.** to travel by [to *take* a bus] **10.** to deal with; consider **11.** to occupy [take a chair] **12.** to require; demand [it *takes* money] **13.** to derive (a name, quality, etc.) from **14.** to excerpt **15.** to study **16.** to write down [take notes] **17.** to make (a photograph, etc.) **18.** to win (a prize, etc.) **19.** to undergo [take punishment] **20.** to engage in [take a nap] **21.** to accept (an offer, bet, etc.) **22.** to react to [to take a joke in earnest] **23.** to contract (a disease, etc.) **24.** to understand **25.** to suppose; presume **26.** to feel [take pity] **27.** to lead, escort, etc. **28.** to carry **29.** to remove as by stealing **30.** to subtract **31.** [Slang] to cheat; trick **32.** *Gram.* to be used with [a transitive verb *takes* an object] *—vi.* **1.** to begin growing: said of a plant **2.** to catch [the fire *took*] **3.** to gain favor; be popular **4.** to be effective [the vaccination *took*] **5.** to go [to *take* to the hills] **6.** [Colloq.] to become (sick) *—n.* **1.** a taking **2.** *a)* the amount taken *b)* [Slang] receipts or profits *—on the take* [Slang] taking bribes, etc. *—take after* to be, act, or look like *—take back* to retract (something said, etc.) *—take down* to put in writing; record *—take in* **1.** to admit; receive **2.** to make smaller **3.** to understand **4.** to cheat; trick *—take off* **1.** to leave the ground, etc. in flight: said of an aircraft **2.** [Colloq.] to start **3.** [Colloq.] to imitate; mimic *—take on* **1.** to acquire; assume **2.** to employ **3.** to undertake (a task, etc.) *—take over* to begin controlling, managing, etc. *—take to* to become fond of *—take up* **1.** to make tighter or shorter **2.** to become interested in (an occupation, study, etc.)

take′off′ *n.* **1.** the act of leaving the ground, as in jumping or flight **2.** [Colloq.] an amusing or mocking imitation

take′o′ver *n.* the usurpation of power in a nation, organization, etc.

tak·ing (tāk′iŋ) *adj.* attractive; winning *—n.* **1.** the act of one that takes **2.** [*pl.*] earnings; profits

talc (talk) *n.* [Fr. < Ar. *talq*] a soft mineral used to make talcum powder, etc.

tal·cum (powder) (tal′kəm) a powder for the body and face made of purified talc

tale (tāl) *n.* [OE. *talu*] **1.** a true or fictitious story; narrative **2.** idle or malicious gossip **3.** a falsehood; lie

tale′bear′er (-ber′ər) *n.* one who gossips, tells secrets, etc. *—tale′bear′ing adj.*

tal·ent (tal′ənt) *n.* [< Gr. *talanton*, a weight] **1.** an ancient unit of weight or money **2.** any natural ability or power **3.** a special, superior ability in an art, etc. **4.** people with talent *—tal′ent·ed adj.*

tal·is·man (tal′is mən, -iz-) *n., pl.* **-mans** [< MGr. *telesma*, a consecrated object] **1.** a ring, stone, etc. bearing engraved figures supposed to bring good luck, avert evil, etc. **2.** any magic charm

talk (tôk) *vi.* [prob. < OE. *talian*, reckon] **1.** to put ideas into words; speak **2.** to express ideas by speech substitutes [to *talk* by signs] **3.** to chatter; gossip **4.** to confer; consult **5.** to confess or inform on someone *—vt.* **1.** to use in speaking [to *talk* Spanish] **2.** to discuss **3.** to put into a specified condition, etc. by talking *—n.* **1.** the act of talking **2.** conversation **3.** a speech **4.** a conference **5.** gossip **6.** the subject of conversation, gossip, etc. **7.** frivolous discussion *—talk back* to answer impertinently *—talk down to* to talk patronizingly to *—talk up* to promote in discussion *—talk′er n.*

talk′a·tive (-ə tiv) *adj.* talking a great deal; loquacious: also **talk′y —talk′a·tive·ness n.**

talk′ing-to′ *n.* [Colloq.] a scolding

tall (tôl) *adj.* [< OE. *(ge)tæl*, swift] **1.** of more than normal stature **2.** having a specified height **3.** [Colloq.] exaggerated [a *tall* tale] **4.** [Colloq.] large [a *tall* drink]

tal·low (tal′ō) *n.* [prob. < MLowG. *talg*] the fat of cattle, sheep, etc., used to make candles, soaps, etc. *—tal′low·y adj.*

tal·ly (tal′ē) *n., pl.* **-lies** [< L. *talea*, a stick (notched to keep accounts)] **1.** anything used as a record for an account **2.** an account, reckoning, etc. **3.** a tag or label *—vt.* **-lied, -ly·ing 1.** to put on or as on a tally **2.** to count (up) *—vi.* **1.** to score in a game **2.** to agree; correspond

tal·ly-ho (tal′ē hō′) *interj.* [< Fr. *taiaut*] the cry of a hunter on sighting the fox

Tal·mud (täl′mood, tal′-; -məd) *n.* [< Heb. *lāmadh*, learn] the writings constituting the Jewish civil and religious law

tal·on (tal′ən) *n.* [< L. *talus*, an ankle] the claw of a bird of prey

tam (tam) *n. short for* TAM-O′-SHANTER

ta·ma·le (tə mä′lē) *n.* [< MexInd. *tamalli*] a Mexican food of minced meat and red peppers cooked in corn husks

tam·a·rack (tam′ə rak′) *n.* [< AmInd.] an American larch tree, usually in swamps

tam·a·rind (tam′ə rind) *n.* [< Sp. < Ar. *tamr hindī*, date of India] **1.** a tropical tree with yellow flowers and brown, acid pods **2.** its fruit, used in foods, medicine, etc.

tam·bou·rine (tam′bə rēn′) *n.* [< Ar. *tanbūr*, stringed instrument] a shallow, single-headed hand drum having jingling metal disks in the rim: played by shaking, hitting, etc.

tame (tām) *adj.* **tam′er, tam′est** [OE. *tam*] **1.**

changed from a wild state for use by man **2.** gentle; docile **3.** without force or spirit; dull — **vt. tamed, tam'ing 1.** to make tame, or domestic **2.** to make gentle, docile, etc. —**tam'a·ble, tame'a·ble** adj. —**tame'ly** adv. —**tame'ness** n.

Tam·il (tam''l, täm''l, tum''l) n. the non-Indo-European language of the Tamils, a people of S India and N Sri Lanka

tam-o'-shan·ter (tam'ə shan'tər) n. [< title character of R. Burns's poem] a Scottish cap with a round, flat top

tamp (tamp) vt. [< ? TAMPON] to pack or pound (down) by a series of taps

tam·per (tam'pər) vi. [< TEMPER] **1.** to make secret, illegal arrangements (with) **2.** to meddle (with), esp. so as to damage

tam·pon (tam'pän) n. [< Fr. tapon, a bung] a plug as of cotton, put into a body cavity, wound, etc., as to stop bleeding

tan (tan) n. [< ML. tannum] **1.** a yellowish-brown color **2.** the color of suntan —adj. **tan'-ner, tan'nest** yellowish-brown —vt. **tanned, tan'-ning 1.** to change (hide) into leather by soaking in tannic acid **2.** to produce a suntan in **3.** [Colloq.] to whip severely —vi. to become tanned

tan'bark' n. any bark containing tannic acid, used to tan hides, etc.

tan·dem (tan'dəm) adv. [< punning use of L. tandem, at length (of time)] one behind the other; in single file

tang (taŋ) n. [ON. tangi, a sting] **1.** a prong on a knife, file, etc. that fits into the handle **2.** a strong, penetrating taste or odor —**tang'y** adj.

tan·ge·lo (tan'jə lō') n., pl. **-los'** [TANG(ERINE) + (pom)elo, grapefruit] a fruit produced by crossing a tangerine with a grapefruit

tan·gent (tan'jənt) adj. [< L. tangere, to touch] **1.** touching **2.** Geom. meeting a curve or surface at one point but not intersecting it —n. a tangent line, curve, or surface —**go off at (or on) a tangent** to change suddenly to another line of action —**tan·gen'tial** (-jen'shəl) adj.

tan·ge·rine (tan'jə rēn') n. [< Tangier, city in N Africa] **1.** a small, loose-skinned, reddish-yellow orange with easily separated segments **2.** reddish yellow

tan·gi·ble (tan'jə b'l) adj. [< L. tangere, to touch] **1.** that can be touched or felt by touch **2.** definite; objective —n. [pl.] property that can be appraised for value —**tan'gi·bil'i·ty** n. —**tan'gi·bly** adv.

tan·gle (taŋ'g'l) vt. **-gled, -gling** [? < ME. taglen, to entangle] **1.** to catch as in a snare; trap **2.** to make a snarl of —vi. **1.** to become tangled **2.** [Colloq.] to argue —n. **1.** an intertwined, confused mass **2.** a confused condition

tan·go (taŋ'gō) n., pl. **-gos** [AmSp.] **1.** a S. American dance with long gliding steps **2.** music for this —vi. **-goed, -go·ing** to dance the tango

tank (taŋk) n. [< Sp. & Port. estancar, stop the flow of] **1.** any large container for liquid or gas **2.** an armored vehicle carrying guns and moving on tractor treads —**tank'ful'** n., pl. **-fuls'**

tank·ard (taŋ'kərd) n. [ME.] a large drinking cup with a handle and a hinged lid

tank'er n. **1.** a ship for carrying oil or other liquids **2.** a plane carrying gasoline for refueling another plane in flight

tank top [orig. worn in swimming tanks] a casual shirt like an undershirt with wide shoulder straps

tan·ner (tan'ər) n. one whose work is tanning hides

tan'ner·y n., pl. **-ies** a place where hides are tanned

tan·nic acid (tan'ik) a yellowish, astringent substance used in tanning, medicine, etc.: also **tan'nin** (-in) n.

tan·ta·lize (tan'tə līz') vt. **-lized', -liz'ing** [< TANTALUS + -IZE] to promise or show something desirable and then withhold it; tease

tan·ta·lum (tan'tə ləm) n. [< TANTALUS: from difficulty in extracting it] a rare, steel-blue metallic chemical element that resists corrosion: symbol, Ta

Tan·ta·lus (tan'tə ləs) Gr. Myth. a king doomed in Hades to stand in water that receded when he tried to drink it and under branches of fruit he could not reach

tan·ta·mount (tan'tə mount') adj. [< L. tantus, so much + OFr. amont, upward] equal (to) in value, effect, etc.

tan·trum (tan'trəm) n. [< ?] a violent, willful outburst of rage, etc.

Tao·ism (dou'iz'm, tou'-) n. [Chin. tao, the way] a Chinese religion and philosophy advocating simplicity, selflessness, etc. —**Tao'ist** n., adj.

tap¹ (tap) vt., vi. **tapped, tap'ping** [prob. echoic] **1.** to strike lightly **2.** to make or do by tapping [to tap a message] **3.** to choose, as for membership in a club —n. a light, rapid blow

tap² (tap) n. [OE. tæppa] **1.** a faucet or spigot **2.** a plug, cork, etc. for stopping a hole in a cask, etc. **3.** a place in an electrical circuit where a connection can be made —vt. **tapped, tap'ping 1.** to put a hole in, or pull the plug from, for drawing off liquid **2.** to draw (liquid) from a container, cavity, etc. **3.** to make use of [to tap new resources] **4.** to make a connection with (an electric circuit, telephone line, etc.)

tape (tāp) n. [OE. tæppe, a fillet] **1.** a strong, narrow strip of cloth, paper, etc. used for binding, tying, etc. **2.** short for: a) TAPE MEASURE b) MAGNETIC TAPE —vt. **taped, tap'ing 1.** to bind, tie, etc. with tape **2.** to record on magnetic tape

tape measure a tape marked in inches, feet, etc. for measuring

ta·per (tā'pər) n. [OE. tapur] **1.** a slender candle **2.** a gradual decrease in width or thickness —vt., vi. **1.** to decrease gradually in width or thickness **2.** to lessen; diminish Often with off

tape recorder a device for recording on magnetic tape

tap·es·try (tap'is trē) n., pl. **-tries** [< Gr. tapēs, a carpet] a heavy woven cloth with decorative designs and pictures, used as a wall hanging, furniture covering, etc.

tape'worm' n. a tapelike worm that lives as a parasite in the intestines

tap·i·o·ca (tap'ē ō'kə) n. [Port. & Sp. < SAmInd.] a starchy substance from cassava roots, used for puddings, etc.

ta·pir (tā'pər) n. [Sp. < SAmInd.] a large, hoglike mammal of tropical America

tap'room' n. same as BARROOM

tap'root' n. [TAP² + ROOT¹] a main root from which branch roots spread out

taps (taps) n. [< TAP¹, because orig. a drum signal] a bugle call to put out the lights for the night, as in an army camp

tar¹ (tär) n. [OE. teru] a thick, sticky, black liquid obtained by the destructive distillation of wood, coal, etc. —vt. **tarred, tar'ring** to cover or smear with tar

tar² (tär) n. [< TAR(PAULIN)] [Colloq.] a sailor

ta·ran·tu·la (tə ran'choo lə) n., pl. **-las, -lae** (-lē) [< Taranto, Italy] a large, hairy, somewhat poisonous spider of S Europe and tropical America

tar·dy (tär'dē) adj. **-di·er, -di·est** [< L. tardus,

slow] **1.** slow in moving, acting, etc. **2.** late, delayed, or dilatory —**tar′di·ly** adv. —**tar′di·ness** n.

tare¹ (ter) n. [< or akin to MDu. tarwe, wheat] **1.** the vetch **2.** Bible a weed

tare² (ter) n. [< It. < Ar. taraḥa, to reject] the weight of a container deducted from the total weight to determine the weight of the contents

tar·get (tär′git) n. [< MFr. targe, a shield] **1.** a) a board, etc. marked as with concentric circles, aimed at in archery, rifle practice, etc. b) any object that is shot at **2.** an objective; goal **3.** an object of attack, criticism, etc.

tar·iff (tar′if) n. [< Ar. ta'rif, information] **1.** a list or system of taxes upon exports or imports **2.** a tax of this kind, or its rate **3.** any list of prices, charges, etc. **4.** [Colloq.] any bill, charge, etc.

tar·nish (tär′nish) vt. [< MFr. ternir, make dim] **1.** to dull the luster of **2.** to sully (a reputation, etc.) —vi. **1.** to lose luster; discolor **2.** to become sullied —n. **1.** dullness **2.** a stain —**tar′nish·a·ble** adj.

ta·ro (tä′rō) n., pl. -ros [Tahitian] a tropical plant with an edible tuber

tar·ot (tar′ō, ta rō′) n. [Fr. < Ar. taraḥa, remove] [often T-] any of a set of fortunetelling cards

tar·pau·lin (tär pô′lin, tär′pə-) n. [< TAR¹ + PALL²] canvas covered with a waterproofing compound, or a protective cover of this

tar·pon (tär′pən, -pän) n. [< ?] a large, silvery game fish of the W Atlantic

tar·ra·gon (tar′ə gän′) n. [Sp. < Gr. drakōn, dragon] **1.** an old-world plant with leaves used for seasoning **2.** these leaves

tar·ry (tar′ē) vi. -ried, -ry·ing [prob. < L. tardus, slow] **1.** to delay, linger, etc. **2.** to stay for a time **3.** to wait

tart¹ (tärt) adj. [OE. teart] **1.** sharp in taste; sour; acid **2.** sharp in meaning; cutting [a tart answer] —**tart′ly** adv. —**tart′ness** n.

tart² (tärt) n. [MFr. tarte] a small shell of pastry filled with fruit, jam, etc.

tart³ (tärt) n. [< prec., orig. slang term of endearment] a prostitute

tar·tan (tär′t'n) n. [prob. < MFr. tiretaine, mixed fabric] a woolen cloth in any of various woven plaid patterns, worn esp. in the Scottish Highlands

Tar·tar (tär′tər) n. same as TATAR

tar·tar (tär′tər) n. [< MGr. tartaron] **1.** a potassium salt forming a reddish, crustlike deposit in wine casks: in purified form called CREAM OF TARTAR **2.** a hard deposit on the teeth

tar·tar sauce (tär′tər) [< Fr.] a sauce of mayonnaise with chopped pickles, olives, etc.

task (task) n. [< L. taxare, to rate] **1.** a piece of work to be done **2.** any difficult undertaking — vt. to put a strain on; tax —**take to task** to reprimand

task force a group, esp. a trained military unit, assigned a specific task

task·mas′ter n. one who assigns tasks to others, esp. when exacting or severe

tas·sel (tas′'l) n. [OFr., a knob] **1.** an ornamental tuft of threads, etc. hanging loosely from a knob or knot **2.** something like this, as a tuft of corn silk

taste (tāst) vt. tast′ed, tast′ing [OFr. taster] **1.** to test the flavor of by putting a little in one's mouth **2.** to detect the flavor of by the sense of taste **3.** to eat or drink a small amount of **4.** to experience [to taste success] —vi. to have a specific flavor —n. **1.** the sense by which flavor

is perceived through stimulation of the taste buds on the tongue **2.** the flavor so perceived **3.** a small amount tasted as a sample **4.** a bit; trace **5.** the ability to appreciate what is beautiful, appropriate, etc. **6.** a liking; inclination —**in bad** (or **good**) **taste** in a style or manner showing a bad (or good) sense of beauty, fitness, etc. —**taste′less** adj.

taste bud any of the cells in the tongue that are the sense organs of taste

taste′ful adj. having or showing good taste (n. 5) —**taste′ful·ly** adv.

tast′y adj. -i·er, -i·est tasting good

tat (tat) vt. tat′ted, tat′ting to make by tatting —vi. to do tatting

Ta·tar (tät′ər) n. **1.** a member of any of the E Asiatic tribes who invaded W Asia and E Europe in the Middle Ages **2.** a Turkic language

tat·ter (tat′ər) n. [prob. < ON. töturr, rags] **1.** a torn and hanging piece, as of a garment **2.** [pl.] torn, ragged clothes —vt., vi. to make or become ragged —**tat′tered** adj.

tat·ting (tat′iŋ) n. [prob. < Brit. dial. tat, to tangle] **1.** a fine lace made by looping and knotting **2.** the act of making this

tat·tle (tat′'l) vi. -tled, -tling [prob. < MDu. tatelen] **1.** to talk idly **2.** to tell others' secrets —n. chatter —**tat′tler** n.

tat′tle·tale′ n. an informer; talebearer

tat·too¹ (ta tōō′) vt. -tooed′, -too′ing [< Tahitian tatau] to make (permanent designs) on (the skin) by puncturing it and inserting indelible colors —n., pl. -toos′ a tattooed mark or design —**tat·too′er** n.

tat·too² (ta tōō′) n., pl. -toos′ [< Du. tap toe, shut the tap: a signal for closing barrooms] **1.** a signal on a drum, bugle, etc. summoning soldiers, etc. to their quarters at night **2.** a drumming, rapping, etc.

tau (tô, tou) n. the nineteenth letter of the Greek alphabet (T, τ)

taught (tôt) pt. & pp. of TEACH

taunt (tônt, tänt) vt. [< ? Fr. tant pour tant, tit for tat] to reproach scornfully or sarcastically —n. a scornful remark

taupe (tōp) n. [Fr. < L. talpa, a mole] a dark, brownish gray, the color of moleskin

Tau·rus (tôr′əs) [L., a bull] the second sign of the zodiac

taut (tôt) adj. [ME. toght, tight] **1.** tightly stretched, as a rope **2.** tense [a taut smile] **3.** trim, tidy, etc. —**taut′ly** adv.

tau·tol·o·gy (tô täl′ə jē) n., pl. -gies [< Gr. to auto, the same + -LOGY] needless repetition of an idea in a different word, phrase, etc.; redundancy

tav·ern (tav′ərn) n. [< L. taberna] **1.** a bar; saloon **2.** an inn

taw·dry (tô′drē) adj. -dri·er, -dri·est [< St. Audrey laces, sold at St. Audrey's fair, Norwich, England] cheap and showy; gaudy

taw·ny (tô′nē) adj. -ni·er, -ni·est [< OFr. tanner, to tan] brownish-yellow; tan —n. a tawny color

tax (taks) vt. [< L. taxare, appraise] **1.** to require to pay a tax **2.** to assess a tax on (income, purchases, etc.) **3.** to put a strain on **4.** to accuse; charge —n. **1.** a compulsory payment, of a percentage of income, property value, etc., for the support of a government **2.** a heavy demand; burden —**tax′a·ble** adj. —**tax·a′tion** n.

tax·i (tak′sē) n., pl. -is short for TAXICAB —vi. tax′ied, tax′i·ing or tax′y·ing **1.** to go in a taxi **2.** to move slowly along the ground or on water as an airplane does before taking off or after landing

tax'i·cab' (-kab') *n.* [< *taxi(meter) cab*] an automobile in which passengers are carried for a fare

tax·i·der·my (tak'si dur'mē) *n.* [< Gr. *taxis*, arrangement + *derma*, a skin] the art of stuffing and mounting animal skins to give a lifelike effect —**tax'i·der'mist** *n.*

tax·i·me·ter (tak'sē mēt'ər) *n.* [< ML. *taxa*, a tax + *-meter*, -METER] an automatic device in taxicabs that registers fares due

tax·on·o·my (tak sän'ə mē) *n.* [< Gr. *taxis*, arrangement + *nomos*, a law] classification, esp. of animals and plants

tax'pay'er *n.* any person who pays taxes

TB, T.B., tb, t.b. tuberculosis

T-bone steak (tē'bōn') a steak from the loin, with a T-shaped bone

tbs., tbsp. tablespoon(s)

TD touchdown: also **td**

tea (tē) *n.* [Chin. dial. *t'e*] 1. an evergreen shrub grown in Asia 2. its dried leaves, steeped in boiling water to make a beverage 3. this beverage 4. a tealike beverage made as from other plants 5. [Chiefly Brit.] a light meal in the late afternoon 6. an afternoon party at which tea, etc. is served

tea'ber'ry *n., pl.* **-ries** 1. *same as* WINTERGREEN (sense 1) 2. a wintergreen berry

teach (tēch) *vt.* **taught, teach'ing** [OE. *tæcan*] 1. to show how to do something; give lessons to 2. to give lessons in (a subject) 3. to give knowledge, insight, etc. to —*vi.* to be a teacher —**teach'ing** *n.*

teach'er *n.* one who teaches, esp. as a profession

tea'cup' *n.* a cup for drinking tea —**tea'cup'ful'** *n., pl.* **-fuls'**

teak (tēk) *n.* [< Port. < native word *tēkka*] 1. an East Indian tree with hard, yellowish-brown wood 2. its wood: also **teak'wood'**

tea'ket'tle *n.* a covered kettle with a spout, used to boil water for tea, etc.

teal (tēl) *n.* [ME. *tele*] 1. a small, short-necked freshwater wild duck 2. a dark greenish blue: also **teal blue**

team (tēm) *n.* [OE., offspring] 1. two or more horses, oxen, etc. harnessed to the same plow, etc. 2. a group of people working or playing together —*vt., vi.* to join together in a team (often with *up*)

team'mate' *n.* a fellow team member

team'ster (-stər) *n.* one whose work is driving teams or trucks for hauling loads

team'work' *n.* the action or effort of people working together as a group

tea'pot' *n.* a pot with a spout, handle, and lid, for brewing and pouring tea

tear' (ter) *vt.* **tore, torn, tear'ing** [OE. *teran*, rend] 1. to pull apart by force; rip 2. to make (a hole, etc.) by tearing 3. to lacerate 4. to split; disrupt *[torn* by dissension*]* 5. to divide by doubt, etc. 6. to remove as by tearing, pulling, etc. (with *out, off*, etc.) —*vi.* 1. to be torn 2. to move with force or speed —*n.* 1. a tearing 2. a torn place; rip —**tear down** to take apart; wreck, demolish, etc.

tear² (tir) *n.* [OE.] 1. a drop of the salty fluid that flows from the eye in weeping 2. [*pl.*] sorrow; grief —**in tears** weeping —**tear'ful** *adj.* —**tear'ful·ly** *adv.*

tear'drop' (tir'-) *n.* a tear

tear gas (tir) a gas that makes the eyes sore and blinds them with tears

tea'room' *n.* a restaurant that serves tea, coffee, light lunches, etc.

tease (tēz) *vt.* **teased, teas'ing** [OE. *tæsan*] 1. *a)* to card or comb (flax, wool, etc.) *b)* to raise a nap on (cloth) with teasels *c)* to fluff (the hair) by combing toward the scalp 2. to annoy by mocking, poking fun, etc. 3. to pester with repeated requests 4. to tantalize —*vi.* to tease someone —*n.* one who teases —**teas'er** *n.*

tea·sel (tē'z'l) *n.* [see TEASE] 1. a bristly plant with prickly, cylindrical flowers 2. the dried flower, or any device, used to raise a nap on cloth

tea'spoon' *n.* a spoon for use at the table and as a measuring unit holding 1/3 tablespoonful —**tea'spoon·ful'** *n., pl.* **-fuls'**

teat (tēt) *n.* [< OFr. *tete*] the nipple of a breast or udder

tech. 1. technical 2. technology

tech·ni·cal (tek'ni k'l) *adj.* [< Gr. *technē*, an art] 1. dealing with the industrial or mechanical arts or the applied sciences 2. of a specific science, art, etc. 3. of or showing technique 4. involving or using technicalities —**tech'ni·cal·ly** *adv.*

tech'ni·cal·i·ty (-nə kal'ə tē) *n., pl.* **-ties** 1. the state or quality of being technical 2. a technical point, term, method, etc. 3. a minute point or detail brought to bear on a main issue

tech·ni·cian (tek nish'ən) *n.* one skilled in the technicalities of an art, science, etc.

Tech·ni·col·or (tek'ni kul'ər) *a trademark for* a certain process of making color motion pictures —*n.* [t-] this process

tech·nique (tek nēk') *n.* [Fr.] 1. the method of procedure in artistic work, scientific operation, etc. 2. the degree of expertness in this 3. any method of doing a thing

tech·noc·ra·cy (tek näk'rə sē) *n.* [< Gr. *technē*, an art + -CRACY] government by scientists and engineers —**tech'no·crat'** (-nə krat') *n.*

tech·nol·o·gy (tek näl'ə jē) *n.* [Gr. *technologia*, systematic treatment] 1. the science of the practical or industrial arts 2. applied science — **tech'no·log'i·cal** (-nə läj'i k'l) *adj.* —**tech·nol'o·gist** *n.*

ted·dy bear (ted'ē) [< *Teddy* (*Theodore*) Roosevelt, 26th President] a child's stuffed toy made to look like a bear

te·di·ous (tē'dē əs) *adj.* full of tedium; tiresome; boring —**te'di·ous·ly** *adv.*

te'di·um (-əm) *n.* [< L. *taedet*, it offends] the condition or quality of being tiresome, boring, or monotonous

tee¹ (tē) *n., pl.* **tees** 1. the letter T, t 2. anything shaped like a T —*adj.* shaped like a T — **to a tee** exactly

tee² (tē) *n.* [prob. < Scot. dial. *teaz*] 1. a small peg from which a golf ball is driven 2. the place at each hole from which a golfer makes his first stroke —**tee off** 1. to play a golf ball from a tee 2. [Slang] to make angry or disgusted

teem (tēm) *vi.* [< OE. *team*, progeny] to be full; abound; swarm

teen (tēn) *n.* [< OE. *tien*, ten] 1. [*pl.*] the years from 13 through 19 2. *same as* TEEN-AGER — *adj. same as* TEEN-AGE

teen'-age' (-āj') *adj.* 1. in one's teens 2. of or for persons in their teens Also **teen'age'** — **teen'-ag'er** *n.*

tee·ny (tē'nē) *adj.* **-ni·er, -ni·est** *colloq. var. of* TINY: also **teen'sy, tee'ny-wee'ny**

tee·pee (tē'pē) *n. alt. sp. of* TEPEE

tee shirt *same as* T-SHIRT

tee·ter (tēt'ər) *vi., vt.* [< ON. *titra*, to tremble] to totter, wobble, etc.

tee'ter-tot'ter (-tät'ər, -tôt'-) *n., vi. same as* SEESAW

teeth (tēth) *n. pl. of* TOOTH

teethe (tēth) *vi.* **teethed, teeth'ing** to grow teeth; cut one's teeth

tee·to·tal·er (tē tōt''l ər) *n.* [< doubling of initial *t* in *total*] one who practices total abstinence from alcoholic liquor: also **tee·to'tal·ler**

Tef·lon (tef'län) *a trademark for* a tough polymer used for nonsticking coatings as on cooking utensils

tel. 1. telegram 2. telephone

tele- *a combining form meaning:* 1. [< Gr. *tēle*, far off] at, over, etc. a distance 2. [< TELE(VISION)] of or by television

tel·e·cast (tel'ə kast') *vt., vi.* **-cast'** or **-cast'ed, -cast'ing** to broadcast by television —*n.* a television broadcast

tel·e·gram (tel'ə gram') *n.* a message transmitted by telegraph

tel'e·graph' (-graf') *n.* [see TELE- & -GRAPH] an apparatus or system for sending messages by electric impulses through a wire or by means of radio waves —*vt., vi.* to send (a message) to (someone) by telegraph —**tel'e·graph'ic** *adj.*

te·leg·ra·phy (tə leg'rə fē) *n.* the operation of telegraph apparatus —**te·leg'ra·pher** *n.*

tel·e·me·ter (tel'ə mēt'ər, tə lem'ə tər) *n.* [TELE- + -METER] a device for measuring and transmitting data about temperature, radiation, etc. to a distant receiver

te·lep·a·thy (tə lep'ə thē) *n.* [TELE- + -PATHY] supposed communication between minds by means other than the normal sensory channels —**tel·e·path·ic** (tel'ə path'ik) *adj.*

tel·e·phone (tel'ə fōn') *n.* [TELE- + -PHONE] an instrument or system for conveying speech over distances by converting sound into electric impulses sent through a wire —*vt., vi.* **-phoned', -phon'ing** to convey (a message) to (a person) by telephone —**tel'e·phon'ic** (-fän'ik) *adj.*

te·leph·o·ny (tə lef'ə nē) *n.* the science of communication by telephone

tel·e·pho·to (tel'ə fōt'ō) *adj.* designating or of a camera lens producing a large image of a distant object

tel'e·pho'to·graph' *n.* 1. a photograph taken with a telephoto lens 2. a photograph sent by wire or radio —*vt., vi.* 1. to take (photographs) with a telephoto lens 2. to transmit (telephotographs) —**tel'e·pho·tog'ra·phy** (-fə täg'rə fē) *n.*

tel'e·scope' (-skōp') *n.* [see TELE- & -SCOPE] an instrument with lenses for making distant objects appear nearer and larger —*vi., vt.* **-scoped', -scop'ing** to slide one into another, as the tubes of a collapsible telescope —**tel'e·scop'ic** (-skäp'ik) *adj.*

tel'e·thon' (-thän') *n.* [TELE(VISION) + (MARA)THON] a campaign, as on a lengthy telecast, asking for support for a cause

Tel·e·type (tel'ə tip') *a trademark for* a form of telegraph in which the receiver prints messages typed on the transmitter

tel·e·vise (tel'ə vīz') *vt., vi.* **-vised', -vis'ing** to transmit by television

tel'e·vi'sion (-vizh'ən) *n.* 1. the process of transmitting images by converting light rays into electric signals: the receiver reconverts the signals so that images are produced on a screen 2. television broadcasting 3. a television receiving set

tell (tel) *vt.* **told, tell'ing** [OE. *tellan*, calculate] 1. orig., to count 2. to narrate; relate 3. to express in words [*tell* the truth] 4. to reveal; dis-

close 5. to recognize; distinguish [I can *tell* the difference] 6. to let know; inform 7. to order [*tell* him to go] —*vi.* 1. to give an account or evidence (*of* something) 2. to be effective —**tell off** [Colloq.] to rebuke severely —**tell on** 1. to tire 2. [Colloq.] to inform against

tell'er *n.* 1. one who tells (a story, etc.) 2. one who counts; specif., a bank clerk who pays out or receives money

tell'ing *adj.* having an effect; forceful

tell'tale' *n.* an outward indication of a secret —*adj.* revealing a secret

Tel·star (tel'stär') a communications satellite, put in earth orbit in 1962

te·mer·i·ty (tə mer'ə tē) *n.* [< L. *temere*, rashly] foolish or rash boldness

temp. 1. temperature 2. temporary

tem·per (tem'pər) *vt.* [< L. *temperare*, regulate] 1. to moderate by mingling with another thing [*temper* blame with praise] 2. *a*) to bring to the proper condition by some treatment [to *temper* steel] *b*) to toughen —*n.* 1. the degree of hardness and resiliency of a metal 2. frame of mind; disposition 3. composure: in **lose** (or **keep**) **one's temper** 4. anger; rage

tem·per·a (tem'pər ə) *n.* [It.: see TEMPER] a way of painting with pigments mixed with size, casein, or egg to produce a dull finish

tem·per·a·ment (tem'prə mənt, -pər ə mənt) *n.* [see TEMPER] 1. one's customary frame of mind 2. a nature that is excitable, moody, etc. —**tem'per·a·men'tal** (-men't'l) *adj.*

tem·per·ance (tem'pər əns, -prəns) *n.* [see TEMPER] 1. moderation; self-restraint 2. moderation in drinking alcoholic liquors or total abstinence from them

tem·per·ate (tem'pər it) *adj.* [see TEMPER] 1. moderate, as in eating or drinking 2. moderate in one's actions, speech, etc. 3. neither very hot nor very cold: said of climate, etc. —**tem'per·ate·ly** *adv.*

Temperate Zone either of two zones (**North** or **South Temperate Zone**) between the tropics and the polar circles

tem·per·a·ture (tem'prə chər, tem'pər ə-) *n.* [< L. *temperatus*, temperate] 1. the degree of hotness or coldness of anything 2. excess of body heat over the normal; fever

tem·pered (tem'pərd) *adj.* 1. having been given the desired texture, hardness, etc. 2. modified by other qualities, etc. 3. having a (specified) temper [bad-*tempered*]

tem·pest (tem'pist) *n.* [< L. *tempus*, time] a violent storm with high winds, esp. one accompanied by rain, snow, etc.

tem·pes·tu·ous (tem pes'choo wəs) *adj.* 1. of or like a tempest; turbulent 2. violent

tem·ple[1] (tem'p'l) *n.* [< L. *templum*] 1. a building for the worship of God or gods 2. a large building for some special purpose

tem·ple[2] (tem'p'l) *n.* [< L. *tempus*] 1. the flat surface beside the forehead, in front of each ear 2. one sidepiece of a pair of glasses

tem·po (tem'pō) *n., pl.* **-pos, -pi** (-pē) [It. < L. *tempus*, time] 1. the speed at which a musical work is played 2. rate of activity

tem·po·ral[1] (tem'pər əl) *adj.* [< L. *tempus*, time] 1. transitory; not eternal 2. of this world; not spiritual 3. secular 4. of or limited by time —**tem'po·ral·ly** *adv.*

tem·po·ral[2] (tem'pər əl) *adj.* of or near the temples (of the head)

tem·po·rar·y (tem'pə rer'ē) *adj.* [< L. *tempus*, time] lasting only for a time; not permanent —**tem'po·rar·i·ly** *adv.*

tem·po·rize (tem'pə rīz') *vi.* **-rized', -riz'ing** to put off making a decision, or to agree for a while, so as to gain time

tempt (tempt) *vt.* [< L. *temptare*, to test] **1.** to entice to do something wrong, etc. **2.** to be inviting to; attract **3.** to provoke or risk provoking (fate, etc.) **4.** to incline strongly /I am *tempted* to go/ —**temp·ta·tion** (temp tā′shən) *n.*

tem·pu·ra (tem′poo rä′, tem poor′ə) *n.* [Jpn.] a Japanese dish of deep-fried seafood or vegetables

ten (ten) *adj., n.* [OE.] one more than nine; 10; X

ten·a·ble (ten′ə b′l) *adj.* [Fr. < L. *tenere*, to hold] that can be held, defended, or believed — **ten′a·bil′i·ty** *n.* —**ten′a·bly** *adv.*

te·na·cious (tə nā′shəs) *adj.* [< L. *tenere*, to hold] **1.** holding firmly /a *tenacious* grip/ **2.** retentive /a *tenacious* memory] **3.** strongly cohesive or adhesive **4.** persistent —**te·nac′i·ty** (-nas′ə tē) *n.*

ten·ant (ten′ənt) *n.* [< L. *tenere*, to hold] **1.** one who pays rent to occupy or use land, a building, etc. **2.** an occupant —*vt.* to occupy as a tenant —**ten′an·cy** *n.*

tenant farmer one who farms land that he pays rent for or sharecrops

Ten Commandments *Bible* the ten laws forming the fundamental moral code of Israel, given to Moses by God: Ex. 20:2–17

tend[1] (tend) *vt.* [see ATTEND] **1.** to take care of **2.** to manage or operate

tend[2] (tend) *vi.* [< L. *tendere*, to stretch] **1.** to be inclined, disposed, etc. (*to*) **2.** to be directed (*to* or *toward*)

tend·en·cy (ten′dən sē) *n., pl.* -**cies** [see prec.] **1.** an inclination to move or act in a particular direction or way **2.** a course toward some purpose, object, or result

ten·der[1] (ten′dər) *adj.* [< L. *tener*, soft] **1.** easily chewed, broken, cut, etc.; soft **2.** physically weak **3.** immature **4.** needing careful handling **5.** gentle or light **6.** *a)* acutely sensitive, as to pain *b)* sensitive to emotions, others' feelings, etc. —**ten′der·ly** *adv.* —**ten′der·ness** *n.*

ten·der[2] (ten′dər) *vt.* [see TEND[2]] to present for acceptance —*n.* **1.** a formal offer **2.** money, etc. offered in payment

tend·er[3] (ten′dər) *n.* **1.** one who tends, or has charge of, something **2.** *a)* a ship for supplying another ship *b)* a boat for carrying passengers, etc. to or from a ship **3.** the railroad car behind a steam locomotive for carrying its coal and water

ten′der·foot′ *n., pl.* -**foots′**, -**feet′** **1.** a newcomer, specif. to the hardships of Western ranching **2.** any novice

ten′der·ize′ *vt.* -**ized′**, -**iz′ing** to make (meat) tender —**ten′der·iz′er** *n.*

ten′der·loin′ *n.* the tenderest muscle of a loin of beef or pork

ten·don (ten′dən) *n.* [< Gr. *teinein*, to stretch] any of the cords of tough, fibrous tissue connecting muscles to bones, etc.; sinew

ten·dril (ten′drəl) *n.* [prob. ult. < L. *tener*, soft] a threadlike, clinging part of a climbing plant, serving to support it

ten·e·ment (ten′ə mənt) *n.* [< L. *tenere*, to hold] **1.** a separately tenanted room or suite **2.** an apartment building, now specif. one in the slums that is run-down and overcrowded: also **tenement house**

ten·et (ten′it) *n.* [L., he holds] a principle, doctrine, or belief held as a truth, as by some group

ten·nis (ten′is) *n.* [prob. < Anglo-Fr. *tenetz*, hold (imperative)] a game in which players

using rackets hit a ball back and forth over a net in a marked area (**tennis court**)

tennis shoe *same as* SNEAKER

ten·on (ten′ən) *n.* [ult. < L. *tenere*, to hold] a part of a piece of wood, etc. cut to stick out so that it will fit into a hole (*mortise*) in another piece to make a joint

ten·or (ten′ər) *n.* [< L. *tenere*, to hold] **1.** general course or tendency **2.** general meaning; drift **3.** *a)* the highest usual adult male voice, or its range *b)* a part for this *c)* a singer or instrument having this range

ten′pins′ *n.pl.* **1.** [*with sing. v.*] the game of bowling in which ten pins are used **2.** the pins

tense[1] (tens) *adj.* **tens′er**, **tens′est** [< L. *tendere*, stretch] **1.** stretched tight; taut **2.** feeling, showing, or causing mental strain —*vt., vi.* **tensed**, **tens′ing** to make or become tense — **tense′ly** *adv.* —**tense′ness** *n.*

tense[2] (tens) *n.* [< L. *tempus*, time] any of the forms of a verb that show the time of the action or condition

ten·sile (ten′s'l) *adj.* **1.** of or under tension **2.** capable of being stretched

ten·sion (ten′shən) *n.* **1.** a tensing or being tensed **2.** mental or nervous strain **3.** a state of strained relations **4.** voltage **5.** stress on a material by forces causing extension

tent (tent) *n.* [< L. *tendere*, stretch] a portable shelter made of canvas, etc. stretched over poles —*vi.* to live in a tent —*vt.* to lodge in tents

ten·ta·cle (ten′tə k'l) *n.* [< L. *tentare*, to touch] a slender, flexible growth near the head or mouth, as of some invertebrates, used to grasp, feel, etc.

ten·ta·tive (ten′tə tiv) *adj.* [< L. *tentare*, try] not definite or final

ten·ter·hook (ten′tər hook′) *n.* [< L. *tendere*, to stretch + HOOK] any of the hooked nails that hold cloth stretched on a frame to dry — **on tenterhooks** in suspense

tenth (tenth) *adj.* preceded by nine others in a series; 10th —*n.* **1.** the one following the ninth **2.** any of the ten equal parts of something; 1/10

ten·u·ous (ten′yoo wəs) *adj.* [< L. *tenuis*, thin] **1.** slender or fine, as a fiber **2.** not dense; rare, as air high up **3.** slight; flimsy

ten·ure (ten′yər, -yoor) *n.* [< MFr. *tenir*, to hold] **1.** the act or right of holding property, an office, etc. **2.** the period or conditions of this

te·pee (tē′pē) *n.* [< Siouan *ti*, to dwell + *pi*, used for] a cone-shaped tent used by American Indians

tep·id (tep′id) *adj.* [< L. *tepere*, be slightly warm] slightly warm; lukewarm —**tep′id·ness** *n.*

te·qui·la (tə kē′lə) *n.* [< *Tequila*, a Mex. district] an alcoholic liquor distilled from a Mexican agave

ter·cen·te·nar·y (tur′sen ten′ər ē, tər sen′tə ner′ē) *adj., n., pl.* -**ies** [L. *ter*, three times + CENTENARY] *same as* TRICENTENNIAL

term (turm) *n.* [< L. *terminus*, a limit] **1.** a set date, as for payment, etc. **2.** a set period of time /school *term*, *term* of office/ **3.** [*pl.*] conditions of a contract, etc. **4.** [*pl.*] mutual relationship between persons /on speaking *terms*/ **5.** a word or phrase, esp. as used in some science, art, etc. **6.** *Math. a)* either quantity of a fraction or ratio *b)* each quantity in a series or algebraic expression —*vt.* to call by a term; name —**bring** (or **come**) **to terms** to force into (or arrive at) an agreement

ter·ma·gant (tur′mə gənt) *n.* [< OFr. *Terva-*

gant, alleged Muslim deity] a quarrelsome, scolding woman

ter·mi·na·ble (tur'mi nə b'l) *adj.* that can be, or is, terminated

ter·mi·nal (tur'mə n'l) *adj.* [L. *terminalis*] **1.** of, at, or forming the end or extremity **2.** concluding; final **3.** of or in the final stages of a fatal disease *[terminal* cancer*]* **4.** of or at the end of a transportation line *—n.* **1.** an end; extremity **2.** a connective point on an electric circuit **3.** either end of a transportation line or a main station on it **—ter'mi·nal·ly** *adv.*

ter'mi·nate' (-nāt') *vt.* -nat'ed, -nat'ing [< L. *terminus,* a limit] **1.** to form the end or limit of **2.** to put an end to; stop *—vi.* to come to an end **—ter'mi·na'tion** *n.*

ter·mi·nol·o·gy (tur'mə näl'ə jē) *n., pl.* -gies the terms used in some science, art, work, etc.

ter·mi·nus (tur'mə nəs) *n., pl.* -nl' (-nī'), -nus·es [L., a limit] **1.** a limit **2.** an end **3.** either end of a transportation line

ter·mite (tur'mīt) *n.* [L. *termes,* wood-boring worm] an antlike insect that is very destructive to wooden structures

tern (turn) *n.* [< ON. *therna]* a sea bird related to the gull, but smaller

ter·race (ter'əs) *n.* [< L. *terra,* earth] **1.** a raised, flat mound of earth with sloping sides, often one in a series on a hillside **2.** an unroofed, paved area next to a house and overlooking a garden **3.** a row of houses on ground raised from the street, or the street below it *— vt.* -raced, -rac·ing to form into a terrace

ter·ra cot·ta (ter'ə kät'ə) [It., lit., baked earth] a hard, brown-red, usually unglazed earthenware, or its color **—ter'ra-cot'ta** *adj.*

terra fir·ma (fur'mə) [L.] firm earth; solid ground

ter·rain (tə rān', ter'ān) *n.* [Fr. < L. *terra,* earth] a tract of ground, esp. with regard to its features or fitness for some use

ter·ra·pin (ter'ə pin) *n.* [< Algonquian] **1.** any of several American freshwater or tidewater turtles **2.** its edible flesh

ter·rar·i·um (tə rer'ē əm) *n., pl.* -i·ums, -i·a (-ə) [< L. *terra,* earth + (AQU)ARIUM] an enclosure in which small plants are grown or small land animals are kept

ter·raz·zo (tə raz'ō) *n.* [It.] flooring of small chips of marble set in cement and polished

ter·res·tri·al (tə res'trē əl) *adj.* [< L. *terra,* earth] **1.** worldly; mundane **2.** of the earth **3.** consisting of land, not water **4.** living on land *—n.* an inhabitant of the earth

ter·ri·ble (ter'ə b'l) *adj.* [< L. *terrere,* frighten] **1.** causing terror; dreadful **2.** extreme; intense **3.** [Colloq.] very bad, unpleasant, etc. **—ter'ri·bly** *adv.*

ter·ri·er (ter'ē ər) *n.* [< MFr. (*chien*) *terrier,* hunting (dog)] any of various breeds of active, typically small dog

ter·rif·ic (tə rif'ik) *adj.* [< L. *terrere,* frighten] **1.** causing great fear **2.** [Colloq.] *a)* unusually great, intense, etc. *b)* unusually fine, enjoyable, etc. **—ter·rif'i·cal·ly** *adv.*

ter·ri·fy (ter'ə fī') *vi.* -fied', -fy'ing to fill with terror; frighten greatly

ter·ri·to·ry (ter'ə tôr'ē) *n., pl.* -ries [< L. *terra,* earth] **1.** an area under the jurisdiction of a nation, ruler, etc. **2.** a part of a country, etc. lacking full status **3.** any large tract of land **4.** an assigned area **5.** a sphere of action, etc. — **ter'ri·to'ri·al** *adj.*

ter·ror (ter'ər) *n.* [< L. *terrere,* frighten] **1.** intense fear **2.** *a)* one causing intense fear *b)* the quality of causing such fear

ter'ror·ism *n.* the use of force and violence to

intimidate, etc., esp. as a political policy **—ter'-ror·ist** *n., adj.* **—ter'ror·is'tic** *adj.*

ter'ror·ize' (-īz') *vt.* -ized', -iz'ing **1.** to fill with terror **2.** to coerce, make submit, etc. by filling with terror

ter·ry (ter'ē) *n., pl.* -ries [prob. < Fr. *tirer,* to draw] cloth having a pile in which the loops are left uncut: also **terry cloth**

terse (turs) *adj.* ters'er, ters'est [< L. *tergere,* to wipe] free of superfluous words; concise; succinct **—terse'ness** *n.*

ter·ti·ar·y (tur'shē er'ē) *adj.* [< L. *tertius,* third] of the third rank, order, etc.

tes·sel·late (tes'ə lāt') *vt.* -lat'ed, -lat'ing [< L. *tessella,* little square stone] to lay out or pave in a mosaic pattern of small, square blocks

test (test) *n.* [< OFr., assaying cup] **1.** *a)* an examination or trial, as of something's value *b)* the method or a criterion used in this **2.** an event, etc. that tries one's qualities **3.** a set of questions, etc. for determining one's knowledge, abilities, etc. **4.** *Chem.* a trial or reaction for identifying a substance *—vt.* to subject to a test; try *—vi.* to be rated by a test *[to test* high*]* **—test'er** *n.*

tes·ta·ment (tes'tə mənt) *n.* [< L. *testis,* a witness] **1.** [T-] either of the two parts of the Bible, the *Old Testament* and the *New Testament* **2.** *a)* a testimonial *b)* an affirmation of beliefs **3.** *Law* a will **—tes'ta·men'ta·ry** (-men'tə rē) *adj.*

tes·tate (tes'tāt) *adj.* [< L. *testari,* make a will] having left a legally valid will

tes'ta·tor *n.* one who has made a will

tes·ti·cle (tes'ti k'l) *n.* [< L. *testis*] either of two oval male sex glands

tes·ti·fy (tes'tə fī') *vi.* -fied', -fy'ing [< L. *testis,* a witness + *facere,* make] **1.** to give evidence, esp. under oath in court **2.** to be evidence *—vt.* **1.** to affirm; declare, esp. under oath in court **2.** to indicate

tes·ti·mo·ni·al (tes'tə mō'nē əl) *n.* **1.** a statement recommending a person or thing **2.** something given or done to show gratitude or appreciation

tes·ti·mo·ny (tes'tə mō'nē) *n., pl.* -nies [< L. *testis,* a witness] **1.** a statement made under oath in court to establish a fact **2.** any declaration **3.** any form of evidence; proof

tes·tis (tes'tis) *n., pl.* -tes (-tēz) [L.] *same as* TESTICLE

tes·tos·ter·one (tes täs'tə rōn') *n.* [see TESTICLE] a male sex hormone

test tube a tube of thin, clear glass closed at one end, used in chemical experiments, etc.

tes·ty (tes'tē) *adj.* -ti·er, -ti·est [< L. *testa,* the head] irritable; touchy

tet·a·nus (tet''n əs) *n.* [< Gr. *tetanos,* spasm] an acute infectious disease, often fatal, caused by a toxin and characterized by spasmodic contractions and rigidity of muscles

tête-à-tête (tāt'ə tāt') *n.* [Fr., head-to-head] a private conversation between two people

teth·er (teth'ər) *n.* [prob. < ON. *tjōthr]* **1.** a rope, etc. fastened to an animal to keep it within bounds **2.** the limit of one's resources, etc. *—vt.* to fasten with a tether

tetra- [< Gr. *tettares,* four] *a combining form meaning* four

tet·ra·eth·yl lead (tet'rə eth''l) a poisonous compound of lead, added to gasoline to increase power and prevent engine knock

tet·ra·he·dron (tet'rə hē'drən) *n., pl.* -drons, -dra (-drə) [see TETRA- & -HEDRON] a solid figure with four triangular faces

Teu·ton·ic (tōō tän'ik) *adj.* designating or of a

group of north European peoples, esp. the German people —**Teu·ton** (tōōt'n) *n.*

text (tekst) *n.* [< L. *texere,* to weave] **1.** the actual words of an author, as distinguished from notes, paraphrase, etc. **2.** any form in which a written work exists **3.** the principal matter on a printed page, as distinguished from notes, pictures, etc. **4.** *a)* a Biblical passage used as the topic of a sermon *b)* any topic or subject **5.** a textbook —**tex·tu·al** (teks'chōō wəl) *adj.*

text'book' *n.* a book giving instructions in a subject of study

tex·tile (teks'tĭl, -t'l) *adj.* [see TEXT] **1.** having to do with weaving **2.** that has been or can be woven —*n.* **1.** a fabric made by weaving, knitting, etc.; cloth **2.** raw material suitable for this

tex·ture (teks'chər) *n.* [see TEXT] **1.** the character of a fabric as determined by the arrangement, size, etc. of its threads **2.** the structure or composition of anything —**tex'tur·al** *adj.*

-th¹ [< OE.] *a suffix meaning:* **1.** the act of [*stealth*] **2.** the state or quality of being or having [*wealth*]

-th² [< OE.] a suffix used in forming ordinal numerals [*fourth*] : also **-eth**

Th *Chem.* thorium

Th. Thursday

Thai (tī) *n.* **1.** a group of languages spoken in central and southeastern Asia **2.** the language of Thailand **3.** *pl.* **Thais, Thai** *a)* a member of a group of Thai-speaking peoples of SE Asia *b)* a native of Thailand —*adj.* of Thailand, its people, culture, etc.

thal·a·mus (thal'ə məs) *n., pl.* **-mi'** (-mī') [< Gr. *thalamos,* inner room] a mass of gray matter at the base of the brain, involved in the transmission of certain sensations

than (than, then) *conj.* [OE. *thenne*] *a particle used* to introduce the second element in a comparison [A is taller *than* B]

thank (thaŋk) *vt.* [OE. *thancian*] **1.** to express appreciation to, as by saying "thank you" **2.** to hold responsible: an ironic use —**thank you** short for I thank you

thank'ful *adj.* feeling or expressing thanks

thank'less *adj.* **1.** not feeling or expressing thanks; ungrateful **2.** unappreciated

thanks (thaŋks) *n.pl.* an expression of gratitude —*interj.* I thank you —**thanks to 1.** thanks be given to **2.** on account of

thanks·giv'ing *n.* **1.** a formal public expression of thanks to God **2.** [T-] a U.S. holiday on the fourth Thursday of November

that (that) *pron., pl.* **those** [OE. *thæt*] **1.** the person or thing mentioned [*that* is John] **2.** the farther one or other one [this is better than *that*] **3.** who, whom, or which [the road (*that*) we took] **4.** where [the place *that* I saw him] **5.** when [the year *that* he died] —*adj., pl.* **those 1.** designating the one mentioned [*that* man is John] **2.** designating the farther one or other one [this house is larger than *that* one] —*conj.* used to introduce: **1.** a noun clause [*that* he's gone is obvious] **2.** an adverbial clause expressing purpose [they died *that* we might live] , result [he ran so fast *that* I lost him] , or cause [I'm sorry *that* I won] **3.** an elliptical sentence expressing surprise, desire, etc. [oh, *that* he were here!] —*adv.* **1.** to that extent; so [I can't see *that* far] **2.** [Colloq.] very [I didn't like the book *that* much] —**all that** [Colloq.] **1.** so very **2.** everything of the same sort —**at that** [Colloq.] **1.** at that point: also **with that 2.** even so —**that is 1.** to be specific **2.** in other words

thatch (thach) *n.* [OE. *thæc*] **1.** a roof of straw,

rushes, palm leaves, etc. **2.** material for such a roof: also **thatch'ing** —*vt.* to cover as with thatch —**thatch'y** *adj.*

thaw (thô) *vi.* [OE. *thawian*] **1.** *a)* to melt, as ice, snow, etc. *b)* to become unfrozen: said of frozen foods **2.** to become warmer, so that ice, snow, etc. melts **3.** to lose coldness of manner —*vt.* to cause to thaw —*n.* **1.** a thawing **2.** a spell of weather warm enough to allow thawing

the (thə; *before vowels* thi, thē) *adj., definite article* [OE. *se,* with *th-* from other forms] *the* (as opposed to *a, an*) refers to: **1.** a particular person or thing [*the* story ended, *the* President] **2.** a person or thing considered generically [*the* cow is a domestic animal, *the* poor] —*adv.* **1.** that much [*the* better to see you] **2.** by how much . . . by that much [*the* sooner *the* better]

the·a·ter, the·a·tre (thē'ə tər) *n.* [< Gr. *theasthai,* to view] **1.** a place or building where plays, motion pictures, etc. are presented **2.** any similar place having ascending rows of seats **3.** any scene of events **4.** *a)* the dramatic art; drama *b)* the theatrical world

the·at·ri·cal (thē at'ri k'l) *adj.* **1.** having to do with the theater **2.** dramatic; esp. (in disparagement), melodramatic

thee (thē) *pron.* [OE. *the*] objective case of THOU: used for *thou* by Friends (Quakers)

theft (theft) *n.* [OE. *thiefth*] the act or an instance of stealing; larceny

their (ther) *possessive pronominal adj.* [ON. *theirra*] of, belonging to, made by, or done by them

theirs (therz) *pron.* that or those belonging to them [*theirs* are better]

the·ism (thē'iz'm) *n.* [< Gr. *theos,* god] **1.** belief in a god or gods **2.** monotheism —**the'ist** *n., adj.* —**the·is'tic** *adj.*

them (them) *pron.* [< ON. *theim*] objective case of THEY

theme (thēm) *n.* [< Gr. *thema,* what is set down] **1.** a topic, as of a lecture **2.** a motif **3.** a short essay **4.** a short melody used as the subject of a musical composition **5.** a recurring or identifying song in a film, musical, TV series, etc.: also **theme song** —**the·mat·ic** (thē mat'ik) *adj.*

them·selves (them selvz') *pron.* **1.** *intensive form* of THEY [they went *themselves*] **2.** *reflexive form* of THEY [they hurt *themselves*] **3.** their true selves [they are not *themselves* today]

then (then) *adv.* [see THAN] **1.** at that time [I did it *then*] **2.** next in time or order [he ate and *then* slept] **3.** in that case; accordingly [if he reads it, *then* he will know] **4.** besides; moreover [I like to walk, and *then* it's cheaper] **5.** at another time [now it's warm, *then* cold] —*adj.* being such at that time [the *then* director] —*n.* that time [by *then,* they were gone]

thence (thens, thens) *adv.* [OE. *thanan*] **1.** from that place **2.** therefore

thence'forth' (-fôrth') *adv.* from that time onward; thereafter: also **thence'for'ward**

the·oc·ra·cy (thē äk'rə sē) *n., pl.* **-cies** [< Gr. *theos,* god + *kratos,* power] (a) government by priests claiming to rule by divine authority —**the'o·crat'ic** *adj.*

the·o·lo·gi·an (thē'ə lō'jən, -jē ən) *n.* a student of or a specialist in theology

the·ol·o·gy (thē äl'ə jē) *n., pl.* **-gies** [< Gr. *theos,* god + -LOGY] the study of God and of religious doctrines and matters of divinity —

the′o·log′i·cal (-ə läj′i k′l) *adj.* —the′o·log′i·cal·ly *adv.*

the·o·rem (thē′ə rəm) *n.* [< Fr. or L. < Gr. *theōrein,* to view] **1.** a proposition that can be proved from accepted premises; law or principle **2.** *Math., Physics* a proposition embodying something to be proved

the·o·ret·i·cal (thē′ə ret′i k′l) *adj.* **1.** limited to or based on theory; hypothetical **2.** tending to theorize; speculative Also the′o·ret′ic — the′o·ret′i·cal·ly *adv.*

the·o·rize (thē′ə rīz′) *vi.* -rized′, -riz′ing to form a theory or theories; speculate —the′o·re·ti′cian (-rə tish′ən), the′o·rist (-rist) *n.*

the·o·ry (thē′ə rē, thir′ē) *n., pl.* -ries [< Fr. < Gr. *theōrein,* to view] **1.** a speculative plan **2.** a formulation of underlying principles of certain observed phenomena which has been verified to some degree **3.** the principles of an art or science rather than its practice **4.** popularly, a guess

ther·a·peu·tic (ther′ə pyo͞ot′ik) *adj.* [< Gr. *therapeuein,* to nurse] serving to cure, heal, or preserve health: also ther′a·peu′ti·cal

ther′a·peu′tics *n.pl.* [*with sing. v.*] the branch of medicine dealing with the treatment and cure of diseases; therapy

ther·a·py (ther′ə pē) *n., pl.* -pies [see THERAPEUTIC] the treatment of any physical or mental disorder by physical or medical means, usually excluding surgery —ther′a·pist *n.*

there (ther) *adv.* [OE. *ther*] **1.** at or in that place: often used as an intensive [John *there* is a good boy] **2.** to or into that place [go *there*] **3.** at that point; then **4.** in that respect [*there* you are wrong] There is also used in clauses in which the real subject follows the verb [*there* is little time] —*n.* that place [we left *there* at six] —*interj.* an exclamation of defiance, dismay, satisfaction, sympathy, etc. —(not) all there [Colloq.] (not) mentally sound

there′a·bouts′ *adv.* **1.** near that place **2.** near that time, number, degree, etc. Also there′a·bout′

there·af′ter *adv.* after that; subsequently

there·at′ *adv.* **1.** at that place; there **2.** at that time **3.** for that reason

there·by′ *adv.* **1.** by that means **2.** connected with that [*thereby* hangs a tale]

there·for′ *adv.* for this; for that; for it

there′fore′ (-fôr′) *adv.* for this or that reason; consequently; hence

there·in′ *adv.* **1.** in or into that place or thing **2.** in that matter, detail, etc.

there·of′ *adv.* **1.** of that **2.** concerning that **3.** from that as a cause, reason, etc.

there·on′ *adv.* **1.** on that **2.** thereupon

there·to′ *adv.* to that place, thing, etc.

there·to·fore′ *adv.* until that time

there′up·on′ *adv.* **1.** immediately following that **2.** as a consequence of that **3.** concerning that subject, etc.

there·with′ *adv.* **1.** along with that **2.** immediately thereafter

ther·mal (thur′m′l) *adj.* [Fr. < Gr. *thermē,* heat] **1.** having to do with heat **2.** designating a loosely knitted material with air spaces for insulation [*thermal* underwear]

thermo- [< Gr. *thermē,* heat] *a combining form meaning* heat

ther·mo·dy·nam·ics (thur′mō dī nam′iks) *n.pl.* [*with sing. v.*] the branch of physics dealing with the reversible transformation of heat into mechanical energy —ther′mo·dy·nam′ic *adj.*

ther·mom·e·ter (thər mäm′ə tər) *n.* [< Fr.: see THERMO- & -METER] an instrument for measuring temperatures, as a graduated glass tube in which mercury, etc. rises or falls as it expands or contracts from changes in temperature

ther·mo·nu·cle·ar (thur′mō no͞o′klē ər) *adj. Physics* **1.** designating a reaction in which light atomic nuclei fuse, at extreme heat, into heavier nuclei **2.** of or employing the heat energy released in nuclear fusion

ther·mo·plas·tic (thur′mə plas′tik) *adj.* soft and moldable when subjected to heat: said of certain plastics —*n.* a thermoplastic substance

ther·mos (thur′məs) *n.* [Gr. *thermos,* hot] a bottle, flask, or jug for keeping liquids at almost their original temperature for several hours: in full thermos bottle

ther·mo·stat (thur′mə stat′) *n.* [THERMO- + -STAT] an apparatus for regulating temperature, esp. one that automatically controls a heating unit —ther′mo·stat′ic *adj.*

the·sau·rus (thi sôr′əs) *n., pl.* -ri (-ī), -rus·es [< Gr. *thēsauros,* a treasure] a book of synonyms and antonyms

these (thēz) *pron., adj. pl. of* THIS

The·seus (thē′so͞os, -syo͞os) *Gr. Legend* a hero who killed the Minotaur

the·sis (thē′sis) *n., pl.* -ses (-sēz) [< Gr. *tithenai,* to put] **1.** a proposition defended in argument **2.** a research paper, esp. one written for a master's degree

Thes·pi·an (thes′pē ən) *adj.* [< Thespis, ancient Gr. poet] [*often* t-] having to do with the drama; dramatic —*n.* [*often* t-] an actor or actress

the·ta (thāt′ə, thēt′ə) *n.* the eighth letter of the Greek alphabet (Θ, θ)

thews (thyo͞oz) *n.pl., sing.* thew [OE. *theaw,* habit] muscles or sinews

they (thā) *pron., for sing. see* HE, SHE, IT [ON. *thei-r*] **1.** the persons, animals, or things previously mentioned **2.** people in general [*they* say it's so]

they'd (thād) **1.** they had **2.** they would

they'll (thāl) **1.** they will **2.** they shall

they're (ther) they are

they've (thāv) they have

thi·a·mine (thī′ə mēn′, -min) *n.* [ult. < Gr. *theion,* brimstone + (VIT)AMIN] vitamin B₁, a compound, found in cereal grains, egg yolk, liver, etc.: also thi′a·min (-min)

thick (thik) *adj.* [OE. *thicce*] **1.** of relatively great extent from side to side **2.** measured between opposite surfaces [one inch *thick*] **3.** close and abundant [*thick* hair] **4.** viscous [*thick* soup] **5.** dense [*thick* smoke] **6.** husky; hoarse; blurred [*thick* speech] **7.** [Colloq.] stupid **8.** [Colloq.] very friendly —*n.* the thickest part —thick′ness *n.*

thick′en *vt., vi.* **1.** to make or become thick or thicker **2.** to make or become more complex or involved —thick′en·er *n.*

thick·et (thik′it) *n.* [see THICK] a thick growth of shrubs or small trees

thick′set′ *adj.* **1.** planted thickly or closely **2.** thick in body; stocky

thick′-skinned′ *adj.* **1.** having a thick skin **2.** not easily hurt by insults, etc.

thief (thēf) *n., pl.* thieves (thēvz) [OE. *theof*] a person who steals, esp. secretly

thieve (thēv) *vt., vi.* thieved, thiev′ing to steal —thiev′ish *adj.*

thiev′er·y *n., pl.* -ies the act or an instance of stealing; theft

thigh (thī) *n.* [OE. *theoh*] the part of the leg between the knee and the hip

thigh'bone' *n.* the bone extending from the hip to the knee; femur: also **thigh bone**

thim·ble (thim'b'l) *n.* [< OE. *thuma,* thumb] a small cap worn to protect the finger that pushes the needle in sewing

thin (thin) *adj.* **thin'ner, thin'nest** [OE. *thynne*] **1.** of relatively little extent from side to side **2.** lean; slender **3.** not dense or compact *[thin hair]* **4.** very fluid or watery *[thin soup]* **5.** not deep and strong *[a thin voice]* **6.** sheer, as a fabric **7.** flimsy or unconvincing *[a thin excuse]* **8.** lacking substance, depth, etc.; weak —*vt., vi.* **thinned, thin'ning** to make or become thin or thinner —**thin'ly** *adv.* —**thin'ness** *n.*

thine (thīn) *pron.* [OE. *thin*] *possessive form of* THOU —*adj.* thy: used before a vowel

thing (thiŋ) *n.* [OE., a council] **1.** any matter, affair, or concern **2.** a happening, act, incident, etc. **3.** a tangible object **4.** an inanimate object **5.** an item, detail, etc. **6.** *a)* [*pl.*] personal belongings *b)* a garment **7.** a person *[poor thing!]* **8.** [Colloq.] a point of dispute; issue **9.** [Colloq.] an irrational liking, fear, etc. **10.** [Colloq.] what one wants to do or is adept at *[do one's own thing]*

think (thiŋk) *vt.* **thought, think'ing** [OE. *thencan*] **1.** to form or have in the mind *[to think good thoughts]* **2.** to judge; consider *[I think her charming]* **3.** to believe; expect *[I think I can go]* —*vi.* **1.** to use the mind; reflect or reason **2.** to have an opinion, belief, etc. (with *of* or *about*) **3.** to remember or consider (with *of* or *about*) **4.** to conceive (*of*) —**think up** to invent, plan, etc. by thinking —**think'er** *n.*

think tank (or **factory**) [Slang] a group or center organized to do intensive research and problem-solving

thin·ner (thin'ər) *n.* a substance added, as turpentine to paint, for thinning

thin'-skinned' *adj.* **1.** having a thin skin **2.** easily hurt by criticism, insults, etc.

third (thurd) *adj.* [OE. *thridda*] preceded by two others in a series; 3d or 3rd —*n.* **1.** the one following the second **2.** any of the three equal parts of something; 1/3

third'-class' *adj.* **1.** of the class, rank, etc. below the second **2.** of a lower-cost class of mail, as for advertisements —*adv.* by third-class mail or travel accommodations

third degree [Colloq.] harsh treatment and questioning to force a confession

third person that form of a pronoun (as *he*) or verb (as *is*) which refers to the person or thing spoken of

third'-rate' *adj.* **1.** third in quality or other rating **2.** very poor

third world [*often* T- W-] the underdeveloped or emergent countries of the world

thirst (thurst) *n.* [OE. *thurst*] **1.** the discomfort caused by a need for water **2.** a strong desire; craving —*vi.* **1.** to feel thirst **2.** to have a strong desire or craving —**thirst'i·ly** *adv.* —**thirst'y** *adj.* **-i·er, -i·est**

thir·teen (thur'tēn') *adj., n.* [OE. *threotyne*] three more than ten; 13; XIII —**thir'teenth'** *adj., n.*

thir·ty (thur'tē) *adj., n., pl.* **-ties** [OE. *thritig*] three times ten; 30; XXX —**the thirties** the numbers or years, as of a century, from 30 through 39 —**thir'ti·eth** (-ith) *adj., n.*

this (this) *pron., adj., pl.* **these** [OE. *thes*] **1.** (designating) the person or thing mentioned *[this* (man) is John]* **2.** (designating) the nearer one or another one *[this* (desk) is older than that]* **3.** (designating) something about to be presented *[hear this* (news)]* —*adv.* to this extent *[it was this big]*

this·tle (this''l) *n.* [OE. *thistel*] a plant with prickly leaves and white, purple, etc. flowers — **this·tly** (this'lē) *adj.*

thith·er (thith'ər, thith'-) *adv.* [OE. *thider*] to or toward that place; there

tho, tho' (thō) *conj., adv.* though

Thom·as (täm'əs) *Bible* one of the twelve Apostles, who doubted at first the resurrection of Jesus

thong (thôŋ) *n.* [OE. *thwang*] a narrow strip of leather, etc. used as a lace, strap, etc.

Thor (thôr) *Norse Myth.* the god of thunder, war, and strength

tho·rax (thôr'aks) *n., pl.* **-rax·es, -ra·ces'** (-ə sēz') [< Gr.] **1.** the part of the body between the neck and the abdomen; chest **2.** the middle one of the three main segments of an insect —**tho·rac·ic** (thô ras'ik) *adj.*

tho·ri·um (thôr'ē əm) *n.* [< THOR] a rare, grayish, radioactive chemical element, used as a nuclear fuel: symbol, Th

thorn (thôrn) *n.* [OE.] **1.** *a)* a very short, hard, leafless stem with a sharp point *b)* any small tree or shrub bearing thorns **2.** a constant source of trouble or irritation —**thorn'y** *adj.* **-i·er, -i·est**

thor·ough (thur'ō) *adj.* [var. of THROUGH] **1.** done or proceeding through to the end; complete **2.** absolute *[a thorough rascal]* **3.** very exact, accurate, or painstaking

thor·ough·bred (thur'ə bred') *adj.* of pure stock; pedigreed —*n.* a thoroughbred animal; specif., [T-] any of a breed of racehorses

thor'ough·fare' (-fer') *n.* a public street open at both ends, esp. a main street

thor'ough·go'ing *adj.* very thorough

those (thōz) *adj., pron. pl. of* THAT

thou (thou) *pron.* [OE. *thu*] you (sing.): in poetic or religious use

though (thō) *conj.* [< OE. *theah*] **1.** in spite of the fact that *[though it rained, he went]* **2.** and yet; however *[they did it, though badly]* **3.** even if *[though he may fail, he will have tried]* —*adv.* however

thought' (thôt) *n.* [OE. *thoht*] **1.** the act or process of thinking **2.** the power of reasoning **3.** an idea, opinion, plan, etc. **4.** attention; consideration **5.** a little; trifle *[be a thought more careful]*

thought² (thôt) *pt. & pp. of* THINK

thought'ful *adj.* **1.** meditative **2.** serious **3.** considerate —**thought'ful·ly** *adv.*

thought'less *adj.* **1.** not stopping to think; careless **2.** ill-considered; rash **3.** inconsiderate —**thought'less·ly** *adv.*

thou·sand (thou'z'nd) *adj., n.* [OE. *thusend*] ten hundred; 1,000; M —**thou'sandth** (-z'ndth) *adj., n.*

thrall (thrôl) *n.* [< ON. *thræl*] **1.** a slave **2.** slavery

thrash (thrash) *vt., vi.* [OE. *therscan*] **1.** to thresh **2.** to beat; flog **3.** to toss about violently **4.** to defeat overwhelmingly —**thrash out** to settle by detailed discussion

thrash·er (thrash'ər) *n.* [E. dial. *thresher*] a thrushlike songbird

thread (thred) *n.* [OE. *thræd*] **1.** a fine, stringlike length of spun cotton, silk, nylon, etc. used in sewing **2.** any thin line, vein, etc. **3.** something like a thread in its length, sequence, etc. *[the thread of a story]* **4.** the spiral ridge of a screw, nut, etc. —*vt.* **1.** to put a thread through (a needle, etc.) **2.** to fashion a thread (sense 4) on or in **3.** to make (one's way) by twisting, weaving, etc. —**thread'er** *n.*

thread'bare' *adj.* **1.** worn down so that the threads show **2.** shabby **3.** stale; trite

threat (thret) *n.* [OE. *threat,* a throng] 1. an expression of intention to hurt, destroy, punish, etc. 2. an indication of, or a source of, imminent danger

threat′en *vt., vi.* 1. to make threats, as of injury (against) 2. to indicate (danger, etc.) 3. to be a source of danger (to)

three (thrē) *adj., n.* [OE. *threo*] one more than two; 3; III

three′-deck′er (-dek′ər) *n.* anything having three levels, layers, etc.

three′-di·men′sion·al *adj.* having or seeming to have depth or thickness

three′fold′ *adj.* 1. having three parts 2. having three times as much or as many —*adv.* three times as much or as many

three·score (thrē′skôr′) *adj.* sixty

thren·o·dy (thren′ə dē) *n., pl.* -**dies** [< Gr. *thrēnos,* lamentation + *ōidē,* song] a dirge

thresh (thresh) *vt., vi.* [earlier form of THRASH] 1. to beat out (grain) from (husks), as with a flail 2. to thrash —**thresh′er** *n.*

thresh·old (thresh′ōld, -hōld) *n.* [OE. *therscwold*] 1. a length of wood, stone, etc. along the bottom of a doorway 2. the beginning point

threw (thrōō) *pt. of* THROW

thrice (thrīs) *adv.* [ME. *thries*] 1. three times 2. threefold 3. greatly; highly

thrift (thrift) *n.* [< ON. *thrifast,* to prosper] careful management of one's money, etc.; frugality —**thrift′i·ly** *adv.* —**thrift′less** *adj.* —**thrift′y** *adj.* -**i·er,** -**i·est**

thrift shop a store where castoff clothes, etc. are sold, as for charity

thrill (thril) *vi., vt.* [< OE. *thurh,* through] 1. to feel or cause to feel emotional excitement 2. to quiver or cause to quiver; tremble —*n.* 1. a thrilling or being thrilled 2. a tremor; quiver —**thrill′er** *n.*

thrive (thrīv) *vi.* **thrived** or **throve, thrived** or **thriv·en** (thriv′'n), **thriv′ing** [< ON. *thrifa,* to grasp] 1. to prosper; be successful 2. to grow vigorously

throat (thrōt) *n.* [OE. *throte*] 1. the front part of the neck 2. the upper passage from the mouth to the stomach and lungs 3. any narrow passage

throat′y *adj.* -**i·er,** -**i·est** produced in the throat, as some sounds; husky

throb (thräb) *vi.* **throbbed, throb′bing** [ME. *throbben*] 1. to beat, pulsate, vibrate, etc., esp. strongly or fast 2. to feel excitement —*n.* 1. a throbbing 2. a strong beat

throe (thrō) *n.* [prob. < OE. *thrawu,* pain] a spasm or pang of pain: *usually used in pl.* [death *throes*]

throm·bo·sis (thräm bō′sis) *n.* [< Gr. *thrombos,* a clot] coagulation of the blood in the heart or a blood vessel, forming a clot, or **throm′bus** (-bəs)

throne (thrōn) *n.* [< Gr. *thronos,* a seat] 1. the chair on which a king, cardinal, etc. sits on formal occasions 2. the power or rank of a king, etc. 3. a sovereign, etc.

throng (thrôn) *n.* [OE. *thringan,* to crowd] 1. a crowd 2. any great number of things considered together —*vi.* to gather together in a throng; crowd —*vt.* to crowd into

throt·tle (thrät′'l) *n.* [< ? THROAT] the valve that regulates the amount of fuel vapor entering an engine, or its control lever or pedal —*vt.* -**tled,** -**tling** 1. to choke; strangle 2. to censor or suppress 3. *a)* to reduce the flow of (fuel vapor) by means of a throttle *b)* to slow by this means

through (thrōō) *prep.* [OE. *thurh*] 1. in one side and out the other side of 2. among 3. by way of 4. around [touring *through* France] 5. *a)* from beginning to end of *b)* up to and including 6. by means of 7. as a result of —*adv.* 1. in one side and out the other 2. from the beginning to the end 3. completely to the end [see it *through*] 4. completely [soaked *through*] —*adj.* 1. extending from one place to another [a *through* street] 2. traveling to the destination without stops [a *through* train] 3. finished

through·out′ *prep.* all the way through —*adv.* in every part; everywhere

through′way′ (-wā′) *n.* an expressway: also **thru′way′**

throve (thrōv) *alt. pt. of* THRIVE

throw (thrō) *vt.* **threw, thrown, throw′ing** [OE. *thrawan,* to twist] 1. to send through the air by a rapid motion of the arm, etc. 2. to cause to fall; upset 3. to send rapidly [to throw troops into battle] 4. to put suddenly into a specified state, etc. [thrown into confusion] 5. to move (a switch, etc.) so as to connect, disconnect, etc. 6. to direct, cast, etc. [throw a glance] 7. [Colloq.] to lose (a game, etc.) deliberately 8. [Colloq.] to give (a party, etc.) 9. [Colloq.] to confuse [the question threw him] —*vi.* to cast or hurl something —*n.* 1. the act of one who throws 2. the distance something is or can be thrown [a stone's *throw*] 3. a spread for a bed, etc. —**throw away** 1. to discard 2. to waste —**throw in** to add extra or free —**throw off** 1. to rid oneself of 2. to mislead or confuse 3. to expel, emit, etc. —**throw oneself at** to try very hard to win the love of —**throw out** 1. to discard 2. to reject —**throw over** 1. to give up; abandon 2. to jilt —**throw together** to make or assemble hurriedly —**throw up** 1. to give up; abandon 2. to vomit

throw′a·way′ *n.* a leaflet, handbill, etc. given out on streets, at houses, etc. —*adj.* designed to be discarded after use

throw′back′ *n.* (a) reversion to an ancestral type

throw rug a small rug for a limited area

thru (thrōō) *prep., adv., adj. shortened sp. of* THROUGH

thrum (thrum) *vt., vi.* **thrummed, thrum′ming** [echoic] 1. to strum (a guitar, banjo, etc.) 2. to drum (on) with the fingers —*n.* a thrumming

thrush (thrush) *n.* [OE. *thrysce*] any of a large group of songbirds, as the robin

thrust (thrust) *vt., vi.* **thrust, thrust′ing** [< ON. *thrysta*] 1. to push with sudden force 2. to stab 3. to force or impose —*n.* 1. a sudden, forceful push 2. a stab 3. continuous pressure, as of a rafter against a wall 4. *a)* the driving force of a propeller *b)* the forward force produced by a jet or rocket engine 5. forward movement 6. the basic meaning or purpose

thud (thud) *vi.* **thud′ded, thud′ding** [prob. < OE. *thyddan,* to strike] to hit with a dull sound —*n.* a dull sound, as of a heavy object dropping on a soft, solid surface

thug (thug) *n.* [Hindi *thag,* swindler] a brutal hoodlum, gangster, etc.

thumb (thum) *n.* [OE. *thuma*] the short, thick finger of the hand —*vt.* 1. to handle, turn, soil, etc. as with the thumb 2. [Colloq.] to ask for or get (a ride) in hitchhiking by gesturing with the thumb —**all thumbs** clumsy —**under one's thumb** under one's influence

thumb′nail′ *n.* the nail of the thumb —*adj.* very small or brief

thumb′screw′ *n.* a screw that can be turned by the thumb and forefinger

thumb′tack′ *n.* a tack with a wide, flat head,

that can be pressed into a board, etc. with the thumb

thump (thump) *n.* [echoic] **1.** a blow with something heavy and blunt **2.** the dull sound made by such a blow —*vt.* to strike with a thump —*vi.* **1.** to hit or fall with a thump **2.** to make a dull, heavy sound; pound; throb — **thump′er** *n.*

thump′ing *adj.* **1.** that thumps **2.** [Colloq.] very large; whopping

thun·der (thun′dər) *n.* [OE. *thunor*] **1.** the sound that is heard after a flash of lightning **2.** any sound like this —*vi.* to produce thunder —*vt.* to utter, etc. with a thundering sound — **thun′der·ous** *adj.*

thun′der·bolt′ (-bōlt′) *n.* **1.** a flash of lightning and the accompanying thunder **2.** something that stuns or acts with sudden force or violence

thun′der·clap′ *n.* a clap, or loud crash, of thunder

thun′der·cloud′ *n.* a storm cloud charged with electricity and producing lightning and thunder

thun′der·show′er *n.* a shower accompanied by thunder and lightning

thun′der·storm′ *n.* a storm accompanied by thunder and lightning

thun′der·struck′ *adj.* struck with amazement, terror, etc.; astonished

Thurs·day (thurz′dē, -dā) *n.* [< THOR] the fifth day of the week: abbrev. **Thur., Thurs.**

thus (*th*us) *adv.* [OE.] **1.** in this or that manner **2.** to this or that degree or extent; so **3.** therefore

thwack (thwak) *vt., n.* [prob. echoic] *same as* WHACK

thwart (thwôrt) *vt.* [< ON. *thvert*, transverse] to obstruct, frustrate, or defeat (a person, plans, etc.)

thy (*th*ī) *possessive pronominal adj.* [< ME. *thin*] of, belonging to, or done by thee: archaic or poet. var. of YOUR

thyme (tīm) *n.* [< Gr. *thymon*] a plant related to the mint, with leaves used for seasoning

thy·mus (thī′məs) *n.* [< Gr. *thymos*] a ductless, glandlike body near the throat

thy·roid (thī′roid) *adj.* [< Gr. *thyreos*, large shield] designating or of a large ductless gland near the trachea, secreting a hormone which regulates growth —*n.* **1.** the thyroid gland **2.** an animal extract of this gland, used in treating goiter, etc.

thy·self (*th*ī self′) *pron.* *reflexive or intensive form of* THOU

ti (tē) *n. Music* a syllable representing the seventh tone of the diatonic scale

Ti *Chem.* titanium

ti·ar·a (tē er′ə, -ar′-) *n.* [< Gr. *tiara*, headdress] a woman's crownlike headdress of jewels or flowers

tib·i·a (tib′ē ə) *n., pl.* **-ae′** (-ē′), **-as** [L.] the inner and thicker of the two bones of the lower leg

tic (tik) *n.* [Fr. < ?] a twitching of a muscle, esp. of the face, that is not consciously controlled

tick¹ (tik) *n.* [prob. echoic] **1.** a light clicking sound, as of a clock **2.** a mark made to check off items —*vi.* to make ticks —*vt.* to record, mark, or check by ticks

tick² (tik) *n.* [OE. *ticia*] any of various blood-sucking arachnids, parasitic on man, cattle, etc.

tick³ (tik) *n.* [ult. < Gr. *thēkē*, a case] the cloth case of a mattress or pillow

tick′er *n.* **1.** one that ticks **2.** a telegraphic device that records stock market quotations, etc. on paper tape (**ticker tape**) **3.** [Slang] the heart

tick·et (tik′it) *n.* [< obs. Fr. *etiquet*, etiquette] **1.** a printed card, etc. that gives one a right, as to attend a theater **2.** a label on merchandise giving size, price, etc. **3.** the list of candidates nominated by a political party in an election **4.** [Colloq.] a court summons for a traffic violation —*vt.* **1.** to label with a ticket **2.** to give a ticket to

tick′ing *n.* a strong, heavy cloth, used for casings of mattresses, pillows, etc.

tick·le (tik′'l) *vt.* **-led, -ling** [ME. *tikelen*] **1.** to please, gratify, delight, etc. **2.** to stroke lightly so as to cause involuntary twitching, laughter, etc. —*vi.* to have or cause a twitching or tingling sensation —*n.* a sensation of being tickled

tick·ler (tik′lər) *n.* a pad, file, etc. for noting things to be tended to later

tick·lish (tik′lish) *adj.* **1.** sensitive to tickling **2.** needing careful handling

tick·tock (tik′täk′) *n.* the sound made by a clock —*vi.* to make this sound

tid·al (tīd′'l) *adj.* of, having, or caused by a tide or tides

tidal wave 1. an unusually great, destructive wave sent inshore by an earthquake or very strong wind **2.** any widespread movement, feeling, etc.

tid·bit (tid′bit′) *n.* [dial. *tid,* tiny object] a choice bit of food, gossip, etc.

tide (tīd) *n.* [OE. *tid,* time] **1.** a period of time [*Eastertide*] **2.** the alternate rise and fall, about twice a day, of the surface of oceans, seas, etc., caused by the attraction of the moon and sun **3.** something that rises and falls like the tide **4.** a current, trend, etc. —*vt.* **tid′ed, tid′ing** to help along temporarily (with *over*)

tide′wa′ter *n.* **1.** water that is affected by the tide **2.** a seaboard —*adj.* of or along a tidewater

ti·dings (tī′diɳz) *n.pl.* [OE. *tidung*] news

ti·dy (tī′dē) *adj.* **-di·er, -di·est** [< OE. *tid,* time] **1.** neat in appearance, arrangement, etc.; orderly **2.** [Colloq.] rather large —*vt., vi.* **-died, -dy·ing** to make (things) tidy (often with *up*)

tie (tī) *vt.* **tied, ty′ing** [< OE. *teag,* rope] **1.** to bind, as with string, rope, etc. **2.** to knot the laces, etc. of **3.** to make (a knot) in **4.** to bind in any way **5.** to equal the score of, as in a contest —*vi.* to make the same score in a contest —*n.* **1.** a string, cord, etc. used to tie things **2.** something that joins, binds, etc. **3.** a necktie **4.** a beam, rod, etc. that holds parts together **5.** any of the crossbeams to which the rails of a railroad are fastened **6.** *a*) an equality of scores *b*) a contest in which this occurs —*adj.* that has been made equal [a tie score] — **tie down** to confine; restrict —**tie up 1.** to wrap up and tie **2.** to moor to a dock **3.** to block or hinder **4.** to cause to be already in use, committed, etc. —**ti′er** *n.*

tie clasp a decorative clasp used for fastening a necktie to the shirt front: also **tie clip, tie bar**

tie′-in′ *n.* a connection or relation

tier (tir) *n.* [< MFr. *tire,* order] any of a series of rows, as of seats, arranged one above or behind another

tie-up (tī′up′) *n.* **1.** a temporary stoppage of production, traffic, etc. **2.** a connection

tiff (tif) *n.* [< ?] **1.** a slight fit of anger **2.** a slight quarrel —*vi.* to be in or have a tiff

ti·ger (tī′gər) *n.* [< Gr. *tigris*] a large, flesh-eating animal of the cat family, native to Asia, having a tawny coat striped with black —**ti′-ger·ish** *adj.*

tight (tīt) *adj.* [< OE. *-thight,* strong] **1.** made

so that water, air, etc. cannot pass through **2.** drawn, packed, etc. closely together **3.** fixed securely; firm **4.** taut **5.** fitting so closely as to be uncomfortable **6.** difficult: esp. in **a tight corner** (or **squeeze,** etc.), a difficult situation **7.** difficult to get; scarce **8.** [Colloq.] stingy **9.** [Slang] drunk —*adv.* **1.** securely **2.** [Colloq.] soundly *[sleep tight]* —**sit tight** to maintain one's position, etc.
tight'en (-'n) *vt., vi.* to make or become tight or tighter —**tight'en·er** *n.*
tight'fist'ed *adj.* stingy; miserly
tight'fit'ting *adj.* fitting very tight
tight'-lipped' (-lipt') *adj.* secretive
tight'rope' *n.* a tightly stretched rope on which acrobats perform
tights *n.pl.* a tightly fitting garment for the lower half of the body
tight'wad' (-wäd', -wôd') *n.* [TIGHT + WAD] [Slang] a stingy person
ti·gress (tī'gris) *n.* a female tiger
til·de (til'də) *n.* [Sp. < L. *titulus,* sign] a diacritical mark (˜) variously used
tile (tīl) *n.* [< L. *tegula*] **1.** a thin piece of fired clay, stone, plastic, etc., used for roofing, flooring, walls, etc. **2.** a drain of earthenware pipe **3.** any of the oblong pieces used in mah-jongg, etc. —*vt.* **tiled, til'ing** to cover with tiles
til'ing *n.* tiles collectively
till[1] (til) *prep., conj.* [OE. *til*] until
till[2] (til) *vt., vi.* [OE. *tilian,* strive for] to work (land) in raising crops, as by plowing
till[3] (til) *n.* [< ? ME. *tillen,* to draw] a drawer for keeping money
till'age (-ij) *n.* **1.** the tilling of land **2.** land that is tilled
till·er (til'ər) *n.* [< ML. *telarium,* weaver's beam] a handle for turning a boat's rudder
tilt (tilt) *vt.* [ME. *tilten,* totter] to cause to slope; tip —*vi.* **1.** to slope; incline **2.** to charge (*at* an opponent) **3.** to engage in a tilt —*n.* **1.** a medieval contest in which two horsemen fight with lances **2.** any spirited contest **3.** a slope — **(at) full tilt** at full speed
tim·ber (tim'bər) *n.* [OE.] **1.** wood for building houses, ships, etc. **2.** a wooden beam used in building **3.** trees collectively **4.** personal quality or character
tim'ber·line' *n.* the line above or beyond which trees do not grow, as on mountains
tim·bre (tam'bər, tim'-) *n.* [Fr. < OFr., a kind of drum] the quality of sound that distinguishes one voice or musical instrument from another
time (tīm) *n.* [OE. *tima*] **1.** every moment there has been or ever will be **2.** a system for measuring duration *[standard time]* **3.** the period during which something exists, happens, etc. **4.** [*usually pl.*] a period of history; age; era **5.** [*usually pl.*] prevailing conditions *[times* are good] **6.** a set period or term, as of work, confinement, etc. **7.** standard rate of pay **8.** rate of speed in marching, driving, etc. **9.** a precise instant, minute, day, etc. **10.** an occasion or repeated occasion *[the fifth time* it's been on TV] **11.** *Music a)* rhythm as determined by the grouping of beats into measures *b)* tempo —*vt.* **timed, tim'ing 1.** to arrange the time of so as to be suitable, opportune, etc. **2.** to adjust, set, etc. so as to coincide with time *[time* our watches] **3.** to record the pace, speed, etc. of —*adj.* **1.** having to do with time **2.** set to explode, open, etc. at a given time **3.** having to do with paying in installments — **ahead of time** early —**at the same time** however —**at times** occasionally —**do time** [Colloq.] to serve a prison term —**for the time being** tem-

porarily —**from time to time** now and then —**in time 1.** eventually **2.** before it is too late **3.** keeping the set tempo, pace, etc. —**make time** to travel, work, etc. rapidly —**on time 1.** at the appointed time **2.** for or by payment by installments —**time after time** again and again: also **time and again**
time clock a clock with a mechanism for recording the time at which an employee begins and ends a work period
time'-hon'ored *adj.* honored because in existence or usage for a long time
time'keep'er *n.* one who keeps account of the hours worked by employees, or of the elapsed time in races, games, etc.
time'less (-lis) *adj.* eternal
time'ly *adj.* **-li·er, -li·est** well-timed; opportune —**time'li·ness** *n.*
time'out' *n. Sports,* etc. any temporary suspension of play, as to discuss strategy, etc.
time'piece' *n.* a clock or watch
tim'er *n.* a device for controlling the timing of a mechanism
times (tīmz) *prep.* multiplied by: symbol, x
time sharing a system for the simultaneous use of a computer by many users at remote locations
time'ta'ble (-tā'b'l) *n.* a schedule of the times of arrival and departure of planes, trains, buses, etc.
time'worn' *adj.* **1.** worn out by long use **2.** trite; hackneyed
time zone *see* STANDARD TIME
tim·id (tim'id) *adj.* [< L. *timere,* to fear] **1.** easily frightened; shy **2.** lacking self-confidence —**ti·mid·i·ty** (tə mid'ə tē) *n.*
tim·ing (tī'miŋ) *n.* the regulation of time or speed so as to achieve the most effective performance
tim·or·ous (tim'ər əs) *adj.* [< L. *timor,* fear] full of fear; timid
tim·o·thy (tim'ə thē) *n.* [< a *Timothy* Hanson, c.1720] a grass with dense spikes, grown for hay
tim·pa·ni (tim'pə nē) *n.pl.* [It.: see TYMPANUM] kettledrums, esp. a set of them played by one performer —**tim'pa·nist** *n.*
tin (tin) *n.* [OE.] **1.** a soft, silver-white, metallic chemical element: symbol, Sn **2.** *same as* TIN PLATE **3.** *a)* a pan, box, etc. made of tin plate *b)* [Chiefly Brit.] *same as* CAN[2] (*n.* 2, 3) —*vt.* **tinned, tin'ning 1.** to plate with tin **2.** [Chiefly Brit.] *same as* CAN[2] (*vt.* 1)
tin can *same as* CAN[2] (*n.* 2)
tinc·ture (tiŋk'chər) *n.* [< L. *tingere,* to dye] **1.** a light color; tinge **2.** a slight trace **3.** a medicinal substance in a solution of alcohol —*vt.* **-tured, -tur·ing** to tinge
tin·der (tin'dər) *n.* [OE. *tynder*] any dry, easily flammable material
tin'der·box' *n.* **1.** formerly, a metal box for holding tinder, flint, and steel **2.** a highly flammable building, etc. **3.** a potential source of war, rebellion, etc.
tine (tīn) *n.* [OE. *tind*] a slender, projecting point; prong *[fork tines]* —**tined** *adj.*
tin'foil' (-foil') *n.* a thin sheet of tin or tin alloy used as a wrapping
tinge (tinj) *n.* [see TINT] **1.** a slight coloring; tint **2.** a slight trace, flavor, etc. —*vt.* **tinged, tinge'ing** or **ting'ing** to give a tinge to
tin·gle (tiŋ'g'l) *vi.* **-gled, -gling** [var. of TINKLE] to have a prickling or stinging feeling, as from cold, excitement, etc. —*n.* this feeling —**tin'gly** *adj.*
tin·ker (tiŋ'kər) *n.* [ME. *tinkere*] **1.** one who mends pots, pans, etc. **2.** a bungler —*vi.* **1.** to

make clumsy attempts to mend something **2.** to putter —**tin′ker·er** *n.*

tin·kle (tiŋ′k'l) *vi.* **-kled, -kling** [echoic] to make a series of light, clinking sounds as of a small bell —*vt.* to cause to tinkle —*n.* a tinkling sound —**tin′kly** *adj.*

tin·ny (tin′ē) *adj.* **-ni·er, -ni·est 1.** of tin **2.** like tin, as in appearance, sound, value, etc. —**tin′-ni·ness** *n.*

tin plate thin sheets of iron or steel that are plated with tin

tin·sel (tin′s'l, -z'l) *n.* [< L. *scintilla,* a spark] **1.** thin strips or threads of tin, metal foil, etc. used for decoration **2.** something that glitters but has little value

tint (tint) *n.* [< L. *tingere,* to dye] **1.** a delicate color **2.** a shade of a color **3.** a hair dye —*vt.* to give a tint to

tin·tin·nab·u·la·tion (tin′ti nab′yoo lā′shən) *n.* [< L. *tintinnabulum,* little bell] the ringing sound of bells

tin·type (tin′tīp′) *n.* an old kind of photograph taken directly as a positive print on a treated plate of tin or iron

ti·ny (tī′nē) *adj.* **-ni·er, -ni·est** [< ME. *tine,* a little] very small —**ti′ni·ness** *n.*

-tion [< Fr. < L.] *a suffix meaning:* **1.** the act of [*correction*] **2.** the state of being [*elation*] **3.** the thing that is [*creation*]

-tious *a suffix used to form adjectives from nouns ending in* -TION [*cautious*]

tip¹ (tip) *n.* [ME. *tippe*] **1.** the point or end of something **2.** something attached to the end, as a cap —*vt.* **tipped, tip′ping 1.** to form a tip on **2.** to cover the tip of

tip² (tip) *vt.* **tipped, tip′ping** [< ?] **1.** to strike lightly and sharply **2.** to give a gratuity to (a waiter, etc.) **3.** [Colloq.] to give secret informa- tion to (often with *off*) —*vi.* to give a tip or tips —*n.* **1.** a light, sharp blow **2.** a piece of se- cret information **3.** a hint, warning, etc. **4.** a gratuity

tip³ (tip) *vt., vi.* **tipped, tip′ping** [< ?] **1.** to over- turn or upset (often with *over*) **2.** to tilt or slant —*n.* a tilt; slant

tip′-off′ *n.* a tip; confidential hint, etc.

tip·ple (tip′'l) *vi., vt.* **-pled, -pling** [< ?] to drink (alcoholic liquor) habitually

tip·ster (tip′stər) *n.* [Colloq.] one who sells tips, as on horse races

tip·sy (tip′sē) *adj.* **-si·er, -si·est 1.** that tips easily; not steady **2.** somewhat drunk

tip′toe′ *n.* the tip of a toe —*vi.* **-toed′, -toe′ing** to walk stealthily or cautiously on one's tiptoes —**on tiptoe 1.** on one's tiptoes **2.** eager(ly) **3.** silently

tip′top′ *n.* [TIP¹ + TOP¹] the highest point — *adj., adv.* **1.** at the highest point **2.** [Colloq.] at the highest point of excellence, health, etc.

ti·rade (tī′rād, tī rād′) *n.* [Fr. < It. *tirare,* to fire] a long vehement speech or denunciation; harangue

tire¹ (tīr) *vt., vi.* **tired, tir′ing** [OE. *tiorian*] to make or become weary, bored, etc.

tire² (tīr) *n.* [prob. < ME. *atir,* equipment] a hoop of iron or rubber, or a rubber tube filled with air, fixed around the wheel of a vehicle to form a tread

tired (tīrd) *adj.* **1.** weary **2.** hackneyed

tire′less *adj.* that does not become tired

tire′some *adj.* tiring; boring

tis·sue (tish′ōō) *n.* [< L. *texere,* to weave] **1.** light, thin cloth **2.** an interwoven mass; mesh; web **3.** a piece of soft, absorbent paper, used as a disposable handkerchief, etc. **4.** *same as* TISSUE PAPER **5.** the substance of an organic

body, consisting of cells and intercellular material

tissue paper very thin, unsized, nearly trans- parent paper for wrapping, etc.

tit¹ (tit) *n. same as* TITMOUSE

tit² (tit) *n.* [OE.] **1.** *same as* TEAT **2.** a breast: in this sense now vulgar

ti·tan (tīt′'n) *n.* [< Gr. *Titan,* a giant deity] any person or thing of great size or power

ti·tan·ic (tī tan′ik) *adj.* of great size, strength, or power

ti·ta·ni·um (tī tā′nē əm, ti-) *n.* [see TITAN] a dark-gray metallic chemical element used for deoxidizing in molten steel, etc.: symbol, Ti

tit for tat [< *tip for tap*] blow for blow

tithe (tīth) *n.* [OE. *teothe,* a tenth] a tenth of one's income paid to a church —*vt., vi.* tithed, **tith′ing** to pay a tithe of (one's income, etc.) — **tith′er** *n.*

ti·tian (tish′ən) *n.* [< *Titian* (1490?-1576), Venetian painter] reddish yellow

tit·il·late (tit′'l āt′) *vt.* **-lat′ed, -lat′ing** [< L. *titillare,* to tickle] to excite pleasurably —**tit′il- la′tion** *n.*

ti·tle (tīt′'l) *n.* [< L. *titulus*] **1.** the name of a poem, book, picture, etc. **2.** an epithet **3.** an appellation indicating one's rank, profession, etc. **4.** a claim or right **5.** *Law a)* a right to ownership, esp. of real estate *b)* a deed **6.** *Mo- tion Pictures, TV* a subtitle, credit, etc. **7.** *Sports, etc.* a championship —*vt.* **-tled, -tling** to give a title to

ti′tled *adj.* having a title, esp. of nobility

tit·mouse (tit′mous′) *n., pl.* **-mice′** (-mīs′) [ME. *titemose*] a small bird with ashy-gray feathers

tit·ter (tit′ər) *vi.* [echoic] to laugh in a half- suppressed way; giggle —*n.* a tittering

tit·tle (tit′'l) *n.* [ME. *title*] a very small parti- cle; iota; jot

tit·u·lar (tich′ə lər) *adj.* [see TITLE] **1.** of a title **2.** being or having a title **3.** in name only [a *titular* leader]

tiz·zy (tiz′ē) *n., pl.* **-zies** [< ?] [Colloq.] a state of frenzied excitement

tn. 1. ton(s) **2.** training

TNT, T.N.T. [< *tri*nitrotoluene] a high explo- sive used for blasting, etc.

to (tōō, too, tə) *prep.* [OE.] **1.** toward [turn *to* the left] **2.** so as to reach [he went *to* Boston] **3.** as far as [wet *to* the skin] **4.** into a condi- tion of [a rise *to* fame] **5.** on, onto, at, etc. [tied *to* a post] **6.** *a)* until [from noon *to* night] *b)* before [the time is 10 *to* 6] **7.** for the pur- pose of [come *to* my aid] **8.** in regard to [open *to* attack] **9.** so as to produce [torn *to* bits] **10.** along with [add this *to* the rest] **11.** belonging with [a key *to* the lock] **12.** as compared with [a score of 7 *to* 0] **13.** in agreement with [not *to* my taste] **14.** constituting [ten *to* a pound] **15.** with (a specified person or thing) as the recipient of the action [give it *to* me] **16.** in honor of [a toast *to* you] *To* is also a sign of the infinitive (Ex.: I want *to* stay) —*adv.* **1.** forward [his hat is on wrong side *to*] **2.** shut or closed [pull the door *to*] **3.** to the matter at hand [fall *to!*] —**to and fro** back and forth

toad (tōd) *n.* [OE. *tade*] a small, froglike ani- mal that lives on moist land

toad′stool′ (-stōōl′) *n.* a mushroom, esp. any poisonous mushroom

toad·y (tōd′ē) *n., pl.* **-ies** [short for *toadeater,* quack doctor's assistant] a servile flatterer — *vt., vi.* **-ied, -y·ing** to be a toady (to) —**toad′y- ism** *n.*

toast¹ (tōst) *vt.* [< L. *torrere,* parch] **1.** to brown the surface of (bread, etc.) by heating

2. to warm thoroughly —*vi.* to become toasted —*n.* sliced bread browned by heat

toast² (tōst) *n.* [< the toasted bread formerly put in wine] **1.** a person or thing in honor of which persons raise their glasses and drink **2.** a proposal to drink, or a drink, in honor of some person, etc. —*vt., vi.* to propose or drink a toast (to) —**toast′er** *n.*

toast′mas′ter *n.* the person at a banquet who proposes toasts, introduces after-dinner speakers, etc.

to·bac·co (tə bak′ō) *n., pl.* **-cos** [< Sp. < WInd. *tabaco,* smoking pipe] **1.** a plant with large leaves that are prepared for smoking, chewing, etc. **2.** the leaves so prepared **3.** cigars, cigarettes, etc.

to·bac′co·nist (-ə nist) *n.* [Chiefly Brit.] a dealer in tobacco

to·bog·gan (tə bäg′ən) *n.* [< AmInd.] a long flat sled without runners, for coasting downhill —*vi.* **1.** to coast downhill on a toboggan **2.** to decline rapidly

toc·sin (täk′sin) *n.* [Fr. < Pr. *toc,* a stroke + *senh,* a bell] an alarm bell

to·day (tə dā′) *adv.* [OE. *to dæg*] **1.** on or during the present day **2.** in the present time —*n.* **1.** the present day **2.** the present time Also, esp. formerly, **to-day**

tod·dle (täd′'l) *vi.* **-dled, -dling** [? < TOTTER] to walk with short, uncertain steps, as a child — **tod′dler** *n.*

tod·dy (täd′ē) *n., pl.* **-dies** [< Hindi] a drink of brandy, whiskey, etc. mixed with hot water, sugar, etc.: also **hot toddy**

to-do (tə dōō′) *n.* [Colloq.] a commotion

toe (tō) *n.* [OE. *ta*] **1.** *a)* any of the digits of the foot *b)* the forepart of the foot **2.** anything like a toe in location, shape, or use —*vt.* **toed, toe′ing** to touch, kick, etc. with the toes —*vi.* to stand, walk, etc. with the toes in a specified position [he *toes* in] —**on one's toes** [Colloq.] alert

toed (tōd) *adj.* having (a specified kind or number of) toes [pigeon-*toed*]

toe′hold′ *n.* **1.** a small space for supporting the toe of the foot **2.** a slight advantage

toe′nail′ *n.* the nail of a toe

tof·fee, tof·fy (tôf′ē, täf′ē) *n.* [< TAFFY] a hard, chewy candy like taffy

to·ga (tō′gə) *n., pl.* **-gas, -gae** (-jē) [L. < *tegere,* to cover] in ancient Rome, a loose outer garment worn in public by citizens

to·geth·er (tə geth′ər) *adv.* [< OE. *to,* to + *gædre,* together] **1.** in or into one group, place, etc. [we ate *together*] **2.** in or into contact, union, etc. [they bumped *together*] **3.** considered collectively [he won more than all of us *together*] **4.** at the same time [shots fired *together*] **5.** continuously [he sulked for three whole days *together*] **6.** in or into agreement, etc. [to get *together* on a deal] —*adj.* [Slang] having a fully integrated personality

to·geth′er·ness *n.* the spending of much time together, in seeking a more unified, stable relationship

tog·gle switch (täg′'l) [prob. < TUG] a switch with a lever moved back and forth to open or close an electric circuit

togs (tägz, tôgz) *n.pl.* [prob. < L. *toga,* TOGA] [Colloq.] clothes

toil (toil) *vi.* [< L. *tudiculare,* stir about] **1.** to work hard and continuously **2.** to proceed laboriously —*n.* hard, exhausting work

toi·let (toi′lit) *n.* [< MFr. *toile,* cloth < L. *tela,* a web] **1.** the act of dressing or grooming oneself **2.** dress; attire **3.** *a)* a room with a bowl-

shaped fixture for defecation or urination *b)* such a fixture

toilet paper (or **tissue**) soft paper for cleaning oneself after evacuation

toi′let·ry (-lə trē) *n., pl.* **-ries** soap, lotion, etc. used in grooming oneself

toi·lette (twä let′, toi-) *n.* [Fr.: see TOILET] **1.** the process of grooming oneself: said of a woman **2.** dress; attire

toilet water a perfumed, slightly alcoholic liquid, applied to the skin

toils (toilz) *n.pl.* [< L. *tela,* a web] any snares suggestive of a net

toil·some (toil′səm) *adj.* laborious

toke (tōk) *n.* [? < TOKEN] [Slang] a puff on a cigarette, esp. one of marijuana

to·ken (tō′kən) *n.* [OE. *tacn*] **1.** a sign, indication, symbol, etc. [a *token* of affection] **2.** a keepsake **3.** a metal disk to be used in place of currency, for transportation fares, etc. —*adj.* merely nominal; slight [*token* resistance] —**by the same** (or **this**) **token** following from this

to′ken·ism (-iz′m) *n.* the making of small, merely formal concessions to a demand, etc.; specif., token integration of Negroes, as in jobs

told (tōld) *pt. & pp. of* TELL —**all told** all (being) counted

tol·er·a·ble (täl′ər ə b'l) *adj.* **1.** endurable **2.** fairly good; passable —**tol′er·a·bly** *adv.*

tol·er·ance (täl′ər əns) *n.* **1.** a being tolerant of others' beliefs, practices, etc. **2.** the amount of variation allowed from a standard, accuracy, etc. **3.** *Med.* the ability to resist the effects of a drug, etc.

tol′er·ant *adj.* having or showing tolerance of others' beliefs, practices, etc.

tol·er·ate (täl′ə rāt′) *vt.* **-at′ed, -at′ing** [< L. *tolerare,* to bear] **1.** to allow; permit **2.** to recognize and respect (others' beliefs, practices, etc.) without sharing them **3.** to put up with **4.** *Med.* to have a tolerance for —**tol′er·a′tion** *n.*

toll¹ (tōl) *n.* [prob. ult. < Gr. *telos,* tax] **1.** a tax or charge for a privilege, as for the use of a bridge **2.** a charge for some service, as for a long-distance telephone call **3.** the number lost, etc. [the storm took a heavy *toll* of lives]

toll² (tōl) *vt.* [ME. *tollen,* to pull] **1.** to ring (a bell, etc.) slowly with regular strokes **2.** to announce, summon, etc. by this —*vi.* to sound or ring slowly: said of a bell —*n.* the sound of a bell tolling

toll′gate′ *n.* a gate for stopping travel at a point where toll is taken

tom (täm) *adj.* [< the name *Tom*] male [a *tom* turkey]

tom·a·hawk (täm′ə hôk′) *n.* [< Algonquian] a light ax used by N. American Indians as a tool and a weapon

to·ma·to (tə mât′ō, -mät′ō) *n., pl.* **-toes** [< Sp. < MexInd.] **1.** a red or yellowish fruit with a juicy pulp, used as a vegetable **2.** the plant that it grows on

tomb (tōōm) *n.* [< Gr. *tymbos*] **1.** a vault or grave for the dead **2.** a burial monument —**the tomb** death

tom·boy (täm′boi′) *n.* a girl who behaves like a boisterous boy —**tom′boy′ish** *adj.*

tomb·stone (tōōm′stōn′) *n.* a stone, as with an inscription, marking a tomb or grave

tom·cat (täm′kat′) *n.* a male cat

tome (tōm) *n.* [< Gr. *tomos,* piece cut off] a book, esp. a large one

tom·fool·er·y (täm′fōōl′ər ē) *n., pl.* **-ies** foolish or silly behavior; nonsense

to·mor·row (tə mär′ō, -môr′ō) *adv.* [OE. *to*

morgen] on the day after today —*n.* the day after today

tom·tit (täm′tit′) *n.* [Chiefly Brit.] a titmouse or other small bird

tom-tom (täm′täm′) *n.* [Hindi *tam-tam*] a simple drum, beaten with the hands

ton (tun) *n.* [var. of TUN] **1.** a unit of weight equal to 2,000 pounds: in full **short ton 2.** a unit of weight equal to 2,240 pounds, commonly used in Great Britain: in full **long ton 3.** *same as* METRIC TON

ton·al (tō′n'l) *adj.* of a tone —**ton′al·ly** *adv.*

to·nal·i·ty (tō nal′ə tē) *n., pl.* **-ties** *Music* **1.** *same as* KEY¹ **2.** tonal character as determined by the relationship of the tones to the keynote

tone (tōn) *n.* [< Gr. *teinein,* to stretch] **1.** a vocal or musical sound or its quality **2.** a manner of expression showing a certain attitude [a friendly *tone*] **3.** style, character, spirit, etc. **4.** elegant style **5.** a quality of color; shade **6.** normal, healthy condition of a muscle, organ, etc. **7.** *Music a*) a sound of distinct pitch *b*) any of the full intervals of a diatonic scale —*vt.* **toned, ton′ing** to give a tone to —**tone down** (or **up**) to give a less (or more) intense tone to — **tone′less** *adj.*

tone arm the pivoted arm containing the pickup on a phonograph

tone′-deaf′ *adj.* not able to distinguish accurately differences in musical pitch

tong (tôŋ, täŋ) *n.* [Chin. *t'ang,* a meeting place] a Chinese association, society, etc.

tongs (tôŋz, täŋz) *n.pl.* [*sometimes with sing. v.*] [OE. *tange*] a device for seizing, lifting, etc., with two hinged arms

tongue (tuŋ) *n.* [OE. *tunge*] **1.** the movable muscular structure in the mouth, used in eating, tasting, and (in man) speaking **2.** talk; speech **3.** a manner of speaking **4.** a language or dialect **5.** something like a tongue in shape, position, use, etc., as the flap under the laces of a shoe

tongue-and-groove joint a kind of joint in which a projection on one board fits exactly into a groove in another

tongue′-tied′ *adj.* speechless from embarrassment, shyness, etc.

ton·ic (tän′ik) *adj.* [see TONE] **1.** of or producing good muscular tone **2.** *Music* designating or based on a keynote —*n.* **1.** anything that invigorates, as a medicine **2.** a quinine-flavored beverage served with gin, vodka, etc. **3.** *Music* a keynote

to·night (tə nīt′) *adv.* [OE. *to niht*] on or during the present or coming night —*n.* the present or the coming night

ton·nage (tun′ij) *n.* **1.** the total shipping, in tons, of a country or port **2.** the amount in tons a ship can carry

ton·sil (tän′s'l) *n.* [L. *tonsillae, pl.*] either of a pair of oval masses of lymphoid tissue, one on each side at the back of the mouth

ton′sil·lec′to·my (-sə lek′tə mē) *n., pl.* **-mies** [see -ECTOMY] the surgical removal of the tonsils

ton′sil·li′tis (-līt′əs) *n.* [see -ITIS] inflammation of the tonsils

ton·so·ri·al (tän sôr′ē əl) *adj.* [< L. *tondere,* to clip] of a barber or his work: often used humorously

ton·sure (tän′shər) *n.* [< L. *tondere,* to clip] **1.** the act of shaving the head or crown of one entering the priesthood or a monastic order **2.** the part so shaven

too (tōō) *adv.* [< TO] **1.** in addition; also **2.** more than enough [the hat is *too* big] **3.** very; extremely [that's *too* bad]

took (took) *pt. of* TAKE

tool (tōōl) *n.* [OE. *tol*] **1.** any hand implement, instrument, etc. used for some work **2.** the working part of a power-driven machine, as a drill **3.** anything that serves as a means **4.** a stooge —*vt.* **1.** to shape or work with a tool **2.** to provide tools or machinery for (a factory, etc.): often with *up* **3.** to impress designs, etc. on (leather, etc.) with tools

toot (tōōt) *vi., vt.* [echoic] to sound (a horn, whistle, etc.) in short blasts —*n.* a short blast of a horn, etc.

tooth (tōōth) *n., pl.* **teeth** [OE. *toth*] **1.** any of the hard, bonelike structures in the jaws, used for biting, chewing, etc. **2.** a toothlike part, as on a saw, comb, gear, etc. **3.** [*pl.*] an effective means of enforcing something —**in the teeth of 1.** directly against **2.** defying —**tooth and nail** with all one's strength —**tooth′less** *adj.*

tooth′ache′ *n.* a pain in or near a tooth

tooth′brush′ *n.* a brush for teeth cleaning

tooth′paste′ *n.* a paste for teeth cleaning

tooth′pick′ *n.* a very small, pointed stick for getting bits of food free from between the teeth

tooth powder a powder used like toothpaste

tooth·some (tōōth′səm) *adj.* tasty

top¹ (täp) *n.* [OE.] **1.** the head or crown **2.** the highest part, point, or surface of anything **3.** the part of a plant above ground **4.** an uppermost part or covering, as a lid, cap, etc. **5.** the highest rank, degree, etc. **6.** a person of highest rank, etc. —*adj.* of or at the top; highest, greatest, etc. —*vt.* **topped, top′ping 1.** to remove the top of (a plant, etc.) **2.** to put a top on **3.** to be a top for **4.** to reach the top of **5.** to exceed in amount, etc. **6.** to surpass; outdo —**on top** successful —**on top of 1.** resting upon **2.** besides **3.** controlling successfully —**top off** to complete with a finishing touch

top² (täp) *n.* [OE.] a child's cone-shaped toy, spun on its pointed end

to·paz (tō′paz) *n.* [< Gr. *topazos*] any of various yellow gems, esp. a variety of aluminum silicate

top′coat′ *n.* a lightweight overcoat

top′-drawer′ *adj.* of first importance

top-flight (täp′flīt′) *adj.* [Colloq.] best

top hat a tall, black, cylindrical silk hat, worn by men in formal dress

top′-heav′y *adj.* too heavy at the top, so as to be unstable —**top′-heav′i·ness** *n.*

top·ic (täp′ik) *n.* [ult. < Gr. *topos,* a place] **1.** the subject of a writing, speech, discussion, etc. **2.** a heading in an outline

top′i·cal *adj.* dealing with topics of the day; of current or local interest

top·knot (täp′nät′) *n.* a tuft of hair or feathers on the top of the head

top′less (-lis) *adj.* without a top, as a costume that exposes the breasts

top′-lev′el *adj.* of the highest office, etc.

top′mast′ *n.* the second mast above the deck of a sailing ship

top·most (täp′mōst′) *adj.* at the very top

top-notch (täp′näch′) *adj.* [Colloq.] first-rate; excellent

to·pog·ra·phy (tə päg′rə fē) *n., pl.* **-phies** [< Gr. *topos,* a place + *graphein,* write] **1.** the science of showing on maps, charts, etc. the surface features of a region **2.** these surface features —**top·o·graph·i·cal** (täp′ə graf′i k'l), **top′o·graph′ic** *adj.*

top′ping (-iŋ) *n.* something put on top of something else, as a sauce on food

top·ple (täp′'l) *vi.* **-pled, -pling** [< TOP¹] to fall (*over*) as from top-heaviness —*vt.* **1.** to cause to topple **2.** to overthrow

top·sail (täp's'l, -sāl') *n.* in a square-rigged vessel, the sail next above the lowest sail on a mast

top'-se'cret *adj.* designating or of the most highly secret information

top'soil' *n.* the upper layer of soil, usually darker and richer than the subsoil

top·sy-tur·vy (täp'sē tur'vē) *adv., adj.* [prob. < *top*, highest part + ME. *terven*, to roll] **1.** upside down; reversed **2.** in confusion or disorder

to·rah, to·ra (tō'rə, tō rä') *n.* [Heb.] **1.** [*also* **T-**] the whole body of Jewish religious literature **2.** [*usually* **T-**] the Pentateuch, or a parchment scroll containing this

torch (tôrch) *n.* [< L. *torquere*, to twist] **1.** a portable flaming light **2.** a source of enlightenment, inspiration, etc. **3.** a device for producing a very hot flame, used as in welding **4.** [Brit.] a flashlight —*vt.* [Slang] to set fire to, as in arson

torch'bear'er *n.* **1.** one who carries a torch **2.** a bringer of truth, inspiration, etc.

torch'light' *n.* the light of a torch or torches — *adj.* done by torchlight

tore (tôr) *pt. of* TEAR[1]

tor·e·a·dor (tôr'ē ə dôr') *n.* [Sp. < L. *taurus*, a bull] a bullfighter

tor·ment (tôr'ment) *n.* [< L. *torquere*, to twist] **1.** great pain; agony **2.** a source of pain, anxiety, or annoyance —*vt.* (tôr ment') **1.** to make suffer greatly in body or mind **2.** to annoy, harass, or tease —**tor·men'tor, torment'er** *n.*

torn (tôrn) *pp. of* TEAR[1]

tor·na·do (tôr nā'dō) *n., pl.* **-does, -dos** [< Sp. < L. *tonare*, to thunder] a rapidly whirling column of air, usually seen as a slender, funnel-shaped cloud that usually destroys everything in its narrow path

tor·pe·do (tôr pē'dō) *n., pl.* **-does** [see TORPID] **1.** a large, cigar-shaped, self-propelled underwater projectile that explodes on contact **2.** any of various explosive devices —*vt.* **-doed, -do·ing** to attack, destroy, etc. as with a torpedo

tor·pid (tôr'pid) *adj.* [< L. *torpere*, to be numb] **1.** dormant; inactive and unfeeling, as a hibernating animal **2.** dull; sluggish

tor·por (tôr'pər) *n.* **1.** a state of being dormant or inactive **2.** dullness; apathy

torque (tôrk) *n.* [< L. *torques*, a twisted metal necklace] *Physics* a force that produces a twisting or wrenching effect

tor·rent (tôr'ənt, tär'-) *n.* [< L. *torrens*, rushing] **1.** a swift, violent stream, esp. of water **2.** a flood or rush of words, etc. —**torren·tial** (tô ren'shəl) *adj.*

tor·rid (tôr'id, tär'-) *adj.* [< L. *torrere*, parch] **1.** subjected to intense heat, esp. of the sun; parched; arid **2.** very hot; scorching **3.** highly passionate, ardent, etc.

tor·sion (tôr'shən) *n.* [< L. *torquere*, to twist] a twisting or being twisted, esp. along the length of an axis

tor·so (tôr'sō) *n., pl.* **-sos, -si** (-sē) [It. < Gr. *thyrsos*, a stem] the trunk of the human body

tort (tôrt) *n.* [< L. *torquere*, to twist] *Law* a wrongful act or damage (not involving a breach of contract), for which civil action can be brought

torte (tôrt) *n.* [G.] a rich cake, variously made, as of eggs, chopped nuts, and crumbs

tor·til·la (tôr tē'ə) *n.* [Sp., dim. of *torta*, a cake] a griddlecake of unleavened cornmeal, or of flour: a staple food of Mexico

tor·toise (tôr'təs) *n.* [prob. < LGr. *tartarouchos*, demon] a turtle, esp. one that lives on land

tortoise shell the hard, mottled, yellow-and-brown shell of some turtles

tor·tu·ous (tôr'choo wəs) *adj.* [< L. *torquere*, to twist] **1.** full of twists and turns; winding; crooked **2.** devious or deceitful

tor·ture (tôr'chər) *n.* [Fr. < L. *torquere*, to twist] **1.** the inflicting of severe pain, as to force information or confession **2.** any severe physical or mental pain —*vt.* **-tured, -tur·ing 1.** to subject to torture **2.** to twist (meaning, etc.)

To·ry (tôr'ē) *n., pl.* **-ries** [< Ir. *tōruidhe*, robber] **1.** formerly, a member of the major conservative party of England **2.** in the American Revolution, one loyal to Great Britain —*adj.* [*also* **t-**] of or being a Tory

toss (tôs, täs) *vt.* [prob. < Scand.] **1.** to throw about [*waves tossed* the boat] **2.** to throw lightly from the hand **3.** to jerk upward [*to toss* one's head] —*vi.* **1.** to be thrown about **2.** to fling oneself about in sleep, etc. —*n.* a tossing or being tossed —**toss up** to toss a coin to decide something according to which side lands up

toss'up' *n.* **1.** the act of tossing up **2.** an even chance

tot (tät) *n.* [prob. < Scand.] **1.** a young child **2.** [Chiefly Brit.] a small drink of alcoholic liquor

to·tal (tōt''l) *adj.* [< L. *totus*, all] **1.** constituting the (or a) whole **2.** complete; utter —*n.* the whole amount or number —*vt.* **-taled** or **-talled, -tal·ing** or **-tal·ling 1.** to find the total of **2.** to add up to **3.** [Slang] to wreck completely —*vi.* to amount (*to*) as a whole —**to'tal·ly** *adv.*

to·tal·i·tar·i·an (tō tal'ə ter'ē ən) *adj.* [TOTAL + (AUTHOR)ITARIAN] designating or of a government in which one political group maintains complete control under a dictator —*n.* one who favors such a government or state —**to·tal'i·tar'i·an·ism** *n.*

to·tal·i·ty (tō tal'ə tē) *n., pl.* **-ties** the total amount or sum

to·tal·i·za·tor (tōt''l i zāt'ər) *n.* a machine for registering parimutuel bets and, usually, computing odds and payoffs

tote' (tōt) *vt.* **tot'ed, tot'ing** [prob. of Afr. origin] [Colloq.] to carry or haul

to·tem (tōt'əm) *n.* [< Algonquian] **1.** among primitive peoples, an animal or natural object taken as the symbol of a family or clan **2.** an image of this

totem pole a pole carved and painted with totems by Indian tribes of NW N. America

tot·ter (tät'ər) *vi.* [prob. < Scand.] **1.** to rock as if about to fall **2.** to be unsteady on one's feet; stagger —**tot'ter·y** *adj.*

tou·can (too'kan) *n.* [SAmInd. *tucana*] a brightly colored bird of tropical America, with a very large beak

touch (tuch) *vt.* [OFr. *tochier*] **1.** to put the hand, etc. on, so as to feel **2.** to bring into contact with something else **3.** to be or come into contact with **4.** to border on **5.** to strike lightly **6.** to give a light tint, aspect, etc. to [*touched* with pink] **7.** to stop at, as a ship **8.** to handle, use, etc. **9.** to come up to; reach **10.** to compare with; equal **11.** to affect; concern **12.** to arouse sympathy, gratitude, etc. in **13.** [Slang] to seek a loan or gift of money from —*vi.* **1.** to touch a person or thing **2.** to be or come in contact **3.** to verge (*on* or *upon*) **4.** to pertain; bear (*on* or *upon*) **5.** to treat in passing (with *on* or *upon*) —*n.* **1.** a touching or being touched; specif., a light tap **2.** the sense by which physical objects are felt **3.** a sensation so caused; feel **4.** a subtle change or addition in a painting, story, etc. **5.** a trace, tinge, etc. **6.** a slight attack *[a touch* of the flu*]* **7.** contact or communication *[keep in touch]* **8.** [Slang] the act of seeking a gift or loan of money **9.** *Music* the manner of striking the keys of a piano, etc. **—touch down** to land: said of an aircraft, etc. **—touch up** to improve or finish (a painting, story, etc.) by minor changes

touch and go an uncertain or dangerous situation **—touch'-and-go'** *adj.*

touch'down' *n. Football* a play, scoring six points, in which a player grounds the ball past the opponent's goal line

tou·che (tōō shā') *interj.* [Fr.] touched: said of a point scored in fencing by a touch, or in acknowledging a witty reply, etc.

touched (tucht) *adj.* **1.** emotionally affected; moved **2.** slightly demented

touch'ing *adj.* arousing tender emotion

touch'stone' *n.* **1.** a stone formerly used to test the purity of gold or silver **2.** any test of genuineness

touch'y *adj.* **-i·er, -i·est 1.** easily offended; irritable **2.** very risky

tough (tuf) *adj.* [OE. *toh*] **1.** that will bend without tearing or breaking **2.** not easily cut or chewed *[tough* steak*]* **3.** strong; hardy **4.** stubborn **5.** brutal or rough **6.** very difficult — *n.* a tough person; thug

tough'en *vt., vi.* to make or become tough or tougher

tou·pee (tōō pā') *n.* [Fr. < OFr. *toup,* tuft of hair] a man's small wig

tour (toor) *n.* [< OFr. *tourner,* to TURN] **1.** a turn, period, etc., as of military duty **2.** a long trip, as for sightseeing **3.** any trip, as for inspection, giving performances, etc. **—vi., vt.** to go on a tour (through)

tour de force (toor' də fôrs') *pl.* **tours' de force'** (toor') [Fr.] an unusually skillful or ingenious production, performance, etc., sometimes a merely clever one

tour'ism *n.* tourist travel, esp. when regarded as a source of income for a country, etc.

tour'ist *n.* one who tours, esp. for pleasure — *adj.* of or for tourists

tour·ma·line (toor'mə lin, -lēn') *n.* [Fr.] a crystalline mineral, used as a gemstone, etc.

tour·na·ment (toor'nə mənt, tur'-) *n.* [< OFr. *tourner,* to TURN] **1.** a contest in which knights on horseback tried to unseat one another with lances **2.** a series of contests in competition for a championship Also **tour'ney** (-nē), *pl.* **-neys**

tour·ni·quet (toor'nə kit, tur'-; -kā') *n.* [Fr. < L. *tunica,* tunic] any device for compressing a blood vessel to stop bleeding, as a bandage twisted tight

tou·sle (tou'z'l) *vt.* **-sled, -sling** [< ME. *tusen,* to pull] to dishevel, muss, etc.

tout (tout) *vi., vt.* [OE. *totian,* to peep] [Colloq.] **1.** to praise or recommend highly **2.** to provide betting tips on (racehorses) **—n.** [Colloq.] a person who touts

tow' (tō) *vt.* [OE. *togian*] to pull as by a rope or chain **—n. 1.** a towing or being towed **2.** something towed **3.** a towline **—in tow 1.** being towed **2.** in one's company or charge

tow² (tō) *n.* [OE. *tow-,* for spinning] the broken fibers of hemp, flax, etc. before spinning

to·ward (tôrd, tə wôrd') *prep.* [see TO & -WARD] **1.** in the direction of **2.** facing **3.** aimed at or tending to *[steps toward* peace*]* **4.** concerning **5.** just before *[toward* noon*]* **6.** in anticipation of *[save toward* a new car*]* Also **towards**

tow·el (tou''l) *n.* [< OFr. *toaille*] a piece of cloth or paper for wiping or drying things

tow'el·ing, tow'el·ling *n.* material for making towels

tow·er (tou'ər) *n.* [< L. *turris*] **1.** a high structure, often part of another building **2.** such a structure used as a fortress **—vi.** to rise high like a tower **—tow'er·ing** *adj.*

tow·head (tō'hed') *n.* **1.** a head of pale-yellow hair **2.** a person with such hair

tow·hee (tou'hē, tō'-) *n.* [echoic] any of various small N. American sparrows

tow'line' *n.* a rope, chain, etc. for towing

town (toun) *n.* [OE. *tun*] **1.** a concentration of houses, etc. somewhat larger than a village **2.** a city **3.** a township **4.** the business center of a city **5.** the people of a town **—go to town** [Slang] **1.** to act fast and efficiently **2.** to be successful **—on the town** [Colloq.] out for a good time

town hall a building in a town, housing the offices of officials, the council chamber, etc.

town house a two-story dwelling, a unit in a complex of such dwellings

town meeting a meeting of the voters of a town, as in New England

town'ship' *n.* **1.** a division of a county, constituting a unit of local government **2.** a unit of territory in the U.S. land survey, generally six miles square

towns·man (tounz'mən) *n., pl.* **-men 1.** a person who lives in a town **2.** a fellow resident of a town

towns'peo'ple *n.pl.* the people of a town: also **towns'folk'**

tow'rope' *n.* a rope used in towing

tox·e·mi·a (täk sē'mē ə) *n.* [see TOXIC] blood poisoning, esp. as caused by toxins from bacteria: also sp. **tox·ae'mi·a**

tox·ic (täk'sik) *adj.* [< L. *toxicum,* a poison] **1.** of, affected by, or caused by a toxin **2.** poisonous **—tox·ic'i·ty** (-sis'ə tē) *n.*

tox·i·col·o·gy (täk'si käl'ə jē) *n.* [see TOXIC & -LOGY] the science of poisons, their effects, antidotes, etc. **—tox'i·col'o·gist** *n.*

tox·in (täk'sin) *n.* [TOX(IC) + -IN¹] **1.** a poison produced by microorganisms and causing certain diseases **2.** any poison secreted by plants or animals

toy (toi) *n.* [< ? MDu. *toi,* finery] **1.** a trifle **2.** a bauble; trinket **3.** a plaything for children — *adj.* **1.** like a toy in size, use, etc. **2.** made as a toy **—vi.** to trifle (*with* food, an idea, etc.)

tr. 1. transpose **2.** treasurer

trace¹ (trās) *n.* [< L. *trahere,* to draw] **1.** a mark, footprint, track, etc. left by a person, animal, or thing **2.** a barely perceptible amount **—vt.** **traced, trac'ing 1.** to follow the trail of; track **2.** *a)* to follow the development or history of *b)* to determine (a source, date, etc.) thus **3.** to draw, outline, etc. **4.** to copy (a drawing, etc.) by following its lines on a transparent sheet placed over it **—trace'a·ble** *adj.* **—trac'er** *n.*

trace² (trās) *n.* [see TRAIT] either of two straps, chains, etc. connecting a draft animal's harness to the vehicle

trac·er·y (trā'sər ē) *n., pl.* **-ies** [TRACE¹ + -(E)RY] ornamental work of interlacing or branching lines

tra·che·a (trā'kē ə) *n., pl.* **-che·ae'** (-ē'), **-che·as** [< Gr. *tracheia (arteria),* rough (windpipe)] the passage that conveys air from the larynx to the bronchi; windpipe **—tra'·che·al** *adj.*

tra·che·ot·o·my (trā'kē ät'ə mē) *n., pl.* **-mies**

[< prec. + Gr. *temnein,* to cut] surgical incision of the trachea

trac·ing (trā'siŋ) *n.* something traced, as a copy of a drawing, a line, etc.

track (trak) *n.* [MFr. *trac*] 1. a mark left in passing, as a footprint or rut 2. a path or trail 3. a course of action or motion 4. a circuit laid out for running, horse racing, etc. 5. a pair of parallel metal rails on which trains, etc. run 6. *a)* sports performed on a track, as running, hurdling, etc. *b)* track and field sports together 7. *a)* the part of a magnetic tape being recorded or played *b)* any of the bands of a phonograph record —*vt.* 1. to follow the track of 2. to trace by means of evidence, etc. 3. to plot the course of, as by radar 4. to leave in the form of tracks *[to track dirt on the floor]* —**in one's tracks** where one is at the moment —**keep** (or **lose**) **track of** to stay (or fail to stay) informed about —**track'er** *n.*

tract[1] (trakt) *n.* [< L. *trahere,* to draw] 1. a continuous expanse of land 2. a system of organs having some special function *[the digestive tract]*

tract[2] (trakt) *n.* [< L. *tractatus,* a treatise] a pamphlet, esp. one on a religious subject

trac·ta·ble (trak'tə b'l) *adj.* [< L. *trahere,* to draw] 1. easily managed; docile 2. easily worked; malleable —**trac'ta·bil'i·ty** *n.*

trac·tion (trak'shən) *n.* [< L. *trahere,* to draw] 1. a pulling or drawing, or a being pulled or drawn 2. the power used by a locomotive, etc. 3. adhesive friction

trac·tor (trak'tər) *n.* [see TRACTION] 1. a powerful, motor-driven vehicle for pulling farm machinery, etc. 2. a driver's cab for hauling one or more large trailers

trade (trād) *n.* [MLowG., a track] 1. an occupation; esp., skilled work; craft 2. all the persons in a particular business 3. buying or selling; commerce 4. customers 5. a purchase or sale 6. an exchange; swap —*vi.* **trad'ed, trad'ing** 1. to carry on a business 2. to have business dealings (*with*) 3. to make an exchange (*with*) 4. [Colloq.] to be a customer (*at* a specified store, etc.) —*vt.* to exchange; barter —**trade on** (or **upon**) to take advantage of

trade'-in' *n.* a used car, etc. given or taken as part payment toward a new one

trade'mark' *n.* a symbol, design, word, etc. used by a manufacturer or dealer to distinguish his products: usually registered and protected by law

trad'er *n.* 1. one who trades; merchant 2. a ship used in trade

trade union *same as* LABOR UNION

trade wind a wind that blows toward the equator from either side of it

trading post a store in an outpost, settlement, etc. where trading is done

trading stamp a stamp given by some merchants as a premium, redeemable in merchandise

tra·di·tion (trə dish'ən) *n.* [< L. *tradere,* deliver] 1. the handing down orally of customs, beliefs, stories, etc. from generation to generation 2. a belief, custom, etc. so handed down

tra·di'tion·al *adj.* of, handed down by, or conforming to tradition

tra·duce (trə dōōs') *vt.* **-duced', -duc'ing** [< L. *trans,* across + *ducere,* to lead] 1. to defame; slander 2. to betray

traf·fic (traf'ik) *n.* [< L. *trans,* across + It. *ficcare,* bring] 1. buying and selling; trade 2. dealings (*with* someone) 3. the movement or number of cars along a street, pedestrians along a sidewalk, etc. 4. the business done by a transportation company —*adj.* of traffic or its regulation —*vi.* **-ficked, -fick·ing** 1. to carry on traffic (*in* something) 2. to have dealings (*with* someone) —**traf'fick·er** *n.*

traffic light (or **signal**) a set of signal lights at intersections of streets to regulate traffic

tra·ge·di·an (trə jē'dē ən) *n.* an actor of tragedy —**tra·ge'di·enne'** (-en') *n.fem.*

trag·e·dy (traj'ə dē) *n., pl.* **-dies** [< Gr. *tragos,* goat + *ōidē,* song] 1. a serious play with an unhappy or disastrous ending 2. a very sad or tragic event

trag·ic (traj'ik) *adj.* 1. of, or having to do with, tragedy 2. very sad, disastrous, etc. Also **trag'i·cal** —**trag'i·cal·ly** *adv.*

trail (trāl) *vt.* [< L. *trahere,* to drag] 1. to drag or let drag behind one 2. to follow the tracks of 3. to hunt by tracking 4. to follow behind —*vi.* 1. to be drawn along behind one 2. to grow along the ground, etc., as some plants 3. to stream behind, as smoke 4. to follow or lag behind; straggle 5. to dwindle, as a sound (with *off* or *away*) —*n.* 1. something that trails behind 2. a mark, scent, etc. left by a person, animal, or thing that has passed 3. a beaten path

trail'er *n.* 1. one that trails 2. *a)* a cart or van designed to be pulled by an automobile or truck *b)* such a vehicle designed to be lived in

train (trān) *n.* [< L. *trahere,* to pull] 1. something that drags along behind, as a trailing skirt 2. a group of followers; retinue 3. a procession; caravan 4. a series of connected things *[a train of thought]* 5. a line of connected railroad cars pulled by a locomotive —*vt.* 1. to guide the growth of (a plant) 2. to guide the mental, moral, etc. development of; rear 3. to instruct so as to make proficient 4. to make fit for some sport 5. to aim (a gun, etc.) —*vi.* to undergo training —**train·ee** (trā nē') *n.* —**train'er** *n.*

train'man *n., pl.* **-men** one who works on a railroad train or in a railroad yard

traipse (trāps) *vi., vt.* **traipsed, traips'ing** [< ?] [Dial. or Colloq.] to walk, wander, tramp, or gad

trait (trāt) *n.* [Fr. < L. *trahere,* to draw] a distinct quality or feature

trai·tor (trāt'ər) *n.* [< L. *tradere,* betray] one who betrays his country, friends, etc. —**trai'tor·ous** *adj.*

tra·jec·to·ry (trə jek'tə rē) *n., pl.* **-ries** [< L. *trans,* across + *jacere,* to throw] the curved path of something hurtling through space, esp. that of a projectile

tram (tram) *n.* [prob. < LowG. *traam,* a beam] 1. an open railway car used in mines 2. [Brit.] a streetcar Also **tram'car'**

tram·mel (tram'l) *n.* [< L. *tres,* three + *macula,* a mesh] [usually *pl.*] something that hinders freedom of action —*vt.* **-meled** or **-melled, -mel·ing** or **-mel·ling** to hinder, restrain, or shackle

tramp (tramp) *vi.* [ME. *trampen*] 1. to walk firmly and heavily 2. to travel about on foot —*vt.* 1. to step on heavily; trample 2. to walk through —*n.* 1. a vagrant; hobo 2. the sound of heavy steps 3. a journey on foot; hike 4. a freight ship without a regular schedule

tram·ple (tram'p'l) *vt.* **-pled, -pling** [see TRAMP] to tread heavily —*vi.* to crush as by treading heavily on —**tram'pler** *n.*

tram·po·line (tram'pə lēn') *n.* [< It. *trampolino,* a springboard] a sheet of strong canvas stretched tightly on a frame, used in acrobatic tumbling

trance (trans) *n.* [< L. *trans*, across + *ire*, go] **1.** a sleeplike state in which consciousness may remain, as in hypnosis **2.** a daze; stupor **3.** the condition of being completely lost in thought or meditation

tran·quil (traŋ′kwəl) *adj.* [L. *tranquillus*] calm, serene, quiet, etc. —**tran·quil′li·ty, tran·quil′i·ty** *n.* —**tran′quil·ly** *adv.*

tran·quil·ize, tran·quil·lize (traŋ′kwə līz′) *vt., vi.* **-ized** or **-lized**, **-iz′ing** or **-liz′ing** to make or become tranquil

tran′quil·iz′er, tran′quil·liz′er *n.* a drug used in calming tense persons

trans- [L. < *trans*, across] *a prefix meaning* over, across, beyond

trans. **1.** translated **2.** translation

trans·act (tran sakt′, -zakt′) *vt.* [< L. *trans*, across + *agere*, to drive] to carry on or complete (business, etc.) —**trans·ac′tor** *n.*

trans·ac′tion *n.* **1.** a transacting **2.** something transacted; specif., *a*) a business deal *b*) [*pl.*] a record of proceedings

trans·at·lan·tic (trans′ət lan′tik) *adj.* **1.** crossing the Atlantic **2.** on the other side of the Atlantic

trans·ceiv·er (tran sē′vər) *n.* a single apparatus functioning alternately as a radio transmitter and receiver

tran·scend (tran send′) *vt.* [< L. *trans-*, over + *scandere*, climb] **1.** to go beyond the limits of; exceed **2.** to surpass; excel —**tran·scend′ent** *adj.*

tran·scen·den·tal (tran′sen den′t′l) *adj.* **1.** *same as* SUPERNATURAL **2.** abstract

trans·con·ti·nen·tal (trans′kän tə nen′t′l) *adj.* **1.** that crosses a continent **2.** on the other side of a continent

tran·scribe (tran skrīb′) *vt.* **-scribed′, -scrib′ing** [< L. *trans*, over + *scribere*, write] **1.** to make a written or typewritten copy of (shorthand notes, etc.) **2.** *Music, Radio, & TV* to make a transcription of

tran·script (tran′skript′) *n.* **1.** a written or typewritten copy **2.** any copy

tran·scrip′tion (-skrip′shən) *n.* **1.** a transcribing **2.** a transcript **3.** an arrangement of a piece of music for some other instrument or voice **4.** a recording made for radio or TV broadcasting

tran·sept (tran′sept) *n.* [< L. *trans-*, across + *septum*, enclosure] the part of a cross-shaped church at right angles to the nave

trans·fer (trans fur′) *vt.* **-ferred′, -fer′ring** [< L. *trans-*, across + *ferre*, to bear] **1.** to carry, send, etc. to another person or place **2.** to make over (property, etc.) to another **3.** to move (a picture, design, etc.) from one surface to another —*vi.* **1.** to transfer oneself or be transferred **2.** to change to another bus, etc. —*n.* (trans′fər) **1.** a transferring or being transferred **2.** one that is transferred **3.** a ticket entitling the bearer to change to another bus, etc.

trans·fig·u·ra·tion (trans fig′yoo rā′shən) *n.* a transfiguring or being transfigured —[T-] **1.** *Bible* the change in the appearance of Jesus on the mountain: Matt. 17 **2.** a church festival (Aug. 6) commemorating this

trans·fig·ure (trans fig′yər) *vt.* **-ured, -ur·ing** [< L. *trans-*, across + *figura*, figure] **1.** to change the form or appearance of; transform **2.** to transform so as to exalt or glorify

trans·fix (trans fiks′) *vt.* [< L. *trans-*, through + *figere*, to fix] **1.** to pierce through; impale **2.** to make motionless, as with horror

trans·form (trans fôrm′) *vt.* [ult. < L. *trans-*, over + *forma*, a shape] **1.** to change the form

or appearance of **2.** to change the condition, character, or function of —**trans′for·ma′tion** *n.*

trans·form′er *n.* **1.** one that transforms **2.** *Elec.* a device for changing electric energy to a different voltage

trans·fuse (trans fyōōz′) *vt.* **-fused′, -fus′ing** [< L. *trans-*, across + *fundere*, pour] **1.** to instill, imbue, permeate, etc. **2.** to transfer (blood, etc.) into a blood vessel, usually a vein —**trans·fu′sion** *n.*

trans·gress (trans gres′) *vt., vi.* [< Fr. < L. *trans-*, over + *gradi*, to step] **1.** to break (a law, commandment, etc.); sin (against) **2.** to go beyond (a limit, etc.) —**trans·gres′sion** (-gresh′ən) *n.* —**trans·gres′sor** *n.*

tran·sient (tran′shənt) *adj.* [< L. *trans-*, over + *ire*, go] **1.** passing away with time; temporary **2.** passing quickly; fleeting **3.** staying for only a short time —*n.* a transient person —**tran′sience, tran′sien·cy** *n.*

tran·sis·tor (tran zis′tər, -sis′-) *n.* [TRAN(SFER) + (RE)SISTOR] a small, solid-state electronic device

tran·sis′tor·ize′ (-tə rīz′) *vt.* **-ized′, -iz′ing** to equip with transistors

trans·it (tran′sit, -zit) *n.* [< L. *trans-*, over + *ire*, go] **1.** passage through or across **2.** a carrying or being carried from one place to another **3.** a surveying instrument for measuring horizontal angles

tran·si·tion (tran zish′ən) *n.* a passing from one condition, place, etc. to another

tran·si·tive (tran′sə tiv) *adj.* taking a direct object to complete the meaning: said of certain verbs —*n.* a transitive verb

tran·si·to·ry (tran′sə tôr′ē) *adj.* not enduring; temporary; fleeting

trans·late (trans lāt′) *vt.* **-lat′ed, -lat′ing** [< L. *translatus*, transferred] **1.** to change from one place or condition to another **2.** to put into the words of a different language **3.** to rephrase —**trans·la′tor** *n.*

trans·la′tion *n.* **1.** a translating or being translated **2.** writing, etc. translated into another language

trans·lit·er·ate (trans lit′ə rāt′) *vt.* **-at′ed, -at′ing** [< TRANS- + L. *litera*, letter] to write or spell (words, etc.) in corresponding characters of another alphabet

trans·lu·cent (trans lōō′sənt) *adj.* [< L. *trans-*, through + *lucere*, to shine] letting light pass through but not transparent

trans·mi·grate (trans mī′grāt) *vi.* **-grat·ed, -grat·ing** [see TRANS- & MIGRATE] in some religions, to pass into another body at death: said of the soul —**trans′mi·gra′tion** *n.*

trans·mis·si·ble (trans mis′ə b′l) *adj.* capable of being transmitted

trans·mis·sion (-mish′ən) *n.* **1.** a transmitting **2.** something transmitted **3.** the part of a motor vehicle that transmits motive force to the wheels, as by gears

trans·mit (trans mit′) *vt.* **-mit′ted, -mit′ting** [< L. *trans-*, over + *mittere*, send] **1.** to cause to go to another person or place; transfer **2.** to hand down by heredity, inheritance, etc. **3.** *a*) to pass (light, heat, etc.) through some medium *b*) to conduct **4.** to convey (force, movement, etc.) to **5.** to send out (radio or television signals)

trans·mit′ter *n.* one that transmits; specif., the apparatus that transmits signals in telephony, radio, etc.

trans·mute (trans myōōt′) *vt., vi.* **-mut′ed, -mut′ing** [< L. *trans-*, over + *mutare*, to change] to change from one form, nature, substance, etc. into another

transoceanic 482 treat

trans·o·ce·an·ic (trans′ō shē an′ik) *adj.* crossing the ocean

tran·som (tran′səm) *n.* [prob. < L. *transtrum*, crossbeam] **1.** a horizontal crossbar, as across the top of a door or window **2.** a small window just above a door or window

trans·par·ent (trans per′ənt) *adj.* [< L. *trans-*, through + *parere*, appear] **1.** transmitting light rays so that objects on the other side may be seen **2.** so fine in texture as to be seen through **3.** easily understood or detected **4.** frank —**trans·par′en·cy** *n., pl.* -**cies** —**trans·par′ent·ly** *adv.*

tran·spire (tran spīr′) *vi.* -**spired′**, -**spir′ing** [< Fr. < L. *trans-*, through + *spirare*, breathe] **1.** to give off moisture, as through pores **2.** to become known **3.** to happen: regarded by some as a loose usage

trans·plant (trans plant′) *vt.* **1.** to remove from one place and plant, resettle, etc. in another **2.** *Surgery* to transfer (tissue or an organ) from one individual or part of the body to another

trans·port (trans pôrt′) *vt.* [< L. *trans-*, over + *portare*, carry] **1.** to carry from one place to another **2.** to carry away with emotion **3.** to banish to a penal colony, etc. —*n.* (trans′pôrt) **1.** a transporting; transportation **2.** rapture **3.** a ship, airplane, etc. used for transporting

trans·por·ta·tion (trans′pər tā′shən) *n.* **1.** a transporting or being transported **2.** a means of conveyance **3.** fare

trans·pose (trans pōz′) *vt., vi.* -**posed′**, -**pos′ing** [see TRANS- & POSE] **1.** to change the usual or relative order or position of; interchange **2.** to rewrite or play (a musical composition) in a different key —**trans′po·si′tion** (-pə zish′ən) *n.*

tran·sub·stan·ti·a·tion (tran′səb stan′shē ā′shən) *n.* [< L. *trans-*, over + *substantia*, substance] *R.C. & Orthodox Eastern Ch.* the doctrine that, in the Eucharist, the whole substances of the bread and wine are changed into the body and blood of Christ

trans·verse (trans vurs′) *adj.* [< L. *trans-*, across + *vertere*, to turn] placed across —*n.* (usually trans′vurs) a transverse part, beam, etc. —**trans·verse′ly** *adv.*

trap (trap) *n.* [OE. *træppe*] **1.** a device for catching animals **2.** any stratagem designed to catch or trick **3.** a device, as a U-shaped part in a drainpipe, for preventing the escape of gas, odors, etc. —*vt.* trapped, trap′ping to catch as in a trap —*vi.* to trap animals, esp. for their furs —**trap′per** *n.*

trap′door′ *n.* a hinged or sliding door in a roof, ceiling, or floor

tra·peze (tra pēz′) *n.* [< Fr.: see TRAPEZOID] a short, horizontal bar, hung at a height by two ropes, on which gymnasts, acrobats, etc. can swing

trap·e·zoid (trap′ə zoid′) *n.* [< Gr. *trapeza*, table] a plane figure with four sides only two of which are parallel

trap·pings (trap′iŋz) *n.pl.* [< OFr. *drap*, cloth] **1.** an ornamental covering for a horse **2.** adornments

trash (trash) *n.* [prob. < Scand.] **1.** discarded or worthless things; rubbish **2.** a disreputable person or people —*vt.* [Slang] to destroy (property) as by vandalism —**trash′y** *adj.* -**i·er**, -**i·est**

trau·ma (trou′mə, trô′-) *n., pl.* -**mas**, -**ma·ta** (-mə tə) [Gr.] **1.** a bodily injury or shock **2.** an emotional shock, often having a lasting psychic effect —**trau·mat′ic** (-mat′ik) *adj.*

trav·ail (trav′āl, trə vāl′) *n.* [< VL. *tria*, three + *palus*, stake: referring to a torture device] **1.** very hard work **2.** intense pain; agony

trav·el (trav′'l) *vi.* -**eled** or -**elled**, -**el·ing** or -**el·ling** [var. of TRAVAIL] **1.** to go from one place to another **2.** to move, pass, or be transmitted —*vt.* to make a journey over or through —*n.* a traveling; trips —**trav′el·er**, **trav′el·ler** *n.*

trav·e·logue, **trav·e·log** (trav′ə lôg′) *n.* an illustrated lecture or motion picture dealing with travels

trav·erse (tra vurs′, trav′ərs) *vt.* -**ersed′**, -**ers′ing** [< L. *trans-*, over + *vertere*, to turn] to pass over, across, or through —*n.* (trav′ərs) something that traverses or crosses, as a crossbar —*adj.* (trav′ərs) **1.** extending across **2.** designating or of drapes drawn by pulling cords at the side —**trav·ers′al** *n.*

trav·es·ty (trav′is tē) *n., pl.* -**ties** [< Fr. < L. *trans-*, over + *vestire*, to dress] **1.** a farcical imitation for purposes of ridicule **2.** a crude or ridiculous representation —*vt.* -**tied**, -**ty·ing** to make a travesty of

trawl (trôl) *n.* [< ? MDu. *traghel*, dragnet] **1.** a large net dragged along the bottom of a fishing bank **2.** a long line supported by buoys, from which many short fishing lines are hung —*vi., vt.* to fish or catch with a trawl

trawl′er *n.* a boat used in trawling

tray (trā) *n.* [OE. *treg*, wooden board] a flat receptacle with raised edges, for holding or carrying things

treach·er·ous (trech′ər əs) *adj.* **1.** characterized by treachery; traitorous **2.** untrustworthy —**treach′er·ous·ly** *adv.*

treach·er·y (trech′ər ē) *n., pl.* -**ies** [< OFr. *trichier*, to cheat] **1.** betrayal of trust; disloyalty **2.** treason

trea·cle (trē′k'l) *n.* [< Gr. *thēriakē*, remedy for venomous bites] [Brit.] molasses

tread (tred) *vt.* **trod**, **trod′den** or **trod**, **tread′ing** [OE. *tredan*] **1.** to walk on, in, along, etc. **2.** to do or follow by walking, dancing, etc. **3.** to press or beat with the feet —*vi.* **1.** to walk **2.** to set one's foot (on, across, etc.) **3.** to trample (on or upon) —*n.* **1.** the manner or sound of treading **2.** something on which a person or thing treads or moves, as a shoe sole, the horizontal surface of a stair step, etc. —**tread water** *pt. & pp.* usually **tread′ed** to stay upright in swimming by moving the legs up and down

trea·dle (tred′'l) *n.* [< OE. *tredan*, to tread] a lever moved by the foot as to turn a wheel

tread′mill′ *n.* a mill wheel turned as by an animal treading an endless belt

treas. **1.** treasurer **2.** treasury

trea·son (trē′z'n) *n.* [< L. *trans-*, over + *dare*, give] betrayal of one's country to an enemy —**trea′son·a·ble**, **trea′son·ous** *adj.*

treas·ure (trezh′ər, trā′zhər) *n.* [< Gr. *thēsauros*] **1.** accumulated wealth, as money, jewels, etc. **2.** any person or thing considered valuable —*vt.* -**ured**, -**ur·ing** **1.** to save up for future use **2.** to value greatly

treas′ur·er *n.* one in charge of a treasury, as of a government, corporation, club, etc.

treas′ure-trove′ (-trōv′) *n.* [*trove* < OFr. *trover*, to find] treasure found hidden, the owner of which is unknown

treas′ur·y (-ē) *n., pl.* -**ies** **1.** a place where treasure or funds are kept **2.** the funds or revenues of a state, corporation, etc. **3.** [T-] the governmental department in charge of revenue, taxation, etc.

treat (trēt) *vi.* [< L. *trahere*, to draw] **1.** to discuss terms (*with*) **2.** to speak or write (*of*) —*vt.* **1.** to deal with (a subject) in a specified manner **2.** to act toward (someone or something) in a specified manner **3.** to pay for the food, entertainment, etc. of (another) **4.** to subject to some process, chemical, etc. **5.** to give medical care to —**n. 1.** a meal, drink, etc. paid for by another **2.** anything that gives great pleasure

trea·tise (trēt'is) **n.** [see TREAT] a formal, systematic article or book on some subject

treat·ment (trēt'mənt) **n. 1.** act, manner, method, etc. of treating **2.** medical or surgical care

trea·ty (trēt'ē) **n., pl.** **-ties** [< L. *trahere*, to draw] a formal agreement between two or more nations, relating to peace, trade, etc.

tre·ble (treb'l) **adj.** [< L. *triplus*, triple] **1.** threefold; triple **2.** of, for, or performing the treble —**n. 1.** the highest part in musical harmony; soprano **2.** a high-pitched voice or sound —**vt., vi.** **-bled, -bling** to make or become threefold

tree (trē) **n.** [OE. *treow*] **1.** a large, woody perennial plant with one main trunk and many branches **2.** anything resembling a tree; specif., a diagram of family descent (**family tree**) —**vt.** **treed, tree'ing** to chase up a tree — **tree'less adj.** —**tree'like' adj.**

tre·foil (trē'foil) **n.** [< L. *tri-*, three + *folium*, leaf] **1.** a plant with leaves divided into three leaflets, as the clover **2.** a design, etc. shaped like such a leaf

trek (trek) **vi.** **trekked, trek'king** [Afrik. < Du. *trekken*, to draw] **1.** to travel slowly and laboriously **2.** [Colloq.] to go on foot —**n. 1.** a journey **2.** a migration

trel·lis (trel'is) **n.** [< L. *trilix*, triple-twilled] a lattice on which vines are trained

trem·ble (trem'b'l) **vi.** **-bled, -bling** [< L. *tremere*] **1.** to shake or shiver, as from cold, fear, etc. **2.** to feel great fear or anxiety **3.** to quiver, vibrate, etc. —**n. 1.** a trembling **2.** [*sometimes pl.*] a fit or state of trembling — **trem'bly adj.**

tre·men·dous (tri men'dəs) **adj.** [< L. *tremere*, tremble] **1.** terrifying; dreadful **2.** *a)* very large; great *b)* [Colloq.] wonderful, amazing, etc. —**tre·men'dous·ly adv.**

trem·o·lo (trem'ə lō') **n., pl.** **-los** [It.] a tremulous effect produced by rapidly repeating the same musical tone

trem·or (trem'ər) **n.** [< L. *tremere*, tremble] **1.** a trembling, shaking, etc. **2.** a vibratory motion **3.** a nervous thrill

trem·u·lous (trem'yoo ləs) **adj.** [< L. *tremere*, tremble] **1.** trembling; quivering **2.** fearful; timid —**trem'u·lous·ly adv.**

trench (trench) **vt.** [< OFr. *trenchier*, to cut] to dig a ditch or ditches in —**n. 1.** a deep furrow **2.** a long, narrow ditch with earth banked in front, used in battle for cover, etc.

trench·ant (tren'chənt) **adj.** [see TRENCH] **1.** penetrating; incisive *[trenchant words]* **2.** forceful; vigorous *[a trenchant argument]*

trench coat a belted raincoat in a military style

trench'er·man (-mən) **n., pl.** **-men** one who eats much and heartily

trench foot a diseased condition of the feet from prolonged exposure to wet and cold, as in trenches

trench mouth an infectious disease of the mucous membranes of the mouth and throat

trend (trend) **vi.** [OE. *trendan*] to have a general direction or tendency —**n. 1.** the general tendency or course; drift **2.** a current style

tre·pan (tri pan') **n.** [< Gr. *trypan*, to bore] an early form of the trephine —**vt.** **-panned', -pan'ning** *same as* TREPHINE

tre·phine (tri fin', -fēn') **n.** [< L. *tres*, three + *fines*, ends] a surgical saw for removing disks

of bone from the skull —**vt.** **-phined', -phin'ing** to operate on with a trephine

trep·i·da·tion (trep'ə dā'shən) **n.** [< L. *trepidus*, disturbed] **1.** trembling movement **2.** fearful uncertainty

tres·pass (tres'pəs, -pas') **vi.** [< L. *trans-*, across + *passus*, a step] **1.** to go beyond the limits of what is considered right; do wrong; transgress **2.** to enter another's property without permission or right —**n.** a trespassing; specif., a moral offense —**tres'pass·er n.**

tress (tres) **n.** [< OFr. *tresce*, braid of hair] **1.** a lock of human hair **2.** [*pl.*] a woman's or girl's hair, esp. when long

tres·tle (tres'l) **n.** [< L. *transtrum*, a beam] **1.** a horizontal beam fastened to two pairs of spreading legs, used as a support **2.** a framework of uprights and crosspieces, supporting a bridge, etc.

trey (trā) **n.** [< L. *tres*, three] a playing card or side of a die with three spots

tri- [< Fr. L., or Gr.] *a combining form meaning:* **1.** having or involving three **2.** three times, into three **3.** every third

tri·ad (trī'ad) **n.** [< Gr. *treis*, three] a group of three

tri·al (trī'əl) **n.** [see TRY] **1.** the act or process of trying, testing, etc.; test; probation **2.** a hardship, suffering, etc. **3.** a source of annoyance **4.** a formal examination by a court of law to decide the validity of a charge or claim **5.** an attempt; effort —**adj. 1.** of a trial **2.** for the purpose of trying, testing, etc.

trial and error a trying or testing again and again until the right result is found

trial balloon something said or done to test public opinion on an issue

tri·an·gle (trī'aŋ'g'l) **n.** [see TRI- & ANGLE¹] **1.** a plane figure having three angles and three sides **2.** any three-sided or three-cornered object, area, etc. **3.** a situation involving three persons *[a love triangle]* —**tri·an'gu·lar** (-gyə lər) **adj.**

tri·an'gu·late' (-gyə lāt') **vt.** **-lat'ed, -lat'ing** to divide into triangles to compute distance or relative positions —**tri·an'gu·la'tion n.**

tribe (trīb) **n.** [< L. *tribus*] **1.** a group of persons or clans believed to have a common ancestor and living under a leader or chief **2.** a natural group of plants or animals —**trib'al adj.** —**tribes'man n., pl.** **-men**

trib·u·la·tion (trib'yə lā'shən) **n.** [< L. *tribulare*, to press] great misery or distress, or the cause of it

tri·bu·nal (trī byōō'n'l, tri-) **n.** [L.: see TRIBUNE] **1.** a seat for a judge in a court **2.** a court of justice

trib·une (trib'yōōn, tri byōōn') **n.** [< L. *tribus*, tribe] **1.** in ancient Rome, a magistrate appointed to protect the rights and interests of the plebians **2.** a champion of the people

trib·u·tar·y (trib'yoo ter'ē) **adj. 1.** paying tribute **2.** subject *[a tributary nation]* **3.** *a)* making additions *b)* flowing into a larger one *[a tributary stream]* —**n., pl.** **-ies 1.** a tributary nation **2.** a tributary stream or river

trib·ute (trib'yōōt) **n.** [< L. *tribuere*, allot] **1.** money paid regularly by one nation to another as acknowledgment of subjugation, for protection, etc. **2.** any forced payment **3.** something given, done, or said that shows gratitude, respect, honor, or praise

tri·cen·ten·ni·al (trī'sen ten'ē əl) **adj.** happening once in 300 years —**n.** a 300th anniversary

tri·ceps (trī'seps) **n., pl.** **-ceps** or **-ceps·es** [< L. *tri-*, three + *caput*, head] a muscle with three points of origin, esp. the large muscle at the back of the upper arm

tri·chi·na (tri kī′nə) *n., pl.* **-nae** (-nē) [< Gr. *trichinos,* hairy] a very small worm whose larvae cause trichinosis

trich·i·no·sis (trik′ə nō′sis) *n.* a disease caused by trichinae in the intestines and muscles and usually acquired by eating undercooked infested pork

trick (trik) *n.* [< OFr. *trichier,* to cheat] **1.** something designed to deceive, cheat, etc. **2.** a practical joke; prank **3.** a clever act intended to amuse **4.** any feat requiring skill **5.** a personal mannerism **6.** a round of duty; shift **7.** *Card Games* the cards in a single round —*vt.* to deceive, cheat, fool, etc. —*adj.* apt to malfunction *[a* trick *knee]* —**do** (or **turn**) **the trick** to produce the desired result —**trick′er·y** *n., pl.* **-ies** —**trick′ster** *n.*

trick·le (trik′'l) *vi.* **-led, -ling** [prob. < ME. *striken,* to strike] **1.** to flow slowly in a thin stream or fall in drops **2.** to move slowly *[the* crowd *trickled* away] —*n.* **1.** a trickling **2.** a slow, small flow

trick′y *adj.* **-i·er, -i·est 1.** given to or characterized by trickery **2.** intricate; difficult —**trick′i·ly** *adv.* —**trick′i·ness** *n.*

tri·col·or (trī′kul′ər) *n.* a flag having three colors in large areas; esp., the flag of France

tri·cy·cle (trī′si k'l) *n.* [Fr.: see TRI- & CYCLE] a child's three-wheeled vehicle operated by pedals

tri·dent (trīd′'nt) *n.* [< L. *tri-,* three + *dens,* tooth] a three-pronged spear

tried (trīd) *pt. & pp. of* TRY —*adj.* **1.** tested; proved **2.** trustworthy; faithful

tri·fle (trī′f'l) *n.* [< OFr. *truffe,* deception] **1.** something of little value or importance **2.** a small amount or sum —*vi.* **-fled, -fling 1.** to talk or act jokingly; deal lightly **2.** to play or toy *(with)* —*vt.* to spend idly; waste (usually with *away*) —**tri′fler** *n.*

tri′fling *adj.* **1.** frivolous; shallow **2.** of little importance; trivial

tri·fo·cals (trī′fō′k'lz) *n.pl.* a pair of glasses like bifocals, but with a third area in the lens ground for intermediate distance

trig·ger (trig′ər) *n.* [< Du. *trekken,* to pull] a lever pulled or pressed to release a catch, etc., esp. one pressed to activate the firing mechanism on a firearm —*vt.* to initiate (an action)

trig·o·nom·e·try (trig′ə näm′ə trē) *n.* [< Gr. *trigōnon,* triangle + *-metria,* measurement] the branch of mathematics dealing with the relations between the sides and angles of triangles —**trig′o·no·met′ric** (-nə met′rik) *adj.*

trill (tril) *n.* [< It., ult. echoic] **1.** a rapid alternation of a musical tone with one just above it **2.** a bird's warble **3.** a rapid vibration of the tongue or uvula, as in pronouncing *r* in some languages —*vt., vi.* to sound, speak, sing, or play with a trill

tril·lion (tril′yən) *n.* [Fr.] **1.** in the U.S. and France, 1 followed by 12 zeros **2.** in Great Britain and Germany, 1 followed by 18 zeros —**tril′lionth** *adj., n.*

tril·o·gy (tril′ə jē) *n., pl.* **-gies** [see TRI- & -LOGY] a set of three plays, novels, etc. which form a related group, although each is a complete work

trim (trim) *vt.* **trimmed, trim′ming** [< OE. *trymman,* make firm] **1.** to put in proper order; make neat or tidy **2.** to clip, lop, cut, etc. **3.** to decorate as by adding ornaments, etc. **4.** *a)* to balance (a ship) by ballasting, shifting cargo, etc. *b)* to put (sails) in order for sailing **5.** to

balance (an aircraft in flight) **6.** [Colloq.] to beat, punish, defeat, cheat, etc. —*vi.* to change one's opinions, policy, etc. in an expedient way —*n.* **1.** order; arrangement **2.** good condition **3.** a trimming **4.** any ornamental accessories — *adj.* **trim′mer, trim′mest 1.** orderly; neat **2.** well-proportioned **3.** in good condition —**trim′ly** *adv.* —**trim′mer** *n.* —**trim′ness** *n.*

trim′ming *n.* **1.** decoration; ornament **2.** [*pl.*] the side dishes of a meal **3.** [*pl.*] parts trimmed off **4.** [Colloq.] a beating, defeat, cheating, etc.

trin·i·ty (trin′ə tē) *n., pl.* **-ties** [< L. *trinus,* triple] **1.** a set of three **2.** [T-] *Christian Theol.* the union of Father, Son, and Holy Spirit in one Godhead

trin·ket (triŋ′kit) *n.* [ME. *trenket*] **1.** a small ornament, piece of jewelry, etc. **2.** a trifle or toy

tri·o (trē′ō) *n., pl.* **-os** [Fr. < It. < L. *tres,* three] **1.** a group of three **2.** *Music a)* a composition for three voices or three instruments *b)* the three performers of such a composition

trip (trip) *vi., vt.* **tripped, trip′ping** [< OFr. *treper*] **1.** to move or perform with light, rapid steps **2.** to stumble or cause to stumble, esp. by catching the foot **3.** to make or cause to make a mistake **4.** to release (a spring, wheel, etc.), as by going past an escapement catch — *n.* **1.** a light, quick tread **2.** a journey, esp. a short one **3.** a stumble or a causing to stumble **4.** [Slang] the experience of being under the influence of a psychedelic drug —**trip up to** catch in a lie, error, etc.

tri·par·tite (trī pär′tīt) *adj.* [< L. *tri-,* three + *partire,* to part] **1.** having three parts **2.** made between three parties, as an agreement

tripe (trīp) *n.* [prob. < Ar. *tharb,* entrails] **1.** part of the stomach of an ox, etc., when used as food **2.** [Slang] anything worthless, etc.; nonsense

trip′ham′mer *n.* a heavy, power-driven hammer, alternately raised and allowed to fall by a tripping device: also **trip hammer**

tri·ple (trip′'l) *adj.* [Fr. < L. *triplus*] **1.** consisting of three; threefold **2.** three times as much or as many —*n.* **1.** an amount three times as much or as many **2.** *Baseball* a hit on which the batter reaches third base —*vt.* **-pled, -pling** to make three times as much or as many —*vi.* **1.** to be tripled **2.** *Baseball* to hit a triple —**tri′ply** *adv.*

tri·plet (trip′lit) *n.* **1.** a group of three, usually of one kind **2.** any of three offspring born at a single birth

trip·li·cate (trip′lə kit) *adj.* [< L. *triplex,* threefold] **1.** threefold **2.** being the last of three identical copies —*n.* any of three identical copies —*vt.* (-kāt′) **-cat′ed, -cat′ing** to make three identical copies of —**in triplicate** in three identical copies

tri·pod (trī′päd) *n.* [< Gr. *tri-,* three + *pous,* a foot] a three-legged caldron, stool, support, etc.

trip·tych (trip′tik) *n.* [< Gr. *tri-,* three + *ptychē,* a fold] a set of three panels with pictures, carvings, etc., often hinged: used as an altarpiece

tri·sect (trī sekt′, trī′sekt) *vt.* [< TRI- + L. *secare,* to cut] to cut into three equal parts

trite (trīt) *adj.* **trit′er, trit′est** [< L. *terere,* wear out] no longer fresh or original; stale —**trite′ly** *adv.* —**trite′ness** *n.*

trit·i·um (trit′ē əm, trish′-) *n.* [< Gr. *tritos,* three] a radioactive isotope of hydrogen having an atomic weight of three

tri·umph (trī′əmf) *n.* [< L. *triumphus*] **1.** a victory; success **2.** exultation or joy over a victory, etc. —**vi. 1.** to gain victory or success **2.** to rejoice over victory, etc. —**tri·um′phal** (-um′f'l) **adj.**

tri·um′phant (-um′fənt) **adj. 1.** victorious; successful **2.** exulting in victory; elated —**tri·um′-phant·ly adv.**

tri·um·vir (trī um′vər) **n., pl.** **-virs, -vi·ri′** (-vi rī′) [L. < *trium virum,* of three men] in ancient Rome, any of three administrators sharing authority

tri·um′vi·rate (-vər it) **n.** government by three men

triv·et (triv′it) **n.** [< L. *tripes,* tripod] **1.** a three-legged stand for holding pots, kettles, etc. near a fire **2.** a short-legged metal or ceramic plate for hot dishes to rest on

triv·i·a (triv′ē ə) **n.pl.** [*often with sing. v.*] [ModL. < TRIVIAL] unimportant matters

triv·i·al (triv′ē əl) **adj.** [< L. *trivialis,* commonplace] unimportant; insignificant — **triv′i·al′i·ty** (-al′ə tē) **n., pl.** **-ties**

-trix *pl.* **-trixes, -trices** an ending of some feminine nouns of agent [*aviatrix*]

tro·che (trō′kē) **n.** [< Fr. < Gr. *trochos,* a wheel] a small medicinal lozenge

tro·chee (trō′kē) **n.** [< Gr. *trechein,* to run] a metrical foot of an accented syllable followed by an unaccented one —**tro·cha′ic** (-kā′ik) **adj.**

trod (träd) *pt. & alt. pp. of* TREAD

trod′den (-'n) *pp. of* TREAD

Tro·jan (trō′jən) **adj.** of Troy, its people, etc. — **n. 1.** a native or inhabitant of Troy **2.** a strong, hard-working, determined person

Trojan horse *Gr. Legend* a huge, hollow wooden horse filled with Greek soldiers: it was taken into Troy as an ostensible gift, thus leading to the destruction of the city

troll¹ (trōl) **vt., vi.** [ME. *trollen,* to roll] **1.** to sing the parts of (a round, etc.) in succession **2.** to sing in a full voice **3.** to fish (for) with a baited line trailed behind a slowly moving boat

troll² (trōl) **n.** [ON.] in Scand. folklore, any of certain supernatural beings, giants or dwarfs, living underground or in caves

trol·ley (träl′ē) **n., pl.** **-leys** [< TROLL¹] **1.** a wheeled carriage, basket, etc. that runs suspended from an overhead track **2.** a device, as a small wheel at the end of a pole, for carrying electric current from an overhead wire to a streetcar, etc. **3.** *same as* TROLLEY CAR

trolley car (or **bus**) an electric streetcar (or bus) powered from an overhead wire by means of a trolley

trol·lop (träl′əp) **n.** [prob. < G. *trolle,* a wench] a prostitute

trom·bone (träm bōn′, träm′bōn) **n.** [It. < *tromba,* a trumpet] a large brass-wind instrument with a bell mouth and a long tube bent parallel to itself twice and having either a section that slides in and out (**slide trombone**) or valves (**valve trombone**) —**trom·bon′ist n.**

troop (trōōp) **n.** [< Fr. < ML. *troppus,* a flock] **1.** a group of persons or animals **2.** [*pl.*] soldiers **3.** a subdivision of a cavalry regiment **4.** a unit of Boy Scouts or Girl Scouts —**vi.** to gather or go as in a group

troop′er n. [TROOP + -ER] **1.** a cavalryman **2.** a mounted policeman **3.** [Colloq.] a State policeman

tro·phy (trō′fē) **n., pl.** **-phies** [< Gr. *tropaion*] a memorial of victory in war, sports competition, etc.; prize

trop·ic (träp′ik) **n.** [< Gr. *tropikos,* of a turn (of the sun at the solstices)] **1.** either of two parallels of latitude, one, the **Tropic of Cancer,** 23°27′ north of the equator, and the other, the

Tropic of Capricorn, 23°27′ south **2.** [*also* T-] [*pl.*] the region between these latitudes, noted for its hot climate —**adj.** of the tropics; tropical

trop′i·cal (-i k'l) **adj.** of, in, characteristic of, or suitable for the tropics

tro·pism (trō′piz'm) **n.** [< Gr. *tropē,* a turn] the tendency of a plant or animal to grow or turn in response to an external stimulus, as light

trot (trät) **vi., vt.** **trot′ted, trot′ting** [< OHG. *trotton,* to tread] **1.** to ride, drive, move, etc. at a trot **2.** to hurry; run —**n. 1.** a gait of a horse, etc. in which the legs are lifted in alternating diagonal pairs **2.** a jogging gait of a person — **trot′ter n.**

troth (trôth, trōth) **n.** [ME. *trouthe*] [Archaic] **1.** faithfulness; loyalty **2.** truth **3.** a promise, esp. to marry

trou·ba·dour (trōō′bə dôr′) **n.** [Fr. < Pr. *tro·bar,* compose in verse] any of a class of poet-musicians of S France and N Italy in the 11th–13th cent.

trou·ble (trub′'l) **vt.** **-bled, -bling** [< L. *turbidus,* turbid] **1.** to disturb or agitate **2.** to worry; harass **3.** to cause inconvenience to [don't *trouble* yourself] —**vi.** to take pains; bother [don't *trouble* to return it] —**n. 1.** a state of mental distress; worry **2.** a misfortune; calamity **3.** a cause of annoyance, distress, etc. **4.** public disturbance **5.** effort; pains [take the *trouble* to listen]

trou′ble·mak′er n. one who incites others to quarrel, rebel, etc.

trou′ble-shoot′er n. one whose work is to find and repair or eliminate mechanical breakdowns or other sources of trouble

trou′ble·some (-səm) **adj.** characterized by or causing trouble

trough (trôf) **n.** [OE. *trog*] **1.** a long, narrow, open container, esp. one for holding water or food for animals **2.** a channel or gutter for carrying off rainwater **3.** a long, narrow hollow, as between waves **4.** a long, narrow area of low barometric pressure

trounce (trouns) **vt.** **trounced, trounc′ing** [< ?] **1.** to beat; thrash **2.** [Colloq.] to defeat soundly

troupe (trōōp) **n.** [Fr.] a troop, esp. of actors, singers, etc.; company —**vi.** **trouped, troup′ing** to travel as a member of a company of actors, etc. —**troup′er n.**

trou·sers (trou′zərz) **n.pl.** [< ScotGael. *triubhas*] a two-legged outer garment, esp. for men and boys, extending from the waist usually to the ankles; pants —**trou′ser adj.**

trous·seau (trōō′sō) **n., pl.** **-seaux** (-sōz), **-seaus** [Fr. < OFr. *trousse,* a bundle] a bride's outfit of clothes, linens, etc.

trout (trout) **n., pl.** **trout, trouts** [< Gr. *trōgein,* gnaw] any of various food and game fishes related to the salmon and found chiefly in fresh water

trow (trō, trou) **vi., vt.** [< OE. *treow,* faith] [Archaic] to believe, think, suppose, etc.

trow·el (trou′əl) **n.** [< L. *trua,* a ladle] **1.** a flat hand tool for smoothing plaster or applying mortar **2.** a pointed, scooplike tool for loosening soil, digging holes, etc. —**vt.** **-eled** or **-elled, -el·ing** or **-el·ling** to spread, smooth, shape, dig, etc. with a trowel

troy weight [< *Troyes,* Fr. city where first used] a system of weights for gold, silver, gems, etc., based on a pound of 12 oz.

tru·ant (trōō′ənt) **n.** [< OFr., beggar] **1.** a pupil who stays away from school without permission **2.** one who shirks his duties —**adj. 1.** that

is a truant 2. errant; straying —**tru'an·cy** *n., pl.*
-cles
truce (trōōs) *n.* [OE. *treow*, faith] 1. a temporary cessation of warfare by agreement between the belligerents 2. any pause in quarreling, conflict, etc.
truck[1] (truk) *n.* [prob. < Gr. *trochos*, a wheel]
1. a kind of two-wheeled barrow or a low,
wheeled frame, for carrying heavy articles 2.
an automotive vehicle for hauling loads 3. a
swiveling frame, with two or more pairs of
wheels, under each end of a railroad car, etc.
—*vt.* to carry on a truck —*vi.* to drive a truck
as one's work —**truck'er** *n.*
truck[2] (truk) *vt., vi.* [MFr. *troquer*] to exchange; barter —*n.* 1. small articles of little
value 2. vegetables raised for sale in markets
3. [Colloq.] dealings 4. [Colloq.] rubbish
truck farm a farm where vegetables are grown
to be marketed —**truck farmer**
truck·le (truk'l) *n.* [< Gr. *trochos*, a wheel]
same as TRUNDLE BED: in full **truckle bed** —*vi.*
-led, -ling to be servile; toady (*to*)
truc·u·lent (truk'yōō lənt) *adj.* [< L. *trux*] 1.
fierce; cruel 2. harsh, scathing, etc. 3. ready to
fight —**truc'u·lence, truc'u·len·cy** *n.* —**truc'u-
lent·ly** *adv.*
trudge (truj) *vi.* **trudged, trudg'ing** [< ?] to
walk, esp. wearily or laboriously —*n.* a walk,
esp. a wearying or tedious one
true (trōō) *adj.* **tru'er, tru'est** [OE. *treowe*] 1.
faithful; loyal 2. in accordance with fact; not
false 3. conforming to a standard, etc.; accurate 4. rightful; lawful 5. accurately fitted,
shaped, etc. 6. real; genuine —*adv.* 1. in a true
way 2. *Biol.* without variation from type —*vt.*
trued, tru'ing or **true'ing** to fit, shape, etc. accurately (often with *up*) —*n.* that which is true
(with *the*) —**come true** to happen as predicted
or expected —**true'ness** *n.*
true'-blue' *adj.* very loyal; staunch
truf·fle (truf'l) *n.* [< Fr. < L. *tuber*, knob] a
fleshy, edible underground fungus
tru·ism (trōō'iz'm) *n.* a statement the truth of
which is obvious and well-known
tru'ly *adv.* 1. in a true manner; accurately,
genuinely, etc. 2. really; indeed 3. sincerely
[yours *truly*]
trump (trump) *n.* [< TRIUMPH] 1. any playing
card of a suit ranked higher than any other
suit for a given hand 2. such a suit —*vt.* to
take (a trick, etc.) with a trump —*vi.* to play a
trump —**trump up** to make up in order to deceive
trump·er·y (trum'pər ē) *n., pl.* **-les** [< MFr.
tromper, deceive] 1. something showy but
worthless 2. nonsense
trum·pet (trum'pit) *n.* [< OFr. *trompe*] 1. a
brass-wind instrument with a blaring tone,
consisting of a looped tube ending in a flared
bell 2. something shaped like a trumpet; esp.,
same as EAR TRUMPET 3. a sound like that of
a trumpet —*vi.* 1. to blow a trumpet 2. to
make a sound like that of a trumpet —*vt.* to
proclaim loudly —**trum'pet·er** *n.*
trun·cate (trun'kāt) *vt.* **-cat·ed, -cat·ing** [< L.
truncus, a stem] to cut off a part of; lop —
trun·ca'tion *n.*
trun·cheon (trun'chən) *n.* [< L. *truncus*, a
stem] a short, thick club
trun·dle (trun'd'l) *vt., vi.* **-dled, -dling** [< OE.
trendan, to roll] to roll along
trundle bed a low bed on casters, that can be
rolled under a higher bed when not in use
trunk (trunk) *n.* [< L. *truncus*] 1. the main
stem of a tree 2. a human or animal body, not
including the head and limbs 3. the main

body of a nerve, blood vessel, etc. 4. a long
snout, as of an elephant 5. a large, reinforced
box to hold clothes, etc. in travel 6. [*pl.*] men's
shorts worn as for athletics 7. a compartment
in an automobile, usually in the rear, for a
spare tire, luggage, etc.
trunk line a main line of a railroad, canal, telephone system, etc.
truss (trus) *vt.* [< OFr. *trousser*, to bundle] 1.
to tie or bind (often with *up*) 2. to support
with a truss —*n.* 1. a bundle or pack 2. a rigid
framework to support a roof, bridge, etc. 3. a
padded device to support a hernia
trust (trust) *n.* [< ON. *traust*] 1. *a*) firm belief
in another's honesty, reliability, etc. *b*) the one
trusted 2. confident expectation, hope, etc. 3.
responsibility arising from confidence placed in
one 4. care; custody 5. something entrusted to
one 6. confidence in one's ability to pay; credit
7. a combination of corporations to establish a
monopoly 8. *Law a*) the fact of having nominal ownership of property to keep, use, or administer for another's benefit *b*) the property
—*vi.* to be confident —*vt.* 1. to have trust in 2.
to entrust 3. to allow, without misgivings, to
do something 4. to believe or suppose 5. to
hope 6. to grant business credit to —*adj.* 1. of a
trust or trusts 2. acting as trustee —**in trust** entrusted to another's care
trus·tee (trus tē') *n.* 1. one to whom another's
property or its management is entrusted 2. a
member of a board managing a school, hospital, etc. —**trus·tee'ship** *n.*
trust'ful *adj.* full of trust; ready to confide
trust fund money, stock, etc. held in trust
trust'ing *adj.* trustful —**trust'ing·ly** *adv.*
trust territory a territory set under a country's
administrative authority by the United Nations
trust'wor·thy *adj.* **-thi·er, -thi·est** worthy of
trust; reliable —**trust'wor'thi·ness** *n.*
trust'y *adj.* **-i·er, -i·est** trustworthy —*n., pl.* **-ies**
a convict granted special privileges as a trust-
worthy person
truth (trōōth) *n., pl.* **truths** (trōōthz, trōōths)
[OE. *treowth*] 1. a being true; specif., *a*) sincerity *b*) conformity with fact *c*) reality *d*) cor-
rectness 2. what is true 3. an established fact,
principle, etc. —**in truth** truly
truth'ful *adj.* 1. telling the truth; honest 2. in
accordance with fact or reality —**truth'ful·ly**
adv. —**truth'ful·ness** *n.*
try (trī) *vt.* **tried, try'ing** [< OFr. *trier*, to sift] 1.
to melt or render (fat, etc.) 2. *a*) to examine
and decide (a case) in a law court *b*) to determine legally the guilt or innocence of 3. to test
4. to subject to difficulties, hardships, suffer-
ings, etc. 5. to experiment with [*try* this
recipe] 6. to endeavor; attempt —*vi.* to make
an effort or attempt at something —*n., pl.* **tries**
a trying; effort or attempt —**try on** to test the
fit or appearance of (something to wear) by
putting it on —**try out** 1. to test; experiment
with 2. to test one's fitness as for a job, team,
role in a play, etc.
try'ing *adj.* that tries; annoying; irksome
try'out' *n.* [Colloq.] a testing of fitness, qualifications, etc.
tryst (trist) *n.* [< OFr. *triste*, hunting station] 1.
an appointment to meet somewhere, esp. one
made secretly by lovers 2. *a*) the meeting *b*)
the place: also **tryst'ing place**
tsar (tsär, zär) *n. alt. sp. of* CZAR
tset·se fly (tset'sē, tsĕt'-) [Afrik. < the native
name] a small fly of C and S Africa: some
species transmit sleeping sickness

T'-shirt' *n.* a collarless pullover undershirt or sport shirt

tsp. 1. teaspoon(s) 2. teaspoonful(s)

T square a T-shaped ruler for drawing parallel lines

tsu·na·mi (tsōō nä'mē) *n.* [Jpn. *tsu*, a harbor + *nami*, a wave] a huge sea wave caused by an underwater disturbance such as an earthquake

tub (tub) *n.* [< MDu. *tubbe*] 1. *a)* a round, open, flat-bottomed wooden container, usually made with staves and hoops *b)* any large, open container, as of metal 2. a bathtub

tu·ba (tōō'bə) *n.* [L., a trumpet] a large brasswind instrument with a deep tone

tub·by (tub'ē) *adj.* -bi·er, -bi·est 1. shaped like a tub 2. short and fat —**tub'bi·ness** *n.*

tube (tōōb, tyōōb) *n.* [Fr. < L. *tubus*, a pipe] 1. *a)* a slender, hollow pipe of metal, glass, rubber, etc., for conveying fluids *b)* any tubelike instrument, part, organ, etc. 2. a cylindrical container for holding toothpaste, glue, etc. 3. *short for: a)* ELECTRON TUBE *b)* VACUUM TUBE 4. [Brit. Colloq.] a subway —**the tube** [Colloq.] television

tu·ber (tōō'bər) *n.* [L., lit., knob] a short, thickened, fleshy part of an underground stem, as a potato —**tu'ber·ous** *adj.*

tu'ber·cle (-k'l) *n.* [see prec.] 1. a small rounded projection as on a bone or on a plant root 2. any abnormal hard nodule or swelling; specif., the lesion of tuberculosis

tu·ber·cu·lin (tōō bur'kyə lin) *n.* a solution injected into the skin as a test for tuberculosis

tu·ber'cu·lo'sis (-lō'sis) *n.* [see TUBERCLE & -OSIS] an infectious bacterial disease characterized by tubercle formations, specif. in the lungs —**tu·ber'cu·lar, tu·ber'cu·lous** *adj.*

tub·ing (tōōb'iŋ) *n.* 1. a system of tubes 2. material in tube form 3. a piece of tube

tu·bu·lar (tōō'byə lər) *adj.* 1. of or like a tube or tubes 2. made with tubes

tuck (tuk) *vt.* [< MDu. *tucken*] 1. to pull or gather up in a fold or folds 2. to sew a fold or folds in (a garment) 3. to push the edges of (a sheet, etc.) under or in so as to secure 4. to press snugly into a small space —*n.* a sewed fold in a garment

tuck·er (tuk'ər) *vt.* [< ?] [Colloq.] to tire; weary

Tues·day (tōōz'dē) *n.* [OE. *Tiwes dæg*, day of the war god Tiu] the third day of the week

tuft (tuft) *n.* [< OFr. *tufe*] 1. a closely bunched group of hairs, feathers, grass, etc. 2. any similar cluster; specif., any one of the small, fluffy balls of thread used decoratively as on a bedspread —*vt.* to provide with tufts

tug (tug) *vi., vt.* tugged, tug'ging [ME. *tuggen*] 1. to pull hard 2. to tow with a tugboat —*n.* 1. a hard pull 2. a tugboat

tug'boat' *n.* a small, powerful boat for towing or pushing ships, barges, etc.

tug of war a contest in which two teams pull at opposite ends of a rope

tu·i·tion (tōō wish'ən) *n.* [< L. *tueri*, protect] the charge for instruction, as at a college

tu·la·re·mi·a (tōō'lə rē'mē ə) *n.* [< *Tulare* County, California] an infectious disease of rodents, esp. rabbits, transmissible to man

tu·lip (tōō'lip) *n.* [< Fr. < Turk. *tülbend*, turban] 1. a bulb plant with a large, cupshaped flower 2. the flower

tulle (tōōl) *n.* [< *Tulle*, city in France] a fine netting of silk, rayon, etc., used as for scarfs

tum·ble (tum'b'l) *vi.* -bled, -bling [OE. *tumbian*, to jump] 1. to do somersaults, handsprings, etc. 2. to fall suddenly; collapse 3. to

toss or roll about 4. to move in a fast, confused way —*vt.* 1. to make tumble 2. to disorder; disarrange —*n.* 1. a fall 2. disorder

tum'ble·down' *adj.* dilapidated

tum'bler (-blər) *n.* 1. one that tumbles; specif., an acrobat or gymnast 2. a drinking glass without foot or stem 3. the lock part moved by a key to release the bolt

tum'ble·weed' *n.* a plant that breaks off near the ground in autumn and is blown about by the wind

tum·brel, tum·bril (tum'brəl) *n.* [< MFr. *tomberel*] a cart that can be tilted for emptying

tu·mid (tōō'mid) *adj.* [< L. *tumere*, to swell] 1. swollen; distended 2. bombastic —**tu·mid'i·ty** *n.*

tum·my (tum'ē) *n., pl.* -mies stomach: a child's word

tu·mor (tōō'mər) *n.* [L., a swelling] a bodily swelling; esp., an independent growth that may or may not be harmful: Brit. sp. **tu'mour**

tu·mult (tōō'mult) *n.* [< L. *tumere*, to swell] 1. uproar; commotion 2. disturbance; agitation

tu·mul'tu·ous (-mul'choo wəs) *adj.* full of tumult; turbulent —**tu·mul'tu·ous·ly** *adv.*

tun (tun) *n.* [< ML. *tunna*] a large cask

tu·na (tōō'nə, tyōō'-) *n., pl.* -na, -nas [AmSp. < Sp., ult. < Gr. *thynnos*] 1. a large, edible fish related to the mackerel 2. its flesh, often canned: also **tuna fish**

tun·dra (tun'drə) *n.* [Russ.] a treeless arctic plain

tune (tōōn) *n.* [see TONE] 1. a catchy, rhythmical succession of musical tones; melody 2. correct musical pitch 3. agreement; concord —*vt.* **tuned, tun'ing** 1. to adjust or adapt to a given musical pitch or key 2. to adapt to a condition, mood, etc. 3. to adjust (a motor, circuit, etc.) for proper performance —**to the tune of** [Colloq.] to the amount of —**tune in** to adjust a radio or television receiver so as to get (a certain station, program, etc.) —**tun'a·ble, tune'a·ble** *adj.* —**tun'er** *n.*

tune'ful *adj.* melodious —**tune'ful·ly** *adv.*

tune'up', tune'-up' *n.* a tuning up, as of an engine

tung·sten (tuŋ'stən) *n.* [Sw. < *tung*, heavy + *sten*, stone] a hard, heavy, gray-white metallic chemical element: symbol, W

tu·nic (tōō'nik) *n.* [L. *tunica*] 1. a loose, gownlike garment worn by men and women in ancient Greece and Rome 2. a blouselike garment extending to the hips

tuning fork a small, two-pronged steel instrument which when struck sounds a fixed tone in perfect pitch

tun·nel (tun'l) *n.* [< OFr. *tonne*, tun] an underground or underwater passageway —*vt., vi.* -neled or -nelled, -nel·ing or -nel·ling to make a tunnel (through or under) —**tun'nel·er, tun'nel·ier** *n.*

tun·ny (tun'ē) *n., pl.* -nies, -ny [< Gr. *thynnos*] *same as* TUNA (sense 1)

tur·ban (tur'bən) *n.* [< Per. *dulbänd*] 1. a Muslim headdress consisting of folded cloth wound about the head 2. any similar headdress

tur·bid (tur'bid) *adj.* [< L. *turba*, a crowd] 1. muddy or cloudy with unsettled sediment 2. thick or dark, as clouds 3. muddled

tur·bine (tur'bin, -bīn) *n.* [Fr. < L. *turbo*, a whirl] an engine driven by pressure, as of steam, against vanes that turn an axle

tur·bo·fan (tur'bō fan') *n.* a turbojet engine developing extra thrust from air that bypasses the engine and is accelerated by a fan

tur'bo·jet' (-jet') *n.* 1. a jet engine in which the energy of the jet operates a turbine which drives the air compressor: in full **turbojet engine 2.** an aircraft having such an engine

tur·bo·prop' (-präp') *n.* **1.** a turbojet engine turning a propeller that develops most of the thrust: in full **turboprop engine 2.** an aircraft having such an engine

tur·bot (tur'bət) *n., pl.* **-bot, -bots** [< OFr. *tourbout*] **1.** a European flatfish esteemed as food **2.** an American flounder or halibut

tur·bu·lent (tur'byə lənt) *adj.* [Fr. < L. *turba*, a crowd] **1.** unruly; boisterous **2.** violently agitated **3.** wildly irregular in motion, as air currents —**tur'bu·lence** *n.* —**tur'bu·lent·ly** *adv.*

tu·reen (too rēn') *n.* [< MFr. *terrine*, earthen vessel] a large, deep dish with a lid, for serving soup, stew, etc.

turf (turf) *n.* [OE.] **1.** *a)* a surface layer of earth containing grass with its roots; sod *b)* a piece of this **2.** peat **3.** a track for horse racing: usually with *the* **4.** [Slang] one's own territory — *vt.* to cover with turf

tur·gid (tur'jid) *adj.* [< L. *turgere*, to swell] **1.** swollen; distended **2.** bombastic —**tur·gid'i·ty** *n.*

Turk (turk) *n.* a native of Turkey

Turk. 1. Turkey **2.** Turkish

tur·key (tur'kē) *n.* [< similarity to a fowl formerly imported through Turkey] **1.** a large N. American bird with a small head and spreading tail **2.** its flesh, used as food

turkey buzzard a dark-colored American vulture with a naked, reddish head

Tur·kic (tur'kik) *adj.* designating or of a group of languages, including Turkish, Tatar, etc. — *n.* this subfamily

Turk·ish (tur'kish) *adj.* of Turkey or the Turks —*n.* the language of Turkey

Turkish bath a bath with steam rooms, showers, massage, etc.

tur·mer·ic (tur'mər ik) *n.* [< ML. *terra merita*, deserving earth] an East Indian plant whose powdered rhizome is used as a yellow dye, a seasoning, etc.

tur·moil (tur'moil) *n.* [< ?] tumult; commotion; confusion

turn (turn) *vt.* [ult. < Gr. *tornos*, lathe] **1.** to rotate (a wheel, etc.) **2.** to move around or partly around *[turn the key]* **3.** to give form to as in a lathe **4.** to change the position or direction of **5.** to ponder **6.** to reverse *[turn the record]* **7.** to upset (the stomach) **8.** to deflect or repel *[to turn a blow]* **9.** to cause to change actions, attitudes, etc. **10.** to go around (a corner, etc.) **11.** to pass (an age, etc.) **12.** to drive, set, let go, etc. *[to turn someone adrift]* **13.** to direct, point, aim, etc. **14.** to change *[to turn cream into butter]* **15.** to make sour **16.** to affect in some way —*vi.* **1.** to revolve or pivot **2.** to whirl or reel **3.** to become curved or bent **4.** to become reversed **5.** to become upset: said of the stomach **6.** to change or reverse course, direction, etc., or one's feelings, allegiance, etc. **7.** to direct or shift one's attention, energy, etc. *[to turn to other matters]* **8.** to make a sudden attack (*on* or *upon*) **9.** to become **10.** to undergo a change **11.** to become sour —*n.* **1.** a turning around; rotation **2.** a single twist, winding, etc. **3.** a change or reversal of course, direction, etc. **4.** a bend or curve, as in a road **5.** a change in trend, events, etc. **6.** *same as* TURNING POINT **7.** a brief shock; start **8.** an action; deed *[a good turn]* **9.** a bout; spell **10.** the right, duty, or chance to do something, esp. as coming in regular order *[it's your turn to speak]* **11.** a distinctive form, detail, etc. *[an odd turn of speech]* **12.** an inclination, aptitude, etc. —**in** (or **out of**) **turn** (not) in proper sequence —**turn down 1.** to reject (a request,

etc.) **2.** to reduce (light, sound, etc.) —**turn in 1.** to deliver; hand in **2.** [Colloq.] to go to bed — **turn off 1.** to shut off; stop from functioning **2.** [Slang] to cause to be bored, annoyed, etc. — **turn on 1.** to make go on or start functioning **2.** to display suddenly (a smile, etc.) **3.** [Slang] to make or become elated, euphoric, etc. —**turn out 1.** to put out (a light) **2.** to put outside **3.** to dismiss **4.** to come or go out, as to a meeting **5.** to produce **6.** to result **7.** to prove to be **8.** to become —**turn over 1.** to ponder **2.** to hand over —**turn up** to happen, arrive, appear, etc.

turn'a·bout' *n.* a shift or reversal of position, allegiance, opinion, etc.

turn'a·round' *n.* **1.** *same as* TURNABOUT **2.** a wide area for turning a vehicle around

turn'buck·le (-buk'l) *n.* a linklike metal coupling having at each end a threaded tubular opening into which a rod or other piece can be screwed, the coupling being turned to tighten or loosen the pieces thus joined

turn'coat' *n.* a renegade or traitor

turning point a point of decisive change; crisis

tur·nip (tur'nip) *n.* [< ?] **1.** *a)* a plant related to the mustard, with edible leaves and a roundish root used as a vegetable *b)* *same as* RUTABAGA **2.** the root of either of these

turn'key' (-kē') *n., pl.* **-keys'** a jailer

turn'off' *n.* **1.** a turning off **2.** a place for turning off; esp., an exit from a highway

turn'out' *n.* **1.** a gathering **2.** a wider part of a road, as for passing

turn'o'ver *n.* **1.** a turning over; upset **2.** a small pie with half the crust folded back over the other **3.** *a)* the selling out and replenishing of a stock of goods *b)* the amount of business done during a given period **4.** the rate of replacement of workers

turn'pike' *n.* [ME. *turnpyke*, spiked road barrier] a toll road, esp. one that is an expressway

turn'stile' *n.* an apparatus such as a post with revolving bars, used at an entrance to admit people one at a time

turn'ta'ble *n.* a circular rotating platform, as for playing a phonograph record

tur·pen·tine (tur'pən tīn') *n.* [< Gr. *terebinthos*, tree yielding such an oleoresin] a colorless, volatile oil distilled from certain coniferous trees, and used in paints, etc.

tur·pi·tude (tur'pə tōōd') *n.* [< L. *turpis*, vile] baseness; vileness; depravity

tur·quoise (tur'koiz, -kwoiz) *n.* [< OFr. *turqueis*, Turkish] **1.** a greenish-blue semiprecious stone **2.** its color; greenish blue —*adj.* greenish-blue

tur·ret (tur'it) *n.* [see TOWER] **1.** a small tower projecting from a building, usually at a corner **2.** a dome or revolving structure for guns, as on a warship, airplane, or tank **3.** a rotating attachment for a lathe, holding several cutting tools for successive use

tur·tle (tur't'l) *n.* [< Fr. < ML. *tortuca*] any of various land and water reptiles having a soft body encased in a hard shell —**turn turtle** to turn upside down

tur'tle·dove' *n.* [< L. *turtur* + DOVE¹] a wild dove with a plaintive call

tur'tle·neck' *n.* **1.** a high, snug, turned-down collar, as on a sweater **2.** a sweater, shirt, etc. with such a collar

tusk (tusk) *n.* [OE. *tucs*] in elephants, walruses, etc., a very long, large, pointed tooth projecting from the mouth

tus·sle (tus''l) *n., vi.* **-sled, -sling** [< ME. *tusen* (in comp.), to pull] struggle; wrestle; scuffle

tu·te·lage (tōōt′'l ij) *n.* [< L. *tutela,* protection] 1. guardianship; care, protection, etc. 2. instruction —**tu′te·lar′y** (-er′ē) *adj.*

tu·tor (tōōt′ər) *n.* [< L. *tueri,* to guard] a private teacher —*vt., vi.* to teach privately —**tu·to·ri·al** (tōō tôr′ē əl) *adj.*

tut·ti-frut·ti (tōōt′ē frōōt′ē) *n.* [It., all fruits] ice cream or other sweet food containing bits of candied fruits

tux (tuks) *n. short for* TUXEDO

tux·e·do (tuk sē′dō) *n., pl.* **-dos** [< country club near *Tuxedo* Lake, N.Y.] a man's semiformal suit with a tailless jacket

TV (tē′vē′) *n.* 1. television 2. *pl.* **TVs, TV's** a television receiving set

TV dinner [because it can conveniently be eaten while watching television] a frozen, precooked dinner packaged in the tray in which it is to be heated and served

twad·dle (twäd′'l) *n.* [earlier *twattle* < ?] foolish, empty talk or writing; nonsense

twain (twān) *adj., n.* [OE. *twegen*] [Archaic] two

twang (twaŋ) *n.* [echoic] 1. a sharp, vibrating sound such as of a taut string plucked 2. a sharply nasal quality —*vi., vt.* to make or cause to make a twang 2. to speak or utter with a twang —**twang′y** *adj.*

'twas (twuz, twäz; *unstressed* twəz) it was

tweak (twēk) *vt.* [OE. *twiccan,* to twitch] to give a sudden, twisting pinch to (someone's nose, cheek, etc.) —*n.* such a pinch

tweed (twēd) *n.* [< misreading of *tweel,* Scot. form of TWILL] 1. a rough wool fabric in a twill weave of two or more colors 2. [*pl.*] clothes of this

twee·dle·dum and twee·dle·dee (twēd′'l dum′ 'n twēd′'l dē′) two persons or things so much alike as to be almost indistinguishable

tweet (twēt) *n., interj.* [echoic] the thin, chirping sound of a small bird —*vi.* to make this sound

tweet′er *n.* in an assembly of two or more loudspeakers, a small speaker for reproducing high sounds

tweez·ers (twēz′ərz) *n.pl.* [*with sing. or pl. v.*] [< obs. *tweeze,* surgical set] small pincers for plucking out hairs, etc.: often **pair of tweezers**

twelfth (twelfth) *adj.* [OE. *twelfta*] preceded by eleven others; 12th —*n.* 1. the one following the eleventh 2. any of the twelve equal parts of something; 1/12

Twelfth Day the twelfth day (Jan. 6) after Christmas; Epiphany: the evening before, or sometimes the evening of, this day is called **Twelfth Night**

twelve (twelv) *adj., n.* [OE. *twelf*] two more than ten; 12; XII

twen·ty (twen′tē) *adj., n., pl.* **-ties** [OE. *twentig*] two times ten; 20; XX —**the twenties** the numbers or years, as of a century, from 20 through 29 —**twen′ti·eth** (-ith) *adj., n.*

twen′ty-one′ *n.* a card game in which the object is to total 21 points

twice (twis) *adv.* [OE. *twiga*] two times

twid·dle (twid′'l) *vt., vi.* **-dled, -dling** [< ?] to twirl or play with (something) idly —**twiddle one's thumbs** to be idle

twig (twig) *n.* [OE. *twigge*] a small branch of a tree or shrub —**twig′gy** *adj.* **-gi·er, -gi·est**

twi·light (twī′līt′) *n.* [ME.] 1. *a)* the light after sunset or before sunrise *b)* the period from sunset to dark 2. a gradual decline

twill (twil) *n.* [OE. *twilic,* double-threaded] a cloth woven with parallel diagonal lines

twin (twin) *adj.* [OE. *twinn,* double] 1. consisting of, or being one of a pair of, two similar

things 2. being a twin or twins —*n.* 1. either of two born at the same birth 2. either of two persons or things much alike

twine (twīn) *n.* [OE. *twin*] strong thread, string, etc. of strands twisted together —*vt., vi.* **twined, twin′ing** 1. to twist together 2. to wind around

twinge (twinj) *vt., vi.* **twinged, twing′ing** [OE. *twengan,* to press] to make have, or to feel, a brief, sharp pain or pang —*n.* such a pain or pang

twin·kle (twiŋ′k'l) *vi.* **-kled, -kling** [OE. *twinclian*] 1. to shine with quick, intermittent flashes 2. to light up as with amusement: said of the eyes 3. to move quickly and lightly, as a dancer's feet —*vt.* to make twinkle —*n.* a twinkling

twin′kling *n.* an instant

twirl (twurl) *vt., vi.* [< ?] 1. to rotate rapidly; spin; whirl 2. to twist [to twirl one's mustache] 3. *Baseball* to pitch —*n.* a twirling or being twirled —**twirl′er** *n.*

twist (twist) *vt.* [OE. *-twist,* a rope] 1. to wind (strands or threads) around one another 2. to wind (thread, rope, etc.) around something 3. to give a spiral shape to 4. *a)* to subject to torsion *b)* to wrench, deform, etc. 5. to contort, distort, etc. 6. to confuse 7. to move, rotate, remove, etc. by subjecting to a turning force —*vi.* 1. to get twisted 2. to wind, coil, spiral, etc. (*around* or *about*) 3. to rotate; revolve 4. to squirm or writhe —*n.* 1. a twisting or being twisted 2. something twisted, as thread or cord, a roll of tobacco, etc. 3. a bend or curve 4. torsional stress 5. a contortion 6. a wrench or sprain 7. a distortion of meaning 8. a distinctive or different meaning, method, slant, etc.

twist′er *n.* 1. one that twists 2. a tornado

twit (twit) *vt.* **twit′ted, twit′ting** [OE. *ætwitan*] to reproach, taunt, etc. —*n.* a reproach or taunt

twitch (twich) *vt., vi.* [OE. *twiccian,* to pluck] to pull (at) or move with a quick, slight jerk —*n.* a twitching; quick, slight jerk

twit·ter (twit′ər) *vi.* [ME. *twiteren*] 1. to chirp continuously 2. *a)* to chatter *b)* to giggle 3. to tremble excitedly —*n.* 1. a twittering 2. nervous excitement

two (tōō) *adj., n.* [OE. *twa*] one more than one; 2; II —**in two** in two parts; asunder

two′-bit′ *adj.* [Slang] cheap

two bits [Colloq.] twenty-five cents

two′-by-four′ *n.* a piece of lumber, originally two inches thick and four inches wide

two′-faced′ *adj.* 1. with two faces 2. hypocritical

two′-fist′ed *adj.* [Colloq.] 1. having, and able to use, both fists 2. vigorous; virile

two′fold′ *adj.* 1. having two parts 2. having twice as much or as many —*adv.* twice as much or as many

two′-hand′ed *adj.* 1. requiring the use of both hands 2. operated, played, etc. by two persons

two-pence (tup′'ns) *n.* 1. two pence 2. a British coin of this value

two′-ply′ *adj.* having two layers, strands, etc.

two′some (-səm) *n.* two people; a couple

two′-time′ *vt.* **-timed′, -tim′ing** [Slang] to be unfaithful to —**two′-tim′er** *n.*

two′-way′ *adj.* 1. allowing movement in two directions 2. involving two persons, groups, etc.

-ty (< L. *-tas*] a suffix meaning quality of, condition of [*novelty*]

ty·coon (tī kōōn′) *n.* [< Jpn. < Chin. *ta,* great + *kiun,* prince] a magnate, as an industrialist

ty·ing (tī′iŋ) *prp. of* TIE

tyke (tīk) *n.* [< ON. *tik,* a bitch] [Colloq.] a tot

tym·pa·ni (tim′pə nē) *n.pl. alt. sp. of* TIMPANI —**tym′pa·nist** *n.*

tympanic membrane a thin membrane that separates the middle ear from the external ear and that vibrates when struck by sound waves; eardrum

tym·pa·num (tim′pə nəm) *n., pl.* -nums, -na (-nə) [< Gr. *tympanon,* a drum] *same as:* 1. MIDDLE EAR 2. TYMPANIC MEMBRANE

type (tīp) *n.* [< Gr. *typos,* a mark] 1. one that represents or symbolizes another 2. the characteristic form, plan, style, etc. of a class, group, etc. 3. a class, group, etc. with characteristics in common 4. one that is representative of a class or group 5. a perfect example or an archetype 6. *a)* a rectangular piece, usually of metal, with a raised letter, figure, etc. in reverse on its top, used in printing *b)* such pieces collectively *c)* a printed or photographically reproduced character or characters —*vt., vi.* typed, typ′ing 1. to classify according to type 2. to typewrite

-type [see prec.] *a combining form meaning* print, printing type *[monotype]*

type′cast′ *vt.* -cast′, -cast′ing to cast (an actor or actress) repeatedly in the same type of part

type′script′ *n.* typewritten matter

type′set′ *vt.* -set′, -set′ting to set in type

type′set′ter *n.* 1. a person who sets type; compositor 2. a machine for setting type

type′write′ *vt., vi.* -wrote′, -writ′ten, -writ′ing to write with a typewriter: now usually **type**

type′writ′er *n.* a writing machine with a keyboard for reproducing letters, figures, etc. that resemble printed ones

ty·phoid (tī′foid) *n.* [TYPH(US) + -OID] an acute infectious disease marked by fever, intestinal disorders, etc. and acquired from con-taminated food or water: in full **typhoid fever**

ty·phoon (tī foon′) *n.* [< Chin. dial. *tai-fung,* great wind] a violent tropical cyclone originating in the W Pacific

ty·phus (tī′fəs) *n.* [< Gr. *typhos,* fever] an acute infectious disease marked by fever, headache, and skin rash and transmitted to man by fleas, lice, etc.: in full **typhus fever**

typ·i·cal (tip′i k′l) *adj.* 1. serving as a type; symbolic 2. having the distinguishing characteristics of a class, group, etc.; representative 3. belonging to a type; characteristic —**typ′i·cal·ly** *adv.*

typ′i·fy′ (-ə fī′) *vt.* -fied′, -fy′ing to be a type of; symbolize, represent, etc.

typ·ist (tīp′ist) *n.* one that typewrites

ty·po (tī′pō) *n., pl.* -pos [Colloq.] an error made in typing or in setting type

ty·pog·ra·phy (tī päg′rə fē) *n.* [see TYPE & -GRAPHY] 1. the setting of, and printing with, type 2. the arrangement or appearance of matter printed from type —**ty·pog′ra·pher** *n.* —**ty′po·graph′i·cal** (-pə graf′i k′l) *adj.* —**ty′po·graph′i·cal·ly** *adv.*

ty·ran·ni·cal (ti ran′i k′l) *adj.* of or like a tyrant; despotic, harsh, unjust, etc.: also **ty·ran′nic** —**ty·ran′ni·cal·ly** *adv.*

tyr·an·nize (tir′ə nīz′) *vi.* -nized′, -niz′ing 1. to govern as a tyrant 2. to use authority harshly or cruelly —*vt.* to oppress

tyr·an·ny (tir′ə nē) *n., pl.* -nies 1. the authority, government, etc. of a tyrant 2. cruel and unjust use of power 3. a tyrannical act

ty·rant (tī′rənt) *n.* [< Gr. *tyrannos*] an absolute ruler, esp. if oppressive, harsh, etc.

ty·ro (tī′rō) *n., pl.* -ros [< L. *tiro,* young soldier] a beginner; novice

tzar (tsär, zär) *n. alt. sp. of* CZAR —**tza·ri·na** (tsä rē′nə, zä-) *n.fem.*

U

U, u (yoo) *n., pl.* **U's, u's** the twenty-first letter of the English alphabet

U *Chem.* uranium

U., U 1. Union 2. United 3. University

U., U, u., u unit; units

u·biq·ui·tous (yoo bik′wə təs) *adj.* [< L. *ubique,* everywhere] (seemingly) present everywhere at the same time —**u·biq′ui·ty** *n.*

U-boat (yoo′bōt′) *n.* [< G. *Unterseeboot,* undersea boat] a German submarine

ud·der (ud′ər) *n.* [OE. *udr*] a large, pendulous, milk-secreting gland with two or more teats, as in cows

UFO (yoo′fō, yoo′ef ō′) *n., pl.* **UFOs, UFO's** an unidentified flying object, esp. one described as saucerlike (*flying saucer*)

ugh (ookh, oo, ug, *etc.*) *interj.* [echoic] an exclamation of horror, disgust, etc.

ug·li (ug′lē) *n.* [< UGLY] an odd-shaped fruit that is a cross between a grapefruit, orange, and tangerine

ug·ly (ug′lē) *adj.* -li·er, -li·est [< ON. *uggr,* fear] 1. unpleasant to look at 2. bad, vile, repulsive, etc. 3. ominous; dangerous 4. [Colloq.] ill-tempered —**ug′li·ness** *n.*

uh (u, un) *interj.* 1. *same as* HUH 2. a sound indicating hesitation

UHF, uhf ultrahigh frequency

u·kase (yoo′kās, -kāz) *n.* [Russ. *ukaz,* edict] a decree, esp. an arbitrary one

U·krain·i·an (yoo krā′nē ən) *adj.* of the Ukraine, a U.S.S.R. republic, its people, their language, etc. —*n.* 1. a native of the Ukraine 2. their Slavic language

u·ku·le·le (yoo′kə lā′lē) *n.* [Haw., flea] a small, four-stringed, guitarlike musical instrument

ul·cer (ul′sər) *n.* [L. *ulcus*] an open sore on the skin or some mucous membrane, discharging pus —**ul′cer·ous** *adj.*

ul′cer·ate′ (-sə rāt′) *vt., vi.* -at′ed, -at′ing to make or become ulcerous —**ul′cer·a′tion** *n.*

ul·na (ul′nə) *n., pl.* -nae (-nē), -nas [L., the elbow] the larger of the two bones of the forearm —**ul′nar** *adj.*

ul·ster (ul′stər) *n.* [< *Ulster,* in Northern Ireland] a long, loose, heavy overcoat

ult. ultimate(ly)

ul·te·ri·or (ul tir′ē ər) *adj.* [L.] 1. lying beyond or on the farther side 2. beyond what is expressed, implied, or evident

ul·ti·mate (ul′tə mit) *adj.* [< L. *ultimus,* last] 1. beyond which it is impossible to go; farthest 2. final; last 3. beyond further analysis; fundamental 4. greatest possible; maximum —*n.* a final point or result

ul·ti·ma·tum (ul′tə māt′əm) *n., pl.* -tums, -ta (-ə) [see prec.] a final offer or demand, as in negotiations

ul·tra (ul′trə) *adj.* [L., beyond] going beyond the usual limit; extreme

ultra- [L.] *a prefix meaning:* 1. beyond

[ultraviolet] **2.** excessively *[ultramodern]* **3.** beyond the range of *[ultramicroscopic]*

ul·tra·high frequency (ul'trə hī') any radio frequency between 300 and 3,000 megahertz

ul'tra·ma·rine' (-mə rēn') *adj.* **1.** beyond the sea **2.** deep-blue —*n.* deep blue

ul'tra·son'ic (-sän'ik) *adj.* above the range of sound audible to the human ear

ul'tra·vi'o·let (-vī'ə lit) *adj.* designating or of those invisible rays just beyond the violet of the visible spectrum

ul·u·late (yōol'yōo lāt', ul'-) *vi.* **-lat'ed, -lat'ing** [L. *ululare*] **1.** to howl or hoot **2.** to wail

U·lys·ses (yōo lis'ēz) *same as* ODYSSEUS

um·bel (um'b'l) *n.* [L. *umbella*, parasol] a cluster of flowers with stalks of nearly equal length growing out from about the same point on a main stem

um·ber (um'bər) *n.* [< It. *(terra d')ombra*, (earth of) shade] **1.** a kind of earth used as a pigment: *raw umber* is yellowish-brown; *burnt umber* is reddish-brown **2.** yellowish brown or reddish brown

um·bil·i·cal (um bil'i k'l) *adj.* of or like an umbilicus or an umbilical cord —*n.* a cable to supply oxygen, power, etc. as to an astronaut outside his craft

umbilical cord 1. a cordlike structure that connects a fetus with the placenta: it is severed at birth **2.** *same as* UMBILICAL (*n.*)

um·bil·i·cus (um bil'i kəs, um'bi li'kəs) *n., pl.* **-ci'** (-sī', -sī) [L.] *same as* NAVEL

um·bra (um'brə) *n., pl.* **-brae** (-brē), **-bras** [L.] shadow; shade

um·brage (um'brij) *n.* [see prec.] offense; resentment

um·brel·la (um brel'ə) *n.* [< L. *umbra*, shade] **1.** a screen on a folding radial frame, used for protection against the rain or sun **2.** any comprehensive, protective alliance, strategy, etc.

u·mi·ak, u·mi·ack (ōō'mē ak') *n.* [Esk.] an open Eskimo boat made of skins stretched on a wooden frame

um·laut (oom'lout) *n.* [G. *um*, about + *laut*, a sound] *Linguis.* **1.** a vowel changed in sound by its assimilation to another vowel **2.** the mark (¨) placed over such a vowel, esp. in German

um·pire (um'pīr) *n.* [< MFr. *nomper*, uneven, hence a third person] **1.** a person chosen to give a decision in a dispute; arbiter **2.** an official who rules on the plays of a game, as in baseball —*vt., vi.* **-pired, -pir·ing** to act as umpire (in or of)

ump·teen (ump'tēn') *adj.* [Slang] very many —**ump'teenth'** *adj.*

un- *either of two prefixes meaning:* **1.** [OE. *un-*] not, lack of, the opposite of *[unhappy, untruth]* **2.** [OE. *un-, on-, and-*] the reverse or removal of *[unfasten, unchain]* The following list includes many of the more common compounds formed with *un-* (either prefix) that do not have special meanings

unabashed	unambiguous
unabated	unannounced
unable	unanswerable
unabridged	unappreciated
unaccented	unashamed
unacceptable	unasked
unaccommodating	unassisted
unaccompanied	unattainable
unacquainted	unattended
unadorned	unattractive
unadulterated	unauthorized
unafraid	unavailable
unaided	unbearable
unalterable	unbefitting

unbiased	unenviable
unbleached	uneventful
unblemished	unexceptional
unbound	unexpired
unbreakable	unexplained
unbuckle	unexplored
unburned	unexpressed
unbusinesslike	unexpurgated
unbutton	unfaded
uncap	unfading
unceasing	unfair
uncensored	unfaltering
unchain	unfashionable
unchallenged	unfasten
unchanged	unfathomable
unchanging	unfavorable
uncharitable	unfettered
uncharted	unflattering
unchaste	unforeseeable
unchecked	unforeseen
uncivilized	unforested
unclaimed	unforgettable
unclassified	unforgivable
uncomplaining	unforgiven
uncompleted	unforgiving
uncomplimentary	unforgotten
unconcealed	unformed
unconfirmed	unfrequented
unconnected	unfruitful
unconquerable	unfulfilled
unconstrained	unfurnished
uncontrollable	ungenerous
uncontrolled	ungentlemanly
unconventional	ungoverned
unconvinced	ungrammatical
uncooked	ungrateful
uncooperative	ungrudging
uncorrupted	unhampered
uncultivated	unhandy
undamaged	unharmed
undated	unharness
undeceive	unhealthful
undecipherable	unheeded
undeclared	unhesitating
undefeated	unhurried
undefended	unhurt
undefiled	unhygienic
undefined	unidentified
undemocratic	unimaginable
undemonstrative	unimaginative
undependable	unimpaired
undeserved	unimportant
undeserving	unimpressed
undesirable	unimproved
undetermined	unincorporated
undeveloped	unindexed
undeviating	uninformed
undifferentiated	uninhabitable
undigested	uninhabited
undiluted	uninhibited
undiminished	uninitiated
undisciplined	uninjured
undiscovered	uninspired
undiscriminating	uninsured
undisguised	unintelligent
undismayed	unintelligible
undisputed	unintended
undistinguished	unintentional
undisturbed	uninterested
undivided	uninteresting
unearned	uninterrupted
uneconomical	unintimidated
uneducated	uninvited
unemotional	uninviting
unending	unjustifiable
unendurable	unknowable
unenlightened	unknowing

unlamented	unregulated
unleavened	unrelated
unlicensed	unreliable
unlined	unrelieved
unlisted	unrepentant
unlit	unrequited
unloved	unresponsive
unlovely	unrestricted
unmanageable	unsafe
unmarked	unsalable
unmarried	unsaleable
unmatched	unsanitary
unmeasurable	unsatisfactory
unmentioned	unsatisfied
unmerited	unscientific
unmindful	unseasoned
unmixed	unseeing
unmolested	unseen
unmoved	unselfish
unmoving	unshaded
unmusical	unshakable
unnamed	unshakeable
unnaturalized	unshaken
unnavigable	unshed
unneeded	unsmiling
unnoted	unsold
unnoticed	unsolicited
unobjectionable	unsought
unobservant	unspoiled
unobserved	unsportsmanlike
unobstructed	unsprung
unobtainable	unstained
unobtrusive	unstrained
unofficial	unstressed
unopened	unsubdued
unopposed	unsuccessful
unorthodox	unsuitable
unostentatious	unsulted
unpaid	unsullied
unpalatable	unsupervised
unpardonable	unsupported
unpardoned	unsure
unpaved	unsurpassed
unperturbed	unsuspected
unplanned	unsuspicious
unpleasing	unsweetened
unplowed	unswept
unpolished	unswerving
unpolluted	unsympathetic
unpredictable	unsympathizing
unprejudiced	untainted
unpremeditated	untarnished
unprepared	untasted
unpretentious	unteachable
unproductive	untenable
unprofitable	untiring
unprogressive	untouched
unpromising	untrained
unpronounceable	untraveled
unprotected	untravelled
unprovided	untried
unprovoked	untrimmed
unpruned	untroubled
unpublished	untrustworthy
unpunished	unuttered
unquenchable	unvaried
unquestioned	unvarying
unquestioning	unverified
unreadable	unvisited
unready	unwanted
unrealized	unwarranted
unreasoned	unwashed
unreceptive	unwavering
unrecognizable	unwed
unrecognized	unworkable
unrecorded	unworkmanlike
unrefined	unyielding

UN, U.N. (yōō′en′) United Nations

un·ac·count·a·ble (un′ə koun′tə b'l) *adj.* **1.** that cannot be explained; strange **2.** not responsible —**un′ac·count′a·bly** *adv.*

un′ac·cus′tomed *adj.* **1.** not accustomed (*to*) **2.** uncommon; strange

un′ad·vised′ (-əd vīzd′) *adj.* **1.** without counsel or advice **2.** indiscreet; hasty

un′af·fect′ed *adj.* **1.** not affected or influenced **2.** without affectation; sincere

un′-A·mer′i·can *adj.* not American; esp., thought of as not conforming to the principles, policies, etc. of the U.S.

u·nan·i·mous (yōō nan′ə məs) *adj.* [< L. *unus*, one + *animus*, mind] agreeing completely; without dissent —**u·na·nim·i·ty** (yōō′nə nim′ə tē) *n.*

un′ap·proach′a·ble *adj.* **1.** not to be approached; inaccessible; aloof **2.** having no equal; unmatched

un·armed′ *adj.* having no weapons

un′as·sum′ing *adj.* not assuming, pretentious, or forward; modest

un′at·tached′ *adj.* **1.** not attached **2.** not engaged or married

un′a·vail′ing *adj.* not availing; useless; futil[

un′a·ware′ *adj.* not aware or conscious —*ad* *same as* UNAWARES

un′a·wares′ (-werz′) *adv.* **1.** without knowin[or being aware **2.** unexpectedly; by surpris[suddenly

un·bal′anced *adj.* **1.** not in balance **2.** n[sane or normal in mind

un·bar′ *vt.* **-barred′, -bar′ring** to unbolt; unlock

un′be·com′ing *adj.* not suited to one's appearance, character, etc.

un′be·lief′ *n.* lack of belief, esp. in religion — **un′be·liev′er** *n.*

un·bend′ *vt.*, *vi.* **-bent′** or **-bend′ed, -bend′ing** **1.** to make or become less tense, less formal, etc. **2.** to make or become straight again

un·bend′ing *adj.* **1.** rigid; stiff **2.** firm; resolute **3.** aloof; austere

un·bid′den *adj.* **1.** not commanded **2.** uninvited

un·bolt′ *vt.*, *vi.* to draw back the bolt or bolts of (a door, etc.); unbar; open

un·born′ *adj.* **1.** not born **2.** still within the mother's womb **3.** yet to come; future

un·bos′om (-booz′əm) *vt.*, *vi.* to tell or reveal (one's feelings, secrets, etc.)

un·bri′dled *adj.* **1.** having no bridle on, as a horse **2.** not controlled; unrestrained

un·bur′den *vt.* **1.** to free from a burden **2.** to relieve (oneself or one's mind) by disclosing (something hard to bear)

un·called′-for′ *adj.* **1.** not required **2.** unnecessary and out of place; impertinent

un·can·ny (un kan′ē) *adj.* **1.** mysterious in an eerie way; weird **2.** so remarkable, acute, etc. as to seem unnatural

un′cer·e·mo′ni·ous 1. not ceremonious; informal **2.** curt; abrupt

un·cer′tain *adj.* **1.** not surely or certainly known **2.** not sure or certain in knowledge; doubtful **3.** vague; not definite **4.** not dependable or reliable —**un·cer′tain·ly** *adv.* —**un·cer′tain·ty** *n.*, *pl.* **-ties**

un·chris′tian *adj.* **1.** not Christian **2.** [Colloq.] outrageous; dreadful

un·cir′cum·cised′ *adj.* **1.** not circumcised; specif., not Jewish; gentile **2.** [Archaic] heathen

un·clasp′ *vt.* **1.** to unfasten the clasp of **2.** to release from a clasp or grasp

un·cle (uŋ′k'l) *n.* [< L. *avunculus*] **1.** the

brother of one's father or mother **2.** the husband of one's aunt

Uncle Sam [< abbrev. *U.S.*] [Colloq.] the U.S. (government or people), personified as a tall man with chin whiskers

un·cloak' *vt., vi.* **1.** to remove a cloak (from) **2.** to reveal; expose

un·clothe' *vt.* **-clothed'** or **-clad'**, **-cloth'ing** to strip of or as of clothes; uncover

un·coil' *vt., vi.* to unwind

un·com'fort·a·ble *adj.* **1.** feeling discomfort **2.** causing discomfort **3.** ill at ease

un·com'mon *adj.* **1.** rare; not common or usual **2.** strange; remarkable

un·com·mu'ni·ca'tive *adj.* not communicative; reserved; silent

un·com'pro·mis'ing *adj.* not yielding; firm; inflexible

un·con·cern' *n.* **1.** lack of interest; indifference **2.** lack of concern or worry

un·con·cerned' *adj.* not solicitous or anxious; not interested

un·con·di'tion·al *adj.* without conditions or stipulations; absolute

un·con·scion·a·ble (un kän'shən ə b'l) *adj.* **1.** not guided or restrained by conscience; unscrupulous **2.** unreasonable

un·con'scious *adj.* **1.** deprived of consciousness **2.** not aware (*of*) **3.** not intended by the person himself [*unconscious* humor] **—the unconscious** *Psychoanalysis* the sum of all memories, thoughts, etc. of which the individual is not conscious but which influence his behavior

un·con·sti·tu'tion·al *adj.* not in accordance with the principles of a constitution

un·cork' *vt.* to pull the cork out of

un·count'ed *adj.* **1.** not counted **2.** too many to be counted; innumerable

un·cou'ple *vt.* **-pled**, **-pling** to unfasten (things coupled); disconnect

un·couth (un kooth') *adj.* [OE. < *un-*, not + *cunnan*, know] **1.** awkward; ungainly **2.** uncultured; crude

un·cov'er *vt.* **1.** to disclose **2.** to remove the cover from **3.** to remove the cap, hat, etc. from (the head) **—vi.** to bare the head, as in respect

unc·tion (uŋk'shən) *n.* [< L. *ungere*, anoint] **1.** the act of anointing, as for medical or religious purposes **2.** the oil, ointment, etc. used for this **3.** anything that soothes or comforts

unc·tu·ous (uŋk'choo wəs) *adj.* [< L. *ungere*, to anoint] **1.** oily or greasy **2.** characterized by a smug, smooth pretense of spiritual feeling or earnestness; too suave

un·cut' *adj.* not cut; specif., *a*) not ground to shape: said of a gem *b*) not abridged

un·daunt'ed *adj.* not daunted; fearless, etc.

un·de·cid'ed *adj.* **1.** not decided **2.** not having come to a decision

un·de·ni'a·ble *adj.* **1.** that cannot be denied **2.** unquestionably good **—un'de·ni'a·bly** *adv.*

un·der (un'dər) *prep.* [OE.] **1.** in, at, or to a position down from; below **2.** beneath the surface of **3.** below and to the other side of [drive *under* the bridge] **4.** covered by [a vest *under* a coat] **5.** lower in authority, position, value, etc. **6.** lower than the required degree of [*under* age] **7.** subject to the control, etc. of **8.** bound by [*under* oath] **9.** undergoing [*under* repair] **10.** with the disguise, etc. of [*under* an alias] **11.** in (the designated category) **12.** during the rule of [France *under* Louis XV] **13.** being the subject of [the question *under* discussion] **14.** because of [*under* the circumstances] **15.** authorized by **—adv. 1.** in or to a lower position; beneath **2.** so as to be cov-

ered or concealed **—adj.** lower in position, authority, amount, etc.

under- *a prefix meaning:* **1.** in, on, to, or from a lower place; beneath [*undershirt*] **2.** in an inferior or subordinate position [*undergraduate*] **3.** too little, not enough, below normal [*underdeveloped*]

un·der·a·chieve' *vi.* **-chieved'**, **-chiev'ing** to fail to do as well in school as might be expected from intelligence tests **—un'der·a·chiev'er** *n.*

un'der·age' *adj.* **1.** not of mature age **2.** below the age required by law

un'der·arm' *adj.* **1.** under the arm; in the armpit **2.** *same as* UNDERHAND (sense 1) **—adv.** *same as* UNDERHAND (sense 1)

un'der·brush' *n.* small trees, shrubs, etc. that grow beneath large trees in woods

un'der·car'riage *n.* a supporting frame or structure, as of an automobile

un'der·charge' *vt., vi.* **-charged'**, **-charg'ing** to charge too low a price (to) **—n.** (un'dər chärj') an insufficient charge

un'der·clothes' *n.pl. same as* UNDERWEAR: also **un'der·cloth'ing** (-klŏth'iŋ)

un'der·coat' *n.* **1.** a tarlike coating applied to the underside of a car, etc. to retard rust, etc. **2.** a coat of paint, etc. applied before the final coat Also **un'der·coat'ing** **—vt.** to apply an undercoat to

un'der·cov'er *adj.* acting or carried out in secret

un'der·cur'rent *n.* **1.** a current flowing beneath the surface **2.** a hidden or underlying opinion, tendency, etc.

un'der·cut' *vt.* **-cut'**, **-cut'ting 1.** to make a cut below or under **2.** to undersell or work for lower wages than

un'der·de·vel'oped *adj.* inadequately developed, esp. industrially

un'der·dog' *n.* one that is underprivileged, unfavored, losing, etc.

un'der·done' *adj.* not cooked enough

un'der·es'ti·mate' *vt., vi.* **-mat'ed**, **-mat'ing** to set too low an estimate on

un'der·foot' *adv., adj.* **1.** under the foot or feet **2.** in the way

un'der·go' *vt.* **-went'**, **-gone'**, **-go'ing** to experience; endure; go through

un'der·grad'u·ate *n.* a college student who does not yet have a degree

un'der·ground' *adj.* **1.** occurring, working, etc. beneath the surface of the earth **2.** secret; undercover **—adv. 1.** beneath the surface of the earth **2.** in or into secrecy or hiding **—n.** (un'dər ground') **1.** the region beneath the surface of the earth **2.** a secret movement organized to oppose the government in power or enemy forces of occupation **3.** [Brit.] a subway

un'der·growth' *n.* underbrush

un'der·hand' *adj.* **1.** done with the hand below the level of the elbow or shoulder **2.** *same as* UNDERHANDED **—adv. 1.** with an underhand motion **2.** slyly; secretly

un'der·hand'ed *adj.* sly, deceitful, etc.

un'der·lie' *vt.* **-lay'**, **-lain'**, **-ly'ing 1.** to lie beneath **2.** to form the foundation of

un'der·line' *vt.* **-lined'**, **-lin'ing 1.** to draw a line beneath **2.** to stress

un·der·ling (un'dər liŋ) *n.* [OE.: see UNDER- & -LING] one in a subordinate position

un'der·ly'ing *adj.* **1.** lying under; placed beneath **2.** fundamental; basic

un'der·mine' *vt.* **-mined'**, **-min'ing 1.** to dig beneath, so as to form a tunnel or mine **2.** to wear away at the foundation **3.** to injure, weaken, etc., esp. in a slow or stealthy way

un·der·most *adj., adv.* lowest in place, position, rank, etc.

un'der·neath' *adv., prep.* under; below

un'der·nour'ish *vt.* to provide with less food than is needed

un'der·pants' *n.pl.* an undergarment of long or short pants

un'der·pass' *n.* a passage under something, as a road under a railway or highway

un'der·pin'ning (-pin'iŋ) *n.* **1.** a support or prop **2.** [*pl.*] [Colloq.] the legs

un'der·play' *vt., vi.* **1.** to act (a role) with restraint **2.** to make seem not too important

un'der·priv'i·leged *adj.* deprived of basic social rights and security through poverty, discrimination, etc.

un'der·rate' *vt.* **-rat'ed, -rat'ing** to rate, assess, or estimate too low

un'der·score' *vt.* **-scored', -scor'ing** *same as* UNDERLINE

un'der·sea' *adj., adv.* beneath the surface of the sea: also **un'der·seas'** *adv.*

un'der·sec're·tar'y *n., pl.* **-ies** an assistant secretary

un'der·sell' *vt.* **-sold', -sell'ing** to sell at a lower price than (another seller)

un'der·shirt' *n.* a usually sleeveless undergarment worn under an outer shirt

un'der·shot' *adj.* **1.** with the lower part jutting out past the upper [an *undershot* jaw] **2.** driven by water flowing along the lower part, as a water wheel

un'der·side' *n.* the side or surface underneath

un'der·sign' *vt.* to sign one's name at the end of (a letter, document, etc.) —**the undersigned** the person or persons undersigning

un'der·skirt' *n.* a skirt worn under another

un'der·stand' *vt.* **-stood', -stand'ing** [OE. *understandan*, stand under] **1.** to get the meaning of **2.** to assume from what is heard, known, etc.; infer **3.** to take as meant; interpret **4.** to take as a fact **5.** to learn **6.** to know the nature, character, etc. of **7.** to be sympathetic with —*vi.* **1.** to have understanding, comprehension, etc. **2.** to be informed; believe —**un'der·stand'a·ble** *adj.*

un'der·stand'ing *n.* **1.** comprehension **2.** the power to think, learn, etc.; intelligence **3.** an explanation or interpretation **4.** an agreement, esp. one that settles differences —*adj.* that understands; sympathetic

un'der·state' *vt.* **-stat'ed, -stat'ing** **1.** to state too weakly **2.** to state in a restrained style —**un'der·state'ment** *n.*

un'der·stud'y *n., pl.* **-ies** an actress or actor prepared to substitute for another —*vt., vi.* **-ied, -y·ing** **1.** to act as an understudy (to) **2.** to learn (a part) as an understudy

un'der·take' *vt.* **-took', -tak'en, -tak'ing** **1.** to take upon oneself (a task, etc.) **2.** to promise; guarantee

un'der·tak'er *n.* earlier term for FUNERAL DIRECTOR

un'der·tak'ing (*also* un'dər tā'kiŋ) *n.* **1.** something undertaken; task; enterprise **2.** a promise; guarantee

un'der-the-count'er *adj.* [Colloq.] done secretly in an unlawful way: also **un'der-the-ta'-ble**

un'der·tone' *n.* **1.** a low tone of voice **2.** a subdued color **3.** any underlying quality, factor, etc.

un'der·tow' (-tō') *n.* a current of water moving beneath the surface water and in a different direction

un'der·wa'ter *adj.* being, done, etc. beneath the surface of the water

un'der·way' *adj.* *Naut.* not at anchor or moored or aground

un'der·wear' *n.* clothing worn under one's outer clothes, usually next to the skin

un'der·weight' *adj.* below the normal weight

un'der·went' *pt. of* UNDERGO

un'der·world' *n.* **1.** Hades; hell **2.** the criminal members of society

un'der·write' *vt.* **-wrote', -writ'ten, -writ'ing** **1.** to agree to market (an issue of securities), guaranteeing to buy any part remaining unsubscribed **2.** to agree to finance (an undertaking, etc.) **3.** to sign one's name to (an insurance policy), thus assuming liability **4.** to insure —**un'der·writ'er** *n.*

un·do' *vt.* **-did', -done', -do'ing** **1.** to untie, open, etc. **2.** to do away with; annul **3.** to ruin or destroy

un·do'ing *n.* **1.** an annulling; reversal **2.** ruin or the cause of ruin

un·done' *adj.* **1.** not done; not performed, accomplished, etc. **2.** ruined

un·doubt'ed *adj.* not doubted or called into question; certain —**un·doubt'ed·ly** *adv.*

un·dress' *vt.* to take off the clothing of —*vi.* to take off one's clothing

un·due' *adj.* **1.** not suitable; improper **2.** too much; excessive

un·du·lant (un'joo lənt) *adj.* undulating

un'du·late' (-lāt') *vi., vt.* **-lat'ed, -lat'ing** [< L. *unda*, a wave] **1.** to move or cause to move in waves **2.** to have or cause to have a wavy form, surface, etc. —**un'du·la'tion** *n.*

un·du·ly (un dōō'lē) *adv.* beyond what is proper or right; excessively

un·dy'ing *adj.* immortal; eternal

un·earth' *vt.* **1.** to dig up from out of the earth **2.** to bring to light; discover or disclose

un·earth'ly *adj.* **1.** supernatural **2.** weird; mysterious **3.** [Colloq.] fantastic, outlandish, etc. —**un·earth'li·ness** *n.*

un·eas'y *adj.* **-i·er, -i·est** **1.** having, showing, or allowing no ease of body or mind; uncomfortable **2.** awkward; constrained **3.** worried; anxious —**un·eas'i·ly** *adv.*

un'em·ployed' *adj.* **1.** not employed; without work **2.** not being used —**un'em·ploy'ment** *n.*

un·e'qual *adj.* **1.** not equal, as in size, strength, ability, value, etc. **2.** not balanced **3.** not even, regular, etc.; variable **4.** not adequate (to) —**un·e'qual·ly** *adv.*

un·e'qualed, un·e'qualled *adj.* not equaled; unmatched; unrivaled; supreme

un'e·quiv'o·cal *adj.* not equivocal; not ambiguous; plain; clear

un·err'ing *adj.* **1.** free from error **2.** not missing or failing; sure; exact

UNESCO (yōō nes'kō) United Nations Educational, Scientific, and Cultural Organization

un·e'ven *adj.* **1.** not even; not level, smooth, etc. **2.** unequal **3.** *Math.* odd —**un·e'ven·ly** *adv.*

un'ex·am'pled *adj.* with nothing like it before; unprecedented

un'ex·pect'ed *adj.* not expected

un·fail'ing *adj.* **1.** not failing **2.** never ceasing or falling short; inexhaustible **3.** always reliable; certain —**un·fail'ing·ly** *adv.*

un·faith'ful *adj.* **1.** failing to stay loyal to or to keep promises, etc. **2.** not true, accurate, etc. **3.** adulterous —**un·faith'ful·ness** *n.*

un'fa·mil'iar *adj.* **1.** not well-known; strange **2.** not acquainted (*with*)

un·feel'ing *adj.* **1.** without feeling **2.** hardhearted; cruel —**un·feel'ing·ly** *adv.*

un·feigned' (-fānd') *adj.* genuine; sincere

un·fin'ished *adj.* **1.** not finished or completed **2.** having no finish, or final coat, as of paint

un·flap'pa·ble (-flap'ə b'l) *adj.* [see FLAP, *n.* 4] [Colloq.] not easily excited or upset; calm

un·flinch'ing *adj.* steadfast; firm

un·fold' *vt.* **1.** to open and spread out (something folded) **2.** to lay open to view —*vi.* **1.** to become unfolded **2.** to develop fully

un·for'tu·nate *adj.* **1.** having or bringing bad luck; unlucky **2.** not suitable —*n.* an unfortunate person

un·found'ed *adj.* **1.** not founded on fact or truth **2.** not established

un·friend'ly *adj.* **1.** not friendly or kind **2.** not favorable —**un·friend'li·ness** *n.*

un·frock' (-fräk') *vt.* to deprive of the rank of priest or minister

un·furl' *vt., vi.* to unfold from a furled state

un·gain·ly (un gān'lē) *adj.* [< ME. < *un-*, not + ON. *gegn*, ready] awkward; clumsy

un·god'ly *adj.* **1.** not godly or religious **2.** [Colloq.] outrageous —**un·god'li·ness** *n.*

un·gov'ern·a·ble *adj.* that cannot be governed or controlled; unruly

un·gra'cious *adj.* **1.** rude; impolite **2.** unpleasant; unattractive

un·guard'ed *adj.* **1.** unprotected **2.** without guile **3.** careless; imprudent

un·guent (uŋ'gwənt) *n.* [< L. *unguere*, anoint] a salve or ointment

un·gu·late (uŋ'gyoo lit, -lāt') *adj.* [< L. *unguis*, a hoof] having hoofs —*n.* a mammal having hoofs

un·hand' *vt.* to loose or release from the hand or hands or one's grasp; let go of

un·hap'py *adj.* **-pi·er, -pi·est** **1.** unfortunate **2.** sad; wretched **3.** not suitable

un·health'y *adj.* **-i·er, -i·est** **1.** sickly; not well **2.** harmful to health **3.** harmful to morals **4.** dangerous

un·heard' *adj.* **1.** not perceived by the ear **2.** not given a hearing

un·heard'-of' *adj.* **1.** not heard of before; unprecedented **2.** outrageous

un·hinge' *vt.* **-hinged', -hing'ing** **1.** to remove from the hinges **2.** to dislodge **3.** to unbalance (the mind)

un·ho'ly *adj.* **-li·er, -li·est** **1.** not sacred, hallowed, etc. **2.** wicked; profane **3.** [Colloq.] outrageous; dreadful

un·horse' *vt.* **-horsed', -hors'ing** to throw (a rider) from a horse

uni- [< L. *unus*, one] *a combining form meaning* having or consisting of one only

u·ni·cam·er·al (yoo'nə kam'ər əl) *adj.* [< UNI- + LL. *camera*, chamber] of or having a single legislative chamber

UNICEF (yoo'nə sef') United Nations International Children's Emergency Fund

u·ni·corn (yoo'nə kôrn') *n.* [< L. *unus*, one + *cornu*, horn] a mythical horselike animal with a single horn in its forehead

u·ni·fi·ca·tion (yoo'nə fi kā'shən) *n.* the act of unifying or the state of being unified

u·ni·form (yoo'nə fôrm') *adj.* [< L. *unus*, one + *-formis*, -FORM] **1.** not varying in form, rate, degree, etc. **2.** like others of the same class —*n.* the distinctive clothes of a particular group, as soldiers —*vt.* to supply with a uniform —**u'ni·form'i·ty** (-fôr'mə tē) *n.*

u·ni·fy (yoo'nə fī') *vt., vi.* **-fied', -fy'ing** [see UNI- & -FY] to become or make united; consolidate —**u'ni·fi'a·ble** *adj.*

u·ni·lat·er·al (yoo'nə lat'ər əl) *adj.* **1.** of, occurring on, or affecting one side only **2.** involving one only of several parties

un·im·peach·a·ble (un'im pēch'ə b'l) *adj.* that cannot be doubted, questioned, or discredited; irreproachable

un·ion (yoon'yən) *n.* [< L. *unus*, one] **1.** a uniting or being united; combination **2.** a grouping together of nations, etc. for some specific purpose **3.** marriage **4.** something united **5.** *short for* LABOR UNION **6.** a design symbolizing political union, used as in a flag **7.** a device for joining together parts

un·ion·ize *vt., vi.* **-ized', -iz'ing** to organize into a labor union

union jack 1. a flag, esp. a national flag, consisting only of a union **2.** [U- J-] the flag of the United Kingdom

u·nique (yoo nēk') *adj.* [Fr. < L. *unicus*, single] **1.** one and only; sole **2.** having no like or equal **3.** very unusual

u·ni·sex (yoo'nə seks') *adj.* [Colloq.] not differentiated for the sexes, as a style of clothing

u·ni·son (yoo'nə sən, -zən) *n.* [< L. *unus*, one + *sonus*, a sound] **1.** identity of musical pitch, as of two or more voices or tones **2.** agreement; concord —**in unison** with all the voices or instruments performing the same part

u·nit (yoo'nit) *n.* [< UNITY] **1.** the smallest whole number; one **2.** a standard basic quantity, measure, etc. **3.** a single person or group, esp. as a part of a whole **4.** a distinct part for a specific purpose

U·ni·tar·i·an (yoo'nə ter'ē ən) *n.* a member of a Christian sect holding that God is one being

u·nite (yoo nīt') *vt., vi.* **-nit'ed, -nit'ing** [< L. *unus*, one] **1.** to put or join together so as to make one; combine **2.** to bring or come together in common cause, etc.

United Nations an international organization for world peace and security: founded 1945

u·ni·ty (yoo'nə tē) *n., pl.* **-ties** [< L. *unus*, one] **1.** the state of being united; oneness **2.** a single, separate thing **3.** harmony; agreement **4.** a complex that is a union of related parts **5.** a harmonious, unified arrangement of parts in an artistic work **6.** constancy or continuity of purpose, action, etc. **7.** *Math.* any quantity, magnitude, etc. identified as a unit, or 1

u·ni·va·lent (yoo'nə vā'lənt) *adj.* *Chem.* **1.** having one valence **2.** having a valence of one

u·ni·ver·sal (yoo'nə vur's'l) *adj.* **1.** of the universe; occurring or present everywhere **2.** of, for, or including all or the whole; unlimited **3.** that can be used for all kinds, sizes, etc. or by all people —**u'ni·ver·sal'i·ty** (-vər sal'ə tē) *n.*

universal joint (or **coupling**) a joint or coupling that permits a swing of limited angle in any direction

u'ni·ver·sal·ly *adv.* **1.** in every instance **2.** in every part or place

u·ni·verse (yoo'nə vurs') *n.* [< L. *unus*, one + *vertere*, to turn] **1.** the totality of all things that exist; the cosmos **2.** the world

u·ni·ver·si·ty (yoo'nə vur'sə tē) *n., pl.* **-ties** [see prec.] an educational institution of the highest level, typically having undergraduate colleges and graduate schools

un·just (un just') *adj.* not just or right; unfair —**un·just'ly** *adv.* —**un·just'ness** *n.*

un·kempt (-kempt') *adj.* [UN- + *kempt* < dial. *kemben*, to comb] **1.** not combed **2.** not tidy or neat; slovenly

un·known' *adj.* **1.** not known; unfamiliar; strange **2.** not discovered, identified, etc. —*n.* an unknown person, thing, or quantity

un·law'ful *adj.* **1.** against the law; illegal **2.** immoral —**un·law'ful·ly** *adv.*

un·lead'ed *adj.* not mixed with tetraethyl lead: said of gasoline

un·learn' *vt., vi.* to forget (something learned) by a conscious effort

un·learn'ed (-lur'nid) *adj.* **1.** not educated; ignorant 2. (-lurnd′) known or acquired without conscious study [*unlearned* tact]

un·leash′ *vt.* to release from or as from a leash

un·less (ən les′) *conj.* [earlier *on lesse that,* at less than] in any case other than; except if

un·let′tered *adj.* 1. uneducated; illiterate 2. not marked with letters

un·like′ *adj.* not alike; different —*prep.* not like; different from —**un·like′ness** *n.*

un·like′ly *adj.* 1. not likely; improbable 2. not likely to succeed —**un·like′li·hood′** *n.*

un·lim·ber (un lim′bər) *vt., vi.* to get ready for use or action

un·lim′it·ed *adj.* 1. without limits or restrictions 2. vast; illimitable

un·load′ *vt., vi.* 1. to remove (a load, cargo, etc.) 2. to take a load from 3. to tell (one's troubles, etc.) without restraint 4. to remove the charge from (a gun) 5. to get rid of

un·lock′ *vt.* 1. to open (a lock) 2. to open the lock of (a door, etc.) 3. to let loose; release 4. to reveal

un·looked′-for′ *adj.* not expected

un·loose′ *vt.* -loosed′, -loos′ing to set loose; loosen, release, etc.: also **un·loos′en**

un·luck′y *adj.* -i·er, -i·est having or bringing bad luck; unfortunate

un·man′ *vt.* -manned′, -man′ning to deprive of manly courage, nerve, etc.

un·manned′ *adj.* without people aboard and operating by automatic or remote control

un·mask′ *vt., vi.* 1. to remove a mask or disguise (from) 2. to show or appear in true character

un·mean′ing *adj.* lacking in meaning

un·men′tion·a·ble *adj.* not fit to be mentioned; not nice to talk about

un·mer′ci·ful *adj.* 1. having or showing no mercy; cruel; pitiless 2. excessive

un·mis·tak′a·ble *adj.* that cannot be mistaken or misinterpreted; clear

un·mit′i·gat′ed *adj.* 1. not lessened or eased 2. out-and-out; absolute

un·mor′al *adj. var. of* AMORAL

un·nat′u·ral *adj.* 1. contrary to nature; abnormal 2. artificial 3. abnormally cruel —**un·nat′u·ral·ly** *adv.*

un·nec′es·sar′y *adj.* not necessary; needless —**un·nec′es·sar′i·ly** *adv.*

un·nerve′ *vt.* -nerved′, -nerv′ing 1. to cause to lose one's courage, etc. 2. to make nervous

un·num′bered *adj.* 1. not counted 2. *same as* INNUMERABLE 3. having no identifying number

un·or′gan·ized′ *adj.* 1. not following any regular order 2. not belonging to a labor union

un·pack′ *vt., vi.* 1. to remove (the contents of a trunk, package, etc.) 2. to take things out of (a trunk, etc.)

un·par′al·leled′ *adj.* that has no parallel, equal, or counterpart

un·pleas′ant *adj.* not pleasant; offensive

un·pop′u·lar *adj.* not liked by the public or the majority —**un′pop·u·lar′i·ty** *n.*

un·prac′ticed *adj.* 1. not habitually or repeatedly done 2. not skilled

un·prec′e·dent′ed *adj.* having no precedent or parallel; unheard-of; novel

un·prin′ci·pled (-p'ld) *adj.* lacking moral principles; unscrupulous

un·print′a·ble *adj.* not fit to be printed, as because of obscenity

un′pro·fes′sion·al *adj.* violating the ethical code of a given profession

un·qual′i·fied′ *adj.* 1. lacking the necessary qualifications 2. not limited; absolute

un·ques′tion·a·ble *adj.* not to be questioned, doubted, or disputed; certain

un′quote′ *interj.* I end the quotation

un·rav′el *vt.* -eled or -elled, -el·ing or -el·ling 1. to separate the threads of (something woven, tangled, etc.) 2. to make clear; solve —*vi.* to become unraveled

un·read′ (-red′) *adj.* 1. not read, as a book 2. having read little or nothing

un·re′al *adj.* not real; imaginary, false, etc.

un·rea′son·a·ble *adj.* 1. not reasonable or rational 2. excessive; immoderate

un·rea′son·ing *adj.* lacking reason or judgment; irrational —**un·rea′son·ing·ly** *adv.*

un′re·gen′er·ate *adj.* 1. not spiritually reborn 2. stubbornly defiant

un′re·lent′ing *adj.* 1. inflexible; relentless 2. without mercy or compassion 3. not relaxing, as in effort, speed, etc.

un′re·mit′ting *adj.* not stopping, relaxing, etc.; incessant; persistent

un′re·served′ *adj.* not reserved; specif., *a)* frank; open *b)* unlimited —**un′re·serv′ed·ly** (-zur′vid lē) *adv.*

un·rest′ *n.* a disturbed state; restlessness; specif., a state of discontent close to revolt

un·ripe′ *adj.* not ripe or mature; green

un·ri′valed, un·ri′valled *adj.* having no rival, equal, or competitor

un·roll′ *vt.* 1. to open or extend (something rolled up) 2. to present to view; display —*vi.* to become unrolled

un·ruf′fled *adj.* not ruffled or disturbed; calm; smooth; serene

un·rul·y (un rōō′lē) *adj.* -i·er, -i·est hard to control, restrain, or keep in order; disobedient, disorderly, etc. —**un·rul′i·ness** *n.*

un·sad′dle *vt.* -dled, -dling to take the saddle off (a horse, etc.)

un·sa′vor·y *adj.* 1. unpleasant to taste or smell 2. morally offensive

un·scathed′ (-skāthd′) *adj.* [< *un-* + ON. *skathi,* harm] not hurt; unharmed

un·scram′ble *vt.* -bled, -bling to cause to be no longer scrambled, disordered, or unintelligible

un·screw′ *vt.* to detach or loosen by removing screws, or by turning

un·scru′pu·lous *adj.* heedless of what is right, just, etc.; unprincipled

un·seal′ *vt.* to break the seal of; open

un·sea′son·a·ble *adj.* 1. not usual for the season 2. coming at the wrong time

un·seat′ *vt.* 1. to throw or dislodge from a seat, saddle, etc. 2. to remove from office

un·seem′ly *adj.* not seemly; not proper; unbecoming —**un·seem′li·ness** *n.*

un·set′tle *vt.* -tled, -tling to make unsettled, insecure, etc. —*vi.* to become unsettled

un·set′tled *adj.* 1. not in order, not stable, etc. 2. not paid, etc., as a debt 3. having no settlers

un·sheathe′ (-shēth′) *vt.* -sheathed′, -sheath′ing to remove (a sword, knife, etc.) from a sheath

un·sight′ly *adj.* not pleasant to look at; ugly

un·skilled′ *adj.* having or requiring no special skill or training

un·skill′ful *adj.* having little or no skill; awkward; clumsy

un·snap′ *vt.* -snapped′, -snap′ping to undo the snaps of, so as to detach

un·snarl′ *vt.* to untangle

un′so·phis′ti·cat′ed *adj.* not sophisticated; artless, simple, etc.

un·sound′ *adj.* not sound; specif., *a)* not normal, safe, or secure *b)* not accurate, sensible, etc.

un·spar'ing *adj.* **1.** not sparing; lavish **2.** not merciful; severe —**un·spar'ing·ly** *adv.*

un·speak'a·ble *adj.* **1.** that cannot be spoken **2.** indescribably bad, evil, etc.

un·sta'ble *adj.* not stable; specif., *a)* easily upset *b)* changeable *c)* unreliable; fickle *d) Chem.* readily decomposing —**un·sta'bly** *adv.*

un·stead'y *adj.* not steady; specif., *a)* not firm or stable *b)* changeable or erratic —**un·stead'i·ly** *adv.* —**un·stead'i·ness** *n.*

un·stop' *vt.* **-stopped'**, **-stop'ping 1.** to remove the stopper from **2.** to clear (an obstructed pipe, etc.)

un·struc'tured *adj.* not formally organized; loose, free, open, etc.

un·strung' *adj.* **1.** nervous, upset, etc. **2.** having the string(s) loosened or detached

un·stud'ied *adj.* **1.** not got by study or conscious effort **2.** spontaneous; natural

un'sub·stan'tial *adj.* **1.** having no material substance **2.** flimsy; light **3.** unreal; visionary

un·sung' *adj.* **1.** not sung **2.** not honored or celebrated, as in song or poetry

un·tan'gle *vt.* **-gled**, **-gling 1.** to free from a snarl or tangle **2.** to put in order

un·taught' *adj.* **1.** not taught or educated **2.** got without being taught; natural

un·think'a·ble *adj.* **1.** inconceivable **2.** not to be considered; impossible

un·think'ing *adj.* thoughtless; heedless

un·ti'dy *adj.* **-di·er, -di·est** not tidy; slovenly; messy

un·tie' *vt.* **-tied'**, **-ty'ing** or **-tie'ing 1.** to loosen or undo (something tied or knotted) **2.** to free, as from restraint —*vi.* to become untied

un·til (un til') *prep.* [ME. *untill*] **1.** up to the time of [*until* payday] **2.** before [not *until* tomorrow] —*conj.* **1.** up to the time when or that [*until* I go] **2.** to the point, degree, etc. that [heat water *until* it boils] **3.** before [don't leave *until* he does]

un·time'ly *adj.* **1.** before the usual time; premature **2.** at the wrong time; inopportune —*adv.* **1.** prematurely **2.** inopportunely

un·to (un'tōō, -too) *prep.* [ME.] *archaic var. of:* **1.** TO **2.** UNTIL

un·told' *adj.* **1.** not told or revealed **2.** too great, numerous, etc. to be counted, described, etc.

un·touch'a·ble *adj.* that cannot or should not be touched —*n.* in India, formerly, a member of the lowest caste

un·to·ward (un tō'ərd, -tôrd') *adj.* **1.** inappropriate, unseemly, etc. **2.** not favorable or fortunate

un·truth' *n.* **1.** falsity **2.** a falsehood; lie —**un·truth'ful** *adj.* —**un·truth'ful·ly** *adv.*

un·tu'tored *adj.* uneducated

un·used' *adj.* **1.** not in use **2.** that has never been used **3.** unaccustomed (*to*)

un·u'su·al *adj.* not usual or common; rare

un·ut'ter·a·ble *adj.* that cannot be expressed or described —**un·ut'ter·a·bly** *adv.*

un·var'nished *adj.* **1.** not varnished **2.** plain; simple; unadorned

un·veil' *vt.* to reveal as by removing a veil from —*vi.* to take off a veil; reveal oneself

un·war'y *adj.* not wary or cautious

un·well' *adj.* not well; ill; sick

un·whole'some *adj.* **1.** harmful to body or mind **2.** unhealthy or unhealthy-looking **3.** morally harmful

un·wield'y *adj.* hard to wield, manage, handle, etc. because of weight, shape, etc.

un·will'ing *adj.* **1.** not willing; reluctant **2.** done, given, etc. against one's will —**un·will'ing·ly** *adv.*

un·wind' *vt.* **-wound'**, **-wind'ing 1.** to wind off or undo (something wound) **2.** to untangle **3.** to relax —*vi.* to become unwound, relaxed, etc.

un·wise' *adj.* not wise; foolish; imprudent

un·wit·ting (un wit'iŋ) *adj.* **1.** not knowing; unaware **2.** unintentional

un·wont'ed (-wun'tid, -wôn'-) *adj.* not common, usual, or habitual

un·wor'thy *adj.* **-thi·er, -thi·est 1.** lacking merit or value; worthless **2.** not deserving (*of*) **3.** not fit or becoming (with *of*) **4.** not deserved —**un·wor'thi·ness** *n.*

un·wrap' *vt.* **-wrapped'**, **-wrap'ping** to take off the wrapping of

un·writ'ten *adj.* **1.** not in writing **2.** operating only through custom or tradition [an *unwritten* law] **3.** not written on; blank

up' (up) *adv.* [OE.] **1.** to, in, or on a higher place or level **2.** in or to a higher condition, amount, etc. **3.** above the horizon **4.** to a later period **5.** *a)* in or into a standing position *b)* out of bed **6.** in or into action, view, consideration, etc. **7.** aside; away [lay *up* grain] **8.** so as to be even with in time, degree, etc. **9.** so as to be tightly closed, bound, etc. [tie it *up*] **10.** completely [eat it *up*] **11.** *Baseball* to one's turn at batting **12.** *Sports*, etc. ahead (by a specified number of points, etc.) The adverb *up* is also used with verbs: *a)* to form combinations having special meanings (Ex.: show *up*) *b)* as an intensive (Ex.: dress *up*) —*prep.* up to, toward, along, through, into, or upon —*adj.* **1.** directed toward a higher position **2.** in a higher place or position **3.** advanced in amount, degree, etc. [rents are *up*] **4.** above the horizon **5.** *a)* in a standing position *b)* out of bed **6.** in an active or excited state **7.** at an end; over [time is *up*] **8.** [Colloq.] going on [what's *up*?] **9.** *Baseball* at bat —*n.* an upward slope, movement, etc. —*vi.* upped, up'ping [Colloq.] to get up; rise —*vt.* [Colloq.] **1.** to put up, lift up, etc. **2.** to raise [to *up* prices] —**on the up and up** [Slang] honest —**up against** [Colloq.] faced with —**up for 1.** presented or considered for (an elective office, sale, etc.) **2.** before a court for (trial) or on (a charge) —**up on** (or **in**) [Colloq.] well-informed about —**ups and downs** good periods and bad periods —**up to** [Colloq.] **1.** doing or scheming **2.** capable of (doing, etc.) **3.** as many as [*up* to four] **4.** as far as [*up* to here] **5.** dependent upon [entirely *up* to her]

up² (up) *adv.* [phonetic respelling of AP(IECE)] apiece; each [the score is seven *up*]

up- *a combining form meaning* up [uphill]

up-and-com·ing (up''n kum'iŋ) *adj.* **1.** enterprising, alert, and promising **2.** gaining in prominence

up'beat' *n. Music* an unaccented beat, esp. when on the last note of a bar —*adj.* cheerful; optimistic

up·braid' (up brād') *vt.* [< OE. *up-*, up + *breg-dan*, to pull] to rebuke severely; censure sharply

up'bring'ing *n.* the training and education received while growing up; rearing; nurture

up'coun'try *adj., adv.* in or toward the interior of a country —*n.* the interior of a country

up·date' *vt.* **-dat'ed**, **-dat'ing** to bring up to date; make current

up·end' *vt., vi.* **1.** to turn or stand on end **2.** to upset or topple

up'grade' *n.* an upward slope —*adj., adv.* uphill —*vt.* (up grād') **-grad'ed**, **-grad'ing** to raise in value, grade, rank, quality, etc.

up·heav·al (up hē'v'l) *n.* **1.** a heaving or lifting up **2.** a sudden, violent change

up·hill' *adj.* **1.** going or sloping up **2.** laborious; tiring —*n.* a sloping rise —*adv.* **1.** upward as on a hillside **2.** with difficulty

up·hold' *vt.* **-held', -hold'ing 1.** to hold up **2.** to keep from falling; support **3.** to confirm; sustain —**up·hold'er** *n.*

up·hol·ster (up hōl'stər) *vt.* [ult. < ME. *upholder*, tradesman] to fit out (furniture, etc.) with covering, padding, springs, etc.

up·hol'ster·y *n., pl.* **-ies 1.** the materials used in upholstering **2.** the work of upholstering

up'keep' *n.* **1.** maintenance **2.** the cost of this **3.** state of repair

up'land (-land) *n.* land elevated above other land —*adj.* of or situated in upland

up·lift' *vt.* **1.** to lift up **2.** to raise to a higher moral, social, or cultural level —*n.* (up'lift') **1.** an uplifting **2.** any influence, movement, etc. aimed at uplifting society

up'most' *adj. same as* UPPERMOST

up·on (ə pän') *prep.* on, or up and on: used interchangeably with *on*

up·per (up'ər) *adj.* **1.** higher in place **2.** higher in rank; superior —*n.* the part of a shoe above the sole —**on one's uppers** [Colloq.] **1.** wearing worn-out shoes **2.** poor

upper case capital-letter type used in printing, as distinguished from small letters (*lower case*) —**up'per-case'** *adj.*

upper class the rich or aristocratic class —**up'-per-class'** *adj.*

up'per·cut' *n. Boxing* a short, swinging blow directed upward

upper hand the position of advantage

up'per·most' *adj.* highest in place, power, etc. —*adv.* in the highest place, rank, etc.

up·pi·ty (up'ə tē) *adj.* [Colloq.] inclined to be arrogant, snobbish, etc.: also **up'pish**

up·raise' *vt.* **-raised', -rais'ing** to raise up

up·rear' *vt.* **1.** to lift up **2.** to erect; build **3.** to exalt **4.** to bring up; rear

up'right' *adj.* **1.** standing or directed straight up; erect **2.** honest and just —*adv.* (also up rīt') in an upright position or direction —*n.* something having an upright position

upright piano a piano with a vertical rectangular body

up'ris'ing *n.* a rising up; specif., a revolt

up·roar (up'rôr') *n.* [Du. *oproer*, a stirring up] **1.** a violent disturbance; tumult **2.** loud, confused noise; din

up·roar'i·ous *adj.* **1.** making, or marked by, an uproar **2.** loud and boisterous, as laughter

up·root' *vt.* **1.** to tear up by the roots **2.** to destroy or remove utterly

up·set' *vt.* **-set', -set'ting 1.** *a)* to tip over; overturn *b)* to defeat unexpectedly **2.** *a)* to disturb the functioning of [to *upset* a schedule] *b)* to disturb emotionally —*vi.* to become overturned or upset —*n.* (up'set') **1.** an upsetting **2.** an unexpected defeat **3.** a disturbance; disorder —*adj.* **1.** tipped over; overturned **2.** overthrown or defeated **3.** disturbed or disordered

up'shot' *n.* [orig., final shot in an archery match] the conclusion; result; outcome

upside down 1. with the top part underneath **2.** in disorder —**up'side-down'** *adj.*

up·si·lon (yōōp'sə län') *n.* the twentieth letter of the Greek alphabet (Υ, υ)

up'stage' *adv., adj.* toward or at the rear of a stage —*vt.* **-staged', -stag'ing** to draw attention away from (another), as by moving upstage

up'stairs' *adv.* **1.** up the stairs **2.** on or to an upper floor —*adj.* on an upper floor —*n.* an upper floor

up·stand'ing *adj.* **1.** erect **2.** upright in character and behavior; honorable

up'start' *n.* one who has recently come into wealth, power, etc., esp. one who is aggressive, presumptuous, etc.

up'state' *adj., adv.* in, to, or from the northerly part of a state

up'stream' *adv., adj.* in the direction against the current of a stream

up'swing' *n.* a swing or trend upward

up'take' *n.* a taking up —**quick** (or **slow**) **on the uptake** [Colloq.] quick (or slow) to understand or comprehend

up'-tight', up'tight' *adj.* [Slang] very tense, nervous, etc.

up'-to-date' *adj.* **1.** extending to the present time **2.** keeping up with what is most recent, modern, etc.

up'town' *adj., adv.* of, in, or toward the upper part of a city or town

up·turn' *vt., vi.* to turn up or over —*n.* (up'turn') an upward turn, curve, or trend

up'ward (-wərd) *adv., adj.* toward a higher place, position, etc.: also **up'wards** *adv.* — **upwards** (or **upward**) **of** more than

u·ra·ni·um (yōō rā'nē əm) *n.* [< G. < URANUS] a very hard, heavy, radioactive metallic chemical element: used in work on atomic energy: symbol, U

U·ra·nus (yoor'ə nəs, yōō rā'nəs) [< Gr. *Ouranos*, heaven] a planet of the solar system: see PLANET

ur·ban (ur'bən) *adj.* [< L. *urbs*, a city] **1.** of, in, or constituting a city **2.** characteristic of cities

ur·bane (ur bān') *adj.* [see prec.] polite and courteous in a smooth, polished way; refined —**ur·ban'i·ty** (-ban'ə tē) *n.*

ur·ban·ize (ur'bə nīz') *vt.* **-ized', -iz'ing** to change from rural to urban —**ur'ban·i·za'tion** *n.*

ur·chin (ur'chin) *n.* [< L. *ericius*, a hedgehog] a small child; esp., a mischievous boy

-ure [Fr. < L. *-ura*] a suffix meaning: **1.** act or result of being [*exposure*] **2.** agent of [*legislature*] **3.** state of being [*composure*]

u·re·a (yōō rē'ə) *n.* [< Fr. < Gr. *ouron*, urine] a soluble, crystalline solid found in urine or produced synthetically

u·re·mi·a (yōō rē'mē ə, -rēm'yə) *n.* [< Gr. *ouron*, urine + *haima*, blood] a toxic condition caused by the presence in the blood of waste products normally eliminated in the urine —**u·re'mic** *adj.*

u·re·ter (yōō rēt'ər) *n.* [< Gr. *ourein*, urinate] a tube carrying urine from a kidney to the bladder

u·re·thra (yōō rē'thrə) *n., pl.* **-thrae** (-thrē), **-thras** [< Gr. *ouron*, urine] the canal through which urine is discharged from the bladder: in the male, also the duct for semen —**u·re'thral** *adj.*

urge (urj) *vt.* **urged, urg'ing** [L. *urgere*, press hard] **1.** *a)* to press upon the attention; advocate *b)* to plead with; ask earnestly **2.** to incite; provoke **3.** to drive or force onward —*n.* **1.** an urging **2.** an impulse

ur·gent (ur'jənt) *adj.* [see prec.] **1.** calling for haste, immediate action, etc. **2.** insistent —**ur'-gen·cy** *n., pl.* **-cies**

-urgy [< Gr. *ergon*, work] *a combining form meaning* a working with or by means of

u·ric (yoor'ik) *adj.* of, in, or from urine

u·ri·nal (yoor'ə n'l) *n.* **1.** a receptacle for urine **2.** a place for urinating

u·ri·nal·y·sis (yoor'ə nal'ə sis) *n.* chemical or microscopic analysis of the urine

u·ri·nar·y (yoor'ə ner'ē) *adj.* **1.** of urine **2.** of the organs that secrete and discharge urine

u·ri·nate (yoor'ə nāt') *vi.* **-nat'ed, -nat'ing** to

discharge urine from the body —**u′ri·na′tion** *n.*

u·rine (yoor′in) *n.* [< L. *urina*] in mammals, the yellowish fluid containing waste products, secreted by the kidneys and discharged through the urethra

urn (urn) *n.* [L. *urna*] **1.** *a)* a vase with a pedestal *b)* such a vase for the ashes of a cremated body **2.** a metal container with a faucet, for making or serving coffee, etc.

ur·ti·car·i·a (ur′tə ker′ē ə) *n.* [< L. *urtica*, a nettle] *same as* HIVES

us (us) *pron.* [OE.] *objective case of* WE

U.S., US United States

USA, U.S.A. 1. United States of America **2.** United States Army

us·a·ble, use·a·ble (yōō′zə b'l) *adj.* that can be used; fit for use

USAF, U.S.A.F. United States Air Force

us·age (yōō′sij, -zij) *n.* **1.** the act, way, or extent of using; treatment **2.** established practice; custom **3.** the way a word, phrase, etc. is used to express a particular idea

USCG, U.S.C.G. United States Coast Guard

use (yōōz; *for n.* yōōs) *vt.* **used, us′ing** [< L. *uti*] **1.** to put into action or service **2.** to exercise *[use* your judgment] **3.** to behave toward; treat **4.** to consume, expend, etc. *[to use* up energy] **5.** to accustom *[used* to the cold] —*vi.* to be accustomed (meaning "did at one time") *[he used* to play golf] —*n.* **1.** a using or being used **2.** the ability to use **3.** the right to use **4.** the need or opportunity to use **5.** way of using **6.** usefulness; utility **7.** the purpose for which something is used **8.** function or service —**us′er** *n.*

used (yōōzd) *adj.* not new; secondhand

use·ful (yōōs′fəl) *adj.* that can be used; serviceable; helpful —**use′ful·ly** *adv.*

use′less *adj.* **1.** worthless **2.** to no purpose

ush·er (ush′ər) *n.* [< L. *ostium*, door] **1.** an official doorkeeper **2.** one who shows people to their seats in a church, theater, etc. **3.** a bridegroom's attendant —*vt.* **1.** to escort (others) to seats, etc. **2.** to herald or bring (in) —*vi.* to act as an usher

USMC, U.S.M.C. United States Marine Corps

USN, U.S.N. United States Navy

U.S.S.R., USSR Union of Soviet Socialist Republics

u·su·al (yōō′zhōō wəl) *adj.* [see USE] such as is most often seen, heard, used, etc.; common; ordinary; customary —**u′su·al·ly** *adv.*

u·surp (yōō surp′, -zurp′) *vt., vi.* [< L. *usus,* use + *rapere,* to seize] to take and hold (power, position, rights, etc.) by force or without right —**u·sur·pa·tion** (yōō′sər pā′shən, -zər-) *n.* —**u·surp′er** *n.*

u·su·ry (yōō′zhōō rē) *n., pl.* **-ries** [see USE] **1.** the lending of money at an excessive rate of interest **2.** interest at such a rate —**u′su·rer** *n.* —**u·su·ri·ous** (yōō zhoor′ē əs) *adj.*

u·ten·sil (yōō ten′s'l) *n.* [< L. *uti,* to use] an implement or container, now esp. one used in a kitchen *[cooking utensils]*

u·ter·us (yōōt′ər əs) *n., pl.* **u′ter·i′** (-ī′) [L.] a hollow organ of female mammals in which the embryo and fetus are developed; womb —**u′ter·ine** (-in, yōō′tə rīn′) *adj.*

u·til·i·tar·i·an (yōō til′ə ter′ē ən) *adj.* **1.** of or having utility; useful **2.** stressing usefulness over beauty, etc.

u·til·i·ty (yōō til′ə tē) *n., pl.* **-ties** [< L. *uti,* to use] **1.** usefulness **2.** something useful, as the service to the public of gas, water, etc. **3.** a company providing such a service

u·ti·lize (yōōt′'l īz′) *vt.* **-lized′, -liz′ing** make use of —**u′ti·li·za′tion** *n.*

ut·most (ut′mōst′) *adj.* [< OE. superl. of *ut,* out] **1.** most extreme or distant; farthest **2.** of the greatest degree, amount, etc.; greatest —*n.* the most that is possible

U·to·pi·a (yōō tō′pē ə) [< Gr. *ou,* not + *topos,* a place] an imaginary island in T. More's *Utopia* (1516), with a perfect political and social system —*n.* [*often* u-] **1.** any idealized place of perfection **2.** any visionary scheme for an ideally perfect society —**U·to′pi·an, u·to′pi·an** *adj., n.*

ut·ter[1] (ut′ər) *adj.* [< OE. compar. of *ut,* out] **1.** complete; total **2.** unqualified; absolute

ut·ter[2] (ut′ər) *vt.* [< ME. *ut,* out] **1.** to speak or express audibly (words, sounds, etc.) **2.** to express in any way **3.** to reveal

ut′ter·ance *n.* **1.** the act, power, or way of uttering **2.** something uttered or said

ut′ter·most′ (-mōst′) *adj., n.* utmost

u·vu·la (yōō′vyə lə) *n., pl.* **-las, -lae′** (-lē′) [< L. *uva,* a grape] the small, fleshy part of the soft palate hanging down above the back of the tongue —**u′vu·lar** *adj.*

V

V, v (vē) *n., pl.* **V's, v's** the twenty-second letter of the English alphabet

V (vē) *n.* **1.** a Roman numeral for 5 **2.** *Chem.* vanadium

V, v 1. velocity **2.** volt(s)

v. 1. verb **2.** versus **3.** voltage **4.** volume

VA, V.A. Veterans Administration

va·can·cy (vā′kən sē) *n., pl.* **-cies 1.** a being vacant **2.** empty or vacant space **3.** an unoccupied position or office **4.** quarters available for rent

va·cant (vā′kənt) *adj.* [< L. *vacare,* be empty] **1.** empty **2.** not held, filled, or occupied, as a position, seat, house, etc. **3.** free from work **4.** without thought, interest, etc. *[a vacant* mind] —**va′cant·ly** *adv.*

va′cate (-kāt) *vt., vi.* **-cat·ed, -cat·ing** [see prec.] **1.** to make (an office, house, etc.) vacant **2.** to make void; annul

va·ca·tion (və kā′shən, vā-) *n.* [< L. *vacatio*] a period of rest from work, study, etc. —*vi.* to take one's vacation

vac·ci·nate (vak′sə nāt′) *vt., vi.* **-nat′ed, -nat′-ing** to inoculate with a vaccine in order to prevent a disease, specif. smallpox —**vac′ci·na′tion** *n.*

vac·cine (vak sēn′) *n.* [< L. *vacca,* a cow: from use of cowpox virus in smallpox vaccine] any preparation of killed microorganisms, living weakened organisms, etc. used to produce immunity to a specific disease

vac·il·late (vas′ə lāt′) *vi.* **-lat·ed, -lat·ing** [< L. *vacillare*] **1.** to sway to and fro; waver **2.** to fluctuate **3.** to show indecision —**vac′il·la′tion** *n.*

va·cu·i·ty (və kyōō′ə tē) *n., pl.* **-ties** [< L. *vacuus,* empty] **1.** emptiness **2.** an empty space; void **3.** lack of intelligence, thought, etc. **4.** inanity

vac·u·ous (vak′yoo wəs) *adj.* [L. *vacuus*] **1.** empty **2.** stupid; senseless

vac·u·um (vak′yoo wəm, vak′yoōm) *n., pl.* **-ums, -a** (-wə) [L.] **1.** a space with nothing at all in it **2.** a space from which most of the air or gas has been taken **3.** a void —*adj.* **1.** of or used to make a vacuum **2.** having or working by a vacuum —*vt., vi.* to clean with a vacuum cleaner

vacuum cleaner a machine for cleaning carpets, floors, upholstery, etc. by suction

vac′u·um-packed′ *adj.* packed in an airtight container to maintain freshness

vacuum tube an electron tube from which the air has been evacuated to the highest possible degree

vag·a·bond (vag′ə bänd′) *adj.* [< L. *vagari*, to wander] **1.** wandering **2.** vagrant; shiftless —*n.* **1.** one who wanders from place to place **2.** a tramp —**vag′a·bond′age** *n.*

va·gar·y (və ger′ē, vā′gər ē) *n., pl.* **-ies** [see prec.] **1.** an odd or eccentric action **2.** an odd, whimsical, or freakish idea

va·gi·na (və jī′nə) *n., pl.* **-nas, -nae** (-nē) [L., a sheath] in female mammals, the canal between the vulva and the uterus —**vag·i·nal** (vaj′ə n'l) *adj.*

va·grant (vā′grənt) *n.* [prob. < OFr. *walcrer*, to wander] one who wanders from place to place; esp., one without a regular job, supporting himself by begging, etc.; tramp —*adj.* **1.** wandering; nomadic **2.** of or like a vagrant **3.** random, wayward, etc. —**va′gran·cy** *n., pl.* **-cies**

vague (vāg) *adj.* [Fr. < L. *vagus*, wandering] **1.** indefinite in shape or form **2.** not sharp, certain, etc. in thought or expression

vain (vān) *adj.* [< L. *vanus*, empty] **1.** having no real value; worthless [*vain* pomp] **2.** without effect; futile [a *vain* attempt] **3.** having an excessively high regard for one's self, looks, etc.; conceited —**in vain 1.** unsuccessfully **2.** profanely

vain′glo′ry (-glôr′ē) *n.* [see VAIN & GLORY] excessive vanity —**vain′glo′ri·ous** *adj.*

val·ance (val′əns, vāl′-) *n.* [< ?] a short drapery or facing of wood, etc. across the top of a window

vale (vāl) *n. poet. var. of* VALLEY

val·e·dic·to·ri·an (val′ə dik tôr′ē ən) *n.* the student who delivers the valedictory at graduation

val′e·dic′to·ry (-tər ē) *n., pl.* **-ries** [< L. *vale*, farewell + *dicere*, to say] a farewell speech, esp. at graduation

va·lence (vā′ləns) *n.* [< L. *valere*, be strong] *Chem.* the combining capacity of an element or radical, as measured by the number of hydrogen or chlorine atoms which one radical or atom of the element will combine with or replace: also **va′len·cy**

val·en·tine (val′ən tīn′) *n.* **1.** a sweetheart chosen or complimented on Saint Valentine's Day **2.** a greeting card or gift sent on this day

val·et (val′it, -ā) *n.* [Fr.] **1.** a personal manservant who takes care of a man's clothes, helps him dress, etc. **2.** a hotel employee who cleans or presses clothes, etc.

Val·hal·la (val hal′ə) *Norse Myth.* the great hall where Odin receives and feasts the souls of heroes slain in battle

val·iant (val′yənt) *adj.* [< L. *valere*, be strong] courageous; brave —**val′iance, val′ian·cy** *n.* —**val′iant·ly** *adv.*

val·id (val′id) *adj.* [< L. *valere*, be strong] **1.** having legal force **2.** well-grounded on principles or evidence, as an argument

val·i·date (val′ə dāt′) *vt.* **-dat′ed, -dat′ing 1.** to

declare legally valid **2.** to prove to be valid —**val′i·da′tion** *n.*

va·lid·i·ty (və lid′ə tē) *n., pl.* **-ties** the state, quality, or fact of being valid in law, argument, etc.

va·lise (və lēs′) *n.* [Fr. < It. *valigia*] a piece of hand luggage

Val·kyr·ie (val kir′ē, val′ki rē) *n. Norse Myth.* any of the maidens of Odin who conduct the souls of heroes slain in battle to Valhalla

val·ley (val′ē) *n., pl.* **-leys** [< L. *vallis*] **1.** low land lying between hills or mountains **2.** the land drained by a river system

val·or (val′ər) *n.* [< L. *valere*, be strong] great courage or bravery: Brit. sp. **val′our** —**val′or·ous** *adj.*

val·u·a·ble (val′yoo b'l, -yoo wə b'l) *adj.* **1.** *a)* being worth money *b)* having great monetary value **2.** highly regarded as precious, useful, etc. —*n.* an article of value: *usually used in pl.*

val·u·a·tion (val′yoo wā′shən) *n.* **1.** the determining of the value of anything **2.** determined or estimated value

val·ue (val′yoō) *n.* [< L. *valere*, be worth] **1.** the worth of a thing in money or goods **2.** estimated worth **3.** purchasing power **4.** that quality of a thing that makes it more or less desirable, useful, etc. **5.** [*pl.*] social principles, standards, etc. **6.** relative duration, intensity, etc. —*vt.* **-ued, -u·ing 1.** to estimate the value of; appraise **2.** to place an estimate of worth on [to *value* health above wealth] **3.** to think highly of; prize —**val′ue·less** *adj.*

val′ued *adj.* highly thought of; esteemed

valve (valv) *n.* [L. *valva*, leaf of a folding door] **1.** *Anat.* a membranous structure which permits body fluids to flow in one direction only, or opens and closes a tube, etc. **2.** any device in a pipe, etc. that regulates the flow by means of a flap, lid, etc. **3.** *Music* a device, as in the trumpet, that changes the tube length so as to change the pitch **4.** *Zool.* one of the parts making up the shell of a mollusk, clam, etc.

va·moose (va moōs′) *vi., vt.* **-moosed′, -moos′-ing** [Sp. *vamos*, let us go] [Old Slang] to leave quickly

vamp (vamp) *n.* [< OFr. *avant*, before + *pié*, a foot] **1.** the part of a boot or shoe covering the instep **2.** *Music* a simple, improvised introduction or interlude —*vt.* **1.** to put a vamp on **2.** *Music* to improvise

vam·pire (vam′pīr) *n.* [Fr. < G. < Slav.] **1.** *Folklore* a corpse that comes alive at night and sucks the blood of sleeping persons **2.** one who preys ruthlessly on others **3.** *short for* VAMPIRE BAT

vampire bat a tropical American bat that lives on the blood of animals

van¹ (van) *n.* the vanguard

van² (van) *n.* [< CARAVAN] a closed truck or wagon for carrying furniture, people, etc.

va·na·di·um (və nā′dē əm) *n.* [< ON. *Vanadis*, goddess of love] a rare, ductile metallic chemical element used in steel alloys: symbol, V

Van·dal (van′d'l) *n.* **1.** a member of a Germanic tribe that sacked Rome (455 A.D.) **2.** [v-] one who purposely destroys works of art, public property, etc. —**van′dal·ism** *n.*

van′dal·ize′ (-īz′) *vt.* **-ized′, -iz′ing** to destroy or damage (property) on purpose

Van·dyke (van dīk′) *n.* a closely trimmed, pointed beard: also **Vandyke beard**

vane (vān) *n.* [OE. *fana*, a flag] **1.** *same as* WEATHER VANE **2.** any of the flat blades set around an axle, usually forming a wheel to be rotated by, or to rotate, air, water, etc. [the *vanes* of a windmill]

van·guard (van′gärd′) *n.* [< OFr. *avant,* before + *garde,* guard] **1.** the front part of an army in an advance; the van **2.** the leading position or persons in a movement

va·nil·la (və nil′ə) *n.* [< Sp. *vaina,* pod] **1.** a climbing tropical American orchid with pod-like capsules (**vanilla beans**) **2.** a flavoring made from these capsules

van·ish (van′ish) *vi.* [see EVANESCENT] **1.** to go or pass suddenly from sight **2.** to cease to exist; come to an end

van·i·ty (van′ə tē) *n., pl.* **-ties** [< L. *vanus,* vain] **1.** anything vain or futile **2.** worthlessness; futility **3.** a being vain, or excessively proud of oneself **4.** a small table with a mirror, for use while putting on cosmetics **5.** a cabinet in a bathroom with a washbowl set in the top

vanity case a woman's small traveling case for carrying cosmetics, etc.

van·quish (vaŋ′kwish, van′-) *vt.* [< L. *vincere*] to conquer or defeat

van·tage (van′tij) *n.* [see ADVANTAGE] **1.** a more advantageous position **2.** a position that allows a clear and broad view: also **vantage point**

vap·id (vap′id) *adj.* [L. *vapidus*] tasteless; flavorless; dull —**va·pid·i·ty** (va pid′ə tē), *pl.* **-ties, vap′id·ness** *n.* —**vap′id·ly** *adv.*

va·por (vā′pər) *n.* [L.] **1.** *a)* visible particles of moisture floating in the air, as fog or steam *b)* smoke, fumes, etc. **2.** the gaseous form of any substance usually a liquid or solid —*vi.* to pass off as vapor; evaporate Brit. sp. **vapour**

va′por·ize′ (-pə rīz′) *vt., vi.* **-ized′, -iz′ing** to change into vapor —**va′por·i·za′tion** *n.* —**va′·por·iz′er** *n.*

va′por·ous *adj.* **1.** forming, full of, or like vapor **2.** fleeting, fanciful, etc.

va·que·ro (vä ker′ō) *n., pl.* **-ros** [Sp. < L. *vacca,* a cow] in the Southwest, a cowboy

var. 1. variant(s) **2.** various

var·i·a·ble (ver′ē ə b′l) *adj.* **1.** apt to change or vary; changeable, inconstant, etc. **2.** that can be changed or varied —*n.* anything changeable; thing that varies —**var′i·a·bil′i·ty** *n.* —**var′i·a·bly** *adv.*

var·i·ance (ver′ē əns) *n.* **1.** a varying or being variant **2.** degree of change or difference —**at variance** disagreeing

var′i·ant (-ənt) *adj.* varying; different in some way from others of the same kind —*n.* anything variant, as a different spelling of the same word

var·i·a·tion (ver′ē ā′shən) *n.* **1.** *a)* a varying; change in form, extent, etc. *b)* the degree of such change **2.** a thing somewhat different from another of the same kind **3.** *Music* the repetition of a theme with changes in harmony, rhythm, key, etc.

var·i·col·ored (ver′i kul′ərd) *adj.* of several or many colors

var·i·cose (var′ə kōs′) *adj.* [< L. *varix,* enlarged vein] abnormally and irregularly swollen [*varicose* veins]

var·ied (ver′ēd) *adj.* **1.** of different kinds; various **2.** changed; altered

var·i·e·gate (ver′ē ə gāt′) *vt.* **-gat′ed, -gat′ing** [< L. *varius,* various] **1.** to make varied in appearance by differences, as in colors **2.** to give variety to

va·ri·e·ty (və rī′ə tē) *n., pl.* **-ties 1.** a being various or varied **2.** any of the various forms of something; sort [*varieties* of cloth] **3.** a number of different kinds

var·i·ous (ver′ē əs) *adj.* [L. *varius,* diverse] **1.**

differing one from another; of several kinds **2.** several or many

var·let (vär′lit) *n.* [OFr., a page] [Archaic] a scoundrel; knave

var·mint, var·ment (vär′mənt) *n.* [dial. var. of VERMIN] [Dial. or Colloq.] a person or animal regarded as objectionable

var·nish (vär′nish) *n.* [< ML. *veronix,* resin] **1.** a preparation of resinous substances dissolved in oil, alcohol, etc., used to give a hard, glossy surface to wood, etc. **2.** this hard, glossy surface **3.** a surface gloss, as of manner —*vt.* to cover with varnish

var·si·ty (vär′sə tē) *n., pl.* **-ties** [< UNIVERSITY] the main team of a university, school, etc., as in an athletic competition

var·y (ver′ē) *vt.* **-ied, -y·ing** [< L. *varius,* various] **1.** to change; alter **2.** to make different from one another **3.** to give variety to —*vi.* **1.** to differ or change **2.** to deviate or depart (*from*)

vas·cu·lar (vas′kyə lər) *adj.* [< L. *vas,* vessel] of or having vessels or special cells for carrying blood, sap, etc.

vase (vās, vāz) *n.* [< L. *vas,* vessel] an open container used for decoration, etc.

vas·ec·to·my (vas ek′tə mē) *n., pl.* **-mies** [< L. *vas,* vessel + -ECTOMY] surgical removal of all, or esp. part, of the ducts carrying sperm from the testicles

Vas·e·line (vas′ə lēn′) [< G. *was(ser),* water + Gr. *el(aion),* oil] *a trademark for* PETROLATUM —*n.* [v-] petrolatum

vas·o·mo·tor (vas′ō mōt′ər) *adj.* [< L. *vas,* vessel + MOTOR] regulating the diameter of blood vessels by causing contraction or dilation, as certain nerves

vas·sal (vas′l) *n.* [< ML. *vassus,* servant] **1.** a person in the feudal system who held land in return for fealty, military help, etc. to an overlord **2.** a subordinate, servant, slave, etc. —**vas′sal·age** (-ij) *n.*

vast (vast) *adj.* [L. *vastus*] very great in size, amount, degree, etc. —**vast′ness** *n.*

vat (vat) *n.* [< OE. *fæt,* cask] a large tank, tub, or cask for liquids

Vat·i·can (vat′i k'n) **1.** the papal palace in Vatican City **2.** the papal government

vaude·ville (vōd′vil, vôd′-) *n.* [Fr. < *Vau-de-Vire,* a valley in Normandy, famous for convivial songs] a stage show consisting of various specialty acts, including songs, dances, comic skits, etc.

vault¹ (vôlt) *n.* [< L. *volvere,* to roll] **1.** an arched roof or ceiling **2.** an arched chamber or space **3.** a cellar room used for storage **4.** a burial chamber **5.** a room for the safekeeping of valuables, as in a bank —*vt.* to cover with, or build as, a vault

vault² (vôlt) *vi.* [< OIt. *voltare*] to leap as over a barrier, esp. putting the hands on the barrier or using a long pole —*vt.* to vault over —*n.* a vaulting

vaunt (vônt, vänt) *vi., vt., n.* [< L. *vanus,* vain] boast or brag —**vaunt′ed** *adj.*

VD, V.D. venereal disease

veal (vēl) *n.* [< OFr. < L. *vitulus,* a calf] the flesh of a young calf, used as food

veer (vir) *vi., vt.* [< Fr. *virer,* to turn around] to change in direction; shift; turn —*n.* a change of direction —**veer′ing·ly** *adv.*

veg·e·ta·ble (vej′tə b'l, vej′ə tə-) *adj.* [see VEGETATE] **1.** of plants in general **2.** of, like, or from vegetables —*n.* **1.** any plant, as distinguished from something animal or inorganic **2.** a plant eaten whole or in part, as with an entree or in a salad, as the tomato, potato, lettuce, etc.

veg·e·tar·i·an (-ter′ē ən) *n.* one who eats no meat —*adj.* **1.** of vegetarians **2.** consisting only of vegetables, fruits, etc.

veg·e·tate (vej′ə tāt′) *vi.* -tat′ed, -tat′ing [< L. *vegere*, to quicken] **1.** to grow as plants **2.** to lead a dull, inactive life

veg·e·ta′tion *n.* **1.** a vegetating **2.** plant life in general

ve·he·ment (vē′ə mənt) *adj.* [< L. *vehere*, to carry] **1.** violent; impetuous **2.** full of or showing very strong feeling —**ve′he·mence, ve′he·men·cy** *n.*

ve·hi·cle (vē′ə k′l) *n.* [< L. *vehere*, to carry] **1.** a means of carrying persons or things, as an automobile **2.** a means of expressing ideas — **ve·hic′u·lar** (-hik′yoo lər) *adj.*

veil (vāl) *n.* [< L. *velum*, cloth] **1.** a piece of light fabric, as net, worn, esp. by women, over the face or head **2.** anything used to conceal, separate, etc. [a *veil* of silence] **3.** a part of a nun's headdress —*vt.* to cover, conceal, etc. with or as with a veil —**take the veil** to become a nun

vein (vān) *n.* [< L. *vena*] **1.** any blood vessel carrying blood to the heart **2.** any of the ribs in an insect wing or in a leaf **3.** a layer of mineral in a fissure of rock; lode **4.** a streak of a different color, etc., as in marble **5.** a distinctive quality **6.** a mood —*vt.* to mark as with veins

veld, veldt (velt) *n.* [Afrik. < MDu. *veld*, a field] in S. Africa, open grassy country

vel·lum (vel′əm) *n.* [< L. *vitulus*, calf] **1.** a fine parchment used for writing on or for binding books **2.** a paper like vellum

ve·loc·i·ty (və läs′ə tē) *n., pl.* -ties [< Fr. < L. *velox*, swift] **1.** quickness of motion; speed **2.** rate of motion in relation to time

ve·lour, ve·lours (və loor′) *n., pl.* -lours′ [Fr.: see VELURE] a fabric with a soft nap like velvet, used for upholstery, etc.

ve·lum (vē′ləm) *n., pl.* -la (-lə) [L., a veil] same as SOFT PALATE

ve·lure (və loor′) *n.* [< Fr. < L. *villus*, shaggy hair] velvet or velvetlike fabric

vel·vet (vel′vit) *n.* [< L. *villus*, shaggy hair] **1.** a rich fabric of silk, rayon, etc. with a soft, thick pile **2.** anything with a surface like velvet —*adj.* **1.** made of velvet **2.** like velvet — **vel′vet·y** *adj.*

vel·vet·een (vel′və tēn′) *n.* a velvetlike cotton cloth

ve·nal (vē′n′l) *adj.* [< L. *venum*, sale] open to, or characterized by, corruption or bribery —**ve·nal′i·ty** (-nal′ə tē) *n., pl.* -ties

vend (vend) *vt., vi.* [< Fr. < L. *venum dare*, offer for sale] to sell, esp. by peddling —**ven′·dor, vend′er** *n.*

ven·det·ta (ven det′ə) *n.* [It. < L. *vindicta*, vengeance] a family feud

vending machine a coin-operated machine for selling certain articles, etc.

ve·neer (və nir′) *vt.* [< Fr. *fournir*, furnish] to cover with a thin layer of finer material; esp., to cover (wood) with wood of a finer quality — *n.* **1.** a thin layer used to veneer something **2.** a surface appearance that hides what is below

ven·er·a·ble (ven′ər ə b'l) *adj.* worthy of respect or reverence because of age, dignity, etc. —**ven′er·a·bil′i·ty** *n.*

ven·er·ate (ven′ə rāt′) *vt.* -at′ed, -at′ing [< L. *venerari*, to worship] to feel deep respect for — **ven′er·a′tion** *n.*

ve·ne·re·al (və nir′ē əl) *adj.* [< L. *venus*, love] **1.** of sexual intercourse **2.** transmitted by sexual intercourse, as syphilis

Ve·ne·tian (və nē′shən) *adj.* of Venice, its people, etc. —*n.* a native of Venice

Venetian blind [*also* **v- b-**] a window blind made of a number of thin, horizontal slats that can be set at any angle

venge·ance (ven′jəns) *n.* [see VINDICATE] the return of an injury for an injury, in punishment; revenge —**with a vengeance 1.** with great force or fury **2.** excessively

venge·ful (venj′fəl) *adj.* seeking revenge; vindictive —**venge′ful·ness** *n.*

ve·ni·al (vē′nē əl, vēn′yəl) *adj.* [< L. *venia*, grace] that can be forgiven or excused

ve·ni·re·man (və nī′rē mən) *n., pl.* -men [< ML. *venire facias*, cause to come] one of a group of people from among whom a jury will be selected

ven·i·son (ven′i s'n, -z'n) *n.* [< L. *venari*, to hunt] the flesh of deer, used as food

ven·om (ven′əm) *n.* [< L. *venenum*, a poison] **1.** the poison secreted by some snakes, spiders, etc. **2.** spite; malice

ven′om·ous *adj.* **1.** full of venom; poisonous **2.** spiteful; malicious

ve·nous (vē′nəs) *adj.* **1.** of or having veins **2.** designating blood carried in veins

vent¹ (vent) *n.* [< L. *ventus*, a wind] **1.** a means of escaping; outlet **2.** expression; release [giving *vent* to emotion] **3.** a small opening to let gas, etc. out —*vt.* **1.** to make a vent in **2.** to let out

vent² (vent) *n.* [< L. *findere*, to split] a vertical slit in a garment

ven·ti·late (ven′t'l āt′) *vt.* -lat′ed, -lat′ing [< L. *ventus*, a wind] **1.** to circulate fresh air in (a room, etc.) **2.** to put a vent in, to let air, gas, etc. escape —**ven′ti·la′tion** *n.*

ven′ti·la′tor *n.* any device for replacing foul air with fresh air

ven·tral (ven′trəl) *adj.* [Fr. < L. *venter*, belly] of, on, or near the belly

ven·tri·cle (ven′tri k'l) *n.* [< L. *venter*, belly] either of the two lower chambers of the heart

ven·tril·o·quism (ven tril′ə kwiz'm) *n.* [< L. *venter*, belly + *loqui*, speak] the art of speaking so that the voice seems to come from some source other than the speaker —**ven·tril′o·quist** *n.*

ven·ture (ven′chər) *n.* [see ADVENTURE] **1.** a risky undertaking, as in business **2.** something on which a risk is taken —*vt.* -tured, -tur·ing **1.** to risk; hazard **2.** to take the risk of; brave **3.** to express (an opinion, etc.) at the risk of being criticized, etc. —*vi.* to do at some risk

ven′ture·some (-səm) *adj.* **1.** inclined to venture; daring **2.** risky; hazardous

ven′tur·ous *adj.* same as VENTURESOME

ven·ue (ven′yōō, -ōō) *n.* [< L. *venire*, to come] *Law* **1.** the locality in which a cause of action or a crime occurs **2.** the locality in which a case is tried

Ve·nus (vē′nəs) **1.** *Rom. Myth.* the goddess of love and beauty **2.** the most brilliant planet in the solar system: see PLANET

ve·ra·cious (və rā′shəs) *adj.* [< L. *verus*, true] **1.** habitually truthful **2.** accurate

ve·rac·i·ty (və ras′ə tē) *n., pl.* -ties **1.** honesty **2.** accuracy or precision **3.** truth

ve·ran·da, ve·ran·dah (və ran′də) *n.* [< Port. *varanda*, a balcony] an open porch, usually roofed

verb (vʉrb) *n.* [< L. *verbum*, a word] a word expressing action, existence, or occurrence

ver·bal (vʉr′b'l) *adj.* **1.** of, in, or by means of

words 2. oral rather than written 3. of, like, or derived from a verb

ver·bal·ize (vur′bə līz′) *vi.* **-ized′, -iz′ing** to communicate in words *—vt.* to express in words **—ver′bal·i·za′tion** *n.*

verbal noun *Gram.* a noun derived from a verb, esp. a gerund or an infinitive (Ex.: *walking* is healthful, *to err* is human)

ver·ba·tim (vər bāt′əm) *adv., adj.* [< L. *verbum*, a word] word for word

ver·bi·age (vur′bē ij) *n.* [< L. *verbum*, a word] an excess of words; wordiness

ver·bose (vər bōs′) *adj.* [< L. *verbum*, a word] using too many words; wordy

ver·dant (vur′d′nt) *adj.* [prob. VERD(URE) + -ANT] covered with green vegetation

ver·dict (vur′dikt) *n.* [< L. *vere*, truly + *dicere*, to say] 1. the decision reached by a jury 2. any decision or judgment

ver·di·gris (vur′di grēs′, -gris) *n.* [< OFr. *verd*, green + *de*, of + *Grece*, Greece] a greenish coating that forms on brass, bronze, or copper

ver·dure (vur′jər) *n.* [< OFr. *verd*, green] 1. the fresh green color of growing things 2. green vegetation

verge[1] (vurj) *n.* [< L. *virga*, rod] the edge, brink, or margin *—vi.* **verged, verg′ing** to be on the edge, brink, or border (usually with *on* or *upon*)

verge[2] (vurj) *vi.* **verged, verg′ing** [L. *vergere*] 1. to tend or incline (*to* or *toward*) 2. to pass gradually (*into*)

ver·i·fy (ver′ə fī′) *vt.* **-fied′, -fy′ing** [< L. *verus*, true + *facere*, to make] 1. to prove to be true by evidence, etc. 2. to test the accuracy of — **ver′i·fi·ca′tion** *n.*

ver·i·ly (ver′ə lē) *adv.* [Archaic] truly

ver·i·si·mil·i·tude (ver′ə si mil′ə tood′) *n.* [< L. *verus*, true + *similis*, like] the appearance of being true or real

ver·i·ta·ble (ver′i tə b′l) *adj.* [< L. *veritas*, truth] true; actual **—ver′i·ta·bly** *adv.*

ver·i·ty (ver′ə tē) *n., pl.* **-ties** [< L. *verus*, true] 1. truth; reality 2. a principle, belief, etc. taken to be fundamentally true

ver·mi·cel·li (vur′mə sel′ē, -chel′ē) *n.* [It., little worms < L. *vermis*, a worm] pasta like spaghetti, but in thinner strings

ver·mi·form (vur′mə fôrm′) *adj.* [< L. *vermis*, worm + -FORM] shaped like a worm

vermiform appendix *see* APPENDIX (sense 2)

ver·mil·ion (vər mil′yən) *n.* [< L. *vermis*, a worm] 1. a bright red pigment 2. a bright red or scarlet *—adj.* of this color

ver·min (vur′min) *n., pl.* **-min** [< L. *vermis*, a worm] 1. any of various destructive insects or small animals, as flies, lice, or rats 2. a vile person **—ver′min·ous** *adj.*

ver·mouth (vər mōōth′) *n.* [Fr. < G. *wermut*, wormwood] a sweet or dry, fortified white wine flavored with aromatic herbs

ver·nac·u·lar (vər nak′yə lər) *adj.* [< L. *vernaculus*, native] 1. of, in, or using the native language of a place 2. native to a place *—n.* 1. the native language or dialect of a country or place 2. the common, everyday language of a people 3. the shoptalk of a profession or trade

ver·nal (vur′n′l) *adj.* [< L. *ver*, spring] 1. of the spring 2. springlike 3. youthful

ver·ni·er (vur′nē ər, -nir) *n.* [< P. *Vernier*, 17th-c. Fr. mathematician] a short scale used to indicate fractional parts of divisions of a longer scale: also **vernier scale**

ver·sa·tile (vur′sə t′l) *adj.* [Fr. < L. *vertere*, to turn] competent in many things **—ver′sa·til′·i·ty** (-til′ə tē) *n.*

verse (vurs) *n.* [< L. *vertere*, to turn] 1. a sin-

gle line of poetry 2. *a)* poetry *b)* poetry of a specified kind 3. a single poem 4. a stanza 5. any of the short divisions of a chapter of the Bible

versed (vurst) *adj.* [< L. *versari*, be busy] skilled or learned (*in* a subject)

ver·si·fy (vur′sə fī′) *vi.* **-fied′, -fy′ing** [< L. *versus*, a VERSE + *facere*, make] to compose verses *—vt.* 1. to tell in verse 2. to put into verse form **—ver′si·fi·ca′tion** (-fi kā′shən) *n.* — **ver′si·fi′er** *n.*

ver·sion (vur′zhən) *n.* [Fr.: see VERSE] 1. a translation, esp. of the Bible 2. an account giving one point of view 3. a particular form [the movie *version* of the novel]

ver·sus (vur′səs) *prep.* [L. < *vertere*, to turn] 1. in contest against 2. in contrast with

ver·te·bra (vur′tə brə) *n., pl.* **-brae′** (-brē′), **-bras** [L. < *vertere*, to turn] any of the single bones of the spinal column

ver′te·brate (-brit, -brāt′) *adj.* 1. having a backbone, or spinal column 2. of the vertebrates *—n.* any of a large group of animals that have a backbone, as mammals

ver·tex (vur′teks) *n., pl.* **-tex·es, -ti·ces′** (-tə sēz′) [L. < *vertere*, to turn] 1. the highest point; top 2. *Geom.* the point where the two sides of an angle intersect

ver·ti·cal (vur′ti k′l) *adj.* 1. of or at the vertex 2. upright; straight up or down *—n.* a vertical line, plane, etc.

ver·tig·i·nous (vər tij′ə nəs) *adj.* of, affected by, or causing vertigo

ver·ti·go (vur′ti gō′) *n.* [L. < *vertere*, to turn] a sensation of dizziness

verve (vurv) *n.* [Fr. < L. *verba*, words] 1. vigor and energy 2. vivacity; dash

ver·y (ver′ē) *adj.* [< L. *verus*, true] 1. complete; utter [the *very* opposite] 2. same [the *very* hat he lost] 3. exactly right, suitable, etc. 4. even [the *very* rafters shook] 5. actual [caught in the *very* act] *—adv.* 1. exceedingly 2. truly; really [the *very* same man]

very high frequency any radio frequency between 30 and 300 megahertz

very low frequency any radio frequency between 10 and 30 kilohertz

ves·i·cle (ves′i k′l) *n.* [< Fr. < L. *vesica*, bladder] a small, membranous cavity, sac, or cyst; specif., a blister **—ve·sic·u·lar** (və sik′yə lər), **ve·sic′u·late** (-lit) *adj.*

ves·per (ves′pər) *n.* [L., evening] [*usually pl.*] an evening prayer or service: also **Vespers**

ves·sel (ves′′l) *n.* [< L. *vas*] 1. a utensil for holding something, as a bowl, pot, etc. 2. a ship or large boat 3. a tube or duct containing or circulating a body fluid

vest (vest) *n.* [< L. *vestis*, garment] a short, sleeveless garment worn, esp. under a suit coat, by men *—vt.* 1. to dress 2. to place (authority) *in* someone 3. to put (a person or group) in control of, as power *—vi.* to become vested (*in* a person), as property

ves·tal (ves′t′l) *adj.* [< L. *Vesta*, goddess of the hearth] chaste; pure *—n.* a virgin priestess of the goddess Vesta: in full **vestal virgin**

vest·ed interest (ves′tid) an established right, as to some future benefit

ves·ti·bule (ves′tə byool′) *n.* [L. *vestibulum*] a small entrance hall, as to a building

ves·tige (ves′tij) *n.* [Fr. < L. *vestigium*, a footprint] 1. a trace, mark, or sign of something that has passed away 2. *Biol.* an organ or part that was more fully developed or functional in an earlier stage **—ves·tig′i·al** (-tij′ē əl) *adj.*

vest·ment (vest'mənt) *n.* [< L. *vestire*, clothe] a garment worn by a clergyman

ves·try (ves'trē) *n., pl.* **-tries** [< L. *vestis*, garment] **1.** a room in a church, where vestments, etc. are kept **2.** a room in a church, used for meetings, Sunday school, etc. **3.** a group of church members who manage the business affairs of the church —**ves'try·man** (-mən) *n., pl.* **-men**

vet¹ (vet) *n. short for* VETERINARIAN

vet² (vet) *n. short for* VETERAN

vetch (vech) *n.* [< L. *vicia*] a plant of the legume family, used chiefly as fodder

vet·er·an (vet'ər ən, vet'rən) *adj.* [< L. *vetus*, old] **1.** old and experienced **2.** of veterans —*n.* **1.** one with much experience in some work **2.** one who has served in the armed forces

Veterans Day a U.S. legal holiday honoring veterans of the armed forces: observed Nov. 11, the date of the armistice of World War I

vet·er·i·nar·i·an (vet'ər ə ner'ē ən) *n.* one who practices veterinary medicine

vet'er·i·nar'y (-ē) *adj.* [< L. *veterina*, beasts of burden] designating or of the medical or surgical treatment of animals —*n., pl.* **-ies** *same as* VETERINARIAN

ve·to (vē'tō) *n., pl.* **-toes** [L., I forbid] **1.** *a)* an order forbidding some act *b)* the power to prevent action thus **2.** *a)* the right of one branch of government to reject bills passed by another *b)* the exercise of this right —*vt.* **-toed, -to·ing 1.** to prevent (a bill) from becoming law by veto **2.** to forbid

vex (veks) *vt.* [< L. *vexare*, agitate] **1.** to disturb, irritate, etc., esp. in a petty, nagging way **2.** to distress or afflict

vex·a·tion (vek sā'shən) *n.* **1.** a vexing or being vexed **2.** something that vexes —**vex·a'tious** (-shəs) *adj.*

VHF, vhf very high frequency

vi., v.i. intransitive verb

vi·a (vī'ə, vē'ə) *prep.* [L., way] by way of

vi·a·ble (vī'ə b'l) *adj.* [Fr. < L. *vita*, life] **1.** developed enough to be able to live outside the uterus **2.** workable; feasible —**vi'a·bil'i·ty** *n.*

vi·a·duct (vī'ə dukt') *n.* [L. *via*, way + (AQUE)DUCT] a bridge consisting of a series of short spans supported on piers or towers

vi·al (vī'əl) *n.* [< Gr. *phialē*, shallow cup] a small bottle, usually of glass, for holding medicine or other liquids

vi·and (vī'ənd) *n.* [< L. *vivere*, to live] **1.** an article of food **2.** [*pl.*] food

vibes (vībz) *n.pl.* **1.** [Colloq.] a vibraphone **2.** [< VIBRATION(S)] [Slang] qualities in a person or thing that arouse good or bad feelings

vi·brant (vī'brənt) *adj.* [< L. *vibrare*, vibrate] **1.** quivering; vibrating **2.** produced by vibration; resonant: said of sound **3.** vigorous, energetic, etc. —**vi'bran·cy** *n.* —**vi'brant·ly** *adv.*

vi·bra·phone (vī'brə fōn') *n.* [VIBRA(TE) + -PHONE] a musical instrument like the marimba, but with electrically operated valves in the resonant tubes

vi·brate (vī'brāt) *vt.* **-brat·ed, -brat·ing** [< L. *vibrare*] to set in to-and-fro motion —*vi.* **1.** to swing back and forth **2.** to move rapidly back and forth; quiver **3.** to resound **4.** to feel very excited; thrill —**vi·bra'tion** *n.* —**vi'bra'tor** *n.*

vi·bra·to (vi brät'ō) *n., pl.* **-tos** [It.] *Music* the pulsating effect of a rapid, hardly noticeable variation in pitch

vic·ar (vik'ər) *n.* [< L. *vicis*, a change] **1.** *Anglican Ch.* a parish priest who receives a stipend instead of the tithes **2.** *R.C.Ch.* a church officer acting as deputy of a bishop —**vic'ar·age** (-ij) *n.*

vi·car·i·ous (vī ker'ē əs) *adj.* [< L. *vicis*, a change] **1.** taking the place of another **2.** delegated **3.** done or undergone by one person in place of another **4.** felt as if one were actually taking part in another's experience [a *vicarious* thrill] —**vi·car'i·ous·ly** *adv.*

vice¹ (vīs) *n.* [< L. *vitium*] **1.** *a)* an evil action or habit *b)* evil conduct; depravity *c)* prostitution **2.** any fault, defect, etc.

vi·ce² (vī'sē) *prep.* [L.: see VICE-] in the place of

vice- [< L. *vicis*, a change] *a prefix meaning* subordinate, deputy [*vice*-president]

vice-pres·i·dent (vīs'prez'i dənt) *n.* an officer next in rank below a president, acting in his place when he is absent: for the U.S. official, usually **Vice President** —**vice'-pres'i·den·cy** *n.*

vice·roy (vīs'roi) *n.* [MFr. < *vice-* (see VICE-) + *roy*, a king] a person ruling a country, etc. as the deputy of a sovereign

vi·ce ver·sa (vī'sē vur'sə, vīs' vur'sə) [L.] the order or relation being reversed

vi·chy·ssoise (vē'shē swäz', vish'ē-) *n.* [Fr.] a thick cream soup of potatoes, onions, etc., usually served cold

vi·cin·i·ty (və sin'ə tē) *n., pl.* **-ties** [< L. *vicinus*, near] **1.** nearness; proximity **2.** a nearby region; neighborhood

vi·cious (vish'əs) *adj.* [< L. *vitium*, vice] **1.** characterized by vice; wicked or depraved **2.** faulty; flawed **3.** unruly [a *vicious* horse] **4.** malicious; spiteful [a *vicious* rumor] **5.** very intense, forceful, etc. [a *vicious* blow] —**vi'cious·ly** *adv.*

vicious circle a situation in which the solution to each problem gives rise to another, eventually bringing back the first problem

vi·cis·si·tudes (vi sis'ə tōōdz') *n.pl.* [< L. *vicis*, a turn] unpredictable changes in life, fortune, etc.; ups and downs

vic·tim (vik'təm) *n.* [L. *victima*] **1.** someone or something killed, destroyed, sacrificed, etc. **2.** one who suffers some loss, esp. by being swindled

vic'tim·ize (-tə mīz') *vt.* **-ized', -iz'ing** to make a victim of —**vic'tim·i·za'tion** *n.*

vic·tor (vik'tər) *n.* [L. < *vincere*, conquer] a winner or conqueror

Vic·to·ri·an (vic tôr'ē ən) *adj.* **1.** of or characteristic of the time of Queen Victoria (1819-1901) **2.** showing the respectability, prudery, etc. attributed to the Victorians —*n.* a person of that time

vic·to·ri·ous (vik tôr'ē əs) *adj.* **1.** having won a victory; triumphant **2.** of or bringing about victory —**vic·to'ri·ous·ly** *adv.*

vic·to·ry (vik'tə rē, -trē) *n., pl.* **-ries** [< L. *vincere*, conquer] **1.** the decisive winning of a battle, etc. **2.** success in any struggle

vict·uals (vit''lz) *n.pl.* [< L. *victus*, food] [Dial. or Colloq.] articles of food

vi·cu·ña (vī kōōn'yə, -kōōn'ə) *n.* [Sp.] **1.** a S. American animal related to the llama **2.** a fabric made from its soft, shaggy wool

‡vi·de (vī'dē) [L.] see; refer to (a certain page, etc.)

vid·e·o (vid'ē ō') *adj.* [L., I see] of television, esp. of the picture portion of a telecast —*n. same as* TELEVISION

vid'e·o'cas·sette' *n.* a cassette containing videotape, as for replay of a TV program

video game an electronic device for producing images on a TV screen, controlled by players of various games

vid'e·o·tape' *n.* **1.** a magnetic tape on which the electronic impulses of a TV program can be recorded **2.** *same as* VIDEOCASSETTE

vie (vī) *vi.* **vied, vy'ing** [< L. *invitare*, invite] to compete (*with* someone)

view (vyōō) *n.* [< L. *videre*, to see] **1.** a seeing or looking, as in inspection **2.** range of vision **3.** mental survey [a correct *view* of the situation] **4.** *a)* a scene or prospect [a room with a *view*] *b)* a picture of such a scene **5.** manner of regarding something; opinion —*vt.* **1.** to inspect; scrutinize **2.** to see; behold **3.** to survey mentally; consider —**in view 1.** in sight **2.** under consideration **3.** as a goal or hope —**in view of** because of —**on view** displayed publicly —**with a view to** with the purpose or hope of — **view'er** *n.*

view'find'er *n.* same as FINDER (sense 2)

view'point' *n.* the mental position from which things are viewed and judged; point of view

vig·il (vij'əl) *n.* [< L. *vigere*, be lively] **1.** a watchful staying awake **2.** a watch kept **3.** the eve of a church festival

vig·i·lant (vij'ə lənt) *adj.* [Fr. < L.: see VIGIL] staying watchful or alert to danger or trouble —**vig'i·lance** *n.*

vig·i·lan·te (vij'ə lan'tē) *n.* [Sp., watchman] one of an unauthorized group organized professedly to keep order and punish crime

vi·gnette (vin yet') *n.* [Fr. < *vigne*, vine] **1.** an ornamental design used as a border, inset, etc. on a page **2.** a picture shading off gradually at the edges **3.** a short, delicate literary sketch

vig·or (vig'ər) *n.* [L. < *vigere*, be strong] active force or strength; vitality or energy: Brit. sp. **vigour** —**vig'or·ous** *adj.*

vik·ing (vī'kiŋ) *n.* [ON. *vikingr*] [*also* V-] any of the Scandinavian pirates of the 8th to 10th centuries

vile (vīl) *adj.* [< L. *vilis*, cheap, base] **1.** morally evil; wicked **2.** repulsive; disgusting **3.** degrading; mean **4.** highly disagreeable; very bad [*vile* weather]

vil·i·fy (vil'ə fī') *vt.* **-fied', -fy'ing** [see VILE & -FY] to use abusive language about or of; defame —**vil'i·fi·ca'tion** *n.*

vil·la (vil'ə) *n.* [It. < L., a farm] a country house or estate, esp. a large one used as a retreat

vil·lage (vil'ij) *n.* [see prec.] **1.** a community smaller than a town **2.** the people of a village, collectively —**vil'lag·er** *n.*

vil·lain (vil'ən) *n.* [< VL. *villanus*, a farm servant] a wicked or evil person, as in a play, etc. —**vil'lain·ous** *adj.*

vil'lain·y *n., pl.* **-ies 1.** wickedness; evil **2.** a villainous act

vim (vim) *n.* [< L. *vis*, strength] vigor

‡**vin** (van; *Anglicized* vin) *n.* [Fr.] wine

vin·di·cate (vin'də kāt') *vt.* **-cat'ed, -cat'ing** [< L. *vis*, force + *dicere*, to say] **1.** to clear from criticism, blame, etc. **2.** to defend against opposition **3.** to justify —**vin'di·ca'tion** *n.* —**vin'di·ca'tor** *n.*

vin·dic·tive (vin dik'tiv) *adj.* [see VINDICATE] **1.** revengeful in spirit **2.** said or done in revenge —**vin·dic'tive·ly** *adv.*

vine (vīn) *n.* [< L. *vinum*, wine] **1.** a plant with a long stem that grows along the ground or climbs a support **2.** a grapevine

vin·e·gar (vin'i gər) *n.* [< MFr. *vin*, wine + *aigre*, sour] a sour liquid containing acetic acid, made by fermenting cider, wine, etc.: it is used to flavor or preserve foods —**vin'e·gar·y** *adj.*

vine·yard (vin'yərd) *n.* a piece of land where grapevines are grown

‡**vin rosé** [Fr.] same as ROSÉ

vin·tage (vin'tij) *n.* [< L. *vinum*, wine + *demere*, to remove] **1.** the crop of grapes in a single season **2.** the wine of a particular region and year **3.** the model of a particular period [a car of prewar *vintage*] —*adj.* **1.** of choice vintage [*vintage* wine] **2.** of a past period [*vintage* clothes]

vint·ner (vint'nər) *n.* [< L. *vinetum*, vineyard] a merchant who sells wine

vi·nyl (vī'n'l) *n.* [< L. *vinum*, wine + -YL] any of various vinyl compounds polymerized to form resins and plastics (**vinyl plastics**)

vi·ol (vī'əl) *n.* [< OPr. *viula* < ?] any of an early family of stringed instruments, usually with six strings, frets, and a flat back

vi·o·la (vē ō'lə, vī-) *n.* [It.] a stringed instrument of the violin family, slightly larger than a violin

vi·o·la·ble (vī'ə lə b'l) *adj.* that can be, or is likely to be, violated

vi·o·late (vī'ə lāt') *vt.* **-lat'ed, -lat'ing** [< L. *violare*, use force] **1.** to break (a law, promise, etc.) **2.** to rape **3.** to desecrate (something sacred) **4.** to break in on; disturb **5.** to offend —**vi'o·la'tor** *n.*

vi·o·la·tion *n.* a violating or being violated; specif., *a)* infringement, as of a law *b)* rape *c)* desecration *d)* disturbance

vi·o·lence (vī'ə ləns) *n.* [< L. *violentus*, violent] **1.** physical force used to cause injury **2.** intense, powerful force, as of a hurricane **3.** the harm done in violating rights, privacy, etc. **4.** a violent deed or act

vi'o·lent (-lənt) *adj.* **1.** acting with or having great physical force **2.** caused by violence **3.** furious [*violent* language] **4.** severe; intense [a *violent* headache]

vi·o·let (vī'ə lit) *n.* [< L. *viola*] **1.** a low plant with white, blue, purple, or yellow flowers **2.** a bluish-purple color —*adj.* bluish-purple

vi·o·lin (vī'ə lin') *n.* [< It. *viola*, viol] any instrument of the modern family of four-stringed instruments played with a bow; specif., the smallest and highest-pitched instrument of this family —**vi'o·lin'ist** *n.*

vi·ol·ist (vī'əl ist; *for 2* vē ō'list) *n.* **1.** a viol player **2.** a viola player

vi·o·lon·cel·lo (vē'ə län chel'ō, vī'ə lən-) *n., pl.* **-los** [It.] same as CELLO

VIP, V.I.P. [Colloq.] very important person

vi·per (vī'pər) *n.* [< L. < ? *vivus*, living + *parere*, to bear] **1.** a venomous snake **2.** a malicious or treacherous person

vi·ra·go (vi rā'gō, vī rä'-) *n., pl.* **-goes, -gos** [< L. *vir*, a man] a quarrelsome, shrewish woman

vi·ral (vī'rəl) *adj.* of or caused by a virus

vir·e·o (vir'ē ō') *n., pl.* **-os'** [L., a type of finch] a small American songbird, with olive-green or gray feathers

vir·gin (vur'jin) *n.* [< L. *virgo*, maiden] a person, esp. a woman, who has never had sexual intercourse —*adj.* **1.** being a virgin **2.** chaste; modest **3.** untouched, unused, pure, etc. [*virgin* snow] —**the Virgin** Mary, the mother of Jesus

vir'gin·al *adj.* same as VIRGIN

Vir·gin·ia creeper (vər jin'yə) same as WOODBINE (sense 2)

Virginia reel an American reel, danced by couples facing in two lines

vir·gin·i·ty (vər jin'ə tē) *n.* the state of being a virgin; maidenhood; chastity

Vir·go (vur'gō) [L., virgin] the sixth sign of the zodiac

vir·ile (vir'əl) *adj.* [< L. *vir*, a man] **1.** of or characteristic of a man; masculine **2.** having manly strength or vigor **3.** capable of copulation —**vi·ril·i·ty** (vi ril'ə tē) *n.*

vir·tu·al (vur'chōō wəl) *adj.* being such practically or in effect, although not in actual fact or name —**vir′tu·al·ly** *adv.*

vir·tue (vur′chōō) *n.* [< L. *virtus*, manliness, worth] 1. general moral excellence 2. a specific moral quality regarded as good 3. chastity 4. *a)* excellence in general *b)* a good quality 5. efficacy, as of a medicine —**by** (or **in**) **virtue of** because of

vir·tu·o·so (vur′chōō wō′sō) *n., pl.* **-sos, -si** (-sē) [It., skilled] a person with great technical skill in some fine art, esp. in music —**vir′tu·os′i·ty** (-wäs′ə tē) *n.*

vir·tu·ous (vur′chōō wəs) *adj.* 1. having, or characterized by, moral virtue 2. chaste: said of a woman —**vir′tu·ous·ly** *adv.*

vir·u·lent (vir′yoo lənt, -oo-) *adj.* [< L. *virus*, a poison] 1. *a)* poisonous; deadly *b)* bitterly antagonistic 2. *Med. a)* violent and rapid in its course: said of a disease *b)* highly infectious — **vir′u·lence** *n.*

vi·rus (vī′rəs) *n.* [L., a poison] 1. *a)* any of a group of very small infective agents that cause various diseases *b)* such a disease 2. a harmful influence

vi·sa (vē′zə) *n.* [Fr. < L. *videre*, to see] an endorsement on a passport, granting entry into a country

vis·age (viz′ij) *n.* [< L. *videre*, to see] 1. the face; countenance 2. appearance; aspect

vis-à-vis (vē′zə vē′) *adj., adv.* [Fr.] face to face; opposite —**prep.** 1. opposite to 2. in relation to

vis·cer·a (vis′ər ə) *n.pl., sing.* **vis′cus** (-kəs) [L.] the internal organs of the body, as the heart, lungs, intestines, etc.

vis′cer·al *adj.* 1. of the viscera 2. intuitive, emotional, etc., not intellectual

vis·cid (vis′id) *adj.* [< L. *viscum*, birdlime] thick, syrupy, and sticky; viscous

vis·cose (vis′kōs) *adj.* [see prec.] 1. *same as* VISCOUS 2. of viscose —*n.* a syruplike solution of cellulose, used in making cellophane and rayon thread and fabric

vis·cos·i·ty (vis käs′ə tē) *n., pl.* **-ties** 1. a viscous quality or state 2. *Physics* the internal friction of a fluid, caused by molecular attraction

vis·count (vī′kount) *n.* [see VICE- & COUNT²] a nobleman next below an earl or count and above a baron —**vis′count·ess** *n.fem.*

vis·cous (vis′kəs) *adj.* [see VISCID] 1. syrupy and sticky 2. *Physics* having viscosity

vise (vīs) *n.* [< L. *vitis*, vine, lit., that which winds] a device having two jaws opened and closed as by a screw, used for holding firmly an object being worked on

Vish·nu (vish′nōō) the second member of the Hindu Trinity (Brahma, Vishnu, and Siva), called "the Preserver"

vis·i·bil·i·ty (viz′ə bil′ə tē) *n., pl.* **-ties** 1. a being visible 2. *a)* the relative possibility of being seen under the prevailing conditions of distance, light, etc. *b)* range of vision

vis·i·ble (viz′ə b′l) *adj.* [< L. *videre*, to see] 1. that can be seen 2. evident —**vis′i·ble·ness** *n.* —**vis′i·bly** *adv.*

vi·sion (vizh′ən) *n.* [< L. *videre*, to see] 1. the power of seeing 2. something supposedly seen in a dream, trance, etc. 3. a mental image [*visions of power]* 4. the ability to foresee or perceive something, as through mental acuteness 5. something or someone of great beauty

vi′sion·ar′y (-er′ē) *adj.* 1. seen in a vision 2. not realistic; impractical *[visionary schemes]* — *n., pl.* **-ies** 1. one who sees visions 2. one who has impractical ideas

vis·it (viz′it) *vt.* [< L. *videre*, to see] 1. to go or come to see 2. to stay with as a guest 3. to af-

flict —*vi.* 1. to make a visit, esp. a social call 2. [Colloq.] to chat —*n.* a visiting; specif., *a)* a social call *b)* a stay as a guest

vis′it·ant (-ənt) *n. same as* VISITOR

vis′it·a′tion (-ə tā′shən) *n.* 1. a visiting; esp., an official visit as to inspect 2. any trouble looked upon as punishment sent by God

vis′i·tor *n.* a person making a visit

vi·sor (vī′zər) *n.* [< OFr. *vis*, a face] 1. the movable part of a helmet, covering the face 2. a projecting brim, as on a cap, for shading the eyes —**vi′sored** *adj.*

vis·ta (vis′tə) *n.* [It. < L. *videre*, to see] 1. a view, esp. as seen through a long passage 2. a mental view of events

vis·u·al (vizh′oo wəl) *adj.* [< L. *videre*, to see] 1. of or used in seeing 2. that is or can be seen; visible —**vis′u·al·ly** *adv.*

vis′u·al·ize′ (-wə līz′) *vt., vi.* **-ized′, -iz′ing** to form a mental image of (something not visible) —**vis′u·al·i·za′tion** *n.*

vi·tal (vīt′′l) *adj.* [< L. *vita*, life] 1. of or concerned with life 2. essential to life 3. fatal *[vital wounds]* 4. *a)* essential; indispensable *b)* of crucial importance 5. full of life; energetic — *n. [pl.]* 1. the vital organs, as the heart, brain, etc. 2. any essential parts —**vi′tal·ly** *adv.*

vi·tal·i·ty (vī tal′ə tē) *n., pl.* **-ties** 1. power to live 2. power to endure or survive 3. mental or physical energy; vigor

vi·tal·ize (vīt′′l īz′) *vt.* **-ized′, -iz′ing** to make vital; give life or vigor to

vital statistics data on births, deaths, marriages, etc.

vi·ta·min (vīt′ə min) *n.* [< L. *vita*, life] any of certain complex substances found variously in foods and essential to good health

vitamin A a fat-soluble alcohol found in fish-liver oil, egg yolk, butter, etc.: a deficiency of this results in imperfect vision in the dark

vitamin B (complex) a group of unrelated water-soluble substances, including: *a)* **vitamin B₁** (*see* THIAMINE) *b)* **vitamin B₂** (*see* RIBOFLAVIN) *c)* NIACIN *d)* **vitamin B₁₂** a vitamin containing cobalt, used in treating anemia

vitamin C *same as* ASCORBIC ACID

vitamin D any of several fat-soluble vitamins found esp. in fish-liver oils, milk, etc.: a deficiency of this produces rickets

vitamin E a group of related oils, necessary to fertility in some animals

vitamin K a substance that clots blood, found in alfalfa leaves, fish meal, etc.

vi·ti·ate (vish′ē āt′) *vt.* **-at′ed, -at′ing** [< L. *vitium*, a vice] 1. to make imperfect; spoil 2. to weaken morally 3. to make legally ineffective —**vi′ti·a′tion** *n.*

vit·re·ous (vit′rē əs) *adj.* [< L. *vitrum*, glass] 1. of or like glass 2. made from glass

vit·ri·fy (vit′rə fī′) *vt., vi.* **-fied′, -fy′ing** [< Fr. < L. *vitrum*, glass + *facere*, make] to change into glass or a glasslike substance by fusion due to heat

vit·ri·ol (vit′rē əl) *n.* [< L. *vitreus*, glassy] 1. any of several sulfates of metals, as of copper (*blue vitriol*) or iron (*green vitriol*) 2. *same as* SULFURIC ACID 3. sharp or bitter speech, etc. — **vit′ri·ol′ic** (-äl′ik) *adj.*

vi·tu·per·ate (vī tōō′pə rāt′, vi-) *vt.* **-at′ed, -at′ing** [< L. *vitium*, fault + *parare*, prepare] to speak abusively to or about —**vi·tu′per·a′tion** *n.*

†vi·va (vē′vä) *interj.* [It., Sp.] (long) live (someone or something specified)!

vi·va·cious (vi vā′shəs, vī-) *adj.* [< L. *vivere*, to live] full of animation; lively

vi·vac·i·ty (-vas′ə tē) *n.* the quality or state of being vivacious; liveliness

‡vive (vēv) *interj.* [Fr.] (long) live (someone or something specified)!

viv·id (viv′id) *adj.* [< L. *vivere*, to live] 1. full of life; lively 2. bright; intense, as colors 3. strong and clear; active *[a vivid imagination]* —**viv′id·ly** *adv.*

viv·i·fy (viv′ə fī′) *vt.* **-fied′, -fy′ing** [< L. *vivus,* alive + *facere,* make] to give life to; animate —**viv′i·fi·ca′tion** *n.*

vi·vip·a·rous (vī vip′ər əs) *adj.* [< L. *vivus,* alive + *parere,* to produce] bearing living young instead of laying eggs

viv·i·sec·tion (viv′ə sek′shən) *n.* [< L. *vivus,* alive + SECTION] medical research that involves surgery on living animals —**viv′i·sect′** *vt., vi.* —**viv′i·sec′tion·ist** *n.*

vix·en (vik′s'n) *n.* [< OE. *fyxe,* she-fox] 1. a female fox 2. an ill-tempered, shrewish woman —**vix′en·ish** *adj.* —**vix′en·ish·ly** *adv.*

viz., **viz** (viz; *often read* "namely") [< contr. for L. *videlicet*] that is; namely

vi·zier, vi·zir (vi zir′, viz′yər) *n.* [< Turk. < Ar. *wazara,* bear a burden] in Muslim countries, a high government official

vi·zor (vī′zər) *n. alt. sp. of* VISOR

vo·cab·u·lar·y (vō kab′yə ler′ē) *n., pl.* **-les** [ult. < L. *vocare,* to call] 1. a list of words, as in a dictionary or glossary 2. all the words used in a language or by a particular person, class, etc.

vo·cal (vō′k'l) *adj.* [< L. *vox,* a voice] 1. uttered by the voice; spoken 2. sung 3. able to make oral sounds 4. speaking freely

vocal cords membranous folds in the larynx that vibrate to produce the voice

vo·cal·ic (vō kal′ik) *adj.* of, or having the nature of, a vowel

vo·cal·ist (vō′k'l ist) *n.* a singer

vo′cal·ize′ (-īz′) *vt., vi.* **-ized′, -iz′ing** to utter, speak, or sing —**vo′cal·i·za′tion** *n.*

vo·ca·tion (vō kā′shən) *n.* [< L. *vocare,* to call] 1. the career toward which one believes oneself to be called 2. any trade, profession, or occupation —**vo·ca′tion·al** *adj.*

voc·a·tive (väk′ə tiv) *adj.* [see VOCATION] *Gram.* designating the case indicating the one addressed

vo·cif·er·ate (vō sif′ə rāt′) *vt., vi.* **-at′ed, -at′ing** [< L. *vox,* voice + *ferre,* to bear] to shout; clamor —**vo·cif′er·a′tion** *n.*

vo·cif·er·ous (-ər əs) *adj.* noisy; clamorous —**vo·cif′er·ous·ly** *adv.*

vod·ka (väd′kə) *n.* [Russ. < *voda,* water] a colorless alcoholic liquor distilled from wheat, rye, etc.

vogue (vōg) *n.* [Fr.] 1. the fashion at any particular time; mode 2. popularity —*adj.* in vogue: also **vogu·ish** (vō′gish)

voice (vois) *n.* [< L. *vox*] 1. sound made through the mouth, esp. by human beings 2. the ability to make such sounds 3. any sound, influence, etc. regarded as like vocal utterance 4. an expressed wish, opinion, etc. 5. the right to express one's wish, etc.; vote 6. expression 7. *Gram.* a form of a verb showing it as active or passive 8. *Music a)* singing ability *b)* any of the parts in a composition —*vt.* **voiced, voic′ing** to utter or express in words

void (void) *adj.* [< L. *vacare,* be empty] 1. containing nothing 2. devoid (of) *[void of sense]* 3. ineffective; useless 4. without legal force; invalid —*n.* 1. an empty space 2. a feeling of emptiness —*vt.* 1. to empty out 2. to discharge (urine or feces) 3. to make void; annul —*vi.* to defecate or, esp., to urinate —**void′a·ble** *adj.*

voile (voil) *n.* [Fr., a veil] a thin, sheer fabric, as of cotton

vol. *pl.* **vols.** volume

vol·a·tile (väl′ə t'l) *adj.* [< L. *volare,* to fly] 1. evaporating quickly 2. unstable or fickle —**vol′a·til′i·ty** (-til′ə tē) *n.* —**vol′a·til·ize′** (-īz′) *vt., vi.* **-ized′, -iz′ing**

vol·can·ic (väl kan′ik) *adj.* 1. of or caused by a volcano 2. like a volcano; violently explosive —**vol·can′i·cal·ly** *adv.*

vol·ca·no (väl kā′nō) *n., pl.* **-noes, -nos** [< L. *Volcanus,* Vulcan] 1. a vent in the earth's crust through which molten rock, rock fragments, ashes, etc. are ejected 2. a cone-shaped mountain of these materials built up around the vent

vo·li·tion (vō lish′ən) *n.* [ult. < L. *velle,* be willing] the act or power of using the will —**vo·li′tion·al** *adj.*

vol·ley (väl′ē) *n., pl.* **-leys** [< L. *volare,* to fly] 1. the simultaneous discharge of a number of weapons 2. the missiles so discharged 3. a rapid burst *[a volley of curses]* 4. *Tennis,* etc. a return of a ball, etc. before it touches the ground —*vt., vi.* **-leyed, -ley·ing** 1. to discharge or be discharged as in a volley 2. *Tennis,* etc. to return (the ball, etc.) as a volley

vol′ley·ball′ *n.* 1. a team game played by hitting a large, light ball back and forth over a high net with the hands 2. the ball

volt (vōlt) *n.* [< A. *Volta* (1745–1827), It. physicist] the unit of electromotive force

volt·age (vōl′tij) *n.* electromotive force expressed in volts

vol·ta·ic (väl tā′ik, vōl-) *adj.* of or producing electricity by chemical action

vol·u·ble (väl′yoo b'l) *adj.* [Fr. < L. *volvere,* to roll] talking very much and easily; talkative —**vol′u·bil′i·ty** *n.* —**vol′u·bly** *adv.*

vol·ume (väl′yoom) *n.* [< L. *volumen,* scroll] 1. *a)* a book *b)* any of the books of a set 2. the amount of space occupied in three dimensions 3. *a)* a quantity, bulk, or amount *b)* a large quantity 4. the loudness of sound

vo·lu·mi·nous (və loo′mə nəs) *adj.* 1. producing or consisting of enough to fill volumes 2. large; bulky; full

vol·un·tar·y (väl′ən ter′ē) *adj.* [< L. *voluntas,* free will] 1. brought about by one's own free choice 2. acting of one's own accord 3. intentional; not accidental 4. controlled by the will *[voluntary muscles]* —**vol′un·tar′i·ly** *adv.*

vol·un·teer (väl′ən tir′) *n.* one who offers to enter into any service, as military service, of his own free will —*adj.* 1. of volunteers 2. serving as a volunteer —*vt.* to offer or give of one's own free will —*vi.* to enter or offer to enter into any service of one's own free will

vo·lup·tu·ar·y (və lup′choo wer′ē) *n., pl.* **-les** [< L. *voluptas,* pleasure] one devoted to luxurious living and sensual pleasures

vo·lup·tu·ous (və lup′choo wəs) *adj.* full of, producing, or fond of sensual pleasures

vo·lute (və loot′) *n.* [< L. *volvere,* to roll] a spiral or whorl

vom·it (väm′it) *n.* [< L. *vomere,* to vomit] matter ejected from the stomach through the mouth —*vt., vi.* 1. to eject (the contents of the stomach) through the mouth 2. to discharge or be discharged with force

voo·doo (vōō′dōō) *n., pl.* **-doos** [Creole Fr. < a WAfr. word] 1. a primitive religion in the West Indies based on a belief in sorcery, etc. 2. a voodoo charm, fetish, etc. —*vt.* to affect by voodoo magic

vo·ra·cious (vô rā′shəs) *adj.* [< L. *vorare,* devour] 1. greedy in eating; ravenous 2. very

eager *[a voracious reader]* —**vo·rac′i·ty** (-ras′ə tē) *n.*

vor·tex (vôr′teks) *n., pl.* **-tex·es, -ti·ces′** (-tə sēz′) [L. < *vertere*, to turn] **1.** a whirlpool **2.** a whirlwind **3.** anything like a whirl in its rush, catastrophic power, etc.

vo·ta·ry (vōt′ə rē) *n., pl.* **-ries** [< L. *vovere*, to vow] **1.** one bound by a vow, esp. by religious vows **2.** one who is devoted to some cause or interest Also **vo′ta·rist**

vote (vōt) *n.* [L. *votum*, a vow] **1.** a decision on a proposal, etc., or a choice between candidates for office **2.** *a)* the expression of such a decision or choice *b)* a ballot, etc. by which it is expressed **3.** the right to vote **4.** votes collectively **5.** a specified group of voters *[the farm vote]* —*vi.* **vot′ed, vot′ing** to give or cast a vote —*vt.* to decide or authorize by vote —**vot′er** *n.*

vo·tive (vōt′iv) *adj.* [see VOTE] given, done, etc. in fulfillment of a vow

vouch (vouch) *vt.* [< L. *vocare*, to call] to uphold by evidence —*vi.* to give, or serve as, assurance, a guarantee, etc. (*for*) *[to vouch for his honesty]*

vouch′er *n.* **1.** one who vouches **2.** a paper serving as evidence or proof, as a receipt for the payment of a debt

vouch·safe′ *vt.* **-safed′, -saf′ing** [< ME. *vouchen safe*, vouch as safe] to be gracious enough to give or grant

vow (vou) *n.* [< L. *votum*] **1.** a solemn promise, esp. one made to God **2.** a promise of love and fidelity *[marriage vows]* —*vt., vi.* to promise or declare solemnly —**take vows** to enter a religious order

vow·el (vou′əl) *n.* [< L. *vocalis*, vocal] **1.** a speech sound made by letting the breath pass in a continuous stream through the open mouth **2.** a letter representing such a sound, as *a, e, i, o, u*

voy·age (voi′ij) *n.* [< L. *via*, way] **1.** a relatively long journey, esp. by water **2.** a journey by aircraft or spacecraft —*vi., vt.* **-aged, -ag·ing** to make a voyage (over or on) —**voy′ag·er** *n.*

vo·yeur (vwä yur′) *n.* [Fr. < *voir*, see] one who has an excessive interest in viewing sexual objects or scenes —**vo·yeur′ism** *n.*

V.P., VP Vice-President

vs. versus

vt., v.t. transitive verb

VTOL [*v(ertical) t(ake)o(ff and) l(anding)*] an aircraft that can take off and land vertically

Vul·can (vul′k'n) *Rom. Myth.* the god of fire and of metalworking

vul·can·ite (vul′kə nīt′) *n.* [< prec. + -ITE] a hard rubber used in combs, etc.

vul′can·ize′ (-nīz′) *vt., vi.* **-ized′, -iz′ing** to treat (crude rubber) with sulfur under great heat to increase its strength and elasticity — **vul′can·i·za′tion** *n.*

vul·gar (vul′gər) *adj.* [< L. *vulgus*, common people] **1.** of people in general; popular **2.** vernacular **3.** lacking culture, taste, etc.; crude **4.** obscene —**vul′gar·ly** *adv.*

vul·gar′i·an (-ger′ē ən) *n.* a rich person with coarse, showy tastes

vul′gar·ism *n.* **1.** a word, phrase, etc. used widely but regarded as nonstandard, coarse, or obscene **2.** vulgarity

vul·gar·i·ty (vul gar′ə tē) *n.* **1.** the state or quality of being vulgar **2.** *pl.* **-ties** a vulgar act, habit, usage in speech, etc.

vul·gar·ize (vul′gə rīz′) *vt.* **-ized′, -iz′ing 1.** to make popular **2.** to make vulgar, coarse, obscene, etc. —**vul′gar·i·za′tion** *n.*

Vulgar Latin the everyday Latin spoken by ancient Romans as distinguished from standard written Latin

Vul·gate (vul′gāt) *n.* [ML. *vulgata (editio)*, popular (edition)] **1.** a Latin version of the Bible, used in the Roman Catholic church **2.** [**v-**] the vernacular

vul·ner·a·ble (vul′nər ə b'l) *adj.* [< L. *vulnus*, a wound] **1.** that can be wounded or injured **2.** open to, or easily hurt by, criticism or attack **3.** *Bridge* subject to increased penalties or bonuses —**vul′ner·a·bil′i·ty** *n.* —**vul′ner·a·bly** *adv.*

vul·pine (vul′pīn) *adj.* [< L. *vulpes*, a fox] of or like a fox; clever; cunning

vul·ture (vul′chər) *n.* [< L. *vultur*] **1.** a large bird that feeds on carrion **2.** a greedy, ruthless person —**vul′tur·ous** *adj.*

vul·va (vul′və) *n.* [L., womb] the external genital organs of the female

vy·ing (vī′iŋ) *adj.* that vies; that competes

W

W, w (dub′'l yōō, -yə) *n., pl.* **W's, w's** the 23d letter of the English alphabet

W *Chem.* tungsten

W, w watt; watts

W, W.., w, w. 1. west **2.** western

W. Wednesday

W.., w. 1. watt(s) **2.** weight **3.** width

w. 1. week(s) **2.** wide **3.** wife **4.** with

Wac (wak) *n.* a member of the Women's Army Corps (**WAC**)

wack·y (wak′ē) *adj.* **-i·er, -i·est** [< ?] [Slang] ŏdd, silly, or crazy

wad (wäd, wôd) *n.* [ML. *wadda*, wadding] **1.** a small, soft mass, as of cotton or paper **2.** a lump or small, compact roll **3.** [Colloq.] a roll of paper money —*vt.* **wad′ded, wad′ding 1.** to compress, or roll up, into a wad **2.** to plug or stuff with a wad

wad′ding *n.* any soft material used in padding, packing, etc.

wad·dle (wäd′'l, wôd′-) *vi.* **-dled, -dling** [< WADE] to walk with short steps, swaying from side to side, as a duck —*n.* a waddling gait — **wad′dler** *n.*

wade (wād) *vi.* **wad′ed, wad′ing** [OE. *waden*, go] **1.** to walk through any resisting substance, as water, mud, etc. **2.** to proceed with difficulty *[wade* through a dull book*]* **3.** [Colloq.] to start with vigor (with *in* or *into*) —*vt.* to cross by wading

wad·er (wād′ər) *n.* **1.** one who wades **2.** *same as* WADING BIRD. **3.** *[pl.]* high waterproof boots, often with trousers

wa·di (wä′dē) *n., pl.* **-dis, -dies** [Ar. *wādī*] in Arabia, N Africa, etc., a river valley that is usually dry: also sp. **wa′dy,** *pl.* **-dies**

wading bird a long-legged shore bird that wades the shallows for food, as the crane

wa·fer (wā′fər) *n.* [MDu. *wafel*] **1.** a thin, flat, crisp cracker or cookie **2.** anything resembling this, as candy

waf·fle (wäf′'l, wôf′-) *n.* [Du. *wafel*] a crisp batter cake baked in a waffle iron

waffle iron a utensil with two flat, studded

plates pressed together so that a waffle bakes between them

waft (waft, wäft) *vt., vi.* [< Du. *wachter*, watcher] to carry or move lightly over water or through the air, as sounds or odors —*n.* 1. an odor, sound, etc. carried through the air 2. a gust of wind 3. a wafting movement

wag¹ (wag) *vt., vi.* **wagged, wag′ging** [prob. < ON. *vaga*] to move rapidly back and forth, up and down, etc. —*n.* a wagging

wag² (wag) *n.* [prob. < obs. *waghalter*, a rogue] a comical person; wit; joker

wage (wāj) *vt.* **waged, wag′ing** [< OFr. *gage*, a pledge] to engage in or carry on (a war, etc.) — *n.* 1. [*often pl.*] money paid for work done 2. [*usually pl.*] what is given in return

wa·ger (wā′jər) *n.* [see WAGE] *same as* BET — *vt., vi. same as* BET

wag·gish (wag′ish) *adj.* 1. of or like a wag; roguishly merry 2. playful; jesting

wag·gle (wag′'l) *vt.* **-gled, -gling** to wag, esp. with short, quick movements —*n.* a waggling

wag·on (wag′ən) *n.* [Du. *wagen*] 1. a four-wheeled vehicle for hauling heavy loads 2. a small cart used by children at play —**on** (or **off**) **the wagon** [Slang] no longer (or once again) drinking alcoholic liquors

waif (wāf) *n.* [prob. < ON.] 1. anything found that is without an owner 2. a homeless person, esp. a child 3. a stray animal

wail (wāl) *vi.* [< ON. *væ*, woe] to make long, loud, sad cries, as in grief or pain —*n.* 1. such a cry 2. a wailing

wain (wān) *n.* [OE. *wægn*] [Archaic] a wagon

wain·scot (wān′skət, -skät′) *n.* [< MDu. *wagenschot*] a paneling of wood, etc. on the walls of a room, often on the lower part only —*vt.* **-scot·ed** or **-scot·ted, -scot·ing** or **-scot·ting** to line (a wall) with wainscoting

wain·scot·ing, wain′scot·ting *n.* 1. *same as* WAINSCOT 2. material used for wainscot

wain·wright (wān′rīt′) *n.* [WAIN + WRIGHT] one who builds or repairs wagons

waist (wāst) *n.* [< OE. *weaxan*, grow] 1. the part of the body between the ribs and the hips 2. the part of a garment that covers the body from the shoulders to the waistline 3. a blouse 4. the middle, narrow part of something

waist′band′ *n.* a band encircling the waist, as at the top of a skirt, trousers, etc.

waist·coat (wes′kət, wāst′kōt′) *n.* [Brit.] a man's vest

waist·line (wāst′līn′) *n.* the line of the waist, between the ribs and the hips

wait (wāt) *vi.* [ONormFr. *waitier*] 1. to remain in readiness or anticipation 2. to be ready [*dinner is waiting*] 3. to remain undone [*it can wait*] 4. to serve food (with *at* or *on*) —*vt.* to be, remain, or delay in expectation of —*n.* the act or a period of waiting —**wait on** (or **upon**) 1. to act as a servant to 2. to serve (a customer, etc.) —**wait up** to delay going to bed while waiting

wait′er *n.* a man who waits on table in a restaurant

wait′ing *adj.* 1. that waits 2. of or for a wait — *n.* 1. the act of one that waits 2. a period of waiting —**in waiting** in attendance, as on a king

waiting room a room in which people wait, as in a railroad station, dentist's office, etc.

wait·ress (wā′tris) *n.* a woman waiter

waive (wāv) *vt.* **waived, waiv′ing** [< ON. *veifa*, fluctuate] 1. to give up or forgo (a right, claim, etc.) 2. to postpone; defer

waiv′er *n. Law* a waiving, or giving up voluntarily, of a right, claim, etc.

wake¹ (wāk) *vi.* **woke** or **waked, waked, wak′ing**

[< OE. *wacian*, be awake & *wacan*, arise] 1. to come out of sleep; awake (often with *up*) 2. to stay awake 3. to become active 4. to become alert [*to wake* to a peril] —*vt.* 1. to cause to wake (often with *up*) 2. to arouse or excite, as passions —*n.* an all-night vigil over a corpse

wake² (wāk) *n.* [< ON. *vök*, hole in the ice] the track left in the water by a moving ship —**in the wake of** following closely

wake′ful *adj.* 1. alert; watchful 2. unable to sleep —**wake′ful·ness** *n.*

wak·en (wāk′'n) *vi., vt.* to wake; rouse

wale (wāl) *n.* [OE. *walu*, a weal] 1. a welt raised by a whip, etc. 2. a ridge on the surface of cloth, as corduroy —*vt.* **waled, wal′ing** to mark (the skin) with wales

walk (wôk) *vi.* [OE. *wealcan*, to roll] 1. to go on foot at a moderate pace 2. to follow a certain course [*to walk* in peace] 3. *Baseball* to go to first base on four balls —*vt.* 1. to walk along, over, etc. 2. to cause (a horse, dog, etc.) to walk 3. to accompany on a walk [I'll *walk* you home] 4. *Baseball* to advance (a batter) to first base by pitching four balls —*n.* 1. the act or manner of walking 2. a stroll or hike 3. a distance to walk [an hour's *walk*] 4. a sphere of activity, station in life, etc. [from all *walks* of life] 5. a path for walking 6. *Baseball* a walking —**walk (all) over** to domineer over — **walk away** (or **off**) **with** 1. to steal 2. to win easily —**walk out** to go on strike —**walk out on** [Colloq.] to leave; desert

walk′er *n.* 1. one that walks 2. a frame on wheels for babies learning to walk 3. a frame without wheels used by convalescents, etc.

walk′ie-talk′ie *n.* a compact radio transmitter and receiver that can be carried by one person

walking stick 1. a stick carried when walking; cane 2. an insect resembling a twig: also **walk′-ing·stick′** *n.*

walk′out′ *n.* 1. a strike of workers 2. an abrupt departure of people as a show of protest

walk′-up′ *n.* an apartment building without an elevator

wall (wôl) *n.* [< L. *vallum*, rampart] 1. an upright structure of wood, stone, etc. serving to enclose, divide, support, or protect 2. something like a wall as in function —*vt.* 1. to divide, enclose, etc. with a wall (often with *off* or *in*) 2. to close (an opening) with a wall (usually with *up*) —**drive** (or **push**) **to the wall** to place in a desperate position —**off the wall** [Slang] 1. insane; crazy 2. very eccentric

wall′board′ *n.* fibrous material in thin slabs for making or covering walls

wal·let (wôl′it, wäl′-) *n.* [ME. *walet*] a flat pocketbook for carrying paper money, cards, etc.; billfold

wall·eye (wôl′ī′) *n.* [< ON. *vagl*, beam + *eygr*, having eyes] 1. an eye that turns outward, showing more white than is normal 2. a fish with large, staring eyes; esp., a N. American freshwater fish: in full **wall′eyed′ pike**

wall′flow′er *n.* [Colloq.] a person who merely looks on at a dance

Wal·loon (wä lōōn′) *n.* 1. a member of a people living in S and SE Belgium 2. the French dialect of the Walloons

wal·lop (wôl′əp, wäl′-) *vt.* [< OFr. *galoper*, to gallop] [Colloq.] 1. to beat or defeat soundly 2. to strike hard —*n.* [Colloq.] 1. a hard blow 2. effective force or power

wal·low (wäl′ō, wôl′-) *vi.* [OE. *wealwian*, roll around] 1. to roll about, as in mud, dust, etc. 2. to indulge oneself fully [to *wallow* in vice] — *n.* 1. a wallowing 2. a place where animals wallow

wall·pa·per *n.* paper for covering the walls —*vt.* to put wallpaper on or in

wal·nut (wôl′nut′, -nət) *n.* [< OE. *wealh*, foreign + *hnutu*, nut] 1. a roundish, edible nut, with a two-lobed seed 2. a tree bearing such a nut, as the *English walnut* 3. the wood of such a tree, used for furniture, etc.

wal·rus (wôl′rəs, wäl′-) *n.* [prob. < ON. *hrosshvalr*, horse whale] a massive sea mammal of the seal family, having two protruding tusks and a heavy layer of blubber

waltz (wôlts, wôls) *n.* [< G. *walzen*, dance about] 1. a ballroom dance for couples, in 3/4 time 2. music for this —*vi.* 1. to dance a waltz 2. to move lightly and nimbly

wam·pum (wäm′pəm) *n.* [< Algonquian] small beads made of shells and used by N. American Indians as money

wan (wän, wôn) *adj.* **wan′ner, wan′nest** [OE. *wann*, dark] 1. sickly pale; pallid [a *wan* complexion] 2. suggesting a sickly condition; feeble [a *wan* smile] —**wan′ly** *adv.*

wand (wänd, wônd) *n.* [ON. *vǫndr*] 1. a rod of authority; scepter 2. a rod of supposed magic power

wan·der (wän′dər, wôn′-) *vi.* [OE. *wandrian*] 1. to roam idly or aimlessly about; ramble 2. to stray (*from* a path, course, etc.) 3. to go astray; specif., to be disjointed, incoherent, etc. 4. to meander, as a river —*vt.* to roam through, in, or over —**wan′der·er** *n.*

wan′der·lust′ (-lust′) *n.* [G.] an impulse, longing, or urge to wander or travel

wane (wän) *vi.* **waned, wan′ing** [OE. *wanian*] 1. to grow gradually less in extent, as the moon after it is full 2. to grow dim, as a light 3. to decline in power, etc. 4. to approach the end — *n.* a waning

wan·gle (waŋ′g'l) *vt.* **-gled, -gling** [< ?] [Colloq.] to get or cause by persuasion, influence, tricks, etc.

Wan·kel engine (väŋ′k'l, waŋ′-) [< F. *Wankel* (1902–), G. engineer] a rotary combustion engine having a spinning piston, needing fewer parts and less fuel than used in a turbine engine

want (wänt, wônt) *vt.* [ON. *vanta*] 1. to lack 2. to crave [to *want* love] 3. to desire [to *want* to travel] 4. to wish to see, talk to, or apprehend [*wanted* by the police] 5. [Chiefly Brit.] to require —*vi.* 1. to have a need or lack (with *for*) 2. to be destitute —*n.* 1. a lack; shortage 2. poverty 3. a craving 4. something needed

want ad [Colloq.] an advertisement for something wanted, as a job

want′ing *adj.* 1. lacking 2. not up to standard —*prep.* 1. lacking (something) 2. minus — **wanting in** deficient in (a quality, etc.)

wan·ton (wän′t'n, wôn′-) *adj.* [< OE. *wan*, lacking + *teon*, bring up] 1. sexually loose 2. [Poet.] playful 3. unprovoked or malicious 4. recklessly ignoring decency, etc. —*n.* a wanton person; esp., a sexually loose woman

wap·i·ti (wäp′ə tē) *n.* [< Algonquian] the American elk, the largest N. American deer, with large, branching antlers and a short tail

war (wôr) *n.* [< ONormFr. *werre*, strife] 1. open armed conflict as between countries 2. any active hostility; strife 3. military operations as a science —*adj.* of, used in, or resulting from war —*vi.* **warred, war′ring** 1. to carry on war 2. to contend; strive

war·ble (wôr′b'l) *vt., vi.* **-bled, -bling** [ONormFr. *werbler*] to sing with trills, quavers, runs, etc., as a bird —*n.* a warbling; trill

war′bler *n.* one that warbles; esp., any of various songbirds

war cry 1. a slogan, etc. shouted in battle 2. a phrase or slogan in any conflict

ward (wôrd) *vt.* [OE. *weardian*, to guard] to turn aside; fend (*off*) —*n.* 1. a being under guard 2. one under the care of a guardian or court 3. a division of a jail, hospital, etc. 4. a division of a city or town, for purposes of voting, etc.

-ward [OE. *-weard*] *a suffix meaning* in a (specified) direction or course [*backward*] : also **-wards**

war·den (wôr′d'n) *n.* [< OFr. *gardein*] 1. one who guards, or has charge of, something [a game *warden*] 2. the head official of a prison

ward′er *n.* a watchman, guard, etc.

ward heeler a follower of a politician, who solicits votes, etc.: contemptuous term

ward·robe (wôrd′rōb′) *n.* 1. a closet, cabinet, etc. for holding clothes 2. one's supply of clothes

ward′room′ *n.* in a warship, a compartment used for eating and lounging by officers

ware (wer) *n.* [OE. *waru*] 1. anything for sale: usually used in pl. 2. pottery

ware′house′ *n.* a building where wares, or goods, are stored —*vt.* **-housed′, -hous′ing** to place or store in a warehouse

war·fare (wôr′fer′) *n.* 1. the action of waging war 2. conflict of any kind

war′head′ *n.* the front part of a torpedo, bomb, etc., containing the explosive charge

war′horse′ *n.* [Colloq.] one who has engaged in many struggles

war·i·ly (wer′ə lē) *adv.* in a wary manner

war′like′ *adj.* 1. fond of or ready for war 2. of war 3. threatening war

warm (wôrm) *adj.* [OE. *wearm*] 1. having, feeling, or giving off a moderate degree of heat 2. that keeps body heat in [*warm* clothing] 3. ardent; enthusiastic 4. lively, vigorous, etc. 5. quick to anger 6. *a)* cordial or sincere [a *warm* welcome] *b)* sympathetic or loving 7. newly made, as a scent or trail 8. [Colloq.] close to discovering something —*vt., vi.* to make or become warm —**warm up** to practice or exercise before a game —**warm′ly** *adv.* —**warm′ness** *n.*

warm′blood′ed *adj.* 1. having warm blood and a constant natural body heat: said of mammals and birds 2. ardent; fervent

warm front *Meteorol.* the forward edge of an advancing mass of warm air replacing colder air

warm′heart′ed *adj.* kind, sympathetic, friendly, etc. —**warm′heart′ed·ly** *adv.*

war·mon·ger (wôr′muŋ′gər) *n.* one that advocates, or tries to bring about, war

warmth (wôrmth) *n.* 1. a being warm 2. mild heat 3. excitement or vigor of feeling; ardor 4. slight anger

warn (wôrn) *vt.* [OE. *wearnian*] 1. to tell (a person) of a danger, coming evil, etc. 2. to caution; admonish [*warned* about smoking] 3. to notify in advance —**warn′er** *n.*

warn′ing *n.* 1. the act of one that warns 2. that which warns —*adj.* that warns

warp (wôrp) *n.* [OE. *weorpan*, to throw] 1. *a)* a distortion, as a twist or bend in wood *b)* any similar distortion 2. a mental quirk, bias, etc. 3. *Weaving* the threads running lengthwise in the loom —*vt.* 1. to bend or twist out of shape 2. to distort, pervert, etc. [a *warped* mind] —*vi.* to become bent

war′path′ *n.* the path taken by American Indians on a warlike expedition —**on the warpath** 1. ready for war 2. angry

war·rant (wôr′ənt, wär′-) *n.* [< OFr. *garant*] 1. *a)* authorization, as by law *b)* justification for some act, belief, etc. **2.** something serving as a guarantee of some event or result **3.** *Law* a writ authorizing an arrest, search, seizure, etc. **4.** *Mil.* the certificate appointing a warrant officer —*vt.* **1.** to authorize **2.** to serve as justification for (an act, belief, etc.) **3.** to guarantee **warrant officer** a military officer ranking above an enlisted man but below a commissioned officer

war′ran·ty (-tē) *n., pl.* **-ties** *same as* GUARANTEE (*n.* 2 *a*)

war·ren (wôr′ən, wär′-) *n.* [< OFr. *warir*, to preserve] **1.** an area in which rabbits breed or are raised **2.** any crowded building or buildings

war·ri·or (wôr′ē ər, wär′-) *n.* [see WAR] a fighting man; soldier

war·ship (wôr′ship′) *n.* any ship for combat use, as a battleship, destroyer, etc.

wart (wôrt) *n.* [OE. *wearte*] **1.** a small, usually hard, tumorous growth on the skin **2.** a small growth on a plant

wart hog a wild African hog with large tusks, and warts below the eyes

war·y (wer′ē) *adj.* **-i·er, -i·est** [OE. *wær*] **1.** cautious **2.** characterized by caution

was (wuz, wäz) [OE. *wæs*] *1st and 3d pers. sing., pt., of* BE

wash (wôsh, wäsh) *vt.* [OE. *wæscan*] **1.** to clean with water or other liquid **2.** to purify **3.** to wet; moisten **4.** to flow over, past, or against: said of a sea, waves, etc. **5.** to soak (*out*), flush (*off*), or carry (*away*) by the action of water **6.** to erode [the flood *washed* out the road] **7.** to cover with a thin coat of paint or metal —*vi.* **1.** to wash oneself **2.** to wash clothes **3.** to undergo washing **4.** to be removed by washing [the stain *washed* out] **5.** to be worn or carried away by the action of water [the bridge *washed* out] —*n.* **1.** a washing **2.** a place where something is washed [an auto *wash*] **3.** a quantity of clothes washed, or to be washed **4.** *a*) the rush or surge of water *b*) the eddy of water or air caused by a propeller, etc. **5.** silt, mud, etc. carried and dropped by running water **6.** a thin coating of paint or metal **7.** a liquid for cosmetic or medicinal use [*mouthwash*] —*adj.* that can be washed without damage [a *wash* dress] —**wash down 1.** to clean by washing **2.** to follow (a bite of food) with a drink —**wash′a·ble** *adj.*

wash′-and-wear′ *adj.* needing little or no ironing after washing

wash′board′ *n.* a ridged board for scrubbing dirt out of clothes

wash′bowl′ *n.* a bowl for use in washing one's hands and face, etc.: also **wash′ba′sin**

wash′cloth′ *n.* a small cloth, usually of terry, used in washing the face or body

washed′-out′ *adj.* **1.** faded **2.** [Colloq.] tired; spiritless **3.** [Colloq.] wan

wash′er *n.* **1.** one who washes **2.** a flat disk or ring of metal, rubber, etc. used to make a seat for a bolt head or for a nut or faucet valve, to provide packing, etc. **3.** a machine for washing

wash′er·wom′an *n., pl.* **-wom′en** a woman whose work is washing clothes

wash′ing *n.* **1.** the act of one that washes **2.** clothes, etc. to be washed, esp. in one batch

washing machine a machine for washing clothes, etc.

wash′out′ *n.* **1.** the washing away of soil, etc. by water **2.** [Slang] a complete failure

wash′room′ *n.* **1.** a room for washing **2.** *same as* RESTROOM

wash′stand′ *n.* a table or plumbing fixture with a washbowl, etc.

wash′tub′ *n.* a tub for washing clothes, etc.

wash′y *adj.* **-i·er, -i·est 1.** watery; diluted **2.** pale **3.** insipid; without force

was·n′t (wuz′nt, wäz′-) was not

WASP, Wasp (wäsp, wôsp) *n.* a white Anglo-Saxon Protestant

wasp (wäsp, wôsp) *n.* [OE. *wæsp*] a winged insect with a slender body and, in the females and workers, a painful sting

wasp′ish *adj.* **1.** of or like a wasp **2.** bad-tempered; snappish —**wasp′ish·ness** *n.*

was·sail (wäs′'l, was′-; -āl) *n.* [< ON. *ves heill*, be hearty] **1.** a former toast in drinking healths **2.** the spiced ale, etc. with which such healths were drunk **3.** a drinking party —*vi., vt.* to drink a wassail (to)

wast·age (wās′tij) *n.* **1.** loss by use, decay, etc. **2.** what is wasted

waste (wāst) *vt.* **wast′ed, wast′ing** [< L. *vastare*, to lay waste] **1.** to destroy; devastate **2.** to wear away; use up **3.** to make weak or feeble [*wasted* by age] **4.** to use up needlessly; squander **5.** to fail to take advantage of [to *waste* a chance] —*vi.* to lose strength, health, etc., as by disease —*adj.* **1.** uncultivated or uninhabited; desolate **2.** left over; no longer of use **3.** excreted from the body **4.** used to carry off or hold waste —*n.* **1.** uncultivated or uninhabited land, as a desert **2.** a devastated area **3.** the act of wasting, or loss by wasting **4.** discarded material, as ashes, garbage, etc. **5.** matter excreted from the body, as feces —**go to waste** to be wasted —**lay waste (to)** to devastate —**wast′er** *n.*

waste′bas′ket *n.* a container for wastepaper, trash, etc.: also **wastepaper basket**

waste′ful *adj.* in the habit of wasting or characterized by waste; squandering; extravagant —**waste′ful·ly** *adv.* —**waste′ful·ness** *n.*

waste′land′ *n.* barren land

waste′pa′per *n.* paper thrown away after use or as useless: also **waste paper**

wast·rel (wās′trəl) *n.* **1.** one who wastes; esp. a spendthrift **2.** a good-for-nothing

watch (wäch, wôch) *n.* [OE. *wæcce*] **1.** a keeping awake, esp. in order to guard **2.** close observation for a time **3.** a guard, or the period of duty of a guard **4.** a small timepiece worn on the wrist or carried in the pocket **5.** *a*) any of the periods of duty (usually four hours) on shipboard *b*) the crew on duty during such a period —*vi.* **1.** to stay awake; keep vigil **2.** to keep guard **3.** to look; observe **4.** to be looking or waiting attentively (*for*) —*vt.* **1.** to guard or tend **2.** to observe carefully **3.** to wait and look for —**watch out** to be alert and careful —**watch′er** *n.*

watch′dog′ *n.* **1.** a dog kept to guard property **2.** a person or group that keeps watch to prevent waste, dishonest practices, etc.

watch′ful *adj.* alert; attentive; vigilant —**watch′ful·ly** *adv.* —**watch′ful·ness** *n.*

watch′man *n., pl.* **-men** a person hired to watch or guard, esp. at night

watch′tow′er *n.* a high tower from which watch is kept, as for forest fires

watch′word′ *n.* **1.** a password **2.** a slogan

wa·ter (wôt′ər, wät′-) *n.* [OE. *wæter*] **1.** the colorless, transparent liquid of rivers, lakes, etc., which falls as rain **2.** water with reference to its depth, surface, or level [under *water*] **3.** a body secretion, as urine, tears, etc. **4.** a wavy, lustrous finish given to linen, silk, metal, etc. —*vt.* **1.** to give (animals) water to drink **2.** to supply (crops, etc.) with water, as by sprinkling **3.** to moisten, soak, or dilute with water **4.** to give a wavy luster to (silk, etc.) —*vi.* **1.** to fill with tears, as the eyes **2.** to fill with saliva [his mouth *watered*] **3.** to take on a supply of water **4.** to drink water —*adj.* of, in, on, near, from, or by water —**hold water** to prove sound, logical, etc.

water bed a heavy vinyl bag filled with water and used as a bed or as a mattress in a special bed frame: also **wa′ter·bed′** *n.*

water buffalo a slow, powerful, oxlike draft animal of S Asia and the Philippine Islands

water chestnut 1. a Chinese sedge, growing in clumps in water **2.** its edible tuber

water closet *same as* TOILET (sense 3)

wa′ter·col′or *n.* **1.** a pigment or coloring matter mixed with water for use as paint **2.** (a) painting done with such paints

wa′ter-cooled′ *adj.* cooled by water circulated around or through it

wa′ter·course′ *n.* **1.** a stream, river, etc. **2.** a channel for water, as a canal

wa′ter·craft′ (-kraft′) *n., pl.* -**craft′** a boat, ship, or other water vehicle

wa′ter·cress′ (-kres′) *n.* a plant of the mustard family, growing generally in running water: its leaves are used in salads, etc.

wa′ter·fall′ *n.* a steep fall of water, as of a stream, from a height; cascade

wa′ter·fowl′ *n.* a water bird, esp. one that swims

wa′ter·front′ *n.* land or docks at the edge of a stream, harbor, etc.

Wa′ter·gate′ (-gāt′) *n.* [< *Watergate,* D.C. building housing Dem. party hdqrs., burglarized (1972) under govt. direction] a scandal that involves officials violating public trust through crime, etc. to maintain their power

water glass 1. a drinking glass **2.** a silicate of sodium or potassium, dissolved in water to form a syrupy liquid used as a preservative for eggs, etc. Also **wa′ter·glass′** *n.*

water hole a pond or pool

wa′ter·lil′y (-lil′ē) *n., pl.* -**les 1.** a water plant with large, flat, floating leaves and showy flowers **2.** the flower

wa′ter·line′ *n.* the line to which the surface of the water comes on the side of a ship

wa′ter·logged′ (-lôgd′, -lägd′) *adj.* soaked or filled with water so as to be heavy and sluggish, as a boat

water main a main pipe in a system of water pipes

wa′ter·mark′ *n.* **1.** a mark showing the limit to which water has risen **2.** a mark in paper, produced by the impression of a design, as in the mold —*vt.* to mark (paper) with a watermark

wa′ter·mel′on *n.* a large, edible fruit with a hard, green rind and juicy, seedy, red pulp

water moccasin a large, poisonous water snake of the SE U.S.

water polo a water game played with a ball by two teams of seven swimmers

water power the power of running or falling water, used to drive machinery, etc.

wa′ter·proof′ (-prōōf′) *adj.* that keeps out water, as a fabric treated with rubber, plastic, etc. —*vt.* to make waterproof

water rat 1. any of various rodents living on banks of streams and ponds **2.** *same as* MUSKRAT

wa′ter-re·pel′lent *adj.* that repels water but is not thoroughly waterproof

wa′ter·shed′ (-shed′) *n.* **1.** a ridge dividing the areas drained by different river systems **2.** the area drained by a river system **3.** a turning point

wa′ter·side′ (-sīd′) *n.* land at the edge of a body of water

wa′ter·ski′ *vi.* -**skied′**, -**ski′ing** to be towed, as

a sport, on skilike boards (**water skis**) by a line attached to a motorboat

wa′ter·spout′ *n.* **1.** a hole, pipe, or spout through which water runs **2.** a tornado occurring over water, appearing as a rapidly rotating column of spray

water table the level below which the ground is saturated with water

wa′ter·tight′ *adj.* **1.** so tight that no water can get in or through **2.** well thought out, with no weak points, as an argument, etc.

water tower an elevated tank for water storage and for equalizing water pressure

wa′ter·way′ *n.* **1.** a channel through which water runs **2.** any body of water on which boats, ships, etc. can travel

water wheel a wheel turned by running water, as for power

water wings a device, inflated with air, used to keep one afloat while learning to swim

wa′ter·works′ *n.pl.* [*often with sing. v.*] a system of reservoirs, pumps, etc. used to bring a water supply to a city, etc.

wa′ter·y *adj.* **1.** of or like water **2.** full of water **3.** thin, diluted, weak, etc. **4.** tearful

watt (wät, wôt) *n.* [< J. *Watt,* 18th-c. Scot. inventor] a unit of electrical power equal to a current of one ampere flowing through a potential difference of one volt

watt′age (-ij) *n.* the amount of watts required to operate a given appliance or device

wat·tle (wät′′l, wôt′-) *n.* [OE. *watul*] **1.** a woven work of sticks intertwined with twigs or branches, used for walls, roofs, etc. **2.** a fleshy flap of skin that hangs from the throat of a cock, turkey, etc. —*vt.* -**tled, -tling 1.** to intertwine (sticks, twigs, etc.) **2.** to construct of wattle

Wave (wāv) *n.* a member of the WAVES

wave (wāv) *vi.* **waved, wav′ing** [OE. *wafian*] **1.** to move or sway to and fro **2.** to signal by moving a hand, arm, etc. to and fro **3.** to have the form of a series of curves —*vt.* **1.** to cause to wave **2.** to brandish, as a weapon **3.** *a)* to move or swing (something) as a signal *b)* to signal (something) to (someone) by doing this **4.** to arrange (hair, etc.) in a series of curves — *n.* **1.** a ridge or swell moving along the surface of a body of water, etc. **2.** a curve or series of curves, as in the hair **3.** a motion to and fro, as with the hand in signaling **4.** something like a wave in effect [*a crime wave*] **5.** *Physics* any of the series of advancing impulses set up by a vibration, etc., as in the transmission of light, sound, etc.

wave′length′ *n. Physics* the distance, measured in the direction of progression of a wave, from any given point to the next point characterized by the same phase

wa·ver (wā′vər) *vi.* [< ME. *waven,* to wave] **1.** to sway to and fro; flutter **2.** to show indecision; vacillate **3.** to falter, flicker, or tremble —*n.* a wavering —**wa′ver·y** *adj.*

WAVES (wāvz) [orig. *W(omen) A(ppointed for) V(oluntary) E(mergency) S(ervice)*] the women's branch of the U.S. Navy

wav·y (wā′vē) *adj.* -**i·er, -i·est 1.** having or like waves **2.** moving in a wavelike motion —**wav′i·ness** *n.*

wax¹ (waks) *n.* [OE. *weax*] **1.** a plastic, dull-yellow substance secreted by bees for building cells; beeswax **2.** any substance like this, as paraffin, etc. —*vt.* to rub, polish, cover, or treat with wax —*adj.* made of wax

wax² (waks) *vi.* [OE. *weaxan,* grow] **1.** to increase in strength, size, etc. **2.** to become

gradually full: said of the moon **3.** to become
[to *wax* old]
wax bean a variety of kidney bean with long,
narrow, yellow pods
wax·en (wak's'n) *adj.* **1.** made of wax **2.** like
wax; smooth, pale, plastic, etc.
wax myrtle a shrub of eastern N. America
with berries coated with a wax used for candles
wax paper paper made moistureproof by a
wax, or paraffin, coating: also **waxed paper**
wax'wing' *n.* a bird with silky-brown plumage,
a showy crest, and scarlet tips on its wings
wax'works' *n.pl.* [*with sing. v.*] an exhibition
of wax figures: also **wax museum**
wax'y *adj.* **-i·er, -i·est** of, full of, or like wax —
wax'i·ness *n.*
way (wā) *n.* [OE. *weg*] **1.** a road, street, path,
etc. **2.** room for passing **3.** a route or course **4.**
a specified route [on the *way* to town] **5.**
habits of life [to fall into evil *ways*] **6.** a
method of doing something **7.** a customary
manner of living, acting, etc. [to change one's
ways] **8.** manner; style **9.** distance [a long *way*
off] **10.** direction of movement, etc. **11.** respect;
particular [right in some *ways*] **12.** wish; will
[I had my *way*] **13.** [*pl.*] a timber framework
on which a ship is built **14.** [Colloq.] *a*) a condition [he's in a bad *way*] *b*) a locality [out
our *way*] —*adv.* away; far [*way* behind] —**by the
way** incidentally —**by way of 1.** passing through
2. as a method, etc. of —**give way 1.** to yield **2.**
to break down —**make way 1.** to clear a passage **2.** to make progress —**under way** moving;
advancing
way'far'er (-fer'ər) *n.* a traveler, esp. on foot —
way'far'ing *adj., n.*
way'lay' *vt.* **-laid', -lay'ing 1.** to lie in wait for
and attack; ambush **2.** to wait for and accost
on the way
way'-out' *adj.* [Colloq.] very unusual or unconventional
-ways [< WAY] *a suffix meaning* in a (specified)
direction, position, or manner [endways]
ways and means methods and resources at
the disposal of a person, company, etc.
way'side' *n.* the edge of a road
way'ward (-wərd) *adj.* [see AWAY & -WARD] **1.**
headstrong, willful, disobedient, etc. **2.** unpredictable; erratic —**way'ward·ness** *n.*
we (wē) *pron., for sing. see* I² [OE.] the persons
speaking or writing: sometimes used by a person in referring to a group of which he is one,
or, in place of *I*, by a monarch, editor, etc.
weak (wēk) *adj.* [ON. *veikr*] **1.** lacking physical
strength; frail; feeble **2.** lacking in moral
strength or willpower **3.** lacking mental power
4. lacking force, power, or authority [*weak*
discipline] **5.** easily torn, broken, etc. [a *weak*
railing] **6.** lacking intensity, etc. [a *weak* voice]
7. diluted [*weak* tea] **8.** unconvincing [a *weak*
argument]
weak'en *vt., vi.* to make or become weak or
weaker
weak'-kneed' *adj.* lacking courage, determination, resistance, etc.
weak'ling *n.* one lacking physical or moral
strength
weak'ly *adj.* **-li·er, -li·est** sickly; feeble; weak —
adv. in a weak way
weak'ness *n.* **1.** a being weak **2.** a weak point;
fault **3.** an immoderate fondness (*for*
something)
weal¹ (wēl) *n.* [< WALE] a mark, line, or ridge
raised on the skin, as by a blow; welt
weal² (wēl) *n.* [OE. *wela*] well-being; welfare
[the public *weal*]

wealth (welth) *n.* [< prec.] **1.** much money or
property; riches **2.** a large amount [a *wealth* of
ideas] **3.** valuable products, contents, etc.
[*wealth* of the oceans] **4.** *Econ.* everything
having value in money
wealth'y *adj.* **-i·er, -i·est** having wealth; rich —
wealth'i·ness *n.*
wean (wēn) *vt.* [OE. *wenian*] **1.** to accustom (a
child or young animal) to take food other than
by suckling **2.** to withdraw (a person) (*from* a
habit, etc.)
weap·on (wep'ən) *n.* [OE. *wæpen*] **1.** any instrument used for fighting **2.** any means of attack or defense
weap'on·ry (-rē) *n.* **1.** the production of
weapons **2.** weapons collectively, esp. of a nation for war use
wear¹ (wer) *vt.* wore, worn, wear'ing [OE.
werian] **1.** to bear (clothing, etc.) on the body
2. to show in one's appearance [she *wore* a
smile] **3.** to impair or diminish by constant
use, friction, etc. **4.** to make by rubbing, flowing, etc. [to *wear* a hole in the rug] **5.** to tire
or exhaust —*vi.* **1.** to become impaired or diminished by constant use, friction, etc. **2.** to
hold up in spite of use [a fabric that *wears*
well] **3.** to have an irritating effect (*on*) —*n.* **1.**
a wearing or being worn **2.** things, esp. clothes,
worn [men's *wear*] **3.** impairment or loss from
use, friction, etc. —**wear off** to diminish by degrees —**wear out 1.** to make or become useless
from continued use **2.** to tire out —**wear'a·ble**
adj. —**wear'er** *n.*
wear and tear loss and damage resulting from
use
wea·ri·some (wir'ē səm) *adj.* causing weariness; tiring; tiresome
wea·ry (wir'ē) *adj.* **-ri·er, -ri·est** [OE. *werig*] **1.**
tired; worn out **2.** no longer liking, patient,
etc.; bored (with *of*) **3.** tiring [*weary* work] —
vt., vi. **-ried, -ry·ing** to make or become weary
—**wea'ri·ly** *adv.* —**wea'ri·ness** *n.*
wea·sel (wē'z'l) *n.* [OE. *wesle*] an agile, flesh-eating mammal, with a long, slender body,
short legs, and a long tail —*vi.* [Colloq.] to
evade a commitment or responsibility (with
out)
weath·er (weth'ər) *n.* [OE. *weder*] **1.** the condition of the atmosphere with regard to temperature, moisture, etc. **2.** storm, rain, etc. —*vt.* **1.**
to expose to the action of weather **2.** to pass
through safely [to *weather* a storm] **3.** *Naut.*
to pass to the windward of —*vi.* to become
worn, discolored, etc. by exposure to the
weather —**under the weather** [Colloq.] ill
weath'er-beat'en *adj.* showing the effect of
exposure to sun, rain, etc.
weath'er·cock' *n.* a weather vane in the form
of a rooster
weath'er-man' *n., pl.* **-men'** one whose work is
forecasting the weather
weath'er·proof' *adj.* that can withstand exposure to the weather without damage —*vt.* to
make weatherproof
weath'er·strip' *n.* a strip of metal, felt, etc.
covering the joint between a door or window
and its casing, to keep out drafts, etc.: also
weath'er·strip'ping —*vt.* **-stripped', -strip'ping**
to provide with this
weather vane a shaped piece of metal, etc. set
up high to show which way the wind is blowing
weave (wēv) *vt.* wove or, chiefly for *vt.* 5 & *vi.*
3, weaved, wo'ven or, chiefly for *vt.* 5
& *vi.* 3, weaved, weav'ing [OE. *wefan*] **1.** to
make (a fabric, basket, etc.) by interlacing
(threads, reeds, etc.), as on a loom **2.** to con-

struct in the mind [to *weave* a tale] **3.** to twist (something) into or through **4.** to spin (a web): said of spiders, etc. **5.** to make (one's way) by moving from side to side or in and out —*vi.* **1.** to do weaving **2.** to become interlaced **3.** to move from side to side or in and out —*n.* a method or pattern of weaving —**weav′er** *n.*

web (web) *n.* [OE. *webb*] **1.** any woven fabric **2.** the network spun by a spider, etc. **3.** a carefully woven trap **4.** a network **5.** a membrane joining the digits of various water birds, animals, etc. —*vt.* **webbed, web′bing** to join by, or cover as with, a web

web′bing *n.* a strong fabric woven in strips and used for belts, in upholstery, etc.

web′foot′ *n., pl.* **-feet′** a foot with the toes webbed —**web′-foot′ed** *adj.*

wed (wed) *vt., vi.* **wed′ded, wed′ded** or **wed, wed′ding** [OE. *weddian*] **1.** to marry **2.** to join closely

we'd (wēd) **1.** we had **2.** we should **3.** we would

Wed. Wednesday

wed·ded (wed′id) *adj.* **1.** married **2.** devoted [*wedded* to one's work] **3.** joined

wed′ding *n.* **1.** the act or ceremony of getting married **2.** a marriage anniversary

wedge (wej) *n.* [OE. *wecg*] **1.** a piece of wood, metal, etc. tapering to a thin edge that can be driven into a narrow opening, as to split wood **2.** anything shaped like a wedge **3.** any act used to open the way for change, etc. —*vt.* **wedged, wedg′ing 1.** to force apart, or fix in place, with a wedge **2.** to pack (*in*) or crowd together —*vi.* to push or be forced as or like a wedge

wedg·ie (wej′ē) *n.* a woman's shoe having a wedgelike piece under the heel so as to form a solid sole, flat from heel to toe

wed·lock (wed′läk′) *n.* [< OE. *wed*, a pledge + *-lac*, an offering] the state of being married

Wednes·day (wenz′dē, -dā) *n.* [< *Woden*, Germanic god] the fourth day of the week

wee (wē) *adj.* **we′er, we′est** [OE. *wege*] **1.** very small; tiny **2.** very early [the *wee* hours]

weed (wēd) *n.* [OE. *weod*] any undesired, uncultivated plant, esp. one crowding out desired plants —*vt., vi.* **1.** to remove weeds from (a garden, etc.) **2.** to remove as useless, harmful, etc.: often with *out* —**weed′er** *n.*

weeds (wēdz) *n.pl.* [< OE. *wæde*, garment] black mourning clothes, esp. of a widow

weed′y *adj.* **-i·er, -i·est 1.** full of weeds **2.** of or like a weed **3.** lean; lanky

week (wēk) *n.* [OE. *wicu*] **1.** a period of seven days, esp. the period from Sunday through Saturday **2.** the hours or days of work in this period

week′day′ *n.* any day of the week except Sunday and, often, Saturday

week′end′, week′-end′ *n.* the period from Friday night or Saturday to Monday morning: also **week end** —*adj.* of, for, or on a weekend —*vi.* to spend the weekend (*at* or *in*)

week′ly *adj.* **1.** of, for, or lasting a week **2.** done, happening, etc. once every week —*adv.* once a week; every week —*n., pl.* **-lies** a periodical published once a week

ween (wēn) *vi., vt.* [OE. *wenan*] [Archaic] to think; suppose; imagine

weep (wēp) *vi., vt.* **wept, weep′ing** [OE. *wepan*] **1.** to shed (tears) **2.** to mourn (*for*) **3.** to drip or exude (water, etc.) —*n.* [*often pl.*] a fit of weeping —**weep′er** *n.*

weep′ing *n.* the act of one who weeps —*adj.* **1.** that weeps **2.** having graceful, drooping branches

weep′y *adj.* **-i·er, -i·est** weeping or inclined to weep

wee·vil (wē′v′l) *n.* [OE. *wifel*] a beetle whose larvae feed on cotton, fruits, grain, etc.

weft (weft) *n.* [< OE. *weftan*, to weave] *same as* WOOF[1]

weigh (wā) *vt.* [OE. *wegan*, carry] **1.** to determine the heaviness of **2.** to have a (specified) weight **3.** to consider and choose carefully [to *weigh* one's words] **4.** to hoist (an anchor) —*vi.* **1.** to have significance, importance, etc. **2.** to be a burden —**weigh down** to burden or bear down on

weight (wāt) *n.* [OE. *wigt*] **1.** a quantity weighing a specified amount **2.** heaviness as a quality; specif., the force of gravity acting on a body **3.** how much a thing weighs **4.** *a*) any unit of heaviness *b*) any system of such units *c*) a piece of metal, etc. of a specific standard heaviness used in weighing **5.** any mass used for its heaviness [a *paperweight*] **6.** a burden, as of sorrow **7.** importance or consequence **8.** influence, power, etc. —*vt.* **1.** to add weight to **2.** to burden

weight′less *adj.* having little or no apparent weight; specif., free of the pull of gravity

weight lifting the athletic exercise or sport of lifting barbells —**weight lifter**

weight′y *adj.* **-i·er, -i·est 1.** very heavy **2.** burdensome **3.** significant; important

weir (wir) *n.* [OE. *wer*] **1.** a low dam built to back up water, as for a mill **2.** a fence, as of brushwood, in a stream, etc., for catching fish

weird (wird) *adj.* [ult. < OE. *wurd*, fate] **1.** suggestive of ghosts, etc.; mysterious **2.** strikingly odd, strange, etc.; bizarre

wel·come (wel′kəm) *adj.* [< OE. *wilcuma*, welcome guest] **1.** gladly received [a *welcome* guest, *welcome* news] **2.** willingly permitted [*welcome* to use the library] **3.** under no obligation [you're *welcome*] —*n.* a welcoming —*vt.* **-comed, -com·ing** to greet or receive with pleasure, etc.

weld (weld) *vt.* [< obs. *well*] **1.** to unite (pieces of metal, etc.) by heating until fused or soft enough to hammer or press together **2.** to unite closely —*vi.* to be welded —*n.* **1.** a welding or being welded **2.** the joint formed by welding —**weld′er** *n.*

wel·fare (wel′fer′) *n.* [see WELL[2] & FARE] **1.** state of health, prosperity, etc.; well-being **2.** aid by government agencies for the poor, unemployed, etc. —**on welfare** receiving government aid because of poverty, etc.

wel·kin (wel′kin) *n.* [OE. *wolcen*] [Archaic or Poet.] the vault of the sky

well[1] *n.* [OE. *wella*] **1.** a natural spring and pool **2.** a hole sunk into the earth to get water, oil, etc. **3.** an abundant source **4.** any shaft like a well —*vi., vt.* to pour forth as from a well; gush

well[2] (wel) *adv.* **bet′ter, best** [OE. *wel*] **1.** in a satisfactory, proper, or skillful manner [treat him *well*, to sing *well*] **2.** prosperously [to live *well*] **3.** with good reason [one may *well* ask] **4.** to a considerable degree [*well* advanced] **5.** thoroughly [stir it *well*] **6.** with certainty; definitely **7.** familiarly [I know him *well*] —*adj.* **1.** suitable, proper, etc. **2.** in good health **3.** in good condition —*interj.* an exclamation of surprise, agreement, etc. —**as well (as) 1.** in addition (to) **2.** equally (with)

we'll (wēl, wil) **1.** we shall **2.** we will

well′-ap·point′ed (-ə poin′tid) *adj.* excellently furnished or equipped

well′-bal′anced *adj.* **1.** carefully adjusted **2.** sane; sensible

well'-be·haved' *adj.* behaving well; polite

well'-be'ing *n.* the state of being well, happy, or prosperous; welfare

well'-bred' *adj.* showing good breeding; courteous and considerate

well'-dis·posed' *adj.* friendly (*toward* a person) or receptive (*to* an idea, etc.)

well'-done' *adj.* 1. performed with skill 2. thoroughly cooked: said esp. of meat

well'-fed' *adj.* plump or fat

well'-fixed' *adj.* [Colloq.] wealthy; rich

well'-found'ed *adj.* based on facts, good evidence, or sound judgment

well'-groomed' *adj.* clean and neat

well'-ground'ed *adj.* having a thorough basic knowledge of a subject

well'-heeled' *adj.* [Slang] rich; prosperous

well'-in·formed' *adj.* having considerable knowledge of a subject or of many subjects

well'-in·ten'tioned *adj.* having or showing good or kindly intentions

well'-knit' *adj.* 1. well constructed 2. having a sturdy body build

well'-known' *adj.* 1. widely known; famous 2. thoroughly known

well'-made' *adj.* 1. skillfully and strongly built 2. skillfully contrived or plotted

well'-man'nered *adj.* polite; courteous

well'-mean'ing *adj.* 1. having good intentions 2. said or done with good intentions, but often with bad results: also **well'-meant'**

well'-nigh' (-nī') *adv.* very nearly; almost

well'-off' *adv.* 1. in a fortunate condition or circumstance 2. prosperous; well-to-do

well'-read' *adj.* having read much

well'-round'ed *adj.* 1. well planned for proper balance 2. showing interest, ability, etc. in many fields 3. shapely

well'-spo'ken *adj.* 1. speaking fluently, graciously, etc. 2. aptly spoken

well'spring' *n.* 1. a spring or fountainhead 2. a source of abundant supply

well'-thought'-of' *adj.* having a good reputation; of good repute

well'-to-do' *adj.* prosperous; wealthy

well'-wish'er *n.* a person who wishes well to another or to a cause, etc.

well'-worn' *adj.* 1. much used 2. overused; trite

Welsh (welsh, welch) *adj.* of Wales, its people, etc. —*n.* the Celtic language of Wales —**the Welsh** the people of Wales —**Welsh'man** (-mən) *n., pl.* -men

welsh (welsh, welch) *vi.* [< ?] [Slang] 1. to fail to pay a debt 2. to evade an obligation Often with *on* —**welsh'er** *n.*

Welsh rabbit a dish of melted cheese, often mixed with ale or beer, served on crackers or toast: also **Welsh rarebit**

welt (welt) *n.* [ME. *welte*] 1. a strip of leather in the seam between the sole and upper of a shoe 2. a ridge raised on the skin by a slash or blow

welt·er (wel'tər) *vi.* [MDu. *welteren*] to roll about or wallow —*n.* a confusion; turmoil

welt·er·weight (wel'tər wāt') *n.* [prob. < WELT] a boxer or wrestler between a lightweight and a middleweight (in boxing, 136-147 lbs.)

wen (wen) *n.* [OE. *wenn*] a harmless skin tumor, esp. of the scalp

wench (wench) *n.* [OE. *wencel*, a child] 1. a girl or young woman: now a derogatory or jocular term 2. [Archaic] a female servant

wend (wend) *vt.* [OE. *wendan*, to turn] to proceed on (one's way)

went (went) *pt. of* GO

wept (wept) *pt. & pp. of* WEEP

were (wur) [OE. *wæron*] *pl. & 2d pers. sing., past indic., and the past subj., of* BE

we're (wir) we are

weren't (wurnt) were not

were·wolf (wir'woolf', wur'-) *n., pl.* -wolves' (-woolvz') [< OE. *wer*, a man + *wulf*, a wolf] *Folklore* a person changed into a wolf

west (west) *n.* [OE.] 1. the direction in which sunset occurs (270° on the compass, opposite east) 2. a region in or toward this direction 3. [W-] the Western Hemisphere and Europe —*adj.* 1. in, of, or toward the west 2. from the west —*adv.* in or toward the west

west'er·ly *adj., adv.* 1. toward the west 2. from the west

west'ern *adj.* 1. in, of, or toward the west 2. from the west 3. [W-] of the West —*n.* a story or motion picture about cowboys, etc. in the western U.S.

west'ern·er *n.* a native of the west

west·ward (west'wərd) *adv., adj.* toward the west: also **west'wards** *adv.*

wet (wet) *adj.* **wet'ter, wet'test** [OE. *wæt*] 1. covered or saturated with water or other liquid 2. rainy; misty 3. not yet dry [*wet* paint] 4. permitting the sale of alcoholic liquor —*n.* 1. water or other liquid 2. rain or rainy weather 3. one who favors the sale of alcoholic liquor —*vt., vi.* **wet** or **wet'ted, wet'ting** to make or become wet —**all wet** [Slang] wrong —**wet'ness** *n.*

wet'back' *n.* [Colloq.] a Mexican who illegally enters the U.S. to work

wet blanket one who dampens or lessens the enthusiasm or gaiety of others

wet nurse a woman hired to suckle another's child —**wet'-nurse'** *vt.* -nursed', -nurs'ing

we've (wēv) we have

whack (hwak) *vt., vi.* [echoic] [Colloq.] to strike or slap with a sharp, resounding blow —*n.* [Colloq.] a sharp, resounding blow, or its sound —**have** (or **take**) **a whack at** [Colloq.] 1. to aim a blow at 2. to make an attempt at —**out of whack** [Colloq.] not in proper condition

whale¹ (hwāl) *n.* [OE. *hwæl*] a large, warm-blooded, fishlike mammal that breathes air —*vi.* **whaled, whal'ing** to hunt whales —**a whale of a** [Colloq.] an exceptionally large, fine, etc. example of

whale² (hwāl) *vt.* **whaled, whal'ing** [prob. var. of WALE] [Colloq.] to beat; thrash

whale'bone' *n.* the horny, elastic material hanging from the upper jaw of some whales used, esp. formerly, for corset stays, etc.

whal'er *n.* 1. a ship used in whaling 2. a man whose work is whaling

wham (hwam) *interj.* a sound imitating a heavy blow, etc. —*n.* a heavy blow or impact —*vt., vi.* **whammed, wham'ming** to strike, etc. loudly

wham·my (hwam'ē) *n., pl.* -mies [Slang] a jinx or the evil eye

wharf (hwôrf) *n., pl.* **wharves** (hwôrvz), **wharfs** [< OE. *hwerf*, a dam] a platform built on the shore, where ships can load or unload

what (hwut, hwät) *pron.* [< OE. *hwa*, who] 1. which thing, event, etc.? [*what* is that object?] 2. that which or those which [do *what* you will] —*adj.* 1. which or which kind of: used interrogatively or relatively 2. as much, or as many, as [take *what* men you need] 3. how great, surprising, etc. [*what* joy!] —*adv.* 1. in what way? how? [*what* does it matter?] 2. partly [*what* with singing and joking, the time passed] 3. how greatly, surprisingly, etc. [*what* sad news!] —*interj.* an exclamation of surprise, anger, etc. [*what!* no dinner?] —**what about**

what do you think, know, etc. concerning? — **what for** why?

what·ev·er (hwət ev'ər) *pron.* 1. what: used for emphasis 2. anything that *[say whatever you like]* 3. no matter what *[whatever you do, don't rush]* 4. [Colloq.] anything of the sort — *adj.* 1. of any kind 2. being who it may be *[whatever man told you that, it isn't true]*

what'not' *n.* 1. a nondescript thing 2. a set of open shelves, as for bric-a-brac

what'so·ev'er (-sō ev'ər) *pron., adj.* whatever: used for emphasis

wheal[1] (hwēl) *n.* [ME. *whele*] a small, raised patch of skin, as from an insect bite

wheal[2] (hwēl) *n. same as* WEAL[1]

wheat (hwēt) *n.* [OE. *hwǣte*] 1. a cereal grass with dense spikes that bear grains 2. such grain, used for flour, cereals, etc.

whee·dle (hwē'd'l) *vt., vi.* **-dled, -dling** [< ?] to influence or persuade (a person) or get (something) by flattery, coaxing, etc.

wheel (hwēl) *n.* [OE. *hweol*] 1. a solid disk or circular frame turning on a central axis 2. anything like a wheel in shape, movement, etc. 3. the steering wheel of a motor vehicle 4. [*pl.*] [Slang] an automobile 5. [*usually pl.*] the moving forces *[the wheels of progress]* 6. a turning movement 7. [Slang] an important person: also **big wheel** —*vt., vi.* 1. to move on or in a wheeled vehicle 2. to turn, revolve, rotate, etc. 3. to turn so as to reverse direction —**at the wheel** steering a motor vehicle, etc. —**wheeled** *adj.*

wheel'bar'row (-bar'ō, -ber'ō) *n.* a shallow, open box for moving small loads, having a wheel in front, and two shafts in back for pushing the vehicle

wheel'base' *n.* in a motor vehicle, the distance in inches from the front axle to the rear axle

wheel'chair' *n.* a chair mounted on large wheels, for persons unable to walk

wheel'er-deal'er (-dēl'ər) *n.* [Slang] one who is showily aggressive, as in arranging business deals

wheel'wright' (-rīt') *n.* one who makes and repairs wagon and carriage wheels

wheeze (hwēz) *vi.* **wheezed, wheez'ing** [ON. *hvaesa*, to hiss] to make a whistling, breathy sound, as in asthma —*n.* a wheezing

whelk (hwelk) *n.* [OE. *wioluc*] any of various large sea snails with spiral shells, esp. those used in Europe for food

whelm (hwelm) *vt.* [ME. *welmen*] 1. to submerge or engulf 2. to overwhelm

whelp (hwelp) *n.* [OE. *hwelp*] the young of a dog, etc. —*vt., vi.* to bring forth (young): said of animals

when (hwen) *adv.* [OE. *hwænne*] 1. at what time? *[when did he leave?]* 2. on what occasion? —*conj.* 1. at the time that *[he told us when we sat down]* 2. at which time *[a time when men must speak out]* 3. as soon as *[come when I call]* 4. at whatever time that *[he rested when he could]* 5. although —*pron.* what time or which time *[until when will you stay?]* —*n.* the time (*of* an event)

whence (hwens) *adv.* [OE. *hwanan*] from what place, source, cause, etc.; from where *[whence do you come?]*

when·ev'er *adv.* [Colloq.] when: used for emphasis —*conj.* at whatever time *[visit us whenever you can]*

where (hwer) *adv.* [OE. *hwær*] 1. in or at what place? *[where is the car?]* 2. to or toward what place? *[where did he go?]* 3. in what respect? *[where is she to blame?]* 4. from what place or

source? *[where did you find out?]* —*conj.* 1. at what place *[he knows where it is]* 2. at which place *[we came home, where we ate]* 3. wherever 4. to the place to which *[we go where you go]* —*pron.* 1. the place at which *[a mile to where he lives]* 2. what place *[where are you from?]* —*n.* the place (*of* an event)

where'a·bouts' (-ə bouts') *adv.* near what place? where? —*n.* the place where a person or thing is *[do you know his whereabouts?]*

where·as' (-az') *conj.* 1. in view of the fact that 2. while on the contrary *[she is slim, whereas he is fat]*

where·at' *conj.* [Archaic] at which point

where·by' *conj.* by which *[a plan whereby to make money]*

where'fore' (-fôr') *adv.* [Archaic] for what reason? why? —*conj.* 1. for which 2. because of which —*n.* the reason; cause

where·in' *conj.* in which

where·of' *adv., conj.* of what, which, or whom

where·on' *conj.* on which

where'up·on' *conj.* 1. upon which 2. at which

wher·ev'er (hwer ev'ər) *adv.* [Colloq.] where: used for emphasis —*conj.* in, at, or to whatever place *[go wherever you like]*

where·with' *conj.* with which

where'with·al' (-with ôl') *n.* the necessary means, esp. money

wher·ry (hwer'ē) *n., pl.* **-ries** [ME. *whery*] a light rowboat

whet (hwet) *vt.* **whet'ted, whet'ting** [< OE. *hwæt*, keen] 1. to sharpen by rubbing or grinding 2. to stimulate (the appetite, etc.)

wheth·er (hweth'ər) *conj.* [OE. *hwæther*] 1. if it be the case or fact that *[ask whether she will help]* 2. in case; in either case: used to introduce alternatives *[whether it rains or snows]*

whet·stone (hwet'stōn') *n.* an abrasive stone for sharpening knives or other edged tools

whew (hyōō) *interj.* [echoic] an exclamation of relief, surprise, dismay, etc.

whey (hwā) *n.* [OE. *hwæg*] the thin, watery part of milk, which separates from the curds

which (hwich) *pron.* [OE. *hwylc*] 1. what one (or ones) of several? *[which do you want?]* 2. the one (or ones) that *[he knows which he wants]* 3. that *[the boat which sank]* 4. any that *[take which you like]* —*adj.* 1. what one or ones *[which man (or men) came?]* 2. whatever

which·ev'er *pron., adj.* 1. any one *[take whichever (desk) you like]* 2. no matter which *[whichever (desk) he chooses, they won't be pleased]*

whiff (hwif) *n.* [echoic] 1. a light puff or gust of air or wind 2. a slight gust of odor

Whig (hwig) *n.* [< *wiggamore* (contemptuous term for Scot. Presbyterians)] 1. a member of a former English political party which championed reform and parliamentary rights 2. a supporter of the American Revolution against Great Britain 3. a member of an American political party (c.1838-1856)

while (hwīl) *n.* [OE. *hwil*] a period of time *[a short while]* —*conj.* 1. during the time that *[we talked while we ate]* 2. a) although *[while she isn't pretty, she is charming]* b) whereas *[the walls are green, while the ceiling is white]* —*vt.* **whiled, whil'ing** to spend (time) pleasantly (often with *away*)

whilst (hwīlst) *conj.* [Dial.] *same as* WHILE

whim (hwim) *n.* [< ?] a sudden fancy; idle and passing notion; caprice

whim·per (hwim'pər) *vi., vt.* [? akin to WHINE] to cry or utter with low, whining, broken sounds —*n.* a whimpering sound

whim·si·cal (hwim′zi k′l) *adj.* 1. full of whims or whimsy 2. different in an odd way —**whim′· si·cal′i·ty** (-kal′ə tē), *pl.* -**ties**

whim·sy (hwim′zē) *n., pl.* -**sies** [< ?] 1. an odd fancy; idle notion; whim 2. fanciful humor Also sp. **whim′sey**, *pl.* -**seys**

whine (hwīn) *vi.* **whined, whin′ing** [OE. *hwinan*] 1. *a)* to utter a high-pitched, nasal sound, as in complaint *b)* to make a prolonged sound like this 2. to complain in a childish way —*n.* 1. a whining 2. a complaint uttered in a whining tone —**whin′y** *adj.*

whin·ny (hwin′ē) *vi.* -**nied, -ny·ing** [prob. < prec.] to neigh in a low, gentle way: said of a horse —*n., pl.* -**nies** a whinnying

whip (hwip) *vt.* **whipped, whip′ping** [MDu. *wippen*, to swing] 1. to move, pull, throw, etc. suddenly [to *whip* out a knife] 2. to strike as with a strap; lash 3. to wind (cord or thread) around a rope to prevent fraying 4. to beat (eggs, cream, etc.) into a froth 5. [Colloq.] to defeat —*vi.* 1. to move quickly and suddenly 2. to flap about in a whiplike manner —*n.* 1. a flexible instrument for striking or flogging 2. a blow, etc. as with a whip 3. an officer of a political party in a legislature who maintains discipline, etc. 4. a whipping motion 5. a dessert of fruit, sugar, whipped cream, etc. —**whip up** to rouse; excite

whip′cord′ *n.* 1. a hard, twisted or braided cord 2. a strong worsted cloth with a diagonally ribbed surface

whip′lash′ *n.* 1. the lash of a whip 2. a sudden, severe jolting of the neck backward and then forward, as caused by the impact of a rear-end automobile collision

whip′per·snap′per *n.* a young or unimportant person who appears presumptuous

whip·pet (hwip′it) *n.* [< WHIP] a swift dog like a small greyhound, used in racing

whip·ple·tree (hwip′′l trē′) *n.* [< WHIP + TREE] *same as* SINGLETREE

whip·poor·will (hwip′ər wil′) *n.* [echoic] a grayish bird of eastern N. America, active at night

whir, whirr (hwur) *vi., vt.* **whirred, whir′ring** [prob. < Scand.] to fly, revolve, vibrate, etc. with a buzzing sound —*n.* such a sound

whirl (hwurl) *vi.* [ON. *hvirfla*] 1. to move rapidly in a circle or orbit 2. to rotate or spin fast 3. to seem to spin [my head is *whirling*] —*vt.* to cause to move, rotate, revolve, etc. rapidly —*n.* 1. a whirling or whirling motion 2. a tumult; uproar 3. a confused or giddy condition —**give it a whirl** [Colloq.] to make an attempt

whirl·i·gig (hwur′li gig′) *n.* a child's toy that whirls or spins

whirl′pool′ *n.* water in violent, whirling motion tending to draw floating objects into its center

whirlpool bath a bath in which an agitating device drives a current of warm or hot water in a swirling motion

whirl′wind′ *n.* 1. a current of air whirling violently in a spiral and moving forward 2. anything like a whirlwind —*adj.* impetuous; speedy

whirl′y·bird′ *n. colloq.* term for HELICOPTER

whisk (hwisk) *n.* [ON. *visk*, a brush] 1. a brushing with a quick, light, sweeping motion 2. such a motion —*vt., vi.* to move, carry, brush (*away, off,* etc.) with a quick, sweeping motion

whisk broom a small, short-handled broom for brushing clothes, etc.

whisk′er *n.* 1. [*pl.*] the hair growing on a man's face, esp. on the cheeks 2. any of the long, bristly hairs on the upper lip of a cat, rat, etc. —**whisk′ered** *adj.*

whis·key (hwis′kē) *n., pl.* -**keys, -kies** [< Ir. & Scot. < IrGael. *uisce*, water + *beathadh*, life] a strong alcoholic liquor distilled from the fermented mash of grain: also, esp. for Brit. and Canad. usage, **whisky**, *pl.* -**kies**

whis·per (hwis′pər) *vi., vt.* [OE. *hwisprian*] 1. to speak or say very softly, esp. without vibration of the vocal cords 2. to talk or tell furtively, as in gossiping 3. to make a soft, rustling sound —*n.* 1. a whispering 2. something whispered 3. a soft, rustling sound —**whis′· per·er** *n.*

whist (hwist) *n.* [< *whisk*] a card game similar to bridge

whis·tle (hwis′′l) *vi.* -**tled, -tling** [OE. *hwistlian*] 1. to make a clear, shrill sound as by forcing breath through the contracted lips 2. to move with a shrill sound, as the wind 3. *a)* to blow a whistle *b)* to have its whistle blown, as a train —*vt.* 1. to produce (a tune, etc.) by whistling 2. to signal, etc. by whistling —*n.* 1. an instrument for whistling 2. a whistling —**whis′tler** *n.*

whit (hwit) *n.* [< OE. *wiht*, a wight] the least bit; jot; iota [not a *whit* the wiser]

white (hwīt) *adj.* **whit′er, whit′est** [OE. *hwīt*] 1. having the color of pure snow or milk 2. of a light or pale color 3. pale; wan 4. pure; innocent 5. having a light-colored skin —*n.* 1. *a)* white color *b)* a white pigment 2. a white or light-colored part, as the albumen of an egg, the white part of the eyeball, etc. 3. a person with a light-colored skin; Caucasoid

white′cap′ *n.* a wave with its crest broken into white foam

white′-col′lar *adj.* designating or of clerical or professional workers or the like

white elephant 1. an albino elephant, held as sacred in SE Asia 2. a thing of little use, but expensive to maintain 3. any object not wanted by its owner, but of possible value to others

white feather a symbol of cowardice

white′fish′ *n., pl.:* see FISH a white or silvery lake fish of the salmon family, found in N U.S.

white flag a white banner hoisted as a signal of truce or surrender

white gold gold alloyed with nickel, zinc, etc., to give it a platinumlike appearance

white goods 1. household linens, as sheets, towels, etc. 2. large household appliances, as refrigerators

white heat 1. the degree of intense heat at which a metal, etc. glows white 2. a state of intense emotion, etc. —**white′-hot′** *adj.*

White House, the 1. official residence of the President of the U.S., in Washington, D.C. 2. the executive branch of the U.S. government

white lead a poisonous, white powder, lead carbonate, used as a paint pigment, etc.

white lie a lie about something unimportant, often told to spare someone's feelings

whit·en (hwīt′′n) *vt., vi.* to make or become white or whiter —**whit′en·er** *n.*

white race loosely, the Caucasoid group of mankind

white sale a store sale of household linens

white slave a woman forced into prostitution for others' profit —**white slavery**

white′wall′ *adj.* designating or of a tire with a white band on the outer sidewall —*n.* a whitewall tire

white′wash′ *n.* 1. a mixture of lime, whiting, water, etc., for whitening walls, etc. 2. a concealing of faults in order to exonerate —*vt.* 1. to cover with whitewash 2. to conceal the faults of **3**. [Colloq.] *Sports* to defeat (an opponent) without permitting him to score — **white'wash'ing** n.

whith-er (hwith'ər) *adv.* [OE. *hwider*] to what place, condition, etc.? where? —*conj.* **1**. to which place, condition, etc. **2**. wherever

whit-ing¹ (hwīt'iŋ) n. [< MDu. *wit*, white] any of many unrelated ocean food fishes of N. America, Europe, and Australia

whit-ing² (hwīt'iŋ) n. [ME. *whytyng*] powdered chalk used in paints, inks, etc.

whit'ish *adj.* somewhat white

Whit-sun-day (hwit'sun'dē, -s'n dā') n. [OE. *Hwita Sunnandæg*, white Sunday] *same as* PENTECOST

whit-tle (hwit''l) *vt.* **-tled, -tling** [OE. *thwitan*, to cut] **1**. *a*) to cut thin shavings from (wood) with a knife *b*) to carve (an object) in this manner **2**. to reduce gradually —*vi.* to whittle wood

whiz, whizz (hwiz) *vi.* **whizzed, whiz'zing** [echoic] **1**. to make the hissing sound of something speeding through the air **2**. to speed by with or as with this sound —n. **1**. this sound **2**. [Slang] an expert [a *whiz* at mathematics]

who (hōō) *pron., obj.* **whom,** *poss.* **whose** [OE. *hwa*] **1**. what or which person or persons [who is he? I know *who* came] **2**. (the, or a, person or persons) that [a man *who* knows]

whoa (hwō, wō) *interj.* [for HO] stop!: used esp. in directing a horse to stand still

who-dun-it (hōō dun'it) n. [Colloq.] a mystery novel, play, etc.

who-ev'er (-ev'ər) *pron.* **1**. any person that **2**. no matter what person [whoever said it, it's not so] **3**. who?: used for emphasis

whole (hōl) *adj.* [OE. *hal*] **1**. not diseased or injured **2**. not broken, damaged, etc.; intact **3**. containing all the parts; complete **4**. not divided up; in a single unit **5**. *Arith.* not a fraction —n. **1**. the entire amount, etc.; totality **2**. a complete organization of parts; unity —**on the whole** all things considered —**whole'ness** n.

whole'heart'ed *adj.* doing or done with all one's energy, enthusiasm, etc.; sincere

whole milk milk from which none of the butterfat, etc. has been removed

whole note *Music* a note (o) having four times the duration of a quarter note

whole'sale' n. the selling of goods in relatively large quantities, esp. to retailers —*adj.* **1**. of or engaged in such selling **2**. extensive or sweeping [wholesale criticism] —*adv.* **1**. at wholesale prices **2**. extensively or sweepingly —*vt., vi.* **-saled', -sal'ing** to sell wholesale —**whole'sal'er** n.

whole-some (hōl'səm) *adj.* [ME. *holsom*] **1**. promoting health or well-being **2**. improving the mind or character **3**. having health and vigor —**whole'some-ness** n.

whole'-wheat' *adj.* made of the entire grain of wheat [whole-wheat flour]

who'll (hōōl) **1**. who shall **2**. who will

whol-ly (hō'lē) *adv.* to the whole amount or extent; totally; entirely

whom (hōōm) *pron. obj. case of* WHO

whom-ev'er (-ev'ər) *pron. obj. case of* WHOEVER

whoop (hōōp, hwōōp) n. [< OFr. *houper*, cry out] **1**. a loud shout, cry, etc., as of joy **2**. the gasping intake of air following a fit of coughing in whooping cough —*vt., vi.* to utter (with) a whoop or whoops

whooping cough an acute infectious disease, esp. of children, with coughing fits that end in a whoop

whop-per (hwäp'ər) n. [< colloq. *whop*, to beat] [Colloq.] **1**. anything extraordinarily large **2**. a great lie —**whop'ping** *adj.*

whore (hôr) n. [< OE. *hore*] a prostitute

whorl (hwôrl, hwurl) n. [dial. var. of WHIRL] anything with a coiled or spiral appearance, as any of the circular ridges that form the design of a fingerprint —**whorled** *adj.*

who's (hōōz) **1**. who is **2**. who has

whose (hōōz) *pron.* [OE. *hwæs*] that or those belonging to whom [whose is this?] —*possessive pronominal adj.* of, belonging to, or done by whom or which

who-so-ev-er (hōō'sō ev'ər) *pron.* whoever: used for emphasis

why (hwī) *adv.* [OE. *hwi* < *hwæt*, what] for what reason, cause, or purpose? [why eat?] —*conj.* **1**. because of which [there is no reason *why* you should go] **2**. the reason for which [that is *why* he went] —n., pl. **whys** the reason, cause, etc. [never mind the *why*] —*interj.* an exclamation of surprise, impatience, etc.

wick (wik) n. [OE. *weoca*] a piece of cord, tape, etc. in a candle, oil lamp, etc., that absorbs the fuel and, when lighted, burns

wick-ed (wik'id) *adj.* [ME. < *wikke*, evil] **1**. morally bad; evil **2**. generally painful, unpleasant, etc. [a *wicked* storm] **3**. mischievous **4**. [Slang] skillful —**wick'ed-ly** *adv.* —**wick'ed-ness** n.

wick-er (wik'ər) n. [< Scand.] **1**. a thin, flexible twig **2**. *a*) such twigs or long, woody strips woven together, as in making baskets or furniture *b*) *same as* WICKERWORK (sense 1) —*adj.* made of wicker

wick'er-work' (-wurk') n. **1**. things made of wicker **2**. *same as* WICKER (sense 2 *a*)

wick-et (wik'it) n. [ONormFr. *wiket*] **1**. a small door or gate, esp. one in or near a larger one **2**. a small window, as in a box office **3**. *Croquet* any of the small wire arches through which the balls must be hit

wide (wīd) *adj.* [OE. *wid*] **1**. extending over a large area, esp. from side to side **2**. of a specified extent from side to side **3**. of great extent [a *wide* variety] **4**. open fully [eyes *wide* with fear] **5**. far from the point, etc. aimed at [wide of the mark] —*adv.* **1**. over a relatively large area **2**. to a large or full extent [wide open] **3**. so as to miss the point, etc. aimed at —**wide'ly** *adv.*

-wide *a combining form meaning* extending throughout [nationwide]

wide'-a-wake' *adj.* **1**. completely awake **2**. alert

wide'-eyed' *adj.* with the eyes wide open

wid-en (wīd''n) *vt., vi.* to make or become wide or wider

wide'spread' *adj.* occurring over a wide area or extent

widg-eon, wi-geon (wij'ən) n. [prob. < MFr. *vigeon*] a wild, freshwater duck

wid-ow (wid'ō) n. [OE. *widewe*] a woman whose husband has died and who has not remarried —*vt.* to cause to become a widow

wid'ow-er n. a man whose wife has died and who has not remarried

width (width) n. **1**. the distance from side to side **2**. a piece of a specified width

wield (wēld) *vt.* [OE. *wealdan*] **1**. to handle (a tool, etc.), esp. with skill **2**. to exercise (power, control, etc.) —**wield'er** n.

wie-ner (wē'nər) n. [< G. *Wiener wurst*, Vienna sausage] a smoked link sausage; frankfurter: also **wie'ner-wurst'** (-wurst')

wife (wīf) n., pl. **wives** (wīvz) [OE. *wif*] a married woman —**wife'ly** *adj.*

wig (wig) *n.* [< PERIWIG] a false covering of hair for the head

wig·gle (wig′'l) *vt., vi.* **-gled, -gling** [ME. *wigelen*] to move with short, jerky motions from side to side —*n.* a wiggling —**wig′gler** *n.* — **wig′gly** *adj.* **-gli·er, -gli·est**

wight (wīt) *n.* [OE. *wiht*] [Archaic] a human being

wig·let (wig′lit) *n.* a small wig

wig·wag (wig′wag′) *vt., vi.* **-wagged′, -wag′ging** [< obs. *wig*, to move + WAG¹] 1. to move back and forth; wag 2. to send (a message) by waving flags, lights, etc. according to a code —*n.* the sending of messages in this way

wig·wam (wig′wäm, -wôm) *n.* [< Algonquian] a N. American Indian shelter consisting of a framework of arched poles covered with bark, leaves, etc.

wild (wīld) *adj.* [OE. *wilde*] 1. living or growing in its original, natural state 2. not lived in or cultivated; waste 3. not civilized; savage 4. not easily controlled [wild children] 5. lacking social or moral restraint; dissolute [a wild party] 6. turbulent; stormy 7. enthusiastic [wild about golf] 8. fantastically impractical; reckless 9. missing the target [a wild pitch] 10. Cards having any value specified by the holder: said of a card —*adv.* in a wild manner —*n.* [usually pl.] a wilderness or wasteland — **wild′ly** *adv.*

wild′cat′ *n.* 1. any fierce, medium-sized, undomesticated animal of the cat family 2. a fierce, aggressive person 3. an oil well drilled in an area not previously known to have oil — *adj.* 1. unsound or risky 2. illegal or unauthorized [a wildcat strike] —*vt.* **-cat′ted, -cat′ting** to drill for oil in an area previously considered unproductive —**wild′cat′ter** *n.*

wil·de·beest (wil′də bēst′, vil′-) *n.* [Afrik.] *same as* GNU

wil·der·ness (wil′dər nis) *n.* [< OE. *wilde*, wild + *deor*, animal] an uncultivated, uninhabited region; waste

wild′-eyed′ *adj.* 1. staring in a wild, distracted way 2. fantastically impractical

wild′fire′ *n.* a fire that spreads fast and is hard to put out

wild′-goose′ chase a futile search, pursuit, or endeavor

wild′life′ *n.* wild animals and birds

wild oats a wild grass common in the W U.S.: also **wild oat** —**sow one's wild oats** to be promiscuous in youth

Wild West [also w- W-] the western U.S. in its early, lawless frontier period

wile (wīl) *n.* [< OE. *wigle*, magic] 1. a sly trick; stratagem 2. a beguiling or coquettish trick: *usually used in pl.* —*vt.* **wiled, wil′ing** to beguile; lure —**wile away** to while away (time, etc.)

will¹ (wil) *n.* [OE. *willa*] 1. the power of making a reasoned choice or of controlling one's own actions 2. determination 3. attitude toward others [good *will*] 4. *a)* a particular desire, choice, etc. of someone *b)* mandate [the *will* of the people] 5. a legal document directing the disposal of one's property after death —*vt.* 1. to desire; want [to *will* to live] 2. to control by the power of the will 3. to bequeath by a will —*vi.* to wish, desire, or choose —**at will** when one wishes

will² (wil) *v., pt.* **would** [OE. *willan*] 1. an auxiliary sometimes used to express futurity in the second and third persons and determination or obligation in the first person See note at SHALL 2. an auxiliary used to express: *a)* willingness [will you go?] *b)* ability or capacity [it

will hold a pint] —*vt., vi.* to wish; desire [do what you *will*]

will·ful (wil′fəl) *adj.* 1. done or said deliberately 2. obstinate; stubborn Also **wil′ful** —**will′ful·ly** *adv.* —**will′ful·ness** *n.*

wil·lies (wil′ēz) *n.pl.* [< ?] [Slang] a state of nervousness; jitters: with *the*

will·ing (wil′iŋ) *adj.* 1. ready or agreeing (*to* do something) 2. doing, giving, etc. or done, given, etc. readily or gladly —**will′ing·ly** *adv.* — **will′ing·ness** *n.*

will-o'-the-wisp (wil′ə *thə* wisp′) *n.* 1. a light seen at night over swamps, etc., believed to be marsh gas burning 2. a delusive hope or goal

wil·low (wil′ō) *n.* [OE. *welig*] 1. a tree with narrow leaves, and flexible twigs used in weaving baskets, etc. 2. its wood

wil·low·y (wil′ə wē) *adj.* like a willow; slender, supple, lithe, etc.

will′pow′er *n.* strength of will, mind, or determination; self-control

wil·ly-nil·ly (wil′ē nil′ē) *adv., adj.* [contr. < *will I, nill I: nill* < OE. *nyllan*, be unwilling] (happening) whether one wishes it or not

wilt (wilt) *vi.* [< obs. *welk*, wither] 1. to become limp, as from heat or lack of water; droop, as a plant 2. to become weak or faint 3. to lose courage —*vt.* to cause to wilt

Wil·ton (carpet or **rug)** (wilt′'n) [< *Wilton*, England] a kind of carpet with a velvety pile

wil·y (wī′lē) *adj.* **-i·er, -i·est** full of wiles; crafty; sly —**wil′i·ness** *n.*

wim·ple (wim′p'l) *n.* [OE. *wimpel*] a nun's head covering so arranged as to leave only the face exposed

win (win) *vi.* **won, win′ning** [OE. *winnan*, to fight] 1. *a)* to gain a victory *b)* to finish first in a race, etc. 2. to succeed with effort; get [to *win* back to health] —*vt.* 1. to get by effort, struggle, etc. 2. to be victorious in (a contest, dispute, etc.) 3. to get to with effort [they *won* the hilltop by noon] 4. to influence; persuade: often with *over* 5. to gain (the sympathy, favor, etc.) of (someone) 6. to persuade to marry one —*n.* [Colloq.] a victory, as in a contest

wince (wins) *vi.* **winced, winc′ing** [< OFr. *guenchir*] to shrink or draw back slightly, usually with a grimace, as in pain

winch (winch) *n.* [OE. *wince*] 1. a crank with a handle for transmitting motion 2. a hoisting or hauling apparatus having a cylinder around which a rope or cable winds when lifting a load

Win·ches·ter (rifle) (win′ches′tər) [< O. F. *Winchester*, U.S. manufacturer] *a trademark for* a type of repeating rifle

wind¹ (wīnd) *vt.* **wound, wind′ing** [OE. *windan*] 1. to turn [wind the crank] 2. to coil into a ball or around something else; twine 3. to cover by entwining 4. *a)* to make (one's way) in a twisting course *b)* to cause to move in a twisting course 5. to tighten the spring of (a clock, etc.) as by turning a stem —*vi.* 1. to move or go in a twisting or curving course 2. to take a devious course 3. to be coiled (*about* or *around* something) —*n.* a turn; twist —**wind up** 1. to wind into a ball, etc. 2. to conclude; settle 3. to make very tense, excited, etc. 4. *Baseball* to swing the arm in getting ready to pitch the ball

wind² (wind) *n.* [OE.] 1. air in motion 2. a strong current of air; gale 3. air bearing a scent, as in hunting 4. air regarded as bearing information, etc. [rumors in the *wind*] 5. breath or the power of breathing 6. empty talk 7. gas in the intestines 8. [pl.] the wind

windbag   520   **wiretap**

instruments in an orchestra —*vt.* **1.** to get the scent of **2.** to put out of breath —**break wind** to expel gas from the bowels —**in the wind** happening or about to happen

wind·bag (wind′bag′) *n.* [Colloq.] one who talks much but says little of importance

wind′break′ *n.* a hedge, fence, or row of trees serving as a protection from wind

wind·ed (win′did) *adj.* out of breath

wind′fall′ *n.* **1.** something blown down by the wind, as fruit from a tree **2.** an unexpected stroke of good luck or personal gain

winding sheet a shroud

wind instrument a musical instrument sounded by blowing air, esp. breath, through it, as a flute

wind·jam·mer (wind′jam′ər) *n. Naut.* a sailing ship or one of its crew

wind·lass (wind′ləs) *n.* [< ON. *vinda,* to WIND¹ + *ass,* a beam] a winch, esp. one worked by a crank

wind′mill′ *n.* a mill operated by the wind's rotation of vanes radiating from a shaft: it provides power for pumping water, etc.

win·dow (win′dō) *n.* [< ON. *vindr,* WIND² + *auga,* eye] **1.** an opening in a building, vehicle, etc. for admitting light and air or for looking through, usually having a pane of glass in a movable frame **2.** a windowpane **3.** an opening resembling a window

window box a long narrow box on or outside a window ledge, for growing plants

window dressing 1. the display of goods in a store window **2.** that which is designed to make something seem better than it really is —**win′dow-dress′** *vt.* —**window dresser**

win′dow-pane′ *n.* a pane of glass in a window

win′dow-shop′ (-shäp′) *vi.* **-shopped′, -shop′-ping** to look at goods in store windows without entering the stores to buy

wind·pipe (wind′pīp′) *n.* the trachea

wind·row (wind′rō′) *n.* a row of hay, etc. raked together to dry

wind′shield′ (-shēld′) *n.* in automobiles, etc., a glass screen in front, to protect the riders from wind, dust, etc.

wind′sock′ (-säk′) *n.* a long, cone-shaped cloth bag flown at an airfield to show wind direction: also **wind sleeve**

wind′storm′ *n.* a storm with a strong wind but little or no rain

wind·up (wīnd′up′) *n.* **1.** a conclusion; end **2.** *Baseball* the swinging of the arm preparatory to pitching the ball

wind·ward (wind′wərd) *n.* the direction from which the wind blows —*adv.* toward the wind —*adj.* **1.** moving windward **2.** on the side from which the wind blows

wind·y (win′dē) *adj.* **-i·er, -i·est 1.** characterized by wind [a *windy* day] **2.** stormy, blustery, etc. **3.** *a)* without substance; flimsy *b)* long-winded, boastful, etc. —**wind′i·ness** *n.*

wine (wīn) *n.* [< L. *vinum*] **1.** the fermented juice of grapes, used as an alcoholic beverage and in cooking, etc. **2.** the fermented juice of other fruits or plants [dandelion *wine*] —*vt., vi.* **wined, win′ing** to provide with or drink wine: usually in **wine and dine,** to entertain lavishly

wine′-col′ored *adj.* having the color of red wine; dark purplish-red

wine′glass′ *n.* a small glass for serving wine

win′er·y (-ər ē) *n., pl.* **-ies** an establishment where wine is made

wing (wiŋ) *n.* [< ON. *vaengr*] **1.** either of the paired organs of flight of a bird, bat, insect, etc. **2.** something like a wing in use, position, etc.; esp., *a)* a (or the) main lateral supporting surface of an airplane *b)* a distinct part of a building, often having a special use *c)* either side of a stage out of sight of the audience **3.** the section of an army, fleet, etc. to the right (or left) of the center **4.** a section, as of a political party, viewed as radical or conservative **5.** a unit in an air force **6.** a flying, or a means of flying —*vt.* **1.** to provide with wings **2.** *a)* to send swiftly as on wings *b)* to make (one's way) by flying *c)* to pass through or over as by flying **3.** to wound in the wing, arm, etc. — *vi.* to go as if on wings; fly —**on the wing** (while) flying —**take wing** to fly away —**under one's wing** under one's protection, etc. —**wing it** [Colloq.] to improvise in acting, speaking, etc. —**winged** (wiŋd; *poet.* wiŋ′id) *adj.*

wing′span′ *n.* the distance between the tips of an airplane's wings

wing′spread′ *n.* **1.** the distance between the tips of a pair of fully spread wings **2.** *same as* WINGSPAN

wink (wiŋk) *vi.* [OE. *wincian*] **1.** to close the eyelids and open them again quickly **2.** to close and open one eyelid quickly, as a signal, etc. **3.** to twinkle —*vt.* to make (an eye) wink — *n.* **1.** a winking, or the instant of time it takes **2.** a signal given by winking **3.** a twinkle — **wink at** to pretend not to see

win·ner (win′ər) *n.* one that wins

win′ning *adj.* **1.** victorious **2.** charming —*n.* **1.** a victory **2.** [*pl.*] something won, esp. money

win·now (win′ō) *vt., vi.* [< OE. *wind,* WIND²] **1.** to blow (the chaff) from (grain) **2.** to scatter **3.** to sort out by sifting

win·o (wīn′ō) *n., pl.* **-os** [Slang] an alcoholic who drinks cheap wine

win·some (win′səm) *adj.* [OE. *wynsum,* pleasant] sweetly attractive; charming

win·ter (win′tər) *n.* [OE.] **1.** the coldest season of the year, following autumn **2.** a period of decline, distress, etc. —*adj.* of, during, or for winter —*vi.* to pass the winter —*vt.* to maintain during the winter

win′ter·green′ *n.* **1.** an evergreen plant with white flowers and red berries **2.** an aromatic oil (**oil of wintergreen**) made from its leaves and used as a flavoring **3.** the flavor

win′ter·ize (-īz′) *vt.* **-ized, -iz′ing** to put into condition for winter

win′ter·time′ *n.* the winter season

win′try (-trē) *adj.* **-tri·er, -tri·est** of or like winter; cold, bleak, etc.

wipe (wīp) *vt.* **wiped, wip′ing** [OE. *wipian*] **1.** to clean or dry by rubbing with a cloth, etc. **2.** to rub (a cloth, etc.) over something **3.** to apply or remove by wiping —*n.* a wiping —**wipe out 1.** to remove; erase **2.** to kill off —**wip′er** *n.*

wire (wīr) *n.* [OE. *wir*] **1.** metal drawn into a long thread **2.** a length of this **3.** *a)* telegraph *b)* a telegram **4.** the finish line of a race —*adj.* made of wire —*vt.* **wired, wir′ing 1.** to furnish, connect, bind, etc. with wire **2.** to telegraph — *vi.* to telegraph —**pull wires** to get what one wants through one's friends' influence

wire′hair′ (-her′) *n.* a fox terrier with a wiry coat: also **wire-haired terrier**

wire′less *adj.* without wire; specif., operating with electromagnetic waves, not with conducting wire —*n.* **1.** wireless telegraphy or telephony **2.** [Chiefly Brit.] radio

Wire′pho′to *a trademark for:* **1.** a system of reproducing photographs at a distance by means of electric impulses transmitted by wire **2.** a photograph so produced

wire′tap′ *vt., vi.* **-tapped′, -tap′ping** to tap (a telephone wire, etc.) to get information secretly —n. 1. a wiretapping 2. a device for wiretapping

wir'ing n. a system of wires, as for carrying electricity

wir'y adj. -i·er, -i·est 1. of wire 2. like wire; stiff 3. lean and strong —**wir'i·ness** n.

wis·dom (wiz'dəm) n. [OE. < wis, WISE¹ + -dom, -DOM] 1. the quality of being wise; good judgment 2. learning; knowledge 3. wise teaching

wisdom tooth the back tooth on each side of each jaw

wise¹ (wīz) adj. **wis'er, wis'est** [OE. wis] 1. having or showing good judgment 2. judicious 3. informed 4. learned 5. shrewd; cunning 6. [Slang] conceited, impudent, fresh, etc.

wise² (wīz) n. [OE.] way; manner

-wise [< prec.] a suffix meaning: 1. in a (specified) direction, position, or manner [sidewise] 2. in a manner characteristic of [clockwise] 3. with regard to [weatherwise]

wise·a·cre (wīz'ā'kər) n. [< OHG. wizzago, prophet] one who pretends to be much wiser than he really is

wise'crack' n. [Slang] a flippant or facetious remark —vi. [Slang] to make wisecracks

wish (wish) vt. [OE. wyscan] 1. to have a longing for; want 2. to express a desire concerning [I wish you well] 3. to request [he wishes her to leave] 4. to impose (with on) [he wished the job on me] —vi. 1. to long; yearn 2. to make a wish —n. 1. a wishing 2. something wished for 3. a request 4. [pl.] expressed desire for a person's well-being, etc. [best wishes]

wish'bone' n. the forked bone in front of a bird's breastbone

wish'ful adj. having or showing a wish; desirous —**wish'ful·ly** adv.

wish·y-wash·y (wish'ē wôsh'ē) adj. [Colloq.] 1. watery; thin 2. a) weak b) vacillating

wisp (wisp) n. [prob. < Scand.] 1. a small bundle, as of straw 2. a thin, filmy bit or puff [a wisp of smoke] 3. something delicate, frail, etc. [a wisp of a girl] —**wisp'y** adj. -i·er, -i·est

wis·te·ri·a (wis tir'ē ə) n. [< C. Wistar, 19th-c. U.S. anatomist] a twining vine with showy clusters of purple, white, or pink flowers: also **wis·tar'i·a** (-ter'-)

wist·ful (wist'fəl) adj. [< earlier wistly, attentive] showing or expressing vague yearnings —**wist'ful·ly** adv. —**wist'ful·ness** n.

wit¹ (wit) n. [OE.] 1. [pl.] powers of thinking; mental faculties 2. good sense 3. the ability to make clever remarks in a surprising or ironic way 4. one having this ability —**at one's wits' end** at a loss as to what to do

wit² (wit) vt., vi. **wist** (wist), **wit'ting** [OE. witan] [Archaic] to know or learn —**to wit** that is to say

witch (wich) n. [OE. wicce] 1. a woman supposedly having supernatural power by a compact with evil spirits 2. an ugly old shrew 3. [Colloq.] a fascinating woman

witch'craft' n. 1. the power or practices of witches 2. bewitching attraction or charm

witch doctor a person who practices primitive medicine involving the use of magic, as among tribes in Africa

witch hazel [< OE. wice] 1. a shrub with yellow flowers 2. a lotion made from its leaves and bark

witch hunt an investigation of political dissenters, conducted with much publicity, supposedly to uncover subversion, etc.

with (with, with) prep. [OE., against] 1. in opposition to [he argued with me] 2. a) alongside of; near to b) in the company of c) into;

among [mix blue with red] 3. as a member of [he plays with a trio] 4. concerning [pleased with her gift] 5. compared to 6. as well as [he can run with the best] 7. of the same opinions as [I'm with you] 8. in the opinion of [it's OK with me] 9. as a result of [faint with hunger] 10. by means of 11. having received [with your consent, he'll go] 12. having or showing [to play with skill] 13. in the keeping, care, etc. of [leave the baby with me] 14. in spite of 15. at the same time as 16. in proportion to [wages varying with skills] 17. to; onto [join this end with that one] 18. from [to part with one's gains] —**with that** after that

with- a combining form meaning: 1. away, back [withdraw] 2. against, from [withhold]

with·al (with ôl') adv. 1. besides 2. despite that

with·draw (with drô', with-) vt. -drew', -drawn', -draw'ing 1. to take back; remove 2. to retract or recall (a statement, etc.) —vi. 1. to move back; go away 2. to remove oneself (from an organization, activity, etc.)

with·draw'al (-əl) n. 1. the act of withdrawing 2. a giving up the use of a habit-forming drug, typically accompanied by physical and mental distress (**withdrawal symptoms**)

with·drawn' adj. shy, reserved, etc.

withe (with, with) n. [OE. withthe] a tough, flexible twig, as of willow, used for binding

with·er (with'ər) vi. [< ME. wederen, to weather] 1. to dry up; shrivel; wilt, as plants 2. to become wasted or decayed 3. to weaken; languish —vt. 1. to cause to wither 2. to cause to feel abashed

with·ers (with'ərz) n.pl. [< OE. wither, against] the part of a horse's back between the shoulder blades

with·hold (with hōld', with-) vt. -held', -hold'ing 1. a) to hold back; restrain b) to deduct (taxes, etc.) from wages 2. to refrain from granting; refuse

withholding tax the amount of income tax withheld from employees' wages or salaries

with·in (with in', with-) adv. [OE. withinnan] 1. on or to the inside 2. indoors 3. inside the body, mind, etc. —prep. 1. in the inner part of 2. not beyond 3. inside the limits of

with·out' (-out') adv. [OE. withutan] 1. on or to the outside 2. outdoors —prep. 1. at, on, or to the outside of 2. beyond 3. lacking 4. free from [without fear] 5. with avoidance of [to pass without speaking]

with·stand (with stand', with-) vt., vi. -stood', -stand'ing to oppose, resist, or endure

wit·less (wit'lis) adj. lacking wit; foolish —**wit'less·ly** adv. —**wit'less·ness** n.

wit·ness (wit'nis) n. [OE. gewitnes, knowledge] 1. evidence; testimony 2. one who saw, or can give a firsthand account, of something 3. one who testifies in court 4. one who observes, and attests to, a signing, etc. —vt. 1. to testify to 2. to serve as evidence of 3. to act as a witness of 4. to be present at —**bear witness** to testify

wit·ti·cism (wit'ə siz'm) n. [< WITTY] a witty remark

wit·ting (wit'iŋ) adj. [ME. wytting] done knowingly; intentional —**wit'ting·ly** adv.

wit·ty (wit'ē) adj. -ti·er, -ti·est [OE. wittig] having or showing wit; cleverly amusing —**wit'ti·ly** adv. —**wit'ti·ness** n.

wives (wīvz) n. pl. of WIFE

wiz·ard (wiz'ərd) n. [ME. wisard] 1. a magician; sorcerer 2. [Colloq.] one very skilled at a certain activity

wiz'ard·ry n. magic; sorcery

wiz·en (wiz''n, wēz'-) vt., vi. [OE. wisnian] to dry up; wither —**wiz'ened** (-'nd) adj.

wk. *pl.* **wks. 1.** week **2.** work
wkly. weekly
wob·ble (wäb''l) *vi.* **-bled, -bling** [prob. < LowG. *wabbeln*] **1.** to move unsteadily from side to side; shake **2.** to vacillate —*vt.* to cause to wobble —*n.* a wobbling motion —**wob'bly** *adj.* **-bli·er, -bli·est** —**wob'bli·ness** *n.*
woe (wō) *n.* [OE. *wa*] **1.** great sorrow; grief **2.** trouble —*interj.* alas!
woe·be·gone (wō'bi gôn', -gän') *adj.* of woeful appearance; looking sad or wretched
woe'ful (-fəl) *adj.* **1.** full of woe; sad; mournful **2.** of, causing, or involving woe **3.** pitiful; wretched —**woe'ful·ly** *adv.*
wok (wäk) *n.* [Chin.] a bowl-shaped pan, as on a ringlike stand, for frying, braising, etc.
woke (wōk) *alt. pt. of* WAKE¹
wolf (woolf) *n., pl.* **wolves** (woolvz) [OE. *wulf*] **1.** a wild, flesh-eating, doglike mammal of the Northern Hemisphere **2.** *a)* a cruel or greedy person *b)* [Slang] a man who flirts with many women —*vt.* to eat greedily —**cry wolf** to give a false alarm —**wolf'ish** *adj.*
wolf'hound' (-hound') *n.* a breed of large dog, once used for hunting wolves
wolf·ram (wool'frəm) *n.* [G.] *same as* TUNGSTEN
wol·ver·ine (wool'və rēn') *n.* [< WOLF] a stocky, ferocious, flesh-eating mammal of N. America and Eurasia
wolves (woolvz) *n. pl. of* WOLF
wom·an (woom'ən) *n., pl.* **wom·en** (wim'in) [< OE. *wif*, a female + *mann*, human being] **1.** an adult female human being **2.** women as a group **3.** a female servant **4.** [Dial.] a wife or sweetheart **5.** womanly qualities
wom'an·hood' *n.* **1.** the state of being a woman **2.** womanly qualities **3.** womankind
wom'an·ish *adj.* like a woman; feminine
wom'an·ize (-īz') *vt.* **-ized, -iz'ing** to make effeminate —*vi.* [Colloq.] to be sexually promiscuous with women
wom'an·kind' *n.* women in general
wom'an·like' *adj.* womanly
wom'an·ly *adj.* **1.** womanish **2.** characteristic of or fit for a woman
womb (woom) *n.* [OE. *wamb*] *same as* UTERUS
wom·bat (wäm'bat) *n.* [< native name] a burrowing Australian marsupial resembling a small bear
wom·en (wim'in) *n. pl. of* WOMAN
wom'en·folk', wom'en·folks' *n.pl.* [Dial. or Colloq.] women
women's rights the rights claimed by and for women, equal to those of men
won (wun) *pt. & pp. of* WIN
won·der (wun'dər) *n.* [OE. *wundor*] **1.** a person, thing, or event causing astonishment, admiration, etc.; marvel **2.** the feeling of surprise, etc. caused by something strange, remarkable, etc. **3.** a miracle —*vi.* **1.** to feel wonder; marvel **2.** to have curiosity, sometimes mixed with doubt —*vt.* to have curiosity or doubt about [I *wonder* what he meant]
won'der·ful *adj.* **1.** that causes wonder; marvelous **2.** [Colloq.] fine; excellent —**won'der·ful·ly** *adv.*
won'der·land' *n.* **1.** an imaginary land full of wonders **2.** a real place like this
won'der·ment *n.* wonder or amazement
won·drous (wun'drəs) *adj.* wonderful —*adv.* wonderfully Now only literary
wont (wônt, wônt) *adj.* [< OE. *wunian*, be used to] accustomed [he was *wont* to rise early] —*n.* usual practice; habit
won't (wônt) will not
wont·ed (wôn'tid, wôn'-) *adj.* customary

woo (woo) *vt.* [OE. *wogian*] **1.** to try to get the love of; court **2.** to seek [she *wooed* fame] **3.** to coax; urge —*vi.* to woo a person —**woo'er** *n.*
wood (wood) *n.* [OE. *wudu*] **1.** [*usually pl.*] a thick growth of trees; forest **2.** the hard, fibrous substance beneath the bark of trees and shrubs **3.** lumber or timber **4.** firewood **5.** a golf club having a wooden head —*adj.* **1.** made of wood; wooden **2.** growing or living in woods —**out of the woods** [Colloq.] out of difficulty, danger, etc. —**wood'ed** *adj.*
wood alcohol a colorless, poisonous liquid obtained by the distillation of wood and used as a fuel, solvent, etc.
wood'bine' (-bīn') *n.* [see WOOD & BIND] **1.** a European climbing honeysuckle **2.** a climbing vine of eastern N. America, with dark-blue berries
wood'chuck' (-chuk') *n.* [< AmInd. name] a N. American burrowing and hibernating marmot; groundhog
wood'cock' (-käk') *n.* a small game bird with short legs and a long bill
wood'craft' *n.* **1.** matters relating to the woods, as camping, hunting, etc. **2.** *same as* WOODWORKING
wood'cut' (-kut') *n.* **1.** a wooden block engraved with a design, etc. **2.** a print made from this
wood'cut'ter *n.* a person who fells trees, cuts wood, etc. —**wood'cut'ting** *n.*
wood'en (-'n) *adj.* **1.** made of wood **2.** stiff, lifeless, etc. **3.** dull; insensitive —**wood'en·ly** *adv.* —**wood'en·ness** *n.*
wood'land' (-land') *n.* land covered with woods —*adj.* (-lənd) of or living in the woods
wood'peck'er (-pek'ər) *n.* a tree-climbing bird with a strong, pointed bill used to drill holes in bark to get insects
wood'shed' *n.* a shed for storing firewood
woods·man (woodz'mən) *n., pl.* **-men 1.** one who lives or works in the woods, as a hunter, etc. **2.** one skilled in woodcraft
wood'wind' (-wind') *n.* any of the wind instruments of an orchestra made, esp. orig., of wood: clarinet, oboe, bassoon, flute, and English horn
wood'work' *n.* **1.** work done in wood **2.** things made of wood, esp. the interior moldings, doors, etc. of a house
wood'work'ing *n.* the art or work of making things out of wood
wood'y *adj.* **-i·er, -i·est 1.** covered with trees **2.** consisting of or forming wood **3.** like wood —**wood'i·ness** *n.*
woof (woof, woof) *n.* [< OE. *wefan*, to weave] the horizontal threads crossing the warp in a woven fabric
woof'er *n.* in an assembly of two or more loudspeakers, a large speaker for reproducing low sounds
wool (wool) *n.* [OE. *wull*] **1.** the soft, curly hair of sheep or of some other animals, as the goat **2.** woolen yarn, cloth, clothing, etc. **3.** anything that looks or feels like wool —*adj.* of wool or woolen goods
wool'en, wool'len (-ən) *adj.* **1.** made of wool **2.** of or relating to wool or woolen cloth —*n.* [*pl.*] woolen goods or clothing
wool'gath'er·ing (-gath'ər iŋ) *n.* absentmindedness or daydreaming
wool·ly (wool'ē) *adj.* **-li·er, -li·est 1.** of or like wool **2.** bearing wool **3.** covered with wool or something like wool **4.** rough and uncivilized: chiefly in **wild and woolly** —*n., pl.* **-lies** a woolen garment Also sp. **wool'y** —**wool'li·ness** *n.*

wooz·y (wōō′zē) *adj.* **-i·er, -i·est** [Colloq.] **1.** dizzy, faint, and sickish **2.** befuddled, as from drink **—wooz′i·ly** *adv.* **—wooz′i·ness** *n.*

word (wurd) *n.* [OE.] **1.** *a)* a speech sound, or series of speech sounds, serving to communicate meaning *b)* the written or printed representation of this **2.** a brief remark [a *word* of advice] **3.** a promise [he gave his *word*] **4.** news; information **5.** *a)* a password or signal *b)* a command; order **6.** [*pl.*] *a)* talk; speech *b)* lyrics; text *c)* a quarrel; dispute **—vt.** to express in words; phrase **—in a word** briefly **—in so many words** precisely **—the Word** the Bible **—word for word** in precisely the same words

word′ing *n.* choice of words

word of honor solemn promise

word processing a computerized system for preparing, storing, or reproducing letters, reports, etc. by use of an electronic typewriter

word·y (wur′dē) *adj.* **-i·er, -i·est** containing or using many or too many words; verbose **—word′i·ly** *adv.* **—word′i·ness** *n.*

wore (wôr) *pt. of* WEAR

work (wurk) *n.* [OE. *weorc*] **1.** effort exerted to do or make something; labor; toil **2.** employment at a job [out of *work*] **3.** occupation, profession, business, trade, etc. **4.** something one is making or doing; task **5.** something made or done; specif., *a)* [*usually pl.*] an act; deed [good *works*] *b)* [*pl.*] collected writings *c)* [*pl.*] engineering structures **6.** [*pl.*] a place where work is done, as a factory **7.** workmanship **—adj.** of, for, or used in work **—vi. worked** or **wrought, work′ing 1.** to do work; labor; toil **2.** to be employed **3.** to function or operate, esp. effectively **4.** to ferment **5.** to move, proceed, etc. slowly and with difficulty **6.** to come or become, as by repeated movement [the handle *worked* loose] **—vt. 1.** to cause; bring about [the mechanic *worked* wonders] **2.** to mold; shape **3.** to sew, embroider, etc. **4.** to solve (a mathematical problem, etc.) **5.** to manipulate; knead **6.** to bring into a specified condition [to *work* a nail loose] **7.** to cultivate (soil) **8.** to operate; use **9.** to cause to work [to *work* a crew hard] **10.** to make (one's way, etc.) by effort **11.** to provoke; rouse [he *worked* her into a rage] **—at work** working **—out of work** unemployed **—the works 1.** the working parts (of a watch, etc.) **2.** [Colloq.] everything **—work off** to get rid of **—work on** (or **upon**) **1.** to influence **2.** to try to persuade **—work out 1.** to accomplish **2.** to solve **3.** to result **4.** to develop **5.** to engage in a workout **—work up 1.** to advance **2.** to develop **3.** to excite

work′a·ble (-ə b'l) *adj.* **1.** that can be worked **2.** practicable; feasible

work·a·day (wur′kə dā′) *adj.* **1.** of workdays; everyday **2.** ordinary

work·a·hol·ic (wur′kə hôl′ik) *n.* [< WORK & ALCOHOLIC] one who has a compulsive need to work

work′bench′ (-bench′) *n.* a table at which work is done, as by a mechanic

work′book′ *n.* a book containing questions and exercises to be worked by students

work′day′ *n.* **1.** a day on which work is done **2.** the part of a day during which work is done **—adj.** *same as* WORKADAY

work·er (wur′kər) *n.* **1.** one who works for a living **2.** one who works for a cause, etc. **3.** any of various sterile female ants, bees, etc. that do work for the colony

work′horse′ *n.* **1.** a horse used for working **2.** a steady, responsible worker

work′house′ *n.* a prison where petty offenders are confined and made to work

work′ing *adj.* **1.** that works **2.** of or used in work **3.** sufficient to get work done [a *working* majority] **—n.** the act of one that works

work′ing·man′ *n., pl.* **-men′** a worker; esp., an industrial or manual worker

work′man (-mən) *n., pl.* **-men 1.** *same as* WORKINGMAN **2.** a craftsman

work′man·like′ *adj.* characteristic of a good workman; skillful: also **work′man·ly**

work′man·ship′ *n.* skill of a workman; craftsmanship

work′out′ *n.* **1.** a training session of physical exercises **2.** any strenuous exercise, work, etc.

work′shop′ *n.* **1.** a room or building where work is done **2.** a seminar or series of meetings for intensive study, work, etc.

world (wurld) *n.* [OE. *werold*] **1.** *a)* the earth *b)* the universe **2.** *a)* mankind *b)* people generally; the public **3.** *a)* [*also* W-] some part of the earth [the Old *World*] *b)* any sphere or domain [the dog *world*] **4.** individual experience, outlook, etc. [his *world* is narrow] **5.** secular life and interests, or people concerned with these **6.** [*often pl.*] a large amount [a *world* of good] **—for all the world** exactly

world′ly *adj.* **-li·er, -li·est 1.** of this world; secular **2.** devoted to the pleasures, etc. of this world **3.** worldly-wise **—world′li·ness** *n.*

world′ly-wise′ *adj.* wise in the ways of the world; sophisticated

world′wide′ *adj.* throughout the world

worm (wurm) *n.* [OE. *wyrm*, serpent] **1.** a long, slender, soft-bodied, creeping animal **2.** popularly, *a)* an insect larva *b)* any wormlike animal **3.** an abject or contemptible person **4.** something wormlike or spiral in shape, as the thread of a screw **5.** [*pl.*] any disease caused by parasitic worms in the intestines, etc. **—vi.** to proceed like a worm, in a winding or devious way **—vt. 1.** to bring about, make, etc. in a winding or devious way **2.** to purge of intestinal worms **—worm′y** *adj.* **-i·er, -i·est**

worm gear a gear consisting of a rotating screw meshed with a toothed wheel

worm′wood′ (-wood′) *n.* [< OE. *wermod*] **1.** any of various strong-smelling plants; esp., a perennial that yields a bitter-tasting oil used in making absinthe **2.** a bitter experience

worn (wôrn) *pp. of* WEAR **—adj. 1.** damaged by use or wear **2.** exhausted

worn′-out′ *adj.* **1.** used until no longer effective, usable, etc. **2.** tired out

wor·ri·some (wur′ē səm) *adj.* **1.** causing worry or anxiety **2.** tending to worry

wor·ry (wur′ē) *vt.* **-ried, -ry·ing** [OE. *wyrgan*, strangle] **1.** to treat roughly, as with continual biting [a dog *worrying* a bone] **2.** to annoy; bother **3.** to make troubled or uneasy **—vi. 1.** to bite or tear (at an object) with the teeth **2.** to be anxious, troubled, etc. **3.** to manage to get (along or through) **—n., pl. -ries 1.** a troubled state of mind; anxiety **2.** a cause of this **—wor′ri·er** *n.*

wor′ry·wart′ (-wôrt′) *n.* [WORRY + WART] [Colloq.] one who tends to worry much

worse (wurs) *adj. compar. of* BAD¹ & ILL [OE. *wiersa*] **1.** *a)* bad, evil, harmful, etc. in a greater degree *b)* of inferior quality **2.** in poorer health; more ill **3.** in a less satisfactory situation **—adv. compar. of** BADLY & ILL in a worse manner; to a worse extent **—n.** that state which is worse **—worse off** in a worse state

wors·en (wur′s'n) *vt., vi.* to make or become worse

wor·ship (wur′ship) *n.* [< OE.: see WORTH & -SHIP] **1.** a service or rite showing reverence for a deity **2.** intense love or admiration **3.** [Chiefly Brit.] a title of honor used in addressing magistrates, etc. —*vt.* **-shiped** or **-shipped, -ship·ing** or **-ship·ping 1.** to show religious reverence for **2.** to have intense love or admiration for —*vi.* to engage in worship —**wor'·ship·er, wor'ship·per** *n.*

wor'ship·ful *adj.* [Brit.] honorable; respected

worst (wurst) *adj. superl. of* BAD¹ & ILL [OE. *wyrsta*] **1.** *a)* bad, evil, harmful, etc. in the greatest degree *b)* of the lowest quality **2.** in the least satisfactory situation —*adv. superl. of* BADLY & ILL in the worst manner; to the worst extent —*n.* that which is worst —*vt.* to defeat —**at worst** under the worst circumstances —**(in) the worst way** [Slang] very much

wor·sted (woos'tid, wur'stid) *n.* [< *Worstead,* England] **1.** a smooth, hard-twisted wool thread or yarn **2.** fabric made from this —*adj.* made of worsted

wort¹ (wurt) *n.* [< OE. *wyrt-*] a liquid prepared with malt which, after fermenting, becomes beer, ale, etc.

wort² (wurt) *n.* [OE. *wyrt,* a root] a plant or herb: now usually in compounds [liverwort]

worth (wurth) *n.* [OE. *weorth*] **1.** material value, esp. as expressed in money **2.** importance, value, merit, etc. **3.** the quantity to be had for a given sum [a dime's *worth* of nuts] **4.** wealth; possessions —*adj.* **1.** deserving or worthy of **2.** equal in value to **3.** having wealth totaling

worth'less (-lis) *adj.* without worth or merit; useless —**worth'less·ness** *n.*

worth'while' (-hwil', -wil') *adj.* worth the time or effort spent

wor·thy (wur'thē) *adj.* **-thi·er, -thi·est 1.** having worth, value, or merit **2.** deserving —*n., pl.* **-thies** a person of outstanding worth, etc. — **wor'thi·ness** *n.*

would (wood) *v.* [OE. *wolde*] **1.** *pt. of* WILL² **2.** an auxiliary used to express: *a)* condition [if you *would*] *b)* futurity [he said he *would* come] *c)* habitual action [Sundays he *would* sleep late] *d)* a request [would you help me?] **3.** I wish [would that I could]

would'-be' *adj.* **1.** wishing or pretending to be **2.** intended to be

would·n't (wood''nt) would not

wound¹ (woond) *n.* [OE. *wund*] **1.** an injury in which the skin or other tissue is cut, torn, etc. **2.** any hurt to the feelings, honor, etc. —*vt., vi.* to inflict a wound (on or upon); injure

wound² (wound) *pt. & pp. of* WIND¹

wove (wōv) *pt. & alt. pp. of* WEAVE

wo'ven (-'n) *alt. pp. of* WEAVE

wow (wou) *Interj.* an exclamation of surprise, pleasure, etc. —*vt.* [Slang] to be a great success with

wrack (rak) *n.* [< OE. *wræc,* misery & MDu. *wrak,* a wreck] ruin; destruction: now chiefly in **wrack and ruin**

wraith (rāth) *n.* [Scot.] a ghost

wran·gle (raŋ'g'l) *vi.* **-gled, -gling** [< ME. *wringen,* to wring] to argue; quarrel, esp. angrily and noisily —*vt.* to herd (livestock) —*n.* an angry, noisy dispute —**wran'gler** *n.*

wrap (rap) *vt.* **wrapped** or **wrapt, wrap'ping** [ME. *wrappen*] **1.** to wind or fold (a covering) around something **2.** to enclose and fasten in paper, etc. —*vi.* to twine, coil, etc. (over, around, etc.) —*n.* an outer covering or garment —**wrapped up in** absorbed in —**wrap up** [Colloq.] to conclude; settle

wrap'per *n.* **1.** one that wraps **2.** that in which something is wrapped **3.** a woman's dressing gown

wrap'ping *n.* [often pl.] the material, as paper, in which something is wrapped

wrap'-up' *n.* [Colloq.] a concluding, summarizing statement, report, etc.

wrath (rath) *n.* [OE., *wroth*] **1.** intense anger; rage **2.** any action of vengeance or punishment —**wrath'ful** *adj.*

wreak (rēk) *vt.* [OE. *wrecan,* to revenge] **1.** to give vent to (anger, etc.) **2.** to inflict (vengeance), etc.

wreath (rēth) *n., pl.* **wreaths** (rēthz) [< OE. *writhan,* to twist] **1.** a twisted ring of leaves, flowers, etc. **2.** something like this in shape [wreaths of smoke]

wreathe (rēth) *vt.* **wreathed, wreath'ing 1.** to form into a wreath **2.** to coil or twist around **3.** to decorate with wreaths

wreck (rek) *n.* [< ON. *vrek,* wreckage] **1.** a shipwreck **2.** the remains of something destroyed or badly damaged **3.** a person in poor health **4.** a wrecking or being wrecked —*vt.* **1.** to destroy **2.** to tear down (a building, etc.) **3.** to overthrow; thwart

wreck'age (-ij) *n.* **1.** a wrecking or being wrecked **2.** the remains of something wrecked

wreck'er *n.* **1.** a person or thing that wrecks **2.** one that salvages or removes wrecks

wren (ren) *n.* [OE. *wrenna*] a small songbird with a long bill and stubby, erect tail

wrench (rench) *n.* [OE. *wrenc,* a trick] **1.** a sudden, sharp twist or pull **2.** an injury caused by a twist or jerk, as to the back **3.** a sudden feeling of grief, anguish, etc. **4.** a tool for holding and turning nuts, bolts, pipes, etc. —*vt.* **1.** to twist or jerk violently **2.** to injure (a part of the body) with a twist **3.** to distort (a meaning, etc.)

wrest (rest) *vt.* [OE. *wræstan*] **1.** to pull or force away violently with a twisting motion **2.** to take by force; usurp —*n.* a wresting; twist; wrench

wres·tle (res''l) *vi., vt.* **-tled, -tling** [< OE. *wræstan,* to twist] **1.** to struggle hand to hand with (an opponent) in an attempt to throw him **2.** to contend (with) —*n.* a wrestling — **wres'tler** *n.*

wres'tling *n.* a sport in which the opponents wrestle, or struggle hand to hand

wretch (rech) *n.* [OE. *wrecca,* an outcast] **1.** a miserable or unhappy person **2.** a person who is despised or scorned

wretch'ed (-id) *adj.* [OE. *wræcc*] **1.** very unhappy; miserable **2.** causing misery **3.** very inferior **4.** deserving to be despised —**wretch'ed·ly** *adv.* —**wretch'ed·ness** *n.*

wrig·gle (rig''l) *vi.* **-gled, -gling** [MLowG. *wriggeln*] **1.** to twist and turn; squirm **2.** to move along with a twisting motion **3.** to make one's way by shifty means —*n.* a wriggling — **wrig'gler** *n.* —**wrig'gly** *adj.*

wright (rīt) *n.* [< OE. *wyrcan,* to work] one who makes, constructs, or repairs: used chiefly in compounds [shipwright]

wring (riŋ) *vt.* **wrung, wring'ing** [OE. *wringan*] **1.** *a)* to squeeze, press, or twist *b)* to force (out water, etc.) **2.** to twist (the hands) in distress **3.** to clasp (another's hand) in greeting **4.** to extract by force; threats, etc. —*n.* a wringing

wring'er *n.* a device with two rollers used for squeezing water from wet clothes

wrin·kle¹ (riŋ'k'l) *n.* [ME. *wrinkel*] **1.** a small ridge or furrow in a normally smooth surface **2.** a crease or pucker in the skin —*vt., vi.* **-kled, -kling** to contract into small ridges or creases — **wrin'kly** *adj.* **-kli·er, -kli·est**

wrin·kle² (riŋ'k'l) *n.* [prob. < OE. *wrenc,* a trick] [Colloq.] a clever trick, idea, etc.

wrist (rist) *n.* [OE.] the joint between the hand and the forearm

wrist′band′ *n.* a band that goes around the wrist, as on the cuff of a sleeve

wrist′watch′ (-wäch′, -wôch′) *n.* a watch worn on a strap or band around the wrist

writ (rit) *n.* [OE. < *writan*, write] a formal legal document ordering or prohibiting some action

write (rīt) *vt.* **wrote, writ′ten, writ′ing** [OE. *writan*] **1.** to form (words, letters, etc.) on a surface, as with a pen **2.** to be the author or composer of (literary or musical material) **3.** to communicate (with) in writing *[he wrote* (me) that he was ill] **4.** to record (information) in a computer —*vi.* to write words, books, etc. —**write off 1.** to remove from accounts (bad debts, etc.) **2.** to drop from consideration —**write up 1.** to put into writing **2.** to write in full —**write up** to write an account of

write′-off′ *n.* something written off, amortized, etc.

writ′er *n.* one who writes, esp. as a business or occupation; author, journalist, etc.

write′-up′ *n.* [Colloq.] a written report, often a favorable account, as for publicity

writhe (rīth) *vt.* **writhed, writh′ing** [OE. *writhan*, to twist] to cause to twist or turn —*vi.* **1.** to twist or turn; squirm **2.** to suffer great emotional distress —*n.* a writhing movement

writ·ing (rīt′iŋ) *n.* **1.** the act of one who writes **2.** something written **3.** written form **4.** *short for* HANDWRITING

writ·ten (rit′'n) *pp. of* WRITE

wrong (rôŋ) *adj.* [< ON. *rangr*, twisted] **1.** not just, moral, etc. **2.** not in accordance with an established standard, etc. **3.** not suitable or appropriate **4.** *a)* contrary to fact, reason, etc.; incorrect *b)* mistaken **5.** not functioning properly **6.** designating the unfinished, inner, or under side, as of a fabric —*adv.* in a wrong manner, direction, etc. —*n.* something wrong; esp., an unjust, immoral, or illegal act —*vt.* to treat badly or unjustly —**in the wrong** wrong

wrong′do′ing (-dōō′iŋ) *n.* any act or behavior that is wrong —**wrong′do′er** *n.*

wrong′ful *adj.* **1.** unjust, unfair, or injurious **2.** unlawful —**wrong′ful·ly** *adv.*

wrong′head′ed (-hed′id) *adj.* stubborn in sticking to wrong opinions, ideas, etc. —**wrong′head′ed·ly** *adv.* —**wrong′head′ed·ness** *n.*

wrote (rōt) *pt. of* WRITE

wroth (rôth; *chiefly Brit.* rōth) *adj.* [OE. *wrath*] angry; wrathful; incensed

wrought (rôt) *alt. pt. & pp. of* WORK —*adj.* **1.** formed; fashioned **2.** shaped by hammering, etc.: said of metals **3.** elaborated with care **4.** ornamented

wrought iron tough, malleable iron containing very little carbon —**wrought′-i′ron** *adj.*

wrought′-up′ *adj.* very disturbed or excited

wrung (ruŋ) *pt. & pp. of* WRING

wry (rī) *adj.* **wri′er, wri′est** [OE. *wrigian*, to turn] **1.** twisted; distorted **2.** made by distorting the features *[a wry face]* —**wry′ly** *adv.* —**wry′ness** *n.*

wry′neck′ *n.* a condition in which the neck is twisted by a muscle spasm

wt. weight

X Y Z

X, x (eks) *n., pl.* **X's, x's** the twenty-fourth letter of the English alphabet

X (eks) *n.* the Roman numeral for 10

X a motion-picture rating meaning that no one under the age of seventeen is to be admitted

x *Math.* a symbol for: **1.** an unknown quantity **2.** times (in multiplication) *[3 x 3 = 9]*

X chromosome a sex-determining chromosome in the germ cells: eggs carry an X chromosome and spermatozoa either an X or Y chromosome, with a female resulting from an XX pairing and a male from an XY

Xe *Chem.* xenon

xe·bec (zē′bek) *n.* [< Fr. < Ar. *shabbāk*] a small, three-masted ship, once common in the Mediterranean

xe·non (zē′nän, zen′än) *n.* [Gr., strange] a colorless gaseous chemical element present in the air in minute quantities: symbol, Xe

xen·o·pho·bi·a (zen′ə fō′bē ə) *n.* [< Gr. *xenos*, strange + -PHOBIA] fear or hatred of strangers or foreigners

xe·rog·ra·phy (zi räg′rə fē) *n.* [< Gr. *xēros*, dry + -GRAPHY] a process for copying printed material, etc. by the action of light on an electrically charged surface

Xe·rox (zir′äks) *a trademark for* a process of xerography —*vt., vi.* to reproduce by this process

xi (zī, sī) *n.* the fourteenth letter of the Greek alphabet (Ξ, ξ)

Xmas (kris′məs) *n. same as* CHRISTMAS

X-ray (eks′rā′) *n.* **1.** an electromagnetic ray or radiation of very short wavelength that can penetrate solid substances: used to study internal body structures and to treat certain disorders **2.** a photograph made by means of X-rays —*vt.* to treat, examine, or photograph with X-rays Also **X ray, x-ray, x ray**

xy·lem (zī′ləm, -lem) *n.* [G. < Gr. *xylon*, wood] the woody tissue of a plant

xy·lo·phone (zī′lə fōn′) *n.* [< Gr. *xylon*, wood + -PHONE] a musical instrument having a series of graduated wooden bars struck with small wooden hammers

Y, y (wī) *n., pl.* **Y's, y's** the twenty-fifth letter of the English alphabet

-y¹ [ME.] *a suffix meaning* little, dear: used to form diminutives, nicknames, etc. *[kitty, Billy]*

-y² [OE. *-ig*] *a suffix meaning:* **1.** having, full of *[dirty]* **2.** somewhat *[chilly]* **3.** tending to *[sticky]* **4.** somewhat like *[wavy]*

-y³ [< L. *-ia*] *a suffix meaning:* **1.** quality or condition of (being) *[jealousy]* **2.** a shop, group, etc. of a specified kind *[bakery]*

-y⁴ [< L. *-ium*] *a suffix meaning* action of *[inquiry]*

yacht (yät) *n.* [Du. *jacht*] a small ship for pleasure cruises, races, etc. —*vi.* to sail in a yacht —**yachts′man** *n., pl.* -men

Ya·hoo (yä′hōō) *n.* in Swift's *Gulliver's Travels,* any of a race of coarse, brutish creatures having the form and vices of man

Yah·weh, Yah·we (yä′we) God: a form of the Hebrew name in the Scriptures

yak¹ (yak) *n.* [Tibetan *gyak*] a long-haired wild ox of Tibet and C Asia

yak² (yak) *vi.* **yakked, yak′king** [echoic] [Slang] to talk much or idly —*n.* [Slang] **1.** a yakking **2.** a laugh

yam (yam) *n.* [Port. *inhame*] **1.** the edible,

starchy root of a tropical climbing plant **2.**
[South] the sweet potato
Yank (yaŋk) *n.* [Slang] a Yankee; esp., a U.S.
soldier in World Wars I and II
yank (yaŋk) *n., vt., vi.* [< ?] [Colloq.] jerk
Yan·kee (yaŋ′kē) *n.* [< ? Du. *Jan Kees,* a disparaging nickname] **1.** a New Englander **2.** a
native of a Northern State **3.** a citizen of the
U.S. *–adj.* of or like Yankees
yap (yap) *vi.* yapped, yap′ping [echoic] **1.** to
make a sharp, shrill bark **2.** [Slang] to talk
noisily and stupidly *–n.* a sharp, shrill bark
yard[1] (yärd) *n.* [OE. *gierd,* a rod] **1.** *a)* a measure of length, equal to 3 feet, or 36 inches *b)* a
cubic yard **2.** *Naut.* a slender rod or spar fastened across a mast to support a sail
yard[2] (yärd) *n.* [OE. *geard,* enclosure] **1.** the
ground around or next to a building **2.** a place
in the open used for a particular purpose [a
navy *yard]* **3.** a railroad center where trains
are made up, switched, etc.
yard·age (yär′dij) *n.* **1.** measurement in yards
2. the extent so measured
yard′arm′ *n. Naut.* either end of a yard supporting a square sail, signal lights, etc.
yard goods textiles made in standard width,
usually sold by the yard
yard′stick′ *n.* **1.** a measuring stick one yard
long **2.** any standard used in judging, comparing, etc.
yar·mul·ke, yar·mal·ke (yär′məl kə) *n.* [Yid.
< Pol.] a skullcap often worn by Jewish men,
as at prayer
yarn (yärn) *n.* [OE. *gearn*] **1.** a continuous
strand of spun wool, cotton, nylon, glass, etc.,
for weaving, knitting, etc. **2.** [Colloq.] a tale,
esp. an exaggerated one
yaw (yô) *vi.* [ON. *jaga,* to sway] **1.** to turn from
the planned course, as a ship **2.** to swing
about the vertical axis, as an aircraft *–n.* a
yawing
yawl (yôl) *n.* [< MLowG. *jolle* or Du. *jol*] a
small, two-masted sailboat rigged fore-and-aft
yawn (yôn) *vi.* [ME. *yanen*] **1.** to open the
mouth widely and breathe in deeply, esp. involuntarily as a result of fatigue or drowsiness
2. to open wide; gape *–n.* a yawning
yaws (yôz) *n.pl.* [*with sing. v.*] [of WInd.
origin] a tropical, infectious skin disease
Y chromosome *see* X CHROMOSOME
y·clept, y·cleped (i klept′) *pp.* [< OE. *clipian,*
to call] [Archaic] called; named
yd. *pl.* **yd., yds.** yard
ye[1] (*tha, thi, thē*; *now often* yē) *adj.* archaic
form of THE
ye[2] (yē) *pron.* [OE. *ge*] [Archaic] you
yea (yā) *adv.* [OE. *gea*] **1.** yes **2.** indeed; truly
–n. an answer or vote of "yes"
yeah (ya, ye, ye′ə, *etc.*) *adv.* [Colloq.] yes
year (yir) *n.* [OE. *gear*] **1.** a period of 365 days
(in leap year, 366 days) beginning Jan. 1 **2.**
the period of time (365 days, 5 hours, 48 minutes, 46 seconds) of one revolution of the
earth around the sun: also **tropical** or **solar
year 3.** a period of 12 calendar months starting
from any date **4.** an annual period of less than
365 days [a school *year]* **5.** [*pl.*] *a)* age [old for
his *years] b)* a long time
year′book′ *n.* an annual book, as one giving
data of the preceding year
year·ling (yir′liŋ, yur′-) *n.* an animal one year
old or in its second year
year′ly *adj.* **1.** lasting a year **2.** once a year or
every year **3.** of a year, or each year *–adv.*
every year
yearn (yurn) *vi.* [< OE. *georn,* eager] **1.** to be

filled with longing or desire **2.** to feel ten-
derness or sympathy *–yearn′ing n., adj.*
yeast (yēst) *n.* [OE. *gist*] **1.** a yellowish, moist
mass of minute fungi that cause fermentation:
used in making beer, whiskey, etc. and as a
leavening in baking **2.** yeast dried in flakes or
granules or compressed into cakes **3.** foam;
froth **4.** ferment; agitation
yeast′y *adj.* **-i-er, -i-est 1.** of, like, or containing
yeast **2.** frothy; light
yegg (yeg) *n.* [Slang] a criminal
yell (yel) *vi., vt.* [OE. *giellan*] to cry out loudly;
shout *–n.* **1.** a loud outcry; scream **2.** a rhythmic cheer given in unison
yel·low (yel′ō) *adj.* [OE. *geolu*] **1.** of the color
of ripe lemons **2.** having a yellowish skin **3.**
[Colloq.] cowardly **4.** cheaply sensational
[*yellow* journalism] *–n.* **1.** a yellow color or
pigment **2.** the yolk of an egg *–vt., vi.* to make
or become yellow *–yel′low·ish adj.*
yellow fever a tropical disease caused by a
virus carried to man by the bite of a certain
mosquito, and marked by fever, jaundice, etc.
yellow jacket a wasp or hornet having bright-
yellow markings
yelp (yelp) *vi., vt.* [OE. *gielpan,* to boast] to
utter or express by a short, sharp cry or bark,
as a dog *–n.* a short, sharp cry or bark
yen[1] (yen) *n., pl.* **yen** [Jpn. < Chin. *yüan,*
round] the monetary unit of Japan
yen[2] (yen) *n.* [Chin. *yăn,* opium] [Colloq.] a
strong longing or desire
yeo·man (yō′mən) *n., pl.* **-men** [ME. *yeman*] **1.**
orig., a freeholder of a class below the gentry
2. *U.S. Navy* a petty officer assigned to clerical
duty
yeo′man·ry (-rē) *n.* yeomen collectively
yes (yes) *adv.* [OE. *gese*] **1.** aye; it is so: used
to express agreement, consent, etc. **2.** not only
that, but more [ready, *yes,* eager to help] *–n.,
pl.* **yes′es** an affirmative reply, vote, etc. *–vt.,
vi.* yessed, yes′sing to say *yes* (to)
yes man [Slang] one who indicates approval of
every idea offered by his superior
yes·ter (yes′tər) *adj.* of yesterday or previous
to this [*yesteryear*]
yes·ter·day (yes′tər dē, -dā′) *n.* [< OE. *geos-
tran,* yesterday + *dæg,* day] **1.** the day before
today **2.** a recent day or time *–adv.* on the
day before today; recently
yet (yet) *adv.* [OE. *giet*] **1.** up to now; thus far
[he hasn't gone *yet*] **2.** at the present time;
now [we can't leave *yet*] **3.** still; even now
[there is *yet* a chance] **4.** in addition; still [he
was *yet* more kind] **5.** nevertheless [he's rich,
yet lonely] *–conj.* nevertheless; however [she
seems well, *yet* she is ill] *–as yet* up to now
yew (yōō) *n.* [OE. *iw*] **1.** an evergreen shrub or
tree with a fine-grained, elastic wood **2.** the
wood
Yid·dish (yid′ish) *n.* [< G. *jüdisch* < L.
Judaeus, a Jew] a language derived from medieval High German, spoken by East European Jews: it is written in the Hebrew alphabet
yield (yēld) *vt.* [OE. *gieldan,* to pay] **1.** to
produce as a crop, result, profit, etc. **2.** to give
up; surrender **3.** to concede; grant *–vi.* **1.** to
produce or bear **2.** to give up; surrender **3.** to
give way to physical force **4.** to lose precedence, etc. (often with *to*) *–n.* the amount
yielded or produced
yield′ing *adj.* **1.** flexible **2.** submissive
yip (yip) *n., vi.* yipped, yip′ping [echoic]
[Colloq.] yelp
-yl [< Gr. *hylē,* wood] *Chem. a combining form*

meaning: **1.** a univalent hydrocarbon radical **2.** a radical containing oxygen

YMCA, Y.M.C.A. Young Men's Christian Association

YMHA, Y.M.H.A. Young Men's Hebrew Association

yo·del (yō′d'l) *vt., vi.* **-deled** or **-delled, -del·ing** or **-del·ling** [G. *jodeln*] to sing with sudden changes back and forth between the normal chest voice and the falsetto —*n.* a yodeling

yo·ga (yō′gə) *n.* [Sans., union] *Hinduism* a discipline by which one seeks union with the universal soul through deep meditation, prescribed postures, controlled breathing, etc.

yo·gi (yō′gē) *n., pl.* **-gis** a person who practices yoga: also **yo′gin** (-gin)

yo·gurt (yō′gərt) *n.* [Turk. *yōghurt*] a thick, semisolid food made from fermented milk: also sp. **yo′ghurt**

yoke (yōk) *n., pl.* **yokes;** for 2, usually **yoke** [OE. *geoc*] **1.** a wooden frame for harnessing together a pair of oxen, etc. **2.** a pair of animals so harnessed **3.** bondage **4.** something that binds, unites, etc. **5.** a part of a garment fitted to the shoulders or hips to support the gathered parts below —*vt.* **yoked, yok′ing 1.** to put a yoke on **2.** to harness (an animal) to (a plow, etc.) **3.** to join together

yo·kel (yō′k'l) *n.* [prob. < dial. *yokel*, woodpecker] a person living in a rural area: a contemptuous term

yolk (yōk) *n.* [OE. *geolca*] the yellow, principal substance of an egg —**yolk′y** *adj.*

Yom Kip·pur (yäm kip′ər; *Heb.* yōm′ kē pōōr′) the Day of Atonement, a Jewish holiday and day of fasting

yon (yän) *adj., adv.* [OE. *geon*] [Archaic or Dial.] yonder

yon·der (yän′dər) *adj.* [ME.] **1.** farther (with *the*) **2.** being at a distance, but within sight —*adv.* over there

yore (yôr) *adv.* [OE. *geara*] [Obs.] long ago —**of yore** formerly

you (yōō) *pron.* [OE. *eow,* dat. of *ge,* YE²] **1.** the person or persons spoken to **2.** a person or people generally [*you* never can tell!]

you'd (yōōd) **1.** you had **2.** you would

you'll (yōōl) **1.** you will **2.** you shall

young (yuŋ) *adj.* [OE. *geong*] **1.** being in an early period of life or growth **2.** youthful; fresh; vigorous **3.** in an early stage **4.** inexperienced; immature —*n.* **1.** young people **2.** offspring, esp. young offspring, collectively —**with young** pregnant —**young′ish** *adj.*

young·ster (yuŋ′stər) *n.* a child or youth

your (yoor, yôr) *possessive pronominal adj.* [OE. *eower*] of, belonging to, or done by you: also used before some titles [*your* Honor]

you're (yoor, yōōr) you are

yours (yoorz, yôrz) *pron.* that or those belonging to you [that book is *yours*]

your·self (yər self′, yoor-) *pron., pl.* **-selves′** (-selvz′) **1.** *the intensive form of* YOU [you *yourself* did it] **2.** *the reflexive form of* YOU [you hurt *yourself*] **3.** your true self [you're not *yourself* today]

yours truly 1. a phrase used before the signature in ending a letter **2.** [Colloq.] I or me

youth (yōōth) *n., pl.* **youths** (yōōths, yōō*th*z) [OE. *geoguthe*]. **1.** the state or quality of being young **2.** the period of adolescence **3.** an early stage of development **4.** young people collectively **5.** a young person; esp., a young man

youth′ful *adj.* **1.** young **2.** of, characteristic of, or suitable for youth **3.** fresh; vigorous **4.** new; early —**youth′ful·ly** *adv.* —**youth′ful·ness** *n.*

you've (yōōv) you have

yowl (youl) *vi., n.* [< ON. *gaula*] howl

yo-yo (yō′yō′) *n.* [< Philippine name] **1.** a spoollike toy attached to one end of a string upon which it may be made to spin up and down **2.** [Slang] a stupid person

yr. 1. year(s) **2.** younger **3.** your

yrs. 1. years **2.** yours

yuc·ca (yuk′ə) *n.* [< Sp. *yuca*] **1.** a plant of the U.S. and Latin America with stiff leaves and white flowers **2.** its flower

yule (yōōl) *n.* [OE. *geol*] Christmas or the Christmas season

yule′tide′ (-tīd′) *n.* Christmas time

yum·my (yum′ē) *adj.* **-mi·er, -mi·est** [echoic] [Colloq.] very tasty; delectable

YWCA, Y.W.C.A. Young Women's Christian Association

YWHA, Y.W.H.A. Young Women's Hebrew Association

Z, z (zē; *Brit. & Canad.* zed) *n., pl.* **Z's, z's** the twenty-sixth and last letter of the English alphabet

za·ny (zā′nē) *n., pl.* **-nies** [< It. *zanni* < *Giovanni,* John] **1.** a clown **2.** a silly or foolish person —*adj.* **-ni·er, -ni·est 1.** comical in a crazy way **2.** foolish —**za′ni·ness** *n.*

zap (zap) *vt., vi.* **zapped, zap′ping** [echoic] [Slang] to move, strike, stun, kill, etc. with sudden speed and force —*n.* [Slang] energy, verve, etc. —*interj.* an exclamation used to express sudden, swift action

zeal (zēl) *n.* [< Gr. *zēlos*] eagerness; enthusiasm

zeal·ot (zel′ət) *n.* one who is zealous, esp. to an excessive degree; fanatic

zeal·ous (zel′əs) *adj.* full of or showing zeal; enthusiastic —**zeal′ous·ly** *adv.*

ze·bra (zē′brə) *n.* [Port., prob. ult. < L.] a swift African mammal related to the horse, with dark stripes on a light body

ze·bu (zē′byōō) *n.* [Fr. *zébu*] an oxlike domestic animal of Asia and Africa: it has a large hump and short, curving horns

Zen (zen) *n.* [Jpn., ult. < Sans. *dhyāna,* meditation] a Japanese Buddhist sect that seeks enlightenment through meditation

ze·nith (zē′nith) *n.* [< Ar. *semt,* road] **1.** the point in the sky directly overhead **2.** the highest point; peak

zeph·yr (zef′ər) *n.* [< Gr. *zephyros*] **1.** the west wind **2.** a soft, gentle breeze

zep·pe·lin (zep′ə lin) *n.* [< F. von *Zeppelin* (1838–1917), G. inventor] [*often* Z-] a type of dirigible airship designed around 1900

ze·ro (zir′ō, zē′rō) *n., pl.* **-ros, -roes** [< Ar. *sifr,* CIPHER]. **1.** the symbol 0; cipher; naught **2.** the point, marked 0, from which quantities are reckoned on a graduated scale **3.** nothing **4.** the lowest point —*adj.* of or at zero —**zero in on** to concentrate on

zero hour the time set for beginning an attack, etc.; crucial point

zest (zest) *n.* [Fr. *zeste,* orange peel] **1.** something that gives flavor or relish **2.** stimulating or exciting quality; piquancy **3.** keen enjoyment [*zest* for life] —**zest′ful** *adj.*

ze·ta (zāt′ə, zēt′ə) *n.* the sixth letter of the Greek alphabet (Z, ζ)

Zeus (zōōs) the supreme deity of the ancient Greeks

zig·zag (zig′zag′) *n.* [Fr.] **1.** a series of short, sharp angles in alternate directions, as in a line or course **2.** a design, path, etc. having such a series —*adj.* having the form of a zigzag —*adv.* in a zigzag course —*vt., vi.* **-zagged′, -zag′ging** to move or form in a zigzag

zil·lion (zil′yən) *n.* [after MILLION] [Colloq.] a very large, indefinite number

zinc (ziŋk) *n.* [G. *zink*] a bluish-white metallic chemical element, used in various alloys, as a protective coating for iron, etc.: symbol, Zn

zinc ointment a zinc-oxide salve

zinc oxide a white powder used in making glass, paints, cosmetics, ointments, etc.

zing (ziŋ) *n.* [echoic] [Slang] 1. a shrill, high-pitched whizzing sound 2. vitality; zest

zin·ni·a (zin′ē ə, zin′yə) *n.* [< J. *Zinn*, 18th-c. G. botanist] an annual plant with colorful, composite flowers

Zi·on (zī′ən) 1. the land of Israel 2. the Jewish people 3. heaven

Zi′on·ism (-iz′m) *n.* a movement formerly for reestablishing, now for supporting, the state of Israel —**Zi′on·ist** *n., adj.*

zip (zip) *n.* [echoic] 1. a short, sharp hissing sound, as of a passing bullet 2. [Colloq.] energy; vim —*vi.* **zipped, zip′ping** 1. to make, or move with, a zip 2. [Colloq.] to move with speed —*vt.* to fasten or unfasten with a zipper

ZIP code (zip) [z(*oning*) i(*mprovement*) p(*lan*)] a system to speed mail deliveries, using a code number for individual areas and places

zip·per (zip′ər) *n.* a device used to fasten and unfasten two edges of material: it has two rows of interlocking tabs worked by a sliding part

zip′py *adj.* -**pi·er**, -**pi·est** [Colloq.] full of vim and energy; brisk; snappy

zir·con (zur′kän) *n.* [< Per. *zar*, gold] a crystalline silicate mineral, often used as a gem

zit (zit) *n.* [Slang] a pimple, esp. on the face

zith·er (zith′ər, zith′-) *n.* [< Gr. *kithara*, lute] a musical instrument with 30 to 40 strings played with a plectrum

Zn *Chem.* zinc

zo·di·ac (zō′dē ak′) *n.* [< Gr. *zōdiakos* (*kyklos*), (circle) of animals] 1. an imaginary belt in the heavens extending on either side of the apparent path of the sun and divided into twelve equal parts, or signs, named for constellations 2. a diagram representing this —**zo·di′a·cal** (-dī′ə k′l) *adj.*

zom·bie (zäm′bē) *n.* [of Afr. origin] 1. in West Indian superstition, a reanimated corpse that moves as ordered: also sp. **zom′bi** 2. [Slang] a weird or eccentric person

zone (zōn) *n.* [< Gr. *zōnē*] 1. an encircling band, stripe, etc. 2. any of the five great latitudinal divisions of the earth's surface: see

TORRID ZONE, TEMPERATE ZONE, and FRIGID ZONE 3. any region or district with reference to a particular use, limitation, etc. [a canal zone, postal zone] —*vt.* **zoned, zon′ing** 1. to divide (a city, etc.) into areas 2. to encircle — **zon′al** *adj.*

zoo (zōō) *n.* [< ZOO(LOGICAL GARDEN)] a place where a collection of wild animals is kept for public showing

zoo- [< Gr. *zōion*, animal] *a combining form meaning* animal(s): also **zoö-, zo-**

zool. 1. zoological 2. zoology

zo·ol·o·gy (zō äl′ə jē) *n.* [see ZOO- & -LOGY] the science that deals with animals and animal life —**zo′o·log′i·cal** (-ə läj′i k′l) *adj.* —**zo·ol′o·gist** *n.*

zoom (zōōm) *vi.* [echoic] 1. to make a loud buzzing noise 2. to climb sharply: said of an airplane 3. to rise rapidly [prices *zoomed*] 4. to focus with a zoom lens —*vt.* to cause to zoom —*n.* 1. a zooming noise 2. a zooming sound

zoom lens a system of lenses, as in a TV camera, that can be rapidly adjusted for close or distant shots while keeping the image in focus

zo·o·phyte (zō′ə fīt′) *n.* [< Gr. *zōion*, animal + *phyton*, plant] any animal, as a sponge, that looks and grows somewhat like a plant — **zo′o·phyt′ic** (-fit′ik) *adj.*

Zou·ave (zōō äv′) *n.* [< Ar. *Zwāwa*, an Algerian tribe] a member of a former French infantry unit with colorful Oriental uniforms

zounds (zoundz) *interj.* [altered < oath *God's wounds*] [Archaic] a mild oath

zuc·chi·ni (zōō kē′nē) *n., pl.* -**ni, -nis** [It.] a cucumberlike summer squash

Zu·lu (zōō′lōō) *n.* 1. *pl.* -**lus, -lu** any member of a people living in South Africa 2. their language —*adj.* of the Zulus, their language, etc.

Zu·ñi (zōōn′yē) *n.* [AmSp. < AmInd.] 1. *pl.* -**ñis, -ñi** any member of a pueblo-dwelling Indian tribe of New Mexico 2. their language

zwie·back (swē′bak, swī′-) *n.* [G. < *zwie-*, twice + *backen*, bake] a kind of biscuit that is sliced and toasted after baking

zy·gote (zī′gōt) *n.* [< Gr. *zygon*, a yoke] a cell formed by the union of male and female gametes; fertilized egg cell

zymo- [< Gr. *zymē*, a leaven] *a combining form meaning* fermentation: also **zym-**

zy·mur·gy (zī′mər jē) *n.* [ZYM(O)- + -URGY] the chemistry of fermentation, as applied in brewing, etc.

TABLES OF WEIGHTS AND MEASURES

Linear Measure

1 mil	=	0.001 inch	=	0.0254 millimeter
1 inch	=	1,000 mils	=	2.54 centimeters
12 inches	=	1 foot	=	0.3048 meter
3 feet	=	1 yard	=	0.9144 meter
5½ yards or 16½ feet	=	1 rod (or perch)	=	5.029 meters
40 rods	=	1 furlong	=	201.168 meters
8 furlongs or 1,760 yards or 5,280 feet	=	1 (statute) mile	=	1.6093 kilometers
3 miles	=	1 (land) league	=	4.83 kilometers

Square Measure

1 square inch			=	6.452 square centimeters
144 square inches	=	1 square foot	=	929.03 square centimeters
9 square feet	=	1 square yard	=	0.8361 square meter
30¼ square yards	=	1 square rod (or square perch)	=	25.292 square meters
160 square rods or 4,840 square yards or 43,560 square feet	=	1 acre	=	0.4047 hectare
640 acres	=	1 square mile	=	259.00 hectares or 2,590 square kilometers

Cubic Measure

1 cubic inch	=	16.387 cubic centimeters		
1,728 cubic inches	=	1 cubic foot	=	0.0283 cubic meter
27 cubic feet	=	1 cubic yard	=	0.7646 cubic meter
(in units for cordwood, etc.)				
16 cubic feet	=	1 cord foot	=	0.453 cubic meter
128 cubic feet or 8 cord feet	=	1 cord	=	3.625 cubic meters

Nautical Measure

6 feet = 1 fathom = 1.829 meters

100 fathoms = 1 cable's length (ordinary) (In the U.S. Navy, 120 fathoms or 720 feet, or 219.456 meters, = 1 cable's length; in the British Navy, 608 feet, or 185.319 meters, = 1 cable's length.)

10 cables' length = 1 international nautical mile (6,076.11549 feet, by international agreement) = 1.852 kilometers (exactly)

1 international nautical mile = 1.150779 statute miles (the length of a minute of longitude at the equator)

3 nautical miles = 1 marine league (3.45 statute miles) = 5.56 kilometers

60 nautical miles = 1 degree of a great circle (i.e., a circle described on the earth's surface by a plane passing through the center of the earth) = 69.047 statute miles

Dry Measure

1 pint	=	33.60 cubic inches	=	0.5506 liter
2 pints	= 1 quart =	67.20 cubic inches	=	1.1012 liters
8 quarts	= 1 peck =	537.61 cubic inches	=	8.8098 liters
4 pecks	= 1 bushel =	2,150.42 cubic inches	=	35.2390 liters

According to United States government standards, the following are the weights avoirdupois for single bushels of the specified grains: for wheat, 60 pounds; for barley, 48 pounds; for oats, 32 pounds; for rye, 56 pounds; for shelled corn, 56 pounds. Some States have specifications varying from these.

The British dry quart = 1.032 U.S. dry quarts

Liquid Measure

1 gill	= 4 fluid ounces (see next table)	=	7.219 cubic inches	= 0.1183 liter
4 gills	= 1 pint	=	28.875 cubic inches	= 0.4732 liter
2 pints	= 1 quart	=	57.75 cubic inches	= 0.9464 liter
4 quarts	= 1 gallon	=	231 cubic inches	= 3.7854 liters

The British imperial gallon (4 imperial quarts) = 277.42 cubic inches = 4.546 liters. The barrel in Great Britain equals 36 imperial gallons, in the United States, usually 31½ gallons.

Apothecaries' Fluid Measure

1 minim	=	0.0038 cubic inch	=	0.0616 milliliter
60 minims	= 1 fluid dram =	0.2256 cubic inch	=	3.6966 milliliters
8 fluid drams	= 1 fluid ounce =	1.8047 cubic inches	=	0.0296 liter
16 fluid ounces	= 1 pint =	28.875 cubic inches	=	0.4732 liter

See table immediately preceding for quart and gallon equivalents. The British pint = 20 fluid ounces.

Circular (or Angular) Measure

60 seconds (″)	=	1 minute (′)
60 minutes	=	1 degree (°)
90 degrees	=	1 quadrant or 1 right angle
180 degrees	=	2 quadrants or 1 straight angle
4 quadrants or 360 degrees	=	1 circle

Avoirdupois Weight

(The grain, equal to 0.0648 gram, is the same in all three tables of weight.)

1 dram or 27.34 grains		=	1.772 grams
16 drams or 437.5 grains	= 1 ounce	=	28.3495 grams
16 ounces or 7,000 grains	= 1 pound	=	453.59 grams
100 pounds	= 1 hundredweight	=	45.36 kilograms
2,000 pounds	= 1 ton	=	907.18 kilograms

In Great Britain, 14 pounds (6.35 kilograms) = 1 stone, 112 pounds (50.80 kilograms) = 1 hundredweight, and 2,240 pounds (1,016.05 kilograms) = 1 long ton.

Troy Weight

(The grain, equal to 0.0648 gram, is the same in all three tables of weight.)

	3.086 grains	= 1 carat	=	200.00 milligrams
	24 grains	= 1 pennyweight	=	1.5552 grams
20 pennyweights or	480 grains	= 1 ounce	=	31.1035 grams
12 ounces or 5,760	grains	= 1 pound	=	373.24 grams

Apothecaries' Weight

(The grain, equal to 0.0648 gram, is the same in all three tables of weight.)

60 grains	= 1 dram	=	3.888 grams
8 drams or 480 grains	= 1 ounce	=	31.1035 grams
12 ounces or 5,760 grains	= 1 pound	=	373.24 grams

THE METRIC SYSTEM

Linear Measure

	1 millimeter	=	0.03937 inch
10 millimeters	= 1 centimeter	=	0.3937 inch
10 centimeters	= 1 decimeter	=	3.937 inches
10 decimeters	= 1 meter	=	39.37 inches or 3.2808 feet
10 meters	= 1 decameter	=	393.7 inches
10 decameters	= 1 hectometer	=	328.08 feet
10 hectometers	= 1 kilometer	=	0.621 mile or 3,280.8 feet
10 kilometers	= 1 myriameter	=	6.21 miles

Square Measure

	1 square millimeter	=	0.00155 square inch
100 square millimeters	= 1 square centimeter	=	0.15499 square inch
100 square centimeters	= 1 square decimeter	=	15.499 square inches
100 square decimeters	= 1 square meter	=	1,549.9 square inches or 1.196 square yards
100 square meters	= 1 square decameter	=	119.6 square yards
100 square decameters	= 1 square hectometer	=	2.471 acres
100 square hectometers	= 1 square kilometer	=	0.386 square mile or 247.1 acres

Land Measure

1 square meter		=	1,549.9 square inches
10,000 square meters	= 1 hectare	=	2.471 acres
100 hectares	= 1 square kilometer	=	0.386 square mile or 247.1 acres

Volume Measure

1,000 cubic millimeters	= 1 cubic centimeter	=	0.06102 cubic inch
1,000 cubic centimeters	= 1 cubic decimeter	=	61.023 cubic inches or 0.0353 cubic foot
1,000 cubic decimeters	= 1 cubic meter	=	35.314 cubic feet or 1.308 cubic yards

As a unit for measuring firewood, the cubic meter is called a *stere.*

Capacity Measure

10 milliliters	= 1 centiliter	=	0.338 fluid ounce
10 centiliters	= 1 deciliter	=	3.38 fluid ounces or 0.1057 liquid quart
10 deciliters	= 1 liter	=	1.0567 liquid quarts or 0.9081 dry quart
10 liters	= 1 decaliter	=	2.64 gallons or 0.284 bushel
10 decaliters	= 1 hectoliter	=	26.418 gallons or 2.838 bushels
10 hectoliters	= 1 kiloliter	=	264.18 gallons or 35.315 cubic feet

Weights

10 milligrams	= 1 centigram	=	0.1543 grain or 0.000353 ounce (avdp.)
10 centigrams	= 1 decigram	=	1.5432 grains
10 decigrams	= 1 gram	=	15.432 grains or 0.035274 ounce (avdp.)
10 grams	= 1 decagram	=	0.3527 ounce
10 decagrams	= 1 hectogram	=	3.5274 ounces
10 hectograms	= 1 kilogram	=	2.2046 pounds

The metric ton = 2,204.6 pounds = 1000 kilograms.

PUNCTUATION

The usages for the marks of punctuation, italics, and capital letters given here are those generally observed by Americans today. The following is a practical, concise treatment of the most important usages. Practice in punctuation often differs in particulars among writers, publishing houses, etc., but the modern trend generally is toward simplification.

PERIOD

The period (.) is used:
1) to mark the end of a declarative or imperative sentence;
   Ex.: The sun has set. Don't wait for us.
2) after many abbreviations;
   Ex.: Colloq. Mr. U.S.
   In much modern practice, the trend is to avoid the use of periods with abbreviations.
3) as one of a series (usually three) to indicate missing material or a break in continuity;
   Ex.: "I pledge allegiance to the flag . . . and to the Republic . . ."

COMMA

The comma (,) is used:
1) between independent clauses of equal value that are short and have no commas within them;
   Ex.: He worked hard, he saved his money, he bought a house.
2) between two independent clauses joined by coordinating conjunctions;
   Ex.: We went to the party, but Ralph wasn't there. Either the fuel pump is broken, or we are out of gas.
3) after a dependent clause, usually a fairly long one, that precedes an independent clause;
   Ex.: When it became apparent that they would not cooperate, we stopped all negotiations.
4) before and after a dependent clause that comes in the middle of a sentence;
   Ex.: The apples, although they had been freshly picked, became spoiled in shipment.
5) to set off a nonrestrictive, as distinguished from a restrictive, clause, phrase, or word;
   Ex.: Dick, who is my brother, is not in town. (But *not* in: The boy who is my brother is sitting on the left.) The President lives in the White House, in Washington. (But *not* in: Many buildings in Washington house government offices.) The planet on which we live, Earth, is between Venus and Mars. (But *not* in: The planet Earth is be-between Venus and Mars.)
6) after a phrase that begins a sentence, especially for emphasis or to prevent misreading;
   Ex.: From this balcony, he spoke to the crowd. In dealing with Frank, Smith was always kind.
7) to set off conjunctive adverbs, such as *however, moreover,* etc., or short transitional phrases;
   Ex.: We are pleased with your suggestion; moreover, we intend to put it into effect.
8) to separate clauses, phrases, or words in a series;
   Ex.: Find out who he is, what he wants, and where he comes from. I proceeded up the stairs, down the hall, and into the office. Ann, Lois, or Jane will be chosen.
   Some writers omit the comma before the *and* connecting the last two elements of a series.

9) after terms (e.g., i.e., namely) that introduce a series or example;
   Ex.: Some of our presidents, e.g., Jefferson, J. Q. Adams, and Buchanan, had previously been secretaries of state.
10) to set of a parenthetical clause, phrase, or word;
   Ex.: By the end of the month, when the bill is due, I will have the money. The family, along with the servants, has left for the summer. Come, please, and bring your wife and children.
11) to set off a word or phrase used in apposition;
   Ex.: Jim, my brother, is here. Cincinnati, the Queen City, is on the Ohio River.
12) between two adjectives which modify the same substantive and can be interchanged in position;
   Ex.: a large, modern building
13) to indicate omitted material;
   Ex.: The infant becomes a child; the child, an adolescent; and the adolescent, an adult.
14) to set off the one spoken to in direct address;
   Ex.: "Go, Dick, and shut the window." "Yes, sir, I'm going."
15) to set off direct quotation;
   Ex.: He said, "Keep to the right." "Thank you," we replied.
16) to set off titles, addresses, names of places, etc.;
   Ex.: R. T. Fisher, Ph.D., Secretary, 110 Elm Street, Akron 6, Ohio, handles all corespondence for the society. He traveled from the Black Forest, Germany, to Paris, France, by bicycle.
17) before, and sometimes after, the year in dates;
   Ex.: Lincoln was born on February 12, 1809, in a log cabin.
18) after the salutation of a personal letter;
   Ex.: Dear Max and Alice,
19) after the complimentary close of letters;
   Ex.: Very truly yours, Peter B. Stewart
20) to separate thousands in numbers of one thousand and over;
   Ex.: The area of the earth is approximately 196,950,000 sq. mi.
21) to separate inverted names, phrases, etc., as in a bibliography, index, or catalogue;
   Ex.: Jones, Harold T.
   Persia, architecture of
   radios, portable

SEMICOLON

The semicolon (;) is used:
1) in compound sentences between independent clauses not joined by connectives, especially if they are long or have commas within them;
   Ex.: The problems of adequately financing and endowing an institution of higher learning have become increasingly difficult; specialists in investing money are needed to assure that the wisest use is made of the funds.
   Detroit, on one side of the river, is in the U.S.; Windsor, on the other side, is in Canada.
2) in compound sentences between independent clauses joined by conjunctive adverbs;
   Ex.: We are pleased with your suggestion; moreover, we intend to put it into effect.
3) in a series where further division than that given by commas is needed;
   Ex.: The contestants came from Albany, New York; Seattle, Washington; and London, England.

COLON

The colon (:) is used:

1) to introduce a list or series, especially in somewhat formal writing;
   Ex.: The following materials will be needed: pencil, pen, eraser, ruler, and notebook.
2) to introduce a part of a sentence that exemplifies, restates, or explains the preceding part;
   Ex.: Some of the greatest creative artists never became wealthy during their lifetime: Mozart died a very poor man and was buried in a pauper's grave.
3) before an extended quotation;
   Ex.: Lincoln arose and spoke as follows: "Fourscore and seven years ago . . ."
4) between the chapter and verse numbers in Biblical references;
   Ex.: The story of Noah begins in Gen. 5:28.
5) between the volume and page numbers in references;
   Ex.: The article is found in *U.S. Encyclopedia* 34:1747.
6) after the salutation of a business letter;
   Ex.: Dear Sir:
7) to separate the hours from the minutes in expressions of time;
   Ex.: The train will depart at 10:47 P.M.
8) to separate the parts of a ratio;
   Ex.: The birth rate and the mortality rate for this region are in the ratio 17:14.

QUESTION MARK

The question mark (?) is used:

1) after a direct question;
   Ex.: Who is the chairman?
2) to express doubt or uncertainty;
   Ex.: Socrates lived 470 ?-399 B.C. Saint Peter lived ?-64? A.D.

EXCLAMATION MARK

The exclamation mark (!) is used after an exclamatory word, phrase, or sentence, to indicate surprise, strong emotion, etc.;
   Ex.: Ouch! That hurt!

HYPHEN

The hyphen (-) is used;

1) to separate the parts of a compound word;
   Ex.: self-control, re-cover (meaning "to cover again", as distinct from *recover*, meaning "to get back"), forty-three, anti-Fascist, reddish-brown, foot-pound
2) to indicate syllabification, as at the end of a line.

DASH

The dash (—) is used:

1) to show a break in continuity or thought in a sentence;
   Ex.: Give it to John—I mean, to George.
2) before and after parenthetical material that is a result of a break in thought or continuity;
   Ex.: I wrote a letter—and what a chore it was—to my lawyer concerning the problem.
3) between numbers, dates, times, etc. that mark limits;
   Ex.: You will find it on pages 89—104. Franklin lived 1706—1790. The hotel is open June—September. The office hours are 8:00—5:00 daily.
4) to indicate the omission of letters, numbers, etc.;
   Ex.: Don't tell Mr. B—.
   One dark winter night in 18— two men were dining together in an inconspicuous restaurant in London's West End.
5) before the citation of the author or source of a quotation, etc.;
   Ex.: "Every dog has his day."—Cervantes. "Great men are not always wise."—Job 32:9.

QUOTATION MARKS

Double quotation marks (" ") are used:

1) to enclose a direct quotation;
   Ex.: I replied, "I will try to help them."
2) in general, to enclose the titles of divisions, parts, chapters, etc. of books, periodicals, etc. Titles of plays, operas, and other works of art are either set off by quotation marks or italicized. Cf. **italics**, 2;
   Ex.: I have just read "The Gold Bug", a short story by Poe. "The Knight's Tale" is one of *The Canterbury Tales*. The motion picture "The Informer" was directed by John Ford.
3) to enclose words out of the grammatical context of the sentence;
   Ex.: The word *silly* originally meant "happy"; now it means "foolish."
4) to enclose terms that are technical, esoteric, ironic, coined, slang, etc.;
   Ex.: The cloud mass was "fractocumulus." The "debate" ended in an angry brawl. Our distinguished patron was well-bred but decidedly "flaky."

Single quotation marks (' ') are used to enclose a direct quotation within other quoted material;
   Ex.: The teacher said, "William Hazlitt's dying words were 'It was a happy life.'"

N.B. Commas and periods are usually placed inside quotation marks;
   Ex.: "I am seven," he said. The answer was "No."
   Colons and semicolons are placed outside quotation marks;
   Ex.: Answer these questions on the "Gettysburg Address": In what year was it given? What was the occasion? How was it received?
   I had not read Francis Bacon's essay "Of Truth"; in fact, I had never heard of it.

A question mark or exclamation mark is placed outside or inside quotation marks according to whether it applies to the entire sentence or just to part of it.
   Ex.: "What did you say?" he repeated. Did I hear you say, "It's snowing"? "Never!" she exclaimed. You had better not call me "yellow"!

APOSTROPHE

The apostrophe (') is used:

1) to indicate an omitted letter or letters in a word or contraction;
   Ex.: He is the town ne'er-do-well. She'll attend if she's in town.
2) with an added s to form the possessive of all nouns that do not end in an s or z sound;
   Ex.: Sam's, Edgar's men's, children's
3) with an added s to form the possessive of monosyllabic, singular nouns that end in an s or z sound and of proper nouns ending in -ce;
   Ex.: lass's, Horace's
4) without an added s to form the possessive case of all nouns that end in an s or z sound except monosyllabic, singular forms and forms ending in -ce;
   Ex.: Moses', wolves', horses'
5) with an added s to indicate the possessive case of some pronouns;
   Ex.: It is everyone's duty to vote.
6) in forming the plural of letters, numbers, etc.
   Ex.: He pronounced his *th*'s like *s*'s. She made her *l*'s look like 7's.

PARENTHESES

Parentheses, ( ), are used:

1) to enclose nonessential material placed in a sentence as explanation or comment;

Ex.: He ran 1500 meters (a little less than a mile).

2) to enclose letters or numbers of references as in an outline form ;
Ex.: The candidate spoke on three subjects: (1) better housing ; (2) improved roads ; (3) expanded recreation facilities.
Sometimes only the closing parenthesis is used, as with letters in this dictionary.

3) to enclose a mathematical expression that is to be considered as one quantity instead of having its individual components treated separately:
Ex.: $(3 + 2)^2 = 25.$

N.B. Periods, commas, etc. are placed inside or outside parentheses depending on the part of the sentence to which they apply ;
Ex.: Veni, vidi, vici. (I came, I saw, I conquered.) I have many faults (as does everybody else).

BRACKETS

Brackets, [ ], are used:
1) for the same purposes as parentheses ; if parenthetical material falls within other parenthetical material, the brackets are used inside of the parentheses ;
Ex.: This is an excellent example of a dichotomy (a continued dividing [or subdividing] into opposed groups).

2) to enclose comments, corrections, etc. inserted in quoted material by a person other than the author of the material ;
Ex.: "Acute anterior poliomyelitis [commonly called polio] is an acute inflammation of the gray matter of the spinal cord." "He was a friend of the nineteenth-century British statesman [Randolph] Churchill."

ITALICS

Italicized type is used:
1) to indicate foreign words:
Ex.: His motto was *omnia vincit amor,* which means "love conquers everything."

2) in general, to set off the titles of books, periodicals, newspapers, etc. Titles of plays, operas, and other works of art are either italicized or set off by quotation marks. Cf. **quotation marks,** 2 ;
Ex.: Charles Dickens' novel *David Copperfield* is to some extent an autobiographical novel. Verdi's *Requiem* requires a large chorus.

3) to indicate words whose meaning is stressed ;
Ex.: Please do *not* use this door.

4) to indicate terms, letters, numbers, etc. used as words instead of for their meanings ;
Ex.: Some people make no distinction between *farther* and *further.* The expression *to wit* is being used less frequently nowadays. He always forgets to dot his *j*'s. The key that types *3* is broken on this typewriter.

CAPITALIZATION

A capital letter is used:
1) for the pronoun *I* and the interjection *O.*
2) as the initial letter of the first word in a sentence ;
Ex.: The books are on the shelves.
3) as the initial letter of the first word in quoted material falling within a sentence ;
Ex.: He called, "Wait a minute and I'll be with you."
4) as the initial letter of the first word in a direct question falling within a sentence ;
Ex.: This story answers the question, Where does true happiness really lie?
5) as the initial letter of the first word in a line of poetry, although a number of modern poets have dispensed with this convention ;
Ex.: "All I could see from where I stood Was three long mountains and a wood ; I turned and looked the other way, And saw three islands in a bay."
6) as the initial letter of every word in all proper nouns or names ;
Ex.: Ronald Jones, London, Germany, Maine, North America, Fifth Avenue, Pacific Ocean, Princeton University, *Atlantic Monthly*
7) as the initial letter of every word, except conjunctions, articles, and short prepositions that are not the first word, in the titles of works of literature, music, art, etc. ;
Ex.: Twelfth Night, The Decline and Fall of the Roman Empire, The Magic Flute, Winger Victory
8) as the initial letter of every word, except conjunctions, articles, and short prepositions, in the names (or derived adjectives, verbs, etc.) of organizations, businesses, agencies, movements, religions, holidays, etc. Sometimes the initial article is capitalized as part of the official name ;
Ex.: the Boy Scouts of America, The Prudential Insurance Company of America, Internal Revenue Service, Humanism, Buddhism, Labor Day
9) as the initial letter of every word in the names of periods of time, as days, months, eras, etc. ;
Ex.: Thursday, June, Iron Age, Palezoic Era
10) in many abbreviations ;
Ex.: B.C., A.D., M.P.
Many abbreviations may be capitalized or not, according to personal preference ;
Ex.: A.M., a.m. ; P.M., p.m.
11) as the initial letter of a symbol for a chemical element ;
Ex.: In chemistry, Au is the symbol for gold.
12) as the initial letter of every word in forms of address ;
Ex.: Your Excellency ; Dear Bishop Hathaway ; The Honorable Edwin Stanton
13) as the initial letter of nouns and, often, pronouns referring to the Deity ;
Ex.: And God is in His heaven.
14) as the initial letter of the names of gods and goddesses of polytheistic religions ;
Ex.: Isis, Zeus, Venus, Thor
15) as the initial letter in the names of all heavenly bodies ;
Ex.: Mars, Sirius, Big Dipper
However, *earth, sun* and *moon* are not capitalized except when cited along with the names of other heavenly bodies ;
Ex.: The moon shines by means of light reflected from the sun. (But: Mercury is the planet closest to the Sun.)
16) as the initial letter in the names of phyla, classes, orders, families, and genera (but not in the names of species) ;
17) as the initial letter of a title, rank, etc. followed by a proper name, or of an epithet used with or in place of a proper name ;
Ex.: Mr. Kauffman, President Wilson, Bishop Butler, Lord Byron, Richard the Lion-hearted, the Great Emancipator
18) as the initial letter in the names of abstract or inanimate things that are personified ;
Ex.: It was the work of Fate. And now Spring wafted her gentle breezes. It has been said that Justice is lame as well as blind.
19) as the initial letter in all salutations and complimentary closes of letters ;
Ex.: Gentlemen, Dear Sir, Very truly yours
20) as the initial letter in names of trademarks ;
Ex.: Kleenex, Vaseline

PRESIDENTS AND VICE PRESIDENTS OF THE UNITED STATES

President	Years in Office	Vice President	Years in Office
1. George Washington	1789-1797	1. John Adams	1789-1797
2. John Adams	1797-1801	2. Thomas Jefferson	1797-1801
3. Thomas Jefferson	1801-1809	3. Aaron Burr	1801-1805
4. James Madison	1809-1817	4. George Clinton[1]	1805-1812
		5. Elbridge Gerry[2]	1813-1814
5. James Monroe	1817-1825	6. Daniel D. Tompkins	1817-1825
6. John Quincy Adams	1825-1829	7. John C. Calhoun[3]	1825-1832
7. Andrew Jackson	1829-1837	8. Martin Van Buren	1833-1837
8. Martin Van Buren	1837-1841	9. Richard M. Johnson	1837-1841
9. William Henry Harrison[2]	1841	10. John Tyler	1841
10. John Tyler	1841-1845		
11. James K. Polk	1845-1849	11. George M. Dallas	1845-1849
12. Zachary Taylor[2]	1849-1850	12. Millard Fillmore	1849-1850
13. Millard Fillmore	1850-1853		
14. Franklin Pierce	1853-1857	13. William R. King[2]	1853
15. James Buchanan	1857-1861	14. John C. Breckinridge	1857-1861
16. Abraham Lincoln[4]	1861-1865	15. Hannibal Hamlin	1861-1865
		16. Andrew Johnson	1865
17. Andrew Johnson	1865-1869		
18. Ulysses S. Grant	1869-1877	17. Schuyler Colfax	1869-1873
		18. Henry Wilson[2]	1873-1875
19. Rutherford B. Hayes	1877-1881	19. William A. Wheeler	1877-1881
20. James A. Garfield[4]	1881	20. Chester A. Arthur	1881
21. Chester A. Arthur	1881-1885		
22. Grover Cleveland	1885-1889	21. Thomas A. Hendricks[5]	1885
23. Benjamin Harrison	1889-1893	22. Levi P. Morton	1889-1893
24. Grover Cleveland	1893-1897	23. Adlai E. Stevenson	1893-1897
25. William McKinley[4]	1897-1901	24. Garret A. Hobart[2]	1897-1899
		25. Theodore Roosevelt	1901
26. Theodore Roosevelt	1901-1909	26. Charles W. Fairbanks	1905-1909
27. William Howard Taft	1909-1913	27. James S. Sherman[2]	1909-1912
28. Woodrow Wilson	1913-1921	28. Thomas R. Marshall	1913-1921
29. Warren G. Harding[2]	1921-1923	29. Calvin Coolidge	1921-1923
30. Calvin Coolidge	1923-1929	30. Charles G. Dawes	1925-1929
31. Herbert C. Hoover	1929-1933	31. Charles Curtis	1929-1933
32. Franklin D. Roosevelt[2]	1933-1945	32. John N. Garner	1933-1941
		33. Henry A. Wallace	1941-1945
		34. Harry S. Truman	1945
33. Harry S. Truman	1945-1953	35. Alben W. Barkley	1949-1953
34. Dwight D. Eisenhower	1953-1961	36. Richard M. Nixon	1953-1961
35. John F. Kennedy[4]	1961-1963	37. Lyndon B. Johnson	1961-1963
36. Lyndon B. Johnson	1963-1969	38. Hubert H. Humphrey	1965-1969
37. Richard M. Nixon[6]	1969-1974	39. Spiro T. Agnew[7]	1969-1973
		40. Gerald R. Ford[8]	1973-1974
38. Gerald R. Ford	1974-1977	41. Nelson A. Rockefeller[9]	1974-1977
39. James E. Carter	1977-1981	42. Walter F. Mondale	1977-1981
40. Ronald Reagan	1981-	43. George Bush	1981-

1. Vice President during Jefferson's second term and during Madison's first term; died in office

2. Died in office (see also note 5)

3. Vice President during Monroe's term and during most of Jackson's first term; resigned to become a U.S. Senator

4. Assassinated

5. His death in office prompted the passage of the Presidential Succession Act (1886), which declared the line of succession to be, in order, after the Vice President, the secretaries of State, Treasury, and War, the Attorney General, and the secretaries of Navy and Interior. In 1947 this act was replaced by one that placed the Speaker of the House of Representatives and the President pro tempore of the Senate ahead of the Secretary of State. Before the enactment of the act of 1886 there was no legally stated line of succession. The only provision for succession had been in Article II of the Constitution — ". . . the Congress may by law provide for the case of removal, death, resignation, or inability of the President and Vice President, declaring what officer shall then act as President . . ." Neither the act of 1886 nor the act of 1947 provided for filling a vacant office of Vice President; when this office became vacant it remained vacant until a new administration was sworn in (see note 8).

6. Resigned under threat of impeachment

7. Resigned after the disclosure of corrupt practices which had taken place while he held political office in Maryland and for which he was allegedly responsible

8. The first nonelected Vice President. He was chosen according to the procedure outlined in the 25th Amendment (ratified 1967), which states that "whenever there is a vacancy in the office of the Vice President, the President shall nominate a Vice President who shall take office upon confirmation by a majority vote of both houses of Congress."

9. Nonelected; chosen in the same manner Ford was chosen (see preceding note)

A DICTIONARY OF GEOGRAPHY

including nations of the world and States of the United States

Abbreviations used in this section: **cap.** capital; **E** eastern; **N** northern; **NE** northeastern; **NW** northwestern; **pop.** population; **S** southern; **SE** southeastern; **sq. mi.** square miles; **SW** southwestern; **U.S.** United States; **U.S.S.R.** Union of Soviet Socialist Republics; **W** western.

Af·ghan·i·stan (af gan'ə stan') a country in SW Asia, between Iran and Pakistan: c. 250,000 sq. mi.; pop. 18,294,000; cap. Kabul

Al·a·bam·a (al'ə bam'ə) a Southern State of the SE U.S., on the Gulf of Mexico: 51,609 sq. mi.; pop. 3,890,000; cap. Montgomery

A·las·ka (ə las'kə) a State of the U.S. in NW North America, on the Pacific and Arctic oceans: 586,400 sq. mi.; pop. 400,000; cap. Juneau

Al·ba·ni·a (al bā'nē ə, -bān'yə) a country in the W Balkan Peninsula, on the Adriatic Sea: 11,099 sq. mi.; pop. 2,188,000; cap. Tirana

Al·ge·ri·a (al jir'ē ə) a country in N Africa, on the Mediterranean: c. 919,000 sq. mi.; pop. 16,776,000; cap. Algiers

An·dor·ra (an dôr'ə, -där'ə) a country in SW Europe, on the border between France and Spain: c. 180 sq. mi.; pop. 27,000; cap. Andorra la Vella

An·go·la (aŋ gō'lə, an-) a country on the SW coast of Africa: 481,351 sq. mi.; pop. 6,761,000; cap. Luanda

An·ti·gua (an tē'gə, -gwə) a country consisting of two islands (*Antigua* and *Barbuda*) in the West Indies: 170 sq. mi.; pop. 75,000; cap. St. John's: official name **Antigua and Barbuda**

Ar·gen·ti·na (är'jən tē'nə) a country in S South America: 1,084,120 sq. mi.; pop. 25,383,000; cap. Buenos Aires

Ar·i·zo·na (ar'ə zō'nə, er'-) a State of the SW U.S., on the Mexican border: 113,909 sq. mi.; pop. 2,718,000; cap. Phoenix

Ar·kan·sas (är'k'n sô') a State of the south central U.S.: 53,104 sq. mi.; pop. 2,286,000; cap. Little Rock

Aus·tral·ia (ô strāl'yə) a country comprising an island continent (also called *Australia*) and an island off its S Pacific and Indian oceans, and an island off its SE coast: 2,971,081 sq. mi.; pop. 13,601,000; cap. Canberra

Aus·tri·a (ôs'trē ə) a country in central Europe: 32,375 sq. mi.; pop. 7,523,000; cap. Vienna

Ba·ha·mas (bə hä'məz, -hä'-) a country on a group of islands in the West Indies, southeast of Florida and north of Cuba: 4,404 sq. mi.; pop. 204,000; cap. Nassau

Bah·rain (bä rān') a country on a group of islands in the Persian Gulf, off the coast of Arabia: 231 sq. mi.; pop. 256,000; cap. Manama

Ban·gla·desh (bäŋ'glə desh') a country in S Asia, at the N end of the Bay of Bengal: 55,134 sq. mi.; pop. 76,815,000; cap. Dacca

Bar·ba·dos (bär bā'dōz, -dōs) a country on the easternmost island of the West Indies: 166 sq. mi.; pop. 245,000; cap. Bridgetown

Be·lau (be lou') a country consisting of a group of islands in the W Pacific, east of the Philippines: c. 180 sq. mi.; pop. 15,000

Bel·gium (bel'jəm) a country in W Europe, on the North Sea: 11,779 sq. mi.; pop. 9,804,000; cap. Brussels

Be·nin (be nēn') a country in west central Africa, on the Atlantic Ocean: 44,696 sq. mi.; pop. 3,112,000; cap. Porto Novo

Bhu·tan (bōō tän') a country in S Asia, north of E India: c. 18,000 sq. mi.; pop. 1,035,000; cap. Thimphu

Bo·liv·i·a (bə liv'ē ə) a country in west central South America: 424,000 sq. mi.; pop. 5,634,000; capitals, La Paz, Sucre

Bot·swa·na (bät swä'nə) a country in S Africa, north of South Africa: 222,000 sq. mi.; pop. 691,000; cap. Gaborone

Bra·zil (brə zil') a country in central and NE South America, on the Atlantic Ocean: 3,287,000 sq. mi.; pop. 107,145,000; cap. Brasília

Bul·gar·i·a (bəl ger'ē ə, bool-) a country in SE Europe, on the Black Sea: 42,796 sq. mi.; pop. 8,722,000; cap. Sofia

Bur·ma (bur'mə) a country in SE Asia, on the peninsula of Indochina: 261,789 sq. mi.; pop. 29,563,000; cap. Rangoon

Bu·run·di (boo roon'dē, -run'-) a country in east central Africa, east of Zaire: 10,745 sq. mi.; pop. 3,763,000; cap. Bujumbura

Cal·i·for·ni·a (kal'ə fôr'nyə, -nē ə) a State of the SW U.S., on the Pacific Ocean: 158,693 sq. mi.; pop. 23,669,000; cap. Sacramento

Cam·e·roon (kam'ə rōōn') a country in west central Africa, on the Atlantic Ocean: 183,000 sq. mi.; pop. 5,836,000; cap. Yaoundé

Can·a·da (kan'ə də) a country in N North America: 3,852,000 sq. mi.; pop. 22,831,000; cap. Ottawa

Cape Verde (vurd) a country on a group of islands in the Atlantic Ocean, west of Senegal: 1,557 sq. mi.; pop. 294,000; cap. Praia

Central African Republic a country in central Africa, north of Zaire and Congo: 238,224 sq. mi.; pop. 2,370,000; cap. Bangui

Chad (chad) a country in north central Africa, south of Libya: c. 495,000 sq. mi.; pop. 4,030,000; cap. N'Djamena

Chil·e (chil'ē) a country on the SW coast of South America: 286,397 sq. mi.; pop. 10,253,000; cap. Santiago

Chi·na (chī'nə) a country in E Asia, south and east of the U.S.S.R. and northeast of India: 3,691,000 sq. mi.; pop. over 700,000,000; cap. Peking

Co·lom·bi·a (kə lum'bē ə) a country in NW South America, on the Pacific Ocean and the Caribbean Sea: 455,335 sq. mi.; pop. 23,542,000; cap. Bogotá

Col·o·rad·o (käl'ə rad'ō, -rä'dō) a Mountain State of the W U.S.: 104,247 sq. mi.; pop. 2,889,000; cap. Denver

Com·o·ros (käm'ə rōs') a country on a group of islands in the Indian Ocean, between Mozambique and Madagascar: 838 sq. mi.; pop. 292,000; cap. Moroni

Con·go (käŋ'gō) a country in west central Africa, on the equator, west of Zaire: 132,046 sq. mi.; pop. 1,300,000; cap. Brazzaville

Con·nect·i·cut (kə net'ə kət) a New England State of the NE U.S.: 5,009 sq. mi.; pop. 3,108,000; cap. Hartford

Cos·ta Ri·ca (käs'tə rē'kə, kôs'-, kōs'-) a country in Central America, northwest of Panama: 19,575 sq. mi.; pop. 1,968,000; cap. San José

Cu·ba (kyōō'bə) a country consisting of a large island and several small nearby islands in the West Indies, south of Florida: 44,218 sq. mi.; pop. 9,090,000; cap. Havana

Cy·prus (sī'prəs) a country that is an island at the E end of the Mediterranean, south of Turkey: 3,572 sq. mi.; pop. 639,000; cap. Nicosia

Czech·o·slo·va·ki·a (chek'ə slō vä'kē ə) a

country in central Europe, south of Poland: 49,367 sq. mi.; pop. 14,862,000; cap. Prague

Del·a·ware (del′ə wer′, -war′) an Eastern State of the U.S., on the Atlantic Ocean: 2,057 sq. mi.; pop. 595,000; cap. Dover

Den·mark (den′märk) a country in Europe, occupying most of a peninsula which separates the North Sea from the Baltic Sea, and several nearby islands in both seas: 16,615 sq. mi.; pop. 5,059,000; cap. Copenhagen

District of Co·lum·bi·a (kə lum′bē ə, -byə) a federal district in the E U.S., on the Potomac River: 69 sq. mi.; pop. 638,000; the city of Washington occupies the same area

Dji·bou·ti (ji boot′ē) a country in E Africa, on the Gulf of Aden: 8,500 sq. mi.; pop. 180,000; cap. Djibouti

Dom·i·ni·ca (däm′ə nē′kə, də min′i kə) a country that is an island of the Windward group in the West Indies: 290 sq. mi.; pop. 81,000; cap. Roseau

Do·min·i·can Republic (də min′i kən) a country occupying the E part of an island in the West Indies, east of Cuba: 18,816 sq. mi.; pop. 4,697,000; cap. Santo Domingo

East Ger·ma·ny (jʉr′mə nē) a country in north central Europe, on the Baltic Sea: c. 41,800 sq. mi.; pop. 16,850,000; cap. East Berlin: official name **German Democratic Republic**

Ec·ua·dor (ek′wə dôr′) a country in NW South America, on the Pacific Ocean: 104,506 sq. mi.; pop. 6,733,000; cap. Quito

E·gypt (ē′jipt) a country in NE Africa, on the Mediterranean and Red seas: c. 386,000 sq. mi.; pop. 37,233,000; cap. Cairo

El Sal·va·dor (el sal′və dôr′) a country in Central America, southwest of Honduras, on the Pacific Ocean: 8,260 sq. mi.; pop. 4,007,000; cap. San Salvador

Equatorial Guin·ea (gin′ē) a country in central Africa, consisting of a region on the coast between Gabon and Cameroon and two islands off the coast of Cameroon: 10,832 sq. mi.; pop. 286,000; cap. Malabo

E·thi·o·pi·a (ē′thē ō′pē ə) a country in E Africa, on the Red Sea: 457,000 sq. mi.; pop. 27,946,000; cap. Addis Ababa

Fi·ji (fē′jē) a country occupying a group of islands in the SW Pacific Ocean, north of New Zealand: c. 7,000 sq. mi.; pop. 573,000; cap. Suva

Fin·land (fin′lənd) a country in N Europe, northeast of the Baltic Sea: 130,119 sq. mi.; pop. 4,729,000; cap. Helsinki

Flor·i·da (flôr′ə də, flär′-) a Southern State of the SE U.S., mostly on a peninsula between the Atlantic Ocean and the Gulf of Mexico: 58,560 sq. mi.; pop. 9,740,000; cap. Tallahassee

France (frans, fräns) a country in W Europe, on the Atlantic Ocean and the Mediterranean Sea: 212,821 sq. mi.; pop. 52,544,000; cap. Paris

Ga·bon (gä bōn′) a country in west central Africa, on the Atlantic Ocean: 103,089 sq. mi.; pop. 500,000; cap. Libreville

Gam·bi·a (gam′bē ə) a country in W Africa, on the Atlantic Ocean, surrounded on three sides by Senegal: c. 4,000 sq. mi.; pop. 524,000; cap. Banjul

Geor·gia (jôr′jə) a Southern State of the SE U.S., on the Atlantic Ocean: 58,876 sq. mi.; pop. 5,464,000; cap. Atlanta

Germany see EAST GERMANY, WEST GERMANY

Gha·na (gä′nə) a country in W Africa, on the Atlantic Ocean: 91,843 sq. mi.; pop. 9,866,000; cap. Accra

Greece (grēs) a country in the S Balkan Peninsula, including many islands in adjoining seas: 50,534 sq. mi.; pop. 9,046,000; cap. Athens

Gre·na·da (grə nā′də) a country consisting of a large island and several small ones in the S West Indies, north of Trinidad: 133 sq. mi.; pop. 95,000; cap. St. George's

Gua·te·ma·la (gwä′tə mä′lə) a country in Central America, south and east of Mexico: 42,042 sq. mi.; pop. 5,540,000; cap. Guatemala City

Guin·ea (gin′ē) a country in W Africa, on the Atlantic Ocean, south of Senegal: 94,925 sq. mi.; pop. 3,702,000; cap. Conakry

Guin·ea-Bis·sau (gin′ē bi sou′) a country in W Africa, on the coast between Guinea and Senegal: 15,505 sq. mi.; pop. 759,000; cap. Madina do Boe

Guy·a·na (gī an′ə, -än′ə) a country in NE South America, on the Atlantic Ocean: 83,000 sq. mi.; pop. 758,000; cap. Georgetown

Hai·ti (hāt′ē) a country occupying the W part of an island in the West Indies, east of Cuba: 10,714 sq. mi.; pop. 4,584,000; cap. Port-au-Prince

Ha·wai·i (hə wä′ē, -yē, -yə) a State of the U.S., consisting of a group of islands in the North Pacific: 6,424 sq. mi.; pop. 965,000; cap. Honolulu

Hon·du·ras (hän door′əs, -dyoor′-) a country in Central America, with coastlines on the Pacific Ocean and the Caribbean Sea: 43,227 sq. mi.; pop. 2,654,000; cap. Tegucigalpa

Hun·ga·ry (hun′gər ē) a country in south central Europe: 35,919 sq. mi.; pop. 10,596,000; cap. Budapest

Ice·land (īs′lənd) a country consisting of an island in the North Atlantic, south of Greenland, and a few small nearby islands: 39,768 sq. mi.; pop. 218,000; cap. Reykjavik

I·da·ho (ī′də hō′) a Mountain State of the NW U.S.: 83,557 sq. mi.; pop. 944,000; cap. Boise

Il·li·nois (il′ə noi′) a State of the east north central U.S.: 56,400 sq. mi.; pop. 11,418,000; cap. Springfield

In·di·a (in′dē ə) a country in S Asia, including a large peninsula between the Arabian Sea and the Bay of Bengal: 1,177,000 sq. mi.; pop. 598,097,000; cap. New Delhi

In·di·an·a (in′dē an′ə) a State of the east north central U.S.: 36,291 sq. mi.; pop. 5,490,000; cap. Indianapolis

In·do·ne·sia (in′də nē′zhə, -shə) a country consisting of a large group of islands between SE Asia and Australia: 736,510 sq. mi.; pop. 130,597,000; cap. Jakarta

I·o·wa (ī′ə wə) a State of the west north central U.S.: 56,290 sq. mi.; pop. 2,913,000; cap. Des Moines

I·ran (i ran′, ī-; ē rän′) a country in SW Asia, between the Caspian Sea and the Persian Gulf: 636,000 sq. mi.; pop. 33,744,000; cap. Tehrán

I·raq (i räk′, i rak′; ē-) a country in SW Asia, at the head of the Persian Gulf: 171,599 sq. mi.; pop. 11,124,000; cap. Baghdad

Ire·land (īr′lənd) a country occupying five sixths of an island (also called *Ireland*) in the NE Atlantic Ocean, just west of Great Britain: 27,136 sq. mi.; pop. 3,127,000; cap. Dublin

Is·ra·el (iz′rē əl) a country at the SE end of the Mediterranean Sea: 7,992 sq. mi.; pop. 3,459,000; cap. Jerusalem

It·a·ly (it′'l ē) a country in S Europe, mostly on a peninsula extending into the Mediterranean Sea: 116,304 sq. mi.; pop. 56,110,000; cap. Rome

Ivory Coast a country in west central Africa, on the Atlantic Ocean, west of Ghana: 124,500 sq. mi.; pop. 6,673,000; cap. Abidjan

Ja·mai·ca (jə mā′kə) a country that is an island in the West Indies, south of Cuba: 4,411 sq. mi.; pop. 2,025,000; cap. Kingston

Ja·pan (jə pan′) a country in the Pacific Ocean, off the E coast of Asia, consisting of four large islands and many smaller ones: 142,726 sq. mi.; pop. 111,934,000; cap. Tokyo

Jor·dan (jôr'd'n) a country in SW Asia, east of Israel: 37,300 sq. mi.; pop. 2,702,000; cap. Amman

Kam·pu·che·a (kam'poo chē'ə) a country of SE Asia, in S Indochina: 69,884 sq. mi.; pop. 8,087,000; cap. Phnom Penh

Kan·sas (kan'zəs) a State of the west north central U.S.: 82,264 sq. mi.; pop. 2,363,000; cap. Topeka

Ken·tuck·y (kən tuk'ē, ken-) a State of the east south central U.S.: 40,395 sq. mi.; pop. 3,661,000; cap. Frankfort

Ken·ya (ken'yə, kēn'-) a country in east central Africa, on the Indian Ocean: 224,960 sq. mi.; pop. 13,399,000; cap. Nairobi

Kir·i·bati (kir'ə bas') a country consisting principally of three groups of atolls in the west central Pacific, east of the Solomon Islands: 264 sq. mi.; pop. 58,000; cap. Tarawa

Korea *see* NORTH KOREA, SOUTH KOREA

Ku·wait (kōō wāt') a country in E Arabia, on the Persian Gulf, between Iraq and Saudi Arabia: 6,000 sq. mi.; pop. 996,000; cap. Kuwait

La·os (lā'ōs, lous, lā'äs) a country of SE Asia, in NW Indochina: 91,429 sq. mi.; pop. 3,257,000; cap. Vientiane

Leb·a·non (leb'ə nən) a country in SW Asia, at the E end of the Mediterranean: c. 4,000 sq. mi.; pop. 2,869,000; cap. Beirut

Le·sot·ho (le sut'hō, -sō'thō) a country in SE Africa, surrounded by South Africa: 11,716 sq. mi.; pop. 1,039,000; cap. Maseru

Li·ber·i·a (lī bir'ē ə) a country on the W coast of Africa, between the Ivory Coast and Sierra Leone: 43,000 sq. mi.; pop. 1,571,000; cap. Monrovia

Lib·y·a (lib'ē ə) a country in N Africa, on the Mediterranean: 679,359 sq. mi.; pop. 2,444,000; cap. Tripoli

Liech·ten·stein (lēk'tən shtīn') a country in west central Europe, between Switzerland and Austria: 61 sq. mi.; pop. 24,000; cap. Vaduz

Lou·i·si·an·a (loo wē'zē an'ə, loo'ə zē-, loo'zē-) a Southern State of the U.S., on the Gulf of Mexico: 48,523 sq. mi.; pop. 4,204,000; cap. Baton Rouge

Lux·em·bourg (luk'səm burg') a country in W Europe, bounded by Belgium, West Germany, and France: 998 sq. mi.; pop. 357,000; cap. Luxembourg

Mad·a·gas·car (mad'ə gas'kər) a country consisting of a large island and several nearby islands in the Indian Ocean, off the SE coast of Africa: 229,930 sq. mi.; pop. 6,750,000; cap. Antananarivo

Maine (mān) a New England State of the U.S., on the Atlantic Ocean: 33,215 sq. mi.; pop. 1,125,000; cap. Augusta

Ma·la·wi (mä'lä wē) a country in SE Africa, between Zambia and Mozambique: 46,066 sq. mi.; pop. 5,044,000; cap. Lilongwe

Ma·lay·sia (mə lā'zhə, -shə) a country in SE Asia occupying most of the Malay Peninsula, and the N portion of the island of Borneo: 128,654 sq. mi.; pop. 11,900,000; cap. Kuala Lumpur

Mal·dives (mal'dīvz) a country on a group of islands in the Indian Ocean, southwest of Sri Lanka: 115 sq. mi.; pop. 143,000; cap. Male

Ma·li (mä'lē) a country in W Africa, south and east of Mauritania: 464,873 sq. mi.; pop. 5,376,000; cap. Bamako

Mal·ta (môl'tə) a country on a group of islands in the Mediterranean Sea, south of Italy: 122 sq. mi.; pop. 319,000; cap. Valletta

Mar·y·land (mer'ə lənd) an Eastern State of

the U.S., on the Atlantic Ocean: 10,577 sq. mi.; pop. 4,216,000; cap. Annapolis

Mas·sa·chu·setts (mas'ə chōō'sits) a New England State of the U.S., on the Atlantic: 8,257 sq. mi.; pop. 5,737,000; cap. Boston

Mau·ri·ta·ni·a (môr'ə tā'nē ə, -tān'yə) a country in W Africa, on the Atlantic: 419,230 sq. mi.; pop. 1,318,000; cap. Nouakchott

Mau·ri·ti·us (mô rish'ē əs, -rish'əs) a country consisting of an island (also called *Mauritius*) and several smaller nearby islands in the Indian Ocean, east of Madagascar: 809 sq. mi.; pop. 872,000; cap. Port Louis

Mex·i·co (mek'si kō') a country in North America, south of the U.S.: 760,373 sq. mi.; pop. 60,145,000; cap. Mexico City

Mich·i·gan (mish'ə gən) a State of the east north central U.S.: 58,216 sq. mi.; pop. 9,258,000; cap. Lansing

Min·ne·so·ta (min'ə sōt'ə) a State of the west north central U.S., on the Canadian border: 84,068 sq. mi.; pop. 4,077,000; cap. St. Paul

Mis·sis·sip·pi (mis'ə sip'ē) a Southern State of the U.S., on the Gulf of Mexico: 47,716 sq. mi.; pop. 2,521,000; cap. Jackson

Mis·sour·i (mi zoor'ē, -ə) a State of the west south central U.S.: 69,686 sq. mi.; pop. 4,917,000; cap. Jefferson City

Mon·a·co (män'ə kō, mə nä'kō) a country in SW Europe, on the Mediterranean, surrounded on three sides by France: 1/2 sq. mi.; pop. 25,000; cap. Monaco-Ville

Mon·go·li·a (mäŋ gō'lē ə, män-; -gōl'yə) a country in east central Asia, north of China: 592,600 sq. mi.; pop. 1,444,000; cap. Ulan Bator

Mon·tan·a (män tan'ə) a Mountain State of the NW U.S., on the Canadian border: 147,138 sq. mi.; pop. 787,000; cap. Helena

Mo·roc·co (mə rä'kō) a country on the NW coast of Africa: c. 171,300 sq. mi.; pop. 17,305,000; cap. Rabat

Mo·zam·bique (mō'zəm bēk') a country in SE Africa, on the Indian Ocean: 302,300 sq. mi.; pop. 9,239,000; cap. Maputo

Na·u·ru (nä ōō'rōō) a country that is an island in the W Pacific, just south of the equator: 8 sq. mi.; pop. 7,000

Ne·bras·ka (nə bras'kə) a State of the west north central U.S.: 77,227 sq. mi.; pop. 1,570,000; cap. Lincoln

Ne·pal (ni pôl', ne-; -päl') a country in S Asia, between India and Tibet: 54,362 sq. mi.; pop. 12,321,000; cap. Katmandu

Neth·er·lands (nethʹər ləndz) a country in W Europe, on the North Sea: 12,978 sq. mi.; pop. 13,763,000; cap. Amsterdam

Ne·vad·a (nə vadʹə, -väʹdə) a Mountain State of the W U.S.: 110,540 sq. mi.; pop. 799,000; cap. Carson City

New Hamp·shire (hampʹshir, hamʹ-) a New England State of the U.S., on the Atlantic: 9,304 sq. mi.; pop. 921,000; cap. Concord

New Jersey (jurʹzē) an Eastern State of the U.S., on the Atlantic Ocean: 7,836 sq. mi.; pop. 7,364,000; cap. Trenton

New Mexico a Mountain State of the SW U.S.: 121,666 sq. mi.; pop. 1,300,000; cap. Santa Fe

New York (yôrk) a State of the NE U.S., on the Atlantic Ocean: 49,576 sq. mi.; pop. 17,557,000; cap. Albany

New Zea·land (zēʹlənd) a country made up of two large islands and several small ones in the South Pacific, southeast of Australia: 103,736 sq. mi.; pop. 3,148,000; cap. Wellington

Nic·a·ra·gua (nikʹə räʹgwə) a country in Central America, on the Caribbean Sea and the Pacific

Ocean: 54,342 sq. mi.; pop. 2,155,000; cap. Managua

Ni·ger (nī′jər) a country in west central Africa, north of Nigeria: c. 458,500 sq. mi.; pop. 4,600,000; cap. Niamey

Ni·ger·i·a (nī jir′ē ə) a country in west central Africa, on the Atlantic Ocean: 327,186 sq. mi.; pop. 74,870,000; cap. Lagos

North Car·o·li·na (kar′ə lī′nə) a Southern State of the SE U.S., on the Atlantic Ocean: 52,712 sq. mi.; pop. 5,874,000; cap. Raleigh

North Da·ko·ta (də kō′tə) a State of the west north central U.S., on the Canadian border: 70,665 sq. mi.; pop. 653,000; cap. Bismarck

North Ko·re·a (kô rē′ə, kō-, kə-) a country in E Asia, on a peninsula extending south from NE China: 47,255 sq. mi.; pop. 15,852,000; cap. Pyongyang: official name **Democratic People's Republic of Korea**

Nor·way (nôr′wā′) a country in N Europe, occupying the western and northern parts of the Scandinavian Peninsula: 125,064 sq. mi.; pop. 4,022,000; cap. Oslo

O·hi·o (ō hī′ō) a State of the east north central U.S.: 41,222 sq. mi.; pop. 10,797,000; cap. Columbus

O·kla·ho·ma (ō′klə hō′mə) a State of the south central U.S.: 69,919 sq. mi.; pop. 3,025,000; cap. Oklahoma City

O·man (ō män′) a country in SE Arabia: 82,000 sq. mi.; pop. 766,000; cap. Muscat

Or·e·gon (ôr′i gən, är′-; -gän′) a State of the NW U.S., on the Pacific Ocean: 96,981 sq. mi.; pop. 2,633,000; cap. Salem

Pa·ki·stan (pä′ki stän′, pak′i stan′) a country in S Asia, on the Arabian Sea: 310,403 sq. mi.; pop. 70,260,000; cap. Islamabad

Pan·a·ma (pan′ə mä′, -mô′) a country in Central America, on a strip of land adjoining South America: 29,201 sq. mi.; pop. 1,668,000; cap. Panama

Pap·u·a New Guinea (pap′yoo wə, pa′poo wə) a country occupying the E half of a large island in the East Indies, north of Australia, and several nearby islands: c. 180,000 sq. mi.; pop. 2,756,000; cap. Port Moresby

Par·a·guay (par′ə gwä′, -gwī′) an inland country in south central South America: 157,042 sq. mi.; pop. 2,647,000; cap. Asunción

Penn·syl·va·ni·a (pen′s'l vän′yə, -vā′nē ə) a State of the NE U.S.: 45,333 sq. mi.; pop. 11,867,000; cap. Harrisburg

Pe·ru (pə rōō′) a country in W South America, on the Pacific Ocean: 496,222 sq. mi.; pop. 15,615,000; cap. Lima

Phil·ip·pines (fil′ə pēnz′) a country occupying a group of c. 7,100 islands in the SW Pacific Ocean off the SE coast of Asia: 114,830 sq. mi.; pop. 43,751,000; cap. Manila

Po·land (pō′lənd) a country in central Europe, on the Baltic Sea: 120,625 sq. mi.; pop. 34,364,000; cap. Warsaw

Por·tu·gal (pôr′chə gəl) a country in SW Europe, on the Atlantic Ocean, and including two groups of islands in the Atlantic: 35,509 sq. mi.; pop. 9,228,000; cap. Lisbon

Puer·to Ri·co (pwer′tə rē′kō, pôr′-) an island in the West Indies, constituting a commonwealth associated with the U.S.: 3,421 sq. mi.; pop. 3,188,000; cap. San Juan

Qa·tar (gut′ər, kä′tär) a country occupying a peninsula of E Arabia, on the Persian Gulf: 6,000 sq. mi.; pop. 180,000; cap. Doha

Rhode Island (rōd) a New England State of the U.S., on the Atlantic: 1,214 sq. mi.; pop. 947,000; cap. Providence

Ro·ma·ni·a (rō män′yə, -mä′nē ə) a country in

SE Europe, on the Black Sea: 91,700 sq. mi.; pop. 21,245,000; cap. Bucharest

Rwan·da (ʉr wän′dä, rōō wän′də) a country in east central Africa, east of Zaire: 10,169 sq. mi.; pop. 4,198,000; cap. Kigali

San Ma·ri·no (san′ mə rē′nō) a country within E Italy: 23 sq. mi.; pop. 20,000; cap. San Marino

São To·mé and Prín·ci·pe (soun tô me′ ənd prin′sə pē′) a country consisting of two main islands, and several islets, in the Atlantic Ocean, west of Gabon and Equatorial Guinea: 372 sq. mi.; pop. 75,000; cap. São Tomé

Sa·u·di Arabia (sä ōō′dē, sou′dē) a country occupying most of Arabia: c. 617,000 sq. mi.; pop. 7,013,000; cap. Riyadh

Sen·e·gal (sen′i gôl′) a country in W Africa, on the Atlantic Ocean: 76,124 sq. mi.; pop. 4,136,000; cap. Dakar

Sey·chelles (sā shel′, -shelz′) a country occupying a group of islands in the Indian Ocean, northeast of Madagascar: 156 sq. mi.; pop. 58,000; cap. Victoria

Si·er·ra Le·one (sē er′ə lē ōn′) a country in W Africa, on the Atlantic Ocean, between Liberia and Guinea: 27,925 sq. mi.; pop. 2,729,000; cap. Freetown

Sin·ga·pore (siŋ′gə pôr′, siŋ′ə-) a country occupying an island off the S tip of the Malay Peninsula, and several nearby islets: 225 sq. mi.; pop. 2,250,000; cap. Singapore

Sol·o·mon Islands (säl′ə mən) a country on a group of islands in the SW Pacific, east of New Guinea: c. 11,500 sq. mi.; pop. 215,000; cap. Honiara

So·ma·li·a (sō mä′lē ə, sə-; -mäl′yə) a country of E Africa, on the Indian Ocean: 246,201 sq. mi.; pop. 2,941,000; cap. Mogadishu

South Africa a country in southernmost Africa: 472,358 sq. mi.; pop. 25,471,000; capitals, Cape Town, Pretoria

South Car·o·li·na (kar′ə lī′nə) a Southern State of the SE U.S., on the Atlantic Ocean: 31,055 sq. mi.; pop. 3,119,000; cap. Columbia

South Da·ko·ta (də kō′tə) a State of the west north central U.S.: 77,047 sq. mi.; pop. 690,000; cap. Pierre

South Ko·re·a (kô rē′ə, kō-, kə-) a country in E Asia, on a peninsula south of North Korea: 38,030 sq. mi.; pop. 34,688,000; cap. Seoul: official name **Republic of Korea**

Spain (spān) a country in SW Europe, on a large peninsula between the Atlantic Ocean and the Mediterranean Sea: 194,346 sq. mi.; pop. 35,472,000; cap. Madrid

Sri Lan·ka (srē läŋ′kə) a country that is an island off the SE tip of India: 25,332 sq. mi.; pop. 13,249,000; cap. Colombo

St. Lu·ci·a (lōō′shē ə, -shə, lōō sē′ə) a country on an island of the Windward group in the West Indies, south of Martinique: 238 sq. mi.; pop. 120,000; cap. Castries

St. Vin·cent (vin′s'nt) a country in the West Indies, consisting of an island of the Windward group and the northern islands of a chain called the Grenadines: 150 sq. mi.; pop. 112,000; cap. Kingstown

Su·dan (sōō dan′) a country in north central Africa, south of Egypt: 967,500 sq. mi.; pop. 17,757,000; cap. Khartoum

Su·ri·name (soor′i näm′, soor′i nam′) a country in NE South America, on the Atlantic Ocean: 55,144 sq. mi.; pop. 385,000; cap. Paramaribo

Swa·zi·land (swä′zē land′) a country in SE Africa, with South Africa on three sides: 6,705 sq. mi.; pop. 494,000; cap. Mbabane

Swe·den (swē′d'n) a country in N Europe, in

the E part of the Scandinavian Peninsula: 173,620 sq. mi.; pop. 8,219,000; cap. Stockholm

Switz·er·land (swit′sər lənd) a country in west central Europe, with France, West Germany, and Italy forming its principal boundaries: 15,941 sq. mi.; pop. 6,333,000; cap. Bern

Syr·i·a (sir′ē ə) a country at the E end of the Mediterranean Sea, south of Turkey: 71,227 sq. mi.; pop. 7,585,000; cap. Damascus

Tai·wan (tī′wän′) a self-governing island province of China, off the SE coast: 13,885 sq. mi.; pop. 16,172,000; cap. Taipei

Tan·za·ni·a (tan′zə nē′ə) a country in E Africa, including a mainland region and a group of islands off the coast: 362,820 sq. mi.; pop. 15,300,000; cap. Dar es Salaam

Ten·nes·see (ten′ə sē′) a State of the east south central U.S.: 42,244 sq. mi.; pop. 4,591,000; cap. Nashville

Tex·as (tek′səs) a State of the SW U.S., on the Gulf of Mexico and the Mexican border: 267,339 sq. mi.; pop. 14,228,000; cap. Austin

Thai·land (tī′land, -lənd) a country in SE Asia, in Indochina and the Malay Peninsula: 198,456 sq. mi.; pop. 41,869,000; cap. Bangkok

To·go (tō′gō) a country in W Africa, on the Atlantic Ocean, east of Ghana: 21,853 sq. mi.; pop. 2,222,000; cap. Lomé

Ton·ga (täŋ′gə) a country occupying a group of islands in the South Pacific, east of Fiji: 270 sq. mi.; pop. 102,000; cap. Nuku'alofa

Trin·i·dad and To·ba·go (trin′ə dad′ ənd tō bā′gō) a country in the West Indies, off the NE coast of Venezuela, consisting of two islands (*Trinidad* and *Tobago*): 1,980 sq. mi.; pop. 1,074,000; cap. Port-of-Spain

Tu·ni·sia (tōō nē′zhə, -nish′ə, -nish′ē ə) a country in N Africa, on the Mediterranean Sea: 48,332 sq. mi.; pop. 5,772,000; cap. Tunis

Tur·key (tʉr′kē) a country occupying Asia Minor and a SE part of the Balkan Peninsula: 301,381 sq. mi.; pop. 39,180,000; cap. Ankara

Tu·va·lu (tōō′və lōō′) a country consisting of a group of nine islands in the west central Pacific: 10 sq. mi.; pop. 6,000; cap. Funafuti

U·gan·da (yōō gan′də, ōō gän′dä) a country in east central Africa, west of Kenya: 93,981 sq. mi.; pop. 11,549,000; cap. Kampala

Union of Soviet Socialist Republics a country in E Europe and N Asia, extending from the Arctic Ocean to the Black Sea and from the Baltic Sea to the Pacific Ocean: 8,603,000 sq. mi.; pop. 254,382,000; cap. Moscow

United Arab Emir·ates (i mir′its, -āts) a country in E Arabia, on the Persian Gulf: c. 32,000 sq. mi.; pop. 335,000; cap. Abu Dhabi

United Kingdom a country in the Atlantic Ocean, just off the W coast of Europe, consisting of the island of Great Britain and the NE portion of the island of Ireland: 94,217 sq. mi.; pop. 55,962,000; cap. London

United States of A·mer·i·ca (ə mer′ə kə) a country made up of the North American area extending from the Atlantic Ocean to the Pacific Ocean between Canada and Mexico, and including Alaska and Hawaii: 3,615,211 sq. mi.; pop. 226,505,000; cap. Washington

Upper Vol·ta (väl′tə) a country in W Africa, north of Ghana: 108,880 sq. mi.; pop. 6,144,000; cap. Ouagadougou

U·ru·guay (yoor′ə gwā′, -gwī′) a country in SE South America, on the Atlantic Ocean: 72,171 sq. mi.; pop. 3,064,000; cap. Montevideo

U·tah (yōō′tô, -tä) a Mountain State of the W U.S.: 84,916 sq. mi.; pop. 1,461,000; cap. Salt Lake City

Van·ua·tu (vän wä tōō′) a country on a group of islands in the SW Pacific, west of Fiji: 5,700 sq. mi.; pop. 112,000

Ven·e·zue·la (ven′i zwā′lə, -zwē′-) a country in N South America, on the Caribbean Sea: 352,143 sq. mi.; pop. 11,993,000; cap. Caracas

Ver·mont (vər mänt′) a New England State of the U.S.: 9,609 sq. mi.; pop. 511,000; cap. Montpelier

Vi·et·nam (vē′ət näm′, vyet′-; -nam′) a country in SE Asia, on the E coast of Indochina: 129,607 sq. mi.; pop. 45,211,000; cap. Hanoi

Vir·gin·ia (vər jin′yə, -ē ə) a Southern State of the U.S., on the Atlantic Ocean: 40,815 sq. mi.; pop. 5,346,000; cap. Richmond

Wash·ing·ton (wôsh′iŋ tən, wäsh′-) a State of the NW U.S., on the Pacific Ocean: 68,192 sq. mi.; pop. 4,130,000; cap. Olympia

Western Sa·mo·a (sə mō′ə) an island country in the South Pacific, north of Tonga: 1,130 sq. mi.; pop. 152,000; cap. Apia

West Ger·ma·ny (jʉr′mə nē) a country in north central Europe, on the North Sea: 95,735 sq. mi.; pop. 61,746,000; cap. Bonn: official name **Federal Republic of Germany**

West Virginia a State of the E U.S., northwest of Virginia: 24,181 sq. mi.; pop. 1,950,000; cap. Charleston

Wis·con·sin (wis kän′s'n) a State of the west north central U.S.: 56,154 sq. mi.; pop. 4,705,000; cap. Madison

Wy·o·ming (wī ō′miŋ) a Mountain State of the W U.S.: 97,914 sq. mi.; pop. 471,000; cap. Cheyenne

Yem·en (yem′ən) **1.** a country in S Arabia, on the Red Sea: c. 75,000 sq. mi.; pop. 6,668,000; cap. San'a: official name **Yemen Arab Republic 2.** a country east of this, on the Indian Ocean: c. 112,000 sq. mi.; pop. 1,690,000; cap. Aden: official name **People's Democratic Republic of Yemen**

Yu·go·sla·vi·a (yōō′gō slä′vē ə, -gə släv′yə) a country in the NW Balkan Peninsula, on the Adriatic Sea: 98,766 sq. mi.; pop. 21,559,000; cap. Belgrade

Za·ire (zä ir′) a country in central Africa, on the equator: 905,563 sq. mi.; pop. 24,902,000; cap. Kinshasa

Zam·bi·a (zam′bē ə) a country in S Africa, south of Zaire: 290,323 sq. mi.; pop. 4,896,000; cap. Lusaka

Zim·ba·bwe (zim bä′bwe) a country in S Africa, north of South Africa: 150,333 sq. mi.; pop. 6,930,000; cap. Salisbury

PRINCIPAL CITIES OF THE UNITED STATES

Population

City	1980 Census	1970 Census	Metropolitan Area 1980 Census*
New York, New York	7,071,000	7,896,000	9,081,000
Chicago, Illinois	3,005,000	3,369,000	7,058,000
Los Angeles, California	2,967,000	2,812,000	7,446,000
Philadelphia, Pennsylvania	1,688,000	1,950,000	4,701,000
Houston, Texas	1,594,000	1,234,000	2,891,000
Detroit, Michigan	1,203,000	1,514,000	4,344,000
Dallas, Texas	904,000	844,000	2,964,000
San Diego, California	876,000	697,000	1,860,000
San Antonio, Texas	785,000	654,000	1,070,000
Baltimore, Maryland	784,000	906,000	2,166,000
Phoenix, Arizona	765,000	584,000	1,512,000
Indianapolis, Indiana	701,000	737,000	1,162,000
San Francisco, California	679,000	716,000	3,227,000
Memphis, Tennessee	646,000	624,000	910,000
Washington, D.C.	638,000	757,000	3,045,000
San Jose, California	637,000	460,000	1,290,000
Milwaukee, Wisconsin	636,000	717,000	1,393,000
Cleveland, Ohio	574,000	751,000	1,896,000
Columbus, Ohio	565,000	540,000	1,089,000
Boston, Massachusetts	563,000	641,000	2,760,000
New Orleans, Louisiana	557,000	593,000	1,184,000
Jacksonville, Florida	541,000	504,000	736,000
Seattle, Washington	494,000	531,000	1,601,000
Denver, Colorado	491,000	515,000	1,615,000
Nashville, Tennessee	456,000	426,000	829,000
St. Louis, Missouri	453,000	622,000	2,345,000
Kansas City, Missouri	448,000	507,000	1,322,000
El Paso, Texas	425,000	322,000	479,000
Atlanta, Georgia	425,000	495,000	2,010,000
Pittsburgh, Pennsylvania	424,000	520,000	2,261,000
Oklahoma City, Oklahoma	403,000	368,000	830,000
Cincinnati, Ohio	385,000	454,000	1,392,000
Fort Worth, Texas	385,000	393,000	(included at Dallas)
Minneapolis, Minnesota	371,000	434,000	2,109,000
Portland, Oregon	366,000	380,000	1,236,000

*Preliminary figures

PRINCIPAL FOREIGN CITIES

City	Population*	City	Population*
Mexico City, Mexico	15,000,000	Madras, India	3,200,000
Shanghai, China	12,000,000	Berlin (East & West), Germany	3,038,000
Tokyo, Japan	11,695,000	Nanking, China	3,000,000
Buenos Aires, Argentina	10,500,000	Melbourne, Australia	2,995,000
Paris, France	8,547,000	Rome, Italy	2,915,000
Peking, China	8,500,000	Bogotá, Colombia	2,881,000
Cairo, Egypt	8,400,000	Toronto, Canada	2,803,000
Moscow, U.S.S.R.	8,011,000	Montreal, Canada	2,802,000
São Paulo, Brazil	8,000,000	Caracas, Venezuela	2,800,000
Seoul, South Korea	7,800,000	Yokohama, Japan	2,686,000
Tientsin, China	7,200,000	Manchester, United Kingdom	2,675,000
Calcutta, India	7,000,000	Osaka, Japan	2,625,000
London, United Kingdom	6,970,000	Ankara, Turkey	2,600,000
Chungking, China	6,000,000	Athens, Greece	2,540,000
Bombay, India	6,000,000	Alexandria, Egypt	2,500,000
Jakarta, Indonesia	5,500,000	Pusan, South Korea	2,454,000
Kwangchow, China	5,200,000	Kinshasa, Zaire	2,444,000
Tehran, Iran	4,950,000	Guadalajara, Mexico	2,400,000
Bangkok, Thailand	4,871,000	Algiers, Algeria	2,200,000
Rio de Janeiro, Brazil	4,858,000	Taipei, Taiwan	2,200,000
Shenyang, China	4,800,000	Casablanca, Morocco	2,173,000
Leningrad, U.S.S.R.	4,588,000	Lahore, Pakistan	2,165,000
Lima, Peru	4,500,000	Kiev, U.S.S.R.	2,144,000
Manila, Philippines	4,500,000	Harbin, China	2,100,000
Wuhan, China	4,400,000	Budapest, Hungary	2,093,000
Lüta, China	4,200,000	Nagoya, Japan	2,078,000
Istanbul, Turkey	3,900,000	Dacca, Bangladesh	2,000,000
Santiago, Chile	3,800,000	Lagos, Nigeria	2,000,000
Rangoon, Burma	3,662,000	Chengtu, China	2,000,000
Delhi, India	3,647,000	Surabaya, Indonesia	2,000,000
Madrid, Spain	3,520,000	Lisbon, Portugal	2,000,000
Karachi, Pakistan	3,500,000	Bucharest, Romania	1,988,000
Baghdad, Iraq	3,500,000	Havana, Cuba	1,800,000
Sydney, Australia	3,474,000	Tashkent, U.S.S.R.	1,779,000
Ho Chi Minh, Vietnam	3,460,000	Barcelona, Spain	1,745,000

*of urban area: in most instances the latest available information makes no distinction between the population of the city proper and that of its urban area